THE GUINNESS RECORD OF

WORLD SOCCER

THE HISTORY OF THE GAME
IN OVER 150 COUNTRIES

GUY OLIVER

GUINNESS PUBLISHING

ACKNOWLEDGEMENTS

Firstly thanks to my family – the Olivers, Greenleaves and Dumases, who have given me every encouragement to complete the book and a sense of proportion when at times I may have been lacking such a quality. My parents, in particular, have been wonderful in their patient proof-reading of much of the information with me, and for that I am particularly grateful as both are far more keen on golf. My mother did, however, take a shine to Red Boys in Luxembourg so perhaps I did kindle a little interest. To Lisa and Chris Dumas for all their translation help – Muy agradecido.

Others without whom you would not be reading this are Tony Willoughby and James Hodgson. Copies are on their way. Thanks also to Simon Duncan and Charles Richards, the main men at Guinness. Special mention must also be given to David Barber at the Football Association in London. To the legal eagle Michael Kirton my thanks also, even if you do support the wrong team. With far better taste, thanks to David Huckle – a fellow Selhurst Eagles! And a big hug for Julie Lamm.

I would like also to thank the following: The Football Associations of Australia, Austria, Argentina, Bangladesh, Belgium, Brazil, Bulgaria, Canada, Chile, Colombia, Costa Rica, Côte d'Ivoire, Cyprus, Denmark, Finland, France, Holland, India, Indonesia, Japan, Luxembourg, Malaysia, Malta, New Zealand, Northern Ireland, Pakistan, Portugal, Republic of Ireland, Romania, Senegal, Singapore, South Korea, Switzerland, Turkey, United Arab Emirates, the United States, Uruguay, Wales and Zimbabwe. Boncho Todorov, Esko Lahtinen, Guillermo Ruiz, Carlos Cure, Peter Pullen, Peter Law, Serge Van Hoof, AW Kanukayi and Dan Cristea. Andreas Herren at FIFA, Zaven Djizmedjian of CAF, Peter Velappan at the AFC and Scott Gleba at CONCACAF.

To write a book of such magnitude, it often takes exceptional circumstances, and this has been the case with this particular work. I would like therefore to dedicate the book to my great friend Tom Chittick who has been unstinting in his support in the time it has taken to write it. He knows how much he has helped, and I will be forever grateful to him. I only hope that in years to come I will be able to show the same generosity of spirit to others as he has shown to me.

Published in Great Britain by Guinness Publishing Ltd,
33 London Road, Enfield, Middlesex

Front cover design by David Roberts

Text design and layout by Kathleen Aldridge

Photographs courtesy of Allsport UK Ltd

Typeset in Goudy and Gill by Ace Filmsetting Ltd, Frome, Somerset

Printed and bound in Great Britain by The Bath Press, Bath

'Guinness' is a registered trademark of Guinness Publishing Ltd

A catalogue record for this book is available from the British Library

ISBN 0–85112–954–4

CONTENTS

Acknowledgements ii
Introduction v
How to use this book vii
List of abbreviations ix

WORLD

Introduction 2
List of FIFA-affiliated nations 4
World Footballer of the Year 4
The World Cup 5
Olympic Football 60
Other FIFA tournaments 79
Other world tournaments 86
The World Club Championship 88

EUROPE

Introduction 94
List of UEFA-affiliated nations . 95
European Footballer of the Year 95
The European Football Championship 98
European club competitions 107
Other European tournaments .. 163

Albania 169
Austria 174
Belgium 188
Bulgaria 200
Cyprus 213
Czechoslovakia 217
Denmark 231
England 243
Faeroe Islands 264
Finland 265
France 276
Germany 289
Greece 311
Holland 319
Hungary 332
Iceland 347
Israel 353
Italy 360
Liechtenstein 374
Luxembourg 375
Malta 383
Northern Ireland 387
Norway 399
Poland 408
Portugal 420
Republic of Ireland 428
Romania 436
San Marino 448
Scotland 448
Soviet Union 463
Spain 476
Sweden 487
Switzerland 502
Turkey 515
Wales 523
Yugoslavia 533

SOUTH AMERICA

Introduction 548
List of CONMEBOL-affiliated nations 548
South American Footballer of the Year 548
The South American Championship 549
South American club competitions 571
Other South American tournaments 592

Argentina 594
Bolivia 611
Brazil 614
Chile 638
Colombia 648
Ecuador 655
Paraguay 658
Peru 667
Uruguay 674
Venezuela 688

AFRICA

Introduction 692
List of CAF-affiliated nations .. 693
African Footballer of the Year . 693
The African Cup of Nations ... 695
All-African Games 710
African club competitions 712

North Africa 731
Algeria 733
Egypt 734
Libya 736
Morocco 736
Tunisia 737

West Africa 739
Benin 741
Burkina Faso 741
Cape Verde 742
Côte d'Ivoire 742
Gambia 743
Ghana 744
Guinea-Bissau 745
Guinea 745
Liberia 746
Mali 746
Mauritania 747
Niger 747
Nigeria 748
Senegal 749
Sierra Leone 750
Togo 751

Central Africa 751
Cameroon 753
Central African Republic 753
Congo 754
Gabon 755
Equatorial Guinea 755
Sao Tome 756
Zaire 756

East Africa 757
Burundi 758
Ethiopia 759
Kenya 759
Rwanda 760
Somalia 761
Sudan 761
Tanzania 762
Uganda 762

Southern Africa 763
Angola 764
Botswana 765
Lesotho 765
Madagascar 766
Malawi 766
Mauritius 767
Mozambique 767
Seychelles 768

South Africa ... 768
Swaziland ... 770
Zambia ... 770
Zimbabwe ... 771

CONCACAF

Introduction ... 774
List of CONCACAF-affiliated nations ... 774
The Central American Championships ... 775
The CONCACAF Champions Cup ... 777
The Copa Inter America ... 778

Canada ... 779
Mexico ... 783
United States of America ... 788

Central America ... 795
Belize ... 796
Costa Rica ... 796
El Salvador ... 797
Guatemala ... 797
Honduras ... 798
Nicaragua ... 798
Panama ... 798

The Caribbean ... 798
Antigua and Barbuda ... 799
Aruba ... 799
Bahamas ... 799
Barbados ... 800
Bermuda ... 800
Cuba ... 800
Dominican Republic ... 800
Grenada ... 801
Guyana ... 801
Haiti ... 801
Jamaica ... 801
Netherlands Antilles ... 802
Puerto Rico ... 802
St Lucia ... 802
St Vincent and the Grenadines ... 802
Surinam ... 803
Trinidad and Tobago ... 803

ASIA

Introduction ... 806
List of AFC-affiliated nations ... 808
The Asian Cup ... 809
The Asian Games ... 813
The Far Eastern Games ... 817
Asian club competitions ... 817
Other Asian tournaments ... 823

Afghanistan ... 837
Bahrain ... 837
Bangladesh ... 838
Brunei ... 838
China ... 838
Hong Kong ... 839
India ... 840
Indonesia ... 841
Iran ... 841
Iraq ... 842
Japan ... 843
Jordan ... 844
Kampuchea ... 844
Kuwait ... 845
Laos ... 845
Lebanon ... 846
Macau ... 846
Malaysia ... 846
Maldives ... 847
Myanmar ... 847
Nepal ... 848
North Korea ... 848
Oman ... 849
Pakistan ... 849
Philippines ... 849
Qatar ... 850
Saudi Arabia ... 850
Singapore ... 851
South Korea ... 851
Sri Lanka ... 855
Syria ... 855
Taiwan ... 856
Thailand ... 856
United Arab Emirates ... 857
Vietnam ... 857
Yemen ... 857

OCEANIA

Introduction ... 860
List of OFC-affiliated nations ... 861
The Oceania Cup ... 861

Australia ... 862
Fiji ... 863
New Zealand ... 863
Papua New Guinea ... 864
Solomon Islands ... 864
French Polynesia 'Tahiti' ... 864
Vanuatu ... 864
Western Samoa ... 864

Bibliography ... 865
Appendix 1 ... 867
Appendix 2 ... 870

INTRODUCTION

Listening to the radio one Saturday morning wondering if all the effort in writing this book had been worthwhile, I heard Bryon Butler interviewed on *Sport on Four*. Asked why he had written his book, *The History of the Football Association*, he replied that without its history, football would have little appeal. Fixtures like Liverpool against Manchester United or Holland against Germany would lose all their significance as events, because there would be no context. True, one could watch football and enjoy its aesthetic beauty; but the pleasure, he argued, would be shallow.

Football plays a large part in the cultural life of the world. Millions of people play the game and even more watch regularly. It is the 'king of sports', if not the sport of kings, and it has a rich history. There have been many fine writers on the game in the English language. Geoffrey Green, for years the chief football correspondent of *The Times*, has told many a tale, as have others like Brian Glanville, Hugh McIlvanney, Willy Meisl and Simon Inglis, to name but a few. The emphasis in this book is to give football a proper historical perspective within which such stories occur. If this book can complement their prose, I will consider it a job well worth having done.

In writing it, curiosity was my great motivator. For example, in his book, *Great Moments in Sport: Soccer*, Geoffrey Green gives us a wonderful description of arriving late for an England–Brazil match in Rio in 1964, a match in which England were soundly beaten 5–1. The match was part of a four-team tournament also involving Argentina and Portugal. I always wondered what happened in the other matches. What was the score of the Argentina versus Portugal game for instance?

Every country has its own publications, and naturally they tend to focus very little on football elsewhere. Thus in Germany there are books listing the matches for the German national side, but in English publications? No chance. In compiling the book, I have therefore had to distil information from many different publications from around the world. I hope I have given credit where it is due, but much of the documentation from the various associations appears authorless.

I would, however, like to mention two books at this juncture. *European International Football* by Gordon Jeffrey and *The Encyclopedia of World Soccer* by Richard Henshaw are both seminal works on the history of football around the world, and I have drawn heavily upon them. Gordon Jeffrey wrote his book 30 years ago and he did much of the spade-work in drawing up the first basic list of international matches played by the nations of Europe, as well as researching much of their early history. Remarkably, much of his information remains unchallenged. Richard Henshaw covered a much more extensive field and built upon a work edited by Norman Barrett called *World Soccer from A to Z*. Credit also to *World Soccer* and *France Football* for keeping us up to date with developments worldwide.

It is also worth mentioning at this point that writing a history of football is not an exact science. 'Facts' can often be challenged. Different sources tell a different story and until recently no-one much cared for keeping extensive records. When is a goal an own goal, for example? Obviously when a defender kicks the ball into his own net, but what about deflected shots? You have to draw the line at some point, and I have where possible used information from official sources.

I recently came across a book on American Football that was unbelievable in its statistical coverage. It had everything, right down to the number of punted yards each season since the league began for every team. Football is just not like that. People do collect detailed records, but if you are not careful you lose sense in a morass of facts. In an ideal book on World Football, the international results section of each country would include the players who appeared in each international game, the name of the referee, the minute of the substitutions, the number of spectators, match receipts, kick-off time and so on. To compile such a book would take a whole team of compilers an inordinate length of time to do. For some South American countries it has been hard enough trying to find even a list of games they have played let alone any further information, so I hope I have struck a fair balance.

The emphasis is on Europe and South America because it is here that football is best known. However, compiling the sections on Africa, Asia and Central America has given me the greatest pleasure. Without them, the book would not be the same.

My sincere hope is that this book is not a requiem for the world of football that we now know. There are conflicting pressures on football. Should the sport be 'only a game' in the traditional amateur sense, is it about right as it is at the moment, or should it run with the flow and follow the lead set by teams like Milan who are taking it into the realms of a multinational business? Geoffrey Green once described football as 'the people's game'. It is a phrase that is well worth heeding. Those involved in the sport must take stock and decide on a course of action that is in the interest of all concerned with the game, not just a minority with a vested interest. Football is too important a cultural asset to be tampered with on a whim.

Football is a simple game, but one example illustrates the delicate balance that exists within it. In 1925, the directors of the top English football clubs, seeing a decline in crowds at their grounds and therefore a fall in revenue, decided the cause was a decrease in the number of goals being scored at games. The answer? Change the offside law. Instead of requiring three players of the opposing side to be in front of the attacking player when the ball was played, it was decided that it should be two, in order to give the forwards an extra advantage.

The directors could not believe their wisdom. The number of goals increased overnight and their bank managers were happy again, but at the time they did not grasp the effects of what they had done. In the long term, the number of goals scored dropped to lower than the 1925 level as defences became better organised to deal with the new threat. Herbert Chapman devised the legendary third-back game, introducing a third defender.

The roots of the defensive football of the second half of the century can be traced back to the decision of 1925. Chapman's own implementation of this tactic was not so disastrous, as he had the players at Arsenal in the 1930s to have a spectacular team, but football suffered from the cheap imitations that other teams adopted. A simple decision that seemed such a good idea at the time had effects that no one could have dreamed of, many years after the fact.

In more recent times, the penalty shoot-out has been introduced to decide drawn games in important competitions. After the World Cup in Italy in 1990 there were complaints by FIFA that the tournament was too defensive and that coaches should encourage attacking football. The extraordinary thing was that FIFA failed to see that it was they who were encouraging the defensive football. The coaches were merely reacting to the set of circumstances they found themselves in. A team which knows it is inferior to the opposition will of course play defensively if there is a get-out clause at the end of the game in the form of penalties.

Other pronouncements of those in control of the sport defy belief. For someone to suggest widening the goalposts to allow more goals simply shows a lack of understanding of the game. When UEFA can suggest that drawn matches should be decided on the fewest yellow cards shown in a match, it is time to start worrying. Penalties may not be ideal but at least they have some connection with the art of playing football. Yellow cards have absolutely no relation to the flow of a game. What on earth is wrong with having a replay? Make teams scared of drawing matches for a change.

The need is for a strong administration that can guide change along a desirable course. The rules of the game itself need little alteration, but the forces at work within it need controlling. Football has had many innovations – the World Cup, the European Cup, the Copa Libertadores, the African Cup of Nations to name but a few. All have on the whole added to football because they have not destroyed existing structures.

The most worrying potential innovation of them all, a European Superleague geared primarily for television audiences, would be a prime case of a new idea destroying an existing institution. For Milan to play full-time in a league other than the Italian league would signal the end of that venerable organisation. Milan and a few other clubs would be happy, but what about the rest? It has been said that Silvio Berlusconi, the Italian industrial magnate and owner of Milan, does not believe in the concept of national teams, only club football, and only a few clubs at that. Where does this leave us? Apparently nearly 125 years of international football means nothing to a man who stands to earn millions from a superleague through his television station.

What happens when people tire of seeing five games of football a week and the whole superleague breaks up because of overkill? The television stations will not give a damn and will move on to the next fad, and football will be left to pick up the pieces.

Kerry Packer, an Australian television magnate, tried the same thing with another game in the 1970s, with his 'World Series Cricket'. In this case it transformed a sport that had all but lost its way. Players and supporters alike ultimately benefited from his innovations. Football does not need the same shot in the arm. It is in a healthy enough condition as it is. The emphasis should be on gradual not revolutionary change as was the case with the Packer Revolution.

Ultimately the football supporter holds the trump card. Football just cannot do without them, and when they are threatened they have a powerful voice. Margaret Thatcher, the British Prime Minister during the 1980s, did not care for or understand the game. After the Bradford City fire and the Heysel riot she pounced on those she held responsible, the infamous English hooligans. An identity-card system was put forward by her government. In all her time in power she was only ever forced to retreat on one major issue, the identity-card scheme. By grouping together and forming a common bond, football supporters saw to it that the policy was never implemented.

Ironically, British football as a result has Margaret Thatcher to thank for the new spirit that prevails in the game, and it is a lead that may well need to be followed elsewhere in the future if the moguls have their way and football is threatened. United by a common cause, supporters can forget on-the-pitch rivalries to pose a powerful force against those who would seek to destroy an institution they cherish. Improbable though it may sound, football holds a grip on the emotions of millions of people that is both hard to define and unlike anything else in the world. Their loyalty is to the game, their club and their national side, not to a superleague or a television station.

HOW TO USE THIS BOOK

The results and tables in the book should not be too difficult to follow, though some areas need further explanation:

1 – Tables of match results.

Below I have listed as an example a section of the results for the 1992 Copa Libertadores.

Cerro Porteño — *Nacional* — *Defensor* — *Sol de America* — *Games played* — *Won* — *Drawn* — *Lost* — *Goals scored* — *Goals against* — *Points scored*

Group 5

	CP	Na	De	SA	Pl	W	D	L	F	A	Pts
Cerro Porteño	–	1–1	1–1	2–0	6	3	3	0	9	4	9
Nacional Mont'deo	0–0	–	1–0	2–2	6	2	3	1	9	7	6
Defensor	2–3	3–2	–	1–2	6	1	2	3	7	9	5
Sol de America	0–2	1–3	0–0	–	6	1	2	3	5	10	4

Final position of teams in the group

Home game for Defensor
Away game for Sol de America
Sol de America won 2–1

2 – Results of individual matches.

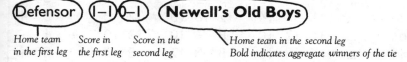

Defensor 1–1 0–1 **Newell's Old Boys**

Home team in the first leg — *Score in the first leg* — *Score in the second leg* — *Home team in the second leg. Bold indicates aggregate winners of the tie*

3 – Details of a particular match.

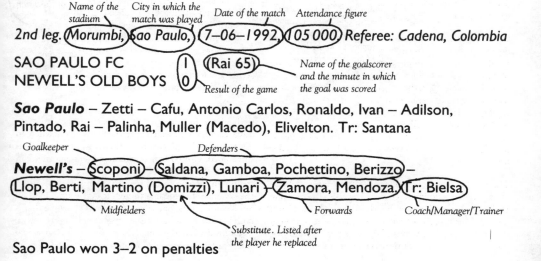

Name of the stadium — *City in which the match was played* — *Date of the match* — *Attendance figure*

2nd leg. *Morumbi, Sao Paulo, 7–06–1992, 105 000 Referee: Cadena, Colombia*

SAO PAULO FC 1 (Rai 65)
NEWELL'S OLD BOYS 0

Result of the game — *Name of the goalscorer and the minute in which the goal was scored*

Sao Paulo – Zetti – Cafu, Antonio Carlos, Ronaldo, Ivan – Adilson, Pintado, Rai – Palinha, Muller (Macedo), Elivelton. Tr: Santana

Goalkeeper — *Defenders*

Newell's – Scoponi – Saldana, Gamboa, Pochettino, Berizzo – Llop, Berti, Martino (Domizzi), Lunari – Zamora, Mendoza. Tr: Bielsa

Midfielders — *Forwards* — *Coach/Manager/Trainer*

Substitute. Listed after the player he replaced

Sao Paulo won 3–2 on penalties

4 – The international matches of each country. These two matches are taken from the list of international matches played by Bulgaria.

Competition. See list of abbreviations

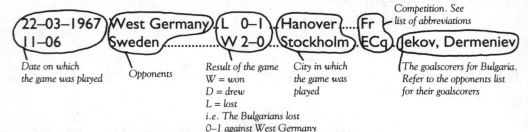

22–03–1967 West Germany ....L 0–1 ...Hanover .....Fr
11–06 Sweden ....W 2–0 ...Stockholm ...ECq ...Jekov, Dermeniev

Date on which the game was played

Opponents

Result of the game
W = won
D = drew
L = lost
i.e. The Bulgarians lost 0–1 against West Germany but beat the Swedes 2–0

City in which the game was played

The goalscorers for Bulgaria. Refer to the opponents list for their goalscorers

5 – The club medals table.

Combination of league championship, National Cup and European tournament totals

G = Number of wins in the championship
S = Number of second places
B = Number of third places

G = Number of Cup wins
S = Number of times losing cup finalists

	Team	All G	All S	All B	League G	League S	League B	Cup G	Cup S	Europe G	Europe S	Europe B
1	Real Madrid	49	35	13	25	13	6	16	17	8	5	7
2	Barcelona	41	31	14	12	18	10	22	8	7	5	4
3	Athletic Bilbao	31	17	10	8	6	10	23	10	–	1	–
4	Atlético Madrid	17	18	16	8	8	12	8	7	1	3	4
5	Valencia	12	14	5	4	5	5	5	8	3	1	–

Valencias 12 honours won consists of 4 league championship 5 Spanish Cup wins and 3 European triumphs (2 in the Fairs Cup & 1 in the Cup Winners Cup)

G = Number of European trophies won
S = Number of times losing finalists
B = Number of times losing semi-finalists

List Of Abbreviations

International Federations

FIFA .... Fédération Internationale de Football Association
International Federation of Association Football

UEFA .... Union Européenne de Football Association
European Union of Association Football

CONMEBOL .... Confederación Sudamericana de Fútbol
South American Football Confederation

CAF .... Confederation Africaine de Football
African Football Confederation

CONCACAF .... Confederación Norte-Centroamericano y del Caribe de Fútbol
North-Central American and Caribbean Football Confederation

AFC .... Asian Football Confederation

OFC .... Oceania Football Confederation

Europe

ALB .... Albania
AUT .... Austria
BEL .... Belgium
BUL .... Bulgaria
CYP .... Cyprus
DEN .... Denmark
ESP .... Spain
EST .... Estonia
FIN .... Finland
FRA .... France
FRG .... West Germany
GDR .... East Germany
GER .... Germany
GRE .... Greece
HOL .... Holland
HUN .... Hungary
IRE .... Republic of Ireland
ISL .... Iceland
ITA .... Italy
LAT .... Latvia
LIE .... Liechtenstein
LIT .... Lithuania
LUX .... Luxembourg
MLT .... Malta
NIR .... Northern Ireland
NOR .... Norway
POL .... Poland
POR .... Portugal
ROM .... Romania
SAN .... San Marino
SCO .... Scotland
SWE .... Sweden
SUI .... Switzerland
TCH .... Czechoslovakia
TUR .... Turkey
URS .... Soviet Union
WAL .... Wales
YUG .... Yugoslavia

South America

ARG .... Argentina
BOL .... Bolivia
BRA .... Brazil
CHI .... Chile
COL .... Colombia
ECU .... Ecuador
PAR .... Paraguay
PER .... Peru
URU .... Uruguay
VEN .... Venezuela

Africa

ALG .... Algeria
ANG .... Angola
BEN .... Benin
BFA .... Burkina Faso
BIS .... Guinea-Bissau
BOT .... Botswana
BUR .... Burundi
CAR .... Central African Republic
CVT .... Cape Verde
CHD .... Chad
CGO .... Congo
CIV .... Côte d'Ivoire
CMR .... Cameroon
EGY .... Egypt
EQG .... Equatorial Guinea
ETH .... Ethiopia
GAB .... Gabon
GAM .... Gambia
GHA .... Ghana
GUI .... Guinea
KEN .... Kenya
LES .... Lesotho
LBA .... Libya
LBR .... Liberia
MAD .... Madagascar
MAR .... Morocco
MAW .... Malawi
MLI .... Mali
MRT .... Mauritania
MRI .... Mauritius
MOZ .... Mozambique
NAM .... Namibia
NIG .... Niger
NGR .... Nigeria
RWA .... Rwanda
STM .... Sao Tome
SEN .... Senegal
SEY .... Seychelles
SLE .... Sierra Leone
SOM .... Somalia
SAF .... South Africa
SUD .... Sudan
SWZ .... Swaziland
TAN .... Tanzania
TOG .... Togo
TUN .... Tunisia
UGA .... Uganda
ZAI .... Zaire
ZAM .... Zambia

CONCACAF

ANT .... Antigua and Barbuda
ARU .... Aruba
BHM .... Bahamas
BAR .... Barbados
BEL .... Belize
BER .... Bermuda
CAN .... Canada
CAY .... Cayman Islands
CRC .... Costa Rica
CUB .... Cuba
DOM .... Dominican Republic
ELS .... El Salvador
GRE .... Grenada
GDP .... Guadeloupe
GUA .... Guatemala
GUY .... Guyana
HAI .... Haiti
HON .... Honduras
JAM .... Jamaica
MTQ .... Martinique
MEX .... Mexico

AHO .... Netherlands Antilles
NIC .... Nicaragua
PAN .... Panama
PUR .... Puerto Rico
STL .... St Lucia
STV .... St Vincent and the Grenadines
SUR .... Surinam
TRN .... Trinidad and Tobago
USA .... United States

Asia

AFG .... Afghanistan
ARS .... Saudi Arabia
BAH .... Bahrain
BAN .... Bangladesh
BRU .... Brunei
PRC .... China
TAI .... Chinese Taipei
HKG .... Hong Kong
INA .... Indonesia
IND .... India
IRN .... Iran
IRQ .... Iraq
ISR .... Israel
JAP .... Japan
JOR .... Jordan
CAM .... Kampuchea
KOR .... South Korea
KUW .... Kuwait
LAO .... Laos
LIB .... Lebanon
MAC .... Macao
MAL .... Malaysia
MLD .... Maldives
MYA .... Myanmar
NEP .... Nepal
NYM .... North Yemen
OMN .... Oman
PAK .... Pakistan
PHI .... Philippines
PRK .... North Korea
QAT .... Qatar
SIN .... Singapore
SRL .... Sri Lanka
SVM .... South Vietnam
SYM .... South Yemen
SYR .... Syria
THA .... Thailand
UAE .... United Arab Emirates
VIE .... Vietnam
YEM .... Yemen

Oceania

AUS .... Australia
FIJ .... Fiji
NZD .... New Zealand
PNG .... Papua New Guinea
SOL .... Solomon Islands
TAH .... French Polynesia 'Tahiti'
VAN .... Vanuatu
SAM .... Western Samoa

Competitions

Every international match can be assigned a category of competition. (The games listed for each country are commonly referred to as 'full internationals', in other words games where the strongest side took the field. Youth games, matches between second or 'B' teams and, in most cases, matches in the Olympic Games, are not listed. The various competitions that countries take part in are as follows:

WCq .... World Cup qualifying game
WCr1 .... World Cup Final Tournament – first round
WCr2 .... World Cup Final Tournament – second round
WCqf .... World Cup Final Tournament – quarter-final
WCsf .... World Cup Final Tournament – semi-final
WCf .... World Cup Final Tournament – final

The same system applies to the Olympic Games and European Championship
OGq .... Olympic Games qualifying game
OGr1 .... Olympic Games Final Tournament – first round etc
ECq .... European Championship qualifying game
ECr1 .... European Championship Final Tournament – first round etc

Other tournaments include

SC .... South American Championship – 1910–67
SCr1 .... South American Championship – first round etc, from 1975
PAC .... Pan American Championship
CC .... CONCACAF Championship
BG .... Bolivar Games
CG .... Central American and Caribbean Games
DGC .... Dr Gerö Cup
HC .... Home International (British) Championship
BC .... Balkan/Baltic Cup
BCE .... Balkan and Central European Championship
CI .... Copa Independencia do Brasil
ML .... Copa d'Oro (Mundialito)
AFT .... Artemo Cup
JNC .... Nehru Cup
KC .... Kirin Cup
TN .... Taça de Naçoes

South American Tournaments

LC .... Lipton Cup
NC .... Newton Cup
RC .... Roca Cup
CA .... Atlantic Cup
PC .... Pacific Cup
RBC .... Rio Branco Cup
RCB .... Rosa Chevallier Boutell Cup
JMC .... Juan Mignaburu Cup
HGC .... Hector Gomez Cup
MEA .... Argentine Ministry of Education Trophy
MEU .... Uruguayan Ministry of Education Trophy
RGP .... Roque Gomez Pena Cup
OCC .... Osvaldo Cruz Cup
SPC .... Saenz Peña Cup
AC .... Artigas Cup
MC .... Montevideo Cup
PDC .... Pinto Duran Cup (CHI/URU)
OHC .... O'Higgins Cup
RCC .... Ramon Castilla Cup
PDC .... Paz del Chaco Cup (BOL/PAR)

And last but certainly not least, the most common of them all

Fr .... A friendly match

THE WORLD

West Germany v Argentina, World Cup 1990

WORLD

The origin of the football we play today can be traced to a series of five meetings between 26 October and 8 December 1863. The first of these, the historic occasion at the Freemasons Tavern in London's Great Queen Street, was where the Football Association was formed and the initial set of rules drawn up. The split with rugby occurred in the last of the meetings as supporters of that code, led by the Blackheath club, withdrew, leaving the way free for the adoption of the first laws of Association Football.

The ancient origins of the game are more difficult to define, however, for kicking an object such as a stone on the ground is a natural thing to do. Exactly when this simple action of kicking was turned into a game involving more than one person has been the source of much study, and various ancient civilisations can lay claim to a game that resembles football.

The Ancient Chinese had a game called Tsu Chu, Tsu referring to the action of kicking, Chu to a stuffed ball of animal skin. Kemari was a Japanese game played at roughly the same time as Tsu Chu, nearly 3000 years ago. Its resemblance to modern-day football is strong – in pictures drawn of the game there are two bamboo posts which the players seem to be trying to kick the ball between.

The Romans and the Greeks also played ball games, the former playing a sport called Harpastum, the latter a sport called Episkyros. It has to be assumed that wherever the Greeks or Romans went they took the game with them and there is an argument that Harpastum is the origin of football in the British Isles.

Football of a kind was being played all around the world by the Middle Ages. William Fitzstephen in 1175 gives us the first account of 'the famous game of ball' on a Shrove Tuesday in London, a tradition that remains to this day in some parts of England.

Elsewhere, in Brittany there was a game called *la soule*, in Italy *giuoco del calcio fiorentino*, in Chile *pilimatun*, in Patagonia *tchoekah* whilst the eskimos are known to have played a game called *aqsaqtuk*.

It was in Britain, however, that these often chaotic games were transformed into a pastime more resembling the modern-day version, and this happened in the public schools of Victorian England. These aristocratic and very exclusive schools, there to educate the children of the English gentry, developed the game as a form of exercise.

Each school tended to have their own rules, and as pupils went on to university they found that they did not have any common rules to play by. In 1848 students at Cambridge, perplexed by all the different codes, drew up their own code and it is this that the rules of 1863 are loosely based on.

Football is now the most popular sport in the world due to a culmination of events. The Football Association in London helped spread the new game around Britain at a time when the country was in the midst of an industrial revolution. The rural population was moving into the cities and they needed a form of entertainment. Football was, to borrow one of its own clichés, in the right place at the right time.

Even more crucial, however, was the fact that Britain was an imperial power and was spreading its influence around the world. The tradesmen and workers who had learnt the game in the cities were in high demand around the world for their skills as other countries sought to industrialise. Thus the railway workers, engineers, clerks and business owners were responsible for the spread of the game to Europe, South America and elsewhere.

Perhaps most important was the fact that football is in essence a simple game and, unlike rugby or cricket, easy to learn. Only in the countries which the British colonised such as India, Australia, New Zealand and parts of Africa, especially South Africa, did they take to rugby or cricket because the British presence was much more imposing. Football remained a sport much more associated with the British merchant class than its ruling class.

The formation in 1904 of the Fédération Internationale de Football Association, or FIFA as it is more commonly known, was a recognition of the inroads the game had made around the world. FIFA is now one of the largest international bodies, having as it does, ten more members than the United Nations. Some even claim that it has done a better job than the United Nations in bringing the world closer together. In football terms, it has been instrumental in making the game the world's favourite pastime, not just through staging events like the World Cup but also through its coaching courses which are taken to every corner of the globe.

As football spread out of Great Britain at the turn of the century, the French in particular were quick to recognise the need for a controlling organisation in order that all countries played to the same rules, and so on 21 May 1904, representatives from Belgium, France, Holland, Denmark, Spain, Sweden and Switzerland met in Paris and founded FIFA. None of the four British Associations were present, being somewhat sceptical of the level of football in these countries compared to that at home.

At the outset, FIFA's tasks were somewhat limited. In particular, it did not control the law-making process, and technically it still does not. This is left to the International Football Association Board, a strange body made up of 20 seats, 16 of which are reserved permanently for the four British Associations. The four remaining seats are filled by election for a fixed term from amongst other FIFA members.

As FIFA's membership has grown, so have its responsibilities. From being an organisation representing a small corner of Europe, with responsibilities amounting to the organisation of the Olympic Games football tournament, it is now a worldwide body with many different powers. These range from the control of the movement of players and administering referees to the organisation of various tournaments at both senior and youth level, as well as administering a range of Standing Committees that look into topics as diverse as sports medicine and proposed changes in the laws of the game.

By the beginning of the Second World War, membership had grown to just over 50 countries, the bulk of whom were from either Europe or South America. After 1945 however, as the shackles of colonialism were thrown off by the countries of Asia and Africa, membership began to rise dramatically and by 1966 it had reached 130.

The leadership of FIFA mirrored this shifting trend. Stanley Rous, president from 1961 to 1974, had come to represent the old world, and although a very capable administrator and a man who devoted his life to spreading the game worldwide, he was eventually undone by those forces he helped unleash. In 1974, Joao Havelange was elected under the banner of change, with the backing of the African and Asian countries. FIFA is now a more overtly commercial organisation, and the 'New World' has become an integral part of the organisation, where once it was marginalised.

In the early 1950s, FIFA sanctioned the formation of continental football confederations for countries within defined geographical zones, and these have also helped increase the profile of the less well-established nations of the world, as well as providing a vehicle through which FIFA's policies can be implemented.

The 'parliament' of FIFA is its biennial congress, held at the venue of either the World Cup or Olympic Games. Issues are decided here on a one vote per country basis, irrespective of size or population. A three-fourths majority must be obtained in each vote. It is FIFA's intention to remain politically neutral, and given the turmoil of the 20th century, she has coped admirably.

The major problems for FIFA have been Israel and China. The Asian Football Confederation has been the most overtly political of the regional confederations. In 1976 both Israel and Taiwan were expelled 'with regret', but they were felt to be holding up progress. Israel's presence was causing a rift with the Arab nations who were starting to join the AFC in the 1970s, whilst Taiwan's membership meant the exclusion of China.

FIFA was not in favour of expelling either, but was very keen to include China in its membership, containing as it did one quarter of the world's population, and so no action was taken against the AFC, leaving Taiwan and Israel to fend for themselves – Taiwan is now back in the AFC and Israel has found what it hopes will be a permanent home in Europe.

South Africa and the former Rhodesia proved to be another thorn in FIFA's side; both were eventually expelled in the early 1970s for contravening FIFA's anti-discrimination code.

FIFA is best known for the World Cup, the final tournament of which is held every four years in a designated country. It is open to every member of FIFA to participate, but despite this, not every country does enter. Many of the smaller nations prefer to take part in the Olympic Games or in FIFA's two junior tournaments. Part of the problem may be the fact that although African, Asian and Central American nations are afforded seven places in the final tournament of the World Cup, these three continents have 112 members between them. The qualifying competition is therefore a long process with, for many, very little prospect of reward at the end of it.

The unequal distribution of places does not occur in the Under-17 championship. Europe is restricted to just three entries, as are Africa, Asia and Central America, and it is worth noting that given equal opportunity, Africa has won two tournaments to Europe's one.

The two junior championships and the World Cup for Women are indicative of the attempt since the 1970s to spread football to parts of the world where the game is less established. Tournaments have been staged in locations as diverse as China and Saudi Arabia, though when the World Cup itself will be staged in an African or Asian country is open to conjecture.

THE WORLD GOVERNING BODY

FÉDÉRATION INTERNATIONALE DE FOOTBALL ASSOCIATION
FIFA House, PO Box 85, Hitzigweg 11, CH-8030 Zürich, Switzerland
Tel: (010 41) 1 3849595 Fax: (010 41) 1 3849696
Telex: 817240 FIF CH

Year of formation: 1904

PRESIDENTS OF FIFA: 7

Robert Guérin	France	1904–06
Daniel Woolfall	England	1906–18
Jules Rimet	France	1921–54
Rodolphe Seeldrayers	Belgium	1954–55
Arthur Drewry	England	1956–61
Stanley Rous	England	1961–74
Joao Havelange	Brazil	1974–

MEMBERS: 179

Afghanistan – Albania – Algeria – Angola – Antigua and Barbuda – Argentina – Armenia – Aruba – Australia – Austria – Bahamas – Bahrain – Bangladesh – Barbados – Belgium – Belize – Belorussia – Benin – Bermuda – Bolivia – Botswana – Brazil – Brunei – Bulgaria – Burkina Faso – Burundi – Cameroon – Canada – Cape Verde Islands – Cayman Islands – Central African Republic – Chad – Chile – China – Chinese Taipei – Colombia – Congo – Costa Rica – Cote d'Ivoire – Croatia – Cuba – Cyprus – Czechoslovakia – Denmark – Dominican Republic – Ecuador – Egypt – El Salvador – England – Equatorial Guinea – Estonia – Ethiopia – Faeroe Islands – Fiji – Finland – France – French Polynesia 'Tahiti' – Gabon – Gambia – Georgia – Germany – Ghana – Greece – Grenada – Guatemala – Guinea – Guinea-Bissau – Guyana – Haiti – Honduras – Hong Kong – Hungary – Iceland – India – Indonesia – Iran – Iraq – Northern Ireland – Republic of Ireland – Israel – Italy – Jamaica – Japan – Jordan – Kampuchea – Kenya – North Korea – South Korea – Kuwait – Laos – Latvia – Lebanon – Lesotho – Liberia – Libya – Liechtenstein – Lithuania – Luxembourg – Macao – Madagascar – Malawi – Malaysia – Maldives – Mali – Malta – Mauritania – Mauritius – Mexico – Morocco – Mozambique – Myanmar – Namibia – Nepal – Netherlands – Netherlands Antilles – New Zealand – Nicaragua – Niger – Nigeria – Norway – Oman – Pakistan – Panama – Papua New Guinea – Paraguay – Peru – Philippines – Poland – Portugal – Puerto Rico – Qatar – Romania – Russia – Rwanda – Saint Kitts and Nevis – Saint Lucia – Saint Vincent and the Grenadines – San Marino – Sao Tomé e Principe – Saudi Arabia – Scotland – Senegal – Seychelles – Sierra Leone – Singapore – Slovenia – Solomon Islands – Somalia – South Africa – Spain – Sri Lanka – Sudan – Surinam – Swaziland – Sweden – Switzerland – Syria – Tanzania – Thailand – Togo – Trinidad and Tobago – Tunisia – Turkey – Uganda – Ukraine – United Arab Emirates – United States of America – Uruguay – Vanuatu – Venezuela – Vietnam – Wales – Western Samoa – Yemen – Yugoslavia – Zaire – Zambia – Zimbabwe

NON-MEMBERS: 44

American Samoa – Andorra – Anguilla – Bhutan – British Virgin Islands – Christmas Island – Cocos Islands – Comoros – Cook Islands – Djibouti – Dominica – Falkland Islands – French Guiana – Gibraltar – Greenland – Guadeloupe – Guam – Guernsey – Isle of Man – Jersey – Kiribati – Marshall Islands – Martinique – Mayotte – Micronesia – Monaco – Mongolia – Montserrat – Nauru – New Caledonia – Niue – Norfolk Island – Northern Marianas – Palau – Pitcairn Island – Réunion – Saint Helena – Saint Pierre and Miquelon – Tokelau – Tonga – Turks and Caicos Islands – Tuvalu – Virgin Islands of the U.S. – Wallis and Fotuna

WORLD FOOTBALLER OF THE YEAR

From World Soccer

1982

				%
1	Paolo Rossi	Juventus	ITA	23
2	Karl-Heinz Rummenigge	Bayern München	FRG	14
3	Falcao	Roma	BRA	12
4	Zico	Flamengo	BRA	10
5	Socrates	Corinthians	BRA	9
6	Dino Zoff	Juventus	ITA	6
7	Bruno Conti	Roma	ITA	4
8	Johan Cruyff	Ajax	HOL	3
9	Gaetano Scirea	Juventus	ITA	3
10	Zbigniew Boniek	Juventus	POL	2

1983

				%
1	Zico	Udinese	BRA	28
2	Michel Platini	Juventus	FRA	24
3	Falcao	Roma	BRA	18
4	Diego Maradona	Barcelona	ARG	6
5	Karl-Heinz Rummenigge	Bayern München	FRG	4
6	Kenny Dalglish	Liverpool	SCO	3
7	Felix Magath	Hamburger SV	FRG	3
8	Bryan Robson	Manchester United	ENG	3
9	Charlie Nicholas	Arsenal	SCO	2
10	Erwin Vandenbergh	RSC Anderlecht	BEL	2

1984

				%
1	Michel Platini	Juventus	FRA	54
2	Ian Rush	Liverpool	WAL	9
3	Zico	Udinese	BRA	7
4	Fernando Chalana	Bordeaux	POR	5
5	Jean Tigana	Bordeaux	FRA	2
6	Morten Olsen	RSC Anderlecht	DEN	2
7	Renato	Gremio	BRA	1
8	Paolo Rossi	Juventus	ITA	1
9	Graeme Souness	Sampdoria	SCO	1
10	Bryan Robson	Manchester United	ENG	1

1985

				%
1	Michel Platini	Juventus	FRA	20
2	Preben Elkjaer-Larsen	Verona	DEN	11
3	Diego Maradona	Napoli	ARG	7
4	Peter Reid	Everton	ENG	6
5	Bernd Schuster	Barcelona	FRG	5
6	Rudi Voller	Werder Bremen	FRG	4
7	Neville Southall	Everton	WAL	3
8	Hans-Peter Briegel	Verona	FRG	3
9	Karl-Heinz Rummenigge	Internazionale	FRG	3
10	Andy Gray	Everton	SCO	2

1986

				%
1	Diego Maradona	Napoli	ARG	35
2	Igor Belanov	Dynamo Kiev	URS	6
3	Gary Lineker	Barcelona	ENG	5
4	Emilio Butragueño	Real Madrid	ESP	4
5	Jan Ceulemans	Club Brugge	BEL	4
6	Michael Laudrup	Juventus	DEN	4
7	Preben Elkjaer-Larsen	Verona	DEN	3
8	Careca	Sao Paulo FC	BRA	3
9	Jean-Marie Pfaff	Bayern München	BEL	3
10	Jorge Burruchaga	Nantes	ARG	3

1987

				%
1	Ruud Gullit	Milan	HOL	38
2	Diego Maradona	Napoli	ARG	13
3	Marco Van Basten	Milan	HOL	8
4	Emilio Butragueño	Real Madrid	ESP	6
5	Paulo Futre	Atlético Madrid	POR	5
6	Ian Rush	Juventus	WAL	3
7	Gary Lineker	Barcelona	ENG	3
8	Hugo Sanchez	Real Madrid	MEX	2
9	Michel Platini	Juventus	FRA	1
10	Rabah Madjer	FC Porto	ALG	1

1988

				%
1	Marco Van Basten	Milan	HOL	43
2	Ruud Gullit	Milan	HOL	21
3	Frank Rijkaard	Milan	HOL	7

4	Ronald Koeman	PSV Eindhoven	HOL	6
5	Alexei Mikhailichenko	Dynamo Kiev	URS	5
6	Diego Maradona	Napoli	ARG	2
7	Gianluca Vialli	Sampdoria	ITA	2
8	Alexander Zavarov	Juventus	URS	2
9	John Barnes	Liverpool	ENG	2
10	Romario	PSV Eindhoven	BRA	1

1989				%
1	Ruud Gullit	Milan	HOL	24
2	Marco Van Basten	Milan	HOL	18
3	Bebeto	Flamengo	BRA	10
4	Diego Maradona	Napoli	ARG	7
5	Franco Baresi	Milan	ITA	6
6	Peter Shilton	Derby County	ENG	6
7	Romario	PSV Eindhoven	ITA	5
8	Michael Laudrup	Barcelona	DEN	4
9	Lothar Matthäus	Internazionale	FRG	3
10	Ruben Sosa	Lazio	URU	2

1990				%
1	Lothar Matthäus	Internazionale	FRG	21
2	Salvatore Schillaci	Juventus	ITA	12
3	Diego Maradona	Napoli	ARG	6
4	Jurgen Klinsmann	Internazionale	FRG	6
5	Paul Gascoigne	Tottenham Hotspur	ENG	5
6	Roberto Baggio	Juventus	ITA	5
7	Andreas Brehme	Internazionale	FRG	5
8	Roger Milla		CMR	4
9	Franco Baresi	Milan	ITA	4
10	John Barnes	Liverpool	ENG	4

1991				%
1	Jean-Pierre Papin	Olympique Marseille	FRA	25
2	Robert Prosinecki	Real Madrid	YUG	15
3	Darko Pancev	Crvena Zvezda Beograd	YUG	13
4	Mark Hughes	Manchester United	ENG	8
5	Lothar Matthäus	Internazionale	GER	6
6	Gianluca Vialli	Sampdoria	ITA	5
7	Gabriel Batistuta	Boca Juniors	ARG	4
8	Sergio Goycochea	Brest	ARG	4
9	Stuart Pearce	Nottingham Forest	ENG	3
10	Gary Lineker	Tottenham Hotspur	ENG	3

THE WORLD CUP

The World Cup is the pre-eminent tournament not only in football but perhaps in all sports. Only the Olympic Games can rival it for prestige and spectator interest. The final of each tournament reaches a worldwide audience, through television, of hundreds of millions in every corner of the globe.

The idea of a World Cup, mooted as early as 1904 when FIFA was formed, was 26 years in the making. With amateurism dominant in all but a select few countries, the football tournament of the Olympic Games was in most people's eyes the world championship of football, and this held true right up until the first World Cup was played.

The winners of the Olympic Tournament were regarded as World Champions, and with the possible exception of Belgium in 1920, the winners deserved that honour. Without doubt England were the pre-eminent world power prior to 1914, and they duly won the 1908 and 1912 Olympic titles. In the 1920s Uruguay twice won the Olympic title, and as if to prove a point, she won the very first World Cup, thus officially confirming her world superiority.

After the First World War, amateurism as the dominant concept in football was increasingly under threat. Countries such as Czechoslovakia in 1925 and Austria and Hungary in 1926, all major football powers at the time, introduced professionalism and therefore could no longer send their full international sides to the Olympics. There were also doubts as to the true amateur nature of the South American entrants, and the issue of 'shamateurism' did much to damage the credibility of the tournament.

By the time of the 1928 FIFA congress in Amsterdam, Jules Rimet, the president of FIFA, knew that more countries would soon follow the example of Czechoslovakia, Austria and Hungary, and so along with Henri Delaunay, the general-secretary of the French Football Federation, he moved a motion that FIFA should organise a quadrennial championship, open to anyone, and this was passed by 25 votes to 5. Hugo Meisl along with Delaunay, Bonnet and Linnemann drew up the regulations and set about organising the first tournament. The French sculptor, Albert Lafleur, was commissioned to design a trophy, and the venue of the first tournament was decided upon at the 1929 FIFA congress in Barcelona.

Italy, Spain, Holland and Sweden all applied for the right to stage the tournament. Uruguay, however, were chosen ahead of the European quartet – they offered to pay everyone's travel and accommodation expenses, they were the current Olympic champions, and 1930, the date set for the tournament, would mark Uruguay's centenary as an independent nation.

In retrospect, the decision seems to have been a mistake. One by one the European nations withdrew citing domestic commitments and the long journey time as their reasons. When the tournament opened only four remained, and they were not considered to be amongst the strongest on the continent. None of the powerful central Europeans were represented, nor were the British.

Only France, Yugoslavia, Belgium and Romania made the journey, and they were joined by nine countries from the Americas. Of the South American contingent Uruguay, the hosts, were overwhelming favourites to reach the final along with Argentina. Brazil had not yet developed into the powerhouse that it would later become, whilst the other South Americans, Paraguay and Chile apart, had played little competitive football.

Uruguay had struggled to build a brand new stadium for the championships, and as the tournament got underway, the 93 000 capacity Centenary Stadium was not completely finished. The first match, however, was not scheduled to be played there, but in Penarol's Pocitos stadium, where on 13 July 1930 a crowd of 1000 turned up to see France defeat Mexico 4–1.

The 13 nations were divided into four groups, and the four winners of each of these would advance to the semi-finals. This combination of a league and cup format was decided upon when it was realised that due to the withdrawals, a wholly knock-out system was not possible. A precedent had been set that was to shape the pattern of future World Cups.

In the event the semi-final line-up was a surprising one. Despite their opening win, the French did not make it past the first round, due mainly to a problem that would plague the entire history of the World Cup: bad refereeing decisions. After falling behind to an 81st minute goal in their next match, against Argentina, they seemed certain to score through Langiller only for the Brazilian referee to blow for full time some six minutes early! Realising his mistake, he restarted the game, but by then it was too late for the French. A defeat by Chile in their next game in a near-empty Centenary Stadium saw them sail for home unrewarded.

Argentina, after their good fortune against France, qualified with some ease for the last four. Playing a blend of rugged and skilful football, they cruised past the Mexicans, winning 6–3 having been 5–1 up, and beat Chile 3–1 in the crucial last game of the group. Before only 1000 supporters in the Centenary Stadium, Guillermo Stabile, the goalscoring sensation of the tournament, scored twice in the first 14 minutes to effectively seal the match.

The attendances were no better in Group 2. Only 800 turned up at Central Park, home of Nacional, to see Yugoslavia beat the Bolivians who were clearly out of their depth. Yugoslavia qualified after winning 2-1 against the Brazilians in the first game of the group. Both were relatively inexperienced sides, but Brazil were the seeded side in the group and had been expected to win.

Group 3 did not produce any surprises. By 18 July the Centenary Stadium was ready for use and 70 000 turned up for its inauguration on Independence day to witness a difficult 1–0 victory for the Uruguayans over Peru, who had already lost to Romania. The deciding game of the group was played four days later before a crowd of 80 000 and by half-time, playing what was to be regarded as the best football of the whole tournament, the Uruguayans had swept the Romanians aside scoring four goals without reply.

The semi-final line-up was completed by the real surprise of the tournament, the United States. In perhaps the first case of a World Cup side containing foreign nationals to boost its chances, the United States team seemed almost to be a 'Scottish XI' as the names of players like McGhee, Gallacher and Auld will testify. Belgium were easily disposed of in their first game, as were Paraguay in the second.

The semi-finals were both well-attended and one-sided affairs, and the results meant that the final would be a repeat of the 1928 Olympic Games. Argentina defeated the Americans 6–1 in the first of the games, but their tactics were not to everybody's liking: Raphael Tracy, the American centre-half, had his leg broken after 10 minutes. Only 1–0 down at half-time, the United States collapsed in the second half in the face of some scintillating football from the Argentines.

Uruguay, on the other hand, had a much tougher game against Yugoslavia who scored first, were unlucky to have a goal disallowed when 2–1 down, and conceded their third after the ball had seemingly gone out of play. Like the Americans however, they collapsed in the second half. It was to become a familiar sight: the Yugoslavs so close to winning a tournament but falling just short of the finishing post.

The final could have gone either way. The two teams were very familiar with each other, playing as they had more times against each other than even England and Scotland had managed. Uruguay were the Olympic champions, but Argentina were the current South American champions. Home advantage in the end swayed the tie. Boats had been hired by large numbers of Argentines to take them the short trip across the River Plate from Buenos Aires to Montevideo, but the majority of fans in the Centenary Stadium were Uruguayans.

Despite the encouragement given to the home team, Argentina had the better of the first half and they led 2-1 at half time, though Stabile's goal after 37 minutes should have been disallowed for offside. The second half was a different story. Playing the type of football that had made them famous in Europe, Uruguay broke down the Argentine defence three times to steal a victory and Jose Nasazzi became the first captain to lift sport's most coveted trophy.

THE FIRST WORLD CUP

Held in Uruguay, 13th–30th July 1930

FIRST ROUND

Group 1 (Pocitos, Central Park, Centenario – Montevideo)

	Ar	Ch	Fr	Me	Pl	W	D	L	F	A	Pts
ARGENTINA	–	3–1	1–0	6–3	3	3	0	0	10	4	6
CHILE	–	–	1–0	3–0	3	2	0	1	5	3	4
FRANCE	–	–	–	4–1	3	1	0	2	4	3	2
MEXICO	–	–	–	–	3	0	0	3	4	13	0

Group 2 (Central Park, Centenario – Montevideo)

	Yu	Br	Bo	Pl	W	D	L	F	A	Pts
YUGOSLAVIA	–	2–1	4–0	2	2	0	0	6	1	4
BRAZIL	–	–	4–0	2	1	0	1	5	2	2
BOLIVIA	–	–	–	2	0	0	2	0	8	0

Group 3 (Pocitos, Centenario – Montevideo)

	Ur	Ro	Pe	Pl	W	D	L	F	A	Pts
URUGUAY	–	4–0	1–0	2	2	0	0	5	0	4
ROMANIA	–	–	3–1	2	1	0	1	3	5	2
PERU	–	–	–	2	0	0	2	1	4	0

Group 4 (Central Park, Centenario – Montevideo)

	US	Pa	Be	Pl	W	D	L	F	A	Pts
UNITED STATES	–	3–0	3–0	2	2	0	0	6	0	4
PARAGUAY	–	–	1–0	2	1	0	1	1	3	2
BELGIUM	–	–	–	2	0	0	2	0	4	0

SEMI-FINALS

Centenario, Montevideo, 26–07–1930, 80 000

ARGENTINA	6	(Monti 20, Scopelli 56, Stábile 69 87, Peucelle 80 85)
UNITED STATES	1	(Brown 88)

Centenario, Montevideo, 27–07–1930, 93 000

URUGUAY	6	(Cea 18 67 72, Anselmo 20 31, Iriarte 60)
YUGOSLAVIA	1	(Sekulic 4)

FINAL

Centenario, Montevideo, 30–07–1930, 93 000

URUGUAY	4	(Dorado 12, Cea 58, Iriarte 68, Castro 89)
ARGENTINA	2	(Peucelle 20, Stábile 37)

Referee: Langenus, Belgium

Uruguay – Ballesteros – Nasazzi, Mascheroni – Andrade J, Fernández, Gestido – Dorado, Scarone, Castro, Cea, Iriarte

Argentina – Botasso – Della Torre, Paternóster – Evaristo J, Monti, Suárez – Peucelle, Varallo, Stábile, Ferreira, Evaristo M

Top scorers: Guillermo Stábile, Argentina 8
Pedro Cea, Uruguay 5
Guillermo Subiabre, Chile 4

Total goals scored: 70
Average per game: 3.9

1934

Italy was chosen as host for the 1934 competition at FIFA's 1932 congress in Stockholm. Again it was a strange choice of venue. If Montevideo had been too far away for most of the European nations, Italy posed another problem. Like all dictators, Mussolini was always on the lookout for a propaganda opportunity, and the World Cup provided him with the perfect vehicle.

FIFA's insistence that the World Cup was too big for one city alone swung the balance in favour of Italy. The Italian government offered to foot what promised to be a hefty bill. The political motives of the Italian government seemed to be a small price to pay for an efficient and well-run tournament. Mussolini was not to be disappointed either. Fortunately for him Italy were at the height of their powers: between June 1930 and May 1948 they lost only one match played on home soil, and during the 1930s only seven altogether. It seemed predestined that Italy would win, and they did.

Home advantage was not Italy's sole advantage. Uruguay, still upset that so few Europeans had bothered to come to her tournament, refused to take part thus robbing the tournament of the defending champions. The losing finalists in 1930, Argentina, weakened the line-up further by sending a virtual 'C' team, in response to the Italians poaching three of their best players, Monti, Orsi and Guaita. Monti had even played in the 1930 final for Argentina. This time he would go one better and win in the final for Italy. Vittorio Pozzo, Italy's trainer, justified their inclusion on the grounds that they were of Italian ancestry, but Argentina were quite naturally unimpressed. They did not want to risk losing their best players to the Italian game so they simply were not sent.

The British were again not present. It is possible that either England or Scotland would have won the tournament, but both had suffered losses against Continental sides. Two weeks before the World Cup began England lost to both Hungary and Czechoslovakia in Budapest and Prague respectively, whilst Scotland, on their last trip to the continent in 1931, had lost 5–0 to the Austrians and 3–0 to the Italians.

Stockholm saw the first World Cup game played on European soil. On 11 June 1933 Sweden kicked off the World Cup qualifiers with a convincing 6–2 win over Estonia. Because the number of entrants was 31, qualifying rounds were needed to reduce the number of teams to 16 for the final tournament which was to be played on a purely knock-out basis. There were few surprises in the qualifying rounds except Yugoslavia's elimination at the hands of Switzerland and Romania. This meant that two of the 1930 semi-finalists were not represented in Italy. March 16th 1934 was also an historic date as Egypt met Palestine in the first World Cup match to be played on African soil, whilst the return in Tel Aviv three weeks later saw the first on Asian soil.

On 27 May 1934 the final tournament got underway, and all of the first round games were completed. After one day of competition there were no American representatives left. Argentina, Brazil and the USA all left for home, the first two having played just one match in the whole competition, their opponents in their qualifying groups having withdrawn. The USA had at least played two games in Italy. Apart from their defeat by the hosts in the first round, they had played a qualifying game against Mexico in Rome three days before the tournament started. Mexico had therefore made the trip across the Atlantic only to be denied the opportunity to play in the competition proper.

The quarter-finals were played three days after the first round, and the hosts were lucky to qualify for the semi-finals. Having gone a goal behind to Spain, their equaliser seemed to have an element of foul play about it, as did most of the Italian play. In the replay the following day, Spain were forced to make seven changes due to injury and unsurprisingly lost 1–0, their cause again not being helped by a referee who seemed to favour the Italians.

The most intriguing tie of the round was that between Austria and Hungary. Both teams would have graced the final, but it was the Austrian 'Wunderteam' who stole the honours. In the previous three years, they had lost only to England and Czechoslovakia and were many people's favourites to win the title. The best game of the round, however, was Czechoslovakia's 3–2 win over Switzerland, the result of which was in doubt right until the final whistle.

The semi-finals pitted Italy against Austria and Czechoslovakia against Germany. The Italians had their Argentine forward Guaita to thank for their victory over the Austrians. Despite heavy pressure, Austria could not level his 19th minute goal. Italy were playing their third game in four days and were not expected to win, but win they did in front of a delighted Mussolini.

At the same time in Rome before a small crowd, Czechoslovakia were having little trouble in disposing of the Germans who could not match their skill or the goalscoring prowess of Oldrich Nejedly who scored a hat-trick. The final between Italy and Czechoslovakia was not played until a week later, but in the meantime that most dubious of fixtures, the third place play-off was used for the first time in a tournament. The Austrians did not have the heart for the game, a feature that has blighted so many of them since. Certainly the public of Naples could see little point in the game as only 7000 bothered to turn up to see the Germans win 3–2.

For the final, Italy, with the crowd behind them and the great tactical awareness of Pozzo binding together some talented individuals, were slight favourites. In the event they almost lost. The Czechs had played and beaten the Italians often enough before not to be intimidated, and when they took the lead 20 minutes from time it looked all over for the Italians. Both Svoboda and Sobotka could have sealed the match shortly after, the latter hitting the post, but after 82 minutes Italy were again saved by an Argentinian. Orsi scored a freakish goal with a shot that he tried to repeat the following day for photographers but couldn't. The match turned against the Czechs and in extra-time Schiavio scored the winner.

Stamina had in the end been the telling factor. The Italian captain, their goalkeeper Giampiero Combi, gratefully received the cup from an admiring Mussolini. All was well with Fascism it seemed. Two years later this myth would be further reinforced when it was Hitler's turn to host a propaganda event, the 1936 Berlin Olympics. Privately most wondered how good the Italians really were and if they would have won the tournament anywhere else and without their Argentine imports who had played so crucial a role.

THE SECOND WORLD CUP

11th June 1933–10th May 1934

QUALIFYING TOURNAMENT

Group 1

First round
Haiti .... 1–3 0–6 1–1 .. Cuba

Second round
Mexico .... 3–2 5–0 4–1 .. Cuba

Third round
UNITED STATES .... 4–2 ...... Mexico

Group 2

BRAZIL qualified as Peru withdrew

Group 3

ARGENTINA qualified as Chile withdrew

Group 4

EGYPT .... 7–1 4–1 ...... Palestine

Group 5

	Sd	Li	Es	Pl	W	D	L	F	A	Pts
SWEDEN	–	–	6–2	2	2	0	0	8	2	4
LITHUANIA	0–2	–	–	1	0	0	1	0	2	0
ESTONIA	–	–	–	1	0	0	1	2	6	0

Group 6

SPAIN .... 9–0 2–1 .... Portugal

Group 7

ITALY .... 4–0 .... Greece

Group 8

	Hu	Au	Bu	Pl	W	D	L	F	A	Pts
HUNGARY	–	–	4–1	2	2	0	0	8	2	4
AUSTRIA	–	–	6–1	1	1	0	0	6	1	2
BULGARIA	1–4	–	–	3	0	0	3	3	14	0

Group 9

Poland .... 1–2 0–2 .... CZECHOSLOVAKIA

Group 10

	Sz	Ro	Yu	Pl	W	D	L	F	A	Pts
SWITZERLAND	–	2–0*	–	2	1	1	0	4	2	3
ROMANIA	–	–	2–1	2	1	0	1	2	3	2
YUGOSLAVIA	2–2	–	–	2	0	1	1	3	4	1

* Awarded to Switzerland 2–0 after the game had ended 2–2

Group 11

	Ho	Be	RI	Pl	W	D	L	F	A	Pts
HOLLAND	–	–	5–2	2	2	0	0	9	4	4
BELGIUM	2–4	–	–	2	0	1	1	6	8	1
REP. IRELAND	–	4–4	–	2	0	1	1	6	9	1

Group 12

	Ge	Fr	Lu	Pl	W	D	L	F	A	Pts
GERMANY	–	–	–	1	1	0	0	9	1	2
FRANCE	–	–	–	1	1	0	0	6	1	2
LUXEMBOURG	1–9	1–6	–	2	0	0	2	2	15	0

FINAL TOURNAMENT

Held in Italy 27th May – 10th June 1934

FIRST ROUND

ITALY .... 7–1 ...... UNITED STATES *(PNF – Rome)*
SPAIN .... 3–1 ...... BRAZIL *(Luigi Ferraris – Genoa)*
HUNGARY .... 4–2 ...... EGYPT *(Ascarelli – Naples)*
AUSTRIA .... 3–2 ...... FRANCE *(Mussolini – Turin)*
GERMANY .... 5–2 ...... BELGIUM *(Giovanni Berta – Florence)*
SWEDEN .... 3–2 ...... ARGENTINA *(Littoriale – Bologna)*
SWITZERLAND .... 3–2 ...... HOLLAND *(San Siro – Milan)*
CZECHOSLOVAKIA ..... 2–1 ...... ROMANIA *(Littorio – Trieste)*

QUARTER-FINALS

Giovanni Berta, Florence, 31–05–1934, 35 000
ITALY 1 (Ferrari 47)
SPAIN 1 (Regueiro 31)

Replay: Giovanni Berta, Florence, 1–06–1934, 43 000
ITALY 1 (Meazza 12)
SPAIN 0

Littoriale, Bologna, 31–05–1934
AUSTRIA 2 (Horvath 5, Zischek 53)
HUNGARY 1 (Sárosi 67)

San Siro, Milan, 31–05–1934, 3000
GERMANY 2 (Hohmann 60 63)
SWEDEN 1 (Dunker 83)

Mussolini, Turin, 31–05–1934
CZECHOSLOVAKIA 3 (Svoboda 24, Sobotka 49, Nejedly 83)
SWITZERLAND 2 (Kielholz 18, Abegglen A 71)

SEMI-FINALS

San Siro, Milan, 3–06–1934, 60 000
ITALY 1 (Guaita 19)
AUSTRIA 0

PNF, Rome, 3–06–1934, 10 000
CZECHOSLOVAKIA 3 (Nejedly 21 60 81)
GERMANY 1 (Noack 50)

3RD PLACE

Ascarelli, Naples, 7–06–1934, 7000
GERMANY 3 (Lehner 1 42, Conen 29)
AUSTRIA 2 (Horvath 30, Sesta 55)

FINAL

PNF, Rome, 10–06–1934, 55 000
ITALY 2 (Orsi 81, Schiavio 95)
CZECHOSLOVAKIA 1 (Puc 71)
Referee: Eklind, Sweden
Italy – Combi – Monzeglio, Allemandi – Ferraris IV, Monti, Bertolini – Guaita, Meazza, Schiavio, Ferrari, Orsi. Tr: Pozzo
Czechoslovakia – Plánicka – Zenisek, Ctyroky – Kostálek, Cambal, Krcil – Junek, Svoboda, Sobotka, Nejedly, Puc. Tr: Petru

Top scorers: Oldrich Nejedly, Czechoslovakia 5
Angelo Schiavio, Italy 4
Edmund Conen, Germany 4
Total goals scored: 70
Average per game: 4.1

1938

The practice of alternating the World Cup between South America and Europe was broken at the 1936 FIFA congress in Berlin. Both Argentina and France had applied to host the next event. The Argentines were upset that the French were chosen and it would be another 20 years before they entered a team. With some justification they felt that Europe had let them down again. If nothing else, however, awarding the World Cup to France was a tacit recognition of their services to the competition.

The tournament was not, however, trouble free, held as it was under the shadow of war. The Spanish Civil War was at its height, Italy had invaded Abyssinia, whilst the Germans had marched into and taken the Rhineland and Austria. Austria had even qualified for the final tournament but was now no longer a separate country. They were withdrawn and as a result Sweden received a bye in the first round. The tournament also proved to be the most unrepresentative of all the World Cups ever held. Only three non-European countries entered. Two of them, Cuba and the Dutch East Indies, had no football heritage whatsoever. Only Brazil were serious contenders. Missing again were the 1930 champions Uruguay, as well as the British quartet who despite pleas from FIFA still would not enter.

Sweden once more got the qualifying tournament underway in Stockholm, this time beating the Finns 4–0. Again, the only surprise of the qualifiers was the elimination of the Yugoslavs, at the hands of Poland. Not surprisingly, no qualifying games were needed outside Europe and so after the shortest qualifying tournament in the history of the World Cup, the 16 teams gathered in France at the beginning of June 1938.

Once again the Fascist states were confident of victory, through either Germany or Italy. The Germans were involved in the opening game on 4 June but were outplayed by the Swiss who were unlucky not to win at the first attempt. Despite the presence in the German team of the best Austrians, Germany put in their worst World Cup performance to date in the replay, where they were beaten 4–2. In a round full of shocks and surprises, Cuba's 2–1 victory over Romania after a 3–3 draw was perhaps the biggest.

The defending champions Italy nearly fell at the first hurdle, but a goal in extra-time by Silvio Piola saved their blushes against the plucky Norwegians, who had almost knocked them out in the semi-finals of the Olympic

Games two years previously. The Italian team had only three survivors from the 1934 winning side, Monzeglio, Ferrari and Meazza, and it was undoubtedly a much better one, as they would prove in the latter rounds. The most sensational game of the tournament, perhaps even in the entire history of the competition, was the first round clash between Brazil and Poland. Two players scored four goals: Leonidas, Brazil's 'Black Diamond', scored a hat-trick before half-time, then Ernst Willimowski undid all of Leonidas' good work by himself scoring a hat-trick, his third after 88 minutes making the score 4–4. Both scored again in extra-time, but Romeo snatched the winner for Brazil.

The quarter-finals were less full of surprises though no less exciting than the previous round. The giant-killers of Switzerland and Cuba were both knocked out, Switzerland by the stylish Hungarians, the Cubans 8-0 by Sweden, thereby putting Romania's first round performance into perspective. At Colombes in Paris, before the largest crowd of the tournament, the holders knocked out the hosts. France were not a very strong side at the time and not even home advantage could give them the edge over Italy for whom Piola scored twice in the second half.

One game did stand out, however: the first of the two matches between Czechoslovakia and Brazil, a game which has become known as the 'Battle of Bordeaux'. Zeze Precopio of Brazil had been sent off early in the first half and the match never recovered. Both Machado of Brazil and Riha of Czechoslovakia were sent off just before half-time; Nejedly, Czechoslovakia's star forward, had his leg broken, whilst Planicka played in goal for the Czechs with a broken arm. Both were missing from the replay and this told as Brazil ran out 2–1 winners in a much milder game.

In the semi-finals Brazil were drawn against the Italians and so confident of victory were they that they rested Leonidas. This proved to be their downfall because without him they lacked any punch in front of goal. The Italians could hardly believe their luck and went on to win 2–1 with Meazza inspirational at the heart of the team, Brazil's only goal coming three minutes before the end. Not for the last time would Brazil suffer through overconfidence.

As Czechoslovakia had done in 1934, Hungary represented the finer side of football in the 1938 tournament. Zsengeller, Sarosi and Tikos were among the best pre-war footballers on the continent and all three scored in their impressive 5–1 victory in the other semi-final over the Swedes, who were simply outclassed as had Switzerland and the Dutch East Indies been in the previous rounds.

Hopes were high that the Hungarians could inflict on Italy their first World Cup defeat. They were certainly the more skilful side, but were often accused of lacking the killer punch, and so it proved in the final. Italy had put the game out of Hungary's reach by half-time, Colaussi's two goals and one from the star of the tournament, Piola, giving them a 3–1 lead. Though Sarosi reduced the Italian lead midway through the second half, the Hungarians could not break down a stout Italian defence again. In a foretaste of the way they would play later on in the century, the Italians had simply 'shut up shop'. Forced to attack, the Hungarians gave away a fourth goal eight minutes from time, Piola's second of the game and fifth of the tournament. Pozzo's tactical genius had triumphed again as Meazza became the third different man to collect the famous trophy. Italy had now won the last three major championships they had entered. Two World Cups and the intervening Olympic Games had proved their worth as the top continental side, if not necessarily the best in the world.

THE THIRD WORLD CUP

16th June 1937 – 19th June 1938

QUALIFYING TOURNAMENT

Group 1

	Ge	Sd	Es	Fi	Pl	W	D	L	F	A	Pts
GERMANY	–	5–0	4–1	–	3	3	0	0	11	1	6
SWEDEN	–	–	7–2	4–0	3	2	0	1	11	7	4
ESTONIA	–	–	–	–	3	1	0	2	4	11	2
FINLAND	0–2	–	0–1	–	3	0	0	3	0	7	0

Group 2

NORWAY .... 3–2 3–3 .... Rep. Ireland
POLAND .... 4–0 0–1 .... Yugoslavia

Group 3

ROMANIA qualified as Egypt withdrew

Group 4

SWITZERLAND ...... 2–1 .... Portugal

Group 5

First round
Palestine .... 1–3 0–1 .... Greece

Second round
HUNGARY .... 11–1 .... Greece

Group 6

Bulgaria .... 1–1 0–6 .... CZECHOSLOVAKIA

Group 7

First round
Latvia .... 4–2 5–1 .... Lithuania

Second round
AUSTRIA .... 2–1 .... Latvia

Group 8

	Ho	Be	Lu	Pl	W	D	L	F	A	Pts
HOLLAND	–	–	4–0	2	1	1	0	5	1	3
BELGIUM	1–1	–	–	2	1	1	0	4	3	3
LUXEMBOURG	–	2–3	–	2	0	0	2	2	7	0

Group 9

BRAZIL and CUBA qualified

Group 10

DUTCH EAST INDIES qualified as Japan withdrew

Group 11

ITALY qualified as holders

Group 12

FRANCE qualified as hosts

FINAL TOURNAMENT

Held in France 4th–19th June 1938

FIRST ROUND

ITALY	2–1	NORWAY	*(Vélodrome – Marseilles)*
FRANCE	3–1	BELGIUM	*(Colombes – Paris)*
CZECHOSLOV.	3–0	HOLLAND	*(Cavée Verte – Le Havre)*
BRAZIL	6–5	POLAND	*(Meinau – Strasbourg)*
SWEDEN	W–O	AUSTRIA	
CUBA	3–3 2–1	ROMANIA	*(Chapou – Toulouse)*
SWITZERLAND	1–1 4–2	GERMANY	*(Parc des Princes – Paris)*
HUNGARY	6–0	DUTCH EAST INDIES	*(Vélodrome – Reims)*

QUARTER-FINALS

Colombes, Paris, 12–06–1938, 58 000
ITALY 3 (Colaussi 9, Piola 52 72)
FRANCE 1 (Heisserer 10)

Parc de Lescure, Bordeaux, 12–06–1938, 25 000
BRAZIL 1 (Leónidas 30)
CZECHOSLOVAKIA 1 (Nejedly 64)

Replay: Parc de Lescure, Bordeaux, 14–06–1938
BRAZIL 2 (Leónidas 57, Roberto 89)
CZECHOSLOVAKIA 1 (Kopecky 30)

Fort Carré, Antibes, 12–06–1938
SWEDEN 8 (Andersson 15, Jonasson 32, Wetterström 38 41 53 89, Keller 55, Nyberg 60)
CUBA 0

Victor Boucquey, Lille, 12–06–1938
HUNGARY 2 (Zsengeller 42 68)
SWITZERLAND 0

SEMI-FINALS

Vélodrome, Marseilles, 16–06–1938, 35 000
ITALY 2 (Colaussi 55, Meazza 60)
BRAZIL 1 (Romeo 87)

Parc des Princes, Paris, 16–06–1938, 17 000
HUNGARY 5 (Zsengeller 18 38 86, Titkos 26, Sárosi 61)
SWEDEN 1 (Nyberg 1)

3RD PLACE

Parc de Lescure, Bordeaux, 19–06–1938
BRAZIL 4 (Romeo 43, Leónidas 63 73, Peracio 80)
SWEDEN 2 (Jonasson 18, Nyberg 38)

FINAL

Colombes, Paris, 19–06–1938, 55 000
ITALY 4 (Colaussi 5 35, Piola 16 82)
HUNGARY 2 (Titkos 7, Sárosi 70)
Referee: Capdeville, France
Italy – Olivieri – Foni, Rava – Serantoni, Andreolo, Locatelli – Biavati, Meazza, Piola, Ferrari, Colaussi. Tr: Pozzo
Hungary – Szabó – Polgar, Bíró – Szalay, Szücs, Lázár – Sas, Vincze, Sárosi, Zsengeller, Titkos. Tr: Dietz

Top scorers: Leónidas da Silva, Brazil 8
Gyula Zsengeller, Hungary 7
Silvio Piola, Italy 4
Total goals scored: 84
Average per game: 4.7

1950

The Second World War put paid to the World Cup for 12 years. Brazil, Argentina and Germany had all made a bid for the 1942 tournament at FIFA's 1938 congress in Paris, but no decision was taken. At the next congress in Luxembourg in 1946, FIFA decided to hold the next tournament in 1949. They also decided to change the name of the tournament from the World Cup to the World Championship. The trophy was given the name of the Jules Rimet Cup in honour of its instigator. Legend has it that during the war, Rimet kept the trophy under his bed to hide it from the Germans.

As Brazil were the only applicants they were given the task of organising the 1949 tournament. Unlike Europe, football had carried on unabated in South America during the war years. Indeed, between the 1938 and 1950 World Cups, seven South American Championships had been played, the last of which, held in Brazil in May 1949, occupied the time originally intended for the World Cup but instead acted as a dress rehearsal for the tournament which had been put back a year.

The qualifying competition was the most disorganised ever and was plagued by withdrawals. Originally there were 32 entries, but Argentina, Ecuador and Peru pulled out before a ball had been kicked, as did Belgium and Austria. Turkey withdrew after they had qualified, as did Scotland. The Scots had come second in the British Home Championship, which acted as a qualifying group, but decided that as they had not finished top they would not enter. This would be the last World Cup where the British could afford to be so disdainful.

Uruguay returned, 20 years after their previous appearance, and for the first time the British quartet entered. For the first time also, the Far East was represented, though both Burma and India later withdrew. For the third World Cup running, Stockholm saw the first encounter of the competition, the Swedes this time playing host to the Republic of Ireland. Notable for their absence were the Communist countries of Europe, especially Hungary and

Czechoslovakia. Germany, the defeated power in the European war, was also absent, due to the chaos overrunning the country.

Because of the withdrawals, FIFA invited France and Portugal, both of whom had been eliminated, to play in the final tournament. France accepted and were grouped with Uruguay and Bolivia but pulled out once they had seen their itinerary and the amount of travel it involved. The Brazilian organisers were roundly criticised, and the complaints were largely justified. Yugoslavia in particular were unhappy about their programme. Their first match against Switzerland was in Belo Horizonte, their second four days later in Porto Alegre and their third, the all-important game against Brazil, two days after that in Rio.

The other groups were not much better, Italy being the only team who did not have to change cities. The withdrawals had also left the ridiculous situation where one group had only two teams, despite the fact that two other groups both had four teams. Apart from these problems, the atmosphere of the tournament was good. The huge Maracana stadium had been specially built, though like the Centenary stadium in Uruguay 20 years before, it was not finished in time for the opening match between Brazil and Mexico.

A crowd of 81 000 were in a carnival mood as they welcomed Brazil, the overwhelming favourites to win the tournament, onto the pitch. There, a 21-gun salute awaited them as well as a firework display. In the game itself, the hosts had no trouble in sweeping aside the Mexicans, the hero of the side, Ademir, scoring two of their four goals. Switzerland and Mexico were no match for either Brazil or Yugoslavia, although the Swiss did hold the hosts to a draw in Sao Paulo. That result meant that Brazil had to beat the Yugoslavs to qualify for the next round. In Yugoslavia's previous appearance in a World Cup finals, in Montevideo in 1930, they had beaten Brazil to qualify for the semi-finals. The biggest crowd that had ever gathered for a World Cup game, 147 000, packed into the Maracana. This time the Brazilians were triumphant. Ademir after three minutes and Zizinho on the hour ensured their progression to the next round.

Group 2 produced one of the biggest upsets ever in the World Cup. England, regarded by many as the World's number one, had started the tournament well, beating Chile 2–0. In their next game they faced the United States, who in their first game had almost defeated Spain but conceded three goals in the last ten minutes to lose 3–1. In Belo Horizonte a small crowd of 10 000 gathered to see the 'inevitable' English victory. Instead they witnessed a result that was so unlikely that on receiving the news, some British newspapers thought there had been a printing mistake and listed the score as 10–1! Larry Gaetjens scored the only goal, and unlike their 1930s semi-final team, the American team in Brazil was almost entirely composed of American-born players. Haitian born Gaetjens was a notable exception.

Going into the last game both England and America still had a chance to qualify for the next round, but the Americans lost heavily to Chile whilst England went down to a Zarra goal in the game against Spain.

The other two groups comprised only four games in total, out of which Sweden and Uruguay qualified for the final pool. Sweden, relying on only three of their superb Olympic Games winning side of two years previously, inflicted a first World Cup defeat on the reigning champions Italy, whose squad had been decimated the previous year by the Superga air crash. It was the decisive game as Paraguay, who drew with the Swedes in the second match of the group, lost to Italy in the last. Uruguay had the easiest first round any team has ever had or is likely to have. Their record against Bolivia consisted of five wins out of six with a goal difference of 27 for and 5 against. The game in Belo Horizonte saw the Uruguayans add another eight to that total in convincing fashion.

Unlike any other World Cup, the 1950 tournament did not have a knock-out element and as a result did not actually have a final. Instead, the second round consisted of another group where the four 'semi-finalists' played each other once. It is fortunate therefore that the final game in the group also proved to be the decisive game and so is treated as the final.

Brazil were positively spellbinding in their first two games in the group. Sweden and Spain were swept aside with such arrogant ease that everyone was certain they would lift the Jules Rimet Trophy. Ademir, Zizinho, Jair, Chico and Friaca were in stunning form in front of goal. Uruguay, perceived to be their greatest threat, started off badly, drawing with Spain and only just beating Sweden.

Sweden beat Spain in a meaningless match in Sao Paulo to finish third in the tournament, whilst on the same day, a world record crowd of 199 000 gathered in the Maracana expecting to see Brazil lift the cup in a game they did not even have to win. A draw, and therefore five points, would have been enough to see them through. After two minutes of the second half it looked as if they were home and dry. A pass from Ademir put Friaca through to open the scoring, but the dreaded over-confidence crept into the Brazilian game, a fact the Uruguayans exploited splendidly. The Brazilians could have fallen back into defence but they continued to attack. Obdulio Varela, the Uruguayan captain, and Victor Andrade, nephew of Jose Andrade of the 1930 winning team, were inspirational, as was Maspoli in goal. Uruguay equalised when Schiaffino converted a pass from Ghiggia who was having an excellent game on the wing. Technically Brazil were still winning, but 11 minutes from the end the unimaginable happened. Running in from the touchline Ghiggia scored a lovely individual goal to seal the match for the Uruguayans.

Uruguay had only entered the World Cup twice, but had won both times. Brazil had entered all four but were still without a title to their name. Nobody inside Brazil, or Montevideo for that matter, could quite believe it.

THE FOURTH WORLD CUP

2nd June 1949 – 16th July 1950

QUALIFYING TOURNAMENT

Group 1

	En	Sc	Wa	NI	Pl	W	D	L	F	A	Pts
ENGLAND	–	–	–	9–2	3	3	0	0	14	3	6
SCOTLAND	0–1	–	2–0	–	3	2	0	1	10	3	4
WALES	1–4	–	–	0–0	3	0	1	2	1	6	1
NTH. IRELAND	–	2–8	–	–	3	0	1	2	4	17	1

Scotland withdrew

Group 2

TURKEY .... 7–0 .... Syria

Both Turkey and Austria withdrew

Group 3

First round

Yugoslavia .... 6–0 5–2 .... Israel

Second round

YUGOSLAVIA .. 1–1 1–1 3–2* ..... France

*Play-off in Florence

Group 4

SWITZERLAND .. 5–2 3–2 .... Luxembourg

Belgium withdrew

Group 5

	Sd	RI	Fi	Pl	W	D	L	F	A	Pts
SWEDEN	–	3–1	–	2	2	0	0	6	2	4
REP. IRELAND	1–3	–	3–0	4	1	1	2	6	7	3
FINLAND	–	1–1	–	2	0	1	1	1	4	1

Group 6

SPAIN .... 5–1 2–2 .... Portugal

Group 7

BOLIVIA and CHILE qualified as Argentina withdrew

Group 8

URUGUAY and PARAGUAY qualified as Ecuador and Peru withdrew

Group 9

	Me	US	Cu	Pl	W	D	L	F	A	Pts
MEXICO	–	6–0	2–0	4	4	0	0	17	2	8
UNITED STATES	2–6	–	1–1	4	1	1	2	8	15	3
CUBA	0–3	2–5	–	4	0	1	3	3	11	1

Group 10

Both India and Burma withdrew

Group 11

BRAZIL qualified as hosts

Group 12

ITALY qualified as holders

FINAL TOURNAMENT

Held in Brazil 24th June–16th July 1950

FIRST ROUND

Group 1 (Maracana – Rio, Sete de Setembro – Belo Horizonte, Pacaembu – Sao Paulo, Beira-Rio – Porto Alegre)

	Br	Yu	Sz	Me	Pl	W	D	L	F	A	Pts
BRAZIL	–	2–0	2–2	4–0	3	2	1	0	8	2	5
YUGOSLAVIA	–	–	3–0	4–1	3	2	0	1	7	3	4
SWITZERLAND	–	–	–	2–1	3	1	1	1	4	6	3
MEXICO	–	–	–	–	3	0	0	3	2	10	0

Group 2 (Maracana – Rio, Brito – Curitiba, Mineiro – Belo Horizonte, Ilha de Retiro – Recife)

	Sp	En	Ch	US	Pl	W	D	L	F	A	Pts
SPAIN	–	1–0	2–0	3–1	3	3	0	0	6	1	6
ENGLAND	–	–	2–0	0–1	3	1	0	2	2	2	2
CHILE	–	–	–	5–2	3	1	0	2	5	6	2
UNITED STATES	–	–	–	–	3	1	0	2	4	8	2

Group 3 (Pacaembu – Sao Paulo, Brito – Curitiba)

	Sd	It	Pa	Pl	W	D	L	F	A	Pts
SWEDEN	–	3–2	2–2	2	1	1	0	5	4	3
ITALY	–	–	2–0	2	1	0	1	4	3	2
PARAGUAY	–	–	–	2	0	1	1	2	4	1

Group 4 (Mineiro – Belo Horizonte)

	Ur	Bo	Pl	W	D	L	F	A	Pts
URUGUAY	–	8–0	1	1	0	0	8	0	2
BOLIVIA	–	–	1	0	0	1	0	8	0

FINAL ROUND

	Ur	Br	Sd	Sp	Pl	W	D	L	F	A	Pts
URUGUAY	–	2–1	3–2	2–2	3	2	1	0	7	5	5
BRAZIL	–	–	7–1	6–1	3	2	0	1	14	4	4
SWEDEN	–	–	–	3–1	3	1	0	2	6	11	2
SPAIN	–	–	–	–	3	0	1	2	4	11	1

Maracana, Rio de Janeiro, 3–07–1950, 138 000

BRAZIL 7 (Ademir Menezes 17 36 52 54, Chico 39 88, Maneca 85)

SWEDEN 1 (Andersson 67)

Pacaembu, Sao Paulo, 9–07–1950, 44 000

SPAIN 2 (Basora 38 40)

URUGUAY 2 (Ghiggia 30, Varela 73)

Maracana, Rio de Janeiro, 13–07–1950, 152 000

BRAZIL 6 (Ademir Menezes 15 71, Jair R Pinto 21, Chico 30 55, Zizinho 67)

SPAIN 1 (Igoa 57)

Pacaembu, Sao Paulo, 13–07–1950, 7000

URUGUAY 3 (Ghiggia 39, Míguez 77 85)

SWEDEN 2 (Palmer 5, Sundqvist 40)

Pacaembu, Sao Paulo, 16–07–1950, 11 000

SWEDEN 3 (Sundqvist 15, Mellberg 33, Palmer 80)

SPAIN 1 (Zarra 82)

Though not technically a final tie, the last game in the group, between Brazil and Uruguay, decided the outcome of the tournament and is regarded as the final

FINAL

Maracana, Rio de Janeiro, 16–07–1950, 199000
URUGUAY 2 (Schiaffino 66, Ghiggia 79)
BRAZIL 1 (Friaça 48)
Referee: Reader, England
Uruguay – Máspoli – Gonzáles, Tejera – Gambetta, Varela O, Andrade V – Ghiggia, Peréz, Míguez, Schiaffino, Morán. Tr: Lopez
Brazil – Barbosa – Augusto, Juvenal – Bauer, Danilo Alvim, Bigode – Friaça, Zizinho, Ademir Menezes, Jair R Pinto, Chico. Tr: Flavio Costa

Top scorers: Ademir Menezes, Brazil 9
Juan Schiaffino, Uruguay 5
Estanislao Basora, Spain 5
Total goals scored: 88
Average per game: 4

1954

Switzerland was chosen to host the 1954 tournament at the same time that Brazil was awarded the 1950 tournament, at the 1946 FIFA congress in Luxembourg. Given the state of Europe at the time, Switzerland, which had remained neutral during the war, was the only candidate. Zurich was also the headquarters of FIFA, and 1954 marked their 50th anniversary. More teams entered than in 1950, but representation was still low outside Europe.

West Germany returned as did the Eastern European bloc with the exception of the Soviet Union and Poland, but amongst the American nations the entries were few and far between. All but Venezuela had taken part in recent South American Championships, but only four could see fit to enter the World Cup. Argentina were again noticeable by their absence, their continued persecution complex denying the world the opportunity to see some of that continent's best footballers.

In Asia, both South Korea and Japan entered, but it is strange that more did not enter given that a month before their appearance in the World Cup, the Koreans starred in the 1954 Asian Games football tournament in Manila where 11 other countries were represented as well. If so many teams could make the trip to Manila, why did more not enter the world's premier football tournament?

Asia's reluctance to join in may be mysterious, but Africa's was wholly understandable. Egypt was the only independent country that had organised football. Other countries tended to be part of either the French or British football associations, given their colonial status, and therefore were not entitled to enter. Furthermore, in an extraordinary episode, FIFA refused the entries of India, Peru, Vietnam, Cuba, Iceland, Bolivia and Costa Rica because their entries were either received too late or on the wrong forms!

Belgrade saw the first match of a qualifying tournament that saw several surprises, the most notable of which was the elimination of Spain by Turkey. The two countries were all square after three matches and for the first time lots were used to decide a tie. Spain were just beginning to dominate European club football, but as far as their national side was concerned, the 1950s was not to be their most successful era. Sweden were the other surprise elimination, losing both home and away to Belgium. This meant that both the third and fourth placed sides from the 1950 World Cup would not be present in Switzerland. Perhaps the third surprise was that although Scotland came second in their qualifying group behind England, this time they eagerly sent a team.

The formula adopted at the finals reverted to that of the 1930 tournament with two differences. Instead of just the group winners qualifying for the next round, they were joined by the runners-up. With eight teams left, a knockout competition would then begin. This system would also be used for the next four World Cups. Curiously though, in Switzerland each team played only two first round matches. Each group had two seeds both of whose matches would be against the non-seeds in the group.

Not surprisingly, with each team playing only two first round games, play-offs were needed in two of the four groups. In Group 2, Hungary easily qualified for the quarter-finals having resoundingly thrashed both the South Koreans and the Germans. The Germans were accused of not playing to the spirit of the game by fielding a weakened team against the Hungarians, a match in which, crucially as it turned out, Puskas the Hungarian captain was injured. The Germans gambled that after losing to Hungary they could beat the Turks, who they had beaten in their first match, in a play-off. By doing this they would almost certainly avoid playing the fancied Brazilians, and this turned out to be the case.

Group 4 was a little less controversial, and for the second successive World Cup, Italy flopped. The Swiss surprisingly beat them 2–1 in an ill-tempered game; not for the first or last time, with luck not having gone their way, the Italians resorted to intimidatory tactics. Victory over Belgium and England's victory over Switzerland meant a play-off between the Italians and the Swiss, and once again the hosts surprised everyone. Tactically more advanced, they outplayed the Italians, and their 4–1 victory was far more convincing and deserved than their triumph of the previous week.

The other two groups were far more straightforward. Uruguay and Austria simply outplayed their opponents, Czechoslovakia and Scotland. Scotland's 7–0 defeat at the hands of the champions Uruguay was a particularly salutary experience for them, brushing away the last vestiges of their 'Ivory Tower' attitude.

In Group 1, the French never recovered from losing the opening game of the tournament to the talented Yugoslavs, whose team consisted almost entirely of the one that had reached the final of the Helsinki Olympic Games two years previously. Brazil easily defeated Mexico in their opening game, which meant that a draw between the Yugoslavs and the Brazilians when they met in the next game would be sufficient to see them both through. Surprise surprise, the result? A draw.

The quarter-finals continued the high scoring pattern of the tournament. The most extraordinary game of them all was Austria's 7–5 victory over the hosts. Losing 3–0 after 23 minutes, the Austrians must have thought it was all over, but ten minutes later they were winning 5–3! All 12 goals came in the space of an hour. The Austrian team, considered too young to enter the previous World Cup, were putting on a splendid performance in Switzerland.

Yugoslavia, faced for the first time in a World Cup by their jinx team, West Germany, dominated the game but could not break down a solid German defence. The Germans scored right at the beginning and the end of a match they really did not deserve to win. The other two quarter-finals pitted Europe against South America.

In the first encounter Uruguay, playing better football than they had done in winning the 1950 tournament, beat an English side handicapped by poor goalkeeping 4–2 in an entertaining game. The following day in Berne, Hungary beat Brazil by the same score but in a game marked by some disgraceful scenes. Commonly called the 'Battle of Berne', the game was plagued by vicious tackling from both sides, three sending-offs and a dressing-room brawl afterwards. Much of the blame was pinned on the Brazilians, fearful and finally distressed at their exit from the World Cup, but the Hungarians were not blameless.

The semi-finals thankfully were much calmer affairs, though no less intriguing. Germany reached the final and no one could understand quite how. Their 6–1 victory over Austria was very convincing but totally unexpected. The Austrians, marshalled by the excellent Ernst Ocwirk, one of the finest players in Europe, fell apart at the seams and the Germans swept up the pieces. Much of the blame has been laid at the feet of their goalkeeper Zeman who had previously been dropped because of lost confidence, but the Germans played some excellent football in the second half to totally demoralise the Austrians who had no answer.

The semi-final between Uruguay and Hungary has been called the finest game of football ever played by many of those present. Indeed it saw the Hungarians at their staggering best, and in the sort of form that had seen them undefeated since May 1950. Without doubt the Hungarian team was the finest to have played in the first five editions of the World Cup. The four goals scored against the Uruguayans took their total to 27 for the tournament in only four games played. Kocsis, Czibor and Hidegkuti were in devastating form and all three contributed to the goals. Against anyone else, the Uruguayans would surely have qualified for the final. Schiaffino in particular had an excellent game, but there was nothing he or his team mates could do about Hungary's extra-time victory. With the score at 2–2 after 90 minutes and the South Americans visibly tiring, Hungary stole a victory. Nine minutes from the end, with Andrade receiving treatment for cramp, Kocsis put the Hungarians into the lead and he sealed it five minutes later with his second. Uruguay had lost for the first time in a World Cup match. They lost for the second time three days later in the dreaded third place play-off against Austria.

There have probably never been greater favourites to win the World Cup than Hungary in 1954, and yet amazingly they failed to do so. From 1950 to 1956 Hungary lost only one match and that was the most important of them all, the World Cup Final, against the apparent no-hopers from West Germany. After eight minutes of the game, even the Germans must have wondered why they had turned up. They were trailing 2–0 and on the precipice of a thrashing, but eight minutes later they were level. Puskas, who had insisted on playing in the final despite injury, seemed to justify his inclusion at the expense of Budai when he put Hungary into the lead after six minutes, latching on to a Kocsis shot that had rebounded off a defender. Hungary's second goal two minutes later was the result of a dreadful mix-up between the German goalkeeper Turek and his defender Kohlmeyer who had tried to pass back to him. Czibor dispossessed them both and scored from close range.

Three minutes later Morlock was on the lucky end of a deflection by Bozsik. Schafer crossed from the left wing, Bozsik went for the ball but only succeeded in pushing it into Morlock's path and the German forward had no trouble in scoring. After 16 minutes, Rahn, the hero of the day, scored from a corner after Grosics in the Hungarian goal had misjudged the flight of the ball. Germany were level. For the rest of the game, played in pouring rain, Hungary attacked the German goal. Turek was in fine form making save after save. The post saved the Germans on two occasions, as did Kohlmeyer who cleared a Toth shot off the line. Five minutes before the end, Schafer broke away down the left wing. His cross was cleared but the ball fell to Rahn, who with four defenders in front of him made for goal. Before he could be tackled he drove the ball perfectly into the corner of the goal. Grosics even at full stretch could not reach it. Totally against the run of play the West Germans had gone into the lead. Two minutes later Puskas was sure he had scored, but controversially it was ruled out for offside. West Germany were the new world champions. For the second successive tournament the overwhelming favourites had been beaten in the final.

THE FIFTH WORLD CUP

9th May 1953 – 4th July 1954

QUALIFYING TOURNAMENT

Group 1

	WG	Sa	No	Pl	W	D	L	F	A	Pts
WEST GERMANY	–	3–0	5–1	4	3	1	0	12	3	7
SAAR	1–3	–	0–0	4	1	1	2	4	8	3
NORWAY	1–1	2–3	–	4	0	2	2	4	9	2

Group 2

	Be	Sd	Fi	Pl	W	D	L	F	A	Pts
BELGIUM	–	2–0	2–2	4	3	1	0	11	6	7
SWEDEN	2–3	–	4–0	4	1	1	2	9	8	3
FINLAND	2–4	3–3	–	4	0	2	2	7	13	2

Group 3

	En	Sc	NI	Wa	Pl	W	D	L	F	A	Pts
ENGLAND	–	–	3–1	–	3	3	0	0	11	4	6
SCOTLAND	2–4	–	–	3–3	3	1	1	1	8	8	3
NTH. IRELAND	–	1–3	–	–	3	1	0	2	4	7	2
WALES	1–4	–	1–2	–	3	0	1	2	5	9	1

Group 4

	Fr	RI	Lu	Pl	W	D	L	F	A	Pts
FRANCE	–	1–0	8–0	4	4	0	0	20	4	8
REP. IRELAND	3–5	–	4–0	4	2	0	2	8	6	4
LUXEMBOURG	1–6	0–1	–	4	0	0	4	1	19	0

Group 5

AUSTRIA .... 9–1 0–0 .... Portugal

Group 6

Spain .... 4–1 0–1 2–2* .. TURKEY

*Play-off in Rome. Turkey won on lots

Group 7

HUNGARY qualified as Poland withdrew

Group 8

	Cz	Ro	Bu	Pl	W	D	L	F	A	Pts
CZECHOSLOVAKIA	–	2–0	0–0	4	3	1	0	5	1	7
ROMANIA	0–1	–	3–1	4	2	0	2	5	5	4
BULGARIA	1–2	1–2	–	4	0	1	3	3	7	1

Group 9

Egypt .... 1–2 1–5 .... ITALY

Group 10

	Yu	Gr	Is	Pl	W	D	L	F	A	Pts
YUGOSLAVIA	–	1–0	1–0	4	4	0	0	4	0	8
GREECE	0–1	–	1–0	4	2	0	2	3	2	4
ISRAEL	0–1	0–2	–	4	0	0	4	0	5	0

Group 11

	Me	US	Ha	Pl	W	D	L	F	A	Pts
MEXICO	–	3–1	8–0	4	4	0	0	19	1	8
UNITED STATES	0–4	–	3–0	4	2	0	2	7	9	4
HAITI	0–4	2–3	–	4	0	0	4	2	18	0

Group 12

	Br	Pa	Ch	Pl	W	D	L	F	A	Pts
BRAZIL	–	4–1	1–0	4	4	0	0	8	1	8
PARAGUAY	0–1	–	4–0	4	2	0	2	8	6	4
CHILE	0–2	1–3	–	4	0	0	4	1	10	0

Group 13

Japan .... 1–5 2–2 .... SOUTH KOREA

Both games played in Tokyo

Taiwan withdrew

Group 14

SWITZERLAND qualified as hosts

Group 15

URUGUAY qualified as holders

FINAL TOURNAMENT

Held in Switzerland 16th June–4th July 1954

FIRST ROUND

Group 1 (La Pontaise – Lausanne, Les Charmilles – Geneva)

	Br	Yu	Fr	Me	Pl	W	D	L	F	A	Pts
BRAZIL	–	1–1	–	5–0	2	1	1	0	6	1	3
YUGOSLAVIA	–	–	1–0	–	2	1	1	0	2	1	3
FRANCE	–	–	–	3–2	2	1	0	1	3	3	2
MEXICO	–	–	–	–	2	0	0	2	2	8	0

Group 2 (Hardturm – Zürich, Wankdorf – Berne, St Jakob – Basle, Les Charmilles – Geneva)

	Hu	Tu	WG	SK	Pl	W	D	L	F	A	Pts
HUNGARY	–	–	8–3	9–0	2	2	0	0	17	3	4
TURKEY	–	–	1–4	7–0	2	1	0	1	8	4	2
WEST GERMANY	–	–	–	–	2	1	0	1	7	9	2
SOUTH KOREA	–	–	–	–	2	0	0	2	0	16	0

Play-off

West Germany 7–2 Turkey

Group 3 (Hardturm – Zürich, Wankdorf – Berne, St Jakob – Basle)

	Ur	Au	Cz	Sc	Pl	W	D	L	F	A	Pts
URUGUAY	–	–	2–0	7–0	2	2	0	0	9	0	4
AUSTRIA	–	–	5–0	1–0	2	2	0	0	6	0	4
CZECHOSLOVAKIA	–	–	–	–	2	0	0	2	0	7	0
SCOTLAND	–	–	–	–	2	0	0	2	0	8	0

Group 4 (St Jakob – Basle, La Pontaise – Lausanne, Wankdorf – Berne, Cornaredo – Lugano)

	En	It	Sz	Be	Pl	W	D	L	F	A	Pts
ENGLAND	–	–	2–0	4–4	2	1	1	0	6	4	3
ITALY	–	–	1–2	4–1	2	1	0	1	5	3	2
SWITZERLAND	–	–	–	–	2	1	0	1	2	3	2
BELGIUM	–	–	–	–	2	0	1	1	5	8	1

Play-off

Switzerland .... 4–1 .... Italy

QUARTER-FINALS

Les Charmilles, Geneva, 27–06–1954, 17 000

WEST GERMANY 2 (OG 9, Rahn 85)
YUGOSLAVIA 0

La Pontaise, Lausanne, 26–06–1954, 31 000

AUSTRIA 7 (Wagner 27 29 52, Körner 28 34, Ocwirk 32, Probst 76)
SWITZERLAND 5 (Ballaman 16 41, Hügi 17 23 58)

St Jakob, Basle, 26–06–1954, 50 000

URUGUAY 4 (Borges 5, Varela 43, Schiaffino 47, Ambrois 78)
ENGLAND 2 (Lofthouse 16, Finney 67)

Wankdorf, Berne, 27–06–1954, 40 000

HUNGARY	4	(Hidegkuti 4, Kocsis 7 89, Lantos 54)
BRAZIL	2	(Santos D 18, Julinho 66)

SEMI-FINALS

St Jakob, Basle, 30–06–1954, 58 000

WEST GERMANY	6	(Schäfer 30, Morlock 49, Walter F 54 65, Walter O 60 89)
AUSTRIA	1	(Probst 51)

La Pontaise, Lausanne, 30–06–1954, 37 000

HUNGARY	4	(Czibor 13, Hidegkuti 47, Kocsis 111 116)
URUGUAY	2	(Hohberg 75 86)

3RD PLACE

Hardturm, Zurich, 3–07–1954, 31 000

AUSTRIA	3	(Stojaspal 16, OG 59, Ocwirk 79)
URUGUAY	1	(Hohberg 21)

FINAL

Wankdorf, Berne, 4–07–1954, 60 000

WEST GERMANY	3	(Morlock 11, Rahn 16 83)
HUNGARY	2	(Puskás 6, Czibor 8)

Referee: Ling, England

West Germany – Turek – Posipal, Liebrich, Kohlmeyer – Eckel, Mai – Rahn, Morlock, Walter O, Walter F, Schäfer Tr: Herberger

Hungary – Grosics – Buzánszky, Lóránt, Lantos – Bozsik, Zakariás – Czibor, Kocsis, Hidegkuti, Puskás, Tóth Tr: Sebes

Top scorers:	Sandor Kocsis, Hungary	11
	Maximilian Morlock, West Germany	6
	Josef Hügi, Switzerland	6

Total goals scored: 140
Average per game: 5.4

1958

Sweden was chosen to host the 1958 World Cup and so once again the Europe–South America pattern had been broken. Indeed, out of the first six tournaments only two were held in South America. The entry was the biggest yet, but still represented under half of FIFA's total membership. Forty-eight countries played in the tournament as opposed to 36 four years previously. The qualifying rounds were once more full of shocks and this time political turmoil. Both Italy and Uruguay, who between them had won four of the five competitions played, failed to qualify. Portugal and ultimately Northern Ireland put paid to Italy's hopes, whilst Paraguay and Colombia between them saw that the Uruguayans did not make the trip to Sweden. Paraguay's 5–0 victory over Uruguay in Asuncion marked one of their best international performances ever.

The Uruguayans must have rued the return of the Argentines after a 24-year absence. Had their traditional enemies not returned, their passage to the finals would have been more likely because Paraguay would have been seeded into a different group. Argentina's return was generally welcomed, especially by those who had admired their victory in the 1957 South American Championship. That side, however, was disgracefully torn to pieces by the vulture-like Italian clubs and federation as yet again they ate up the best Argentina had to offer. Sivori, Angelillo, Maschio and Grillo all left their native land, and inexcusably the first three were picked to play for Italy. The loss of Sivori hurt Argentina most and they only just managed to qualify, having lost to Bolivia in the process.

Spain were the third of the big names not to qualify. With Di Stefano, another star Argentina had lost to Europe, and half of the all-conquering Real Madrid team in the side, they came second in their group behind Scotland. It was ironic that FIFA, having been put under pressure to change the system whereby the British Home Championship was used as a qualifying group because it guaranteed at least two places for British teams, sanctioned a change that ultimately led to all four of the British nations qualifying, a feat never since repeated.

Wales were the luckiest of the quartet. They had finished second in their group and been eliminated but political troubles in the Asia–Africa group soon gave them a second chance. South Korea and Ethiopia had both tried to enter the tournament but FIFA refused on the grounds that they had not applied properly. Now trouble involving Israel provided Wales with a second bite at the cherry. In 1954, Israel had taken part in the European qualifying rounds. This time they did not and it turned out to be a mistake the organising committee should have avoided. One by one their opponents pulled out. Turkey, Indonesia, Egypt and Sudan, all Muslim countries, refused to play them. Only a year previously Egypt and Israel had been at war with each other! Israel had therefore qualified for the finals without playing a game. This had happened to Hungary in the previous World Cup, and to others before that, but a new rule disallowed this. Lots were drawn among the European group runners-up to meet Israel in a play-off and Wales were the lucky winners.

The dominant forces in the European qualifying rounds had been the British and Eastern European sides, both of whom had four qualifiers each. A novel system was therefore used to construct the four groups for the final tournament. Each group would have one British, one Eastern European, one Western European and one South American team as there were four of each. This slightly arbitrary system produced groups of varying strengths. The strongest without doubt was Group 4 which contained Brazil, the Soviet Union, England and Austria, all in good form although England had suffered a cruel blow losing vital players in the Munich air crash only four months previously. The weakest group contained the hosts, Wales, Mexico and a Hungary side depleted by mass defections after the 1956 uprising.

As the tournament got underway no-one was really quite prepared for the emergence of the team who were to steal most of the limelight. Brazil, adopting a tactical awareness not previously evident in their game, had moulded together a side of outstanding ball artists. One player however caught the headlines, further promoting the mystique of the Brazilian side. Pele, at the age of 17 then the youngest player to appear in the World Cup finals, became the first of football's worldwide superstars. Helped by the fact that television was covering the event for the first time, he was soon a household name around the world.

Winning their first game easily against the Austrians with two goals from another star in the making, Altafini, who would play for Italy in the next World Cup, they drew their next against England against whom they could not score – the first match, incidentally, ever to finish 0–0 in the World Cup finals. For their final game, against the Soviets who had drawn with England and beaten Austria, the Brazilians brought in Pele, Garrincha and Zito for the first time. Before the highest attendance of the tournament, 51 000 in Gothenburg's Ullevi Stadium, Brazil made everyone sit up and take notice of them. Didi, the main creator of a team playing to a new 4–2–4 formation, led Brazil to a convincing victory, Vava scoring both of the goals. Brazil's revolutionary new tactics took the Europeans in the group, who were still stuck on the old 2–3–5 system or variations of it, by surprise. Though they lost to Brazil, the Soviets qualified for the second round after a play-off victory over England.

Groups 1 and 3 also needed play-offs to see who would join the group winners in the quarter-finals, and in both ties British teams qualified at the expense of Eastern European sides. Wales beat Hungary, whilst Northern Ireland defeated Czechoslovakia. Britain was therefore represented by two teams, but not the two that everyone would have predicted. Scotland had a second successive disastrous tournament, finishing bottom of their group.

Argentina, whose disappointments continued, also finished bottom of their group, obviously missing the players languishing in Italy. Yugoslavia and France, though, qualified for the quarter-finals in style. Both were playing excellent football and were tipped to at least reach the semi-finals. This France did, destroying the Irish in a convincing performance in Norrköping. Fontaine, having scored six goals in the first round, added two more to his tally. Danny Blanchflower, the Irish captain, could do nothing to hold the rampant French at bay.

Yugoslavia, facing West Germany in the quarter-finals again, lost again. As in 1954 they were the better side, but the holders refused to give up their title without a struggle. An early Rahn goal meant that the Germans sat back and protected their lead for most of the match, but they were lucky to survive a penalty appeal for a foul on Milutinovic nine minutes before the end.

The Welsh, inspired by their goalkeeper Kelsey, and without the injured John Charles, put up the bravest fight of the round, holding the Brazilian attack for most of the match but eventually losing to a Pele goal 13 minutes from time. Sweden completed the semi-final line-up. They beat a weary Soviet side in the half-full Rasunda Stadium in Stockholm. One would have expected the Swedish public to be fully behind their team, but crowds in the tournament had generally been poor with the exception of Gothenburg.

Fortunately for Sweden that was where they played their semi-final against the Germans. Had the game been in Stockholm, they might never have recovered from Schafer's 21st minute goal, but the crowd, egged on by cheerleaders, got behind the team, which sufficiently intimidated the Germans. Skogland equalised after half an hour, but the turning point came when Juskowiak was sent off after 58 minutes. Sweden began to exploit the defensive gaps this created and the crowd, sensing a victory, urged them on. They had to wait until nine minutes from time, but two quick goals saw them through.

In the other semi-final, Brazil and France, the two most entertaining teams of the tournament, served up an excellent game. An injury to Jonquet, their centre-half, did not help the French cause, but the Brazilians were playing sensational football, and a 20-minute second-half hat-trick from the magnificent Pele sealed the game for Brazil.

The final therefore matched the hosts with the favourites. It seemed certain that the Brazilians would be the first team to win the prize outside of their own continent. Sweden, however, were starting to impress. The decision to let professional footballers playing abroad represent Sweden was paying dividends. Players like Nils Liedholm, Gunnar Gren, Kurt Hamrin, Nacka Skoglund, Gunnar Nordahl and Julli Gustavsson who had made the exodus to Italy after the 1948 Olympics and 1950 World Cup and had not been selected since were invited back to play in the team, once again under the control of the Englishman George Raynor. Without them, despite the presence of new talents like Agne Simonsson, they almost certainly would not have reached the final.

Brazil in the event were much too good for them once they got there, though they did fall behind to a fourth minute Liedholm goal. Worried that the Swedish crowd would be as intimidatory as in the semi-final, the Brazilians were pleasantly surprised by the quiet, friendly atmosphere in Stockholm and they took advantage of it. Five minutes after Sweden's goal, they equalised through Vava after Garrincha had crossed well. After half an hour Brazil scored an almost identical goal involving the same players to go into half-time leading 2–1.

As he had done in the semi-final against France, Pele stole the show in the second half. After 56 minutes, collecting the ball on his chest in the penalty area, he flicked the ball over the head of a Swedish defender, rounded the man and, the ball only having bounced once, shot Brazil into a 3–1 lead. Zagalo, destined to be Brazil's manager in the 1970 tournament, scored the fourth goal, running in from the left and beating two defenders in the process, but Pele was to have the last word. Zagalo, having provided the pass for Pele's first goal, did the same for his second, but not until he had first received the ball from the 17 year old courtesy of an arrogant backheel. This time Pele looped it into the net with his head. Sweden had put together a final rally before Pele scored during which Simonsson had reduced the deficit, but it was too little too late.

Brazil had won playing football to a standard rarely witnessed before. They won the admiration of all the Swedes in the stadium and as a gesture paraded a huge Swedish flag around the stadium at the end. They and France, who the previous day had beaten West Germany 6–3 to finish third, had both lit up what was by and large a lacklustre tournament played before relatively small crowds.

THE SIXTH WORLD CUP
30th September 1956–29th June 1958

QUALIFYING TOURNAMENT

EUROPE

Group 1

	En	Ri	De	Pl	W	D	L	F	A	Pts
ENGLAND	–	5–1	5–2	4	3	1	0	15	5	7
Rep. Ireland	1–1	–	2–1	4	2	1	1	6	7	5
Denmark	1–4	0–2	–	4	0	0	4	4	13	0

Group 2

	Fr	Be	Ic	Pl	W	D	L	F	A	Pts
FRANCE	–	6–3	8–0	4	3	1	0	19	4	7
Belgium	0–0	–	8–3	4	2	1	1	16	11	5
Iceland	1–5	2–5	–	4	0	0	4	6	26	0

Group 3

	Hu	Bu	No	Pl	W	D	L	F	A	Pts
HUNGARY	–	4–1	5–0	4	3	0	1	12	4	6
Bulgaria	1–2	–	7–0	4	2	0	2	11	7	4
Norway	2–1	1–2	–	4	1	0	3	3	15	2

Group 4

	Cz	Wa	EG	Pl	W	D	L	F	A	Pts
CZECHOSLOVAKIA	–	2–0	3–1	4	3	0	1	9	3	6
Wales	1–0	–	4–1	4	2	0	2	6	5	4
East Germany	1–4	2–1	–	4	1	0	3	5	12	2

Wales qualified to meet Israel in play-off after the drawing of lots

Group 5

	Au	Ho	Lu	Pl	W	D	L	F	A	Pts
AUSTRIA	–	3–2	7–0	4	3	1	0	14	3	7
Holland	1–1	–	4–1	4	2	1	1	12	7	5
Luxembourg	0–3	2–5	–	4	0	0	4	3	19	0

Group 6

	SU	Pd	Fi	Pl	W	D	L	F	A	Pts
SOVIET UNION	–	3–0	2–1	4	3	0	1	16	3	6
Poland	2–1	–	4–0	4	3	0	1	9	5	6
Finland	0–10	1–3	–	4	0	0	4	2	19	0

Play-off in Leipzig
Soviet Union .... 2–0 .... Poland

Group 7

	Yu	Ro	Gr	Pl	W	D	L	F	A	Pts
YUGOSLAVIA	–	2–0	4–1	4	2	2	0	7	2	6
Romania	1–1	–	3–0	4	2	1	1	6	4	5
Greece	0–0	1–2	–	4	0	1	3	2	9	1

Group 8

	NI	It	Pt	Pl	W	D	L	F	A	Pts
Nth. IRELAND	–	2–1	3–0	4	2	1	1	6	3	5
Italy	1–0	–	3–0	4	2	0	2	5	5	4
Portugal	1–1	3–0	–	4	1	1	2	4	7	3

Group 9

	Sc	Sp	Sz	Pl	W	D	L	F	A	Pts
SCOTLAND	–	4–2	3–2	4	3	0	1	10	9	6
Spain	4–1	–	2–2	4	2	1	1	12	8	5
Switzerland	1–2	1–4	–	4	0	1	3	6	11	1

SOUTH AMERICA

Group 1

Peru .... 1–1 0–1 ...... BRAZIL

Group 2

	Ar	Bo	Ch	Pl	W	D	L	F	A	Pts
ARGENTINA	–	4–0	4–0	4	3	0	1	10	2	6
Bolivia	2–0	–	3–0	4	2	0	2	6	6	4
Chile	0–2	2–1	–	4	1	0	3	2	10	2

Group 3

	Pa	Ur	Co	Pl	W	D	L	F	A	Pts
PARAGUAY	–	5–0	3–0	4	3	0	1	11	4	6
Uruguay	2–0	–	1–0	4	2	1	1	4	6	5
Colombia	2–3	1–1	–	4	0	1	3	3	8	1

CENTRAL AND NORTH AMERICA

FIRST ROUND
Group 1

	CR	Cu	Gu	Pl	W	D	L	F	A	Pts
Costa Rica	–	4–0	3–1	4	4	0	0	15	4	8
Curacao	1–2	–	–	4	1	0	2	4	7	2
Guatemala	2–6	1–3	–	4	0	0	3	4	12	0

Group 2

	Me	Ca	US	Pl	W	D	L	F	A	Pts
Mexico	–	2–0	6–0	4	4	0	0	18	2	8
Canada	0–3	–	5–1	4	2	0	2	8	8	4
United States	2–7	2–3	–	4	0	0	4	5	21	0

SECOND ROUND
MEXICO .... 2–0 1–1 ...... Costa Rica

ASIA–AFRICA

FIRST ROUND
Group 1

Indonesia .... 2–0 3–4 .... Taiwan

Play-off in Rangoon
Indonesia .... * 0–0 .... Taiwan

* Indonesia qualified for the next round on goal average

Group 2

Israel qualified for the next round as Turkey withdrew

Group 3

Egypt qualified for the next round as Cyprus withdrew

Group 4

Sudan .... 1–0 1–1 .... Syria

SECOND ROUND
Sudan and Israel qualified for the next round as Indonesia and Egypt withdrew

THIRD ROUND
Israel qualified as Sudan withdrew. However, a FIFA ruling that no team could qualify without playing a match meant that Israel had to meet Wales in a play-off

Israel .... 0–2 0–2 .... WALES

SWEDEN qualified as hosts

WEST GERMANY qualified as holders

FINAL TOURNAMENT

Held in Sweden 8th–29th June 1958

FIRST ROUND

Group 1 (Örjans Vall – Halmstad, Malmö Stadium – Malmö, Olympia – Helsingborg)

	WG	Cz	NI	Ar	Pl	W	D	L	F	A	Pts
WEST GERMANY	–	2–2	2–2	3–1	3	1	2	0	7	5	4
CZECHOSLOVAKIA	–	–	0–1	6–1	3	1	1	1	8	4	3
NTH. IRELAND	–	–	–	1–3	3	1	1	1	4	5	3
ARGENTINA	–	–	–	–	3	1	0	2	5	10	2

Play-off
Nth. Ireland .... 2–1 .... Czechoslovakia

Group 2 (Arosvallen – Västerås, Idrottspark – Norrköping, Eyravallen – Örebro, Tunavallen – Eskilstuna)

	Fr	Yu	Pa	Sc	Pl	W	D	L	F	A	Pts
FRANCE	–	2–3	7–3	2–1	3	2	0	1	11	7	4
YUGOSLAVIA	–	–	3–3	1–1	3	1	2	0	7	6	4
PARAGUAY	–	–	–	3–2	3	1	1	1	9	12	3
SCOTLAND	–	–	–	–	3	0	1	2	4	6	1

Group 3 (Råsunda – Stockholm, Jernvallen – Sandviken)

	Sd	Hu	Wa	Me	Pl	W	D	L	F	A	Pts
SWEDEN	–	2–1	0–0	3–0	3	2	1	0	5	1	5
HUNGARY	–	–	1–1	4–0	3	1	1	1	6	3	3
WALES	–	–	–	1–1	3	0	3	0	2	2	3
MEXICO	–	–	–	–	3	0	1	2	1	8	1

Play-off
Wales .... 2–1 .... Hungary

Group 4 (Rimnersvallen – Uddevalla, Nya Ullevi – Gothenburg, Ryavallen – Borås)

	Br	En	SU	Au	Pl	W	D	L	F	A	Pts
BRAZIL	–	0–0	2–0	3–0	3	2	1	0	5	0	5
ENGLAND	–	–	2–2	2–2	3	0	3	0	4	4	3
SOVIET UNION	–	–	–	2–0	3	1	1	1	4	4	3
AUSTRIA	–	–	–	–	3	0	1	2	2	7	1

Play-off
Soviet Union .... 1–0 .... England

QUARTER-FINALS

Nya Ullevi, Gothenburg, 19–06–1958, 25 000
BRAZIL 1 (Pelé 73)
WALES 0

Idrottspark, Norrköping, 19–06–1958, 11 000
FRANCE 4 (Wisnieski 44, Fontaine 56 64, Piantoni 68)
NTH. IRELAND 0

Malmö Stadium, Malmö, 19–06–1958, 20 000
WEST GERMANY 1 (Rahn 12)
YUGOSLAVIA 0

Råsunda, Stockholm, 19–06–1958, 31 000
SWEDEN 2 (Hamrin 49, Simonsson 88)
SOVIET UNION 0

SEMI-FINALS

Råsunda, Stockholm, 24–06–1958, 27 000
BRAZIL 5 (Vava 2, Didi 38, Pele 53 64 76)
FRANCE 2 (Fontaine 8, Piantoni 83)

Nya Ullevi, Gothenburg, 24–06–1958, 49 000
SWEDEN 3 (Skogland 30, Gren 81, Hamrin 88)
WEST GERMANY 1 (Schäfer 21)

3RD PLACE

Nya Ullevi, Gothenburg, 28–06–1958, 32 000
FRANCE 6 (Fontaine 16 36 78 89, Kopa 27, Douis 50)
WEST GERMANY 3 (Cieslarczyk 18, Rahn 52, Schäfer 83)

FINAL

Råsunda, Stockholm, 29–06–1958, 49 000
BRAZIL 5 (Vava 10 32, Pele 56 89, Zagalo 68)
SWEDEN 2 (Liedholm 4, Simonsson 80)
Referee: Guigue, France
Brazil – Gilmar – Djalma Santos, Bellini, Orlando Peçanha, Nilton Santos – Zito, Didi – Garrincha, Vava, Pele, Zagalo. Tr: Feola
Sweden – Svensson – Bergmark, Gustavsson, Axbom – Börjesson, Parling – Hamrin, Gren G, Simonsson, Liedholm, Skoglund. Tr: Raynor

Top scorers: Juste Fontaine, France 13
Pele, Brazil 6
Helmut Rahn, West Germany 6
Total goals scored: 126
Average per game: 3.6

1962

Chile was awarded the 1962 World Cup at the 1956 FIFA congress in Lisbon in preference to both Argentina and Germany. It was a surprising choice. Both Uruguay and Brazil had hosted the tournament, and as the other member of the continent's 'big three', Argentina was confident of success. She had the stadiums, Chile did not; she had an eager football public, Chile did not; and most important of all, she had a proud footballing heritage, Chile did not. Not even a serious earthquake in May 1960, during which the damage and loss of life was widespread, could put the Chileans off their task. Carlos Dittborn, the president of the Chilean Football Federation, claimed, 'We have nothing, that is why we must have the World Cup,' when FIFA thought it might be a good idea to relocate the tournament, a phrase that has been immortalised in World Cup folklore. Unfortunately for Dittborn, he died a month before the tournament he had done so much to organise got off the ground. In his memory they named the stadium in Arica after him.

For the first time a non-European city saw the opening qualifying game, Costa Rica beating their traditional rivals Guatemala in San Jose, but again Mexico qualified from the Central American group. In one of a series of intercontinental play-offs, the Mexicans had to beat Paraguay to qualify for Chile and this they did.

The idea of playing qualification matches on an intercontinental basis has long been argued as being fairer and in the 1990s where standards have equalled out to a great degree this is probably true. In the 1962 tournament however, it left Africa and Asia without a representative. Spain defeated Morocco, Italy beat Israel and Yugoslavia knocked out the South Koreans. Yet again the World Cup finals did not have a representative from two continents that contained the majority of the world's population.

With Chile as hosts and Brazil as holders only six qualifying games were needed in South America to whittle six countries down to three. Argentina and Uruguay had little trouble in disposing of Ecuador and Bolivia respectively, whilst Colombia, thanks to a 1–0 win in Bogota, knocked out Peru to qualify for the first time.

The European section did see a couple of shocks as the teams who had finished second and third in 1958 both failed to qualify. Sweden were knocked out after a play-off with Switzerland, despite having a better goal difference, whilst France lost to the fast emerging Bulgarians who forced a play-off after scoring a last minute goal in their last group match against the French. Otherwise those who were expected to qualify did. Britain was represented only by England this time, Scotland losing in a play-off with Czechoslovakia and Wales to Spain, whilst Northern Ireland finished second in their group behind West Germany. Of the eight quarter-finalists in Sweden, four failed to qualify for Chile. The only change in the format of the final tournament was the abolition of play-offs for teams that finished equal on points in second and third places. Instead goal difference would be used.

Group 1 was the most entertaining, played in far away Arica. The Soviet Union, the European champions, topped the standings followed by Yugoslavia, the team they had beaten to win the European title two years previously. Both were scoring freely, though the Soviets did have a scare in their second match against Colombia. Racing into a 3–0 lead after 11 minutes and leading 4–1 just into the second half, they then conceded three goals in the last 25 minutes and were lucky not to lose the game.

Group 2 was interesting, not for entertaining games but for the bad atmosphere amongst the teams, which sparked off the 'Battle of Santiago'. At the centre of the controversy were the Italians. Due to the constant poaching of players from the South American continent, the Italians were not the most popular team in Chile. Scouts from Italian clubs constantly plagued the training camps of other teams, while most controversially two Italian journalists covering the tournament sent home articles that were scathing about life in Chile.

Italy had begun the tournament against West Germany with a stale 0–0 draw before a large hostile crowd in Santiago. Three of their team were South Americans. Altafini had played for Brazil in 1958, whilst Sivori and Maschio were members of the famous 1957 Argentine side which had won the South American Championship.

In their next game the Italians faced the hosts before 66000 extremely hostile fans in the Estadio Nacional. The game dissolved into absolute chaos which even the experienced referee, Ken Aston, could do little to control. He sent off the Italian Ferrini after eight minutes for retaliation but for 10 minutes Ferrini refused to leave the field, until FIFA officials and the police removed him. This was just the start of the trouble. A violent tackle by Maschio on Sanchez resulted in the Chilean forward breaking Maschio's nose with a punch seen on television around the world, but amazingly he stayed on the pitch as Aston had not seen it.

The tackling and histrionics were so bad that at one point Aston nearly abandoned the game. David the Italian full back was sent off in the second half for a head tackle on Sanchez, but it was not until 15 minutes from time that Chile could exploit their numerical advantage. Much to the crowd's delight Ramirez and Toro both scored to give the hosts a victory which ensured their qualification for the next round. Despite victory over Switzerland in their last game, the Battle of Santiago proved decisive for the Italians and they left for home. The World Cup was not proving a happy hunting ground for them in the post-war period.

Perhaps the most picturesque stadium the World Cup has ever seen is the Sausalito Stadium in Viña del Mar. Surrounded by woods on two sides and by the Pacific Ocean on the other two, the stadium played host to the group which contained both the eventual finalists as well as Spain and Mexico. Spain, like Italy, contained non-Spaniards in the team. Alfredo di Stefano finally had the chance to appear on the world stage that his talents so richly deserved. Alongside him was Puskas, the captain of the Hungary team eight years before. In the event an injury kept Di Stefano out of all three of Spain's games. Despite having a team of household names due to Real Madrid's exploits in the European Cup, Spain failed to perform and finished bottom of the group.

Brazil, with an almost unchanged team from Sweden, ran out easy winners despite losing Pele in their second match, against Czechoslovakia, with a torn muscle. The star of 1958 missed the rest of the tournament, though as Brazil proved, they had many replacements up their sleeve.

Attendances were low in all of the groups with the exception of Group 2 in Santiago. The lowest of them all occurred in Rancagua at the stadium of the Braden Copper Company, where the average crowd was 7000, as opposed to 8000 in Arica and 13 000 at Viña del Mar. Hungary, regaining some of their pre-1956 strength, easily won the group. The tie that decided the other qualifier from the group was England's 3–1 victory over Argentina.

The Eastern Europeans were having a particularly fine tournament. Four of the quarter-finalists hailed from behind the Iron Curtain, whilst only two came from each of Western Europe and South America. Both of the Western European sides lost. For the third tournament running Yugoslavia faced West Germany in the quarter-finals, only on this occasion they won. It was a close run thing but a Radakovic goal three minutes from time saw the Slavs through, much to their relief.

As this match was progressing the large crowd in the Estadio Nacional were all paying more attention via radios to Chile's match against the Soviet Union being played at the same time in Arica. Lev Yashin, the Soviet goalkeeper, played another bad game to follow that against Colombia in the first round. He was blamed for both of the goals that Chile scored, both of which were long range shots from Sanchez and Rojas respectively. Though it may have appeared a shock result, Reira, the trainer of Chile, had prepared the side for five years for the tournament, and although they had been inconsistent in their build-up, victories over West Germany and Hungary had hinted at the success that lay ahead in the finals.

Had Yashin played as well for the Soviets as Schroiff did for Czechoslovakia, the Soviets might well have progressed to the semi-finals, for Schroiff, generally regarded as an able but not brilliant goalkeeper, kept Hungary at bay for the whole match, which they should easily have won. Having taken an early lead, the Czechs were under pressure for the rest of the game. Hungary seemed to have equalised after 78 minutes, but Tichy's goal was surprisingly disallowed for offside.

The fourth quarter-final, between Brazil and England at Viña del Mar, was lit up by a dazzling display from Garrincha, no longer playing in the shadow of Pele. He was responsible for all three of Brazil's goals, scoring the first and third and creating the second. Hitchens equalised Garrincha's first-half goal to send the teams in level at half-time, but in the second half England were no match for the Brazilians who were beginning to sense that the World Cup would be theirs again, and that this game would represent their toughest test.

Brazil's game in the semi-final, in contrast to their quarter-final, was a one-sided affair. The hosts were no match for the champions, despite the largest crowd of the tournament willing them on. After half an hour Brazil were 2–0 up, both goals coming from Garrincha, and although Toro pulled a goal back just before half-time, Vava put the issue beyond doubt just after the break. A Sanchez penalty on the hour gave the Chilean fans a brief moment of hope but Vava soon ended that with his second goal. Brazil had Garrincha sent off near the end for retaliation and for a while it seemed as though he might miss the final.

The other semi-final was inexplicably played before the second lowest crowd of the tournament. Only 5890 people turned out in Viña del Mar to watch Czechoslovakia double the amount of goals they had scored in the tournament. Again their defence was solid and Schroiff inspired. After a goalless first half, Kadraba put the Czechs into the lead just after the restart. When Jerkovic levelled the scores for Yugoslavia they seemed set to win, but Schroiff kept them at bay as he had done with the Hungarians in the quarter-finals. Two goals in the last ten minutes by Scherer, the second a penalty, took the Yugoslavs by surprise. Having scored with ease in the first round group, the Yugoslavs' old disease of dominating a match but never finishing the opposition off returned.

Undoubtedly Czechoslovakia were surprising finalists. Unlike their counterparts who had lost the 1934 final to Italy, they were not the most entertaining team in the tournament. Instead their strength was based on defence. Novak, Pluskal, Popluhar, Pospichal, Scherer and Masopust were all fine players but they were not a great attacking side. Brazil were, and with Garrincha reprieved after his sending-off, no-one gave the Czechs much hope. As they had done in Stockholm, Brazil conceded the first goal of the game: Masopust scored after 15 minutes, receiving a lovely defence-splitting pass from Scherer; but the Czech lead lasted only two minutes.

The hero of the previous two rounds, Schroiff, turned villain in the final. Amarildo scored Brazil's first goal from the edge of the penalty area and at the most acute of angles. Schroiff, expecting a cross, did not react fast enough. He was also out of position for Brazil's second goal which came midway through the second half. Up until then the Czechs had just about matched the Brazilians, but Zito's goal spelled their downfall. Amarildo was again involved. It was his lobbed cross from inside the penalty area which gave Zito a free header to score. The goal for which the Czechoslovakian keeper had to take most blame, however, was the third. Djalma Santos, out on the right wing, crossed the ball hopefully and high into the penalty area. Schroiff was there to collect it but he let it fall out of his hands straight to the feet of Vava who touched it into an empty net, and Brazil had won. Four years previously Bellini had collected the trophy as captain. This time it was Mauro who had the honour.

THE SEVENTH WORLD CUP

21st August 1960–17th June 1962

QUALIFYING TOURNAMENT

EUROPE

Group 1

	Sz	Sd	Be	Pl	W	D	L	F	A	Pts
SWITZERLAND	–	3–2	2–1	4	3	0	1	9	9	6
SWEDEN	4–0	–	2–0	4	3	0	1	10	3	6
BELGIUM	2–4	0–2	–	4	0	0	4	3	10	0

Play-off in Berlin
Switzerland .... 2–1 .... Sweden

Group 2

	Bu	Fr	Fi	Pl	W	D	L	F	A	Pts
BULGARIA	–	1–0	3–1	4	3	0	1	6	4	6
FRANCE	3–0	–	5–1	4	3	0	1	10	3	6
FINLAND	0–2	1–2	–	4	0	0	4	3	12	0

Play-off in Milan
Bulgaria .... 1–0 .... France

Group 3

	WG	NI	Gr	Pl	W	D	L	F	A	Pts
WEST GERMANY	–	2–1	2–1	4	4	0	0	11	5	8
NTH. IRELAND	3–4	–	2–0	4	1	0	3	7	8	2
GREECE	0–3	2–1	–	4	1	0	3	3	8	2

Group 4

	Hu	Ho	EG	Pl	W	D	L	F	A	Pts
HUNGARY	–	3–3	2–0	4	3	1	0	11	5	7
HOLLAND	0–3	–	–	3	0	2	1	4	7	2
EAST GERMANY	2–3	1–1	–	3	0	1	2	3	6	2

Group 5

	SU	Tu	No	Pl	W	D	L	F	A	Pts
SOVIET UNION	–	1–0	5–2	4	4	0	0	11	3	8
TURKEY	1–2	–	2–1	4	2	0	2	4	4	4
NORWAY	0–3	0–1	–	4	0	0	4	3	11	0

Group 6

	En	Pt	Lu	Pl	W	D	L	F	A	Pts
ENGLAND	–	2–0	4–1	4	3	1	0	16	2	7
PORTUGAL	1–1	–	6–0	4	1	1	2	9	7	3
LUXEMBOURG	0–9	4–2	–	4	1	0	3	5	21	2

Group 7

First round
Cyprus .... 1–1 1–6 .... Israel

Second round
Israel .... 1–0 3–2 .... Ethiopia

Third round
Israel received a bye as Romania withdrew

Fourth round
Israel .... 2–4 0–6 .... ITALY

Group 8

	Cz	Sc	RI	Pl	W	D	L	F	A	Pts
CZECHOSLOVAKIA	–	4–0	7–1	4	3	0	1	16	5	6
SCOTLAND	3–2	–	4–1	4	3	0	1	10	7	6
REP. IRELAND	1–3	0–3	–	4	0	0	4	3	17	0

Play-off in Brussels
Czechoslovakia .... 4–2 .... Scotland

Group 9

First round
Morocco .... 2–1 1–2 .... Tunisia
Ghana .... 4–1 2–2 .... Nigeria

Play-off in Palermo
Morocco .... * 1–1 .... Tunisia

* Morocco qualified on lots

Second round
Ghana .... 0–0 0–1 .... Morocco
Wales .... 1–2 1–1 .... Spain

Third round
Morocco .... 0–1 2–3 .... SPAIN

Group 10

First round
South Korea .... 2–1 2–0 .... Japan
Yugoslavia .... 2–1 1–1 .... Poland

Second round
YUGOSLAVIA ..... 5–1 3–1 .... South Korea

SOUTH AMERICA

Group 1

Ecuador .... 3–6 0–5 .... ARGENTINA

Group 2

Bolivia .... 1–1 1–2 .... URUGUAY

Group 3

COLOMBIA .... 1–0 1–1 .... Peru

CENTRAL AND NORTH AMERICA

FIRST ROUND

Group 1

United States .... 3–3 0–3 .... Mexico

Group 2

	CR	Ho	Gu	Pl	W	D	L	F	A	Pts
COSTA RICA	–	5–0	3–2	4	2	1	1	13	8	5
HONDURAS	2–1	–	1–1	3	1	1	1	3	7	5
GUATEMALA	4–4	*	–	3	0	2	1	7	8	2

* Match abandoned with Honduras leading 2–0. Honduras awarded both points

Play-off in Guatemala City
Costa Rica .... 1–0 .... Honduras

Group 3

Surinam .... 1–2 0–0 ..... Neth. Antilles

SECOND ROUND

	Me	CR	NA	Pl	W	D	L	F	A	Pts
MEXICO	–	4–1	7–0	4	2	1	1	11	2	5
COSTA RICA	1–0	–	6–0	4	2	0	2	8	6	4
NETH. ANTILLES	0–0	2–0	–	4	1	1	2	2	12	3

THIRD ROUND
MEXICO .... 1–0 0–0 .... Paraguay

CHILE qualified as hosts

BRAZIL qualified as holders

FINAL TOURNAMENT

Held in Chile 30th May–17th June 1962

FIRST ROUND

Group 1 (Carlos Dittborn – Arica)

	SU	Yu	Ur	Co	Pl	W	D	L	F	A	Pts
SOVIET UNION	–	2–0	2–1	4–4	3	2	1	0	8	5	5
YUGOSLAVIA	–	–	3–1	5–0	3	2	0	1	8	3	4
URUGUAY	–	–	–	2–1	3	1	0	2	4	6	2
COLOMBIA	–	–	–	–	3	0	1	2	5	11	1

Group 2 (Estadio Nacional – Santiago)

	WG	Ch	It	Sz	Pl	W	D	L	F	A	Pts
WEST GERMANY	–	2–0	0–0	2–1	3	2	1	0	4	1	5
CHILE	–	–	2–0	3–1	3	2	0	1	5	3	4
ITALY	–	–	–	3–0	3	1	1	1	3	2	3
SWITZERLAND	–	–	–	–	3	0	0	3	2	8	0

Group 3 (Sausalito – Viña del Mar)

	Br	Cz	Me	Sp	Pl	W	D	L	F	A	Pts
BRAZIL	–	0–0	2–0	2–1	3	2	1	0	4	1	5
CZECHOSLOVAKIA	–	–	1–3	1–0	3	1	1	1	2	3	3
MEXICO	–	–	–	0–1	3	1	0	2	3	4	2
SPAIN	–	–	–	–	3	1	0	2	2	3	2

Group 4 (Braden – Rancagua)

	Hu	En	Ar	Bu	Pl	W	D	L	F	A	Pts
HUNGARY	–	2–1	0–0	6–1	3	2	1	0	8	2	5
ENGLAND	–	–	3–1	0–0	3	1	1	1	4	3	3
ARGENTINA	–	–	–	1–0	3	1	1	1	2	3	3
BULGARIA	–	–	–	–	3	0	1	2	1	7	1

QUARTER-FINALS

Sausalito, Viña del Mar, 10–06–1962, 17000
BRAZIL 3 (Garrincha 31 59, Vavá 53)
ENGLAND 1 (Hitchens 38)

Carlos Dittborn, Arica, 10–06–1962, 17000
CHILE 2 (Sánchez 11, Rojas 27)
SOVIET UNION 1 (Chislenko 26)

Estadio Nacional, Santiago, 10–06–1962, 63000
YUGOSLAVIA 1 (Radakovic 87)
WEST GERMANY 0

Braden, Rancagua, 10–06–1962, 11000
CZECHOSLOVAKIA 1 (Scherer 12)
HUNGARY 0

SEMI-FINALS

Estadio Nacional, Santiago, 13–06–1962, 76000
BRAZIL 4 (Garrincha 9 31, Vavá 49 77)
CHILE 2 (Toro 41, Sánchez 61)

Sausalito, Viña del Mar, 13–06–1962, 5000
CZECHOSLOVAKIA 3 (Kadraba 49, Scherer 80 86)
YUGOSLAVIA 1 (Jerkovic 69)

3RD PLACE

Estadio Nacional, Santiago, 16–06–1962, 66000
CHILE 1 (Rojas 89)
YUGOSLAVIA 0

FINAL

Estadio Nacional, Santiago, 17–06–1962, 68000
BRAZIL 3 (Amarildo 18, Zito 69, Vavá 77)
CZECHOSLOVAKIA 1 (Masopust 16)
Referee: Latichev, Soviet Union
Brazil – Gilmar – Djalma Santos, Mauro R Oliveira, Zózimo, Nilton Santos – Zito, Didi – Garrincha, Vava, Amarildo, Zagalo. Tr: Moreira
Czechoslovakia – Schrojf – Tichy, Pluskal, Popluhár, Novák – Kvasnák, Masopust – Pospíchal, Scherer, Kadraba, Jelínek. Tr: Vytlacil

Top scorers: Florian Albert, Hungary 4
Garrincha, Brazil 4
Valentin Ivanov, Soviet Union 4
Drazen Jerkovic, Yugoslavia 4
Leonel Sánchez, Chile 4
Vava, Brazil 4

Total goals scored: 89
Average per game: 2.8

1966

For the first time post-war, the major Western European football nations put in serious bids to stage the World Cup. England emerged as the favourites over both Spain and West Germany, and at FIFA's 1960 congress in Rome they were chosen in a close vote over the Germans, the Spanish having withdrawn their bid at the last moment. The year 1963 marked the centenary of the founding of modern association football in London, so in a way England was being honoured for her part in the development of the game.

The number of entries totalled seventy, 21 more than for Chile. At last it seemed the world outside Europe and the Americas was beginning to take an interest in the competition. Alas, it was a false dawn. Out of the whole of Asia and Africa just North Korea and Australia ended up playing a game. The point of conflict was the allocation of just one finals place to cover the two continents. Justified in their anger to the extent that as a World Cup, the competition should represent the world and not just Europe and South America, the representatives of the two continents withdrew en masse. It is interesting to note, however, that only four teams from Asia had entered in the first place. One of these, North Korea, were the eventual qualifiers.

Holland kicked off the qualifying tournament with a match against Albania in Rotterdam. The Dutch had not qualified since 1938 and their luck was not about to change. The Swiss, one of Europe's weaker nations, qualified from this group. It would have been interesting to see how an African nation like Ghana or Nigeria would have fared in Switzerland's place, given their poor performance in the final tournament. Not that this group was the only weak-looking European group. To lose in the final of the World Cup seemed to be a bad omen for the next competition as Czechoslovakia, like Sweden before them, failed to qualify for England. Losing semi-finalists Yugoslavia, who seemed to blow either hot or cold, blew cold in this tournament, and they too failed to qualify. The rest of the groups went much to plan in Europe as they did in South America, where there were no surprises. No surprises either in Central America where Mexico once again qualified at the expense of her smaller neighbours.

Four months before the final tournament started, the Jules Rimet trophy was stolen whilst on display in Westminster. For a week it could not be located, but a dog called Pickles found it hidden it under a bush in a London suburb. Who had stolen it and why they had hidden it under a bush will never be known, but Pickles became an overnight hero. It was a shame that when the same trophy was stolen again in 1984 from the offices of the Brazilian Football Federation, Pickles was not still alive! Instead, the thief, who was later caught, admitted that he had melted it down.

In the finals, the greatest talking point of the first round again involved Italy, and again they failed to qualify for the quarter-finals. Their conquerors this time were the North Koreans. The country that liked to think itself at the top of the football tree was humbled by a group of players who had no experience of competitive football in Asia, let alone at world level. The crowds in the North-East of England, where the Koreans were based, warmed to their guests, even though it looked certain after the first round of games in Group 4 that the Soviet Union and Italy would qualify. The Korean victory over Italy, courtesy of a goal by Pak Doo-ik, was possibly the greatest upset the World Cup has seen, and on their return to Italy, the Italian team were pelted with all manner of objects by disgusted fans.

The other groups produced only one surprise, the elimination of the champions Brazil. England was not a happy tournament for the Brazilians. Regarded as favourites, they never adapted to the conditions in the North-West or the tackling of the Bulgarian and Portuguese defenders. Although they defeated Bulgaria, Pele was injured and missed the next match against the Hungarians, a game in which the Magyars outplayed their South American opponents. Indeed the Hungarians had recovered from the traumas of ten years previously and were amongst the best teams in Europe. Portugal, making their World Cup debut, were also an outstanding side. Eusebio, a naturalised Mozambican, emerged as the star and top scorer of the tournament. He was instrumental in Portugal's victory over Brazil, a game in which Pele was again on the receiving end of some disgraceful tackles. After the game he threatened never to play again in the World Cup. Thankfully he was back four years later.

Group 2 did not manage the excitement of Brazil's group, but it contained three very highly-rated teams. Spain were the unlucky ones not to qualify, defeats by the two qualifiers, West Germany and Argentina, sealing their fate. Like Italy, the Spaniards were learning that success at club level could be a positive hindrance at national level, a fact England would learn in the 1970s.

England looked comfortable enough in qualifying from Group 1, probably the weakest of the four. None of their opponents were tipped to proceed far and after a sterile opening game with Uruguay, both France and Mexico were defeated with ease by the hosts in front of full houses at Wembley. In the quarter-finals they played Argentina who were confident of victory, but in a show of temper they spoiled what was potentially an excellent game. Their captain Rattín, in particular, behaved deplorably and when sent off he refused to go. Playing against ten men, all of whom seemed intent on avenging Rattín's dismissal, England deservedly won the game when Hurst headed home a cross from Martin Peters 12 minutes from time. That an Argentinian team containing players of the quality of Artime, Rattín, Onega, Albrecht and Mas should resort to intimidatory tactics was a shame, but it was to be a familiar sight over the next few years, particularly at club level.

South American cries of conspiracy against them were heightened further after the match between West Germany and Uruguay during which two Uruguayans were sent off. It was a match Uruguay could have won, but they reacted badly to German provocation, and with only nine men for most of the second half, they conceded three goals to add to the one the Germans had scored in the first. All manner of rumour circulated in South America following these two games. A German referee in the England–Argentina game had sent off an Argentinian, and an English referee in the West Germany–Uruguay game had sent off two Uruguayans. Not surprisingly, two and two was put together and the South American press came up with five.

Two of the strongest teams met at Roker Park, Sunderland, where two defensive errors by the Hungarians let the Soviets in to win. The Soviet Union defended well and Yashin in particular made up for the errors he had made four years previously with a fine performance to deny the Hungarians, who had most of the play.

Goodison Park in Liverpool witnessed an extraordinary game. After 22 minutes North Korea led Portugal 3–0, and had victory in their grasp. Had they had more international experience they might well have won, but instead of concentrating more on defence they went out for more goals. Marshalled by the brilliant Eusebio, Portugal regrouped and exploited the gaps in the Korean defence. After an hour the Portuguese led 4–3, all of the goals scored by Eusebio. The 5–3 victory was comfortable enough in the end, but if ever a match sealed two reputations, that of the Koreans and of Eusebio, this was it.

The semi-finals starkly contrasted each other. The Goodison Park spectators had witnessed two excellent matches, between Hungary and Brazil and North Korea and Portugal, but the semi-final encounter between the Soviet Union and West Germany was not in the same class. Haller scored for the Germans just before half-time and Beckenbauer made it 2–0 halfway through the second half, and although Porkujan scored just before the end, the game was never exciting.

Not so the game at Wembley between England and Portugal, which was an open encounter and one of the best games of the tournament. Bobby Charlton, the scorer of both England's goals, was in superb form. His second goal even merited handshakes from a couple of the Portuguese players. The final ten minutes were especially tense, after Bobby's brother Jackie handled the ball on the line and Eusebio scored from the penalty spot. Try as they might, Portugal could not equalise, and the sight of Eusebio leaving the field in tears after the game is one of the most poignant pictures in World Cup history.

West Germany were back for their first final in 12 years. For England it was their first in 54 years. Not since the 1912 Olympic Games had they progressed so far. Home advantage was being made to tell: Italy in 1934 had been the last host nation to win the tournament and England were to become the second, in somewhat controversial style. After Haller had put the Germans ahead on 12 minutes following a poor clearance from Wilson, England applied the pressure and six minutes later they were on level terms after a quickly taken free-kick by Bobby Moore was headed home by Geoff Hurst. It was not until 12 minutes from time that the English pressure told when Peters scored, following in after a shot from Hurst.

It looked as though the game was beyond West Germany and they left it very late to equalise. From a free-kick blasted into the penalty area by Emmerich, Weber prodded the ball home seconds before the final whistle was blown. In extra-time the match was effectively decided by one of the most talked about goals in the history of the World Cup. From a cross by Ball, Hurst, with his back to the goal, controlled the ball, turned and shot. The ball hit the underside of the bar and came down. Hunt, who was following in, turned away in celebration. Dienst, the Swiss referee, after consulting his Soviet linesman Bakhramov, blew his whistle for a goal. The Germans hotly disputed the decision and still do to this day. They point to the fact that Bakhramov was not really in a position to give a proper verdict.

The issue was put beyond doubt seconds before the end of extra-time when Hurst ran on to a long clearance and scored with a lovely left-footed shot. England had deservedly won the World Cup in what had proved to be a very exciting game, and brought the highest honour the game has back to the country that gave the world the game in the first place.

THE EIGHTH WORLD CUP

24th May 1964–30th July 1966

QUALIFYING TOURNAMENT

EUROPE

Group 1

	Be	Bu	Is	Pl	W	D	L	F	A	Pts
BELGIUM	–	5–0	1–0	4	3	0	1	11	3	6
BULGARIA	3–0	–	4–0	4	3	0	1	9	6	6
ISRAEL	0–5	1–2	–	4	0	0	4	1	12	0

Play-off in Florence

Bulgaria .... 2–1 .... Belgium

Group 2

	WG	Sd	Cy	Pl	W	D	L	F	A	Pts
WEST GERMANY	–	1–1	5–0	4	3	1	0	14	2	7
SWEDEN	1–2	–	3–0	4	2	1	1	10	3	5
CYPRUS	0–6	0–5	–	4	0	0	4	0	19	0

Group 3

	Fr	No	Yu	Lu	Pl	W	D	L	F	A	Pts
FRANCE	–	1–0	1–0	4–1	6	5	0	1	9	2	10
NORWAY	0–1	–	3–0	4–2	6	3	1	2	10	5	7
YUGOSLAVIA	1–0	1–1	–	3–1	6	3	1	2	10	8	7
LUXEMBOURG	0–2	0–2	2–5	–	6	0	0	6	6	20	0

Group 4

	Pt	Cz	Ro	Tu	Pl	W	D	L	F	A	Pts
PORTUGAL	–	0–0	2–1	5–1	6	4	1	1	9	4	9
CZECHOSLOVAKIA	0–1	–	3–1	3–1	6	3	1	2	12	4	7
ROMANIA	2–0	1–0	–	3–0	6	3	0	3	9	7	6
TURKEY	0–1	0–6	2–1	–	6	1	0	5	4	19	2

Group 5

	Sz	NI	Ho	Al	Pl	W	D	L	F	A	Pts
SWITZERLAND	–	2–1	2–1	1–0	6	4	1	1	7	3	9
NTH. IRELAND	1–0	–	2–1	4–1	6	3	2	1	9	5	8
HOLLAND	0–0	0–0	–	2–0	6	2	2	2	6	4	6
ALBANIA	0–2	1–1	0–2	–	6	0	1	5	2	12	1

Group 6

	Hu	EG	Au	Pl	W	D	L	F	A	Pts
HUNGARY	–	3–2	3–0	4	3	1	0	8	5	7
EAST GERMANY	1–1	–	1–0	4	1	2	1	5	5	4
AUSTRIA	0–1	1–1	–	4	0	1	3	3	6	1

Group 7

	SU	Wa	Gr	De	Pl	W	D	L	F	A	Pts
SOVIET UNION	–	2–1	3–1	6–0	6	5	0	1	19	6	10
WALES	2–1	–	4–1	4–2	6	3	0	3	11	9	6
GREECE	1–4	2–0	–	4–2	6	2	1	3	10	14	5
DENMARK	1–3	1–0	1–1	–	6	1	1	4	7	18	3

Group 8

	It	Sc	Pd	Fi	Pl	W	D	L	F	A	Pts
ITALY	–	3–0	6–1	6–1	6	4	1	1	17	3	9
SCOTLAND	1–0	–	1–2	3–1	6	3	1	2	8	8	7
POLAND	0–0	1–1	–	7–0	6	2	2	2	11	10	6
FINLAND	0–2	1–2	2–0	–	6	1	0	5	5	20	2

Group 9

Rep. Ireland .... 1–0 1–4 .... Spain

Syria withdrew

Play-off in Paris

SPAIN .... 1–0 .... Rep Ireland

SOUTH AMERICA

Group 1

	Ur	Pe	Ve	Pl	W	D	L	F	A	Pts
URUGUAY	–	2–1	5–0	4	4	0	0	11	2	8
PERU	0–1	–	1–0	4	2	0	2	8	6	4
VENEZUELA	1–3	3–6	–	4	0	0	4	4	15	0

Group 2

	Ch	Ec	Co	Pl	W	D	L	F	A	Pts
CHILE	–	3–1	7–2	4	2	1	1	12	7	5
ECUADOR	2–2	–	2–0	4	2	1	1	6	5	5
COLOMBIA	2–0	0–1	–	4	1	0	3	4	10	2

Play-off in Lima

Chile .... 2–1 .... Ecuador

Group 3

	Ar	Pa	Bo	Pl	W	D	L	F	A	Pts
ARGENTINA	–	3–0	4–1	4	3	1	0	9	2	7
PARAGUAY	0–0	–	2–0	4	1	1	2	3	5	3
BOLIVIA	1–2	2–1	–	4	1	0	3	4	9	2

CENTRAL AND NORTH AMERICA

FIRST ROUND

Group 1

	Ja	NA	Cu	Pl	W	D	L	F	A	Pts
JAMAICA	–	2–0	2–0	4	2	1	1	5	2	5
NETH. ANTILLES	0–0	–	1–0	4	1	2	1	2	3	4
CUBA	2–1	1–1	–	4	1	1	2	3	5	3

Group 2

	CR	Su	Tr	Pl	W	D	L	F	A	Pts
COSTA RICA	–	1–0	4–0	4	4	0	0	9	1	8
SURINAM	1–3	–	6–1	4	1	0	3	8	9	2
TRINIDAD	0–1	4–1	–	4	1	0	3	5	12	2

Group 3

	Me	US	Ho	Pl	W	D	L	F	A	Pts
MEXICO	–	2–0	3–0	4	3	1	0	8	2	7
UNITED STATES	2–2	–	1–1	4	1	2	1	4	5	4
HONDURAS	0–1	0–1	–	4	0	1	3	1	6	1

SECOND ROUND

	Me	CR	Ja	Pl	W	D	L	F	A	Pts
MEXICO	–	1–0	8–0	4	3	1	0	12	2	7
COSTA RICA	0–0	–	7–0	4	1	2	1	8	2	4
JAMAICA	2–3	1–1	–	4	0	1	3	3	19	1

AFRICA–ASIA

NORTH KOREA .... 6–1 3–1 ..... Australia

All of the African entries and all bar North Korea of the Asian entries withdrew over the allocation of just one place for them in the final tournament

ENGLAND qualified as hosts

BRAZIL qualified as holders

FINAL TOURNAMENT

Held in England 11th–30th July 1966

FIRST ROUND

Group 1 (Wembley – London, White City – London)

	En	Ur	Me	Fr	Pl	W	D	L	F	A	Pts
ENGLAND	–	0–0	2–0	2–0	3	2	1	0	4	0	5
URUGUAY	–	–	0–0	2–1	3	1	2	0	2	1	4
MEXICO	–	–	–	1–1	3	0	2	1	1	3	2
FRANCE	–	–	–	–	3	0	1	2	2	5	1

Group 2 (Hillsborough – Sheffield, Villa Park – Birmingham)

	WG	Ar	Sp	Sz	Pl	W	D	L	F	A	Pts
WEST GERMANY	–	0–0	2–1	5–0	3	2	1	0	7	1	5
ARGENTINA	–	–	2–1	2–0	3	2	1	0	4	1	5
SPAIN	–	–	–	2–1	3	1	0	2	4	5	2
SWITZERLAND	–	–	–	–	3	0	0	3	1	9	0

Group 3 (Goodison Park – Liverpool, Old Trafford – Manchester)

	Pt	Hu	Br	Bu	Pl	W	D	L	F	A	Pts
PORTUGAL	–	3–1	3–1	3–0	3	3	0	0	9	2	6
HUNGARY	–	–	3–1	3–1	3	2	0	1	7	5	4
BRAZIL	–	–	–	2–0	3	1	0	2	4	6	2
BULGARIA	–	–	–	–	3	0	0	3	1	8	0

Group 4 (Ayresome Park – Middlesbrough, Roker Park – Sunderland)

	SU	NK	It	Ch	Pl	W	D	L	F	A	Pts
SOVIET UNION	–	3–0	1–0	2–1	3	3	0	0	6	1	6
NORTH KOREA	–	–	1–0	1–1	3	1	1	1	2	4	3
ITALY	–	–	–	2–0	3	1	0	2	2	2	2
CHILE	–	–	–	–	3	0	1	2	2	5	1

QUARTER-FINALS

Wembley, London, 23–07–1966, 90 000

ENGLAND 1 (Hurst 78)
ARGENTINA 0

Goodison Park, Liverpool, 23–07–1966, 51 000

PORTUGAL 5 (Eusebio 27 42 56 59, Augusto 78)
NORTH KOREA 3 (Seung-zin 1, Dong-woon 21, Seung-kook 22)

Roker Park, Sunderland, 23–07–1966, 26 000

SOVIET UNION 2 (Chislenko 5, Porkujan 48)
HUNGARY 1 (Bene 50)

Hillsborough, Sheffield, 23–07–1966, 33 000

WEST GERMANY 4 (Held 11, Beckenbauer 65, Seeler 76, Haller 83)
URUGUAY 0

SEMI-FINALS

Goodison Park, Liverpool, 25–07–1966, 43 000

WEST GERMANY 2 (Haller 44, Beckenbauer 68)
SOVIET UNION 1 (Porkujan 88)

Wembley, London, 26–07–1966, 94 000

ENGLAND 2 (Charlton B 30 79)
PORTUGAL 1 (Eusebio 82)

3RD PLACE

Wembley, London, 28–07–1966, 87 000

PORTUGAL 2 (Eusebio 12, Torres 88)
SOVIET UNION 1 (Metreveli 43)

FINAL

Wembley, London, 30–07–1966, 96 000
ENGLAND 4 (Hurst 19 100 119, Peters 77)
WEST GERMANY 2 (Haller 13, Weber 89)
Referee: Dienst, Switzerland
England – Banks – Cohen, Charlton J, Moore, Wilson – Stiles, Charlton B – Ball, Hunt, Hurst, Peters. Tr: Ramsey
West Germany – Tilkowski – Höttges, Schulz, Weber, Schnellinger – Haller, Beckenbauer – Seeler, Held, Overath, Emmerich. Tr: Schoen

Top scorers	Eusebio, Portugal	9
	Helmut Haller, West Germany	5
	Franz Beckenbauer, West Germany	4
	Ferenc Bene, Hungary	4
	Geoff Hurst, England	4
	Valeri Porkujan, Soviet Union	4

Total goals scored: 89
Average per game: 2.8

1970

At the FIFA congress in Tokyo in 1964, FIFA surprisingly gave the 1970 World Cup to Mexico. Once again Argentina was overlooked and their delegation was furious. The conditions in Mexico were thought by many to be unsuitable, both in terms of the heat and altitude, but the persistent lobbying by the Mexican delegation won the day.

As it turned out, the 1970 Mexican World Cup will be remembered as perhaps the best tournament ever to be staged. For those who were not there, it was the first chance to see the tournament not only live on the television but also in colour, definitely a contributing factor to the mystique which has surrounded the tournament since.

After failing to secure the staging of the tournament, Argentina failed even to qualify. This perhaps was a blessing in disguise. The three previous World Club Championships between European and Argentinian sides had been marred by brutal behaviour on the pitch, mainly by the Argentines, though not exclusively. Mexico was spared such confrontations. Instead, South America was represented by three supremely gifted teams in Brazil, Uruguay and Peru. Peru in particular were a welcome sight. Managed by Didi, the former Brazilian midfielder, they were responsible for Argentina's demise thanks to a 1–0 victory in Lima and a 2–2 draw in Buenos Aires.

Peru's presence in the final tournament was threatened by an earthquake just before the tournament began, but that was nothing compared to the traumas of the CONCACAF qualifying tournament, where full-scale war was declared as a result of three matches between El Salvador and Honduras. Relations had been tense for many months between the two countries. Border disputes and the problems of Salvadorean migrant workers in Honduras just needed a spark to start the fire. That spark was provided when the two countries were drawn to play each other in the semi-finals of the qualifying group. After all three games that were played, rioting and border skirmishes ensued and finally all-out war, though remarkably there was little trouble during the games themselves. Known as the Fútbol War, over 2000 lives were lost in the fighting.

There were disputes elsewhere in the qualifying competition, but thankfully not on the same scale. The North Koreans, hoping to repeat their 1966 success in Mexico, were forced to withdraw after refusing to play Israel, the eventual qualifiers from Asia. The Asian entry was again rather low, considering the fact that the Asian Games, Asian Cup and Asian Club Championship were regularly attracting a high number of entries. Only Japan and South Korea from the AFC bothered to enter.

For the first time since 1934, Africa was represented at the final tournament, this time by Morocco, who won a close run play-off against Nigeria and Sudan. Ghana, without question the best team on the continent, having appeared in the four previous Cup of Nations final ties, did not live up to their billing as favourites, Nigeria defeating them 2–1 in a crucial game in Ibadan.

Europe was full of surprises too. Eusebio could do no more than inspire Portugal to finish bottom of their qualifying group behind Romania. Also out were Hungary, the fourth of the quarter-finalists in 1966 who did not qualify for Mexico. They lost to Czechoslovakia, 4–1 in a play-off in Marseille. Spain once again failed to live up to her clubs' reputation, finishing third in a group which Yugoslavia, runners-up two years previously in the European Championships, were expected to win. Belgium surprised both countries by qualifying with some ease.

The final tournament was played at the hottest time of the year in Mexico, and quite inexcusably, due to television commitments, many of the games kicked off at midday. That the tournament produced any good football at all is a wonder, but it did: the standard was of the highest quality. Group 3 in particular served up a feast of games, the best of which was the game between the holders and Brazil in Guadalajara. England had a team that was regarded as better than their 1966 side, and the predictions were that the first round game with the Brazilians would be a rehearsal for the final. They were unlucky to lose to a goal by Jairzinho, but Banks had earlier kept a Pele header out by producing one of the best saves ever witnessed. Both teams qualified for the quarter-finals by beating both the Czechs and Romanians, who were no match.

Group 4 produced lots of goals and some excellent football. Morocco put up excellent displays against West Germany and Bulgaria, whilst Peru with Chumpitaz and Cubillas in excellent form saw off both the Moroccans and the Bulgarians. Bulgaria, often criticised as one of the most negative teams in Europe, even played their part, though they could not match the skill shown by the Germans for whom Gerd Müller was in devastating form. His seven goals in three games included hat-tricks against both Bulgaria and Peru.

Group 1, played in the most imposing football stadium in the world, the newly constructed Azteca, got off to a poor start with a tedious 0–0 draw between the hosts and the Soviet Union in the opening game of the tournament. El Salvador and Belgium, the other two teams in the group, were no match for the Soviets or the Mexicans. Mexico, for years the whipping boys at each World Cup, were enjoying home advantage and were determined to make the most of it.

Group 2 was the poorest. Both Uruguay and Italy were expected to qualify, and this they did without much trouble. Italy, after beating Sweden 1–0, simply shut up shop and played out two 0–0 draws. The Italians were determined that there would be no repeat of the fiascos of the previous five World Cups. Uruguay were very tight defensively and although they lost against the Swedes in the last game, the Scandinavians needed to win by two goals to qualify. The one goal they did score came in the last minute.

The quarter-finals threw up a repeat of the 1966 final, and this time the West Germans gained a measure of revenge. England, missing Banks in goal through food poisoning, lead 2–0 with 22 minutes remaining, but the Germans fought back magnificently and eventually won with a goal from Müller in the second period of extra-time. Ramsey, the England manager, has been blamed for substituting Bobby Charlton instead of Cooper, as has Peter Bonetti, Banks' replacement in goal, for a poor display, but West Germany, forced into attack, never lost the initiative once they had scored.

In Guadalajara, Brazil continued to delight the public there with another inspired display against Peru. Pele, in his fourth World Cup, was proving why he was regarded as the best footballer ever to play the game, but he was not the only star in the side. Rivelino, Tostao, Jairzinho and Gerson with Pele represented an attacking unit that has rarely, if ever, been equalled. Peru might well have qualified against any other of the quarter-finalists, and against Brazil, Cubillas scored a stunning goal after an excellent run by Sotil, but they could not match the overall quality of the Brazilians.

Uruguay, Brazil's opponents in the semi-finals, beat the Soviet Union in the quarter-finals with a hotly disputed goal three minutes from the end of extra-time. The Soviets were adamant that the ball went out of play before Esparrago put it in the net to win a game in which the Soviets were frustrated by the excellent Uruguayan defence. The game was played in a half-full Azteca stadium, and it would have made more sense to have moved the game to Toluca were Mexico and Italy played their quarter-final. Had the Mexicans played in the Azteca, not only would it have been a sell-out, but their chances of winning would have been improved. Instead, in front of only 24 000 in Toluca they floundered and lost badly, despite taking an early lead, to an Italian side that showed it could attack as well as it could defend. Rivera and Riva were in particularly fine form.

In the semi-final against West Germany three days later, the Italians continued in this vein, scoring four more goals. That they also let in three was astonishing given that Italian football was dominated by *catenaccio* at the time. Every tournament seems to throw up a real thriller of a game, and in Mexico this was it. The Italians scored after seven minutes and went on the defensive for the rest of the game, only for Schnellinger to score right at the death for the Germans. In extra-time the game came alive. Müller, the tournament's top scorer, put West Germany ahead only for Burgnich to equalise. Just before the end of the first period Riva put the Italians ahead again only for Müller to equalise. When Rivera scored to put Italy into the lead for the third time, West Germany had nothing left to give.

Brazil, still playing in Guadalajara in front of a crowd that were fiercely behind them, won the other semi-final in some style. Uruguay had played Brazil often enough not to be intimidated, and they took the lead through Cubilla after 19 minutes, a lead they kept right up to half-time. Just before the interval, however, the inevitable happened and Clodoaldo equalized. It was not until the last quarter of an hour that the Brazilian pressure paid off. Brazil were on a roll and there was nothing the Uruguayans could do to stop them. First Jairzinho and then Rivelino scored the goals that won the match for them.

The final, before a full house in the Azteca, was a match that showed football at its best. At stake was the permanent possession of the Jules Rimet trophy, both sides having won it twice before. Pele opened the scoring, thus matching Vava, the only other man who had scored in two World Cup Finals, when he headed home from Rivelino's cross. Italy pulled level just before half-time after careless play in the Brazilian defence let in Boninsegna to score, but Italian optimism that they could win the game proved a false hope.

Again Brazil left it to the last quarter of the match to convert their supremacy into goals. A brilliant left-footed shot by Gerson from outside the area put the Brazilians ahead. Gerson was again involved in the third goal as his high cross was headed down by Pele for Jairzinho to score a goal that made him the only player ever to have scored in every round of the World Cup. In fact he scored in every game Brazil played in Mexico. Brazil's last goal, just before the end, remains one of the best goals ever scored. Working the ball cleverly out from defence, a long ball found Jairzinho on the wing. He passed to Pele who with arrogant ease slipped the ball into the path of Carlos Alberto the captain. The first Albertosi in the Italian goal saw of the ball was when he retrieved it from the net.

A remarkable goal finished off a remarkable tournament for Brazil. They had conceded seven goals, but worked to the philosophy that as long as you scored more than you conceded you would win. The World Cup in Mexico should have been the spur to break the defensive mentality that was becoming prevalent in the game. Instead, systems were devised by coaches all over the world to stop the threat of a team playing like Brazil had done. Indeed Brazil themselves, four years later in an attempt to keep their crown played a defensive game designed to snuff out their opponents. The World Cup in Mexico therefore will be remembered as an oasis of attacking football in a time when the 0–0 draw was an ever more familiar scoreline.

THE NINTH WORLD CUP

19th May 1968–21st June 1970

QUALIFYING TOURNAMENT

EUROPE

Group 1

	Ro	Gr	Sz	Pt	Pl	W	D	L	F	A	Pts
ROMANIA	–	1–1	2–0	1–0	6	3	2	1	7	6	8
GREECE	2–2	–	4–1	4–2	6	2	3	1	13	9	7
SWITZERLAND	0–1	1–0	–	1–1	6	2	1	3	5	8	5
PORTUGAL	3–0	2–2	0–2	–	6	1	2	3	8	10	4

Group 2

	Cz	Hu	De	RI	Pl	W	D	L	F	A	Pts
CZECHOSLOVAKIA	–	3–3	1–0	3–0	6	4	1	1	12	6	9
HUNGARY	2–0	–	3–0	4–0	6	4	1	1	16	7	9
DENMARK	0–3	3–2	–	2–0	6	2	1	3	6	10	5
REP. IRELAND	1–2	1–2	1–1	–	6	0	1	5	3	14	1

Play-off in Marseilles
Czechoslovakia .... 4–1 .... Hungary

Group 3

	It	EG	Wa	Pl	W	D	L	F	A	Pts
ITALY	–	3–0	4–1	4	3	1	0	10	3	7
EAST GERMANY	2–2	–	2–1	4	2	1	1	7	7	5
WALES	0–1	1–3	–	4	0	0	4	3	10	0

Group 4

	SU	NI	Tu	Pl	W	D	L	F	A	Pts
SOVIET UNION	–	2–0	3–0	4	3	1	0	8	1	7
NTH. IRELAND	0–0	–	4–1	4	2	1	1	7	3	5
TURKEY	1–3	0–3	–	4	0	0	4	2	13	0

Group 5

	Sd	Fr	No	Pl	W	D	L	F	A	Pts
SWEDEN	–	2–0	5–0	4	3	0	1	12	5	6
FRANCE	3–0	–	0–1	4	2	0	2	6	4	4
NORWAY	2–5	1–3	–	4	1	0	3	4	13	2

Group 6

	Be	Yu	Sp	Fi	Pl	W	D	L	F	A	Pts
BELGIUM	–	3–0	2–1	6–1	6	4	1	1	14	8	9
YUGOSLAVIA	4–0	–	0–0	9–1	6	3	1	2	19	7	7
SPAIN	1–1	2–1	–	6–0	6	2	2	2	10	6	6
FINLAND	1–2	1–5	2–0	–	6	1	0	5	6	28	2

Group 7

	WG	Sc	Au	Cy	Pl	W	D	L	F	A	Pts
WEST GERMANY	–	3–2	1–0	12–0	6	5	1	0	20	3	11
SCOTLAND	1–1	–	2–1	8–0	6	3	1	2	18	7	7
AUSTRIA	0–2	2–0	–	7–1	6	3	0	3	12	7	6
CYPRUS	0–1	0–5	1–2	–	6	0	0	6	2	35	0

Group 8

	Bu	Pd	Ho	Lu	Pl	W	D	L	F	A	Pts
BULGARIA	–	4–1	2–0	2–1	6	4	1	1	12	7	9
POLAND	3–0	–	2–1	8–1	6	4	0	2	19	8	8
HOLLAND	1–1	1–0	–	4–0	6	3	1	2	9	5	7
LUXEMBOURG	1–3	1–5	0–2	–	6	0	0	6	4	24	0

SOUTH AMERICA

Group 1

	Pe	Bo	Ar	Pl	W	D	L	F	A	Pts
PERU	–	3–0	1–0	4	2	1	1	7	4	5
BOLIVIA	2–1	–	3–1	4	2	0	2	5	6	4
ARGENTINA	2–2	1–0	–	4	1	1	2	4	6	3

Group 2

	Br	Pa	Co	Ve	Pl	W	D	L	F	A	Pts
BRAZIL	–	1–0	6–2	6–0	6	6	0	0	23	2	12
PARAGUAY	0–3	–	2–1	1–0	6	4	0	2	6	5	8
COLOMBIA	0–2	0–1	–	3–0	6	1	1	4	7	12	3
VENEZUELA	0–5	0–2	1–1	–	6	0	1	5	1	18	1

Group 3

	Ur	Ch	Ec	Pl	W	D	L	F	A	Pts
URUGUAY	–	2–0	1–0	4	3	1	0	5	0	7
CHILE	0–0	–	4–1	4	1	2	1	5	4	4
ECUADOR	0–2	1–1	–	4	0	1	3	2	8	1

CENTRAL AND NORTH AMERICA

FIRST ROUND

Group 1

	Ho	CR	Ja	Pl	W	D	L	F	A	Pts
HONDURAS	–	1–0	3–1	4	3	1	0	7	2	7
COSTA RICA	1–1	–	3–0	4	2	1	1	7	3	5
JAMAICA	0–2	1–3	–	4	0	0	4	2	11	0

Group 2

	Ha	Gu	Tr	Pl	W	D	L	F	A	Pts
HAITI	–	2–0	2–4	4	2	1	1	8	4	5
GUATEMALA	1–1	–	4–0	4	1	2	1	5	3	4
TRINIDAD	0–4	0–0	–	4	1	1	2	4	10	3

Group 3

	ES	Su	NA	Pl	W	D	L	F	A	Pts
EL SALVADOR	–	6–0	1–0	4	3	0	1	10	5	6
SURINAM	4–1	–	6–0	4	2	0	2	10	9	4
NETH. ANTILLES	1–2	2–0	–	4	1	0	3	3	9	2

Group 4

	US	Ca	Be	Pl	W	D	L	F	A	Pts
UNITED STATES	–	1–0	6–2	4	3	0	1	11	6	6
CANADA	4–2	–	4–0	4	2	0	2	8	3	5
BERMUDA	0–2	0–0	–	4	0	1	3	2	12	1

SECOND ROUND

Haiti .... 2–0 1–0 .... United States
Honduras .... 1–0 0–3 .... El Salvador

Play-off in Mexico City
El Salvador .... 3–2 .... Honduras

THIRD ROUND
Haiti .... 1–2 3–0 .... El Salvador
Play-off in Kingston, Jamaica
EL SALVADOR .... 1–0 .... Haiti

ASIA–OCEANIA

FIRST ROUND
Group 1

First round

	Au	SK	Ja	Pl	W	D	L	F	A	Pts
Australia	–	2–1	1–1	4	2	2	0	7	4	6
South Korea	1–1	–	2–2	4	1	2	1	6	5	4
Japan	1–3	0–2	–	4	0	2	2	4	8	2

Second round
Australia .... 1–1 0–0 3–1 .... Rhodesia
All three matches played in Lourenço Marques, Mozambique

Group 2
Israel .... 4–0 2–0 .... New Zealand
North Korea withdrew

SECOND ROUND
ISRAEL .... 1–0 1–1 .... Australia

AFRICA

FIRST ROUND
Algeria .... 1–2 0–0 .... Tunisia
Morocco .... 1–0 1–2 2–0* ... Senegal
Libya .... 2–0 1–5 .... Ethiopia
Zambia .... 4–2 2–4** ...... Sudan
Nigeria .... 1–1 3–2 .... Cameroon
Ghana .... Bye

* Play-off in Las Palmas, Spain
** Sudan qualified having scored more goals in the second game

SECOND ROUND
Tunisia .... 0–0 0–0 2–2* ... Morocco
Ethiopia .... 1–1 1–3 .... Sudan
Nigeria .... 2–1 1–1 .... Ghana

* Morocco qualified on toss of a coin after a play-off in Marseilles

THIRD ROUND

	Mo	Ni	Su	Pl	W	D	L	F	A	Pts
MOROCCO	–	2–1	3–0	4	2	1	1	5	3	5
Nigeria	2–0	–	2–2	4	1	2	1	8	7	4
Sudan	0–0	3–3	–	4	0	3	1	5	8	3

MEXICO qualified as hosts

ENGLAND qualified as holders

FINAL TOURNAMENT

Held in Mexico 31st May–21st June 1970

FIRST ROUND

Group 1 (Azteca – Mexico City)

	SU	Me	Be	ES	Pl	W	D	L	F	A	Pts
SOVIET UNION	–	0–0	4–1	2–0	3	2	1	0	6	1	5
MEXICO	–	–	1–0	4–0	3	2	1	0	5	0	5
BELGIUM	–	–	–	3–0	3	1	0	2	4	5	2
EL SALVADOR	–	–	–	–	3	0	0	3	0	9	0

Group 2 (Cuauhtemoc – Puebla, Luis Dosal – Toluca)

	It	Ur	Sd	Is	Pl	W	D	L	F	A	Pts
ITALY	–	0–0	1–0	0–0	3	1	2	0	1	0	4
URUGUAY	–	–	0–1	2–0	3	1	1	1	2	1	3
SWEDEN	–	–	–	1–1	3	1	1	1	2	2	3
ISRAEL	–	–	–	–	3	0	2	1	1	3	2

Group 3 (Jalisco – Guadalajara)

	Br	En	Ro	Cz	Pl	W	D	L	F	A	Pts
BRAZIL	–	1–0	3–2	4–1	3	3	0	0	8	3	6
ENGLAND	–	–	1–0	1–0	3	2	0	1	2	1	4
ROMANIA	–	–	–	2–1	3	1	0	2	4	5	2
CZECHOSLOVAKIA	–	–	–	–	3	0	0	3	2	7	0

Group 4 (Guanajuato – León)

	WG	Pe	Bu	Mo	Pl	W	D	L	F	A	Pts
WEST GERMANY	–	3–1	5–2	2–1	3	3	0	0	10	4	6
PERU	–	–	3–2	3–0	3	2	0	1	7	5	4
BULGARIA	–	–	–	1–1	3	0	1	2	5	9	1
MOROCCO	–	–	–	–	3	0	1	2	2	6	1

QUARTER-FINALS

Jalisco, Guadalajara, 14–06–1970, 54 000
BRAZIL 4 (Rivelino 11, Tostao 15 52, Jairzinho 77)
PERU 2 (Gallardo 27, Cubillas 64)

Azteca, Mexico City, 14–06–1970, 45 000
URUGUAY 1 (Esparrago 117)
SOVIET UNION 0

Guanajuato, León, 14–06–1970, 24 000
WEST GERMANY 3 (Beckenbauer 68, Seeler 81, Müller 108)
ENGLAND 2 (Mullery 31, Peters 49)

Luis Dosal, Toluca, 14–06–1970, 24 000
ITALY 4 (Domenghini 25, Riva 64 75, Rivera 69)
MEXICO 1 (González 13)

SEMI-FINALS

Jalisco, Guadalajara, 17–06–1970, 51 000
BRAZIL 3 (Clodoaldo 45, Jairzinho 76, Rivelino 88)
URUGUAY 1 (Cubilla 19)

Azteca, Mexico City, 17–06–1970, 80 000
ITALY 4 (Boninsegna 7, Burgnich 99, Riva 104, Rivera 111)
WEST GERMANY 3 (Schnellinger 90, Muller 95 110)

3RD PLACE

Azteca, Mexico City, 20–06–1970, 104 000
WEST GERMANY 1 (Overath 26)
URUGUAY 0

FINAL

Azteca, Mexico City, 21–06–1970, 107 000
BRAZIL 4 (Pele 18, Gerson 66, Jairzinho 71, Carlos Alberto 86)
ITALY 1 (Boninsegna 37)
Referee: Glöckner, East Germany
Brazil – Félix – Carlos Alberto, Brito, Piazza, Everaldo – Clodoaldo, Gerson – Jairzinho, Tostao, Pele, Rivelino. Tr: Zagalo
Italy – Albertosi – Burgnich, Cera, Rosato, Facchetti – Bertini (Juliano),

Mazzola, De Sisti – Domenghini, Boninsegna (Rivera), Riva Tr: Valcareggi

Top scorers: Gerd Müller, West Germany 10
Jairzinho, Brazil 7
Teófilo Cubillas, Peru 5
Total goals scored: 95
Average per game: 3

1974

As it was the turn of Europe to stage the 1974 World Cup, West Germany were the clear favourites and they were awarded the tournament at FIFA's 1968 congress in Mexico City. As with Mexico in 1968 and 1970, Germany had the honour of staging both the Olympic Games and then the World Cup within two years of each other. The space-age Olympic stadium in Munich was designated to stage the final, so there were no worries about the final venue being ready on time. The main worry was that of terrorism. During the Olympic Games in 1972, eleven Israeli athletes had been murdered by Palestinian terrorists, and consequently, even though Israel was not represented at the World Cup, security throughout the tournament was on a level never witnessed before.

A new trophy was also necessary, Brazil having been given permanent possession of the Jules Rimet Trophy. Football therefore lost, as did the Brazilians, literally, six years later, a beautiful, simple trophy and gained an ugly replacement, an 18 carat gold globe on an 18 carat gold pedestal.

Many famous names were not in Germany to fight for the new trophy, the most famous of whom were England. Grouped with the Olympic champions Poland, England could do no more than draw with them at home, in a game marked by some fine goalkeeping by Tomaszewski in the Polish goal. Spain were also absent once again. Having finished level on points with Yugoslavia in their group they lost a play-off 1–0 in Frankfurt.

Hungary, Czechoslovakia, Austria, France and Portugal, all semi-finalists in previous tournaments, failed to qualify along with the Soviet Union, though the latter's exit from the competition was controversial. Forced to play-off against Chile, they drew the first leg in Moscow 0–0. The return leg, however, was due to be staged in the National Stadium in Santiago, and with some justification the Soviets refused to play there. Earlier in the year, during the coup which saw the Marxist President Allende ousted by the right-wing General Pinochet, thousands of people had been herded into the stadium and never seen again. Many, though not all, were communists, and the Soviets did not feel happy about playing a game of football in such surroundings. Despite pleas to play the game elsewhere, the Chileans refused, and on the appointed day took to the field in the National Stadium. In one of the most bizarre sights the World Cup has ever seen, Chile kicked off the game and scored in the empty net. As the Soviets were not there to restart the game, it was abandoned and awarded to Chile.

There were not many other surprises in the qualifying tournament, except perhaps the elimination of Mexico by Haiti in the CONCACAF group. Bolstered by countries from the Arab world, the number of entrants in Asia rose dramatically, though ultimately they were all disappointed as Australia won through the qualifying tournament after being given a hard fight by Iran, the Asian champions, and South Korea, who took the more robust Australians to a play-off in Hong Kong in the final round before losing to a solitary goal.

The number of entries in Africa rose dramatically as well, as sub-Saharan Africa joined in for the first time in numbers. The Arab countries of North Africa had always been the part of Africa most taken note of by the rest of the world given its proximity to Europe, but with the qualification of Zaire the focus shifted further south. The Zaireans won a final group against Morocco and Zambia, and they were considered to be among the best on the continent. Three months before the final tournament in West Germany began, they were crowned African champions after beating Zambia in the final of the African Cup of Nations in Cairo.

The format of the final tournament was changed in an attempt to increase revenue. Instead of eight games from the second round onwards there would now be fourteen. Gone were the quarter-finals and semi-finals which were replaced by two groups of four, the winners of which would qualify for the final, with the runners-up contesting the third place play-off. The system was heavily criticised as there would only be one knock-out game, the final.

Also changed, three days before the finals began, was the presidency of FIFA. Out went Sir Stanley Rous and in came Joao Havelange who had the support of the majority of members from Africa and Asia.

The first round threw up a very interesting pairing in Group 1. East Germany, appearing in the finals for the first time, were drawn in the same group as West Germany. Since the division of Germany after the war, the two had never met in an international. Surprisingly, the men from the East won the day through a Jurgen Sparwasser goal, though both sides had already qualified for the second round at the expense of the weak Australians and Chileans. It was the only time the two countries ever played each other in 45 years of separate existence.

The defending champions Brazil were not the same team as they had been four years previously. Gone were Pele, Gerson and Tostao, and gone also was the free-flowing football and spirit of 1970. Brazil did not go out to win the tournament, instead they tried to prevent the opposition from taking a title they thought was rightfully theirs. Goalless draws against both Yugoslavia and Scotland set the tone and although they qualified with Yugoslavia at the expense of Scotland it was only on goal difference, and one goal at that. Zaire performed creditably against both Brazil and Scotland, but unfortunately will always be remembered for their drubbing at the hands of Yugoslavia, who although they scored nine could easily have taken the total well into double figures.

If the 1974 World Cup is remembered for one aspect in particular, it is for the introduction into the vocabulary of the phrase 'Total Football'. The masters at playing it were Holland, who had qualified for the World Cup for the first time since 1938. It was not a form of tactics as such, but a system whereby players would not be stuck to one position on the pitch. To make it work, players had to be very versatile and Holland had such men. They were by general consent the most talented team in the tournament and they qualified for the second round with ease, along with Sweden. Uruguay failed to qualify as they, like Brazil, seemed intent on playing hard, defensive football.

Not so Argentina, South America's third representatives, who played attractive, open football in their group matches. They qualified along with Poland, the real surprise package of the tournament, in what was an exciting group. Haiti in particular nearly caused an upset when they raced into an early second-half lead against Italy, but the thought of North Korea no doubt spurred the Italians on and they eventually ran out winners. They did not qualify for the next round, however. In their third game they had to beat the Poles, who were much too good for them. If any solace for England was to be found, this was it.

The second round separated the two arch-exponents of total football, Holland and West Germany. Holland now had to get past the challenge of Brazil, who were considered their greatest threat. Argentina, though full of promise, had not matured into a world-beating side just yet, and they lost to both Holland and Brazil in their first two matches. East Germany did likewise, which meant that although technically there was no semi-final, the final tie of the group between Brazil and Holland was just that, though a superior goal difference meant that Holland only had to draw to qualify for the final.

Holland were not to be denied by the champions. Goals by Neeskens and Cruyff in the second half of a game that saw some over-the-top tackling from both sides, gave Holland their place in the final, a place they richly deserved. Krol, Neeskens, Van Hanegem, Rep, Haan and Cruyff were all masters of their trade, but they needed the dominating figure of Rinus Michels, the manager, to make them function as a unit. Without him they might not have even reached the finals. Larger than life egos among the players had threatened to destroy the very basis of the team, that of combining together.

The other second round group saw a similar 'semi-final' situation develop. Both Poland and West Germany won their first two matches, leaving the game between the two of them as the decider. Like Holland, however, the Germans knew they could rely on a draw, and this gave them the advantage. Poland, who had been considered fortunate to beat both the Swedes and Yugoslavia, were this time unfortunate to lose to the Germans. The game was played on a rain-soaked Frankfurt pitch and only some excellent goalkeeping by Maier kept Lato at bay. Twelve minutes from time, however, Müller, who had not played as well as he had in Mexico, scored the killer goal that saw the hosts through.

The final therefore matched two perfectly balanced teams and was built up as a contest between Cruyff and Beckenbauer, both of whom vied to inherit the title of the world's greatest footballer, a position Pele had held for what seemed like an eternity. Beckenbauer was building a fearsome reputation as a *libero*, a sweeper who unlike the Italian model was not confined to defensive duties. Instead Beckenbauer was used as a springboard for attacking moves as well as clearing up in defence. Cruyff was regarded as the more skilful of the two, a player who could either make or score goals.

Beckenbauer was the one who emerged triumphant on this occasion, though not before Cruyff had given the game a start that would not be forgotten. Holland kicked off and before a German player had touched the ball they were a goal up. A superb run by Cruyff from outside the penalty area ended up with him being upended by Hoeness in it. Neeskens scored from the penalty spot with barely a minute gone.

For the first quarter of the game West Germany simply were not in it, and had the Dutch bothered to press home their advantage, Germany would have been out of the game completely. After 25 minutes, however, they were back in it when Breitner scored from the second penalty of the game after Holzenbein had been tripped by Jansen. Two minutes before half-time West Germany took the lead. Müller, receiving the ball from Bonhof, showed lightning reactions in first stopping the pass and then retrieving the ball when it looked as though it had gone behind him. Before any of the Dutch defenders had a chance to clear, the ball was in the back of the net.

Try as they might in the second half, the Dutch could not score. Again Maier showed why he was considered to be the best goalkeeper in the world, saving well from Neeskens, but Holland had lost the momentum they had built up in the first half, and for the second time the World Cup was West Germany's. Beckenbauer became the first captain to lift the new FIFA trophy.

THE TENTH WORLD CUP
14th November 1971–7th July 1974

QUALIFYING TOURNAMENT

EUROPE

Group 1

	Sd	Au	Hu	Ma	Pl	W	D	L	F	A	Pts
SWEDEN	–	3–2	0–0	7–0	6	3	2	1	14	7	8
Austria	2–0	–	2–2	4–0	6	3	2	1	15	8	8
Hungary	3–3	2–2	–	3–0	6	2	4	0	12	7	8
Malta	1–2	0–2	0–2	–	6	0	0	6	1	20	0

Play-off in Gelsenkirchen
Sweden .... 2–1 .... Austria

Group 2

	It	Tu	Sz	Lu	Pl	W	D	L	F	A	Pts
ITALY	–	0–0	2–0	5–0	6	4	2	0	12	0	10
Turkey	0–1	–	2–0	3–0	6	2	2	2	5	3	6
Switzerland	0–0	0–0	–	1–0	6	2	2	2	2	4	6
Luxembourg	0–4	2–0	0–1	–	6	1	0	5	2	14	2

Group 3

	Ho	Be	No	Ic	Pl	W	D	L	F	A	Pts
HOLLAND	–	0–0	9–0	8–1	6	4	2	0	24	2	10
Belgium	0–0	–	2–0	4–0	6	4	2	0	12	0	10
Norway	1–2	0–2	–	4–1	6	2	0	4	9	16	4
Iceland	0–5	0–4	0–4	–	6	0	0	6	2	29	0

Group 4

	EG	Ro	Fi	Al	Pl	W	D	L	F	A	Pts
EAST GERMANY	–	2–0	5–0	2–0	6	5	0	1	18	3	10
Romania	1–0	–	9–0	2–0	6	4	1	1	17	4	9
Finland	1–5	1–1	–	1–0	6	1	1	4	3	21	3
Albania	1–4	1–4	1–0	–	6	1	0	5	3	13	2

Group 5

	Pd	En	Wa	Pl	W	D	L	F	A	Pts
POLAND	–	2–0	3–0	4	2	1	1	6	3	5
England	1–1	–	1–1	4	1	2	1	3	4	4
Wales	2–0	0–1	–	4	1	1	2	3	5	3

Group 6

	Bu	Pt	NI	Cy	Pl	W	D	L	F	A	Pts
BULGARIA	–	2–1	3–0	2–0	6	4	2	0	13	3	10
Portugal	2–2	–	1–1	4–0	6	2	3	1	10	6	7
Nth. Ireland	0–0	1–1	–	3–0	6	1	3	2	5	6	5
Cyprus	0–4	0–1	1–0	–	6	1	0	5	1	14	2

Group 7

	Sp	Yu	Gr	Pl	W	D	L	F	A	Pts
Spain	–	2–2	3–1	4	2	2	0	8	5	6
YUGOSLAVIA	0–0	–	1–0	4	2	2	0	7	4	6
Greece	2–3	2–4	–	4	0	0	4	5	11	0

Play-off in Frankfurt
Yugoslavia .... 1–0 .... Spain

Group 8

	Sc	Cz	De	Pl	W	D	L	F	A	Pts
SCOTLAND	–	2–1	2–0	4	3	0	1	8	3	6
Czechoslovakia	1–0	–	6–0	4	2	1	1	9	3	5
Denmark	1–4	1–1	–	4	0	1	3	2	13	1

Group 9

	SU	RI	Fr	Pl	W	D	L	F	A	Pts
Soviet Union	–	1–0	2–0	4	3	0	1	5	2	6
Rep. Ireland	1–2	–	2–1	4	1	1	2	4	5	3
France	1–0	1–1	–	4	1	1	2	3	5	3

Soviet Union qualified for play-off against South American Group 3 winners Chile

SOUTH AMERICA

Group 1

	Ur	Co	Ec	Pl	W	D	L	F	A	Pts
URUGUAY	–	0–1	4–0	4	2	1	1	6	2	5
Colombia	0–0	–	1–1	4	1	3	0	3	2	5
Ecuador	1–2	1–1	–	4	0	2	2	3	8	2

Group 2

	Ar	Pa	Bo	Pl	W	D	L	F	A	Pts
ARGENTINA	–	3–1	4–0	4	3	1	0	9	2	7
Paraguay	1–1	–	4–0	4	2	1	1	8	5	5
Bolivia	0–1	1–2	–	4	0	0	4	1	11	0

Group 3

Peru .... 2–0 0–2 .. Chile

Play-off in Montevideo
Chile .... 2–1 ...... Peru

Chile qualified for a play-off with Soviet Union

Soviet Union .... 0–0 * ... CHILE

* Soviet Union refused to play the second leg and were disqualified

CENTRAL AND NORTH AMERICA

FIRST ROUND

Group 1

	Me	Ca	US	Pl	W	D	L	F	A	Pts
Mexico	–	2–1	3–1	4	4	0	0	8	3	8
Canada	0–1	–	3–2	4	1	1	2	6	7	3
United States	1–2	2–2	–	4	0	1	3	6	10	1

Group 2

Guatemala .... 1–0 1–0 .... El Salvador

Group 3

Honduras .... 2–1 3–3 .... Costa Rica

Group 4

Netherlands Antilles received a bye as Jamaica withdrew

Group 5

Haiti .... 7–0 5–0 .... Puerto Rico

Group 6

	Tr	Su	An	Pl	W	D	L	F	A	Pts
Trinidad	–	1–1	11–1	4	3	1	0	16	4	7
Surinam	1–2	–	3–1	4	2	1	1	11	4	5
Antigua	1–2	0–6	–	4	0	0	4	3	22	0

SECOND ROUND

Tournament held in Haiti

	Ha	Tr	Me	Ho	Gu	NA	Pl	W	D	L	F	A	Pts
HAITI	–	2–1	0–1	1–0	2–1	3–0	5	4	0	1	8	3	8
Trinidad	–	–	4–0	1–2	1–0	4–0	5	3	0	2	11	4	6
Mexico	–	–	–	1–1	0–0	8–0	5	2	2	1	10	5	6
Honduras	–	–	–	–	1–1	2–2	5	1	3	1	6	6	5
Guatemala	–	–	–	–	–	2–2	5	0	3	2	4	6	3
Neth. Antilles	–	–	–	–	–	–	5	0	2	3	4	19	2

AFRICA

FIRST ROUND

Morocco .... 0–0 2–1 .... Senegal
Algeria .... 1–0 1–5 .... Guinea
Egypt .... 2–1 0–2 .... Tunisia
Sierra Leone .... 0–1 0–2 .... Côte d'Ivoire
Kenya .... 2–0 0–1 .... Sudan
Mauritius .... W–O .... Madagascar
Ethiopia .... 1–1 0–0 3–0* .. Tanzania
Lesotho .... 0–0 1–6 .... Zambia
Nigeria .... 2–1 1–1 .... Congo
Dahomey .... 0–5 1–5 .... Ghana
Togo .... 0–0 0–4 .... Zaire
Cameroon .... W–O .... Gabon

* Play-off in Addis Ababa

SECOND ROUND

Kenya .... 3–1 2–2 .... Mauritius
Guinea .... 1–1 0–2 .... Morocco
Tunisia .... 1–1 1–2 .... Côte d'Ivoire
Nigeria .... 0–2 1–1** ... Ghana
Cameroon .... 0–1 1–0 0–2* . Zaire
Ethiopia .... 0–0 2–4 .... Zambia

* Play-off in Kinshasa
** First match abandoned with Ghana leading 3–2. Ghana awarded the game 2–0

THIRD ROUND

Côte d'Ivoire .... 1–1 1–4 .... Morocco
Zambia .... 2–0 2–2 .... Kenya
Ghana .... 1–0 1–4 .... Zaire

FOURTH ROUND

	Zr	Zm	Mo	Pl	W	D	L	F	A	Pts
ZAIRE	–	2–1	3–0	4	4	0	0	9	1	8
ZAMBIA	0–2	–	4–0	4	1	0	3	5	6	2
MOROCCO	0–2*	2–0	–	4	1	0	3	2	9	2

* Morocco against Zaire was not played. Tie awarded to Zaire 2–0

ASIA

FIRST ROUND

Group A

Preliminary round (To determine group placements)

South Vietnam .... 1–0 .. Thailand
Israel .... 2–1 .. Japan
Hong Kong .... 1–0 .. Malaysia

First Round

Sub Group 1

	HK	Ja	SV	Pl	W	D	L	F	A	Pts
HONG KONG	–	1–0	1–0	2	2	0	0	2	0	4
JAPAN	–	–	4–0	2	1	0	1	4	1	2
SOUTH VIETNAM	–	–	–	2	0	0	2	0	5	0

Sub Group 2

	Is	SK	Ma	Th	Pl	W	D	L	F	A	Pts
ISRAEL	–	0–0	3–0	6–0	3	2	1	0	9	0	5
SOUTH KOREA	–	–	0–0	4–0	3	1	2	0	4	0	4
MALAYSIA	–	–	–	2–0	3	1	1	1	2	3	3
THAILAND	–	–	–	–	3	0	0	3	0	12	0

Semi-Finals

Israel .... 1–0 .... Japan
South Korea .... 3–1 .... Hong Kong

Final

South Korea .... 1–0 .... Israel

Group B

First round

Sub Group 1

	Au	Ir	Id	NZ	Pl	W	D	L	F	A	Pts
AUSTRALIA	–	3–1	2–1	3–3	6	3	3	0	15	6	9
IRAQ	0–0	–	1–1	2–0	6	3	2	1	11	6	8
INDONESIA	0–6	2–3	–	1–1	6	1	2	3	6	13	4
NEW ZEALAND	1–1	0–4	0–1	–	6	0	3	3	5	12	3

Sub Group 2

	Ir	Sy	NK	Ku	Pl	W	D	L	F	A	Pts
IRAN	–	1–0	0–0	2–1	6	4	1	1	7	3	9
SYRIA	1–0	–	1–1	2–1	6	3	1	2	6	6	7
NORTH KOREA	1–2	3–0	–	0–0	6	1	3	2	5	5	5
KUWAIT	0–2	0–2	2–0	–	6	1	1	4	4	8	3

Final

Australia .... 3–0 0–2 .... Iran

SECOND ROUND

Australia .... 0–0 2–2 .... South Korea

Play-off in Hong Kong

AUSTRALIA .... 1–0 .... South Korea

WEST GERMANY qualified as hosts

BRAZIL qualified as holders

FINAL TOURNAMENT

Held in West Germany 13th June–7th July 1974

FIRST ROUND

Group 1 (Olympiastadion – Berlin, Volksparkstadion – Hamburg)

	EG	WG	Ch	Au	Pl	W	D	L	F	A	Pts
EAST GERMANY	–	1–0	1–1	2–0	3	2	1	0	4	1	5
WEST GERMANY	–	–	1–0	3–0	3	2	0	1	4	1	4
CHILE	–	–	–	0–0	3	0	2	1	1	2	2
AUSTRALIA	–	–	–	–	3	0	1	2	0	5	1

Group 2 (Waldstadion – Frankfurt, Westfalenstadion – Dortmund, Parkstadion – Gelsenkirchen)

	Yu	Br	Sc	Zr	Pl	W	D	L	F	A	Pts
YUGOSLAVIA	–	0–0	1–1	9–0	3	1	2	0	10	1	4
BRAZIL	–	–	0–0	3–0	3	1	2	0	3	0	4
SCOTLAND	–	–	–	2–0	3	1	2	0	3	1	4
ZAIRE	–	–	–	–	3	0	0	3	0	14	0

Group 3 (Niedersachsenstadion – Hanover, Rheinstadion – Düsseldorf, Westfalenstadion – Dortmund)

	Ho	Sd	Bu	Ur	Pl	W	D	L	F	A	Pts
HOLLAND	–	0–0	4–1	2–0	3	2	1	0	6	1	5
SWEDEN	–	–	0–0	3–0	3	1	2	0	3	0	4
BULGARIA	–	–	–	1–1	3	0	2	1	2	5	2
URUGUAY	–	–	–	–	3	0	1	2	1	6	1

Group 4 (Olympiastadion – Munich, Neckarstadion – Stuttgart)

	Pd	Ar	It	Ha	Pl	W	D	L	F	A	Pts
POLAND	–	3–2	2–1	7–0	3	3	0	0	12	3	6
ARGENTINA	–	–	1–1	4–1	3	1	1	1	7	5	3
ITALY	–	–	–	3–1	3	1	1	1	5	4	3
HAITI	–	–	–	–	3	0	0	3	2	14	0

SECOND ROUND

GROUP A

Niedersachsenstadion, Hanover, 26–06–1974, 59 000
BRAZIL 1 (Rivelino 60)
EAST GERMANY 0

Parkstadion, Gelsenkirchen, 26–06–1974, 55 000
HOLLAND 4 (Cruyff 11 89, Krol 25, Rep 72)
ARGENTINA 0

Parkstadion, Gelsenkirchen, 30–06–1974, 69 000
HOLLAND 2 (Neeskens 8, Rensenbrink 61)
EAST GERMANY 0

Niedersachsenstadion, Hanover, 30–06–1974, 39 000
BRAZIL 2 (Rivelino 31, Jairzinho 48)
ARGENTINA 1 (Brindisi 34)

Parkstadion, Gelsenkirchen, 3–07–1974, 54 000
EAST GERMANY 1 (Streich 14)
ARGENTINA 1 (Houseman 20)

Westfalenstadion, Dortmund, 3–07–1974, 53 000
HOLLAND 2 (Neeskens 50, Cruyff 65)
BRAZIL 0

	Pl	W	D	L	F	A	Pts
HOLLAND	3	3	0	0	8	0	6
BRAZIL	3	2	0	1	3	3	4
EAST GERMANY	3	0	1	2	1	4	1
ARGENTINA	3	0	1	2	2	7	1

GROUP B

Neckarstadion, Stuttgart, 26–06–1974, 45 000
POLAND 1 (Lato 43)
SWEDEN 0

Rheinstadion, Düsseldorf, 26–06–1974, 67 000
WEST GERMANY 2 (Breitner 39, Müller 77)
YUGOSLAVIA 0

Waldstadion, Frankfurt, 30–06–1974, 53 000
POLAND 2 (Deyna 25, Lato 62)
YUGOSLAVIA 1 (Karasi 43)

Rheinstadion, Düsseldorf, 30–06–1974, 67 000
WEST GERMANY 4 (Overath 50, Bonhof 51, Grabowski 78, Hoeness 89)
SWEDEN 2 (Edström 26, Sandberg 53)

Rheinstadion, Düsseldorf, 3–07–1974, 37 000
SWEDEN 2 (Edström 30, Torstensson 86)
YUGOSLAVIA 1 (Surjak 27)

Waldstadion, Frankfurt, 3–07–1974, 62 000
WEST GERMANY 1 (Müller 76)
POLAND 0

	Pl	W	D	L	F	A	Pts
WEST GERMANY	3	3	0	0	7	2	6
POLAND	3	2	0	1	3	2	4
SWEDEN	3	1	0	2	4	6	2
YUGOSLAVIA	3	0	0	3	2	6	0

3RD PLACE

Olympiastadion, Munich, 6–07–1974, 69 000
POLAND 1 (Lato 76)
BRAZIL 0

FINAL

Olympiastadion, Munich, 7–07–1974, 77 000
WEST GERMANY 2 (Breitner 25, Müller 43)
HOLLAND 1 (Neeskens 1)
Referee: Taylor, England
West Germany – Maier – Vogts, Schwarzenbeck, Beckenbauer, Breitner – Bonhof, Hoeness, Overath – Grabowski, Müller, Hölzenbein. Tr: Schoen
Holland – Jongbloed – Suurbier, Rijsbergen (De Jong), Haan, Krol – Jansen, Neeskens, Van Hanegem – Rep, Cruyff, Rensenbrink (Van de Kerkhof R). Tr: Michels

Top scorers: Grzegorz Lato, Poland 7
Andrzej Szarmach, Poland 5
Johan Neeskens, Holland 5
Total goals scored: 97
Average per game: 2.6

1978

In 1978 the World Cup finally came to the home of South American football, Argentina. They had been awarded the tournament 12 years previously when no-one could foresee the problems that were to face the country in 1978. A brutal right-wing dictatorship under General Videla was busy terrorising its own people, many of whom simply 'disappeared' and were never seen again. Left-wing guerillas were in turn fighting back, and the country seemed to be on the verge of collapse. At one stage it seemed likely that the tournament would be relocated to Holland and Belgium as the threat of withdrawals became evident.

Despite these political problems, and concern that some of the stadia might not be ready on time, in the event the tournament passed off without incident off the field, helped by a truce tacitly agreed between the government and guerillas.

Both Uruguay and England failed to qualify. The former lost out to Bolivia in one of the biggest shocks in South American football history, the latter to Italy in a group that was decided on goal difference. Questions were asked about a system that allowed two former world champions to be grouped together in one group whilst another could contain Sweden, Switzerland and Norway, none of whom were relatively strong at the time. The Soviet Union were another established nation to miss out for the second time in a row, Hungary returning to the fold at their expense after a 12-year absence. The European champions Czechoslovakia were another surprise failure, and apart from West Germany, Holland and Italy, the European representation in Argentina did not look to be that strong.

Brazil were forced to play in the qualifying competition for the first time in 20 years and along with Peru, qualified with relative ease. Despite knocking out the Uruguayans, who were rueing the missed chance to play so close to home, Bolivia could not beat off the challenge of Hungary in the intercontinental play-off – indeed they were trounced 6–0 in Budapest.

In Central America, Mexico made no mistake in qualifying, winning a tournament held in Mexico. To reach the finals, the Mexicans had to play nine games. Tunisia, who qualified from Africa, had to play ten, whilst Iran, Asia's representatives, had to play 12, double, and in some cases three times, the number required by most European nations. As the number of entries rose, it was evident that the number of places afforded Africa and Asia would have to rise in the future, and the 1978 World Cup was the last to be played to the 16-team formula.

Iran and Tunisia, especially, both strengthened the case for increased representation by playing well once in Argentina. Tunisia comfortably beat Mexico, narrowly lost against Poland and held the world champions West Germany to a goalless draw in a match that the North Africans needed to win to qualify for the second round. Instead it was the Poles and West Germans who qualified, but no longer would European teams play African sides and expect scores similar to Yugoslavia's 9–0 win four years previously.

Iran were expected to do better than Tunisia, dominating Asian football as they had for over ten years, but unfortunately for them they were grouped with Holland, who although they were without Cruyff who had temporarily retired, were still the favourites, along with the hosts, to win the tournament. Two penalties in a Rensenbrink hat-trick saw the Dutch beat Iran in the opening game of Group 4, but in their next game against Scotland, Iran, but for an extraordinary own goal, would have won. The much-fancied Peru made up the teams in Group 4 and they made sure the Iranians did not progress further.

Group 4 was in the event the most dramatic of the first round. Scotland needed to beat the Dutch by three clear goals in the final group game to qualify at their expense, and at one stage in the match, leading 3–1, they looked set to do it. After having played badly in the first two games, the Scots were turning on the style. The third goal in particular, a mazy dribble and shot by Gemmill, was possibly the best of the tournament. But a Rep goal 20 minutes from time put paid to any hopes they may have had.

Group 3 was the most dour, but was enlivened by an extraordinary refereeing decision in the match between Sweden and Brazil. With the scores at 1–1, Zico headed home a corner to seemingly win the match, but as the ball was sailing into the net, Clive Thomas the referee blew the whistle for full time. The Brazilians were furious but the result stood. Playing to much the same style that they had done in West Germany, Brazil drew their next game 0–0 with Spain, who once again did not have a happy tournament. The Austrians proved to be the surprise package, and although beaten by Brazil in the final game, they were already assured of their qualification.

Argentina, based in the impressive River Plate stadium which had been completely refurbished, beat both Hungary and France, as did the Italians, based further down the coast in Mar del Plata. France however were no push-overs and with a young Platini in the side, showed promise that would stand them in good stead for the following World Cup. Argentina were spurred on by a fiercely partisan crowd, though in the final game against Italy, with nothing to play for, they lost 1–0 in an ill-tempered game, a result that left them in what looked like a marginally easier group for the second round, though the Argentine fans in the River Plate stadium had hoped for a win to keep their team in Buenos Aires.

Following the same system as four years previously, the second round was played in two groups of four, the winners of which would contest the final. The groups were divided almost exactly on continental lines. Along with Argentina were grouped Brazil and Peru as well as one European team, Poland, whilst Group A was a totally European affair.

Neither West Germany or Poland were of the same strength that had taken them to first and third places in 1974 and both flopped badly. Holland roundly disposed of the Austrians in their opening game whilst the Italians played out a 0–0 draw with the Germans, and although the Germans still had a mathematical chance of reaching the final going into the last game, courtesy of a draw against the Dutch, Austria saw to it that they would not. The game between Italy and Holland was therefore in effect a semi-final. Italy needed to win, whereas Holland could rely on a draw, and after 19 minutes a Brandts own goal put the Italians in the driving seat. The same player made amends early in the second half with a long range shot, an effort that Haan bettered after 75 minutes from even further out.

Group B was full of controversy as both Brazil and Argentina finished level on five points. Both had beaten Peru and Poland respectively in the opening games of the group, and they met in Rosario in the second set of games. No goals were scored in a highly charged game, which meant that if, as expected, Brazil beat Poland and Argentina beat Peru, goal difference would be needed to decide the finalists. In a piece of crass organisation, the Brazil–Poland game kicked off before the Argentina–Peru game which meant that the Argentinians knew exactly the result they needed.

The Brazilians cried cheat and they were largely justified. The organisers put the case that if Argentina played at the same time, no-one would go to the Brazil–Poland match, and they had a point; but the fact remained that the hosts derived a clear advantage. Knowing that they needed to win 4–1 at the very least, Argentina went even further than that, winning 6–0. To the accusations of bad organisation those of foul play were added, though Brazilian claims that the Peruvians had been bribed were totally unfounded.

The final therefore was between the hosts and the runners-up of four years previously. Unfortunately for the Dutch, they joined both Czechoslovakia and Hungary as nations who had reached two finals and lost them both. Holland's misfortune was that on both occasions they lost to the hosts. Had either of the finals been staged on neutral ground, they might well have won them.

Ernst Happel was their manager in Argentina, and despite the absence of Cruyff, Van Hanegem, Van Beveren and Geels, he fashioned a side that looked capable of beating the Argentines, despite their home advantage. Argentina meanwhile, managed by the chain-smoking Menotti, had suffered the usual Argentine disease, players leaving Argentina for Europe. Of the exiles, only Kempes was recalled. Menotti decided to rely on home-based players, and the ploy worked.

Argentina won the final before a passionate crowd in the River Plate stadium in Buenos Aires. So much light blue and white confetti had been used to celebrate the home team's arrival on the pitch that at both ends it looked as if it had been snowing. Mario Kempes, leading the Argentine attack, played one of the best games of his life, and he opened the scoring in the 38th minute, cleverly touching home a pass from Luque. The Dutch, annoyed by Argentina's late arrival on the pitch at the beginning of the game, and by a protest about a bandage Rene Van de Kerkhof was wearing, did not approach the game with the right attitude. The match was plagued by fouls and the referee seemed to have lost control, but Argentina hung onto their lead.

In the last ten minutes, however, the Dutch nearly stole the match. Rene Van de Kerkhof beat the offside trap after an excellent through ball by Haan. He crossed and the substitute Nanninga was there to head home the equaliser. In the very last seconds of the game, Rensenbrink hit the post from close range after receiving a perfectly weighted long ball from Krol, and Holland's chance was gone. In extra-time, with the crowd roaring them on, Argentina regrouped and went into the lead again. Kempes it was who scored, this time after a dazzling run from outside the penalty area during which he took on and beat three players, including the goalkeeper. Kempes was involved in Argentina's third goal as well. Setting off on another run he flicked the ball to Bertoni, Bertoni knocked it back, and it fortuitously came back off Kempes' chest for Bertoni to sweep it home.

Argentina had won a colourful and sometimes controversial tournament and deservedly so. None of the threatened problems had materialised. Having contributed so much to the game over the years, they finally had some tangible reward.

THE ELEVENTH WORLD CUP

7th March 1976–25th June 1978

QUALIFYING TOURNAMENT

EUROPE

Group 1

	Pd	Pt	De	Cy	Pl	W	D	L	F	A	Pts
POLAND	–	1–1	4–1	5–0	6	5	1	0	17	4	11
PORTUGAL	0–2	–	1–0	4–0	6	4	1	1	12	6	9
DENMARK	1–2	2–4	–	5–0	6	2	0	4	14	12	4
CYPRUS	1–3	1–2	1–5	–	6	0	0	6	3	24	0

Group 2

	It	En	Fi	Lu	Pl	W	D	L	F	A	Pts
ITALY	–	2–0	6–1	3–0	6	5	0	1	18	4	10
ENGLAND	2–0	–	2–1	5–0	6	5	0	1	15	4	10
FINLAND	0–3	1–4	–	7–1	6	2	0	4	11	16	4
LUXEMBOURG	1–4	0–2	0–1	–	6	0	0	6	2	22	0

Group 3

	Au	EG	Tu	Ma	Pl	W	D	L	F	A	Pts
AUSTRIA	–	1–1	1–0	9–0	6	4	2	0	14	2	10
EAST GERMANY	1–1	–	1–1	9–0	6	3	3	0	15	4	9
TURKEY	0–1	1–2	–	4–0	6	2	1	3	9	5	5
MALTA	0–1	0–1	0–3	–	6	0	0	6	0	27	0

Group 4

	Ho	Be	NI	Ic	Pl	W	D	L	F	A	Pts
HOLLAND	–	1–0	2–2	4–1	6	5	1	0	11	3	11
BELGIUM	0–2	–	2–0	4–0	6	3	0	3	7	6	6
NTH. IRELAND	0–1	3–0	–	2–0	6	2	1	3	7	6	5
ICELAND	0–1	0–1	1–0	–	6	1	0	5	2	12	2

Group 5

	Fr	Bu	RI	Pl	W	D	L	F	A	Pts
FRANCE	–	3–1	2–0	4	2	1	1	7	4	5
BULGARIA	2–2	–	2–1	4	1	2	1	5	6	4
REP. IRELAND	1–0	0–0	–	4	1	1	2	2	4	3

Group 6

	Sd	No	Sz	Pl	W	D	L	F	A	Pts
SWEDEN	–	2–0	2–1	4	3	0	1	7	4	6
NORWAY	2–1	–	1–0	4	2	0	2	3	4	4
SWITZERLAND	1–2	1–0	–	4	1	0	3	3	5	2

Group 7

	Sc	Cz	Wa	Pl	W	D	L	F	A	Pts
SCOTLAND	–	3–1	1–0	4	3	0	1	6	3	6
CZECHOSLOVAKIA	2–0	–	1–0	4	2	0	2	4	6	4
WALES	0–2	3–0	–	4	1	0	3	3	4	2

Group 8

	Sp	Ro	Yu	Pl	W	D	L	F	A	Pts
SPAIN	–	2–0	1–0	4	3	0	1	4	1	6
ROMANIA	1–0	–	4–6	4	2	0	2	7	8	4
YUGOSLAVIA	0–1	0–2	–	4	1	0	3	6	8	2

Group 9

	Hu	SU	Gr	Pl	W	D	L	F	A	Pts
HUNGARY	–	2–1	3–0	4	2	1	1	6	4	5
SOVIET UNION	2–0	–	2–0	4	2	0	2	5	3	4
GREECE	1–1	1–0	–	4	1	1	2	2	6	3

Hungary qualified to meet the 3rd placed team in the South American group final, Bolivia

SOUTH AMERICA

FIRST ROUND

Group 1

	Br	Pa	Co	Pl	W	D	L	F	A	Pts
BRAZIL	–	1–1	6–0	4	2	2	0	8	1	6
PARAGUAY	0–1	–	1–1	4	1	2	1	3	3	4
COLOMBIA	0–0	0–1	–	4	0	2	2	1	8	2

Group 2

	Bo	Ur	Ve	Pl	W	D	L	F	A	Pts
BOLIVIA	–	1–0	2–0	4	3	1	0	8	3	7
URUGUAY	2–2	–	2–0	4	1	2	1	5	4	4
VENEZUELA	1–3	1–1	–	4	0	1	3	2	8	1

Group 3

	Pe	Ch	Ec	Pl	W	D	L	F	A	Pts
PERU	–	2–0	4–0	4	2	2	0	8	2	6
CHILE	1–1	–	3–0	4	2	1	1	5	3	5
ECUADOR	1–1	0–1	–	4	0	1	3	1	9	1

SECOND ROUND

Tournament in Cali, Colombia

	Br	Pe	Bo	Pl	W	D	L	F	A	Pts
BRAZIL	–	1–0	8–0	4	2	0	0	9	0	4
PERU	–	–	5–0	4	1	0	1	5	1	2
BOLIVIA	–	–	–	4	0	0	2	0	13	0

Bolivia qualified to meet the winners of Europe Group 9, Hungary

HUNGARY .... 6–0 3–2 .... Bolivia

CENTRAL AND NORTH AMERICA

FIRST ROUND

Group 1

	Me	US	Ca	Pl	W	D	L	F	A	Pts
MEXICO	–	3–0	0–0	4	1	2	1	3	1	4
UNITED STATES	0–0	–	2–0	4	1	2	1	3	4	4
CANADA	1–0	1–1	–	4	1	2	1	2	3	4

Play-off in Port-au-Prince

Canada .... 3–0 .... United States

Group 2

	Gu	ES	CR	Pa	Pl	W	D	L	F	A	Pts
GUATEMALA	–	3–1	1–1	7–0	6	3	2	1	15	6	8
EL SALVADOR	2–0	–	1–1	4–1	6	2	3	1	10	7	7
COSTA RICA	0–0	1–1	–	3–0	6	1	4	1	8	6	6
PANAMA	2–4	1–1	3–2	–	6	1	1	4	7	21	3

Group 3

First round

Dominican Rep. ... 0–3 0–3 .... Haiti

Second round

Guyana .... 2–0 0–3 .... Surinam
Neth. Antilles .... 1–2 0–7 .... Haiti
Jamaica .... 1–3 0–2 .... Cuba
Barbados .... 2–1 0–1 1–3* .. Trinidad

* Play-off in Port of Spain, Trinidad

Third round

Surinam .... 1–1 2–2 3–2* .. Trinidad
Cuba .... 1–1 1–1 0–2** .. Haiti

* Play-off in Cayenne, Surinam
** Play-off in Panama City

SECOND ROUND

Tournament in Mexico City and Monterrey

	Me	Ha	Ca	ES	Gu	Su	Pl	W	D	L	F	A	Pts
MEXICO	–	4–1	3–1	3–1	2–1	8–1	5	5	0	0	20	5	10
HAITI	–	–	1–1	1–0	2–1	1–0	5	3	1	1	6	6	7
CANADA	–	–	–	1–2	2–1	2–1	5	2	1	2	7	8	5
EL SALVADOR	–	–	–	–	2–2	3–2	5	2	1	2	8	9	5
GUATEMALA	–	–	–	–	–	3–2	5	1	1	3	8	10	3
SURINAM	–	–	–	–	–	–	5	0	0	5	6	17	0

AFRICA

PRELIMINARY ROUND

Sierra Leone .... 5–1 1–2 .... Niger
Upper Volta .... 1–1 2–0 .... Mauritania

FIRST ROUND

Algeria .... 1–0 0–0 .... Libya
Zambia .... 4–1 1–0 .... Malawi
Upper Volta .... 1–1 0–2 .... Côte d'Ivoire
Sierra Leone .... 0–0 2–6 .... Nigeria
Togo .... 1–0 1–1 .... Senegal
Congo .... 2–2 2–1 .... Cameroon
Egypt .... 3–0 2–1 .... Ethiopia
Morocco .... 1–1 1–1 (2–4p) .. Tunisia
Ghana .... 2–1 1–2 0–2* .... Guinea
Zaire .... W–O .... Cent. African Rep.
Kenya .... W–O .... Sudan
Uganda .... W–O .... Tanzania

* Play-off in Lome, Togo

SECOND ROUND

Tunisia .... 2–0 1–1 .... Algeria
Togo .... 0–2 1–2 .... Guinea
Côte d'Ivoire .... 3–2 3–1 .... Congo
Kenya .... 0–0 0–1 .... Egypt
Uganda .... 1–0 2–4 .... Zambia
Nigeria .... W–O .... Zaire

THIRD ROUND

Guinea .... 1–0 1–3 .... Tunisia
Nigeria .... 4–0 2–2 .... Côte d'Ivoire
Egypt .... 2–0 0–0 .... Zambia

FOURTH ROUND

	Tu	Eg	Ni	Pl	W	D	L	F	A	Pts
TUNISIA	–	4–1	0–0	4	2	1	1	7	4	5
EGYPT	3–2	–	3–1	4	2	0	2	7	11	4
NIGERIA	0–1	4–0	–	4	1	1	2	5	4	3

ASIA–OCEANIA

FIRST ROUND

Oceania

	Au	Nz	Ta	Pl	W	D	L	F	A	Pts
AUSTRALIA	–	3–1	3–0	4	3	1	0	9	3	7
NEW ZEALAND	1–1	–	6–0	4	2	1	1	14	4	5
TAIWAN	1–2	0–6	–	4	0	0	4	1	17	0

Both Australia–Taiwan matches played in Suva, Fiji
Both New Zealand–Taiwan matches played in Wellington, New Zealand

Asia

Group 1

Tournament in Singapore

	HK	Si	Ma	Id	Th	Pl	W	D	L	F	A	Pts
HONG KONG	–	2–2	1–1	4–1	2–1	4	2	2	0	9	5	6

SINGAPORE	–	–	1–0	0–4	2–0	4	2	1	1	5	6	5
MALAYSIA	–	–	–	0–0	6–4	4	1	2	1	7	6	4
INDONESIA	–	–	–	–	2–3	4	1	1	2	7	7	3
THAILAND	–	–	–	–	–	4	1	0	3	8	12	2

Final

Singapore .... 0–1 .... Hong Kong

Group 2

	SK	Is	Ja	Pl	W	D	L	F	A	Pts
SOUTH KOREA	–	3–1	1–0	4	2	2	0	4	1	6
ISRAEL	0–0	–	2–0	4	2	1	1	5	3	5
JAPAN	0–0	0–2*	–	4	0	1	3	0	5	1

* Played in Tel Aviv, Israel

Group 3

	Ir	SA	Sy	Pl	W	D	L	F	A	Pts
IRAN	–	2–0	2–0*	4	4	0	0	8	0	8
SAUDI ARABIA	0–3	–	2–0	4	1	0	3	3	7	2
SYRIA	0–1	2–1	–	4	1	0	3	2	6	2

* Game awarded to Iran 2–0

Group 4

Tournament in Doha, Qatar

	Ku	Ba	Qa	Pl	W	D	L	F	A	Pts
KUWAIT	–	2–0	2–0	4	4	0	0	10	2	8
BAHRAIN	1–2	–	0–2	4	1	0	3	4	6	2
QATAR	1–4	0–3	–	4	1	0	3	3	9	2

SECOND ROUND

	Ir	SK	Ku	Au	HK	Pl	W	D	L	F	A	Pts
IRAN	–	2–2	1–0	1–0	3–0	8	6	2	0	12	3	14
SOUTH KOREA	0–0	–	1–0	0–0	5–2	8	3	4	1	12	8	10
KUWAIT	1–2	2–2	–	1–0	4–0	8	4	1	3	13	8	9
AUSTRALIA	0–1	2–1	1–2	–	3–0	8	3	1	4	11	8	7
HONG KONG	0–2	0–1	1–3	2–5	–	8	0	0	8	5	26	0

ARGENTINA qualified as hosts

WEST GERMANY qualified as holders

FINAL TOURNAMENT

Held in Argentina 1st–25th June 1978

FIRST ROUND

Group 1 (Monumental – Buenos Aires, Estadio Mar del Plata, Mar del Plata)

	It	Ar	Fr	Hu	Pl	W	D	L	F	A	Pts
ITALY	–	1–0	2–1	3–1	3	3	0	0	6	2	6
ARGENTINA	–	–	2–1	2–1	3	2	0	1	4	3	4
FRANCE	–	–	–	3–1	3	1	0	2	5	5	2
HUNGARY	–	–	–	–	3	0	0	3	3	8	0

Group 2 (Rosario Central – Rosario, Estadio Córdoba – Córdoba, Monumental – Buenos Aires)

	Pd	WG	Tu	Me	Pl	W	D	L	F	A	Pts
POLAND	–	0–0	1–0	3–1	3	2	1	0	4	1	5
WEST GERMANY	–	–	0–0	6–0	3	1	2	0	6	0	4
TUNISIA	–	–	–	3–1	3	1	1	1	3	2	3
MEXICO	–	–	–	–	3	0	0	3	2	12	0

Group 3 (Estadio Mar del Plata – Mar del Plata, José Amalfitani – Buenos Aires)

	Au	Br	Sp	Sd	Pl	W	D	L	F	A	Pts
AUSTRIA	–	0–1	2–1	1–0	3	2	0	1	3	2	4
BRAZIL	–	–	0–0	1–1	3	1	2	0	2	1	4
SPAIN	–	–	–	1–0	3	1	1	1	2	2	3
SWEDEN	–	–	–	–	3	0	1	2	1	3	1

Group 4 (San Martin – Mendoza, Estadio Córdoba – Córdoba)

	Pe	Ho	Sc	Ir	Pl	W	D	L	F	A	Pts
PERU	–	0–0	3–1	4–1	3	2	1	0	7	2	5
HOLLAND	–	–	2–3	3–0	3	1	1	1	5	3	3
SCOTLAND	–	–	–	1–1	3	1	1	1	5	6	3
IRAN	–	–	–	–	3	0	1	2	2	8	1

SECOND ROUND

GROUP A

Monumental, Buenos Aires, 14–06–1978, 60 000

ITALY 0

WEST GERMANY 0

Estadio Córdoba, Córdoba, 14–06–1978, 15 000

HOLLAND 5 (Brandts 6, Rensenbrink 35, Rep 36 53, Van de Kerkof W 83)

AUSTRIA 1 (Obermayer 80)

Estadio Córdoba, Córdoba, 18–06–1978, 46 000

HOLLAND 2 (Haan 26, Van de Kerkof R 83)

WEST GERMANY 2 (Abramczik 3, Müller D 70)

Monumental, Buenos Aires, 18–06–1978, 50 000

ITALY 1 (Rossi 13)

AUSTRIA 0

Estadio Córdoba, Córdoba, 21–06–1978, 20 000

AUSTRIA 3 (OG 60, Krankl 67 88)

WEST GERMANY 2 (Rummenigge 19, Hölzenbein 72)

Monumental, Buenos Aires, 21–06–1978, 70 000

HOLLAND 2 (Brandts 51, Haan 75)

ITALY 1 (OG 19)

	Pl	W	D	L	F	A	Pts
HOLLAND	3	2	1	0	9	4	5
ITALY	3	1	1	1	2	2	3
WEST GERMANY	3	0	2	1	4	5	2
AUSTRIA	3	1	0	2	4	8	2

GROUP B

San Martin, Mendoza, 14–06–1978, 40 000

BRAZIL 3 (Dirceu 14 27, Zico 70)

PERU 0

Rosario Central, Rosario, 14–06–1978, 40 000

ARGENTINA 2 (Kempes 15 70)

POLAND 0

San Martin, Mendoza, 18–06–1978, 35 000

POLAND 1 (Szarmach 64)

PERU 0

Rosario Central, Rosario, 18–06–1978, 46 000

ARGENTINA 0

BRAZIL 0

San Martin, Mendoza, 21–06–1978, 44 000

BRAZIL 3 (Nelinho 12, Roberto 57 62)

POLAND 1 (Lato 44)

Rosario Central, Rosario, 21–06–1978, 40 000

ARGENTINA 6 (Kempes 20 48, Tarantini 43, Luque 49 72, Houseman 66)

PERU 0

	Pl	W	D	L	F	A	Pts
ARGENTINA	3	2	1	0	8	0	5
BRAZIL	3	2	1	0	6	1	5
POLAND	3	1	0	2	2	5	2
PERU	3	0	0	3	0	10	0

3RD PLACE

Monumental, Buenos Aires, 24–06–1978, 76 000
BRAZIL 2 (Nelinho 64, Dirceu 71)
ITALY 1 (Causio 38)

FINAL

Monumental, Buenos Aires, 25–06–1978, 77 000
ARGENTINA 3 (Kempes 37 104, Bertoni 114)
HOLLAND 1 (Nanninga 81)
Referee: Gonella, Italy
Argentina – Fillol – Olguín, Galván, Passarella, Tarantini – Ardiles (Larrosa), Gallego, Kempes – Bertoni, Luque, Ortíz (Houseman). Tr: Menotti
Holland – Jongbloed – Krol, Poortvliet, Brandts, Jansen (Suurbier) – Van de Kerkhof W, Neeskens, Haan – Rep (Nanninga), Rensenbrink, Van de Kerkhof R. Tr: Happel

Top scorers: Mario Kempes, Argentina 6
Teófilo Cubillas, Peru 5
Rob Rensenbrink, Holland 5
Total goals scored: 102
Average per game: 2.7

1982

As the hosts had won three of the previous four World Cups, Spain were regarded as among the favourites for the 1982 tournament. The Spanish league was among the best in the world, and although their track record in the tournament was not good, many felt that this could be the year when the Spanish national team finally made their mark, and that the run of home victories would continue.

Joao Havelange kept his promise to increase the number of competitors in the final tournament, made at the time of his election. From 16 teams in most of the previous tournaments, the total rose to 24, a highly questionable number in that although it gave more representation to the developing world, the final tournament became protracted and unwieldy. Two rounds of league groups would be used to thin the number of competitors down to four semi-finalists, and then two finalists, all over the period of a month.

Africa and Asia might have each gained another place in the finals, but the real beneficiary of the increased size of the tournament was Europe which gained an extra four places to take its total to 13. As two teams instead of one now qualified from each group, the scope for surprises was drastically reduced. There was one, though: Holland's failure to make it to the finals. Suffering a downward turn in their fortunes after the successes of the 1970s, they missed out by a point to France and Belgium, though the Republic of Ireland were even more unlucky. They failed to qualify for their first finals on goal difference behind the French.

England and the Soviet Union both made welcome returns after missing West Germany and Argentina, and for the first time since 1958 more than one country from the British Isles was represented. Scotland and Northern Ireland came first and second respectively in their group and so only Wales were missing.

From South America, Uruguay were again absent despite the continent having four places in the finals, whilst from CONCACAF, Mexico were surprisingly eliminated by Honduras and El Salvador.

Both Africa and Asia had their representation doubled – to two each! Of the four who qualified, the Asian pair looked the weaker and so it proved. Kuwait were the current Asian champions. Oil money had seen a succession of European and South American coaches visit the rich city state and this had made the difference in turning them from an ordinary side into a good one, but one which was slightly out of its depth in Spain. New Zealand had qualified after defeating China in a play-off, but like the Kuwaitis, the All-Whites, as the New Zealand footballers were known, were clearly outclassed.

Not so Algeria or Cameroon. Neither qualified for the second round in the finals, but both deserved to. Cameroon, playing in Group 1 in the north-western towns of Vigo and La Coruña, were grouped with Italy, Poland and Peru. Poland were enjoying something of a revival. Zmuda, Lato and Boniek were still instrumental in the team and courtesy of a heavy win over a weak Peru, for whom Cubillas was still the most influential player, they won the group. All the other games finished as draws, but because Italy had been involved in two 1–1 draws as opposed to Cameroon's one, they qualified at the Africans' expense. That Cameroon should lose out to the eventual champions only on goal difference served as a warning that Africa had arrived.

Events in Group 2 provided further proof, if any were needed. Algeria were denied a place in the second round courtesy of inexcusably inept organisation on FIFA's behalf and a blatant piece of cheating by the West Germans and the Austrians. Algeria beat the Germans in the opening game of the group in Gijón, a result likened to North Korea's victory over Italy and America's victory over England in previous World Cups. In their second game the Algerians faltered, losing to Austria who thus effectively qualified having beaten the hapless Chileans in their first game. West Germany's victory over Chile left them with two points from their first two games, like Algeria.

FIFA obviously had not learnt the lessons of the Argentina–Peru match four years previously, because Algeria played against Chile the day before the Germans and the Austrians met. Chile were beaten in an exciting game, once again marked by the quality of the Algerian players. Missing Belloumi, the star of the game against Germany, they were now inspired by Madjer and raced into a 3–0 half-time lead. Had the result stayed that way, all of the controversy of the following day would have been avoided, but the Algerians conceded two second-half goals.

The following day therefore, West Germany knew that a 1–0 win would put them through whilst the same score would also see the Austrians through. What has become known as the 'Great Gijón Swindle' or 'Anschluss' saw the game finish with just that result. After the Germans had taken an early lead, both teams might just as well have left the field, so little football was played. The Algerians were outraged. They immediately appealed to FIFA, who limply did nothing, knowing full well that ultimately it was they who were the culprits, for not insisting that the final games in each group were played simultaneously. Mindful of their mistake they implemented just such a policy four years later in Mexico.

In Group 3, the champions Argentina were beaten in the opening game of the tournament by Belgium, but both these two qualified at the expense of Hungary who, despite a 10–1 victory over El Salvador and a draw with Belgium, could not find a passage to the next round. In Group 4 both England and France qualified. Kuwait, having drawn against Czechoslovakia, lost heavily to the French, who for the only time in the first round showed the form that would take them to the semi-finals. The game was marred when Prince Fahed, the president of the Kuwaiti FA, who years later was killed defending his country against the invasion by Iraq, came onto the pitch to protest about a French goal. The referee then extraordinarily reversed his decision! Fahed not only had the money to hire the best coaches in the world but also, it seems, was a very persuasive man!

The hosts struggled to qualify for the next round from Group 5. Only a dubious penalty saved them from defeat at the hands of Honduras with whom they drew 1–1. Honduras were unlucky not to qualify. They also drew with Northern Ireland, and although they lost to Yugoslavia, it was only courtesy of a goal three minutes from time. Northern Ireland went into the last game needing a victory or a high-scoring draw against the Spaniards, who had beaten Yugoslavia 2–1 with the help of another penalty. Again the hosts looked overwhelmed by the pressure and their defeat at the hands of the Irish meant that they qualified for the second round but went into a much harder group containing both England and West Germany. The defeat also dispelled any notions the Spanish public might have had that their team could win the Cup.

Group 6 was the best of the first round. Brazil were back on song, playing lovely open football. After 12 years of living in the shadow of Pele, they had found their self-belief again. Based in the southern city of Seville, Socrates, Junior, Falcao, Eder, Zico and co put on a marvellous show, scoring 10 goals in their three games, and became the favourites for the title. Scotland, for the third tournament running, missed out on qualification on goal difference, but if their performance in Argentina had been inept, they could salvage some pride this time from their excellent contribution to a fascinating group.

The second round was left with four groups of unequal strength. Group C was especially strong, containing as it did the holders, the favourites and the ultimate winners. Both Brazil and Italy beat Argentina, who despite having Maradona in their side could not match the achievements of four years before. This left a decider between Brazil and Italy in the final game of the group. The match was a classic, and it saw the re-emergence of the man who was to win Italy the Cup, Paolo Rossi. Reprieved from a ban imposed after a match-fixing and bribery scandal, he suddenly burst into life in the game, scoring a hat-trick.

Brazil would rue the fact that, needing only a draw to qualify, they went out to win the game with the scores level at 2–2. Had they played more defensively after they levelled the scores they might not have let Rossi in for the winner 15 minutes from time. Out they went, but despite not winning the tournament they certainly made the biggest impression.

The other strong group on paper contained West Germany, the hosts and England. Spain bowed out after their defeat by Germany who had already drawn a sterile game with the English. England therefore had to beat Spain by two clear goals in the Bernabeu, but Spain, with the pressure off, were determined not to be humiliated and they defended admirably. England, who had come close on a number of occasions, went out. They had conceded just one goal and remained unbeaten, a record the West Germans could not match, but it was they who were in the semi-finals.

In Group D France began to play to the best of their ability. With a powerhouse midfield of Platini, Ghengini, Giresse and Tigana they outplayed both Austria and the Northern Irish to set up a semi-final meeting with West Germany.

The first semi-final saw Italy meet Poland. The latter had qualified due to the fact that they had beaten Belgium by more goals than the Soviets, but they were without Boniek for the semi-finals and it told. Playing before a half-full Nou Camp in Barcelona, Paolo Rossi was again the difference, scoring both the goals that saw Italy through to their second final in twelve years.

The France–West Germany match, held before a full house in Seville, was a much better game altogether, and vindicated the return to the use of semi-finals instead of group winners meeting in the final. The game saw the French at their very best, and the Germans at their most tenacious. The French, playing the fluent, outstanding football that made them European Champions two years later, quickly equalised a first-half Littbarski goal, and for the rest of normal time the score did not change. A crucial incident occurred in the second half which was ultimately to turn the game. Minutes after coming on as a substitute, Patrick Battiston, the French defender, was wickedly felled by Schumacher in the German goal. The Frenchman was carried off unconscious. West Germany were awarded a goal kick.

After scoring two goals early in extra time, France looked set for their first major final appearance, but in a show of Gallic extravagance they went forward in search of more goals. Had Battiston been on the field to shore up a weary defence this might not have mattered, but the Germans brought on Karl-Heinz Rummenigge and at his instigation they pulled level. For the first time in the World Cup, penalties were used to decide a game, a most unsatisfactory way of deciding the finalists for a competition of such importance. Unfortunately for France, after five kicks each and with the scores at 4–4, Schumacher saved from Bossis and Hrubesch scored the winner.

West Germany were without doubt the most unpopular finalists ever. They had lost to Algeria, been accused of a flagrant act of gamesmanship, and had now beaten the team most neutrals wanted to win, on penalties. Before the final Poland and France were involved in that most rare of events, an entertaining third place play-off. The French gave the rest of their squad an outing and lost 3–2 in the process, but for Poland third place capped a remarkable ten year spell in world football which had seen them crowned Olympic Champions in 1972 and runners-up in 1976, achieve third place in the 1974 World Cup and reach the second round in 1978.

There are few better sights in football than a full Bernabeu stadium lit up against the night sky, and as Italy lifted the World Cup at the end of the final they knew they had graced the grand setting with some equally lovely football. The Germans were simply outclassed, although when Antonio Cabrini missed a first-half penalty many Italians must have thought it was not to be their day. After all, West Germany had progressed thus far against all the odds.

Once again it was Paolo Rossi who turned Italian domination into a goal, diving to head home a Gentile cross ten minutes into the second half. Tardelli had been quick to see Gentile free on the wing at a free kick and given him the ball before the Germans had time to react. Unusually for the Germans, their heads sank and Italy took over. Tardelli scored their second ten minutes later, after Rossi and Scirea had played a one-two in the area, and substitute Altobelli made sure of victory nine minutes from the end, Conti having run almost the full length of the pitch to cross it to him.

Breitner scored a consolation goal for West Germany right at the death, thus becoming only the third man after Vava and Pele to score in two finals. Italy, having played some dreadfully dour football in the first round, had suddenly sprung to life in the second and played attractive and entertaining football. For once they forgot about defence and concentrated on attack, and it won them the World Cup.

THE TWELFTH WORLD CUP

26th March 1980–11th July 1982

QUALIFYING TOURNAMENT

EUROPE

Group 1

	WG	Au	Bu	Al	Fi	Pl	W	D	L	F	A	Pts
W GERMANY	–	2–0	4–0	8–0	7–1	8	8	0	0	33	3	16
AUSTRIA	1–3	–	2–0	5–0	5–1	8	5	1	2	16	6	11
Bulgaria	1–3	0–0	–	2–1	4–0	8	4	1	3	11	10	9
Albania	0–2	0–1	0–2	–	2–0	8	1	0	7	4	22	2
Finland	0–4	0–2	0–2	2–1	–	8	1	0	7	4	27	2

Group 2

	Be	Fr	RI	Ho	Cy	Pl	W	D	L	F	A	Pts
BELGIUM	–	2–0	1–0	1–0	3–2	8	5	1	2	12	9	11
FRANCE	3–2	–	2–0	2–0	4–0	8	5	0	3	20	8	10
Rep. Ireland	1–1	3–2	–	2–1	6–0	8	4	2	2	17	11	10
Holland	3–0	1–0	2–2	–	3–0	8	4	1	3	11	7	9
Cyprus	0–2	0–7	2–3	0–1	–	8	0	0	8	4	29	0

Group 3

	SU	Cz	Wa	Ic	Tu	Pl	W	D	L	F	A	Pts
SOVIET UNION	–	2–0	3–0	5–0	4–0	8	6	2	0	20	2	14
CZECHOSLOV.	1–1	–	2–0	6–1	2–0	8	4	2	2	15	6	10
Wales	0–0	1–0	–	2–2	4–0	8	4	2	2	12	7	10
Iceland	1–2	1–1	0–4	–	2–0	8	2	2	4	10	21	6
Turkey	0–3	0–3	0–1	1–3	–	8	0	0	8	1	22	0

Group 4

	Hu	En	Ro	Sz	No	Pl	W	D	L	F	A	Pts
HUNGARY	–	1–3	1–0	3–0	4–1	8	4	2	2	13	8	10
ENGLAND	1–0	–	0–0	2–1	4–0	8	4	1	3	13	8	9
Romania	0–0	2–1	–	1–2	1–0	8	2	4	2	5	5	8
Switzerland	2–2	2–1	0–0	–	1–2	8	2	3	3	9	12	7
Norway	1–2	2–1	1–1	1–1	–	8	2	2	4	8	15	6

Group 5

	Yu	It	De	Gr	Lu	Pl	W	D	L	F	A	Pts
YUGOSLAVIA	–	1–1	2–1	5–1	5–0	8	6	1	1	22	7	13
ITALY	2–0	–	2–0	1–1	1–0	8	5	2	1	12	5	12
Denmark	1–2	3–1	–	0–1	4–0	8	4	0	4	14	11	8
Greece	1–2	0–2	2–3	–	2–0	8	3	1	4	10	13	7
Luxembourg	0–5	0–2	1–2	0–2	–	8	0	0	8	1	23	0

Group 6

	Sc	NI	Sd	Pt	Is	Pl	W	D	L	F	A	Pts
SCOTLAND	–	1–1	2–0	0–0	3–1	8	4	3	1	9	4	11
NTH. IRELAND	0–0	–	3–0	1–0	1–0	8	3	3	2	6	3	9

						Pl	W	D	L	F	A	Pts
SWEDEN	0–1	1–0	–	3–0	1–1	8	3	2	3	7	8	8
PORTUGAL	2–1	1–0	1–2	–	3–0	8	3	1	4	8	11	7
ISRAEL	0–1	0–0	0–0	4–1	–	8	1	3	4	6	10	5

Group 7

	Pd	EG	Ma	Pl	W	D	L	F	A	Pts
POLAND	–	1–0	6–0	4	4	0	0	12	2	8
EAST GERMANY	2–3	–	5–1	4	2	0	2	9	6	4
MALTA	0–2	1–2	–	4	0	0	4	2	15	0

SOUTH AMERICA

Group 1

	Br	Bo	Ve	Pl	W	D	L	F	A	Pts
BRAZIL	–	3–1	5–0	4	4	0	0	11	2	8
BOLIVIA	1–2	–	3–0	4	1	0	3	5	6	2
VENEZUELA	0–1	1–0	–	4	1	0	3	1	9	2

Group 2

	Pe	Ur	Co	Pl	W	D	L	F	A	Pts
PERU	–	0–0	2–0	4	2	2	0	5	2	6
URUGUAY	1–2	–	3–2	4	1	2	1	5	5	4
COLOMBIA	1–1	1–1	–	4	0	2	2	4	7	2

Group 3

	Ch	Ec	Pa	Pl	W	D	L	F	A	Pts
CHILE	–	2–0	3–0	4	3	1	0	6	0	7
ECUADOR	0–0	–	1–0	4	1	1	2	2	5	3
PARAGUAY	0–1	3–1	–	4	1	0	3	3	6	2

AFRICA

FIRST ROUND

Ethiopia .... 0–0 0–4 .... Zambia
Sierra Leone .... 2–2 1–3 .... Algeria
Libya .... 2–1 0–0 .... Gambia
Guinea .... 3–1 1–1 .... Lesotho
Senegal .... 0–1 0–0 .... Morocco
Tunisia .... 2–0 0–2 (3–4p) .. Nigeria
Kenya .... 3–1 0–5 .... Tanzania
Cameroon .... 3–0 1–1 .... Malawi
Zaire .... 5–2 2–1 .... Mozambique
Niger .... 0–0 1–1 .... Somalia
Egypt .... W–O .... Ghana
Madagascar .... W–O .... Uganda
Zimbabwe .... Bye
Sudan .... Bye
Liberia .... Bye
Togo .... Bye

SECOND ROUND

Cameroon .... 2–0 0–1 .... Zimbabwe
Morocco .... 2–0 0–2 (5–4p) .. Zambia
Nigeria .... 1–1 2–0 .... Tanzania
Madagascar .... 1–1 2–3 .... Zaire
Liberia .... 0–0 0–1 .... Guinea
Algeria .... 2–0 1–1 .... Sudan
Niger .... 0–1 2–1 .... Togo
Egypt .... W–O .... Libya

THIRD ROUND

Guinea .... 1–1 0–1 .... Nigeria
Zaire .... 1–0 1–6 .... Cameroon
Morocco .... 1–0 0–0 .... Egypt
Algeria .... 4–0 0–1 .... Niger

FOURTH ROUND

Nigeria .... 0–2 1–2 .... ALGERIA
Morocco .... 0–2 1–2 .... CAMEROON

CENTRAL AND NORTH AMERICA

FIRST ROUND

Group 1

	Ca	Me	US	Pl	W	D	L	F	A	Pts
CANADA	–	1–1	2–1	4	1	3	0	4	3	5
MEXICO	1–1	–	5–1	4	1	2	1	8	5	4
UNITED STATES	0–0	2–1	–	4	1	1	2	4	8	3

Group 2

	Ho	ES	Gu	CR	Pa	Pl	W	D	L	F	A	Pts
HONDURAS	–	2–0	0–0	1–1	5–0	8	5	2	1	15	5	12
EL SALVADOR	2–1	–	1–0	2–0*	4–1	8	5	2	1	12	5	12
GUATEMALA	0–1	0–0	–	0–0	5–0	8	3	3	2	10	2	9
COSTA RICA	2–3	0–0	0–3	–	2–0	8	1	4	3	6	10	6
PANAMA	0–2	1–3	0–2	1–1	–	8	0	1	7	3	24	1

* El Salvador awarded match 2–0

Group 3

Preliminary round

Guyana .... 5–2 3–2 .... Grenada

GROUP A

	Cu	Su	Gu	Pl	W	D	L	F	A	Pts
CUBA	–	3–0	1–0	4	3	1	0	7	0	7
SURINAM	0–0	–	4–0	4	2	1	1	5	3	5
GUYANA	0–3	0–1	–	4	0	0	4	0	9	0

GROUP B

	Ha	Tr	NA	Pl	W	D	L	F	A	Pts
HAITI	–	2–0	1–0	4	2	1	1	4	2	5
TRINIDAD	1–0	–	0–0	4	1	2	1	1	2	4
NETH. ANTILLES	1–1	0–0	–	4	0	3	1	1	2	3

SECOND ROUND

Tournament in Tegucigalpa, Honduras

	Ho	ES	Me	Ca	Cu	Ha	Pl	W	D	L	F	A	Pts
HONDURAS	–	0–0	0–0	2–1	2–0	4–0	5	3	2	0	8	1	8
EL SALVADOR	–	–	1–0	0–1	0–0	1–0	5	2	2	1	2	1	6
MEXICO	–	–	–	1–1	4–0	1–1	5	1	3	1	6	3	5
CANADA	–	–	–	–	2–2	1–1	5	1	3	1	6	6	5
CUBA	–	–	–	–	–	2–0	5	1	2	2	4	8	4
HAITI	–	–	–	–	–	–	5	0	2	3	2	9	2

ASIA–OCEANIA

FIRST ROUND

Group 1

	NZ	Au	Id	Ta	Fi	Pl	W	D	L	F	A	Pts
NEW ZEALAND	–	3–3	5–0	2–0	13–0	8	6	2	0	31	3	14
AUSTRALIA	0–2	–	2–0	3–2	10–0	8	4	2	2	22	9	10
INDONESIA	0–2	1–0	–	1–0	3–3	8	2	2	4	5	14	6
TAIWAN	0–0	0–0	2–0	–	0–0	8	1	3	4	5	8	5
FIJI	0–4	1–4	0–0	2–1	–	8	1	3	4	6	35	5

Group 2

Tournament in Riyadh, Saudi Arabia

	SA	Iq	Qa	Ba	Sy	Pl	W	D	L	F	A	Pts
SAUDI ARABIA	–	1–0	1–0	1–0	2–0	4	4	0	0	5	0	8
IRAQ	–	–	1–0	2–0	2–1	4	3	0	1	5	2	6
QATAR	–	–	–	3–0	2–1	4	2	0	2	5	3	4
BAHRAIN	–	–	–	–	1–0	4	1	0	3	1	6	2
SYRIA	–	–	–	–	–	4	0	0	4	2	7	0

Group 3

Tournament in Kuwait City

	Ku	SK	Ma	Th	Pl	W	D	L	F	A	Pts
KUWAIT	–	2–0	4–0	6–0	3	3	0	0	12	0	6

					Pl	W	D	L	F	A	Pts
SOUTH KOREA	–	–	2–1	5–1	3	2	0	1	7	4	4
MALAYSIA	–	–	–	2–2	3	0	1	2	3	8	1
THAILAND	–	–	–	–	3	0	1	2	3	13	1

Group 4

Tournament in Hong Kong

Preliminary round (to determine group placements)

Hong Kong .... 0–1 .... China
North Korea .... 3–0 .... Macao
Singapore .... 0–1 .... Japan

First Round

Group A

	Ch	Ja	Mc	Pl	W	D	L	F	A	Pts
CHINA	–	1–0	3–0	2	2	0	0	4	0	4
JAPAN	–	–	3–0	2	1	0	1	3	1	2
MACAO	–	–	–	2	0	0	2	0	6	0

Group B

	NK	HK	Si	Pl	W	D	L	F	A	Pts
NORTH KOREA	–	2–2	1–0	2	1	1	0	3	2	3
HONG KONG	–	–	1–1	2	0	2	0	3	3	2
SINGAPORE	–	–	–	2	0	1	1	1	2	1

Semi-finals

North Korea .... 1–0 .... Japan
China .... 0–0 (5–4p) ..... Hong Kong

Final

China .... 4–2 .... North Korea

SECOND ROUND

	Ku	NZ	Ch	SA	Pl	W	D	L	F	A	Pts
KUWAIT	–	2–2	1–0	2–0	6	4	1	1	8	6	9
NEW ZEALAND	1–2	–	1–0	2–2	6	2	3	1	11	6	7
CHINA	3–0	0–0	–	2–0*	6	3	1	2	9	4	7
SAUDI ARABIA	0–1	0–5	2–4*	–	6	0	1	5	4	16	1

* Played in Kuala Lumpur, Malaysia

Play-off in Singapore

New Zealand .... 2–1 .... China

SPAIN qualified as hosts

ARGENTINA qualified as holders

FINAL TOURNAMENT

Held in Spain 13th June–11th July 1982

FIRST ROUND

Group 1 (Balaidos – Vigo, Riazor – La Coruña)

	Pd	It	Ca	Pe	Pl	W	D	L	F	A	Pts
POLAND	–	0–0	0–0	5–1	3	1	2	0	5	1	4
ITALY	–	–	1–1	1–1	3	0	3	0	2	2	3
CAMEROON	–	–	–	0–0	3	0	3	0	1	1	3
PERU	–	–	–	–	3	0	2	1	2	6	2

Group 2 (El Molinón – Gijón, Carlos Tartiere – Oviedo)

	WG	Au	Al	Ch	Pl	W	D	L	F	A	Pts
WEST GERMANY	–	1–0	1–2	4–1	3	2	0	1	6	3	4
AUSTRIA	–	–	2–0	1–0	3	2	0	1	3	1	4
ALGERIA	–	–	–	3–2	3	2	0	1	5	5	4
CHILE	–	–	–	–	3	0	0	3	3	8	0

Group 3 (Nou Camp – Barcelona, José Rico Perez – Alicante, Manuel Martínez Valero – Elche)

	Be	Ar	Hu	ES	Pl	W	D	L	F	A	Pts
BELGIUM	–	1–0	1–1	1–0	3	2	1	0	3	1	5
ARGENTINA	–	–	4–1	2–0	3	2	0	1	6	2	4
HUNGARY	–	–	–	10–1	3	1	1	1	12	6	3
EL SALVADOR	–	–	–	–	3	0	0	3	1	13	0

Group 4 (San Mamés – Bilbao, José Zorrilla – Valladolid)

	En	Fr	Cz	Ku	Pl	W	D	L	F	A	Pts
ENGLAND	–	3–1	2–0	1–0	3	3	0	0	6	1	6
FRANCE	–	–	1–1	4–1	3	1	1	1	6	5	3
CZECHOSLOVAKIA	–	–	–	1–1	3	0	2	1	2	4	2
KUWAIT	–	–	–	–	3	0	1	2	2	6	1

Group 5 (Luis Casanova – Valencia, La Romereda – Zaragoza)

	NI	Sp	Yu	Ho	Pl	W	D	L	F	A	Pts
NTH. IRELAND	–	1–0	0–0	1–1	3	1	2	0	2	1	4
SPAIN	–	–	2–1	1–1	3	1	1	1	3	3	3
YUGOSLAVIA	–	–	–	1–0	3	1	1	1	2	2	3
HONDURAS	–	–	–	–	3	0	2	1	2	3	2

Group 6 (La Rosaleda – Málaga, Sánchez Pizjuán – Seville, Benito Villamarín – Seville)

	Br	SU	Sc	NZ	Pl	W	D	L	F	A	Pts
BRAZIL	–	2–1	4–1	4–0	3	3	0	0	10	2	6
SOVIET UNION	–	–	2–2	3–0	3	1	1	1	6	4	3
SCOTLAND	–	–	–	5–2	3	1	1	1	8	8	3
NEW ZEALAND	–	–	–	–	3	0	0	3	2	12	0

SECOND ROUND

GROUP A

Nou Camp, Barcelona, 28–06–1982, 65 000

POLAND 3 (Boniek 4 26 53)
BELGIUM 0

Nou Camp, Barcelona, 1–07–1982, 45 000

SOVIET UNION 1 (Oganesian 50)
BELGIUM 0

Nou Camp, Barcelona, 4–07–1982, 65 000

POLAND 0
SOVIET UNION 0

	Pl	W	D	L	F	A	Pts
POLAND	2	1	1	0	3	0	3
SOVIET UNION	2	1	1	0	1	0	3
BELGIUM	2	0	0	2	0	4	0

GROUP B

Bernabeu, Madrid, 29–06–1982, 75 000

WEST GERMANY 0
ENGLAND 0

Bernabeu, Madrid, 2–07–1982, 90 000

WEST GERMANY 2 (Littbarski 51, Fischer 75)
SPAIN 1 (Zamora 81)

Bernabeu, Madrid, 5–07–1982, 75 000

ENGLAND 0
SPAIN 0

	Pl	W	D	L	F	A	Pts
WEST GERMANY	2	1	1	0	2	1	3
ENGLAND	2	0	2	0	0	0	2
SPAIN	2	0	1	1	1	2	1

GROUP C

Sarriá, Barcelona, 29–06–1982, 43 000
ITALY 2 (Tardelli 57, Cabrini 67)
ARGENTINA 1 (Passarella 83)

Sarriá, Barcelona, 2–07–1982, 44 000
BRAZIL 3 (Zico 12, Serginho 67, Junior 72)
ARGENTINA 1 (Díaz 89)

Sarriá, Barcelona, 5–07–1982, 44 000
ITALY 3 (Rossi 5 25 74)
BRAZIL 2 (Socrates 12, Falcao 68)

	Pl	W	D	L	F	A	Pts
ITALY	2	2	0	0	5	3	4
BRAZIL	2	1	0	1	5	4	2
ARGENTINA	2	0	0	2	2	5	0

GROUP D

Vicente Calderón, Madrid, 28–06–1982, 37 000
FRANCE 1 (Genghini 39)
AUSTRIA 0

Vicente Calderón, Madrid, 1–07–1982, 20 000
AUSTRIA 2 (Pezzey 51, Hintermaier 67)
NTH. IRELAND 2 (Hamilton 27 74)

Vicente Calderón, Madrid, 4–07–1982, 37 000
FRANCE 4 (Giresse 33 80, Rochetau 48 63)
NTH. IRELAND 1 (Armstrong 75)

	Pl	W	D	L	F	A	Pts
FRANCE	2	2	0	0	5	1	4
AUSTRIA	2	0	1	1	2	3	1
NTH. IRELAND	2	0	1	1	3	6	1

SEMI-FINALS

Nou Camp, Barcelona, 8–07–1982, 50 000
ITALY 2 (Rossi 22 73)
POLAND 0

Sánchez Pizjuán, Seville, 8–07–1982, 63 000
WEST GERMANY 3 (Littbarski 18, Rummenigge 102, Fischer 107)
FRANCE 3 (Platini 27, Trésor 93, Giresse 97)
West Germany won 5–4 on penalties

3RD PLACE

José Rico Perez, Alicante, 10–07–1982, 28 000
POLAND 3 (Szarmach 41, Majewski 44, Kupcewicz 47)
FRANCE 2 (Girard 14, Couriol 75)

FINAL

Bernabeu, Madrid, 11–07–1982, 90 000
ITALY 3 (Rossi 56, Tardelli 69, Altobelli 80)
WEST GERMANY 1 (Breitner 82)
Referee: Coelho, Brazil
Italy – Zoff – Cabrini, Scirea, Gentile, Collovati – Oriali, Bergomi, Tardelli – Conti, Rossi, Graziani (Altobelli) (Causio). Tr: Bearzot
West Germany – Schumacher – Kaltz, Stielike, Förster K-H, Förster B – Breitner, Briegel, Dremmler (Hrubesch) – Rummenigge (Müller H), Littbarski, Fischer. Tr: Derwall

Top scorers: Paolo Rossi, Italy 6
Karl-Heinz Rummenigge, West Germany 5
Zbigniew Boniek, Poland 4
Zico, Brazil 4

Total goals scored: 146
Average per game: 2.8

1986

The common pattern for the World Cup had been to alternate it between Europe and South America, and the 1986 tournament looked set to follow that pattern when Colombia were chosen as hosts. But in 1982, four years before the event, a combination of events forced them to withdraw, not least the fact that when they were awarded the tournament it was to comprise only 16 teams. Even with that number, a poor economic situation, as well as the violence associated with the drug trade, meant that it was not possible for them to go ahead and stage the event.

Brazil, the United States and Mexico all applied for the right to stage the tournament, and somewhat surprisingly Mexico emerged as the victors, becoming the first country to stage the tournament twice. A terrible earthquake in Mexico City a year before the finals nearly caused a second relocation but the tournament went ahead as planned. The problems with heat, altitude and an ever-worsening pollution problem, especially in the large sprawling capital, did not make conditions ideal, but like the 1970 tournament the 1986 World Cup was a success, despite these problems.

A record 121 countries entered initially, although after withdrawals only 113 nations set out on a qualification road that contained relatively few surprises. In Europe, Portugal qualified for only the second time and made a piece of history into the bargain when they inflicted on West Germany their first and only defeat to date in the World Cup qualifying tournament, with a 1–0 victory in Stuttgart.

All of the other major European powers qualified, although Holland, who would be crowned European Champions two years later, saw their revival cut short by Belgium in a play-off. There were few surprises in South America either as the 'big three' all made it to the finals for the first time since 1974. They were joined by Paraguay who made their first appearance since 1958.

North Africa provided both of the representatives for that continent as both Algeria and Morocco qualified. Such was the supremacy of that part of Africa that all five nations north of the Sahara made it to the quarter-finals of the qualifying competition and only Egypt missed out on the semi-finals.

The Asian qualifying group was divided into East and West which ensured that both the Middle East with Iraq and the Far East with South Korea were represented in Mexico. As by far and away the most powerful nation in the region, South Korea finally qualified for the first time since 1954 after so many near misses. Iraq's qualification was all the more remarkable in that all of their matches were played away from home due to the war with Iran.

CONCACAF were only given one berth in the finals due to the fact that Mexico as hosts qualified automatically, and it was to general surprise that the previously unknown Canadians won through at the expense of the supposedly superior Costa Rica and Honduras. With the demise of the North American Soccer League in the early 1980s, it had seemed as though football in that part of the world was on the decline.

The final tournament opened with a game between Italy and Bulgaria in the magnificent Azteca Stadium in Mexico City, the scene of the 1970 final. From the outset, the finals were regarded as the most open since they were last held in Mexico. There were no clear favourites. Mexico were not expected to win, despite a fanatical home following. West Germany, France, England, Italy and the Soviet Union were seen as potential winners from Europe whilst Brazil and Argentina were tipped from South America. If there were favourites, it was Argentina who took the fancy, largely due to the presence of Maradona who was at the peak of his career and playing football unrivalled since Pele had graced the World Cup 16 years previously.

Argentina duly won Group A, drawing 1–1 with the Italians in the big game of the group. The Italians, however, were at times given the run-around by South Korea in their final match. Fearful of another defeat by a Korean team, remembering their 1966 humiliation at the hands of the North, they eventually won 3–2. The new format of playing knock-out games from the second round meant that four of the third-placed teams with the best records in the six groups would qualify to make the numbers up to a workable 16. Italy's win over South Korea meant that the extremely dour Bulgarians qualified from Group A instead of the entertaining if somewhat cynical Koreans.

The effect of this format change was double-edged. Few doubted that knock-out games were potentially more exciting than group matches, but to achieve 16 second round qualifiers meant playing 36 first round games to eliminate just eight teams. The increase in the number of knock-out games also increased the spectre of the penalty shoot-out, as teams played for a draw in the hope of winning on spot-kicks.

Group B also saw three teams qualifying for the second round as Asia's other representatives, Iraq, were knocked out after playing some very sterile football. Mexico, playing to capacity crowds in the Azteca, were good value for their first place in the group. Inspired by their Real Madrid striker Hugo Sanchez, they beat ultimate semi-finalists Belgium 2–1 in their opening match after which qualification was virtually assured.

Group C saw the Soviet Union and France both finishing on five points, but having beaten Hungary 6–0 in their opening game the Soviets had a much better goal difference. Despite beating the weak Canadians 2–0, Hungary were disappointing after having initially been seen as a possible dark horse, and they were one of the two third-placed sides who failed to qualify. They deserve some credit, however. In their six games in the 1982 and 1986 finals, 29 goals had been scored in total. In an era when goals were beginning to dry up drastically, this was achievement of sorts.

The third-placed team in Group D also failed to qualify for the second round as both Northern Ireland and Algeria were outclassed by Spain and Brazil in the most uneven first round group. Four years are a long time in football, and neither could live up to the reputations built in Spain in 1982. Northern Ireland's defeat by Brazil did have one event of note, however. Pat Jennings, the Irish goalkeeper, won his 119th and last cap, making him then the most capped player in history.

Called the 'group of death' by journalists, Group E was the hardest of the first round. All four teams were capable of qualifying and it was Scotland who were the unlucky team when for the fourth time running they failed to reached the second round. Denmark were in devastating form, winning all three of their games including a 6–1 annihilation of Uruguay, after which they were widely tipped as potential winners.

The last of the groups was by contrast called the 'group of sleep'. Based in the faraway and low-lying Monterrey, the first four games produced just two goals. Despite beating England in their opening game, Portugal were surprisingly eliminated when the group suddenly sprang into life with the final two fixtures. England recovered from a torpid start to the tournament when Gary Lineker scored three first-half goals in Monterrey against the mesmerised Poles to ensure England progressed to the second round when it had seemed likely that they would be returning home in disgrace. Even greater events were unfolding in Guadalajara where Morocco made sure of finishing top of the group with a stunning 3–1 victory over the hapless Portuguese. Thus for the first time an African nation had qualified for the second round. Nobody could now deny the growing strength of that continent.

The second round got underway in the Azteca when Mexico took on the Bulgarians. Looking for their first win in 16 games in the finals, Bulgaria were never in danger of breaking that most dubious of records, and they feebly succumbed to a spectacular overhead kick by Negrete and a header from Servin.

Later that afternoon the public of León were treated to an absolute thriller in what was undoubtedly the game of the tournament. With the score at 2–2 after full time, Belgium eventually beat the Soviet Union 4–3 after extra-time having twice been behind. Igor Belanov, later to be voted European Footballer of the Year, scored a hat-trick for the Soviets, but it was not enough and one of the best and most entertaining sides in the tournament bowed out of the competition.

The following day it was the turn of the South Americans to hold centre stage, and after having been thrashed by England, Poland were on the receiving end of another big score. Try as he might, Boniek could not inspire his team-mates to the same form which had seen them finish third in Spain. Instead, Brazil with Alemao, Junior, Zico and the irrepressible Socrates in midfield and the excellent Muller and Careca in attack, easily swept aside the Polish challenge to win 4–0.

If Brazil were beginning to look like champions, Argentina increased the prospect of an all-South American final by overcoming a potentially difficult tie against their neighbours and fierce rivals Uruguay, in a repeat of the 1930 final. This was also the first time the two teams had met in the World Cup since then, and in difficult conditions Argentina gained some semblance of revenge for the defeat in 1930 when Pasculli scored the winner for them just before half-time.

World Champions Italy faced European Champions France in the Olympic Stadium in the next match of the tournament. For Italy, gone was Rossi and much of their inspiration, and they meekly lost to the French, for whom Platini was still the driving force in a team with which it was hard to find much fault. Giresse, Tigana and Fernandez were brilliant alongside Platini in midfield, whilst Battiston, Amoros and Bossis were firm in defence. If there was a weakness it was in attack, where Jean-Pierre Papin was still a rising star and unable to command a regular place.

France would ultimately lose again in the semi-finals to West Germany, who scraped through the second round against Morocco courtesy of a last-minute winner from a Matthäus free-kick. The Germans were looking as unconvincing as they had done in 1982 yet they seemed to get the results. Morocco returned home to a heroes' welcome, and had they not been a little too much in awe of the Germans they might well have progressed further.

The last day of the second round saw England take on Paraguay and Spain play Belgium. In a near-capacity Azteca, England carried on where they had left off against Poland. Lineker, this time with two goals, was the star of the show as the English staked their claim to be seen as serious title contenders. Both Hoddle and Beardsley were in fine form and the latter scored the other England goal to take their total to six in two games after having failed to score in their first two.

The real surprise of the round was Denmark's defeat at the hands of Spain in Queretaro. Defeat in itself was not so surprising – the Spanish had, after all, beaten the Danes in the semi-finals of the European Championships two years previously – but the manner in which Denmark fell apart after having taken the lead after half an hour was extraordinary. Emilio Butragueño scored four goals in the space of 46 minutes as Spain walked away with the match 5–1 before the bewildered Danes.

The unsatisfactory side of the knock-out tournament reared its ugly head in the quarter-finals when three of the four ties were settled on penalties, whilst the fourth was settled by an incident that will forever live in World Cup folklore.

In a good game between France and Brazil in Guadalajara, where as in 1970 Brazil were based, France reached their second successive semi-final. The game was not without incident. Muller had given the South Americans an early lead but Platini equalised just before half-time. In the second half, Zico, the hero of Brazilian football, temporarily became a villain when he missed a penalty after having just come on as a substitute and Brazil's chance had gone.

Carlos, their goalkeeper, was lucky to stay on the field after a wild challenge outside the area on Bellone just before the finish. The French striker had managed to stay on his feet but was off balance and could not make the advantage the referee had played count. French nerves at the prospect of losing a second penalty shoot-out were calmed after Socrates missed from Brazil's first effort and they eventually won 4–3.

West Germany and Mexico played out a sterile draw in the match later on in the day. After 120 minutes of no goals, it may have been something of a relief for the crowd to see the ball hit the back of the net even if it was from penalties. In 1970, Mexico had lost at home to Italy in the quarter-finals. They were to go no further this time either. Playing in Monterrey and not in the Azteca, the Mexicans' game suffered and even in the penalty shoot-out they could only score once. The Germans could hardly believe their luck. Once again they were in the semi-finals and no one could quite understand how.

The third quarter-final, played the following day, was potentially the most explosive, involving as it did England and Argentina. Four years previously the two countries had fought a war over the Falkland Islands and emotions were still running high. In the event it will be remembered as one of the most controversial matches in World Cup history. The football rivalry between the two countries had always been intense, no more so than in the 1966 World Cup when controversy surrounded England's victory in the quarter-final of that tournament. In that match, the sending-off of Rattin, the Argentine captain, had been a crucial factor. Maradona, the captain in 1986, was also to be a key figure.

His first goal early in the second half has become known as 'The Hand of God' goal, which is how Maradona described it after the match. As he went for a high ball in the area with Peter Shilton, the England goalkeeper, Maradona cleared fisted the ball into the net, but despite vehement protests from Shilton, the Tunisian referee would not change his mind and the goal stood. Four minutes later the English, still smarting at the goal, were two down. This time it was Maradona at his most brilliant. Collecting the ball in his own half he simply strode through a mesmerised English defence to score one of the best goals football, let alone the World Cup, has ever seen. Lineker scored a consolation for England to make him the top scorer in the tournament, but the Argentines won through and the English somewhat unluckily bowed out of a tournament they could have won.

The last quarter-final saw Belgium reach the semi-finals for the first time in their history as once again the World Cup jinx hit Spain. The Spaniards came closer to reaching their first semi-final than they had ever done before but were denied 5–4 on penalties. Butragueño and Michel were the stars of the side but they had to thank Señor for equalising a first-half Begium goal just five minutes from time. Not so fortunate was Eloy, whose miss proved vital in the shoot-out.

The France–West Germany semi-final was a repeat of 1982 and again the Germans triumphed, although this time they did not need penalties to reach the final. It also failed to live up to the pedigree of the 1982 match as France performed strangely below par, never recovering from conceding an eighth-minute Brehme free-kick. Only in the final stages of the game did the French really threaten the German goal, and it was not surprising that with a minute left Völler scored a vital second goal on the breakaway.

In the other semi-final, Maradona was again turning on the magic, but this time without any of the controversy. As in the quarter-final with England, he scored his two goals early in the second half, the second of which was almost as good as his outstanding effort against the English. The Belgians, no doubt delighted to have proceeded so far, knew they had been beaten by a far superior team. Argentina, meanwhile, knew that they were overwhelming favourites to win their second world title, and win it they did.

Having lost the third place play-off in Spain, France made no mistake this time, beating Belgium 4–2 in Puebla, but once again the value of such a fixture was brought into question as the French gave a run out to those players who had not featured heavily in the previous matches.

Throughout the tournament, Franz Beckenbauer, the West German coach, had been saying his team was not good enough to win the tournament. They had reached the final largely due to the tournament mentality so prevalent in German sportsmen. They also undoubtedly had some fine players. Karl-Heinz Rummenigge was once again the inspiration, but alongside him were players of the calibre of Lothar Matthäus and Felix Magath in midfield, Andreas Brehme, Thomas Berthold and Karl-Heinz Förster in defence, and Klaus Allofs and Rudi Völler in attack.

Argentina were obviously reliant on Maradona for much of their inspiration, but they were by no means a one-man team. In midfield, Sergio Batista, Ricardo Giusti, Hector Enrique and Jorge Burruchaga were all in excellent form, whilst Oscar Ruggeri was proving to be one of the best defenders Argentina had ever had. Alongside Maradona in attack, Jorge Valdano was also at the top of his game.

In a packed Azteca with the majority of the crowd behind Argentina, a slightly nervous performance by both sides in the first half saw Brown, the Argentine defender, give his side the lead after 22 minutes with a header from a Burruchaga free-kick. Ten minutes into the second half, Argentina were 2–0 up when Valdano, put clean through by Enrique, coolly slotted the ball past Schumacher. The Argentines were coasting to victory, but the Germans rose to the occasion and gave them a nasty shock.

With 17 minutes left the Germans pulled a goal back from a corner when Rummenigge prodded the ball home after it had been headed down by Völler, and from an almost identical situation eight minutes later it was Völler himself who sensationally levelled the scores, heading home after Berthold had played on a Brehme corner. It was anybody's game, but Maradona was not going to let his hour of glory slip away. With an exquisite pass he found Burruchaga in acres in space, and the Argentine midfielder had no trouble in finishing off a glorious move to seal the title for the South Americans.

Though he had not managed to score in the final, there was no doubt who the man of the tournament had been, and as he went up to collect the trophy, Maradona knew he had inherited Pele's title of the world's best footballer. Argentina had played the most consistent football throughout the tournament and had won all but one of their matches. Their manager Carlos Bilardo had built a side that complemented Maradona well and they fully deserved their victory. If there had been some lingering doubts about their victory eight years previously on home soil, few begrudged them their triumph in Mexico.

THE THIRTEENTH WORLD CUP

2nd May 1984–29th June 1986

QUALIFYING TOURNAMENT

EUROPE

Group 1

	Pd	Be	Al	Gr	Pl	W	D	L	F	A	Pts
POLAND	–	0–0	2–2	3–1	6	3	2	1	10	6	8
Belgium	2–0	–	3–1	2–0	6	3	2	1	7	3	8
Albania	0–1	2–0	–	1–1	6	1	2	3	6	9	4
Greece	1–4	0–0	2–0	–	6	1	2	3	5	10	4

Belgium qualified to meet the runners–up of Group 5, Holland, in a play-off

Group 2

	WG	Pt	Sd	Cz	Ma	Pl	W	D	L	F	A	Pts
WEST GERMANY	–	0–1	2–0	2–2	6–0	8	5	2	1	22	9	12
PORTUGAL	1–2	–	1–3	2–1	3–2	8	5	0	3	12	10	10
Sweden	2–2	0–1	–	2–0	4–0	8	4	1	3	14	9	9
Czechoslovakia	1–5	1–0	2–1	–	4–0	8	3	2	3	11	12	8
Malta	2–3	1–3	1–2	0–0	–	8	0	1	7	6	25	1

Group 3

	En	NI	Ro	Fi	Tu	Pl	W	D	L	F	A	Pts
ENGLAND	–	0–0	1–1	5–0	5–0	8	4	4	0	21	2	12
NTH. IRELAND	0–1	–	3–2	2–1	2–0	8	4	2	2	8	5	10
Romania	0–0	0–1	–	2–0	3–0	8	3	3	2	12	7	9
Finland	1–1	1–0	1–1	–	1–0	8	3	2	3	7	12	8
Turkey	0–8	0–0	1–3	1–2	–	8	0	1	7	2	24	1

Group 4

	Fr	Bu	EG	Yu	Lu	Pl	W	D	L	F	A	Pts
FRANCE	–	1–0	2–0	2–0	6–0	8	5	1	2	15	4	11
BULGARIA	2–0	–	1–0	2–1	4–0	8	5	1	2	13	5	11
East Germany	2–0	2–1	–	2–3	3–1	8	5	0	3	19	9	10
Yugoslavia	0–0	0–0	1–2	–	1–0	8	3	2	3	7	8	8
Luxembourg	0–4	1–3	0–5	0–1	–	8	0	0	8	2	27	0

Group 5

	Hu	Ho	Au	Cy	Pl	W	D	L	F	A	Pts
HUNGARY	–	0–1	3–1	2–0	6	5	0	1	12	4	10
Holland	1–2	–	1–1	7–1	6	3	1	2	11	5	7
Austria	0–3	1–0	–	4–0	6	3	1	2	9	8	7
Cyprus	1–2	0–1	1–2	–	6	0	0	6	3	18	0

Holland qualified to meet the runners–up of Group 1, Belgium, in a play-off

BELGIUM .... 1–0 1–2 ..... Holland

Group 6

	De	SU	Sz	RI	No	Pl	W	D	L	F	A	Pts
DENMARK	–	4–2	0–0	3–0	1–0	8	5	1	2	17	6	11
SOVIET UNION	1–0	–	4–0	2–0	1–0	8	4	2	2	13	8	10
Switzerland	1–0	2–2	–	0–0	1–1	8	2	4	2	5	10	8
Rep. Ireland	1–4	1–0	3–0	–	0–0	8	2	2	4	5	10	6
Norway	1–5	1–1	0–1	1–0	–	8	1	3	4	4	10	5

Group 7

	Sp	Sc	Wa	Ic	Pl	W	D	L	F	A	Pts
SPAIN	–	1–0	3–0	2–1	6	4	0	2	9	8	8
Scotland	3–1	–	0–1	3–0	6	3	1	2	8	4	7
Wales	3–0	1–1	–	2–1	6	3	1	2	7	6	7
Iceland	1–2	0–1	1–0	–	6	1	0	5	4	10	2

Scotland qualified to meet the winners of the Oceania group, Australia, in a play-off

SOUTH AMERICA

Group 1

	Ar	Pe	Co	Ve	Pl	W	D	L	F	A	Pts
ARGENTINA	–	2–2	1–0	3–0	6	4	1	1	12	6	9
Peru	1–0	–	0–0	4–1	6	3	2	1	8	4	8
Colombia	1–3	1–0	–	2–0	6	2	2	2	6	6	6
Venezuela	2–3	0–1	2–2	–	6	0	1	5	5	15	1

Peru and Colombia qualified for South American play-offs

Group 2

	Ur	Ch	Ec	Pl	W	D	L	F	A	Pts
URUGUAY	–	2–1	2–1	4	3	0	1	6	4	6
Chile	2–0	–	6–2	4	2	1	1	10	5	5
Ecuador	0–2	1–1	–	4	0	1	3	4	11	1

Chile qualified for South American play-offs

Group 3

	Br	Pa	Bo	Pl	W	D	L	F	A	Pts
BRAZIL	–	1–1	1–1	4	2	2	0	6	2	6
Paraguay	0–2	–	3–0	4	1	2	1	5	4	4
Bolivia	0–2	1–1	–	4	0	2	2	2	7	2

Paraguay qualified for South American play-offs

Play-offs

First round

Paraguay .... 3–0 1–2 .... Colombia
Chile .... 4–2 1–0 .... Peru

Final

PARAGUAY ..... 3–0 2–2 .... Chile

CENTRAL AND NORTH AMERICA

FIRST ROUND

El Salvador .... 5–0 3–0 .... Puerto Rico
Neth. Antilles .... 0–0 0–4 .... United States
Canada .... W–O .... Jamaica
Panama .... 0–3 0–1 .... Honduras
Costa Rica .... W–O .... Barbados
Guatemala .... Bye
Trinidad .... W–O .... Grenada
Haiti .... 4–0 1–2* ..... Antigua
Surinam .... 1–0 1–1 .... Guyana

* Both legs played in Haiti

SECOND ROUND

Group 1

	Ho	Es	Su	Pl	W	D	L	F	A	Pts
Honduras	–	0–0	2–1	4	2	2	0	5	3	6
El Salvador	1–2	–	3–0	4	2	1	1	7	2	5
Surinam*	1–1	0–3	–	4	0	1	3	2	9	1

* Surinam played all games away from home

Group 2

	Ca	Gu	Ha	Pl	W	D	L	F	A	Pts
Canada	–	2–1	2–0	4	3	1	0	7	2	7
Guatemala	1–1	–	4–0	4	2	1	1	7	3	5
Haiti	0–2	0–1	–	4	0	0	4	0	9	0

Group 3

	CR	US	Tr	Pl	W	D	L	F	A	Pts
Costa Rica	–	1–1	1–1	4	2	2	0	6	2	6
United States	0–1	–	1–0	4	2	1	1	4	3	5
Trinidad *	0–3	1–2	–	4	0	1	3	2	7	1

* Trinidad played all games away from home

THIRD ROUND

	Ca	Ho	CR	Pl	W	D	L	F	A	Pts
CANADA	–	2–1	1–1	4	2	2	0	4	2	6
HONDURAS	0–1	–	3–1	4	1	1	2	6	6	3
COSTA RICA	0–0	2–2	–	4	0	3	1	4	6	3

AFRICA

FIRST ROUND

Egypt .... 1–0 1–1 .... Zimbabwe
Kenya .... 2–1 3–3 .... Ethiopia
Mauritius .... 0–1 0–4 .... Malawi
Zambia .... 3–0 0–1 .... Uganda
Madagascar .... W–O .... Lesotho
Tanzania .... 1–1 0–0 .... Sudan
Sierra Leone ...... 0–1 0–4 .... Morocco
Libya .... W–O .... Niger
Benin .... 0–2 0–4 .... Tunisia
Guinea .... W–O .... Togo
Côte d'Ivoire ..... 4–0 2–3 .... Gambia
Nigeria .... 3–0 1–0 .... Liberia
Angola .... 1–0 0–1 (4–3p) .. Senegal
Algeria .... Bye
Cameroon .... Bye
Ghana .... Bye

SECOND ROUND

Zambia .... 4–1 1–1 .... Cameroon
Morocco .... 2–0 0–0 .... Malawi
Angola .... 0–0 2–3 .... Algeria
Kenya .... 0–3 1–3 .... Nigeria
Egypt .... 1–0 0–1 (4–2p) .. Madagascar
Guinea .... 1–0 0–2 .... Tunisia
Sudan .... 0–0 0–4 .... Libya
Côte d'Ivoire ..... 0–0 0–2 .... Ghana

THIRD ROUND

Algeria .... 2–0 1–0 .... Zambia
Ghana .... 0–0 0–2 .... Libya
Nigeria .... 1–0 0–2 .... Tunisia
Egypt .... 0–0 0–2 .... Morocco

FOURTH ROUND

Tunisia .... 1–4 0–3 .... ALGERIA
MOROCCO ..... 3–0 0–1 .... Libya

ASIA

FIRST ROUND

Group 1

Saudi Arabia ...... 0–0 0–1 .... Arab Emirates

Group 2

	Iq	Qa	Jo	Pl	W	D	L	F	A	Pts
IRAQ	–	2–1	2–0	4	3	0	1	7	6	6
QATAR	3–0	–	2–0	4	2	0	2	6	3	4
JORDAN	2–3	1–0	–	4	1	0	3	3	7	2

Iraq played Jordan in Kuwait City, and Qatar in Calcutta, India

Group 3

	Sy	Ku	NY	Pl	W	D	L	F	A	Pts
SYRIA	–	1–0	3–0	4	3	1	0	5	0	7
KUWAIT	0–0	–	5–0	4	2	1	1	8	2	5
NORTH YEMEN	0–1	1–3	–	4	0	0	4	1	12	0

Group 4

South Yemen .... 1–4 3–3 .... Bahrain

Group 5

	SK	Ma	Ne	Pl	W	D	L	F	A	Pts
SOUTH KOREA	–	2–0	4–0	4	3	0	1	8	1	6
MALAYSIA	1–0	–	5–0	4	2	1	1	6	2	5
NEPAL	0–2	0–0	–	4	0	1	3	0	11	1

Group 6

	Id	In	Th	Ba	Pl	W	D	L	F	A	Pts
INDONESIA	–	2–1	1–0	2–0	6	4	1	1	8	4	9
INDIA	1–1	–	1–1	2–1	6	2	3	1	7	6	7
THAILAND	0–1	0–0	–	3–0	6	1	2	3	4	4	4
BANGLADESH	2–1	1–2	1–0	–	6	2	0	4	5	10	4

Group 7

	HK	Ch	Mc	Br	Pl	W	D	L	F	A	Pts
HONG KONG	–	0–0	2–0	8–0	6	5	1	0	19	2	11
CHINA	1–2	–	6–0	8–0**	6	4	1	1	23	2	9
MACAO	0–2	0–4	–	2–0	6	2	0	4	4	15	4
BRUNEI	1–5	0–4*	1–2	–	6	0	0	6	2	29	0

* Played in Hong Kong ** Played in Macao

Group 8

	Ja	NK	Si	Pl	W	D	L	F	A	Pts
JAPAN	–	1–0	5–0	4	3	1	0	9	1	7
NORTH KOREA	0–0	–	2–0	4	1	2	1	3	2	4
SINGAPORE	1–3	1–1	–	4	0	1	3	2	11	1

SECOND ROUND

Arab Emirates ... 2–3 2–1* ... Iraq
Bahrain .... 1–1 0–1 ..... Syria
South Korea .... 2–0 4–1 ..... Indonesia
Japan .... 3–0 2–1 ..... Hong Kong

* Second leg played in Ta'if, Saudi Arabia

THIRD ROUND

Syria .... 0–0 1–3 * ... IRAQ
Japan .... 1–2 0–1 .... SOUTH KOREA

* Second leg played in Ta'if, Saudi Arabia

OCEANIA

	Au	Is	NZ	Ta	Pl	W	D	L	F	A	Pts
AUSTRALIA	–	1–1	2–0	7–0	6	4	2	0	20	2	10
ISRAEL	1–2	–	3–0	6–0	6	3	1	2	17	6	7
NEW ZEALAND	0–0	3–1	–	5–1	6	3	1	2	13	7	7
TAIWAN*	0–8	0–5	0–5	–	6	0	0	6	1	36	0

* Taiwan played all matches away from home

Australia qualified to meet the runners–up of European group 7, Scotland, in a play-off

Play-off

SCOTLAND ..... 2–0 0–0 .... Australia

MEXICO qualified as hosts

ITALY qualified as holders

FINAL TOURNAMENT

Held in Mexico 31st May–29th June 1986

FIRST ROUND

Group 1 (Azteca – Mexico City, Olimpico – Mexico City, Cuauhtemoc – Puebla)

	Ar	It	Bu	SK	Pl	W	D	L	F	A	Pts
ARGENTINA	–	1–1	2–0	3–1	3	2	1	0	6	2	5

					Pl	W	D	L	F	A	Pts
ITALY	–	–	1–1	3–2	3	1	2	0	5	4	4
BULGARIA	–	–	–	1–1	3	0	2	1	2	4	2
SOUTH KOREA	–	–	–	–	3	0	1	2	4	7	1

Group 2 (Azteca – Mexico City, Luis Dosal – Toluca)

	Me	Pa	Be	Iq	Pl	W	D	L	F	A	Pts
MEXICO	–	1–1	2–1	1–0	3	2	1	0	4	2	5
PARAGUAY	–	–	2–2	1–0	3	1	2	0	4	3	4
BELGIUM	–	–	–	2–1	3	1	1	1	5	5	3
IRAQ	–	–	–	–	3	0	0	3	1	4	0

Group 3 (Nou Camp – León, Estadio Irapuato – Irapuato)

	SU	Fr	Hu	Ca	Pl	W	D	L	F	A	Pts
SOVIET UNION	–	1–1	6–0	2–0	3	2	1	0	9	1	5
FRANCE	–	–	3–0	1–0	3	2	1	0	5	1	5
HUNGARY	–	–	–	2–0	3	1	0	2	2	9	2
CANADA	–	–	–	–	3	0	0	3	0	5	0

Group 4 (Jalisco – Guadalajara, 3 de Marzo – Guadalajara, Tecnológico – Monterrey)

	Br	Sp	NI	Al	Pl	W	D	L	F	A	Pts
BRAZIL	–	1–0	3–0	1–0	3	3	0	0	5	0	6
SPAIN	–	–	2–1	3–0	3	2	0	1	5	2	4
NTH. IRELAND	–	–	–	1–1	3	0	1	2	2	6	1
ALGERIA	–	–	–	–	3	0	1	2	1	5	1

Group 5 (La Corregidora – Querétaro, Neza 86 – Nezahualcoyotl)

	De	WG	Ur	Sc	Pl	W	D	L	F	A	Pts
DENMARK	–	2–0	6–1	1–0	3	3	0	0	9	1	6
WEST GERMANY	–	–	1–1	2–1	3	1	1	1	3	4	3
URUGUAY	–	–	–	0–0	3	0	2	1	2	7	2
SCOTLAND	–	–	–	–	3	0	1	2	1	3	1

Group 6 (Universitario – Monterrey, Tecnológico – Monterrey, 3 de Marzo – Guadalajara)

	Mo	En	Pd	Pt	Pl	W	D	L	F	A	Pts
MOROCCO	–	0–0	0–0	3–1	3	1	2	0	3	1	4
ENGLAND	–	–	3–0	0–1	3	1	1	1	3	1	3
POLAND	–	–	–	1–0	3	1	1	1	1	3	3
PORTUGAL	–	–	–	–	3	1	0	2	2	4	2

SECOND ROUND

Cuauhtemoc, Puebla, 16–06–1986, 26 000
ARGENTINA 1 (Pasculli 41)
URUGUAY 0

Azteca, Mexico City, 18–06–1986, 98 000
ENGLAND 3 (Lineker 31 72, Beardsley 55)
PARAGUAY 0

La Corregidora, Querétaro, 18–06–1986, 38 000
SPAIN 5 (Butragueño 43 57 79 88, Goicoechea 68)
DENMARK 1 (Olsen J 32)

Nou Camp, León, 15–06–1986, 32 000
BELGIUM 4 (Scifo 54, Ceulemans 75, Demol 102, Claesen 108)
SOVIET UNION 3 (Belanov 27 69 111)

Olimpico, Mexico City, 17–06–1986, 70 000
FRANCE 2 (Platini 13, Stopyra 56)
ITALY 0

Jalisco, Guadalajara, 16–06–1986, 45 000
BRAZIL 4 (Socrates 29, Josimar 56, Edinho 78, Careca 82)
POLAND 0

Azteca, Mexico City, 15–06–1986, 114 000
MEXICO 2 (Negrete 34, Servin 60)
BULGARIA 0

Universitario, Monterrey, 17–06–1986, 19 000
WEST GERMANY 1 (Matthäus 89)
MOROCCO 0

QUARTER-FINALS

Azteca, Mexico City, 22–06–1986, 114 000
ARGENTINA 2 (Maradona 51 55)
ENGLAND 1 (Lineker 81)

Cuauhtemoc, Puebla, 22–06–1986, 45 000
BELGIUM 1 (Ceulemans 34)
SPAIN 1 (Señor 85)
Belgium won 5–4 on penalties

Jalisco, Guadalajara, 21–06–1986, 65 000
FRANCE 1 (Platini 41)
BRAZIL 1 (Careca 18)
France won 4–3 on penalties

Universitario, Monterrey, 21–06–1986, 44 000
WEST GERMANY 0
MEXICO 0
West Germany won 4–1 on penalties

SEMI-FINALS

Azteca, Mexico City, 25–06–1986, 110 000
ARGENTINA 2 (Maradona 51 62)
BELGIUM 0

Jalisco, Guadalajara, 25–06–1990, 45 000
WEST GERMANY 2 (Brehme 9, Völler 90)
FRANCE 0

3RD PLACE

Cuauhtemoc, Puebla, 28–06–1986, 21 000
FRANCE 4 (Ferreri 27, Papin 42, Genghini 103, Amoros 108)
BELGIUM 2 (Ceulemans 10, Claesen 73)

FINAL

Azteca, Mexico City, 29–07–1986, 114 000
ARGENTINA 3 (Brown 22, Valdano 56, Burruchaga 84)
WEST GERMANY 2 (Rummenigge 73, Völler 82)
Referee: Arppi Filho, Brazil
Argentina – Pumpido – Cuciuffo, Brown, Ruggeri, Olarticoechea – Batista, Giusti, Enrique, Burruchaga (Trobbiani) – Maradona, Valdano. Tr: Bilardo

West Germany – Schumacher – Jakobs, Förster K-H, Briegel, Brehme – Eder, Berthold, Matthäus, Magath (Hoeness D) – Rummenigge, Allofs (Völler). Tr: Beckenbauer

Top scorers: Gary Lineker, England 6
Emilio Butragueño, Spain 5
Careca, Brazil 5
Diego Maradona, Argentina 5
Total goals scored: 132
Average per game: 2.5

1990

For the first time since 1950, the number of countries taking part in the World Cup fell, perhaps in anticipation of the poor tournament that was to result at the end of the qualifying matches. Italia '90 will be remembered for dull, defensive football, and ultimately proved a test not of footballing prowess but of penalty-taking technique. Italy were awarded the tournament in 1984 during the FIFA congress at the Los Angeles Olympic Games. Their only competition was from the Soviet Union whose case was shot to pieces by their boycott of those very Games.

Italy therefore became the second nation to be awarded the tournament twice. They promised a host of new facilities, and although it looked like a close call at times, with a number of building workers being killed in the process, the tournament started as planned with 10 refurbished stadiums and two totally new ones, in Bari and Turin.

The qualifying tournament produced a couple of surprises, the major one being the elimination of France. Coached by the star of their three previous World Cup campaigns, Michel Platini, they were busy restructuring their team and came third in their group behind Yugoslavia and Scotland. The rest of the European zone went much to form. Of the countries who finished in second place in the three groups containing four sides, Denmark were the unfortunate ones to miss out on Italy as only the two with the best records, England and West Germany, qualified. Like France the Danes were a team in transition but the finals would have undoubtedly benefited from their flair.

Making their first appearance in the finals were the Republic of Ireland. Following on from their success in qualifying for the European Championships two years previously, they inherited the mantle left by their neighbours in the North whom they eliminated. They also made sure Hungary were not present for the first time since 1974, and also missing were Portugal and Bulgaria both of whom had been finalists four years previously.

South America saw no surprises, but a huge scandal instead. In one of the most outrageous pieces of cheating ever seen, Chile left the field in the final and crucial group match with Brazil when they were losing 1–0 and on their way out of the competition. The reason for their departure was a flare thrown from the crowd at Rojas, their goalkeeper, and they claimed to fear for their safety. At first sight it looked as though he was badly injured as his teammates carried him off, but it soon transpired that the flare had not hit him and that the bleeding conveniently visible to the television cameras was self-inflicted.

For their rather ridiculous efforts, the perpetrators of this pre-arranged plan were given lengthy bans and Chile were barred from the 1994 tournament. Banned from the 1990 tournament were Mexico, for cheating in the World Youth Cup by fielding over-age players. This left the CONCACAF field wide open and for the first time ever Costa Rica made it to the finals. Traditionally the second power in the region behind Mexico, it was surprising that it had taken them so long to qualify, but they did so with ease. That was not the case with the United States, who accompanied them to Italy. A 1–0 victory in Port of Spain meant that they and not the colourful Trinidadians qualified, much to the relief of FIFA who had just awarded America the staging of the 1994 tournament.

Asia was once again represented by South Korea, who won a tournament staged in Singapore for the six first round group winners. They were expected to be joined by either China or Saudi Arabia, two growing continental powers. Instead it was the tiny oil-rich United Arab Emirates who joined the Koreans in Italy. It seems remarkable that a country with a population of under two million could humble a country like China with over 500 times the population, but the Emirates showed the benefits that good organisation and a few petro-dollars can bring.

The number of teams taking part from Africa was at its lowest level since 1970. Undoubtedly the difficult economic situation on the continent affected the entry, but there was also continued resentment at the allocation of just two places, and some of the smaller nations, with little chance of qualifying, decided not to enter or pulled out at a later date. Having generally been run on a knock-out basis, the competition now saw group matches used in the first round, from which four teams emerged.

Once again North Africa was strongly represented, with three of the four teams. Egypt qualified for the first time since 1934 at the expense of Algeria who were attempting to make it three final tournaments in a row, but it was the other qualifiers, Cameroon, who were to make all the headlines in Italy. By beating Tunisia 3–0 on aggregate, they made their second appearance in the finals and once there, were minutes away from becoming the first African nation to reach the semi–finals. Their performance in Italy had one major benefit for the rest of African football in that FIFA found it hard to resist the African demands for an extra finals place which they were duly awarded for the 1994 tournament.

The build up for the finals in Italy promised much more than the tournament delivered. The Italian league had the majority of the top players in the world playing there and the shackles of *catenaccio* were slowly but surely being thrown off. The hosts were capable of playing some excellent football and with home advantage they were overwhelming favourites to win the tournament.

The 1986 champions, Argentina, were also regarded as likely challengers before the tournament started, but after the opening game, staged in the beautifully revamped Giuseppe Meazza Stadium in Milan, they were regarded in an entirely different light. The champions were humbled by Cameroon, despite the Africans having two men sent off. Francois Oman Biyik scored the only goal of the game five minutes after his brother, Kana Biyik, had been sent off. Roared on by the crowd, Cameroon held on to their lead and scored one of the most sensational victories the World Cup had ever seen.

Cameroon followed up this victory with another one in their second game, against Romania. The hero of that performance was the 38-year-old Roger Milla who came on as a substitute with 15 minutes remaining and scored two goals to qualify his side for the next round. The surprise failures of Group B were the Soviet Union who were strongly fancied at the start of the tournament. They showed their potential by beating Cameroon 4–0 in a final game that ultimately had no bearing on the outcome of the group. Romania finished second and Argentina qualified as one of the four best third-placed teams.

Group A was very clear cut. Italy won all three of their games in fine style and were joined by Czechoslovakia in the next round. Both Austria and the United States had miserable World Cups. Austria were expected to do much better; the same could not be said about the United States. Alarmingly for FIFA, interest in the tournament back home in America was limited to the numerous ethnic communities who usually followed the fortunes of other teams, most notably the Irish. The one consolation for the Americans was a fine goal scored by Caligiuri against Czechoslovakia which many rated as one of the best of the tournament.

Brazil were easy winners of Group C even if their coach Lazaroni did come in for much criticism for adopting too 'European' an approach. What was surprising in the group was that Costa Rica finished second and eliminated both Scotland and Sweden, both of whom they defeated in some style. With much of the attention focused on Cameroon, the achievements of Costa Rica have largely been forgotten. Scotland were eliminated in the first round for the fifth consecutive tournament.

Three teams qualified from Group D which was won by West Germany, who looked in very good form. Having demolished both Yugoslavia and the United Arab Emirates, they let their form slip against the Colombians, whose presence in the tournament had provoked a huge operation by America's Drug Enforcement Agency. At times it seemed as though they ought not to look any further than the Colombian goalkeeper, Rene Higuita, so strange were some of his antics. The majority of the crowds loved him for his cavalier attitude, though he did have his critics.

This was not Asia's tournament. The Emirates were obviously outclassed in Group D, whilst in Group E, South Korea could not rekindle the spirit that had seen them perform well four years previously in Mexico. The group was won by Spain who were hoping to win on Italian soil just as the Italians had won on Spanish soil in 1982. The side had matured well since reaching the quarter-finals in Mexico and they had little trouble in beating both Belgium and the Koreans and drawing with Uruguay, who won through to the next round in third place courtesy of a last-minute winner against South Korea.

The most closely fought group in the first round was Group F containing England, Holland, the Republic of Ireland and Egypt, the outcome of which was in doubt right to the very end. Five of the six games were drawn, the only exception being England's victory over Egypt in the final match. This result meant that England won the group and Egypt were eliminated. Lots had to be drawn to decide the placings of Holland and Ireland and it was kind to the Irish who were pitted against Romania in the next round instead of West Germany.

Much of the football in the first round had been predictable, and if not exactly boring, it had lacked the passion to bring the tournament to life. In every match apart from Costa Rica's 2–1 win over Sweden, the side who scored first either went on to win or at least draw the game. Much more criticism was to follow in the rest of the tournament, particularly in relation to the use of penalties to decide drawn games.

It looked as if the opening game of the second round would be decided in just that way when after 90 minutes and one period of extra-time, both Colombia and Cameroon had failed to muster a goal. Just as in the game against Romania in the first round, however, it was to be Roger Milla's day as again he scored two goals after having come on as a substitute. The second of these goals was in no small part down to Higuita who was robbed of the ball way outside of his penalty area. Although Redin scored for the Colombians just before the end, the Cameroons went one further than Morocco in 1986 and became the first African nation to reach the quarter-finals.

Later the same night another side from the Americas was dumped out of the tournament when the Czechs beat Costa Rica 4–1 in Bari. The Costa Ricans were not disgraced. Trailing 2–1 with 15 minutes to go they let Czechoslovakia in twice as they pushed forward for an equaliser.

The South American agony continued the following day in Turin and it was the turn of Brazil to exit the tournament at the hands of their fierce rivals Argentina. Despite dominating most of the match and coming close on several occasions, they were beaten by a Caniggia goal after a clever through pass by Maradona, his only really noteworthy contribution to the tournament. Once again the Brazilians had failed, and the result only served to enhance the perception that the Brazilians were a fading world power. They may have won the tournament on three occasions, but with each successive World Cup these victories are consigned further into the annals of history.

The best match of the second round was between Holland and West Germany in Milan. The Germans faced potentially their biggest threat in the form of the European Champions. Six of the players on the pitch plied their trade in that very stadium in Milan: Brehme, Klinsmann and Matthäus of West Germany with Inter, the Dutch trio of Gullit, Rijkaard and Van Basten for Milan.

The Dutch had been rather subdued in the first round, but the game burst into life after 20 minutes when both Rijkaard and Völler were sent off after a bad-tempered exchange. The incident gave the match a cutting edge that most of the other games in the tournament lacked, and in a pulsating second half Klinsmann and Brehme scored to give the Germans victory. Ronald Koeman's reply for Holland came too late.

There was no such excitement the following day in Genoa, except for the penalty shoot-out in which the Irish knocked out Romania. Neither side managed to score in 120 minutes of open play but were remarkably efficient at the spot kicks. Only Timofte failed to convert his, but that was enough to see Ireland through to the quarter-finals, even though in the four games they had played they had failed to win at all and had only scored two goals in the process.

Italy's progress to the quarter-finals had been far more confident and assured and against Uruguay in the Stadio Olimpico in Rome they chalked up another comfortable win. Their new hero, Salvatore Schillaci, scored their first midway through the second half and Serena made sure of the game just before the end. The Italians were the only quarter-finalists to have won all of their games and they had not conceded a goal either. In the quarter-finals they were pitted against the Irish whose record could not have been more different.

The final day of the second round saw Yugoslavia take on Spain in Verona and England play Belgium in Bologna. Spain yet again failed to live up to their promise and were beaten by the ever-improving Yugoslavs, thanks in no small part to some excellent finishing by Dragan Stojkovic. His two goals were the decisive factor in a close-fought tie that went to extra-time.

Extra-time was also needed in Bologna and it was not until the very last minute, when David Platt coolly finished off a Paul Gascoigne free-kick, that the two sides could be separated. Belgium, inspired by the brilliant Enzo Scifo and the ageless Ceulemans and Gerets, came close on a couple of occasions, but they were not to repeat their success of four year previously and England qualified to meet the Cameroons in the next round.

The first three quarter-finals produced just two goals between them. In one of the worst games of the tournament, Argentina and Yugoslavia played out a tedious 0–0 draw in Florence which was only enlivened by the penalty-kicks at the end. Sergio Goycochea, who was Pumpido's replacement in goal after the first-choice keeper had broken his leg in the match against the Soviet Union, was Argentina's hero as they triumphed 3–2 after both sides had at one point been ahead.

Argentina were to come in for great criticism on their route to the final. They rarely offered any positive football and seemed content to take their chances on post-match penalties. In 1986, though Maradona played a crucial role, he was only one of a very good team. In Italy, the Argentinians seemed to abdicate all responsibility to him, and as he was not one hundred percent fit the team suffered as a result.

Italy took on the Republic of Ireland later on in the day in Rome and again Schillaci was the telling factor, although the Irish put up their best performance in defeat. Italy's victory was hardly surprising. They looked threatening whenever they attacked and should have scored more goals. It was the end of the road for the Irish whose fans had made the most of their first World Cup appearance and certainly added much colour to the occasion.

The following day in Milan, the West Germans moved relentlessly into the semi-finals even if it did take a somewhat dubious penalty for them to do so. Despite their fine football some of the Germans' antics were beginning to raise questions about their excessive will to win. A disturbing feature of the tournament had been the number of times referees were prompted into giving decisions that resulted from play-acting by the players, and unfortunately the Germans were more guilty than most. The Czechs, who had played good football throughout the tournament, could have won the game had they made their early pressure count, but in the end, with two goal-line clearances by Hasek and Bilek, they were fortunate to lose only 1–0.

The last quarter-final between England and Cameroon in Naples was by far the best game of the tournament. Cameroon came within ten minutes of a semi-final place and only lack of experience told against them. The match was unique in Italia '90 in that it was the only time that the lead in a game changed hands twice. England went ahead through a David Platt header midway through the first half, only for Cameroon to equalise after fifteen minutes of the second half with a Kunde penalty after Roger Milla was felled in the area.

Both sides were playing fluent, open football and it was no surprise when Milla and Ekeke combined well for the latter to put the Africans ahead four minutes later, but the drama was not over yet. Cameroon appeared to be coping well with containing England in the last 25 minutes, but nine minutes from the end they gave away a silly penalty which Gary Lineker converted. England had been given a considerable fright coming so close to elimination, but they made sure of qualifying for their first semi-final since 1966 when Lineker was again brought down in the area and converted his second penalty in extra-time. Cameroon had without question been one of the highlights of the tournament and in Roger Milla certainly had the star of the show.

The semi-finals were surrounded with controversy as both finalists were decided on penalty kicks. In Naples, Argentina knocked the hosts and favourites out after a 1–1 draw. Italy went into the lead after 17 minutes when Schillaci scored his fifth goal of the series. It seemed as though they would cruise through the game, but Argentina were forced to take the game to the Italians who inexcusably tried to sit back on their lead.

Had they attacked with more enterprise they might well have won with ease but instead Walter Zenga in the Italian goal was forced to pick the ball out of his own net for the first time in the tournament when midway through the second half Caniggia headed home an Olarticoechea cross. Neither side thereafter seemed to have enough imagination to win the game in open play and the Argentinians, thanks once more to the skill of Goycochea in goal, won the ensuing shoot-out. It was a desperately unsatisfactory end to Italy's campaign.

Turin was the location for the second of the semi-finals the following day. England and West Germany took to the field in the new Stadio Delle Alpi and served up an excellent game. Like the previous evening, however, it ended 1–1, and the Germans qualified for their third successive final, the second time they had done so courtesy of penalty kicks. Like the England–Cameroon match, the game was open and flowing and full of incident. England were much on top, but against the run of play the Germans took the lead on the hour when a Brehme free-kick was deflected over Shilton by Parker's attempted block.

Again England left it late and with only ten minutes remaining, Lineker, who had had a quiet first round in the tournament, was again on hand to rescue his side with a well-taken goal from a Parker cross. Both sides hit the post in extra-time but no further goals were scored. In the penalties that followed, West Germany scored all four of theirs with clinical precision, but first Stuart Pearce and then England's best player in the tournament, Chris Waddle, missed their kicks and England were out.

To have both semi-finals decided on penalties was totally unsatisfactory in such an important tournament, and since then the whole concept of penalties has been brought into question. Many regard them as responsible for dull and tedious football, as weaker teams pack their defences in the knowledge that even if they don't score, as long as the other side does not either they still have a fighting chance of winning the match. It is perhaps no coincidence that in the earlier years of the World Cup, draws were less frequent in the knock-out stages because there was no such escape clause. In 40 later-stage games between 1954 and 1970, not one single match was drawn!

If the final had been decided on a penalty shoot-out, it would not have been inappropriate. Instead it was decided by a penalty in normal time, and the Germans won the world's highest honour having scored just one goal from open play in their final three games, and that came from a set piece. The final itself was a disgrace and both sides were equally responsible. Argentina clearly played for penalties whilst the Germans indulged in gamesmanship that saw two of their opponents sent off.

It was also the first final that saw less than three goals scored. Without fail, finals in the past had always lived up to their billing as the showpiece of world football. The best teams had not necessarily always reached the final nor won, but they had all been entertaining affairs. The third-place match between Italy and England might well have produced a much better final. Certainly, in the later stages, the matches those teams had been involved in were amongst the best in the tournament, and the third-place match itself was a most engaging game, even if the pressure was off.

West Germany were expected to win with ease. Lothar Matthäus was at the peak of his game, whilst Maradona was a mere shadow of his former self. Only seven players remained from when the two teams had met in the final four years previously but both coaches were the same. Beckenbauer was out to become the first man to captain and coach a winning side whilst Carlos Bilardo was determined to follow in the footsteps of Vittorio Pozzo and become only the second coach to retain the title.

Few expected it to be a good game and sure enough the world had to witness 90 minutes of the most uninspiring football imaginable. The only goal came five minutes from the end, much to the relief of the crowd who were spared another 30 minutes' tedium. Völler was brought down in the penalty area and Brehme's kick won the game for Germany. Ten minutes previously, however, Calderon had been brought down in the German area in a not dissimilar incident, but Argentine appeals went unnoticed by the Mexican referee.

If Argentina thought they had been hard done by in that incident, neither were their feelings towards the referee improved by the two sendings-off which reduced them to nine men by the end. After 68 minutes, Klinsmann acted as though he had stepped on a landmine when tackled by Monzon and got the Argentine sent off for his troubles, whilst with three minutes to go Dezotti was dismissed after trying to retrieve the ball from Köhler, who acted as though he had been kicked by a bull. On their performance throughout the tournament, a West Germany win was far more preferable than an Argentinian one, but the 1990 final left a bad taste in the mouth.

THE FOURTEENTH WORLD CUP
17th April 1988–8th July 1990

QUALIFYING TOURNAMENT

EUROPE

Group 1

	Ro	De	Gr	Bu	Pl	W	D	L	F	A	Pts
ROMANIA	–	3–1	3–0	1–0	6	4	1	1	10	5	9
DENMARK	3–0	–	7–1	1–1	6	3	2	1	15	6	8
GREECE	0–0	1–1	–	1–0	6	1	2	3	3	15	4
BULGARIA	1–3	0–2	4–0	–	6	1	1	4	6	8	3

Group 2

	Sd	En	Pd	Al	Pl	W	D	L	F	A	Pts
SWEDEN	–	0–0	2–1	3–1	6	4	2	0	9	3	10
ENGLAND	0–0	–	3–0	5–0	6	3	3	0	10	0	9
POLAND	0–2	0–0	–	1–0	6	2	1	3	4	8	5
ALBANIA	1–2	0–2	1–2	–	6	0	0	6	3	15	0

Group 3

	SU	Au	Tu	EG	Ic	Pl	W	D	L	F	A	Pts
SOVIET UNION	–	2–0	2–0	3–0	1–1	8	4	3	1	11	4	11
AUSTRIA	0–0	–	3–2	3–0	2–1	8	3	3	2	9	9	9
TURKEY	0–1	3–0	–	3–1	1–1	8	3	1	4	12	10	7
EAST GERMANY	2–1	1–1	0–2	–	2–0	8	3	1	4	9	13	7
ICELAND	1–1	0–0	2–1	0–3	–	8	1	4	3	6	11	6

Group 4

	Ho	WG	Fi	Wa	Pl	W	D	L	F	A	Pts
HOLLAND	–	1–1	3–0	1–0	6	4	2	0	8	2	10
WEST GERMANY	0–0	–	6–1	2–1	6	3	3	0	13	3	9
FINLAND	0–1	0–4	–	1–0	6	1	1	4	4	16	3
WALES	1–2	0–0	2–2	–	6	0	2	4	4	8	2

Group 5

	Yu	Sc	Fr	No	Cy	Pl	W	D	L	F	A	Pts
YUGOSLAVIA	–	3–1	3–2	1–0	4–0	8	6	2	0	16	6	14
SCOTLAND	1–1	–	2–0	1–1	2–1	8	4	2	2	12	12	10
FRANCE	0–0	3–0	–	1–0	2–0	8	3	3	2	10	7	9
NORWAY	1–2	1–2	1–1	–	3–1	8	2	2	4	10	9	6
CYPRUS	1–2	2–3	1–1	0–3	–	8	0	1	7	6	20	1

Group 6

	Sp	RI	Hu	NI	Ma	Pl	W	D	L	F	A	Pts
SPAIN	–	2–0	4–0	4–0	4–0	8	6	1	1	20	3	13
REP. IRELAND	1–0	–	2–0	3–0	2–0	8	5	2	1	10	2	12
HUNGARY	2–2	0–0	–	1–0	1–1	8	2	4	2	8	12	8
NTH. IRELAND	0–2	0–0	1–2	–	3–0	8	2	1	5	6	12	5
MALTA	0–2	0–2	2–2	0–2	–	8	0	2	6	3	18	2

Group 7

	Be	Cz	Pt	Sz	Lu	Pl	W	D	L	F	A	Pts
BELGIUM	–	2–1	3–0	1–0	1–1	8	4	4	0	15	5	12
CZECHOSLOVAKIA	0–0	–	2–1	3–0	4–0	8	5	2	1	13	3	12
PORTUGAL	1–1	0–0	–	3–1	1–0	8	4	2	2	11	8	10
SWITZERLAND	2–2	0–1	1–2	–	2–1	8	2	1	5	10	14	5
LUXEMBOURG	0–5	0–2	0–3	1–4	–	8	0	1	7	3	22	1

SOUTH AMERICA

Group 1

	Ur	Bo	Pe	Pl	W	D	L	F	A	Pts
URUGUAY	–	2–0	2–0	4	3	0	1	7	2	6
BOLIVIA	2–1	–	2–1	4	3	0	1	6	5	6
PERU	0–2	1–2	–	4	0	0	4	2	8	0

Group 2

	Co	Pa	Ec	Pl	W	D	L	F	A	Pts
COLOMBIA	–	2–1	2–0	4	2	1	1	5	3	5
PARAGUAY	2–1	–	2–1	4	2	0	2	6	7	4
ECUADOR	0–0	3–1	–	4	1	1	2	4	5	3

Colombia qualified to meet the winners of the Oceania group, Israel, in a play-off

Group 3

	Br	Ch	Ve	Pl	W	D	L	F	A	Pts
BRAZIL	–	2–0*	6–0	4	3	1	0	13	1	7
CHILE	1–1	–	5–0**	4	2	1	1	9	4	5
VENEZUELA	0–4	1–3	–	4	0	0	4	1	18	0

* Match abandoned after 65 minutes with Brazil leading 1–0. Brazil awarded game 2–0.
** Played in Mendoza, Argentina

OCEANIA

FIRST ROUND

Taiwan .... 0–4 1–4 .... New Zealand
Fiji .... 1–0 1–5 .... Australia
Israel .... Bye

SECOND ROUND

	Is	Au	NZ	Pl	W	D	L	F	A	Pts
ISRAEL	–	1–1	1–0	4	1	3	0	5	4	5
AUSTRALIA	1–1	–	4–1	4	1	2	1	6	5	4
NEW ZEALAND	2–2	2–0	–	4	1	1	2	5	7	3

Israel qualified to meet winners of South America Group 2, Colombia, in a play-off.

COLOMBIA ..... 1–0 0–0 .... Israel

CENTRAL AND NORTH AMERICA

FIRST ROUND

Guyana .... 0–4 0–1 .... Trinidad
Cuba .... 0–1 1–1 .... Guatemala
Jamaica .... 1–0 2–1 .... Puerto Rico
Antigua .... 0–1 1–3 .... Neth. Antilles
Costa Rica .... 1–1 2–0 .... Panama
Mexico .... Bye
United States .... Bye
Canada .... Bye
El Salvador .... Bye
Honduras .... Bye

SECOND ROUND

Jamaica .... 0–0 1–5 .... United States
Guatemala .... 1–0 2–3 .... Canada
Neth. Antilles .... 0–1 0–5 .... El Salvador
Trinidad .... 0–0 1–1 .... Honduras
Costa Rica .... W–O .... Mexico

THIRD ROUND

	CR	US	Tr	Gu	ES	Pl	W	D	L	F	A	Pts
COSTA RICA	–	1–0	1–0	2–1	1–0	8	5	1	2	10	6	11
UNITED STATES	1–0	–	1–1	2–1	0–0	8	4	3	1	6	3	11
Trinidad	1–1	0–1	–	2–1	2–0	8	3	3	2	7	5	9
Guatemala	1–0	0–0	0–1	–	–	6	1	1	4	4	7	3
El Salvador	2–4	0–1	0–0	–	–	6	0	2	4	2	8	2

AFRICA

FIRST ROUND

Uganda .... 1–0 1–3 .... Malawi
Angola .... 0–0 2–1 .... Sudan
Zimbabwe .... W–O .... Lesotho
Zambia .... W–O .... Rwanda
Libya .... 3–0 0–2 .... Burkina Faso
Ghana .... 0–0 0–2 .... Liberia
Tunisia .... 5–0 0–3 .... Guinea
Gabon .... W–O .... Togo
Algeria .... Bye
Côte d'Ivoire .... Bye
Egypt .... Bye
Kenya .... Bye
Cameroon .... Bye
Nigeria .... Bye
Zaire .... Bye
Morocco .... Bye

SECOND ROUND

Group A

	Al	CI	Zi	Pl	W	D	L	F	A	Pts
Algeria	–	1–0	3–0	4	3	1	0	6	1	7
Côte d'Ivoire	0–0	–	5–0	4	1	2	1	5	1	4
Zimbabwe	1–2	0–0	–	4	0	1	3	1	10	1

Libya played one match and then withdrew

Group B

	Eg	Li	Ma	Ke	Pl	W	D	L	F	A	Pts
Egypt	–	2–0	1–0	2–0	6	3	2	1	6	2	8
Liberia	1–0	–	1–0	0–0	6	2	2	2	2	3	6
Malawi	1–1	0–0	–	1–0	6	1	3	2	3	4	5
Kenya	0–0	1–0	1–1	–	6	1	3	2	2	4	5

Group C

	Cm	Ni	An	Ga	Pl	W	D	L	F	A	Pts
Cameroon	–	1–0	1–1	2–1	6	4	1	1	9	6	9
Nigeria	2–0	–	1–0	1–0	6	3	1	2	7	5	7
Angola	1–2	2–2	–	2–0	6	1	2	3	6	7	4
Gabon	1–3	2–1	1–0	–	6	2	0	4	5	9	4

Group D

	Tu	Zm	Zr	Mo	Pl	W	D	L	F	A	Pts
Tunisia	–	1–0	1–0	2–1	6	3	1	2	5	5	7
Zambia	1–0	–	4–2	2–1	6	3	0	3	7	6	6
Zaire	3–1	1–0	–	0–0	6	2	2	2	7	7	6
Morocco	0–0	1–0	1–1	–	6	1	3	2	4	5	5

THIRD ROUND

Algeria .... 0–0 0–1 .... EGYPT
CAMEROON ... 2–0 1–0 .... Tunisia

ASIA

FIRST ROUND

Group 1

	Qa	Iq	Jo	Om	Pl	W	D	L	F	A	Pts
Qatar	–	1–0	1–0	3–0	6	3	3	0	8	3	9
Iraq	2–2	–	4–0	3–1	6	3	2	1	11	5	8
Jordan	1–1	0–1	–	2–0	6	2	1	3	5	7	5
Oman	0–0	1–1	0–2	–	6	0	2	4	2	11	2

Group 2

	SA	Sy	NY	Pl	W	D	L	F	A	Pts
Saudi Arabia	–	5–4	1–0	4	3	1	0	7	4	7
Syria	0–0	–	2–0	4	2	1	1	7	5	5
North Yemen	0–1	0–1	–	4	0	0	4	0	5	0

Group 3

	Em	Ku	Pa	Pl	W	D	L	F	A	Pts
Arab Emirates	–	1–0	5–0	4	3	0	1	12	4	6
Kuwait	3–2	–	2–0	4	3	0	1	6	3	6
Pakistan	1–4	0–1	–	4	0	0	4	1	12	0

Group 4

Tournaments held in Seoul and Singapore

	SK	Ma	Si	Ne	Pl	W	D	L	F	A	Pts
South Korea	–	3–0	3–0	9–0	6	6	0	0	25	0	12
Malaysia	0–3	–	1–0	2–0	6	3	1	2	8	8	7
Singapore	0–3	2–2	–	7–0	6	2	1	3	12	9	5
Nepal	0–4	0–3	0–3	–	6	0	0	6	0	28	0

Group 5

	Ch	Ir	Ba	Th	Pl	W	D	L	F	A	Pts
China	–	2–0	2–0	2–0	6	5	0	1	13	3	10
Iran	3–2	–	1–0	3–0	6	5	0	1	12	5	10
Bangladesh	0–2	1–2	–	3–1	6	1	0	5	4	9	2
Thailand	0–3	0–3	1–0	–	6	1	0	5	2	14	2

Group 6

	NK	Ja	Id	HK	Pl	W	D	L	F	A	Pts
North Korea	–	2–0	2–1	4–1	6	4	1	1	11	5	9
Japan	2–1	–	5–0	0–0	6	2	3	1	7	3	7
Indonesia	0–0	0–0	–	3–2	6	1	3	2	5	10	5
Hong Kong	1–2	0–0	1–1	–	6	0	3	3	5	10	3

SECOND ROUND

Tournament held in Singapore

	Em	Qa	Ch	SA	NK	Pl	W	D	L	F	A	Pts
SOUTH KOREA	1–1	0–0	1–0	2–0	1–0	5	3	2	0	5	1	8
ARAB EMIRATES	–	1–1	2–1	0–0	0–0	5	1	4	0	4	3	6
QATAR	–	–	2–1	1–1	0–2	5	1	3	1	4	5	5
China	–	–	–	2–1	1–0	5	2	0	3	5	6	4
Saudi Arabia	–	–	–	–	2–0	5	1	2	2	4	5	4
North Korea	–	–	–	–	–	5	1	1	3	2	4	3

ARGENTINA qualified as holders

ITALY qualified as hosts

FINAL TOURNAMENT

Held in Italy 8th June–8th July 1990

FIRST ROUND

Group A (Olimpico – Rome, Comunale – Florence)

	It	Cz	Au	US	Pl	W	D	L	F	A	Pts
ITALY	–	2–0	1–0	1–0	3	3	0	0	4	0	6
CZECHOSLOVAKIA	–	–	1–0	5–1	3	2	0	1	6	3	4
AUSTRIA	–	–	–	2–1	3	1	0	2	2	3	2
UNITED STATES	–	–	–	–	3	0	0	3	2	8	0

Group B (Giuseppe Meazza – Milan, Sant Nicola – Bari, San Paolo – Naples)

	Ca	Ro	Ar	SU	Pl	W	D	L	F	A	Pts
CAMEROON	–	2–1	1–0	0–4	3	2	0	1	3	5	4

ROMANIA	–	–	1–1	2–0	3	1	1	1	4	3	3
ARGENTINA	–	–	–	2–0	3	1	1	1	3	2	3
SOVIET UNION	–	–	–	–	3	1	0	2	4	4	2

Group C (Delle Alpi – Turin, Luigi Ferraris – Genoa)

	Br	CR	Sc	Sd	Pl	W	D	L	F	A	Pts
BRAZIL	–	1–0	1–0	2–1	3	3	0	0	4	1	6
COSTA RICA	–	–	1–0	2–1	3	2	0	1	3	2	4
SCOTLAND	–	–	–	2–1	3	1	0	2	2	3	2
SWEDEN	–	–	–	–	3	0	0	3	3	6	0

Group D (Giuseppe Meazza – Milan, Dall'Ara – Bologna)

	WG	Yu	Co	AE	Pl	W	D	L	F	A	Pts
WEST GERMANY	–	4–1	1–1	5–1	3	2	1	0	10	3	5
YUGOSLAVIA	–	–	1–0	4–1	3	2	0	1	6	5	4
COLOMBIA	–	–	–	2–0	3	1	1	1	3	2	3
UAE	–	–	–	–	3	0	0	3	2	11	0

Group E (Bentegodi – Verona, Friuli – Udine)

	Sp	Be	Ur	SK	Pl	W	D	L	F	A	Pts
SPAIN	–	2–1	0–0	3–1	3	2	1	0	5	2	5
BELGIUM	–	–	3–1	2–0	3	2	0	1	6	3	4
URUGUAY	–	–	–	1–0	3	1	0	2	2	3	2
SOUTH KOREA	–	–	–	–	3	0	0	3	1	6	0

Group F (Sant 'Elia – Cagliari, Della Favorita – Palermo)

	En	RI	Ho	Eg	Pl	W	D	L	F	A	Pts
ENGLAND	–	1–1	0–0	1–0	3	1	2	0	2	1	4
REP. IRELAND	–	–	1–1	0–0	3	0	3	0	2	2	3
HOLLAND	–	–	–	1–1	3	0	3	0	2	2	3
EGYPT	–	–	–	–	3	0	2	1	1	2	2

SECOND ROUND

Giuseppe Meazza, Milan, 24–06–1990, 74 000
WEST GERMANY 2 (Klinsmann 50, Brehme 84)
HOLLAND 1 (Koeman R 88)

Sant Nicola, Bari, 23–06–1990, 47 000
CZECHOSLOVAKIA 4 (Skuhravy 11 62 82, Kubik 77)
COSTA RICA 1 (Gonzalez 56)

San Paolo, Naples, 23–06–1990, 50 000
CAMEROON 2 (Milla 106 108)
COLOMBIA 1 (Redin 116)

Dall'Ara, Bologna, 26–06–1990, 34 000
ENGLAND 1 (Platt 119)
BELGIUM 0

Olimpico, Rome, 25–06–1990, 73 000
ITALY 2 (Schillaci 65, Serena 82)
URUGUAY 0

Luigi Ferraris, Genoa, 25–06–1990, 31 000
REP. IRELAND 0
ROMANIA 0
Rep. Ireland won 5–4 on penalties

Bentegodi, Verona, 26–06–1990, 35 000
YUGOSLAVIA 2 (Stojkovic 77 92)
SPAIN 1 (Salinas 83)

Delle Alpi, Turin, 24–06–1990, 61 000
ARGENTINA 1 (Caniggia 82)
BRAZIL 0

QUARTER-FINALS

Giuseppe Meazza, Milan, 1–07–1990, 73 000
WEST GERMANY 1 (Matthäus 24)
CZECHOSLOVAKIA 0

San Paolo, Naples, 1–07–1990, 55 000
ENGLAND 3 (Platt 25, Lineker 82 105)
CAMEROON 2 (Kunde 61, Ekeke 64)

Olimpico, Rome, 30–06–1990, 73 000
ITALY 1 (Schillaci 37)
REP. IRELAND 0

Comunale, Florence, 30–06–1990, 38 000
ARGENTINA 0
YUGOSLAVIA 0
Argentina won 3–2 on penalties

SEMI-FINALS

Delle Alpi, Turin, 4–07–1990, 62 000
WEST GERMANY 1 (Brehme 59)
ENGLAND 1 (Lineker 80)
West Germany won 4–3 on penalties

San Paolo, Naples, 3–07–1990, 59 000
ARGENTINA 1 (Schillaci 17)
ITALY 1 (Caniggia 67)
Argentina won 4–3 on penalties

3RD PLACE

Sant Nicola, Bari, 7–07–1990, 51 000
ITALY 2 (Baggio 71, Schillaci 84)
ENGLAND 1 (Platt 80)

FINAL

Olimpico, Rome, 8–07–1990, 73 000
WEST GERMANY 1 (Brehme 85)
ARGENTINA 0
Referee: Codesal, Mexico
West Germany – Illgner – Berthold (Reuter), Kohler, Augenthaler, Buchwald, Brehme – Hässler, Matthäus, Littbarski – Völler, Klinsmann. Tr: Beckenbauer
Argentina – Goycochea – Ruggeri (Monzon), Simón, Serrizuela – Sensini, Basualdo, Burruchaga (Calderon), Troglio, Lorenzo – Maradona, Dezotti. Tr: Bilardo

Top scorers: Salvatore Schillaci, Italy 6
Tomás Skuhravy, Czechoslovakia 5
Gary Lineker, England 4
Lothar Matthäus, West Germany 4
Michel, Spain 4
Roger Milla, Cameroon 4
Total goals scored: 115
Average per game: 2.2

And so to the United States in 1994. The Americans have promised to serve up an excellent tournament, and if the football tournament of the 1984 Olympic Games in Los Angeles is anything to go by, they should have no trouble. There is, however, increasing alarm at the lack of

WORLD CUP MEDALS TABLE

	Country	G	S	B	Finals	Semis
1	Germany	3	3	2	6	9
2	Brazil	3	1	2	4	5
3	Italy	3	1	1	4	4
4	Argentina	2	2	–	4	4
5	Uruguay	2	–	–	2	4
6	England	1	–	–	1	2
7	Czechoslovakia	–	2	–	2	2
	Holland	–	2	–	2	2
	Hungary	–	2	–	2	2
10	Sweden	–	1	1	1	2
11	France	–	–	2	–	3
12	Poland	–	–	2	–	1
13	Austria	–	–	1	–	2
	Yugoslavia	–	–	1	–	2
15	Chile	–	–	1	–	1
	Portugal	–	–	1	–	1
	USA	–	–	1	–	1
18	Belgium	–	–	–	–	1
	Soviet Union	–	–	–	–	1

1930	Uruguay	4–2	Argentina
1934	Italy	2–1	Czechoslovakia
1938	Italy	4–2	Hungary
1950	Uruguay	2–1	Brazil
1954	West Germany	3–2	Hungary
1958	Brazil	5–2	Sweden
1962	Brazil	3–1	Czechoslovakia
1966	England	4–2	West Germany
1970	Brazil	4–1	Italy
1974	West Germany	2–1	Holland
1978	Argentina	3–1	Holland
1982	Italy	3–1	West Germany
1986	Argentina	3–2	West Germany
1990	West Germany	1–0	Argentina

interest shown by the American public in the event. Few American journalists were present at the draw held in New York, and the poor response from newspapers and television in promoting the event has been at the root of rumours that FIFA were at one stage on the verge of giving the tournament to either Argentina or West Germany.

There are many vested interests in the native American sports of baseball and American football and they tend to see soccer as a potential threat. From the journalists to the players and owners of baseball and American football teams, they all see their livelihoods threatened by this new sport. FIFA was hoping to break through this barrier with the World Cup, reasoning that it was too big to be ignored. After all, the World Cup rivals the Olympic Games as the top event in world sport. This logic seems to have fallen on deaf ears if the draw for the qualifying tournament is anything to go by.

One major problem that FIFA has had to deal with, and it will become far more focused in future events, is the new political map of the world. Africa gained a place in the final competition at the expense of Europe, who at the same time were admitting new members from the now deceased Soviet Union and Yugoslavia. With the possibility of up to nearly 20 new members, FIFA will have to address the question of changing the structure of not only the qualifying tournament, but also the final tournament.

Already in Europe there are groups of seven teams in the 1994 qualifiers and with the new countries from Yugoslavia and the Soviet Union, a system which already puts a strain on the professional commitments of clubs and players will have to be changed. Perhaps the fairest system of all would be to increase the number of finalists to 32 and play the tournament as a straight knock-out affair, with scope for replays after drawn games. This would get rid of two of the prevailing problems: a plethora of meaningless first round games and the penalty shoot-outs.

For many years leading journalists have also advocated changing the system of qualifying teams for the final tournament away from a regional-based system to an intercontinental one. Thus if they were good enough, ten African nations could make it to the finals. On the other hand, none might make it. It would seem to be the fairest system of finding the best teams throughout the world.

Whatever the future and the associated problems, the World Cup will always remain one of the most eagerly anticipated sports events the world over. So far the domain of only six countries, there are over 150 more out there eager to get their hands on it. After all it is every footballer's ambition to be the one who lifts the coveted trophy above his head at the end of the final.

OLYMPIC FOOTBALL

Theoretically open only to amateur players, the football tournament of the Olympic Games has been a source of much controversy down the years and has gone through three distinct phases: from 1908–28, during which time it could legitimately be regarded as the world championship; 1952–76, when it was the domain of the Eastern European state amateurs; and post-1976, when it was opened up to professional players who had not competed in World Cup games.

The 1992 tournament in Barcelona heralded the birth of a fourth era. Olympic officials had wanted to turn it into a tournament open to everyone, but fearful that the World Cup would lose its pre-eminence, FIFA insisted it became the official Under-23 tournament of the world.

The birth of the real football tournament was in 1908. Before that date football had been played at the Games as an exhibition sport on three occasions with England, Canada and Denmark emerging as victors. A tournament of sorts was held in 1896 between a Danish XI and a team from each of Izmir and Athens, but the only result known is a 15–0 victory for Denmark over the Izmir XI.

The 1908 football tournament, held in London after the main Games had finished, was won by the England amateur team as distinct from a side representing the United Kingdom. Containing many of the best players in the country, the side could lay claim to being the first world champions even if the entry was restricted to just five countries.

Led by one of the outstanding personalities of English football at that time, Vivian Woodward, England retained their title four years later in Stockholm, again beating the poor Danes who were by far the best side on the continent. The entry this time more than doubled to eleven as the tournament established itself as one of the main attractions of the Games.

The 1912 tournament saw the start of a practice subsequently followed at most pre-Second World War Games: a consolation tournament for the teams beaten early on, so that they did not have to travel home after having played just one game. It was during this that the German Gottfried Fuchs scored 10 of his side's 16 goals against Czarist Russia matching a similar feat by Sophus Nielsen of Denmark at the previous Games.

The 1920s will chiefly be rembered for the dazzling skills of the South Americans, which many Europeans were seeing for the first time, and the debates over the definition of amateurism which led to the withdrawal of the four British associations from FIFA in 1928, over the introduction of 'broken time' payments to players, i.e. payments made to make up for loss of income from their regular jobs whilst taking part in the tournament.

Belgium won a bad-tempered match in the final of the 1920 tournament against Czechoslovakia, who felt the referee was favouring the hosts and so walked off the field in the second half. They were promptly banned by FIFA and a tournament for the silver and bronze medals had to be hastily arranged. Spain, having won the consolation tournament, beat Holland in a play-off to decide the medal placings.

In 1924 came the appearance for the first time of a South American team on European soil and in a wonderful display of football that took the European sides by surprise, Uruguay won the tournament with ease; in 1928 they were back with more of the same. This time they were joined by their rivals Argentina who if anything played better than them en route to the final.

The final itself was the last hurrah for football in the Olympic Games. Professionalism was rapidly spreading and by the time football was next held at the Games, in Berlin in 1936, the majority of the major nations taking part could not send their full-strength squads.

Since 1928 the Olympic football tournament has become an outdated concept for both South America and Western Europe, and although they have continued to enter teams, they have had no realistic chance of success against the state-sponsored amateur sides of post-war Eastern Europe. Scandinavia, for so long a bastion of the amateur game, has been the only threat to the communist sides, none more so than Sweden, victors in 1948.

OLYMPIC FOOTBALL MEDALS TABLE

	Country	G	S	B	Finals	Semis
1	Hungary	3	1	1	4	4
2	Soviet Union	2	–	3	2	4
3	England	2	–	–	2	2
4	Uruguay	2	–	–	2	2
5	Yugoslavia	1	3	1	4	6
6	East Germany	1	1	2	2	3
7	Czechoslovakia	1	1	–	3	3
8	Poland	1	1	–	2	2
9	Italy	1	–	1	1	5
10	Sweden	1	–	2	1	3
11	France	1	–	–	1	3
12	Belgium	1	–	–	1	1
13	Denmark	–	3	1	3	4
14	Brazil	–	2	–	2	3
15	Bulgaria	–	1	1	1	2
16	Argentina	–	1	–	1	1
	Austria	–	1	–	1	1
	Switzerland	–	1	–	1	1
19	Spain	–	1	–	–	–
20	Holland	–	–	3	–	4
21	West Germany	–	–	1	–	2
22	Japan	–	–	1	–	1
	Norway	–	–	1	–	1
24	Egypt	–	–	–	–	2
25	Finland	–	–	–	–	1
	Great Britain	–	–	–	–	1
	India	–	–	–	–	1
	Mexico	–	–	–	–	1

Not including 1992 medals

The final tournament of 1952 was the last not to be preceded by a qualifying tournament and it was won by Hungary, who would probably have won whoever had entered. The Olympic title was the only major honour won by the Magic Magyars in their heyday, and the side was almost identical to that which appeared in the 1954 World Cup Final. On no occasion after 1952 could the winners claim to be the best team in the world as the Hungarians could.

Held in Melbourne, the 1956 tournament was almost a non-event as nation after nation pulled out at the pros-

THE FOOTBALL TOURNAMENT OF THE OLYMPIC GAMES

1908	England	2–0	Denmark
1912	England	4–2	Denmark
1920	Belgium	2–0	Czechoslovakia
1924	Uruguay	3–0	Switzerland
1928	Uruguay	1–1 2–1	Argentina
1936	Italy	2–1	Austria
1948	Sweden	3–1	Yugoslavia
1952	Hungary	2–0	Yugoslavia
1956	Soviet Union	1–0	Yugoslavia
1960	Yugoslavia	3–1	Denmark
1964	Hungary	2–1	Czechoslovakia
1968	Hungary	4–1	Bulgaria
1972	Poland	2–1	Hungary
1976	East Germany	3–1	Poland
1980	Czechoslovakia	1–0	East Germany
1984	France	2–0	Brazil
1988	Soviet Union	2–1	Brazil

pect of travelling to Australia. The gold medal was won by the daddy of all the Eastern European nations, the Soviet Union, still very new to international competition, and for the third time in a row Yugoslavia lost in the final.

They won at the fourth attempt in 1960 in a tournament that was rapidly changing. The qualifying tournament for 1956 had involved only ten games. For 1960 it was divided along continental lines and consisted of just under 100 games. Both Africa and Asia were given two entries each to the finals and in many respects the Olympic football tournament has been just as important to these continents as the World Cup, given the low number of professional players there.

In 1964 they were both afforded three entries each. Compared to the World Cup where they were allocated just one, it is not surprising to find that the Olympic tournament often attracted more entrants, and became a regular feature on the fixture list for both continents.

The 1960s and 1970s were dominated by Hungary, Poland, Czechoslovakia and East Germany, who entered sides identical to those fielded in normal internationals, but for the 1980 tournament FIFA changed the eligibility rules to prevent anyone who had taken part in a World Cup qualifier from playing. This was a bizarre rule at best, in that it stopped many genuine amateurs from taking part in what was supposed to be an amateur tournament.

It did break the Eastern European stranglehold, as France won the gold medal in Los Angeles, but it threw the tournament into disrepute. Had it not been for the huge crowds which attended matches at each Games, football may well have been ditched long ago. At Los Angeles and Seoul for example, more spectators turned up to see the football than any other event including the athletics, and the revenue was important for the success of the Games as a whole.

The International Olympic Committee has tried to persuade FIFA to organise a tournament open to the full national sides of every country, but to no avail. The under-23 age limit smacks of compromise, but at least the playing field is now level for all nations, for the first time since the 1920s. There are many who feel that with a gap of four years, the World Cup is not representative of the shifts in power among the top football nations, and that a full-strength Olympic Games football tournament would be a good idea, though the increase in fixtures may prove to be an insurmountable problem. The current status quo looks set to stay with us, at least for the time being.

I. OLYMPIAD, ATHENS 1896

A Danish XI beat an Izmir XI 15–0. The results involving an Athens XI are not known

II. OLYMPIAD, PARIS 1900

England, represented by Upton Park FC, defeated France 4–0 in a demonstration game

III. OLYMPIAD, ST LOUIS 1904

Canada were represented by Galt FC of Ontario, USA (1) by the Christian Brothers College, St Louis, and USA (2) by the St Rose Kickers, St Louis

	Ca	U1	U2	Pl	W	D	L	F	A	Pts
Canada	–	7–0	4–0	2	2	0	0	11	0	4
USA (1)	–	–	2–0*	2	1	0	1	2	7	2
USA (2)	–	–	–	2	0	0	2	0	6	0

* After two 0–0 draws

INTERMEDIATE GAMES, ATHENS 1906

	De	Iz	At	Sa	Pl	W	D	L	F	A	Pts
Denmark XI	–	5–2	9–0	–	2	2	0	0	14	2	4
Izmir XI	–	–	–	3–0	2	1	0	1	5	5	2
Athens XI	–	–	–	5–0	2	1	0	1	5	9	2
Salonica XI	–	–	–	–	2	0	0	2	0	8	0

IV. OLYMPIAD LONDON 1908

1st football tournament, 19th–24th October

FIRST ROUND

England	12–1	Sweden
Holland	Bye	
France 'A'	Bye	
Denmark	9–0	France 'B'

SEMI-FINALS

England	4–0	Holland
Denmark	17–1	France 'A'

3RD PLACE

Holland .... 2–0 .... Sweden

FINAL

White City, London, 24–10–1908

ENGLAND 2 (Chapman 20, Woodward 46)

DENMARK 0

Referee: Lewis, England

England – Bailey – Corbett, Smith – Hunt, Chapman, Hawkes – Berry, Woodward, Stapley, Purnell, Hardman

Denmark – Drescher – Buchwald, Hansen – Bohr, Middleboe N, Middleboe O – Nielsen-Norland, Lindgren, Nielsen, Wolffhagen, Rasmussen

V. OLYMPIAD STOCKHOLM 1912

2nd football tournament, 29th June–4th July

PRELIMINARY ROUND

Finland .... 3–2 .... Italy
Holland .... 4–3 .... Sweden
Austria .... 5–1 .... Germany

FIRST ROUND

England .... 7–0 .... Hungary
Finland .... 2–1 .... Czarist Russia
Holland .... 3–1 .... Austria
Denmark .... 7–0 .... Norway

SEMI-FINALS

England .... 4–0 .... Finland
Denmark .... 4–1 .... Holland

3RD PLACE

Holland .... 9–0 .... Finland

FINAL

Stockholms Stadion, Stockholm, 4–07–1912

ENGLAND 4 (Berry, Walden, Hoare 2)

DENMARK 2 (Olsen 2)

Referee: Groothoff, Holland

England – Brebner – Burn, Knight – McWhirter, Littlewort, Dines – Berry, Woodward, Walden, Hoare, Sharpe

Denmark – Hansen S – Middleboe N, Hansen H – Buchwald, Jorgensen, Berth – Nielsen-Norland, Thufvason, Olsen, Nielsen, Wolffhagen

CONSOLATION TOURNAMENT

FIRST ROUND

Hungary .... Bye
Germany .... 16–0 .... Czarist Russia
Italy .... 1–0 .... Sweden
Austria .... 1–0 .... Norway

SEMI-FINALS

Hungary .... 3–1 .... Germany
Austria .... 5–1 .... Italy

FINAL

Hungary .... 3–0 .... Austria

VI. OLYMPIAD, BERLIN 1916

Cancelled

VII. OLYMPIAD ANTWERP 1920

3rd football tournament, 28th August–5th September

FIRST ROUND

Belgium .... Bye
Spain .... 1–0 .... Denmark
Holland .... 3–0 .... Luxembourg
Sweden .... 9–0 .... Greece
France .... Bye
Italy .... 2–1 .... Egypt
Norway .... 3–1 .... England
Czechoslovakia .... 7–0 .... Yugoslavia

QUARTER-FINALS

Belgium .... 3–1 .... Spain
Holland .... 5–4 .... Sweden
France .... 3–1 .... Italy
Czechoslovakia .... 4–0 .... Norway

SEMI-FINALS

Belgium .... 3–0 .... Holland
Czechoslovakia .... 4–1 .... France

FINAL

Olympisch (Kielstadion), Antwerp, 5–09–1920

BELGIUM 2 (Coppée 32, Larnoe 78)

CZECHOSLOVAKIA 0

Referee: Lewis, England

Belgium – De Bie – Swartenbroeks, Verbeeck – Musch, Hense, Fierens – Van Hege, Larnoe, Bragard, Coppée, Bastin

Czechoslovakia – Klapka – Hojer, Steiner – Kolenaty, Kada, Seifert – Sedlacek, Janda, Vanik, Mazal, Placek

Play-off for second and third places after Czechoslovakia were disqualified for leaving the field during the final

Spain .... 2–1 .... Sweden
Italy .... 2–1 .... Norway
Spain .... 2–0 .... Italy

Spain qualified to meet Holland

Spain .... 3–1 .... Holland

VIII. OLYMPIAD PARIS 1924

4th football tournament, 25th May–9th June

PRELIMINARY ROUND

Uruguay .... 7–0 .... Yugoslavia
United States .... 1–0 .... Estonia
Hungary .... 5–0 .... Poland
Italy .... 1–0 .... Spain
Czechoslovakia .... 5–2 .... Turkey
Switzerland .... 9–0 .... Lithuania

FIRST ROUND

Uruguay	3–0	United States
France	7–0	Latvia
Holland	6–0	Romania
Rep. Ireland	1–0	Bulgaria
Sweden	8–1	Belgium
Egypt	3–0	Hungary
Italy	2–0	Luxembourg
Switzerland	1–1 1–0	Czechoslovakia

QUARTER-FINALS

Uruguay	5–1	France
Holland	2–1	Rep. Ireland
Sweden	5–0	Egypt
Switzerland	2–1	Italy

SEMI-FINALS

Uruguay	2–1	Holland
Switzerland	2–1	Sweden

3RD PLACE

Sweden	1–1 3–1	Holland

FINAL

Colombes, Paris, 9–06–1924, 41 000
URUGUAY 3 (Petrone 27, Cea 63, Romano 81)
SWITZERLAND 0
Referee: Slawick, France
Uruguay – Mazzali – Nasazzi, Arispe – Andrade, Vidal, Ghierra – Urdinaran, Scarone, Petrone, Cea, Romano
Switzerland – Pulver – Reymond, Ramseyer – Oberhauser, Schmiedlin, Pollitz – Ehrenbolger, Pache, Dietrich, Abegglen, Fassler

IX. OLYMPIAD AMSTERDAM 1928

5th football tournament, 27th May–13th June

PRELIMINARY ROUND

Portugal	4–2	Chile

FIRST ROUND

Uruguay	2–0	Holland
Germany	4–0	Switzerland
Italy	4–3	France
Spain	7–1	Mexico
Egypt	7–1	Turkey
Portugal	2–1	Yugoslavia
Belgium	5–3	Luxembourg
Argentina	11–2	United States

QUARTER-FINALS

Uruguay	4–1	Germany
Italy	1–1 7–1	Spain
Egypt	2–1	Portugal
Argentina	6–3	Belgium

SEMI-FINALS

Uruguay	3–2	Italy
Argentina	6–0	Egypt

3RD PLACE

Italy	11–3	Egypt

FINAL

Olympisch Stadion, Amsterdam, 10–06–1928
URUGUAY 1 (Ferreira)
ARGENTINA 1 (Petrone)
Referee: Mutler, Holland
Uruguay – Mazzali – Nasazzi, Arispe – Andrade, Fernandez, Gestido – Urdinarrain, Castro H, Petrone, Cea, Campolo
Argentina – Bossio – Bidoglio, Paternoster – Medici, Monti, Evaristo J – Carricaberry, Tarasconi, Ferreira, Gainzarain, Orsi

Replay. Olympisch Stadion, Amsterdam, 13–06–1928
URUGUAY 2 (Figueroa, Scarone H)
ARGENTINA 1 (Monti)
Referee: Mutler, Holland
Uruguay – Mazzali – Nasazzi, Arispe – Andrade, Piriz, Gestido – Arremond, Scarone H, Borjas, Cea, Figueroa
Argentina – Bossio – Bidoglio, Paternoster – Medici, Monti, Evaristo J – Carricaberry, Tarasconi, Ferreira, Perducca, Orsi

CONSOLATION TOURNAMENT

FIRST ROUND

Holland	3–1	Belgium
Chile	3–1	Mexico

FINAL

Holland	2–2	Chile

Holland won on lots

X. OLYMPIAD, LOS ANGELES 1932

No football tournament was held

XI. OLYMPIAD BERLIN 1936

6th football tournament, 3rd–15th August

FIRST ROUND

Italy	1–0	United States
Japan	3–2	Sweden
Norway	4–0	Turkey
Germany	9–0	Luxembourg
Poland	3–0	Hungary
Great Britain	2–0	China
Peru	7–3	Finland
Austria	3–1	Egypt

QUARTER-FINALS

Italy	8–0	Japan
Norway	2–0	Germany
Poland	5–4	Great Britain
Austria	2–4*	Peru

* Match abandoned. Peru failed to turn up for rearranged game

SEMI-FINALS

Italy	2–1	Norway
Austria	3–1	Poland

3RD PLACE

Norway	3–2	Poland

FINAL

Olympiastadion, Berlin, 15–08–1936, 90 000
ITALY 2 (Frossi 70 92)
AUSTRIA 1 (Kainberger K 80)
Referee: Bauwens, Germany
Italy – Venturini – Foni, Rava – Baldo, Piccini, Locatelli – Frossi, Marchini, Bertoni, Biagi, Gabriotti
Austria – Kainberger E – Kunz, Kargl – Krenn, Wahlmuller, Hofmeister – Warginz, Laudon, Steinmetz, Kainberger K, Fuchsberger

XII. OLYMPIAD, TOKYO/HELSINKI 1940

Cancelled

XIII. OLYMPIAD, LONDON 1944

Cancelled

XIV. OLYMPIAD LONDON 1948

7th football tournament

31st July–13th August

PRELIMINARY ROUND

Holland	3–1	Rep. Ireland
Luxembourg	6–0	Afghanistan

FIRST ROUND

Sweden	3–0	Austria
Korea	5–3	Mexico
Denmark	3–1	Egypt
Italy	9–0	United States
Great Britain	4–3	Holland
France	2–1	India
Turkey	4–0	China
Yugoslavia	6–1	Luxembourg

QUARTER-FINALS

Sweden	12–0	Korea
Denmark	5–3	Italy
Great Britain	1–0	France
Yugoslavia	3–1	Turkey

SEMI-FINALS

Sweden	4–2	Denmark
Yugoslavia	3–1	Great Britain

3RD PLACE

Denmark	5–3	Great Britain

FINAL

Wembley, London, 13–08–1948, 60 000
SWEDEN 3 (Gren 24 67, Nordahl G 48)
YUGOSLAVIA 1 (Bobek)
Referee: Ling, England
Sweden – Lindberg – Nordahl K, Nilsson E – Rosengren, Nordahl B, Andersson – Rosén, Gren, Nordahl G, Carlsson, Liedholm
Yugoslavia – Lovric – Brozovic, Stankovic – Cajkovski Ze, Jovanovic – Atanackovic, Cimermancic, Mitic, Bobek, Cajkovski Zl, Vukas

XV. OLYMPIAD HELSINKI 1952

8th football tournament

19th July–2nd August

PRELIMINARY ROUND

Hungary	2–1	Romania
Italy	8–0	United States
Egypt	5–4	Chile
Brazil	5–1	Holland
Luxembourg	5–3	Great Britain
Denmark	2–1	Greece
Poland	2–1	France
Soviet Union	2–1	Bulgaria
Yugoslavia	10–1	India

FIRST ROUND

Hungary	3–0	Italy
Turkey	2–1	Dutch W.Indies
Sweden	4–1	Norway
Austria	4–3	Finland
West Germany	3–1	Egypt
Brazil	2–1	Luxembourg
Denmark	2–1	Poland
Yugoslavia	5–5 3–1	Soviet Union

QUARTER-FINALS

Hungary	7–1	Turkey
Sweden	3–1	Austria
West Germany	4–2	Brazil
Yugoslavia	5–3	Denmark

SEMI-FINALS

Hungary	6–0	Sweden
Yugoslavia	3–1	West Germany

3RD PLACE

Sweden	2–0	West Germany

FINAL

Olympiastadion, Helsinki, 2–08–1952, 60 000
HUNGARY 2 (Puskás 25, Czibor 88)
YUGOSLAVIA 0
Referee: Ellis, England
Hungary – Grosics – Buzánszky, Lantos – Bozsik, Lóránt, Zakariás – Hidegkuti, Kocsis, Palotás, Puskás, Czibor
Yugoslavia – Beara – Stankovic, Crnkovic – Cajkovski Zl, Horvat, Boskov – Ognjanov, Mitic, Vukas, Bobek, Zebec

XVI. OLYMPIAD MELBOURNE 1956

9th football tournament

QUALIFYING TOURNAMENT

Ethiopia	1–4 2–5	EGYPT
SOVIET UNION	5–0 2–1	Israel
BULGARIA	2–0 3–3	GREAT BRITAIN

VIETNAM	5–2 4–3	Cambodia
JAPAN	2–0 0–2 *	Korea
CHINA	W–O	Philippines
INDONESIA	W–O	Taiwan
UNITED STATES	W–O	Mexico
YUGOSLAVIA	W–O	Romania
Hungary	W–O	East Germany
AUSTRALIA	Bye	
INDIA	Bye	
POLAND	Bye	
THAILAND	Bye	
TURKEY	Bye	
WEST GERMANY	Bye	

Egypt, Vietnam, China, Hungary, Poland and Turkey withdrew from finals. Both Iran and Afghanistan withdrew before they were due to play each other.

FINAL TOURNAMENT

24th November–8th December 1956

PRELIMINARY ROUND

Soviet Union	2–1	West Germany
Great Britain	9–0	Thailand
Australia	2–0	Japan

FIRST ROUND

Soviet Union	0–0 4–0	Indonesia
Bulgaria	6–1	Great Britain
India	4–2	Australia
Yugoslavia	9–1	United States

SEMI-FINALS

Soviet Union	2–1	Bulgaria
Yugoslavia	4–1	India

3RD PLACE

Bulgaria	3–0	India

FINAL

Melbourne Cricket Ground, Melbourne, 8–12–1956, 120 000

SOVIET UNION 1 (Ilyin 48)
YUGOSLAVIA 0

Referee: Wright, Australia

Soviet Union – Yashin – Baschaschkin, Ogognikov – Kuznetsov, Netto, Maslenkin – Tatushin, Isaev, Simonian, Salinikov, Ilyin

Yugoslavia – Radenkovic – Koscak, Radovic – Santek, Spajic, Krstic – Sekularac, Antic, Papek, Veselinovic, Mujic

XVII. OLYMPIAD ROME 1960

10th football tournament

QUALIFYING TOURNAMENT

EUROPE

Group 1

	De	Ic	No	Pl	W	D	L	F	A	Pts
DENMARK	–	1–1	2–1	4	3	1	0	11	6	7
Iceland	2–4	–	1–0	4	1	1	2	5	7	3
NORWAY	2–4	2–1	–	4	1	0	3	5	8	2

Group 2

	Pd	WG	Fi	Pl	W	D	L	F	A	Pts
POLAND	–	3–1	6–2	4	4	0	0	15	4	8
West Germany	0–3	–	2–1	4	1	0	3	5	10	2
FINLAND	1–3	3–2	–	4	1	0	3	7	13	2

Group 3

	Bu	SU	Ro	Pl	W	D	L	F	A	Pts
BULGARIA	–	1–0	2–1	4	2	1	1	4	3	5
Soviet Union	1–1	–	2–0	4	1	2	1	3	2	4
ROMANIA	1–0	0–0	–	4	1	1	2	2	4	3

Group 4

	Yu	Is	Gr	Pl	W	D	L	F	A	Pts
YUGOSLAVIA	–	1–2	4–0	4	2	1	1	12	4	5
Israel	2–2	–	2–1	4	2	1	1	7	6	5
GREECE	0–5	2–1	–	4	1	0	3	3	12	2

Group 5

	GB	RI	Ho	Pl	W	D	L	F	A	Pts
GREAT BRITAIN	–	3–2	2–2	4	3	1	0	13	6	7
Rep. Ireland	1–3	–	6–3	4	1	1	2	9	9	3
HOLLAND	1–5	0–0	–	4	0	2	2	6	13	2

Group 6

	Fr	Lu	Sz	Pl	W	D	L	F	A	Pts
FRANCE	–	1–0	1–0	4	3	1	0	7	6	7
Luxembourg	5–3	–	0–0	4	1	2	1	7	6	4
SWITZERLAND	1–2	2–2	–	4	0	2	2	3	5	2

Group 7

	Hu	Cz	Au	Pl	W	D	L	F	A	Pts
HUNGARY	–	2–1	2–1	4	4	0	0	10	3	8
Czechoslovakia	1–2	–	2–1	4	1	1	2	4	5	3
AUSTRIA	0–4	0–0	–	4	0	1	3	2	8	1

THE AMERICAS

FIRST ROUND

Brazil	7–1 0–2	Colombia
Chile	1–5 0–6	Argentina
Mexico	2–0 1–1	United States
Peru	6–0 3–2	Uruguay
Surinam	4–1 2–2	Neth. Antilles

SECOND ROUND

Tournament in Lima

	Ar	Pe	Br	Me	Su	Pl	W	D	L	F	A	Pts
ARGENTINA	–	2–1	3–1	3–1	6–2	4	4	0	0	14	5	8
PERU	–	–	2–0	1–0	3–1	4	3	0	1	7	3	6
BRAZIL	–	–	–	2–1	4–1	4	2	0	2	7	7	4
MEXICO	–	–	–	–	4–0	4	1	0	3	6	6	2
SURINAM	–	–	–	–	–	4	0	0	4	4	17	0

AFRICA

FIRST ROUND

Group 1

	Tu	Mo	Ma	Pl	W	D	L	F	A	Pts
TUNISIA	–	2–0	2–0	4	2	1	1	5	3	5
MOROCCO	3–1	–	2–1	4	2	1	1	7	6	5
MALTA	0–0	2–2	–	4	0	2	2	3	6	2

Group 2

	Eg	Gh	Ni	Pl	W	D	L	F	A	Pts
EGYPT	–	2–1	3–0	4	3	0	1	11	5	6
GHANA	2–0	–	4–1	4	2	0	2	8	6	4
NIGERIA	2–6	3–1	–	4	1	0	3	6	14	2

Group 3

	Su	Et	Ug	Pl	W	D	L	F	A	Pts
SUDAN	–	3–1	1–0	4	3	1	0	6	2	7
ETHIOPIA	1–1	–	1–1	4	1	2	1	5	6	4
UGANDA	0–1	1–2	–	4	0	1	3	2	5	1

SECOND ROUND

	Eg	Tu	Su	Pl	W	D	L	F	A	Pts
EGYPT	–	3–1	3–0	4	3	1	0	7	1	7
TUNISIA	0–0	–	2–0	4	1	1	2	3	4	3
SUDAN	0–1	1–0	–	4	1	0	3	1	6	2

ASIA

FIRST ROUND

Afghanistan .... 2–5 .... India
Indonesia .... W–O .... Australia
South Korea .... 2–0 0–1 .... Japan
Thailand .... 1–3 1–3 .... Taiwan

SECOND ROUND

INDIA .... 4–2 2–0 .... Indonesia
TAIWAN .... 1–2 * .... South Korea

* South Korea suspended

NEAR EAST

Iraq .... 2–3 1–7 .... TURKEY

Lebanon withdrew from group

ITALY qualified as hosts

FINAL TOURNAMENT

26th August–10th September 1960

FIRST ROUND

Group 1

	Yu	Bu	Eg	Tu	Pl	W	D	L	F	A	Pts
YUGOSLAVIA	–	3–3	6–1	4–0	3	2	1	0	13	4	5
BULGARIA	–	–	2–0	3–0	3	2	1	0	8	3	5
EGYPT	–	–	–	3–3	3	0	1	2	4	11	1
TURKEY	–	–	–	–	3	0	1	2	3	10	1

Group 2

	It	Br	GB	Ta	Pl	W	D	L	F	A	Pts
ITALY	–	3–1	2–2	4–1	3	2	1	0	9	4	5
BRAZIL	–	–	4–3	5–0	3	2	0	1	10	6	4
GREAT BRITAIN	–	–	–	3–2	3	1	1	1	8	8	3
TAIWAN	–	–	–	–	3	0	0	3	3	12	0

Group 3

	De	Ar	Po	Tu	Pl	W	D	L	F	A	Pts
DENMARK	–	3–2	2–1	3–1	3	3	0	0	8	4	6
ARGENTINA	–	–	2–0	2–1	3	2	0	1	6	4	4
POLAND	–	–	–	6–1	3	1	0	2	7	5	2
TUNISIA	–	–	–	–	3	0	0	3	3	11	0

Group 4

	Hu	Fr	Pe	In	Pl	W	D	L	F	A	Pts
HUNGARY	–	7–0	6–2	2–1	3	3	0	0	15	3	6
FRANCE	–	–	2–1	1–1	3	1	1	1	3	9	3
PERU	–	–	–	3–1	3	1	0	2	6	9	2
INDIA	–	–	–	–	3	0	1	2	3	6	1

SEMI-FINALS

Yugoslavia .... 1–1 * .... Italy
Denmark .... 2–0 .... Hungary

* Yugoslavia won on lots

3RD PLACE

Hungary .... 2–1 .... Italy

FINAL

Flamino, Rome, 10–09–1960, 40 000

YUGOSLAVIA 3 (Galic, Matus, Kostic)
DENMARK 1 (Nielsen F)

Referee: Lo Bello, Italy

Yugoslavia – Vidinic – Roganovic, Jusufi – Perusic, Durkovic, Zanetic – Ankovic, Matus, Galic, Knez, Kostic

Denmark – Froem – Andersen, Jensen – Hansen, Nielsen Hn, Nielsen F – Pedersen, Troelsen, Nielsen Hr, Enoksen, Sorensen

XVIII. OLYMPIAD
TOKYO 1964
11th football tournament

QUALIFYING TOURNAMENT

EUROPE

PRELIMINARY ROUND

Albania .... 0–1 0–1 .... Bulgaria
Iceland .... 0–6 4–0 .... Great Britain

FIRST ROUND

Czechoslovakia .... 4–0 4–2 .... France
Bulgaria .... W–O .... Luxembourg
Denmark .... 2–3 3–2 1–2 ... Romania
Great Britain .... 2–1 1–4 .... Greece
Holland .... 0–1 1–3 .... East Germany
Hungary .... 4–0 2–2 .... Sweden
Poland .... Bye
Soviet Union .... 7–0 4–0 .... Finland
Switzerland .... 0–1 0–6 .... Spain
Turkey .... 2–2 1–7 .... Italy

SECOND ROUND

EAST GERMANY .... 1–1 1–1 4–1 ... Soviet Union
CZECHOSLOVAKIA ... W–O .... Greece
ITALY .... 3–0 1–0 .... Poland
ROMANIA .... 2–1 1–0 .... Bulgaria
Spain .... 1–2 0–3 .... HUNGARY

Italy withdrew before the finals

SOUTH AMERICA

Tournament in Lima

	Pe	Br	Co	Ch	Ur	Ec	Pl	W	D	L	F	A	Pts
ARGENTINA	1–0*	–	2–0	4–0	3–1	1–0	5	5	0	0	11	1	10
PERU	–	–	3–0	–	2–0	1–1	4	2	1	1	6	2	5
BRAZIL	–	–	1–1	2–0	–	3–1	3	2	1	0	6	2	5
COLOMBIA	–	–	–	0–2	1–1	4–1	6	1	2	3	6	10	4
CHILE	–	–	–	–	0–0	–	4	1	1	2	2	6	4
URUGUAY	–	–	–	–	–	1–1	5	0	3	2	3	7	3
ECUADOR	–	–	–	–	–	–	5	0	2	3	4	10	2

* The tournament was abandoned after the death of 300 spectators during this match. Brazil and Peru played a decider in Rio the following month for the second place available.

BRAZIL .... 4–1 .... Peru

AFRICA

FIRST ROUND

Dahomey .... 2–2 1–1 1–1* .. Tunisia
Kenya .... 4–3 1–7 .... Ethiopia
Liberia .... 4–5 0–1 .... Ghana
Nigeria .... 3–0 1–4 1–2 ... Morocco
Sudan .... W–O .... Rhodesia
Uganda .... 1–4 1–3 .... Egypt

SECOND ROUND

EGYPT .... 4–1 3–3 .... Sudan
Ethiopia .... 0–1 0–1 .... MOROCCO
GHANA .... 2–0 1–2 .... Tunisia

ASIA

PRELIMINARY ROUND

Iran .... 4–1 0–1 .... Pakistan
Malaysia .... 1–1 2–3 .... Thailand
South Korea .... 2–1 0–1 .... Taiwan
Sri Lanka .... 3–5 1–7 .... India

FIRST ROUND

Burma .... 0–0 0–1 .... North Korea
India .... W–O .... Lebanon
Iran .... 4–0 0–0 .... Iraq
South Korea .... W–O .... Philippines
South Vietnam .... 0–1 2–0 .... Israel
Thailand .... W–O .... Indonesia

SECOND ROUND

IRAN .... 3–0 3–1 .... India
NORTH KOREA .... 2–0 5–0 .... Thailand
SOUTH KOREA .... 3–0 2–2 .... South Vietnam

North Korea withdrew before the finals

CENTRAL AND NORTH AMERICA

PRELIMINARY ROUND

Neth. Antilles .... 2–1 0–3 .... Surinam

FINAL ROUND

Tournament in Mexico City

	Me	Su	US	Pa	Pl	W	D	L	F	A	Pts
MEXICO	–	6–0	2–1	5–1	3	3	0	0	13	2	6
SURINAM	–	–	1–0	6–1	3	2	0	1	7	7	4
UNITED STATES	–	–	–	4–2	3	1	0	2	5	5	2
PANAMA	–	–	–	–	3	0	0	3	4	15	0

JAPAN qualified as hosts

YUGOSLAVIA qualified as holders

FINAL TOURNAMENT

11th–23rd October 1964

FIRST ROUND

Group 1

	EG	Ro	Me	Ir	Pl	W	D	L	F	A	Pts
EAST GERMANY	–	1–1	2–0	4–0	3	2	1	0	7	1	5
ROMANIA	–	–	3–1	1–0	3	2	1	0	5	2	5
MEXICO	–	–	–	1–1	3	0	1	2	2	6	1
IRAN	–	–	–	–	3	0	1	2	1	6	1

Group 2

	Hu	Yu	Mo	Pl	W	D	L	F	A	Pts
HUNGARY	–	6–5	6–0	2	2	0	0	12	5	4
YUGOSLAVIA	–	–	3–1	2	1	0	1	8	7	2
MOROCCO	–	–	–	2	0	0	2	1	9	0

Group 3

	Cz	Eg	Br	SK	Pl	W	D	L	F	A	Pts
CZECHOSLOVAKIA	–	5–1	1–0	6–1	3	3	0	0	12	2	6
EGYPT	–	–	1–1	10–0	3	1	1	1	12	6	3
BRAZIL	–	–	–	4–0	3	1	1	1	5	2	3
SOUTH KOREA	–	–	–	–	3	0	0	3	1	20	0

Group 4

	Gh	Ja	Ar	Pl	W	D	L	F	A	Pts
GHANA	–	3–2	1–1	2	1	1	0	4	3	3
JAPAN	–	–	3–2	2	1	0	1	5	5	2
ARGENTINA	–	–	–	2	0	1	1	3	4	1

QUARTER-FINALS

Hungary .... 2–0 .... Romania
Egypt .... 5–1 .... Ghana
East Germany .... 1–0 .... Yugoslavia
Czechoslovakia .... 4–0 .... Japan

SEMI-FINALS

Hungary .... 6–0 .... Egypt
Czechoslovakia .... 2–1 .... East Germany

5TH–8TH PLACE

Romania .... 4–2 .... Ghana
Yugoslavia .... 6–1 .... Japan
Romania .... 3–0 .... Yugoslavia

3RD PLACE

East Germany .... 3–1 .... Egypt

FINAL

National Stadium, Tokyo, 23–10–1964

HUNGARY 2 (OG 47, Bene 60)
CZECHOSLOVAKIA 1 (Brumovsky 80)

Referee: Ashkenazi, Israel

Hungary – Szentimihályi (Gelei) – Novák, Ihász, Szepesi (Palotai), Orban, Nogradi, Farkas, Csernai, Bene, Komora, Katona

Czechoslovakia – Schmucker – Urban, Picman, Vojta, Weiss, Geleta, Brumovsky, Mraz, Lichtnegl, Masny, Valosek

XIX. OLYMPIAD
MEXICO CITY 1968
12th football tournament

QUALIFYING TOURNAMENT

EUROPE

PRELIMINARY ROUND

Finland .... 0–0 1–0 .... Holland
Greece .... 0–5 0–5 .... East Germany
Iceland .... 1–1 3–5 .... Spain
Soviet Union .... W–O .... Albania

FIRST ROUND

Czechoslovakia .... W–O .... Yugoslavia
East Germany .... 1–0 1–0 .... Romania
Finland .... 1–1 1–3 .... France
Poland .... 0–1 1–2 .... Soviet Union
Spain .... W–O .... Italy
Switzerland .... 1–0 1–4 .... Austria

Turkey .... 2–3 0–3 .... Bulgaria
West Germany .... 0–2 1–0 .... Great Britain

SECOND ROUND
BULGARIA .... 4–1 2–3 .... East Germany
FRANCE .... 3–1 1–1 .... Austria
Soviet Union .... 3–2 0–3 .... CZECHOSLOVAKIA
SPAIN .... 1–0 0–0 .... Great Britain

SOUTH AMERICA

Tournament in Colombia
FIRST ROUND

Group 1

	Pa	Br	Ch	Ve	Pl	W	D	L	F	A	Pts
Paraguay	–	0–0	1–0	3–0	3	2	1	0	4	0	5
Brazil	–	–	0–0	3–0	3	1	2	0	3	0	4
Chile	–	–	–	1–0	3	1	1	1	1	1	3
Venezuela	–	–	–	–	3	0	0	3	0	7	0

Group 2

	Co	Ur	Pe	Ec	Pl	W	D	L	F	A	Pts
Colombia	–	1–1	2–1	1–0	3	2	1	0	4	2	5
Uruguay	–	–	0–0	2–0	3	1	2	0	3	1	4
Peru	–	–	–	1–1	3	0	2	1	2	3	2
Ecuador	–	–	–	–	3	0	1	2	1	4	1

SECOND ROUND

	Br	Co	Ur	Pa	Pl	W	D	L	F	A	Pts
BRAZIL	–	3–0	1–2	2–0	3	2	0	1	6	2	4
COLOMBIA	–	–	2–0	4–2	3	2	0	1	6	5	4
Uruguay	–	–	–	3–3	3	1	1	1	5	6	3
Paraguay	–	–	–	–	3	0	1	2	5	9	1

AFRICA

PRELIMINARY ROUND
Cameroon .... W–O .... Mali
Gabon .... 0–0 1–6 .... Guinea
Libya .... 2–0 2–2 .... Niger
Madagascar .... 4–2 2–0 .... Tanzania
Nigeria .... W–O .... Uganda

FIRST ROUND
Cameroon .... 1–0 2–3 * ...... Ghana
Guinea .... W–O .... Egypt
Libya .... 1–1 1–2 .... Algeria
Madagascar .... 1–0 3–8 .... Ethiopia
Morocco .... 1–1 0–0** ..... Tunisia
Nigeria .... 1–0 1–2** ..... Sudan

* Cameroon withdrew from play–off
** Morocco and Nigeria won on lots

SECOND ROUND
GUINEA .... 2–2 3–2 .... Algeria
MOROCCO .... 1–1 2–1 .... Ghana
NIGERIA .... 3–1 0–1 .... Ethiopia

Morocco withdrew from the finals and were replaced by Ghana

ASIA

Group 1

Tournament in Japan

	Ja	SK	Le	SV	Ta	Ph	Pl	W	D	L	F	A	Pts
JAPAN	–	3–3	3–1	1–0	4–0	15–0	5	4	1	0	26	4	9
South Korea	–	–	2–0	3–0	4–2	5–0	5	4	1	0	17	5	9
Lebanon	–	–	–	1–1	5–2	11–1	5	2	1	2	18	9	5
South Vietnam	–	–	–	–	3–0	10–0	5	2	1	2	14	5	5
Taiwan	–	–	–	–	–	7–2	5	1	0	4	11	18	2
Philippines	–	–	–	–	–	–	5	0	0	5	3	48	0

Group 2

Tournament in Thailand

	Th	Iq	Id	Pl	W	D	L	F	A	Pts
THAILAND	–	2–1	1–0	4	3	0	1	5	6	6
Iraq	4–0	–	1–1	4	1	1	2	7	5	3
Indonesia	1–2	2–1	–	4	1	1	2	4	5	3

Hong Kong, Malaysia and Pakistan withdrew

Group 3

ISRAEL* .... 7–0 4–0 .... Sri Lanka

* Both matches played in Israel. Burma, India, Iran and North Korea withdrew

CENTRAL AND NORTH AMERICA

FIRST ROUND
Bermuda .... 0–1 1–1 .... United States
Canada .... 1–1 1–2 .... Cuba
Dominican Rep. .... 0–8 0–6 .... Haiti
El Salvador .... W–O .... Honduras
Trinidad .... 1–0 2–5 * ...... Surinam
Costa Rica .... Bye
Guatemala .... Bye
Neth. Antilles .... Bye

* Surinam withdrew. Trinidad qualified for the next round

SECOND ROUND
Costa Rica .... 3–1 2–3 .... Haiti
El Salvador .... 3–0 2–1 .... Cuba
Guatemala .... 1–1 2–1 .... Bermuda
Neth. Antilles .... 3–0 0–4 .... Trinidad

THIRD ROUND
EL SALVADOR .... 2–0 2–1 .... Trinidad
GUATEMALA .... 1–0 2–3* ...... Costa Rica

* Guatemala qualified on lots

MEXICO qualified as hosts

HUNGARY qualified as holders

FINAL TOURNAMENT

13th–26th October 1968

FIRST ROUND

Group 1

	Fr	Me	Co	Gu	Pl	W	D	L	F	A	Pts
FRANCE	–	4–1	1–2	3–1	3	2	0	1	8	4	4
MEXICO	–	–	1–0	4–0	3	2	0	1	6	4	4
Colombia	–	–	–	2–3	3	1	0	2	4	5	2
Guinea	–	–	–	–	3	1	0	2	4	9	2

Group 2

	Sp	Ja	Br	Ni	Pl	W	D	L	F	A	Pts
SPAIN	–	0–0	1–0	3–0	3	2	1	0	4	0	5
JAPAN	–	–	1–1	3–1	3	1	2	0	4	2	4
Brazil	–	–	–	3–3	3	0	2	1	4	5	2
Nigeria	–	–	–	–	3	0	1	2	4	9	1

Group 3

	Hu	Is	Gh	ES	Pl	W	D	L	F	A	Pts
HUNGARY	–	2–0	2–2	4–0	3	2	1	0	8	2	5
ISRAEL	–	–	5–3	3–1	3	2	0	1	8	6	4

GHANA	–	–	–	1–1	3	0	2	1	6	8	2
EL SALVADOR	–	–	–	–	3	0	1	2	2	8	1

Group 4

	Bu	Gu	Cz	Th	Pl	W	D	L	F	A	Pts
BULGARIA	–	2–1	2–2	7–0	3	2	1	0	11	4	5
GUATEMALA	–	–	1–0	4–1	3	2	0	1	6	3	4
CZECHOSLOVAKIA	–	–	–	8–0	3	1	1	1	10	3	3
THAILAND	–	–	–	–	3	0	0	3	2	19	0

QUARTER-FINALS

Hungary .... 1–0 .... Guatemala
Japan .... 3–1 .... France
Mexico .... 2–0 .... Spain
Bulgaria .... 1–1 * .... Israel

* Won on the toss of a coin

SEMI-FINALS

Hungary .... 5–0 .... Japan
Bulgaria .... 3–2 .... Mexico

3RD PLACE

Japan .... 2–0 .... Mexico

FINAL

Azteca, Mexico City, 26–10–1968
HUNGARY 4 (Menczel 40 48, Dunai A 41 61)
BULGARIA 1 (Dimitrov 20)
Referee: De Leo, Mexico
Hungary – Fater – Novák, Dunai L, Páncsics, Menczel, Szücs, Fazekas, Dunai A, Nagy, Noskó, Juhász
Bulgaria – Yordanov – Guerov, Christakiev, Gadarski, Ivkov, Georgiev, Dimitrov, Yantchovski (Christov K), Jekov, Christov A, Donev (Ivanov)

XX. OLYMPIAD MUNICH 1972

13th football tournament

QUALIFYING TOURNAMENT

EUROPE

FIRST ROUND

East Germany .... 4–0 1–0 .... Italy
Great Britain .... 1–0 0–5 .... Bulgaria
Iceland .... 0–0 0–1 .... France
Luxembourg .... 1–0 2–3 0–2 ... Austria
Poland .... 7–0 0–1 .... Greece
Rep. Ireland .... 0–1 0–2 .... Yugoslavia
Romania .... 2–1 2–1 .... Albania
Soviet Union .... 4–0 0–0 .... Holland
Spain .... 1–0 1–0 .... Turkey
Switzerland .... 2–1 0–4 .... Denmark

SECOND ROUND

Group 1

	SU	Fr	Au	Pl	W	D	L	F	A	Pts
SOVIET UNION	–	5–1	4–0	4	4	0	0	13	2	8
FRANCE	1–3	–	5–1	4	2	0	2	10	9	4
AUSTRIA	0–1	0–3	–	4	0	0	4	1	13	0

Group 2

	Pd	Bu	Sp	Pl	W	D	L	F	A	Pts
POLAND	–	3–0	2–0	4	3	0	1	9	3	6
BULGARIA	3–2	–	8–3	4	2	1	1	14	11	5
SPAIN	0–2	3–3	–	4	0	1	3	6	15	1

Group 3

EAST GERMANY .... 2–0 0–0 .... Yugoslavia

Group 4

DENMARK .... 2–1 3–2 .... Romania

SOUTH AMERICA

Tournament in Colombia
FIRST ROUND

Group 1

	Br	Ar	Bo	Ec	Ch	Pl	W	D	L	F	A	Pts
BRAZIL	–	0–0	2–1	1–1	1–0	4	2	2	0	4	2	6
ARGENTINA	–	–	1–1	2–2	2–0	4	1	3	0	5	3	5
BOLIVIA	–	–	–	2–1	1–1	4	1	2	1	5	5	4
ECUADOR	–	–	–	–	0–0	4	0	3	1	4	5	3
CHILE	–	–	–	–	–	4	0	2	2	1	4	2

Group 2

	Pe	Co	Pa	Ur	Ve	Pl	W	D	L	F	A	Pts
PERU	–	1–1	2–1	1–0	3–0	4	3	1	0	7	2	7
COLOMBIA	–	–	0–0	2–1	2–0	4	2	2	0	5	2	6
PARAGUAY	–	–	–	1–1	4–1	4	1	2	1	6	4	4
URUGUAY	–	–	–	–	2–0	4	1	1	2	4	4	3
VENEZUELA	–	–	–	–	–	4	0	0	4	1	11	0

SECOND ROUND

	Br	Co	Ar	Pe	Pl	W	D	L	F	A	Pts
BRAZIL	–	1–1	1–0	1–0	3	2	1	0	3	1	5
COLOMBIA	–	–	1–1	0–0	3	0	3	0	2	2	3
ARGENTINA	–	–	–	1–1	3	0	2	1	2	3	2
PERU	–	–	–	–	3	0	2	1	1	2	2

AFRICA

FIRST ROUND

Ethiopia .... 6–3 1–0 .... Zambia
Gabon .... 2–3 .... Cameroon
Ghana .... 2–1 1–0 .... Liberia
Malawi .... 1–2 2–4 .... Madagascar
Mali .... 1–0 2–2 .... Algeria
Morocco .... 5–2 3–1 .... Niger
Nigeria .... 1–1 1–2 .... Senegal
Sudan .... 4–0 1–1 .... Uganda
Togo .... 1–1 5–4 .... Guinea
Tunisia .... 3–0 0–2 .... Egypt

SECOND ROUND

Group 1

	Mo	Tu	Ml	Pl	W	D	L	F	A	Pts
MOROCCO	–	0–0	2–1	4	2	2	0	9	5	6
TUNISIA	3–3	–	4–0	4	1	2	1	7	5	4
MALI	1–4	2–0	–	4	1	0	3	4	10	2

Group 2

	Gh	Cm	Se	To	Pl	W	D	L	F	A	Pts
GHANA	–	0–0	1–0	1–1	6	3	2	1	7	3	8
CAMEROON	0–3	–	3–2	1–0	6	3	2	1	7	7	8
SENEGAL	2–0	1–1	–	0–0	6	2	2	2	8	6	6
TOGO	0–2	1–2	1–3	–	6	0	2	4	3	9	2

Group 3

	Su	Et	Md	Pl	W	D	L	F	A	Pts
SUDAN	–	2–2	3–0	4	2	2	0	9	4	6
ETHIOPIA	2–2	–	3–2	4	2	2	0	9	7	6
MADAGASCAR	0–2*	1–2	–	4	0	0	4	3	10	0

* Game awarded to Sudan 2–0

ASIA

Group 1

Tournament in Seoul, South Korea

	Ma	Sk	Ja	Ph	Ta	Pl	W	D	L	F	A	Pts
MALAYSIA	–	1–0	3–0	5–0	3–0	4	4	0	0	12	0	8
SOUTH KOREA	–	–	2–1	6–0	8–0	4	3	0	1	16	2	6
JAPAN	–	–	–	8–1	5–1	4	2	0	2	14	7	4
PHILIPPINES	–	–	–	–	3–0	4	1	0	3	4	19	2
TAIWAN	–	–	–	–	–	4	0	0	4	1	19	0

Group 2

Tournament in Rangoon, Burma

FIRST ROUND

	Bu	Is	Id	Th	In	SL	Pl	W	D	L	F	A	Pts
BURMA	–	–	–	7–0	4–3	5–1	3	3	0	0	16	4	6
ISRAEL	–	–	1–0	–	1–0	3–0	3	3	0	0	5	0	6
INDONESIA	–	–	–	4–0	4–2	–	3	2	0	1	8	3	4
THAILAND	–	–	–	–	–	5–0	3	1	0	2	5	11	2
INDIA	–	–	–	–	–	–	3	0	0	3	5	9	0
SRI LANKA	–	–	–	–	–	–	3	0	0	3	1	13	0

SEMI-FINALS

Burma .... 3–0 .... Indonesia
Thailand .... 0–0 (4–2p) ..... Israel

FINAL

BURMA .... 1–0 .... Thailand

Group 3

FIRST ROUND

Lebanon .... 1–0 0–1 1–2 ... Iraq
Syria .... 0–0 0–1 .... North Korea

SECOND ROUND

Iran .... 2–0 2–0 .... Kuwait
Iraq .... 1–0 0–3 .... North Korea

THIRD ROUND

North Korea .... 0–0 0–0 0–2 ... IRAN

CENTRAL AND NORTH AMERICA

FIRST ROUND

Group 1

	Me	Ca	Be	Pl	W	D	L	F	A	Pts
Mexico	–	1–0	3–0	4	3	0	1	6	1	6
Canada	1–0	–	1–1	4	2	1	1	5	2	5
Bermuda	0–2	0–3	–	4	0	1	3	1	9	1

Group 2

	Gu	Su	Pa	Pl	W	D	L	F	A	Pts
Guatemala	–	2–2	4–1	3	2	1	0	7	3	5
Surinam	0–1	–	3–0	4	1	1	2	6	7	3
Panama	–	4–1	–	3	1	0	2	5	8	2

Group 3

	US	ES	Ba	Pl	W	D	L	F	A	Pts
United States	–	1–1	3–0	4	2	2	0	8	3	6
El Salvador	1–1	–	4–2	4	2	2	0	9	4	6
Barbados	1–3	0–3	–	4	0	0	4	3	13	0

Group 4

Jamaica .... 2–1 1–1 .... Neth. Antilles

SECOND ROUND

	Me	US	Gu	Ja	Pl	W	D	L	F	A	Pts
MEXICO	–	1–1	3–1	4–0	6	3	2	1	12	6	8
UNITED STATES	2–2	–	2–1	2–1	6	2	3	1	10	9	7
GUATEMALA	1–2	3–2	–	1–0	6	2	1	3	7	9	5
JAMAICA	1–0	1–1	0–0	–	6	1	2	3	3	8	4

WEST GERMANY qualified as hosts

HUNGARY qualified as holders

FINAL TOURNAMENT

28th August–10th September 1972

FIRST ROUND

Group 1

	WG	Mo	Ma	US	Pl	W	D	L	F	A	Pts
WEST GERMANY	–	3–0	3–0	7–0	3	3	0	0	13	0	6
MOROCCO	–	–	6–0	0–0	3	1	1	1	6	3	3
MALAYSIA	–	–	–	3–0	3	1	0	2	3	9	2
UNITED STATES	–	–	–	–	3	0	1	2	0	10	0

Group 2

	SU	Me	Bu	Su	Pl	W	D	L	F	A	Pts
SOVIET UNION	–	4–1	1–0	2–1	3	3	0	0	7	2	6
MEXICO	–	–	1–0	1–0	3	2	0	1	3	4	4
BURMA	–	–	–	2–0	3	1	0	2	2	2	2
SUDAN	–	–	–	–	3	0	0	3	1	5	0

Group 3

	Hu	De	Ir	Br	Pl	W	D	L	F	A	Pts
HUNGARY	–	2–0	5–0	2–2	3	2	1	0	9	2	5
DENMARK	–	–	4–0	3–2	3	2	0	1	7	4	4
IRAN	–	–	–	1–0	3	1	0	2	1	9	2
BRAZIL	–	–	–	–	3	0	1	2	4	6	1

Group 4

	Po	EG	Co	Gh	Pl	W	D	L	F	A	Pts
POLAND	–	2–1	5–1	4–0	3	3	0	0	11	2	6
EAST GERMANY	–	–	6–1	4–0	3	2	0	1	11	3	4
COLOMBIA	–	–	–	3–1	3	1	0	2	5	12	2
GHANA	–	–	–	–	3	0	0	3	1	11	0

SECOND ROUND

Group A

	Hu	EG	WG	Me	Pl	W	D	L	F	A	Pts
HUNGARY	–	2–0	4–1	2–0	3	3	0	0	8	1	6
EAST GERMANY	–	–	3–2	7–0	3	2	0	1	10	4	4
WEST GERMANY	–	–	–	1–1	3	0	1	2	4	8	1
MEXICO	–	–	–	–	3	0	1	2	1	10	1

Group B

	Po	SU	De	Mo	Pl	W	D	L	F	A	Pts
POLAND	–	2–1	1–1	5–0	3	2	1	0	8	2	5
SOVIET UNION	–	–	4–0	3–0	3	2	0	1	8	2	4
DENMARK	–	–	–	3–1	3	1	1	1	4	6	3
MOROCCO	–	–	–	–	3	0	0	3	1	11	0

3RD PLACE

Soviet Union .... 2–2 .... East Germany

Bronze medal shared

FINAL

Olympiastadion, Munich, 10–09–1972, 50 000

POLAND 2 (Deyna 47 68)

HUNGARY 1 (Varadi 42)

Referee: Tschenscher, West Germany

Poland – Kostka – Gut, Cmikiewski, Gorgon, Anczok, Szoltyski, Deyna (Szymczak) Kraska, Maszczyk, Lubanski, Gadocha

Hungary – Géczi – Vépi, Pancsics, Juhasz, Szücs, Kozma, Dunai A (Tóth), Kü (Kocsis), Varadi, Dunai E, Bálint

XXI. OLYMPIAD MONTREAL 1976

14th football tournament

QUALIFYING TOURNAMENT

EUROPE

FIRST ROUND

Yugoslavia	1–1 0–3	Soviet Union
Finland	3–5 1–1	Norway
Greece	0–1 0–4	East Germany
Rep. Ireland	1–2 0–1	Czechoslovakia
West Germany	0–0 2–3	Spain
Hungary	2–0 0–4	Bulgaria
Luxembourg	0–1 1–2	Holland
Romania	4–0 2–1	Denmark

SECOND ROUND

Group 1

	SU	No	Ic	Pl	W	D	L	F	A	Pts
SOVIET UNION	–	4–0	1–0	4	4	0	0	10	1	8
Norway	1–3	–	3–2	4	1	1	2	5	10	3
Iceland	0–2	1–1	–	4	0	1	3	3	7	1

Group 2

	EG	Cz	Au	Pl	W	D	L	F	A	Pts
EAST GERMANY	–	0–0	1–0	4	2	2	0	4	1	6
Czechoslovakia	1–1	–	5–0	4	1	3	0	6	1	5
Austria	0–2	0–0	–	4	0	1	3	0	8	1

Group 3

	Sp	Bu	Tu	Pl	W	D	L	F	A	Pts
SPAIN	–	2–1	2–0	4	2	2	0	5	2	6
Bulgaria	1–1	–	3–0	4	2	1	1	7	3	5
Turkey	0–0	0–2	–	4	0	1	3	0	7	1

Group 4

	Fr	Ro	Ho	Pl	W	D	L	F	A	Pts
FRANCE	–	4–0	4–2	4	3	0	1	11	5	6
Romania	1–0	–	5–1	4	3	0	1	9	5	6
Holland	2–3	0–3	–	4	0	0	4	5	15	0

SOUTH AMERICA

Tournament in Recife, Brazil

	Br	Ur	Ar	Co	Ch	Pe	Pl	W	D	L	F	A	Pts
BRAZIL	–	1–1	2–0	4–0	2–1	3–0	5	4	1	0	12	2	9
Uruguay	–	–	2–0	2–2	1–1	3–0	5	2	3	0	9	4	7
Argentina	–	–	–	2–2	2–1	3–1	5	2	1	2	7	8	5
Colombia	–	–	–	–	1–0	0–1	5	1	2	2	5	9	4
Chile	–	–	–	–	–	2–1	5	1	1	3	5	7	3
Peru	–	–	–	–	–	–	5	1	0	4	3	11	2

AFRICA

FIRST ROUND

Algeria	1–1 1–2	Tunisia
Egypt	1–1 0–1	Sudan
Ethiopia	0–0 0–3	Tanzania
Gambia	0–1 0–6	Guinea
Ghana	6–0 4–1	Liberia
Malawi	W–O	Madagascar
Mali	6–0 1–0	Mauritania
Morocco	2–1 1–0	Libya
Nigeria	W–O	Cameroon
Senegal	1–0 1–1	Togo
Zaire	4–1 2–1	Upper Volta
Zambia	5–0 4–0	Mauritius

SECOND ROUND

Guinea	1–0 2–6	Ghana
Malawi	1–1 1–4	Zambia
Nigeria	W–O	Mali
Senegal	3–1 0–2 (5–4p)	Zaire
Tanzania	1–0 0–2	Sudan
Tunisia	1–0 0–1	Morocco

THIRD ROUND

NIGERIA	3–1 0–1	Morocco
Senegal	0–0 1–2	GHANA
ZAMBIA	2–2 0–0 (5–4p)	Sudan

Nigeria, Ghana and Zambia all withdrew from the final tournament and were not replaced

ASIA

Group 1

Tournament in Tehran

	Ir	Ku	Iq	SA	Ba	Pl	W	D	L	F	A	Pts
IRAN	–	1–1	1–0	3–0	3–0	4	3	1	0	8	1	7
Kuwait	–	–	1–2	4–2	2–1	4	2	1	1	8	6	5
Iraq	–	–	–	0–2	4–0	4	2	0	2	6	4	4
Saudi Arabia	–	–	–	–	1–0	4	2	0	2	5	7	4
Bahrain	–	–	–	–	–	4	0	0	4	1	10	0

Group 2

Tournament in Djakarta, Indonesia

	NK	Id	Ma	Si	PN	Pl	W	D	L	F	A	Pts
North Korea	–	2–1	2–0	2–0	4–0	4	4	0	0	10	1	8
Indonesia	–	–	2–1	0–0	8–2	4	2	1	1	11	5	5
Malaysia	–	–	–	6–0	10–1	4	2	0	2	17	5	4
Singapore	–	–	–	–	7–0	4	1	1	2	7	8	3
Papua N Guinea	–	–	–	–	–	4	0	0	4	3	29	0

NORTH KOREA ...... 0–0 (5–4p) ..... Indonesia

Group 3

First round

Japan	3–0 3–0	Philippines
Taiwan	0–2 0–3	South Korea
Israel	W–O	Vietnam

Second round

	Is	SK	Ja	Pl	W	D	L	F	A	Pts
ISRAEL	–	0–0	4–1	4	3	1	0	10	2	7
South Korea	1–3	–	2–2	4	1	2	1	5	5	4
Japan	0–3	0–2	–	4	0	1	3	3	11	1

CENTRAL AND NORTH AMERICA

PRELIMINARY ROUND

Barbados .... 1–1 0–0 1–3 ... Trinidad
El Salvador .... 4–0 1–2 .... Nicaragua
Jamaica .... 1–0 2–1 .... Dominican Rep.

FIRST ROUND

Bermuda .... 3–2 0–2 .... United States
Costa Rica .... 1–0 2–1 .... El Salvador
Cuba .... 1–0 0–1 4–1 ... Jamaica
Honduras .... 0–0 0–2 .... Guatemala
Surinam .... 2–0 1–1 .... Trinidad

SECOND ROUND

Costa Rica .... 1–1 1–2 .... Guatemala
Mexico .... 8–0 4–2 .... United States
Surinam .... 0–1 1–6 .... Cuba

THIRD ROUND

	Me	Gu	Cu	Pl	W	D	L	F	A	Pts
MEXICO	–	4–1	4–2	4	2	1	1	11	7	5
GUATEMALA	3–2	–	1–1	4	1	2	1	6	8	4
CUBA	1–1	1–1	–	4	0	3	1	5	7	3

CANADA qualified as hosts

POLAND qualified as holders

FINAL TOURNAMENT

18th–31st July 1976

FIRST ROUND

Group 1

	Br	EG	Sp	Pl	W	D	L	F	A	Pts
BRAZIL	–	0–0	2–1	2	1	1	0	2	1	3
EAST GERMANY	–	–	1–0	2	1	1	0	1	0	3
SPAIN	–	–	–	2	0	0	2	1	3	0

Group 2

	Fr	Is	Me	Gu	Pl	W	D	L	F	A	Pts
FRANCE	–	1–1	4–1	4–1	3	2	1	0	9	3	5
ISRAEL	–	–	2–2	0–0	3	0	3	0	3	3	3
MEXICO	–	–	–	1–1	3	0	2	1	4	7	2
GUATEMALA	–	–	–	–	3	0	2	1	2	5	2

Group 3

	Po	Ir	Cu	Pl	W	D	L	F	A	Pts
POLAND	–	3–2	0–0	2	1	1	0	3	2	3
IRAN	–	–	1–0	2	1	0	1	3	3	2
CUBA	–	–	–	2	0	1	1	0	1	1

Group 4

	SU	NK	Ca	Pl	W	D	L	F	A	Pts
SOVIET UNION	–	3–0	2–1	2	2	0	0	5	1	4
NORTH KOREA	–	–	3–1	2	1	0	1	3	4	2
CANADA	–	–	–	2	0	0	2	2	5	0

QUARTER-FINALS

East Germany .... 4–0 .... France
Soviet Union .... 2–1 .... Iran
Brazil .... 4–1 .... Israel
Poland .... 5–0 .... North Korea

SEMI-FINALS

East Germany .... 2–1 .... Soviet Union
Poland .... 2–0 .... Brazil

3RD PLACE

Soviet Union .... 2–0 .... Brazil

FINAL

Olympic Stadium, Montreal. 31–07–1976, 71 000
EAST GERMANY 3 (Schade 7, Hoffmann 14, Häfner 79)
POLAND 1 (Lato 59)
Referee: Barreto, Uruguay
East Germany – Croy – Lauck, Weise, Dorner, Kurbjuweit – Schade, Riediger (Bransch), Häfner – Kische, Lowe (Grobner), Hoffmann
Poland – Tomaszewski (Mowlik) – Symanowski, Wieczorek, Zmuda, Wawrowski – Maszczyk, Deyna, Kasperczak – Lato, Szarmach, Kmiecik

XXII. OLYMPIAD MOSCOW 1980

15th football tournament

QUALIFYING TOURNAMENT

EUROPE

FIRST ROUND

Group 1

Bulgaria .... 1–0 0–4 .... Czechoslovakia
Romania .... 2–0 0–3 .... Hungary

Group 2

Greece .... 1–0 0–4 .... Italy
Austria .... 1–0 1–2 (3–4p) . Turkey

Group 3

	Be	Sp	Is	Ho	Pl	W	D	L	F	A	Pts
BELGIUM	–	3–1	0–0	1–0	6	4	2	0	9	3	10
SPAIN	1–1	–	1–1	3–0	6	2	3	1	10	6	7
ISRAEL	0–2	0–3	–	1–1	6	1	3	2	6	10	5
HOLLAND	1–2	1–1	3–4	–	6	0	2	4	6	12	2

Group 4

Rep. Ireland .... 0–0 1–2 .... Norway
Denmark .... 1–1 1–4 .... Finland

SECOND ROUND

Group 1

	Cz	Hu	Pd	Pl	W	D	L	F	A	Pts
CZECHOSLOVAKIA	–	3–2	1–0	4	3	0	1	5	5	6
HUNGARY	3–0	–	2–0	4	2	0	2	7	4	4
POLAND	0–1	1–0	–	4	1	0	3	1	4	2

Group 2

	Yu	It	Tu	Pl	W	D	L	F	A	Pts
YUGOSLAVIA	–	5–2	3–0	4	3	0	1	9	3	6
ITALY	1–0	–	5–0	4	3	0	1	10	5	6
TURKEY	0–1	0–2	–	4	0	0	4	0	11	0

Group 3

	Sp	Be	Fr	Pl	W	D	L	F	A	Pts
SPAIN	–	3–0	3–1	4	2	1	1	7	4	5
BELGIUM	2–0	–	4–2	4	2	0	2	7	8	4
FRANCE	1–1	3–1	–	4	1	1	2	7	9	3

Group 4

	No	WG	Fi	Pl	W	D	L	F	A	Pts
NORWAY	–	2–0	1–1	4	3	1	0	5	1	7
WEST GERMANY	0–1	–	2–0	4	1	1	2	2	3	3
FINLAND	0–1	0–0	–	4	0	2	2	1	4	2

Norway withdrew from the final tournament and were replaced by Finland

SOUTH AMERICA

Tournament in Colombia

	Co	Pe	Ve	Br	Ch	Bo	Pl	W	D	L	F	A	Pts
ARGENTINA	0–0	4–1	1–0	3–1	1–0	4–0	6	5	1	0	13	2	11
COLOMBIA	–	2–1	0–1	5–1	3–1	0–1	6	3	1	2	10	5	7
PERU	–	–	2–0	3–0	1–0	1–1	6	3	1	2	9	7	7
VENEZUELA	–	–	–	1–2	0–0	5–1	6	2	1	3	7	6	5
BRAZIL	–	–	–	–	0–0	4–0	6	2	1	3	8	12	5
CHILE	–	–	–	–	–	2–0	6	1	2	3	3	5	4
BOLIVIA	–	–	–	–	–	–	6	1	1	4	3	16	3

Argentina withdrew from the final tournament and were replaced by Venezuela

AFRICA

FIRST ROUND

Algeria .... 1–0 4–2 .... Mali
Egypt .... W–O .... Tanzania
Kenya .... W–O .... Sudan
Lesotho .... 4–1 3–2 .... Mauritius
Liberia .... W–O .... Côte d'Ivoire
Madagascar .... 2–1 1–1 .... Ethiopia
Morocco .... 1–0 0–1 (6–5p) . Senegal
Sierra Leone .... W- O .... Guinea
Tunisia .... 1–0 0–3 .... Libya

SECOND ROUND

Algeria .... 5–1 3–0 .... Morocco
Ghana .... 4–1 1–0 .... Kenya
Lesotho .... 0–0 0–5 .... Zambia
Liberia .... W–O .... Sierra Leone
Madagascar .... 1–1 1–1 (3–4p) . Egypt
Libya .... Bye

THIRD ROUND

ALGERIA .... W–O .... Libya
EGYPT .... 4–1 1–1 .... Zambia
Liberia .... 0–2 2–2 .... GHANA

Ghana and Egypt withdrew from the final tournament and were replaced by Zambia and Nigeria

ASIA

Group 1

Tournament in Iraq

	Iq	Ku	Sy	Ye	Jo	Pl	W	D	L	F	A	Pts
IRAQ	–	0–0	1–0	3–0	4–0	4	3	1	0	8	0	7
KUWAIT	–	–	1–0	5–1	1–0	4	3	1	0	7	1	7
SYRIA	–	–	–	2–1	2–0	4	2	0	2	4	3	4
YEMEN	–	–	–	–	2–1	4	1	0	3	4	11	2
JORDAN	–	–	–	–	–	4	0	0	4	1	9	0

Final

KUWAIT .... 3–2 .... Iraq

Group 2

Tournament in Malaysia

	Ma	SK	Ja	Br	Id	Ph	Pl	W	D	L	F	A	Pts
MALAYSIA	–	3–0	1–1	3–1	6–1	8–0	5	4	1	0	21	3	9
SOUTH KOREA	–	–	3–1	3–0	1–0	8–0	5	4	0	1	15	4	8
JAPAN	–	–	–	2–1	2–0	10–0	5	3	1	1	16	5	7
BRUNEI	–	–	–	–	3–2	2–0	5	2	0	3	7	10	4
INDONESIA	–	–	–	–	–	4–0	5	1	0	4	7	12	2
PHILIPPINES	–	–	–	–	–	–	5	0	0	5	0	32	0

Final

MALAYSIA .... 2–1 .... South Korea

Malaysia withdrew from the final tournament and were replaced by Iraq

Group 3

Tournament in Singapore

	Ir	Si	Ch	NK	In	SL	Pl	W	D	L	F	A	Pts
IRAN	–	3–0	2–2	0–0	2–0	11–0	5	3	2	0	18	2	8
SINGAPORE	–	–	1–0	3–1	1–0	3–0	5	4	0	1	8	4	8
CHINA	–	–	–	1–1	1–0	7–0	5	2	2	1	11	4	6
NORTH KOREA	–	–	–	–	2–1	7–0	5	2	2	1	11	5	6
INDIA	–	–	–	–	–	4–0	5	1	0	4	5	6	2
SRI LANKA	–	–	–	–	–	–	5	0	0	5	0	32	0

Final

IRAN .... 4–0 .... Singapore

Iran withdrew from the final tournament and were replaced by Syria

CENTRAL AND NORTH AMERICA

FIRST ROUND

Haiti .... 4–1 3–0 .... Dominican Rep.
Jamaica .... 0–3 0–2 .... Cuba
Bermuda .... 3–0 5–2 .... Canada
Mexico .... 4–0 2–0 *..... United States
Costa Rica .... 4–0 2–0 .... Panama
Guatemala .... 2–0 0–1 .... El Salvador
Barbados .... 1–2 1–5 .... Surinam
Neth. Antilles .... 2–3 1–6 .... Trinidad

* Mexico withdrew after protest from the USA over the status of Mexican players

SECOND ROUND

Bermuda .... 0–3 0–5 .... United States
Costa Rica .... 1–2 1–0 1–0 ... Guatemala
Cuba .... 0–1 0–0 .... Haiti
Trinidad .... 2–0 1–3 0–2 ... Surinam

THIRD ROUND

Haiti .... 2–0 0–2 0–2 ... Surinam

FOURTH ROUND

	CR	US	Su	Pl	W	D	L	F	A	Pts
COSTA RICA	–	0–1	3–2	4	2	1	1	7	6	5
UNITED STATES	1–1	–	2–1	4	2	1	1	6	6	5
SURINAM	2–3	4–2	–	4	1	0	3	9	10	2

The United States withdrew from the final tournament and were replaced by Cuba

SOVIET UNION qualified as hosts

EAST GERMANY qualified as holders

FINAL TOURNAMENT
20th July–2nd August 1980

FIRST ROUND

Group 1

	SU	Cu	Ve	Zm	Pl	W	D	L	F	A	Pts
SOVIET UNION	–	8–0	4–0	3–1	3	3	0	0	15	1	6
CUBA	–	–	2–1	1–0	3	2	0	1	3	9	4
VENEZUELA	–	–	–	2–1	3	1	0	2	3	7	2
ZAMBIA	–	–	–	–	3	0	0	3	2	6	0

Group 2

	Cz	Ku	Co	Ni	Pl	W	D	L	F	A	Pts
CZECHOSLOVAKIA	–	0–0	3–0	1–1	3	1	2	0	4	1	4
KUWAIT	–	–	1–1	3–1	3	1	2	0	4	2	4
COLOMBIA	–	–	–	1–0	3	1	1	1	2	4	3
NIGERIA	–	–	–	–	3	0	1	2	2	5	1

Group 3

	EG	Al	Sp	Sy	Pl	W	D	L	F	A	Pts
EAST GERMANY	–	1–0	1–1	5–0	3	2	1	0	7	1	5
ALGERIA	–	–	1–1	3–0	3	1	1	1	4	2	3
SPAIN	–	–	–	0–0	3	0	3	0	2	2	3
SYRIA	–	–	–	–	3	0	1	2	0	8	1

Group 4

	Yu	Iq	Fi	CR	Pl	W	D	L	F	A	Pts
YUGOSLAVIA	–	1–1	2–0	3–2	3	2	1	0	6	3	5
IRAQ	–	–	0–0	3–0	3	1	2	0	4	1	4
FINLAND	–	–	–	3–0	3	1	1	1	3	2	3
COSTA RICA	–	–	–	–	3	0	0	3	2	9	0

QUARTER-FINALS

Czechoslovakia .... 3–0 .... Cuba
Yugoslavia .... 3–0 .... Algeria
Soviet Union .... 2–1 .... Kuwait
East Germany .... 4–0 .... Iraq

SEMI-FINALS

Czechoslovakia .... 2–0 .... Yugoslavia
East Germany .... 1–0 .... Soviet Union

3RD PLACE

Soviet Union .... 2–0 .... Yugoslavia

FINAL

Centralny Lenina, Moscow, 2–08–1980, 70 000
CZECHOSLOVAKIA 1 (Svoboda 77)
EAST GERMANY 0
Referee: Azim Zade, Soviet Union
Czechoslovakia – Seman – Mazura, Macela, Radimec, Rygel – Rott, Berger, Stambachr – Vízek (Svoboda), Licka, Pokluda (Nemec)
East Germany – Rudwaleit – Muller, Hause (Liebers), Trieloff, Ullrich – Schnuphase, Terletzki, Steinbach – Baum, Netz, Kuhn

XXIII. OLYMPIAD
LOS ANGELES 1984
16th football tournament

QUALIFYING TOURNAMENT

EUROPE

Group 1

	SU	Hu	Bu	Gr	Pl	W	D	L	F	A	Pts
SOVIET UNION	–	0–1	0–0	3–0	6	3	2	1	9	4	8
HUNGARY	0–1	–	1–1	3–1	6	3	2	1	8	5	8
BULGARIA	2–2	1–1	–	0–0	6	1	5	0	7	5	7
GREECE	1–3	1–2	1–3	–	6	0	1	5	4	14	1

Soviet Union withdrew and were replaced by West Germany

Group 2

	EG	Pd	No	De	Fi	Pl	W	D	L	F	A	Pts
EAST GERMANY	–	3–1	1–0	4–0	1–0	8	6	1	6	14	5	13
Poland	2–1	–	1–0	0–0	3–2	8	6	1	1	13	6	13
Norway	1–1	0–1	–	1–1	4–2	8	1	4	3	9	10	6
Denmark	1–2	0–1	2–2	–	3–0	8	1	4	3	7	10	6
Finland	0–1	0–4	1–1	0–0	–	8	0	2	6	5	17	2

East Germany withdrew and were replaced by Norway

Group 3

Liechtenstein .... 0–3 1–3 .... Holland

	Yu	Ro	It	Ho	Pl	W	D	L	F	A	Pts
YUGOSLAVIA	–	4–1	5–1	2–1	6	4	1	1	14	6	9
ROMANIA	1–0	–	0–0	3–0	6	3	2	1	7	5	8
ITALY	2–2	1–2	–	2–2	6	0	4	2	7	12	4
HOLLAND	0–1	0–0	1–1	–	6	0	3	3	4	9	3

Group 4

Sub–group A

	Wg	Pt	Is	Pl	W	D	L	F	A	Pts
WEST GERMANY	–	3–0	2–0	4	3	0	1	7	3	6
PORTUGAL	3–1	–	2–1	4	2	0	2	5	6	4
ISRAEL	0–1	1–0	–	4	1	0	3	2	5	2

Sub–group B

	Fr	Be	Sp	Pl	W	D	L	F	A	Pts
FRANCE	–	2–0	3–1	4	3	1	0	7	2	7
BELGIUM	1–1	–	0–0	4	0	3	1	1	3	3
SPAIN	0–1	0–0	–	4	0	2	2	1	4	2

FRANCE .... 1–1 1–0 .... West Germany

Czechoslovakia, the holders, withdrew and were replaced by Italy

SOUTH AMERICA

Tournament in Ecuador
FIRST ROUND

Group 1

	Ec	Br	Co	Pl	W	D	L	F	A	Pts
ECUADOR	–	0–0	3–0	2	1	1	0	3	0	3
BRAZIL	–	–	2–1	2	1	1	0	2	1	3
COLOMBIA	–	–	–	2	0	0	2	1	5	0

Group 2

	Pa	Ch	Ve	Pl	W	D	L	F	A	Pts
PARAGUAY	–	0–0	4–0	2	1	1	0	4	0	3
CHILE	–	–	1–0	2	1	1	0	1	0	3
VENEZUELA	–	–	–	2	0	0	2	0	5	0

SECOND ROUND

	Br	Ch	Pa	Ec	Pl	W	D	L	F	A	Pts
BRAZIL	–	3–2	2–0	2–0	3	3	0	0	7	2	6
CHILE	–	–	2–3	2–0	3	2	0	1	6	6	4
PARAGUAY	–	–	–	2–3	3	1	0	2	5	7	2
ECUADOR	–	–	–	–	3	1	0	2	3	6	2

AFRICA

PRELIMINARY ROUND

Angola .... W–O .... Niger
Benin .... W–O .... Sierra Leone
Mauritania .... 1–3 1–3 .... Gambia
Mauritius .... W–O .... Madagascar
Mozambique .... 3–0 0–0 .... Lesotho
Uganda .... W–O .... Congo

FIRST ROUND

Angola .... 1–1 2–3 .... Cameroon
Ethiopia .... W–O .... Tanzania
Gambia .... 0–2 0–1 .... Ghana
Guinea .... 0–0 0–3 .... Morocco
Kenya .... 1–0 0–2 .... Libya
Mozambique .... 0–1 0–2 .... Zimbabwe
Nigeria .... 2–1 1–1 .... Togo
Senegal .... 2–0 2–0 .... Benin
Sudan .... 0–0 1–2 .... Egypt
Tunisia .... 3–0 1–1 .... Gabon
Uganda .... 4–1 0–3 .... Algeria
Zambia .... W–O .... Mauritius

SECOND ROUND

Cameroon .... W–O .... Tunisia
Libya .... 2–1 0–2 .... Algeria
Morocco .... 1–0 1–1 .... Senegal
Nigeria .... 0–0 2–1 .... Ghana
Zambia .... 1–0 0–2 .... Egypt
Zimbabwe .... 3–2 0–1 .... Ethiopia

THIRD ROUND

Algeria .... 1–1 0–1 .... EGYPT
CAMEROON .... 4–0 1–1 .... Ethiopia
Nigeria .... 0–0 0–0 (3–4p) . MOROCCO

ASIA

FIRST ROUND

Group 1

	Ku	Qa	Sy	Jo	Pl	W	D	L	F	A	Pts
Kuwait	–	2–2	1–3	3–0	6	3	2	1	11	6	8
Qatar	0–0	–	1–0	2–1	6	2	4	0	6	4	8
Syria	1–3	1–1	–	3–2	6	3	1	2	9	8	7
JORDAN	0–2	0–0	0–1	–	6	0	1	5	3	11	1

Group 2

	Iq	Ba	Em	Pl	W	D	L	F	A	Pts
Iraq	–	0–0	0–0	4	1	3	0	4	3	5
Bahrain	1–2	–	0–0	4	1	2	1	3	3	4
ARAB EMIRATES	2–2	1–2	–	4	0	3	1	3	4	3

Group 3

	SA	Ma	In	Si	Id	Pl	W	D	L	F	A	Pts
SAUDI ARABIA	–	2–0	5–0	5–0	3–0	8	6	1	1	22	5	13
MALAYSIA	3–1	–	3–3	2–0	1–1	8	5	2	1	14	7	12
INDIA	1–2	0–2	–	1–2	4–0	8	3	1	4	11	14	7
SINGAPORE	0–3	0–1	0–1	–	1–0	8	2	1	5	4	14	5
INDONESIA	1–1	0–2	0–1	1–1	–	8	0	3	5	3	14	3

Saudi played a normal fixture list. The games between the other four nations were played in Singapore and Kuala Lumpur, Malaysia

Group 4

Tournament in Bangkok, Thailand

	Th	SK	Ch	HK	Pl	W	D	L	F	A	Pts
THAILAND	–	2–1	0–0	1–0	6	4	1	1	7	3	9
SOUTH KOREA	2–0	–	3–3	4–0	6	3	2	1	12	5	8
CHINA	0–1	0–0	–	4–0	6	2	3	1	10	5	7
HONG KONG	0–3	0–2	1–3	–	6	0	0	6	1	17	0

Group 5

Preliminary game

Japan .... 7–0 10–1 .... Philippines

Final round

	NZ	Ja	Ta	Pl	W	D	L	F	A	Pts
NEW ZEALAND	–	3–1	2–0	4	3	1	0	7	2	7
JAPAN	0–1	–	2–0	4	1	1	2	4	5	3
TAIWAN	1–1	1–1	–	4	0	2	2	2	6	2

SECOND ROUND

Tournament in Singapore

Group 1

	SA	SK	Ku	Ba	NZ	Pl	W	D	L	F	A	Pts
SAUDI ARABIA	–	5–4	4–1	1–1	3–1	4	3	1	0	13	7	7
SOUTH KOREA	–	–	0–0	1–0	2–0	4	2	1	1	7	5	5
KUWAIT	–	–	–	2–0	2–0	4	2	1	1	5	4	5
BAHRAIN	–	–	–	–	1–0	4	1	1	2	2	4	3
NEW ZEALAND	–	–	–	–	–	4	0	0	4	1	8	0

Group 2

	Qa	Iq	Th	Ma	Ja	Pl	W	D	L	F	A	Pts
QATAR	–	2–0	1–0	2–0	2–1	4	4	0	0	7	1	8
IRAQ	–	–	2–1	2–0	2–1	4	3	0	1	6	4	6
THAILAND	–	–	–	0–0	5–2	4	1	1	2	6	5	3
MALAYSIA	–	–	–	–	2–1	4	1	1	2	2	5	3
JAPAN	–	–	–	–	–	4	0	0	4	5	11	0

IRAQ .... 1–0 .... South Korea

CENTRAL AND NORTH AMERICA

PRELIMINARY ROUND

Antigua .... 0–1 1–2 .... Barbados
Jamaica .... 0–1 1–4 .... Cuba
Cuba .... 2–0 0–0 .... Barbados

FIRST ROUND

Canada .... 6–0 1–1 .... Bermuda
Mexico .... 6–0 0–0 .... Bahamas
El Salvador .... 0–2 1–4 .... Guatemala
Honduras .... 0–1 2–3 .... Costa Rica
Surinam .... 1–0 0–3 .... Cuba
Trinidad .... W–O .... Neth. Antilles

SECOND ROUND

Cuba .... 2–0 1–0 .... Trinidad
Canada .... 1–0 1–2 1–0 ... Mexico
Costa Rica .... 1–0 1–1 .... Guatemala

THIRD ROUND

	CR	Ca	Cu	Pl	W	D	L	F	A	Pts
COSTA RICA	–	0–0	1–0	4	1	3	0	1	0	5
CANADA	0–0	–	3–0	3	1	2	0	3	0	4
CUBA	0–0	–	–	3	0	1	2	0	4	1

UNITED STATES qualified as hosts

FINAL TOURNAMENT

29th July–11th August 1984

FIRST ROUND

Group 1

	Fr	Ch	No	Qa	Pl	W	D	L	F	A	Pts
FRANCE	–	1–1	2–1	2–2	3	1	2	0	5	4	4
CHILE	–	–	0–0	1–0	3	1	2	0	2	1	4
NORWAY	–	–	–	2–0	3	1	1	1	3	2	3
QATAR	–	–	–	–	3	0	1	2	2	5	1

Group 2

	Yu	Ca	Cm	Iq	Pl	W	D	L	F	A	Pts
YUGOSLAVIA	–	1–0	2–1	4–2	3	3	0	0	7	3	6
CANADA	–	–	3–1	1–1	3	1	1	1	4	3	3
CAMEROON	–	–	–	1–0	3	1	0	2	3	5	2
IRAQ	–	–	–	–	3	0	1	2	3	6	1

Group 3

	Br	WG	Mo	SA	Pl	W	D	L	F	A	Pts
BRAZIL	–	1–0	2–0	3–1	3	3	0	0	6	1	6
WEST GERMANY	–	–	2–0	6–0	3	2	0	1	8	1	4
MOROCCO	–	–	–	1–0	3	1	0	2	1	4	2
SAUDI ARABIA	–	–	–	–	3	0	0	3	1	10	0

Group 4

	It	Eg	US	CR	Pl	W	D	L	F	A	Pts
ITALY	–	1–0	1–0	0–1	3	2	0	1	2	1	4
EGYPT	–	–	1–1	4–1	3	1	1	1	5	3	3
UNITED STATES	–	–	–	3–0	3	1	1	1	4	2	3
COSTA RICA	–	–	–	–	3	1	0	2	2	7	2

QUARTER-FINALS

France .... 2–0 .... Egypt
Yugoslavia .... 5–2 .... West Germany
Italy .... 1–0 .... Chile
Brazil .... 1–1 (4–2p) ..... Canada

SEMI-FINALS

France .... 4–2 .... Yugoslavia
Brazil .... 2–1 .... Italy

3RD PLACE

Yugoslavia .... 2–1 .... Italy

FINAL

Rose Bowl, Pasadena, 11–08–1984, 101 000

FRANCE 2 (Brisson 55, Xuereb 62)
BRAZIL 0

Referee: Keizer, Holland

France – Rust – Ayache, Bibard, Jeannol, Zanon – Lemoult, Rohr, Lacombe G – Bijotat, Xuereb (Cubaynes), Brisson (Garande)

Brazil – Gilmar R – Ronaldo, Pinga, Mauro Galvao, André Luís – Ademir, Dunga, Gilmar – Tonho (Mílton Cruz), Kita (Chicao), Silvinho

XXIV. OLYMPIAD SEOUL 1988

17th football tournament

QUALIFYING TOURNAMENT

EUROPE

PRELIMINARY ROUND

Cyprus .... 1–2 0–2 .... Greece
Liechtenstein .... 0–10 0–9 ...... Switzerland

FINAL ROUND

Group 1

	WG	De	Pd	Ro	Gr	Pl	W	D	L	F	A	Pts
WEST GERMANY	–	1–1	5–1	3–0	3–0	8	5	2	1	16	4	12
DENMARK	0–1	–	3–0	8–0	4–0	8	5	1	2	23	5	11
POLAND	1–1	2–0*	–	1–0	5–1	8	4	2	2	11	10	10
ROMANIA	1–0	1–2	0–0	–	0–1	8	2	1	5	5	17	5
GREECE	0–2	0–5	0–1	2–3	–	8	1	0	7	4	23	2

* Denmark won the game 2–0 but fielded an ineligible player, and thus forfeited the game 0–2

Group 2

	It	EG	Pt	Ho	Ic	Pl	W	D	L	F	A	Pts
ITALY	–	1–1	1–0	3–0	2–0	8	5	3	0	11	1	13
EAST GERMANY	0–0	–	3–0	4–2	3–0	8	4	3	1	12	5	11
PORTUGAL	0–0	0–0	–	1–1	2–1	8	2	4	2	4	6	8
HOLLAND	0–1	0–1	0–0	–	1–0	8	1	3	4	6	12	5
ICELAND	0–3	2–0	0–1	2–2	–	8	1	1	6	5	14	3

Group 3

	Sd	Hu	Sp	RI	Fr	Pl	W	D	L	F	A	Pts
SWEDEN	–	1–0	2–0	1–0	4–2	8	6	1	1	13	6	13
HUNGARY	2–1	–	2–1	3–1	2–2	8	5	1	2	13	8	11
SPAIN	1–1	1–0	–	2–2	1–2	8	1	4	3	9	12	6
REP. IRELAND	0–1	1–2	2–2	–	3–0	8	1	3	4	10	12	5
FRANCE	1–2	0–2	1–1	1–1	–	8	1	3	4	9	16	5

Group 4

	SU	Bu	Sz	No	Tu	Pl	W	D	L	F	A	Pts
SOVIET UNION	–	2–0	0–0	1–0	2–0	8	6	2	0	12	2	14
BULGARIA	0–1	–	2–0	4–0	3–1	8	4	2	2	13	5	10
SWITZERLAND	2–4	1–1	–	1–0	2–0	8	2	3	3	8	10	7
NORWAY	0–0	0–0	0–0	–	1–1	8	0	5	3	1	7	5
TURKEY	0–2	0–3	3–2	0–0	–	8	1	2	5	5	15	4

Group 5

	Yu	Cz	Be	Au	Fi	Pl	W	D	L	F	A	Pts
YUGOSLAVIA	–	1–0	4–0	2–1	5–0	8	6	1	1	17	5	13
CZECHOSLOVAKIA	1–0	–	2–0	1–0	2–0	8	6	0	2	10	3	12
BELGIUM	2–2	0–2	–	2–3	1–0	8	3	1	4	8	13	7
AUSTRIA	0–1	2–0	0–1	–	0–2	8	2	0	6	7	11	4
FINLAND	1–2	0–2	0–2	2–1	–	8	2	0	6	5	15	4

SOUTH AMERICA

Tournament in Bolivia

FIRST ROUND

Group 1

	Co	Br	Pa	Ur	Pe	Pl	W	D	L	F	A	Pts
COLOMBIA	–	2–0	1–0	0–0	1–0	4	3	1	0	4	0	7
BRAZIL	–	–	3–1	1–1	1–1	4	1	2	1	5	5	4
PARAGUAY	–	–	–	1–0	2–0	4	2	0	2	4	4	4
URUGUAY	–	–	–	–	1–0	4	1	2	1	2	2	4
PERU	–	–	–	–	–	4	0	1	3	1	5	1

Group 2

	Ar	Bo	Ch	Ec	Ve	Pl	W	D	L	F	A	Pts
ARGENTINA	–	3–0	1–1	0–0	2–0	4	2	2	0	6	1	6
BOLIVIA	–	–	1–0	1–0	3–0	4	3	0	1	5	3	6
CHILE	–	–	–	2–1	3–1	4	2	1	1	6	4	5
ECUADOR	–	–	–	–	1–0	4	1	1	2	2	3	3
VENEZUELA	–	–	–	–	–	4	0	0	4	1	9	0

SECOND ROUND

	Br	Ar	Bo	Co	Pl	W	D	L	F	A	Pts
BRAZIL	–	0–2	2–1	2–1	3	2	0	1	4	4	4
ARGENTINA	–	–	0–0	0–1	3	1	1	1	2	1	3

Bolivia	–	–	–	2–1	3	1	1	1	3	3	3
Colombia	–	–	–	–	3	1	0	2	3	4	2

AFRICA

PRELIMINARY ROUND

Botswana	W–O	Madagascar
Rwanda	2–5 0–3	Malawi
Swaziland	W–O	Mauritius

FIRST ROUND

Botswana	0–4 0–3	Zambia
Egypt	4–0 3–1	Kenya
Ghana	2–0 1–0	Senegal
Côte d'Ivoire	W–O	Guinea
Liberia	2–1 1–4	Nigeria
Libya	W–O	Ethiopia
Malawi	1–1 0–3	Cameroon
Morocco	W–O	Gambia
Sierra Leone	1–0 0–2	Tunisia
Swaziland	0–2 1–6	Zimbabwe
Sudan	1–1 1–3	Algeria
Uganda	4–1 2–1	Mozambique

SECOND ROUND

Algeria	W–O	Libya
Ghana	0–0 2–2	Cameroon
Côte d'Ivoire	0–0 1–2	Morocco
Tunisia	0–0 1–0	Egypt
Uganda	2–1 0–5	Zambia
Zimbabwe	0–0 0–2	Nigeria

THIRD ROUND

Algeria	1–0 0–2	NIGERIA
TUNISIA	1–0 2–2	Morocco
ZAMBIA	2–0 0–1	Ghana

ASIA

WEST ASIA

FIRST ROUND

Group 1

	SA	Ba	Om	Pl	W	D	L	F	A	Pts
Saudi Arabia	–	2–0	1–0	4	4	0	0	8	1	8
Bahrain	1–2	–	2–0	4	1	0	3	4	6	2
Oman	0–3	2–1	–	4	1	0	3	2	7	2

Group 2

	Iq	Em	Jo	Pl	W	D	L	F	A	Pts
Iraq	–	1–1*	2–0*	4	3	1	0	8	2	7
Arab Emirates	0–3	–	3–0	4	1	2	1	5	5	4
Jordan	1–2	1–1	–	4	0	1	3	2	8	1

* Matches played in Kuwait

Group 3

Qatar	2–0 0–1	Syria

Group 4

Iran	* 2–1 0–1	Kuwait

* Both matches played in Doha, Qatar

SECOND ROUND

	Iq	Ku	Qa	SA	Pl	W	D	L	F	A	Pts
IRAQ	–	1–0*	4–1*	1–1*	6	3	2	1	10	5	8
Kuwait	2–1	–	0–0	1–0	6	2	3	1	3	2	7
Qatar	1–3	0–0	–	1–0	6	1	3	2	4	8	5
Saudi Arabia	0–0	0–0	1–1	–	6	0	4	2	2	4	4

* Played in Muscat, Oman

EAST ASIA

FIRST ROUND

Group 1

Pakistan	2–2 0–1	Nepal

Both matches played in Kathmandu, Nepal

Group 2

Malaysia	0–1 2–2	Thailand

Both matches played in Kuala Lumpur, Malaysia.

North Korea withdrew

Group 3

	Ja	Si	Id	Pl	W	D	L	F	A	Pts
Japan	–	1–0	3–0	4	4	0	0	7	1	8
Singapore	0–1	–	2–0	4	1	0	3	3	4	2
Indonesia	1–2	2–1	–	4	1	0	3	3	8	2

Group 4

	Ch	HK	Ph	Pl	W	D	L	F	A	Pts
China	–	1–0	10–0	4	3	1	0	20	0	7
Hong Kong	0–0	–	7–0	4	2	1	1	12	1	5
Philippines*	0–9	0–5	–	4	0	0	4	0	31	0

* Philippines played all matches away from home

SECOND ROUND

	Ch	Ja	Th	Ne	Pl	W	D	L	F	A	Pts
CHINA	–	0–1	2–0	12–0	6	5	0	1	25	1	10
Japan	0–2	–	1–0	9–0	6	4	1	1	16	2	9
Thailand	0–1	0–0	–	3–0	6	2	1	3	5	5	5
Nepal*	0–8	0–5	1–2	–	6	0	0	6	1	39	0

* Nepal played all matches away from home

OCEANIA

FIRST ROUND

Taiwan	0–3 0–3	Australia
Western Samoa	0–7 0–12	New Zealand

Play-off between two losers for a place in the next round

Taiwan	5–0	Western Samoa

SECOND ROUND

Tournament in Australia and New Zealand

	Au	Is	NZ	Ta	Pl	W	D	L	F	A	Pts
AUSTRALIA	–	2–0	3–1	3–2	6	4	2	0	12	4	10
Israel	0–0	–	2–0	5–1	6	4	1	1	17	3	9
New Zealand	1–1	0–1	–	2–0	6	2	1	3	5	7	5
Taiwan	0–3	0–9	0–1	–	6	0	0	6	3	23	0

CENTRAL AND NORTH AMERICA

PRELIMINARY ROUND

Bahamas	1–3 0–3	Guyana
Antigua	1–1 0–0	Dominican Rep.
Trinidad	W–O	Surinam
Barbados	0–0 1–0	Jamaica

FIRST ROUND

Bermuda	2–1 0–6	Mexico
Canada	2–0 0–3	United States
Guyana	4–0 2–1	Dominican Rep.
Honduras	1–2 2–2	Guatemala
Panama	1–1 2–3	El Salvador
Trinidad	2–0 1–1	Barbados

SECOND ROUND

Group 1

	US	Tr	ES	Pl	W	D	L	F	A	Pts
UNITED STATES	–	4–1	4–1	4	4	0	0	13	4	8
TRINIDAD	0–1	–	–	3	1	0	2	2	5	2
EL SALVADOR	2–4	0–1	–	3	0	0	3	3	9	0

Group 2

	Me	Gu	Gu	Pl	W	D	L	F	A	Pts
MEXICO	–	2–1	2–0*	4	4	0	0	16	1	8
GUATEMALA	0–3	–	6–0	4	2	0	2	10	5	4
GUYANA	0–9	0–3	–	4	0	0	4	0	20	0

* Mexico awarded game 2–0

Mexico withdrew and were replaced by Guatemala in the final tournament

SOUTH KOREA qualified as hosts

FINAL TOURNAMENT

17th September–1st October 1988

FIRST ROUND

Group 1

	Sd	WG	Tu	Ch	Pl	W	D	L	F	A	Pts
SWEDEN	–	2–1	2–2	2–0	3	2	1	0	6	3	5
WEST GERMANY	–	–	4–1	3–0	3	2	0	1	8	3	4
TUNISIA	–	–	–	0–0	3	0	2	1	3	6	2
CHINA	–	–	–	–	3	0	1	2	0	5	1

Group 2

	Zm	It	Iq	Gu	Pl	W	D	L	F	A	Pts
ZAMBIA	–	4–0	2–2	4–0	3	2	1	0	10	2	5
ITALY	–	–	2–0	5–2	3	2	0	1	7	6	4
IRAQ	–	–	–	3–0	3	1	1	1	5	4	3
GUATEMALA	–	–	–	–	3	0	0	3	2	12	0

Group 3

	SU	Ar	SK	US	Pl	W	D	L	F	A	Pts
SOVIET UNION	–	2–1	0–0	4–2	3	2	1	0	6	3	5
ARGENTINA	–	–	2–1	1–1	3	1	1	1	4	4	3
SOUTH KOREA	–	–	–	0–0	3	0	2	1	1	2	2
UNITED STATES	–	–	–	–	3	0	2	1	3	5	2

Group 4

	Br	Au	Yu	Ni	Pl	W	D	L	F	A	Pts
BRAZIL	–	3–0	2–1	4–0	3	3	0	0	9	1	6
AUSTRALIA	–	–	1–0	1–0	3	2	0	1	2	3	4
YUGOSLAVIA	–	–	–	3–1	3	1	0	2	4	4	2
NIGERIA	–	–	–	–	3	0	0	3	1	8	0

QUARTER-FINALS

Soviet Union .... 3–0 .... Australia
Italy .... 2–1 .... Sweden
West Germany .... 4–0 .... Zambia
Brazil .... 1–0 .... Argentina

SEMI-FINALS

Soviet Union .... 3–2 .... Italy
Brazil .... 1–1 (3–2p) ..... West Germany

3RD PLACE

West Germany .... 3–0 .... Italy

FINAL

Olympic Stadium, Seoul, 1–10–1988, 73 000

SOVIET UNION 2 (Dobrovolski 62, Savichev 104)
BRAZIL 1 (Romario 30)

Referee: Biguet, France

Soviet Union – Kharin – Ketashvili, Yarovenko, Gorlukvich, Losev – Kuznetsov, Dobrovolski, Mikhailichenko, Tatarchuk – Liuti (Skliyarov), Narbekovas (Savichev)

Brazil – Taffarel – Luís Carlos, Aloísio, André Cruz, Jorginho – Andrade, Mílton, Neto (Edmar) – Careca II, Bebeto (Joao Paulo), Romario

OTHER FIFA TOURNAMENTS

Aside from the World Cup and the football tournament of the Olympic Games, FIFA organises the Under-17 World Championship, the World Youth Cup for the Under-20s and the World Cup for women.

FIFA is very keen to promote football at the grass roots level and although often criticised as bringing competitive football to players at too young an age, it feels that the two junior tournaments serve that ideal. Both are relatively new tournaments, and the under-17 championship has shown that levels of skill are relatively even around the world. Africa has won two of the four editions and Asia one.

It is after that age where the disparity begins to show and the fact that the under-20 Youth Cup has been won on each occasion by a European or South American country shows how the more stable club situation on those two continents helps the development of players, many of whom are already established in a first division team at that age.

A major problem with the under-17 event especially has been the question of over-age players, and despite the heavy punishments handed out by FIFA, most notably the suspension of Mexico from the 1990 World Cup, accusations still fly after each event.

The Women's World Cup, although only introduced in 1991, looks set to tap into one of the biggest growth sports in the world. It is not impossible that eventually the tournament will become an equal partner to the men's event as has happened in tennis and athletics.

Certainly, with half the world's population to account for, FIFA is taking the challenge seriously. If they can change football to a sport both played and watched by women as equal partners to men, from a bastion of male culture they will have achieved a magnificent feat. It should certainly be one of their top priorities for the 21st century and the World Cup is just the first step on what promises to be a long but exciting road.

THE FIFA UNDER-17 WORLD CHAMPIONSHIPS

1985	Nigeria	2–0	West Germany
1987	Soviet Union	1–1 (4–2p)	Nigeria
1989	Saudi Arabia	2–2 (5–4p)	Scotland
1991	Ghana	1–0	Spain

WORLD UNDER-17 MEDALS TABLE

		G	S	B	Finals	Semis
1	Nigeria	1	1	–	2	2
2	Ghana	1	–	–	1	1
	Saudi Arabia	1	–	–	1	1
	Soviet Union	1	–	–	1	1
5	Scotland	–	1	–	1	1
	Spain	–	1	–	1	1
	West Germany	–	1	–	1	1
8	Argentina	–	–	1	–	1
	Brazil	–	–	1	–	1
	Côte d'Ivoire	–	–	1	–	1
	Portugal	–	–	1	–	1
12	Bahrain	–	–	–	–	1
	Guinea	–	–	–	–	1
	Italy	–	–	–	–	1
	Qatar	–	–	–	–	1

First Edition, China, 31st July–11th August 1985

FIRST ROUND

Group 1

	Ch	Gu	US	Bo	Pl	W	D	L	F	A	Pts
CHINA	–	2–1	3–1	1–1	3	2	1	0	6	3	5
GUINEA	–	–	1–0	3–0	3	2	0	1	5	2	4
UNITED STATES	–	–	–	2–1	3	1	0	2	3	5	2
BOLIVIA	–	–	–	–	3	0	1	2	2	6	1

Group 2

	Au	WG	Ar	Co	Pl	W	D	L	F	A	Pts
AUSTRALIA	–	1–0	1–0	2–1	3	3	0	0	4	1	6
WEST GERMANY	–	–	1–1	4–1	3	1	1	1	5	3	3
ARGENTINA	–	–	–	4–2	3	1	1	1	5	4	3
CONGO	–	–	–	–	3	0	0	3	4	10	0

Group 3

	SA	Ni	It	CR	Pl	W	D	L	F	A	Pts
SAUDI ARABIA	–	0–0	3–1	4–1	3	2	1	0	7	2	5
NIGERIA	–	–	1–0	3–0	3	2	1	0	4	0	5
ITALY	–	–	–	2–0	3	1	0	2	3	4	2
COSTA RICA	–	–	–	–	3	0	0	3	1	9	0

Group 4

	Hu	Br	Me	Qa	Pl	W	D	L	F	A	Pts
HUNGARY	–	1–0	0–0	3–0	3	2	1	0	4	0	5
BRAZIL	–	–	2–0	2–1	3	2	0	1	4	2	4
MEXICO	–	–	–	3–1	3	1	1	1	3	3	3
QATAR	–	–	–	–	3	0	0	3	2	8	0

QUARTER-FINALS

NIGERIA	3–1	HUNGARY
GUINEA	0–0 (4–2p)	AUSTRALIA
BRAZIL	2–1	SAUDI ARABIA
WEST GERMANY	4–2	CHINA

SEMI-FINALS

NIGERIA	1–1 (4–2p)	GUINEA
WEST GERMANY	4–3	BRAZIL

3RD PLACE

BRAZIL	4–1	GUINEA

FINAL

Workers' Stadium, Beijing, 11–08–1985, 80 000

NIGERIA 2 (Akpoborire, Adamu)
WEST GERMANY 0

Second Edition, Canada, 12th–25th July 1987

FIRST ROUND

Group 1

	It	Qa	Eg	Ca	Pl	W	D	L	F	A	Pts
ITALY	–	1–1	1–0	3–0	3	2	1	0	5	1	5
QATAR	–	–	1–0	2–1	3	2	1	0	4	2	5
EGYPT	–	–	–	3–0	3	1	0	2	3	2	2
CANADA	–	–	–	–	3	0	0	3	1	8	0

Group 2

	CI	SK	Ec	US	Pl	W	D	L	F	A	Pts
CÔTE D'IVOIRE	–	1–1	1–0	1–0	3	2	1	0	3	1	5
SOUTH KOREA	–	–	0–1	4–2	3	1	1	1	5	4	3
ECUADOR	–	–	–	0–1	3	1	0	2	1	2	2
UNITED STATES	–	–	–	–	3	1	0	2	3	5	2

Group 3

	Au	Fr	SA	Br	Pl	W	D	L	F	A	Pts
AUSTRALIA	–	1–4	1–0	1–0	3	2	0	1	3	4	4
FRANCE	–	–	0–2	0–0	3	1	1	1	4	3	3
SAUDI ARABIA	–	–	–	0–0	3	1	1	1	2	1	3
BRAZIL	–	–	–	–	3	0	2	1	0	1	2

Group 4

	SU	Ni	Me	Bo	Pl	W	D	L	F	A	Pts
SOVIET UNION	–	1–1	7–0	4–2	3	2	1	0	12	3	5
NIGERIA	–	–	0–1	3–2	3	1	1	1	4	4	3
MEXICO	–	–	–	2–2	3	1	1	1	3	9	3
BOLIVIA	–	–	–	–	3	0	1	2	6	9	1

QUARTER-FINALS

SOVIET UNION	3–2	FRANCE
CÔTE D'IVOIRE	3–0	QATAR
ITALY	2–0	SOUTH KOREA
NIGERIA	1–0	AUSTRALIA

SEMI-FINALS

SOVIET UNION	5–1	CÔTE D'IVOIRE
NIGERIA	1–0	ITALY

3RD PLACE

CÔTE D'IVOIRE	2–1	ITALY

FINAL

Varsity Stadium, Toronto, 25–07–1987, 15 000

SOVIET UNION 1 (Nikiforov)
NIGERIA 1 (Osundu)

Soviet Union won 3–1 on penalties

Third Edition, Scotland, 10th–24th June 1989

FIRST ROUND

Group 1

	Ba	Sc	Gh	Cu	Pl	W	D	L	F	A	Pts
BAHRAIN	–	1–1	1–0	3–0	3	2	1	0	5	1	5
SCOTLAND	–	–	0–0	3–0	3	1	2	0	4	1	4
GHANA	–	–	–	2–2	3	0	2	1	2	3	2
CUBA	–	–	–	–	3	0	1	2	2	8	1

Group 2

	EG	Br	US	Au	Pl	W	D	L	F	A	Pts
EAST GERMANY	–	1–2	5–2	1–0	3	2	0	1	7	4	4
BRAZIL	–	–	0–1	3–1	3	2	0	1	5	3	4
UNITED STATES	–	–	–	2–2	3	1	1	1	5	7	3
AUSTRALIA	–	–	–	–	3	0	1	2	3	6	1

Group 3

	Ni	Ar	Ch	Ca	Pl	W	D	L	F	A	Pts
NIGERIA	–	0–0	3–0	4–0	3	2	1	0	7	0	5
ARGENTINA	–	–	0–0	4–1	3	1	2	0	4	1	4
CHINA	–	–	–	1–0	3	1	1	1	1	3	3
CANADA	–	–	–	–	3	0	0	3	1	9	0

Group 4

	Po	SA	Gu	Co	Pl	W	D	L	F	A	Pts
PORTUGAL	–	2–2	1–1	3–2	3	1	2	0	6	5	4
SAUDI ARABIA	–	–	2–2	1–0	3	1	2	0	5	4	4
GUINEA	–	–	–	1–1	3	0	3	0	4	4	3
COLOMBIA	–	–	–	–	3	0	1	2	3	5	1

QUARTER-FINALS

SAUDI ARABIA .... 0–0 (2–0p) ..... NIGERIA
BAHRAIN .... 0–0 (4–1p) ..... BRAZIL
PORTUGAL .... 2–1 .... ARGENTINA
SCOTLAND .... 1–0 .... EAST GERMANY

SEMI-FINALS

SAUDI ARABIA .... 1–0 .... BAHRAIN
SCOTLAND .... 1–0 .... PORTUGAL

3RD PLACE

PORTUGAL .... 3–0 .... BAHRAIN

FINAL

Hampden Park, Glasgow, 24–06–1989, 51 000

SAUDI ARABIA 2 (Al-Reshoudi, Al-Terair)
SCOTLAND 2 (Downie, Dickov)

Saudi Arabia won 5–4 on penalties

Fourth Edition, Italy, 15th–31st August 1991

FIRST ROUND

Group 1

	US	Ar	It	Ch	Pl	W	D	L	F	A	Pts
UNITED STATES	–	1–0	1–0	3–1	3	3	0	0	5	1	6
ARGENTINA	–	–	0–0	2–1	3	1	1	1	2	2	3
ITALY	–	–	–	2–2	3	0	2	1	2	3	2
CHINA	–	–	–	–	3	0	1	2	4	7	1

Group 2

	Au	Qa	Co	Me	Pl	W	D	L	F	A	Pts
AUSTRALIA	–	0–1	2–0	4–3	3	2	0	1	6	4	4
QATAR	–	–	0–0	0–1	3	1	1	1	1	1	3
CONGO	–	–	–	2–1	3	1	1	1	2	3	3
MEXICO	–	–	–	–	3	1	0	2	5	6	2

Group 3

	Br	Ge	Su	Em	Pl	W	D	L	F	A	Pts
BRAZIL	–	2–0	1–0	4–0	3	3	0	0	7	0	6
GERMANY	–	–	3–1	2–2	3	1	1	1	5	5	3
SUDAN	–	–	–	4–1	3	1	0	2	5	5	2
ARAB EMIRATES	–	–	–	–	3	0	1	2	3	10	1

Group 4

	Sp	Gh	Ur	Cu	Pl	W	D	L	F	A	Pts
SPAIN	–	1–1	1–0	7–2	3	2	1	0	9	3	5
GHANA	–	–	2–0	2–1	3	2	1	0	5	2	5
URUGUAY	–	–	–	1–0	3	1	0	2	1	3	2
CUBA	–	–	–	–	3	0	0	3	3	10	0

QUARTER-FINALS

GHANA .... 2–1 .... BRAZIL
QATAR .... 1–1 (5–4p) ..... UNITED STATES
ARGENTINA .... 2–1 .... AUSTRALIA
SPAIN .... 3–1 .... GERMANY

SEMI-FINALS

GHANA .... 0–0 (4–2p) ..... QATAR
SPAIN .... 1–0 .... ARGENTINA

3RD PLACE

ARGENTINA .... 1–1 (4–1p) ..... QATAR

FINAL

Comunale, Florence, 31–08–1991, 5000

GHANA 1 (Duah)
SPAIN 0

THE FIFA WORLD YOUTH CHAMPIONSHIP FOR UNDER 20'S

1977	Soviet Union	2–2 (9–8p)	Mexico
1979	Argentina	3–1	Soviet Union
1981	West Germany	4–0	Qatar
1983	Brazil	1–0	Argentina
1985	Brazil	1–0	Spain
1987	Yugoslavia	1–1 (5–4p)	West Germany
1989	Portugal	2–0	Nigeria
1991	Portugal	0–0 (4–2p)	Brazil

First Edition, Tunisia, 27th June–10th July 1977

FIRST ROUND

Group 1

	Me	Sp	Fr	Tu	Pl	W	D	L	F	A	Pts
MEXICO	–	1–1	1–1	6–0	3	1	2	0	8	2	4
SPAIN	–	–	2–1	0–1	3	1	1	1	3	3	3
FRANCE	–	–	–	1–0	3	1	1	1	3	3	3
TUNISIA	–	–	–	–	3	1	0	2	1	7	2

WORLD YOUTH MEDALS TABLE

	Country	G	S	B	Finals	Semis
1	Brazil	2	1	2	3	5
2	Portugal	2	–	–	2	2
3	Soviet Union	1	1	1	2	4
4	Argentina	1	1	–	2	2
	West Germany	1	1	–	2	2
6	Yugoslavia	1	–	–	1	1
7	Nigeria	–	1	1	1	2
8	Mexico	–	1	–	1	1
	Qatar	–	1	–	1	1
	Spain	–	1	–	1	1
11	Poland	–	–	1	–	2
	Uruguay	–	–	1	–	2
13	East Germany	–	–	1	–	1
	Romania	–	–	1	–	1
15	Australia	–	–	–	–	1
	Chile	–	–	–	–	1
	England	–	–	–	–	1
	South Korea	–	–	–	–	1
	United States	–	–	–	–	1

Group 2

	Ur	Ho	Hu	Mo	Pl	W	D	L	F	A	Pts
URUGUAY	–	1–0	2–1	3–0	3	3	0	0	6	1	6
HONDURAS	–	–	2–0	1–0	3	2	0	1	3	1	4
HUNGARY	–	–	–	2–0	3	1	0	2	3	4	2
MOROCCO	–	–	–	–	3	0	0	3	0	6	0

Group 3

	Br	Ir	It	Cl	Pl	W	D	L	F	A	Pts
BRAZIL	–	5–1	2–0	1–1	3	2	1	0	8	2	5
IRAN	–	–	0–0	3–0	3	1	1	1	4	5	3
ITALY	–	–	–	1–1	3	0	2	1	1	3	2
CÔTE D'IVOIRE	–	–	–	–	3	0	2	1	2	5	2

Group 4

	SU	Pa	Iq	Au	Pl	W	D	L	F	A	Pts
SOVIET UNION	–	2–1	3–1	0–0	3	2	1	0	5	2	5
PARAGUAY	–	–	4–0	1–0	3	2	0	1	6	2	4
IRAQ	–	–	–	5–1	3	1	0	2	6	8	2
AUSTRIA	–	–	–	–	3	0	1	2	1	6	1

SEMI-FINALS

SOVIET UNION .... 0–0 (4–3p) ..... URUGUAY
MEXICO .... 1–1 (5–3p) ..... BRAZIL

3RD PLACE

BRAZIL .... 4–0 .... URUGUAY

FINAL

Tunis, 10–07–1977, 5000
SOVIET UNION 2 (Bessonov 2)
MEXICO 2 (Garduno, Manzo)
Soviet Union won 9–8 on penalties

Second Edition, Japan, 25th August–7th September 1979

FIRST ROUND

Group 1

	Sp	Al	Me	Ja	Pl	W	D	L	F	A	Pts
SPAIN	–	0–1	2–1	1–0	3	2	0	1	3	2	4
ALGERIA	–	–	1–1	0–0	3	1	2	0	2	1	4
MEXICO	–	–	–	1–1	3	0	2	1	3	4	2
JAPAN	–	–	–	–	3	0	2	1	1	2	2

Group 2

	Ar	Po	Yu	Id	Pl	W	D	L	F	A	Pts
ARGENTINA	–	4–1	1–0	5–0	3	3	0	0	10	1	6
POLAND	–	–	2–0	6–0	3	2	0	1	9	4	4
YUGOSLAVIA	–	–	–	5–0	3	1	0	2	5	3	2
INDONESIA	–	–	–	–	3	0	0	3	0	16	0

Group 3

	Pa	Po	SK	Ca	Pl	W	D	L	F	A	Pts
PARAGUAY	–	0–1	3–0	3–0	3	2	0	1	6	1	4
PORTUGAL	–	–	0–0	1–3	3	1	1	1	2	3	3
SOUTH KOREA	–	–	–	1–0	3	1	1	1	1	3	3
CANADA	–	–	–	–	3	1	0	2	3	5	2

Group 4

	Ur	SU	Hu	Gu	Pl	W	D	L	F	A	Pts
URUGUAY	–	1–0	2–0	5–0	3	3	0	0	8	0	6
SOVIET UNION	–	–	5–1	3–0	3	2	0	1	8	2	4
HUNGARY	–	–	–	2–0	3	1	0	2	3	7	2
GUINEA	–	–	–	–	3	0	0	3	0	10	0

QUARTER-FINALS

ARGENTINA .... 5–0 .... ALGERIA
URUGUAY .... 1–0 .... PORTUGAL
POLAND .... 0–0 (4–3p) ..... SPAIN
SOVIET UNION .... 2–2 (6–5p) ..... PARAGUAY

SEMI-FINALS

ARGENTINA .... 2–0 .... URUGUAY
SOVIET UNION .... 1–0 .... POLAND

3RD PLACE

URUGUAY .... 1–1 (5–3p) ..... POLAND

FINAL

National Stadium, Tokyo, 7–09–1979
ARGENTINA 3 (Alves, Diaz, Maradona)
SOVIET UNION 1 (Ponomarev)

Third Edition, Australia, 3rd–18th October 1981

FIRST ROUND

Group 1

	Ur	Qa	Po	US	Pl	W	D	L	F	A	Pts
URUGUAY	–	1–0	1–0	3–0	3	3	0	0	5	0	6
QATAR	–	–	1–0	1–1	3	1	1	1	2	2	3
POLAND	–	–	–	4–0	3	1	0	2	4	2	2
UNITED STATES	–	–	–	–	3	0	1	2	1	8	1

Group 2

	Br	Ro	SK	It	Pl	W	D	L	F	A	Pts
BRAZIL	–	1–1	3–0	1–0	3	2	1	0	5	1	5
ROMANIA	–	–	1–0	1–0	3	2	1	0	3	1	5
SOUTH KOREA	–	–	–	4–1	3	1	0	2	4	5	2
ITALY	–	–	–	–	3	0	0	3	1	6	0

Group 3

	WG	Eg	Me	Sp	Pl	W	D	L	F	A	Pts
WEST GERMANY	–	1–2	1–0	4–2	3	2	0	1	6	4	4
EGYPT	–	–	3–3	2–2	3	1	2	0	7	6	4

					Pl	W	D	L	F	A	Pts
MEXICO	–	–	–	1–1	3	0	2	1	4	5	2
SPAIN	–	–	–	–	3	0	2	1	5	7	2

Group 4

	En	Au	Ar	Cm	Pl	W	D	L	F	A	Pts
ENGLAND	–	1–1	1–1	2–0	3	1	2	0	4	2	4
AUSTRALIA	–	–	2–1	3–3	3	1	2	0	6	5	4
ARGENTINA	–	–	–	1–0	3	1	1	1	3	3	3
CAMEROON	–	–	–	–	3	0	1	2	3	6	1

QUARTER-FINALS

WEST GERMANY .... 1–0 .... AUSTRALIA
ROMANIA .... 2–1 .... URUGUAY
ENGLAND .... 4–2 .... EGYPT
QATAR .... 3–2 .... BRAZIL

SEMI-FINALS

WEST GERMANY .... 1–0 .... ROMANIA
QATAR .... 2–1 .... ENGLAND

3RD PLACE

ROMANIA .... 1–0 .... ENGLAND

FINAL

Sydney Cricket Ground, Sydney, 18–10–1981, 19 000
WEST GERMANY 4 (Loose 2, Wohlfarth, Anthes)
QATAR 0

Fourth Edition, Mexico, 4th–19th June 1983

FIRST ROUND

Group 1

	Sc	SK	Au	Me	Pl	W	D	L	F	A	Pts
SCOTLAND	–	2–0	1–2	1–0	3	2	0	1	4	2	4
SOUTH KOREA	–	–	2–1	2–1	3	2	0	1	4	4	4
AUSTRALIA	–	–	–	1–1	3	1	1	1	4	4	3
MEXICO	–	–	–	–	3	0	1	2	2	4	1

Group 2

	Ur	Pd	US	CI	Pl	W	D	L	F	A	Pts
URUGUAY	–	3–1	3–2	0–0	3	2	1	0	6	3	5
POLAND	–	–	2–0	7–2	3	2	0	1	10	5	4
UNITED STATES	–	–	–	1–0	3	1	0	2	3	5	2
CÔTE D'IVOIRE	–	–	–	–	3	0	1	2	2	8	1

Group 3

	Ar	Cz	Ch	Au	Pl	W	D	L	F	A	Pts
ARGENTINA	–	2–0	5–0	3–0	3	3	0	0	10	0	6
CZECHOSLOVAKIA	–	–	3–2	4–0	3	2	0	1	7	4	4
CHINA	–	–	–	3–0	3	1	0	2	5	8	2
AUSTRIA	–	–	–	–	3	0	0	3	0	10	0

Group 4

	Br	Ho	Ni	SU	Pl	W	D	L	F	A	Pts
BRAZIL	–	1–1	3–0	2–1	3	2	1	0	6	2	5
HOLLAND	–	–	0–0	3–2	3	1	2	0	4	3	4
NIGERIA	–	–	–	1–0	3	1	1	1	1	3	3
SOVIET UNION	–	–	–	–	3	0	0	3	3	6	0

QUARTER-FINALS

BRAZIL.............................. 4–1 .... CZECHOSLOVAKIA
SOUTH KOREA .... 2–1 .... URUGUAY
POLAND .... 1–0 .... SCOTLAND
ARGENTINA .... 2–1 .... HOLLAND

SEMI-FINALS

BRAZIL.............................. 2–1 .... SOUTH KOREA
ARGENTINA .... 1–0 .... POLAND

3RD PLACE

POLAND .... 2–1 .... SOUTH KOREA

FINAL

Azteca, Mexico City, 19–06–1983, 110 000
BRAZIL 1 (Silva)
ARGENTINA 0

Fifth Edition, Soviet Union, 24th August–7th September 1985

FIRST ROUND

Group 1

	Bu	Co	Hu	Tu	Pl	W	D	L	F	A	Pts
BULGARIA	–	1–1	1–1	2–0	3	1	2	0	4	2	4
COLOMBIA	–	–	2–2	2–1	3	1	2	0	5	4	4
HUNGARY	–	–	–	2–1	3	1	2	0	5	4	4
TUNISIA	–	–	–	–	3	0	0	3	2	6	0

Colombia qualified on lots

Group 2

	Br	Sp	SA	RI	Pl	W	D	L	F	A	Pts
BRAZIL	–	2–0	1–0	2–1	3	3	0	0	5	1	6
SPAIN	–	–	0–0	4–2	3	1	1	1	4	4	3
SAUDI ARABIA	–	–	–	1–0	3	1	1	1	1	1	3
REP. IRELAND	–	–	–	–	3	0	0	3	3	7	0

Group 3

	SU	Ni	Au	Ca	Pl	W	D	L	F	A	Pts
SOVIET UNION	–	2–1	0–0	5–0	3	2	1	0	7	1	5
NIGERIA	–	–	3–2	2–0	3	2	0	1	6	4	4
AUSTRALIA	–	–	–	0–0	3	0	2	1	2	3	2
CANADA	–	–	–	–	3	0	1	2	0	7	1

Group 4

	Me	Ch	Pa	En	Pl	W	D	L	F	A	Pts
MEXICO	–	3–1	2–0	1–0	3	3	0	0	6	1	6
CHINA	–	–	2–1	2–0	3	2	0	1	5	4	4
PARAGUAY	–	–	–	2–2	3	0	1	2	3	6	1
ENGLAND	–	–	–	–	3	0	1	2	2	5	1

QUARTER-FINALS

BRAZIL.............................. 6–0 .... COLOMBIA
NIGERIA .... 2–1 .... MEXICO
SOVIET UNION .... 1–0 .... CHINA
SPAIN .... 2–1 .... BULGARIA

SEMI-FINALS

BRAZIL.............................. 2–0 .... NIGERIA
SPAIN .... 2–2 (4–3p) ..... SOVIET UNION

3RD PLACE

NIGERIA .... 0–0 (3–1p) ..... SOVIET UNION

FINAL

Centralny Lenina, Moscow, 7–09–1985, 45 000

BRAZIL	1	(Henrique)
SPAIN	0	

Sixth Edition, Chile, 10th–25th October 1987

FIRST ROUND

Group 1

	Yu	Ch	Au	To	Pl	W	D	L	F	A	Pts
YUGOSLAVIA	–	4–2	4–0	4–1	3	3	0	0	12	3	6
CHILE	–	–	2–0	3–0	3	2	0	1	7	4	4
AUSTRALIA	–	–	–	2–0	3	1	0	2	2	6	2
TOGO	–	–	–	–	3	0	0	3	1	9	0

Group 2

	It	Br	Ca	Ni	Pl	W	D	L	F	A	Pts
ITALY	–	1–0	2–2	2–0	3	2	1	0	5	2	5
BRAZIL	–	–	1–0	4–0	3	2	0	1	5	1	4
CANADA	–	–	–	2–2	3	0	2	1	4	5	2
NIGERIA	–	–	–	–	3	0	1	2	2	8	1

Group 3

	EG	Sc	Co	Ba	Pl	W	D	L	F	A	Pts
EAST GERMANY	–	1–2	3–1	2–0	3	2	0	1	6	3	4
SCOTLAND	–	–	2–2	1–1	3	1	2	0	5	4	4
COLOMBIA	–	–	–	1–0	3	1	1	1	4	5	3
BAHRAIN	–	–	–	–	3	0	1	2	1	4	1

Group 4

	WG	Bu	US	SA	Pl	W	D	L	F	A	Pts
WEST GERMANY	–	3–0	2–1	3–0	3	3	0	0	8	1	6
BULGARIA	–	–	1–0	2–0	3	2	0	1	3	3	4
UNITED STATES	–	–	–	1–0	3	1	0	2	2	3	2
SAUDI ARABIA	–	–	–	–	3	0	0	3	0	6	0

QUARTER-FINALS

YUGOSLAVIA .... 2–1 .... BRAZIL
EAST GERMANY .... 2–0 .... BULGARIA
CHILE .... 1–0 .... ITALY
WEST GERMANY .... 1–1 (4–3p) ..... SCOTLAND

SEMI-FINALS

YUGOSLAVIA .... 2–1 .... EAST GERMANY
WEST GERMANY .... 4–0 .... CHILE

3RD PLACE

EAST GERMANY ...... 1–1 (3–1p) ..... CHILE

FINAL

Estadio Nacional, Santiago. 25–10–1987, 68 000

YUGOSLAVIA	1	(Boban)
WEST GERMANY	1	(Witeczek)

Yugoslavia won 5–4 on penalties

Seventh Edition, Saudi Arabia, 16th February–3rd March 1989

FIRST ROUND

Group 1

	Po	Ni	Cz	SA	Pl	W	D	L	F	A	Pts
PORTUGAL	–	1–0	1–0	0–3	3	2	0	1	2	3	4
NIGERIA	–	–	1–1	2–1	3	1	1	1	3	3	3
CZECHOSLOVAKIA	–	–	–	1–0	3	1	1	1	2	2	3
SAUDI ARABIA	–	–	–	–	3	1	0	2	4	3	2

Group 2

	SU	Co	Sy	CR	Pl	W	D	L	F	A	Pts
SOVIET UNION	–	3–1	3–1	1–0	3	3	0	0	7	2	6
COLOMBIA	–	–	2–0	0–1	3	1	0	2	3	4	2
SYRIA	–	–	–	3–1	3	1	0	2	4	6	2
COSTA RICA	–	–	–	–	3	1	0	2	2	4	2

Group 3

	Br	US	EG	Ml	Pl	W	D	L	F	A	Pts
BRAZIL	–	3–1	2–0	5–0	3	3	0	0	10	1	6
UNITED STATES	–	–	2–0	1–1	3	1	1	1	4	4	3
EAST GERMANY	–	–	–	3–0	3	1	0	2	3	4	2
MALI	–	–	–	–	3	0	1	2	1	9	1

Group 4

	Iq	Ar	No	Sp	Pl	W	D	L	F	A	Pts
IRAQ	–	1–0	1–0	2–0	3	3	0	0	4	0	6
ARGENTINA	–	–	2–0	1–2	3	1	0	2	3	3	2
NORWAY	–	–	–	4–2	3	1	0	2	4	5	2
SPAIN	–	–	–	–	3	1	0	2	4	7	2

QUARTER-FINALS

PORTUGAL .... 1–0 .... COLOMBIA
BRAZIL .... 1–0 .... ARGENTINA
UNITED STATES .... 2–1 .... IRAQ
NIGERIA .... 4–4 (5–3p) ..... SOVIET UNION

SEMI-FINALS

PORTUGAL .... 1–0 .... BRAZIL
NIGERIA .... 2–1 .... UNITED STATES

3RD PLACE

BRAZIL .... 2–0 .... UNITED STATES

FINAL

King Fahd International Stadium, Riyadh, 3–03–1989, 65 000

PORTUGAL	2	(Abel, Jorge Couto)
NIGERIA	0	

Eighth Edition, Portugal, 14th–30th June 1991

FIRST ROUND

Group 1

	Pt	Ko	RI	Ar	Pl	W	D	L	F	A	Pts
PORTUGAL	–	1–0	2–0	3–0	3	3	0	0	6	0	6
KOREA	–	–	1–1	1–0	3	1	1	1	2	2	3
REP. IRELAND	–	–	–	2–2	3	0	2	1	3	5	2
ARGENTINA	–	–	–	–	3	0	1	2	2	6	1

Group 2

	Br	Me	Sw	CI	Pl	W	D	L	F	A	Pts
BRAZIL	–	2–2	2–0	2–1	3	2	1	0	6	3	5
MEXICO	–	–	3–0	1–1	3	1	2	0	6	3	4
SWEDEN	–	–	–	4–1	3	1	0	2	4	6	2
CÔTE D'IVOIRE	–	–	–	–	3	0	1	2	3	7	1

Group 3

	Au	SU	Eg	Tr	Pl	W	D	L	F	A	Pts
AUSTRALIA	–	1–0	1–0	2–0	3	3	0	0	4	0	6

SOVIET UNION	–	–	1–0	4–0	3	2	0	1	5	1	4
EGYPT	–	–	–	6–0	3	1	0	2	6	2	2
TRINIDAD	–	–	–	–	3	0	0	3	0	12	0

Group 4

	Sp	Sy	En	Ur	Pl	W	D	L	F	A	Pts
SPAIN	–	0–0	1–0	6–0	3	2	1	0	7	0	5
SYRIA	–	–	3–3	1–0	3	1	2	0	4	3	4
ENGLAND	–	–	–	0–0	3	0	2	1	3	4	2
URUGUAY	–	–	–	–	3	0	1	2	0	7	1

QUARTER-FINALS

PORTUGAL .... 2–1 .... MEXICO
AUSTRALIA .... 1–1 (5–4p) ..... SYRIA
SOVIET UNION .... 3–1 .... SPAIN
BRAZIL .... 5–1 .... KOREA

SEMI-FINALS

PORTUGAL .... 1–0 .... AUSTRALIA
BRAZIL .... 3–0 .... SOVIET UNION

3RD PLACE

SOVIET UNION .... 1–1 (5–4p) ..... AUSTRALIA

FINAL

Estádio da Luz, Lisbon, 30–06–1991, 120 000
PORTUGAL 0
BRAZIL 0
Portugal won 4–2 on penalties

COMBINED YOUTH AND UNDER-17 MEDALS TABLE

		G	S	B	Finals	Semis
1	Brazil	2	1	3	3	6
2	Portugal	2	–	1	2	3
3	Soviet Union	2	1	1	3	5
4	Nigeria	1	2	1	3	4
5	West Germany	1	2	–	3	3
6	Argentina	1	1	1	2	3
7	Ghana	1	–	–	1	1
	Saudi Arabia	1	–	–	1	1
	Yugoslavia	1	–	–	1	1
10	Spain	–	2	–	2	2
11	Qatar	–	1	–	1	2
12	Mexico	–	1	–	1	1
	Scotland	–	1	–	1	1
14	Poland	–	–	1	–	2
	Uruguay	–	–	1	–	2
16	Côte d'Ivoire	–	–	1	–	1
	East Germany	–	–	1	–	1
	Romania	–	–	1	–	1
19	Australia	–	–	–	–	1
	Bahrain	–	–	–	–	1
	Chile	–	–	–	–	1
	England	–	–	–	–	1
	Guinea	–	–	–	–	1
	Italy	–	–	–	–	1
	South Korea	–	–	–	–	1
	United States	–	–	–	–	1

THE WORLD CUP FOR WOMEN
First Edition

QUALIFYING TOURNAMENT

EUROPE

The fourth European Championship was used as the qualifying tournament. WEST GERMANY, NORWAY, DENMARK, ITALY and SWEDEN qualified for the finals.

SOUTH AMERICA

	Br	Ch	Ve	Pl	W	D	L	F	A	Pts
BRAZIL	–	6–1	6–0	2	2	0	0	12	1	4
Chile	–	–	1–0	2	1	0	1	2	6	2
Venezuela	–	–	–	2	0	0	2	0	7	0

CENTRAL AND NORTH AMERICA

FIRST ROUND

Group A

	US	Tr	Me	Ma	Pl	W	D	L	F	A	Pts
United States	–	0–0	12–0	12–0	3	2	1	0	24	0	5
Trinidad	–	–	3–1	1–1	3	1	2	0	4	2	4
Mexico	–	–	–	8–1	3	1	0	2	9	16	2
Martinique	–	–	–	–	3	0	1	2	2	21	1

Group B

	Ca	Ha	CR	Ja	Pl	W	D	L	F	A	Pts
Canada	–	2–0	6–0	9–0	3	3	0	0	17	0	6
Haiti	–	–	4–0	1–0	3	2	0	1	5	2	4
Costa Rica	–	–	–	2–1	3	1	0	2	2	11	2
Jamaica	–	–	–	–	3	0	0	3	1	12	0

SEMI-FINALS

United States .... 10–0 .... Haiti
Canada .... 6–0 .... Trinidad

3RD PLACE

Trinidad .... 4–2 .... Haiti

FINAL

UNITED STATES .... 5–0 .... Canada

AFRICA

FIRST ROUND

Nigeria .... 5–1 2–1 .... Ghana
Guinea .... W–O .... Senegal
Zambia .... W–O .... Zimbabwe
Cameroon .... W–O .... Congo

SEMI-FINALS

Nigeria .... 3–0 4–0 .... Guinea
Cameroon .... W–O .... Zambia

FINAL

NIGERIA .... 2–0 4–0 .... Cameroon

ASIA

FIRST ROUND

Group A

	Ch	Ta	Th	SK	Pl	W	D	L	F	A	Pts
China	–	3–0	10–1	10–0	3	3	0	0	23	1	6
Taiwan	–	–	0–0	9–0	3	1	1	1	9	3	3
Thailand	–	–	–	3–0	3	1	1	1	4	10	3
South Korea	–	–	–	–	3	0	0	3	0	22	0

Group B

	Ja	NK	HK	Ma	Si	Pl	W	D	L	F	A	Pts
Japan	–	1–0	4–1	12–0	10–0	4	4	0	0	27	1	8
North Korea	–	–	5–0	12–0	8–0	4	3	0	1	25	1	6
Hong Kong	–	–	–	0–0	2–0	4	1	1	2	3	9	3
Malaysia	–	–	–	–	1–0	4	1	1	2	1	24	3
Singapore	–	–	–	–	–	4	0	0	4	0	21	0

SEMI-FINALS

China .... 1–0 .... North Korea
Japan .... 0–0 (5–4p) ..... Taiwan

3RD PLACE

Taiwan .... 0–0 (5–4p) ..... North Korea

FINAL

China .... 5–0 .... Japan

CHINA, JAPAN and TAIWAN qualified for the finals

OCEANIA

	NZ	Au	PN	Pl	W	D	L	F	A	Pts
NEW ZEALAND		1–0	11–0	4	3	0	1	28	1	6
Australia	1–0	–	12–0	4	3	0	1	21	1	6
Papua New Guinea	0–16	0–8	–	4	0	0	4	0	47	0

Finals, China, 16th–30th November 1991

FIRST ROUND

Group 1 (Guangzhou/Foshan/Punya)

	Ch	No	De	NZ	Pl	W	D	L	F	A	Pts
CHINA	–	4–0	2–2	4–1	3	2	1	0	10	3	5
NORWAY	–	–	2–1	4–0	3	2	0	1	6	5	4
DENMARK	–	–	–	3–0	3	1	1	1	6	4	3
NEW ZEALAND	–	–	–	–	3	0	0	3	1	11	0

Group 2 (Foshan/Punya)

	US	Sd	Br	Ja	Pl	W	D	L	F	A	Pts
UNITED STATES	–	3–2	5–0	3–0	3	3	0	0	11	2	6
SWEDEN	–	–	2–0	8–0	3	2	0	1	12	3	4
BRAZIL	–	–	–	1–0	3	1	0	2	1	7	2
JAPAN	–	–	–	–	3	0	0	3	0	12	0

Group 3 (Jiangmen/Zhongshan)

	Ge	It	Ta	Ng	Pl	W	D	L	F	A	Pts
GERMANY	–	2–0	3–0	4–0	3	3	0	0	9	0	6
ITALY	–	–	5–0	1–0	3	2	0	1	6	2	4
TAIWAN	–	–	–	2–0	3	1	0	2	2	8	2
NIGERIA	–	–	–	–	3	0	0	3	0	7	0

QUARTER-FINALS

UNITED STATES .... 7–0 .... TAIWAN
GERMANY .... 2–1 .... DENMARK
SWEDEN .... 1–0 .... CHINA
NORWAY .... 3–2 .... ITALY

SEMI-FINALS

UNITED STATES .... 5–2 .... GERMANY
NORWAY .... 4–1 .... SWEDEN

3RD PLACE

SWEDEN .... 4–0 .... GERMANY

FINAL

Tianhe Stadium, Guangzhou, 30–11–1991, 65 000
UNITED STATES 2 (Akers-Stahl 20 77)
NORWAY 1 (Medalen 28)
Referee: Zhuk, Soviet Union
United States – Harvey, Heinrichs, Higgins, Werden, Hamilton, Hamm, Akers-Stahl, Foudy, Jennings, Lilly, Biefeld
Norway – Seth, Zaborowski, Espeseth, Nyborg, Carleen, Haugen, Stoere, Riise, Medalen, Hedstad, Svensson

OTHER WORLD TOURNAMENTS

COPA INDEPENDENCIA DO BRAZIL

11th June–9th July 1972

The South Americans love to celebrate an anniversary. Argentina celebrated the centenary of her independence in 1916 with the first properly recognised South American Championship. In 1930 Uruguay went one better by staging the first World Cup. Since 1972 did not present any such opportunities for the Brazilians to celebrate 150 years of independence, they simply organised their own one-off tournament. The fact that they were the newly-crowned world champions meant that the event would be taken seriously.

All ten South American nations were invited to take part, and all agreed. The organisers had more trouble with regard to the European invitations. The problem lay in the fact that the final stages of the 1972 European Championships were due to take place during May and June. This ruled out all the big European powers. West Germany, England, Italy and Spain all declined the invitations sent out, leaving the European contingent looking somewhat depleted.

To give the event a worldwide flavour, representative teams from Africa, Asia and CONCACAF were invited. The Asian Football Confederation decided that the winners of its continental championship would represent Asia and in the event this turned out to be Iran. Both Africa and CONCACAF chose representative XIs.

The organisation of the competition was rather curious.

Five sides were given byes into the second round, whilst the 15 remaining sides were divided into three groups of five, the winners of which qualified to join the five given byes. An excellent aspect of the competition was the country-wide allocation of fixtures. Manaus, Natal, Macejo, Aracaju, Campo Grande and Salvador all witnessed international football for the first time and many of them had new stadia to celebrate the fact.

All three first round had close finishes. Argentina drew with France in their last game but qualified on goal difference, whilst Portugal's victory over the Republic of Ireland in the last game in Group 2 ensured their qualification. Having reached the quarter-finals of the World Cup two years previously, Peru were hot favourites in Group 3, but they lost to Paraguay who in turn lost to Yugoslavia, who qualified.

The second round consisted of two groups of four, the winners of which qualified for the final. The tournament moved away from the first round centres to the more established footballing cities of Rio, Sao Paulo, Belo Horizonte and Porto Alegre. Over two weeks after the tournament had started, Brazil made their entrance with a 0–0 draw against Czechoslovakia in the Maracana. They had little trouble in reaching the final. Scotland could have made it instead had they beaten the Brazilians in the last game, but they lost 1–0 and did not even make the 3rd place match.

Portugal made it an all-Portuguese speaking final when they won Group 2. That the final should be between Brazil and Portugal was ironic in that the tournament was to celebrate 150 years of Brazilian independence from . . . Portugal; and as if to prove a point the Brazilians won the match through a goal by Jairzinho.

Brazil, without Pele, were playing only their fourth match compared to Portugal who were playing in their eighth game of the tournament. There was nothing Portugal, with Eusebio still at the helm, could do to stop the Brazilians as they reinforced their position as the world's best team.

In retrospect, the final can be seen as a final hurrah for two great teams who were to see a dramatic decline in their fortunes in the ensuing years. Portugal failed to qualify for a major tournament for 12 years, whilst two years later in West Germany the Brazilians saw their world crown slip away to mark the end of a golden era.

FIRST ROUND

Group 1 (Aracaju, Salvador, Macejo)

	Ar	Fr	Af	Co	CN	Pl	W	D	L	F	A	Pts
ARGENTINA	–	0–0	2–0	4–1	7–0	4	3	1	0	13	1	7
France	–	–	2–0	3–2	5–0	4	3	1	0	10	2	7
African XI	–	–	–	3–0	0–0	4	1	1	2	3	4	3
Colombia	–	–	–	–	4–3	4	1	0	3	7	13	2
CONMEBOL XI	–	–	–	–	–	4	0	1	3	3	16	1

Group 2 (Natal, Recife)

	Pt	RI	Ch	Ec	Ir	Pl	W	D	L	F	A	Pts
PORTUGAL	–	2–1	4–1	3–0	3–0	4	4	0	0	12	2	8
Rep. Ireland	–	–	2–1	3–2	2–1	4	3	0	1	8	6	6
Chile	–	–	–	2–1	2–1	4	2	0	2	6	8	4
Ecuador	–	–	–	–	1–1	4	0	1	3	4	9	1
Iran	–	–	–	–	–	4	0	1	3	3	8	1

Group 3 (Curitiba, Campo Grande, Manaus)

	Yu	Pa	Pe	Bo	Ve	Pl	W	D	L	F	A	Pts
YUGOSLAVIA	–	2–1	2–1	1–1	10–0	4	3	1	0	15	3	7
Paraguay	–	–	1–0	6–1	4–1	4	3	0	1	12	4	6
Peru	–	–	–	3–0	1–0	4	2	0	2	5	3	4
Bolivia	–	–	–	–	2–2	4	0	2	2	4	12	2
Venezuela	–	–	–	–	–	4	0	1	3	3	17	1

SECOND ROUND

Group 1 (Rio de Janeiro, Sao Paulo, Belo Horizonte, Porto Alegre)

	Br	Yu	Sc	Cz	Pl	W	D	L	F	A	Pts
BRAZIL	–	3–0	1–0	0–0	3	2	1	0	4	0	5
Yugoslavia	–	–	2–2	2–1	3	1	1	1	4	4	3
Scotland	–	–	–	0–0	3	0	2	1	2	3	2
Czechoslovakia	–	–	–	–	3	0	2	1	1	2	2

Group 2 (Rio de Janeiro, Sao Paulo, Belo Horizonte, Porto Alegre)

	Pt	Ar	SU	Ur	Pl	W	D	L	F	A	Pts
PORTUGAL	–	3–1	1–0	1–1	3	2	1	0	5	2	5
Argentina	–	–	1–0	1–0	3	2	0	1	3	3	4
Soviet Union	–	–	–	1–0	3	1	0	2	1	2	2
Uruguay	–	–	–	–	3	0	1	2	1	3	1

3RD PLACE

Yugoslavia .... 4–2 .... Argentina

FINAL

Maracana, Rio de Janeiro, 9–07–1972

BRAZIL 1 (Jairzinho)

PORTUGAL 0

Brazil – Leao – Zé Maria, Brito, Vantuir, Marco Antonio (Rodrigues Neto) – Clodoaldo, Gerson – Jairzinho, Leivinha (Dario-Dada), Tostao, Rivelino

Portugal – Marques – Correia, Humberto Coelho, Timula, Calisto – Toni, Jaime Graça – Peres, Jordao (Jorge), Eusebio, Dinis

COPA DE ORO

Montevideo, 30th December 1980–10th January 1981

The Uruguayan Football Association could not let the 50th anniversary of the first World Cup pass without celebrating the occasion and so they organised a tournament involving all the previous winners. All took part with the exception of the English, who declined the invitation on the grounds of an overcrowded domestic fixture list. Holland, losing finalists in the two previous World Cups, replaced them.

The six teams were split into two groups and from these Uruguay and Brazil emerged to contest the final in the Centenario Stadium, where all the games were played. Home advantage paid off for the Uruguayans as a 2–1 victory saw them win the 'Mundialito' – little World Cup – as the tournament was also known.

FIRST ROUND

Group A

	Ur	It	Ho	Pl	W	D	L	F	A	Pts
Uruguay	–	2–0	2–0	2	2	0	0	4	0	4
Italy	–	–	1–1	2	0	1	1	1	3	1
Holland	–	–	–	2	0	1	1	1	3	1

Group B

	Br	Ar	WG	Pl	W	D	L	F	A	Pts
Brazil	–	1–1	4–1	2	1	1	0	5	2	3
Argentina	–	–	2–1	2	1	1	0	3	2	3
West Germany	–	–	–	2	0	0	2	2	6	0

FINAL

Centenario, 10–01–1981, 70 000

URUGUAY	2	(Barrios, Victorino)
BRAZIL	1	(Socrates)

WORLD CLUB CHAMPIONSHIP

The World Club Championship is actually nothing of the sort as it involves only the winners of the European Champion Clubs' Cup and the Copa Libertadores. None of the African, Asian or CONCACAF champion teams are involved. Until this happens the title will remain a misnomer, despite the fact that in the event of a tournament involving all of the continents, a European or South American winner would be the most likely outcome.

A letter from Henri Delaunay, the general secretary of UEFA, to CONMEBOL suggesting a meeting between the winners of both the European Cup and any South American tournament they might organise was the spur needed to get the Copa Libertadores off the ground.

At first the idea of an annual challenge match seemed a good one, but after a promising start the event became embroiled in controversy, and has only settled down as a worthwhile event since the fixture was moved to neutral Tokyo in 1980. Until that point games had been played on a home and away basis and more often than not resembled a battleground.

The tournament has gone through three distinct phases coinciding with the three decades of its existence. Real Madrid were unfortunately coming to the end of their supremacy when the tournament started but they appeared in the first edition and in a pulsating match in Madrid thrashed Peñarol 5–1. The following year Peñarol recovered their self-respect with a 5–0 victory over Benfica in the Centenario and a 2–1 win in the play-off two days later. Santos were responsible for another five-goal extravaganza against Benfica the following year, but the honeymoon was nearly over.

The 1963 Milan–Santos series was marred by several incidents and it became increasingly common for the intense rivalries between the two continents to spill over into violence on the field. There was no better example than in the 1967 and 1968 series, which involved Argentine and British clubs, and in 1969 when Milan played Estudiantes.

Feelings were running high in Argentina over their quarter-final exit in the 1966 World Cup against England, and in the play-off between Racing Club and Celtic a fight on the pitch led to five players being sent off after Basile had spat at Lennox. Manchester United and Estudiantes played a bad-tempered series the following year after which Stanley Rous, the president of FIFA, was moved to write a letter of complaint to the management of Estudiantes.

The whole justification of the tournament came into question the following year as Estudiantes embarked on a hostile campaign against the players of Milan, the net result of which was that three of their players landed up in jail for their behaviour in the second leg. Estudiantes were simply not concerned with playing football and their attitude ultimately led to the European sides giving the tournament the cold shoulder.

Throughout the 1970s the World Club Championship turned into a non-event as one after another of the European Cup winners decided they could not be bothered to play in the matches. Ajax, Bayern Munich and Liverpool on two occasions each refused to take part whilst Nottingham Forest in 1979 made it seven editions that had not contained the top European side.

Had it not been for the intervention in 1980 of the Japanese, who offered to stage the event, and Toyota, who offered to sponsor it, the World Club Championship would have almost certainly been assigned to the scrap heap. Instead it has become a stable, annual event that has been contested over a single leg in the National Stadium in Tokyo, and on each occasion since has seen the European Cup and Copa Libertadores winners take part.

Some of the games have even been entertaining, a feature not really in evidence since the first three series. South America has a better overall record, despite a succession of European wins in the late 1980s and the fact that it is not uncommon to see a South American playing for a European side but not the other way around.

The World Club Championship looks set to stay. FIFA, who at the moment are not involved with the event, may wish to see it expanded to include Africa, Asia and Central America, at which point they would give it offical sanction, but that does not seem to be on the cards just yet.

WORLD CLUB CHAMPIONSHIP MEDALS TABLE

	Team	Country	G	S
1	Peñarol	URU	3	2
2	Milan	ITA	3	1
3	Nacional Montevideo	URU	3	–
4	Independiente	ARG	2	4
5	Internazionale	ITA	2	–
	Santos	BRA	2	–
7	Estudiantes LP	ARG	1	2
8	Real Madrid	ESP	1	1
	Juventus	ITA	1	1
	Olimpia	PAR	1	1
11	Ajax	HOL	1	–
	Atlético Madrid	ESP	1	–
	Bayern München	FRG	1	–
	Boca Juniors	ARG	1	–
	Crvena Zvezda Beograd	YUG	1	–
	Feyenoord	HOL	1	–
	Flamengo	BRA	1	–
	Gremio	BRA	1	–
	FC Porto	POR	1	–
	Racing Club	ARG	1	–
	River Plate	ARG	1	–
22	Benfica	POR	–	2
	Liverpool	ENG	–	2
24	Argentinos Juniors	ARG	–	1
	Aston Villa	ENG	–	1
	Bor. Mönchengladbach	FRG	–	1
	Glasgow Celtic	SCO	–	1
	Colo Colo	CHI	–	1
	Cruzeiro	BRA	–	1
	Manchester United	ENG	–	1
	At. Nacional Medellin	COL	–	1
	Malmö FF	SWE	–	1
	Nottingham Forest	ENG	–	1
	Panathinaikos	GRE	–	1
	PSV Eindhoven	HOL	–	1
	Steaua Bucuresti	RUM	–	1
	Hamburger SV	FRG	–	1

1960	Real Madrid	0–0 5–1	Peñarol
1961	Peñarol	0–1 5–0 2–1	Benfica
1962	Santos	3–2 5–2	Benfica
1963	Santos	2–4 4–2 1–0	Milan
1964	Internazionale	0–1 2–0 1–0	Independiente
1965	Internazionale	3–0 0–0	Independiente
1966	Peñarol	2–0 2–0	Real Madrid
1967	Racing Club	0–1 2–1 1–0	Glasgow Celtic
1968	Estudiantes LP	1–0 1–1	Manchester United
1969	Milan	3–0 1–2	Estudiantes LP
1970	Feyenoord	2–2 1–0	Estudiantes LP
1971	Nacional Montevideo	1–1 2–1	Panathinaikos
1972	Ajax	1–1 3–0	Independiente
1973	Independiente	1–0	Juventus
1974	Atlético Madrid	0–1 2–0	Independiente
1975	–		
1976	Bayern München	2–0 0–0	Cruzeiro
1977	Boca Juniors	2–2 3–0	B. Mönchengladbach
1978	–		
1979	Olimpia	1–0 2–1	Malmö FF
1980	Nacional Montevideo	1–0	Nottingham Forest
1981	Flamengo	3–0	Liverpool
1982	Peñarol	2–0	Aston Villa
1983	Gremio	2–1	Hamburger SV
1984	Independiente	1–0	Liverpool
1985	Juventus	2–2 (4–2p)	Argentinos Juniors
1986	River Plate	1–0	Steaua Bucuresti
1987	FC Porto	2–1	Peñarol
1988	Nacional Montevideo	2–2 (7–6p)	PSV Eindhoven
1989	Milan	1–0	At. Nacional Medellin
1990	Milan	3–0	Olimpia
1991	Crvena Zvezda Beograd	3–0	Colo Colo

1960 *1st leg. Centenario, Montevideo, 3–07–1960, 75 000*
PENAROL 0
REAL MADRID 0
Referee: Praddaude, Argentina
Peñarol – Maidana – Martinez, Aguerre, Pino – Salvador, Goncalves – Cubilla, Linazza, Hohberg, Spencer, Borges
Real Madrid – Dominguez – Marquitos, Santamaria, Pachín – Vidal, Zarraga – Canario, Del Sol, Di Stefano, Puskás, Bueno

2nd leg. Bernabeu, Madrid, 4–09–1960, 125 000
REAL MADRID 5 (Puskás 3 9, Di Stefano 4, Herrera 44, Gento 54)
PENAROL 1 (Borges 69)
Referee: Aston, England
Real Madrid – Dominguez – Marquitos, Santamaria, Pachín – Vidal, Zarraga – Herrera, Del Sol, Di Stefano, Puskás, Gento. Tr: Munoz
Peñarol – Maidana – Pino, Mayewski, Martinez – Aguerre, Salvador – Cubilla, Linazza, Hohberg, Spencer, Borges. Tr: Scarone

1961 *1st leg. Estádio da Luz, Lisbon, 4–09–1961, 50 000*
BENFICA 1 (Coluna 60)
PENAROL 0
Referee: Ebert, Switzerland
Benfica – Costa Pereira – Angelo, Saraiva, Joao – Neto, Cruz – Augusto, Santana, Aguas, Coluna, Cavem
Peñarol – Maidana – Gonzales, Martinez, Aguerre, Cano – Goncalvez, Ledesma – Spencer, Cubilla, Cabrera, Sasia

2nd leg. Centenario, Montevideo, 17–09–1961, 56 000
PENAROL 5 (Sasia 10, Joya 18 28, Spencer 42 60)
BENFICA 0
Referee: Nalfoino, Argentina
Peñarol – Maidana – Gonzales, Martinez, Cano, Aguerre – Goncalvez, Ledesma – Cubilla, Sasia, Spencer, Joya
Benfica – Costa Pereira – Angelo, Saraiva, Joao – Neto, Cruz – Augusto, Santana, Mendes, Coluna, Cavem

Play-off. Centenario, Montevideo, 19–09–1961, 62 000
PENAROL 2 (Sasia 6 41)
BENFICA 1 (Eusebio 35)
Referee: Praddaude, Argentina
Peñarol – Maidana – Gonzales, Martinez, Aguerre, Cano – Goncalvez, Cabrera – Cubilla, Ledesma, Sasia, Spencer. Tr:
Benfica – Costa Pereira – Angelo, Humberto, Cruz – Neto, Coluna – Augusto, Eusebio, Aguas, Cavem, Simoes. Tr: Guttmann

1962 *1st leg. Maracana, Rio de Janeiro, 19–09–1962, 90 000*
SANTOS 3 (Pele 31 86, Coutinho 64)
BENFICA 2 (Santana 58 87)
Referee: Ramirez, Paraguay
Santos – Gilmar – Lima, Mauro, Calvet, Dalmo – Zito, Mengalvio – Dorval, Coutinho, Pele, Pepe
Benfica – Costa Pereira – Jacinto, Raul, Humberto, Cruz – Cavem, Coluna – Augusto, Santana, Eusebio, Simoes

2nd leg. Estádio da Luz, Lisbon, 11–10–1962, 75 000
BENFICA 2 (Eusebio 87, Santana 89)
SANTOS 5 (Pele 17 28 64, Coutinho 49, Pepe 77)
Referee: Scwinte, France
Benfica – Costa Pereira – Jacinto, Raul, Humberto, Cruz – Cavem, Coluna – Augusto, Santana, Eusebio, Simoes. Tr: Reira
Santos – Gilmar – Olavo, Mauro, Calvet, Dalmo – Lima, Zito – Dorval, Coutinho, Pele, Pepe. Tr: Lula

WORLD CLUB MEDALS BY COUNTRY

	Country	G	S		Country	G	S
1	Argentina	6	7	12	Chile	–	1
2	Italy	6	2		Colombia	–	1
	Uruguay	6	2		Greece	–	1
4	Brazil	4	1		Rumania	–	1
5	Holland	2	1		Scotland	–	1
	Spain	2	1		Sweden	–	1
7	Portugal	1	2				
	West Germany	1	2		Continent	G	S
9	Paraguay	1	1				
10	Yugoslavia	1	–	1	South America	17	13
11	England	–	5	2	Europe	13	17

1963 *1st leg. San Siro, Milan, 16–10–1963, 80 000*
MILAN 4 (Trapattoni 4, Amarildo 15 65, Mora 80)
SANTOS 2 (Pele 59 87)
Referee: Haberfellner, Austria
Milan – Ghezzi – David, Maldini, Trapattoni, Trebbi – Pelagalli, Lodetti, Rivera – Mora, Altafini, Amarildo
Santos – Gilmar – Lima, Haroldo, Calvet, Geraldino – Zito, Mengalvio – Dorval, Coutinho, Pele, Pepe
2nd leg. Maracana, Rio de Janeiro, 14–11–1963, 150 000
SANTOS 4 (Pepe 50 67, Almir 60, Lima 63)
MILAN 2 (Altafini 12, Mora 17)
Referee: Brozzi, Argentina
Santos – Gilmar – Ismael, Dalmo, Mauro, Haroldo – Lima, Mengalvio – Dorval, Coutinho, Pele, Pepe
Milan – Ghezzi – David, Maldini, Trapattoni, Trebbi – Pelagalli, Lodetti, Rivera – Mora, Altafini, Amarildo
Play-off. Maracana, Rio de Janeiro, 16–11–1963, 121 000
SANTOS 1 (Dalmo 26)
MILAN 0
Referee: Brozzi, Argentina
Santos – Gilmar – Ismael, Dalmo, Mauro, Haroldo – Lima, Mengalvio – Dorval, Coutinho, Almir, Pepe. Tr: Lula
Milan – Balzarini (Barluzzi) – Pelagalli, Maldini, Trebbi, Benitez – Lodetti, Trapattoni – Mora, Altafini, Amarildo, Fortunato. Tr: Carniglia

1964 *1st leg. Cordero, Avellaneda, 9–09–1964, 70 000*
INDEPENDIENTE 1 (Rodriguez 60)
INTERNAZIONALE 0
Referee: Marques, Brazil
Independiente – Santoro – Ferreiro, Guzman, Maldonado, Rolan – Acevedo, Mura – Bernao, Prospitti, Rodriguez, Savoy.
Internazionale – Sarti – Burgnich, Guarneri, Picchi, Facchetti – Tagnin, Suárez, Corso – Jair, Mazzola, Peiro
2nd leg. San Siro, Milan, 23–09–1964, 70 000
INTERNAZIONALE 2 (Mazzola 8, Corso 39)
INDEPENDIENTE 0
Referee: Gere, Hungary
Internazionale – Sarti – Burgnich, Guarneri, Picchi, Facchetti – Malatrasi, Suárez, Corso – Jair, Mazzola, Milani
Independiente – Santoro – Ferreiro, Paflik, Maldonado, Decaria – Acevedo, Prospitti, Suarez – Mura, Rodriguez, Savoy
Play-off. Bernabeu, Madrid, 26–09–1964, 45 000
INTERNAZIONALE 1 (Corso 120)
INDEPENDIENTE 0
Referee: De Mendibil, Spain
Internazionale – Sarti – Malatrasi, Guarneri, Picchi, Facchetti – Tagnin, Suárez, Corso – Domenghini, Peiro, Milani. Tr: Herrera
Independiente – Santoro – Guzman, Paflik, Decaria, Maldonado – Acevedo, Prospitti, Suarez – Bernao, Rodriguez, Savoy. Tr: Guidice

1965 *1st leg. San Siro, Milan, 8–09–1965, 70 000*
INTERNAZIONALE 3 (Peiro 3, Mazzola 23 61)
INDEPENDIENTE 0
Referee: Kreitlein, West Germany
Internazionale – Sarti – Burgnich, Guarneri, Picchi, Facchetti – Bedin, Suárez, Corso – Jair, Mazzola, Peiro
Independiente – Santoro – Pavoni, Guzman, Navarro, Ferreiro – Acevedo, De La Mata, Avalay – Bernao, Rodriguez, Savoy.

2nd leg. Cordero, Avellaneda, 15–09–1965, 70 000
INDEPENDIENTE 0
INTERNAZIONALE 0
Referee: Yamasaki, Peru
Independiente – Santoro – Navarro, Pavoni, Guzman, Ferreiro – Rolan, Mori – Bernao, Mura, Avalay, Savoy. Tr: Guidice
Internazionale – Sarti, Burgnich, Guarneri, Picchi, Facchetti – Bedin, Suárez, Corso – Jair, Mazzola, Peiro. Tr: Herrera

1966 *1st leg. Centenario, Montevideo, 12–10–1966, 70 000*
PENAROL 2 (Spencer 39 82)
REAL MADRID 0
Referee: Vicuña, Chile
Peñarol – Mazurkiewicz – Forlan, Lezcano, Varela, Gonzales – Goncalvez, Cortes, Rocha – Abbadie, Spencer, Joya
Real Madrid – Betancort – Pachín, De Felipe, Zoco, Sanchís – Ruiz, Pirri, Velasquez – Serena, Amancio, Bueno

2nd leg. Bernabeu, Madrid, 26–10–1966, 70 000
REAL MADRID 0
PENAROL 2 (Rocha 28, Spencer 37)
Referee: Lo Bello, Italy
Real Madrid – Betancort – Calpe, De Felipe, Zoco, Sanchís – Pirri, Grosso, Velasquez – Serena, Amancio, Gento. Tr: Munoz
Peñarol – Mazurkiewicz – Gonzales, Lezcano, Varela, Caetano – Rocha, Goncalvez, Cortes – Abbadie, Spencer, Joya. Tr: Maspoli

1967 *1st leg. Hampden Park, Glasgow, 18–10–1967, 103 000*
CELTIC 1 (McNeill 67)
RACING CLUB 0
Referee: Gardeazabal, Spain
Celtic – Simpson – Craig, McNeill, Gemmell – Murdoch, Clark – Johnstone, Lennox, Wallace, Auld, Hughes
Racing Club – Cejas – Martin, Perfumo, Basile, Diaz – Rulli, Mori, Maschio – Cardenas, Rodriguez, Raffo

2nd leg. Mozart y Cuyo, Avellaneda, 1–11–1967, 80 000
RACING CLUB 2 (Raffo 32, Cardenas 48)
CELTIC 1 (Gemmell 20)
Referee: Esteban, Spain
Racing Club – Cejas – Perfumo, Chabay, Basile, Martin – Rulli, Maschio – Raffo, Cardoso, Cardenas, Rodriguez
Celtic – Fallon – Craig, Clark, McNeill, Gemmell – Murdoch, O'Neill – Johnstone, Wallace, Chalmers, Lennox

Play-off. Centenario, Montevideo, 4–11–1967, 65 000
RACING CLUB 1 (Cardenas 55)
CELTIC 0
Referee: Osorio, Paraguay
Racing Club – Cejas – Perfumo, Chabay, Martin, Basile – Rulli, Maschio – Raffo, Cardoso, Cardenas, Rodriguez. Tr: Pizzuti
Celtic – Fallon – Craig, Clark, McNeill, Gemmell – Murdoch, Auld – Johnstone, Lennox, Wallace, Hughes. Tr: Stein

1968 *1st leg. Bonbonera, Buenos Aires, 25–09–1968, 65 000*
ESTUDIANTES LP 1 (Conigliaro 28)
MANCHESTER UNITED 0
Referee: Miranda, Paraguay
Estudiantes – Poletti – Malbernat, Aguirre-Suarez, Medina, Pachame – Madero, Ribaudo, Bilardo – Togneri, Conigliaro, Veron

Manchester United – Stepney – Dunne, Sadler, Foulkes, Burns – Stiles, Crerand, Charlton – Morgan, Law, Best.

2nd leg. Old Trafford, Manchester, 16–10–1968, 60 000
MANCHESTER UNITED 1 (Morgan 8)
ESTUDIANTES LP 1 (Veron 5)
Referee: Machin, France
Manchester United – Stepney – Dunne, Foulkes, Brennan, Sadler – Crerand, Charlton – Morgan, Kidd, Law (Sartori), Best. Tr: Busby
Estudiantes – Poletti – Malbernat, Aguirre-Suarez, Medina, Bilardo – Pachame, Madero – Togneri, Ribaudo, Conigliaro, Veron (Echecopar). Tr: Zubeldia

1969 *1st leg. San Siro, Milan, 8–10–1969, 80 000*
MILAN 3 (Sormani 8 73, Combin 44)
ESTUDIANTES LP 0
Referee: Machin, France
Milan – Cudicini – Malatrasi, Anquilletti, Rosato, Schnellinger – Lodetti, Rivera, Fogli – Sormani, Combin (Rognoni), Prati
Estudiantes – Poletti – Aguirre-Suarez, Manera, Madero, Malbernat – Bilardo, Togneri, Echecopar (Ribaudo) – Flores, Conigliaro, Veron

2nd leg. Bonbonera, Buenos Aires, 22–10–1969, 65 000
ESTUDIANTES LP 2 (Conigliaro 43, Aguirre-Suarez 44)
MILAN 1 (Rivera 30)
Referee: Massaro, Chile
Estudiantes – Poletti – Manera, Aguirre-Suarez, Madero, Malbernat – Bilardo (Echecopar), Romero, Togneri – Conigliaro, Taverna, Veron. Tr: Zubeldia
Milan – Cudicini – Malatrasi (Maldera), Anquilletti, Rosato, Schnellinger – Foglio, Lodetti, Rivera – Sormani, Combin, Prati (Rognoni). Tr: Rocco

1970 *1st leg. Bonbonera, Buenos Aires, 26–08–1970, 65 000*
ESTUDIANTES LP 2 (Echecopar 6, Veron 10)
FEYENOORD 2 (Kindvall 21, Van Hanegem 65)
Referee: Glöckner, East Germany
Estudiantes – Errea – Pagnanini, Spadaro, Togneri, Malbernat – Bilardo (Solari), Pachame, Echecopar (Rudzki) – Conigliaro, Flores, Veron
Feyenoord – Treytel – Romeyn, Israel, Laseroms, Van Duivenbode – Hasil, Jansen, Van Henegem (Boskamp) – Wery, Kindvall, Moulijn

2nd leg. Feyenoord Stadion, Rotterdam, 9–09–1970, 70 000
FEYENOORD 1 (Van Deale 65)
ESTUDIANTES LP 0
Referee: Tejada, Peru
Feyenoord – Treytel – Romeyn, Israel, Laseroms, Van Duivenbode – Hasil (Boskamp), Van Henegem, Jansen – Wery, Kindvall, Moulijn (Van Deale). Tr: Happel
Estudiantes – Pezzano – Malbernat, Spadaro, Togneri, Medina (Pagnanini) – Bilardo, Pachame, Romero – Conigliaro (Rudzki), Flores, Veron. Tr: Zubeldia

1971 European champions Ajax declined to play Nacional. Their place was taken by the European Cup finalists, Panathinaikos.

1st leg. Athens, 15–12–1971, 60 000
PANATHINAIKOS 1 (Filakouris 48)
NACIONAL MONTEVIDEO 1 (Artime 50)

2nd leg. Centenario, Montevideo, 29–12–1971, 70 000
NACIONAL MONTEVIDEO 2 (Artime 34 75)
PANATHINAIKOS 1 (Filakouris 89)

1972 *1st leg. Mozart y Cuyo, Avellaneda, 6–09–1972, 65 000*
INDEPENDIENTE 1 (Sa 82)
AJAX 1 (Cruyff 6)
Referee: Bakhramov, Soviet Union
Independiente – Santoro – Commisso, Lopez, Sa, Pavoni – Pastoriza, Semenewicz, Raimondo (Bulla) – Balbuena, Maglioni, Mircoli
Ajax – Stuy – Suurbier, Hulshoff, Blankenburg, Krol – Haan, Neeskens, Muhren G – Swart, Cruyff (Muhren A), Keizer

2nd leg. Olympisch Stadion, Amsterdam, 28–09–1972, 60 000
AJAX 3 (Neeskens 12, Rep 16 78)
INDEPENDIENTE 0
Referee: Romey, Paraguay
Ajax – Stuy – Suurbier, Hulshoff, Blankenburg, Krol – Haan, Neeskens, Muhren G – Swart (Rep), Cruyff, Keizer. Tr: Kovacs
Independiente – Santoro – Commisso, Sa, Lopez, Pavoni – Pastoriza, Garisto (Magan), Semenewicz – Balbuena, Maglioni, Mircoli (Bulla).

1973 European champions Ajax declined to play Independiente. Their place was taken by the European Cup finalists, Juventus.

Stadio Olimpico, Rome, 28–11–1973, 35 000
INDEPENDIENTE 1 (Bochini 40)
JUVENTUS 0

1974 European champions Bayern Munich declined to play Independiente. Their place was taken by the European Cup finalists, Atletico Madrid.

1st leg. Mozart y Cuyo, Buenos Aires, 12–03–1975, 60 000
INDEPENDIENTE 1 (Balbuena 33)
ATLETICO MADRID 0

2nd leg. Vicente Calderón, Madrid, 10–04–1975, 45 000
ATLETICO MADRID 2 (Irureta 21, Ayala 86)
INDEPENDIENTE 0

1975 No dates could be agreed between Independiente and Bayern Munich, so no games took place.

1976 *1st leg. Olympiastadion, Munich, 23–11–1976, 22 000*
BAYERN MUNCHEN 2 (Müller 80, Kapellmann 83)
CRUZEIRO 0
Referee: Pestarino, Argentina
Bayern München – Maier – Andersson, Beckenbauer, Schwarzenbeck, Horsmann – Durnberger, Kapellmann – Torstensson, Hoeness, Müller, Rummenigge
Cruzeiro – Raul – Nelinho, Moraes, Osiris, Vanderlay – Ze Carlos, Piazza, Eduardo – Jairzinho, Palinha, Joaozinho

2nd leg. Magalhaes Pinto-Mineirao, Belo Horizonte, 21–12–1976, 114 000
CRUZEIRO 0
BAYERN MUNCHEN 0
Referee: Partridge, England
Cruzeiro – Raul – Moraes, Osiris, Piazza (Eduardo), Nelinho – Vanderlay, Dirceu (Forlan) Ze Carlos – Jairzinho, Palinha, Joaozinho.
Bayern München – Maier – Andersson, Beckenbauer, Schwarzenbeck, Horsmann – Weiss, Hoeness, Kapellmann – Torstensson, Müller, Rummenigge. Tr: Lattek

1977 European champions Liverpool declined to play Boca Juniors. Their place was taken by the European Cup finalists, Borussia Monchengladbach.

1st leg. Bonbonera, Buenos Aires, 22–03–1978, 50 000
BOCA JUNIORS 2 (Mastrangelo 16, Ribolzi 51)
BOR. MONCHENGLADBACH 2 (Hannes 24, Bonhof 29)

2nd leg. Wildpark Stadion, Karlsruhe, 26–07–1978, 21 000

BOR. MONCHENGLADBACH 0
BOCA JUNIORS 3 (Zanabria 2, Mastrangelo 33, Salinas 35)

1978 Boca Juniors and Liverpool declined to play each other.

1979 European champions Nottingham Forest declined to play Olimpia. Their place was taken by European Cup finalists, Malmö

1st leg. Malmö Stadion, Malmö, 18–11–1979, 4000
MALMÖ FF 0
OLIMPIA 1 (Isasi 41)

2nd leg. Manuel Ferreira, Asuncion, 3–03–1980, 35000
OLIMPIA 2 (Solalinde 40, Michelagnoli 71)
MALMÖ FF 1 (Earlandsson 48)

1980 *National Stadium, Tokyo, 11–02–1981, 62000*
NACIONAL MONTEVIDEO 1 (Victorino 10)
NOTTINGHAM FOREST 0
Referee: Klein, Israel
Nacional – Rodriguez – Moreira, Blanco, Enriquez, Gonzalez – Milar, Esparrago, Luzardo, Morales – Bica, Victorino. Tr: Mujica
Nottingham Forest – Shilton – Anderson, Lloyd, Burns, Gray F – Ponte (Ward), O'Neill, Gray S, Robertson – Francis, Wallace. Tr: Clough

1981 *National Stadium, Tokyo, 13–12–1981, 62000*
FLAMENGO 3 (Nunes 13 41, Adilio 34)
LIVERPOOL 0
Referee: Vasquez, Mexico
Flamengo – Raul – Leandro, Junior, Mozer, Marinho – Adilio, Tita, Andrade – Zico, Lico, Nunes. Tr: Paolo Cesar Carpegiani
Liverpool – Grobbelaar – Neal, Lawrenson, Hansen, Thompson – Kennedy R, Lee, McDermott (Johnson), Souness – Dalglish, Johnston. Tr: Paisley

1982 *National Stadium, Tokyo, 12–12–1982, 62000*
PENAROL 2 (Jair 27, Charrua 68)
ASTON VILLA 0
Referee: Calderon, Costa Rica
Peñarol – Fernandez – Diogo, Oliveira, Morales, Gutierrez – Saralegui, Bossio, Jair – Ramos (Charrua), Morena, Silva. Tr: Bagnulo
Aston Villa – Rimmer – Jones, Evans, McNaught, Williams – Bremner, Mortimer, Cowans – Shaw, Withe, Morley. Tr: Barton

1983 *National Stadium, Tokyo, 11–12–1983, 62000*
GREMIO 2 (Renato 37, 93)
HAMBURGER SV 1 (Schröder 85)
Referee: Vautrot, France
Gremio – Mazaropi – Paulo Roberto, Baidek, De Leon, Magalhaes – Sergio, Paulo Cesar (Caio), Osvaldo (Bonamigo), China – Renato, Tarciso. Tr: Valdir Espinosa
HSV – Stein – Wehmeyer, Jakobs, Hieronymus, Schröder – Hartwig, Groh, Rolff, Magath – Wuttke, Hansen. Tr: Happel

1984 *National Stadium, Tokyo, 9–12–1984, 62000*
INDEPENDIENTE 1 (Percudani 6)
LIVERPOOL 0
Referee: Romualdo, Brazil
Independiente – Goyen – Villaverde (Monzon), Enrique, Clausen, Trossero – Marangoni, Burruchaga, Giusti, Bochini – Percudani, Barberon. Tr: Pastoriza
Liverpool – Grobbelaar – Neal, Kennedy A, Gillespie, Hansen – Nicol, Dalglish, Molby, Wark (Whelan) – Rush, Johnston. Tr: Fagan

1985 *National Stadium, Tokyo, 8–12–1985, 62000*
JUVENTUS 2 (Platini 63, Laudrup 82)
ARGENTINOS JUNIORS 2 (Ereros 55, Castro 75)
Juventus won 4–2 on penalties
Referee: Roth, West Germany
Juventus – Tacconi – Favero, Brio, Scirea (Pioli), Cabrini – Bonini, Manfredonia, Platini – Mauro (Briaschi), Serena, Laudrup. Tr: Trapattoni
Argentinos Juniors – Vidallé – Villalba, Pavoni, Olguin, Domenech – Videla, Batista, Commisso (Corsi) – Castro, Borghi, Ereros (Lopez). Tr: Yudica

1986 *National Stadium, Tokyo, 14–12–1986, 62000*
RIVER PLATE 1 (Alzamendi 28)
STEAUA BUCURESTI 0
Referee: Martinez-Bazan, Uruguay
River Plate – Pumpido – Gordillo, Gutierrez, Montenegro, Ruggeri – Alfaro (Sperandio), Alonso, Enrique – Gallego, Alzamendi, Funes. Tr: Vieira
Steaua Bucuresti – Stimgaciu – Iovan, Bumbescu, Belodedici, Barbulescu (Majaru) – Weisenbacher, Stoica, Balint, Balan – Lacatus, Piturca. Tr: Iordanescu

1987 *National Stadium, Tokyo, 13–12–1987, 45000*
FC PORTO 2 (Gomes 41, Madjer 108)
PENAROL 1 (Viera 80)
Referee: Wöhrer, Austria
Porto – Mlynarczyk – Joao Pinto, Geraldao, Lima Periera, Inacio – Rui Barros (Quim), Magalhaes, Andre, Sousa – Gomes, Madjer. Tr: Ivic
Peñarol – Periera – Herrera (Goncalves), Rotti, Trasante, Dominguez – Perdomo, Viera, Aguirre, Cabrera (Matosas) – Vidal, Da Silva. Tr: Tabarez

1988 *National Stadium, Tokyo, 11–12–1988, 62000*
NACIONAL MONTEVIDEO 2 (Ostolaza 7 119)
PSV EINDHOVEN 2 (Romario 75, Koeman 109)
Nacional won 7–6 on penalties
Referee: Palacios, Colombia
Nacional – Sere – Gomez, De Leon, Revelez, Saldana – Ostolaza, Vargas (Moran), Lemos, De Lima – Cardaccio (Carreno), Castro. Tr: Fleitas
PSV Eindhoven – Van Breukelen – Gerets, Koot, Koeman, Heintze (Valckx) – Lerby, Van Aerle, Vanenburg (Gillhaus) – Romario, Kieft, Ellerman. Tr: Hiddink

1989 *National Staium, Tokyo, 17–12–1989, 62000*
MILAN 1 (Evani 118)
NACIONAL MEDELLIN 0
Referee: Fredriksson, Sweden
Milan – Galli – Baresi, Tassoti, Maldini, Fuser (Evani) – Costacurta, Donadoni, Rijkaard, Ancelotti – Van Basten, Massaro (Simone). Tr: Sacchi
Nacional – Higuita – Escobar, Gomez, Herrera, Cassiani – Perez, Arango (Restrepo), Alvarez, Arboleda (Uzurriaga) – Garcia, Trellez. Tr: Maturana

1990 *National Stadium, Tokyo, 9–12–1990, 60000*
MILAN 3 (Rijkaard 43 65, Stroppa 62)
OLIMPIA 0
Referee: Wright, Brazil
Milan – Pazzagli – Baresi, Tassotti, Costacurta, Maldini (Galli) – Carbone, Donadoni (Guerreiri), Rijkaard, Stroppa – Gullit, Van Basten. Tr: Sacchi
Olimpia – Almeida – Fernandez, Caceres, Guasch, Ramirez (Chamac) – Suarez, Hoyn (Cubilla), Balbuena, Monzon – Amarilla, Samaniego. Tr: Cubilla

1991 *National Stadium, Tokyo, 8–12–1991, 60000*
CRVENA ZVEZDA BEOGRAD 3 (Jugovic 19 58, Pancev 72)
COLO COLO 0
Referee: Rothlisberger, Switzerland
Crvena Zvezda – Milojevic – Radinovic, Vasilijevic, Belodedic, Najdoski – Jugovic, Stosic, Ratkovic, Savicevic – Mikhailovic, Pancev. Tr: Popovic
Colo Colo – Moron – Garrido, Margas, Ramirez.M, Salvatierra (Dabrowski) – Mendoza, Vilches, Barticciotto, Pizarro – Yanez, Martinez (Rubio). Tr: Jozic

EUROPE

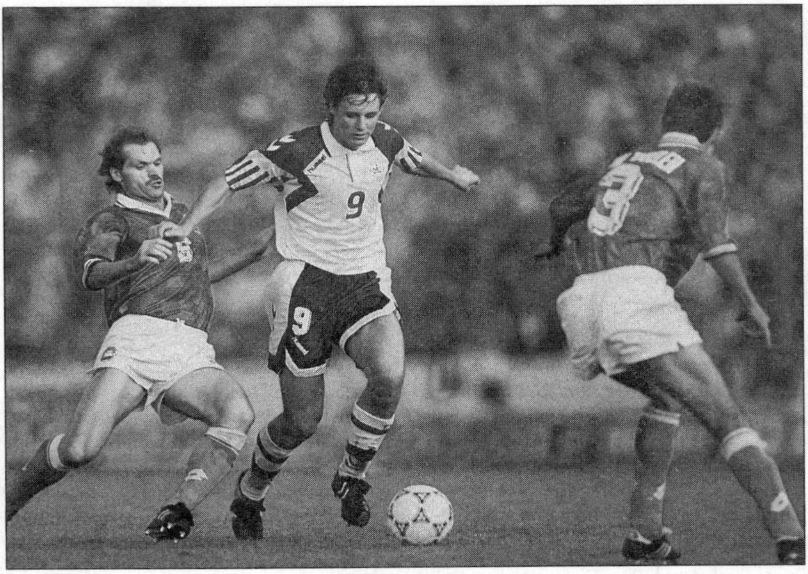

Denmark v Holland, European Championship 1992

WORLD SOCCER

EUROPE

Europe is without question the centre of world football. It has seen football played there in its modern form for longer than anywhere else, it boasts six times more registered clubs than both South America and Asia, its nearest rivals, and for many years now, players from all over the world have migrated to Europe to play their football.

From very austere beginnings in the North of England, competitive club football in Europe has grown into a huge business that occupies many television hours a week not just within Europe but also in the rest of the world. One can travel to almost anywhere on the globe and still see the odd snippet of Italian, English, German or Spanish league football on the local television screens.

The British, having founded the modern game in 1863, were instrumental in its spread accross the continent. Many of the great English amateur teams of the late 19th century such as the Middlesex Wanderers undertook tours of the continent, whilst British residents were always willing to play a game wherever they lived. It is perhaps fortunate that Britain and France, who took to the game from a very early stage, were the major world powers at the time and not America, for we might now all be playing American football and baseball and not football. Baseball's 'World Series' might have been just that, instead of just the championship for North American teams.

FIFA, at the time of its foundation, was very much a European affair, and it was perhaps this heavy European bias that delayed the formation of UEFA until 1954, 50 years after FIFA's birth. Although many international matches both at club and national level were played before 1954, the real growth of competitive games took place after that date. Tournaments like the British and Scandinavian Championships had been organised by the relevant national associations, whilst special committees were set up to run tournaments like the Mitropa Cup and the International (later Dr Gerö) Cup.

The introduction of the European Champion Clubs' Cup, known commonly as the European Cup, was the real turning point in the history of European football, and it was followed in 1958 by the European Nations Cup, later known as the European Football Championship. For the first time a rigid structure for both club and international football was set in place. This has meant countries embarking on two-year playing schedules for the World Cup alternating with the European Championship.

The European Cup, the Cup-Winners Cup and the Fairs/UEFA Cup have also added a much more competitive edge to club football in each country. The chance to play in one of the European competitions is every footballer's ambition, but it also means more revenue for the clubs involved. All these competitions have helped keep European football in the limelight. Players' reputations are gained or lost in them, whilst the European Cup Final every May is the highlight of the season's calendar.

Europe is now, however, at a crossroads. The break-up of Eastern Europe is likely to lead to a big increase in the number of countries belonging to UEFA, whilst the big clubs, ever anxious to increase revenues to enable them to sign more players, are openly talking of the creation of a European Super League. Many of the stadia around the continent are also in dire need of improvement, after the events at Bradford, Heysel, Hillsborough and Furiani have shown, in the most cruel way possible, their often fatal shortcomings. The FIFA directive on all-seated grounds will not be cheap to implement.

UEFA will have a vital role to play over the next few years. It is up to them to find a solution that is in the interests of all the member countries with regard to the 'super league'. The dangers are that if many of the top clubs break away from their national associations, what will be left will not be worth much, and so apart from a few clubs that will thrive, the rest of football on the continent will stagnate. After all, who is going to be interested in the Italian championship without the two Milan clubs or Juventus!

UEFA also faces a challenge from the European Community. Not only would a European Super League seem to be right in line with the political integration which is the aim of the Community, but on a far more practical level, the EC insists on free movement of labour within its boundaries. This is a potentially explosive issue, both from the point of view of a player drain from some countries and the recipient countries' fear for the development of their own players who will inevitably be squeezed out by more glamorous imports. Though only one third of European countries are in the EC, all the major leagues are located within.

Europe faces an interesting and challenging future, not least in that there will be some intriguing ties thrown up in future competitions. Already in the 1994 World Cup, Latvia, Lithuania and Estonia have joined in the throng, but in future editions, who will relish a trip to Kazan to take on the mighty Tartars of Tartarstan?

THE EUROPEAN GOVERNING BODY

UNION OF EUROPEAN FOOTBALL ASSOCIATIONS
Jupiterstrasse 33, PO Box 16, 3000 Berne 15, Switzerland
Tel: (010 41) 31 9414121 Fax: (010 41) 31 9411838
Telex: 912037 UEF CH Cable: UEFA BERNE

Year of formation: 1954
Registered clubs: 243 733
Registered players: 18 244 000
Registered referees: 386 392

MEMBERS: 37
Albania – Austria – Belgium – Bulgaria – Cyprus – Czechoslovakia – Denmark – England – Estonia – Faeroe Islands – Finland – France – Germany – Greece – Hungary – Iceland – Northern Ireland – Republic of Ireland – Italy – Latvia – Liechtenstein – Lithuania – Luxembourg – Malta – Netherlands – Norway – Poland – Portugal – Romania – San Marino – Scotland – Spain – Sweden – Switzerland – Turkey – Wales – Yugoslavia

INDEPENDENT FIFA MEMBER: 1
Israel

PROVISIONAL MEMBERS: 5
Croatia – Georgia – Russia – Slovenia – Ukraine

EUROPEAN FOOTBALLER OF THE YEAR

From France Football

1956

1	Stanley Matthews	Blackpool	ENG	47
2	Alfredo Di Stéfano	Real Madrid	ESP	44
3	Raymond Kopa	Stade de Reims	FRA	33
4	Ferenc Puskas	Honved	HUN	32
5	Lev Yashin	Dynamo Moskva	URS	19
6	Jozsef Bozsik	Honved	HUN	15
7	Ernst Ocwirk	Sampdoria	AUT	9
8	Sandor Kocsis	Honved	HUN	6
9	Ivan Kolev	CDNA Sofia	BUL	4
	Billy Wright	Wolverhampton Wdrs	ENG	4
	Thadée Cisowski	Racing Club Paris	FRA	4

1957

1	Alfredo Di Stéfano	Real Madrid	ESP	72
2	Billy Wright	Wolverhampton Wdrs	ENG	19
3	Raymond Kopa	Real Madrid	FRA	16
	Duncan Edwards	Manchester United	ENG	16
5	Lazslo Kubala	Barcelona	ESP	15
6	John Charles	Juventus	WAL	14
7	Edward Strelitsov	Torpedo Moskva	URS	12
8	Tommy Taylor	Manchester United	ENG	10
9	Jozsef Bozsik	Honved	HUN	9
	Igor Netto	Dynamo Moskva	URS	9

1958

1	Raymond Kopa	Real Madrid	FRA	71
2	Helmut Rahn	Rot-Weiss Essen	FRG	40
3	Just Fontaine	Stade de Reims	FRA	23
4	Kurt Hamrin	Fiorentina	SWE	15
6	Billy Wright	Wolverhampton Wdrs	ENG	9
7	Johnny Haynes	Fulham	ENG	7
8	Harry Gregg	Manchester United	IRE	6
	Horst Szymaniak	Wuppertaler SV	FRG	6
	Nils Liedholm	Milan	SWE	6

1959

1	Alfredo Di Stéfano	Real Madrid	ESP	80
2	Raymond Kopa	Stade de Reims	FRA	42
3	John Charles	Juventus	WAL	24
4	Luis Suárez	Barcelona	ESP	22
5	Agne Simonsson	Örgryte IS Göteborg	SWE	20
6	Lajos Tichy	Honved	HUN	18
7	Ferenc Puskas	Real Madrid	HUN	16
8	Francisco Gento	Real Madrid	ESP	12
9	Helmut Rahn	1.FC Köln	FRG	11
10	Horst Szymaniak	Karlsruher SC	FRG	8

1960

1	Luis Suárez	Barcelona	ESP	54
2	Ferenc Puskas	Real Madrid	HUN	37
3	Uwe Seeler	Hamburger SV	FRG	33
4	Alfredo Di Stéfano	Real Madrid	ESP	32
5	Lev Yashin	Dynamo Moskva	URS	28
6	Raymond Kopa	Stade de Reims	FRA	14
7	John Charles	Juventus	WAL	11
	Bobby Charlton	Manchester United	ENG	11
9	Omar Sivori	Juventus	ITA	9
	Horst Szymaniak	Karlsruher SC	FRG	9

1961

1	Omar Sivori	Juventus	ITA	46
2	Luis Suárez	Internazionale	ESP	40
3	Johnny Haynes	Fulham	ENG	22
4	Lev Yashin	Dynamo Moskva	URS	21
5	Ferenc Puskas	Real Madrid	ESP	16
6	Alfredo Di Stéfano	Real Madrid	ESP	13
	Uwe Seeler	Hamburger SV	FRG	13
8	John Charles	Juventus	WAL	10
9	Francisco Gento	Real Madrid	ESP	8
10	Seven players on 5 votes			

1962

1	Josef Masopust	Dukla Praha	TCH	65
2	Eusébio	Benfica	POR	
3	Karl-Heinz Schnellinger	1.FC Köln	FRG	
4	Dragoslav Sekularac	Crvena Zvezda Beograd	YUG	
5	Joseph Jurion	RSC Anderlecht	BEL	
6	Gianni Rivera	Milan	ITA	
7	Jimmy Greaves	Tottenham Hotspur	ENG	
8	John Charles	Roma	WAL	
	Milan Galic	Partizan Beograd	YUG	
10	Janos Gorocs	Ujpesti Dózsa	HUN	

1963

1	Lev Yashin	Dynamo Moskva	URS	73
2	Gianni Rivera	Milan	ITA	56
3	Jimmy Greaves	Tottenham Hotspur	ENG	51
4	Denis Law	Manchester United	SCO	45
5	Eusébio	Benfica	POR	19
6	Karl-Heinz Schnellinger	Mantova	FRG	16
7	Uwe Seeler	Hamburger SV	FRG	9
8	Luis Suárez	Internazionale	ESP	5
	Giovanni Trapattoni	Milan	ITA	5
	Bobby Charlton	Manchester United	ENG	5

1964

1	Denis Law	Manchester United	SCO	61
2	Luis Suárez	Internazionale	ESP	43
3	Amancio	Real Madrid	ESP	38
4	Eusébio	Benfica	POR	31
5	Paul Van Himst	RSC Anderlecht	BEL	28
6	Jimmy Greaves	Tottenhan Hotspur	ENG	19
7	Mario Corso	Internazionale	ITA	17
8	Lev Yashin	Dynamo Moskva	URS	15
9	Gianni Rivera	Milan	ITA	14
10	Valerie Voronin	Torpedo Moskva	URS	13

1965

1	Eusébio	Benfica	POR	
2	Giacinto Facchetti	Internazionale	ITA	
3	Luis Suárez	Internazionale	ITA	

1966

1	Bobby Charlton	Manchester United	ENG	81
2	Eusébio	Benfica	POR	80
3	Franz Beckenbauer	Bayern München	FRG	59
4	Bobby Moore	West Ham United	ENG	31
5	Florian Albert	Ferencváros	HUN	23
6	Ferenc Bene	Ujpesti Dózsa	HUN	8
7	Lev Yashin	Dynamo Moskva	URS	6
	Alan Ball	Everton	ENG	6
	János Farkas	Vasas Budapest	HUN	6
10	José Torres	Benfica	POR	5

1967

1	Florian Albert	Ferencváros	HUN	68
2	Bobby Charlton	Manchester United	ENG	40
3	Jimmy Johnstone	Glasgow Celtic	SCO	39
4	Franz Beckenbauer	Bayern München	FRG	37
5	Eusébio	Benfica	POR	26
6	Tommy Gemmell	Glasgow Celtic	SCO	21
7	Gerd Müller	Bayern München	FRG	19
8	George Best	Manchester United	NIR	18
9	Igor Chislenko	Torpedo Moskva	URS	9
10	Three players on 8 points			

1968

1	George Best	Manchester United	NIR	61
2	Bobby Charlton	Manchester United	ENG	53
3	Dragan Dzajic	Crvena Zvezda Beograd	YUG	46
4	Franz Beckenbauer	Bayern München	FRG	36
5	Giacinto Facchetti	Internazionale	ITA	30
6	Gigi Riva	Cagliari	ITA	22
7	Amancio	Real Madrid	ESP	21
8	Eusébio	Benfica	POR	15
9	Gianni Rivera	Milan	ITA	13
10	Jimmy Greaves	Tottenham Hotspur	ENG	8
	Pirri	Real Madrid	ESP	8

1969

1	Gianni Rivera	Milan	ITA	83
2	Gigi Riva	Cagliari	ITA	79
3	Gerd Müller	Bayern München	FRG	38
4	Johan Cruyff	Ajax	HOL	30
	Ove Kindvall	Feyenoord	SWE	30
6	George Best	Manchester United	ENG	21
7	Franz Beckenbauer	Bayern München	FRG	18
8	Pierino Prati	Milan	ITA	17
9	Peter Jekov	CSKA Sofia	BUL	14
10	Jackie Charlton	Leeds United	ENG	10

1970

1	Gerd Müller	Bayern München	FRG	77
2	Bobby Moore	West Ham United	ENG	69
3	Gigi Riva	Cagliari	ITA	65
4	Franz Beckenbauer	Bayern München	FRG	32
5	Wolfgang Overath	1.FC Köln	FRG	29
6	Dragan Dzajic	Crvena Zvezda Beograd	YUG	24
7	Johan Cruyff	Ajax	HOL	
8	Gordon Banks	Stoke City	ENG	8
	Sandro Mazzola	Internazionale	ITA	8
10	Four players on 7 points			

1971

1	Johan Cruyff	Ajax	HOL	116
2	Sandro Mazzola	Internazionale	ITA	57
3	George Best	Manchester United	NIR	56
4	Gunter Netzer	Bor. Mönchengladbach	FRG	30
5	Franz Beckenbauer	Bayern München	FRG	27
6	Gerd Müller	Bayern München	FRG	18
	Josip Skoblar	Olympique Marseille	YUG	18
8	Martin Chivers	Tottenham Hotspur	ENG	13
9	Piet Keizer	Ajax	HOL	9
10	Ferenc Bene	Ujpesti Dózsa	HUN	7
	Bobby Moore	West Ham United	ENG	7

1972

1	Franz Beckenbauer	Bayern München	FRG	81
2	Gerd Müller	Bayern München	FRG	79
	Gunter Netzer	Bor. Mönchengladbach	FRG	79
4	Johan Cruyff	Ajax	HOL	73
5	Piet Keizer	Ajax	HOL	13
6	Kazimierz Deyna	Legia Warszawa	POL	6
7	Gordon Banks	Stoke City	ENG	4
	Barry Hulshoff	Ajax	HOL	4
	Wlodzmierz Lubánski	Gornik Zabrze	POL	4
	Bobby Moore	West Ham United	ENG	4

1973

1	Johan Cruyff	Barcelona	HOL	96
2	Dino Zoff	Juventus	ITA	47
3	Gerd Müller	Bayern München	FRG	44
4	Franz Beckenbauer	Bayern München	FRG	30
5	Billy Bremner	Leeds United	SCO	22
6	Kazimierz Deyna	Legia Warszawa	POL	16
7	Eusébio	Benfica	POR	14
8	Gianni Rivera	Milan	ITA	12
9	Ralf Edström	PSV Eindhoven	SWE	11
	Uli Hoeness	Bayern München	FRG	11

1974

1	Johan Cruyff	Barcelona	HOL	116
2	Franz Beckenbauer	Bayern München	FRG	105
3	Kazimierz Deyna	Legia Warszawa	POL	35
4	Paul Breitner	Real Madrid	FRG	32
5	Johan Neeskens	Barcelona	HOL	21
6	Grzegorz Lato	Stal Mielec	POL	16
7	Gerd Müller	Bayern München	FRG	14
8	Robert Gadocha	Legia Warszawa	POL	11
9	Billy Bremner	Leeds United	SCO	9
10	Ralf Edström	PSV Eindhoven	SWE	4
	Jurgen Sparwasser	1.FC Magdeburg	GDR	4
	Berti Vogts	Bor. Mönchengladbach	FRG	4

1975

1	Oleg Blokhin	Dynamo Kiev	URS	122
2	Franz Beckenbauer	Bayern München	FRG	42
3	Johan Cruyff	Barcelona	HOL	27
4	Berti Vogts	Bor. Mönchengladbach	FRG	25
5	Sepp Maier	Bayern München	FRG	20

6	Ruud Geels	Ajax	HOL	18
7	Jupp Heynckes	Bor. Mönchengladbach	FRG	17
8	Paul Breitner	Real Madrid	FRG	14
9	Colin Todd	Derby County	ENG	12
10	Dudu Georgescu	Dinamo Bucuresti	RUM	11

1976

1	Franz Beckenbauer	Bayern München	FRG	91
2	Robby Rensenbrink	RSC Anderlecht	HOL	75
3	Ivo Viktor	Dukla Praha	TCH	52
4	Kevin Keegan	Liverpool	ENG	32
5	Michel Platini	AS Nancy	FRA	19
6	Anton Ondrus	Slovan Bratislava	TCH	16
7	Johan Cruyff	Barcelona	HOL	12
	Ivan Curkovic	AS Saint Étienne	YUG	12
9	Rainer Bonhof	Bor. Mönchengladbach	FRG	9
	Marian Masny	Slovan Bratislava	TCH	9
	Gerd Müller	Bayern München	FRG	9

1977

1	Allan Simonsen	Bor. Mönchengladbach	DEN	74
2	Kevin Keegan	Liverpool	ENG	71
3	Michel Platini	AS Nancy	FRA	70
4	Roberto Bettega	Juventus	ITA	39
5	Johan Cruyff	Barcelona	HOL	23
6	Klaus Fischer	Schalke 04	FRG	21
7	Tibor Nyilasi	Ferencváros	HUN	13
	Robby Rensenbrink	RSC Anderlecht	HOL	13
9	Dudu Georgescu	Dinamo Bucuresti	RUM	6
10	Steve Heighway	Liverpool	ENG	5
	Emlyn Hughes	Liverpool	ENG	5
	Berti Vogts	Bor. Mönchengladbach	FRG	5

1978

1	Kevin Keegan	Hamburger SV	ENG	87
2	Hans Krankl	SK Rapid Wien	AUT	81
3	Robby Rensenbrink	RSC Anderlecht	HOL	50
4	Roberto Bettega	Juventus	ITA	28
5	Paolo Rossi	Lanerossi-Vicenza	ITA	23
6	Ronnie Hellstrom	I.FC Kaiserslautern	SWE	20
	Ruud Krol	Ajax	HOL	20
8	Kenny Dalglish	Liverpool	SCO	10
	Allan Simonsen	Bor. Mönchengladbach	DEN	10
10	Peter Shilton	Nottingham Forest	ENG	9

1979

1	Kevin Keegan	Hamburger SV	ENG	118
2	Karl-Heinz Rummenigge	Bayern München	FRG	52
3	Ruud Krol	Ajax	HOL	41
4	Manni Kaltz	Hamburger SV	FRG	27
5	Michel Platini	AS Saint Étienne	FRA	23
6	Paolo Rossi	Perugia	ITA	16
7	Liam Brady	Arsenal	IRL	13
	Trevor Francis	Nottingham Forest	ENG	13
9	Zbigniew Boniek	Wisla Krakow	POL	9
	Zdenek Nehoda	Dukla Praha	TCH	9

1980

1	Karl-Heinz Rummenigge	Bayern München	FRG	122
2	Bernd Schuster	Barcelona	FRG	34
3	Michel Platini	AS Saint Étienne	FRA	33
4	Wilfred Van Moer	SK Beveren	BEL	27
5	Jan Ceulemans	Club Brugge	BEL	20
6	Horst Hrubesch	Hamburger SV	FRG	18
7	Herbert Prohaska	Internazionale	AUT	16
8	Hansi Müller	VfB Stuttgart	FRG	11
	Liam Brady	Juventus	IRL	11
10	Manni Kaltz	Hamburger SV	FRG	10

1981

1	Karl-Heinz Rummenigge	Bayern München	FRG	106
2	Paul Breitner	Bayern München	FRG	64
3	Bernd Schuster	Barcelona	FRG	39
4	Michel Platini	AS Saint Étienne	FRA	36
5	Oleg Blokhin	Dynamo Kiev	URS	14
6	Dino Zoff	Juventus	ITA	13
7	Ramas Shengelia	Dynamo Tbilisi	URS	10
8	Alexander Chivadze	Dynamo Tbilisi	URS	9
9	Liam Brady	Juventus	IRL	7
	John Wark	Ipswich Town	SCO	7

1982

1	Paolo Rossi	Juventus	ITA	115
2	Alain Giresse	Girondins Bordeaux	FRA	64
3	Zbigniew Boniek	Juventus	POL	53
4	Karl-Heinz Rummenigge	Bayern München	FRG	51
5	Bruno Conti	Roma	ITA	48
6	Rinat Dasayev	Spartak Moskva	URS	17
7	Pierre Littbarski	I.FC Köln	FRG	10
8	Dino Zoff	Juventus	ITA	9
9	Michel Platini	Juventus	FRA	5
10	Bernd Schuster	Barcelona	FRG	4

1983

1	Michel Platini	Juventus	FRA	110
2	Kenny Dalglish	Liverpool	SCO	26
3	Allan Simonsen	Vejle BK	DEN	25
4	Gordon Strachan	Aberdeen	SCO	24
5	Felix Magath	Hamburger SV	FRG	20
6	Rinat Dasayev	Spartak Moskva	URS	15
	Jean-Marie Pfaff	Bayern München	BEL	15
8	Jesper Olsen	Ajax	DEN	14
	Karl-Heinz Rummenigge	Bayern München	FRG	14
10	Bryan Robson	Manchester United	ENG	13

1984

1	Michel Platini	Juventus	FRA	128
2	Jean Tigana	Girondins Bordeaux	FRA	57
3	Preben Elkjaer-Larsen	Hellas Verona	DEN	48
4	Ian Rush	Liverpool	WAL	44
5	Chalana	Girondins Bordeaux	POR	18
6	Graeme Souness	Sampdoria	SCO	16
7	Harald Schumacher	I.FC Köln	FRG	12
8	Karl-Heinz Rummenigge	Internazionale	FRG	10
9	Alain Giresse	Girondins Bordeaux	FRA	9
10	Bryan Robson	Manchester United	ENG	7

1985

1	Michel Platini	Juventus	FRA	127
2	Preben Elkjaer-Larsen	Hellas Verona	DEN	71
3	Bernd Schuster	Barcelona	FRG	46
4	Michael Laudrup	Juventus	DEN	14
5	Karl-Heinz Rummenigge	Internazionale	FRG	13
6	Zbigniew Boniek	Roma	POL	12
7	Oleg Protasov	Dnepr Dnepropetrovsk	URS	10
8	Hans-Peter Briegel	Hellas Verona	FRG	9
9	Rinat Dasayev	Spartak Moskva	URS	8
	Bryan Robson	Manchester United	ENG	8

1986

1	Igor Belanov	Dynamo Kiev	URS	84
2	Gary Lineker	Barcelona	ENG	62
3	Emilio Butragueño	Real Madrid	ESP	59
4	Manuel Amoros	AS Monaco	FRA	22
	Preben Elkjaer-Larsen	Hellas Verona	DEN	22
6	Ian Rush	Liverpool	ENG	20
	Alexander Zavarov	Dynamo Kiev	URS	20
8	Marco Van Basten	Ajax	HOL	10

	Helmut Ducadam	Steaua Bucuresti	ROM	10
10	Alessandro Altobelli	Internazionale	ITA	9

1987

1	Ruud Gullit	Milan	HOL	106
2	Paolo Futre	Atlético Madrid	POR	91
3	Emilio Butragueño	Real Madrid	ESP	61
4	Gonzales Michel	Real Madrid	ESP	29
5	Gary Lineker	Barcelona	ENG	13
6	John Barnes	Liverpool	ENG	10
	Marco Van Basten	Milan	HOL	10
8	Gianluca Vialli	Sampdoria	ITA	9
9	Bryan Robson	Manchester United	ENG	7
10	Klaus Allofs	Olympique Marseille	FRG	6
	Glen Hysen	Fiorentina	SWE	6

1988

1	Marco Van Basten	Milan	HOL	129
2	Ruud Gullit	Milan	HOL	88
3	Frank Rijkaard	Milan	HOL	45
4	Alexei Mikhailichenko	Dynamo Kiev	URS	41
5	Ronald Koeman	PSV Eindhoven	HOL	39
6	Lothar Matthäus	Bayern München	FRG	10
7	Gianluca Vialli	Sampdoria	ITA	7
8	Franco Baresi	Milan	ITA	5
	Jurgen Klinsmann	VfB Stuttgart	FRG	5
	Alexander Zavarov	Juventus	URS	5

1989

1	Marco Van Basten	Milan	HOL	119
2	Franco Baresi	Milan	HOL	80
3	Frank Rijkaard	Milan	HOL	43
4	Lothar Matthäus	Internazionale	FRG	24
5	Peter Shilton	Derby County	ENG	22
6	Dragan Stojkovic	Crvena Zvezda Beograd	YUG	19
7	Ruud Gullit	Milan	HOL	16
8	Georgi Hagi	Steaua Bucuresti	ROM	11
	Jurgen Klinsmann	Internazionale	FRG	11
10	Michel Preud'homme	KV Mechelen	BEL	10
	Jean-Pierre Papin	Olympique Marseille	FRA	10

1990

1	Lothar Matthäus	Internazionale	FRG	137
2	Salvatore Schillaci	Juventus	ITA	84
3	Andreas Brehme	Internazionale	FRG	68
4	Paul Gascoigne	Tottenham Hotspur	ENG	43
5	Franco Baresi	Milan	ITA	37
6	Jurgen Klinsmann	Internazionale	FRG	12
	Enzo Scifo	AJ Auxerre	BEL	12
8	Roberto Baggio	Juventus	ITA	8
9	Frank Rijkaard	Milan	HOL	7
10	Guido Buchwald	VfB Stuttgart	FRG	6

1991

1	Jean-Pierre Papin	Olympique Marseille	FRA	141
2	Darko Pancev	Crvena Zvezda Beograd	YUG	42
	Dejan Savicevic	Crvena Zvezda Beograd	YUG	42
	Lothar Matthäus	Internazionale	FRG	42
5	Robert Prosinecki	Real Madrid	YUG	34
6	Gary Lineker	Tottenham Hotspur	ENG	33
7	Gianluca Vialli	Sampdoria	ITA	18
8	Miodrag Belodedic	Crvena Zvezda Beograd	YUG	15
9	Mark Hughes	Manchester United	WAL	12
10	Chris Waddle	Olympique Marseille	ENG	11

THE EUROPEAN FOOTBALL CHAMPIONSHIP

Europe was the last continent to organise a championship for its members, just pipped to the post by Africa and Asia, but some way behind both South and Central America. This seems odd given the opportunities that were available before it finally got underway in 1958. Odder still was the fact that West Germany, Italy, Belgium, Holland, Switzerland, Sweden, Finland, Luxembourg and the four British nations did not enter the first edition. Scotland and West Germany did not enter the second edition either.

Originally called the European Nations Cup, the competition's trophy was named after Henri Delaunay, the French football administrator and former general secretary of UEFA, whose idea the competition was. With seven qualifying groups and only eight places in the final tournament, with the hosts, but not the holders, getting a bye, it is a more difficult tournament to qualify for than the World Cup, in which two from each group qualify.

Held every four years, it has developed into the second most important tournament in the world after the World Cup. As the shape of Europe changes with the break-up of the Soviet Union, it will not be long before drastic changes in the tournament are effected. With the possibility of perhaps over 15 new members, the final tournament will certainly have to grow from the present eight finalists to sixteen in the future so as to not overload already busy playing schedules.

A return to the system used in the first two tournaments would not be out of place. Then it was a straight knock-out with all of the ties until the semi-final held on a home and away basis. Indeed the four-team final tournament was a feature of the first five editions, even though qualifying groups were introduced in the third series.

The early dominant powers were the countries from the Eastern bloc. Three of the four semi-finalists in 1960 were from behind the Iron Curtain, and the biggest of them all, the Soviet Union, won, beating Yugoslavia 2–1 in the final. France hosted the final stages, but despite home advantage lost a thrilling semi-final 5–4 to Yugoslavia.

The Soviet Union again reached the final four years later but lost to Spain, who in 1960 had pulled out of their quarter-final tie with the Soviets, who were regarded as politically unsuitable by the right-wing Franco government. Thankfully there were no such problems the second time around as Spain had been chosen to host the final tournament. Home advantage was made to count with a 2–1 extra-time victory over Hungary in the semi-finals and there was a repeat scoreline in the final against the Soviets.

The 1968 tournament saw the introduction of eight qualifying groups. Scotland at last entered, as did West Germany. The biggest surprise was the elimination of Portugal by Bulgaria, but the Bulgarians then lost in the quarter-finals to Italy who were then awarded the hosting of the final tournament. Italy's semi-final victory over the Soviet Union was somewhat fortuitous in that after a 0–0 draw, they won on the toss of a coin. The world champions England were meanwhile losing to a late goal against Yugoslavia and had to be content with a third place victory over the Soviets. A replay was needed in the final, but the Italians eventually triumphed, leaving the poor Yugoslavs to collect yet another runners-up medal.

The 1972 tournament again saw the Eastern Europeans put in a strong challenge, and again the Soviet Union reached the final. This was the tournament of the West Germans, however. They were at their very best and reached the final by beating England in the quarter-finals and Belgium in the semis. The Belgians had been chosen to host the tournament having beaten Italy, but they were no match for the Germans. Gerd Müller was in devastating form, and his goals sealed the title for his team and set them up nicely for the World Cup two years later on home soil.

Neither Italy nor England made it past the qualifying stage in 1976, but as the tournament progressed it all looked set for a repeat of the World Cup Final of two years previously. But in the semi-finals, Czechoslovakia, England's conquerors in the qualifying round, put a spanner in the works by defeating the Dutch with two very late goals in extra-time. West Germany also needed two goals in the second period of extra-time to beat the hosts Yugoslavia, who earlier in the match had looked as if they would run away with the game. The final is one of only two occasions on which penalties have ever been used in the European Championships. The Germans again left it very late in the match to score their equalising goal but lost in the penalty shoot-out to the Czechs who were crowned as Europe's unlikely champions. In five tournaments, five different nations had won Europe's top prize.

A new format was adopted for the 1980 championship. The hosts, Italy, were chosen at the outset, instead of after the quarter-final round as had been the practice, and were given a bye to the final tournament. The quarter-finals were done away with, the seven group winners now proceeding to a final tournament consisting of two groups of four, the winners of which would contest the final. The Soviet Union was the surprise absentee, and Yugoslavia did not make the trip either. West Germany became the only nation to win the tournament twice when they beat the surpise package, Belgium, in the final.

The group matches were marred by violence on the terraces involving the England supporters, and it was to the great relief of the authorities that they were knocked out in the first round. Italy could not make the final either and had to be content with a third place play-off with the Czechs as Belgium topped Group 2. In Group 1, the Germans had little trouble in seeing off the holders and the Dutch, who were past their best. Their only point dropped was against Greece, who were making their only appearance ever in the finals of a major tournament. The Germans' old trick of leaving it late surfaced again in the final, Hrubesch's second and winning goal coming two minutes from time.

The list of big names failing to qualify for the 1984 tournament included England, Holland, the Soviet Union and Italy. England were once again grouped with a strong emerging nation, Denmark, as they had been with Czechoslovakia in 1976, whilst Italy surprisingly finished behind Romania, who did not perform well in the finals. France were chosen as hosts and they put a lot of effort into staging the event. Unlike any of the previous competitions, new stadia were built and old ones refurbished in preparation, and in the end it proved worthwhile as the public were treated to the best ever championship. The French team in particular were brilliant, and their victory partially compensated for their unlucky semi-final loss in the 1982 World Cup. Michel Platini was particularly inspired and his incredible total of nine goals in five matches was the crucial factor in their success.

Spain and Portugal qualified for the semi-finals from Group 2, and Spain, unfancied at the start, made it to the final courtesy of penalties against Denmark, who had been in fine form in the first round. In the other semi-final, the Portuguese, making their first appearance in the finals, more than held their own against France for most of the game, but lost in extra-time to a last-minute Platini goal. The final was a more straightforward affair; with France on a roll there was very little the Spaniards could do to stop them, and for the third time in seven tournaments the hosts were victorious.

The Dutch made it seven different winners in eight tournaments with victory in West Germany in 1988. England, despite being among the favourites, were a disappointment as were the Spaniards and Danes, and it was Holland and the Soviet Union who qualified from Group 2 to meet the hosts, West Germany, and Italy in the semi-finals. Marco Van Basten, the star of the tournament, scored to put the hosts out with two minutes of the semi-final remaining and was on target again in the final against the Soviets. Playing football reminiscent of their golden age in the 1970s, Holland thrilled the crowd in Munich with their display and at last won an international honour.

Four years later, in perhaps the most extraordinary championships ever, Denmark, to the surprise of everyone, won the tournament in neighbouring Sweden after not having initially qualified. Yugoslavia were expelled and their place given to the Danes, who had finished second behind them in their qualifying group. Also absent were Italy and Spain, and it was not a good tournament for the established powers. Both France and England bowed out in the first round, and the Germans might easily have joined them. Holland, after a fine first round, fell under the Danish spell and were knocked out in the semi-finals. No-one believed that the injury-hit Danes could repeat the feat against Germany in the final, but they did. In a splendid display of defence and counter-attack they ran out 2–0 winners.

EUROPEAN CHAMPIONSHIP MEDALS TABLE

	Country	G	S	B	Finals	Semis
1	Germany	2	2	1	4	5
2	Soviet Union	1	3	–	4	5
3	Spain	1	1	–	2	2
4	Holland	1	–	2	1	3
5	Czechoslovakia	1	–	2	1	2
6	Denmark	1	–	1	1	2
7	Italy	1	–	1	1	2
8	France	1	–	–	1	2
9	Yugoslavia	–	2	–	2	3
10	Belgium	–	1	1	1	2
	Hungary	–	–	1	–	2
12	England	–	–	1	–	1
	Portugal	–	–	1	–	1
	Sweden	–	–	1	–	1

1960	Soviet Union	2–1	Yugoslavia
1964	Spain	2–1	Soviet Union
1968	Italy	1–1 2–0	Yugoslavia
1972	West Germany	3–0	Soviet Union
1976	Czechoslovakia	2–2 (5–4p)	West Germany
1980	West Germany	2–1	Belgium
1984	France	2–0	Spain
1988	Holland	2–0	Soviet Union
1992	Denmark	2–0	Germany

FIRST EDITION

28th September 1958–10th July 1960

PRELIMINARY ROUND

REP. IRELAND	2–0 0–4	CZECHOSLOVAKIA

FIRST ROUND

FRANCE	7–1 1–1	GREECE
SOVIET UNION	3–1 1–0	HUNGARY
ROMANIA	3–0 0–2	TURKEY
NORWAY	0–1 2–5	AUSTRIA
YUGOSLAVIA	2–0 1–1	BULGARIA
EAST GERMANY	0–2 2–3	PORTUGAL
DENMARK	2–2 1–5	CZECHOSLOVAKIA
POLAND	2–4 0–3	SPAIN

QUARTER-FINALS

SOVIET UNION	W–O	SPAIN
ROMANIA	0–2 0–3	CZECHOSLOVAKIA
FRANCE	5–2 4–2	AUSTRIA
PORTUGAL	2–1 1–5	YUGOSLAVIA

SEMI-FINALS

Vélodrome, Marseille, 6–07–1960, 23 000
SOVIET UNION 3 (Ivanov V 35 58, Ponedelnik 64)
CZECHOSLOVAKIA 0

Parc des Princes, Paris, 6–07–1990, 26 000
YUGOSLAVIA 5 (Galic 11, Zanetic 55, Knez 75, Jerkovic 77 78)
FRANCE 4 (Vincent 12, Heutte 43 62, Wisnieski 52)

3RD PLACE

Vélodrome, Marseille, 9–07–1960, 9000
CZECHOSLOVAKIA 2 (Bubernik 58, Pavlovic 88)
FRANCE 0

FINAL

Parc des Princes, Paris, 10–07–1960, 18 000
SOVIET UNION 2 (Metreveli 49, Ponedelnik 113)
YUGOSLAVIA 1 (Galic 41)
Referee: Ellis, England
Soviet Union – Yashin – Tchekeli, Maslenkin, Kroutikov – Voinov, Netto – Metreveli, Ivanov V, Ponedelnik, Bubukin, Meshki. Tr: Katchalin
Yugoslavia – Vidinic – Durkovic, Miladinovic, Jusufi – Zanetic, Perusic – Sekularac, Jerkovic, Galic, Matus, Kostic. Tr: Ciric

SECOND EDITION

1962–64

FIRST ROUND

SPAIN	6–0 1–3	ROMANIA
POLAND	0–2 0–2	NTH. IRELAND
DENMARK	6–1 3–1	MALTA
EAST GERMANY	2–1 1–1	CZECHOSLOVAKIA
HUNGARY	3–1 1–1	WALES
ITALY	6–0 1–0	TURKEY
HOLLAND	3–1 1–1	SWITZERLAND
NORWAY	0–2 1–1	SWEDEN
REP. IRELAND	4–2 1–1	ICELAND
YUGOSLAVIA	3–2 1–0	BELGIUM
BULGARIA	3–1 1–3 1–0*	PORTUGAL
ENGLAND	1–1 2–5	FRANCE
ALBANIA	W–O	GREECE
AUSTRIA	Bye	
LUXEMBOURG	Bye	
SOVIET UNION	Bye	

* Play–off in Rome

SECOND ROUND

SPAIN	1–1 1–0	NTH. IRELAND
DENMARK	4–0 0–1	ALBANIA
AUSTRIA	0–0 2–3	REP. IRELAND
EAST GERMANY	1–2 3–3	HUNGARY
SOVIET UNION	2–0 1–1	ITALY
HOLLAND	1–1 1–2	LUXEMBOURG
YUGOSLAVIA	0–0 2–3	SWEDEN
BULGARIA	1–0 1–3	FRANCE

QUARTER-FINALS

SPAIN .... 5–1 2–0 .... REP. IRELAND
FRANCE .... 1–3 1–2 .... HUNGARY
LUXEMBOURG ...... 3–3 2–2 0–1* .. DENMARK
SWEDEN .... 1–1 1–3 .... SOVIET UNION

* Play-off in Amsterdam

SEMI-FINALS

Bernabeu, Madrid, 17–06–1964, 75 000
SPAIN 2 (Pereda 39, Amancio 115)
HUNGARY 1 (Bene 85)

Nou Camp, Barcelona, 17–06–1964, 50 000
SOVIET UNION 3 (Voronin 19, Ponedelnik 40, Ivanov V 88)
DENMARK 0

3RD PLACE

Nou Camp, Barcelona, 20–06–1964, 3000
HUNGARY 3 (Bene 11, Novák 107 110)
DENMARK 1 (Bertelsen 81)

FINAL

Bernabeu, Madrid, 21–06–1964, 105 000
SPAIN 2 (Pereda 6, Marcelino 83)
SOVIET UNION 1 (Khusainov 8)
Referee: Holland, England
Spain – Iríbar – Rivilla, Olivella, Calleja – Zoco, Fusté – Amancio, Pereda, Marcelino, Suárez, Lapetra. Tr: Villalonga
Soviet Union – Yashin – Chustikov, Shesterniev, Anitchkin, Mudrik – Voronin, Korniev – Chislenko, Ivanov V, Ponedelnik, Khusainov. Tr: Beskov

THIRD EDITION
1966–68

QUALIFYING TOURNAMENT

Group 1

	Sp	Cz	RI	Tu	Pl	W	D	L	F	A	Pts
SPAIN	–	2–1	2–0	2–0	6	3	2	1	6	2	8
CZECHOSLOV.	1–0	–	1–2	3–0	6	3	1	2	8	4	7
REP. IRELAND	0–0	0–2	–	2–1	6	2	1	3	5	8	5
TURKEY	0–0	0–0	2–1	–	6	1	2	3	3	8	4

Group 2

	Bu	Pt	Sd	No	Pl	W	D	L	F	A	Pts
BULGARIA	–	1–0	3–0	4–2	6	4	2	0	10	2	10
PORTUGAL	0–0	–	1–2	2–1	6	2	2	2	6	6	6
SWEDEN	0–2	1–1	–	5–2	6	2	1	3	9	12	5
NORWAY	0–0	1–2	3–1	–	6	1	1	4	9	14	3

Group 3

	SU	Gr	Au	Fi	Pl	W	D	L	F	A	Pts
SOVIET UNION	–	4–0	4–3	2–0	6	5	0	1	16	6	10
GREECE	0–1	–	4–1	2–1	6	2	2	2	8	9	6
AUSTRIA	1–0	1–1	–	2–1	6	2	2	2	8	10	6
FINLAND	2–5	1–1	0–0	–	6	0	2	4	5	12	2

Group 4

	Yu	WG	Al	Pl	W	D	L	F	A	Pts
YUGOSLAVIA	–	1–0	4–0	4	3	0	1	8	3	6
WEST GERMANY	3–1	–	6–0	4	2	1	1	9	2	5
ALBANIA	0–2	0–0	–	4	0	1	3	0	12	1

Group 5

	Hu	EG	Ho	De	Pl	W	D	L	F	A	Pts
HUNGARY	–	3–1	2–1	6–0	6	4	1	1	15	5	9
EAST GERMANY	1–0	–	4–3	3–2	6	3	1	2	10	10	7
HOLLAND	2–2	1–0	–	2–0	6	2	1	3	11	11	5
DENMARK	0–2	1–1	3–2	–	6	1	1	4	6	16	3

Group 6

	It	Ru	Sz	Cy	Pl	W	D	L	F	A	Pts
ITALY	–	3–1	4–0	5–0	6	5	1	0	17	3	11
ROMANIA	0–1	–	4–2	7–0	6	3	0	3	18	14	6
SWITZERLAND	2–2	7–1	–	5–0	6	2	1	3	17	13	5
CYPRUS	0–2	1–5	2–1	–	6	1	0	5	3	25	2

Group 7

	Fr	Be	Pd	Lu	Pl	W	D	L	F	A	Pts
FRANCE	–	1–1	2–1	3–1	6	4	1	1	14	6	9
BELGIUM	2–1	–	2–4	3–0	6	3	1	2	14	9	7
POLAND	1–4	3–1	–	4–0	6	3	1	2	13	9	7
LUXEMBOURG	0–3	0–5	0–0	–	6	0	1	5	1	18	1

Group 8

	En	Sc	Wa	NI	Pl	W	D	L	F	A	Pts
ENGLAND	–	2–3	5–1	2–0	6	4	1	1	15	5	9
SCOTLAND	1–1	–	3–2	2–1	6	3	2	1	10	8	8
WALES	0–3	1–1	–	2–0	6	1	2	3	6	12	4
NTH. IRELAND	0–2	1–0	0–0	–	6	1	1	4	2	8	3

QUARTER-FINALS

ENGLAND .... 1–0 2–1 .... SPAIN
BULGARIA .... 3–2 0–2 .... ITALY
FRANCE .... 1–1 1–5 .... YUGOSLAVIA
HUNGARY .... 2–0 0–3 .... SOVIET UNION

SEMI-FINALS

San Paolo, Naples, 5–06–1968, 75 000
ITALY 0
SOVIET UNION 0

Italy won on the toss of a coin

Comunale, Florence, 5–06–1968, 21 000
YUGOSLAVIA 1 (Dzajic 85)
ENGLAND 0

3RD PLACE

Stadio Olimpico, Rome, 8–06–1968, 50 000
ENGLAND 2 (Charlton B 39, Hurst 63)
SOVIET UNION 0

FINAL

Stadio Olimpico, Rome, 8–06–1968, 85 000
ITALY 1 (Domenghini 80)
YUGOSLAVIA 1 (Dzajic 39)
Referee: Dienst, Switzerland
Italy – Zoff – Burgnich, Guarneri, Facchetti – Ferrini, Castano – Domenghini, Juliano, Anastasi, Lodetti, Prati
Yugoslavia – Pantelic – Fazlagic, Paunovic, Holcer, Damjanovic – Pavlovic, Trivic – Petkovic, Musemic, Acimovic, Dzajic

Replay. *Stadio Olimpico, Rome, 10–06–1968, 50 000*
ITALY 2 (Riva 11, Anastasi 32)
YUGOSLAVIA 0
Referee: De Mendibil, Spain
Italy – Zoff – Burgnich, Guarneri, Facchetti – Rosato, Salvadore – Domenghini, Mazzola, Anastasi, De Sisti, Riva. Tr: Valcareggi
Yugoslavia – Pantelic – Fazlagic, Paunovic, Holcer, Damjanovic – Pavlovic, Trivic – Acimovic, Musemic, Hosic, Dzajic. Tr: Mitic

FOURTH EDITION
1970–72

QUALIFYING TOURNAMENT

Group 1

	Ro	Cz	Wa	Fi	Pl	W	D	L	F	A	Pts
ROMANIA	–	2–1	2–0	3–0	6	4	1	1	11	2	9
Czechoslovakia	1–0	–	1–0	1–1	6	4	1	1	11	4	9
Wales	0–0	1–3	–	3–0	6	2	1	3	5	6	5
Finland	0–4	0–4	0–1	–	6	0	1	5	1	16	1

Group 2

	Hu	Bu	Fr	No	Pl	W	D	L	F	A	Pts
HUNGARY	–	2–0	1–1	4–0	6	4	1	1	12	5	9
Bulgaria	3–0	–	2–1	1–1	6	3	1	2	11	7	7
France	0–2	2–1	–	3–1	6	3	1	2	10	8	7
Norway	1–3	1–4	1–3	–	6	0	1	5	5	18	1

Group 3

	En	Sz	Gr	Ma	Pl	W	D	L	F	A	Pts
ENGLAND	–	1–1	3–0	5–0	6	5	1	0	15	3	11
Switzerland	2–3	–	1–0	5–0	6	4	1	1	12	5	9
Greece	0–2	0–1	–	2–0	6	1	1	4	3	8	3
Malta	0–1	1–2	1–1	–	6	0	1	5	2	16	1

Group 4

	SU	Sp	NI	Cy	Pl	W	D	L	F	A	Pts
SOVIET UNION	–	2–1	1–0	6–1	6	4	2	0	13	4	10
Spain	0–0	–	3–0	7–0	6	3	2	1	14	3	8
Nth. Ireland	1–1	1–1	–	5–0	6	2	2	2	10	6	6
Cyprus	1–3	0–2	0–3	–	6	0	0	6	2	26	0

Group 5

	Be	Pt	Sc	De	Pl	W	D	L	F	A	Pts
BELGIUM	–	3–0	3–0	2–0	6	4	1	1	11	3	9
Portugal	1–1	–	2–0	5–0	6	3	1	2	10	6	7
Scotland	1–0	2–1	–	1–0	6	3	0	3	4	7	6
Denmark	1–2	0–1	1–0	–	6	1	0	5	2	11	2

Group 6

	It	Au	Sd	RI	Pl	W	D	L	F	A	Pts
ITALY	–	2–2	3–0	3–0	6	4	2	0	12	4	10
Austria	1–2	–	1–0	6–0	6	3	1	2	14	6	7
Sweden	0–0	1–0	–	1–0	6	2	2	2	3	5	6
Rep. Ireland	1–2	1–4	1–1	–	6	0	1	5	3	17	1

Group 7

	Yu	Ho	EG	Lu	Pl	W	D	L	F	A	Pts
YUGOSLAVIA	–	2–0	0–0	0–0	6	3	3	0	7	2	9
Holland	1–1	–	3–2	6–0	6	3	1	2	18	6	7
East Germany	1–2	1–0	–	2–1	6	3	1	2	11	6	7
Luxembourg	0–2	0–8	0–5	–	6	0	1	5	1	23	1

Group 8

	WG	Pd	Tu	Al	Pl	W	D	L	F	A	Pts
WEST GERMANY	–	0–0	1–1	2–0	6	4	2	0	10	2	10
Poland	1–3	–	5–1	3–0	6	2	2	2	10	6	6
Turkey	0–3	1–0	–	2–1	6	2	1	3	5	13	5
Albania	0–1	1–1	3–0	–	6	1	1	4	5	9	3

QUARTER-FINALS

ENGLAND .... 1–3 0–0 .... WEST GERMANY
ITALY .... 0–0 1–2 .... BELGIUM
HUNGARY .... 1–1 2–2 2–1* .. ROMANIA
YUGOSLAVIA .... 0–0 0–3 .... SOVIET UNION

* Play-off in Belgrade

SEMI-FINALS

Bosuil, Antwerp, 14–06–1972, 60 000
WEST GERMANY 2 (Müller 24 72)
BELGIUM 1 (Polleunis 83)

Parc Astrid, Brussels, 14–06–1972, 3000
SOVIET UNION 1 (Konkov 53)
HUNGARY 0

3RD PLACE

Liège, 17–06–1972, 10 000
BELGIUM 2 (Lambert, Van Himst)
HUNGARY 1 (Kü)

FINAL

Heysel, Brussels, 18–06–1972, 65 000
WEST GERMANY 3 (Müller 27 58, Wimmer 52)
SOVIET UNION 0
Referee: Marschall, Austria
West Germany – Maier – Höttges, Schwarzenbeck, Beckenbauer, Breitner – Wimmer, Hoeness, Netzer – Heynckes, Müller, Kremmers. Tr: Schoen
Soviet Union – Rudakov – Dzodzuashvili, Khurtsilava, Kaplichny, Istomin – Kolotov, Troshkin, Konkov (Dolmatov) – Baidachni, Banishevski (Kozinkievits), Onishenko. Tr: Ponomarev

FIFTH EDITION
1974–76

QUALIFYING TOURNAMENT

Group 1

	Cz	En	Pt	Cy	Pl	W	D	L	F	A	Pts
CZECHOSLOVAKIA	–	2–1	5–0	4–0	6	4	1	1	15	5	9
England	3–0	–	0–0	5–0	6	3	2	1	11	3	8
Portugal	1–1	1–1	–	1–0	6	2	3	1	5	7	7
Cyprus	0–3	0–1	0–2	–	6	0	0	6	0	16	0

Group 2

	Wa	Hu	Au	Lu	Pl	W	D	L	F	A	Pts
WALES	–	2–0	1–0	5–0	6	5	0	1	14	4	10
Hungary	1–2	–	2–1	8–1	6	3	1	2	15	8	7
Austria	2–1	0–0	–	6–2	6	3	1	2	11	7	7
Luxembourg	1–3	2–4	1–2	–	6	0	0	6	7	28	0

Group 3

	Yu	NI	Sd	No	Pl	W	D	L	F	A	Pts
YUGOSLAVIA	–	1–0	3–0	3–1	6	5	0	1	12	4	10
Nth. Ireland	1–0	–	1–2	3–0	6	3	0	3	8	5	6
Sweden	1–2	0–2	–	3–1	6	3	0	3	8	9	6
Norway	1–3	2–1	0–2	–	6	1	0	5	5	15	2

Group 4

	Sp	Ru	Sc	De	Pl	W	D	L	F	A	Pts
SPAIN	–	1–1	1–1	2–0	6	3	3	0	10	6	9
Romania	2–2	–	1–1	6–1	6	1	5	0	11	6	7
Scotland	1–2	1–1	–	3–1	6	2	3	1	8	6	7
Denmark	1–2	0–0	0–1	–	6	0	1	5	3	14	1

Group 5

	Ho	Pl	It	Fi	Pl	W	D	L	F	A	Pts
HOLLAND	–	3–0	3–1	4–1	6	4	0	2	14	8	8
POLAND	4–1	–	0–0	3–0	6	3	2	1	9	5	8
ITALY	1–0	0–0	–	0–0	6	2	3	1	3	3	7
FINLAND	1–3	1–2	0–1	–	6	0	1	5	3	13	1

Group 6

	SU	RI	Tu	Sz	Pl	W	D	L	F	A	Pts
SOVIET UNION	–	2–1	3–0	4–1	6	4	0	2	10	6	8
REP. IRELAND	3–0	–	4–0	2–1	6	3	1	2	11	5	7
TURKEY	1–0	1–1	–	2–1	6	2	2	2	5	10	6
SWITZERLAND	0–1	1–0	1–1	–	6	1	1	4	5	10	3

Group 7

	Be	EG	Fr	Ic	Pl	W	D	L	F	A	Pts
BELGIUM	–	1–2	2–1	1–0	6	3	2	1	6	3	8
EAST GERMANY	0–0	–	2–1	1–1	6	2	3	1	8	7	7
FRANCE	0–0	2–2	–	3–0	6	1	3	2	7	6	5
ICELAND	0–2	2–1	0–0	–	6	1	2	3	3	8	4

Group 8

	WG	Gr	Bu	Ma	Pl	W	D	L	F	A	Pts
WEST GERMANY	–	1–1	1–0	8–0	6	3	3	0	14	4	9
GREECE	2–2	–	2–1	4–0	6	2	3	1	12	9	7
BULGARIA	1–1	3–3	–	5–0	6	2	2	2	12	7	6
MALTA	0–1	2–0	0–2	–	6	1	0	5	2	20	2

QUARTER-FINALS

CZECHOSLOVAKIA . 2–0 2–2 .... SOVIET UNION
HOLLAND .... 5–0 2–1 .... BELGIUM
YUGOSLAVIA .... 2–0 1–1 .... WALES
SPAIN .... 1–1 0–2 .... WEST GERMANY

SEMI-FINALS

Zagreb, 16–06–1976, 40 000
CZECHOSLOVAKIA 3 (Ondrus 20, Nehoda 115, Vesely F 118)
HOLLAND 1 (OG 75)

Belgrade, 17–06–1976, 75 000
WEST GERMANY 4 (Flohe 65, Müller D 80 114 119)
YUGOSLAVIA 2 (Popivoda 20, Dzajic 30)

3RD PLACE

Stadion Dinamo, Zagreb, 19–06–1976, 18 000
HOLLAND 3 (Geels (2), Van de Kerkof W)
YUGOSLAVIA 2 (Katalinski, Dzajic)

FINAL

Crvena Zvezda, Belgrade, 20–06–1976, 45 000
CZECHOSLOVAKIA 2 (Svehlík 8, Dobiás 25)
WEST GERMANY 2 (Müller D 28, Hölzenbein 89)
Czechoslovakia won 5–4 on penalties
Referee: Gonella, Italy

Czechoslovakia – Viktor – Pivarník, Ondrus, Capkovic, Gögh – Dobiás (Vesely F), Móder, Panenka – Masny, Svehlík (Jurkemik), Nehoda. Tr: Jezek

West Germany – Maier – Vogts, Schwarzenbeck, Beckenbauer, Dietz – Wimmer (Flohe), Beer (Bongartz), Bonhof – Hoeness, Müller D, Hölzenbein. Tr: Schoen

SIXTH EDITION
1978–80

QUALIFYING TOURNAMENT

Group 1

	En	NI	RI	Bu	De	Pl	W	D	L	F	A	Pts
ENGLAND	–	4–0	2–0	2–0	1–0	8	7	1	0	22	5	15
NTH. IRELAND	1–5	–	1–0	2–0	2–1	8	4	1	3	8	14	9
REP. IRELAND	1–1	0–0	–	3–0	2–0	8	2	3	3	9	8	7
BULGARIA	0–3	0–2	1–0	–	3–0	8	2	1	5	6	14	5
DENMARK	3–4	4–0	3–3	2–2	–	8	1	2	5	13	17	4

Group 2

	Be	Au	Pt	Sc	No	Pl	W	D	L	F	A	Pts
BELGIUM	–	1–1	2–0	2–0	1–1	8	4	4	0	12	5	12
AUSTRIA	0–0	–	1–2	3–2	4–0	8	4	3	1	14	7	11
PORTUGAL	1–1	1–2	–	1–0	3–1	8	4	1	3	10	11	9
SCOTLAND	1–3	1–1	4–1	–	3–2	8	3	1	4	15	13	7
NORWAY	1–2	0–2	0–1	0–4	–	8	0	1	7	5	20	1

Group 3

	Sp	Yu	Ro	Cy	Pl	W	D	L	F	A	Pts
SPAIN	–	0–1	1–0	5–0	6	4	1	1	13	5	9
YUGOSLAVIA	1–2	–	2–1	5–0	6	4	0	2	14	6	8
ROMANIA	2–2	3–2	–	2–0	6	2	2	2	9	8	6
CYPRUS	1–3	0–3	1–1	–	6	0	1	5	2	19	1

Group 4

	Ho	Pd	EG	Sz	Ic	Pl	W	D	L	F	A	Pts
HOLLAND	–	1–1	3–0	3–0	3–0	8	6	1	1	20	6	13
POLAND	2–0	–	1–1	2–0	2–0	8	5	2	1	13	4	12
EAST GERMANY	2–3	2–1	–	5–2	3–1	8	5	1	2	18	11	11
SWITZERLAND	1–3	0–2	0–2	–	2–0	8	2	0	6	7	18	4
ICELAND	0–4	0–2	0–3	1–2	–	8	0	0	8	2	21	0

Group 5

	Cz	Fr	Sd	Lu	Pl	W	D	L	F	A	Pts
CZECHOSLOVAKIA	–	2–0	4–1	4–0	6	5	0	1	17	4	10
FRANCE	2–1	–	2–2	3–0	6	4	1	1	13	7	9
SWEDEN	1–3	1–3	–	3–0	6	1	2	3	9	13	4
LUXEMBOURG	0–3	1–3	1–1	–	6	0	1	5	2	17	1

Group 6

	Gr	Hu	Fi	SU	Pl	W	D	L	F	A	Pts
GREECE	–	4–1	8–1	1–0	6	3	1	2	13	7	7
HUNGARY	0–0	–	3–1	2–0	6	2	2	2	9	9	6
FINLAND	3–0	2–1	–	1–1	6	2	2	2	10	15	6
SOVIET UNION	2–0	2–2	2–2	–	6	1	3	2	7	8	5

Group 7

	WG	Tu	Wa	Ma	Pl	W	D	L	F	A	Pts
WEST GERMANY	–	2–0	5–1	8–0	6	4	2	0	17	1	10
TURKEY	0–0	–	1–0	2–1	6	3	1	2	5	5	7
WALES	0–2	1–0	–	7–0	6	3	0	3	11	8	6
MALTA	0–0	1–2	0–2	–	6	0	1	5	2	21	1

ITALY qualified as hosts

FINAL TOURNAMENT
Held in Italy 11th–22nd June 1980

FIRST ROUND

Group 1
Stadio Olimpico, Rome, 11–06–1980, 15 000

WEST GERMANY 1 (Rummenigge 55)
CZECHOSLOVAKIA 0

San Paolo, Naples, 11–06–1980, 10 000
HOLLAND 1 (Kist 56)
GREECE 0

San Paolo, Naples, 14–06–1980, 50 000
WEST GERMANY 3 (Allofs 15 60 67)
HOLLAND 2 (Rep 75, Van de Kerkof W 86)

Stadio Olimpico, Rome, 14–06–1980
CZECHOSLOVAKIA 3 (Panenka 5, Vízek 25, Nehoda 63)
GREECE 1 (Anastopoulos 11)

Giuseppe Meazza, Milan, 17–06–1980, 11 000
CZECHOSLOVAKIA 1 (Nehoda 13)
HOLLAND 1 (Kist 58)

Comunale, Turin, 17–06–1980, 13 000
WEST GERMANY 0
GREECE 0

	Pl	W	D	L	F	A	Pts
WEST GERMANY	3	2	1	0	4	2	5
CZECHOSLOVAKIA	3	1	1	1	4	3	3
HOLLAND	3	1	1	1	4	4	3
GREECE	3	0	1	2	1	4	1

Group 2
Comunale, Turin, 12–06–1980, 7000
BELGIUM 1 (Ceulemans 38)
ENGLAND 1 (Wilkins 32)

Giuseppe Meazza, Milan, 12–06–1980, 55 000
ITALY 0
SPAIN 0

Giuseppe Meazza, Milan, 15–06–1980, 11 000
BELGIUM 2 (Gerets 17, Cools 64)
SPAIN 1 (Quini 35)

Comunale, Turin, 15–06–1980, 59 000
ITALY 1 (Tardelli 79)
ENGLAND 0

Stadio Olimpico, Rome, 18–06–1980, 69 000
ITALY 0
BELGIUM 0

San Paolo, Naples, 18–06–1980, 14 000
ENGLAND 2 (Brooking 18, Woodcock 62)
SPAIN 1 (Dani 48)

	Pl	W	D	L	F	A	Pts
BELGIUM	3	1	2	0	3	2	4
ITALY	3	1	2	0	1	0	4
ENGLAND	3	1	1	1	3	3	3
SPAIN	3	0	1	2	2	4	1

3RD PLACE

San Paolo, Naples, 21–06–1980, 25 000
CZECHOSLOVAKIA 1 (Jurkemik 48)
ITALY 1 (Graziani 74)

Czechoslovakia won 9–8 on penalties

FINAL

Stadio Olimpico, Rome, 22–06–1980, 48 000
WEST GERMANY 2 (Hrubesch 10 88)
BELGIUM 1 (Vandereycken 72)
Referee: Rainea, Romania
West Germany – Schumacher – Kaltz, Förster K–H, Stielike, Dietz – Briegel (Cullmann), Schuster, Müller H – Rummenigge, Hrubesch, Allofs. Tr: Derwall
Belgium – Pfaff – Gerets, Millecamps, Meeuws, Renquin – Cools, Vandereycken, Van Moer – Mommens, Vander Elst, Ceulemans. Tr: Thys

SEVENTH EDITION
1982–84

QUALIFYING TOURNAMENT

Group 1

	Be	Sz	EG	Sc	Pl	W	D	L	F	A	Pts
BELGIUM	–	3–0	2–1	3–2	6	4	1	1	12	8	9
SWITZERLAND	3–1	–	0–0	2–0	6	2	2	2	7	9	6
EAST GERMANY	1–2	3–0	–	2–1	6	2	1	3	7	7	5
SCOTLAND	1–1	2–2	2–0	–	6	1	2	3	8	10	4

Group 2

	Pt	SU	Pd	Fi	Pl	W	D	L	F	A	Pts
PORTUGAL	–	1–0	2–1	5–0	6	5	0	1	11	6	10
SOVIET UNION	5–0	–	2–0	2–0	6	4	1	1	11	2	9
POLAND	0–1	1–1	–	1–1	6	1	2	3	6	9	4
FINLAND	0–2	0–1	2–3	–	6	0	1	5	3	14	1

Group 3

	De	En	Gr	Hu	Lu	Pl	W	D	L	F	A	Pts
DENMARK	–	2–2	1–0	3–1	6–0	8	6	1	1	17	5	13
ENGLAND	0–1	–	0–0	2–0	9–0	8	5	2	1	23	3	12
GREECE	0–2	0–3	–	2–2	1–0	8	3	2	3	8	10	8
HUNGARY	1–0	0–3	2–3	–	6–2	8	3	1	4	18	17	7
LUXEMBOURG	1–2	0–4	0–2	2–6	–	8	0	0	8	5	36	0

Group 4

	Yu	Wa	Bu	No	Pl	W	D	L	F	A	Pts
YUGOSLAVIA	–	4–4	3–2	2–1	6	3	2	1	12	11	8
WALES	1–1	–	1–0	1–0	6	2	3	1	7	6	7
BULGARIA	0–1	1–0	–	2–2	6	2	1	3	7	8	5
NORWAY	3–1	0–0	1–2	–	6	1	2	3	7	8	4

Group 5

	Ru	Sd	Cz	It	Cy	Pl	W	D	L	F	A	Pts
ROMANIA	–	2–0	0–1	1–0	3–1	8	5	2	1	9	3	12
SWEDEN	0–1	–	1–0	2–0	5–0	8	5	1	2	14	5	11
CZECHOSLOVAKIA	1–1	2–2	–	2–0	6–0	8	3	4	1	15	7	10
ITALY	0–0	0–3	2–2	–	3–1	8	1	3	4	6	12	5
CYPRUS	0–1	0–1	1–1	1–1	–	8	0	2	6	4	21	2

Group 6

	WG	NI	Au	Tu	Al	Pl	W	D	L	F	A	Pts
WEST GERMANY	–	0–1	3–0	5–1	2–1	8	5	1	2	15	5	11
NTH. IRELAND	1–0	–	3–1	2–1	1–0	8	5	1	2	8	5	11
AUSTRIA	0–0	2–0	–	4–0	5–0	8	4	1	3	15	10	9
TURKEY	0–3	1–0	3–1	–	1–0	8	3	1	4	8	16	7
ALBANIA	1–2	0–0	1–2	1–1	–	8	0	2	6	4	14	2

Group 7

	Sp	Ho	RI	Ic	Ma	Pl	W	D	L	F	A	Pts
SPAIN	–	1–0	2–0	1–0	12–1	8	6	1	1	24	8	13
HOLLAND	2–1	–	2–1	3–0	5–0	8	6	1	1	22	6	13
REP. IRELAND	3–3	2–3	–	2–0	8–0	8	4	1	3	20	10	9
ICELAND	0–1	1–1	0–3	–	1–0	8	1	1	6	3	13	3
MALTA	2–3	0–6	0–1	2–1	–	8	1	0	7	5	37	2

FRANCE qualified as hosts

FINAL TOURNAMENT

Held in France 12th–27th June 1984

FIRST ROUND

Group 1

Parc des Princes, Paris, 12–06–1984, 47 000
FRANCE 1 (Platini 77)
DENMARK 0

Félix Bollaert, Lens, 13–06–1984, 45 000
BELGIUM 2 (Vandenbergh 27, Grun 44)
YUGOSLAVIA 0

Beaujoire, Nantes, 16–06–1984, 51 000
FRANCE 5 (Platini 3 74 88, Giresse 32, Fernandez 43)
BELGIUM 0

Gerland, Lyon, 16–06–1984, 25 000
DENMARK 5 (OG 7, Berggren 16, Arnesen 68, Elkjaer 81, Lauridsen 83)
YUGOSLAVIA 0

Geoffroy Guichard, Saint Etienne, 19–06–1984, 50 000
FRANCE 3 (Platini 59 61 76)
YUGOSLAVIA 2 (Sestic 31, Stojkovic 80)

Meinau, Strasbourg, 19–06–1984, 36 000
DENMARK 3 (Arnesen 40, Brylle 60, Elkjaer 83)
BELGIUM 2 (Ceulemans 25, Vercauteren 38)

	Pl	W	D	L	F	A	Pts
FRANCE	3	3	0	0	9	2	6
DENMARK	3	2	0	1	8	3	4
BELGIUM	3	1	0	2	4	8	2
YUGOSLAVIA	3	0	0	3	2	10	0

Group 2

Meinau, Strasbourg, 14–06–1984, 47 000
PORTUGAL 0
WEST GERMANY 0

Geoffroy Guichard, Saint Etienne, 14–06–1984, 15 000
SPAIN 1 (Carrasco 20)
ROMANIA 1 (Bölöni 34)

Félix Bollaert, Lens, 17–06–1984, 35 000
WEST GERMANY 2 (Völler 24 65)
ROMANIA 1 (Coras 46)

Vélodrome, Marseille, 17–06–1984, 30 000
PORTUGAL 1 (Sousa 51)
SPAIN 1 (Santillana 72)

Parc des Princes, Paris, 20–06–1984, 40 000
SPAIN 1 (Maceda 89)
WEST GERMANY 0

Beaujoire, Nantes, 20–06–1984, 20 000
PORTUGAL 1 (Nene 80)
ROMANIA 0

	Pl	W	D	L	F	A	Pts
SPAIN	3	1	2	0	3	2	4
PORTUGAL	3	1	2	0	2	1	4
WEST GERMANY	3	1	1	1	2	2	3
ROMANIA	3	0	1	2	2	4	1

SEMI-FINALS

Vélodrome, Marseille, 23–06–1984, 55 000
FRANCE 3 (Domergue 24 114, Platini 119)
PORTUGAL 2 (Jordao 73 97)

Gerland, Lyon, 24–06–1984, 48 000
SPAIN 1 (Maceda 66)
DENMARK 1 (Lerby 6)
Spain won 5–4 on penalties

FINAL

Parc des Princes, Paris, 27–06–1984, 47 000
FRANCE 2 (Platini 57, Bellone 90)
SPAIN 0
Referee: Christov, Czechoslovakia
France – Bats – Battiston (Amoros), Le Roux, Bossis, Domergue – Giresse, Tigana, Fernandez, Platini – Lacombe (Genghini), Bellone. Tr: Hidalgo
Spain – Arconada – Urquiaga, Salva (Roberto), Gallego – Señor, Francisco, Víctor, Camacho, Julio Alberto (Sarabia) – Santillana, Carrasco. Tr: Muñoz

EIGHTH EDITION
1986–88

QUALIFYING TOURNAMENT

Group 1

	Sp	Ru	Au	Al	Pl	W	D	L	F	A	Pts
SPAIN	–	1–0	2–0	5–0	6	5	0	1	14	6	10
ROMANIA	3–1	–	4–0	5–1	6	4	1	1	13	3	9
AUSTRIA	2–3	0–0	–	3–0	6	2	1	3	6	9	5
ALBANIA	1–2	0–1	0–1	–	6	0	0	6	2	17	0

Group 2

	It	Sd	Pt	Sz	Ma	Pl	W	D	L	F	A	Pts
ITALY	–	2–1	3–0	3–2	5–0	8	6	1	1	16	4	13
SWEDEN	1–0	–	0–1	2–0	1–0	8	4	2	2	12	5	10
PORTUGAL	0–1	1–1	–	0–0	2–2	8	2	4	2	6	8	8
SWITZERLAND	0–0	1–1	1–1	–	4–1	8	1	5	2	9	9	7
MALTA	0–2	0–5	0–1	1–1	–	8	0	2	6	4	21	2

Group 3

	SU	EG	Fr	Ic	No	Pl	W	D	L	F	A	Pts
SOVIET UNION	–	2–0	1–1	2–0	4–0	8	5	3	0	14	3	13
EAST GERMANY	1–1	–	0–0	2–0	3–1	8	4	3	1	13	4	11
FRANCE	0–2	0–1	–	2–0	1–1	8	1	4	3	4	7	6
ICELAND	1–1	0–6	0–0	–	2–1	8	2	2	4	4	14	6
NORWAY	0–1	0–0	2–0	0–1	–	8	1	2	5	5	12	4

Group 4

	En	Yu	NI	Tu	Pl	W	D	L	F	A	Pts
ENGLAND	–	2–0	3–0	8–0	6	5	1	0	19	1	11
YUGOSLAVIA	1–4	–	3–0	4–0	6	4	0	2	13	9	8
NTH. IRELAND	0–2	1–2	–	1–0	6	1	1	4	2	10	3
TURKEY	0–0	2–3	0–0	–	6	0	2	4	2	16	2

Group 5

	Ho	Gr	Hu	Pd	Cy	Pl	W	D	L	F	A	Pts
HOLLAND	–	1–1	2–0	0–0	4–0*	8	6	2	0	15	1	14
GREECE	0–3	–	2–1	1–0	3–1	8	4	1	3	12	13	9
HUNGARY	0–1	3–0	–	5–3	1–0	8	4	0	4	13	11	8
POLAND	0–2	2–1	3–2	–	0–0	8	3	2	3	9	11	8
CYPRUS	0–2	2–4	0–1	0–1	–	8	0	1	7	3	16	1

* After 8–0 win declared void

Group 6

	De	Cz	Wa	Fi	Pl	W	D	L	F	A	Pts
DENMARK	–	1–1	1–0	1–0	6	3	2	1	4	2	8
CZECHOSLOVAKIA	0–0	–	2–0	3–0	6	2	3	1	7	5	7
WALES	1–0	1–1	–	4–0	6	2	2	2	7	5	6
FINLAND	0–1	3–0	1–1	–	6	1	1	4	4	10	3

Group 7

	RI	Bu	Be	Sc	Lu	Pl	W	D	L	F	A	Pts
REP. IRELAND	–	2–0	0–0	0–0	2–1	8	4	3	1	10	5	11
BULGARIA	2–1	–	2–0	0–1	3–0	8	4	2	2	12	6	10
BELGIUM	2–2	1–1	–	4–1	3–0	8	3	3	2	16	8	9
SCOTLAND	0–1	0–0	2–0	–	3–0	8	3	3	2	7	5	9
LUXEMBOURG	0–2	1–4	0–6	0–0	–	8	0	1	7	2	23	1

WEST GERMANY qualified as hosts

FINAL TOURNAMENT

Held in West Germany 10th–25th June 1988

FIRST ROUND

Group 1

Rheinstadion, Düsseldorf, 10–06–1988, 68 000
WEST GERMANY 1 (Brehme 55)
ITALY 1 (Mancini 51)

Niedersachsenstadion, Hanover, 11–06–1988, 60 000
SPAIN 3 (Michel 5, Butragueño 52, Gordillo 67)
DENMARK 2 (Laudrup 25, Povlsen 85)

Parkstadion, Gelsenkirchen, 14–06–1988, 70 000
WEST GERMANY 2 (Klinsmann 9, Thon 85)
DENMARK 0

Waldstadion, Frankfurt, 14–06–1988, 51 000
ITALY 1 (Vialli 73)
SPAIN 0

Olympiastadion, Munich, 17–06–1988, 72 000
WEST GERMANY 2 (Völler 30 51)
SPAIN 0

Müngersdorfer, Cologne, 17–06–1988, 60 000
ITALY 2 (Altobelli 65, De Agostini 87)
DENMARK 0

	Pl	W	D	L	F	A	Pts
WEST GERMANY	3	2	1	0	5	1	5
ITALY	3	2	1	0	4	1	5
SPAIN	3	1	0	2	3	5	2
DENMARK	3	0	0	3	2	7	0

Group 2

Neckarstadion, Stuttgart, 12–06–1988, 53 000
REP. IRELAND 1 (Houghton 5)
ENGLAND 0

Müngersdorfer, Cologne, 12–06–1988, 60 000
SOVIET UNION 1 (Rats 53)
HOLLAND 0

Rheinstadion, Düsseldorf, 15–06–1988, 65 000
HOLLAND 3 (Van Basten 23 71 75)
ENGLAND 1 (Robson 53)

Niedersachsenstadion, Hanover, 15–06–1988, 52 000
SOVIET UNION 1 (Protasov 74)
REP. IRELAND 1 (Whelan 38)

Waldstadion, Frankfurt, 18–06–1988, 53 000
SOVIET UNION 3 (Aleinikov 3, Mikhailichenko 28, Pasulko 72)
ENGLAND 1 (Adams 16)

Parkstadion, Gelsenkirchen, 18–06–1988, 70 000
HOLLAND 1 (Kieft 81)
REP. IRELAND 0

	Pl	W	D	L	F	A	Pts
SOVIET UNION	3	2	1	0	5	2	5
HOLLAND	3	2	0	1	4	2	4
REP. IRELAND	3	1	1	1	2	2	3
ENGLAND	3	0	0	3	2	7	0

SEMI-FINALS

Volksparkstadion, Hamburg, 21–06–1988, 60 000
HOLLAND 2 (Koeman R 73, Van Basten 88)
WEST GERMANY 1 (Matthäus 54)

Neckarstadion, Stuttgart, 22–06–1988, 70 000
SOVIET UNION 2 (Litovchenko 59, Protasov 62)
ITALY 0

FINAL

Olympiastadion, Munich, 25–06–1988, 72 000
HOLLAND 2 (Gullit 32, Van Basten 53)
SOVIET UNION 0
Referee: Vautrot, France

Holland – Van Breukelen – Van Aerle, Rijkaard, Koeman R, Van Tiggelen – Vanenburg, Wouters, Muhren, Koeman E – Gullit, Van Basten. Tr: Michels

Soviet Union – Dasayev – Demianenko, Aleinikov, Khidiatulin, Rats – Litovchenko, Zavarov, Mikhailichenko, Gotsmanov (Baltacha) – Protasov (Pasulko), Belanov. Tr: Lobanovsky

NINTH EDITION
1990–92

QUALIFYING TOURNAMENT

Group 1

	Fr	Cz	Sp	Ic	Al	Pl	W	D	L	F	A	Pts
FRANCE	–	2–1	3–1	3–1	5–0	8	8	0	0	20	6	16
CZECHOSLOVAKIA	1–2	–	3–2	1–0	2–1	8	5	0	3	12	9	10
SPAIN	1–2	2–1	–	2–1	9–0	7	3	0	4	17	12	6
ICELAND	1–2	0–1	2–0	–	2–0	8	2	0	6	7	10	4
ALBANIA	0–1	0–2	–	1–0	–	7	1	0	6	2	21	2

Group 2

	Sc	Sz	Ro	Bu	SM	Pl	W	D	L	F	A	Pts
SCOTLAND	–	2–1	2–1	1–1	4–0	8	4	3	1	14	7	11
SWITZERLAND	2–2	–	0–0	2–0	7–0	8	4	2	2	19	7	10
ROMANIA	1–0	1–0	–	0–3	6–0	8	4	2	2	13	7	10
BULGARIA	1–1	2–3	1–1	–	4–0	8	3	3	2	15	8	9
SAN MARINO	0–2	0–4	1–3	0–3	–	8	0	0	8	1	33	0

Group 3

	SU	It	No	Hu	Cy	Pl	W	D	L	F	A	Pts
SOVIET UNION	–	0–0	2–0	2–2	4–0	8	5	3	0	13	2	13
ITALY	0–0	–	1–1	3–1	2–0	8	3	4	1	12	5	10
NORWAY	0–1	2–1	–	0–0	3–0	8	3	3	2	9	5	9
HUNGARY	0–1	1–1	0–0	–	4–2	8	2	4	2	10	9	8
CYPRUS	0–3	0–4	0–3	0–2	–	8	0	0	8	2	25	0

Group 4

	Yu	De	NI	Au	FI	Pl	W	D	L	F	A	Pts
YUGOSLAVIA	–	1–2	4–1	4–1	7–0	8	7	0	1	24	4	14
DENMARK	0–2	–	2–1	2–1	4–1	8	6	1	1	18	7	13
NTH. IRELAND	0–2	1–1	–	2–1	1–1	8	2	3	3	11	11	7
AUSTRIA	0–2	0–3	0–0	–	3–0	8	1	1	6	6	14	3
FAEROE ISL.	0–2	0–4	0–5	1–0	–	8	1	1	6	3	26	3

Group 5

	Ge	Wa	Be	Lu	Pl	W	D	L	F	A	Pts
GERMANY	–	4–1	1–0	4–0	6	5	0	1	13	4	10
WALES	1–0	–	3–1	1–0	6	4	1	1	8	6	9
BELGIUM	0–1	1–1	–	3–0	6	2	1	3	7	6	5
LUXEMBOURG	2–3	0–1	0–2	–	6	0	0	6	2	14	0

Group 6

	Ho	Pt	Gr	Fi	Ma	Pl	W	D	L	F	A	Pts
HOLLAND	–	1–0	2–0	2–0	1–0	8	6	1	1	17	2	13
PORTUGAL	1–0	–	1–0	1–0	5–0	8	5	1	2	11	4	11
GREECE	0–2	3–2	–	2–0	4–0	8	3	2	3	11	9	8
FINLAND	1–1	0–0	1–1	–	2–0	8	1	4	3	5	8	6
MALTA	0–8	0–1	1–1	1–1	–	8	0	2	6	2	23	2

Group 7

	En	RI	Pd	Tu	Pl	W	D	L	F	A	Pts
ENGLAND	–	1–1	2–0	1–0	6	3	3	0	7	3	9
REP. IRELAND	1–1	–	0–0	5–0	6	2	4	0	13	6	8
POLAND	1–1	3–3	–	3–0	6	2	3	1	8	6	7
TURKEY	0–1	1–3	0–1	–	6	0	0	6	1	14	0

SWEDEN qualified as hosts

FINAL TOURNAMENT
Held in Sweden 10th June–26th June

FIRST ROUND

Group 1

Råsunda Stadion, Stockholm, 10–06–1992, 29 000
SWEDEN 1 (Eriksson 26)
FRANCE 1 (Papin 59)

Malmo Stadion, Malmo, 11–06–1992, 26 000
DENMARK 0
ENGLAND 0

Malmo Stadion, Malmo, 14–06–1992, 26 000
FRANCE 0
ENGLAND 0

Råsunda, Stockholm, 14–06–1992, 29 000
SWEDEN 1 (Brolin 58)
DENMARK 0

Råsunda Stadion, Stockholm, 17–06–1992, 30 000
SWEDEN 2 (Eriksson 51, Brolin 84)
ENGLAND 1 (Platt 3)

Malmo Stadion, Malmo, 17–06–1992, 17 000
DENMARK 2 (Larsen 7, Elstrup 78)
FRANCE 1 (Papin 59)

	Pl	W	D	L	F	A	Pts
SWEDEN	3	2	1	0	4	2	5
DENMARK	3	1	1	1	2	2	3
FRANCE	3	0	2	1	2	3	2
ENGLAND	3	0	2	1	1	2	2

Group 2

Nya Ullevi, Gothenburg, 12–06–1992, 35 000
HOLLAND 1 (Bergkamp 77)
SCOTLAND 0

Idraetspark, Norrkoping, 12–06–1992, 17 000
GERMANY 1 (Hässler 90)
CIS 1 (Dobrovolski 63)

Idraetspark, Norrkoping, 15–06–1992, 17 000
GERMANY 2 (Riedle 29, Effenberg 47)
SCOTLAND 0

Nya Ullevi, Gothenburg, 15–06–1992, 34 000
HOLLAND 0
CIS 0

Idraetspark, Norrkoping, 18–06–1992, 17 000
SCOTLAND 3 (OG 7, McClair 17, McAllister 83)
CIS 0

Nya Ullevi, Gothenburg, 18–06–1992, 35 000
HOLLAND 3 (Rijkaard 3, Witschge 15, Bergkamp 73)
GERMANY 1 (Klinsmann 53)

	Pl	W	D	L	F	A	Pts
HOLLAND	3	2	1	0	4	1	5
GERMANY	3	1	1	1	4	4	3
SCOTLAND	3	1	0	2	3	3	2
CIS	3	0	2	1	1	4	2

SEMI-FINALS

Råsunda Stadion, Stockholm, 21–06–1992, 28 000
GERMANY 3 (Hässler 11, Riedle 59 88)
SWEDEN 2 (Brolin 64, Andersson 89)

Nya Ullevi, Gothenburg, 22–06–1992, 35 000
DENMARK 2 (Larsen 5 32)
HOLLAND 2 (Bergkamp 23, Rijkaard 85)

FINAL

Nya Ullevi, Gothenburg, 26–06–1992, 37 000
DENMARK 2 (Jensen 18, Vilfort 78)
GERMANY 0
Referee: Galler, Switzerland

Denmark – Schmeichel – Sivebaek (Christiansen), Nielsen K, Olsen L, Piechnik – Christofte, Jensen J, Vilfort, Larsen H – Povlsen, Laudrup B. *Tr:* Möller Nielsen

Germany – Illgner – Helmer, Reuter, Kohler, Buchwald – Brehme, Hässler, Sammer (Doll), Effenberg (Thom) – Riedle, Klinsmann. *Tr:* Vogts

THE EUROPEAN CLUB TOURNAMENTS

Europe has three major club competitions. The European Champion Clubs' Cup is reserved for the winners of the league championship in each of UEFA's member countries. The Cup Winners Cup is reserved for the winners of the knock-out competition in each country whilst the UEFA Cup is for the best of the rest. The number of entries into this last tournament is determined by a UEFA coefficient table and is based upon past results in all three tournaments. A country like Italy or Spain will therefore usually have the maximum four entrants whilst the likes of Malta and Luxembourg are restricted to one.

The European Champion Clubs' Cup, or European Cup as it is more usually known, was the first of the three to get underway. In early 1955, Gabriel Hanot, then editor of *L'Equipe*, a French daily sports paper, invited representatives to a meeting in Paris to sound out the idea of creating a championship for the major clubs of Europe. Fifteen clubs responded to his invitation by attending the meeting and it was agreed to organise a tournament for the 1955–56 season.

FIFA were willing to support the idea and so UEFA gave the tournament its blessing, and has organised it ever since. The first tournament was curious in that only half of the clubs which took part were the champions of their respective countries. Not until the following season did UEFA manage to restrict it to the current practice of champions and the previous season's winners only.

Fortunately for the long-term success of the competition, Real Madrid were maturing into one of the best sides club football had ever seen and in a feat which is almost certain never to be repeated, they won five consecutive editions of the tournament and wrote themselves into football folklore. Ever since these triumphs, the competition has had a special aura about it.

This was not the case with the other two tournaments. At roughly the same time as the meeting arranged by Hanot, Ernst Thommen, a Swiss vice-president of UEFA, invited representatives to Basle, with a view to organising a tournament for representative sides from cities in Europe that regularly organised trade fairs. This may have been a somewhat tenuous reason for a tournament, but it was agreed upon, and a tournament called the International Industries Fairs Inter-Cities Cup was launched in the autumn of 1955.

Commonly known as the Fairs Cup, it drew entrants from ten cities that organised such events. The original idea was for these cities to field representative sides from all of the teams located in the city, but this idea did not hold out for very long. Barcelona, the winners of the first edition, fielded a team based purely on players from CF Barcelona, whilst Birmingham entered Birmingham City. Originally conceived as a two-year tournament, the first lasted for three years during which time only 23 games were played.

The Cup Winners Cup did not have a particularly auspicious start either. To begin with, not every country in Europe had a cup competition. Many did not see the need for one, and it was only in countries like Britain where the cup goes further back than the league that it enjoyed any real support. Nevertheless the organising committee of the Mitropa Cup launched the competition for the 1960–61 season, and Europe's trio of cups was on the road.

The European Cup has stayed uniform in size after the initial years, but it took longer for the Cup Winners Cup to reach its full complement as domestic cup tournaments were either initiated or old ones were brought out of storage. The Fairs Cup, renamed the UEFA Cup in 1972, eventually reached twice the size of both the European and Cup Winners Cup and has in a strange sense become the hardest of the three to win as there are usually more top quality clubs taking part than in the other two.

The UEFA Cup is the only one of the three tournaments whose final is played on a home and away basis. Both the others have a single game final tie in a neutral city. To qualify for the final, the rounds of all three are generally played on a home and away basis with the highest aggregate scorers qualifying for the next round. If the scores are level, the team which has scored more goals away from home qualifies, and if it is still all square after that, penalty kicks are used to seperate the sides. The away goals system was first used in 1967, before which an extra game was often played. Penalty kicks were introduced in 1971 to replace the very arbitrary toss of a coin. In 1992 the European Cup replaced the knock-out quarter-final and semi-final stages with a 'league' format. There were two groups of four teams, with the group winners going on to contest the final.

There have been three distinct phases in these European competitions. The first, lasting until the late 1960s, was the period of domination by clubs from the south of Europe, notably Spain, Italy and Portugal. Not until Glasgow Celtic won the European Cup in 1967 was that trophy won by a non-Latin side, whilst southern teams were also dominant in the Fairs Cup. The most notable sides of this period were of course Real Madrid, as well as Barcelona, Valencia and Real Zaragoza from Spain, the two Milan clubs and Roma from Italy and the two Lisbon clubs, Benfica and Sporting, from Portugal.

The European Cup produced some exciting encounters in these early years, none better than the 1960 final between Real Madrid and Eintracht Frankfurt. Scorer of a hat-trick that day was Alfredo Di Stéfano, and he was without question the leading personality in the tournament until he left Real in 1964. His 49 goals, scored in 58 matches, in the European Cup, the only one of the competitions in which he competed, is never likely to be equalled.

Eusébio took over Di Stéfano's mantle in the 1960s as his Benfica side reached five finals, winning two of them. In the 1962 clash between Benfica and Real, Eusébio's two goals were instrumental in helping overcome the Madrid giants in what was another scintillating game.

Italy was determined not to be left out and for three seasons running in the first half of the 1960s, the city of Milan ruled Europe. Northern Europe was beginning to mount a challenge, however. In 1963 Tottenham Hotspur won the Cup Winners Cup followed by West Ham United two years later. Celtic's European Cup win against Internazionale in 1967 signalled a dramatic decline for the established powers, as Britain, Holland and Germany began to flex their muscles.

This second phase saw two hat-tricks of European Cup successes, first by Ajax of Holland and then Bayern Munich of West Germany. These followed on from wins by Manchester United in 1968 and Feyenoord in 1970. The same was happening in the Cup Winners Cup and Fairs Cup. Milan won the Cup Winners Cup in 1968 and 1973, but they were the only Latin side to do so from 1965 until Barcelona won it for the first time in 1979.

The UEFA Cup was becoming very much an English affair by the late 1960s with six victories on the trot. It was in the late 1970s, however, that English clubs really came into their own, especially in the European Cup. Seven victories in eight years by three teams from England, most notably Liverpool, tells the story, but this period also heralded a decline in the number of goals scored, especially in the finals. In the 18 finals of the European Cup since 1975, only 25 goals have been scored, one less than the total scored in the first five finals.

The year 1985 marked a turning point in European football. For many years the game had been plagued by hooliganism from the supporters. The 1975 European Cup final was marred by supporters of Leeds United tearing the stadium to pieces in Paris, after their defeat by Bayern Munich, whilst the previous year supporters of Tottenham and Feyenoord had wrecked the UEFA Cup final. Whenever the English travelled abroad, they seemed to leave a trail of destruction behind them, and soon the Europeans copied.

The whole sordid problem came to a head at the 1985 European Cup final between Liverpool and Juventus. Thirty-nine supporters, mainly Italians, were crushed to death at the Heysel stadium in Brussels. The English paid the price for years of neglect of their supporters. Only two weeks prior to the Heysel tragedy, 53 supporters had died in a fire at Bradford City. The image of the English game could not have been any worse and they were banned from all European club competition indefinitely.

Though free of English hooligans, the European competitions suffered without the English clubs who had done so well until 1985. The hooligan problem did not go away either, as there seemed to be an active element in most countries. This third phase has been marked by the rise of the Latin countries again, especially Italy, whose clubs, free from a ban on importing players, bought up the best.

Milan especially have revived past glories, but Juventus, Internazionale, Napoli and Sampdoria all won one or other of the competitions, but apart from Milan's 4–0 demolition of Steaua Bucharest in 1989, goals in the final of the European Cup have dried up even further. Three finals have finished 0–0 and had to be settled by penalties, and so bad was the 1986 final between Steaua and Barcelona that only two penalties out of seven were scored.

The Cup Winners Cup and UEFA Cup have not suffered such poor finals, but they have not exactly been brimming with good football. The return of English clubs in 1991 will hopefully mark the onset of a more adventurous phase; Manchester United's victory in the 1991 Cup Winners Cup was one of the best finals Europe had seen for a few years.

COMBINED EUROPEAN CLUB RECORDS BY COUNTRY

		G	S	B	Finals	Semis
1	England	23	12	20	35	55
2	Spain	20	17	19	37	55
3	Italy	17	16	20	33	52
4	Germany	12	13	33	25	58
5	Holland	9	4	10	13	23
6	Belgium	4	7	13	11	24
7	Portugal	4	7	4	11	15
8	Scotland	3	4	14	7	21
9	Soviet Union	3	1	6	4	10
10	Yugoslavia	2	3	11	5	16
11	Sweden	2	1	1	3	4
12	Hungary	1	5	7	6	13
13	East Germany	1	2	5	3	8
14	Romania	1	1	4	2	6
15	Czechoslovakia	1	–	6	1	7
16	France	–	6	9	6	15
17	Austria	–	2	4	2	6
18	Poland	–	1	3	1	4
19	Greece	–	1	2	1	3
20	Switzerland	–	–	5	–	5
21	Bulgaria	–	–	4	–	4
22	Turkey	–	–	2	–	2
23	Denmark	–	–	1	–	1
	Wales	–	–	1	–	1
24	Albania/Cyprus/Finland/Iceland/Malta N.Ireland/Luxembourg/Norway/ Republic of Ireland	–	–	–	–	–

COMBINED EUROPEAN CLUB RECORDS

	Team	Country	G	S	B
1	Real Madrid	ESP	8	5	8
2	Barcelona	ESP	7	5	4
3	Liverpool	ENG	6	2	2
	Milan	ITA	6	2	2
5	Ajax	HOL	5	2	2
6	Juventus	ITA	4	4	5
7	Bayern München	FRG	4	2	8
8	RSC Anderlecht	BEL	3	4	2

9	Internazionale	ITA	3	2	6
10	Tottenham Hotspur	ENG	3	1	3
11	Valencia	ESP	3	1	–
12	Benfica	POR	2	6	2
13	Bor. Mönchengladbach	FRG	2	3	3
14	Hamburger SV	FRG	2	3	2
	Leeds United	ENG	2	3	2
16	Manchester United	ENG	2	–	6
17	PSV Eindhoven	HOL	2	–	3
	Feyenoord	HOL	2	–	3
19	Dinamo Kiev	URS	2	–	2
20	Nottingham Forest	ENG	2	–	1
	IFK Göteborg	SWE	2	–	1
22	Atlético Madrid	ESP	1	3	4
23	Fiorentina	ITA	1	3	–
24	Ferencváros	HUN	1	2	2
	Glasgow Rangers	SCO	1	2	2
	Roma	ITA	1	2	2
27	Sampdoria	ITA	1	2	–
28	Glasgow Celtic	SCO	1	1	4
	Crvena Zvezda Beograd	YUG	1	1	4
30	Eintracht Frankfurt	FRG	1	1	2
	Real Zaragoza	ESP	1	1	2
32	HASK Gradanski Zagreb	YUG	1	1	1
	Steaua Bucuresti	ROM	1	1	1
	West Ham United	ENG	1	1	1
35	Arsenal	ENG	1	1	–
	FC Porto	POR	1	1	–
37	Sporting CP	POR	1	–	2
	Werder Bremen	FRG	1	–	2
39	Aberdeen	SCO	1	–	1
	Borussia Dortmund	FRG	1	–	1
	Chelsea	ENG	1	–	1
	Dinamo Tbilisi	URS	1	–	1
	Manchester City	ENG	1	–	1
	KV Mechelen	BEL	1	–	1
	Napoli	ITA	1	–	1
46	Aston Villa	ENG	1	–	–
	Bayer Leverkusen	FRG	1	–	–
	Everton	ENG	1	–	–
	Ipswich Town	ENG	1	–	–
	1.FC Magdeburg	GDR	1	–	–
	Newcastle United	ENG	1	–	–
	Slovan Bratislava	TCH	1	–	–
53	Birmingham City	ENG	–	2	1
	Club Brugge	BEL	–	2	1
55	Stade de Reims	FRA	–	2	–
56	1.FC Köln	FRG	–	1	7
57	Standard CL	BEL	–	1	2
	FK Austria	AUT	–	1	2
	FC Twente Enschede	HOL	–	1	2
	Olympique Marseille	FRA	–	1	2
	Dinamo Moskva	URS	–	1	2
	VfB Stuttgart	FRG	–	1	2
	Ujpesti TE	HUN	–	1	2
64	Carl Zeiss Jena	GDR	–	1	1
	Dundee United	SCO	–	1	1
	VfB Leipzig	GDR	–	1	1
	AS Monaco	FRA	–	1	1
	MTK-VM Budapest	HUN	–	1	1
	Panathinaikos	GRE	–	1	1
	SK Rapid Wien	AUT	–	1	1
	AS Saint-Etienne	FRA	–	1	1
	Torino	ITA	–	1	1
	Wolverhampton Wdrs	ENG	–	1	1
74	AZ Alkmaar	HOL	–	1	–
	Athletic Bilbao	ESP	–	1	–
	SEC Bastia	FRA	–	1	–
	RCD Español	ESP	–	1	–

	Fortuna Düsseldorf	FRG	–	1	–
	Górnik Zabrze	POL	–	1	–
	Malmö FF	SWE	–	1	–
	TSV München 1860	FRG	–	1	–
	Partizan Beograd	YUG	–	1	–
	Videoton SC	HUN	–	1	–
	London Select XI	ENG	–	1	–
85	CSKA Sofia	BUL	–	–	3
86	Girondins Bordeaux	FRA	–	–	2
	Dinamo Bucuresti	ROM	–	–	2
	Dukla Praha	TCH	–	–	2
	Dundee	SCO	–	–	2
	Legia Warszawa	POL	–	–	2
	Hajduk Split	YUG	–	–	2
	Hibernian Edinburgh	SCO	–	–	2
	FC Zürich	SUI	–	–	2
94	AEK Athens	GRE	–	–	1
	Atalanta	ITA	–	–	1
	Baník Ostrava	TCH	–	–	1
	Bayer Uerdingen	FRG	–	–	1
	Belgrade Select XI	YUG	–	–	1
	SK Beveren	BEL	–	–	1
	Bologna	ITA	–	–	1
	Brondbyernes IF	DEN	–	–	1
	Cardiff City	WAL	–	–	1
	Derby County	ENG	–	–	1
	MSV Duisburg	FRG	–	–	1
	Bohemians Praha	TCH	–	–	1
	Dunfermline Athletic	SCO	–	–	1
	Berliner FC	GDR	–	–	1
	1.FC Dynamo Dresden	GDR	–	–	1
	Genoa 1893	ITA	–	–	1
	Galatasaray	TUR	–	–	1
	Göztepe Izmir	TUR	–	–	1
	Grasshopper-Club	SUI	–	–	1
	Hertha BSC Berlin	FRG	–	–	1
	1.FC Kaiserslautern	FRG	–	–	1
	Kilmarnock	SCO	–	–	1
	Lausanne-Sports	SUI	–	–	1
	RFC Liège	BEL	–	–	1
	Olympique Lyon	FRA	–	–	1
	RWD Molenbeek	BEL	–	–	1
	FC Nantes	FRA	–	–	1
	1.FC Nürnberg	FRG	–	–	1
	OFK Beograd	YUG	–	–	1
	Radnicki Nis	YUG	–	–	1
	Real Sociedad	ESP	–	–	1
	FSV Zwickau	GDR	–	–	1
	FC Schalke 04	FRG	–	–	1
	Slavia Sofia	BUL	–	–	1
	FC Sochaux	FRA	–	–	1
	Sparta Praha	TCH	–	–	1
	Spartak Moskva	URS	–	–	1
	Spartak Trnava	TCH	–	–	1
	FC Tirol	AUT	–	–	1
	Union St. Gilloise	BEL	–	–	1
	Universitatea Craiova	ROM	–	–	1
	Vasas Budapest	HUN	–	–	1
	Rába ETO Györ	HUN	–	–	1
	KSV Waregem	BEL	–	–	1
	Racing Club Genk	BEL	–	–	1
	Widzew Lódz	POL	–	–	1
	BSC Young Boys Berne	SUI	–	–	1
	Zeljeznicar Sarajevo	YUG	–	–	1

To the end of the 1991–92 season

THE EUROPEAN CHAMPIONS CLUBS' CUP

1956	Real Madrid	4–3	Stade de Reims
1957	Real Madrid	2–0	Fiorentina
1958	Real Madrid	3–2	Milan
1959	Real Madrid	2–0	Stade de Reims
1960	Real Madrid	7–3	Eintracht Frankfurt
1961	Benfica	3–2	Barcelona
1962	Benfica	5–3	Real Madrid
1963	Milan	2–1	Benfica
1964	Internazionale	3–1	Real Madrid
1965	Internazionale	1–0	Benfica
1966	Real Madrid	2–1	Partizan Beograd
1967	Glasgow Celtic	2–1	Internazionale
1968	Manchester United	4–1	Benfica
1969	Milan	4–1	Ajax
1970	Feyenoord	2–1	Glasgow Celtic
1971	Ajax	2–0	Panathinaikos
1972	Ajax	2–0	Milan
1973	Ajax	1–0	Juventus
1974	Bayern München	1–1 4–0	Atlético Madrid
1975	Bayern München	2–0	Leeds United
1976	Bayern München	1–0	AS Saint-Étienne
1977	Liverpool	3–1	Bor. Mönchenglad.
1978	Liverpool	1–0	Club Brugge
1979	Nottingham Forest	1–0	Malmö FF
1980	Nottingham Forest	1–0	Hamburger SV
1981	Liverpool	1–0	Real Madrid
1982	Aston Villa	1–0	Bayern München
1983	Hamburger SV	1–0	Juventus
1984	Liverpool	1–1 (4–2p)	Roma
1985	Juventus	1–0	Liverpool
1986	Steaua Bucuresti	0–0 (2–0p)	Barcelona
1987	FC Porto	2–1	Bayern München
1988	PSV Eindhoven	0–0 (6–5p)	Benfica
1989	Milan	4–0	Steaua Bucuresti
1990	Milan	1–0	Benfica
1991	Crvena Zvezda	0–0 (5–3p)	Olympique Marseille
1992	Barcelona	1–0	Sampdoria

COUNTRIES IN EUROPEAN CUP

		G	S	B	Finals	Semis
1	England	8	2	8	10	18
2	Italy	7	8	5	15	19
3	Spain	7	6	12	13	24
4	Holland	5	1	3	6	9
5	Germany	4	5	7	9	16
6	Portugal	3	5	1	8	9
7	Scotland	1	1	6	2	8
8	Romania	1	1	2	2	4
	Yugoslavia	1	1	2	2	4
10	France	–	4	3	4	7
11	Belgium	–	1	3	1	4
12	Greece	–	1	1	1	2
	Sweden	–	1	1	1	2
14	Hungary	–	–	3	–	3
	Soviet Union	–	–	3	–	3
	Switzerland	–	–	3	–	3
17	Austria	–	–	2	–	2
	Bulgaria	–	–	2	–	2
	Czechoslovakia	–	–	2	–	2
	Poland	–	–	2	–	2
21	Turkey	–	–	1	–	1

CLUB RECORDS IN EUROPEAN CUP

			G	S	B
1	Real Madrid	ESP	6	3	7
2	Liverpool	ENG	4	1	1
	Milan	ITA	4	1	1
4	Bayern München	FRG	3	2	3
5	Ajax	HOL	3	1	1
6	Benfica	POR	2	5	1
7	Internazionale	ITA	2	2	2
8	Nottingham Forest	ENG	2	–	–
9	Juventus	ITA	1	2	2
	Barcelona	ESP	1	2	2
11	Glasgow Celtic	SCO	1	1	2
12	Hamburger SV	FRG	1	1	1
	Steaua Bucuresti	ROM	1	1	1
14	Manchester United	ENG	1	–	4
15	Crvena Zvezda Beograd	YUG	1	–	2
16	Feyenoord	HOL	1	–	1
	PSV Eindhoven	HOL	1	–	1
18	Aston Villa	ENG	1	–	–
	FC Porto	POR	1	–	–
20	Stade de Reims	FRA	–	2	–
21	Atlético Madrid	ESP	–	1	2
22	Bor. Mönchengladbach	FRG	–	1	1
	Leeds United	ENG	–	1	1
	Olympique Marseille	FRA	–	1	1
	Panathinaikos	GRE	–	1	1
	AS Saint-Étienne	FRA	–	1	1
27	Eintracht Frankfurt	FRG	–	1	–
	Club Brugge	BEL	–	1	–
	Fiorentina	ITA	–	1	–
	Malmö FF	SWE	–	1	–
	Partizan Beograd	YUG	–	1	–
	Roma	ITA	–	1	–
	Sampdoria	ITA	–	1	–
34	RSC Anderlecht	BEL	–	–	2
	CSKA Sofia	BUL	–	–	2
	Dinamo Kiev	URS	–	–	2
	FC Zürich	SUI	–	–	2
38	FK Austria	AUT	–	–	1
	Girondins Bordeaux	FRA	–	–	1
	Borussia Dortmund	FRG	–	–	1
	1.FC Köln	FRG	–	–	1
	Derby County	ENG	–	–	1
	Dinamo Bucuresti	ROM	–	–	1
	Dukla Praha	TCH	–	–	1
	Dundee	SCO	–	–	1
	Dundee United	SCO	–	–	1
	Galatasaray	TUR	–	–	1
	IFK Göteborg	SWE	–	–	1
	Hibernian Edinburgh	SCO	–	–	1
	Legia Warszawa	POL	–	–	1
	Glasgow Rangers	SCO	–	–	1
	SK Rapid Wien	AUT	–	–	1
	Real Sociedad	ESP	–	–	1
	Spartak Moskva	URS	–	–	1
	Spartak Trnava	TCH	–	–	1
	Standard CL	BEL	–	–	1
	Tottenham Hotspur	ENG	–	–	1
	Ujpesti TE	HUN	–	–	1
	Vasas Budapest	HUN	–	–	1
	Rába ETO Györ	HUN	–	–	1
	Widzew Lódz	POL	–	–	1
	BSC Young Boys Berne	SUI	–	–	1

THE EUROPEAN CUP WINNERS CUP

1961	Fiorentina	2–0 2–1	Glasgow Rangers
1962	Atlético Madrid	1–1 3–0	Fiorentina
1963	Tottenham Hotspur	5–1	Atlético Madrid
1964	Sporting CP	3–3 1–0	MTK Budapest
1965	West Ham United	2–0	TSV 1860 München
1966	Borussia Dortmund	2–1	Liverpool
1967	Bayern München	1–0	Glasgow Rangers
1968	Milan	2–0	Hamburger SV
1969	Slovan Bratislava	3–2	Barcelona
1970	Manchester City	2–1	Gornik Zabrze
1971	Chelsea	1–1 2–1	Real Madrid
1972	Glasgow Rangers	3–2	Dynamo Moskva
1973	Milan	1–0	Leeds United
1974	1.FC Magdeburg	2–0	Milan
1975	Dynamo Kiev	3–0	Ferencváros
1976	RSC Anderlecht	4–2	West Ham United
1977	Hamburger SV	2–0	RSC Anderlecht
1978	RSC Anderlecht	4–0	FK Austria
1979	Barcelona	4–3	Fortuna Düsseldorf
1980	Valencia	0–0 (5–4p)	Arsenal
1981	Dynamo Tbilisi	2–1	Carl Zeiss Jena
1982	Barcelona	2–1	Standard CL
1983	Aberdeen	2–1	Real Madrid
1984	Juventus	2–1	FC Porto
1985	Everton	3–1	SK Rapid Wien
1986	Dynamo Kiev	3–0	Atlético Madrid
1987	Ajax	1–0	Lokomotive Leipzig
1988	KV Mechelen	1–0	Ajax
1989	Barcelona	2–0	Sampdoria
1990	Sampdoria	2–0	RSC Anderlecht
1991	Manchester United	2–1	Barcelona
1992	Werder Bremen	2–0	AS Monaco

COUNTRIES IN CUP WINNERS CUP

	Team	G	S	B	Finals	Semis
1	England	6	4	5	10	15
2	Spain	5	6	3	11	14
3	Italy	5	3	6	8	14
4	Germany	4	3	9	7	16
5	Belgium	3	3	5	6	11
6	Soviet Union	3	1	3	4	7
7	Scotland	2	2	4	4	8
8	East Germany	1	2	3	3	6
9	Holland	1	1	5	2	7
10	Portugal	1	1	2	2	4
11	Czechoslovakia	1	–	3	1	4
12	Austria	–	2	1	2	3
	Hungary	–	2	1	2	3
14	France	–	1	5	1	6
15	Poland	–	1	1	1	2
16	Yugoslavia	–	–	4	–	4
17	Bulgaria	–	–	2	–	2
18	Romania	–	–	1	–	1
	Wales	–	–	1	–	1

CLUB RECORDS IN CUP WINNERS CUP

	Team	Country	G	S	B
1	Barcelona	ESP	3	2	–
2	RSC Anderlecht	BEL	2	2	–
3	Milan	ITA	2	1	–
4	Dinamo Kiev	URS	2	–	–
5	Atlético Madrid	ESP	1	2	1
6	Glasgow Rangers	SCO	1	2	–
7	West Ham United	ENG	1	1	1
8	Fiorentina	ITA	1	1	–
	Hamburger SV	FRG	1	1	–
	Ajax	HOL	1	1	–
	Sampdoria	ITA	1	1	–
12	Bayern München	FRG	1	–	3
13	Juventus	ITA	1	–	2
14	Aberdeen	SCO	1	–	1
	Dinamo Tbilisi	URS	1	–	1
	Manchester City	ENG	1	–	1
	Manchester United	ENG	1	–	1
	KV Mechelen	BEL	1	–	1
	Sporting CP	POR	1	–	1
	Tottenham Hotspur	ENG	1	–	1
21	Borussia Dortmund	FRG	1	–	–
	Chelsea	ENG	1	–	–
	Everton	ENG	1	–	–
	1.FC Magdeburg	GDR	1	–	–
	Slovan Bratislava	TCH	1	–	–
	Valencia	ESP	1	–	–
	Werder Bremen	FRG	1	–	–
28	Real Madrid	ESP	–	2	–
29	Dinamo Moskva	URS	–	1	2
30	FK Austria	AUT	–	1	1
	Carl Zeiss Jena	GDR	–	1	1
	AS Monaco	FRA	–	1	1
	Standard CL	BEL	–	1	1
34	Arsenal	ENG	–	1	–
	Ferencváros	HUN	–	1	–
	Fortuna Düsseldorf	FRG	–	1	–
	Górnik Zabrze	POL	–	1	–
	Leeds United	ENG	–	1	–
	Liverpool	ENG	–	1	–
	VfB Leipzig	GDR	–	1	–
	MTK–VM Budapest	HUN	–	1	–
	TSV München 1860	FRG	–	1	–
	FC Porto	POR	–	1	–
	SK Rapid Wien	AUT	–	1	–
45	Glasgow Celtic	SCO	–	–	2
	Feyenoord	HOL	–	–	2
	PSV Eindhoven	HOL	–	–	2
	Real Zaragoza	ESP	–	–	2
49	Atalanta	ITA	–	–	1
	Baník Ostrava	TCH	–	–	1
	Bayer Uerdingen	FRG	–	–	1
	Benfica	POR	–	–	1
	SK Beveren	BEL	–	–	1
	Girondins Bordeaux	FRA	–	–	1
	Bor. Mönchengladbach	FRG	–	–	1
	Cardiff City	WAL	–	–	1
	Club Brugge	BEL	–	–	1
	CSKA Sofia	BUL	–	–	1
	1.FC Köln	FRG	–	–	1
	Dukla Praha	TCH	–	–	1
	Dunfermline Athletic	SCO	–	–	1
	Berliner FC	GDR	–	–	1
	Dinamo Bucuresti	ROM	–	–	1
	HASK Gradanski Zagreb	YUG	–	–	1

Eintracht Frankfurt	FRG	–	–	1
Hajduk Split	YUG	–	–	1
Legia Warszawa	POL	–	–	1
Olympique Lyon	FRA	–	–	1
Olympique Marseille	FRA	–	–	1
FC Nantes	FRA	–	–	1
Napoli	ITA	–	–	1
1.FC Nürnberg	FRG	–	–	1
OFK Beograd	YUG	–	–	1
Crvena Zvezda Beograd	YUG	–	–	1
Roma	ITA	–	–	1
FSV Zwickau	GDR	–	–	1
FC Schalke 04	FRG	–	–	1
Slavia Sofia	BUL	–	–	1
Sparta Praha	TCH	–	–	1
Torino	ITA	–	–	1
FC Twente Enschede	HOL	–	–	1
Ujpesti TE	HUN	–	–	1
Racing Club Genk	BEL	–	–	1
Wolverhampton Wdrs	ENG	–	–	1

THE INTER CITIES FAIRS CUP

1958	Barcelona	2–2 6–0	London Select XI
1960	Barcelona	0–0 4–1	Birmingham City
1961	Roma	2–2 2–0	Birmingham City
1962	Valencia	6–2 1–1	Barcelona
1963	Valencia	2–1 2–0	Dinamo Zagreb
1964	Real Zaragoza	2–1	Valencia
1965	Ferencváros	1–0	Juventus
1966	Barcelona	0–1 4–2	Real Zaragoza
1967	Dinamo Zagreb	2–0 0–0	Leeds United
1968	Leeds United	1–0 0–0	Ferencváros
1969	Newcastle United	3–0 3–2	Ujpesti Dózsa
1970	Arsenal	1–3 3–0	RSC Anderlecht
1971	Leeds United	2–2 1–1	Juventus

THE UEFA CUP

1972	Tottenham Hotspur	2–1 1–1	Wolverhampton Wdrs
1973	Liverpool	3–0 0–2	B. Mönchengladbach
1974	Feyenoord	2–2 2–0	Tottenham Hotspur
1975	B. Mönchengladbach	0–0 5–1	FC Twente Enschede
1976	Liverpool	3–2 1–1	Club Brugge
1977	Juventus	1–0 1–2	Athletic Bilbao
1978	PSV Eindhoven	0–0 3–0	SEC Bastia
1979	B. Mönchengladbach	1–1 1–0	Crvena Zvezda
1980	Eintracht Frankfurt	2–3 1–0	B. Mönchengladbach
1981	Ipswich Town	3–0 2–4	AZ 67 Alkmaar
1982	IFK Göteborg	1–0 3–0	Hamburger SV
1983	RSC Anderlecht	1–0 1–1	Benfica
1984	Tottenham Hotspur	1–1 1–1 (4–3p)	RSC Anderlecht
1985	Real Madrid	3–0 0–1	Videoton SC
1986	Real Madrid	5–1 0–2	1.FC Köln
1987	IFK Göteborg	1–0 1–1	Dundee United
1988	Bayer Leverkusen	0–3 3–0 (3–2p)	Español
1989	Napoli	2–1 3–3	VfB Stuttgart
1990	Juventus	3–1 0–0	Fiorentina
1991	Internazionale	2–0 0–1	Roma
1992	Ajax	2–2 0–0	Torino

COUNTRIES IN FAIRS/UEFA CUP

		G	S	B	Finals	Semis
1	England	9	6	7	15	22
2	Spain	8	5	4	13	17
3	Italy	5	5	9	10	19
4	Germany	4	5	17	9	26
5	Holland	3	2	2	5	7
6	Sweden	2	–	–	2	2
7	Belgium	1	3	5	4	9
8	Hungary	1	3	3	4	7
9	Yugoslavia	1	2	5	3	8
10	Scotland	–	1	4	1	5
11	France	–	1	1	1	2
	Portugal	–	1	1	1	2
13	East Germany	–	–	2	–	2
	Switzerland	–	–	2	–	2
15	Austria	–	–	1	–	1
	Czechoslovakia	–	–	1	–	1
	Denmark	–	–	1	–	1
	Greece	–	–	1	–	1
	Romania	–	–	1	–	1
	Turkey	–	–	1	–	1

CLUB RECORDS IN FAIRS/UEFA CUP

			G	S	B
1	Barcelona	ESP	3	1	2
2	Bor. Mönchengladbach	FRG	2	2	1
	Juventus	ITA	2	2	1
4	Leeds United	ENG	2	1	1
	Tottenham Hotspur	ENG	2	1	1
6	Valencia	ESP	2	1	–
7	Liverpool	ENG	2	–	1
	Real Madrid	ESP	2	–	1
9	IFK Göteborg	SWE	2	–	–
10	RSC Anderlecht	BEL	1	2	–
11	Ferencváros	HUN	1	1	2
12	Roma	ITA	1	1	1
13	HASK Gradanski Zagreb	YUG	1	1	–
	Real Zaragoza	ESP	1	1	–
15	Internazionale	ITA	1	–	4
16	Ajax	HOL	1	–	1
	Eintracht Frankfurt	FRG	1	–	1
18	Arsenal	ENG	1	–	–
	Bayer Leverkusen	FRG	1	–	–
	Feyenoord	HOL	1	–	–
	Ipswich Town	ENG	1	–	–
	Napoli	ITA	1	–	–
	Newcastle United	ENG	1	–	–
	PSV Eindhoven	HOL	1	–	–
25	Birmingham City	ENG	–	2	1
26	1.FC Köln	FRG	–	1	5
27	VfB Stuttgart	FRG	–	1	2
28	Club Brugge	BEL	–	1	1
	Hamburger SV	FRG	–	1	1
	Crvena Zvezda Beograd	YUG	–	1	1
	FC Twente Enschede	HOL	–	1	1
32	AZ Alkmaar	HOL	–	1	–
	Athletic Bilbao	ESP	–	1	–
	SEC Bastia	FRA	–	1	–
	Benfica	POR	–	1	–
	Dundee United	SCO	–	1	–
	RCD Español	ESP	–	1	–
	Fiorentina	ITA	–	1	–

	London Select XI	ENG	–	1	–
	Torino	ITA	–	1	–
	Ujpesti TE	HUN	–	1	–
	Videoton SC	HUN	–	1	–
	Wolverhampton Wdrs	ENG	–	1	–
44	Bayern München	FRG	–	–	2
	Werder Bremen	FRG	–	–	2
46	AEK Athens	GRE	–	–	1
	Atlético Madrid	ESP	–	–	1
	Belgrade Select XI	YUG	–	–	1
	Bologna	ITA	–	–	1
	Brondbyernes IF	DEN	–	–	1
	Chelsea	ENG	–	–	1
	MSV Duisburg	FRG	–	–	1
	Bohemians Praha	TCH	–	–	1
	Dundee	SCO	–	–	1
	1.FC Dynamo Dresden	GDR	–	–	1
	Genoa	ITA	–	–	1
	Grasshopper–Club	SUI	–	–	1
	Göztepe Izmir	TUR	–	–	1
	Hibernian Edinburgh	SCO	–	–	1
	Hajduk Split	YUG	–	–	1
	Hertha BSC Berlin	FRG	–	–	1
	1.FC Kaiserslautern	FRG	–	–	1
	Kilmarnock	SCO	–	–	1
	RFC Liège	BEL	–	–	1
	Lausanne–Sports	SUI	–	–	1
	VfB Leipzig	GDR	–	–	1
	Manchester United	ENG	–	–	1
	Milan	ITA	–	–	1
	MTK–VM Budapest	HUN	–	–	1
	RWD Molenbeek	BEL	–	–	1
	Nottingham Forest	ENG	–	–	1
	Radnicki Nis	YUG	–	–	1
	Glasgow Rangers	SCO	–	–	1
	FC Sochaux	FRA	–	–	1
	Sporting CP	POR	–	–	1
	FC Tirol	AUT	–	–	1
	Universitatea Craiova	ROM	–	–	1
	Union St. Gilloise	BEL	–	–	1
	KSV Waregem	BEL	–	–	1
	Zeljeznicar Sarajevo	YUG	–	–	1

RESULTS HISTORY OF THE EUROPEAN CUPS

Teams in bold progressed to the following round – See Appendix 1 for all clubs' country of origin – Asterisk * indicates a tie decided by the toss of a coin.

1955–56

EUROPEAN CUP

FIRST ROUND

Servette FC 0–2 0–5 **Real Madrid**
Sporting CP 3–3 2–5 **Partizan Beograd**
SK Rapid Wien 6–1 0–1 PSV Eindhoven
Milan 3–4 4–1 1.FC Saarbrücken
Rot-Weiss Essen 0–4 1–1 **Hibernian Edinburgh**
Djurgårdens IF 0–0 4–1 Gwardia Warszawa
Vörös Lobogó 6–3 4–1 RSC Anderlecht
ÅGF Åarhus 0–2 2–2 **Stade de Reims**

QUARTER-FINALS

Real Madrid 4–0 0–3 Partizan Beograd
SK Rapid Wien 1–1 2–7 **Milan**
Hibernian Edinburgh 3–1 1–0 Djurgårdens IF
Stade de Reims 4–2 4–4 Vörös Lobogó

SEMI-FINALS

Real Madrid 4–2 1–2 Milan
Stade de Reims 2–0 1–0 Hibernian Edinburgh

FINAL

Parc des Princes, Paris, 13–06–1956, 38 000. Referee: Ellis, England

REAL MADRID 4 (Di Stefano 14, Rial 30 79, Marquitos 67)
STADE DE REIMS 3 (Leblond 6, Templin 10, Hidalgo 62)

Real Madrid – Alonso – Atienza, Marquitos, Lesmes – Munoz, Zarraga – Joseito, Marchal, Di Stefano, Rial, Gento. Tr: Villalonga

Stade de Reims – Jacquet – Zimny, Jonquet, Giraudo – Leblond, Siatka – Hidalgo, Glovacki, Kopa, Bliard, Templin. Tr: Batteux

Top scorers: Glovacki, Stade de Reims 7
Milutinovic, Partizan Beograd 7

1956–57

EUROPEAN CUP

PRELIMINARY ROUND

ÅGF Åarhus 1–1 1–5 **OGC Nice**
FC Porto 1–2 2–3 **Athletic Bilbao**
RSC Anderlecht 0–2 0–10 **Manchester United**
Borussia Dortmund 4–3 1–2 7–0 AC Spora
Dinamo Bucuresti 3–1 1–2 Galatasaray
Slovan Bratislava 4–0 0–2 CWKS Warszawa
Real Madrid Bye
SK Rapid Wien Bye
Glasgow Rangers Bye
Honvéd Bye
Rapid JC Heerlen Bye
Crvena Zvezda Beograd Bye
CDNA Sofia Bye
Grasshopper-Club Bye
IFJ Norrköping Bye
Fiorentina Bye

FIRST ROUND

Real Madrid 4–2 1–3 2–0 SK Rapid Wien
Glasgow Rangers 2–1 1–2 1–3 **OGC Nice**
Athletic Bilbao 3–2 3–3 Honvéd
Manchester United 3–2 0–0 Borussia Dortmund
Rapid JC Heerlen 3–4 0–2 **Crvena Zvezda Beograd**
CDNA Sofia 8–1 2–3 Dinamo Bucuresti
Slovan Bratislava 1–0 0–2 **Grasshopper-Club**
Fiorentina 1–1 1–0 IFK Norrköping

QUARTER-FINALS

Real Madrid 3–0 3–2 OGC Nice
Athletic Bilbao 5–3 0–3 **Manchester United**
Crvena Zvezda Beograd 3–1 1–2 CDNA Sofia
Fiorentina 3–1 2–2 Grasshopper-Club

SEMI-FINALS

Real Madrid 3–1 2–2 Manchester United
Crvena Zvezda Beograd 0–1 0–0 **Fiorentina**

FINAL

Bernabeu, Madrid, 30–05–1957, 124 000. Referee: Horn, Holland

REAL MADRID 2 (Di Stefano 70, Gento 76)
FIORENTINA 0

Real Madrid – Alonso – Torres, Marquitos, Lesmes – Munoz, Zarraga – Kopa, Mateos, Di Stefano, Rial, Gento. Tr: Villalonga

Fiorentina – Sarti – Magnini, Orzan, Cervato – Scaramucci, Segato – Julinho, Gratton, Virgili, Montuori, Bizzarri. Tr: Bernardini

Top scorer: Violet, Manchester United 9

1957–58

EUROPEAN CUP

PRELIMINARY ROUND

Sevilla .... 3–1 0–0 .... Benfica
ÅGF Åarhus .... 0–0 3–0 .... Glenavon
CDNA Sofia .... 2–1 1–6 .... **Vasas Budapest**
Gwardia Warszawa .... 3–1 1–3 1–1* .. **Wismut Karl-Marx-S.**
Shamrock Rovers .... 0–6 2–3 .... **Manchester United**
Stade Dudelange .... 0–5 1–9 .... **Crvena Zvezda Beograd**
Glasgow Rangers .... 3–1 1–2 .... AS Saint-Étienne
Milan .... 4–1 2–5 4–2 ... SK Rapid Wien
Real Madrid .... Bye
Royal Antwerp FC .... Bye
Ajax .... Bye
BSC Young Boys .... Bye
Dukla Praha .... Bye
IFK Norrköping .... Bye
Borussia Dortmund .... Bye
CCA Bucuresti .... Bye

FIRST ROUND

Royal Antwerp FC .... 1–2 0–6 .... **Real Madrid**
Sevilla .... 4–0 0–2 .... ÅGF Åarhus
Wismut Karl–Marx–Stadt .. 1–3 0–1 .... **Ajax**
BSC Young Boys .... 1–1 1–2 .... **Vasas Budapest**
Manchester United .... 3–0 0–1 .... Dukla Praha
IFK Norrköping .... 2–2 1–2 .... **Crvena Zvezda Beograd**
Borussia Dortmund ... 4–2 1–3 3–1 ... CCA Bucuresti
Glasgow Rangers .... 1–4 0–2 .... **Milan**

QUARTER-FINALS

Real Madrid .... 8–0 2–2 .... Sevilla
Ajax .... 2–2 0–4 .... **Vasas Budapest**
Manchester United .... 2–1 3–3 .... Crvena Zvezda Beograd
Borussia Dortmund .... 1–1 1–4 .... **Milan**

SEMI-FINALS

Real Madrid .... 4–0 0–2 .... Vasas Budapest
Manchester United .... 2–1 0–4 .... **Milan**

FINAL

Heysel, Brussels, 28–05–1958, 67 000. Referee: Alsteen, Belgium

REAL MADRID 3 (Di Stefano 74, Rial 79, Gento 107)
MILAN 2 (Schiaffino 69, Grillo 78)

Real Madrid – Alonso – Atienza, Santamaria, Lesmes – Santisteban, Zarraga – Kopa, Joseito, Di Stefano, Rial, Gento. Tr: Carniglia

Milan – Soldan – Fontana, Maldini, Beraldo – Bergamaschi, Radice – Danova, Liedholm, Schiaffino, Grillo, Cucchiaroni. Tr: Viani

Top scorer: Di Stefano, Real Madrid 10

FAIRS CUP (1955–58)

FIRST ROUND

Group A

	Ba	St	W	D	L	F	A	Pts
Barcelona	–	6–2	1	1	0	7	3	3
Staevnet Select XI	1–1	–	0	1	1	3	7	1
Vienna Select XI	Withdrew							

Group B

	BC	In	Za	W	D	L	F	A	Pts
Birmingham City	–	2–1	3–0	3	1	0	6	1	7
Internazionale	0–0	–	4–0	2	1	1	6	2	5
Zagreb Select XI	0–1	0–1	–	0	0	4	0	9	0

Group C

	LS	Le	W	D	L	F	A	Pts
Lausanne-Sports	–	7–3	1	0	1	10	9	2
Leipzig Select XI	6–3	–	1	0	1	9	10	2
Cologne Select XI	Withdrew							

Group D

	Lo	Fr	Ba	W	D	L	F	A	Pts
London Select XI	–	3–2	1–0	3	0	1	9	3	6
Frankfurt Select XI	1–0	–	5–1	2	0	2	10	10	4
Basle Select XI	0–5	6–2	–	1	0	3	7	13	2

SEMI-FINALS

Birmingham City .... 4–3 0–1 1–2 ... **Barcelona**
Lausanne–Sports .... 2–1 0–2 .... **London Select XI**

FINAL

1st leg

Stamford Bridge, London, 5–03–1958, 45 000. Referee: Dusch, West Germany

LONDON SELECT XI 2 (Greaves 5, Langley 83)
BARCELONA 2 (Tejada 4, Martinez 43)

London – Kelsey, Sillett, Langley, Blanchflower, Norman, Koot, Groves, Greaves, Smith, Haynes, Robb

Barcelona – Estrems, Olivella, Segarra, Gracia, Gensana, Ribelles, Basora, Evaristo, Martinez, Villaverde, Tejada

2nd leg

Nou Camp, Barcelona, 1–05–1958, 62 000. Referee: Dusch, West Germany

BARCELONA 6 (Suarez 2, Evaristo 2, Martinez, Verges)
LONDON SELECT XI 0

Barcelona – Ramallets – Olivella, Segarra, Verges, Brugue, Gensana, Tejada, Evaristo, Martinez, Suarez, Basora

London – Kelsey – Wright, Cantwell, Blanchflower, Brown, Bowen, Medwin, Groves, Smith, Bloomfield, Lewis

1958–59

EUROPEAN CUP

PRELIMINARY ROUND

Real Madrid .... Bye
Besiktas .... W–O .... Olympiakos
Juventus .... 3–1 0–7 .... **Wiener Sport-Club**
Dinamo Zagreb .... 2–2 1–2 .... **Dukla Praha**
KB Kobenhavn .... 3–0 2–5 1–3 ... **FC Schalke 04**
Wolverhampton W. .... Bye
CDNA Sofia .... Bye
Atlético Madrid .... 8–0 5–1 .... Drumcondra
Wismut K-M-S .... 4–2 0–2 4–0 ... Petrolul Ploiesti
IFK Göteborg .... 2–1 0–1 5–1 ... Jeunesse Esch
Polonia Bytom .... 0–3 0–3 .... **MTK Budapest**.
DOS Utrecht .... 3–4 1–2 .... **Sporting CP**
BSC Young Boys .... W–O .... Manchester United
Standard CL .... 5–1 1–2 .... Heart of Midlothian
HPS Helsinki .... Bye
Ards .... 1–4 2–6 .... **Stade de Reims**

FIRST ROUND

Real Madrid .... 2–0 1–1 .... Besiktas
Wiener Sport-Club .... 3–1 0–1 .... Dukla Praha

Wolverhampton Wand. ..... 2–2 1–2 .... **FC Schalke 04**
Atlético Madrid .... 2–1 0–1 3–1 ... CDNA Sofia
MTK Budapest .... 1–2 1–4 .... **BSC Young Boys**
Wismut Karl-Marx-S. ... 4–0 2–2 .... IFK Göteborg
Sporting CP .... 2–3 0–3 .... **Standard CL**
Stade de Reims .... 4–0 3–0 .... HPS Helsinki

QUARTER–FINALS
Wiener Sport-Club .... 0–0 1–7 .... **Real Madrid**
Atlético Madrid .... 3–0 1–1 .... FC Schalke 04
BSC Young Boys .... 2–2 0–0 2–1 ... Wismut Karl-Marx-Stadt
Standard CL .... 2–0 0–3 .... **Stade de Reims**

SEMI–FINALS
Real Madrid .... 2–1 0–1 2–1 ... Atlético Madrid
BSC Young Boys .... 1–0 0–3 .... **Stade de Reims**

FINAL
Neckarstadion, Stuttgart, 3–06–1959, 80 000. Referee: Dusch, West Germany
REAL MADRID 2 (Mateos 2, Di Stefano 47)
STADE DE REIMS 0
Real Madrid – Dominguez – Marquitos, Santamaria, Zarraga – Santisteban, Ruiz – Kopa, Mateos, Di Stefano, Rial, Gento. Tr: Carniglia
Stade de Reims – Colonna – Rodzik, Jonquet, Giraudo – Penverne, Leblond – Lamartine, Bliard, Fontaine, Piantoni, Vincent. Tr: Batteux

Top scorer: Fontaine, Stade de Reims 10

1959–60

EUROPEAN CUP

PRELIMINARY ROUND
Real Madrid .... Bye
Jeunesse Esch. .... 5–0 1–2 .... LKS Lódz
Fenerbahçe .... 1–1 3–2 .... Csepel SC
OGC Nice .... 3–2 1–1 .... Shamrock Rovers
Vorwärts Berlin .... 2–1 0–2 .... **Wolverhampton W.**
Crvena Zvezda Beograd .... Bye
Olympiakos .... 2–2 1–3 .... **Milan**
CDNA Sofia .... 2–2 2–6 .... **Barcelona**
Glasgow Rangers .... 5–2 2–0 .... RSC Anderlecht
CH Bratislava .... 2–1 2–0 .... FC Porto
Linfield .... 2–1 1–6 .... **IFK Göteborg**
Sparta Rotterdam .... Bye
Wiener Sport-Club .... 0–0 2–1 .... Petrolul Ploiesti
B 1909 Odense .... Bye
BSC Young Boys .... Bye
Eintracht Frankfurt .... W–O .... KuPS Kuopio

FIRST ROUND
Real Madrid. .... 7–0 5–2 .... Jeunesse Esch
Fenerbahçe .... 2–1 1–2 1–5 ... **OGC Nice**
Crvena Zvezda Beograd ..... 1–1 0–3 .... **Wolverhampton Wand.**
Milan .... 0–2 1–5 .... **Barcelona**
Glasgow Rangers .... 4–3 1–1 .... CH Bratislava
Sparta Rotterdam ..... 3–1 1–3 3–1 ... IFK Göteborg
B 1909 Odense .... 0–3 2–2 .... **Wiener Sport–Club**
BSC Young Boys .... 1–4 1–1 .... **Eintracht Frankfurt**

QUARTER–FINALS
OGC Nice .... 3–2 0–4 .... **Real Madrid**
Barcelona .... 4–0 5–2 .... Wolverhampton Wand.
Sparta Rotterdam .... 2–3 1–0 2–3 ... **Glasgow Rangers**
Eintracht Frankfurt .... 2–1 1–1 .... Wiener Sport–Club

SEMI–FINALS
Real Madrid .... 3–1 3–1 .... Barcelona
Eintracht Frankfurt .... 6–1 6–3 .... Glasgow Rangers

FINAL
Hampden Park, Glasgow, 18–05–1960, 135 000. Referee: Mowat, Scotland
REAL MADRID 7 (Di Stefano 27 30 75, Puskas 45 56 60 71)
EINTRACHT FRANKFURT 3 (Kress 10, Stein 64 72)
Real Madrid – Dominguez – Marquitos, Santamaria, Pachin – Vidal, Zarraga – Canario, Del Sol, Di Stefano, Puskas, Gento. Tr: Munoz
Eintracht – Loy – Lutz, Eigenbrodt, Hofer – Weilbacher, Stinka – Kress, Lindner, Stein, Pfaff, Meier. Tr: Oswald

Top scorer: Puskas, Real Madrid 12

FAIRS CUP (1958–1960)

FIRST ROUND
Basle Select XI .... 1–2 2–5 .... **Barcelona**
Internazionale .... 7–0 1–1 .... Olympique Lyon
Frem Kobenhavn .... 1–3 1–4 .... **Chelsea**
Belgrade Select XI .... 6–1 5–3 .... Lausanne-Sports
Union St Gilloise .... 6–1 0–1 .... Leipzig Select XI
Hannover 96 .... 1–3 1–1 .... **Roma**
Zagreb Select XI .... 4–2 0–1 .... Ujpesti Dózsa
Cologne Select XI .... 2–2 0–2 .... **Birmingham City**

QUARTER–FINALS
Barcelona .... 4–0 4–2 .... Internazionale
Chelsea .... 1–0 1–4 .... **Belgrade Select XI**
Union St Gilloise .... 2–0 1–1 .... Roma
Birmingham City .... 1–0 3–3 .... Zagreb Select XI

SEMI–FINALS
Belgrade Select XI .... 1–1 1–3 .... **Barcelona**
Union St Gilloise .... 2–4 2–4 .... **Birmingham City**

FINAL
1st leg
St Andrews, Birmingham, 29–03–1960, 40 000. Referee: Van Nuffel, Belgium
BIRMINGHAM CITY 0
BARCELONA 0
Birmingham City – Schofield – Farmer, Allen, Watts, Smith, Neal, Astall, Gordon, Weston, Orritt, Hooper
Barcelona – Ramallets – Olivella, Gracia, Segarra, Rodri, Gensana, Coll, Kocsis, Martinez, Ribelles, Villaverde

2nd leg
Nou Camp, Barcelona, 4–05–1960, 70 000. Referee: Van Nuffel, Belgium
BARCELONA 4 (Martinez 3, Czibor 6 48, Coll 78)
BIRMINGHAM CITY 1 (Hooper 82)
Barcelona – Ramallets – Olivella, Gracia, Verges, Rodri, Segarra, Coll, Ribelles, Martinez, Kubala, Czibor
Birmingham City – Schofield – Farmer, Allen, Watts, Smith, Neal, Astall, Gordon, Weston, Murphy, Hooper

1960–61

EUROPEAN CUP

FIRST ROUND
Heart of Midlothian .... 1–2 0–3 .... **Benfica**
Crvena Zvezda Beograd ..... 1–2 0–3 .... **Ujpesti Dózsa**
Fredrikstad FK .... 4–3 0–0 .... Ajax
ÅGF Åarhus .... 3–0 0–1 .... Legia Warszawa
Juventus .... 2–0 1–4 .... **CDNA Sofia**
HIFK Helsinki .... 1–3 1–2 .... **IFK Malmö**
Wismut K-M-S .... W–O .... Glenavon
SK Rapid Wien .... 4–0 0–1 .... Besiktas
Hamburger SV .... Bye

Limerick FC .... 0–5 2–4 ...... **BSC Young Boys**
Stade de Reims .... 6–1 5–0 ...... Jeunesse Esch
Burnley .... Bye
CCA Bucuresti .... 0–3 ...... **Spartak Králové**
Panathinaikos .... Bye
Real Madrid .... Bye
Barcelona .... 2–0 3–0 ...... Lierse SK

SECOND ROUND
Benfica .... 6–2 1–2 ...... Ujpesti Dózsa
ÅGF Åarhus .... 3–0 1–0 ...... Fredrikstad FK
IFK Malmö .... 1–0 1–1 ...... CDNA Sofia
SK Rapid Wien .... 3–1 0–2 1–0 ... Wismut Karl–Marx–Stadt
BSC Young Boys .... 0–5 3–3 ...... **Hamburger SV**
Burnley .... 2–0 2–3 ...... Stade de Reims
Spartak Králové .... 1–0 0–0 ...... Panathinaikos
Real Madrid .... 2–2 1–2 ...... **Barcelona**

QUARTER–FINALS
Benfica .... 3–1 4–1 ...... ÅGF Åarhus
SK Rapid Wien .... 2–0 2–0 ...... IFK Malmö
Burnley .... 3–1 1–4 ...... **Hamburger SV**
Barcelona .... 4–0 1–1 ...... Spartak Králové

SEMI–FINALS
Benfica .... 3–0 1–1 ...... SK Rapid Wien
Barcelona .... 1–0 1–2 1–0 ... Hamburger SV

FINAL
Wankdorf, Berne, 31–05–1961, 27000. Referee: Dienst, Switzerland
BENFICA 3 (Aguas 30, OG 32, Coluna 55)
BARCELONA 2 (Kocsis 20, Czibor 75)
Benfica – Costa Pereira – Joao, Germano, Angelo – Neto, Cruz – Augusto, Santana, Aguas, Coluna, Cavem. Tr: Guttmann
Barcelona – Ramallets – Foncho, Gensana, Gracia – Verges, Garay – Kubala, Kocsis, Evaristo, Suarez, Czibor. Tr: Orizaola

Top scorer: José Aguas, Benfica 10

FAIRS CUP

FIRST ROUND
Union St Gilloise .... 0–0 1–4 ...... **Roma**
Olympique Lyon .... 1–3 2–1 ...... **1.FC Köln**
Zagreb Select XI .... 1–1 3–4 ...... **Barcelona**
Lausanne-Sports .... 0–2 ...... **Hibernian Edinburgh**
Internazionale .... 8–2 6–1 ...... Hannover 96
Leipzig Select XI .... 5–2 1–4 0–2 ... **Belgrade Select XI**
Frem Kobenhavn .... 8–1 3–3 ...... Basle Select XI
Birmingham City .... 3–2 2–1 ...... Ujpesti Dózsa

QUARTER–FINALS
1.FC Köln .... 0–2 2–0 1–4 ... **Roma**
Barcelona .... 4–4 2–3 ...... **Hibernian Edinburgh**
Internazionale .... 5–0 0–1 ...... Belgrade Select XI
Frem Kobenhavn .... 4–4 0–5 ...... **Birmingham City**

SEMI–FINALS
Hibernian Edinburgh .... 2–2 3–3 0–6 ... **Roma**
Internazionale .... 1–2 1–2 ...... **Birmingham City**

FINAL
1st leg
St Andrews, Birmingham, 27–09–1961, 21000. Referee: Davidson, Scotland
BIRMINGHAM CITY 2 (Hellawell 78, Orritt 85)
ROMA 2 (Manfredini 30 56)
Birmingham City – Schofield – Farmer, Sissons, Hennessey, Foster, Beard, Hellawell, Bloomfield, Harris, Orritt, Auld
Roma – Cudicini – Fontana, Corsini, Guiliano, Losi, Carpanesi, Orlando, Da Costa, Manfredini, Angelillo, Menichelli

2nd leg
Stadio Olimpico, Rome, 11–10–1961, 60000. Referee: Schwinte, France
ROMA 2 (OG 56, Pestrin 90)
BIRMINGHAM CITY 0
Roma – Cudicini – Fontana, Corsini, Carpanesi, Losi, Pestrin, Orlando, Angelillo, Manfredini, Lojacono, Menichelli
Birmingham City – Schofield – Farmer, Sissons, Hennessey, Smith, Beard, Hellawell, Bloomfield, Harris, Singer, Orritt

CUP WINNERS CUP

PRELIMINARY ROUND
Vorwärts Berlin .... 2–1 0–2 ...... **Red Star Brno**
Glasgow Rangers .... 4–2 1–2 ...... Ferencváros

QUARTER-FINALS
FC Luzern .... 0–3 2–6 ...... **Fiorentina**
Red Star Brno .... 0–0 0–2 ...... **Dinamo Zagreb**
FK Austria .... 2–0 0–5 ...... **Wolverhampton Wand.**
B. Mönchengladbach .... 0–3 0–8 ...... **Glasgow Rangers**

SEMI-FINALS
Fiorentina .... 3–0 1–2 ...... Dinamo Zagreb
Glasgow Rangers .... 2–0 1–1 ...... Wolverhampton Wand.

FINAL
1st leg
Ibrox, Glasgow, 17–05–1961, 80000. Referee: Steiner, Austria
GLASGOW RANGERS 0
FIORENTINA 2 (Milani 12 88)
Rangers – Ritchie – Shearer, Caldow, Davis – Paterson, Baxter – Wilson, McMillan, Scott, Brand, Hume
Fiorentina – Albertosi – Robotti, Castelletti, Gonfiantini – Orzan, Rimbaldo – Hamrin, Micheli, Da Costa, Milani, Petris

2nd leg
Comunale, Florence, 27–05–1961, 50000. Referee: Hernadi, Hungary
FIORENTINA 2 (Milani 12, Hamrin 86)
GLASGOW RANGERS 1 (Scott 60)
Fiorentina – Albertosi – Robotti, Castelletti, Gonfiantini – Orzan, Rimbaldo – Hamrin, Micheli, Da Costa, Milani, Petris
Rangers – Ritchie – Shearer, Caldow, Davis – Paterson, Baxter – Scott, McMillan, Millar, Brand, Wilson

1961–62

EUROPEAN CUP

FIRST ROUND
Benfica .... Bye
CCA Bucuresti .... 0–0 0–2 ...... **FK Austria**
Fenerbahçe .... Bye
1.FC Nürnberg .... 5–0 4–1 ...... Drumcondra
Servette FC .... 5–0 2–1 ...... Hibernians Paola
CDNA Sofia .... 4–4 1–2 ...... **Dukla Praha**
IFK Göteborg .... 0–3 2–8 ...... **Feyenoord**
Górnik Zabrze .... 4–2 1–8 ...... **Tottenham Hotspur**
Standard CL .... 2–1 2–0 ...... Fredrikstad FK
Haka Valkeakoski .... Bye
Vorwärts Berlin .... 3–0 ...... Linfield
AS Monaco .... 2–3 2–3 ...... **Glasgow Rangers**
Sporting CP .... 1–1 0–2 ...... **Partizan Beograd**
Panathinaikos .... 1–1 1–2 ...... **Juventus**
AC Spora .... 0–6 2–9 ...... **B 1913 Odense**
Vasas Budapest .... 0–2 1–3 ...... **Real Madrid**

SECOND ROUND
FK Austria .... 1–1 1–5 ...... **Benfica**
Fenerbahçe .... 1–2 0–1 ...... **1.FC Nürnberg**
Servette FC .... 4–3 0–2 ...... **Dukla Praha**

Feyenoord .... 1–3 1–1 .... **Tottenham Hotspur**
Vorwärts Berlin .... 1–2 1–4 .... **Glasgow Rangers**
Standard CL .... 5–1 2–0 .... Haka Valkeakoski
Partizan Beograd .... 1–2 0–5 .... **Juventus**
B 1913 Odense .... 0–3 0–9 .... **Real Madrid**

QUARTER-FINALS
1.FC Nürnberg .... 3–1 0–6 .... **Benfica**
Dukla Praha .... 1–0 1–4 .... **Tottenham Hotspur**
Standard CL .... 4–1 0–2 .... Glasgow Rangers
Juventus .... 0–1 1–0 1–3 ... **Real Madrid**

SEMI-FINALS
Benfica .... 3–1 1–2 .... Tottenham Hotspur
Real Madrid .... 4–0 2–0 .... Standard CL

FINAL
Olympisch Stadion, Amsterdam, 2–05–1962, 65 000. Referee: Horn, Holland
BENFICA 5 (Aguas 25, Cavem 34, Coluna 51, Eusebio 65 68)
REAL MADRID 3 (Puskas 17 23 38)
Benfica – Costa Pereira – Joao, Germano, Angelo – Cavem, Cruz – Augusto, Eusebio, Aguas, Coluna, Simoes. Tr: Guttmann
Real Madrid – Araquistain – Casado, Santamaria, Miera – Felo, Pachin – Tejada, Del Sol, Di Stefano, Puskas, Gento. Tr: Munoz

Top scorers: Di Stefano, Real Madrid 7
Puskas, Real Madrid 7
Tejada, Real Madrid 7

FAIRS CUP

FIRST ROUND
Valencia .... 2–0 5–1 .... Nottingham Forest
Lausanne-Sports .... Bye
Union St Gilloise .... 1–3 0–2 .... **Heart of Midlothian**
1.FC Köln .... 4–2 0–2 3–5 ... **Internazionale**
Milan .... 0–0 0–2 .... **Novi Sad Select XI**
Iraklis Salonica .... Bye
Spartak Brno .... 2–2 1–4 .... **Leipzig Select XI**
RC Strasbourg .... 1–3 2–10 .... **MTK Budapest**
Basle Select XI .... 1–1 1–4 .... **Crvena Zvezda Beograd**
OS Belenenses .... 3–3 1–3 .... **Hibernian Edinburgh**
Hannover 96 .... 0–1 0–2 .... **RCD Español**
Birmingham City .... Bye
Olympique Lyon .... 4–2 2–5 .... **Sheffield Wednesday**
Roma .... Bye
Dinamo Zagreb .... 7–2 2–2 .... Staevnet Select XI
West Berlin XI .... 1–0 0–3 .... **Barcelona**

SECOND ROUND
Lausanne-Sports .... 3–4 .... **Valencia**
Heart of Midlothian .... 0–1 0–4 .... **Internazionale**
Iraklis Salonica .... 2–1 1–9 .... **Novi Sad Select XI**
MTK Budapest .... 3–0 0–3 2–0 ... Leipzig Select XI
Crvena Zvezda Beo. ..... 4–0 1–0 .... Hibernian Edinburgh
RCD Español .... 5–2 0–1 .... Birmingham City
Sheffield Wednesday .... 4–0 0–1 .... Roma
Barcelona .... 5–1 2–2 .... Dinamo Zagreb

QUARTER-FINALS
Valencia .... 2–0 3–3 .... Internazionale
Novi Sad Select XI .... 1–4 1–2 .... **MTK Budapest**
RCD Español .... 2–1 0–5 .... **Crvena Zvezda Beograd**
Sheffield Wednesday .... 3–2 0–2 .... **Barcelona**

SEMI-FINALS
Valencia .... 3–0 7–3 .... MTK Budapest
Barcelona .... 2–0 4–1 .... Crvena Zvezda Beograd

FINAL
1st leg
Luis Casanova, Valencia, 8–09–1962, 65 000. Referee: Barberan, France
VALENCIA 6 (Yosu 14 42, Guillot 35 54 67, Nunez 74)
BARCELONA 2 (Kocsis 4 20)
Valencia – Zamora – Piquer, Mestre, Sastre, Quincoces, Chicao, Nunez, Ribelles, Waldo, Guillot, Yosu
Barcelona – Pesudo – Benitez, Rodri, Olivella, Verges, Gracia, Cubilla, Kocsis, Re, Villaverde, Camps

2nd leg
Nou Camp, Barcelona, 12–09–1962, 60 000. Referee: Campanati, Italy
BARCELONA 1 (Kocsis 46)
VALENCIA 1 (Guillot 87)
Barcelona – Pesudo – Benitez, Garay, Fuste, Verges, Gracia, Cubilla, Kocsis, Goyvaerts, Villaverde, Camps
Valencia – Zamora – Piquer, Mestre, Sastre, Quincoces, Chicao, Nunez, Urtiaga, Waldo, Guillot, Yosu

CUP WINNERS CUP

PRELIMINARY ROUND
FC Sedan .... 2–3 1–4 .... **Atlético Madrid**
Glenavon .... 1–4 1–3 .... **Leicester City**
La Chaux-de-Fonds .... 6–2 0–5 .... **Leixoes SC**
Swansea Town .... 2–2 1–5 .... **Motor Jena**
Floriana .... 2–5 2–10 ...... **Ujpesti Dózsa**
Dunfermline Athletic ... 4–1 4–0 .... St Patrick's Athletic
SK Rapid Wien .... 0–0 5–2 .... Spartak Varna
Fiorentina .... Bye
Werder Bremen .... Bye
ÅGF Åarhus .... Bye
Alliance Dudelange .... Bye
Progresul Oradea .... Bye
Ajax .... Bye
Vardar Skopje .... Bye
Olympiakos .... Bye
Dynamo Zilina .... Bye

FIRST ROUND
Leicester City .... 1–1 0–2 .... **Atlético Madrid**
Werder Bremen .... 2–0 3–2 .... ÅGF Åarhus
Leixoes SC .... 1–1 1–0 .... Progresul Oradea
Motor Jena .... 7–0 2–2 .... Alliance Dudelange
Ajax .... 2–1 1–3 .... **Ujpesti Dózsa**
Dunfermline Athletic ... 5–0 0–2 .... Vardar Skopje
Olympiakos .... 2–3 0–1 .... **Dynamo Zilina**
Fiorentina .... 3–1 6–2 .... SK Rapid Wien

QUARTER-FINALS
Werder Bremen .... 1–1 1–3 .... **Atlético Madrid**
Motor Jena .... 1–1 3–1 .... Leixoes SC
Ujpesti Dózsa .... 4–3 1–0 .... Dunfermline Athletic
Dynamo Zilina .... 3–2 0–2 .... **Fiorentina**

SEMI-FINALS
Motor Jena .... 0–1 0–4 .... **Atlético Madrid**
Fiorentina .... 2–0 1–0 .... Ujpesti Dózsa

FINAL
Hampden Park, Glasgow, 10–05–1962, 27 000. Referee: Wharton, Scotland
ATLÉTICO MADRID 1 (Peiro 11)
FIORENTINA 1 (Hamrin 27)
Atlético – Madinabeytia – Rivilla, Calleja, Ramirez – Griffa, Glaria – Jones, Adelardo, Mendonca, Peiro, Collar
Fiorentina – Albertosi – Robotti, Castelletti, Malatrasi – Orzan, Marchesi – Hamrin, Ferretti, Milani, Dell-Angelo, Petris

Replay. Neckarstadion, Stuttgart, 5–09–1962, 38 000. Referee: Tschenscher, West Germany

ATLÉTICO MADRID 3 (Jones 8, Mendonca 27, Peiro 59)
FIORENTINA 0

Atlético – Madinabeytia – Rivilla, Calleja, Ramirez – Griffa, Glaria – Jones, Adelardo, Mendonca, Peiro, Collar

Fiorentina – Albertozi – Robotti, Castelletti, Malatrasi – Orzan, Marchesi – Hamrin, Ferretti, Milani, Dell-Angelo, Petris

1962–63

EUROPEAN CUP

FIRST ROUND

Milan	8–0 6–0	Union Luxembourg
Floriana	1–4 0–10	**Ipswich Town**
Dinamo Bucuresti	1–1 0–3	**Galatasaray**
Polonia Bytom	2–1 4–1	Panathinaikos
CDNA Sofia	2–1 4–1	Partizan Beograd
Real Madrid	3–3 0–1	**RSC Anderlecht**
Shelbourne	0–2 1–5	**Sporting CP**
Dundee	8–1 0–4	1.FC Köln
Servette FC	1–3 3–1 1–3	**Feyenoord**
Fredrikstad FK	1–4 0–7	**Vasas Budapest**
FK Austria	5–3 2–0	HIFK Helsinki
Stade de Reims	Bye	
Vorwärts Berlin	0–3 0–1	**Dukla Praha**
Linfield	1–2 0–0	**Esbjerg FB**
IFK Norrköping	2–0 1–1	Partizani Tiranë
Benfica	Bye	

SECOND ROUND

Milan	3–0 1–2	Ipswich Town
Galatasaray	4–1 0–1	Polonia Bytom
CDNA Sofia	2–2 0–2	**RSC Anderlecht**
Sporting CP	1–0 1–4	**Dundee**
Feyenoord	1–1 2–2 1–0	Vasas Budapest
FK Austria	3–2 0–5	**Stade de Reims**
Esbjerg FB	0–0 0–5	**Dukla Praha**
IFK Norrköping	1–1 1–5	**Benfica**

QUARTER-FINALS

Galatasaray	1–3 0–5	**Milan**
RSC Anderlecht	1–4 1–2	**Dundee**
Stade de Reims	0–1 1–1	**Feyenoord**
Benfica	2–1 0–0	Dukla Praha

SEMI-FINALS

Milan	5–1 0–1	Dundee
Feyenoord	0–0 1–3	**Benfica**

FINAL

Wembley, London, 22–05–1963, 45 000. Referee: Holland, England

MILAN 2 (Altafini 58 70)
BENFICA 1 (Eusebio 19)

Milan – Ghezzi – David, Maldini, Trebbi – Benitez, Trapattoni – Pivatelli, Sani, Altafini, Rivera, Mora. Tr: Rocco

Benfica – Costa Pereira – Cavem, Cruz, Humberto, Raul – Coluna, Santana – Augusto, Torres, Eusebio, Simoes. Tr: Riera

Top scorer: Altafini, Milan 14

FAIRS CUP

FIRST ROUND

Valencia	4–2 2–2	Glasgow Celtic
Everton	1–0 0–2	**Dunfermline Athletic**
Utrecht Select XI	3–2 2–1	Tasmania Berlin
Hibernian Edinburgh	4–0 3–2	Staevnet Select XI
SK Rapid Wien	1–1 0–1	**Crvena Zvezda Beograd**
Barcelona	1–1 1–1 3–2	OS Belenenses
Glentoran	0–2 2–6	**Real Zaragoza**
Altay Izmir	2–3 1–10	**Roma**
Viktoria Köln	4–3 1–4	**Ferencváros**
Sampdoria	1–0 2–0	Aris Bonnevoie
Vojvodina Novi Sad	1–0 0–2	**Leipzig Select XI**
Petrolul Ploiesti	4–2 0–1	Spartak Brno
Basle Select XI	0–3	**Bayern München**
Drumcondra	4–1 2–4	Odense Select XI
Olympique Marseille	1–0 2–4	**Union St Gilloise**
FC Porto	1–2 0–0	**Dinamo Zagreb**

SECOND ROUND

Valencia	4–0 2–6 1–0	Dunfermline Athletic
Utrecht Select XI	0–1 1–2	**Hibernian Edinburgh**
Crvena Zvezda	3–2 0–1 1–0	Barcelona
Roma	4–2 2–1	Real Zaragoza
Sampdoria	1–0 0–6	**Ferencváros**
Petrolul Ploiesti	1–0 0–1 1–0	Leipzig Select XI
Bayern München	6–0 0–1	Drumcondra
Dinamo Zagreb	2–1 0–1 3–2	Union St Gilloise

QUARTER-FINALS

Valencia	5–0 1–2	Hibernian Edinburgh
Roma	3–0 0–2	Crvena Zvezda Beograd
Ferencváros	2–0 0–1	Petrolul Ploiesti
Bayern München	0–0 1–4	**Dinamo Zagreb**

SEMI-FINALS

Valencia	3–0 0–1	Roma
Ferencváros	0–1 1–2	**Dinamo Zagreb**

FINAL

1st leg

Dinamo Stadion, Zagreb, 12–06–1963, 40 000. Referee: Adami, Italy

DINAMO ZAGREB 1 (Zambata 13)
VALENCIA 2 (Waldo 64, Urtiaga 67)

Dinamo Zagreb – Skoric – Belin, Braun, Biscam, Markovic, Perusic, Kobesnac, Zambata, Knez, Matus, Lamza

Valencia – Zamora – Piquer, Chicao, Paquito, Quincoces, Sastre, Manio, Sanchez-Lage, Waldo, Ribelles, Urtiaga

2nd leg

Luis Casanova, Valencia, 26–06–1963, 55 000. Referee: Howley, England

VALENCIA 2 (Manio 68, Nunez 78)
DINAMO ZAGREB 0

Valencia – Zamora – Piquer, Chicao, Paquito, Quincoces, Sastre, Manio, Sanchez–Lage, Waldo, Ribelles, Nunez

Dinamo Zagreb – Skoric – Belin, Braun, Matus, Markovic, Perusic, Kobesnac, Lamza, Raus, Zambata, Knez

CUP WINNERS CUP

PRELIMINARY ROUND

Tottenham Hotspur	Bye	
Glasgow Rangers	4–0 0–2	Sevilla
Lausanne-Sports	3–0 2–4	Sparta Rotterdam
Slovan Bratislava	Bye	
Bangor City	2–0 1–3 1–2	**Napoli**
Ujpesti Dózsa	5–0 0–0	Zaglebie Sosnowiec
Portadown	Bye	
OFK Beograd	2–0 3–3	Chemie Halle
1.FC Nürnberg	Bye	
AS Saint-Étienne	1–1 3–0	Vitória FC Setúbal
SK Sturm Graz	Bye	
Alliance Dudelange	1–1 1–8	**B 1909 Odense**
Steaua Bucuresti	3–2 1–5	**Botev Plovdiv**
Shamrock Rovers	Bye	
Hibernians Paola	W–O	Olympiakos
Atlético Madrid	Bye	

FIRST ROUND

Tottenham Hotspur	5–2 3–2	Glasgow Rangers
Lausanne-Sports	1–1 0–1	**Slovan Bratislava**
Ujpesti Dózsa	1–1 1–1 1–3	**Napoli**
OFK Beograd	5–1 2–3	Portadown
AS Saint-Étienne	0–0 0–3	**1.FC Nürnberg**
SK Sturm Graz	1–1 3–5	**B 1909 Odense**
Shamrock Rovers	0–4 0–1	**Botev Plovdiv**
Atlético Madrid	4–0 1–0	Hibernians Paola

QUARTER-FINALS

Slovan Bratislava	2–0 0–6	**Tottenham Hotspur**
OFK Beograd	2–0 1–3 3–1	Napoli
B 1909 Odense	0–1 0–6	**1.FC Nürnberg**
Botev Plovdiv	1–1 0–4	**Atlético Madrid**

SEMI-FINALS

OFK Beograd	1–2 1–3	**Tottenham Hotspur**
1.FC Nürnberg	2–1 0–2	**Atlético Madrid**

FINAL

Feyenoord Stadion, Rotterdam, 15–05–1963, 49 000. Referee: Van Leuwen, Holland

TOTTENHAM HOTSPUR 5 (Greaves 16 80, White 35, Dyson 67 85)

ATLÉTICO MADRID 1 (Collar 47)

Tottenham – Brown – Baker, Norman, Henry – Blanchflower, Marchi – Jones, White, Smith, Greaves, Dyson

Atlético – Madinabeytia – Rivilla, Griffa, Rodriguez – Ramiro, Glaria – Jones, Adelardo, Chuzo, Mendonca, Collar,

1963–64

EUROPEAN CUP

FIRST ROUND

Everton	0–0 0–1	**Internazionale**
AS Monaco	7–2 1–1	AEK Athens
Haka Valkeakoski	4–1 0–4	**Jeunesse Esch**
Partizan Beograd	3–0 3–1	Anorthosis Famagusta
Górnik Zabrze	1–0 0–1 2–1	FK Austria
Dukla Praha	6–0 2–0	Valletta
Distillery	3–3 0–5	**Benfica**
SOFK Lyn Oslo	2–4 1–3	**Borussia Dortmund**
Dundalk	0–3 2–1	**FC Zürich**
Galatasaray	4–0 0–2	Ferencváros
Partizani Tiranë	1–0 1–3	**Spartak Plovdiv**
Esbjerg FB	3–4 1–7	**PSV Eindhoven**
Milan	Bye	
Standard CL	1–0 0–2	**IFK Norrköping**
Dinamo Bucuresti	2–0 1–0	Motor Jena
Glasgow Rangers	0–1 0–6	**Real Madrid**

SECOND ROUND

Internazionale	1–0 3–1	AS Monaco
Jeunesse Esch	2–1 2–6	**Partizan Beograd**
Górnik Zabrze	2–0 1–4	**Dukla Praha**
Benfica	2–1 0–5	**Borussia Dortmund**
FC Zürich	* 2–0 0–2 2–2	Galatasaray
Spartak Plovdiv	0–1 0–0	**PSV Eindhoven**
IFK Norrköping	1–1 2–5	**Milan**
Dinamo Bucuresti	1–3 3–5	**Real Madrid**

QUARTER-FINALS

Partizan Beograd	0–2 1–2	**Internazionale**
Dukla Praha	0–4 3–1	**Borussia Dortmund**
PSV Eindhoven	1–0 1–3	**FC Zürich**
Real Madrid	4–1 0–2	Milan

SEMI-FINALS

Borussia Dortmund	2–2 0–2	**Internazionale**
FC Zürich	1–2 0–6	**Real Madrid**

FINAL

Prater, Vienna, 27–05–1964, 72 000. Referee: Stoll, Austria

INTERNAZIONALE 3 (Mazzola 43 76, Milani 61)

REAL MADRID 1 (Felo 70)

Internazionale – Sarti – Burgnich, Guarneri, Facchetti – Tagnin, Picchi – Jair, Mazzola, Milani, Suarez, Corso. Tr: Herrera

Real Madrid – Vicente – Isidro, Santamaria, Pachin – Zoco, Muller – Amancio, Felo, Di Stefano, Puskas, Gento. Tr: Munoz

Top scorers:	Kovacevic, Partizan Beograd	7
	Mazzola, Internazionale	7
	Puskas, Real Madrid	7

FAIRS CUP

FIRST ROUND

Real Zaragoza	6–1 3–0	Iraklis Salonica
Lausanne-Sports	2–2 4–4 3–2	Heart of Midlothian
Atlético Madrid	2–1 0–0	FC Porto
Juventus	2–1 1–2 1–0	OFK Beograd
Spartak Brno	5–0 2–1	Servette FC
Glentoran	1–4 0–3	**Partick Thistle**
Staevnet Select XI	1–7 3–2	**Arsenal**
Aris Bonnevoie	0–2 0–0	**RFC Liège**
1.FC Köln	3–1 1–1	AA Gent
DOS Utrecht	1–4 1–4	**Sheffield Wednesday**
Tresnjevka Zagreb	0–2 1–2	**OS Belenenses**
Hertha BSC Berlin	1–3 0–2	**Roma**
Ujpesti Dózsa	3–2 0–0	SC Leipzig
Steagul Rosu Brasov	1–3 1–2	**Lokomotiv Plovdiv**
SK Rapid Wien	1–0 3–2	Racing Club Paris
Shamrock Rovers	0–1 2–2	**Valencia**

SECOND ROUND

Lausanne-Sports	1–2 0–3	**Real Zaragoza**
Juventus	1–0 2–1	Atlético Madrid
Partick Thistle	3–2 0–4	**Spartak Brno**
Arsenal	1–1 1–3	**RFC Liège**
1.FC Köln	3–2 2–1	Sheffield Wednesday
Roma	2–1 1–0	OS Belenenses
Ujpesti Dózsa	0–0 3–1	Lokomotiv Plovdiv
SK Rapid Wien	0–0 2–3	**Valencia**

QUARTER-FINALS

Real Zaragoza	3–2 0–0	Juventus
RFC Liège	2–0 0–2 1–0	Spartak Brno
Roma	3–1 0–4	**1.FC Köln**
Valencia	5–2 1–3	Ujpesti Dózsa

SEMI-FINALS

RFC Liège	1–0 1–2 0–2	**Real Zaragoza**
Valencia	4–1 0–2	1.FC Köln

FINAL

Nou Camp, Barcelona, 25–06–1964, 50 000. Referee, De Campos, Portugal

REAL ZARAGOZA 2 (Villa 40, Marcelino 83)

VALENCIA 1 (Urtiaga 42)

Real Zaragoza – Yarza, Cortizo, Santamaria, Reija, Isasi, Pais, Canario, Duca, Marcelino, Villa, Lapetra

Valencia – Zamora, Arnal, Villegani, Paquito, Quincoces, Roberto, Suco, Guillot, Waldo, Urtiaga, Ficha

CUP WINNERS CUP

FIRST ROUND

Atalanta	2–0 1–3 1–3	**Sporting CP**
Apoel Nicosia	6–0 0–1	Gjovik Lyn

Tottenham Hotspur	Bye	
Willem II Tilburg	1–1 1–6	**Manchester United**
Hamburger SV	4–0 3–2	Union Luxembourg
Shelbourne	0–2 1–3	**Barcelona**
Olympiakos	2–1 0–1 2–0	Zaglebie Sosnowiec
Olympique Lyon	3–1 3–1	B 1913 Odense
FC Basel	1–5 0–5	**Glasgow Celtic**
Linzer ASK	1–0 0–1 1–1*	**Dinamo Zagreb**
HPS Helsinki	1–4 1–8	**Slovan Bratislava**
Sliema Wanderers	0–0 0–2	**Borough United**
Fenerbahçe	4–1 0–1	Petrolul Ploiesti
Linfield	Bye	
Motor Zwickau	Bye	
MTK Budapest	1–0 1–1	Slavia Sofia

SECOND ROUND

Sporting CP	16–1 2–0	Apoel Nicosia
Tottenham Hotspur	2–0 1–4	**Manchester United**
Barcelona	4–4 0–0 2–3	**Hamburger SV**
Olympique Lyon	4–1 1–2	Olympiakos
Glasgow Celtic	3–0 1–2	Dinamo Zagreb
Borough United	0–1 0–3	**Slovan Bratislava**
Fenerbahçe	4–1 0–2	Linfield
Motor Zwickau	1–0 0–2	**MTK Budapest**

QUARTER-FINALS

Manchester United	4–1 0–5	**Sporting CP**
Hamburger SV	1–1 0–2	**Olympique Lyon**
Glasgow Celtic	1–0 1–0	Slovan Bratislava
MTK Budapest	2–0 1–3 1–0	Fenerbahçe

SEMI-FINALS

Olympique Lyon	0–0 1–1 0–1	**Sporting CP**
Glasgow Celtic	3–0 0–4	**MTK Budapest**

FINAL

Heysel, Brussels, 13–05–1964, 3000. Referee: Van Nuffel, Belgium

SPORTING CLUB PORTUGAL 3 (Mascaranha 40, Figueiredo 45 80)

MTK BUDAPEST 3 (Sandor 19 75, Kuti 73)

Sporting – Carvalho – Gomez, Perdis, Battista, Carlos – Geo, Mendes – Oswaldo, Mascaranhas, Figueiredo, Morais

MTK Budapest – Kovalik – Keszei, Dansky, Jenei – Nagy, Kovacs – Sandor, Vasas, Kuti, Bodor, Halapi

Replay. Bosuil, Antwerp, 15–05–1964, 19 000. Referee: Versyp, Belgium

SPORTING CLUB PORTUGAL 1 (Morais 19)

MTK BUDAPEST 0

Sporting – Carvalho – Gomez, Perdis, Battista, Carlos – Geo, Mendes – Oswaldo, Mascaranhas, Figueiredo, Morais

MTK Budapest – Kovalik – Keszei, Dansky, Jenei – Nagy, Kovacs – Sandor, Vasas, Kuti, Bodor, Halapi

1964–65

EUROPEAN CUP

FIRST ROUND

Internazionale	Bye	
Sliema Wanderers	0–2 0–5	**Dinamo Bucuresti**
Glasgow Rangers	3–1 2–4 3–1	Crvena Zvezda Beograd
SK Rapid Wien	3–0 2–0	Shamrock Rovers
Glentoran	2–2 2–3	**Panathinaikos**
Partizani Tiranë	0–0 0–2	**1.FC Köln**
RSC Anderlecht	*1–0 1–2 0–0	Bologna
KR Reykjavík	0–5 1–6	**Liverpool**
Chemie Leipzig	0–2 2–4	**Vasas ETO Györ**
Lokomotiv Sofia	8–3 0–2	Malmö FF
DWS Amsterdam	3–1 1–0	Fenerbahçe
Reipas Lahti	2–1 0–3	**SOFK Lyn Oslo**
B 1909 Odense	2–5 0–4	**Real Madrid**
Dukla Praha	*4–1 0–3 0–0	Górnik Zabrze
AS Saint-Étienne	2–2 1–2	**La Chaux-de-Fonds**
Aris Bonnevoie	1–5 1–5	**Benfica**

SECOND ROUND

Internazionale	6–0 1–0	Dinamo Bucuresti
Glasgow Rangers	1–0 2–0	SK Rapid Wien
Panathinaikos	1–1 1–2	**1.FC Köln**
Liverpool	3–0 1–0	RSC Anderlecht
Vasas ETO Györ	5–3 3–4	Lokomotiv Sofia
DWS Amsterdam	5–0 3–1	SOFK Lyn Oslo
Real Madrid	4–0 2–2	Dukla Praha
La Chaux-de-Fonds	1–1 0–5	**Benfica**

QUARTER-FINALS

Internazionale	3–1 0–1	Glasgow Rangers
1.FC Köln	0–0 0–0 2–2*	**Liverpool**
DWS Amsterdam	1–1 0–1	**Vasas ETO Györ**
Benfica	5–1 1–2	Real Madrid

SEMI-FINALS

Liverpool	3–1 0–3	**Internazionale**
Vasas ETO Györ	0–1 0–4	**Benfica**

FINAL

San Siro, Milan, 27–05–1965, 85 000. Referee: Dienst, Switzerland

INTERNAZIONALE 1 (Jair 42)

BENFICA 0

Internazionale – Sarti – Burgnich, Guarneri, Facchetti – Bedin, Picchi – Jair, Mazzola, Peiro, Suarez, Corso. Tr: Herrera

Benfica – Costa Pereira – Cavem, Cruz, Germano, Raul – Neto, Coluna – Augusto, Eusebio, Torres, Simoes. Tr: Schwartz

Top scorer: Torres, Benfica 9

FAIRS CUP

FIRST ROUND

Ferencváros	2–0 0–1	Spartak Brno
Wiener Sport-Club	2–1 1–0	SC Leipzig
Aris Salonica	0–0 0–3	**Roma**
NK Zagreb	3–2 6–0	Grazer AK
Dunfermline Athletic	4–2 0–0	Örgryte IS
B 1913 Odense	1–3 0–1	**VfB Stuttgart**
Hertha BSC Berlin	2–1 0–2	**Royal Antwerp FC**
Athletic Bilbao	2–2 2–0	OFK Beograd
Vålerengens Oslo	2–5 2–4	**Everton**
Eintracht Frankfurt	3–0 1–5	**Kilmarnock**
Manchester United	6–1 1–1	Djurgårdens IF
Borussia Dortmund	4–1 0–2	Girondins Bordeaux
Leixoes SC	1–1 0–3	**Glasgow Celtic**
Barcelona	0–1 2–0	Fiorentina
RC Strasbourg	2–0 0–1	Milan
FC Basel	2–0 0–1	AC Spora
Servette FC	2–2 1–6	**Atlético Madrid**
OS Belenenses	1–1 0–0 1–2	**Shelbourne**
Valencia	1–1 1–3	**RFC Liège**
KB Kobenhavn	3–4 1–2	**DOS Utrecht**
Vojvodina Novi Sad	1–1 1–1 0–2	**Lokomotiv Plovdiv**
Göztepe Izmir	0–1 1–2	**Petrolul Ploiesti**
Real Betis	1–1 0–2	**Stade Français**
Union St Gilloise	0–1 0–1	**Juventus**

SECOND ROUND

Ferencváros	2–1 0–1 2–0	Wiener Sport-Club
NK Zagreb	1–1 0–1	**Roma**
Dunfermline Athletic	1–0 0–0	VfB Stuttgart
Athletic Bilbao	2–0 1–0	Royal Antwerp FC
Kilmarnock	0–2 1–4	**Everton**

Borussia Dortmund .... 1–6 0–4 .... **Manchester United**
Barcelona .... 3–1 0–0 .... Glasgow Celtic
FC Basel .... 0–1 2–5 .... **RC Strasbourg**
Shelbourne .... 0–1 0–1 .... **Atlético Madrid**
DOS Utrecht .... 0–2 0–2 .... **RFC Liège**
Petrolul Ploiesti .... 1–0 0–2 .... **Lokomotiv Plovdiv**
Stade Français .... 0–0 0–1 .... **Juventus**

THIRD ROUND

Roma .... 1–2 0–1 .... **Ferencváros**
Athletic Bilbao .... 1–0 0–1 2–1 ... Dunfermline Athletic
RC Strasbourg .... *0–0 2–2 0–0 .. Barcelona
Manchester United .... 1–1 2–1 .... Everton
RFC Liège .... 1–0 0–2 .... **Atlético Madrid**
Juventus .... 1–1 1–1 2–1 ... Lokomotiv Plovdiv

QUARTER-FINALS

Ferencváros .... 1–0 1–2 3–0 ... Athletic Bilbao
RC Strasbourg .... 0–5 0–0 .... **Manchester United**
Atlético Madrid .... Bye
Juventus .... Bye

SEMI-FINALS

Manchester United .... 3–2 0–1 1–2 ... **Ferencváros**
Atlético Madrid .... 3–1 1–3 1–3 ... **Juventus**

FINAL

Comunale, Turin, 23–06–1965, 25 000. Referee: Dienst, Switzerland
FERENCVAROS 1 (Fenyvesi 74)
JUVENTUS 0
Ferencváros – Geczi, Novak, Horvath, Juhasz, Matrai, Orosz, Karaba, Varga, Albert, Rakosi, Fenyvesi
Juventus – Anzolin, Gori, Sarti, Bercellino, Castano, Leoncini, Stachini, Del Sol, Combin, Mazzia, Menichelli

CUP WINNERS CUP

FIRST ROUND

AA Gent .... 0–1 1–1 .... **West Ham United**
Sparta Praha .... 10–0 6–0 ...... Anorthosis Famagusta
Slavia Sofia .... 1–1 2–0 .... Cork Celtic
Lausanne-Sports .... 2–0 0–1 .... Honvéd
Esbjerg FB .... 0–0 0–1 .... **Cardiff City**
Sporting CP .... Bye
Dundee .... Bye
Valletta .... 0–3 1–5 .... **Real Zaragoza**
Torino .... 3–1 2–2 .... Fortuna 54 Geleen
FK Skeid Oslo .... 1–0 0–2 .... **Haka Valkeakoski**
AEK Athens .... 2–0 0–3 .... **Dinamo Zagreb**
Steaua Bucuresti .... 3–0 2–0 .... Derry City
Admira Wien .... 1–3 0–1 .... **Legia Warszawa**
Aufbau Magdeburg .... 1–1 1–1 1–1* .. **Galatasaray**
FC Porto .... 3–0 1–0 .... Olympique Lyon
Union Luxembourg .... 0–4 0–6 .... **TSV München 1860**

SECOND ROUND

West Ham United .... 2–0 1–2 .... Sparta Praha
Slavia Sofia .... 1–0 1–2 2–3 ... **Lausanne-Sports**
Sporting CP .... 1–2 0–0 .... **Cardiff City**
Dundee .... 2–2 1–2 .... **Real Zaragoza**
Torino .... 5–0 1–0 .... Haka Valkeakoski
Steaua Bucuresti .... 1–3 0–2 .... **Dinamo Zagreb**
Legia Warszawa .... 2–1 0–1 1–0 ... Galatasaray
FC Porto .... 0–1 1–1 .... **TSV München 1860**

QUARTER-FINALS

Lausanne-Sports .... 1–2 3–4 .... **West Ham United**
Real Zaragoza .... 2–1 1–0 .... Cardiff City
Torino .... 1–1 2–1 .... Dinamo Zagreb
Legia Warszawa .... 0–4 0–0 .... **TSV München 1860**

SEMI-FINALS

West Ham United .... 2–1 1–1 .... Real Zaragoza
Torino .... 2–0 1–3 0–2 ... **TSV München 1860**

FINAL

Wembley, London, 19–05–1965, 100 000. Referee: Zsolt, Hungary
WEST HAM UNITED 2 (Sealey 70 72)
TSV MUNCHEN 1860 0
West Ham – Standen – Kirkup, Burkett, Moore – Peters, Brown – Sealey, Boyce, Hurst, Dear, Sissons
München 1860 – Radenkovic – Wagner, Kohlars, Reich – Bena, Luttrop – Heiss, Kuppers, Brunnenmeier, Grosser, Rebele

1965–66

EUROPEAN CUP

FIRST ROUND

Feyenoord .... 2–1 0–5 .... **Real Madrid**
17 Nëntori Tiranë .... 0–0 0–1 .... **Kilmarnock**
Fenerbahçe .... 0–0 1–5 .... **RSC Anderlecht**
SOFK Lyn Oslo .... 5–3 1–5 .... **Derry City**
Panathinaikos .... 4–1 0–1 .... Sliema Wanderers
IBK Keflavík .... 1–4 1–9 .... **Ferencváros**
Dinamo Bucuresti .... 4–0 3–2 .... B 1909 Odense
Internazionale .... Bye
HJK Helsinki .... 2–3 0–6 .... **Manchester United**
Drumcondra .... 1–0 0–3 .... **Vorwärts Berlin**
Stade Dudelange .... 0–8 0–10 ..... **Benfica**
Djurgårdens IF .... 2–1 0–6 .... **Levski Sofia**
Lausanne-Sports .... 0–0 0–4 .... **Sparta Praha**
Linzer ASK .... 1–3 1–2 .... **Górnik Zabrze**
Apoel Nicosia .... 0–5 0–5 .... **Werder Bremen**
Partizan Beograd .... 2–0 2–2 .... FC Nantes

SECOND ROUND

Kilmarnock .... 2–2 1–5 .... **Real Madrid**
RSC Anderlecht .... 9–0 .... Derry City
Ferencváros .... 0–0 3–1 .... Panathinaikos
Dinamo Bucuresti .... 2–1 0–2 .... **Internazionale**
Vorwärts Berlin .... 0–2 1–3 .... **Manchester United**
Levski Sofia .... 2–2 2–3 .... **Benfica**
Sparta Praha .... 3–0 2–1 .... Górnik Zabrze
Partizan Beograd .... 3–0 0–1 .... Werder Bremen

QUARTER-FINALS

RSC Anderlecht .... 1–0 2–4 .... **Real Madrid**
Internazionale .... 4–0 1–1 .... Ferencváros
Manchester United .... 3–2 5–1 .... Benfica
Sparta Praha .... 4–1 0–5 .... **Partizan Beograd**

SEMI-FINALS

Real Madrid .... 1–0 1–1 .... Internazionale
Partizan Beograd .... 2–0 0–1 .... Manchester United

FINAL

Heysel, Brussels, 11–05–1966, 55 000. Referee: Kreitlein, West Germany
REAL MADRID 2 (Amancio 70, Serena 75)
PARTIZAN BEOGRAD 1 (Vasovic 55)
Real Madrid – Araquistain – Pachin, De Felipe, Zoco, Sanchis – Pirri, Velazquez – Serena, Amancio, Grosso, Gento. Tr: Munoz
Partizan – Soskic – Jusufi, Rasovic, Vasovic, Milhailovic – Kovacevic, Becejac – Bajic, Hasanagic, Galic, Pirmajer. Tr: Gegic

Top scorer: Eusebio, Benfica 8

FAIRS CUP

FIRST ROUND

DOS Utrecht .... 0–0 1–7 .... **Barcelona**
Royal Antwerp FC .... 1–0 3–3 .... Glentoran
Stade Français .... 0–0 0–1 .... **FC Porto**
Girondins Bordeaux .... 0–4 1–6 .... **Sporting CP**
RFC Liège .... 1–0 0–2 .... **NK Zagreb**
Malmö FF .... 0–3 0–4 .... **TSV München 1860**
AIK Stockholm .... 3–1 0–0 .... Daring CB
Milan .... *1–0 1–2 1–1 .. RC Strasbourg
Wiener Sport-Club .... 6–0 1–2 .... PAOK Salonica
Chelsea .... 4–1 0–0 .... Roma
Leeds United .... 2–1 0–0 .... Torino
Hibernian Edinburgh .... 2–0 0–2 0–3 ... **Valencia**
Union Luxembourg .... 0–4 0–13 ...... **1.FC Köln**
1.FC Nürnberg .... 1–1 0–1 .... **Everton**
Crvena Zvezda Beograd ..... 0–4 1–3 .... **Fiorentina**
Spartak Brno .... 2–0 0–1 .... Lokomotiv Plovdiv
Hannover 96 .... Bye
RCD Español .... Bye
Steagul Rosu Brasov .... Bye
Göztepe Izmir .... Bye
Servette FC .... Bye
GD Cuf Barreiro .... Bye
SC Leipzig .... Bye
FC Basel .... Bye
Aris Salonica .... Bye
Ujpesti Dózsa .... Bye
Dunfermline Athletic .... Bye
KB Kobenhavn .... Bye
Heart of Midlothian .... Bye
Vålerengens Oslo .... Bye
Shamrock Rovers .... Bye
Real Zaragoza .... Bye

SECOND ROUND

Royal Antwerp FC .... 2–1 0–2 .... **Barcelona**
Hannover 96 .... 5–0 1–2 .... FC Porto
NK Zagreb .... 2–2 0–1 .... **Steagul Rosu Brasov**
Sporting CP .... 2–1 3–4 1–2 .. **RCD Español**
Göztepe Izmir .... 2–1 1–9 .... **TSV München 1860**
AIK Stockholm .... 2–1 1–4 .... **Servette FC**
GD Cuf Barreiro .... 2–0 0–2 0–1 ... **Milan**
Wiener Sport-Club .... 1–0 0–2 .... **Chelsea**
SC Leipzig .... 1–2 0–0 .... **Leeds United**
FC Basel .... 1–3 1–5 .... **Valencia**
Aris Salonica .... 2–1 0–2 .... **1.FC Köln**
Ujpesti Dózsa .... 3–0 1–2 .... Everton
Dunfermline Athletic ..... 5–0 4–2 .... KB Kobenhavn
Fiorentina .... 2–0 0–4 .... **Spartak Brno**
Heart of Midlothian ...... 1–0 3–1 .... Vålerengens IF Oslo
Shamrock Rovers .... 1–1 1–2 .... **Real Zaragoza**

THIRD ROUND

Hannover 96 .... 2–1 0–1 1–1* .. **Barcelona**
RCD Español .... 3–1 2–4 1–0 ... Steagul Rosu Brasov
Servette FC .... 1–1 1–4 .... **TSV München 1860**
Milan .... 2–1 1–2 1–1 * .. **Chelsea**
Leeds United .... 1–1 1–0 .... Valencia
1.FC Köln .... 3–2 0–4 .... **Ujpesti Dózsa**
Dunfermline Athletic ... 2–0 0–0 .... Spartak Brno
Heart of Midlothian .... 3–3 2–2 0–1 ... **Real Zaragoza**

QUARTER-FINALS

Barcelona .... 1–0 1–0 .... RCD Español
TSV München 1860 .... 2–2 0–1 .... **Chelsea**
Leeds United .... 4–1 1–1 .... Ujpesti Dózsa
Dunfermline Athletic .... 1–0 2–4 .... **Real Zaragoza**

SEMI-FINALS

Barcelona .... 2–0 0–2 5–0 ... Chelsea
Real Zaragoza .... 1–0 1–2 3–1 ... Leeds United

FINAL

1st leg

Nou Camp, Barcelona, 14–09–1966, 70 000. Referee: Zsolt, Hungary

BARCELONA 0
REAL ZARAGOZA 1 (Canario 30)

Barcelona – Sadurni – Benitez, Eladio, Montesinos, Gallego, Torres, Zaballa, Muller, Zaldua, Fuste, Vidal
Real Zaragoza – Yarza – Irusquieta, Reija, Pais, Santamaria, Violeta, Canario, Santos, Marcelino, Villa, Lapetra

2nd leg

La Romareda, Zaragoza, 21–09–1966, 35000. Referee: Lo Bello, Italy

REAL ZARAGOZA 2 (Marcelino 24 87)
BARCELONA 4 (Pujol 3 86 120, Zaballa 89)

Real Zaragoza – Yarza – Irusquieta, Reija, Pais, Santamaria, Violeta, Canario, Santos, Marcelino, Villa, Lapetra
Barcelona – Sadurni – Foncho, Eladio, Montesinos, Gallego, Torres, Zaballa, Mas, Zaldua, Fuste, Pujol

CUP WINNERS CUP

FIRST ROUND

Floriana .... 1–5 0–8 .... **Borussia Dortmund**
Limerick FC .... 1–2 0–2 .... **CSKA-CZ Sofia**
Wiener Neustadt .... 0–1 0–2 .... **Stiinta Cluj**
Atlético Madrid .... 4–0 1–0 .... Dinamo Zagreb
FC Sion .... 5–1 1–2 .... Galatasaray
1.FC Magdeburg .... 1–0 2–0 .... AC Spora
Omonia Nicosia .... 0–1 1–1 .... **Olympiakos**
West Ham United .... Bye
Go Ahead Deventer .... 0–6 0–1 .... **Glasgow Celtic**
ÅGF Åarhus .... 2–1 2–1 .... Vitória FC Setúbal
KR Reykjavík .... 1–3 1–3 .... **Rosenborg BK**
Coleraine .... 1–6 0–4 .... **Dinamo Kiev**
Reipas Lahti .... 2–10 0–6 ...... **Honvéd**
Dukla Praha .... 2–0 0–0 .... Stade Rennes
Cardiff City .... 1–2 0–1 .... **Standard CL**
Juventus .... 1–0 0–2 .... **Liverpool**

SECOND ROUND

Borussia Dortmund ...... 3–0 2–4 .... CSKA-CZ Sofia
Stiinta Cluj .... 0–2 0–4 .... **Atlético Madrid**
1.FC Magdeburg .... 8–1 2–2 .... FC Sion
West Ham United .... 4–0 2–2 .... Olympiakos
ÅGF Åarhus .... 0–1 0–2 .... **Glasgow Celtic**
Rosenborg BK .... 1–4 0–2 .... **Dynamo Kiev**
Dukla Praha .... 2–3 2–1 .... **Honvéd**
Liverpool .... 3–1 2–1 .... Standard Liege

QUARTER-FINALS

Atlético Madrid .... 1–1 0–1 .... **Borussia Dortmund**
West Ham United .... 1–0 1–1 .... 1.FC Magdeburg
Glasgow Celtic .... 3–0 1–1 .... Dynamo Kiev
Honvéd .... 0–0 0–2 .... **Liverpool**

SEMI-FINALS

West Ham United .... 1–2 1–3 .... **Borussia Dortmund**
Glasgow Celtic .... 1–0 0–2 .... **Liverpool**

FINAL

Hampden Park, Glasgow, 5–05–1966, 41 000. Referee: Schwinte, France

BORUSSIA DORTMUND 2 (Held 62, Libuda 109)
LIVERPOOL 1 (Hunt 68)

Borussia – Tilkowski – Cyliax, Paul, Redder – Kurrat, Assauer – Libuda, Schmidt, Held, Sturm, Emmerich
Liverpool – Lawrence – Lawler, Yeats, Byrne – Milne, Stevenson – Callaghan, Hunt, St John, Smith, Thompson

Top scorer: Emmerich, Borussia Dortmund 14

1966–67

EUROPEAN CUP

PRELIMINARY ROUND

Sliema Wanderers .... 1–2 0–4 .... **CSKA-CZ Sofia**
Waterford FC .... 1–6 0–6 .... **Vorwärts Berlin**

FIRST ROUND

Glasgow Celtic .... 2–0 3–0 .... FC Zürich
KR Reykjavík .... 2–3 2–5 .... **FC Nantes**
Malmö FF .... 0–2 1–3 .... **Atlético Madrid**
Admira Wien .... 0–1 0–0 .... **Vojvodina Novi Sad**
Liverpool .... 2–0 1–3 2–0 ... Petrolul Ploiesti
Ajax .... 2–0 2–1 .... Besiktas
Haka Valkeakoski .... 1–10 0–2 ..... **RSC Anderlecht**
Esbjerg FB .... 0–2 0–4 .... **Dukla Praha**
Aris Bonnevoie .... 3–3 1–6 .... **Linfield**
Vålerengens Oslo .... W–O .... 17 Nëntori Tiranë
Górnik Zabrze .... 2–1 1–2 3–1 ... Vorwärts Berlin
CSKA-CZ Sofia .... 3–1 0–1 .... Olympiakos
Real Madrid .... Bye
TSV München 1860 .... 8–0 2–1 .... Omonia Nicosia
Vasas Budapest .... 5–0 2–0 .... Sporting CP
Internazionale .... 1–0 0–0 .... Torpedo Moskva

SECOND ROUND

FC Nantes .... 1–3 1–3 .... **Glasgow Celtic**
Vojvodina Novi Sad ... 3–1 0–2 3–2 ... Atlético Madrid
Ajax .... 5–1 2–2 .... Liverpool
Dukla Praha .... 4–1 2–1 .... RSC Anderlecht
CSKA-CZ Sofia .... 4–0 0–3 .... Górnik Zabrze
Vålerengens IF Oslo .... 1–4 1–1 .... **Linfield**
TSV München 1860 .... 1–0 1–3 .... **Real Madrid**
Internazionale .... 2–1 2–0 .... Vasas Budapest

QUARTER-FINALS

Vojvodina Novi Sad .... 1–0 0–2 .... **Glasgow Celtic**
Ajax .... 1–1 1–2 .... **Dukla Praha**
Linfield .... 2–2 0–1 .... **CSKA-CZ Sofia**
Internazionale .... 1–0 2–0 .... Real Madrid

SEMI-FINALS

Glasgow Celtic .... 3–1 0–0 .... Dukla Praha
Internazionale .... 1–1 1–1 1–0 ... CSKA-CZ Sofia

FINAL

Estádio Nacional, Lisbon, 25–05–1967, 54 000. Referee: Tschenscher, West Germany

GLASGOW CELTIC 2 (Gemmell 63, Chalmers 85)
INTERNAZIONALE 1 (Mazzola 8)

Celtic – Simpson, Craig, McNeill, Gemmell – Murdoch, Clark – Johnstone, Wallace, Chalmers, Auld, Lennox. Tr: Stein

Internazionale – Sarti – Burgnich, Guarneri, Facchetti – Bedin, Picchi – Domenghini, Mazzola, Cappellini, Bicicli, Corso. Tr: Herrera

Top scorer: Piepenburg, Vorwärts Berlin 6
Van Himst, Anderlecht 6

FAIRS CUP

FIRST ROUND

Spartak Brno .... 2–0 0–2 * ...... **Dinamo Zagreb**
Frigg SK Oslo .... 1–3 1–3 .... **Dunfermline Ath.**
Dinamo Pitesti .... 2–0 2–2 .... Sevilla
Juventus .... 5–0 2–0 .... Aris Salonica
Wiener Sport-Club .... 1–2 1–3 .... **Napoli**
VfB Stuttgart .... 1–1 0–2 .... **Burnley**
Olimpia Ljubljana .... 3–3 0–3 .... **Ferencváros**
OGC Nice .... 2–2 1–2 .... **Örgryte IS**
Drumcondra .... 0–2 1–6 .... **Eintracht Frankfurt**
FC Porto .... 2–1 1–2* ...... **Girondins Bordeaux**
Union Luxembourg .... 0–1 0–1 .... **Royal Antwerp FC**
Djurgårdens IF .... 1–3 1–2 .... **Lokomotive Leipzig**
Bologna .... 2–1 3–1 .... Göztepe Izmir
DOS Utrecht .... 2–1 2–2 .... FC Basel
Crvena Zvezda Beo. ...... 5–0 0–2 .... Athletic Bilbao
1.FC Nürnberg .... 1–2 0–2 .... **Valencia**
Toulouse FC .... Bye
Dundee United .... Bye
Barcelona .... Bye
Vitória FC Setúbal .... Bye
B 1909 Odense .... Bye
Lausanne-Sports .... Bye
Hvidovre BK .... Bye
AA Gent .... Bye
Kilmarnock .... Bye
Spartak Plovdiv .... Bye
Benfica .... Bye
RFC Liège .... Bye
Sparta Praha .... Bye
West Bromwich Albion .. Bye
DWS Amsterdam .... Bye
Leeds United .... Bye

SECOND ROUND

Dunfermline Athletic .... 4–2 0–2 .... **Dinamo Zagreb**
Toulouse FC .... 3–0 1–5 .... **Dinamo Pitesti**
Barcelona .... 1–2 0–2 .... **Dundee United**
Juventus .... 3–1 2–0 .... Vitória FC Setúbal
Lausanne-Sports .... 1–3 0–5 .... **Burnley**
B 1909 Odense .... 1–4 1–2 .... **Napoli**
Örgryte IS .... 0–0 1–7 .... **Ferencváros**
Eintracht Frankfurt .... 5–1 2–2 .... Hvidovre BK
Royal Antwerp FC .... 0–1 2–7 .... **Kilmarnock**
AA Gent .... 1–0 0–0 .... Girondins Bordeaux
Spartak Plovdiv .... 1–1 0–3 .... **Benfica**
Lokomotive Leipzig ...... 0–0 2–1 .... RFC Liège
Sparta Praha .... 2–2 1–2 .... **Bologna**
DOS Utrecht .... 1–1 2–5 .... **West Bromwich Albion**
Valencia .... 1–0 2–1 .... Crvena Zvezda Beograd
DWS Amsterdam .... 1–3 1–5 .... **Leeds United**

THIRD ROUND

Dinamo Pitesti .... 0–1 0–0 .... **Dinamo Zagreb**
Juventus .... 3–0 0–1 .... Dundee United
Burnley .... 3–0 0–0 .... Napoli
Eintracht Frankfurt .... 4–1 1–2 .... Ferencváros
Kilmarnock .... 1–0 2–1 .... AA Gent
Lokomotive Leipzig ...... 3–1 1–2 .... Benfica
Bologna .... 3–0 3–1 .... West Bromwich Albion
Leeds United .... 1–1 2–0 .... Valencia

QUARTER-FINALS

Juventus .... 2–2 0–3 .... **Dinamo Zagreb**
Eintracht Frankfurt .... 1–1 2–1 .... Burnley
Lokomotive Leipzig .... 1–0 0–2 .... **Kilmarnock**
Bologna .... 1–0 0–1* ...... **Leeds United**

SEMI-FINALS

Eintracht Frankfurt .... 3–0 0–4 .... **Dinamo Zagreb**
Leeds United .... 4–2 0–0 .... Kilmarnock

FINAL

1st leg

Dinamo Stadion, Zagreb, 30–08–1967, 40 000. Referee: Bueno Perales, Spain

DINAMO ZAGREB 2 (Cercek 39 59)
LEEDS UNITED 0

Dinamo Zagreb – Skoric – Gracanin, Brncic, Belin, Ramljak – Blaskovic, Cercek – Piric, Zambata, Gucmirtl, Rora

Leeds Utd – Sprake – Reaney, Cooper, Bremner, Charlton, Hunter, Bates, Lorimer, Belfitt, Gray, O'Grady

2nd leg

Elland Road, Leeds, 6–09–1967, 35 000. Referee: Lo Bello, Italy

LEEDS UNITED 0
DINAMO ZAGREB 0

Leeds Utd – Sprake – Bell, Cooper, Bremner, Charlton, Hunter, Reaney, Belfitt, Greenhoff, Giles, O'Grady

Dinamo Zagreb – Skoric – Gracanin, Brncic, Belin, Ramljak – Blaskovic, Cercek – Piric, Zambata, Gucmirtl, Rora

CUP WINNERS CUP

PRELIMINARY ROUND

Valur Reykjavík	1–1 1–8	**Standard CL**

FIRST ROUND

Tatran Presov	1–1 2–3	**Bayern München**
Shamrock Rovers	4–1 4–1	AC Spora
OFK Beograd	1–3 0–3	**Spartak Moskva**
SK Rapid Wien	4–0 5–3	Galatasaray
Fiorentina	1–0 2–4	**Vasas ETO Györ**
AEK Athens	0–1 2–3	**Sporting Braga**
Chemie Leipzig	3–0 2–2	Legia Warszawa
Standard CL	5–1 1–0	Apollon Limassol
Swansea Town	1–1 0–4	**Slavia Sofia**
RC Strasbourg	1–0 1–1	Steaua Bucuresti
Floriana	1–1 0–6	**Sparta Rotterdam**
Servette FC	1–1 2–1	AIFK Abo
FK Skeid Oslo	3–2 1–3	**Real Zaragoza**
ÅAB Åalborg	0–0 1–2	**Everton**
Borussia Dortmund	Bye	
Glentoran	1–1 0–4	**Glasgow Rangers**

SECOND ROUND

Shamrock Rovers	1–1 2–3	**Bayern München**
Spartak Moskva	1–1 0–1	**SK Rapid Wien**
Vasas ETO Györ	3–0 0–2	Sporting Braga
Chemie Leipzig	2–1 0–1	**Standard CL**
RC Strasbourg	1–0 0–2	**Slavia Sofia**
Servette FC	2–0 0–1	Sparta Rotterdam
Real Zaragoza	2–0 0–1	Everton
Glasgow Rangers	2–1 0–0	Borussia Dortmund

QUARTER-FINALS

SK Rapid Wien	1–0 0–2	**Bayern München**
Vasas ETO Györ	2–1 0–2	**Standard CL**
Servette FC	1–0 0–3	**Slavia Sofia**
Glasgow Rangers	*2–0 0–2	Real Zaragoza

SEMI-FINALS

Bayern München	2–0 3–1	Standard CL
Slavia Sofia	0–1 0–1	**Glasgow Rangers**

FINAL

Nürnbergerstadion, Nuremberg, 31–05–1967, 69 000. Referee: Lo Bello, Italy

BAYERN MUNCHEN 1 (Roth 108)
GLASGOW RANGERS 0

Bayern München – Maier – Nowak, Kupferschmidt, Beckenbauer, Olk – Roth, Koulmann – Nafziger, Ohlhauser, Muller, Brenninger

Rangers – Martin – Johansen, Provan, McKinnon, Greig – Jardine, Smith D – Henderson, Hynd, Smith A, Johnston

Top scorer: Müller, Bayern München 9

1967–68

EUROPEAN CUP

FIRST ROUND

Manchester United	4–0 0–0	Hibernians Paola
Olympiakos Nicosia	2–2 1–3	**FK Sarajevo**
Górnik Zabrze	3–0 1–0	Djurgårdens IF
Glasgow Celtic	1–2 1–1	**Dynamo Kiev**
Ajax	1–1 1–2	**Real Madrid**
FC Basel	1–2 3–3	**Hvidovre BK**
FK Skeid Oslo	0–1 1–1	**Sparta Praha**
FC Karl-Marx-Stadt	1–3 1–2	**RSC Anderlecht**
Olympiakos	0–0 0–2	**Juventus**
Botev Plovdiv	2–0 0–3	**Rapid Bucuresti**
Eint.Braunschweig	W–O	Dinamo Tiranë
Besiktas	0–1 0–3	**SK Rapid Wien**
Dundalk	0–1 1–8	**Vasas Budapest**
Valur Reykjavík	1–1 3–3	Jeunesse Esch
AS Saint-Étienne	2–0 3–0	KuPS Kuopio
Glentoran	1–1 0–0	**Benfica**

SECOND ROUND

FK Sarajevo	0–0 1–2	**Manchester United**
Dynamo Kiev	1–2 1–1	**Górnik Zabrze**
Sparta Praha	3–2 3–3	RSC Anderlecht
Hvidovre	2–2 1–4	**Real Madrid**
Juventus	1–0 0–0	Rapid Bucuresti
SK Rapid Wien	1–0 0–2	**Eintracht Braunschweig**
Vasas Budapest	6–0 5–1	Valur Reykjavík
Benfica	2–0 0–1	AS Saint-Étienne

QUARTER-FINALS

Manchester United	2–0 0–1	Górnik Zabrze
Real Madrid	3–0 1–2	Sparta Praha
Eint. Braunschweig	3–2 0–1 0–1	**Juventus**
Vasas Budapest	0–0 0–3	**Benfica**

SEMI-FINALS

Manchester United	1–0 3–3	Real Madrid
Benfica	2–0 1–0	Juventus

FINAL

Wembley, London, 29–05–1968, 100 000. Referee: Lo Bello, Italy

MANCHESTER UNITED 4 (Charlton 53 99, Best 93, Kidd 94)
BENFICA 1 (Graca 75)

Manchester Utd – Stepney – Brennan, Stiles, Foulkes, Dunne – Crerand, Charlton, Sadler – Best, Kidd, Aston. Tr: Busby

Benfica – Henrique – Adolfo, Humberto, Jacinto, Cruz – Graca, Coluna, Augusto – Eusebio, Torres, Simoes. Tr: Otto Gloria

Top scorer: Eusebio, Benfica 6

FAIRS CUP

FIRST ROUND

AC Spora	0–9 0–7	**Leeds United**
Partizan Beograd	5–1 1–1	Lokomotiv Plovdiv
Hibernian Edinburgh	3–0 1–3	FC Porto
Napoli	4–0 1–1	Hannover 96
OGC Nice	0–1 0–4	**Fiorentina**
Club Brugge	0–0 1–2	**Sporting CP**
1.FC Köln	2–0 2–2	Slavia Praha
Dynamo Dresden	1–1 1–2	**Glasgow Rangers**
FC Zürich	3–1 0–1	Barcelona
Eintracht Frankfurt	0–1 0–4	**Nottingham Forest**
PAOK Salonica	0–2 2–3	**RFC Liège**
DWS Amsterdam	2–1 0–3	**Dundee**
Bologna	2–0 0–0	SOFK Lyn Oslo

Dinamo Zagreb	5–0 0–2	Petrolul Ploiesti
Wiener Sport-Club	2–5 1–2	**Atlético Madrid**
Royal Antwerp FC	1–2 0–0	**Göztepe Izmir**
Lokomotive Leipzig	5–1 0–1	Linfield
Vojvodina Novi Sad	1–0 3–1	GD Cuf Barreiro
Frem Kobenhavn	0–1 2–3	**Athletic Bilbao**
St Patrick's Athletic	1–3 3–6	**Girondins Bordeaux**
Malmö FF	0–2 1–2	**Liverpool**
Servette FC	2–2 0–4	**TSV München 1860**
DOS Utrecht	3–2 1–3	**Real Zaragoza**
FC Arges Pitesti	3–1 0–4	**Ferencváros**

SECOND ROUND

Partizan Beograd	1–2 1–1	**Leeds United**
Napoli	4–1 0–5	**Hibernian Edinburgh**
Fiorentina	1–1 1–2	**Sporting CP**
Glasgow Rangers	3–0 1–3	1.FC Köln
Nottingham Forest	2–1 0–1	**FC Zürich**
Dundee	3–1 4–1	RFC Liège
Bologna	0–0 2–1	Dinamo Zagreb
Vojvodina Novi Sad	0–0 2–0	Lokomotive Leipzig
Atlético Madrid	2–0 0–3	**Göztepe Izmir**
Girondins Bordeaux	1–3 0–1	**Athletic Bilbao**
Liverpool	8–0 1–2	TSV München 1860
Real Zaragoza	2–1 0–3	**Ferencváros**

THIRD ROUND

Leeds United	1–0 1–1	Hibernian Edinburgh
Glasgow Rangers	Bye	
FC Zürich	3–0 0–1	Sporting CP
Dundee	Bye	
Bologna	Bye	
Vojvodina Novi Sad	1–0 1–0	Göztepe Izmir
Athletic Bilbao	Bye	
Ferencváros	1–0 1–0	Liverpool

QUARTER-FINALS

Glasgow Rangers	0–0 0–2	**Leeds United**
Dundee	1–0 1–0	FC Zürich
Bologna	0–0 2–0	Vojvodina Novi Sad
Ferencváros	2–1 2–1	Athletic Bilbao

SEMI-FINALS

Dundee	1–1 0–1	**Leeds United**
Ferencváros	3–2 2–2	Bologna

FINAL

1st leg

Elland Road, Leeds, 7–08–1968, 25 000. Referee: Scheurer, Switzerland

LEEDS UNITED 1 (Jones 41)
FERENCVAROS 0

Leeds Utd – Sprake – Reaney, Cooper, Bremner, Charlton, Hunter, Lorimer, Madeley, Jones (Belfitt), Giles (Greenhoff), Gray
Ferencváros – Geczi – Novak, Pancsics, Havasi, Juhasz, Szucs, Szoke, Varga, Albert, Rakosi, Fenyvesi (Balint)

2nd leg

Népstadion, Budapest, 11–09–1968, 76 000. Referee: Schulemburg, West Germany

FERENCVAROS 0
LEEDS UNITED 0

Ferencváros – Geczi – Novak, Pancsics, Havasi, Juhasz, Szucs, Rakosi, Szoke (Karaba), Varga, Albert, Katona
Leeds Utd – Sprake – Reaney, Cooper, Bremner, Charlton, Hunter, O'Grady, Lorimer, Jones, Madeley, Hibbitt (Bates)

CUP WINNERS CUP

FIRST ROUND

Milan	5–1 1–1	Levski Sofia
Vasas ETO Györ	5–0 4–0	Apollon Nicosia
Aberdeen	10–0 4–1	KR Reykjavík
Altay Izmir	2–3 0–0	**Standard CL**
Valencia	4–0 4–2	Crusaders
FK Austria	0–2 1–2	**Steaua Bucuresti**
Fredrikstad FK	1–5 1–2	**Vitória FC Setúbal**
Bayern München	5–0 2–1	Panathinaikos
Shamrock Rovers	1–1 0–2	**Cardiff City**
Floriana	1–2 0–1	**NAC Breda**
Lausanne-Sports	3–2 0–2	**Spartak Trnava**
Torpedo Moskva	0–0 1–0	Sachsenring Zwickau
Aris Bonnevoie	0–3 1–2	**Olympique Lyon**
Hajduk Split	0–2 3–4	**Tottenham Hotspur**
HJK Helsinki	1–4 0–4	**Wisla Kraków**
Hamburger SV	5–3 2–0	Randers Freja

SECOND ROUND

Vasas ETO Györ	2–2 1–1	**Milan**
Standard CL	3–0 0–2	Aberdeen
Valencia	3–0 0–1	Steaua Bucuresti
Bayern München	6–2 1–1	Vitória FC Setúbal
NAC Breda	1–1 1–4	**Cardiff City**
Torpedo Moskva	3–0 3–1	Spartak Trnava
Olympique Lyon	1–0 3–4	Tottenham Hotspur
Wisla Kraków	0–1 0–4	**Hamburger SV**

QUARTER-FINALS

Standard CL	1–1 1–1 0–2	**Milan**
Valencia	1–1 0–1	**Bayern München**
Cardiff City	1–0 0–1 1–0	Torpedo Moskva
Hamburger SV	2–0 0–2 2–0	Olympique Lyon

SEMI-FINALS

Milan	2–0 0–0	Bayern München
Hamburger SV	1–1 3–2	Cardiff City

FINAL

Feyenoord Stadion, Rotterdam, 23–05–1968, 53 000. Ortiz de Mendebil, Spain

MILAN 2 (Hamrin 3 19)
HAMBURGER SV 0

Milan – Cudicini – Anquilletti, Schnellinger, Rosato, Scala – Trapattoni, Lodetti – Hamrin, Sormani, Rivera, Prati
Hamburg – Ozcan – Sandmann, Schulx, Horst, Kurbjuhn – Dieckmann, Kramer – Dorfel B, Seeler, Honig, Dorfel G

Top scorer: Seeler, Hamburger SV 6

1968–69

EUROPEAN CUP

FIRST ROUND

Malmö FF	2–1 1–4	**Milan**
Crvena Zvezda Beo.	W–O	Carl Zeiss Jena
AS Saint-Étienne	2–0 0–4	**Glasgow Celtic**
RSC Anderlecht	3–0 2–2	Glentoran
Waterford FC	1–3 1–7	**Manchester United**
Rosenborg BK	1–3 3–3	**SK Rapid Wien**
Real Madrid	6–0 6–0	AEL Limassol
Steaua Bucuresti	3–1 0–4	**Spartak Trnava**
Floriana	1–1 0–2	**Reipas Lahti**
AEK Athens	3–0 2–3	Jeunesse Esch
FC Zürich	1–3 2–1	**Akademisk Kobenhavn**
Valur Reykjavík	0–0 1–8	**Benfica**
Manchester City	0–0 1–2	**Fenerbahçe**
1.FC Nürnberg	1–1 0–4	**Ajax**
Levski Sofia	Withdrew	
Ferencváros	Withdrew	

Dynamo Kiev	Withdrew	
Ruch Chorzów	Withdrew	

SECOND ROUND

Milan	Bye	
Glasgow Celtic	5–1 1–1	Crvena Zvezda Beograd
SK Rapid Wien	1–0 1–2	Real Madrid
Manchester United	3–0 1–3	RSC Anderlecht
Reipas Lahti	1–9 1–7	**Spartak Trnava**
AEK Athens	0–0 2–0	Akademisk Kobenhavn
Benfica	Bye	
Ajax	2–0 2–0	Fenerbahçe

QUARTER-FINALS

Milan	0–0 1–0	Glasgow Celtic
Manchester United	3–0 0–0	SK Rapid Wien
Spartak Trnava	2–1 1–1	AEK Athens
Ajax	1–3 3–1 3–0	Benfica

SEMI-FINALS

Milan	2–0 0–1	Manchester United
Ajax	3–0 0–2	Spartak Trnava

FINAL

Bernabeu, Madrid, 28–05–1969, 31 000. Referee: Ortiz de Mendebil, Spain

MILAN 4 (Prati 7 40 75, Sormani 67)
AJAX 1 (Vasovic 60)

Milan – Cudicini – Malatrasi, Anquilletti, Schnellinger, Rosato, Trapattoni – Lodetti, Rivera – Hamrin, Sormani, Prati. Tr: Rocco

Ajax – Bals – Suurbier (Muller), Hulshoff, Vasovic, Van Duivenbode – Pronk, Groot (Nuninga) – Swart, Cruyff, Danielsson, Keizer. Tr: Michels

Top scorer: Law, Manchester United 9

FAIRS CUP

FIRST ROUND

Newcastle United	4–0 0–2	Feyenoord
Sporting CP	4–0 1–4	Valencia
Slavia Sofia	0–0 0–2	**Aberdeen**
Trakia Plovdiv	3–1 0–2	**Real Zaragoza**
Dinamo Zagreb	1–1 1–2	**Fiorentina**
Hansa Rostock	3–0 1–2	OGC Nice
Olympique Lyon	* 1–0 0–1	Académica Coimbra
Vitória FC Setúbal	3–0 3–1	Linfield
Athletic Bilbao	* 2–1 1–2	Liverpool
Daring CB	2–1 0–2	**Panathinaikos**
Lausanne-Sports	0–2 0–2	**Juventus**
Wacker Innsbruck	2–2 0–3	**Eint. Frankfurt**
Beerschot VAV	1–1 1–2	**DWS Amsterdam**
Chelsea	5–0 4–3	Morton
DOS Utrecht	1–1 1–2	**Dundalk**
Glasgow Rangers	2–0 0–1	Vojvodina Novi Sad
Göztepe Izmir	* 2–0 0–2	Olympique Marseille
Leixoes SC	1–1 0–0	**FC Arges Pitesti**
Bologna	4–1 2–1	FC Basel
Rapid Bucuresti	3–1 1–6	**OFK Beograd**
Olimpia Ljubljana	0–3 1–2	**Hibernian Edinburgh**
Lokomotive Leipzig	W–O	KB Kobenhavn
Wiener Sport-Club	1–0 0–5	**Slavia Praha**
FC Metz	1–4 2–3	**Hamburger SV**
Standard CL	0–0 2–3	**Leeds United**
Napoli	3–1 0–1	Grasshopper-Club
FK Skeid Oslo	1–1 1–2	**AIK Stockholm**
Hannover 96	3–2 1–0	B 1909 Odense
Legia Warszawa	6–0 3–2	TSV München 1860
Atlético Madrid	2–1 0–1	**KSV Waregem**
Aris Salonica	1–0 6–0	Hibernians Paola
Ujpesti Dózsa	W–O	Union Luxembourg

SECOND ROUND

Sporting CP	1–1 0–1	**Newcastle United**
Aberdeen	2–1 0–3	**Real Zaragoza**
Hansa Rostock	3–2 1–2	**Fiorentina**
Vitória FC Setúbal	5–0 2–1	Olympique Lyon
Panathinaikos	0–0 0–1	**Athletic Bilbao**
Juventus	0–0 0–1	**Eintracht Frankfurt**
Chelsea	0–0 0–0*	**DWS Amsterdam**
Glasgow Rangers	6–1 3–0	Dundalk
Göztepe Izmir	3–0 2–3	FC Arges Pitesti
OFK Beograd	1–0 1–1	Bologna
Hibernian Edinburgh	3–1 1–0	Lokomotive Leipzig
Hamburger SV	4–1 1–3	Slavia Praha
Leeds United	*2–0 0–2	Napoli
AIK Stockholm	4–2 2–5	**Hannover 96**
KSV Waregem	1–0 0–2	**Legia Warszawa**
Aris Salonica	1–2 1–9	**Ujpesti Dózsa**

THIRD ROUND

Real Zaragoza	3–2 1–2	**Newcastle United**
Vitória FC Setúbal	3–0 1–2	Fiorentina
Eintracht Frankfurt	1–1 0–1	**Athletic Bilbao**
DWS Amsterdam	0–2 1–2	**Glasgow Rangers**
OFK Beograd	3–1 0–2	**Göztepe Izmir**
Hamburger SV	1–0 1–2	Hibernian Edinburgh
Leeds United	5–1 2–1	Hannover 96
Legia Warszawa	0–1 2–2	**Ujpesti Dózsa**

QUARTER-FINALS

Newcastle United	5–1 1–3	Vitória FC Setúbal
Glasgow Rangers	4–1 0–2	Athletic Bilbao
Göztepe Izmir	W–O	Hamburger SV
Leeds United	0–1 0–2	**Ujpesti Dózsa**

SEMI-FINALS

Glasgow Rangers	0–0 0–2	**Newcastle United**
Göztepe Izmir	1–4 0–4	**Ujpesti Dózsa**

FINAL

1st leg

St James' Park, Newcastle, 29–05–1969, 60 000. Referee: Hannet, France

NEWCASTLE UNITED 3 (Moncur 63 72, Scott 83)
UJPESTI DOZSA 0

Newcastle – McFaul, Craig, Clark, Gibb, Burton, Moncur, Scott, Robson, Davies, Arentoft, Sinclair (Foggon)

Ujpesti Dózsa – Szentmihalyi, Kaposzta, Solymosi, Bankuti, Nosko, Dunai E, Fazekas, Gorocs, Bene, Dunai A, Zambo

2nd leg

Budapest, 11–06–69, 37 000. Referee: Heymann, Switzerland

UJPESTI DOZSA 2 (Bene 31, Gorocs 44)
NEWCASTLE UNITED 3 (Moncur 46, Arentoft 50, Foggon 74)

Ujpesti Dózsa – Szentmihalyi, Kaposzta, Solymosi, Bankuti, Nosko, Dunai E, Fazekas, Gorocs, Bene, Dunai A, Zambo

Newcastle – McFaul, Craig, Clark, Gibb, Burton, Moncur, Scott (Foggon), Arentoft, Robson, Davies, Sinclair

CUP WINNERS CUP

FIRST ROUND

Slovan Bratislava	3–0 0–2	FK Bor
Cardiff City	2–2 1–2	**FC Porto**
Partizani Tiranë	1–0 1–3	**Torino**
Club Brugge	3–1 0–2	**West Bromwich Albion**
Dinamo Bucuresti	W–O	Vasas ETO Györ
Olympiakos	2–0 2–0	Fram Reykjavík
Dunfermline Athletic	10–1 2–0	Apoel Nicosia
Girondins Bordeaux	2–1 0–3	**1.FC Köln**
Altay Izmir	3–1 1–4	**SOFK Lyn Oslo**
US Rumelange	2–1 0–1	**Sliema Wanderers**
Randers Freja	1–0 2–1	Shamrock Rovers

ADO Den Haag	4–1 2–1	Grazer AK
Crusaders	2–2 1–4	**IFK Norrköping**
FC Lugano	0–1 0–3	**Barcelona**
Spartak Sofia	Withdrew	
Union Berlin	Withdrew	
Górnik Zabrze	Withdrew	
Dynamo Moskva	Withdrew	

SECOND ROUND

FC Porto	1–0 0–4	**Slovan Bratislava**
Torino	Bye	
Dinamo Bucuresti	1–1 0–4	**West Bromwich Albion**
Dunfermline Athletic	4–0 0–3	Olympiakos
ADO Den Haag	0–1 0–3	**1.FC Köln**
Randers Freja	6–0 2–0	Sliema Wanderers
SOFK Lyn Oslo	2–0 2–3	IFK Norrköping
Barcelona	Bye	

QUARTER-FINALS

Torino	0–1 1–2	**Slovan Bratislava**
Dunfermline Athletic	0–0 1–0	West Bromwich Albion
1.FC Köln	2–1 3–0	Randers Freja
Barcelona	3–2 2–2	SOFK Lyn Oslo

SEMI-FINALS

Dunfermline Athletic	1–1 0–1	**Slovan Bratislava**
1.FC Köln	2–2 1–4	**Barcelona**

FINAL

St Jakob, Basle, 21–05–1969, 19 000. Referee: Van Raveszn, Holland

SLOVAN BRATISLAVA 3 (Cvetler 2, Hrivnak 30, Jan Capkovic 42)

BARCELONA 2 (Zaldua 16, Rexach 52)

Slovan – Vencel – Filo, Horvath, Hrivnak – Zlocha, Hrdlicka, Josef Capkovic – Cvetler, Moder (Hatar), Jokl, Jan Capkovic

Barcelona – Sadurni – Franch (Pereda), Eladio, Rife – Olivella, Zabalza, Pellicer – Castro (Mendoza), Zaldua, Fuste, Rexach

Top scorer: Rühl, 1.FC Köln 6

1969–70

EUROPEAN CUP

PRELIMINARY ROUND

TPS Turku	0–1 0–4	**KB Kobenhavn**

FIRST ROUND

Feyenoord	12–2 4–0	KR Reykjavík
Milan	5–0 3–0	Avenir Beggen
Crvena Zvezda Beo.	8–0 4–2	Linfield
Vorwärts Berlin	2–0 1–1	Panathinaikos
Galatasaray	2–0 3–2	Waterford FC
Hibernians Paola	2–2 0–4	**Spartak Trnava**
Bayern München	2–0 0–3	**AS Saint-Étienne**
UT Arad	1–2 0–8	**Legia Warszawa**
Leeds United	10–0 6–0	SOFK Lyn Oslo
CSKA Sofia	2–1 1–4	**Ferencváros**
Real Madrid	8–0 6–1	Olympiakos Nicosia
Standard CL	3–0 1–1	17 Nëntori Tiranë
Fiorentina	1–0 2–1	Östers IF Växjö
FK Austria	1–2 1–3	**Dynamo Kiev**
Benfica	2–0 3–2	KB Kobenhavn
FC Basel	0–0 0–2	**Glasgow Celtic**

SECOND ROUND

Milan	1–0 0–2	**Feyenoord**
Vorwärts Berlin	2–1 2–3	Crvena Zvezda Beograd
Galatasaray	*1–0 0–1	Spartak Trnava
Legia Warszawa	2–1 1–0	AS Saint-Étienne
Leeds United	3–0 3–0	Ferencváros
Standard CL	1–0 3–2	Real Madrid
Dynamo Kiev	1–2 0–0	**Fiorentina**
Glasgow Celtic	*3–0 0–3	Benfica

QUARTER-FINALS

Vorwärts Berlin	1–0 0–2	**Feyenoord**
Galatasaray	1–1 0–2	**Legia Warszawa**
Standard CL	0–1 0–1	**Leeds United**
Glasgow Celtic	3–0 0–1	Fiorentina

SEMI-FINALS

Legia Warszawa	0–0 0–2	**Feyenoord**
Leeds United	0–1 1–2	**Glasgow Celtic**

FINAL

San Siro, Milan, 6–05–1970, 53 000. Referee: Lo Bello, Italy

FEYENOORD 2 (Israel 31, Kindvall 117)

GLASGOW CELTIC 1 (Gemmell 29)

Feyenoord – Pieters Graafland – Romeijn (Haak), Laseroms, Israel, Van Duivenbode – Hasil, Jansen – Van Hanegem, Wery, Kindvall, Moulijn. Tr: Happel

Celtic – Williams – Hay, Brogan, McNeill, Gemmell – Murdoch, Auld (Connelly) – Johnstone, Lennox, Wallace, Hughes. Tr: Stein

Top scorer: Jones, Leeds United 8

FAIRS CUP

FIRST ROUND

Arsenal	3–0 0–1	Glentoran
Sporting CP	4–0 2–2	Linzer ASK
RSC Charleroi	2–1 3–1	NK Zagreb
FC Rouen	2–0 0–1	FC Twente Enschede
FC Zürich	3–2 1–3	**Kilmarnock**
Slavia Sofia	2–0 1–1	Valencia
TSV München 1860	2–2 1–2	**FK Skeid Oslo**
Dinamo Bacau	6–0 1–0	Floriana
Carl Zeiss Jena	1–0 0–0	Altay Izmir
Aris Salonica	1–1 0–3	**Cagliari**
Partizan Beograd	2–1 0–2	**Ujpesti Dózsa**
FC Metz	1–1 1–2	**Napoli**
VfB Stuttgart	3–0 1–1	Malmö FF
Sabadell	2–0 1–5	**Club Brugge**
Wiener Sport-Club	4–2 1–4	**Ruch Chorzów**
Hannover 96	2–1 0–3	**Ajax**
Internazionale	3–0 1–0	Sparta Praha
Hansa Rostock	3–0 0–2	Panionios
Lausanne-Sports	1–2 1–2	**Rába ETO Györ**
Barcelona	4–0 2–0	B 1909 Odense
Vitória FC Setúbal	3–1 4–1	Rapid Bucuresti
Liverpool	10–0 4–0	Dundalk
Juventus	3–1 2–1	Lokomotiv Plovdiv
Las Palmas	0–0 0–1	**Hertha BSC Berlin**
Dundee United	1–2 0–1	**Newcastle United**
Hvidovre BK	1–2 0–2	**FC Porto**
Vitória Guimaraes	1–0 1–1	Baník Ostrava
Rosenborg BK	1–0 0–2	**Southampton**
Dunfermline Athletic	4–0 0–2	Girondins Bordeaux
Gwardia Warszawa	1–0 1–1	Vojvodina Novi Sad
Jeunesse Esch	3–2 0–4	**Coleraine**
Valur Reykjavík	0–6 0–2	**RSC Anderlecht**

SECOND ROUND

Sporting CP	0–0 0–3	**Arsenal**
RSC Charleroi	3–1 0–2	**FC Rouen**
Kilmarnock	4–1 0–2	Slavia Sofia
FK Skeid Oslo	0–0 0–2	**Dinamo Bacau**
Carl Zeiss Jena	2–0 1–0	Cagliari

Club Brugge 5–2 0–3 **Ujpesti Dózsa**
VfB Stuttgart 0–0 0–1 **Napoli**
Ajax 7–0 2–1 Ruch Chorzów
Hansa Rostock 2–1 0–3 **Internazionale**
Rába ETO Györ 2–3 0–2 **Barcelona**
Vitória FC Setúbal 1–0 2–3 Liverpool
Hertha BSC Berlin 3–1 0–0 Juventus
FC Porto 0–0 0–1 **Newcastle United**
Vitória SC Guimaraes 3–3 1–5 **Southampton**
Dunfermline Athletic 2–1 1–0 Gwardia Warszawa
RSC Anderlecht 6–1 7–3 Coleraine

THIRD ROUND
FC Rouen 0–0 0–1 **Arsenal**
Kilmarnock 1–1 0–2 **Dinamo Bacau**
Carl Zeiss Jena 1–0 3–0 Ujpesti Dózsa
Napoli 1–0 0–4 **Ajax**
Barcelona 1–2 1–1 **Internazionale**
Vitória FC Setúbal 1–1 0–1 **Hertha BSC Berlin**
Newcastle United 0–0 1–1 Southampton
RSC Anderlecht 1–0 2–3 Dunfermline Athletic

QUARTER-FINALS
Dinamo Bacau 0–2 1–7 **Arsenal**
Carl Zeiss Jena 3–1 1–5 **Ajax**
Hertha BSC Berlin 1–0 0–2 **Internazionale**
RSC Anderlecht 2–0 1–3 Newcastle United

SEMI-FINALS
Arsenal 3–0 0–1 Ajax
RSC Anderlecht 0–1 2–0 Internazionale

FINAL
1st leg
Parc Astrid, Brussels, 22–04–1970, 37 000. Referee: Scheurer, Switzerland
RSC ANDERLECHT 3 (Devrindt 25, Mulder 30 74)
ARSENAL 1 (Kennedy 82)
Anderlecht – Trappeniers, Heylens, Velkeneers, Kialunda, Cornelis (Peeters), Nordahl, Desanghere, Puis, Devrindt, Van Himst, Mulder
Arsenal – Wilson, Storey, McNab, Kelly, McLintock, Simpson, Armstrong, Sammels, Radford, George (Kennedy), Graham

2nd leg
Highbury, London, 28–04–1970, 51 000. Referee: Kunze, East Germany
ARSENAL 3 (Kelly 25, Radford 75, Sammels 76)
RSC ANDERLECHT 0
Arsenal – Wilson, Storey, McNab, Kelly, McLintock, Simpson, Armstrong, Sammels, Radford, George, Graham
Anderlecht – Trappeniers, Heylens, Velkeneers, Kialunda, Martens, Nordahl, Desanghere, Puis, Devrindt, Mulder, Van Himst

CUP WINNERS CUP

PRELIMINARY ROUND
SK Rapid Wien 0–0 1–1 Torpedo Moskva

FIRST ROUND
Athletic Bilbao 3–3 0–3 **Manchester City**
Lierse SK 10–1 1–0 Apoel Nicosia
1.FC Magdeburg 1–0 1–1 MTK Budapest
Académica Coimbra 0–0 1–0 KuPS Kuopio
Dinamo Zagreb 3–0 0–0 Slovan Bratislava
Dukla Praha 1–0 0–2 **Olymp. Marseille**
IFK Norrköping 5–1 0–1 Sliema Wanderers
Shamrock Rovers 2–1 0–3 **FC Schalke 04**
Ards 0–0 1–3 **Roma**
SK Rapid Wien 1–2 2–4 **PSV Eindhoven**
Mjondalen IF 1–7 1–5 **Cardiff City**
Göztepe Izmir 3–0 3–2 Union Luxembourg
IBV Vestmannaeyjar 0–4 0–4 **Levski-Spartak**
Frem Kobenhavn 2–1 0–1 **FC St Gallen**
Glasgow Rangers 2–0 0–0 Steaua Bucuresti
Olympiakos 2–2 0–5 **Górnik Zabrze**

SECOND ROUND
Lierse SK 0–3 0–5 **Manchester City**
1.FC Magdeburg 1–0 0–2 **Académica Coimbra**
Olympique Marseille 1–1 0–2 **Dinamo Zagreb**
IFK Norrköping 0–0 0–1 **FC Schalke 04**
Roma *1–0 0–1 PSV Eindhoven
Göztepe Izmir 3–0 0–1 Cardiff City
Levski-Spartak 4–0 0–0 FC St Gallen
Górnik Zabrze 3–1 3–1 Glasgow Rangers

QUARTER-FINALS
Académica Coimbra 0–0 0–1 **Manchester City**
Dinamo Zagreb 1–3 0–1 **FC Schalke 04**
Roma 2–0 0–0 Göztepe Izmir
Levski-Spartak 3–2 1–2 **Górnik Zabrze**

SEMI-FINALS
FC Schalke 04 1–0 1–5 **Manchester City**
Roma 1–1 2–2 1–1* **Górnik Zabrze**

FINAL
Prater, Vienna, 29–04–1970, 8000. Referee: Schiller, Austria
MANCHESTER CITY 2 (Young 11, Lee 43)
GORNIK ZABRZE 1 (Oslizlo 70)
Manchester City – Corrigan – Book, Booth, Heslop, Pardoe – Doyle (Bowyer), Towers, Oakes – Bell, Lee, Young
Górnik Zabrze – Kostka – Oslizlo, Florenski (Deja), Gorgon, Olek – Latocha, Szoltysik, Wilczek (Skowronek) – Szarynski, Banas, Lubanski

Top scorer: Lubanski, Górnik Zabrze 8

1970–71

EUROPEAN CUP

PRELIMINARY ROUND
Levski–Spartak 3–1 0–3 **FK Austria**

FIRST ROUND
17 Nëntori Tiranë 2–2 0–2 **Ajax**
Spartak Moskva 3–2 1–2 **FC Basel**
Glentoran 1–3 0–1 **Waterford FC**
Glasgow Celtic 9–0 5–0 KPV Kokkola
IFK Göteborg 0–4 1–2 **Legia Warszawa**
Rosenborg BK 0–2 0–5 **Standard CL**
Cagliari 3–0 0–1 AS Saint–Étienne
Atlético Madrid 2–0 2–1 FK Austria
Ujpesti Dózsa 2–0 0–4 **Crvena Zvezda Beograd**
Feyenoord 1–1 0–0 **UT Arad**
Sporting CP 5–0 4–0 Floriana
Fenerbahçe 0–4 0–1 **Carl Zeiss Jena**
Everton 6–2 3–0 IBK Keflavík
B. Mönchengladbach 6–0 10–0 EPA Larnaca
Slovan Bratislava 2–1 2–2 B 1903 Kobenhavn
Jeunesse Esch 1–2 0–5 **Panathinaikos**

SECOND ROUND
Ajax 3–0 2–1 FC Basel
Waterford FC 0–7 2–3 **Glasgow Celtic**
Standard CL 1–0 0–2 **Legia Warszawa**
Cagliari 2–1 0–3 **Atlético Madrid**
Crvena Zvezda Beo. 3–0 3–1 UT Arad
Carl Zeiss Jena 2–1 2–1 Sporting CP
B. Mönchengladbach 1–1 1–1 (3–4p) **Everton**
Panathinaikos 3–0 1–2 Slovan Bratislava

QUARTER-FINALS

Ajax 3–0 0–1 Glasgow Celtic
Atlético Madrid 1–0 1–2 Legia Warszawa
Carl Zeiss Jena 3–2 0–4 **Crvena Zvezda Beograd**
Everton 1–1 0–0 **Panathinaikos**

SEMI-FINALS

Atlético Madrid 1–0 0–3 **Ajax**
Crvena Zvezda Beograd 4–1 0–3 **Panathinaikos**

FINAL

Wembley, London, 2–06–1971, 83 000. Referee: Taylor, England
AJAX 2 (Van Dijk 5, OG 87)
PANATHINAIKOS 0

Ajax – Stuy – Neeskens, Hulshoff, Vasovic, Suurbier – Rijnders (Blankenburg), Muhren G – Swart (Haan), Cruyff, Van Dijk, Keizer. Tr: Michels

Panathinaikos – Oeconomopoulos – Tomaras, Kapsis, Sourpis, Vlahos – Kamaras, Elefterakis – Grammos, Antoniadis, Domazos, Filakouris. Tr: Puskas

Top scorer: Antoniadis, Panathinaikos 10

FAIRS CUP

FIRST ROUND

FK Sarpsborg 0–1 0–5 **Leeds United**
Partizan Beograd 0–0 0–6 **Dynamo Dresden**
Dundee United 3–2 0–0 Grasshopper-Club
Sparta Praha 2–0 1–1 Athletic Bilbao
Zeljeznicar Sarajevo 3–4 4–5 **RSC Anderlecht**
Akademisk Kob'havn 7–0 3–2 Sliema Wanderers
Hajduk Split 3–0 0–1 Slavia Sofia
Lausanne-Sports 0–2 1–2 **Vitória FC Setúbal**
Bayern München 1–0 1–1 Glasgow Rangers
Trakia Plovdiv 1–4 0–2 **Coventry City**
Coleraine 1–1 3–2 Kilmarnock
Sparta Rotterdam 6–0 9–0 IA Akranes
Hibernian Edinburgh 6–0 3–2 Malmö FF
Vitória Guimaraes 3–0 1–3 AS Angouleme
Dinamo Bucuresti 5–0 0–1 PAOK Salonica
Liverpool 1–0 1–1 Ferencváros
1.FC Köln 5–1 0–1 RCP Sedan
Ruch Chorzów 1–1 0–2 **Fiorentina**
B 1901 Nykobing 2–4 1–4 **Hertha BSC Berlin**
Spartak Trnava 2–0 0–2 (4–3p) Olympique Marseille
Wiener Sport-Club 0–2 0–3 **SK Beveren**
Cork Hibernians 0–3 1–3 **Valencia**
Ilves Tampere 4–2 0–3 **SK Sturm Graz**
Lazio 2–2 0–2 **Arsenal**
AEK Athens 0–1 0–3 **FC Twente Enschede**
Sevilla 1–0 1–3 **Eskisehirspor**
AA Gent 0–1 1–7 **Hamburger SV**
FC Barreirense 2–0 1–6 **Dinamo Zagreb**
Universitatea Craiova 2–1 0–3 **Pécsi Dózsa**
Internazionale 1–1 0–2 **Newcastle United**
GKS Katowice 0–1 2–3 **Barcelona**
Juventus 7–0 4–0 Union Luxembourg

SECOND ROUND

Leeds United 1–0 1–2 Dynamo Dresden
Sparta Praha 3–1 0–1 Dundee United
Akademisk Kobenhavn 1–3 0–4 **RSC Anderlecht**
Vitória FC Setúbal 2–0 1–2 Hajduk Split
Bayern München 6–1 1–2 Coventry City
Sparta Rotterdam 2–0 2–1 Coleraine
Hibernian Edinburgh 2–0 1–2 Vitória SC Guimaraes
Liverpool 3–0 1–1 Dinamo Bucuresti
Fiorentina 1–2 0–1 **1.FC Köln**
Hertha BSC Berlin 1–0 1–3 **Spartak Trnava**
Valencia 0–1 1–1 **SK Beveren**
SK Sturm Graz 1–0 0–2 **Arsenal**
Eskisehirspor 3–2 1–6 **FC Twente Enschede**
Dinamo Zagreb 4–0 0–1 Hamburger SV
Newcastle United 2–0 0–2 (3–5p) **Pécsi Dózsa**
Barcelona 1–2 1–2 **Juventus**

THIRD ROUND

Leeds United 6–0 3–2 Sparta Praha
RSC Anderlecht 2–1 1–3 **Vitória FC Setúbal**
Bayern München 2–1 3–1 Sparta Rotterdam
Hibernian Edinburgh 0–1 0–2 **Liverpool**
Spartak Trnava 0–1 0–3 **1.FC Köln**
Arsenal 4–0 0–0 SK Beveren
Dinamo Zagreb 2–2 0–1 **FC Twente Enschede**
Pécsi Dózsa 0–1 0–2 **Juventus**

QUARTER–FINALS

Leeds United 2–1 1–1 Vitória FC Setúbal
Liverpool 3–0 1–1 Bayern München
Arsenal 2–1 0–1 **1.FC Köln**
Juventus 2–0 2–2 FC Twente Enschede

SEMI–FINALS

Liverpool 0–1 0–0 **Leeds United**
1.FC Köln 1–1 0–2 **Juventus**

FINAL

1st leg
Comunale, Turin, 28–05–1971, 65 000. Referee: Van Ravens, Holland
JUVENTUS 2 (Bettega 27, Capello 55)
LEEDS UNITED 2 (Madeley 48, Bates 77)

Juventus – Piloni, Spinosi, Salvadore, Marchetti, Furino, Morini, Haller, Capello, Causio, Anastasi (Novellini), Bettega

Leeds Utd – Sprake, Reaney, Cooper, Bremner, Charlton, Hunter, Lorimer, Clarke, Jones (Bates), Giles, Madeley

2nd leg
Elland Road, Leeds, 3–06–1971, 42 000. Referee: Glöckner, East Germany
LEEDS UNITED 1 (Clarke 12)
JUVENTUS 1 (Anastasi 20)

Leeds Utd – Sprake, Reaney, Cooper, Bremner, Charlton, Hunter, Lorimer, Clarke, Jones, Giles, Madeley (Bates)

Juventus – Tancredi, Spinosi, Salvadore, Marchetti, Furino, Morini, Haller, Capello, Causio, Anastasi, Bettega

CUP WINNERS CUP

PRELIMINARY ROUND

Bohemians Dublin 1–2 2–2 **TJ Gottwaldov**
Åtvidabergs FF 1–1 0–2 **Partizani Tiranë**

FIRST ROUND

Aris Salonica 1–1 1–5 **Chelsea**
CSKA Sofia 9–0 2–1 Haka Valkeakoski
IBA Akureyri 1–7 0–7 **FC Zürich**
Kickers Offenbach 2–1 0–2 **Club Brugge**
ÅAB Åalborg 0–1 1–8 **Górnik Zabrze**
Göztepe Izmir 5–0 0–1 Union Luxembourg
Aberdeen 3–1 1–3 (4–5p) **Honvéd**
Manchester City 1–0 1–2 Linfield
TJ Gottwaldov 2–1 0–1 **PSV Eindhoven**
Steaua Bucuresti 1–0 3–3 Karpati Lvov
Olimpia Ljubljana 1–1 1–8 **Benfica**
Vorwärts Berlin 0–0 1–1 Bologna
Cardiff City 8–0 0–0 Pezoporikos
IF Stromsgodset 0–5 3–2 **FC Nantes**
Wacker Innsbruck 3–2 2–1 Partizani Tiranë
Hibernians Paola 0–0 0–5 **Real Madrid**

SECOND ROUND

CSKA Sofia 0–1 0–1 **Chelsea**
Club Brugge 2–0 2–3 FC Zürich

Göztepe Izmir	0–1 0–3	**Górnik Zabrze**
Honvéd	0–1 0–2	**Manchester City**
PSV Eindhoven	4–0 3–0	Steaua Bucuresti
Benfica	2–0 0–2 (3–5p)	**Vorwärts Berlin**
Cardiff City	5–1 2–1	FC Nantes
Real Madrid	0–1 2–0	Wacker Innsbruck

QUARTER-FINALS

Club Brugge	2–0 0–4	**Chelsea**
Manchester City	2–0 0–2 3–1	Górnik Zabrze
PSV Eindhoven	2–0 0–1	Vorwärts Berlin
Cardiff City	1–0 0–2	**Real Madrid**

SEMI-FINALS

Chelsea	1–0 1–0	Manchester City
PSV Eindhoven	0–0 1–2	**Real Madrid**

FINAL

Karaiskaki, Piraeus, 19–05–1971, 42 000. Referee: Scheurer, Switzerland

CHELSEA 1 (Osgood 55)
REAL MADRID 1 (Zoco 30)

Chelsea – Bonetti – Boyle, Dempsey, Webb, Harris – Hollins (Mulligan), Hudson, Cooke – Weller, Osgood (Baldwin), Houseman

Real Madrid – Borja – Jose Luis, Benito, Zoco, Zunzunegui – Pirri, Grosso, Velazquez – Perez (Fleitas), Amancio, Gento (Grande)

Replay. Karaiskaki, Piraeus, 21–05–1971, 35 000. Referee: Bucheli, Switzerland

CHELSEA 2 (Dempsey 32, Osgood 38)
REAL MADRID 1 (Fleitas 74)

Chelsea – Bonetti – Boyle, Dempsey, Webb, Harris – Cooke, Hudson, Weller – Baldwin, Osgood (Smethurst), Houseman

Real Madrid – Borja – Jose Luis, Benito, Zoco, Zunzunegui – Pirri, Grosso, Velazquez (Gento) – Fleitas, Amancio, Bueno (Grande)

Top scorer: Lubanski, Górnik Zabrze 8

1971–72

EUROPEAN CUP

PRELIMINARY ROUND

Valencia	3–1 1–0	Union Luxembourg

FIRST ROUND

Ajax	2–0 0–0	Dynamo Dresden
Olympique Marseille	2–1 1–1	Górnik Zabrze
Reipas Lahti	1–1 0–8	**Grasshopper-Club**
IF Stromsgodset	1–3 0–4	**Arsenal**
Feyenoord	8–0 9–0	Olympiakos Nicosia
Dinamo Bucuresti	0–0 2–2	Spartak Trnava
CSKA Sofia	3–0 1–0	Partizani Tiranë
Wacker Innsbruck	0–4 1–3	**Benfica**
B 1903 Kobenhavn	2–1 0–3	**Glasgow Celtic**
IA Akranes	0–4 0–0	**Sliema Wanderers**
Valencia	0–0 1–1	Hajduk Split
Ujpesti Dózsa	4–0 0–1	Malmö FF
Standard CL	2–0 3–2	Linfield
Galatasaray	1–1 0–3	**CSKA Moskva**
Cork Hibernians	0–5 1–2	**B. Mönchengladbach**
Internazionale	4–1 2–3	AEK Athens

SECOND ROUND

Olympique Marseille	1–2 1–4	**Ajax**
Grasshopper-Club	0–2 0–3	**Arsenal**
Dinamo Bucuresti	0–3 0–2	**Feyenoord**
Benfica	2–1 0–0	CSKA Sofia
Glasgow Celtic	5–0 2–1	Sliema Wanderers
Valencia	0–1 1–2	**Ujpesti Dózsa**
CSKA Moskva	1–0 0–2	**Standard CL**
Internazionale	4–2 0–0	Borussia Mönchengladbach

QUARTER-FINALS

Ajax	2–1 1–0	Arsenal
Feyenoord	1–0 1–5	**Benfica**
Ujpesti Dózsa	1–2 1–1	**Glasgow Celtic**
Internazionale	1–0 1–2	Standard CL

SEMI-FINALS

Ajax	1–0 0–0	Benfica
Internazionale	0–0 0–0 (5–4p)	Glasgow Celtic

FINAL

Feyenoord Stadion, Rotterdam, 31–05–1972, 61 000. Referee: Héliès, France

AJAX 2 (Cruyff 47 78)
INTERNAZIONALE 0

Ajax – Stuy – Suurbier, Blankenburg, Hulshoff, Krol – Neeskens, Haan, Muhren G – Swart, Cruyff, Keizer. Tr: Kovacs

Internazionale – Bordon – Burgnich, Facchetti, Bellugi, Oriali – Giubertoni (Bertini), Bedin, Frustalupi – Jair (Pellizarro), Mazzola, Boninsegna. Tr: Invernizzi

Top scorers: Cruyff, Ajax 5
Macari, Celtic 5
Takac, Standard CL 5

UEFA CUP

IBK Keflavík	1–6 0–9	**Tottenham Hotspur**
FC Porto	0–2 1–1	**FC Nantes**
FC Lugano	1–3 0–0	**Legia Warszawa**
Napoli	1–0 0–2	**Rapid Bucuresti**
Vitória FC Setúbal	1–0 1–2	Nîmes Olympique
Spartak Moskva	2–0 1–2	VSS Kosice
Zaglebie Walbrzych	1–0 3–2	Union Teplice
UT Arad	4–1 1–3	Austria Salzburg
Lierse SK	0–2 4–0	Leeds United
Rosenborg BK	3–0 1–0	HIFK Helsinki
FC Basel	1–2 1–2	**Real Madrid**
Chemie Halle (*withdrew*)	0–0	PSV Eindhoven
Dundee	4–2 1–0	Akademisk Kobenhavn
AS Saint-Étienne	1–1 1–2	**1.FC Köln**
Hertha BSC Berlin	3–1 4–1	IF Elfsborg Borås
Milan	4–0 3–0	Digenis Morphou
Fenerbahçe	1–1 1–3	**Ferencváros**
Atlético Madrid	2–1 0–1	**Panionios**
Southampton	2–1 0–2	**Athletic Bilbao**
Glentoran	0–1 1–6	**Eintracht Braunschweig**
Hamburger SV	2–1 0–3	**St Johnstone**
Vasas Budapest	1–0 1–1	Shelbourne
Bologna	1–1 2–0	RSC Anderlecht
Zeljeznicar Sarajevo	3–0 1–3	Club Brugge
Marsa	0–6 0–5	**Juventus**
Celta	0–2 0–1	**Aberdeen**
Dinamo Zagreb	6–1 2–1	Botev Vratza
SK Rapid Wien	W–O	Vllaznia Shkodër
Carl Zeiss Jena	3–0 1–3	Lokomotiv Plovdiv
OFK Beograd	4–1 2–2	Djurgårdens IF
FC Den Haag	5–0 1–1	Aris Bonnevoie
Wolverhampton W.	3–0 4–1	Académica Coimbra

SECOND ROUND

FC Nantes	0–0 0–1	**Tottenham Hotspur**
Rapid Bucuresti	4–0 0–2	Legia Warszawa
Spartak Moskva	0–0 0–4	**Vitória FC Setúbal**
Zaglebie Walbrzych	1–1 1–2	**UT Arad**
Rosenborg BK	4–1 0–3	**Lierse SK**
Real Madrid	3–1 0–2	**PSV Eindhoven**
1.FC Köln	2–1 2–4	**Dundee**
Milan	4–2 1–2	Hertha BSC Berlin
Ferencváros	6–0	Panionios (*disqualified*)

Eintracht Braunschweig	2–1 2–2	Athletic Bilbao
St Johnstone	2–0 0–1	Vasas Budapest
Zeljeznicar Sarajevo	1–1 2–2	Bologna
Juventus	2–0 1–1	Aberdeen
Dinamo Zagreb	2–2 0–0	**SK Rapid Wien**
OFK Beograd	1–1 0–4	**Carl Zeiss Jena**
FC Den Haag	1–3 0–4	**Wolverhampton Wand.**

THIRD ROUND

Tottenham Hotspur	3–0 2–0	Rapid Bucuresti
UT Arad	3–0 0–1	Vitória FC Setúbal
PSV Eindhoven	1–0 0–4	**Lierse SK**
Milan	3–0 0–2	Dundee
Eintracht Braunschweig	1–1 2–5	**Ferencváros**
St Johnstone	1–0 1–5	**Zeljeznicar Sarajevo**
SK Rapid Wien	0–1 1–4	**Juventus**
Carl Zeiss Jena	0–1 0–3	**Wolverhampton Wand.**

QUARTER-FINALS

UT Arad	0–2 1–1	**Tottenham Hotspur**
Milan	2–0 1–1	Lierse SK
Ferencváros	1–2 2–1 (5–4p)	Zeljeznicar Sarajevo
Juventus	1–1 1–2	**Wolverhampton Wand.**

SEMI-FINALS

Tottenham Hotspur	2–1 1–1	Milan
Ferencváros	2–2 1–2	**Wolverhampton Wand.**

FINAL

1st leg

Molineux, Wolverhampton, 3–05–1972, 38000. Referee: Bakhramov, Soviet Union

WOLVERHAMPTON WANDERERS 1 (McCalliog 72)
TOTTENHAM HOTSPUR 2 (Chivers 57 87)

Wolves – Parkes, Shaw, Taylor, Hegan, Munro, McAlle, McCalliog, Hibbitt, Richards, Dougan, Wagstaffe

Tottenham – Jennings, Kinnear, Knowles, Mullery, England, Beal, Gilzean, Perryman, Chivers, Peters, Coates (Pratt)

2nd leg

White Hart Lane, London, 17–05–1972, 54000. Referee: Van Ravens, Holland

TOTTENHAM HOTSPUR 1 (Mullery 30)
WOLVERHAMPTON WANDERERS 1 (Wagstaffe 41)

Tottenham – Jennings, Kinnear, Knowles, Mullery, England, Beal, Gilzean, Perryman, Chivers, Peters, Coates

Wolves – Parkes, Shaw, Taylor, Hegan, Munro, McAlle, McCalliog, Hibbitt (Bailey), Richards, Dougan (Curran), Wagstaffe

CUP WINNERS CUP

PRELIMINARY ROUND

B 1909 Odense	4–2 0–2	**FK Austria**
Hibernians Paola	3–0 0–2	Fram Reykjavík

FIRST ROUND

Stade Rennes	1–1 0–1	**Glasgow Rangers**
Sporting CP	4–0 3–0	SOFK Lyn Oslo
Dinamo Tiranë	1–1 0–1	**FK Austria**
Limerick FC	0–1 0–4	**Torino**
Hibernians Paola	0–0 0–1	**Steaua Bucuresti**
Distillery	1–3 0–4	**Barcelona**
Servette FC	2–1 0–2	**Liverpool**
Skoda Plzen	0–1 1–6	**Bayern München**
Dynamo Berlin	1–1 1–1 (5–4p)	Cardiff City
Beerschot VAV	7–0 1–0	Anorthosis Famagusta
Jeunesse Hautcharage	0–8 0–13	**Chelsea**
Zaglebie Sosnowiec	3–4 1–1	**Åtvidabergs FF**
Komló Bányász	2–7 2–1	**Crvena Zvezda Beograd**
Levski-Spartak	1–1 0–2	**Sparta Rotterdam**
MP Mikkeli	0–0 0–4	**Eskisehirspor**
Olympiakos	0–2 2–1	**Dynamo Moskva**

SECOND ROUND

Glasgow Rangers	3–2 3–4	Sporting CL
Torino	1–0 0–0	FK Austria
Barcelona	0–1 1–2	**Steaua Bucuresti**
Liverpool	0–0 1–3	**Bayern München**
Beerschot VAV	1–3 1–3	**Dynamo Berlin**
Åtvidabergs FF	0–0 1–1	Chelsea
Sparta Rotterdam	1–1 1–2	**Crvena Zvezda Beograd**
Eskisehirspor	0–1 0–1	**Dynamo Moskva**

QUARTER-FINALS

Torino	1–1 0–1	**Glasgow Rangers**
Steaua Bucuresti	1–1 0–0	**Bayern München**
Åtvidabergs FF	0–2 2–2	**Dynamo Berlin**
Crvena Zvezda Beograd	1–2 1–1	**Dynamo Moskva**

SEMI-FINALS

Bayern München	1–1 0–2	**Glasgow Rangers**
Dynamo Berlin	1–1 1–1 (1–4p)	**Dynamo Moskva**

FINAL

Nou Camp, Barcelona, 24–05–1972, 24000. Referee: Ortiz de Mendebil, Spain

GLASGOW RANGERS 3 (Stein 23, Johnston 40 49)
DYNAMO MOSKVA 2 (Estrekov 60, Makovikov 87)

Rangers – McCloy – Jardine, Johnstone, Smith, Mathieson – Greig, Conn, MacDonald – McLean, Stein, Johnston

Dynamo Moskva – Pilgui – Basalev, Dolmatov, Zikov, Dobonosov (Gerschkovitch) – Zhukov, Yakubik (Estrekov), Sabo – Baidatchini, Makovikov, Evriuschkin

Top scorer: Osgood, Chelsea 8

EUROPEAN SUPERCUP 1972

1st leg

Ibrox, Glasgow, 16–01–1973. Referee: MacKenzie, Scotland

GLASGOW RANGERS 1 (MacDonald 39)
AJAX 3 (Rep 31, Cruyff 43, Haan 44)

2nd leg

Amsterdam, 24–01–1973. Referee: Weyland, West Germany

AJAX 3 (Haan 9, Muhren 39, Cruyff 78)
GLASGOW RANGERS 2 (MacDonald 7 26)

1972–73

EUROPEAN CUP

FIRST ROUND

Ajax	Bye	
CSKA Sofia	2–1 2–0	Panathinaikos
Waterford FC	2–1 0–2	**Omonia Nicosia**
Galatasaray	1–1 0–6	**Bayern München**
Wacker Innsbruck	0–1 0–2	**Dynamo Kiev**
Sliema Wanderers	0–5 0–5	**Górnik Zabrze**
Aris Bonnevoie	0–2 0–4	**FC Arges Pitesti**
Real Madrid	3–0 1–0	IBK Keflavík
Derby County	2–0 2–1	Zeljeznicar Sarajevo
Malmö FF	1–0 1–4	**Benfica**
RSC Anderlecht	4–2 3–0	Vejle BK
Spartak Trnava	Bye	
Ujpesti Dózsa	2–0 2–3	FC Basel
Glasgow Celtic	2–1 3–1	Rosenborg BK
1.FC Magdeburg	6–0 3–1	TPS Turku
Olympique Marseille	1–0 0–3	**Juventus**

SECOND ROUND

CSKA Sofia	1–3 0–3	**Ajax**
Omonia Nicosia	0–9 0–4	**Bayern München**

Dynamo Kiev	2–0 1–2	Górnik Zabrze
FC Arges Pitesti	2–1 1–3	**Real Madrid**
Derby County	3–0 0–0	Benfica
Spartak Trnava	1–0 1–0	RSC Anderlecht
Glasgow Celtic	2–1 0–3	**Ujpesti Dózsa**
Juventus	1–0 1–0	1.FC Magdeburg

QUARTER-FINALS

Ajax	4–0 1–2	Bayern München
Dynamo Kiev	0–0 0–3	**Real Madrid**
Spartak Trnava	1–0 0–2	**Derby County**
Juventus	0–0 2–2	Ujpesti Dózsa

SEMI-FINALS

Ajax	2–1 1–0	Real Madrid
Juventus	3–1 0–0	Derby County

FINAL

Crvena Zvezda, Belgrade, 30–05–1973, 89 000. Referee: Gugulovic, Yugoslavia

AJAX 1 (Rep 4)
JUVENTUS 0

Ajax – Stuy – Suurbier, Hulshoff, Blankenburg, Krol – Neeskens, Muhren G, Haan – Rep, Cruyff, Keizer. Tr: Kovacs

Juventus – Zoff – Salvadore, Marchetti, Morini, Longobucco – Causio (Cuccureddu), Furino, Capello – Altafini, Anastasi, Bettega (Haller). Tr: Vycpalek

Top scorer: Müller, Bayern München 11

UEFA CUP

FIRST ROUND

Liverpool	2–0 0–0	Eintracht Frankfurt
AEK Athens	3–1 1–1	Salgótarján BTC
Universitatea Cluj	4–1 1–5	**Levski-Spartak**
SC Angers	1–1 1–2	**Dynamo Berlin**
FC Porto	3–1 1–0	Barcelona
Åtvidabergs FF	3–5 2–1	**Club Brugge**
Ruch Chorzów	3–0 0–1	Fenerbahçe
Dynamo Dresden	2–0 2–2	VÖEST Linz
Vitória FC Setúbal	6–1 0–1	Zaglebie Sosnowiec
Eskisehirspor	1–2 0–3	**Fiorentina**
UT Arad	1–2 0–2	**IFK Norrköping**
Internazionale	6–1 1–0	Valletta
Crvena Zvezda Beo.	5–1 2–3	Lausanne-Sports
Manchester City	2–2 1–2	**Valencia**
Olympiakos	2–1 1–0	Cagliari
SOFK Lyn Oslo	3–6 0–6	**Tottenham Hotspur**
Dynamo Tbilisi	3–2 0–2	**FC Twente Enschede**
FC Sochaux	1–3 1–2	**Frem Kobenhavn**
Slovan Bratislava	6–0 2–1	Vojvodina Novi Sad
Torino	2–0 0–4	**Las Palmas**
Beroe Stara Zagora	7–0 3–1	FK Austria
Honvéd	1–0 3–0	Partick Thistle
Feyenoord	9–0 12–0	US Rumelange
Dukla Praha	2–2 1–3	**OFK Beograd**
Stoke City	3–1 0–4	**1.FC Kaiserslautern**
Racing White	0–1 0–2	**GD Cuf Barreiro**
Grasshopper-Club	2–1 2–1	Nîmes Olympique
EPA Larnaca	0–1 0–1	**Ararat Yerevan**
1.FC Köln	2–1 3–0	Bohemians Dublin
Viking Stavanger	1–0 0–0	IBV Vestmannaeyjar
Hvidovre BK	W–O	HIFK Helsinki
Aberdeen	2–3 3–6	**B. Mönchengladbach**

SECOND ROUND

Liverpool	3–0 3–1	AEK Athens
Dynamo Berlin	3–0 0–2	Levski-Spartak
FC Porto	3–0 2–3	Club Brugge
Ruch Chorzów	0–1 0–3	**Dynamo Dresden**
Vitória FC Setúbal	1–0 1–2	Fiorentina
Internazionale	2–2 2–0	IFK Norrköping
Crvena Zvezda Beo.	3–1 1–0	Valencia
Tottenham Hotspur	4–0 0–1	Olympiakos
Frem Kobenhavn	0–5 0–4	**FC Twente Enschede**
Las Palmas	2–2 1–0	Slovan Bratislava
Beroe Stara Zagora	3–0 0–1	Honvéd
Feyenoord	4–3 1–2	**OFK Beograd**
GD Cuf Barreiro	1–3 1–0	**1.FC Kaiserslautern**
Grasshopper-Club	1–3 2–4	**Ararat Yerevan**
Viking FK Stavanger	1–0 1–9	**1.FC Köln**
B. Mönchengladbach	3–0 3–1	Hvidovre BK

THIRD ROUND

Dynamo Berlin	0–0 1–3	**Liverpool**
FC Porto	1–2 0–1	**Dynamo Dresden**
Vitória FC Setúbal	2–0 0–1	Internazionale
Tottenham Hotspur	2–0 0–1	Crvena Zvezda Beograd
FC Twente Enschede	3–0 1–2	Las Palmas
OFK Beograd	0–0 3–1	Beroe Stara Zagora
Ararat Yerevan	2–0 0–2 (4–5p)	**1.FC Kaiserslautern**
1.FC Köln	0–0 0–5	**B. Mönchengladbach**

QUARTER-FINALS

Liverpool	2–0 1–0	Dynamo Dresden
Tottenham Hotspur	1–0 1–2	Vitória FC Setúbal
OFK Beograd	3–2 0–2	**FC Twente Enschede**
1.FC Kaiserslautern	1–2 1–7	**B. Mönchengladbach**

SEMI-FINALS

Liverpool	1–0 1–2	Tottenham Hotspur
B. Mönchengladbach	3–0 2–1	FC Twente Enschede

FINAL

1st leg

Anfield, Liverpool, 10–05–1973, 41 000. Referee: Linemayr, Austria

LIVERPOOL 3 (Keegan 21 32, Lloyd 61)
BOR. MÖNCHENGLADBACH 0

Liverpool – Clemence, Lawler, Lindsay, Smith, Lloyd, Hughes, Keegan, Cormack, Toshack, Heighway (Hall), Callaghan

Borussia – Kleff, Michallik, Netzer, Bonhof, Vogts, Wimmer, Danner, Kulik, Jensen, Rupp (Simonsen), Heynckes

2nd leg

Bökelbergstadion, Mönchengladbach, 23–05–1973, 35 000. Referee: Kazakov, Soviet Union

BOR. MÖNCHENGLADBACH 2 (Heynckes 29 40)
LIVERPOOL 0

Borussia – Kleff, Surau, Netzer, Bonhof, Vogts, Wimmer, Danner, Kulik, Jensen, Rupp, Heynckes

Liverpool – Clemence, Lawler, Lindsay, Smith, Lloyd, Hughes, Keegan, Cormack, Heighway (Boersma), Toshack, Callaghan

CUP WINNERS CUP

FIRST ROUND

Red Boys	1–4 0–3	**Milan**
Víkingur Reykjavík	0–2 0–9	**Legia Warszawa**
SEC Bastia	0–0 1–2	**Atlético Madrid**
Spartak Moskva	1–0 0–0	FC Den Haag
FC Schalke 04	2–1 3–1	Slavia Sofia
Pezoporikos	1–2 1–4	**Cork Hibernians**
Floriana	1–0 0–6	**Ferencváros**
Standard CL	1–0 2–4	**Sparta Praha**
Hajduk Split	1–0 1–0	Fredrikstad FK
FC Zürich	1–1 1–2	**Wrexham**
Fremad Amager	1–1 0–0	**Besa Kavajë**
Sporting CP	2–1 1–6	**Hibernian Edinburgh**
Rapid Bucuresti	3–0 0–1	Landskrona BoIS
SK Rapid Wien	0–0 2–2	PAOK Salonica

Carl Zeiss Jena	6–1 2–3	MP Mikkeli
MKE Ankaragücü	1–1 0–1	**Leeds United**

SECOND ROUND

Legia Warszawa	1–1 1–2	**Milan**
Atlético Madrid	3–4 2–1	**Spartak Moskva**
Cork Hibernians	0–0 0–3	**FC Schalke 04**
Ferencváros	2–0 1–4	**Sparta Praha**
Wrexham	3–1 0–2	**Hajduk Split**
Hibernian Edinburgh	7–1 1–1	Besa Kavajë
SK Rapid Wien	1–1 1–3	**Rapid Bucuresti**
Carl Zeiss Jena	0–0 0–2	**Leeds United**

QUARTER-FINALS

Spartak Moskva	0–1 1–1	**Milan**
FC Schalke 04	2–1 0–3	**Sparta Praha**
Hibernian Edinburgh	4–2 0–3	**Hajduk Split**
Leeds United	5–0 3–1	Rapid Bucuresti

SEMI-FINALS

Milan	1–0 1–0	Sparta Praha
Leeds United	1–0 0–0	Hajduk Split

FINAL

Salonica, 16–05–73, 45 000. Referee: Michas, Greece

MILAN 1 (Chiarugi 5)
LEEDS UNITED 0

Milan – Vecchi – Sabadini, Zignoli, Anquilletti, Turone – Rosato (Dolci), Rivera, Benetti – Sogliano, Bigon, Chiarugi

Leeds Utd – Harvey – Reaney, Cherry, Bates, Madeley – Hunter, Gray E, Yorath (McQueen) – Lorimer, Jordan, Jones

Top scorer: Chiarugi, Milan 7

EUROPEAN SUPERCUP 1973

1st leg

San Siro, Milan, 9–01–1974. Referee: Scheurer, Switzerland

MILAN 1 (Chiarugi 77)
AJAX 0

2nd leg

Amsterdam, 16–01–1974. Referee: Glöckner, East Germany

AJAX 6 (Mulder 26, Keizer 35, Neeskens 71, Rep 81, Muhren 84, Haan 87)
MILAN 0

1973–74

EUROPEAN CUP

FIRST ROUND

Bayern München	3–1 1–3 (4–3p)	Åtvidabergs FF
Dynamo Dresden	2–0 2–3	Juventus
Ajax	Bye	
CSKA Sofia	3–0 1–0	Wacker Innsbruck
Viking Stavanger	1–2 0–1	**Spartak Trnava**
Zarja Voroschilovgrad	2–0 1–0	Apoel Nicosia
Benfica	1–0 1–0	Olympiakos
Waterford FC	2–3 0–3	**Ujpesti Dózsa**
TPS Turku	1–6 0–3	**Glasgow Celtic**
Vejle BK	2–2 1–0	FC Nantes
Club Brugge	8–0 2–0	Floriana
Fram Reykjavík	0–5 2–6	**FC Basel**
Crvena Zvezda Beo.	2–1 1–0	Stal Mielec
Jeunesse Esch	1–1 0–2	**Liverpool**
Crusaders	0–1 0–11	**Dinamo Bucuresti**
Atlético Madrid	0–0 1–0	Galatasaray

SECOND ROUND

Bayern München	4–3 3–3	Dynamo Dresden
Ajax	1–0 0–2	**CSKA Sofia**
Spartak Trnava	0–0 1–0	Zarja Voroschilovgrad
Benfica	1–1 0–2	**Ujpesti Dózsa**
Glasgow Celtic	0–0 1–0	Vejle BK
Club Brugge	2–1 4–6	**FC Basel**
Crvena Zvezda Beo.	2–1 2–1	Liverpool
Dinamo Bucuresti	0–2 2–2	**Atlético Madrid**

QUARTER-FINALS

Bayern München	4–1 1–2	CSKA Sofia
Spartak Trnava	1–1 1–1 (3–4p)	**Ujpesti Dózsa**
FC Basel	3–2 2–4	**Glasgow Celtic**
Crvena Zvezda Beograd	0–2 0–0	**Atlético Madrid**

SEMI-FINALS

Ujpesti Dózsa	1–1 0–3	**Bayern München**
Glasgow Celtic	0–0 0–2	**Atlético Madrid**

FINAL

Heysel, Brussels, 15–05–1974, 49 000. Referee: Loraux, Belgium

BAYERN MUNCHEN 1 (Schwarzenbeck 119)
ATLÉTICO MADRID 1 (Luis 114)

Bayern – Maier – Hansen, Breitner, Schwarzenbeck, Beckenbauer – Roth, Zobel, Hoeness – Torstensson (Durnberger), Muller, Kapellmann

Atlético – Reina – Melo, Capon, Adelardo, Heredia – Luis, Eusebio, Irureta – Ufarte (Becerra), Garate, Salcedo (Alberto)

Replay. Heysel, Brussels, 17–05–1974, 23 000. Referee: Delcourt, Belgium

BAYERN MUNCHEN 4 (Hoeness 28 83, Muller 58 71)
ATLÉTICO MADRID 0

Bayern – Maier – Hansen, Breitner, Schwarzenbeck, Beckenbauer – Roth, Zobel, Hoeness – Torstensson, Muller, Kapellmann. Tr: Lattek

Atlético – Reina – Melo, Capon, Adelardo (Benegas), Heredia – Luis, Eusebio, Alberto (Ufarte) – Garate, Salcedo, Becerra. Tr: Lorenzo

Top scorer: Müller, Bayern München 9

UEFA CUP

FIRST ROUND

Östers IF Växjö	1–3 1–2	**Feyenoord**
Ferencváros	0–1 1–2	**Gwardia Warszawa**
Fiorentina	0–0 0–1	**Universitatea Craiova**
Ards	3–2 1–6	**Standard CL**
Sliema Wanderers	0–2 0–1	**Lokomotiv Plovdiv**
VSS Kosice	1–0 2–5	**Honvéd**
Carl Zeiss Jena	3–0 3–0	MP Mikkeli
Ruch Chorzów	4–1 4–5	Wuppertaler SV
Vitória FC Setúbal	2–0 2–0	Beerschot VAV
RCD Español	0–3 2–1	**RWD Molenbeek**
Hibernian Edinburgh	2–0 1–1	IBK Keflavík
IF Stromsgodset	1–1 1–6	**Leeds United**
Fredrikstad FK	0–1 0–4	**Dynamo Kiev**
B 1903 Kobenhavn	2–1 1–1	AIK Stockholm
Tatran Presov	4–2 1–1	Velez Mostar
VfB Stuttgart	9–0 4–0	Olympiakos Nicosia
Torino	1–2 1–2	**Lokomotive Leipzig**
OS Belenenses	0–2 1–2	**Wolverhampton Wand**
Fortuna Düsseldorf	1–0 2–2	Naestved IF
Admira-Wacker	1–0 1–2	Internazionale
Panahaiki Patras	2–1 1–0	Grazer AK
Dundee	1–3 2–4	**FC Twente Enschede**
Lazio	3–0 1–3	FC Sion
Ipswich Town	1–0 0–0	Real Madrid
Union Luxembourg	0–5 1–7	**Olympique Marseille**
Eskisehirspor	0–0 0–2	**1.FC Köln**
Fenerbahçe	5–1 1–1	FC Arges Pitesti
OGC Nice	3–0 0–2	Barcelona
Dynamo Tbilisi	4–1 0–2	Slavia Sofia

Panathinaikos .... 1–2 1–0 .... **OFK Beograd**
Aberdeen .... 4–1 3–1 .... Finn Harps
Grasshopper-Club .... 1–5 1–4 .... **Tottenham Hotspur**

SECOND ROUND
Feyenoord .... 3–1 0–1 .... Gwardia Warszawa
Standard CL .... 2–0 1–1 .... Universitatea Craiova
Lokomotiv Plovdiv .... 3–4 2–3 .... **Honvéd**
Ruch Chorzów .... 3–0 0–1 .... Carl Zeiss Jena
Vitória FC Setúbal .... 1–0 1–2 .... RWD Molenbeek
Leeds United .... 0–0 0–0 (5–4p) . Hibernian Edinburgh
Dynamo Kiev .... 1–0 2–1 .... B 1903 Kobenhavn
VfB Stuttgart .... 3–1 5–3 .... Tatran Presov
Lokomotive Leipzig .... 3–0 1–4 .... Wolverhampton Wand.
Admira-Wacker .... 2–1 0–3 .... **Fortuna Düsseldorf**
Panahaiki Patras .... 1–1 0–7 .... **FC Twente Enschede**
Ipswich Town .... 4–0 2–4 .... Lazio
Olympique Marseille .... 2–0 0–6 .... **1.FC Köln**
OGC Nice .... 4–0 0–2 .... Fenerbahçe
Dynamo Tbilisi .... 3–0 5–1 .... OFK Beograd
Aberdeen .... 1–1 1–4 .... **Tottenham Hotspur**

THIRD ROUND
Standard CL .... 3–1 0–2 .... **Feyenoord**
Honvéd .... 2–0 0–5 .... **Ruch Chorzów**
Leeds United .... 1–0 1–3 .... **Vitória FC Setúbal**
Dynamo Kiev .... 2–0 0–3 .... **VfB Stuttgart**
Fortuna Düsseldorf .... 2–1 0–3 .... **Lokomotive Leipzig**
Ipswich Town .... 1–0 2–1 .... FC Twente Enschede
OGC Nice .... 1–0 0–4 .... **1.FC Köln**
Dynamo Tbilisi .... 1–1 1–5 .... **Tottenham Hotspur**

QUARTER-FINALS
Ruch Chorzów .... 1–1 1–3 .... **Feyenoord**
VfB Stuttgart .... 1–0 2–2 .... Vitória FC Setúbal
Ipswich Town .... 1–0 0–1 (3–4p) . **Lokomotive Leipzig**
1.FC Köln .... 1–2 0–3 .... **Tottenham Hotspur**

SEMI-FINALS
Feyenoord .... 2–1 2–2 .... VfB Stuttgart
Lokomotive Leipzig .... 1–2 0–2 .... **Tottenham Hotspur**

FINAL
1st leg
White Hart Lane, London, 21–05–1974, 46 000. Referee: Scheurer, Switzerland
TOTTENHAM HOTSPUR 2 (England 39, OG 64)
FEYENOORD 2 (Van Hanegem 43, De Jong 85)
Tottenham – Jennings – Evans, Naylor, Pratt, England – Beal, McGrath, Perryman, Peters – Chivers, Coates
Feyenoord – Treytel – Rijsbergen, Van Daele, Israel, Vos – De Jong, Jansen, Van Hanegem, Ressel – Schoenmaker, Kristensen

2nd leg
Feyenoord Stadion, Rotterdam, 29–05–1974, 59 000. Referee: Lo Bello, Italy
FEYENOORD 2 (Rijsbergen 43, Ressel 84)
TOTTENHAM HOTSPUR 0
Feyenoord – Treytel – Rijsbergen, Van Daele, Israel, Vos – Ramljak, Jansen, De Jong, Ressel – Schoenmaker, Kristensen (Boskamp) (Wery)
Tottenham – Jennings – Evans, Naylor, Pratt (Holder), England – Beal, McGrath, Perryman Peters – Chivers, Coates

CUP WINNERS CUP

FIRST ROUND
NAC Breda .... 0–0 0–2 .... **1.FC Magdeburg**
Baník Ostrava .... 1–0 2–1 .... Cork Hibernians
Torpedo Moskva .... 0–0 0–2 .... **Athletic Bilbao**
Fola Esch .... 0–7 1–4 .... **Beroe Stara Zagora**
RSC Anderlecht .... 3–2 0–1 .... **FC Zürich**
Pezoporikos .... 0–0 0–11 .... **Malmö FF**
Vasas Budapest .... 0–2 0–1 .... **Sunderland**
Cardiff City .... 0–0 1–2 .... **Sporting CP**
IBV Vestmannaeyjar .... 0–7 1–9 .... **B. Mönchengladbach**
MKE Ankaragücü .... 0–2 0–4 .... **Glasgow Rangers**
Gzira United .... 0–2 0–7 .... **SK Brann Bergen**
Chimea Rimnicu .... 2–2 0–2 .... **Glentoran**
Legia Warszawa .... 1–1 0–1 .... **PAOK Salonica**
Reipas Lahti .... 0–0 0–2 .... **Olympique Lyon**
Randers Freja .... 0–0 1–2 .... **SK Rapid Wien**
Milan .... 3–1 1–0 .... Dinamo Zagreb

SECOND ROUND
Baník Ostrava .... 2–0 0–3 .... **1.FC Magdeburg**
Beroe Stara Zagora .... 3–0 0–1 .... Athletic Bilbao
FC Zürich .... 0–0 1–1 .... Malmö FF
Sunderland .... 2–1 0–2 .... **Sporting CP**
B. Mönchengladbach .... 3–0 2–3 .... Glasgow Rangers
SK Brann Bergen .... 1–1 1–3 .... **Glentoran**
Olympique Lyon .... 3–3 0–4 .... **PAOK Salonica**
Milan .... 0–0 2–0 .... SK Rapid Wien

QUARTER-FINALS
1.FC Magdeburg .... 2–0 1–1 .... Beroe Stara Zagora
Glentoran .... 0–2 0–5 .... **B. Mönchengladbach**
Sporting CP .... 3–0 1–1 .... FC Zürich
Milan .... 3–0 2–2 .... PAOK Salonica

SEMI-FINALS
Sporting CP .... 1–1 1–2 .... **1.FC Magdeburg**
Milan .... 2–0 0–1 .... Borussia Mönchengladbach

FINAL
Feyenoord Stadion, Rotterdam, 8–05–1974, 4000. Referee: Van Gemert, Holland
1.FC MAGDEBURG 2 (OG 43, Seguin 74)
MILAN 0
Magdeburg – Schulze – Enge, Zapf, Tyll, Abraham – Seguin, Pommerenke, Gaube – Raugust, Sparwasser, Hoffmann
Milan – Pizzaballa – Sabadini, Anquilletti, Lanzi, Schnellinger – Benetti, Maldera, Rivera – Tresoldi, Bigon, Bergamaschi (Turini)

Top scorer: Heynckes, Borussia Mönchengladbach 10

1974–75

EUROPEAN CUP

FIRST ROUND
Bayern München .... Bye
1.FC Magdeburg .... Bye
Cork Celtic .... W–O .... Omonia Nicosia
Viking Stavanger .... 0–2 0–4 .... **Ararat Yerevan**
Hvidovre BK .... 0–0 1–2 .... **Ruch Chorzów**
Jeunesse Esch .... 2–3 0–2 .... **Fenerbahçe**
Hajduk Split .... 7–1 2–0 .... IBK Keflavík
AS Saint-Étienne .... 2–0 1–1 .... Sporting CP
VÖEST Linz .... 0–0 0–5 .... **Barcelona**
Feyenoord .... 7–0 4–1 .... Coleraine
Valletta .... 1–0 1–4 .... **HJK Helsinki**
Universitatea Craiova .... 2–1 1–3 .... **Åtvidabergs FF**
Slovan Bratislava .... 4–2 1–3 .... **RSC Anderlecht**
Glasgow Celtic .... 1–1 0–2 .... **Olympiakos**
Levski-Spartak .... 0–3 1–4 .... **Ujpesti Dózsa**
Leeds United .... 4–1 1–2 .... FC Zürich

SECOND ROUND
Bayern München .... 3–2 2–1 .... 1.FC Magdeburg
Cork Celtic .... 1–2 0–5 .... **Ararat Yerevan**
Ruch Chorzów .... 2–1 2–0 .... Fenerbahçe

Hajduk Split	4–1 1–5	**AS Saint-Étienne**
Feyenoord	0–0 0–3	**Barcelona**
HJK Helsinki	0–3 0–1	**Åtvidabergs FF**
RSC Anderlecht	5–1 0–3	Olympiakos
Ujpesti Dózsa	1–2 0–3	**Leeds United**

QUARTER-FINALS

Bayern München	2–0 0–1	Ararat Yerevan
Ruch Chorzów	3–2 0–2	**AS Saint-Étienne**
Barcelona	2–0 3–0	Åtvidabergs FF
Leeds United	3–0 1–0	RSC Anderlecht

SEMI-FINALS

AS Saint-Étienne	0–0 0–2	**Bayern München**
Leeds United	2–1 1–1	Barcelona

FINAL

Parc des Princes, Paris, 28–05–1975, 48 000. Referee: Kitabdjian, France

BAYERN MUNCHEN 2 (Roth 71, Müller 81)
LEEDS UNITED 0

Bayern – Maier – Beckenbauer, Schwarzenbeck, Durnberger, Andersson (Weiss) – Zobel, Roth, Kapellmann – Hoeness (Wunder), Müller, Torstensson. Tr: Cramer

Leeds Utd – Stewart – Reaney, Gray F, Madeley, Hunter – Bremner, Giles, Yorath (Gray E) – Lorimer, Clarke, Jordan. Tr: Armfield

Top scorer: Müller, Bayern München 6

UEFA CUP

FIRST ROUND

Wacker Innsbruck	2–1 0–3	**B. Mönchengladbach**
Olympique Lyon	7–0 4–1	Red Boys
Grasshopper-Club	2–0 1–2	Panathinaikos
Vitória FC Setúbal	1–1 0–4	**Real Zaragoza**
Napoli	2–0 1–1	Videoton SC
FC Porto	4–1 1–3	Wolverhampton Wan.
FC Nantes	2–2 1–0	Legia Warszawa
Real Sociedad	0–1 0–4	**Baník Ostrava**
FC Amsterdam	5–0 7–0	Hibernians Paola
Etar Veliko Tarnovo	0–0 0–3	**Internazionale**
Lokomotiv Plovdiv	3–1 1–3 (4–5p)	**Rába ETO Györ**
Torino	1–1 1–3	**Fortuna Düsseldorf**
Górnik Zabrze	2–2 0–3	**Partizan Beograd**
Valur Reykjavík	0–0 1–2	**Portadown**
Boluspor	0–1 0–3	**Dinamo Bucuresti**
1.FC Köln	5–1 4–1	KPV Kokkola
Vorwärts Frankfurt	2–1 0–3	**Juventus**
Rosenborg BK	2–3 1–9	**Hibernian Edinburgh**
SK Sturm Graz	2–1 0–1	**Royal Antwerp FC**
Stoke City	1–1 0–0	**Ajax**
Randers Freja	1–1 0–0	**Dynamo Dresden**
Östers IF Växjö	3–2 1–2	**Dynamo Moskva**
Besiktas	2–0 0–3	**Steagul Rosu Brasov**
Hamburger SV	3–0 1–0	Bohemians Dublin
Spartak Moskva	3–1 0–2	**Velez Mostar**
SK Rapid Wien	3–1 0–1	Aris Salonica
KB Kobenhavn	3–2 0–4	**Atlético Madrid**
Derby County	4–1 2–1	Servette FC
Dukla Praha	W–O	Pezoporikos
Start Kristiansand	1–2 0–5	**Djurgårdens IF**
RWD Molenbeek	1–0 4–2	Dundee
Ipswich Town	2–2 1–1	**FC Twente Enschede**

SECOND ROUND

B. Mönchengladbach	1–0 5–2	Olympique Lyon
Grasshopper-Club	2–1 0–5	**Real Zaragoza**
Napoli	1–0 1–0	FC Porto
FC Nantes	1–0 0–2	**Baník Ostrava**
Internazionale	1–2 0–0	**FC Amsterdam**
Rába ETO Györ	2–0 0–3	**Fortuna Düsseldorf**
Partizan Beograd	5–0 1–1	Portadown
Dinamo Bucuresti	1–1 2–3	**1.FC Köln**
Hibernian Edinburgh	2–4 0–4	**Juventus**
Ajax	1–0 1–2	Royal Antwerp FC
Dynamo Dresden	1–0 0–1 (4–3p)	Dynamo Moskva
Hamburger SV	8–0 2–1	Steagul Rosu Brasov
SK Rapid Wien	1–1 0–1	**Velez Mostar**
Derby County	2–2 2–2 (7–6p)	Atlético Madrid
Djurgårdens IF	0–2 1–3	**Dukla Praha**
FC Twente Enschede	2–1 1–0	RWD Molenbeek

THIRD ROUND

B. Mönchengladbach	5–0 4–2	Real Zaragoza
Napoli	0–2 1–1	**Baník Ostrava**
FC Amsterdam	3–0 2–1	Fortuna Düsseldorf
Partizan Beograd	1–0 1–5	**1.FC Köln**
Juventus	1–0 1–2	Ajax
Hamburger SV	4–1 2–2	Dynamo Dresden
Derby County	3–1 1–4	**Velez Mostar**
Dukla Praha	3–1 0–5	**FC Twente Enschede**

QUARTER-FINALS

Baník Ostrava	0–1 1–3	**B. Mönchengladbach**
1.FC Köln	5–1 3–2	FC Amsterdam
Juventus	2–0 0–0	Hamburger SV
Velez Mostar	1–0 0–2	**FC Twente Enschede**

SEMI-FINALS

1.FC Köln	1–3 0–1	**B. Mönchengladbach**
FC Twente Enschede	3–1 1–0	Juventus

FINAL

1st leg

Rheinstadion, Dusseldorf, 7–05–1975, 42 000. Referee: Palotai, Hungary

BOR. MÖNCHENGLADBACH 0
FC TWENTE ENSCHEDE 0

Borussia – Kleff – Wittkamp, Stielike, Vogts, Surau – Bonhof, Wimmer, Danner (Del'Haye), Kulik (Schaffer) – Simonsen, Jensen

FC Twente – Gross – Drost, Van Ierssel, Overweg, Oranen – Thijssen, Pahlplatz, Van der Vall, Bos – Jeuring (Achterberg), Zuidema

2nd leg

Diekman, Enschede, 21–05–1975, 21 000. Referee: Schiller, Austria

FC TWENTE ENSCHEDE 1 (Drost 76)
BOR. MÖNCHENGLADBACH 5 (Simonsen 2 86, Heynckes 9 50 60)

FC Twente – Gross – Drost, Van Ierssel, Overweg, Oranen, Bos (Muhren), Thijssen, Pahlplatz (Achterberg), Van der Vall, Jeuring, Zuidema

Borussia – Kleff – Wittkamp, Vogts, Surau (Schaffer), Klinkhammer – Bonhof, Wimmer (Koppel), Danner – Simonsen, Jensen, Heynckes

CUP WINNERS CUP

FIRST ROUND

Dynamo Kiev	1–0 1–0	CSKA Sofia
Eintracht Frankfurt	3–0 2–2	AS Monaco
Dundee United	3–0 0–2	Jiul Petrosani
Bursaspor	4–2 0–0	Finn Harps
Benfica	4–0 4–1	Vanlose BK
Slavia Praha	1–0 0–1 (2–3p)	**Carl Zeiss Jena**
Gwardia Warszawa	2–1 1–2 (5–3p)	Bologna
PSV Eindhoven	10–0 4–1	Ards
PAOK Salonica	1–0 0–2	**Crvena Zvezda Beograd**
Avenir Beggen	W–O	Union Paralimni
KSV Waregem	2–1 1–4	**FK Austria**
Fram Reykjavík	0–2 0–6	**Real Madrid**
Malmö FF	1–0 0–1 (5–4p)	FC Sion
Sliema Wanderers	2–0 1–4	**Reipas Lahti**
Liverpool	11–0 1–0	IF Stromsgodset
Ferencváros	2–0 4–1	Cardiff City

SECOND ROUND

Eintracht Frankfurt	2–3	1–2	**Dynamo Kiev**
Dundee United	0–0	0–1	**Bursaspor**
Carl Zeiss Jena	1–1	0–0	**Benfica**
Gwardia Warszawa	1–5	0–3	**PSV Eindhoven**
Avenir Beggen	1–6	1–5	**Crvena Zvezda Beograd**
Real Madrid	3–0	2–2	FK Austria
Malmö FF	3–1	0–0	Reipas Lahti
Liverpool	1–1	0–0	**Ferencváros**

QUARTER-FINALS

Bursaspor	0–1	0–2	**Dynamo Kiev**
PSV Eindhoven	0–0	2–1	Benfica
Real Madrid	2–0	0–2 (5–6p)	**Crvena Zvezda Beograd**
Malmö FF	1–3	1–1	**Ferencváros**

SEMI-FINALS

Dynamo Kiev	3–0	1–2	PSV Eindhoven
Ferencváros	2–1	2–2	Crvena Zvezda Beograd

FINAL

St Jakobs, Basle, 14–05–1975, 10 000. Referee: Davidson, Scotland

DYNAMO KIEV 3 (Onischenko 18 39, Blokhin 67)
FERENCVAROS 0

Dynamo Kiev – Rudakov – Troshkin, Matvienko, Reshko, Fomenko – Muntjan, Konkov, Burjak, Kolotov – Onischenko, Blokhin
Ferencváros – Geczi – Martos, Megyesi, Pataki, Rab – Nyilasi (Onhaus), Juhasz, Mucha – Szabo, Mate, Magyar

Top scorer: Onischenko, Dynamo Kiev 7

EUROPEAN SUPERCUP 1975

1st leg

Olympiastadion, Munich, 9–09–1975. Referee: Gonella, Italy

BAYERN MÜNCHEN 0
DYNAMO KIEV 1 (Blokhin 66)

2nd leg

Republican Stadium, Kiev, 6–10–1975. Referee: Babaçan, Turkey

DYNAMO KIEV 2 (Blokhin 40 53)
BAYERN MÜNCHEN 0

1975–76

EUROPEAN CUP

FIRST ROUND

Jeunesse Esch	0–5	1–3	**Bayern München**
Malmö FF	2–1	1–2 (2–1p)	1.FC Magdeburg
Ujpesti Dózsa	4–0	1–5	FC Zürich
Benfica	7–0	0–1	Fenerbahçe
B. Mönchengladbach	1–1	6–1	Wacker Innsbruck
CSKA Sofia	2–1	0–2	**Juventus**
Slovan Bratislava	1–0	0–3	**Derby County**
Real Madrid	4–1	0–1	Dinamo Bucuresti
Linfield	1–2	0–8	**PSV Eindhoven**
Ruch Chorzów	5–0	2–2	KuPS Kuopio
RWD Molenbeek	3–2	1–0	Viking Stavanger
Floriana	0–5	0–3	**Hajduk Split**
Olympiakos	2–2	0–1	**Dynamo Kiev**
Omonia Nicosia	2–1	0–4	**IA Akranes**
Glasgow Rangers	4–1	1–1	Bohemians Dublin
KB Kobenhavn	0–2	1–3	**AS Saint-Étienne**

SECOND ROUND

Malmö FF	1–0	0–2	**Bayern München**
Benfica	5–2	1–3	Ujpesti Dózsa
B. Mönchengladbach	2–0	2–2	Juventus
Derby County	4–1	1–5	**Real Madrid**
Ruch Chorzów	1–3	0–4	**PSV Eindhoven**
Hajduk Split	4–0	3–2	RWD Molenbeek
Dynamo Kiev	3–0	2–0	IA Akranes
AS Saint-Étienne	2–0	2–1	Glasgow Rangers

QUARTER-FINALS

Benfica	0–0	1–5	**Bayern München**
Borussia Mönchengladbach	2–2	1–1	**Real Madrid**
Hajduk Split	2–0	0–3	**PSV Eindhoven**
Dynamo Kiev	2–0	0–3	**AS Saint-Étienne**

SEMI-FINALS

Real Madrid	1–1	0–2	**Bayern München**
AS Saint-Étienne	1–0	0–0	PSV Eindhoven

FINAL

Hampden Park, Glasgow, 12–05–1976, 63 000. Referee: Palotai, Hungary

BAYERN MUNCHEN 1 (Roth 57)
AS SAINT-ÉTIENNE 0

Bayern – Maier – Hansen, Schwarzenbeck, Beckenbauer, Horsmann – Roth, Durnberger, Kapellmann, Rummenigge – Muller, Hoeness. Tr: Cramer
St-Étienne – Curkovic – Repellini, Piazza, Lopez, Janvion – Bathenay, Santini, Larque – Revelli P, Revelli H, Sarramagna (Rocheteau). Tr: Herbin

Top scorers: Heynckes, Borussia Mönchengladbach 6
Santillana, Real Madrid 6

UEFA CUP

FIRST ROUND

Hibernian Edinburgh	1–0	1–3	**Liverpool**
Grasshopper-Club	3–3	1–1	**Real Sociedad**
Royal Antwerp FC	4–1	1–0	Aston Villa
GAIS Göteborg	2–1	2–4	**Slask Wroclaw**
Torpedo Moskva	4–1	1–1	Napoli
SK Rapid Wien	1–0	1–3	**Galatasaray**
Bohemians Praha	1–2	1–1	**Honvéd**
ASA Tîrgu Mures	2–2	1–4	**Dynamo Dresden**
Levski-Spartak	3–0	4–1	Eskisehirspor
MSV Duisburg	7–1	3–2	Union Paralimni
Hertha BSC Berlin	4–1	2–1	HJK Helsinki
Glentoran	1–6	0–8	**Ajax**
VÖEST Linz	2–0	0–4	**Vasas Budapest**
Sliema Wanderers	1–2	1–3	**Sporting CP**
Chernomorets Odessa	1–0	0–3	**Lazio**
PAOK Salonica	1–0	1–6	**Barcelona**
BSC Young Boys	0–0	2–4	**Hamburger SV**
Universitatea Craiova	1–3	1–1	**Crvena Zvezda Beograd**
IBK Keflavík	0–2	0–4	**Dundee United**
FC Porto	7–0	3–0	Avenir Beggen
TJ Internacional	5–0	3–2	Real Zaragoza
Vojvodina Novi Sad	0–0	1–3	**AEK Athens**
Carl Zeiss Jena	3–0	1–0	Olympique Marseille
Holbaek BK	0–1	1–2	**Stal Mielec**
Everton	0–0	0–1	**Milan**
Athlone Town	3–1	1–1	Vålerengens Oslo
1.FC Köln	2–0	3–2	B 1903 Kobenhavn
AIK Stockholm	1–1	0–1	**Spartak Moskva**
Roma	2–0	0–1	Dunav Ruse
Molde FK	1–0	0–6	**Östers IF Växjö**
Feyenoord	1–2	0–2	**Ipswich Town**
Olympique Lyon	4–3	0–3	**Club Brugge**

SECOND ROUND

Real Sociedad	1–3	0–6	**Liverpool**
Slask Wroclaw	1–1	2–1	Royal Antwerp FC
Galatasaray	2–4	0–3	**Torpedo Moskva**
Honvéd	2–2	0–1	**Dynamo Dresden**
MSV Duisburg	3–2	1–2	**Levski-Spartak**

Hertha BSC Berlin 1–0 1–4 **Ajax**
Vasas Budapest 3–1 1–2 Sporting CP
Lazio 0–3 0–4 **Barcelona**
Crvena Zvezda Beograd 1–1 0–4 **Hamburger SV**
Dundee United 1–2 1–1 **FC Porto**
TJ Internacional 2–0 1–3 AEK Athens
Carl Zeiss Jena 1–0 0–1 (2–3p) **Stal Mielec**
Athlone Town 0–0 0–3 **Milan**
Spartak Moskva 2–0 1–0 1.FC Köln
Östers IF Växjö 1–0 0–2 **Roma**
Ipswich Town 3–0 0–4 **Club Brugge**

THIRD ROUND

Slask Wroclaw 1–2 0–3 **Liverpool**
Dynamo Dresden 3–0 1–3 Torpedo Moskva
Ajax 2–1 1–2 (3–5p) **Levski-Spartak**
Barcelona 3–1 1–0 Vasas Budapest
Hamburger SV 2–0 1–2 FC Porto
TJ Internacional 1–0 0–2 **Stal Mielec**
Milan 4–0 0–2 Spartak Moskva
Club Brugge 1–0 1–0 Roma

QUARTER-FINALS

Dynamo Dresden 0–0 1–2 **Liverpool**
Barcelona 4–0 4–5 Levski-Spartak
Hamburger SV 1–1 1–0 Stal Mielec
Club Brugge 2–0 1–2 Milan

SEMI-FINALS

Barcelona 0–1 1–1 **Liverpool**
Hamburger SV 1–1 0–1 **Club Brugge**

FINAL

1st leg

Anfield, Liverpool, 28–04–1976, 49 000. Referee: Biwersi, Austria

LIVERPOOL 3 (Kennedy 59, Case 61, Keegan 65)
CLUB BRUGGE 2 (Lambert 5, Cools 15)

Liverpool – Clemence – Smith, Neal, Thompson, Hughes – Keegan, Kennedy, Callaghan – Fairclough, Heighway, Toshack (Case)

Brugge – Jensen – Bastijns, Krieger, Leekens, Volders – Cools, Vandereycken, Decubber – Van Gool, Lambert, Lefevre

2nd leg

Olympiastadion, Bruges, 19–05–1976, 32 000. Referee: Glöckner, East Germany

CLUB BRUGGE 1 (Lambert 11)
LIVERPOOL 1 (Keegan 15)

Brugge – Jensen – Bastijns, Krieger, Leekens, Volders – Cools, Vandereycken, Decubber (Hinderyckx) – Van Gool, Lambert (Sanders), Lefevre

Liverpool – Clemence – Smith, Neal, Thompson, Hughes, Keegan, Kennedy, Callaghan – Case, Heighway, Toshack (Fairclough)

CUP WINNERS CUP

FIRST ROUND

Rapid Bucuresti 1–0 0–2 **RSC Anderlecht**
Borac Banja Luka 9–0 5–1 US Rumelange
FK Skeid Oslo 1–4 0–4 **Stal Rzeszów**
Wrexham 2–1 1–1 Djurgårdens IF
Valur Reykjavík 0–2 0–7 **Glasgow Celtic**
Spartak Trnava 0–0 0–3 **Boavista FC**
Besiktas 0–3 0–3 **Fiorentina**
Panathinaikos 0–0 0–2 **Sachsenring Zwickau**
Eintracht Frankfurt 5–1 6–2 Coleraine
FC Basel 1–2 1–1 **Atlético Madrid**
Haladás VSE 7–0 1–1 Valletta
SK Sturm Graz 3–1 0–1 Slavia Sofia
Vejle BK 0–2 0–2 **FC Den Haag**
Home Farm 1–1 0–6 **RC Lens**
Ararat Yerevan 9–0 1–1 Anorthosis Famagusta
Reipas Lahti 2–2 0–3 **West Ham United**

SECOND ROUND

RSC Anderlecht 3–0 0–1 Borac Banja Luka
Wrexham 2–0 1–1 Stal Rzeszów
Boavista FC 0–0 1–3 **Glasgow Celtic**
Fiorentina 1–0 0–1 (4–5p) **Sachsenring Zwickau**
Atlético Madrid 1–2 0–1 **Eintracht Frankfurt**
SK Sturm Graz 2–0 1–1 Haladás VSE Sombathely
FC Den Haag 3–2 3–1 RC Lens
Ararat Yerevan 1–1 1–3 **West Ham United**

QUARTER-FINALS

RSC Anderlecht 1–0 1–1 Wrexham
Glasgow Celtic 1–1 0–1 **Sachsenring Zwickau**
SK Sturm Graz 0–2 0–1 **Eintracht Frankfurt**
FC Den Haag 4–2 1–3 **West Ham United**

SEMI-FINALS

Sachsenring Zwickau 0–3 0–2 **RSC Anderlecht**
Eintracht Frankfurt 2–1 1–3 **West Ham United**

FINAL

Heysel, Brussels, 5–05–1976, 58 000. Referee: Wurtz, France

RSC ANDERLECHT 4 (Rensenbrink 42 73, Vander Elst 48 87)
WEST HAM UNITED 2 (Holland 28, Robson 68)

Anderlecht – Ruiter – Lomme, Van Binst, Thissen, Broos – Dockx, Coeck (Vercauteren), Haan, Vander Elst – Ressel, Rensenbrink

West Ham – Day – Coleman, Lampard (Taylor A), Taylor T, McDowell – Bonds, Brooking, Paddon – Holland, Jennings, Robson

Top scorer: Rensenbrink, Anderlecht 8

EUROPEAN SUPERCUP 1976

1st leg

Olympiastadion, Munich, 17–08–1976. Referee: Burns, England

BAYERN MÜNCHEN 2 (Müller 58 88)
RSC ANDERLECHT 1 (Haan 16)

2nd leg

Parc Astrid, Brussels, 30–08–1976. Referee: Schiller, Austria

RSC ANDERLECHT 4 (Rensenbrink 20 82, Vander Elst 25, Haan 59)
BAYERN MÜNCHEN 1 (Müller 63)

1976–77

EUROPEAN CUP

FIRST ROUND

Liverpool 2–0 5–0 Crusaders
IA Akranes 1–3 2–3 **Trabzonspor**
Dundalk 1–1 0–6 **PSV Eindhoven**
CSKA Sofia 0–0 0–1 **AS Saint-Étienne**
Dynamo Dresden 2–0 0–0 Benfica
Ferencváros 5–1 6–2 Jeunesse Esch
Sliema Wanderers 2–1 0–1 **TPS Turku**
Glasgow Rangers 1–1 0–1 **FC Zürich**
Dynamo Kiev 3–0 2–0 Partizan Beograd
Omonia Nicosia 0–2 1–1 **PAOK Salonica**
Viking Stavanger 2–1 0–2 **Baník Ostrava**
Koge BK 0–5 1–2 **Bayern München**
Club Brugge 2–1 1–1 Steaua Bucuresti
Stal Mielec 1–2 0–1 **Real Madrid**
Torino 2–1 1–1 Malmö FF
FK Austria 1–0 0–3 **B. Mönchengladbach**

SECOND ROUND

Trabzonspor 1–0 0–3 **Liverpool**
AS Saint-Étienne 1–0 0–0 PSV Eindhoven
Ferencváros 1–0 0–4 **Dynamo Dresden**

FC Zürich .... 2–0 1–0 .... TPS Turku
Dynamo Kiev .... 4–0 2–0 .... PAOK Salonica
Baník Ostrava .... 2–1 0–5 .... **Bayern München**
Real Madrid .... 0–0 0–2 .... **Club Brugge**
Torino .... 1–2 0–0 .... **B. Mönchengladbach**

QUARTER-FINALS
AS Saint-Étienne .... 1–0 1–3 .... **Liverpool**
FC Zürich .... 2–1 2–3 .... Dynamo Dresden
Bayern München .... 1–0 0–2 .... **Dynamo Kiev**
B. Mönchengladbach .... 2–2 1–0 .... Club Brugge

SEMI-FINALS
FC Zürich .... 1–3 0–3 .... **Liverpool**
Dynamo Kiev .... 1–0 0–2 .... **B. Mönchengladbach**

FINAL
Stadio Olimpico, Rome, 25–05–1977, 52 000. Referee: Wurtz, France
LIVERPOOL 3 (McDermott 29, Smith 67, Neal 85)
B. MÖNCHENGLADBACH 1 (Simonsen 50)
Liverpool – Clemence – Neal, Jones, Smith, Hughes – Case, Kennedy, Callaghan, McDermott – Keegan, Heighway. Tr: Paisley
Borussia – Kneib – Vogts, Klinkhammer, Wittkamp, Schaffer – Wohlers (Hannes), Wimmer (Kulik), Stielike, Bonhof – Simonsen, Heynckes. Tr: Lattek

Top scorers: Cucinotta, FC Zürich 5
Müller, Bayern München 5

UEFA CUP

FIRST ROUND
Manchester City .... 1–0 0–2 .... **Juventus**
Ajax .... 1–0 0–2 .... **Manchester United**
Internazionale .... 0–1 1–1 .... **Honvéd**
Shachter Donetsk .... 3–0 1–1 .... Dynamo Berlin
Fenerbahçe .... 2–1 0–4 .... **Videoton SC**
Wacker Innsbruck .... 2–1 5–0 .... Start Kristiansand
ASA Tîrgu Mures .... 0–1 0–3 .... **Dinamo Zagreb**
1.FC Magdeburg .... 3–0 1–3 .... Cesena
Queen's Park Rangers . 4–0 7–0 .... SK Brann Bergen
Fram Reykjavík .... 0–3 0–5 .... **Slovan Bratislava**
Grasshopper-Club .... 7–0 2–0 .... Hibernians Paola
1.FC Köln .... 2–0 1–1 .... GKS Tychy
Lokomotiv Plovdiv .... 2–1 1–4 .... **Crvena Zvezda Beograd**
Austria Salzburg .... 5–0 0–2 .... Adanaspor
Derby County .... 12–0 4–1 .... Finn Harps
AEK Athens .... 2–0 1–2 .... Dynamo Moskva
Naestved IF .... 0–3 0–4 .... **RWD Molenbeek**
Glasgow Celtic .... 2–2 0–2 .... **Wisla Kraków**
Sportul Studentesc .... 3–0 1–2 .... Olympiakos
FC Porto .... 2–2 2–3 .... **FC Schalke 04**
RCD Español .... 3–1 1–2 .... OGC Nice
Eintract Braunschweig 7–0 0–1 .... Holbaek BK
Union Paralimni .... 1–3 0–8 .... **1.FC Kaiserslautern**
Feyenoord .... 3–0 1–2 .... Djurgårdens IF
OS Belenenses .... 2–2 2–3 .... **Barcelona**
Red Boys .... 0–3 1–3 .... **KSC Lokeren**
Hibernian Edinburgh .... 1–0 0–0 .... FC Sochaux
KuPS Kuopio .... 3–2 0–2 .... **Östers IF Växjö**
Dinamo Bucuresti .... 0–0 1–2 .... **Milan**
Slavia Praha .... 2–0 0–3 .... **Akademic Sofia**
Glentoran .... 3–2 0–3 .... **FC Basel**
Ujpesti Dózsa .... 1–0 0–5 .... **Athletic Bilbao**

SECOND ROUND
Manchester United .... 1–0 0–3 .... **Juventus**
Shachter Donetsk .... 3–0 3–2 .... Honvéd
Wacker Innsbruck .... 1–1 0–1 .... **Videoton SC**
1.FC Magdeburg .... 2–0 2–2 .... Dinamo Zagreb
Slovan Bratislava .... 3–3 2–5 .... **Queen's Park Rangers**
1.FC Köln .... 2–0 3–2 .... Grasshopper-Club
Austria Salzburg .... 2–1 0–1 .... **Crvena Zvezda Beograd**
AEK Athens .... 2–0 3–2 .... Derby County
Wisla Kraków .... 1–1 1–1 (4–5p) . **RWD Molenbeek**
Sportul Studentesc .... 0–1 0–4 .... **FC Schalke 04**
Eintracht Braunschweig .... 2–1 0–2 .... **RCD Español**
1.FC Kaiserslautern .... 2–2 0–5 .... **Feyenoord**
Barcelona .... 2–0 1–2 .... KSC Lokeren
Hibernian Edinburgh .... 2–0 1–4 .... **Östers IF Växjö**
Akademic Sofia .... 4–3 0–2 .... **Milan**
FC Basel .... 1–1 1–3 .... **Athletic Bilbao**

THIRD ROUND
Juventus .... 3–0 0–1 .... Shachter Donetsk
1.FC Magdeburg .... 5–0 0–1 .... Videoton SC
Queen's Park Rangers . 3–0 1–4 .... 1.FC Köln
AEK Athens .... 2–0 1–3 .... Crvena Zvezda Beograd
RWD Molenbeek .... 1–0 1–1 .... FC Schalke 04
RCD Español .... 0–1 0–2 .... **Feyenoord**
Östers IF Växjö .... 0–3 1–5 .... **Barcelona**
Athletic Bilbao .... 4–1 1–3 .... Milan

QUARTER-FINALS
1.FC Magdeburg .... 1–3 0–1 .... **Juventus**
Queen's Park Rangers .. 3–0 0–3 (6–7p) . **AEK Athens**
Feyenoord .... 0–0 1–2 .... **RWD Molenbeek**
Athletic Bilbao .... 2–1 2–2 .... Barcelona

SEMI-FINALS
Juventus .... 4–1 1–0 .... AEK Athens
RWD Molenbeek .... 1–1 0–0 .... **Athletic Bilbao**

FINAL
1st leg
Comunale, Turin, 4–05–1977, 75 000. Referee: Corver, Holland
JUVENTUS 1 (Tardelli 15)
ATHLETIC BILBAO 0
Juventus – Zoff – Cuccureddu, Gentile, Scirea, Morini – Tardelli, Furino, Benetti – Causio, Boninsegna (Gori), Bettega
Athletic Bilbao – Iribar – Quaderra, Escalza, Guoicoechea, Guisasola – Villar, Irureta, Rojo M, Churruca – Dani, Rojo J

2nd leg
San Mamés, Bilbao, 18–05–1977, 43 000. Referee: Linemayr, Austria
ATHLETIC BILBAO 2 (Churruca 11, Carlos 78)
JUVENTUS 1 (Bettega 7)
Athletic Bilbao – Iribar – Lasa (Carlos), Guisasola, Alesanco, Escalza – Villar, Churruca, Irureta – Amarrortu, Dani, Rojo J
Juventus – Zoff, Cuccureddu, Morini, Scirea, Gentile – Causio, Tardelli, Furino, Benetti – Boninsegna (Spinosi), Bettega

Top scorer: Bowles, Queen's Park Rangers 11

CUP WINNERS CUP

PRELIMINARY ROUND
Cardiff City .... 1–0 1–2 .... Servette FC

FIRST ROUND
Hamburger SV .... 3–0 1–1 .... IBK Keflavík
Lokomotive Leipzig .... 2–0 1–5 .... **Heart of Midlothian**
Cardiff City .... 1–0 0–3 .... **Dynamo Tbilisi**
MTK-VM Budapest .... 3–1 1–1 .... Sparta Praha
Levski-Spartak .... 12–2 7–1 .... Reipas Lahti
CSU Galati .... 2–3 0–2 .... **Boavista FC**
Lierse SK .... 1–0 0–3 .... **Hajduk Split**
SK Rapid Wien .... 1–2 1–1 .... **Atlético Madrid**
SOFK Bodo-Glimt .... 0–2 0–1 .... **Napoli**
Iraklis Salonica .... 0–0 0–2 .... **Apoel Nicosia**
Bohemians Dublin .... 2–1 1–0 .... Esbjerg FB
Floriana .... 1–4 0–2 .... **Slask Wroclaw**

Southampton 4–0 1–2 Olympique Marseille
Carrick Rangers 3–1 1–2 Aris Bonnevoie
AIK Stockholm 1–2 1–1 **Galatasaray**
RSC Anderlecht 2–1 3–2 Roda JC Kerkrade

SECOND ROUND
Hamburger SV 4–2 4–1 Heart of Midlothian
Dynamo Tbilisi 1–4 0–1 **MTK-VM Budapest**
Boavista FC 3–1 0–2 **Levski-Spartak**
Atlético Madrid 1–0 2–1 Hajduk Split
Apoel Nicosia 1–1 0–2 **Napoli**
Slask Wroclaw 3–0 1–0 Bohemians Dublin
Carrick Rangers 2–5 1–4 **Southampton**
RSC Anderlecht 5–1 5–1 Galatasaray

QUARTER-FINALS
MTK-VM Budapest 1–1 1–4 **Hamburger SV**
Levski-Spartak 2–1 0–2 **Atlético Madrid**
Slask Wroclaw 0–0 0–2 **Napoli**
RSC Anderlecht 2–0 1–2 Southampton

SEMI-FINALS
Atlético Madrid 3–1 0–3 **Hamburger SV**
Napoli 1–0 0–2 **RSC Anderlecht**

FINAL
Olympisch Stadion, Amsterdam, 11–05–1977, 66 000. Referee: Partridge, England
HAMBURGER SV 2 (Volkert 78, Magath 88)
RSC ANDERLECHT 0
Hamburg – Kargus – Kaltz, Ripp, Nogly, Hidien – Memering, Magath, Keller – Steffenhagen, Reimann, Volkert
Anderlecht – Ruiter – Van Binst, Van Den Daele, Thissen, Broos – Dockx (Van Poucke), Coeck, Haan, Vander Elst – Ressel, Rensenbrink

Top scorer: Milanov, Levski–Spartak 13

EUROPEAN SUPERCUP 1977

1st leg
Volksparkstadion, Hamburg, 22–11–1977. Referee: Da Silva Garrido, Portugal
HAMBURGER SV 1 (Keller 29)
LIVERPOOL 1 (Fairclough 65)

2nd leg
Anfield, Liverpool, 6–12–1977. Referee: Eriksson, Sweden
LIVERPOOL 6 (Thompson 21, McDermott 40 56 57, Fairclough 84, Dalglish 88)
HAMBURGER SV 0

1977–78

EUROPEAN CUP

FIRST ROUND
Liverpool Bye
Dynamo Dresden 2–0 1–2 Halmstad BK
Trabzonspor 1–0 0–2 **B 1903 Kobenhavn**
Benfica 0–0 0–0 (4–1p) Torpedo Moskva
FC Basel 1–3 1–0 **Wacker Innsbruck**
Glasgow Celtic 5–0 6–1 Jeunesse Esch
Crvena Zvezda Beo. 3–0 3–0 Sligo Rovers
Vasas Budapest 0–3 1–1 **B. Mönchengladbach**
Omonia Nicosia 0–3 0–2 **Juventus**
Valur Reykjavík 1–0 0–2 **Glentoran**
Levski-Spartak 3–0 2–2 Slask Wroclaw
Lillestrom SK 2–0 0–4 **Ajax**
Dinamo Bucuresti 2–1 0–2 **Atlético Madrid**
Dukla Praha 1–1 0–0 **FC Nantes**
Floriana 1–1 0–4 **Panathinaikos**
KuPS Kuopio 0–4 2–5 **Club Brugge**

SECOND ROUND
Liverpool 5–1 1–2 Dynamo Dresden
Benfica 1–0 1–0 B 1903 Kobenhavn
Glasgow Celtic 2–1 0–3 **Wacker Innsbruck**
Crvena Zvezda Beograd 0–3 1–5 **B. Mönchengladbach**
Glentoran 0–1 0–5 **Juventus**
Levski-Spartak 1–2 1–2 **Ajax**
FC Nantes 1–1 1–2 **Atlético Madrid**
Club Brugge 2–0 0–1 Panathinaikos

QUARTER-FINALS
Benfica 1–2 1–4 **Liverpool**
Wacker Innsbruck 3–1 0–2 **B. Mönchengladbach**
Ajax 1–1 1–1 (0–3p) **Juventus**
Club Brugge 2–0 2–3 Atlético Madrid

SEMI-FINALS
B. Mönchengladbach 2–1 0–3 **Liverpool**
Juventus 1–0 0–2 **Club Brugge**

FINAL
Wembley, London, 10–05–1978, 92 000. Referee: Corver, Holland
LIVERPOOL 1 (Dalglish 64)
CLUB BRUGGE 0
Liverpool – Clemence – Neal, Thompson, Hansen, Hughes – McDermott, Kennedy, Souness – Case (Heighway), Fairclough, Dalglish. Tr: Paisley
Brugge – Jensen – Bastijns, Krieger, Leekens, Maes (Volders) – Cools, Decubber, Vandereycken, Ku (Sanders) – Simoen, Sorensen. Tr: Happel

Top scorer: Simonsen, Borussia Mönchengladbach 5

UEFA CUP

FIRST ROUND
Glenavon 2–6 0–5 **PSV Eindhoven**
Manchester City 2–2 0–0 **Widzew Lódz**
Start Kristiansand 6–0 2–0 Fram Reykjavík
Dynamo Kiev 1–1 0–0 **Eintracht Braunschweig**
Boavista FC 1–0 0–5 **Lazio**
RC Lens 4–1 0–2 Malmö FF
Fiorentina 0–0 1–2 **FC Schalke 04**
Odra Opole 1–2 1–1 **1.FC Magdeburg**
Aston Villa 4–0 2–0 Fenerbahçe
Górnik Zabrze 5–3 0–0 Haka Valkeakoski
Linzer ASK 3–2 0–7 **Ujpesti Dózsa**
Servette FC 1–0 0–2 **Athletic Bilbao**
Landskrona BoIS 0–1 0–5 **Ipswich Town**
Las Palmas 5–0 3–4 Sloboda Tuzla
AZ 67 Alkmaar 11–1 5–0 Red Boys
Barcelona 5–1 3–1 Steaua Bucuresti
Frem Kobenhavn 0–2 1–6 **Grasshopper-Club**
SK Rapid Wien 1–0 0–3 **TJ Internacional**
Dundee United 1–0 0–3 **KB Kobenhavn**
Internazionale 0–1 0–0 **Dynamo Tbilisi**
Bayern München 8–0 4–0 Mjondalen IF
Marek Stanke Dim. 3–0 0–2 Ferencváros
FC Zürich 1–0 1–1 CSKA Sofia
Eintracht Frankfurt 5–0 0–0 Sliema Wanderers
RWD Molenbeek 0–0 2–1 Aberdeen
Carl Zeiss Jena 5–1 1–4 Altay Izmir
Standard CL 1–0 2–3 Slavia Praha
ASA Tîrgu Mures 1–0 0–3 **AEK Athens**
Torino 3–0 1–1 Apoel Nicosia
Olympiakos 3–1 1–5 **Dinamo Zagreb**

Bohemians Dublin 0–0 0–4 **Newcastle United**
SEC Bastia 3–2 2–1 Sporting CP

SECOND ROUND

Widzew Lódz 3–5 0–1 **PSV Eindhoven**
Start Kristiansand 1–0 0–4 **Eintracht Braunschweig**
Lazio 2–0 0–6 **RC Lens**
1.FC Magdeburg 4–2 3–1 FC Schalke 04
Aston Villa 2–0 1–1 Górnik Zabrze
Ujpesti Dózsa 2–0 0–3 **Athletic Bilbao**
Ipswich Town 1–0 3–3 Las Palmas
AZ 67 Alkmaar 1–1 1–1 (4–5p) **Barcelona**
TJ Internacional 1–0 1–5 **Grasshopper-Club**
KB Kobenhavn 1–4 1–2 **Dynamo Tbilisi**
Bayern München 3–0 0–2 Marek Stanke Dimitrov
FC Zürich 0–3 3–4 **Eintracht Frankfurt**
RWD Molenbeek 1–1 1–1 (5–6p) **Carl Zeiss Jena**
AEK Athens 2–2 1–4 **Standard CL**
Torino 3–1 0–1 Dinamo Zagreb
SEC Bastia 2–1 3–1 Newcastle United

THIRD ROUND

PSV Eindhoven 2–0 2–1 Eintracht Braunschweig
1.FC Magdeburg 4–0 0–2 RC Lens
Aston Villa 2–0 1–1 Athletic Bilbao
Ipswich Town 3–0 0–3 (1–3p) **Barcelona**
Dynamo Tbilisi 1–0 0–4 **Grasshopper-Club**
Eintracht Frankfurt 4–0 2–1 Bayern München
Carl Zeiss Jena 2–0 2–1 Standard CL
SEC Bastia 2–1 3–2 Torino

QUARTER-FINALS

1.FC Magdeburg 1–0 2–4 **PSV Eindhoven**
Aston Villa 2–2 1–2 **Barcelona**
Eintracht Frankfurt 3–2 0–1 **Grasshopper-Club**
SEC Bastia 7–2 2–4 Carl Zeiss Jena

SEMI-FINALS

PSV Eindhoven 3–0 1–3 Barcelona
Grasshopper-Club 3–2 0–1 **SEC Bastia**

FINAL

1st leg

Furiani, Bastia, 26–04–1978, 15 000. Referee: Maksimovis, Yugoslavia

SEC BASTIA 0
PSV EINDHOVEN 0

Bastia – Hiard – Burkhard, Guesdon, Orlanducci, Cazes – Papi, Lacuesta (Felix), Larios – Rep, Krimau, Mariot

PSV Eindhoven – Van Beveren – Van Kraay, Krijgh, Stevens, Brandts, Poortvliet – Van der Kuijlen, Van de Kerkhof W, Deijkers – Van de Kerkhof R, Lubse

2nd leg

Philips Stadion, Eindhoven, 9–05–1978, 27 000. Referee: Rainea, Romania

PSV EINDHOVEN 3 (Van der Kerkhof W 24, Deijkers 67, Van der Kuijlen 69)
SEC BASTIA 0

PSV Eindhoven – Van Beveren – Krijgh, Stevens, Van Kraay (Deacy), Brandts – Van de Kerkhof W, Poortvliet, Van der Kuijlen – Lubse, Deijkers, Van de Kerkhof R

Bastia – Hiard (Weller) – Marchioni, Orlanducci, Guesdon, Cazes – Lacuesta, Larios, Papi – Rep, Krimau, Mariot (De Zerbi)

Top scorers: Deykers, PSV Eindhoven 8
Ponte, Grasshopper–Club 8

CUP WINNERS CUP

PRELIMINARY ROUND

Glasgow Rangers 1–0 2–2 BSC Young Boys

FIRST ROUND

Lokomotiv Sofia 1–6 0–2 **RSC Anderlecht**
Hamburger SV 8–1 5–2 Reipas Lahti
AS Saint-Étienne 1–1 0–2 **Manchester United**
1.FC Köln 2–2 0–1 **FC Porto**
Progres Niedercorn 0–1 0–9 **Vejle BK**
PAOK Salonica 2–0 2–0 Zaglebie Sosnowiec
SK Brann Bergen 1–0 4–0 IA Akranes
Glasgow Rangers 0–0 0–3 **FC Twente Enschede**
Valletta 0–2 0–5 **Dynamo Moskva**
Olympiakos Nicosia 1–6 0–2 **Universitatea Craiova**
Coleraine 1–4 2–2 **Lokomotive Leipzig**
Real Betis 2–0 1–2 Milan
Dundalk 1–0 0–4 **Hajduk Split**
Besiktas 2–0 0–5 **Diósgyöri VTK**
Lokomotiva Kosice 0–0 2–2 Östers IF Växjö
Cardiff City 0–0 0–1 **FK Austria**

SECOND ROUND

Hamburger SV 1–2 1–1 **RSC Anderlecht**
FC Porto 4–0 2–5 Manchester United
Vejle BK 3–0 1–2 PAOK Salonica
FC Twente Enschede 2–0 2–1 SK Brann Bergen
Dynamo Moskva 2–0 0–2 (3–0p) Universitatea Craiova
Lokomotive Leipzig 1–1 1–2 **Real Betis**
Diósgyöri VTK 2–1 1–2 (3–4p) **Hajduk Split**
FK Austria 0–0 1–1 Lokomotiva Kosice

QUARTER-FINALS

FC Porto 1–0 0–3 **RSC Anderlecht**
Vejle BK 0–3 0–4 **FC Twente Enschede**
Real Betis 0–0 0–3 **Dynamo Moskva**
FK Austria 1–1 1–1 (3–0p) Hajduk Split

SEMI-FINALS

FC Twente Enschede 0–1 0–2 **RSC Anderlecht**
Dynamo Moskva 2–1 1–2 (4–5p) **FK Austria**

FINAL

Parc des Princes, Paris, 3–05–1978, 48 000. Referee: Alginder, West Germany

RSC ANDERLECHT 4 (Rensenbrink 13 41, Van Binst 45 80)
FK AUSTRIA 0

Anderlecht – De Bree – Van Binst, Thissen, Dusbaba, Broos – Vander Elst, Haan, Nielsen, Coeck, Vercauteren (Dockx) – Rensenbrink

FK Austria – Baumgartner – Sara R, Sara J, Obermayer, Baumeister – Prohaska, Daxbacher (Martinez), Gasselich, Morales (Drazen) – Pirkner, Parits

Top scorer: Gritter, FC Twente Enschede 7

EUROPEAN SUPERCUP 1978

1st leg

Parc Astrid, Brussels, 4–12–1978. Referee: Palotai, Hungary

RSC ANDERLECHT 3 (Vercauteren 17, Vander Elst 38, Rensenbrink 87)
LIVERPOOL 1 (Case 27)

2nd leg

Anfield, Liverpool, 19–12–1978. Referee: Rainea, Romania

LIVERPOOL 2 (Hughes 13, Fairclough 85)
RSC ANDERLECHT 1 (Vander Elst 71)

1978–79

EUROPEAN CUP

PRELIMINARY ROUND

AS Monaco 3–0 0–2 Steaua Bucuresti

FIRST ROUND

Nottingham Forest 2–0 0–0 Liverpool
AEK Athens 6–1 1–4 FC Porto
Real Madrid 5–0 7–0 Progres Niedercorn
Grasshopper-Club 8–0 5–3 Valletta
Juventus 1–0 0–2 **Glasgow Rangers**
Fenerbahçe 2–1 1–6 **PSV Eindhoven**
B 1909 Odense 2–2 1–2 **Lokomotiv Sofia**
1.FC Köln 4–1 1–1 IA Akranes
Vllaznia Shkodër 2–0 1–4 **FK Austria**
Linfield 0–0 0–1 **Lillestrom SK**
Omonia Nicosia 2–1 0–1 **Bohemians Dublin**
Partizan Beograd 2–0 0–2 (4–5p) **Dynamo Dresden**
Club Brugge 2–1 1–3 **Wisla Kraków**
Zbrojovka Brno 2–2 2–0 Ujpesti Dózsa
Haka Valkeakoski 0–1 1–3 **Dynamo Kiev**
Malmö FF 0–0 1–0 AS Monaco

SECOND ROUND

AEK Athens 1–2 1–5 **Nottingham Forest**
Real Madrid 3–1 0–2 **Grasshopper-Club**
Glasgow Rangers 0–0 3–2 PSV Eindhoven
Lokomotiv Sofia 0–1 0–4 **1.FC Köln**
FK Austria 4–1 0–0 Lillestrom SK
Bohemians Dublin 0–0 0–6 **Dynamo Dresden**
Zbrojovka Brno 2–2 1–1 **Wisla Kraków**
Dynamo Kiev 0–0 0–2 **Malmö FF**

QUARTER-FINALS

Nottingham Forest 4–1 1–1 Grasshopper-Club
1.FC Köln 1–0 1–1 Glasgow Rangers
FK Austria 3–1 0–1 Dynamo Dresden
Wisla Kraków 2–1 1–4 **Malmö FF**

SEMI-FINALS

Nottingham Forest 3–3 1–0 1.FC Köln
FK Austria 0–0 0–1 **Malmö FF**

FINAL

Olympiastadion, Munich, 30–05–1979, 57 000. Referee: Linemayr, Austria

NOTTINGHAM FOREST 1 (Francis 45)
MALMÖ FF 0

Nottm. Forest – Shilton – Anderson, Lloyd, Burns, Clark – Francis, McGovern, Bowyer, Robertson – Woodcock, Birtles. Tr. Clough

Malmö – Moller – Andersson R, Jonsson, Andersson M, Erlandsson – Tapper (Malmberg), Ljungberg, Prytz, Kinnvall – Hansson (Andersson T), Cervin. Tr: Houghton

Top scorer: Sulser, Grasshopper-Club 11

UEFA CUP

FIRST ROUND

B. Mönchengladbach 5–1 2–1 SK Sturm Graz
FC Nantes 0–2 0–0 **Benfica**
IBV Vestmannaeyjar 0–0 1–1 Glentoran
Pezoporikos 2–2 1–5 **Slask Wroclaw**
Milan 1–0 0–1 (8–7p) Lokomotiva Kosice
Olympiakos 2–1 1–3 **Levski-Spartak**
Standard CL 1–0 0–0 Dundee United
FC Twente Enschede 1–1 2–3 **Manchester City**
Honvéd 6–0 2–2 Adanaspor
Politehnica Timisoara 2–0 1–2 MTK-VM Budapest
Jeunesse Esch 0–0 0–2 **Lausanne-Sports**
Athletic Bilbao 2–0 0–3 **Ajax**
IF Elfsborg Borås 2–0 1–4 **RC Strasbourg**
Sporting Braga 5–0 2–3 Hibernians Paola
Carl Zeiss Jena 1–0 2–2 Lierse SK
MSV Duisburg 5–0 5–2 Lech Poznan
Hertha BSC Berlin 0–0 2–1 Trakia Plovdiv
Dynamo Tbilisi 2–0 1–1 Napoli
KuPS Kuopio 2–1 4–4 B 1903 Kobenhavn
Start Kristiansand 0–0 0–1 **Esbjerg FB**
FC Basel 2–3 1–4 **VfB Stuttgart**
Torpedo Moskva 4–0 3–3 Molde FK
Finn Harps 0–5 0–5 **Everton**
Dukla Praha 1–0 1–1 Lanerossi-Vicenza
Galatasaray 1–3 1–3 **West Bromwich Albion**
Hibernian Edinburgh 3–2 0–0 IFK Norrköping
FC Arges Pitesti 3–0 2–1 Panathinaikos
CSKA Sofia 2–1 1–4 **Valencia**
Hajduk Split 2–0 1–2 SK Rapid Wien
Arsenal 3–0 4–1 Lokomotive Leipzig
Sporting Gijón 3–0 0–1 Torino
Dynamo Berlin 5–2 1–4 **Crvena Zvezda Beograd**

SECOND ROUND

Benfica 0–0 0–2 **B. Mönchengladbach**
IBV Vestmannaeyjar 0–2 1–2 **Slask Wroclaw**
Levski-Spartak 1–1 0–3 **Milan**
Manchester City 4–0 0–2 Standard CL
Honvéd 4–0 0–2 Politehnica Timisoara
Ajax 1–0 4–0 Lausanne-Sports
RC Strasbourg 2–0 0–1 Hibernian Edinburgh
Carl Zeiss Jena 0–0 0–3 **MSV Duisburg**
Hertha BSC Berlin 2–0 0–1 Dynamo Tbilisi
KuPS Kuopio 0–2 1–4 **Esbjerg FB**
Torpedo Moskva 2–1 0–2 **VfB Stuttgart**
Everton 2–1 0–1 **Dukla Praha**
Sporting Braga 0–2 0–1 **West Bromwich Albion**
FC Arges Pitesti 2–1 2–5 **Valencia**
Hajduk Split 2–1 0–1 **Arsenal**
Sporting Gijón 0–1 1–1 **Crvena Zvezda Beograd**

THIRD ROUND

B. Mönchengladbach 1–1 4–2 Slask Wroclaw
Milan 2–2 0–3 **Manchester City**
Honvéd 4–1 0–2 Ajax
RC Strasbourg 0–0 0–4 **MSV Duisburg**
Esbjerg FB 2–1 0–4 **Hertha BSC Berlin**
VfB Stuttgart 4–1 0–4 **Dukla Praha**
Valencia 1–1 0–2 **West Bromwich Albion**
Crvena Zvezda Beo. 1–0 1–1 Arsenal

QUARTER-FINALS

Manchester City 1–1 1–3 **B. Mönchengladbach**
Honvéd 2–3 2–1 **MSV Duisburg**
Hertha BSC Berlin 1–1 2–1 Dukla Praha
Crvena Zvezda Beo. 1–0 1–1 West Bromwich Albion

SEMI-FINALS

MSV Duisburg 2–2 1–4 **B. Mönchengladbach**
Crvena Zvezda Beo. 1–0 1–2 Hertha BSC Berlin

FINAL

1st leg

Crvena Zvezda, Belgrade, 9–05–1979, 87 000. Referee: Foote, England

CRVENA ZVEZDA BEOGRAD 1 (Sestic 21)
BOR. MÖNCHENGLADBACH 1 (OG 60)

Red Star – Stojanovic – Jovanovic, Miletovic, Jurisic, Jovin – Muslin (Krmpotic), Petrovic, Blagojevic, Milosavljevic (Milovanovic) – Savic, Sestic

Borussia – Kneib – Vogts, Hannes, Schaffer, Ringels – Schafer, Kulik, Nielsen (Danner), Wohlers (Gores) – Simonsen, Lienen

2nd leg

Rheinstadion, Dusseldorf, 23–05–1979, 45 000. Referee: Michelotti, Italy

BOR. MÖNCHENGLADBACH 1 (Simonsen 15)
CRVENA ZVEZDA BEOGRAD 0

Borussia – Kneib – Vogts, Hannes, Schaffer, Ringels – Schafer, Kulik (Koppel), Gores, Wohlers – Simonsen, Lienen

Red Star – Stojanovic – Jovanovic, Miletovic, Jurisic, Jovin – Muslin

Petrovic, Blagojevic, Milovanovic (Sestic) – Savic, Milosavljevic

Top scorer: Simonsen, Borussia Mönchengladbach 9

CUP WINNERS CUP

FIRST ROUND

Barcelona	3–0	1–1	Shachter Donetsk
RSC Anderlecht	Bye		
Zaglebie Sosnowiec	2–3	1–1	**Wacker Innsbruck**
AZ 67 Alkmaar	0–0	0–2	**Ipswich Town**
Floriana	1–3	0–5	**Internazionale**
SOFK Bodo-Glimt	4–1	0–1	Union Luxembourg
NK Rijeka	3–0	0–2	Wrexham
SK Beveren	3–0	3–0	Ballymena United
Sporting CP	0–1	0–1	**Baník Ostrava**
Apoel Nicosia	0–2	0–1	**Shamrock Rovers**
Ferencváros	2–0	2–2	Kalmar FF
Valur Reykjavík	1–1	0–4	**1.FC Magdeburg**
PAOK Salonica	2–0	0–4	**Servette FC**
Frem Kobenhavn	2–0	0–4	**AS Nancy-Lorraine**
Marek Stanke Dimitrov	3–2	0–3	**Aberdeen**
Universitatea Craiova	3–4	1–1	**Fortuna Düsseldorf**

SECOND ROUND

RSC Anderlecht	3–0	0–3 (1–4p)	**Barcelona**
Ipswich Town	1–0	1–1	Wacker Innsbruck
Internazionale	5–0	2–1	SOFK Bodo-Glimt
NK Rijeka	0–0	0–2	**SK Beveren**
Baník Ostrava	3–0	3–1	Shamrock Rovers
1.FC Magdeburg	1–0	1–2	Ferencváros
Servette FC	2–1	2–2	AS Nancy-Lorraine
Fortuna Düsseldorf	3–0	0–2	Aberdeen

QUARTER-FINALS

Ipswich Town	2–1	0–1	**Barcelona**
Internazionale	0–0	0–1	**SK Beveren**
1.FC Magdeburg	2–1	2–4	**Baník Ostrava**
Fortuna Düsseldorf	0–0	1–1	Servette FC

SEMI-FINALS

Barcelona	1–0	1–0	SK Beveren
Fortuna Düsseldorf	3–1	1–2	Baník Ostrava

FINAL

St Jakobs, Basle, 16–05–1979, 58 000. Referee: Palotai, Hungary

BARCELONA 4 (Sanchez 5, Asensi 34, Rexach 104, Krankl 111)

FORTUNA DUSSELDORF 3 (Allofs K 8, Seel 41 114)

Barcelona – Artola – Zuviria, Migueli, Costas (Martinez), Albaladejo (De la Cruz) – Sanchez, Neeskens, Asensi – Rexach, Krankl, Carrasco

Fortuna – Daniel – Baltes, Zewe, Zimmermann (Lund), Brei (Weikl) – Kohnen, Schmitz, Bommer – Allofs T, Allofs K, Seel

Top scorer: Altobelli, Internazionale 7

EUROPEAN SUPERCUP 1979

1st leg

City Ground, Nottingham, 30–01–1980. Referee: Prokop, East Germany

NOTTINGHAM FOREST 1 (George 9)

BARCELONA 0

2nd leg

Nou Camp, Barcelona, 5–02–1980. Referee: Eschweiler, West Germany

BARCELONA 1 (Roberto 25)

NOTTINGHAM FOREST 1 (Burns 42)

1979–80

EUROPEAN CUP

PRELIMINARY ROUND

Dundalk	1–1	2–0	Linfield

FIRST ROUND

Nottingham Forest	2–0	1–1	Östers IF Växjö
FC Arges Pitesti	3–0	0–2	AEK Athens
Servette FC	3–1	1–1	SK Beveren
Dynamo Berlin	4–1	0–0	Ruch Chorzów
Start Kristiansand	1–2	0–4	**RC Strasbourg**
Ujpesti Dózsa	3–2	0–2	**Dukla Praha**
Red Boys	2–1	1–6	**Omonia Nicosia**
HJK Helsinki	1–8	1–8	**Ajax**
Levski-Spartak	0–1	0–2	**Real Madrid**
FC Porto	0–0	1–0	Milan
Dundalk	2–0	0–1	Hibernians Paola
Partizani Tiranë	1–0	1–4	**Glasgow Celtic**
Hajduk Split	1–0	1–0	Trabzonspor
Vejle BK	3–2	1–1	FK Austria
Liverpool	2–1	0–3	**Dynamo Tbilisi**
Valur Reykjavík	0–3	1–2	**Hamburger SV**

SECOND ROUND

Nottingham Forest	2–0	2–1	FC Arges Pitesti
Dynamo Berlin	2–1	2–2	Servette FC
Dukla Praha	1–0	0–2	**RC Strasbourg**
Ajax	10–0	0–4	Omonia Nicosia
FC Porto	2–1	0–1	**Real Madrid**
Glasgow Celtic	3–2	0–0	Dundalk
Vejle BK	0–3	2–1	**Hajduk Split**
Hamburger SV	3–1	3–2	Dynamo Tbilisi

QUARTER-FINALS

Nottingham Forest	0–1	3–1	Dynamo Berlin
RC Strasbourg	0–0	0–4	**Ajax**
Glasgow Celtic	2–0	0–3	**Real Madrid**
Hamburger SV	1–0	2–3	Hajduk Split

SEMI-FINALS

Nottingham Forest	2–0	0–1	Ajax
Real Madrid	2–0	1–5	**Hamburger SV**

FINAL

Bernabeu, Madrid, 28–05–1980, 50 000. Referee: Garrido, Portugal

NOTTINGHAM FOREST 1 (Robertson 21)

HAMBURGER SV 0

Nottm. Forest – Shilton – Anderson, Gray (Gunn), Lloyd, Burns – O'Neill, McGovern, Bowyer, Mills (O'Hare), Robertson – Birtles. Tr: Clough

Hamburg – Kargus – Kaltz, Nogly, Buljan, Jakobs – Hieronymus (Hrubesch), Magath, Memering – Keegan, Reimann, Milewski. Tr: Zebec

Top scorer: Lerby, Ajax 10

UEFA CUP

FIRST ROUND

Aberdeen	1–1	0–1	**Eintracht Frankfurt**
Dinamo Bucuresti	3–0	9–0	Alki Larnaca
KuPS Kuopio	1–2	0–2	**Malmö FF**
Feyenoord	1–0	1–0	Everton
Glenavon	0–1	0–1	**Standard CL**
Napoli	2–0	0–1	Olympiakos
Kalmar FF	2–1	0–1	**IBK Keflavík**
Zbrojovka Brno	6–0	1–1	Esbjerg FB
FC Zürich	1–3	1–5	**1.FC Kaiserslautern**

Sporting CP	2–0 0–0	Bohemians Dublin
Dundee United	0–0 1–1	RSC Anderlecht
SK Rapid Wien	0–1 2–3	**Diósgyöri VTK**
Galatasaray	0–0 1–3	**Crvena Zvezda Beograd**
Carl Zeiss Jena	2–0 2–1	West Bromwich Albion
ÅGF Åarhus	1–1 1–0	Stal Mielec
Bohemians Praha	0–2 2–2	**Bayern München**
VfB Stuttgart	1–0 1–2	Torino
Atlético Madrid	1–2 0–3	**Dynamo Dresden**
FK Skeid Oslo	1–3 0–7	**Ipswich Town**
Progres Niedercorn	0–2 0–4	**Grasshopper-Club**
Dynamo Kiev	2–1 1–1	CSKA Sofia
Orduspor	2–0 0–6	**Baník Ostrava**
Shachter Donetsk	2–1 0–2	**AS Monaco**
Lokomotiv Sofia	3–0 0–2	Ferencváros
Widzew Lódz	2–1 0–3	**AS Saint-Étienne**
Sporting Gijón	0–0 0–1	**PSV Eindhoven**
Perugia	1–0 0–0	Dinamo Zagreb
Aris Salonica	3–1 1–2	Benfica
Wiener Sport-Club	0–0 1–3	**Universitatea Craiova**
Valletta	0–4 0–3	**Leeds United**
Internazionale	3–0 0–2	Real Sociedad
B. Mönchengladbach	3–0 1–1	Viking Stavanger

SECOND ROUND

Dinamo Bucuresti	2–0 0–3	**Eintracht Frankfurt**
Feyenoord	4–0 1–1	Malmö FF
Standard CL	2–1 1–1	Napoli
Zbrojovka Brno	3–1 2–1	IBK Keflavík
Sporting CP	1–1 0–2	**1.FC Kaiserslautern**
Dundee United	0–1 1–3	**Diósgyöri VTK**
Crvena Zvezda Beo.	3–2 3–2	Carl Zeiss Jena
ÅGF Åarhus	1–2 1–3	**Bayern München**
Dynamo Dresden	1–1 0–0	**VfB Stuttgart**
Grasshopper-Club	0–0 1–1	Ipswich Town
Baník Ostrava	1–0 0–2	**Dynamo Kiev**
Lokomotiv Sofia	4–2 1–2	AS Monaco
PSV Eindhoven	2–0 0–6	**AS Saint-Étienne**
Aris Salonica	1–1 3–0	Perugia
Universitatea Craiova	2–0 2–0	Leeds United
B. Mönchengladbach	1–1 3–2	Internazionale

THIRD ROUND

Eintracht Frankfurt	4–1 0–1	Feyenoord
Standard CL	1–2 2–3	**Zbrojovka Brno**
Diósgyöri VTK	0–2 1–6	**1.FC Kaiserslautern**
Bayern München	2–0 2–3	Crvena Zvezda Beograd
Grasshopper-Club	0–2 0–3	**VfB Stuttgart**
Lokomotiv Sofia	1–0 1–2	Dynamo Kiev
AS Saint-Étienne	4–1 3–3	Aris Salonica
B. Mönchengladbach	2–0 0–1	Universitatea Craiova

QUARTER-FINALS

Eintracht Frankfurt	4–1 2–3	Zbrojovka Brno
1.FC Kaiserslautern	1–0 1–4	**Bayern München**
VfB Stuttgart	3–1 1–0	Lokomotiv Sofia
AS Saint-Étienne	1–4 0–2	**B. Mönchengladbach**

SEMI-FINALS

Bayern München	2–0 1–5	**Eintracht Frankfurt**
VfB Stuttgart	2–1 0–2	**B. Mönchengladbach**

FINAL

1st leg

Bökelberg, Mönchengladbach, 7–05–80, 25 000. Referee: Gurucheta, Spain

BOR. MÖNCHENGLADBACH 3 (Kulik 44 88, Matthaus 76)
EINTRACHT FRANKFURT 2 (Karger 37, Holzenbein 71)

Borussia – Kneib – Hannes, Schafer, Schaffer, Ringels – Matthaus, Kulik, Nielsen (Thychosen) – Del'Haye (Bodeker), Nickel, Lienen

Eintracht – Pahl – Pezzey, Neuberger, Korbel, Ehrmanntraut – Lorant, Holzenbein (Nachtweih), Borchers, Nickel – Tscha, Karger (Trapp)

2nd leg

Waldstadion, Frankfurt, 21–05–1980, 59 000. Referee: Ponnet, Belgium

EINTRACHT FRANKFURT 1 (Schaub 81)
BOR. MÖNCHENGLADBACH 0

Eintracht – Pahl – Pezzey, Neuberger, Korbel, Ehrmanntraut – Lorant, Holzenbein, Borchers, Nickel – Tscha, Nachtweih (Schaub)

Borussia – Kneib – Bodecker, Hannes, Schafer, Ringels – Matthaus (Thychosen), Fleer, Kulik, Nielsen (Del'Haye) – Nickel, Lienen

Top scorers: Hoeness, Bayern München 7
Nickel, Borussia Mönchengladbach 7

CUP WINNERS CUP

PRELIMINARY ROUND

B 1903 Kobenhavn	6–0 1–0	Apoel Nicosia
Glasgow Rangers	1–0 2–0	Lillestrom SK

FIRST ROUND

B 1903 Kobenhavn	2–2 0–4	**Valencia**
Glasgow Rangers	2–1 0–0	Fortuna Düsseldorf
Reipas Lahti	0–1 0–1	**Aris Bonnevoie**
IA Akranes	0–1 0–5	**Barcelona**
Dynamo Moskva	W–O	Vllaznia Shkodër
Sliema Wanderers	2–1 0–8	**Boavista FC**
BSC Young Boys	2–2 0–6	**Steaua Bucuresti**
Cliftonville	0–1 0–7	**FC Nantes**
Juventus	2–0 1–2	Rába ETO Györ
Arka Gdynia	3–2 0–2	**Beroe Stara Zagora**
Wacker Innsbruck	1–2 0–1	**Lokomotiva Kosice**
Beerschot VAV	0–0 1–2	**NK Rijeka**
IFK Göteborg	1–0 1–1	Waterford FC
Panionios	4–0 1–3	FC Twente Enschede
Wrexham	3–2 2–5	**1.FC Magdeburg**
Arsenal	2–0 0–0	Fenerbahçe

SECOND ROUND

Valencia	1–1 3–1	Glasgow Rangers
Aris Bonnevoie	1–4 1–7	**Barcelona**
Dynamo Moskva	0–0 1–1	Boavista FC
FC Nantes	3–2 2–1	Steaua Bucuresti
Beroe Stara Zagora	1–0 0–3	**Juventus**
Lokomotiva Kosice	2–0 0–3	**NK Rijeka**
Panionios	1–0 0–2	**IFK Göteborg**
Arsenal	2–1 2–2	1.FC Magdeburg

QUARTER-FINALS

Barcelona	0–1 3–4	**Valencia**
Dynamo Moskva	0–2 3–2	**FC Nantes**
NK Rijeka	0–0 0–2	**Juventus**
Arsenal	5–1 0–0	IFK Göteborg

SEMI-FINALS

FC Nantes	2–1 0–4	**Valencia**
Arsenal	1–1 1–0	Juventus

FINAL

Heysel, Brussels, 15–05–1980, 36000. Referee: Christov, Czechoslovakia

VALENCIA 0
ARSENAL 0

Valencia won 5–4 on penalties

Valencia – Pereira – Carrette, Botubot, Arias, Tendillo – Solsona, Saura, Bonhof, Subirates (Castellanos), Kempes, Pablo

Arsenal – Jennings – Rice, Nelson, O'Leary, Young – Rix, Talbot, Price (Hollins), Brady – Sunderland, Stapleton

Top scorer: Kempes, Valencia 9

EUROPEAN SUPERCUP 1980

1st leg

City Ground, Nottingham, 25–11–1980. Referee: Ponnet, Belgium

NOTTINGHAM FOREST 2 (Bowyer 57 89)
VALENCIA 1 (Felman 47)

2nd leg
Luis Casanova, Valencia, 17–12–1980. Referee: Wöhrer, Austria
VALENCIA 1 (Morena 51)
NOTTINGHAM FOREST 0

1980–81

EUROPEAN CUP

PRELIMINARY ROUND

Honvéd	8–0	3–0	Valletta

FIRST ROUND

OPS Oulu	1–1	1–10	**Liverpool**
Aberdeen	1–0	0–0	FK Austria
Trabzonspor	2–1	0–3	**Szombierki Bytom**
CSKA Sofia	1–0	1–0	Nottingham Forest
IBV Vestmannaeyjar	1–1	0–1	**Baník Ostrava**
Dynamo Berlin	3–0	1–2	Apoel Nicosia
Dinamo Tiranë	0–2	0–1	**Ajax**
Olympiakos	2–4	0–3	**Bayern München**
Internazionale	2–0	1–1	Universitatea Craiova
Linfield	0–1	0–2	**FC Nantes**
Club Brugge	0–1	1–4	**FC Basel**
Viking Stavanger	2–3	1–4	**Crvena Zvezda Beograd**
Jeunesse Esch	0–5	0–4	**Spartak Moskva**
Halmstad BK	0–0	2–3	**Esbjerg FB**
Sporting CP	0–2	0–1	**Honvéd**
Limerick United	1–2	1–5	**Real Madrid**

SECOND ROUND

Aberdeen	0–1	0–4	**Liverpool**
CSKA Sofia	4–0	1–0	Szombierki Bytom
Baník Ostrava	0–0	1–1	Dynamo Berlin
Bayern München	5–1	1–2	Ajax
FC Nantes	1–2	1–1	**Internazionale**
FC Basel	1–0	0–2	**Crvena Zvezda Beograd**
Spartak Moskva	3–0	0–2	Esbjerg FB
Real Madrid	1–0	2–0	Honvéd

QUARTER-FINALS

Liverpool	5–1	1–0	CSKA Sofia
Bayern München	2–0	4–2	Baník Ostrava
Internazionale	1–1	1–0	Crvena Zvezda Beograd
Spartak Moskva	0–0	0–2	**Real Madrid**

SEMI-FINALS

Liverpool	0–0	1–1	Bayern München
Real Madrid	2–0	0–1	Internazionale

FINAL

Parc des Princes, Paris, 27–05–1981, 48 000. Referee: Palotai, Hungary
LIVERPOOL 1 (Kennedy A 82)
REAL MADRID 0

Liverpool – Clemence – Neal, Thompson, Hansen, Kennedy A – Lee, McDermott, Souness, Kennedy R – Dalglish (Case), Johnson. Tr: Paisley

Real Madrid – Agustin – Cortes (Pineda), Navajas, Sabido – Del Bosque, Angel, Camacho, Stielike – Juanito, Santillana, Cunningham. Tr: Boskov

Top scorer:	Rummenigge, Bayern München	6
	McDermott, Liverpool	6
	Souness, Liverpool	6

UEFA CUP

FIRST ROUND

Ipswich Town	5–1	1–3	Aris Salonica
Bohemians Praha	3–1	1–2	Sporting Gijón
Juventus	4–0	2–4	Panathinaikos
Manchester United	1–1	0–0	**Widzew Lódz**
Hamburger SV	4–2	3–3	FK Sarajevo
PSV Eindhoven	3–1	0–1	Wolverhampton Wan.
IF Elfsborg Borås	1–2	0–0	**St Mirren**
KuPS Kuopio	0–7	0–7	**AS Saint-Étienne**
Standard CL	1–1	2–1	Steaua Bucuresti
1.FC Kaiserslautern	1–0	2–3	RSC Anderlecht
FC Twente Enschede	5–1	0–2	IFK Göteborg
Dynamo Dresden	1–0	1–0	Napredak Krusevac
VfB Stuttgart	6–0	4–1	Pezoporikos
Ballymena United	2–1	0–3	**Vorwärts Frankfurt**
Sliema Wanderers	0–2	0–1	**Barcelona**
IA Akranes	0–4	0–6	**1.FC Köln**
FC Sochaux	2–0	1–2	Servette FC
Vasas Budapest	0–2	1–0	**Boavista FC**
FC Arges Pitesti	0–0	0–2	**FC Utrecht**
Shachter Donetsk	1–0	0–3	**Eintracht Frankfurt**
RWD Molenbeek	1–2	2–2	**Torino**
1.FC Magdeburg	2–1	3–2	Moss FK
FC Porto	1–0	0–0	Dundalk
Grasshopper-Club	3–1	5–2	B 1903 Kobenhavn
KSC Lokeren	1–1	1–0	Dynamo Moskva
Slask Wroclaw	0–0	2–7	**Dundee United**
Zbrojovka Brno	3–1	2–0	VÖEST Linz
Ujpesti Dózsa	1–1	0–1	**Real Sociedad**
Linzer ASK	1–2	1–4	**Radnicki Nis**
Fenerbahçe	0–1	1–2	**Beroe Stara Zagora**
Dynamo Kiev	1–1	0–0	**Levski-Spartak**
AZ 67 Alkmaar	6–0	4–0	Red Boys

SECOND ROUND

Ipswich Town	3–0	0–2	Bohemians Praha
Widzew Lódz	3–1	1–3 (4–1p)	Juventus
PSV Eindhoven	1–1	1–2	**Hamburger SV**
St Mirren	0–0	0–2	**AS Saint-Étienne**
1.FC Kaiserslautern	1–2	1–2	**Standard CL**
FC Twente Enschede	1–1	0–0	**Dynamo Dresden**
VfB Stuttgart	5–1	2–1	Vorwärts Frankfurt
1.FC Köln	0–1	4–0	Barcelona
FC Sochaux	2–2	1–0	Boavista FC
FC Utrecht	2–1	1–3	**Eintracht Frankfurt**
Torino	3–1	0–1	1.FC Magdeburg
FC Porto	2–0	0–3	**Grasshopper-Club**
Dundee United	1–1	0–0	**KSC Lokeren**
Zbrojovka Brno	1–1	1–2	**Real Sociedad**
Beroe Stara Zagora	0–1	1–2	**Radnicki Nis**
Levski-Spartak	1–1	0–5	**AZ 67 Alkmaar**

THIRD ROUND

Ipswich Town	5–0	0–1	Widzew Lódz
Hamburger SV	0–5	0–1	**AS Saint-Étienne**
Standard CL	1–1	4–1	Dynamo Dresden
VfB Stuttgart	3–1	1–4	**1.FC Köln**
Eintracht Frankfurt	4–2	0–2	**FC Sochaux**
Grasshopper-Club	2–1	1–2 (4–3p)	Torino
KSC Lokeren	1–0	2–2	Real Sociedad
Radnicki Nis	2–2	0–5	**AZ 67 Alkmaar**

QUARTER-FINALS

AS Saint-Étienne	1–4	1–3	**Ipswich Town**
Standard CL	0–0	2–3	**1.FC Köln**
Grasshopper-Club	0–0	1–2	**FC Sochaux**
AZ 67 Alkmaar	2–0	0–1	KSC Lokeren

SEMI-FINALS
Ipswich Town .... 1–0 1–0 .... 1.FC Köln
FC Sochaux .... 1–1 2–3 .... **AZ 67 Alkmaar**

FINAL
1st leg
Portman Road, Ipswich, 6–05–1981, 27 000. Referee: Prokop, East Germany
IPSWICH TOWN 3 (Wark 28, Thijssen 46, Mariner 56)
AZ 67 ALKMAAR 0
Ipswich Town – Cooper – Mills, Osman, Butcher, McCall – Thijssen, Wark, Muhren – Mariner, Brazil, Gates
AZ 67 Alkmaar – Treytel – Van der Meer, Spelbos, Metgod, Hovenkamp – Peters, Jonker, Arntz, Nygaard (Welzl) – Kist, Tol
2nd leg
Olympisch Stadion, Amsterdam, 20–05–1981, 28 000. Referee: Eschweiler, West Germany
AZ 67 ALKMAAR 4 (Welzl 7, Metgod 25, Tol 40, Jonker 74)
IPSWICH TOWN 2 (Thijssen 4, Wark 32)
AZ 67 Alkmaar – Treytel – Reijnders, Spelbos, Metgod, Hovenkamp – Peters, Arntz, Jonker, Nygaard – Welzl (Van den Dungen), Tol (Kist)
Ipswich Town – Cooper – Mills, Osman, Butcher, McCall – Thijssen, Wark, Muhren – Mariner, Brazil, Gates

Top scorer: Wark, Ipswich Town 14

CUP WINNERS CUP

PRELIMINARY ROUND
Glasgow Celtic .... 6–0 1–2 .... Diósgyöri VTK
Altay Izmir .... 0–0 0–4 .... **Benfica**

FIRST ROUND
Kastoria .... 0–0 0–2 .... **Dynamo Tbilisi**
Hibernians Paola .... 1–0 0–4 .... **Waterford FC**
Glasgow Celtic .... 2–1 0–1 .... **Politehnica Timisoara**
Castilla .... 3–1 1–5 .... **West Ham United**
Slavia Sofia .... 3–1 0–1 .... Legia Warszawa
AC Spora .... 0–6 0–6 .... **Sparta Praha**
Hvidovre BK .... 1–0 2–0 .... Fram Reykjavík
Ilves Tampere .... 1–3 2–4 .... **Feyenoord**
Dinamo Zagreb .... 0–0 0–2 .... **Benfica**
Malmö FF .... 1–0 0–0 .... Partizani Tiranë
Omonia Nicosia .... 1–3 0–4 .... **Waterschei THOR**
Fortuna Düsseldorf .... 5–0 3–0 .... Austria Salzburg
Newport County .... 4–0 0–0 .... Crusaders
FC Sion .... 1–1 0–2 .... **SK Haugar**
Valencia .... 2–0 3–3 .... AS Monaco
Roma .... 3–0 0–4 .... **Carl Zeiss Jena**

SECOND ROUND
Waterford .... 0–1 0–4 .... **Dynamo Tbilisi**
West Ham United .... 4–0 0–1 .... Politehnica Timisoara
Sparta Praha .... 2–0 0–3 .... **Slavia Sofia**
Hvidovre BK .... 1–2 0–1 .... **Feyenoord**
Malmö FF .... 1–0 0–2 .... **Benfica**
Waterschei THOR .... 0–0 0–1 .... **Fortuna Düsseldorf**
SK Haugar .... 0–0 0–6 .... **Newport County**
Carl Zeiss Jena .... 3–1 0–1 .... Valencia

QUARTER-FINALS
West Ham United .... 1–4 1–0 .... **Dynamo Tbilisi**
Slavia Sofia .... 3–2 0–4 .... **Feyenoord**
Fortuna Düsseldorf .... 2–2 0–1 .... **Benfica**
Carl Zeiss Jena .... 2–2 1–0 .... Newport County

SEMI-FINALS
Dynamo Tbilisi .... 3–0 0–2 .... Feyenoord
Carl Zeiss Jena .... 2–0 0–1 .... Benfica

FINAL
Rheinstadion, Dusseldorf, 13–05–1981, 9000. Referee: Lattanzi, Italy
DYNAMO TBILISI 2 (Gutsayev 67, Daraselia 86)
CARL ZEISS JENA 1 (Hoppe 63)
Dynamo Tbilisi – Gabelia – Kostava, Chivadze, Khisanishvili, Tavadze – Svanadze (Kakilashvili), Sulakvelidze, Daraselia – Gutsayev, Kipiani, Shengelia
Carl Zeiss Jena – Grapenthin – Brauer, Kurbjuweit, Schnuphase, Schilling – Hoppe (Overmann), Krause, Lindemann – Bielau (Topfer), Raab, Vogel

Top scorer: Cross, West Ham United 6

1981–82

EUROPEAN CUP

PRELIMINARY ROUND
AS Saint-Étienne .... 1–1 0–2 .... **Dynamo Berlin**

FIRST ROUND
Aston Villa .... 5–0 2–0 .... Valur Reykjavík
Dynamo Berlin .... 2–0 1–3 .... FC Zürich
FK Austria .... 3–1 0–1 .... Partizani Tiranë
Dynamo Kiev .... 1–0 1–1 .... Trabzonspor
Hibernians Paola .... 1–2 1–8 .... **Crvena Zvezda Beograd**
Ferencváros .... 3–2 0–3 .... **Baník Ostrava**
Glasgow Celtic .... 1–0 0–2 .... **Juventus**
Widzew Lódz .... 1–4 1–2 .... **RSC Anderlecht**
CSKA Sofia .... 1–0 0–0 .... Real Sociedad
Progres Niedercorn .... 1–1 0–4 .... **Glentoran**
Start Kristiansand .... 1–3 0–1 .... **AZ 67 Alkmaar**
OPS Oulu .... 0–1 0–7 .... **Liverpool**
Universitatea Craiova .. 3–0 0–2 .... Olympiakos
KB Kobenhavn .... 1–1 2–2 .... Athlone Town
Benfica .... 3–0 1–0 .... Omonia Nicosia
Östers IF Växjö .... 0–1 0–5 .... **Bayern München**

SECOND ROUND
Dynamo Berlin .... 1–2 1–0 .... **Aston Villa**
FK Austria .... 0–1 1–1 .... **Dynamo Kiev**
Baník Ostrava .... 3–1 0–3 .... **Crvena Zvezda Beograd**
RSC Anderlecht .... 3–1 1–1 .... Juventus
CSKA Sofia .... 2–0 1–2 .... Glentoran
AZ 67 Alkmaar .... 2–2 2–3 .... **Liverpool**
KB Kobenhavn .... 1–0 1–4 .... **Universitatea Craiova**
Benfica .... 0–0 1–4 .... **Bayern München**

QUARTER-FINALS
Dynamo Kiev .... 0–0 0–2 .... **Aston Villa**
RSC Anderlecht .... 2–1 2–1 .... Crvena Zvezda Beograd
Liverpool .... 1–0 0–2 .... **CSKA Sofia**
Universitatea Craiova .... 0–2 1–1 .... **Bayern München**

SEMI-FINALS
Aston Villa .... 1–0 0–0 .... RSC Anderlecht
CSKA Sofia .... 4–3 0–4 .... **Bayern München**

FINAL
Feyenoord, Rotterdam, 26–05–1982, 46 000. Referee: Konrath, France
ASTON VILLA 1 (Withe 67)
BAYERN MUNCHEN 0
Aston Villa – Rimmer (Spink) – Swain, Evans, McNaught, Williams – Bremner, Cowans, Mortimer – Shaw, Withe, Morley. Tr: Barton
Bayern – Muller – Dremmler, Weiner, Augenthaler, Horsmann – Mathy (Guttler), Breitner, Kraus (Niedermayer), Durnberger – Rummenigge, Hoeness. Tr: Csernai

Top scorer: Hoeness, Bayern München 7
Geurts, Anderlecht 7

UEFA CUP

FIRST ROUND

Haka Valkeakoski	2–3 0–4	**IFK Göteborg**
SK Sturm Graz	1–0 1–2	CSKA Moskva
Adanaspor	1–3 1–4	**Internazionale**
Dinamo Bucuresti	3–0 1–2	Levski-Spartak
Hajduk Split	3–1 2–2	VfB Stuttgart
SK Beveren	3–0 5–0	Linfield
Boavista FC	4–1 1–3	Atlético Madrid
Bohemians Praha	0–1 0–1	**Valencia**
Tatabánya Bányász	2–1 0–1	**Real Madrid**
Dinamo Tiranë	1–0 0–4	**Carl Zeiss Jena**
PSV Eindhoven	7–0 1–2	Naestved IF
SK Rapid Wien	2–2 2–0	Videoton SC
FC Nantes	1–1 2–4	**KSC Lokeren**
Aris Salonica	4–0 4–2	Sliema Wanderers
Spartak Moskva	3–1 3–1	Club Brugge
1.FC Kaiserslautern	1–0 2–1	Akademic Sofia
Napoli	2–2 0–0	**Radnicki Nis**
Grasshopper-Club	1–0 3–1	West Bromwich Albion
Zenit Leningrad	1–2 1–4	**Dynamo Dresden**
Feyenoord	2–0 1–1	Szombierki Bytom
Byrne IL Stavanger	0–2 2–1	**SV Winterslag**
Panathinaikos	0–2 0–1	**Arsenal**
1.FC Magdeburg	3–1 0–2	**B. Mönchengladbach**
AS Monaco	2–5 2–1	**Dundee United**
Neuchâtel Xamax	4–0 2–3	Sparta Praha
Malmö FF	2–0 3–1	Wisla Kraków
Limerick United	0–3 1–1	**Southampton**
Sporting CP	4–0 7–0	Red Boys
Ipswich Town	1–1 1–3	**Aberdeen**
Apoel Nicosia	1–1 0–4	**FC Arges Pitesti**
Víkingur Reykjavík	0–4 0–4	**Girondins Bordeaux**
Hamburger SV	0–1 6–3	FC Utrecht

SECOND ROUND

SK Sturm Graz	2–2 2–3	**IFK Göteborg**
Internazionale	1–1 2–3	**Dinamo Bucuresti**
SK Beveren	2–3 2–1	**Hajduk Split**
Valencia	2–0 0–1	Boavista FC
Real Madrid	3–2 0–0	Carl Zeiss Jena
SK Rapid Wien	1–0 1–2	PSV Eindhoven
Aris Salonica	1–1 0–4	**KSC Lokeren**
Spartak Moskva	2–1 0–4	**1.FC Kaiserslautern**
Grasshopper-Club	2–0 0–2 (0–3p)	**Radnicki Nis**
Feyenoord	2–1 1–1	Dynamo Dresden
SV Winterslag	1–0 1–2	Arsenal
Borussia Möncheng'bach	2–0 0–5	**Dundee United**
Malmö FF	0–1 0–1	**Neuchâtel Xamax**
Southampton	2–4 0–0	**Sporting CP**
Aberdeen	3–0 2–2	FC Arges Pitesti
Girondins Bordeaux	2–1 0–2	**Hamburger SV**

THIRD ROUND

IFK Göteborg	3–1 1–0	Dinamo Bucuresti
Valencia	5–1 1–4	Hajduk Split
SK Rapid Wien	0–1 0–0	**Real Madrid**
KSC Lokeren	1–0 1–4	**1.FC Kaiserslautern**
Radnicki Nis	2–0 0–1	Feyenoord
SV Winterslag	0–0 0–5	**Dundee United**
Sporting CP	0–0 0–1	**Neuchâtel Xamax**
Aberdeen	3–2 1–3	**Hamburger SV**

QUARTER-FINALS

Valencia	2–2 0–2	**IFK Göteborg**
Real Madrid	3–1 0–5	**1.FC Kaiserslautern**
Dundee United	2–0 0–3	**Radnicki Nis**
Hamburger SV	3–2 0–0	Neuchâtel Xamax

SEMI-FINALS

1.FC Kaiserslautern	1–1 1–2	**IFK Göteborg**
Radnicki Nis	2–1 1–5	**Hamburger SV**

FINAL

1st leg

Nya Ullevi, Gothenburg, 5–05–1982, 42 000. Referee: Carpenter, Ireland

IFK GÖTEBORG 1 (Tord Holmgren 87)
HAMBURGER SV 0

IFK Göteborg – Wernersson – Svensson, Hysen, Karlsson C, Fredriksson – Tord Holmgren, Karlsson J, Stromberg – Corneliusson, Nilsson (Sandberg), Tommy Holmgren (Schiller)

Hamburg – Stein – Kaltz, Jakobs, Hieronymus, Groh – Hartwig, Wehmeyer, Magath – Von Heesen (Memering), Bastrup, Hrubesch

2nd leg

Volksparkstadion, Hamburg, 19–05–1982, 60 000. Referee: Courtney, England

HAMBURGER SV 0
IFK GÖTEBORG 3 (Corneliusson 26, Nilsson 61, Fredriksson 63)

Hamburg – Stein – Kaltz (Hidien), Hieronymus, Groh, Wehmeyer – Hartwig, Memering, Magath, Von Heesen – Hrubesch, Bastrup

IFK Göteborg – Wernersson – Svensson, Hysen (Schiller), Karlsson C, Fredriksson – Tord Holmgren, Stromberg, Karlsson J – Corneliusson (Sandberg), Nilsson, Tommy Holmgren

Top scorer: Nilsson, IFK Göteborg 9

CUP WINNERS CUP

PRELIMINARY ROUND

Politehnica Timisoara	2–0 0–5	**Lokomotive Leipzig**

FIRST ROUND

Barcelona	4–1 0–1	Trakia Plovdiv
Dukla Praha	3–0 1–2	Glasgow Rangers
Jeunesse Esch	1–1 1–6	**Velez Mostar**
Swansea City	0–1 1–2	**Lokomotive Leipzig**
Eintracht Frank.	2–0 0–2 (5–4p)	PAOK Salonica
SKA Rostov-na-Donu	3–0 2–0	MKE Ankaragücü
Fram Reykjavík	2–1 0–4	**Dundalk**
Ajax	1–3 0–3	**Tottenham Hotspur**
Dynamo Tbilisi	2–0 2–2	Grazer AK
KTP Kotka	0–0 0–5	**SEC Bastia**
Lausanne-Sports	2–1 2–3	Kalmar FF
Vålerengens Oslo	2–2 1–4	**Legia Warszawa**
Vejle BK	2–1 0–3	**FC Porto**
Ballymena United	0–2 0–4	**Roma**
Union Paralimni	1–0 0–8	**Vasas Budapest**
Floriana	1–3 0–9	**Standard CL**

SECOND ROUND

Dukla Praha	1–0 0–4	**Barcelona**
Lokomotive Leipzig	1–1 1–1 (3–0p)	Velez Mostar
SKA Rostov-na-Donu	1–0 0–2	**Eintracht Frankfurt**
Dundalk	1–1 0–1	**Tottenham Hotspur**
SEC Bastia	1–1 1–3	**Dynamo Tbilisi**
Legia Warszawa	2–1 1–1	Lausanne-Sports
FC Porto	2–0 0–0	Roma
Vasas Budapest	0–2 1–2	**Standard CL**

QUARTER-FINALS

Lokomotive Leipzig	0–3 2–1	**Barcelona**
Tottenham Hotspur	2–0 1–2	Eintracht Frankfurt
Legia Warszawa	0–1 0–1	**Dynamo Tbilisi**
Standard CL	2–0 2–2	FC Porto

SEMI-FINALS

Tottenham Hotspur	1–1 0–1	**Barcelona**
Dynamo Tbilisi	0–1 0–1	**Standard CL**

FINAL

Nou Camp, Barcelona, 12–05–1982, 100 000. Referee: Eschweiler, West Germany

BARCELONA 2 (Simonsen 44, Quini 63)
STANDARD CL 1 (Vandermissen 7)

Barcelona – Urruti – Gerardo, Migueli, Alesanco, Manolo – Sanchez, Moratalla, Esteban – Simonsen, Quini, Carrasco
Standard – Preud'homme – Gerets, Poel, Meeuws, Plessers – Vandermissen, Daerden, Haan, Botteron – Tahamata, Wendt

Top scorer: Shengelia, Dynamo Tbilisi 6
Voordeckers, Standard CL 6

EUROPEAN SUPERCUP 1982

1st leg

Nou Camp, Barcelona, 19–01–1983. Referee: Galler, Switzerland

BARCELONA 1 (Marcos 52)
ASTON VILLA 0

2nd leg

Villa Park, Birmingham, 26–01–1983. Referee: Ponnet, Belgium

ASTON VILLA 3 (Shaw 80, Cowans 99, McNaught 104)
BARCELONA 0

1982–83

EUROPEAN CUP

PRELIMINARY ROUND

Dinamo Bucuresti	3–1 1–2	Vålerengens Oslo

FIRST ROUND

Dynamo Berlin	1–1 0–2	**Hamburger SV**
Olympiakos	2–0 0–1	Östers IF Växjö
17 Nëntori Tiranë	1–0 1–2	Linfield
Grasshopper-Club	0–1 0–3	**Dynamo Kiev**
Dinamo Zagreb	1–0 0–3	**Sporting CP**
AS Monaco	0–0 0–2	**CSKA Sofia**
Glasgow Celtic	2–2 2–1	Ajax
Víkingur Reykjavík	0–1 2–3	**Real Sociedad**
Hibernians Paola	1–4 1–3	**Widzew Lódz**
Avenir Beggen	0–5 0–8	**SK Rapid Wien**
Omonia Nicosia	2–0 0–3	**HJK Helsinki**
Dundalk	1–4 0–1	**Liverpool**
Aston Villa	3–1 0–0	Besiktas
Dinamo Bucuresti	2–0 1–2	Dukla Praha
Standard CL	5–0 0–3	Rába ETO Györ
Hvidovre BK	1–4 3–3	**Juventus**

SECOND ROUND

Hamburger SV	1–0 4–0	Olympiakos
Dynamo Kiev	W–O	17 Nëntori Tiranë
CSKA Sofia	2–2 0–0	**Sporting CP**
Real Sociedad	2–0 1–2	Glasgow Celtic
SK Rapid Wien	2–1 3–5	**Widzew Lódz**
HJK Helsinki	1–0 0–5	**Liverpool**
Dinamo Bucuresti	0–2 2–4	**Aston Villa**
Standard CL	1–1 0–2	**Juventus**

QUARTER-FINALS

Dynamo Kiev	0–3 2–1	**Hamburger SV**
Sporting CP	1–0 0–2	**Real Sociedad**
Widzew Lódz	2–0 2–3	Liverpool
Aston Villa	1–2 1–3	**Juventus**

SEMI-FINALS

Real Sociedad	1–1 1–2	**Hamburger SV**
Juventus	2–0 2–2	Widzew Lódz

FINAL

Olympiako Stadio, Athens, 25–05–1983, 75 000. Referee: Rainea, Romania

HAMBURGER SV 1 (Magath 7)
JUVENTUS 0

Hamburg – Stein – Kaltz, Hieronymous, Jakobs, Wehmeyer – Groh, Rolff, Magath, Milewski – Bastrup (Von Heesen), Hrubesch. Tr: Happel
Juventus – Zoff – Gentile, Brio, Scirea, Cabrini – Bonini, Tardelli, Bettega – Platini, Rossi (Marocchino), Boniek. Tr: Trapattoni

Top scorer: Rossi, Juventus 6

UEFA CUP

FIRST ROUND

RSC Anderlecht	3–0 3–1	Koparit Kuopio
FC Utrecht	0–1 0–2	**FC Porto**
Grazer AK	1–1 0–3	**Corvinul Hunedoara**
Slavia Sofia	2–2 2–4	**FK Sarajevo**
Spartak Moskva	3–2 5–2	Arsenal
Haarlem	2–1 3–3	AA Gent
Glentoran	1–3 0–1	**Baník Ostrava**
Manchester United	0–0 1–2	**Valencia**
Dundee United	1–1 2–0	PSV Eindhoven
Viking Stavanger	1–0 2–3	Lokomotive Leipzig
Lyngby BK	1–2 2–2	**IK Brage Borlange**
Vorwärts Frankfurt	1–3 2–0	**Werder Bremen**
Progres Niedercorn	0–1 0–3	**Servette FC**
Slask Wroclaw	2–2 1–0	Dynamo Moskva
AS Saint-Étienne	4–1 0–0	Tatabánya Bányász
Bohemians Praha	5–0 2–1	Admira-Wacker
Universitatea Craiova	3–1 0–1	Fiorentina
Fram Reykjavík	0–3 0–4	**Shamrock Rovers**
Zurrieq	1–4 0–4	**Hajduk Split**
Carl Zeiss Jena	3–1 0–5	**Girondins Bordeaux**
Sevilla	3–1 3–0	Levski-Spartak
PAOK Salonica	1–0 1–2	FC Sochaux
Dynamo Tbilisi	2–1 0–1	**Napoli**
1.FC Kaiserslautern	3–0 3–0	Trabzonspor
Roma	3–0 1–3	Ipswich Town
Southampton	2–2 0–0	**IFK Norrköping**
Borussia Dortmund	0–0 0–2	**Glasgow Rangers**
AEK Athens	0–1 0–5	**1.FC Köln**
Pezoporikos	2–2 0–1	**FC Zürich**
Ferencváros	2–1 1–1	Athletic Bilbao
Stal Mielec	1–1 0–0	**KSC Lokeren**
Benfica	2–1 2–1	Real Betis

SECOND ROUND

RSC Anderlecht	4–0 2–3	FC Porto
Corvinul Hunedoara	4–4 0–4	**FK Sarajevo**
Spartak Moskva	2–0 3–1	Haarlem
Valencia	1–0 0–0	Baník Ostrava
Viking FK Stavanger	1–3 0–0	**Dundee United**
Werder Bremen	2–0 6–2	IK Brage Borlange
Slask Wroclaw	0–2 1–5	**Servette FC**
AS Saint-Étienne	0–0 0–4	**Bohemians Praha**
Shamrock Rovers	0–2 0–3	**Universitatea Craiova**
Hajduk Split	4–1 0–4	**Girondins Bordeaux**
PAOK Salonica	2–0 0–4	**Sevilla**
Napoli	1–2 0–2	**1.FC Kaiserslautern**
Roma	1–0 0–1 (4–2p)	IFK Norrkoping
Glasgow Rangers	2–1 0–5	**1.FC Köln**
Ferencváros	1–1 0–1	**FC Zürich**
Benfica	2–0 2–1	KSC Lokeren

THIRD ROUND

RSC Anderlecht	6–1 0–1	FK Sarajevo
Spartak Moskva	0–0 0–2	**Valencia**
Dundee United	2–1 1–1	Werder Bremen

Servette FC	2–2 1–2	**Bohemians Praha**
Girondins Bordeaux	1–2 0–2	**Universitatea Craiova**
Sevilla	1–0 0–4	**1.FC Kaiserslautern**
1.FC Köln	1–0 0–2	**Roma**
FC Zürich	1–1 0–4	**Benfica**

QUARTER-FINALS

Valencia	1–2 1–3	**RSC Anderlecht**
Bohemians Praha	1–0 0–0	Dundee United
1.FC Kaiserslautern	3–2 0–1	**Universitatea Craiova**
Roma	1–2 1–1	**Benfica**

SEMI-FINALS

Bohemians Praha	0–1 1–3	**RSC Anderlecht**
Benfica	0–0 1–1	Universitatea Craiova

FINAL

1st leg

Heysel, Brussels, 4–05–1983, 55 000. Referee: Dotschev, Bulgaria

RSC ANDERLECHT 1 (Brylle 29)
BENFICA 0

Anderlecht – Munaron – Hofkens, Peruzovic, Olsen, De Groote – Frimann, Coeck, Vercauteren, Lozano – Vandenbergh (Czerniatynski), Brylle

Benfica – Bento – Pietra, Alvaro, Humberto Coelho, Jose Luis – Sheu (Bastos Lopes), Frederico, Carlos Manuel, Chalana (Nene) – Diamantino, Filipovic

2nd leg

Estádio da Luz, Lisbon, 18–05–1983, 80000. Referee: Corver, Holland

BENFICA 1 (Sheu 36)
RSC ANDERLECHT 1 (Lozano 38)

Benfica – Bento – Pietra, Humberto Coelho, Bastos Lopes, Veloso (Alves) – Carlos Manuel, Stromberg, Sheu (Filipovic), Chalana – Nene, Diamantino

Anderlecht – Munaron – Peruzovic, De Greef, Broos, Olsen, De Groot – Frimann, Lozano, Coeck, Vercauteren – Vandenbergh (Brylle)

Top scorers: Vandenburgh, Anderlecht 7
Giresse, Bordeaux 7

CUP WINNERS CUP

PRELIMINARY ROUND

Aberdeen	7–0 4–1	FC Sion
Swansea City	3–0 0–1	Sporting Braga

FIRST ROUND

Aberdeen	1–0 0–0	Dinamo Tiranë
IBV Vestmannaeyjar	0–1 0–3	**Lech Poznan**
Coleraine	0–3 0–4	**Tottenham Hotspur**
Torpedo Moskva	1–1 0–0	**Bayern München**
Lokomotiv Sofia	1–0 1–5	**Paris St Germain**
Swansea City	12–0 5–0	Sliema Wanderers
Dynamo Dresden	3–2 1–2	**B 93 Kobenhavn**
Waterschei THOR	7–1 1–0	Red Boys
FK Austria	2–0 1–2	Panathinaikos
Galatasaray	2–1 1–1	Kuusysi Lahti
Lillestrom SK	0–4 0–3	**Crvena Zvezda Beograd**
Barcelona	8–0 1–1	Apollon Limassol
Internazionale	2–0 1–2	Slovan Bratislava
Limerick United	1–1 0–1	**AZ 67 Alkmaar**
IFK Göteborg	1–1 1–3	**Ujpesti Dózsa**
FC Baia Mare	0–0 2–5	**Real Madrid**

SECOND ROUND

Aberdeen	2–0 1–0	Lech Poznan
Tottenham Hotspur	1–1 1–4	**Bayern München**
Swansea City	0–1 0–2	**Paris Saint Germain**
B 93 Kobenhavn	0–2 1–4	**Waterschei THOR**
Galatasaray	2–4 1–0	**FK Austria**
Crvena Zvezda Beograd	2–4 1–2	**Barcelona**
AZ 67 Alkmaar	1–0 0–2	**Internazionale**
Real Madrid	3–1 1–0	Ujpesti Dózsa

QUARTER-FINALS

Bayern München	0–0 2–3	**Aberdeen**
Paris Saint Germain	2–0 0–3	**Waterschei THOR**
FK Austria	0–0 1–1	Barcelona
Internazionale	1–1 1–2	**Real Madrid**

SEMI-FINALS

Aberdeen	5–1 0–1	Waterschei THOR
FK Austria	2–2 1–3	**Real Madrid**

FINAL

Nya Ullevi, Gothenburg, 11–05–1983, 17000. Referee: Menegali, Italy

ABERDEEN 2 (Black 4, Hewitt 112)
REAL MADRID 1 (Juanito 15)

Aberdeen – Leighton – Rougvie, McLeish, Miller, McMaster – Cooper, Strachan, Simpson – McGhee, Black (Hewitt), Weir

Real Madrid – Agustin – Juan Jose, Metgod, Bonet, Camacho (San Jose) – Angel, Gallego, Stielike, Isidro (Salguero) – Juanito, Santillana

Top scorer: Santillana, Real Madrid 8

EUROPEAN SUPERCUP 1983

1st leg

Volksparkstadion, Hamburg, 22–11–1983. Referee: Christov, Czechoslovakia

HAMBURGER SV 0
ABERDEEN 0

2nd leg

Pittodrie, Aberdeen, 20–12–1983. Referee: Brunmeier, Austria

ABERDEEN 2 (Simpson 47, McGhee 65)
HAMBURGER SV 0

1983–84

EUROPEAN CUP

FIRST ROUND

OB Odense	0–1 0–5	**Liverpool**
Lech Poznan	2–0 0–4	**Athletic Bilbao**
Ajax	0–0 0–2	**Olympiakos**
Benfica	3–0 3–2	Linfield
Dynamo Minsk	1–0 2–2	Grasshopper-Club
Rába ETO Györ	2–1 2–0	Víkingur Reykjavík
Hamburger SV	W–O	Vllaznia Shkodër
Kuusysi Lahti	0–1 0–3	**Dinamo Bucuresti**
Hamrun Spartans	0–3 0–3	**Dundee United**
Athlone Town	2–3 2–8	**Standard CL**
Fenerbahçe	0–1 0–4	**Bohemians Praha**
SK Rapid Wien	3–0 1–3	FC Nantes
Dynamo Berlin	4–1 2–0	Jeunesse Esch
Partizan Beograd	5–1 0–0	Viking Stavanger
CSKA Sofia	3–0 1–4	Omonia Nicosia
Roma	3–0 1–2	IFK Göteborg

SECOND ROUND

Liverpool	0–0 1–0	Athletic Bilbao
Olympiakos	1–0 0–3	**Benfica**
Rába ETO Györ	3–6 1–3	**Dynamo Minsk**
Dinamo Bucuresti	3–0 2–3	Hamburger SV
Standard CL	0–0 0–4	**Dundee United**
Bohemians Praha	2–1 0–1	**SK Rapid Wien**
Dynamo Berlin	2–0 0–1	Partizan Beograd
CSKA Sofia	0–1 0–1	**Roma**

QUARTER-FINALS

Liverpool	1–0 4–1	Benfica
Dynamo Minsk	1–1 0–1	**Dinamo Bucuresti**
SK Rapid Wien	2–1 0–1	**Dundee United**
Roma	3–0 1–2	Dynamo Berlin

SEMI-FINALS

Liverpool	1–0 2–1	Dinamo Bucuresti
Dundee United	2–0 0–3	**Roma**

FINAL

Stadio Olimpico, Rome, 30–05–1984, 69 000. Referee: Fredriksson, Sweden

LIVERPOOL 1 (Neal 13)
ROMA 1 (Pruzzo 42)
Liverpool won 4–2 on penalties

Liverpool – Grobbelaar – Neal, Lawrenson, Hansen, Kennedy A – Johnston (Nicol), Lee, Souness, Whelan – Dalglish (Robinson), Rush. Tr: Fagan

Roma – Tancredi – Nappi, Bonetti, Righetti, Nela – Di Bartolomei, Falcao, Cerezo (Strukelj) – Conti, Pruzzo (Chierico), Graziani. Tr: Liedholm

Top scorer: Sokol, Dynamo Minsk ... 6

UEFA CUP

FIRST ROUND

Drogheda United	0–6 0–8	**Tottenham Hotspur**
St Mirren	0–1 0–2	**Feyenoord**
Lokomotiv Plovdiv	1–2 1–3	**PAOK Salonica**
Anorthosis Famagusta	0–1 0–10	**Bayern München**
Trabzonspor	1–0 0–2	**Internazionale**
Atlético Madrid	2–1 0–3	**FC Groningen**
Dynamo Kiev	0–0 0–1	**Stade Lavallois**
Aris Bonnevoie	0–5 0–10	**FK Austria**
Sparta Praha	3–2 1–1	Real Madrid
Widzew Lódz	0–0 2–2	IF Elfsborg Borås
VfB Stuttgart	1–1 0–1	**Levski-Spartak**
1.FC Kaiserslautern	3–1 0–3	**Watford**
Radnicki Nis	3–0 2–1	FC St Gallen
Rabat Ajax	0–10 0–6	**TJ Internacional**
Larissa	2–0 0–3	**Honvéd**
Universitatea Craiova	1–0 0–1 (1–3p)	**Hajduk Split**
Nottingham Forest	2–0 1–0	Vorwärts Frankfurt
PSV Eindhoven	4–2 2–0	Ferencváros
Sevilla	1–1 2–3	**Sporting CP**
Glasgow Celtic	1–0 4–1	ÅGF Åarhus
Girondins Bordeaux	2–3 0–4	**Lokomotive Leipzig**
Werder Bremen	1–1 2–1	Malmö FF
Hellas-Verona	1–0 3–2	Crvena Zvezda Beograd
Sportul Studentesc	1–2 0–0	**SK Sturm Graz**
Spartak Moskva	2–0 5–0	HJK Helsinki
Vitoria Guimaraes	1–0 0–5	**Aston Villa**
IBV Vestmannaeyjar	0–0 0–3	**Carl Zeiss Jena**
Sparta Rotterdam	4–0 1–1	Coleraine
AA Gent	1–1 1–2	**RC Lens**
FC Zürich	1–4 2–4	**Royal Antwerp FC**
Baník Ostrava	5–0 1–1	B 1903 Kobenhavn
Byrne IL Stavanger	0–3 1–1	**RSC Anderlecht**

SECOND ROUND

Tottenham Hotspur	4–2 2–0	Feyenoord
PAOK Salonica	0–0 0–0 (8–9p)	**Bayern München**
FC Groningen	2–0 1–5	**Internazionale**
FK Austria	2–0 3–3	Stade Lavallois
Widzew Lódz	1–0 0–3	**Sparta Praha**
Watford	1–1 3–1	Levski-Spartak
Radnicki Nis	4–0 2–3	TJ Internacional
Honvéd	3–2 0–3	**Hajduk Split**
PSV Eindhoven	1–2 0–1	**Nottingham Forest**
Sporting CP	2–0 0–5	**Glasgow Celtic**
Lokomotive Leipzig	1–0 1–1	Werder Bremen
Hellas-Verona	2–2 0–0	**SK Sturm Graz**
Spartak Moskva	2–2 2–1	Aston Villa
Sparta Rotterdam	3–2 1–1	Carl Zeiss Jena
RC Lens	2–2 3–2	Royal Antwerp FC
RSC Anderlecht	2–0 2–2	Baník Ostrava

THIRD ROUND

Bayern München	1–0 0–2	**Tottenham Hotspur**
FK Austria	2–1 1–1	Internazionale
Watford	2–3 0–4	**Sparta Praha**
Radnicki Nis	0–2 0–2	**Hajduk Split**
Nottingham Forest	0–0 2–1	Glasgow Celtic
SK Sturm Graz	2–0 0–1	Lokomotive Leipzig
Sparta Rotterdam	1–1 0–2	**Spartak Moskva**
RC Lens	1–1 0–1	**RSC Anderlecht**

QUARTER-FINALS

Tottenham Hotspur	2–0 2–2	FK Austria
Sparta Praha	1–0 0–2	**Hajduk Split**
Nottingham Forest	1–0 1–1	SK Sturm Graz
RSC Anderlecht	4–2 0–1	Spartak Moskva

SEMI-FINALS

Hajduk Split	2–1 0–1	**Tottenham Hotspur**
Nottingham Forest	2–0 0–3	**RSC Anderlecht**

FINAL

1st leg

Parc Astrid, Brussels, 9–05–1984, 35 000. Referee: Galler, Switzerland

RSC ANDERLECHT 1 (Olsen 85)
TOTTENHAM HOTSPUR 1 (Miller 57)

Anderlecht – Munaron – Grun, De Greef, Olsen, De Groot – Hofkens, Vandereycken, Scifo, Brylle – Vandenbergh (Arnesen), Czerniatynski (Vercauteren)

Tottenham – Parks – Thomas, Roberts, Hughton, Perryman – Miller, Stevens (Mabbutt), Hazard, Galvin – Archibald, Falco

2nd leg

White Hart Lane, London, 23–05–1984, 46000. Referee: Roth, West Germany

TOTTENHAM HOTSPUR 1 (Roberts 84)
RSC ANDERLECHT 1 (Czerniatynski 60)
Tottenham won 4–3 on penalties

Tottenham – Parks – Thomas, Hughton, Roberts, Miller (Ardiles) – Mabbutt (Dick), Hazard, Stevens, Galvin – Archibald, Falco

Anderlecht – Munaron – Hofkens, Grun, De Greef, Olsen, De Groot – Arnesen (Gudjohnsen), Vercauteren, Scifo – Czerniatynski (Brylle), Vandereycken

Top scorer: Nyilasi, FK Austria ... 9

CUP WINNERS CUP

PRELIMINARY ROUND

Swansea City	1–1 0–1	**1.FC Magdeburg**

FIRST ROUND

Juventus	7–0 3–2	Lechia Gdansk
Glentoran	1–2 1–2	**Paris St Germain**
Hammarby IF	4–0 1–2	17 Nëntori Tiranë
Sligo Rovers	0–1 0–3	**Haka Valkeakoski**
1.FC Magdeburg	1–5 0–2	**Barcelona**
NEC Nijmegen	1–1 1–0	SK Brann Bergen
Mersin Idman Yurdu	0–0 0–1	**Spartak Varna**
Manchester United	1–1 2–2	Dukla Praha
IA Akranes	1–2 1–1	**Aberdeen**
Union Paralimni	2–4 1–3	**SK Beveren**
Wacker Innsbruck	1–0 1–7	**1.FC Köln**
AEK Athens	2–0 1–4	**Ujpesti Dózsa**
B 1901 Nykobing	1–5 2–4	**Shachter Donetsk**

Servette FC	4–0 5–1	Avenir Beggen
Valletta	0–8 0–10	**Glasgow Rangers**
Dinamo Zagreb	2–1 0–1	**FC Porto**

SECOND ROUND

Paris Saint Germain	2–2 0–0	**Juventus**
Hammarby IF	1–1 1–2	**Haka Valkeakoski**
NEC Nijmegen	2–3 0–2	**Barcelona**
Spartak Varna	1–2 0–2	**Manchester United**
SK Beveren	0–0 1–4	**Aberdeen**
Ujpesti Dózsa	3–1 2–4	1.FC Köln
Shachter Donetsk	1–0 2–1	Servette FC
Glasgow Rangers	2–1 0–1	**FC Porto**

QUARTER-FINALS

Haka Valkeakoski	0–1 0–1	**Juventus**
Barcelona	2–0 0–3	**Manchester United**
Ujpesti Dózsa	2–0 0–3	**Aberdeen**
FC Porto	3–2 1–1	Shachter Donetsk

SEMI-FINALS

Manchester United	1–1 1–2	**Juventus**
FC Porto	1–0 1–0	Aberdeen

FINAL

St Jakobs, Basle, 16–05–1984, 60 000. Referee: Prokop, East Germany

JUVENTUS	2	(Vignola 12, Boniek 41)
FC PORTO	1	(Sousa 29)

Juventus – Tacconi – Gentile, Brio, Scirea, Cabrini – Tardelli, Bonini, Vignola (Caricola), Platini – Rossi, Boniek

Porto – Ze Beto – Joao Pinto, Lima Pereira, Enrico, Eduardo Luis (Costa) – Magalhaes (Walsh), Frasco, Pacheco, Sousa – Gomes, Vermelinho

Top scorer: McGhee, Aberdeen 5

EUROPEAN SUPERCUP 1984

Comunale, Turin, 16–01–1985. Referee: Pauly, West Germany

JUVENTUS	2	(Boniek 39 79)
LIVERPOOL	0	

1984–85

EUROPEAN CUP

FIRST ROUND

Ilves Tampere	0–4 1–2	**Juventus**
Grasshopper-Club	3–1 1–2	Honvéd
Labinoti Elbasan	0–3 0–3	**Lyngby BK**
Vålerengens Oslo	3–3 0–2	**Sparta Praha**
Trabzonspor	1–0 0–3	**Dnepr Dnepropetrovsk**
Levski-Spartak	1–1 2–2	VfB Stuttgart
Dinamo Bucuresti	4–1 1–2	Omonia Nicosia
Girondins Bordeaux	3–2 0–0	Athletic Bilbao
Feyenoord	0–0 1–2	**Panathinaikos**
Linfield	0–0 1–1	Shamrock Rovers
IA Akranes	2–2 0–5	**SK Beveren**
Avenir Beggen	0–8 0–9	**IFK Göteborg**
FK Austria	4–0 4–0	Valletta
Aberdeen	2–1 1–2 (4–5p)	**Dynamo Berlin**
Crvena Zvezda Beograd	3–2 0–2	**Benfica**
Lech Poznan	0–1 0–4	**Liverpool**

SECOND ROUND

Juventus	2–0 4–2	Grasshopper-Club
Sparta Praha	0–0 2–1	Lyngby BK
Levski-Sofia	3–1 0–2	**Dnepr Dnepropetrovsk**
Girondins Bordeaux	1–0 1–1	Dinamo Bucuresti
Panathinaikos	2–1 3–3	Linfield
IFK Göteborg	1–0 1–2	SK Beveren
Dynamo Berlin	3–3 1–2	**FK Austria**
Liverpool	3–1 0–1	Benfica

QUARTER-FINALS

Juventus	3–0 0–1	Sparta Praha
Girondins Bordeaux	1–1 1–1 (5–3p)	Dnepr Dnepropetrovsk
IFK Göteborg	0–1 2–2	**Panathinaikos**
FK Austria	1–1 1–4	**Liverpool**

SEMI-FINALS

Juventus	3–0 0–2	Girondins Bordeaux
Liverpool	4–0 1–0	Panathinaikos

FINAL

Heysel, Brussels, 29–05–1985, 58 000. Referee: Daina, Switzerland

JUVENTUS	1	(Platini 56)
LIVERPOOL	0	

Juventus – Tacconi – Favero, Cabrini, Brio, Scirea – Bonini, Platini, Tardelli – Briaschi (Prandelli), Rossi (Vignola), Boniek. Tr: Trapattoni

Liverpool – Grobbelaar – Neal, Beglin, Lawrenson (Gillespie), Hansen – Nicol, Dalglish, Whelan, Wark – Rush, Walsh (Johnston). Tr: Fagan

Top scorers:	Platini, Juventus	7
	Nilsson, IFK Göteborg	7

UEFA CUP

FIRST ROUND

Real Madrid	5–0 0–2	Wacker Innsbruck
Real Valladolid	1–0 1–4	**NK Rijeka**
Fenerbahçe	0–1 0–2	**Fiorentina**
RSC Anderlecht	1–0 1–2	**Werder Bremen**
Bohemians Praha	6–1 2–2	Apollon Limassol
Red Boys	0–0 0–14	**Ajax**
Nottingham Forest	0–0 0–1	**Club Brugge**
Sporting Braga	0–3 0–6	**Tottenham Hotspur**
1.FC Köln	2–1 1–0	Pogon Szczecin
Glentoran	1–1 0–2	**Standard CL**
Lokomotive Leipzig	7–0 0–3	Lillestrom SK
OB Odense	1–5 1–2	**Spartak Moskva**
Southampton	0–0 0–2	**Hamburger SV**
AS Monaco	2–2 1–2	**CSKA Sofia**
Bohemians Dublin	3–2 0–2	**Glasgow Rangers**
Sportul Studentesc	1–0 0–2	**Internazionale**
Sliven	1–0 1–5	**Zeljeznicar Sarajevo**
FC Sion	1–0 3–2	Atlético Madrid
Olympiakos	1–0 2–2	Neuchâtel Xamax
Real Betis	1–0 0–1 (3–5p)	**Universitatea Craiova**
Widzew Lódz	2–0 0–1	ÅGF Århus
Dukla B. Bystrica	2–3 1–4	**B. Mönchengladbach**
Sporting CP	2–0 2–2	AJ Auxerre
Dynamo Minsk	4–0 6–0	HJK Helsinki
Manchester United	3–0 2–2	Rába ETO Györ
Vorwärts Frankfurt	2–0 0–3	**PSV Eindhoven**
Östers IF Växjö	0–1 0–1	**Linzer ASK**
AIK Stockholm	1–0 0–3	**Dundee United**
Rabat Ajax	0–2 0–2	**Partizan Beograd**
KR Reykjavík	0–3 0–4	**Queens Park Rangers**
Paris St Germain	4–0 2–2	Heart of Midlothian
Videoton SC	1–0 0–0	Dukla Praha

SECOND ROUND

NK Rijeka	3–1 0–3	**Real Madrid**
Fiorentina	1–1 2–6	**RSC Anderlecht**
Ajax	1–0 0–1 (2–4p)	**Bohemians Praha**
Club Brugge	2–1 0–3	**Tottenham Hotspur**
Standard CL	0–2 1–2	**1.FC Köln**
Lokomotive Leipzig	1–1 0–2	**Spartak Moskva**
Hamburger SV	4–0 2–1	CSKA Sofia

Internazionale	3–0 1–3	Glasgow Rangers
Zeljeznicar Sarajevo	2–1 1–1	FC Sion
Universitatea Craiova	1–0 1–0	Olympiakos
Borussia Möncheng'bach	3–2 0–1	**Widzew Lódz**
Sporting CP	2–0 0–2 (3–5p)	**Dynamo Minsk**
PSV Eindhoven	0–0 0–1	**Manchester United**
Linzer ASK	1–2 1–5	**Dundee United**
Queens Park Rangers	6–2 0–4	**Partizan Beograd**
Paris Saint Germain	2–4 0–1	**Videoton SC**

THIRD ROUND

RSC Anderlecht	3–0 1–6	**Real Madrid**
Tottenham Hotspur	2–0 1–1	Bohemians Praha
Spartak Moskva	1–0 0–2	**1.FC Köln**
Hamburger SV	2–1 0–1	**Internazionale**
Universitatea Craiova	2–0 0–4	**Zeljeznicar Sarajevo**
Widzew Lódz	0–2 1–0	**Dynamo Minsk**
Manchester United	2–2 3–2	Dundee United
Videoton SC	5–0 0–2	Partizan Beograd

QUARTER–FINALS

Tottenham Hotspur	0–1 0–0	**Real Madrid**
Internazionale	1–0 3–1	1.FC Köln
Zeljeznicar Sarajevo	2–0 1–1	Dynamo Minsk
Manchester United	1–0 0–1 (4–5p)	**Videoton SC**

SEMI–FINALS

Internazionale	2–0 0–3	**Real Madrid**
Videoton SC	3–1 1–2	Zeljeznicar Sarajevo

FINAL

1st leg

Sóstói, Székesfehérvár, 8–05–1985, 30 000. Referee: Vautrot, France

VIDEOTON SC 0
REAL MADRID 3 (Michel 31, Santillana 77, Valdano 89)

Videoton – Disztl P – Borsanyi, Disztl L, Csuhay, Horvath – Palkovics, Vegh, Wittman, Vadasz – Novath (Gyenti), Burcsa

Real Madrid – Miguel Angel – Chendo, Sanchis, Stielike, Camacho – San Jose, Michel, Gallego – Butragueno (Juanito), Santillana (Salguero), Valdano

2nd leg

Bernabeu, Madrid, 22–05–1985, 90 000. Referee: Ponnet, Belgium

REAL MADRID 0
VIDEOTON SC 1 (Majer 86)

Real Madrid – Miguel Angel – Chendo, Sanchis, Stielike, Camacho – San Jose, Michel, Gallego – Butragueno, Santillana, Valdano (Juanito)

Videoton – Disztl P – Csuhay, Disztl L, Vegh, Horvath – Burcsa, Csongradi (Wittman), Vadasz – Szabo, Majer, Novath (Palkovics)

Top scorers: Bannister, Queen's Park Rangers 7
Bahtic, Zeljeznicar 7

CUP WINNERS CUP

FIRST ROUND

University College	0–0 0–1	**Everton**
TJ Internacional	2–1 0–0	Kuusysi Lahti
Wisla Kraków	4–2 3–1	IBV Vestmannaeyjar
B 1903 Kobenhavn	0–0 0–3	**Fortuna Sittard**
Roma	1–0 0–0	Steaua Bucuresti
Wrexham	1–0 3–4	FC Porto
Trakia Plovdiv	4–0 1–1	Union Luxembourg
Bayern München	4–1 2–1	Moss FK
Dynamo Moskva	1–0 5–2	Hajduk Split
Ballymena United	0–1 1–2	**Hamrun Spartans**
Apoel Nicosia	0–3 1–3	**Servette FC**
Siófoki Bányász	1–1 0–2	**Larissa**
Malmö FF	2–0 1–4	**Dynamo Dresden**
FC Metz	2–4 4–1	Barcelona
AA Gent	1–0 0–3	**Glasgow Celtic**
SK Rapid Wien	4–1 1–1	Besiktas

SECOND ROUND

TJ Internacional	0–1 0–3	**Everton**
Fortuna Sittard	2–0 1–2	Wisla Kraków
Roma	2–0 1–0	Wrexham
Bayern München	4–1 0–2	Trakia Plovdiv
Dynamo Moskva	5–0 1–0	Hamrun Spartans
Larissa	2–1 1–0	Servette FC
Dynamo Dresden	3–1 0–0	FC Metz
SK Rapid Wien	3–1 1–0	Glasgow Celtic

QUARTER-FINALS

Everton	3–0 2–0	Fortuna Sittard
Bayern München	2–0 2–1	Roma
Larissa	0–0 0–1	**Dynamo Moskva**
Dynamo Dresden	3–0 0–5	**SK Rapid Wien**

SEMI-FINALS

Bayern München	0–0 1–3	**Everton**
SK Rapid Wien	3–1 1–1	Dynamo Moskva

FINAL

Feyenoord Stadion, Rotterdam, 15–05–1985, 50 000. Referee: Casarin, Italy

EVERTON 3 (Gray 57, Steven 72, Sheedy 85)
SK RAPID WIEN 1 (Krankl 83)

Everton – Southall – Stevens, Van den Hauwe, Ratcliffe, Mountfield – Reid, Steven, Bracewell, Sheedy – Gray, Sharp

Rapid – Konsel – Lainer, Weber, Garger, Brauneder – Hrstic, Kranjcar, Kienast, Weinhofer (Panenka) – Pacult (Gross), Krankl

Top scorers: Gray, Everton 5
Panenka, Rapid Wein 5
Gazaev, Dynamo Moskva 5

1985–86

EUROPEAN CUP

FIRST ROUND

Vejle BK	1–1 1–4	**Steaua Bucuresti**
Honvéd	2–0 3–1	Shamrock Rovers
Zenit Leningrad	2–0 2–0	Vålerengens Oslo
Kuusysi Lahti	2–1 2–1	FK Sarajevo
Górnik Zabrze	1–2 1–4	**Bayern München**
Dynamo Berlin	0–2 1–2	**FK Austria**
Rabat Ajax	0–5 0–5	**Omonia Nicosia**
RSC Anderlecht	Bye	
IFK Göteborg	3–2 2–1	Trakia Plovdiv
Girondins Bordeaux	2–3 0–0	**Fenerbahçe**
Linfield	2–2 1–2	**Servette FC**
IA Akranes	1–3 1–4	**Aberdeen**
Jeunesse Esch	0–5 1–4	**Juventus**
Hellas-Verona	3–1 2–1	PAOK Salonica
FC Porto	2–0 0–0	Ajax
Sparta Praha	1–2 1–0	**Barcelona**

SECOND ROUND

Honvéd	1–0 1–4	**Steaua Bucuresti**
Zenit Leningrad	2–1 1–3	**Kuusysi Lahti**
Bayern München	4–2 3–3	FK Austria
RSC Anderlecht	1–0 3–1	Omonia Nicosia
IFK Göteborg	4–0 1–2	Fenerbahçe
Servette FC	0–0 0–1	**Aberdeen**
Hellas-Verona	0–0 0–2	**Juventus**
Barcelona	2–0 1–3	FC Porto

QUARTER-FINALS

Steaua Bucuresti	0–0 1–0	Kuusysi Lahti
Bayern München	2–1 0–2	**RSC Anderlecht**

Aberdeen .... 2–2 0–0 .... **IFK Göteborg**
Barcelona .... 1–0 1–1 .... Juventus

SEMI-FINALS
RSC Anderlecht .... 1–0 0–3 .... **Steaua Bucuresti**
IFK Göteborg .... 3–0 0–3 (4–5p) . **Barcelona**

FINAL
Sánchez Pizjuán, Sevilla, 7–05–1986, 70 000. Referee: Vautrot, France
STEAUA BUCURESTI 0
BARCELONA 0
Steaua won 2–0 on penalties
Steaua – Ducadam – Iovan, Belodedici, Bumbescu, Barbulescu – Balint, Balan (Iordanescu), Boloni, Majaru – Lacatus, Piturca (Radu). Tr: Jenei
Barcelona – Urruti – Gerardo, Migueli, Alesanco, Julio Alberto – Victor, Marcos, Schuster (Moratalla), Pedraza – Archibald (Pichi Alonso), Carrasco. Tr: Venables

Top scorer: Nilsson, IFK Göteborg 6

UEFA CUP

FIRST ROUND
AEK Athens .... 1–0 0–5 .... **Real Madrid**
Chernomorets Odessa 2–1 2–3 .... Werder Bremen
Sparta Rotterdam ... 2–0 0–2 (4–3p) . Hamburger SV
B. Mönchengladbach .... 1–1 2–0 .... Lech Poznan
Bohemians Dublin .... 2–5 2–2 .... **Dundee United**
Dinamo Bucuresti .... 2–1 0–1 .... **Vardar Skopje**
Apoel Nicosia .... 2–2 2–4 .... **Lokomotiv Sofia**
Neuchâtel Xamax .... 3–0 4–4 .... Sportul Studentesc
Valur Reykjavík .... 2–1 0–3 .... **FC Nantes**
Portimonense SC .... 1–0 0–4 .... **Partizan Beograd**
Boavista FC .... 4–3 1–3 .... **Club Brugge**
Spartak Moskva .... 1–0 3–1 .... TPS Turku
Legia Warszawa .... 3–0 1–1 .... Viking Stavanger
Videoton SC .... 1–0 2–3 .... Malmö FF
Linzer ASK .... 2–0 1–0 .... Baník Ostrava
Internazionale .... 5–1 0–0 .... FC St Gallen
KSV Waregem .... 5–2 1–0 .... ÅGF Aarhus
Glasgow Rangers .... 1–0 0–2 .... **Osasuna**
Coleraine .... 1–1 0–5 .... **Lokomotive Leipzig**
AJ Auxerre .... 3–1 0–3 .... **Milan**
Wismut Aue .... 1–3 1–2 .... **Dnepr Dnepretrovsk**
Avenir Beggen .... 0–2 0–4 .... **PSV Eindhoven**
Torino .... 2–1 1–1 .... Panathinaikos
Hajduk Split .... 5–1 2–2 .... FC Metz
Sporting CP .... 3–1 1–2 .... Feyenoord
Dinamo Tiranë .... 1–0 0–0 .... Hamrun Spartans
RFC Liège .... 1–0 3–1 .... Wacker Innsbruck
Athletic Bilbao .... 4–1 1–0 .... Besiktas
Pirin Blagoevgrad .... 1–3 0–4 .... **Hammarby IF**
Slavia Praha .... 1–0 0–3 .... **St Mirren**
Rába ETO Györ .... 3–1 1–4 .... **Bohemians Praha**
1.FC Köln .... 0–0 2–1 .... Sporting Gijón

SECOND ROUND
Real Madrid .... 2–1 0–0 .... Chernomorets Odessa
Sparta Rotterdam .... 1–1 1–5 .... **B. Mönchengladbach**
Dundee United .... 2–0 1–1 .... Vardar Skopje
Lokomotiv Sofia .... 1–1 0–0 .... **Neuchâtel Xamax**
Partizan Beograd .... 1–1 0–4 .... **FC Nantes**
Spartak Moskva .... 1–0 3–1 .... Club Brugge
Videoton .... 0–1 1–1 .... **Legia Warszawa**
Linzer ASK .... 1–0 0–4 .... **Internazionale**
KSV Waregem .... 2–0 1–2 .... Osasuna
Milan .... 2–0 1–3 .... Lokomotive Leipzig
PSV Eindhoven .... 2–2 0–1 .... **Dnepr Dnepropetrovsk**
Torino .... 1–1 1–3 .... **Hajduk Split**
Dinamo Tiranë .... 0–0 0–1 .... **Sporting CP**
RFC Liège .... 0–1 1–3 .... **Athletic Bilbao**
Hammarby IF .... 3–3 2–1 .... St Mirren
1.FC Köln .... 4–0 4–2 .... Bohemians Praha

THIRD ROUND
B. Mönchengladbach .... 5–1 0–4 .... **Real Madrid**
Dundee United .... 2–1 1–3 .... **Neuchâtel Xamax**
Spartak Moskva .... 0–1 1–1 .... **FC Nantes**
Internazionale .... 0–0 1–0 .... Legia Warszawa
KSV Waregem .... 1–1 2–1 .... Milan
Dnepr Dnepropetrovsk ...... 0–1 0–2 .... **Hajduk Split**
Athletic Bilbao .... 2–1 0–3 .... **Sporting CP**
Hammarby .... 2–1 1–3 .... **1.FC Köln**

QUARTER-FINALS
Real Madrid .... 3–0 0–2 .... Neuchâtel Xamax
Internazionale .... 3–0 3–3 .... FC Nantes
Hajduk Split .... 1–0 0–1 (4–5p) . **KSV Waregem**
Sporting CP .... 1–1 0–2 .... **1.FC Köln**

SEMI-FINALS
Internazionale .... 3–1 1–5 .... **Real Madrid**
1.FC Köln .... 4–0 3–3 .... KSV Waregem

FINAL
1st leg
Bernabeu, Madrid, 30–04–1986, 85 000. Referee: Courtney, England
REAL MADRID 5 (Sanchez 38, Gordillo 42, Valdano 51 84, Santillana 89)
1.FC KÖLN 1 (Allofs 29)
Real Madrid – Agustin – Salguero, Solana, Camacho – Martin Vazquez (Santillana), Michel, Juanito, Gordillo – Butragueno, Sanchez, Valdano
Köln – Schumacher – Geils, Gielchen, Steiner, Prestin – Geilenkirchen, Honerbach, Bein (Hässler), Janssen – Littbarski (Dickel), Allofs

2nd leg
Olympiastadion, Berlin, 6–05–1986, 15000. Referee: Valentine, Scotland
1.FC KÖLN 2 (Bein 22, Geilenkirchen 72)
REAL MADRID 0
Köln – Schumacher – Prestin, Gielchen, Geils (Schmitz) – Geilenkirchen, Steiner, Bein, Honerbach – Janssen (Pisanti), Littbarski, Allofs
Real Madrid – Agustin – Chendo, Maceda, Solana, Camacho – Michel, Gallego, Valdano, Gordillo – Butragueno (Juanito), Sanchez (Santillana)

Top scorer: Allofs, 1.FC Köln 9

CUP WINNERS CUP

FIRST ROUND
FC Utrecht .... 2–1 1–4 .... **Dynamo Kiev**
AS Monaco .... 2–0 0–3 .... **Universitatea Craiova**
Fram Reykjavík .... 3–1 0–1 .... Glentoran
SK Rapid Wien .... 5–0 1–1 .... Tatabánya Bányász
Benfica .... Bye
Larissa .... 1–1 0–1 .... **Sampdoria**
AIK Stockholm .... 8–0 5–0 .... Red Boys
AEL Limassol .... 2–2 0–4 .... **Dukla Praha**
Zurrieq .... 0–3 0–9 .... **Bayer Uerdingen**
Galatasaray .... 1–0 1–2 .... Widzew Lódz
HJK Helsinki .... 3–2 2–1 .... Flamurtari Vlorë
Cercle Brugge .... 3–2 1–2 .... **Dynamo Dresden**
Crvena Zvezda Beo. ..... 2–0 2–2 .... FC Aarau
Lyngby BK .... 1–0 3–2 .... Galway United
Fredrikstad FK .... 1–1 0–0 .... **Bangor City**
Atlético Madrid .... 1–1 2–1 .... Glasgow Celtic

SECOND ROUND
Universitatea Craiova .... 2–2 0–3 .... **Dynamo Kiev**
SK Rapid Wien .... 3–0 1–2 .... Fram Reykjavík
Benfica .... 2–0 0–1 .... Sampdoria
Dukla Praha .... 1–0 2–2 .... AIK Stockholm

Bayer Uerdingen	2–0 1–1	Galatasaray
HJK Helsinki	1–0 2–7	**Dynamo Dresden**
Lyngby BK	2–2 1–3	**Crvena Zvezda Beograd**
Bangor City	0–2 0–1	**Atlético Madrid**

QUARTER-FINALS

SK Rapid Wien	1–4 1–5	**Dynamo Kiev**
Dukla Praha	1–0 1–2	Benfica
Dynamo Dresden	2–0 3–7	**Bayer Uerdingen**
Crvena Zvezda Beograd	0–2 1–1	**Atlético Madrid**

SEMI-FINALS

Dynamo Kiev	3–0 1–1	Dukla Praha
Atlético Madrid	1–0 3–2	Bayer Uerdingen

FINAL

Stade de Gerland, Lyon, 2–05–1986, 39 000. Referee: Wöhrer, Austria

DYNAMO KIEV 3 (Zavarov 5, Blokhin 85, Yevtushenko 88)
ATLÉTICO MADRID 0

Dynamo Kiev – Chanov – Baltacha (Bal), Bessonov, Kuznetsov, Demianenko – Rats, Yakovenko, Yaremchuk, Zavarov (Yevtushenko) – Belanov, Blokhin

Atlético – Fillol – Tomas, Arteche, Ruiz, Villaverde – Prieto, Ramos, Marina, Landaburu (Setien) – Cabrera, Da Silva

Top scorers: Yaremchuk, Dynamo Kiev 6
Funkel, Bayer Uerdingen 6

EUROPEAN SUPERCUP 1986

Stade Louis II, Monte Carlo, 24–02–1987. Referee: Agnolin, Italy

STEAUA BUCURESTI 1 (Hagi 44)
DYNAMO KIEV 0

1986–87

EUROPEAN CUP

FIRST ROUND

FC Porto	9–0 1–0	Rabat Ajax
Paris St Germain	2–2 0–1	**TJ Vitkovice**
Örgryte IS	2–3 1–4	**Dynamo Berlin**
Brondbyernes IF	4–1 2–2	Honvéd
Besiktas	2–0 1–0	Dinamo Tiranë
Apoel Nicosia	1–0 2–3	HJK Helsinki
Shamrock Rovers	0–1 0–2	**Glasgow Celtic**
Beroe Stara Zagora	1–1 0–2	**Dynamo Kiev**
BSC Young Boys	1–0 0–5	**Real Madrid**
Juventus	7–0 4–0	Valur Reykjavík
Rosenborg BK	1–0 1–1	Linfield
Crvena Zvezda Beo.	3–0 1–2	Panathinaikos
RSC Anderlecht	2–0 1–1	Górnik Zabrze
Steaua Bucuresti	Bye	
Avenir Beggen	0–3 0–3	**FK Austria**
PSV Eindhoven	0–2 0–0	**Bayern München**

SECOND ROUND

TJ Vitkovice	1–0 0–3	**FC Porto**
Brondbyernes IF	2–1 1–1	Dynamo Berlin
Besiktas	W–O	Apoel Nicosia
Glasgow Celtic	1–1 1–3	**Dynamo Kiev**
Real Madrid	1–0 0–1 (3–1p)	Juventus
Rosenborg BK	0–3 1–4	**Crvena Zvezda Beograd**
RSC Anderlecht	3–0 0–1	Steaua Bucuresti
Bayern München	2–0 1–1	FK Austria

QUARTER-FINALS

FC Porto	1–0 1–1	Brondbyernes IF
Besiktas	0–5 0–2	**Dynamo Kiev**
Crvena Zvezda Beograd	4–2 0–2	**Real Madrid**
Bayern München	5–0 2–2	RSC Anderlecht

SEMI-FINALS

FC Porto	2–1 2–1	Dynamo Kiev
Bayern München	4–1 0–1	Real Madrid

FINAL

Prater, Vienna, 27–05–1987, 56 000. Referee: Ponnet, Belgium

FC PORTO 2 (Madjer 77, Juary 79)
BAYERN MUNCHEN 1 (Kogl 24)

Porto – Mlynaraczyk – Joao Pinto, Eduardo Luis, Celso, Inacio (Frasco) – Quim (Juary), Magalhaes, Madjer, Sousa, Andre – Futre. Tr: Jorge

Bayern – Pfaff – Winklhofer, Nachtweih, Eder, Pfluger – Flick (Lunde), Brehme, Matthaus, Rummenigge – Hoeness, Kogl. Tr: Lattek

Top scorer: Cvetkovic, Crvena Zvezda Beograd 7

UEFA CUP

FIRST ROUND

Sigma Olomouc	1–1 0–4	**IFK Göteborg**
Coleraine	1–1 0–1	**Stahl Brandenburg**
Sportul Studentesc	1–0 1–1	Omonia Nicosia
Jeunesse Esch	1–2 1–1	**AA Gent**
Heart of Midlothian	3–2 0–1	**Dukla Praha**
Kalmar FF	1–4 0–3	**Bayer Leverkusen**
Legia Warszawa	0–0 1–0	Dnepr Dnepretrovsk
Internazionale	2–0 1–0	AEK Athens
FC Nantes	0–4 1–1	**Torino**
Dynamo Minsk	2–4 1–0	**Rába ETO Györ**
Athletic Bilbao	2–0 0–1	1.FC Magdeburg
SK Beveren	1–0 0–0	Vålerengens Oslo
Spartak Moskva	0–0 1–0	FC Luzern
Napoli	1–0 0–1 (3–4p)	**Toulouse FC**
NK Rijeka	0–1 1–1	**Standard CL**
FC Tirol	3–0 0–2	Sredets Sofia
B. Mönchengladbach	1–0 3–1	Partizan Beograd
Pécsi MSC	1–0 0–2	**Feyenoord**
Fiorentina	1–0 0–1 (1–3p)	**Boavista FC**
Glasgow Rangers	4–0 0–2	Ilves Tampere
FC Groningen	5–1 3–1	Galway United
Neuchâtel Xamax	2–0 3–1	Lyngby BK
Atlético Madrid	2–0 1–2	Werder Bremen
Sparta Praha	1–1 1–2	**Vitória Guimaraes**
Flamurtari Vlorë	1–1 0–0	Barcelona
IA Akranes	0–9 0–6	**Sporting CP**
Linzer ASK	1–1 0–1	**Widzew Lódz**
Bayer Uerdingen	3–0 4–0	Carl Zeiss Jena
OFI Crete	1–0 0–4	**Hajduk Split**
Hibernians Paola	0–2 0–8	**Trakia Plovdiv**
Universitatea Craiova	2–0 1–2	Galatasaray
RC Lens	1–0 0–2	**Dundee United**

SECOND ROUND

IFK Göteborg	2–0 1–1	Stahl Brandenburg
Sportul Studentesc	0–3 1–1	**AA Gent**
Dukla Praha	0–0 1–1	Bayer Leverkusen
Legia Warszawa	3–2 0–1	**Internazionale**
Torino	4–0 1–1	Rába ETO Györ
SK Beveren	3–1 1–2	Athletic Bilbao
Toulouse FC	3–1 1–5	**Spartak Moskva**
FC Tirol	2–1 2–3	Standard CL
B. Mönchengladbach	5–1 2–0	Feyenoord
Glasgow Rangers	2–1 1–0	Boavista FC
FC Groningen	0–0 1–1	Neuchâtel Xamax
Vitória SC Guimaraes	2–0 0–1	Atlético Madrid
Barcelona	1–0 1–2	Sporting CP
Widzew Lódz	0–0 0–2	**Bayer Uerdingen**
Hajduk Split	3–1 2–2	Trakia Plovdiv
Dundee United	3–0 0–1	Universitatea Craiova

THIRD ROUND

AA Gent	0–1 0–4	**IFK Göteborg**
Dukla Praha	0–1 0–0	**Internazionale**
Torino	2–1 1–0	SK Beveren
Spartak Moskva	1–0 0–2	**FC Tirol**
Glasgow Rangers	1–1 0–0	**B. Mönchengladbach**
FC Groningen	1–0 0–3	**Vitória SC Guimaraes**
Bayer Uerdingen	0–2 0–2	**Barcelona**
Dundee United	2–0 0–0	Hajduk Split

QUARTER-FINALS

IFK Göteborg	0–0 1–1	Internazionale
Torino	0–0 1–2	**FC Tirol**
B. Mönchengladbach	3–0 2–2	Vitória SC Guimaraes
Dundee United	1–0 2–1	Barcelona

SEMI-FINALS

IFK Göteborg	4–1 1–0	FC Tirol
Dundee United	0–0 2–0	Borussia Mönchengladbach

FINAL

1st leg

Nya Ullevi, Gothenburg, 6–05–1987, 50 000. Referee: Kirschen, East Germany

IFK GÖTEBORG 1 (Pettersson 38)
DUNDEE UNITED 0

IFK Göteborg – Wernersson – Carlsson, Hysen, Larsson, Fredriksson – Johansson (Nilsson R), Tord Holmgren (Zetterlund), Andersson, Tommy Holmgren – Pettersson, Nilsson L

Dundee United – Thompson – Malpas, Narey, Hegarty (Clark), Holt – McInally, Kirkwood, Bowman, Bannon – Sturrock (Beaumont), Redford

2nd leg

Tannadice Park, Dundee, 20–05–1987, 21 000. Referee: Igna, Romania

DUNDEE UNITED 1 (Clark 60)
IFK GÖTEBORG 1 (Nilsson L 22)

Dundee United – Thompson – Malpas, Clark, Narey, Holt (Hegarty) – McInally, Ferguson, Kirkwood, Sturrock, Redford (Bannon), Gallacher

IFK Göteborg – Wernersson – Carlsson, Hysen, Larsson, Fredriksson – Nilsson R (Johansson), Tord Holmgren, Andersson, Tommy Holmgren (Mordt) – Pettersson, Nilsson L

Top scorers: Rantanen, IFK Göteborg 5
Houtman, FC Groningen 5
Kieft, Torino 5
Cascavel, Vitória SC Guimaraes 5

CUP WINNERS CUP

FIRST ROUND

Bursaspor	0–2 0–5	**Ajax**
Olympiakos	3–0 3–0	Union Luxembourg
17 Nëntori Tiranë	1–0 2–1	Dinamo Bucuresti
Malmö FF	6–0 1–2	Apollon Limassol
B 1903 Kobenhavn	1–0 0–2	**Vitosha Sofia**
Vasas Budapest	2–2 2–3	**Velez Mostar**
Zurrieq	0–3 0–4	**Wrexham**
Roma	2–0 0–2 (3–4p)	**Real Zaragoza**
Waterford United	1–2 0–4	**Girondins Bordeaux**
Benfica	2–0 2–1	Lillestrom SK
Haka Valkeakoski	2–2 1–3	**Torpedo Moskva**
VfB Stuttgart	1–0 0–0	Spartak Trnava
Aberdeen	2–1 0–3	**FC Sion**
Fram Reykjavík	0–3 0–1	**GKS Katowice**
SK Rapid Wien	4–3 3–3	Club Brugge
Glentoran	1–1 0–2	**Lokomotive Leipzig**

SECOND ROUND

Ajax	4–0 1–1	Olympiakos
17 Nëntori Tiranë	0–3 0–0	**Malmö FF**
Vitosha Sofia	2–0 3–4	Velez Mostar
Real Zaragoza	0–0 2–2	Wrexham
Benfica	1–1 0–1	**Girondins Bordeaux**
Torpedo Moskva	2–0 5–3	VfB Stuttgart
GKS Katowice	2–2 0–3	**FC Sion**
SK Rapid Wien	1–1 1–2	**Lokomotive Leipzig**

QUARTER-FINALS

Malmö FF	1–0 1–3	**Ajax**
Real Zaragoza	2–0 2–0	Vitosha Sofia
Girondins Bordeaux	1–0 2–3	Torpedo Moskva
Lokomotive Leipzig	2–0 0–0	FC Sion

SEMI-FINALS

Real Zaragoza	2–3 0–3	**Ajax**
Girondins Bordeaux	0–1 1–0 (5–6p)	**Lokomotive Leipzig**

FINAL

Olympiako Stadio, Athens, 13–05–1987, 35 000. Referee: Agnolin, Italy

AJAX 1 (Van Basten 21)
LOKOMOTIVE LEIPZIG 0

Ajax – Menzo – Silooy, Rijkaard, Verlaat, Boeve – Wouters, Winter, Muhren (Scholten) – Van't Schip, Van Basten, Witschge (Bergkamp)

Lokomotive – Muller – Kreer, Baum, Lindner, Zotzsche – Scholz, Liebers (Kuhn), Bredow, Marschal – Richter, Edmond (Leitzke)

Top scorer: Bosman, Ajax 8

EUROPEAN SUPERCUP 1987

1st leg

Amsterdam, 24–11–1987. Referee: Valentine, Scotland

AJAX 0
FC PORTO 1 (Rui Barros 5)

2nd leg

Das Antas, Oporto, 13–01–1988. Referee: Schmidhuber, West Germany

FC PORTO 1 (Sousa 70)
AJAX 0

1987–88

EUROPEAN CUP

FIRST ROUND

PSV Eindhoven	3–0 0–2	Galatasaray
SK Rapid Wien	6–0 1–0	Hamrun Spartans
Lillestrom SK	1–1 4–2	Linfield
Girondins Bordeaux	2–0 2–0	Dynamo Berlin
Bayern München	4–0 1–0	CFKA Sredets Sofia
Neuchâtel Xamax	5–0 1–2	Kuusysi Lahti
FC Porto	3–0 3–0	Vardar Skopje
Real Madrid	2–0 1–1	Napoli
Steaua Bucuresti	4–0 0–2	MTK-VM Budapest
Shamrock Rovers	0–1 0–0	**Omonia Nicosia**
Olympiakos	1–1 1–2	**Górnik Zabrze**
Dynamo Kiev	1–0 0–2	**Glasgow Rangers**
Malmö FF	0–1 1–1	**RSC Anderlecht**
Fram Reykjavík	0–2 0–8	**Sparta Praha**
ÅGF Åarhus	4–1 0–1	Jeunesse Esch
Benfica	4–0	Partizani Tiranë

SECOND ROUND

SK Rapid Wien	1–2 0–2	**PSV Eindhoven**
Lillestrom SK	0–0 0–1	**Girondins Bordeaux**
Neuchâtel Xamax	2–1 0–2	**Bayern München**
Real Madrid	2–1 2–1	FC Porto
Steaua Bucuresti	3–1 2–0	Omonia Nicosia
Glasgow Rangers	3–1 1–1	Górnik Zabrze
Sparta Praha	1–2 0–1	**RSC Anderlecht**
ÅGF Åarhus	0–0 0–1	**Benfica**

QUARTER-FINALS

Girondins Bordeaux	1–1 0–0	**PSV Eindhoven**
Bayern München	3–2 0–2	**Real Madrid**
Steaua Bucuresti	2–0 1–2	Glasgow Rangers
Benfica	2–0 0–1	RSC Anderlecht

SEMI-FINALS

Real Madrid	1–1 0–0	**PSV Eindhoven**
Steaua Bucuresti	0–0 0–2	**Benfica**

FINAL

Neckarstadion, Stuttgart, 25–05–1988, 55 000. Referee: Agnolin, Italy

PSV EINDHOVEN 0
BENFICA 0
PSV Eindhoven won 6–5 on penalties

PSV Eindhoven – Van Breukelen – Gerets, Van Aerle, Koeman R, Nielsen, Heintze – Vanenburg, Linskens, Lerby – Kieft, Gillhaus (Janssen). Tr: Hiddink

Benfica – Silvino – Veloso, Dito, Mozer, Alvaro – Elzo, Sheu, Chiquinho, Pacheco – Rui Aguas (Vando), Magnusson (Hajiri). Tr: Toni

Top scorers:		
	Rui Aguas, Benfica	4
	Ferreri, Bordeaux	4
	Madjer, FC Porto	4
	McCoist, Rangers	4
	Michel, Real Madrid	4
	Hagi, Steaua Bucharesti	4

UEFA CUP

FIRST ROUND

FK Austria	0–0 1–5	**Bayer Leverkusen**
Toulouse FC	5–1 1–0	Panionios
Bohemians Dublin	0–0 0–1	**Aberdeen**
Feyenoord	5–0 5–2	AC Spora
Flamurtari Vlorë	2–0 1–2	Partizan Beograd
Wismut Aue	0–0 1–1	Valur Reykjavík
Grasshopper-Club	0–4 0–1	**Dynamo Moskva**
Barcelona	2–0 0–1	OS Belenenses
Pogon Szczecin	1–1 1–3	**Hellas-Verona**
Linzer ASK	0–0 0–2	**FC Utrecht**
Brondbyernes IF	2–1 0–0	IFK Göteborg
Sportul Studentesc	1–0 2–1	GKS Katowice
Lokomotiv Sofia	3–1 0–3	**Dynamo Tbilisi**
EPA Larnaca	0–1 0–3	**Victoria Bucuresti**
Spartak Moskva	3–0 0–1	Dynamo Dresden
Mjondalen IF	0–5 1–0	**Werder Bremen**
Zenit Leningrad	2–0 0–5	**Club Brugge**
Crvena Zvezda Beo.	3–0 2–2	Trakia Plovdiv
Velez Mostar	5–0 0–3	FC Sion
Glasgow Celtic	2–1 0–2	**Borussia Dortmund**
Honvéd	1–0 0–0	KSC Lokeren
Universitatea Craiova	3–2 1–2	**GD Chaves**
Valletta	0–4 0–3	**Juventus**
Panathinaikos	2–0 2–3	AJ Auxerre
TJ Vitkovice	1–1 2–0	AIK Stockholm
Coleraine	0–1 1–3	**Dundee United**
SK Beveren	2–0 0–1	Bohemians Praha
Tatabánya Bányász	1–1 0–1	**Vitória Guimaraes**
Besiktas	0–0 1–3	**Internazionale**
TPS Turku	0–1 2–0	Admira-Wacker
Sporting Gijón	1–0 0–3	**Milan**
B. Mönchengladbach	0–1 1–4	**RCD Español**

SECOND ROUND

Toulouse FC	1–1 0–1	**Bayer Leverkusen**
Aberdeen	2–1 0–1	**Feyenoord**
Wismut Aue	1–0 0–2	**Flamurtari Vlorë**
Barcelona	2–0 0–0	Dynamo Moskva
FC Utrecht	1–1 1–2	**Hellas-Verona**
Brondbyernes IF	3–0 0–3 (0–3p)	**Sportul Studentesc**
Victoria Bucuresti	1–2 0–0	**Dynamo Tbilisi**
Spartak Moskva	4–1 2–6	**Werder Bremen**
Crvena Zvezda Beograd	3–1 0–4	**Club Brugge**
Borussia Dortmund	2–0 1–2	Velez Mostar
GD Chaves	1–2 1–3	**Honvéd**
Panathinaikos	1–0 2–3	Juventus
Dundee United	1–2 1–1	**TJ Vitkovice**
Vitória Guimaraes	1–0 0–1 (5–4p)	SK Beveren
Internazionale	0–1 2–0	TPS Turku
Milan	0–2 0–0	**RCD Español**

THIRD ROUND

Feyenoord	2–2 0–1	**Bayer Leverkusen**
Barcelona	4–1 0–1	Flamurtari Vlorë
Hellas-Verona	3–1 1–0	Sportul Studentesc
Werder Bremen	2–1 1–1	Dynamo Tbilisi
Borussia Dortmund	3–0 0–5	**Club Brugge**
Honvéd	5–2 1–5	**Panathinaikos**
Vitória SC Guimaraes	2–0 0–2 (4–5p)	**TJ Vitkovice**
Internazionale	1–1 0–1	**RCD Español**

QUARTER-FINALS

Bayer Leverkusen	0–0 1–0	Barcelona
Hellas-Verona	0–1 1–1	**Werder Bremen**
Panathinaikos	2–2 0–1	**Club Brugge**
RCD Español	2–0 0–0	TJ Vitkovice

SEMI-FINALS

Bayer Leverkusen	1–0 0–0	Werder Bremen
Club Brugge	2–0 0–3	**RCD Español**

FINAL

1st leg

Sarriá, Barcelona, 4–05–1988, 42 000. Referee: Krchnak, Czechoslovakia

ESPANOL 3 (Losada 45 56, Soler 49)
BAYER LEVERKUSEN 0

Español – N'Kono – Job, Miguel Angel, Gallart – Soler, Orejuela (Golobart), Urquiaga, Inaki – Valverde, Pichi Alonso (Lauridsen), Losada

Bayer – Vollborn – Rolff, De Kayser, Reinhardt A, Hinterberger – Cha-Bum-Kun (Gotz), Tita, Buncol, Falkenmayer (Reinhardt K) – Waas, Tauber

2nd leg

Ulrich Haberland Stadion, Leverkusen, 18–05–1988, 22000. Referee: Keizer, Holland

BAYER LEVERKUSEN 3 (Tita 57, Gotz 63, Cha-Bum-Kun 81)
ESPANOL 0
Bayer won 3–2 on penalties

Bayer – Vollborn – Rolff, Seckler, Reinhardt A, Reinhardt K – Schreier (Waas), Buncol, Falkenmayer – Cha-Bum-Kun, Gotz, Tita (Tauber)

Español – N'Kono – Miguel Angel, Golobart (Zuniga), Urquiaga – Job, Orejuela (Zubillaga), Inaki, Soler – Pichi Alonso, Losada

Top scorers:		
	Brylle, Club Brugge	6
	Saravakos, Panathinaikos	6

CUP WINNERS CUP

PRELIMINARY ROUND

AEL Limassol	0–1 1–5	**Dunajska Streda**

FIRST ROUND

KV Mechelen	1–0 2–0	Dinamo Bucuresti
St Mirren	1–0 0–0	Tromso IL
Real Sociedad	0–0 2–0	Slask Wroclaw
Dynamo Minsk	2–0 2–1	Gençlerbirligi
Sporting CP	4–0 2–4	FC Tirol
IA Akranes	0–0 0–1	**Kalmar FF**
Vitosha Sofia	1–0 1–3	**OFI Crete**
Merthyr Tydfil	2–1 0–2	**Atalanta**

Lokomotive Leipzig	0–0 0–1	**Olympique Marseille**
ÅAB Ålborg	1–0 0–1 (2–4p)	**Hajduk Split**
Vllaznia Shkodër	2–0 4–0	Sliema Wanderers
RoPS Rovaniemi	0–0 1–1	Glentoran
Dunajska Streda	2–1 1–3	**BSC Young Boys**
Ujpesti Dózsa	1–0 1–3	**FC Den Haag**
Avenir Beggen	0–5 0–3	**Hamburger SV**
Ajax	4–0 2–0	Dundalk

SECOND ROUND

KV Mechelen	0–0 2–0	St Mirren
Real Sociedad	1–1 0–0	**Dynamo Minsk**
Kalmar FF	1–0 0–5	**Sporting CP**
OFI Crete	1–0 0–2	**Atalanta**
Olympique Marseille	4–0 0–2	Hajduk Split
Vllaznia Shkodër	0–1 0–1	**RoPS Rovaniemi**
FC Den Haag	2–1 0–1	**BSC Young Boys**
Hamburger SV	0–1 0–2	**Ajax**

QUARTER-FINALS

KV Mechelen	1–0 1–1	Dynamo Minsk
Atalanta	2–0 1–1	Sporting CP
RoPS Rovaniemi	0–1 0–3	**Olympique Marseille**
BSC Young Boys	0–1 0–1	**Ajax**

SEMI-FINALS

KV Mechelen	2–1 2–1	Atalanta
Olympique Marseille	0–3 2–1	**Ajax**

FINAL

Stade de la Meinau, Strasbourg, 11–05–1988, 40 000. Referee: Pauly, West Germany

KV MECHELEN 1 (Den Boer 53)
AJAX 0

Mechelen – Preud'Homme – Clijsters, Sanders, Rutjes, Deferm – Hofkens (Theunis), Emmers, Koeman, De Wilde (Demesmeker) – Den Boer, Ohana

Ajax – Menzo – Blind, Wouters, Larsson, Verlaat (Meijer) – Van't Schip (Bergkamp), Winter, Muhren, Scholten – Bosman, Witschge

Top scorer: Cascavel, Sporting CP 6

EUROPEAN SUPERCUP 1988

1st leg

Achter de Kazerne, Mechelen, 1–02–1989. Referee: Kirschen, East Germany

KV MECHELEN 3 (Bosman 16 50, OG 17)
PSV EINDHOVEN 0

2nd leg

Philips Stadion, Eindhoven, 8–02–1989. Referee: Fredriksson, Sweden

PSV EINDHOVEN 1 (Gilhaus 78)
KV MECHELEN 0

1988–89

EUROPEAN CUP

FIRST ROUND

Vitosha Sofia	0–2 2–5	**Milan**
Dundalk	0–5 0–3	**Crvena Zvezda Beograd**
Honvéd	1–0 0–4	**Glasgow Celtic**
Dynamo Berlin	3–0 0–5	**Werder Bremen**
PSV Eindhoven	Bye	
FC Porto	3–0 0–2	HJK Helsinki
Górnik Zabrze	3–0 4–1	Jeunesse Esch
Real Madrid	3–0 1–0	Moss FK
SK Rapid Wien	2–1 0–2	**Galatasaray**
Larissa	2–1 1–2 (0–3p)	**Neuchâtel Xamax**
Club Brugge	1–0 1–2	Brondbyernes IF
Valur Reykjavík	1–0 0–2	**AS Monaco**
Pezoporikos	1–2 1–5	**IFK Göteborg**
Hamrun Spartans	2–1 0–2	**17 Nëntori Tiranë**
Spartak Moskva	2–0 1–1	Glentoran
Sparta Praha	1–5 2–2	**Steaua Bucuresti**

SECOND ROUND

Milan	1–1 1–1 (4–2p)	Crvena Zvezda Beograd
Glasgow Celtic	0–1 0–0	**Werder Bremen**
PSV Eindhoven	5–0 0–2	FC Porto
Górnik Zabrze	0–1 2–3	**Real Madrid**
Neuchâtel Xamax	3–0 0–5	**Galatasaray**
Club Brugge	1–0 1–6	**AS Monaco**
17 Nëntori Tiranë	0–3 0–1	**IFK Göteborg**
Steaua Bucuresti	3–0 2–1	Spartak Moskva

QUARTER-FINALS

Werder Bremen	0–0 0–1	**Milan**
PSV Eindhoven	1–1 1–2	**Real Madrid**
AS Monaco	0–1 1–1	**Galatasaray**
IFK Göteborg	1–0 1–5	**Steaua Bucuresti**

SEMI-FINALS

Real Madrid	1–1 0–5	**Milan**
Steaua Bucuresti	4–0 1–1	Galatasaray

FINAL

Nou Camp, Barcelona, 24–05–1989, 97 000. Referee: Tritscher, West Germany

MILAN 4 (Gullit 17 38, Van Basten 26 46)
STEAUA BUCURESTI 0

Milan – Galli G – Tassotti, Costacurta (Galli F), Baresi, Maldini – Colombo, Rijkaard, Ancelotti, Donadoni – Gullit (Virdis), Van Basten. Tr: Sacchi

Steaua – Lung – Iovan, Petrescu, Bumbescu, Ungureanu – Hagi, Stoica, Minea, Rotariu (Balaci) – Lacatus, Piturca. Tr: Iordanescu

Top scorer: Van Basten, Milan 10

UEFA CUP

FIRST ROUND

Napoli	1–0 1–1	PAOK Salonica
FC Aarau	0–3 0–4	**Lokomotive Leipzig**
IA Akranes	0–0 1–2	**Ujpesti Dózsa**
Dnepr Dnepropetrovsk	1–1 1–2	**Girondins Bordeaux**
Union Luxembourg	1–7 0–4	**RFC Liège**
SCP Montpellier	0–3 1–3	**Benfica**
AEK Athens	1–0 0–2	**Athletic Bilbao**
Otelul Galati	1–0 0–5	**Juventus**
St Patrick's Athletic	0–2 0–2	**Heart of Midlothian**
First Vienna FC	1–0 1–2	Ikast BK
Velez Mostar	1–0 5–2	Apoel Nicosia
Bayer Leverkusen	0–1 0–1	**OS Belenenses**
Internazionale	2–1 2–1	Sporting Braga
Malmö FF	2–0 1–2	Torpedo Moskva
Östers IF Växjö	2–0 0–6	**Dunajska Streda**
Bayern München	3–1 7–3	Legia Warszawa
Aberdeen	0–0 0–2	**Dynamo Dresden**
Molde FK	0–0 1–5	**KSV Waregem**
Partizan Beograd	5–0 5–0	Slavia Sofia
Roma	1–2 3–1	1.FC Nürnberg
TPS Turku	0–0 1–1	Linfield
Zalgiris Vilnius	2–0 2–5	**FK Austria**
Trakia Plovdiv	1–2 0–0	**Dynamo Minsk**
Sliema Wanderers	0–2 1–6	**Victoria Bucuresti**
Real Sociedad	2–1 2–3	Dukla Praha
Sporting CP	4–2 2–1	Ajax
Glasgow Rangers	1–0 4–2	GKS Katowice
Royal Antwerp FC	2–4 1–2	**1.FC Köln**

FC Groningen	1–0 1–2	Atlético Madrid
Servette FC	1–0 0–0	SK Sturm Graz
Besiktas	1–0 0–2	**Dinamo Zagreb**
VfB Stuttgart	2–0 1–2	Tatabánya Bányász

SECOND ROUND

Lokomotive Leipzig	1–1 0–2	**Napoli**
Ujpesti Dózsa	0–1 0–1	**Girondins Bordeaux**
RFC Liège	2–1 1–1	Benfica
Juventus	5–1 2–3	Athletic Bilbao
Heart of Midlothian	0–0 1–0	First Vienna FC
Velez Mostar	0–0 0–0 (4–3p)	OS Belenenses
Malmö FF	0–1 1–1	**Internazionale**
Bayern München	3–1 2–0	Dunajska Streda
Dynamo Dresden	4–1 1–2	KSV Waregem
Partizan Beograd	4–2 0–2	**Roma**
FK Austria	2–1 0–1	**TPS Turku**
Dynamo Minsk	2–1 0–1	Victoria Bucuresti
Sporting CP	1–2 0–0	**Real Sociedad**
1.FC Köln	2–0 1–1	Glasgow Rangers
FC Groningen	2–0 1–1	Servette FC
Dinamo Zagreb	1–3 1–1	**VfB Stuttgart**

THIRD ROUND

Girondins Bordeaux	0–1 0–0	**Napoli**
RFC Liège	0–1 0–1	**Juventus**
Heart of Midlothian	3–0 1–2	Velez Mostar
Bayern München	0–2 3–1	Internazionale
Dynamo Dresden	2–0 2–0	Roma
Victoria Bucuresti	1–0 2–3	TPS Turku
Real Sociedad	1–0 2–2	1.FC Köln
FC Groningen	1–3 0–2	**VfB Stuttgart**

QUARTER-FINALS

Juventus	2–0 0–3	**Napoli**
Heart of Midlothian	1–0 0–2	**Bayern München**
Victoria Bucuresti	1–1 0–4	**Dynamo Dresden**
VfB Stuttgart	1–0 0–1 (4–2p)	Real Sociedad

SEMI-FINALS

Napoli	2–0 2–2	Bayern München
VfB Stuttgart	1–0 1–1	Dynamo Dresden

FINAL

1st leg

San Paolo, Naples, 3–05–1989, 83 000. Referee: Germanakos, Greece

NAPOLI 2 (Maradona 68, Careca 87)
VfB STUTTGART 1 (Gaudino 17)

Napoli – Giuliani – Renica, Ferrera, Francini, Corradini (Crippa) – Alemao, Fusi, De Napoli – Careca, Maradona, Carnevale
Stuttgart – Immel – Allgower, Schmaler N, Hartmann, Buchwald – Schafer, Katanec, Sigurvinnson, Schroder – Walter (Zietsch), Gaudino

2nd leg

Neckarstadion, Stuttgart, 17–05–1989, 67 000. Referee: Sanchez Arminio, Spain

VfB STUTTGART 3 (Klinsmann 27, OG 70, Schmaler O 89)
NAPOLI 3 (Alemao 18, Ferrera 39, Careca 62)

Stuttgart – Immel – Allgower, Schmaler N, Hartmann – Schafer, Katanec, Sigurvinnson, Schroder – Walter (Schmaler O), Klinsmann, Gaudino
Napoli – Giuliani – Renica, Ferrera, Francini, Corradini – Alemao (Carranante), Fusi, De Napoli – Careca (Bigliardi), Maradona, Carnevale

Top scorers: Careca, Napoli 6
Gutschow, Dynamo Dresden 6

CUP WINNERS CUP

PRELIMINARY ROUND

Békéscaba ESSC	3–0 1–2	Byrne IL Stavanger

FIRST ROUND

Fram Reykjavík	0–2 0–5	**Barcelona**
Flamurtari Vlorë	2–3 0–1	**Lech Poznan**
Derry City	0–0 0–4	**Cardiff City**
Glenavon	1–4 1–3	**ÅGF Åarhus**
Roda JC Kerkrade	2–0 0–1	Vitória Guimaraes
Borac Banja Luka	2–0 0–4	**Metalist Kharkov**
Omonia Nicosia	0–1 0–2	**Panathinaikos**
Internacional ZTS	2–3 0–5	**CFKA Sredets Sofia**
KV Mechelen	5–0 3–1	Avenir Beggen
FC Metz	1–3 0–2	**RSC Anderlecht**
Sakaryaspor	2–0 0–1	Békéscaba ESSC
Grasshopper-Club	0–0 0–1	**Eintracht Frankfurt**
Dinamo Bucuresti	3–0 3–0	Kuusysi Lahti
Floriana	0–0 0–1	**Dundee United**
Carl Zeiss Jena	5–0 0–1	Kremser SC
IFK Norrköping	2–1 0–2	**Sampdoria**

SECOND ROUND

Barcelona	1–1 1–1 (5–4p)	Lech Poznan
Cardiff City	1–2 0–4	**ÅGF Åarhus**
Roda JC Kerkrade	1–0 0–0	Metalist Kharkov
CFKA Sredets Sofia	2–0 1–0	Panathinaikos
KV Mechelen	1–0 2–0	RSC Anderlecht
Eintracht Frankfurt	3–1 3–0	Sakaryaspor
Dundee United	0–1 1–1	**Dinamo Bucuresti**
Carl Zeiss Jena	1–1 1–3	**Sampdoria**

QUARTER-FINALS

ÅGF Åarhus	0–1 0–0	**Barcelona**
CFKA Sredets Sofia	2–1 1–2 (4–3p)	Roda JC Kerkrade
Eintracht Frankfurt	0–0 0–1	**KV Mechelen**
Dinamo Bucuresti	1–1 0–0	**Sampdoria**

SEMI-FINALS

Barcelona	4–2 2–1	CFKA Sredets Sofia
KV Mechelen	2–1 0–3	**Sampdoria**

FINAL

Wankdorf, Berne, 10–05–1989, 45 000. Referee: Courtney, England

BARCELONA 2 (Salinas 4, Recarte 79)
SAMPDORIA 0

Barcelona – Zubizarreta – Aloisio, Alesanco, Urbano – Milla (Soler), Amor, Eusebio, Roberto – Lineker, Salinas, Beguiristain (Recarte)
Sampdoria – Pagliuca – Pellegrini L (Bonomi), Mannini (Pellegrini S), Lanna, Salsano – Pari, Victor, Cerezo, Dossena – Vialli, Mancini

Top scorer: Stoichkov, CFKA Sredets Sofia 7

EUROPEAN SUPERCUP 1989

1st leg

Nou Camp, Barcelona, 23–11–1989. Referee: Quiniou, France

BARCELONA 1 (Amor 67)
MILAN 1 (Van Basten 44)

2nd leg

Giuseppe Meazza, Milan, 7–12–1989. Referee: Kohl, Austria

MILAN 1 (Evani 55)
BARCELONA 0

1989–90

EUROPEAN CUP

FIRST ROUND

Milan	4–0 1–0	HJK Helsinki
AC Spora	0–3 0–6	**Real Madrid**
Malmö FF	1–0 1–1	Internazionale

Rosenborg BK 0–0 0–5 **KV Mechelen**
PSV Eindhoven 3–0 2–0 FC Luzern
Steaua Bucuresti 4–0 1–0 Fram Reykjavík
Sliema Wanderers 1–0 0–5 **17 Nëntori Tiranë**
Glasgow Rangers 1–3 0–0 **Bayern München**
Olympique Marseille 3–0 1–1 Brondbyernes IF
Dynamo Dresden 1–0 3–5 **AEK Athens**
Sparta Praha 3–1 2–1 Fenerbahçe
Ruch Chórzow 1–1 1–5 **CSKA Sofia**
Linfield 1–2 0–1 **Dnepr Dnepropetrovsk**
FC Tirol 6–0 3–2 Omonia Nicosia
Honvéd 1–0 1–2 Vojvodina Novi Sad
Derry City 1–2 0–4 **Benfica**

SECOND ROUND

Milan 2–0 0–1 Real Madrid
Malmö FF 0–0 1–4 **KV Mechelen**
Steaua Bucuresti 1–0 1–5 **PSV Eindhoven**
Bayern München 3–1 3–0 17 Nëntori Tiranë
Olympique Marseille 2–0 1–1 AEK Athens
Sparta Praha 2–2 0–3 **CSKA Sofia**
Dnepr Dnepropetrovsk 2–0 2–2 FC Tirol
Honvéd 0–2 0–7 **Benfica**

QUARTER-FINALS

KV Mechelen 0–0 0–2 **Milan**
Bayern München 2–1 1–0 PSV Eindhoven
CSKA Sofia 0–1 1–3 **Olympique Marseille**
Benfica 1–0 3–0 Dnepr Dnepropetrovsk

SEMI-FINALS

Milan 1–0 1–2 Bayern München
Olympique Marseille 2–1 0–1 **Benfica**

FINAL

Prater, Vienna, 23–05–1990, 57 000. Referee: Kohl, Austria

MILAN 1 (Rijkaard 68)
BENFICA 0

Milan – Galli G – Tassotti, Costacurta, Baresi, Maldini – Colombo (Galli F), Rijkaard, Ancelotti (Massaro), Evani – Gullit, Van Basten. Tr: Sacchi

Benfica – Silvino – Jose Carlos, Aldair, Ricardo, Samuel – Vitor Paneira (Garcia), Valdo, Thern, Hernani – Magnusson, Pacheco (Brito). Tr: Eriksson

Top scorers: Papin, Olympique Marseille 6
Romario, PSV Eindhoven 6

UEFA CUP

PRELIMINARY ROUND

AJ Auxerre 0–1 3–1 Dinamo Zagreb

FIRST ROUND

Górnik Zabrze 0–1 2–4 **Juventus**
Kuusysi Lahti 0–0 2–3 **Paris St Germain**
Iraklis Salonica 1–0 0–2 **FC Sion**
FC Karl-Marx-Stadt 1–0 2–2 Boavista FC
FC Porto 2–0 2–1 Flacara Moreni
Valencia 3–1 1–1 Victoria Bucuresti
Apollon Limassol 0–3 1–1 **Real Zaragoza**
Örgryte IS 1–2 1–5 **Hamburger SV**
Levski Sofia 0–0 3–4 **Royal Antwerp FC**
Glentoran 1–3 0–2 **Dundee United**
Zenit Leningrad 3–1 0–0 Naestved IF
VfB Stuttgart 2–0 1–2 Feyenoord
Galatasaray 1–1 0–2 **Crvena Zvezda Beograd**
Zalgiris Vilnius 2–0 0–1 IFK Göteborg
Atalanta 0–0 0–2 **Spartak Moskva**
1.FC Köln 4–1 1–0 Plastika Nitra
Lillestrom SK 1–3 0–2 **Werder Bremen**
FK Austria 1–0 1–1 Ajax
FC Wettingen 3–0 2–0 Dundalk
Sporting CP 0–0 0–0 (3–4p) **Napoli**
Aberdeen 2–1 0–1 **SK Rapid Wien**
FC Twente Enschede 0–0 1–4 **Club Brugge**
Hibernian Edinburgh 1–0 3–0 Videoton SC
IA Akranes 0–2 1–4 **RFC Liège**
AJ Auxerre 5–0 3–0 Apolonia Fier
RoPS Rovaniemi 1–1 1–0 GKS Katowice
Valletta 1–4 0–3 **First Vienna FC**
Rad Beograd 2–1 0–2 **Olympiakos**
Dynamo Kiev 4–0 2–1 MTK-VM Budapest
Hansa Rostock 2–3 0–4 **Baník Ostrava**
FC Sochaux 7–0 5–0 Jeunesse Esch
Atlético Madrid 1–0 0–1 (1–3p) **Fiorentina**

SECOND ROUND

Paris Saint Germain 0–1 1–2 **Juventus**
FC Sion 2–1 1–4 **FC Karl-Marx-Stadt**
FC Porto 3–1 2–3 Valencia
Real Zaragoza 1–0 0–2 **Hamburger SV**
Royal Antwerp FC 4–0 2–3 Dundee United
Zenit Leningrad 0–1 0–5 **VfB Stuttgart**
Crvena Zvezda Beo. 4–1 1–0 Zalgiris Vilnius
1.FC Köln 3–1 0–0 Spartak Moskva
Werder Bremen 5–0 0–2 FK Austria
FC Wettingen 0–0 1–2 **Napoli**
Club Brugge 1–2 3–4 **SK Rapid Wien**
Hibernian Edinburgh 0–0 0–1 **RFC Liège**
RoPS Rovaniemi 0–5 0–3 **AJ Auxerre**
First Vienna FC 2–2 1–1 **Olympiakos**
Dynamo Kiev 3–0 1–1 Baník Ostrava
Fiorentina 0–0 1–1 FC Sochaux

THIRD ROUND

Juventus 2–1 1–0 FC Karl-Marx-Stadt
Hamburger SV 1–0 1–2 FC Porto
Royal Antwerp FC 1–0 1–1 VfB Stuttgart
Crvena Zvezda Beograd 2–0 0–3 **1.FC Köln**
Napoli 2–3 1–5 **Werder Bremen**
SK Rapid Wien 1–0 1–3 **RFC Liège**
Olympiakos 1–1 0–0 **AJ Auxerre**
Fiorentina 1–0 0–0 Dynamo Kiev

QUARTER-FINALS

Hamburger SV 0–2 2–1 **Juventus**
1.FC Köln 2–0 0–0 Royal Antwerp FC
RFC Liège 1–4 2–0 **Werder Bremen**
Fiorentina 1–0 1–0 AJ Auxerre

SEMI-FINALS

Juventus 3–2 0–0 1.FC Köln
Werder Bremen 1–1 0–0 **Fiorentina**

FINAL

1st leg

Comunale, Turin, 2–05–1990, 45 000. Referee: Soriano Aladren, Spain

JUVENTUS 3 (Galia 3, Casiraghi 59, De Agostini 73)
FIORENTINA 1 (Buso 10)

Juventus – Tacconi – Napoli, De Agostini, Galia, Bruno (Alessio) – Bonetti, Aleinikov, Barros, Marocchi – Casiraghi, Schillaci

Fiorentina – Landucci – Dell'Oglio, Volpecina, Pin, Battistini – Dunga, Nappi, Kubik (Malusci), Baggio – Buso, Di Chiara

2nd leg

Stadio Partenio, Avellino, 16–05–1990, 32 000. Referee: Schmidhuber, West Germany

FIORENTINA 0
JUVENTUS 0

Fiorentina – Landucci – Dell'Oglio, Volpecina, Pin, Battistini – Dunga, Nappi (Zironelli), Kubik, Baggio – Buso, Di Chiara

Juventus – Tacconi – Napoli, De Agostini, Galia, Bruno – Alessio, Aleinikov, Barros (Avallone), Marocchi – Casiraghi (Rosa), Schillaci

Top scorers:	Gotz, 1.FC Köln	6
	Riedle, Werder Bremen	6

CUP WINNERS CUP

PRELIMINARY ROUND

Chernomorets Burgas	3–1 0–4	**Dinamo Tiranë**

FIRST ROUND

SK Brann Bergen	0–2 0–1	**Sampdoria**
Besiktas	0–1 1–2	**Borussia Dortmund**
Torpedo Moskva	5–0 1–0	Cork City
Slovan Bratislava	3–0 0–4	**Grasshopper-Club**
Real Valladolid	5–0 1–0	Hamrun Spartans
Union Luxembourg	0–0 0–5	**Djurgårdens IF**
Valur Reykjavík	1–2 1–2	**Dynamo Berlin**
OS Belenenses	1–1 0–3	**AS Monaco**
Dinamo Tiranë	1–0 0–2	**Dinamo Bucuresti**
Panathinaikos	3–2 3–3	Swansea City
FC Groningen	1–0 2–1	Ikast BK
Partizan Beograd	2–1 4–5	Glasgow Celtic
Admira-Wacker	3–0 0–1	AEL Limassol
Ferencváros	5–1 1–1	Haka Valkeakoski
Barcelona	1–1 1–0	Legia Warszawa
RSC Anderlecht	6–0 4–0	Ballymena United

SECOND ROUND

Borussia Dortmund	1–1 0–2	**Sampdoria**
Torpedo Moskva	1–1 0–3	**Grasshopper-Club**
Real Valladolid	2–0 2–2	Djurgårdens IF
AS Monaco	0–0 1–1	Dynamo Berlin
Panathinaikos	0–2 1–6	**Dinamo Bucuresti**
FC Groningen	4–3 1–3	**Partizan Beograd**
Admira-Wacker	1–0 1–0	Ferencváros
RSC Anderlecht	2–0 1–2	Barcelona

QUARTER-FINALS

Sampdoria	2–0 2–1	Grasshopper-Club
Real Valladolid	0–0 0–0 (1–3p)	**AS Monaco**
Dinamo Bucuresti	2–1 2–0	Partizan Beograd
RSC Anderlecht	2–0 1–1	Admira-Wacker

SEMI-FINALS

AS Monaco	2–2 0–2	**Sampdoria**
RSC Anderlecht	1–0 1–0	Dinamo Bucuresti

FINAL

Nya Ullevi, Gothenburg, 9–05–1990, 20 000. Referee: Galler, Switzerland

SAMPDORIA 2 (Vialli 105 107)
RSC ANDERLECHT 0

Sampdoria – Pagliuca – Pellegrini L, Mannini, Vierchwood, Carboni – Pari, Katanec (Salsano), Invernizzi (Lombardo), Dossena – Vialli, Mancini

Anderlecht – De Wilde – Grun, Marchoul, Keshi, Kooiman – Vervoort, Musonda, Gudjohnson, Jankovic (Oliveira) – Degryse (Nilis), Van der Linden

Top scorer: Vialli, Sampdoria 7

EUROPEAN SUPERCUP 1990

1st leg

Luigi Ferraris, Genoa, 10–10–1990

SAMPDORIA 1 (Mikhailichenko 31)
MILAN 1 (Evani 31)

2nd leg

Giuseppe Meazza, Milan, 29–11–1990

MILAN 2 (Gullit 45, Rijkaard 76)
SAMPDORIA 0

1990–91

EUROPEAN CUP

FIRST ROUND

Crvena Zvezda Beo.	1–1 4–1	Grasshopper–Club
Valletta	0–4 0–6	**Glasgow Rangers**
Malmö FF	3–2 2–2	Besiktas
Union Luxembourg	1–3 0–3	**Dynamo Dresden**
FC Porto	5–0 8–1	Portadown
Dinamo Bucuresti	4–0 1–1	St Patrick's Athletic
KA Akureyri	1–0 0–3	**CSKA Sofia**
Apoel Nicosia	2–3 0–4	**Bayern München**
Sparta Praha	0–2 0–2	**Spartak Moskva**
Napoli	3–0 2–0	Ujpesti Dózsa
FC Tirol	5–0 2–1	Kuusysi Lahti
OB Odense	1–4 0–6	**Real Madrid**
Milan	Bye	
Lillestrom SK	1–1 0–2	**Club Brugge**
Lech Poznan	3–0 2–1	Panathinaikos
Olympique Marseille	5–1 0–0	Dinamo Tiranë

SECOND ROUND

Crvena Zvezda Beo.	3–0 1–1	Glasgow Rangers
Dynamo Dresden	1–1 1–1 (5–4p)	Malmö FF
Dinamo Bucuresti	0–0 0–4	**FC Porto**
Bayern München	4–0 3–0	CSKA Sofia
Napoli	0–0 0–0 (3–5p)	**Spartak Moskva**
Real Madrid	9–1 2–2	FC Tirol
Milan	0–0 1–0	Club Brugge
Lech Poznan	3–2 1–6	**Olympique Marseille**

QUARTER-FINALS

Crvena Zvezda Beo.	3–0 2–1	Dynamo Dresden
Bayern München	1–1 2–0	FC Porto
Spartak Moskva	0–0 3–1	Real Madrid
Milan	1–1 0–1	**Olympique Marseille**

SEMI-FINALS

Bayern München	1–2 2–2	**Crvena Zvezda Beograd**
Spartak Moskva	1–3 1–2	**Olympique Marseille**

FINAL

San Nicola, Bari, 29–05–1991, 50 000. Referee: Lanese, Italy

CRVENA ZVEZDA BEOGRAD 0
OLYMPIQUE MARSEILLE 0

Red Star – Stojanovic – Belodedici, Najdoski, Sabanadzovic, Jugovic, Marovic, Mihajlovic – Binic, Savicevic (Stosic), Prosinecki – Pancev. Tr: Petrovic

Marseille – Olmeta – Amoros, Boli, Mozer, Di Meco (Stojkovic) – Fournier (Vercruysse), Germain, Casoni, Pele – Papin, Waddle. Tr: Goethals

Red Star Belgrade won 5–3 on penalties

Top scorers:	Papin, Olympique Marseille	6
	Pacult, FC Tirol	6

UEFA CUP

FIRST ROUND

SK Rapid Wien	2–1 1–3	**Internazionale**
Aston Villa	3–1 2–1	Baník Ostrava
Lausanne-Sports	3–2 0–1	**Real Sociedad**
Hibernians Paola	0–3 0–2	**Partizan Beograd**
IFK Norrköping	0–0 1–3	**1.FC Köln**
Avenir Beggen	2–1 0–5	**Internacional ZTS**
Fenerbahçe	3–0 3–2	Vitória Guimaraes
Atalanta	0–0 1–1	Dinamo Zagreb
Zaglebie Lubin	0–1 0–1	**Bologna**
Dnepr Dnepropetrovsk	1–1 1–3	**Heart of Midlothian**
MTK-VM Budapest	1–1 1–2	**FC Luzern**

Vejle BK	0–1 0–3	**Admira-Wacker**
Derry City	0–1 0–0	**Vitesse Arnhem**
FH Hafnarfjördur	1–3 2–2	**Dundee United**
Politehnica Timisoara	2–0 0–1	Atlético Madrid
Sporting CP	1–0 2–2	KV Mechelen
Brondbyernes IF	5–0 1–4	Eintracht Frankfurt
Royal Antwerp FC	0–0 1–3	**Ferencváros**
GKS Katowice	3–0 1–0	TPS Turku
Bayer Leverkusen	1–0 1–1	FC Twente Enschede
Roda JC Kerkrade	1–3 1–3	**AS Monaco**
Chernomorets Odessa	3–1 1–2	Rosenborg BK
Sevilla	0–0 0–0 (4–3p)	PAOK Salonica
Torpedo Moskva	4–1 1–1	GAIS Göteborg
RSC Anderlecht	2–0 2–0	Petrolul Ploiesti
Slavia Sofia	2–1 2–4	**Omonia Nicosia**
Partizani Tiranë	0–1 0–1	**Universitatea Craiova**
Borussia Dortmund	2–0 2–0	Chemnitzer FC
Glenavon	0–0 0–2	**Girondins Bordeaux**
1.FC Magdeburg	0–0 1–0	RoPS Rovaniemi
Iraklis Salonica	0–0 0–2	**Valencia**
Roma	1–0 1–0	Benfica

SECOND ROUND

Aston Villa	2–0 0–3	**Internazionale**
Real Sociedad	1–0 0–1 (4–5p)	**Partizan Beograd**
1.FC Köln	0–1 2–0	Internacional ZTS
Fenerbahçe	0–1 1–4	**Atalanta**
Heart of Midlothian	3–1 0–3	**Bologna**
FC Luzern	0–1 1–1	**Admira-Wacker**
Vitesse Arnhem	1–0 4–0	Dundee United
Sporting CP	7–0 0–2	Politehnica Timisoara
Brondbyernes IF	3–0 1–0	Ferencváros
GKS Katowice	1–2 0–4	**Bayer Leverkusen**
Chernomorets Odessa	0–0 0–1	**AS Monaco**
Torpedo Moskva	3–1 1–2	Sevilla
Omonia Nicosia	1–1 0–3	**RSC Anderlecht**
Universitatea Craiova	0–3 0–1	**Borussia Dortmund**
1.FC Magdeburg	0–1 0–1	**Girondins Bordeaux**
Valencia	1–1 1–2	**Roma**

THIRD ROUND

Internazionale	3–0 1–1	Partizan Beograd
1.FC Köln	1–1 0–1	**Atalanta**
Admira-Wacker	3–0 0–3 (5–6p)	**Bologna**
Vitesse Arnhem	0–2 1–2	**Sporting CP**
Brondbyernes IF	3–0 0–0	Bayer Leverkusen
Torpedo Moskva	2–1 2–1	AS Monaco
RSC Anderlecht	1–0 1–2	Borussia Dortmund
Roma	5–0 2–0	Girondins Bordeaux

QUARTER-FINALS

Atalanta	0–0 0–2	**Internazionale**
Bologna	1–1 0–2	**Sporting CP**
Brondbyernes IF	1–0 0–1 (4–2p)	Torpedo Moskva
Roma	3–0 3–2	RSC Anderlecht

SEMI-FINALS

Sporting CP	0–0 0–2	**Internazionale**
Brondbyernes IF	0–0 1–2	**Roma**

FINAL

1st leg

Giuseppe Meazza, Milan, 8–05–1991, 75 000. Referee: Spirin, Soviet Union

INTERNAZIONALE	2	(Matthäus 55, Berti 67)
ROMA	0	

Internazionale – Zenga – Bergomi, Brehme, Battistini, Ferri – Paganin (Baresi), Bianchi, Berti, Matthäus – Klinsmann, Serena (Pizzi)
Roma – Cervone – Tempestilli, Nela, Berthold, Aldair (Carboni) – Comi (Muzzi), Gerolin, Di Mauro, Giannini – Voller, Rizzitelli

2nd leg

Stadio Olimpico, Rome, 22–05–1991, 71 000. Referee: Quiniou, France

ROMA	1	(Rizzitelli 81)
INTERNAZIONALE	0	

Roma – Cervone – Tempestilli (Salsano), Gerolin, Berthold, Aldair – Nela, Desideri (Muzzi), Di Mauro, Giannini – Völler, Rizzitelli
Internazionale – Zenga – Bergomi, Brehme, Battistini, Ferri – Paganin, Bianchi, Berti, Matthäus – Klinsmann, Pizzi (Mandorlini)

Top scorer: Völler, Roma 10

CUP WINNERS CUP

PRELIMINARY ROUND

Bray Wanderers	1–1 0–2	**Trabzonspor**

FIRST ROUND

Manchester United	2–0 1–0	Pécsi MSC
Wrexham	0–0 1–0	Lyngby BK
Glentoran	1–1 0–5	**Steaua Bucuresti**
SCP Montpellier	1–0 0–0	PSV Eindhoven
1.FC Kaiserslautern	1–0 0–2	**Sampdoria**
Olympiakos	3–1 2–0	Flamurtari Vlorë
NEA Salamis	0–2 0–3	**Aberdeen**
Legia Warszawa	3–0 3–0	Swift Hesperange
Sliven	0–2 1–6	**Juventus**
PSV Schwerin	0–2 0–0	**FK Austria**
Estrela da Amadora	1–1 1–1 (4–3p)	Neuchâtel Xamax
Viking Stavanger	0–2 0–3	**RFC Liège**
KuPS Kuopio	2–2 0–4	**Dynamo Kiev**
Sliema Wanderers	1–2 0–2	**Dukla Praha**
Fram Reykjavík	3–0 1–1	Djurgårdens IF
Trabzonspor	1–0 2–7	**Barcelona**

SECOND ROUND

Manchester United	3–0 2–0	Wrexham
SCP Montpellier	5–0 3–0	Steaua Bucuresti
Olympiakos	0–1 1–3	**Sampdoria**
Aberdeen	0–0 0–1	**Legia Warszawa**
FK Austria	0–4 0–4	**Juventus**
RFC Liège	2–0 0–1	Estrela da Amadora
Dynamo Kiev	1–0 2–2	Dukla Praha
Fram Reykjavík	1–2 0–3	**Barcelona**

QUARTER-FINALS

Manchester United	1–1 2–0	SCP Montpellier
Legia Warszawa	1–0 2–2	Sampdoria
RFC Liège	1–3 0–3	**Juventus**
Dynamo Kiev	2–3 1–1	**Barcelona**

SEMI-FINALS

Legia Warszawa	1–3 1–1	**Manchester United**
Barcelona	3–1 0–1	Juventus

FINAL

Feyenoord Stadion, Rotterdam, 15–05–1991, 42 000. Referee: Karlsson, Sweden

MANCHESTER UNITED	2	(Bruce 67, Hughes 74)
BARCELONA	1	(Koeman 79)

Manchester United – Sealey, Irwin, Bruce, Pallister, Blackmore – Phelan, Robson, Ince, Sharpe – Hughes, McClair
Barcelona – Busquets – Alexanco (Pinilla), Nando, Koeman R, Ferrer – Goikoetxea, Eusebio, Baquero, Beguiristain – Salinas, Laudrup M

Top scorer: Baggio, Juventus 9

EUROPEAN SUPERCUP 1991

Old Trafford, Manchester, 19–11–1991. Referee: Vander Ende, Holland

MANCHESTER UNITED	1	(McClair 67)
CRVENA ZVEZDA BEOGRAD	0	

1991–92

EUROPEAN CUP

FIRST ROUND

Barcelona	3–0 0–1	Hansa Rostock
1.FC Kaiserslautern	2–0 1–1	Etar V. Tirnovo
Union Luxembourg	0–5 0–5	**Olympique Marseille**
Sparta Praha	1–0 1–2	Glasgow Rangers
Hamrun Spartans	0–6 0–4	**Benfica**
Arsenal	6–1 0–1	FK Austria
Brondbyernes IF	3–0 1–2	Zaglebie Lubin
HJK Helsinki	0–1 0–3	**Dynamo Kiev**
Fram Reykjavík	2–2 0–0	**Panathinaikos**
IFK Göteborg	0–0 1–1	Flamurtari
Besiktas	1–1 1–2	**PSV Eindhoven**
RSC Anderlecht	1–1 3–0	Grasshopper–Club
Crvena Zvezda Beo.	4–0 4–0	Portadown
Universitatea Craiova	2–0 0–3	**Apollon Limassol**
Kispest-Honvéd	1–1 2–0	Dundalk
Sampdoria	5–0 2–1	Rosenborg BK

SECOND ROUND

Barcelona	2–0 1–3	1.FC Kaiserslautern
Olympique Marseille	3–2 1–2	**Sparta Praha**
Benfica	1–1 3–1	Arsenal
Dynamo Kiev	1–1 1–0	Brondbyernes IL
Panathinaikos	2–0 2–2	IFK Göteborg
PSV Eindhoven	0–0 0–2	**RSC Anderlecht**
Crvena Zvezda Beo.	3–1 2–0	Apollon Limassol
Kispest-Honved	2–1 1–3	**Sampdoria**

QUARTER-FINAL GROUPS

GROUP 1

	Sa	CZ	An	Pa	Pl	W	D	L	F	A	Pts
Sampdoria	–	2–0	2–0	1–1	6	3	2	1	10	5	8
Crvena Zvezda Beo.	1–3	–	3–2	1–0	6	3	0	3	9	10	6
Anderlecht	3–2	3–2	–	0–0	6	2	2	2	8	9	6
Panathinaikos	0–0	0–2	0–0	–	6	0	4	2	1	4	4

GROUP 2

	Ba	SP	Be	DK	Pl	W	D	L	F	A	Pts
Barcelona	–	3–2	2–1	3–0	6	4	1	1	10	4	9
Sparta Praha	1–0	–	1–1	2–1	6	2	2	2	7	7	6
Benfica	0–0	1–1	–	5–0	6	1	3	2	8	5	5
Dynamo Kiev	0–2	1–0	1–0	–	6	2	0	4	3	12	4

FINAL

Wembley, London, 20–05–1992, 71 000. Referee: Schmidhuber, Germany

BARCELONA 1 (Koeman R 112)
SAMPDORIA 0

Barcelona – Zubizarreta – Eusebio, Ferrer, Koeman R, Muñoz, Juan Carlos – Baquero, Guardiola (Alexanco), Laudrup M – Salinas (Goikoetxea), Stoichkov. Tr: Cruyff

Sampdoria – Pagliuca – Mannini, Lanna, Vierchowod, Katanec – Lombardo, Pari, Cerezo, Bonetti I (Invernizzi) – Vialli (Buso), Mancini. Tr: Boskov

Top scorer: Papin, Olympique Marseille 7

UEFA CUP

FIRST ROUND

Ajax	3–0 0–1	Örebro SK
FC Groningen	0–1 0–1	**Rot-Weiss Erfurt**
VfB Stuttgart	4–1 2–2	Pecsi MSC
Slavia Sofia	1–0 0–4	**Osasuna**
Vaci Izzo MTE	1–0 1–4	**Dynamo Moskva**
SC Salgueiros	1–0 0–1 (2–4p)	**AS Cannes**
Eintracht Frankfurt	6–1 5–0	Spora Luxembourg
AA Gent	0–1 1–0 (4–1p)	Lausanne–Sports
Liverpool	6–1 0–1	Kuusysi Lahti
Ikast FS	0–1 1–5	**AJ Auxerre**
PAOK Salonica	1–1 1–0	KV Mechelen
FC Tirol	2–1 1–1	Tromso IL
Anorthosis Famagusta	1–2 2–2	**Steaua Bucuresti**
Sporting Gijón	2–0 0–2 (3–2p)	Partizan Beograd
Sporting CP	0–0 0–2	**Dinamo Bucuresti**
Real Oviedo	1–0 1–3	**Genoa 1893**
Slovan Bratislava	1–2 1–1	**Real Madrid**
SK Sturm Graz	0–1 1–3	**FC Utrecht**
Glasgow Celtic	2–0 1–1	Germinal Ekeren
Neuchâtel Xamax	2–0 0–0	Floriana
Hamburger SV	1–1 3–0	Górnik Zabrze
CSKA Sofia	0–0 1–1	Parma
Hallescher FC	2–1 0–3	**Torpedo Moskva**
Bangor	0–3 0–3	**Sigma Olomouc**
Aberdeen	0–1 0–2	**B 1903 Kobenhavn**
Cork City	1–1 0–2	**Bayern München**
Olympique Lyon	1–0 1–1	Östers IF Växjö
HASK Gradanski	2–3 1–1	**Trabzonspor**
Vllaznia Shkoder	0–1 0–2	**AEK Athens**
MP Mikkeli	0–2 1–3	**Spartak Moskva**
Boavista FC	2–1 0–0	Internazionale
KR Reykjavík	0–2 1–6	**Torino**

SECOND ROUND

Rot–Weiss Erfurt	1–2 0–3	**Ajax**
Osasuna	0–0 3–2	VfB Stuttgart
AS Cannes	0–1 1–1	**Dynamo Moskva**
AA Gent	0–0 1–0	Eintracht Frankfurt
AJ Auxerre	2–0 0–3	**Liverpool**
PAOK Salonica	0–2 0–2	**FC Tirol**
Sporting Gijón	2–2 0–1	**Steaua Bucuresti**
Genoa 1893	3–1 2–2	Dinamo Bucuresti
FC Utrecht	1–3 0–1	**Real Madrid**
Neuchâtel Xamax	5–1 0–1	Glasgow Celtic
Hamburger SV	2–0 4–1	CSKA Sofia
Sigma Olomouc	2–0 0–0	Torpedo Moskva
B 1903 Kobenhavn	6–2 0–1	Bayern München
Olympique Lyon	3–4 1–4	**Trabzonspor**
Spartak Moscow	0–0 1–2	**AEK Athens**
Torino	2–0 0–0	Boavista FC

THIRD ROUND

Osasuna	0–1 0–1	**Ajax**
AA Gent	2–0 0–0	Dynamo Moskva
FC Tirol	0–2 0–4	**Liverpool**
Steaua Bucuresti	0–1 0–1	**Genoa 1893**
Neuchâtel Xamax	1–0 0–4	**Real Madrid**
Hamburger SV	1–2 1–4	**Sigma Olomouc**
B 1903 Kobenhavn	1–0 0–0	Trabzonspor
AEK Athens	2–2 0–1	**Torino**

QUARTER-FINALS

AA Gent	0–0 0–3	**Ajax**
Genoa 1893	2–0 2–1	Liverpool
Sigma Olomouc	1–1 0–1	**Real Madrid**
B 1903 Kobenhavn	0–2 0–1	**Torino**

SEMI-FINALS

Genoa 1893	2–3 1–1	**Ajax**
Real Madrid	2–1 0–2	**Torino**

FINAL

1st leg

Delle Alpi, Turin, 29–04–1992, 65 000. Referee: Worral, England

TORINO 2 (Casagrande 65 82)
AJAX 2 (Jonk 17, Pettersson 73)

Torino – Marchegiani – Bruno, Annoni, Cravero (Bresciani), Mussi (Sordo) – Benedetti, Scifo, Martin Vasquez, Venturin – Lentini, Casagrande

Ajax – Menzo – Silooy, Blind, Jonk, De Boer – Winter, Kreek, Bergkamp – Van't Schip, Pettersson, Roy)

2nd leg

Olympisch Stadion, Amsterdam, 13–05–1992, 42 000. Referee: Petrovic, Yugoslavia

AJAX 0
TORINO 0

Ajax – Menzo – Silooy, Blind, Jonk, De Boer – Winter, Kreek (Vink), Alflen – Van't Schip, Pettersson, Roy (Van Loen)

Torino – Marchegiani – Mussi, Cravero (Sordo), Benedetti, Fusi, Policano – Martin Vasquez, Scifo (Bresciani), Venturin – Casagrande, Lentini

Top scorer: Saunders, Liverpool 9

CUP WINNERS CUP

PRELIMINARY ROUND

SV Stockerau	0–1 0–1	**Tottenham Hotspur**
Galway United	0–3 0–4	**OB Odense**

FIRST ROUND

FC Bacau	0–6 0–5	**Werder Bremen**
Levski Sofia	2–3 1–4	**Ferencváros**
OB Odense	0–2 1–2	**Baník Ostrava**
Stahl Eisenh'stadt	1–2 0–3	**Galatasaray**
Fyllingen IL	0–1 2–7	**Atlético Madrid**
Athinaikos	0–0 0–2	**Manchester United**
GKS Katowice	2–0 1–3	Motherwell
Omonia Nicosia	0–2 0–2	**Club Brugge**
Partizani Tiranë	0–0 0–1	**Feyenoord**
Valur Reykjavík	0–1 1–1	**FC Sion**
Valletta	0–3 0–1	**FC Porto**
Hajduk Split	1–0 0–2	**Tottenham Hotspur**
CSKA Moskva	1–2 1–0	**Roma**
Glenavon	3–2 0–1	**Ilves Tampere**
IFK Norrköping	4–0 2–1	Jeunesse Esch
Swansea City	1–2 0–8	**AS Monaco**

SECOND ROUND

Werder Bremen	3–2 1–0	Ferencváros
Galatasaray	0–1 2–1	Baník Ostrava
Atlético Madrid	3–0 1–1	Manchester United
GKS Katowice	0–1 0–3	**Club Brugge**
FC Sion	0–0 0–0 (3–5p)	**Feyenoord**
Tottenham Hotspur	3–1 0–0	FC Porto
Ilves Tampere	1–1 2–5	**Roma**
IFK Norrköping	1–2 0–1	**AS Monaco**

QUARTER-FINALS

Werder Bremen	2–1 0–0	Galatasaray
Atlético Madrid	3–2 1–2	**Club Brugge**
Feyenoord	1–0 0–0	Tottenham Hotspur
Roma	0–0 0–1	**AS Monaco**

SEMI-FINALS

Club Brugge	1–0 0–2	**Werder Bremen**
AS Monaco	1–1 2–2	Feyenoord

FINAL

Estádio da Luz, Lisbon, 6–05–1992, 15 000. Referee: D'Elia, Italy

WERDER BREMEN 2 (Allofs 41, Rufer 54)
AS MONACO 0

Werder Bremen – Rollmann – Wolter (Schaaf), Borowka, Bratseth, Bode – Bockenfeld, Eilts, Votova, Neubarth – Rufer, Allofs

Monaco – Ettori – Valery (Djorkaeff), Petit, Mendy, Sonor – Dib, Gnako, Passi, Barros – Weah, Fofana (Clement)

Top scorer: Lipcsei, Ferencváros 6

OTHER EUROPEAN TOURNAMENTS

The Dr Gerö Cup

The International Cup, as it was originally known, was the brainchild of Hugo Meisl, one of the dominant personalities of inter-war European football administration. The competition brought together four of the most powerful European nations of the time, Italy, Austria, Czechoslovakia and Hungary, as well as Switzerland and in the final edition, Yugoslavia. It was ranked with the British International Championship as the most important of the regional competitions of the time ahead of the Scandinavian, Balkan and Baltic Cups.

Usually played over two years, six editions of the tournament were started, but only five finished, the 1936–37 series being cut short by the hostile political climate of the time and the annexation of Austria by Germany. Twice it was played after the Second World War, both tournaments taking a marathon five years to complete, and when the European Championship was introduced in 1958, the organisers felt that much of the justification for the tournament was gone and it was discontinued in 1960.

Honours were evenly spread over the years. Italy was the only nation to win twice, a fair reflection of its inter-war strength, whilst the Austrian 'Wunderteam' gained just recognition for its good football by winning the second series. Not unsurprisingly the great Hungarian team of the late 1940s and early 1950s won the first post-war edition from 1948–53 and it was the other Eastern bloc country, Czechoslovakia, who won the last title. Only Switzerland did not manage to win a least one tournament, and they finished last in each series.

The British International Championship

Until England and Scotland decided in 1984 that they could no longer justify playing the annual championship with Northern Ireland and Wales on the grounds of an overcrowded fixture list and dwindling interest in the matches, the Home Internationals, as they were called, were the longest running of all the world's competitions.

Started in 1884 as a natural progression from the annual friendly matches that had taken place between the four British nations, the championship was the major feature in all four nations' fixture list until after the Second World War. Organised either over the length of the season or over a week at the end of it, the highlight was the England–Scotland game, played alternately in Glasgow and London.

On two occasions the championship was used as a qualifying group for the World Cup and once for the European Championships, but other members of UEFA were unhappy that this guaranteed Britain a place, although in 1958 after these complaints, placed in four separate groups, all four qualified for the World Cup in Sweden that year! Over the years England and Scotland have totally dominated the tournament, and after 1984 carried on their annual fixture under the guise of the Rous Cup in which a country, usually from South America, was invited to make up a threesome. After repeated incidents of hooliganism between the English and the Scots, even this tournament went by the board, and in 1990, for the first time ever in peacetime, the most famous 'derby' match of them all was not played.

Other regional European tournaments

Scandinavia boasted the strongest of the remaining regional tournaments , but this too has been dropped as an ever-increasing fixture list crowded it out. Played consecutively from 1924 until 1971, each series lasted four years. Every nation played each other once a year and after having played each opponent twice at home and twice away the winner was the nation with most points. Denmark, Norway and Finland all won one edition but Sweden were easily the strongest of the four as their seven titles suggests.

The Balkan Cup, played in the 1930s and briefly revived in the 1970s, was a major factor in helping the development of the game in south-eastern Europe. Though none of the entrants were a force to be reckoned with during the 1930s, Yugoslavia, Romania and Bulgaria have all enjoyed successful spells since 1945. The Balkan Cup remains notable for affording Albania her only international honour to date.

The Baltic Championships may have remained a historical curiosity had it not been for the re-emergence of Latvia, Lithuania and Estonia as independent nations again in 1991. Played over the course of a few days in a designated city, the cup was not particularly notable as all three entrants were among the weakest nations in Europe at that time.

The Mitropa Cup

The Mitropa Cup was the most glamorous competition in Europe in the inter-war years and was the forerunner of today's European club competitions. The idea to have clubs from different countries playing a knock-out cup had been touted for some years and Hugo Meisl, as well as launching the International Cup for national sides, launched the Mitropa Cup the same year. Mitropa is a shortened form of Mittel Europa, meaning middle Europe, and entry was restricted to Italy, Austria, Hungary, Czechoslovakia, Switzerland and occasionally Romania and Yugoslavia. Initially only the champion team of each country was allowed to enter but this was increased to the top two, and at one point, the top four.

The Mitropa Cup was suspended after 1939 and did not get underway again properly until 1955, but with the new European Cup, it lost much of its significance. None of the best sides were ever entered and in 1980 entry was restricted to the second division champions of the participating countries.

At its height in the inter-war years, the Mitropa Cup drew large crowds and sealed the reputations of many teams. The possibility of taking part certainly helped spice up club football in the area. Large fees were paid for players in a bid to win the tournament, especially by the Italian clubs, who apart from Bologna, were surprisingly unsuccessful. Instead it was the cities of Prague, Budapest and Vienna who stole the honours winning all of the titles except for the two won by Bologna. Slavia and Sparta Prague won three titles between them, Ferencváros and Ujpesti Budapest won two apiece whilst Vienna clubs won the other four titles.

The Latin Cup

Played between the champions of Spain, Italy, Portugal and France, the Latin Cup replaced the Mitropa Cup as the top club competition in the immediate post-war period, but it too suffered at the hands of the new UEFA-sponsored tournaments and was discontinued in 1957. Played in a single city every year, the tournament was curious in that there was not a cup presentation at the end of each edition. Instead, four points were awarded to the winners down to one for the fourth-placed team, and after four years the cup itself was awarded to the country with the highest number of combined points.

THE DR GERÖ/ INTERNATIONAL CUP

1927–29	Italy
1931–32	Austria
1933–35	Italy
1936–37	–
1948–53	Hungary
1955–60	Czechoslovakia

FIRST EDITION 1927–30

	It	Au	Cz	Hu	Sz	Pl	W	D	L	F	A	Pts
ITALY	–	0–1	4–2	4–3	3–2	8	5	1	2	21	15	11
Austria	3–0	–	0–1	5–1	2–0	8	5	0	3	17	10	10
Czechoslovakia	2–2	2–0	–	1–1	5–0	8	4	2	2	17	10	10
Hungary	0–5	5–3	2–0	–	3–1	8	4	1	3	20	23	9
Switzerland	2–3	1–3	1–4	4–5	–	8	0	0	8	11	28	0

Decisive match. Ulloi ut, Budapest, 11–05–1930, 40 000

HUNGARY 0

ITALY 5 (Meazza 17, 65, 70, Magnozzi 72, Costantino 84)

Hungary – Aknai – Korányi, Fogl – Borsányi, Turay, Vig – Markos, Takács, Opata, Hirzer, Titkos

Italy – Combi – Monzeglio, Caligaris – Colombari, Ferraris, Pitto – Costantino, Baloncieri, Meazza, Magnozzi, Orsi

Champions: Italy

SECOND EDITION 1931–32

	Au	It	Hu	Cz	Sz	Pl	W	D	L	F	A	Pts
AUSTRIA	–	2–1	0–0	2–1	3–1	8	4	3	1	19	9	11
Italy	2–1	–	3–2	2–2	3–0	8	3	3	2	14	11	9
Hungary	2–2	1–1	–	2–1	6–2	8	2	4	2	17	15	8
Czechoslovakia	1–1	2–1	3–3	–	7–3	8	2	3	3	18	19	7
Switzerland	1–8	1–1	3–1	5–1	–	8	2	1	5	16	30	5

Decisive game. Prater, Vienna, 20–03–1932, 63 000

AUSTRIA 2 (Sindelar 56, 58)

ITALY 1 (Meazza 66)

Austria – Hiden – Schramseis, Blum – Mock, Hoffmann, Nausch – Zischek, Gschweidl, Sindelar, Müller, Vogel
Italy – Sclavi – Rosetta, Allemandi – Pitto, Ferraris, Bertolini – Costantino, Sansone, Meazza, Magnozzi, Orsi

Champions: Austria

THIRD EDITION 1933–35

	It	Au	Hu	Cz	Sz	Pl	W	D	L	F	A	Pts
ITALY	–	2–4	2–2	2–0	5–2	8	5	1	2	18	10	11
Austria	0–2	–	4–4	2–2	3–0	8	3	3	2	17	15	9
Hungary	0–1	3–1	–	1–0	3–0	8	3	3	2	17	16	9
Czechoslovakia	2–1	0–0	2–2	–	3–1	8	2	4	2	11	11	8
Switzerland	0–3	2–3	6–2	2–2	–	8	1	1	6	13	24	3

Decisive game. Prater, Vienna, 24–03–1935, 60 000
AUSTRIA 0
ITALY 2 (Piola 51, 81)
Austria – Platzer – Pavlicek, Sesta – Wagner, Smistik, Skoumal – Zischek, Gschweidl, Sindelar, Kaburek, Pesser
Italy – Ceresoli – Monzeglio, Mascheroni – Pitto, Faccio, Corsi – Guaita, Demaria, Piola, Ferrari Giovanni, Orsi

Champions: Italy

FOURTH EDITION 1936–37, UNFINISHED

	Hu	It	Cz	Au	Sz	Pl	W	D	L	F	A	Pts
Hungary	–	–	8–3	5–3	2–0	7	5	0	2	24	15	10
Italy	2–0	–	–	–	4–2	4	3	1	0	9	4	7
Czechoslovakia	5–2	0–1	–	2–1	5–3	7	3	1	3	16	20	7
Austria	1–2	–	1–1	–	4–3	6	2	1	3	13	14	5
Switzerland	1–5	2–2	4–0	1–3	–	8	1	1	6	16	25	3

FIFTH EDITION 1948–1953

	Hu	Cz	Au	It	Sz	Pl	W	D	L	F	A	Pts
HUNGARY	–	2–1	6–1	1–1	7–4	8	5	1	2	27	17	11
Czechoslovakia	5–2	–	3–1	2–0	5–0	8	4	1	3	18	12	9
Austria	3–2	3–1	–	1–0	3–3	8	3	1	4	15	19	9
Italy	0–3	3–0	3–1	–	2–0	8	3	2	2	10	9	8
Switzerland	2–4	1–1	1–2	1–1	–	8	1	3	4	12	25	3

Decisive match. Ulloi ut, Budapest, 23–05–1948, 37 000
HUNGARY 2 (Egresi, Deák)
CZECHOSLOVAKIA 1 (Subert)
Hungary – Henni – Rudas, Nagy – Balogh, Kovács (Kéri), Nagymarosi – Egresi, Szusza, Deák, Puskás, Tóth
Czechoslovakia – Havlícek (Capek) – Senecky, Vedral – Pokorny, Marko, Karel – Kokstein, Rygr, Malatinsky, Subert, Klimek

Champions: Hungary

SIXTH EDITION 1955–60

	Cz	Hu	Au	Yu	It	Sz	Pl	W	D	L	F	A	Pts
CZECHOSLOV.	–	1–3	3–2	1–0	2–1	3–2	10	7	2	1	25	15	16
Hungary	2–4	–	6–1	2–2	2–0	8–0	10	6	3	1	34	16	15
Austria	2–2	2–2	–	2–1	3–2	4–0	10	4	3	3	21	21	11
Yugoslavia	1–2	1–3	1–1	–	6–1	0–0	10	3	3	4	21	13	9
Italy	1–1	1–1	2–1	0–4	–	3–0	10	2	3	5	12	21	7
Switzerland	1–6	4–5	2–3	1–5	1–1	–	10	0	2	8	11	38	2

Decisive match. Nep, Budapest, 20–05–1956, 90 000
HUNGARY 2 (Machos 32, Bozsik 65)
CZECHOSLOVAKIA 4 (Feureisl 8, Moravcík 27 55 Pazdera 75)
Hungary – Gellér – Kárpáti, Kotász, Szojka – Teleki, Bozsik – Budai (Tichy), Kocsis, Machos, Hidegkuti, Fenyvesi
Czechoslovakia – Dolejsí – Hertl, Hledik, Novík – Pluskal, Masopust – Pazdera, Moravcík, Feureisl (Práda), Borovicka, Kraus

Champions: Czechoslovakia

THE MITROPA CUP

1927	Sparta Praha	TCH	6–2 1–2	Rapid Wien	AUT
1928	Ferencváros	HUN	7–1 3–5	Rapid Wien	AUT
1929	Ujpesti Dózsa	HUN	5–1 2–2	Slavia Praha	TCH
1930	Rapid Wien	AUT	2–0 2–3	Sparta Praha	TCH
1931	First Vienna	AUT	3–2 2–1	Wien AC	AUT
1932	Bologna	ITA	Walk–over		
1933	FK Austria	AUT	1–2 3–1	Ambrosiana–Inter	ITA
1934	Bologna	ITA	2–3 5–1	Admira Wien	AUT
1935	Sparta Praha	TCH	1–2 3–0	Ferencváros	HUN
1936	FK Austria	AUT	0–0 1–0	Sparta Praha	TCH
1937	Ferencváros	HUN	4–2 5–4	Lazio	ITA
1938	Slavia Praha	TCH	2–2 2–0	Ferencváros	HUN
1939	Ujpesti Dózsa	HUN	4–1 2–2	Ferencváros	HUN
1940–50 – *No competition*					
1951	Rapid Wien	AUT	3–2	Wacker Wien	AUT
1952–54 – *No competition*					
1955	Voros Lobogo	HUN	6–0 2–1	UDA Prague	TCH
1956	Vasas Budapest	HUN	3–3 1–1 9–2	Rapid Wien	AUT
1957	Vasas Budapest	HUN	4–0 1–2	Vojvodina	YUG
1958 – *No competition*					
1959	Honved	HUN	4–3 2–1	MTK Budapest	HUN
1960	Hungary (Ujpest Dozsa, Ferencvaros, MTK and Vasas)				
1961	Bologna	ITA	2–2 3–0	Slovan Nitra	TCH
1962	Vasas Budapest	HUN	5–1 1–2	Bologna	ITA
1963	MTK Budapest	HUN	2–1 1–1	Vasas Budapest	HUN
1964	Spartak Sokolovo	TCH	0–0 2–0	Slovan Bratislava	TCH
1965	Vasas Budapest	HUN	1–0	Fiorentina	ITA
1966	Fiorentina	ITA	1–0	Jednota Trencin	TCH
1967	Spartak Trnava	HUN	2–3 3–1	Ujpesti Dózsa	HUN
1968	Crvena Zvezda	YUG	0–1 4–1	Spartak Trnava	TCH
1969	TJ Internacional	TCH	4–1 0–0	Union Teplice	TCH
1970	Vasas Budapest	HUN	1–2 4–1	Internazionale	ITA
1971	Celik Zenica	YUG	3–1	Austria Salzburg	AUT
1972	Celik Zenica	YUG	0–0 1–0	Fiorentina	ITA
1973	Tatabanya Banyasz	HUN	2–1 2–1	Celik Zenica	YUG
1974	Tatabanya Banyasz	HUN	3–2 2–0	Jednota Zilina	TCH
1975	Wacker Innsbruck	AUT	3–1 2–1	Honved	HUN
1976	Wacker Innsbruck	AUT	3–1 3–1	Velez Mostar	YUG
1977	Vojvodina	YUG			
1978	Partizan Beograd	YUG	1–0	Honved	HUN
1979 – *No competition*					
1980	Udinese	ITA			
1981	Tatran Presov	TCH			
1982	Milan	ITA			
1983	Vasas Budapest	HUN			
1984	SC Eisenstadt	AUT			
1985	Iskra Bugojno	YUG			
1986	Pisa	ITA			
1987	Ascoli	ITA			
1988	Pisa	ITA			
1989	Baník Ostrava	TCH			
1990	Bari	ITA			
1991	Torino	ITA			

1927 FIRST ROUND

Sparta Praha	5–1 3–5	Admira Wien
Hungária	4–2 4–0	BSK Beograd
Slavia Praha	4–0 2–2	Ujpesti Dózsa
Rapid Wien	8–1 1–0	Hajduk Split

SEMI–FINALS

Hungária	2–2 0–0	Sparta Praha
Slavia Praha	2–2 1–2	Rapid Wien

FINAL

Sparta Praha	6–2 1–2	Rapid Wien

Sparta – Hochmann – Burger, Perner – Kolenaty, Kada, Hajny – Patek, Sima, Miclik, Sylny, Horeja

1928 FIRST ROUND

BSK Beograd .... 0–7 1–6 .... Ferencváros
Admira Wien .... 3–1 3–3 .... Slavia Praha
Gradjanski Zagreb ...... 3–2 1–6 .... Viktoria Zizkov
Rapid Wien .... 6–4 1–0 .... Hungária

SEMI-FINALS

Admira Wien .... 1–2 0–1 .... Ferencváros
Viktoria Zizkov .... 4–3 2–3 1–3 .... Rapid Wien

FINAL

Ferencváros 7–1 3–5 Rapid Wien

Ferencváros – Amsel – Takács I, Hungler – Lyka, Bukovi, Berkessi – Rászó, Takács II, Turay, Sedlaczek, Kohuth

1929 FIRST ROUND

Ujpesti Dózsa .... 6–1 0–2 .... Sparta Praha
Rapid Wien .... 5–1 0–0 .... Genoa
Hungária .... 1–4 1–2 .... First Vienna
Juventus .... 1–0 0–3 .... Slavia Praha

SEMI-FINAL

Ujpesti Dózsa .... 2–1 2–3 3–1 .... Rapid Wien
First Vienna .... 3–2 2–4 .... Slavia Praha

FINAL

Ujpesti Dózsa .... 5–1 2–2 .... Slavia Praha

Ujpesti Dózsa – Acht – Kövágó, Fogl III – Borsányi, Köves, Wilhelm – Ströck, Auer, Meszaros, Spitz, Szabó

1930 FIRST ROUND

Genoa .... 1–1 1–6 .... Rapid Wien
Slavia Praha .... 2–2 0–1 .... Ferencváros
Ujpesti Dózsa .... 2–4 4–2 1–1 3–5 .... Ambrosiana–Inter
Sparta Praha .... 2–1 3–2 .... First Vienna

SEMI-FINALS

Rapid Wien .... 5–1 0–1 .... Ferencváros
Ambrosiana–Inter .... 2–2 1–6 .... Sparta Praha

FINAL

Sparta Praha .... 0–2 3–2 .... Rapid Wien

Rapid Wien – Bugala – Schramseis, Cejka – Rappan, Smistik, Wana – Kirbes, Wesselik, Kaburek, Luef, Wessely

1931 FIRST ROUND

First Vienna .... 3–0 4–0 .... Bocskai Debrecen
Slavia Praha .... 2–2 1–2 .... Roma
Juventus .... 2–1 0–1 2–3 .... Sparta Praha
Hungária .... 1–5 3–1 .... Wien AC

SEMI–FINALS

Roma .... 2–3 1–2 .... First Vienna
Wien AC .... 2–3 4–3 2–0 .... Sparta Praha

FINAL

First Vienna .... 3–2 2–1 .... Wien AC

First Vienna – Horeschofsky – Rainer, Blum – Schmaus, Hoffmann, Machu – Brosenbauer, Adelbrecht, Gschweidl, Togel, Erdl

1932 FIRST ROUND

Bologna .... 5–0 0–3 .... Sparta Praha
First Vienna .... 5–3 1–1 .... Ujpesti Dózsa
Juventus .... 4–0 3–3 .... Ferencváros
Slavia Praha .... 3–0 0–1 .... Admira Wien

SEMI-FINALS

Bologna .... 2–0 0–1 .... First Vienna
Slavia Praha .... 4–0 0–2 * .... Juventus

* Both teams disqualified. Bologna were declared tournament winners

Bologna – Gianni – Monzeglio, Gasperi – Montesanto, Baldi, Martelli – Maini, Sansone, Schiavio, Fedullo, Reguzzoni

1933 FIRST ROUND

Slavia Praha .... 3–1 0–3 .... FK Austria
Ujpesti Dózsa .... 2–1 2–6 .... Juventus
Hungária .... 2–3 1–2 .... Sparta Praha
First Vienna .... 1–0 0–4 .... Ambrosiana-Inter

SEMI-FINALS

FK Austria .... 3–0 1–1 .... Juventus
Ambrosiana-Inter .... 4–1 2–2 .... Sparta Praha

FINAL

Ambrosiana-Inter .... 2–1 1–3 .... FK Austria

FK Austria – Billich – Graf, Nausch – Majemnik, Mock, Gall – Milzer, Stroh, Sindelar, Jerusalem, Viertl

1934 FIRST ROUND

Bologna .... 2–0 1–2 .... Bocskai Debrecen
Slavia Praha .... 1–3 1–1 .... Rapid Wien
SK Kladno .... 1–1 3–2 .... Ambrosiana-Inter
Ferencváros .... 8–0 2–1 .... Floridsdorfer AC
Juventus .... 4–2 1–0 .... Teplice FK
FK Austria .... 1–2 1–2 .... Ujpesti Dózsa
Hungária .... 4–5 2–1 2–5 .... Sparta Praha
2–1 1–2 1–1*
Admira Wien .... 0–0 2–2 5–0 .... Napoli

* Sparta qualified on lots

QUARTER-FINALS

Bologna .... 6–1 1–4 .... Rapid Wien
Ferencváros .... 6–0 1–4 .... SK Kladno
Ujpesti Dózsa .... 1–3 1–1 .... Juventus
Admira Wien .... 4–0 2–3 .... Sparta Praha

SEMI-FINALS

Ferencváros .... 1–1 1–5 .... Bologna
Admira Wien .... 3–1 1–2 .... Juventus

FINAL

Admira Wien .... 3–2 1–5 .... Bologna

Bologna – Gianni – Monzeglio, Gasperi – Montesanto, Donati, Corsi – Maini, Sansone, Schiavio, Fedullo, Reguzzoni

1935 FIRST ROUND

First Vienna .... 1–1 3–5 .... Sparta Praha
Ujpesti Dózsa .... 0–2 3–4 .... Fiorentina
Admira Wien .... 3–2 1–7 .... Hungária
Viktoria Plzen .... 3–3 1–5 .... Juventus
Ambrosiana-Inter .... 2–5 1–3 .... FK Austria
Bástya Szeged .... 1–4 0–1 .... Slavia Praha
SK Zidenice .... 3–2 2–2 .... Rapid Wien
Roma .... 3–1 0–8 .... Ferencváros

QUARTER-FINALS

Sparta Praha .... 7–1 1–3 .... Fiorentina
Hungária .... 1–3 1–1 .... Juventus
Slavia Praha .... 1–0 1–2 2–5 .... FK Austria
SK Zidenice .... 4–2 1–6 .... Ferencváros

SEMI–FINALS

Sparta Praha .... 2–0 1–3 5–1 .... Juventus
Ferencváros .... 4–2 2–3 .... FK Austria

FINAL

Ferencváros .... 2–1 0–3 .... Sparta Praha

Sparta – Klenovec – Burger, Ctyrocky – Kostalek, Boucek, Srbk – Faszinek, Zajicek, Braine, Nejedly, Kalocsai

1936 QUALIFYING ROUND

SK Zidenice .... 5–0 1–2 .... Lausanne-Sports
BSC Young Boys .... 1–4 1–7 .... Torino
FK Austria .... 3–1 1–1 .... Grasshopper-Club
Young Fellows .... 0–3 2–6 .... Phoebus Budapest

FIRST ROUND

Bologna .... 2–1 0–4 .... FK Austria
Ferencváros .... 5–2 0–4 .... Slavia Praha
Admira Wien .... 0–4 3–2 .... SK Prostejov
Torino .... 2–0 0–5 .... Ujpesti Dózsa
SK Zidenice .... 2–3 1–8 .... Ambrosiana-Inter
Hungária .... 0–2 1–5 .... First Vienna
Rapid Wien .... 3–1 1–5 .... Roma
Sparta Praha .... 5–2 2–4 .... Phoebus Budapest

QUARTER-FINALS

FK Austria .... 3–0 0–1 .... Slavia Praha
SK Prostejov .... 0–1 0–2 .... Ujpesti Dózsa
First Vienna .... 2–0 1–4 .... Ambrosiana-Inter
Sparta Praha .... 3–0 1–1 .... Roma

SEMI-FINALS

Ujpesti Dózsa .... 1–2 2–5 .... FK Austria
Ambrosiana–Inter .... 3–5 2–3 .... Sparta Praha

FINAL

FK Austria .... 0–0 1–0 .... Sparta Praha
FK Austria – Zohrer – Andritz, Seszta – Adamek, Mock, Nausch – Riegler, Stroh, Sindelar, Jerusalem, Viertl

1937 FIRST ROUND

Slavia Praha .... 2–2 1–3 .... Ferencváros
First Vienna .... 2–1 0–1 2–0 .... Young Fellows
Venus Bucuresti .... 4–6 1–4 .... Ujpesti Dózsa
Bologna .... 1–2 1–5 .... FK Austria
Admira Wien .... 1–1 2–2 2–0 .... Sparta Praha
Genoa .... 3–1 3–0 .... Gradjanski Zagreb
Grasshopper-Club .... 4–3 2–2 .... SK Prostejov
Hungária .... 1–1 2–3 .... Lazio

QUARTER-FINALS

Ferencváros .... 2–1 0–1 2–1 .... First Vienna
FK Austria .... 5–4 2–1 .... Ujpesti Dózsa
Admira Wien .... 2–2 * .... Genoa
Lazio .... 6–1 2–3 .... Grasshopper–Club
* Both teams disqualified

SEMI-FINALS

FK Austria .... 4–1 1–6 .... Ferencváros
Lazio .... Bye

FINAL

Ferencváros .... 4–2 5–4 .... Lazio
Ferencváros – Háda – Tátrai, Korányi I – Magda, Polgár, Szekely – Tänzer, Kiss, Sárosi, Toldi, Kemény

1938 FIRST ROUND

SK Beograd .... 2–3 1–2 .... Slavia Praha
Ambrosiana-Inter .... 4–2 1–1 .... Kispest AC
Ujpesti Dózsa .... 4–1 0–4 .... Rapid Bucuresti
Genoa .... 4–2 1–1 .... Sparta Praha
Hungária .... 3–3 1–6 .... Juventus
SK Kladno .... 3–1 1–2 .... HASK Zagreb
Ripensia Timisoara .... 3–0 1–3 .... Milan
SK Zidenice .... 3–1 0–3 .... Ferencváros

QUARTER-FINALS

Slavia Praha .... 9–0 1–3 .... Ambrosiana-Inter
Genoa .... 3–0 1–2 .... Rapid Bucharest
Juventus .... 4–2 2–1 .... SK Kladno
Ripensia Timisoara .... 4–5 1–4 .... Ferencváros

SEMI-FINALS

Genoa .... 4–2 0–4 .... Slavia Praha
Juventus .... 3–2 0–2 .... Ferencváros

FINAL

Slavia Praha .... 2–2 2–0 .... Ferencváros
Slavia – Boskai – Cerny, Daucik I – Prucha, Daucik II, Kopecky – Horak, Simonek, Bican, Bradac, Vytlacil

1939 FIRST ROUND

Ambrosiana-Inter .... 2–1 1–3 .... Ujpesti Dózsa
SK Beograd .... 3–0 1–2 .... Slavia Praha
Venus Bucuresti .... 1–1 0–5 .... Bologna
Ferencváros .... 2–3 2–0 .... Sparta Praha

SEMI-FINALS

SK Beograd .... 4–2 1–7 .... Ujpesti Dózsa
Bologna .... 3–1 1–4 .... Ferencváros

FINAL

Ferencváros .... 1–4 2–2 .... Ujpesti Dózsa
Ujpesti Dózsa – Sziklai – Futó, Fekete – Szalay, Szücs, Balogh I – Adám, Vincze, Kállai, Zsengellér, Kocsis

THE LATIN CUP

1949	Barcelona	ESP	2–1	Sporting CP	POR
1950	Benfica	POR	3–3 2–1	Bordeaux	FRA
1951	Milan	ITA	5–0	OSC Lille	FRA
1952	Barcelona	ESP	1–0	OGC Nice	FRA
1953	Stade de Reims	FRA	3–0	Milan	ITA
1954	*– No competition*				
1955	Real Madrid	ESP	2–0	Stade de Reims	FRA
1956	Milan	ITA	2–1	Athletic Bilbao	ESP
1957	Real Madrid	ESP	1–0	Benfica	POR

1949 Held in Barcelona

FIRST ROUND

Sporting CP .... 3–1 .... Torino
Barcelona .... 5–0 .... Stade de Reims

3rd PLACE

Torino .... 5–3 .... Stade de Reims

FINAL

Barcelona .... 2–1 .... Sporting CP

1950 Held in Lisbon

FIRST ROUND

Bordeaux .... 4–2 .... Atlético Madrid
Benfica .... 3–0 .... Lazio

3rd PLACE

Atlético Madrid .... 2–1 .... Lazio

FINAL

Benfica .... 3–3 2–1 .... Bordeaux

1951 Held in Milan

FIRST ROUND

Milan .... 4–1 .... Atlético Madrid
OSC Lille .... 1–1 6–4 .... Sporting CP

3rd PLACE

Atlético Madrid .... 3–1 .... Sporting CP

FINAL

Milan .... 5–0 .... OSC Lille

1952 Held in Paris

FIRST ROUND
Barcelona .... 4–2 .... Juventus
OGC Nice .... 4–2 .... Sporting CP

3rd PLACE
Juventus .... 3–2 .... Sporting CP

FINAL
Barcelona .... 1–0 .... OGC Nice

The standings at the end of the first edition of the Latin Cup (1949–52) were:
1 Spain 12
2 France 10
3 Italy 9
Portugal 9

1953 Held in Lisbon

FIRST ROUND
Stade de Reims .... 2–1 .... Valencia
Milan .... 4–2 .... Sporting CP

3rd PLACE
Sporting CP .... 4–1 .... Valencia

FINAL
Stade de Reims .... 3–0 .... Milan

1955 Held in Paris

FIRST ROUND
Real Madrid .... 2–0 .... OS Belenenses
Stade de Reims .... 3–2 .... Milan

3rd PLACE
Milan .... 3–1 .... OS Belenenses

FINAL
Real Madrid .... 2–0 .... Stade de Reims

1956 Held in Milan

FIRST ROUND
Milan .... 4–2 .... Benfica
Athletic Bilbao .... 2–0 .... OGC Nice

3rd PLACE
Benfica .... 2–1 .... OGC Nice

FINAL
Milan .... 2–1 .... Athletic Bilbao

1957 Held in Madrid

FIRST ROUND
Real Madrid .... 5–1 .... Milan
Benfica .... 1–0 .... AS Saint Étienne

3rd PLACE
Milan .... 4–3 .... AS Saint Étienne

FINAL
Real Madrid .... 1–0 .... Benfica

The standings at the end of the second edition were:
1 Spain 12
2 Italy 11
3 France 9
4 Portugal 8

THE BRITISH INTERNATIONAL CHAMPIONSHIP

1884 Scotland
1985 Scotland
1886 England/Scotland
1887 Scotland
1888 England
1889 Scotland
1890 Scotland/England
1891 England
1892 England
1893 England
1894 Scotland
1895 England
1896 Scotland
1897 Scotland
1898 England
1899 England
1900 Scotland
1901 England
1902 Scotland
1903 England/Ireland/Scotland
1904 England
1905 England
1906 England/Scotland
1907 Wales
1908 Scotland/England
1909 England
1910 Scotland
1911 England
1912 England/Scotland
1913 England
1914 Ireland
1915–19 No championship
1920 Wales
1921 Scotland
1922 Scotland
1923 Scotland
1924 Wales
1925 Scotland
1926 Scotland
1927 Scotland/England
1928 Wales
1929 Scotland
1930 England
1931 Scotland/England
1932 England
1933 Wales
1934 Wales
1935 England/Scotland
1936 Scotland
1937 Wales
1938 England
1939 England/Scotland/Wales
1940–46 No championship
1947 England
1948 England
1949 Scotland
1950 England
1951 Scotland
1952 Wales/England
1953 England/Scotland
1954 England
1955 England
1956 England/Scotland/Wales/Nth. Ireland
1957 England
1958 England/Nth. Ireland
1959 Nth. Ireland/England
1960 England/Scotland/Wales
1961 England
1962 Scotland
1963 Scotland
1964 Scotland/England/Nth. Ireland
1965 England
1966 England
1967 Scotland
1968 England
1969 England
1970 England/Scotland/Wales
1971 England
1972 England/Scotland
1973 England
1974 England
1975 England
1976 Scotland
1977 Scotland
1978 England
1979 England
1980 Nth. Ireland
1981 –
1982 England
1983 England
1984 Nth. Ireland

England .... 54 wins
Scotland .... 40 wins
Wales .... 12 wins
Ireland/Nth. Ireland .... 8 wins

THE SCANDINAVIAN CHAMPIONSHIP

1924–29 .... Denmark
1929–32 .... Norway
1933–36 .... Sweden
1937–47 .... Sweden
1948–51 .... Sweden
1952–55 .... Sweden
1956–59 .... Sweden
1960–63 .... Finland
1964–67 .... Sweden
1968–71 .... Sweden

THE BALTIC CUP

1928 .... Latvia
1929 .... Estonia
1930 .... Lithuania
1931 .... Estonia
1932 .... Latvia
1933 .... –
1934 .... –
1935 .... Lithuania
1936 .... Latvia
1937 .... Latvia
1938 .... Estonia

THE BALKAN CUP

1929–31	Romania
1932	Bulgaria
1933	Romania
1934	Yugoslavia
1934–35	Bulgaria
1936	Romania
1946	Albania
1947	Hungary
1948	–
1973–76	Bulgaria
1977–80	Romania

EUROPEAN JUNIOR CHAMPIONSHIP

1948	England
1949	France
1950	Austria
1951	Yugoslavia
1952	Spain
1953	Hungary
1954	Spain
1955	No final
1956	No final
1957	Austria
1958	Italy
1959	Bulgaria
1960	Hungary
1961	Portugal
1962	Romania
1963	England
1964	England
1965	East Germany
1966	Soviet Union & Italy
1967	Soviet Union
1968	Czechoslovakia
1969	Bulgaria
1970	East Germany
1971	England
1972	England
1973	England
1974	Bulgaria
1975	England
1976	Soviet Union
1977	Belgium
1978	Soviet Union
1979	Yugoslavia
1980	England

EUROPEAN YOUTH CHAMPIONSHIP

1981	West Germany	1–0	Poland
1982	Scotland	3–1	Czechoslovakia
1983	France	1–0	Czechoslovakia
1984	Hungary	0–0 (3–2p)	Soviet Union
1986	East Germany	3–1	Italy
1988	Soviet Union	3–1	Portugal
1990	Soviet Union	0–0 (4–2p)	Portugal

EUROPEAN UNDER-23 CHAMPIONSHIP

1972	Czechoslovakia	2–2 3–1	Soviet Union
1974	Hungary	2–3 4–0	East Germany
1976	Soviet Union	1–1 2–1	Hungary

EUROPEAN UNDER-21 CHAMPIONSHIP

1978	Yugoslavia	1–0 4–4	East Germany
1980	Soviet Union	0–0 1–0	East Germany
1982	England	3–1 2–3	West Germany
1984	England	1–0 2–0	Spain
1986	Spain	1–2 2–1 (3–0p)	Italy
1988	France	0–0 3–0	Greece
1990	Soviet Union	4–2 3–1	Yugoslavia
1992	Italy	2–0 0–1	Sweden

EUROPEAN UNDER-16 CHAMPIONSHIP

1982	Italy	1–0	West Germany
1984	West Germany	2–0	Soviet Union
1985	Soviet Union	4–0	Greece
1986	Spain	2–1	Italy
1987	Italy*	1–0	Soviet Union
1988	Spain	0–0 (4–2p)	Portugal
1989	Portugal	4–1	East Germany
1990	Czechoslovakia	3–2	Yugoslavia
1991	Spain	2–0	Germany
1992	Germany	2–1	Spain

* Italy's title was later taken away for fielding over-age players

EUROPEAN CHAMPIONSHIP FOR WOMEN

1984	Sweden	1–0 0–1 (4–3p)	England
1987	Norway	2–1	Sweden
1989	West Germany	4–1	Norway
1991	West Germany	3–1	Norway

ALBANIA

This small Balkan country for years shunned her European neighbours, both in everyday life and in football, preferring instead the company of the equally hard-line Communist Chinese. Indeed many matches were played between the two countries, either by the full or representative sides, but as the Chinese were not members of FIFA, none of these 'full' internationals are recognised as such.

After World War II, things began promisingly. In 1946, full of Communist vigour, Albania won their only honour to date, The Balkan Cup, and it was achieved on their international debut. Despite losing to Yugoslavia in the first match of the tournament, they defeated both Romania and Bulgaria to lift the cup on their own soil.

		All			League			Cup		Europe		
	Team	G	S	B	G	S	B	G	S	G	S	B
1	Dinamo Tiranë	27	11	7	15	8	7	12	3	–	–	–
2	Partizani Tiranë	26	26	3	14	18	3	12	8	–	–	–
3	SK Tiranë	20	12	11	14	8	11	6	4	–	–	–
4	Vllaznia Shkodër	12	11	12	7	7	12	5	4	–	–	–
5	Flamurtari Vlorë	3	12	1	1	6	1	2	6	–	–	–
6	SK Elbasani	3	1	1	1	–	1	2	1	–	–	–
7	Skënderbeu Korçë	1	6	2	1	3	2	–	3	–	–	–
8	Besa Kavajë	–	7	8	–	1	8	–	6	–	–	–
9	Teuta Durrës	–	3	4	–	1	4	–	2	–	–	–
10	Luftëtari Gjirokastër	–	1	–	–	1	–	–	–	–	–	–
	Tomori Berat	–	1	–	–	–	–	–	1	–	–	–
	Traktori Lushnjë	–	1	–	–	–	–	–	1	–	–	–

To the end of the 1991–92 season

Since then success has been muted to say the least, and despite impressive victories over the Czechs in 1952 and Belgium in 1984, Albania have amassed one of the poorest records in international football. Not until the 1980s did they enter European competitions at either national or club level on a regular basis, and a total of just two victories by the national side in the 1980s tells the whole story.

Albania, like her Balkan neighbours, was for centuries under Turkish rule, and at the beginning of the 20th century, although football was played by foreign residents in Tirana, the Turks did all they could to stop the locals playing it. It was not until 1930 therefore, that an association was formed and a league competition introduced.

The stability was short-lived however; in 1939 Mussolini annexed Albania and all competition stopped. In the turbulent year of 1944, the country was taken over by the communists under Enver Hoxha, and until the death of Stalin in 1953, Albania looked to be entering into the mainstream of European football. Hoxha did not agree with the new Soviet leaders, however, and so Albania cut herself off from the Eastern Bloc as well as the rest of Europe, and between 1954 and 1963 played only one international, against East Germany.

In 1963, Albania unexpectedly entered the European Championship but unfortunately for the organisers they were drawn against Greece, who refused to play them. Albanian clubs also made their debut in the European Cup that season, but the good relations did not last long, and they and the national side soon went back into obscurity.

Whether Albanian football will be able to develop further is open to debate. Increasingly foreign sides are finding it harder and harder to play there, as Barcelona have found to their cost, but unless the structure of the clubs is changed to meet the demands of the new Europe, Albania may struggle to keep up with even the weakest nations. Gone are the days when the clubs could rely on the government to meet their every need in the name of mother Albania.

Population: 3 262 000
Area, sq km: 28 748
% in urban areas: 35.8%
Capital city: Tirana

Federata Shqiptarë Futbollit
Rruga Dervish Hima #31
Tirana
Albania
Tel: (010 355) 42 7556
Fax: (010 355) 42 28198
Telex: 2228 BFSSH AB
Cable: ALBSPORT TIRANA
Languages for correspondence: English, French

Year of formation: 1930
Affiliation to FIFA: 1932
Affiliation to UEFA: 1954
Registered clubs: 51
Registered players: 2500
Registered coaches: 191
Registered referees: 328
National stadium: Qemal Stafa, Tirana 24 000
National colours: Shirts: Red/Shorts: Red/Socks: Red
Reserve colours: Shirts: White/Shorts: White/Socks: White
Season: August–June

THE RECORD

WORLD CUP

1930–62 ...... Did not enter
1966 .... QT 4th/4 in group 5
1970 .... Did not enter
1974 .... QT 4th/4 in group 4
1978 .... Did not enter
1982 .... QT 4th/5 in group 1
1986 .... QT 3rd/4 in group 1
1990 .... QT 4th/4 in group 2

EUROPEAN CHAMPIONSHIP

1960 .... Did not enter
1964 .... 2nd round
1968 .... QT 3rd/3 in group 4
1972 .... QT 4th/4 in group 8
1976 .... Did not enter
1980 .... Did not enter
1984 .... QT 5th/5 in group 6
1988 .... QT 4th/4 in group 1
1992 .... QT 5th/5 in group 1

OLYMPIC GAMES

1908–60 ..... Did not enter
1964 .... QT Failed to qualify
1968 .... Did not enter
1972 .... QT Failed to qualify
1976–88 ..... Did not enter
1992 .... QT Failed to qualify

BALKAN CUP

1946 .... Winners

EUROPEAN CLUB COMPETITIONS

EUROPEAN CUP: 2nd round – 17 Nëntori 1983, 1989, 1990

CUP WINNERS CUP: 2nd round – Partizan 1971, Besa Kavajë 1973, 17 Nëntori 1987, Vllaznia 1988

UEFA CUP: 3rd round – Flamurtari 1988

CLUB DIRECTORY

TIRANË (Population – 238 000)

Klubi Sportiv Dinamo
Stadium: Dinamo 12 000
Founded: 1950
Colours: Blue/Blue

Klubi Sportiv Partizani
Stadium: Qemal Stafa 24 000
Founded: 1946
Colours: Red/Red

SK Tiranë
Stadium: Qemal Stafa 24 000
Founded: 1920
Colours: Blue and white stripes/White
Previous names: Agmi 1920–27, SK Tiranë 1927–39, Shprefeja 1939–45, 17 Nëntori 1945–50, Tiranë 1950–51, Puna Tiranë 1951–58, 17 Nëntori 1958–91

DURRËS (Population – 80 000)
Klubi Sportiv Teuta
Stadium: Lokomotiva 10 000
Founded: 1925
Colours: Blue with white sleeves/Blue
Previous names: Teuta 1925–45, Yllikuq 1945–49, Puna 1950–57, Lokomotiva 1957–91

ELBASAN (Population 80 000)
Klubi Sportiv Elbasani
Stadium: Labinoti 10 000
Founded: 1929 Colours: Yellow/Blue
Previous names: Urani 1923–34, Bashkimi 1934–49, Puna 1950–56, Labinoti 1956–91

SHKODËR (Population – 79 000)
Clubi Sportiv Vllaznia
Stadium: Vllaznia 16 000

Founded: 1919
Colours: Blue with red sleeves/Blue
Previous names: Bashkimi 1919–35, Vllaznia 1935–49, Puna 1950–57

VLORË (Population – 71000)
Klubi Sportiv Flamurtari
Stadium: Flamurtari 15000
Founded: 1923
Colours: White with a red and black panel/White
Previous names: Vlorë 1923–35, Ismail Qemali 1935–45, Flamurtari 1945–49, Puna 1950–57

KORCË (Population 57000)
Klubi Sportiv Skënderbeu
Stadium: Skënderbeu
Founded: 1926
Colours: Red and white stripes/White
Previous names: Skëndederbeu 1923–46, Dinamo 1946–49, Puna 1950–57

KAVAJË
Klubi Sportiv Besa
Stadium: Besa 10000
Founded: 1930
Colours: Yellow and black stripes/Black
Previous names: Kavajë 1930–35, Besa 1935–49, Puna 1950–57

FIER
Klubi Sportiv Apolonia
Stadium: Apolonia 10000
Founded: 1925
Colours: Green and white stripes/White
Previous names: Apolonia 1925–49, Puna 1950–57

LEZHË
Klubi Sportiv Besëlidhja
Stadium: Besëlidhja 6000
Founded: 1930
Colours: White with blue sleeves/Red
Previous names: Bardhyli 1930–37, Lezhë 1937–50, Puna 1950–57

GJIROKASTER
Klubi Sportiv Luftëtari
Stadium: Subi Bakiri 8000
Founded: 1929
Colours: Blue/White
Previous names: Luftëtari 1929–45, Shqiponja 1945–48, Luftëtari 1948–51, Puna 1951–57

BERAT
Klubi Sportiv Tomori
Stadium: Tomori 13000
Founded: 1923
Colours: White/White
Previous names: Muzeka 1923–31, Tomori 1931–49, Puna 1949–57

LUSHNJË
Klubi Sportiv Traktori
Stadium: Traktori 8000
Founded: 1926
Colours: Green/White
Previous names: Traktori 1926–49, Puna 1950–57

All clubs with the exception of Dinamo Tiranë and Partizani were known only by the name of their town from 1949–50

ALBANIAN LEAGUE CHAMPIONSHIP

Year	Champions		Runners up		3rd	
1930	SK Tiranë	14*	Skënderbeu Korçë	14	Bashkimi Shkodër	13
1931	SK Tiranë	1–1 3–1	Teuta Durrës			
1932	SK Tiranë	13	Bashkimi Shkodër	11	Teuta Durrës	11
1933	Skënderbeu Korçë	12	Bashkimi Shkodër	10	Teuta Durrës	8
1934	SK Tiranë	19	Skënderbeu Korçë	18	Bashkimi Shkodër	16
1935						–
1936	SK Tiranë	25	Vllaznia Shkodër	23	Besa Kavajë	13
1937	SK Tiranë	35	Vllaznia Shkodër	29	Besa Kavajë	22
1938–44 – No championship						
1945	Vllaznia Shkodër	2–1 2–1	SK Tiranë			
1946	Vllaznia Shkodër	3–0 2–0	Flamurtari Vlorë			
1947	Partizani Tiranë	29	Vllaznia Shkodër	28	Dinamo Korçë	24
1948	Partizani Tiranë	6–2	Flamurtari Vlorë			
1949	Partizani Tiranë	30	Vllaznia Shkodër	26	Yllikuq Durrës	20
1950	Dinamo Tiranë	29	Partizani Tiranë	29	Vllaznia Shkodër	21
1951	Dinamo Tiranë	50	Partizani Tiranë	48	Puna Tiranë	35
1952	Dinamo Tiranë	16	Partizani Tiranë	15	Puna Shkodër	12
1953	Dinamo Tiranë	30	Partizani Tiranë	29	Puna Tiranë	29
1954	Partizani Tiranë	43	Dinamo Tiranë	36	Puna Tiranë	31
1955	Dinamo Tiranë	55	Partizani Tiranë	55	Puna Tiranë	37
1956	Dinamo Tiranë	29	Partizani Tiranë	23	Puna Tiranë	17
1957	Partizani Tiranë	23	Dinamo Tiranë	23	Puna Korçë	17
1958	Partizani Tiranë	19	Besa Kavajë	18	17 Nëntori Tiranë	17
1959	Partizani Tiranë	23	17 Nëntori Tiranë	19	Dinamo Tiranë	14
1960	Dinamo Tiranë	32	Partizani Tiranë	28	17 Nëntori Tiranë	20
1961	Partizani Tiranë	30	Dinamo Tiranë	30	17 Nëntori Tiranë	23
1962	–					
1963	Partizani Tiranë	36	Dinamo Tiranë	32	Besa Kavajë	31
1964	Partizani Tiranë	37	Dinamo Tiranë	32	Besa Kavajë	29
1965	17 Nëntori Tiranë	31	Partizani Tiranë	30	Dinamo Tiranë	30
1966	17 Nëntori Tiranë	38	Partizani Tiranë	38	Dinamo Tiranë	29
1967	Dinamo Tiranë	38	17 Nëntori Tiranë	33	Besa Kavajë	26
1968	17 Nëntori Tiranë	45	Partizani Tiranë	44	Dinamo Tiranë	38
1969	–					
1970	17 Nëntori Tiranë	44	Partizani Tiranë	38	Vllaznia Shkodër	35
1971	Partizani Tiranë	40	Dinamo Tiranë	39	Vllaznia Shkodër	34
1972	Vllaznia Shkodër	40	17 Nëntori Tiranë	37	Dinamo Tiranë	36

* Play-off: SK Tiranë 0–0 2–0 Skënderbeu Korçë

1973	Dinamo Tiranë	41	Partizani Tiranë	34	Besa Kavajë	34
1974	Vllaznia Shkodër	37	Partizani Tiranë	36	Besa Kavajë	30
1975	Dinamo Tiranë	44	Vllaznia Shkodër	39	Partizani Tiranë	34
1976	Dinamo Tiranë	28	17 Nëntori Tiranë	26	Vllaznia Shkodër	25
1977	Dinamo Tiranë	44	Skënderbeu Korçë	40	Vllaznia Shkodër	37
1978	Vllaznia Shkodër	29	Luftëtari	26	Partizani Tiranë	25
1979	Partizani Tiranë	36	17 Nëntori Tiranë	35	Besa Kavajë	31
1980	Dinamo Tiranë	37	17 Nëntori Tiranë	32	Vllaznia Shkodër	31
1981	Partizani Tiranë	37	Dinamo Tiranë	36	17 Nëntori Tiranë	35
1982	17 Nëntori Tiranë	37	Flamurtari Vlorë	33	Dinamo Tiranë	32
1983	Vllaznia Shkodër	34	Partizani Tiranë	34	17 Nëntori Tiranë	32
1984	Labinoti Elbasan	37	17 Nëntori Tiranë	34	Partizani Tiranë	30
1985	17 Nëntori Tiranë	39	Dinamo Tiranë	33	Vllaznia Shkodër	29
1986	Dinamo Tiranë	38	Flamurtari Vlorë	38	17 Nëntori Tiranë	37
1987	Partizani Tiranë	36	Flamurtari Vlorë	33	Vllaznia Shkodër	32
1988	17 Nëntori Tiranë	48	Flamurtari Vlorë	41	Labinoti Elbasan	39
1989	17 Nëntori Tiranë	48	Partizani Tiranë	45	Dinamo Tiranë	42
1990	Dinamo Tiranë	50	Partizani Tiranë	49	Flamurtari Vlorë	39
1991	Flamurtari Vlorë	54	Partizani Tiranë	48	Vllaznia Shkodër	45
1992	Vllaznia Shkodër	44	Partizani Tiranë	38	Teuta Durrës	33

ALBANIAN CUP FINALS

Year	Winners	Score	Runners–up
1948	Partizani Tiranë	5–2	17 Nëntori Tiranë
1949	Partizani Tiranë	1–0	17 Nëntori Tiranë
1950	Dinamo Tiranë	2–1	Partizani Tiranë
1951	Dinamo Tiranë	3–2	Partizani Tiranë
1952	Dinamo Tiranë	4–1	Puna Tiranë
1953	Dinamo Tiranë	2–0	Partizani Tiranë
1954	Dinamo Tiranë	2–1	Partizani Tiranë
1955–56	– No competition		
1957	Partizani Tiranë	2–0	Lokomotiva Durrës
1958	Partizani Tiranë	4–0	Skënderbeu Korçë
1959	–		
1960	Dinamo Tiranë	1–0 1–0	Flamurtari Vlorë
1961	Partizani Tiranë	1–1 1–0	Besa Kavajë
1962	– No competition		
1963	17 Nëntori Tiranë	1–0 2–3	Besa Kavajë
1964	Partizani Tiranë	3–0	Tomori Berat
1965	Vllaznia Shkodër	1–0	Skënderbeu Korçë
1966	Partizani Tiranë	2–1 4–3	Vllaznia Shkodër
1967	– No competiton		
1968	Partizani Tiranë	4–1	Vllaznia Shkodër
1969	– No competition		
1970	Partizani Tiranë	4–0 0–1	Vllaznia Shkodër
1971	Dinamo Tiranë	2–0	Besa Kavajë
1972	Vllaznia Shkodër	2–0 0–2	Besa Kavajë
1973	Partizani Tiranë	1–0	Dinamo Tiranë
1974	Dinamo Tiranë	1–0	Partizani Tiranë
1975	Labinoti Elbasan	1–0 1–0	Lokomotiva Durrës
1976	17 Nëntori Tiranë	3–1 1–0	Skënderbeu Korçë
1977	17 Nëntori Tiranë	2–1 1–2	Dinamo Tiranë
1978	Dinamo Tiranë	0–0 1–0	Traktori Lushnjë
1979	Vllaznia Shkodër	1–1 2–1	Dinamo Tiranë
1980	Partizani Tiranë	1–1 1–0	Labinoti Elbasan
1981	Vllaznia Shkodër	5–1 1–2	Besa Kavajë
1982	Dinamo Tiranë	1–0 2–3	17 Nëntori Tiranë
1983	17 Nëntori Tiranë	1–0	Flamurtari Vlorë
1984	17 Nëntori Tiranë	2–1	Flamurtari Vlorë
1985	Flamurtari Vlorë	2–1	Partizani Tiranë
1986	17 Nëntori Tiranë	3–1	Vllaznia Shkodër
1987	Vllaznia Shkodër	3–0 1–3	Flamurtari Vlorë
1988	Flamurtari Vlorë	1–0	Partizani Tiranë
1989	Dinamo Tiranë	0–0 3–1	Partizani Tiranë
1990	Dinamo Tiranë	1–1 (4–2p)	Flamurtari Vlorë
1991	Partizani Tiranë	1–1 (4–3p)	Flamurtari Vlorë
1992	SK Elbasani	2–1	Besa Kavajë

INTERNATIONAL MATCHES PLAYED BY ALBANIA

Date	Opponents	Result		Venue	Compet	Scorers
7–10–1946	Yugoslavia	L	2–3	Tirana	BC	Begeja, Teliti
9–10	Bulgaria	W	3–1	Tirana	BC	Borici 2, Mirashi
13–10	Rumania	W	1–0	Tirana	BC	Teliti
25–05–1947	Rumania	L	0–4	Tirana	BCE	
15–06	Bulgaria	L	0–2	Sofia	BCE	
20–08	Hungary	L	0–3	Budapest	BCE	
14–09	Yugoslavia	L	2–4	Tirana	BCE	Borici, Parapani
2–05–1948	Rumania	W	1–0	Bucharest	BCE	Mirashi
23–05	Hungary	D	0–0	Tirana	BCE	
27–06	Yugoslavia	D	0–0	Belgrade	BCE	
23–10–1949	Rumania	D	1–1	Bucharest	Fr	Teliti
6–11	Poland	L	1–2	Warsaw	Fr	Gjinali
17–11	Bulgaria	D	0–0	Sofia	Fr	

29–11	Rumania	L	1–4	Tirana	Fr	Mirashi
1–05–1950	Poland	D	0–0	Tirana	Fr	
4–06	Bulgaria	W	2–1	Tirana	Fr	Borici, Bichaku
1–09	Czechoslovakia	L	0–3	Prague	Fr	
24–09	Hungary	L	0–12	Budapest	Fr	
8–10	Rumania	L	0–6	Bucharest	Fr	
29–11–1952	Czechoslovakia	W	3–2	Tirana	Fr	Gjinali, Teliti, Jareci
9–12	Czechoslovakia	W	2–1	Tirana	Fr	Gjinali, Borici
29–11–1953	Poland	W	2–0	Tirana	Fr	Borici, Resmja
1–05–1958	East Germany	D	1–1	Tirana	Fr	Kraga
2–06–1963	Bulgaria	L	0–1	Tirana	OGq	
16–06	Bulgaria	L	0–1	Sofia	OGq	
29–06	Denmark	L	0–4	Copenhagen	ECr2	
30–10	Denmark	W	1–0	Tirana	ECr2	Pana
24–05–1964	Holland	L	0–2	Rotterdam	WCq	
25–10	Holland	L	0–2	Tirana	WCq	
11–04–1965	Switzerland	L	0–2	Tirana	WCq	
2–05	Switzerland	L	0–1	Geneva	WCq	
7–05	Nth. Ireland	L	1–4	Belfast	WCq	Gashari
24–11	Nth. Ireland	D	1–1	Tirana	WCq	Haxhiu
8–04–1967	West Germany	L	0–6	Dortmund	ECq	
14–05	Yugoslavia	L	0–2	Tirana	ECq	
12–11	Yugoslavia	L	0–4	Belgrade	ECq	
17–12	West Germany	D	0–0	Tirana	ECq	
14–10–1970	Poland	L	0–3	Chorzow	ECq	
13–12	Turkey	L	1–2	Istanbul	ECq	Ziu
17–02–1971	West Germany	L	0–1	Tirana	ECq	
18–04	Romania	L	1–2	Bucharest	OGq	
12–05	Poland	D	1–1	Tirana	ECq	Zegha
26–05	Romania	L	1–2	Tirana	OGq	
12–06	West Germany	L	0–2	Karlsruhe	ECq	
14–11	Turkey	W	3–0	Tirana	ECq	Pernaska 2, Pano
21–06–1972	Finland	L	0–1	Helsinki	WCq	
29–10	Rumania	L	0–2	Bucharest	WCq	
7–04–1973	East Germany	L	0–2	Magdeburg	WCq	
6–05	Rumania	L	1–4	Tirana	WCq	Bizi
10–10	Finland	W	1–0	Tirana	WCq	Ragani
3–11	East Germany	L	1–4	Tirana	WCq	Ghika
10–10–1976	Algeria	W	3–0	Tirana	Fr	Ballgina, Pernaska 2
3–09–1980	Finland	W	2–0	Tirana	WCq	Braho, Baci
19–10	Bulgaria	L	1–2	Sofia	WCq	Pernaska
15–11	Austria	L	0–5	Vienna	WCq	
6–12	Austria	L	0–1	Tirana	WCq	
1–04–1981	West Germany	L	0–2	Tirana	WCq	
2–09	Finland	L	1–2	Kotka	WCq	Targaj
14–10	Bulgaria	L	0–2	Tirana	WCq	
18–11	West Germany	L	0–8	Dortmund	WCq	
22–09–1982	Austria	L	0–5	Vienna	ECq	
27–10	Turkey	L	0–1	Izmir	ECq	
15–12	Nth. Ireland	D	0–0	Tirana	ECq	
30–03–1983	West Germany	L	1–2	Tirana	ECq	Targaj
27–04	Nth. Ireland	L	0–1	Belfast	ECq	
11–05	Turkey	D	1–1	Tirana	ECq	OG
8–06	Austria	L	1–2	Tirana	ECq	Targaj
20–11	West Germany	L	1–2	Saarbrucken	ECq	Tomori
17–10–1984	Belgium	L	1–3	Brussels	WCq	Omuri
31–10	Poland	D	2–2	Mielic	WCq	Minga, Kola
22–12	Belgium	W	2–0	Tirana	WCq	Josa, Minga
27–02–1985	Greece	L	0–2	Athens	WCq	
28–03	Turkey	D	0–0	Tirana	Fr	
30–05	Poland	L	0–1	Tirana	WCq	
30–10	Greece	D	1–1	Tirana	WCq	Omuri
15–10–1986	Austria	L	0–3	Graz	ECq	
3–12	Spain	L	1–2	Tirana	ECq	Minga
25–03–1987	Rumania	L	1–5	Bucharest	ECq	Muca
29–04	Austria	L	0–1	Tirana	ECq	
28–10	Rumania	L	0–1	Vlore	ECq	
18–11	Spain	L	0–5	Seville	ECq	
6–08–1988	Cuba	D	0–0	Beirat	Fr	

LEADING INTERNATIONAL GOALSCORERS		
1	Teliti	6
	Borici	6
3	Pernaska	5
4	Mirashi	4
	Kushta	4
6	Gjinali	3
	Omuri	3
	Pano	3
	Targaj	3

LEADING INTERNATIONAL APPEARANCES		
1	Demollari	30
2	Minga	28
3	Josa	27
4	Zmijani	26
5	Borici	24
	Pano	24
7	Targaj	22
8	Hodja	21
	Musta	21

20–09	Rumania	L	0–3	Constantza	Fr	
19–10	Poland	L	0–1	Chorzow	WCq	
5–11	Sweden	L	1–2	Tirana	WCq	Shehu
18–01–1989	Greece	D	1–1	Tirana	Fr	Minga
8–03	England	L	0–2	Tirana	WCq	
26–04	England	L	0–5	London	WCq	
8–10	Sweden	L	1–3	Stockholm	WCq	Kushta
15–11	Poland	L	1–2	Tirana	WCq	Kushta
30–05–1990	Iceland	L	0–2	Reykjavik	ECq	
5–09	Greece	L	0–1	Patras	Fr	
17–11	France	L	0–1	Tirana	ECq	
19–12	Spain	L	0–9	Seville	ECq	
30–03–1991	France	L	0–5	Paris	ECq	
1–05	Czechoslovakia	L	0–2	Tirana	ECq	
26–05	Iceland	W	1–0	Tirana	ECq	Abazi
4–09	Greece	W	2–0	Athens	Fr	Kushta 2
16–10	Czechoslovakia	L	1–2	Olomouz	ECq	Zmijani
29–01–1992	Greece	W	1–0	Tirana	Fr	Raklli
22–04	Spain	L	0–3	Seville	WCq	
26–05	Rep. Ireland	L	0–2	Dublin	WCq	
3–06	Lithuania	W	1–0	Tirana	WCq	Abazi

AUSTRIA

September 12th, 1991 will go down as a landmark in Austrian football. Before a handful of spectators in Landskrona, Sweden, the national side lost to a Faeroe Islands team that was playing its very first competitive international match. How the mighty have fallen! For Vienna, in the first half of the 20th century, was at the very hub of European football. Now it is little more than a side show.

The very first international match on mainland Europe took place on Viennese soil and until the 1960s Austria lived up to this proud tradition. Vienna was one of the three great cities of the Austro–Hungarian empire along with Budapest and Prague, and the legend of the 'Danubian school of football' was born even before the three cities became the capitals of their own separate countries after the First World War. Austrian teams became synonymous with skilful ball players who combined clever short passing movements with innovative tactics. Austria was also innovative off the field. The great Hugo Meisl was one of the game's greatest administrators, and it was largely due to his efforts that football became so popular in central Europe.

The large British community in Vienna formed the basis from which football developed. Naturally, English teams were invited to play there and in 1900 Southampton visited and gave a display that greatly encouraged the development of the game, beating a Vienna selection 6–0. A cup had been introduced for teams from Vienna three years previously, and as the name of the first winners, Cricketers, suggests, the British influence was strong. It was to Budapest, however, that Austrian teams turned for more regular opposition. Hungarian clubs were invited to take part in Der Challenge-Cup, and it was on 12 October 1902 that the most significant event to that date on mainland Europe took place. Before 500 spectators and an English referee, Austria beat Hungary 5–0 in an international match that was to be the first of thousands on the continent.

The Hungary match became an annual event but opposition was also found in matches against Germany and Italy. In 1912 Austria entered the Stockholm Olympics and although Germany were well beaten in the first round, a strong Dutch side won 3–1 in the quarter-finals. In a consolation tournament organised for the teams that did not reach the semi-finals, Austria lost in the final to Hungary.

At the same time that international football was gaining a foothold, clubs were being created across the country but especially in Vienna. Along with the Cricketers, who are no longer in existence, 1894 also saw the founding of First Vienna who to this day retain the English spelling of their name. In 1898 Sportklub Rapid arrived on the scene as a workers' club, and they were joined in 1911 by their greatest rivals Amateure, who later became known as FK Austria. The governing body of Austrian football was formed in 1904 and joined FIFA in 1905, a year after FIFA's own formation. A league was set up in 1911, taking over from Der Challenge-Cup as the source of competition in Vienna. The league was contested entirely by teams from Vienna, and it was not until 1949 that clubs from other cities were invited to take part. The same was true of the of the Vienna Cup introduced in 1919.

The inter-war period was Austria's most successful era. Success in the Mitropa Cup and the International Cup helped seal her reputation. The Mitropa Cup especially caught the imagination of the public and huge crowds turned up to see the annual games. Rapid, FK Austria and First Vienna all won the tournament, whilst in the International Cup, the national team finished as runners-up in the first tournament and won the second. Victory in the 1930–32 edition saw the Austrians at their very best. Dubbed as the 'Wunderteam' the exploits of this side are never likely to be equalled by another Austrian side. After losing to Italy in early 1931, Austria enjoyed a spell lasting until June 1934 when they took on all-comers and generally beat them convincingly – 101 goals were scored in 30 games, and though Austria did not stay undefeated in this time, one of the two defeats suffered was at the hands of England, in London, a game in which the English were lucky not to lose their unbeaten home record 20 years before they finally did.

The names of the members of the 'Wunderteam' will echo down through the ages. The forward line was one of the most fearsome ever fielded, spearheaded by a man called der Papierne, 'the man of paper', due to his slight build. This was Matthias Sindelar, until the emergence of Hans Krankl in the 1970s Austria's most celebrated player. He scored 27 goals for his country as did his forward partner Schall, who along with Gschweidl, Zischek, Vogel and later Binder and Bican were the terror of defences across the continent. Sadly however, aside from the International Cup victory, there was to be no lasting honour to mark the quality of this side. The 1934 World Cup was there for the taking and had it been played anywhere other than Italy, Austria might well have won it. Instead, after having disposed of both France and Hungary, they met Italy in the semi-finals in Milan. Home advantage and a muddy pitch settled the match 1–0 in favour of the more robust Italians. Demoralised by the defeat, the Austrians also lost the third place play-off to Germany four days later.

Italy were again Austria's downfall two years later in the 1936 Olympic Games, this time in the final. That Austria reached the final at all, however, is something of a mystery. Playing without all their well-known players, who by this time were all professionals and therefore ineligible, the Austrians were not expected to progress far. Indeed they nearly didn't. Having beaten Egypt, they faced Peru in the quarter-finals. The Olympic Games had never seen a game like it, nor has it since. The Peruvians were leading 4–2 with 10 minutes left when an Austrian player, having left the field for treatment to an injury, returned to the field with a clean shirt on. The Peruvians took him to be a substitute and protested. There followed a melée in which spectators and players alike were involved. The game was abandoned, but so furious were the Peruvians at having victory snatched from them that they refused to turn up for the replay. The Austrians were therefore given a bye to the semi-finals and met Poland, who, clearly exhausted after their extraordinary 5–4 win over Great Britain in the previous round, succumbed easily. Austria were defeated 2–1 in the final, but the fact that they got so far was partly attributable to a man who had helped mould the Austrian game for over 20 years. Jimmy Hogan, an Englishman who felt more at home away from England, a country that never appreciated his talents, had coached in Austria on and off since 1912, as well as working in Germany and Hungary. His work as coach of the team for the 1936 Olympics was his crowning glory and to this day the Olympic Final remains the only major final the Austrians have ever played in.

Hitler soon put paid to any aspirations the Austrians may have had of winning the 1938 World Cup. United into a greater Germany in March 1938, 'Austrian' football ceased to exist, and although three international matches were played by the Germans in Vienna, all three were during the war. Austrian club sides were not so easily submerged, however. Rapid won the German Cup in 1938 and were German champions in 1941, whilst First Vienna won the Cup in 1943.

Remarkably, when the Austrians next took the field for an international match, on 19 August 1945 in a match against Hungary, four of the side were survivors from the previous game in October 1937 against Czechoslovakia. Sindelar was not amongst them, however. He was Jewish and had disappeared even before the war had broken out. In 1948 Austria entered the London Olympics but there was no repeat of their previous success as they lost 3–0 in the first round against Sweden, who went on to win the tournament. Like most other European countries, Austria shunned the 1950 World Cup, but in the meantime, under Walter Nausch a new team was being moulded. The dynamos of the side were Ernst Ocwirk and Gerhard Hanappi and they inspired the Austrians to the semi-finals of the 1954 World Cup in Switzerland. Poor Portugal were beaten 9–1 in the qualifiers and in the final tournament the goals carried on flowing. That so many goals were scored in the tournament was in no small part due to a remarkable game between Austria and their hosts. The final score of 7–5 in favour of the Austrians is the highest ever score in the World Cup finals and is unlikely to be beaten. Their 6–1 defeat at the hands of Germany in the semi-finals, however, surprised even the Germans. Once again the Austrians had fallen at a hurdle they were expected to conquer with ease. There was to be no third attempt at winning a World Cup semi-final. From 1954 onwards, the Austrians became increasing happy just to qualify for the finals.

Austria's triumphs until the early 1950s are best seen in the light of what was still very much an amateur game, but at which they were professionals. With a population of only seven million, the increasing commercialisation of the game was bound to leave them behind. A none too happy outing at the 1958 World Cup was followed by failure to qualify again until 1978, and seven attempts to qualify for the European Championship finals have all ended in disappointment. Club football has suffered too. As the league was extended to include provincial teams, many of the great club sides of the 1920s and 1930s either fell by the wayside or merged with others in an effort to stay solvent. Austrian clubs have also fared badly in the European club competitions, although FK Austria and Rapid both reached the final of the Cup Winners Cup.

Austria does, however, continue to produce fine players, although they rarely stay in Austria for their club football. The late 1970s and early 1980s saw some success at international level. Hans Krankl along with Walter Schachner, Herbert Prohaska, Bruno Pezzey and Kurt Jara led the Austrians to two World Cup qualifications, in 1978 and 1982. In 1978, victories over Spain and Sweden ensured a place in the second round, where despite beating the reigning champions West Germany, they lost to both the Dutch and the Italians. The 1982 tournament will always be remembered for the great Gijón swindle in which the West Germans and Austrians contrived a result that saw both teams through at the expense of Algeria. Once in the second round the Austrians came up against France who ensured their elimination with a 1–0 victory in Madrid.

		All			League			Cup		Europe		
	Team	G	S	B	G	S	B	G	S	G	S	B
1	FK Austria Wien	45	28	18	21	16	16	24	11	–	1	2
2	SK Rapid Wien	42	29	18	29	18	17	13	10	–	1	1
3	Admira-Wacker	15	17	9	9	13	9	6	4	–	–	–
4	FC Tirol	13	10	6	7	5	5	6	5	–	–	1
5	First Vienna FC	9	12	10	6	7	10	3	5	–	–	–
6	Wiener Sport-Club	4	14	5	3	7	5	1	7	–	–	–
7	Linzer ASK	2	4	4	1	1	4	1	3	–	–	–
8	Wiener AF	2	2	3	1	2	3	1	–	–	–	–
9	FAC Wien	1	3	1	1	3	1	–	–	–	–	–
	FC Stahl Linz	1	3	1	1	2	1	–	1	–	–	–
11	Grazer AK	1	2	2	–	–	2	1	2	–	–	–
12	Hakoah Wien	1	1	–	1	1	–	–	–	–	–	–
13	Kremser SC	1	–	–	–	–	–	1	–	–	–	–
	SV Stockerau	1	–	–	–	–	–	1	–	–	–	–
15	SV Austria Salzburg	–	5	–	–	2	–	–	3	–	–	–
16	SK Sturm Graz	–	3	3	–	1	3	–	2	–	–	–
17	BAC Wien	–	2	–	–	1	–	–	1	–	–	–
18	Rudolfshugel FC	–	1	2	–	1	2	–	–	–	–	–
19	FC Wien	–	1	–	–	1	–	–	–	–	–	–
	Slovan Wien	–	1	–	–	–	–	–	1	–	–	–
	Wiener Neustadt	–	1	–	–	–	–	–	1	–	–	–
	Vorwärts Steyr	–	1	–	–	–	–	–	1	–	–	–
23	I.SC Simmering	–	–	1	–	–	1	–	–	–	–	–

To the end of the 1991–92 season

Failure to qualify for the 1986 Mexico World Cup due to the presence of their eternal rivals Hungary, was followed by qualification for Italy in 1990. Though much was expected of a forward line that included Polster, Rodax and Ogris, Austria could not proceed beyond the first round. If that was perhaps to be expected, what happened the following September in their European Championship match against the Faeroes was not. The defeat at the hands of the part-timers was deeply embarrassing and ensured that once again the European Championship would bring no joy to the Austrians.

Population: 7 623 000
Area, sq km: 83 856
% in urban areas: 57.7%
Capital city: Vienna

Österreichischer Fussball-Bund
Praterstadion, Sektor A/F
Meiereistrasse, Postfach 340
A-1020 Wien
Austria
Tel: (010 43) 1 217180
Fax: (010 43) 1 2181632
Telex: 111919 OEFB A
Cable: FOOTBAL WIEN
Languages for correspondence: German, English, French

Year of formation: 1904
Affiliation to FIFA: 1905
Affiliation to UEFA: 1954
Registered clubs: 2009
Registered players: 252 600
Professional players: 380
Registered coaches: 2814
Registered referees: 1982
National stadium: Wiener Stadion (Prater) 62 000
National colours: Shirts: White/Shorts: Black/Socks: Black
Reserve colours: Shirts: Red/Shorts: White/Socks: Red
Season: August–June with a mid-season break in January and February

THE RECORD

WORLD CUP

1930 .... Did not enter
1934 .... QT 2nd/3 in group 8 – Final Tournament/Semi-finalists/4th Place
1938 .... Did not enter
1950 .... Did not enter
1954 .... QT 1st/2 in group 5 – Final Tournament/Semi-finalists/3rd Place
1958 .... QT 1st/3 in group 5 – Final Tournament/1st round
1962 .... Did not enter
1966 .... QT 3rd/3 in group 6
1970 .... QT 3rd/4 in group 7
1974 .... QT 2nd/4 in group 1
1978 .... QT 1st/4 in group 3 – Final Tournament/2nd round
1982 .... QT 2nd/5 in group 1 – Final Tournament/2nd round
1986 .... QT 3rd/4 in group 5
1990 .... QT 2nd/5 in group 3 – Final Tournament/1st round

EUROPEAN CHAMPIONSHIP

1960 .... Quarter-finalists
1964 .... Did not enter
1968 .... QT 3rd/4 in group 3
1972 .... QT 2nd/4 in group 6
1976 .... QT 3rd/4 in group 2
1980 .... QT 2nd/5 in group 2
1984 .... QT 3rd/5 in group 6
1988 .... QT 3rd/4 in group 1
1992 .... QT 4th/5 in group 4

OLYMPIC GAMES

1908 .... Did not enter
1912 .... Quarter-finals
1920 .... Did not enter
1924 .... Did not enter
1928 .... Did not enter
1936 .... Runners-up
1948 .... 1st round
1952 .... Quarter-finalists
1956 .... Did not enter
1960 .... QT Failed to qualify
1964 .... Did not enter
1968 .... QT Failed to qualify
1972 .... QT Failed to qualify
1976 .... QT Failed to qualify
1980 .... QT Failed to qualify
1984 .... Did not enter
1988 .... QT Failed to qualify
1992 .... QT Failed to qualify

DR GERO CUP

1929 .... 2nd
1932 .... Winners
1935 .... 2nd
1953 .... 3rd
1960 .... 3rd

EUROPEAN CLUB COMPETITIONS

EUROPEAN CUP: Semi-finalists – SK Rapid Wien 1961, FK Austria 1979

CUP WINNERS CUP: Finalists – FK Austria 1978, SK Rapid Wien 1985

UEFA CUP: Semi-finalists – FC Tirol 1987

MITROPA CUP: Winners – SK Rapid Wien 1930, First Vienna 1931, FK Austria 1933, 1936
Finalists – SK Rapid Wien 1927 1928, Wiener AC 1931, Admira 1934

CLUB DIRECTORY

VIENNA (Population – 1 875 000)

FK Austria
Stadium: Franz Horr 10 000
Founded: 1911
Colours: Violet/White
Previous names: Amateure until 1926. Merged with Wiener Athletik Club (WAC) in 1972

First Vienna FC
Stadium: Hohe Warte 10 000
Founded: 1894
Colours: Yellow/Blue

SK Rapid Wien
Stadium: Gerhard Hanappi 19 000
Founded: 1898
Colours: Green and white stripes/Green

Wiener Sport-Club
Stadium: Sport-Club Platz 10 000
Founded: 1893
Colours: Black and white stripes/Black

Vienna clubs that are no longer in existence: Cricket FV 1894–1939, Hakaoh 1901–39, Hertha 1904–40, Rudolfshügel 1902–35, Wien AF 1912–35, FC Wien 1918– 56 (Previously known as Nicholson 1918–32)

LINZ (Population – 335 000)

Linzer ASK
Stadium: Linzer 22 000
Founded: 1908
Colours: Black and white stripes/Black

FC Stahl Linz (1949)
Stadium: Linzer 22 000
Founded: 1949
Colours: Blue/Blue
Previous names: VÖEST merged with SV Stickstoff in 1964, SK VÖEST Linz 1964–91

GRAZ (Population – 325 000)

Grazer AK
Stadium: Liebenau 9000
Founded: 1902
Colours: Red/Red

SK Sturm Graz
Stadium: Strurm-Platz 11 000
Founded: 1909
Colours: White/Black

SALZBURG (Population 220 000)
SV Austria Salzburg
Stadium: Salzburger 22 000
Founded: 1933
Colours: White/Violet
Previous names: Formed when Hertha and Rapid Salzburg merged in 1933

INNSBRUCK (Population – 185 000)
FC Tirol
Stadium: Tivoli 17 000
Founded: 1914
Colours: White/White
Previous names: Wacker Innsbruck until 1986

KLAGENFURT (Population – 115 000)
SK Austria
Stadium: Wörthersee 12 000
Founded: 1920
Colours: Violet/White

ST PÖLTEN (Population – 67 000)
VSE St Pölten
Stadium: Voith-Platz 12 000
Founded: 1920
Colours: Red/Red

STEYR (Population – 65 000)
SK Vorwärts Steyr
Stadium: Steyr-Volksstrasse 7000
Founded: 1919
Colours: Red/White

MARIA ENZERSDORF
FC Admira-Wacker
Stadium: Südstadt 18 000
Founded: 1971
Colours: White with blue sleeves/White
Previous names: Admira Wien (1905) and Wacker Wien (1908) merged in 1971

MÖDLING
VfB Mödling
Stadium: Mödling 8000
Founded: 1911
Colours: Red/White

KREMS
Kremser SC
Stadium: Kremser 15 000
Founded: 1919
Colours: White with black sleeves and shoulders/White

DER CHALLENGE-CUP

Year	Winners
1897	Cricketers
1898	Cricketers
1899	First Vienna FC
1900	First Vienna FC
1901	Wiener AC
1902	Cricketers
1903	Wiener AC
1904	Wiener AC
1905	Wiener Sport-Club
1906–08	–
1909	Ferencvaros Budapest
1910	–
1911	Wiener Sport-Club
1912–18	–

AUSTRIAN LEAGUE CHAMPIONSHIP

Year	Champions		Runners up		3rd	
1912	SK Rapid Wien	31	Wiener Sport-Club	30	Wiener AF	29
1913	SK Rapid Wien	33	Wiener AF	26	Wiener Sport-Club	21
1914	Wiener AF	27	SK Rapid Wien	27	Wiener AC	23
1915	Wiener AC	16	Wiener AF	15	SK Rapid Wien	10
1916	SK Rapid Wien	31	FAC Wien	29	Wiener AF	26
1917	SK Rapid Wien	29	FAC Wien	27	Rudolfshügel FC	27
1918	FAC Wien	24	SK Rapid Wien	24	Wiener AF	22
1919	SK Rapid Wien	31	Rudolfshügel FC	24	Wiener AC	23
1920	SK Rapid Wien	33	Amateure	33	Wiener Sport-Club	30
1921	SK Rapid Wien	40	Amateure	34	Rudolfshügel FC	26
1922	Wiener Sport-Club	34	Hakoah Wien	32	SK Rapid Wien	31
1923	SK Rapid Wien	36	Amateure	32	Admira Wien	27
1924	Amateure	36	First Vienna FC	32	Wiener Sport-Club	30
1925	Hakoah Wien	26	Amateure	24	First Vienna FC	23
1926	Amateure	35	First Vienna FC	31	I.SC Simmering	29
1927	Admira Wien	36	BAC Wien	33	SK Rapid Wien	31
1928	Admira Wien	39	SK Rapid Wien	36	First Vienna FC	32
1929	SK Rapid Wien	33	Admira Wien	30	Wiener AC	30
1930	SK Rapid Wien	30	Admira Wien	29	First Vienna FC	28
1931	First Vienna FC	29	Admira Wien	27	SK Rapid Wien	26
1932	Admira Wien	33	First Vienna FC	31	SK Rapid Wien	31
1933	First Vienna FC	35	SK Rapid Wien	32	Admira Wien	25
1934	Admira Wien	33	SK Rapid Wien	31	FK Austria	27
1935	SK Rapid Wien	40	Admira Wien	34	First Vienna FC	27
1936	Admira Wien	37	First Vienna FC	32	SK Rapid Wien	26
1937	Admira Wien	35	FK Austria	35	First Vienna FC	30
1938	SK Rapid Wien	30	Wiener Sport-Club	23	FK Austria	21
1939	Admira Wien	28	Wacker Wien	26	SK Rapid Wien	25
1940	SK Rapid Wien	20	Wacker Wien	17	Wiener Sport-Club	16
1941	SK Rapid Wien	28	Wacker Wien	24	First Vienna FC	24
1942	First Vienna FC	25	FC Wien	21	SK Rapid Wien	19
1943	First Vienna FC	30	Wiener AC	27	FAC Wien	25
1944	First Vienna FC	27	FAC Wien	22	Wiener AC	16
1945	–					
1946	SK Rapid Wien	35	FK Austria	34	Wacker Wien	31
1947	Wacker Wien	30	SK Rapid Wien	28	First Vienna FC	27
1948	SK Rapid Wien	28	Wacker Wien	27	FK Austria	22
1949	FK Austria	27	SK Rapid Wien	25	Admira Wien	24
1950	FK Austria	38	SK Rapid Wien	36	Wacker Wien	33
1951	SK Rapid Wien	43	Wacker Wien	38	FK Austria	32
1952	SK Rapid Wien	41	FK Austria	39	First Vienna FC	32
1953	FK Austria	45	Wacker Wien	44	SK Rapid Wien	39
1954	SK Rapid Wien	39	FK Austria	38	Wacker Wien	31
1955	First Vienna FC	39	Wiener Sport-Club	39	SK Rapid Wien	36
1956	SK Rapid Wien	43	Wacker Wien	41	First Vienna FC	40
1957	SK Rapid Wien	40	First Vienna FC	39	FK Austria	38
1958	Wiener Sport-Club	45	SK Rapid Wien	43	First Vienna FC	30
1959	Wiener Sport-Club	46	SK Rapid Wien	44	First Vienna FC	32
1960	SK Rapid Wien	42	Wiener Sport-Club	38	Wiener AC	38
1961	FK Austria	39	First Vienna FC	32	Wiener AC	32
1962	FK Austria	42	Linzer ASK	38	Admira Wien	36
1963	FK Austria	38	Admira Wien	34	Wiener Sport-Club	33
1964	SK Rapid Wien	43	FK Austria	37	Linzer ASK	33
1965	Linzer ASK	36	SK Rapid Wien	35	Admira Wien	35
1966	Admira Wien	43	SK Rapid Wien	40	FK Austria	35
1967	SK Rapid Wien	41	Wacker Innsbruck	41	FK Austria	35
1968	SK Rapid Wien	44	Wacker Innsbruck	37	FK Austria	35
1969	FK Austria	46	Wiener Sport-Club	38	SK Rapid Wien	35
1970	FK Austria	45	Wiener Sport-Club	38	SK Sturm Graz	36
1971	Wacker Innsbruck	44	Austria Salzburg	43	SK Rapid Wien	41
1972	Wacker Innsbruck	39	FK Austria	38	SK VÖEST Linz	35
1973	Wacker Innsbruck	43	SK Rapid Wien	40	Grazer AK	36
1974	SK VÖEST Linz	47	Wacker Innsbruck	46	SK Rapid Wien	45
1975	Wacker Innsbruck	51	SK VÖEST Linz	42	SK Rapid Wien	41
1976	FK Austria	52	Wacker Innsbruck	45	SK Rapid Wien	40

1977	Wacker Innsbruck 53	SK Rapid Wien 47	FK Austria 45
1978	FK Austria 56	SK Rapid Wien 42	Wacker Innsbruck 39
1979	FK Austria 55	Wiener Sport-Club 41	SK Rapid Wien 39
1980	FK Austria 50	SK VÖEST Linz 43	Linzer ASK 43
1981	FK Austria 46	SK Sturm Graz 45	SK Rapid Wien 43
1982	SK Rapid Wien 47	FK Austria 44	Grazer AK 38
1983	SK Rapid Wien 48	FK Austria 48	Wacker Innsbruck 38
1984	FK Austria 47	SK Rapid Wien 47	Linzer ASK 42
1985	FK Austria 54	SK Rapid Wien 45	Linzer ASK 38
1986	FK Austria 58	SK Rapid Wien 56	Wacker Innsbruck 39
1987	SK Rapid Wien 52	FK Austria 52	FC Tirol 45
1988	SK Rapid Wien 54	FK Austria 46	SK Sturm Graz 42
1989	FC Tirol 39	Admira-Wacker 33	FK Austria 39
1990	FC Tirol 38	FK Austria 31	Admira-Wacker 29
1991	FK Austria 36	FC Tirol 35	SK Sturm Graz 32
1992	FK Austria 33	Austria Salzburg 33	FC Tirol 33

AUSTRIAN CUP FINALS

Year	Winners	Score	Runners-up
1919	SK Rapid Wien	3–0	Wiener Sport-Club
1920	SK Rapid Wien	5–2	Amateure
1921	Amateure	2–1	Wiener Sport-Club
1922	Wiener AF	2–1	Amateure
1923	Wiener Sport-Club	3–1	Wacker Wien
1924	Amateure	8–6	Slovan Wien
1925	Amateure	3–1	First Vienna FC
1926	Amateure	4–3	First Vienna FC
1927	SK Rapid Wien	3–0	FK Austria
1928	Admira Wien	2–1	Wiener AC
1929	First Vienna FC	3–2	SK Rapid Wien
1930	First Vienna FC	1–0	FK Austria
1931	Wiener AC declared winners		
1932	Admira Wien	6–1	Wiener AC
1933	FK Austria	1–0	BAC Wien
1934	Admira Wien	8–0	SK Rapid Wien
1935	FK Austria	5–1	Wiener AC
1936	FK Austria	3–0	First Vienna FC
1937	First Vienna FC	2–0	Wiener Sport-Club
1938	Wiener AC	1–0	Wiener Sport-Club
1939–45		–	
1946	SK Rapid Wien	2–1	First Vienna FC
1947	Wacker Wien	4–3	FK Austria
1948	FK Austria	2–0	SK Sturm Graz
1949	FK Austria	5–2	Vorwärts Steyr
1950–58		–	
1959	Wiener AC	2–0	SK Rapid Wien
1960	FK Austria	4–2	SK Rapid Wien
1961	SK Rapid Wien	3–1	First Vienna FC
1962	FK Austria	4–1	Grazer AK
1963	FK Austria	1–0	Linzer ASK
1964	Admira Wien	1–0	FK Austria
1965	Linzer ASK	1–1 1–0	Wiener Neustadt
1966	Admira Wien	1–0	SK Rapid Wien
1967	FK Austria	1–0	Linzer ASK
1968	SK Rapid Wien	2–0	Grazer AK
1969	SK Rapid Wien	2–1	Wiener Sport-Club
1970	Wacker Innsbruck	1–0	Linzer ASK
1971	FK Austria	2–1	SK Rapid Wien
1972	SK Rapid Wien	1–2 3–1	Wiener Sport-Club
1973	Wacker Innsbruck	1–0 1–2	SK Rapid Wien
1974	FK Austria	2–1 1–1	Austria Salzburg
1975	Wacker Innsbruck	3–0 0–2	SK Sturm Graz
1976	SK Rapid Wien	1–0 1–2	Wacker Innsbruck
1977	FK Austria	1–0 3–0	Wiener Sport-Club
1978	Wacker Innsbruck	1–1 2–1	SK VÖEST Linz
1979	Wacker Innsbruck	1–0 1–1	Admira-Wacker
1980	FK Austria	0–1 2–0	Austria Salzburg
1981	Grazer AK	0–1 2–0	Austria Salzburg
1982	FK Austria	1–0 3–1	Wacker Innsbruck
1983	SK Rapid Wien	3–0 5–0	Wacker Innsbruck
1984	SK Rapid Wien	1–3 2–0	FK Austria
1985	SK Rapid Wien	3–3 (6–5p)	FK Austria
1986	FK Austria	6–4	SK Rapid Wien
1987	SK Rapid Wien	2–0 2–2	FC Tirol
1988	Kremser SC	2–0 1–3	FC Tirol
1989	FC Tirol	0–2 6–2	Admira-Wacker
1990	FK Austria	3–1	SK Rapid Wien
1991	SV Stockerau	2–1	SK Rapid Wien
1992	FK Austria	1–0	Admira Wacker

INTERNATIONAL MATCHES PLAYED BY AUSTRIA

Date	Opponents	Result	Venue	Compet	Scorers
12–10–1902	Hungary	W 5–0	Vienna	Fr	Studnicka 3, Huber, Taurer
10–06–1903	Hungary	L 2–3	Budapest	Fr	Studnicka, Pulchert
11–10	Hungary	W 4–2	Vienna	Fr	Studnicka 3, Huber
2–06–1904	Hungary	L 0–3	Budapest	Fr	
9–11	Hungary	W 5–4	Vienna	Fr	Stansfield 4, Bugno
9–04–1905	Hungary	D 0–0	Budapest	Fr	
4–11–1906	Hungary	L 1–3	Budapest	Fr	Hussack
5–05–1907	Hungary	W 3–1	Vienna	Fr	Schediwy, Dünnmann, Wolf
3–11	Hungary	L 1–4	Budapest	Fr	Dünnmann
3–05–1908	Hungary	W 4–0	Vienna	Fr	Hussack, Kubik, Kohn, Andres
6–06	England	L 1–6	Vienna	Fr	Schmieger

7–06	Germany	W 3–2	Vienna	Fr	Dlabac, Studnicka, Andres
8–06	England	L 1–11	Vienna	Fr	Hirschl
1–11	Hungary	L 3–5	Budapest	Fr	Fischera 2, Studnicka
2–05–1909	Hungary	L 3–4	Vienna	Fr	Neubauer L 2, Schmieger
30–05	Hungary	D 1–1	Budapest	Fr	Schrenk
1–06	England	L 1–8	Vienna	Fr	Neubauer L
9–11	Hungary	D 2–2	Budapest	Fr	Schmieger 2
1–05–1910	Hungary	W 2–1	Vienna	Fr	Hussack, Fischer
6–11	Hungary	L 0–3	Budapest	Fr	
7–05–1911	Hungary	W 3–1	Vienna	Fr	Merz 2, Hussack
9–10	Germany	W 2–1	Dresden	Fr	Schmieger, Neumann
5–11	Hungary	L 0–2	Budapest	Fr	
5–05–1912	Hungary	D 1–1	Vienna	Fr	Fisch
29–06	Germany	W 5–1	Stockholm	OGr1	Merz 2, Cimera, Studnicka, Neubauer L
30–06	Holland	L 1–3	Stockholm	OGqf	Muller A
1–07	Norway	W 1–0	Stockholm	OGct	OG
3–07	Italy	W 5–1	Stockholm	OGct	Grundwald 2, Müller A, Hussak, Studnicka
5–07	Hungary	L 0–3	Stockholm	OGct	
3–11	Hungary	L 0–4	Budapest	Fr	
22–12	Italy	W 3–1	Genoa	Fr	Schmieger, Kuthan, Kohn
27–04–1913	Hungary	L 1–4	Vienna	Fr	Studnicka
15–06	Italy	W 2–0	Vienna	Fr	Brandstätter 2
26–10	Hungary	L 3–4	Budapest	Fr	Merz, Schwarz J, Dittrich
11–01–1914	Italy	D 0–0	Milan	Fr	
3–05	Hungary	W 2–0	Vienna	Fr	Fischera 2
4–10	Hungary	D 2–2	Budapest	Fr	Studnicka, Swatosch F
8–11	Hungary	L 1–2	Vienna	Fr	Kuthan
2–05–1915	Hungary	W 5–2	Budapest	Fr	Studnicka 2, Swatosch F, Ehrlich, Hoel
30–05	Hungary	L 1–2	Vienna	Fr	
3–10	Hungary	W 4–2	Vienna	Fr	Bauer E 2, Heinzl 2
7–11	Hungary	L 2–6	Budapest	Fr	Studnicka, Kuthan
7–05–1916	Hungary	W 3–1	Vienna	Fr	Bauer E 2, Studnicka
4–06	Hungary	L 1–2	Budapest	Fr	Bauer E
1–10	Hungary	W 3–2	Budapest	Fr	Bauer E 2, Grundwald
5–11	Hungary	D 3–3	Vienna	Fr	Bauer E, Kraus J
6–05–1917	Hungary	D 1–1	Vienna	Fr	
3–06	Hungary	L 2–6	Budapest	Fr	Bauer E, Heinzl
15–07	Hungary	L 1–4	Vienna	Fr	Prousek
7–10	Hungary	L 1–2	Budapest	Fr	Sedlacek J
4–11	Hungary	L 1–2	Vienna	Fr	Wilda
23–12	Switzerland	W 1–0	Basle	Fr	Bauer E
26–12	Switzerland	L 2–3	Zurich	Fr	Bauer E, Neubauer
14–04–1918	Hungary	L 0–2	Budapest	Fr	
9–05	Switzerland	W 5–1	Vienna	Fr	Wilda 2, Heinlein, Kozeluh, OG
2–06	Hungary	L 0–2	Vienna	Fr	
6–10	Hungary	L 0–3	Vienna	Fr	
6–04–1919	Hungary	L 1–2	Budapest	Fr	Wondrak
5–10	Hungary	W 2–0	Vienna	Fr	Uridil, Bauer E
9–11	Hungary	L 2–3	Budapest	Fr	Hansl, Treml
2–05–1920	Hungary	D 2–2	Vienna	Fr	Swatosch, Wieser
26–09	Germany	W 3–2	Vienna	Fr	Swatosch 3
7–11	Hungary	W 2–1	Budapest	Fr	Swatosch, Kuthan
25–03–1921	Sweden	D 2–2	Vienna	Fr	Kuthan 2
24–04	Hungary	W 4–1	Budapest	Fr	Kuthan 2, Wondrak, Neubauer K
1–05	Switzerland	D 2–2	St Gallen	Fr	Kuthan, Neubauer K
5–05	Germany	D 3–3	Dresden	Fr	Kuthan, Wondrak, Uridil
24–07	Sweden	W 3–1	Stockholm	Fr	Kuthan 2, Uridil
31–07	Finland	W 3–2	Helsinki	Fr	Uridil 2, Neumann
15–01–1922	Italy	D 3–3	Milan	Fr	Hansl 2, Köck
23–04	Germany	L 0–2	Vienna	Fr	
30–04	Hungary	D 1–1	Budapest	Fr	Jiszda
11–06	Switzerland	W 7–1	Vienna	Fr	Uridil 3, Kuthan 2, Fischera 2
24–09	Hungary	D 2–2	Vienna	Fr	Kuthan, Wessely
26–11	Hungary	W 2–1	Budapest	Fr	Swatosch, Kowanda
21–12	Switzerland	L 0–2	Geneva	Fr	
15–04–1923	Italy	D 0–0	Vienna	Fr	
6–05	Hungary	W 1–0	Vienna	Fr	Swatosch
10–06	Sweden	L 2–4	Gothenburg	Fr	Swatosch, Wieser
15–08	Finland	W 2–1	Vienna	Fr	Wieser 2

23–09	Hungary	L 0–2	Budapest	Fr	
13–01–1924	Germany	L 3–4	Nuremburg	Fr	Swatosch, Seidl, Jiszda
20–01	Italy	W 4–0	Genoa	Fr	Wieser 2, Swatosch, Jiszda
10–02	Yugoslavia	W 4–1	Zagreb	Fr	Wieser 3, Hofbauer
4–05	Hungary	D 2–2	Budapest	Fr	Wieser, Horvath
20–05	Rumania	W 4–1	Vienna	Fr	Kanhäuser 3, Häusler
21–05	Bulgaria	W 6–0	Vienna	Fr	Horvath 3, Grünwald, Danis
22–06	Egypt	W 3–1	Vienna	Fr	Horvath, Höss, Wessely
14–09	Hungary	W 2–1	Vienna	Fr	Horvath, Wessely
9–11	Sweden	D 1–1	Vienna	Fr	Wessely
21–12	Spain	L 1–2	Barcelona	Fr	Horvath
22–03–1925	Switzerland	W 2–0	Vienna	Fr	Horvath, Gschweidl
19–04	France	W 4–0	Paris	Fr	Swatosch 2, Wieser, Cutti
5–05	Hungary	W 3–1	Vienna	Fr	Haftl, Häusler
24–05	Czechoslovakia	L 1–3	Prague	Fr	Swatosch
5–07	Sweden	W 4–2	Stockholm	Fr	Horvath 3, Swatosch
10–07	Finland	W 2–1	Helsinki	Fr	Wessely, Dumser
20–09	Hungary	D 1–1	Budapest	Fr	OG
27–09	Spain	L 0–1	Vienna	Fr	
8–11	Switzerland	L 0–2	Berne	Fr	
13–12	Belgium	W 4–3	Liege	Fr	Cutti 2, Wieser, Hierländer
14–03–1926	Czechoslovakia	W 2–0	Vienna	Fr	Cutti, Hierländer
2–05	Hungary	W 3–0	Budapest	Fr	Cutti, Hanel, Eckl
30–05	France	W 4–1	Vienna	Fr	Hanel, Wesely, Ivramitsch 2
19–09	Hungary	L 2–3	Vienna	Fr	Wessely, Höss
28–09	Czechoslovakia	W 2–1	Prague	Fr	Sindelar, Wortmann
10–10	Switzerland	W 7–1	Vienna	Fr	Horvath 3, Sindelar 2, Wessely, Klima
7–11	Sweden	W 3–1	Vienna	Fr	Horvath, Sindelar, Klima
11–03–1927	Czechoslovakia	L 1–2	Vienna	Fr	Blum
10–04	Hungary	W 6–0	Vienna	Fr	Jiszda 2, Horvath, Sindelar, Wessely, Rappan
22–05	Belgium	W 4–1	Vienna	Fr	Schall 2, Wessely, Jiszda
29–05	Switzerland	W 4–1	Zurich	Fr	Jiszda, Blum, Giebisch, OG
18–09	Czechoslovakia	L 0–2	Prague	DGC	
25–09	Hungary	L 3–5	Budapest	DGC	Wessely 2, Siegl
6–11	Italy	W 1–0	Bologna	DGC	Runge
8–01–1928	Belgium	W 2–1	Brussels	Fr	Wessely, Hierländer
1–04	Czechoslovakia	L 0–1	Vienna	DGC	
6–05	Hungary	D 5–5	Budapest	Fr	Weselik 3, Wessely, Kirbes
29–07	Sweden	W 3–2	Stockholm	Fr	Gschweidl, Seidl, Smistik
7–10	Hungary	W 5–1	Vienna	DGC	Siegl 2, Weselik, Wessely, Gschweidl
28–10	Switzerland	W 2–0	Vienna	DGC	Tandler 2
11–11	Italy	D 2–2	Rome	Fr	Runge, Tandler
17–03–1929	Czechoslovakia	D 3–3	Prague	Fr	Weselik 2, Siegl
7–04	Italy	W 3–0	Vienna	DGC	Horvath 2, Weselik
5–05	Hungary	D 2–2	Vienna	Fr	Weselik, Siegl
15–09	Czechoslovakia	W 2–1	Vienna	Fr	Weselik, Gschweidl
6–10	Hungary	L 1–2	Budapest	Fr	Klima
27–10	Switzerland	W 3–1	Berne	DGC	Horvath, Schall, Stoiber
23–03–1930	Czechoslovakia	D 2–2	Prague	Fr	Horvath 2
14–05	England	D 0–0	Vienna	Fr	
1–06	Hungary	L 1–2	Budapest	Fr	Adelbrecht
21–09	Hungary	L 2–3	Vienna	Fr	Weselik, Gschweidl
16–11	Sweden	W 4–1	Vienna	Fr	Weselik, Wessely, Gschweidl, Schall
22–02–1931	Italy	L 1–2	Milan	DGC	Horvath
12–04	Czechoslovakia	W 2–1	Vienna	DGC	Horvath, Nausch
3–05	Hungary	D 0–0	Vienna	DGC	
16–05	Scotland	W 5–0	Vienna	Fr	Zischek 2, Sindelar, Schall, Vogl A
24–05	Germany	W 6–0	Berlin	Fr	Schall 3, Vogl A, Gschweidl, Zischek
16–06	Switzerland	W 2–0	Vienna	Fr	Gschweidl, Schall
13–09	Germany	W 5–0	Vienna	Fr	Sindelar 3, Schall, Gschweidl
4–10	Hungary	D 2–2	Budapest	DGC	Zischek 2
29–11	Switzerland	W 8–1	Basle	DGC	Schall 3, Vogl A 2, Sindelar, Gschweidl, Zischek
20–03–1932	Italy	W 2–1	Vienna	DGC	Sindelar 2
24–04	Hungary	W 8–2	Vienna	Fr	Schall 4, Sindelar 3, Gschweidl
22–05	Czechoslovakia	D 1–1	Prague	DGC	Sindelar
17–07	Sweden	W 4–3	Stockholm	Fr	Sindelar, Vogl A, Waitz, Molzer
2–10	Hungary	W 3–2	Budapest	Fr	Schall, Müller H, Braun

23–10	Switzerland	W	3–1	Vienna	DGC	Schall 2, Müller H
7–12	England	L	3–4	London	Fr	Zischek 2, Sindelar
11–12	Belgium	W	6–1	Brussels	Fr	Schall 4, Weselik, Zischek
12–02–1933	France	W	4–0	Paris	Fr	Sindelar, Zischek, Weselik, Vogl A
9–04	Czechoslovakia	L	1–2	Vienna	Fr	Smistik
30–04	Hungary	D	1–1	Budapest	Fr	Ostermann
11–06	Belgium	W	4–1	Vienna	Fr	Binder F 2, Sindelar, Erdl
17–09	Czechoslovakia	D	3–3	Prague	Fr	Sindelar 2, Müller H
1–10	Hungary	D	2–2	Vienna	Fr	Schall, Müller H
29–11	Scotland	D	2–2	Glasgow	Fr	Schall, Zischek
10–12	Holland	W	1–0	Amsterdam	Fr	Bican
11–02–1934	Italy	W	4–2	Turin	DGC	Zischek 3, Binder F
25–03	Switzerland	W	3–2	Geneva	DGC	Bican 2, Kaburek M
15–04	Hungary	W	5–2	Vienna	Fr	Bican 2, Schall, Zischek, Viertl
25–04	Bulgaria	W	6–1	Vienna	WCq	Horvath 3, Sindelar, Zischek, Viertl
27–05	France	W	3–2	Turin	WCr1	Sindelar, Schall, Bican
31–05	Hungary	W	2–1	Bologna	WCr2	Horvath, Zischek
3–06	Italy	L	0–1	Milan	WCsf	
7–06	Germany	L	2–3	Naples	WC3p	Horvath, Sesta
23–09	Czechoslovakia	D	2–2	Vienna	DGC	Binder F, Vogl A
7–10	Hungary	L	1–3	Budapest	DGC	Zischek
11–11	Switzerland	W	3–0	Vienna	DGC	Zischek, Skoumal, Kaburek M
24–03–1935	Italy	L	0–2	Vienna	DGC	
14–04	Czechoslovakia	D	0–0	Prague	DGC	
12–05	Hungary	L	3–6	Budapest	Fr	Zischek 2, Durspekt
12–05	Poland	W	5–2	Vienna	Fr	Stoiber 2, Vogel L, Pesser, Hahnemann
6–10	Hungary	D	4–4	Vienna	DGC	Bican 3, Hofmann L
6–10	Poland	L	0–1	Warsaw	Fr	
19–01–1936	Spain	W	5–4	Madrid	Fr	Hanreiter 2, Zischek, Bican, Binder F
26–01	Portugal	W	3–2	Oporto	Fr	Bican, Binder F, Zischek
22–03	Czechoslovakia	D	1–1	Vienna	DGC	Bican
5–04	Hungary	L	3–5	Vienna	Fr	Bican 2, Zische
6–05	England	W	2–1	Vienna	Fr	Viertl, Geiter
17–05	Italy	D	2–2	Rome	Fr	Jerusalem, Viertl
27–09	Hungary	L	3–5	Budapest	DGC	Sindelar 2, Binder F
8–11	Switzerland	W	3–1	Zurich	DGC	Binder F, Hahnemann
24–01–1937	France	W	2–1	Paris	Fr	Stroh J, Binder F
21–03	Italy	W	2–0	Vienna	Fr	Stroh, Jerusalem
	Match abandoned after 73 mins					
9–05	Scotland	D	1–1	Vienna	Fr	Jerusalem
23–05	Hungary	D	2–2	Budapest	Fr	Pesser 2
19–09	Switzerland	W	4–3	Vienna	DGC	Jerusalem 2, Sindelar, Geiter
5–10	Latvia	W	2–1	Vienna	WCq	Jerusalem, Binder F
10–10	Hungary	L	1–2	Vienna	DGC	Stroh J
24–10	Czechoslovakia	L	1–2	Prague	DGC	Neumer
19–08–1945	Hungary	L	0–2	Budapest	Fr	
20–08	Hungary	L	2–5	Budapest	Fr	Kominek, Decker
6–12	France	W	4–1	Vienna	Fr	Decker 3, Neumer
14–04–1946	Hungary	W	3–2	Vienna	Fr	Decker 2, Melchior E
5–05	France	L	1–3	Paris	Fr	Hahnemann
6–10	Hungary	L	0–2	Budapest	Fr	
27–10	Czechoslovakia	L	3–4	Vienna	Fr	Binder F 2, Kaspirek
10–11	Switzerland	L	0–1	Berne	Fr	
1–12	Italy	L	2–3	Milan	Fr	Epp, Stojaspal
4–05–1947	Hungary	L	2–5	Budapest	Fr	Epp 2
14–09	Hungary	W	4–3	Vienna	Fr	Binder F 2, Körner A, Hahnemann
5–10	Czechoslovakia	L	2–3	Prague	Fr	Binder F, Stojaspal
9–11	Italy	W	5–1	Vienna	Fr	Brinek T 2, Körner A, Ocwirk, Stojaspal
18–04–1948	Switzerland	W	3–1	Vienna	Fr	Epp 2, Melchior E
2–05	Hungary	W	3–2	Vienna	DGC	Körner A, Wagner T, Melchior E
30–05	Turkey	W	1–0	Istanbul	Fr	Körner A
11–07	Sweden	L	2–3	Stockholm	Fr	Habitzl 2
2–08	Sweden	L	0–3	London	OGr1	
3–10	Hungary	L	1–2	Budapest	Fr	Melchior E
31–10	Czechoslovakia	L	1–3	Bratislava	DGC	Stroh J
14–11	Sweden	W	2–1	Vienna	Fr	Habitzl, Wagner T
20–03–1949	Turkey	W	1–0	Vienna	Fr	Decker
3–04	Switzerland	W	2–1	Lausanne	DGC	Habitzl 2
8–05	Hungary	L	1–6	Budapest	DGC	Melchior E

22–05	Italy	L 1–3	Florence	DGC	Huber A
25–09	Czechoslovakia	W 3–1	Vienna	DGC	Decker 2, Huber A
16–10	Hungary	L 3–4	Vienna	Fr	Decker 2, Dienst
13–11	Yugoslavia	W 5–2	Belgrade	Fr	Decker 3, Huber A 2
19–03–1950	Switzerland	D 3–3	Vienna	DGC	Decker, Körner R, Huber A
2–04	Italy	W 1–0	Vienna	DGC	Melchior E
14–05	Hungary	W 5–3	Vienna	Fr	Decker 2, Melchior E, Dienst, Aurenik
8–10	Yugoslavia	W 7–2	Vienna	Fr	Stojaspal 2, Melchior E 2, Decker, Wagner T, Aurednik
29–10	Hungary	L 3–4	Budapest	Fr	Wagner T 2, Melchior E
5–11	Denmark	W 5–1	Vienna	Fr	Wagner T 3, Melchior E, Aurednik
13–12	Scotland	W 1–0	Glasgow	Fr	Melchior E
27–05–1951	Scotland	W 4–0	Vienna	Fr	Wagner T 2, Hanappi 2
17–06	Denmark	D 3–3	Copenhagen	Fr	Melchior E, Wagner T, Riegler J
23–09	West Germany	L 0–2	Vienna	Fr	
14–10	Belgium	W 8–1	Brussels	Fr	Huber A 3, Stojaspal 2, Melchior E 2, Hanappi
1–11	France	D 2–2	Paris	Fr	Körner A, Stojaspal
28–11	England	D 2–2	London	Fr	Melchior E, Stojaspal
23–03–1952	Belgium	W 2–0	Vienna	Fr	Stojaspal 2
7–05	Rep. Ireland	W 6–0	Vienna	Fr	Huber A 3, Dienst 2, Haummer
25–05	England	L 2–3	Vienna	Fr	Huber A, Dienst
22–06	Switzerland	D 1–1	Geneva	Fr	Decker
21–09	Yugoslavia	L 2–4	Belgrade	Fr	Körner A, Cejka F
19–10	France	L 1–2	Vienna	Fr	Walzhofer O
23–11	Portugal	D 1–1	Oporto	Fr	Halla
22–03–1953	West Germany	D 0–0	Cologne	Fr	
25–03	Rep Ireland	L 0–4	Dublin	Fr	
26–04	Hungary	D 1–1	Budapest	Fr	Hinesser
27–09	Portugal	W 9–1	Vienna	WCq	Probst E 5, Dienst, Wagner T, Ocwirk, Happel
11–10	Hungary	L 2–3	Vienna	Fr	Wagner T, Happel
29–11	Portugal	D 0–0	Lisbon	WCq	
11–04–1954	Hungary	L 0–1	Vienna	Fr	
9–05	Wales	W 2–0	Vienna	Fr	Dienst, Halla
30–05	Norway	W 5–0	Vienna	Fr	Probst E 2, Happel, Schleger
16–06	Scotland	W 1–0	Zurich	WCr1	Probst E
19–06	Czechoslovakia	W 5–0	Zurich	WCr1	Probst E 3, Stojaspal 2
26–06	Switzerland	W 7–5	Lausanne	WCqf	Wagner T 3, Körner A 2, Probst E, Ocwirk
30–06	West Germany	L 1–6	Basle	WCsf	Stojaspal
3–07	Uruguay	W 3–1	Zurich	WC3p	Stojaspal, Ocwirk, OG
3–10	Yugoslavia	D 2–2	Vienna	Fr	Walzhofer O, Haummer
31–10	Sweden	L 1–2	Stockholm	Fr	Wagner T
14–11	Hungary	L 1–4	Budapest	Fr	Hanappi
27–03–1955	Czechoslovakia	L 2–3	Brno	DGC	Probst E, Dienst
24–04	Hungary	D 2–2	Vienna	DGC	Probst E 2
1–05	Switzerland	W 3–2	Berne	DGC	Probst E, Brousek R, Hofbauer O
19–05	Scotland	L 1–4	Vienna	Fr	Ocwirk
16–10	Hungary	L 1–6	Budapest	DGC	Grohs
30–10	Yugoslavia	W 2–1	Vienna	DGC	Hanappi, Grohs
23–11	Wales	W 2–1	Wrexham	Fr	Hanappi, Wagner T
25–03–1956	France	L 1–3	Paris	Fr	Hanappi
15–04	Brazil	L 2–3	Vienna	Fr	Sabetzer 2
2–05	Scotland	D 1–1	Glasgow	Fr	Wagner T
17–06	Yugoslavia	D 1–1	Zagreb	DGC	Koller
30–09	Luxembourg	W 7–0	Vienna	WCq	Wagner T 2, Hanappi 2, Haummer, Walzhofer O, Kozlicek E
14–10	Hungary	L 0–2	Vienna	Fr	
9–12	Italy	L 1–2	Genoa	DGC	Körner A
10–03–1957	West Germany	L 2–3	Vienna	Fr	Wagner T, Buzek
14–04	Switzerland	W 4–0	Vienna	DGC	Buzek 2, Haummer, Koller
5–05	Sweden	W 1–0	Vienna	Fr	Dienst
26–05	Holland	W 3–2	Vienna	WCq	Buzek, Koller, Stotz
15–09	Yugoslavia	D 3–3	Belgrade	Fr	Dienst 2, Happel
25–09	Holland	D 1–1	Amsterdam	WCq	Hanappi
29–09	Luxembourg	W 3–0	Luxembourg	WCq	Dienst, Kozlicek E, Senekowitsch
13–10	Czechoslovakia	D 2–2	Vienna	DGC	Körner A, Senekowitsch
23–03–1958	Italy	W 3–2	Vienna	DGC	Kozlicek P, Körner A, Buzek

14–05	Rep Ireland	W	3–1	Vienna	Fr	Körner A, Buzek, Hamerl
8–06	Brazil	L	0–3	Uddevalla	WCr1	
11–06	Soviet Union	L	0–2	Boras	WCr1	
15–06	England	D	2–2	Boras	WCr1	Körner A, Koller
14–09	Yugoslavia	L	3–4	Vienna	Fr	Körner A, Happel, Ninaus H
5–10	France	L	1–2	Vienna	Fr	Hof E
19–11	West Germany	D	2–2	Berlin	Fr	Knoll, Hora
20–05–1959	Norway	W	1–0	Oslo	ECr1	Hof E
24–05	Belgium	W	2–0	Brussels	Fr	Skerlan, Huberts
14–06	Belgium	W	4–2	Vienna	Fr	Hof E 2, Horak, Skerlan
23–09	Norway	W	5–2	Vienna	ECr1	Hof E 2, Nemec 2, Skerlan
22–11	Spain	L	3–6	Valencia	Fr	Hof E, Knoll, Senekowitsch
13–12	France	L	2–5	Paris	ECqf	Horak, Pichler R
27–03–1960	France	L	2–4	Vienna	ECqf	Nemec, Probst E
1–05	Czechoslovakia	L	0–4	Prague	Fr	
29–05	Scotland	W	4–1	Vienna	Fr	Hof E 2, Hanappi 2
22–06	Norway	W	2–1	Oslo	Fr	Hof E, Hamerl
4–09	Soviet Union	W	3–1	Vienna	Fr	Hof E 2, Flögel
30–10	Spain	W	3–0	Vienna	Fr	Hof E, Senekowitsch, Nemec
20–11	Hungary	L	0–2	Budapest	Fr	
10–12	Italy	W	2–1	Naples	Fr	Hof E, Kaltenbrunner E
27–05–1961	England	W	3–1	Vienna	Fr	Hof E, Senekowitsch, Nemec
11–06	Hungary	W	2–1	Budapest	Fr	Nemec, Rafreider
10–09	Soviet Union	W	1–0	Moscow	Fr	Rafreider
8–10	Hungary	W	2–1	Vienna	Fr	Hof E, Oslansk
19–11	Yugoslavia	L	1–2	Zagreb	Fr	Nemec
5–01–1962	Egypt	L	0–1	Cairo	Fr	
4–04	England	L	1–3	London	Fr	Buzek
8–04	Rep Ireland	W	3–2	Dublin	Fr	Hof E, Buzek, Hirnschrodt
6–05	Bulgaria	W	2–0	Vienna	Fr	Hof E, OG
24–06	Hungary	L	1–2	Vienna	Fr	Nemec
16–09	Czechoslovakia	L	0–6	Vienna	Fr	
28–10	Hungary	L	0–2	Budapest	Fr	
11–11	Italy	L	1–2	Vienna	Fr	Nemec
25–11	Bulgaria	D	1–1	Sofia	Fr	Nemec
24–04–1963	Czechoslovakia	W	3–1	Vienna	Fr	Nemec 3
8–05	Scotland	L	1–4	Glasgow	Fr	Linhart
9–06	Italy	L	0–1	Vienna	Fr	
25–09	Rep Ireland	D	0–0	Vienna	ECr1	
13–10	Rep Ireland	L	2–3	Dublin	ECr1	Koleznik, Flogel
27–10	Hungary	L	1–2	Budapest	Fr	Viehböck
14–12	Italy	L	0–1	Turin	Fr	
12–04–1964	Holland	D	1–1	Amsterdam	Fr	Flögel
3–05	Hungary	W	1–0	Vienna	Fr	Nemec
14–05	Uruguay	L	0–2	Vienna	Fr	
27–09	Yugoslavia	W	3–2	Vienna	Fr	Nemec 2, Hasil
11–10	Soviet Union	W	1–0	Vienna	Fr	Glechner
24–03–1965	France	W	2–1	Paris	Fr	Koller, Seitl
25–04	East Germany	D	1–1	Vienna	WCq	Hof E
16–05	Soviet Union	D	0–0	Moscow	Fr	
13–06	Hungary	L	0–1	Vienna	WCq	
5–09	Hungary	L	0–3	Budapest	WCq	
9–10	West Germany	L	1–4	Stuttgart	Fr	Buzek
20–10	England	W	3–2	London	Fr	Fritsch 2, Flögel
31–10	East Germany	L	0–1	Leipzig	WCq	
24–04–1966	Soviet Union	L	0–1	Vienna	Fr	
22–05	Rep. Ireland	W	1–0	Vienna	Fr	Seitl
18–06	Italy	L	0–1	Milan	Fr	
18–09	Holland	W	2–1	Vienna	Fr	Sara, Viehböck
2–10	Finland	D	0–0	Helsinki	ECq	
5–10	Sweden	L	1–4	Stockholm	Fr	Flögel
30–10	Hungary	L	1–3	Budapest	Fr	Wolny
27–05–1967	England	L	0–1	Vienna	Fr	
11–06	Soviet Union	L	3–4	Moscow	ECq	Hof E, Wolny, Siber
6–09	Hungary	L	1–3	Vienna	Fr	Hof E
24–09	Finland	W	2–1	Vienna	ECq	Flögel, Grausam
4–10	Greece	L	1–4	Athens	ECq	Grausam
15–10	Soviet Union	W	1–0	Vienna	ECq	Grausam
5–11	Greece	D	1–1	Vienna	ECq	Siber

1-05-1968	Rumania	D	1-1	Linz	Fr	Siber
19-05	Cyprus	W	7-1	Vienna	WCq	Hof E 5, Redl, Siber
16-06	Soviet Union	L	1-3	Leningrad	Fr	Hof E
22-09	Switzerland	L	0-1	Berne	Fr	
13-10	West Germany	L	0-2	Vienna	WCq	
6-11	Scotland	L	1-2	Glasgow	WCq	Starek
10-11	Rep. Ireland	D	2-2	Dublin	Fr	Hof E, Redl
19-04-1969	Cyprus	W	2-1	Nicosia	WCq	Kreuz, Redl
23-04	Israel	D	1-1	Tel Aviv	Fr	Kreuz
27-04	Malta	W	3-1	Gzira	Fr	Köglberger 2, Kreuz
10-05	West Germany	L	0-1	Nuremberg	WCq	
21-09	West Germany	D	1-1	Vienna	Fr	Pirkner
5-11	Scotland	W	2-0	Vienna	WCq	Redl 2
8-04-1970	Yugoslavia	D	1-1	Sarajevo	Fr	Redl
12-04	Czechoslovakia	L	1-3	Vienna	Fr	OG
29-04	Brazil	L	0-1	Rio de Janeiro	Fr	
10-09	Yugoslavia	L	0-1	Graz	Fr	
27-09	Hungary	D	1-1	Budapest	Fr	Redl
7-10	France	W	1-0	Vienna	Fr	Kreuz
31-10	Italy	L	1-2	Vienna	ECq	Parits
4-04-1971	Hungary	L	0-2	Vienna	Fr	
26-05	Sweden	L	0-1	Stockholm	ECq	
30-05	Rep. Ireland	W	4-1	Dublin	ECq	Kodat, Starek, Schmidradner, OG
11-07	Brazil	D	1-1	Sao Paulo	Fr	Jara
4-09	Sweden	W	1-0	Vienna	ECq	Stering
10-10	Rep. Ireland	W	6-0	Linz	ECq	Parits 3, Jara 2, Pirkner
20-11	Italy	D	2-2	Rome	ECq	Jara, Sara
8-04-1972	Czechoslovakia	L	0-2	Brno	Fr	
30-04	Malta	W	4-0	Vienna	WCq	Hickersberger 3, Hof N
10-06	Sweden	W	2-0	Vienna	WCq	Parits, Pumm
3-09	Rumania	D	1-1	Craiova	Fr	Hickersberger
15-10	Hungary	D	2-2	Vienna	WCq	Hasil, Jara
25-11	Malta	W	2-0	Gzira	WCq	Köglberger, OG
28-03-1973	Holland	W	1-0	Vienna	Fr	Köglberger
29-04	Hungary	D	2-2	Budapest	WCq	Starek, Jara
23-05	Sweden	L	2-3	Gothenberg	WCq	Jara, Starek
13-06	Brazil	D	1-1	Vienna	Fr	Kreuz
26-09	England	L	0-7	London	Fr	
10-10	West Germany	L	0-4	Hannover	Fr	
27-11	Sweden	L	1-2	Gelsenkirchen	WCq	Hattenberger
27-03-1974	Holland	D	1-1	Rotterdam	Fr	Krankl
1-05	Brazil	D	0-0	Sao Paulo	Fr	
8-06	Italy	D	0-0	Vienna	Fr	
4-09	Wales	W	2-1	Vienna	ECq	Kreuz, Krankl
28-09	Hungary	W	1-0	Vienna	Fr	Krankl
13-11	Turkey	W	1-0	Istanbul	Fr	Stering
16-03-1975	Luxembourg	W	2-1	Luxembourg	ECq	Köglberger, Krankl
2-04	Hungary	D	0-0	Vienna	ECq	
7-06	Czechoslovakia	D	0-0	Vienna	Fr	
3-09	West Germany	L	0-2	Vienna	Fr	
24-09	Hungary	L	1-2	Budapest	ECq	Krankl
15-10	Luxembourg	W	6-2	Vienna	ECq	Welzl 2, Krankl 2, Jara, Prohaska
19-11	Wales	L	0-1	Wrexham	ECq	
28-04-1976	Sweden	W	1-0	Vienna	Fr	Pirkner
12-06	Hungary	L	0-2	Budapest	Fr	
23-06	Soviet Union	L	1-2	Vienna	Fr	Rinker
22-09	Switzerland	W	3-1	Linz	Fr	Krankl, Köglberger, Kreuz
13-10	Hungary	L	2-4	Vienna	Fr	Krankl 2
10-11	Greece	W	3-0	Kavalla	Fr	Hickersberger, Krankl, Pezzey
5-12	Malta	W	1-0	Gzira	WCq	Krankl
15-12	Israel	W	3-1	Tel Aviv	Fr	Prohaska, Schachner, Krankl
9-03-1977	Greece	W	2-0	Vienna	Fr	Sara, Schachner
17-04	Turkey	W	1-0	Vienna	WCq	Schachner
30-04	Malta	W	9-0	Salzburg	WCq	Krankl 6, Stering 2, Pirkner
1-06	Czechoslovakia	D	0-0	Ostrava	Fr	
24-08	Poland	W	2-1	Vienna	Fr	Stering, Krankl
24-09	East Germany	D	1-1	Vienna	WCq	Kreuz
12-10	East Germany	D	1-1	Leipzig	WCq	Hattenberger

30–10	Turkey	W	1–0	Izmir	WCq	Prohaska
15–02–1978	Greece	D	1–1	Athens	Fr	Krankl
22–03	Belgium	L	0–1	Charleroi	Fr	
4–04	Switzerland	W	1–0	Basle	Fr	Jara
20–05	Holland	L	0–1	Vienna	Fr	
3–06	Spain	W	2–1	Buenos Aires	WCr1	Schachner, Krankl
7–06	Sweden	W	1–0	Buenos Aires	WCr1	Krankl
11–06	Brazil	L	0–1	Mar del Plata	WCr1	
14–06	Holland	L	1–5	Cordoba	WCr2	Obermayer
18–06	Italy	L	0–1	Buenos Aires	WCr2	
21–06	West Germany	W	3–2	Cordoba	WCr2	OG, Krankl 2
30–08	Norway	W	2–0	Oslo	ECq	Pezzey, Krankl
20–09	Scotland	W	3–2	Vienna	ECq	Pezzy, Schachner, Kreuz
15–11	Portugal	L	1–2	Vienna	ECq	Schachner
30–01–1979	Israel	W	1–0	Tel Aviv	Fr	Oberacher
28–03	Belgium	D	1–1	Brussels	ECq	Krankl
2–05	Belgium	D	0–0	Vienna	ECq	
13–06	England	W	4–3	Vienna	Fr	Pezzey 2, Welzl 2
29–08	Norway	W	4–0	Vienna	ECq	Jara, Prohaska, Kreuz, Krankl
26–09	Hungary	W	3–1	Vienna	Fr	Prohaska 2, Steinkogler
17–10	Scotland	D	1–1	Glasgow	ECq	Krankl
21–11	Portugal	W	2–1	Lisbon	ECq	Welzl, Schachner
2–04–1980	West Germany	L	0–1	Munich	Fr	
21–05	Argentina	L	1–5	Vienna	Fr	Jara
4–06	Hungary	D	1–1	Budapest	Fr	Jara
24–09	Finland	W	2–0	Helsinki	WCq	Jara, Welzl
8–10	Hungary	W	3–1	Vienna	Fr	Welzl, Keglevits 2
15–11	Albania	W	5–0	Vienna	WCq	Pezzey, Schachner 2, Welzl, Krankl
6–12	Albania	W	1–0	Tirana	WCq	Welzl
29–04–1981	West Germany	L	0–2	Hamburg	WCq	
28–05	Bulgaria	W	2–0	Linz	WCq	Krankl, Jara
17–06	Finland	W	5–1	Vienna	WCq	Prohaska 2, Krankl, Welzl, Jurtin
23–09	Spain	D	0–0	Vienna	Fr	
14–10	West Germany	L	1–3	Vienna	WCq	Schachner
11–11	Bulgaria	D	0–0	Sofia	WCq	
24–03–1982	Hungary	W	3–2	Budapest	Fr	Krankl, Schachner, Hattenberger
28–04	Czechoslovakia	W	2–1	Vienna	Fr	Schachner 2
19–05	Denmark	W	1–0	Vienna	Fr	Degeorgi
17–06	Chile	W	1–0	Oviedo	WCr1	Schachner
21–06	Algeria	W	2–0	Oviedo	WCr1	Schachner, Krankl
25–06	West Germany	L	0–1	Gijon	WCr1	
28–06	France	L	0–1	Madrid	WCr2	
1–07	Nth Ireland	D	2–2	Madrid	WCr2	Pezzey, Hintermaier
22–09	Albania	W	5–0	Vienna	ECq	Hagmayr, Gasselich, Weber, Brauneder, OG
13–10	Nth Ireland	W	2–0	Vienna	ECq	Schachner 2
17–11	Turkey	W	4–0	Vienna	ECq	Polster, Pezzey, Prohaska, Schachner
27–04–1983	West Germany	D	0–0	Vienna	ECq	
17–05	Soviet Union	D	2–2	Vienna	Fr	Gasselich, Pezzey
8–06	Albania	W	2–1	Tirana	ECq	Schachner 2
21–09	Nth Ireland	L	1–3	Belfast	ECq	Gasselich
5–10	West Germany	L	0–3	Gelsenkirchen	ECq	
16–11	Turkey	L	1–3	Istanbul	ECq	Baumeister
28–03–1984	France	L	0–1	Bordeaux	Fr	
18–04	Greece	D	0–0	Vienna	Fr	
2–05	Cyprus	W	2–1	Nicosia	WCq	Gisinger, Prohaska
12–09	Denmark	L	1–3	Copenhagen	Fr	Gisinger
26–09	Hungary	L	1–3	Budapest	WCq	Schachner
14–11	Holland	W	1–0	Vienna	WCq	Jara
27–03–1985	Soviet Union	L	0–2	Tbilisi	Fr	
17–04	Hungary	L	0–3	Vienna	WCq	
1–05	Holland	D	1–1	Rotterdam	WCq	Schachner
7–05	Cyprus	W	4–0	Graz	WCq	Hrstic, Polster, Schachner, Willfurth
16–10	Yugoslavia	L	0–3	Linz	Fr	
20–11	Spain	D	0–0	Zaragoza	Fr	
26–03–1986	Italy	L	1–2	Udine	Fr	Polster
14–05	Sweden	W	1–0	Salzburg	Fr	Kienast
27–08	Switzerland	D	1–1	Innsbruck	Fr	Polster
10–09	Rumania	L	0–4	Bucharest	ECq	

15–10	Albania	W 3–0	Graz	ECq	Ogris A, Polster, Linzmaier
29–10	West Germany	W 4–1	Vienna	Fr	Polster 2, Kienast 2
25–03–1987	Yugoslavia	L 0–4	Banja Luka	Fr	
1–04	Spain	L 2–3	Vienna	ECq	Linzmaier, Polster
29–04	Albania	W 1–0	Tirana	ECq	Polster
18–08	Switzerland	D 2–2	St Gallen	Fr	Ogris A, Zsak
14–10	Spain	L 0–2	Seville	ECq	
18–11	Rumania	D 0–0	Vienna	ECq	
5–02–1988	Switzerland	L 1–2	Monaco	Fr	OG
6–04	Greece	D 2–2	Athens	Fr	Zsak, Willfurth
7–04	Denmark	W 1–0	Vienna	Fr	OG
17–05	Hungary	W 4–0	Budapest	Fr	Marko 3, Hasenhüttl
3–08	Brazil	L 0–2	Vienna	Fr	
31–08	Hungary	D 0–0	Linz	Fr	
20–09	Czechoslovakia	L 2–4	Prague	Fr	Pacult, Willfurth
19–10	Soviet Union	L 0–2	Kiev	WCq	
2–11	Turkey	W 3–2	Vienna	WCq	Polster, Herzog 2
25–03–1989	Italy	L 0–1	Vienna	Fr	
11–04	Czechoslovakia	L 1–2	Graz	Fr	Herzog
20–05	East Germany	D 1–1	Leipzig	WCq	Polster
31–05	Norway	L 1–4	Oslo	Fr	Ogris A
14–06	Iceland	D 0–0	Reykjavik	WCq	
23–08	Iceland	W 2–1	Salzburg	WCq	Pfeifenberger, Zsak
6–09	Soviet Union	D 0–0	Vienna	WCq	
4–10	Malta	W 2–1	Ta'Quali	Fr	Glatzmayer, Rodax
25–10	Turkey	L 0–3	Istanbul	WCq	
15–11	East Germany	W 3–0	Vienna	WCq	Polster 3
28–02–1990	Egypt	D 0–0	Cairo	Fr	
28–03	Spain	W 3–2	Malaga	Fr	Polster, Rodax, Hörtnagl
11–04	Hungary	W 3–0	Salzburg	Fr	Ogris A, Artner, Keglevits
3–05	Argentina	D 1–1	Vienna	Fr	Zsak
30–05	Holland	W 3–2	Vienna	Fr	Zsak, Pecl, Pfeffer
9–06	Italy	L 0–1	Rome	WCr1	
15–06	Czechoslovakia	L 0–1	Florence	WCr1	
19–06	USA	W 2–1	Florence	WCr1	Rodax, Ogris A
21–08	Switzerland	L 1–3	Vienna	Fr	Ogris A
12–09	Faeroe Islands	L 0–1	Landskrona	ECq	
31–10	Yugoslavia	L 1–4	Belgrade	ECq	Ogris A
14–11	Nth Ireland	D 0–0	Vienna	ECq	
17–04–1991	Norway	D 0–0	Vienna	Fr	
1–05	Sweden	L 0–6	Stockholm	Fr	
22–05	Faeroe Islands	W 3–0	Salzburg	ECq	Pfeifenberger, Streiter, Wetl
5–06	Denmark	L 1–2	Odense	ECq	Ogris E
4–09	Portugal	D 1–1	Oporto	Fr	Kockler
9–10	Denmark	L 0–3	Vienna	ECq	
16–10	Nth. Ireland	L 1–2	Belfast	ECq	Lainer
13–11	Yugoslavia	L 0–2	Vienna	ECq	
25–03–1992	Hungary	L 1–2	Budapest	Fr	Polster
14–04	Lithuania	W 4–0	Vienna	Fr	Ogris A, Prosenik, Polster, Hutti
29–04	Wales	D 1–1	Vienna	Fr	Baur
19–05	Poland	L 2–4	Salzburg	Fr	Hasenhutti, Waldhoer
27–05	Holland	L 2–3	Sittard	Fr	Polster, Schinkels

LEADING INTERNATIONAL GOALSCORERS

1	Krankl	34
2	Hof	28
	Horvath	28
4	Sindelar	27
	Schall	27
6	Zischek	24
7	Schachner	23
8	Wagner	22
9	Decker	19
10	Polster	18
11	Probst	17
	Swatosch	17
	Studnicka	17
	Wessely	17
15	Binder	16
	Melchior	16
	Nemec	16
18	Kuthan	15
	Stojaspal	15
20	Bican	14
	Jara	14
	Körner	14
23	Weselik	13
	Bauer	13
25	Dienst	12
	Hanappi	12
	Wieser	12
28	Huber	11
	Kreuz	11
30	Gschweidl	10
	Welzl	10
	Prohaska	10

LEADING INTERNATIONAL APPEARANCES

1	Hanappi	93	7	Weber	68	13	Blum	51
2	Koller	86	8	Schachner	63		Happel	51
3	Koncilia	84	9	Ocwirk	62		Hattenberger	51
	Pezzey	84	10	Jara	59	16	Obermayer	50
5	Prohaska	83	11	Kreuz	56			
6	Krankl	69	12	Sara	55			

BELGIUM

Belgium is a country that has matured with age on the football field. As founder members of FIFA they have been playing for longer than most, but, hidebound by tradition, were held back for years from modernising their domestic game. Since the restrictions were thrown off in the 1960s, the Belgians have proved to be one of the more enduring forces of both European and world football.

Belgium has always been a focal point of Europe. Waterloo was fought on its soil, as was the majority of the First World War. Now in the late 20th century it is the centre for many functions of the EEC, so it is not surprising that the Belgians were in the forefront of organised football on the continent. The Association was formed in 1895, and a league started the following year, thus making it, along with Sweden, the oldest league in Europe outside of Great Britain.

Naturally the Belgians were prime movers in the formation of FIFA in 1904, and in the same year played their first international, making their debut against France who were also playing their first game. The following year, Belgium met Holland in Antwerp. Over the course of the first half of the century, the Belgium–France match became an annual event, whilst the Belgium–Holland game was usually played twice a year, one at home and one away. The latter fixture has become as famous a 'derby' match as either the Austria–Hungary or England–Scotland encounters.

A large number of clubs had been formed by the turn of the century, the oldest of them, Royal Antwerp, having been founded in 1880. RFC Liege won the inaugural championship, and although some of the famous clubs of this time no longer survive as separate entities, they survive as combinations that have since merged. Although teams were very active in the league, they remained true to the amateur spirit. The sport was seen very much as a pastime, and this meant that progress at both club and national level was slow.

In 1920, Belgium won the only title the national team has ever won, beating Czechoslovakia in the final of the Olympic Games. At the time only the British Isles were professional, so with some justification the Belgians regarded themselves as world champions. The fact that the tournament was held in Belgium and occurred in the immediate aftermath of World War I does take some shine off the honour, and in subsequent years Belgium did not live up to the reputation gained by winning the tournament.

Results in the inter-war period were poor and saw defeats in the first round of every tournament entered, with the exception of the 1928 Olympic Games where they beat Luxembourg in the first round only to lose heavily to Argentina in the quarter-finals. The Belgian FA was heavily involved in promoting the idea of the World Cup, and so when it was launched they were one of the few European nations to make the trip to Uruguay. They were spectacularly unsuccessful once there, but one Belgian did make an impression. Jean Langenus became the first man to referee the World Cup Final, resplendent as he was in knickerbockers and cap.

Very few players of this period can be regarded as of the highest class. Two who were, however, were the Braine brothers, Raymond and Pierre. Raymond has often been regarded as one of the all-time greats of Belgian football, and in its amateur state, it could not keep him. He helped Beerschot to four titles in five years in the 1920s, playing alongside his brother, and after being refused a work permit to play in England he joined Sparta Prague in 1931 as a professional, winning many honours.

The post-war years saw no dramatic improvement in Belgian football. Anderlecht became the dominant club and by the 1960s were at the forefront of a movement to modernise the game, which they felt was decaying at the roots. Semi-professionalism was grudgingly introduced and foreigners known as 'Independents' were brought in to pep up a flagging club scene. The process eventually paid off with qualification for the 1970 World Cup.

Although famous names such as Jef Mermans, Pol Anoul, Rik Coppens, Jef Jurion and most of all Paul Van Himst had represented their country during the 1950s and 1960s, they never achieved any lasting results. Indeed the 1970 World Cup was the first time since 1954 that they had qualified for the final tournament, and once there they again made little impression.

The introduction of full professionalism in 1972 gave the country the impetus it needed to perform at the highest level. Clubs like Anderlecht, Club Brugge and Standard Liege all found that they could compete with the best when on an equal footing, something they had been denied for so long. Anderlecht especially took advantage of the new conditions and in 1976 won the Cup Winners Cup, the first honour for any Belgian side since 1920. They followed up with victory in the same competition two years later, and have done well on a regular basis since.

The benefits were bound to be felt by the national side eventually, and from 1972 to 1984 Belgium reached the last eight of four successive European Championship tournaments. Semi-finalists in 1972, they went one better in 1980 by reaching the final itself before losing to the West Germans. The 1980 team was remarkable in that it formed the nucleus of the side that was to represent Belgium over the next ten years. Rarely has a team been so closely moulded as the team Guy Thys had charge of from 1976.

Jean-Marie Pfaff was probably the best goalkeeper in Belgian history, whilst in defence Eric Gerets has provided the backbone around whom players like Michel Renquin, Leo Clijsters and Georges Grun have slotted in well. Frankie Vercauteren, Rene Vandereycken and Jan Ceulemans have been consistent influences in midfield, whilst Enzo Scifo is widely regarded as Belgium's best player ever. In attack Erwin Vandenbergh proved to be one of the most consistent scorers ever for Belgium, and although Jan Ceulemans overtook him in the scoring chart for the national team, this was done in twice the number of games.

The side's greatest achievement came in the 1986 World Cup where they were eventually beaten in the semi-finals by two brilliant Maradona goals. After years of under-achieving Belgium finally had a team capable of pushing for the highest honours, and there is no reason to see why this should change in the future.

	All			League			Cup		Europe		
Team	G	S	B	G	S	B	G	S	G	S	B
1 RSC Anderlecht	31	21	7	21	15	5	7	2	3	4	2
2 Club Brugge KV	14	15	10	9	10	8	5	3	–	2	2
3 RWD Molenbeek*	13	11	12	12	9	11	1	2	–	–	1
4 Union Saint Gilloise	13	8	8	11	8	7	2	–	–	–	1
5 Standard Club Liège	12	14	17	8	7	15	4	6	–	1	2
6 Beerschot VAV	9	8	5	7	7	5	2	1	–	–	–
7 Royal Antwerp FC	6	13	7	4	12	7	2	1	–	–	–
8 KV Mechelen	6	8	3	4	5	2	1	3	1	–	1
9 RFC Liège	6	4	5	5	3	4	1	1	–	–	1
10 Cercle Brugge	5	2	6	3	–	6	2	2	–	–	–
11 Lierse SK	4	3	2	3	2	2	1	1	–	–	–
12 SK Beveren	4	2	1	2	–	–	2	2	–	–	1
13 AA Gent	2	1	5	–	1	5	2	–	–	–	–
14 Racing Club Genk	2	1	2	–	–	1	2	1	–	–	1
15 KSV Waregem	1	1	1	–	–	–	1	1	–	–	1
16 Racing Tournai	1	–	–	–	–	–	1	–	–	–	–
17 Berchem Sport	–	3	1	–	3	1	–	–	–	–	–
18 Racing Mechelen	–	2	4	–	1	4	–	1	–	–	–
19 RSC Charelroi	–	2	–	–	1	–	–	1	–	–	–
KSC Lokeren	–	2	–	–	1	–	–	1	–	–	–
St. Truidense VV	–	2	–	–	1	–	–	1	–	–	–
22 Leopold CB	–	1	3	–	1	3	–	–	–	–	–
23 Olympic Charleroi	–	1	1	–	1	1	–	–	–	–	–
24 FC Beringen	–	1	–	–	1	–	–	–	–	–	–
FC Diest	–	1	–	–	–	–	–	1	–	–	–
FC Germinal Ekeren	–	1	–	–	–	–	–	1	–	–	–
Racing Gent	–	1	–	–	–	–	–	1	–	–	–
Tubantia Borgerhout	–	1	–	–	–	–	–	1	–	–	–
SK Tongeren	–	1	–	–	–	–	–	1	–	–	–
CS Verviers	–	1	–	–	–	–	–	1	–	–	–
30 Athletic Brussels	–	–	1	–	–	1	–	–	–	–	–
SC Brussels	–	–	1	–	–	1	–	–	–	–	–

* Includes 11 championships and one cup win by Racing White and Daring CB

To the end of the 1991–92 season

Population: 9958000
Area, sq km: 30518
% in urban areas: 96.5%
Capital city: Brussels

Union Royale Belge des Sociétés de Football-Association
Avenue Houba de Strooper #145
B-1020 Brussels
Belgium
Tel: (010 32) 2 477 1211
Fax: (010 32) 2 478 2391
Telex: BVBFBF B 23257
Cable: URBSFA BRUXELLES
Languages for correspondence: French, Dutch, English, German

Year of formation: 1895
Affiliation to FIFA: 1904
Affiliation to UEFA: 1954

Registered clubs: 2112
Registered players: 423 100
Professional players: 1260
Registered coaches: 2765
Registered referees: 7080

National stadium: Stade du Heysel 35 000
National colours: Shirts: Red/Shorts: Red/Socks: Red
Reserve colours: Shirts: White/Shorts: White/Socks: White
Season: September–May

THE RECORD

WORLD CUP

1930 .... Final Tournament/1st round
1934 .... QT 2nd/3 in group 11 – Final Tournament/1st round
1938 .... QT 2nd/3 in group 8 – Final Tournament/1st round
1950 .... Did not enter
1954 .... QT 1st/3 in group 2 – Final Tournament/1st round
1958 .... QT 2nd/3 in group 2
1962 .... QT 3rd/3 in group 1
1966 .... QT 2nd/3 in group 1
1970 .... QT 1st/4 in group 6 – Final

Tournament/1st round
1974 .... QT 2nd/4 in group 3
1978 .... QT 2nd/4 in group 4
1982 .... QT 1st/5 in group 2 – Final Tournament/2nd round
1986 .... QT 2nd/4 in group 1 – Final Tournament/Semi-finalists/4th place
1990 .... QT 1st/5 in group 7 – Final Tournament/2nd round

EUROPEAN CHAMPIONSHIP

1960 .... Did not enter
1964 .... 1st round
1968 .... QT 2nd/4 in group 7
1972 .... QT 1st/4 in group 5 – Final Tournament/Semi-finalists/3rd place
1976 .... QT 1st/4 in group 7 – Final Tournament/Quarter-finalists
1980 .... QT 1st/5 in group 2 – Final Tournament/Finalists
1984 .... QT 1st/4 in group 1 – Final Tournament/1st round
1988 .... QT 3rd/5 in group 7
1992 .... QT 3rd/4 in group 5

OLYMPIC GAMES

1908 .... Did not enter
1912 .... Did not enter
1920 .... Winners
1924 .... 1st round
1928 .... Quarter-finalists
1936–76 ..... Did not enter
1980 .... QT Failed to qualify
1984 .... QT Failed to qualify
1988 .... QT Failed to qualify
1992 .... QT Failed to qualify

EUROPEAN CLUB COMPETITIONS

EUROPEAN CUP: Finalists – Club Brugge 1978

CUP WINNERS CUP: Winners – RSC Anderlecht 1976 1978, KV Mechelen 1988
Finalists – RSC Anderlecht 1977 1990, Standard CL 1982

UEFA CUP: Winners – RSC Anderlecht 1983
Finalists – RSC Anderlecht 1970 1984, Club Brugge 1976

CLUB DIRECTORY

BRUSSELS (Population – 2 385 000)

RSC Anderlecht
Stadium: Stade Constant Vanden Stock 'Parc Astrid' 32 000
Founded: 1908
Colours: White with violet sleeves/White

RWD Molenbeek
Stadium: Edmond Machtens 31 000
Founded: 1973
Colours: White/Black
Previous names: Merger in 1973 of Racing White Brussels (1963) and Daring CB (1895). Racing White was the result of a merger in 1963 between Racing CB (1891) and White Star AC (1910)

ANTWERP (Population – 1 100 000)

Royal Antwerp FC
Stadium: Bosuil 35 000
Founded: 1880
Colours: White/Red

Beerschot VAV
Stadium: Kiel 25000
Founded: 1899
Colours: Violet/White

FC Germinal Ekeren
Stadium: Veltwijkpark 10000
Founded: 1942
Colours: Yellow with red sleeves and shoulders/Yellow

LIEGE (Population – 750 000)

Standard Club Liège
Stadium: Sclessin 30 000
Founded: 1898
Colours: Red/White

RFC Liège
Stadium: Jules Georges 35 000
Founded: 1892
Colours: Red and blue stripes/Blue
Previous names: RFC Liègeois 1892–1989

CHARLEROI (Population – 480 000)

RSC Charleroi
Stadium: Communal 27 000
Founded: 1904
Colours: Black and white stripes/White

Olympic Charleroi
Stadium: La Neuville
Founded: 1912
Colours: White/Black
Previous name: Olympic Montignies 1971–80

GENT (Population – 465 000)
AA Gent
Stadium: Ottenstadion 25 000
Founded: 1896
Colours: White/White

HASSELT (Population – 290 000)
Racing Club Genk
Stadium: Tyl Gheyselinck 16000
Founded: 1988
Colours: Blue/White
Previous names: Merger in 1988 of SV Winterslag (1923) and Waterschei THOR (1925)

BRUGES (Population – 223 000)
Club Brugge KV
Stadium: Olympiastadion 30 000
Founded: 1891
Colours: Blue/Black

KSV Cercle Brugge
Stadium: Olympiastadion 30 000
Founded: 1899
Colours: White with green sleeves and shoulders/Green

KORTRIJK (Population – 202 000)
KV Kortrijk
Stadium: Gulden Sporen 16 000
Founded: 1971
Colours: White/Red
Previous names: Merger in 1971 of Kortrijk Sport (1901) and Stade Kortrijk

MECHELEN (Population – 121 000)

KV Mechelen
Stadium: Achter de Kazerne 20 000
Founded: 1904
Colours: Red and yellow stripes/Black

Racing Club Mechelen
Stadium: Oscar Vankesbeeckstadium 12 000
Founded: 1904
Colours: Green/White

BEVEREN
SK Beveren
Stadium: Freethial 22 000
Founded: 1935
Colours: Blue and yellow stripes/Blue
Previous names: Formed when Amical and Standard merged in 1935

LOKEREN
KSC Lokeren
Stadium: Daknam 18 000
Founded: 1970
Colours: White/black
Previous names: Merger in 1970 of Racing and Standard Lokeren

SAINT–TRUIDEN
St. Truidense VV
Stadium: Staaien 18 000
Founded: 1922
Colours: Yellow/Blue

WAREGEM
KSV Waregem
Stadium: Regenboogstadion 20 000
Founded: 1946
Colours: Red with white sleeves/White
Previous names: Merger in 1946 of Red Star and Sportif

LIER
Lierse SK
Stadium: Herman Vanderpoortenstadium 20 000
Founded: 1908
Colours: Yellow/Black

BELGIAN LEAGUE CHAMPIONSHIP

Year	Champions		Runners up		3rd	
1896	RFC Liège	20	Royal Antwerp FC	14	SC Brussels	13
1897	Racing CB	16	RFC Liège	12	Royal Antwerp FC	11
1898	RFC Liège	14	Racing CB	10	Leopold CB	6
1899	RFC Liège	16	Racing CB	8	Leopold CB	7
1900	Racing CB	14	Royal Antwerp FC	14	Athletic Brussels	12
1901	Racing CB	26	Beerschot	25	Leopold CB	23
1902	Racing CB	9	Leopold CB	9	Union St. Gilloise	4
1903	Racing CB	11	Union St. Gilloise	6	Beerschot	6
1904	Union St. Gilloise	12	Racing CB	6	Club Brugge	4
1905	Union St. Gilloise	35	Racing CB	30	Club Brugge	28
1906	Union St. Gilloise	33	Club Brugge	29	Racing CB	24
1907	Union St. Gilloise	34	Racing CB	25	Club Brugge	24
1908	Racing CB	35	Union St. Gilloise	30	Club Brugge	26
1909	Union St. Gilloise	41	Daring CB	34	Club Brugge	33
1910	Union St. Gilloise	38	Club Brugge	38	Cercle Brugge	36
1911	Cercle Brugge	35	Club Brugge	34	Daring CB	27
1912	Daring CB	38	Union St. Gilloise	36	Racing CB	29
1913	Union St. Gilloise	38	Daring CB	38	Racing CB	31
1914	Daring CB	36	Union St. Gilloise	33	Cercle Brugge	30
1915–19	–					
1920	Club Brugge	34	Union St. Gilloise	32	Daring CB	31
1921	Daring CB	36	Union St. Gilloise	31	Beerschot	27
1922	Beerschot	39	Union St. Gilloise	39	Royal Antwerp FC	37
1923	Union St. Gilloise	42	Beerschot	37	Cercle Brugge	37
1924	Beerschot	38	Union St. Gilloise	37	Cercle Brugge	33
1925	Beerschot	40	Royal Antwerp FC	34	Union St. Gilloise	32
1926	Beerschot	40	Standard CL	33	Daring CB	32
1927	Cercle Brugge	35	Beerschot	33	Standard CL	32
1928	Beerschot	48	Standard CL	37	Cercle Brugge	34
1929	Royal Antwerp FC	39	Beerschot	39	Racing Mechelen	31
1930	Cercle Brugge	37	Royal Antwerp FC	36	Racing Mechelen	31
1931	Royal Antwerp FC	37	KV Mechelen	34	Berchem Sport	33
1932	Lierse SK	37	Royal Antwerp FC	36	Union St. Gilloise	29
1933	Union St. Gilloise	43	Royal Antwerp FC	36	Cercle Brugge	33
1934	Union St. Gilloise	43	Daring CB	35	Standard CL	35
1935	Union St. Gilloise	45	Lierse SK	40	Daring CB	35
1936	Daring CB	37	Standard CL	34	Union St. Gilloise	32
1937	Daring CB	39	Beerschot	38	Union St. Gilloise	36
1938	Beerschot	41	Daring CB	36	Union St. Gilloise	31
1939	Beerschot	41	Lierse SK	34	Olympic Charleroi	33
1940–41	–					
1942	Lierse SK	39	Beerschot	35	Royal Antwerp FC	33
1943	KV Mechelen	46	Beerschot	44	Lierse SK	39
1944	Royal Antwerp FC	49	RSC Anderlecht	42	Beerschot	37
1945	–					
1946	KV Mechelen	55	Royal Antwerp FC	49	RSC Anderlecht	46
1947	RSC Anderlecht	50	Olympic Charleroi	48	KV Mechelen	45
1948	KV Mechelen	43	RSC Anderlecht	38	RFC Liège	36
1949	RSC Anderlecht	41	Berchem Sport	38	Standard CL	38
1950	RSC Anderlecht	45	Berchem Sport	40	Racing Mechelen	38
1951	RSC Anderlecht	38	Berchem Sport	38	Racing Mechelen	36
1952	RFC Liège	44	Racing Mechelen	40	Royal Antwerp FC	40
1953	RFC Liège	42	RSC Anderlecht	41	Beerschot	36
1954	RSC Anderlecht	37	KV Mechelen	36	AA Gent	36
1955	RSC Anderlecht	41	AA Gent	38	Standard CL	37
1956	RSC Anderlecht	42	Royal Antwerp FC	39	Union St. Gilloise	37
1957	Royal Antwerp FC	46	RSC Anderlecht	40	AA Gent	39
1958	Standard CL	44	Royal Antwerp FC	44	AA Gent	41
1959	RSC Anderlecht	44	RFC Liège	43	Standard CL	42
1960	Lierse SK	38	RSC Anderlecht	37	Waterschei THOR	35
1961	Standard CL	45	RFC Liège	41	RSC Anderlecht	37
1962	RSC Anderlecht	49	Standard CL	40	Royal Antwerp FC	40
1963	Standard CL	44	Royal Antwerp FC	40	RSC Anderlecht	37
1964	RSC Anderlecht	45	FC Beringen	41	Standard CL	40
1965	RSC Anderlecht	51	Standard CL	39	Beerschot	35

1966	RSC Anderlecht	47	St. Truidense VV	40	Standard CL	40
1967	RSC Anderlecht	47	Club Brugge	45	RFC Liège	39
1968	RSC Anderlecht	46	Club Brugge	45	Standard CL	40
1969	Standard CL	45	RSC Charleroi	40	Lierse SK	36
1970	Standard CL	49	Club Brugge	45	AA Gent	39
1971	Standard CL	47	Club Brugge	46	RSC Anderlecht	41
1972	RSC Anderlecht	45	Club Brugge	45	Standard CL	41
1973	Club Brugge	45	Standard CL	38	Racing White	37
1974	RSC Anderlecht	41	Royal Antwerp FC	39	RWD Molenbeek	39
1975	RWD Molenbeek	61	Royal Antwerp FC	52	RSC Anderlecht	52
1976	Club Brugge	52	RSC Anderlecht	48	RWD Molenbeek	47
1977	Club Brugge	52	RSC Anderlecht	48	Standard CL	45
1978	Club Brugge	51	RSC Anderlecht	50	Standard CL	49
1979	SK Beveren	49	RSC Anderlecht	45	Standard CL	44
1980	Club Brugge	53	Standard CL	49	RWD Molenbeek	48
1981	RSC Anderlecht	57	KSC Lokeren	46	Standard CL	42
1982	Standard CL	48	RSC Anderlecht	46	AA Gent	45
1983	Standard CL	50	RSC Anderlecht	49	Royal Antwerp FC	46
1984	SK Beveren	51	RSC Anderlecht	47	Club Brugge	44
1985	RSC Anderlecht	59	Club Brugge	48	RFC Liège	46
1986	RSC Anderlecht	52	Club Brugge	52	Standard CL	42
1987	RSC Anderlecht	57	KV Mechelen	55	Club Brugge	45
1988	Club Brugge	51	KV Mechelen	49	Royal Antwerp FC	49
1989	KV Mechelen	57	RSC Anderlecht	53	RFC Liège	46
1990	Club Brugge	57	RSC Anderlecht	53	KV Mechelen	50
1991	RSC Anderlecht	53	KV Mechelen	50	Club Brugge	47
1992	Club Brugge	53	RSC Anderlecht	49	Standard CL	46

BELGIAN CUP FINALS

Year	Winners	Score	Runners–up
1912	Racing CB	1–0	Racing Gent
1913	Union St. Gilloise	3–2	Cercle Brugge
1914	Union St. Gilloise	4–1	Club Brugge
1915–26	–		
1927	Cercle Brugge	2–1	Tubantia Borgerhout
1928–53	–		
1954	Standard CL	3–1	Racing Mechelen
1955	Royal Antwerp FC	4–0	Waterschei THOR
1956	Racing Tournai	2–1	CS Verviers
1957–63	–		
1964	AA Gent	4–2	FC Diest
1965	RSC Anderlecht	3–2	Standard CL
1966	Standard CL	1–0	RSC Anderlecht
1967	Standard CL	3–1	KV Mechelen
1968	Club Brugge	1–1 4–4 (4–2p)	Beerschot
1969	Lierse SK	2–0	Racing White
1970	Club Brugge	6–1	Daring CB
1971	Beerschot	2–1	St. Truidense VV
1972	RSC Anderlecht	1–0	Standard CL
1973	RSC Anderlecht	2–1	Standard CL
1974	KSV Waregem	4–1	SK Tongeren
1975	RSC Anderlecht	1–0	Royal Antwerp FC
1976	RSC Anderlecht	4–0	Lierse SK
1977	Club Brugge	4–3	RSC Anderlecht
1978	SK Beveren	2–0	RSC Charleroi
1979	Beerschot	1–0	Club Brugge
1980	Waterschei THOR	2–1	SK Beveren
1981	Standard CL	4–0	KSC Lokeren
1982	Waterschei THOR	2–0	KSV Waregem
1983	SK Beveren	3–1	Club Brugge
1984	AA Gent	2–0	Standard CL
1985	Cercle Brugge	1–1 (5–4p)	SK Beveren
1986	Club Brugge	3–0	Cercle Brugge
1987	KV Mechelen	1–0	RFC Liège
1988	RSC Anderlecht	2–0	Standard CL
1989	RSC Anderlecht	2–0	Standard CL
1990	RFC Liège	2–1	FC Germinal Ekeren
1991	Club Brugge	3–1	KV Mechelen
1992	Royal Antwerp	2–2 (9–8p)	KV Mechelen

INTERNATIONAL MATCHES PLAYED BY BELGIUM

Date	Opponents	Result	Venue	Compet	Scorers
1–05–1904	France	D 3–3	Brussels	Fr	Destrebecq, Quéritet 2
30–04–1905	Holland	L 1–4	Antwerp	Fr	OG
7–05	France	W 7–0	Brussels	Fr	Van Hoorden 2, Destrebecq 3, Theunen 2
14–05	Holland	L 0–4	Rotterdam	Fr	
22–04–1906	France	W 5–0	Paris	Fr	Feye 2, Van Hoorden, Deveen 2
29–04	Holland	W 5–0	Antwerp	Fr	Vanden Eynde G, Goetinck, De Veen 3
13–05	Holland	W 3–2	Rotterdam	Fr	Cambier 2, Destrebecq
14–04–1907	Holland	L 1–3	Antwerp	Fr	Feye
21–04	France	L 1–2	Brussels	Fr	OG
9–05	Holland	W 2–1	Haarlem	Fr	Feye, Goetinck
29–03–1908	Holland	L 1–4	Antwerp	Fr	Vertongen
12–04	France	W 2–1	Paris	Fr	De Veen 2

18-04	England*	L	2-8	Brussels	Fr	De Veen 2
26-04	Holland	L	1-3	Rotterdam	Fr	Saeys
26-10	Sweden	W	2-1	Brussels	Fr	Kavorkian, Goossens
21-03-1909	Holland	L	1-4	Antwerp	Fr	Poelmans
17-04	England*	L	2-11	London	Fr	De Veen 2
25-04	Holland	L	1-4	Rotterdam	Fr	Goossens
9-05	France	W	5-2	Brussels	Fr	De Veen 3, Van Hoorden, Theunen
13-03-1910	Holland	W	3-2	Antwerp	Fr	De Veen 2, Six
26-03	England*	D	2-2	Brussels	Fr	Six, Paternoster
3-04	France	W	4-0	Gentilly	Fr	Six 2, Saeys, De Veen
10-04	Holland	L	0-7	Haarlem	Fr	
16-05	Germany	W	3-0	Duisburg	Fr	Saeys 2, Van Staceghem
4-03-1911	England*	L	0-4	London	Fr	
19-03	Holland	L	1-5	Antwerp	Fr	Paternoster
2-04	Holland	L	1-3	Dordrecht	Fr	Six
23-04	Germany	W	2-1	Liege	Fr	Van Houtte, Saeys
30-04	France	W	7-1	Brussels	Fr	De Veen 5, Saeys, Bouttiau
28-01-1912	France	D	1-1	Paris	Fr	Hubin
20-02	Switzerland	W	9-2	Antwerp	Fr	Van Cant 2, Saeys 3, Six 2, De Veen 2
10-03	Holland	L	1-2	Antwerp	Fr	Nizot
8-04	England*	L	1-2	Brussels	Fr	Nizot
28-04	Holland	L	3-4	Dordrecht	Fr	Musch, Nizot 2
9-11	England*	L	0-4	Swindon	Fr	
16-02-1913	France	W	3-0	Brussels	Fr	Nizot 2, Bessens
9-03	Holland	D	3-3	Antwerp	Fr	De Veen 2, Nizot
20-04	Holland	W	4-2	Zwolle	Fr	Suetens, Musch 2, Nizot
1-05	Italy	L	0-1	Turin	Fr	
4-05	Switzerland	W	2-1	Basle	Fr	Saeys, Brébart
2-11	Switzerland	W	2-0	Verviers	Fr	Wertz, Nizot
23-11	Germany	W	6-2	Antwerp	Fr	Brébart 3, Van Cant 3
25-01-1914	France	L	3-4	Lille	Fr	Van Cant, Brébart, Thys
24-02	England*	L	1-8	Brussels	Fr	Brébart
15-03	Holland	L	2-4	Antwerp	Fr	Brébart 2
26-04	Holland	L	2-4	Amsterdam	Fr	Van Cant, Nizot
9-03-1919	France	D	2-2	Brussels	Fr	Coppée, Hebdin
17-02-1920	England*	W	3-1	Brussels	Fr	
28-03	France	L	1-2	Paris	Fr	Vlaminck
5-05	England*	W	3-0	Brussels	Fr	
29-08	Spain	W	3-1	Antwerp	OGqf	Coppée 3
31-08	Holland	W	3-0	Antwerp	OGsf	Larnoe, Van Hege, Bragard
2-09	Czechoslovakia	W	2-0	Antwerp	OGf	Coppée, Larnoe
6-03-1921	France	W	3-1	Brussels	Fr	Bragard 2, Van Hege
5-05	Italy	L	2-3	Antwerp	Fr	Larnoe, Bragard
15-05	Holland	D	1-1	Antwerp	Fr	Bragard
21-05	England	L	0-2	Brussels	Fr	
9-10	Spain	L	0-2	Bilbao	Fr	
15-01-1922	France	L	1-2	Paris	Fr	Michel
26-03	Holland	W	4-0	Antwerp	Fr	Larnoe 2, Vandevelde, Coppée
15-04	Denmark	D	0-0	Liege	Fr	
7-05	Holland	W	2-1	Amsterdam	Fr	OG, Michel
21-05	Italy	L	2-4	Milan	Fr	Larnoe, Thys
4-02-1923	Spain	W	1-0	Antwerp	Fr	Coppée
25-02	France	W	4-1	Brussels	Fr	Gillis 2, Larnoe 2
19-03	England	L	1-6	London	Fr	Vlaminck
29-04	Holland	D	1-1	Amsterdam	Fr	Thys
1-11	England	D	2-2	Antwerp	Fr	Larnoe, Schelstraete
13-01-1924	France	L	0-2	Paris	Fr	
23-03	Holland	D	1-1	Amsterdam	Fr	Coppée
27-04	Holland	D	1-1	Antwerp	Fr	Thys
29-05	Sweden	L	1-8	Paris	OGr1	
5-10	Denmark	L	1-2	Copenhagen	Fr	Adams
11-11	France	W	3-0	Brussels	Fr	Braine P, Dupac 2
8-12	England	L	0-4	West Bromwich	Fr	
15-03-1925	Holland	L	0-1	Antwerp	Fr	
3-05	Holland	L	0-5	Amsterdam	Fr	
21-05	Hungary	W	3-1	Budapest	Fr	Houet, Adams, Thys
24-05	Switzerland	D	0-0	Lausanne	Fr	
13-12	Austria	L	3-4	Liege	Fr	Thys, Gillis, Braine P
14-02-1926	Hungary	L	0-2	Brussels	Fr	

* Amateur side fielded by England

14–03	Holland	D	1–1	Antwerp	Fr	Adams
11–04	France	L	3–4	Paris	Fr	Vanderbouwhelde, Thys, Devos
2–05	Holland	W	5–1	Amsterdam	Fr	Braine R 2, Diddens, Adams, Gillis
24–05	England	L	3–5	Antwerp	Fr	Thys, Braine R 2
20–06	France	D	2–2	Brussels	Fr	Gillis, Adams
2–01–1927	Czechoslovakia	L	2–3	Liege	Fr	Bierna, Gillis
13–03	Holland	W	2–0	Antwerp	Fr	Bierna, Adams
3–04	Sweden	W	2–1	Brussels	Fr	Braine R, Adams
1–05	Holland	L	2–3	Amsterdam	Fr	Diddens, Braine R
11–05	England	L	1–9	Brussels	Fr	Van Halme
22–05	Austria	L	1–4	Vienna	Fr	Braine P
26–05	Czechoslovakia	L	0–4	Prague	Fr	
4–09	Sweden	L	0–7	Stockholm	Fr	
8–01–1928	Austria	L	1–2	Brussels	Fr	Ledent
12–02	Rep. Ireland	L	2–4	Liege	Fr	Braine R, Ledent
11–03	Holland	D	1–1	Amsterdam	Fr	Braine R
1–04	Holland	W	1–0	Antwerp	Fr	Moeschal
15–04	France	W	3–2	Paris	Fr	Devos, Braine R 2
19–05	England	L	1–3	Antwerp	Fr	Moeschal
27–05	Luxembourg	W	5–3	Amsterdam	OGr1	Braine R 2, Versyp, Moeschal 2
2–06	Argentina	L	3–6	Amsterdam	OGqf	Braine R, Van Halme, Moeschal
5–06	Holland	L	1–3	Rotterdam	OGct	Braine P
4–11	Holland	D	1–1	Amsterdam	Fr	Braine R
20–04–1929	Rep. Ireland	L	0–4	Dublin	Fr	
5–05	Holland	W	3–1	Antwerp	Fr	Braine R 2, Vandenbawhede
11–05	England	L	1–5	Brussels	Fr	Moeschal
26–05	France	W	4–1	Liege	Fr	Vandenbawhede, Braine R, Bastin 2
13–04–1930	France	W	6–1	Paris	Fr	Versyp 2, Adams, Vandenbawhede 3
4–05	Holland	D	2–2	Amsterdam	Fr	Bastin, Adams
11–05	Rep. Ireland	L	1–3	Brussels	Fr	Bastin
18–05	Holland	W	3–1	Antwerp	Fr	Voorhoof, Bastin, OG
25–05	France	L	1–2	Liege	Fr	Adams
8–06	Portugal	W	2–1	Antwerp	Fr	Vandenbawhede, Bastin
13–07	United States	L	0–3	Montevideo	WCr1	
20–07	Paraguay	L	0–1	Montevideo	WCr1	
21–09	Czechoslovakia	L	2–3	Antwerp	Fr	Versyp, Voorhoof
28–09	Sweden	D	2–2	Liege	Fr	Secrétin, Braine P
7–12	France	D	2–2	Paris	Fr	Van Beeck, Voorhoof
29–03–1931	Holland	L	2–3	Amsterdam	Fr	Versyp, Voorhoof
3–05	Holland	W	4–2	Antwerp	Fr	Voorhoof 2, Vanden Eynde S, Versyp
16–05	England	L	1–4	Brussels	Fr	Capelle
31–05	Portugal	L	2–3	Lisbon	Fr	Van Beeck, Hellemans
11–10	Poland	W	2–1	Brussels	Fr	Hellemans, Voorhoof
6–12	Switzerland	W	2–1	Brussels	Fr	Capelle 2
20–03–1932	Holland	L	1–4	Antwerp	Fr	Bastin
17–04	Holland	L	1–2	Amsterdam	Fr	Capelle
1–05	France	W	5–2	Brussels	Fr	Brichaut, Vanden Eynde S 2, Capelle, Van Beeck
5–06	Denmark	W	4–3	Copenhagen	Fr	Capelle 3, Van Beeck
12–06	Sweden	L	1–3	Stockholm	Fr	Vanden Eynde S
11–12	Austria	L	1–6	Brussels	Fr	Van Landegem
12–02–1933	Italy	L	2–3	Brussels	Fr	Voorhoof 2
12–03	Switzerland	D	3–3	Zurich	Fr	Desmedt, Voorhoof 2
26–03	France	L	0–3	Paris	Fr	
9–04	Holland	L	1–3	Antwerp	Fr	Saeys A
7–05	Holland	W	2–1	Amsterdam	Fr	Desmedt, Voorhoof
4–06	Poland	W	1–0	Warsaw	Fr	Brichaut
11–06	Austria	L	1–4	Vienna	Fr	Voorhoof
22–10	Germany	L	1–8	Duisburg	Fr	Lamoot
26–11	Denmark	D	2–2	Brussels	Fr	Versyp, Vanden Eynde S
21–01–1934	France	L	2–3	Brussels	Fr	Voorhoof, Van Den Eynde F
25–02	Rep. Ireland	D	4–4	Dublin	WCq	Capelle, Vanden Eynde S, Van Den Eynde F 2
11–03	Holland	L	3–9	Amsterdam	Fr	Voorhoof, Brichaut, Versyp
29–04	Holland	L	2–4	Antwerp	WCq	Grimonprez, Voorhoof
27–05	Germany	L	2–5	Florence	WCr1	Voorhoof 2
31–03–1935	Holland	L	2–4	Amsterdam	Fr	Van Beeck, Voorhoof
14–04	France	D	1–1	Brussels	Fr	Van Beeck
28–04	Germany	L	1–6	Brussels	Fr	Isemborghs
12–05	Holland	L	0–2	Brussels	Fr	

30–05	Switzerland	D 2–2	Brussels	Fr	OG 2
17–11	Sweden	W 5–1	Brussels	Fr	Van Caelenberghe, Capelle 2, Isemborghs 2
16–02–1936	Poland	L 0–2	Brussels	Fr	
8–03	France	L 0–3	Paris	Fr	
29–03	Holland	L 0–8	Amsterdam	Fr	
3–05	Holland	D 1–1	Brussels	Fr	Braine R
9–05	England	W 3–2	Brussels	Fr	Isemborghs 2, Fiévez
24–05	Switzerland	D 1–1	Basle	Fr	Capelle
21–02–1937	France	W 3–1	Brussels	Fr	Braine R, Ceuleers, Vanden Eynde S
4–04	Holland	W 2–1	Antwerp	Fr	Ceuleers, Fiévez
18–04	Switzerland	L 1–2	Brussels	Fr	Voorhoof
25–04	Germany	L 0–1	Hanover	Fr	
2–05	Holland	L 0–1	Rotterdam	Fr	
6–06	Yugoslavia	D 1–1	Belgrade	Fr	Capelle
10–06	Romania	L 1–2	Bucharest	Fr	Voorhoof
30–01–1938	France	L 3–5	Paris	Fr	Braine R, Voorhoof, Vanden Eynde S
27–02	Holland	L 2–7	Rotterdam	Fr	Braine R, Voorhoof
13–03	Luxembourg	W 3–2	Luxembourg	WCq	Voorhoof 2, Braine R
3–04	Holland	D 1–1	Antwerp	WCq	Isemborghs
8–05	Switzerland	W 3–0	Lausanne	Fr	Voorhoof 2, Capelle
15–05	Italy	L 1–6	Milan	Fr	Capelle
29–05	Yugoslavia	D 2–2	Brussels	Fr	Capelle, Vandenwouwer
5–06	France	L 1–3	Paris	WCr1	Isemborghs
29–01–1939	Germany	L 1–4	Brussels	Fr	Stijnen
19–03	Holland	W 5–4	Antwerp	Fr	Capelle 3, Fievez, Braine R
23–04	Holland	L 2–3	Amsterdam	Fr	Braine R, Buyle
14–05	Switzerland	L 1–2	Liege	Fr	Voorhoof
18–05	France	L 1–3	Brussels	Fr	Lamoot
27–05	Poland	D 3–3	Lodz	Fr	Fiévez, Braine R, Isemborghs
17–03–1940	Holland	W 7–1	Antwerp	Fr	Nelis, Voorhoof, Van Craen 3, Vandenwouwer, OG
21–04	Holland	L 2–4	Amsterdam	Fr	Van Craen, Nelis
24–12–1944	France	L 1–3	Paris	Fr	De Wael
13–05–1945	Luxembourg	L 1–4	Luxembourg	Fr	Gillaux
15–12	France	W 2–1	Brussels	Fr	Sermon 2
19–01–1946	England*	L 0–2	London	Fr	
23–01	Scotland*	D 2–2	Glasgow	Fr	Lemberechts, Chaves
23–02	Luxembourg	W 7–0	Charleroi	Fr	De Cleyn 5, Coppens H, Lemberechts
12–05	Holland	L 3–6	Amsterdam	Fr	De Cleyn 2, Coppens H
30–05	Holland	D 2–2	Antwerp	Fr	Lemberechts, Van Vaerenbergh
7–04–1947	Holland	L 1–2	Amsterdam	Fr	Thirifays
4–05	Holland	L 1–2	Antwerp	Fr	Anoul
18–05	Scotland	W 2–1	Brussels	Fr	Anoul 2
1–06	France	L 2–4	Paris	Fr	De Cleyn, Coppens H
21–09	England	L 2–5	Brussels	Fr	Mermans, De Cleyn
2–11	Switzerland	L 0–4	Geneva	Fr	
14–03–1948	Holland	D 1–1	Antwerp	Fr	Van Steenlant
18–04	Holland	D 2–2	Rotterdam	Fr	Mermans, Van Steenlant
28–04	Scotland	L 0–2	Glasgow	Fr	
6–06	France	W 4–2	Brussels	Fr	Chaves 2, Govard, Mermans
17–10	France	D 3–3	Paris	Fr	Mermans, Anoul, Chaves
21–11	Holland	D 1–1	Antwerp	Fr	Chaves
2–01–1949	Spain	D 1–1	Barcelona	Fr	Coppens H
13–03	Holland	D 3–3	Amsterdam	Fr	Mermans 2, OG
24–04	Rep. Ireland	W 2–0	Dublin	Fr	Lemberechts, Mermans
22–05	Wales	W 3–1	Liege	Fr	Govard 2, De Hert
2–10	Switzerland	W 3–0	Brussels	Fr	Verbruggen, Mermans, ?
6–11	Holland	W 1–0	Rotterdam	Fr	Govard
23–11	Wales	L 1–5	Cardiff	Fr	Coppens R
5–03–1950	Italy	L 1–3	Bologna	Fr	Chaves
16–04	Holland	W 2–0	Antwerp	Fr	Mermans, De Hert
10–05	Rep. Ireland	W 5–1	Brussels	Fr	Mermans 3, De Hert, Chaves
18–05	England	L 1–4	Brussels	Fr	Mermans
4–06	France	W 4–1	Brussels	Fr	Mermans 3, Mordant
1–11	France	D 3–3	Paris	Fr	Lemberechts, Mermans 2
12–11	Holland	W 7–2	Antwerp	Fr	Lemberechts 3, Mermans 2, Anoul 2
15–04–1951	Holland	L 4–5	Amsterdam	Fr	Mermans, Chaves, Vaillant
20–05	Scotland	L 0–5	Brussels	Fr	

* Not considered full internationals by England and Scotland

10–06	Spain	D	3–3	Brussels	Fr	Van Gestel 2, Van Steenlant
17–06	Portugal	D	1–1	Lisbon	Fr	Givard
14–10	Austria	L	1–8	Brussels	Fr	Lemberechts
25–11	Holland	W	7–6	Rotterdam	Fr	Anoul 3, Verbruggen, Moës 2, Van Steen
24–02–1952	Italy	W	2–0	Brussels	Fr	Moës 2
23–03	Austria	L	0–2	Vienna	Fr	
6–04	Holland	W	4–2	Antwerp	Fr	Anoul, Coppens R 2, Lemberechts
22–05	France	L	1–2	Brussels	Fr	Mermans
19–10	Holland	W	2–1	Antwerp	Fr	Anoul, Mermans
26–11	England	L	0–5	London	Fr	
25–12	France	W	1–0	Paris	Fr	Straetmans
19–03–1953	Spain	L	1–3	Barcelona	Fr	Lemberechts
19–04	Holland	W	2–0	Amsterdam	Fr	Coppens R, Janssens.
14–05	Yugoslavia	L	1–3	Brussels	Fr	Anoul
25–05	Finland	W	4–2	Helsinki	WCq	Coppens R 3, Anoul
28–05	Sweden	W	3–2	Stockholm	WCq	Anoul, Straetmans, Lemberechts
23–09	Finland	D	2–2	Brussels	WCq	Bollen M 2
8–10	Sweden	W	2–0	Brussels	WCq	Coppens R, Mees
25–10	Holland	L	0–1	Rotterdam	Fr	
22–11	Switzerland	D	2–2	Zurich	Fr	Vanden Bosch H 2
14–03–1954	Portugal	D	0–0	Brussels	Fr	
4–04	Holland	W	4–0	Antwerp	Fr	Mermans, Coppens R 2, OG
9–05	Yugoslavia	W	2–0	Zagreb	Fr	Coppens R, Mermans
30–05	France	D	3–3	Brussels	Fr	Mermans, Anoul 2
17–06	England	D	4–4	Basle	WCr1	Anoul 2, Coppens R, OG
20–06	Italy	L	1–4	Lugano	WCr1	Anoul
26–09	West Germany	W	2–0	Brussels	Fr	Coppens R, Anoul
24–10	Holland	W	4–3	Antwerp	Fr	Lemberechts, Coppens R 2, Houf
11–11	France	D	2–2	Paris	Fr	OG, Lemberechts
16–01–1955	Italy	L	0–1	Bari	Fr	
3–04	Holland	L	0–1	Amsterdam	Fr	
5–06	Czechoslovakia	L	1–3	Brussels	Fr	OG
25–09	Czechoslovakia	L	2–5	Prague	Fr	Coppens R, Orlans
28–09	Romania	L	0–1	Bucharest	Fr	
16–10	Holland	D	2–2	Rotterdam	Fr	Jacquemijns 2
25–12	France	W	2–1	Brussels	Fr	Jadot, Vanden Bosch H
11–03–1956	Switzerland	L	1–3	Brussels	Fr	Mermans
8–04	Holland	L	0–1	Antwerp	Fr	
3–06	Hungary	W	5–4	Brussels	Fr	Van Kerkhoven, Vandewaeyer R, Orlans 2, Houf
14–10	Holland	L	2–3	Antwerp	Fr	Willems M, Houf
11–11	France	L	3–6	Paris	WCq	Houf, Willems M 2
23–12	West Germany	L	1–4	Cologne	Fr	Moyson
31–03–1957	Spain	L	0–5	Brussels	Fr	
28–04	Holland	D	1–1	Amsterdam	Fr	Vandenberg P
26–05	Romania	W	1–0	Brussels	Fr	Vandenberg P
5–06	Iceland	W	8–3	Brussels	WCq	Orlans 2, Piters, Vandenberg P, Coppens R 2, Mees 2
4–09	Iceland	W	5–2	Reykjavik	WCq	Van Herpe, Vandenberg P 3, Willems M
27–10	France	D	0–0	Brussels	WCq	
17–11	Holland	L	2–5	Rotterdam	Fr	Vandenberg P, Houf
8–12	Turkey	D	1–1	Ankara	Fr	Jurion
2–03–1958	West Germany	L	0–2	Brussels	Fr	
13–04	Holland	L	2–7	Antwerp	Fr	Coppens R 2
26–05	Switzerland	W	2–0	Zurich	Fr	Stockman, Paeschen
28–09	Holland	L	2–3	Antwerp	Fr	Hanon, Piters
26–10	Turkey	D	1–1	Brussels	Fr	Piters
23–11	Hungary	L	1–3	Budapest	Fr	Mallants
1–03–1959	France	D	2–2	Paris	Fr	Lippens, Piters
19–04	Holland	D	2–2	Amsterdam	Fr	Wegria, Goyvaerts
24–05	Austria	L	0–2	Brussels	Fr	
14–06	Austria	L	2–4	Vienna	Fr	Vanden Voer, Coppens R
4–10	Holland	L	1–9	Rotterdam	Fr	Delire
28–02–1960	France	W	1–0	Brussels	Fr	Piters
27–03	Switzerland	W	3–1	Brussels	Fr	Dirickx, Jadot, Ritzen
13–04	Chile	D	1–1	Brussels	Fr	Vandenberg P
24–04	Holland	W	2–1	Antwerp	Fr	Lippens, Piters
22–05	Bulgaria	L	1–4	Sofia	Fr	Piters
2–10	Holland	L	1–4	Antwerp	Fr	Wegria

19–10	Sweden	L	0–2	Stockholm	WCq	
30–10	Hungary	W	2–1	Brussels	Fr	Van Himst, Hanon
20–11	Switzerland	L	2–4	Brussels	WCq	Van Himst, Paeschen
8–03–1961	West Germany	L	0–1	Frankfurt	Fr	
15–03	France	D	1–1	Paris	Fr	Paeschen
22–03	Holland	L	2–6	Rotterdam	Fr	Paeschen, Van Himst
20–05	Switzerland	L	1–2	Lausanne	WCq	Claessen R
4–10	Sweden	L	0–2	Brussels	WCq	
18–10	France	W	3–0	Brussels	Fr	Hanon, Vandenberg P, Claessen R
12–11	Holland	W	4–0	Amsterdam	Fr	Claessen R 2, Vandenberg P, Van Himst
24–12	Bulgaria	W	4–0	Brussels	Fr	Stockman, Jurion, Van Himst 2
1–04–1962	Holland	W	3–1	Antwerp	Fr	Jurion, Vandenberg P 2
13–05	Italy	L	1–3	Brussels	Fr	Van Himst
17–05	Portugal	W	2–1	Lisbon	Fr	Stockman, Jurion
23–05	Poland	L	0–2	Warsaw	Fr	
14–10	Holland	W	2–0	Antwerp	Fr	Stockman, Van Himst
4–11	Yugoslavia	L	2–3	Belgrade	ECr1	Stockman, Jurion
2–12	Spain	D	1–1	Brussels	Fr	Jurion
3–03–1963	Holland	W	1–0	Rotterdam	Fr	Vandenberg P
31–03	Yugoslavia	L	0–1	Brussels	ECr1	
24–04	Brazil	W	5–1	Brussels	Fr	Stockman 3, Van Himst, OG
20–10	Holland	D	1–1	Amsterdam	Fr	Vandenberg P
1–12	Spain	W	2–1	Valencia	Fr	Vandenberg P
25–12	France	W	2–1	Paris	Fr	Vandenberg P, Puis
22–03–1964	Holland	D	0–0	Antwerp	Fr	Van Himst 2
15–04	Switzerland	L	0–2	Geneva	Fr	
3–05	Portugal	L	1–2	Brussels	Fr	Vandenberg P
30–09	Holland	W	1–0	Antwerp	Fr	Jurion
21–10	England	D	2–2	London	Fr	Cornelis, Van Himst
2–12	France	W	3–0	Brussels	Fr	Van Himst, Vermeyen 2
24–03–1965	Rep. Ireland	W	2–0	Dublin	Fr	OG, Jurion
7–04	Poland	D	0–0	Brussels	Fr	
9–05	Israel	W	1–0	Brussels	WCq	Jurion
2–06	Brazil	L	0–5	Rio de Janeiro	Fr	
26–09	Bulgaria	L	0–3	Sofia	WCq	
27–10	Bulgaria	W	5–0	Brussels	WCq	Van Himst 2, Thio 2, Stockman
10–11	Israel	W	5–0	Tel Aviv	WCq	Van Himst 3, Thio, Puis
29–12	Bulgaria	L	1–2	Florence	WCq	OG
17–04–1966	Holland	L	1–3	Rotterdam	Fr	Spronck
20–04	France	W	3–0	Paris	Fr	Lambert, Stockman, Thio
22–05	Soviet Union	L	0–1	Brussels	Fr	
25–05	Rep. Ireland	L	2–3	Liege	Fr	Van Himst, Vanden Boer
22–10	Switzerland	W	1–0	Bruges	Fr	Claessen R
11–11	France	W	2–1	Brussels	ECq	Van Himst 2
19–03–1967	Luxembourg	W	5–0	Luxembourg	ECq	Van Himst 2, Stockman 3
16–04	Holland	W	1–0	Antwerp	Fr	Puis
21–05	Poland	L	1–3	Chorzow	ECq	Puis
8–10	Poland	L	2–4	Brussels	ECq	Devrindt 2
28–10	France	D	1–1	Nantes	ECq	Claessen R
22–11	Luxembourg	W	3–0	Bruges	ECq	Thio 2, Claessen R
10–01–1968	Israel	W	2–0	Tel Aviv	Fr	Devrindt, Puis
6–03	West Germany	L	1–3	Brussels	Fr	Devrindt
7–04	Holland	W	2–1	Amsterdam	Fr	Polleunis 2
24–04	Soviet Union	L	0–1	Moscow	Fr	
19–06	Finland	W	2–1	Helsinki	WCq	Devrindt, Polleunis
9–10	Finland	W	6–1	Waregem	WCq	Polleunis 3, Puis 2, Semmeling
16–10	Yugoslavia	W	3–0	Brussels	WCq	Devrindt 2, Polleunis
11–12	Spain	D	1–1	Madrid	WCq	Devrindt
23–02–1969	Spain	W	2–1	Liege	WCq	Devrindt 2
16–04	Mexico	W	2–0	Brussels	Fr	Puis, Van Himst
19–10	Yugoslavia	L	0–4	Skopje	WCq	
5–11	Mexico	L	0–1	Mexico City	Fr	
25–02–1970	England	L	1–3	Brussels	Fr	Dockx
3–06	El Salvador	W	3–0	Mexico City	WCr1	Van Moer 2, Lambert
6–06	Soviet Union	L	1–4	Mexico City	WCr1	Lambert
11–06	Mexico	L	0–1	Mexico City	WCr1	
15–11	France	L	1–2	Brussels	Fr	Van Moer
25–11	Denmark	W	2–0	Bruges	ECq	Devrindt 2
3–02–1971	Scotland	W	3–0	Liege	ECq	Van Himst 2, OG

17–02	Portugal	W 3–0	Brussels	ECq	Lambert 2, Denul
20–05	Luxembourg	W 4–0	Luxembourg	Fr	Denul, Van Himst, Semmeling, Van Moer
26–05	Denmark	W 2–1	Copenhagen	ECq	Devrindt 2
7–11	Luxembourg	W 1–0	Verviers	Fr	Van Den Daele
10–11	Scotland	L 0–1	Aberdeen	ECq	
21–11	Portugal	D 1–1	Lisbon	ECq	Lambert
29–04–1972	Italy	D 0–0	Milan	ECqf	
13–05	Italy	W 2–1	Brussels	ECqf	Van Moer, Van Himst
18–05	Iceland	W 4–0	Liege	WCq	Van Himst, Polleunis 3
22–05	Iceland	W 4–0	Bruges	WCq	Janssens F, Lambert 2, Dockx
14–06	West Germany	L 1–2	Antwerp	ECsf	Polleunis
17–06	Hungary	W 2–1	Liege	EC3p	Lambert, Van Himst
4–10	Norway	W 2–0	Oslo	WCq	Dolmans, Lambert,
19–11	Holland	D 0–0	Antwerp	WCq	
18–04–1973	East Germany	W 3–0	Antwerp	Fr	Lambert 2, Dockx
31–10	Norway	W 2–0	Brussels	WCq	Dolmans, Lambert
18–11	Holland	D 0–0	Amsterdam	WCq	
13–03–1974	East Germany	L 0–1	Berlin	Fr	
17–04	Poland	D 1–1	Liege	Fr	Van Moer
1–05	Switzerland	W 1–0	Geneva	Fr	Van Herp
1–06	Scotland	W 2–1	Bruges	Fr	Henrotay, Lambert
8–09	Iceland	W 2–0	Reykjavik	ECq	Van Moer, Teugels
12–10	France	W 2–1	Brussels	ECq	Martens, Vander Elst
7–12	East Germany	D 0–0	Leipzig	ECq	
30–04–1975	Holland	W 1–0	Antwerp	Fr	Lambert
6–09	Iceland	W 1–0	Liege	ECq	Lambert
27–09	East Germany	L 1–2	Brussels	ECq	Pius
15–11	France	D 0–0	Paris	ECq	
25–04–1976	Holland	L 0–5	Rotterdam	ECqf	
22–05	Holland	L 1–2	Brussels	ECqf	Van Gool
5–09	Iceland	W 1–0	Reykjavik	WCq	Vander Elst
10–11	Nth. Ireland	W 2–0	Liege	WCq	Van Gool, Lambert
26–01–1977	Italy	L 1–2	Rome	Fr	Piot
26–03	Holland	L 0–2	Antwerp	WCq	
3–09	Iceland	W 4–0	Brussels	WCq	Van Binst, Martens, Courant, Lambert
26–10	Holland	L 0–1	Amsterdam	WCq	
16–11	Nth. Ireland	L 0–3	Belfast	WCq	
21–12	Italy	L 0–1	Liege	Fr	
22–03–1978	Austria	W 1–0	Charleroi	Fr	Geurts
19–04	East Germany	D 0–0	Magdeburg	Fr	
20–09	Norway	D 1–1	Lokeren	ECq	Cools
11–10	Portugal	D 1–1	Lisbon	ECq	Vercauteren
15–11	Israel	L 0–1	Tel Aviv	Fr	
28–03–1979	Austria	D 1–1	Brussels	ECq	Vandereycken
2–05	Austria	D 0–0	Vienna	ECq	
12–09	Norway	W 2–1	Oslo	ECq	Janssens J, Vander Elst
26–09	Holland	L 0–1	Rotterdam	Fr	
17–10	Portugal	W 2–0	Brussels	ECq	Van Moer, Vander Elst
21–11	Scotland	W 2–0	Brussels	ECq	Vander Elst, Voordeckers
19–12	Scotland	W 3–1	Glasgow	ECq	Vandenbergh E, Vander Elst 2
27–02–1980	Luxembourg	W 5–0	Brussels	Fr	Vandenbergh E 2, Vandereycken, Vander Elst 2
18–03	Uruguay	W 2–0	Brussels	Fr	Verheyen, Vander Elst
2–04	Poland	W 2–1	Brussels	Fr	Coeck, Vandenbergh E
6–06	Romania	W 2–1	Brussels	Fr	Ceulemans, Vander Elst
12–06	England	D 1–1	Turin	ECr1	Ceulemans
15–06	Spain	W 2–1	Milan	ECr1	Gerets, Cools
18–06	Italy	D 0–0	Rome	ECr1	
22–06	West Germany	L 1–2	Rome	ECf	Vandereycken
15–10	Rep. Ireland	D 1–1	Dublin	WCq	Cluytens
19–11	Holland	W 1–0	Brussels	WCq	Vandenbergh E
21–12	Cyprus	W 2–0	Nicosia	WCq	Vandenbergh E, Ceulemans
18–02–1981	Cyprus	W 3–2	Brussels	WCq	Plessers, Vandenbergh E, Ceulemans
25–03	Rep. Ireland	W 1–0	Brussels	WCq	Ceulemans
29–04	France	L 2–3	Paris	WCq	Vandenbergh E, Ceulemans
9–09	France	W 2–0	Brussels	WCq	Czerniatynski, Vandenbergh E
14–10	Holland	L 0–3	Rotterdam	WCq	
16–12	Spain	L 0–2	Valencia	Fr	
24–03–1982	Romania	W 4–1	Brussels	Fr	Verheyen 2, Czerniatynski 2

28–04	Bulgaria	W 2–1	Brussels	Fr	Vandenbergh E, Van Moer
27–05	Denmark	L 0–1	Copenhagen	Fr	
13–06	Argentina	W 1–0	Barcelona	WCr1	Vandenbergh E
19–06	El Salvador	W 1–0	Elche	WCr1	Coeck
22–06	Hungary	D 1–1	Elche	WCr1	Czerniatynski
28–06	Poland	L 0–3	Barcelona	WCr2	
1–07	Soviet Union	L 0–1	Barcelona	WCr2	
22–09	West Germany	D 0–0	Munich	Fr	
6–10	Switzerland	W 3–0	Brussels	ECq	Vercauteren, Coeck, Vandenbergh E
15–12	Scotland	W 3–2	Brussels	ECq	Vandenbergh E, Vander Elst 2
30–03–1983	East Germany	W 2–1	Leipzig	ECq	Vander Elst, Vandenbergh E
27–04	East Germany	W 2–1	Brussels	ECq	Ceulemans, Coeck
31–05	France	D 1–1	Luxembourg	Fr	Voordeckers
21–09	Holland	D 1–1	Brussels	Fr	Voordeckers
12–10	Scotland	D 1–1	Glasgow	ECq	Vercauteren
9–11	Switzerland	L 1–3	Berne	ECq	Vandenbergh E
29–02–1984	West Germany	L 0–1	Brussels	Fr	
17–04	Poland	W 1–0	Warsaw	Fr	Czerniatynski
6–06	Hungary	D 2–2	Brussels	Fr	Ceulemans 2
13–06	Yugoslavia	W 2–0	Lens	ECr1	Vandenbergh E, Grün
16–06	France	L 0–5	Nantes	ECr1	
19–06	Denmark	L 2–3	Strasbourg	ECr1	Ceulemans, Vercauteren
5–09	Argentina	L 0–2	Brussels	Fr	
17–10	Albania	W 3–1	Brussels	WCq	Claesen N, Scifo, Voordeckers
19–12	Greece	D 0–0	Athens	WCq	
22–12	Albania	L 0–2	Tirana	WCq	
27–03–1985	Greece	W 2–0	Brussels	WCq	Vercauteren, Scifo
1–05	Poland	W 2–0	Brussels	WCq	Vandenbergh E, Vercauteren
11–09	Poland	D 0–0	Chorzow	WCq	
16–10	Holland	W 1–0	Brussels	WCq	Vercauteren
20–11	Holland	L 1–2	Rotterdam	WCq	Grün
19–02–1986	Spain	L 0–3	Elche	Fr	
23–04	Bulgaria	W 2–0	Brussels	Fr	De Smet, Vandenbergh E
19–05	Yugoslavia	L 1–3	Brussels	Fr	Claesen N
3–06	Mexico	L 1–2	Mexico City	WCr1	Vandenbergh E
8–06	Iraq	W 2–1	Toluca	WCr1	Scifo, Claesen N
11–06	Paraguay	D 2–2	Toluca	WCr1	Vercauteren, Veyt
15–06	Soviet Union	W 4–3	Leon	WCr2	Scifo, Ceulemans, Demol, Claesen N
22–06	Spain	D 1–1	Puebla	WCqf	Ceulemans
25–06	Argentina	L 0–2	Mexico City	WCsf	
28–06	France	L 2–4	Puebla	WC3p	Ceulemans, Claesen N
10–09	Rep. Ireland	D 2–2	Brussels	ECq	Claesen N, Scifo
14–10	Luxembourg	W 6–0	Luxembourg	ECq	Gerets, Claesen N 3, Vercauteren, Ceulemans
19–11	Bulgaria	D 1–1	Brussels	ECq	Janssen
4–02–1987	Portugal	L 0–1	Braga	Fr	
1–04	Scotland	W 4–1	Brussels	ECq	Claesen N 3, Vercauteren
29–04	Rep. Ireland	D 0–0	Dublin	ECq	
9–09	Holland	D 0–0	Rotterdam	Fr	
23–09	Bulgaria	L 0–2	Sofia	ECq	
14–10	Scotland	L 0–2	Glasgow	ECq	
11–11	Luxembourg	W 3–0	Brussels	ECq	Ceulemans, De Gryse, Creve
19–01–1988	Israel	W 3–2	Tel Aviv	Fr	De Gryse, Van der Linden, Grün
26–03	Hungary	W 3–0	Brussels	Fr	Ceulemans, OG, Severeyns
4–06	Denmark	L 1–3	Odense	Fr	Ceulemans
12–10	Brazil	L 1–2	Antwerp	Fr	Clijsters
19–10	Switzerland	W 1–0	Brussels	WCq	Vervoort
16–11	Czechoslovakia	D 0–0	Bratislava	WCq	
15–02–1989	Portugal	D 1–1	Lisbon	WCq	Gerets
29–04	Czechoslovakia	W 2–1	Brussels	WCq	De Gryse 2
27–05	Yugoslavia	W 1–0	Brussels	Fr	Van der Linden
1–06	Luxembourg	W 5–0	Lille	WCq	Van der Linden 4, Vervoort
8–06	Canada	W 2–0	Ottowa	Fr	Ceulemans, De Gryse
24–08	Denmark	W 3–0	Bruges	Fr	De Gryse, Ceulemans 2
6–09	Portugal	W 3–0	Brussels	WCq	Ceulemans, Van der Linden 2
11–10	Switzerland	D 2–2	Basle	WCq	De Gryse, OG
25–10	Luxembourg	D 1–1	Brussels	WCq	Versavel
17–01–1990	Greece	L 0–2	Athens	Fr	
21–02	Sweden	D 0–0	Brussels	Fr	

LEADING INTERNATIONAL GOALSCORERS

1	Voorhoof	30		Braine R	26		Vandenbergh E	20
	Van Himst	30	6	Ceulemans	22	10	Capelle	19
3	Mermans	27	7	Coppens.R	21	11	Lambert	18
4	De Veen	26	8	Anoul	20	12	Vandenberg	16

LEADING INTERNATIONAL APPEARANCES

1	Ceulemans	96		Pfaff	64		Mermans	56
2	Gerets	86	8	Vercauteren	63	14	Renquin	55
3	Van Himst	82	9	Voorhoof	61	15	Braine R	54
4	Mees	68	10	Grün	60		Scifo	54
5	Heylens	67	11	Van Moer	57	17	Swartenbroeks	53
6	Jurion	64	12	Carre	56	18	Vander Elst F	51

26–05	Romania	D 2–2	Brussels	Fr	Scifo, Clijsters
2–06	Mexico	W 3–0	Brussels	Fr	De Gryse 2, Versavel
6–06	Poland	D 1–1	Brussels	Fr	Emmers
12–06	South Korea	W 2–0	Verona	WCr1	De Gryse, De Wolf
17–06	Uruguay	W 3–1	Verona	WCr1	Clijsters, Scifo, Ceulemans
21–06	Spain	L 1–2	Verona	WCr1	Vervoort
26–06	England	L 0–1	Bologna	WCr2	
12–09	East Germany	L 0–2	Brussels	Fr	
17–10	Wales	L 1–3	Cardiff	ECq	Versavel
13–02–1991	Italy	D 0–0	Terni	Fr	
27–02	Luxembourg	W 3–0	Brussels	ECq	Vandenbergh E, Ceulemans, Scifo
27–03	Wales	D 1–1	Brussels	ECq	De Gryse
1–05	Germany	L 0–1	Hanover	ECq	
11–09	Luxembourg	W 2–0	Luxembourg	ECq	Scifo, De Gryse
9–10	Hungary	W 2–0	Szekesfehervar	Fr	Emmens, Scifo
20–11	Germany	L 0–1	Brussels	ECq	
26–02–1992	Tunisia	L 1–2	Tunis	Fr	Oliveira
25–03	France	D 3–3	Paris	Fr	Albert, Scifo, Wilmots
22–04	Cyprus	W 1–0	Brussels	WCq	Wilmots
3–06	Faeroe Islands	W 3–0	Toftir	WCq	Albert, Wilmots 2

BULGARIA

Like most of the former Eastern Bloc countries, Bulgarian football benefited enormously from the communist take-over in 1944. Before, the standard was very poor and the game was not taken very seriously. There had been a league and a cup for clubs, and the national team took part regularly in the Balkan Cup, but it was not until after 1944 that the first grass pitch was laid. In typical communist fashion, football was organised from top to bottom. New training techniques were introduced and players became 'professionals', if not in name then in outlook.

In common with their comrades behind the Iron Curtain, this approach was ultimately to lead to the stagnation of the game, but not before Bulgaria had qualified for four consecutive World Cups between 1962 and 1974. 'The system' produced many fine footballers, and the Bulgars were almost impossible to beat in Sofia in the 1960s, but as these players cast their eyes to the fabulous sums being earned by their colleagues in the West, a decline set in that left the game once again among the weakest on the continent.

Popular legend has it that football first made an appearance in the country when a certain Georges de Regibus came to Bulgaria in 1894. He was a Swiss physical education teacher, and he used football as part of his warm-up routine at the boys' middle school in Varna. Indeed the Black Sea resort of Varna has always been regarded as the hotbed of Bulgarian football in these early years.

Political events in the Balkan region, however, held up the development of the game. For centuries Bulgaria had been a province in the Ottoman Empire. After independence in 1908, she became involved in the two Balkan Wars of 1912 and 1913, first against the Turks and then against her other neighbours. The area was referred to as the 'powder keg of Europe', so it was not surprising that sport did not have a very high priority. Indeed any sports club was officially frowned upon, so great credit must go to players like Stefan Naumov, a prominent figure in Sofia, for their perseverance. He organised the first inter-town match in 1912, a team from Plovdiv beating his Sofia side 4–0.

Sofia, due to its size and importance, began to take over from Varna as the leading force behind the game. In 1913, a group of the leading Sofia players, led by Dimiter Blagoyev and Boris Sharankov, formed Slavia, the oldest surviving club in the league, whilst in 1914 a group of teenage enthusiasts started Levski, a team that was destined to become one of the most successful and best supported clubs in the country. By the early 1920s, the political situation in the Balkans had stabilised, and the mounting popularity of the game meant that proper organisation was required. In 1923 the Bulgarian National Sports Federation was founded, of which the Football Federation formed a part, and the following year a successful application to FIFA was submitted.

By 1923 numerous clubs had sprung up around the country and disorganised regional leagues had already been formed. On 31 July 1921, ten clubs in Sofia created the Sofia sports league, whilst on the same day the Northern league was formed in Varna. After an abortive attempt at a national championship in 1924, a competition took place the following year involving the winners of the leagues from Sofia, Plovdiv, Varna, Burgas, Kyustendil and Vratsa. It was won by Vladislav Varna.

This formula continued until 1937 when for the first time a single league of the top 10 clubs was introduced. This lasted only 3 seasons, however, before the war forced a return to the regional leagues. In 1944 football was suspended altogether when Russian troops marched into the country. The period from 1925 to 1943 was an era of great equality in terms of honours won in the league. No fewer than nine teams won the title, though all bar one of them came from either Sofia or Varna.

In 1938 a knockout competition was introduced. Formulated along the lines of the English cup in that any team could compete, it has, unlike those of many other countries, always been a very popular tournament. Five editions of it were played before it was suspended in 1943 and all five were won by teams from Sofia.

Bulgaria's baptism in international football can only be described as disastrous. They lost their first match 6–0 away to a powerful Austrian team, proceeded to lose their next six, and failed to win until their 15th game some six years later. Most of their games before 1943 were played against their neighbours in the Balkans and when they did venture out they were usually given sound thrashings by Europe's strongest nations. Results like the 13–0 defeat by Spain meant that the team were unwilling to take on the more advanced nations any more than necessary. Instead the Balkan Cup proved a popular arena for games.

In the first tournament in 1931, Bulgaria finished last in the table, losing six of their eight games. The second tournament, held over the course of a week in Belgrade the following year, was altogether a different matter, as Bulgaria won all three of their games to take the trophy, a feat they repeated in the fifth tournament held in Sofia in 1935.

The lure of the World Cup proved too hard to resist even though the Bulgarians knew they were one of the weakest sides. An application was made to take part in the second tournament in 1934 and they were drawn in a qualifying group that included Austria and Hungary, both major powers in Europe. The gulf in class was illustrated as the Bulgarians crashed twice to the Hungarians and once to the Austrians. In the 1938 competition their opponents were this time Czechoslovakia, the runners–up in 1934. The first match in Sofia was probably Bulgaria's finest pre-war result. They held the Czechs to a 1–1 draw but alas to no avail as they were humbled 6–0 in the return in Prague five months later. The most famous player of this era was Luibomir Angelov. He scored 23 goals but overall Bulgaria's pre–war record was very poor.

After falling into the hands of the Nazis early on in the war, Bulgaria was 'liberated' by the Soviets in 1944. The revolution that took place in all sports and not just football firmly put the country on the sporting map. The high priority given by the Communist government to sport slowly transformed the football scene as large funds were made available for facilities and coaching.

The championship was resumed in 1945, but in 1948 the whole system was reorganised. A single first division of 10 teams was established, though this has crept up over the years to 16. This formed the apex of a league pyramid that included every team in the country right down to the junior teams.

The other enormous influence state socialism had was in the actual composition of the clubs themselves. As was common behind the Iron Curtain, football clubs formed only one arm of a much bigger sports club, albeit the most important. After the war each club came under the control of one official body or another. The most remarkable of these was the Army club. Taking over an unknown club in 1948, the army turned Septemvri CDW into national champions the following year. Though they have often changed their name, CSKA, as they are known now, have never given up this pre-eminent position.

All other clubs were reorganised as well. Each city had their representative for the Army, the Police, the railway workers and other industries, but Sofia clubs have always remained dominant. Levski, the team of the Interior Ministry, struggled to maintain a challenge to CSKA, but the Army team, as they formed the basis of the national team, were given every advantage. In their first 15 years they won the title a staggering 12 times. Indeed they have only once ever finished outside the top five, a disastrous 11th in 1964. They are a very poorly supported club and are the main reason why the league is not as popular as it could be. There is simply not enough competition.

The CSKA side of the 1950s is regarded as the best club side the country has ever produced. It included such great names as Ivan Kolev, widely acclaimed as the best footballer Bulgaria has ever known, as well as Stefan Bojkov, Manol Manolov, Georgy Naidenov and Dimiter Milanov to name but a few. All good things must come to an end, however, and by the early 1960s CSKA were forced to rebuild. The mid-1960s therefore proved to be the only time since the war that the league was an open affair. In five consecutive seasons five different teams triumphed, whilst in the space of seven years five different teams won the cup. By the end of the decade, however, events were back to normal with CSKA and Levski-Spartak passing the title back and forth between them.

In 1985 the calm was shattered when the cup final between Levski and CSKA erupted into mayhem. CSKA had won a game marred by three sendings off, 2–1. All hell broke loose as the two teams started fighting one another as the match finished. The Central Committee of the Communist Party was so appalled that it ordered both teams to be disbanded. All the officials were suspended and various players received life bans. The cup was withheld from CSKA and the league title was stripped from Levski and awarded to Trakia Plovdiv who had finished third. There were also allegations of financial misdoings in both clubs, but in the event both were reformed under new names, Sredets and Vitosha, and many of the officials and players were reprieved.

	All			League			Cup		SAC		Europe		
Team	G	S	B	G	S	B	G	S	G	S	G	S	B
1 CSKA Sofia	46	20	4	27	11	1	5	3	14	6	–	–	3
2 Levski Sofia	41	33	7	16	25	7	8	2	17	6	–	–	–
3 Slavia Sofia	12	11	12	6	9	11	–	–	6	2	–	–	1
4 Lokomotiv Sofia	7	9	6	4	6	6	–	–	3	3	–	–	–
5 Botev Plovdiv	5	9	7	3	2	7	–	2	2	5	–	–	–
6 Cherno More Varna	4	8	2	4	6	2	–	–	–	2	–	–	–
7 Spartak Plovdiv	2	4	–	1	1	–	–	–	1	3	–	–	–
8 Etar Veliko Tarnovo	2	–	1	1	–	1	–	–	1	–	–	–	–
9 AC 23 Sofia	2	–	–	1	–	–	1	–	–	–	–	–	–
10 Lokomotiv Plovdiv	1	5	2	–	1	2	–	–	1	4	–	–	–
11 Beroe Stara Zagora	1	4	1	1	–	1	–	–	–	4	–	–	–
12 Spartak Varna	1	4	1	1	2	1	–	1	–	1	–	–	–
13 SC Sofia	1	1	–	1	1	–	–	–	–	–	–	–	–
14 Marek Stanke Dimitrov	1	–	1	–	–	1	–	–	1	–	–	–	–
Shipka Sofia	1	–	1	–	–	1	1	–	–	–	–	–	–
Sliven	1	–	1	–	–	1	1	–	–	–	–	–	–
17 Dunav Ruse	–	5	–	–	1	–	–	3	–	1	–	–	–
18 Pirin Blagoevgrad	–	2	1	–	–	1	–	1	–	1	–	–	–
19 Sportclub Plovdiv	–	2	–	–	–	–	–	2	–	–	–	–	–
20 Akademic Sofia	–	1	2	–	–	2	–	–	–	1	–	–	–
21 Spartak Pleven	–	1	1	–	–	1	–	–	–	1	–	–	–
22 Chernomorets Burgas	–	1	–	–	–	–	–	1	–	–	–	–	–
Chernomorets Popovo	–	1	–	–	–	–	–	–	–	1	—	–	
Chirpan	–	1	–	–	–	–	–	–	–	1	–	–	–
Dorostol	–	1	–	–	–	–	–	–	–	1	–	–	–
Macedonia Skoplje	–	1	–	–	1	–	–	–	–	–	–	–	–
Maritsa Istok Radnevo	–	1	–	–	–	–	–	–	–	1	–	–	–
Minyor Pernik	–	1	–	–	–	–	–	–	–	1	–	–	–
Neftokhimik Burgas	–	1	–	–	–	–	–	–	–	1	–	–	–
Sportclub Sofia	–	1	–	–	1	–	–	–	–	–	–	–	–
31 Botev Vratsa	–	–	1	–	–	1	–	–	–	–	–	–	–

To the end of the 1991–92 season

In a hint of the 'Glasnost' that was to come, all clubs were made independent bodies and forced to survive on their own. In the search for income, many clubs have opted to sell their best players abroad, and the exodus has turned into a flood.

Since the war Bulgaria has taken great strides in international football. For a 15-year spell in the 1960s and 1970s, they were one of the top dozen countries in Europe. After the war, games were at first confined to other communist countries – not until a World Cup match in 1957 against Norway did Bulgaria leave the seclusion of Eastern Europe. It was a time when Bulgaria found her footballing feet. The approach was to build physically strong teams that could conform to a set pattern of play that comprised a slow build-up from defence with a passing game. As a result Bulgaria have always been tricky opponents, but they have been accused of lacking the flair and flexibility that could have made them a very successful team.

Their post-war record illustrates this point perfectly. They have qualified for 5 of the last 8 World Cup finals, a tremendous achievement, but once there their game falters. Out of the 16 games played in these final stages, 6 have been drawn and 10 lost. No team has such a poor record with so many games played. At home they have a very good record even against the strongest of teams, but away from home they just do not seem to be able to rise to the challenge.

During the 1950s, the national team was in essence the CSKA team with Ivan Kolev, and Stefan Bojkov the captain, at the helm. Their results varied. Failure to qualify for the 1954 and 1958 World Cups due to the presence of first Czechoslovakia and then Hungary was countered by some very creditable performances especially against the Hungarians when the latter were at their peak. A bronze medal was won at the Melbourne Olympics in 1956 but it was not until the end of the decade that the first real signs came that all the effort being afforded to football was beginning to pay off.

The World Cup to be held in Chile in 1962 saw Bulgaria's dreams of qualifying for the first time come true as a fine run of 10 victories in 12 games culminated in a 1–0 win over France in Milan. It was to be the first of four consecutive appearances in the finals, but each time the team was to prove a severe disappointment. A new breed of player was emerging led by the inspirational Georgi Asparuhov whom many Bulgarians rate above Ivan Kolev. He was to score Bulgaria's only goal in Chile – in a 6–1 defeat by Hungary. Their poor showing in Chile was put down to inexperience on the big occasion, but matters did not improve four years later in the finals in England. Bad tactics and an injury to Asparuhov sent the team home after three defeats.

The late 1960s probably saw the side at its peak. The prolific Hristo Bonev broke into the team in this period along with players such as Petar Jekov. An unfortunate defeat at the hands of Italy in the quarter-finals of the 1968 European Championships was partly recompensed by winning the silver medal at the Mexico Olympics later that summer, and qualification for their third successive World Cup finals in Mexico in 1970 was greeted with real optimism and hope. Their performance this time was far more creditable and although they failed to win, their tally of 5 goals from 3 games helped ease the disappointment of not qualifying for the next round. If Asparuhov, again carrying an injury, had been fully fit matters may have turned out differently, but at least they made their contribution to the general spirit in which this tournament was played.

The game was dealt a body blow in 1971, however, when Asparuhov was killed in a car crash along with his international team-mate Nikola Kotkov, and although the team managed to qualify for the next World Cup in West Germany thanks largely to the presence of Bonev, the game in Bulgaria was entering a period of decline. Players such as Jekov began to lose interest, and one suspects that as state amateurs they were looking enviously at the large sums of money players were earning in Western Europe. Bulgaria left West Germany without much credit, again failing to win a match.

Since 1974 Bulgaria's record has been miserable: qualification for the 1986 World Cup finals has been the only achievement of note. Matters came to a head after their worst performance yet, in the 1980 European Championship, when they finished fourth in a relatively weak group, prompting the sacking of the entire governing body. At the 1986 World Cup Finals in Mexico it was to the general outrage that they qualified for the second round at the expense of the more ebullient South Koreans. Eventually a lacklustre defeat at the hands of Mexico sent them home empty handed, devoid of any inspiration and ideas.

It is hoped that the sudden liberalisation of the game at home and the experience being gained by the large numbers of players abroad will help revitalise Bulgarian football. Until it is, that first ever win at a World Cup finals will remain as elusive as ever.

Population: 8 997 000
Area, sq km: 110 994
% in urban areas: 67.6%
Capital city: Sofia

Bulgarski Futbolen Soius
Gotcho Gopin #19
1000 Sofia
Bulgaria
Tel: (010 359) 2 877490
Fax: (010 359) 2 803237
Telex: 23145 BFS BG
Cable: BULFUTBOL SOFIA
Languages for correspondence: German, English, French, Spanish

Year of formation: 1923
Affiliation to FIFA: 1924
Affiliation to UEFA: 1954
Registered clubs: 4328
Registered players: 441 300
Professional players: 600
Registered coaches: 2390
Registered referees: 325
National stadium: Stadion Vasilij Levski 55 000
National colours: Shirts: White/Shorts: Green/Socks: Red
Reserve colours: Shirts: Red/Shorts: Green/Socks: White
Season: August–June with a mid-season break in January and February

THE RECORD

WORLD CUP

1930 .... Did not enter
1934 .... QT 3rd/3 in group 8
1938 .... QT Failed to qualify
1950 .... Did not enter
1954 .... QT 3rd/3 in group 8
1958 .... QT 2nd/3 in group 3
1962 .... QT 1st/3 in group 2 – Final Tournament/1st round
1966 .... QT 1st/3 in group 1 – Final Tournament/1st round
1970 .... QT 1st/4 in group 8 – Final Tournament/1st round
1974 .... QT 1st/4 in group 6 – Final Tournament/1st round
1978 .... QT 2nd/4 in group 5
1982 .... QT 3rd/5 in group 1
1986 .... QT 2nd/5 in group 4 – Final Tournament/2nd round
1990 .... QT 4th/4 in group 1

EUROPEAN CHAMPIONSHIP

1960 .... 1st round
1964 .... 2nd round
1968 .... QT 1st/4 in group 2 – Final Tournament/Quarter-finalists
1972 .... QT 2nd/4 in group 2
1976 .... QT 3rd/4 in group 8
1980 .... QT 4th/5 in group 1
1984 .... QT 3rd/4 in group 4
1988 .... QT 2nd/5 in group 7
1992 .... QT 4th/5 in group 2

OLYMPIC GAMES

1908–20 ..... Did not enter
1924 .... 1st round
1928–48 ..... Did not enter
1952 .... 1st round
1956 .... Final Tournament/Semi-finalists/3rd place
1960 .... Final Tournament/1st round
1964 .... QT Failed to qualify
1968 .... Final Tournament/Runners-up
1972 .... QT Failed to qualify
1976 .... QT Failed to qualify
1980 .... QT Failed to qualify
1984 .... QT Failed to qualify
1988 .... QT Failed to qualify
1992 .... QT Failed to qualify

EUROPEAN CLUB COMPETITIONS

EUROPEAN CUP: Semi-finalists – CSKA Sofia 1967 1982

CUP WINNERS CUP: Semi-finalists – Slavia Sofia 1967, CSKA Sofia 1989

UEFA Cup: Quarter-finalists – Levski-Spartak 1976, Lokomotiv Sofia 1980

CLUB DIRECTORY

SOFIA (Population – 1 217 000)

CSKA Sofia
Stadium: CSKA 35 000
Founded: 1948
Colours: Red/White
Previous names: Septemvri CDW 1948–49, Narodna Voiska 1949–50, CDNA 1950–64, CSKA–CZ 1964–69, CSKA 1969–85, Sredets 1985–87, CFKA Sredets 1987–1989. Septemvri CDW split away in 1957 but rejoined in 1969

FC Levski
Stadium: Georgi Asparuhov 45 000
Founded: 1914
Colours: Blue/Blue
Previous names: Levski 1914–49, Dinamo 1949–57, Levski 1957–69, Levski–Spartak 1969–85, Vitosha 1985–1989. Spartak Sofia with whom Levski merged in 1969 were called Iskra 1907–11, Rakovski 1911–13, FK 13 1913–45, Rakovski 1945–47, Spartak 1947–69

FC Lokomotiv Sofia
Stadium: Lokomotiv 35 000
Founded: 1929
Colours: Red and black stripes/Black
Previous names: JSK Sofia 1929–45, Lokomotiv 1945–49, Torpedo 1949–50. In 1969 Lokomotiv merged with Slavia to become Lokomotiv JSK, but the two clubs separated in 1971

FC Slavia Sofia
Stadium: Slavia 35 000
Founded: 1913
Colours: White/White
Previous names: Slavia 1913–49, Strojtel 1949–51, Udarnik 1951–57

PLOVDIV (Population – 364 000)
FC Botev Plovdiv
Stadium: Cristo Botev 40 000
Founded: 1912
Colours: Yellow/Black
Previous names: Botev 1912–44, Shipka 1944–47, Botev 1947–51, DNW 1951–55, SKNA 1955–56, 1956–67 Botev, Trakia 1967–1990. Botev merged with Spartak and Akademik in 1967, but Spartak broke away in 1982

FC Lokomotiv Plovdiv
Stadium: Lokomotiv 25 000
Founded: 1936
Colours: Black and white stripes/Black
Previous names: JSK, JSK Levski, Slavia and Torpedo

FC Spartak Plovdiv
Stadium: 9 Septemvri
Founded: 1947
Colours: Blue and white stripes/Blue
Previous names: Levski and Udarnik. Merged with Botev as Trakia from 1967–82

VARNA (Population – 306 000)

FC Cherno More Varna
Stadium: Yuri Gregarin
Founded: 1912
Colours: Green/White
Previous names: Ticha (1912) and Vladislav (1921) merged in 1945 to become TV'45. Botev Varna 1948–50, VUS 1950–56, SKNA 1956–57

FC Spartak Varna
Stadium: Spartak 15 000
Founded: 1914
Colours: Blue/White
Previous names: Shipenski Sokol. Merged in 1969 with Lokomotiv to become JSK Spartak, but broke away in 1986

BURGAS (Population – 200 000)
FC Chernomorets Burgas
Stadium: Chernomorets 25 000
Founded: 1916
Colours: Blue/Blue
Previous names: Merger in 1969 of Lokomotiv and Botev

RUSE (Population – 190 000)
FC Dunav Ruse
Stadium: Gradski 25 000
Founded: 1919
Colours: Blue/Blue
Previous names: Cava, Levski and Napradek

STARA ZAGORA (Population – 158 000)
FC Beroe Stara Zagora
Stadium: Beroe 24 000
Founded: 1916
Colours: Green/White
Previous names: Merger in 1958 between Lokomotiv and Botev

PLEVEN (Population – 136 000)
FC Spartak Pleven
Stadium: Slavi Aleksejev 20000
Founded: 1919
Colours: Blue/White
Previous names: Skobelev, Pobeda, SP'39

SLIVEN (Population – 104 000)
FC Sliven
Stadium: Hadji Dimitar 25000
Founded: 1914
Colours: Orange/Blue
Previous names: Sportist, DNA, SKNA

PERNIK (Population – 96 000)
FC Minyor Pernik
Stadium: Minyor 20000
Founded: 1919
Colours: Yellow/Black
Previous names: Minyor 1952–62, Krakara 1962–70, Pernik 1970–73

VELIKO TARNOVO (Population – 70 000)
FC Etar Veliko Tarnovo
Stadium: Ivailo 20000
Founded: 1924
Colours: Violet/White
Previous names: Trapezita, Udarnik, Cerweno Zname, Spartak and DNA

GORNA ORIAHOVISTA
FC Lokomotiv GO
Stadium: Dimitar Dylguerov 16 000
Founded: 1922
Colours: Red and black stripes/Black
Previous names: Levski, JSK, Nikolo Petrov, Torpedo

BLAGOEVGRAD (Population – 67 000)
FC Pirin Blagoevgrad
Stadium: Christo Botev 20 000
Founded: 1934
Colours: Green/White
Previous names: Botev, Macedonia, Torpedo, Strojtel

BULGARIAN CUPS

BULGARIAN CUP

Year	Winners	Score	Runners-up
1938	FK 13 Sofia	3–0	Levski Ruse
1939	Shipka Sofia	2–0	Levski Ruse
1940	FK 13 Sofia	2–0	Sportclub Plovdiv
1941	AC 23 Sofia	4–2	Napradek Ruse
1942	Levski Sofia	3–0	Sportclub Plovdiv
1943–45	–		

SOVIET ARMY CUP

1946	Levski Sofia	4–1	Chernomorets Popovo
1947	Levski Sofia	1–0	Botev Plovdiv
1948	Lokomotiv Sofia	1–0	Slavia Plovdiv
1949	Dinamo Sofia	1–1 2–2 2–1	Narodna Voiska
1950	Dinamo Sofia	1–1 1–1 1–0	Narodna Voiska
1951	CDNA Sofia	1–0	Academic Sofia
1952	Udarnik Sofia	3–1	Spartak Sofia
1953	Lokomotiv Sofia	2–1	Dinamo Sofia
1954	CDNA Sofia	2–1	Udarnik Sofia

1955	CDNA Sofia	5–2	Spartak Plovdiv
1956	Dinamo Sofia	5–2	Botev Plovdiv
1957	Levski Sofia	2–1	Spartak Pleven
1958	Spartak Plovdiv	1–0	Minyor Pernik
1959	Levski Sofia	1–0	Spartak Plovdiv
1960	Septemvri CDW Sofia	4–3	Lokomotiv Plovdiv
1961	CDNA Sofia	3–0	Spartak Varna
1962	Botev Plovdiv	3–0	Dunav Ruse
1963	Slavia Sofia	2–0	Botev Plovdiv
1964	Slavia Sofia	3–2	Botev Plovdiv
1965	CSKA-CZ Sofia	3–2	Levski Sofia
1966	Slavia Sofia	1–0	CSKA-CZ Sofia
1967	Levski Sofia	3–0	Spartak Sofia
1968	Spartak Sofia	3–2	Beroe Stara Zagora
1969	CSKA Sofia	2–1	Levski-Spartak
1970	Levski-Spartak	2–1	CSKA Sofia
1971	Levski-Spartak	3–0	Lokomotiv Plovdiv
1972	CSKA Sofia	3–0	Slavia Sofia
1973	CSKA Sofia	2–1	Beroe Stara Zagora
1974	CSKA Sofia	2–1	Levski-Spartak
1975	Slavia Sofia	3–2	Lokomotiv Sofia
1976	Levski-Spartak	4–3	CSKA Sofia
1977	Levski-Spartak	2–1	Lokomotiv Sofia
1978	Marek St. Dimitrov	1–0	CSKA Sofia
1979	Levski-Spartak	4–1	Beroe Stara Zagora
1980	Slavia Sofia	3–1	Beroe Stara Zagora
1981	Trakia Plovdiv	1–0	Pirin Blagoevgrad
1982	Lokomotiv Sofia	2–1	Lokomotiv Plovdiv
1983	Lokomotiv Plovdiv	3–1	Chirpan
1984	Levski-Spartak	4–0	Dorostol
1985	CSKA Sofia	4–0	Cherno More Varna
1986	CFKA Sredets	2–0	Lokomotiv Sofia
1987	Vitosha Sofia	3–2	Spartak Plovdiv
1988	Vitosha Sofia	2–0	Cherno More Varna
1989	CFKA Sredets	6–1	Maritsa IstokRadnevo
1990	CSKA Sofia	2–1	Botev Plovdiv
1991	Etar Veliko Tarnovo	2–1	Neftokhimik Burgas

BULGARIAN CUP OF THE REPUBLIC

1981	CSKA Sofia *(league format)*		
1982	Levski-Spartak	4–0	CSKA Sofia
1983	CSKA Sofia	4–0	Spartak Varna
1984	Levski-Spartak	1–0	Trakia Plovdiv
1985	CSKA Sofia	2–1	Levski Spartak *(void)*
1986	Vitosha Sofia	2–1	CFKA Sredets
1987	CFKA Sredets	2–1	Vitosha Sofia
1988	CFKA Sredets	4–1	Vitosha Sofia
1989	CFKA Sredets	3–0	Chernomorets Burgas
1990	Sliven	2–0	CSKA Sofia
1991	Levski Sofia	2–1	Botev Plovdiv
1992	Levski Sofia	5–0	Pirin Blagoevgrad

BULGARIAN LEAGUE CHAMPIONSHIP

Year	Champions		Finalists
1925	Vladislav Varna	2–0	Levski Sofia
1926	Vladislav Varna	1–1	Slavia Sofia
1927	–		
1928	Slavia Sofia	4–0	Vladislav Varna
1929	Botev Plovdiv	1–0	Levski Sofia
1930	Slavia Sofia	4–1	Vladislav Varna
1931	AC 23 Sofia	3–0	Shipenski Sokol
1932	Shipenski Sokol	2–1	Slavia Sofia
1933	Levski Sofia	3–1	Shipenski Sokol
1934	Vladislav Varna	2–0	Slavia Sofia
1935	SC Sofia	4–0	Ticha Varna
1936	Slavia Sofia	2–0	Ticha Varna
1937	Levski Sofia	1–1 3–0	Levski Ruse

	Champions		Runners–up		3rd	
1938	Ticha Varna	25	Vladislav Varna	22	Shipka Sofia	22
1939	Slavia Sofia	23	Vladislav Varna	22	Ticha Varna	22
1940	JSK Sofia	23	Levski Sofia	22	Slavia Sofia	22

	Champions		Finalists
1941	Slavia Sofia	0–0 2–1	JSK Sofia
1942	Levski Sofia	2–0 1–0	Macedonia Skoplje
1943	Slavia Sofia	1–0 1–0	Levski Sofia
1944	–		
1945	Lokomotiv Sofia	3–1 1–1	SC Sofia
1946	Levski Sofia	1–0 1–0	Lokomotiv Sofia
1947	Levski Sofia	1–1 1–0	Lokomotiv Sofia
1948	Septemvri CDW	1–2 3–1	Levski Sofia

	Champions		Runners–up		3rd	
1949	Levski Sofia	33	Septemvri CDW	24	Lokomotiv Sofia	21
1950	Dinamo Sofia	29	Strojtel Sofia	27	Akademic Sofia	22
1951	CDNA Sofia	37	Spartak Sofia	36	Dinamo Sofia	26
1952	CDNA Sofia	33	Spartak Sofia	26	Lokomotiv Sofia	25
1953	Dinamo Sofia	43	CDNA Sofia	42	VUS Varna	31

1954	CDNA Sofia	45	Udarnik Sofia	38	Lokomotiv Sofia	36
1955	CDNA Sofia	37	Udarnik Sofia	31	Spartak Varna	28
1956	CDNA Sofia	31	Dinamo Sofia	26	SKNA Plovdiv	25
1957	CDNA Sofia	34	Lokomotiv Sofia	33	Levski Sofia	30
1958	CDNA Sofia	18	Levski Sofia	14	Spartak Pleven	14
1959	CDNA Sofia	32	Slavia Sofia	27	Levski Sofia	24
1960	CDNA Sofia	32	Levski Sofia	28	Lokomotiv Sofia	23
1961	CDNA Sofia	40	Levski Sofia	30	Botev Plovdiv	29
1962	CDNA Sofia	41	Spartak Plovdiv	35	Levski Sofia	30
1963	Spartak Plovdiv	43	Botev Plovdiv	40	CDNA Sofia	37
1964	Lokomotiv Sofia	44	Levski Sofia	41	Slavia Sofia	35
1965	Levski Sofia	42	Lokomotiv Sofia	39	Slavia Sofia	35
1966	CSKA-CZ Sofia	42	Levski Sofia	41	Slavia Sofia	39
1967	Botev Plovdiv	38	Slavia Sofia	37	Levski Sofia	36
1968	Levski Sofia	45	CSKA-CZ Sofia	42	Lokomotiv Sofia	40
1969	CSKA Sofia	47	Levski-Spartak	40	Lokomotiv Plovdiv	39
1970	Levski-Spartak	48	CSKA Sofia	44	Slavia Sofia	34
1971	CSKA Sofia	48	Levski-Spartak	48	Botev Vratsa	38
1972	CSKA Sofia	58	Levski-Spartak	50	Beroe Stara Zagora	42
1973	CSKA Sofia	51	Lokomotiv Plovdiv	43	Slavia Sofia	43
1974	Levski-Spartak	47	CSKA Sofia	46	Lokomotiv Plovdiv	34
1975	CSKA Sofia	39	Levski-Spartak	38	Slavia Sofia	36
1976	CSKA Sofia	43	Levski-Spartak	41	Akademic Sofia	37
1977	Levski-Spartak	43	CSKA Sofia	39	Marek St. Dimitrov	38
1978	Lokomotiv Sofia	42	CSKA Sofia	41	Levski-Spartak	38
1979	Levski-Spartak	43	CSKA Sofia	40	Lokomotiv Sofia	37
1980	CSKA Sofia	46	Slavia Sofia	45	Levski-Spartak	37
1981	CSKA Sofia	40	Levski-Spartak	36	Trakia Plovdiv	35
1982	CSKA Sofia	47	Levski-Spartak	46	Slavia Sofia	35
1983	CSKA Sofia	45	Levski-Spartak	42	Trakia Plovdiv	36
1984	Levski-Spartak	47	CSKA Sofia	45	Sliven	31
1985	Trakia Plovdiv	33	Lokomotiv Sofia	33	Pirin Blagoevgrad	31
1986	Beroe Stara Zagora	43	Trakia Plovdiv	41	Slavia Sofia	36
1987	CFKA Sredets	47	Vitosha Sofia	44	Trakia Plovdiv	39
1988	Vitosha Sofia	48	CFKA Sredets	46	Trakia Plovdiv	39
1989	CFKA Sredets	48	Vitosha Sofia	39	Etar Veliko Tarnovo	34
1990	CSKA Sofia	47	Levski-Spartak	36	Slavia Sofia	36
1991	Etar Veliko Tarnovo	44	CSKA Sofia	37	Slavia Sofia	37
1992	CSKA Sofia	47	Levski Sofia	45	Botev Plovdiv	37

INTERNATIONAL MATCHES PLAYED BY BULGARIA

Date	Opponents	Result	Venue	Compet	Scorers
21-05-1924	Austria	L 0-6	Vienna	Fr	
28-05	Rep. Ireland	L 0-1	Paris	OGr1	
10-04-1925	Turkey	L 1-2	Istanbul	Fr	Mutafchiev
31-05	Romania	L 2-4	Sofia	Fr	Ivanov A, Dimitriev
25-04-1926	Romania	L 1-6	Bucharest	Fr	Denev K
30-05	Yugoslavia	L 1-3	Zagreb	Fr	Staikov
15-05-1927	Yugoslavia	L 0-2	Sofia	Fr	
17-07	Turkey	D 3-3	Sofia	Fr	Liutzkanov 2, Stoyanov
14-10	Turkey	L 1-3	Istanbul	Fr	Manolov D
21-04-1929	Romania	L 0-3	Bucharest	Fr	
30-06	Greece	D 1-1	Sofia	Fr	Staikov
15-09	Romania	L 2-3	Sofia	Fr	Staikov 2,
13-04-1930	Yugoslavia	L 1-6	Belgrade	Fr	Staikov
15-06	Yugoslavia	D 2-2	Sofia	Fr	Staikov, Stoyanov
12-10	Romania	W 5-3	Sofia	BC	Staikov 2, Stoyanov, Peshev, Vasilev V
16-11	Yugoslavia	L 0-3	Sofia	BC	
7-12	Greece	L 1-6	Athens	BC	Peshev
19-04-1931	Yugoslavia	L 0-1	Belgrade	BC	
10-05	Romania	L 2-5	Bucharest	BC	Lozanov, Panchev
27-09	Turkey	W 5-1	Sofia	Fr	Panchev 2, Lozanov, Peshev, Stoyanov
4-10	Yugoslavia	W 3-2	Sofia	Fr	Lozanov, Angelov, Panchev
25-10	Greece	W 2-1	Sofia	BC	Peshev, Angelov
27-03-1932	Greece	W 2-1	Athens	Fr	Panchev, Angelov
9-06	France	L 3-5	Sofia	Fr	Panchev 3
26-06	Romania	W 2-0	Belgrade	BC	Panchev, Peshev

30–06	Yugoslavia	W	3–2	Belgrade	BC	Angelov, Panchev, Lozanov
2–07	Greece	W	2–0	Belgrade	BC	Peshev, Angelov
5–11	Turkey	W	3–2	Istanbul	Fr	Staikov, Peshev, Angelov
21–05–1933	Spain	L	0–13	Madrid	Fr	
4–06	Romania	L	0–7	Bucharest	BC	
7–06	Yugoslavia	L	0–4	Bucharest	BC	
10–06	Greece	W	2–0	Bucharest	BC	Todorov 2
4–02–1934	Greece	L	0–1	Athens	Fr	
18–03	Yugoslavia	L	1–2	Sofia	Fr	Angelov
25–03	Hungary	L	1–4	Sofia	WCq	Baikushev
1–04	Yugoslavia	W	3–2	Belgrade	Fr	Baikushev 2, Angelov
25–04	Austria	L	1–6	Vienna	WCq	Lozanov
29–04	Hungary	L	1–4	Budapest	WCq	Todorov
25–12	Yugoslavia	L	3–4	Athens	BC	Peshev, Todorov, Panchev
30–12	Romania	L	2–3	Athens	BC	Angelov 2
1–01–1935	Greece	W	2–1	Athens	BC	Lozanov, Panchev
16–06	Greece	W	5–2	Sofia	BC	Angelov 2, Yordanov V 2, Peshev
19–06	Romania	W	4–0	Sofia	BC	Lozanov, Yordanov V, Peshev, OG
24–06	Yugoslavia	D	3–3	Sofia	BC	Angelov 3
20–10	Germany	L	2–4	Leipzig	Fr	Panchev, Stoichkov K
21–05–1936	Greece	W	5–4	Bucharest	BC	Panchev 2, Rafailov, Angelov, Lozanov
24–05	Romania	L	1–4	Bucharest	BC	Angelov
11–07–1937	Yugoslavia	W	4–0	Sofia	Fr	Angelov 2, Yordanov V, Rafailov
12–09	Poland	D	3–3	Sofia	Fr	Iliev K, Angelov, Yordanov V
7–11	Czechoslovakia	D	1–1	Sofia	WCq	Pachedjiev
24–03–1938	France	L	1–6	Paris	Fr	Lozanov
24–04	Czechoslovakia	L	0–6	Prague	WCq	
24–05–1939	Lithuania	W	3–0	Sofia	Fr	Bobev, Angelov, Pachedjiev
22–10	Germany	L	1–3	Sofia	Fr	Yordanov V
6–06–1940	Slovakia	L	1–4	Sofia	Fr	Stoyanov
20–10	Germany	L	3–7	Munich	Fr	Evtimov 2, Angelov
11–04–1942	Croatia	L	0–6	Zagreb	Fr	
19–07	Germany	L	0–3	Sofia	Fr	
6–06–1943	Hungary	L	2–4	Sofia	Fr	Milev, Spassov V
8–10–1946	Romania	D	2–2	Tirana	BC	Milev, OG
9–10	Albania	L	1–3	Tirana	BC	Spassov V
12–10	Yugoslavia	L	1–2	Tirana	BC	Laskov
15–06–1947	Albania	W	2–0	Sofia	BCE	Stankov T 2
6–07	Romania	L	2–3	Sofia	BCE	Stankov T, Yordanov V
17–08	Hungary	L	0–9	Budapest	BCE	
12–10	Yugoslavia	L	1–2	Zagreb	BCE	Stankov T
4–04–1948	Poland	D	1–1	Sofia	BCE	Stankov T
20–06	Romania	L	2–3	Bucharest	BCE	Argirov, Tzetkov
4–07	Yugoslavia	L	1–3	Sofia	BCE	Argirov
29–08	Czechoslovakia	W	1–0	Sofia	BCE	Milev
7–11	Hungary	W	1–0	Sofia	BCE	Milanov D
4–09–1949	Czechoslovakia	W	3–1	Prague	Fr	Laskov, Spassov V, Milanov D
2–10	Poland	L	2–3	Warsaw	Fr	Spassov V, Bojkov
30–10	Hungary	L	0–5	Budapest	Fr	
17–11	Albania	D	0–0	Sofia	Fr	
4–06–1950	Albania	L	1–2	Tirana	Fr	Spassov V
27–08	Czechoslovakia	L	1–2	Sofia	Fr	Trandafilov
30–10	Poland	L	0–1	Sofia	Fr	
12–11	Hungary	D	1–1	Sofia	Fr	Dimitrov A
18–05–1952	Poland	W	1–0	Warsaw	Fr	Milanov D
15–07	Soviet Union	L	1–2	Kotka	OGr1	Kolev I
14–06–1953	East Germany	D	0–0	Dresden	Fr	
28–06	Romania	L	1–3	Bucharest	WCq	Tashkov
6–09	Czechoslovakia	L	1–2	Sofia	WCq	Bojkov
13–09	Poland	D	2–2	Sofia	Fr	Dimitrov G 2
4–10	Hungary	D	1–1	Sofia	Fr	Kolev I
11–10	Romania	L	1–2	Sofia	WCq	Kolev I
8–11	Czechoslovakia	D	0–0	Bratislava	WCq	
8–08–1954	Poland	D	2–2	Warsaw	Fr	Kolev I, Milanov D
24–10	East Germany	W	3–1	Sofia	Fr	Kolev I 2, Yanev
7–01–1955	Egypt	L	0–1	Cairo	Fr	
23–01	Lebanon	W	3–2	Beirut	Fr	Milanov D 3
22–05	Egypt	W	2–1	Sofia	Fr	Milanov D, Gugalov
26–06	Poland	D	1–1	Sofia	Fr	Bojkov
9–10	Romania	D	1–1	Bucharest	Fr	Panayotov
13–11	Czechoslovakia	W	3–0	Sofia	Fr	Kolev I, Bojkov, Diev
20–11	East Germany	L	0–1	Berlin	Fr	
26–08–1956	Poland	W	2–1	Wroclaw	Fr	Milanov D, Kolev I
10–09	Romania	W	2–0	Sofia	Fr	Milanov D, Yanev

14–10	East Germany	W	3–1	Sofia	Fr	Kolev I 2, Panayotov
5–12	Soviet Union	L	1–2	Melbourne	OGsf	Kolev I
7–12	India	W	3–0	Melbourne	OG3p	Diev 2, Milanov D
22–05–1957	Norway	W	2–1	Oslo	WCq	Dimitrov G 2
26–05	Denmark	D	1–1	Copenhagen	Fr	Kovachev
23–06	Hungary	L	1–4	Budapest	WCq	Dimitrov G
21–07	Soviet Union	L	0–4	Sofia	Fr	
15–09	Hungary	L	1–2	Sofia	WCq	Diev
29–09	Poland	D	1–1	Sofia	Fr	Milanov D
3–11	Norway	W	7–0	Sofia	WCq	Iliev C 3, Panayotov 2, Yanev, Debarski
25–12	France	D	2–2	Paris	Fr	Diev, Nestorov
14–05–1958	Brazil	L	0–4	Rio de Janeiro	Fr	
18–05	Brazil	L	1–3	Sao Paulo	Fr	Diev
5–10	East Germany	D	1–1	Berlin	Fr	Milanov D
12–10	Czechoslovakia	W	1–0	Ostrava	Fr	Milanov D
7–12	Turkey	D	0–0	Ankara	Fr	
21–12	West Germany	L	0–3	Augsburg	Fr	
13–05–1959	Holland	W	3–2	Sofia	Fr	Vasilev A 2, Kolev I
31–05	Yugoslavia	L	0–2	Belgrade	ECr1	
27–06	Soviet Union	D	1–1	Moscow	OGq	Milanov D
13–09	Soviet Union	W	1–0	Sofia	OGq	Kolev I
11–10	France	W	1–0	Sofia	Fr	Kolev I
25–10	Yugoslavia	D	1–1	Sofia	ECr1	Diev
8–11	Romania	L	0–1	Bucharest	OGq	
6–12	Denmark	W	2–1	Sofia	Fr	Abadjiev, Dimitrov I
3–04–1960	Holland	L	2–4	Amsterdam	Fr	Yakimov, Panayotov
1–05	Romania	W	2–1	Sofia	OGq	Yordanov D, Kovachev
22–05	Belgium	W	4–1	Sofia	Fr	Kolev I 2, Yordanov D, Diev
26–06	Poland	L	0–4	Chorzow	Fr	
10–07	East Germany	W	2–0	Sofia	Fr	Iliev C, Yakimov
26–08	Turkey*	W	3–0	Grossetto	OGr1	Diev 2, Iliev C
29–08	Egypt	W	2–0	Aquila	OGr1	Yordanov D, Diev
1–09	Yugoslavia	D	3–3	Rome	OGr1	Debarski 2, Rakarov
23–11	West Germany	W	2–1	Sofia	Fr	Kolev I 2
27–11	Turkey	W	2–1	Sofia	Fr	Kolev I, Iliev C
11–12	France	L	0–3	Paris	WCq	
16–06–1961	Finland	W	2–0	Helsinki	WCq	Iliev C, Kolev I
29–10	Finland	W	3–1	Sofia	WCq	Yakimov, Diev, Velichkov P
12–11	France	W	1–0	Sofia	WCq	Iliev C
16–12	France	W	1–0	Milan	WCq	Yakimov
24–12	Belgium	L	0–4	Brussels	Fr	
6–05–1962	Austria	L	0–2	Vienna	Fr	
30–05	Argentina	L	0–1	Rancagua	WCr1	
3–06	Hungary	L	1–6	Rancagua	WCr1	Asparuhov
7–06	England	D	0–0	Rancagua	WCr1	
30–09	Poland	W	2–1	Sofia	Fr	Diev, Apostolov
7–11	Portugal	W	3–1	Sofia	ECr1	Asparuhov 2, Diev
25–11	Austria	D	1–1	Sofia	Fr	Kolev I
16–12	Portugal	L	1–3	Lisbon	ECr1	Iliev C
6–01–1963	Algeria	L	1–2	Algiers	Fr	Asparuhov
23–01	Portugal	W	1–0	Rome	ECr1	Asparuhov
28–04	Czechoslovakia	W	1–0	Sofia	Fr	Yakimov
2–06	Albania	W	1–0	Tirana	OGq	
16–06	Albania	W	1–0	Sofia	OGq	
4–09	East Germany	D	1–1	Magdeburg	Fr	Dermendjiev
18–09	Sudan	D	1–1	Sofia	Fr	Kotkov
29–09	France	W	1–0	Sofia	ECr2	Diev
26–10	France	L	1–3	Paris	ECr2	Yakimov
3–05–1964	Romania	L	1–2	Bucharest	OGq	
31–05	Romania	L	0–1	Sofia	OGq	
29–11	Soviet Union	D	0–0	Sofia	Fr	
20–12	Turkey	D	0–0	Istanbul	Fr	
24–02–1965	Greece	W	2–1	Athens	Fr	Apostolov, Debarski
9–05	Turkey	W	4–1	Sofia	Fr	Debarski 3, Penev D
16–05	Poland	D	1–1	Krakow	Fr	Debarski
13–06	Israel	W	4–0	Sofia	WCq	Kotkov 2, Asparuhov, Kitov
4–09	East Germany	W	3–2	Varna	Fr	Kotkov 2, Diev
26–09	Belgium	W	3–0	Sofia	WCq	Kotkov 2, Asparuhov
27–10	Belgium	L	0–5	Brussels	WCq	
21–11	Israel	W	2–1	Tel Aviv	WCq	Kolev I, Asparuhov
29–12	Belgium	W	2–1	Florence	WCq	Asparuhov 2
25–02–1966	Egypt	D	2–2	Cairo	Fr	Kostov, Jekov
1–06	Yugoslavia	W	2–0	Belgrade	Fr	Jekov 2
14–06	Italy	L	1–6	Bologna	Fr	Asparuhov

* Not considered full International

12–07	Brazil	L	0–2	Liverpool	WCr1	
16–07	Portugal	L	0–3	Manchester	WCr1	
20–07	Hungary	L	1–3	Manchester	WCr1	Asparuhov
6–11	Yugoslavia	W	6–1	Sofia	Fr	Jekov 2, Dimitrov Y 2, Vasilev A, Dermendjiev
13–11	Norway	W	4–2	Sofia	ECq	Tzanev 2, Jekov 2
22–03–1967	West Germany	L	0–1	Hanover	Fr	
11–06	Sweden	W	2–0	Stockholm	ECq	Jekov, Dermendjiev
29–06	Norway	D	0–0	Oslo	ECq	
8–10	Soviet Union	L	1–2	Sofia	Fr	Dermendjiev
12–11	Sweden	W	3–0	Sofia	ECq	Kotkov, Mitkov, Asparuhov
26–11	Portugal	W	1–0	Sofia	ECq	Dermendjiev
17–12	Portugal	D	0–0	Lisbon	ECq	
6–04–1968	Italy	W	3–2	Sofia	ECqf	Kotkov, Dermendjiev, Jekov
10–04	East Germany*	W	4–1	Stara Zagora	OGq	
20–04	Italy	L	0–2	Naples	ECqf	
24–04	East Germany*	L	2–3	Leipzig	OGq	
14–10	Thailand*	W	7–0	Leon	OGr1	Christov 2, Giuonine, Jekov, Zafirov, Donev, Ivkov
16–10	Czechoslovakia*	D	2–2	Guadalajara	OGr1	Gueroguiev, Jekov
18–10	Guatemala*	W	2–1	Leon	OGr1	Donev, Jekov
20–10	Israel*	D	1–1 *(won on lots)*	Leon	OGqf	Christakiev
22–10	Mexico*	W	3–2	Guadalajara	OGsf	Jekov, Christov, Dimitrov
26–10	Hungary*	L	1–4	Mexico City	OGf	Dimitrov
9–10	Turkey	W	2–0	Istanbul	Fr	Dermendjiev, Bonev
27–10	Holland	W	2–0	Sofia	WCq	Bonev, Asparuhov
11–12	England	D	1–1	London	Fr	Asparuhov
23–04–1969	Luxembourg	W	2–1	Sofia	WCq	Asparuhov 2
24–05	Italy	D	0–0	Turin	Fr	
15–06	Poland	W	4–1	Sofia	WCq	Bonev, Dermendjiev, Penev D, Asparuhov
24–09	West Germany	L	0–1	Sofia	Fr	
22–10	Holland	D	1–1	Rotterdam	WCq	Bonev
9–11	Poland	L	0–3	Warsaw	WCq	
7–12	Luxembourg	W	3–1	Luxembourg	WCq	Dermendjiev, Yakimov, Bonev
28–12	Morocco	L	0–3	Casablanca	Fr	
15–02–1970	Mexico	D	1–1	Mexico City	Fr	Marashliev
18–02	Mexico	L	0–2	Leon	Fr	
21–02	Peru	W	3–1	Lima	Fr	Nikodimov, Marashliev, Mihaylov
24–02	Peru	L	3–5	Lima	Fr	Dermendjiev, Asparuhov, Marashliev
8–04	France	D	1–1	Rouen	Fr	Jekov
5–05	Soviet Union	D	3–3	Sofia	Fr	Jekov 2, Bonev
6–05	Soviet Union	D	0–0	Sofia	Fr	
2–06	Peru	L	2–3	Leon	WCr1	Dermendjiev, Bonev
7–06	West Germany	L	2–5	Leon	WCr1	Nikodimov, Kolev T
11–06	Morocco	D	1–1	Leon	WCr1	Jechev
15–11	Norway	D	1–1	Sofia	ECq	Atanasov
7–04–1971	Greece	W	1–0	Athens	Fr	Vasilev M
28–04	Soviet Union	D	1–1	Sofia	Fr	Mitkov
19–05	Hungary	W	3–0	Sofia	ECq	Kolev B, Petkov, Velichkov S
9–06	Norway	W	4–1	Oslo	ECq	Bonev 2, Jekov, Vasilev M
25–09	Hungary	L	0–2	Budapest	ECq	
10–11	France	L	1–2	Nantes	ECq	Bonev
17–11	Greece	D	2–2	Sofia	Fr	Vasiliev M, Kirilov
4–12	France	W	2–1	Sofia	ECq	Jekov, Mihaylov
29–03–1972	Soviet Union	D	1–1	Sofia	Fr	Bonev
16–04	Poland	W	3–1	Stara Zagora	OGq	Bonev 2, Dermendjiev
7–05	Poland	L	0–3	Warsaw	OGq	
7–06	Soviet Union	L	0–1	Moscow	Fr	
21–06	Italy	D	1–1	Sofia	Fr	Bonev
18–10	Nth. Ireland	W	3–0	Sofia	WCq	Bonev 2, Kolev B
19–11	Cyprus	W	4–0	Nicosia	WCq	Mihaylov, Bonev, Denev G 2
28–01–1973	Cyprus	W	3–0	Nicosia	Fr	Denev G 2, A Mihaylov
31–01	Greece	D	2–2	Athens	Fr	Petkov, Bonev
4–02	Indonesia	W	4–0	Djakarta	Fr	Mihaylov 2, Dermendjiev 2
8–02	New Caledonia	W	5–3	Noumea	Fr	Vasilev G, Yakimov, Dermendjiev, Mihaylov 2
14–02	Australia	D	2–2	Sydney	Fr	Vasilev G, Mihaylov
16–02	Australia	W	3–1	Adelaide	Fr	Bogomilov, Pritargov, Mihaylov
18–02	Australia	W	2–0	Melbourne	Fr	Pritargov, Dermendjiev
28–03	Soviet Union	W	1–0	Plovdiv	Fr	Dermendjiev
18–04	Turkey	L	2–5	Izmir	BC	Panov, Milanov K
2–05	Portugal	W	2–1	Sofia	WCq	Denev G, Bonev
12–05	West Germany	L	0–3	Hamburg	Fr	

19–08	Poland	L	0–2	Varna	Fr	
26–09	Nth. Ireland	D	0–0	Sheffield	WCq	
13–10	Portugal	D	2–2	Lisbon	WCq	Bonev 2
18–11	Cyprus	W	2–0	Sofia	WCq	Kolev B, Denev G
6–02–1974	Cyprus	W	4–1	Morphou	Fr	Kolev B, Bonev 3
8–02	Kuwait	W	3–1	Kuwait City	Fr	Denev G, Bonev, Petkov
10–02	Kuwait	W	2–1	Kuwait City	Fr	Bonev 2
31–03	Hungary	L	1–3	Zalaegerzeg	Fr	Bonev
13–04	Czechoslovakia	L	0–1	Plovdiv	Fr	
14–04	Brazil	L	0–1	Rio de Janeiro	Fr	
8–05	Turkey	W	5–1	Sofia	BC	Bonev, OG, Jechev, Panov, Grigorov
25–05	North Korea	W	6–1	Sofia	Fr	Bonev 3, Mihaylov, Panov, Borisov
1–06	England	L	0–1	Sofia	Fr	
15–06	Sweden	D	0–0	Dusseldorf	WCr1	
19–06	Uruguay	D	1–1	Hanover	WCr1	Bonev
23–06	Holland	L	1–4	Dortmund	WCr1	OG
25–09	Romania	D	0–0	Sofia	Fr	
13–10	Greece	D	3–3	Sofia	ECq	Bonev, Denev G 2
10–11	Hungary	D	0–0	Varna	Fr	
18–12	Greece	L	1–2	Athens	ECq	Kolev B
29–12	Italy	D	0–0	Genoa	Fr	
26–03–1975	East Germany	D	0–0	Berlin	Fr	
27–04	West Germany	D	1–1	Sofia	ECq	Kolev B
11–06	Malta	W	5–0	Sofia	ECq	Dimitrov B, Denev G, Panov, Bonev, Milanov K
19–11	West Germany	L	0–1	Stuttgart	ECq	
21–12	Malta	W	2–0	Gzira	ECq	Panov, Yordanov J
25–01–1976	Japan	W	3–1	Tokyo	Fr	Bonev, Tzvetkov C, Iliev S
28–01	Japan	D	1–1	Osaka	Fr	Bonev
1–02	Japan	W	3–0	Tokyo	Fr	Simov, Djevizov, Hristov
24–03	Soviet Union	L	0–3	Sofia	Fr	
5–05	North Korea	W	3–0	Sofia	Fr	Bonev 2, Jelyzkov
12–05	Romania	W	1–0	Veliko Tarnovo	BC	Vasilev T
17–08	Switzerland	D	2–2	Lucerne	Fr	Vasilev T, Yordanov J
22–09	Turkey	D	2–2	Sofia	Fr	Bonev, Jelyzkov
9–10	France	D	2–2	Sofia	WCq	Bonev, Panov
27–10	East Germany	L	0–4	Sliven	Fr	
28–11	Romania	L	2–3	Bucharest	BC	Jelyzkov, Garabski
11–01–1977	Algeria	D	1–1	Algiers	Fr	Dermendjiev
23–01	Brazil	L	0–1	Sao Paulo	Fr	
30–01	Cyprus	W	2–1	Nicosia	Fr	Panov, Milanov K
16–02	Turkey	L	0–2	Istanbul	BC	
13–04	Denmark	W	3–1	Sofia	Fr	Tzvetkov C, Jelyzkov, Borsov
1–06	Rep. Ireland	W	2–0	Sofia	WCq	Panov, Jelyzkov
21–09	Turkey	W	3–1	Sofia	BC	Jelyzkov, Alexandrov A, Djevizov
12–10	Rep. Ireland	D	0–0	Dublin	WCq	
26–10	Greece	D	0–0	Sofia	Fr	
16–11	France	L	1–3	Paris	WCq	Tzvetkov C
22–02–1978	Scotland	L	1–2	Glasgow	Fr	Mladenov
29–03	Argentina	L	1–3	Buenos Aires	Fr	Grantcharov
1–04	Peru	D	1–1	Lima	Fr	Manolov K
5–04	Mexico	L	0–3	Mexico City	Fr	
23–04	Czechoslovakia	D	0–0	Brno	Fr	
26–04	Poland	L	0–1	Warsaw	Fr	
26–04	Iran	D	1–1	Tehran	Fr	Sokolov
3–05	Romania	L	0–2	Bucharest	BC	
31–05	Romania	D	1–1	Sofia	BC	Mladenov
30–08	East Germany	D	2–2	Erfurt	Fr	Panov, Stankov A
20–09	Italy	L	0–1	Turin	Fr	
11–10	Denmark	D	2–2	Copenhagen	ECq	Panov, Iliev I
29–11	Nth. Ireland	L	0–2	Sofia	ECq	
26–02–1979	East Germany	W	1–0	Burgas	Fr	R Gochev
28–03	Soviet Union	L	1–3	Simferopol	Fr	Panov
25–04	Argentina	L	1–2	Buenos Aires	Fr	Bonev
2–05	Nth. Ireland	L	0–2	Belfast	ECq	
19–05	Rep. Ireland	W	1–0	Sofia	ECq	Tzvetkov C
6–06	England	L	0–3	Sofia	ECq	
17–10	Rep. Ireland	L	0–3	Dublin	ECq	
31–10	Denmark	W	3–0	Sofia	ECq	Jelyzkov, Tzvetkov C 2
22–11	England	L	0–2	London	ECq	
8–03–1980	Kuwait	D	1–1	Kuwait City	Fr	Jelyzkov
26–03	Soviet Union	L	1–3	Sofia	Fr	Tzvetkov C
14–05	Greece	D	0–0	Athens	Fr	
22–05	Norway	L	0–1	Oslo	Fr	

4–06	Finland	W 2–0	Helsinki	WCq	Markov P, Kostadinov K
10–09	Romania	L 1–2	Varna	Fr	Slavkov
24–09	Sweden	L 2–3	Burgas	Fr	Tzvetkov C, Markov P
9–10	Argentina	L 0–2	Buenos Aires	Fr	
19–10	Albania	W 2–1	Sofia	WCq	Jelyzkov, Slavkov
3–12	West Germany	L 1–3	Sofia	WCq	Yonchev
20–01–1981	Mexico	D 1–1	Mexico City	Fr	Kostadinov K
27–01	Ecuador	W 3–1	Quito	Fr	Slavkov, Tzvetkov C, Kostadinov K
1–02	Bolivia	W 3–1	La Paz	Fr	Slavkov, Tzvetkov C, Kostadinov K
11–02	Peru	W 2–1	Lima	Fr	Zehtinski, Tzvetkov C
25–03	Yugoslavia	L 1–2	Subotica	Fr	Slavkov
15–04	Portugal	D 1–1	Oporto	Fr	Tzvetkov C
29–04	Norway	W 1–0	Pleven	Fr	Tzvetkov P
13–05	Finland	W 4–0	Sofia	WCq	Slavkov 2, Kostadinov K, Tzvetkov C
28–05	Austria	L 0–2	Vienna	WCq	
12–08	Sweden	L 0–1	Uddevalla	Fr	
9–09	Romania	W 2–1	Bucharest	Fr	Yonchev, Kostadinov K
23–09	Italy	L 2–3	Bologna	Fr	Mladenov, Blonghev
14–10	Albania	W 2–0	Tirana	WCq	Slavkov 2
28–10	Brazil	L 0–3	Porto Alegre	Fr	
11–11	Austria	D 0–0	Sofia	WCq	
22–11	West Germany	L 0–4	Dusseldorf	WCq	
16–12	Portugal	W 5–2	Haskovo	Fr	Yonchev 2, Zdravkov 2, OG
14–04–1982	Romania	L 1–2	Ruse	Fr	Lovtschev
28–04	Belgium	L 1–2	Brussels	Fr	Mladenov
5–05	Argentina	L 1–2	Buenos Aires	Fr	Mladenov
15–05	France	D 0–0	Lyon	Fr	
7–09	Switzerland	L 2–3	St Gallen	Fr	Yonchev, Zdravkov
22–09	East Germany	D 2–2	Burgas	Fr	Zdravkov 2
14–10	Malta	W 7–0	Sofia	Fr	Kerimov, Blonghev, Velichkov B, Dimitrov G, Slavkov 3
27–10	Norway	D 2–2	Sofia	ECq	Velichkov B, Nikolov
17–11	Yugoslavia	L 0–1	Sofia	ECq	
7–03–1983	Switzerland	D 1–1	Varna	Fr	Getov
23–03	Poland	L 1–3	Lodz	Fr	Naidenov
13–04	East Germany	L 0–3	Gera	Fr	
27–04	Wales	L 0–1	Wrexham	ECq	
4–05	Cuba	W 5–2	Sofia	Fr	Valtchev, Spassov E, Gospodinov 2, Pashev
8–08	Algeria	W 3–2	Paris	Fr	Zdravkov, Sadkov 2
7–09	Norway	W 2–1	Oslo	ECq	Mladenov, Sirakov
26–10	Czechoslovakia	W 2–1	Prague	Fr	Mladenov, Iskrenov
16–11	Wales	W 1–0	Sofia	ECq	Gochev
21–12	Yugoslavia	L 2–3	Split	ECq	Iskrenov, Dimitrov G
4–02–1984	Morocco	D 1–1	Casablanca	Fr	Mladenov
15–02	West Germany	L 2–3	Varna	Fr	Iskrenov 2
4–04	Kuwait	D 1–1	Kuwait City	Fr	Gospodinov
8–06	Denmark	D 1–1	Copenhagen	Fr	Zdravkov
6–09	Portugal	L 0–1	Lisbon	Fr	
29–09	Yugoslavia	D 0–0	Belgrade	WCq	
16–10	Turkey	D 0–0	Istanbul	Fr	
21–11	France	L 0–1	Paris	WCq	
5–12	Luxembourg	W 4–0	Sofia	WCq	Sirakov, Velichkov B, Mladenov, Dimitrov G
5–02–1985	Switzerland	W 1–0	Queretaro	Fr	Zdravkov
7–02	Poland	D 2–2	Queretaro	Fr	Dimitrov G, Zdravkov
6–04	East Germany	W 1–0	Sofia	WCq	Mladenov
17–04	West Germany	L 1–4	Augsburg	Fr	Zdravkov
2–05	France	W 2–0	Sofia	WCq	Dimitrov G, Sirakov
1–06	Yugoslavia	W 2–1	Sofia	WCq	Getov 2
27–08	Mexico	D 1–1	Los Angeles	Fr	Iskrenov
4–09	Holland	L 0–1	Heerenveen	Fr	
25–09	Luxembourg	W 3–1	Luxembourg	WCq	Dimitrov G, OG 2
16–10	Greece	W 2–0	Salonica	Fr	Kolev H, Sadkov
16–11	East Germany	L 1–2	Karl Marx Stadt	WCq	Gochev
18–12	Spain	L 0–2	Valencia	Fr	
9–02–1986	East Germany	L 1–2	Queretaro	Fr	Pashev
19–02	Morocco	D 0–0	Rabat	Fr	
9–04	Denmark	W 3–0	Sofia	Fr	Sirakov 2, Velichkov B
23–04	Belgium	L 0–2	Brussels	Fr	
30–04	North Korea	W 3–0	Sofia	Fr	Dragolov, Markov A 2
31–05	Italy	D 1–1	Mexico City	WCr1	Sirakov
6–06	South Korea	D 1–1	Mexico City	WCr1	Getov
10–06	Argentina	L 0–2	Mexico City	WCr1	
15–06	Mexico	L 0–2	Mexico City	WCr2	

10–09	Scotland	D 0–0	Glasgow	ECq	
7–10	East Germany	W 2–0	Sofia	Fr	Stoichkov H 2
29–10	Tunisia	D 3–3	Tunis	Fr	Alexandrov P, Sirakov, Markov P
19–11	Belgium	D 1–1	Brussels	ECq	Tanev
29–01–1987	China	W 4–0	Sofia	Fr	Dragolov, Penev L 2, Eranosyan
1–04	Rep. of Ireland	W 2–1	Sofia	ECq	Sadkov, Tanev
30–04	Luxembourg	W 4–1	Luxembourg	ECq	Sadkov, Sirakov, Tanev, Kolev H
20–05	Luxembourg	W 3–0	Sofia	ECq	Sirakov, Yordanov G, Kolev H
23–09	Belgium	W 2–0	Sofia	ECq	Sirakov, Tanev
14–10	Rep. of Ireland	L 0–2	Dublin	ECq	
11–11	Scotland	L 0–1	Sofia	ECq	
21–01–1988	UAE	W 3–2	Dubai	Fr	Kirov, Alexandrov P, Stoichkov H
23–01	UAE	W 3–0	Dubai	Fr	Iliev N, Kolev H, Sadkov
25–01	UAE	W 3–1	Sharjah	Fr	Sadkov, Kolev H, Alexandrov P
29–01	Egypt	L 0–1	Cairo	Fr	
23–03	Czechoslovakia	W 2–0	Sofia	Fr	Sirakov, Penev L
13–04	East Germany	D 1–1	Burgas	Fr	Ivanov T
24–05	Holland	W 2–1	Rotterdam	Fr	Ivanov T, Penev L
4–08	Finland	D 1–1	Vaasa	Fr	Pashev
7–08	Iceland	W 3–2	Reykjavik	Fr	Yordanov G, Penev L, Alexandrov P
9–08	Norway	D 1–1	Oslo	Fr	Stoichkov H
24–08	Poland	L 2–3	Bialystok	Fr	Stoichkov H, Penev L
19–10	Romania	L 1–3	Sofia	WCq	Kolev H
2–11	Denmark	D 1–1	Copenhagen	WCq	Sadkov
22–12	UAE	W 1–0	Sharjah	Fr	Kostadinov E
21–02–1989	Soviet Union	L 1–2	Sofia	Fr	Kostadinov E
22–03	West Germany	L 1–2	Sofia	Fr	Stoichkov H
26–04	Denmark	L 0–2	Sofia	WCq	
10–05	Romania	L 0–1	Bucharest	WCq	
23–08	East Germany	D 1–1	Erfurt	Fr	Yordanov G
20–09	Italy	L 0–4	Cesena	Fr	
11–10	Greece	W 4–0	Varna	WCq	Ivanov Z, Barkov, Iskrenov, Stoichkov H
15–11	Greece	L 0–1	Athens	WCq	
5–05–1990	Brazil	L 1–2	Campinas	Fr	Kostadinov E
12–09	Switzerland	L 0–2	Geneva	ECq	
26–09	Sweden	L 0–2	Stockholm	Fr	
17–10	Romania	W 3–0	Bucharest	ECq	Sirakov, Todorov 2
14–11	Scotland	D 1–1	Sofia	ECq	Todorov
27–03–1991	Scotland	D 1–1	Glasgow	ECq	Kostadinov E
9–04	Denmark	D 1–1	Odense	Fr	Alexandrov P
1–05	Switzerland	L 2–3	Sofia	ECq	Kostadinov E, Sirakov
22–05	San Marino	W 3–0	Serravalle	ECq	Ivanov Z, Sirakov, Penev L
28–05	Brazil	L 0–3	Uberlandia	Fr	
21–08	Turkey	D 0–0	Stara Zagora	Fr	
25–09	Italy	W 2–1	Sofia	Fr	Kostadinov E, Stoichkov H
16–10	San Marino	W 4–0	Sofia	ECq	Penev L, Stoichkov H, Yankov, Iliev N
20–11	Romania	D 1–1	Sofia	ECq	Sirakov
28–04–1992	Switzerland	W 2–0	Berne	Fr	Sirakov, Kostadinov E
14–05	Finland	W 3–0	Helsinki	WCq	Balakov, Kostadinov E 2

LEADING INTERNATIONAL APPEARANCES

1	Bonev	96	7	Zdravkov	71	13	Rakarov	58	20	Jelyzkov	54
2	Penev	90	8	Dimitrov I	70		Dermendjiev	58	21	Bojkov	53
3	Sadkov	80	9	Yakimov	67	16	Manolov	57	22	Naidenov	51
4	Dimitrov G	77	10	Kolev B	60		Tzvetkov	57		Gaganelov	51
5	Kolev I	75	11	Mladenov	59	18	Nikolov	55	24	Asparuhov	50
6	Jetchev	73		Mikhailov B	59		Diev	55		Zafirov	50

LEADING INTERNATIONAL GOALSCORERS

1	Bonev	47		Jekov	25	7	Asparuhov	19	10	Diev	16
2	Angelov	25	5	Mihaylov	23		Dermendjiev	19		Sirakov	16
	Kolev I	25	6	Milanov	20	9	Panchev	18			

CYPRUS

It is often assumed that either Malta or Luxembourg is the weakest of the European nations, but Cyprus has a record that rivals both! Victory against the Faroe Islands in June 1992 was the first by the national side in a competitive international match for almost 20 years.

In 1974 Turkish troops invaded and occupied the north of the country, and although the north is not recognised by anyone except for Turkey, the island effectively operates as two separate countries. Though this cannot be used as an excuse for the poor showing of the national side, the division has had an effect on football, not least in that the Greek clubs which found themselves on Turkish territory had to up and move south. Famagusta, now in the northern sector of the island, was home to two Greek clubs, Anorthosis and Nea Salamis, but they both relocated to Larnaca.

The Greeks have always been the more football-orientated of the two communities, and as a British colony, football caught on easily amongst the locals. The Cyprus Football Association was formed in 1934, and a league as well as a cup competition was introduced the following year. In 1948 this association was affiliated to the one in London and membership of FIFA was granted. An international was played against Israel the following year, but it was not until the 1962 World Cup qualifiers that another Cypriot team took the field.

Since Cyprus became a member of UEFA in 1962, they have regularly entered teams into competitions at both national and club level. Success in the European club competitions has been as spectacularly absent as it has been for the national side. Apoel, traditionally the strongest side on the island, have been on the receiving end of a 16–1 thrashing by Sporting from Portugal as well as conceding double figures against both Dunfermline and Lierse SK.

	All			League			Cup		Europe		
Team	G	S	B	G	S	B	G	S	G	S	B
1 Apoel Nicosia	27	23	10	15	16	10	12	7	–	–	–
2 Omonia Nicosia	25	11	4	16	8	4	9	3	–	–	–
3 AEL Limassol	12	4	4	6	1	4	6	3	–	–	–
4 Anorthosis of Famagusta	10	8	4	6	5	4	4	3	–	–	–
5 EPA Larnaca	7	9	4	2	6	4	5	3	–	–	–
6 Apollon Limassol	5	5	2	1	2	2	4	3	–	–	–
7 Olympiakos Nicosia	4	6	2	3	3	2	1	3	–	–	–
8 Trust AC	4	3	–	1	2	–	3	1	–	–	–
9 Pezoporikos Larnaca	3	15	14	2	8	14	1	7	–	–	–
10 Chetin Kaya	3	4	3	1	1	3	2	3	–	–	–
11 NEA Salamis	1	1	2	–	–	2	1	1	–	–	–
12 Union Paralimni	–	5	2	–	1	2	–	4	–	–	–
13 Alki Larnaca	–	5	1	–	–	1	–	5	–	–	–
14 Aris Limassol	–	1	1	–	–	1	–	1	–	–	–
15 Digenis Morphou	–	1	–	–	1	–	–	–	–	–	–

To the end of the 1991–92 season

Only one predominantly Turkish club, Chetin Kaya, has ever achieved any success in the league or cup, and although an effort was made by the north to join world football, FIFA would have nothing to do with it, and to all intents and purposes, football lies dormant north of the green line. The possibilities for trouble are there, but thankfully only once has a Cypriot club drawn a side from Turkey. As they rarely progress beyond the first round, the likelihood of a meeting, given that Turkish clubs are usually not seeded either, is remote, but in 1987, Apoel beat HJK Helsinki and were drawn against Besiktas in the second round, and so promptly withdrew.

Population: 568 000
Area, sq km: 5896
% in urban areas: 63.6%
Capital city: Nicosia

Cyprus Football Association
Stasinos Str #1, Engomi 152
PO Box 5071
Nicosia
Cyprus
Tel: (010 357) 2 445341
Fax: (010 357) 2 472544
Telex: 3880 FOOTBALL CY
Cable: FOOTBALL CYPRUS
Languages for correspondence: English

Year of formation: 1934
Affiliation to FIFA: 1948
Affiliation to UEFA: 1954
Registered clubs: 91
Registered players: 23 500
Registered coaches: 250
Registered referees: 159
National stadium: Makarion Athletic Centre 20 000
National colours: Shirts: Blue/Shorts: White/Socks: Blue
Reserve colours: Shirts: White/Shorts: Blue/Socks: White
Season: October–June

THE RECORD

WORLD CUP

1930–58 ..... Did not enter
1962 .... QT 1st round in group 7
1966 .... QT 3rd/3 in group 2
1970 .... QT 4th/4 in group 7
1974 .... QT 4th/4 in group 6
1978 .... QT 4th/4 in group 1
1982 .... QT 5th/5 in group 2
1986 .... QT 4th/4 in group 5
1990 .... QT 5th/5 in group 5

EUROPEAN CHAMPIONSHIP

1960 .... Did not enter
1964 .... Did not enter
1968 .... QT 4th/4 in group 6
1972 .... QT 4th/4 in group 4
1976 .... QT 4th/4 in group 1
1980 .... QT 4th/4 in group 3
1984 .... QT 5th/5 in group 5
1988 .... QT 5th/5 in group 5
1992 .... QT 5th/5 in group 3

OLYMPIC GAMES

1908–84 ..... Did not enter
1988 .... QT Failed to qualify
1992 .... QT Failed to qualify

EUROPEAN CLUB COMPETITIONS

EUROPEAN CUP: 2nd round – Omonia

1973 1980 1986 1988, Apollon 1992

CUP WINNERS CUP: 2nd round – Apoel 1964 1977

UEFA CUP: 2nd round – Omonia 1991

CLUB DIRECTORY

NICOSIA (Population – 185 000 plus 37000 in the Turkish sector)

Omonia Nicosia
Stadium: Makarion 20 000
Founded: 1948
Colours: White/Green

Apoel Nicosia
Stadium: Makarion 20 000
Founded: 1926
Colours: Yellow/Blue

Olympiakos Nicosia
Stadium: Pancypria 10 000
Founded: 1931
Colours: Green/Black

LIMASSOL (Population – 120 000)

AEL Limassol
Stadium: Tsirion 20 000
Founded: 1930
Colours: Yellow/Blue

Apollon Limassol
Stadium: Tsirion 20 000
Founded: 1954
Colours: Blue/White

Aris Limassol
Stadium: Tsirion 20 000
Founded: 1930
Colours: Green/White

APEP Limassol
Stadium: Tsirion 20 000
Founded: 1979
Colours: Blue with White top and sleeves/ Blue

LARNACA (Population – 48 000)

Anorthosis of Famagusta
Stadium: Antonis Papadopoulos 8000
Founded: 1911
Colours: Blue/Blue

Pezoporikos Larnaca
Stadium: Zenon 8000
Founded: 1927
Colours: Green with white sleeves/Green

Alki Larnaca
Stadium: Zenon 8000
Founded: 1948
Colours: Blue with red sleeves/Red

EPA Larnaca
Stadium: Zenon 8000
Founded: 1932
Colours: Yellow/Black

NEA Salamis of Famagusta
Stadium: Antonis Papadopoulos 8000
Founded: 1948
Colours: White with Red top/White

Trust AC
Stadium: Old Gymnastica
Founded: 1896–1944
Colours: Blue/White

PARALIMNI

Union of Paralimni
Stadium: Paralimni 7000
Founded: 1936
Colours: Claret/Blue

PAPHOS

APOP Paphos
Stadium: Paphiako 8000
Founded: 1953
Colours: White/White

Evagoras Paphos
Stadium: Paphiako 8000
Founded: 1961
Colours: Blue/Blue

CYPRIOT LEAGUE CHAMPIONSHIP

Year	Champions		Runners up		3rd	
1935	Trust AC	24	LTSK Nicosia	16	Apoel Nicosia	15
1936	Apoel Nicosia	24	Trust AC	20	LTSK Nicosia	19
1937	Apoel Nicosia	20	Trust AC	19	LTSK Nicosia	16
1938	AEL Limassol	16	Apoel Nicosia	14	Aris Limassol	8
1939	Apoel Nicosia	20	EPA Larnaca	18	AEL Limassol	12
1940	Apoel Nicosia	16	Pezoporikos Larnaca	14	EPA Larnaca	11
1941	AEL Limassol	12	Apoel Nicosia	12	EPA Larnaca	4
1942–44	–					
1945	Apoel Nicosia	17	EPA Larnaca	17	AEL Limassol	13
1946	EPA Larnaca	17	Apoel Nicosia	15	Pezoporikos Larnaca	9
1947	Apoel Nicosia	24	EPA Larnaca	18	Pezoporikos Larnaca	11
1948	Apoel Nicosia	15	AEL Limassol	11	Olympiakos Nicosia	8
1949	Apoel Nicosia	28	Anorthosis Famag.	21	Pezoporikos Larnaca	19
1950	Anorthosis Famag.	23	EPA Larnaca	22	Apoel Nicosia	17
1951	LTSK Nicosia	20	Apoel Nicosia	18	Anorthosis Famag.	17
1952	Apoel Nicosia	22	EPA Larnaca	17	Chetin Kaya	17
1953	AEL Limassol	23	Pezoporikos Larnaca	21	Apoel Nicosia	17
1954	Pezoporikos Larnaca	26	Apoel Nicosia	22	Anorthosis Famag.	18
1955	AEL Limassol	29	Pezoporikos Larnaca	24	Apoel Nicosia	23
1956	AEL Limassol	23	Apoel Nicosia	21	NEA Salamis	19
1957	Anorthosis Famag.	29	Pezoporikos Larnaca	21	Omonia Nicosia	21
1958	Anorthosis Famag.	27	Pezoporikos Larnaca	21	EPA Larnaca	20
1959	–					
1960	Anorthosis Famag.	30	Omonia Nicosia	29	Apoel Nicosia	23
1961	Omonia Nicosia	44	Anorthosis Famag.	35	Pezoporikos Larnaca	29
1962	Anorthosis Famag.	35	Omonia Nicosia	31	Pezoporikos Larnaca	30
1963	Anorthosis Famag.	37	Apoel Nicosia	32	Omonia Nicosia	27
1964	–					
1965	Apoel Nicosia	54	Olympiakos Nicosia	47	AEL Limassol	47
1966	Omonia Nicosia	50	Olympiakos Nicosia	49	NEA Salamis	48
1967	Olympiakos Nicosia	55	Apoel Nicosia	55	Anorthosis Famag.	54

1968	AEL Limassol	58	Omonia Nicosia	54	Pezoporikos Larnaca	52
1969	Olympiakos Nicosia	55	Omonia Nicosia	52	Pezoporikos Larnaca	50
1970	EPA Larnaca	53	Pezoporikos Larnaca	53	Omonia Nicosia	53
1971	Olympiakos Nicosia	31	Digenis Morphou	27	Apoel Nicosia	26
1972	Omonia Nicosia	32	EPA Larnaca	30	Union Paralimni	25
1973	Apoel Nicosia	42	Olympiakos Nicosia	34	Pezoporikos Larnaca	31
1974	Omonia Nicosia	44	Pezoporikos Larnaca	42	AEL Limassol	33
1975	Omonia Nicosia	43	Union Paralimni	39	Olympiakos Nicosia	39
1976	Omonia Nicosia	50	Apoel Nicosia	42	Union Paralimni	42
1977	Omonia Nicosia	54	Apoel Nicosia	51	Pezoporikos Larnaca	40
1978	Omonia Nicosia	51	Apoel Nicosia	41	Pezoporikos Larnaca	37
1979	Omonia Nicosia	45	Apoel Nicosia	44	Alki Larnaca	33
1980	Apoel Nicosia	48	Omonia Nicosia	48	Pezoporikos Larnaca	33
1981	Omonia Nicosia	38	Apoel Nicosia	36	Pezoporikos Larnaca	34
1982	Omonia Nicosia	44	Pezoporikos Larnaca	34	Apoel Nicosia	34
1983	Omonia Nicosia	36	Anorthosis Famag.	35	Apoel Nicosia	32
1984	Omonia Nicosia	42	Apollon Limassol	37	Pezoporikos Larnaca	34
1985	Omonia Nicosia	43	Apoel Nicosia	34	Anorthosis Famag.	33
1986	Apoel Nicosia	47	Omonia Nicosia	40	Apollon Limassol	37
1987	Omonia Nicosia	52	Apoel Nicosia	47	EPA Larnaca	43
1988	Pezoporikos Larnaca	48	Apoel Nicosia	47	Omonia Nicosia	37
1989	Omonia Nicosia	43	Apollon Limassol	40	Apoel Nicosia	34
1990	Apoel Nicosia	41	Omonia Nicosia	35	Pezoporikos Larnaca	31
1991	Apollon Limassol	44	Anorthosis Famag.	41	Apoel Nicosia	35
1992	Apoel Nicosia	60	Anorthosis Famag.	58	Apollon Limassol	53

CYPRIOT CUP FINALS

Year	Winners	Score	Runners–up
1935	Trust AC	0–0 1–0	Apoel Nicosia
1936	Trust AC	4–1	LTSK Nicosia
1937	Apoel Nicosia	2–1	Trust AC
1938	Trust AC	1–0	LTSK Nicosia
1939	AEL Limassol	3–1	Apoel Nicosia
1940	AEL Limassol	3–1	Pezoporikos Larnaca
1941	Apoel Nicosia	2–1	AEL Limassol
1942–44	–		
1945	EPA Larnaca	3–1	Apoel Nicosia
1946	EPA Larnaca	2–1	Apoel Nicosia
1947	Apoel Nicosia	4–1	Anorthosis Famagusta
1948	AEL Limassol	2–0	Apoel Nicosia
1949	Anorthosis Famagusta	3–0	Apoel Nicosia
1950	EPA Larnaca	2–0	Anorthosis Famagusta
1951	Apoel Nicosia	7–0	EPA Larnaca
1952	Chetin Kaya	4–1	Pezoporikos Larnaca
1953	EPA Larnaca	2–1	Chetin Kaya
1954	Chetin Kaya	2–1	Pezoporikos Larnaca
1955	EPA Larnaca	2–1	Pezoporikos Larnaca
1956–61	–		
1962	Anorthosis Famagusta	5–2	Olympiakos Nicosia
1963	Apoel Nicosia	1–1 2–0	Anorthosis Famagusta
1964	–		
1965	Omonia Nicosia	5–1	Apollon Limassol
1966	Apollon Limassol	4–2	NEA Salamis
1967	Apollon Limassol	1–0	Alki Larnaca
1968	Apoel Nicosia	2–1	EPA Larnaca
1969	Apoel Nicosia	1–0	Omonia Nicosia
1970	Pezoporikos Larnaca	2–1	Alki Larnaca
1971	Anorthosis Famag.	1–1 1–0	Omonia Nicosia
1972	Omonia Nicosia	3–1	Pezoporikos Larnaca
1973	Apoel Nicosia	1–0	Pezoporikos Larnaca
1974	Omonia Nicosia	3–2	Union Paralimni
1975	Anorthosis Famagusta	3–2	Union Paralimni
1976	Apoel Nicosia	6–0	Alki Larnaca
1977	Olympiakos Nicosia	2–0	Alki Larnaca
1978	Apoel Nicosia	3–0	Olympiakos Nicosia
1979	Apoel Nicosia	1–0	AEL Limassol
1980	Omonia Nicosia	3–1	Alki Larnaca
1981	Omonia Nicosia	1–1 3–0	Union Paralimni
1982	Omonia Nicosia	2–2 4–1	Apollon Limassol
1983	Omonia Nicosia	2–1	Union Paralimni
1984	Apoel Nicosia	1–1 3–1	Pezoporikos Larnaca
1985	AEL Limassol	1–0	EPA Larnaca
1986	Apollon Limassol	2–0	Apoel Nicosia
1987	AEL Limassol	1–0	Apollon Limassol
1988	Omonia Nicosia	2–1	AEL Limassol
1989	AEL Limassol	3–2	Aris Limassol
1990	NEA Salamis	3–2	Omonia Nicosia
1991	Omonia Nicosia	1–0	Olympiakos Nicosia
1992	Apollon Limassol	1–0	Omonia Nicosia

INTERNATIONAL MATCHES PLAYED BY CYPRUS

Date	Opponents	Result		Venue	Compet	Scorers
30–07–1949	Israel	L	1–3	Tel Aviv	Fr	Yiasemis
13–11–1960	Israel	D	1–1	Nicosia	WCq	Yiasemis
27–11	Israel	L	1–6	Tel Aviv	WCq	Yiasemis
27–11–1963	Greece	W	3–1	Nicosia	Fr	Pakkos 2, Kristallis
20–03–1965	Lebanon	W	2–0	Nicosia	Fr	Pakkos, Kristallis
24–04	West Germany	L	0–5	Karlsruhe	WCq	
5–05	Sweden	L	0–3	Norrkoping	WCq	
7–11	Sweden	L	0–5	Famagusta	WCq	
14–11	West Germany	L	0–6	Nicosia	WCq	
3–12–1966	Rumania	L	1–5	Nicosia	ECq	Pierides

22-03-1967	Italy	L	0–2	Nicosia	ECq	
23-04	Rumania	L	0–7	Bucharest	ECq	
1-11	Italy	L	0–5	Cosenza	ECq	
8-11	Switzerland	L	0–5	Lugano	ECq	
17-02-1968	Switzerland	W	2–1	Nicosia	ECq	Asproy, Papadopoulos
19-05	Austria	L	1–7	Vienna	WCq	Kantzilieris
23-11	West Germany	L	0–1	Nicosia	WCq	
11-12	Scotland	L	0–5	Nicosia	WCq	
25-03-1969	Greece	L	0–1	Athens	Fr	
19-04	Austria	L	1–2	Nicosia	WCq	Efthymiadis
17-05	Scotland	L	0–8	Glasgow	WCq	
21-05	West Germany	L	0–12	Essen	WCq	
15-11-1970	Soviet Union	L	1–3	Nicosia	ECq	Charalambous
9-12	Greece	D	1–1	Athens	Fr	Pamboulis
3-02-1971	Nth. Ireland	L	0–3	Nicosia	ECq	
21-04	Nth. Ireland	L	0–5	Belfast	ECq	
9-05	Spain	L	0–2	Nicosia	ECq	
7-06	Soviet Union	L	1–6	Moscow	ECq	Stefanis
24-11	Spain	L	0–7	Granada	ECq	
29-03-1972	Portugal	L	0–4	Lisbon	WCq	
10-05	Portugal	L	0–1	Nicosia	WCq	
19-11	Bulgaria	L	0–4	Nicosia	WCq	
28-01-1973	Bulgaria	L	0–3	Nicosia	Fr	
14-02	Nth. Ireland	W	1–0	Nicosia	WCq	Antoniou
8-05	Nth. Ireland	L	0–3	London	WCq	
18-11	Bulgaria	L	0–2	Sofia	WCq	
6-02-1974	Bulgaria	L	1–4	Morphou	Fr	Haris
15-11	Greece	L	1–3	Athens	Fr	Papadopoulos
1-04-1975	Greece	L	1–2	Nicosia	Fr	Constantinou
16-04	England	L	0–5	London	ECq	
20-04	Czechoslovakia	L	0–4	Prague	ECq	
11-05	England	L	0–1	Limassol	ECq	
8-06	Portugal	L	0–2	Limassol	ECq	
23-11	Czechoslovakia	L	0–3	Limassol	ECq	
3-12	Portugal	L	0–1	Setubal	ECq	
23-05-1976	Denmark	L	1–5	Limassol	WCq	Stefanis
27-10	Denmark	L	0–5	Copenhagen	WCq	
31-10	Poland	L	0–5	Warsaw	WCq	
5-12	Portugal	L	1–2	Limassol	WCq	Stavros
30-01-1977	Bulgaria	L	1–2	Nicosia	Fr	Savva
15-05	Poland	L	1–3	Nicosia	WCq	Antoniou
16-11	Portugal	L	0–4	Lisbon	WCq	
11-01-1978	Greece	L	0–2	Limassol	Fr	
16-11	Saudi Arabia	D	2–2	Nicosia	Fr	Timotheoy, Economolis
13-12	Spain	L	0–5	Salamanca	ECq	
1-04-1979	Yugoslavia	L	0–3	Nicosia	ECq	
13-05	Rumania	D	1–1	Limassol	ECq	Kaiafas
14-11	Yugoslavia	L	0–5	Novi Sad	ECq	
18-11	Rumania	L	0–2	Bucharest	ECq	
9-12	Spain	L	1–3	Limassol	ECq	Vrahimis
16-01-1980	Greece	D	1–1	Nicosia	Fr	Kitzas
26-03	Rep. Ireland	L	2–3	Nicosia	WCq	Pantziaras, Kaiafas
11-10	France	L	0–7	Limassol	WCq	
19-11	Rep. Ireland	L	0–6	Dublin	WCq	
21-12	Belgium	L	0–2	Nicosia	WCq	
18-02-1981	Belgium	L	2–3	Brussels	WCq	Lysandrou, Firos
22-02	Holland	L	0–3	Groningen	WCq	
15-04	Greece	L	0–1	Nicosia	Fr	
29-04	Holland	L	0–1	Nicosia	WCq	

LEADING INTERNATIONAL APPEARANCES

1	Yiangoudakis	48
2	Pantziaras	46
3	Nicoloau	40
4	Stylianou	37
5	Stefanis	35

LEADING INTERNATIONAL GOALSCORERS

1	Vrahimis	8
2	Kaifas	6
3	Papadopoulos	5

5–12	France	L	0–4	Paris	WCq	
14–04–1982	Syria	W	1–0	Damascus	Fr	Vrahimis
1–05	Rumania	L	1–3	Hunedoara	ECq	Vrahimis
27–10	Greece	D	1–1	Nicosia	Fr	Yiangoudakis
13–11	Sweden	L	0–1	Nicosia	ECq	
22–12	Greece	L	0–1	Yanina	Fr	
12–02–1983	Italy	D	1–1	Limassol	ECq	Mavris
27–03	Czechoslovakia	D	1–1	Nicosia	ECq	Theofanus
16–04	Czechoslovakia	L	0–6	Prague	ECq	
15–05	Sweden	L	0–5	Malmo	ECq	
12–11	Rumania	L	0–1	Limassol	ECq	
22–12	Italy	L	1–3	Perugia	ECq	Tsinghis
11–04–1984	Greece	D	1–1	Athens	Fr	Theofanus
2–05	Austria	L	1–2	Nicosia	WCq	Christophorou
30–09	Greece	L	0–2	Limassol	Fr	
30–10	Canada	D	0–0	Nicosia	Fr	
17–11	Hungary	L	1–2	Limassol	WCq	Fotis
17–12	Luxembourg	W	1–0	Nicosia	Fr	Tsikos
23–12	Holland	L	0–1	Nicosia	WCq	
27–02–1985	Holland	L	1–7	Amsterdam	WCq	Marangos
3–04	Hungary	L	0–2	Budapest	WCq	
7–05	Austria	L	0–4	Graz	WCq	
19–02–1986	Greece	D	0–0	Athens	Fr	
3–12	Greece	L	2–4	Nicosia	ECq	Christofi, Savvides
21–12	Holland	L	0–2	Nicosia	ECq	
14–01–1987	Greece	L	1–3	Athens	ECq	Savva
8–02	Hungary	L	0–1	Nicosia	ECq	
25–03	Jordan	L	1–2	Amman	Fr	Taziadoros
12–04	Poland	D	0–0	Gdansk	ECq	
28–10	Holland	L	0–8	Rotterdam	ECq	Declared Void
11–11	Poland	L	0–1	Limassol	ECq	
2–12	Hungary	L	0–1	Budapest	ECq	
9–12	Holland	L	0–4	Amsterdam	ECq	
12–10–1988	Malta	L	0–1	Limassol	Fr	
22–10	France	D	1–1	Nicosia	WCq	Pittas
2–11	Norway	L	0–3	Limassol	WCq	
23–11	Malta	D	1–1	Ta'Qali	Fr	Ioannou
11–12	Yugoslavia	L	0–4	Belgrade	WCq	
8–02–1989	Scotland	L	2–3	Limassol	WCq	Koliandris, Ioannou
26–04	Scotland	L	1–2	Glasgow	WCq	Nicolaou
21–05	Norway	L	1–3	Oslo	WCq	Koliandris
11–10	Malta	D	0–0	Nicosia	Fr	
28–10	Yugoslavia	L	1–2	Athens	WCq	Pittas
18–11	France	L	0–2	Toulouse	WCq	
31–10–1990	Hungary	L	2–4	Budapest	ECq	Xiouroupas, Tsolakis
14–11	Norway	L	0–3	Nicosia	ECq	
22–12	Italy	L	0–4	Limassol	ECq	
27–02–1991	Greece	D	1–1	Limassol	Fr	Nicolaou
3–04	Hungary	L	0–2	Limassol	ECq	
1–05	Norway	L	0–3	Oslo	ECq	
29–05	Soviet Union	L	0–4	Moscow	ECq	
13–11	Soviet Union	L	0–3	Larnaca	ECq	
21–12	Italy	L	0–2	Foggia	ECq	
3–03–1992	Israel	L	1–2	Tel Aviv	Fr	Pittas
25–03	Greece	L	1–3	Limassol	Fr	Larku
22–04	Belgium	L	0–1	Brussels	WCq	
17–06	Faeroe Islands	W	2–0	Toftir	WCq	Soririou, Papavassiliou

CZECHOSLOVAKIA

If it can be said that football in Bulgaria, Romania and Poland benefited from forty years of communist rule, the opposite would be the case in both Czechoslovakia and Hungary, for although in the 1950s and early 1960s it looked as if football behind the Iron Curtain was in a healthy state, success at that time merely papered over the cracks that were to appear later.

At the beginning of the century, Czechoslovakia, along with Hungary and Austria, was the powerhouse of football on the European continent. Had clubs like Sparta or Slavia Prague been allowed to develop along the lines of the major western European clubs after World War II, they might have grown to be amongst the best on the continent. Now, in the wake of the overthrow of their communist leaders, all Czech clubs are struggling financially and the flow of players westwards has become alarming.

In the 1930s, the process worked in the opposite direction. Success in the Mitropa Cup meant that both Slavia and Sparta could bring famous players, the likes of the Belgian Raymond Braine, to Prague. Three wins and three runners-up spots in the Mitropa Cup sealed the reputation of the Czechs as did reaching the World Cup Final in 1934. Had they played Italy in that final anywhere other than in Italy, they may well even have been world champions.

Prior to 1918, Czechoslovakia did not exist, but Bohemia, a province in the Austro-Hungarian empire with its capital Prague, took to football from the start. Both Slavia and Sparta were formed in 1893 and a provincial league was set up three years later, followed in 1906 by the Charity Cup. As Bohemia, a representative side took the field against Hungary in 1903 for the their first international match. Five years later they took on England in the last game of England's first tour abroad with their full international side. Though beaten 4–0 in Prague, they did better than either Hungary or Austria did against the tourists.

Czechoslovakia was born as an independent state in 1918 but it was not until 1925 that a national league was set up catering for all three republics of Bohemia, Moravia and Slovakia. The national team entered the Olympic Games in 1920 and reached the first of the four major finals they have appeared in, but they lost 2–0 to the hosts and were not even awarded the silver medal as they walked off the field in the second half, complaining about the bias of the referee.

Throughout the 1920s and 1930s, Czechoslovakia produced some fabulous players and sides. Sparta won the first Mitropa Cup in 1927, a feat they repeated in 1935, whilst Slavia were victorious in 1938. In 1934 the national side played some of the best football in the World Cup in Italy and contained players such as Antonin Puc, who today remains the leading goalscorer for the national side, Frantisek Planicka, who was regarded as the finest goalkeeper of the pre-war era, and Oldrich Nejedly, another prolific goalscorer, as were Frantisek Svoboda and Josef Silny, whilst Josef Kostalek, Stefan Cambal and Rudolf Krcil were a formidable midfield.

Professionalism, which had been introduced in 1925, formed the basis for the success of Czechoslovakian sides. After World War II, however, all clubs reverted to amateur status, and were incorporated into various government bodies such as the army and police.

	All			League			Cup		Europe		
Team	G	S	B	G	S	B	G	S	G	S	B
1 Sparta Praha	40	31	8	20	18	7	20	13	–	–	1
2 Slavia Praha	24	16	7	13	10	7	11	6	–	–	–
3 Dukla Praha	19	9	5	11	7	3	8	2	–	–	2
4 Slovan Bratislava	18	18	2	12	12	2	5	6	1	–	–
5 Spartak Trnava	9	2	3	5	1	2	4	1	–	–	1
6 Baník Ostrava	6	8	2	3	6	1	3	2	–	–	1
7 Viktoria Zizkov	5	3	3	1	1	3	4	2	–	–	–
8 Bohemians Praha	2	5	12	1	1	11	1	4	–	–	1
9 Lokomotiva Kosice	2	1	2	–	–	2	2	1	–	–	–
10 TJ Internacional	1	6	5	1	3	5	–	3	–	–	–
11 AC Bystrica	1	1	2	1	1	2	–	–	–	–	–
12 Zbrojovka Brno	1	1	1	1	1	1	–	–	–	–	–
13 OAP Bratislava	1	1	–	1	1	–	–	–	–	–	–
TJ Vítkovice	1	1	–	1	1	–	–	–	–	–	–
15 SK Zlin	1	–	2	–	–	2	1	–	–	–	–
16 DAC Dunajská Streda	1	–	1	–	–	1	1	–	–	–	–
17 ASO Olomouc	1	–	–	–	–	–	1	–	–	–	–
Spartak Hradec Králové	1	–	–	1	–	–	–	–	–	–	–
19 Jednota VSS Kosice	–	4	2	–	1	2	–	3	–	–	–
20 Tatran Presov	–	4	1	–	2	1	–	2	–	–	–
21 Skoda Plzen	–	3	1	–	–	1	–	3	–	–	–
22 SONP Kladno	–	2	2	–	–	2	–	2	–	–	–
SK Prostejov	–	2	2	–	1	2	–	1	–	–	–
24 Jednota Trencin	–	2	1	–	1	1	–	1	–	–	–
25 CAFC Vinohrady	–	2	–	–	–	–	–	2	–	–	–
Vrutky	–	2	–	–	2	–	–	–	–	–	–
27 Synthesia Pardubice	–	1	3	–	–	3	–	1	–	–	–
SK Zilina	–	1	3	–	–	3	–	1	–	–	–
29 Sklo Union Teplice	–	1	2	–	–	2	–	1	–	–	–
30 FC Nitra	–	1	1	–	1	1	–	–	–	–	–
SK Plzen	–	1	1	–	1	1	–	–	–	–	–
32 Cechie Karlin	–	1	–	–	–	–	–	1	–	–	–
Dukla Banská Bystrica	–	1	–	–	–	–	–	1	–	–	–
SS Plincner	–	1	–	–	–	–	–	1	–	–	–
SK Rakovnic	–	1	–	–	–	–	–	1	–	–	–
36 SK Zidenice	–	–	2	–	–	2	–	–	–	–	–
37 Sigma Olomouc	–	–	1	–	–	1	–	–	–	–	–

To the end of the 1992–92 season. This table includes the Stredocesky Cup finals, the Czech Cup finals 1940–46 and the Slovak League 1939–45. It does not include any tournaments pre-1925.

The immediate effect was to break the Sparta–Slavia stranglehold. Dukla Prague, the team of the army, and sides from Bratislava and other provincial towns began to make their presence felt. Slavia went into a decline from which they have never recovered, and the same looked set to happen to Sparta, but they pulled themselves round and remained one of the most successful teams. Clubs such as Slovan Bratislava, Banik Ostrava, and Spartak Trnava have all had successful spells in the league and cup.

For a while it looked as if the change in government had seriously weakened the Czech national side. A poor performance in the 1954 and 1958 World Cups was followed by an upturn in fortunes. Based around the now powerful Dukla team, Czechoslovakia finished third in the inaugural European Championship and followed this success by reaching the World Cup Final again in 1962. In that side was Josef Masopust, who remains one of the most famous Czech footballers of all time, and he was joined in midfield by Andrej Kvasnak, whilst in defence Ladislav Novak, for a long time after his retirement the most capped player for the national side, formed a good partnership with Svatopluk Pluskal and Jan Popluhar. Goals had often been a problem in the 1950s but Adolf Scherer, Tomas Pospichal, Josef Kabraba and Jozef Adamec all helped spice up the attack.

There were those who claimed that the post-war generation did not match up to their pre-war counterparts, and there was a grain of truth in this. Failure to qualify for the 1966 World Cup as well as defeat in the first round of the 1964 European Championship by East Germany lent credence to the belief that had it not been for Viliam Schroif, their goalkeeper who was in inspirational form until the final in Chile, the Czechs would not have got as far as they did.

Slovan Bratislava won the Cup Winners Cup in 1969, but this remains the only success that has been achieved by any Czechoslovakian club. The slide continued throughout the 1970s despite one brief interlude. In the 1976 European Championship, England were beaten into second place in the qualifying group and the quarter-finals saw victory over the Soviet Union. But when they travelled to Yugoslavia for the final stages, of the four teams the Czechs were the least fancied.

In the semi-finals they beat Holland 3–1, in a match the Dutch were expected to win easily, to qualify for their fourth major international final. Having defeated the runners-up of the previous World Cup, for which they had not even qualified, Czechoslovakia now faced the world champions. The sides could not be separated after extra-time had been played and so the game was decided on penalty kicks. Perhaps not the most satisfactory of means to become European Champions, but the Czechs deserved their title in what proved to be a most entertaining final tournament.

This team can perhaps be regarded as the third great Czech team following on from the team of the 1930s and early 1960s. Once again it was based upon outstanding goalkeeping. Ivo Viktor rivals Planicka as the best goalkeeper to play for the national side and remains the only Czech to have won the European Footballer of the Year award. In defence Anton Ondrus was particularly strong whilst in midfield Antonin Panenka and Karol Dobias combined well together. Zdenek Nehoda in attack was a prolific goalscorer, and although not equalling Puc's record tally of goals, he was only three short, at a time when goals were much harder to come by.

Third place was achieved in the 1980 European Championship, but results since then have been poor, both at club and national level. Czechoslovakia now faces a difficult challenge. The infrastructure and support for football is there if the clubs can stand up to the challenge facing them. The flow of players out of the country will only be halted if clubs like Sparta and Slavia can become as prestigious again as they once were.

All this of course depends on whether Czechoslovakia will remain as a unified country, or whether the Czechs and the Slovaks will go their separate ways. It happened during the war and even now the Czechoslovakian Cup final is contested between the winners of the Czech Cup and the Slovak Cup. It may not be unreasonable to assume that in the future, the winners of both will be represented in the European Cup Winners Cup.

Population: 15 664 000
Area, sq km: 127 900
% in urban areas: 75.7%
Capital city: Prague

Ceskoslovensky Fotbalovy Svaz
NA Porici #12
11530 Prague 1
Czechoslovakia
Tel: (010 42) 2 355358
Fax: (010 42) 2 352784
Telex: 122650 CSTV C
Cable: SPORTSVAZ PRAHA
Languages for correspondence: German, English, French

Year of formation: 1901
Affiliation to FIFA: 1906
Affiliation to UEFA: 1954
Registered clubs: 5943
Registered players: 561 700
Registered coaches: 28 876
Registered referees: 11 736
National stadium: The Strahov 36 000
National colours: Shirts: Red/Shorts: White/Socks: Blue
Reserve colours: Shirts: White/Shorts: White/Socks: White
Season: August–June with a mid-season break in January and February

THE RECORD

WORLD CUP

1930 .... Did not enter
1934 .... QT 1st/2 in group 9 – Final Tournament/Finalists
1938 .... QT 1st/2 in group 6 – Final Tournament/Quarter-finalists
1950 .... Did not enter
1954 .... QT 1st/3 in group 8 – Final Tournament/1st round
1958 .... QT 1st/3 in group 4 – Final Tournament/1st round
1962 .... QT 1st/3 in group 8 – Final Tournament/Finalists
1966 .... QT 2nd/4 in group 4
1970 .... QT 1st/4 in group 2 – Final Tournament/1st round
1974 .... QT 2nd/3 in group 8
1978 .... QT 2nd/3 in group 7
1982 .... QT 2nd/5 in group 3 – Final Tournament/1st round
1986 .... QT 4th/5 in group 2
1990 .... QT 2nd/5 in group 7 – Final Tournament/Quarter-finalists

EUROPEAN CHAMPIONSHIP

1960 .... Semi-finalists/3rd place
1964 .... 1st round
1968 .... QT 2nd/4 in group 1

1972	QT 2nd/4 in group 1
1976	QT 1st/4 in group 1
	– Final Tournament/Winners
1980	QT 1st/4 in group 5
	– Final Tournament/3rd place
1984	QT 3rd/5 in group 5
1988	QT 2nd/4 in group 6
1992	QT 2nd/5 in group 1

OLYMPIC GAMES

1908	Did not enter
1912	Did not enter
1920	Runners-up
1924	1st round
1928–56	Did not enter
1960	Failed to qualify
1964	Final Tournament/Runners-up
1968	Final Tournament/1st round
1972	Did not enter
1976	Failed to qualify
1980	Final Tournament/Winners
1984	Did not enter
1988	Failed to qualify
1992	Failed to qualify

DR GERO/INTERNATIONAL CUP

1929	3rd
1932	4th
1935	4th
1953	2nd
1960	Winners

EUROPEAN CLUB COMPETITIONS

EUROPEAN CUP: Semi-finalists – Dukla Praha 1967, Spartak Trnava 1969

EUROPEAN CUP WINNERS CUP: Winners – Slovan Bratislava 1969

UEFA CUP: Semi-finalists – Bohemians Praha 1983

MITROPA CUP: Winners – Sparta 1927 1935, Slavia 1938
Finalists – Slavia 1929, Sparta 1930 1936

CLUB DIRECTORY

PRAGUE (Population – 1 325 000)

Bohemians Praha
Stadium: Vrsovice 18 000
Founded: 1903
Colours: Green and white stripes/Green
Previous names: AFK Vrsovice 1903–27, Bohemians 1927–39, AFK Bohemia 1939–49, Zeleznicari 1949–51, Spartak Stalingrad 1951–61, Bohemians CKD 1961–90

ASVS Dukla Praha
Stadium: Juliska 28 000
Founded: 1948
Colours: Yellow/Yellow
Previous names: ATK 1948–52, UDA 1952–56

SK Slavia Praha
Stadium: Dr Vacka 35 000
Founded: 1893
Colours: Red and white halves/White
Previous names: SK Slavia 1893–1949, Dynamo Slavia 1949–51, TJ Slavia 1951–90

AC Sparta Praha
Stadium: Letná 36 000
Founded: 1893
Colours: Red/White
Previous names: AC Sparta 1893–1949, Sparta Bratrstvi 1949–51, Sparta Sokolovo 1951–53, Spartak Sokolovo 1953–64, TJ Sparta CKD 1964–90

OSTRAVA (Population – 760 000)

FC Baník Ostrava OKD
Stadium: Bazaly 32 000
Founded: 1922
Colours: Light blue/Blue
Previous names: Slezska 1922–48, Trojice 1948–50, OKD 1950–53, TJ Baník OKD 1953–90

TJ Vitkovice
Stadium: Vitkovice 22 000
Founded: 1922
Colours: Blue/Blue
Previous names: Zelezarni 1934–39 & 1945–52, Baník Vitkovice 1952–57

BRNO (Population – 450 000)
FC Zbrojovka Brno
Stadium: Luzankani 35 000
Founded: 1913
Colours: Red/White
Previous names: Zidenice 1913–49, Zbrojovka Zidenice 1949–52, MEZ Zidenice 1952–53, Red Star 1953–61, Spartak 1961–65, TJ Zbrojovka 1965–90

BRATISLAVA (Population – 435 000)

TJ Internacionál Slovnaft Bratislava
Stadium: Petrzalka 25000
Founded: 1942
Colours: Yellow with black sleeves and shoulders/Black
Previous names: CH Bratislava 1942–62, Slonaft 1962–65, TJ Internacionál 1965–86. Merged in 1986 with ZTS Petrzalka (1892) to become Internacionál ZTS. Adopted present name in 1990

SK Slovan Bratislava
Stadium: Tehelné Pole 50 000
Founded: 1919
Colours: Blue/Blue
Previous names: ICSSK 1919–40, SK 1940–49, NV 1949–52, TJ Slovan CHZJD 1952–90

KOSICE (Population – 232 000)

TJ Lokomotiva Kosice
Stadium: Jeho Cermell 35 000
Founded: 1946
Colours: Blue/White
Previous names: Zeleznicari 1946–48, Sparta 1948–49, Dynamo 1949–52. Merged with VSZ in 1963, but kept Lokomotiva

Jednota VSS Kosice
Stadium: Ligovy 20 000
Founded: 1952
Colours: Yellow/Blue
Previously names: Spartak Kosice 1952–56, Jednota Kosice 1956–62, VSS Kosice 1962–79, ZTS Kosice 1977–90

PLZEN (Population – 210 000)
TJ Skoda Plzen
Stadium: Skoda 33 000
Founded: 1911
Colours: Blue/White
Previous names: Viktoria 1911–48, Skoda 1948–53, Spartak 1953–65

OLOMOUC (Population – 126 000)
SK Sigma Olomouc MZ
Stadium: Miru 15 000
Founded: 1919
Colours: Sky blue/White
Previous names: Sokol Moravska Zelezarny 1919–53, Banik 1953–56, Spartak 1956–61, Moravske Zelezarny 1961–66, TJ Sigma ZTS 1966–90

ZLIN (Population – 124 000)
FC Svit Zlin
Stadium: Zlin
Founded: 1919
Colours: Blue/Yellow
Previous names: FK Zlin 1919–24, Bata Zlin 1924–48, Botostroj Zlin 1948–49, Svit Gottwaldov 1949–53, Iskra Gottwaldov 1953–58, TJ Gottwaldov 1958–90

HRADEC KRALOVE (Population – 113 000)
SKP Spartak Hradec Králové
Stadium: Spartak 27 000
Founded: 1905
Colours: White with black sleeves and shoulders/White
Previous names: SK 1905–48, Sokol Skoda 1948–53, RH Spartak ZVU 1953–90

ZILINA (Population – 96 000)
SK Zilina
Stadium: ZVL 19 000
Founded: 1908
Colours: Green/Green
Previous names: ZTK 1908–19, SK 1919–48, Slovena 1948–53, ISKRA 1953–56, Dynamo 1956–63, Jednota 1963–67, TJ ZVL Zilina 1967–90

PARDUBICE (Population – 95 000)
Synthesia Pardubice
Stadium: VCHZ
Founded: 1925
Colours: Blue/White
Previous name: Explosie 1925–49, VCHZ Pardubice 1949–90

TEPLICE (Population – 94 000)
Sklo Union Teplice
Stadium: Na Stinadlech
Founded: 1945
Colours: Yellow/Blue
Previous names: Technomat 1945–51, Vodotechna 1951–52, Ingstav 1952, Tatran 1952–60, Slovan 1960–66

NITRA (Population – 89 000)
FC Nitra
Stadium: Nitra 12 000
Founded: 1911
Colours: Sky blue/White
Pevious names: NTVE 1911–19, NSE 1919–23, AC 1923–48, Sokol 1948–53, Slavoj 1953–56, Slovan 1956–66, AC 1966–76, TJ Plastika 1976–90

KLADNO (Population – 88 000)
SONP Kladno
Stadium: Kladno
Founded: 1903
Colours: Blue/White
Previous names: SK KLadno 1903–49 and Banik Kladno 1953–57

PRESOV (Population – 87 000)
TJ Tatran Agro Presov
Stadium: Tatran 16 000
Founded: 1931
Colours: Green/White
Previous names: Slavia 1931–45, PTS 1945–47, Sparta 1947–50, Dukla 1950–53, TJ Tatran 1953–89

BANSKA BYSTRICA (Population – 85 000)
ASVS Dukla Banská Bystrica
Stadium: SNP 13 000
Founded: 1965
Colours: White/White

TRNAVA (Population – 72 000)
TJ Spartak TAZ Trnava
Stadium: Spartak 25 000
Founded: 1925
Colours: Red and black stripes/Black
Previous names: Rapid 1925–39, TSS Trnava 1939–48, Kovosmalt 1948–53

CHEB
SKP Union Cheb
Stadium: Lokomotiva 12 000
Founded: 1951
Colours: Blue/Blue
Previous names: Sokolovo 1951–53, Red Star 1953–66, Dukla Hranicar 1966–71, Red Star Cheb (Rudá Hvezda) 1971–90

DUNAJSKA STREDA
DAC Dunajská Streda
Stadium: DAC 11 000
Founded: 1905
Colours: Yellow/Blue

CZECHOSLOVAKIAN LEAGUE CHAMPIONSHIP

Year	Champions		Runners up		3rd	
1925	Slavia Praha	15	Sparta Praha	15		
1926	Sparta Praha	39	Slavia Praha	38	Viktoria Zizkov	11
1927	Sparta Praha	13	Slavia Praha	11	Viktoria Zizkov	35
1928	Viktoria Zizkov	18	Slavia Praha	16	AFK Vrsovice	8
1929	Slavia Praha	21	Viktoria Zizkov	18	Sparta Praha	14
1930	Slavia Praha	28	Sparta Praha	18	Sparta Praha	13
1931	Slavia Praha	24	Sparta Praha	21	Viktoria Zizkov	16
1932	Sparta Praha	27	Slavia Praha	22	Bohemians Praha	18
1933	Slavia Praha	26	Sparta Praha	24	Bohemians Praha	18
1934	Slavia Praha	30	Sparta Praha	25	Viktoria Plzen	22
1935	Slavia Praha	36	Sparta Praha	35	SK Kladno	21
1936	Sparta Praha	41	Slavia Praha	41	SK Zidenice	26
1937	Slavia Praha	38	Sparta Praha	31	SK Prostejov	36
1938	Sparta Praha	36	Slavia Praha	29	SK Prostejov	29
1939	Sparta Praha	32	Slavia Praha	31	SK Zidenice	26
1940	Slavia Praha	36	Sparta Praha	35	SK Pardubice	28
1941	Slavia Praha	32	SK Plzen	26	SK Pardubice	23
1942	Slavia Praha	37	SK Prostejov	28	SK Pardubice	24
1943	Slavia Praha	32	Sparta Praha	29	SK Plzen	24
1944	Sparta Praha	48	Slavia Praha	45	Bata Zlin	25
1945	–				Bata Zlin	32
1946	Sparta Praha	4–2 5–0	Slavia Praha			
1947	Slavia Praha	40	Sparta Praha	39		
1948	Sparta Praha	27	Slavia Praha	27	SK Kladno	32
1948*	Dynamo Slavia	18	Viktoria Plzen	18	SK Bratislava	24
1949	NV Bratislava	41	Bratrstvi Sparta	37	Bratrstvi Sparta	17
1950	NV Bratislava	35	Bratrstvi Sparta	35	Zeleznicari	33
1951	NV Bratislava	33	Sparta Sokolovo	33	Zeleznicari	35
1952	Sparta Sokolovo	41	NV Bratislava	40	Dynamo Kosice	33
1953	UDA Praha	22	Sparta Sokolovo	19	Ingstav Teplice	33
1954	Spartak Sokolovo	30	Baník Ostrava	28	CH Bratislava	18
1955	Slovan Bratislava	31	UDA Praha	29	CH Bratislava	27
1956	Dukla Praha	32	Slovan Bratislava	27	Spartak Sokolovo	27
1957	–				Spartak Sokolovo	26
1958	Dukla Praha	40	Spartak Sokolovo	40	CH Bratislava	38
1959	CH Bratislava	40	Dukla Praha	31	Dynamo Praha	31
1960	Spartak Hradec Králové	34	Slovan Bratislava	32	Dukla Praha	32
1961	Dukla Praha	39	CH Bratislava	32	Slovan Bratislava	29
1962	Dukla Praha	35	Slovan Nitra	32	CH Bratislava	30

* Unofficial tournament

1963	Dukla Praha 35	Jednota Trencin 32	Baník Ostrava 31
1964	Dukla Praha 37	Slovan Bratislava 35	Tatran Presov 31
1965	Sparta Praha 42	Tatran Presov 33	VSS Kosice 30
1966	Dukla Praha 33	Sparta Praha 33	Slavia Praha 33
1967	Sparta Praha 39	Slovan Bratislava 35	Spartak Trnava 34
1968	Spartak Trnava 35	Slovan Bratislava 30	Jednota Trencin 30
1969	Spartak Trnava 39	Slovan Bratislava 34	Sparta Praha 29
1970	Slovan Bratislava 43	Spartak Trnava 40	Sparta Praha 38
1971	Spartak Trnava 40	VSS Kosice 36	Union Teplice 35
1972	Spartak Trnava 44	Slovan Bratislava 42	Dukla Praha 35
1973	Spartak Trnava 39	Tatran Presov 38	VSS Kosice 35
1974	Slovan Bratislava 37	Dukla Praha 35	Slavia Praha 34
1975	Slovan Bratislava 39	TJ Internacional 37	Bohemians Praha 36
1976	Baník Ostrava 37	Slovan Bratislava 36	Slavia Praha 36
1977	Dukla Praha 42	TJ Internacional 38	Slavia Praha 36
1978	Zbrojovka Brno 43	Dukla Praha 41	Lokomotiva Kosice 39
1979	Dukla Praha 41	Baník Ostrava 41	Zbrojovka Brno 35
1980	Baník Ostrava 41	Zbrojovka Brno 36	Bohemians Praha 34
1981	Baník Ostrava 40	Dukla Praha 38	Bohemians Praha 36
1982	Dukla Praha 42	Baník Ostrava 38	Bohemians Praha 38
1983	Bohemians Praha 42	Baník Ostrava 40	Sparta Praha 36
1984	Sparta Praha 46	Dukla Praha 44	Bohemians Praha 40
1985	Sparta Praha 43	Bohemians Praha 43	Slavia Praha 39
1986	TJ Vítkovice 40	Sparta Praha 37	Dukla Praha 34
1987	Sparta Praha 42	TJ Vítkovice 37	Bohemians Praha 35
1988	Sparta Praha 49	Dukla Praha 39	Dunajská Streda 35
1989	Sparta Praha 45	Baník Ostrava 42	Plastika Nitra 34
1990	Sparta Praha 46	Baník Ostrava 41	Internacional ZTS 36
1991	Sparta Praha 39	Slovan Bratislava 38	Sigma Olomouc 37
1992	Slovan Bratislava 51	Sparta Praha 47	Slavia Praha 43

SLOVAK LEAGUE

1939	AC Bystrica 15	SK Bratislava 15	SK Zilina 12
1940	SK Bratislava 37	AC Bystrica 33	SK Zilina 28
1941	SK Bratislava 32	Vrutky 31	AC Bystrica 26
1942	SK Bratislava 31	Vrutky 29	SK Zilina 24
1943	OAP Bratislava 37	SK Bratislava 30	AC Bystrica 26
1944	SK Bratislava 38	OAP Bratislava 31	TSS Trnava 25

CZECHOSLOVAKIAN CUP FINALS

STREDOCESKY CUP

Year	Winners	Score	Runners-up
1918	Sparta Praha	4–1	Slavia Praha
1919	Sparta Praha	2–0	Viktoria Zizkov
1920	Sparta Praha	5–1	Viktoria Zizkov
1921	Viktoria Zizkov	3–0	Sparta Praha
1922	Slavia Praha	3–2	Cechie Karlin
1923	Sparta Praha	3–1	Slavia Praha
1924	Sparta Praha	5–1	AFK Vrsovice
1925	Sparta Praha	7–0	CAFC Vinohrady
1926	Slavia Praha	10–0	CAFC Vinohrady
1927	Slavia Praha	1–0	Sparta Praha
1928	Slavia Praha	1–1 1–1 3–2	Sparta Praha
1929	Viktoria Zizkov	3–1	SK Liben
1930	Slavia Praha	4–2	SK Kladno
1931	Sparta Praha	3–1	Slavia Praha
1932	Slavia Praha	2–1	Sparta Praha
1933	Viktoria Zizkov	2–1	Sparta Praha
1934	Sparta Praha	6–0	SK Kladno
1935	Slavia Praha	4–1	Bohemians Praha
1936	Sparta Praha	1–1 1–0	Slavia Praha
1937–39	–		
1940	Viktoria Zizkov	5–3	Sparta Praha
1941	Slavia Praha	13–2	SS Plincner
1942	Bohemians Praha	8–6	Sparta Praha

CZECH CUP

Year	Winners	Score	Runners-up
1940	ASO Olomouc	3–1 2–1	SK Prostejov
1941	Slavia Praha	2–3 6–3	Sparta Praha
1942	Slavia Praha	5–2 5–5	Bohemians Praha
1943	Sparta Praha	3–1 7–1	Viktoria Plzen
1944	Sparta Praha	4–2 4–3	Viktoria Plzen
1945	Slavia Praha	1–1 5–2	SK Rakovnik
1946	Sparta Praha	6–0 3–0	Slezka Ostrava
1947–1950	–		
1951	Kovosmalt Trnava	1–0	Armaturka Usti
1952	ATK Praha	4–3	Skoda Hradec Králové

CZECHOSLOVAKIAN CUP

Year	Winners	Score	Runners-up
1961	Dukla Praha	3–0	Dynamo Zilina
1962	Slovan Bratislava	1–1 4–1	Dukla Praha
1963	Slovan Bratislava	0–0 9–0	Dynamo Praha
1964	Sparta Sokolovo	4–1	VSS Kosice
1965	Dukla Praha	0–0 (5–3p)	Slovan Bratislava
1966	Dukla Praha	2–1 4–0	Tatran Presov
1967	Spartak Trnava	2–4 2–0 (5–4p)	Sparta Praha
1968	Slovan Bratislava	0–1 2–0	Dukla Praha
1969	Dukla Praha	1–1 1–0	VCHZ Pardubice
1970	TJ Gottwaldov	3–3 0–0 (4–3p)	Slovan Bratislava
1971	Spartak Trnava	2–1 5–1	Skoda Plzen

1972	Sparta Praha	0–1 4–3 (4–2p)	Slovan Bratislava
1973	Baník Ostrava	1–2 3–1	VSS Kosice
1974	Slovan Bratislava	0–1 1–0 (4–3p)	Slavia Praha
1975	Spartak Trnava	3–1 1–0	Sparta Praha
1976	Sparta Praha	3–2 1–0	Slovan Bratislava
1977	Lokomotiva Kosice	2–1	Union Teplice
1978	Baník Ostrava	1–0	Jednota Trencin
1979	Lokomotiva Kosice	2–1	Baník Ostrava
1980	Sparta Praha	2–0	ZTS Kosice
1981	Dukla Praha	4–1	Dukla Banská Bystrica
1982	Slovan Bratislava	0–0 (4–2p)	Bohemians Praha
1983	Dukla Praha	2–1	Slovan Bratislava
1984	Sparta Praha	4–2	TJ Internacional
1985	Dukla Praha	3–2	Lokomotiva Kosice
1986	Spartak Trnava	1–1 (4–3p)	Sparta Praha
1987	DAC Dunajská Streda	0–0 (3–2p)	Sparta Praha
1988	Sparta Praha	2–0	Internacional ZTS
1989	Sparta Praha	3–0	Slovan Bratislava
1990	Dukla Praha	1–1 (5–4p)	Internacional ZTS
1991	Baník Ostrava	6–1	Spartak Trnava
1992	Sparta Praha	2–1	Tatran Presov

CZECH LEAGUE

1896	FC Kickers
	DFC Praha
1897	Slavia Praha
1898	Slavia Praha
1899	Slavia Praha
1902	CAFC Vinohrady
1912	Sparta Praha
1913	Sparta Praha
1917	Sparta Praha
1919	Sparta Praha
1922	Sparta Praha

CHARITY CUP

1906	SK Smichov
1907	SK Smichov
1908	Slavia Praha 'B'
1909	Sparta Praha
1910	Slavia Praha
1911	Slavia Praha
1912	Slavia Praha
1913	Viktoria Zizkov
1914	Viktoria Zizkov
1915	Sparta Praha
1916	Viktoria Zizkov

STREDOCESKY LEAGUE

1915	Slavia Praha
1918	Slavia Praha
1919	Sparta Praha
1920	Sparta Praha
1921	Sparta Praha
1922	Sparta Praha
1923	Sparta Praha
1924	Slavia Praha

INTERNATIONAL MATCHES PLAYED BY CZECHOSLOVAKIA

Date	Opponents	Result		Venue	Compet	Scorers
5-04-1903	Hungary	L	1–2	Budapest	Fr	
1-04-1906	Hungary	D	1–1	Budapest	Fr	Setela
7-10	Hungary	D	4–4	Prague	Fr	Horvath, Baumruk, Vanek, Kosek
7-04-1907	Hungary	L	2–5	Budapest	Fr	Pelikan, Milka
6-10	Hungary	W	5–3	Prague	Fr	Kosek 3, Belka 2
5-04-1908	Hungary	L	2–5	Budapest	Fr	Belka
13-06	England	L	0–4	Prague	Fr	
28-08-1920	Yugoslavia	W	7–0	Antwerp	OGr1	Janda 3, Vaník 3, Sedlácek
29-08	Norway	W	4–0	Brussels	OGqf	Janda 3, Vaník
31-08	France	W	4–1	Antwerp	OGsf	Mazal 3, Steiner
2-09	Belgium	L	0–2	Antwerp	OGf	
28-10-1921	Yugoslavia	W	6–1	Prague	Fr	Vaník 4, Janda 2
13-11	Sweden	D	2–2	Prague	Fr	Janda 2
26-02-1922	Italy	D	1–1	Turin	Fr	Janda
11-06	Denmark	W	3–0	Copenhagen	Fr	Dvorácek 2, Pilat
28-06	Yugoslavia	L	3–4	Zagreb	Fr	Plodr, Vaník, Dvorácek
13-08	Sweden	W	2–0	Stockholm	Fr	Stapl, Dvorácek
6-05-1923	Denmark	W	2–0	Prague	Fr	Stapl, Císar
27-05	Italy	W	5–1	Prague	Fr	Sedlácek 3, Kozeluh K, Dvorácek
1-07	Romania	W	6–0	Kluj	Fr	Stapl 2, Capek 2, Vlcek 2
28-10	Yugoslavia	D	4–4	Prague	Fr	Stapl 2, Capek 2
25-05-1924	Turkey	W	5–2	Paris	OGr1	Sedlácek 2, Stapl, Novák J, Capek
28-05	Switzerland	D	1–1	Paris	OGr2	Stapl
30-05	Switzerland	L	0–1	Paris	OGr2	
31-08	Romania	W	4–1	Prague	Fr	Rysavy, Dvorácek, Zd'ársky K, Kolenaty
28-09	Yugoslavia	W	2–0	Zagreb	Fr	Lastovicka, Jelínek
23-05-1925	Poland	W	2–1	Prague	Fr	Mraz, Polacek
24-05	Austria	W	3–1	Prague	Fr	Sedlácek, Capek, Severin
11-10	Hungary	W	2–0	Prague	Fr	Dvorácek, Perner
28-10	Yugoslavia	W	7–0	Prague	Fr	Dvorácek 3, Silny, Soltys, Wimmer, Steiner
17-01-1926	Italy	L	1–3	Turin	Fr	Kristál
14-03	Austria	L	0–2	Vienna	Fr	
6-06	Poland	W	2–1	Krakow	Fr	Polacek, Dolejsi
6-06	Hungary	L	1–2	Budapest	Fr	Silny
13-06	Sweden	D	2–2	Stockholm	Fr	Novák O 2
28-06	Yugoslavia	W	6–2	Zagreb	Fr	Silny 4, Puc, Wimmer
3-07	Sweden	W	4–2	Prague	Fr	Jelínek, Meduna, Novák O, Mares
28-09	Austria	L	1–2	Prague	Fr	Jelínek
28-10	Italy	W	3–1	Prague	Fr	Capek 2, Puc
2-01-1927	Belgium	W	3–2	Liege	Fr	Svoboda 2, Podrazil
20-02	Italy	D	2–2	Milan	Fr	Puc, Silny
11-03	Austria	W	2–1	Vienna	Fr	Puc, Maloun
24-04	Hungary	W	4–1	Prague	Fr	Puc, Silny, Svoboda, Steiner

26–05	Belgium	W	4–0	Prague	Fr	Puc 2, Silny, Fleischmann
30–07	Yugoslavia	D	1–1	Belgrade	Fr	Puc
18–09	Austria	W	2–0	Prague	DGC	Kratochvíl, Podrazil
9–10	Hungary	W	2–1	Budapest	Fr	Silny, Podrazil
23–10	Italy	D	2–2	Prague	DGC	Svoboda 2
28–10	Yugoslavia	W	5–3	Prague	Fr	Bejbl 2, Svoboda 2, Soltys
1–04–1928	Austria	W	1–0	Vienna	DGC	Silny
22–04	Hungary	L	0–2	Budapest	DGC	
13–05	France	W	2–0	Paris	Fr	Puc 2
23–09	Hungary	W	6–1	Prague	Fr	Bejbl 2, Kratochvíl, Puc, Podrazil, Káda
27–10	Poland	W	3–2	Prague	Fr	Puc 2, Bejbl
28–10	Yugoslavia	W	7–1	Prague	Fr	Puc 2, Silny 2, Bejbl 2, Soltys
3–03–1929	Italy	L	2–4	Bologna	DGC	Silny, Svoboda
17–03	Austria	D	3–3	Prague	Fr	Silny, Svoboda, Soltys
5–05	Switzerland	W	4–1	Lausanne	DGC	Silny 2, Puc, Podrazil
8–06	Yugoslavia	D	3–3	Zagreb	Fr	Silny, Madelon, Hojer A
8–09	Hungary	D	1–1	Prague	DGC	Hojer A
15–09	Austria	L	1–2	Vienna	Fr	Kratochvíl
6–10	Switzerland	W	5–0	Prague	DGC	Puc 2, Kratochvíl, Svoboda, Junek
28–10	Yugoslavia	W	4–3	Prague	Fr	Silny 2, Kloz, Thaut
1–01–1930	Spain	L	0–1	Barcelona	Fr	
12–01	Portugal	L	0–1	Lisbon	Fr	
2–03	Austria	D	2–2	Prague	Fr	Junek, Svoboda
1–05	Hungary	D	1–1	Prague	Fr	Hojer A
11–05	France	W	3–2	Paris	Fr	Silny, Kostálek, Junek
14–06	Spain	W	2–0	Prague	Fr	Svoboda, Hojer A
21–09	Belgium	W	3–2	Antwerp	Fr	Hejma, Soltys, Junek
26–10	Hungary	D	1–1	Budapest	Fr	Soltys
15–02–1931	France	W	2–1	Paris	Fr	Novák A 2
22–03	Hungary	D	3–3	Prague	DGC	Svoboda 2, Junek
12–04	Austria	L	1–2	Vienna	DGC	Silny
13–06	Switzerland	W	7–3	Prague	DGC	Bejbl 3, Silny 2, Bradác V 2
14–06	Poland	W	4–0	Warsaw	Fr	Pelcner 2, Bára, Nejedly
2–08	Yugoslavia	L	1–2	Belgrade	Fr	Puc
20–09	Hungary	L	0–3	Budapest	Fr	
15–11	Italy	D	2–2	Rome	DGC	Svoboda 2
20–03–1932	Hungary	L	1–3	Prague	Fr	Silny
17–04	Switzerland	L	1–5	Zurich	DGC	Bradác V
22–05	Austria	D	1–1	Prague	DGC	Svoboda
29–05	Holland	W	2–1	Amsterdam	Fr	Silny, Nejedly
18–09	Hungary	L	1–2	Budapest	DGC	Puc
9–10	Yugoslavia	W	2–1	Prague	Fr	Puc, Nejedly
28–10	Italy	W	2–1	Prague	DGC	Nejedly, Bradác V
19–03–1933	Hungary	L	0–2	Budapest	Fr	
9–04	Austria	W	2–1	Vienna	Fr	Puc 2
7–05	Italy	L	0–2	Florence	DGC	
10–06	France	W	4–0	Prague	Fr	Puc, Nejedly, Svoboda, Junek
6–08	Yugoslavia	L	1–2	Zagreb	Fr	Kocsis
17–09	Austria	D	3–3	Prague	Fr	Puc 2, Silny
15–10	Poland	W	2–1	Warsaw	WCq	Silny, Pelcner
25–03–1934	France	W	2–1	Paris	Fr	Sobotka, Svoboda
29–04	Hungary	D	2–2	Prague	DGC	Puc, Subotka
16–05	England	W	2–1	Prague	Fr	Puc, Nejedly
27–05	Romania	W	2–1	Trieste	WCr1	Puc, Nejedly
31–05	Switzerland	W	3–2	Turin	WCqf	Nejedly, Svoboda, Sobotka
3–06	Germany	W	3–1	Rome	WCsf	Nejedly 3
10–06	Italy	L	1–2	Rome	WCf	Puc
2–09	Yugoslavia	W	3–1	Prague	Fr	Nejedly, Sobotka, Junek
23–09	Austria	D	2–2	Vienna	DGC	Cech 2
14–10	Switzerland	D	2–2	Geneva	DGC	Nejedly 2
17–03–1935	Switzerland	W	3–1	Prague	DGC	Nejedly 2, Horák
14–04	Austria	D	0–0	Prague	DGC	
26–05	Germany	L	1–2	Dresden	Fr	Hruska
6–09	Yugoslavia	D	0–0	Belgrade	Fr	
22–09	Hungary	L	0–1	Budapest	DGC	
27–10	Italy	W	2–1	Prague	DGC	Horák 2
9–02–1936	France	W	3–0	Paris	Fr	Puc, Nejedly, Boucek
22–03	Austria	D	1–1	Vienna	DGC	Zajícek
26–04	Spain	W	1–0	Prague	Fr	Zajícek

27–09	Germany	L	1–2	Prague	Fr	Cech
18–10	Hungary	W	5–2	Prague	DGC	Kloz 4, Kopecky
13–12	Italy	L	0–2	Genoa	Fr	
21–02–1937	Switzerland	W	5–3	Prague	DGC	Kopecky 2, Puc, Svoboda, Horák
18–04	Romania	D	1–1	Bucharest	Fr	Nejedly
22–05	Scotland	L	1–3	Prague	Fr	Puc
23–05	Italy	L	0–1	Prague	DGC	
19–09	Hungary	L	3–8	Budapest	DGC	Nejedly, Rulc, Ríha
3–10	Yugoslavia	W	5–4	Prague	Fr	Nejedly, Rulc, Sobotka, Senecky, Ríha
13–10	Latvia	W	4–0	Prague	Fr	Sobotka 3, Senecky
24–10	Austria	W	2–1	Prague	DGC	Kloz, Ríha
7–11	Bulgaria	D	1–1	Sofia	WCq	Ríha
1–12	England	L	4–5	London	Fr	Nejedly 2, Puc, Zeman
8–12	Scotland	L	0–5	Glasgow	Fr	
3–04–1938	Switzerland	L	0–4	Basle	DGC	
24–04	Bulgaria	W	6–0	Prague	WCq	Simunek 3, Nejedly 2, Ludl
18–05	Rep. Ireland	D	2–2	Prague	Fr	Nejedly 2
5–06	Holland	W	3–0	Le Havre	WCr1	Nejedly, Zeman, Kostálek
12–06	Brazil	D	1–1	Bordeaux	WCqf	Nejedly
14–06	Brazil	L	1–2	Bordeaux	WCqf	Kopecky
7–08	Sweden	W	6–2	Stockholm	Fr	Bican 3, Senecky 2, Horák
28–08	Yugoslavia	W	3–1	Zagreb	Fr	Bican, Bradác V, Seneky
4–12	Romania	W	6–2	Prague	Fr	Bican 4, Ludl, Kopecky
7–04–1946	France	L	0–3	Paris	Fr	
9–05	Yugoslavia	L	0–2	Prague	Fr	
14–09	Switzerland	W	3–2	Prague	Fr	Janík, Ríha, Klimek
29–09	Yugoslavia	L	2–4	Belgrade	Fr	Klimek, Plánicky
27–10	Austria	W	4–3	Vienna	Fr	Cejp 2, Zechar 2
11–05–1947	Yugoslavia	W	3–1	Prague	Fr	Bican 2, Cejp
20–06	Denmark	D	2–2	Copenhagen	Fr	Zachar 2
22–06	Holland	W	2–1	Amsterdam	Fr	Kubala 2
31–08	Poland	W	6–3	Prague	Fr	Kubala 2, Bican 2, Cejp, Ludl
21–09	Romania	W	6–2	Bucharest	Fr	Kubala 2, Cejp 2, Simansky 2
5–10	Austria	W	3–2	Prague	Fr	Ríha 2, Balázi
14–12	Italy	L	1–3	Bari	Fr	Ríha
18–04–1948	Poland	L	1–3	Warsaw	BCE	Kokstein
23–05	Hungary	L	1–2	Budapest	DGC/BCE	Subert
12–06	France	L	0–4	Prague	Fr	
4–07	Romania	L	1–2	Bucharest	BCE	Menclík
29–08	Bulgaria	L	0–1	Sofia	BCE	
10–10	Switzerland	D	1–1	Basle	DGC	Cejp
31–10	Austria	W	3–1	Bratislava	DGC	Hemele 2, Hlavácek
23–03–1949	Luxembourg	D	2–2	Bratislava	Fr	Hemele 2
10–04	Hungary	W	5–2	Prague	DGC	Hlavácek 2, Pazicky, Preis, Simansky
22–05	Romania	W	3–2	Prague	Fr	Pazicky, Preis, Simansky
4–09	Bulgaria	L	1–3	Prague	Fr	Marko
25–09	Austria	L	1–3	Vienna	DGC	Simansky
30–10	Poland	W	2–0	Vitkowice	Fr	Pazicky, Preis
13–11	France	L	0–1	Paris	Fr	
30–04–1950	Hungary	L	0–5	Budapest	Fr	
21–05	Romania	D	1–1	Bucharest	Fr	Zd'árský J
27–08	Bulgaria	W	2–1	Sofia	Fr	Hlavácek, Preis
1–09	Albania	W	3–0	Prague	Fr	Zd'árský, Hlavácek, Cejp
22–10	Poland	W	4–1	Warsaw	Fr	Preis 3, Cejp
20–05–1951	Romania	D	2–2	Prague	Fr	Vlk, Cejp
14–10	Hungary	L	1–2	Vitkowice	Fr	Vejvoda
11–05–1952	Romania	L	1–3	Bucharest	Fr	Pluskal
14–09	Poland	D	2–2	Prague	Fr	Zd'árský, Müller
19–10	Hungary	L	0–5	Budapest	Fr	
29–11	Albania	L	2–3	Tirana	Fr	Müller, Kvapil
9–12	Albania	L	1–2	Tirana	Fr	Dvorák
26–04–1953	Italy	W	2–0	Prague	DGC	Pazicky 2
10–05	Poland	D	1–1	Wroclaw	Fr	Simansky
14–06	Romania	W	2–0	Prague	WCq	Vlk, Pazicky
6–09	Bulgaria	W	2–1	Sofia	WCq	Vlk 2
20–09	Switzerland	W	5–0	Prague	DGC	Trnka 2, Kraus, Hertl, Pazicky
4–10	Hungary	L	1–5	Prague	Fr	Kacáni
25–10	Romania	W	1–0	Bucharest	WCq	Safránek
8–11	Bulgaria	D	0–0	Bratislava	WCq	

13–12	Italy	L	0–3	Genoa	DGC	
16–06–1954	Uruguay	L	0–2	Berne	WCr1	
19–06	Austria	L	0–5	Zurich	WCr1	
24–10	Hungary	L	1–4	Budapest	Fr	Pazdera
27–03–1955	Austria	W	3–2	Brno	DGC	Procházka, Crha, Pesek
5–06	Belgium	W	3–1	Brussels	Fr	Trnka, Crha, Kraus
25–09	Belgium	W	5–2	Prague	Fr	Práda 2, Pazdera, Crha, Simansky
2–10	Hungary	L	1–3	Prague	DGC	Práda
13–11	Bulgaria	L	0–3	Sofia	Fr	
21–04–1956	Brazil	D	0–0	Prague	Fr	
10–05	Switzerland	W	6–1	Geneva	DGC	Feureisl 4, Masopust, Borovicka
20–05	Hungary	W	4–2	Budapest	DGC	Moravcík 2, Feureisl, Pazdera
5–08	Brazil	W	1–0	Rio de Janeiro	Fr	Moravcík
8–08	Brazil	L	1–4	Sao Paulo	Fr	Moravcík
12–08	Uruguay	L	1–2	Montevideo	Fr	Masopust
19–08	Argentina	L	0–1	Buenos Aires	Fr	
26–08	Chile	L	0–3	Santiago	Fr	
30–09	Yugoslavia	W	2–1	Belgrade	DGC	Práda
25–11	Turkey	D	1–1	Prague	Fr	Feureisl
1–05–1957	Wales	L	0–1	Cardiff	WCq	
18–05	Yugoslavia	W	1–0	Bratislava	DGC	Borovicka
26–05	Wales	W	2–0	Prague	WCq	Kraus, OG
16–06	East Germany	W	3–1	Brno	WCq	Bubník, Molnár, Kraus
13–10	Austria	D	2–2	Vienna	DGC	Moravcík 2
27–10	East Germany	W	4–1	Leipzig	WCq	Kraus 2, Moravcík, Novák L
13–12	Egypt	W	2–1	Cairo	Fr	Moravcík, Kacáni
2–04–1958	West Germany	W	3–2	Prague	Fr	Molnár
8–06	Nth Ireland	L	0–1	Halmstad	WCr1	
11–06	West Germany	D	2–2	Halsingborg	WCr1	Zikán, Dvorák
15–06	Argentina	W	6–1	Halsingborg	WCr1	Zikán 2, Hovorka 2, Feureisl, Dvorák
17–06	Nth Ireland	L	1–2	Malmo	WCr1	Zikán
30–08	Soviet Union	L	1–2	Prague	Fr	Masopust
20–09	Switzerland	W	2–1	Bratislava	DGC	Moravcík, Scherer
12–10	Bulgaria	L	0–1	Ostrava	Fr	
13–12	Italy	D	1–1	Genoa	DGC	Masopust
18–12	Turkey	L	0–1	Istanbul	Fr	
5–04–1959	Rep. Ireland	L	0–2	Dublin	ECpr	
10–05	Rep. Ireland	W	4–0	Bratislava	ECpr	Dolinsky, Pavlovic L, Buberník, Stacho
6–09	Soviet Union	L	1–3	Moscow	Fr	Molnár
23–09	Denmark	D	2–2	Copenhagen	ECr1	Dolinsky, Kacáni
18–10	Denmark	W	5–1	Brno	ECr1	Buberník 2, Scherer 2, Dolinsky
1–11	Italy	W	2–1	Prague	DGC	Dolinsky, Scherer
1–05–1960	Austria	W	4–0	Prague	Fr	Dolinsky, Kvasnák, Moravcík, Masopust
22–05	Romania	W	2–0	Bucharest	ECqf	Masopust, Bubník
29–05	Romania	W	3–0	Bratislava	ECqf	Buberník 2, Bubník
6–07	Soviet Union	L	0–3	Marseille	ECsf	
9–07	France	W	2–0	Marseille	EC3p	Bubník, Pavlovic L
30–10	Holland	W	4–0	Prague	Fr	Scherer 3, Kadraba
26–03–1961	Sweden	W	2–1	Prague	Fr	Adamec, Kadraba
29–04	Mexico	W	2–1	Ostrava	Fr	Scherer, Kadraba
14–05	Scotland	W	4–0	Bratislava	WCq	Pospíchal 2, Kadraba, Kvasnák
19–06	Argentina	D	3–3	Brno	Fr	Masek, Kadraba, Kvasnák
26–09	Scotland	L	2–3	Glasgow	WCq	Scherer, Kvasnák
8–10	Rep. Ireland	W	3–1	Dublin	WCq	Kvasnák 2, Scherer
29–10	Rep. Ireland	W	7–1	Prague	WCq	Scherer 2, Kvasnák 2, Masopust, Pospíchal, Jelínek (II)
29–11	Scotland	W	4–2	Brussels	WCq	Scherer, Pospíchal, Kvasnák, Hledík
7–04–1962	Sweden	L	1–3	Gothenburg	Fr	Pospíchal
22–04	Uruguay	W	3–1	Prague	Fr	Scherer, Kadraba, Jelínek (II)
31–05	Spain	W	1–0	Vina del Mar	WCr1	Stibrányi
2–06	Brazil	D	0–0	Vina del Mar	WCr1	
7–06	Mexico	L	1–3	Vina del Mar	WCr1	Masek
10–06	Hungary	W	1–0	Rancagua	WCqf	Scherer
13–06	Yugoslavia	W	3–1	Vina del Mar	WCsf	Scherer 2, Kadraba
17–06	Brazil	L	1–3	Santiago	WCf	Masopust
16–09	Austria	W	6–0	Vienna	Fr	Masopust 2, Kucera 2, Scherer, Kadraba
28–10	Poland	W	2–1	Bratislava	Fr	Scherer, Láfa
21–11	East Germany	L	1–2	Berlin	ECr1	Kucera
31–03–1963	East Germany	D	1–1	Prague	ECr1	Masek

24–04	Austria	L	1–3	Vienna	Fr	Masek
28–04	Bulgaria	L	0–1	Sofia	Fr	
29–05	England	L	2–4	Bratislava	Fr	Scherer, Kadraba
2–06	Hungary	D	2–2	Prague	Fr	Scherer, Kvasnák
3–11	Yugoslavia	L	0–2	Zagreb	Fr	
11–04–1964	Italy	D	0–0	Florence	Fr	
29–04	West Germany	W	4–3	Ludwigshaven	Fr	Mráz 2, Pospíchal, Scherer
17–05	Yugoslavia	L	2–3	Prague	Fr	Mráz, Masny
13–09	Poland	L	1–2	Warsaw	Fr	Masek
11–10	Hungary	D	2–2	Budapest	Fr	Pospíchal 2
25–04–1965	Portugal	L	0–1	Bratislava	WCq	
30–05	Romania	L	0–1	Bucharest	WCq	
19–09	Romania	W	3–1	Prague	WCq	Knebort, Jokl
9–10	Turkey	W	6–0	Istanbul	WCq	Knebort 2, Jokl 2, Kabát, Kvasnák
31–10	Portugal	D	0–0	Oporto	WCq	
21–11	Turkey	W	3–1	Brno	WCq	Mráz 2, Horváth
18–05–1966	Soviet Union	L	1–2	Prague	Fr	Adamec
12–06	Brazil	L	1–2	Rio de Janeiro	Fr	Masny
15–06	Brazil	D	2–2	Rio de Janeiro	Fr	Popluhár, Szikora
19–10	Yugoslavia	L	0–1	Belgrade	Fr	
2–11	England	D	0–0	London	Fr	
6–11	Holland	W	2–1	Amsterdam	Fr	Hrdlicka, Geleta
3–05–1967	Switzerland	W	2–1	Basle	Fr	Jokl, Geleta
21–05	Rep. Ireland	W	2–0	Dublin	ECq	Masny V, Szikora
18–06	Turkey	W	3–0	Bratislava	ECq	Adamec 2, Jurkanin
1–10	Spain	W	1–0	Prague	ECq	Horváth
22–10	Spain	L	1–2	Madrid	ECq	Kuna
15–11	Turkey	D	0–0	Ankara	ECq	
22–11	Rep. Ireland	L	1–2	Prague	ECq	OG
27–04–1968	Yugoslavia	W	3–0	Bratislava	Fr	Adamec, Kuna, Jokl
23–06	Brazil	W	3–2	Bratislava	Fr	Adamec 3
25–09	Denmark	W	3–0	Copenhagen	WCq	Jokl, Kuna, Hagara
20–10	Denmark	W	1–0	Bratislava	WCq	Jokl
16–04–1969	Holland	L	0–2	Rotterdam	Fr	
4–05	Rep. Ireland	W	2–1	Dublin	WCq	Kabát, Adamec
25–05	Hungary	L	0–2	Budapest	WCq	
14–09	Hungary	D	3–3	Prague	WCq	Hagara, Kvasnák, Kuna
7–10	Rep. Ireland	W	3–0	Prague	WCq	Adamec 3
3–12	Hungary	W	4–1	Marseilles	WCq	Kvasnák, Vesely B, Adamec, Jokl
12–04–1970	Austria	W	3–1	Vienna	Fr	Adamec, Albrecht, Hrdlicka
9–05	Luxembourg	W	1–0	Luxembourg	Fr	Jurkanin
13–05	Norway	W	2–0	Oslo	Fr	Kuna, Horváth
3–06	Brazil	L	1–4	Guadalajara	WCr1	Petrás
6–06	Romania	L	1–2	Guadalajara	WCr1	Petrás
11–06	England	L	0–1	Guadalajara	WCr1	
5–09	France	L	0–3	Nice	Fr	
7–10	Finland	D	1–1	Prague	ECq	Albrecht
25–10	Poland	D	2–2	Prague	Fr	Stratil 2
21–04–1971	Wales	W	3–1	Swansea	ECq	Capkovic J 2, Táborsky
16–05	Romania	W	1–0	Bratislava	ECq	Vesely F
16–06	Finland	W	4–0	Helsinki	ECq	Karkó 2, Capkovic J, Pollák
14–07	Brazil	L	0–1	Rio de Janeiro	Fr	
25–09	East Germany	D	1–1	Berlin	Fr	Kuna
27–10	Wales	W	1–0	Prague	ECq	Kuna
14–11	Romania	L	1–2	Bucharest	ECq	Capkovic J
8–04–1972	Austria	W	2–0	Brno	Fr	Petrás, Térnenyi
26–04	Luxembourg	W	6–0	Pilsen	Fr	Kuna 2, Capkovic J 2, Jokl, Dobiás
14–05	Sweden	W	2–1	Gothenburg	Fr	Jokl 2
28–06	Brazil	D	0–0	Rio de Janeiro	Clr2	
2–07	Scotland	D	0–0	Porto Alegre	Clr2	
6–07	Yugoslavia	L	1–2	Sao Paulo	Clr2	Hrusecky
30–08	Holland	L	1–2	Prague	Fr	Hagara
15–10	Poland	L	0–3	Bydgoszcz	Fr	
1–11	East Germany	L	1–3	Bratislava	Fr	Pekárik
28–03–1973	West Germany	L	0–3	Dusseldorf	Fr	
2–05	Denmark	D	1–1	Copenhagen	WCq	Petrás
27–05	England	D	1–1	Prague	Fr	Novák I
6–06	Denmark	W	6–0	Prague	WCq	Nehoda, Vesely B 3, Bicovsky, Hagara
26–09	Scotland	L	1–2	Glasgow	WCq	Nehoda

17–10	Scotland	W	1–0	Bratislava	WCq	Nehoda
27–03–1974	East Germany	L	0–1	Dresden	Fr	
7–04	Brazil	L	0–1	Rio de Janeiro	Fr	
13–04	Bulgaria	W	1–0	Plovdiv	Fr	Dobiás
27–04	France	D	3–3	Prague	Fr	Pivarník, Bicovsky, Panenka
20–05	Soviet Union	W	1–0	Odessa	Fr	Nehoda
25–09	East Germany	W	3–1	Prague	Fr	Bicovsky 2, Ondrus
13–10	Sweden	W	4–0	Bratislava	Fr	Svehlík 2, Masny M, Bicovsky
30–10	England	L	0–3	London	ECq	
13–11	Poland	D	2–2	Prague	Fr	Svehlík, Masny M
8–12	Indonesia	D	1–1	Djakarta	Fr	Kroupa
20–12	Iran	W	1–0	Tehran	Fr	Ondrus
31–03–1975	Romania	D	1–1	Prague	Fr	Nehoda
20–04	Cyprus	W	4–0	Prague	ECq	Panenka 3, Masny M
30–04	Portugal	W	5–0	Prague	ECq	Bicovsky 2, Nehoda 2, Petrás
7–06	Austria	D	0–0	Vienna	Fr	
24–09	Switzerland	D	1–1	Brno	Fr	Masny M
15–10	Hungary	D	1–1	Bratislava	Fr	Nehoda
30–10	England	W	2–1	Bratislava	ECq	Nehoda, Gallis
12–11	Portugal	D	1–1	Porto	ECq	Ondrus
19–11	East Germany	D	1–1	Brno	OGq	Bicovsky
23–11	Cyprus	W	3–0	Limassol	ECq	Nehoda, Bicovsky, Masny M
10–03–1976	Soviet Union	D	2–2	Kosice	Fr	Ondrus, Nehoda
27–03	France	D	2–2	Paris	Fr	Ondrus, Dobiás
7–04	East Germany	D	0–0	Leipzig	OGq	
24–04	Soviet Union	W	2–0	Bratislava	ECqf	Móder, Panenka
22–05	Soviet Union	D	2–2	Kiev	ECqf	Móder 2
16–06	Holland	W	3–1	Zagreb	ECsf	Ondrus, Nehoda, Vesely F
20–06	West Germany	D	2–2	Belgrade	ECf	Svehlík, Dobiás Won 5–3 pens
22–09	Romania	D	1–1	Bucharest	Fr	Panenka
6–10	Romania	W	3–2	Prague	Fr	Panenka, Dobiás, Ondrus
13–10	Scotland	W	2–0	Prague	WCq	Panenka, Petrás
17–11	West Germany	L	0–2	Hannover	Fr	
23–03–1977	Greece	W	4–0	Prague	Fr	Panenka, Nehoda, Gögh, Masny M
30–03	Wales	L	0–3	Wrexham	WCq	
20–04	Hungary	L	0–2	Budapest	Fr	
24–05	Switzerland	L	0–1	Basle	Fr	
1–06	Austria	D	0–0	Ostrava	Fr	
7–09	Turkey	W	1–0	Bratislava	Fr	Gajdusek
21–09	Scotland	L	1–3	Glasgow	WCq	Gajdusek
9–11	Hungary	D	1–1	Prague	Fr	Nehoda
16–11	Wales	W	1–0	Prague	WCq	Nehoda
22–03–1978	Greece	W	1–0	Salonika	Fr	Kroupa
15–04	Hungary	L	1–2	Budapest	Fr	Kroupa
23–04	Bulgaria	D	0–0	Brno	Fr	
17–05	Brazil	L	0–2	Rio de Janeiro	Fr	
21–05	Sweden	D	0–0	Stockholm	Fr	
6–09	East Germany	L	1–2	Leipzig	Fr	Ondrus
4–10	Sweden	W	3–1	Stockholm	ECq	Masny 2, Nehoda
11–10	West Germany	L	3–4	Prague	Fr	Stambachr 2, Masny
8–11	Italy	W	3–0	Bratislava	Fr	Jarusek, Panenka, Masny
29–11	England	L	0–1	London	Fr	
14–03–1979	Spain	W	1–0	Bratislava	Fr	Masny
4–04	France	W	2–0	Bratislava	ECq	Panenka, Stambachr
1–05	Luxembourg	W	3–0	Luxembourg	ECq	Masny, Gajdusek, Stambachr
5–05	Soviet Union	L	0–3	Moscow	Fr	
12–09	Hungary	L	1–2	Nyiregyhaza	Fr	Panenka
26–09	Rep. Ireland	W	4–1	Prague	Fr	Ondrus, Nehoda, Kroupa, Masny
10–10	Sweden	W	4–1	Prague	ECq	Nehoda, Kozák, Vízek 2
17–11	France	L	1–2	Paris	ECq	Kozák
24–11	Luxembourg	W	4–0	Prague	ECq	Panenka, Masny 2, Vízek
23–01–1980	Mexico	L	0–1	Leon	Fr	
27–01	Australia	W	4–0	Canberra	Fr	Jurkemik, Vízek, Nehoda, Kozák
3–02	Australia	W	5–0	Sydney	Fr	Masny 2, Gajdusek, Kroupa, Kozák
9–02	Australia	D	2–2	Melbourne	Fr	Dobiás, Nehoda
6–03	Switzerland	L	0–2	Basle	Fr	
16–04	Spain	D	2–2	Gijon	Fr	Nehoda 2
30–04	Hungary	W	1–0	Kosice	Fr	Nehoda
16–05	Romania	W	2–1	Brno	Fr	Vízek 2

11-06	West Germany	L	0-1	Rome	ECr1	
14-06	Greece	W	3-1	Rome	ECr1	Panenka, Vízek, Nehoda
17-06	Holland	D	1-1	Milan	ECr1	Nehoda
21-06	Italy	D	1-1	Naples	EC3p	Jurkemik Won 9-8 pens
24-09	Poland	D	1-1	Chorzow	Fr	Nehoda
8-10	East Germany	L	0-1	Prague	Fr	
15-10	Argentina	L	0-1	Buenos Aires	Fr	
19-11	Wales	L	0-1	Cardiff	WCq	
3-12	Turkey	W	2-0	Prague	WCq	Nehoda 2
25-01-1981	Bolivia	L	1-2	La Paz	Fr	Janecka
30-01	Bolivia	W	5-2	Santa Cruz	Fr	Daneska, Nehoda 2, Kozák, Vízek
4-02	Peru	W	3-1	Lima	Fr	Vízek 2, Jakubec
24-03	Switzerland	L	0-1	Bratislava	Fr	
15-04	Turkey	W	3-0	Istanbul	WCq	Janecka, Kozák, Vízek
29-04	Rep. Ireland	L	1-3	Dublin	Fr	Masny
27-05	Iceland	W	6-1	Bratislava	WCq	Vízek, Panenka, Nehoda, Kozák 2, Janecka
9-09	Wales	W	2-0	Prague	WCq	OG, Licka
23-09	Iceland	D	1-1	Reykjavik	WCq	Kozák
28-10	Soviet Union	L	0-2	Tbilisi	WCq	
11-11	Argentina	D	1-1	Buenos Aires	Fr	Valek
29-11	Soviet Union	D	1-1	Bratislava	WCq	Vojacek
3-03-1982	Brazil	D	1-1	Sao Paulo	Fr	Janecka
9-03	Argentina	D	0-0	Mar del Plata	Fr	
24-03	Greece	W	2-1	Prague	Fr	Radimec, Jarolim
14-04	West Germany	L	1-2	Cologne	Fr	Bicovsky
28-04	Austria	L	1-2	Vienna	Fr	Jakkubec
17-06	Kuwait	D	1-1	Valladolid	WCr1	Panenka
20-06	England	L	0-2	Bilbao	WCr1	
24-06	France	D	1-1	Valladolid	WCr1	Panenka
6-10	Sweden	D	2-2	Bratislava	ECq	Janecka 2
27-10	Denmark	W	3-1	Copenhagen	Fr	Cermak, Fiala, Choupka
13-11	Italy	D	2-2	Milan	ECq	Sloup, Chaloupka
27-03-1983	Cyprus	D	1-1	Nicosia	ECq	Bicovsky
16-04	Cyprus	W	6-0	Prague	ECq	Danek 2, Vízek 2, Prokes, Jurkemik
15-05	Romania	W	1-0	Bucharest	ECq	Vízek (p)
7-09	Switzerland	D	0-0	Neuchatel	Fr	
21-09	Sweden	L	0-1	Stockholm	ECq	
26-10	Bulgaria	L	1-2	Prague	Fr	Stambacher
16-11	Italy	W	2-0	Prague	ECq	Rada 2
30-11	Romania	D	1-1	Bratislava	ECq	Luhovy
28-03-1984	East Germany	L	1-2	Erfurt	Fr	Griga
7-04	Italy	D	1-1	Verona	Fr	Griga
16-05	Denmark	W	1-0	Prague	Fr	Knoflicek
5-09	Greece	W	1-0	Athens	Fr	Berger
14-10	Portugal	L	1-2	Oporto	WCq	Jarolim
31-10	Malta	W	4-0	Prague	WCq	Janecka 2, Jarolim, Berger
27-03-1985	Switzerland	L	0-2	Sion	Fr	
21-04	Malta	D	0-0	Ta'Qali	WCq	
30-04	West Germany	L	1-5	Prague	WCq	Griga
5-06	Sweden	L	0-2	Stocholm	WCq	
4-09	Poland	W	3-1	Brno	Fr	Berger, Kubik, OG
25-09	Portugal	W	1-0	Prague	WCq	Hruska
16-10	Sweden	W	2-1	Prague	WCq	Vízek 2
17-11	West Germany	D	2-2	Munich	WCq	Novák J, Lauda
23-04-1986	East Germany	W	2-0	Nitra	Fr	Knoflicek, Luhovy
27-05	Rep. Ireland	L	0-1	Reykjavik	Fr	
29-05	Iceland	W	2-1	Reykjavik	Fr	Kula, Chovanec
3-08	Australia	D	1-1	Melbourne	Fr	Novák J
6-08	Australia	W	1-0	Adelaide	Fr	Griga
10-08	Australia	W	3-0	Sydney	Fr	Kula, Kubik 2
10-09	Holland	W	1-0	Prague	Fr	Knoflicek
15-10	Finland	W	3-0	Brno	ECq	Janecka, Knoflicek, Kula
12-11	Denmark	D	0-0	Bratislava	ECq	
25-03-1987	Switzerland	W	2-1	Bellinzona	Fr	Kubik 2
29-04	Wales	D	1-1	Wrexham	ECq	Knoflicek
13-05	East Germany	L	0-2	Brandenburg	Fr	
3-06	Denmark	D	1-1	Copenhagen	ECq	Hasek
9-09	Finland	L	0-3	Helsinki	ECq	
27-10	Poland	W	3-1	Bratislava	Fr	Danek, Micinec, Bilek

11-11	Wales	W	2–0	Prague	ECq	Knoflicek, Bilek
12-01-1988	Finland	L	0–2	Las Palmas	Fr	
15-01	East Germany	W	1–0	Las Palmas	Fr	Hasek
24-02	Spain	W	2–1	Malaga	Fr	Knoflicek, Kubik
23-03	Bulgaria	L	0–2	Sofia	Fr	
27-04	Soviet Union	D	1–1	Trnava	Fr	Vlk
1-06	Denmark	W	1–0	Copenhagen	Fr	Kubik
24-08	France	D	1–1	Paris	Fr	Danek
20-09	Austria	W	4–2	Prague	Fr	Luhovy, Bilek, Danek 2
18-10	Luxembourg	W	2–0	Esch	WCq	Hasek, Chovanec
4-11	Norway	W	3–2	Bratislava	Fr	Griga, Weiss, Luhovy
16-11	Belgium	D	0–0	Bratislava	WCq	
11-04-1989	Austria	W	2–1	Graz	Fr	Griga 2
29-04	Belgium	L	1–2	Brussels	WCq	Luhovy
9-05	Luxembourg	W	4–0	Prague	WCq	Griga, Skuhravy 2, Bilek
7-06	Switzerland	W	1–0	Berne	WCq	Skuhravy
5-09	Romania	W	2–0	Nitra	Fr	Vlk, Bilek
6-10	Portugal	W	2–1	Prague	WCq	Bilek 2
25-10	Switzerland	W	3–0	Prague	WCq	Skuhravy, Bilek, Moravcik
15-11	Portugal	D	0–0	Lisbon	WCq	
21-02-1990	Spain	L	0–1	Alicante	Fr	
4-04	Egypt	L	0–1	Brno	Fr	
25-04	England	L	2–4	London	Fr	Skuhravy, Kubik
26-05	West Germany	L	0–1	Dusseldorf	Fr	
10-06	United States	W	5–1	Florence	WCr1	Skuhravy 2, Bilek, Hasek, Luhovy
15-06	Austria	W	1–0	Florence	WCr1	Bilek
19-06	Italy	L	0–2	Rome	WCr1	
23-06	Costa Rica	W	4–1	Bari	WCr2	Skuhravy 3, Kubik
1-07	West Germany	L	0–1	Milan	WCqf	
29-08	Finland	D	1–1	Kuusankoski	Fr	Kuka
26-09	Iceland	W	1–0	Kosice	ECq	Danek
13-10	France	L	1–2	Paris	ECq	Skuhravy
14-11	Spain	W	3–2	Prague	ECq	Danek 2, Moravcik
30-01-1991	Australia	W	1–0	Melbourne	Fr	Kristofik
6-02	Australia	W	2–0	Sydney	Fr	Kula, Grussmann
27-03	Poland	W	4–0	Olomouc	Fr	Kuka, Moravcik, Pecko, Danek
1-05	Albania	W	2–0	Tirana	ECq	Kubik, Kuka
5-06	Iceland	W	1–0	Reykjavik	ECq	Hasek
21-08	Switzerland	D	1–1	Prague	Fr	Luhovy
4-09	France	L	1–2	Bratislava	ECq	OG
25-09	Norway	W	3–2	Oslo	Fr	Nemecek, Moravcik, Kuka
16-10	Albania	W	2–1	Olomouc	ECq	Kula, Lancz
13-11	Spain	L	1–2	Seville	ECq	Nemecek
18-12	Brazil	L	1–2	Goiana	Fr	Skuhravy
4-01-1992	Egypt	L	0–2	Cairo	Fr	
25-03	England	D	2–2	Prague	Fr	Skuhravy, Nemecek
22-04	Germany	D	1–1	Prague	Fr	Bilek
27-05	Poland	L	0–1	Jastrzebie	Fr	

LEADING INTERNATIONAL GOALSCORERS

1	Puc	34
2	Nehoda	31
3	Nejedly	28
	Silny	28
5	Scherer	22
6	Svoboda	21
7	Masny	18
8	Vízek	17
	Panenka	17
10	Adamec	14
11	Kvasnák	13
12	Bican	12
	Janda-Ocko	12
	Skuhravy	12

LEADING INTERNATIONAL APPEARANCES

1	Nehoda	90
2	Novák	75
	Masny	75
4	Plánicka	73
5	Dobiás	67
6	Masopust	63
	Viktor	63
8	Popluhár	62
9	Ondrus	59
	Puc	59

DENMARK

Denmark was among the very first continental nations to take up football, and of these early proponents of the game they were certainly the best. As the game spread, however, they were left behind, firmly ensconced in the tradition that to be an amateur was the only way to play the game. This might have continued uninterrupted had not a collection of fine players all come to prominence in the late 1970s and early 1980s. Success at international level forced change at home, and Danish football is currently in the throes of reorganisation that could shape its continued success in the 21st century, building on their amazing win in the 1992 European Championships.

Scandinavia was a popular location for tours by British sides at the turn of the century. Staevnet, a combination of the four main Copenhagen sides, KB, B 93, Akademisk and Frem, were specially formed to take on these tourists and the experienced gained launched the Danes to the forefront of the European game. KB Copenhagen, formed in 1876, are even older than most English and Scottish clubs, but although there were numerous clubs by the turn of the century, a league did not come into operation until 1913.

The 1908 and 1912 Olympic Games were a particular triumph for the Danish national side. As a fortress of the amateur game, players came from unlikely backgrounds. The Bohr brothers, for example, were both professors at Copenhagen University, and one of them, Niels, later won the Nobel Prize for physics! Coached by Charlie Williams, the Manchester City goalkeeper, for the 1908 Games, they beat the French 17–1 and 9–0 in a clear indication of their superiority to qualify for the final. Against England in the final at White City the Danes played very well and an England side that represented the best the country had to offer, despite being amateur, struggled to win 2–0.

Four years later in Stockholm, the same two teams faced each other again in the final. In the semi-finals, the Danes had disposed of their biggest rivals, Holland, with an easy victory and in the final were on top for much of the game against England, eventually losing 4–2. The England players were all regular players in the Football League and their experience told. The stars of these early Danish teams included Nils Middleboe and his three brothers, Hans Hansen, Charles Buchwald, S and N Nielsen as well as Wolffhagen. Nils Middleboe joined Chelsea in 1913 and became one of their most famous players ever.

As professionalism was adopted throughout Europe, the focus of football shifted towards Central and Southern Europe and away from Scandinavia. The decline in Denmark's performances in the inter-war period was startling as even Norway caught up and for a while overtook them in terms of success on the field. Only Finland remained

		All			League			Cup		Europe		
	Team	G	S	B	G	S	B	G	S	G	S	B
1	KB Kobenhavn	17	19	8	15	15	8	2	4	–	–	–
2	ÅGF Åarhus	13	7	10	5	4	10	8	3	–	–	–
3	B 93 Kobenhavn	11	5	9	10	5	9	1	–	–	–	–
4	Vejle BK	11	3	2	5	2	2	6	1	–	–	–
5	Akademisk Kobenhavn	9	13	9	9	11	9	–	2	–	–	–
6	B 1903 Kobenhavn	9	10	8	7	8	8	2	2	–	–	–
7	Frem Kobenhavn	8	15	9	6	12	9	2	3	–	–	–
8	Esbjerg FB	7	7	1	5	3	1	2	4	–	–	–
9	Brondbyernes IF	6	3	1	5	2	–	1	1	–	–	1
10	Lyngby BK	5	5	3	2	3	3	3	2	–	–	–
11	OB Odense	5	3	3	3	2	3	2	1	–	–	–
12	B 1909 Odense	4	1	1	2	–	1	2	1	–	–	–
	Hvidovre BK	4	1	1	3	1	1	1	–	–	–	–
14	Randers Freja	3	1	–	–	1	–	3	–	–	–	–
15	ÅAB Åalborg	2	3	2	–	–	2	2	3	–	–	–
16	Koge BK	2	3	–	2	1	–	–	2	–	–	–
17	B 1913 Odense	1	2	1	–	2	1	1	–	–	–	–
18	Vanlose BK	1	–	–	–	–	–	1	–	–	–	–
19	Fremad Amager	–	3	1	–	2	1	–	1	–	–	–
	Ikast BK	–	3	1	–	1	1	–	2	–	–	–
21	Holbaek BK	–	3	–	–	1	–	–	2	–	–	–
22	Naestved IF	–	2	4	–	2	4	–	–	–	–	–
23	B 1901 Nykobing	–	2	–	–	–	–	–	2	–	–	–
	Åalborg Chang	–	1	–	–	–	–	–	1	–	–	–
	Frem Sakskobing	–	1	–	–	–	–	–	1	–	–	–
	Odense KFUM	–	1	–	–	–	–	–	1	–	–	–
	Skovshoved IF	–	1	–	–	1	–	–	–	–	–	–
28	Horsens FS	–	–	1	–	–	1	–	–	–	–	–

To the end of the 1991–92 season

weaker and even victory against them was no longer assured.

With a reputation for producing a number of talented players, such as Karl and John Hansen and Karl Praest, Denmark was able to stage a mini-revival after the war, and these three players helped them achieve third place in the 1948 Olympics. As a result, all three were signed by Juventus and a rule which kept foreign-based professionals out of the national side meant that no lasting progress was made.

Twelve years later, after the Danes had finished runners-up in the Rome Olympics, the same happened again. Club football as a result was not exactly vibrant. Copenhagen's hegemony was broken in the 1950s as the provincial clubs began to win honours, but the game was seen as little more than a pastime and spectators were few and far between.

The 1970s saw the beginnings of change, and the national side gave the lead. One player in particular, Allan Simonsen, seemed to set an example for others to follow. Playing for Borussia Mönchengladbach and Barcelona, his profile was higher than any Dane before him. There followed a flood of players leaving Denmark for the clubs of Western Europe. The likes of Michael Laudrup, Preben Elkjaer-Larsen, John Sivebaek, Jesper Olsen, Jan Molby and Soren Lerby all left home to play professional football abroad.

With the rule barring these players from representing Denmark thrown out in 1976, the effect on the national team was not long in coming. In the 1984 European Championships, England were knocked out in the qualifying tournament and beaten 1–0 at Wembley. This Danish victory is all the more remarkable in that it represents one of only three competitive defeats that the English have ever suffered at home.

In the final tournament, the Danes won many admirers for their skilful and entertaining brand of football, as did their supporters who added much colour and humour to the event. Following a semi-final appearance in France where they lost on penalties to Spain, Denmark qualified for their only World Cup finals appearance to date, in the 1986 Mexico tournament.

A stunning 6–1 victory over Uruguay in the first round saw the team being talked about as possible world champions. Once again, however, Spain put paid to any hopes in the second round as the Danes collapsed. As the original generation of players who had been part of this revolution began to retire, it was predicted that the game in Denmark would once again float back to obscurity and a poor performance in the 1988 European Championship finals seemed to support this theory.

Talented players continued to emerge, however. Professionalism was introduced in 1978, but was never exploited to the full until the late 1980s. A new superleague played over the winter period as opposed to the traditional summer season, in order to be in line with the major European powers, got underway in 1991 and was the spark that took the game to even greater heights, culminating in the national side's historic victory in the European Championships in Sweden, with over half the squad based at Danish clubs.

Whether Denmark can develop into a consistent European power at both club and international level, along say the lines of Holland or Belgium, only time will tell.

Population: 5139000
Area, sq km: 43093
% in urban areas: 86.4%
Capital city: Copenhagen

Dansk Boldspil–Union
Ved Amagerbanen #15
DK–2300 Copenhagen S
Denmark
Tel: (010 45) 31950511
Fax: (010 45) 31950588
Telex: 15545 DBU DK
Cable: DANSKBOLDSPIL COPENHAGEN
Languages for correspondence: English, German

Year of formation: 1889
Affiliation to FIFA: 1904
Affiliation to UEFA: 1954
Registered clubs: 1514
Registered players: 236000
Professional players: 350
Registered coaches: 4550
Registered referees: 7969
National stadium: Idrætspark, Copenhagen 48000
National colours: Shirts: Red/Shorts: White/Socks: Red
Reserve colours: Shirts: White/Shorts: White/Socks: Red
Season: April–November

THE RECORD

WORLD CUP

1930–54 ..... Did not enter
1958 .... QT 3rd/3 in group 1
1962 .... Did not enter
1966 .... QT 4th/4 in group 7
1970 .... QT 3rd/4 in group 2
1974 .... QT 3rd/3 in group 8
1978 .... QT 3rd/4 in group 1
1982 .... QT 3rd/5 in group 5
1986 .... QT 1st/5 in group 6 – Final Tournament/2nd round
1990 .... QT 2nd/4 in group 1

EUROPEAN CHAMPIONSHIP

1960 .... 1st round
1964 .... Semi-finalists/4th place
1968 .... QT 4th/4 in group 5
1972 .... QT 4th/4 in group 5
1976 .... QT 4th/4 in group 4
1980 .... QT 5th/5 in group 1
1984 .... QT 1st/5 in group 3 – Final Tournament/Semi-finalists
1988 .... QT 1st/4 in group 6 – Final Tournament/1st round
1992 .... QT 2nd/5 in group 4 – Final Tournament/Winners

OLYMPIC GAMES

1906 .... Winners
1908 .... Runners–up
1912 .... Runners–up
1920 .... 1st round
1924–36 ..... Did not enter
1948 .... Semi-finalists/3rd place
1952 .... Quarter-finalists
1956 .... Did not enter
1960 .... Final Tournament/ Finalists
1964 .... QT Failed to qualify
1968 .... Did not enter
1972 .... Final Tournament/2nd round
1976 .... QT Failed to qualify
1980 .... QT Failed to qualify
1984 .... QT Failed to qualify
1988 .... QT Failed to qualify
1992 .... Final Tournament

EUROPEAN CLUB COMPETITIONS

EUROPEAN CUP: Quarter-finalists – ÅGF Århus 1961

CUP WINNERS CUP: Quarter-finalists – Randers Freja 1969, Vejle BK 1978, ÅGF Århus 1989

UEFA CUP: Semi-finalists – Brondby 1991

CLUB DIRECTORY

COPENHAGEN (Population – 1 685 000)

Akademisk Boldklub Kobenhavn
Stadium: Gladsaxe Idrætspark 10 000
Founded: 1889
Colours: Green and white stripes/White

Boldklubben 93 (B 93 Kobenhavn)
Stadium: Osterbrö 7000
Founded: 1893
Colours: White/Blue

Boldklubben 1903 (B 1903 Kobenhavn)
Stadium: Gentofte 18 000
Founded: 1903
Colours: White/White

Brondbyernes Idrætsförening
Stadium: Brondby Stadion 14000
Founded: 1964
Colours: Yellow/Blue

Bronshoj Boldklub
Stadium: Vanlose Idrætspark 8000
Founded: 1919
Colours: Yellow and black stripes/White

Boldklubben Frem Kobenhavn
Stadium: Valby Idrætspark 12000
Founded: 1886
Colours: Blue with two red hoops/White

Fremad Amager
Stadium: Sundby Idrætspark 9000
Founded: 1910
Colours: Blue/White
Hvidovre Boldklub
Stadium: Hvidovre Stadion 15000
Founded: 1925
Colours: Red/Blue

Kastrup Boldklub
Stadium: Tårnby 12000
Founded: 1933
Colours: White/Blue

Kobenhavens Boldklub (KB Kobenhavn)
Stadium: Frederiksberg 7000
Founded: 1876
Colours: Blue and white stripes/White

Lyngby Boldklub
Stadium: Lyngby Stadion 15000
Founded: 1921
Colours: Blue/White

Skovshoved Idrætsförening
Stadium: Krojersved
Founded: 1909
Colours: Blue/Blue

Vanlose Boldklub
Stadium: Vanlose Idrætspark 8000
Founded: 1921
Colours: White/Black

ÅARHUS (Population – 258000)

Åarhus Gimnastic Förening (ÅGF Åarhus)
Stadium: Århus 23000
Founded: 1880
Colours: White with blue sleeves/Blue

Arbejdernes Idrætsklub Århus (AIÅ Åarhus)
Stadium: Tranbjerg
Founded: 1918
Colours: Blue/White

Skovbakken Idrætsklub
Stadium: Vojlby Risskov
Founded: 1927
Colours: Yellow/Blue

ODENSE (Population – 178000)

Boldklubben 1909 (B 1909 Odense)
Stadium: Gillostedvej
Founded: 1909
Colours: Red/White

Boldklubben 1913 (B 1913 Odense)
Stadium: Campusvej
Founded: 1913
Colours: Blue/White

Odense Boldklub (OB Odense)
Stadium: Odense Stadion 24000
Founded: 1887
Colours: Blue and white stripes/White

ÅALBORG (Population – 154000)
Åalborg Boldspilklub (ÅAB Åalborg)
Stadium: Åalborg Stadion 20000
Founded: 1885
Colours: Red and white stripes/White

ESBJERG (Population – 81000)
Esbjerg Förenede Boldklub
Stadium: Esbjerg Idrætsparken 20000
Founded: 1924
Colours: Blue and white stripes/Blue

RANDERS (Population – 61000)
Randers Freja
Stadium: Randers Stadion 20000
Founded: 1898
Colours: Blue and white stripes/Blue

HORSENS (Population – 54000)
Horsens Förene Sportsklub
Stadium: Horsens Idrætspark
Founded: 1915
Colours: Yellow/Blue

VEJLE (Population – 50000)
Vejle Boldklub
Stadium: Vejle Stadion 18000
Founded: 1891
Colours: Red/White

NAESTVED
Naestved Idræts Förening
Stadium: Naestved Stadion 20000
Founded: 1939
Colours: Green/White

IKAST
Ikast Forenede Sportsklubber
Stadium: Ikast Stadion 14000
Founded: 1935
Colours: Yellow/Blue

KOGE
Koge Boldklub
Stadium: Koge 14000
Founded: 1927
Colours: Black and white stripes/Black

SILKEBORG
Silkeborge Idræts Förening
Stadium: Silkeborge 12000
Founded: 1917
Colours: Red/White

HERFOLGE
Herfolge Boldklub
Stadium: Herfolge 6000
Founded: 1921
Colours: Yellow/Blue

VIBORG
Viborg Fodsport Förening
Stadium: Viborg Stadion 15000
Founded: 1896
Colours: Green/White

DANISH LEAGUE CHAMPIONSHIP

Year	Champions		Runners up		3rd	
1913	KB Kobenhavn	17	B 93 Kobenhavn	14	Frem Kobenhavn	10
1914	KB Kobenhavn	18	B 93 Kobenhavn	12	Frem Kobenhavn	12
1915	–					
1916	B 93 Kobenhavn	15	KB Kobenhavn	15	Akademisk	15
1917	KB Kobenhavn	15	Akademisk	13	B 93 Kobenhavn	12
1918	KB Kobenhavn	17	Frem Kobenhavn	12	B 93 Kobenhavn	11
1919	Akademisk	22	B 93 Kobenhavn	18	KB Kobenhavn	17
1920	B 1903 Kobenhavn	17	KB Kobenhavn	16	Akademisk	16
1921	Akademisk	11	B 1903 Kobenhavn	11	B 93 Kobenhavn	10
1922	KB Kobenhavn	14	Frem Kobenhavn	8	B 1903 Kobenhavn	8
1923	Frem Kobenhavn	12	B 93 Kobenhavn	10	KB Kobenhavn	10
1924	B 1903 Kobenhavn	15	KB Kobenhavn	13	B 93 Kobenhavn	12
1925	KB Kobenhavn	18	Akademisk	12	B 93 Kobenhavn	10
1926	B 1903 Kobenhavn	15	B 93 Kobenhavn	13	Frem Kobenhavn	12
1927	B 93 Kobenhavn	18	B 1903 Kobenhavn	12	Akademisk	9

1928	B 93 Kobenhavn	6	Frem Kobenhavn	6	B 1903 Kobenhavn	6
1929	B 93 Kobenhavn	7	KB Kobenhavn	5	Akademisk	3
1930	B 93 Kobenhavn	17	Frem Kobenhavn	15	B 1903 Kobenhavn	14
1931	Frem Kobenhavn	17	KB Kobenhavn	13	B 93 Kobenhavn	12
1932	KB Kobenhavn	18	Akademisk	15	B 93 Kobenhavn	12
1933	Frem Kobenhavn	16	B 1903 Kobenhavn	14	ÅGF Åarhus	12
1934	B 93 Kobenhavn	14	B 1903 Kobenhavn	14	Frem Kobenhavn	13
1935	B 93 Kobenhavn	13	Frem Kobenhavn	12	KB Kobenhavn	12
1936	Frem Kobenhavn	15	Akademisk	15	ÅAB Åalborg	10
1937	Akademisk	28	Frem Kobenhavn	26	B 93 Kobenhavn	25
1938	B 1903 Kobenhavn	27	Frem Kobenhavn	27	KB Kobenhavn	22
1939	B 93 Kobenhavn	31	KB Kobenhavn	24	Akademisk	20
1940	KB Kobenhavn	24	Fremad Amager	22	B 93 Kobenhavn	20
1941	Frem Kobenhavn	4–2	Fremad Amager			
1942	B 93 Kobenhavn	3–2	Akademisk			
1943	Akademisk	2–1	KB Kobenhavn			
1944	Frem Kobenhavn	4–2	Akademisk			
1945	Akademisk	1–1	ÅGF Åarhus			
1946	B 93 Kobenhavn	28	KB Kobenhavn	24	Akademisk	21
1947	Akademisk	28	KB Kobenhavn	26	Fremad Amager	22
1948	KB Kobenhavn	33	Frem Kobenhavn	29	Akademisk	26
1949	KB Kobenhavn	27	Akademisk	22	ÅGF Åarhus	19
1950	KB Kobenhavn	28	Akademisk	27	ÅGF Åarhus	26
1951	Akademisk	28	OB Odense	19	ÅGF Åarhus	18
1952	Akademisk	26	Koge BK	21	B 1909 Odense	20
1953	KB Kobenhavn	30	Skovshoved IF	23	OB Odense	21
1954	Koge BK	23	KB Kobenhavn	20	Akademisk	19
1955	ÅGF Åarhus	25	Akademisk	23	Frem Kobenhavn	21
1956	ÅGF Åarhus	26	Esbjerg FB	22	Akademisk	22
1957	ÅGF Åarhus	39	Akademisk	37	Frem Kobenhavn	32
1958	Vejle BK	30	Frem Kobenhavn	29	OB Odense	28
1959	B 1909 Odense	33	KB Kobenhavn	31	Vejle BK	29
1960	ÅGF Åarhus	32	KB Kobenhavn	29	Vejle BK	29
1961	Esbjerg FB	33	KB Kobenhavn	33	B 1913 Odense	28
1962	Esbjerg FB	37	B 1913 Odense	29	ÅGF Åarhus	27
1963	Esbjerg FB	33	B 1913 Odense	25	B 1903 Kobenhavn	25
1964	B 1909 Odense	31	ÅGF Åarhus	30	KB Kobenhavn	29
1965	Esbjerg FB	31	Vejle BK	30	B 1903 Kobenhavn	28
1966	Hvidovre BK	31	Frem Kobenhavn	27	KB Kobenhavn	25
1967	Akademisk	31	Frem Kobenhavn	29	Horsens FS	28
1968	KB Kobenhavn	29	Esbjerg FB	29	Frem Kobenhavn	29
1969	B 1903 Kobenhavn	34	KB Kobenhavn	30	ÅAB Åalborg	29
1970	B 1903 Kobenhavn	27	Akademisk	27	Hvidovre BK	26
1971	Vejle BK	29	Hvidovre BK	24	Frem Kobenhavn	24
1972	Vejle BK	33	B 1903 Kobenhavn	27	Naestved IF	26
1973	Hvidovre BK	27	Randers Freja	26	KB Kobenhavn	26
1974	KB Kobenhavn	33	Vejle BK	25	B 1903 Kobenhavn	24
1975	Koge BK	41	Holbaek BK	41	Naestved IF	38
1976	B 1903 Kobenhavn	40	Frem Kobenhavn	39	KB Kobenhavn	39
1977	OB Odense	47	B 1903 Kobenhavn	39	Esbjerg FB	34
1978	Vejle BK	44	Esbjerg FB	40	ÅGF Åarhus	39
1979	Esbjerg FB	46	KB Kobenhavn	40	B 1903 Kobenhavn	38
1980	KB Kobenhavn	40	Naestved IF	40	OB Odense	38
1981	Hvidovre BK	40	Lyngby BK	39	Naestved IF	38
1982	OB Odense	41	ÅGF Åarhus	40	B 1903 Kobenhavn	35
1983	Lyngby BK	40	OB Odense	38	ÅGF Åarhus	36
1984	Vejle BK	41	ÅGF Åarhus	40	Lyngby BK	38
1985	Brondbyernes IF	43	Lyngby BK	37	ÅGF Åarhus	36
1986	ÅGF Åarhus	41	Brondbyernes IF	37	Naestved IF	35
1987	Brondbyernes IF	47	Ikast BK	38	ÅGF Åarhus	36
1988	Brondbyernes IF	40	Naestved IF	35	Lyngby BK	35
1989	OB Odense	41	Brondbyernes IF	38	Lyngby BK	38
1990	Brondbyernes IF	42	B 1903 Kobenhavn	31	Ikast BK	30
1991	Brondbyernes IF	26	Lyngby BK	24	ÅGF Åarhus	20
1992	Lyngby BK	32	B 1903 Kobenhavn	29	Frem Kobenhavn	26

DANISH CUP FINALS

Year	Winners	Score	Runners–up
1955	ÅGF Åarhus	4–0	Aalborg Chang
1956	Frem Kobenhavn	1–0	Akademisk
1957	ÅGF Åarhus	2–0	Esbjerg FB
1958	Vejle BK	3–2	ÅGF Åarhus
1959	Vejle BK	1–1 2–0	ÅGF Åarhus
1960	ÅGF Åarhus	2–0	Frem Sakskobing
1961	ÅGF Åarhus	2–0	KB Kobenhavn
1962	B 1909 Odense	1–0	Esbjerg FB
1963	B 1913 Odense	2–1	Koge BK
1964	Esbjerg FB	2–1	Odense KFUM
1965	ÅGF Åarhus	1–0	KB Kobenhavn
1966	ÅAB Åalborg	3–1	KB Kobenhavn
1967	Randers Freja	1–0	ÅAB Åalborg
1968	Randers Freja	3–1	Vejle BK
1969	KB Kobenhavn	3–0	Frem Kobenhavn
1970	ÅAB Åalborg	2–1	Lyngby BK
1971	B 1909 Odense	1–0	Frem Kobenhavn
1972	Vejle BK	2–0	Fremad Amager
1973	Randers Freja	2–0	B 1901 Nykobing
1974	Vanlose BK	5–2	OB Odense
1975	Vejle BK	1–0	Holbaek BK
1976	Esbjerg FB	2–1	Holbaek BK
1977	Vejle BK	2–1	B 1909 Odense
1978	Frem Kobenhavn	1–1 1–1 (6–5p)	Esbjerg FB
1979	B 1903 Kobenhavn	1–0	Koge BK
1980	Hvidovre BK	5–3	Lyngby BK
1981	Vejle BK	2–1	Frem Kobenhavn
1982	B 93 Kobenhavn	3–3 1–0	B 1903 Kobenhavn
1983	OB Odense	3–0	B 1901 Nykobing
1984	Lyngby BK	2–1	KB Kobenhavn
1985	Lyngby BK	3–2	Esbjerg FB
1986	B 1903 Kobenhavn	2–1	Ikast BK
1987	ÅGF Åarhus	3–0	ÅAB Åalborg
1988	ÅGF Åarhus	2–1	Brondbyernes IF
1989	Brondbyernes IF	6–3	Ikast BK
1990	Lyngby BK	0–0 6–1	ÅGF Åarhus
1991	OB Odense	0–0 0–0 (4–3p)	ÅAB Åalborg
1992	ÅGF Åarhus	3–0	B 1903 Kobenhavn

INTERNATIONAL MATCHES PLAYED BY DENMARK

Date	Opponents	Result		Venue	Compet	Scorers
19–10–1908	France	W	9–0	London	OGr1	
22–10	France	W	17–1	London	OGsf	
24–10	England*	L	0–2	London	OGf	
5–05–1910	England*	W	2–1	Copenhagen	Fr	
21–10–1911	England*	L	0–3	London	Fr	
30–06–1912	Norway	W	7–0	Stockholm	OGqf	
2–07	Holland	W	4–1	Stockholm	OGsf	
4–07	England*	L	2–4	Stockholm	OGf	
6–10	Germany	W	3–1	Copenhagen	Fr	
25–05–1913	Sweden	W	8–0	Copenhagen	Fr	
5–10	Sweden	W	10–0	Stockholm	Fr	
26–10	Germany	W	4–1	Hamburg	Fr	
17–05–1914	Holland	W	4–3	Copenhagen	Fr	
5–06	England*	W	3–0	Copenhagen	Fr	
6–06–1915	Sweden	W	2–0	Copenhagen	Fr	
19–09	Norway	W	8–1	Copenhagen	Fr	
1–10	Sweden	W	2–0	Stockholm	Fr	
4–06–1916	Sweden	W	2–0	Copenhagen	Fr	
25–06	Norway	W	2–0	Oslo	Fr	
8–10	Sweden	L	0–4	Stockholm	Fr	
15–10	Norway	W	8–0	Copenhagen	Fr	
3–06–1917	Sweden	D	1–1	Copenhagen	Fr	
17–06	Norway	W	2–1	Oslo	Fr	
7–10	Norway	W	12–0	Copenhagen	Fr	
14–10	Sweden	W	2–1	Stockholm	Fr	
2–06–1918	Sweden	W	3–0	Copenhagen	Fr	
16–06	Norway	L	1–3	Oslo	Fr	
6–10	Norway	W	4–0	Copenhagen	Fr	
20–10	Sweden	W	2–1	Gothenberg	Fr	
5–06–1919	Sweden	W	3–0	Copenhagen	Fr	
12–06	Norway	W	5–1	Copenhagen	Fr	
21–09	Norway	L	2–3	Oslo	Fr	
12–10	Sweden	L	0–3	Stockholm	Fr	
5–04–1920	Holland	L	0–2	Amsterdam	Fr	
13–06	Norway	D	1–1	Oslo	Fr	
28–08	Spain	L	0–1	Brussels	OGr1	
10–10	Sweden	W	2–0	Stockholm	Fr	
12–06–1921	Holland	D	1–1	Copenhagen	Fr	
2–10	Norway	W	3–1	Copenhagen	Fr	
9–10	Sweden	D	0–0	Stockholm	Fr	
15–04–1922	Belgium	D	0–0	Liege	Fr	

* Amateur side

17–04	Holland	L	0–2	Amsterdam	Fr
11–06	Czechoslovakia	L	0–3	Copenhagen	Fr
10–09	Norway	D	3–3	Fredrikstad	Fr
1–10	Sweden	L	1–2	Copenhagen	Fr
6–05–1923	Czechoslovakia	L	0–2	Prague	Fr
17–06	Switzerland	W	3–2	Copenhagen	Fr
30–09	Norway	W	2–1	Copenhagen	Fr
14–10	Sweden	W	3–1	Stockholm	Fr
21–04–1924	Switzerland	L	0–2	Basle	Fr
15–06	Sweden	L	2–3	Copenhagen	Fr
14–09	Norway	W	3–1	Oslo	Fr
5–10	Belgium	W	2–1	Copenhagen	Fr
14–06–1925	Sweden	W	2–0	Stockholm	Fr
21–06	Norway	W	5–1	Copenhagen	Fr
27–09	Finland	D	3–3	Aarhus	Fr
25–10	Holland	L	2–4	Amsterdam	Fr
13–06–1926	Holland	W	4–1	Copenhagen	Fr
20–06	Finland	L	2–3	Helsinki	Fr
19–09	Norway	D	2–2	Oslo	Fr
3–10	Sweden	W	2–0	Copenhagen	Fr
29–05–1927	Norway	W	1–0	Oslo	Fr
12–06	Holland	D	1–1	Copenhagen	Fr
19–06	Sweden	D	0–0	Stockholm	Fr
2–10	Germany	W	3–1	Copenhagen	Fr
30–10	Norway	W	3–1	Copenhagen	Fr
22–04–1928	Holland	L	0–2	Amsterdam	Fr
17–06	Norway	W	3–2	Oslo	Fr
16–09	Germany	L	1–2	Nuremberg	Fr
7–10	Sweden	W	3–1	Copenhagen	Fr
16–06–1929	Sweden	L	2–3	Gothenberg	Fr
23–06	Norway	L	2–5	Copenhagen	Fr
13–10	Finland	W	8–0	Copenhagen	Fr
16–06–1930	Finland	W	6–1	Helsinki	Fr
22–06	Sweden	W	6–1	Copenhagen	Fr
7–09	Germany	W	6–3	Copenhagen	Fr
21–09	Norway	L	0–1	Oslo	Fr
25–05–1931	Norway	W	3–1	Copenhagen	Fr
14–06	Holland	L	0–2	Copenhagen	Fr
28–06	Sweden	L	1–3	Stockholm	Fr
27–09	Germany	L	2–4	Hanover	Fr
11–10	Finland	L	2–3	Copenhagen	Fr
5–06–1932	Belgium	L	3–4	Copenhagen	Fr
19–06	Sweden	W	3–1	Copenhagen	Fr
30–08	Finland	L	2–4	Helsinki	Fr
25–09	Norway	W	2–1	Oslo	Fr
11–06–1933	Norway	D	2–2	Copenhagen	Fr
18–06	Sweden	W	3–2	Stockholm	Fr
8–10	Finland	W	2–0	Copenhagen	Fr
26–11	Belgium	D	2–2	Brussels	Fr
21–05–1934	Poland	W	4–2	Copenhagen	Fr
17–06	Sweden	L	3–5	Copenhagen	Fr
3–07	Finland	L	1–2	Helsinki	Fr
23–09	Norway	L	1–3	Oslo	Fr
7–10	Germany	L	2–5	Copenhagen	Fr
16–06–1935	Sweden	L	1–3	Gothenberg	Fr
23–06	Norway	W	1–0	Copenhagen	Fr
6–10	Finland	W	5–1	Copenhagen	Fr
3–11	Holland	L	0–3	Amsterdam	Fr
14–06–1936	Sweden	W	4–3	Copenhagen	Fr
30–06	Finland	W	4–1	Helsinki	Fr
30–09	Norway	D	3–3	Oslo	Fr
4–10	Poland	W	2–1	Copenhagen	Fr
16–05–1937	Germany	L	0–8	Breslau	Fr
13–06	Norway	W	5–1	Copenhagen	Fr
12–09	Poland	L	1–3	Warsaw	Fr
3–10	Sweden	W	2–1	Stockholm	Fr
17–10	Finland	W	2–1	Copenhagen	Fr
21–06–1938	Sweden	L	0–1	Copenhagen	Fr
31–08	Finland	L	1–2	Helsinki	Fr

18–09	Norway	D	1–1	Oslo	Fr
23–10	Holland	D	2–2	Copenhagen	Fr
15–06–1939	Finland	W	5–0	Copenhagen	Fr
18–06	Norway	W	6–3	Copenhagen	Fr
25–06	Germany	L	0–2	Copenhagen	Fr
17–09	Finland	W	8–1	Copenhagen	Fr
1–10	Sweden	L	1–4	Stockholm	Fr
22–10	Norway	W	4–1	Copenhagen	Fr
6–10–1940	Sweden	D	1–1	Stockholm	Fr
20–10	Sweden	D	3–3	Copenhagen	Fr
17–11	Germany	L	0–1	Hamburg	Fr
14–09–1941	Sweden	D	2–2	Stockholm	Fr
19–10	Sweden	W	2–1	Copenhagen	Fr
16–11	Germany	D	1–1	Dresden	Fr
28–06–1942	Sweden	L	0–3	Copenhagen	Fr
4–10	Sweden	L	1–2	Stockholm	Fr
20–06–1943	Sweden	W	3–2	Copenhagen	Fr
24–06–1945	Sweden	L	1–2	Stockholm	Fr
1–07	Sweden	L	3–4	Copenhagen	Fr
26–08	Norway	W	4–2	Copenhagen	Fr
9–09	Norway	W	5–1	Oslo	Fr
30–09	Sweden	L	1–4	Stockholm	Fr
16–06–1946	Norway	L	1–2	Oslo	Fr
24–06	Sweden	W	3–1	Copenhagen	Fr
8–07	Norway	W	2–0	Copenhagen	Fr
17–07	Iceland	W	3–0	Reykjavik	Fr
1–09	Finland	W	5–2	Helsinki	Fr
6–10	Sweden	D	3–3	Gothenberg	Fr
20–10	Norway	W	7–1	Copenhagen	Fr
15–06–1947	Sweden	L	1–4	Copenhagen	Fr
20–06	Czechoslovakia	D	2–2	Copenhagen	Fr
26–06	Sweden	L	1–6	Stockholm	Fr
21–09	Norway	W	5–3	Oslo	Fr
5–10	Finland	W	4–1	Aarhus	Fr
12–06–1948	Norway	L	1–2	Copenhagen	Fr
15–06	Finland	W	3–0	Helsinki	Fr
26–06	Poland	W	8–0	Copenhagen	Fr
31–07	Egypt	W	3–1	London	OGr1
10–08	Sweden	L	2–4	London	OGsf
26–09	England	D	0–0	Copenhagen	Fr
10–10	Sweden	L	0–1	Stockholm	Fr
12–06–1949	Holland	L	1–2	Copenhagen	Fr
19–06	Poland	W	2–1	Warsaw	Fr
7–08	Iceland	W	5–1	Aarhus	Fr
11–09	Norway	W	2–0	Oslo	Fr
11–09	Finland	L	0–2	Copenhagen	Fr
23–10	Sweden	W	3–2	Copenhagen	Fr
11–12	Holland	W	1–0	Amsterdam	Fr
28–05–1950	Yugoslavia	L	1–5	Belgrade	Fr
22–06	Norway	W	4–0	Copenhagen	Fr
27–08	Finland	W	2–1	Helsinki	Fr
10–09	Yugoslavia	L	1–4	Copenhagen	Fr
15–10	Sweden	L	0–4	Stockholm	Fr
5–11	Austria	L	1–5	Vienna	Fr
12–05–1951	Scotland	L	1–3	Glasgow	Fr
17–06	Austria	D	3–3	Copenhagen	Fr
16–09	Norway	L	0–2	Oslo	Fr
30–09	Finland	W	1–0	Copenhagen	Fr
21–10	Sweden	W	3–1	Copenhagen	Fr
25–05–1952	Scotland	L	1–2	Copenhagen	Fr
11–06	Sweden	L	0–2	Oslo	Fr
22–06	Sweden	L	3–4	Stockholm	Fr
15–07	Greece	W	2–1	Tammerfors	OGr1
21–07	Poland	W	2–0	Turku	OGr2
25–07	Yugoslavia	L	3–5	Helsinki	OGqf
21–09	Holland	W	3–2	Copenhagen	Fr
5–10	Finland	L	1–2	Helsinki	Fr
19–10	Norway	L	1–3	Copenhagen	Fr
7–03–1953	Holland	W	2–1	Rotterdam	Fr

21–06	Sweden	L	1–3	Copenhagen	Fr
27–06	Switzerland	W	4–1	Basle	Fr
9–08	Iceland	W	4–0	Copenhagen	Fr
13–09	Norway	W	1–0	Oslo	Fr
4–10	Finland	W	6–1	Copenhagen	Fr
4–06–1954	Norway	L	1–2	Malmo	Fr
13–06	Finland	D	2–2	Helsinki	Fr
19–09	Switzerland	D	1–1	Copenhagen	Fr
10–10	Sweden	L	2–5	Stockholm	Fr
31–10	Norway	L	0–1	Copenhagen	Fr
13–03–1955	Holland	D	1–1	Amsterdam	Fr
15–05	Hungary	L	0–6	Copenhagen	Fr
19–06	Finland	W	2–1	Copenhagen	Fr
3–07	Iceland	W	4–0	Reykjavik	Fr
11–09	Norway	D	1–1	Oslo	Fr
2–10	England	L	1–5	Copenhagen	Fr
16–10	Sweden	D	3–3	Copenhagen	Fr
23–05–1956	Soviet Union	L	1–5	Moscow	Fr
24–06	Norway	L	2–3	Copenhagen	Fr
1–07	Soviet Union	L	2–5	Copenhagen	Fr
16–09	Finland	W	4–0	Helsinki	Fr
3–10	Rep. Ireland	L	1–2	Dublin	WCq
21–10	Sweden	D	1–1	Stockholm	Fr
4–11	Holland	D	2–2	Copenhagen	Fr
5–12	England	L	2–5	Wolverhampton	WCq
15–05–1957	England	L	1–4	Copenhagen	WCq
26–05	Bulgaria	D	1–1	Copenhagen	Fr
18–06	Finland	L	0–2	Helsinki	Fr
19–06	Norway	W	2–0	Tammerfors	Fr
30–06	Sweden	L	1–2	Copenhagen	Fr
10–07	Iceland	W	6–2	Reykjavik	Fr
22–09	Norway	D	2–2	Oslo	Fr
2–10	Rep. Ireland	L	0–2	Copenhagen	WCq
13–10	Finland	W	3–0	Copenhagen	Fr
15–05–1958	Neth Antilles	W	3–2	Aarhus	Fr
25–05	Poland	W	3–2	Copenhagen	Fr
29–06	Norway	L	1–2	Copenhagen	Fr
14–09	Finland	W	4–1	Helsinki	Fr
24–09	West Germany	D	1–1	Copenhagen	Fr
15–10	Holland	L	1–5	Rotterdam	Fr
26–10	Sweden	D	4–4	Stockholm	Fr
21–06–1959	Sweden	L	0–6	Copenhagen	Fr
26–06	Iceland	W	4–2	Reykjavik	OGq
2–07	Norway	W	2–1	Copenhagen	OGq
18–08	Iceland	D	1–1	Copenhagen	OGq
13–09	Norway	W	4–2	Oslo	OGq
23–09	Czechoslovakia	D	2–2	Copenhagen	ECr1
4–10	Finland	W	4–0	Copenhagen	Fr
18–10	Czechoslovakia	L	1–5	Brno	ECr1
2–12	Greece	W	3–1	Athens	Fr
6–12	Bulgaria	L	1–2	Sofia	Fr
10–05–1960	Brazil	L	3–4	Copenhagen	Fr
26–05	Norway	W	3–0	Copenhagen	Fr
3–07	Greece	W	7–2	Copenhagen	Fr
27–07	Hungary	W	1–0	Copenhagen	Fr
10–08	Finland	W	2–1	Copenhagen	Fr
29–08	Poland	W	2–1	Livorno	OGr1
1–09	Tunisia	W	3–1	Aquilla	OGr1
10–09	Yugoslavia	L	1–3	Rome	OGf
23–10	Sweden	L	0–2	Gothenberg	Fr
28–05–1961	East Germany	D	1–1	Copenhagen	Fr
18–06	Sweden	L	1–2	Copenhagen	Fr
17–09	Norway	W	4–0	Oslo	Fr
20–09	West Germany	L	1–5	Dusseldorf	Fr
15–10	Finland	W	9–1	Copenhagen	Fr
5–11	Poland	L	0–5	Chorzow	Fr
23–05–1962	East Germany	L	1–4	Leipzig	Fr
11–06	Norway	W	6–1	Copenhagen	Fr
28–06	Malta	W	6–1	Copenhagen	ECr1

11-09	Neth Antilles	W	3-1	Odense	Fr	
16-09	Finland	W	6-1	Helsingfors	Fr	
26-09	Holland	W	4-1	Copenhagen	Fr	
28-10	Sweden	L	2-4	Stockholm	Fr	
8-12	Malta	W	3-1	Gzira	ECr1	
12-12	Turkey	D	1-1	Istanbul	Fr	
19-05-1963	Hungary	L	0-6	Budapest	Fr	
3-06	Finland	D	1-1	Copenhagen	Fr	
23-06	Romania	L	2-3	Copenhagen	OGq	
29-06	Albania	W	4-0	Copenhagen	ECr2	
15-09	Norway	W	4-0	Oslo	Fr	
6-10	Sweden	D	2-2	Copenhagen	Fr	
30-10	Albania	L	0-1	Tirana	ECr2	
3-11	Romania	W	3-2	Bucharest	OGq	
28-11	Romania	L	1-2	Turin	OGq	
4-12	Luxembourg	D	3-3	Luxembourg	ECqf	
10-12	Luxembourg	D	2-2	Copenhagen	ECqf	
18-12	Luxembourg	W	1-0	Amsterdam	ECqf	
17-06-1964	Soviet Union	L	0-3	Barcelona	ECsf	
20-06	Hungary	L	1-3	Barcelona	EC3p	
28-06	Sweden	L	1-4	Malmo	Fr	
6-09	Finland	L	1-2	Helsinki	Fr	
11-10	Norway	W	2-0	Copenhagen	Fr	
21-10	Wales	W	1-0	Copenhagen	WCq	
29-11	Greece	L	2-4	Athens	WCq	
1-12	Israel	W	1-0	Tel Aviv	Fr	
5-12	Italy	L	1-3	Bologna	Fr	
9-06-1965	Finland	W	3-1	Copenhagen	Fr	
20-06	Sweden	W	2-1	Copenhagen	Fr	
27-06	Soviet Union	L	0-6	Moscow	WCq	
5-07	Iceland	W	3-1	Reykjavik	Fr	
26-09	Norway	D	2-2	Oslo	Fr	
17-10	Soviet Union	L	1-3	Copenhagen	WCq	
27-10	Greece	D	1-1	Copenhagen	WCq	
1-12	Wales	L	2-4	Wrexham	WCq	
30-05-1966	Turkey	D	0-0	Copenhagen	Fr	
17-06	Argentina	L	0-2	Copenhagen	Fr	
21-06	Portugal	L	1-3	Esbjerg	Fr	
26-06	Norway	L	0-1	Copenhagen	Fr	
3-07	England	L	0-2	Copenhagen	Fr	
18-09	Finland	L	1-2	Helsinki	Fr	
21-09	Hungary	L	0-6	Budapest	ECq	
26-10	Israel	W	3-1	Copenhagen	Fr	
6-11	Sweden	L	1-2	Stockholm	Fr	
30-11	Holland	L	0-2	Rotterdam	ECq	
24-05-1967	Hungary	L	0-2	Copenhagen	ECq	
4-06	East Germany	D	1-1	Copenhagen	ECq	
25-06	Sweden	D	1-1	Copenhagen	Fr	
23-08	Iceland	W	14-2	Copenhagen	Fr	
24-09	Norway	W	5-0	Oslo	Fr	
4-10	Holland	W	3-2	Copenhagen	ECq	
11-10	East Germany	L	2-3	Leipzig	ECq	
22-10	Finland	W	3-0	Copenhagen	Fr	
4-06-1968	Finland	W	3-1	Helsinki	Fr	
23-06	Norway	W	5-1	Copenhagen	Fr	
27-06	Sweden	L	1-2	Stockholm	Fr	
25-09	Czechoslovakia	L	0-3	Copenhagen	WCq	
16-10	Scotland	L	0-1	Copenhagen	Fr	
20-10	Czechoslovakia	L	0-1	Bratislava	WCq	
20-11	Luxembourg	W	5-1	Copenhagen	Fr	
22-01-1969	Mexico	L	0-3	Mexico City	Fr	
6-05	Mexico	W	3-1	Copenhagen	Fr	
27-05	Rep Ireland	W	2-0	Copenhagen	WCq	Sorensen O 2
15-06	Hungary	W	3-2	Copenhagen	WCq	Sorensen O, Le Fevre, Madsen O
25-06	Sweden	L	0-1	Copenhagen	Fr	
10-09	Finland	W	5-2	Copenhagen	Fr	
21-09	Norway	L	0-2	Oslo	Fr	
15-10	Rep. Ireland	D	1-1	Dublin	WCq	Jensen B
22-10	Hungary	L	0-3	Budapest	WCq	

19-05-1970	Poland	L	0–2	Copenhagen	Fr	
3-06	Finland	D	1–1	Helsinki	Fr	
25-06	Sweden	D	1–1	Gothenburg	Fr	
7-07	Iceland	D	0–0	Reykjavik	Fr	
2-09	Poland	L	0–5	Warsaw	Fr	
21-09	Norway	L	0–1	Copenhagen	Fr	
14-10	Portugal	L	0–1	Copenhagen	ECq	
11-11	Scotland	L	0–1	Glasgow	ECq	
25-11	Belgium	L	0–2	Bruges	ECq	
12-05-1971	Portugal	L	0–5	Oporto	ECq	
26-05	Belgium	L	1–2	Copenhagen	ECq	
9-06	Scotland	W	1–0	Copenhagen	ECq	
20-06	Sweden	L	1–3	Copenhagen	Fr	
30-06	West Germany	L	1–3	Copenhagen	Fr	
8-09	Finland	D	0–0	Copenhagen	Fr	
26-09	Norway	W	4–1	Oslo	Fr	
10-10	Romania	W	2–1	Copenhagen	OGq	
21-05-1972	Romania	W	3–2	Bucharest	OGq	
7-06	Finland	W	3–0	Copenhagen	Fr	Kristensen 2, Bjerre
29-06	Sweden	L	0–2	Malmo	Fr	
3-07	Iceland	W	5–2	Reykjavik	Fr	
4-10	Switzerland	D	1–1	Copenhagen	Fr	Hansen H
18-10	Scotland	L	1–4	Copenhagen	WCq	Laudrup F
15-11	Scotland	L	0–2	Glasgow	WCq	
26-04-1973	Sweden	L	1–2	Copenhagen	Fr	Dahl
2-05	Czechoslovakia	D	1–1	Copenhagen	WCq	Bjornmose
6-06	Czechoslovakia	L	0–6	Prague	WCq	
20-06	Norway	W	1–0	Copenhagen	Fr	
23-09	Norway	W	1–0	Trondheim	Fr	Hansen H
13-10	Hungary	D	2–2	Copenhagen	Fr	Jensen H, Stendahl
21-11	France	L	0–3	Paris	Fr	
6-03-1974	Togo	W	2–0	Lome	Fr	Pettersson 2
10-03	Benin	L	0–2	Cotonou	Fr	
3-06	Sweden	L	0–2	Copenhagen	Fr	
6-06	Finland	D	1–1	Oulu	Fr	Pettersson
3-09	Indonesia	W	9–0	Copenhagen	Fr	Holmstrom 3, Jensen H 3, Nygaard, Simonsen, Sorensen N
25-09	Spain	L	1–2	Copenhagen	ECq	Nygaard
9-10	Iceland	W	2–1	Aalborg	Fr	Lund, Le Fevre
13-10	Rumania	D	0–0	Copenhagen	ECq	
10-05-1975	Rumania	L	1–6	Bucharest	ECq	Dahl
25-06	Finland	W	2–0	Copenhagen	Fr	Bjornmose, OG
3-09	Scotland	L	0–1	Copenhagen	ECq	
25-09	Sweden	D	0–0	Malmo	Fr	
12-10	Spain	L	0–2	Barcelona	ECq	
29-10	Scotland	L	1–3	Glasgow	ECq	Bastrup
4-02-1976	Israel	W	1–0	Tel Aviv	Fr	
11-05	Sweden	W	2–1	Gothenberg	Fr	Bastrup, Bjerg
23-05	Cyprus	W	5–1	Limassol	WCq	Bastrup 2, Simonsen, Hansen T, Rasmussen
24-06	Norway	D	0–0	Bergen	Fr	
25-08	Norway	W	3–0	Copenhagen	Fr	
1-09	France	D	1–1	Copenhagen	Fr	Rontved
22-09	Italy	L	0–1	Copenhagen	Fr	
27-10	Cyprus	W	5–0	Copenhagen	WCq	Jensen H 2, Nielsen, Rontved, Kristensen
17-11	Portugal	L	0–1	Lisbon	WCq	
30-01-1977	Ghana	W	4–1	Banjul	Fr	
2-02	Senegal	W	3–2	Dakar	Fr	
13-04	Bulgaria	L	1–3	Sofia	Fr	Sorensen
1-05	Poland	L	1–2	Copenhagen	WCq	Simonsen
1-06	Norway	W	2–0	Oslo	Fr	Lund, Sorensen
15-06	Sweden	W	2–1	Copenhagen	Fr	Simonsen
22-06	Finland	W	2–1	Helsinki	Fr	Elkjaer 2
21-09	Poland	L	1–4	Chorzow	WCq	Nygaard
5-10	Sweden	L	0–1	Malmo	Fr	
9-10	Portugal	L	2–4	Copenhagen	WCq	Rontved, Hansen A
8-02-1978	Israel	L	0–2	Tel Aviv	Fr	
24-05	Rep. Ireland	D	3–3	Copenhagen	ECq	Jensen H, Nielsen B, Lerby

31–05	Norway	W	2–1	Oslo	Fr	Sorensen J, Larsen
28–06	Iceland	D	0–0	Reykjavik	Fr	
16–08	Sweden	W	2–1	Copenhagen	Fr	Nielsen B, Rontved
20–09	England	L	3–4	Copenhagen	ECq	Simonsen, Arnesen, Rontved
11–10	Bulgaria	D	2–2	Copenhagen	ECq	Nielsen B, Lerby
25–10	Nth. Ireland	L	1–2	Belfast	ECq	Jensen H
2–05–1979	Rep. Ireland	L	0–2	Dublin	ECq	
9–05	Sweden	D	2–2	Copenhagen	Fr	Nielsen B, Lerby
6–06	Nth. Ireland	W	4–0	Copenhagen	ECq	Elkjaer 3, Simonsen
27–06	Soviet Union	L	1–2	Copenhagen	Fr	Andersson T
29–08	Finland	D	0–0	Mikkeli	Fr	
12–09	England	L	0–1	London	ECq	
26–09	Finland	W	1–0	Copenhagen	Fr	Elkjaer
31–10	Bulgaria	L	0–3	Sofia	ECq	
14–11	Spain	W	3–1	Cadiz	Fr	Elkjaer 2, Bethelsen
7–05–1980	Sweden	W	1–0	Gothenberg	Fr	Steffensen
21–05	Spain	D	2–2	Copenhagen	Fr	Simonsen, Bastrup
4–06	Norway	W	3–1	Copenhagen	Fr	Nielsen B, Arnesen, Elkjaer
12–07	Soviet Union	L	0–2	Moscow	Fr	
27–08	Switzerland	D	1–1	Lausanne	Fr	Bastrup
27–09	Yugoslavia	L	1–2	Ljubljana	WCq	Arnesen
15–10	Greece	L	0–1	Copenhagen	WCq	
1–11	Italy	L	0–2	Rome	WCq	
19–11	Luxembourg	W	4–0	Copenhagen	WCq	Arnesen 2, Elkjaer, Simonsen
15–04–1981	Rumania	W	2–1	Copenhagen	Fr	Simonsen, Bastrup
1–05	Luxembourg	W	2–1	Luxembourg	WCq	Elkjaer, Arnesen
14–05	Sweden	W	2–1	Malmo	Fr	Bastrup, Elkjaer
3–06	Italy	W	3–1	Copenhagen	WCq	Rontved, Arnesen, Bastrup
12–08	Finland	W	2–1	Tammerfors	Fr	Madsen Ol, Eigenbrod
26–08	Iceland	W	3–0	Copenhagen	Fr	Simonsen 2, Lundqvist
9–09	Yugoslavia	L	1–2	Copenhagen	WCq	Elkjaer
23–09	Norway	W	2–1	Copenhagen	Fr	Elkjaer, Arnesen
14–10	Greece	W	3–2	Salonika	WCq	Lerby, Arnesen, Elkjaer
5–05–1982	Sweden	D	1–1	Copenhagen	Fr	Arnesen
19–05	Austria	L	0–1	Vienna	Fr	
27–05	Belgium	W	1–0	Copenhagen	Fr	Larsen E
15–06	Norway	L	1–2	Oslo	Fr	Laudrup M
11–08	Finland	W	3–2	Copenhagen	Fr	Bastrup, Lerby, Busk
1–09	Rumania	L	0–1	Bucharest	Fr	
22–09	England	D	2–2	Copenhagen	ECq	Hansen A, Olsen J
27–10	Czechoslovakia	L	1–3	Copenhagen	Fr	Laudrup M
10–11	Luxembourg	W	2–1	Luxembourg	ECq	Lerby, Bergren
27–04–1983	Greece	W	1–0	Copenhagen	ECq	Busk
1–06	Hungary	W	3–1	Copenhagen	ECq	Elkjaer, Olsen J, Simonsen
7–09	France	W	3–1	Copenhagen	Fr	Laudrup M 2, Brylle
21–09	England	W	1–0	London	ECq	Simonsen
12–10	Luxembourg	W	6–0	Copenhagen	ECq	Laudrup M 3, Elkjaer 2, Simonsen
26–10	Hungary	L	0–1	Budapest	ECq	
16–11	Greece	W	2–0	Athens	ECq	Elkjaer, Simonsen
14–03–1984	Holland	L	0–6	Amsterdam	Fr	
2–04	Spain	L	1–2	Valencia	Fr	Eriksen
16–05	Czechoslovakia	L	0–1	Prague	Fr	
6–06	Sweden	W	1–0	Gothenberg	Fr	Elkjaer
8–06	Bulgaria	D	1–1	Copenhagen	Fr	Laudrup M
12–06	France	L	0–1	Paris	ECr1	
16–06	Yugoslavia	W	5–0	Lyon	ECr1	Arnesen 2, Berggreen, Elkjaer, Lauridsen
19–06	Belgium	W	3–2	Strasbourg	ECr1	Arnesen, Brylle, Elkjaer
24–06	Spain	D	1–1 (4–5p)	Lyon	ECsf	Lerby
12–09	Austria	W	3–1	Copenhagen	Fr	Laudrup M, Christensen, Eigenbrod
26–09	Norway	W	1–0	Copenhagen	WCq	Elkjaer
17–10	Switzerland	L	0–1	Berne	WCq	
14–11	Rep. Ireland	W	3–0	Copenhagen	WCq	Elkjaer 2, Lerby
27–01–1985	Honduras	L	0–1	Tegucigalpa	Fr	
8–05	East Germany	W	4–1	Copenhagen	Fr	Laudrup M 2, Lauridsen, Berggreen
5–06	Soviet Union	W	4–2	Copenhagen	WCq	Elkjaer 2, Laudrup M 2
11–09	Sweden	L	0–3	Copenhagen	Fr	

25–09	Soviet Union	L	0–1	Moscow	WCq	
9–10	Switzerland	D	0–0	Copenhagen	WCq	
16–10	Norway	W	5–1	Oslo	WCq	Berggreen 2, Laudrup M, Lerby, Elkjaer
13–11	Rep. Ireland	W	4–1	Dublin	WCq	Elkjaer 2, Laudrup, Sivabaek
26–03–1986	Nth. Ireland	D	1–1	Belfast	Fr	Christensen F
9–04	Bulgaria	L	0–3	Sofia	Fr	
13–05	Norway	L	0–1	Oslo	Fr	
16–05	Poland	W	1–0	Copenhagen	Fr	Elkjaer
20–05	Paraguay	L	1–2	Bogota	Fr	Andersen
4–06	Scotland	W	1–0	Nezahualcoytl	WCr1	Elkjaer
8–06	Uruguay	W	6–1	Nezahualcoytl	WCr1	Elkjaer 3, Lerby, Laudrup M, Olsen J
13–06	West Germany	W	2–0	Queretaro	WCr1	Olsen J, Eriksen
18–06	Spain	L	1–5	Queretaro	WCr2	Olsen J
10–09	East Germany	W	1–0	Leipzig	Fr	Eriksen
24–09	West Germany	L	0–2	Copenhagen	Fr	
29–10	Finland	W	1–0	Copenhagen	ECq	Bertelsen
12–11	Czechoslovakia	D	0–0	Bratislava	ECq	
29–04–1987	Finland	W	1–0	Helsinki	ECq	Molby
3–06	Czechoslovakia	D	1–1	Copenhagen	ECq	Molby
26–08	Sweden	L	0–1	Stockholm	Fr	
9–09	Wales	L	0–1	Cardiff	ECq	
23–09	West Germany	L	0–1	Hamburg	Fr	
14–10	Wales	W	1–0	Copenhagen	ECq	Elkjaer
27–04–1988	Austria	L	0–1	Vienna	Fr	
10–05	Hungary	D	2–2	Budapest	Fr	Frimann, Eriksen
1–06	Czechoslovakia	L	0–1	Copenhagen	Fr	
4–06	Belgium	W	3–1	Odense	Fr	Eriksen 2, Olsen M
11–06	Spain	L	2–3	Hannover	ECr1	Laudrup M, Povlsen
14–06	West Germany	L	0–2	Gelsenkirchen	ECr1	
17–06	Italy	L	0–2	Cologne	ECr1	
31–08	Sweden	W	2–1	Stockholm	Fr	Elstrup 2
14–09	England	L	0–1	London	Fr	
28–09	Iceland	W	1–0	Copenhagen	Fr	Bartram
19–10	Greece	D	1–1	Athens	WCq	Povlsen
2–11	Bulgaria	D	1–1	Copenhagen	WCq	Elstrup
8–02–1989	Malta	W	2–0	Ta'Qali	Fr	Elstrup, Larsen H
10–02	Finland	D	0–0	Ta'Qali	Fr	
12–02	Algeria	D	0–0	Ta'Qali	Fr	
22–02	Italy	L	0–1	Pisa	Fr	
12–04	Canada	W	2–0	Aalborg	Fr	Elstrup, Vilfort
26–04	Bulgaria	W	2–0	Sofia	WCq	Povlsen, Laudrup B
17–05	Greece	W	7–1	Copenhagen	WCq	Laudrup B, Bartram, Nielsen K, Povlsen, Vilfort, Andersen H, Laudrup M
7–06	England	D	1–1	Copenhagen	Fr	Elstrup
14–06	Sweden	W	6–0	Copenhagen	Fr	Elstrup 2, Povlsen, Andersen H, Bartram, Laudrup M
18–06	Brazil	W	4–0	Copenhagen	Fr	Laudrup M 2, Olsen M, Olsen L
24–08	Belgium	L	0–3	Bruges	Fr	
6–09	Holland	D	2–2	Amsterdam	Fr	Bartram, Heintze
11–10	Rumania	W	3–0	Copenhagen	WCq	Nielsen K, Laudrup B, Povlsen
15–11	Rumania	L	1–3	Bucharest	WCq	Povlsen
29–01–1990	Iraq	D	1–1	Baghdad	Fr	
1–02	Iraq	L	0–1	Baghdad	Fr	
5–02	UAE	D	1–1	Dubai	Fr	Larsen J
9–02	UAE	W	5–0	Dubai	Fr	Jakobsen, Larsen J, Svingaard, Risom, Hogh
12–02	Bahrain	W	2–1	Manama	Fr	Jakobsen 2
14–02	Egypt	D	0–0	Cairo	Fr	
11–04	Turkey	W	1–0	Copenhagen	Fr	Jakobsen
15–05	England	L	0–1	London	Fr	
30–05	West Germany	L	0–1	Gelsenkirchen	Fr	
6–06	Norway	W	2–1	Trondheim	Fr	Povlsen, Laudrup M
5–09	Sweden	W	1–0	Vasteras	Fr	Christensen
11–09	Wales	W	1–0	Copenhagen	Fr	Laudrup B
10–10	Faeroe Islands	W	4–1	Copenhagen	ECq	Laudrup M 2, Elstrup, Povlsen
17–10	Nth Ireland	D	1–1	Belfast	ECq	Bartram

LEADING INTERNATIONAL GOALSCORERS	
1 Nielsen P 52	5 Enoksen 29
2 Jorgensen 44	6 Laudrup M 26
3 Madsen 43	7 Rohde 22
4 Elkjaer-Larssen 38	8 Simonsen 21

LEADING INTERNATIONAL APPEARANCES	
1 Olsen M 102	Elkjaer-Larsen 69
2 Sivebaek 82	6 Lerby 67
3 Rontved 75	7 Laudrup M 64
4 Bertelsen 69	8 Jensen H 62

14-11	Yugoslavia	L	0-2	Copenhagen	ECq	
9-04-1991	Bulgaria	D	1-1	Odense	Fr	Hoegh
1-05	Yugoslavia	W	2-1	Belgrade	ECq	Christensen B 2
5-06	Austria	W	2-1	Odense	ECq	Christensen B 2
12-06	Italy	L	0-2	Malmo	Fr	
15-06	Sweden	L	0-4	Norrkoping	Fr	
4-09	Iceland	D	0-0	Reykjavik	Fr	
25-09	Faeroe Islands	W	4-0	Landskrona	ECq	Christofte, Christensen B, Pingel, Vilfort
9-10	Austria	W	3-0	Vienna	ECq	OG, Povlsen, Christensen B
13-11	Nth. Ireland	W	2-1	Odense	ECq	Povlsen 2
8-04-1992	Turkey	L	1-2	Ankara	Fr	Christensen B
29-04	Norway	W	1-0	Aarhus	Fr	Elstrup
3-06	CIS	D	1-1	Copenhagen	Fr	Christensen B
11-06	England	D	0-0	Malmo	ECr1	
14-06	Sweden	L	0-1	Stockholm	ECr1	
17-06	France	W	2-1	Malmo	ECr1	Larsen L, Elstrup
22-06	Holland	D	2-2 (5-4p)	Gothenburg	ECsf	Larsen L 2
26-06	Germany	W	2-0	Gothenburg	ECf	Jensen J, Vilfort

ENGLAND

The playing fields of Eton and the other major Public Schools of 19th century England should have a treasured place in the hearts of the world, for out of these exclusive establishments came the embryonic versions of all the major codes of modern-day football. For many centuries, in different parts of the world, a haphazard and often violent form of 'Foote-balle' had been practised by the population at large, but the Public Schools were the first to adopt binding rules and mark out a definitive area of play.

The rules varied from school to school but in 1848, pupils at Cambridge University, in an attempt to unify these different methods of play, drew up the 'Cambridge Rules'. Based primarily on the dribbling game, these rules formed the basis of those adopted in 1863 by the newly formed Football Association. The historic meeting on 26 October that year marks the birth of Association Football proper. The handling code went its separate way, giving rise to the birth of rugby, and although various regions like Sheffield did not immediately adopt the new rules, the new association gradually became the pre-eminent body in England. Four events of tremendous significance happened before the turn of the century. In 1871 the Football Association launched the Challenge Cup. In 1872 the first international match was played, between England and Scotland. In 1885 professionalism was legalised, whilst in 1888 league football was introduced.

The Football Association Challenge Cup, or FA Cup as it is more commonly known, is the oldest and still the most famous football tournament played in the world. The 'little tin idol', as the Cup itself was called, was instrumental in the development of the game. It brought into focus the issue of professionalism by pitting the 'old schoolboy' amateur sides of the South against the rapidly forming 'works' sides of the industrial North. Football, though initially a pastime of the privileged elite, was fast becoming a major recreation in the drab industrial cities. Factory workers enjoyed both playing and watching the game as a diversion from the harsh realities of 19th century life. The increasingly widespread practice of finishing work at lunchtime on a Saturday left the afternoon free, and many workers used the time to watch football, a tradition that survives to this day in England. By 1880 rumours were rife that many of these Northern sides were paying members of their teams, and as they became more successful in the Cup, the issue of professionalism was brought to a head.

In 1883 Blackburn Olympic beat Old Etonians 2-1 in the final and never again would the amateur sides of the South triumph. In 1884 having just drawn with Preston North End in the fourth round of the Cup, Upton Park protested that Preston were employing professionals. Major Sudell, the architect of the great Preston side of the late 1880s, openly admitted that this was the case but maintained that it was common practice amongst all the northern clubs. Preston were disqualified but a year later, realising that fighting the tide was futile, the Football Association legalised professionalism.

Professionalism, once established, then had a big influence on the next major development in the game, the formation of the Football League in 1888. The regular

		All			League			Cup		Europe			L Cup	
	Team	G	S	B	G	S	B	G	S	G	S	B	G	S
1	Liverpool	33	19	4	18	10	2	5	5	6	2	2	4	2
2	Aston Villa	18	13	2	7	9	2	7	2	1	–	–	3	2
3	Manchester United	17	16	9	7	10	3	7	4	2	–	6	1	2
4	Arsenal	17	13	4	10	3	4	5	6	1	1	–	1	3
5	Tottenham Hotspur	15	7	12	2	4	9	8	1	3	1	3	2	1
6	Everton	14	16	7	9	7	7	4	7	1	–	–	–	2
7	Newcastle United	11	6	2	4	–	2	6	5	1	–	–	–	1
8	Wolverhampton Wanderers	9	10	7	3	5	6	4	4	–	1	1	2	–
9	Manchester City	9	8	4	2	3	3	4	4	1	–	1	2	1
10	Nottingham Forest	9	5	4	1	2	3	2	1	2	–	1	4	2
11	Sunderland	8	8	8	6	5	8	2	2	–	–	–	–	1
12	Sheffield Wednesday	8	3	7	4	1	7	3	2	–	–	–	1	–
13	Blackburn Rovers	8	2	3	2	–	3	6	2	–	–	–	–	–
14	Leeds United	7	11	3	3	5	1	1	3	2	3	2	1	–
15	West Bromwich Albion	7	9	1	1	2	1	5	5	–	–	–	1	2
16	Sheffield United	5	4	–	1	2	–	4	2	–	–	–	–	–
17	The Wanderers	5	–	–	–	–	–	5	–	–	–	–	–	–
18	Preston North End	4	11	2	2	6	2	2	5	–	–	–	–	–
19	Huddersfield Town	4	7	3	3	3	3	1	4	–	–	–	–	–
20	West Ham United	4	4	2	–	–	1	3	1	1	1	1	–	2
21	Chelsea	4	3	4	1	–	3	1	2	1	–	1	1	1
22	Bolton Wanderers	4	3	3	–	–	3	4	3	–	–	–	–	–
23	Derby County	3	6	5	2	3	4	1	3	–	–	1	–	–
24	Burnley	3	4	5	2	2	5	1	2	–	–	–	–	–
25	Ipswich Town	3	2	3	1	2	3	1	–	1	–	–	–	–
26	Portsmouth	3	2	1	2	–	1	1	2	–	–	–	–	–
27	Old Etonians	2	4	–	–	–	–	2	4	–	–	–	–	–
28	Norwich City	2	2	–	–	–	–	–	–	–	–	–	2	2
29	Bury	2	–	–	–	–	–	2	–	–	–	–	–	–
30	Leicester City	1	6	1	–	1	1	–	4	–	–	–	1	1
31	Birmingham City	1	4	1	–	–	–	–	2	–	2	1	1	–
32	Southampton	1	4	–	–	1	–	1	2	–	–	–	–	1
33	Blackpool	1	3	1	–	1	1	1	2	–	–	–	–	–
34	Oxford University	1	3	–	–	–	–	1	3	–	–	–	–	–
	Queens Park Rangers	1	3	–	–	1	–	–	1	–	–	–	1	1
	Royal Engineers	1	3	–	–	–	–	1	3	–	–	–	–	–
37	Cardiff	1	2	1	–	1	–	1	1	–	–	1	–	–
	Charlton Athletic	1	2	1	–	1	1	1	1	–	–	–	–	–
39	Luton Town	1	2	–	–	–	–	–	1	–	–	–	1	1
40	Notts County	1	1	2	–	–	2	1	1	–	–	–	–	–
41	Stoke City	1	1	–	–	–	–	–	–	–	–	–	1	1
	Clapham Rovers	1	1	–	–	–	–	1	1	–	–	–	–	–
	Barnsley	1	1	–	–	–	–	1	1	–	–	–	–	–
44	Swindon Town	1	–	–	–	–	–	–	–	–	–	–	1	–
	Old Carthusians	1	–	–	–	–	–	1	–	–	–	–	–	–
	Coventry City	1	–	–	–	–	–	1	–	–	–	–	–	–
	Oxford United	1	–	–	–	–	–	–	–	–	–	–	1	–
	Blackburn Olympic	1	–	–	–	–	–	1	–	–	–	–	–	–
	Bradford City	1	–	–	–	–	–	1	–	–	–	–	–	–
	Wimbledon	1	–	–	–	–	–	1	–	–	–	–	–	–
51	Watford	–	2	–	–	1	–	–	1	–	–	–	–	–
	Bristol City	–	2	–	–	1	–	–	1	–	–	–	–	–
	Oldham Athletic	–	2	–	–	1	–	–	–	–	–	–	–	1
	Queens Park Glasgow	–	2	–	–	–	–	–	2	–	–	–	–	–
55	Crystal Palace	–	1	1	–	–	–	–	1	–	–	–	–	–
56	Fulham	–	1	–	–	–	–	–	1	–	–	–	–	–
	Brighton & Hove Albion	–	1	–	–	–	–	–	1	–	–	–	–	–
	London Select XI	–	1	–	–	–	–	–	–	–	1	–	–	–
	Rochdale	–	1	–	–	–	–	–	–	–	–	–	–	1
	Rotherham United	–	1	–	–	–	–	–	–	–	–	–	–	1
60	Middlesbrough	–	–	1	–	–	1	–	–	–	–	–	–	–

Correct to the end of the 1991–92 season

payment of players necessitated playing regular fixtures. As the Cup did not afford this, William McGregor of the Aston Villa club proposed, in a letter to interested parties, the arranging of home and away fixtures each season as occurred in cricket. The idea was adopted at a meeting in the Anderton Hotel in Fleet Street on 22 March 1888. All of the 12 clubs involved in the new league were from the North or the Midlands, and not until the 1930s were any teams from the South to feature prominently in either the Cup or the League. Football had found its roots, and they lay mainly in the North.

On Saturday 30 November 1872 at the West of Scotland cricket ground in Glasgow, England met Scotland in the first ever international football match played in the world. It would be another 30 years before any non-British sides took up the idea. By then the annual fixture was equal in importance to any other sporting fixture in the calendar and served as an excellent model for these countries to follow. It also became a means whereby professionals could play alongside their amateur colleagues. After the events of 1885 this was crucial in uniting the game and keeping the Football Association as the ultimate governing body in English football. The first professional to play for England was the Blackburn Rovers half-back James Forrest, against Scotland in 1885, but despite the growing strength of the professional game, amateurs continued to represent England well into the next century.

In 1879 Wales were added to the fixture list as were Ireland in 1882. In 1884 these fixtures were formalised into the British International Championship, and until 1923 this was the basis of England's international programme. It was not until 1908, when the side made a tour of central Europe, that teams from outside Britain were first encountered, although representative English sides had toured Germany in 1896 and 1899, and France in the early years of the 20th century, whilst numerous English club sides had made trips to all four corners of the world in an effort to spread the game. The British Championship however, remained at the pinnacle of world football.

Many fine club sides emerged in these early years, the first being the Wanderers. They won the Cup five times in the first seven years. Their major rivals, the Old Etonians, won twice and were the losing side on four occasions. A leading figure of this time was the redoubtable Lord Kinnaird who appeared in nine of the first twelve finals for both the Wanderers and Old Etonians. His five winners' medals remains a record and he later went on to become president of the Football Association. Two teams emerged to take the limelight away from these Southern amateur sides. First Blackburn Rovers, who themselves won the Cup five times between 1884 and 1891. James Forrest appeared in all five of their triumphs, thus equalling the feat of both Wollaston of the Wanderers and Lord Kinnaird.

Along with Blackburn, Preston reinforced the supremacy of the North. Often labelled 'the Invincibles', Preston revolutionised the game in England. Using the 2–3–5 formation, they recognised the need for a more scientific approach to their play. The team became the most feared in the land and in 1889 they did the coveted League and Cup 'double' without losing a game. Their star player was undoubtedly John Goodall, the outstanding centre-forward of his generation. Soon, however, other teams from the North began to make their presence felt, notably Aston Villa, Sunderland and Newcastle United. Until 1921 only one team from the South managed to win a trophy: Tottenham Hotspur won the Cup in 1901 as a Southern League side.

Before the First World War, many great players helped spread the popularity of the game to the extent that by 1914 it had become the national sport. Crowds of over 100 000 had watched the Cup Final, whilst even in the South the professional teams of the Southern League gained in popularity. Chief among these great players, curiously, was an amateur, GO Smith. He played for the last great amateur side, the Corinthians, and won 20 caps for England at a time when only three internationals were played every season. Steve Bloomer of Derby County, Billy Bassett of West Brom, Ernest Needham of Sheffield United and Vivian Woodward, an amateur with Tottenham, also stand out as the great pre-war players, the latter leading England to two Olympic gold medals in 1908 and 1912. Woodward was also the star of England's first official foreign tour in 1908 and again the next year. He scored 15 goals in the seven matches against Austria, Hungary and Bohemia.

Along with Scotland, there can be no doubt that England were a class above the rest of the football world during this period. Huge victories over Ireland (13–2 in 1899), Austria (11–1 in 1908), France (15–0, 12–0, 11–0 and 10–1 between 1906 and 1910) and Germany (9–0 in 1909) confirm this fact, though the victories against the last two are not recorded as official games. The rivalry with Scotland, however, was a different matter, with the honours evenly shared. The Scots played an enormous part in the development of the game in England. Most notably they were responsible for the adoption of the passing game, which gradually took over from the dribbling game as the norm. This happened due to the large numbers of Scots who came to play their football south of the border. Successful teams such as Sunderland in the 1890s relied heavily on their contribution as did teams like Preston. Even William McGregor, the father of the Football League, originally hailed from north of the border.

When football resumed after the break caused by the war, it seemed as though things were back to normal. England and the rest of the Home Unions were, however, beginning on a course of gradual isolation. The world was taking up football with a passion, and becoming rather good at it. The Football Association had joined FIFA in 1905, but had always adopted a rather paternal attitude towards it. They withdrew in 1920 because they refused to fraternise with their wartime adversaries, and having rejoined in 1924 they withdrew again in 1928 over the definition of the word 'amateur' in relation to the Olympic Games. This action meant that England could not compete in any of the first three World Cups which were played during the inter-war period. Even if they had been members of FIFA it is doubtful that would have deigned to compete anyway. Judging by the interest shown in the English newspapers at the time of these tournaments, most Englishmen cannot have even been aware that they were being played.

The consequences of this self-imposed 'splendid isolation' did not immediately become apparent. England's first defeat against foreign opposition did not come until they were beaten by Spain in 1929 in Madrid. Defeats by France in 1930, Hungary and Czechoslovakia in 1934, Austria and Belgium in 1936, Switzerland in 1938 and Yugoslavia in 1939, all away from home, did little to dent England's self–belief, but the cracks were beginning to appear. Even the 4–3 victory over the Austrian 'Wunderteam' at Chelsea in 1932 only disguised the fact that the Austrians were the better team. Most Englishmen assume that they would have won the three World Cups of the 1930s, but even Vittorio Pozzo, the Italian manager and a great admirer of English football, stated that away from England, the English would have been lucky to have reached the quarter-finals of either the 1934 or 1938 tournaments.

The English League, however, continued to be strong between the wars. It produced two sides of outstanding quality, Huddersfield Town in the 1920s and Arsenal in the 1930s. Both won the League three years in succession, and both had a common guiding force, Herbert Chapman. He was a revolutionary figure, the first modern-day manager. He had an astute tactical brain with which he devised methods of play and then bought players who would fit into this system. Along with Charlie Buchan, his skilful centre-forward at Arsenal, he introduced the 'third-back game' following the change in the offside law in 1925. To counter the increased number of goals being scored as a result of this change, he pulled the centre–half back into the role of a stopper as well as introducing a deep-lying centre-forward, both of whose roles would be to initiate effective counter attacks. Arsenal played this system to great effect, the key player being Alex James. It often seemed that Arsenal were under pressure for most of a match but a key pass from James, deep in defence, regularly brought goals on the counter. Arsenal always had an excellent forward line with players like Ted Drake, Cliff Bastin and David Jack, along with Buchan, playing for them in the 1930s. Their five League Championships and two Cup wins are testament to the skills of Herbert Chapman, though he did not live to see all of his team's triumphs.

The inter-war period also produced many other great players. Dixie Dean achieved fame for his 60 goals for Everton during the 1928 season, and his scoring record of 379 goals in 437 league matches bears few comparisons. George Camsell of Middlesbrough and Raich Carter of Sunderland were both prolific scorers whilst Eddie Hapgood was a key man in defence for both Arsenal and England. The inter-war years also produced the greatest star of them all, Stanley Matthews. His career spanned the Second World War, after which his fame grew to even greater heights.

Football did not cease during the war. It was thought to be a good diversion during troubled times, though none of the international or domestic results are counted as official. The interest shown in the game directly after the war has never been surpassed. Huge crowds turned out every week, but what they were witnessing was a decline that had set in before the war, especially with regard to the national side. Again, however, results disguised the true state of the game. A 4–0 win over the World Cup holders Italy in Turin was hailed as a world-beating performance, as was the 10–0 victory over Portugal in Lisbon the year previously. The 1950 World Cup in Brazil did little to bring the team down to earth. Defeats by America and Spain were dismissed as flukes and it was not until one famous Wednesday afternoon in November 1953 that the English team realised that tactically they were stale, the state of coaching in the country was poor and that technically players from elsewhere were superior to them. The 6–3 victory by Hungary that day, the first by a foreign team on English soil, had far-reaching repercussions. Slowly the English began to learn from the experience, to adapt foreign methods and styles to the English game. This defeat and those that followed in the 1954, 1958, and 1962 World Cups paved the way for their triumph in the 1966 competition, by forcing the English team to find out where the faults lay and what their strengths were.

England was not devoid of talent in these post-war years. Stanley Matthews seemed to get better with age and there were players such as Tom Finney of Preston, Billy Wright of Wolves and Nat Lofthouse of Bolton all of whom were excellent players. Stan Cullis, the Wolves manager, built a successful team based more on hard work and rudimentary tactics than on skill, but one which dominated the league in the 1950s and achieved notable victories in friendly matches against Honved and Spartak Moscow. One team, however, paved the way for the English revival. Matt Busby, a former Scottish international, created the Manchester United legend. In his time at the club he moulded together four excellent sides, the greatest of which was possibly the 'Busby Babes' team. Spearheaded by Duncan Edwards, the boy genius, they seemed destined to become as fine a team as the famous Real Madrid who were dominating the European Cup in the latter half of the 1950s. Tragically, however, the team was wiped out by an air crash at Munich airport on their way back to England from a European Cup tie in February 1958. Duncan Edwards, Roger Byrne and Tommy Taylor, all established England internationals, perished in the disaster. One survivor who formed the link with the next great Manchester United team was Bobby Charlton. He also played a crucial role in England's re-emergence as a world power in the 1960s, playing alongside the likes of Jimmy Greaves, Gordon Banks, Bobby Moore and Martin Peters. Charlton and the rest of the England team, ably managed by the dour Alf Ramsey, won the World Cup at home in 1966.

England's victory formed the basis from which the game, especially at club level, developed. Manchester United's victory in the 1968 European Cup was not the first win by an English club in a European competition – Tottenham and West Ham had won the Cup Winners Cup in 1963 and 1965 respectively – but it fired a warning shot that the game in England was in a healthy state and that the World Cup victory was no fluke. For the next 17 years, clubs from England dominated the European scene. From 1977 until 1984 three different English teams won the European Cup in seven of the eight seasons. The UEFA Cup was won six years in succession, by five different clubs, between 1968 and 1974. The strength in depth of the Football League could not be matched by any other European nation. A very English style of game had emerged that was quick and penetrative and best epitomised by first Leeds United and then Liverpool. Between them they won nine European finals and appeared in 13.

This astounding success can partially be traced back to 1963, when the maximum wage limit imposed on English players was removed. It allowed the top clubs to sign and pay handsomely all the top players in the country. A league of superclubs began to emerge. Up until 1963 the championship and the Cup had been open affairs, and anybody had a chance to win. This allowed small clubs like Burnley to win the League as late as 1960. But by the late 1960s Liverpool, Everton, Manchester United, Arsenal, Leeds and Tottenham came to dominate the domestic scene. By the end of the 1980s Liverpool had become pre-eminent. A single statistic sums up their stunning success. Since 1973 they have finished outside of the top two in the league on only two occasions, a miserable fifth in 1980 and sixth in 1992. During this time they won the championship an incredible 10 times.

Achievement at club level did not, however, translate itself into success at international level. Third place in the European Championship in 1968 and fourth place in the 1990 World Cup have been the only achievements of note since the World Cup victory in 1966. An unlucky defeat in the quarter-finals of the 1970 World Cup in Mexico, with what many rate as a better team than the 1966 side, proved to be the beginning of a traumatic time for the national side as England failed to qualify for both the 1974 and 1978 World Cup Finals. In the 1974 tournament they fell victim to an impressive Polish side who would later finish in third place. In the final game of the qualifying tournament, with a single goal victory over Poland needed, England did everything but score the decisive goal needed, much to the disappointment of the Wembley crowd. Four years later it was Italy who qualified on goal difference at the expense of England, though quite what England and Italy were doing in the same group with only one possible qualifier has never been understood. The irony of the situation was that England's side in the 1970s, though not world beaters, was never a bad one. Players such as Colin Bell, Tony Currie, Mike Channon and Kevin Keegan deserved to have their talents displayed on a World Cup stage.

By the 1980s the team had settled down and were unlucky not to progress further than they did in the 1982 World Cup, as was the case in 1986 when Maradona's 'Hand of God' sealed their fate in the quarter-finals. However, the events at the Heysel stadium in Brussels during the 1985 European Cup final between Liverpool and Juventus, where 39 Italians fans died as a result of hooliganism, left English clubs banned from European competition and isolated, and their consequent lack of European experience inevitably had its effect on the national side as the disastrous performance in the finals of the 1988 European Championship showed. Indeed the game as a whole was seriously tarnished by a series of tragedies and continued hooliganism. In May 1985, 45 people lost their lives in a fire at Bradford City Football Club, whilst in April 1989 95 fans were crushed at Hillsborough in Sheffield at the FA Cup semi-final between Liverpool and Nottingham Forest.

Football is slowly coming to terms with the problem and a recent cash award of £100 million by the government has set the restructuring on its path. As the home of football, it is no less than game in England deserves.

Population: 47254000
Area, sq km: 130439
% in urban areas: 91.5%
Capital city: London

The Football Association
16 Lancaster Gate
London, W2 3LW
England
Tel: (010 44) 71 2624542
Fax: (010 44) 71 4020486
Telex: 261110 FALONG
Cable: FOOTBALL ASSOCIATION LONDON W2
Languages for correspondence: English, French, German, Spanish

Year of formation: 1863
Affiliation to FIFA: 1905–1920, 1924–28, 1946
Affiliation to UEFA: 1954
Registered clubs: 41 750
Registered players: 3 258 000
Professional Players: 5000
Registered coaches: 41 600
Registered referees: 30 000
National stadium: Empire Stadium, Wembley, London 80 000
National colours: Shirts: White/Shorts: Blue/Socks: White
Reserve colours: Shirts: Red/Shorts: White/Socks: Red
Season: August–May

THE RECORD

WORLD CUP

1930–38 ..... Did not enter
1950 .... QT 1st/4 in group 1 – Final Tournament/1st round
1954 .... QT 1st/4 in group 3 – Final Tournament/Quarter-finalists
1958 .... QT 1st/3 in group 1 – Final Tournament/1st round
1962 .... QT 1st/3 in group 6 – Final Tournament/Quarter-finalists
1966 .... QT Automatic – Final Tournament/Winners
1970 .... QT Automatic – Final Tournament/Quarter-finalists
1974 .... QT 2nd/3 in group 5
1978 .... QT 2nd/4 in group 2
1982 .... QT 2nd/5 in group 4 – Final Tournament/2nd round
1986 .... QT 1st/5 in group 3 – Final Tournament/Quarter-finalists
1990 .... QT 2nd/4 in group 2 – Final Tournament/Semi-finalists/4th place

EUROPEAN CHAMPIONSHIP

1960 .... Did not enter
1964 .... 1st round
1968 .... QT 1st/4 in group 8 – Final Tournament/Semi-finalists/3rd place
1972 .... QT 1st/4 in group 3 – Final Tournament/Quarter-finalists
1976 .... QT 2nd/4 in group 1
1980 .... QT 1st/5 in group 1 – Final Tournament/1st round
1984 .... QT 2nd/5 in group 3
1988 .... QT 1st/4 in group 4 – Final Tournament/1st round
1992 .... QT 1st/4 in group 7 – Final Tournament/1st round

OLYMPIC GAMES

1908 .... Winners
1912 .... Winners
1920 .... 1st round
1924 .... Did not enter
1928 .... Did not enter
1936 .... Quarter–finalists
1948 .... Semi–finalists/4th place
1952 .... Preliminary round
1956 .... Final Tournament/1st round
1960 .... Final Tournament/1st round
1964 .... QT Failed to qualify
1968 .... QT Failed to qualify
1972 .... QT Failed to qualify
1976–92 ..... Did not enter
From 1936 the participating team was a Great Britain XI

EUROPEAN CLUB COMPETITIONS

EUROPEAN CUP: Winners – Manchester United 1968, Liverpool 1977 1978 1981 1984, Nottingham Forest 1979 1980, Aston Villa 1982
Finalists – Leeds United 1975, Liverpool 1985
CUP WINNERS CUP: Winners – Tottenham Hotspur 1963, West Ham United 1965, Manchester City 1970, Chelsea 1971, Everton 1985, Manchester United 1991
Finalists – Liverpool 1966, Leeds United 1973, West Ham United 1976, Arsenal 1980
UEFA CUP: Winners – Leeds United 1968 1971, Newcastle United 1969, Arsenal 1970, Tottenham Hotspur 1972 1984, Liverpool 1973 1976, Ipswich Town 1981
Finalists – Birmingham City 1960 1961, Leeds United 1967, Wolverhampton Wanderers 1972, Tottenham Hotspur 1974

CLUB DIRECTORY

LONDON (Population – 11 100 000)

Arsenal Football Club
Stadium: Highbury 42 000
Founded: 1886
Colours: Red with white sleeves/White
Previous names: Dial Square 1886, Royal Arsenal 1886–92, Woolwich Arsenal 1892–1913

Brentford Football Club
Stadium: Griffin Park 12 000
Founded: 1889
Colours: Red and white stripes/Black

Charlton Athletic Footbal Club
Stadium: The Valley 12 000
Founded: 1905
Colours: Red/White

Chelsea Football Club
Stadium: Stamford Bridge 35 000
Founded: 1905
Colours: Blue/Blue

Crystal Palace Football Club
Stadium: Selhurst Park 30 000
Founded: 1905
Colours: Red and blue stripes/Red

Fulham Football Club
Stadium: Craven Cottage 20 000
Founded: 1879
Colours: White/Black
Previous name: Fulham St Andrew's 1879–98

Leyton Orient Football Club
Stadium: Brisbane Road 18 000
Founded: 1881
Colours: Red/Red
Previous names: Glyn Cricket and Football Club 1881–86, Eagle FC 1886–88, Orient FC 1888–98 and 1966–87, Clapton Orient FC 1898–1946, Leyton Orient FC 1946–66, Orient 1966–87

Millwall Football Club
Stadium: The Den 18 000
Founded: 1885
Colours: Blue/White
Previous names: Millwall Rovers 1885, Millwall Athletic 1889

Queen's Park Rangers Football Club
Stadium: Loftus Road 23 000
Founded: 1885
Colours: Blue and white hoops/White

Tottenham Hotspur
Stadium: White Hart Lane 35 000
Founded: 1882
Colours: White/Black
Previous name: Hotspur FC 1882–85

Watford Football Club
Stadium: Vicarage Road 24 000
Founded: 1891
Colours: Yellow/Black

West Ham United Football Club
Stadium: Upton Park 29 000
Founded: 1895
Colours: Claret with blue sleeves/White
Previous name: Thames Ironworks 1895–1900

Wimbledon Football Club
Stadium: Selhurst Park 30 000
Founded: 1889
Colours: Blue/Blue
Previous name: Wimbledon Old Centrals 1889–1905

MANCHESTER (Population – 2 775 000)

Manchester City Football Club
Stadium: Maine Road 44 000
Founded: 1887
Colours: Sky blue/White
Previous name: Ardwick FC 1887–94

Manchester United Football Club
Stadium: Old Trafford 47 000
Founded: 1878
Colours: Red/White
Previous name: Newton Heath FC 1880–92

Oldham Athletic Association Football Club
Stadium: Boundary Park 17 000
Founded: 1894
Colours: Blue/Blue
Previous name: Pine Villa 1894

Bolton Wanderers Football Club
Stadium: Burnden Park 25 000
Founded: 1874
Colours: White/Blue
Previous name: Christ Church FC 1874–77

Bury Football Club
Stadium: Gigg Lane 8000
Founded: 1885
Colours: White/Blue

BIRMINGHAM (Population – 2 675 000)

Aston Villa Football Club
Stadium: Villa Park 41 000
Founded: 1874
Colours: Claret with blue sleeves/White

Birmingham City Football Club
Stadium: St Andrews 28 000
Founded: 1875
Colours: Blue/White
Previous names: Small Heath Alliance 1875–88, Small Heath 1888–1905, Birmingham FC 1905–45

West Bromwich Albion Football Club
Stadium: The Hawthorns 31 000
Founded: 1879
Colours: Blue and white stripes/Blue

Wolverhampton Wanderers Football Club
Stadium: Molineux 25 000
Founded: 1877
Colours: Gold/Black

LEEDS (Population – 1 540 000)

Bradford City Football Club
Stadium: Valley Parade 15 000
Founded: 1903
Colours: Claret and amber stripes/Black

Bradford Park Avenue
Stadium: Park Avenue
Founded: 1907
Colours: Red, Amber and black hoops/Black
Dissolved in 1974

Leeds United Association Football Club
Stadium: Elland Road 32 000
Founded: 1904
Colours: White/White
Previous name: Leeds City 1904–19

LIVERPOOL (Population – 1 525 000)

Everton Football Club
Stadium: Goodison Park 38 000
Founded: 1878
Colours: Blue/White

Liverpool Football Club
Stadium: Anfield 39 000
Founded: 1892
Colours: Red/Red

NEWCASTLE UPON TYNE (Population – 1 300 000)

Newcastle United Football Club
Stadium: St James' Park 33 000
Founded: 1882
Colours: Black and white stripes/Black

Sunderland Association Football Club
Stadium: Roker Park 31 000
Founded: 1879
Colours: Red and white stripes/Black

SHEFFIELD (Population – 710 000)

Sheffield United Football Club
Stadium: Bramall Lane 32 000
Founded: 1889
Colours: Red and white stripes/Black

Sheffield Wednesday Football Club
Stadium: Hillsborough 38 000
Founded: 1867
Colours: Blue and white stripes/White

NOTTINGHAM (Population – 655 000)

Nottingham Forest Football Club
Stadium: City Ground 31 000
Founded: 1865
Colours: Red/White

Notts County Football Club
Stadium: Meadow Lane 20 000
Founded: 1862 (The oldest club in the world)
Colours: Black and white stripes/Black

COVENTRY (Population – 645 000)
Coventry City Football Club
Stadium: Highfield Road 25 000
Founded: 1883
Colours: Sky blue and white stripes/White

BRISTOL (Population – 630 000)
Bristol City Football Club

Stadium: Ashton Gate 25 000
Founded: 1894
Colours: Red/White

MIDDLESBROUGH (Population – 580 000)
Middlesbrough Football Club
Stadium: Ayresome Park 26 000
Founded: 1876
Colours: Red/White

LEICESTER (Population – 495 000)
Leicester City Football Club
Stadium: Filbert Street 27 000
Founded: 1884
Colours: Blue/White
Previous name: Leicester Fosse 1884–1919

PORTSMOUTH (Population – 485 000)
Portsmouth Football Club
Stadium: Fratton Park 26 000
Founded: 1898
Colours: Blue/White

STOKE-ON-TRENT (Population – 440 000)
Stoke City Football Club
Stadium: Victoria Ground 25 000
Founded: 1863
Colours: Red and white stripes/White

BRIGHTON (Population – 420 000)
Brighton and Hove Albion Football Club
Stadium: Goldstone Ground 18 000
Founded: 1900
Colours: Blue and white stripes/Blue

SOUTHAMPTON (Population – 415 000)
Southampton Football Club
Stadium: The Dell 20 000
Founded: 1885
Colours: Red and white stripes/Black
Previous name: Southampton St Mary's 1885–97

HUDDERSFIELD (Population 377 000)
Huddersfield Town Association Football Club
Stadium: Leeds Road 15000
Founded: 1908
Colours: Blue and white stripes/White

BLACKPOOL (Population – 280 000)
Blackpool Football Club
Stadium: Bloomfield Road 9500
Founded: 1887
Colours: Orange/Orange

DERBY (Population – 275 000)
Derby County Football Club
Stadium: Baseball Ground 24 000
Founded: 1884
Colours: White/Black

PRESTON (Population 250 000)
Preston North End Football Club
Stadium: Deepdale 15 000
Founded: 1881
Colours: White/White

NORWICH (Population – 230 000)
Norwich City Football Club
Stadium: Carrow Road 24 000
Founded: 1905
Colours: Yellow/Green

OXFORD (Population – 230 000)
Oxford United Football Club
Stadium: Manor Ground 11 000
Founded: 1893
Colours: Yellow/Blue
Previous name: Headington United 1893–1960

BLACKBURN (Population – 221 000)
Blackburn Rovers Football Club
Stadium: Ewood Park 19 500
Founded: 1875
Colours: Blue and white halves/White

LUTON (Population – 220 000)
Luton Town Football Club
Stadium: Kenilworth Road 14 000
Founded: 1885
Colours: White/Blue

BURNLEY (Population – 160 000)
Burnley Football Club
Stadium: Turf Moor 20 000 Founded: 1882
Colours: Claret with blue sleeves/White

NORTHAMPTON (Population – 154 000)
Northampton Town Football Club
Stadium: County Ground 10 000
Founded: 1897
Colours: Claret/White

GRIMSBY (Population – 145 000)
Grimsby Town Football Club
Stadium: Blundell Park 18 000
Founded: 1878
Colours: Black and white stripes/Black

IPSWICH (Population – 129 000)
Ipswich Town Football Club
Stadium: Portman Road 27 000
Founded: 1878 Colours: Blue/White

CARLISLE (Population – 72 000)
Carlisle United Football Club
Stadium: Brunton Park 16 000
Founded: 1904
Colours: Blue/Blue

ACCRINGTON (Population – 36 000)
Accrington Stanley Football Club
Stadium: Peel Park
Founded: 1872 Colours: Red/Red
Previous name: Accrington FC 1872–1968

DARWEN (Population – 30 000)
Darwen Football Club
Stadium: Anchor Ground
Founded: 1875
Colours: Maroon/Blue

GLOSSOP (Population – 29 000)
Glossop North End
Stadium: Surrey Street
Founded: 1886
Colours: Blue/Blue

Other major towns never represented by a first division side: Hull 350 000, Bournemouth 315 000, Plymouth 290 000, Reading 200 000, Mansfield 198 000.

ENGLISH LEAGUE CHAMPIONSHIP

Year	Champions		Runners up		3rd	
1889	Preston North End	40	Aston Villa	29	Wolverhampton Wand.	28
1890	Preston North End	33	Everton	31	Blackburn Rovers	27
1891	Everton	29	Preston North End	27	Notts County	26
1892	Sunderland	42	Preston North End	37	Bolton Wanderers	36
1893	Sunderland	48	Preston North End	37	Everton	36
1894	Aston Villa	44	Sunderland	38	Derby County	36
1895	Sunderland	47	Everton	42	Aston Villa	39
1896	Aston Villa	45	Derby County	41	Everton	39
1897	Aston Villa	47	Sheffield United	36	Derby County	36
1898	Sheffield United	42	Sunderland	37	Wolverhampton Wand.	35
1899	Aston Villa	45	Liverpool	43	Burnley	39
1900	Aston Villa	50	Sheffield United	48	Sunderland	41
1901	Liverpool	45	Sunderland	43	Notts County	40
1902	Sunderland	44	Everton	41	Newcastle United	37

1903	Sheffield Wednesday	42	Aston Villa	41	Sunderland	41
1904	Sheffield Wednesday	47	Manchester City	44	Everton	43
1905	Newcastle United	48	Everton	47	Manchester City	46
1906	Liverpool	51	Preston North End	47	Sheffield Wednesday	44
1907	Newcastle United	51	Bristol City	48	Everton	45
1908	Manchester United	52	Aston Villa	43	Manchester City	43
1909	Newcastle United	53	Everton	46	Sunderland	44
1910	Aston Villa	53	Liverpool	48	Blackburn Rovers	45
1911	Manchester United	52	Aston Villa	51	Sunderland	45
1912	Blackburn Rovers	49	Everton	46	Newcastle United	44
1913	Sunderland	54	Aston Villa	50	Sheffield Wednesday	49
1914	Blackburn Rovers	51	Aston Villa	44	Middlesbrough	43
1915	Everton	46	Oldham Athletic	45	Blackburn Rovers	43
1916–19 –						
1920	West Bromwich Albion	60	Burnley	51	Chelsea	49
1921	Burnley	59	Manchester City	54	Bolton Wanderers	52
1922	Liverpool	57	Tottenham Hotspur	51	Burnley	49
1923	Liverpool	60	Sunderland	54	Huddersfield Town	53
1924	Huddersfield Town	57	Cardiff City	57	Sunderland	53
1925	Huddersfield Town	58	West Bromwich Albion	56	Bolton Wanderers	55
1926	Huddersfield Town	57	Arsenal	52	Sunderland	48
1927	Newcastle United	56	Huddersfield Town	51	Sunderland	49
1928	Everton	53	Huddersfield Town	51	Leicester City	48
1929	Sheffield Wednesday	52	Leicester City	51	Aston Villa	50
1930	Sheffield Wednesday	60	Derby County	50	Manchester City	47
1931	Arsenal	66	Aston Villa	59	Sheffield Wednesday	52
1932	Everton	56	Arsenal	54	Sheffield Wednesday	50
1933	Arsenal	58	Aston Villa	54	Sheffield Wednesday	51
1934	Arsenal	59	Huddersfield Town	56	Tottenham Hotspur	49
1935	Arsenal	58	Sunderland	54	Sheffield Wednesday	49
1936	Sunderland	56	Derby County	48	Huddersfield Town	48
1937	Manchester City	57	Charlton Athletic	54	Arsenal	52
1938	Arsenal	52	Wolverhampton Wand.	51	Preston North End	49
1939	Everton	59	Wolverhampton Wand.	55	Charlton Athletic	50
1940–46 –						
1947	Liverpool	57	Manchester United	56	Wolverhampton Wand.	56
1948	Arsenal	59	Manchester United	52	Burnley	52
1949	Portsmouth	58	Manchester United	53	Derby County	53
1950	Portsmouth	53	Wolverhampton Wand.	53	Sunderland	52
1951	Tottenham Hotspur	60	Manchester United	56	Blackpool	50
1952	Manchester United	57	Tottenham Hotspur	53	Arsenal	53
1953	Arsenal	54	Preston North End	54	Wolverhampton Wand.	51
1954	Wolverhampton Wand.	57	West Bromwich Albion	53	Huddersfield Town	51
1955	Chelsea	52	Wolverhampton Wand.	48	Portsmouth	48
1956	Manchester United	60	Blackpool	49	Wolverhampton Wand.	49
1957	Manchester United	64	Tottenham Hotspur	56	Preston North End	56
1958	Wolverhampton Wand.	64	Preston North End	59	Tottenham Hotspur	51
1959	Wolverhampton Wand.	61	Manchester United	55	Arsenal	50
1960	Burnley	55	Wolverhampton Wand.	54	Tottenham Hotspur	53
1961	Tottenham Hotspur	66	Sheffield Wednesday	58	Wolverhampton Wand.	57
1962	Ipswich Town	56	Burnley	53	Tottenham Hotspur	52
1963	Everton	61	Tottenham Hotspur	55	Burnley	54
1964	Liverpool	57	Manchester United	53	Everton	52
1965	Manchester United	61	Leeds United	61	Chelsea	56
1966	Liverpool	61	Leeds United	55	Burnley	55
1967	Manchester United	60	Nottingham Forest	56	Tottenham Hotspur	56
1968	Manchester City	58	Manchester United	56	Liverpool	55
1969	Leeds United	67	Liverpool	61	Everton	57
1970	Everton	66	Leeds United	57	Chelsea	55
1971	Arsenal	65	Leeds United	64	Tottenham Hotspur	52
1972	Derby County	58	Leeds United	57	Liverpool	57
1973	Liverpool	60	Arsenal	57	Leeds United	53
1974	Leeds United	62	Liverpool	57	Derby County	48
1975	Derby County	53	Liverpool	51	Ipswich Town	51
1976	Liverpool	60	Queens Park Rangers	59	Manchester United	56
1977	Liverpool	57	Manchester City	56	Ipswich Town	52
1978	Nottingham Forest	64	Liverpool	57	Everton	55
1979	Liverpool	68	Nottingham Forest	60	West Bromwich Albion	59
1980	Liverpool	60	Manchester United	58	Ipswich Town	53

1981	Aston Villa	60	Ipswich Town	56	Arsenal	53
1982	Liverpool	87	Ipswich Town	83	Manchester United	78
1983	Liverpool	82	Watford	71	Manchester United	70
1984	Liverpool	80	Southampton	77	Nottingham Forest	74
1985	Everton	90	Liverpool	77	Tottenham Hotspur	77
1986	Liverpool	88	Everton	86	West Ham United	84
1987	Everton	86	Liverpool	77	Tottenham Hotspur	71
1988	Liverpool	90	Manchester United	81	Nottingham Forest	73
1989	Arsenal	76	Liverpool	76	Nottingham Forest	64
1990	Liverpool	79	Aston Villa	70	Tottenham Hotspur	63
1991	Arsenal	83	Liverpool	76	Crystal Palace	69
1992	Leeds United	82	Manchester United	78	Sheffield Wednesday	75

ENGLISH CUP FINALS

Year	Winners	Score	Runners-up
1872	Wanderers	1–0	Royal Engineers
1873	Wanderers	2–0	Oxford University
1874	Oxford University	2–0	Royal Engineers
1875	Royal Engineers	1–1 2–0	Old Etonians
1876	Wanderers	1–1 3–0	Old Etonians
1877	Wanderers	2–1	Oxford University
1878	Wanderers	3–1	Royal Engineers
1879	Old Etonians	1–0	Clapham Rovers
1880	Clapham Rovers	1–0	Oxford University
1881	Old Carthusians	3–0	Old Etonians
1882	Old Etonians	1–0	Blackburn Rovers
1883	Blackburn Olympic	2–1	Old Etonians
1884	Blackburn Rovers	2–1	Queen's Park Glasgow
1885	Blackburn Rovers	2–0	Queen's Park Glasgow
1886	Blackburn Rovers	0–0 2–0	West Bromwich Albion
1887	Aston Villa	2–0	West Bromwich Albion
1888	West Bromwich Albion	2–1	Preston North End
1889	Preston North End	3–0	Wolverhampton Wanderers
1890	Blackburn Rovers	6–1	Sheffield Wednesday
1891	Blackburn Rovers	3–1	Notts County
1892	West Bromwich Albion	3–0	Aston Villa
1893	Wolverhampton Wand.	1–0	Everton
1894	Notts County	4–1	Bolton Wanderers
1895	Aston Villa	1–0	West Bromwich Albion
1896	Sheffield Wednesday	2–1	Wolverhampton Wanderers
1897	Aston Villa	3–2	Everton
1898	Nottingham Forest	3–1	Derby County
1899	Sheffield United	4–1	Derby County
1900	Bury	4–0	Southampton
1901	Tottenham Hotspur	2–2 3–1	Sheffield United
1902	Sheffield United	1–1 2–1	Southampton
1903	Bury	6–0	Derby County
1904	Manchester City	1–0	Bolton Wanderers
1905	Aston Villa	2–0	Newcastle United
1906	Everton	1–0	Newcastle United
1907	Sheffield Wednesday	2–1	Everton
1908	Wolverhampton Wand.	3–1	Newcastle United
1909	Manchester United	1–0	Bristol City
1910	Newcastle United	1–1 2–0	Barnsley
1911	Bradford City	0–0 1–0	Newcastle United
1912	Barnsley	0–0 1–0	West Bromwich Albion
1913	Aston Villa	0–0 1–0	Sunderland
1914	Burnley	1–0	Liverpool
1915	Sheffield United	3–0	Chelsea
1916–19 –			
1920	Aston Villa	1–0	Huddersfield Town
1921	Tottenham Hotspur	1–0	Wolverhampton Wanderers
1922	Huddersfield Town	1–0	Preston North End
1923	Bolton Wanderers	2–0	West Ham United
1924	Newcastle United	2–0	Aston Villa
1925	Sheffield United	1–0	Cardiff City
1926	Bolton Wanderers	1–0	Manchester City
1927	Cardiff City	1–0	Arsenal
1928	Blackburn Rovers	3–1	Huddersfield Town
1929	Bolton Wanderers	2–0	Portsmouth
1930	Arsenal	2–0	Huddersfield Town
1931	West Bromwich Albion	2–1	Birmingham City
1932	Newcastle United	2–1	Arsenal
1933	Everton	3–0	Manchester City
1934	Manchester City	2–1	Portsmouth
1935	Sheffield Wednesday	4–2	West Bromwich Albion
1936	Arsenal	1–0	Sheffield United
1937	Sunderland	3–1	Preston North End
1938	Preston North End	1–0	Huddersfield Town
1939	Portsmouth	4–1	Wolverhampton Wanderers
1940–1945 –			
1946	Derby County	4–1	Charlton Athletic
1947	Charlton Athletic	1–0	Burnley
1948	Manchester United	4–2	Blackpool
1949	Wolverhampton Wand.	3–1	Leicester City
1950	Arsenal	2–0	Liverpool
1951	Newcastle United	2–0	Blackpool
1952	Newcastle United	1–0	Arsenal
1953	Blackpool	4–3	Bolton Wanderers
1954	West Bromwich Albion	3–2	Preston North End
1955	Newcastle United	3–1	Manchester City
1956	Manchester City	3–1	Birmingham City
1957	Aston Villa	2–1	Manchester United
1958	Bolton Wanderers	2–0	Manchester United
1959	Nottingham Forest	2–1	Luton Town
1960	Wolverhampton Wand.	3–0	Blackburn Rovers
1961	Tottenham Hotspur	2–0	Leicester City
1962	Tottenham Hotspur	3–1	Burnley
1963	Manchester United	3–1	Leicester City
1964	West Ham United	3–2	Preston North End
1965	Liverpool	2–1	Leeds United
1966	Everton	3–2	Sheffield Wednesday
1967	Tottenham Hotspur	2–1	Chelsea
1968	West Bromwich Albion	1–0	Everton
1969	Manchester City	1–0	Leicester City
1970	Chelsea	2–2 2–1	Leeds United
1971	Arsenal	2–1	Liverpool
1972	Leeds United	1–0	Arsenal
1973	Sunderland	1–0	Leeds United
1974	Liverpool	3–0	Newcastle United
1975	West Ham United	2–0	Fulham
1976	Southampton	1–0	Manchester United
1977	Manchester United	2–1	Liverpool
1978	Ipswich Town	1–0	Arsenal
1979	Arsenal	3–2	Manchester United
1980	West Ham United	1–0	Arsenal
1981	Tottenham Hotspur	1–1 3–2	Manchester City

1982	Tottenhan Hotspur	1–1 1–0	Queens Park Rangers
1983	Manchester United	2–2 4–0	Brighton & Hove Albion
1984	Everton	2–0	Watford
1985	Manchester United	1–0	Everton
1986	Liverpool	3–1	Everton
1987	Coventry City	3–2	Tottenham Hotspur
1988	Wimbledon	1–0	Liverpool
1989	Liverpool	3–2	Everton
1990	Manchester United	3–3 1–0	Crystal Palace
1991	Tottenham Hotspur	2–1	Nottingham Forest
1992	Liverpool	2–0	Sunderland

ENGLISH LEAGUE CUP FINALS

Year	Winners	Score	Runners–up
1961	Aston Villa	0–2 3–0	Rotherham United
1962	Norwich City	3–0 1–0	Rochdale
1963	Birmingham City	3–1 0–0	Aston Villa
1964	Leicester City	1–1 3–2	Stoke City
1965	Chelsea	3–2 0–0	Leicester City
1966	West Bromwich Alb.	1–2 4–1	West Ham United
1967	Queens Park Rangers	3–2	West Bromwich Albion
1968	Leeds United	1–0	Arsenal
1969	Swindon Town	3–1	Arsenal
1970	Manchester City	2–1	West Bromwich Albion
1971	Tottenham Hotspur	2–0	Aston Villa
1972	Stoke City	2–1	Chelsea
1973	Tottenham Hotspur	1–0	Norwich City
1974	Wolverhampton Wand.	2–1	Manchester City
1975	Aston Villa	1–0	Norwich City
1976	Manchester City	2–1	Newcastle United
1977	Aston Villa	0–0 1–1 3–2	Everton
1978	Nottingahm Forest	0–0 1–0	Liverpool
1979	Nottingham Forest	3–2	Southampton
1980	Wolverhampton Wand.	1–0	Nottingham Forest
1981	Liverpool	1–1 2–1	West Ham United
1982	Liverpool	3–1	Tottenham Hotspur
1983	Liverpool	2–1	Manchester United
1984	Liverpool	0–0 1–0	Everton
1985	Norwich City	1–0	Sunderland
1986	Oxford United	3–0	Queens Park Rangers
1987	Arsenal	2–1	Liverpool
1988	Luton Town	3–2	Arsenal
1989	Nottingham Forest	3–1	Luton Town
1990	Nottingham Forest	1–0	Oldham Athletic
1991	Sheffield Wednesday	1–0	Manchester United
1992	Manchester United	1–0	Nottingham Forest

INTERNATIONAL MATCHES PLAYED BY ENGLAND

Date	Opponents	Result	Venue	Compet	Scorers
30–11–1872	Scotland	D 0–0	Glasgow	Fr	
8–03–1873	Scotland	W 4–2	London	Fr	Chenery, Bonsor, Kenyon–Slaney 2
7–03–1874	Scotland	L 1–2	Glasgow	Fr	Kingsford
6–03–1875	Scotland	D 2–2	London	Fr	Alcock, Wollaston
4–03–1876	Scotland	L 0–3	Glasgow	Fr	
3–03–1877	Scotland	L 1–3	London	Fr	Lyttleton
2–03–1878	Scotland	L 2–7	Glasgow	Fr	Cursham A, Wylie
18–01–1879	Wales	W 2–1	London	Fr	Sorby, Whitfield
5–04	Scotland	W 5–4	London	Fr	Bailey, Goodyer, Mosforth, Bambridge E 2
13–03–1880	Scotland	L 4–5	Glasgow	Fr	Sparks, Mosforth, Bambridge E 2
15–03	Wales	W 3–2	Wrexham	Fr	Brindle, Sparks 2
26–02–1881	Wales	L 0–1	Blackburn	Fr	
12–03	Scotland	L 1–6	London	Fr	Bambridge E
18–02–1882	Ireland	W 13–0	Belfast	HC	Bambridge E, Brown A 4, Brown J 2, Vaughton 5, Cursham H
11–03	Scotland	L 1–5	Glasgow	HC	Vaughton
13–03	Wales	L 3–5	Wrexham	HC	Parry E, Cursham H, Mosforth
3–02–1883	Wales	W 5–0	London	HC	Cursham A, Mitchell 3, Bambridge E
24–02	Ireland	W 7–0	Liverpool	HC	Whateley 2, Pawson, Dunn 2, Cobbold 2
10–03	Scotland	L 2–3	Sheffield	HC	Cobbold, Mitchell
23–02–1884	Ireland	W 8–1	Belfast	HC	Johnson E 2, Bambridge A, Bambridge E 2, Cursham H 3
15–03	Scotland	L 0–1	Glasgow	HC	
17–03	Wales	W 4–0	Wrexham	HC	Bailey, Gunn, Bromley–Davenport 2
28–02–1885	Ireland	W 4–0	Manchester	HC	Lofthouse J, Spilsbury, Brown J, Bambridge E
14–03	Wales	D 1–1	Blackburn	HC	Mitchell
21–03	Scotland	D 1–1	London	HC	Bambridge E
13–03–1886	Ireland	W 6–1	Belfast	HC	Spilsbury 4, Dewhurst, Lindley
27–03	Scotland	D 1–1	Glasgow	HC	Lindley
29–03	Wales	W 3–1	Wrexham	HC	Dewhurst, Bambridge E, Lindley
5–02–1887	Ireland	W 7–0	Sheffield	HC	Cobbold 2, Lindley 3, Dewhurst 2
26–02	Wales	W 4–0	London	HC	Cobbold 2, Lindley 2
19–03	Scotland	L 2–3	Blackburn	HC	Dewhurst, Lindley
4–02–1888	Wales	W 5–1	Crewe	HC	Dewhurst 2, Woodhall, Goodall, Lindley
17–03	Scotland	W 5–0	Glasgow	HC	Lindley, Hodgetts, Dewhurst 2, Goodall
31–03	Ireland	W 5–1	Belfast	HC	Dewhurst, Allen G 3, Lindley

23-02-1889	Wales	W	4-1	Stoke	HC	Bassett, Goodall, Southworth, Dewhurst
2-03	Ireland	W	6-1	Liverpool	HC	Weir, Yates 3, Lofthouse J, Brodie
13-04	Scotland	L	2-3	London	HC	Bassett, Weir
15-03-1890	Wales	W	3-1	Wrexham	HC	Currey 2, Lindley
15-03	Ireland	W	9-1	Belfast	HC	Townley 2, Davenport 2, Geary 3, Lofthouse J, Barton
5-04	Scotland	D	1-1	Glasgow	HC	Wood
7-03-1891	Wales	W	4-1	Sunderland	HC	Goodall, Southworth, Chadwick, Milward
7-03	Ireland	W	6-1	Wolverhampton	HC	Cotterill, Daft, Henfrey, Lindley 2, Bassett
6-04	Scotland	W	2-1	Blackburn	HC	Goodall, Chadwick
5-03-1892	Wales	W	2-0	Wrexham	HC	Henfrey, Sandilands
5-03	Ireland	W	2-0	Belfast	HC	Daft 2
2-04	Scotland	W	4-1	Glasgow	HC	Southworth, Goodall 2, Chadwick
25-02-1893	Ireland	W	6-1	Birmingham	HC	Sandilands, Gilliatt 3, Winckworth, Smith G
13-03	Wales	W	6-0	Stoke	HC	Spiksley 2, Goodall, Bassett, Schofield, Reynolds
1-04	Scotland	W	5-2	London	HC	Spiksley 2, Gosling, Cotterill, Reynolds
3-03-1894	Ireland	D	2-2	Belfast	HC	Devey, Spiksley
12-03	Wales	W	5-1	Wrexham	HC	Veitch 3, Gosling, OG
7-04	Scotland	D	2-2	Glasgow	HC	Goodall, Reynolds
9-03-1895	Ireland	W	9-0	Derby	HC	Bloomer 2, Goodall 2, Bassett, Howell, Becton 2, OG
18-03	Wales	D	1-1	London	HC	Smith G
6-04	Scotland	W	3-0	Liverpool	HC	Bloomer, Smith G, OG
7-03-1896	Ireland	W	2-0	Belfast	HC	Bloomer, Smith G
16-03	Wales	W	9-1	Cardiff	HC	Bloomer 5, Smith G 2, Goodall, Bassett
4-04	Scotland	L	1-2	Glasgow	HC	Bassett
20-02-1897	Ireland	W	6-0	Nottingham	HC	Bloomer 2, Wheldon 3, Athersmith
29-03	Wales	W	4-0	Sheffield	HC	Bloomer, Needham, Milward 2
3-04	Scotland	L	1-2	London	HC	Bloomer
5-03-1898	Ireland	W	3-2	Belfast	HC	Morren, Athersmith, Smith G
28-03	Wales	W	3-0	Wrexham	HC	Smith G, Wheldon 2
2-04	Scotland	W	3-1	Glasgow	HC	Bloomer 2, Wheldon
18-02-1899	Ireland	W	13-2	Sunderland	HC	Forman F (I), Bloomer 2, Athersmith, Settle 3, Smith G 4, Forman F (II) 2
20-03	Wales	W	4-0	Bristol	HC	Bloomer 2, Forman F (II), Needham
8-04	Scotland	W	2-1	Birmingham	HC	Smith G, Settle
17-03-1900	Ireland	W	2-0	Dublin	HC	Johnson W, Sagar
26-03	Wales	D	1-1	Cardiff	HC	Wilson G
7-04	Scotland	L	1-4	Glasgow	HC	Bloomer
9-03-1901	Ireland	W	3-0	Southampton	HC	Foster, Crawshaw
18-03	Wales	W	6-0	Newcastle	HC	Bloomer 4, Foster, Needham
30-03	Scotland	D	2-2	London	HC	Blackburn, Bloomer
3-03-1902	Wales	D	0-0	Wrexham	HC	
22-03	Ireland	W	1-0	Belfast	HC	Settle
3-05	Scotland	D	2-2	Birmingham	HC	Wilkes, Settle
14-02-1903	Ireland	W	4-0	Wolverhampton	HC	Sharp, Davis H, Woodward 2
2-03	Wales	W	2-1	Portsmouth	HC	Bache, Woodward
4-04	Scotland	L	1-2	Sheffield	HC	Woodward
29-02-1904	Wales	D	2-2	Wrexham	HC	Common, Bache
12-03	Ireland	W	3-1	Belfast	HC	Common, Bache, Davis G
9-04	Scotland	W	1-0	Glasgow	HC	Bloomer
25-02-1905	Ireland	D	1-1	Middlesbrough	HC	Bloomer
27-03	Wales	W	3-1	Liverpool	HC	Woodward 2, Harris
1-04	Scotland	W	1-0	London	HC	Bache
17-02-1906	Ireland	W	5-0	Belfast	HC	Bond 2, Day, Harris, Brown A
19-03	Wales	W	1-0	Cardiff	HC	Day
7-04	Scotland	L	1-2	Glasgow	HC	Shepherd
1-11	France*	W	15-0	Paris	Fr	
16-02-1907	Ireland	W	1-0	Liverpool	HC	Hardman
18-03	Wales	D	1-1	London	HC	Stewart
1-04	Holland*	W	8-1	The Hague	Fr	
6-04	Scotland	D	1-1	Newcastle	HC	Bloomer
21-12	Holland*	W	12-2	Darlington	Fr	
15-02-1908	Ireland	W	3-1	Belfast	HC	Woodward, Hilsdon 2
16-03	Wales	W	7-1	Wrexham	HC	Wedlock, Windridge, Hilsdon 2, Woodward 3
23-03	France*	W	12-0	Ipswich	Fr	

* England Amateur team against non-British countries: not considered full internationals by the English FA.

4–04	Scotland	D	1–1	Glasgow	HC	Windridge
18–04	Belgium*	W	8–2	Brussels	Fr	
20–04	Germany*	W	5–1	Berlin	Fr	
6–06	Austria	W	6–1	Vienna	Fr	Hilsdon 2, Windridge 2, Bridget Woodward
8–06	Austria	W	11–1	Vienna	Fr	Woodward 4, Bridgett, Bradshaw 3, Warren, Rutherford, Windridge
10–06	Hungary	W	7–0	Budapest	Fr	Hilsdon 4, Windridge, Woodward, Rutherford
13–06	Bohemia	W	4–0	Prague	Fr	Hilsdon 2, Windridge, Rutherford
8–09	Sweden*	W	6–1	Gothenburg	Fr	
20–10	Sweden*	W	12–1	London	OGr1	
22–10	Holland*	W	4–0	London	OGsf	
24–10	Denmark*	W	2–0	London	OGf	
13–02–1909	Ireland	W	4–0	Bradford	HC	Hilsdon 2, Woodward 2
16–03	Germany*	W	9–0	Oxford	Fr	
15–03	Wales	W	2–0	Nottingham	HC	Holley, Freeman
3–04	Scotland	W	2–0	London	HC	Walesl 2
12–04	Holland*	W	4–0	Amsterdam	Fr	
17–04	Belgium*	W	11–2	London	Fr	
20–05	Switzerland*	W	9–0	Basle	Fr	
22–05	France*	W	11–0	Gentily	Fr	
29–05	Hungary	W	4–2	Budapest	Fr	Woodward 2, Fleming, Bridgett
31–05	Hungary	W	8–2	Budapest	Fr	Woodward 4, Fleming 2, Holley 2
1–06	Austria	W	8–1	Vienna	Fr	Woodward 3, Warren, Halse 2, Holley 2
6–11	Sweden*	W	7–0	Hull	Fr	
11–12	Holland*	W	9–1	London	Fr	
12–02–1910	Ireland	D	1–1	Belfast	HC	Fleming
14–03	Wales	W	1–0	Cardiff	HC	Ducat
26–03	Belgium*	D	2–2	Brussels	Fr	
2–04	Scotland	L	0–2	Glasgow	HC	
9–04	Switzerland*	W	6–1	London	Fr	
16–04	France*	W	10–1	Brighton	Fr	
5–05	Denmark*	L	1–2	Copenhagen	Fr	
11–02–1911	Ireland	W	2–1	Derby	HC	Shepherd, Evans
4–03	Belgium*	W	4–0	London	Fr	
13–03	Wales	W	3–0	London	HC	Woodward 2, Webb G
23–03	France*	W	3–0	Paris	Fr	
1–04	Scotland	D	1–1	Liverpool	HC	Stewart
14–04	Germany*	D	2–2	Berlin	Fr	
17–04	Holland*	W	1–0	Amsterdam	Fr	
25–05	Switzerland*	W	4–1	Berne	Fr	
21–10	Denmark*	W	3–0	London	Fr	
10–02–1912	Ireland	W	6–1	Dublin	HC	Fleming 3, Freeman, Holley, Simpson
11–03	Wales	W	2–0	Wrexham	HC	Holley, Freeman
16–03	Holland*	W	4–0	Hull	Fr	
23–03	Scotland	D	1–1	Glasgow	HC	Holley
8–04	Belgium*	W	2–1	Brussels	Fr	
30–06	Hungary*	W	7–0	Stockholm	OGqf	
2–07	Finland*	W	4–0	Stockholm	OGsf	
4–07	Denmark*	W	4–2	Stockholm	OGf	
9–11	Belgium*	W	4–0	Swindon	Fr	
15–02–1913	Ireland	L	1–2	Belfast	HC	Buchan
27–02	France*	W	4–1	Paris	Fr	
21–03	Germany*	W	3–0	Berlin	Fr	
17–03	Wales	W	4–3	Bristol	HC	Flemming, McCall, Latheron, Hampton
24–03	Holland*	L	1–2	The Hague	Fr	
5–04	Scotland	W	1–0	London	HC	Hampton
15–11	Holland*	W	2–1	Hull	Fr	
14–02–1914	Ireland	L	0–3	Middlesbrough	HC	
24–02	Belgium*	W	8–1	Brussels	Fr	
16–03	Wales	W	2–0	Cardiff	HC	Smith J (I), Wedlock
4–04	Scotland	L	1–3	Glasgow	HC	Fleming
5–06	Denmark*	L	0–3	Copenhagen	Fr	
10–06	Sweden*	W	5–1	Stockholm	Fr	
25–10–1919	Ireland	D	1–1	Belfast	HC	Cock
17–02–1920	Belgium*	L	1–3	Brussels	Fr	
15–03	Wales	L	1–2	London	HC	Buchan
10–04	Scotland	W	5–4	Sheffield	HC	Kelly 2, Cock, Morris F, Quantrill

28-08	Norway*	L	1-3	Antwerp	OGr1	
23-10	Ireland	W	2-0	Sunderland	HC	Kelly, Walker
14-03-1921	Wales	D	0-0	Cardiff	HC	
9-04	Scotland	L	0-3	Glasgow	HC	
21-05	Belgium	W	2-0	Brussels	Fr	Buchan, Chambers
22-10	Ireland	D	1-1	Belfast	HC	Kirton
13-03-1922	Wales	W	1-0	Liverpool	HC	Kelly
8-04	Scotland	L	0-1	Birmingham	HC	
21-10	Ireland	W	2-0	West Bromwich	HC	Chambers 2
5-03-1923	Wales	D	2-2	Cardiff	HC	Chambers, Watson V
19-03	Belgium	W	6-1	London	Fr	Hegan 2, Chambers, Mercer, Seed, Bullock
14-04	Scotland	D	2-2	Glasgow	HC	Kelly, Watson V
5-05	Belgium*	L	0-3	Brussels	Fr	
10-05	France	W	4-1	Paris	Fr	Hegan 2, Buchan, Creek
21-05	Sweden	W	4-2	Stockhlom	Fr	Walker 2, Moore J, Thornewell
20-10	Ireland	L	1-2	Belfast	HC	Bradford J
1-11	Belgium	D	2-2	Antwerp	Fr	Brown W, Roberts W
3-03-1924	Wales	L	1-2	Blackburn	HC	Roberts W
12-04	Scotland	D	1-1	London	HC	Walker
17-05	France	W	3-1	Paris	Fr	Gibbins 2, Storer
22-10	Nth. Ireland	W	3-1	Liverpool	HC	Kelly, Bedford, Walker
8-12	Belgium	W	4-0	West Bromwich	Fr	Bradford J 2, Walker 2
28-02-1925	Wales	W	2-1	Swansea	HC	Roberts F 2
4-04	Scotland	L	0-2	Glasgow	HC	
21-05	France	W	3-2	Paris	Fr	Gibbins, Dorrell, OG
24-10	Nth. Ireland	D	0-0	Belfast	HC	
1-03-1926	Wales	L	1-3	London	HC	Walker
17-04	Scotland	L	0-1	Manchester	HC	
24-05	Belgium	W	5-3	Antwerp	HC	Osborne 3, Carter J, Johnson T
20-10	Nth. Ireland	D	3-3	Liverpool	HC	Brown G, Spence, Bullock
12-02-1927	Wales	D	3-3	Wrexham	HC	Dean 2, Walker
2-04	Scotland	W	2-1	Glasgow	HC	Dean 2
11-05	Belgium	W	9-1	Brussels	Fr	Dean 3, Brown G 2, Rigby 2, Page, Hulme
21-05	Luxembourg	W	5-2	Luxembourg	Fr	Dean 3, Kelly, Bishop
26-05	France	W	6-0	Paris	Fr	Dean 2, Brown G 2, Rigby, OG
22-10	Nth. Ireland	L	0-2	Belfast	HC	
28-11	Wales	L	1-2	Burnley	HC	OG
31-03-1928	Scotland	L	1-5	London	HC	Kelly
17-05	France	W	5-1	Paris	Fr	Stephenson 2, Dean 2, Jack
19-05	Belgium	W	3-1	Antwerp	Fr	Dean 2, Matthews V
22-10	Nth. Ireland	W	2-1	Liverpool	HC	Hulme, Dean
17-11	Wales	W	3-2	Swansea	HC	Hulme 2, Hine
13-04-1929	Scotland	L	0-1	Glasgow	HC	
9-05	France	W	4-1	Paris	Fr	Kail 2, Camsell 2
11-05	Belgium	W	5-1	Brussels	Fr	Camsell 4, Carter J
15-05	Spain	L	3-4	Madrid	Fr	Carter J 2, Bradford J
19-10	Nth. Ireland	W	3-0	Belfast	HC	Camsell 2, Hine
20-11	Wales	W	6-0	London	HC	Adcock, Camsell 3, Johnson T 2,
5-04-1930	Scotland	W	5-2	London	HC	Jack, Watson V 2, Rimmer 2
10-05	Germany	D	3-3	Berlin	Fr	Bradford J 2, Jack
14-05	Austria	D	0-0	Vienna	Fr	
20-10	Nth. Ireland	W	5-1	Sheffield	HC	Burgess 2, Crooks, Hampson, Houghton
22-11	Wales	W	4-0	Wrexham	HC	Hodgson, Bradford J, Hampson 2
28-03-1931	Scotland	L	0-2	Glasgow	HC	
14-05	France	L	2-5	Paris	Fr	Crooks, Waring
16-05	Belgium	W	4-1	Brussels	Fr	Burgess 2, Houghton, Roberts H
17-10	Nth. Ireland	W	6-2	Belfast	HC	Waring 2, Smith J (II), Hine, Houghton 2
18-11	Wales	W	3-1	Liverpool	HC	Smith J (II), Crooks, Hine
9-12	Spain	W	7-1	London	Fr	Smith J (II) 2, Johnson T 2, Crooks 2, Dean
9-04-1932	Scotland	W	3-0	London	HC	Waring, Crooks, Barclay
17-10	Nth. Ireland	W	1-0	Blackpool	HC	Barclay
16-11	Wales	D	0-0	Wrexham	HC	
7-12	Austria	W	4-3	London	Fr	Hampson 2, Houghton, Crooks
1-04-1933	Scotland	L	1-2	Glasgow	HC	Hunt G
13-05	Italy	D	1-1	Rome	Fr	Bastin
20-05	Switzerland	W	4-0	Berne	Fr	Bastin 2, Richardson 2
14-10	Nth. Ireland	W	3-0	Belfast	HC	Brook, Grosvenor, Bowers
15-11	Wales	L	1-2	Newcastle	HC	Brook
6-12	France	W	4-1	London	Fr	Camsell 2, Brook, Grosvenor

14–04–1934	Scotland	W	3–0	London	HC	Brook, Bastin, Bowers
10–05	Hungary	L	1–2	Budapest	Fr	Tilson
16–05	Czechoslovakia	L	1–2	Prague	Fr	Tilson
29–09	Wales	W	4–0	Cardiff	HC	Tilson 2, Brook, Matthews S
14–11	Italy	W	3–2	London	Fr	Brook 2, Drake
6–02–1935	Nth. Ireland	W	2–1	Liverpool	HC	Bastin 2
6–04	Scotland	L	0–2	Glasgow	HC	
18–05	Holland	W	1–0	Amsterdam	Fr	Worrall
19–10	Nth. Ireland	W	3–1	Belfast	HC	Tilson 2, Brook
4–12	Germany	W	3–0	London	Fr	Camsell 2, Bastin
5–02–1936	Wales	L	1–2	Wolverhampton	HC	Bowden
4–04	Scotland	D	1–1	London	HC	Camsell
6–05	Austria	L	1–2	Vienna	Fr	Camsell
9–05	Belgium	L	2–3	Brussels	Fr	Camsell, Hobbis
17–10	Wales	L	1–2	Cardiff	HC	Bastin
18–11	Nth. Ireland	W	3–1	Stoke	HC	Carter H, Bastin, Worrall
2–12	Hungary	W	6–2	London	Fr	Drake 3, Brook, Britton, Carter H
17–04–1937	Scotland	L	1–3	Glasgow	HC	Steele
14–05	Norway	W	6–0	Oslo	Fr	Steele 2, Kirchen, Galley, Goulden, OG
17–05	Sweden	W	4–0	Stockholm	Fr	Steele 3, Johnson J
20–05	Finland	W	8–0	Helsinki	Fr	Payne 2, Steele 2, Kirchen, Willingham, Johnson J, Robinson
23–10	Nth. Ireland	W	5–1	Belfast	HC	Mills 3, Hall, Brook
17–11	Wales	W	2–1	Middlesbrough	HC	Matthews S, Hall
1–12	Czechoslovakia	W	5–4	London	Fr	Crayston, Morton, Matthews S 3
9–04–1938	Scotland	L	0–1	London	HC	
14–05	Germany	W	6–3	Berlin	Fr	Robinson 2, Bastin, Broome, Matthews S, Goulden
21–05	Switzerland	L	1–2	Zurich	Fr	Bastin
26–05	France	W	4–2	Paris	Fr	Drake 2, Broome, Bastin
22–10	Wales	L	2–4	Cardiff	HC	Lawton, Matthews S
9–11	Norway	W	4–0	Newcastle	Fr	Smith J (III) 2, Dix, Lawton
16–11	Nth. Ireland	W	7–0	Manchester	HC	Hall 5, Lawton, Matthews S
15–04–1939	Scotland	W	2–1	Glasgow	HC	Beasley, Lawton
13–05	Italy	D	2–2	Milan	Fr	Lawton, Hall
18–05	Yugoslavia	L	1–2	Belgrade	Fr	Broome
24–05	Romania	W	2–0	Bucharest	Fr	Goulden, Welsh
19–01–1946	Belgium*	W	2–0	London	Fr	Brown, Pye
11–05	Switzerland*	W	4–1	London	Fr	Carter 2, Brown, Lawton
19–05	France*	L	1–2	Paris	Fr	Hagan
28–09	Nth. Ireland	W	7–2	Belfast	HC	Carter H, Mannion 3, Finney, Lawton, Langton
30–09	Rep. Ireland	W	1–0	Dublin	Fr	Finney
13–11	Wales	W	3–0	Manchester	HC	Mannion 2, Lawton
27–11	Holland	W	8–2	Huddersfield	Fr	Lawton 4, Carter H 2, Mannion, Finney
12–04–1947	Scotland	D	1–1	London	HC	Carter H
3–05	France	W	3–0	London	Fr	Finney, Mannion, Carter H
18–05	Switzerland	L	0–1	Zurich	Fr	
25–05	Portugal	W	10–0	Lisbon	Fr	Lawton 4, Mortensen 4, Finney, Matthews
21–09	Belgium	W	5–2	Brussels	Fr	Lawton 2, Mortensen, Finney 2
18–10	Wales	W	3–0	Cardiff	HC	Finney, Mortensen, Lawton
5–11	Nth. Ireland	D	2–2	Liverpool	HC	Mannion, Lawton
19–11	Sweden	W	4–2	London	Fr	Mortensen 3, Lawton
10–04–1948	Scotland	W	2–0	Glasgow	HC	Finney, Mortensen
16–05	Italy	W	4–0	Turin	Fr	Mortensen, Lawton, Finney 2
26–09	Denmark	D	0–0	Copenhagen	Fr	
9–10	Nth. Ireland	W	6–2	Belfast	HC	Matthews S, Mortensen 3, Milburn, Pearson S
10–11	Wales	W	1–0	Birmingham	HC	Finney
2–12	Switzerland	W	6–0	London	Fr	Haines 2, Hancocks 2, Rowley, Milburn
9–04–1949	Scotland	L	1–3	London	HC	Milburn
13–05	Sweden	L	1–3	Stockholm	Fr	Finney
18–05	Norway	W	4–1	Oslo	Fr	Mullen, Finney, OG, Morris J
22–05	France	W	3–1	Paris	Fr	Morris J 2, Wright
21–09	Rep. Ireland	L	0–2	Liverpool	Fr	
15–10	Wales	W	4–1	Cardiff	HC/WCq	Mortensen, Milburn 3
16–11	Nth. Ireland	W	9–2	Manchester	HC/WCq	Rowley 4, Froggatt J, Pearson S 2, Mortensen 2

30–11	Italy	W	2–0	London	Fr	Rowley, Wright
15–04–1950	Scotland	W	1–0	Glasgow	HC/WCq	Bentley
14–05	Portugal	W	5–3	Lisbon	Fr	Finney 4, Mortensen
18–05	Belgium	W	4–1	Brussels	Fr	Mullen, Mortensen, Mannion, Bentley
25–06	Chile	W	2–0	Rio de Janeiro	WCr1	Mortensen, Mannion
29–06	United States	L	0–1	Belo Horizonte	WCr1	
2–07	Spain	L	0–1	Rio de Janeiro	WCr1	
7–10	Nth. Ireland	W	4–1	Belfast	HC	Baily 2, Lee J, Wright
15–11	Wales	W	4–2	Sunderland	HC	Baily 2, Mannion, Milburn
22–11	Yugoslavia	D	2–2	London	Fr	Lofthouse N 2
14–04–1951	Scotland	L	2–3	London	HC	Hassall, Finney
9–05	Argentina	W	2–1	London	Fr	Mortensen 2
19–05	Portugal	W	5–2	Liverpool	Fr	Nicholson, Milburn 2, Finney, Hassall
3–10	France	D	2–2	London	Fr	OG, Medley
20–10	Wales	D	1–1	Cardiff	HC	Baily
14–11	Nth. Ireland	W	2–0	Birmingham	HC	Lofthouse N 2
28–11	Austria	D	2–2	London	Fr	Ramsey, Lofthouse N
5–04–1952	Scotland	W	2–1	Glasgow	HC	Pearson S 2
18–05	Italy	D	1–1	Florence	Fr	Broadis
25–05	Austria	W	3–2	Vienna	Fr	Lofthouse N 2, Sewell
28–05	Switzerland	W	3–0	Zurich	Fr	Sewell, Lofthouse N 2
4–10	Nth. Ireland	D	2–2	Belfast	HC	Lofthouse N, Elliott
12–11	Wales	W	5–2	London	HC	Finney, Lofthouse N 2, Froggatt J, Bentley
26–11	Belgium	W	5–0	London	Fr	Elliott 2, Lofthouse N 2, Froggatt R
18–04–1953	Scotland	D	2–2	London	HC	Broadis 2
17–05	Argentina	D	0–0	Buenos Aires	Fr	Abandoned after 21 minutes
24–05	Chile	W	2–1	Santiago	Fr	Taylor T, Lofthouse N
31–05	Uruguay	L	1–2	Montevideo	Fr	Taylor T
8–06	United States	W	6–3	New York	Fr	Broadis, Finney 2, Lofthouse N 2, Froggatt R
10–10	Wales	W	4–1	Cardiff	HC/WCq	Wilshaw 2, Lofthouse N 2
11–11	Nth. Ireland	W	3–1	Liverpool	HC/WCq	Hassall 2, Lofthouse N
25–11	Hungary	L	3–6	London	Fr	Sewell, Mortensen, Ramsey
3–04–1954	Scotland	W	4–2	Glasgow	HC/WCq	Broadis, Nicholls, Allen R, Mullen
16–05	Yugoslavia	L	0–1	Belgrade	Fr	
23–05	Hungary	L	1–7	Budapest	Fr	Broadis
17–06	Belgium	D	4–4	Basle	WCr1	Broadis 2, Lofthouse N 2
20–06	Switzerland	W	2–0	Berne	WCr1	Wilshaw, Mullen
26–06	Uruguay	L	2–4	Basle	WCqf	Lofthouse N, Finney
2–10	Nth. Ireland	W	2–0	Belfast	HC	Haynes, Revie
10–11	Wales	W	3–2	London	HC	Bentley 3
1–12	West Germany	W	3–1	London	Fr	Bentley, Allen R, Shackleton
2–04–1955	Scotland	W	7–2	London	HC	Wilshaw 4, Lofthouse N 2, Revie
15–05	France	L	0–1	Paris	Fr	
18–05	Spain	D	1–1	Madrid	Fr	Bentley
22–05	Portugal	L	1–3	Oporto	Fr	Bentley
2–10	Denmark	W	5–1	Copenhagen	Fr	Revie 2, Lofthouse N 2, Bradford G
22–10	Wales	L	1–2	Cardiff	HC	OG
2–11	Nth. Ireland	W	3–0	London	HC	Wilshaw 2, Finney
30–11	Spain	W	4–1	London	Fr	Atyeo, W Perry 2, Finney
14–04–1956	Scotland	D	1–1	Glasgow	HC	Haynes
9–05	Brazil	W	4–2	London	Fr	Taylor T 2, Grainger 2
16–05	Sweden	D	0–0	Stockholm	Fr	
20–05	Finland	W	5–1	Helsinki	Fr	Wilshaw, Haynes, Astall, Lofthouse N 2
25–05	West Germany	W	3–1	Berlin	Fr	Edwards, Grainger, Haynes
6–10	Nth. Ireland	D	1–1	Belfast	HC	Matthews S
14–11	Wales	W	3–1	London	HC	Haynes, Brooks, Finney
28–11	Yugoslavia	W	3–0	London	Fr	Brooks, Taylor T 2
5–12	Denmark	W	5–2	Wolverhampton	WCq	Taylor T 3, Edwards 2
6–04–1957	Scotland	W	2–1	London	HC	Kevan, Edwards
8–05	Rep. Ireland	W	5–1	London	WCq	Taylor T 3, Atyeo 2
15–05	Denmark	W	4–1	Copenhagen	WCq	Haynes, Taylor T 2, Atyeo
19–05	Rep. Ireland	D	1–1	Dublin	WCq	Atyeo
19–10	Wales	W	4–0	Cardiff	HC	OG, Haynes 2, Finney
6–11	Nth. Ireland	L	2–3	London	HC	A'Court, Edwards
27–11	France	W	4–0	London	Fr	Taylor T 2, Robson R
19–04–1958	Scotland	W	4–0	Glasgow	HC	Douglas, Kevan 2, Charlton R
7–05	Portugal	W	2–1	London	Fr	Charlton R 2
11–05	Yugoslavia	L	0–5	Belgrade	Fr	

18–05	Soviet Union	D	1–1	Moscow	Fr	Kevan
8–06	Soviet Union	D	2–2	Gothenburg	WCr1	Kevan, Finney
11–06	Brazil	D	0–0	Gothenburg	WCr1	
15–06	Austria	D	2–2	Boras	WCr1	Haynes, Kevan
17–06	Soviet Union	L	0–1	Gothenburg	WCr1	
4–10	Nth. Ireland	D	3–3	Belfast	HC	Charlton R 2, Finney
22–10	Soviet Union	W	5–0	London	Fr	Haynes 3, Charlton R, Lofthouse N
26–11	Wales	D	2–2	Birmingham	HC	Broadbent 2
11–04–1959	Scotland	W	1–0	London	HC	Charlton R
6–05	Italy	D	2–2	London	Fr	Charlton R, Bradley
13–05	Brazil	L	0–2	Rio de Janeiro	Fr	
17–05	Peru	L	1–4	Lima	Fr	Greaves
24–05	Mexico	L	1–2	Mexico City	Fr	Kevan
28–05	United States	W	8–1	Los Angeles	Fr	Charlton R 3, Flowers 2, Bradley, Kevan, Haynes
17–10	Wales	D	1–1	Cardiff	HC	Greaves
28–10	Sweden	L	2–3	London	Fr	Connelly, Charlton R
18–11	Nth. Ireland	W	2–1	London	HC	Baker, Parry R
9–04–1960	Scotland	D	1–1	Glasgow	HC	Charlton R
11–05	Yugoslavia	D	3–3	London	Fr	Douglas, Greaves, Baker
15–05	Spain	L	0–3	Madrid	Fr	
22–05	Hungary	L	0–2	Budapest	Fr	
8–10	Nth. Ireland	W	5–2	Belfast	HC	Smith R, Greaves 2, Charlton R, Douglas
19–10	Luxembourg	W	9–0	Luxembourg	WCq	Greaves 3, Charlton R 3, Smith R 2, Haynes
26–10	Spain	W	4–2	London	Fr	Greaves, Douglas, Smith R 2
23–11	Wales	W	5–1	London	HC	Greaves 2, Charlton R, Smith R, Haynes
15–04–1961	Scotland	W	9–3	London	HC	Robson R, Greaves 3, Douglas, Smith R 2, Haynes 2
10–05	Mexico	W	8–0	London	Fr	Hitchens, Charlton R 3, Robson R, Douglas 2, Flowers
21–05	Portugal	D	1–1	Lisbon	WCq	Flowers
24–05	Italy	W	3–2	Rome	Fr	Hitchens 2, Greaves
27–05	Austria	L	1–3	Vienna	Fr	Greaves
28–09	Luxembourg	W	4–1	London	WCq	Pointer, Viollet, Charlton R 2
14–10	Wales	D	1–1	Cardiff	HC	Douglas
25–10	Portugal	W	2–0	London	WCq	Connelly, Pointer
22–11	Nth. Ireland	D	1–1	London	HC	Charlton R
4–04–1962	Austria	W	3–1	London	Fr	Crawford, Flowers, Hunt R
14–04	Scotland	L	0–2	Glasgow	HC	
9–05	Switzerland	W	3–1	London	Fr	Flowers, Hitchens, Connelly
20–05	Peru	W	4–0	Lima	Fr	Flowers, Greaves 3
31–05	Hungary	L	1–2	Rancagua	WCr1	Flowers
2–06	Argentina	W	3–1	Rancagua	WCr1	Flowers, Charlton R, Greaves
7–06	Bulgaria	D	0–0	Rancagua	WCr1	
10–06	Brazil	L	1–3	Vina del Mar	WCqf	Hitchens
3–10	France	D	1–1	Sheffield	ECr1	Flowers
20–10	Nth. Ireland	W	3–1	Belfast	HC	Greaves, O'Grady 2
21–11	Wales	W	4–0	London	HC	Connelly, Peacock 2, Greaves
27–02–1963	France	L	2–5	Paris	ECr1	Smith R, Tambling
6–04	Scotland	L	1–2	London	HC	Douglas
8–05	Brazil	D	1–1	London	Fr	Douglas
29–05	Czechoslovakia	W	4–2	Bratislava	Fr	Greaves 2, Smith R, Charlton R
2–06	East Germany	W	2–1	Leipzig	Fr	Hunt R, Charlton R
5–06	Switzerland	W	8–1	Basle	Fr	Charlton R 3, Byrne 2, Douglas, Kay, Melia
12–10	Wales	W	4–0	Cardiff	HC	Smith R 2, Greaves, Charlton R
20–11	Nth. Ireland	W	8–3	London	HC	Greaves 4, Paine 3, Smith R
11–04–1964	Scotland	L	0–1	Glasgow	HC	
6–05	Uruguay	W	2–1	London	Fr	Byrne 2
17–05	Portugal	W	4–3	Lisbon	Fr	Byrne 3, Charlton R
24–05	Rep. Ireland	W	3–1	Dublin	Fr	Eastham, Byrne, Greaves
27–05	United States	W	10–0	New York	Fr	Hunt R 4, Pickering 3, Paine 2, Charlton R
30–05	Brazil	L	1–5	Rio de Janeiro	CN	Greaves
4–06	Portugal	D	1–1	Sao Paulo	CN	Hunt R
6–06	Argentina	L	0–1	Rio de Janeiro	CN	
3–10	Nth. Ireland	W	4–3	Belfast	HC	Pickering, Greaves 3
21–10	Belgium	D	2–2	London	Fr	Pickering, Hinton
18–11	Wales	W	2–1	London	HC	Wignall 2
9–12	Holland	D	1–1	Amsterdam	Fr	Greaves

10-04-1965	Scotland	D	2-2	London	HC	Charlton R, Greaves
5-05	Hungary	W	1-0	London	Fr	Greaves
9-05	Yugoslavia	D	1-1	Belgrade	Fr	Bridges
12-05	West Germany	W	1-0	Nuremburg	Fr	Paine
16-05	Sweden	W	2-1	Gothenburg	Fr	Ball, Connolly
2-10	Wales	D	0-0	Cardiff	HC	
20-10	Austria	L	2-3	London	Fr	Charlton R, Connolly
10-11	Nth. Ireland	W	2-1	London	HC	Baker, Peacock
8-12	Spain	W	2-0	Madrid	Fr	Baker, Hunt R
5-01-1966	Poland	D	1-1	Liverpool	Fr	Moore R
23-02	West Germany	W	1-0	London	Fr	Stiles
2-04	Scotland	W	4-3	Glasgow	HC	Hurst, Hunt R 2, Charlton R
4-05	Yugoslavia	W	2-0	London	Fr	Greaves, Charlton R
26-06	Finland	W	3-0	Helsinki	Fr	Peters, Hunt R, Charlton J
29-06	Norway	W	6-1	Oslo	Fr	Greaves 4, Connolly, Moore R
3-07	Denmark	W	2-0	Copenhagen	Fr	Charlton J, Eastham
5-07	Poland	W	1-0	Chorzow	Fr	Hunt R
11-07	Uruguay	D	0-0	London	WCr1	
16-07	Mexico	W	2-0	London	WCr1	Charlton R, Hunt R
20-07	France	W	2-0	London	WCr1	Hunt R 2
23-07	Argentina	W	1-0	London	WCqf	Hurst
26-07	Portugal	W	2-1	London	WCsf	Charlton R 2
30-07	West Germany	W	4-2	London	WCf	Hurst 3, Peters
22-10	Nth. Ireland	W	2-0	Belfast	HC/ECq	Hunt R, Peters
2-11	Czechoslovakia	D	0-0	London	Fr	
16-11	Wales	W	5-1	London	HC/ECq	Hurst 2, Charlton R, Charlton J, OG
15-04-1967	Scotland	L	2-3	London	HC/ECq	Charlton J, Hurst
24-05	Spain	W	2-0	London	Fr	Greaves, Hunt R
27-05	Austria	W	1-0	Vienna	Fr	Ball
21-10	Wales	W	3-0	Cardiff	HC/ECq	Peters, Charlton R, Ball
22-11	Nth. Ireland	W	2-0	London	HC/ECq	Hurst, Charlton R
6-12	Soviet Union	D	2-2	London	Fr	Ball, Peters
24-02-1968	Scotland	D	1-1	Glasgow	HC/ECq	Peters
3-04	Spain	W	1-0	London	ECqf	Charlton R
8-05	Spain	W	2-1	Madrid	ECqf	Peters, Hunter
22-05	Sweden	W	3-1	London	Fr	Peters, Charlton R, Hunt R
1-06	West Germany	L	0-1	Hanover	Fr	
5-06	Yugoslavia	L	0-1	Florence	ECsf	
8-06	Soviet Union	W	2-0	Rome	EC3p	Charlton R, Hurst
6-11	Romania	D	0-0	Bucharest	Fr	
11-12	Bulgaria	D	1-1	London	Fr	Hurst
15-01-1969	Romania	D	1-1	London	Fr	Charlton J
12-03	France	W	5-0	London	Fr	Hurst 3, O'Grady, Lee F
3-05	Nth. Ireland	W	3-1	Belfast	HC	Peters, Lee F, Hurst
7-05	Wales	W	2-1	London	HC	Charlton R, Lee F
10-05	Scotland	W	4-1	London	HC	Peters 2, Hurst 2
1-06	Mexico	D	0-0	Mexico City	Fr	
8-06	Uruguay	W	2-1	Montevideo	Fr	Lee F, Hurst
12-06	Brazil	L	1-2	Rio de Janeiro	Fr	Bell
5-11	Holland	W	1-0	Amsterdam	Fr	Bell
10-12	Portugal	W	1-0	London	Fr	Charlton J
14-01-1970	Holland	D	0-0	London	Fr	
25-02	Belgium	W	3-1	Brussels	Fr	Ball, Hurst
18-04	Wales	D	1-1	Cardiff	HC	Lee F
21-04	Nth. Ireland	W	3-1	London	HC	Peters, Hurst, Charlton R
25-04	Scotland	D	0-0	Glasgow	HC	
20-05	Colombia	W	4-0	Bogota	Fr	Peters 2, Charlton R, Ball
24-05	Ecuador	W	2-0	Quito	Fr	Lee F, Kidd
2-06	Romania	W	1-0	Guadalajara	WCr1	Hurst
7-06	Brazil	L	0-1	Guadalajara	WCr1	
11-06	Czechoslovakia	W	1-0	Guadalajara	WCr1	Clarke
14-06	West Germany	L	2-3	Leon	WCqf	Mullery, Peters
25-11	East Germany	W	3-1	London	Fr	Lee F, Peters, Clarke
3-02-1971	Malta	W	1-0	Gzira	ECq	Peters
21-04	Greece	W	3-0	London	ECq	Chivers, Hurst, Lee F
12-05	Malta	W	5-0	London	ECq	Chivers 2, Lee F, Clarke, Lawler
15-05	Nth. Ireland	W	1-0	Belfast	HC	Clarke
19-05	Wales	D	0-0	London	HC	
22-05	Scotland	W	3-1	London	HC	Peters, Chivers 2

13–10	Switzerland	W	3–2	Basle	ECq	Hurst, Chivers, OG
10–11	Switzerland	D	1–1	London	ECq	Summerbee
1–12	Greece	W	2–0	Athens	ECq	Hurst, Chivers
29–04–1972	West Germany	L	1–3	London	ECqf	Lee F
13–05	West Germany	D	0–0	Berlin	ECqf	
20–05	Wales	W	3–0	Cardiff	HC	Hughes, Bell, Marsh
23–05	Nth. Ireland	L	0–1	London	HC	
27–05	Scotland	W	1–0	Glasgow	HC	Ball
11–10	Yugoslavia	D	1–1	London	Fr	Royle
15–11	Wales	W	1–0	Cardiff	WCq	Bell
24–01–1973	Wales	D	1–1	London	WCq	Hunter
14–02	Scotland	W	5–0	Glasgow	Fr	OG, Clarke 2, Channon, Chivers
12–05	Nth. Ireland	W	2–1	Liverpool	HC	Chivers 2
15–05	Wales	W	3–0	London	HC	Chivers, Channon, Peters
19–05	Scotland	W	1–0	London	HC	Peters
27–05	Czechoslovakia	D	1–1	Prague	Fr	Clarke
6–06	Poland	L	0–2	Chorzow	WCq	
10–06	Soviet Union	W	2–1	Moscow	Fr	OG, Chivers
14–06	Italy	L	0–2	Turin	Fr	
26–09	Austria	W	7–0	London	Fr	Channon 2, Clarke 2, Chivers, Currie, Bell
17–10	Poland	D	1–1	London	WCq	Clarke
14–11	Italy	L	0–1	London	Fr	
3–04–1974	Portugal	D	0–0	Lisbon	Fr	
11–05	Wales	W	2–0	Cardiff	HC	Bowles, Keegan
15–05	Nth. Ireland	W	1–0	London	HC	Weller
18–05	Scotland	L	0–2	Glasgow	HC	
22–05	Argentina	D	2–2	London	Fr	Channon, Worthington
29–05	East Germany	D	1–1	Leipzig	Fr	Channon
1–06	Bulgaria	W	1–0	Sofia	Fr	Worthigton
5–06	Yugoslavia	D	2–2	Belgrade	Fr	Channon, Keegan
30–10	Czechoslovakia	W	3–0	London	ECq	Channon, Bell 2
20–11	Portugal	D	0–0	London	ECq	
12–03–1975	West Germany	W	2–0	London	Fr	Bell, Macdonald
16–04	Cyprus	W	5–0	London	ECq	Macdonald 5
11–05	Cyprus	W	1–0	Limassol	ECq	Keegan
17–05	Nth. Ireland	D	0–0	Belfast	HC	
21–05	Wales	D	2–2	London	HC	Johnson D 2
24–05	Scotland	W	5–1	London	HC	Francis G 2, Beattie, Bell, Johnson D
3–09	Switzerland	W	2–1	Basle	Fr	Keegan, Channon
30–10	Czechoslovakia	L	1–2	Bratislava	ECq	Channon
19–11	Portugal	D	1–1	Lisbon	ECq	Channon
24–03–1976	Wales	W	2–1	Wrexham	Fr	Kennedy, Taylor P
8–05	Wales	W	1–0	Cardiff	HC	Taylor P
11–05	Nth. Ireland	W	4–0	London	HC	Francis G, Channon 2, Pearson J
15–05	Scotland	L	1–2	Glasgow	HC	Channon
23–05	Brazil	L	0–1	Los Angeles	Fr	
28–05	Italy	W	3–2	New York	Fr	Channon 2, Thompson
13–06	Finland	W	4–1	Helsinki	WCq	Keegan 2, Channon, Pearson J
8–09	Rep. Ireland	D	1–1	London	Fr	Pearson J
13–10	Finland	W	2–1	London	WCq	Tueart, Royle
17–11	Italy	L	0–2	Rome	WCq	
9–02–1977	Holland	L	0–2	London	Fr	
30–03	Luxembourg	W	5–0	London	WCq	Keegan, Francis T, Kennedy, Channon 2
28–05	Nth. Ireland	W	2–1	Belfast	HC	Channon, Tueart
31–05	Wales	L	0–1	London	HC	
4–06	Scotland	L	1–2	London	HC	Channon
8–06	Brazil	D	0–0	Rio de Janeiro	Fr	
12–06	Argentina	D	1–1	Buenos Aires	Fr	Pearson J
15–06	Uruguay	D	0–0	Montevideo	Fr	
7–09	Switzerland	D	0–0	London	Fr	
12–10	Luxembourg	W	2–0	Luxembourg	WCq	Kennedy, Mariner
16–11	Italy	W	2–0	London	WCq	Keegan, Brooking
22–02–1978	West Germany	L	1–2	Munich	Fr	Pearson J
19–04	Brazil	D	1–1	London	Fr	Keegan
13–05	Wales	W	3–1	Cardiff	HC	Latchford, Currie, Barnes P
16–05	Nth. Ireland	W	1–0	London	HC	Neal
20–05	Scotland	W	1–0	Glasgow	HC	Coppell
24–05	Hungary	W	4–1	London	Fr	Barnes P, Neal, Francis T, Currie
20–09	Denmark	W	4–3	Copenhagen	Fr	Keegan 2, Latchford, Neal

25–10	Rep. Ireland	D	1–1	Dublin	ECq	Latchford
29–11	Czechoslovakia	W	1–0	London	Fr	Coppell
7–02–1979	Nth. Ireland	W	4–0	London	ECq	Keegan, Latchford 2, Watson D
19–05	Nth. Ireland	W	2–0	Belfast	HC	Watson D, Coppell
23–05	Wales	D	0–0	London	HC	
26–05	Scotland	W	3–1	London	HC	Barnes P, Coppell, Keegan,
6–06	Bulgaria	W	3–0	Sofia	ECq	Keegan, Watson D, Barnes P
10–06	Sweden	D	0–0	Stockholm	Fr	
13–06	Austria	L	3–4	Vienna	Fr	Keegan, Coppell, Wilkins
12–09	Denmark	W	1–0	London	ECq	Keegan
17–10	Nth. Ireland	W	5–1	Belfast	ECq	Francis T 2, Woodcock 2, Og
22–11	Bulgaria	W	2–0	London	ECq	Watson D, Hoddle
6–02–1980	Rep. Ireland	W	2–0	London	ECq	Keegan 2
26–03	Spain	W	2–0	Barcelona	Fr	Woodcock, Francis T
13–05	Argentina	W	3–1	London	Fr	Johnson D 2, Keegan
17–05	Wales	L	1–4	Wrexham	HC	Mariner
20–05	Nth. Ireland	D	1–1	London	HC	OG
24–05	Scotland	W	2–0	Glasgow	HC	Brooking, Coppell
31–05	Australia	W	2–1	Sydney	Fr	Hoddle, Mariner
12–06	Belgium	D	1–1	Turin	ECr1	Wilkins
15–06	Italy	L	0–1	Turin	ECr1	
18–06	Spain	W	2–1	Naples	ECr1	Brooking, Woodcock
10–09	Norway	W	4–0	London	WCq	McDermott 2, Woodcock, Mariner
15–10	Romania	L	1–2	Bucharest	WCq	Woodcock
19–11	Switzerland	W	2–1	London	WCq	OG, Mariner
25–03–1981	Spain	L	1–2	London	Fr	Hoddle
29–04	Romania	D	0–0	London	WCq	
12–05	Brazil	L	0–1	London	Fr	
20–05	Wales	D	0–0	London	HC	
23–05	Scotland	L	0–1	London	HC	
30–05	Switzerland	L	1–2	Basle	WCq	McDermott
6–06	Hungary	W	3–1	Budapest	WCq	Brooking 2, Keegan
9–09	Norway	L	1–2	Oslo	WCq	Robson B
18–11	Hungary	W	1–0	London	WCq	Mariner
23–02–1982	Nth. Ireland	W	4–0	London	HC	Robson B, Keegan, Wilkins, Hoddle
27–04	Wales	W	1–0	Cardiff	HC	Francis T
25–05	Holland	W	2–0	London	Fr	Woodcock, Mariner
29–05	Scotland	W	1–0	Glasgow	HC	Mariner
2–06	Iceland	D	1–1	Reykjavik	Fr	Goddard
3–06	Finland	W	4–1	Helsinki	Fr	Mariner 2, Robson B 2
16–06	France	W	3–1	Bilbao	WCr1	Robson B 2, Mariner
20–06	Czechoslovakia	W	2–0	Bilbao	WCr1	Francis T, Mariner
25–06	Kuwait	W	1–0	Bilbao	WCr1	Francis T
29–06	West Germany	D	0–0	Madrid	WCr2	
5–07	Spain	D	0–0	Madrid	WCr2	
22–09	Denmark	D	2–2	Copenhagen	ECq	Francis T 2
13–10	West Germany	L	1–2	London	Fr	Woodcock
17–11	Greece	W	3–0	Salonika	ECq	Woodcock 2, Lee S
15–12	Luxembourg	W	9–0	London	ECq	OG, Coppell, Woodcock, Blissett 3, Chamberlain, Hoddle, Neal
23–02–1983	Wales	W	2–1	London	HC	Butcher, Neal
30–03	Greece	D	0–0	London	ECq	
27–04	Hungary	W	2–0	London	ECq	Francis T, Withe
28–05	Nth. Ireland	D	0–0	Belfast	HC	
1–06	Scotland	W	2–0	London	HC	Robson B, Cowans
12–06	Australia	D	0–0	Sydney	Fr	
15–06	Australia	W	1–0	Brisbane	Fr	Walsh
19–06	Australia	D	1–1	Melbourne	Fr	Francis T
21–09	Denmark	L	0–1	London	ECq	
12–10	Hungary	W	3–0	Budapest	ECq	Hoodle, Lee S, Mariner
16–11	Luxembourg	W	4–0	Luxembourg	ECq	Robson B 2, Mariner, Butcher
29–02–1984	France	L	0–2	Paris	Fr	
4–04	Nth. Ireland	W	1–0	London	HC	Woodcock
2–05	Wales	L	0–1	Wrexham	HC	
26–05	Scotland	D	1–1	Glasgow	HC	Woodcock
2–06	Soviet Union	L	0–2	London	Fr	
10–06	Brazil	W	2–0	Rio de Janeiro	Fr	Barnes J, Hateley
13–06	Uruguay	L	0–2	Montevideo	Fr	
17–06	Chile	D	0–0	Santiago	Fr	

12–09	East Germany	W	1–0	London	Fr	Robson B
17–10	Finland	W	5–0	London	WCq	Sansom, Robson B, Hateley 2, Woodcock
14–11	Turkey	W	8–0	Istanbul	WCq	Anderson, Robson B 3, Woodcock 2, Barnes J 2
27–02–1985	Nth. Ireland	W	1–0	Belfast	WCq	Hateley
26–03	Rep. Ireland	W	2–1	London	Fr	Lineker, Steven
1–05	Romania	D	0–0	Bucharest	WCq	
22–05	Finland	D	1–1	Helsinki	WCq	Hateley
25–05	Scotland	L	0–1	Glasgow	Fr	
6–06	Italy	L	1–2	Mexico City	Fr	Hateley
9–06	Mexico	L	0–1	Mexico City	Fr	
12–06	West Germany	W	3–0	Mexico City	Fr	Robson B, Dixon K 2
16–06	United States	W	5–0	Los Angeles	Fr	Lineker 2, Dixon K 2, Steven
11–09	Romania	D	1–1	London	WCq	Hoddle
16–10	Turkey	W	5–0	London	WCq	Waddle, Lineker 3, Robson B
13–11	Nth. Ireland	D	0–0	London	WCq	
29–01–1986	Egypt	W	4–0	Cairo	Fr	Steven, OG, Wallace, Cowans
26–02	Israel	W	2–1	Tel Aviv	Fr	Robson B 2
26–03	Soviet Union	W	1–0	Tbilisi	Fr	Waddle
23–04	Scotland	W	2–1	London	Fr	Butcher, Hoddle
17–05	Mexico	W	3–0	Los Angeles	Fr	Hateley 2, Beardsley
24–05	Canada	W	1–0	Vancouver	Fr	Hateley
3–06	Portugal	L	0–1	Monterrey	WCr1	
8–06	Morocco	D	0–0	Monterrey	WCr1	
11–06	Poland	W	3–0	Monterrey	WCr1	Lineker 3
18–06	Paraguay	W	3–0	Mexico City	WCr2	Lineker 2, Beardsley
22–06	Argentina	L	1–2	Mexico City	WCqf	Lineker
10–09	Sweden	L	0–1	Stockholm	Fr	
15–10	Nth. Ireland	W	3–0	London	ECq	Lineker 2, Waddle
12–11	Yugoslavia	W	2–0	London	ECq	Mabbutt, Anderson
18–02–1987	Spain	W	4–2	Madrid	Fr	Lineker 4
1–04	Nth. Ireland	W	2–0	Belfast	ECq	Robson B, Waddle
29–04	Turkey	D	0–0	Izmir	ECq	
19–05	Brazil	D	1–1	London	Fr	Lineker
23–05	Scotland	D	0–0	Glasgow	Fr	
9–09	West Germany	L	1–3	Dusseldorf	Fr	Lineker
14–10	Turkey	W	8–0	London	ECq	Barnes J 2, Lineker 3, Robson B, Beardsley, Webb
11–11	Yugoslavia	W	4–1	Belgrade	ECq	Beardsley, Barnes J, Robson B, Adams
17–02–1988	Israel	D	0–0	Tel Aviv	Fr	
23–03	Holland	D	2–2	London	Fr	Lineker, Adams
27–04	Hungary	D	0–0	Budapest	Fr	
21–05	Scotland	W	1–0	London	Fr	Beardsley
24–05	Colombia	D	1–1	London	Fr	Lineker
28–05	Switzerland	W	1–0	Lausanne	Fr	Lineker
12–06	Rep. Ireland	L	0–1	Stuttgart	ECr1	
15–06	Holland	L	1–3	Dusseldorf	ECr1	Robson B
18–06	Soviet Union	L	1–3	Frankfurt	ECr1	Adams
14–09	Denmark	W	1–0	London	Fr	Webb N
19–10	Sweden	D	0–0	London	WCq	
16–11	Saudi Arabia	D	1–1	Riyadh	Fr	Adams

LEADING INTERNATIONAL GOALSCORERS

1	Charlton R	49
2	Lineker	48
3	Greaves	44
4	Finney	30
	Lofthouse N	30
6	Woodward	29
7	Bloomer	28
8	Robson B	26
9	Hurst	24
10	Mortensen	23
11	Lawton	22
	Own Goals	22
13	Keegan	21
	Channon	21
15	Peters	20
16	Camsell	18
	Dean	18
	Haynes	18
	Hunt R	18
20	Taylor T	16
	Woodcock	16
22	Lindley	15
23	Hilsdon	14
24	Chivers	13
	Mariner	13
	Smith R	13
27	Bambridge E	12
	Bastin	12
	Francis T	12
	Goodall	12
	Smith GO	12
32	Dewhurst	11
	Douglas	11
	Mannion	11
	Matthews S	11
	Platt	11

LEADING INTERNATIONAL APPEARANCES

1	Shilton	125
2	Moore R	108
3	Charlton R	106
4	Wright W	105
5	Robson B	90
6	Sansom	86
7	Wilkins	84
8	Lineker	80
9	Butcher	77
10	Finney	76
11	Banks	73
12	Ball	72
13	Peters	67
	Barnes J	67
15	Watson D	65
16	Keegan	63
	Wilson R	63
18	Hughes E	62
	Waddle	62
20	Clemence	61
21	Greaves	57
22	Haynes	56
23	Matthews S	54
24	Hoddle	53
25	Francis T	52
26	Neal P	50
	Pearce	50

8-02-1989	Greece	W	2-1	Athens	Fr	Barnes J, Robson B
8-03	Albania	W	2-0	Tirana	WCq	Barnes J, Robson B
26-04	Albania	W	5-0	London	WCq	Lineker, Beardsley 2, Waddle, Gascoigne
23-05	Chile	D	0-0	London	Fr	
27-05	Scotland	W	2-0	Glasgow	Fr	Waddle, Bull
3-06	Poland	W	3-0	London	WCq	Lineker, Barnes J, Webb N
7-06	Denmark	D	1-1	Copenhagen	Fr	Lineker
6-09	Sweden	D	0-0	Stockholm	WCq	
11-10	Poland	D	0-0	Chorzow	WCq	
15-11	Italy	D	0-0	London	Fr	
13-12	Yugoslavia	W	2-1	London	Fr	Robson B 2
28-03-1990	Brazil	W	1-0	London	Fr	Lineker
25-04	Czechoslovakia	W	4-2	London	Fr	Bull 2, Pearce, Gascoigne
15-05	Denmark	W	1-0	London	Fr	Lineker
22-05	Uruguay	L	1-2	London	Fr	Barnes J
2-06	Tunisia	D	1-1	Tunis	Fr	Bull
11-06	Rep. Ireland	D	1-1	Cagliari	WCr1	Lineker
16-06	Holland	D	0-0	Cagliari	WCr1	
21-06	Egypt	W	1-0	Cagliari	WCr1	Wright M
26-06	Belgium	W	1-0	Bologna	WCr2	Platt
1-07	Cameroon	W	3-2	Naples	WCqf	Lineker 2, Platt
4-07	West Germany	D	1-1(3-4p)	Turin	WCsf	Lineker
7-07	Italy	L	1-2	Bari	WC3p	Platt
12-09	Hungary	W	1-0	London	Fr	Lineker
17-10	Poland	W	2-0	London	ECq	Lineker, Beardsley
14-11	Rep. Ireland	D	1-1	Dublin	ECq	Platt
6-02-1991	Cameroon	W	2-0	London	Fr	Lineker 2
27-03	Rep. Ireland	D	1-1	London	ECq	OG
1-05	Turkey	W	1-0	Izmir	ECq	Wise
21-05	Soviet Union	W	3-1	London	Fr	Smith A, Platt 2
25-05	Argentina	D	2-2	London	Fr	Lineker, Platt
1-06	Australia	W	1-0	Sydney	Fr	OG
3-06	New Zealand	W	1-0	Auckland	Fr	Lineker
8-06	New Zealand	W	2-0	Wellington	Fr	Pearce, Hirst
12-06	Malaysia	W	4-2	Kuala Lumpur	Fr	Lineker 4
11-09	Germany	L	0-1	London	Fr	
16-10	Turkey	W	1-0	London	ECq	Smith A
13-11	Poland	D	1-1	Poznan	ECq	Lineker
19-02-1992	France	W	2-0	London	Fr	Shearer, Lineker
25-03	Czechoslovakia	D	2-2	Prague	Fr	Merson, Keown
29-04	Commonwealth IS	D	2-2	Moscow	Fr	Lineker, Steven
12-05	Hungary	W	1-0	Budapest	Fr	OG
17-05	Brazil	D	1-1	London	Fr	Platt
3-06	Finland	W	2-1	Helsinki	Fr	Platt 2
11-06	Denmark	D	0-0	Malmo	ECr1	
14-06	France	D	0-0	Malmo	ECr1	
17-06	Sweden	L	1-2	Stockholm	ECr1	Platt

FAEROE ISLANDS

The Faeroe Islands could hardly be more remote from Europe. They are a collection of windswept and storm-ridden islands with a tiny population that has a reputation for slaughtering large quantities of whales every year. Few people outside of Greenpeace ever really took any notice of them, until, that is, they suddenly arrived on the European football scene with a bang in September 1990.

In years of regularly playing matches in international competitions, Cyprus, Malta and Luxembourg had chalked up only 8 wins between them, and yet the Faeroes, playing their first competitive game, won it. Austria were the hapless victims of the biggest shock the European Championship has ever seen, and they could not even claim that the game was played away from home, taking place as it did in neutral Sweden.

Knudsen, the Faeroe goalkeeper, playing throughout the game in a bobble hat, became an instant hero as did Morkore, the scorer of the goal that sank the Austrians. This result was followed up by an equally impressive draw away to Northern Ireland in Belfast, and the Faeroe Islanders finished the group with three points, an achievement no-one would have thought possible at the start.

A league was started in 1942 and a Cup competition has been played since 1967, but neither of the winners see fit to enter either the European or Cup Winners Cup. Perhaps the success of the national team will be the spur that is needed to tempt them to perhaps join in at club level.

The national side has often played matches against Iceland but as the Faeroes did not join FIFA until 1988, technically these cannot be regarded as full internationals; likewise the games played against Greenland and the Shetland Isles. The Faeroe Islands now look set to become regular contestants at national level. The question is can they repeat the successes of their initial outing?

Population: 46 986
Area, sq km: 1339
% in urban areas: 30%
Capital city: Tórshavn

Fotboltssambund Foroya, The Faroes' Football Association
Gundadalur
PO Box 1028
FR–110 Tórshavn
Faeroe Islands
Tel: (010 298) 16707
Fax: (010 298) 19079
Telex: 81332 ITROTT FA
Cable: None
Languages for correspondence: English

Year of formation: 1979
Affiliation to FIFA: 1988
Affiliation to UEFA: 1988
Registered clubs: 172
Registered players: 2900
Registered referees: 84
National stadium: Gundadulur 8000
National colours: Shirts: White/Shorts: Blue/Socks: White
Season: April–October

THE RECORD

WORLD CUP

1930–90 ..... Did not enter

EUROPEAN CHAMPIONSHIP

1960–88 ..... Did not enter
1992 .... QT 5th/5 in group 4

OLYMPIC GAMES

1908–92 ..... Did not enter

CLUB DIRECTORY

TORSHAVN (Population – 14000)
HB Tórshavn
B 36 Tórshavn
Fram Tórshavn

Other clubs are:
EB Eidi – IF Fuglafjordur – GI Gotu – Royn Hvalba – Streymur Hvalvik – LIF Lorvik – KI Klakksvik – MB Midvag – NSI Runavik – SIF Sandavagur – B 71 Sandur – Skala – SI Sorvag – Sumba – B 68 Toftir – TB Tvoroyri – VB Vagur

FAEROE ISLANDS CUP FINALS

Year	Winners	Score	Runners–up
1967	KI Klaksvik	6–2	B'36 Tórshavn
1968	HB Tórshavn	2–1	B'36 Tórshavn
1969–72 – No competition			
1973	HB Tórshavn	2–1	KI Klaksvik
1974	VB Vagur	7–5	HB Tórshavn
1975	HB Tórshavn	7–2	IF Fuglafjordur
1976	HB Tórshavn	3–1	TB Tvoroyri
1977	TB Tvoroyri	4–3	VB Vagur
1978	TB Tvoroyri	5–2	HB Tórshavn
1979	TB Tvoroyri	5–0	KI Klaksvik
1980	TB Tvoroyri	2–1	NSI Runavik
1981	HB Tórshavn	5–2	TB Tvoroyri
1982	HB Tórshavn	2–1	IF Fuglafjordur
1983	GI Gotu	5–1	Royn Valba
1984	HB Tórshavn	2–0	GI Gotu
1985	GI Gotu	4–2	NSI Runavik
1986	NSI Runavik	3–1	LIF Lorvik
1987	HB Tórshavn	2–2 3–0	IF Fuglafjordur
1988	HB Tórshavn	1–0	NSI Runavik
1989	HB Tórshavn	1–1 2–0	B'71
1990	KI Klaksvik	6–1	GI Gotu
1991	B'36 Tórshavn	1–0	HB Tórshavn

NUMBER OF WINS

HB Tórshavn	10
TB Tvoroyri	4
GI Gotu	2
KI Klaksvik	2
NSI Runavik	1
VB Vagur	1
B'36 Tórshavn	1

FAEROE ISLANDS LEAGUE CHAMPIONSHIP

Year	Champions
1942	KI Klaksvik
1943	TB Tvoroyri
1944	–
1945	TB Tvoroyri
1946	B'36 Tórshavn
1947	SI Sorvag
1948	B'36 Tórshavn
1949	TB Tvoroyri
1950	B'36 Tórshavn
1951	TB Tvoroyri
1952	KI Klaksvik
1953	KI Klaksvik
1954	KI Klaksvik
1955	HB Tórshavn
1956	KI Klaksvik
1957	KI Klaksvik
1958	KI Klaksvik
1959	B'36 Tórshavn
1960	HB Tórshavn
1961	KI Klaksvik
1962	B'36 Tórshavn
1963	HB Tórshavn
1964	HB Tórshavn
1965	HB Tórshavn
1966	KI Klaksvik
1967	KI Klaksvik
1968	KI Klaksvik
1969	KI Klaksvik
1970	KI Klaksvik
1971	HB Tórshavn
1972	KI Klaksvik
1973	HB Tórshavn
1974	HB Tórshavn
1975	HB Tórshavn
1976	TB Tvoroyri
1977	TB Tvoroyri
1978	HB Tórshavn
1979	IF Fuglafjordur
1980	TB Tvoroyri
1981	HB Tórshavn
1982	HB Tórshavn
1983	GI Gotu
1984	B'68 Toftir
1985	B'68 Toftir
1986	GI Gotu
1987	GI Gotu
1988	HB Tórshavn
1989	B'71 Sandur
1990	HB Tórshavn
1991	KI Klaksvik

NUMBER OF WINS

KI Klaksvik	15
HB Tórshavn	14
TB Tvoroyri	7
B'36 Tórshavn	5
GI Gotu	3
B'68 Toftir	2
SI Sorvag	1
IF Fuglafjordur	1
B'71 Sandur	1

INTERNATIONAL MATCHES PLAYED BY THE FAEROE ISLANDS

Date	Opponents	Result	Venue	Compet
–1930	Iceland	L 0–1	Tórshavn	Fr
	Shetland Isl	L 1–5	Lerwick	Fr
	Shetland Isl	D 1–1	Lerwick	Fr
	Shetland Isl	L 0–3	Lerwick	Fr
–1935	Shetland Isl	L 2–5	Lerwick	Fr
–1948	Shetland Isl	W 4–1	Tórshavn	Fr
–1951	Shetland Isl	W 7–2	Lerwick	Fr
–1953	Shetland Isl	W 5–0	Tórshavn	Fr
–1955	Shetland Isl	L 0–1	Lerwick	Fr
–1957	Shetland Isl	W 4–1	Tórshavn	Fr
–1959	Shetland Isl	W 4–1	Lerwick	Fr
–1961	Shetland Isl	W 6–1	Tórshavn	Fr
–1963	Shetland Isl	W 3–2	Lerwick	Fr
–1967	Shetland Isl	W 1–0	Tórshavn	Fr
–1969	Shetland Isl	W 2–1	Lerwick	Fr
–1970	Orkney Isl	W 4–3	Tórshavn	Fr
	Shetland Isl	L 0–3	Tórshavn	Fr
–1972	Shetland Isl	W 6–2	Tórshavn	Fr
12–07	Iceland	L 0–3	Reykjavik	Fr
8–06–1973	Iceland	L 0–4	Klaksvik	Fr
	Shetland Isl	L 1–5	Lerwick	Fr
	Orkney Isl	L 1–2	Kirkwall	Fr
3–07–1974	Iceland	L 2–3	Tórshavn	Fr
23–06–1975	Iceland	L 0–6	Reykjavik	Fr
16–06–1976	Iceland	L 1–6	Tórshavn	Fr
30–06–1980	Iceland	L 1–2	Akureyri	Fr
–06	Greenland	W 6–0	Akureyri	Fr
–1981	Shetland Isl	W 3–0	Tvaera	Fr
	Shetland Isl	W 4–1	Fuglefjord	Fr
	Shetland Isl	D 2–2	Tórshavn	Fr
1–08–1982	Iceland	L 1–4	Tórshavn	Fr
2–08	Iceland	L 0–4	Gotu	Fr
–1983	Greenland	D 0–0	Godthaab	Fr
–1983	Greenland	W 3–2	Godthaab	Fr
8–08	Iceland	L 0–6	Njardvik	Fr
1–08–1984	Iceland	D 0–0	Tórshavn	Fr
	Greenland	W 1–0	Tórshavn	Fr
	Greenland	W 4–2	Tórshavn	Fr
–1985	Shetland Isl	W 1–0	Lerwick	Fr
10–07	Iceland	L 0–9	Keflavik	Fr
12–07	Iceland	L 0–1	Akranes	Fr
24–08–1988	Iceland	L 0–1	Akranes	Fr
–1989	Anglesey	W 6–0	Gotu	Fr
	Shetland Isl	W 4–0	Tórshavn	Fr
	Greenland	W 3–0	Fuglefjord	Fr
	Aland Isl	W 7–1	Tórshavn	Fr
12–06–1990	Shetland Isl	W 2–0	Lerwick	Fr
8–08	Iceland	L 2–3	Tórshavn	Fr
	Morkore, Hansen O			
12–09	Austria	W 1–0	Landskrona	ECq
	Nielsen T			
10–10	Denmark	L 1–4	Copenhagen	ECq
	Morkore			
1–05–1991	Nth. Ireland	D 1–1	Belfast	ECq
	Reynheim			
16–05	Yugoslavia	L 0–7	Belgrade	ECq
22–05	Austria	L 0–3	Salzburg	ECq
15–07	Turkey	D 1–1	Tórshavn	Fr
	Jonsson			
11–09	Nth. Ireland	L 0–5	Landskrona	ECq
25–09	Denmark	L 0–4	Landskrona	ECq
16–10	Yugoslavia	L 0–2	Landskrona	ECq
6–05–1992	Romania	L 0–7	Bucharest	WCq
13–05	Norway	L 0–2	Oslo	Fr
3–06	Belgium	L 0–3	Toftir	WCq
17–06	Cyprus	L 0–2	Toftir	WCq

FINLAND

Football is not the national sport in Finland, and trails in popularity well behind the likes of skiing, ski jumping, and ice hockey. Finnish athletes like Lassie Viren, the world's best long-distance runner in the 1970s, have always received far more attention than footballers. Consequently, football is not up to much in the land of lakes, and does not look as though it ever will be.

The football association, formed in 1907, instigated a league in the following year, but this was based almost

	Team	All G	All S	All B	League G	League S	League B	Cup G	Cup S	Europe G	Europe S	Europe B
1	HJK Helsinki	20	11	8	17	9	8	3	2	–	–	–
2	Haka Valkeakoski	13	8	8	4	5	8	9	3	–	–	–
3	Reipas Lahti	10	10	3	3	6	3	7	4	–	–	–
4	HPS Helsinki	10	7	2	9	6	2	1	1	–	–	–
5	TPS Turku	9	14	5	8	12	5	1	2	–	–	–
6	HIFK Helsinki	7	8	4	7	7	4	–	1	–	–	–
7	KuPS Kuopio	7	8	1	5	8	1	2	–	–	–	–
8	Kuusysi Lahti	7	6	–	5	3	–	2	3	–	–	–
9	KTP Kotka	6	2	1	2	–	1	4	2	–	–	–
10	Abo IFK	4	5	1	3	5	1	1	–	–	–	–
11	KIF Helsinki	4	2	3	4	1	3	–	1	–	–	–
12	Ilves Tampere	4	2	–	2	1	–	2	1	–	–	–
13	IFK Vaasa	3	2	2	3	2	2	–	–	–	–	–
14	VPS Vaasa	2	4	1	2	3	1	–	1	–	–	–
15	MP Mikkeli	2	3	–	–	3	–	2	–	–	–	–
16	OPS Oulu	2	–	–	2	–	–	–	–	–	–	–
17	KPV Kokkola	1	2	2	1	1	2	–	1	–	–	–
18	Sudet Kouvola	1	1	4	1	1	4	–	–	–	–	–
19	RoPS Rovaniemi	1	1	2	–	–	2	1	1	–	–	–
20	PP Voikka	1	1	–	–	–	–	1	1	–	–	–
	PUS Helsinki	1	1	–	1	1	–	–	–	–	–	–
22	Helsinki Toverit	1	–	3	1	–	3	–	–	–	–	–
23	Pyrkiva Turku	1	–	1	1	–	1	–	–	–	–	–
24	Unitas Helsinki	1	–	–	1	–	–	–	–	–	–	–
	Drott	1	–	–	–	–	–	1	–	–	–	–
26	Koparit Kuopio	–	4	–	–	2	–	–	2	–	–	–
27	OTP Oulu	–	3	–	–	–	–	–	3	–	–	–
28	Assat Pori	–	2	–	–	1	–	–	1	–	–	–
	ViPS Viipuri	–	2	–	–	2	–	–	–	–	–	–
	SePS Seinajoken	–	2	–	–	–	–	–	2	–	–	–
31	Janteva Kotka	–	1	–	–	1	–	–	–	–	–	–
	KePS Kemi	–	1	–	–	–	–	–	1	–	–	–
	LaPA Lappenranta	–	1	–	–	–	–	–	1	–	–	–
	IF Sport Vaasa	–	1	–	–	–	–	–	1	–	–	–
	Tapion Honka	–	1	–	–	–	–	–	1	–	–	–
	Turun Toverit	–	1	–	–	1	–	–	–	–	–	–
	TKT Tampere	–	1	–	–	–	–	–	1	–	–	–
	TPV Tampere	–	1	–	–	1	–	–	–	–	–	–
39	TaPa Tampere	–	–	1	–	–	1	–	–	–	–	–
	TuPK Turku	–	–	1	–	–	1	–	–	–	–	–

To the end of the 1991 season

exclusively around Helsinki, the distances between towns being too great to allow the participation of provincial teams until later on.

In the international field Finland did not venture far either. Except for a tour to Austria, Hungary and Germany in 1923, the national side rarely left northern Europe and Scandinavia until after the Second World War. In 1912 Finland entered the Stockholm Olympic Games and reached the semi-finals, beating Italy and what was Tsarist Russia on the way. In the semis, however, they were drawn against England and lost, as they did in the bronze medal play-off match against Holland.

The achievements in Stockholm proved to be a false dawn and even high-scoring victories over the Baltic states could not disguise the weakness of the game. On five occasions since, the Finns have been on the receiving end of a double-figure defeat. Even Norway, who are in many ways in a similar position to Finland, managed to score 12 against them.

The Scandinavian Championship provided the Finns' staple diet of international games until well into the 1970s when World Cup and European Championship commitments forced its abandonment, and apart from the 1960–63 edition which they rather surprisingly won, Finland were accustomed to finishing last on most occasions. Playing football only in the summer months does not make playing fixtures against those countries who play on a winter timetable very easy, although tours abroad in the early months of the year are now common practice.

Finnish clubs have been involved in the European competitions from the earliest years and there have been some suprising successes, especially from the provincial clubs, who after the war began to make their presence felt both in the league and cup. In 1986, Kuusysi Lahti reached the quarter-finals of the European Cup with victories over Sarajevo and Zenit Leningrad and only lost to Steaua Bucharest, the eventual winners, by the odd goal.

The national side is also capable on its day of causing an upset or two, and in the 1980 European Championship Finland were only one point off qualifying for the final tournament, finishing above the Soviet Union but behind Greece.

Such exploits are what the Finns have come rely on for their entertainment, as crowds at league games are usually very poor. Instead they prefer to watch the local ice hockey team or the national team whose success rate far outstrips that of their football counterparts.

Population: 4 978 000
Area, sq km: 338 145
% in urban areas: 61.7%
Capital city: Helsinki

Suomen Palloliito Finlands Bollfoerbund
Kuparitie #1
PO Box 29
SF–00441 Helsinki
Finland
Tel: (010 358) 0 905626233
Fax: (010 358) 0 5626413

Telex: 126033 SPLSF
Cable: SUOMIFOTBOLL HELSINKI
Languages for correspondence: English, German
Year of formation: 1907
Affiliation to FIFA: 1908
Affiliation to UEFA: 1954
Registered clubs: 1128
Registered players: 54 100
Registered coaches: 4100
Registered referees: 2500
National stadium: Olympiastadion 50 000

National colours: Shirts: White/Shorts: Blue/Socks: White
Reserve colours: Shirts: Blue/Shorts: White/Socks: Blue
Season: April–October

THE RECORD

WORLD CUP

1930 .... Did not enter
1934 .... Did not enter

1938 .... QT 4th/4 in group 1
1950 .... QT 3rd/3 in group 5
1954 .... QT 3rd/3 in group 2
1958 .... QT 3rd/3 in group 6
1962 .... QT 3rd/3 in group 2
1966 .... QT 4th/4 in group 8
1970 .... QT 4th/4 in group 6
1974 .... QT 3rd/4 in group 4
1978 .... QT 3rd/4 in group 2
1982 .... QT 5th/5 in group 1
1986 .... QT 4th/5 in group 3
1990 .... QT 3rd/4 in group 4

EUROPEAN CHAMPIONSHIP

1960 .... Did not enter
1964 .... Did not enter
1968 .... QT 4th/4 in group 3
1972 .... QT 4th/4 in group 1
1976 .... QT 4th/4 in group 5
1980 .... QT 3rd/4 in group 6
1984 .... QT 4th/4 in group 2
1988 .... QT 4th/4 in group 6
1992 .... QT 4th/5 in group 6

OLYMPIC GAMES

1908 .... Did not enter
1912 .... Semi-finalists/4th place
1920–28 ..... Did not enter
1936 .... 1st round
1948 .... Did not enter
1952 .... 1st round
1956 .... Did not enter
1960 .... QT Failed to qualify
1964 .... QT Failed to qualify
1968 .... QT Failed to qualify
1972 .... Did not enter
1976 .... QT Failed to qualify
1980 .... 1st round
1984 .... QT Failed to qualify
1988 .... QT Failed to qualify
1992 .... QT Failed to qualify

EUROPEAN CLUB COMPETITIONS

EUROPEAN CUP: Quarter-finalists – Kuusysi Lahti 1986

CUP WINNERS CUP: Quarter-finalists – Haka Valkeakosken 1984, RoPS Rovaniemi 1988

UEFA CUP: 3rd round – TPS Turku 1989

CLUB DIRECTORY

HELSINKI (Population – 990 000)

Helsingen Idrotts Förening Kamraterna (HIFK Helsinki)
Stadium: Helsingen Pallokenttä 7000
Founded: 1897
Colours: Red/White

Helsingin Jalkapallo Klubi (HJK Helsinki)
Stadium: Olympiastadion 50 000
Founded: 1907
Colours: Blue and white stripes/Blue

Helsingen Palloseura (HPS Helsinki)
Stadium: Helsingen Pallokenttä 7000
Founded: 1917
Colours: Green/White

TAMPERE (Population – 241 000)

Ilves Tampere
Stadium: Ratina 25 000
Founded: 1931
Colours: Yellow/Yellow
Previous name: Ilves Kissat 1931–70

TURKU (Population – 221 000)

Turun Palloseura (TPS Turku)
Stadium: Kupittaan 10 000
Founded: 1922
Colours: Black and white stripes/White

OULU (Population – 112 000)

Oulun Palloseura (OPS Oulu)
Stadium: Raatti 10 000
Founded: 1925
Colours: Yellow/Blue

Oulun Työväen Palloilijat (OTP Oulu)
Stadium: Raatti 10 000
Founded: 1946
Colours: White/Red

LAHTI (Population – 109 000)

FC Kuusysi Lahti
Stadium: Keskusurheilukenttä 10 000
Founded: 1934
Colours: White/White
Previous names: UP Lahti 1934–69, Lahti'69 1969–74

Reipas Lahti
Stadium: Keskusurheilukenttä 10 000
Founded: 1891
Colours: Orange and black stripes/Black

KUOPIO (Population – 78 000)

Kuopion Palloseura (KuPS Kuopio)
Stadium: Väinölänniemi 12 000
Founded: 1923
Colours: Yellow/Black

Koparit Kuopio
Stadium: Väinölänniemi 12 000
Founded: 1931
Colours: Green/White
Previous name: KPT 1931–82

PORI (Population – 77 000)
Porin Pallotoverit (PPT Pori)
Stadium: Porin 10 000
Founded: 1934
Colours: Red/White

KOUVOLA (Population – 55 000)
Sudet Kouvola
Stadium: Keskuskenttä
Founded: 1912
Colours: Red/White

VAASA (Population – 53 000)
Idrotts Förening Kamraterna (Vassa IFK)
Stadium: Vaskiluoto
Founded: 1900
Colours: Blue/White

KOTKA
Kotkan Työväen Palloilijat (KTP Kotka)
Stadium: Ureheilukeskus 6000
Founded: 1927
Colours: Green and black stripes/White

MIKKELI
Mikkelin Palloilijat (MP Mikkeli)
Stadium: Urheilupuisto 10 000
Founded: 1929
Colours: Blue/White

KOKKOLA
Kokkolan Palloveikot (KPV Kokkola)
Stadium: Keskuskenttä
Founded: 1930
Colours: Green/Green

KEMI
Kemin Palloseura (KePS Kemi)
Stadium: Sauvosaari 4000
Founded: 1932
Colours: Red/White

VALKEAKOSKI
FC Haka
Stadium: Tehtaan Kenttä 6000
Founded: 1932
Colours: White/Black

ROVANIEMI
Rovaniemen Palloseura (RoPS Rovaniemi)
Stadium: Keskuskenttä 4000
Founded: 1950
Colours: Blue/White

FINNISH LEAGUE CHAMPIONSHIP

Year	Champions		Finalists
1908	Unitas Helsinki	4–1	PUS Helsinki
1909	PUS Helsinki	4–0	HIFK Helsinki
1910	Abo IFK	4–2	ViPS Viipuri
1911	HJK Helsinki	7–1	Abo IFK
1912	HJK Helsinki	7–1	HIFK Helsinki
1913	KIF Helsinki	5–3	Abo IFK
1914	–		
1915	KIF Helsinki	1–0	Abo IFK

1916	KIF Helsinki	3–2	Abo IFK
1917	HJK Helsinki	4–2	Abo IFK
1918	HJK Helsinki	3–0	ViPS Viipuri
1919	HJK Helsinki	1–0	Reipas Lahti
1920	Abo IFK	2–1	HPS Helsinki
1921	HPS Helsinki	1–1 2–1	HJK Helsinki
1922	HPS Helsinki	4–2	Reipas Lahti
1923	HJK Helsinki	3–1	TPS Turku
1924	Abo IFK	4–3	HPS Helsinki
1925	HJK Helsinki	3–2	TPS Turku
1926	HPS Helsinki	5–2	TPS Turku
1927	HPS Helsinki	6–0	Reipas Lahti
1928	TPS Turku	1–1 3–2	HIFK Helsinki
1929	HPS Helsinki	4–0	HIFK Helsinki

	Champions		Runners–up		Third	
1930	HIFK Helsinki	12	TPS Turku	12	HPS Helsinki	9
1931	HIFK Helsinki	14	HPS Helsinki	10	TPS Turku	8
1932	HPS Helsinki	20	VPS Vaasa	19	HIFK Helsinki	17
1933	HIFK Helsinki	27	HJK Helsinki	16	Sudet Kouvola	16
1934	HPS Helsinki	24	HIFK Helsinki	23	Helsinki Toverit	15
1935	HPS Helsinki	22	HIFK Helsinki	17	Helsinki Toverit	15
1936	HJK Helsinki	19	HPS Helsinki	17	HIFK Helsinki	16
1937	HIFK Helsinki	21	HJK Helsinki	20	Sudet Kouvola	16
1938	HJK Helsinki	20	TPS Turku	16	VPS Vaasa	16
1939	TPS Turku	20	HJK Helsinki	18	Helsinki Toverit	13
1940	Sudet Kouvola	2–1	TPS Turku			
1941	TPS Turku	21	VPS Vaasa	19	Sudet Kouvola	17
1942	Helsinki Toverit	6–4	Sudet Kouvola			
1943	–					
1944	IFK Vaasa	5–1	TPS Turku			
1945	VPS Vaasa	2–0	HPS Helsinki			
1946	IFK Vaasa	5–2 0–1 5–1	TPV Tampere			
1947	HIFK Helsinki	3–2	Turun Toverit			
1948	VPS Vaasa	24	TPS Turku	24	HPS Helsinki	21
1949	TPS Turku	34	VPS Vaasa	33	KIF Helsinki	32
1950	Ilves Kissat	25	KuPS Kuopio	22	IFK Vaasa	20
1951	KTP Kotka	27	IFK Vaasa	26	TuPK Turku	23
1952	KTP Kotka	26	IFK Vaasa	22	Pyrkiva Turku	21
1953	IFK Vaasa	24	Janteva Kotka	24	KuPS Kuopio	21
1954	Pyrkiva Turku	26	KuPS Kuopio	22	HJK Helsinki	22
1955	KIF Helsinki	25	Haka Valkeakoski	23	IFK Vaasa	21
1956	KuPS Kuopio	27	HJK Helsinki	21	KIF Helsinki	20
1957	HPS Helsinki	26	Haka Valkeakoski	25	TPS Turku	21
1958	KuPS Kuopio	26	HPS Helsinki	26	HIFK Helsinki	21
1959	HIFK Helsinki	27	RU '38 Pori	25	Haka Valkeakoski	21
1960	Haka Valkeakoski	41	TPS Turku	28	KIF Helsinki	27
1961	HIFK Helsinki	31	KIF Helsinki	30	Haka Valkeakoski	29
1962	Haka Valkeakoski	32	Reipas Lahti	27	TaPA Tampere	26
1963	Reipas Lahti	32	Haka Valkeakoski	31	Abo IFK	25
1964	HJK Helsinki	34	KuPS Kuopio	30	KTP Kotka	28
1965	Haka Valkeakoski	31	HJK Helsinki	29	Reipas Lahti	25
1966	KuPS Kuopio	29	HJK Helsinki	27	Haka Valkeakoski	24
1967	Reipas Lahti	32	KuPS Kuopio	30	TPS Turku	28
1968	TPS Turku	32	Reipas Lahti	30	HJK Helsinki	29
1969	KPV Kokkola	35	KuPS Kupio	32	HJK Helsinki	27
1970	Reipas Lahti	32	MP Mikkeli	29	HIFK Helsinki	28
1971	TPS Turku	34	HIFK Helsinki	33	KPV Kokkola	33
1972	TPS Turku	31	MP Mikkeli	30	Reipas Lahti	28
1973	HJK Helsinki	33	KPV Kokkola	31	Reipas Lahti	30
1974	KuPS Kuopio	33	Reipas Lahti	30	HJK Helsinki	28
1975	TPS Turku	32	KuPS Kupio	30	KPV Kokkola	27
1976	KuPS Kuopio	32	Haka Valkeakoski	30	HJK Helsinki	29
1977	Haka Valkeakoski	33	KuPS Kuopio	26	TPS Turku	25
1978	HJK Helsinki	33	KPT Kuopio	32	Haka Valkeakoski	31
1979	OPS Oulu	41	KuPS Kuopio	40	HJK Helsinki	35
1980	OPS Oulu	26	Haka Valkeakoski	25	HJK Helsinki	24
1981	HJK Helsinki	25	KPT Kuopio	23	Haka Valkeakoski	23
1982	Kuusysi Lahti	24	HJK Helsinki	22	Haka Valkeakoski	22
1983	Ilves Tampere	27	HJK Helsinki	25	Haka Valkeakoski	25
1984	Kuusysi Lahti	4–0 4–4	TPS Turku			
1985	HJK Helsinki	4–1 0–1	Ilves Tampere			
1986	Kuusysi Lahti	32	TPS Turku	30	HJK Helsinki	30
1987	HJK Helsinki	33	Kuusysi Lahti	30	TPS Turku	28

1988	HJK Helsinki 43	Kuusysi Lahti 34	RoPS Rovaniemi 31
1989	Kuusysi Lahti 41	TPS Turku 39	RoPS Rovaniemi 34
1990	HJK Helsinki 1–1 1–0	Kuusysi Lahti	
1991	Kuusysi Lahti 59	MP Mikkeli 58	Haka Valkeakoski 54

FINNISH CUP FINALS

Year	Winners	Score	Runners–up
1955	Haka Valkeakoski	5–1	HPS Helsinki
1956	PP Voikka	2–1	TKT Tampere
1957	Drott	2–1	KPT Kuopio
1958	KTP Kotka	4–1	KIF Helsinki
1959	Haka Valkeakoski	2–1	HIFK Helsinki
1960	Haka Valkeakoski	3–1	RU '38 Pori
1961	KTP Kotka	5–2	PP Voikka
1962	HPS Helsinki	5–0	RoPS Rovaniemi
1963	Haka Valkeakoski	1–0	Reipas Lahti
1964	Reipas Lahti	1–0	LaPa Lappenranta
1965	Abo IFK	1–0	TPS Turku
1966	HJK Helsinki	6–1	KTP Kotka
1967	KTP Kotka	2–0	Reipas Lahti
1968	KuPS Kuopio	2–1	KTP Kotka
1969	Haka Valkeakoski	2–0	Tapion Honka
1970	MP Mikkeli	2–0	Reipas Lahti
1971	MP Mikkeli	4–1	IF Sport Vaasa
1972	Reipas Lahti	2–0	VPS Vaasa
1973	Reipas Lahti	1–0	SePS Seinajoki
1974	Reipas Lahti	1–0	OTP Oulu
1975	Reipas Lahti	6–2	HJK Helsinki
1976	Reipas Lahti	2–0	Ilves Tampere
1977	Haka Valkeakoski	3–1	SePS Seinajoki
1978	Reipas Lahti	1–1 3–1	KPT Kuopio
1979	Ilves Tampere	2–0	TPS Turku
1980	KTP Kotka	3–2	Haka Valkeakoski
1981	HJK Helsinki	4–0	Kuusysi Lahti
1982	Haka Valkeakoski	3–2	KPV Kokkola
1983	Kuusysi Lahti	2–0	Haka Valkeakoski
1984	HJK Helsinki	2–1	Kuusysi Lahti
1985	Haka Valkeakoski	1–0	Reipas Lahti
1986	RoPS Rovaniemi	2–0	KePS Kemi
1987	Kuusysi Lahti	5–4	OTP Oulu
1988	Haka Valkeakoski	1–0	OTP Oulu
1989	KuPS Kuopio	3–2	Haka Valkeakoski
1990	Ilves Tampere	2–1	HJK Helsinki
1991	TPS Turku	0–0 (5–3p)	Kuusysi Lahti

INTERNATIONAL MATCHES PLAYED BY FINLAND

Date	Opponents	Result		Venue	Compet	Scorers
22-10-1911	Sweden	L	2–5	Helsinki	Fr	Lindback, Jerima
27-06-1912	Sweden	L	1–7	Stockholm	Fr	Wiberg
29–06	Italy	W	3–2	Stockholm	OGr1	Ohman J, Soinio E, Wiberg
30–06	Tsarist Russia	W	2–1	Stockholm	OGqf	Wiberg, Ohman J
2–07	England *	L	0–4	Stockholm	OGsf	
4–07	Holland	L	0–9	Stockholm	OG3p	
24–05-1914	Sweden	L	3–4	Stockholm	Fr	Schybergsson 2, Johansson K
29–05-1919	Sweden	L	0–1	Stockholm	Fr	
28–09	Sweden	D	3–3	Helsinki	Fr	Wickstrom 2, Thorn
30–05-1920	Sweden	L	0–4	Stockholm	Fr	
19–09	Sweden	W	1–0	Helsinki	Fr	Ohman J
17–10	Estonia	W	6–0	Helsinki	Fr	Tanner 2, Eklof 2, Ohman G, Osterholm
25–05-1921	Norway	L	2–3	Oslo	Fr	Eklof, Mantila
29–05	Sweden	W	3–0	Stockholm	Fr	Kelin, Ohman G
31–07	Austria	L	2–3	Helsinki	Fr	Mantila, OG
28–08	Estonia	W	3–0	Tallinn	Fr	Grannas, Hirvonen, Eklof
18–09	Germany	D	3–3	Helsinki	Fr	Eklof, Thorn, Ohman G
5–06-1922	Sweden	L	1–4	Helsinki	Fr	Kataiavoori
13–07	Hungary	L	1–5	Helsinki	Fr	Kelin
11–08	Estonia	W	10–2	Helsinki	Fr	Ohman J 6, Mantila 2, Eklof 2
26–08	Norway	L	1–3	Helsinki	Fr	Eklof
17–06-1923	Norway	L	0–3	Oslo	Fr	
20–06	Sweden	L	4–5	Gavle	Fr	Linna 2, Kelin, Eklof
12–08	Germany	W	2–1	Dresden	Fr	Linna, OG
15–08	Austria	L	1–2	Vienna	Fr	Eklof
19–08	Hungary	L	1–3	Budapest	Fr	Linna
23–09	Poland	W	5–3	Helsinki	Fr	Eklof 2, Korma 2, Linna
30–09	Estonia	L	1–2	Tallinn	Fr	Österlund T (I)
17–06-1924	Turkey	L	2–4	Helsinki	Fr	Kelin, Korma
28–07	Sweden	L	5–7	Helsinki	Fr	Korma 2, Eklof, Koponen, Karjagin A
10–08	Poland	L	0–1	Warsaw	Fr	
14–08	Latvia	W	2–0	Riga	Fr	Korma, Koponen
23–08	Norway	W	2–0	Helsinki	Fr	Kanerva, Korma
14–09	Estonia	W	4–0	Helsinki	Fr	Koponen 2, Kanerva, Soinio
7–06-1925	Norway	L	0–1	Oslo	Fr	
9–06	Sweden	L	0–4	Gothenberg	Fr	

26–06	Germany	L	3–5	Helsinki	Fr	Koponen 2, Kelin
5–07	Estonia	L	0–2	Tallinn	Fr	
10–07	Austria	L	1–2	Helsinki	Fr	Eklof
9–08	Latvia	W	3–1	Helsinki	Fr	Korma 2, Eklof
30–08	Poland	D	2–2	Helsinki	Fr	Linna, Kulmala
27–09	Denmark	D	3–3	Aarhus	Fr	Eklof 2, Koponen
6–06–1926	Norway	L	2–5	Helsinki	Fr	Kanerva 2
20–06	Denmark	W	3–2	Helsinki	Fr	Lonnberg 2, Kelin
26–07	Sweden	L	2–3	Helsinki	Fr	Kanerva, Saario
8–08	Poland	L	1–7	Poznan	Fr	Laaksonen
12–08	Latvia	W	4–1	Riga	Fr	Koponen 2, Silve, Lonnberg
5–09	Estonia	D	1–1	Helsinki	Fr	Saario
12–06–1927	Sweden	L	2–6	Stockholm	Fr	Åström 2
15–06	Norway	L	1–3	Oslo	Fr	Åström
10–08	Estonia	L	1–2	Tallinn	Fr	Kulmala
11–09	Latvia	W	3–1	Helsinki	Fr	Korma, Koponen, OG
3–06–1928	Norway	L	0–6	Helsinki	Fr	
12–08	Estonia	D	2–2	Helsinki	Fr	Åström, Kanerva
19–08	Latvia	L	1–2	Riga	Fr	Lonnberg
2–09	Sweden	L	2–3	Helsinki	Fr	Kanerva, Malmgren
14–06–1929	Sweden	L	1–3	Stockholm	Fr	Koponen
18–06	Norway	L	0–4	Oslo	Fr	
25–07	Estonia	D	1–1	Tallinn	Fr	Koponen
27–08	Estonia	W	2–1	Helsinki	Fr	Koponen, Lonnberg
15–09	Latvia	W	3–1	Helsinki	Fr	Svanström, Närvänen, Suontausta
13–10	Denmark	L	0–8	Copenhagen	Fr	
20–10	Germany	L	0–4	Hamburg	Fr	
1–06–1930	Norway	L	2–6	Oslo	Fr	Åström, Saario
16–06	Denmark	L	1–6	Helsinki	Fr	Kanerva
4–08	Latvia	L	0–3	Riga	Fr	
6–08	Estonia	L	0–4	Tallinn	Fr	
28–09	Sweden	D	4–4	Helsinki	Fr	Lehtinen L 3, Koponen
17–06–1931	Estonia	W	3–1	Helsinki	Fr	Åström 2, Strömsten
3–07	Sweden	L	2–8	Stockholm	Fr	Lintamo, Grönlund
19–08	Latvia	W	4–0	Helsinki	Fr	Grönlund 2, Malmgren, Åström
6–09	Norway	D	4–4	Helsinki	Fr	Åström 2, Kanerva, Salin
11–10	Denmark	W	3–2	Copenhagen	Fr	Strömsten 2, Åström
16–05–1932	Sweden	L	1–7	Stockholm	Fr	Kanerva
10–06	Sweden	L	1–3	Helsinki	Fr	Grönlund
17–06	Norway	L	1–2	Oslo	Fr	Grönlund
1–07	Germany	L	1–4	Helsinki	Fr	Åström
17–08	Estonia	W	3–0	Tallinn	Fr	Lintamo, Salin, OG
30–08	Denmark	W	4–2	Helsinki	Fr	Malmgren 2, Lintamo 2
14–07–1933	Sweden	L	0–2	Stockholm	Fr	
9–08	Lithuania	W	9–2	Helsinki	Fr	Ronkanen 2, Grönlund 2, Karjagin L 2, Åström 2, Viinioksa
16–08	Estonia	W	2–1	Helsinki	Fr	Weckström, OG
3–09	Norway	L	1–5	Helsinki	Fr	Åström
8–10	Denmark	L	0–2	Copenhagen	Fr	
3–07–1934	Denmark	W	2–1	Helsinki	Fr	Salin, Taipale
8–08	Estonia	D	1–1	Tallinn	Fr	Taipale
14–08	Latvia	D	1–1	Riga	Fr	Kylmälä
16–08	Lithuania	L	0–1	Kaunas	Fr	
2–09	Norway	L	2–4	Oslo	Fr	Lonnberg 2
23–09	Sweden	W	5–4	Helsinki	Fr	Koponen 2, Lintamo 2, Åström
5–06–1935	Latvia	W	4–1	Helsinki	Fr	Weckström 2, Kanerva, Lintamo
12–06	Sweden	D	2–2	Stockholm	Fr	Weckström 2
7–08	Estonia	D	2–2	Helsinki	Fr	Larvo 2
18–08	Germany	L	0–6	Munich	Fr	
8–09	Norway	L	1–5	Helsinki	Fr	Larvo
6–10	Denmark	L	1–5	Copenhagen	Fr	Grönlund
30–06–1936	Denmark	L	1–4	Helsinki	Fr	Salin
6–08	Peru	L	3–7	Berlin	OGr1	Kanerva, Grönlund, Larvo
20–08	Estonia	D	2–2	Tallinn	Fr	Grönlund, Weckström
6–09	Norway	W	2–0	Oslo	Fr	Weckström, Lehtonen
27–09	Sweden	L	1–2	Helsinki	Fr	Kanerva
20–05–1937	England	L	0–8	Helsinki	Fr	
16–06	Sweden	L	0–4	Stockholm	WCq	
29–06	Germany	L	0–2	Helsinki	WCq	

19–08	Estonia	L	0–1	Turku	WCq	
5–09	Norway	L	0–2	Helsinki	Fr	
17–10	Denmark	L	1–2	Copenhagen	Fr	Mäkelä
15–06–1938	Sweden	L	0–2	Stockholm	Fr	
17–06	Norway	L	0–9	Oslo	Fr	
4–07	Sweden	L	2–4	Helsinki	Fr	Lintamo, Granström
17–08	Estonia	W	3–1	Tallinn	Fr	Weckström, Eronen, Lehtonen
31–08	Denmark	W	2–1	Helsinki	Fr	Lintamo, Lehtonen
18–09	Lithuania	W	3–1	Helsinki	Fr	Lehtonen 3
9–06–1939	Sweden	L	1–5	Stockholm	Fr	OG
15–06	Denmark	L	0–5	Copenhagen	Fr	
20–07	Italy	L	2–3	Helsinki	Fr	Lehtonen, Weckström
4–08	Estonia	W	4–2	Helsinki	Fr	Kylmälä 3, Eronen
3–09	Norway	L	1–2	Helsinki	Fr	Eronen
17–09	Denmark	L	1–8	Copenhagen	Fr	Granström
24–09	Latvia	L	0–3	Helsinki	Fr	
29–08–1940	Sweden	L	2–3	Helsinki	Fr	Weckström, Beijar
1–09	Germany	L	0–13	Leipzig	Fr	
22–09	Sweden	L	0–5	Stockholm	Fr	
5–10–1941	Germany	L	0–6	Helsinki	Fr	
15–09–1943	Hungary	L	0–3	Helsinki	Fr	
3–10	Sweden	D	1–1	Helsinki	Fr	Teräs
26–08–1945	Sweden	L	2–7	Gothenberg	Fr	Beijar 2
30–09	Sweden	L	1–6	Helsinki	Fr	Sotiola
28–06–1946	Norway	L	0–12	Bergen	Fr	
1–09	Denmark	L	2–5	Helsinki	Fr	Svahn, Beijar
15–09	Sweden	L	0–7	Helsinki	Fr	
26–06–1947	Norway	L	1–2	Helsinki	Fr	Hasso
24–08	Sweden	L	0–7	Boras	Fr	
7–09	Norway	D	3–3	Helsinki	Fr	Myntti 2, Reunanen
17–09	Poland	L	1–4	Helsinki	Fr	Forsman
5–10	Denmark	L	1–4	Aarhus	Fr	Stolpe
15–06–1948	Denmark	L	0–3	Helsinki	Fr	
2–07	Iceland	L	0–2	Reykjavik	Fr	
5–09	Norway	L	0–2	Oslo	Fr	
19–09	Sweden	D	2–2	Helsinki	Fr	Lehtovirta, Rytkönen
17–10	Poland	L	0–1	Warsaw	Fr	
16–06–1949	Holland	L	1–4	Helsinki	Fr	Reunanen
8–07	Norway	D	1–1	Helsinki	Fr	Vaihela
8–09	Rep. Ireland	L	0–3	Dublin	WCq	
11–09	Denmark	W	2–0	Copenhagen	Fr	
2–10	Sweden	L	1–8	Malmo	Fr	Vaihela
9–10	Rep Ireland	D	1–1	Helsinki	WCq	Vaihela
11–06–1950	Holland	W	4–1	Helsinki	Fr	Myntti, Asikainen, Rytkönen, Vaihela
27–08	Denmark	L	1–2	Helsinki	Fr	Asikainen
7–09	Yugoslavia	W	3–2	Helsinki	Fr	Vaihela, Asikainen, Lehtovirta
10–09	Norway	L	1–4	Oslo	Fr	Lilja
24–09	Sweden	L	0–1	Helsinki	Fr	
16–08–1951	Norway	D	1–1	Helsinki	Fr	Vaihela
2–09	Sweden	L	2–3	Stockholm	Fr	Vaihela, Lehtovirta
30–09	Denmark	L	0–1	Copenhagen	Fr	
27–10	Holland	D	4–4	Rotterdam	Fr	Lehtovirta 2, Vaihela, Rytkonen
4–11	Luxembourg	L	0–3	Luxembourg	Fr	
18–11	Hungary	L	0–8	Budapest	Fr	
10–06–1952	Norway	W	2–1	Oslo	Fr	Rikberg 2
13–06	Sweden	W	3–1	Oslo	Fr	Rikberg 2, Vaihela
22–06	Hungary	L	1–6	Helsinki	Fr	Lehtovirta
4–08	China	W	4–0	Helsinki	Fr	Vaihela 2, Pelkonen, Stolpe
31–08	Norway	L	2–7	Oslo	Fr	Lehtovirta, Rikberg
21–09	Sweden	L	1–8	Helsinki	Fr	Pelkonen
5–10	Denmark	W	2–1	Helsinki	Fr	Rikberg, Rytkönen
25–05–1953	Belgium	L	2–4	Helsinki	WCq	Lehtovirta 2
5–08	Sweden	D	3–3	Helsinki	WCq	Lehtovirta, Lahtinen, Rikberg
16–08	Sweden	L	0–4	Stockholm	WCq	
30–08	Norway	L	1–4	Helsinki	Fr	Lahtinen
23–09	Belgium	D	2–2	Brussels	WCq	Lahtinen, Vaihela
4–10	Denmark	L	1–6	Copenhagen	Fr	OG
25–05–1954	Scotland	L	1–2	Helsinki	Fr	Lahtinen
4–06	Sweden	L	0–6	Gothenberg	Fr	

13–06	Denmark	D	2–2	Helsinki	Fr	Myntti, Hiltunen
15–08	Sweden	L	1–10	Helsinki	Fr	Lahtinen
29–08	Norway	L	1–3	Oslo	Fr	Hiltunen
19–05–1955	Hungary	L	1–9	Helsinki	Fr	Hiltunen
19–06	Denmark	L	1–2	Copenhagen	Fr	Lehmusvirta
14–08	Norway	L	1–3	Helsinki	Fr	Hiltunen
28–08	Sweden	L	0–3	Halsingborg	Fr	
11–09	Poland	L	1–3	Helsinki	Fr	Asikainen
20–05–1956	England	L	1–5	Helsinki	Fr	Forsgren
10–06	Sweden	L	1–3	Helsinki	Fr	Lahtinen
29–06	Iceland	W	2–1	Helsinki	Fr	Forsgren 2
26–08	Norway	D	1–1	Oslo	Fr	Forsgren
16–09	Denmark	L	0–4	Helsinki	Fr	
4–11	Poland	L	0–5	Krakow	Fr	
18–06–1957	Denmark	W	2–0	Helsinki	Fr	Pahlman, Vanhanen
19–06	Sweden	L	1–5	Helsinki	Fr	Myntti
5–07	Poland	L	1–3	Helsinki	WCq	Vanhanen
27–07	Soviet Union	L	1–2	Moscow	WCq	Lahtinen
15–08	Soviet Union	L	0–10	Helsinki	WCq	
1–09	Norway	L	0–4	Helsinki	Fr	
22–09	Sweden	L	1–5	Stockholm	Fr	Sundelin
13–10	Denmark	L	0–3	Copenhagen	Fr	
3–11	Poland	L	0–4	Warsaw	WCq	
15–06–1958	Norway	L	0–2	Oslo	Fr	
20–08	Sweden	L	1–7	Helsinki	Fr	Korpela
14–09	Denmark	L	1–4	Helsinki	Fr	Pahlman
28–06–1959	Norway	L	2–4	Helsinki	Fr	Kankkonen 2
2–08	Sweden	L	1–3	Malmo	Fr	Nevalainen
6–09	East Germany	W	3–2	Helsinki	Fr	Pahlman, Hiltunen, Rosqvist
4–10	Denmark	L	0–4	Copenhagen	Fr	
18–10	Poland	L	1–3	Helsinki	OGq	Kankkonen
8–11	Poland	L	2–6	Chorzow	OGq	Österlund T (II), Peltonen
22–06–1960	Sweden	L	0–3	Helsinki	Fr	
10–08	Denmark	L	1–2	Copenhagen	Fr	OG
28–08	Norway	L	3–6	Oslo	Fr	Kankkonen 2, Pahlman
25–09	France	L	1–2	Helsinki	WCq	Pahlman
30–10	East Germany	L	1–5	Rostock	Fr	Rytkönen
16–06–1961	Bulgaria	L	0–2	Helsinki	WCq	
27–06	Norway	W	4–1	Helsinki	Fr	Pahlman, Holmqvist, Mäkelä, Nuovanen
9–08	Sweden	L	0–4	Norrkoping	Fr	
28–09	France	L	1–5	Paris	WCq	Pahlman
15–10	Denmark	L	1–9	Copenhagen	Fr	Österlund T (II)
29–10	Bulgaria	L	1–3	Sofia	WCq	Pietiläinen
19–06–1962	Sweden	L	0–3	Helsinki	Fr	
26–08	Norway	L	1–2	Bergen	Fr	Mäkelä
16–09	Denmark	L	1–6	Helsinki	Fr	Virtanen
3–06–1963	Denmark	D	1–1	Copenhagen	Fr	Pahlman
27–06	Norway	W	2–0	Helsinki	Fr	Pahlman, Lyytikäinen
14–08	Sweden	D	0–0	Stockholm	Fr	
7–06–1964	West Germany	L	1–4	Helsinki	Fr	Peltonen
2–08	Sweden	W	1–0	Helsinki	Fr	Järvi
20–08	Norway	L	0–2	Trondheim	Fr	
23–08	Iceland	W	2–0	Reykjavik	Fr	Järvi, Kestilä
6–09	Denmark	W	2–1	Helsinki	Fr	Järvi, Peltonen
21–10	Scotland	L	1–3	Glasgow	WCq	Peltonen
4–11	Italy	L	1–6	Genoa	WCq	Peltonen
27–05–1965	Scotland	L	1–2	Helsinki	WCq	Hyvärinen
9–06	Denmark	L	1–3	Copenhagen	Fr	Tolsa
23–06	Italy	L	0–2	Helsinki	WCq	
8–08	Norway	W	4–0	Helsinki	Fr	Pahlman, Mäkilä, Kumpulampi, Lindholm
22–08	Sweden	D	2–2	Lulea	Fr	Pahlman, Mäkilä
26–09	Poland	W	2–0	Helsinki	WCq	Peltonen, Nuoranen
24–10	Poland	L	0–7	Szczecin	WCq	
8–05–1966	Israel	L	0–3	Helsinki	Fr	
4–06	Sweden	W	1–0	Helsinki	Fr	Lindholm
26–06	England	L	0–3	Helsinki	Fr	
14–08	Norway	D	1–1	Stavanger	Fr	Lindholm
18–09	Denmark	W	2–1	Helsinki	Fr	Mäkipää, Laine
2–10	Austria	D	0–0	Helsinki	ECq	

16–10	Greece	L	1–2	Salonica	ECq	Mäkipää
10–05–1967	Greece	D	1–1	Helsinki	ECq	Peltonen
1–06	Norway	L	0–2	Helsinki	Fr	
10–08	Sweden	L	0–2	Stockholm	Fr	
30–08	Soviet Union	L	0–2	Moscow	ECq	
6–09	Soviet Union	L	2–5	Turku	ECq	Peltonen, Syriävaara
24–09	Austria	L	1–2	Vienna	ECq	Peltonen
22–10	Denmark	L	0–3	Copenhagen	Fr	
4–06–1968	Denmark	L	1–3	Helsinki	Fr	Tolsa
19–06	Belgium	L	1–2	Helsinki	WCq	Flink
18–08	Norway	L	1–4	Oslo	Fr	Tolsa
11–09	Sweden	L	0–3	Helsinki	Fr	
25–09	Yugoslavia	L	1–9	Belgrade	WCq	Tolsa
9–10	Belgium	L	1–6	Waregem	WCq	Lindholm
22–05–1969	Sweden	L	0–4	Vaxjo	Fr	
4–06	Yugoslavia	L	1–5	Helsinki	WCq	Tolsa
25–06	Spain	W	2–0	Helsinki	WCq	Lindholm, Tolsa
24–07	Iceland	W	3–1	Helsinki	Fr	Lindholm, Rissanen, OG
24–08	Norway	D	2–2	Helsinki	Fr	Lindholm, Tolsa
10–09	Denmark	L	2–5	Copenhagen	Fr	Lindholm, Tolsa
15–10	Spain	L	0–6	La Concepcion	WCq	
3–06–1970	Denmark	D	1–1	Helsinki	Fr	Tolsa
17–06	Norway	L	0–2	Bergen	Fr	
26–08	Sweden	L	1–2	Helsinki	Fr	Lindholm
7–10	Czechoslovakia	D	1–1	Prague	ECq	Paatelainen
11–10	Rumania	L	0–3	Bucharest	ECq	
20–05–1971	Sweden	L	1–4	Boras	Fr	Paatelainen
26–05	Wales	L	0–1	Helsinki	ECq	
16–06	Czechoslovakia	L	0–4	Helsinki	ECq	
24–08	Norway	D	1–1	Helsinki	Fr	Suhonen
8–09	Denmark	D	0–0	Copenhagen	Fr	
22–09	Rumania	L	0–4	Helsinki	ECq	
13–10	Wales	L	0–3	Swansea	ECq	
31–05–1972	Norway	D	0–0	Turku	Fr	
7–06	Denmark	L	0–3	Copenhagen	Fr	
21–06	Albania	W	1–0	Helsinki	WCq	Toivola
16–07	Soviet Union	D	1–1	Vaasa	Fr	Rissanen
20–09	Rumania	D	1–1	Helsinki	WCq	Rissanen
7–10	East Germany	L	0–5	Dresden	WCq	
6–06–1973	East Germany	L	1–5	Tampere	WCq	Manninen
8–07	Sweden	D	1–1	Halmstad	Fr	Suomalainen
29–08	Sweden	L	1–2	Helsinki	Fr	Suhonen
10–10	Albania	L	0–1	Tirana	WCq	
14–10	Rumania	L	0–9	Bucharest	WCq	
6–06–1974	Denmark	D	1–1	Oulu	Fr	Paatelainen
15–08	Norway	W	2–1	Oslo	Fr	Tiovola, Linholm
19–08	Iceland	D	2–2	Reykjavik	Fr	Paatelainen, Laine
1–09	Poland	L	1–2	Helsinki	ECq	Rahja
25–09	Holland	L	1–3	Helsinki	ECq	Rahja
9–10	Poland	L	0–3	Poznan	ECq	
5–06–1975	Italy	L	0–1	Helsinki	ECq	
25–05	Denmark	L	0–2	Copenhagen	Fr	
3–09	Holland	L	1–4	Nijmegen	ECq	Paatelainen
27–09	Italy	D	0–0	Rome	ECq	
19–05–1976	Switzerland	W	1–0	Kuopio	Fr	Jantunen
1–06	Sweden	L	0–2	Helsinki	Fr	
13–06	England	L	1–4	Helsinki	WCq	Paatelainen
14–07	Iceland	W	1–0	Helsinki	Fr	Heiskanen H
11–08	Sweden	L	0–6	Malmo	Fr	
25–08	Turkey	W	2–1	Helsinki	Fr	Heiskanen A, Paatelainen
8–09	Scotland	L	0–6	Glasgow	Fr	
22–09	Luxembourg	W	7–1	Helsinki	WCq	Rissanen 2, Heiskanen E 2, Heiskanen A, Heikkinen, Maekynen
13–10	England	L	1–2	London	WCq	Nieminen
6–04–1977	Turkey	W	2–1	Ankara	Fr	Paatelainen, Nieminen
26–05	Luxembourg	W	1–0	Luxembourg	WCq	Heiskanen A
8–06	Italy	L	0–3	Helsinki	WCq	
22–06	Denmark	L	1–2	Helsinki	Fr	Nieminen
18–08	Norway	D	1–1	Oslo	Fr	Paatelainen

7–09	West Germany	L	0–1	Helsinki	Fr	
5–10	Switzerland	L	0–2	Zurich	Fr	
15–10	Italy	L	1–6	Turin	WCq	Haaskivi
5–04–1978	Soviet Union	L	2–10	Erevan	Fr	Heiskanen A, Nieminen
3–05	Mexico	L	0–1	Helsinki	Fr	
24–05	Greece	W	3–0	Helsinki	ECq	Ismail 2, Nieminen
28–06	Sweden	L	1–2	Boras	Fr	Ismail
9–08	Norway	D	1–1	Helsinki	Fr	Ismail
30–08	Poland	L	0–1	Helsinki	Fr	
20–09	Hungary	W	2–1	Helsinki	ECq	Ismail, Pyykko
11–10	Greece	L	1–8	Athens	ECq	Heiskanen A
5–02–1979	Iraq	L	0–1	Baghdad	Fr	
7–02	Iraq	L	0–2	Baghdad	Fr	
9–02	Bahrain	W	1–0	Manama	Fr	Backman
4–07	Soviet Union	D	1–1	Helsinki	ECq	Ismail
21–08	Norway	L	0–1	Kuopio	OGq	
29–08	Denmark	D	0–0	Mikkeli	Fr	
26–09	Denmark	L	0–1	Copenhagen	Fr	
17–10	Hungary	L	1–3	Debrecen	ECq	Toivola
26–10	Norway	D	1–1	Stavanger	OGq	Rautiainen
31–10	Soviet Union	D	2–2	Moscow	ECq	Hakala, Haaskivi
21–11	Mexico	D	1–1	Mexico City	Fr	Nieminen
26–11	Bermuda	W	2–0	Hamilton	Fr	Nieminen, Himanka
22–05–1980	Sweden	L	0–2	Helsinki	Fr	
4–06	Bulgaria	L	0–2	Helsinki	WCq	
25–06	Iceland	D	1–1	Reykjavik	Fr	Tissari
21–08	Norway	L	1–6	Oslo	Fr	Himanka
3–09	Albania	L	0–2	Tirana	WCq	
24–09	Austria	L	0–2	Helsinki	WCq	
30–11	Bolivia	L	0–3	La Paz	Fr	
4–12	Bolivia	D	2–2	Santa Cruz	Fr	Jaakonsaari, Valvee
8–12	Uruguay	L	0–6	Montevideo	Fr	
1–03–1981	Sweden	W	2–1	Lahti	Fr	
13–05	Bulgaria	L	0–4	Sofia	WCq	
24–05	West Germany	L	0–4	Lahti	WCq	
17–06	Austria	L	1–5	Linz	WCq	Valvee
2–07	Norway	W	3–1	Helsinki	Fr	Kousa, Rajaniemi, Turunen
29–07	Sweden	L	0–1	Halmstad	Fr	
12–08	Denmark	L	1–2	Tampere	Fr	Valvee
2–09	Albania	W	2–1	Kotka	WCq	Houtsonen, Kousa
23–09	West Germany	L	1–7	Bochum	WCq	Turunen
20–02–1982	Sweden	D	2–2	Lahti	Fr	Jaakonsaari 2
21–02	Sweden	W	2–1	Lahti	Fr	Jaakonsaari, Ikalainen
28–04	Norway	D	1–1	Stavanger	Fr	Nieminen
3–06	England	L	1–4	Helsinki	Fr	Haaskivi
11–07	Iceland	W	3–2	Helsinki	Fr	Ismail, Himanka, Kousa
11–08	Denmark	L	2–3	Copenhagen	Fr	Valvee, Turunen
8–09	Poland	L	2–3	Kuopio	ECq	Valvee, Kousa
22–09	Portugal	L	0–2	Helsinki	ECq	
13–10	Soviet Union	L	0–2	Moscow	ECq	
16–03–1983	East Germany	L	1–3	Magdeburg	Fr	Hjelm
17–04	Poland	D	1–1	Warsaw	ECq	OG
1–06	Soviet Union	L	0–1	Helsinki	ECq	
7–09	Sweden	L	0–3	Helsinki	Fr	
21–09	Portugal	L	0–5	Lisbon	ECq	
9–03–1984	Kuwait	L	0–1	Kuwait	Fr	
15–05	Soviet Union	L	1–3	Kouvola	Fr	Rantanen
27–05	Nth. Ireland	W	1–0	Pori	WCq	Valvee
16–08	Mexico	L	0–3	Helsinki	Fr	
12–09	Poland	L	0–2	Helsinki	Fr	
17–10	England	L	0–5	London	WCq	

LEADING INTERNATIONAL APPEARANCES

1 Tolsa	76	4 Turunen	66
2 Ranta	69	Hjelm	66
3 Peltonen	68	6 Petäjä	65

LEADING INTERNATIONAL GOALSCORERS

1	Eklöf	17	4	Vaihela	13
2	Koponen	16		Kanerva	13
	Aström	16			

31–10	Turkey	W 2–1	Antalya	WCq	Hjelm, Lipponen
14–11	Nth. Ireland	L 1–2	Belfast	WCq	Lipponen
20–11	Saudi Arabia	L 1–2	Jubayl	Fr	Hjelm
22–11	Qatar	D 2–2	Doha	Fr	Pekonen, Remes
24–11	Qatar	D 1–1	Doha	Fr	Hjelm
23–01–1985	Spain	L 1–3	Alicante	Fr	Lipponen
8–02	Chile	L 0–2	Vina del Mar	Fr	
14–02	Uruguay	L 1–2	Montevideo	Fr	Valvee
17–02	Ecuador	L 1–3	Ambato	Fr	Nieminen
26–02	Mexico	L 1–2	Acapulco	Fr	Pekonen
17–04	Poland	L 1–2	Opole	Fr	Ukkonen
22–05	England	D 1–1	Helsinki	WCq	Rantanen
6–06	Rumania	D 1–1	Helsinki	WCq	Lipponen
28–08	Rumania	L 0–2	Timisoara	WCq	
25–09	Turkey	W 1–0	Tampere	WCq	Rantenen
22–01–1986	Portugal	D 1–1	Leiria	Fr	Hjelm
22–02	Bahrain	D 0–0	Manama	Fr	
24–02	Bahrain	W 4–0	Manama	Fr	Valvee, Tornvall, Ikalainen, Rasimus
17–04	Brazil	L 0–3	Brasilia	Fr	
7–05	Soviet Union	D 0–0	Moscow	Fr	
6–08	Sweden	L 1–3	Helsinki	Fr	Lipponen
20–08	East Germany	W 1–0	Lahti	Fr	Hjelm
10–09	Wales	D 1–1	Helsinki	ECq	Hjelm
15–10	Czechoslovakia	L 0–3	Brno	ECq	
29–10	Denmark	L 0–1	Copenhagen	ECq	
18–03–1987	Poland	L 1–3	Rybnik	Fr	Ikalainen
1–04	Wales	L 0–4	Wrexham	ECq	
29–04	Denmark	L 0–1	Helsinki	ECq	
28–05	Brazil	L 2–3	Helsinki	Fr	Hjelm, Lius
9–09	Czechoslovakia	W 3–0	Helsinki	ECq	Hjelm, Lius, Tiainen
12–01–1988	Czechoslovakia	W 2–0	Las Palmas	Fr	Paatelainen M, Alatensio
15–01	Sweden	L 0–1	Las Palmas	Fr	
7–02	Malta	L 0–2	Ta'Qali	Fr	
13–02	Tunisia	W 3–0	Ta'Qali	Fr	Lipponen 3
19–05	Colombia	L 1–3	Helsinki	Fr	Rantanen
4–08	Bulgaria	D 1–1	Vaasa	Fr	Myyry
17–08	Soviet Union	D 0–0	Turku	Fr	
31–08	West Germany	L 0–4	Helsinki	WCq	
19–10	Wales	D 2–2	Swansea	WCq	Ukkonen, Paatelainen M
3–11	Kuwait	D 0–0	Kuwait	Fr	
6–11	Kuwait	D 0–0	Kuwait	Fr	
11–01–1989	Egypt	L 1–2	El Mehalla	Fr	Paatelainen M
13–01	Egypt	L 1–2	Cairo	Fr	Tarkkio
8–02	Algeria	L 0–2	Ta'Qali	Fr	
10–02	Denmark	D 0–0	Ta'Qali	Fr	
12–02	Malta	D 0–0	Ta'Qali	Fr	
22–03	East Germany	D 1–1	Dresden	Fr	Lipponen
31–05	Holland	L 0–1	Helsinki	WCq	
23–08	Yugoslavia	D 2–2	Kuopio	Fr	Tarkkio, Ukkonen
6–09	Wales	W 1–0	Helsinki	WCq	Lipponen
4–10	West Germany	L 1–6	Dortmund	WCq	Lipponen
22–10	Trinidad	W 1–0	Port of Spain	Fr	Lius
25–10	Trinidad	L 0–2	Port of Spain	Fr	
15–11	Holland	L 0–3	Rotterdam	WCq	
12–02–1990	UAE	D 1–1	Dubai	Fr	Tiainen
15–02	Kuwait	W 1–0	Cairo	Fr	Aaltonen M
10–03	USA	L 1–2	Tampa	Fr	Tarkkio
16–05	Rep Ireland	D 1–1	Dublin	Fr	Tauriainen
27–05	Sweden	L 0–6	Stockholm	Fr	
29–08	Czechoslovakia	D 1–1	Kuusankoski	Fr	Jarvinen
12–09	Portugal	D 0–0	Helsinki	ECq	

11–11	Tunisia	W	2–1	Tunis	Fr	Paatelainen M, Tegelberg
25–11	Malta	D	1–1	Ta'Qali	ECq	Holmgren
13–03–1991	Poland	D	1–1	Warsaw	Fr	Paatelainen M
17–04	Holland	L	0–2	Rotterdam	ECq	
16–05	Malta	W	2–0	Helsinki	ECq	Jarvinen, Litmanen
5–06	Holland	D	1–1	Helsinki	ECq	Holmgren
11–09	Portugal	L	0–1	Oporto	ECq	
9–10	Greece	D	1–1	Helsinki	ECq	Ukkonen
30–10	Greece	L	0–2	Athens	ECq	
12–02–1992	Turkey	D	1–1	Adana	Fr	Jarvinen
25–03	Scotland	D	1–1	Glasgow	Fr	Litmanen
15–04	Brazil	L	1–3	Cuiaba	Fr	Vanhala
14–05	Bulgaria	L	0–3	Helsinki	WCq	
3–06	England	L	1–2	Helsinki	Fr	Hjelm

FRANCE

France are a football enigma. Along with England, Italy, Germany, the Soviet Union and Spain, Europe's other dominant countries, they have the capability to become a world power but so far have not fulfilled this potential. This is particularly true at club level where low attendances and general apathy have left France trailing behind the likes of Sweden in the European club competitions. Most embarrassingly for the French, their neighbours Belgium and Holland both have a more vibrant club scene.

The national side has had its moments, however. They finished in third place in the 1958 World Cup, and the team they had in the 1980s was amongst the most exciting Europe has seen in recent years, peaking with a victory in the 1984 European Championship.

If the English were responsible for inventing modern football and taking it around the world, we have the French to thank for organising it into a coherent structure and creating both the World Cup and European Championship. It is somewhat surprising therefore that the prime movers behind the formation of both FIFA and UEFA produced nothing but chaos in the organisation of the game at home.

No fewer than five different bodies vied for control of the game before the present body was founded in 1918. Rugby was by far the more popular game at the turn of the century, and football clubs were often offshoots of rugby clubs. The oldest club, Le Havre Athletic Club, was an example of this. Formed in 1872, it remains the oldest club in the country, but it was not until 1892 that a football section was formed. Up until that point it only played rugby.

Racing Club de France were another such club. Formed in 1882, they remain the standard bearers of French rugby, but it was not until 1932 that they formed a professional football section, Racing Club de Paris, and became involved in the round ball game. White Rovers, Gordon and Club Francais, the first clubs devoted entirely to football, were founded in 1892.

The north of France was a popular venue for tours by English teams before the turn of the century and it was here that the game was played most, but football (and rugby) spread throughout the country, notably in the South. Various leagues were formed by the different bodies who claimed responsibility for the game, but the first proper competition, the French Cup, was not launched until 1918 with the formation of the Federation Francaise de Football. Open to teams from the whole of France, it proved a huge success.

Professionalism became an issue in the early 1930s, and although attempts to form a national league had been made in the late 1920s and early 1930s it was not until the FFF sanctioned professionalism in 1932 that a proper league structure was set up.

France had more success in organising a national side in the early years than creating a settled club structure. Many unofficial games had taken place against sides from England, Belgium and Holland, but the first official match did not take place until 1904 against Belgium in Brussels. Four years later France entered the London Olympic Games but were resoundingly thrashed 17–1 by Denmark. The turmoil in club football obviously did not help matters, but even after the war results did not improve. An all-time low was reached in 1927 when the national side lost 13–1 to Hungary in Budapest.

Professionalism did help to improve results, but all three pre-war World Cups were a disaster for the French, not least in 1938 when they were chosen to host the event. Not before or since has a host country made so little impact on a tournament.

The first signs of real progress in French football came after the war with the emergence of Stade de Reims, until recently the best team France had produced. It contained names like Albert Batteux, who in 1950 became its manager, Roger Marché, Robert Jonquet, Roger Piantoni,

Jean Vincent, Raymond Kopa and Just Fontaine. Twice they lost to Real Madrid in the final of the European Cup, but these players also formed the basis for the national side that played so well to finish third in the 1958 World Cup.

Inconsistency then let the French down. Instead of building on this success, the game went into decline. France only qualified for one of the next four World Cups and apart from reaching the semi-finals of the first European Championships in 1960 and the quarter-finals in 1968, they barely made an impression either in this tournament or the European club competitions. Saint-Étienne did their best to halt the decline in the 1970s, reaching the European Cup final in 1976 before losing to Bayern Munich, but not until the 1980s was the decline really reversed.

In the late 1970s, Michel Platini emerged as the greatest player in French history, and as one of the best in the world. He soon left for the Italian league and an illustrious career with Juventus and so the French league did not see much benefit, but the national side did.

At the 1978 World Cup in Argentina, had they not been grouped with Argentina and Italy who won the tournament and came fourth respectively, France would undoubtedly have progressed further than they did. Four years later, the side was reaching maturity and along with Brazil was considered the best team present. The midfield of Jean Tigana, Alain Giresse, Bernard Genghini and Platini was especially gifted. They should have beaten West Germany in the semi-final, and it was inexperience and a desire for more goals that led to their downfall. Leading 3–1 in extra-time, they did not sit back and defend the lead and so let the Germans score twice. In the penalty shoot-out that followed, poor Maxim Bossis fired his kick at Schumacher and France were out.

Two years later in the European Championships, justice was done as France won her first and only honour. Admittedly they were playing at home, but the French were without question the best side in Europe, if not the world, at that time. With Luis Fernandez added to the midfield, the team was not significantly different from two years previously, and consisted of Joel Bats in goal, a defence of Manuel Amoros, Bossis, Patrick Battiston and Yvon Le Roux, whilst the attack was led by Bernard Lacombe, Didier Six or Bruno Bellone.

For Michel Platini, the tournament was a personal triumph that elevated his reputation to the level of players like Pele, Maradona, Beckenbauer and Cruyff. He scored nine goals in the five games that ultimately saw France beat Spain 2–0 in the final at Parc des Princes. In the same year he won the second of three European Footballer of the Year titles and the first of two World Footballer of the Year titles. Add this to his success in the European club competitions with Juventus, and the 1980s seemed to belong to him.

	All			League			Cup		Europe		
Team	G	S	B	G	S	B	G	S	G	S	B
1 Olympique Marseille	18	12	5	8	5	3	10	6	–	1	2
2 AS Saint–Étienne	16	7	3	10	3	2	6	3	–	1	1
3 AS Monaco	10	8	6	5	4	5	5	3	–	1	1
4 OSC Lille	8	10	1	3	6	1	5	4	–	–	–
5 Stade de Reims	8	6	4	6	3	4	2	1	–	2	–
6 Girondins Bordeaux	7	13	6	4	7	4	3	6	–	–	2
7 FC Nantes	7	11	2	6	7	1	1	4	–	–	1
8 Racing Club Paris	6	4	5	1	2	5	5	2	–	–	–
9 OGC Nice	6	4	–	4	3	–	2	1	–	–	–
10 Red Star Paris	5	1	–	–	–	–	5	1	–	–	–
11 FC Sete	4	4	1	2	–	1	2	4	–	–	–
12 FC Sochaux	3	6	5	2	3	4	1	3	–	–	1
13 Olympique Lyon	3	3	3	–	–	2	3	3	–	–	1
14 Racing Club Strasbourg	3	3	3	1	1	3	2	2	–	–	–
15 Paris Saint Germain	3	2	2	1	1	2	2	1	–	–	–
16 CO Roubaix–Tourcoing	2	2	1	1	–	1	1	2	–	–	–
17 Stade de Rennes	2	2	–	–	–	–	2	2	–	–	–
18 US Sedan–Torcy	2	1	2	–	–	2	2	1	–	–	–
19 FC Metz	2	1	1	–	–	1	2	1	–	–	–
20 CAS Generaux	2	–	–	–	–	–	2	–	–	–	–
21 SEC Bastia	1	2	1	–	–	1	1	1	–	1	–
22 Le Havre AC	1	1	1	–	–	1	1	1	–	–	–
Toulouse FC	1	1	1	–	1	1	1	–	–	–	–
24 AS Cannes	1	1	–	–	1	–	1	–	–	–	–
CA Paris	1	1	–	–	–	–	1	1	–	–	–
SO Montpellier	1	1	–	–	–	–	1	1	–	–	–
27 SCP Montpellier	1	–	1	–	–	1	1	–	–	–	–
28 Club Francais	1	–	–	–	–	–	1	–	–	–	–
Nancy–Lorraine XI	1	–	–	–	–	–	1	–	–	–	–
AS Nancy–Lorraine	1	–	–	–	–	–	1	–	–	–	–
Olympique Pantin	1	–	–	–	–	–	1	–	–	–	–
32 Nîmes Olympique	–	6	1	–	4	1	–	2	–	–	–
33 Racing Club Lens	–	5	2	–	3	2	–	2	–	–	–
34 FC Nancy	–	2	–	–	–	–	–	2	–	–	–
Olympique Paris	–	2	–	–	–	–	–	2	–	–	–
36 AJ Auxerre	–	1	2	–	–	2	–	1	–	–	–
US Valenciennes	–	1	2	–	–	2	–	1	–	–	–
38 SC Angers	–	1	1	–	–	1	–	1	–	–	–
39 US Charleville	–	1	–	–	–	–	–	1	–	–	–
FC Lyon	–	1	–	–	–	–	–	1	–	–	–
US Orléans	–	1	–	–	–	–	–	1	–	–	–
US Quevilly	–	1	–	–	–	–	–	1	–	–	–
Racing Club France	–	1	–	–	–	–	–	1	–	–	–
Reims–Champagne XI	–	1	–	–	–	–	–	1	–	–	–
FC Rouen	–	1	–	–	–	–	–	1	–	–	–
FC Troyes–Aube	–	1	–	–	–	–	–	1	–	–	–
AS Valentigney	–	1	–	–	–	–	–	1	–	–	–

To the end of the 1991–92 season

The 1986 World Cup in Mexico saw the French reach the semi-finals again, and once more they were undone by the Germans at the crucial stage having already knocked out the champions, Italy, and many people's favourites, Brazil. Of the teams in the two tournaments held in the 1980s, France were perhaps the most unlucky. That the Germans appeared in two finals was certainly a victory of unspectacular yet consistent play over a far more exciting, beautiful brand.

Failure to qualify for the 1988 European Championships as well as the 1990 World Cup seemed to signal another decline in French fortunes. The backbone of the 1980s team had gone, but the national team, now managed by Platini, was only in temporary decline, and in the 1992 European Championship became the first team ever to win all of its qualifying games.

The new hero of the side, Jean-Pierre Papin, also helped create an upsurge in the club game. As part of the Marseille side owned by the millionaire Bernard Tapie, he took a French side to a European Cup Final for only the fourth time, although yet again it ended in defeat. If there is one area of the game French teams should improve, it has to be their penalty-taking, as yet again they lost out via the dreaded spot-kicks.

Marseille, it is hoped, will lead French clubs into a new era where they can match their undoubted spending power with success on the fields of Europe. The national team has done it. It is now the turn of the clubs and the French public to follow suit.

Population: 56 647 000
Area, sq km: 543 965
% in urban areas: 73.4%
Capital city: Paris

Fédération Française de Football
60 bis, Avenue d'Iéna
F–75783 Paris Cédex 16
France
Tel: (010 33) 1 44317300
Fax: (010 33) 1 47208296
Telex: 640000 FEDFOOT F
Cable: CEFI PARIS 034
Languages for correspondence: French, English, German, Spanish

Year of formation: 1918
Affiliation to FIFA: 1904
Affiliation to UEFA: 1954
Registered clubs: 22 772
Registered players: 1 588 500
Professional Players: 1400
Registered coaches: 600
Registered referees: 22 772
National stadium: Parc des Princes 49 000
National colours: Shirts: Blue/Shorts: White/Socks: Red
Reserve colours: Shirts: White/Shorts: Blue/Socks: Red
Season: August–June with a mid season break in December and January

THE RECORD

WORLD CUP

1930 .... QT Automatic – Final Tournament/1st round
1934 .... QT 2nd/3 in group 12 – Final Tournament/1st round
1938 .... QT Automatic – Final Tournament/2nd round
1950 .... QT 2nd rd in group 3
1954 .... QT 1st/3 in group 4 – Final Tournament/1st round
1958 .... QT 1st/3 in group 2 – Final Tournament/Semi-finalists/3rd place 1962 QT 2nd/3 in group 2
1966 .... QT 1st/4 in group 3 – Final Tournament/1st round
1970 .... QT 2nd/3 in group 5
1974 .... QT 3rd/3 in group 9
1978 .... QT 1st/3 in group 5 – Final Tournament/1st round
1982 .... QT 2nd/5 in group 2 – Final Tournament/Semi-finalists/4th place
1986 .... QT 1st/5 in group 4 – Final Tournament/Semi-finalists/3rd place 1990 QT 3rd/5 in group 5

EUROPEAN CHAMPIONSHIP

1960 .... Semi-finalists/4th place
1964 .... Quarter-finalists
1968 .... QT 1st/4 in group 7 – Final Tournament/Quarter-finalists
1972 .... QT 3rd/4 in group 2
1976 .... QT 3rd/4 in group 7
1980 .... QT 2nd/4 in group 5
1984 .... QT Automatic – Final Tournament/Winners
1988 .... QT 3rd/5 in group 3
1992 .... QT 1st/5 in group 1 – Final Tournament/First round

OLYMPIC GAMES

1908 .... Semi-finalists
1912 .... Did not enter
1920 .... Semi-finalists
1924 .... Quarter-finalists
1928 .... 1st round
1936 .... Did not enter
1948 .... Quarter-finalists
1952 .... Preliminary round
1956 .... Did not enter
1960 .... Final Tournament/1st round
1964 .... QT Failed to qualify
1968 .... Final Tournament/Quarter-finalists
1972 .... QT Failed to qualify
1976 .... Final Tournament/Quarter-finalists
1980 .... QT Failed to qualify
1984 .... Final Tournament/Winners
1988 .... QT Failed to qualify
1992 .... QT Failed to qualify

EUROPEAN CLUB COMPETITIONS

EUROPEAN CUP: Finalists – Stade de Reims 1956 1959, Saint-Étienne 1976, Olympique Marseille 1991

CUP WINNERS CUP: Finalists – AS Monaco 1992

UEFA CUP: Finalists – Bastia 1978

CLUB DIRECTORY

PARIS (Population – 9 775 000)

Paris FC
Stadium: Stade Montreuil
Founded: 1968
Colours: Blue/White

Paris Saint-Germain
Stadium: Parc des Princes 49 000
Founded: 1973
Colours: White with a single red and blue side band/White
Previous name: Paris FC 1971–73

Racing Club de Paris
Stadium: Colombes
Founded: 1932–66 as the professional section of Racing Club de France
Colours: Sky blue and white hoops/White
A separate club called Racing Club de Paris, also known as Matra Racing, was formed in 1982. It was reconstituted in 1991 as Racing 92

Red Star
Stadium: St Ouen
Founded: 1897
Colours: Green/White
Previous names: Merged with Olympique de Paris to form Red Star Olympique 1926–46, Red Star Olympique Audonien 1946–48, Merged with Stade Français to form Stade Red Star 1948–50, Red Star Olympique Audonien 1950–67, Merged with FC Toulouse to form Red Star FC 1967–70

Stade Français
Stadium: Stade Mathieu
Founded: 1883–1985
Colours: Blue/Red
Previous name: Stade Red Star 1948–50. Dissolved in 1985

LYON (Population – 1 275 000)
Olympique Lyonnais
Stadium: Stade de Gerland 51 000

Founded: 1950
Colours: White with a red and blue V on the front/White

MARSEILLE (Population – 1 225 000)
Olympique de Marseille
Stadium: Stade Vélodrome 45 000
Founded: 1898
Colours: White/White

LILLE (Population – 1 020 000)

Lille Olympique Sporting Club
Stadium: Grimomprez-Jooris 25 000
Founded: 1945
Colours: White/Blue
Previous names: Merger in 1945 of SC Fives (1908) and Olympique Lille (1910)

Club Olympique Roubaix–Tourcoing
Stadium: Amade Prouvost
Founded: 1945
Colours: Red and black stripes/White
Previous name: Merger in 1945 of Racing, Excelsior and US Tourcoing

BORDEAUX (Population – 640 000)
Les Girondins de Bordeaux
Stadium: Parc de Lescure 51 000
Founded: 1881
Colours: Blue/Blue

TOULOUSE (Population – 541 000)
Toulouse Football Club
Stadium: Municipal 34 000
Founded: 1937
Colours: White with violet sleeves/Violet
Previous name: Merged with Red Star as Red Star FC 1967–70

NANTES (Population – 464 000)
Football Club de Nantes
Stadium: Stade de la Beaujoire 52 000
Founded: 1943
Colours: Yellow/Yellow

NICE (Population – 449 000)
Olympique Gymnaste Club de Nice
Stadium: Municipal du Ray 29 000
Founded: 1904
Colours: Red and black stripes/White

TOULON (Population – 410 000)
Sporting Club Toulon
Stadium: Mayol 18 000
Founded: 1945
Colours: Yellow/Blue

STRASBOURG (Population – 400 000)
Racing Club de Strasbourg
Stadium: Stade de Meinau 42 000
Founded: 1906
Colours: Blue with white sleeves/White

GRENOBLE (Population – 392 000)
Football Club Grenoble Dauphiné
Stadium: Charles Berli
Founded: 1892
Colours: Red/Blue

ROUEN (Population – 379 000)
Football Club de Rouen
Stadium: Robert Diochon
Founded: 1923
Colours: White/Red

VALENCIENNES (Population – 349 000)
Union Sportive Valenciennes
Stadium: Roland Nungesser
Founded: 1913
Colours: Red/White

LENS (Population – 327 000)
Racing Club de Lens
Stadium: Félix Bollaert 51 000
Founded: 1906
Colours: Yellow/Red

SAINT-ÉTIENNE (Population – 317 000)
Association Sportive Saint–Étienne
Stadium: Geoffroy Guichard 48 000
Founded: 1920
Colours: Green/White

NANCY (Population 306 000)
Association Sportive Nancy-Lorraine
Stadium: Marcel Picot 37000
Founded: 1935
Colours: White/White
Previous name: FC Nancy 1935–67

CANNES (Population – 295 000)
Association Sportive de Cannes
Stadium: Pièrre de Coubertin 20 000
Founded: 1902
Colours: White with red sleeves/White

LE HAVRE (Population – 254 000)
Le Havre Athletic Club
Stadium: Jules Deschaseaux 22 000
Founded: 1872
Colours: Sky blue/Blue

RENNES (Population – 234 000)
Stade Rennais Football Club
Stadium: Route de Orient 25 000
Founded: 1901
Colours: Red/Black

MONTPELLIER (Population – 221 000)
Montpellier Paillade Sports-Club
Stadium: La Mosson 18 000
Founded: 1974
Colours: White/Orange
Previous name: Sports Olympique Montpellier 1919–69. The club was disolved in 1969, but was the forerunner of the present club

BREST (Population – 201 000)
Brest Amorique Football Club
Stadium: Franci Le Blé
Founded: 1912
Colours: White/White
Previous name: Stade de Brest 1912–86

REIMS (Population – 199 000)
Stade de Reims
Stadium: Auguste Delaune 18 000
Founded: 1931
Colours: Red with white sleeves/White

METZ (Population – 186 000)
Football Club Metz
Stadium: Saint Symphorien 30 000
Founded: 1932
Colours: Claret/Claret

CAEN (Population – 183 000)
Stade Malherbe de Caen
Stadium: Venoix 11 000
Founded: 1913
Colours: Blue with red shoulders and sleeves/Blue

NIMES (Population – 132 000)
Nîmes Olympique
Stadium: Stade des Costières 26 000
Founded: 1901
Colours: Red/Red
Previous name: SC Nîmes 1901–37

MONTBELIARD (Population – 128 000)
Football Club Sochaux-Montbéliard
Stadium: Bonal 17 000
Founded: 1928
Colours: Yellow/Blue

MONACO (Population – 87 000)
Association Sportive de Monaco
Stadium: Louis II 20 000
Founded: 1924
Colours: Red and white diagonal halves/Red

LAVAL (Population – 55 000)
Stade Lavallois
Stadium: Francis Le Basser 18 000
Founded: 1902
Colours: Tangerine/Black

BASTIA (Population – 50 000)
Sporting Etoile Club Bastia
Stadium: Armand-Césari de Furiani 12 000
Founded: 1962
Colours: Blue/Blue

AUXERRE (Population – 40 000)
Association de la Jeunesse Auxerroise
Stadium: Abbé-Deschamps 22 000
Founded: 1905
Colours: White/White

SETE
Football Club de Sète
Stadium: Georges Bayrou 11 000
Founded: 1914
Colours: Green and white stripes/Black

FRENCH LEAGUE CHAMPIONSHIP

Year	Champions		Runners up		3rd	
1933	Olympique Lille	4–3	AS Cannes			
1934	FC Sete	34	SC Fives	33	Olympique Marseille	33
1935	FC Sochaux	48	RC Strasbourg	47	Racing Club Paris	37
1936	Racing Club Paris	44	Olympique Lille	41	RC Strasbourg	39
1937	Olympique Marseille	38	FC Sochaux	38	Racing Club Paris	37
1938	FC Sochaux	44	Olympique Marseille	42	FC Sete	41
1939	FC Sete	42	Olympique Marseille	40	Racing Club Paris	38
1940–1945 –						
1946	OSC Lille	45	AS Saint-Étienne	44	CO Roubaix	41
1947	CO Roubaix	53	Stade de Reims	49	RC Strasbourg	49
1948	Olympique Marseille	48	OSC Lille	47	Stade de Reims	46
1949	Stade de Reims	48	OSC Lille	47	Olympique Marseille	42
1950	Girondins Bordeaux	51	OSC Lille	45	Stade de Reims	44
1951	OGC Nice	41	OSC Lille	41	Le Havre AC	40
1952	OGC Nice	46	Girondins Bordeaux	45	OSC Lille	44
1953	Stade de Reims	48	FC Sochaux	44	Girondins Bordeaux	43
1954	OSC Lille	47	Stade de Reims	46	Girondins Bordeaux	46
1955	Stade de Reims	44	Toulouse FC	40	RC Lens	38
1956	OGC Nice	43	RC Lens	42	AS Monaco	41
1957	AS Saint-Étienne	49	RC Lens	45	Stade de Reims	43
1958	Stade de Reims	48	Nîmes Olympique	41	AS Monaco	41
1959	OGC Nice	56	Nîmes Olympique	53	Racing Club Paris	49
1960	Stade de Reims	60	Nîmes Olympique	53	Racing Club Paris	49
1961	AS Monaco	57	Racing Club Paris	56	Stade de Reims	50
1962	Stade de Reims	48	Racing Club Paris	48	Nîmes Olympique	47
1963	AS Monaco	50	Stade de Reims	47	FC Sedan	46
1964	AS Saint-Étienne	44	AS Monaco	41	RC Lens	40
1965	FC Nantes	43	Girondins Bordeaux	41	US Valenciennes	40
1966	FC Nantes	60	Girondins Bordeaux	53	US Valenciennes	52
1967	AS Saint-Étienne	54	FC Nantes	50	SC Angers	44
1968	AS Saint-Étienne	57	OGC Nice	46	FC Sochaux	43
1969	AS Saint-Étienne	53	Girondins Bordeaux	51	FC Metz	42
1970	AS Saint-Étienne	56	Olympique Marseille	45	RCP Sedan	42
1971	Olympique Marseille	55	AS Saint-Étienne	51	FC Nantes	46
1972	Olympique Marseille	56	Nîmes Olympique	51	FC Sochaux	47
1973	FC Nantes	55	OGC Nice	50	Olympique Marseille	48
1974	AS Saint-Étienne	66	FC Nantes	58	Olympique Lyon	55
1975	AS Saint-Étienne	58	Olympique Marseille	49	Olympique Lyon	48
1976	AS Saint-Étienne	57	OGC Nice	54	FC Sochaux	52
1977	FC Nantes	58	RC Lens	49	SEC Bastia	47
1978	AS Monaco	53	FC Nantes	52	RC Strasbourg	50
1979	RC Strasbourg	56	FC Nantes	54	AS Saint-Étienne	54
1980	FC Nantes	57	FC Sochaux	54	AS Saint-Étienne	54
1981	AS Saint-Étienne	57	FC Nantes	55	Girondins Bordeaux	49
1982	AS Monaco	55	AS Saint-Étienne	54	FC Sochaux	49
1983	FC Nantes	58	Girondins Bordeaux	48	Paris Saint-Germain	47
1984	Girondins Bordeaux	54	AS Monaco	54	AJ Auxerre	49
1985	Girondins Bordeaux	59	FC Nantes	56	AS Monaco	48
1986	Paris Saint-Germain	56	FC Nantes	53	Girondins Bordeaux	49
1987	Girondins Bordeaux	53	Olympique Marseille	49	Toulouse FC	48
1988	AS Monaco	52	Girondins Bordeaux	46	SCP Montpellier	45
1989	Olympique Marseille	73	Paris Saint-Germain	70	AS Monaco	68
1990	Olympique Marseille	53	Girondins Bordeaux	51	AS Monaco	46
1991	Olympique Marseille	55	AS Monaco	51	AJ Auxerre	48
1992	Olympique Marseille	58	AS Monaco	52	Paris Saint-Germain	47

FRENCH CUP FINALS

Year	Winners	Score	Runners–up
1918	Olympique de Pantin	3–0	FC Lyon
1919	CAS Generaux	3–2	Olympique Paris
1920	CA Paris	2–1	Le Havre AC
1921	Red Star Paris	2–1	Olympique Paris
1922	Red Star Paris	2–0	Stade de Rennes
1923	Red Star Paris	4–2	FC Sete
1924	Olympique Marseille	3–2	FC Sete
1925	CAS Generaux	1–1 3–2	FC Rouen
1926	Olympique Marseille	4–1	AS Valentigney
1927	Olympique Marseille	3–0	US Quevilly
1928	Red Star Paris	3–1	CA Paris
1929	SO Montpellier	2–0	FC Sete
1930	FC Sete	3–1	Racing Club France

1931	Club Francais	3–0	SO Montpellier
1932	AS Cannes	1–0	Racing Club Roubaix
1933	Excelsior Roubaix	3–1	Racing Club Roubaix
1934	FC Sete	2–1	Olympique Marseille
1935	Olympique Marseille	3–0	Stade de Rennes
1936	Racing Club Paris	1–0	US Charleville
1937	FC Sochaux	2–1	RC Strasbourg
1938	Olympique Marseille	2–1	FC Metz
1939	Racing Club Paris	3–1	Olympique Lille
1940	Racing Club Paris	2–1	Olympique Marseille
1941	Girondins Bordeaux	2–0	SC Fives
1942	Red Star Paris	2–0	FC Sete
1943	Olympique Marseille	2–2 4–0	Girondins Bordeaux
1944	Nancy-Lorraine XI	4–0	Reims-Champagne XI
1945	Racing Club Paris	3–0	OSC Lille
1946	OSC Lille	4–2	Red Star Paris
1947	OSC Lille	2–0	RC Strasbourg
1948	OSC Lille	3–2	RC Lens
1949	Racing Club Paris	5–2	OSC Lille
1950	Stade de Reims	2–0	Racing Club Paris
1951	RC Strasbourg	3–0	US Valenciennes
1952	OGC Nice	5–3	Girondins Bordeaux
1953	OSC Lille	2–1	FC Nancy
1954	OGC Nice	2–1	Olympique Marseille
1955	OSC Lille	5–2	Girondins Bordeaux
1956	FC Sedan	3–1	FC Troyes-Aube
1957	FC Toulouse	6–3	SC Angers
1958	Stade de Reims	3–1	Nîmes Olympique
1959	Le Havre AC	2–2 3–0	FC Sochaux
1960	AS Monaco	4–2	AS Saint-Étienne
1961	FC Sedan	3–1	Nîmes Olympique
1962	AS Saint-Étienne	1–0	FC Nancy
1963	AS Monaco	0–0 2–0	Olympique Lyon
1964	Olympique Lyon	2–0	Girondins Bordeaux
1965	Stade de Rennes	2–2 3–1	FC Sedan
1966	RC Strasbourg	1–0	FC Nantes
1967	Olympique Lyon	3–1	FC Sochaux
1968	AS Saint-Étienne	2–1	Girondins Bordeaux
1969	Olympique Marseille	2–0	Girondins Bordeaux
1970	AS Saint-Étienne	5–0	FC Nantes
1971	Stade de Rennes	1–0	Olympique Lyon
1972	Olympique Marseille	2–1	SEC Bastia
1973	Olympique Lyon	2–1	FC Nantes
1974	AS Saint-Étienne	2–1	AS Monaco
1975	AS Saint-Étienne	2–0	RC Lens
1976	Olympique Marseille	2–0	Olympique Lyon
1977	AS Saint-Étienne	2–1	Stade de Reims
1978	AS Nancy	1–0	OGC Nice
1979	FC Nantes	4–1	AJ Auxerre
1980	AS Monaco	3–1	US Orléans
1981	SEC Bastia	2–1	AS Saint-Étienne
1982	Paris Saint-Germain	2–2 (6–5p)	AS Saint-Étienne
1983	Paris Saint-Germain	3–2	FC Nantes
1984	FC Metz	2–0	AS Monaco
1985	AS Monaco	1–0	Paris Saint-Germain
1986	Girondins Bordeaux	2–1	Olympique Marseille
1987	Girondins Bordeaux	2–0	Olympique Marseille
1988	FC Metz	1–1 (5–4p)	FC Sochaux
1989	Olympique Marseille	4–3	AS Monaco
1990	SCP Montpellier	2–1	Racing Club Paris
1991	AS Monaco	1–0	Olympique Marseille
1992	–		

INTERNATIONAL MATCHES PLAYED BY FRANCE

Date	Opponents	Result	Venue	Compet	Scorers
1–05–1904	Belgium	D 3–3	Brussels	Fr	Mesnier, Royet, Cypres
12–02–1905	Switzerland	W 1–0	Paris	Fr	Cypres
7–05	Belgium	L 0–7	Brussels	Fr	
22–04–1906	Belgium	L 0–5	Paris	Fr	
1–11	England*	L 0–15	Paris	Fr	
21–04–1907	Belgium	W 2–1	Brussels	Fr	Royet, Puget
8–03–1908	Switzerland	W 2–1	Geneva	Fr	Sartorius, Francois
23–03	England*	L 0–12	Ipswich	Fr	
12–04	Belgium	L 1–2	Paris	Fr	Verlet
10–05	Holland	L 1–4	Rotterdam	Fr	Francois
19–10	Denmark	L 0–9	London	OGr1	
22–10	Denmark	L 1–17	London	OGsf	Sartorius
9–05–1909	Belgium	L 2–5	Brussels	Fr	
22–05	England*	L 0–11	Gentilly	Fr	
3–04–1910	Belgium	L 0–4	Gentilly	Fr	
16–04	England*	L 1–10	Brighton	Fr	Mouton
15–05	Italy	L 2–6	Milan	Fr	Sellier, Ducret
1–01–1911	Hungary	L 0–3	Paris	Fr	
23–03	England*	L 0–3	Paris	Fr	
9–04	Italy	D 2–2	Paris	Fr	Maes 2
23–04	Switzerland	L 2–5	Geneva	Fr	Triboulet, Maes
30–04	Belgium	L 1–7	Brussels	Fr	Maes
29–10	Luxembourg	W 4–1	Luxembourg	Fr	Mesnier 2, Viallemonteil, Gravier
28–01–1912	Belgium	D 1–1	Paris	Fr	Maes
18–02	Switzerland	W 4–1	Paris	Fr	Maes
17–03	Italy	W 4–3	Turin	Fr	Mesnier, Triboulet, Vialmonteil, Maes
12–01–1913	Italy	W 1–0	Paris	Fr	Maes 3, Mesnier
16–02	Belgium	L 0–3	Paris	Fr	Maes
27–02	England*	L 1–4	Brussels	Fr	
9–03	Switzerland	W 4–1	Paris	Fr	Poulain
20–04	Luxembourg	W 8–0	Geneva	Fr	Dubly 2, Montagne, Eloy
25–01–1914	Belgium	W 4–3	Paris	Fr	Maes 5, Poulain 2, Romano
			Lille	Fr	Hanot, Jourde 2, Dubly

8–02	Luxembourg	L 4–5	Luxembourg	Fr	Bard, Ducret, Geromini, Triboulet
8–03	Switzerland	D 2–2	Paris	Fr	Devic, Gastiger
29–03	Italy	L 0–2	Turin	Fr	
31–05	Hungary	L 1–5	Budapest	Fr	Brouzes
9–03–1919	Belgium	D 2–2	Brussels	Fr	Hanot 2
18–01–1920	Italy	L 4–9	Milan	Fr	Bard 2, Dubly, Nicolas P
29–02	Switzerland	W 2–0	Geneva	Fr	Dewaquez, Nicolas P
28–03	Belgium	W 2–1	Paris	Fr	Nicolas P 2
29–08	Italy	W 3–1	Antwerp	OGqf	Bard 2, Boyer
31–08	Czechoslovakia	L 1–4	Antwerp	OGsf	Boyer
20–02–1921	Italy	L 1–2	Marseilles	Fr	Devic
6–03	Belgium	L 1–3	Brussels	Fr	
13–11	Holland	L 0–5	Paris	Fr	
15–01–1922	Belgium	W 2–1	Paris	Fr	Darques, Dewaquez
30–04	Spain	L 0–4	Bordeaux	Fr	
28–01–1923	Spain	L 0–3	San Sebastian	Fr	
25–02	Belgium	L 1–4	Brussels	Fr	Isbecque
2–04	Holland	L 1–8	Amsterdam	Fr	Bard
22–04	Switzerland	D 2–2	Paris	Fr	Dubly, Nicolas P
10–05	England	L 1–4	Paris	Fr	Dewaquez
28–10	Norway	L 0–2	Paris	Fr	
13–01–1924	Belgium	W 2–0	Paris	Fr	Gross, Renier
23–03	Switzerland	L 0–3	Geneva	Fr	
17–05	England	L 1–3	Paris	Fr	Dewaquez
27–05	Estonia	W 7–0	Paris	OGr1	Crut 3, Nicolas P 2, Boyer 2
1–06	Uruguay	L 1–5	Paris	OGqf	Nicolas P
4–06	Hungary	L 0–1	Le Havre	Fr	
11–11	Belgium	L 0–3	Brussels	Fr	
22–03–1925	Italy	L 0–7	Turin	Fr	
19–04	Austria	L 0–4	Paris	Fr	
21–05	England	L 2–3	Paris	Fr	Boyer, Dewaquez
11–04–1926	Belgium	W 4–3	Paris	Fr	Crut 2, Dewaquez, Leveugle
18–04	Portugal	W 4–2	Toulouse	Fr	Salvano, Brunel 2, Bonello
25–04	Switzerland	W 1–0	Paris	Fr	Nicolas P
30–05	Austria	L 1–4	Vienna	Fr	Gallay
13–06	Yugoslavia	W 4–1	Paris	Fr	Gallay, Nicolas P 3
20–06	Belgium	D 2–2	Brussels	Fr	Accard, Dewaquez
16–03–1927	Portugal	L 0–4	Lisbon	Fr	
24–04	Italy	D 3–3	Paris	Fr	Taisne 2, Sottiault
22–05	Spain	L 1–4	Paris	Fr	Boyer
26–05	England	L 0–6	Paris	Fr	
12–06	Hungary	L 1–13	Budapest	Fr	Dewaquez
11–03–1928	Switzerland	L 3–4	Lausanne	Fr	Lieb, Seyler, Nicolas P
15–04	Belgium	L 2–3	Paris	Fr	Bardot
29–04	Portugal	D 1–1	Paris	Fr	Nicolas P
13–05	Czechoslovakia	L 0–2	Paris	Fr	
17–05	England	L 1–5	Paris	Fr	Brouzes
29–05	Italy	L 3–4	Amsterdam	OGr1	Brouzes, Pavillard 2
24–02–1929	Hungary	W 3–0	Paris	Fr	Banide, Nicolas P, Lieb
24–03	Portugal	W 2–0	Paris	Fr	Nicolas P, Galey
14–04	Spain	L 1–8	Zaragoza	Fr	Veinante
9–05	England	L 1–4	Paris	Fr	Dewaquez
19–05	Yugoslavia	L 1–3	Paris	Fr	Cheuva
26–05	Belgium	L 1–4	Liege	Fr	Dewaquez
23–02–1930	Portugal	L 0–2	Oporto	Fr	
23–03	Switzerland	D 3–3	Paris	Fr	Cheuva, Anatol, Liberati
13–04	Belgium	L 1–6	Paris	Fr	Dubus
11–05	Czechoslovakia	L 2–3	Paris	Fr	Delfour, Korb
18–05	Scotland	L 0–2	Paris	Fr	
25–05	Belgium	W 2–1	Liege	Fr	Pinel 2
13–07	Mexico	W 4–1	Montevideo	WCr1	Langiller, Laurent L, Maschinot 2
15–07	Argentina	L 0–1	Montevideo	WCr1	
19–07	Chile	L 0–1	Montevideo	WCr1	
7–12	Belgium	D 2–2	Paris	Fr	Pinel 2
25–01–1931	Italy	L 0–5	Bologna	Fr	
15–02	Czechoslovakia	L 1–2	Paris	Fr	Langiller
15–03	Germany	W 1–0	Paris	Fr	OG
14–05	England	W 5–2	Paris	Fr	Laurent L, Mercier, Langiller, Delfour, Liberati

29–11	Holland	L	3–4	Paris	Fr	Veinante
20–03–1932	Switzerland	D	3–3	Berne	Fr	Liberati, Veinante, Bardot
10–04	Italy	L	1–2	Paris	Fr	Liberati
1–05	Belgium	L	2–5	Brussels	Fr	Pavillard, Cesember
8–05	Scotland	L	1–3	Paris	Fr	Langiller
5–06	Yugoslavia	L	1–2	Belgrade	Fr	Alcazar
9–06	Bulgaria	W	5–3	Sofia	Fr	Rodriguez, Cesember 4
12–06	Rumania	L	3–6	Bucharest	Fr	Chardar, Rolhion
12–02–1933	Austria	L	0–4	Paris	Fr	
19–03	Germany	D	3–3	Berlin	Fr	Rio, Gerard 2
26–03	Belgium	W	3–0	Paris	Fr	Rio, Langiller, Nicolas J
23–04	Spain	W	1–0	Paris	Fr	Nicolas J
25–05	Wales	D	1–1	Paris	Fr	Nicolas J
10–06	Czechoslovakia	L	0–4	Prague	Fr	
6–12	England	L	1–4	London	Fr	Veinante
21–01–1934	Belgium	W	3–2	Brussels	Fr	Nicolas J 2, Veinante
11–03	Switzerland	L	0–1	Paris	Fr	
25–03	Czechoslovakia	L	1–2	Paris	Fr	Korb
15–04	Luxembourg	W	6–1	Luxembourg	WCq	Aston, Nicolas J 4, Liberati
10–05	Holland	W	5–4	Amsterdam	Fr	Keller, Nicolas J 3, Alcazar
27–05	Austria	L	2–3	Turin	WCr1	Nicolas J, Verriest
16–12	Yugoslavia	W	3–2	Paris	Fr	Nicolas J 2, Courtois
24–01–1935	Spain	L	0–2	Madrid	Fr	
17–02	Italy	L	1–2	Rome	Fr	Keller
17–03	Germany	L	1–3	Paris	Fr	Duhart
14–04	Belgium	D	1–1	Brussels	Fr	Courtois
19–05	Hungary	W	2–0	Paris	Fr	Courtois 2
27–10	Switzerland	L	1–2	Geneva	Fr	OG
10–11	Sweden	W	2–0	Paris	Fr	OG, Courtois
12–01–1936	Holland	L	1–6	Paris	Fr	Courtois
9–02	Czechoslovakia	L	0–3	Paris	Fr	
8–03	Belgium	W	3–0	Paris	Fr	Courtois 2, Rio
13–12	Yugoslavia	W	1–0	Paris	Fr	Keller
24–01–1937	Austria	L	1–2	Paris	Fr	Novicki
21–02	Belgium	L	1–3	Brussels	Fr	Rio
21–03	Germany	L	0–4	Stuttgart	Fr	
23–05	Rep. Ireland	L	0–2	Paris	Fr	
10–10	Switzerland	W	2–1	Paris	Fr	Veinante 2
31–10	Holland	W	3–2	Amsterdam	Fr	Nicolas J, Langiller, Courtois
5–12	Italy	D	0–0	Paris	Fr	
30–01–1938	Belgium	W	5–3	Paris	Fr	Courtois, Veinante 2, Heisserer, Ignace
24–03	Bulgaria	W	6–1	Paris	Fr	Nicolas J 2, Aston 2, Aznar, Veinante
26–05	England	L	2–4	Paris	Fr	Jordan, Nicolas J
5–06	Belgium	W	3–1	Paris	WCr1	Veinante, Nicolas J 2
12–06	Italy	L	1–3	Paris	WCqf	Heisserer
4–12	Italy	L	0–1	Naples	Fr	
22–01–1939	Poland	W	4–0	Paris	Fr	Veinante 2, Heisserer, Zatelli
16–03	Hungary	D	2–2	Paris	Fr	Ben Barek, Heisserer
18–05	Belgium	W	3–1	Brussels	Fr	Koranyi 2, Mathe
20–05	Wales	W	2–1	Paris	Fr	Bigot, Veinante
28–01–1940	Portugal	W	3–2	Paris	Fr	Koranyi 2, Hiltl
8–03–1942	Switzerland	L	0–2	Marseille	Fr	
15–03	Spain	L	0–4	Seville	Fr	
24–12–1944	Belgium	W	3–1	Paris	Fr	Simonyi, Arnaudeau, Aston
8–04–1945	Switzerland	L	0–1	Lausanne	Fr	
6–12	Austria	L	1–4	Vienna	Fr	Bongiorni
15–12	Belgium	L	1–2	Brussels	Fr	Aston
7–04–1946	Czechoslovakia	W	3–0	Paris	Fr	Ben Barek, Vaast, Heisserer
14–04	Portugal	L	1–2	Lisbon	Fr	Vaast
5–05	Austria	W	3–1	Paris	Fr	Vaast, Heisserer, Leduc
19–05	England	W	2–1	Paris	Fr	Prouff, Vaast
23–03–1947	Portugal	W	1–0	Paris	Fr	Bihel
3–05	England	L	0–3	London	Fr	
26–05	Holland	W	4–0	Paris	Fr	Alpsteg, Baratte 2, Dard
1–06	Belgium	W	4–2	Paris	Fr	Vaast 2, Baratte, Dard
8–06	Switzerland	W	2–1	Lausanne	Fr	Alpsteg, Baratte
23–11	Portugal	W	4–2	Lisbon	Fr	Vaast 3, Ben Barek
4–04–1948	Italy	L	1–3	Paris	Fr	Baratte
23–05	Scotland	W	3–0	Paris	Fr	Bongiorne, Flamion, Baratte

6–06	Belgium	L 2–4	Brussels	Fr	Cuissard, Ben Barek
12–06	Czechoslovakia	W 4–0	Prague	Fr	Baillot, Baratte 2, Batteux
17–10	Belgium	D 3–3	Paris	Fr	Flamion 2, Baratte
23–04–1949	Holland	L 1–4	Rotterdam	Fr	Baratte
27–04	Scotland	L 0–2	Glasgow	Fr	
22–05	England	L 1–3	Paris	Fr	Moreel
4–06	Switzerland	W 4–2	Paris	Fr	Baillot, Grumellon, Baratte 2
19–06	Spain	L 1–5	Paris	Fr	Baratte
9–10	Yugoslavia	D 1–1	Belgrade	WCq	Baillot
30–10	Yugoslavia	D 1–1	Paris	WCq	Baillot
13–11	Czechoslovakia	W 1–0	Paris	Fr	Baratte
11–12	Yugoslavia	L 2–3	Forence	WCq	Walter, Luciano
27–05–1950	Scotland	L 0–1	Paris	Fr	
4–06	Belgium	L 1–4	Brussels	Fr	Kargu
1–11	Belgium	D 3–3	Paris	Fr	Doye, Baratte, Kargu
10–12	Holland	W 5–2	Paris	Fr	Flamion, Baratte 2, Doye
6–02–1951	Yugoslavia	W 2–1	Paris	Fr	Strappe, Flamion
12–05	Nth. Ireland	D 2–2	Belfast	Fr	Baratte, Bonifaci
16–05	Scotland	L 0–1	Glasgow	Fr	
3–06	Italy	L 1–4	Genoa	Fr	Grumellon
3–10	England	D 2–2	London	Fr	Doye, Alpsteg
14–10	Switzerland	W 2–1	Geneva	Fr	Doye, Grumellon
1–11	Austria	D 2–2	Paris	Fr	Grumellon 2
26–03–1952	Sweden	L 0–1	Paris	Fr	
20–04	Portugal	W 3–0	Paris	Fr	Alpsteg, Strappe 2
22–05	Belgium	W 2–1	Brussels	Fr	Doye, Deladeriere
5–10	West Germany	W 3–1	Paris	Fr	Ujlaki, Cisowski, Strappe
19–10	Austria	W 2–1	Vienna	Fr	Baratte, Penverne
11–11	Nth. Ireland	W 3–1	Paris	Fr	Ujlaki, Kopa
16–11	Rep. Ireland	D 1–1	Dublin	Fr	Piantoni
25–12	Belgium	L 0–1	Paris	Fr	
14–05–1953	Wales	W 6–1	Paris	Fr	Gardien 2, Kopa 2, Bonifaci, Ujlaki
11–06	Sweden	L 0–1	Stockholm	Fr	
20–09	Luxembourg	W 6–1	Luxembourg	WCq	Piantoni, Kopa, Cicci, Glovacki, Kargu, Flamion
4–10	Rep. Ireland	W 5–3	Dublin	WCq	Glovacki, Penverne, Ujlaki 2, Flamion
18–10	Yugoslavia	L 1–3	Zagreb	Fr	Marcel
11–11	Switzerland	L 2–4	Paris	Fr	Ujlaki 2
25–11	Rep. Ireland	W 1–0	Paris	WCq	Piantoni
17–12	Luxembourg	W 8–0	Paris	WCq	Desgranges 2, Vincent 2, Fontaine 3, Foix
11–04–1954	Italy	L 1–3	Paris	Fr	Piantoni
30–05	Belgium	D 3–3	Brussels	Fr	Vincent, OG, Kopa
16–06	Yugoslavia	L 0–1	Lausanne	WCr1	
19–06	Mexico	W 3–2	Geneva	WCr1	Vincent, OG, Kopa
16–10	West Germany	W 3–1	Hanover	Fr	Foix 2, Vincent
11–11	Belgium	D 2–2	Paris	Fr	Kopa 2
17–03–1955	Spain	W 2–1	Madrid	Fr	Kopa, Vincent
3–04	Sweden	W 2–0	Paris	Fr	Oliver, Glovacki
15–05	England	W 1–0	Paris	Fr	Kopa
9–10	Switzerland	W 2–1	Basle	Fr	Kopa, Piantoni
23–10	Soviet Union	D 2–2	Moscow	Fr	Kopa, Piantoni
11–11	Yugoslavia	D 1–1	Paris	Fr	Piantoni
25–12	Belgium	L 1–2	Brussels	Fr	Piantoni
15–02–1956	Italy	L 0–2	Bologna	Fr	
25–03	Austria	W 3–1	Paris	Fr	Leblond, Vincent, Piantoni
7–10	Hungary	L 1–2	Paris	Fr	Cisowski
21–10	Soviet Union	W 2–1	Paris	Fr	Tellechea, Vincent
11–11	Belgium	W 6–3	Paris	WCq	Cisowski 5, Vincent
24–03–1957	Portugal	W 1–0	Lisbon	Fr	Piantoni
2–06	Iceland	W 8–0	Nantes	WCq	Oliver 2, Vincent 2, Dereuddre, Piantoni 2, Brahimi
1–09	Iceland	W 5–1	Rejkjavik	WCq	Cisowski 2, Ujlaki 2, Wisnieski
6–10	Hungary	L 0–2	Budapest	Fr	
27–10	Belgium	D 0–0	Brussels	WCq	
27–11	England	L 0–4	London	Fr	
25–12	Bulgaria	D 2–2	Paris	Fr	Wisnieski, Douis
13–03–1958	Spain	D 2–2	Paris	Fr	Fontaine, Piantoni
16–04	Switzerland	D 0–0	Paris	Fr	
8–06	Paraguay	W 7–3	Norrkoping	WCr1	Fontaine 3, Piantoni, Wisnieski, Kopa, Vincent

11-06	Yugoslavia	L	2-3	Vasteras	WCr1	Fontaine 2,
15-06	Scotland	W	2-1	Orebro	WCr1	Kopa, Fontaine
19-06	Nth. Ireland	W	4-0	Norrkoping	WCqf	Wisnieski, Fontaine 2, Piantoni
24-06	Brazil	L	2-5	Stockholm	WCsf	Fontaine, Piantoni
28-06	West Germany	W	6-3	Gothenburg	WC3p	Fontaine 4, Kopa, Douis
1-10	Greece	W	7-1	Paris	ECr1	Kopa, Fontaine 2, Cisowski 2, Vincent 2
5-10	Austria	W	2-1	Vienna	Fr	Deladeriere, Fontaine
26-10	West Germany	D	2-2	Paris	Fr	Deladeriere, Douis
9-11	Italy	D	2-2	Paris	Fr	Vincent, Fontaine
3-12	Greece	D	1-1	Athens	ECr1	Bruey
1-03-1959	Belgium	D	2-2	Paris	Fr	Vincent 2
11-10	Bulgaria	L	0-1	Sofia	Fr	
11-11	Portugal	W	5-3	Paris	Fr	Fontaine 3, Grillet, Muller
13-12	Austria	W	5-2	Paris	ECr2	Fontaine 3, Vincent 2
17-12	Spain	W	4-3	Paris	Fr	Muller, Fontaine, Vincent, Marche
28-02-1960	Belgium	L	0-1	Brussels	Fr	
16-03	Chile	W	6-0	Paris	Fr	Kaelbel, Vincent, Grillet, Fontaine 2, Muller
27-03	Austria	W	4-2	Vienna	ECr2	Marcel, Rahis, Heutte, Kopa
6-07	Yugoslavia	L	4-5	Paris	ECsf	Vincent, Heutte 2, Wisnieski
9-07	Czechoslovakia	L	0-2	Marseilles	EC3p	
25-09	Finland	W	2-1	Helsinki	WCq	Wisnieski, Ujlaki
28-09	Poland	D	2-2	Warsaw	Fr	Guillas, Wisnieski
12-10	Switzerland	L	2-6	Basle	Fr	Goujon 2
30-10	Sweden	L	0-1	Stockholm	Fr	
11-12	Bulgaria	W	3-0	Paris	WCq	Wisnieski, Marcel, Cossou
15-03-1961	Belgium	D	1-1	Paris	Fr	Piantoni
2-04	Spain	L	0-2	Madrid	Fr	
28-09	Finland	W	5-1	Paris	WCq	Faivre 2, Wisnieski, Piantoni, Schultz
18-10	Belgium	L	0-3	Brussels	Fr	
12-11	Bulgaria	L	0-1	Sofia	WCq	
10-12	Spain	D	1-1	Paris	Fr	Heutte
16-12	Bulgaria	L	0-1	Milan	WCq	
11-04-1962	Poland	L	1-3	Paris	Fr	De Bourgoing
5-05	Italy	L	1-2	Florence	Fr	Piumi
20-10	England	D	1-1	Sheffield	ECr1	Goujon
24-10	West Germany	D	2-2	Stuttgart	Fr	Stako, Goujon
11-11	Hungary	L	2-3	Paris	Fr	Di Nallo
9-01-1963	Spain	D	0-0	Barcelona	Fr	
27-02	England	W	5-2	Paris	ECr1	Wisnieski 2, Douis, Cossou 2
17-04	Holland	L	0-1	Rotterdam	Fr	
28-04	Brazil	L	2-3	Paris	Fr	Wisnieski, Di Nallo
29-09	Bulgaria	L	0-1	Sofia	ECr2	
26-10	Bulgaria	W	3-1	Paris	ECr2	Goujon 2, Herbin
11-11	Switzerland	D	2-2	Paris	Fr	Buron, Lech
25-12	Belgium	L	1-2	Paris	Fr	Masnaghetti
25-04-1964	Hungary	L	1-3	Paris	ECqf	Cossou
23-05	Hungary	L	1-2	Budapest	ECqf	Combin
4-10	Luxembourg	W	2-0	Luxembourg	WCq	Guy, Artelesa
11-11	Norway	W	1-0	Paris	WCq	Rambert
2-12	Belgium	L	0-3	Brussels	Fr	
24-03-1965	Austria	L	1-2	Paris	Fr	Hausser
18-04	Yugoslavia	L	0-1	Belgrade	WCq	
3-06	Argentina	D	0-0	Paris	Fr	
15-09	Norway	W	1-0	Oslo	WCq	Combin
9-10	Yugoslavia	W	1-0	Paris	WCq	Gondet
6-11	Luxembourg	W	4-1	Marseilles	WCq	Gondet 2, Combin 2
19-03-1966	Italy	D	0-0	Paris	Fr	
20-04	Belgium	L	0-3	Paris	Fr	
5-06	Soviet Union	D	3-3	Moscow	Fr	Blanchet, Gondet, Bonnel

LEADING INTERNATIONAL APPEARANCES

1	Amoros	82
2	Bossis	76
3	Platini	72
4	Tresor	65
5	Marche R	63
6	Fernandez	60
7	Jonquet	58
	Michel H	58
8	Battiston	56

13–07	Mexico	D	1–1	London	WCr1	Hausser
15–07	Uruguay	L	1–2	London	WCr1	De Bourgoing
20–07	England	L	0–2	London	WCr1	
28–09	Hungary	L	2–4	Budapest	Fr	Gondet, Revelli H
22–10	Poland	W	2–1	Paris	ECq	Di Nallo, Lech
11–11	Belgium	L	1–2	Brussels	ECq	Lech
26–11	Luxembourg	W	3–0	Luxembourg	ECq	Herbet, Revelli H, Lech
22–03–1967	Rumania	L	1–2	Paris	Fr	Dogliani
3–06	Soviet Union	L	2–4	Paris	Fr	Gondet, Simon
17–09	Poland	W	4–1	Warsaw	ECq	Herbin, Di Nallo 2, Guy
27–09	West Germany	L	1–5	Berlin	Fr	Bosquier
28–10	Belgium	D	1–1	Nantes	ECq	Herbin
23–12	Luxembourg	W	3–1	Paris	ECq	Loubet 3
6–04–1968	Yugoslavia	D	1–1	Marseilles	ECqf	Di Nallo
24–04	Yugoslavia	L	1–5	Belgrade	ECqf	Di Nallo
25–09	West Germany	D	1–1	Marseilles	Fr	Bosquier
17–10	Spain	L	1–3	Lyon	Fr	Blanchet
6–11	Norway	L	0–1	Strasbourg	WCq	
12–03–1969	England	L	0–5	Wembley	Fr	
10–09	Norway	W	3–1	Oslo	WCq	Revelli H 3
15–10	Sweden	L	0–2	Stockholm	WCq	
1–11	Sweden	W	3–0	Paris	WCq	Bras 2, Djorkaeff
8–04–1970	Bulgaria	D	1–1	Rouen	Fr	Michel
28–04	Rumania	W	2–0	Reims	Fr	Loubet, Djorkaeff
3–05	Switzerland	L	1–2	Basle	Fr	Revelli H
5–09	Czechoslovakia	W	3–0	Nice	Fr	Gondet, Loubet, Bosquier
7–10	Austria	L	0–1	Vienna	Fr	
11–11	Norway	W	3–1	Lyon	ECq	Floch, Lech, Mezy
15–11	Belgium	W	2–1	Brussels	Fr	Molitor
8–01–1971	Argentina	W	4–3	Buenos Aires	Fr	Loubet, Djorkaeff, Lech, Revelli H
13–01	Argentina	L	0–2	Mar del Plata	Fr	
17–03	Spain	D	2–2	Valencia	Fr	Revelli H 2
24–04	Hungary	D	1–1	Budapest	ECq	Revelli H
8–09	Norway	W	3–1	Oslo	ECq	Vergnes, Loubet, Blanchet
9–10	Hungary	L	0–2	Paris	ECq	
10–11	Bulgaria	W	2–1	Nantes	ECq	Lech, Loubet
4–12	Bulgaria	L	1–2	Sofia	ECq	Blanchet
8–04–1972	Rumania	L	0–2	Bucharest	Fr	
18–06	Colombia	W	3–2	Salvador	Clr1	Loubet 2, Molitor
25–06	Argentina	D	0–0	Salvador	Clr1	
2–09	Greece	W	3–1	Athens	Fr	Michel Revelli H, Larque
13–10	Soviet Union	W	1–0	Paris	WCq	Bereta
15–11	Rep. Ireland	L	1–2	Dublin	WCq	Larque
3–03–1973	Portugal	L	1–2	Paris	Fr	Molitor
19–05	Rep. Ireland	D	1–1	Paris	WCq	Chiesa
26–05	Soviet Union	L	0–2	Moscow	WCq	
8–09	Greece	W	3–1	Paris	Fr	Jouve, Berdoll, Chiesa
13–10	West Germany	L	1–2	Gelsenkirchen	Fr	Tresor
21–11	Denmark	W	3–0	Paris	Fr	Bereta, Revelli P, Revelli H
23–03–1974	Rumania	W	1–0	Paris	Fr	Bereta
27–04	Czechoslovakia	D	3–3	Prague	Fr	Chiesa, Lacombe 2
18–05	Argentina	L	0–1	Paris	Fr	
7–09	Poland	W	2–0	Wroclaw	Fr	Coste, Jodar
12–10	Belgium	L	1–2	Brussels	ECq	Coste
16–11	East Germany	D	2–2	Paris	ECq	Guillou, Gallice
26–03–1975	Hungary	W	2–0	Paris	Fr	Michel, Parizon
26–04	Portugal	L	0–2	Paris	Fr	
25–05	Iceland	D	0–0	Reykjavik	ECq	
3–09	Iceland	W	3–0	Nantes	ECq	Guillou 2, Berdoll
12–10	East Germany	L	1–2	Leipzig	ECq	Bathenay
15–11	Belgium	D	0–0	Paris	ECq	
27–03–1976	Czechoslovakia	D	2–2	Paris	Fr	Soler, Platini
24–04	Poland	W	2–0	Lens	Fr	Pintenat, Revelli P
22–05	Hungary	L	0–1	Budapest	Fr	
1–09	Denmark	D	1–1	Copenhagen	Fr	Platini
9–10	Bulgaria	D	2–2	Sofia	WCq	Platini, Lacombe
17–11	Rep. Ireland	W	2–0	Paris	WCq	Platini, Bathenay
23–02–1977	West Germany	W	1–0	Paris	Fr	Rouyer
30–03	Rep. Ireland	L	0–1	Dublin	WCq	

23–04	Switzerland	W 4–0	Geneva	Fr	Platini, Six, Rocheteau, Rouyer
26–06	Argentina	D 0–0	Buenos Aires	Fr	
30–06	Brazil	D 2–2	Rio de Janeiro	Fr	Six, Tresor
8–10	Soviet Union	D 0–0	Paris	Fr	
16–11	Bulgaria	W 3–1	Paris	WCq	Rocheteau, Platini, Dalger
8–02–1978	Italy	D 2–2	Naples	Fr	Bathenay, Platini
8–03	Portugal	W 2–0	Paris	Fr	Baronchelli, Berdoll
1–04	Brazil	W 1–0	Paris	Fr	Platini
11–05	Iran	W 2–1	Toulouse	Fr	Gemmrich, Six
19–05	Tunisia	W 2–0	Lille	Fr	Platini, Dalger
2–06	Italy	L 1–2	Mar del Plata	WCr1	Lacombe
6–06	Argentina	L 1–2	Buenos Aires	WCr1	Platini
10–06	Hungary	W 3–1	Mar del Plata	WCr1	Lopez, Berdoll, Rocheteau
1–09	Sweden	D 2–2	Paris	ECq	Berdoll, Six
7–10	Luxembourg	W 3–1	Luxembourg	ECq	Six, Tresor, Gemmrich
8–11	Spain	W 1–0	Paris	Fr	Specht
25–02–1979	Luxembourg	W 3–0	Paris	ECq	Petit, Emon, Larios
4–04	Czechoslovakia	L 0–2	Bratislava	ECq	
2–05	USA	W 6–0	New York	Fr	Lacombe 3, OG, Amisse, Six
5–09	Sweden	W 3–1	Stockholm	ECq	Lacombe, Platini, Battiston
10–10	USA	W 3–0	Paris	Fr	Platini, Wagner, Amisse
17–11	Czechoslovakia	W 2–1	Paris	ECq	Pecout, Rampillon
27–02–1980	Greece	W 5–1	Paris	Fr	Bathenay, Platini 2, Christophe, Stopyra
26–03	Holland	D 0–0	Paris	Fr	
23–05	Soviet Union	L 0–1	Moscow	Fr	
11–10	Cyprus	W 7–0	Limassol	WCq	Lacombe, Platini 2, Larios 2, Six, Zimako
28–10	Rep. Ireland	W 2–0	Paris	WCq	Platini, Zimako
19–11	West Germany	L 1–4	Hanover	Fr	Larios
18–02–1981	Spain	L 0–1	Madrid	Fr	
25–03	Holland	L 0–1	Rotterdam	WCq	
29–04	Belgium	W 3–2	Paris	WCq	Soler 2, Six
15–05	Brazil	L 1–3	Paris	Fr	Six
9–09	Belgium	L 0–2	Brussels	WCq	
14–10	Rep. Ireland	L 2–3	Dublin	WCq	Bellone, Platini
18–11	Holland	W 2–0	Paris	WCq	Platini, Six
5–12	Cyprus	W 4–0	Paris	WCq	Rocheteau, Lacombe 2, Genghini
23–02–1982	Italy	W 2–0	Paris	Fr	Platini, Bravo
24–03	Nth. Ireland	W 4–0	Paris	Fr	Zenier, Couriol, Larios, Genghini
28–04	Peru	L 0–1	Paris	Fr	
15–05	Bulgaria	D 0–0	Lyon	Fr	
2–06	Wales	L 0–1	Toulouse	Fr	
16–06	England	L 1–3	Bilbao	WCr1	Soler
21–06	Kuwait	W 4–1	Valladolid	WCr1	Genghini, Platini, Six, Bossis
24–06	Czechoslovakia	D 1–1	Valladolid	WCr1	Six
28–06	Austria	W 1–0	Madrid	WCr2	Genghini
4–07	Nth. Ireland	W 4–1	Madrid	WCr2	Giresse 2, Rocheteau 2
8–07	West Germany	D 3–3	Seville	WCsf	Platini, Tresor, Giresse Lost 4–5 pens
10–07	Poland	L 2–3	Alicante	WC3p	Girard, Couriol
31–08	Poland	L 0–4	Paris	Fr	
6–10	Hungary	W 1–0	Paris	Fr	Roussey
10–11	Holland	W 2–1	Rotterdam	Fr	Battiston, Platini
16–02–1983	Portugal	W 3–0	Guimaraes	Fr	Stopyra 2, Ferreri
23–03	Soviet Union	D 1–1	Paris	Fr	Fernandez
23–04	Yugoslavia	W 4–0	Paris	Fr	Le Roux, Rocheteau 2, Toure
31–05	Belgium	D 1–1	Luxembourg	Fr	Six
7–09	Denmark	L 1–3	Copenhagen	Fr	Platini
5–10	Spain	D 1–1	Paris	Fr	Rocheteau
12–11	Yugoslavia	D 0–0	Zagreb	Fr	
29–02–1984	England	W 2–0	Paris	Fr	Platini 2
28–03	Austria	W 1–0	Bordeaux	Fr	Rocheteau
18–04	West Germany	W 1–0	Strasbourg	Fr	Genghini
1–06	Scotland	W 2–0	Marseilles	Fr	Giresse, Lacombe
12–06	Denmark	W 1–0	Paris	ECr1	Platini
16–06	Belgium	W 5–0	Nantes	ECr1	Platini 3, Giresse, Fernandez
19–06	Yugoslavia	W 3–2	St-Etienne	ECr1	Platini 3
23–06	Portugal	W 3–2	Marseilles	ECsf	Domergue 2, Platini
27–06	Spain	W 2–0	Paris	ECf	Platini, Bellone
13–10	Luxembourg	W 4–0	Luxembourg	WCq	Battiston, Platini, Stopyra 2
21–11	Bulgaria	W 1–0	Paris	WCq	Platini

LEADING INTERNATIONAL GOALSCORERS

1 Platini	41	3 Papin	22	Nicholas P	20
2 Fontaine	27	4 Nicolas J	20	Vincent	20

8–12	East Germany	W	2–0	Paris	WCq	Stopyra, Anziani
3–04–1985	Yugoslavia	D	0–0	Sarajevo	WCq	
2–05	Bulgaria	L	0–2	Sofia	WCq	
21–08	Uruguay	W	2–0	Paris	AFT	Rocheteau, Toure
11–09	East Germany	L	0–2	Leipzig	WCq	
30–10	Luxembourg	W	6–0	Paris	WCq	Rocheteau 3, Toure, Giresse, Fernandez
16–11	Yugoslavia	W	2–0	Paris	WCq	Platini 2
26–02–1986	Nth. Ireland	D	0–0	Paris	Fr	
26–05	Argentina	W	2–0	Paris	Fr	Ferreri, Vercruysse
5–06	Canada	W	1–0	Leon	WCr1	Papin
9–06	Soviet Union	D	1–1	Leon	WCr1	Fernandez
10–06	Hungary	W	3–0	Leon	WCr1	Stopyra, Tigana, Rocheteau
17–06	Italy	W	2–0	Mexico City	WCr2	Platini, Stopyra
21–06	Brazil	D	1–1	Guadalajara	WCqf	Platini Won 4–3 pens
25–06	West Germany	L	0–2	Guadalajara	WCsf	
28–06	Belgium	W	4–2	Puebla	WC3p	Ferreri, Papin, Genghini, Amoros
19–08	Switzerland	L	0–2	Lausanne	Fr	
10–09	Iceland	D	0–0	Reykjavik	ECq	
11–10	Soviet Union	L	0–2	Paris	ECq	
19–11	East Germany	D	0–0	Leipzig	ECq	
29–04–1987	Iceland	W	2–0	Paris	ECq	Micciche, Stopyra
16–06	Norway	L	0–2	Oslo	ECq	
12–08	West Germany	L	1–2	Berlin	Fr	Cantona
9–09	Soviet Union	D	1–1	Moscow	ECq	Toure
14–10	Norway	D	1–1	Paris	ECq	Fargeon
18–11	East Germany	L	0–1	Paris	ECq	
27–01–1988	Israel	D	1–1	Tel Aviv	Fr	Stopyra
2–02	Switzerland	W	2–1	Toulouse	Fr	Passi, Fargeon
5–02	Morocco	W	2–1	Monaco	Fr	OG, Stopyra
23–03	Spain	W	2–1	Bordeaux	Fr	Passi, Fernandez
27–04	Nth. Ireland	D	0–0	Belfast	Fr	
24–08	Czechoslovakia	D	1–1	Paris	Fr	Paille
28–09	Norway	W	1–0	Paris	WCq	Papin
22–10	Cyprus	D	1–1	Nicosia	WCq	Xuereb
19–11	Yugoslavia	L	2–3	Belgrade	WCq	Perez, Sauzee
7–02–1989	Rep. Ireland	D	0–0	Dublin	Fr	
8–03	Scotland	L	0–2	Glasgow	WCq	
29–04	Yugoslavia	D	0–0	Paris	WCq	
16–08	Sweden	W	4–2	Malmo	Fr	Cantona 2, Papin 2
5–09	Norway	D	1–1	Oslo	WCq	Papin
11–10	Scotland	W	3–0	Paris	WCq	Deschamps, Cantona, OG
18–11	Cyprus	W	2–0	Toulouse	WCq	Deschamps, Blanc
21–01–1990	Kuwait	W	1–0	Kuwait	Fr	Blanc
24–01	East Germany	W	3–0	Kuwait	Fr	Cantona 2, Deschamps
28–02	West Germany	W	2–1	Montpellier	Fr	Papin, Cantona
28–03	Hungary	W	3–1	Budapest	Fr	Cantona 2, Sauzee
15–08	Poland	D	0–0	Paris	Fr	
5–09	Iceland	W	2–1	Reykjavik	ECq	Papin, Cantona
13–10	Czechoslovakia	W	2–1	Paris	ECq	Papin 2
17–11	Albania	W	1–0	Tirana	ECq	Boli
20–02–1991	Spain	W	3–1	Paris	ECq	Sauzee, Papin, Blanc
30–03	Albania	W	5–0	Paris	ECq	Sauzee 2, Papin 2, OG
14–08	Poland	W	5–1	Poznan	Fr	Sauzee, Papin, Simba, Blanc, Perez
4–09	Czechoslovakia	W	2–1	Bratislava	ECq	Papin 2
12–10	Spain	W	2–1	Seville	ECq	Fernandez, Papin
20–11	Iceland	W	3–1	Paris	ECq	Simba, Cantona 2
19–02–1992	England	L	0–2	London	Fr	
25–03	Belgium	D	3–3	Paris	Fr	Papin, Vahirua
27–05	Switzerland	L	1–2	Lausanne	Fr	Divert
5–06	Holland	D	1–1	Lens	Fr	Papin
10–06	Sweden	D	1–1	Stockholm	ECr1	Papin
14–06	England	D	0–0	Malmo	ECr1	
17–06	Denmark	L	1–2	Malmo	ECr1	Papin

GERMANY

Like their cars, German football is solid, well built, often unspectacular and seems to go on and on running. Three World Cup victories and appearances in five of the last seven finals is a phenomenal record that not even Brazil can match. Now with the talent of the former East Germany at their disposal, who knows what new levels the Germans will rise to?

Given the enormous propaganda boost a successful team would have given Hitler, it is perhaps fortunate that much of this success is a post-1945 phenomenon. So instead of a victorious German team at the biggest propaganda show of them all, the 1936 Olympic Games, Hitler witnessed a humiliating defeat by Norway. In the 1938 match with England where the English players were forced to give the Nazi salute, the Fuhrer still could gain no satisfaction, as Germany lost heavily before a capacity crowd in Berlin.

By the turn of the century football had been played in Germany for over 20 years and the majority of today's major clubs had been formed by then. In 1875 Oxford University made a tour of Germany, the first by a British side abroad, but football was often given a hostile reception. As was common in East Germany in the second half of the 20th century, the emphasis was often on individual sports, but this did not stop the growth of football.

The first club devoted entirely to football was SC Germania Hamburg, formed in 1887. As was often the case in France, some clubs such as TSV 1860 Munich were formed earlier but did not start football sections until later. Hamburg, as the major port in the country, was the first centre of football, but it soon spread to the other regions and Berlin especially became dominant. In 1896, in the first inter-city match, they beat Hamburg 13–0.

In 1898 regional leagues had been set up in Southern Germany and Berlin, and to help create an organised structure the Deutscher Fussball-Bund was formed in 1900. Two years later it was decided to invite the winners of the regional leagues to take part in an end of season play-off to determine the national champions. This system remained until 1963, when rather belatedly the West Germans became the last European country to institute a single national league.

Unofficial international matches were played against their neighbours and especially against England, but it was not until 1908 that a proper national side was instituted and a game played against Switzerland in Basle. The record leading up to the First World War was not very impressive with only six wins in 30 games. One game was remarkable, however: in the consolation tournament for teams that had lost in the early stages of the 1912 Stockholm Olympic Games, the Germans defeated Tsarist Russia 16–0, and Gottfried Fuchs scored 10 of the goals.

The inter-war period did not see an immediate rise in German fortunes and there was a surprising reluctance to join in with the main stream of European football, even allowing for Britain's opposition to Germany remaining a member of FIFA. In the 1928 Olympic Games, Germany were beaten by Uruguay in the quarter-finals, and their next appearance in a competition was in the 1934 World Cup.

It would have made sense for the Germans to have entered the International Cup or for the clubs to have joined in the Mitropa Cup. The two great club sides from this era, Schalke 04 and 1.FC Nürnberg, would probably have been a match for the leading Austrian, Czech, Italian and Hungarian sides, although as German football was still strictly amateur, they may well have been at a crucial disadvantage.

After Hitler came to power results for the national team began to improve drastically, though it can be seen from the records that weaker teams were played to bolster this record. The 1934 World Cup was something of a triumph, with Germany winning a third place play-off over the 'Wunderteam' of the Austrians. With a reputation of being robust footballers rather than skilful, the Germans had taken their first steps in a competition that was to bring them great success after the war, when they combined this physique with tactical awareness and a level of skill that teams like the Austrians displayed in the 1930s.

Both the 1936 Olympic Games and the 1938 World Cup were a disaster for Germany. On both occasions they were beaten by supposedly inferior opponents. In 1938, not even with the best of Austria's players, who after the 'Anchluss' were eligible to play for the fatherland, could they beat Switzerland. The outbreak of war did not stop internationals being played. As the Germans conquered more and more of Europe, it was common for games to be played against both these countries and those that remained neutral.

The aftermath of war brought about great change, not least in that there were now two Germanys. With Germany having been thrown out of FIFA in 1946, football all but ceased in the territory held by the Americans, British and French, which became known as West Germany, as it did in the Eastern sector held by the Soviets.

In 1948 the Deutscher Fussball-Verband der DDR (East Germany) was formed and a national championship was organised in the East. The east had never been very powerful in pre-war football and teams from that area had won only five championships, two of those in the war years. The pattern continued throughout the GDR's existence as a separate nation. Never did East Germany's

	Team	All G	All S	All B	League G	League S	League B	Cup G	Cup S	Europe G	Europe S	Europe B
1	Bayern München	24	6	11	12	3	3	8	1	4	2	8
2	1.FC Nürnberg	12	5	1	9	3	–	3	2	–	–	1
3	Hamburger SV	11	16	2	6	9	–	3	4	2	3	2
4	FC Schalke 04	9	11	1	7	5	–	2	6	–	–	1
5	Borussia Mönchengladbach	9	7	8	5	2	5	2	2	2	3	3
6	1.FC Köln	7	15	9	3	8	2	4	6	–	1	7
7	VfB Stuttgart	6	5	5	4	3	3	2	1	–	1	2
8	Borussia Dortmund	6	5	3	3	4	2	2	1	1	–	1
9	Eintracht Frankfurt	6	3	6	1	1	4	4	1	1	1	2
10	Werder Bremen	5	6	4	2	4	2	2	2	1	–	2
11	1.FC Kaiserslautern	4	7	3	3	3	2	1	4	–	–	1
12	VfB Leipzig	4	2	–	3	2	–	1	–	–	–	–
13	Dresdener SC	4	1	–	2	1	–	2	–	–	–	–
14	Fortuna Düsseldorf	3	7	2	1	1	2	2	5	–	1	–
15	TSV München 1860	3	3	–	1	2	–	2	–	–	1	–
16	Karlsruher SC	3	2	–	1	1	–	2	1	–	–	–
17	SpVgg Fürth	3	1	–	3	1	–	–	–	–	–	–
18	Hannover 96	3	–	–	2	–	–	1	–	–	–	–
19	Hertha BSC Berlin	2	7	4	2	5	3	–	2	–	–	1
20	Viktoria Berlin	2	2	–	2	2	–	–	–	–	–	–
21	Rapid Wien (Austria)	2	–	–	1	–	–	1	–	–	–	–
	Rot-Weiss Essen	2	–	–	1	–	–	1	–	–	–	–
23	Holstein Kiel	1	2	–	1	2	–	–	–	–	–	–
	Karlsruher FV	1	2	–	1	2	–	–	–	–	–	–
	Kickers Offenbach	1	2	–	–	2	–	1	–	–	–	–
26	First Vienna (Austria)	1	1	–	–	1	–	1	–	–	–	–
27	Bayer Uerdingen	1	–	2	–	–	1	1	–	–	–	1
28	Eintracht Braunschweig	1	–	1	1	–	1	–	–	–	–	–
29	Bayer Leverkusen	1	–	–	–	–	–	–	–	1	–	–
	SC Freiburg	1	–	–	1	–	–	–	–	–	–	–
	VfR Mannheim	1	–	–	1	–	–	–	–	–	–	–
	Schwarz-Weiss Essen	1	–	–	–	–	–	1	–	–	–	–
	Union 92 Berlin	1	–	–	1	–	–	–	–	–	–	–
34	MSV Duisburg	–	4	1	–	2	–	–	2	–	–	1
35	Alemania Aachen	–	3	–	–	1	–	–	2	–	–	–
36	VfL Bochum	–	2	–	–	–	–	–	2	–	–	–
	FSV Frankfurt	–	2	–	–	1	–	–	1	–	–	–
	1.FC Saarbrücken	–	2	–	–	2	–	–	–	–	–	–
	Stuttgarter Kickers	–	2	–	–	1	–	–	1	–	–	–
40	Fortuna Köln	–	1	–	–	–	–	–	1	–	–	–
	Borussia Neunkirchen	–	1	–	–	–	–	–	1	–	–	–
	Preußen Münster	–	1	–	–	1	–	–	–	–	–	–
	SV Waldhof Mannheim	–	1	–	–	–	–	–	1	–	–	–
	Union Berlin	–	1	–	–	1	–	–	–	–	–	–
	Vorwärts Berlin	–	1	–	–	1	–	–	–	–	–	–
	Phorzheim	–	1	–	–	1	–	–	–	–	–	–
	Admira Wien (Austria)	–	1	–	–	1	–	–	–	–	–	–
	DFC Prague (Czechos)	–	1	–	–	1	–	–	–	–	–	–

To the end of the 1991–92 season

footballers match the achievements of its athletes and swimmers, either at club or international level.

Their first international was played in 1952 against Poland, but it was not until the 1958 World Cup that East Germany entered an official competition. Many countries were unhappy about the presence of the GDR in FIFA and it was not until 1963 that a friendly game was played against a major Western power, with the visit of England to Leipzig.

During their 45-year history, the East Germans built up a phenomenal reputation in the sports field. There was a major sports university in Leipzig, and any children that were perceived to have any potential were given a special education and training. As a result, East Germany, even with a population that was one twentieth of the United States', managed to finish ahead of the Americans in the medal rankings at the 1976 Olympic Games in Montreal.

The main problem for football, however, was the special emphasis given to individual sports and the lesser known team sports. Football never benefited from the East German emphasis on sporting achievement, and in many ways suffered because of it. Firstly, gifted athletes were more often than not syphoned off into other sports, but more importantly, the level of official interference in the clubs often reached ludicrous proportions.

Like all Eastern bloc countries, football teams were part of government institutions, and as none of them dated to pre-1945, there was very little identification with the supporters. Teams frequently changed their names and sometimes even moved town. Dynamo Berlin in particular came to represent the worst side of East German football. As the team of the Stasi secret police, they were universally disliked but managed to 'win' 10 league championships in a row in the 1970s and 1980s. Their biggest fan was the Stasi chief Miekle, who let it be known that he wanted to see them win, and so they did. Known as the 'offside' champions due to the number of opponents' goals that were mysteriously disallowed for that offence, even their players on occasions were known to be acutely embarrassed by events on the field.

The national side did see some success in the 1970s, but nobody was that impressed. The East Germans qualified for the 1974 World Cup Finals in neighbouring West Germany, and as luck would have it were drawn in the same group as their western counterparts. Jurgen Sparwasser's goal has gone down in legend as the winner in the only game ever played between the two countries and East Germany won the group. In the second round, however, they were no match for the Dutch or the Brazilians who ended any hopes they may have had of reaching the final.

Two years later, in the Montreal Olympics, they won the gold medal, but by this time the Olympic football tournament had lost most of its credibility. The runners-up spot four years later did nothing to improve the image of the East Germans, and it was with little regret that with reunification in 1990 the East German association was disbanded, as was the national side and the league structure. The state that it was in was summed up by the award of just two places to East German clubs in the unified Bundesliga, and many felt that even this was too generous an act.

As East Germany excelled at the individual sports, what became known as West Germany excelled in team sports and in particular at football. They were readmitted to FIFA in 1950, and four years later were world champions. Relying on a few players from the pre-war era and managed by Sepp Herberger, West Germany entered the 1954 World Cup in Switzerland and pulled off the biggest shock football has ever seen.

The Hungarian side of 1954 was the best side the world had seen, and many would argue that it has not been bettered since, and yet the Germans managed to beat them in the final, inflicting on the Hungarians their only defeat in six years. Not only did they beat the Hungarians but they also disposed of the fancied Austrians and Yugoslavs. The hero of the team was Helmut Rahn, but their success was more down to teamwork and the presence of the Walter brothers, along with Morlock and the inspirational Turek in goal.

From 1954 the Germans did not look back. A comprehensive coaching network was set up throughout the country and the flow of excellent footballers has continued unabated. Semi-finalists in 1958 and quarter-finalists in the 1962 World Cup, they reached the final again in 1966, but this time lost to the hosts England at Wembley. Along with Rahn, the most famous players of this era were Uwe Seeler, Hans Schäfer, Helmut Haller, Hans Tilkowski, and Karl-Heinz Schnellinger.

As their fortunes rose on the pitch, it became evident that the league structure of the German game was becoming out of date, and so in 1963 a new single national league was created along with a second division, instead of the regional leagues which were relegated to the status of third division. Just as importantly, full-time professionalism was introduced, remarkably for the first time in the history of German football. Until 1963, most players had played on a semi-professional basis.

This was the spur that the game needed and by the late 1960s one team in particular was showing the way forward. Bayern Munich won the Bundesliga in 1969 with a team of players that have since become household names. They have dominated club football since and formed the basis of the national side that was without question the dominant force in world football in the 1970s.

In goal Sepp Maier has never been equalled, although the defence in front of him consisting of Schwarzenbeck, Beckenbauer and Breitner would have made an average goalkeeper look good. Beckenbauer, in particular, was regarded, along with Cruyff, as the heir apparent to the title left vacant by Pele as the world's greatest player. It was not just in defence and midfield that Bayern and West Germany were blessed with gifted players. Along with Pele and Puskas, there has never been a more prolific goalscorer than Gerd Müller. His 68 goals in just 62 international matches was an extraordinary achievement that will take some beating. Also scoring goals for Bayern and Germany was Uli Hoeness. The other dominant club during the 1970s, Borussia Moenchengladbach, also contributed their share of players with the likes of Berti Vogts, Rainer Bonhof, Herbert Wimmer, Uli Stielike, Jupp Heynckes and Gunter Netzer.

The record at national and club level since 1970 speaks for itself. Twice world champions, twice European champions as well as 19 appearances in finals of European club competitions. After the break-up of the 1970s side, new players have simply replaced those that have retired. Karl-Heinz Rummenigge took over the mantle of Beckenbauer as the star of German football and captain of the national side, and he in turn passed it on to Lothar Matthäus. Strikers like Klaus Allofs and Rudi Völler have taken over the role vacated by Müller, and now with the former East German players available for selection, there is an embarrassment of riches.

Nobody does it better. The Germans are the perfect example of how to run football, and barring a major catastrophe, will be winning just as many honours in 20 or 50 years time as they are now.

Population: 79 070 000
Area, sq km: 356 954
% in urban areas: 85.5%
Capital city: Berlin

Deutscher Fussball–Bund
Otto–Fleck–Schneise 6
Postfach 710265
D–6000 Frankfurt am Main
Germany
Tel: (010 49) 69 67880
Fax: (010 49) 69 6788266
Telex: 416815 DFB D
Cable: FUSSBALL FRANKFURT
Languages for correspondence: German, English & French

Year of formation: 1900 (1948 for the East German DFB)
Affiliation to FIFA: 1904–1946, 1950 (1952–90 for the East German DFB) Affiliation to UEFA: 1954
Registered clubs: 27 049
Registered players: 5 305 700
Professional players: 700
Registered coaches: 63 950
Registered referees: 87 922
National stadium: Olympiastadion, Munich 73 000
National colours: Shirts: White/Shorts: Black/Socks: White
Reserve colours: Shirts: Green/Shorts: White/Socks: White

Season: August–June with a mid-season break in January and February

THE RECORD FOR GERMANY AND WEST GERMANY

WORLD CUP

1930 .... Did not enter
1934 .... QT 1st/3 in group 12 – Final Tournament/Semi-finalists/3rd place
1938 .... QT 1st/4 in group 1 – Final Tournament/1st round
1950 .... Did not enter
1954 .... QT 1st/3 in group 1 – Final Tournament/Winners
1958 .... QT Automatic – Final Tournament/Semi-finalists/4th place
1962 .... QT 1st/3 in group 3 – Final Tournament/Quarter-finalists
1966 .... QT 1st/3 in group 2 – Final Tournament/Finalists
1970 .... QT 1st/4 in group 7 – Final Tournament/Semi-finalists/3rd place
1974 .... QT Automatic – Final Tournament/Winners
1978 .... QT Automatic – Final Tournament/2nd round
1982 .... QT 1st/5 in group 1 – Final Tournament/Finalists
1986 .... QT 1st/5 in group 2 – Final Tournament/Finalists
1990 .... QT 2nd/4 in group 4 – Final Tournament/Winners

EUROPEAN CHAMPIONSHIP

1960 .... Did not enter
1964 .... Did not enter
1968 .... QT 2nd/3 in group 4
1972 .... QT 1st/4 in group 8 – Final Tournament/Winners
1976 .... QT 1st/4 in group 8 – Final Tournament/Finalists
1980 .... QT 1st/4 in group 7 – Final Tournament/Winners
1984 .... QT 1st/5 in group 6 – Final Tournament/1st round
1988 .... QT Automatic – Final Tournament/Semi-finalists
1992 .... QT 1st/4 in group 5 – Final Tournament/Finalists

OLYMPIC GAMES

1908 .... Did not enter
1912 .... Preliminary round
1920 .... Did not enter
1924 .... Did not enter
1928 .... Quarter-finalists
1936 .... Quarter-finalists
1948 .... Did not enter
1952 .... Semi-finalists/4th place
1956 .... Final Tournament/Preliminary round
1960 .... QT Failed to qualify
1964 .... Did not enter
1968 .... QT Failed to qualify
1972 .... Final Tournament/2nd round
1976 .... QT Failed to qualify
1980 .... QT Failed to qualify
1984 .... Final Tournament/Quarter-finalists
1988 .... Final Tournament/Semi-finalists/3rd place
1992 .... QT Failed to qualify

EUROPEAN CLUB COMPETITIONS

EUROPEAN CUP: Winners – Bayern Munich 1974 1975 1976, SV Hamburg 1983
Finalists – Eintracht Frankfurt 1960, Bor. Monchengladbach 1977, SV Hamburg 1980, Bayern Munich 1982 1987

CUP WINNERS CUP: Winners – Borussia Dortmund 1966, Bayern Munich 1967, SV Hamburg 1977, Werder Bremen 1992
Finalists – TSV Munich 1860 1965, SV Hamburg 1968, Fortuna Düsseldorf 1979

UEFA CUP: Winners – Bor. Monchengladbach 1975 1979, Eintracht Frankfurt 1980, Bayer Leverkusen 1988
Finalists – Bor. Monchengladbach 1973 1980, SV Hamburg 1982, 1.FC Köln 1986, VfB Stuttgart 1989

THE RECORD FOR EAST GERMANY

WORLD CUP

1950 .... Did not enter
1954 .... Did not enter
1958 .... QT 3rd/3 in group 4
1962 .... QT 3rd/3 in group 4
1966 .... QT 2nd/3 in group 6
1970 .... QT 2nd/3 in group 3
1974 .... QT 1st/4 in group 4 – Final Tournament/2nd round
1978 .... QT 2nd/4 in group 3
1982 .... QT 2nd/3 in group 7
1986 .... QT 3rd/5 in group 4
1990 .... QT 4th/5 in group 3

EUROPEAN CHAMPIONSHIP

1960 .... 1st round
1964 .... 2nd round
1968 .... QT 2nd/4 in group 5
1972 .... QT 3rd/3 in group 7
1976 .... QT 2nd/4 in group 7
1980 .... QT 3rd/5 in group 4
1984 .... QT 3rd/4 in group 1
1988 .... QT 2nd/5 in group 3

OLYMPIC GAMES

1948–60 ..... Did not enter
1964 .... Final Tournament/Semi-finalists/3rd place
1968 .... QT Failed to qualify
1972 .... Final Tournament/2nd round/3rd place
1976 .... Final Tournament/Winners
1980 .... Final Tournament/Runners–up
1984 .... Qualified but withdrew
1988 .... QT Failed to qualify

EUROPEAN CLUB COMPETITIONS

EUROPEAN CUP: Quarter-finalists – Wismut Karl-Marx-Stadt 1959, Vorwärts Berlin 1970, Carl Zeiss Jena 1971, Dynamo Dresden 1977 1979, Dynamo Berlin 1980 1984

CUP WINNERS CUP: Winners – 1.FC Magdeburg 1974
Finalists – Carl Zeiss Jena 1981, Lokomotive Leipzig 1987

UEFA CUP: Semi-finalists – Lokomotive Leipzig 1974, Dynamo Dresden 1989

CLUB DIRECTORY

BERLIN (Population – 5061000)

Berliner Fussball Club
Stadium: Friedrich Ludwig Jahn Sportpark 14000
Founded: 1952
Colours: Red/White
Previous name: BFC Dynamo Berlin 1952–90

Blau–Weiss 90
Stadium: Olympiastadion 76000
Founded: 1890
Colours: Blue/White
Previous name: Merger in 1925 of Union 92 and Vorwärts 90

Hertha Berliner Sports Club (BSC)
Stadium: Olympiastadion 76000
Founded: 1892
Colours: White with blue sleeves and shoulders/Blue

1.FC Union Berlin
Stadium: Alte Försterei 25000
Founded: 1945
Colours: Red/White
Previous names: SG Union Oberschöneweide 1945–51, BSG Motor Oberschöneweide 1951–55, SC Motor Berlin 1955–57, TSC Oberschöneweide 1957–63, TSC Berlin 1963–66

Tasmania Berlin
Stadium: Olympiastadion 76000
Founded: 1900
Colours: Red/White

Tennis Borussia Berlin
Stadium: Olympiastadion 76000
Founded: 1902
Colours: Violet/White

ESSEN (Population – 4 950 000)

Verein fuer Leibesuebung (VfL) Bochum
Stadium: Ruhrstadion 49 000
Founded: 1938
Colours: Blue/White
Previous name: merger in 1938 of Bochum '08, TG Bochum and Germania

Ballspiel Verein Borussia Dortmund
Stadium: Westfalenstadion 53 000
Founded: 1909
Colours: Yellow/Black

Meiderichher Sport Verein (MSV) Duisburg
Stadium: Wedaustadion 30 000
Founded: 1902
Colours: Blue and white hoops/White

Rot-Weiss Essen
Stadium: Georg Melches 36 000
Founded: 1907
Colours: White/Red

Rot-Weiss Oberhausen
Stadium: Niederrhein
Founded: 1904
Colours: Red/White

Fussball Club Schalke 04 Gelsenkirchen
Stadium: Parkstadion 70 000
Founded: 1904
Colours: Blue/White

Fussball Club Bayer 05 Uerdingen
Stadium: Grotenburg 34 000
Founded: 1905
Colours: Blue and red stripes/Blue

SG Wattenscheid 09
Stadium: Lohrheide 14 000
Founded: 1909
Colours: White with red sleeves/White

HAMBURG (Population – 2 225 000)

Hamburger Sport–Verein
Stadium: Volksparkstadion 61 000
Founded: 1887
Colours: White/Red
Previous name: Merger in 1919 of Germania '87, Falke '87 and Hamburger SC '87

Fussball Club St. Pauli
Stadium: Wilhelm Koch 20 000
Founded: 1910
Colours: White/White

MUNICH (Population – 1 955 000)

Fussball Club Bayern München
Stadium: Olympiastadion 73 000
Founded: 1900
Colours: Red/Red

Turn & Sport Verein (TSV) München 1860
Stadium: Grünwalder Strasse 35 000
Founded: 1899
Colours: Blue/White

STUTTGART (Population 1 925 000)
Verein fuer Ballspiele (VfB) Stuttgart
Stadium: Neckarstadion 67 000
Founded: 1893
Colours: White with a red band on chest/White

Stuttgarter Kickers
Stadium: Waldau 10 000
Founded: 1899
Colours: Blue/Blue

FRANKFURT AM MAIN (Population – 1 885 000)

Sport Gemeinde Eintracht Frankfurt
Stadium: Waldstadion 61 000
Founded: 1899
Colours: Red and black stripes/Black

Offenbacher Fussball Club (OFC) Kickers Offenbach
Stadium: Bieberer Berg
Founded: 1901
Colours: Red/White

COLOGNE (Population – 1 760 000)

Fussball Club Bayer 04 Leverkusen
Stadium: Ulrich Haberland Stadion 30 000
Founded: 1904
Colours: White/Red

I.FC Köln
Stadium: Müngersdorfer 60 000
Founded: 1948
Colours: White/White
Previous name: Merger in 1948 of Kölner BC (1901) and FC Sülz (1907)

Fortuna Köln
Stadium: Bezirkssportanlage 15 000
Founded: 1948
Colours: Red and white stripes/Red
Previous name: Merger in 1948 of SV Köln (1927), Viktoria (1911) and Bayenthaler (1920)

MANNHEIM (Population – 1 400 000)
Sport Verein Waldhof Mannheim
Stadium: Südwest stadion 41 000
Founded: 1907
Colours: Blue and black stripes/Blue

DUSSELDORF (Population – 1 190 000)
Fortuna Düsseldorf
Stadium: Rheinstadion 68 000
Founded: 1895
Colours: White with red sleeves/Red

NUREMBERG (Population – 1 030 000)
I.FC Nürnberg
Stadium: Nürnberger Stadion 55 000
Founded: 1900
Colours: Red and white stripes/Black

HANNOVER (Population – 1 000 000)
Sport Verein Hannover '96
Stadium: Niedersachsenstadion 60 000
Founded: 1896
Colours: Red/Black

WUPPERTAL (Population – 830 000)
Wuppertaler Sport Verein
Stadium: Stadion am Zoo
Founded: 1954
Colours: Orange/Blue
Previous name: Merger in 1954 of Vohwinkel and WSV

BREMEN (Population – 800 000)
Sport Verein Werder Bremen
Stadium: Weserstadion 40 000
Founded: 1899
Colours: White/Green

LEIPZIG (Population – 700 000)

Verein fuer Ballspiele (VfB) Leipzig
Stadium: Bruno Plache Stadion 22 000
Founded: 1945
Colours: Yellow and blue stripes/Blue
Previous names: SG Probstheida 1945–48, BSG Erich Zeigner 1948, BSG Einheit Ost 1949–54, SC Rotation 1954–63, SC Leipzig 1963–66, I.FC Lokomotive Leipzig 1966–91

Fussball Club Sachsen Leipzig
Stadium: Georg Schwarz Sportpark 22 000
Founded: 1945
Colours: White/Green
Previous names: SG Leipzig–Leutzsch 1945–48, ZSG Industrie 1948–50, BSG Chemie 1950–54, SC Lokomotive 1954–63, BSG Chemie Leipzig 1963–90

DRESDEN (Population – 670 000)

I.FC Dynamo Dresden
Stadium: Rudolf Harbig Stadion 32 000
Founded: 1953
Colours: Yellow/Black
Previous name: SG VP Dresden 1945–52, SG Dynamo Dresden 1953–90

FSV Lokomotive Dresden
Stadium: Sportplatz Pieschener Allee 3000
Founded: 1950
Colours: White/Black
Previous names: SG Mickten 1950, BSG Sachsenverlag 1950, BSG Rotation Dresden 1951–54, SC Einheit Dresden 1954–65

AACHEN (Population – 535 000)
Turn & Sport Verein (TSV) Alemannia
Stadium: Tivoli 26 000
Founded: 1900
Colours: Yellow/Black

BIELEFELD (Population – 515 000)
Deutscher Sport Club (DSC) Arminia
Stadium: Stadion der Alm
Founded: 1905
Colours: Blue/White

KARLSRUHE (Population – 485 000)
Karlsruher Sport Club
Stadium: Wildpark Stadion 46 000
Founded: 1894
Colours: White/Blue
Previous name: Merger in 1952 of Mülburg and Phönix '94

HALLE (Population – 475 000)
Hallescher Fussball Club
Stadium: Kurt Wabbel 23 000
Founded: 1945
Colours: White/Red
Previous names: SG Freiimfelde Halle 1945–49, ZSG Union Halle 1949–50, BSG Turbine Halle 1950–54, SC Chemie Halle–Leuna 1958–66, HFC Chemie 1966–91

CHEMNITZ (Population – 450 000)
Chemnitzer Fussball Club
Stadium: Sportforum Chemnitz 24 000
Founded: 1965
Colours: Sky blue/Sky blue
Previous names: SG Chemnitz Nord until 1950, BSG Fewa 1950–51, BSG Chemie Chemnitz 1951–53, BSG Chemie Karl-Marx-Stadt 1953–56, SC Motor Karl-Marx-Stadt 1956–63, SC Karl-Marx-Stadt 1963–65, FC Karl-Marx-Stadt 1965–90

MÖNCHENGLADBACH (Population – 410 000)
Borussia Mönchengladbach
Stadium: Bökelberg 34 000
Founded: 1900 Colours: White/White

MAGDEBURG (Population – 400 000)
1.FC Magdeburg
Stadium: Ernst Grube Stadion 35 000
Founded: 1965
Colours: White/White
Previous names: SG Einheit Sudenburg until 1951, BSG Krupp 1951, BSG Stahl 1951–52, BSG Motor Mitte 1952–57, SC Aufbau 1957–65

SAARBRUCKEN (Population – 385 000)
1.FC Saarbrücken
Stadium: Ludwigspark 38 000
Founded: 1903
Colours: Blue and black stripes/White

BRAUNSCHWEIG (Population – 330 000)
Braunschweiger Turn & Sport Verein Eintracht
Stadium: Eintracht Stadion 32 000
Founded: 1895
Colours: Yellow/Blue

DARMSTADT (Population – 305 000)
Sport Verein Darmstadt '98
Stadium: Böllenfalltor 30 000
Founded: 1898
Colours: Blue/White

MUNSTER (Population 267 000)
SC Preussen Münster
Stadium: Hammer Strasse 28 000
Founded: 1906
Colours: Green/Black

ROSTOCK (Population – 249 000)
Fussball Club Hansa Rostock
Stadium: Ostseestadion 25 000
Founded: 1965
Colours: White/White
Previous names: Rostock until 1949, Empor Lauter 1949–54, SC Empor 1954–65, FC Rostock 1965–66

ERFURT (Population – 217 000)
Fussball Club Rot-Weiss Erfurt
Stadium: Steigerwaldstadion 28 000
Founded: 1946
Colours: White/Red
Previous names: Erfurt West 1946–48, SG Fortuna Erfurt 1948–49, KWU Erfurt 1949–50, Turbine Erfurt 1950–54, SC Turbine 1954–65

ZWICKAU (Population – 165 000)
FSV Zwickau
Stadium: Georgi Dimitroff 35 000
Founded: 1949
Colours: Red/White
Previous names: SG Planitz 1949, Horch Zwickau 1949–50, Motor Zwickau 1950–67, BSG Sachsenring Zwickau 1967–90

KAISERSLAUTERN (Population – 138 000)
1.FC Kaiserslautern
Stadium: Fritz Walter 38 000
Founded: 1900
Colours: Red/Red

NEUENKIRCHEN (Population – 135 000)
Borussia Neunkirchen
Stadium: Borussia Stadion
Founded: 1905
Colours: White/Black

GERA (Population – 132 000)
FSV Wismut Gera
Stadium: Freundschaft 35 000
Founded: 1949
Colours: Orange/Black
Previous names: Gera–Süd 1949–50, BSG Motor Gera 1950–52, BSG Wismut Gera 1952–90

JENA (Population – 107 000)
Fussball Club Carl Zeiss Jena
Stadium: Ernst Abbe Sportfeld 9000
Founded: 1946
Colours: Blue/White
Previous names: SG Ernst Abbe 1946–48, SG Stadion Jena 1948–49, BSG Carl Zeiss Jena 1949–51, BSG Mechanik Jena 1951, BSG Motor Jena 1951– 54, SC Motor Jena 1954–66

BRANDENBURG (Population – 94 000)
BSV Stahl Brandenburg
Stadium: Stahlstadion 15 000
Founded: 1950
Colours: White/Blue

FRANKFURT AN DER ODER (Population – 86 000)
Fussball Club Victoria 91 Frankfurt/Oder
Stadium: Freundschaft 16 000
Founded: 1951
Colours: Yellow/White
Previous names: SV Vorwärts Leipzig 1951–53, ASK Vorwärts Berlin 1954–71, FC Vorwärts Frankfurt/Oder 1971–91

HOMBURG
FC 08 Homburg/Saar
Stadium: Waldstadion 25 000
Founded: 1908
Colours: Green/White

AUE
Fussbal Club Wismut Aue
Stadium: Otto Grotewohl 20 000
Founded: 1946
Colours: Violet/White
Previous names: Pneumatik Aue 1946–49, Zentra Wismut Aue 1949–51, Wismut Aue 1951–54, SC Wismut Karl-Marx-Stadt 1954–63, BSG Wismut Aue 1963–90

THE GERMAN LEAGUE CHAMPIONSHIP

	Champions		Runners up
1903	VfB Leipzig	7–2	DFC Prague
1904	–		
1905	Union 92 Berlin	2–0	Karlsruher FV
1906	VfB Leipzig	2–1	Pforzheim
1907	SC Freiburg	3–1	Viktoria Berlin
1908	Viktoria Berlin	3–1	Stuttgarter Kickers
1909	Phönix Karlsruhe	4–2	Viktoria Berlin
1910	Karlsruher FV	1–0	Holstein Kiel
1911	Viktoria Berlin	3–1	VfB Leipzig
1912	Holstein Kiel	1–0	Karlsruher FV
1913	VfB Leipzig	3–1	MSV Duisburg
1914	SPVGG Fürth	3–2	VfB Leipzig
1915–1919		–	
1920	1.FC Nürnberg	2–0	SPVGG Fürth
1921	1.FC Nürnberg	5–0	Vorwärts Berlin
1922	–		
1923	Hamburger SV	3–0	Union Berlin
1924	1.FC Nürnberg	3–0	Hamburger SV
1925	1.FC Nürnberg	1–0	FSV Frankfurt
1926	SPVGG Fürth	4–1	Hertha BSC Berlin
1927	1.FC Nürnberg	2–0	Hertha BSC Berlin
1928	Hamburger SV	5–2	Hertha BSC Berlin
1929	SPVGG Fürth	3–2	Hertha BSC Berlin
1930	Hertha BSC Berlin	5–4	Holstein Kiel
1931	Hertha BSC Berlin	3–2	TSV München 1860

1932	Bayern München	2–0	Eintracht Frankfurt	
1933	Fortuna Düsseldorf	3–0	FC Schalke 04	
1934	FC Schalke 04	2–1	1.FC Nürnberg	
1935	FC Schalke 04	6–4	VfB Stuttgart	
1936	1.FC Nürnberg	2–1	Fortuna Düsseldorf	
1937	FC Schalke 04	2–0	1.FC Nürnberg	
1938	Hannover 96	3–3 4–3	FC Schalke 04	
1939	FC Schalke 04	9–0	Admira Wien	
1940	FC Schalke 04	1–0	Dresdener SC	
1941	Rapid Wien	4–3	FC Schalke 04	
1942	FC Schalke 04	2–0	First Vienna FC	
1943	Dresdener SC	3–0	1.FC Saarbrücken	
1944	Dresdener SC	4–0	Hamburger SV	

THE WEST GERMAN CHAMPIONSHIP

1948	1.FC Nürnberg	2–1	1.FC Kaiserslautern
1949	VfR Mannheim	3–2	Borussia Dortmund
1950	VfB Stuttgart	2–1	Kickers Offenbach
1951	1.FC Kaiserslautern	2–1	Preussen Münster
1952	VfB Stuttgart	3–2	1.FC Saarbrücken
1953	1.FC Kaiserslautern	4–1	VfB Stuttgart
1954	Hannover 96	5–1	1.FC Kaiserslautern
1955	Rot–Weiss Essen	4–3	1.FC Kaiserslautern
1956	Borussia Dortmund	4–2	Karlsruher SC
1957	Borussia Dortmund	4–1	Hamburger SV
1958	FC Schalke 04	3–0	Hamburger SV
1959	Eintracht Frankfurt	5–3	Kickers Offenbach
1960	Hamburger SV	3–2	1.FC Köln
1961	1.FC Nürnberg	3–0	Borussia Dortmund
1962	1.FC Köln	4–0	1.FC Nürnberg
1963	Borussia Dortmund	3–1	1.FC Köln

THE WEST GERMAN BUNDESLIGA

	Champions		Runners–up		3rd	
1964	1.FC Köln	45	MSV Duisburg	39	Eintracht Frankfurt	39
1965	Werder Bremen	41	1.FC Köln	38	Borussia Dortmund	36
1966	TSV München 1860	50	Borussia Dortmund	47	Bayern München	47
1967	Eintr. Braunschweig	43	TSV München 1860	41	Borussia Dortmund	39
1968	1.FC Nürnberg	47	Werder Bremen	44	B. Mönchengladbach	42
1969	Bayern München	46	Alemania Aachen	38	B. Mönchengladbach	37
1970	B. Mönchengladbach	51	Bayern München	47	Hertha BSC Berlin	45
1971	B. Mönchengladbach	50	Bayern München	48	Hertha BSC Berlin	41
1972	Bayern München	55	FC Schalke 04	52	B. Mönchengladbach	43
1973	Bayern München	54	1.FC Köln	43	Fortuna Düsseldorf	42
1974	Bayern München	49	B. Mönchengladbach	48	Fortuna Düsseldorf	41
1975	B. Mönchengladbach	50	Hertha BSC Berlin	44	Eintracht Frankfurt	43
1976	B. Mönchengladbach	45	Hamburger SV	41	Bayern München	40
1977	B. Mönchengladbach	44	FC Schalke 04	43	Eintr. Braunschweig	43
1978	1.FC Köln	48	B. Mönchengladbach	48	Hertha BSC Berlin	40
1979	Hamburger SV	49	VfB Stuttgart	48	1.FC Kaiserslautern	43
1980	Bayern München	50	Hamburger SV	48	VfB Stuttgart	41
	....		....		1.FC Kaiserslautern	41
1981	Bayern München	53	Hamburger SV	49	VfB Stuttgart	46
1982	Hamburger SV	48	1.FC Köln	45	Bayern München	43
1983	Hamburger SV	52	Werder Bremen	52	VfB Stuttgart	48
1984	VfB Stuttgart	48	Hamburger SV	48	B. Mönchengladbach	48
1985	Bayern München	50	Werder Bremen	46	1.FC Köln	40
1986	Bayern München	49	Werder Bremen	49	Bayer Uerdingen	45
1987	Bayern München	53	Hamburger SV	47	B. Mönchengladbach	43
1988	Werder Bremen	52	Bayern München	48	1.FC Köln	48
1989	Bayern München	50	1.FC Köln	45	Werder Bremen	44
1990	Bayern München	49	1.FC Köln	43	Eintracht Frankfurt	43
1991	1.FC Kaiserslautern	48	Bayern München	45	Werder Bremen	42
1992	VfB Stuttgart	52	Borussia Dortmund	52	Eintracht Frankfurt	50

GERMAN CUP FINALS

Year	Winners	Score	Runners–up
1935	1.FC Nürnberg	2–0	FC Schalke 04
1936	VFB Leipzig	2–1	FC Schalke 04
1937	Schalke 04	2–1	Fortuna Düsseldorf
1938	Rapid Wien	3–1	FSV Frankfurt
1939	1.FC Nürnberg	2–0	SV Waldhof Mannheim
1940	Dresdener SC	2–1	1.FC Nürnberg
1941	Dresdener SC	2–1	FC Schalke 04
1942	TSV Munich 1860	2–0	FC Schalke 04
1943	First Vienna FC	3–2	Hamburger SV
1953	Rot-Weiss Essen	2–1	Alemania Aachen
1954	VfB Stuttgart	1–0	1.FC Cologne
1955	Karlsruher SC	3–2	FC Schalke 04
1956	Karlsruher SC	3–1	Hamburger SV
1957	Bayern München	1–0	Fortuna Düsseldorf
1958	VfB Stuttgart	4–3	Fortuna Düsseldorf
1959	Schwarz-Weiss Essen	5–2	Borussia Neunkirchen
1960	B. Mönchengladbach	3–2	Karlsruher SC
1961	Werder Bremen	2–0	1.FC Kaiserslautern
1962	1.FC Nürnberg	2–1	Fortuna Düsseldorf
1963	Hamburger SV	3–0	Borussia Dortmund
1964	TSV Munich 1860	2–0	Eintracht Frankfurt
1965	Borussia Dortmund	2–0	Alemannia Aachen
1966	Bayern München	4–2	MSV Duisburg
1967	Bayern München	4–0	Hamburger SV
1968	1.FC Köln	4–1	VfL Bochum
1969	Bayern München	2–1	FC Schalke 04
1970	Kickers Offenbach	2–1	1.FC Köln
1971	Bayern München	2–1	1.FC Köln
1972	FC Schalke 04	5–0	1.FC Kaiserslautern
1973	B. Mönchengladbach	2–1	1.FC Köln
1974	Eintracht Frankfurt	3–1	Hamburger SV

1975	Eintracht Frankfurt	1–0	MSV Duisburg
1976	Hamburger SV	2–0	1.FC Kaiserslautern
1977	1.FC Köln	1–1 1–0	Hertha BSC Berlin
1978	1.FC Köln	2–0	Fortuna Düsseldorf
1979	Fortuna Düsseldorf	1–0	Hertha BSC Berlin
1980	Fortuna Düsseldorf	2–1	1.FC Köln
1981	Eintracht Frankfurt	3–1	1.FC Kaiserslautern
1982	Bayern München	4–2	1.FC Nürnberg
1983	1.FC Köln	1–0	Fortuna Köln
1984	Bayern München	1–1 (7–6p)	B. Mönchengladbach
1985	Bayer Uerdingen	2–1	Bayern München
1986	Bayern München	5–2	VfB Stuttgart
1987	Hamburger SV	3–1	Stuttgarter Kickers
1988	Eintracht Frankfurt	1–0	VfL Bochum
1989	Borussia Dortmund	4–1	Werder Bremen
1990	1.FC Kaiserslautern	3–2	Werder Bremen
1991	Werder Bremen	1–1 (4–3p)	1.FC Köln
1992	Hannover 96	0–0 (4–3p)	B. Mönchengladbach

EAST GERMAN LEAGUE CHAMPIONSHIP

Year	Champions		Runners up		3rd	
1948	SG Planitz	1–0	Freiimfelde Halle			
1949	ZSG Halle	4–1	Fortuna Erfurt			
1950	Horch Zwickau	41	SG Friederichstadt	39	Waggonbau Dessau	37
1951	Chemie Leipzig	50	Turbine Erfurt	50	Motor Zwickau	43
1952	Turbine Halle	53	Polizei Dresden	49	Chemie Leipzig	47
1953	Dynamo Dresden	38	Wismut Aue	38	Motor Zwickau	37
1954	Turbine Erfurt	39	Chemie Leipzig	35	Dynamo Dresden	34
1955	Turbine Erfurt	34	Wismut K-M-S	33	Rotor Leipzig	30
1956	Wismut K-M-S	38	Brieske-Senftenberg	36	SC Lokomotive Leipzig	34
1957	Wismut K-M-S	36	Vorwärts Berlin	33	Rotor Leipzig	32
1958	Vorwärts Berlin	38	Motor Jena	32	Brieske-Senftenberg	30
1959	Wismut K-M-S	39	Vorwärts Berlin	35	Dynamo Berlin	33
1960	Vorwärts Berlin	41	Dynamo Berlin	32	SC Lokomotive Leipzig	32
1961	–					
1962	Vorwärts Berlin	50	Empor Rostock	47	Dynamo Berlin	45
1963	Motor Jena	39	Empor Rostock	33	Vorwärts Berlin	31
1964	Chemie Leipzig	35	Empor Rostock	33	SC Leipzig	32
1965	Vorwärts Berlin	37	Motor Jena	32	Chemie Leipzig	31
1966	Vorwärts Berlin	34	Motor Jena	32	Lokomotive Leipzig	28
1967	FC Karl-Marx-Stadt	37	Lokomotive Leipzig	30	Motor Zwickau	27
1968	Carl-Zeiss Jena	39	Hansa Rostock	34	1.FC Magdeburg	33
1969	Vorwärts Berlin	34	Carl-Zeiss Jena	32	1.FC Magdeburg	31
1970	Carl-Zeiss Jena	39	Vorwärts Berlin	32	Dynamo Dresden	31
1971	Dynamo Dresden	39	Carl-Zeiss Jena	33	Chemie Halle	30
1972	1.FC Magdeburg	38	Dynamo Berlin	35	Dynamo Dresden	33
1973	Dynamo Dresden	42	Carl-Zeiss Jena	39	1.FC Magdeburg	34
1974	1.FC Magdeburg	39	Carl-Zeiss Jena	36	Dynamo Dresden	35
1975	1.FC Magdeburg	41	Carl-Zeiss Jena	38	Dynamo Dresden	32
1976	Dynamo Dresden	43	Dynamo Berlin	37	1.FC Magdeburg	36
1977	Dynamo Dresden	38	1.FC Magdeburg	34	Carl-Zeiss Jena	33
1978	Dynamo Dresden	41	1.FC Magdeburg	38	Dynamo Berlin	35
1979	Dynamo Berlin	46	Dynamo Dresden	39	Carl-Zeiss Jena	34
1980	Dynamo Berlin	43	Dynamo Dresden	42	Carl-Zeiss Jena	32

	All			League			Cup		Europe		
Team	G	S	B	G	S	B	G	S	G	S	B
1 1.FC Dynamo Dresden	14	12	8	8	8	6	7	4	–	–	1
2 Berliner FC	13	10	4	10	4	3	3	6	–	–	1
3 1.FC Magdeburg	11	2	6	3	2	6	7	–	1	–	–
4 FC Victoria 91 Frankfurt	8	7	1	6	4	1	2	3	–	–	–
5 FC Carl Zeiss Jena	7	13	6	3	9	5	4	3	–	1	1
6 FSV Zwickau	5	1	4	2	–	3	3	1	–	–	1
7 VfB Leipzig	4	8	9	–	3	8	4	4	–	1	1
8 FC Wismut Aue	4	3	–	3	2	–	1	1	–	–	–
9 FC Sachsen Leipzig	4	2	4	2	1	4	2	1	–	–	–
10 Hallescher FC	4	1	1	2	1	1	2	–	–	–	–
11 FC Hansa Rostock	2	9	–	1	4	–	1	5	–	–	–
12 FC Rot–Weiss Erfurt	2	4	1	2	2	1	–	2	–	–	–
13 Chemnitzer FC	1	4	1	1	1	1	–	3	–	–	–
14 1.FC Union Berlin	1	1	–	–	–	–	1	1	–	–	–
15 SG Motor Dessau	1	–	1	–	–	1	1	–	–	–	–
16 EHW Thale	1	–	–	–	–	–	1	–	–	–	–
FSV Lokomotive Dresden	1	–	–	–	–	–	1	–	–	–	–
18 BSG Aktivist Senftenberg	–	1	1	–	1	1	–	–	–	–	–
19 BSG Chemie Zeitz	–	1	–	–	–	–	–	1	–	–	–
BSG Einheit Pankow	–	1	–	–	–	–	–	1	–	–	–
Eisenhüttenstadt FC Stahl	–	1	–	–	–	–	–	1	–	–	–
FSV Wismut Gera	–	1	–	–	–	–	–	1	–	–	–
BSG Lokomotive Stendal	–	1	–	–	–	–	–	1	–	–	–
SG Friederichstadt	–	1	–	–	1	–	–	–	–	–	–
PSV Schwerin	–	1	–	–	–	–	–	1	–	–	–

1981	Dynamo Berlin	39	Carl-Zeiss Jena	36	I.FC Magdeburg	34
1982	Dynamo Berlin	41	Dynamo Dresden	34	Lokomotive Leipzig	33
1983	Dynamo Berlin	46	Vorwärts Frankfurt	34	Carl-Zeiss Jena	34
1984	Dynamo Berlin	39	Dynamo Dresden	37	Lokomotive Leipzig	37
1985	Dynamo Berlin	44	Dynamo Dresden	38	Lokomotive Leipzig	38
1986	Dynamo Berlin	34	Lokomotive Leipzig	32	Carl-Zeiss Jena	31
1987	Dynamo Berlin	42	Dynamo Dresden	36	Lokomotive Leipzig	34
1988	Dynamo Berlin	37	Lokomotive Leipzig	37	Dynamo Dresden	33
1989	Dynamo Dresden	40	Dynamo Berlin	32	FC Karl-Marx-Stadt	30
1990	Dynamo Dresden	36	Chemnitzer FC	36	I.FC Magdeburg	34
1991	Hansa Rostock	35	Dynamo Dresden	32	Rot-Weiss Erfurt	31

Championship play-offs: 1951 Chemie Leipzig 2–0 Turbine Erfurt, 1953 Dynamo Dresden 3–2 Wismut Aue

EAST GERMAN CUP FINALS

Year	Winners	Score	Runners–up
1949	Waggonbau Dessau	1–0	Gera Süd
1950	EHW Thale	4–0	KWU Erfurt
1951	–		
1952	VP Dresden	3–0	SC Einheit Pankow
1953	–		
1954	Vorwärts Berlin	2–1	Motor Zwickau
1955	Wismut K-M-S	3–2	Empor Rostock
1956	Chemie Halle	2–1	Vorwärts Berlin
1957	SC Lokomotive Leipzig	2–1	Empor Rostock
1958	Einheit Dresden	2–1	SC Lokomotive Leipzig
1959	Dynamo Berlin	0–0 3–2	Wismut K-M-S
1960	Motor Jena	3–2	Empor Rostock
1961	–		
1962	Chemie Halle	3–1	Dynamo Berlin
1963	Motor Zwickau	3–0	Chemie Zeitz
1964	Aufbau Magdeburg	3–2	SC Leipzig
1965	Aufbau Magdeburg	2–1	Motor Jena
1966	Chemie Leipzig	1–0	Lokomotive Stendal
1967	Motor Zwickau	3–0	Hansa Rostock
1968	I.FC Union Berlin	2–1	Carl-Zeiss Jena
1969	I.FC Magdeburg	4–0	FC Karl-Marx-Stadt
1970	Vorwärts Berlin	4–2	Lokomotive Leipzig
1971	Dynamo Dresden	2–1	Dynamo Berlin
1972	Carl-Zeiss Jena	2–1	Dynamo Dresden
1973	I.FC Magdeburg	3–2	Lokomotive Leipzig
1974	Carl-Zeiss Jena	3–1	Dynamo Dresden
1975	Sachsenring Zwickau	2–2 4–3p	Dynamo Dresden
1976	Lokomotive Leipzig	3–0	Vorwärts Frankfurt
1977	Dynamo Dresden	3–2	Lokomotive Leipzig
1978	I.FC Magdeburg	1–0	Dynamo Dresden
1979	I.FC Magdeburg	1–0	Dynamo Berlin
1980	Carl-Zeiss Jena	3–1	Rot-Weiss Erfurt
1981	Lokomotive Leipzig	4–1	Vorwärts Frankfurt
1982	Dynamo Dresden	1–1 5–4p	Dynamo Berlin
1983	I.FC Magdeburg	4–0	FC Karl-Marx-Stadt
1984	Dynamo Dresden	2–1	Dynamo Berlin
1985	Dynamo Dresden	3–2	Dynamo Berlin
1986	Lokomotive Leipzig	5–1	I.FC Union Berlin
1987	Lokomotive Leipzig	4–1	Hansa Rostock
1988	Dynamo Berlin	2–0	Carl-Zeiss Jena
1989	Dynamo Berlin	1–0	FC Karl-Marx-Stadt
1990	Dynamo Dresden	2–1	PSV Schwerin
1991	Hansa Rostock	1–0	Stahl Eisenhüttenstadt

INTERNATIONAL MATCHES PLAYED BY GERMANY

Date	Opponents	Result		Venue	Compet	Scorers
5–04–1908	Switzerland	L	3–5	Basle	Fr	Becker 2, Förderer
20–04	England*	L	1–5	Berlin	Fr	Förderer
7–06	Austria	L	2–3	Vienna	Fr	Jäger, Kipp
16–03–1909	England*	L	0–9	Oxford	Fr	
4–04	Hungary	D	3–3	Budapest	Fr	Worpitzky 2, Ugi
4–04	Switzerland	W	1–0	Karlsruhe	Fr	Kipp
3–04–1910	Switzerland	W	3–2	Basle	Fr	Kipp, Hiller
24–04	Holland	L	2–4	Arnhem	Fr	Kipp, Fick
16–05	Belgium	L	0–3	Duisburg	Fr	
16–10	Holland	L	1–2	Kleve	Fr	Queck
26–03–1911	Switzerland	W	6–2	Stuttgart	Fr	Förderer 2, Fuchs 2, Kipp, Breunig
14–04	England*	D	2–2	Berlin	Fr	Möller E 2
23–04	Belgium	L	1–2	Liege	Fr	Förderer
18–06	Sweden	W	4–2	Stockholm	Fr	Dumke 3, Kipp
9–10	Austria	L	1–2	Dresden	Fr	Worpitzky
29–10	Sweden	L	1–3	Hamburg	Fr	Möller E
17–12	Hungary	L	1–4	Munich	Fr	Worpitzky
24–03–1912	Holland	D	5–5	Zwolle	Fr	Hirsch 4, Fuchs
14–04	Hungary	D	4–4	Budapest	Fr	Worpitzky, Kipp, Möller E, Jäger
5–05	Switzerland	W	2–1	St Gallen	Fr	Kipp, Mechling
29–06	Austria	L	1–5	Stockholm	OGct	Jäger
1–07	Tsarist Russia	W	16–0	Stockholm	OGct	Fuchs 10, Förderer 4, Oberle, Burger
3–07	Hungary	L	1–3	Stockholm	OGct	Förderer
6–10	Denmark	L	1–3	Copenhagen	Fr	Jäger
17–11	Holland	L	2–3	Leipzig	Fr	Jäger 2
21–03–1913	England*	L	0–3	Berlin	Fr	

* Amateur side

18–05	Switzerland	L	1–2	Freiburg	Fr	Kipp
26–10	Denmark	L	1–4	Hamburg	Fr	Jäger
23–11	Belgium	L	2–6	Antwerp	Fr	Fuchs
5–04	Holland	D	4–4	Amsterdam	Fr	Jäger, Wegele, Harder, Queck
27–06–1920	Switzerland	L	1–4	Zurich	Fr	Jäger
26–09	Austria	L	2–3	Vienna	Fr	Sutor, Seiderer
24–10	Hungary	W	1–0	Berlin	Fr	Jäger
5–05–1921	Austria	D	3–3	Dresden	Fr	Seiderer, Träg, Popp
5–06	Hungary	L	0–3	Budapest	Fr	
18–09	Finland	D	3–3	Helsinki	Fr	Herberger 2, Kalb
26–03–1922	Switzerland	D	2–2	Frankfurt	Fr	Seiderer, Franz
23–04	Austria	W	2–0	Vienna	Fr	Jäger, Weissenbacher
2–07	Hungary	D	0–0	Bochum	Fr	
1–01–1923	Italy	L	1–3	Milan	Fr	Seiderer
10–05	Holland	D	0–0	Hamburg	Fr	
3–06	Switzerland	W	2–1	Basle	Fr	Hartmann 2
28–06	Sweden	L	1–2	Stockholm	Fr	Seiderer
12–08	Finland	L	1–2	Dresden	Fr	Claus–Oehler
4–11	Norway	W	1–0	Hamburg	Fr	Harder
13–01–1924	Austria	W	4–3	Nuremberg	Fr	Franz 3, Auer
21–04	Holland	W	1–0	Amsterdam	Fr	Auer
15–06	Norway	W	2–0	Oslo	Fr	Sutor, Wieder
31–08	Sweden	L	1–4	Berlin	Fr	Harder
21–09	Hungary	L	1–4	Budapest	Fr	Harder
23–11	Italy	L	0–1	Duisburg	Fr	
14–12	Switzerland	D	1–1	Stuttgart	Fr	Harder
29–03–1925	Holland	L	1–2	Amsterdam	Fr	Voss
21–06	Sweden	L	0–1	Stockholm	Fr	
26–06	Finland	W	5–3	Helsinki	Fr	Paulsen 3, Ruch, Voss
25–10	Switzerland	W	4–0	Basle	Fr	Harder 3, Hochgesang
18–04–1926	Holland	W	4–2	Dusseldorf	Fr	Pöttinger 3, Harder
20–06	Sweden	D	3–3	Nuremberg	Fr	Harder 3
31–10	Holland	W	3–2	Amsterdam	Fr	Harder 2, Wieder
12–12	Switzerland	L	2–3	Munich	Fr	Hochgesang, K Scherm
2–10–1927	Denmark	L	1–3	Copenhagen	Fr	Kiessling
23–10	Norway	W	6–2	Hamburg	Fr	Hochgesang 2, Pöttinger 2, Hofmann L, Kalb
20–11	Holland	D	2–2	Cologne	Fr	Pöttinger 2
15–04–1928	Switzerland	W	3–2	Berne	Fr	Hofmann R, Hornauer, Albrecht
28–05	Switzerland	W	4–0	Amsterdam	OGr1	Hofmann R 3, Hornauer
3–06	Uruguay	L	1–4	Amsterdam	OGqf	Hofmann R
16–09	Denmark	W	2–1	Nuremberg	Fr	Hofmann L, Heidkamp
23–09	Norway	W	2–0	Oslo	Fr	Kuzorra, Schmitt J
30–09	Sweden	L	0–2	Stockholm	Fr	
10–02–1929	Switzerland	W	7–1	Mannheim	Fr	Frank 4, Sobek 2, Pöttinger
28–04	Italy	W	2–1	Turin	Fr	Frank, Hornauer
1–06	Scotland	D	1–1	Berlin	Fr	Ruch
23–06	Sweden	W	3–0	Cologne	Fr	Hofmann R 3
20–10	Finland	W	4–0	Hamburg	Fr	Sackenheim 2, Hofmann R, Szepan
2–03–1930	Italy	L	0–2	Frankfurt	Fr	
4–05	Switzerland	W	5–0	Zurich	Fr	Kuzorra 3, Hofmann R 2
10–05	England	D	3–3	Berlin	Fr	Hofmann R 3
7–09	Denmark	L	3–6	Copenhagen	Fr	Hofmann R, Kund, Hohmann
28–09	Hungary	W	5–3	Dresden	Fr	Hofmann L 2, Hofmann R, Ludwig, Lachner
2–11	Norway	D	1–1	Breslau	Fr	Hanke
15–03–1931	France	L	0–1	Paris	Fr	
26–04	Holland	D	1–1	Amsterdam	Fr	Schlösser
24–05	Austria	L	0–6	Berlin	Fr	
17–06	Sweden	D	0–0	Stockholm	Fr	
21–06	Norway	D	2–2	Oslo	Fr	Ludwig, Bergmaier
13–09	Austria	L	0–5	Vienna	Fr	
27–09	Denmark	W	4–2	Hanover	Fr	Hofmann R 3, Kuzorra
6–03–1932	Switzerland	W	2–0	Leipzig	Fr	Hofmann R 2
1–07	Finland	W	4–1	Helsinki	Fr	Hofmann R 3, Rutz
25–09	Sweden	W	4–3	Nuremberg	Fr	Rohr 2, Kobierski, Krumm
30–10	Hungary	L	1–2	Budapest	Fr	Malik
4–12	Holland	L	0–2	Dusseldorf	Fr	
1–01–1933	Italy	L	1–3	Bologna	Fr	Rohr
19–03	France	D	3–3	Berlin	Fr	Rohr 2, Lachner

22–10	Belgium	W	8–1	Duisburg	Fr	Hohmann 3, Wigold 2, Kobierski, Rasselnberg, Albrecht
5–11	Norway	D	2–2	Magdeburg	Fr	Hohmann, Albrecht
19–11	Switzerland	W	2–0	Zurich	Fr	Hohmann, Lachner
3–12	Poland	W	1–0	Berlin	Fr	Rasselnberg
14–01–1934	Hungary	W	3–1	Frankfurt	Fr	Conen, Lachner, Stubb
11–03	Luxembourg	W	9–1	Luxembourg	WCq	Rasselnberg 4, Hohmann 3, Wigold, Albrecht
27–05	Belgium	W	5–2	Florence	WCr1	Conen 3, Kobierski, Siffling
31–05	Sweden	W	2–1	Milan	WCqf	Hohmann 2
3–06	Czechoslovakia	L	1–3	Rome	WCsf	Noack
7–06	Austria	W	3–2	Naples	WC3p	Lehner 2, E Conen
9–09	Poland	W	5–2	Warsaw	Fr	Lehner 2, Hohmann, Siffling, Szepan
7–10	Denmark	W	5–2	Copenhagen	Fr	Fath 3, Hohmann, Rohwedder
27–01–1935	Switzerland	W	4–0	Stuttgart	Fr	Conen 3, Lehner
17–02	Holland	W	3–2	Amsterdam	Fr	Hohmann, Conen, Kobierski
17–03	France	W	3–1	Paris	Fr	Hohmann, Kobierski, Lehner
28–04	Belgium	W	6–1	Brussels	Fr	Lenz 2, Damminger 2, Fath 2
8–05	Rep. Ireland	W	3–1	Dortmund	Fr	Damminger 2, Lehner
12–05	Spain	L	1–2	Cologne	Fr	Conen
26–05	Czechoslovakia	W	2–1	Dresden	Fr	Lenz 2
27–06	Norway	D	1–1	Oslo	Fr	Lenz
30–06	Sweden	L	1–3	Stockholm	Fr	Rohwedder
18–08	Finland	W	6–0	Munich	Fr	Conen 3, Lehner 3
18–08	Luxembourg	W	1–0	Luxembourg	Fr	Günther
25–08	Romania	W	4–2	Erfurt	Fr	Lenz, Hohmann, Rasselnberg, Simetsreiter
15–09	Poland	W	1–0	Breslau	Fr	Conen
15–09	Estonia	W	5–0	Stettin	Fr	Simetsreiter 2, Rasselnberg, Damminger, Malecki
13–10	Latvia	W	3–0	Konigsberg	Fr	Langenbein, Lenz, Panse
20–10	Bulgaria	W	4–2	Leipzig	Fr	Simetsreiter 2, Lehner, Pörtgen
4–12	England	L	0–3	London	Fr	
23–02–1936	Spain	W	2–1	Barcelona	Fr	Fath 2
27–02	Portugal	W	3–1	Lisbon	Fr	Hohmann, Lehner, Kitzinger
15–03	Hungary	L	2–3	Budapest	Fr	Lenz, Urban
4–08	Luxembourg	W	9–0	Berlin	OGr1	Simetsreiter 3, Urban 3, Gauchel 2, Elbern
7–08	Norway	L	0–2	Berlin	OGqf	
13–09	Poland	D	1–1	Warsaw	Fr	Hohmann
27–09	Czechoslovakia	W	2–1	Prague	Fr	Elbern, Siffling
27–09	Luxembourg	W	7–2	Krefeld	Fr	Pörtgen 3, Kuzorra 2, Günther, Malecki
14–10	Scotland	L	0–2	Glasgow	Fr	
17–10	Rep. Ireland	L	2–5	Dublin	Fr	Kobierski, Szepan
15–11	Italy	D	2–2	Berlin	Fr	Siffling 2
31–01–1937	Holland	D	2–2	Dusseldorf	Fr	Lehner 2
21–03	France	W	4–0	Stuttgart	Fr	Urban 2, Lehner, Lenz
21–03	Luxembourg	W	3–2	Luxembourg	Fr	Striebinger 2, Pörtgen
25–04	Belgium	W	1–0	Hanover	Fr	Hohmann
2–05	Switzerland	W	1–0	Zurich	Fr	Kitzinger
16–05	Denmark	W	8–0	Breslau	Fr	Siffling 5, Urban, Szepan, Lehner
25–06	Latvia	W	3–1	Riga	Fr	Berndt 2, Hohmann
29–06	Finland	W	2–0	Helsinki	WCq	Lehner, Urban
29–08	Estonia	W	4–1	Konigsberg	WCq	Lehner 2, Gauchel 2
24–10	Norway	W	3–0	Berlin	Fr	Siffling 3
21–11	Sweden	W	5–0	Hamburg	WCq	Siffling 2, Schön 2, Szepan
6–02–1938	Switzerland	D	1–1	Cologne	Fr	Szepan
20–03	Hungary	D	1–1	Nuremberg	Fr	Siffling
20–03	Luxembourg	W	2–1	Wuppertal	Fr	Gauchel 2
24–04	Portugal	D	1–1	Frankfurt	Fr	Siffling
14–05	England	L	3–6	Berlin	Fr	Gellesch, Gauchel, Pesser

GERMANY AND WEST GERMANY LEADING INTERNATIONAL GOALSCORERS

1	Müller G	68
2	Rummenigge	45
3	Seeler	43
4	Völler	43
5	Walter F	33
6	Fischer	32
7	Lehner	30
8	Conen	27
9	Hofmann R	24
10	Matthäus	23
11	Morlock	21
	Rahn H	21
13	Hohmann	20
14	Littbarski	18
15	Allofs K	17
	Overath	17
	Schön	17
	Siffling	17

GERMANY AND WEST GERMANY LEADING INTERNATIONAL APPEARANCES

1	Beckenbauer	103
2	Vogts	96
3	Maier	95
	Rummenigge	95
5	Matthäus	93
6	Völler	84
7	Förster K	81
	Overath	81
9	Schumacher	76
10	Brehme	75
11	Littbarski	73
12	Briegel	72
	Seeler	72
14	Janes	71
15	Kaltz	69
16	Höttges	66
	Schulz	66
18	Lehner	65
19	Müller G	62
20	Walter F	61
21	Allofs K	56
	Buchwald	56
23	Bonhof	53
	Dietz	53
	Weber	53
26	Erhardt	50

4–06	Switzerland	D	1–1	Paris	WCr1	Gauchel
9–06	Switzerland	L	2–4	Paris	WCr1	Hahnemann, OG
18–09	Poland	W	4–1	Chemnitz	Fr	Gauchel 3, Schön
25–09	Romania	W	4–1	Bucharest	Fr	Stroh, Schön, Pesser, OG
29–01–1939	Belgium	W	4–1	Brussels	Fr	Lehner, Hahnemann, Binder, Schön
26–02	Yugoslavia	W	3–2	Berlin	Fr	Janes, Urban, Biallas
26–03	Italy	L	2–3	Florence	Fr	Hahnemann, Janes
26–03	Luxembourg	L	1–2	Differdange	Fr	Hänel
23–05	Rep. Ireland	D	1–1	Bremen	Fr	Schön
22–06	Norway	W	4–0	Oslo	Fr	Schön 2, Urban, Janes
25–06	Denmark	W	2–0	Copenhagen	Fr	Conen, Gauchel
29–06	Estonia	W	2–0	Tallin	Fr	Lehner, R Schaletzki
27–08	Slovakia	L	0–2	Pressburg	Fr	
24–09	Hungary	L	1–5	Budapest	Fr	Lehner
15–10	Yugoslavia	W	5–1	Zagreb	Fr	Schön 3, Szepan 2
22–10	Bulgaria	W	2–1	Sofia	Fr	Conen, Urban
12–11	Bohemia	D	4–4	Breslau	Fr	Binder 3, Janes
26–11	Italy	W	5–2	Berlin	Fr	Binder 3, Lehner, Conen
3–12	Slovakia	W	3–1	Chemnitz	Fr	Schön, Lehner, Fiederer
7–04–1940	Hungary	D	2–2	Berlin	Fr	Binder, Gauchel
14–04	Yugoslavia	L	1–2	Vienna	Fr	Lehner
5–05	Italy	L	2–3	Milan	Fr	Binder 2
14–07	Romania	W	9–3	Frankfurt	Fr	Walter F 3, Plener 2, Hahnemann 2, Fiederer 2
1–09	Finland	W	13–0	Leipzig	Fr	Hahnemann 6, Conen 4, Walter F 2, Arlt
15–09	Slovakia	W	1–0	Pressburg	Fr	Durek
6–10	Hungary	D	2–2	Budapest	Fr	Hahnemann, Lehner
20–10	Bulgaria	W	7–3	Munich	Fr	Conen 4, Lehner, Kupfer, Gärtner
3–11	Yugoslavia	L	0–2	Zagreb	Fr	
17–11	Denmark	W	1–0	Hamburg	Fr	Schön
9–03–1941	Switzerland	W	4–2	Stuttgart	Fr	Schön 2, Walter F, Kobierski
6–04	Hungary	W	7–0	Cologne	Fr	Schön 2, Hahnemann 2, Kobierski, Walter F, Janes
20–04	Switzerland	L	1–2	Berne	Fr	Hahnemann
1–06	Romania	W	4–1	Bucharest	Fr	Willimowski 2, Walter F, Kobierski
15–06	Croatia	W	5–1	Vienna	Fr	Walter F 2, Lehner 2, Willinowski
5–10	Sweden	L	2–4	Stockholm	Fr	Walter F, Lehner
5–10	Finland	W	6–0	Helsinki	Fr	Willimowski 3, Eppenhoff 3
16–11	Denmark	D	1–1	Dresden	Fr	Hahnemann
7–12	Slovakia	W	4–0	Breslau	Fr	Conen 2, Walter F, Durek
18–01–1942	Croatia	W	2–0	Agram	Fr	Decker, OG
1–02	Switzerland	L	1–2	Vienna	Fr	Decker
12–04	Spain	D	1–1	Berlin	Fr	Decker
3–05	Hungary	W	5–3	Budapest	Fr	Walter F 2, Dörfel F, Janes, Sing
19–07	Bulgaria	W	3–0	Sofia	Fr	Decker 2, Arlt
16–08	Romania	W	7–0	Bytom	Fr	Walter F 3, Willimowski, Klingler, Burdenski, Decker
20–09	Sweden	L	2–3	Berlin	Fr	Decker, Klingler
18–10	Switzerland	W	5–3	Berne	Fr	Willimowski 4, Walter F
1–11	Croatia	W	5–1	Stuttgart	Fr	Willimowski 2, Walter F, Klingler, Janes
22–11	Slovakia	W	5–2	Pressburg	Fr	Klingler 3, Decker, Adamkiewicz

MATCHES OF THE WEST GERMAN NATIONAL TEAM

22–11–1950	Switzerland	W	1–0	Stuttgart	Fr	Burdenski
15–04–1951	Switzerland	W	3–2	Zurich	Fr	Gerritzen, Walter F, Walter O
17–06	Turkey	L	1–2	Berlin	Fr	Haferkamp
23–09	Austria	W	2–0	Vienna	Fr	Haferkamp, Morlock
17–10	Rep. Ireland	L	2–3	Dublin	Fr	Morlock, Walter F
21–11	Turkey	W	2–0	Istanbul	Fr	Morlock 2
23–12	Luxembourg	W	4–1	Essen	Fr	Rahn H, Stollenwerk, Termath 2
20–04–1952	Luxembourg	W	3–0	Luxembourg	Fr	Klodt, Stollenwerk, Zeitler
4–05	Rep. Ireland	W	3–0	Cologne	Fr	Posipal, Walter O, Termath
5–10	France	L	1–3	Paris	Fr	Walter O
9–11	Switzerland	W	5–1	Augsburg	Fr	Morlock, Walter O, Walter F, Schäfer 2
21–12	Yugoslavia	W	3–2	Ludwigshafen	Fr	Rahn H, Morlock, Walter F
28–12	Spain	D	2–2	Madrid	Fr	Walter O, Termath
22–03–1953	Austria	D	0–0	Cologne	Fr	
19–08	Norway	D	1–1	Oslo	WCq	Walter F
11–10	Saar	W	3–0	Stuttgart	WCq	Morlock 2, Schade
22–11	Norway	W	5–1	Hamburg	WCq	Morlock 2, Rahn H, Walter O, Walter F
28–03–1954	Saar	W	3–1	Saarbrucken	WCq	Morlock 2, Schäfer
25–04	Switzerland	W	5–3	Basle	Fr	Walter F 2, Schäfer 2, Morlock
17–06	Turkey	W	4–1	Berne	WCr1	Klodt, Morlock, Walter O, Schäfer
20–06	Hungary	L	3–8	Basle	WCr1	Rahn H, Pfaff, Herrmann R
23–06	Turkey	W	7–2	Zurich	WCr1	Morlock 3, Schäfer 2, Walter O, Walter F
27–06	Yugoslavia	W	2–0	Geneva	WCqf	Rahn H, OG
30–06	Austria	W	6–1	Basle	WCsf	Walter O 2, Walter F 2, Morlock, Schäfer
4–07	Hungary	W	3–2	Berne	WCf	Rahn H 2, Morlock
26–09	Belgium	L	0–2	Brussels	Fr	
16–10	France	L	1–3	Hanover	Fr	Stürmer
1–12	England	L	1–3	London	Fr	Beck
19–12	Portugal	W	3–0	Lisbon	Fr	Pfaff, Juskowiak, Erhardt
30–03–1955	Italy	L	1–2	Stuttgart	Fr	Juskowiak
28–05	Rep. Ireland	W	2–1	Hamburg	Fr	Mai, Waldner
21–08	Soviet Union	L	2–3	Moscow	Fr	Walter F, Schäfer
25–09	Yugoslavia	L	1–3	Belgrade	Fr	Morlock
16–11	Norway	W	2–0	Karlsruhe	Fr	Walter F, Röhrig
18–12	Italy	L	1–2	Rome	Fr	Röhrig
14–03–1956	Holland	L	1–2	Dusseldorf	Fr	OG
25–05	England	L	1–3	Berlin	Fr	Walter F
13–06	Norway	W	3–1	Oslo	Fr	Bäumler, Biesinger, Schönhoft
30–06	Sweden	D	2–2	Stockholm	Fr	Schröder, Biesinger
15–09	Soviet Union	L	1–2	Hanover	Fr	Schröder
21–11	Switzerland	L	1–3	Frankfurt	Fr	Neuschäfer
25–11	Rep. Ireland	L	0–3	Dublin	Fr	
23–12	Belgium	W	4–1	Cologne	Fr	Kelbassa, Schröder, Vollmar, Wewers
10–03–1957	Austria	W	3–2	Vienna	Fr	Rahn H 2, Kraus
3–04	Holland	W	2–1	Amsterdam	Fr	Schmidt, Siedl
22–05	Scotland	L	1–3	Stuttgart	Fr	Siedl
20–11	Sweden	W	1–0	Hamburg	Fr	Schmidt
22–12	Hungary	W	1–0	Hanover	Fr	Kelbassa
2–03–1958	Belgium	W	2–0	Brussels	Fr	Schmidt, Schäfer
19–03	Spain	W	2–0	Frankfurt	Fr	Klodt, Cieslarczyk
2–04	Czechoslovakia	L	2–3	Prague	Fr	Cieslarczyk, OG
8–06	Argentina	W	3–1	Malmo	WCr1	Rahn H 2, Seeler
11–06	Czechoslovakia	D	2–2	Halsingborg	WCr1	Rahn H, Schäfer
15–06	Nth. Ireland	D	2–2	Malmo	WCr1	Rahn H, Seeler
19–06	Yugoslavia	W	1–0	Malmo	WCqf	Rahn H
24–06	Sweden	L	1–3	Gothenburg	WCsf	Schäfer
28–06	France	L	3–6	Gothenburg	WC3p	Rahn H, Schäfer, Cieslarczyk
24–09	Denmark	D	1–1	Copenhagen	Fr	Rahn H
26–10	France	D	2–2	Paris	Fr	Rahn H, Seeler
19–11	Austria	D	2–2	Berlin	Fr	Rahn H 2
21–12	Bulgaria	W	3–0	Augsburg	Fr	Seeler 2, Waldner
28–12	Egypt	L	1–2	Cairo	Fr	Morlock
6–05–1959	Scotland	L	2–3	Glasgow	Fr	Seeler, Juskowiak
20–05	Poland	D	1–1	Hamburg	Fr	Stein
4–10	Switzerland	W	4–0	Berne	Fr	Rahn H, Juskowiak, Brülls, Vollmar
21–10	Holland	W	7–0	Cologne	Fr	Seeler 3, Schmidt 2, Brülls, Siedl

8–11	Hungary	L	3–4	Budapest	Fr	Seeler 2, Brülls
20–12	Yugoslavia	D	1–1	Hanover	Fr	Schmidt
23–03–1960	Chile	W	2–1	Stuttgart	Fr	Haller, Seeler
27–04	Portugal	W	2–1	Ludwigshaven	Fr	Rahn H, Seeler
11–05	Rep. Ireland	L	0–1	Dusseldorf	Fr	
3–08	Iceland	W	5–0	Reykjavik	Fr	Dörfel G 2, Seeler, Marx, Reitgassl
26–10	Nth. Ireland	W	4–3	Belfast	WCq	Dörfel G 2, Brülls, Seeler
20–11	Greece	W	3–0	Athens	WCq	Dörfel G, Brülls, Haller
23–11	Bulgaria	L	1–2	Sofia	Fr	Vollmar
8–03–1961	Belgium	W	1–0	Frankfurt	Fr	Dörfel G
26–03	Chile	L	1–3	Santiago	Fr	Herrmann G
10–05	Nth. Ireland	W	2–1	Berlin	WCq	Brülls, Kress
20–09	Denmark	W	5–1	Dusseldorf	Fr	Seeler 3, Kress, Brülls
8–10	Poland	W	2–0	Warsaw	Fr	Brülls, Haller
22–10	Greece	W	2–1	Augsburg	WCq	Seeler 2
11–04–1962	Uruguay	W	3–0	Hamburg	Fr	Koslowski, Haller, Schäfer
31–05	Italy	D	0–0	Santiago	WCr1	
3–06	Switzerland	W	2–1	Santiago	WCr1	Seeler, Brülls
6–06	Chile	W	2–0	Santiago	WCr1	Seeler, Szymaniak
10–06	Yugoslavia	L	0–1	Santiago	WCqf	
30–09	Yugoslavia	W	3–2	Zagreb	Fr	Strehl
24–10	France	D	2–2	Stuttgart	Fr	Konietzka, Steinmann
23–12	Switzerland	W	5–1	Karlsruhe	Fr	Schütz 2, Küppers, Kraus, Werner
5–05–1963	Brazil	L	1–2	Hamburg	Fr	Werner
28–09	Turkey	W	3–0	Frankfurt	Fr	Seeler 3
3–11	Sweden	L	1–2	Stockholm	Fr	Dörfel G
29–12	Morocco	W	4–1	Casablanca	Fr	Konietzka 2, Krämer, Schmidt
1–01–1964	Algeria	L	0–2	Algiers	Fr	
29–04	Czechoslovakia	L	3–4	Ludwigshaven	Fr	Seeler 2, Geiger
12–05	Scotland	D	2–2	Hanover	Fr	Seeler 2
7–06	Finland	W	4–1	Helsinki	Fr	Schmidt, Kraus, Geiger, Overath
4–11	Sweden	D	1–1	Berlin	WCq	Brunnenmeier
13–03–1965	Italy	D	1–1	Hamburg	Fr	Sieloff
24–04	Cyprus	W	5–0	Karlsruhe	WCq	Overath 2, Sieloff 2, Strehl
12–05	England	L	0–1	Nuremberg	Fr	
26–05	Switzerland	W	1–0	Basle	Fr	Rodekamp
6–06	Brazil	L	0–2	Rio de Janeiro	Fr	
26–09	Sweden	W	2–1	Stockholm	WCq	Seeler, Krämer
9–10	Austria	W	4–1	Stuttgart	Fr	Ulsass 3, Sieloff
14–11	Cyprus	W	6–0	Nicosia	WCq	Brunnenmeier 2, Szymaniak, Heiss, Krämer, OG
23–02–1966	England	L	0–1	London	Fr	
23–03	Holland	W	4–2	Rotterdam	Fr	Beckenbauer 2, Seeler, Emmerich
4–05	Rep. Ireland	W	4–0	Dublin	Fr	Overath 2, Beckenbauer, Haller
7–05	Nth. Ireland	W	2–0	Belfast	Fr	Seeler, Heiss
1–06	Romania	W	1–0	Ludwigshaven	Fr	Seeler
23–06	Yugoslavia	W	2–0	Hanover	Fr	Seeler, Overath
12–07	Switzerland	W	5–0	Sheffield	WCr1	Beckenbauer 2, Haller 2, Held
16–07	Argentina	D	0–0	Birmingham	WCr1	
20–07	Spain	W	2–1	Birmingham	WCr1	Seeler, Emmerich
23–07	Uruguay	W	4–0	Sheffield	WCqf	Haller 2, Seeler, Beckenbauer
25–07	Soviet Union	W	2–1	Liverpool	WCsf	Beckenbauer, Haller
30–07	England	L	2–4	London	WCf	Weber, Haller
12–10	Turkey	W	2–0	Ankara	Fr	Rupp, Küppers
19–11	Norway	W	3–0	Cologne	Fr	Ulsass 2, Seeler
22–02–1967	Morocco	W	5–1	Karlsruhe	Fr	Ulsass 2, Heynckes, Zaczyk, Löhr
22–03	Bulgaria	W	1–0	Hanover	Fr	Heynckes
8–04	Albania	W	6–0	Dortmund	ECq	Müller G 4, Löhr 2
3–05	Yugoslavia	L	0–1	Belgrade	ECq	
27–09	France	W	5–1	Berlin	Fr	Siemensmeyer 2, Müller G, Overath, Libuda
7–10	Yugoslavia	W	3–1	Hamburg	ECq	Seeler, Müller G, Löhr
22–11	Romania	L	0–1	Bucharest	Fr	
17–12	Albania	D	0–0	Tirana	ECq	
6–03–1968	Belgium	W	3–1	Brussels	Fr	Volkert 2, Laumen
17–04	Switzerland	D	0–0	Basle	Fr	
8–05	Wales	D	1–1	Cardiff	Fr	Overath
1–06	England	W	1–0	Hanover	Fr	Beckenbauer
16–06	Brazil	W	2–1	Stuttgart	Fr	Dörfel B, Held

25–09	France	D	1–1	Marseille	Fr	Overath
13–10	Austria	W	2–0	Vienna	WCq	Müller G, OG
23–11	Cyprus	W	1–0	Nicosia	WCq	Müller G
14–12	Brazil	D	2–2	Rio de Janeiro	Fr	Held, Gerwien
18–12	Chile	L	1–2	Santiago	Fr	Ulsass
22–12	Mexico	D	0–0	Mexico City	Fr	
26–03–1969	Wales	D	1–1	Frankfurt	Fr	Müller G
16–04	Scotland	D	1–1	Glasgow	WCq	Müller G
10–05	Austria	W	1–0	Nuremberg	WCq	Müller G
21–05	Cyprus	W	12–0	Essen	WCq	Müller G 4, Overath 3, Haller 2, Höttges, Lorenz, Held
21–09	Austria	D	1–1	Vienna	Fr	Müller G
24–09	Bulgaria	W	1–0	Sofia	Fr	Dörfel B
22–10	Scotland	W	3–2	Hamburg	WCq	Müller G, Libuda, Fichtel
11–02–1970	Spain	L	0–2	Seville	Fr	
8–04	Romania	D	1–1	Stuttgart	Fr	Overath
9–05	Rep. Ireland	W	2–1	Berlin	Fr	Seeler, Löhr
13–05	Yugoslavia	W	1–0	Hanover	Fr	Seeler
3–06	Morocco	W	2–1	Leon	WCr1	Seeler
7–06	Bulgaria	W	5–2	Leon	WCr1	Müller G 3, Seeler, Libuda
10–06	Peru	W	3–1	Leon	WCr1	Müller G 3
14–06	England	W	3–2	Leon	WCqf	Müller G, Seeler, Beckenbauer
17–06	Italy	L	3–4	Mexico City	WCsf	Müller G 2, Schnellinger
20–06	Uruguay	W	1–0	Mexico City	WC3p	Overath
9–09	Hungary	W	3–1	Nuremberg	Fr	Müller G 2, Sieloff
17–10	Turkey	D	1–1	Cologne	ECq	Müller G
18–11	Yugoslavia	L	0–2	Zagreb	Fr	
22–11	Greece	W	3–1	Athens	Fr	Beckenbauer, Netzer, Grabowski
17–02–1971	Albania	W	1–0	Tirana	ECq	Müller G
25–04	Turkey	W	3–0	Istanbul	ECq	Müller G 2, Köppel
12–06	Albania	W	2–0	Karlsruhe	ECq	G Netzer, Grabowski
22–06	Norway	W	7–1	Oslo	Fr	Müller G 3, Netzer, Overath, Beckenbauer, Held
27–06	Sweden	L	0–1	Gothenburg	Fr	
30–06	Denmark	W	3–1	Copenhagen	Fr	Müller G, Beckenbauer, Flohe
8–09	Mexico	W	5–0	Hanover	Fr	Müller G 3, Netzer, Köppel
10–10	Poland	W	3–1	Warsaw	ECq	Müller G 2, Grabowski
17–11	Poland	D	0–0	Hamburg	ECq	
29–03–1972	Hungary	W	2–0	Budapest	Fr	Hoeness U, Breitner
29–04	England	W	3–1	London	ECqf	Müller G, Hoeness U, Netzer
13–05	England	D	0–0	Berlin	ECqf	
26–05	Soviet Union	W	4–1	Munich	Fr	Müller G 4
14–06	Belgium	W	2–1	Antwerp	ECsf	Müller G 2
18–06	Soviet Union	W	3–0	Brussels	ECf	Müller G 2, Wimmer
15–11	Switzerland	W	5–1	Dusseldorf	Fr	Müller G 4, Netzer
14–02–1973	Argentina	L	2–3	Munich	Fr	Heynckes, Cullmann
28–03	Czechoslovakia	W	3–0	Dusseldorf	Fr	Müller G 2, Kremers
9–05	Yugoslavia	L	0–1	Munich	Fr	
12–05	Bulgaria	W	3–0	Hamburg	Fr	Cullmann, Beckenbauer, OG
16–06	Brazil	L	0–1	Berlin	Fr	
5–09	Soviet Union	W	1–0	Moscow	Fr	Müller G
10–10	Austria	W	4–0	Hanover	Fr	Müller G 2, Weber, Kremers
13–10	France	W	2–1	Gelsenkirchen	Fr	Müller G 2
14–11	Scotland	D	1–1	Glasgow	Fr	Hoeness U
24–11	Spain	W	2–1	Stuttgart	Fr	Heynckes 2
23–02–1974	Spain	L	0–1	Barcelona	Fr	
26–02	Italy	D	0–0	Rome	Fr	
27–03	Scotland	W	2–1	Frankfurt	Fr	Grabowski, Breitner
17–04	Hungary	W	5–0	Dortmund	Fr	Müller G 2, Wimmer, Kremers, Hölzenbein
1–05	Sweden	W	2–0	Hamburg	Fr	Heynckes 2
14–06	Chile	W	1–0	Berlin	WCr1	Breitner
18–06	Australia	W	3–0	Hamburg	WCr1	Cullmann, Müller G, Overath
22–06	East Germany	L	0–1	Hamburg	WCr1	
26–06	Yugoslavia	W	2–0	Dusseldorf	WCr2	Müller G, Breitner
30–06	Sweden	W	4–2	Dusseldorf	WCr2	Bonhoff, Hoeness, Overath, Grabowski
3–07	Poland	W	1–0	Frankfurt	WCr2	Müller G
7–07	Holland	W	2–1	Munich	WCf	Müller G, Breitner
4–09	Switzerland	W	2–1	Basle	Fr	Cullmann, Geye

20–11	Greece	D	2–2	Athens	ECq	Cullmann, Wimmer
22–12	Malta	W	1–0	Gzira	ECq	Cullmann
12–03–1975	England	L	0–2	London	Fr	
27–04	Bulgaria	D	1–1	Sofia	ECq	Ritschel
17–05	Holland	D	1–1	Frankfurt	Fr	Wimmer
3–09	Austria	W	2–0	Vienna	Fr	Beer 2
11–10	Greece	D	1–1	Dusseldorf	ECq	Heynckes
19–11	Bulgaria	W	1–0	Stuttgart	ECq	Heynckes
20–12	Turkey	W	5–0	Istanbul	Fr	Heynckes 2, Worm 2, Beer
28–02–1976	Malta	W	8–0	Dortmund	ECq	Heynckes 2, Worm 2, Beer 2, Vogts, Hölzenbein
24–04	Spain	D	1–1	Madrid	ECqf	Beer
22–05	Spain	W	2–0	Munich	ECqf	Hoeness U, Toppmöller
17–06	Yugoslavia	W	4–2	Belgrade	ECsf	Müller D 3, Flohe
20–06	Czechoslovakia	D	2–2 (4–5p)	Belgrade	ECf	Müller D, Hölzenbein
6–10	Wales	W	2–0	Cardiff	Fr	Beckenbauer, Heynckes
17–11	Czechoslovakia	W	2–0	Hanover	Fr	Beer, Flohe
23–02–1977	France	L	0–1	Paris	Fr	
27–04	Nth. Ireland	W	5–0	Cologne	Fr	Fischer 2, Bonhof, Flohe, Müller D
30–04	Yugoslavia	W	2–1	Belgrade	Fr	Müller D, Bonhof
5–06	Argentina	W	3–1	Buenos Aires	Fr	Fischer 2, Hölzenbein
8–06	Uruguay	W	2–0	Montevideo	Fr	Müller D, Flohe
12–06	Brazil	D	1–1	Rio de Janeiro	Fr	Fischer
14–06	Mexico	D	2–2	Mexico City	Fr	Fischer 2
7–09	Finland	W	1–0	Helsinki	Fr	Fischer
8–10	Italy	W	2–1	Berlin	Fr	Rummenigge, Kaltz
16–11	Switzerland	W	4–1	Stuttgart	Fr	Fischer 2, Flohe, OG
14–12	Wales	D	1–1	Dortmund	Fr	Fischer
22–02–1978	England	W	2–1	Munich	Fr	Bonhof, Worm
8–03	Soviet Union	W	1–0	Frankfurt	Fr	Rüssmann
5–04	Brazil	L	0–1	Hamburg	Fr	
19–04	Sweden	L	1–3	Stockholm	Fr	Bonhof
1–06	Poland	D	0–0	Buenos Aires	WCr1	
6–06	Mexico	W	6–0	Cordoba	WCr1	Rummenigge 2, Flohe 2, Müller D, Müller H
10–06	Tunisia	D	0–0	Cordoba	WCr1	
14–06	Italy	D	0–0	Buenos Aires	WCr2	
18–06	Holland	D	2–2	Cordoba	WCr2	Müller D, Abramczik
21–06	Austria	L	2–3	Cordoba	WCr2	Hölzenbein, Rummenigge
11–10	Czechoslovakia	W	4–3	Prague	Fr	Bonhof 2, Müller H, Abramczik
15–11	Hungary	D	0–0	Frankfurt	Fr	*Abandoned 60 mins*
20–12	Holland	W	3–1	Dusseldorf	Fr	Bonhof, Fischer, Rummenigge
25–02–1979	Malta	D	0–0	Gzira	ECq	
1–04	Turkey	D	0–0	Izmir	ECq	
2–05	Wales	W	2–0	Wrexham	ECq	Fischer, Zimmermann
22–05	Rep. Ireland	W	3–1	Dublin	Fr	Rummenigge, Hoeness D, Kelsch
26–05	Iceland	W	3–1	Reykjavik	Fr	Hoeness D 2, Kelsch
12–09	Argentina	W	2–1	Berlin	Fr	Rummenigge, Allofs
17–10	Wales	W	5–1	Cologne	ECq	Fischer 2, Förster K, Rummenigge, Kaltz
21–11	Soviet Union	W	3–1	Tbilisi	Fr	Rummenigge 2, Fischer
22–12	Turkey	W	2–0	Gelsenkirchen	ECq	Fischer, Zimmermann
27–02–1980	Malta	W	8–0	Bremen	ECq	Allofs 2, Fischer 2, Bonhof, Kelsch, Rummenigge, OG
2–04	Austria	W	1–0	Munich	Fr	Müller H
13–05	Poland	W	3–1	Frankfurt	Fr	Allofs, Rummenigge, Schuster
11–06	Czechoslovakia	W	1–0	Rome	ECr1	Rummenigge
14–06	Holland	W	3–2	Naples	ECr1	Allofs 3
17–06	Greece	D	0–0	Turin	ECr1	
22–06	Belgium	W	2–1	Rome	ECf	Hrubesch 2
10–09	Switzerland	W	3–2	Basle	Fr	Müller H 2, Magath
11–10	Holland	D	1–1	Eindhoven	Fr	Hrubesch
19–11	France	W	4–1	Hanover	Fr	Allofs, Hrubesch, Briegel, Kaltz
3–12	Bulgaria	W	3–1	Sofia	WCq	Kaltz 2, Rummenigge
1–01–1981	Argentina	L	1–2	Montevideo	ML	Hrubesch
7–01	Brazil	L	1–4	Montevideo	ML	Allofs
1–04	Albania	W	2–0	Tirana	WCq	Schuster 2
29–04	Austria	W	2–0	Hamburg	WCq	Fischer, OG
19–05	Brazil	L	1–2	Stuttgart	Fr	Fischer
24–05	Finland	W	4–0	Lahti	WCq	Fischer 2, Kaltz, Briegel

2–09	Poland	W	2–0	Chorzow	Fr	Fischer, Rummenigge
23–09	Finland	W	7–1	Bochum	WCq	Rummenigge 3, Breitner 2, Fischer, Dremmler
14–10	Austria	W	3–1	Vienna	WCq	Littbarski 2, Magath
18–11	Albania	W	8–0	Dortmund	WCq	Rummenigge 3, Fischer 2, Littbarski, Breitner, Kaltz
22–11	Bulgaria	W	4–0	Dusseldorf	WCq	Rummenigge 2, Fischer, Kaltz
17–02–1982	Portugal	W	3–1	Hanover	Fr	Fischer 2, OG
21–03	Brazil	L	0–1	Rio de Janeiro	Fr	
24–03	Argentina	D	1–1	Buenos Aires	Fr	Dremmler
14–04	Czechoslovakia	W	2–1	Cologne	Fr	Littbarski, Breitner
12–05	Norway	W	4–2	Oslo	Fr	Rummenigge 2, Littbarski 2
16–06	Algeria	L	1–2	Gijon	WCr1	Rummenigge
20–06	Chile	W	4–1	Gijon	WCr1	Rummenigge 3, Reinders
25–06	Austria	W	1–0	Gijon	WCr1	Hrubesch
29–06	England	D	0–0	Madrid	WCr2	
2–07	Spain	W	2–1	Madrid	WCr2	Fischer, Littbarski
8–07	France	D	3–3 (5–4p)	Seville	WCsf	Fischer, Littbarski, Rummenigge
11–07	Italy	L	1–3	Madrid	WCf	Breitner
22–09	Belgium	D	0–0	Munich	Fr	
13–10	England	W	2–1	London	Fr	Rummenigge 2
17–11	Nth. Ireland	L	0–1	Belfast	ECq	
23–02–1983	Portugal	L	0–1	Lisbon	Fr	
30–03	Albania	W	2–1	Tirana	ECq	Rummenigge, Völler
23–04	Turkey	W	3–0	Izmir	ECq	Rummenigge 2, Dremmler
27–04	Austria	D	0–0	Vienna	ECq	
7–06	Yugoslavia	W	4–2	Luxembourg	Fr	Meier 2, Rummenigge, Schuster
7–09	Hungary	D	1–1	Budapest	Fr	Völler
5–10	Austria	W	3–0	Gelsenkirchen	ECq	Völler 2, Rummenigge
26–10	Turkey	W	5–1	Berlin	ECq	Völler 2, Rummenigge 2, Stielike
16–11	Nth. Ireland	L	0–1	Hamburg	ECq	
20–11	Albania	W	2–1	Saarbrucken	ECq	Rummenigge, Strack
15–02–1984	Bulgaria	W	3–2	Varna	Fr	Stielike 2, Völler
29–02	Belgium	W	1–0	Brussels	Fr	Völler
28–03	Soviet Union	W	2–1	Hanover	Fr	Völler, Brehme
18–04	France	L	0–1	Strasbourg	Fr	
22–05	Italy	W	1–0	Zurich	Fr	Briegel
14–06	Portugal	D	0–0	Strasbourg	ECr1	
17–06	Romania	W	2–1	Lens	ECr1	Völler 2
20–06	Spain	L	0–1	Paris	ECr1	
12–09	Argentina	L	1–3	Dusseldorf	Fr	Jakobs
17–10	Sweden	W	2–0	Cologne	WCq	Rummenigge, Rahn U
16–12	Malta	W	3–2	Ta'Qali	WCq	Allofs 2, Förster K
29–01–1985	Hungary	L	0–1	Hamburg	Fr	
24–02	Portugal	W	2–1	Lisbon	WCq	Littbarski, Völler
27–03	Malta	W	6–0	Saarbrucken	WCq	Rummenigge 2, Rahn U 2, Littbarski, Magath
17–04	Bulgaria	W	4–1	Augsburg	Fr	Völler 2, Littbarski, Rahn U
30–04	Czechoslovakia	W	5–1	Prague	WCq	Littbarski, Allofs, Matthäus, Herget, Berthold
12–06	England	L	0–3	Mexico City	Fr	
15–06	Mexico	L	0–2	Mexico City	Fr	
28–08	Soviet Union	L	0–1	Moscow	Fr	
25–09	Sweden	D	2–2	Stockholm	WCq	Völler, Herget
16–10	Portugal	L	0–1	Stuttgart	WCq	
17–11	Czechoslovakia	D	2–2	Munich	WCq	Rummenigge, Herget
5–02–1986	Italy	W	2–1	Avellino	Fr	M Herget, Matthäus
12–03	Brazil	W	2–0	Frankfurt	Fr	Allofs, Briegel
9–04	Switzerland	W	1–0	Basle	Fr	Hoeness D
11–05	Yugoslavia	D	1–1	Bochum	Fr	Völler
14–05	Holland	W	3–1	Dortmund	Fr	Völler 2, Herget
4–06	Uruguay	D	1–1	Queretaro	WCr1	Allofs
8–06	Scotland	W	2–1	Queretaro	WCr1	Völler, Allofs
13–06	Denmark	L	0–2	Queretaro	WCr1	
17–06	Morocco	W	1–0	Monterrey	WCr2	Matthäus
21–06	Mexico	D	0–0	Monterrey	WCqf	
25–06	France	W	2–0	Guadalajara	WCsf	Brehme, Völler
29–06	Argentina	L	2–3	Mexico City	WCf	Rummenigge, Völler
24–09	Denmark	W	2–0	Copenhagen	Fr	Allofs, Thon

15–10	Spain	D	2–2	Hanover	Fr	Rahn U, Waas
29–10	Austria	L	1–4	Vienna	Fr	Völler
25–03–1987	Israel	W	2–0	Tel Aviv	Fr	Thon, Matthäus
18–04	Italy	D	0–0	Cologne	Fr	
12–08	France	W	2–1	Berlin	Fr	Völler 2
9–09	England	W	3–1	Dusseldorf	Fr	Littbarski 2, Wuttke
23–09	Denmark	W	1–0	Hamburg	Fr	Völler
13–10	Sweden	D	1–1	Gelsenkirchen	Fr	Littbarski
18–11	Hungary	D	0–0	Budapest	Fr	
12–12	Brazil	D	1–1	Brasilia	Fr	Reuter
16–12	Argentina	L	0–1	Buenos Aires	Fr	
31–03–1988	Sweden	D	1–1 (2–4p)	Berlin	Fr	Allofs
2–04	Argentina	W	1–0	Berlin	Fr	Matthäus
27–04	Switzerland	W	1–0	Kaiserslautern	Fr	Klinsmann
4–06	Yugoslavia	D	1–1	Bremen	Fr	Matthäus
10–06	Italy	D	1–1	Dusseldorf	ECr1	Brehme
14–06	Denmark	W	2–0	Gelsenkirchen	ECr1	Thon, Klinsmann
17–06	Spain	W	2–0	Munich	ECr1	Völler 2
21–06	Holland	L	1–2	Hamburg	ECsf	Matthäus
31–08	Finland	W	4–0	Helsinki	WCq	Völler 2, Matthäus, Riedle
21–09	Soviet Union	W	1–0	Dusseldorf	Fr	OG
19–10	Holland	D	0–0	Munich	WCq	
22–03–1989	Bulgaria	W	2–1	Sofia	Fr	Völler, Littbarski
26–04	Holland	D	1–1	Rotterdam	WCq	Riedle
31–05	Wales	D	0–0	Cardiff	WCq	
6–09	Rep. Ireland	D	1–1	Dublin	Fr	Dorfner
4–10	Finland	W	6–1	Dortmund	WCq	Moller A 2, Littbarski, Völler, Klinsmann, Matthäus
15–11	Wales	W	2–1	Cologne	WCq	Völler, Hassler
28–02–1990	France	L	1–2	Montpellier	Fr	Moller A
25–04	Uruguay	D	3–3	Stuttgart	Fr	Matthäus, Völler, Klinsmann
26–05	Czechoslovakia	W	1–0	Dusseldorf	Fr	Bein
30–05	Denmark	W	1–0	Gelsenkirchen	Fr	Völler
10–06	Yugoslavia	W	4–1	Milan	WCr1	Matthäus 2, Klinsmann, Völler
15–06	UAE	W	5–1	Milan	WCr1	Völler 2, Klinsmann, Matthäus, Bein
19–06	Colombia	D	1–1	Milan	WCr1	Littbarski
24–06	Holland	W	2–1	Milan	WCr2	Klinsmann, Brehme
1–07	Czechoslovakia	W	1–0	Milan	WCqf	Matthäus
4–07	England	D	1–1 (4–3p)	Turin	WCsf	Brehme
8–07	Argentina	W	1–0	Rome	WCf	Brehme
29–08	Portugal	D	1–1	Lisbon	Fr	Matthäus
10–10	Sweden	W	3–1	Stockholm	Fr	Klinsmann, Völler, Brehme
31–10	Luxembourg	W	3–2	Luxembourg	ECq	Klinsmann, Bein, Völler

MATCHES OF THE GERMAN NATIONAL TEAM

19–12–1990	Switzerland	W	4–0	Stuttgart	Fr	Völler, Riedle, Thom, Matthäus
27–03–1991	Soviet Union	W	2–1	Frankfurt	Fr	Reuter, Matthäus
1–05	Belgium	W	1–0	Hanover	ECq	Matthäus
5–06	Wales	L	0–1	Cardiff	ECq	
11–09	England	W	1–0	London	Fr	Riedle
16–10	Wales	W	4–1	Nuremberg	ECq	Möller, Völler, Riedle, Doll
20–11	Belgium	W	1–0	Brussels	ECq	Völler
18–12	Luxembourg	W	4–0	Leverkusen	ECq	Matthäus, Buchwald, Riedle, Hässler
25–03–1992	Italy	L	0–1	Turin	Fr	
22–04	Czechoslovakia	D	1–1	Prague	Fr	Hässler
30–05	Turkey	W	1–0	Gelsenkirchen	Fr	Völler
2–06	Nth. Ireland	D	1–1	Bremen	Fr	Binz
12–06	CIS	D	1–1	Norrkoping	ECr1	Hässler
15–06	Scotland	W	2–0	Norrkoping	ECr1	Riedle, Effenberg
18–06	Holland	L	1–3	Gothenburg	ECr1	Klinsmann
21–06	Sweden	W	3–2	Stockholm	ECsf	Hässler, Riedle 2
26–06	Denmark	L	0–2	Gothenburg	ECf	

INTERNATIONAL MATCHES PLAYED BY EAST GERMANY

Date	Opponents	Result		Venue	Compet	Scorers
21-09-1952	Poland	L	0-3	Warsaw	Fr	
26-10	Romania	L	1-3	Bucharest	Fr	Schnieke
14-06-1953	Bulgaria	D	0-0	Dresden	Fr	
8-05-1954	Romania	L	0-1	Berlin	Fr	
26-09	Poland	L	0-1	Rostock	Fr	
24-10	Bulgaria	L	1-3	Sofia	Fr	Meier
18-09-1955	Romania	W	3-2	Bucharest	Fr	Tröger 2, Wirth
20-11	Bulgaria	W	1-0	Berlin	Fr	Tröger
22-07-1956	Poland	W	2-0	Chorzow	Fr	Tröger, Assmy
20-09	Indonesia	W	3-1	Karl-Marx-Stadt	Fr	Tröger 2, Wirth
14-10	Bulgaria	L	1-3	Sofia	Fr	Wirth
10-03-1957	Luxembourg	W	3-0	Berlin	Fr	Tröger 2, Schröter
19-05	Wales	W	2-1	Leipzig	WCq	Wirth, Tröger
16-06	Czechoslovakia	L	1-3	Brno	WCq	Wirth
25-09	Wales	L	1-4	Cardiff	WCq	Kaiser
27-10	Czechoslovakia	L	1-4	Leipzig	WCq	Müller H
1-05-1958	Albania	D	1-1	Tirana	Fr	Tröger
28-06	Poland	D	1-1	Rostock	Fr	Klingbiel
13-08	Norway	L	5-6	Oslo	Fr	Schröter, Wirth, Assmy
14-09	Romania	W	3-2	Leipzig	Fr	Schröter, Assmy, Wirth
5-10	Bulgaria	D	1-1	Berlin	Fr	Tröger
2-11	Norway	W	4-1	Leipzig	Fr	Müller H 2, Assmy, Schröter
11-02-1959	Indonesia	D	2-2	Djakarta	Fr	Wirth, Ducke R
1-05	Hungary	L	0-1	Dresden	Fr	
21-06	Portugal	L	0-2	Berlin	ECr1	
28-06	Portugal	L	2-3	Oporto	ECr1	Vogt, Kohle
6-09	Finland	L	2-3	Helsinki	Fr	Franz R, Schröter
10-07-1960	Bulgaria	L	0-2	Sofia	Fr	
17-08	Soviet Union	L	0-1	Leipzig	Fr	
30-10	Finland	W	5-1	Rostock	Fr	Nöldner 2, Erler, Ducke P, Heine
4-12	Tunisia	W	3-0	Tunis	Fr	Nöldner, Müller H, Meyer
11-12	Morocco	W	3-2	Casablanca	Fr	Meyer, Ducke P, Müller H
16-04-1961	Hungary	L	0-2	Budapest	WCq	
14-05	Holland	D	1-1	Leipzig	WCq	Erler
28-05	Denmark	D	1-1	Copenhagen	Fr	Mühlbächer
21-06	Morocco	L	1-2	Erfurt	Fr	Nöldner
10-09	Hungary	L	2-3	Berlin	WCq	Erler, Ducke P
22-10	Poland	L	1-3	Wroclaw	Fr	Erler
10-12	Morocco	L	0-2	Casablanca	Fr	
3-05-1962	Soviet Union	L	1-2	Moscow	Fr	Erler
16-05	Yugoslavia	L	1-3	Belgrade	Fr	Ducke R
23-05	Denmark	W	4-1	Leipzig	Fr	Schröter 3, Ducke R
16-09	Yugoslavia	D	2-2	Leipzig	Fr	Wirth, Schröter
14-10	Romania	W	3-2	Dresden	Fr	Wirth, Schröter, Nachtigall
21-11	Czechoslovakia	W	2-1	Berlin	ECr1	Erler, Liebrecht
9-12	Mali	W	2-1	Bamoko	Fr	Erler 2
16-12	Guinea	W	3-2	Conakry	Fr	Frenzel 2, Vogel
31-03-1963	Czechoslovakia	D	1-1	Prague	ECr1	Ducke P
12-05	Romania	L	2-3	Bucharest	Fr	Ducke P, Nöldner
2-06	England	L	1-2	Leipzig	Fr	Ducke P
4-09	Bulgaria	D	1-1	Magdeburg	Fr	Nachtigall
19-10	Hungary	L	1-2	Berlin	ECr2	
3-11	Hungary	D	3-3	Budapest	ECr2	
17-12	Burma	W	5-1	Rangoon	Fr	Backhaus, Stöcker, Kleiminger, Körner, Frässdorf
12-01-1964	Ceylon	W	12-1	Colombo	Fr	Kleiminger 4, Stöcker 3, Barthels 2, Nöldner, Backhaus, Frässdorf
23-02	Ghana	L	0-3	Accra	Fr	
3-01-1965	Uruguay	W	2-0	Montevideo	Fr	Frenzel, Ducke P
25-04	Austria	D	1-1	Vienna	WCq	Nöldner
23-05	Hungary	D	1-1	Leipzig	WCq	Vogel
4-09	Bulgaria	L	2-3	Varna	Fr	Vogel, Nöldner
9-10	Hungary	L	2-3	Budapest	WCq	Ducke P 2
31-10	Austria	W	1-0	Leipzig	WCq	Nöldner
27-04-1966	Sweden	W	4-1	Leipzig	Fr	Nöldner 2, Ducke R, Frenzel

2-07	Chile	W	5-2	Leipzig	Fr	Nöldner, Frenzel, Vogel, Frässdorf, Geisler
4-09	Egypt	W	6-0	Karl-Marx-Stadt	Fr	Erler 2, Pankau, Vogel, Irmscher, Engelhardt
11-09	Poland	W	2-0	Erfurt	Fr	Erler, Körner
21-09	Romania	W	2-0	Gera	Fr	Nöldner, Frenzel
23-10	Soviet Union	D	2-2	Moscow	Fr	Frässdorf, Nöldner
5-04-1967	Holland	W	4-3	Leipzig	ECq	Frenzel 3, Vogel
17-05	Sweden	W	1-0	Halsingborg	Fr	Nöldner
4-06	Denmark	D	1-1	Copenhagen	ECq	Löwe
13-09	Holland	L	0-1	Amsterdam	ECq	
27-09	Hungary	L	1-3	Budapest	ECq	Frenzel
11-10	Denmark	W	3-2	Leipzig	ECq	Pankau 2, Körner
29-10	Hungary	W	1-0	Leipzig	ECq	Frenzel
18-11	Romania	W	1-0	Berlin	OGq	Pankau
6-12	Romania	W	1-0	Bucharest	OGq	Irmscher
20-10-1968	Poland	D	1-1	Szczecin	Fr	Löwe
29-03-1969	Italy	D	2-2	Berlin	WCq	Vogel, Kreische
16-04	Wales	W	2-1	Dresden	WCq	Löwe, Rock
22-06	Chile	L	0-1	Magdeburg	Fr	
9-07	Egypt	W	7-0	Rostock	Fr	Frenzel 3, Sparwasser 2, Vogel, Löwe
25-07	Soviet Union	D	2-2	Leipzig	Fr	Löwe, Frenzel
22-10	Wales	W	3-1	Cardiff	WCq	Vogel, Löwe, Frenzel
22-11	Italy	L	0-3	Naples	WCq	
8-12	Iraq	D	1-1	Baghdad	Fr	Körner
19-12	Egypt	W	3-1	Cairo	Fr	Kreische 2, Sparwasser
16-05-1970	Poland	D	1-1	Krakow	Fr	Vogel
26-07	Iraq	W	5-0	Jena	Fr	Ducke P 2, Kreische, Vogel, Weise
6-09	Poland	W	5-0	Rostock	Fr	Kreische 2, Stempel, Stein, Vogel
11-11	Holland	W	1-0	Dresden	ECq	Ducke P
15-11	Luxembourg	W	5-0	Luxembourg	ECq	Kreische 4, Vogel
25-11	England	L	1-3	London	Fr	Vogel
2-02-1971	Chile	W	1-0	Santiago	Fr	Kreische
8-02	Uruguay	W	3-0	Montevideo	Fr	Stein 2, Richter
10-02	Uruguay	D	1-1	Montevideo	Fr	Frenzel
24-04	Luxembourg	W	2-1	Gera	ECq	Kreische, Frenzel
9-05	Yugoslavia	L	1-2	Leipzig	ECq	Löwe
16-08	Mexico	W	1-0	Guadalajara	Fr	Sparwasser
18-09	Mexico	D	1-1	Leipzig	Fr	Löwe
25-09	Czechoslovakia	D	1-1	Berlin	Fr	Streich
10-10	Holland	L	2-3	Rotterdam	ECq	Vogel 2
16-10	Yugoslavia	D	0-0	Belgrade	ECq	
27-05-1972	Uruguay	W	1-0	Leipzig	Fr	Irmscher
31-05	Uruguay	D	0-0	Rostock	Fr	
28-08	Ghana	W	4-0	Munich	OGr1	Kreische 2, Sparwasser, Streich
30-08	Colombia*	W	6-1	Passau	OGr1	
1-09	Poland	L	1-2	Nuremberg	OGr1	Streich
3-09	Hungary*	L	0-2	Passau	OGr2	
5-09	Mexico*	W	7-0	Ingolstadt	OGr2	
8-09	West Germany*	W	3-2	Munich	OGr2	
10-09	Soviet Union	D	2-2	Munich	OG3p	Kreische, Vogel
7-10	Finland	W	5-0	Dresden	WCq	Kreische, Sparwasser 2, Streich 2
1-11	Czechoslovakia	W	3-1	Bratislava	Fr	Kreische 2, Ducke P
15-02-1973	Colombia	W	2-0	Bogota	Fr	Streich, Kurbjuweit
18-02	Ecuador	D	1-1	Quito	Fr	Kreische
7-04	Albania	W	2-0	Magdeburg	WCq	Streich, Sparwasser
18-04	Belgium	L	0-3	Antwerp	Fr	
16-05	Hungary	W	2-1	Karl-Marx-Stadt	Fr	Streich 2
27-05	Romania	L	0-1	Bucharest	WCq	
6-06	Finland	W	5-1	Tampere	WCq	Streich 2, Löwe, Ducke P, Kreische
17-07	Iceland	W	2-1	Reykjavik	Fr	
19-07	Iceland	W	2-0	Reykjavik	Fr	
26-09	Romania	W	2-0	Leipzig	WCq	Bransch 2
17-10	Soviet Union	W	1-0	Leipzig	Fr	Streich
3-11	Albania	W	4-1	Tirana	WCq	Streich 2, Löwe, Sparwasser
21-11	Hungary	W	1-0	Budapest	Fr	Lauck
26-02-1974	Tunisia	W	4-0	Tunis	Fr	Lauck 2, Frenzel, Dörner
28-02	Algeria	W	3-1	Algiers	Fr	Streich, Matoul, Löwe
13-03	Belgium	W	1-0	Berlin	Fr	Streich
27-03	Czechoslovakia	W	1-0	Dresden	Fr	Streich

22–05	Norway	W	1–0	Rostock	Fr	Sparwasser
29–05	England	D	1–1	Leipzig	Fr	Streich
14–06	Australia	W	2–0	Hamburg	WCr1	OG, Streich
18–06	Chile	D	1–1	Berlin	WCr1	Hoffman
22–06	West Germany	W	1–0	Hamburg	WCr1	Sparwasser
26–06	Brazil	L	0–1	Hanover	WCr2	
30–06	Holland	L	0–2	Gelsenkirchen	WCr2	
3–07	Argentina	D	1–1	Gelsenkirchen	WCr2	Streich
4–09	Poland	W	3–1	Warsaw	Fr	Kurbjuweit, Vogel, Dörner
25–09	Czechoslovakia	L	1–3	Prague	Fr	Hoffman
9–10	Canada	W	2–0	Frankfurt	Fr	Hoffman, Dörner
12–10	Iceland	D	1–1	Magdeburg	ECq	Hoffman
30–10	Scotland	L	0–3	Glasgow	Fr	
16–11	France	D	2–2	Paris	ECq	Sparwasser, Kreische
7–12	Belgium	D	0–0	Leipzig	ECq	
26–03–1975	Bulgaria	D	0–0	Berlin	Fr	
28–05	Poland	L	1–2	Halle	Fr	Vogel
5–06	Iceland	L	1–2	Reykjavik	ECq	Pommerenke
29–07	Canada	W	3–0	Toronto	Fr	Vogel, OG, Bransch
31–07	Canada	W	7–1	Ottowa	Fr	Vogel 3, Streich 2, Riediger, Pommerenke
27–09	Belgium	W	2–1	Brussels	ECq	Ducke P, Häfner
12–10	France	W	2–1	Leipzig	ECq	Streich, Vogel
19–11	Czechoslovakia	D	1–1	Brno	OGq	Weise
7–04–1976	Czechoslovakia	D	0–0	Leipzig	OGq	
21–04	Algeria	W	5–0	Cottbus	Fr	Kotte 2, Riediger, Heidler, Dörner
18–07	Brazil*	D	0–0	Toronto	OGr1	
22–07	Spain*	W	1–0	Montreal	OGr1	
25–07	France*	W	4–0	Ottawa	OGqf	
27–07	Soviet Union	W	2–1	Montreal	OGsf	Kurbjuweit, Dörner
31–07	Poland	W	3–1	Montreal	OGf	Häfner, Schade, Hoffmann
22–09	Hungary	D	1–1	Berlin	Fr	Riediger
27–10	Bulgaria	W	4–0	Sliven	Fr	Streich 2, Heidler, Schade
17–11	Turkey	D	1–1	Dresden	WCq	Kotte
2–04–1977	Malta	W	1–0	Gzira	WCq	Streich
27–04	Romania	D	1–1	Bucharest	Fr	Kurbjuweit
12–07	Argentina	L	0–2	Buenos Aires	Fr	
28–07	Soviet Union	W	2–1	Leipzig	Fr	Häfner, Sparwasser
17–08	Sweden	W	1–0	Stockholm	Fr	Dörner
7–09	Scotland	W	1–0	Berlin	Fr	Schade
24–09	Austria	D	1–1	Vienna	WCq	Hoffmann
12–10	Austria	D	1–1	Leipzig	WCq	Löwe
29–10	Malta	W	9–0	Babelsberg	WCq	Streich 3, Hoffmann 3, Weber, Schade, Sparwasser
16–11	Turkey	W	2–1	Izmir	WCq	Schade, Hoffmann
8–03–1978	Switzerland	W	3–1	Karl–Marx–Stadt	Fr	Riediger, Hoffmann 2
4–04	Sweden	L	0–1	Leipzig	Fr	
19–04	Belgium	D	0–0	Magdeburg	Fr	
30–08	Bulgaria	D	2–2	Erfurt	Fr	Eigendorf 2
6–09	Czechoslovakia	W	2–1	Leipzig	Fr	Pommerenke, Eigendorf
4–10	Iceland	W	3–1	Halle	ECq	Peter, Riediger, Hoffmann
15–11	Holland	L	0–3	Rotterdam	ECq	
9–02–1979	Iraq	D	1–1	Baghdad	Fr	Streich
12–02	Iraq	L	1–2	Baghdad	Fr	Kühn
26–02	Bulgaria	L	0–1	Burgas	Fr	
28–03	Hungary	L	0–3	Budapest	Fr	
18–04	Poland	W	2–1	Leipzig	ECq	Lindemann, Streich
5–05	Switzerland	W	2–0	St Gallen	ECq	Lindemann, Streich
1–06	Romania	W	1–0	Berlin	Fr	Streich
5–09	Soviet Union	L	0–1	Moscow	Fr	
12–09	Iceland	W	3–0	Reykjavik	ECq	Weber 2, Riediger
26–09	Poland	D	1–1	Chorzow	ECq	Häfner
13–10	Switzerland	W	5–2	Berlin	ECq	Hoffmann 3, Weber, Schnuphase
21–11	Holland	L	2–3	Leipzig	ECq	Schnuphase, Streich
13–02–1980	Spain	W	1–0	Malaga	Fr	Streich
2–04	Romania	D	2–2	Bucharest	Fr	Streich, Schmuck
16–04	Greece	W	2–0	Leipzig	Fr	Weber, Streich
7–05	Soviet Union	D	2–2	Rostock	Fr	Kühn, Terletzki
8–10	Czechoslovakia	W	1–0	Prague	Fr	Streich
15–10	Spain	D	0–0	Leipzig	Fr	

19–11	Hungary	W	2–0	Halle	Fr	Trocha, Streich
4–04–1981	Malta	W	2–1	Gzira	WCq	Schnuphase, Häfner
19–04	Italy	D	0–0	Udine	Fr	
2–05	Poland	L	0–1	Chorzow	WCq	
19–05	Cuba	W	5–0	Senftenberg	Fr	Heun 2, Schnuphase, Streich, OG
10–10	Poland	L	2–3	Leipzig	WCq	Schnuphase, Streich
11–11	Malta	W	5–1	Jena	WCq	Krause, Streich, Heun, Liebers, OG
26–02–1982	Brazil	L	1–3	Natal	Fr	Dörner
10–02	Greece	W	1–0	Athens	Fr	Liebers
2–03	Iraq	D	0–0	Baghdad	Fr	
14–04	Italy	W	1–0	Leipzig	Fr	Hause
5–05	Soviet Union	L	0–1	Moscow	Fr	
19–05	Sweden	D	2–2	Halmstad	Fr	Jarosin, Dörner
8–09	Iceland	W	1–0	Reykjavik	Fr	Streich
22–09	Bulgaria	D	2–2	Burgas	Fr	Dörner, Riediger
13–10	Scotland	L	0–2	Glasgow	ECq	
17–11	Romania	W	4–1	Karl-Marx-Stadt	Fr	Kühn 2, Schnuphase, Heun
10–02–1983	Tunisia	W	2–0	Tunis	Fr	Streich, Kühn
23–02	Greece	W	2–1	Dresden	Fr	Richter, Streich
16–03	Finland	W	3–1	Magdeburg	Fr	Streich, Richter 2
30–03	Belgium	L	1–2	Leipzig	ECq	Streich
13–04	Bulgaria	W	3–0	Gera	Fr	Steinbach, Streich, Busse
27–04	Belgium	L	1–2	Brussels	ECq	Streich
14–05	Switzerland	D	0–0	Geneva	ECq	
26–07	Soviet Union	L	1–3	Leipzig	Fr	Streich
24–08	Romania	L	0–1	Bucharest	Fr	
12–10	Switzerland	W	3–0	Berlin	ECq	Richter, Ernst, Streich
16–11	Scotland	W	2–1	Halle	ECq	Kreer, Streich
15–02–1984	Greece	W	3–1	Athens	Fr	Döschner, Raab, Gütschow
28–03	Czechoslovakia	W	2–1	Erfurt	Fr	Minge, Ernst
11–08	Mexico	D	1–1	Berlin	Fr	Backs
29–08	Romania	W	2–1	Dresden	Fr	Minge, Liebers
12–09	England	L	0–1	London	Fr	
12–09	Greece	W	1–0	Zwickau	Fr	Gütschow
10–10	Algeria	W	5–2	Aue	Fr	Ernst 2, Stahmann, Rohde, Streich
20–10	Yugoslavia	L	2–3	Leipzig	WCq	Glowatzky, Ernst
17–11	Luxembourg	W	5–0	Esch	WCq	Ernst 3, Minge 2
8–12	France	L	0–2	Paris	WCq	
29–01–1985	Uruguay	L	0–3	Montevideo	Fr	
6–02	Ecuador	W	3–2	Guayaquil	Fr	Ernst 2, Thom
13–03	Algeria	D	1–1	Batna	Fr	Schulz
6–04	Bulgaria	L	0–1	Sofia	WCq	
17–04	Norway	W	1–0	Frankfurt	Fr	Krause
8–05	Denmark	L	1–4	Copenhagen	Fr	Zötzsche
18–05	Luxembourg	W	3–1	Babelsberg	WCq	Minge 2, Ernst
14–08	Norway	W	1–0	Oslo	Fr	Kirsten
11–09	France	W	2–0	Leipzig	WCq	Ernst, Kreer
28–09	Yugoslavia	W	2–1	Belgrade	WCq	Thom 2
16–10	Scotland	D	0–0	Glasgow	Fr	
16–11	Bulgaria	W	2–1	Karl-Marx-Stadt	WCq	Zötzsche, Liebers
9–02–1986	Bulgaria	W	2–1	Queretaro	Fr	Liebers, Zötzsche
14–02	Mexico	W	2–1	San Jose	Fr	Zötzsche 2
19–02	Portugal	W	3–1	Braga	Fr	Thom, Kirsten, Ernst
12–03	Holland	L	0–1	Leipzig	Fr	
26–03	Greece	L	0–2	Athens	Fr	

EAST GERMANY LEADING INTERNATIONAL APPEARANCES

1	Streich	102	4	Weise	86	7	Ducke	68	10	Kreer	65
2	Dörner	100	5	Vogel	74	8	Kurbjuweit	66	11	Kische	63
3	Croy	94	6	Bransch	72		Hoffmann	66	12	Liebers	59

EAST GERMANY LEADING INTERNATIONAL GOALSCORERS

1	Streich	55	5	Frenzel	19	9	Sparwasser	15	13	Löwe	12
2	Kreische	25	6	Nöldner	16		Ducke	15		Erler	12
	Vogel	25		Hoffmann	16	11	Kirsten	14	15	Tröger	11
4	Ernst	20		Thom	16	12	Schröter	13	16	Wirth	10

8-04	Brazil	L	0-3	Goiana	Fr	
23-04	Czechoslovakia	L	0-2	Nitra	Fr	
20-08	Finland	L	0-1	Lahti	Fr	
10-09	Denmark	L	0-1	Leipzig	Fr	
24-09	Norway	D	0-0	Oslo	ECq	
7-10	Bulgaria	L	0-2	Sofia	Fr	
29-10	Iceland	W	2-0	Karl-Marx-Stadt	ECq	Thom, Kirsten
19-11	France	D	0-0	Leipzig	ECq	
25-03-1987	Turkey	L	1-3	Istanbul	Fr	Minge
29-04	Soviet Union	L	0-2	Kiev	ECq	
13-05	Czechoslovakia	W	2-0	Brandenburg	Fr	Raab, Ernst
3-06	Iceland	W	6-0	Reykjavik	ECq	Thom 3, Minge, Doll, Döschner
28-07	Hungary	D	0-0	Leipzig	Fr	
19-08	Poland	L	0-2	Lublin	Fr	
23-09	Tunisia	W	2-0	Gera	Fr	Doll, Kirsten
10-10	Soviet Union	D	1-1	Berlin	ECq	Kirsten
28-10	Norway	W	3-1	Magdeburg	ECq	Kirsten 2, Thom
18-11	France	W	1-0	Paris	ECq	Ernst
13-01-1988	Sweden	L	1-4	Las Palmas	Fr	Thom
15-01	Czechoslovakia	L	0-1	Las Palmas	Fr	
27-01	Spain	D	0-0	Valencia	Fr	
3-03	Morocco	L	1-2	Mohammedia	Fr	Ernst
30-03	Romania	D	3-3	Halle	Fr	Ernst, Zötzsche, Stahmann
13-04	Bulgaria	D	1-1	Burgas	Fr	Stübner
31-08	Greece	W	1-0	Berlin	Fr	Sammer
21-09	Poland	L	1-2	Cottbus	Fr	Ernst
19-10	Iceland	W	2-0	Berlin	WCq	Thom 2
30-11	Turkey	L	1-3	Istanbul	WCq	Thom
13-02-1989	Egypt	W	4-0	Cairo	Fr	Thom 2, Kirsten 2
8-03	Greece	L	2-3	Athens	Fr	Thom, Halata
22-03	Finland	D	1-1	Dresden	Fr	Trautmann
12-04	Turkey	L	0-2	Magdeburg	WCq	
26-04	Soviet Union	L	0-3	Kiev	WCq	
20-05	Austria	D	1-1	Leipzig	WCq	Kirsten
23-08	Bulgaria	D	1-1	Erfurt	Fr	Kirsten
6-09	Iceland	W	3-0	Reykjavik	WCq	Sammer, Ernst, Doll
8-10	Soviet Union	W	2-1	Karl-Marx-Stadt	WCq	Thom, Sammer
25-10	Malta	W	4-0	Ta'Qali	Fr	Doll 2, Steinmann 2
15-11	Austria	L	0-3	Vienna	WCq	
24-01-1990	France	L	0-3	Kuwait City	Fr	
26-01	Kuwait	W	2-1	Kuwait City	Fr	Wuckel 2
28-03	USA	W	3-2	Berlin	Fr	Kirsten 3
11-04	Egypt	W	2-0	Karl-Marx-Stadt	Fr	Peschke, Sammer
25-04	Scotland	W	1-0	Glasgow	Fr	Doll
13-05	Brazil	D	3-3	Rio de Janeiro	Fr	Doll, Ernst, Steinmann
28-07	USA	W	2-1	Milwaukee	Fr	Gerlach, Rische
12-09	Belgium	W	2-0	Brussels	Fr	Sammer 2

* Not full internationals

GREECE

Greece have a curious footballing history. At times they seem to be amongst the most passionate of footballing nations, and yet success for the national team has been non-existent. Their clubs spend large amounts of money on foreign players and yet they to have nothing to show for it. Qualification for the 1980 European Championships is the one success in a history of unbridled failure.

Civil war and political instability in the first half of the 20th century certainly did not help the situation. The Balkan conflicts at the turn of the century meant that it was not until 1926 that the football association was formed.

A league championship was started two years after the formation of the association, based on clubs from Athens and Salonica. Not until 1960, however, was there a single national league open to anybody. Instead, play-offs between various league winners were organised to determine the national champions in what was surely one of Europe's most complicated league structures.

Steeped in the history of the Olympic Games, Greek clubs reflected this heritage, not only through names of clubs like Olympiakos but also in their adherence to the amateur ethic. It was not until 1979 that full-time professionalism was introduced, 20 years exactly after the formation of the national league. This perhaps explains their lack of success.

The giants of the club game, Panathinaikos and AEK from Athens, Olympiakos from Piraeus and Aris and PAOK from Salonica, are now all highly professional outfits, but they all suffer from a further problem. The image of the game in Greece has been more seriously affected than anywhere, with the possible exception of Britain and Holland, by hooliganism. Until this problem is alleviated, progress can only be limited.

Immediately after World War II, civil war broke out as the communists tried to seize power. The fighting lasted until 1950 with their defeat, but it left Greece on a limb in south-eastern Europe. Surrounded by communist countries, as well as Turkey, her traditional foe, the Greeks looked to the near-east for international matches. The Mediterranean Games was a popular source of competition, but most of these games did not count as full internationals. Greece have entered every World Cup since 1954 and every European Championship since its inception, but it was not until the 1970s that regular friendly matches were played against top sides so that players could gain experience.

Qualification for the 1980 European Championship finals seemed to herald the dawn of a new age, and their performances in Italy won them many friends. Since then, however, things have been disappointing, but given time Greek football could develop into a force to be reckoned with in Europe, both at club and international level.

	All			League			Cup		Europe		
Team	G	S	B	G	S	B	G	S	G	S	B
1 Olympiakos Piraeus	44	21	7	25	14	7	19	7	–	–	–
2 Panathinaikos	28	19	12	16	12	11	12	6	–	1	1
3 AEK Athens	17	15	10	9	12	9	8	3	–	–	1
4 PAOK Salonica	4	16	6	2	4	6	2	12	–	–	–
5 Aris Salonica	4	7	8	3	3	8	1	4	–	–	–
6 Larissa	2	3	–	1	1	–	1	2	–	–	–
7 Iraklis Salonika	1	7	2	–	3	2	1	4	–	–	–
8 Panionios Athens	1	6	3	–	2	3	1	4	–	–	–
9 OFI Crete	1	2	1	–	1	1	1	1	–	–	–
10 Ethnikos Piraeus	1	2	–	–	2	–	1	–	–	–	–
11 Kastoria	1	–	–	–	–	–	1	–	–	–	–
12 Doxa Drama	–	3	–	–	–	–	–	3	–	–	–
13 Apollon Athens	–	2	5	–	2	5	–	–	–	–	–
14 Athinaikos Athens	–	1	–	–	–	–	–	1	–	–	–
Pierikos Katerini	–	1	–	–	–	–	–	1	–	–	–
16 Atromitos Athens	–	–	1	–	–	1	–	–	–	–	–

To the end of the 1991–92 season

Population: 10 038 000
Area, sq km: 131 957
% in urban areas: 57.7%
Capital city: Athens

Elliniki Podosfairiki Omnospondia
Singrou Avenue #137
Athens
Greece
Tel: (010 30) 1 9338850
Fax: (010 30) 1 9359666
Telex: 215328 EPOGR
Cable: FOOTBALL ATHENS
Languages for correspondence: English & French

Year of formation: 1926
Affiliation to FIFA: 1927
Affiliation to UEFA: 1954
Registered clubs: 3678
Registered players: 402 500
Professional players: 500
Registered coaches: 3950
Registered referees: 2921
National stadium: OAKA Spiros Louis Athens 74 000
National colours: Shirts: White/Shorts: Blue/Socks: White
Reserve colours: Shirts: Blue/Shorts: White/Socks: Blue
Season: September–June

THE RECORD

WORLD CUP

1930 .... Did not enter
1934 .... QT 2nd/2 in group 7
1938 .... QT 2nd/3 in group 5
1950 .... Did not enter
1954 .... QT 2nd/3 in group 10
1958 .... QT 3rd/3 in group 7
1962 .... QT 3rd/3 in group 3
1966 .... QT 3rd/4 in group 7
1970 .... QT 2nd/4 in group 1
1974 .... QT 3rd/3 in group 7
1978 .... QT 3rd/3 in group 9
1982 .... QT 4th/5 in group 5
1986 .... QT 4th/4 in group 1
1990 .... QT 3rd/4 in group 1

EUROPEAN CHAMPIONSHIP

1960 .... 1st round
1964 .... Did not enter
1968 .... QT 2nd/4 in group 3
1972 .... QT 3rd/4 in group 3
1976 .... QT 2nd/4 in group 8
1980 .... QT 1st/4 in group 6 – Final Tournament/1st round
1984 .... QT 3rd/5 in group 3
1988 .... QT 2nd/5 in group 5
1992 .... QT 3rd/5 in group 6

OLYMPIC GAMES

1908 .... Did not enter
1912 .... Did not enter
1920 .... 1st round
1924–48 ..... Did not enter
1952 .... Preliminary round
1956 .... Did not enter
1960 .... QT Failed to qualify
1964 .... QT Failed to qualify
1968 .... QT Failed to qualify
1972 .... QT Failed to qualify
1976 .... QT Failed to qualify
1980 .... QT Failed to qualify
1984 .... QT Failed to qualify
1988 .... QT Failed to qualify
1992 .... QT Failed to qualify

EUROPEAN CLUB COMPETITIONS

EUROPEAN CUP: Finalists – Panathinaikos 1971

CUP WINNERS CUP: Quarter-finalists – PAOK Salonica 1974, Larissa 1985

UEFA CUP: Semi-finalists – AEK Athens 1977

CLUB DIRECTORY

ATHENS (Population – 3 027 000)
AEK Athens
Stadium: Nea Filadelphia 33 000
Founded: 1924
Colours: Yellow/Black

Apollon Athens
Stadium: Gipedo Rizopoleos 17 000
Founded: 1891
Colours: Blue and white stripes/Blue

Athinaikos
Stadium: Vironos 7000
Founded: 1917
Colours: Red/Red

Atromitos Athens
Stadium: Gipedo Peristeriou
Founded: 1923
Colours: Blue/White

Ethnikos Piraeus
Stadium: Karaiskaki 34 000

Founded: 1925
Colours: Blue/Blue

Olympiakos Pireaus
Stadium: Karaiskaki 34000
Founded: 1925
Colours: Red and white stripes/White

Panathinaikos Athens
Stadium: Apostolos Nikolaidis 26000
Founded: 1908
Colours: Green/Green

Panionios Athens
Stadium: Nea Smyrni 16000
Founded: 1890
Colours: Red and blue stripes/Red

SALONICA (Population – 706000)

Apollon Kalamarias
Stadium: Kalamarias 12000
Founded: 1925
Colours: Red and black stripes/Black

Aris Salonica
Stadium: Harilaou 26000
Founded: 1914
Colours: Yellow/Black

Iraklis Salonica
Stadium: Kaftantzoglio 42000
Founded: 1908
Colours: Sky blue with white sleeves/Sky blue

PAOK Salonica
Stadium: Toumbas 41000
Founded: 1926
Colours: Black and white stripes/White

PATRAS (Population – 154000)
Panahaiki Patras
Stadium: Patron 18000
Founded: 1923
Colours: Red and black stripes/Black

IRAKLION (Population – 110000)
OFI Crete
Stadium: Irakliou 14000
Founded: 1925
Colours: White/Black

VOLOS (Population – 107000)
Olympiakos Volos
Stadium: Volos 15000
Founded: 1934
Colours: Red and white/White

LARISSA (Population – 102000)
Larissa FC
Stadium: Alkazar 18000
Founded: 1964
Colours: White/White

RHODES (Population – 40000)
Diagoras Rhodes
Stadium: Diagoras 20000
Founded: 1905
Colours: Claret/Blue

VEROIA (Population – 37000)
Veroia
Stadium: Verias 10000
Founded: 1958
Colours: Red/Red

DRAMA
Doxa Drama
Stadium: Dramas 10000
Founded: 1918
Colours: Black/Black

LIVADIA
Levadiakos
Stadium: Livadias 8000
Founded: 1926
Colours: Green and blue stripes/Blue

SERRES
Panserraikos
Stadium: Serron 12000
Founded: 1964
Colours: Red and white sleeves/Red

GREEK LEAGUE CHAMPIONSHIP

Year	Champions		Runners up		3rd	
1928	Aris Salonica	6	Ethnikos Piraeus	5	Atromitos Athens	1
1929	–					
1930	Panathinaikos	7	Aris Salonica	3	Olympiakos	2
1931	Olympiakos	24	Panathinaikos	19	Aris Salonica	19
1932	Aris Salonica	22	Panathinaikos	18	Apollon Athens	16
1933	Olympiakos	8	Aris Salonica	2	AEK Athens	0
1934	Olympiakos	3–2 2–1	Iraklis Salonica			
1935	–					
1936	Olympiakos	37	Panathinaikos	33	Apollon Athens	31
1937	Olympiakos	12	PAOK Salonica	6	Panathinaikos	4
1938	Olympiakos	12	Apollon Athens	8	Aris Salonica	4
1939	AEK Athens	3–1 4–2	Iraklis Salonica			
1940	AEK Athens	1–0 4–3	PAOK Salonica			
1941–1945	–					
1946	Aris Salonica	9	AEK Athens	8	Olympiakos	7
1947	Olympiakos	25	Iraklis Salonica	24	Panionios	23
1948	Olympiakos	11	Apollon Athens	8	PAOK Salonica	5
1949	Panathinaikos	9	Olympiakos	9	Aris Salonica	4
1950	–					
1951	Olympiakos	11	Panionios	8	Iraklis Salonica	2
1952	–					
1953	Panathinaikos	10	Olympiakos	9	Aris Salonica	5
1954	Olympiakos	28	Panathinaikos	25	AEK Athens	21
1955	Olympiakos	29	Panathinaikos	25	Apollon Athens	22
1956	Olympiakos	23	Ethnikos Piraeus	22	Panathinaikos	22
1957	Olympiakos	46	Panathinaikos	46	Apollon Athens	42
1958	Olympiakos	55	AEK Athens	53	Panathinaikos	53
1959	Olympiakos	48	AEK Athens	46	Panionios	37
1960	Panathinaikos	79	AEK Athens	79	Olympiakos	70
1961	Panathinaikos	80	Olympiakos	73	Panionios	70
1962	Panathinaikos	81	Olympiakos	78	Apollon Athens	74
1963	AEK Athens	77	Panathinaikos	77	Olympiakos	75
1964	Panathinaikos	84	Olympiakos	77	AEK Athens	71
1965	Panathinaikos	79	AEK Athens	76	Olympiakos	71

1966	Olympiakos	80	Panathinaikos	79	AEK Athens	71
1967	Olympiakos	79	AEK Athens	76	Panathinaikos	71
1968	AEK Athens	84	Olympiakos	80	Panathinaikos	79
1969	Panathinaikos	90	Olympiakos	88	Aris Salonica	79
1970	Panathinaikos	93	AEK Athens	85	Olympiakos	84
1971	AEK Athens	88	Panionios	83	Panathinaikos	82
1972	Panathinaikos	88	Olympiakos	83	AEK Athens	82
1973	Olympiakos	94	PAOK Salonica	92	Panathinaikos	82
1974	Olympiakos	59	Panathinaikos	55	Aris Salonica	48
1975	Olympiakos	57	AEK Athens	55	PAOK Salonica	46
1976	PAOK Salonica	49	AEK Athens	44	Olympiakos	41
1977	Panathinaikos	54	Olympiakos	52	PAOK Salonica	52
1978	AEK Athens	53	PAOK Salonica	46	Panathinaikos	45
1979	AEK Athens	56	Olympiakos	56	Aris Salonica	50
1980	Olympiakos	47	Aris Salonica	47	Panathinaikos	45
1981	Olympiakos	49	AEK Athens	44	Aris Salonica	43
1982	Olympiakos	50	Panathinaikos	50	PAOK Salonica	46
1983	Olympiakos	50	Larissa	45	AEK Athens	45
1984	Panathinaikos	46	Olympiakos	43	Iraklis Salonica	42
1985	PAOK Salonica	46	Panathinaikos	43	AEK Athens	43
1986	Panathinaikos	43	OFI Crete	38	AEK Athens	36
1987	Olympiakos	49	Panathinaikos	39	OFI Crete	38
1988	Larissa	43	AEK Athens	40	PAOK Salonica	39
1989	AEK Athens	44	Olympiakos	41	Panathinaikos	37
1990	Panathinaikos	53	AEK Athens	50	PAOK Salonica	46
1991	Panathinaikos	54	Olympiakos	46	AEK Athens	42
1992	AEK Athens	54	Olympiakos	51	Panathinaikos	48

GREEK CUP FINALS

Year	Winners	Score	Runners-up
1932	AEK Athens	5–3	Aris Salonica
1933	Ethnikos Piraeus	2–2 2–1	Aris Salonica
1934–1938	–		
1939	AEK Athens	2–1	PAOK Salonica
1940	Panathinaikos	3–1	Aris Salonica
1941–1946	–		
1947	Olympiakos	5–0	Iraklis Salonica
1948	Panathinaikos	2–1	AEK Athens
1949	AEK Athens	0–0 2–1	Panathinaikos
1950	AEK Athens	4–0	Aris Salonica
1951	Olympiakos	4–0	PAOK Salonica
1952	Olympiakos	2–2 2–0	Panionios
1953	Olympiakos	3–2	AEK Athens
1954	Olympiakos	2–0	Doxa Drama
1955	Panathinaikos	2–0	PAOK Salonica
1956	AEK Athens	2–1	Olympiakos
1957	Olympiakos	2–0	Iraklis Salonica
1958	Olympiakos	5–1	Doxa Drama
1959	Olympiakos	2–1	Doxa Drama
1960	Olympiakos	1–1 3–0	Panathinaikos
1961	Olympiakos	3–0	Panionios
1962	–		
1963	Olympiakos	3–0	Pierikos Katerini
1964	–		
1965	Olympiakos	1–0	Panathinaikos
1966	AEK Athens	2–0	Olympiakos
1967	Panathinaikos	1–0	Panionios
1968	Olympiakos	1–0	Panathinaikos
1969	Panathinaikos*	1–1	Olympiakos
1970	Aris Salonica	1–0	PAOK Salonica
1971	Olympiakos	3–1	PAOK Salonica
1972	PAOK Salonica	2–1	Panathinaikos
1973	Olympiakos	1–0	PAOK Salonica
1974	PAOK Salonica	2–2 (4–3p)	Olympiakos
1975	Olympiakos	1–0	Panathinaikos
1976	Iraklis Salonica	4–4 (6–5p)	Olympiakos
1977	Panathinaikos	2–1	PAOK Salonica
1978	AEK Athens	2–0	PAOK Salonica
1979	Panionios	3–1	AEK Athens
1980	Kastoria	5–2	Iraklis Salonica
1981	Olympiakos	3–1	PAOK Salonica
1982	Panathinaikos	1–0	Larissa
1983	AEK Athens	2–0	PAOK Salonica
1984	Panathinaikos	2–0	Larissa
1985	Larissa	4–1	PAOK Salonica
1986	Panathinaikos	4–0	Olympiakos
1987	OFI Crete	1–1 (3–1p)	Iraklis Salonica
1988	Panathinaikos	2–2 (4–3p)	Olympiakos
1989	Panathinaikos	3–1	Panionios
1990	Olympiakos	4–2	OFI Crete
1991	Panathinaikos	3–0 2–1	Athinaikos
1992	Olympiakos	1–1 2–0	PAOK Salonica

* Won on toss of coin

INTERNATIONAL MATCHES PLAYED BY GREECE

Date	Opponents	Result	Venue	Compet	Scorers
28-08-1920	Sweden	L 0–9	Antwerp	OGr1	
30-06-1929	Bulgaria	D 1–1	Sofia	Fr	Andrianopoulos V
26-01-1930	Yugoslavia	W 2–1	Athens	BC	Andrianopoulos Y, Andrianopoulos K
25-05	Romania	L 1–8	Bucharest	BC	Andrianopoulos V
7-12	Bulgaria	W 6–1	Athens	BC	Tsolinas 4, Mesaris 2
15-03-1931	Yugoslavia	L 1–4	Belgrade	BC	Miyakis
25-10	Bulgaria	L 1–2	Sofia	BC	Kitsos

29–11	Romania	L	2–4	Athens	BC	Angelakis 2
27–03–1932	Bulgaria	L	1–2	Athens	Fr	Simeonidis
26–06	Yugoslavia	L	1–7	Belgrade	BC	Kitsos
28–06	Romania	L	0–3	Belgrade	BC	
2–07	Bulgaria	L	0–2	Belgrade	BC	
3–06–1933	Yugoslavia	L	3–5	Bucharest	BC	Simeonidis, Ragos, Pierakos
6–06	Romania	L	0–1	Bucharest	BC	
10–06	Bulgaria	L	0–2	Bucharest	BC	
4–02–1934	Bulgaria	W	1–0	Athens	Fr	Danelian
25–03	Italy	L	0–4	Milan	WCq	
23–12	Yugoslavia	W	2–1	Athens	BC	Vazos, Andrianopoulos L
27–12	Romania	D	2–2	Athens	BC	Andrianopoulos L, Humis
1–01–1935	Bulgaria	L	1–2	Athens	BC	Vazos
16–06	Bulgaria	L	2–5	Sofia	BC	Humis 2
21–06	Yugoslavia	L	1–6	Sofia	BC	Baltasis
24–06	Romania	D	2–2	Sofia	BC	Humis 2
17–05–1936	Romania	L	2–5	Bucharest	BC	Vazos, Simeonidis
21–05	Bulgaria	L	4–5	Bucharest	BC	Miyakis, Humis, Vazos, Simeonidis
19–06	Egypt	L	1–3	Cairo	Fr	Humis
22–01–1938	Palestine	W	3–1	Tel Aviv	WCq	Vikelidis 2, Miyakis
20–02	Palestine	W	1–0	Athens	WCq	Vikelidis
25–03	Hungary	L	1–11	Budapest	WCq	Makris
23–04–1948	Turkey	L	1–3	Athens	Fr	Vikelidis
28–11	Turkey	L	1–2	Istanbul	Fr	Filaktos
15–05–1949	Turkey	L	1–2	Athens	MC	Xenos
18–05	Egypt	L	1–3	Athens	MC	Hatzistavridis
25–11	Syria	W	8–0	Athens	MC	Papandoniou 3, Vasiliadis 2, Maropoulos, Nembidis 2
17–02–1950	Egypt	L	0–2	Cairo	Fr	
14–10–1951	Syria	W	4–0	Alexandria	Fr	Lekatsas 3, Muratis
18–10	Egypt	W	2–0	Alexandria	Fr	Kotridis, Lekatsas
21–10	Egypt	L	0–3	Cairo	Fr	
25–11	Egypt	W	1–0	Athens	Fr	Darivas
15–07–1952	Denmark	L	1–2	Tammerfors	OGr1	Emanuilidis
28–11	Egypt	D	2–2	Athens	Fr	
9–05–1953	Yugoslavia	L	0–1	Belgrade	WCq	
1–11	Israel	W	1–0	Athens	WCq	Bembis
8–03–1954	Israel	W	2–0	Tel Aviv	WCq	Kokinakis, Kamaras
28–03	Yugoslavia	L	0–1	Athens	WCq	
7–11	Egypt	D	1–1	Athens	Fr	Kuirukidis
21–01–1955	Egypt	D	1–1	Cairo	Fr	Panakis
5–05–1957	Yugoslavia	D	0–0	Athens	WCq	
16–06	Romania	L	1–2	Athens	WCq	Panakis
3–11	Romania	L	0–3	Bucharest	WCq	
10–11	Yugoslavia	L	1–4	Belgrade	WCq	Nestoridis
1–10–1958	France	L	1–7	Paris	ECr1	Ifandis
3–12	France	D	1–1	Athens	ECr1	Papaemanuil
15–11–1959	Yugoslavia	L	0–4	Belgrade	OGq	
2–12	Denmark	L	1–3	Athens	Fr	Serafidis
6–03–1960	Israel	L	1–2	Tel Aviv	OGq	Linoxilakis
3–04	Israel	W	2–1	Athens	OGq	Serafidis 2
24–04	Yugoslavia	L	0–5	Athens	OGq	
3–07	Denmark	L	2–7	Copenhagen	Fr	Lukanidis 2
20–11	West Germany	L	0–3	Athens	WCq	
3–05–1961	Nth. Ireland	W	2–1	Athens	WCq	Papaemanuil 2
17–10	Nth. Ireland	L	0–2	Belfast	WCq	
22–10	West Germany	L	1–2	Augsburg	WCq	Papaemanuil
18–10–1962	Ethiopia	W	3–2	Athens	Fr	Papaemanuil, Nestoridis, Deimezis
22–05–1963	Poland	L	0–4	Warsaw	Fr	
16–10	Poland	W	3–1	Athens	Fr	Lukanidis, Sideris, Petridis
27–11	Cyprus	L	1–3	Nicosia	Fr	Domazos
13–05–1964	Ethiopia	W	3–1	Athens	Fr	Papazoglou 2, Taktikos
29–11	Denmark	W	4–2	Athens	WCq	Sideris 2, Papaioanou 2
9–12	Wales	W	2–0	Athens	WCq	Papaioanou, Papaemanuil
24–02–1965	Bulgaria	L	1–2	Athens	Fr	Papaemanuil
17–03	Wales	L	1–4	Cardiff	WCq	Papaioanou
23–05	Soviet Union	L	1–3	Moscow	WCq	Papaioanou
3–10	Soviet Union	L	1–4	Athens	WCq	Papaioanou
27–10	Denmark	D	1–1	Copenhagen	WCq	Sideris

16-10-1966	Finland	W 2-1	Salonika	ECq	Alexiadis 2
15-02-1967	Libya	W 4-0	Athens	Fr	Sideris 2, Yutsos 2
8-03	Romania	L 1-2	Bucharest	Fr	Sideris
10-05	Finland	D 1-1	Helsinki	ECq	Haitas
16-07	Soviet Union	L 0-4	Tbilisi	ECq	
4-10	Austria	W 4-1	Athens	ECq	Sideris 3, Papaioanou
31-10	Soviet Union	L 0-1	Athens	ECq	
5-11	Austria	D 1-1	Vienna	ECq	Sideris
12-10-1968	Switzerland	L 0-1	Basle	WCq	
20-11	Egypt	W 4-1	Athens	Fr	Papaioanou, Aidiniou, Dedes 2
11-12	Portugal	W 4-2	Athens	WCq	Papaioanou, Dedes, OG, Sideris
12-03-1969	Israel	D 3-3	Tel Aviv	Fr	Yutsos 3
25-03	Cyprus	W 1-0	Athens	Fr	
16-04	Romania	D 2-2	Athens	WCq	Sideris, Dedes
4-05	Portugal	D 2-2	Oporto	WCq	Botinos, Eleftherakis
19-07	Australia	L 0-1	Sydney	Fr	
23-07	Australia	D 2-2	Brisbane	Fr	Dedes 2
26-07	Australia	W 2-0	Melbourne	Fr	Dedes, Papaioanou
15-10	Switzerland	W 4-1	Salonika	WCq	Kudas, Botinos 2, Sideris
16-11	Romania	D 1-1	Bucharest	WCq	Domazos
11-10-1970	Malta	D 1-1	Gzira	ECq	Kritikopoulos
28-10	Spain	L 1-2	Zaragoza	Fr	Papaioanou
19-11	Australia	L 1-3	Athens	Fr	Eleftherakis
22-11	West Germany	L 1-3	Athens	Fr	Yutsos
9-12	Cyprus	D 1-1	Athens	Fr	Papaioanou
16-12	Switzerland	L 0-1	Athens	ECq	
7-04-1971	Bulgaria	L 0-1	Athens	Fr	
21-04	England	L 0-3	London	ECq	
12-05	Switzerland	L 0-1	Berne	ECq	
18-06	Malta	W 2-0	Athens	ECq	Davurlis, Aidiniou
6-07	Mexico	D 1-1	Mexico City	Fr	Davurlis
30-09	Mexico	L 0-1	Salonika	Fr	
17-11	Bulgaria	D 2-2	Sofia	Fr	Andoniadis, Papaioanou
1-12	England	L 0-2	Athens	ECq	
16-02-1972	Holland	L 0-5	Athens	Fr	
4-03	Italy	W 2-1	Athens	Fr	Andoniadis, Pomonis
12-04	Spain	D 0-0	Salonika	Fr	
7-05	Ethiopia	W 1-0	Addis Ababa	Fr	Spiridon
2-09	France	L 1-3	Athens	Fr	Sarafis
19-11	Yugoslavia	L 0-1	Belgrade	WCq	
17-01-1973	Spain	L 2-3	Athens	WCq	Kudas, Domazos
31-01	Bulgaria	D 2-2	Athens	Fr	Sarafis, Eleftherakis
21-02	Spain	L 1-3	Malaga	WCq	Andoniadis
8-09	France	L 1-3	Paris	Fr	Aidiniou
19-12	Yugoslavia	L 2-4	Athens	WCq	Eleftherakis, OG
28-04-1974	Brazil	D 0-0	Rio de Janeiro	Fr	
15-05	Poland	L 0-2	Warsaw	Fr	
29-05	Romania	L 1-3	Bucharest	BC	Sarafis
13-10	Bulgaria	D 3-3	Sofia	ECq	Andoniadis, Papaioanou, Glezos
15-11	Cyprus	W 3-1	Athens	Fr	Papaioanou, Sarafis, Terzanidis
20-11	West Germany	D 2-2	Athens	ECq	Delikaris, Eleftherakis
18-12	Bulgaria	W 2-1	Athens	ECq	Sarafis, Andoniadis
23-02-1975	Malta	L 0-2	Gzira	ECq	
1-04	Cyprus	W 2-1	Nicosia	Fr	Kritikopoulos, Anastasiadis
4-06	Malta	W 4-0	Salonika	ECq	Mavros, Andoniadis, Iosifidis, Papaioannou
24-09	Romania	D 1-1	Salonika	BC	Sarafis
11-10	West Germany	D 1-1	Dusseldorf	ECq	Delikaris
30-12	Italy	L 2-3	Florence	Fr	Kritikopoulos, Sarafis
6-05-1976	Poland	W 1-0	Athens	Fr	Kudas
22-09	Israel	L 0-1	Patras	Fr	
9-10	Hungary	D 1-1	Athens	WCq	Papaioanou
10-11	Austria	L 0-3	Kavala	Fr	
26-01-1977	Israel	D 1-1	Tel Aviv	Fr	Galakos
9-03	Austria	L 0-2	Vienna	Fr	
23-03	Czechoslovakia	L 0-4	Prague	Fr	
24-04	Soviet Union	L 0-2	Moscow	WCq	
10-05	Soviet Union	W 1-0	Salonika	WCq	Papaioanou
28-05	Hungary	L 0-3	Budapest	WCq	
21-09	Romania	L 1-6	Bucharest	Fr	Karavitis

26-10	Bulgaria	D	0-0	Sofia	Fr	
16-11	Yugoslavia	D	0-0	Salonika	BC	
11-01-1978	Cyprus	W	2-0	Limassol	Fr	Delikaris, Livathinos
15-02	Austria	D	1-1	Athens	Fr	Galakos
22-03	Czechoslovakia	L	0-1	Salonika	Fr	
5-04	Poland	L	2-5	Poznan	Fr	Karavitis, Mavros
24-05	Finland	L	0-3	Helsinki	ECq	
11-06	Australia	W	2-1	Melbourne	Fr	Ifandidis 2
14-06	Australia	W	1-0	Adelaide	Fr	Ifandidis
17-06	Australia	D	1-1	Sydney	Fr	Karavitis
20-09	Soviet Union	L	0-2	Erevan	ECq	
11-10	Finland	W	8-1	Athens	ECq	Mavros 3, Delikaris 2, Nikoludis 2, Galakos
29-10	Hungary	W	4-1	Salonika	ECq	Galakos 2, Ardizoglou, Mavros
15-11	Yugoslavia	L	1-4	Skoplje	BC	Mavros
13-12	Romania	W	2-1	Athens	Fr	Kudas, Nikoludis
14-02-1979	Israel	L	1-4	Tel Aviv	Fr	Delikaris
21-03	Romania	L	0-3	Bucharest	Fr	
2-05	Hungary	D	0-0	Budapest	ECq	
12-09	Soviet Union	W	1-0	Athens	ECq	Nikoludis
16-01-1980	Cyprus	D	1-1	Nicosia	Fr	Anastopoulos
27-02	France	L	1-5	Paris	Fr	Mavros
1-04	Switzerland	L	0-2	Zurich	Fr	
16-04	East Germany	L	0-2	Leipzig	Fr	
14-05	Bulgaria	D	0-0	Athens	Fr	
11-06	Holland	L	0-1	Naples	ECr1	
14-06	Czechoslovakia	L	1-3	Rome	ECr1	Anastopoulos
17-06	West Germany	D	0-0	Turin	ECr1	
15-10	Denmark	W	1-0	Copenhagen	WCq	Kuis
11-11	Australia	D	3-3	Athens	Fr	Damanakis, Domazos, Delikaris
6-12	Italy	L	0-2	Athens	WCq	
28-01-1981	Luxembourg	W	2-0	Salonika	WCq	Kuis, Kostikos
11-03	Luxembourg	W	2-0	Luxembourg	WCq	Kuis, Mavros
15-04	Cyprus	W	1-0	Nicosia	Fr	Iosifidis
29-04	Yugoslavia	L	1-5	Split	WCq	Kostikos
23-09	Sweden	W	2-1	Salonika	Fr	Anastopoulos, Kuis
14-10	Denmark	L	2-3	Salonika	WCq	Anastopoulos, Kuis
14-11	Italy	D	1-1	Turin	WCq	Kuis
29-11	Yugoslavia	L	1-2	Athens	WCq	Mavros
20-01-1982	Portugal	L	1-2	Athens	Fr	Anastopoulos
10-02	East Germany	L	0-1	Athens	Fr	
10-03	Soviet Union	L	0-2	Athens	Fr	
24-03	Czechoslovakia	L	1-2	Prague	Fr	Kuis
14-04	Holland	L	0-1	Eindhoven	Fr	
9-10	Luxembourg	W	2-0	Luxembourg	ECq	Anastopoulos 2
27-10	Cyprus	D	1-1	Nicosia	Fr	Mavros
17-11	England	L	0-3	Salonika	ECq	
1-12	Switzerland	L	1-3	Athens	Fr	Anastopoulos
22-12	Cyprus	W	1-0	Yanina	Fr	Semertzidis
2-02-1983	Romania	L	1-3	Larissa	Fr	Kusulakis
23-02	East Germany	L	1-2	Dresden	Fr	Ardizoglou
30-03	England	D	0-0	London	ECq	
27-04	Denmark	L	0-1	Copenhagen	ECq	
15-05	Hungary	W	3-2	Budapest	ECq	Anastopoulos, Kostikos, Papaioanou A
31-08	Bulgaria	L	2-3	Athens	Fr	Chaghielefteriu, Guerino
5-10	Italy	L	0-3	Bari	Fr	
16-11	Denmark	L	0-2	Athens	ECq	
3-12	Hungary	D	2-2	Salonika	ECq	Anastopoulos 2
14-12	Luxembourg	W	1-0	Athens	ECq	Saravakos
15-02-1984	East Germany	L	1-3	Athens	Fr	Anastopoulos
7-03	Romania	L	0-2	Craiova	Fr	

LEADING INTERNATIONAL APPEARANCES

1	Anastopoulos	73	6	Kofidis	57
2	Saravakos	70	7	Manolas	56
3	Papaioanou D	61	8	Firos	52
	Mitropoulos	61	9	Mihos	51
5	Sarganis	58		Iosifidis	51

11–04	Cyprus	D	1–1	Athens	Fr	Anastopoulos
18–04	Austria	D	0–0	Vienna	Fr	
5–09	Czechoslovakia	L	0–1	Athens	Fr	
12–09	East Germany	L	0–1	Zwickau	Fr	
30–09	Cyprus	W	2–0	Limassol	Fr	Mitsimbonas, Anastopoulos
9–10	Israel	D	2–2	Athens	Fr	Semertzidis, Manolas
17–10	Poland	L	1–3	Zabrze	WCq	Mitropoulos
19–12	Belgium	D	0–0	Athens	WCq	
9–01–1985	Israel	W	2–0	Tel Aviv	Fr	Anastopoulos, Kofidis
27–02	Albania	W	2–0	Athens	WCq	Saravakos, Antoniou
13–03	Italy	D	0–0	Athens	Fr	
27–03	Belgium	L	0–2	Brussels	WCq	
19–05	Poland	L	1–4	Athens	WCq	Anastopoulos
16–10	Bulgaria	L	0–2	Salonika	Fr	
30–10	Albania	D	1–1	Tirana	WCq	Skartados
17–01–1986	Qatar	W	1–0	Doha	Fr	Saravakos
19–02	Cyprus	D	0–0	Athens	Fr	
26–03	East Germany	W	2–0	Athens	Fr	Anastopoulos, Saravakos
1–05	Sweden	D	0–0	Malmo	Fr	
24–09	Spain	L	1–3	Gijon	Fr	Skartados
8–10	Italy	L	0–2	Bologna	Fr	
15–10	Poland	L	1–2	Poznan	ECq	Anastopoulos
12–11	Hungary	W	2–1	Athens	ECq	Mitropoulos, Anastopoulos
3–12	Cyprus	W	4–2	Nicosia	ECq	Antoniou, Batsinilas, Anastopoulos, Papaioanou A
7–01–1987	Portugal	D	1–1	Portalegre	Fr	Batsinilas
14–01	Cyprus	W	3–1	Athens	ECq	Anastopoulos 2, Bonovas
11–03	Romania	D	1–1	Athens	Fr	Saravakos
25–03	Holland	D	1–1	Rotterdam	ECq	Saravakos
29–04	Poland	W	1–0	Athens	ECq	Saravakos
23–09	Soviet Union	L	0–3	Moscow	Fr	
7–10	Romania	D	2–2	Bucharest	Fr	Anastopoulos, Xanthopoulos
14–10	Hungary	L	0–3	Budapest	ECq	
16–12	Holland	L	0–3	Rhodes	ECq	
17–02–1988	Nth. Ireland	W	3–2	Athens	Fr	Manolas 2, Mitropoulos
23–03	Soviet Union	L	0–4	Athens	Fr	
6–04	Austria	D	2–2	Athens	Fr	Saravakos, Skartados
19–05	Canada	W	1–0	Montreal	Fr	Tsiolis
21–05	Canada	W	3–0	Toronto	Fr	Anastopoulos 2, Mitropoulos
23–05	Chile	W	1–0	Toronto	Fr	Anastopoulos
28–05	Canada	D	0–0	Toronto	Fr	
31–08	East Germany	L	0–1	Berlin	Fr	
21–09	Turkey	L	1–3	Istanbul	Fr	Anastopoulos
19–10	Denmark	D	1–1	Athens	WCq	Mitropoulos
2–11	Romania	L	0–3	Bucharest	WCq	
15–11	Hungary	W	3–0	Athens	Fr	Tsaluhidis 2, Lagonidis
18–01–1989	Albania	D	1–1	Tirana	Fr	Tsiandakis
25–01	Portugal	L	1–2	Athens	Fr	Borbokis
8–02	England	L	1–2	Athens	Fr	Saravakos
22–02	Norway	W	4–2	Athens	Fr	Samaras, Vakalopoulos, Tsaluhidis, Saravakos
8–03	East Germany	W	3–2	Athens	Fr	Saravakos 2, OG
29–03	Turkey	L	0–1	Athens	Fr	
5–04	Yugoslavia	L	1–4	Athens	Fr	Mitropoulos
26–04	Romania	D	0–0	Athens	WCq	
17–05	Denmark	L	1–7	Copenhagen	WCq	Mavridis
23–08	Norway	D	0–0	Oslo	Fr	
5–09	Poland	L	0–3	Warsaw	Fr	
20–09	Yugoslavia	L	0–3	Novi Sad	Fr	
11–10	Bulgaria	L	0–4	Varna	WCq	

LEADING INTERNATIONAL GOALSCORERS

1 Anastopoulos	29	4 Sideris	14
2 Papaioanou	21	5 Mavros	11
3 Saravakos	20	6 Tsaluhidis	9

25–10	Hungary	D 1–1	Budapest	Fr	Borbokis
15–11	Bulgaria	W 1–0	Athens	WCq	Nioplias
17–01–1990	Belgium	W 2–0	Athens	Fr	Tsaluhidis, Apostolakis
28–03	Israel	W 2–1	Athens	Fr	Manolas 2
30–05	Italy	D 0–0	Perugia	Fr	
5–09	Albania	W 1–0	Patras	Fr	Dimitriadis
10–10	Egypt	W 6–1	Athens	Fr	Tsaluhidis, Saravakos 5
31–10	Malta	W 4–0	Athens	ECq	Tsiandakis, Karapialis, Saravakos, Borbokis
21–11	Holland	L 0–2	Rotterdam	ECq	
19–12	Poland	L 1–2	Volos	Fr	Tsaluhidis
23–01–1991	Portugal	W 3–2	Athens	ECq	Borbokis, Manolas, Tsaluhidis
27–02	Cyprus	D 1–1	Limassol	Fr	Saravakos
27–03	Morocco	D 0–0	Rabat	Fr	
17–04	Sweden	D 2–2	Athens	Fr	OG, Borbokis
4–09	Albania	L 0–2	Athens	Fr	
9–10	Finland	D 1–1	Helsinki	ECq	Tsaluhidis
30–10	Finland	W 2–0	Athens	ECq	Saravakos, Borbokis
21–11	Portugal	L 0–1	Lisbon	ECq	
4–12	Holland	L 0–2	Salonika	ECq	
22–12	Malta	D 1–1	Ta'Qali	ECq	Marinakis
29–01–1992	Albania	L 0–1	Tirana	Fr	
12–02	Romania	W 1–0	Athens	Fr	Tsaluhidis
25–03	Cyprus	W 3–1	Limassol	Fr	Tursunidis, Karapialis, Donis
13–05	Iceland	W 1–0	Athens	WCq	Sofianopoulos

HOLLAND

At once the best, and at another time among the worst, the Dutch it seems are capable of anything. Along with Denmark they were the first European country to play the game with any degree of success and reached the semi-finals of four successive Olympic Games from 1908. As the amateur ideal started to fade in the 1920s, a long period of decline set in and not until the 1960s, with success at both club and international level, was the decline reversed.

Proximity to Great Britain ensured the early development of the game in Holland and by the turn of the century there were numerous clubs playing either football or rugby, though rugby never became as popular as it did further south in France. In 1889 the football association was formed making it, after Denmark, the second oldest on mainland Europe. Tours by English sides were common, and in 1898 a league championship was instituted, along with a cup competition the following year.

At this time there were numerous clubs, many of which no longer exist, or if they do are now playing in the local amateur leagues, and of the original clubs who made an impact only Sparta Rotterdam remain of any consequence. Of the major present-day clubs, Ajax were not formed until 1900 and did not win their first championship until 1918, Feyenoord were formed in 1908 and became champions for the first time in 1924, whilst PSV Eindhoven were formed as late as 1913. They did not win the league until 1929.

If the club scene was somewhat confused, the national team were very quick to set their stall out. After playing their first match, against Belgium, in 1905, the Dutch entered the 1908 Olympic Games in London. Given a bye to the semi-finals, they lost against the hosts but won the third place play-off against Sweden. Four years later in Stockholm they again won the bronze medal, after having lost to the Danes in the semi-finals. When the Olympics resumed after the First World War, Holland once again reached the semi-finals, this time losing to Belgium. In Paris in 1924, for the fourth consecutive tournament they lost in the semi-finals, Uruguay winning 2–1, but when Amsterdam was chosen to host the 1928 tournament it looked as if the Dutch might at last reach the final. Unfortunately they drew Uruguay in the first round, losing 2–0, and their Olympic dream was over for good.

Apart from twice-yearly matches against Belgium, Holland's international programe was very limited until the 1960's. Defeats in the first round of both the 1934 and 1938 World Cups did little to encourage the game. After World War II, a dreadful sequence of results lasting over five years in which just one game was won, helped to bring about the modernisation of the game. Fas Wilkes, perhaps the first great name in Dutch football, left to play for Valencia in Spain, and it was felt that if change was not instituted more would leave; and so in 1957, along with the creation of a national league for the first time, professionalism was sanctioned.

The immediate effect was the rise of the big clubs, Feyenoord, Ajax and PSV who since 1957 have dominated Dutch football. In an attempt to stay alive in the new professional league, there were a spate of mergers between clubs who could not face the challenge alone, but none have managed to rise to the levels of the big three. In 1970 Feyenoord won the European Cup. The following year it was won by their great rivals Ajax, in the first of three consecutive wins. The Dutch had arrived.

Feyenoord won the UEFA Cup in 1974 and PSV did the same in 1978.

One of the most talented generations of footballers appeared for Holland in the 1970s. The most famous was Johan Cruyff, whom many regard as the greatest player of his day, but he was not the only Dutch star at the time. At Ajax, Johan Neeskens, Ruud Krol, Arie Haan, Johnny Rep, Willem Suurbier, Barrie Hulshoff and Gerry Muhren all joined him in the national side at one time or another. Along with the Feyenoord pair of Willem Van Hanegem and Willem Jansen they formed the basis of the team which so nearly won the 1974 World Cup. Under manager Rinus Michels, a key figure in modern Dutch football, the team played 'Total football'. They were all comfortable on the ball, could play in most positions on the pitch and were highly skilful individuals who moulded well into a team structure.

A consequence of their impressive display was the dispersal of the team around Europe. Cruyff had gone to Barcelona in the first million-dollar deal in 1973, and the rest of the team soon followed, tempted by large offers from the Italians and Spanish. Despite this Holland very nearly won the following World Cup in Argentina, but once again lost to the hosts in the final. If ever a team deserved a world title it was the Dutch in the 1970s. They could not even manage a win in the European Championship in 1976, finishing third after losing to Czechoslovakia in the semi-finals.

Had Cruyff made the trip to Argentina Holland might well have won. As it was, only the width of the post saw them fail at the last hurdle. In the last seconds of the final, with the score at 1–1, Rob Rensenbrink was put through, but hit the post.

It seemed as if the Dutch dream was coming to an end with the failure to qualify for the 1982 and 1986 World Cups, but further success was just around the corner. A revival, this time lead by PSV and Ajax, took place in the mid-1980s. PSV won the European Cup in 1988, whilst Ajax won their first European trophy for 14 years, the Cup Winners Cup, in 1987. In 1992 they became only the second team, after Juventus, to have won all three European trophies with their victory in the UEFA Cup.

A new generation of players, brought up on the success of the 1970s team, started to play the game. Ruud Gullit, Marco Van Basten and Frank Rijkaard all achieved lasting fame as the Dutch trio in the dominant Milan side of the late 1980s, but they also led Holland to their only international success to date in the 1988 European Championships in Germany.

Once again under Rinus Michels, they stuttered in the first round but beat the Germans in the semi-finals and then destroyed the Soviets in a scintillating final in Munich. After years of coming so close, they had at last won a major title.

	All			League			Cup		Europe		
Team	G	S	B	G	S	B	G	S	G	S	B
1 Ajax Amsterdam	39	23	10	23	16	8	11	5	5	2	2
2 Feyenoord Rotterdam	22	18	9	12	16	6	8	2	2	–	3
3 PSV Eindhoven	21	12	12	13	8	9	6	4	2	–	3
4 HVV Den Haag	9	3	–	8	–	–	1	–	–	–	–
5 Sparta Rotterdam	9	1	5	6	–	5	3	1	–	–	–
6 HBS Den Haag	5	5	–	3	–	–	2	5	–	–	–
7 Willem II Tilburg	5	–	5	3	–	5	2	–	–	–	–
8 Quick Den Haag	5	–	–	1	–	–	4	–	–	–	–
9 FC Den Haag	4	6	4	2	–	4	2	6	–	–	–
Go Ahead Eagles Deventer	4	6	4	4	5	4	–	1	–	–	–
11 AZ Alkmaar	4	2	3	1	1	3	3	–	–	1	–
12 RCH Haarlem	4	–	–	2	–	–	2	–	–	–	–
13 Haarlem	3	3	1	1	–	1	2	3	–	–	–
14 RAP Amsterdam	3	1	–	2	–	–	1	1	–	–	–
15 HFC Haarlem	3	–	–	–	–	–	3	–	–	–	–
16 FC Twente Enschede	2	5	12	1	2	10	1	2	–	1	2
17 NAC Breda	2	7	2	1	4	2	1	3	–	–	–
18 VOC Rotterdam	2	3	–	–	1	–	2	2	–	–	–
19 FC Utrecht	2	2	2	1	1	2	1	1	–	–	–
20 Fortuna Sittard	2	2	1	–	1	1	2	1	–	–	–
21 Eindhoven VV	2	2	–	1	2	–	1	–	–	–	–
DFC Dordrecht	2	2	–	–	–	–	2	2	–	–	–
23 Heracles Almelo	2	1	1	2	1	1	–	–	–	–	–
24 Wageningen	2	–	–	–	–	–	2	–	–	–	–
25 Roda JC Kerkrade	1	4	–	1	1	–	–	3	–	–	–
26 DWS Amsterdam	1	3	1	1	3	1	–	–	–	–	–
27 SC Telstar	1	2	1	–	1	1	1	1	–	–	–
28 FC Den Bosch	1	2	–	1	1	–	–	1	–	–	–
Be Quick Groningen	1	2	–	1	2	–	–	–	–	–	–
VUC Den Haag	1	2	–	–	1	–	1	1	–	–	–
31 Velocitas Breda	1	1	–	–	1	–	1	–	–	–	–
Quick Nijmegan	1	1	–	–	1	–	1	–	–	–	–
33 LONGA Lichtenvoorde	1	–	1	–	–	1	1	–	–	–	–
VVV Venlo	1	–	1	–	–	1	1	–	–	–	–
Velocitas Groningen	1	–	1	–	–	1	1	–	–	–	–
36 De Volewijckers	1	–	–	1	–	–	–	–	–	–	–
Limburg Brunssue	1	–	–	1	–	–	–	–	–	–	–
SVV Schiedam	1	–	–	1	–	–	–	–	–	–	–
Concordia	1	–	–	–	–	–	1	–	–	–	–
CVV	1	–	–	–	–	–	1	–	–	–	–
Roermund	1	–	–	–	–	–	1	–	–	–	–
Schoten	1	–	–	–	–	–	1	–	–	–	–
ZFC	1	–	–	–	–	–	1	–	–	–	–
44 Vitesse Arnhem	–	8	–	–	5	–	–	3	–	–	–
31 teams with a combined total of	–	40	11	–	20	11	–	20	–	–	–

To the end of the 1991–92 season

If there had been a criticism of the 1970s team it was that the players had become too big for their boots. The fame went to their heads and they thought they knew best. The same happened to the 1990 World Cup team, and they paid for it, luckily qualifying for the second round at the expense of Egypt, but losing to their old bogey team, West Germany, in the second round.

Population: 14 934 000
Area, sq km: 41 863
% in urban areas: 88.6%
Capital city: Amsterdam, The Hague

Koninklijke Nederlandsche Voetbalbond (KNVB)
Woudenbergseweg #56
Postbus 515
NL–3700 Am Zeist
Netherlands
Tel: (010 31) 34399211
Fax: (010 31) 34391397
Telex: 40497 KNVB NL
Cable: VOETBAL ZEIST
Languages for correspondence: English & German

Year of formation: 1889
Affiliation to FIFA: 1904
Affiliation to UEFA: 1954
Registered clubs: 7079
Registered players: 965 300
Professional players: 600
Registered coaches: 4100
Registered referees: 11 991
National stadium: Olympisch Stadion Amsterdam 59 000
National colours: Shirts: Orange/Shorts: White/Socks: Orange
Reserve colours: Shirts: White/Shorts: White/Socks: White
Season: August–June

THE RECORD

WORLD CUP

1930 .... Did not enter
1934 .... QT 1st/3 in group 11 – Final Tournament/1st round
1938 .... QT 1st/3 in group 8 – Final Tournament/1st round
1950 .... Did not enter
1954 .... Did not enter
1958 .... QT 2nd/3 in group 5
1962 .... QT 2nd/3 in group 4
1966 .... QT 3rd/4 in group 5
1970 .... QT 3rd/4 in group 8
1974 .... QT 1st/4 in group 3 – Final Tournament/Finalists
1978 .... QT 1st/4 in group 4 – Final Tournament/Finalists
1982 .... QT 4th/5 in group 2
1986 .... QT 2nd/4 in group 5
1990 .... QT 1st/4 in group 4 – Final Tournament/2nd round

EUROPEAN CHAMPIONSHIP

1960 .... Did not enter
1964 .... 2nd round
1968 .... QT 3rd/4 in group 5
1972 .... QT 2nd/4 in group 7
1976 .... QT 1st/4 in group 5 – Final Tournament/Semi-finalists/3rd place
1980 .... QT 1st/5 in group 4 – Final Tournament/1st round
1984 .... QT 2nd/5 in group 7
1988 .... QT 1st/5 in group 5 – Final Tournament/Winners
1992 .... QT 1st/5 in group 6 – Final Tournament/Semi-finals

OLYMPIC GAMES

1908 .... Semi-finalists/3rd place
1912 .... Semi-finalists/3rd place
1920 .... Semi-finalists/4th place
1924 .... Semi-finalists/4th place
1928 .... 1st round
1936 .... Did not enter
1948 .... 1st round
1952 .... Preliminary round
1956 .... Did not enter
1960 .... QT Failed to qualify
1964 .... QT Failed to qualify
1968 .... QT Failed to qualify
1972 .... QT Failed to qualify
1976 .... QT Failed to qualify
1980 .... QT Failed to qualify
1984 .... QT Failed to qualify
1988 .... QT Failed to qualify
1992 .... QT Failed to qualify

EUROPEAN CLUB COMPETITIONS

EUROPEAN CUP: Winners – Feyenoord 1970, Ajax 1971 1972 1973, PSV Eindhoven 1988
Finalists – Ajax 1969

CUP WINNERS CUP: Winners – Ajax 1987
Finalists – Ajax 1988

UEFA CUP: Winners – Feyenoord 1974, PSV Eindhoven 1978, Ajax 1992
Finalists – Twente Enschede 1975, AZ '67 Alkmaar 1981

CLUB DIRECTORY

AMSTERDAM (Population – 1 860 000)

Ajax
Stadium: De Meer 20 000
Founded: 1900
Colours: White with a broad red stripe/White

FC Amsterdam
Stadium: Olympisch Stadion 59 000
Founded: 1972–1983
Colours: White/Red
Previous names: Merger in 1972 of Blauw Wit (1902), DWS (1907) and Volewijckers (1920). The club was dissolved in 1983 when all three teams split away to operate as amateurs

Haarlem
Stadium: Haarlem Stadion 14 000
Founded: 1889
Colours: Blue with red sleeves/Red

SC Telstar IJmuiden
Stadium: Schoonenberg
Founded: 1962
Colours: White/White
Previous names: Merger in 1962 of Stormvogels and VSV

ROTTERDAM (Population – 1 110 000)

Excelsior
Stadium: Woudensteyn
Founded: 1902
Colours: Red/Black

Feyenoord
Stadium: Feyenoord Stadion 56 000
Founded: 1908
Colours: Red and white halves/Black

Sparta Rotterdam
Stadium: Spangen 18 000
Founded: 1888
Colours: Red and white stripes/Black

THE HAGUE (Population – 770 000)
FC Den Haag
Stadium: Zuiderparkstadion 15 000
Founded: 1971
Colours: Yellow/Green
Previous names: Merger in 1971 of ADO Den Haag (1905) and Holland Sport (1954)

UTRECHT (Population – 511 000)
FC Utrecht
Stadium: Galgenwaard 20 000
Founded: 1970
Colours: Red/White
Previous names: Merger in 1970 of DOS Utrecht (1902), Velox and Elinkwijk (1919)

EINDHOVEN (Population – 376000)

Philips Sport Vereniging (PSV) Eindhoven
Stadium: Philips Stadion 27000
Founded: 1913
Colours: Red and thin white stripes/White

Eindhoven
Stadium: Aalsterweg
Founded: 1909
Colours: Blue and white stripes/Black

ARNHEM (Population – 294 000)
Vitesse Arnhem
Stadium: Monnikenhuize 11 000
Founded: 1892
Colours: Yellow and black stripes/White

ENSCHEDE (Population – 288 000)
FC Twente Enschede
Stadium: Diekman 18 000
Founded: 1965
Colours: Red/White
Previous names: Merger in 1965 of SC Enschede (1910) and Enschede Boys

HEERLEN (Population – 266 000)
Roda JC Kerkrade
Stadium: Kaalheide 23 000
Founded: 1914
Colours: Yellow/Black

Previous names: Merged with Rapid Heerlen (1954) in 1962

NIJMEGEN (Population – 238 000)
NEC Nijmegan (Nijmegan Eendracht Combinatie)
Stadium: Goffert Stadion 29 000
Founded: 1900
Colours: Red with a black and green hoop/Black

TILBURG (Population – 223 000)
Willem II Tilburg
Stadium: Gemeentelijk Sportpark 18 000
Founded: 1896
Colours: Red white and blue stripes/White

GRONINGEN (Population – 207 000)
FC Groningen
Stadium: Oosterpark 20 000
Founded: 1921
Colours: White with green shoulders and green hoop/White
Previous name: GVAV 1921–71

DORDRECHT (Population – 200 000)
SVV Dordrecht
Stadium: Krommedijk 12 000
Founded: 1904
Colours: Red and green halves/White
Previous names: DFC until 1974, FC Dordrecht 1974–79, DS '79 1979–1990. Merged with Schiedamse Voetbal Vereniging (SVV) (1904) in 1991

HERTOGENBOSCH (Population – 189 000)
FC Den Bosch
Stadium: De Vliert 25 000
Founded: 1967
Colours: Blue/White
Previous name: BVV 1906–67

GELEEN (Population – 177 000)
Fortuna Sittard
Stadium: De Baandaert 16 000
Founded: 1968
Colours: Green with yellow sleeves and yellow hoop/Green
Previous names: Merger of Fortuna '54 Geleen and Sittardia (1950) in 1968 to form FSC, FSC 1968–79

MAASTRICHT (Population – 158 000)
Maastrichtse Voetbal Vereniging (MVV)
Stadium: De Geusselt 10 000
Founded: 1902
Colours: Red/White

BREDA (Population – 154 000)
Noad Advendo Combinatie (NAC) Breda
Stadium: NAC Stadion
Founded: 1912
Colours: Yellow/Black

ALKMAAR (Population – 121 000)
AZ Alkmaar (Alkmaar–Zaanstreek)
Stadium: Alkmaarderhout 18 000
Founded: 1967
Colours: Red/White
Previous name: Almaar 1954–67, AZ '67 Alkmaar 1967–86

ZWOLLE (Population – 88 000)
FC Zwolle
Stadium: Gemeentelijk 14 000
Founded: 1910
Colours: Green/White
Previous name: PEC Zwolle 1910–90

VENLO (Population – 87 000)
Venlose Voetbal Vereniging (VVV)
Stadium: De Koel 20 000
Founded: 1903
Colours: Yellow/Black

DEVENTER (Population 64 000)
Go Ahead Eagles
Stadium: Adelaarshorsi
Founded: 1971
Colours: Yellow/Red
Previous name: Go Ahead Deventer 1902–71

HELMOND (Population – 63 000)
Helmond Sport
Stadium: De Braak
Founded: 1967
Colours: Red/White
Previous name: Helmondia until 1967

VOLENDAM
FC Volendam
Stadium: Sportpark Volendam 12 000
Founded: 1920
Colours: Orange/Black

DUTCH LEAGUE CHAMPIONSHIP

Year	Champions		Runners up		3rd	
1898	RAP Amsterdam	4	Vitesse Arnhem	0		
1899	RAP Amsterdam	4	PW Enschede	0		
1900	HVV Den Haag	2	Victoria Wageningen	2		
1901	HVV Den Haag	2	Victoria Wageningen	2		
1902	HVV Den Haag	3	Victoria Wageningen	1		
1903	HVV Den Haag	8	Vitesse Arnhem	2	Volharding	2
1904	HBS Den Haag	5	Velocitas Breda	4	PW Enschede	3
1905	HVV Den Haag	4	PW Enschede	0		
1906	HBS Den Haag	4	PW Enschede	0		
1907	HVV Den Haag	4	PW Enschede	0		
1908	Quick Den Haag	2	UD	2		
1909	Sparta Rotterdam	4	Wilhelmina	0		
1910	HVV Den Haag	4	Quick Nijmegen	0		
1911	Sparta Rotterdam	4	GVC	0		
1912	Sparta Rotterdam	4	GVC	0		
1913	Sparta Rotterdam	4	Vitesse Arnhem	0		
1914	HVV Den Haag	6	Vitesse Arnhem	6		
1915	Sparta Rotterdam	2	Vitesse Arnhem	2		
1916	Willem II Tilburg	5	Go Ahead Deventer	4	Sparta Rotterdam	3
1917	Go Ahead Deventer	11	UVV	7	Willem II Tilburg	5
1918	Ajax	13	Go Ahead Deventer	10	Willem II Tilburg	9
1919	Ajax	13	Go Ahead Deventer	9	AFC Amsterdam	9
1920	Be Quick Groningen	10	VOC Rotterdam	7	Go Ahead Deventer	5
1921	NAC Breda	8	Be Quick Groningen	7	Ajax	6
1922	Go Ahead Eagles	7	Blauw–Wit Amsterdam	7	NAC Breda	6
1923	RCH Haarlem	8	Be Quick Groningen	5	Go Ahead Deventer	5
1924	Feyenoord	13	Stormvogels Velsen	12	NAC Breda	7
1925	HBS Den Haag	15	NAC Breda	11	Sparta Rotterdam	9

1926	SC Enschede	14	MVV Maastricht	10	Feyenoord	8
1927	Heracles Almelo	14	NAC Breda	10	Ajax	8
1928	Feyenoord	12	Ajax	10	NOAD Tilburg	8
1929	PSV Eindhoven	12	Go Ahead Deventer	10	Feyenoord	8
1930	Go Ahead Deventer	10	Ajax	9	Velocitas Groningen	9
1931	Ajax	12	Feyenoord	8	PSV Eindhoven	8
1932	Ajax	13	Feyenoord	12	SC Enschede	9
1933	Go Ahead Deventer	11	Feyenoord	10	Stormvogels Velsen	8
1934	Ajax	10	KFC Alkmaar	10	Willem II Tilburg	10
1935	PSV Eindhoven	13	Go Ahead Deventer	12	Ajax	8
1936	Feyenoord	12	Ajax	10	SC Enschede	10
1937	Ajax	14	Feyenoord	10	PSV Eindhoven	6
1938	Feyenoord	14	Heracles Almelo	12	DWS Amsterdam	7
1939	Ajax	12	DWS Amsterdam	10	SC Nijmegen	8
1940	Feyenoord	11	Blauw–Wit Amsterdam	9	Heracles Almelo	9
1941	Heracles Almelo	13	PSV Eindhoven	9	ADO Den Haag	7
1942	ADO Den Haag	10	Eindhoven VV	9	AGOVV	8
1943	ADO Den Haag	11	Feyenoord	9	Willem II Tilburg	8
1944	De Volewijckers	12	VUC Den Haag	10	LONGA Lichtenvoorde	9
1945	–					
1946	Haarlem	15	Ajax	14	SC Heerenveen	10
1947	Ajax	17	SC Heerenveen	14	SC Nijmegen	9
1948	BVV Hertogenbosch	14	SC Heerenveen	13	Go Ahead Deventer	12
1949	SVV Schiedam	15	BVV Hertogenbosch	13	AGOVV	11
1950	Limburg Brunssue	15	Blauw–Wit Amsterdam	14	Maurits	10
1951	PSV Eindhoven	13	DWS Amsterdam	10	Willem II Tilburg	9
1952	Willem II Tilburg	12	Hermes Schiedam	7	Haarlem	4
1953	RCH Haarlem	7	Eindhoven VV	7	Sparta Rotterdam	6
1954	Eindhoven VV	8	DOS Utrecht	6	PSV Eindhoven	5
1955	Willem II Tilburg	8	NAC Breda	6	PSV Eindhoven	6
1956	Rapid JC Heerlen	8	NAC Breda	8	Elikwijk Utrecht	5

DUTCH NATIONAL LEAGUE

1957	Ajax	49	Fortuna '54 Geleen	45	SC Enschede	41
1958	DOS Utrecht	47	SC Enschede	47	Ajax	42
1959	Sparta Rotterdam	51	Rapid JC Heerlen	48	Fortuna '54 Geleen	44
1960	Ajax	50	Feyenoord	50	PSV Eindhoven	45
1961	Feyenoord	53	Ajax	51	VVV Venlo	42
1962	Feyenoord	50	PSV Eindhoven	49	Blauw–Wit Amsterdam	41
1963	PSV Eindhoven	42	Ajax	39	Sparta Rotterdam	39
1964	DWS Amsterdam	43	PSV Eindhoven	41	SC Enschede	39
1965	Feyenoord	45	DWS Amsterdam	40	ADO Den Haag	33
1966	Ajax	52	Feyenoord	45	ADO Den Haag	39
1967	Ajax	56	Feyenoord	51	Sparta Rotterdam	48
1968	Ajax	58	Feyenoord	55	Go Ahead Deventer	42
1969	Feyenoord	57	Ajax	54	FC Twente Enschede	47
1970	Ajax	60	Feyenoord	55	PSV Eindhoven	46
1971	Feyenoord	57	Ajax	53	ADO Den Haag	50
1972	Ajax	63	Feyenoord	55	FC Twente Enschede	48
1973	Ajax	60	Feyenoord	58	FC Twente Enschede	50
1974	Feyenoord	56	FC Twente Enschede	54	Ajax	51
1975	PSV Eindhoven	55	Feyenoord	53	Ajax	49
1976	PSV Eindhoven	53	Feyenoord	52	Ajax	50
1977	Ajax	52	PSV Eindhoven	47	AZ 67 Alkmaar	46
1978	PSV Eindhoven	53	Ajax	49	AZ 67 Alkmaar	47
1979	Ajax	54	Feyenoord	51	PSV Eindhoven	49
1980	Ajax	50	AZ 67 Alkmaar	47	PSV Eindhoven	44
1981	AZ 67 Alkmaar	60	Ajax	48	FC Utrecht	45
1982	Ajax	56	PSV Eindhoven	51	AZ 67 Alkmaar	47
1983	Ajax	58	Feyenoord	54	PSV Eindhoven	51
1984	Feyenoord	57	PSV Eindhoven	52	Ajax	51
1985	Ajax	54	PSV Eindhoven	48	Feyenoord	48
1986	PSV Eindhoven	60	Ajax	52	Feyenoord	44
1987	PSV Eindhoven	59	Ajax	53	Feyenoord	42
1988	PSV Eindhoven	59	Ajax	50	FC Twente Enschede	41
1989	PSV Eindhoven	53	Ajax	50	FC Twente Enschede	40
1990	Ajax	49	PSV Eindhoven	48	FC Twente Enschede	42
1991	PSV Eindhoven	53	Ajax	53	FC Groningen	46
1992	PSV Eindhoven	58	Ajax	55	Feyenoord	49

DUTCH CUP FINALS

Year	Winners	Score	Runners–up
1899	RAP Amsterdam	1–0	HVV Den Haag
1900	Velocitas Breda	3–1	Ajax
1901	HBS Den Haag	4–3	RAP Amsterdam
1902	Haarlem	2–1	HBS Den Haag
1903	HVV Den Haag	6–1	HBS Den Haag
1904	HFC Haarlem	3–1	HVV Den Haag
1905	VOC Rotterdam	3–0	HBS Den Haag
1906	Concordia	3–2	Volharding
1907	VOC Rotterdam	4–3	Voorwaarts
1908	HBS Den Haag	3–1	VOC Rotterdam
1909	Quick Den Haag	2–0	VOC Rotterdam
1910	Quick Den Haag	2–0	HVV Den Haag
1911	Quick Den Haag	1–0	Haarlem
1912	Haarlem	2–0	Vitesse Arnhem
1913	HFC Haarlem	4–1	DFC Dordrecht
1914	DFC Dordrecht	3–2	Haarlem
1915	HFC Haarlem	1–0	HBS Den Haag
1916	Quick Den Haag	2–1	HBS Den Haag
1917	Ajax	5–0	VSV Velsen
1918	RCH Haarlem	2–1	VVA
1919	–		
1920	CVV	2–1	VUC Den Haag
1921	Schoten	2–1	RFC
1922–24	–		
1925	ZFC	5–1	Xerxes
1926	LONGA Lichtenvoorde	5–2	De Spartan
1927	VUC Den Haag	3–1	Vitesse Arnhem
1928	RCH Haarlem	2–0	PEC Zwolle
1929	–		
1930	Feyenoord	1–0	Excelsior
1931	–		
1932	DFC Dordrecht	5–4	PSV Eindhoven
1933	–		
1934	Velocitas Groningen	3–2	Feyenoord
1935	Feyenoord	5–2	Helmondia
1936	Roermond	4–2	KFC Alkmaar
1937	Eindhoven VV	1–0	De Spartan
1938	VSV Velsen	4–1	AGOVV
1939	Wageningen	2–1	PSV Eindhoven
1940–42	–		
1943	Ajax	3–2	DFC Dordrecht
1944	Willem II Tilburg	9–2	Groene Ster
1945–47	–		
1948	Wageningen	0–0*	DWV
1949	Quick Nijmegen	1–1*	Helmondia
1950	PSV Eindhoven	4–3	Haarlem
1951–56	–		
1957	Fortuna '54 Geleen	4–2	Feyenoord
1958	Sparta Rotterdam	4–3	Volendam
1959	VVV Venlo	4–1	ADO Den Haag
1960	–		
1961	Ajax	3–0	NAC Breda
1962	Sparta Rotterdam	1–0	DHC
1963	Willem II Tilburg	3–0	ADO Den Haag
1964	Fortuna '54 Geleen	0–0*	ADO Den Haag
1965	Feyenoord	1–0	Go Ahead Deventer
1966	Sparta Rotterdam	1–0	ADO Den Haag
1967	Ajax	2–1	NAC Breda
1968	ADO Den Haag	2–1	Ajax
1969	Feyenoord	1–1 2–0	PSV Eindhoven
1970	Ajax	2–0	PSV Eindhoven
1971	Ajax	2–2 2–1	Sparta Rotterdam
1972	Ajax	3–2	FC Den Haag
1973	NAC Breda	2–0	NEC Nijmegen
1974	PSV Eindhoven	6–0	NAC Breda
1975	FC Den Haag	1–0	FC Twente Enschede
1976	PSV Eindhoven	1–0	Roda JC Kerkrade
1977	FC Twente Enschede	3–0	PEC Zwolle
1978	AZ 67 Alkmaar	1–0	Ajax
1979	Ajax	1–1 3–0	FC Twente Enschede
1980	Feyenoord	3–1	Ajax
1981	AZ 67 Alkmaar	3–1	Ajax
1982	AZ 67 Alkmaar	5–1 0–1	FC Utrecht
1983	Ajax	3–1 3–1	NEC Nijmegan
1984	Feyenoord	1–0	Fortuna Sittard
1985	FC Utrecht	1–0	Helmond Sport
1986	Ajax	3–0	RBC Roosendaal
1987	Ajax	4–2	FC Den Haag
1988	PSV Eindhoven	3–2	Roda JC Kerkrade
1989	PSV Eindhoven	4–1	FC Groningen
1990	PSV Eindhoven	1–0	Vitesse Arnhem
1991	Feyenoord	1–0	BVV Den Bosch
1992	Feyenoord	3–0	Roda Jc Kerkrade

* Won on penalties

INTERNATIONAL MATCHES PLAYED BY HOLLAND

Date	Opponents	Result	Venue	Compet	Scorers
30–04–1905	Belgium	W 4–1	Antwerp	Fr	De Neve 4
14–05	Belgium	W 4–0	Rotterdam	Fr	De Neve 2, Hesselink, Lutjens
29–04–1906	Belgium	L 0–5	Antwerp	Fr	
13–05	Belgium	L 2–3	Rotterdam	Fr	Vinne, Muller
1–04–1907	England*	L 1–8	The Hague	Fr	Blume
14–04	Belgium	W 3–1	Antwerp	Fr	Van Gogh 2, Feith
9–05	Belgium	L 1–2	Haarlem	Fr	Feith
21–12	England	L 2–12	Darlington	Fr	Ruffelse 2
29–03–1908	Belgium	W 4–1	Antwerp	Fr	Thomée 2, Ruffelse, De Korver
26–04	Belgium	W 3–1	Rotterdam	Fr	Thomée 2, Snethlage,
10–05	France	W 4–1	Rotterdam	Fr	Snethlage 2, Thomée, Akkersdijk
22–10	England*	L 0–4	London	OGsf	
23–10	Sweden	W 2–0	London	OG3p	Snethlage, Reeman
25–10	Sweden	W 5–3	The Hague	Fr	Snethlage 2, Welcker, Francken, Thomée
21–03–1909	Belgium	W 4–1	Antwerp	Fr	Snethlage, Welcker, Lutjens, Kessler J
12–04	England*	L 0–4	Amsterdam	Fr	
25–04	Belgium	W 4–1	Rotterdam	Fr	Snethlage 3, Lutjens
11–12	England*	L 1–9	London	Fr	Kessler H (I)
13–03–1910	Belgium	L 2–3	Antwerp	Fr	Lutjens, Kessler J

10–04	Belgium	W 7–0	Haarlem	Fr	Francken 3, Thomée 2, Welcker 2
24–04	Germany	W 4–2	Arnhem	Fr	Thomée 2, Lutjens, OG
16–10	Germany	W 2–1	Kleve	Fr	Thomée, Van Berckel
19–03–1911	Belgium	W 5–1	Antwerp	Fr	Francken 3, Thomée, Welcker
2–04	Belgium	W 3–1	Dordrecht	Fr	Francken 2, Van Breda Kolff
17–04	England*	L 0–1	Amsterdam	Fr	
10–03–1912	Belgium	W 2–1	Antwerp	Fr	Thomée 2
16–03	England*	L 0–4	Hull	Fr	
24–03	Germany	D 5–5	Zwolle	Fr	Thomée 2, Francken 2, OG
28–04	Belgium	W 4–3	Dordrecht	Fr	Francken 3, Van Berckel
29–06	Sweden	W 4–3	Stockholm	OGr1	Vos 2, Bouvy 2
30–06	Austria	W 3–1	Stockholm	OGqf	Vos, Bouvy, Ten Cate
2–07	Denmark	L 1–4	Stockholm	OGsf	OG
4–07	Finland	W 9–0	Stockholm	OG3p	Vos 5, De Groot 2, Sluis 2
17–11	Germany	W 3–2	Leipzig	Fr	Francken 2, Haak
9–03–1913	Belgium	D 3–3	Antwerp	Fr	Francken, Haak, Bosschart
24–03	England*	W 2–1	The Hague	Fr	De Groot 2
20–04	Belgium	L 2–4	Zwolle	Fr	De Groot, Bouvy
15–11	England*	L 1–2	Hull	Fr	Boutmy
15–03–1914	Belgium	W 4–2	Antwerp	Fr	Kessler J 2, Francken, Van Holthe
5–04	Germany	D 4–4	Amsterdam	Fr	Buitenweg 2, Vos, ?
26–04	Belgium	W 4–2	Amsterdam	Fr	Buitenweg 2, Vos, Kessler J
17–05	Denmark	L 3–4	Copenhagen	Fr	Buitenweg 2, De Groot
9–06–1919	Sweden	W 3–1	Amsterdam	Fr	Kessler J, Gupffert, Brokmann
24–08	Sweden	L 1–4	Stockholm	Fr	Buitenweg
31–08	Norway	D 1–1	Oslo	Fr	Buitenweg
5–04–1920	Denmark	W 2–0	Amsterdam	Fr	Kessler H (II), De Natris
13–05	Italy	D 1–1	Genoa	Fr	Kessler J
16–05	Switzerland	L 1–2	Basle	Fr	De Natris
28–08	Luxembourg	W 3–0	Brussels	OGr1	Groosjohan 2, Bulder
29–08	Sweden	W 5–4	Antwerp	OGqf	Groosjohan 2, Bulder 2, De Natris
31–08	Belgium	L 0–3	Antwerp	OGsf	
5–09	Spain	L 1–3	Antwerp	OG2p	Groosjohan
28–03–1921	Switzerland	W 2–0	Amsterdam	Fr	Kessler J, Gupffert
8–05	Italy	D 2–2	Amsterdam	Fr	Kessler J, Van Gendt
15–05	Belgium	D 1–1	Antwerp	Fr	Kessler J
12–06	Denmark	D 1–1	Copenhagen	Fr	Van Gendt
13–11	France	W 5–0	Paris	Fr	Van Gendt 3, Rodermond 2
26–03–1922	Belgium	L 0–4	Antwerp	Fr	
17–04	Denmark	W 2–0	Amsterdam	Fr	Rodermond, Groen
7–05	Belgium	L 1–2	Amsterdam	Fr	Bulder
19–11	Switzerland	L 0–5	Berne	Fr	
2–04–1923	France	W 8–1	Amsterdam	Fr	Bulder 2, Addicks 2, Roetert 2, Van Linge 2
29–04	Belgium	D 1–1	Amsterdam	Fr	Heijnen
10–05	Germany	D 0–0	Hamburg	Fr	
25–11	Switzerland	W 4–1	Amsterdam	Fr	Verlegh 2, Sigmond, Krom
23–03–1924	Belgium	D 1–1	Amsterdam	Fr	Pijl
21–04	Germany	L 0–1	Amsterdam	Fr	
27–04	Belgium	D 1–1	Antwerp	Fr	Visser
27–05	Romania	W 6–0	Paris	OGr2	Pijl 4, De Natris, Hurgronje
2–06	Rep. Ireland	W 2–1	Paris	OGqf	Formenoy 2
6–06	Uruguay	L 1–2	Paris	OGsf	Pijl
8–06	Sweden	D 1–1	Paris	OG3p	Le Fèvre
9–06	Sweden	L 1–3	Paris	OG3p	Formenoy
2–11	South Africa	W 2–1	Amsterdam	Fr	De Natris, Volkers
15–03–1925	Belgium	W 1–0	Antwerp	Fr	Volkers
29–03	Germany	W 2–1	Amsterdam	Fr	Volkers, De Haas
19–04	Switzerland	L 1–4	Zurich	Fr	Buitenweg
3–05	Belgium	W 5–0	Amsterdam	Fr	Buitenweg 3, Van Slangenburgh 2
25–10	Denmark	W 4–2	Amsterdam	Fr	Van Slangenburgh 2, Buitenweg, Tap
14–03–1926	Belgium	D 1–1	Antwerp	Fr	Tap
28–03	Switzerland	W 5–0	Amsterdam	Fr	Ruisch 2, Pijl, Gielens, Van Linge
18–04	Germany	L 2–4	Dusseldorf	Fr	Tap, Küchlin
2–05	Belgium	L 1–5	Amsterdam	Fr	Tap
13–06	Denmark	L 1–4	Copenhagen	Fr	Buitenweg
31–10	Germany	L 2–3	Amsterdam	Fr	Tap 2
13–03–1927	Belgium	L 0–2	Antwerp	Fr	
1–05	Belgium	W 3–2	Amsterdam	Fr	Tap 2, Massy
12–06	Denmark	D 1–1	Copenhagen	Fr	Elfring

* Amateur side

13–11	Sweden	W	1–0	Amsterdam	Fr	Ghering
20–11	Germany	D	2–2	Cologne	Fr	Smeets, Weber
11–03–1928	Belgium	D	1–1	Amsterdam	Fr	Tap
1–04	Belgium	L	0–1	Antwerp	Fr	
22–04	Denmark	W	2–0	Amsterdam	Fr	Elfring, Kools
6–05	Switzerland	L	1–2	Basle	Fr	Smeets
30–05	Uruguay	L	0–2	Amsterdam	OGr1	
5–06	Belgium	W	3–1	Rotterdam	OGct	Tap, Smeets, Ghering
8–06	Chile	D	2–2	Rotterdam	OGct	Smeets, Ghering Won on lots
14–06	Egypt	L	1–2	Rotterdam	Fr	Grobbe
4–11	Belgium	D	1–1	Amsterdam	Fr	Van Kol
2–12	Italy	L	2–3	Milan	Fr	Tap 2
17–03–1929	Switzerland	W	3–2	Amsterdam	Fr	Van Kol, Bakhuys, OG
5–05	Belgium	L	1–3	Antwerp	Fr	Bakhuys
4–06	Scotland	L	0–2	Amsterdam	Fr	
9–06	Sweden	L	2–6	Stockholm	Fr	Smeets 2
12–06	Norway	D	4–4	Oslo	Fr	Kools 2, Tap, Landaal
3–11	Norway	L	1–4	Amsterdam	Fr	Broek
6–04–1930	Italy	D	1–1	Amsterdam	Fr	Broek
4–05	Belgium	D	2–2	Amsterdam	Fr	Tap, Van Kol
18–05	Belgium	L	1–3	Antwerp	Fr	Broek
8–06	Hungary	L	2–6	Budapest	Fr	Landaal, Heijden
2–11	Switzerland	L	3–6	Zurich	Fr	Van Nellen, Mulders, Lagendaal
29–03–1931	Belgium	W	3–2	Amsterdam	Fr	Lagendaal 2, Formenoy
26–04	Germany	D	1–1	Amsterdam	Fr	Tap
3–05	Belgium	L	2–4	Antwerp	Fr	Van Kol, Adam
14–06	Denmark	W	2–0	Copenhagen	Fr	Lagendaal 2
29–11	France	W	4–3	Paris	Fr	Lagendaal 3, Mol
20–03–1932	Belgium	W	4–1	Antwerp	Fr	Lagendaal 4
17–04	Belgium	W	2–1	Amsterdam	Fr	Adam 2
8–05	Rep. Ireland	L	0–2	Amsterdam	Fr	
29–05	Czechoslovakia	L	1–2	Amsterdam	Fr	Bonsema
4–12	Germany	W	2–0	Dusseldorf	Fr	Adam 2
22–01–1933	Switzerland	L	0–2	Amsterdam	Fr	
5–03	Hungary	L	1–2	Amsterdam	Fr	Broek
9–04	Belgium	W	3–1	Antwerp	Fr	Bonsema 2, Van Nellen
7–05	Belgium	L	1–2	Amsterdam	Fr	Adam
10–12	Austria	L	0–1	Amsterdam	Fr	
11–03	Belgium	W	9–3	Amsterdam	Fr	Vente 5, Smit 2, Bakhuys 2
8–04–1934	Rep. Ireland	W	5–2	Amsterdam	WCq	Smit 2, Bakhuys 2, Vente
29–04	Belgium	W	4–2	Antwerp	WCq	Bakhuys 2, Smit, Vente
10–05	France	L	4–5	Amsterdam	Fr	Bakhuys 2, Smit, Vente
27–05	Switzerland	L	2–3	Milan	WCr1	Smit, Vente
4–11	Switzerland	W	4–2	Berne	Fr	Bakhuys 2, Smit, Van Gelder
17–02–1935	Germany	L	2–3	Amsterdam	Fr	Smit, Bakhuys
31–03	Belgium	W	4–2	Amsterdam	Fr	Bakhuys 3, Lagendaal
12–05	Belgium	W	2–0	Brussels	Fr	Bakhuys, Smit
18–05	England	L	0–1	Amsterdam	Fr	
3–11	Denmark	W	3–0	Amsterdam	Fr	Bakhuys, Smit, Wels
8–12	Rep. Ireland	W	5–3	Dublin	Fr	Van Nellen 2, Bakhuys, Smit, Drok
12–01–1936	France	W	6–1	Paris	Fr	Bakhuys 3, Wels, Drok, Van Nellen
29–03	Belgium	W	8–0	Amsterdam	Fr	Bakhuys 3, Van Nellen 2, Smit, Wels, Drok
3–05	Belgium	D	1–1	Brussels	Fr	Bakhuys
1–11	Norway	D	3–3	Amsterdam	Fr	Bakhuys, Smit, De Bock
31–01–1937	Germany	D	2–2	Dusseldorf	Fr	Van Spaandonck 2
7–03	Switzerland	W	2–1	Amsterdam	Fr	Bakhuys, Vrauwdeunt
4–04	Belgium	L	1–2	Antwerp	Fr	Wels
2–05	Belgium	W	1–0	Rotterdam	Fr	Vente
31–10	France	L	2–3	Amsterdam	Fr	Smit 2
28–11	Luxembourg	W	4–0	Rotterdam	WCq	De Boer 3, Smit
27–02–1938	Belgium	W	7–2	Rotterdam	Fr	Smit 4, Vente, Wels, Van Spaandonck
3–04	Belgium	D	1–1	Antwerp	WCq	Van Spaandonck
21–05	Scotland	L	1–3	Amsterdam	Fr	Vente
5–06	Czechoslovakia	L	0–3	Le Havre	WCr1	
23–10	Denmark	D	2–2	Copenhagen	Fr	Van Leur, Veen
26–02–1939	Hungary	W	3–2	Rotterdam	Fr	Vente 2, De Harder
19–03	Belgium	L	4–5	Antwerp	Fr	Vente 2, Smit, Dräger
23–04	Belgium	W	3–2	Amsterdam	Fr	Vente 2, Dräger
7–05	Switzerland	L	1–2	Berne	Fr	Smit

17–03–1940	Belgium	L	1–7	Antwerp	Fr	Smit
31–03	Luxembourg	L	4–5	Rotterdam	Fr	Lenstra, Bergman, Drok, Paauwe
21–04	Belgium	W	4–2	Amsterdam	Fr	De Harder 2, Vente, Engel
10–03–1946	Luxembourg	W	6–2	Luxembourg	Fr	Wilkes 4, Rijvers, Bergman
12–05	Belgium	W	6–3	Amsterdam	Fr	Wilkes 3, Smit, Rijvers, Dräger
30–05	Belgium	D	2–2	Antwerp	Fr	Wilkes 2
27–11	England	L	2–8	Huddersfield	Fr	Smit, Bergman
7–04–1947	Belgium	W	2–1	Amsterdam	Fr	Bergman 2
4–05	Belgium	W	2–1	Antwerp	Fr	Dräger, Roozen
26–05	France	L	0–4	Paris	Fr	
22–06	Czechoslovakia	L	1–2	Amsterdam	Fr	
21–09	Switzerland	W	6–2	Amsterdam	Fr	Wilkes 2, Rijvers 2, Dräger, Lenstra
14–03–1948	Belgium	D	1–1	Antwerp	Fr	Lenstra
18–04	Belgium	D	2–2	Rotterdam	Fr	Lenstra, Engelsman
26–05	Norway	W	2–1	Oslo	Fr	Clavan, Tuyn
9–06	Sweden	W	1–0	Amsterdam	Fr	Wilkes
21–11	Belgium	D	1–1	Antwerp	Fr	Clavan
13–03–1949	Belgium	D	3–3	Amsterdam	Fr	Lenstra, Clavan, Brandes
23–04	France	W	4–1	Rotterdam	Fr	Timmermans 3, Wilkes
12–06	Denmark	W	2–1	Copenhagen	Fr	Wilkes, Lenstra
16–06	Finland	W	4–1	Helsinki	Fr	Van Roessel 2, Schaap, Van Schijndel
6–11	Belgium	L	0–1	Rotterdam	Fr	
11–12	Denmark	L	0–1	Amsterdam	Fr	
16–04–1950	Belgium	L	0–2	Antwerp	Fr	
8–06	Sweden	L	1–4	Stockholm	Fr	Clavan
11–06	Finland	L	1–4	Helsinki	Fr	Lenstra
15–10	Switzerland	L	5–7	Basle	Fr	Clavan, Rijvers, Van Melis, De Graaf, OG
12–11	Belgium	L	2–7	Antwerp	Fr	Van Melis, De Graaf
10–12	France	L	2–5	Paris	Fr	Van Melis, Tuyn
15–04–1951	Belgium	W	5–4	Amsterdam	Fr	Van Melis 3, Lenstra 2
6–06	Norway	L	2–3	Rotterdam	Fr	Van Melis, Lenstra
27–10	Finland	D	4–4	Rotterdam	Fr	Van Melis 3, Lenstra
25–11	Belgium	L	6–7	Rotterdam	Fr	Lenstra 3, Van Melis, Clavan, Bennaars
6–04–1952	Belgium	L	2–4	Antwerp	Fr	Van Melis, Clavan
14–05	Sweden	D	0–0	Amsterdam	Fr	
16–07	Brazil	L	1–5	Turku	OGr1	Van Roessel
21–09	Denmark	L	2–3	Copenhagen	Fr	Lenstra, Van Roessel
19–10	Belgium	L	1–2	Antwerp	Fr	Lenstra
7–03–1953	Denmark	L	1–2	Rotterdam	Fr	Lenstra
22–03	Switzerland	L	1–2	Amsterdam	Fr	Lenstra
19–04	Belgium	L	0–2	Amsterdam	Fr	
27–09	Norway	L	0–4	Oslo	Fr	
25–10	Belgium	W	1–0	Rotterdam	Fr	Van Beurden
4–04–1954	Belgium	L	0–4	Antwerp	Fr	
19–05	Sweden	L	1–6	Stockholm	Fr	Louer
30–05	Switzerland	L	1–3	Zurich	Fr	Dillen
24–10	Belgium	L	3–4	Antwerp	Fr	Dillen, De Bruyckere, Gijp
13–03–1955	Denmark	D	1–1	Amsterdam	Fr	Lenstra
3–04	Belgium	W	1–0	Amsterdam	Fr	Dillen
1–05	Rep. Ireland	L	0–1	Dublin	Fr	
19–05	Switzerland	W	4–1	Rotterdam	Fr	Wilkes 2, Timmermans, De Bruyckere
16–10	Belgium	D	2–2	Rotterdam	Fr	Appel 2
6–11	Norway	W	3–0	Amsterdam	Fr	Bosselaar 2, Appel
16–11	Saar	W	2–1	Saarbrucken	Fr	Brusselers, Hart
14–03–1956	West Germany	W	2–1	Dusseldorf	Fr	Lenstra 2
8–04	Belgium	W	1–0	Antwerp	Fr	Koopal
10–05	Rep. Ireland	L	1–4	Rotterdam	Fr	Appel
6–06	Saar	W	3–2	Amsterdam	Fr	Lenstra, Wilkes, Koopal
15–09	Switzerland	W	3–2	Lausanne	Fr	Lenstra, Bosselaar, Gijp
14–10	Belgium	W	3–2	Antwerp	Fr	Appel 2, Notermans
4–11	Denmark	D	2–2	Copenhagen	Fr	Appel 2
30–01–1957	Spain	L	1–5	Madrid	Fr	Bosselaar
20–03	Luxembourg	W	4–1	Rotterdam	WCq	Gijp 2, Dillen, Brusselers
3–04	West Germany	L	1–2	Amsterdam	Fr	Wilkes
28–04	Belgium	D	1–1	Amsterdam	Fr	Carlier
26–05	Austria	L	2–3	Vienna	WCq	Van Melis 2
11–09	Luxembourg	W	5–2	Rotterdam	WCq	Lenstra 2, Wilkes, Van Melis, Rijvers
25–09	Austria	D	1–1	Amsterdam	WCq	Lenstra
17–11	Belgium	W	5–2	Rotterdam	Fr	Wilkes 2, Kruiver, Carlier, Van Wissen

LEADING INTERNATIONAL GOALSCORERS

1 Wilkes	35	Van der Linden	17	17 Lagendaal	13
2 Lenstra	33	Tap	17	18 Groot H	12
Cruyff	33	Neeskens	17	Kruiver	12
4 Bakhuys	28	12 Thomée	16	Rep	12
5 Smit	26	13 Van Melis	15	Geels	12
6 Van Basten	24	Gullit	15	22 Keizer	11
7 Vente	19	15 Buitenweg	14	Kieft	11
8 Francken	17	Rensenbrink	14		

13-04-1958	Belgium	W 7-2	Antwerp	Fr	Wilkes 2, Lenstra 2, Moulijn, Van Wissen, Notermans
23-04	Curacao	W 8-1	Rotterdam	Fr	Wilkes 2, Lenstra 2, Van Wissen 2, Moulijn, Kuil
4-05	Turkey	L 1-2	Amsterdam	Fr	Wilkes
28-05	Norway	D 0-0	Oslo	Fr	
28-09	Belgium	W 3-2	Antwerp	Fr	Linden, Kruiver, Hart
15-10	Denmark	W 5-1	Rotterdam	Fr	Lenstra 2, Linden, Kruiver, Kuil
2-11	Switzerland	W 2-0	Rotterdam	Fr	Kruiver 2
19-04-1959	Belgium	D 2-2	Amsterdam	Fr	Lenstra, Linden
10-05	Turkey	D 0-0	Istanbul	Fr	
13-05	Bulgaria	L 2-3	Sofia	Fr	Canjels 2
27-05	Scotland	L 1-2	Amsterdam	Fr	Gijp
4-10	Belgium	W 9-1	Rotterdam	Fr	Wilkes 3, Kuil 3, Linden, Rijvers, Klaassens
21-10	West Germany	L 0-7	Cologne	Fr	
4-11	Norway	W 7-1	Rotterdam	Fr	Linden 3, Wilkes 2, Rijvers, Kuil
3-04-1960	Bulgaria	W 4-2	Amsterdam	Fr	Linden 3, Groot
24-04	Belgium	L 1-2	Antwerp	Fr	Rijvers
18-05	Switzerland	L 1-3	Zurich	Fr	Rijvers
26-06	Mexico	L 1-3	Mexico City	Fr	Gijp
29-06	Neth. Antilles	D 0-0	Willemstad	Fr	
3-07	Suriname	W 4-3	Paramaribo	Fr	Kruiver 3, Swart
2-10	Belgium	W 4-1	Antwerp	Fr	Groot 2, Kuil, OG
30-10	Czechoslovakia	L 0-4	Prague	Fr	
22-03-1961	Belgium	W 6-2	Rotterdam	Fr	Groot 2, Kruiver 2, Swart, Moulijn
19-04	Mexico	L 1-2	Amsterdam	Fr	Wilkes
30-04	Hungary	L 0-3	Rotterdam	WCq	
14-05	East Germany	D 1-1	Leipzig	WCq	Groot
22-10	Hungary	D 3-3	Budapest	WCq	Linden 2, Groot
12-11	Belgium	L 0-4	Amsterdam	Fr	
1-04-1962	Belgium	L 1-3	Antwerp	Fr	Linden
9-05	Nth. Ireland	W 4-0	Rotterdam	Fr	Linden 2, Swart, Kuil
16-05	Norway	L 1-2	Oslo	Fr	Linden
5-09	Neth. Antilles	W 8-0	Amsterdam	Fr	Groot 3, Prins 2, Swart 2, Keizer
26-09	Denmark	L 1-4	Copenhagen	Fr	Prins
14-10	Belgium	L 0-2	Antwerp	Fr	
11-11	Switzerland	W 3-1	Amsterdam	ECr1	Linden, Groot, Swart
3-03-1963	Belgium	L 0-1	Rotterdam	Fr	
31-03	Switzerland	D 1-1	Berne	ECr1	Kruiver
17-04	France	W 1-0	Rotterdam	Fr	Groot
2-05	Brazil	W 1-0	Amsterdam	Fr	Petersen
11-09	Luxembourg	D 1-1	Amsterdam	ECr2	Nuninga
20-10	Belgium	D 1-1	Amsterdam	Fr	Keizer
30-10	Luxembourg	L 1-2	Rotterdam	ECr2	Kruiver
22-03-1964	Belgium	D 0-0	Antwerp	Fr	
12-04	Austria	D 1-1	Amsterdam	Fr	Nuninga
29-04	Sweden	L 0-1	Rotterdam	Fr	
24-05	Albania	W 2-0	Rotterdam	WCq	Schrijvers, Muller
30-09	Belgium	L 0-1	Antwerp	Fr	
25-10	Albania	W 2-0	Tirana	WCq	Van Nee, Geurtsen
9-12	England	D 1-1	Amsterdam	Fr	Moulijn
26-01-1965	Israel	W 1-0	Tel Aviv	Fr	Fransen
17-03	Nth. Ireland	L 1-2	Belfast	WCq	Van Nee
7-04	Nth. Ireland	D 0-0	Rotterdam	WCq	
17-10	Switzerland	D 0-0	Amsterdam	WCq	
14-11	Switzerland	L 1-2	Berne	WCq	Laseroms
23-03-1966	West Germany	L 2-4	Rotterdam	Fr	Nuninga, Swart

17–04	Belgium	W 3–1	Rotterdam	Fr	Keizer, Muller, Kuijlen
11–05	Scotland	W 3–0	Glasgow	Fr	Kuijlen 2, Nuninga
7–09	Hungary	D 2–2	Rotterdam	ECq	Cruyff, Pijs
18–09	Austria	L 1–2	Vienna	Fr	OG
6–11	Czechoslovakia	L 1–2	Amsterdam	Fr	Swart
30–11	Denmark	W 2–0	Rotterdam	ECq	Swart, Kuijlen
5–04–1967	East Germany	L 3–4	Leipzig	ECq	Keizer 2, Mulder
16–04	Belgium	L 0–1	Antwerp	Fr	
10–05	Hungary	L 1–2	Budapest	ECq	Suurbier
13–09	East Germany	W 1–0	Amsterdam	ECq	Cruyff
4–10	Denmark	L 2–3	Copenhagen	ECq	Suurbier, Israël
1–11	Yugoslavia	L 1–2	Rotterdam	Fr	Swart
29–11	Soviet Union	W 3–1	Rotterdam	Fr	Wery 2, Romeijn
7–04–1968	Belgium	L 1–2	Amsterdam	Fr	Klijnjan
1–05	Poland	D 0–0	Warsaw	Fr	
30–05	Scotland	D 0–0	Amsterdam	Fr	
5–06	Romania	D 0–0	Bucharest	Fr	
4–09	Luxembourg	W 2–0	Rotterdam	WCq	Van Hanegem, Jansen
27–10	Bulgaria	L 0–2	Sofia	WCq	
26–03–1969	Luxembourg	W 4–0	Rotterdam	WCq	Pahlplatz 2, Cruyff, Van Dijk
16–04	Czechoslovakia	W 2–0	Rotterdam	Fr	Roggeveen 2
7–05	Poland	W 1–0	Rotterdam	WCq	Roggeveen
7–09	Poland	L 1–2	Chorzow	WCq	Wery
22–10	Bulgaria	D 1–1	Rotterdam	WCq	Veenstra
5–11	England	L 0–1	Amsterdam	Fr	
14–01–1970	England	D 0–0	London	Fr	
28–01	Israel	W 1–0	Tel Aviv	Fr	Brokamp
11–10	Yugoslavia	D 1–1	Rotterdam	ECq	Israël
11–11	East Germany	L 0–1	Dresden	ECq	
2–12	Romania	W 2–0	Amsterdam	Fr	Cruyff 2
24–02–1971	Luxembourg	W 6–0	Rotterdam	ECq	Cruyff 2, Keizer 2, Lippens, Suurbier
4–04	Yugoslavia	L 0–2	Split	ECq	
10–10	East Germany	W 3–2	Rotterdam	ECq	Keizer 2, Hulshoff
17–11	Luxembourg	W 8–0	Eindhoven	ECq	Cruyff 3, Keizer, Hoekema, Pahlplatz, Hulshoff, Israël
1–12	Scotland	W 2–1	Amsterdam	Fr	Cruyff, Hulshoff
16–02–1972	Greece	W 5–0	Athens	Fr	Cruyff 2, Hulshoff 2, Neeskens
3–05	Peru	W 3–0	Rotterdam	Fr	Van Hanegem, Klijnjan, Schneider
30–08	Czechoslovakia	W 2–1	Prague	Fr	Cruyff, Neeskens
1–11	Norway	W 9–0	Rotterdam	WCq	Neeskens 3, Cruyff 2, Brokamp 2, Keizer, De Jong
19–11	Belgium	D 0–0	Antwerp	WCq	
28–03–1973	Austria	L 0–1	Vienna	Fr	
2–05	Spain	W 3–2	Amsterdam	Fr	Cruyff, Rep, OG
22–08	Iceland	W 5–0	Amsterdam	WCq	Cruyff 2, Haan, Van Hanegem, Brokamp
29–08	Iceland	W 8–1	Deventer	WCq	Cruyff 2, Brokamp 2, Neeskens, Van Hanegem, Van de Kerkhof R, Schneider
12–09	Norway	W 2–1	Oslo	WCq	Cruyff, Hulshoff
10–10	Poland	D 1–1	Rotterdam	Fr	De Jong
18–11	Belgium	D 0–0	Amsterdam	WCq	
27–03–1974	Austria	D 1–1	Rotterdam	Fr	Krol
26–05	Argentina	W 4–1	Amsterdam	Fr	Neeskens, Rensenbrink, Strik, Haan
5–06	Romania	D 0–0	Rotterdam	Fr	
15–06	Uruguay	W 2–0	Hanover	WCr1	Rep.2
19–06	Sweden	D 0–0	Dortmund	WCr1	
23–06	Bulgaria	W 4–1	Dortmund	WCr1	Neeskens 2, Rep, De Jong
26–06	Argentina	W 4–0	Gelsenkirchen	WCr2	Cruyff 2, Krol, Rep
30–06	East Germany	W 2–0	Gelsenkirchen	WCr2	Neeskens, Rensenbrink
3–07	Brazil	W 2–0	Dortmund	WCr2	Neeskens, Cruyff
7–07	West Germany	L 1–2	Munich	WCf	Neeskens
4–09	Sweden	W 5–1	Stockholm	Fr	Neeskens 3, Cruyff, Rensenbrink
25–09	Finland	W 3–1	Helsinki	ECq	Cruyff 2, Neeskens
9–10	Switzerland	W 1–0	Rotterdam	Fr	Geels
20–11	Italy	W 3–1	Rotterdam	ECq	Cruyff 2, Rensenbrink
30–04–1975	Belgium	L 0–1	Antwerp	Fr	
17–05	West Germany	D 1–1	Frankfurt	Fr	Van Hanegem
31–05	Yugoslavia	L 0–3	Belgrade	Fr	
3–09	Finland	W 4–1	Nijmegen	ECq	Van der Kuylen 3, Lubse
10–09	Poland	L 1–4	Chorzow	ECq	Van de Kerkhof R

15–10	Poland	W	3–0	Amsterdam	ECq	Neeskens, Geels, Thijssen
22–11	Italy	L	0–1	Rome	ECq	
25–04–1976	Belgium	W	5–0	Rotterdam	ECqf	Rensenbrink 3, Rijsbergen, Neeskens
22–05	Belgium	W	2–1	Brussels	ECqf	Rep, Cruyff
16–06	Czechoslovakia	L	1–3	Zagreb	ECsf	OG
19–06	Yugoslavia	W	3–2	Zagreb	EC3p	Geels 2, Van de Kerkhof W
8–09	Iceland	W	1–0	Reykjavik	WCq	Geels
13–10	Nth. Ireland	D	2–2	Rotterdam	WCq	Krol, Cruyff
9–02–1977	England	W	2–0	London	Fr	Peters 2
26–03	Belgium	W	2–0	Antwerp	WCq	Rep, Cruyff
31–08	Iceland	W	4–1	Nijmegen	WCq	Geels 2, Van Hanegem, Rep
5–10	Soviet Union	D	0–0	Rotterdam	Fr	
12–10	Nth. Ireland	W	1–0	Belfast	WCq	Van de Kerkhof W
26–10	Belgium	W	1–0	Amsterdam	WCq	Van de Kerkhof R
22–02–1978	Israel	W	2–1	Tel Aviv	Fr	Rensenbrink, La Ling
5–04	Tunisia	W	4–0	Tunis	Fr	Nanninga 2, Van Leeuwen, OG
20–05	Austria	W	1–0	Vienna	Fr	Haan
3–06	Iran	W	3–0	Mendoza	WCr1	Rensenbrink 3
7–06	Peru	D	0–0	Mendoza	WCr1	
11–06	Scotland	L	2–3	Mendoza	WCr1	Rensenbrink, Rep
14–06	Austria	W	5–1	Cordoba	WCr2	Rep.2, Brandts, Rensenbrink, Van de Kerkhof W
18–06	West Germany	D	2–2	Cordoba	WCr2	Haan, Van de Kerkhof R
21–06	Italy	W	2–1	Buenos Aires	WCr2	Brandts, Haan
25–06	Argentina	L	1–3	Buenos Aires	WCf	Nanninga
20–09	Iceland	W	3–0	Nijmegen	ECq	Krol, Brandts, Rensenbrink
11–10	Switzerland	W	3–1	Berne	ECq	Wildschut, Brandts, Geels
15–11	East Germany	W	3–0	Rotterdam	ECq	Geels 2, OG
20–12	West Germany	L	1–3	Dusseldorf	Fr	La Ling
24–02–1979	Italy	L	0–3	Milan	Fr	
28–03	Switzerland	W	3–0	Eindhoven	ECq	Kist, Metgod, Peters
2–05	Poland	L	0–2	Chorzow	ECq	
22–05	Argentina	D	0–0	Berne	Fr	
5–09	Iceland	W	4–0	Reykjavik	ECq	Nanninga 2, Metgod, Van de Kerkhof W
26–09	Belgium	W	1–0	Rotterdam	Fr	Poortvliet
17–10	Poland	D	1–1	Amsterdam	ECq	Stevens
21–11	East Germany	W	3–2	Leipzig	ECq	Thijssen, Kist, Van de Kerkhof R
23–01–1980	Spain	L	0–1	Vigo	Fr	
26–03	France	D	0–0	Paris	Fr	
11–06	Greece	W	1–0	Naples	ECr1	Kist
14–06	West Germany	L	2–3	Naples	ECr1	Rep, Van de Kerkhof W
17–06	Czechoslovakia	D	1–1	Milan	ECr1	Kist
10–09	Rep. Ireland	L	1–2	Dublin	WCq	Tahamata
11–10	West Germany	D	1–1	Eindhoven	Fr	Brandts
19–11	Belgium	L	0–1	Brussels	WCq	
30–12	Uruguay	L	0–2	Montevideo	ML	
6–01–1981	Italy	D	1–1	Montevideo	ML	Peters
22–02	Cyprus	W	3–0	Groningen	WCq	Hovenkamp, Schapendonk, Nanninga
25–03	France	W	1–0	Rotterdam	WCq	Muhren
29–04	Cyprus	W	1–0	Nicosia	WCq	Van Kooten
1–09	Switzerland	L	1–2	Zurich	Fr	Metgod
9–09	Rep. Ireland	D	2–2	Rotterdam	WCq	Thijssen, Muhren
14–10	Belgium	W	3–0	Rotterdam	WCq	Metgod, Van Kooten, Geels
18–11	France	L	0–2	Paris	WCq	
23–03–1982	Scotland	L	1–2	Glasgow	Fr	Kieft
14–04	Greece	W	1–0	Eindhoven	Fr	Ophof
25–05	England	L	0–2	London	Fr	
1–09	Iceland	D	1–1	Reykjavik	ECq	Schoenaker
22–09	Rep. Ireland	W	2–1	Rotterdam	ECq	Schoenaker, Gullit
10–11	France	L	1–2	Rotterdam	Fr	Tahamata

LEADING INTERNATIONAL APPEARANCES

1 Krol	83	5 Van de Kerkhof W	63	9 Klaassens	57
2 Van Breukelen	72	6 Suurbier	60	10 Dénis	56
3 Jansen	65	Gullit	60	Rijkaard	56
4 Van Heel	64	8 Koeman R	59		

19–12	Malta	W 6–0	Aachen	ECq	Van Kooten 2, Schoenaker 2, Ophof, Hovenkamp
16–02–1983	Spain	L 0–1	Seville	ECq	
27–04	Sweden	L 0–3	Utrecht	Fr	
7–09	Iceland	W 3–0	Groningen	ECq	Koeman R, Gullit, Houtman
21–09	Belgium	D 1–1	Brussels	Fr	Van Basten
12–10	Rep. Ireland	W 3–2	Dublin	ECq	Gullit 2, Van Basten
16–11	Spain	W 2–1	Rotterdam	ECq	Houtman, Gullit
17–12	Malta	W 5–0	Rotterdam	ECq	Rijkaard 2, Vanenburg, Wijnstekers, Houtman
14–03–1984	Denmark	W 6–0	Amsterdam	Fr	Van der Gijp 2, Houtman 2, Kieft, Hoekstra
17–10	Hungary	L 1–2	Rotterdam	WCq	Kieft
14–11	Austria	L 0–1	Vienna	WCq	
23–12	Cyprus	W 1–0	Nicosia	WCq	Houtman
27–02–1985	Cyprus	W 7–1	Amsterdam	WCq	Kieft 2, Schoenaker 2, Koeman E, Van Basten, OG
1–05	Austria	D 1–1	Rotterdam	WCq	Kieft
14–05	Hungary	W 1–0	Budapest	WCq	De Wit
4–09	Bulgaria	W 1–0	Heerenven	Fr	De Wit
16–10	Belgium	L 0–1	Brussels	WCq	
20–11	Belgium	W 2–1	Rotterdam	WCq	Houtman, De Wit
12–03–1986	East Germany	W 1–0	Leipzig	Fr	Van Basten
29–04	Scotland	D 0–0	Eindhoven	Fr	
14–05	West Germany	L 1–3	Dortmund	Fr	Van der Gijp
10–09	Czechoslovakia	L 0–1	Prague	Fr	
15–10	Hungary	W 1–0	Budapest	ECq	Van Basten
19–11	Poland	D 0–0	Amsterdam	ECq	
21–12	Cyprus	W 2–0	Nicosia	ECq	Gullit, Bosman
21–01–1987	Spain	D 1–1	Barcelona	Fr	Gullit
25–03	Greece	D 1–1	Rotterdam	ECq	Van Basten
29–04	Hungary	W 2–0	Rotterdam	ECq	Gullit, Muhren
9–09	Belgium	D 0–0	Rotterdam	Fr	
14–10	Poland	W 2–0	Zabrze	ECq	Gullit 2
28–10	Cyprus	W 8–0	Rotterdam	ECq	Bosman 5, Gullit, Spelbos, Van't Schip
Match declared Void					
9–12	Cyprus	W 4–0	Amsterdam	ECq	Bosman 3, Koeman R
16–12	Greece	W 3–0	Rhodes	ECq	Gillhaus 2, Koeman R
23–03–1988	England	D 2–2	London	Fr	Bosman, OG
24–05	Bulgaria	L 1–2	Rotterdam	Fr	Wouters
1–06	Romania	W 2–0	Amsterdam	Fr	Bosman, Kieft
12–06	Soviet Union	L 0–1	Cologne	ECr1	
15–06	England	W 3–1	Dusseldorf	ECr1	Van Basten 3
18–06	Rep. Ireland	W 1–0	Gelsenkirchen	ECr1	Kieft
21–06	West Germany	W 2–1	Hamburg	ECsf	Koeman R, Van Basten
25–06	Soviet Union	W 2–0	Munich	ECf	Gullit, Van Basten
14–09	Wales	W 1–0	Amsterdam	WCq	Gullit
19–10	West Germany	D 0–0	Munich	WCq	
16–11	Italy	L 0–1	Rome	Fr	
4–01–1989	Israel	W 2–0	Tel Aviv	Fr	Wouters, Van Loen
22–03	Soviet Union	W 2–0	Eindhoven	Fr	Van Basten, Koeman R
26–04	West Germany	D 1–1	Rotterdam	WCq	Van Basten
31–05	Finland	W 1–0	Helsinki	WCq	Kieft
6–09	Denmark	D 2–2	Amsterdam	Fr	Koeman R, Wouters
11–10	Wales	W 2–1	Wrexham	WCq	Rutjers, Bosman
15–11	Finland	W 3–0	Rotterdam	WCq	Bosman, Koeman E, Koeman R
20–12	Brazil	L 0–1	Rotterdam	Fr	
21–02–1990	Italy	D 0–0	Rotterdam	Fr	
28–03	Soviet Union	L 1–2	Kiev	Fr	Koeman R
30–05	Austria	L 2–3	Vienna	Fr	Koeman R, Van Basten
3–06	Yugoslavia	W 2–0	Zagreb	Fr	Rijkaard, Van Basten
12–06	Egypt	D 1–1	Palermo	WCr1	Kieft
16–06	England	D 0–0	Cagliari	WCr1	
21–06	Rep. Ireland	D 1–1	Palermo	WCr1	Gullit
24–06	West Germany	L 1–2	Milan	WCr2	Koeman R
26–09	Italy	L 0–1	Palermo	Fr	
17–10	Portugal	L 0–1	Oporto	ECq	
21–11	Greece	W 2–0	Rotterdam	ECq	Bergkamp, Van Basten
19–12	Malta	W 8–0	Ta'Qali	ECq	Van Basten 5, Winter, Bergkamp 2

13-03-1991	Malta	W 1-0	Rotterdam	ECq	Van Basten
17-04	Finland	W 2-0	Rotterdam	ECq	Van Basten, Gullit
5-06	Finland	D 1-1	Helsinki	ECq	De Boer
11-09	Poland	D 1-1	Eindhoven	Fr	Bergkamp
16-10	Portugal	W 1-0	Rotterdam	ECq	Witschge
4-12	Greece	W 2-0	Salonica	ECq	Bergkamp, Blind
12-02-1992	Portugal	L 0-2	Faro	Fr	
25-03	Yugoslavia	W 2-0	Amsterdam	Fr	Kieft, Wouters
27-05	Austria	W 3-2	Sittard	Fr	Rijkaard, Bergkamp, Gullit
30-05	Wales	W 4-0	Utrecht	Fr	Roy, Van Basten, Winter, Jonk
5-06	France	D 1-1	Lens	Fr	Roy
12-06	Scotland	W 1-0	Gothenburg	ECr1	Bergkamp
15-06	CIS	D 0-0	Gothenburg	ECr1	
18-06	Germany	W 3-1	Gothenburg	ECr1	Rijkaard, Witschge, Bergkamp
22-06	Denmark	D 2-2 (4-5p)	Gothenburg	ECsf	Bergkamp, Rijkaard

HUNGARY

Proud Hungary! Never has a country come so close to winning the World Cup and yet been so cruelly denied as the Hungarians were in 1954. Regarded as the best team the world had ever seen the 'Magic Magyars', as they were known, lost only one game in six years of international football, and that game was the World Cup final.

The 1950s team, although only one of three great teams Hungary have produced over the years, will always be the one present Hungarian teams are compared to, a burden that will not go away until a team of equal stature is built. Given the state that Hungarian football finds itself in now, this could be a long time in coming.

Hungarian football was very quick to develop, especially in Budapest which along with Vienna and Prague formed the first focus of organised football in central Europe. Among the first clubs formed were Ujpesti in 1885, MTK in 1888 and Ferencvaros in 1899, all of whom remain in the forefront of Hungarian football today, but as was traditional in central Europe, football sections were often added on to already existing clubs, and in Hungary these tended to be Gymnastic clubs.

In 1901 the football association was formed and Southampton, the first English professional club to travel abroad, came to Hungary. It was a very significant tour, and although Budapest selections lost 8–0 and 13–0, it was the spur the Hungarians needed to develop their game. A league was formed in the same year, whilst the following year, a national selection travelled to Vienna to take part in the very first international match on the continent.

Although beaten 5–0 on that historic day, the Hungarians developed into a highly original and prolific side, noted for some remarkable individuals. The first of the great Hungarian players was Imre Schlosser. His 58 goals either side of and during the First World War made him the outstanding player of his time and the leading scorer on mainland Europe, a position he held for many years.

Hungarian football flourished in the inter-war period, especially after professionalism was introduced in 1926. Ferencvaros, Ujpest and Hungaria, who had changed their name from MTK in 1927, were among the most feared clubs on the continent. MTK won a staggering 10 consecutive championships in the years up until 1925, but it was in the Mitropa Cup in the 1930s that Ferencvaros and Ujpest, especially, made their mark. The former appeared in five finals, winning three, whilst the latter won on two occasions.

With the demise of the national side that had contained Schlosser and the great Alfred Schaffer, who had moved to Germany and had become known as the 'Fussballkönig' – Football king – by his fans at 1.FC Nürnberg, another equally good, if not better, team was not long in developing. France were beaten 13–1 in Budapest in 1927, and by the 1934 World Cup Hungary were regarded as being among the favourites. In Italy, however, they came up against the Austrian 'Wunderteam' and lost to them in the quarter-finals.

In 1938 they reached the final. The stars of this side were Gyorgy Sarosi and Gyula Zsengeller. Sarosi in particular was an influential figure. He had scored in a victory over England in Budapest just prior to the 1934 World Cup and scored a remarkable seven goals against Czechoslovakia in 1937.

After the defeat against Italy in the 1938 final, the Hungarians were accused of being too pretty and lacking the steel to win. Certainly they were much more gifted than the Italians, but the Italian will to win and robust approach to the game proved decisive. It was a lesson that was learnt by the Hungarians when once again, after the war, they produced another great side to uphold the tradition started by Schlosser and continued by Sarosi.

The aftermath of the war saw a communist takeover in Hungary, but despite interference by the political authorities in the club structure, football flourished. To a great extent it was seen as a propaganda weapon and no club epitomised this as much as the Honved side of the

1950s. Though nominally amateur, their approach was very professional and they formed the basis of the national side that went for six years and 48 games with only one defeat, a truly remarkable record.

The players that this team regularly used are worth noting. There was the reliable Grosics in goal, Jeno Buzansky and Mihaly Lantos in defence, the midfield had Gyula Lorant at centre-half along with Jozsef Bozsik the captain and record cap winner, whilst the forward line was truely fearsome. Zoltan Czibor and Jozsef Toth operated down the wings whilst Nandor Hidegkuti operated slightly behind Sandor Kocsis and Ferenc Puskas, probably the most deadly striking partnership football has ever seen. Between them they scored an extraordinary 158 goals for the national side, more than some countries have scored full stop!

After winning the 1952 Olympic title in Helsinki, they sealed their reputation with a 6–3 victory over England at Wembley. The victory was significant because it marked England's first defeat on home soil by a non-British side. A 7–1 victory in the return in Budapest the following year confirmed the Hungarians as possibly the most overwhelming favourites the World Cup has ever seen.

How they failed in the final against Germany has never properly been explained, particularly after they had taken an early two-goal lead. In their six year run they had played many better sides than the Germans and beaten them with consummate ease. To lose only one match in six years and for that match to be the World Cup Final was a cruel disappointment to the Hungarians, and as it transpired, the team did not have another bite at the cherry four years later.

The Hungarian uprising and its subsequent crushing by the Soviet army split the side up. Fortunately for Puskas, Kocsis and Czibor, and unfortunately for Hungary, they were on a tour when the uprising broke out, and all three decided to stay and make their fortunes in the West, Czibor and Kocsis with Barcelona, Puskas with Real Madrid. If one person had epitomised Hungary at this time it was Puskas, the 'Galloping Major' as he was known due to his rank in the army. He was without question the greatest Hungarian player of all time, and many would rank him as one of the best the world has ever seen.

The loss of the heart of the team would have caused a major decline in the fortunes of most countries, but the football infrastructure in the country was such that by the early 1960s another supremely gifted side had been created. Talented players, it seemed, simply poured off the production line. Added to this was the reputation Hungary had built up as a nation of top coaches. Bela Guttmann, for example, was only a modestly known player, yet he coached the successful Benfica side of the early 1960s.

Chief among the new generation of players were Florian Albert and Ferenc Bene. Hungary were quarter-finalists

		All			League			Cup		Europe		
	Team	G	S	B	G	S	B	G	S	G	S	B
1	Ferencváros	40	39	20	24	29	18	15	8	1	2	2
2	MTK–VM Budapest	28	21	14	19	18	13	9	2	–	1	1
3	Ujpesti TE	26	22	18	19	16	16	7	5	–	1	2
4	Kispest-Honvéd	16	18	5	12	11	5	4	7	–	–	–
5	Vasas Budapest	10	3	11	6	2	10	4	1	–	–	1
6	Rába ETO Györ	7	4	4	3	2	3	4	2	–	–	1
7	Csepel SC	4	–	2	4	–	2	–	–	–	–	–
8	Diósgyöri VTK	2	3	1	–	–	1	2	3	–	–	–
9	Budapest TC	2	2	3	2	1	3	–	1	–	–	–
10	Pécsi MSC	1	3	1	–	1	1	1	2	–	–	–
11	Nagyváradi AC	1	1	–	1	1	–	–	–	–	–	–
12	Bocskai Debrecen	1	–	1	–	–	1	1	–	–	–	–
	Szolnoki MAV	1	–	1	–	–	1	1	–	–	–	–
14	Békéscsaba ESC	1	–	–	–	–	–	1	–	–	–	–
	Siófoki Bányász	1	–	–	–	–	–	1	–	–	–	–
	Soroksár Erzsebet	1	–	–	–	–	–	1	–	–	–	–
	111 Kerület TVE	1	–	–	–	–	–	1	–	–	–	–
18	Tatabánya Bányász	–	4	4	–	2	4	–	2	–	–	–
19	Magyar AC	–	4	1	–	2	1	–	2	–	–	–
	Salgótárjan BTC	–	4	1	–	–	1	–	4	–	–	–
21	Videoton–Waltham SC	–	3	2	–	1	2	–	1	–	1	–
22	Vaci Izzo MTE	–	3	–	–	1	–	–	2	–	–	–
23	VSC Budapest	–	2	–	–	1	–	–	1	–	–	–
	Komló Bányász	–	2	–	–	–	–	–	2	–	–	–
25	Törekvés SE	–	1	3	–	1	3	–	–	–	–	–
26	Budapest AK	–	1	1	–	–	1	–	1	–	–	–
	Szeged SC	–	1	1	–	–	1	–	1	–	–	–
	Kolozsvári AC	–	1	1	–	–	1	–	1	–	–	–
29	Atilla Miskolc	–	1	–	–	–	–	–	1	–	–	–
	Budapest EAC	–	1	–	–	–	–	–	1	–	–	–
	Dorogi AC	–	1	–	–	–	–	–	1	–	–	–
	Haladás VSE	–	1	–	–	–	–	–	1	–	–	–
	Magyar UE	–	1	–	–	1	–	–	–	–	–	–
34	Nemzeti SC	–	–	1	–	–	1	–	–	–	–	–
	33 FC	–	–	1	–	–	1	–	–	–	–	–

To the end of the 1991–92 season

at both the 1962 and 1966 World Cups, a final standing which did not do them justice on either occasion. The shadow of their predecessors has always limited the recognition given to this side.

Club football had been dominated by Honved in the 1950s, but Ferencvaros managed to regain some of their former glories with four titles and a UEFA Cup victory in the 1960s. The 1970s, however, belonged to Ujpest who won a remarkable 9 titles in 11 years. The national side did not fare so well and entered a period of decline that set in with failure to qualify for the 1970 World Cup, and from which they have yet to escape. Hungary still produces players of the highest quality, such as Tibor Nyilasi and Lajos Detari, but the game seems to have lost its way.

Betting scandals, match fixing and general apathy have characterised recent years, but it is to be hoped that the new political freedoms will be an incentive for the clubs to develop along western lines so that they can compete with the best that Europe has to offer. They have the tradition and the set-up to achieve this, the question is, do they have the will?

Population: 10437000
Area, sq km: 93031
% in urban areas: 62.0%
Capital city: Budapest

Magyar Labdarugó Szövetség
Népstadion, Toronyépület
'Tower' Bldg, Istvanm. ut 3–5
H-1146 Budapest
Hungary
Tel: (010 36) 1 2529296
Fax: (010 36) 1 2529986
Telex: 225782 MLSZ H
Cable: MLSZ BUDAPEST NEPSTADION
Languages for correspondence: German & English

Year of formation: 1901
Affiliation to FIFA: 1906
Affiliation to UEFA: 1954
Registered clubs: 2503
Registered players: 143600
Registered referees: 4670
National stadium: Népstadion Budapest 72000
National colours: Shirts: Red/Shorts: White/Socks: Green
Reserve colours: Shirts: White/Shorts: White/Socks: White
Season: August–June with a mid season break in January and February

THE RECORD

WORLD CUP

1930 .... Did not enter
1934 .... QT 1st/3 in group 8 – Final Tournament/Quarter-finalists
1938 .... QT 1st/3 in group 5 – Final Tournament/Runners-up
1950 .... Did not enter
1954 .... QT Walk-over – Final Tournament/Runners-up
1958 .... QT 1st/3 in group 3 – Final Tournament/1st round
1962 .... QT 1st/3 in group 4 – Final Tournament/Quarter-finalists
1966 .... QT 1st/3 in group 6 – Final Tournament/Quarter-finalists
1970 .... QT 2nd/4 in group 2
1974 .... QT 3rd/4 in group 1
1978 .... QT 1st/3 in group 9 – Final Tournament/1st round
1982 .... QT 1st/5 in group 4 – Final Tournament/1st round
1986 .... QT 1st/4 in group 5 – Final Tournament/1st round
1990 .... QT 3rd/5 in group 6

EUROPEAN CHAMPIONSHIP

1960 .... 1st round
1964 .... Semi-finalists/3rd place
1968 .... QT 1st/4 in group 5 – Final Tournament/Quarter-finalists
1972 .... QT 1st/4 in group 2 – Final Tournament/Semi-finalists/4th place
1976 .... QT 2nd/4 in group 2
1980 .... QT 2nd/4 in group 6
1984 .... QT 4th/5 in group 3
1988 .... QT 3rd/5 in group 5
1992 .... QT 4th/5 in group 3

OLYMPIC GAMES

1908 .... Did not enter
1912 .... 1st round
1920 .... Did not enter
1924 .... 1st round
1928 .... Did not enter
1936 .... 1st round
1948 .... Did not enter
1952 .... Winners
1956 .... Did not enter
1960 .... Final Tournament/Semi-finalists/4th place
1964 .... Final Tournament/Winners
1968 .... Final Tournament/Winners
1972 .... Final Tournament/Finalists
1976 .... QT Failed to qualify
1980 .... QT Failed to qualify
1984 .... QT Failed to qualify
1988 .... QT Failed to qualify
1992 .... QT Failed to qualify

DR. GERO CUP

1929 .... 4th
1932 .... 3rd
1935 .... 3rd
1953 .... Winners
1960 .... 2nd

EUROPEAN CLUB COMPETITIONS

EUROPEAN CUP: Semi-finalists – Vasas Budapest 1958, Vasas ETO Gyór 1965, Ujpest Dózsa 1974

CUP WINNERS CUP: Finalists – MTK Budapest 1964, Ferencváros 1975

UEFA CUP: Winners – Ferencváros 1965
Finalists – Ferencváros 1968, Ujpest Dózsa 1969, Videoton 1985

MITROPA CUP: Winners – Ferencváros 1928 1937, Ujpest Dózsa 1929 1939
Finalists – Ferencváros 1935 1938 1939

CLUB DIRECTORY

BUDAPEST (Population – 2565000)

Csepel SC
Stadium: Csepel 16000
Founded: 1912
Colours: Blue and cherry halves/Red

Ferencváros Torna Club
Stadium: Üllöi Ut 28000
Founded: 1899
Colours: Green/Green
Previous names: Ferencváros TC 1899–1950, ÉDOSZ 1950–51, Kinizsi 1951–56

Kispest–Honvéd Football Club
Stadium: József Bozsik Stadion 20000
Founded: 1909
Colours: Red/Red
Previous names: Kispest AC 1909–49, Honvéd SE 1949–91

Magyar Testgyakorlók Köre Vörös Meteor (MTK–VM)
Stadium: MTK Stadion 23000
Founded: 1888
Colours: Blue/White
Previous names: MTK 1888–1926, Hungária 1926–40, MTK 1940–50, Textilés 1950–51, Bástya 1951–53, Vörös Lobogó 1953–56, MTK 1956–75. Merged with VM Egyetértés in 1975 to become MTK–VM

Ujpesti Torna Egylet
Stadium: Dózsa Stadion 32000
Founded: 1885
Colours: Violet/White
Previous names: Ujpest TE 1885–1949, Budapest Dózsa 1949–57, Ujpesti Dózsa SC 1957–90

Vasas Sport Club
Stadium: Vasas Stadion 20000
Founded: 1911
Colours: Red/Blue
Previous names: Vasas 1911–43, Kinizsi Vasas 1943–45

DEBRECEN (Population 219000)
Debreceni Vasutas Sport Club (VSC)
Stadium: Nagyerdei 12000
Founded: 1902
Colours: Red and white checks/Red
Previous names: Merger in 1979 of Debrecen VSE and Debrecen MTE

MISKOLC (Population – 207000)
Diósgyöri Vasgyárak Testgyakorlo Köre (VTK)
Stadium: Vasgyári Sporttélep 30000
Founded: 1910
Colours: Red/Red
Previous name: Diósgyör 1910–38, DIMAVAG 1938–45

SZEGED (Population – 189000)
Szeged Sport Club
Stadium: Felsötiszaparti 18000
Founded: 1899
Colours: Blue and black stripes/Blue
Previous names: Szak 1899–1926, Bástya Szeged 1926–31, Szeged FC 1931–40, Szeged AK 1940–49, Petöfi 1950–57, Szak 1957–77. In 1977 Szak merged with SZEOL (1921) under SZEOL. SZEOL Became Szeged in 1987

PECS (Population – 183000)
Pécsi Munkas Sport Club (MSC)
Stadium: PMSC 16000
Founded: 1973 Colours: Red/Black
Previous names: Merger in 1973 of Pécsi Dózsa, Pécs Bányász, Ercbányász, Helypar and Pécs Epitök

GYÖR (Population – 131 000)
Györi Rába ETO (Egyetértés Torna Osztálya)
Stadium: Rába ETO Stadion 28 000
Founded: 1904
Colours: White/White
Previous names: ETO Györ 1904–46, Vasas ETO Györ 1946–68

SZÉKESFEHÉRVAR (Population – 113 000)
Videoton–Waltham Sport Club
Stadium: Sóstói 30 000
Founded: 1941
Colours: Red and blue halves/Blue
Previous names: Vadásztöltényár 1941–48, Dolgozók 1949–50, Vasas 1950–68, Videoton SC 1968–89

SZOMBATHELY (Population – 87 000)
Haladás Vasutas Sport Egytemi (VSE)
Stadium: Haladás 20 000
Founded: 1919
Colours: White/White
Previous names: Haladás 1919–26, Szombathely MAV 1926–36, Haladás 1936–48, Szombathely VSE 1948–49, Lokomotiv 1949–54, Törekvés 1954–56

SZOLNOK (Population – 87 000)
Szolnoki MAV MTE
Stadium: Tiszaligeti
Founded: 1910
Colours: Blue/White
Previous names: Szolnok MAV 1910–49 1956–79, Lokomotiv 1949–55, Törekvés 1955–56. Merged with Szolnok MTE in 1979

KAPOSVAR (Population – 76 000)
Kaposvári Rákóczi SC
Stadium: Rákóczi 18 000
Founded: 1923
Colours: Red/White
Previous names: Kinizsi Kaposvár 1951–56 & 1957–70

TATABANYA (Population – 76 000)
Tatabányai Bányász Sport Club
Stadium: Bányász Stadion 22 000
Founded: 1910
Colours: White/White
Previous name: Tatabánya SC 1910–49

BÉKÉSCSABA (Population – 70 000)
Békéscsabai Elöre Football Club
Stadium: Békéscsaba 20 000
Founded: 1912
Colours: Violet/Violet

VESZPRÉM (Population 66 000)
Veszprémi Football Club
Stadium: Municipal 10 000
Founded: 1912
Colours: White/White

ZALAEGERSZEG (Population – 63 000)
Zalaegerszegi Torna Egylet
Stadium: Zalaegerszegi 20 000
Founded: 1920
Colours: White/Sky blue

SALGOTARJAN (Population – 48 000)
Salgótárjan Bányász Torna Club (BTC)
Stadium: Malinovszkij
Founded: 1920
Colours: White/Black

VAC (Population – 36 000)
Váci Izzó MTE
Stadium: Városi 15 000
Founded: 1951
Colours: White/Blue

SIOFOK
Siófoki Bányász
Stadium: Siófok 12 000
Founded: 1921
Colours: Red and black stripes/Red

HUNGARIAN LEAGUE CHAMPIONSHIP

Year	Champions		Runners up		3rd	
1901	Budapest TC	16	Magyar UE	10	Ferencváros	7
1902	Budapest TC	15	Ferencváros	9	33 FC	9
1903	Ferencváros	21	Budapest TC	19	MTK Budapest	18
1904	MTK Budapest	25	Ferencváros	24	Budapest TC	22
1905	Ferencváros	26	Postás Budapest	26	MTK Budapest	23
1906	–					
1907	Ferencváros	24	Magyar AC	22	MTK Budapest	22
1908	MTK Budapest	28	Ferencváros	25	Magyar AC	24
1909	Ferencváros	28	Magyar AC	22	Budapest TC	21
1910	Ferencváros	27	MTK Budapest	25	Nemzeti SC	18
1911	Ferencváros	32	MTK Budapest	24	Törekvés SE	22
1912	Ferencváros	30	MTK Budapest	22	Budapest AK	20
1913	Ferencváros	33	MTK Budapest	26	Budapest TC	24
1914	MTK Budapest	33	Ferencváros	27	Törekvés SE	23
1915–16	–					
1917	MTK Budapest	42	Törekvés SE	34	Ujpesti TE	27
1918	MTK Budapest	43	Ferencváros	31	Törekvés SE	30
1919	MTK Budapest	39	Ferencváros	35	Ujpesti TE	30
1920	MTK Budapest	53	Kispest AC	43	Ferencváros	40
1921	MTK Budapest	44	Ujpesti TE	36	Ferencváros	30
1922	MTK Budapest	37	Ferencváros	36	Ujpesti TE	32
1923	MTK Budapest	37	Ujpesti TE	34	Ferencváros	32
1924	MTK Budapest	40	Ferencváros	30	Ujpesti TE	28
1925	MTK Budapest	38	Ferencváros	30	Vasas Budapest	27
1926	Ferencváros	33	MTK Budapest	31	Vasas Budapest	29
1927	Ferencváros	30	Ujpesti TE	23	Hungária	19
1928	Ferencváros	39	Hungária	35	Ujpesti TE	34
1929	Hungária	37	Ferencváros	36	Ujpesti TE	30
1930	Ujpesti TE	38	Ferencváros	36	Hungária	27
1931	Ujpesti TE	35	Hungária	30	Ferencváros	29
1932	Ferencváros	44	Ujpesti TE	36	Hungária	35
1933	Ujpesti TE	37	Hungária	36	Ferencváros	35
1934	Ferencváros	39	Ujpesti TE	37	Bocskai Debrecen	27
1935	Ujpesti TE	35	Ferencváros	33	Hungária	29

1936	Hungária	48	Ujpesti TE	43	Ferencváros	39
1937	Hungária	43	Ferencváros	42	Ujpesti TE	37
1938	Ferencváros	47	Ujpesti TE	44	Hungária	40
1939	Ujpesti TE	44	Ferencváros	43	Hungária	41
1940	Ferencváros	39	Hungária	39	Ujpesti TE	38
1941	Ferencváros	45	Ujpesti TE	34	Szeged AK	32
1942	Csepel SC	48	Ujpesti TE	44	Szolnoki MAV	41
1943	Csepel SC	45	Nagyváradi AC	42	Ferencváros	36
1944	Nagyváradi AC	49	Ferencváros	36	Kolozsvári AC	36
1945	Ujpesti TE	37	Ferencváros	34	Csepel SC	32
1946	Ujpesti TE	31	Vasas Budapest	24	Csepel SC	20
1947	Ujpesti TE	47	Kispest AC	41	Vasas Budapest	39
1948	Csepel SC	52	Vasas Budapest	51	Ferencváros	50
1949	Ferencváros	53	MTK Budapest	42	Kispest AC	41
1950	Honvéd	50	EDOSZ	46	Textiles Budapest	44
1950	Honvéd	27	Textiles Budapest	24	Budapest Dózsa	21
1951	Bástya Budapest	46	Honvéd	42	Budapest Dózsa	31
1952	Honvéd	47	Bástya Budapest	45	Budapest Dózsa	36
1953	Vörös Lobogó	46	Honvéd	43	Vasas Budapest	32
1954	Honvéd	40	Vörös Lobogó	35	Kinizsi	33
1955	Honvéd	45	Vörös Lobogó	41	Kinizsi	37
1956	–					
1957	Vasas Budapest	17	MTK Budapest	16	Ujpesti Dózsa	14
1958	MTK Budapest	35	Honvéd	34	Ferencváros	33
1959	Csepel SC	34	MTK Budapest	34	Honvéd	33
1960	Ujpesti Dózsa	40	Ferencváros	35	Vasas Budapest	32
1961	Vasas Budapest	38	Ujpesti Dózsa	34	MTK Budapest	32
1962	Vasas Budapest	38	Ujpesti Dózsa	36	Ferencváros	33
1963	Ferencváros	37	MTK Budapest	31	Ujpesti Dózsa	30
1963	Györ Vasas ETO	17	Honvéd	17	Ferencváros	17
1964	Ferencváros	41	Honvéd	38	Tatabánya Bányász	33
1965	Vasas Budapest	39	Ferencváros	36	Ujpesti Dózsa	33
1966	Vasas Budapest	43	Ferencváros	37	Tatabánya Bányász	32
1967	Ferencváros	52	Ujpesti Dózsa	44	Györ Vasas ETO	39
1968	Ferencváros	49	Ujpesti Dózsa	48	Vasas Budapest	42
1969	Ujpesti Dózsa	48	Honvéd	44	Ferencváros	39
1970*	Ujpesti Dózsa	23	Ferencváros	20	Honvéd	18
1971	Ujpesti Dózsa	51	Ferencváros	49	Vasas Budapest	47
1972	Ujpesti Dózsa	46	Honvéd	39	Salgótarján BTC	39
1973	Ujpesti Dózsa	46	Ferencváros	41	Vasas Budapest	40
1974	Ujpesti Dózsa	42	Ferencváros	39	Rába ETO Györ	38
1975	Ujpesti Dózsa	45	Honvéd	42	Ferencváros	33
1976	Ferencváros	46	Videoton SC	44	Ujpesti Dózsa	42
1977	Vasas Budapest	53	Ujpesti Dózsa	50	Ferencváros	47
1978	Ujpesti Dózsa	51	Honvéd	50	MTK–VM Budapest	47
1979	Ujpesti Dózsa	52	Ferencváros	47	Diósgyöri VTK	44
1980	Honvéd	48	Ujpesti Dózsa	45	Vasas Budapest	44
1981	Ferencváros	51	Tatabánya Bányász	48	Vasas Budapest	46
1982	Rába ETO Györ	49	Ferencváros	44	Tatabánya Bányász	43
1983	Rába ETO Györ	44	Ferencváros	43	Honvéd	42
1984	Honvéd	45	Rába ETO Györ	37	Videoton SC	37
1985	Honvéd	46	Rába ETO Györ	36	Videoton SC	36
1986	Honvéd	45	Pécsi MSC	39	Rába ETO Györ	37
1987	MTK–VM Budapest	43	Ujpesti Dózsa	40	Tatabánya Bányász	35
1988	Honvéd	41	Tatábanya Bányász	37	Ujpesti Dózsa	37
1989	Honvéd	61	Ferencváros	59	MTK–VM Budapest	59
1990	Ujpesti Dózsa	58	MTK–VM Budapest	58	Ferencváros	48
1991	Honvéd	45	Ferencváros	40	Pécsi MSC	37
1992	Ferencvaros	46	Vaci Izzo	45	Kispest-Honved	40

* Honvéd beat MTK 3–1 and 3–1 to take third place. Ujpesti beat Ferencvaros 3–2 1–1 to take first place.

HUNGARIAN CUP FINALS

Year	Winners	Score	Runners–up
1910	MTK Budapest	1–1 3–1	Budapest TC
1911	MTK Budapest	1–0	Magyar AC
1912	MTK Budapest	W–O	Ferencváros
1913	Ferencváros	2–1	Budapest AK
1914	MTK Budapest	4–0	Magyar AC
1915–21	–		
1922	Ferencváros	2–2 1–0	Ujpesti TE
1923	MTK Budapest	4–1	Ujpesti TE

1924	–		
1925	MTK Budapest	4–0	Ujpesti TE
1926	Kispest AC	1–1 3–2	Budapest EAC
1927	Ferencváros	3–0	Ujpesti TE
1928	Ferencváros	5–1	Attila Miskolc
1929	–		
1930	Bocskai Debrecen	5–1	Bástya Szeged
1931	111 Kerület TVE	4–1	Ferencváros
1932	Hungária	1–1 4–3	Ferencváros
1933	Ferencváros	11–1	Ujpesti TE
1934	Soroksár	2–2 1–1 2–0	BSZKRT
1935	Ferencváros	2–1	Hungária
1936–40	–		
1941	Szolnoki MAV	3–0	Salgótarján BTC
1942	Ferencváros	6–2	DIMAVAG
1943	Ferencváros	3–0	Salgótarján BTC
1944	Ferencváros	2–2 3–1	Kolozsvári AC
1945–51	–		
1952	Bástya Budapest	3–2	Dorogi AC
1953–54	–		
1955	Vasas Budapest	3–2	Honvéd
1956	Ferencváros	2–1	Salgótarján BTC
1957–63	–		
1964	Honvéd	1–0	Vasas ETO Györ
1965	Vasas ETO Györ	4–0	Diósgyöri VTK
1966	Vasas ETO Györ	1–1 3–2	Ferencváros
1967	Vasas ETO Györ	1–0	Salgótarján BTC
1968	MTK Budapest	2–1	Honvéd
1969	Ujpesti Dózsa	3–1	Honvéd
1970	Ujpesti Dózsa	3–2	Komló Bányász
1971	–		
1972	Ferencváros	2–1	Tatabánya Bányász
1973	Vasas Budapest	4–3	Honvéd
1974	Ferencváros	3–1	Komló Bányósz
1975	Ujpesti Dózsa	3–2	Haladás VSE
1976	Ferencváros	1–0	MTK–VM Budapest
1977	Diósgyöri VTK	*	Ferencváros
1978	Ferencváros	4–2	Pécsi MSC
1979	Rába ETO Györ	1–0	Ferencváros
1980	Diósgyöri VTK	3–1	Vasas Budapest
1981	Vasas Budapest	1–0	Diósgyöri VTK
1982	Ujpesti Dózsa	2–0	Videoton SC
1983	Ujpesti Dózsa	3–2	Honvéd
1984	Siófoki Bányász	2–1	Rába ETO Györ
1985	Honvéd	5–0	Tatabánya Bányász
1986	Vasas Budapest	0–0 5–4p	Ferencváros
1987	Ujpesti Dózsa	3–2	Pécsi MSC
1988	Békéscsaba ESSC	3–2	Honvéd
1989	Honvéd	1–0	Ferencváros
1990	Pécsi MSC	2–0	Honvéd
1991	Ferencváros	1–0	Vaci Izzo MTE
1992	Ujpesti TE	1–0	Vaci Izzo

* League format used for the final rounds of the 1977 competition

INTERNATIONAL MATCHES PLAYED BY HUNGARY

Date	Opponents	Result		Venue	Compet	Scorers
12-10-1902	Austria	L	0–5	Vienna	Fr	
5-04-1903	Bohemia	W	2–1	Budapest	Fr	Borbás, Minder
10–06	Austria	W	3–2	Budapest	Fr	Pokorny 2, Buda
11–10	Austria	L	2–4	Vienna	Fr	Borbás 2
2–06–1904	Austria	W	3–0	Budapest	Fr	Pokorny, Koch, Borbás
9–10	Austria	L	4–5	Vienna	Fr	Pokorny 2, Borbás, Károly
9–04–1905	Austria	D	0–0	Budapest	Fr	
1–04–1906	Bohemia	D	1–1	Budapest	Fr	Borbás
7–10	Bohemia	D	4–4	Prague	Fr	Horváth 2, Károly, Molnár I
4–11	Austria	W	3–1	Budapest	Fr	Molnár I, Schlosser, Károly
7–04–1907	Bohemia	W	5–2	Budapest	Fr	Horváth 3, Borbás, Molnár I
5–05	Austria	L	1–3	Vienna	Fr	Károly
6–10	Bohemia	L	3–5	Prague	Fr	Gorszky, Szednicsek, Weisz
3–11	Austria	W	4–1	Budapest	Fr	Borbás 2, Károly, OG
5–04–1908	Bohemia	W	5–2	Budapest	Fr	Károly 3, Schlosser 2
3–05	Austria	L	0–4	Vienna	Fr	
10–06	England	L	0–7	Budapest	Fr	
1–11	Austria	W	5–3	Budapest	Fr	Krempels, Koródy, Schlosser 2, OG
4–04–1909	Germany	D	3–3	Budapest	Fr	Borbás, Schlosser, Sebestyén
2–05	Austria	W	4–3	Vienna	Fr	Schlosser 3, Biró G
29–05	England	L	2–4	Budapest	Fr	Késmárky, Grósz
30–05	Austria	D	1–1	Budapest	Fr	Borbás
31–05	England	L	2–8	Budapest	Fr	Schlosser, Mészáros
9–11	Austria	D	2–2	Budapest	Fr	Schlosser 2
1–05–1910	Austria	L	1–2	Vienna	Fr	Dobó
26–05	Italy	W	6–1	Budapest	Fr	Schlosser 2, Weisz, Károly, Dobó, Koródy
6–11	Austria	W	3–0	Budapest	Fr	Koródy 2, Bodnár
1–01–1911	France	W	3–0	Paris	Fr	Schlosser 3
6–01	Italy	W	1–0	Milan	Fr	Schlosser
8–01	Switzerland	L	0–2	Zurich	Fr	
7–05	Austria	L	1–3	Vienna	Fr	Bodnár
29–10	Switzerland	W	9–0	Budapest	Fr	Schlosser 6, Koródy, Biró G, Bodnár
5–11	Austria	W	2–0	Budapest	Fr	Koródy, Bodnár
17–12	Germany	W	4–1	Munich	Fr	Schlosser 2, Sebestyén, Bodnár
14–04–1912	Germany	D	4–4	Budapest	Fr	Bodnár 3, Schlosser
5–05	Austria	D	1–1	Vienna	Fr	Bodnár

20–06	Sweden	D	2–2	Gothenburg	Fr	Bodnár, Pataki
23–06	Norway	W	6–0	Oslo	Fr	Bodnár 3, Schlosser 2, Tóth I
30–06	England *	L	0–7	Stockholm	OGqf	
3–07	Germany	W	3–1	Stockholm	OGct	Schlosser 3
5–07	Austria	W	3–0	Stockholm	OGct	Schlosser, Pataki, Bodnár
12–07	Tsarist Russia	W	9–0	Moscow	Fr	Pataki 4, Kertész V 3, Schlosser 2
14–07	Tsarist Russia	W	12–0	Moscow	Fr	Schlosser 5, Kertész V 3, Pataki 2, Tóth I, Bródy
3–11	Austria	W	4–0	Budapest	Fr	Schlosser 2, Bodnár, Pataki
27–04–1913	Austria	W	4–1	Vienna	Fr	Pataki 2, Tóth I, Biró G
18–05	Sweden	W	2–0	Budapest	Fr	Pataki, Schlosser
26–10	Austria	W	4–3	Budapest	Fr	Kertész V 2, Hlavay, Pataki
3–05–1914	Austria	L	0–2	Vienna	Fr	
31–05	France	W	5–1	Budapest	Fr	Bodnár 3, Payer, Pataki
21–06	Sweden	D	1–1	Stockholm	Fr	Schlosser
4–10	Austria	D	2–2	Budapest	Fr	Pótz, Schlosser
8–11	Austria	W	2–1	Vienna	Fr	Konrád II, Bodnár
2–05–1915	Austria	L	2–5	Budapest	Fr	Patakai, OG
30–05	Austria	W	2–1	Vienna	Fr	Schlosser, Borbás
3–10	Austria	L	2–4	Vienna	Fr	Schlosser, Kertész II
7–11	Austria	W	6–2	Budapest	Fr	Schaffer 3, Tóth 2, Kertész
7–05–1916	Austria	L	1–3	Vienna	Fr	Kertész II
4–06	Austria	W	2–1	Budapest	Fr	Schaffer, Schlosser
1–10	Austria	L	2–3	Budapest	Fr	Tóth, Schaffer
5–11	Austria	D	3–3	Vienna	Fr	Schaffer, Konrád II, Schlosser
6–05–1917	Austria	D	1–1	Vienna	Fr	Schlosser
3–06	Austria	W	6–2	Budapest	Fr	Schaffer 2, Schlosser 2, Urik, Weisz
15–07	Austria	W	4–1	Vienna	Fr	Schaffer 3, Schlosser
7–10	Austria	W	2–1	Budapest	Fr	Schaffer, Taussig
4–11	Austria	W	2–1	Vienna	Fr	Schaffer 2
14–04–1918	Austria	W	2–0	Budapest	Fr	Schlosser, Schaffer
12–05	Switzerland	W	2–1	Budapest	Fr	Schaffer, Schlosser
2–06	Austria	W	2–0	Vienna	Fr	Schlosser, Schaffer
6–10	Austria	W	3–0	Vienna	Fr	Payer 2, Braun
6–04–1919	Austria	W	2–1	Budapest	Fr	Orth, Braun
5–10	Austria	L	0–2	Vienna	Fr	
9–11	Austria	W	3–2	Budapest	Fr	Pataki 2, Orth
2–05–1920	Austria	D	2–2	Vienna	Fr	Tóth I, Pataki
24–10	Germany	L	0–1	Berlin	Fr	
7–11	Austria	L	1–2	Budapest	Fr	Braun
24–04–1921	Austria	L	1–4	Vienna	Fr	Orth
5–06	Germany	W	3–0	Budapest	Fr	Schlosser, Guttmann, Braun
6–11	Sweden	W	4–2	Budapest	Fr	Orth 3, Schlosser
18–12	Poland	W	1–0	Budapest	Fr	Szabó J
30–04–1922	Austria	D	1–1	Budapest	Fr	Molnár G
14–05	Poland	W	3–0	Krakow	Fr	Solti M 2, OG
15–06	Switzerland	D	1–1	Budapest	Fr	Blum
2–07	Germany	D	0–0	Bochum	Fr	
9–07	Sweden	D	1–1	Stockholm	Fr	Hirzer
13–07	Finland	W	5–1	Helsinki	Fr	Schwarz 2, Pataki 2, Fogel
24–09	Austria	D	2–2	Vienna	Fr	Priboj 2
26–11	Austria	L	1–2	Budapest	Fr	Molnár G
4–03–1923	Italy	D	0–0	Genoa	Fr	
11–03	Switzerland	W	6–1	Lausanne	Fr	Orth 2, Molnár G 2, Hirzer 2
6–05	Austria	L	0–1	Vienna	Fr	
19–08	Finland	W	3–1	Budapest	Fr	Braun 2, Hirzer
23–09	Austria	W	2–0	Budapest	Fr	Molnár G, Jeszmás
28–10	Sweden	W	2–1	Budapest	Fr	Eisenhoffer 2
6–04–1924	Italy	W	7–1	Budapest	Fr	Molnár G 3, Braun 2, Eisenhoffer, Opata
4–05	Austria	D	2–2	Budapest	Fr	Eisenhoffer 2
18–05	Switzerland	L	2–4	Zurich	Fr	Braun, Opata
26–05	Poland	W	5–0	Paris	OGr1	Hirzer 2, Opata 2, Eisenhoffer
29–05	Egypt	L	0–3	Paris	OGr2	
4–06	France	W	1–0	Le Havre	Fr	Eisenhoffer
31–08	Poland	W	4–0	Budapest	Fr	Takács 2, Orth, OG
14–09	Austria	L	1–2	Vienna	Fr	Orth
21–09	Germany	W	4–1	Budapest	Fr	Takács 2, Szentmiklóssy, OG
18–01–1925	Italy	W	2–1	Milan	Fr	Spitz, Takács
25–03	Switzerland	W	5–0	Budapest	Fr	Molnár G 2, Jeny 2, Takács

5–05	Austria	L	1–3	Vienna	Fr	Takács
21–05	Belgium	L	1–3	Budapest	Fr	Jeny
12–07	Sweden	L	2–6	Stockholm	Fr	Takács 2
19–07	Poland	W	2–0	Krakow	Fr	Winkler, Holzbauer
20–09	Austria	D	1–1	Budapest	Fr	Priboj
4–10	Spain	L	0–1	Budapest	Fr	
11–10	Czechoslovakia	L	0–2	Prague	Fr	
8–11	Italy	D	1–1	Budapest	Fr	Molnár G
14–02–1926	Belgium	W	2–0	Brussels	Fr	Pipa, Rémay
2–05	Austria	L	0–3	Budapest	Fr	
6–06	Czechoslovakia	W	2–1	Budapest	Fr	Takács, Kohut
20–08	Poland	W	4–1	Budapest	Fr	Kautzky, Horváth, Fogel, Senkey
19–09	Austria	W	3–2	Vienna	Fr	Holzbauer, Jeszmás, Kohut
14–11	Sweden	W	3–1	Budapest	Fr	Braun, Opata, Kohut
19–12	Spain	L	2–4	Vigo	Fr	Opata, Braun
26–12	Portugal	D	3–3	Oporto	Fr	
10–04–1927	Austria	L	0–6	Vienna	Fr	
10–04	Yugoslavia	W	3–0	Budapest	Fr	Siklóssy, Orth, Szabó P
24–04	Czechoslovakia	L	1–4	Prague	Fr	Mészáros
12–06	France	W	13–1	Budapest	Fr	Takács 6, Kohut 2, Orth 2, Skvarek 2, OG
25–09	Austria	W	5–3	Budapest	DGC	Takács, Kohut, Ströck, Holzbauer, Hirzer
9–10	Czechoslovakia	L	1–2	Budapest	Fr	
25–03–1928	Italy	L	3–4	Rome	DGC	Kohut, Hirzer, Takács
25–03	Yugoslavia	W	2–1	Budapest	Fr	Stofián 2
22–04	Czechoslovakia	W	2–0	Budapest	DGC	Hirzer, Kohut
6–05	Austria	D	5–5	Budapest	Fr	Kohut 3, Hirzer, Ströck
23–09	Czechoslovakia	L	1–6	Prague	Fr	
7–10	Austria	L	1–5	Vienna	DGC	Hirzer
1–11	Switzerland	W	3–1	Budapest	DGC	Turay, Hirzer, Stöck
24–02–1929	France	L	0–3	Paris	Fr	
14–04	Switzerland	W	5–4	Berne	DGC	Takács 2, Toldi, Hirzer, OG
5–05	Austria	D	2–2	Vienna	Fr	Takács 2
8–09	Czechoslovakia	D	1–1	Prague	DGC	Kalmár
6–10	Austria	W	2–1	Budapest	Fr	Takács, Avar
13–04–1930	Switzerland	D	2–2	Basle	Fr	Toldi 2
1–05	Czechoslovakia	D	1–1	Prague	Fr	Hirzer
11–05	Italy	L	0–5	Budapest	DGC	
1–06	Austria	W	2–1	Budapest	Fr	Kohut, Turay
8–06	Holland	W	6–2	Budapest	Fr	Avar 3, Turay 2, Toldi
21–09	Austria	W	3–2	Vienna	Fr	Turay 2, Titkos
28–09	Germany	L	3–5	Dresden	Fr	Takács 3
26–10	Czechoslovakia	D	1–1	Budapest	Fr	Titkos
22–03–1931	Czechoslovakia	D	3–3	Prague	DGC	Avar 3
12–04	Switzerland	W	6–2	Budapest	DGC	Avar 3, Szabó P, Kalmár, Táncos
3–05	Austria	D	0–0	Vienna	DGC	
21–05	Yugoslavia	L	2–3	Belgrade	Fr	Avar 2
20–09	Czechoslovakia	W	3–0	Budapest	Fr	Turay, Avar, Kalmár
4–10	Austria	D	2–2	Budapest	DGC	Szabó P, Spitz
8–11	Sweden	W	3–1	Budapest	Fr	Avar 2, Spitz
13–12	Italy	L	2–3	Turin	DGC	Avar 2
19–02–1932	Egypt	D	0–0	Cairo	Fr	
20–03	Czechoslovakia	W	3–1	Prague	Fr	Turay, Závodi, Toldi
24–04	Austria	L	2–8	Vienna	Fr	Cseh 2
8–05	Italy	D	1–1	Budapest	DGC	Toldi
19–06	Switzerland	L	1–3	Berne	DGC	OG
18–09	Czechoslovakia	W	2–1	Budapest	DGC	Titkos, Toldi
2–10	Austria	L	2–3	Budapest	Fr	Kalmár, Déri
30–10	Germany	W	2–1	Budapest	Fr	Déri, Turay
27–11	Italy	L	2–4	Milan	Fr	Bihámy, Markos
29–01–1933	Portugal	L	0–1	Lisbon	Fr	
5–03	Holland	W	2–1	Amsterdam	Fr	Bihámy, Teleki
19–03	Czechoslovakia	W	2–0	Budapest	Fr	Turay, Cseh
30–04	Austria	D	1–1	Budapest	Fr	Markos
2–07	Sweden	L	2–5	Stockholm	Fr	Toldi, Sárosi G
17–09	Switzerland	W	3–0	Budapest	DGC	Avar 2, OG
1–10	Austria	D	2–2	Vienna	Fr	Avar, Polgár
22–10	Italy	L	0–1	Budapest	DGC	
14–01–1934	Germany	L	1–3	Frankfurt	Fr	Polgár
25–03	Bulgaria	W	4–1	Sofia	WCq	Sárosi G, Toldi, Szabó P, Markos

15–04	Austria	L	2–5	Vienna	Fr	Sárosi G 2
29–04	Bulgaria	W	4–1	Budapest	WCq	Szabó P 2, Solti J 2
29–04	Czechoslovakia	D	2–2	Prague	DGC	Sárosi G 2
10–05	England	W	2–1	Budapest	Fr	Sárosi G, Avar
27–05	Egypt	W	4–2	Naples	WCr1	Toldi 2, Teleki, Vincze J
31–05	Austria	L	1–2	Bologna	WCqf	Sárosi G
7–10	Austria	W	3–1	Budapest	DGC	Sárosi G 2, Toldi
9–12	Italy	L	2–4	Milan	Fr	Sárosi G, Avar
15–12	Rep. Ireland	W	4–2	Dublin	Fr	Avar 2, Vincze J, Markos
14–04–1935	Switzerland	L	2–6	Zurich	DGC	Cseh 2
12–05	Austria	W	6–3	Budapest	Fr	Sárosi G 3, Titkos 2, Toldi
19–05	France	L	0–2	Paris	Fr	
22–09	Czechoslovakia	W	1–0	Budapest	DGC	Markos
6–10	Austria	D	4–4	Vienna	DGC	Vincze J 2, Sárosi G, Toldi
10–11	Switzerland	W	6–1	Budapest	Fr	Sárosi G 2, Vincze J 2, Toldi, Cseh
24–11	Italy	D	2–2	Milan	DGC	Sárosi G 2
15–03–1936	Germany	W	3–2	Budapest	Fr	Titkos, Cseh, Sárosi G
5–04	Austria	W	5–3	Vienna	Fr	Kállai 3, Cseh 2
3–05	Rep. Ireland	D	3–3	Budapest	Fr	Sárosi G 2, Sas
31–05	Italy	L	1–2	Budapest	Fr	Turay
27–09	Austria	W	5–3	Budapest	DGC	Toldi 3, Cseh, Titkos
4–10	Romania	W	2–1	Bucharest	Fr	Lázár, Toldi
18–10	Czechoslovakia	L	2–5	Prague	DGC	Titkos, Toldi
2–12	England	L	2–6	London	Fr	Vincze J, Cseh
6–12	Rep. Ireland	W	3–2	Dublin	Fr	Titkos, Cseh, Toldi
11–04–1937	Switzerland	W	5–1	Basle	DGC	Zsengellér 3, Sárosi G, Dudás
25–04	Italy	L	0–2	Turin	DGC	
9–05	Yugoslavia	D	1–1	Budapest	Fr	Cseh
23–05	Austria	D	2–2	Budapest	Fr	Sas, Cseh
19–09	Czechoslovakia	W	8–3	Budapest	DGC	Sárosi G 7, Zsengellér
10–10	Austria	W	2–1	Vienna	DGC	Sárosi G, Cseh
14–11	Switzerland	W	2–0	Budapest	DGC	Sárosi G, Toldi
9–01–1938	Portugal	L	0–4	Lisbon	Fr	
16–01	Luxembourg	W	6–0	Luxembourg	Fr	Szendrödi 3, Kállai, Zsengellér, Miklósi
20–03	Germany	D	1–1	Nuremburg	Fr	Toldi
25–03	Greece	W	11–1	Budapest	WCq	Zsengellér 5, Nemes 3, Titkos 2, Vincze J
5–06	Dutch E. Indies	W	6–0	Reims	WCr1	Sárosi G 2, Zsengellér 2, Kohut, Toldi
12–06	Switzerland	W	2–0	Lille	WCqf	Sárosi G, Zsengellér
16–06	Sweden	W	5–1	Paris	WCsf	Zsengellér 2, Titkos, Sárosi G, OG
19–06	Italy	L	2–4	Paris	WCf	Titkos, Sárosi G
7–12	Scotland	L	1–3	Glasgow	Fr	Sárosi G
26–02–1939	Holland	L	2–3	Rotterdam	Fr	Zsengellér, Gyetvai
16–03	France	D	2–2	Paris	Fr	Kiszely 2
19–03	Rep. Ireland	D	2–2	Cork	Fr	Zsengellér, Kolláth
2–04	Switzerland	L	1–3	Zurich	Fr	Déri
18–05	Rep. Ireland	D	2–2	Budapest	Fr	Kolláth 2
8–06	Italy	L	1–3	Budapest	Fr	Kiszely
27–08	Poland	L	2–4	Warsaw	Fr	Zsengellér, Adám
24–09	Germany	W	5–1	Budapest	Fr	Zsengellér 3, Kincses, Dudás
22–10	Romania	D	1–1	Bucharest	Fr	Tóth M
12–11	Yugoslavia	W	2–0	Belgrade	Fr	Sárosi G, Tóth M
31–03–1940	Switzerland	W	3–0	Budapest	Fr	Sárosi G 2, Sütö
7–04	Germany	D	2–2	Berlin	Fr	Toldi, Sárosi B
2–05	Croatia	W	1–0	Budapest	Fr	Dudás
19–05	Romania	W	2–0	Budapest	Fr	Sárosi G, Gyetvai
29–09	Yugoslavia	D	0–0	Budapest	Fr	
6–10	Germany	D	2–2	Budapest	Fr	
1–12	Italy	D	1–1	Genoa	Fr	Bodola
8–12	Croatia	D	1–1	Zagreb	Fr	Sárvári
23–03–1941	Yugoslavia	D	1–1	Belgrade	Fr	Gyetvai
6–04	Germany	L	0–7	Cologne	Fr	
16–11	Switzerland	W	2–1	Zurich	Fr	Kovacs I, Olajkár II
3–05–1942	Germany	L	3–5	Budapest	Fr	Nagymarosi, Zsengellér, Tihanyi II
14–06	Croatia	D	1–1	Budapest	Fr	Szusza
1–11	Switzerland	W	3–0	Budapest	Fr	Bodola, Németh, Tóth M
16–05–1943	Switzerland	W	3–1	Geneva	Fr	Bodola 2, Zsengellér
6–06	Bulgaria	W	4–2	Sofia	Fr	Zsengellér 4
12–09	Sweden	W	3–2	Stockholm	Fr	Zsengellér, Sárvári, OG
15–09	Finland	W	3–0	Helsinki	Fr	Tóth M 2, Sárvári

7–11	Sweden	L	2–7	Budapest	Fr	Szusza 2
19–08–1945	Austria	W	2–0	Budapest	Fr	Rudas, Zsengellér
20–08	Austria	W	5–2	Budapest	Fr	Szusza 2, Puskás, Zsengellér, Vincze G
30–09	Romania	W	7–2	Budapest	Fr	Hidgekuti 2, Puskás 2, Zsengellér, Rudas, Nyers
14–04–1946	Austria	L	2–3	Vienna	Fr	Nyers, Zsengellér
6–10	Austria	W	2–0	Budapest	Fr	Deák 2
30–10	Luxembourg	W	7–2	Esch	Fr	Deák 3, Puskás 3, Nagymarosi
4–05–1947	Austria	W	5–2	Budapest	Fr	Szusza 2, Puskás, Egresi, OG
11–05	Italy	L	2–3	Turin	Fr	Szusza, Puskás
29–06	Yugoslavia	W	3–2	Belgrade	BCE	Szilágy, Puskás, Mike
17–08	Bulgaria	W	9–0	Budapest	BCE	Deák 4, Hidegkuti 3, Zsolnai, Nagymarosi
20–08	Albania	W	3–0	Budapest	BCE	Zsolnai, Egresi, Deák
14–09	Austria	L	3–4	Vienna	Fr	Szusza 3
12–10	Romania	W	3–0	Bucharest	BCE	Puskás 2, Egresi
21–04–1948	Switzerland	W	7–4	Budapest	DGC	Puskás 2, Deák 2, Göcze, Egresi, Szusza
2–05	Austria	L	2–3	Vienna	DGC	Szusza, Deák
23–05	Czechoslovakia	W	2–1	Budapest	DGC	Egresi, Deák
23–05	Albania	D	0–0	Tirana	BCE	
6–06	Romania	W	9–0	Budapest	BCE	Egresi 3, Mészáros 2, Puskás 2, Kocsis 2
19–09	Poland	W	6–2	Warsaw	BCE	Hidegkuti 2, Bozsik, Szusza, Deák, Tóth M
3–10	Austria	W	2–1	Budapest	Fr	Deák, Szusza
24–10	Romania	W	5–1	Bucharest	BCE	Puskás 3, Deák 2
7–11	Bulgaria	L	0–1	Sofia	BCE	
10–04–1949	Czechoslovakia	L	2–5	Prague	DGC	Puskás, Szusza
8–05	Austria	W	6–1	Budapest	DGC	Puskás 3, Deák 2, Kocsis
12–06	Italy	D	1–1	Budapest	DGC	Deák
19–06	Sweden	D	2–2	Stockholm	Fr	Budai, Kocsis
10–07	Poland	W	8–2	Debrecen	Fr	Deák 4, Puskás 2, Egresi, Keszthelyi
16–10	Austria	W	4–3	Vienna	Fr	Puskás 2, Deák 2
30–10	Bulgaria	W	5–0	Budapest	Fr	Puskás 2, Deák, Budai, Rudas
20–11	Sweden	W	5–0	Budapest	Fr	Kocsis 3, Puskás, Deák
30–04–1950	Czechoslovakia	W	5–0	Budapest	Fr	Puskás 2, Kocsis 2, Szilágyi
14–05	Austria	L	3–5	Vienna	Fr	Kocsis, Puskás, Szilágyi
4–06	Poland	W	5–2	Warsaw	Fr	Szilágyi 3, Puskás 2
24–09	Albania	W	12–0	Budapest	Fr	Puskás 4, Budai 4, Palotás 2, Kocsis 2
29–10	Austria	W	4–3	Budapest	Fr	Puskás 3, Szilágyi
12–11	Bulgaria	D	1–1	Sofia	Fr	Szilágyi
27–05–1951	Poland	W	6–0	Budapest	Fr	Kocsis 2, Puskás 2, Sándor, Czibor
14–10	Czechoslovakia	W	2–1	Vitkovice	Fr	Kocsis 2
18–11	Finland	W	8–0	Budapest	Fr	Hidegkuti 3, Kocsis 2, Puskás 2, Czibor
15–06–1952	Poland	W	5–1	Warsaw	Fr	Kocsis 2, Puskás 2, Hidegkuti
22–06	Finland	W	6–1	Helsinki	Fr	Kocsis 3, Puskás, Bozsik, Palotás
15–07	Romania	W	2–1	Turku	OGr1	Kocsis, Czibor
21–07	Italy *	W	3–0	Helsinki	OGr2	Palotás 2, Kocsis
24–07	Turkey *	W	7–1	Kotka	OGqf	Kocsis 2, Puskás 2, Palotás, Lantos, Bozsik
28–07	Sweden	W	6–0	Helsinki	OGsf	Kocsis 2, Puskás, Palotás, Hidegkuti, OG
2–08	Yugoslavia	W	2–0	Helsinki	OGf	Puskás, Czibor
20–09	Switzerland	W	4–2	Berne	DGC	Puskás 2, Kocsis, Hidegkuti
19–10	Czechoslovakia	W	5–0	Budapest	Fr	Kocsis 3, Egresi, Hidegkuti
26–04–1953	Austria	D	1–1	Budapest	Fr	Czibor
17–05	Italy	W	3–0	Rome	DGC	Puskás 2, Hidegkuti
5–07	Sweden	W	4–2	Stockholm	Fr	Puskás, Budai, Kocsis, Hidegkuti
4–10	Czechoslovakia	W	5–1	Prague	Fr	Csordás 2, Hidegkuti, Tóth M (II), Puskás
4–10	Bulgaria	D	1–1	Sofia	Fr	Szilágy
11–10	Austria	W	3–2	Vienna	Fr	Hidegkuti 2, Csordás
15–11	Sweden	D	2–2	Budapest	Fr	Palotás, Czibor
25–11	England	W	6–3	London	Fr	Hidegkuti 3, Puskás 2, Bozsik
12–02–1954	Egypt	W	3–0	Cairo	Fr	Puskás 2, Hidegkuti
11–04	Austria	W	1–0	Vienna	Fr	OG
23–05	England	W	7–1	Budapest	Fr	Puskás 2, Kocsis 2, Lantos, Hidegkuti, Tóth J
17–06	South Korea	W	9–0	Zurich	WCr1	Kocsis 3, Puskás 2, Palotás 2, Lantos, Czibor
20–06	West Germany	W	8–3	Basle	WCr1	Kocsis 4, Hidegkuti 2, Puskás, Tóth J
27–06	Brazil	W	4–2	Berne	WCqf	Kocsis 2, Hidegkuti, Lantos
30–06	Uruguay	W	4–2	Lausanne	WCsf	Kocsis 2, Czibor, Hidegkuti
4–07	West Germany	L	2–3	Berne	WCf	Puskás, Czibor
19–09	Romania	W	5–1	Budapest	Fr	Kocsis 2, Hidegkuti 2, Budai

26–09	Soviet Union	D	1–1	Moscow	Fr	Kocsis
10–10	Switzerland	W	3–0	Budapest	Fr	Kocsis 2, Bozsik
24–10	Czechoslovakia	W	4–1	Budapest	Fr	Kocsis 3, Sándor
14–11	Austria	W	4–1	Budapest	Fr	Czibor, Palotás, Kocsis, Sándor
8–12	Scotland	W	4–2	Glasgow	Fr	Bozsik, Hidegkuti, Sándor, Kocsis
24–04–1955	Austria	D	2–2	Vienna	DGC	Fenyvesi, Hidegkuti
8–05	Norway	W	5–0	Oslo	Fr	Palotás 2, Kocsis, Puskás, Tichy
11–05	Sweden	W	7–3	Stockholm	Fr	Kocsis 3, Puskás 2, Szojka, Hidegkuti
15–05	Denmark	W	6–0	Copenhagen	Fr	Sándor 3, Kocsis 2, Palotás
19–05	Finland	W	9–1	Helsinki	Fr	Palotás 3, Csordás 2, Tichy 2, Puskás, Tóth J
29–05	Scotland	W	3–1	Budapest	Fr	Hidegkuti, Kocsis, Fenyvesi
17–09	Switzerland	W	5–4	Lausanne	DGC	Machos 2, Puskás 2, Kocsis
25–09	Soviet Union	D	1–1	Budapest	Fr	Puskás
2–10	Czechoslovakia	W	3–1	Prague	DGC	Kocsis, Czibor, Tichy
16–10	Austria	W	6–1	Budapest	DGC	Czibor 2, Tichy, Kocsis, Tóth J, Puskás
13–11	Sweden	W	4–2	Budapest	Fr	Czibor 2, Tichy, Puskás
27–11	Italy	W	2–0	Budapest	DGC	Puskás, Tóth J
19–02–1956	Turkey	L	1–3	Istanbul	Fr	Puskás
29–04	Yugoslavia	D	2–2	Budapest	DGC	Fenyvesi, Bozsik
20–05	Czechoslovakia	L	2–4	Budapest	DGC	Machos, Bozsik
3–06	Belgium	L	4–5	Brussels	Fr	Kocsis 2, Puskás, Budai
9–06	Portugal	D	2–2	Lisbon	Fr	Kocsis 2
15–07	Poland	W	4–1	Budapest	Fr	Kocsis 2, Szusza, Machos
16–09	Yugoslavia	W	3–1	Belgrade	DGC	Czibor, Kocsis, Puskás
23–09	Soviet Union	W	1–0	Moscow	Fr	Czibor
7–10	France	W	2–1	Paris	Fr	Machos, Kocsis
14–10	Austria	W	2–0	Vienna	Fr	Puskás, Sándor
12–06–1957	Norway	L	1–2	Oslo	WCq	Tichy
16–06	Sweden	D	0–0	Stockholm	Fr	
23–06	Bulgaria	W	4–1	Budapest	WCq	Machos 3, Bozsik
15–09	Bulgaria	W	2–1	Sofia	WCq	Hidegkuti 2
22–09	Soviet Union	L	1–2	Budapest	Fr	Hidegkuti
6–10	France	W	2–0	Budapest	Fr	Aspirány 2
10–11	Norway	W	5–0	Budapest	WCq	Csordás 2, Sándor, Machos, OG
22–12	West Germany	L	0–1	Hanover	Fr	
20–04–1958	Yugoslavia	W	2–0	Budapest	Fr	Sándor, Vasas
7–05	Scotland	D	1–1	Glasgow	Fr	Fenyvesi
8–06	Wales	D	1–1	Sandviken	WCr1	Bozsik
12–06	Sweden	L	1–2	Stockholm	WCr1	Tichy
15–06	Mexico	W	4–0	Sandviken	WCr1	Tichy 2, Sándor, Bencsics
17–06	Wales	L	1–2	Stockholm	WCr1	Tichy
14–09	Poland	W	3–1	Chorzow	Fr	Csordás, Tichy, Budai
28–09	Soviet Union	L	1–3	Moscow	ECr1	Göröcs
5–10	Yugoslavia	D	4–4	Zagreb	Fr	Sándor 3, Tichy
26–10	Romania	W	2–1	Bucharest	Fr	Vasas, Tichy
23–11	Belgium	W	3–1	Budapest	Fr	Tichy 2, Göröcs
19–04–1959	Yugoslavia	W	4–0	Budapest	Fr	Tichy 2, Sándor, Pál
1–05	East Germany	W	1–0	Dresden	Fr	Göröcs
28–06	Sweden	W	3–2	Budapest	Fr	Göröcs 2, Sándor
27–09	Soviet Union	L	0–1	Budapest	ECr1	
11–10	Yugoslavia	W	4–2	Belgrade	Fr	Albert 3, Bundzsák
25–10	Switzerland	W	8–0	Budapest	DGC	Tichy 4, Göröcs, Sándor, Albert
8–11	West Germany	W	4–3	Budapest	Fr	Tichy 2, Albert, Sándor
29–11	Italy	D	1–1	Florence	DGC	Tichy
22–05–1960	England	W	2–0	Budapest	Fr	Albert 2
5–06	Scotland	D	3–3	Budapest	Fr	Sándor, Göröcs, Tichy
27–07	Denmark	L	0–1	Copenhagen	Fr	
9–10	Yugoslavia	D	1–1	Budapest	Fr	Göröcs
30–10	Belgium	L	1–2	Brussels	Fr	Tichy
13–11	Poland	W	4–1	Budapest	Fr	Monostori 2, Göröcs, Sándor
20–11	Austria	W	2–0	Budapest	Fr	Göröcs, Machos
17–02–1961	Egypt	W	2–0	Cairo	Fr	Albert 2
16–04	East Germany	W	2–0	Budapest	WCq	Albert, Göröcs
30–04	Holland	W	3–0	Rotterdam	WCq	Sándor, Fenyvesi, Tichy
7–05	Yugoslavia	W	4–2	Belgrade	Fr	Tichy 2, Albert, OG
28–05	Wales	W	3–2	Budapest	Fr	Tichy 2, Solymosi
11–06	Austria	L	1–2	Budapest	Fr	Göröcs
10–09	East Germany	W	3–2	Berlin	WCq	Solymosi, Sándor, Tichy

8–10	Austria	L	1–2	Vienna	Fr	Tichy
22–10	Holland	D	3–3	Budapest	WCq	Monostori, Göröcs, Tichy
9–12	Chile	L	1–5	Santiago	Fr	Tichy
13–12	Chile	D	0–0	Santiago	Fr	
23–12	Uruguay	D	1–1	Montevideo	Fr	Solymosi
18–04–1962	Uruguay	D	1–1	Budapest	Fr	Bozsik
29–04	Turkey	W	2–1	Budapest	Fr	Solymosi, Göröcs
31–05	England	W	2–1	Rancagua	WCr1	Tichy, Albert
3–06	Bulgaria	W	6–1	Rancagua	WCr1	Albert 3, Tichy 2, Solymosi
6–06	Argentina	D	0–0	Rancagua	WCr1	
10–06	Czechoslovakia	L	0–1	Rancagua	WCqf	
24–06	Austria	W	2–1	Vienna	Fr	Tichy 2
2–09	Poland	W	2–0	Poznan	Fr	Tichy, Göröcs
14–10	Yugoslavia	L	0–1	Budapest	Fr	
28–10	Austria	W	2–0	Budapest	Fr	Göröcs, Sándor
7–11	Wales	W	3–1	Budapest	ECr1	Albert, Tichy, Sándor
11–11	France	W	3–2	Paris	Fr	Tichy 2, Rákosi
20–03–1963	Wales	D	1–1	Cardiff	ECr1	Tichy
5–05	Sweden	L	1–2	Stockholm	Fr	Albert
19–05	Denmark	W	6–0	Budapest	Fr	Göröcs, Fenyvesi, Monostori, Albert, Rákosi, Solymosi
2–06	Czechoslovakia	D	2–2	Prague	Fr	Tichy, Machos
22–09	Soviet Union	D	1–1	Moscow	Fr	Machos
6–10	Yugoslavia	L	0–2	Belgrade	Fr	
19–10	East Germany	W	2–1	Berlin	ECr2	Bene, Rákosi
27–10	Austria	W	2–1	Budapest	Fr	Albert, Sándor
3–11	East Germany	D	3–3	Budapest	ECr2	Bene, Sándor, Solymosi
25–04–1964	France	W	3–1	Paris	ECqf	Tichy 2, Albert
3–05	Austria	L	0–1	Vienna	Fr	
23–05	France	W	2–1	Budapest	ECqf	Sipos, Bene
17–06	Spain	L	1–2	Madrid	ECsf	Bene
20–06	Denmark	W	3–1	Barcelona	EC3p	Novák 2, Bene
4–10	Switzerland	W	2–0	Berne	Fr	Albert 2
11–10	Czechoslovakia	D	2–2	Budapest	Fr	Albert 2
25–10	Yugoslavia	W	2–1	Budapest	Fr	Albert 2
5–05–1965	England	L	0–1	London	Fr	
23–05	East Germany	D	1–1	Leipzig	WCq	Bene
13–06	Austria	W	1–0	Vienna	WCq	Fenyvesi
27–06	Italy	W	2–1	Budapest	Fr	Albert, Bene
5–09	Austria	W	3–0	Budapest	WCq	Farkas, Fenyvesi, Mészöly
9–10	East Germany	W	3–2	Budapest	WCq	Rákosi, Novák, Farkas
3–05–1966	Poland	D	1–1	Chorzow	Fr	Bene
8–05	Yugoslavia	L	0–2	Zagreb	Fr	
5–06	Switzerland	W	3–1	Budapest	Fr	Bene 2, Farkas
13–07	Portugal	L	1–3	Manchester	WCr1	Bene
15–07	Brazil	W	3–1	Liverpool	WCr1	Bene, Farkas, Mészöly
20–07	Bulgaria	W	3–1	Manchester	WCr1	Meszoly, Bene, OG
23–07	Soviet Union	L	1–2	Sunderland	WCqf	Bene
7–09	Holland	D	2–2	Rotterdan	ECq	Molnár D, Mészöly
21–09	Denmark	W	6–0	Budapest	ECq	Albert 2, Mészöly, Bene, Farkas, Varga Z
28–09	France	W	4–2	Budapest	Fr	Farkas 4
30–10	Austria	W	3–1	Budapest	Fr	Farkas 3
23–04–1967	Yugoslavia	W	1–0	Budapest	Fr	Bene
10–05	Holland	W	2–1	Budapest	ECq	Mészöly, Farkas
24–05	Denmark	W	2–0	Copenhagen	ECq	Albert, Bene
6–09	Austria	W	3–1	Vienna	Fr	Bene, Farkas, Varga Z
27–09	East Germany	W	3–1	Budapest	ECq	Farkas 3
29–10	East Germany	L	0–1	Leipzig	ECq	
4–05–1968	Soviet Union	W	2–0	Budapest	ECqf	Farkas, Göröcs
11–05	Soviet Union	L	0–3	Moscow	ECqf	
25–05–1969	Czechoslovakia	W	2–0	Budapest	WCq	Dunai, Albert
8–06	Rep. Ireland	W	2–1	Dublin	WCq	Dunai, Bene
15–06	Denmark	L	2–3	Copenhagen	WCq	Bene, Farkas
14–09	Czechoslovakia	D	3–3	Prague	WCq	Bene, Dunai, Fazekas
24–09	Sweden	L	0–2	Stockholm	Fr	
22–10	Denmark	W	3–0	Budapest	WCq	Bene 2, Szücs
5–11	Rep. Ireland	W	4–0	Budapest	WCq	Halmosi, Bene, Puskás L, Kocsis L
3–12	Czechoslovakia	L	1–4	Marseille	WCq	Kocsis L
12–04–1970	Yugoslavia	D	2–2	Belgrade	Fr	Fazekas, Bene

2–05	Poland	W	2–0	Budapest	Fr	Fazekas, Karsai
16–05	Sweden	L	1–2	Budapest	Fr	Fazekas
9–09	West Germany	L	1–3	Nuremberg	Fr	Fazekas
27–09	Austria	D	1–1	Budapest	Fr	Vidáts
7–10	Norway	W	3–1	Oslo	ECq	Bene, Nagy L, OG
15–11	Switzerland	W	1–0	Basle	Fr	Fazekas
4–04–1971	Austria	W	2–0	Vienna	Fr	Bene
24–04	France	D	1–1	Budapest	ECq	Kocsis L
19–05	Bulgaria	L	0–3	Sofia	ECq	
21–07	Brazil	D	0–0	Rio de Janeiro	Fr	
1–09	Yugoslavia	W	2–1	Budapest	Fr	Szöke, OG
25–09	Bulgaria	W	2–0	Budapest	ECq	Juhász P, Vidáts
9–10	France	W	2–0	Paris	ECq	Bene, Zámbó
27–10	Norway	W	4–0	Budapest	ECq	Bene 2, Dunai, Szücs
14–11	Malta	W	2–0	Gzira	WCq	Bene 2
12–01–1972	Spain	L	0–1	Madrid	Fr	
29–03	West Germany	L	0–2	Budapest	Fr	
29–04	Romania	D	1–1	Budapest	ECqf	Branikovits
6–05	Malta	W	3–0	Budapest	WCq	Kocsis L, Bene, Juhász I
14–05	Romania	D	2–2	Bucharest	ECqf	Szöke, Kocsis L
17–05	Romania	W	2–1	Belgrade	ECqf	Kocsis L, Szöke
25–05	Sweden	D	0–0	Stockholm	WCq	
14–06	Soviet Union	L	0–1	Brussels	ECsf	
17–06	Belgium	L	1–2	Liege	EC3p	Kü
15–10	Austria	D	2–2	Vienna	WCq	Dunai, Kocsis L
29–04–1973	Austria	D	2–2	Budapest	WCq	Zámbó, Bálint
16–05	East Germany	L	1–2	Karl–Marx Stadt	Fr	OG
13–06	Sweden	D	3–3	Budapest	WCq	Kozma, Vidáts, Zámbó
26–09	Yugoslavia	D	1–1	Belgrade	Fr	Bene
13–10	Denmark	D	2–2	Copenhagen	Fr	Fazekas 2
21–11	East Germany	L	0–1	Budapest	Fr	
31–03–1974	Bulgaria	W	3–1	Zalaegerszeg	Fr	Fazekas 2, Bene
17–04	West Germany	L	0–5	Dortmund	Fr	
29–05	Yugoslavia	W	3–0	Szekesfehervar	Fr	Máté 2, Fazekas
28–09	Austria	L	0–1	Vienna	Fr	
13–10	Luxembourg	W	4–2	Luxembourg	ECq	Nagy L 2, Horváth, Bálint
30–10	Wales	L	0–2	Cardiff	ECq	
10–11	Bulgaria	D	0–0	Varna	Fr	
4–12	Switzerland	W	1–0	Szolnok	Fr	Fazekas
26–03–1975	France	L	0–2	Paris	Fr	
2–04	Austria	D	0–0	Vienna	ECq	
16–04	Wales	L	1–2	Budapest	ECq	Branikovits
10–08	Iran	W	2–1	Tehran	Fr	Váradi, Nagy L
24–09	Austria	W	2–1	Budapest	ECq	Nyilasi, Pusztai
8–10	Poland	L	2–4	Lodz	Fr	Nagy L, Pusztai
15–10	Czechoslovakia	D	1–1	Bratislava	Fr	Váradi
19–10	Luxembourg	W	8–1	Szombathely	ECq	Nyilasi 5, Pintér, Wollek, Váradi
27–03–1976	Argentina	W	2–0	Budapest	Fr	Nyilasi, Fazekas
17–04	Yugoslavia	D	0–0	Banja Luka	Fr	
30–04	Switzerland	W	1–0	Lausanne	Fr	Fazekas
22–05	France	W	1–0	Budapest	Fr	Fekete
26–05	Soviet Union	D	1–1	Budapest	Fr	Fekete
12–06	Austria	W	2–0	Budapest	Fr	Magyar, Váradi
8–09	Sweden	D	1–1	Stockholm	Fr	Ebedli
22–09	East Germany	D	1–1	Berlin	Fr	Fazekas
9–10	Greece	D	1–1	Athens	WCq	Kereki
13–10	Austria	W	4–2	Vienna	Fr	Nyilasi 2, Kereki 2
9–02–1977	Peru	L	2–3	Lima	Fr	Töröcsik, Kereki
22–02	Mexico	D	1–1	Mexico City	Fr	Töröcsik
27–02	Argentina	L	1–5	Buenos Aires	Fr	Zombori
15–03	Iran	W	2–0	Tehran	Fr	Fazekas, Nyilasi
27–03	Spain	D	1–1	Alicante	Fr	Pusztai
13–04	Poland	W	2–1	Budapest	Fr	Nyilasi 2
20–04	Czechoslovakia	W	2–0	Budapest	Fr	Váradi, Kovács I
30–04	Soviet Union	W	2–1	Budapest	WCq	Nyilasi, Kereki
18–05	Soviet Union	L	0–2	Tbilisi	WCq	
28–05	Greece	W	3–0	Budapest	WCq	Pusztai, Nyilasi, Fazekas
5–10	Yugoslavia	W	4–3	Budapest	Fr	Töröcsik 2, Váradi, Kereki

12–10	Sweden	W	3–0	Budapest	Fr	Nyilasi, Váradi, Töröcsik
29–10	Bolivia	W	6–0	Budapest	WCq	Nyilasi, Töröcsik, Zombori, Váradi, Pintér, Nagy L
9–11	Czechoslovakia	D	1–1	Prague	Fr	Halász
30–11	Bolivia	W	3–2	La Paz	WCq	Töröcsik, Halász, OG
15–04–1978	Czechoslovakia	W	2–1	Budapest	Fr	Nyilasi, OG
24–05	England	L	1–4	London	Fr	Nagy L
2–06	Argentina	L	1–2	Buenos Aires	WCr1	Csapó
6–06	Italy	L	1–3	Mar del Plata	WCr1	Tóth A
10–06	France	L	1–3	Mar del Plata	WCr1	Zombori
20–09	Finland	L	1–2	Helsinki	ECq	Tieber
11–10	Soviet Union	W	2–0	Budapest	ECq	Váradi, Szokolai
29–10	Greece	L	1–4	Salonika	ECq	Váradi
15–11	West Germany	D	0–0	Frankfurt	Fr	Abandoned after 60 Mins
28–03–1979	East Germany	W	3–0	Budapest	Fr	Töröcsik, Tieber, Tatar
4–04	Poland	D	1–1	Chorzow	Fr	Tatár
2–05	Greece	D	0–0	Budapest	ECq	
19–05	Soviet Union	D	2–2	Tbilisi	ECq	Tatár, Pusztai
12–09	Czechoslovakia	W	2–1	Nyiregyhaza	Fr	Tatár, Kuti
26–09	Austria	L	1–3	Vienna	Fr	Fekete
17–10	Finland	W	3–1	Debrecen	ECq	Fekete 2, Tatár
26–10	United States	L	0–2	Budapest	Fr	
26–03–1980	Poland	W	2–1	Budapest	Fr	Fazekas, Töröcsik
30–04	Czechoslovakia	L	0–1	Kosice	Fr	
31–05	Scotland	W	3–1	Budapest	Fr	Töröcsik 2, Kereki
4–06	Austria	D	1–1	Budapest	Fr	Kiss L
20–08	Sweden	W	2–0	Budapest	Fr	Burcsa, OG
27–08	Soviet Union	L	1–4	Budapest	Fr	Pásztor
24–09	Spain	D	2–2	Budapest	Fr	Kiss L, Bodonyi
8–10	Austria	L	1–3	Vienna	Fr	Bodonyi
19–11	East Germany	L	0–2	Halle	Fr	
15–04–1981	Spain	W	3–0	Valencia	Fr	Kiss L, Bodonyi, Nyilasi
28–04	Switzerland	D	2–2	Lucerne	WCq	Bálint, Müller
13–05	Romania	W	1–0	Budapest	WCq	Fazekas
20–05	Norway	W	2–1	Oslo	WCq	Kiss L 2
6–06	England	L	1–3	Budapest	WCq	Garaba
23–09	Romania	D	0–0	Bucharest	WCq	
14–10	Switzerland	W	3–0	Budapest	WCq	Nyilasi 2, Fazekas
31–10	Norway	W	4–1	Budapest	WCq	Kiss L 2, Bálint, Fazekas
18–11	England	L	0–1	London	WCq	
11–02–1982	New Zealand	W	2–1	Auckland	Fr	Izsó, Bodonyi
14–02	New Zealand	W	2–1	Christchurch	Fr	Pölöskei, Izsó
24–03	Austria	L	2–3	Budapest	Fr	Váradi, Nyilasi
18–04	Peru	L	1–2	Budapest	Fr	Szentes
15–06	El Salvador	W	10–1	Elche	WCr1	Kiss L 3, Fazekas 2, Nyilasi 2, Tóth J, Szentes, Pölöskei
18–06	Argentina	L	1–4	Alicante	WCr1	Pölöskei
22–06	Belgium	D	1–1	Elche	WCr1	Varga J
22–09	Turkey	W	5–0	Gyor	Fr	Garaba, Burcsa, Budavári, Kiss S, Póczik
6–10	France	L	0–1	Paris	Fr	
27–03–1983	Luxembourg	W	6–2	Luxembourg	ECq	Póczik 3, Nyilasi, Pölöskei, Hannich
13–04	Portugal	D	0–0	Coimbra	Fr	
17–04	Luxembourg	W	6–2	Budapest	ECq	Nyilasi 2, Hajszán, Kiss L, Szentes, Burcsa
27–04	England	L	0–2	London	ECq	
15–05	Greece	L	2–3	Budapest	ECq	Nyilasi, Hajszán
1–06	Denmark	L	1–3	Copenhagen	ECq	Nyilasi
7–09	West Germany	D	1–1	Budapest	Fr	Nyilasi

LEADING INTERNATIONAL APPEARANCES

1	Bozsik	100		Bene	76		Hidegkuti	68
2	Fazekas	92		Bálint	76	18	Göröcs	62
3	Grosics	86	11	Sándor	75	19	Sárosi G	61
4	Puskás	84		Albert	75		Mészöly K	61
5	Garaba	82	13	Tichy	71	21	Tóth.J	56
6	Mátrai	80	14	Nyilasi	70	22	Sallai	55
7	Sipos	77	15	Schlosser	68	23	Biró	53
8	Fenyvesi	76		Kocsis	68		Kiprich	53

LEADING INTERNATIONAL GOALSCORERS

1	Puskás	83	7	Bene	36	13	Takács II	26
2	Kocsis	75	8	Zsengellér	32	14	Toldi	25
3	Schlosser	58		Nyilasi	32	15	Avar	24
4	Tichy	49	10	Albert	31		Fazekas	24
5	Sárosi G	42	11	Deák	29	17	Kiprich	23
6	Hidegkuti	39	12	Sándor	27	18	Pataki	20

12–10	England	L	0–3	Budapest	ECq	
26–10	Denmark	W	1–0	Budapest	ECq	Kiss S
3–12	Greece	D	2–2	Salonika	ECq	Kardos J, Töröcsik
18–01–1984	Spain	W	1–0	Cadiz	Fr	Garaba
31–03	Yugoslavia	L	1–2	Subotica	Fr	Gyimesi
4–04	Turkey	W	6–0	Istanbul	Fr	Mészáros 2, Esterházy 2, Kardos J, Bodonyi
23–05	Norway	D	0–0	Szekesfehervar	Fr	
31–05	Spain	D	1–1	Budapest	Fr	Nagy A
6–06	Belgium	D	2–2	Brussels	Fr	Hajszán, Nyilasi
22–08	Switzerland	W	3–0	Budapest	Fr	Esterházy 2, Bodonyi
25–08	Mexico	L	0–2	Budapest	Fr	
26–09	Austria	W	3–1	Budapest	WCq	Nagy A, Esterházy, Kardos J
17–10	Holland	W	2–1	Rotterdam	WCq	Détári, Esterházy
17–11	Cyprus	W	2–1	Limassol	WCq	Róth, Nyilasi
29–01–1985	West Germany	W	1–0	Hamburg	Fr	Péter
3–04	Cyprus	W	2–0	Budapest	WCq	Nyilasi, Szokolai
17–04	Austria	W	3–0	Vienna	WCq	Kiprich 2, Détári
14–05	Holland	L	0–1	Budapest	WCq	
16–10	Wales	W	3–0	Cardiff	Fr	Esterházy, Hajszan, Détári
8–12	South Korea	W	1–0	Irapuato	Fr	Kiprich
11–12	Algeria	W	3–1	Monterrey	Fr	Zoltan, Kovács K, Détári
14–12	Mexico	L	0–2	Mexico City	Fr	
2–02–1986	Qatar	W	3–0	Doha	Fr	Hannich, Kiprich, Détári
16–03	Brazil	W	3–0	Budapest	Fr	Détári, Kovács K, Esterházy
2–06	Soviet Union	L	0–6	Irapuato	WCr1	
6–06	Canada	W	2–0	Irapuato	WCr1	Esterházy, Détári
9–06	France	L	0–3	Leon	WCr1	
9–09	Norway	D	0–0	Oslo	Fr	
15–10	Holland	L	0–1	Budapest	ECq	
12–11	Greece	L	1–2	Athens	ECq	Boda
8–02–1987	Cyprus	W	1–0	Nicosia	ECq	Boda
29–04	Holland	L	0–2	Rotterdam	ECq	
17–05	Poland	W	5–3	Budapest	ECq	Détári 2, Vincze I, Péter, Preszeller
28–07	East Germany	D	0–0	Leipzig	Fr	
9–09	Scotland	L	0–2	Glasgow	Fr	
23–09	Poland	L	2–3	Warsaw	ECq	Bognár, Mészáros
14–10	Greece	W	3–0	Budapest	ECq	Détári, Bognár, Mészáros
18–11	West Germany	D	0–0	Budapest	Fr	
2–12	Cyprus	W	1–0	Budapest	ECq	Kiprich
16–03–1988	Turkey	W	1–0	Budapest	Fr	Kiprich
26–03	Belgium	L	0–3	Brussels	Fr	
27–04	England	D	0–0	Budapest	Fr	
4–05	Iceland	W	3–0	Budapest	Fr	Vincze I, Sallai, Kovács K
10–05	Denmark	D	2–2	Budapest	Fr	Kiprich, Bognár
17–05	Austria	L	0–4	Budapest	Fr	
31–08	Austria	D	0–0	Linz	Fr	
21–09	Iceland	W	3–0	Reykjavik	Fr	Kiprich 2, Vincze I
19–10	Nth. Ireland	W	1–0	Budapest	WCq	Vincze I
15–11	Greece	L	0–3	Athens	Fr	
11–12	Malta	D	2–2	Ta'Qali	WCq	Vincze I, Kiprich
8–03–1989	Rep. Ireland	D	0–0	Budapest	WCq	
4–04	Switzerland	W	3–0	Budapest	Fr	Détári, Kovács E, Bognár
12–04	Malta	D	1–1	Budapest	WCq	Boda
26–04	Italy	L	0–4	Taranto	Fr	
4–06	Rep. Ireland	L	0–2	Dublin	WCq	
6–09	Nth. Ireland	W	2–1	Belfast	WCq	Kovács K, Bognár
11–10	Spain	D	2–2	Budapest	WCq	Pinter 2
25–10	Greece	D	1–1	Budapest	Fr	Szekeres

15–11	Spain	L	0–4	Seville	WCq	
20–03–1990	United States	W	2–0	Budapest	Fr	Petres, Limperger
28–03	France	L	1–3	Budapest	Fr	Pinter
11–04	Austria	L	0–3	Salzburg	Fr	
28–05	Arab Emirates	W	3–0	Nimes	Fr	Kovács K 3
2–06	Colombia	W	3–1	Budapest	Fr	Kovács K 2, Bognár
5–09	Turkey	W	4–1	Budapest	Fr	Kovács K, Kozma, Kiprich 2
12–09	England	L	0–1	London	Fr	
10–10	Norway	D	0–0	Bergen	ECq	
17–10	Italy	D	1–1	Budapest	ECq	Disztl
31–10	Cyprus	W	4–2	Budapest	ECq	Lorincz, OG, Kiprich 2
19–02–1991	Argentina	L	0–2	Rosario	Fr	
27–03	Spain	W	4–2	Santander	Fr	Kiprich 2, Lórincz 2
3–04	Cyprus	W	2–0	Limassol	ECq	Szalma, Kiprich
17–04	Soviet Union	L	0–1	Budapest	ECq	
1–05	Italy	L	1–3	Salerno	ECq	Bognár
11–09	Rep. Ireland	L	1–2	Gyor	Fr	Kovacs K
25–09	Soviet Union	D	2–2	Moscow	ECq	Kiprich 2
9–10	Belgium	L	0–2	Szekesfehervar	Fr	
30–10	Norway	D	0–0	Szombathely	Fr	
5–12	Mexico	L	0–3	Leon	Fr	
8–12	El Salvador	D	1–1	San Salvador	Fr	Hamori
25–03–1992	Austria	W	2–1	Budapest	Fr	Kiprich, Kovacs K
29–04	Ukraine	W	3–1	Uzgorod	Fr	Sallai, Kiprich 2
12–05	England	L	0–1	Budapest	Fr	
27–05	Sweden	L	1–2	Stockholm	Fr	Marton
3–06	Iceland	L	1–2	Budapest	WCq	Kiprich

ICELAND

A small population in a remote island that is closer to Greenland than to mainland Europe would seem to be a poor recipe for football. Added to this is the fact that football can only be played in the summer months, given that in winter it is either too cold or too dark to contemplate playing.

For years this stereotype did hold true, but in recent years Iceland has emerged, if not as a football power, then as a nation capable of causing an upset, not at club level, but against the very best national selections Europe has to offer.

League football does, however, predate the formation of the national side by some 34 years, though it has never been of a very high standard. Reykjavik, dominating the island as it does, provided all of the winners until IA Akranes broke the stranglehold in 1951, and since then teams from the smaller towns have always fared quite reasonably. Football is a very popular game and crowds of over 2000 are not uncommon for league games, though the average is nearer 500.

For international matches it is not uncommon to see the Laugardalsvöllur full to capacity, and in recent years they have been treated to some excellent games. The national side first made an appearance in a match against Denmark in 1946, but for the next quarter of a century matches were not that regular. The 1958 World Cup and 1964 European Championship were both entered, but it was not until the 1970s that Iceland regularly took part in these two competitions.

Results were not impressive at first, but as experience was gained results began to improve. East Germany, Wales, Northern Ireland, Norway, Austria, Turkey and most recently Spain have all been beaten in Reykjavik. Some very good players have played for the national side, and most are eager to join clubs on the continent or in England and Scotland. Internationals who have followed the latter path include Siggi Jonsson of Arsenal and Gudni Bergsson of Spurs, whilst Arnor Gudjohnsen and Asgeir Sigurvinsson have known success with Anderlecht and Stuttgart respectively, both appearing in the finals of European club competitions with their clubs.

They may not ever qualify for a major tournament, but more and more, Iceland are affecting the outcome of the qualifying groups. As Spain found to their cost in the 1992 European Championships, they are no longer the pushovers they were once seen to be. More than anything else, though, Iceland serves as a model for countries like Malta, Luxembourg and Cyprus on how the future of their game could be.

	All			League			Cup		Europe		
Team	G	S	B	G	S	B	G	S	G	S	B
1 KR Reykjavík	27	24	12	20	21	12	7	3	–	–	–
2 Valur Reykjavík	26	19	17	19	16	17	7	3	–	–	–
3 Fram Reykjavík	25	23	15	18	17	15	7	6	–	–	–
4 IA Akranes	17	19	8	12	11	8	5	8	–	–	–
5 Víkingur Reykjavík	6	8	8	5	7	8	1	1	–	–	–
6 IBK Keflavík	5	6	5	4	2	5	1	4	–	–	–
7 IBV Vestmannaeyjar	4	6	6	1	3	6	3	3	–	–	–
8 IBA Akureyri	1	–	4	–	–	4	1	–	–	–	–
9 KA Akureyri	1	–	–	1	–	–	–	–	–	–	–
10 FH Hafnarfjördhur	–	3	–	–	1	–	–	2	–	–	–
11 UBK Kópavogur	–	1	1	–	–	1	–	1	–	–	–
12 Vídir Gardur	–	1	–	–	–	–	–	1	–	–	–
13 Thór Akureyri	–	–	1	–	–	1	–	–	–	–	–

Correct to the end of the 1991 season

Population: 256 000
Area, sq km: 103 000
% in urban areas: 90.5%
Capital city: Reykjavík

Knattspyrnusamband Island
PO Box 8511
IS-104 Reykjavík
Iceland
Tel: (010 354) 1 84444
Fax: (010 354) 1 689793
Telex: 2314 ISI IS
Cable: KSI REYKJAVIK
Languages for correspondence: English & German

Year of formation: 1947
Affiliation to FIFA: 1929
Affiliation to UEFA: 1954
Registered clubs: 110
Registered players: 20 400
Registered coaches: 120
Registered referees: 524
National stadium: Laugardalsvöllur, Reykjavik 14 000
National colours: Shirts: Blue/Shorts: White/Socks: Blue
Reserve colours: Shirts: White/Shorts: Blue/Socks: White
Season: April–October

THE RECORD

WORLD CUP

1930–54 ..... Did not enter
1958 .... QT 3rd/3 in group 2
1962–70 ..... Did not enter
1974 .... QT 4th/4 in group 3
1978 .... QT 4th/4 in group 4
1982 .... QT 4th/5 in group 3
1986 .... QT 4th/4 in group 7
1990 .... QT 5th/5 in group 3

EUROPEAN CHAMPIONSHIP

1960 .... Did not enter
1964 .... 1st round
1968 .... Did not enter
1972 .... Did not enter
1976 .... QT 4th/4 in group 7
1980 .... QT 5th/5 in group 4
1984 .... QT 4th/5 in group 7
1988 .... QT 4th/5 in group 3
1992 .... QT 4th/5 in group 1

OLYMPIC GAMES

1908–56 ..... Did not enter
1960 .... QT Failed to qualify
1964 .... QT Failed to qualify
1968 .... QT Failed to qualify
1972 .... QT Failed to qualify
1976 .... QT Failed to qualify
1980 .... Did not enter
1984 .... Did not enter
1988 .... QT Failed to qualify
1992 .... QT Failed to qualify

EUROPEAN CLUB COMPETITIONS

EUROPEAN CUP: 2nd round – Valur 1968, IA Akranes 1976

CUP WINNERS CUP: 2nd round – Fram 1986 1991

UEFA Cup: 2nd round – IBV Vestmannaeyjar 1979, IBK Keflavik 1980

CLUB DIRECTORY

REYKJAVIK (Population – 137 000)

Knattspyrnufélagid Fram
Stadium: Laugardalsvöllur 14 000
Founded: 1908
Colours: Blue/White

Fylkir
Stadium: Fylkisvöllur
Founded: 1967
Colours: Red/Black

Idróttafélag Reykjavikur (IR)
Stadium: IR–völlur
Founded: 1907
Colours: White/Blue

Knattspyrnufélag Reykjavikur (KR)
Stadium: KR–völlur 2000
Founded: 1899
Colours: Black and white stripes/Black

Thróttur
Stadium: Thróttur–völlur
Founded: 1949
Colours: Red and white stripes/White

Knattspyrnufélagid Valur
Stadium: Hlidarendi 3000
Founded: 1911
Colours: Red/White

Knattspyrnufélagid Víkingur
Stadium: Víkingsvöllur 2000
Founded: 1908
Colours: Red and black stripes/White

KOPAVOGUR (Population – 15 000)
Ungmennafélagid Breidablik Kópavogur (UBK)
Stadium: Idróttsvöllur
Founded: 1950
Colours: Green/White

AKUREYRI (Population – 14 000)

Knattspyrnufélag Akureyri (KA)
Stadium: Akureyrivöllur 4000
Founded: 1974
Colours: Yellow/Blue
Previous name: IBA Akureyri until 1974

Idrottafélagid Thór
Stadium: Akureyrivöllur 4000
Founded: 1974
Colours: White/Red
Previous name: IBA Akureyri until 1974

HAFNARFJÖRDUR (Population – 14 000)

Fimleikafélag Hafnarfjördur (FH)
Stadium: FH–völlur 3000
Founded: 1929
Colours: White/Black
Previous name: IBH Hafnarfjördur until 1961

Hauker
Stadium: Idróttsvöllur
Founded: 1961
Colours: Red/White
Previous name: IBH Hafnarfjördur until 1961

KEFLAVIK (Population – 13 000)
Idrótta Bandelag Keflavíkur (IBK)
Stadium: Keflavíkurvöllur 5000
Founded: 1946
Colours: Yellow/Blue

VESTMANNAEYJAR
Idrótta Bandelag Vestmannaeyjar (IBV)
Stadium: Hásteinvöllur 1000
Founded: 1946
Colours: White/White

AKRANES
Idróttabandalag Akranes (IA)
Stadium: Akranesvöllur 3000
Founded: 1946
Colours: Yellow/Black

OLAFSFJÖRDUR
Idróttafélagig Leiftur
Stadium: Idróttsvöllur 1000
Founded: 1931
Colours: Yellow/Green

GARDUR
Knattspyrnufélagid Vídir
Stadium: Gardurvöllur 1000
Founded: 1936
Colours: Blue/White

HUSAVIK
Idróttafélagid Völsungur
Stadium: Idróttsvöllur 2000
Founded: 1927
Colours: Green and white halves/Green

GARDABÆR
Ungemennafélagid Stjarnan
Stadium: Stjarnanvöllur 2000
Founded: 1960
Colours: Blue/White

ICELANDIC LEAGUE CHAMPIONSHIP

Year	Champions		Runners up		3rd	
1912	KR Reykjavik	3	Fram Reykjavík	3	IBV Vestmannaeyjar	0
1913	Fram Reykjavík declared winners					
1914	Fram Reykjavík declared winners					
1915	Fram Reykjavík	4	KR Reykjavík	2	Valur Reykjavík	0
1916	Fram Reykjavík	3	KR Reykjavík	3	Valur Reykjavík	0
1917	Fram Reykjavík	4	KR Reykjavík	2	Valur Reykjavík	0
1918	Fram Reykjavík	6	Víkingur Reykjavík	4	Valur Reykjavík	2
1919	KR Reykjavík	5	Fram Reykjavík	4	Víkingur Reykjavík	3
1920	Víkingur Reykjavík	4	KR Reykjavík	2	Fram Reykjavík	0
1921	Fram Reykjavík	4	Víkingur Reykjavík	2	KR Reykjavík	0
1922	Fram Reykjavík	4	Víkingur Reykjavík	1	KR Reykjavík	1
1923	Fram Reykjavík	6	KR Reykjavík	4	Valur Reykjavík	1
1924	Víkingur Reykjavík	6	Fram Reykjavík	4	KR Reykjavík	1
1925	Fram Reykjavík	5	Víkingur Reykjavík	4	KR Reykjavík	3
1926	KR Reykjavík	7	Fram Reykjavík	7	Víkingur Reykjavík	4
1927	KR Reykjavík	6	Valur Reykjavík	4	Víkingur Reykjavík	2
1928	KR Reykjavík	4	Valur Reykjavík	2	Fram Reykjavík	0
1929	KR Reykjavík	8	Valur Reykjavík	4	IBV Vestmannaeyjar	4
1930	Valur Reykjavík	8	KR Reykjavík	6	IBV Vestmannaeyjar	4
1931	KR Reykjavík	6	Valur Reykjavík	4	Víkingur Reykjavík	2
1932	KR Reykjavík	7	Valur Reykjavík	5	IBA Akureyri	4
1933	Valur Reykjavík	6	KR Reykjavík	4	Fram Reykjavík	2
1934	KR Reykjavík	7	Valur Reykjavík	6	Fram Reykjavík	5
1935	Valur Reykjavík	5	KR Reykjavík	4	Fram Reykjavík	3
1936	Valur Reykjavík	5	KR Reykjavík	4	Fram Reykjavík	3
1937	Valur Reykjavík	4	KR Reykjavík	2	Fram Reykjavík	0
1938	Valur Reykjavík	5	Víkingur Reykjavík	3	Fram Reykjavík	2
1939	Fram Reykjavík	4	KR Reykjavík	3	Víkingur Reykjavík	3
1940	Valur Reykjavík	5	Víkingur Reykjavík	4	KR Reykjavík	2
1941	KR Reykjavík	7	Valur Reykjavík	6	Víkingur Reykjavík	3
1942	Valur Reykjavík	6	Fram Reykjavík	6	KR Reykjavík	4
1943	Valur Reykjavík	8	KR Reykjavík	4	Fram Reykjavík	4
1944	Valur Reykjavík	5	KR Reykjavík	4	Víkingur Reykjavík	2
1945	Valur Reykjavík	6	KR Reykjavík	4	Fram Reykjavík	1
1946	Fram Reykjavík	9	KR Reykjavík	8	Valur Reykjavík	7
1947	Fram Reykjavík	7	Valur Reykjavík	6	KR Reykjavík	5
1948	KR Reykjavík	5	Víkingur Reykjavík	4	Valur Reykjavík	2
1949	KR Reykjavík	5	Fram Reykjavík	5	Valur Reykjavík	4
1950	KR Reykjavík	6	Fram Reykjavík	5	IA Akranes	3
1951	IA Akranes	6	Valur Reykjavík	4	KR Reykjavík	4
1952	KR Reykjavík	7	IA Akranes	6	Fram Reykjavík	4
1953	IA Akranes	3–2	Valur Reykjavík			
1954	IA Akranes	9	KR Reykjavík	8	Fram Reykjavík	5
1955	KR Reykjavík	9	IA Akranes	8	Valur Reykjavík	6
1956	Valur Reykjavík	9	KR Reykjavík	8	IA Akranes	7
1957	IA Akranes	10	Fram Reykjavík	7	Valur Reykjavík	6
1958	IA Akranes	9	KR Reykjavík	8	Valur Reykjavík	6
1959	KR Reykjavík	20	IA Akranes	11	Valur Reykjavík	11
1960	IA Akranes	15	KR Reykjavík	13	Fram Reykjavík	11
1961	KR Reykjavík	17	IA Akranes	15	Valur Reykjavík	12
1962	Fram Reykjavík	13	Valur Reykjavík	13	IA Akranes	12
1963	KR Reykjavík	15	IA Akranes	13	Valur Reykjavík	10
1964	IBK Keflavík	15	IA Akranes	12	KR Reykjavík	10
1965	KR Reykjavík	13	IA Akranes	13	IBK Keflavík	11
1966	Valur Reykjavík	14	IBK Keflavík	14	IBA Akureyri	12
1967	Valur Reykjavík	14	Fram Reykjavík	14	IBA Akureyri	13
1968	KR Reykjavík	15	Fram Reykjavík	12	IBA Akureyri	10
1969	IBK Keflavík	15	IA Akranes	14	KR Reykjavík	12
1970	IA Akranes	20	Fram Reykjavík	16	IBK Keflavík	16
1971	IBK Keflavík	20	IBV Vestmannaeyjar	20	Fram Reykjavík	15
1972	Fram Reykjavík	22	IBV Vestmannaeyjar	18	IBK Keflavík	15
1973	IBK Keflavík	26	Valur Reykjavík	21	IBV Vestmannaeyjar	17
1974	IA Akranes	23	IBK Keflavík	19	Valur Reykjavík	14
1975	IA Akranes	19	Fram Reykjavík	17	Valur Reykjavík	16
1976	Valur Reykjavík	25	Fram Reykjavík	24	IA Akranes	21

1977	IA Akranes	28	Valur Reykjavík	27	IBV Vestmannaeyjar	21
1978	Valur Reykjavík	35	IA Akranes	28	IBK Keflavík	20
1979	IBV Vestmannaeyjar	24	IA Akranes	23	Valur Reykjavík	23
1980	Valur Reykjavík	28	Fram Reykjavík	25	Víkingur Reykjavík	20
1981	Víkingur Reykjavík	25	Fram Reykjavík	23	IA Akranes	22
1982	Víkingur Reykjavík	23	IBV Vestmannaeyjar	22	KR Reykjavík	21
1983	IA Akranes	24	KR Reykjavík	20	UBK Kópavogur	19
1984	IA Akranes	38	Valur Reykjavík	28	IBK Keflavík	27
1985	Valur Reykjavík	38	IA Akranes	36	Thór Akureyri	35
1986	Fram Reykjavík	38	Valur Reykjavík	38	IA Akranes	30
1987	Valur Reykjavík	37	Fram Reykjavík	32	IA Akranes	30
1988	Fram Reykjavík	49	Valur Reykjavík	41	IA Akranes	32
1989	KA Akureyri	34	FH Hafnarfjördhur	32	Fram Reykjavík	32
1990	Fram Reykjavík	38	KR Reykjavík	38	IBV Vestmannaeyjar	37
1991	Vikingur Reykjavik	37	Fram Reykjavik	37	KR Reykjavik	28

CHAMPIONSHIP PLAY-OFF MATCHES

1912	KR	3–1	Fram
1916	Fram	3–1	KR
1926	KR	8–2	Fram
1942	Valur	0–0 1–0	Fram
1949	KR	2–1	Fram
1962	Fram	1–0	Valur
1965	KR	2–1	IA Akranes
1966	Valur	2–2 2–1	IB Keflavík
1967	Valur	2–0	Fram
1971	IB Keflavík	4–0	IB Vestmannaeyjar

ICELANDIC CUP FINALS

Year	Winners	Score	Runners-up
1960	KR Reykjavík	2–0	Fram Reykjavík
1961	KR Reykjavík	4–3	IA Akranes
1962	KR Reykjavík	3–0	Fram Reykjavík
1963	KR Reykjavík	4–1	IA Akranes
1964	KR Reykjavík	4–0	IA Akranes
1965	Valur Reykjavík	5–3	IA Akranes
1966	KR Reykjavík	1–0	Valur Reykjavík
1967	KR Reykjavík	3–0	Víkingur Reykjavík
1968	IBV Vestmannaeyjar	2–1	KR Reykjavík
1969	IBA Akureyri	1–1 3–2	IA Akranes
1970	Fram Reykjavík	2–1	IBV Vestmannaeyjar
1971	Víkingur Reykjavík	1–0	UBK Kópavogur
1972	IBV Vestmannaeyjar	2–0	FH Hafnarfjördhur
1973	Fram Reykjavík	2–1	IBK Keflavík
1974	Valur Reykjavík	4–1	IA Akranes
1975	IBK Keflavík	1–0	IA Akranes
1976	Valur Reykjavík	3–0	IA Akranes
1977	Valur Reykjavík	2–1	Fram Reykjavík
1978	IA Akranes	1–0	Valur Reykjavík
1979	Fram Reykjavík	1–0	Valur Reykjavík
1980	Fram Reykjavík	2–1	IBV Vestmannaeyjar
1981	IBV Vestmannaeyjar	3–2	Fram Reykjavík
1982	IA Akranes	2–1	IBK Keflavík
1983	IA Akranes	2–1	IBV Vestmannaeyjar
1984	IA Akranes	2–1	Fram Reykjavík
1985	Fram Reykjavík	3–1	IBK Keflavík
1986	IA Akranes	2–1	Fram Reykjavík
1987	Fram Reykjavík	5–0	Vídir Gardur
1988	Valur Reykjavík	1–0	IBK Keflavík
1989	Fram Reykjavík	3–1	KR Reykjavík
1990	Valur Reykjavík	1–1 0–0 (5–4p)	KR Reykjavík
1991	Valur Reykjavik	2–1	FH Hafnarfjördhur

INTERNATIONAL MATCHES PLAYED BY ICELAND

Date	Opponents	Result	Venue	Compet	Scorers
17-07-1946	Denmark	L 0–3	Reykjavik	Fr	
24-07-1947	Norway	L 2–4	Reykjavik	Fr	Gudmundsson A 2
2-07-1948	Finland	W 2–0	Reykjavik	Fr	Jónsson R 2
7-08-1949	Denmark	L 1–5	Aarhus	Fr	Halldórsson
29-06-1951	Sweden	W 4–3	Reykjavik	Fr	Jónsson R 4
26-07	Norway	L 1–3	Trondheim	Fr	Jónsson R
9-08-1953	Denmark	L 0–4	Copenhagen	Fr	
13-08	Norway	L 1–3	Bergen	Fr	Gunnarsson G
4-07-1954	Norway	W 1–0	Reykjavik	Fr	Thórdarson Th
24-08	Sweden	L 2–3	Kalmar	Fr	Thórdarson Th, Jónsson R
3-07-1955	Denmark	L 0–4	Reykjavik	Fr	
25-08	USA	W 3–2	Reykjavik	Fr	Gudmannsson G 2, Thórdarson Th
29-06-1956	Finland	L 1–2	Helsinki	Fr	Jónsson R
2-06-1957	France	L 0–8	Nantes	WCq	
5-06	Belgium	L 3–8	Brussels	WCq	Thórdarson Th 2, Jónsson R
8-07	Norway	L 0–3	Reykjavik	Fr	
10-07	Denmark	L 2–6	Reykjavik	Fr	Jónsson R, Thórdarson Th

1-09	France	L	1-5	Reykjavik	WCq	Jónsson T
4-09	Belgium	L	2-5	Reykjavik	WCq	Jónsson R, Thórdarson Th
26-06-1959	Denmark	L	2-4	Reykjavik	OGq	Beck, Jónsson S
7-07	Norway	W	1-0	Reykjavik	OGq	Jónsson R
18-08	Denmark	D	1-1	Copenhagen	OGq	Teitsson
21-08	Norway	L	1-2	Oslo	OGq	Steinsen
9-06-1960	Norway	L	0-4	Oslo	Fr	
3-08	West Germany	L	0-5	Reykjavik	Fr	
9-07-1962	Norway	L	1-3	Reykjavik	Fr	Jónsson R
12-08	Rep. Ireland	L	2-4	Dublin	ECr1	Jónsson R 2
2-09	Rep. Ireland	D	1-1	Reykjavik	ECr1	Arnason
10-08-1964	Bermuda	W	4-3	Reykjavik	Fr	Beck 2, Schram 2
23-08	Finland	L	0-2	Reykjavik	Fr	
5-07-1965	Denmark	L	1-3	Reykjavik	Fr	Baldvinsson
23-08-1967	Denmark	L	2-14	Copenhagen	Fr	Gunnarsson H, Numason
18-07-1968	Norway	L	0-4	Reykjavik	Fr	
23-06-1969	Bermuda	W	2-1	Reykjavik	Fr	Schram, Hallgrimsson
21-07	Norway	L	1-2	Trondheim	Fr	Schram
24-07	Finland	L	1-3	Helsinki	Fr	Schram
11-11	Bermuda	L	2-3	Hamilton	Fr	Hallgrimsson, Lárusson
7-07-1970	Denmark	D	0-0	Reykjavik	Fr	
20-07	Norway	W	2-0	Reykjavik	Fr	Gunnarsson H 2
26-05-1971	Norway	L	1-3	Bergen	Fr	Gunnarsson H
13-08	Japan	L	0-2	Reykjavik	Fr	
18-05-1972	Belgium	L	0-4	Liege	WCq	
22-05	Belgium	L	0-4	Bruges	WCq	
3-07	Denmark	L	2-5	Reykjavik	Fr	Pálsson T, Hafsteinsson
12-07	Faeroe Islands	W	3-0	Reykjavik	Fr	Hafsteinsson, Pálsson T, OG
3-08	Norway	L	1-4	Stavanger	WCq	Öskarsson
8-06-1973	Faeroe Islands	W	4-0	Klakksvik	Fr	Geirsson M 2, Jóhannson S, Hallgrimsson
11-07	Sweden	L	0-1	Uddevalla	Fr	
17-07	East Germany	L	1-2	Reykjavik	Fr	Juliusson
19-07	East Germany	L	0-2	Reykjavik	Fr	
2-08	Norway	L	0-4	Reykjavik	WCq	
22-08	Holland	L	0-5	Amsterdam	WCq	
29-08	Holland	L	1-8	Deventer	WCq	Geirsson E
3-07-1974	Faeroe Islands	W	3-2	Torshafn	Fr	Björnsson K, Eliásson, Hallgrimsson
19-08	Finland	D	2-2	Reykjavik	Fr	Geirsson M, Thórdarson Te
8-09	Belgium	L	0-2	Reykjavik	ECq	
9-10	Denmark	L	1-2	Aalborg	Fr	Hallgrimsson
12-10	East Germany	D	1-1	Magdeburg	ECq	Hallgrimsson
25-05-1975	France	D	0-0	Reykjavik	ECq	
5-06	East Germany	W	2-1	Reykjavik	ECq	Edvaldsson J, Sigurvinsson A
23-06	Faeroe Islands	W	6-0	Reykjavik	Fr	Thórdarson Te 3, Hallgrimsson 2, Hilmarsson
7-07	Norway	D	1-1	Reykjavik	OGq	Sveinsson
17-07	Norway	L	2-3	Bergen	OGq	Thórdarson Te, Edvaldsson J
3-09	France	L	0-3	Nantes	ECq	
6-09	Belgium	L	0-1	Liege	ECq	
19-05-1976	Norway	W	1-0	Oslo	Fr	Sigurvinsson A
16-06	Faeroe Islands	W	6-1	Torshafn	Fr	Thorbjörnsson 2, Hallgrimsson 2, Danivalsson, Thórdarson Te
14-07	Finland	L	0-1	Helsinki	Fr	
21-08	Luxembourg	W	3-1	Reykjavik	Fr	Thorbjörnsson 2, Sveinsson
5-09	Belgium	L	0-1	Reykjavik	WCq	
8-09	Holland	L	0-1	Reykjavik	WCq	
11-06-1977	Nth. Ireland	W	1-0	Reykjavik	WCq	Albertsson

LEADING INTERNATIONAL APPEARANCES

1 Edvaldsson A	70
2 Geirsson M	67
3 Jónsson Sa	65
4 Gislason	50
Sveinsson	50
6 Hallgrímsson	45
Sigurvinsson A	45
8 Thórdarson O	45
9 Bergsson G	44
Margeirsson	44
11 Grétarsson	42
Gudjohnsen A	42
13 Ormslev	41
Pétursson P	41
Sigurdsson	41
16 Leifsson	39
Thórdarson Te	39
Torfason	39
19 Edvaldsson J	34
Gudlaugsson	34
21 Jónsson R	33
22 Kjartansson	31
23 Sigurvinsson O	30

LEADING INTERNATIONAL GOALSCORERS					
1 Jónsson R	17	Gudjohnsen A	9	Grétarsson	7
2 Pétursson P	11	7 Steinsson	8	12 Gunnarsson H	6
Hallgrímsson M	11	Edvaldsson A	8	Schram	6
4 Thórdarson Th	9	Geirsson M	8	14 Margeirsson	5
Thórdarson Te	9	10 Thorbjörnsson	7	Sigurvinsson	5

30–06	Norway	W	2–1	Reykjavik	Fr	Albertsson, Thórdarson Te
20–07	Sweden	L	0–1	Reykjavik	Fr	
31–08	Holland	L	1–4	Nijmegen	WCq	Sigurvinsson
3–09	Belgium	L	0–4	Brussels	WCq	
21–09	Nth. Ireland	L	0–2	Belfast	WCq	
28–06–1978	Denmark	D	0–0	Reykjavik	Fr	
3–09	USA	D	0–0	Reykjavik	Fr	
6–09	Poland	L	0–2	Reykjavik	ECq	
20–09	Holland	L	0–3	Nijmegen	ECq	
4–10	East Germany	L	1–3	Halle	ECq	Pétursson P
22–05–1979	Switzerland	L	0–2	Berne	ECq	
26–05	West Germany	L	1–3	Reykjavik	Fr	Edvaldsson E
9–06	Switzerland	L	1–2	Reykjavik	ECq	Gudlaugsson
5–09	Holland	L	0–4	Reykjavik	ECq	
12–09	East Germany	L	0–3	Reykjavik	ECq	
10–10	Poland	L	0–2	Krakow	ECq	
2–06–1980	Wales	L	0–4	Reykjavik	WCq	
25–06	Finland	D	1–1	Reykjavik	Fr	Pétursson P
30–06	Faeroe Islands	W	2–1	Akureyri	Fr	Geirsson M, Thorleifsson
3–07	Greenland	W	4–1	Husavik	Fr	Geirsson M, Ölafsson P, Gudmundsson L, Steinsson
14–07	Norway	L	1–3	Oslo	Fr	Thorleifsson
17–07	Sweden	D	1–1	Halmstad	Fr	Thorbjörnsson
3–09	Soviet Union	L	1–2	Reykjavik	WCq	Sveinsson
24–09	Turkey	W	3–1	Izmir	WCq	Gudlaugsson, Gudmundsson A, Thórdarson Te
15–10	Soviet Union	L	0–5	Moscow	WCq	
27–05–1981	Czechoslovakia	L	1–6	Bratislava	WCq	Bergs
22–08	Nigeria	W	3–0	Reykjavik	Fr	Sveinsson, Geirsson M, Gudmundsson L
26–08	Denmark	L	0–3	Copenhagen	Fr	
9–09	Turkey	W	2–0	Reykjavik	WCq	Gudmundsson L, Edvaldsson A
23–09	Czechoslovakia	D	1–1	Reykjavik	WCq	Ormslev
14–10	Wales	D	2–2	Swansea	WCq	Sigurvinsson A 2
14–03–1982	Kuwait	D	0–0	Kuwait	Fr	
2–06	England	D	1–1	Reykjavik	Fr	Gudjohnsen A
5–06	Malta	L	1–2	Messina	ECq	Geirsson M
11–07	Finland	L	2–3	Helsinki	Fr	Geirsson M, Edvaldsson A
1–08	Faeroe Islands	W	4–1	Torshafn	Fr	Grétarsson 2, Karlsson H, Kristjánsson
2–08	Faeroe Islands	W	4–0	Gotu	Fr	Grétarsson 2, Kristjánsson
1–09	Holland	D	1–1	Reykjavik	ECq	Edvaldsson A
8–09	East Germany	L	0–1	Reykjavik	Fr	
13–10	Rep. Ireland	L	0–2	Dublin	ECq	
27–10	Spain	L	0–1	Malaga	ECq	
29–05–1983	Spain	L	0–1	Reykjavik	ECq	
5–06	Malta	W	1–0	Reykjavik	ECq	Edvaldsson A
8–08	Faeroe Islands	W	6–0	Njardvik	Fr	Magnusson 2, Gudmundsson S 2, Gislason, Margeirsson
17–08	Sweden	L	0–4	Reykjavik	Fr	
7–09	Holland	L	0–3	Groningen	ECq	
21–09	Rep. Ireland	L	0–3	Reykjavik	ECq	
20–06–1984	Norway	L	0–1	Reykjavik	Fr	
1–08	Faeroe Islands	D	0–0	Torshafn	Fr	
3–08	Greenland	W	1–0	Fuglafirdi	Fr	Birgirsson
12–09	Wales	W	1–0	Reykjavik	WCq	Bergs
25–09	Saudi Arabia	W	2–1	Dhahran	Fr	Gislason, Steinsson
17–10	Scotland	L	0–3	Glasgow	WCq	
14–11	Wales	L	1–2	Cardiff	WCq	Pétursson P
31–03–1985	Kuwait	D	1–1	Kuwait City	Fr	Steinsson
24–04	Luxembourg	D	0–0	Ettelbruck	Fr	

28-05	Scotland	L	0-1	Reykjavik	WCq	
12-06	Spain	L	1-2	Reykjavik	WCq	Thórdarson Te
10-07	Faeroe Islands	W	9-0	Keflavik	Fr	Margeirsson 3, Steinsson 2, Gislason, Hákonarson, Thorbjörnsson, Jónsson Sa
12-07	Faeroe Islands	W	1-0	Akranes	Fr	Pétursson P
25-09	Spain	L	1-2	Seville	WCq	Thorbjörnsson
11-03-1986	Bahrian	L	1-2	Manama	Fr	Askelsson
15-03	Bahrain	W	2-0	Manama	Fr	Askelsson, Steinsson
19-03	Kuwait	L	0-1	Kuwait City	Fr	
25-05	Rep. Ireland	L	1-2	Reykjavik	Fr	Gudjohnsen A
29-05	Czechoslovakia	L	1-2	Reykjavik	Fr	Steinsson
10-09	France	D	0-0	Reykjavik	ECq	
24-09	Soviet Union	D	1-1	Reykjavik	ECq	Gudjohnsen A
29-10	East Germany	L	0-2	Karl-Marx-Stadt	ECq	
26-02-1987	Kuwait	D	1-1	Kuwait City	Fr	Askelsson
28-02	Kuwait	W	1-0	Kuwait City	Fr	Olafsson L
29-04	France	L	0-2	Paris	ECq	
3-06	East Germany	L	0-6	Reykjavik	ECq	
9-09	Norway	W	2-1	Reykjavik	ECq	Pétursson P, Ormslev
23-09	Norway	W	1-0	Oslo	ECq	Edvaldsson A
28-10	Soviet Union	L	0-2	Simferopol	ECq	
4-05-1988	Hungary	L	0-3	Budapest	Fr	
7-08	Bulgaria	L	2-3	Reykjavik	Fr	Ormslev 2
24-08	Faeroe Islands	W	1-0	Akranes	Fr	Torfason
31-08	Soviet Union	D	1-1	Reykjavik	WCq	Grétarsson
21-09	Hungary	L	0-3	Reykjavik	Fr	
12-10	Turkey	D	1-1	Istanbul	WCq	Torfason
19-10	East Germany	L	0-2	Berlin	WCq	
31-05-1989	Soviet Union	D	1-1	Moscow	WCq	Askelsson
14-06	Austria	D	0-0	Reykjavik	WCq	
23-08	Austria	L	1-2	Salzburg	WCq	Margeirsson
6-09	East Germany	L	0-3	Reykjavik	WCq	
20-09	Turkey	W	2-1	Reykjavik	WCq	Petursson P 2
28-03-1990	Luxembourg	W	2-1	Esch	Fr	Petursson P, Thórdarson O
3-04	Bermuda	W	4-0	Hamilton	Fr	Petursson P 2, Ormslev, Einarsson
8-04	USA	L	1-4	St Louis	Fr	Petursson P
30-05	Albania	W	2-0	Reykjavik	ECq	Gudjohnsen, Edvaldsson A
8-08	Faeroe Islands	W	3-2	Torshafn	Fr	Gregory 2, Gudjohnsen A
5-09	France	L	1-2	Reykjavik	ECq	Edvaldsson A
26-09	Czechoslovakia	L	0-1	Kosice	ECq	
10-10	Spain	L	1-2	Seville	ECq	Jónsson Si
1-05-1991	Wales	L	0-1	Cardiff	Fr	
7-05	Malta	W	4-1	Ta'Qali	Fr	Kristinsson 2, Gretarsson, Morteinsson
26-05	Albania	L	0-1	Tirana	ECq	
5-06	Czechoslovakia	L	0-1	Reykjavik	ECq	
17-07	Turkey	W	5-1	Reykjavik	Fr	Gretarsson, Gudjohnsen 4
4-09	Denmark	D	0-0	Reykjavik	Fr	
25-09	Spain	W	2-0	Reykjavik	ECq	Orlygsson, Sverrisson
20-11	France	L	1-3	Paris	ECq	Sverrisson
13-05-1992	Greece	L	0-1	Athens	WCq	
3-06	Hungary	W	2-1	Budapest	WCq	Orlygsson, Magnusson

ISRAEL

Israel was for many years amongst the strongest of nations in Asia, but since the rise to prominence in the 1970s of the Arab states, she has led a strange and often lonely existence. Cast out from the Asian Confederation in 1976 'with regret' – but no doubt considerable relief – Israel has flitted from Europe to Oceania in search of a home, and is the only country to have played a World Cup qualifying match in every continent of the world.

There is now cause for hope as the Israelis finally seem set to have a permanent home – Europe. Both the clubs and the national side have been accepted into European competitions on a permanent basis. Often seen as a location to bask in some winter sun by touring sides, visits to Israel will now take on a far more serious aspect.

How Israel will fare in this new competitive environment is unknown. The years in the wilderness have not had a healthy effect on the development of the game, as the association has struggled to maintain a regular fixture list for the national side, whilst nothing has been seen of the club sides since their brief flurry in the Asian Champion Teams' Cup in the late 1960s. Another huge disadvantage is its small population. With only four million inhabitants, Israel is unlikely ever to become a major power.

Israel did not exist as a nation until 1948 when the United

Nations founded the state in what was then Palestine, but football predates the founding of the country. Growing Jewish immigration to Palestine from Europe had encouraged the growth of the game and in 1928 the Palestine Football Association was formed in Tel Aviv. The presence of British soldiers and officials also gave the game a boost and the winners of the first championship in 1932 were the British Police.

The National Cup competition preceded the championship by four years during which time it was won by both Hapoel and Maccabi Tel Aviv, both of whom have been a major force in the game since. Domestic football in Israel has been relatively unaffected by the constant state of hostilities with her neighbours although the invasion by the Arabs in 1948 and the Suez crisis in 1956 did bring about a temporary halt to the game.

A Palestinian side took part in the 1934 World Cup and was drawn against Egypt in the qualifiers. In later years this match would not have been possible, but as it predated the formation of Israel there was no problem, even if the Palestinian team was made up entirely of Jews. These two games, along with the unsuccessful attempt to qualify for the 1938 World Cup and a friendly against the Lebanon, were the only games that Palestine played and it was not until 1949 that the national side was revived.

The Israelis always knew it would be difficult to find opponents among their neighbours, and in the first few years after 1948 matches were confined to World Cup qualifying games and the odd friendly match. This World Cup experience did give Israel an advantage when they took part in the 1956 Asian Cup, but although they were regarded as favourites for the tournament, South Korea proved too clever for them and the Israelis had to be content with second place, a position they secured again four years later when the Koreans themselves hosted the tournament.

The 1958 World Cup saw the first hint of the disruption that Israel's position was to cause world football when each of their opponents withdrew from the Asia–Africa section. This left the Israelis as the winners without having played a match, but a new FIFA law that no side except the holders and hosts could qualify without playing a game forced a play-off against Wales. Both matches were lost 2–0. Had the original games taken place, Israel may well have qualified without the need to play Wales, who were therefore the unwitting benificiaries of political machinations in the Middle East.

Further controversy surrounded Israel's involvement at the 1962 Asian Games. The Indonesian hosts, mindful of their large Moslem population, refused to invite an Israeli team for any of the sports, in a move that nearly broke the Asian Games movement apart. The decision of the Asian Confederation to award Israel the staging of the 1964 Asian Cup may have been foolhardy under such conditions, but the Israelis made full use of home advantage to win their only honour to date.

By beating India, a weakened South Vietnamese team and their fierce rivals South Korea, they won the tournament at the third attempt. Although this was not their last appearance – they came third in 1968 – the emergence of the Arab states as a footballing bloc suggested that the Israelis were to become a fading power in Asian football.

From the mid-1960s, Israel began to rely on visits by touring European sides for their players to gain experience, although there was a final hurrah in Asian football when they finished second behind Iran in the 1974 Asian Games in Tehran. Even here controversy abounded. In their semi-final group, both North Korea and Kuwait refused to take the field against Israel and as a result forfeited the points and their hopes of making it to the final.

The Asian Football Confederation clearly needed to sort out the situation and in 1976 Israel were thrown out. The AFC faced a dilema. Either they bowed to pressure from a vocal section of their members or they stood firm and put at risk the future development of the game in the continent, which Israel's presence was beginning to disrupt. They took the former course to howls of protest from the world football community who regarded the decision as a political act.

With some justification, the Israelis felt that they were being discriminated against on racial lines. Many of the nations who supported their expulsion were at the same time condemning South Africa for their organisation of sport on racial lines, and the hypocrisy of their seemingly conflicting positions was not lost on the world at large. But it is difficult to see how else the AFC could have acted and in the long run their decision may well act in Israel's favour. Asia is the weakest of all the continents and both Israel's national side and the clubs will face a much higher standard of opposition in Europe.

Not until 1991 was Israel formally welcomed into Europe and for 15 years, the national side led a nomadic existence. In 1970 Israel had qualified for the World Cup finals in Mexico, confirming their status as one of the strongest nations in Asia. That they have not qualified again since is largely due to the fact that they were adopted as an associate member of Oceania, which was not afforded an automatic berth in the finals.

In the 1990 World Cup, for instance, they were forced to play off against Colombia after having won the Oceania section, and it was no surprise when the stronger South Americans won through to Italy. Israel's future prospects for qualification do not look much better in Europe, but with more regular competition the hope is that they can emulate a small country like Denmark and make their presence felt.

Population: 4 666 000
Area, sq km: 20 700
% in urban areas: 89%
Capital city: Jerusalem

Hitachdut Lekaduregel Beisrael
Israel Football Association
12 Carlibach Street
PO Box 20188
Tel Aviv 61201
Israel
Tel: (010 972) 3 5610888
Fax: (010 972) 3 5618693
Telex: 361353 FA
Cable: CADUREGEL TEL AVIV
Languages for correspondence: English, French & German

Year of formation: 1928
Affiliation to FIFA: 1929
Registered clubs: 544
Registered players: 45 500
Registered referees: 634
National stadium: Ramat Gan, Tel Aviv 55 000
National colours: Shirts: White/Shorts: Blue/Socks: White
Reserve colours: Shirts: Blue/Shorts: White/Socks: White
Season: September–June

THE RECORD

WORLD CUP

1930 .... Did not enter
1934 .... QT 2nd/2 in group 4
1938 .... QT 3rd/3 in group 5
1950 .... QT 3rd/3 in group 3
1954 .... QT 3rd/3 in group 10
1958 .... QT Lost play-off Asia
1962 .... QT 2nd/4 in group 7 Europe
1966 .... QT 3rd/3 in group 1 Europe
1970 .... QT R1 1st/2, R2 1st/2 Asia – Final tournament/1st round
1974 .... QT 2nd/7 in group B Asia
1978 .... QT 2nd/3 in group 2 Asia
1982 .... QT 5th/5 in group 6 Europe
1986 .... QT R1 2nd/4 Oceania
1990 .... QT R1 –, R2 1st/3, R3 2nd/2 Oceania

OLYMPIC GAMES

1908–52 ..... Did not enter
1956 .... QT Failed to qualify
1960 .... QT 2nd/3 in group 4 Europe
1964 .... QT 1st round Asia
1968 .... QT 1st/2 in group 3 Asia – Final tournament/Quarter-finalists
1972 .... QT 2nd/6 in group 2 Asia
1976 .... QT 1st/6 in group 3 Asia – Final tournament/Quarter-finalists
1980 .... QT 3rd/4 in group 3 Europe
1984 .... QT 5th/6 in group 4 Europe
1988 .... QT R1 –, R2 2nd/4 Oceania
1992 .... QT 2nd/4 in group 8 Europe

ASIAN CHAMPIONSHIP

1956 .... QT Walk-over in group 1 – Final tournament/2nd place
1960 .... QT 1st/4 in group 1 – Final tournament/2nd place
1964 .... QT Automatic – Final tournament/Winners
1968 .... QT Automatic – Final tournament/3rd place
1972–92 ..... Did not enter

ASIAN GAMES

1951 .... Did not enter
1954 .... Did not enter
1958 .... Quarter-finalists
1962–70 ..... Did not enter
1974 .... Finalists
1978–90 ..... Did not enter

ASIAN CHAMPIONS CLUB CUP

Winners – Hapoel Tel Aviv 1967, Maccabi Tel Aviv 1969 1971
Finalists – Hapoel Tel Aviv 1970

CLUB DIRECTORY

TEL AVIV (Population – 1 553 000)
Beitar Tel Aviv
Colours: Blue/blue

Hakoah Maccabi Ramat Gan

Hapoel Kfar Saba

Hapoel Petah Tikva
Colours: Blue/white

Hapoel Tel Aviv
Colours: Red/red

Maccabi Yaffo

Maccabi Tel Aviv
Colours: Yellow/blue

Maccabi Petah Tikva
Colours: White/white

Shimson Tel Aviv

JERUSALEM (Population – 493 000)
Beitar Jerusalem
Colours: Yellow/black

Hapoel Jerusalem
Colours: White/red

HAIFA (Population – 435 000)
Hapoel Haifa

Maccabi Haifa
Colours: Green/green

NETANYA (Population – 117 000)
Maccabi Netanya
Colours: Yellow/yellow

BEERSHEBA (Population – 113 000)
Hapoel Beersheba
Colours: Red/white

ISRAELI CHAMPIONS

1932 .... British Police
1933 .... –
1934 .... Hapoel Tel Aviv
1935 .... Hapoel Tel Aviv
1936 .... Hapoel Tel Aviv
1937 .... Maccabi Tel Aviv
1938 .... Hapoel Tel Aviv
1939 .... Maccabi Tel Aviv
1940 .... Hapoel Tel Aviv
1941 .... Maccabi Tel Aviv
1942 .... –
1943 .... Hapoel Tel Aviv
1944–46 .... –
1947 .... Maccabi Tel Aviv
1948–49 .... –
1950 .... Maccabi Tel Aviv
1951 .... –
1952 .... Maccabi Tel Aviv
1953 .... –
1954 .... Maccabi Tel Aviv
1955 .... Hapoel Petah Tikva
1956 .... Maccabi Tel Aviv
1957 .... Hapoel Tel Aviv
1958 .... Maccabi Tel Aviv
1959 .... Hapoel Petah Tikva
1960 .... Hapoel Petah Tikva
1961 .... Hapoel Petah Tikva
1962 .... Hapoel Petah Tikva
1963 .... Hapoel Petah Tikva
1964 .... Hapoel Ramat Gan
1965 .... Hakoah Ramat Gan
1966 .... Hapoel Tel Aviv
1967 .... Maccabi Tel Aviv
1968 .... Maccabi Tel Aviv
1969 .... Hapoel Tel Aviv
1970 .... Maccabi Tel Aviv
1971 .... Maccabi Netanya
1972 .... Maccabi Tel Aviv
1973 .... Hakoah Ramat Gan
1974 .... Maccabi Netanya
1975 .... Hapoel Beersheba
1976 .... Hapoel Beersheba
1977 .... Maccabi Tel Aviv
1978 .... Maccabi Netanya
1979 .... Maccabi Tel Aviv
1980 .... Maccabi Netanya
1981 .... Hapoel Tel Aviv
1982 .... Hapoel Kfar Sava
1983 .... Maccabi Netanya
1984 .... Maccabi Haifa
1985 .... Maccabi Haifa
1986 .... Hapoel Tel Aviv
1987 .... Beitar Jerusalem
1988 .... Hapoel Tel Aviv
1989 .... Maccabi Haifa
1990 .... Bnei Yehoudah
1991 .... Maccabi Haifa
1992 .... Maccabi Tel Aviv

ISRAELI CUP WINNERS

1928 .... Hapoel Tel Aviv
1929 .... Maccabi Tel Aviv
1930 .... Maccabi Tel Aviv

1931	–
1932	British Police
1933	Maccabi Tel Aviv
1934	Hapoel Tel Aviv
1935	Maccabi Petah Tikva
1936	–
1937	Hapoel Tel Aviv
1938	Hapoel Tel Aviv
1939	Hapoel Tel Aviv
1940	Betar Tel Aviv
1941	Maccabi Tel Aviv
1942	Betar Tel Aviv
1943–45	–
1946	Maccabi Tel Aviv
1947	Maccabi Tel Aviv
1948–51	–
1952	Maccabi Petah Tikva
1953	–
1954	Maccabi Tel Aviv
1955	Maccabi Tel Aviv
1956	–
1957	Petah Tikva Hapoel
1958	Maccabi Tel Aviv
1959	Maccabi Tel Aviv
1960	Hapoel Tel Aviv
1961	–
1962	Maccabi Haifa
1963	Hapoel Haifa
1964	Maccabi Tel Aviv
1965	Maccabi Tel Aviv
1966	Hapoel Haifa
1967	Maccabi Tel Aviv
1968	Bney Yehuda Tel Aviv
1969	Hakoah Ramat Gan
1970	Maccabi Tel Aviv
1971	Hakoah Ramat Gan
1972	Hapoel Tel Aviv
1973	Hapoel Jerusalem
1974	Hapoel Haifa
1975	Hapoel Kfar Sava
1976	Beitar Jeusalem
1977	Maccabi Tel Aviv
1978	Maccabi Netanya
1979	Beitar Jerusalem
1980	Hapoel Kfar Sava
1981	Hapoel Tel Aviv
1982	Bney Yehuda Tel Aviv
1983	Hapoel Tel Aviv
1984	Hapoel Lod
1985	Beitar Jerusalem
1986	Beitar Jerusalem
1987	Maccabi Tel Aviv
1988	Maccabi Tel Aviv
1989	Beitar Jerusalem
1990	Hapoel Kfar Saba
1991	Maccabi Haifa
1992	Hapoel Petah Tikva

INTERNATIONAL MATCHES PLAYED BY ISRAEL

Date	Opponents	Result	Venue	Compet	Scorers
16–03–1934	Egypt	L 1–7	Cairo	WCq	Neudelmann
6–04	Egypt	L 1–4	Tel Aviv	WCq	Suknik
22–01–1938	Greece	L 1–3	Tel Aviv	WCq	Neufeld
20–02	Greece	L 0–1	Athens	WCq	
27–04–1940	Lebanon	W 5–1	Tel Aviv	Fr	Meitner, Scheindrowitch, Maclis, Caspi 2
30–07–1949	Cyprus	W 3–1	Tel Aviv	Fr	Weinberger 2, Yalovski
21–08	Yugoslavia	L 0–6	Belgrade	WCq	
18–09	Yugoslavia	L 2–5	Tel Aviv	WCq	Glazer 2
28–10–1950	Turkey	W 5–1	Tel Aviv	Fr	Gambasch 2, Glazer 3
3–12	Turkey	L 2–3	Istanbul	Fr	Glazer 2
1–11–1953	Greece	L 0–1	Athens	WCq	
8–11	Yugoslavia	L 0–1	Skoplje	WCq	
8–03–1954	Greece	L 0–2	Tel Aviv	WCq	
21–03	Yugoslavia	L 0–1	Tel Aviv	WCq	
1–05	South Africa	L 1–2	Johannesburg	Fr	Glazer
11–07–1956	Soviet Union	L 0–5	Moscow	OGq	
31–07	Soviet Union	L 1–2	Tel Aviv	OGq	Stelmach
1–09	Hong Kong	W 3–2	Hong Kong	AC	Glazer 2, Stelmach
8–09	South Korea	L 1–2	Hong Kong	AC	Stelmach
12–09	South Vietnam	W 2–1	Hong Kong	AC	Stelmach 2
15–01–1958	Wales	L 0–2	Tel Aviv	WCq	
5–02	Wales	L 0–2	Cardiff	WCq	
26–05	Iran	W 4–0	Tokyo	AGr1	Glazer, Stelmach 2, Reznik
28–05	Singapore	W 2–1	Tokyo	AGr1	Nahari, Stelmach
30–05	Taiwan	L 0–2	Tokyo	AGqf	
21–06–1959	Poland	L 2–7	Wroclaw	Fr	Goldstein, Stelmach
21–10	Yugoslavia	D 2–2	Tel Aviv	OGq	Stelmach 2
29–11	Poland	D 1–1	Tel Aviv	Fr	Levy R
5–12	Iran	L 0–3	Cochin	ACq	
8–12	India	W 3–1	Cochin	ACq	Levy R 3
10–12	Pakistan	W 2–0	Cochin	ACq	Levy R, Stelmach
12–12	Iran	D 1–1	Cochin	ACq	Mentchel
14–12	India	W 2–1	Cochin	ACq	Stelmach, Levy R
17–12	Pakistan	D 2–2	Cochin	ACq	Mentchel, Ratzabi
6–03–1960	Greece	W 2–1	Tel Aviv	OGq	Mentchel, Glazer
3–04	Greece	L 1–2	Athens	OGq	Glazer
10–04	Yugoslavia	W 2–1	Belgrade	OGq	Levy R 2
17–10	South Korea	L 0–3	Seoul	AC	
19–10	South Vietnam	W 5–1	Seoul	AC	Levy R, Stelmach, Levy S, Mentchel, Aaronskind
20–10	Taiwan	W 1–0	Seoul	AC	Levy S
13–11	Cyprus	D 1–1	Nicosia	WCq	Kaufmann
27–11	Cyprus	W 6–1	Tel Aviv	WCq	Levy S 3, Nahari, Stelmach 2
14–03–1961	Ethiopia	W 1–0	Tel Aviv	WCq	Glazer

19–03	Ethiopia	W 3–2	Tel Aviv	WCq	Glazer 2, Stelmach
15–10	Italy	L 2–4	Tel Aviv	WCq	Stelmach, Young
22–10	South Korea	D 1–1	Tel Aviv	Fr	Stelmach
4–11	Italy	L 0–6	Turin	WCq	
14–12	Yugoslavia	L 0–2	Tel Aviv	Fr	
16–05–1962	Turkey	L 0–1	Istanbul	Fr	
7–10	Ethiopia	W 3–0	Tel Aviv	Fr	Levkowitch, Mentchel, Stelmach
13–11	Sweden	L 0–4	Tel Aviv	Fr	
25–11	Turkey	L 0–2	Tel Aviv	Fr	
19–05–1963	Brazil	L 0–5	Tel Aviv	Fr	
28–12	South Vietnam	W 1–0	Saigon	OGq	Young
2–01–1964	Hong Kong	W 3–0	Hong Kong	Fr	Mahalal 2, Spiegler
17–03	South Vietnam	L 0–2	Tel Aviv	OGq	
26–05	Hong Kong	W 1–0	Tel Aviv	AC	Spiegler
29–05	India	W 2–0	Tel Aviv	AC	Spiegler, Aharoni
3–06	South Korea	W 2–1	Tel Aviv	AC	Leon, Tisch
28–10	Yugoslavia	W 2–0	Tel Aviv	Fr	Spiegler, Cohen S
1–12	Denmark	L 0–1	Tel Aviv	Fr	
26–01–1965	Holland	L 0–1	Tel Aviv	Fr	
9–05	Belgium	L 0–1	Brussels	WCq	
13–06	Bulgaria	L 0–4	Sofia	WCq	
10–11	Belgium	L 0–5	Tel Aviv	WCq	
21–11	Bulgaria	L 1–2	Tel Aviv	WCq	Talbi
8–05–1966	Finland	W 3–0	Helsinki	Fr	Young, Stelmach 2
15–06	Uruguay	L 1–2	Tel Aviv	Fr	Spiegler
12–10	Yugoslavia	L 1–3	Tel Aviv	Fr	Spiegler
26–10	Denmark	L 1–3	Copenhagen	Fr	Assis
7–12	Rumania	L 1–2	Tel Aviv	Fr	Borba
10–01–1968	Belgium	L 0–2	Tel Aviv	Fr	
14–02	Switzerland	W 2–1	Tel Aviv	Fr	Spiegler 2
19–02	Sweden	L 0–3	Tel Aviv	Fr	
17–03	Ceylon	W 7–0	Tel Aviv	OGq	Borba 2, Spiegler 3, OG, Spiegel
22–03	Ceylon	W 4–0	Tel Aviv	OGq	Spiegel, Talbi, Rosenthal, Borba
12–05	Hong Kong	W 6–1	Tehran	AC	Spiegler 2, Spiegel 2, Romano 2
14–05	Burma	L 0–1	Tehran	AC	
17–05	Taiwan	W 4–1	Tehran	AC	Romano 2, Rosenthal, Spiegel
19–05	Iran	L 1–2	Tehran	AC	Spiegel
10–09	Nth. Ireland	L 2–3	Tel Aviv	Fr	Spiegler, Talbi
13–10	Ghana	W 5–3	Leon	OGr1	Spiegel 2, Feygenbaum 3
15–10	El Salvador	W 3–1	Leon	OGr1	Talbi, Spiegler, Bar S
17–10	Hungary	L 0–2	Guadalajara	OGr1	
20–10	Bulgaria	D 1–1	Leon	OGqf	Feygenbaum
	Lost on toss of coin				
19–02–1969	Sweden	L 2–3	Tel Aviv	Fr	Spiegel, Young
12–03	Greece	D 3–3	Tel Aviv	Fr	Young, Talbi, Feygenbaum
23–04	Austria	D 1–1	Tel Aviv	Fr	Feygenbaum
25–08	Sweden	L 1–3	Stockholm	Fr	Talbi
28–09	New Zealand	W 4–0	Tel Aviv	WCq	Spiegler, Spiegel, Feygenbaum 2
1–10	New Zealand	W 2–0	Tel Aviv	WCq	Spiegler, Spiegel
4–12	Australia	W 1–0	Tel Aviv	WCq	Spiegel
14–12	Australia	D 1–1	Sydney	WCq	Spiegler
28–01–1970	Holland	L 0–1	Tel Aviv	Fr	
22–03	Ethiopia	W 5–1	Addis Ababa	Fr	Feygenbaum 3, Spiegler 2
2–06	Uruguay	L 0–2	Puebla	WCr1	
7–06	Sweden	D 1–1	Toluca	WCr1	Spiegler
11–06	Italy	D 0–0	Toluca	WCr1	
10–11	Australia	L 0–1	Tel Aviv	Fr	
12–03–1971	Sweden	W 2–1	Tel Aviv	Fr	Feygenbaum, Spiegel
11–11	Australia	D 2–2	Brisbane	Fr	Borba, Spiegler
14–11	Australia	L 0–1	Sydney	Fr	
21–11	Australia	W 3–1	Melbourne	Fr	Rosen, Sharabani 2
16–02–1972	Norway	W 2–1	Tel Aviv	Fr	Bar Nur 2
22–03	Ceylon	W 3–0	Rangoon	OGq	Calderon, Bar Nur, Borba
28–03	India	W 1–0	Rangoon	OGq	Spiegler
30–03	Indonesia	W 1–0	Rangoon	OGq	Sarussi
1–04	Thailand	D 0–0 (2–4p)	Rangoon	OGq	
20–02–1973	Argentina	D 1–1	Tel Aviv	Fr	Shum
16–05	Japan	W 2–1	Seoul	WCq	Onana 2
19–05	Malaysia	W 3–0	Seoul	WCq	Farkas, Shum, Onana

21–05	Thailand	W 6–0	Seoul	WCq	Borba, Spiegler, Shum, Rosen 2, Onana
23–05	South Korea	D 0–0	Seoul	WCq	
26–05	Japan	W 1–0	Seoul	WCq	Onana
28–05	South Korea	L 0–1	Seoul	WCq	
19–07	Uruguay	L 1–2	Tel Aviv	Fr	Damti
13–11	United States	W 3–1	Tel Aviv	Fr	Peretz, Rosen, Macmel
15–11	United States	W 2–0	Beersheba	Fr	Damti, Peretz
28–05–1974	Australia	W 2–1	Tel Aviv	Fr	Feygenbaum 2
3–09	Malaysia	W 8–3	Tehran	AGr1	Onana 2, Schwartz, Feygenbaum, Damti 3, Massuari
5–09	Philippines	W 6–0	Tehran	AGr1	Schweitzer 2, Damti, Shum, Onana, Feygenbaum
7–09	Japan	W 3–1	Tehran	AGr1	Feygenbaum 2, Damti
10–09	Burma	W 3–0	Tehran	AGr2	Feygenbaum, Schweitzer, Damti
12–09	North Korea	W 2–0		AGr2	
	North Korea refused to play. Israel awarded game 2–0				
14–09	Kuwait	W 2–0		AGr2	
	Kuwait refused to play. Israel awarded game 2–0				
16–09	Iran	L 0–1	Tehran	AGf	
4–12	Rumania	L 0–1	Tel Aviv	Fr	
20–10–1975	Mexico	W 1–0	Tel Aviv	Fr	Schweitzer
4–02–1976	Denmark	L 0–1	Tel Aviv	Fr	
3–03	Nth. Ireland	D 1–1	Tel Aviv	Fr	Damti
31–03	Japan	W 3–0	Seoul	OGq	Damti, Peretz, Oz
4–04	South Korea	W 3–1	Seoul	OGq	Schweitzer, Damti 2
11–04	Japan	W 4–1	Tel Aviv	OGq	Schweitzer, Damti, Shum 2
28–04	South Korea	D 0–0	Tel Aviv	OGq	
19–07	Guatemala	D 0–0	Toronto	OGr1	
21–07	Mexico*	D 2–2	Montreal	OGr1	Oz, Shum
23–07	France*	D 1–1	Montreal	OGr1	Peretz
25–07	Brazil*	L 1–4	Toronto	OGqf	Peretz
22–09	Greece	W 1–0	Patras	Fr	Tabak
3–11	Australia	D 1–1	Tel Aviv	Fr	Damti
15–12	Austria	L 1–3	Tel Aviv	Fr	Peretz
26–01–1977	Greece	D 1–1	Tel Aviv	Fr	Schweitzer
12–02	Australia	D 1–1	Melbourne	Fr	Damti
16–02	Australia	D 1–1	Sydney	Fr	Schweitzer
27–02	South Korea	D 0–0	Tel Aviv	WCq	
6–03	Japan	W 2–0	Tel Aviv	WCq	Machness O, Bar H
10–03	Japan	W 2–0	Tel Aviv	WCq	Machness O, Peretz
20–03	South Korea	L 1–3	Seoul	WCq	Malmilian
8–02–1978	Denmark	W 2–0	Tel Aviv	Fr	Cohen Y, Machness G
22–02	Holland	L 1–2	Tel Aviv	Fr	Peretz
15–11	Belgium	W 1–0	Tel Aviv	Fr	Peretz
19–12	Romania	D 1–1	Tel Aviv	Fr	Malmilian
30–01–1979	Austria	L 0–1	Tel Aviv	Fr	
14–02	Greece	W 4–1	Tel Aviv	Fr	Shum, Peretz 3
26–03–1980	Nth. Ireland	D 0–0	Tel Aviv	WCq	
18–06	Sweden	D 1–1	Stockholm	WCq	Damti
12–11	Sweden	D 0–0	Tel Aviv	WCq	
2–12	Australia	L 0–1	Beersheba	Fr	
17–12	Portugal	L 0–3	Lisbon	WCq	
25–02–1981	Scotland	L 0–1	Tel Aviv	WCq	
8–04	Romania	W 2–1	Tel Aviv	Fr	Sinai, Mizrahi
28–04	Scotland	L 1–3	Glasgow	WCq	Sinai
28–10	Portugal	W 4–1	Tel Aviv	WCq	Tabak 3, Damti
18–11	Nth Ireland	L 0–1	Belfast	WCq	
26–09–1983	Uruguay	D 2–2	Tel Aviv	Fr	Armeli, Levy S
8–11	Romania	D 1–1	Tel Aviv	Fr	Malmilian

LEADING INTERNATIONAL GOALSCORERS

1 Spiegler 24	7 Spiegel 13	13 Armeli 7
2 Stelmach 22	8 Ohana 11	Borba 7
Feygenbaum 22	9 Peretz 10	Sinai 7
4 Damti 17	10 Levy R 9	Shum 7
5 Glazer 16	11 Onana 8	
Malmilian 16	Schweitzer 8	

LEADING INTERNATIONAL APPEARANCES			
1 Spiegler 79	Malmilian 61	Sinai 47	19 Primo 38
2 Shum 75	8 Rosen 55	14 Talbi 43	20 Tisch 36
3 Visoker 68	9 Bello 54	15 Levkowitch 42	21 Glazer 35
4 Damti 67	10 Bar H 49	16 Rosenthal S 41	22 Schwager 35
5 Cohen Av 65	11 Feygenbaum 48	Spiegel 41	
6 Stelmach 61	12 Young 47	18 Peretz 39	

4-04-1984	Rep. Ireland	W 3-0	Tel Aviv	Fr	Ohana, Armeli, Sinai
11-04	Romania	D 0-0	Oradea	Fr	
10-06	Wales	D 0-0	Tel Aviv	Fr	
6-09	Malta	W 2-1	Tel Aviv	Fr	Malmilian 2
9-10	Greece	D 2-2	Athens	Fr	Cohen Av, Ohana
16-10	Nth. Ireland	L 0-3	Belfast	Fr	
21-11	Romania	D 1-1	Tel Aviv	Fr	Ohana
19-12	Luxembourg	W 2-0	Tel Aviv	Fr	Malmilian, Ohana
9-01-1985	Greece	L 0-2	Tel Aviv	Fr	
27-02	Rep. Ireland	D 0-0	Tel Aviv	Fr	
1-05	Sweden	D 1-1	Tel Aviv	Fr	Ohana
3-09	Taiwan	W 6-0	Tel Aviv	WCq	Turk 3, Armeli, Malmilian 2
8-09	Taiwan	W 5-0	Tel Aviv	WCq	Cohen Av, Armeli, Ohana 3
8-10	Australia	L 1-2	Tel Aviv	WCq	Armeli
20-10	Australia	D 1-1	Melbourne	WCq	Malmilian
26-10	New Zealand	L 1-3	Auckland	WCq	Armeli
10-11	New Zealand	D 3-3	Tel Aviv	WCq	Cohen N, Selekter, Armeli
28-01-1986	Scotland	L 0-1	Tel Aviv	Fr	
26-02	England	L 1-2	Tel Aviv	Fr	Ohana
4-05	Argentina	L 2-7	Tel Aviv	Fr	Sinai, Malmilian
8-10	Romania	L 2-4	Tel Aviv	Fr	Malmilian, Cohen N
18-02-1987	Nth. Ireland	D 1-1	Tel Aviv	Fr	Marili
25-03	West Germany	L 0-2	Tel Aviv	Fr	
8-04	Romania	L 2-3	Brasov	Fr	Brailovsky, Tikva
19-05	Switzerland	L 0-1	Aarau	Fr	
1-06	Brazil	L 0-4	Tel Aviv	Fr	
10-11	Rep. Ireland	L 0-5	Dublin	Fr	
2-12	Malta	D 1-1	Tel Aviv	Fr	Ovadia
16-12	Switzerland	L 0-2	Tel Aviv	Fr	
19-01-1988	Belgium	L 2-3	Tel Aviv	Fr	Malmilian, Tikva
27-01	France	D 1-1	Tel Aviv	Fr	Cohen Ab
3-02	Romania	L 0-2	Haifa	Fr	
10-02	Poland	L 1-3	Tel Aviv	Fr	Rosenthal R
17-02	England	D 0-0	Tel Aviv	Fr	
7-03	Australia	L 0-2	Melbourne	OGq	
9-03	New Zealand	W 2-0	Adelaide	OGq	Cohen E, Iwanir
13-03	Taiwan	W 5-1	Sydney	OGq	Brailovsky 2, Malmilian 2, Levin
20-03	Australia	D 0-0	Christchurch	OGq	
23-03	Taiwan	W 9-0	Wellington	OGq	Tikva 3, Levin 3, Rosenthal R, Cohen E, Malmilian
27-03	New Zealand	W 1-0	Auckland	OGq	Levin
18-10	Malta	W 2-0	Beersheba	Fr	Sinai, Dryks
23-11	Romania	L 0-3	Sibiu	Fr	
4-01-1989	Holland	L 0-2	Tel Aviv	Fr	
11-01	Malta	W 2-1	Ta'Qali	Fr	Menahem, Sinai
8-02	Wales	D 3-3	Tel Aviv	Fr	Klinger, Alon, Dryks
5-03	New Zealand	W 1-0	Tel Aviv	WCq	Rosenthal R
19-03	Australia	D 1-1	Tel Aviv	WCq	Ohana
9-04	New Zealand	D 2-2	Auckland	WCq	Rosenthal R, Klinger
16-04	Australia	D 1-1	Sydney	WCq	Ohana
15-10	Colombia	L 0-1	Barranquilla	WCq	
30-10	Colombia	D 0-0	Tel Aviv	WCq	
28-03-1990	Greece	L 1-2	Athens	Fr	Sinai
25-04	Romania	L 1-4	Haifa	Fr	Aharoni
16-05	Soviet Union	W 3-2	Tel Aviv	Fr	Malmilian, Levin, Banin
22-05	Argentina	L 1-2	Tel Aviv	Fr	Banin
9-10	Soviet Union	L 0-3	Moscow	Fr	
12-02-1992	CIS	L 1-2	Tel Aviv	Fr	Dryks
3-03	Cyprus	W 2-1	Tel Aviv	Fr	Berkovitz, Cohen A

* Not full Internationals

ITALY

Love them or hate them, the Italians will always be big news in football. Their league has more players of quality than any other, their fans are amongst the most passionate in the world, and they have won the World Cup a record-equalling three times.

Yet at the same time, they evoke deep feelings of resentment from countries all over the world. South America in particular has had cause to rue the agents of the big Italian clubs. Player after player has been lured away from Argentina, Brazil and Uruguay, so that what is left often resembles the runt of the pack.

Italian football has also been at the forefront of the demise of the game as an entertaining spectacle. During the 1960s and 1970s, *catenaccio*, or defensive football motivated by the fear of defeat, spread right across the globe. Under the maxim that if you don't concede a goal you can't lose, free-flowing football became the exception rather than the rule. It was perhaps apt that the 1990 World Cup, without question the most sterile tournament ever staged, should take place in the birthplace of *catenaccio*.

Despite these criticisms, Italy can be the perfect setting for football, and it has contributed greatly to the development of the game. The first clubs were formed in the three main cultural and industrial centres in Northern Italy. Internazionale Torino, the forerunners of the present day Torino, were formed in 1890; Genoa Football Club was formed in 1893 as Genoa Cricket and Football Club; whilst in Milan, Milan Football and Cricket Club, later simply known as Milan, were formed in 1899. The English influence was obvious, and some clubs to this day still retain the title Football Club rather than the Italian Associazione Calcio.

To call Genoa the first league champions is perhaps stretching the point in that the first competition in 1898 consisted of only three games and until 1910, the number of matches played in each championship remained limited. It was the common practice to play eliminating games by region, often between only two clubs, to qualify for a round robin play-off.

The year 1910 proved to be a watershed for the Italians. Not only did the Italian football association try to set league football on a more firm footing, but a national side was fielded for the first time. Although an impressive debut saw a 6–0 win over the French, results well into the 1920s were not outstanding. Italy's first official competition, the 1912 Olympic Games, ended with first round defeat at the hands of Finland.

The 1910 league championship saw a dramatic increase in the number of games played and for the first time a single league was used but the following year it reverted to regional groupings. As more and more clubs were formed and wanted to join in, these regional leagues became ever more complicated, but not until 1930 was a single league reintroduced. When it was, it proved to be exactly the boost the game needed to project itself to the Italian population, and neither have had cause to look back since. These early years were often marked by disorganisation. Although an association had been formed in 1898 its authority was always being challenged, whilst rivalries between the different towns meant that at times it had its headquarters in Turin, Milan, Turin again and Bologna before finally settling in Rome in 1929. In 1921 matters seemed to have got out of hand as the championship consisted of 18 regional leagues of vastly different strengths. The big clubs felt at the mercy of their smaller counterparts and in 1922 set up a rival organisation, but that only lasted a year.

The 1930s were exciting times for Italian football. Under the guidance of Vittorio Pozzo the national team reached dizzy heights of success that they have been hard pressed to match since. They won the 1934 World Cup, then won the gold medal at the 1936 Olympics before setting the seal on a remarkable decade with victory in the 1938 World Cup. Only seven games were lost throughout the whole of the 1930s as the Italians confirmed themselves as the giants of the game.

The game was still deemed amateur, though for the most part it was nothing of the sort. Huge incentives were given to players, especially at club level, where the Mitropa Cup was proving to be a rewarding challenge both on the field and financially. Clubs like Juventus, in a bid to give themselves an advantage in the championship, started to import players from abroad in a tradition that persists to this day. Luisito Monti and Raimundo Orsi were perhaps the most famous. Both were Argentinian, Monti having played in the 1930 World Cup final. That he played for Italy in the 1934 final gives a small indication why among some nations the Italians are not the most popular of people in the football world!

The greatest star of the period was Giuseppe Meazza, one of only two players – the other being Ferrari – who played in both World Cup winning teams. Meazza played for Internazionale, who along with Bologna and Juventus dominated league football at this time. Bologna however were the only ones who could turn this domination into success in the Mitropa Cup, winning it in 1932 and 1934. The first victory was achieved by a walk-over after a riot in the other semi-final between Juventus and Slavia Prague had led to both teams being disqualified. In the 1934 final however, after losing 3–2 in the first leg to Admira Wien, they pulled off a 5–1 victory, inspired by another of Italy's great players, Angelo Schiavio.

The immediate post-war football story is dominated by the Superga aircrash in 1949. Torino were at the time probably the best team Italy had seen and almost without exception formed the national side. On a return trip from Lisbon, however, the aircraft carrying the team crashed into the Superga hill in the suburbs of Turin, killing everyone on board. Among those killed were 10 Italian internationals, the most famous of whom was Valentin Mazzola, father of Sandro Mazzola who achieved such fame in the 1960s.

Neither the national side nor Torino recovered quickly from the tragedy, and throughout the 1950s Italy faltered. Poor performances in the 1950 and 1954 World Cups were followed by failure to qualify for the 1958 tournament in Sweden, in what was seen as a national disaster. Although they qualified for both the 1962 and 1966 World Cups, on both occasions the performances were once again extremely disappointing. The defeat by North Korea in 1966 was especially humiliating

Many blamed the number of 'Oriundi' or foreigners that were playing in the league. Throughout the 1950s, Swedes, Danes, Argentinians, Uruguayans, Brazilians, Englishmen and more were tempted into the Italian game by the vast salaries on offer. Milan had forced their way back to the top of the league after years in the wilderness, largely on the back of the Gre-No-Li trio of Swedes, Gren, Nordahl and Liedholm, whilst Juventus sealed their reputation as the biggest club in the country with players such as John Charles of Wales and the Danish pair Hansen and Praest.

In 1964 it was decided to ban the importation of any more foreigners in order to let the Italian players develop. For so long in the shadow of their foreign counterparts, they were no less skilful but they simply did not get the attention they deserved. The effect of the ban was two-fold. Over the period of more than 20 years that the ban was in place, a new generation of Italian stars came to the fore, which ultimately led to the World Cup win in 1982.

On the domestic scene, however, a little of the gloss was taken off the large clubs who with their foreigners had looked as if they would dominate European football for good. Milan had won the European Cup in 1963, and were emulated by their local rivals Internazionale the following two years. Inter, in particular, relied heavily on the likes of the Brazilian Jair and the Spaniard Suarez. For Italian clubs, denied access to players like this, the 1970s proved to be a barren time in European competitions.

Tactics did not help the Italian cause either. Because of the money at stake in the Italian league, and the prestige that went with winning the title, ever more pressure was put on coaches. Catenaccio became the accepted style of play, reinforcing the image of the Italian game as a sterile, moribund game.

This description applied less to the national side. Beaten finalists in the 1970 World Cup, the Italians proved that given the motivation they were as good if not better than most teams. After scoring just one goal in the three group matches, they turned on the style in the quarter and semi-finals scoring eight goals against the hosts and West Germany. The same thing happened when they finally won the World Cup again in 1982. After three tedious perfomances in the opening group matches, they played four brilliant games and in the end were deserved winners.

The 1990 World Cup saw the reverse happen. Starting off the tournament as if their very lives depended on winning, they were superb up until the semi-final against Argentina. Clearly the far superior side in that game, they even took an early lead, but then seemed to want to protect their lead rather than to reinforce their superiority. That age-old cautiousness finally undid them when it mattered most, and they had only themselves to blame for not reaching the final.

The 1980s saw a tremendous boom in club football. With the relaxation of the ban on foreigners, Italian clubs once again sought the cream of the world's footballers. Michel

		All			League			Cup		Europe		
	Team	G	S	B	G	S	B	G	S	G	S	B
1	Juventus	34	21	16	22	15	11	8	8	4	4	5
2	Milan	22	19	15	12	12	13	4	5	6	2	2
3	Internazionale	19	15	17	13	10	11	3	3	3	2	6
4	Torino	12	17	7	8	9	6	4	7	–	1	1
5	Roma	10	9	7	2	5	5	7	2	1	2	2
6	Genoa 1893	10	5	2	9	4	1	1	1	–	–	1
7	Bologna	9	4	4	7	4	3	2	–	–	–	1
8	Fiorentina	7	10	4	2	5	4	4	2	1	3	–
9	Pro Vercelli	7	1	–	7	1	–	–	–	–	–	–
10	Napoli	6	7	7	2	4	6	3	3	1	–	1
11	Sampdoria	5	5	2	1	1	2	3	2	1	2	–
12	Lazio	2	5	2	1	4	2	1	1	–	–	–
13	Hellas-Verona	1	3	–	1	–	–	–	3	–	–	–
14	Venezia	1	2	1	–	1	1	1	1	–	–	–
15	Atalanta	1	1	1	–	–	–	1	1	–	–	1
16	Cagliari	1	1	–	1	1	–	–	–	–	–	–
17	Casale	1	–	–	1	–	–	–	–	–	–	–
	Novese	1	–	–	1	–	–	–	–	–	–	–
	Parma	1	–	–	1	–	–	–	–	–	–	–
	Vado	1	–	–	–	–	–	1	–	–	–	–
21	US Milanese	–	2	1	–	2	1	–	–	–	–	–
22	Alba	–	2	–	–	2	–	–	–	–	–	–
	Livorno	–	2	–	–	2	–	–	–	–	–	–
	Palermo	–	2	–	–	–	–	–	2	–	–	–
	Udinese	–	2	–	–	1	–	–	1	–	–	–
	Lanerossi-Vicenza	–	2	–	–	2	–	–	2	–	–	–
27	Alessandria	–	1	1	–	–	1	–	1	–	–	–
	Padova	–	1	1	–	–	1	–	1	–	–	–
29	Catanzaro	–	1	–	–	–	–	–	1	–	–	–
	Fortitudo	–	1	–	–	1	–	–	–	–	–	–
	Novara	–	1	–	–	–	–	–	1	–	–	–
	Perugia	–	1	–	–	1	–	–	–	–	–	–
	Pisa	–	1	–	–	1	–	–	–	–	–	–
	Savoia	–	1	–	–	1	–	–	–	–	–	–
	SPAL Ferrara	–	1	–	–	–	–	–	1	–	–	–
36	Modena	–	–	1	–	–	1	–	–	–	–	–

To the end of the 1991–92 season

Platini was signed by Juventus and led them to many honours both at home and in Europe in the first half of the 1980s, whilst perhaps most significantly Diego Maradona was lured by Napoli from Barcelona. The Italians could now claim that theirs was the strongest league in the world, for without question they had most of the world's top players playing there. In the 1960s, they had failed to engage Pele, but with Maradona they now had the best player in the world.

As the number of foreigners allowed grew from one per team to the present three, a tradition started with the Gre-No-Li trio continued as Milan went Dutch with Gullit, Rijkaard and Van Basten, and Internazionale went German with Klinsmann, Brehme and Matthäus. The influence of the foreigners – and perhaps the ban on English clubs from Europe – saw the Italian clubs at their most prolific in Europe at the end of the decade. Milan won the European Cup twice, whilst Napoli, Juventus, Internazionale and Sampdoria were all winners of one of the other two competitions.

Whether another decline in the national side has set in due to the emergence of the 'Oriundi' is open to debate, but failure to qualify for the 1992 European Championships is not an encouraging sign for the Italians. With freedom of movement for labour in the European Community, in no country will the battle between club and country be more pronounced in the future. Perhaps Italian players ought to buck the trend and move abroad themseives to countries like Spain, Germany or England, in order to increase their profile!

Population: 57 512 000
Area, sq km: 301 277
% in urban areas: 65.0%
Capital city: Rome

Federazione Italiana Giuoco Calcio
Via Gregorio Allegri #14
CP 2450
I–00198 Rome
Italy
Tel: (010 39) 6 84911
Fax: (010 39) 6 84912239
Telex: 611483 CALCIO I
Cable: FEDERCALCIO ROMA
Languages for correspondence: French, English, German & Spanish

Year of formation: 1898
Affiliation to FIFA: 1905
Affiliation to UEFA: 1954
Registered clubs: 19966
Registered players: 1 390 000
Professional players: 4250
Registered coaches: 33 057
Registered referees: 28 455
National stadium: Stadio Olimpico, Rome 80 000
National colours: Shirts: Blue/Shorts: White/Socks: Blue
Reserve colours: Shirts: White/Shorts: Blue/Socks: Blue
Season: September–June

THE RECORD

WORLD CUP

1930 Did not enter
1934 .... QT 1st/2 in group 7 – Final Tournament/Winners
1938 .... QT Automatic – Final Tournament/Winners
1950 .... QT Automatic – Final Tournament/1st round
1954 .... QT 1st/2 in group 9 – Final Tournament/1st round
1958 .... QT 2nd/3 in group 8
1962 .... QT 1st/4 in group 7 – Final Tournament/1st round
1966 .... QT 1st/4 in group 8 – Final Tournament/1st round
1970 .... QT 1st/3 in group 3 – Final Tournament/Finalists
1974 .... QT 1st/4 in group 2 – Final Tournament/1st round
1978 .... QT 1st/4 in group 2 – Final Tournament/2nd round/4th place
1982 .... QT 2nd/5 in group 4 – Final Tournament/Winners
1986 .... QT Automatic – Final Tournament/2nd round
1990 .... QT Automatic – Final Tournament/Semi-finalists/3rd place

EUROPEAN CHAMPIONSHIP

1960 .... Did not enter
1964 .... 2nd round
1968 .... QT 1st/4 in group 6 – Final Tournament/Winners
1972 .... QT 1st/4 in group 6 – Final Tournament/Quarter-finalists
1976 .... QT 3rd/4 in group 5
1980 .... QT Automatic – Final Tournament/4th place
1984 .... QT 4th/5 in group 5
1988 .... QT 1st/5 in group 2 – Final Tournament/Semi-finalists
1992 .... QT 2nd/5 in group 3

OLYMPIC GAMES

1908 .... Did not enter
1912 .... Preliminary round
1920 .... Quarter-finalists
1924 .... Quarter-finalists
1928 .... Semi-finalists/3rd place
1936 .... Winners
1948 .... Quarter-finalists
1952 .... 1st round
1956 .... Did not enter
1960 .... Final Tournament/Semi-finalists/3rd place
1964 .... QT Qualified but withdrew
1968 .... Did not enter
1972 .... QT Failed to qualify
1976 .... Did not enter
1980 .... QT Failed to qualify
1984 .... Final Tournament/Semi-finalists/4th place
1988 .... Final Tournament/Semi-finalists/4th place
1992 .... Final Tournament

DR. GERO CUP

1929 .... Winners
1932 .... 2nd
1935 .... Winners
1953 .... 4th
1960 .... 5th

EUROPEAN CLUB COMPETITIONS

EUROPEAN CUP: Winners – Milan 1963 1969 1989 1990, Internazionale 1964 1965, Juventus 1985
Finalists – Fiorentina 1957, Milan 1958, Internazionale 1967, 1972, Juventus 1973 1983, Roma 1984, Sampdoria 1992

CUP WINNERS CUP: Winners – Fiorentina 1961, Milan 1968 1973, Juventus 1984, Sampdoria 1990
Finalists – Fiorentina 1962, Milan 1974, Sampdoria 1989

UEFA CUP: Winners – Roma 1961, Juventus 1977, Napoli 1989, Juventus 1990, Internazionale 1991
Finalists – Juventus 1965 1971, Fiorentina 1990, Roma 1991, Torino 1992

MITROPA CUP: Winners – Bologna 1932 1934
Finalists – Ambrosiana-Inter 1933, Lazio 1937

CLUB DIRECTORY

ROME (Population – 3 175 000)

Lazio Societa Sportiva
Stadium: Stadio Olimpico 82 000
Founded: 1900
Colours: Sky blue/White
Previous name: SP Lazio 1900–25

Roma Associazione Sportiva
Stadium: Stadio Olimpico 82 000
Founded: 1927
Colours: Red/Red
Previous names: Merger in 1927 of Fortitudo, Pro Roma, Roman and Alba

MILAN (Population – 3 750 000)

Internazionale Milano Football Club
Stadium: Giuseppe Meazza 76 000
Founded: 1908
Colours: Black and blue stripes/Black
Previous name: Ambrosiana-Inter 1929–46

Milan Associazione Calcio
Stadium: Giuseppe Meazza 76 000
Founded: 1899
Colours: Red and black stripes/White
Previous name: Milan Cricket and Football Club 1899–1905, Milan Football Club 1905–38

NAPLES (Population – 2 875 000)
Napoli Societa Sportiva Calcio
Stadium: San Paolo 85 000
Founded: 1926
Colours: Sky blue/White
Previous names: Merger in 1926 of Internaples and Naples

TURIN (Population – 1 550 000)

Juventus Football Club
Stadium: Della Alpi 70 000
Founded: 1897
Colours: Black and white stripes/White
Previous name: SC Juventus 1897–99

Torino Calcio
Stadium: Della Alpi 70 000
Founded: 1906
Colours: Grenadine/White
Previous names: Merger in 1906 of FC Torinense and dissatified members of Juventus. FC Torinense had merged with Internazionale Torino in 1900. FC Torino 1906–36

GENOA (Population – 805 000)

Genoa 1893
Stadium: Luigi Ferraris 44 000
Founded: 1893
Colours: Red and blue halves/Blue
Previous names: Genoa Football and Cricket Club 1893–99, Genoa FC 1899–1929, Genova 1893 1929–45

Sampdoria Unione Calcio
Stadium: Luigi Ferraris 44 000
Founded: 1946
Colours: Blue with a white, red, black and white hoop/White
Previous names: Merger in 1946 of Andrea Doria and Sampierdarenese

PALERMO (Population – 723 000)
Palermo Unione Sportiva
Stadium: Della Favorita 40 000
Founded: 1898
Colours: Pink/Black
Previous names: US Palermo 1892–42, Palermo–Juve 1942–45, SSC Palermo 1945–87

FLORENCE (Population – 640 000)
Fiorentina Associazione Calcio
Stadium: Comunale 44 000
Founded: 1926
Colours: Violet/White
Previous manes: Merger in 1926 of Polisportiva and CS Firenze

CATANIA (Population – 550 000)
Catania Calcio
Stadium: Cibali 12 000
Founded: 1946
Colours: Red and blue stripes/Blue
Previous names: Merger in 1946 of Virtus and US Catanese (1908)

BOLOGNA (Population – 525 000)
Bologna Football Club
Stadium: Renato Dall'Aria 40 000
Founded: 1909
Colours: Red and blue stripes/White

BARI (Population – 475 000)
Bari Associazione Sportiva
Stadium: San Nicola 60 000
Founded: 1928
Colours: Red and white stripes/White
Previous names: Merger in 1928 of FC Bari and US Ideale as US Bari. US Bari 1928–45

VENICE (Population – 420 000)
Venezia Calcio
Stadium: Penzo 15 000
Founded: 1907
Colours: Green, black and orange stripes/Black
Previous names: Venezia-Mestre 1980–89

BERGAMO (Population – 345 000)
Atalanta Bergamasca Calcio
Stadium: Comunale 32 000
Founded: 1907
Colours: Black and blue stripes/Black

CAGLIARI (Population – 305 000)
Cagliari Calcio
Stadium: Sant'Elia 43 000
Founded: 1920
Colours: Red and blue halves/Blue
Previous names: Cagliari FC 1920–24, CS Cagliari 1924–34

PADUA (Population – 270 000)
Padova Calcio
Stadium: Silvio Appiani 22 000
Founded: 1910
Colours: White/White

MESSINA (Population – 268 000)
Messina Associazioni Calcio Riunite
Stadium: Giovanni Celeste 15 000
Founded: 1945
Colours: White/Black

VERONA (Population – 259 000)
Hellas-Verona
Stadium: Bentegodi 50 000
Founded: 1903
Colours: Blue/Blue
Previous names: Hellas 1903–19, Hellas-Verona 1919–28, AC Verona 1928–69

SALERNO (Population – 250 000)
Salernitana Sport
Stadium: Stadio Vestuti 12 000
Founded: 1919
Colours: Grenadine/Grenadine
Previous name: US Salernitana 1919–79

TARANTO (Population – 244 000)
Taranto Football Club
Stadium: Erasmo Jacovone 30 000
Founded: 1926
Colours: Red and blue stripes/Blue

TRIESTE (Population – 239 000)
Triestina Unione Sportiva Calcio
Stadium: Primo Grezar 24 000
Founded: 1918
Colours: Red/Red

BRESCIA (Population – 199 000)
Brescia Calcio
Stadium: Mario Rigamonti 25 000
Founded: 1911
Colours: Blue/White

MODENA (Population – 176 000)
Modena Football Club
Stadium: Alberto Braglia 20 000
Founded: 1912
Colours: Yellow/Blue
Previous name: Zenit Modena 1957–59

PARMA (Population – 175 000)
Parma Associazione Calcio
Stadium: Ennio Tardini 20 000
Founded: 1968
Colours: White/White

LIVORNO (Population – 174 000)
Pro Livorno Calcio
Stadium: Armando Picchi 20 000
Founded: 1915
Colours: Cherry/White
Previous name: US Livorno 1915–88

COMO (Population – 165 000)
Como Calcio
Stadium: Giuseppe Sinigaglia 28 000
Founded: 1907
Colours: Blue/Blue
Previous names: FC Como 1907–25, AC Comense 1925–37

FOGGIA (Population – 155 000)
Foggia Calcio
Stadium: Pino Zaccheria 24 000
Founded: 1920
Colours: Red and black stripes/Black
Previous names: SC Foggia 1920–24, US Foggia 1924–85

PERUGIA (Population – 146 000)
Perugia Associazione Calcio
Stadium: Renato Curi 40 000
Founded: 1905
Colours: Red/White
Previous name: SS Perugia 1913–19

FERRARA (Population – 143 000)
Societa Polisportiva Ars et Labor (SPAL)
Stadium: Paolo Meazza 21 000
Founded: 1907
Colours: Blue and white stripes/White

PESCARA (Population – 131 000)
Pescara Calcio
Stadium: Adriatico 26 000
Founded: 1936
Colours: Blue and white stripes/Blue

UDINE (Population – 126 000)
Udinese Calcio
Stadium: Friuli 42 000
Founded: 1896
Colours: White/White

TERNI (Population – 111 000)
Ternana Polisportiva Calcio
Stadium: Liberati 38 000
Founded: 1929
Colours: Red/Green

VICENZA (Population – 110 000)
Lanerossi-Vicenza Societa Sportiva
Stadium: Romeo Menti 28 000
Founded: 1902
Colours: Red and white stripes/White
Previous name: AC Vicenzia 1902–53

PISA (Population – 104 000)
Pisa Sporting Club
Stadium: Arena Garibaldi 31 000
Founded: 1909
Colours: Blue and black stripes/Black
Previous name: AC Pisa 1931–43

CATANZARO (Population – 102 000)
Catanzaro Unione Sportiva
Stadium: Nicola Ceravolo 30 000
Founded: 1929
Colours: Red and yellow stripes/White

NOVARA (Population – 102 000)
Novara Calcio
Stadium: Comunale 14 000
Founded: 1908
Colours: Blue/Blue
Previous names: Novara FC 1908–34. Merged with US Novarese as Novara Calcio in 1934

LEECE (Population – 100 000)
Leece Unione Sportiva
Stadium: Via del Mare 55 000
Founded: 1908
Colours: Red and yellow stripes/Red

ALESSANDRIA (Population – 96 000)
Alessandria Unione Sportiva Calcio
Stadium: Moccagatta 12 000
Founded: 1920
Colours: Grey/Black
Previous names: Merger in 1920 of US Alessandria and Alessandria FC

CESENA (Population – 90 000)
Cesena Associazione Calcio
Stadium: Dino Manuzzi 28 000
Founded: 1940 Colours: White/Black

PISTOIA (Population – 90 000)
Nuova Pistoiese
Stadium: Comunale
Founded: 1921
Colours: Orange/Orange
Previous name: US Pistoiese 1921–88

LUCCA (Population – 88 000)
Lucchese-Libertas Associazione Sportiva
Stadium: Porta Elisa 9000
Founded: 1905
Colours: Red and black stripes/Black

VARESE (Population – 88 000)
Varese Football Club
Stadium: Franco Ossola 23 000
Founded: 1910 Colours: White/Red
Previous names: AS Varesina 1924–26, Varese Sportiva 1926–46

BUSTO ARSIZIO (Population 78 000)
Pro Patria et Libertate
Stadium: Carlo Speroni 20 000
Founded: 1919
Colours: Blue and white hoops/White

CREMONA (Population – 76 000)
Cremonese Unione Sportiva
Stadium: Giovanni Zini 14 000
Founded: 1903
Colours: Grey and red stripes/Red
Previous name: AC Cremona 1903–13

AVELLINO (Population – 56 000)
Avellino Unione Sportiva
Stadium: Partenio 42 000
Founded: 1912
Colours: Green and white stripes/White

MANTOVA (Population – 56 000)
Montova Nuova Associazione Calcio
Stadium: Danilo Martelli 25 000
Founded: 1911
Colours: Red/White

VERCELLI (Population – 51 000)
Pro Vercelli Unione Sportiva Calcio
Stadium: Leonida Robbiano 12 000
Founded: 1892
Colours: White/White

LECCO (Population – 48 000)
Lecco Calcio
Stadium: Rigamonti Ceppi 9000
Founded: 1910
Colours: White/White

LEGNANO (Population 48 000)
Legnano Associazione Calcio
Stadium: Giovanni Mari 7000
Founded: 1913
Colours: Lilac/Lilac

EMPOLI (Population – 43 000)
Empoli Football Club
Stadium: Carlo Castellani 19 000
Founded: 1921
Colours: Blue/White

ASCOLI
Ascoli Calcio 1898
Stadium: Cino e Lillo Del Duca 34 000
Founded: 1898
Colours: Black and white stripes/White
Previous names: SS Vigor 1898–1905, CS Vigor 1905–11, SS Ascoli 1911–55

CASALE
Casale Associazione Sportiva
Stadium: Natale Palli 8000
Founded: 1909
Colours: Black/Black

ITALIAN LEAGUE CHAMPIONSHIP

Year	Champions		Runners up			
1898	Genoa	2–1	Internazionale Torino			
1899	Genoa	2–0	Internazionale Torino			
1900	Genoa	1–0	FC Torinese			
1901	Milan	1–0	Genoa			
1902	Genoa	2–0	Milan			
1903	Genoa	3–0	Juventus			
1904	Genoa	1–0	Juventus			
1905	Juventus	6	Genoa	5	US Milanese	1

1906	Milan 5	Juventus 5	Genoa 2
1907	Milan 6	Torino 5	Andrea Doria 1
1908	Pro Vercelli 6	US Milanese 5	Andrea Doria 1
1909	Pro Vercelli 2–0 1–1	US Milanese	
1910	Internazionale 25	Pro Vercelli 25	Juventus 20
	Internazionale won the play–off with Pro Vercelli 10–3		
1911	Pro Vercelli 3–0 2–1	Vicenza	
1912	Pro Vercelli 6–0 7–0	Venezia	
1913	Pro Vercelli 6–0	Lazio	
1914	Casale 7–1 2–0	Lazio	
1915	Genoa declared winners		
1916–19 –			
1920	Internazionale 3–2	Livorno	
1921	Pro Vercelli 2–1	Pisa	
1922	Novese 0–0 0–0 2–1	Sampierdarenese	
1922	Pro Vercelli 3–0 5–2	Fortitudo	
1923	Genoa 4–1 2–0	Lazio	
1924	Genoa 3–1 1–1	Savoia	
1925	Bologna 4–0 2–0	Alba	
1926	Juventus 7–1 5–0	Alba	
1927	Torino 14	Bologna 12	Juventus 11
1928	Torino 19	Genoa 17	Juventus/Alessandria 16
1929	Bologna 3–1 0–1 1–0	Torino	

NATIONAL CHAMPIONSHIP

	Champions	Runners–up	3rd
1930	Ambrosiana–Inter 50	Genova 48	Juventus 45
1931	Juventus 55	Roma 51	Bologna 48
1932	Juventus 54	Bologna 50	Roma 40
1933	Juventus 54	Ambrosiana-Inter 46	Bologna 42
1934	Juventus 53	Ambrosiana-Inter 49	Napoli 46
1935	Juventus 44	Ambrosiana-Inter 42	Fiorentina 39
1936	Bologna 40	Roma 39	Torino 38
1937	Bologna 42	Lazio 39	Torino 38
1938	Ambrosiana-Inter 41	Juventus 39	Milan 38
1939	Bologna 42	Torino 38	Ambrosiana-Inter 37
1940	Ambrosiana-Inter 44	Bologna 41	Juventus 36
1941	Bologna 39	Ambrosiana-Inter 35	Milan 34
1942	Roma 42	Torino 39	Venezia 38
1943	Torino 44	Livorno 43	Juventus 37
1944–45 –			
1946	Torino 22	Juventus 21	Milan 16
1947	Torino 63	Juventus 53	Modena 51
1948	Torino 65	Milan 49	Juventus 49
1949	Torino 60	Internazionale 55	Milan 50
1950	Juventus 62	Milan 57	Internazionale 49
1951	Milan 60	Internazionale 59	Juventus 54
1952	Juventus 60	Milan 53	Internazionale 49
1953	Internazionale 47	Juventus 45	Milan 43
1954	Internazionale 51	Juventus 50	Milan 44
1955	Milan 48	Udinese 44	Roma 41
1956	Fiorentina 53	Milan 41	Internazionale 39
1957	Milan 48	Fiorentina 42	Lazio 41
1958	Juventus 51	Fiorentina 43	Padova 42
1959	Milan 52	Fiorentina 49	Internazionale 46
1960	Juventus 55	Fiorentina 47	Milan 44
1961	Juventus 49	Milan 45	Internazionale 44
1962	Milan 53	Internazionale 48	Fiorentina 46
1963	Internazionale 49	Juventus 45	Milan 43
1964	Bologna 54	Internazionale 54	Milan 51
1965	Internazionale 54	Milan 51	Torino 44
1966	Internazionale 50	Bologna 46	Napoli 45
1967	Juventus 49	Internazionale 48	Bologna 45
1968	Milan 46	Napoli 37	Juventus 36
1969	Fiorentina 45	Cagliari 41	Milan 41
1970	Cagliari 45	Internazionale 41	Juventus 38
1971	Internazionale 46	Milan 42	Napoli 39

1972	Juventus	43	Milan	42	Torino	42
1973	Juventus	45	Milan	44	Lazio	43
1974	Lazio	43	Juventus	41	Napoli	36
1975	Juventus	43	Napoli	41	Roma	39
1976	Torino	45	Juventus	43	Milan	38
1977	Juventus	51	Torino	50	Fiorentina	35
1978	Juventus	44	Lanerossi-Vicenza	39	Torino	39
1979	Milan	44	Perugia	41	Juventus	37
1980	Internazionale	41	Juventus	38	Milan	36
1981	Juventus	44	Roma	42	Napoli	38
1982	Juventus	46	Fiorentina	45	Roma	38
1983	Roma	43	Juventus	39	Internazionale	38
1984	Juventus	43	Roma	41	Fiorentina	36
1985	Hellas–Verona	43	Torino	39	Internazionale	38
1986	Juventus	45	Roma	41	Napoli	39
1987	Napoli	42	Juventus	39	Internazionale	38
1988	Milan	45	Napoli	42	Roma	38
1989	Internazionale	58	Napoli	47	Milan	46
1990	Napoli	51	Milan	49	Internazionale	44
1991	Sampdoria	51	Milan	46	Internazionale	46
1992	Milan	56	Juventus	48	Torino	43

ITALIAN CUP FINALS

Year	Winners	Score	Runners–up
1922	Vado	1–0	Udinese
1923–35	–		
1936	Torino	5–1	Alessandria
1937	Genoa	1–0	Roma
1938	Juventus	2–1	Torino
1939	Ambrosiana-Inter	2–1	Novara
1940	Fiorentina	1–0	Genova
1941	Venezia	3–3 1–0	Roma
1942	Juventus	1–1 4–1	Milan
1943	Torino	4–0	Venezia
1944–57	–		
1958	Lazio	1–0	Fiorentina
1959	Juventus	4–1	Internazionale
1960	Juventus	3–2	Fiorentina
1961	Fiorentina	2–0	Lazio
1962	Napoli	2–1	SPAL Ferrara
1963	Atalanta	3–1	Torino
1964	Roma	0–0 1–0	Torino
1965	Juventus	1–0	Internazionale
1966	Fiorentina	2–1	Catanzaro
1967	Milan	1–0	Padova
1968	Torino	*	
1969	Roma	*	
1970	Bologna	*	
1971	Torino	0–0 (5–3p)	Milan
1972	Milan	2–0	Napoli
1973	Milan	1–1 (5–2p)	Juventus
1974	Bologna	0–0 (5–4p)	Palermo
1975	Fiorentina	3–2	Milan
1976	Napoli	4–0	Hellas-Verona
1977	Milan	2–0	Internazionale
1978	Internazionale	2–1	Napoli
1979	Juventus	2–1	Palermo
1980	Roma	0–0 (3–2p)	Torino
1981	Roma	1–1 1–1 (5–3p)	Torino
1982	Internazionale	1–0 1–1	Torino
1983	Juventus	0–2 3–0	Hellas-Verona
1984	Roma	1–1 1–0	Hellas-Verona
1985	Sampdoria	1–0 2–1	Milan
1986	Roma	1–2 2–0	Sampdoria
1987	Napoli	3–0 1–0	Atalanta
1988	Sampdoria	2–0 1–2	Torino
1989	Sampdoria	0–1 4–0	Napoli
1990	Juventus	0–0 1–0	Milan
1991	Roma	3–1 1–1	Sampdoria
1992	Parma	0–1 2–0	Juventus

* League format

INTERNATIONAL MATCHES PLAYED BY ITALY

Date	Opponents	Result		Venue	Compet	Scorers
15–05–1910	France	W	6–2	Milan	Fr	Lana 3, Fossati, Rizzi, Debernardi
26–05	Hungary	L	1–6	Budapest	Fr	Rizzi
6–01–1911	Hungary	L	0–1	Milan	Fr	
9–04	France	D	2–2	Paris	Fr	Rampini, Boiocchi
7–05	Switzerland	D	2–2	Milan	Fr	Carrer, Boiocchi
21–05	Switzerland	L	0–3	Chaux-de-Fonds	Fr	
17–03–1912	France	L	3–4	Turin	Fr	Rampini 2, Cevenini A
29–06	Finland	L	2–3	Stockholm	OGr1	Bontadini, Sardi
1–07	Sweden	W	1–0	Stockholm	OGct	Bontadini
3–07	Austria	L	1–5	Stockholm	OGct	Berardo
22–12	Austria	L	1–3	Genoa	Fr	Sardi
12–01–1913	France	L	0–1	Paris	Fr	
1–05	Belgium	W	1–0	Turin	Fr	Ara
15–06	Austria	L	0–2	Vienna	Fr	
11–01–1914	Austria	D	0–0	Milan	Fr	

29–03	France	W	2–0	Turin	Fr	Berardo, Cevenini A
5–04	Switzerland	D	1–1	Genoa	Fr	Mattea
17–05	Switzerland	W	1–0	Berne	Fr	Barbesino
31–01–1915	Switzerland	W	3–1	Turin	Fr	Cevenini A 2, Cevenini L
18–01–1920	France	W	9–4	Milan	Fr	Cevenini L 2, Aebi 3, Brezzi 3, Carcano
28–03	Switzerland	L	0–3	Berne	Fr	
13–05	Holland	D	1–1	Genoa	Fr	Sardi
28–08	Egypt	W	2–1	Ghent	OGr1	Baloncieri, Brezzi
29–08	France	L	1–3	Antwerp	OGqf	Brezzi
31–08	Norway	W	2–1	Antwerp	OGct	Sardi, Badini
2–09	Spain	L	0–2	Antwerp	OGct	
20–02–1921	France	W	2–1	Marseille	Fr	Cevenini L, Santamaria
6–03	Switzerland	W	2–1	Milan	Fr	Migliavacca, Cevenini L
5–05	Belgium	W	3–2	Antwerp	Fr	Migliavacca, Forlivesi, Ferraris P (I)
8–05	Holland	D	2–2	Amsterdam	Fr	Forlivesi, Cevenini L
6–11	Switzerland	D	1–1	Geneva	Fr	Moscardini
15–01–1922	Austria	D	3–3	Milan	Fr	Moscardini 2, Santamaria
26–02	Czechoslovakia	D	1–1	Turin	Fr	Baloncieri
21–05	Belgium	W	4–2	Milan	Fr	Baloncieri 2, Moscardini, Burlando
3–12	Switzerland	D	2–2	Bologna	Fr	Cevenini L 2
1–01–1923	Germany	W	3–1	Milan	Fr	Cevenini L, Santamaria, Migliavacca
4–03	Hungary	D	0–0	Genoa	Fr	
15–04	Austria	D	0–0	Vienna	Fr	
27–05	Czechoslovakia	L	1–5	Prague	Fr	Moscardini
20–01–1924	Austria	L	0–4	Genoa	Fr	
9–03	Spain	D	0–0	Milan	Fr	
6–04	Hungary	L	1–7	Budapest	Fr	Cevenini L
25–05	Spain	W	1–0	Paris	OGr1	Og
29–05	Luxembourg	W	2–0	Paris	OGr2	Baloncieri, Della Valle
2–06	Switzerland	L	1–2	Paris	OGqf	Della Valle
16–11	Sweden	D	2–2	Milan	Fr	Magnozzi 2
23–11	Germany	W	1–0	Duisburg	Fr	Janni
18–01–1925	Hungary	L	1–2	Milan	Fr	Conti L
22–03	France	W	7–0	Turin	Fr	Conti L, Baloncieri 2, Levratto 2, Moscardini 2
14–06	Spain	L	0–1	Valencia	Fr	
18–06	Portugal	L	0–1	Lisbon	Fr	
4–11	Yugoslavia	W	2–1	Padua	Fr	Schiavio 2
8–11	Hungary	D	1–1	Budapest	Fr	Della Valle
17–01–1926	Czechoslovakia	W	3–1	Turin	Fr	Della Valle, Conti L, Magnozzi
21–03	Rep. Ireland	W	3–0	Turin	Fr	Baloncieri, Magnozzi, Bernardini
18–04	Switzerland	D	1–1	Zurich	Fr	Magnozzi
9–05	Switzerland	W	3–2	Milan	Fr	Della Valle 2, Schiavio
18–07	Sweden	L	3–5	Stockholm	Fr	Levratto 2, Cevenini L
28–10	Czechoslovakia	L	1–3	Prague	Fr	Levratto
30–01–1927	Switzerland	W	5–1	Geneva	Fr	Baloncieri 3, Libonatti, Rossetti
20–02	Czechoslovakia	D	2–2	Milan	Fr	Libonatti, Baloncieri
17–04	Portugal	W	3–1	Turin	Fr	Levratto 2, Baloncieri
24–04	France	D	3–3	Paris	Fr	Libonatti 2, Conti L
29–05	Spain	W	2–0	Bologna	Fr	Baloncieri, OG
23–10	Czechoslovakia	D	2–2	Prague	DGC	Libonatti 2
6–11	Austria	L	0–1	Bologna	DGC	
1–01–1928	Switzerland	W	3–2	Genoa	DGC	Libonatti 2, Magnozzi
25–03	Hungary	W	4–3	Rome	DGC	Conti L 2, Rossetti, Libonatti
15–04	Portugal	L	1–4	Oporto	Fr	Libonatti
22–04	Spain	D	1–1	Gijon	Fr	Libonatti
29–05	France	W	4–3	Amsterdam	OGr1	Rossetti, Levratto, Banchero, Baloncieri
1–06	Spain	D	1–1	Amsterdam	OGqf	Baloncieri
4–06	Spain	W	7–1	Amsterdam	OGqf	Magnozzi, Schiavio, Baloncieri, Bernardini, Rivolta, Levratto 2
7–06	Uruguay	L	2–3	Amsterdam	OGsf	Baloncieri, Levratto
10–06	Egypt	W	11–3	Amsterdam	OG3p	Schiavio 3, Baloncieri 2, Banchero 3, Magnozzi 3
14–10	Switzerland	W	3–2	Zurich	DGC	Rossetti 2, Baloncieri
11–11	Austria	D	2–2	Rome	Fr	Conti L 2
2–12	Holland	W	3–2	Milan	Fr	Libonatti 2, Baloncieri
3–03–1929	Czechoslovakia	W	4–2	Bologna	DGC	Rossetti 3, Libonatti
7–04	Austria	L	0–3	Vienna	DGC	
28–04	Germany	L	1–2	Turin	Fr	Rossetti

1–12	Portugal	W	6–1	Milan	Fr	Mihalic 2, Orsi 2, Baloncieri, Sallustro
9–02–1930	Switzerland	W	4–2	Rome	Fr	Magnozzi, Orsi, Meazza 2
2–03	Germany	W	2–0	Frankfurt	Fr	Baloncieri, Meazza
6–04	Holland	D	1–1	Amsterdam	Fr	Baloncieri
11–05	Hungary	W	5–0	Budapest	DGC	Meazza 3, Magnozzi, Costantino
22–06	Spain	L	2–3	Bologna	Fr	Costantino 2
25–01–1931	France	W	5–0	Bologna	Fr	Meazza 3, Cesarini, Cattaneo
22–02	Austria	W	2–1	Milan	DGC	Meazza, Orsi
29–03	Switzerland	D	1–1	Berne	DGC	Cesarini
12–04	Portugal	W	2–0	Oporto	Fr	Orsi, Ferrari
19–04	Spain	D	0–0	Bilbao	Fr	
20–05	Scotland	W	3–0	Rome	Fr	Costantino, Meazza, Orsi
15–11	Czechoslovakia	D	2–2	Rome	DGC	Pitto, Bernardini
13–12	Hungary	W	3–2	Turin	DGC	Libonatti, Orsi, Cesarini
14–02–1932	Switzerland	W	3–0	Naples	DGC	Fedullo 3
20–03	Austria	L	1–2	Vienna	DGC	Meazza
10–04	France	W	2–1	Paris	Fr	Magnozzi, Costantino
8–05	Hungary	D	1–1	Budapest	DGC	Costantino
28–10	Czechoslovakia	L	1–2	Prague	DGC	Ferrari
27–11	Hungary	W	4–2	Milan	Fr	Orsi 2, Meazza, Ferrari
1–01–1933	Germany	W	3–1	Bologna	Fr	Meazza, Costantino, Schiavio
12–02	Belgium	W	3–2	Brussels	Fr	Meazza 2, Costantini
2–04	Switzerland	W	3–0	Geneva	DGC	Schiavio 2, Meazza
7–05	Czechoslovakia	W	2–0	Florence	DGC	Ferrari, Schiavio
13–05	England	D	1–1	Rome	Fr	Ferrari
22–10	Hungary	W	1–0	Budapest	DGC	Borel
3–12	Switzerland	W	5–2	Florence	DGC	Ferrari, Pizziolo, Orsi, Meazza, Monti
11–02–1934	Austria	L	2–4	Turin	DGC	Guaita 2
25–03	Greece	W	4–0	Milan	WCq	Guarisi, Meazza 2, Ferrari
27–05	USA	W	7–1	Rome	WCr1	Schiavio 3, Orsi 2, Ferrari, Meazza
31–05	Spain	D	1–1	Florence	WCqf	Ferrari
1–06	Spain	W	1–0	Florence	WCqf	Meazza 2
3–06	Austria	W	1–0	Milan	WCsf	Guaita
10–06	Czechoslovakia	W	2–1	Rome	WCf	Orsi, Schiavio
14–11	England	L	2–3	London	Fr	Meazza 2
9–12	Hungary	W	4–2	Milan	Fr	Guaita 2, Ferrari, Meazza
17–02–1935	France	W	2–1	Rome	Fr	Meazza 2
24–03	Austria	W	2–0	Vienna	DGC	Piola
27–10	Czechoslovakia	L	1–2	Prague	DGC	Pitto
24–11	Hungary	D	2–2	Milan	DGC	Colaussi, Ferrari
5–04–1936	Switzerland	W	2–1	Zurich	Fr	Demaria, Colaussi
17–05	Austria	D	2–2	Rome	Fr	Demaria, Pasinati
31–05	Hungary	W	2–1	Budapest	Fr	Pasinati, Meazza
3–08	United States	W	1–0	Berlin	OGr1	Frossi
7–08	Japan	W	8–0	Berlin	OGqf	Frossi 3, Biagi 4, Cappelli
10–08	Norway	W	2–1	Berlin	OGsf	Negro, Frossi
15–08	Austria	W	2–1	Berlin	OGf	Frossi 2
25–10	Switzerland	W	4–2	Milan	DGC	Meazza, Piola 2, Pasinati
15–11	Germany	D	2–2	Berlin	Fr	Colaussi, Ferrari
13–12	Czechoslovakia	W	2–0	Genoa	Fr	Pasinati, Ferrari
25–04–1937	Hungary	W	2–0	Turin	DGC	Colaussi, Frossi
23–05	Czechoslovakia	W	1–0	Prague	DGC	Piola
27–05	Norway	W	3–1	Oslo	Fr	Meazza, Piola 2
31–10	Switzerland	D	2–2	Geneva	DGC	Piola 2
5–12	France	D	0–0	Paris	Fr	
15–05–1938	Belgium	W	6–1	Milan	Fr	Meazza, Andreolo, Pasinati, Piola 3
22–05	Yugoslavia	W	4–0	Genoa	Fr	Colaussi, Piola, Meazza, Ferrari
5–06	Norway	W	2–1	Marseille	WCr1	Ferraris P (II), Piola
12–06	France	W	3–1	Paris	WCqf	Colaussi, Piola 2
16–06	Brazil	W	2–1	Marseille	WCsf	Colaussi, Meazza
19–06	Hungary	W	4–2	Paris	WCf	Colaussi 2, Piola 2
20–11	Switzerland	W	2–0	Bologna	Fr	Colaussi, OG
4–12	France	W	1–0	Naples	Fr	Biavati
26–03–1939	Germany	W	3–2	Florence	Fr	Piola 2, Biavati
13–05	England	D	2–2	Milan	Fr	Biavati, Piola
4–06	Yugoslavia	W	2–1	Belgrade	Fr	Piola, Colaussi
8–06	Hungary	W	3–1	Budapest	Fr	Piola, Colaussi 2
11–06	Rumania	W	1–0	Bucharest	Fr	Colaussi
20–07	Finland	W	3–2	Helsinki	Fr	Piola 3

12–11	Switzerland	L	1–3	Zurich	Fr	Puricelli
26–11	Germany	L	2–5	Berlin	Fr	Neri, Demaria
3–03–1940	Switzerland	D	1–1	Turin	Fr	Corbelli
14–04	Rumania	W	2–1	Rome	Fr	Biavati, Piola
5–05	Germany	W	3–2	Milan	Fr	Colaussi, Bertoni I, Biavati
1–12	Hungary	D	1–1	Genoa	Fr	Trevisan
5–04–1942	Croatia	W	4–0	Genoa	Fr	Gabetto, Ferraris P (II), Biavati, OG
19–04	Spain	W	4–0	Milan	Fr	Mazzola V, Ferraris P (II), Piola, Loik
11–11–1945	Switzerland	D	4–4	Zurich	Fr	Piola, Loik, Biavati 2
1–12–1946	Austria	W	3–2	Milan	Fr	Castigliano, Mazzola V, Piola
27–04–1947	Switzerland	W	5–2	Florence	Fr	Mazzola V, Loik, Menti 3
11–05	Hungary	W	3–2	Turin	Fr	Gabetto 2, Loik
9–11	Austria	L	1–5	Vienna	Fr	Carapellese
14–12	Czechoslovakia	W	3–1	Bari	Fr	Menti, Gabetto, Carapellese
4–04–1948	France	W	3–1	Paris	Fr	Carapellese 2, Gabetto
16–05	England	L	0–4	Turin	Fr	
27–02–1949	Portugal	W	4–1	Genoa	Fr	Menti, Carapellese, Mazzola V, Maroso
27–03	Spain	W	3–1	Madrid	Fr	Lorenzi, Carapellese, Amadei
22–05	Austria	W	3–1	Florence	DGC	Cappello, Amadei, Boniperti
12–06	Hungary	D	1–1	Budapest	DGC	Carapellese
30–11	England	L	0–2	London	Fr	
5–03–1950	Belgium	W	3–1	Bologna	Fr	Muccinelli 2, Amadei
2–04	Austria	L	0–1	Vienna	DGC	
25–06	Sweden	L	2–3	Sao Paulo	WCr1	Carapellese, Muccinelli
2–07	Paraguay	W	2–0	Sao Paulo	WCr1	Carapellese, Pandolfini
8–04–1951	Portugal	W	4–1	Lisbon	Fr	Pandolfini, Burini, Amadei, Cappello
6–05	Yugoslavia	D	0–0	Milan	Fr	
3–06	France	W	4–1	Genoa	Fr	Lorenzi 2, Amadei, Cappello
11–11	Sweden	D	1–1	Florence	Fr	Amadei
25–11	Switzerland	D	1–1	Lugano	DGC	Boniperti
24–02–1952	Belgium	L	0–2	Brussels	Fr	
18–05	England	D	1–1	Florence	Fr	Amadei
26–10	Sweden	D	1–1	Stockholm	Fr	Vivolo
28–12	Switzerland	W	2–0	Palermo	DGC	Pandolfini, Frignani
26–04–1953	Czechoslovakia	L	0–2	Prague	DGC	
17–05	Hungary	L	0–3	Rome	DGC	
13–11	Egypt	W	2–1	Cairo	WCq	Frignani, Muccinelli
13–12	Czechoslovakia	W	3–0	Genoa	DGC	Cervato, Ricagni, Pandolfini
24–01–1954	Egypt	W	5–1	Milan	WCq	Pandolfini, Frignani, Boniperti 2, Ricagni
11–04	France	W	3–1	Paris	Fr	Pandolfini, Galli 2
17–06	Switzerland	L	1–2	Lausanne	WCr1	Boniperti
20–06	Belgium	W	4–1	Lugano	WCr1	Pandolfini, Galli, Frignani, Lorenzi
23–06	Switzerland	L	1–4	Basle	WCr1	Nesti
5–12	Argentina	W	2–0	Rome	Fr	Frignani, Galli
16–01–1955	Belgium	W	1–0	Bari	Fr	Boniperti
30–03	West Germany	W	2–1	Stuttgart	Fr	Frignani, Pivatelli
29–05	Yugoslavia	L	0–4	Turin	DGC	
27–11	Hungary	L	0–2	Budapest	DGC	
18–12	West Germany	W	2–1	Rome	Fr	OG, Boniperti
15–02–1956	France	W	2–0	Bologna	Fr	Carapellese, Gratton
25–04	Brazil	W	3–0	Milan	Fr	Virgili 2, OG
24–06	Argentina	L	0–1	Buenos Aires	Fr	
1–07	Brazil	L	0–2	Rio de Janeiro	Fr	
11–11	Switzerland	D	1–1	Berne	DGC	Firmani
9–12	Austria	W	2–1	Genoa	DGC	Longoni 2
25–04–1957	Nth. Ireland	W	1–0	Rome	WCq	Cervato
12–05	Yugoslavia	L	1–6	Zagreb	DGC	Cervato
26–05	Portugal	L	0–3	Lisbon	WCq	
4–12	Nth. Ireland	D	2–2	Belfast	Fr	Ghiggia, Montuori
22–12	Portugal	W	3–0	Milan	WCq	Gratton 2, Pivatelli
15–01–1958	Nth. Ireland	L	1–2	Belfast	WCq	Da Costa
23–03	Austria	L	2–3	Vienna	DGC	Petris, Firmani
9–11	France	D	2–2	Paris	Fr	Nicole 2
13–12	Czechoslovakia	D	1–1	Genoa	DGC	Galli
28–02–1959	Spain	D	1–1	Rome	Fr	Lojacono
6–05	England	D	2–2	London	Fr	Brighenti, Mariani
1–11	Czechoslovakia	L	1–2	Prague	DGC	Lojacono
29–11	Hungary	D	1–1	Florence	DGC	Cervato
6–01–1960	Switzerland	W	3–0	Naples	DGC	OG, Stacchini, Montuori

13–03	Spain	L	1–3	Barcelona	Fr	Lojacono
10–12	Austria	L	1–2	Naples	Fr	Boniperti
25–04–1961	Nth. Ireland	W	3–2	Bologna	Fr	Stacchini 2, Sivori
24–05	England	L	2–3	Rome	Fr	Sivori, Brighenti
15–06	Argentina	W	4–1	Florence	Fr	Lojacono, Sivori 2, Mora
15–10	Israel	W	4–2	Tel Aviv	WCq	Lojacono, Altafini, Corso 2
4–11	Israel	W	6–0	Turin	WCq	Sivori 4, Corso, Angelillo
5–05–1962	France	W	2–1	Florence	Fr	Altafini 2
13–05	Belgium	W	3–1	Brussels	Fr	Menichelli, Altafini 2
31–05	West Germany	D	0–0	Santiago	WCr1	
2–06	Chile	L	0–2	Santiago	WCr1	
7–06	Switzerland	W	3–0	Santiago	WCr1	Mora, Bulgarelli 2
11–11	Austria	W	2–1	Vienna	Fr	Pascutti 2
2–12	Turkey	W	6–0	Bologna	ECr1	Rivera 2, Orlando 4
27–03–1963	Turkey	W	1–0	Istanbul	ECr1	Sormani
12–05	Brazil	W	3–0	Milan	Fr	Sormani, Mazzola A, Bulgarelli
9–06	Austria	W	1–0	Vienna	Fr	Trapattoni
13–10	Soviet Union	L	0–2	Moscow	ECr2	
10–11	Soviet Union	D	1–1	Rome	ECr2	Rivera
14–12	Austria	W	1–0	Turin	Fr	Rivera
11–04–1964	Czechoslovakia	D	0–0	Florence	Fr	
10–05	Switzerland	W	3–1	Lausanne	Fr	Mazzola A, Corso, Rivera
4–11	Finland	W	6–1	Genoa	WCq	Facchetti, OG, Rivera, Bulgarelli, Mazzola A 2
5–12	Denmark	W	3–1	Bologna	Fr	Pascutti 2, Bulgarelli
13–03–1965	West Germany	D	1–1	Hamburg	Fr	Mazzola A
18–04	Poland	D	0–0	Warsaw	WCq	
1–05	Wales	W	4–1	Florence	Fr	Lodetti 2, Barison, Nocera
16–06	Sweden	D	2–2	Malmo	Fr	Pascutti, Mazzola A
23–06	Finland	W	2–0	Helsinki	WCq	Mazzola A 2
27–06	Hungary	L	1–2	Budapest	Fr	Mazzola A
1–11	Poland	W	6–1	Rome	WCq	Mazzola A, Barison 3, Rivera, Mora
9–11	Scotland	L	0–1	Glasgow	WCq	
7–12	Scotland	W	3–0	Naples	WCq	Pascutti, Facchetti, Mora
19–03–1966	France	D	0–0	Paris	Fr	
14–06	Bulgaria	W	6–1	Bologna	Fr	Mazzola A, Perani, Rizzo 2, Barison, Meroni
18–06	Austria	W	1–0	Milan	Fr	Burgnich
22–06	Argentina	W	3–0	Turin	Fr	Pascutti 2, Meroni
29–06	Mexico	W	5–0	Florence	Fr	Bulgarelli 2, Rivera 2, Mazzola A
13–07	Chile	W	2–0	Sunderland	WCr1	Mazzola A, Barison
16–07	Soviet Union	L	0–1	Sunderland	WCr1	
19–07	North Korea	L	0–1	Middlesbrough	WCr1	
1–11	Soviet Union	W	1–0	Milan	Fr	Guarneri
26–11	Rumania	W	3–1	Naples	ECq	Mazzola A 2, Depaoli
22–03–1967	Cyprus	W	2–0	Nicosia	ECq	Domenghini, Facchetti
27–03	Portugal	D	1–1	Rome	Fr	Cappellini
25–06	Rumania	W	1–0	Bucharest	ECq	Bertini
1–11	Cyprus	W	5–0	Cosenza	ECq	Mazzola A 2, Riva 3
18–11	Switzerland	D	2–2	Berne	ECq	Riva 2
23–12	Switzerland	W	4–0	Cagliari	ECq	Mazzola A, Riva, Domenghini
6–04–1968	Bulgaria	L	2–3	Sofia	ECqf	OG, Prati
20–04	Bulgaria	W	2–0	Naples	ECqf	Prati, Domenghini
5–06	Soviet Union	D	0–0	Naples	ECsf	
8–06	Yugoslavia	D	1–1	Rome	ECf	Domenghini
10–06	Yugoslavia	W	2–0	Rome	ECf	Riva, Anastasi
23–10	Wales	W	1–0	Cardiff	WCq	Riva
1–01–1969	Mexico	W	3–2	Mexico City	Fr	Riva 2, Anastasi
5–01	Mexico	D	1–1	Mexico City	Fr	Bertini
29–03	East Germany	D	2–2	Berlin	WCq	Riva
24–05	Bulgaria	D	0–0	Turin	Fr	
4–11	Wales	W	4–1	Rome	WCq	Riva 3, Mazzola A
22–11	East Germany	W	3–0	Naples	WCq	Mazzola A, Domenghini, Riva
21–02–1970	Spain	D	2–2	Madrid	Fr	Anastasi, Riva
10–05	Portugal	W	2–1	Lisbon	Fr	Riva 2
3–06	Sweden	W	1–0	Toluca	WCr1	Domenghini
6–06	Uruguay	D	0–0	Puebla	WCr1	
11–06	Israel	D	0–0	Toluca	WCr1	
14–06	Mexico	W	4–1	Toluca	WCqf	OG, Riva 2, Rivera

17–06	West Germany	W	4–3	Mexico City	WCsf	Boninsegna, Burgnich, Riva, Rivera
21–06	Brazil	L	1–4	Mexico City	WCf	Boninsegna
17–10	Switzerland	D	1–1	Berne	Fr	Mazzola A
31–10	Austria	W	2–1	Vienna	ECq	De Sisti, Mazzola A
8–12	Rep. Ireland	W	3–0	Florence	ECq	De Sisti, Boninsegna, Prati
20–02–1971	Spain	L	1–2	Cagliari	Fr	De Sisti
10–05	Rep. Ireland	W	2–1	Dublin	ECq	Boninsegna, Prati
9–06	Sweden	D	0–0	Stockholm	ECq	
25–09	Mexico	W	2–0	Genoa	Fr	Boninsegna 2
9–10	Sweden	W	3–0	Milan	ECq	Riva 2, Boninsegna
20–11	Austria	D	2–2	Rome	ECq	Prati, De Sisti
4–03–1972	Greece	L	1–2	Athens	Fr	Boninsegna
29–04	Belgium	D	0–0	Milan	ECqf	
13–05	Belgium	L	1–2	Brussels	ECqf	Riva
17–06	Rumania	D	3–3	Bucharest	Fr	Prati 2, Causio
21–06	Bulgaria	D	1–1	Sofia	Fr	Chinaglia
20–09	Yugoslavia	W	3–1	Turin	Fr	Riva, Chinaglia, Anastasi
7–10	Luxembourg	W	4–0	Luxembourg	WCq	Chinaglia, Riva 2, Capello
21–10	Switzerland	D	0–0	Berne	WCq	
13–01–1973	Turkey	D	0–0	Naples	WCq	
25–02	Turkey	W	1–0	Istanbul	WCq	Anastasi
31–03	Luxembourg	W	5–0	Genoa	WCq	Riva 4, Rivera
9–06	Brazil	W	2–0	Rome	Fr	Riva, Capello
14–06	England	W	2–0	Turin	Fr	Anastasi, Capello
29–09	Sweden	W	2–0	Milan	Fr	Anastasi, Riva
20–10	Switzerland	W	2–0	Rome	WCq	Rivera, Riva
14–11	England	W	1–0	London	Fr	Capello
26–02–1974	West Germany	D	0–0	Rome	Fr	
8–06	Austria	D	0–0	Vienna	Fr	
15–06	Haiti	W	3–1	Munich	WCr1	Rivera, OG, Anastasi
19–06	Argentina	D	1–1	Stuttgart	WCr1	OG
23–06	Poland	L	1–2	Stuttgart	WCr1	Capello
28–09	Yugoslavia	L	0–1	Zagreb	Fr	
20–11	Holland	L	1–3	Rotterdam	ECq	Boninsegna
29–12	Bulgaria	D	0–0	Genoa	Fr	
19–04–1975	Poland	D	0–0	Rome	ECq	
5–06	Finland	W	1–0	Helsinki	ECq	Chinaglia
8–06	Soviet Union	L	0–1	Moscow	Fr	
27–09	Finland	D	0–0	Rome	ECq	
26–10	Poland	D	0–0	Warsaw	ECq	
22–11	Holland	W	1–0	Rome	ECq	Capello
30–12	Greece	W	3–2	Florence	Fr	Pulici 2, Savoldi
7–04–1976	Portugal	W	3–1	Turin	Fr	Antognoni, Graziani, Pulici
28–05	England	L	2–3	New York	Fr	Graziani 2
31–05	Brazil	L	1–4	New Haven	Fr	Capello
5–06	Rumania	W	4–2	Milan	Fr	Graziani, Antognoni, Bettega 2
22–09	Denmark	W	1–0	Copenhagen	Fr	Pulici
25–09	Yugoslavia	W	3–0	Rome	Fr	Bettega 2, Graziani
16–10	Luxembourg	W	4–1	Luxembourg	WCq	Graziani, Bettega 2, Antognoni
17–11	England	W	2–0	Rome	WCq	Antognoni, Bettega
22–12	Portugal	L	1–2	Lisbon	Fr	Bettega
26–01–1977	Belgium	W	2–1	Rome	Fr	Graziani, OG
8–06	Finland	W	3–0	Helsinki	WCq	Gentile, Bettega, Benetti
8–10	West Germany	L	1–2	Berlin	Fr	Antognoni
15–10	Finland	W	6–1	Turin	WCq	Bettega 4, Graziani, Zaccarelli
16–11	England	L	0–2	London	WCq	
3–12	Luxembourg	W	3–0	Rome	WCq	Bettega, Graziani, Causio
21–12	Belgium	W	1–0	Liege	Fr	Antognoni
25–01–1978	Spain	L	1–2	Madrid	Fr	Tardelli

LEADING INTERNATIONAL GOALSCORERS

1	Riva	35
2	Meazza	33
3	Piola	30
4	Baloncieri	25
	Altobelli	25
6	Graziani	23
7	Mazzola A	22
8	Rossi	20
9	Bettega	19

8–02	France	D	2–2	Naples	Fr	Graziani 2
18–05	Yugoslavia	D	0–0	Rome	Fr	
2–06	France	W	2–1	Mar del Plata	WCr1	Rossi, Zaccarelli
6–06	Hungary	W	3–1	Mar del Plata	WCr1	Rossi, Bettega, Benetti
10–06	Argentina	W	1–0	Buenos Aires	WCr1	Bettega
14–06	West Germany	D	0–0	Buenos Aires	WCr2	
18–06	Austria	W	1–0	Buenos Aires	WCr2	Rossi
21–06	Holland	L	1–2	Buenos Aires	WCr2	OG
24–06	Brazil	L	1–2	Buenos Aires	WC3p	Causio
20–09	Bulgaria	W	1–0	Turin	Fr	Cabrini
23–09	Turkey	W	1–0	Florence	Fr	Graziani
8–11	Czechoslovakia	L	0–3	Bratislava	Fr	
21–12	Spain	W	1–0	Rome	Fr	Rossi
24–02–1979	Holland	W	3–0	Milan	Fr	Bettega, Rossi, Tardelli
26–05	Argentina	D	2–2	Rome	Fr	Causio, Rossi
13–06	Yugoslavia	L	1–4	Zagreb	Fr	Rossi
26–09	Sweden	W	1–0	Florence	Fr	Oriali
17–11	Switzerland	W	2–0	Udinese	Fr	Graziani, Tardelli
16–02–1980	Rumania	W	2–1	Naples	Fr	Collovati, Causio
15–03	Uruguay	W	1–0	Milan	Fr	Graziani
19–04	Poland	D	2–2	Turin	Fr	Causio, Scirea
12–06	Spain	D	0–0	Milan	ECr1	
15–06	England	W	1–0	Turin	ECr1	Tardelli
18–06	Belgium	D	0–0	Rome	ECr1	
21–06	Czechoslovakia	D	1–1 (8–9p)	Naples	EC3p	Graziani
24–09	Portugal	W	3–1	Genoa	Fr	Altobelli 2, Graziani
11–10	Luxembourg	W	2–0	Luxembourg	WCq	Collovati, Bettega
1–11	Denmark	W	2–0	Rome	WCq	Graziani 2
15–11	Yugoslavia	W	2–0	Turin	WCq	Cabrini, Conti B
6–12	Greece	W	2–0	Athens	WCq	Antognoni, Scirea
3–01–1981	Uruguay	L	0–2	Montevideo	ML	
6–01	Holland	D	1–1	Montevideo	ML	Ancelotti
19–04	East Germany	D	0–0	Udine	Fr	
3–06	Denmark	L	1–3	Copenhagen	WCq	Graziani
23–09	Bulgaria	W	3–2	Bologna	Fr	Graziani 2, Dossena
17–10	Yugoslavia	D	1–1	Belgrade	WCq	Bettega
14–11	Greece	D	1–1	Turin	WCq	Conti B
5–12	Luxembourg	W	1–0	Naples	WCq	Collovati
23–02–1982	France	L	0–2	Paris	Fr	
14–04	East Germany	L	0–1	Leipzig	Fr	
28–05	Switzerland	D	1–1	Geneva	Fr	Cabrini
14–06	Poland	D	0–0	Vigo	WCr1	
18–06	Peru	D	1–1	Vigo	WCr1	Conti B
23–06	Cameroon	D	1–1	Vigo	WCr1	Graziani
29–06	Argentina	W	2–1	Barcelona	WCr2	Tardelli, Cabrini
5–07	Brazil	W	3–2	Barcelona	WCr2	Rossi 3
8–07	Poland	W	2–0	Barcelona	WCsf	Rossi 2
11–07	West Germany	W	3–1	Madrid	WCf	Rossi, Tardelli, Altobelli
27–10	Switzerland	L	0–1	Rome	Fr	
13–11	Czechoslovakia	D	2–2	Milan	ECq	Altobelli, OG
4–12	Rumania	D	0–0	Florence	ECq	
12–02–1983	Cyprus	D	1–1	Limassol	ECq	OG
16–04	Rumania	L	0–1	Bucharest	ECq	
29–05	Sweden	L	0–2	Gothenburg	ECq	
5–10	Greece	W	3–0	Bari	Fr	Giordano, Cabrini, Rossi
15–10	Sweden	L	0–3	Naples	ECq	
16–11	Czechoslovakia	L	0–2	Prague	ECq	
22–12	Cyprus	W	3–1	Perugia	ECq	Altobelli, Cabrini, Rossi
4–02–1984	Mexico	W	5–0	Rome	Fr	Bagni, Rossi 3, Conti B
3–03	Turkey	W	2–1	Istanbul	Fr	Altobelli, Cabrini
7–04	Czechoslovakia	D	1–1	Verona	Fr	Bagni
22–05	West Germany	L	0–1	Zurich	Fr	
26–05	Canada	W	2–0	Toronto	Fr	Altobelli, Battistini
30–05	USA	D	0–0	New York	Fr	
26–09	Sweden	W	1–0	Milan	Fr	Cabrini
3–11	Switzerland	D	1–1	Lausanne	Fr	Cabrini
8–12	Poland	W	2–0	Pescara	Fr	Altobelli, Di Gennaro
5–02–1985	Rep. Ireland	W	2–1	Dublin	Fr	Rossi, Altobelli
13–03	Greece	D	0–0	Athens	Fr	

LEADING INTERNATIONAL APPEARANCES

1 Zoff	112	12 Causio	63	23 Collovati	50
2 Facchetti	94	Baresi F	63	24 Rossi	48
3 Tardelli	81	14 Altobelli	61	25 Baloncieri	47
4 Scirea	78	15 Rivera	60	Combi	47
5 Bergomi	77	16 Caligaris	59	Conti	47
6 Antognoni	73	17 Zenga	58	Giannini	47
Cabrini	73	18 Vialli	56	29 Ferrari G	44
8 Gentile	71	19 Benetti	55	Ferri	44
9 Mazzola A	70	20 Meazza	53	31 De Vecchi	43
10 Burgnich	66	21 Rosetta	52	32 Bettega	42
11 Graziani	64	De Napoli	52	Riva	42

3–04	Portugal	W	2–0	Ascoli	Fr	Conti B, Rossi
2–06	Mexico	D	1–1	Mexico City	Fr	Di Gennaro
6–06	England	W	2–1	Mexico City	Fr	Bagni, Altobelli
25–09	Norway	L	1–2	Lecce	Fr	Altobelli
16–11	Poland	L	0–1	Chorzow	Fr	
5–02–1986	West Germany	L	1–2	Avellino	Fr	Serena
26–03	Austria	W	2–1	Udine	Fr	Altobelli, Di Gennaro
11–05	China	W	2–0	Naples	Fr	Di Gennaro, Altobelli
31–05	Bulgaria	D	1–1	Mexico City	WCr1	Altobelli
5–06	Argentina	D	1–1	Puebla	WCr1	Altobelli
10–06	South Korea	W	3–2	Puebla	WCr1	Altobelli 2, OG
17–06	France	L	0–2	Mexico City	WCr2	
8–10	Greece	W	2–0	Bologna	Fr	Bergomi 2
15–11	Switzerland	W	3–2	Milan	ECq	Donadoni, Altobelli 2
6–12	Malta	W	2–0	Ta'Qali	ECq	Ferri, Altobelli
24–01–1987	Malta	W	5–0	Bergamo	ECq	Bagni, Bergomi, Altobelli 2, Vialli
14–02	Portugal	W	1–0	Lisbon	ECq	Altobelli
18–04	West Germany	D	0–0	Cologne	Fr	
28–05	Norway	D	0–0	Oslo	Fr	
3–06	Sweden	L	0–1	Stockholm	ECq	
10–06	Argentina	W	3–1	Zurich	Fr	De Napoli, OG, Vialli
23–09	Yugoslavia	W	1–0	Pisa	Fr	Altobelli
17–10	Switzerland	D	0–0	Berne	ECq	
14–11	Sweden	W	2–1	Naples	ECq	Vialli 2
5–12	Portugal	W	3–0	Milan	ECq	Vialli, Giannini, De Agostini
20–02–1988	Soviet Union	W	4–1	Bari	Fr	Baresi, Vialli 2, Bergomi
31–03	Yugoslavia	D	1–1	Split	Fr	Vialli
27–04	Luxembourg	W	3–0	Luxembourg	Fr	Ferri, Bergomi, L De Agostini
4–06	Wales	L	0–1	Brescia	Fr	
10–06	West Germany	D	1–1	Dusseldorf	ECr1	Mancini
14–06	Spain	W	1–0	Frankfurt	ECr1	Vialli
17–06	Denmark	W	2–0	Cologne	ECr1	Altobelli, De Agostini
22–06	Soviet Union	L	0–2	Stuttgart	ECsf	
19–10	Norway	W	2–1	Pescara	Fr	Giannini, Ferri
16–11	Holland	W	1–0	Rome	Fr	Vialli
22–12	Scotland	W	2–0	Perugia	Fr	Giannini, Berti
22–02–1989	Denmark	W	1–0	Pisa	Fr	Bergomi
25–03	Austria	W	1–0	Vienna	Fr	Berti
29–03	Rumania	L	0–1	Sibiu	Fr	
22–04	Uruguay	D	1–1	Verona	Fr	Baggio
26–04	Hungary	W	4–0	Taranto	Fr	Vialli, Ferri, Berti, Carnevale
20–09	Bulgaria	W	4–0	Cesena	Fr	Baggio 2, Carnevale, OG
14–10	Brazil	L	0–1	Bologna	Fr	
11–11	Algeria	W	1–0	Vicenza	Fr	Serena
15–11	England	D	0–0	London	Fr	
21–12	Argentina	D	0–0	Cagliari	Fr	
21–02–1990	Holland	D	0–0	Rotterdam	Fr	
31–03	Switzerland	W	1–0	Basle	Fr	De Agostini
30–05	Greece	D	0–0	Perugia	Fr	
9–06	Austria	W	1–0	Rome	WCr1	Schillaci
14–06	USA	W	1–0	Rome	WCr1	Giannini
19–06	Czechoslovakia	W	2–0	Rome	WCr1	Schillaci, Baggio
25–06	Uruguay	W	2–0	Rome	WCr2	Schillaci, Serena

30–06	Rep. Ireland	W	1–0	Rome	WCqf	Schillaci
3–07	Argentina	D	1–1 (3–4p)	Naples	WCsf	Schillaci
7–07	England	W	2–1	Bari	WC3p	Baggio, Schillaci
26–09	Holland	W	1–0	Palermo	Fr	Baggio
17–10	Hungary	D	1–1	Budapest	ECq	Baggio
3–11	Soviet Union	D	0–0	Rome	ECq	
22–12	Cyprus	W	4–0	Limassol	ECq	Vierchowod, Serena 2, Lombardo
13–02–1991	Belgium	D	0–0	Terni	Fr	
1–05	Hungary	W	3–1	Salerno	ECq	Donadoni 2, Vialli
5–06	Norway	L	1–2	Oslo	ECq	Schillaci
12–06	Denmark	W	2–0	Malmo	Fr	Rizzitelli, Vialli
16–06	Soviet Union	D	1–1	Stockholm	Fr	Giannini
25–09	Bulgaria	L	1–2	Sofia	Fr	Giannini
12–10	Soviet Union	D	0–0	Moscow	ECq	
13–11	Norway	D	1–1	Genoa	ECq	Rizzitelli
21–12	Cyprus	W	2–0	Foggia	ECq	Vialli, Baggio
19–02–1992	San Marino	W	4–0	Cesena	Fr	Baggio 2, Donadoni, Casiraghi
25–03	Germany	W	1–0	Turin	Fr	Baggio
31–05	Portugal	D	0–0	New Haven	Fr	
4–06	Rep. Ireland	W	2–0	Boston	Fr	Signori, Costacurta
6–06	USA	D	1–1	Chicago	Fr	Baggio

LIECHTENSTEIN

That this tiny principality, squeezed in between Austria and Switzerland, should have a national team at all is quite remarkable. The population is just 27 000 and its citizens are more usually concerned with banking and finance rather than playing football.

The country's football association dates from 1933 and in 1974 joined both FIFA and UEFA, but over this time few matches have been played. In 1981 a trip was made to Korea and the results in the President's Cup were very impressive, especially the victory over Indonesia. The best result to date, however, is the 2–0 victory over China in 1982. To think that a country with a population of just 27 000 could beat another whose population totals over 1000 million!

There is no league in Liechtenstein and what teams there are compete in the lower divisions of Swiss football. There is an annual Cup competition and the winners now enter the Cup Winners Cup. The national team may decide that a crack at the European Championship or World Cup is worth a try in the near future, although both attempts to qualify for the Olympic Games have ended in heavy defeat. Thirty-five goals against in only four matches and none scored does not bode too well for matches against the full national sides.

Population: 27 000 Area, sq km: 160
Capital city: Vaduz
Liechtensteiner Fussball-Verband
Postfach 165, FL–9490 Vaduz, Liechtenstein
Tel: (010 41) 75 23344
Fax: (010 41) 75 28265 Telex: 889 261
Cable: FUSSBALLVERBAND VADUZ
Languages for correspondence: German, English & French
Year of formation: 1933
Affiliation to FIFA: 1974
Affiliation to UEFA: 1974
Registered clubs: 7
Registered players: 1200
Registered coaches: 36
Registered referees: 36
National colours: Shirts: Blue/Shorts: Red/Socks: Blue
Reserve colours: Shirts: Yellow/Shorts: Red/Socks: Yellow
Season: Teams compete in the Swiss league

THE RECORD

WORLD CUP
1930–90 ..... Did not enter

EUROPEAN CHAMPIONSHIP
1960–92 ..... Did not enter

OLYMPIC GAMES
1908–84 ..... Did not enter
1988 .... QT Failed to qualify
1992 .... QT Failed to qualify

INTERNATIONAL MATCHES PLAYED BY LIECHTENSTEIN

Date	Opponents	Result		Venue	Compet	Scorers
14–06–1981	Malta	D	1–1	Seoul	PC	
16–06	Thailand	L	0–2	Seoul	PC	
22–06	Indonesia	W	3–2	Seoul	PC	
6–10	Malaysia	W	1–0	Balzers	Fr	
6–06–1982	China	W	2–0	Vaduz	Fr	Moser 2
6–06–1984	Austria	L	0–6	Vaduz	Fr	
30–05–1990	United States	L	1–4	Eschen	Fr	Marxer
12–03–1991	Switzerland	L	0–6	Balzers	Fr	

LUXEMBOURG

Ten out of ten for effort, but Luxembourg fail to score at all for achievement. They have entered every World Cup bar the first and have without fail finished last in their qualifying group. Added to this is the fact that since two victories were gained against Thailand and South Korea in the 1980 Marah Halim Cup, Luxembourg have set off on a stunning run of 60 games with only three draws to break the losing sequence, and which at one point included 32 straight losses.

Leaving aside the Marah Halim Cup, which was of dubious 'A' grade status anyway, the run without a win dates back a further 22 matches and seven years. The last time Luxembourg won a game against European opposition was in a 1973 friendly match against Norway. The last win in a competitive match dates to the previous year and a 2–0 victory against Turkey.

The Federation Luxembourgeoise de Football was formed in 1908 and became a member of FIFA two years later, when a league was also started. Luxembourg is a small country traditionally involved in both finance and heavy industry, and it was as a form of leisure for the workers in the latter that football gained a foothold. Nowadays the structure remains amateur, and players are attracted from all walks of life, but a few players do manage to make a name for themselves abroad as professionals, usually in France or Belgium.

The three dominant towns in the league are Luxembourg itself, Differdange and Esch. The latter has produced the best known club in the country, Jeunesse Esch, and they remain the only club to have reached the second round of the European Cup, where in 1964 they even managed to beat Partizan Belgrade 2–1 at home, although they lost the tie 4–7 on aggregate. Heavy defeats are the norm for most clubs in Europe, and these include a 14–0 victory by Ajax over Red Boys, a 13–0 win by Chelsea over Jeunesse Hautcharage, another 13–0 scoreline by 1.FC Köln over US Luxembourg and perhaps most embarrassingly of all, a 12–0 loss *at home* by US Rumelingen at the hands of Feyenoord.

The first international match was played in 1911 against France, and Luxembourg have been very active in international games since. Most of the games, however, have been played against amateur or 'B' selections, and therefore do not show up on their record. This was especially true in the years up until the 1960s, during which time regular matches were contested with both Holland and Belgium in particular, but also against selections from other European countries.

		All			League			Cup		Europe		
	Team	G	S	B	G	S	B	G	S	G	S	B
1	Jeunesse Esch/ Alzette	30	19	10	21	11	10	9	8	–	–	–
2	AC Spora Luxembourg	23	21	15	14	13	15	9	8	–	–	–
3	Red Boys Differdange	21	19	14	6	10	14	15	9	–	–	–
4	Union Luxembourg	19	19	10	10	10	10	9	9	–	–	–
5	Stade Dudeldange	14	13	6	10	6	6	4	7	–	–	–
6	Avenir Beggen	9	7	1	5	4	1	4	3	–	–	–
7	Fola Esch/Alzette	8	8	4	5	7	4	3	1	–	–	–
8	Progres Niedercorn	7	8	8	3	5	8	4	3	–	–	–
9	Aris Bonnevoie	4	6	2	3	1	2	1	5	–	–	–
10	US Rumelange	2	5	1	–	3	1	2	2	–	–	–
11	The National Schifflange	2	3	–	1	2	–	1	1	–	–	–
12	Alliance Dudelange	2	2	–	–	1	–	2	1	–	–	–
13	US Dudelange	1	5	3	–	4	3	1	1	–	–	–
14	Jeunesse Hautcharage	1	–	–	–	–	–	1	–	–	–	–
	Swift Hesperange	1	–	–	–	–	–	1	–	–	–	–
	SC Tetange	1	–	–	–	–	–	1	–	–	–	–
16	CS Grevenmacher	–	4	1	–	–	1	–	4	–	–	–
17	AS Differdange	–	1	–	–	–	–	–	1	–	–	–
	Olympique Eischen	–	1	–	–	–	–	–	1	–	–	–
	CS Petange	–	1	–	–	–	–	–	1	–	–	–
	Racing Rodange	–	1	–	–	–	–	–	1	–	–	–
	Red Star Merl	–	1	–	–	–	–	–	1	–	–	–

To the end of the 1991–92 season

Just occasionally, Luxembourg has tasted success. France, Belgium and Holland have been beaten in full internationals, but the most impressive victories were against Portugal in 1961 in the World Cup, and against Holland in the 1964 European Championship. A 2–2 draw in Amsterdam and a 2–1 win in Rotterdam saw Luxembourg qualify for the quarter-finals and a tie against Denmark, which the Danes eventually won in a play-off in Amsterdam after a 3–3 and 2–2 draw.

Since then wins, or even draws, have been so rare that it would seem sensible to play an annual contest with Malta, Cyprus, San Marino and Liechtenstein in order to drastically improve the winning percentage in games. Until that happens it seems Luxembourg will go on losing and losing and . . .

Population: 379 000
Area, sq km: 2586
% in urban areas: 77.6%
Capital city: Luxembourg

Federation Luxembourgeoise de Football
50 Rue de Strasbourg
L–2560 Luxembourg
Tel: (010 352) 488665
Fax: (010 352) 400201
Telex: 2426 FLFLU
Cable: FOOTBALL LUXEMBOURG

Languages for correspondence: French, German & English

Year of formation: 1908
Affiliation to FIFA: 1910
Affiliation to UEFA: 1954

Registered clubs: 129
Registered players: 23 300
Registered referees: 279
National stadium: Stade Municipal 10 000
National colours: Shirts: Red Shorts: White Socks: Blue
Reserve colours: Shirts: Blue/Shorts: White/Socks: Blue
Season: August–May

THE RECORD

WORLD CUP

1930 .... Did not enter
1934 .... QT 3rd/3 in group 12
1938 .... QT 3rd/3 in group 8
1950 .... QT 2nd/2 in group 4
1954 .... QT 3rd/3 in group 4
1958 .... QT 3rd/3 in group 5
1962 .... QT 3rd/3 in group 6
1966 .... QT 4th/4 in group 3
1970 .... QT 4th/4 in group 8
1974 .... QT 4th/4 in group 2
1978 .... QT 4th/4 in group 2
1982 .... QT 5th/5 in group 5
1986 .... QT 5th/5 in group 4
1990 .... QT 5th/5 in group 7

EUROPEAN CHAMPIONSHIP

1960 .... Did not enter
1964 .... Quarter-finalists
1968 .... QT 4th/4 in group 7
1972 .... QT 4th/4 in group 7
1976 .... QT 4th/4 in group 2
1980 .... QT 4th/4 in group 5
1984 .... QT 5th/5 in group 3
1988 .... QT 5th/5 in group 7
1992 .... QT 4th/4 in group 5

OLYMPIC GAMES

1908 .... Did not enter
1912 .... Did not enter
1920 .... 1st round
1924 .... 1st round
1928 .... 1st round
1936 .... 1st round
1948 .... 1st round
1952 .... 1st round
1956 .... Did not enter
1960 .... QT Failed to qualify
1964 .... Did not enter
1968 .... Did not enter
1972 .... QT Failed to qualify
1976 .... QT Failed to qualify
1980–92 ..... Did not enter

EUROPEAN CLUB COMPETITIONS

EUROPEAN CUP: 2nd round – Jeunesse Esch 1964

CUP WINNERS CUP: 2nd round – Alliance Dudelange 1962, Aris Bonnevoie1980

UEFA CUP: Never past the first round

CLUB DIRECTORY

LUXEMBOURG CITY (Population – 133 000)

FC Aris Bonnevoie
Stadium: Camille Polfer 3000
Founded: 1922
Colours: White/Black

FC Avenir Beggen
Stadium: Beggen 4000
Founded: 1915
Colours: Yellow and black stripes/Black

AC Spora Luxembourg
Stadium: Municipal 10 000
Founded: 1923
Colours: Blue/Yellow
Previous names: Merger of Sporting Club (1908) and Racing Club (1907) in 1923

FC Union Sportive Luxembourg
Stadium: Achille Hammerel 6000
Founded: 1908
Colours: White/Blue
Previous name: US Hollerich 1908–20

ESCH-SUR-ALZETTE (Population – 83 000)

CS FOLA Esch (Football and Lawn Tennis Club)
Stadium: Émile Mayerisch 10 000
Founded: 1906
Colours: Red and white stripes/Blue

AS La Jeunesse d'Esch
Stadium: De La Frontière 7000
Founded: 1907
Colours: Black and white stripes/Black

DIFFERDANGE (Population – 16 000)

AS Differdange
Stadium: Henri Jungers
Founded: 1921
Colours: White/White

FA Red Boys Differdange
Stadium: Thillenberg 6000
Founded: 1907
Colours: Red/White

DUDELANGE (Population – 14 000)

CS Alliance Dudelange
Stadium: Amadeo Barozzi 3000
Founded: 1916
Colours: Red/Black

US Dudelange
Stadium: Jos Nosbaum
Founded: 1912
Colours: Blue/White

Stade Dudelange
Stadium: Alois Mayer
Founded: 1913
Colours: White/Black

PÉTANGE (Population – 11 000)
CS Pétange
Stadium: Antoine Nangeroni 3000
Founded: 1909
Colours: Blue/White

FC Progrés Niedercorn
Stadium: Jos Haupert 3000
Founded: 1919
Colours: Yellow/Blue

RUMELANGE
Union Sportive Rumelange
Stadium: Municipal 3000
Founded: 1908
Colours: Blue/White

GREVENMACHER
CS Grevenmacher
Stadium: Flohr 3000
Founded: 1909
Colours: Blue/Blue

EISCHEN
Olympique Eischen
Stadium: Am Freschepul 2000
Founded: 1917
Colours: Red/Blue

HESPERANGE
FC Swift Hesperange
Stadium: Holleschbierg 2000
Founded: 1916
Colours: Red/Yellow

WILTZ
FC Wiltz 71
Stadium: Getzt 3000
Founded: 1971
Colours: Red and white diagonal halves/Red

TETANGE
SC Tétange
Stadium: Gommerwiese
Founded: 1914
Colours: Green/White

SCHIFFLANGE
The National Schifflange
Stadium: National
Founded: 1912
Colours: Yellow/Black

HAUTCHARAGE
Jeunesse Hautcharage
Stadium: Umbechel
Founded: 1919
Colours: White/Black

LUXEMBOURG LEAGUE CHAMPIONSHIP

Year	Champions	Runners up	3rd
1910	Racing Club 3–2	US Hollerich	
1911	Sporting Club 9	SC Differdange 9	US Hollerich 6
1912	US Hollerich 8	Sporting Club 8	Racing Club 7
1913			–
1914	US Hollerich 16	Sporting Club 15	Racing Club 10
1915	US Hollerich 8–1	Jeunesse Esch	
1916	US Hollerich 16	Sporting Club 12	Fola Esch 11
1917	US Hollerich 20	Fola Esch 12	Racing Club 8
1918	Fola Esch 16	US Hollerich 13	Sporting Club 10
1919	Sporting Club 16	Fola Esch 13	Jeunesse Esch 12
1920	Fola Esch 17	Stade Dudelange 13	Sporting Club 10
1921	Jeunesse Esch 20	Fola Esch 19	Union Luxembourg 18
1922	Fola Esch 22	Union Luxembourg 20	Jeunesse Esch 16
1923	Red Boys 23	Stade Dudelange 22	Fola Esch 16
1924	Fola Esch 23	AC Spora 20	Red Boys 18
1925	AC Spora 21	Stade Dudelange 20	Jeunesse Esch 18
1926	Red Boys 22	AC Spora 21	Fola Esch 18
1927	Union Luxembourg 21	Red Boys 18	AC Spora 17
1928	AC Spora 24	Stade Dudelange 16	Red Boys 15
1929	AC Spora 19	Fola Esch 18	Red Boys 17
1930	Fola Esch 20	AC Spora 19	Red Boys 17
1931	Red Boys 25	AC Spora 20	Progres Niedercorn 14
1932	Red Boys 21	Progres Niedercorn 21	AC Spora 14
1933	Red Boys 27	AC Spora 16	Progres Niedercorn 15
1934	AC Spora 23	Red Boys 18	US Dudelange 14
1935	AC Spora 20	Red Boys 17	Jeunesse Esch 14
1936	AC Spora 28	Jeunesse Esch 26	Red Boys 22
1937	Jeunesse Esch 26	Progres Niedercorn 26	US Dudelange 26
1938	AC Spora 26	Jeunesse Esch 24	Stade Dudelange 22
1939	Stade Dudelange 31	US Dudelange 28	AC Spora 23
1940	Stade Dudelange 31	US Dudelange 24	Progres Niedercorn 22
1941–44 –			
1945	Stade Dudelange 6–0	AC Spora	
1946	Stade Dudelange 32	US Dudelange 24	Progres Niedercorn 21
1947	Stade Dudelange 40	US Dudelange 28	Fola Esch 25
1948	Stade Dudelange 38	Union Luxembourg 27	Red Boys 27
1949	AC Spora 38	Fola Esch 34	Stade Dudelange 29
1950	Stade Dudelange 35	Nat. Schifflange 34	AC Spora 25
1951	Jeunesse Esch 32	Nat. Schifflange 30	Red Boys 26
1952	Nat. Schifflange 24	AC Spora 23	Stade Dudelange 21
1953	Progres Niedercorn 32	Jeunesse Esch 31	Stade Dudelange 27
1954	Jeunesse Esch 33	Fola Esch 28	Progres Niedercorn 24
1955	Stade Dudelange 34	Fola Esch 25	Union Luxembourg 24
1956	AC Spora 33	Stade Dudelange 32	Progres Niedercorn 30
1957	Stade Dudelange 37	Jeunesse Esch 31	Red Boys 27
1958	Jeunesse Esch 35	Red Boys 30	Stade Dudelange 28
1959	Jeunesse Esch 32	AC Spora 26	Red Boys 26
1960	Jeunesse Esch 34	Stade Dudelange 28	CS Grevenmacher 26
1961	AC Spora 33	Jeunesse Esch 33	Union Luxembourg 30
1962	Union Luxembourg 39	Alliance Dudelange 32	AC Spora 24
1963	Jeunesse Esch 35	Union Luxembourg 29	Red Boys 28
1964	Aris Bonnevoie 33	Union Luxembourg 31	Stade Dudelange 30
1965	Stade Dudelange 32	Union Luxembourg 31	Jeunesse Esch 28
1966	Aris Bonnevoie 35	Union Luxembourg 28	US Dudelange 28
1967	Jeunesse Esch 36	AC Spora 30	Union Luxembourg 27
1968	Jeunesse Esch 35	US Rumelange 31	Union Luxembourg 28
1969	Avenir Beggen 34	Jeunesse Esch 34	Aris Bonnevoie 30
1970	Jeunesse Esch 36	US Rumelange 31	AC Spora 30
1971	Union Luxembourg 37	Aris Bonnevoie 29	Jeunesse Esch 29
1972	Aris Bonnevoie 31	US Rumelange 30	Red Boys 26
1973	Jeunesse Esch 38	Union Luxembourg 30	Red Boys 27
1974	Jeunesse Esch 38	Red Boys 32	AC Spora 30
1975	Jeunesse Esch 33	Avenir Beggen 31	Union Luxembourg 27
1976	Jeunesse Esch 34	Red Boys 30	US Rumelange 25
1977	Jeunesse Esch 34	Progres Niedercorn 32	Red Boys 27

1978	Progres Niedercorn	32	Jeunesse Esch	26	Red Boys	25
1979	Red Boys	34	Progres Niedercorn	34	Union Luxembourg	25
1980	Jeunesse Esch	33	Red Boys	32	Progres Niedercorn	30
1981	Progres Niedercorn	35	Red Boys	34	Jeunesse Esch	31
1982	Avenir Beggen	36	Progres Niedercorn	32	Jeunesse Esch	29
1983	Jeunesse Esch	34	Avenir Beggen	29	Aris Bonnevoie	28
1984	Avenir Beggen	33	Red Boys	32	Progres Niedercorn	27
1985	Jeunesse Esch	37	Red Boys	32	Avenir Beggen	28
1986	Avenir Beggen	33	Jeunesse Esch	32	AC Spora	31
1987	Jeunesse Esch	38	Avenir Beggen	35	AC Spora	30
1988	Jeunesse Esch	25	Avenir Beggen	23	Union Luxembourg	20.5
1989	AC Spora	29	Jeunesse Esch	25.5	Union Luxembourg	24
1990	Union Luxembourg	29.5	Avenir Beggen	27.5	Jeunesse Esch	26.5
1991	Union Luxembourg	28	Jeunesse Esch	25	AC Spora	22.5
1992	Avenir Beggen	26	Union Luxembourg	26	Jeunesse Esch	23

LUXEMBOURG CUP FINALS

Year	Winners	Score	Runners–up
1922	Racing Club	2–0	Jeunesse Esch
1923	Fola Esch	3–0	Union Luxembourg
1924	Fola Esch	2–0	Red Boys
1925	Red Boys	1–1 3–0	AC Spora
1926	Red Boys	5–2	Union Luxembourg
1927	Red Boys	3–2	Jeunesse Esch
1928	AC Spora	2–2 3–3 5–2	Stade Dudelange
1929	Red Boys	5–3	AC Spora
1930	Red Boys	2–1	AC Spora
1931	Red Boys	5–3	AC Spora
1932	AC Spora	2–1	Red Boys
1933	Progres Niedercorn	4–1	Union Luxembourg
1934	Red Boys	5–2	AC Spora
1935	Jeunesse Esch	4–2	Red Boys
1936	Red Boys	2–0	Stade Dudelange
1937	Jeunesse Esch	3–0	Union Luxembourg
1938	Stade Dudelange	1–0	Nat. Schifflange
1939	US Dudelange	2–1	Stade Dudelange
1940	AC Spora	6–2	Stade Dudelange
1941–44	–		
1945	Progres Niedercorn	2–0	AC Spora
1946	Jeunesse Esch	3–1	Progres Niedercorn
1947	Union Luxembourg	2–1	Stade Dudelange
1948	Stade Dudelange	1–0	Red Boys
1949	Stade Dudelange	1–0	Racing Rodange
1950	AC Spora	5–1	Red Boys
1951	SC Tetange	1–1 2–0	CS Grevenmacher
1952	Red Boys	1–0	Red Star Merl
1953	Red Boys	2–1	CS Grevenmacher
1954	Jeunesse Esch	5–0	CS Grevenmacher
1955	Fola Esch	1–1 4–1	Red Boys
1956	Stade Dudelange	3–1	Progres Niedercorn
1957	AC Spora	2–1	Stade Dudelange
1958	Red Boys	3–1	US Dudelange
1959	Union Luxembourg	3–1	CS Grevenmacher
1960	Nat. Schifflange	3–0	Stade Dudelange
1961	Alliance Dudelange	3–2	Union Luxembourg
1962	Alliance Dudelange	1–0	Union Luxembourg
1963	Union Luxembourg	2–1	AC Spora
1964	Union Luxembourg	1–0	Aris Bonnevoie
1965	AC Spora	1–0	Jeunesse Esch
1966	AC Spora	2–0	Jeunesse Esch
1967	Aris Bonnevoie	1–0	Union Luxembourg
1968	US Rumelange	0–0 1–0	Aris Bonnevoie
1969	Union Luxembourg	5–2	Alliance Dudelange
1970	Union Luxembourg	1–0	Red Boys
1971	Jeunesse Hautcharage	4–1	Jeunesse Esch
1972	Red Boys	4–3	Aris Bonnevoie
1973	Jeunesse Esch	3–2	Fola Esch
1974	Jeunesse Esch	4–1	Avenir Beggen
1975	US Rumelange	2–0	Jeunesse Esch
1976	Jeunesse Esch	2–1	Aris Bonnevoie
1977	Progres Niedercorn	4–4 3–1	Red Boys
1978	Progres Niedercorn	2–1	Union Luxembourg
1979	Red Boys	4–1	Aris Bonnevoie
1980	AC Spora	3–2	Progres Niedercorn
1981	Jeunesse Esch	5–0	Olympique Eischen
1982	Red Boys	2–1	US Rumelange
1983	Avenir Beggen	4–2	Union Luxembourg
1984	Avenir Beggen	4–1	US Rumelange
1985	Red Boys	1–0	Jeunesse Esch
1986	Union Luxembourg	4–1	Red Boys
1987	Avenir Beggen	6–0	AC Spora
1988	Jeunesse Esch	1–0	Avenir Beggen
1989	Union Luxembourg	2–0	Avenir Beggen
1990	Swift Hesperange	3–3 7–1	AS Differdange
1991	Union Luxembourg	3–0	Jeunesse Esch
1992	Avenir Beggen	1–0	CS Petange

INTERNATIONAL MATCHES PLAYED BY LUXEMBOURG

Date	Opponents	Result		Venue	Compet	Scorers
29–10–1911	France	L	1–4	Luxembourg	Fr	Elter
20–04–1913	France	L	0–8	Paris	Fr	
8–02–1914	France	W	5–4	Luxembourg	Fr	Massard 4, Bernard
28–08–1920	Holland	L	0–3	Brussels	OGr1	
29–05–1924	Italy	L	0–2	Paris	OGr2	
21–05–1927	England	L	2–5	Esch	Fr	Hubert, Lefevre
27–05–1928	Belgium	L	3–5	Amsterdam	OGr1	Schutz, Weisgerber, Theissen
28–06	Egypt	D	1–1	Esch	Fr	Theissen
11–03–1934	Germany	L	1–9	Luxembourg	WCq	Mengel

15–04	France	L	1–6	Luxembourg	WCq	Speicher
18–08–1935	Germany	L	0–1	Luxembourg	Fr	
9–05–1936	Rep. Ireland	L	1–5	Luxembourg	Fr	Mart
27–09	Germany	L	2–7	Krefeld	Fr	Kemp 2
4–08	Germany	L	0–9	Berlin	OGr1	
21–03–1937	Germany	L	2–3	Luxembourg	Fr	Kemp, Stamet
28–11	Holland	L	0–4	Rotterdam	WCq	
16–01–1938	Hungary	L	0–6	Luxembourg	Fr	
13–03	Belgium	L	2–3	Luxembourg	WCq	Libar, Kemp
20–03	Germany	L	1–2	Wuppertal	Fr	Libar
26–03–1939	Germany	W	2–1	Differdange	Fr	Mart 2
31–03–1940	Holland	W	5–4	Rotterdam	Fr	Kemp 2, Libar, Feller P, Everard
13–05–1945	Belgium	W	4–1	Luxembourg	Fr	Mart 2, Libar, Kemp
23–02–1946	Belgium	L	0–7	Charleroi	Fr	
10–03	Holland	L	2–6	Luxembourg	Fr	Lahure, Feller P
28–07	Norway	W	3–2	Luxembourg	Fr	Schumacher 2, Pauly
30–10	Hungary	L	2–7	Esch	Fr	
24–05–1947	Scotland	L	0–6	Luxembourg	Fr	
26–07–1948	Afghanistan	W	6–0	London	OGr1	Konter 2, Kremer 2, Wagner, Feller V
31–07	Yugoslavia	L	1–6	London	OGr2	Schammel
23–03–1949	Czechoslovakia	D	2–2	Bratislava	Fr	
26–06	Switzerland	L	2–5	Zurich	WCq	Wagner, Reuter
18–09	Switzerland	L	2–3	Luxembourg	WCq	Muller, Kremer
15–08–1950	Norway	D	2–2	Bergen	Fr	Letsch, Muller
4–11–1951	Finland	W	3–0	Luxembourg	Fr	Muller, Nurenberg, OG
23–12	West Germany	L	1–4	Essen	Fr	Muller
20–04–1952	West Germany	L	0–3	Luxembourg	Fr	
20–09–1953	France	L	1–6	Luxembourg	WCq	Kohn
28–10	Rep. Ireland	L	0–4	Dublin	WCq	
17–12	France	L	0–8	Paris	WCq	
7–03–1954	Rep. Ireland	L	0–1	Luxembourg	WCq	
30–09–1956	Austria	L	0–7	Vienna	WCq	
20–03–1957	Holland	L	1–4	Rotterdam	WCq	Halsdorf
11–09	Holland	L	2–5	Rotterdam	WCq	Fiedler, Letsch
29–09	Austria	L	0–3	Luxembourg	WCq	
17–06–1959	Norway	L	0–1	Oslo	Fr	
19–10–1960	England	L	0–9	Luxembourg	WCq	
19–03–1961	Portugal	L	0–6	Lisbon	WCq	
28–09	England	L	1–4	London	WCq	Dimmer
8–10	Portugal	W	4–2	Luxembourg	WCq	Schmit 3, Hoffmann
11–04–1962	Soviet Union	L	1–3	Luxembourg	Fr	Schmit
11–09–1963	Holland	D	1–1	Amsterdam	ECr2	May
30–10	Holland	W	2–1	Rotterdam	ECr2	Dimmer 2
4–12	Denmark	D	3–3	Luxembourg	ECqf	Pilot, Klein H 2
10–12	Denmark	D	2–2	Copenhagen	ECqf	Leonard, Schmit
18–12	Denmark	L	0–1	Amsterdam	ECqf	
20–09–1964	Yugoslavia	L	1–3	Belgrade	WCq	Schmit
4–10	France	L	0–2	Luxembourg	WCq	
8–11	Norway	L	0–2	Luxembourg	WCq	
27–05–1965	Norway	L	2–4	Trondheim	WCq	Brenner, Dublin
19–09	Yugoslavia	L	2–5	Luxembourg	WCq	Pilot 2
6–11	France	L	1–4	Marseille	WCq	Pilot
2–10–1966	Poland	L	0–4	Szezecin	ECq	
26–11	France	L	0–3	Luxembourg	ECq	
19–03–1967	Belgium	L	0–5	Luxembourg	ECq	
16–04	Poland	D	0–0	Luxembourg	ECq	
22–11	Belgium	L	0–3	Bruges	ECq	
23–12	France	L	1–3	Paris	ECq	Klein J
4–09–1968	Holland	L	0–2	Rotterdam	WCq	
20–11	Denmark	L	1–5	Copenhagen	Fr	Klein J
26–03–1969	Holland	L	0–4	Rotterdam	WCq	
10–04	Mexico	W	2–1	Luxembourg	Fr	Leonard, Philipp
20–04	Poland	L	1–8	Krakow	WCq	Leonard
23–04	Bulgaria	L	1–2	Sofia	WCq	Leonard
12–10	Poland	L	1–5	Luxembourg	WCq	
7–12	Bulgaria	L	1–3	Luxembourg	WCq	Philipp
4–01–1970	Malta	D	1–1	Gzira	Fr	Hoffmann N
9–05	Czechoslovakia	L	0–1	Luxembourg	Fr	
14–10	Yugoslavia	L	0–2	Luxembourg	ECq	

15–11	East Germany	L	0–5	Luxembourg	ECq	
24–02–1971	Holland	L	0–6	Rotterdam	ECq	
24–04	East Germany	L	1–2	Gera	ECq	Dussier
20–05	Belgium	L	0–4	Luxembourg	Fr	
27–10	Yugoslavia	D	0–0	Titograd	ECq	
7–11	Belgium	L	0–1	Verviers	Fr	
17–11	Holland	L	0–8	Eindhoven	ECq	
26–04–1972	Czechoslovakia	L	0–6	Pilsen	Fr	
7–10	Italy	L	0–4	Luxembourg	WCq	
22–10	Turkey	W	2–0	Esch	WCq	Dussier, Braun
10–12	Turkey	L	0–3	Istanbul	WCq	
31–03–1973	Italy	L	0–5	Genoa	WCq	
8–04	Switzerland	L	0–1	Luxembourg	WCq	
26–09	Switzerland	L	0–1	Lucerne	WCq	
7–10	Canada	L	0–2	Luxembourg	Fr	
4–11	Norway	W	2–1	Luxembourg	Fr	Monacelli, Langers
13–10–1974	Hungary	L	2–4	Luxembourg	ECq	Dussier 2
20–11	Wales	L	0–5	Swansea	ECq	
16–03–1975	Austria	L	1–2	Luxembourg	ECq	Braun
1–05	Wales	L	1–3	Luxembourg	ECq	Philipp
15–10	Austria	L	2–6	Vienna	ECq	Braun, Philipp
19–10	Hungary	L	1–8	Szombathely	ECq	Dussier
21–08–1976	Iceland	L	1–3	Reykjavik	Fr	Braun
22–09	Finland	L	1–7	Helsinki	WCq	Zender G
16–10	Italy	L	1–4	Luxembourg	WCq	Braun
30–03–1977	England	L	0–5	London	WCq	
26–05	Finland	L	0–1	Luxembourg	WCq	
12–10	England	L	0–2	Luxembourg	WCq	
3–12	Italy	L	0–3	Rome	WCq	
22–03–1978	Poland	L	1–3	Luxembourg	Fr	Reiter
7–10	France	L	1–3	Luxembourg	ECq	Michaux
25–02–1979	France	L	0–3	Paris	ECq	
1–05	Czechoslovakia	L	0–3	Luxembourg	ECq	
7–06	Sweden	L	0–3	Malmo	ECq	
23–10	Sweden	D	1–1	Esch	ECq	Braun
24–11	Czechoslovakia	L	0–4	Prague	ECq	
27–02–1980	Belgium	L	0–5	Brussels	Fr	
26–03	Uruguay	L	0–1	Esch	Fr	
1–05	Thailand	W	1–0	Medan	Fr	Clemens
9–05	South Korea	W	3–2	Medan	Fr	Di Domenico, Reiter 2
11–05	Japan	L	0–1	Medan	Fr	
13–05	Burma	L	0–2	Medan	Fr	
14–05	South Korea	L	0–3	Medan	Fr	
10–09	Yugoslavia	L	0–5	Luxembourg	WCq	
4–10	USA	L	0–2	Dudelange	Fr	
11–10	Italy	L	0–2	Luxembourg	WCq	
19–11	Denmark	L	0–4	Copenhagen	WCq	
28–01–1981	Greece	L	0–2	Salonika	WCq	
11–03	Greece	L	0–2	Luxembourg	WCq	
1–05	Denmark	L	1–2	Luxembourg	WCq	Nurenberg
14–10	Spain	L	0–3	Valencia	Fr	
21–11	Yugoslavia	L	0–5	Novi Sad	WCq	
5–12	Italy	L	0–1	Naples	WCq	
9–10–1982	Greece	L	0–2	Luxembourg	ECq	
10–11	Denmark	L	1–2	Luxembourg	ECq	Di Domenico

LEADING INTERNATIONAL APPEARANCES

1 Konter	77	Weis	63
2 Brenner	67	5 Bossi M	58
3 Dresch	63	Including 'B' Internationals	

LEADING INTERNATIONAL GOALSCORERS

1 Mart	16	3 Libar	14
2 Kemp	15	4 Kettel	13

15-12	England	L	0-9	London	ECq	
27-03-1983	Hungary	L	2-6	Luxembourg	ECq	Reiter, Schreiner
17-04	Hungary	L	2-6	Budapest	ECq	Reiter, Malget
12-10	Denmark	L	0-6	Copenhagen	ECq	
16-11	England	L	0-4	Luxembourg	ECq	
14-12	Greece	L	0-1	Athens	ECq	
29-02-1984	Spain	L	0-1	Luxembourg	Fr	
11-03	Turkey	L	1-3	Esch	Fr	Dresch
1-05	Norway	L	0-2	Ettelbruck	Fr	
9-06	Portugal	L	1-2	Luxembourg	Fr	Wagner
13-10	France	L	0-4	Luxembourg	WCq	
17-11	East Germany	L	0-5	Esch	WCq	
5-12	Bulgaria	L	0-4	Sofia	WCq	
17-12	Cyprus	L	0-1	Nicosia	Fr	
19-12	Israel	L	0-2	Tel Aviv	Fr	
22-12	Turkey	L	0-1	Istanbul	Fr	
27-03-1985	Yugoslavia	L	0-1	Zenica	WCq	
24-04	Iceland	D	0-0	Ettelbruck	Fr	
1-05	Yugoslavia	L	0-1	Luxembourg	WCq	
18-05	East Germany	L	1-3	Babelsberg	WCq	Langers R
25-09	Bulgaria	L	1-3	Luxembourg	WCq	Langers R
30-10	France	L	0-6	Paris	WCq	
5-02-1986	Portugal	L	0-2	Portimao	Fr	
14-10	Belgium	L	0-6	Luxembourg	ECq	
12-11	Scotland	L	0-3	Glasgow	ECq	
30-04-1987	Bulgaria	L	1-4	Luxembourg	ECq	Langers R
20-05	Bulgaria	L	0-3	Sofia	ECq	
28-05	Rep. Ireland	L	0-2	Luxembourg	ECq	
9-09	Rep. Ireland	L	1-2	Dublin	ECq	Krings
23-09	Spain	L	0-2	Castellon	Fr	
11-11	Belgium	L	0-3	Brussels	ECq	
2-12	Scotland	D	0-0	Esch	ECq	
27-04-1988	Italy	L	0-3	Luxembourg	Fr	
21-09	Switzerland	L	1-4	Luxembourg	WCq	Langers R
18-10	Czechoslovakia	L	0-2	Esch	WCq	
16-11	Portugal	L	0-1	Oporto	WCq	
9-05-1989	Czechoslovakia	L	0-4	Prague	WCq	
1-06	Belgium	L	0-5	Lille	WCq	
11-10	Portugal	L	0-3	Saarbrucken	WCq	
25-10	Belgium	D	1-1	Brussels	WCq	Hellers
15-11	Switzerland	L	1-2	St Gallen	WCq	Malget
28-03-1990	Iceland	L	1-2	Esch	Fr	Malget
31-10	Germany	L	2-3	Luxembourg	ECq	Girres, Langers R
14-11	Wales	L	0-1	Luxembourg	ECq	
27-02-1991	Belgium	L	0-3	Brussels	ECq	
11-09	Belgium	L	0-2	Luxembourg	ECq	
12-10	Portugal	D	1-1	Luxembourg	Fr	Weis
13-11	Wales	L	0-1	Cardiff	ECq	
18-12	Germany	L	0-4	Leverkusen	ECq	

MALTA

With a population of only 300 000, Malta will never have a large enough pool of players to call upon to have a good team, but it is disappointing that they have not done better. Almost all of their victories have come from games against African or Asian opposition, and of the middle-ranking European powers only Greece have been defeated.

The Malta Football Association was formed as far back as 1900, and as a British colony, was affiliated to the Football Association in London. The obvious British influence led to the formation of a league in 1910, and for many years, with a cup competition introduced in 1935, the Maltese were content to chug along in relative obscurity.

In 1959, with the permission of the FA in London, Malta decided the time was right to start playing international football and was granted membership of FIFA. They entered the 1960 Olympic Games qualifiers, not in Europe, but in Africa. The venture did not turn out successfully, as although they held both Morocco and Tunisia to draws at home, they lost to both away.

It was not until the 1970s that Malta began regularly

entering either the World Cup or European Championship, but Maltese clubs have been steadfast competitors in the three European club competitions since the early 1960s. As would be expected, results have not been good despite the professional status of many of the players. In 1983, Valletta FC were on the end of an 18–0 aggregate thrashing by Glasgow Rangers and other double-figure defeats are not uncommon.

The club scene has traditionally been dominated by Floriana and Sliema Wanderers, although Valletta FC, Hamrun Spartans and Hibernians Paola make up the traditional big five. Since the inauguration of the Ta'Qali national stadium in 1980, all of the games in the premier league take place there, so technically there are no home games. There is little justification in having any more stadia given that the island is only 316 square kilometres big and that full to capacity, Ta'Qali will hold one tenth of the island's population.

The only occasions when the national stadium does fill up is for the visits of the major foreign clubs, or national sides. If there has been little to cheer about at club level, the record of the Maltese national eleven brings little relief either. Bottom of every qualifying group they have ever taken part in, they have occasionally achieved an honourable draw against the likes of Czechoslovakia and Portugal, but the last win in competition was in 1982 against Iceland in neutral Messina. The one possible advantage they did have in the past, a dreadful pitch at the old Empire Stadium in Gzira, has now gone as well.

		All			League			Cup		Europe		
	Team	G	S	B	G	S	B	G	S	G	S	B
1	Floriana	40	21	11	24	10	11	16	11	–	–	–
2	Sliema Wanderers	39	39	17	22	25	17	17	14	–	–	–
3	Valletta	20	22	15	14	13	15	6	9	–	–	–
4	Hamrun Spartans	13	10	13	7	9	13	6	1	–	–	–
5	Hibernians	11	18	7	6	9	7	5	9	–	–	–
6	Rabat Ajax	3	2	1	2	1	1	1	1	–	–	–
7	St. Georges	1	6	5	1	4	5	–	2	–	–	–
8	Zurrieq	1	2	2	–	–	2	1	2	–	–	–
9	Melita St. Julians	1	2	1	–	1	1	1	1	–	–	–
10	Gzira United	1	–	1	–	–	1	1	–	–	–	–
11	KOMR Militia	1	–	–	1	–	–	–	–	–	–	–
12	Birkana United	–	3	–	–	1	–	–	2	–	–	–
13	Marsa	–	2	–	–	2	–	–	–	–	–	–
14	Hamrun Liberty	–	1	–	–	–	–	–	1	–	–	–
	Hamrun United	–	1	–	–	1	–	–	–	–	–	–
	Sengla Athletic	–	1	–	–	–	–	–	1	–	–	–
	Vittoriosa Rovers	–	1	–	–	1	–	–	–	–	–	–
18	ASC Militia	–	–	1	–	–	1	–	–	–	–	–
	Civil Police	–	–	1	–	–	1	–	–	–	–	–
	St Joseph's	–	–	1	–	–	1	–	–	–	–	–

To the end of the 1991–92 season

Malta will continue to contribute to the European game for many years to come, and in the future may well cause an upset or two, but her best hope for prestige is to continue to invite Asian and African teams to friendly tournaments like the Rothmans International Tournament, or to take part in the President's Cup tournament in Seoul, or others like it; on both occasions when Malta have taken part, impressive wins have been scored.

Population: 353 000
Area, sq km: 316
% in urban areas: 85.3%
Capital city: Valletta

Malta Football Association
280 St. Paul Street
Valletta
Malta
Tel: (010 356) 222697
Fax: (010 356) 245136
Telex: 1752 MALFA MW
Cable: FOOTBALL MALTA VALLETTA
Languages for correspondence: English

Year of formation: 1900
Affiliation to FIFA: 1959
Affiliation to UEFA: 1960
Registered clubs: 47
Registered players: 7100
Professional players: 370
Registered coaches: 71
Registered referees: 55
National stadium: Ta'Qali Stadium 30 000
National colours: Shirts: Red/Shorts: White/Socks: Red
Reserve colours: Shirts: White/Shorts: White/Socks: Red
Season: September–May

THE RECORD

WORLD CUP

1930–70 ..... Did not enter
1974 .... QT 4th/4 in group 1
1978 .... QT 4th/4 in group 3
1982 .... QT 3rd/3 in group 7
1986 .... QT 5th/5 in group 2
1990 .... QT 5th/5 in group 6

EUROPEAN CHAMPIONSHIP

1960 .... Did not enter
1964 .... 1st round
1968 .... Did not enter
1972 .... QT 4th/4 in group 3
1976 .... QT 4th/4 in group 8
1980 .... QT 4th/4 in group 7
1984 .... QT 5th/5 in group 7
1988 .... QT 5th/5 in group 2
1992 .... QT 5th/5 in group 6

OLYMPIC GAMES

1908–56 ..... Did not enter
1960 .... QT Failed to qualify
1964–88 ..... Did not enter
1992 .... QT Failed to qualify

EUROPEAN CLUB COMPETITIONS

EUROPEAN CUP: 2nd round – Sliema Wanderers 1972

CUP WINNERS CUP: 2nd round – Hibernians 1963 1972, Sliema Wanderers 1969, Hamrun Spartans 1985

UEFA CUP: Never past the first round

CLUB DIRECTORY

VALLETTA (Population – 9000)
Valletta Football Club
Stadium: Ta'Qali 35 000
Founded: 1904
Colours: White/White
Previous names: Valletta United 1904–39

BIRKIRKARA (Population – 20 000)
Birkirkara Football Club
Stadium: Ta'Qali 35 000
Founded: 1934
Colours: Red and yellow diagonal halves/Red

QORMI (Population – 19 000)
Qormi Football Club
Stadium: Ta'Qali 35 000
Founded: 1918
Colours: Yellow/Black

HAMRUM (Population – 13 000)
Hamrun Spartans Football Club
Stadium: Ta'Qali 35000
Founded: 1907
Colours: Red and black stripes/Black

SLIEMA (Population – 13 000)
Sliema Wanderers Football Club
Stadium: Ta'Qali 35 000
Founded: 1909
Colours: Blue and black checks/Black

FLORIANA
Floriana Football Club
Stadium: Ta'Qali 35 000
Founded: 1900
Colours: Green and white stripes/Green

PAOLA
Hibernians Football Club
Stadium: Ta'Qali 35 000
Founded: 1931
Colours: White/Black

MOSTA
Mosta Football Club
Stadium: Ta'Qali 35 000
Founded: 1935
Colours: Blue/Blue

NAXXAR
Naxxar Lions Football Club
Stadium: Ta'Qali 35 000
Founded: 1920
Colours: Red with white sleeves/White

RABAT
Rabat Ajax Football Club
Stadium: Ta'Qali 35 000
Founded: 1930
Colours: Black and white stripes/White
Previous name: Rabat FC 1929–81

ZURRIEQ
Zurrieq Football Club
Stadium: Ta'Qali 35 000
Founded: 1949
Colours: Red and white stripes/White

MQABBA
Mqabba Hajduks Football Club
Stadium: Ta'Qali 35 000
Founded: 1957
Colours: Red/White

ZEBBUG
Zebbug Rangers Football Club
Stadium: Ta'Qali 35 000
Founded: 1946
Colours: Yellow/Green

TARXIEN
Tarxien Rainbows Football Club
Stadium: Ta'Qali 35 000
Founded: 1949
Colours: Blue and white stripes/White

COSPICUA
St. Georges Football Club
Stadium: Ta'Qali 35 000
Founded: 1899
Colours: Blue/White
Previous names: Merged in 1930 with Old St. Georges

MSIDA
St. Joseph's Football Club
Stadium: Ta'Qali 35 000
Founded: 1911
Colours: Red/White
Previous name: Merged with Msida Rovers in 1924 as St. Joseph's

ST. JULIANS
Melita St. Julians Football Club
Stadium: Ta'Qali 35 000
Founded: 1906
Colours: Red/White
Previous name: BEL St. Julian's

MARSA
Marsa Football Club
Stadium: Ta'Qali 35 000
Founded: 1910
Colours: Blue and red stripes/Blue
Previous name: Marsa United 1910–31

GZIRA
Gzira United Football Club
Stadium: Ta'Qali 35 000
Founded: 1950
Colours: Brown/White

SENGLEA
Senglea Athletic Football Club
Stadium: Ta'Qali 35 000
Founded: 1945
Colours: Yellow/Red

MALTESE LEAGUE CHAMPIONSHIP

Year	Champions		Runners up		3rd	
1910	Floriana	8	Sliema Wanderers	5	St Joseph's	4
1911	–					
1912	Floriana	8	Hamrun Spartans	4	St George's	3
1913	Floriana	12	Hamrun Spartans	10	Sliema Wanderers	8
1914	Hamrun Spartans	10	St George's	10	Valletta United	8
1915	Valletta United	9	Hamrun Spartans	7	Sliema Wanderers	6
1916	–					
1917	St George's	8	Sliema Wanderers	8	Hamrun Spartans	7
1918	Hamrun Spartans	12	St George's	12	Sliema Wanderers	11
1919	KOMR Militia	8	Hamrun United	6	ASC Militia	2
1920	Sliema Wanderers	9	Hamrun Spartans	7	Valletta United	6
1921	Floriana	16	Marsa United	13	Hamrun Spartans	13
1922	Floriana	10	Sliema Wanderers	9	Civil Police	8
1923	Sliema Wanderers	10	Floriana	8	Sliema Rangers	4
1924	Sliema Wanderers	8	Vittoriosa Rovers	4	Valletta United	4
1925	Floriana	13	Sliema Wanderers	11	Valletta United	8
1926	Sliema Wanderers	12	Floriana	9	Valletta United	6
1927	Floriana	5	Sliema Wanderers	3	St George's	2
1928	Floriana	10	Valletta United	9	St George's	6
1929	Floriana	7	Sliema Wanderers	4	Valletta United	1
1930	Sliema Wanderers	7	Old St George's	7	Valletta United	3
1931	Floriana	12	Sliema Wanderers	6	Valletta United	4
1932	Valletta United	5	Sliema Wanderers	4	Sliema Rangers	2
1933	Sliema Wanderers	5	Hibernians	5	Sliema Rangers	2
1934	Sliema Wanderers	5	Hibernians	3		

1935	Floriana	11	Sliema Wanderers	10	Hibernians	9
1936	Sliema Wanderers	6	Floriana	5	Hibernians	1
1937	Floriana	8	Hibernians	6	Sliema Wanderers	5
1938	Sliema Wanderers	10	Floriana	8	Valletta	3
1939	Sliema Wanderers	11	Melita St Julians	5	St George's	4
1940	Sliema Wanderers	16	St George's	16	Melita St Julians	10
1941–44	–					
1945	Valletta	4	Sliema Wanderers	3	Floriana	3
1946	Valletta	19	Sliema Wanderers	17	Floriana	16
1947	Hamrun Spartans	21	Valletta	20	Floriana	17
1948	Valletta	23	Hamrun Spartans	21	Sliema Wanderers	19
1949	Sliema Wanderers	22	Hamrun Spartans	20	Valletta	19
1950	Floriana	23	Hamrun Spartans	22	Sliema Wanderers	19
1951	Floriana	23	Hibernians	20	Valletta	18
1952	Floriana	24	Hamrun Spartans	20	Sliema Wanderers	19
1953	Floriana	21	Birkirkara United	20	Valletta	19
1954	Sliema Wanderers	20	Floriana	19	Hamrun Spartans	16
1955	Floriana	26	Sliema Wanderers	21	Hamrun Spartans	18
1956	Sliema Wanderers	24	Floriana	19	Hamrun Spartans	14
1957	Sliema Wanderers	26	Valletta	20	Floriana	19
1958	Floriana	24	Sliema Wanderers	21	Hamrun Spartans	19
1959	Valletta	23	Sliema Wanderers	18	Hamrun Spartans	15
1960	Valletta	24	Hibernians	20	Floriana	16
1961	Hibernians	25	Valletta	22	Sliema Wanderers	20
1962	Floriana	28	Valletta	24	Sliema Wanderers	17
1963	Valletta	23	Hibernians	21	Sliema Wanderers	21
1964	Sliema Wanderers	26	Valletta	22	Hibernians	17
1965	Sliema Wanderers	20	Valletta	18	Hibernians	16
1966	Sliema Wanderers	17	Floriana	11	Hibernians	10
1967	Hibernians	17	Sliema Wanderers	16	Floriana	10
1968	Floriana	25	Sliema Wanderers	20	Hibernians	18
1969	Hibernians	21	Valletta	18	Floriana	18
1970	Floriana	22	Sliema Wanderers	19	Valletta	17
1971	Sliema Wanderers	20	Marsa	20	Gzira United	17
1972	Sliema Wanderers	26	Floriana	26	Valletta	24
1973	Floriana	26	Sliema Wanderers	25	Hamrun Spartans	25
1974	Valletta	28	Hibernians	24	Sliema Wanderers	21
1975	Floriana	31	Sliema Wanderers	24	St George's	23
1976	Sliema Wanderers	26	Floriana	25	Hibernians	20
1977	Floriana	33	Sliema Wanderers	27	Valletta	25
1978	Valletta	28	Hibernians	26	Sliema Wanderers	24
1979	Hibernians	11	Valletta	6	Sliema Wanderers	4
1980	Valletta	31	Sliema Wanderers	28	Floriana	28
1981	Hibernians	26	Sliema Wanderers	23	Floriana	15
1982	Hibernians	26	Sliema Wanderers	18	Floriana	16
1983	Hamrun Spartans	24	Valletta	16	Rabat Ajax	16
1984	Valletta	11	Rabat Ajax	10	Hamrun Spartans	9
1985	Rabat Ajax	17	Hamrun Spartans	16	Sliema Wanderers	15
1986	Rabat Ajax	23	Hibernians	18	Hamrun Spartans	17
1987	Hamrun Spartans	25	Valletta	16	Zurrieq	16
1988	Hamrun Spartans	22	Sliema Wanderers	19	Zurrieq	18
1989	Sliema Wanderers	26	Valletta	23	Hamrun Spartans	20
1990	Valletta	28	Sliema Wanderers	24	Hamrun Spartans	23
1991	Hamrun Spartans	24	Valletta	19	Floriana	18
1992	Valletta	33	Floriana	24	Hamrun Spartans	23

MALTESE CUP FINALS

Year	Winners	Score	Runners–up
1935	Sliema Wanderers	4–0	Floriana
1936	Sliema Wanderers	2–1	Floriana
1937	Sliema Wanderers	2–1	St George's
1938	Floriana	2–1	Sliema Wanderers
1939	Melita St Julians	4–0	Sliema Wanderers
1940	Sliema Wanderers	3–2	Melita St Julians
1941–44	–		
1945	Floriana	2–1	Sliema Wanderers
1946	Sliema Wanderers	2–1	Hamrun Liberty
1947	Floriana	3–0	Valletta
1948	Sliema Wanderers	2–2 1–0	Hibernians
1949	Floriana	5–1	Sliema Wanderers
1950	Floriana	3–1	St George's
1951	Sliema Wanderers	5–0	Hibernians
1952	Sliema Wanderers	3–3 1–1 1–0	Hibernians
1953	Floriana	1–0	Sliema Wanderers
1954	Floriana	5–1	Rabat FC
1955	Floriana	1–0	Sliema Wanderers
1956	Sliema Wanderers	1–0	Floriana

1957	Floriana	2–0	Valletta
1958	Floriana	2–0	Sliema Wanderers
1959	Sliema Wanderers	1–1 1–0	Valletta
1960	Valletta	3–0	Floriana
1961	Floriana	2–0	Hibernians
1962	Hibernians	1–0	Valletta
1963	Sliema Wanderers	2–0	Hibernians
1964	Valletta	1–0	Sliema Wanderers
1965	Sliema Wanderers	4–2	Floriana
1966	Floriana	2–1	Hibernians
1967	Floriana	1–0	Hibernians
1968	Sliema Wanderers	3–2	Hibernians
1969	Sliema Wanderers	3–1	Hamrun Spartans
1970	Hibernians	1–1 2–1	Valletta
1971	Hibernians	1–1 2–0	Sliema Wanderers
1972	Floriana	3–1	Sliema Wanderers
1973	Gzira United	0–0 0–0 2–0	Birkirkara United
1974	Sliema Wanderers	1–0	Floriana
1975	Valletta	1–0	Hibernians
1976	Floriana	2–0	Valletta
1977	Valletta	1–0	Floriana
1978	Valletta	3–2	Floriana
1979	Sliema Wanderers	2–1	Floriana
1980	Hibernians	2–1	Sliema Wanderers
1981	Floriana	2–1	Senglea Athletic
1982	Hibernians	2–0	Sliema Wanderers
1983	Hamrun Spartans	2–0	Valletta
1984	Hamrun Spartans	0–0 1–0	Zurrieq
1985	Zurrieq	0–0 2–1	Valletta
1986	Rabat Ajax	2–0	Zurrieq
1987	Hamrun Spartans	2–1	Sliema Wanderers
1988	Hamrun Spartans	4–2	Floriana
1989	Hamrun Spartans	1–0	Floriana
1990	Sliema Wanderers	1–0	Birkirkara United
1991	Valletta	2–1	Sliema Wanderers
1992	Hamrun Spartans	3–3 (2–1p)	Valletta

INTERNATIONAL MATCHES PLAYED BY MALTA

Date	Opponents	Result		Venue	Compet	Scorers
8-03-1959	Tunisia	D	0–0	Tunis	Fr	
8-12-1960	Tunisia	W	1–0	Gzira	Fr	Borg
5-11-1961	Norway	D	1–1	Gzira	Fr	Demanuele P
28-06-1962	Denmark	L	1–6	Copenhagen	ECr1	Theobald
3-07	Norway	L	0–5	Trondheim	Fr	
8-12	Denmark	L	1–3	Gzira	ECr1	Urpani
20-09-1963	Egypt	L	0–6	Caserta	MG	
23-09	Lebanon	L	0–2	Salerno	MG	
13-02-1966	Libya	W	1–0	Gzira	Fr	Aquilina E
27-03	Libya	W	1–0	Tripoli	Fr	Cocks
27-04-1969	Austria	L	1–3	Gzira	Fr	Cini
4-01-1970	Luxembourg	D	1–1	Gzira	Fr	Cini
11-10	Greece	D	1–1	Gzira	ECq	Vassallo
20-12	Switzerland	L	1–2	Gzira	ECq	Theobald
3-02-1971	England	L	0–1	Gzira	ECq	
21-04	Switzerland	L	0–5	Lucerne	ECq	
12-05	England	L	0–5	London	ECq	
18-06	Greece	L	0–2	Athens	ECq	
14-11	Hungary	L	0–2	Gzira	WCq	
8-12	Algeria	D	1–1	Gzira	Fr	Vassallo
15-03-1972	Algeria	L	0–1	Algiers	Fr	
30-04	Austria	L	0–4	Vienna	WCq	
6-05	Hungary	L	0–3	Budapest	WCq	
15-10	Sweden	L	0–7	Gothenburg	WCq	
25-11	Austria	L	0–2	Gzira	WCq	
28-09-1973	Canada	W	2–0	Gzira	Fr	Xuereb R, Arpa
11-11	Sweden	L	1–2	Gzira	WCq	Camilleri
24-08-1974	Libya	L	0–1	Gzira	Fr	
4-09	Libya	D	0–0	Tripoli	Fr	
22-12	West Germany	L	0–1	Gzira	ECq	
23-02-1975	Greece	W	2–0	Gzira	ECq	Aquilina R, Magro
4-06	Greece	L	0–4	Salonika	ECq	
11-06	Bulgaria	L	0–5	Sofia	ECq	
21-12	Bulgaria	L	0–2	Gzira	ECq	
28-02-1976	West Germany	L	0–8	Dortmund	ECq	
10-03	Libya	D	2–2	Gzira	Fr	Losco 2
31-10	Turkey	L	0–4	Istanbul	WCq	
24-11	Tunisia	D	1–1	Gzira	Fr	Magro
5-12	Austria	L	0–1	Gzira	WCq	
5-03-1977	Tunisia	W	1–0	Tunis	Fr	Xuereb R
2-04	East Germany	L	0–1	Gzira	WCq	
30-04	Austria	L	0–9	Salzburg	WCq	
6-09	Tunisia	L	1–2	Tunis	Fr	Xuereb G
29-10	East Germany	L	0–9	Babelsberg	WCq	
27-11	Turkey	L	0–3	Gzira	WCq	

14–05–1978	Libya	L	0–1	Tripoli	Fr	
25–10	Wales	L	0–7	Wrexham	ECq	
25–02–1979	West Germany	D	0–0	Gzira	ECq	
18–03	Turkey	L	1–2	Izmir	ECq	Spiteri–Gonzi
2–06	Wales	L	0–2	Gzira	ECq	
28–08	Tunisia	L	0–4	Tunis	Fr	
28–10	Turkey	L	1–2	Gzira	ECq	Farrugia Em
27–02–1980	West Germany	L	0–8	Bremen	ECq	
7–12	Poland	L	0–2	Gzira	WCq	
	Abandoned after 82 mins					
4–04–1981	East Germany	L	1–2	Gzira	WCq	Fabri
14–06	Liechtenstein	D	1–1	Seoul	PC	
23–06	Indonesia	W	1–0	Seoul	PC	
27–06	Thailand	W	2–0	Seoul	PC	
24–10	Tunisia	W	1–0	Tunis	Fr	Tortell
11–11	East Germany	L	1–5	Jena	WCq	Spiteri-Gonzi
15–11	Poland	L	0–6	Wroclaw	WCq	
5–06–1982	Iceland	W	2–1	Messina	ECq	Spiteri-Gonzi, Fabri
14–10	Bulgaria	L	0–7	Sofia	Fr	
19–12	Holland	L	0–6	Aachen	ECq	
1–02–1983	Tunisia	L	1–2	Marsa	Fr	Fabri
30–03	Rep. Ireland	L	0–1	Ta'Qali	ECq	
15–05	Spain	L	2–3	Ta'Qali	ECq	Busuttil 2
5–06	Iceland	L	0–1	Reykjavik	ECq	
9–10	Libya	L	0–4	Tripoli	Fr	
16–11	Rep. Ireland	L	0–8	Dublin	ECq	
17–12	Holland	L	0–5	Rotterdam	ECq	
21–12	Spain	L	1–12	Seville	ECq	Demanuele S
23–05–1984	Sweden	L	0–4	Norrkoping	WCq	
6–09	Israel	L	1–2	Tel Aviv	Fr	Muscat
31–10	Czechoslovakia	L	0–4	Prague	WCq	
16–12	West Germany	L	2–3	Ta'Qali	WCq	Busuttil, Xuereb R
10–02–1985	Portugal	L	1–3	Ta'Qali	WCq	Farrugia N
27–03	West Germany	L	0–6	Saarbrucken	WCq	
3–04	Jordan	W	3–1	Ta'Qali	Fr	Xuereb R 3
21–04	Czechoslovakia	D	0–0	Ta'Qali	WCq	
12–10	Portugal	L	2–3	Lisbon	WCq	Degiorgio, OG
17–11	Sweden	L	1–2	Ta'Qali	WCq	Farrugia N
16–11–1986	Sweden	L	0–5	Ta'Qali	ECq	
6–12	Italy	L	0–2	Ta'Qali	ECq	
24–01–1987	Italy	L	0–5	Bergamo	ECq	
29–03	Portugal	D	2–2	Funchal	ECq	Mizzi, Busuttil
15–04	Switzerland	L	1–4	Neuchatel	ECq	Busuttil
24–05	Sweden	L	0–1	Gothenburg	ECq	
15–11	Switzerland	D	1–1	Ta'Qali	ECq	Busuttil
2–12	Israel	D	1–1	Tel Aviv	Fr	Mizzi
20–12	Portugal	L	0–1	Ta'Qali	ECq	
7–02–1988	Finland	W	2–0	Ta'Qali	Fr	Busuttil 2
10–02	Tunisia	W	2–1	Ta'Qali	Fr	Vella R, Busuttil
22–03	Scotland	D	1–1	Ta'Qali	Fr	Busuttil
21–05	Nth. Ireland	L	0–3	Belfast	WCq	
1–06	Wales	L	2–3	Ta'Qali	Fr	Busuttil 2
12–10	Cyprus	W	1–0	Limassol	Fr	Busuttil
18–10	Israel	L	0–2	Beersheba	Fr	
23–11	Cyprus	D	1–1	Ta'Qali	Fr	Carabott
11–12	Hungary	D	2–2	Ta'Qali	WCq	Busuttil 2
11–01–1989	Israel	L	1–2	Ta'Qali	Fr	Carabott
22–01	Spain	L	0–2	Ta'Qali	WCq	

LEADING INTERNATIONAL APPEARANCES

1 Degeorgio 69	7 Azzopardi 43	13 Cluett 30
2 Holland 59	Xuereb R 43	Farrugia Em 30
3 Vella R 52	9 Farrugia E 39	15 Bonello 29
4 Busuttil 47	10 Camilleri 37	Darmanin 29
5 Buttigieg 45	11 Carabott 35	Xuereb G 29
6 Scerri 44	12 Gregory 33	

LEADING INTERNATIONAL GOALSCORERS								
1	Busuttil	16		Xuereb G	3		Mizzi	2
2	Xuereb R	6	8	Carabott	2		Theobald	2
3	Suda	5		Cini	2		Vassallo	2
4	Degiorgio	4		Farrugia N	2		Scerri	2
5	Spiteri-Gonzi	3		Losco	2		Brincat	2
	Fabri	3		Magro	2		Sultana	2

8–02	Denmark	L	0–2	Ta'Qali	Fr	
10–02	Algeria	L	0–1	Ta'Qali	Fr	
12–02	Finland	D	0–0	Ta'Qali	Fr	
23–03	Spain	L	0–4	Seville	WCq	
12–04	Hungary	D	1–1	Budapest	WCq	Busuttil
26–04	Nth. Ireland	L	0–2	Ta'Qali	WCq	
28–05	Rep. Ireland	L	0–2	Dublin	WCq	
4–10	Austria	L	1–2	Ta'Qali	Fr	Zarb
11–10	Cyprus	D	0–0	Nicosia	Fr	
25–10	East Germany	L	0–4	Ta'Qali	Fr	
15–11	Rep. Ireland	L	0–2	Ta'Qali	WCq	
7–02–1990	Norway	D	1–1	Ta'Qali	Fr	Scerri
10–02	South Korea	L	1–2	Ta'Qali	Fr	Laferla
5–05	United States	L	0–1	Piscataway	Fr	
28–05	Scotland	L	1–2	Ta'Qali	Fr	Degiorgio
2–06	Rep. Ireland	L	0–3	Ta'Qali	Fr	
31–10	Greece	L	0–4	Athens	ECq	
25–11	Finland	D	1–1	Ta'Qali	ECq	Suda
19–12	Holland	L	0–8	Ta'Qali	ECq	
9–02–1991	Portugal	L	0–1	Ta'Qali	ECq	
20–02	Portugal	L	0–5	Oporto	ECq	
13–03	Holland	L	0–1	Rotterdam	ECq	
7–05	Iceland	L	1–4	Ta'Qali	Fr	Suda
16–05	Finland	L	0–2	Helsinki	ECq	
7–06	Indonesia	W	3–0	Seoul	PC	Degiorgio, Suda, Scerri
9–06	Egypt	L	2–5	Seoul	PC	Brincat, Suda
11–06	South Korea	D	1–1	Seoul	PC	Suda
27–11	Libya	W	2–0	Psyala	Fr	Brincat, Sultana
22–12	Greece	D	1–1	Ta'Qali	Fr	Sultana

NORTHERN IRELAND

The fourth oldest football association in the world; a permanent seat on the International Board, the world's rule-making body; the third oldest league in the world and a history of international matches that stretches back 110 years. This is the heritage of football in Northern Ireland but one which is increasingly under threat. How long will a Northern Ireland team last before it is either swallowed up into a British XI, or alternatively into a United Ireland XI which seems more likely?

The Irish Football Association, not to be confused with the Football Association of Ireland which rules the game in the Republic, until 1923 controlled football throughout the island of Ireland. Until that time, however, the game was a predominantly Northern sport. The association was based in Belfast, and on only six occasions in 40 years did the Irish team play a match in Dublin. Shelbourne and Bohemians of Dublin had the odd cup success, but the real football base was in the North.

The civil war in the early 1920s and the partition of the country led to bitter disputes between the association in the North and its new rival in the South. There were major defections to the Southern body, even from those clubs located in the six provinces which constituted Northern Ireland. A meeting of the four British associations in 1923 decided to recognise the Dublin association, but ordered that clubs located within the six provinces should rejoin the association in Belfast.

With the Irish Free State in the South embarking on international matches and running its own league and cup, Irish football was split into two camps, although it was not until 1948 that the North abstained from selecting players for the national side who were from the South.

Along with Wales, Ireland has had to compete fiercely with rugby for the affections of the public. The first football playing club was Ulster FC, a rugby club who formed a football section after an exhibition match between two Scottish clubs, Queen's Park and Caledonian,

		All			League			Cup		Europe		
	Team	G	S	B	G	S	B	G	S	G	S	B
1	Linfield	73	35	13	40	16	13	33	19	–	–	–
2	Glentoran	34	37	19	19	20	20	15	17	–	–	–
3	Belfast Celtic	22	8	8	14	4	8	8	4	–	–	–
4	Distillery	18	15	8	6	8	8	12	7	–	–	–
5	Cliftonville	10	13	4	2	5	4	8	8	–	–	–
6	Glenavon	7	16	4	3	8	4	4	8	–	–	–
7	Ballymena United	6	10	5	–	2	5	6	8	–	–	–
8	Coleraine	5	11	8	1	7	8	4	4	–	–	–
9	Ards	5	2	8	1	1	8	4	1	–	–	–
10	Derry City	4	10	3	1	7	3	3	3	–	–	–
11	Crusaders	4	1	2	2	–	2	2	1	–	–	–
12	Portadown	3	10	3	2	6	3	1	4	–	–	–
13	Shelbourne Dublin	3	4	1	–	1	1	3	3	–	–	–
14	Queen's Island	3	3	–	1	3	–	2	–	–	–	–
15	Bohemians Dublin	1	5	–	–	–	–	1	5	–	–	–
16	Ulster FC	1	3	–	–	1	–	1	2	–	–	–
17	Carrick Rangers	1	1	–	–	–	–	1	1	–	–	–
	Willowfield	1	1	–	–	–	–	1	1	–	–	–
19	Dundela	1	–	–	–	–	–	1	–	–	–	–
	Moyola Park	1	–	–	–	–	–	1	–	–	–	–
	Gordon Highlanders	1	–	–	–	–	–	1	–	–	–	–
22	Larne	–	4	1	–	–	1	–	4	–	–	–
23	Bangor	–	2	1	–	1	1	–	1	–	–	–
24	Limavady	–	2	–	–	–	–	–	2	–	–	–
25	The Black Watch	–	1	–	–	–	–	–	1	–	–	–
	Derry Celtic	–	1	–	–	–	–	–	1	–	–	–
	Freebooters	–	1	–	–	–	–	–	1	–	–	–
	St Columbs Hall Celtic	–	1	–	–	–	–	–	1	–	–	–
	Sherwood Foresters	–	1	–	–	–	–	–	1	–	–	–
	Wellington Park	–	1	–	–	–	–	–	1	–	–	–
	YMCA Belfast	–	1	–	–	–	–	–	1	–	–	–
32	Lancashire Fusiliers	–	–	1	–	–	1	–	–	–	–	–
	Newry Town	–	–	1	–	–	1	–	–	–	–	–

To the end of the 1991–92 season

in 1878 in Belfast. Soon football clubs began to spring up in and around Belfast. The first of these devoted entirely to football, Cliftonville FC, was formed in 1879 by JM McAlery, who was instrumental in the formation of the Irish Football Association in the following year.

Club football in Ireland has never been particularly strong and has always suffered from the loss of its best players to either England or Scotland, but in these early years most of the players appearing for Irish clubs were Scottish. That not many Irish people were playing football can be seen from their early results in international matches. A match against England was organised for 1882 in Belfast and the 13–0 defeat remains their record loss. Heavy defeats were the order of the day until the turn of the century, and although the Irish fairly soon reached the standard of the Welsh, who had had a four year headstart in international matches, it was not until 1903 that Scotland were beaten for the first time, whilst a further ten years were needed to inflict a defeat on England.

The Home International Championship for 68 years provided Ireland and subsequently Northern Ireland with their only international opposition. Not until 1951 when France visited Belfast did they play a non-British side. During these years, the Home International Championship was won just twice. In 1914 Ireland won it outright, whilst in 1903 it was shared with both England and Scotland.

After 1951, the increase in competitive matches revitalised the Irish and until the competition's demise in 1984, Northern Ireland either won or shared the title on six occasions. Most importantly, in 1958, victories over Italy and Portugal saw them qualify for the World Cup Finals in Sweden. With perhaps the best international team the country has ever had, the Irish reached the quarter-finals, further than either England or Scotland. Danny Blanchflower, the man who led Tottenham to the English League and Cup double three years later, was the linchpin of the side which also contained Billy Bingham, who later achieved great feats as manager of the side, Jimmy McIlroy, Jackie Blanchflower, Danny's brother, a very young Derek Dougan and Peter McParland whose goals in Sweden contributed so greatly to the fine results achieved there.

Of the World Cup team only Peacock did not play his club football in England, and he was a regular for Glasgow Celtic. This highlights the weakness of the league in Northern Ireland. Another weakness that in many ways is even more damaging is the sectarian nature of football in the country. The most successful club, Linfield, are associated with the Protestant community, and in a country where religious violence is an everyday occurrence, this leads football down a very dangerous path. Before the Second World War, the main challenge to the supremacy of Linfield came from Belfast Celtic, which as the name suggests was a Catholic-based club, modelled on their mentors from Glasgow.

The matches between Linfield and Celtic became the scene of increasing violence between the two sets of supporters and after a particularly nasty incident in 1948, Celtic withdrew from the league and folded not long after. They are not the only victims of the Troubles. Derry City withdrew from the league in 1972, and now play in the Republic of Ireland's league. In recent years Cliftonville have become the focus for Catholic support, but trouble has also occurred in games between Linfield and another staunchly Protestant club Glentoran. Glentoran supporters have even been known to wear the green and white of Celtic to goad their opponents.

Amidst all this, the Irish Football Association has striven to remain neutral in the conflict, and it is perhaps fortunate for them that the best players do play abroad, thus avoiding disputes with clubs alleging biased selection policy for the national side. One player who would have been picked no matter where he played was George Best, the most talented Irishman ever to have played football.

Indeed he would have walked into the national side of any country in the world. It is unfortunate for him that at his peak he was denied a world stage to display his talents, for the Northern Irish team of the late 1960s was perhaps at its lowest ebb.

The 1980s saw a dramatic rise in their fortunes, but by then it was too late for Best. Outright champions in the Home International Championship for only the second time in 1980, Northern Ireland qualified for the 1982 World Cup thanks largely to the increase in the number of places given to Europe after the expansion of the final tournament. Once there, however, they impressed everyone with their spirit which saw them finish top of their first round group after beating the hosts, Spain, 1–0 in Valencia. Unfortunately they were drawn in the same group as France in the second round and lost 4–1 against them in the decisive match.

They qualified again for the 1986 World Cup in Mexico, and although drawn again with Spain they could not repeat the victory of four years previously, whilst a defeat by Brazil saw to it that they did not qualify for the second round. Since 1986 the Northern Irish team has been in decline. In 1984 they had won the last Home International Championship, but deprived of the income from the folding of the championship, times are hard, and matches now consist mainly of European Championship and World Cup qualifiers.

Financial pressure, and the rise of football in the Republic of Ireland, has led to calls for the unification of Irish football. There is a united team in rugby union so why not for football? Such a move would seem to make sense, but whether football in this troubled island could rise above the fighting and sectarian hatreds like rugby is open to question.

Population: 1 567 000
Area, sq km: 14 120
% in urban areas: 91.5%
Capital city: Belfast

Irish Football Association
20 Winsor Avenue
Belfast BT9 6EG
Northern Ireland
Tel: (010 44) 232 669458
Fax: (010 44) 232 667620
Telex: 747317 IFANIG
Cable: FOOTBALL BELFAST
Languages for correspondence: English

Year of formation: 1880
Affiliation to FIFA: 1911–20, 1924–28, 1946
Affiliation to UEFA: 1954
Registered clubs: 700
Registered players: 15 900
Professional players: 230
Registered coaches: 90
Registered referees: 291
National stadium: Windsor Park 28 000
National colours: Shirts: Green/Shorts: White/Socks: Green
Reserve colours: Shirts: White/Shorts: Green/Socks: Green
Season: August–May

THE RECORD

WORLD CUP

1930–38 ..... Did not enter
1950 .... QT 4th/4 in group 1
1954 .... QT 3rd/4 in group 2
1958 .... QT 1st/3 in group 8 – Final Tournament/Quarter-finalists
1962 .... QT 2nd/3 in group 3
1966 .... QT 2nd/4 in group 5
1970 .... QT 2nd/3 in group 4
1974 .... QT 3rd/4 in group 6
1978 .... QT 3rd/4 in group 4
1982 .... QT 2nd/5 in group 6 – Final Tournament/2nd round
1986 .... QT 2nd/5 in group 3 – Final Tournament/1st round
1990 .... QT 4th/5 in group 6

EUROPEAN CHAMPIONSHIP

1960 .... Did not enter
1964 .... 2nd round
1968 .... QT 4th/4 in group 8
1972 .... QT 3rd/4 in group 4
1976 .... QT 2nd/4 in group 3
1980 .... QT 2nd/5 in group 1
1984 .... QT 2nd/5 in group 6
1988 .... QT 3rd/4 in group 4
1992 .... QT 3rd/5 in group 4

EUROPEAN CLUB COMPETITIONS

EUROPEAN CUP: Quarter-finals – Linfield 1967

CUP WINNERS CUP: Quarter-finals – Glentoran 1974

UEFA CUP: 2nd round – Coleraine 1970 1971, Portadown 1975

CLUB DIRECTORY

BELFAST (Population – 303 000)
Belfast Celtic
Stadium: Celtic Park
Founded: 1891. Dissolved in 1949
Colours: Green/White

Crusaders Football Club
Stadium: Seaview 9000
Founded: 1909
Colours: Red and black stripes/White

Distillery Football Club
Stadium: New Grosvenor 14 000
Founded: 1880
Colours: White with blue sleeves/Blue

Glentoran Football Club
Stadium: The Oval 30 000
Founded: 1882
Colours: Green/Black

Linfield Football Club
Stadium: Windsor Park 30 000
Founded: 1886
Colours: Blue/White

LONDONDERRY (Population – 97 000)
Derry City Football Club
Stadium: Brandywell Park 11 000
Founded: 1928
Colours: Red and white stripes/Black
Previous name: Derry Celtic 1892–1915

Derry City now play in the Republic of Ireland League

NEWTOWNABBEY (Population – 72 000)
Cliftonville Football Club
Stadium: Solitude 15000
Founded: 1879
Colours: Red/White

BANGOR (Population – 70 000)
Bangor Football Club
Stadium: Clandeboye Park 5000
Founded: 1918
Colours: Yellow/Blue

BALLYMENA
Ballymena United
Stadium: The Showgrounds 8000
Founded: 1928
Colours: Blue/Blue
Previous name: Ballymena FC 1928–34

CARRICKFERGUS
Carrick Rangers Football Club
Stadium: Taylor's Avenue 5000
Founded: 1939
Colours: Gold/Black

COLERAINE
Coleraine Football Club
Stadium: The Showgrounds 10 000
Founded: 1927
Colours: Blue and white stripes/Blue

LARNE
Larne Football Club
Stadium: Inver Park 12 000
Founded: 1889
Colours: Red/Red

LURGAN (Population – 63 000)
Glenavon Football Club
Stadium: Mourneview Park 12 000
Founded: 1889
Colours: Blue/White

NEWRY
Newry Town Football Club
Stadium: The Showground 15000
Founded: 1923
Colours: Blue and white stripes/White

NEWTOWNARDS
Ards Football Club
Stadium: Castlereagh Park 10 000
Founded: 1902
Colours: Red and blue stripes/Blue

PORTADOWN
Portadown Football Club
Stadium: Shamrock Park 12 000
Founded: 1924
Colours: Red/Red

OMAGH
Omagh Town Football Club
Stadium: St. Julian's Road 8000
Founded: 1964
Colours: White/Black

ALL-IRELAND LEAGUE CHAMPIONSHIP

Year	Champions		Runners up		3rd	
1891	Linfield	25	Distillery	21	Glentoran	19
1892	Linfield	30	Ulster	24	Lancashire Fus.	23
1893	Linfield	18	Cliftonville	15	Distillery	11
1894	Glentoran	16	Linfield	14	Cliftonville	10
1895	Linfield	10	Distillery	7	Glentoran	4
1896	Distillery	8	Cliftonville	8	Linfield	5
1897	Glentoran	17	Cliftonville	11	Linfield	11
1898	Linfield	17	Cliftonville	13	Glentoran	13
1899	Distillery	15	Linfield	15	Cliftonville	12
1900	Celtic	11	Linfield	10	Cliftonville	9
1901	Distillery	16	Glentoran	15	Celtic	10
1902	Linfield	24	Glentoran	21	Distillery	19
1903	Distillery	20	Linfield	19	Glentoran	17
1904	Linfield	26	Distillery	20	Glentoran	20
1905	Glentoran	21	Celtic	21	Linfield	16
1906	Cliftonville	19			Linfield	17
	Distillery	19				
1907	Linfield	23	Shelbourne	19	Distillery	16
1908	Linfield	22	Cliftonville	17	Glentoran	17
1909	Linfield	21	Glentoran	19	Shelbourne	15
1910	Cliftonville	20	Celtic	18	Linfield	15
1911	Linfield	22	Glentoran	22	Celtic	15
1912	Glentoran	24	Distillery	21	Celtic	20
1913	Glentoran	26	Distillery	24	Linfield	23
1914	Linfield	24	Glentoran	19	Celtic	17
1915	Celtic	23	Glentoran	21	Linfield	17
1916–19 – No championship						
1920	Celtic	23	Distillery	20	Glentoran	19

NORTHERN IRISH LEAGUE CHAMPIONSHIP

Year	Champions		Runners up		3rd	
1921	Glentoran	14	Glenavon	12	Linfield	9
1922	Linfield	17	Glentoran	13	Distillery	11
1923	Linfield	16	Queen's Island	12	Glentoran	11
1924	Queen's Island	26	Distillery	20	Glenavon	20
1925	Glentoran	37	Queen's Island	32	Celtic	27
1926	Celtic	33	Glentoran	30	Larne	27
1927	Celtic	37	Queen's Island	30	Distillery	29
1928	Celtic	45	Linfield	41	Newry Town	33
1929	Celtic	48	Linfield	39	Glentoran	33
1930	Linfield	42	Glentoran	36	Coleraine	32
1931	Glentoran	47	Linfield	38	Celtic	36
1932	Linfield	42	Derry City	38	Celtic	32
1933	Celtic	41	Distillery	39	Linfield	38
1934	Linfield	46	Celtic	37	Glentoran	35
1935	Linfield	46	Derry City	40	Celtic	37
1936	Celtic	43	Derry City	41	Linfield	38
1937	Celtic	44	Derry City	43	Linfield	42
1938	Celtic	41	Derry City	41	Portadown	37

1939	Celtic	40	Ballymena United	35	Derry City	33
1940	Celtic	45	Portadown	41	Glentoran	39
1941–47	– No championship					
1948	Celtic	39	Linfield	35	Ballymena United	27
1949	Linfield	36	Celtic	31	Glentoran	29
1950	Linfield	38	Glentoran	38	Distillery	29
1951	Glentoran	38	Linfield	34	Glenavon	31
1952	Glenavon	37	Glentoran	27	Coleraine	27
1953	Glentoran	33	Linfield	31	Ballymena United	29
1954	Linfield	36	Glentoran	35	Glenavon	28
1955	Linfield	36	Glenavon	36	Ards	24
1956	Linfield	40	Glenavon	29	Bangor City	27
1957	Glenavon	35	Linfield	34	Ards	30
1958	Ards	36	Glenavon	34	Ballymena United	28
1959	Linfield	34	Glenavon	31	Glentoran	27
1960	Glenavon	35	Glentoran	32	Distillery	29
1961	Linfield	32	Portadown	32	Ards	31
1962	Linfield	31	Portadown	31	Ballymena United	29
1963	Distillery	31	Linfield	29	Portadown	28
1964	Glentoran	33	Coleraine	32	Derry City	29
1965	Derry City	35	Coleraine	30	Crusaders	27
1966	Linfield	34	Derry City	32	Glentoran	32
1967	Glentoran	34	Linfield	33	Derry City	27
1968	Glentoran	37	Linfield	36	Coleraine	35
1969	Linfield	35	Derry City	32	Glentoran	30
1970	Glentoran	34	Coleraine	27	Ards	27
1971	Linfield	38	Glentoran	35	Distillery	30
1972	Glentoran	33	Portadown	30	Ards	29
1973	Crusaders	32	Ards	31	Portadown	29
1974	Coleraine	35	Portadown	30	Crusaders	30
1975	Linfield	37	Coleraine	32	Glentoran	31
1976	Crusaders	36	Glentoran	32	Coleraine	31
1977	Glentoran	36	Glenavon	31	Linfield	28
1978	Linfield	40	Glentoran	34	Glenavon	28
1979	Linfield	34	Glenavon	28	Ards	27
1980	Linfield	39	Ballymena United	30	Glentoran	27
1981	Glentoran	37	Linfield	35	Ballymena United	28
1982	Linfield	37	Glentoran	33	Coleraine	31
1983	Linfield	35	Glentoran	30	Coleraine	28
1984	Linfield	45	Glentoran	42	Cliftonville	31
1985	Linfield	39	Coleraine	36	Glentoran	34
1986	Linfield	43	Coleraine	35	Ards	31
1987	Linfield	57	Coleraine	53	Ards	48
1988	Glentoran	62	Linfield	60	Coleraine	52
1989	Linfield	65	Glentoran	55	Coleraine	50
1990	Portadown	55	Glenavon	54	Glentoran	44
1991	Portadown	71	Bangor City	61	Glentoran	60
1992	Glentoran	77	Portadown	65	Linfield	60

ALL-IRELAND CUP FINALS

Year	Winners	Score	Runners–up
1881	Moyola Park	1–0	Cliftonville
1882	Queen's Island	2–1	Cliftonville
1883	Cliftonville	5–0	Ulster
1884	Distillery	5–0	Wellington Park
1885	Distillery	2–0	Limavady
1886	Distillery	1–0	Limavady
1887	Ulster	3–0	Cliftonville
1888	Cliftonville	2–1	Distillery
1889	Distillery	5–4	YMCA
1890	Gordon Highlanders	3–1	Cliftonville
1891	Linfield	4–2	Ulster
1892	Linfield	7–0	The Black Watch
1893	Linfield	5–1	Cliftonville
1894	Distillery	3–2	Linfield
1895	Linfield	10–1	Bohemians
1896	Distillery	3–1	Glentoran
1897	Cliftonville	3–1	Sherwood Foresters
1898	Linfield	2–0	St Columbs Hall Celtic
1899	Linfield	2–1	Glentoran
1900	Cliftonville	2–1	Bohemians
1901	Cliftonville	1–0	Freebooters
1902	Linfield	5–1	Distillery
1903	Distillery	3–1	Bohemians
1904	Linfield	5–1	Derry Celtic
1905	Distillery	3–0	Shelbourne
1906	Shelbourne	2–0	Celtic
1907	Cliftonville	1–0	Shelbourne
1908	Bohemians	3–1	Shelbourne
1909	Cliftonville	2–1	Bohemians
1910	Distillery	1–0	Cliftonville
1911	Shelbourne	2–1	Bohemians
1912	Linfield	W–O	
1913	Linfield	2–0	Glentoran
1914	Glentoran	3–1	Linfield
1915	Linfield	1–0	Celtic

1916	Linfield	1–0	Glentoran
1917	Glentoran	2–0	Celtic
1918	Celtic	2–0	Linfield
1919	Linfield	2–1	Glentoran
1920	Shelbourne	W–O	
1921	Glentoran	2–0	Glenavon

NORTHERN IRISH CUP FINALS

Year	Winners	Score	Runners-up
1922	Linfield	2–0	Glenavon
1923	Linfield	2–0	Glentoran
1924	Queen's Island	1–0	Willowfield
1925	Distillery	2–1	Glentoran
1926	Celtic	3–2	Linfield
1927	Ards	3–2	Cliftonville
1928	Willowfield	1–0	Larne
1929	Ballymena United	2–1	Celtic
1930	Linfield	4–3	Ballymena United
1931	Linfield	3–0	Ballymena United
1932	Glentoran	2–1	Linfield
1933	Glentoran	3–1	Distillery
1934	Linfield	5–0	Cliftonville
1935	Glentoran	1–0	Larne
1936	Linfield	2–1	Derry City
1937	Celtic	3–0	Linfield
1938	Celtic	2–0	Bangor City
1939	Linfield	2–0	Ballymena United
1940	Ballymena United	2–0	Glenavon
1941	Celtic	1–0	Linfield
1942	Linfield	3–1	Glentoran
1943	Celtic	1–0	Glentoran
1944	Celtic	3–1	Linfield
1945	Linfield	4–2	Glentoran
1946	Linfield	3–0	Distillery
1947	Celtic	1–0	Glentoran
1948	Linfield	3–0	Coleraine
1949	Derry City	3–1	Glentoran
1950	Linfield	2–1	Distillery
1951	Glentoran	3–1	Ballymena United
1952	Ards	1–0	Glentoran
1953	Linfield	5–0	Coleraine
1954	Derry City	2–2 0–0 1–0	Glentoran
1955	Dundela	3–0	Glenavon
1956	Distillery	2–2 0–0 1–0	Glentoran
1957	Glenavon	2–0	Derry City
1958	Ballymena United	2–0	Linfield
1959	Glenavon	1–1 2–0	Ballymena United
1960	Linfield	5–1	Ards
1961	Glenavon	5–1	Linfield
1962	Linfield	4–0	Portadown
1963	Linfield	2–1	Distillery
1964	Derry City	2–0	Glentoran
1965	Coleraine	2–1	Glenavon
1966	Glentoran	2–0	Linfield
1967	Crusaders	3–1	Glentoran
1968	Crusaders	2–0	Linfield
1969	Ards	0–0 4–2	Distillery
1970	Linfield	2–1	Ballymena United
1971	Distillery	3–0	Derry City
1972	Coleraine	2–1	Portadown
1973	Glentoran	3–2	Linfield
1974	Ards	2–1	Ballymena United
1975	Coleraine	1–1 0–0 1–0	Linfield
1976	Carrick Rangers	2–1	Linfield
1977	Coleraine	4–1	Linfield
1978	Linfield	3–1	Ballymena United
1979	Cliftonville	3–2	Portadown
1980	Linfield	2–0	Crusaders
1981	Ballymena United	1–0	Glenavon
1982	Linfield	2–1	Coleraine
1983	Glentoran	1–1 2–1	Linfield
1984	Ballymena United	4–1	Carrick Rangers
1985	Glentoran	1–1 1–0	Linfield
1986	Glentoran	2–1	Coleraine
1987	Glentoran	1–0	Larne
1988	Glentoran	1–0	Glenavon
1989	Ballymena United	1–0	Larne
1990	Glentoran	3–0	Portadown
1991	Portadown	2–1	Glenavon
1992	Glenavon	2–1	Linfield

INTERNATIONAL MATCHES PLAYED BY ALL-IRELAND TEAM

Date	Opponents	Result		Venue	Compet	Scorers
18-02-1882	England	L	0–13	Belfast	Fr	
25-02	Wales	L	1–7	Wrexham	Fr	Johnston S
24-02-1883	England	L	0–7	Liverpool	Fr	
17-03	Wales	D	1–1	Belfast	Fr	Morrow
26-01-1884	Scotland	L	0–5	Belfast	HC	
9-02	Wales	L	0–6	Wrexham	HC	
23-02	England	L	1–8	Belfast	HC	McWha
28-02-1885	England	L	0–4	Manchester	HC	
14-03	Scotland	L	2–8	Glasgow	HC	Gibb J 2
11-04	Wales	L	2–8	Belfast	HC	Molyneux, Dill
27-02-1886	Wales	L	0–5	Wrexham	HC	
13-03	England	L	1–6	Belfast	HC	Williams
20-03	Scotland	L	2–7	Belfast	HC	Condy, Johnston S
5-02-1887	England	L	0–7	Sheffield	HC	
19-02	Scotland	L	1–4	Glasgow	HC	Browne
12-03	Wales	W	4–1	Belfast	HC	Stanfield, Browne, Peden, Sherrard
3-03-1888	Wales	L	0–11	Wrexham	HC	
24-03	Scotland	L	2–10	Belfast	HC	Lemon, Dalton
31-03	England	L	1–5	Belfast	HC	Crone
2-03-1889	England	L	1–6	Liverpool	HC	Wilton
9-03	Scotland	L	0–7	Glasgow	HC	
27-04	Wales	L	1–3	Belfast	HC	Lemon

8-02-1890	Wales	L	2-5	Shrewsbury	HC	Dalton 2
15-03	England	L	1-9	Belfast	HC	Reynolds
29-03	Scotland	L	1-4	Belfast	HC	Peden
7-02-1891	Wales	W	7-2	Belfast	HC	Dalton 3, Stanfield 2, Gaffikin 2
7-03	England	L	1-6	Wolverhampton	HC	Whiteside T
28-03	Scotland	L	1-2	Glasgow	HC	Stanfield
27-02-1892	Wales	D	1-1	Bangor	HC	Stanfield
5-03	England	L	0-2	Belfast	HC	
19-03	Scotland	L	2-3	Belfast	HC	Williamson, Gaffikin
25-02-1893	England	L	1-6	Birmingham	HC	Gaffikin
25-03	Scotland	L	1-6	Glasgow	HC	Gaffikin
5-04	Wales	W	4-3	Belfast	HC	Peden 3, Wilton
24-02-1894	Wales	L	1-4	Swansea	HC	Stanfield
3-03	England	D	2-2	Belfast	HC	Stanfield, Gibson
31-03	Scotland	L	1-2	Belfast	HC	Stanfield
9-03-1895	England	L	0-9	Derby	HC	
16-03	Wales	D	2-2	Belfast	HC	Gawkrodger, Sherrard
30-03	Scotland	L	1-3	Glasgow	HC	Sherrard
29-02-1896	Wales	L	1-6	Wrexham	HC	Turner
7-03	England	L	0-2	Belfast	HC	
28-03	Scotland	D	3-3	Belfast	HC	Barron 2, Milne
20-02-1897	England	L	0-6	Nottingham	HC	
6-03	Wales	W	4-3	Belfast	HC	Barron, Stanfield, Pyper J (1), Peden
27-03	Scotland	L	1-5	Glasgow	HC	Pyper J (11)
19-02-1898	Wales	W	1-0	Llandudno	HC	Peden
5-03	England	L	2-3	Belfast	HC	Pyper J (11), Mercer
26-03	Scotland	L	0-3	Belfast	HC	
18-02-1899	England	L	2-13	Sunderland	HC	McAllen, Campbell J
4-03	Wales	W	1-0	Belfast	HC	Meldon
25-03	Scotland	L	1-9	Glasgow	HC	Goodall
24-02-1900	Wales	L	0-2	Llandudno	HC	
3-03	Scotland	L	0-3	Belfast	HC	
17-03	England	L	0-2	Dublin	HC	
23-02-1901	Scotland	L	0-11	Glasgow	HC	
9-03	England	L	0-3	Southampton	HC	
23-03	Wales	L	0-1	Belfast	HC	
22-02-1902	Wales	W	3-0	Cardiff	HC	Gara 3
1-03	Scotland	L	1-3	Belfast	HC	Milne
22-03	England	L	0-1	Belfast	HC	
14-02-1903	England	L	0-4	Wolverhampton	HC	
21-03	Scotland	W	2-0	Glasgow	HC	Connor, Kirwan
28-03	Wales	W	2-0	Belfast	HC	Goodall, Sheridan
12-03-1904	England	L	1-3	Belfast	HC	Kirwan
21-03	Wales	W	1-0	Bangor	HC	McCracken
26-03	Scotland	D	1-1	Dublin	HC	Sheridan
25-02-1905	England	D	1-1	Middlesbrough	HC	OG
18-03	Scotland	L	0-4	Glasgow	HC	
8-04	Wales	D	2-2	Belfast	HC	Murphy, O'Hagan
17-02-1906	England	L	0-5	Belfast	HC	
17-03	Scotland	L	0-1	Dublin	HC	
2-04	Wales	D	4-4	Wrexham	HC	Maxwell 2, Sloan 2
16-02-1907	England	L	0-1	Liverpool	HC	
23-02	Wales	L	2-3	Belfast	HC	O'Hagan, Sloan
16-03	Scotland	L	0-3	Glasgow	HC	
15-02-1908	England	L	1-3	Belfast	HC	Hannon
14-03	Scotland	L	0-5	Dublin	HC	
11-04	Wales	W	1-0	Aberdare	HC	Sloan
13-02-1909	England	L	0-4	Bradford	HC	
15-03	Scotland	L	0-5	Glasgow	HC	
20-03	Wales	L	2-3	Belfast	HC	Lacey, Hunter A (I)
12-02-1910	England	D	1-1	Belfast	HC	Thompson
19-03	Scotland	W	1-0	Belfast	HC	Thompson
11-04	Wales	L	1-4	Wrexham	HC	Darling
28-01-1911	Wales	L	1-2	Belfast	HC	Halligan
11-02	England	L	1-2	Derby	HC	McAuley
18-03	Scotland	L	0-2	Glasgow	HC	
10-02-1912	England	L	1-6	Dublin	HC	Hamill
16-03	Scotland	L	1-4	Belfast	HC	McKnight
13-04	Wales	W	3-2	Cardiff	HC	McCandless 2, Brennan B

18–01–1913	Wales	L	0–1	Belfast	HC	
15–02	England	W	2–1	Belfast	HC	Gillespie 2
15–03	Scotland	L	1–2	Dublin	HC	McKnight
19–01–1914	Wales	W	2–1	Wrexham	HC	Young, Gillespie
14–02	England	W	3–0	Middlesbrough	HC	Lacey 2, Gillespie
14–03	Scotland	D	1–1	Belfast	HC	Young
25–10–1919	England	D	1–1	Belfast	HC	Ferris J
14–02–1920	Wales	D	2–2	Belfast	HC	McCandless, Emerson
13–03	Scotland	L	0–3	Glasgow	HC	
23–10	England	L	0–2	Sunderland	HC	
26–02–1921	Scotland	L	0–2	Belfast	HC	
9–04	Wales	L	1–2	Swansea	HC	Chambers
22–10	England	D	1–1	Belfast	HC	Gillespie
4–03–1922	Scotland	L	1–2	Glasgow	HC	Gillespie
1–04	Wales	D	1–1	Belfast	HC	Gillespie
21–10	England	L	0–2	West Bromwich	HC	
3–03–1923	Scotland	L	0–1	Belfast	HC	
14–04	Wales	W	3–0	Wrexham	HC	Irvine R 2, Gillespie

INTERNATIONAL MATCHES PLAYED BY NORTHERN IRELAND

20–10–1923	England	W	2–1	Belfast	HC	Gillespie, Croft
1–03–1924	Scotland	L	0–2	Glasgow	HC	
15–03	Wales	L	0–1	Belfast	HC	
22–10	England	L	1–3	Liverpool	HC	Gillespie
28–02–1925	Scotland	L	0–3	Belfast	HC	
18–04	Wales	D	0–0	Wrexham	HC	
24–10	England	D	0–0	Belfast	HC	
13–02–1926	Wales	W	3–0	Belfast	HC	Gillespie, Curran 2
27–02	Scotland	L	0–4	Glasgow	HC	
20–10	England	D	3–3	Liverpool	HC	Gillespie, Davey, Irvine R
26–02–1927	Scotland	L	0–2	Belfast	HC	
9–04	Wales	D	2–2	Cardiff	HC	Johnston H 2
22–10	England	W	2–0	Belfast	HC	OG, Mahood
4–02–1928	Wales	L	1–2	Belfast	HC	Chambers
25–02	Scotland	W	1–0	Glasgow	HC	Chambers
22–10	England	L	1–2	Liverpool	HC	Bambrick
2–02–1929	Wales	D	2–2	Wrexham	HC	Mahood, McCluggage
23–02	Scotland	L	3–7	Belfast	HC	Bambrick 2, Rowley
19–10	England	L	0–3	Belfast	HC	
1–02–1930	Wales	W	7–0	Belfast	HC	Bambrick 6, McCluggage
22–02	Scotland	L	1–3	Glasgow	HC	McCaw
20–10	England	L	1–5	Sheffield	HC	Dunne
21–02–1931	Scotland	D	0–0	Belfast	HC	
22–04	Wales	L	2–3	Wrexham	HC	Dunne, Rowley
19–09	Scotland	L	1–3	Glasgow	HC	Dunne
17–10	England	L	2–6	Belfast	HC	Dunne, Kelly
5–12	Wales	W	4–0	Belfast	HC	Kelly 2, Millar, Bambrick
17–09–1932	Scotland	L	0–4	Belfast	HC	
17–10	England	L	0–1	Blackpool	HC	
7–12	Wales	L	1–4	Wrexham	HC	English
16–09–1933	Scotland	W	2–1	Glasgow	HC	Martin 2
14–10	England	L	0–3	Belfast	HC	
4–11	Wales	D	1–1	Belfast	HC	Jones S
20–10–1934	Scotland	W	2–1	Belfast	HC	Martin, Coulter
6–02–1935	England	L	1–2	Liverpool	HC	Stevenson
27–03	Wales	L	1–3	Wrexham	HC	Bambrick
19–10	England	L	1–3	Belfast	HC	Brown
13–11	Scotland	L	1–2	Edinburgh	HC	Kelly
11–03–1936	Wales	W	3–2	Belfast	HC	Gibb T, Stevenson, Kernaghan
31–10	Scotland	L	1–3	Belfast	HC	Kernaghan
18–11	England	L	1–3	Stoke	HC	Davis
17–03–1937	Wales	L	1–4	Wrexham	HC	Stevenson
23–10	England	L	1–5	Belfast	HC	Stevenson
10–11	Scotland	D	1–1	Aberdeen	HC	Doherty P
16–03–1938	Wales	W	1–0	Belfast	HC	Bambrick
8–10	Scotland	L	0–2	Belfast	HC	
16–11	England	L	0–7	Manchester	HC	
15–03–1939	Wales	L	1–3	Wrexham	HC	Milligan

28-09-1946	England	L	2-7	Belfast	HC	Lockhart 2
27-11	Scotland	D	0-0	Glasgow	HC	
16-04-1947	Wales	W	2-1	Belfast	HC	Stevenson, Doherty P
4-10	Scotland	W	2-0	Belfast	HC	Smyth 2
5-11	England	D	2-2	Liverpool	HC	Doherty P, Walsh
10-03-1948	Wales	L	0-2	Wrexham	HC	
9-10	England	L	2-6	Belfast	HC	Walsh 2
17-11	Scotland	L	2-3	Glasgow	HC	Walsh 2
9-03-1949	Wales	L	0-2	Belfast	HC	
1-10	Scotland	L	2-8	Belfast	HC/WCq	Smyth 2
16-11	England	L	2-9	Manchester	HC/WCq	Smyth, Brennan R
8-03-1950	Wales	D	0-0	Wrexham	HC/WCq	
7-10	England	L	1-4	Belfast	HC	McMorran
1-11	Scotland	L	1-6	Glasgow	HC	McGarry
7-03-1951	Wales	L	1-2	Belfast	HC	Simpson
12-05	France	D	2-2	Belfast	Fr	Ferris R, Simpson
6-10	Scotland	L	0-3	Belfast	HC	
14-11	England	L	0-2	Birmingham	HC	
19-03-1952	Wales	L	0-3	Swansea	HC	
4-10	England	D	2-2	Belfast	HC	Tully 2
5-11	Scotland	D	1-1	Glasgow	HC	D'Arcy
11-11	France	L	1-3	Paris	Fr	Tully
15-04-1953	Wales	L	2-3	Belfast	HC	McMorran 2
3-10	Scotland	L	1-3	Belfast	HC/WCq	Lockhart
11-11	England	L	1-3	Liverpool	HC/WCq	McMorran
31-03-1954	Wales	W	2-1	Wrexham	HC/WCq	McParland 2
2-10	England	L	0-2	Belfast	HC	
3-11	Scotland	D	2-2	Glasgow	HC	Bingham, McAdams
20-04-1955	Wales	L	2-3	Belfast	HC	Crossan E, Walker
8-10	Scotland	W	2-1	Belfast	HC	Blanchflower J, Bingham
2-11	England	L	0-3	London	HC	
11-04-1956	Wales	D	1-1	Cardiff	HC	Jones J
6-10	England	D	1-1	Belfast	HC	McIlroy J
7-11	Scotland	L	0-1	Glasgow	HC	
16-01-1957	Portugal	D	1-1	Lisbon	WCq	Bingham
10-04	Wales	D	0-0	Belfast	HC	
25-04	Italy	L	0-1	Rome	WCq	
1-05	Portugal	W	3-0	Belfast	WCq	Simpson, McIlroy J, Casey
5-10	Scotland	D	1-1	Belfast	HC	Bingham
6-11	England	W	3-2	London	HC	McIlroy J, McCrory, Simpson
4-12	Italy	D	2-2	Belfast	Fr	Cush 2
15-01-1958	Italy	W	2-1	Belfast	WCq	McIlroy J, Cush
16-04	Wales	D	1-1	Cardiff	HC	Simpson
8-06	Czechoslovakia	W	1-0	Halmstad	WCr1	Cush
11-06	Argentina	L	1-3	Halmstad	WCr1	McParland
15-06	West Germany	D	2-2	Malmo	WCr1	McParland 2
17-06	Czechoslovakia	W	2-1	Malmo	WCr1	McParland 2
19-06	France	L	0-4	Norrkoping	WCqf	
4-10	England	D	3-3	Belfast	HC	Cush, Peacock, Casey
15-10	Spain	L	2-6	Madrid	Fr	Bingham, McIlroy J
5-11	Scotland	D	2-2	Glasgow	HC	OG, McIlroy J
22-04-1959	Wales	W	4-1	Belfast	HC	McParland 2, Peacock, McIlroy J
3-10	Scotland	L	0-4	Belfast	HC	
18-11	England	L	1-2	London	HC	Bingham
6-04-1960	Wales	L	2-3	Wrexham	HC	Bingham, Blanchflower D
8-10	England	L	2-5	Belfast	HC	McAdams 2
26-10	West Germany	L	3-4	Belfast	WCq	McAdams 3
9-11	Scotland	L	2-5	Glasgow	HC	Blanchflower D, McParland
12-04-1961	Wales	L	1-5	Belfast	HC	Dougan
25-04	Italy	L	2-3	Bologna	Fr	Dougan, McAdams
3-05	Greece	L	1-2	Athens	WCq	McIlroy J
10-05	West Germany	L	1-2	Berlin	WCq	McIlroy J
7-10	Scotland	L	1-6	Belfast	HC	McLaughlin
17-10	Greece	W	2-0	Belfast	WCq	McLaughlin 2
22-11	England	D	1-1	London	HC	McIlroy J
11-04-1962	Wales	L	0-4	Cardiff	HC	
9-05	Holland	L	0-4	Rotterdam	Fr	
10-10	Poland	W	2-0	Chorzow	ECr1	Dougan, Humphries
20-10	England	L	1-3	Belfast	HC	Barr

7–11	Scotland	L	1–5	Glasgow	HC	Bingham
28–11	Poland	W	2–0	Belfast	ECr1	Crossan J, Bingham
3–04–1963	Wales	L	1–4	Belfast	HC	Harvey
30–05	Spain	D	1–1	Bilbao	ECr2	Irvine W
12–10	Scotland	W	2–1	Belfast	HC	Bingham, Wilson S
30–10	Spain	L	0–1	Belfast	ECr2	
20–11	England	L	3–8	London	HC	Crossan J, Wilson S 2
15–04–1964	Wales	W	3–2	Swansea	HC	McLaughlin, Wilson S, Harvey
29–04	Uruguay	W	3–0	Belfast	Fr	Crossan J 2, Wilson S
3–10	England	L	3–4	Belfast	HC	Wilson S, McLaughlin 2
14–10	Switzerland	W	1–0	Belfast	WCq	Crossan J
14–11	Switzerland	L	1–2	Lausanne	WCq	Best
25–11	Scotland	L	2–3	Glasgow	HC	Best, Irvine W
17–03–1965	Holland	W	2–1	Belfast	WCq	Crossan J, Neill
31–03	Wales	L	0–5	Belfast	HC	
7–04	Holland	D	0–0	Rotterdam	WCq	
7–05	Albania	W	4–1	Belfast	WCq	Crossan J, Best
2–10	Scotland	W	3–2	Belfast	HC	Dougan, Crossan J, Irvine W
10–11	England	L	1–2	London	HC	Irvine W
24–11	Albania	D	1–1	Tirana	WCq	Irvine W
30–03–1966	Wales	W	4–1	Cardiff	HC	Irvine W, Wilson S, Welsh, Harvey
7–05	West Germany	L	0–2	Belfast	Fr	
22–06	Mexico	W	4–1	Belfast	Fr	Johnston W, Elder, Nicholson, Ferguson
22–10	England	L	0–2	Belfast	HC/ECq	
16–11	Scotland	L	1–2	Glasgow	HC/ECq	Nicholson
12–04–1967	Wales	D	0–0	Belfast	HC/ECq	
21–10	Scotland	W	1–0	Belfast	HC/ECq	Clements
22–11	England	L	0–2	London	HC/ECq	
28–02–1968	Wales	L	0–2	Wrexham	HC/ECq	
10–09	Israel	W	3–2	Tel Aviv	Fr	Irvine W 2, Dougan
23–10	Turkey	W	4–1	Belfast	WCq	Best, McMordie, Dougan, Campbell W
11–12	Turkey	W	3–0	Istanbul	WCq	Harkin 2, Nicholson
3–05–1969	England	L	1–3	Belfast	HC	McMordie
6–05	Scotland	D	1–1	Glasgow	HC	McMordie
10–05	Wales	D	0–0	Belfast	HC	
10–09	Soviet Union	D	0–0	Belfast	WCq	
22–10	Soviet Union	L	0–2	Moscow	WCq	
18–04–1970	Scotland	L	0–1	Belfast	HC	
21–04	England	L	1–3	London	HC	Best
25–04	Wales	L	0–1	Swansea	HC	
11–11	Spain	L	0–3	Seville	ECq	
3–02–1971	Cyprus	W	3–0	Nicosia	ECq	Nicholson, Dougan, Best
21–04	Cyprus	W	5–0	Belfast	ECq	Dougan, Best 3, Nicholson
15–05	England	L	0–1	Belfast	HC	
18–05	Scotland	W	1–0	Glasgow	HC	OG
22–05	Wales	W	1–0	Belfast	HC	Hamilton B
22–09	Soviet Union	L	0–1	Moscow	ECq	
13–10	Soviet Union	D	1–1	Belfast	ECq	Nicholson
16–02–1972	Spain	D	1–1	Hull	ECq	Morgan
20–05	Scotland	L	0–2	Glasgow	HC	
23–05	England	W	1–0	London	HC	Neill
27–05	Wales	D	0–0	Wrexham	HC	
18–10	Bulgaria	L	0–3	Sofia	WCq	
14–02–1973	Cyprus	L	0–1	Nicosia	WCq	
28–03	Portugal	D	1–1	Coventry	WCq	O'Neill M (I)
8–05	Cyprus	W	3–0	London	WCq	Morgan, Anderson 2
12–05	England	L	1–2	Liverpool	HC	Clements
16–05	Scotland	W	2–1	Glasgow	HC	O'Neill M (I), Anderson
19–05	Wales	W	1–0	Liverpool	HC	Hamilton B
26–09	Bulgaria	D	0–0	Sheffield	WCq	
14–11	Portugal	D	1–1	Lisbon	WCq	O'Kane
11–05–1974	Scotland	W	1–0	Glasgow	HC	Cassidy
15–05	England	L	0–1	London	HC	
18–05	Wales	L	0–1	Wrexham	HC	
4–09	Norway	L	1–2	Oslo	ECq	Finney
30–10	Sweden	W	2–0	Stockholm	ECq	O'Neill M (I), Nicholl C
16–03–1975	Yugoslavia	W	1–0	Belfast	ECq	Hamilton B
17–05	England	D	0–0	Belfast	HC	
20–05	Scotland	L	0–3	Glasgow	HC	

23–05	Wales	W	1–0	Belfast	HC	Finney
3–09	Sweden	L	1–2	Belfast	ECq	Hunter A (II)
29–10	Norway	W	3–0	Belfast	ECq	Morgan, McIlroy S, Hamilton B
19–11	Yugoslavia	L	0–1	Belgrade	ECq	
3–03–1976	Israel	D	1–1	Tel Aviv	Fr	OG
8–05	Scotland	L	0–3	Glasgow	HC	
11–05	England	L	0–4	London	HC	
14–05	Wales	L	0–1	Swansea	HC	
13–10	Holland	D	2–2	Rotterdam	WCq	McGrath, Spence
10–11	Belgium	L	0–2	Liege	WCq	
27–04–1977	West Germany	L	0–5	Cologne	Fr	
28–05	England	L	1–2	Belfast	HC	McGrath
1–06	Scotland	L	0–3	Glasgow	HC	
3–06	Wales	D	1–1	Belfast	HC	Nelson
11–06	Iceland	L	0–1	Reykjavik	WCq	
21–09	Iceland	W	2–0	Belfast	WCq	McGrath, McIlroy S
12–10	Holland	L	0–1	Belfast	WCq	
16–11	Belgium	W	3–0	Belfast	WCq	Armstrong 2, McGrath
13–05–1978	Scotland	D	1–1	Glasgow	HC	O'Neill M (I)
16–05	England	L	0–1	London	HC	
19–05	Wales	L	0–1	Wrexham	HC	
20–09	Rep. Ireland	D	0–0	Dublin	ECq	
25–10	Denmark	W	2–1	Belfast	ECq	Spence, Anderson
29–11	Bulgaria	W	2–0	Sofia	ECq	Armstrong, Casey
7–02–1979	England	L	0–4	London	ECq	
2–05	Bulgaria	W	2–0	Belfast	ECq	Nicholl C, Armstrong
19–05	England	L	0–2	Belfast	HC	
22–05	Scotland	L	0–1	Glasgow	HC	
26–05	Wales	D	1–1	Belfast	HC	Spence
6–06	Denmark	L	0–4	Copenhagen	ECq	
17–10	England	L	1–5	Belfast	ECq	Moreland
21–11	Rep. Ireland	W	1–0	Belfast	ECq	Armstrong
26–03–1980	Israel	D	0–0	Tel Aviv	WCq	
16–05	Scotland	W	1–0	Belfast	HC	Hamilton W
20–05	England	D	1–1	London	HC	Cochrane
23–05	Wales	W	1–0	Cardiff	HC	Brotherston
11–06	Australia	W	2–1	Sydney	Fr	Nicholl C, O'Neill M (I)
15–06	Australia	D	1–1	Melbourne	Fr	O'Neill M (I)
18–06	Australia	W	2–1	Adelaide	Fr	Brotherston, McCurdy
15–10	Sweden	W	3–0	Belfast	WCq	Brotherston, McIlroy S, Nicholl J
19–11	Portugal	L	0–1	Lisbon	WCq	
25–03–1981	Scotland	D	1–1	Glasgow	WCq	Hamilton W
29–04	Portugal	W	1–0	Belfast	WCq	Armstrong
19–05	Scotland	L	0–2	Glasgow	HC	
3–06	Sweden	L	0–1	Stockholm	WCq	
14–10	Scotland	D	0–0	Belfast	WCq	
18–11	Israel	W	1–0	Belfast	WCq	Armstrong
23–02–1982	England	L	0–4	London	HC	
24–03	France	L	0–4	Paris	Fr	
28–04	Scotland	D	1–1	Belfast	HC	McIlroy S
27–05	Wales	L	0–3	Wrexham	HC	
17–06	Yugoslavia	D	0–0	Zaragoza	WCr1	
21–06	Honduras	D	1–1	Zaragoza	WCr1	Armstrong
25–06	Spain	W	1–0	Valencia	WCr1	Armstrong
1–07	Austria	D	2–2	Madrid	WCr2	Hamilton W 2

LEADING INTERNATIONAL APPEARANCES

1	Jennings	119
2	McIlroy S	88
3	Donaghy	75
4	Nichol J	73
5	McCreery D	67
6	O'Neill M (I)	64
7	Armstrong	63
8	Neill	59
9	Bingham	56
	Blanchflower	56
11	McIlroy J	55
12	Hunter	53
	McClelland J	53
14	Nelson	51
	Nichol C	51
16	Hamilton B	50
17	Rice	49
18	Clements	48
19	Dougan	43
20	Hamilton W	42
21	Nicholson J	41
22	Elder	40
	McMichael	40

LEADING INTERNATIONAL GOALSCORERS

1	Armstrong	12		McParland	10	15	McAdams	7
	Bambrick	12	9	Best	9		Peden	7
	Clarke C	12		O'Neill M (I)	9		Wilson S	7
	Gillespie	12		Stanfield	9	18	Dalton	6
5	Bingham	10		Whiteside	9		McLaughlin J	6
	Crossan J	10	13	Dougan	8		Nicolson J	6
	McIlroy J	10		Irvine W	8		Quinn J	6

4–07	France	L	1–4	Madrid	WCr2	Armstrong
13–10	Austria	L	0–2	Vienna	ECq	
17–11	West Germany	W	1–0	Belfast	ECq	Stewart
15–12	Albania	D	0–0	Tirana	ECq	
30–03–1983	Turkey	W	2–1	Belfast	ECq	O'Neill M (I), McClelland
27–04	Albania	W	1–0	Belfast	ECq	Stewart
24–05	Scotland	D	0–0	Glasgow	HC	
28–05	England	D	0–0	Belfast	HC	
31–05	Wales	L	0–1	Belfast	HC	
21–09	Austria	W	3–1	Belfast	ECq	Hamilton W, Whiteside N, O'Neill M (I)
12–10	Turkey	L	0–1	Ankara	ECq	
16–11	West Germany	W	1–0	Hamburg	ECq	Whiteside N
13–12	Scotland	W	2–0	Glasgow	HC	Whiteside N, McIlroy S
4–04–1984	England	L	0–1	London	HC	
22–05	Wales	D	1–1	Swansea	HC	Armstrong
27–05	Finland	L	0–1	Pori	WCq	
12–09	Romania	W	3–2	Belfast	WCq	Whiteside N, O'Neill M (I), OG
16–10	Israel	W	3–0	Belfast	Fr	Whiteside N, Doherty L, Quinn
14–11	Finland	W	2–1	Belfast	WCq	O'Neill J, Armstrong
27–02–1985	England	L	0–1	Belfast	WCq	
27–03	Spain	D	0–0	Palma	Fr	
1–05	Turkey	W	2–0	Belfast	WCq	Whiteside N 2
11–09	Turkey	D	0–0	Izmir	WCq	
16–10	Romania	W	1–0	Bucharest	WCq	Quinn
13–11	England	D	0–0	London	WCq	
26–02–1986	France	D	0–0	Paris	Fr	
26–03	Denmark	D	1–1	Belfast	Fr	McDonald
23–04	Morocco	W	2–1	Belfast	Fr	Clarke, Quinn
3–06	Algeria	D	1–1	Guadalajara	WCr1	Whiteside N
7–06	Spain	L	1–2	Guadalajara	WCr1	Clarke
12–06	Brazil	L	0–3	Guadalajara	WCr1	
15–10	England	L	0–3	London	ECq	
12–11	Turkey	D	0–0	Izmir	ECq	
18–02–1987	Israel	D	1–1	Tel Aviv	Fr	Penney
1–04	England	L	0–2	Belfast	ECq	
29–04	Yugoslavia	L	1–2	Belfast	ECq	Clarke
14–10	Yugoslavia	L	0–3	Sarajevo	ECq	
11–11	Turkey	W	1–0	Belfast	ECq	Quinn
17–02–1988	Greece	L	2–3	Athens	Fr	Clarke 2
23–03	Poland	D	1–1	Belfast	Fr	Wilson D
27–04	France	D	0–0	Belfast	Fr	
21–05	Malta	W	3–0	Belfast	WCq	Clarke, Penney, Quinn
14–09	Rep. Ireland	D	0–0	Belfast	WCq	
19–10	Hungary	L	0–1	Budapest	WCq	
21–12	Spain	L	0–4	Seville	WCq	
8–02–1989	Spain	L	0–2	Belfast	WCq	
26–04	Malta	W	2–0	Ta'Qali	WCq	Clarke, O'Neill M (II)
26–05	Chile	L	0–1	Belfast	Fr	
6–09	Hungary	L	1–2	Belfast	WCq	Whiteside N
11–10	Rep. Ireland	L	0–3	Dublin	WCq	
27–03–1990	Norway	L	2–3	Belfast	Fr	Quinn, Wilson K
18–05	Uruguay	W	1–0	Belfast	Fr	Wilson K
12–09	Yugoslavia	L	0–2	Belfast	ECq	
17–10	Denmark	D	1–1	Belfast	ECq	Clarke
14–11	Austria	D	0–0	Vienna	ECq	
6–02–1991	Poland	W	3–1	Belfast	Fr	Taggart 2, Magilton

27–03	Yugoslavia	L	1–4	Belgrade	ECq	Hill
1–05	Faeroe Islands	D	1–1	Belfast	ECq	Clarke
11–09	Faeroe Islands	W	5–0	Landskrona	ECq	Wilson K, Clarke 3, McDonald
16–10	Austria	W	2–1	Belfast	ECq	Dowie, Black
13–11	Denmark	L	1–2	Odense	ECq	Taggart
19–02–1992	Scotland	L	0–1	Glasgow	Fr	
28–04	Lithuania	D	2–2	Belfast	WCq	Wilson K, Taggart
2–06	Germany	D	1–1	Bremen	Fr	Hughes

NORWAY

Norway are one of Europe's perennial underdogs and they look set to stay that way. Despite the odd shock caused at international level, none greater than the defeat of Italy in the 1992 European Championships which led to the Italians' premature exit from the competition, club football remains relatively undeveloped.

Norway is a large elongated country in which mountains make communications difficult. It is therefore surprising to see how well distributed football is when it might have been expected to have developed only in and around the capital. Oslo, Bergen, Trondheim and Stavanger of the major towns all have successful clubs whilst even smaller and more remote towns have played a part in the development of the game.

The Norges Fotballforbund initiated a cup competition in 1902, the year in which it was founded, and for the next 34 years this remained the sole source of competition. Norway's oldest club, Odds BK of Skein, founded in 1894, were the dominant force in the early years of the competition and set the trend for the success of non-Oslo clubs.

The national team first took to the field in 1908. An 11–3 defeat at the hands of Sweden was not the best of starts and it was not until ten years later that Norway won their first game. Throughout the years, matches against their Scandinavian neighbours, especially in the Scandinavian Championship, have provided the bulk of the international programme. Usually much stronger than Finland, Norway is traditionally the third strongest country in this competition. The 1930s, however, saw the Norwegians at their height and they won the 1929–32 edition.

The 1936 Olympic Games represents Norway's greatest achievement. Against all the odds they reached the semi-finals and only lost to the Italian 'professionals' in extra-time. On the way they caused one of the biggest upsets ever in football by beating the hosts, Germany. Given the backdrop to the game the victory is remarkable. With the Germans roared on by a fanatical crowd which included Hitler, Norway, according to the script, should have crumbled. Instead they played the game of their lives to win 2–0. In a scene reminiscent of the snub to Jesse Owens

		All			League			Cup		Europe		
	Team	G	S	B	G	S	B	G	S	G	S	B
1	Fredrikstad FK	19	15	1	9	8	1	10	7	–	–	–
2	Viking FK Stavanger	12	6	3	8	2	3	4	4	–	–	–
3	Rosenborg BK Trondheim	11	9	1	6	5	1	5	4	–	–	–
4	Odd SK Skien	11	9	–	–	2	–	11	7	–	–	–
5	SOFK Lyn Oslo	10	8	2	2	4	2	8	4	–	–	–
6	Lillestrom SK	9	10	2	5	5	2	4	5	–	–	–
8	FK Skeid Oslo	9	8	1	1	5	1	8	3	–	–	–
9	SK Brann Bergen	7	8	1	2	2	1	5	6	–	–	–
10	FK Sarpsborg	6	6	2	–	–	2	6	6	–	–	–
11	Vålerengens IF Oslo	5	3	2	4	1	2	1	2	–	–	–
12	IF Stromsgodset	5	–	2	1	–	2	4	–	–	–	–
13	Orn FK Horten	4	4	–	–	–	–	4	4	–	–	–
14	Mjondalen IF	3	7	–	–	2	–	3	7	–	–	–
15	Frigg SK Oslo	3	3	–	–	–	–	3	3	–	–	–
16	Larvik Turn IF	3	1	–	3	–	–	–	1	–	–	–
17	Moss FK	2	2	–	1	1	–	1	1	–	–	–
18	SOFK Mercantile Oslo	2	1	–	–	–	–	2	1	–	–	–
19	IK Start Kristiansand	2	–	6	2	–	6	–	–	–	–	–
20	SOFK Bodo–Glimt	1	2	–	–	1	–	1	1	–	–	–
	Bryne IL Stavanger	1	2	–	–	2	–	1	–	–	–	–
	Kvik Halden	1	2	–	–	–	–	1	2	–	–	–
23	Tromso IL	1	1	1	–	1	1	1	–	–	–	–
24	Fram Larvik	1	1	–	1	–	–	–	1	–	–	–
	Gjovik Lyn	1	1	–	–	–	–	1	1	–	–	–
	Grand Nordstrand	1	1	–	–	–	–	1	1	–	–	–
	Sparta Sarpsborg	1	1	–	–	1	–	1	–	–	–	–
28	Freidig SK	1	–	–	1	–	–	–	–	–	–	–
29	Molde FK	–	4	3	–	2	3	–	2	–	–	–
30	SK Hauger	–	2	–	–	–	–	–	2	–	–	–
	Sandefjord BK	–	2	–	–	–	–	–	2	–	–	–
	IF Uraed	–	2	–	–	–	–	–	2	–	–	–
	SK Vard Haugesand	–	2	–	–	–	–	–	2	–	–	–
34	Akademisk SK Oslo	–	1	–	–	–	–	–	1	–	–	–
	Asker	–	1	–	–	–	–	–	1	–	–	–
	Drafn SK	–	1	–	–	–	–	–	1	–	–	–
	Drammens BK	–	1	–	–	–	–	–	1	–	–	–
	IF Eik	–	1	–	–	1	–	–	–	–	–	–
	Fyllingen	–	1	–	–	–	–	–	1	–	–	–
	Sogndal IL	–	1	–	–	–	–	–	1	–	–	–
	Solberg	–	1	–	–	–	–	–	1	–	–	–
	Steinkjer IFK	–	1	–	–	1	–	–	–	–	–	–
43	Kongsvinger IL	–	–	2	–	–	2	–	–	–	–	–
44	Hamarkameratene	–	–	1	–	–	1	–	–	–	–	–

Correct to the end of the 1991 season

in the same Games, Hitler stormed out of the stadium in a rage. A 3–2 victory over Poland in the third place play-off gave Norway the bronze medal.

Qualification for the 1938 World Cup remains the only occasion on which the Norwegians have been present in the final tournament of the competition, and to their misfortune they drew Italy in the first round. They lost in extra-time by the same score as they had done two years previously in Berlin.

Olympic year, 1936, had seen the introduction of a national league for the clubs, although the winner was decided in a series of knock-out games until 1961, at which point a single league was introduced. Not many Norwegians have made their name abroad and this remains one of the strengths of the league. Thorbjorn Svenssen, for example, was in the 1950s one of the most famous names in Europe, representing his country on 104 occasions, yet he played all his football for Sandefjord BK. Likewise, Jurgen Juve, the most prolific scorer for the national team with 30 goals, played only for SOFK Lyn Oslo.

Over the last ten years or so players have moved abroad, but not in any great numbers like Denmark or Sweden. Erik Thorstvedt, the best goalkeeper in Norwegian history, has, for example, played for Borussia Monchengladbach, IFK Göteborg and Tottenham, and players like him have given the national team an extra cutting edge. They may remain underdogs, but they are capable of beating anyone on their day at home. England, Yugoslavia, Argentina, France and Italy have all met with defeat in Oslo in important matches.

It may take a while for a second appearance in the World Cup finals to materialise, and an appearance in the European Championship would appear to be even more unlikely, but teams should beware of Norway if drawn in the same group. What Norway must try and achieve next is to give their clubs the same aura of unpredictability in European competitions.

Population: 4 246 000
Area, sq km: 323 878
% in urban areas: 72.8%
Capital city: Oslo

Norges Fotballforbund
Ullevaal Stadion
Postboks 3823
Ullevaal Hageby
N-0805 Oslo 8
Norway
Tel: (010 47) 2 469830
Fax: (010 47) 2 608222
Telex: 71722 NFF N
Cable: FOTBALLFORBUND OSLO
Languages for correspondence: English, German & French

Year of formation: 1902
Affiliation to FIFA: 1908
Affiliation to UEFA: 1954
Registered clubs: 1857
Registered players: 573 500
Registered coaches: 9222
Registered referees: 3866
National stadium: Ullevål Stadion 27 000
National colours: Shirts: Red/Shorts: White/Socks: Blue
Reserve colours: Shirts: Blue/Shorts: White/Socks: Blue
Season: April–November

THE RECORD

WORLD CUP

1930 .... Did not enter
1934 .... Did not enter
1938 .... QT 1st/2 in group 2 – Final Tournament/1st round
1950 .... Did not enter
1954 .... QT 3rd/3 in group 1
1958 .... QT 3rd/3 in group 3
1962 .... QT 3rd/3 in group 5
1966 .... QT 2nd/4 in group 3
1970 .... QT 3rd/3 in group 5
1974 .... QT 3rd/4 in group 3
1978 .... QT 2nd/3 in group 6
1982 .... QT 5th/5 in group 4
1986 .... QT 5th/5 in group 6
1990 .... QT 4th/5 in group 5

EUROPEAN CHAMPIONSHIP

1960 .... 1st round
1964 .... 1st round
1968 .... QT 4th/4 in group 2
1972 .... QT 4th/4 in group 2
1976 .... QT 4th/4 in group 3
1980 .... QT 5th/5 in group 2
1984 .... QT 4th/4 in group 4
1988 .... QT 5th/5 in group 3
1992 .... QT 3rd/5 in group 3

OLYMPIC GAMES

1908 .... Did not enter
1912 .... 1st round
1920 .... Quarter-finalists
1924 .... Did not enter
1928 .... Did not enter
1936 .... Semi-finalists/3rd place
1948 .... Did not enter
1952 .... 1st round
1956 .... Did not enter
1960 .... QT Failed to qualify
1964–72 ..... Did not enter
1976 .... QT Failed to qualify
1980 .... Qualified but withdrew
1984 .... Final Tournament/1st round
1988 .... QT Failed to qualify
1992 .... QT Failed to qualify

EUROPEAN CLUB COMPETITIONS

EUROPEAN CUP: 2nd round – Fredrikstad 1961, Lyn Oslo 1965, Vålerengens 1967, Lillestrom 1979, Rosenborg 1987

CUP WINNERS CUP: Quarter-finals – Lyn Oslo 1969

UEFA CUP: 2nd round – Valerengens 1966, Skeid Oslo 1970, Rosenborg 1972, Viking Stavanger 1973 1983, Start Kristiansand 1978

CLUB DIRECTORY

OSLO (Population – 720 000)

Frigg Sport Klubben Oslo
Stadium: Voldslokka 4000
Founded: 1904
Colours: Blue/White

Ski og Fotball Klubb Lyn (SOFK Lyn Oslo)
Stadium: Ullevål 27000
Founded: 1896
Colours: Red with a broad white stripe/Blue

Fotball Klubben Skeid Oslo
Stadium: Ullevål 27 000
Founded: 1915
Colours: Red/Black

Vålerengens Idretts Förening Oslo
Stadium: Bislett 23 000
Founded: 1913
Colours: Blue/White

BERGEN (Population – 239 000)
Sports Klubben Brann Bergen

Stadium: Brann 25 000
Founded: 1908
Colours: Red/Red

TRONDHEIM (Population – 134 000)
Rosenborg Ball Klubb Trondheim
Stadium: Lerkendal 28 000
Founded: 1917
Colours: White/Black

STAVANGER (Population – 132 000)

Bryne Idretts Laget Stavanger
Stadium: Bryne 12 000
Founded: 1926
Colours: Red with white sleeves/White

Viking Fotball Klubb Stavanger
Stadium: Stavanger 18 000
Founded: 1899
Colours: Blue/White

SKIEN (Population – 77 000)
Odd Sport Klubben Skien
Stadium: Falkum
Founded: 1894
Colours: White/Black

DRAMMEN (Population – 73 000)
Stromgodset Idretts Förening
Stadium: Marienlyst 15 000
Founded: 1907
Colours: Blue/White

KRISTIANSAND (Population – 62 000)
Idretts Klubben Start Kristiansand
Stadium: Kristiansand 15 000
Founded: 1905
Colours: Yellow/Black

FREDRIKSTAD (Population – 52 000)
Fredrikstad Fotball Klubben
Stadium: Fredrikstad 16 000
Founded: 1903
Colours: White/Red

TROMSO (Population – 47 000)
Tromso Idrettslag
Stadium: Alfheim 10 000
Founded: 1920
Colours: Red and white stripes/White

LILLESTROM
Lillestrom Sports Klubb
Stadium: Åråsen 14 000
Founded: 1917
Colours: Yellow/Black

MOSS
Moss Fotball Klubb
Stadium: Mellos 12 000
Founded: 1906
Colours: Yellow/Black

KONGSVINGER
Kongsvinger Idrettslag
Stadium: Gjemselund 7000
Founded: 1892
Colours: Red/White

MJONDALEN
Mjondalen Idretts Förening
Stadium: Nedre Eiker 15 000
Founded: 1910
Colours: Brown/White

MOLDE
Molde Fotball Klubb
Stadium: Molde 15 000
Founded: 1911
Colours: Blue/White

SARPSBORG
Fotball Klubben Sarpsborg
Stadium: Sarpsborg 20 000
Founded: 1903
Colours: Blue/White

BODO
Ski og Fotball Klubb (SOFK) Bodo–Glimt
Stadium: Aspmyra 12 000
Founded: 1916
Colours: Yellow/White

HORTEN
Orn Fotball Klubben
Stadium: Lystlunden
Founded: 1904
Colours: Brown/White

GJOVIK
Gjovik Lyn
Stadium: Gjovik Founded: 1902
Colours: Red/White

LARVIK
Larvik Turn Idretts Förening
Stadium: Luisenlund Founded: 1906
Colours: White/Blue

NORWEGIAN LEAGUE CHAMPIONSHIP

Year	Champions	Score	Runners-up
1938	Fredrikstad FK	0–0 4–0	SOFK Lyn Oslo
1939	Fredrikstad FK	2–1	FK Skeid Oslo
1940–47	– No championship		
1948	Freidig SK	2–1	Sparta Sarpsborg
1949	Fredrikstad FK	3–1 3–0	Vålerengens IF Oslo
1950	Fram Larvik	1–1 1–0	Fredrikstad FK
1951	Fredrikstad FK	4–2 3–1	Odd SK Skien
1952	Fredrikstad FK	3–1	SK Brann Bergen
1953	Larvik Turn IF	3–2	FK Skeid Oslo
1954	Fredrikstad FK	2–1	FK Skeid Oslo
1955	Larvik Turn IF	4–2	Fredrikstad FK
1956	Larvik Turn IF	3–2	Fredrikstad FK
1957	Fredrikstad FK	6–1	Odd SK Skien
1958	Viking FK Stavanger	2–0	FK Skeid Oslo
1959	Lillestrom SK	2–2 4–1	Fredrikstad FK
1960	Fredrikstad FK	6–2	Lillestrom SK
1961	Fredrikstad FK	2–0	IF Eik

Year	Champions	Pts	Runners–up	Pts	3rd	Pts
1962	SK Brann Bergen	46	Steinkjer IFK	41	Fredrikstad FK	41
1963	SK Brann Bergen	24	SOFK Lyn Oslo	23	FK Skeid Oslo	20
1964	SOFK Lyn Oslo	26	Fredrikstad FK	24	FK Sarpsborg	23
1965	Vålerengens IF Oslo	27	SOFK Lyn Oslo	26	FK Sarpsborg	23
1966	FK Skeid Oslo	25	Fredrikstad FK	24	SOFK Lyn Oslo	21
1967	Rosenborg BK	25	FK Skeid Oslo	22	SOFK Lyn Oslo	21
1968	SOFK Lyn Oslo	28	Rosenborg BK	24	Viking FK Stavanger	21
1969	Rosenborg BK	27	Fredrikstad FK	22	IF Stromgodset	22
1970	IF Stromgodset	25	Rosenborg BK	24	Hamarkameratene	23
1971	Rosenborg BK	24	SOFK Lyn Oslo	23	Viking FK Stavanger	22
1972	Viking FK Stavanger	34	Fredrikstad FK	34	IF Stromgodset	27
1973	Viking FK Stavanger	32	Rosenborg BK	27	Start Kristiansand	26
1974	Viking FK Stavanger	31	Molde FK	30	Vålerengens IF Oslo	28
1975	Viking FK Stavanger	30	SK Brann Bergen	27	Start Kristiansand	27
1976	Lillestrom SK	31	Mjondalen IF	30	SK Brann Bergen	28
1977	Lillestrom SK	36	SOFK Bodo–Glimt	28	Molde FK	27

1978	Start Kristiansand ... 33	Lillestrom SK ... 31	Viking FK Stavanger ... 31
1979	Viking FK Stavanger ... 32	Moss FK ... 30	Start Kristiansand ... 27
1980	Start Kristiansand ... 29	Bryne IL ... 29	Lillestrom SK ... 27
1981	Vålerengens IF Oslo ... 29	Viking FK Stavanger ... 28	Rosenborg BK ... 26
1982	Viking FK Stavanger ... 29	Bryne IL ... 26	Lillestrom SK ... 25
1983	Vålerengens IF Oslo ... 31	Lillestrom SK ... 28	Start Kristiansand ... 27
1984	Vålerengens IF Oslo ... 32	Viking FK Stavanger ... 25	Start Kristiansand ... 25
1985	Rosenberg BK ... 33	Lillestrom SK ... 32	Vålerengens IF Oslo ... 24
1986	Lillestrom SK ... 33	Mjondalen IF ... 27	Kongsvinger IL ... 27
1987	Moss FK ... 44	Molde FK ... 41	Kongsvinger IL ... 39
1988	Rosenborg BK ... 45	Lillestrom SK ... 40	Molde FK ... 39
1989	Lillestrom SK ... 52	Rosenborg BK ... 44	Tromso IL ... 37
1990	Rosenborg BK ... 44	Tromso IL ... 42	Molde FK ... 40
1991	Viking Stavanger ... 41	Rosenborg BK ... 36	Start Kristiansand ... 34

NORWEGIAN CUP FINALS

Year	Winners	Score	Runners–up
1902	Grand Nordstrand	2–0	Odd SK Skien
1903	Odd SK Skien	1–0	Grand Nordstrand
1904	Odd SK Skien	4–0	IF Uraed
1905	Odd SK Skien	2–1	Akademisk FK Oslo
1906	Odd SK Skien	1–0	FK Sarpsborg
1907	Mercantile	3–0	FK Sarpsborg
1908	SOFK Lyn Oslo	3–2	Odd SK Skien
1909	SOFK Lyn Oslo	4–3	Odd SK Skien
1910	SOFK Lyn Oslo	4–2	Odd SK Skien
1911	SOFK Lyn Oslo	5–2	IF Uraed
1912	Mercantile	6–0	Fram Larvik
1913	Odd SK Skien	2–1	Mercantile
1914	Frigg SK Oslo	4–2	Gjovik Lyn
1915	Odd SK Skien	2–1	Kvik Halden
1916	Frigg SK Oslo	2–0	Orn FK Horten
1917	FK Sarpsborg	4–1	SK Brann Bergen
1918	Kvik Halden	4–0	SK Brann Bergen
1919	Odd SK Skien	1–0	Frigg SK Oslo
1920	Orn FK Horten	1–0	Frigg SK Oslo
1921	Frigg SK Oslo	2–0	Odd SK Skien
1922	Odd SK Skien	5–1	Kvik Halden
1923	SK Brann Bergen	2–1	SOFK Lyn Oslo
1924	Odd SK Skien	3–0	Mjondalen IF
1925	SK Brann Bergen	3–0	FK Sarpsborg
1926	Odd SK Skien	3–0	Orn FK Horten
1927	Orn FK Horten	4–0	Drafn SK
1928	Orn FK Horten	2–1	SOFK Lyn Oslo
1929	FK Sarpsborg	2–1	Orn FK Horten
1930	Orn FK Horten	4–2	Drammens BK
1931	Odd SK Skien	3–1	Mjondalen IF
1932	Fredrikstad FK	6–1	Orn FK Horten
1933	Mjondalen IF	3–1	Viking FK Stavanger
1934	Mjondalen IF	2–1	FK Sarpsborg
1935	Fredrikstad FK	4–0	FK Sarpsborg
1936	Fredrikstad FK	2–0	Mjondalen IF
1937	Mjondalen IF	4–2	Odd SK Skien
1938	Fredrikstad SK	3–2	Mjondalen IF
1939	FK Sarpsborg	2–1	FK Skeid Oslo
1940	Fredrikstad FK	3–0	FK Skeid Oslo
1941–44 – No competition			
1945	SOFK Lyn Oslo	1–1 1–1 4–0	Fredrikstad FK
1946	SOFK Lyn Oslo	3–2	Fredrikstad FK
1947	FK Skeid Oslo	2–0	Viking FK Stavanger
1948	FK Sarpsborg	1–0	Fredrikstad SK
1949	FK Sarpsborg	3–1	FK Skeid Oslo
1950	Fredrikstad FK	3–0	SK Brann Bergen
1951	FK Sarpsborg	3–2	Asker
1952	Sparta Sarpsborg	3–2	Solberg
1953	Viking FK Stavanger	2–1	Lillestrom SK
1954	FK Skeid Oslo	3–0	Fredrikstad FK
1955	FK Skeid Oslo	5–0	Lillestrom SK
1956	FK Skeid Oslo	2–1	Larvik Turn IF
1957	Fredrikstad FK	4–0	Sandefjord BK
1958	FK Skeid Oslo	1–0	Lillestrom SK
1959	Viking FK Stavanger	2–1	Sandefjord BK
1960	Rosenborg BK	3–3 3–2	Odd SK Skien
1961	Fredrikstad FK	7–0	SK Hauger
1962	Gjovik Lyn	2–0	SK Vard Haugesund
1963	FK Skeid Oslo	2–1	Fredrikstad FK
1964	Rosenborg BK	2–1	FK Sarpsborg
1965	FK Skeid Oslo	2–2 1–1 2–1	Frigg SK Oslo
1966	Fredrikstad FK	3–2	SOFK Lyn Oslo
1967	SOFK Lyn Oslo	4–1	Rosenborg BK
1968	SOFK Lyn Oslo	3–0	Mjondalen IF
1969	IF Stromsgodset	2–2 5–3	Fredrikstad FK
1970	IF Stromsgodset	4–2	SOFK Lyn Oslo
1971	Rosenborg BK	4–1	Fredrikstad FK
1972	SK Brann Bergen	1–0	Rosenborg BK
1973	IF Stromgodset	1–0	Rosenborg BK
1974	FK Skeid Oslo	3–1	Viking FK Stavanger
1975	SOFK Bodo–Glimt	2–0	SK Vard Haugesund
1976	SK Brann Bergen	2–1	Sogndal IL
1977	Lillestrom SK	1–0	SOFK Bodo–Glimt
1978	Lillestrom SK	2–1	SK Brann Bergen
1979	Viking FK Stavanger	2–1	SK Hauger
1980	Vålerengens IF Oslo	4–1	Lillestrom SK
1981	Lillestrom SK	3–1	Moss FK
1982	SK Brann Bergen	3–2	Molde FK
1983	Moss FK	2–0	Vålerengens IF Oslo
1984	Fredrikstad FK	3–3 3–2	Viking FK Stavanger
1985	Lillestrom SK	4–1	Vålerengens IF Oslo
1986	Tromso IL	4–1	Lillestrom SK
1987	Bryne IL Stavanger	1–0	SK Brann Bergen
1988	Rosenborg BK	2–2 2–0	SK Brann Bergen
1989	Viking FK Stavanger	2–2 2–1	Molde FK
1990	Rosenborg BK	5–1	Fyllingen
1991	IF Stromgodset	3–2	Rosenborg BK

LEADING INTERNATIONAL GOALSCORERS

1	Juve	33
2	Gundersen	26
3	Hennum	25
4	Thoresen	22
5	Iversen	19
	Nilsen O	19

INTERNATIONAL MATCHES PLAYED BY NORWAY

Date	Opponents	Result	Venue	Compet
12–07–1908	Sweden	L 3–11	Gothenburg	Fr
11–09–1910	Sweden	L 0–4	Oslo	Fr
17–09–1911	Sweden	L 1–4	Stockholm	Fr
16–06–1912	Sweden	L 1–2	Oslo	Fr
23–06	Hungary	L 0–6	Oslo	Fr
30–06	Denmark	L 0–7	Stockholm	OGqf
1–07	Austria	L 0–1	Stockholm	OGct
3–11	Sweden	L 2–4	Gothenburg	Fr
8–06–1913	Sweden	L 0–9	Stockholm	Fr
14–09	Tsarist Russia	D 1–1	Moscow	Fr
26–10	Sweden	D 1–1	Oslo	Fr
28–06–1914	Sweden	L 0–1	Oslo	Fr
12–07	Tsarist Russia	D 1–1	Oslo	Fr
25–10	Sweden	L 0–7	Stockholm	Fr
27–06–1915	Sweden	D 1–1	Oslo	Fr
19–09	Denmark	L 1–8	Copenhagen	Fr
24–10	Sweden	L 2–5	Stockholm	Fr
25–06–1916	Denmark	L 0–2	Oslo	Fr
2–07	Sweden	L 0–6	Stockholm	Fr
3–09	USA	D 1–1	Oslo	Fr
1–10	Sweden	D 0–0	Oslo	Fr
15–10	Denmark	L 0–8	Copenhagen	Fr
17–06–1917	Denmark	L 1–2	Oslo	Fr
19–08	Sweden	D 3–3	Halsingborg	Fr
16–09	Sweden	L 0–2	Oslo	Fr
7–10	Denmark	L 0–12	Copenhagen	Fr
26–05–1918	Sweden	L 0–2	Stockholm	Fr
16–06	Denmark	W 3–1	Oslo	Fr
15–09	Sweden	W 2–1	Oslo	Fr
6–10	Denmark	L 0–4	Copenhagen	Fr
12–06–1919	Denmark	L 1–5	Copenhagen	Fr
29–06	Sweden	W 4–3	Oslo	Fr
31–08	Holland	D 1–1	Oslo	Fr
14–09	Sweden	W 5–1	Gothenburg	Fr
21–09	Denmark	W 3–2	Oslo	Fr
13–06–1920	Denmark	D 1–1	Oslo	Fr
27–06	Sweden	L 0–3	Oslo	Fr
28–08	England*	W 3–1	Antwerp	OGr1
29–08	Czechoslovakia	L 0–4	Brussels	OGqf
31–08	Italy	L 1–2	Antwerp	OGct
26–09	Sweden	D 0–0	Stockholm	Fr
25–05–1921	Finland	W 3–2	Oslo	Fr
19–06	Sweden	W 3–1	Oslo	Fr
18–09	Sweden	W 3–0	Stockholm	Fr
2–10	Denmark	L 1–3	Copenhagen	Fr
23–08–1922	Sweden	D 0–0	Stockholm	Fr
26–08	Finland	W 3–1	Helsinki	Fr
10–09	Denmark	D 3–3	Fredrikstad	Fr
24–09	Sweden	L 0–5	Oslo	Fr
17–06–1923	Finland	W 3–0	Oslo	Fr
21–06	Switzerland	D 2–2	Oslo	Fr
16–09	Sweden	L 2–3	Oslo	Fr
30–09	Denmark	L 1–2	Copenhagen	Fr
28–10	France	W 2–0	Paris	Fr
4–11	Germany	L 0–1	Hamburg	Fr
15–06–1924	Germany	L 0–2	Oslo	Fr
23–08	Finland	L 0–2	Helsinki	Fr
14–09	Denmark	L 1–3	Oslo	Fr
21–09	Sweden	L 1–6	Stockholm	Fr
7–06–1925	Finland	W 1–0	Oslo	Fr
21–06	Denmark	L 1–5	Copenhagen	Fr
23–08	Sweden	L 3–7	Oslo	Fr
6–06–1926	Finland	W 5–2	Helsinki	Fr
9–06	Sweden	L 2–3	Stockholm	Fr
19–09	Denmark	D 2–2	Oslo	Fr
7–10	Poland	L 3–4	Fredrikstad	Fr
29–05–1927	Denmark	L 0–1	Oslo	Fr
15–06	Finland	W 3–1	Oslo	Fr
26–06	Sweden	L 3–5	Oslo	Fr
23–10	Germany	L 2–6	Hamburg	Fr
30–10	Denmark	L 1–3	Copenhagen	Fr
3–06–1928	Finland	W 6–0	Helsinki	Fr
7–06	Sweden	L 1–6	Stockholm	Fr
17–06	Denmark	L 2–3	Oslo	Fr
23–09	Germany	L 0–2	Oslo	Fr
28–05–1929	Scotland	L 3–7	Oslo	Fr
12–06	Holland	D 4–4	Oslo	Fr
18–06	Finland	W 4–0	Oslo	Fr
23–06	Denmark	W 5–2	Copenhagen	Fr
29–09	Sweden	W 2–1	Oslo	Fr
3–11	Holland	W 4–1	Amsterdam	Fr
1–06–1930	Finland	W 6–2	Oslo	Fr
9–06	Switzerland	W 3–0	Oslo	Fr
6–07	Sweden	L 3–6	Stockholm	Fr
21–09	Denmark	W 1–0	Oslo	Fr
2–11	Germany	D 1–1	Breslau	Fr
25–05–1931	Denmark	L 1–3	Copenhagen	Fr
21–06	Germany	D 2–2	Oslo	Fr
6–09	Finland	D 4–4	Helsinki	Fr
27–09	Sweden	W 2–1	Oslo	Fr
5–06–1932	Estonia	W 3–0	Oslo	Fr
17–06	Finland	W 2–1	Oslo	Fr
1–07	Sweden	W 4–1	Gothenburg	Fr
25–09	Denmark	L 1–2	Oslo	Fr
11–06–1933	Denmark	D 2–2	Copenhagen	Fr
3–09	Finland	W 5–1	Helsinki	Fr
24–09	Sweden	L 0–1	Oslo	Fr
5–11	Germany	D 2–2	Magdeburg	Fr
1–07–1934	Sweden	D 3–3	Stockholm	Fr
2–09	Finland	W 4–2	Oslo	Fr
23–09	Denmark	W 3–1	Oslo	Fr
23–06–1935	Denmark	L 0–1	Copenhagen	Fr
27–06	Germany	D 1–1	Oslo	Fr
8–09	Finland	W 5–1	Helsinki	Fr
22–09	Sweden	L 0–2	Oslo	Fr
3–11	Switzerland	L 0–2	Zurich	Fr
18–06–1936	Switzerland	L 1–2	Oslo	Fr
5–07	Sweden	L 0–2	Gothenburg	Fr
26–07	Sweden	W 4–3	Stockholm	Fr
3–08	Turkey	W 4–0	Berlin	OGr1
7–08	Germany	W 2–0	Berlin	OGqf
10–08	Italy	L 1–2	Berlin	OGsf
13–08	Poland	W 3–2	Berlin	OG3p
6–09	Finland	L 0–2	Oslo	Fr
30–09	Denmark	D 3–3	Oslo	Fr
1–11	Holland	D 3–3	Amsterdam	Fr
14–05–1937	England	L 0–6	Oslo	Fr
27–05	Italy	L 1–3	Oslo	Fr
13–06	Denmark	L 1–5	Copenhagen	Fr
5–09	Finland	W 2–0	Helsinki	Fr
19–09	Sweden	W 3–2	Oslo	Fr
10–10	Rep. Ireland	W 3–2	Oslo	WCq
24–10	Germany	L 0–3	Berlin	Fr
7–11	Rep. Ireland	D 3–3	Dublin	WCq
31–05–1938	Estonia	W 1–0	Oslo	Fr
5–06	Italy	L 1–2	Marseilles	WCr1
17–06	Finland	W 9–0	Oslo	Fr
4–09	Sweden	W 2–1	Oslo	Fr
18–09	Denmark	D 1–1	Oslo	Fr
2–10	Sweden	W 3–2	Stockholm	Fr
23–10	Poland	D 2–2	Warsaw	Fr
9–11	England	L 0–4	Newcastle	Fr

* Amateur side

LEADING INTERNATIONAL APPEARANCES

1 Svenssen T	104	5 Thoresen	64
2 Grondalen	77	6 Nilsen O	62
3 Thorstvedt	70	7 Johansen R	61
4 Kojedal	66	8 Karlsen H	58

3–06–1939	Sweden	L	2–3	Stockholm	Fr
14–06	Sweden	W	1–0	Copenhagen	Fr
18–06	Denmark	L	3–6	Copenhagen	Fr
22–06	Germany	L	0–4	Oslo	Fr
3–09	Finland	W	2–1	Helsinki	Fr
17–09	Sweden	L	2–3	Oslo	Fr
22–10	Denmark	L	1–4	Copenhagen	Fr
26–08–1945	Denmark	L	2–4	Copenhagen	Fr
9–09	Denmark	L	1–5	Oslo	Fr
21–10	Sweden	L	0–10	Stockholm	Fr
16–06–1946	Denmark	W	2–1	Oslo	Fr
28–06	Finland	W	12–0	Bergen	Fr
8–07	Denmark	L	0–2	Copenhagen	Fr
28–07	Luxembourg	L	2–3	Luxembourg	Fr
15–09	Sweden	L	0–3	Oslo	Fr
20–10	Denmark	L	1–7	Copenhagen	Fr
11–06–1947	Poland	W	3–1	Oslo	Fr
26–06	Finland	W	2–1	Helsinki	Fr
28–06	Sweden	L	1–5	Helsinki	Fr
24–07	Iceland	W	4–2	Reykjavik	Fr
7–09	Finland	D	3–3	Helsinki	Fr
21–09	Denmark	L	3–5	Oslo	Fr
5–10	Sweden	L	1–4	Stockholm	Fr
6–05–1948	Holland	L	1–2	Oslo	Fr
12–06	Denmark	W	2–1	Copenhagen	Fr
6–08	USA	W	11–0	Oslo	Fr
5–09	Finland	W	2–0	Oslo	Fr
19–09	Sweden	L	3–5	Oslo	Fr
24–12	Egypt	D	1–1	Cairo	Fr
18–05–1949	England	L	1–4	Oslo	Fr
19–06	Yugoslavia	L	1–3	Oslo	Fr
8–07	Finland	D	1–1	Helsinki	Fr
11–09	Denmark	L	0–2	Oslo	Fr
2–10	Sweden	D	3–3	Stockholm	Fr
22–06–1950	Denmark	L	0–4	Copenhagen	Fr
15–08	Luxembourg	D	2–2	Bergen	Fr
10–09	Finland	W	4–1	Oslo	Fr
24–09	Sweden	L	1–3	Oslo	Fr
5–11	Yugoslavia	L	0–4	Belgrade	Fr
26–11	Rep. Ireland	D	2–2	Dublin	Fr
30–05–1951	Rep. Ireland	L	2–3	Oslo	Fr
6–06	Holland	W	3–2	Rotterdam	Fr
26–07	Iceland	W	3–1	Trondheim	Fr
16–08	Finland	D	1–1	Helsinki	Fr
23–08	Yugoslavia	L	2–4	Oslo	Fr
16–09	Denmark	W	2–0	Oslo	Fr
30–09	Sweden	W	4–3	Gothenburg	Fr
10–06–1952	Finland	L	1–2	Oslo	Fr
25–06	Yugoslavia	L	1–4	Zagreb	Fr
21–07	Sweden	L	1–4	Tammerfors	OGr2
31–08	Finland	W	7–2	Oslo	Fr
5–10	Sweden	L	1–2	Oslo	Fr
19–10	Denmark	W	3–1	Copenhagen	Fr
24–06–1953	Saar	L	2–3	Oslo	WCq
13–08	Iceland	W	3–1	Bergen	Fr
19–08	West Germany	D	1–1	Oslo	WCq
30–08	Finland	W	4–1	Helsinki	Fr
13–09	Denmark	L	0–1	Oslo	Fr
27–09	Holland	W	4–0	Oslo	Fr
18–10	Sweden	D	0–0	Stockholm	Fr
8–11	Saar	D	0–0	Saarbrucken	WCq
22–11	West Germany	L	1–5	Hamburg	WCq
5–05–1954	Scotland	L	0–1	Glasgow	Fr
19–05	Scotland	D	1–1	Oslo	Fr
30–05	Austria	L	0–5	Vienna	Fr
4–06	Denmark	W	2–1	Malmo	Fr
7–06	Sweden	L	0–3	Stockholm	Fr
4–07	Iceland	L	0–1	Reykjavik	Fr
29–08	Finland	W	3–1	Oslo	Fr
19–09	Sweden	D	1–1	Oslo	Fr
31–10	Denmark	W	1–0	Copenhagen	Fr
8–11	Rep. Ireland	L	1–2	Dublin	Fr
8–05–1955	Hungary	L	0–5	Oslo	Fr
25–05	Rep. Ireland	L	1–3	Oslo	Fr
12–06	Rumania	L	0–1	Oslo	Fr
14–08	Finland	W	3–1	Helsinki	Fr
11–09	Denmark	D	1–1	Oslo	Fr
25–09	Sweden	D	1–1	Stockholm	Fr
6–11	Holland	L	0–3	Amsterdam	Fr
16–11	West Germany	L	0–2	Karlsruhe	Fr
30–05–1956	Poland	D	0–0	Oslo	Fr
13–06	West Germany	L	1–3	Oslo	Fr
24–06	Denmark	W	3–2	Copenhagen	Fr
26–06	Rumania	L	0–2	Bucharest	Fr
26–08	Finland	D	1–1	Oslo	Fr
16–09	Sweden	W	3–1	Oslo	Fr
28–10	Poland	L	3–5	Warsaw	Fr
22–05–1957	Bulgaria	L	1–2	Oslo	WCq
12–06	Hungary	W	2–1	Oslo	WCq
18–06	Sweden	D	0–0	Turku	Fr
19–06	Denmark	L	0–2	Tammerfors	Fr
8–07	Iceland	W	3–0	Reykjavik	Fr
1–09	Finland	W	4–0	Helsinki	Fr
22–09	Denmark	D	2–2	Oslo	Fr
13–10	Sweden	L	2–5	Stockholm	Fr
3–11	Bulgaria	L	0–7	Sofia	WCq
10–11	Hungary	L	0–5	Budapest	WCq
28–05–1958	Holland	D	0–0	Oslo	Fr
15–06	Finland	W	2–0	Oslo	Fr
29–06	Denmark	W	2–1	Copenhagen	Fr
13–08	East Germany	W	6–5	Oslo	Fr
14–09	Sweden	L	0–2	Oslo	Fr
2–11	East Germany	L	1–4	Leipzig	Fr
20–05–1959	Austria	L	0–1	Oslo	ECr1
17–06	Luxembourg	W	1–0	Oslo	Fr
28–06	Finland	W	4–2	Helsinki	Fr
2–07	Denmark	L	1–2	Copenhagen	OGq
7–07	Iceland	L	0–1	Reykjavik	OGq
21–08	Iceland	W	2–1	Oslo	OGq
13–09	Denmark	L	2–4	Oslo	OGq
23–09	Austria	L	2–5	Vienna	ECr1
18–10	Sweden	L	2–6	Gothenburg	Fr
4–11	Holland	L	1–7	Rotterdam	Fr
26–05–1960	Denmark	L	0–3	Copenhagen	Fr
9–06	Iceland	W	4–0	Oslo	Fr
22–06	Austria	L	1–2	Oslo	Fr
28–08	Finland	W	6–3	Oslo	Fr
18–09	Sweden	W	3–1	Oslo	Fr
6–11	Rep. Ireland	L	1–3	Dublin	Fr
16–05–1961	Mexico	D	1–1	Bergen	Fr
1–06	Turkey	L	0–1	Oslo	WCq
27–06	Finland	L	1–4	Helsinki	Fr

1–07	Soviet Union	L	2–5	Moscow	WCq
23–08	Soviet Union	L	0–3	Oslo	WCq
17–09	Denmark	L	0–4	Oslo	Fr
22–10	Sweden	L	0–2	Gothenburg	Fr
29–10	Turkey	L	1–2	Istanbul	WCq
5–11	Malta	D	1–1	Gzira	Fr
16–05–1962	Holland	W	2–1	Oslo	Fr
11–06	Denmark	L	1–6	Copenhagen	Fr
21–06	Sweden	L	0–2	Oslo	ECr1
3–07	Malta	W	5–0	Trondheim	Fr
9–07	Iceland	W	3–1	Reykjavik	Fr
26–08	Finland	W	2–1	Bergen	Fr
16–09	Sweden	W	2–1	Oslo	Fr
4–11	Sweden	D	1–1	Malmo	ECr1
15–05–1963	Poland	L	2–5	Oslo	Fr
4–06	Scotland	W	4–3	Bergen	Fr
27–06	Finland	L	0–2	Helsinki	Fr
14–08	Sweden	D	0–0	Gothenburg	Fr
4–09	Poland	L	0–9	Szezecin	Fr
15–09	Denmark	L	0–4	Oslo	Fr
3–11	Switzerland	W	2–0	Zurich	Fr
7–11	Scotland	L	1–6	Glasgow	Fr
13–05–1964	Rep. Ireland	L	1–4	Oslo	Fr
1–07	Switzerland	W	3–2	Bergen	Fr
20–08	Finland	W	2–0	Trondheim	Fr
20–09	Sweden	D	1–1	Oslo	Fr
11–10	Denmark	L	0–2	Copenhagen	Fr
8–11	Luxembourg	W	2–0	Luxembourg	WCq
11–11	France	L	0–1	Paris	WCq
19–05–1965	Thailand	W	7–0	Bergen	Fr
27–05	Luxembourg	W	4–2	Trondheim	WCq
16–06	Yugoslavia	W	3–0	Oslo	WCq
8–08	Finland	L	0–4	Helsinki	Fr
15–09	France	L	0–1	Oslo	WCq
26–09	Denmark	D	2–2	Oslo	Fr
31–10	Sweden	D	0–0	Stockholm	Fr
7–11	Yugoslavia	D	1–1	Belgrade	WCq
12–06–1966	Portugal	L	0–4	Lisbon	Fr
26–06	Denmark	W	1–0	Copenhagen	Fr
29–06	England	L	1–6	Oslo	Fr
14–08	Finland	D	1–1	Stavanger	Fr
18–09	Sweden	L	2–4	Oslo	Fr
13–11	Bulgaria	L	2–4	Sofia	ECq
19–11	West Germany	L	0–3	Cologne	Fr
1–06–1967	Finland	W	2–0	Helsinki	Fr
8–06	Portugal	L	1–2	Oslo	ECq
29–06	Bulgaria	D	0–0	Oslo	ECq
3–09	Sweden	W	3–1	Oslo	ECq
24–09	Denmark	L	0–5	Oslo	Fr
5–11	Sweden	L	2–5	Stockholm	ECq
12–11	Portugal	L	1–2	Oporto	ECq
9–06–1968	Poland	L	1–6	Oslo	Fr
23–06	Denmark	L	1–5	Copenhagen	Fr
18–07	Iceland	W	4–0	Reykjavik	Fr
18–08	Finland	W	4–1	Oslo	Fr
15–09	Sweden	D	1–1	Oslo	Fr
9–10	Sweden	L	0–5	Stockholm	WCq
6–11	France	W	1–0	Strasbourg	WCq
8–05–1969	Mexico	L	0–2	Oslo	Fr
1–06	Sweden	L	2–4	Gothenburg	Fr
19–06	Sweden	L	2–5	Oslo	WCq
3–07	Bermuda	W	2–0	Stavanger	Fr
21–07	Iceland	W	2–1	Trondheim	Fr
24–08	Finland	D	2–2	Helsinki	Fr
27–08	Poland	L	1–6	Lodz	Fr
10–09	France	L	1–3	Oslo	WCq
21–09	Denmark	W	2–0	Oslo	Fr
11–11	Mexico	L	0–4	Mexico City	Fr
16–11	Guatemala	W	3–1	Guatemala City	Fr
13–05–1970	Czechoslovakia	L	0–2	Oslo	Fr
17–06	Finland	W	2–0	Bergen	Fr
20–07	Iceland	L	0–2	Reykjavik	Fr
13–09	Sweden	L	2–4	Oslo	Fr
21–09	Denmark	W	1–0	Copenhagen	Fr
7–10	Hungary	L	1–3	Oslo	ECq
11–11	France	L	1–3	Lyon	ECq
15–11	Bulgaria	D	1–1	Sofia	ECq
26–05–1971	Iceland	W	3–1	Bergen	Fr
9–06	Bulgaria	L	1–4	Oslo	ECq
22–06	West Germany	L	1–7	Oslo	Fr
8–08	Sweden	L	0–3	Malmo	Fr
24–08	Finland	D	1–1	Helsinki	Fr
8–09	France	L	1–3	Oslo	ECq
26–09	Denmark	L	1–4	Oslo	Fr
27–10	Hungary	L	0–4	Budapest	ECq
23–02–1972	Israel	L	1–2	Tel Aviv	Fr
31–05	Finland	D	0–0	Turku	Fr
14–06	Uruguay	L	0–1	Oslo	Fr

Date	Opponents	Result		Venue	Compet	Scorers
3–08	Iceland	W	4–1	Stavanger	WCq	Fuglset, Turmlund, Hestad, Johannson T
17–09	Sweden	L	1–3	Oslo	Fr	Fuglset
4–10	Belgium	L	0–2	Oslo	WCq	
1–11	Holland	L	0–9	Rotterdam	WCq	
6–06–1973	Rep. Ireland	D	1–1	Oslo	Fr	Paulsen
20–06	Denmark	L	0–1	Copenhagen	Fr	
25–07	North Korea	W	3–0	Bergen	Fr	
2–08	Iceland	W	4–0	Reykjavik	WCq	Sunde, Lunx, Petterson, Johannessen
12–09	Holland	L	1–2	Oslo	WCq	Hestad
23–09	Denmark	L	0–1	Trondheim	Fr	
31–10	Belgium	L	0–2	Brussels	WCq	
4–11	Luxembourg	L	1–2	Luxembourg	Fr	Sunde
22–05–1974	East Germany	L	0–1	Rostock	Fr	
6–06	Scotland	L	1–2	Oslo	Fr	Lund
8–08	Sweden	L	1–2	Gothenburg	Fr	Hestad
15–08	Finland	L	1–2	Oslo	Fr	Johansen T
4–09	Nth. Ireland	W	2–1	Oslo	ECq	Lund 2
30–10	Yugoslavia	L	1–3	Belgrade	ECq	Lund
9–06–1975	Yugoslavia	L	1–3	Oslo	ECq	Thunberg
30–06	Sweden	L	1–3	Stockholm	ECq	Olsen
7–07	Iceland	D	1–1	Reykjavik	OGq	
17–07	Iceland	W	3–2	Bergen	OGq	
13–08	Sweden	L	0–2	Oslo	ECq	

29–10	Nth. Ireland	L	0–3	Belfast	ECq	
24–03–1976	Rep. Ireland	L	0–3	Dublin	Fr	
19–05	Iceland	L	0–1	Oslo	Fr	
16–06	Sweden	L	0–2	Stockholm	WCq	
24–06	Denmark	D	0–0	Bergen	Fr	
25–08	Denmark	L	0–3	Copenhagen	Fr	
8–09	Switzerland	W	1–0	Oslo	WCq	Lund
22–09	Sweden	W	3–2	Oslo	Fr	Thunberg 2, Jacobsen P
26–05–1977	Sweden	L	0–1	Gothenburg	Fr	
1–06	Denmark	L	0–2	Oslo	Fr	
30–06	Iceland	L	1–2	Reykjavik	Fr	Iversen
18–08	Finland	D	1–1	Oslo	Fr	
7–09	Sweden	W	2–1	Oslo	WCq	Ottensen, Iversen
30–10	Switzerland	L	0–1	Berne	WCq	
29–03–1978	Spain	L	0–3	Gijon	Fr	
21–05	Rep. Ireland	D	0–0	Oslo	Fr	
31–05	Denmark	L	1–2	Oslo	Fr	Thoresen
9–08	Finland	D	1–1	Helsinki	Fr	Johansen
30–08	Austria	L	0–2	Oslo	ECq	
20–09	Belgium	D	1–1	Lokeren	ECq	Larsen-Okland
25–10	Scotland	L	2–3	Glasgow	ECq	Aas, Larsen-Okland
9–05–1979	Portugal	L	0–1	Oslo	ECq	
7–06	Scotland	L	0–4	Oslo	ECq	
28–06	Sweden	L	0–2	Gothenburg	Fr	
15–08	Sweden	W	2–0	Oslo	Fr	Mathiesen, Larsen-Okland
21–08	Finland	W	1–0	Kuopio	OGq	Davidsen
29–08	Austria	L	0–4	Vienna	ECq	
12–09	Belgium	L	1–2	Oslo	ECq	Jacobsen
26–10	Finland	D	1–1	Stavanger	OGq	Rein
1–11	Portugal	L	1–3	Lisbon	ECq	Hammer
22–05–1980	Bulgaria	W	1–0	Oslo	Fr	Jacobsen
4–06	Denmark	L	1–3	Copenhagen	Fr	Kollshaugen
14–07	Iceland	W	3–1	Oslo	Fr	Kollshaugen, Jacobsen, Erlandsen
21–08	Finland	W	6–1	Oslo	Fr	Jacobsen 4, Dokken, Aas
10–09	England	L	0–4	London	WCq	
24–09	Romania	D	1–1	Oslo	WCq	Hareide
29–10	Switzerland	W	2–1	Berne	WCq	Hareide, Mathiesen
29–04–1981	Bulgaria	L	0–1	Pleven	Fr	
20–05	Hungary	L	1–2	Oslo	WCq	Thoresen
3–06	Romania	L	0–1	Bucharest	WCq	
17–06	Switzerland	D	1–1	Oslo	WCq	Davidsen
2–07	Finland	L	1–3	Helsinki	Fr	Davidsen
12–08	Nigeria	D	2–2	Oslo	Fr	Jacobsen, Lund
9–09	England	W	2–1	Oslo	WCq	Albertsen, Thoresen
23–09	Denmark	L	1–2	Copenhagen	Fr	Krujedal
31–10	Hungary	L	1–4	Budapest	WCq	Lund
28–04–1982	Finland	D	1–1	Stavanger	Fr	Thoresen
12–05	West Germany	L	2–4	Oslo	Fr	Larsen-Okland, Albertsen
15–06	Denmark	W	2–1	Oslo	Fr	Hareida, Hansen V
11–08	Sweden	W	1–0	Olso	Fr	Lund
22–09	Wales	L	0–1	Swansea	ECq	
13–10	Yugoslavia	W	3–1	Oslo	ECq	Lund, Larsen-Okland, Hareide
27–10	Bulgaria	D	2–2	Sofia	ECq	Larsen-Okland, Thoresen
13–11	Kuwait	L	0–1	Kuwait	Fr	
10–08–1983	Romania	D	0–0	Oslo	Fr	
7–09	Bulgaria	L	1–2	Oslo	ECq	Hareide
21–09	Wales	D	0–0	Oslo	ECq	
12–10	Yugoslavia	L	1–2	Belgrade	ECq	Thoresen
1–05–1984	Luxembourg	W	2–0	Ettelbruck	Fr	Thoresen, Dokken
23–05	Hungary	D	0–0	Szekesfehervar	Fr	
6–06	Wales	W	1–0	Trondheim	Fr	Larsen-Okland
20–06	Iceland	W	1–0	Reykjavik	Fr	Johansen E
29–08	Poland	D	1–1	Drammen	Fr	Danielsen
12–09	Switzerland	L	0–1	Oslo	WCq	
26–09	Denmark	L	0–1	Copenhagen	WCq	
10–10	Soviet Union	D	1–1	Oslo	WCq	Thoresen
17–10	Rep. Ireland	W	1–0	Oslo	WCq	Jacobsen
18–12	Egypt	W	1–0	Cairo	Fr	
21–12	Egypt	W	1–0	Ismailia	Fr	
26–02–1985	Wales	D	1–1	Wrexham	Fr	Ahlsen

17–04	East Germany	L	0–1	Frankfurt	Fr	
1–05	Rep. Ireland	D	0–0	Dublin	WCq	
22–05	Sweden	L	0–1	Gothenburg	Fr	
5–06	Wales	W	4–2	Bergen	Fr	Sollied, Larsen-Okland, Jacobsen, OG
14–08	East Germany	L	0–1	Oslo	Fr	
10–09	Egypt	W	3–0	Oslo	Fr	Andersen, Soler, Jacobsen
25–09	Italy	W	2–1	Leece	Fr	Larsen-Okland, Davidsen
16–10	Denmark	L	1–5	Oslo	WCq	Sundby
30–10	Soviet Union	L	0–1	Moscow	WCq	
13–11	Switzerland	D	1–1	Lucerne	WCq	Sundby
26–02–1986	Grenada	W	2–1	St George's	Fr	Sundby, Skogheim
30–04	Argentina	W	1–0	Oslo	Fr	Osvold
13–05	Denmark	W	1–0	Oslo	Fr	Thoresen
4–06	Rumania	L	1–3	Bucharest	Fr	Sundby
20–08	Rumania	D	2–2	Oslo	Fr	Larsen-Okland 2
9–09	Hungary	D	0–0	Oslo	Fr	
24–09	East Germany	D	0–0	Oslo	ECq	
29–10	Soviet Union	L	0–4	Simferopol	ECq	
24–03–1987	Poland	L	1–4	Wroclaw	Fr	Sundby
28–05	Italy	D	0–0	Oslo	Fr	
3–06	Soviet Union	L	0–1	Oslo	ECq	
16–06	France	W	2–0	Oslo	ECq	Mordt, Andersen
12–08	Sweden	D	0–0	Oslo	Fr	
9–09	Iceland	L	1–2	Reykjavik	ECq	Andersen
23–09	Iceland	L	0–1	Oslo	ECq	
14–10	France	D	1–1	Paris	ECq	Sundby
28–10	East Germany	L	1–3	Magdeburg	ECq	Fjerestad
1–06–1988	Rep. Ireland	D	0–0	Oslo	Fr	
28–07	Brazil	D	1–1	Oslo	Fr	Fjortoft
9–08	Bulgaria	D	1–1	Oslo	Fr	Sorloth
14–09	Scotland	L	1–2	Oslo	WCq	Fjortoft
28–09	France	L	0–1	Paris	WCq	
19–10	Italy	L	1–2	Pescara	Fr	Brandhaug
2–11	Cyprus	W	3–0	Limassol	WCq	Sorloth 2, Osvold
4–11	Czechoslovakia	L	2–3	Bratislava	Fr	Sorloth, Adgestein
22–02–1989	Greece	L	2–4	Athens	Fr	Bratseth, Sorloth
2–05	Poland	L	0–3	Oslo	Fr	
21–05	Cyprus	W	3–1	Oslo	WCq	Osvold, Sorloth, Bratseth
31–05	Austria	W	4–1	Oslo	Fr	Halle, Fjortoft, Loken, Kojedal
14–06	Yugoslavia	L	1–2	Oslo	WCq	Fjortoft
23–08	Greece	D	0–0	Oslo	Fr	
5–09	France	D	1–1	Oslo	WCq	Bratseth
11–10	Yugoslavia	L	0–1	Sarajevo	WCq	
25–10	Kuwait	D	2–2	Kuwait City	Fr	Sorloth, Fjortoft
15–11	Scotland	D	1–1	Glasgow	WCq	Johnsen
5–02–1990	South Korea	W	3–2	Ta'Qali	Fr	Berg O, Skammelsrund, Tangen
7–02	Malta	D	1–1	Ta'Qali	Fr	Fjortoft
27–03	Nth. Ireland	W	3–2	Belfast	Fr	Skammelsrund, Andersen, Johnsen E
6–06	Denmark	L	1–2	Trondheim	Fr	Andersen
22–08	Sweden	L	1–2	Stavanger	Fr	Ahlsen
12–09	Soviet Union	L	0–2	Moscow	ECq	
10–10	Hungary	D	0–0	Bergen	ECq	
31–10	Cameroon	W	6–1	Oslo	Fr	Bratseth, Bohinen, Dahlum, Fjortoft 2, Sorloth
7–11	Tunisia	W	3–1	Bizerte	Fr	Dahlum 2, Ingebrigtsen
14–11	Cyprus	W	3–0	Nicosia	ECq	Sorloth, Bohinen, Brandhaug
17–04–1991	Austria	D	0–0	Vienna	Fr	
1–05	Cyprus	W	3–0	Oslo	ECq	Lydersen, Dahlum, Sorloth
22–05	Romania	W	1–0	Oslo	Fr	Fjortoft
5–06	Italy	W	2–1	Oslo	ECq	Dahlum, Bohinen
8–08	Sweden	L	1–2	Oslo	Fr	Leonhardsen
28–08	Soviet Union	L	0–1	Oslo	ECq	
25–09	Czechoslovakia	L	2–3	Oslo	Fr	Jakobsen, Fjortoft
30–10	Hungary	D	0–0	Szombathely	ECq	
13–11	Italy	D	1–1	Genoa	ECq	Jakobsen
7–01–1992	Egypt	D	0–0	Cairo	Fr	
4–02	Bermuda	W	3–1	Hamilton	Fr	Leonhardsen 3
29–04	Denmark	L	0–1	Aarhus	Fr	
13–05	Faeroe Islands	W	2–0	Oslo	Fr	Sorloth, Bohinen
3–06	Scotland	D	0–0	Oslo	Fr	

POLAND

Poland is a country whose boundaries have chopped and changed more than any other European country in recent history. In the 17th century Poland was roughly three times the size it is today and stretched south to include even Kiev, whilst in the 19th century it had shrunk to include only the area around Warsaw, Krakow and Lublin. In the period from 1874 to 1918, when football first started on the continent, it did not even exist at all.

Poland was part of both the German and Russian Empires at this time, and it was the German areas that took most to football at the turn of the century. Königsberg (now Kalliningrad in the Soviet Union), Danzig (now Gdansk), Stettin (now Szczecin) and Breslau (now Wroclaw) were all centres of German football prior to 1945. Warsaw, Lodz, Lwow and Lublin, as part of Russia until 1918, formed the basis of the Polish state that was created in 1921, along with Krakow from Germany.

The Polish Football Federation was formed in 1919 and admitted to FIFA four years later. In 1921 a championship was started, and as if to prove the flimsy nature of politics at the time, one of the early dominant clubs, Pogon Lwow, would today find itself back in the Soviet Union – if the latter still existed that is!

Polish football took great strides in the inter-war years and a number of clubs from around this time still exist. Wisla Krakow and LKS Lodz, formed in 1906 and 1908 respectively, remain two of the oldest clubs still playing football at the highest level in Poland, and along with Legia Warsaw, formed in 1916, and Ruch Chorzow, in 1920, these clubs dominated football until the Second World War.

		All			League			Cup		Europe		
	Team	G	S	B	G	S	B	G	S	G	S	B
1	Górnik Zabrze	20	11	6	14	4	6	6	6	–	1	–
2	Ruch Chorzów	15	8	6	13	5	6	2	3	–	–	–
3	Legia Warszawa	13	10	10	4	5	8	9	5	–	–	2
4	Wisla Kraków	8	12	8	6	8	8	2	4	–	–	–
5	Lech Poznan	7	1	3	4	–	3	3	1	–	–	–
6	Cracovia	5	2	–	5	2	–	–	–	–	–	–
7	Zaglebie Sosnowiec	4	5	2	–	4	2	4	1	–	–	–
8	Pogon Lwow	4	3	–	4	3	–	–	–	–	–	–
9	Widzew Lódz	3	6	4	2	5	3	1	–	–	–	1
10	Slask Wroclaw	3	2	1	1	2	1	2	–	–	–	–
11	Polonia Bytom	2	7	2	2	4	2	–	3	–	–	–
12	GKS Katowice	2	6	2	–	3	2	2	3	–	–	–
13	Warta Poznan	2	5	6	2	5	6	–	–	–	–	–
14	Stal Mielec	2	2	3	2	1	3	–	1	–	–	–
15	Polonia Warszawa	2	2	–	1	2	–	1	–	–	–	–
16	LKS Lódz	2	1	1	1	1	1	1	–	–	–	–
17	Gwardia Warszawa	1	2	2	–	1	2	1	1	–	–	–
18	Lechia Gdansk	1	1	1	–	–	1	1	1	–	–	–
	Szombierki Bytom	1	1	1	1	1	1	–	–	–	–	–
20	Garbarnia Kraków	1	1	–	1	1	–	–	–	–	–	–
	Zaglebie Lubin	1	1	–	1	1	–	–	–	–	–	–
22	Arka Gdynia	1	–	–	–	–	–	1	–	–	–	–
	Miedz Legnica	1	–	–	–	–	–	1	–	–	–	–
	Stal Rzeszów	1	–	–	–	–	–	1	–	–	–	–
25	Pogon Szczecin	–	3	1	–	1	1	–	2	–	–	–
26	Piast Gliwice	–	2	–	–	–	–	–	2	–	–	–
27	AKS Chorzów	–	1	2	–	1	2	–	–	–	–	–
28	Czarni Zagan	–	1	–	–	–	–	–	1	–	–	–
	Górnik Radlin	–	1	–	–	1	–	–	–	–	–	–
	Jagiellonia Bialystok	–	1	–	–	–	–	–	1	–	–	–
	I.FC Katowice	–	1	–	–	1	–	–	–	–	–	–
	Rakow Czestochowa	–	1	–	–	–	–	–	1	–	–	–
	ROW II Rybnik	–	1	–	–	–	–	–	1	–	–	–
	Sparta Lwow	–	1	–	–	–	–	–	1	–	–	–
	GKS Tychy	–	1	–	–	1	–	–	–	–	–	–
	Wawel Kraków	–	1	–	–	1	–	–	–	–	–	–
37	Odra Opole	–	–	1	–	–	1	–	–	–	–	–
	Zaglebie Walbrzych	–	–	1	–	–	1	–	–	–	–	–

To the end of the 1991–92 season

In December 1921 a national side took to the field for the first time in a match against Hungary, and although the record up to 1939 was not outstanding, the Poles managed to hold their own against most sides. The finest player of this generation was Ernest Wilimowski of Ruch Chorzow and he will always be remembered for what turned out to be a personal duel with the Brazilian Leonidas in the 1938 World Cup match in Strasbourg. Both scored four goals, but sadly for Wilimowski and his team-mates, Poland lost 6–5 in what remains one of the great matches of World Cup history.

Two years previously Poland had reached the semi-finals of the Berlin Olympics only to lose to Austria. In the event, their disappointment was not eased with a bronze medal as they also lost the third place play-off to Norway.

The war and its aftermath brought wholesale changes not only to the boundaries of Poland once again, setting them as they remain to this day, but also to the set-up of club football. In true communist fashion, football was organised from head to toe. The control of clubs passed to various government bodies, whilst at the same time new clubs were created.

Of the clubs formed, Górnik Zabrze, were to have the biggest impact on the game, dominating the league from the late 1950s to early 1970s. In 1963 a young Wlodzimierz Lubanski made his debut for Górnik, joining Ernest Pol who until Lubanski took over his mantle was Poland's most prolific marksman. Lubanski was the spark that ignited Polish football which in the post-war period had progressed steadily but not spectacularly.

By the end of the 1960s Poland was embarked on era of success that lasted the best part of 15 years and included Olympic gold and silver medals as well as third place in the 1974 World Cup and a semi-final appearance in 1982.

With a population of over 30 million perhaps this success was long overdue, as of all the large countries in Europe Poland had achieved the least.

Central to the side that won the 1972 Olympic Games was Lubanski, but alongside him were Kazimierz Deyna and Robert Gadocha, both prolific goalscorers. Unfortunately for Poland, Lubanski was injured and did not play in the 1974 World Cup but Deyna and Gadocha were joined by Grzegorz Lato and Andrzej Szarmach, two more players who seemed to be able to score with ease. Not only was the attack formidable, the defence was also particularly strong, dominated as it was by the giant Jan Tomaszewski in goal along with Wladislav Zmuda and Jerzy Gorgon in front of him.

Lato especially emerged as a star after the World Cup where his seven goals were instrumental in taking Poland to third place. Each tournament Poland entered seemed to throw up a new goalscoring sensation. Deyna had scored nine in the 1972 Olympics, whilst Szarmach chipped in with eight in the Montreal Olympics which saw the Poles lose in the final to East Germany. Remarkably the team kept together for most of the 1970s. Lubanski finally bowed out after the 1978 World Cup, but by this time Zbigniew Boniek, perhaps Poland's best known player, had made his debut.

The side that entered the World Cup in Argentina was perhaps the most complete ever to have represented Poland: Tomaszewski, Szymanowski, Zmuda, Gorgon, Maculeewicz, Kasperczak, Deyna, Nawalka, Lato, Lubanski, Boniek and Szarmach should have been able to take on and beat the rest of the world, but although they reached the second round, they were disappointing against both Brazil and Argentina.

The 1982 World Cup side did not seem to be so strong on paper but it fared better, reaching the semi-finals before losing to Italy. Boniek, Lato, Zmuda and the evergreen Szarmach remained, but all apart from Boniek were reaching the end of their careers, and the achievements to a large extent papered over the cracks that were appearing in Polish football.

Many of the well-known players were given permission to move abroad: Boniek to Juventus, Zmuda to Verona, Lato to Lokeren and Szarmach to Auxerre for example, and this exodus left the domestic game in a poor state with low crowds and a general apathy that was so prevalent in the Eastern Bloc countries at that time. Since the fall of the communist government, matters have if anything become worse. Left to fight for their existence in the commercial world, the sole source of money seems to be the sale of players to clubs in the West, and this in turn lessens interest.

With so many players gaining experience abroad, the national side may well benefit and on their day they are capable of beating anyone. However, if interest is to be sustained at home, the sooner Poland is able to throw off the legacy of 40 years of economic stagnation the better. When it does, given the size of the country, there is no reason why clubs such as Górnik Zabrze and Legia Warsaw should not be regarded as among the best on the continent.

Population: 38 064 000
Area, sq km: 312 683
% in urban areas: 61.2%
Capital city: Warsaw

Polski Zwlazek Pilki Noznej
Al. Ujazdowskie #22
00–478 Warsaw
Tel: (010 48) 22 292489
Fax: (010 48) 22 219175
Telex: 815320 PZPN PL
Cable: PEZETPEEN WARSZAWA
Languages for correspondence: French, German & English

Year of formation: 1919
Affiliation to FIFA: 1923
Affiliation to UEFA: 1954
Registered clubs: 4103
Registered players: 281 400
Registered coaches: 3918
Registered referees: 7215
National stadium: Stadion Slaski, Chorzów, 70 000
National colours: Shirts: White/Shorts: Red/Socks: White
Reserve colours: Shirts: Red/Shorts: White/Socks: Red

Season: August – June with a mid-season break in December, January and February

THE RECORD

WORLD CUP

1930 .... Did not enter
1934 .... QT 2nd/2 in group 9
1938 .... QT 1st/2 in group 2 – Final Tournament/1st round
1950 .... Did not enter
1954 .... Did not enter
1958 .... QT 2nd/3 in group 6
1962 .... QT 1st rd in group 10
1966 .... QT 3rd/4 in group 8
1970 .... QT 2nd/4 in group 8
1974 .... QT 1st/3 in group 5 – Final Tournament/2nd round/3rd place
1978 .... QT 1st/4 in group 1 – Final Tournament/2nd round
1982 .... QT 1st/3 in group 7 – Final Tournament/Semi-Finalists/3rd place
1986 .... QT 1st/4 in group 1 – Final Tournament/2nd round
1990 .... QT 3rd/4 in group 2

EUROPEAN CHAMPIONSHIP

1960 .... 1st round
1964 .... 1st round
1968 .... QT 3rd/4 in group 7
1972 .... QT 2nd/4 in group 8
1976 .... QT 2nd/4 in group 5
1980 .... QT 2nd/5 in group 4
1984 .... QT 3rd/4 in group 2
1988 .... QT 4th/5 in group 5
1992 .... QT 3rd/4 in group 7

OLYMPIC GAMES

1908–20 ..... Did not enter
1924 .... Preliminary round
1928 .... Did not enter
1936 .... Semi-finalists/4th place
1948 .... Did not enter
1952 .... 1st round
1956 .... Did not enter
1960 .... Final Tournament/1st round
1964 .... QT Failed to qualify
1968 .... QT Failed to qualify

1972 .... Final Tournament/Winners
1976 .... Final Tournament/Runners-up
1980 .... QT Failed to qualify
1984 .... QT Failed to qualify
1988 .... QT Failed to qualify
1992 .... Final Tournament

EUROPEAN CLUB COMPETITIONS

EUROPEAN CUP: Semi-finalists – Legia Warsaw 1970, Widzew Lódz 1983

CUP WINNERS CUP: Finalists – Górnik Zabrze 1970

UEFA CUP: Quarter-finalists – Ruch Chorzów 1974, Stal Mielec 1976

CLUB DIRECTORY

WARSAW (Population – 2323000)

CWKS Legia Warszawa
Stadium: Wojska Polskiego 21000
Founded: 1916
Colours: Green/Green
Previous names: WKS 1016–20, Legia 1920–50, CWKS 1950–57

Gwardia Warszawa
Stadium: Gwardia 12000
Founded: 1948
Colours: Blue/White

Polonia Warszawa
Stadium: Konwiktorska
Founded: 1915
Colours: Black/White
Previous name: Kolejarz 1948–56

KATOWICE (Population – 2778000)

Amatorski Klub Sportowy (AKS) Chorzów
Stadium: I Maja
Founded: 1910
Colours: Green/White
Previous name: Budowlani 1948–55

Górniczy Klub Sportowy (GKS) Katowice
Stadium: GKS 11000
Founded: 1964
Colours: Yellow/Black

KS Górnik Zabrze
Stadium: Górnik 23000
Founded: 1948
Colours: Red/Blue

KS Polonia Bytom
Stadium: Koniewa
Founded: 1920
Colours: Blue/Red
Previous name: Ogniwo 1948–55

KS Ruch Chorzów
Stadium: Ruch 40000
Founded: 1920
Colours: Blue/White
Previous name: Unia 1950–55

GKS Szombierki Bytom
Stadium: Frycza Modrzewskiego
Founded: 1919
Colours: Green and black stripes/Black
Previous names: Górnik Bytom 1948–56

LODZ (Population – 1061000)

Lodzkie Klub Sportowy (LKS) Lódz
Stadium: LKS 30000
Founded: 1908
Colours: Red/Red
Previous names: Wlokniarz 1948–54

RTS Widzew Lódz
Stadium: Widzew 22000
Founded: 1910
Colours: White/Red

GDANSK (Population – 909000)
BKS Lechia Gdansk
Stadium: Lechia 18000
Founded: 1945
Colours: White/Green
Previous names: Budowlany 1949–56

KRAKOW (Population – 828000)

KS Cracovia
Stadium: Cracovia 12000
Founded: 1906
Colours: Red and white stripes/White
Previous names: Ogniwo 1949–54, Sparta 1954–55

Garbarnia Kraków
Stadium: Parkowa
Founded: 1921
Colours: Claret/White
Previous names: Zwiazkowiec 1949–50, Wlokniarz 1950–55

KS Hutnik Kraków
Stadium: Hutnik 15000
Founded: 1950
Colours: White/Blue

GTS Wisla Kraków
Stadium: Wisla 28000
Founded: 1906
Colours: Blue/Red
Previous names: Gwardia 1949–55

POZNAN (Population – 672000)

KKS Lech Poznan
Stadium: Lech 23000
Founded: 1922
Colours: Blue/Blue
Previous names: Kolejarz 1947–56

GKS Olimpia Poznan
Stadium: Olimpia 25000
Founded: 1945
Colours: Blue/White

KS Warta Poznan
Stadium: Warta 50000
Founded: 1912
Colours: White/Green
Previous names: Zwiazkowiec 1949–55

WROCLAW (Population – 640000)
WKS Slask Wroclaw
Stadium: Slask 14000
Founded: 1947
Colours: Green/White
Previous names: Ogniwo 1948–56

SZCZECIN (Population – 449000)
MKS Pogon Szczecin
Stadium: Pogon 17000
Founded: 1948
Colours: Claret and Blue stripes/White

LUBLIN (Population – 389000)
RKS Motor Lublin
Stadium: Motor 20000
Founded: 1950
Colours: Yellow/Blue

BYDGOSZCZ (Population – 372000)
WKS Zawisza Bydgoszcz
Stadium: Zawisza 45000
Founded: 1946
Colours: Blue/Black
Previous names: OWKS 1948–56

BIALYSTOK (Population – 259000)
MK Jagiellonia Bialystok
Stadium: Gwardia 23000
Founded: 1927
Colours: White/White

SOSNOWIEC (Population – 258000)
GKS Zaglebie Sosnowiec
Stadium: Ludowy 34000
Founded: 1906
Colours: Red/Green
Previous names: Milowice 1906–08, Union 1908–1918, Sosnowiec 1918–21, Victoria 1921–31, Unia 1931–39, RKU 1939–48, Stal 1948–63

WALBRZYCH (Population – 207000)
KS Górnik Walbrzych
Stadium: Górnik 30000
Founded: 1946
Colours: Blue/White

RZESZOW (Population – 147000)
Stal Rzeszów
Founded: 1944
Colours: White/Blue

LUBIN (Population – 77000)
MKS Zaglebie Lubin
Stadium: Zaglebie 34000
Founded: 1946
Colours: White/white

MIELEC (Population – 56000)
FKS Stal Mielec
Stadium: Stal 30000
Founded: 1939
Colours: White/Blue

POLISH LEAGUE CHAMPIONSHIP

Year	Champions	Runners up	3rd
1921	Cracovia 15	Polonia Warszawa 10	Warta Poznan 8
1922	Pogon Lwow 4–3 1–1	Warta Poznan	
1923	Pogon Lwow 3–0 1–2 2–1	Wisla Kraków	
1924	–		
1925	Pogon Lwow 7	Warta Poznan 3	Wisla Kraków 2
1926	Pogon Lwow 6	Polonia Warszawa 3	Warta Poznan 3
1927	Wisla Kraków 40	1.FC Katowice 36	Warta Poznan 32
1928	Wisla Kraków 42	Warta Poznan 40	Legia Warszawa 36
1929	Warta Poznan 33	Garbarnia Kraków 32	Wisla Kraków 30
1930	Cracovia 33	Wisla Kraków 32	Legia Warszawa 30
1931	Garbarnia Krakow 30	Wisla Kraków 29	Legia Warszawa 29
1932	Cracovia 29	Pogon Lwow 28	Warta Poznan 27
1933	Ruch Chorzów 14	Pogon Lwow 13	Wisla Kraków 13
1934	Ruch Chorzów 36	Cracovia 29	Wisla Kraków 28
1935	Ruch Chorzów 26	Pogon Lwow 25	Warta Poznan 24
1936	Ruch Chorzów 24	Wisla Kraków 22	Warta Poznan 21
1937	Cracovia 26	AKS Chorzów 24	Ruch Chorzów 23
1938	Ruch Chorzów 27	Warta Poznan 21	Wisla Kraków 20
1939–45	–		
1946	Polonia Warszawa 9	Warta Poznan 6	AKS Chorzów 5
1947	Warta Poznan 8	Wisla Kraków 4	AKS Chorzów 0
1948	Cracovia 38	Wisla Kraków 38	Ruch Chorzów 30
1949	Gwardia Kraków 30	Ogniwo Kraków 29	Kolejarz Poznan 27
1950	Gwardia Kraków 33	Unia Chorzów 32	Kolejarz Poznan 26
1951	Gwardia Kraków 32	Górnik Radlin 29	CWKS Warszawa 27
1952	Unia Chorzów 7–0 0–0	Ogniwo Bytom	
1953	Unia Chorzów 38	Wawel Kraków 28	Gwardia Kraków 27
1954	Ogniwo Bytom 24	Wlokniarz Lódz 24	Unia Chorzów 24
1955	CWKS Warszawa 28	Stal Sosnowiec 27	Unia Chorzów 25
1956	CWKS Warszawa 34	Unia Chorzów 29	Budowlani Gdansk 27
1957	Górnik Zabrze 33	Gwardia Warszawa 32	LKS Lódz 29
1958	LKS Lódz 32	Polonia Bytom 31	Górnik Zabrze 27
1959	Górnik Zabrze 36	Polonia Bytom 30	Gwardia Warszawa 25
1960	Ruch Chorzów 30	Legia Warszawa 29	Górnik Zabrze 28
1961	Górnik Zabrze 43	Polonia Bytom 35	Legia Warszawa 32
1962	Polonia Bytom 4–1 1–2	Górnik Zabrze	
1963	Górnik Zabrze 42	Ruch Chorzów 37	Stal Sosnowiec 36
1964	Górnik Zabrze 40	Zaglebie Sosnowiec 31	Odra Opole 31
1965	Górnik Zabrze 37	Szombierki Bytom 32	Zaglebie Sosnowiec 31
1966	Górnik Zabrze 42	Wisla Kraków 32	Polonia Bytom 31
1967	Górnik Zabrze 37	Zaglebie Sosnowiec 34	Ruch Chorzów 30
1968	Ruch Chorzów 38	Legia Warszawa 35	Górnik Zabrze 33
1969	Legia Warszawa 39	Górnik Zabrze 37	Polonia Bytom 28
1970	Legia Warszawa 40	Ruch Chorzów 35	Górnik Zabrze 35
1971	Górnik Zabrze 39	Legia Warszawa 34	Zaglebie Walbrzych 27
1972	Górnik Zabrze 37	Zaglebie Sosnowiec 33	Legia Warszawa 32
1973	Stal Mielec 36	Ruch Chorzów 33	Gwardia Warszawa 30
1974	Ruch Chorzów 41	Górnik Zabrze 38	Stal Mielec 37
1975	Ruch Chorzów 44	Stal Mielec 38	Slask Wroclaw 36
1976	Stal Mielec 38	GKS Tychy 38	Wisla Kraków 37
1977	Slask Wroclaw 41	Widzew Lódz 38	Górnik Zabrze 37
1978	Wisla Kraków 39	Slask Wroclaw 38	Lech Poznan 37
1979	Ruch Chorzów 39	Widzew Lódz 39	Stal Mielec 36
1980	Szombierki Bytom 39	Widzew Lódz 36	Legia Warszawa 36
1981	Widzew Lódz 39	Wisla Kraków 37	Szombierki Bytom 36
1982	Widzew Lódz 39	Slask Wroclaw 39	Stal Mielec 35
1983	Lech Poznan 39	Widzew Lódz 38	Ruch Chorzów 35
1984	Lech Poznan 42	Widzew Lódz 42	Pogon Szczecin 38
1985	Górnik Zabrze 42	Legia Warszawa 41	Widzew Lódz 38
1986	Górnik Zabrze 46	Legia Warszawa 42	Widzew Lódz 41
1987	Górnik Zabrze 49	Pogon Szczecin 44	GKS Katowice 43
1988	Górnik Zabrze 51	GKS Katowice 40	Legia Warszawa 39
1989	Ruch Chorzów 52	GKS Katowice 47	Górnik Zabrze 45
1990	Lech Poznan 42	Zaglebie Lubin 40	GKS Katowice 40
1991	Zaglebie Lubin 44	Górnik Zabrze 40	Wisla Kraków 40
1992	Lech Pozan 49	GKS Katowice 44	Widzew Lódz 43

POLISH CUP FINALS

Year	Winners	Score	Runners–up
1926	Wisla Kraków	2–1	Sparta Lvov
1927–50 – No competition			
1951	Unia Chorzów	2–0	Gwardia Kraków
1952	Kolejarz Warszawa	1–0	CWKS Warszawa
1953 – No competition			
1954	Gwardia Warszawa	0–0 3–1	Gwardia Kraków
1955	CWKS Warszawa	5–0	Budowlani Gdansk
1956	CWKS Warszawa	3–0	Górnik Zabrze
1957	LKS Lódz	2–1	Górnik Zabrze
1958–61 – No competition			
1962	Zaglebie Sosnowiec	2–1	Górnik Zabrze
1963	Zaglebie Sosnowiec	2–0	Ruch Chorzów
1964	Legia Warszawa	2–1	Polonia Bytom
1965	Górnik Zabrze	4–0	Czarni Zagan
1966	Legia Warszawa	2–1	Górnik Zabrze
1967	Wisla Kraków	2–0	Rakow Czestochowa
1968	Górnik Zabrze	3–0	Ruch Chorzów
1969	Górnik Zabrze	2–0	Legia Warszawa
1970	Górnik Zabrze	3–1	Ruch Chorzów
1971	Górnik Zabrze	3–1	Zaglebie Sosnowiec
1972	Górnik Zabrze	5–2	Legia Warszawa
1973	Legia Warszawa	0–0 (4–2p)	Polonia Bytom
1974	Ruch Chorzów	2–0	Gwardia Warszawa
1975	Stal Rzeszów	0–0 (3–2p)	ROW II Rybnik
1976	Slask Wroclaw	2–0	Stal Mielec
1977	Zaglebie Sosnowiec	1–0	Polonia Bytom
1978	Zaglebie Sosnowiec	2–0	Piast Gliwice
1979	Arka Gdynia	2–1	Wisla Kraków
1980	Legia Warszawa	5–0	Lech Poznan
1981	Legia Warszawa	1–0	Pogon Szczecin
1982	Lech Poznan	1–0	Pogon Szczecin
1983	Lechia Gdansk	2–1	Piast Gliwice
1984	Lech Poznan	3–0	Wisla Kraków
1985	Widzew Lódz	0–0 (3–1p)	GKS Katowice
1986	GKS Katowice	4–1	Górnik Zabrze
1987	Slask Wroclaw	0–0 (4–3p)	GKS Katowice
1988	Lech Poznan	1–1 (3–2p)	Legia Warszawa
1989	Legia Warszawa	5–2	Jagiellonia Bialystok
1990	Legia Warszawa	2–0	GKS Katowice
1991	GKS Katowice	1–0	Legia Warszawa
1992	Miedz Legnica	1–1 (4–3p)	Gornik Zabrze

INTERNATIONAL MATCHES PLAYED BY POLAND

Date	Opponents	Result		Venue	Compet	Scorers
18–12–1921	Hungary	L	0–1	Budapest	Fr	
14–05–1922	Hungary	L	0–3	Krakow	Fr	
28–05	Sweden	W	2–1	Stockholm	Fr	Klotz, Garbien
3–09	Romania	D	1–1	Czernowitz	Fr	Dluzniak
1–10	Yugoslavia	W	3–1	Zagreb	Fr	Kaluza 2, Garbien
3–06–1923	Yugoslavia	L	1–2	Krakow	Fr	Kaluza
2–09	Romania	D	1–1	Lwow	Fr	Kuchar W
23–09	Finland	L	3–5	Helsinki	Fr	Stalinski 2, Miller J
25–09	Estonia	W	4–1	Tallin	Fr	Kowalski W 2, Stalinski, Batsch
1–11	Sweden	D	2–2	Krakow	Fr	Stalinski 2
18–05–1924	Sweden	L	1–5	Stockholm	Fr	Batsch
26–05	Hungary	L	0–5	Paris	OGr1	
10–06	United States	L	2–3	Warsaw	Fr	Czulak, Chruscinski
29–06	Turkey	W	2–0	Lodz	Fr	Balcer, Reyman (I)
10–08	Finland	W	1–0	Warsaw	Fr	Reyman (I)
31–08	Hungary	L	0–4	Budapest	Fr	
23–05–1925	Czechoslovakia	L	1–2	Prague	Fr	Batsch
19–07	Hungary	L	0–2	Krakow	Fr	
30–08	Finland	D	2–2	Helsinki	Fr	Stalinski, Kaluza
2–09	Estonia	D	0–0	Tallin	Fr	
2–10	Turkey	W	2–1	Istanbul	Fr	Adamek, Sperling
1–11	Sweden	L	2–6	Krakow	Fr	Kuchar W, Sperling
6–06–1926	Czechoslovakia	L	1–2	Krakow	Fr	Kuchar W
4–07	Estonia	W	2–0	Warsaw	Fr	Tupalski, Sobota
8–08	Finland	W	7–1	Poznan	Fr	Batsch 4, Stalinski 3
20–08	Hungary	L	1–4	Budapest	Fr	Stalinski
12–09	Turkey	W	6–1	Lwow	Fr	Steuermann 3, Batsch 2, Balcer
3–10	Sweden	L	1–3	Stockholm	Fr	Adamek
7–10	Norway	W	4–3	Fredrikstad	Fr	Kaluza 2, Balcer 2
19–06–1927	Romania	D	3–3	Bucharest	Fr	Kaluza, Wojcik, Pazurek K
10–06–1928	United States	D	3–3	Warsaw	Fr	Kuchar W 2, Steuermann
1–07	Sweden	W	2–1	Katowice	Fr	Kuchar W, Stalinski
27–10	Czechoslovakia	L	2–3	Prague	Fr	Reyman (I) 2
28–09–1930	Sweden	W	3–0	Stockholm	Fr	Ciszewski 2, Smoczek
26–10	Latvia	W	6–0	Warsaw	Fr	Nawrot 4, Malik, Balcer
14–06–1931	Czechoslovakia	L	0–4	Warsaw	Fr	
5–08	Latvia	W	5–0	Riga	Fr	Kossok K 2, Kisielinski 2, Reyman (I)
23–08	Romania	L	2–3	Warsaw	Fr	Wypijewski, Nawrot
11–10	Belgium	L	1–2	Brussels	Fr	Wypijewski
25–10	Yugoslavia	W	6–3	Poznan	Fr	Balcer 3, Kniola 2, Martyna

29-05-1932	Yugoslavia	W	3-0	Zagreb	Fr	Nawrot 2, Ciszewski
10-07	Sweden	W	2-0	Warsaw	Fr	Nawrot, Bator
2-10	Romania	W	5-0	Bucharest	Fr	Nawrot 3, Urban, Matyas M
2-10	Latvia	W	2-1	Warsaw	Fr	Kossok K, Radojewski
4-06-1933	Belgium	L	0-1	Warsaw	Fr	
10-09	Yugoslavia	W	4-3	Warsaw	Fr	Nawrot 2, Majowski, Król
15-10	Czechoslovakia	L	1-2	Warsaw	WCq	Martyna
3-12	Germany	L	0-1	Berlin	Fr	
21-05-1934	Denmark	L	2-4	Copenhagen	Fr	Nawrot 2
23-05	Sweden	L	2-4	Stockholm	Fr	Nawrot, Wilimowski
26-08	Yugoslavia	L	1-4	Belgrade	Fr	Wilimowski
9-09	Germany	L	2-5	Warsaw	Fr	Wilimowski, Pazurek
14-10	Romania	D	3-3	Lwow	Fr	Martyna 2, Urban
14-10	Latvia	W	6-2	Riga	Fr	Wodarz, Lysakowski, Peterek, Pazurek
12-05-1935	Austria	L	2-5	Vienna	Fr	Matyas M 2
18-08	Yugoslavia	L	2-3	Katowice	Fr	Matyas M, Peterek
15-09	Germany	L	0-1	Breslau	Fr	
15-09	Latvia	D	3-3	Lodz	Fr	Malczyk S, Smoczek
6-10	Austria	W	1-0	Warsaw	Fr	Matyas M
3-11	Romania	L	1-4	Bucharest	Fr	Pazurek
16-02-1936	Belgium	W	2-0	Brussels	Fr	Piec T, God
5-08	Hungary	W	3-0	Berlin	OGr1	God 2, Wodarz
8-08	Great Britain	W	5-4	Berlin	OGqf	Wodarz 3, God, Piec T
11-08	Austria	L	1-3	Berlin	OGsf	God
13-08	Norway	L	2-3	Berlin	OG3p	Wodarz, Peterek
6-09	Yugoslavia	L	3-9	Belgrade	Fr	Peterek 2, Wodarz
6-09	Latvia	D	3-3	Riga	Fr	Matyas M, Wostal, Schwarz
13-09	Germany	D	1-1	Warsaw	Fr	Wodarz
4-10	Denmark	L	1-2	Copenhagen	Fr	God
23-06-1937	Sweden	W	3-1	Warsaw	Fr	Wilimowski, Wodarz, Piontek
4-07	Romania	L	2-4	Lodz	Fr	Piontek, Matyas M
12-09	Denmark	W	3-1	Warsaw	Fr	Wilimowski, Król, Piec T
12-09	Bulgaria	D	3-3	Sofia	Fr	Korbas 3
10-10	Yugoslavia	W	4-0	Warsaw	WCq	Piontek 2, Wilimowski, Wostal
10-10	Latvia	W	2-1	Katowice	Fr	Piec T, Pytel
13-03-1938	Switzerland	D	3-3	Zurich	Fr	Wilimowski, Piontek, Wostal
3-04	Yugoslavia	L	0-1	Belgrade	WCq	
22-05	Rep. Ireland	W	6-0	Warsaw	Fr	Piontek 2, Wodarz 2, Wilimowski, Wasiewicz
5-06	Brazil	L	5-6	Strasbourg	WCr1	Wilimowski 4, Scherfke
18-09	Germany	L	1-4	Chemnitz	Fr	Peterek
25-09	Yugoslavia	D	4-4	Warsaw	Fr	Wilimowski 2, Piontek, Korbas
25-09	Latvia	L	1-2	Riga	Fr	Habowski
23-10	Norway	D	2-2	Warsaw	Fr	Wilimowski, Piec T
13-11	Rep. Ireland	L	2-3	Dublin	Fr	Wilimowski, Piontek
22-01-1939	France	L	0-4	Paris	Fr	
27-05	Belgium	D	3-3	Lodz	Fr	Wilimowski 2, Wostal
4-06	Switzerland	D	1-1	Warsaw	Fr	Piontek
27-08	Hungary	W	4-2	Warsaw	Fr	Wilimowski 3, Piontek
11-06-1947	Norway	L	1-3	Oslo	Fr	Jablonski
19-07	Romania	L	1-2	Warsaw	Fr	Cieslik
31-08	Czechoslovakia	L	3-6	Prague	Fr	Cieslik 2, Hogendorf
14-09	Sweden	L	4-5	Stockholm	Fr	Gracz 2, Cieslik, Hogendorf
17-09	Finland	W	4-1	Helsinki	Fr	Cieslik 2, Spodzieja 2
19-10	Yugoslavia	L	1-7	Belgrade	Fr	Cieslik
26-10	Romania	D	0-0	Bucharest	Fr	
4-04-1948	Bulgaria	D	1-1	Sofia	BCE	Parpan T
18-04	Czechoslovakia	W	3-1	Warsaw	BCE	Cieslik, Gracz, Spodzieja
26-06	Denmark	L	0-8	Copenhagen	Fr	
25-08	Yugoslavia	L	0-1	Warsaw	BCE	
19-09	Hungary	L	2-6	Warsaw	BCE	Cieslik, Kohut J
10-10	Romania	D	0-0	Chorzow	BCE	
17-10	Finland	W	1-0	Warsaw	Fr	Cieslik
8-05-1949	Romania	L	1-2	Bucharest	Fr	Mamon
19-06	Denmark	L	1-2	Warsaw	Fr	Kokot A
10-07	Hungary	L	2-8	Debrecen	Fr	Mamon, Spodzieja
2-10	Bulgaria	W	3-2	Warsaw	Fr	Cieslik 2, Alszer
30-10	Czechoslovakia	L	0-2	Vitkovice	Fr	
6-11	Albania	W	2-1	Warsaw	Fr	Cieslik, Kohut J

1-05-1950	Albania	D	0-0	Tirana	Fr	
14-05	Romania	D	3-3	Wroclaw	Fr	Cieslik 3
4-06	Hungary	L	2-5	Warsaw	Fr	Cieslik, Mordarski
22-10	Czechoslovakia	L	1-4	Warsaw	Fr	Gracz
30-10	Bulgaria	W	1-0	Sofia	Fr	Cieslik
27-05-1951	Hungary	L	0-6	Budapest	Fr	
18-05-1952	Bulgaria	L	0-1	Warsaw	Fr	
25-05	Romania	L	0-1	Bucharest	Fr	
15-06	Hungary	L	1-5	Warsaw	Fr	Alszer
21-07	Denmark	L	0-2	Turku	OGr2	
14-09	Czechoslovakia	D	2-2	Prague	Fr	Mordarski, Wisniewski
21-09	East Germany	W	3-0	Warsaw	Fr	Aniola T 2, Trampisz
10-05-1953	Czechoslovakia	D	1-1	Wroclaw	Fr	Kohut J
13-09	Bulgaria	D	2-2	Sofia	Fr	Sobek, Wisniewski
29-11	Albania	L	0-2	Tirana	Fr	
8-08-1954	Bulgaria	D	2-2	Warsaw	Fr	Trampisz 2
26-09	East Germany	W	1-0	Rostock	Fr	Cieslik
29-05-1955	Romania	D	2-2	Bucharest	Fr	Cieslik, Hachorek
26-06	Bulgaria	D	1-1	Sofia	Fr	Brychczy
11-09	Finland	W	3-1	Helsinki	Fr	Cieslik 2, Kempny
30-05-1956	Norway	D	0-0	Oslo	Fr	
15-07	Hungary	L	1-4	Budapest	Fr	Kempny
22-07	East Germany	L	0-2	Chorzow	Fr	
26-08	Bulgaria	L	1-2	Wroclaw	Fr	Pol E
28-10	Norway	W	5-3	Warsaw	Fr	Pol E 4, Kempny
4-11	Finland	W	5-0	Krakow	Fr	Kempny 2, Brychczy, Kowal, Baszkiewicz
16-11	Turkey	D	1-1	Istanbul	Fr	Pol E
19-05-1957	Turkey	L	0-1	Warsaw	Fr	
23-06	Soviet Union	L	0-3	Moscow	WCq	
5-07	Finland	W	3-1	Helsinki	WCq	Jankowski 3
29-09	Bulgaria	D	1-1	Sofia	Fr	Brychczy
20-10	Soviet Union	W	2-1	Chorzow	WCq	Cieslik 2
3-11	Finland	W	4-0	Warsaw	WCq	Brychczy 2, Jankowski, Gawlik
24-11	Soviet Union	L	0-2	Leipzig	WCq	
11-05-1958	Rep. Ireland	D	2-2	Chorzow	Fr	Cieslik, Zientara
25-05	Denmark	L	2-3	Copenhagen	Fr	Cieslik, Lentner
1-06	Scotland	L	1-2	Warsaw	Fr	Cieslik
28-06	East Germany	D	1-1	Rostock	Fr	Kempny
14-09	Hungary	L	1-3	Chorzow	Fr	OG
5-10	Rep. Ireland	D	2-2	Dublin	Fr	Pol E 2
20-05-1959	West Germany	D	1-1	Hamburg	Fr	Baszkiewicz
21-06	Israel	W	7-2	Wroclaw	Fr	Liberda 2, Hachorek 2, Szarzynski 2, Baszkiewicz
28-06	Spain	L	2-4	Chorzow	ECr1	Pol E, Brychczy
30-08	Romania	L	2-3	Warsaw	Fr	Pol E 2
14-10	Spain	L	0-3	Madrid	ECr1	
18-10	Finland	W	3-1	Helsinki	OGq	Pol E, Hachorek, Gawronski
8-11	Finland	W	6-2	Chorzow	OGq	Pol E 3, Hachorek, Sykta, Szarzynski
29-11	Israel	D	1-1	Tel Aviv	Fr	Pol E
4-05-1960	Scotland	W	3-2	Glasgow	Fr	Pol E, Brychczy, Baszkiewicz
19-05	Soviet Union	L	1-7	Moscow	Fr	Pol E
26-06	Bulgaria	W	4-0	Chorzow	Fr	Hachorek 2, Lentner, Zientara
26-08	Tunisia	W	6-1	Rome	OGr1	Pol E 5, Hachorek
29-08	Denmark	L	1-2	Livorno	OGr1	Gadecki
1-09	Argentina	L	0-2	Naples	OGr1	
28-09	France	D	2-2	Warsaw	Fr	Faber, Norkowski M
13-11	Hungary	L	1-4	Budapest	Fr	Pol E
21-05-1961	Soviet Union	W	1-0	Warsaw	Fr	Pol E
4-06	Yugoslavia	L	1-2	Belgrade	WCq	Brychczy
25-06	Yugoslavia	D	1-1	Chorzow	WCq	Schmidt J
8-10	West Germany	L	0-2	Warsaw	Fr	
22-10	East Germany	W	3-1	Wroclaw	Fr	Pol E 2, Lentner
5-11	Denmark	W	5-0	Chorzow	Fr	Pol E 3, Gajda 2
11-04-1962	France	W	3-1	Paris	Fr	Pol E, Lentner, Brychczy
15-04	Morocco	W	3-1	Casablanca	Fr	Brychczy, Jarek, Wilczek
23-05	Belgium	W	2-0	Warsaw	Fr	Brychczy, Lentner
2-09	Hungary	L	0-2	Poznan	Fr	
30-09	Bulgaria	L	1-2	Sofia	Fr	Faber
10-10	Nth. Ireland	L	0-2	Chorzow	ECr1	

11–10	Morocco	D	1–1	Warsaw	Fr	Wilczek
28–10	Czechoslovakia	L	1–2	Bratislava	Fr	Lentner
28–11	Nth. Ireland	L	0–2	Belfast	ECr1	
15–05–1963	Norway	W	5–2	Oslo	Fr	Faber 2, Brychczy 2, Galeczka
22–05	Greece	W	4–0	Warsaw	Fr	Brychczy 2, Galeczka 2
2–06	Romania	D	1–1	Chorzow	Fr	Faber
4–09	Norway	W	9–0	Szczecin	Fr	Faber 2, Bazan 2, Szoltysik 2, Blaut B, Lubanski, Galeczka
22–09	Turkey	D	0–0	Poznan	Fr	
16–10	Greece	L	1–3	Athens	Fr	Musialek
10–05–1964	Rep. Ireland	W	3–1	Krakow	Fr	Faber, Szoltysik, Wilim (I)
13–09	Czechoslovakia	W	2–1	Warsaw	Fr	Pol E 2
27–09	Turkey	W	3–2	Istanbul	Fr	Pol E, Lubanski, Banas
7–10	Sweden	D	3–3	Stockholm	Fr	Liberda 2, Pol E
25–10	Rep. Ireland	L	2–3	Dublin	Fr	Pol E, Lubanski
7–04–1965	Belgium	D	0–0	Brussels	Fr	
18–04	Italy	D	0–0	Warsaw	WCq	
16–05	Bulgaria	D	1–1	Krakow	Fr	Pol E
23–05	Scotland	D	1–1	Chorzow	WCq	Lentner
26–09	Finland	L	0–2	Helsinki	WCq	
13–10	Scotland	W	2–1	Glasgow	WCq	Pol E, Sadek
24–10	Finland	W	7–0	Szczecin	WCq	Lubanski 4, Sadek 2, Pol E
1–11	Italy	L	1–6	Rome	WCq	Lubanski
5–01–1966	England	D	1–1	Liverpool	Fr	Sadek
3–05	Hungary	D	1–1	Chorzow	Fr	Lubanski
18–05	Sweden	D	1–1	Wroclaw	Fr	Oslizlo
5–06	Brazil	L	1–4	Belo Horizonte	Fr	Liberda
8–06	Brazil	L	1–2	Rio de Janeiro	Fr	Liberda
11–06	Argentina	D	1–1	Buenos Aires	Fr	Liberda
5–07	England	L	0–1	Chorzow	Fr	
11–09	East Germany	L	0–2	Erfurt	Fr	
2–10	Luxembourg	W	4–0	Szczecin	ECq	Sadek, Liberda, Jarosik, Grzegorczyk
22–10	France	L	1–2	Paris	ECq	Grzegorczyk
17–11	Romania	L	3–4	Ploesti	Fr	Galeczka, Jarosik, Strzalkowski
16–04–1967	Luxembourg	D	0–0	Luxembourg	ECq	
21–05	Belgium	W	3–1	Chorzow	ECq	Lubanski 2, Szoltysik
20–07	Soviet Union	L	0–1	Warsaw	OGq	
4–08	Soviet Union	L	1–2	Moscow	OGq	Lubanski
17–09	France	L	1–4	Warsaw	ECq	Brychczy
8–10	Belgium	W	4–2	Brussels	ECq	Zmijewski 3, Brychczy
29–10	Romania	D	0–0	Krakow	Fr	
24–04–1968	Turkey	W	8–0	Chorzow	Fr	Faber 3, Lubanski 3, Bula, Zmijewski
1–05	Holland	D	0–0	Warsaw	Fr	
15–05	Rep. Ireland	D	2–2	Dublin	Fr	Lubanski, Jarosik
9–06	Norway	W	6–1	Oslo	Fr	Jarosik 3, Zmijewski 2, Lubanski
20–06	Brazil	L	3–6	Warsaw	Fr	Sadek, Zmijewski, Blaut B
20–10	East Germany	D	1–1	Szczecin	Fr	Gadocha
30–10	Rep. Ireland	W	1–0	Chorzow	Fr	Lubanski
20–04–1969	Luxembourg	W	8–1	Krakow	WCq	Lubanski 5, Deyna 2, Wilim
30–04	Turkey	W	3–1	Ankara	Fr	Wilim 2, Lubanski
7–05	Holland	L	0–1	Rotterdam	WCq	
15–06	Bulgaria	L	1–4	Sofia	WCq	Deyna
27–08	Norway	W	6–1	Lodz	Fr	Lubanski 2, Marx 2, Deyna, Brychczy
7–09	Holland	W	2–1	Chorzow	WCq	Lubanski, Jarosik
12–10	Luxembourg	W	5–1	Luxembourg	WCq	Deyna 2, Lubanski, Jarosik, Bula
9–11	Bulgaria	W	3–0	Warsaw	WCq	Jarosik 2, Deyna
2–05–1970	Hungary	L	0–2	Budapest	Fr	
6–05	Rep. Ireland	W	2–1	Poznan	Fr	Kozerski, Szoltysik
16–05	East Germany	D	1–1	Krakow	Fr	Deyna
19–05	Denmark	W	2–0	Copenhagen	Fr	Jarosik, Banas
22–07	Iraq	W	2–0	Szczecin	Fr	Banas, Szoltysik
2–09	Denmark	W	5–0	Warsaw	Fr	Marx 3, Lubanski, Deyna
6–09	East Germany	L	0–5	Rostock	Fr	
23–09	Rep. Ireland	W	2–0	Dublin	Fr	Szoltysik, Stachurski
14–10	Albania	W	3–0	Chorzow	ECq	Lubanski, Gadocha, Szoltysik
25–10	Czechoslovakia	D	2–2	Prague	Fr	Blaut B, Kozerski
5–05–1971	Switzerland	W	4–2	Lausanne	Fr	Lubanski, Deyna, Szoltysik, Banas
12–05	Albania	D	1–1	Tirana	ECq	Banas
22–09	Turkey	W	5–1	Krakow	ECq	Lubanski 3, Gadocha, Bula

10–10	West Germany	L	1–3	Warsaw	ECq	Gadocha
17–11	West Germany	D	0–0	Hamburg	ECq	
5–12	Turkey	L	0–1	Izmir	ECq	
16–04–1972	Bulgaria	L	1–3	Stara Zagora	OGq	Lubanski
7–05	Bulgaria	W	3–0	Warsaw	OGq	Banao 2, Marx
10–05	Switzerland	D	0–0	Poznan	Fr	
28–08	Colombia*	W	5–1	Ingolstadt	OGr1	Gadocha 3, Deyna 2
30–08	Ghana	W	4–0	Regensburg	OGr1	Gadocha 2, Lubanski, Deyna
1–09	East Germany	W	2–1	Nuremberg	OGr1	Gorgon 2
3–09	Denmark	D	1–1	Regensburg	OGr2	Deyna
5–09	Soviet Union	W	2–1	Augsburg	OGr2	Deyna, Szoltysik
8–09	Morocco	W	5–0	Nuremberg	OGr2	Deyna 2, Kmiecik, Lubanski, Gadocha
10–09	Hungary*	W	2–1	Munich	OGf	Deyna 2
15–10	Czechoslovakia	W	3–0	Bydgoszcz	Fr	Deyna 2, Gadocha
20–03–1973	United States	W	4–0	Lodz	Fr	Lubanski 3, Kasperczak
28–03	Wales	L	0–2	Cardiff	WCq	
13–05	Yugoslavia	D	2–2	Warsaw	Fr	Lubanski, Masztaler
16–05	Rep. Ireland	W	2–0	Wroclaw	Fr	Lubanski 2
6–06	England	W	2–0	Chorzow	WCq	Lubanski, Banas
1–08	Canada	W	3–1	Toronto	Fr	Gadocha 2, Gorgon
3–08	United States	W	1–0	Chicago	Fr	Kasperczak
5–08	Mexico	W	1–0	Los Angeles	Fr	Gorgon
8–08	Mexico	W	2–1	Monterrey	Fr	Gadocha, Gorgon
10–08	United States	W	4–0	San Francisco	Fr	Kmiecik 2, Kasztelan, Szarmach
12–08	United States	L	0–1	New Britain	Fr	
19–08	Bulgaria	W	2–0	Varna	Fr	Lato 2
26–09	Wales	W	3–0	Chorzow	WCq	Lato, Gadocha, Domarski
10–10	Holland	D	1–1	Rotterdam	Fr	Deyna
17–10	England	D	1–1	London	WCq	Domarski
21–10	Rep. Ireland	L	0–1	Dublin	Fr	
17–04–1974	Belgium	D	1–1	Liege	Fr	Deyna
15–05	Greece	W	2–0	Warsaw	Fr	Lato, Jakobczak
15–06	Argentina	W	3–2	Stuttgart	WCr1	Lato 2, Szarmach
19–06	Haiti	W	7–0	Munich	WCr1	Szarmach 3, Lato 2, Deyna, Gorgon
23–06	Italy	W	2–1	Stuttgart	WCr1	Deyna, Szarmach
26–06	Sweden	W	1–0	Stuttgart	WCr2	Lato
30–06	Yugoslavia	W	2–1	Frankfurt	WCr2	Lato, Deyna
3–07	West Germany	L	0–1	Frankfurt	WCr2	
6–07	Brazil	W	1–0	Munich	WC3p	Lato
1–09	Finland	W	2–1	Helsinki	ECq	Lato, Szarmach
4–09	East Germany	L	1–3	Warsaw	Fr	Lato
7–09	France	L	0–2	Wroclaw	Fr	
9–10	Finland	W	3–0	Poznan	ECq	Lato, Gadocha, Kasperczak
31–10	Canada	W	2–0	Warsaw	Fr	Kasalik, Jakobczak
13–11	Czechoslovakia	D	2–2	Prague	Fr	Szarmach, Gadocha
26–03–1975	United States	W	7–0	Poznan	Fr	Deyna 3, Lato 2, Szarmach 2
19–04	Italy	D	0–0	Rome	ECq	
28–05	East Germany	W	2–1	Halle	Fr	Lato, Marx
24–06	United States	W	4–0	Seattle	Fr	Lato, Szarmach, Bula, Wyrobek
6–07	Canada	W	8–1	Montreal	Fr	Lato 3, Deyna 2, Szarmach, Marx, Bula
9–07	Canada	W	4–1	Toronto	Fr	Szarmach 2, Deyna, Kwiatkowski
10–09	Holland	W	4–1	Chorzow	ECq	Szarmach 2, Gadocha, Lato
8–10	Hungary	W	4–2	Lodz	Fr	Marx 2, Kmiecik, Kasperczak
15–10	Holland	L	0–3	Amsterdam	ECq	
26–10	Italy	D	0–0	Warsaw	ECq	
24–03–1976	Argentina	L	1–2	Chorzow	Fr	Kmiecik
24–04	France	L	0–2	Lens	Fr	
6–05	Greece	L	0–1	Athens	Fr	
11–05	Switzerland	L	1–2	Basle	Fr	Boniek
26–05	Rep. Ireland	L	0–2	Poznan	Fr	
18–07	Cuba	D	0–0	Montreal	OGr1	
22–07	Iran	W	3–2	Montreal	OGr1	Szarmach 2, Deyna
25–07	North Korea	W	5–0	Montreal	OGqf	Szarmach 2, Lato 2, Szymanowski
27–07	Brazil*	W	2–0	Toronto	OGsf	Szarmach 2
30–07	East Germany	L	1–3	Montreal	OGf	Lato
16–10	Portugal	W	2–0	Oporto	WCq	Lato 2
31–10	Cyprus	W	5–0	Warsaw	WCq	Deyna 2, Boniek, Szarmach, Terlecki
13–04–1977	Hungary	L	1–2	Budapest	Fr	Nawalka
24–04	Rep. Ireland	D	0–0	Dublin	Fr	

* Not full International

1–05	Denmark	W	2–1	Copenhagen	WCq	Lubanski 2
15–05	Cyprus	W	3–1	Limassol	WCq	Lato, Terlecki, Mazur
29–05	Argentina	L	1–3	Buenos Aires	Fr	Lato
10–06	Peru	W	3–1	Lima	Fr	Szarmach, Deyna, Kasperczak
12–06	Bolivia	W	2–1	La Paz	Fr	Lato, Kapka
19–06	Brazil	L	1–3	Sao Paulo	Fr	Boniek
24–08	Austria	L	1–2	Vienna	Fr	Kmiecik
7–09	Soviet Union	L	1–4	Volgograd	Fr	Lato
21–09	Denmark	W	4–1	Chorzow	WCq	Lato, Deyna, Szarmach, Masztaler
29–10	Portugal	D	1–1	Chorzow	WCq	Deyna
12–11	Sweden	W	2–1	Wroclaw	Fr	Deyna, Kusto
22–03–1978	Luxembourg	W	3–1	Luxembourg	Fr	Szarmach 2, Lubanski
5–04	Greece	W	5–2	Poznan	Fr	Deyna 2, Lato, Boniek, Zmuda
12–04	Rep. Ireland	W	3–0	Lodz	Fr	Deyna, Boniek, Mazur
26–04	Bulgaria	W	1–0	Warsaw	Fr	Lato
1–06	West Germany	D	0–0	Buenos Aires	WCr1	
6–06	Tunisia	W	1–0	Rosario	WCr1	Lato
0–06	Mexico	W	3–1	Rosario	WCr1	Boniek 2, Deyna
14–06	Argentina	L	0–2	Rosario	WCr2	
18–06	Peru	W	1–0	Mendoza	WCr2	Szarmach
21–06	Brazil	L	1–3	Mendoza	WCr2	Lato
30–08	Finland	W	1–0	Helsinki	Fr	Majewski S
6–09	Iceland	W	2–0	Reykjavik	ECq	Lato, Kusto
11–10	Romania	L	0–1	Bucharest	Fr	
15–11	Switzerland	W	2–0	Wroclaw	ECq	Boniek, Ogaza
18–02–1979	Tunisia	W	2–0	Tunis	Fr	Ogaza 2
21–03	Algeria	W	1–0	Algiers	Fr	Lato
4–04	Hungary	D	1–1	Chorzow	Fr	Lato
18–04	East Germany	L	1–2	Leipzig	ECq	Boniek
2–05	Holland	W	2–0	Chorzow	ECq	Boniek, Mazur
19–08	Libya	W	5–0	Slupsk	Fr	Kmiecik, Terlecki, Faber, Janas, Wieczorek
29–08	Romania	W	3–0	Warsaw	Fr	Lato, Boniek, Terlecki
12–09	Switzerland	W	2–0	Lausanne	ECq	Terlecki 2
26–09	East Germany	D	1–1	Chorzow	ECq	Wieczorek
10–10	Iceland	W	2–0	Krakow	ECq	Ogaza 2
17–10	Holland	D	1–1	Amsterdam	ECq	Rudy
27–02–1980	Iraq	D	1–1	Baghdad	Fr	Palasz
26–03	Hungary	L	1–2	Budapest	Fr	Lato
2–04	Belgium	L	1–2	Brussels	Fr	Lato
19–04	Italy	D	2–2	Turin	Fr	Szarmach, Sybis
26–04	Yugoslavia	L	1–2	Borovo	Fr	Sybis
13–05	West Germany	L	1–3	Frankfurt	Fr	Boniek
28–05	Scotland	W	1–0	Poznan	Fr	Boniek
22–06	Iraq	W	3–0	Warsaw	Fr	Lato, Kmiecik, Iwan
29–06	Brazil	D	1–1	Sao Paulo	Fr	Lato
2–07	Bolivia	W	1–0	Santa Cruz	Fr	Iwan
9–07	Colombia	W	4–1	Bogota	Fr	Iwan 3, Terlecki
24–09	Czechoslovakia	D	1–1	Chorzow	Fr	Lubanski
12–10	Argentina	L	1–2	Buenos Aires	Fr	Ciolek
12–11	Spain	W	2–1	Barcelona	Fr	Iwan 2
19–11	Algeria	W	5–1	Krakow	Fr	Iwan 2, Ciolek, Kupcewicz, Dziuba
7–12	Malta	W	2–0	Gzira	WCq	Smolarek, Lipka
25–03–1981	Romania	L	0–2	Bucharest	Fr	
2–05	East Germany	W	1–0	Chorzow	WCq	Buncol
24–05	Rep. Ireland	W	3–0	Bydgoszcz	Fr	Iwan, Ogaza, OG
2–09	West Germany	L	0–2	Chorzow	Fr	
23–09	Portugal	L	0–2	Lisbon	Fr	
10–10	East Germany	W	3–2	Leipzig	WCq	Szarmach 2, Smolarek
28–10	Argentina	W	2–1	Buenos Aires	Fr	Boniek, Buncol

LEADING INTERNATIONAL APPEARANCES

1	Lato	104		Boniek	80
2	Deyna	102	7	Gadocha	65
3	Zmuda	92		Tomaszewski	65
4	Szymanowski	87	9	Kasperczak	63
5	Lubanski	80	10	Dziekanowski	62

15–11	Malta	W	6–0	Wroclaw	WCq	Smolarek 2, Boniek, Buncol, Majewski S, Dziekanowski
18–11	Spain	L	2–3	Lodz	Fr	Boniek, Palasz
14–06–1982	Italy	D	0–0	Vigo	WCr1	
19–06	Cameroon	D	0–0	La Coruna	WCr1	
22–06	Peru	W	5–1	La Coruna	WCr1	Lato, Boniek, Buncol, Smolarek, Ciolek
28–06	Belgium	W	3–0	Barcelona	WCr2	Boniek 3
4–07	Soviet Union	D	0–0	Barcelona	WCr2	
8–07	Italy	L	0–2	Barcelona	WCsf	
10–07	France	W	3–2	Alicante	WC3p	Szarmach, Kupcewicz, Majewski S
31–08	France	W	4–0	Paris	Fr	Kupcewicz 2, Buncol, Locha
8–09	Finland	W	3–2	Kuopio	ECq	Smolarek, Dziekanowski, Kupcewicz
10–10	Portugal	L	1–2	Lisbon	ECq	Król
23–03–1983	Bulgaria	W	3–1	Lodz	Fr	Majewski, Dziekanowski, Okonski
17–04	Finland	D	1–1	Warsaw	ECq	Smolarek
22–05	Soviet Union	D	1–1	Chorzow	ECq	Boniek
7–09	Romania	D	2–2	Krakow	Fr	Ciolek, Iwan
9–10	Soviet Union	L	0–2	Moscow	ECq	
28–10	Portugal	L	0–1	Wroclaw	ECq	
11–01–1984	India	W	2–1	Calcutta	Fr	Dziekanowski, Pawlak
15–01	China	W	1–0	Calcutta	Fr	Adamiec
17–01	Argentina	D	1–1	Calcutta	Fr	Buncol
27–01	China	W	1–0	Calcutta	Fr	Wójcicki
27–03	Switzerland	D	1–1	Zurich	Fr	Boniek
17–04	Belgium	L	0–1	Warsaw	Fr	
23–05	Rep. Ireland	D	0–0	Dublin	Fr	
29–08	Norway	D	1–1	Drammen	Fr	Tarasiewicz
12–09	Finland	W	2–0	Helsinki	Fr	Dziekanowski, Palasz
26–09	Turkey	W	2–0	Slupsk	Fr	Dziekanowski 2
17–10	Greece	W	3–1	Zabrze	WCq	Dziekanowski 2, Smolarek
31–10	Albania	D	2–2	Mielec	WCq	Palasz, Smolarek
8–12	Italy	L	0–2	Pescara	Fr	
5–02–1985	Mexico	L	0–5	Queretaro	Fr	
7–02	Bulgaria	D	2–2	Queretaro	Fr	Dziekanowski, Prusik
10–02	Colombia	W	2–1	Bogota	Fr	Palasz 2
14–02	Colombia	L	0–1	Cali	Fr	
27–03	Romania	D	0–0	Sibiu	Fr	
17–04	Finland	W	2–1	Opole	Fr	Palasz, Zmuda
1–05	Belgium	L	0–2	Brussels	WCq	
19–05	Greece	W	4–1	Athens	WCq	Boniek, Smolarek, Dziekanowski, Ostrowski
30–05	Albania	W	1–0	Tirana	WCq	Boniek
21–08	Sweden	L	0–1	Malmo	Fr	
4–09	Czechoslovakia	L	1–3	Brno	Fr	Prusik
11–09	Belgium	D	0–0	Chorzow	WCq	
16–11	Italy	W	1–0	Chorzow	Fr	Dziekanowski
8–12	Tunisia	L	0–1	Tunis	Fr	
11–12	Turkey	D	1–1	Adana	Fr	Furtok
16–02–1986	Uruguay	D	2–2	Montevideo	Fr	Baran K 2
26–03	Spain	L	0–3	Cadiz	Fr	
16–05	Denmark	L	0–1	Copenhagen	Fr	
2–06	Morocco	D	0–0	Monterrey	WCr1	
7–06	Portugal	W	1–0	Monterrey	WCr1	Smolarek
11–06	England	L	0–3	Monterrey	WCr1	
16–06	Brazil	L	0–4	Guadalajara	WCr2	
7–10	North Korea	D	2–2	Bydgoszcz	Fr	Karas, Tarasiewicz
15–10	Greece	W	2–1	Poznan	ECq	Dziekanowski 2

LEADING INTERNATIONAL GOALSCORERS

1	Lubanski	50
2	Deyna	45
	Lato	45
4	Pol	40
5	Szarmach	33
6	Cieslik	27
7	Boniek	24
8	Wilimowski	21
9	Gadocha	20
10	Dziekanowski	19
11	Brychczy	18
12	Nawrot	16
13	Smolarek	13
14	Kosecki	12

12–11	Rep. Ireland	W	1–0	Warsaw	Fr	Koniarek
19–11	Holland	D	0–0	Amsterdam	ECq	
18–03–1987	Finland	W	3–1	Rybnik	Fr	Lesniak, Furtok, Urban
24–03	Norway	W	4–1	Wroclaw	Fr	Furtok, Urban, Prusik, Król
12–04	Cyprus	D	0–0	Gdansk	ECq	
29–04	Greece	L	0–1	Athens	ECq	
17–05	Hungary	L	3–5	Budapest	ECq	Smolarek, Wójcicki, Marciniak
19–08	East Germany	W	2–0	Lublin	Fr	Prusik, Król
2–09	Romania	W	3–1	Bydgoszcz	Fr	Lesniak 2, Rudy A
23–09	Hungary	W	3–2	Warsaw	ECq	Lesniak, Dziekanowski, Tarasiewicz
14–10	Holland	L	0–2	Zabrze	ECq	
27–10	Czechoslovakia	L	1–3	Bratislava	Fr	Tarasiewicz
11–11	Cyprus	W	1–0	Limassol	ECq	Lesniak
6–02–1988	Romania	D	2–2	Haifa	Fr	Cisek 2
10–02	Israel	W	3–1	Tel Aviv	Fr	Prusik, Kosecki, Kubicki
23–03	Nth. Ireland	D	1–1	Belfast	Fr	Dziekanowski
22–05	Rep. Ireland	L	1–3	Dublin	Fr	Warzycha R
1–06	Soviet Union	L	1–2	Moscow	Fr	Dziekanowski
13–07	United States	W	2–0	New Britain	Fr	Kosecki 2
15–07	Canada	W	2–1	Toronto	Fr	Rudy A Tarasiewicz
24–08	Bulgaria	W	3–2	Bialystok	Fr	Furtok, Rudy A, OG
21–09	East Germany	W	2–1	Cottbus	Fr	Furtok 2
19–10	Albania	W	1–0	Chorzow	WCq	Warzycha K
8–02–1989	Costa Rica	W	2–4	San Jose	Fr	Warzycha K 2, Kosecki, Urban
12–02	Guatemala	W	1–0	Guatemala City	Fr	Warzycha K
14–02	Mexico	L	1–3	Puebla	Fr	Kosecki
12–04	Romania	W	2–1	Warsaw	Fr	Urban, Tarasiewicz
2–05	Norway	W	3–0	Oslo	Fr	Furtok 2, Wdowczyk
3–06	Engand	L	0–3	London	WCq	
7–07	Sweden	L	1–2	Stockholm	WCq	Tarasiewicz
23–08	Soviet Union	D	1–1	Lublin	Fr	Wdowczyk
5–09	Greece	W	3–0	Warsaw	Fr	Warzycha R, Dziekanowski, Ziober
20–09	Spain	L	0–1	La Coruna	Fr	
11–10	England	D	0–0	Chorzow	WCq	
25–10	Sweden	L	0–2	Chorzow	WCq	
15–11	Albania	W	2–1	Tirana	WCq	Tarasiewicz, Ziober
2–02–1990	Iran	W	2–0	Tehran	Fr	Ziober 2
4–02	Iran	W	1–0	Tehran	Fr	Szewczyk
11–02	Kuwait	D	1–1	Cairo	Fr	Kosecki
28–03	Yugoslavia	D	0–0	Lodz	Fr	
4–05	Colombia	L	1–2	Chicago	Fr	Kosecki
6–05	Costa Rica	W	2–0	Chicago	Fr	Pisz, Nowak
10–05	United States	L	1–3	Hershey	Fr	Ziober
19–05	Scotland	D	1–1	Glasgow	Fr	OG
21–05	Arab Emirates	W	4–0	Marseille	Fr	Dziekanowski, Kosecki, Warzycha R 2
6–06	Belgium	D	1–1	Brussels	Fr	Ziober
15–08	France	D	0–0	Paris	Fr	
26–09	Romania	L	1–2	Bucharest	Fr	Warzycha R
10–10	United States	L	2–3	Warsaw	Fr	Kosecki, Ziober
17–10	England	L	0–2	London	ECq	
14–11	Turkey	W	1–0	Istanbul	ECq	Dziekanowski
19–12	Greece	W	2–1	Volos	Fr	Soczynski, Kosecki
6–02–1991	Nth. Ireland	L	1–3	Belfast	Fr	Warzycha R
13–03	Finland	D	1–1	Warsaw	Fr	Lesiak
27–03	Czechoslovakia	L	0–4	Olomouc	Fr	
17–04	Turkey	W	3–0	Warsaw	ECq	Tarasiewicz, Urban, Kosecki
1–05	Rep. Ireland	D	0–0	Dublin	ECq	
29–05	Wales	D	0–0	Radom	Fr	
14–08	France	L	1–5	Poznan	Fr	Ziober
21–08	Sweden	W	2–0	Gdynia	Fr	Kowalczyk, Trzeciak
11–09	Holland	D	1–1	Eindhoven	Fr	Ziober
16–10	Rep. Ireland	D	3–3	Poznan	ECq	Czachowski, Furtok, Urban
13–11	England	D	1–1	Poznan	ECq	Szewczyk
25–03–1992	Lithuania	W	2–0	Katowice	Fr	Kraus, Lesiak
7–05	Sweden	L	0–5	Stockholm	Fr	
19–05	Austria	W	4–2	Salzburg	Fr	Kosecki 2, Warzycha K, Kowalczyk
27–05	Czechoslovakia	W	1–0	Jastrzebie	Fr	Warzycha K

PORTUGAL

Portugal's football fame rests on three laurels: the continued excellence of Benfica, Sporting and FC Porto, the 1966 World Cup and Eusébio. The Portuguese were without doubt one of the great nations of the 1960s. Benfica appeared in five European Cup finals winning two of them, whilst the national side, based as it was on these Benfica players, enjoyed its only prolonged and successful era.

The Federaçao Portuguesa de Futebol was formed in 1914, but it was not until eight years later that it organised a competition for the numerous clubs that had been formed. Until this time, clubs had taken part in local competitions, with the major centres in Lisbon and Oporto. Indeed the Portuguese Federation was formed as a result of the merger of the two associations from these cities.

Most of the clubs still prominent today were formed around the turn of the century. Benfica were founded in 1904 whilst their great rivals Sporting and FC Porto appeared two years later. FC Porto were the winners of the first cup competition in 1922, and since then Portuguese football has been dominated by these three teams in a way that is unique in European football. The league championship, introduced in 1935, has only ever been won by four teams. Apart from the big three, Belenenses in 1948 are the only other team to have won the major prize.

The national team did not have an auspicious start. In December 1921, a friendly match was organised against neighbours Spain. It was not a success and throughout the next three decades matches were fairly infrequent, with Spain providing the only regular opposition. This reluctance to get a national team together more often still persists today. In 1988 only two games were played whilst 1990 saw only four, which is too few to achieve anything at this level.

The early 1960s saw Portugal finally make an impact on the European game. In 1961 Benfica won the European Cup beating Barcelona in the final. The following year they won it again, this time beating Real Madrid in a thriller in Amsterdam. A third final the year after that ended in defeat at the hands of Milan at Wembley, whilst the losses in the 1965 and 1968 finals had more to do with the fact that both games were effectively played away rather than on neutral territory. In 1965 they lost to a sterile Internazionale by the only goal in the San Siro, whilst in 1968, Wembley was the scene of another defeat for them, this time at the hands of Manchester United.

The basis of the Benfica side was also the core of the national side in the 1960s, and the central figure was Eusébio, who along with Mario Coluña was Mozambiquan by birth. Both were spotted young and brought over to Portugal, and both qualified to play for the mother country.

The use of players from their colonies gave Portuguese sides an aura of mystique, as European crowds in the 1960s were still unused to black footballers. Jose Aguas was another African-born player, from Angola, and he, having been a central figure at Benfica in the 1950s, scored two goals, one in each of the finals, that helped Benfica in their European Cup triumphs.

The other great players for both Benfica and Portugal in the 1960s included Costa Pereira in goal and Germano who is often rated as the best centre-half of his generation, with Cavem and Jose Augusto on either wing keeping Eusébio, Coluña and Torres well supplied in the centre. Eusébio, however, was the undoubted star. Qualification for the 1966 World Cup reversed a trend that had seen six previous unsuccessful attempts to qualify, but once there the Portuguese played some of the best football of that or any other tournament, beating Hungary, Bulgaria and Brazil with great style in the first round. The quarter-finals saw them pitted against the North Koreans, who nearly continued on their rather surprising path. Three goals down after half an hour, Portugal looked in serious danger, but one of the most inspired individual performances

		All			League			Cup		Europe		
	Team	G	S	B	G	S	B	G	S	G	S	B
1	Benfica	55	33	10	29	19	8	24	8	2	6	2
2	Sporting Clube Portugal	32	26	20	16	13	18	15	13	1	–	2
3	FC Porto	24	33	9	12	20	9	11	12	1	1	–
4	OS Belenenses	7	10	14	1	3	14	6	7	–	–	–
5	Boavista FC	4	1	1	–	1	1	4	–	–	–	–
6	Vitória FC Setúbal	2	8	3	–	1	3	2	7	–	–	–
7	Académica Coimbra	1	5	–	–	1	–	1	4	–	–	–
8	Atletico Clube Portugal	1	3	2	–	–	2	1	3	–	–	–
9	Sporting Clube Braga	1	2	–	–	–	–	1	2	–	–	–
10	SC Olhanense	1	1	–	–	–	–	1	1	–	–	–
11	Estrela da Amadora	1	–	–	–	–	–	1	–	–	–	–
	Leixoes SC	1	–	–	–	–	–	1	–	–	–	–
	CS Marítimo	1	–	–	–	–	–	1	–	–	–	–
14	Vitória SC Guimaraes	–	4	2	–	–	2	–	4	–	–	–
15	FC Barreirense	–	2	–	–	–	–	–	2	–	–	–
16	SC Beira Mar	–	1	–	–	–	–	–	1	–	–	–
	GD Estoril Praia	–	1	–	–	–	–	–	1	–	–	–
	SC Farense	–	1	–	–	–	–	–	1	–	–	–
	FC Rio Ave	–	1	–	–	–	–	–	1	–	–	–
	Sporting Clube Covilha	–	1	–	–	–	–	–	1	–	–	–
	SC Uniao Torriense	–	1	–	–	–	–	–	1	–	–	–
16	GD Quimigal	–	–	1	–	–	1	–	–	–	–	–

To the end of the 1991–92 season

ever witnessed in the World Cup saw Eusébio score four goals as his side came back to win 5–3.

It is often said that it is worse to lose a semi-final than a final, and for Eusébio, the defeat by England at Wembley provoked the most publicised tears until Paul Gascoigne was moved to the same 24 years later. Despite his nine goals, Eusébio was denied the opportunity to appear in the World Cup final, a stage he richly deserved.

The Portuguese have struggled to live up to the great reputation of this side and the 1970s saw a decline both of the national team and the club sides. Not until 1983, when Benfica lost to Anderlecht in the UEFA Cup, did a Portuguese side appear in another European club final. It sparked a mini-revival and the following year FC Porto reached the Cup Winners Cup final. Qualification for only their second World Cup in 1986 followed, but although the trip to Mexico proved to be a disaster, FC Porto then became the third club from Portugal to win a European honour when they won the 1987 European Cup beating Bayern Munich in the final.

Portuguese football has the makings of being among the best in Europe. Two more European Cup final appearances by Benfica in 1988 and 1990 are testament to the strength of the top Portuguese clubs, and victories in the 1989 and 1991 World Youth Cups show that quality players are still being produced in Portugal. The challenge is to blend the native Portuguese players with the numerous foreign stars playing their league football in Portugal as well as achieving the right balance between club and country. Until the national team is more consistent and given a proper programme which will allow it to fulfil its capabilities, Portugal will remain a curiosity on the European scene.

Population: 10 388 000
Area, sq km: 92 389
% in urban areas: 29.6%
Capital city: Lisbon

Federaçao Portuguesa de Futebol
Praça de Alegría #25
Apartado 21.100
P–1128 Lisbon Codex
Portugal
Tel: (010 351) 1 328207/08/09
Fax: (010 351) 1 3467231
Telex: 13489 FPF P
Cable: FUTEBOL LISBOA
Languages for correspondence: French, Spanish & English

Year of formation: 1914
Affiliation to FIFA: 1926
Affiliation to UEFA: 1954
Registered clubs: 1246
Registered players: 73 900
Professional Players: 1650
Registered coaches: 571
Registered referees: 175
National stadium: Estádio Nacional 60 000
National colours: Shirts: Red/Shorts: GreenSocks: Red
Reserve colours: Shirts: White/Shorts: Red/Socks: White
Season: September–July

THE RECORD

WORLD CUP

1930 .... Did not enter
1934 .... QT 2nd/2 in group 6
1938 .... QT 2nd/2 in group 4
1950 .... QT 2nd/2 in group 6
1954 .... QT 2nd/2 in group 5
1958 .... QT 3rd/3 in group 8
1962 .... QT 2nd/3 in group 6
1966 .... QT 1st/4 in group 4 – Final Tournament/Semi-finalists/3rd place
1970 .... QT 4th/4 in group 1
1974 .... QT 2nd/4 in group 6
1978 .... QT 2nd/4 in group 1
1982 .... QT 4th/5 in group 6
1986 .... QT 2nd/5 in group 2 – Final Tournament/1st round
1990 .... QT 3rd/5 in group 7

EUROPEAN CHAMPIONSHIP

1960 .... Quarter-finalists
1964 .... 1st round
1968 .... QT 2nd/4 in group 2
1972 .... QT 2nd/4 in group 5
1976 .... QT 3rd/4 in group 1
1980 .... QT 3rd/5 in group 2
1984 .... QT 1st/4 in group 2 – Final Tournament/Semi-finalists
1988 .... QT 3rd/5 in group 2
1992 .... QT 2nd/5 in group 6

OLYMPIC GAMES

1908–24 ..... Did not enter
1928 .... Quarter-finalists
1936–80 ..... Did not enter
1984 .... QT Failed to qualify
1988 .... QT Failed to qualify
1992 .... QT Failed to qualify

EUROPEAN CLUB COMPETITIONS

EUROPEAN CUP: Winners – Benfica 1961 1962, FC Porto 1987
Finalists – Benfica 1963 1965 1968 1988 1990

CUP WINNERS CUP: Winners – Sporting CP 1964
Finalists – FC Porto 1984

UEFA CUP: Finalists – Benfica 1983

CLUB DIRECTORY

LISBON (Population – 2 250 000)

Atletico Clube Portugal
Stadium: Tapadinha
Founded: 1942
Colours: Yellow and blue stripes/Blue
Previous names: Formed when Carcavelinhos and Uniao merged in 1942

Futebol Clube Barreirense
Stadium: Manuel de Melo
Founded: 1911
Colours: Red and white chequered/White

Clube de Futebol OS Belenenses
Stadium: Estádio do Restelo 40000
Founded: 1919
Colours: Blue/White

Sport Lisboa Benfica
Stadium: Estádio da Luz 120 000
Founded: 1904
Colours: Red/White

Clube de Futebol Estrela da Amadora
Stadium: Estrela da Amadora 20 000
Founded: 1932
Colours: Red, green and white stripes/White

Grupo Desportivo Quimigal
Stadium: Alfiedo da Silva
Founded: 1937
Colours: Green/White
Previous names: Unidos FC 1937–44, GD Cuf Barreiro 1944–78

Sporting Clube de Portugal
Stadium: José Alvalade 75 000
Founded: 1906
Colours: Green and white hoops/Black

OPORTO (Population – 1 225 000)

Boavista Futebol Clube
Stadium: Estádio do Bessa 28 000
Founded: 1903
Colours: Black and white checks/Black

Futebol Clube do Porto
Stadium: Estádio das Antas 90000
Founded: 1906
Colours: Blue and white stripes/Blue

Sport Commércio E Salgueiros
Stadium: Campo Vidal Pinheiro 20000
Founded: 1911
Colours: Red/White

Leixoes Sport Club
Stadium: Estádio do Mar 20000
Founded: 1907
Colours: Red and white stripes/White

FUNCHAL, Madeira (Population – 273000)

Club Sport Marítimo
Stadium: Estádio dos Barreiros 13000
Founded: 1910
Colours: Red and green stripes/White

Clube Desportivo Nacional
Stadium: Estádio dos Barreiros 13000
Founded: 1910
Colours: Black and white stripes/Black

Clube de Futebol Uniao
Stadium: Estádio dos Barreiros 13000
Founded: 1913
Colours: Yellow with two blue hoops/Blue

SETUBAL (Population – 77000)

Vitória Futebol Clube Setúbal
Stadium: Estádio do Bonfim 30000
Founded: 1910
Colours: Green and white stripes/White

COIMBRA (Population – 74000)

Associacao Académica de Coimbra
Stadium: Municipal 35000
Founded: 1876 Colours: Black/Black

BRAGA (Population – 63000)

Sporting Club de Braga
Stadium: Primeiro de Maio 40000
Founded: 1921
Colours: Red with white sleeves/White

Futebol Clube de Famalicao
Stadium: Municipal 30000
Founded: 1931 Colours: White/Blue

GUIMARAES

Vitória Sport Clube Guimaraes
Stadium: Municipal 30000
Founded: 1922 Colours: White/White

OLHAO

Sporting Clube Olhanense
Stadium: Padinho Founded: 1912
Colours: Red and Black stripes/White

PORTUGUESE LEAGUE CHAMPIONSHIP

Year	Champions		Runners up		3rd	
1935	FC Porto	22	Sporting CP	20	Benfica	19
1936	Benfica	21	FC Porto	20	Sporting CP	18
1937	Benfica	24	OS Belenenses	23	Sporting CP	20
1938	Benfica	23	FC Porto	23	Sporting CP	22
1939	FC Porto	23	Sporting CP	22	Benfica	21
1940	FC Porto	34	Sporting CP	32	OS Belenenses	25
1941	Sporting CP	23	FC Porto	20	OS Belenenses	19
1942	Benfica	38	Sporting CP	34	OS Belenenses	30
1943	Benfica	30	Sporting CP	29	OS Belenenses	28
1944	Sporting CP	31	Benfica	26	Atletico CP	24
1945	Benfica	30	Sporting CP	27	OS Belenenses	27
1946	OS Belenenses	38	Benfica	37	Sporting CP	32
1947	Sporting CP	47	Benfica	41	FC Porto	33
1948	Sporting CP	41	Benfica	41	OS Belenenses	37
1949	Sporting CP	42	Benfica	37	OS Belenenses	35
1950	Benfica	45	Sporting CP	39	Atletico CP	30
1951	Sporting CP	45	FC Porto	34	Benfica	30
1952	Sporting CP	41	Benfica	40	FC Porto	36
1953	Sporting CP	43	Benfica	39	OS Belenenses	36
1954	Sporting CP	43	FC Porto	36	Benfica	32
1955	Benfica	39	OS Belenenses	39	Sporting CP	37
1956	FC Porto	43	Benfica	43	OS Belenenses	37
1957	Benfica	41	FC Porto	40	OS Belenenses	33
1958	Sporting CP	43	FC Porto	43	Benfica	36
1959	FC Porto	41	Benfica	41	OS Belenenses	38
1960	Benfica	45	Sporting CP	43	OS Belenenses	36
1961	Benfica	46	Sporting CP	42	FC Porto	33
1962	Sporting CP	43	FC Porto	41	Benfica	36
1963	Benfica	48	FC Porto	42	Sporting CP	38
1964	Benfica	46	FC Porto	40	Sporting CP	34
1965	Benfica	43	FC Porto	37	CUF Barreiro	35
1966	Sporting CP	42	Benfica	41	FC Porto	34
1967	Benfica	43	Académica Coimbra	40	FC Porto	39
1968	Benfica	41	Sporting CP	37	FC Porto	36
1969	Benfica	39	FC Porto	37	Vitória Guimaraes	36
1970	Sporting CP	46	Benfica	38	Vitória Setúbal	36
1971	Benfica	41	Sporting CP	38	FC Porto	37
1972	Benfica	55	Vitória Setúbal	45	Sporting CP	43
1973	Benfica	58	OS Belenenses	40	Vitória Setúbal	38
1974	Sporting CP	49	Benfica	47	Vitória Setúbal	45
1975	Benfica	49	FC Porto	44	Sporting CP	43
1976	Benfica	50	Boavista FC	48	OS Belenenses	40
1977	Benfica	51	Sporting CP	42	FC Porto	41
1978	FC Porto	51	Benfica	51	Sporting CP	42

1979	FC Porto	50	Benfica	49	Sporting CP	42
1980	Sporting CP	52	FC Porto	50	Benfica	45
1981	Benfica	50	FC Porto	48	Sporting CP	37
1982	Sporting CP	46	Benfica	44	FC Porto	43
1983	Benfica	51	FC Porto	47	Sporting CP	42
1984	Benfica	52	FC Porto	49	Sporting CP	42
1985	FC Porto	55	Sporting CP	47	Benfica	43
1986	FC Porto	49	Benfica	47	Sporting CP	46
1987	Benfica	49	FC Porto	46	Vitória Guimaraes	41
1988	FC Porto	66	Benfica	51	OS Belenenses	48
1989	Benfica	63	FC Porto	56	Boavista FC	49
1990	FC Porto	59	Benfica	55	Sporting CP	46
1991	Benfica	69	FC Porto	67	Sporting CP	56
1992	FC Porto	56	Benfica	46	Sporting CP	44

PORTUGUESE CUP FINALS

Year	Winners	Score	Runners-up
1922	FC Porto	3–1	Sporting CP
1923	Sporting CP	3–0	Académica Coimbra
1924	SC Olhanense	4–2	FC Porto
1925	FC Porto	2–1	Sporting CP
1926	CS Marítimo	2–0	OS Belenenses
1927	OS Belenenses	3–0	Vitória Setúbal
1928	Carcavelinhos	3–1	Sporting CP
1929	OS Belenenses	2–1	Uniao Lisbon
1930	Benfica	3–1	FC Barreirense
1931	Benfica	3–0	FC Porto
1932	FC Porto	2–0	OS Belenenses
1933	OS Belenenses	3–1	Sporting CP
1934	Sporting CP	4–3	FC Barreirense
1935	Benfica	2–1	Sporting CP
1936	Sporting CP	3–1	OS Belenenses
1937	FC Porto	3–2	Sporting CP
1938	Sporting CP	3–1	Benfica
1939	Académica Coimbra	4–3	Benfica
1940	Benfica	3–1	OS Belenenses
1941	Sporting CP	4–1	OS Belenenses
1942	OS Belenenses	2–0	Vitória Guimaraes
1943	Benfica	5–1	Vitória Setúbal
1944	Benfica	8–0	GD Estoril Praia
1945	Sporting CP	1–0	SC Olhanense
1946	Sporting CP	4–2	Atletico CP
1947	–		
1948	Sporting CP	3–1	OS Belenenses
1949	Benfica	2–1	Atletico CP
1950	–		
1951	Benfica	5–1	Académica Coimbra
1952	Benfica	5–4	Sporting CP
1953	Benfica	5–0	FC Porto
1954	Sporting CP	3–2	Vitória Setúbal
1955	Benfica	2–1	Sporting CP
1956	FC Porto	3–0	SC Uniao Torriense
1957	Benfica	3–1	Sporting Covilha
1958	FC Porto	1–0	Benfica
1959	Benfica	1–0	FC Porto
1960	OS Belenenses	2–1	Sporting CP
1961	Leixoes SC	2–0	FC Porto
1962	Benfica	3–0	Vitória Setúbal
1963	Sporting CP	4–0	Vitória Guimaraes
1964	Benfica	6–2	FC Porto
1965	Vitória Setúbal	3–1	Benfica
1966	Sporting Braga	1–0	Vitória Setúbal
1967	Vitória Setúbal	3–2	Academica Coimbra
1968	FC Porto	2–1	Vitória Setúbal
1969	Benfica	2–1	Academica Coimbra
1970	Benfica	3–1	Sporting CP
1971	Sporting CP	4–1	Benfica
1972	Benfica	3–2	Sporting CP
1973	Sporting CP	3–2	Vitória Setúbal
1974	Sporting CP	2–1	Benfica
1975	Boavista FC	2–1	Benfica
1976	Boavista FC	2–1	Vitória Guimaraes
1977	FC Porto	2–1	Sporting Braga
1978	Sporting CP	1–1 2–1	FC Porto
1979	Boavista FC	1–1 1–0	Sporting CP
1980	Benfica	1–0	FC Porto
1981	Benfica	3–1	FC Porto
1982	Sporting CP	4–0	Sporting Braga
1983	Benfica	1–0	FC Porto
1984	FC Porto	4–1	FC Rio Ave
1985	Benfica	3–1	FC Porto
1986	Benfica	2–0	OS Belenenses
1987	Benfica	2–1	Sporting CP
1988	FC Porto	1–0	Vitória Guimaraes
1989	OS Belenenses	2–1	Benfica
1990	Estrela da Amadora	2–0	SC Farense
1991	FC Porto	3–1	SC Beira Mar
1992	Boavista FC	2–1	FC Porto

INTERNATIONAL MATCHES PLAYED BY PORTUGAL

Date	Opponents	Result		Venue	Compet	Scorers
18-12-1921	Spain	L	1–3	Madrid	Fr	Alberto Augusto
17-12-1922	Spain	L	1–2	Lisbon	Fr	Jaime Gonçalves
16-12-1923	Spain	L	0–3	Seville	Fr	
15-05-1925	Spain	L	0–2	Lisbon	Fr	
18-06	Italy	W	1–0	Lisbon	Fr	Joao Maia
18-04-1926	France	L	2–4	Toulouse	Fr	Augusto Silva, Joao Santos
26-12	Hungary	D	3–3	Oporto	Fr	Joao Santos, José Martins, Tiago
16-03-1927	France	W	4–0	Lisbon	Fr	José Martins 2, José Soares 2
17-04	Italy	L	1–3	Turin	Fr	Cambalacho
29-05	Spain	L	0–2	Madrid	Fr	
8-01-1928	Spain	D	2–2	Lisbon	Fr	José Martins, Joao Santos

1–04	Argentina	D	0–0	Lisbon	Fr	
15–04	Italy	W	4–1	Oporto	Fr	Waldemar Mota 3, Victor Silva
29–04	France	D	1–1	Paris	Fr	Armando Martins
27–05	Chile	W	4–2	Amsterdam	OGr1	José Soares 2, Victor Silva, Waldemar Mota
29–05	Yugoslavia	W	2–1	Amsterdam	OGr2	Victor Silva, Augusto Silva
4–06	Egypt	L	1–2	Amsterdam	OGqf	Victor Silva
17–03–1929	Spain	L	0–5	Seville	Fr	
24–03	France	L	0–2	Paris	Fr	
1–12	Italy	L	1–6	Milan	Fr	Victor Silva
12–01–1930	Czechoslovakia	W	1–0	Lisbon	Fr	José Soares
23–02	France	W	2–0	Oporto	Fr	José Soares 2
8–06	Belgium	L	1–2	Antwerp	Fr	Armando Martins
30–11	Spain	L	0–1	Oporto	Fr	
12–04–1931	Italy	L	0–2	Oporto	Fr	
31–05	Belgium	W	3–2	Lisbon	Fr	Armando Martins, Victor Silva, Artur Sousa
3–05–1932	Yugoslavia	W	3–2	Lisbon	Fr	Artur Sousa, Alfredo Valadas, Soeiro Vasques
29–01–1933	Hungary	W	1–0	Lisbon	Fr	Artur Sousa
2–04	Spain	L	0–3	Vigo	Fr	
11–03–1934	Spain	L	0–9	Madrid	WCq	
18–03	Spain	L	1–2	Lisbon	WCq	Victor Silva
5–05–1935	Spain	D	3–3	Lisbon	Fr	Artur Sousa 2, Soeiro Vasques
26–01–1936	Austria	L	2–3	Oporto	Fr	Ferreira Silva, Soeiro Vasques
27–02	Germany	L	1–3	Lisbon	Fr	Victor Silva
9–01–1938	Hungary	W	4–0	Lisbon	Fr	Joao Cruz, Espirito Santo, Artur Sousa
24–04	Germany	D	1–1	Frankfurt	Fr	Artur Sousa
1–05	Switzerland	L	1–2	Milan	WCq	Peyroteo
6–11	Switzerland	L	0–1	Lausanne	Fr	
12–02–1939	Switzerland	L	2–4	Lisbon	Fr	Joao Cruz, Soeiro Vasques
28–01–1940	France	L	2–3	Paris	Fr	Peyroteo 2
12–01–1941	Spain	D	2–2	Lisbon	Fr	Peyroteo 2
16–03	Spain	L	1–5	Bilbao	Fr	Artur Sousa
1–01–1942	Switzerland	W	3–0	Lisbon	Fr	Alberto Gomes, Mourao
11–03–1945	Spain	D	2–2	Lisbon	Fr	Peyroteo 2
6–05	Spain	L	2–4	La Coruña	Fr	Peyroteo 2
21–05	Switzerland	L	0–1	Basle	Fr	
14–04–1946	France	W	2–1	Lisbon	Fr	Araujo, Peyroteo
16–06	Rep. Ireland	W	3–1	Lisbon	Fr	Rogério, Peyroteo 2
5–01–1947	Switzerland	D	2–2	Lisbon	Fr	Rogério, Moreira
26–01	Spain	W	4–1	Lisbon	Fr	Travassos 2, Araujo 2
23–03	France	L	0–1	Paris	Fr	
4–05	Rep. Ireland	W	2–0	Dublin	Fr	Jesus Correia, Araujo
25–05	England	L	0–10	Lisbon	Fr	
23–11	France	L	2–4	Lisbon	Fr	Peyroteo, Araujo
21–03–1948	Spain	L	0–2	Madrid	Fr	
23–05	Rep. Ireland	W	2–0	Lisbon	Fr	Peyroteo, Albano
27–02–1949	Italy	L	1–4	Genoa	Fr	Miguel Lourenço
20–03	Spain	D	1–1	Lisbon	Fr	Peyroteo
15–05	Wales	W	3–2	Lisbon	Fr	Demétrico, José Mota, M Vasques
22–05	Rep. Ireland	L	0–1	Dublin	Fr	
2–04–1950	Spain	L	1–5	Madrid	WCq	Cabrita
9–04	Spain	D	2–2	Lisbon	WCq	Travassos, Jesus Correia
14–05	England	L	3–5	Lisbon	Fr	Ben-David 2, Vasques M
21–05	Scotland	D	2–2	Lisbon	Fr	Travassos, Albano
8–04–1951	Italy	L	1–4	Lisbon	Fr	Jesus Correia
12–05	Wales	L	1–2	Cardiff	Fr	Ben-David
19–05	England	L	2–5	Liverpool	Fr	Demétrico, Albano
17–06	Belgium	D	1–1	Lisbon	Fr	Ben-David
20–04–1952	France	L	0–3	Paris	Fr	
23–11	Austria	D	1–1	Oporto	Fr	Travassos
14–12	Argentina	L	1–3	Lisbon	Fr	Vasques M
27–09–1953	Austria	L	1–9	Vienna	WCq	José Aguas
22–11	South Africa	W	3–1	Lisbon	Fr	Hernâni, José Aguas, Matateu
29–11	Austria	D	0–0	Lisbon	WCq	
14–03–1954	Belgium	D	0–0	Brussels	Fr	
28–11	Argentina	L	1–3	Lisbon	Fr	Travassos
19–12	West Germany	L	0–3	Lisbon	Fr	

4–05–1955	Scotland	L	0–3	Glasgow	Fr	
22–05	England	W	3–1	Oporto	Fr	José Aguas 2, Matateu
20–11	Sweden	L	2–6	Lisbon	Fr	José Aguas 2
18–12	Turkey	L	1–3	Istanbul	Fr	Hernâni
23–12	Egypt	W	4–0	Cairo	Fr	José Aguas 2, Matateu 2
25–03–1956	Turkey	W	3–1	Lisbon	Fr	Vasques M, Matateu, OG
8–04	Brazil	L	0–1	Lisbon	Fr	
3–06	Spain	W	3–1	Lisbon	Fr	Palmeiro 3
9–06	Hungary	D	2–2	Lisbon	Fr	José Aguas, Vasques M
16–01–1957	Nth. Ireland	D	1–1	Lisbon	WCq	Vasques M
24–03	France	L	0–1	Lisbon	Fr	
1–05	Nth. Ireland	L	0–3	Belfast	WCq	
26–05	Italy	W	3–0	Lisbon	WCq	Vasques M, Teixeira, Matateu
11–06	Brazil	L	1–2	Rio de Janeiro	Fr	Matateu
16–06	Brazil	L	0–3	Sao Paulo	Fr	
22–12	Italy	L	0–3	Milan	WCq	
13–04–1958	Spain	L	0–1	Madrid	Fr	
7–05	England	L	1–2	London	Fr	Carlos Duarte
16–05–1959	Switzerland	L	3–4	Geneva	Fr	Hernâni, Cavém, Matateu
21–05	Sweden	L	0–2	Gothenburg	Fr	
3–06	Scotland	W	1–0	Lisbon	Fr	Matateu
21–06	East Germany	W	2–0	Berlin	ECr1	Matateu, Mário Coluna
28–06	East Germany	W	3–2	Oporto	ECr1	Cavém, Mário Coluna 2
11–11	France	L	3–5	Paris	Fr	Matateu 2, Cavém
27–04–1960	West Germany	L	1–2	Ludwigshaven	Fr	Cavém
8–05	Yugoslavia	W	2–1	Lisbon	ECqf	Santana, Matateu
22–05	Yugoslavia	L	1–5	Belgrade	ECqf	Cavém
19–03–1961	Luxembourg	W	6–0	Lisbon	WCq	José Aguas, Yauca 3, Mário Coluna, OG
21–05	England	D	1–1	Lisbon	WCq	José Aguas
4–06	Argentina	L	0–2	Lisbon	Fr	
8–10	Luxembourg	L	2–4	Luxembourg	WCq	Eusébio, Tauca
25–10	England	L	0–2	London	WCq	
6–05–1962	Brazil	L	1–2	Sao Paulo	Fr	Mário Coluna
9–05	Brazil	L	0–1	Rio de Janeiro	Fr	
17–05	Belgium	L	1–2	Lisbon	Fr	Eusébio
7–11	Bulgaria	L	1–3	Sofia	ECr1	Eusébio
16–12	Bulgaria	W	3–1	Lisbon	ECr1	Hernâni 2, Mário Coluna
23–01–1963	Bulgaria	L	0–1	Rome	ECr1	
21–04	Brazil	W	1–0	Lisbon	Fr	José Augusto
29–04–1964	Switzerland	W	3–2	Zurich	Fr	Torres, Simoes, José Augusto
3–05	Belgium	W	2–1	Brussels	Fr	Eusébio, José Augusto
17–05	England	L	3–4	Lisbon	Fr	Torres 2, Eusébio
31–05	Argentina	L	0–2	Rio de Janeiro	CN	
4–06	England	D	1–1	Sao Paulo	CN	Peres
7–06	Brazil	L	1–4	Rio de Janeiro	CN	Mário Coluna
15–11	Spain	W	2–1	Oporto	Fr	Eusebio 2
24–01–1965	Turkey	W	5–1	Lisbon	WCq	Mário Coluna, Eusébio 3, Jaime Graça
19–04	Turkey	W	1–0	Ankara	WCq	Eusébio
25–04	Czechoslovakia	W	1–0	Bratislava	WCq	Eusébio
13–06	Rumania	W	2–1	Lisbon	WCq	Eusébio 2
24–06	Brazil	D	0–0	Oporto	Fr	
31–10	Czechoslovakia	D	0–0	Oporto	WCq	
21–11	Rumania	L	0–2	Bucharest	WCq	
12–06–1966	Norway	W	4–0	Lisbon	Fr	Eusébio 2, José Augusto 2
18–06	Scotland	W	1–0	Glasgow	Fr	Torres
21–06	Denmark	W	3–1	Esbjerg	Fr	Eusébio, Torres 2
26–06	Uruguay	W	3–0	Lisbon	Fr	Torres 3
3–07	Romania	W	1–0	Oporto	Fr	Torres
13–07	Hungary	W	3–1	Manchester	WCr1	José Augusto 2, Torres
16–07	Bulgaria	W	3–0	Manchester	WCr1	Eusébio, Torres, OG
19–07	Brazil	W	3–1	Liverpool	WCr1	Simoes, Eusébio 2
23–07	North Korea	W	5–3	Liverpool	WCqf	Eusébio 4, José Augusto
26–07	England	L	1–2	London	WCsf	Eusébio
28–07	Soviet Union	W	2–1	London	WC3p	Eusébio, Torres
13–11	Sweden	L	1–2	Lisbon	ECq	Jaime Graça
27–03–1967	Italy	D	1–1	Rome	Fr	Eusébio
1–06	Sweden	D	1–1	Stockholm	ECq	Custódio Pinto
8–06	Norway	W	2–1	Oslo	ECq	Eusébio 2
12–11	Norway	W	2–1	Oporto	ECq	Torres, Jaime Graça

26–11	Bulgaria	L	0–1	Sofia	ECq	
17–12	Bulgaria	D	0–0	Lisbon	ECq	
30–06–1968	Brazil	L	0–2	Lourenco Marques	Fr	
27–10	Romania	W	3–0	Lisbon	WCq	Jacinto 2, Joao
11–12	Greece	L	2–4	Athens	WCq	José Augusto, Eusébio
6–04–1969	Mexico	D	0–0	Lisbon	Fr	
16–04	Switzerland	L	0–2	Lisbon	WCq	
4–05	Greece	D	2–2	Oporto	WCq	Eusébio, Peres
12–10	Romania	L	0–1	Bucharest	WCq	
2–11	Switzerland	D	1–1	Berne	WCq	Eusébio
10–12	England	L	0–1	London	Fr	
10–05–1970	Italy	L	1–2	Lisbon	Fr	Humberto Coelho
14–10	Denmark	W	1–0	Copenhagen	ECq	Joao
17–02–1971	Belgium	L	0–3	Brussels	ECq	
21–04	Scotland	W	2–0	Lisbon	ECq	Eusébio, OG
12–05	Denmark	W	5–0	Oporto	ECq	Rui Rodrigues, Eusébio, Batista 2, OG
13–10	Scotland	L	1–2	Glasgow	ECq	Rui Rodrigues
21–11	Belgium	D	1–1	Lisbon	ECq	Peres
29–03–1972	Cyprus	W	4–0	Lisbon	WCq	Humberto Coelho, Nené, Jorge, Jordao
10–05	Cyprus	W	1–0	Nicosia	WCq	Chico Faria
11–06	Ecuador	W	3–0	Natal	Clr1	Eusébio, Dinis, Nené
14–06	Iran	W	3–0	Recife	Clr1	Eusébio, Dinis, Toni
18–06	Chile	W	4–1	Recife	Clr1	Humberto Coelho, Dinis 2, Eusébio
25–06	Rep. Ireland	W	2–1	Recife	Clr1	Peres, Nené
29–06	Argentina	W	3–1	Rio de Janeiro	Clr2	Adolfo, Eusébio, Dinis
2–07	Uruguay	D	1–1	Sao Paulo	Clr2	Peres
6–07	Soviet Union	W	1–0	Belo Horizonte	Clr2	Jordao
9–07	Brazil	L	0–1	Rio de Janeiro	Clf	
3–03–1973	France	W	2–1	Paris	Fr	Eusebio 2
28–03	Nth. Ireland	D	1–1	Coventry	WCq	Eusebio
2–05	Bulgaria	L	1–2	Sofia	WCq	Nené
13–10	Bulgaria	D	2–2	Lisbon	WCq	Simoes, Quaresma
14–11	Nth. Ireland	D	1–1	Lisbon	WCq	Jordao
3–04–1974	England	D	0–0	Lisbon	Fr	
13–11	Switzerland	L	0–3	Berne	Fr	
20–11	England	D	0–0	London	ECq	
26–04–1975	France	W	2–0	Paris	Fr	Nené, Marinho
30–04	Czechoslovakia	L	0–5	Prague	ECq	
13–05	Scotland	L	0–1	Glasgow	Fr	
8–06	Cyprus	W	2–0	Limassol	ECq	Nené, Moinhos
12–11	Czechoslovakia	D	1–1	Oporto	ECq	Nené
19–11	England	D	1–1	Lisbon	ECq	Rui Rodrigues
3–12	Cyprus	W	1–0	Setubal	ECq	Alves
7–04–1976	Italy	L	1–3	Turin	Fr	Fraguito
16–10	Poland	L	0–2	Oporto	WCq	
17–11	Denmark	W	1–0	Lisbon	WCq	Manuel Fernandes
5–12	Cyprus	W	2–1	Limassol	WCq	Chalana, Nené
22–12	Italy	W	2–1	Lisbon	Fr	Nené 2
30–03–1977	Switzerland	W	1–0	Funchal	Fr	Alves
9–10	Denmark	W	4–2	Copenhagen	WCq	Jordao, Nené, Manuel Fernandes, Octavio
29–10	Poland	D	1–1	Chorzow	WCq	Manuel Fernandes
16–11	Cyprus	W	4–0	Lisbon	WCq	Seninho, Chalana, Vital, Manuel Fernandes
8–03–1978	France	L	0–2	Paris	Fr	
20–09	USA	W	1–0	Setubal	Fr	Costa
11–10	Belgium	D	1–1	Lisbon	ECq	Fernando Gomes
15–11	Austria	W	2–1	Vienna	ECq	Nené, Alberto
29–11	Scotland	W	1–0	Lisbon	ECq	Alberto
9–05–1979	Norway	W	1–0	Oslo	ECq	Alves
26–09	Spain	D	1–1	Vigo	Fr	Nené
17–10	Belgium	L	0–2	Brussels	ECq	

LEADING INTERNATIONAL APPEARANCES

1	Nené	66	6	Joao Pinto	52
2	Eusébio	64	7	Fernando Gomes	48
	Humberto Coelho	64	8	Simoes	46
4	Bento	63	9	José Augusto	45
5	Mário Coluna	57	10	Jordao	43

LEADING INTERNATIONAL GOALSCORERS			
1 Eusébio	41	6 Matateu	13
2 Nené	22	Fernando Gomes	13
3 Peyroteo	15	8 José Aguas	11
Jordao	15	9 Artur Sousa	9
5 Torres	14	José Augusto	9

1-11	Norway	W	3-1	Lisbon	ECq	Artur, Nené 2
21-11	Austria	L	1-2	Lisbon	ECq	Reinaldo
26-03-1980	Scotland	L	1-4	Glasgow	ECq	Fernando Gomes
24-09	Italy	L	1-3	Genoa	Fr	Jordao
7-10	USA	D	1-1	Lisbon	Fr	Carlos Manuel
15-10	Scotland	D	0-0	Glasgow	WCq	
19-11	Nth. Ireland	W	1-0	Lisbon	WCq	Jordao
17-12	Israel	W	3-0	Lisbon	WCq	Humberto Coelho 2, Jordao
15-04-1981	Bulgaria	D	1-1	Oporto	Fr	Oliveira
29-04	Nth. Ireland	L	0-1	Belfast	WCq	
20-06	Spain	W	2-0	Oporto	Fr	Nené, Nogueira
24-06	Sweden	L	0-3	Stockholm	WCq	
23-09	Poland	W	2-0	Lisbon	Fr	Nené, Sheu
14-10	Sweden	L	1-2	Lisbon	WCq	Pietra
28-10	Israel	L	1-4	Tel Aviv	WCq	Jordao
18-11	Scotland	W	2-1	Lisbon	WCq	Manuel Fernandes, Oliveira
16-12	Bulgaria	L	2-5	Haskovo	Fr	Oliveira 2
20-01-1982	Greece	W	2-1	Athens	Fr	Oliveira 2
17-02	West Germany	L	1-3	Hanover	Fr	De Matos
24-03	Switzerland	L	1-2	Lugano	Fr	Nené
5-05	Brazil	L	1-3	Sao Luiz	Fr	Nené
22-09	Finland	W	2-0	Helsinki	ECq	Nené, Oliveira
10-10	Poland	W	2-1	Lisbon	ECq	Nené, Fernando Gomes
16-02-1983	France	L	0-3	Guimaraes	Fr	
23-02	West Germany	W	1-0	Lisbon	Fr	Dito
13-04	Hungary	D	0-0	Coimbra	Fr	
27-04	Soviet Union	L	0-5	Moscow	ECq	
8-06	Brazil	L	0-4	Coimbra	Fr	
21-09	Finland	W	5-0	Lisbon	ECq	Jordao, Carlos Manuel, Luis, Oliveira, OG
28-10	Poland	W	1-0	Wroclaw	ECq	Carlos Manuel
13-11	Soviet Union	W	1-0	Lisbon	ECq	Jordao
2-06-1984	Yugoslavia	L	2-3	Lisbon	Fr	Jordao 2
9-06	Luxembourg	W	2-1	Luxembourg	Fr	Eurico, Diamantino
14-06	West Germany	D	0-0	Strasbourg	ECr1	
17-06	Spain	D	1-1	Marseille	ECr1	Sousa
20-06	Romania	W	1-0	Nantes	ECr1	Nené
23-06	France	L	2-3	Marseille	ECsf	Jordao 2
6-09	Bulgaria	W	1-0	Lisbon	Fr	Fernando Gomes
12-09	Sweden	W	1-0	Stockholm	WCq	Fernando Gomes
14-10	Czechoslovakia	W	2-1	Oporto	WCq	Diamantino, Carlos Manuel
14-11	Sweden	L	1-3	Lisbon	WCq	Jordao
30-01-1985	Romania	L	2-3	Lisbon	Fr	Futre, Carlos Manuel
10-02	Malta	W	3-1	Ta'Qali	WCq	Fernando Gomes 2, Carlos Manuel
24-02	West Germany	L	1-2	Lisbon	WCq	Diamantino
3-04	Italy	L	0-2	Ascoli	Fr	
25-09	Czechoslovakia	L	0-1	Pague	WCq	
12-10	Malta	W	3-2	Lisbon	WCq	Fernando Gomes 2, Rafael
16-10	West Germany	W	1-0	Stuttgart	WCq	Carlos Manuel
22-01-1986	Finland	D	1-1	Leiria	Fr	Diamantino
5-02	Luxembourg	W	2-0	Portimao	Fr	Frederico, Fernando Gomes
19-02	East Germany	L	1-3	Braga	Fr	Fernando Gomes
3-06	England	W	1-0	Monterrey	WCr1	Carlos Manuel
7-06	Poland	L	0-1	Monterrey	WCr1	
11-06	Morocco	L	1-3	Guadalajara	WCr1	Diamantino
12-10	Sweden	D	1-1	Lisbon	ECq	Jorge Coelho
29-10	Switzerland	D	1-1	Berne	ECq	Manuel Fernandes
7-01-1987	Greece	D	1-1	Portalegre	Fr	Jorge Coelho
4-02	Belgium	W	1-0	Braga	Fr	Frasco
14-02	Italy	L	0-1	Lisbon	ECq	
29-03	Malta	D	2-2	Funchal	ECq	Placido 2

23–09	Sweden	W	1–0	Stockholm	ECq	Fernando Gomes
11–11	Switzerland	D	0–0	Oporto	ECq	
5–12	Italy	L	0–3	Milan	ECq	
20–12	Malta	W	1–0	Ta'Qali	ECq	Frederico
12–10–1988	Sweden	D	0–0	Gothenburg	Fr	
16–11	Luxembourg	W	1–0	Oporto	WCq	Fernando Gomes
25–01–1989	Greece	W	2–1	Athens	Fr	Nunes, Paneira
15–02	Belgium	D	1–1	Lisbon	WCq	Paneira
29–03	Angola	W	6–0	Lisbon	Fr	Frederico 2, Domingos Oliveira, Andre, Nunes, Semedo
26–04	Switzerland	W	3–1	Lisbon	WCq	Joao Pinto, Frederico, Paneira
8–06	Brazil	L	0–4	Rio de Janeiro	Fr	
31–08	Romania	D	0–0	Setubal	Fr	
6–09	Belgium	L	0–3	Brussels	WCq	
20–09	Switzerland	W	2–1	Neuchatel	WCq	Futre, Rui Aguas
6–10	Czechoslovakia	L	1–2	Prague	WCq	Rui Aguas
11–10	Luxembourg	W	3–0	Saarbrucken	WCq	Rui Aguas 2, Rui Barros
15–11	Czechoslovakia	D	0–0	Lisbon	WCq	
29–08–1990	West Germany	D	1–1	Lisbon	Fr	Rui Aguas
12–09	Finland	D	0–0	Helsinki	ECq	
17–10	Holland	W	1–0	Oporto	ECq	Rui Aguas
19–12	USA	W	1–0	Oporto	Fr	Domingos
16–01–1991	Spain	D	1–1	Castellon	Fr	Oceano
23–01	Greece	L	2–3	Athens	ECq	Rui Aguas, Futre
9–02	Malta	W	1–0	Ta'Qali	ECq	Futre
20–02	Malta	W	5–0	Oporto	ECq	Rui Aguas, Leal, Paneira, OG, Cadete
4–09	Austria	D	1–1	Oporto	Fr	Rui Barros
11–09	Finland	W	1–0	Oporto	ECq	Cesar Brito
12–10	Luxembourg	D	1–1	Luxembourg	Fr	Nogueira
16–10	Holland	L	0–1	Rotterdam	ECq	
21–11	Greece	W	1–0	Lisbon	ECq	Joao Pinto II
15–01–1992	Spain	D	0–0	Torres Novas	Fr	
12–02	Holland	W	2–0	Faro	Fr	Oceano, Cesar Brito
31–05	Italy	D	0–0	New Haven	Fr	
3–06	USA	L	0–1	Chicago	Fr	
7–06	Rep. Ireland	L	0–2	Boston	Fr	

REPUBLIC OF IRELAND

For many years the Republic of Ireland struggled along, not only in the shadow of their neighbours in the North but also as poor cousins of rugby union and the indigenous sports of the island such as Gaelic football and hurling. Ever since Jackie Charlton, a World Cup winner with the English in 1966, took over as manager of the national side in 1986 however, football in the South has risen to a prominence that it never enjoyed before.

Football had never been traditionally strong in the South. The Irish Football Association was located in Belfast and only Shelbourne, Bohemians of Dublin and Shamrock Rovers from the area that now constitutes the Republic of Ireland regularly took part in either the league or the cup before the separation in 1921.

A championship and a cup were initiated the following year but the league has been characterised by the departure of all its best players to either England or Scotland, and has therefore not had the chance to develop. Financial crises and the closure and reformation of clubs have for a long time been the order of the day. Cork, the second largest city in the country, has been represented by five

		All			League			Cup		Europe		
	Team	G	S	B	G	S	B	G	S	G	S	B
1	Shamrock Rovers	38	19	11	14	12	11	24	7	–	–	–
2	Dundalk	16	14	6	8	10	6	8	4	–	–	–
3	Shelbourne	14	19	8	8	8	8	6	11	–	–	–
4	Bohemians Dublin	13	19	11	7	9	11	6	10	–	–	–
5	Cork Athletic	13	9	2	7	2	2	6	7	–	–	–
6	Home Farm Drumcondra	11	9	4	5	5	4	6	4	–	–	–
7	Waterford United	8	10	8	6	4	8	2	6	–	–	–
8	St Patrick's Athletic	6	6	1	4	2	1	2	4	–	–	–
9	Limerick City	4	5	3	2	2	3	2	3	–	–	–
10	St James' Gate	4	3	–	2	1	–	2	2	–	–	–
11	Sligo Rovers	3	7	4	2	2	4	1	5	–	–	–
12	Cork Hibernians	3	3	3	1	1	3	2	2	–	–	–
13	Athlone Town	3	1	3	2	1	3	1	–	–	–	–
14	Derry City	2	3	–	1	2	–	1	1	–	–	–
15	Cork Celtic	1	7	2	1	4	2	–	3	–	–	–
	Finn Harps	1	3	1	–	3	1	1	–	–	–	–
17	Dolphin	1	3	–	1	1	–	–	2	–	–	–
18	Galway United	1	2	–	–	1	–	1	1	–	–	–
19	Alton United	1	–	–	–	–	–	1	–	–	–	–
	Bray Wanderers	1	–	–	–	–	–	1	–	–	–	–
	Transport	1	–	–	–	–	–	1	–	–	–	–
	University College	1	–	–	–	–	–	1	–	–	–	–
23	Drogheda United	–	3	3	–	1	3	–	2	–	–	–
	Cork City	–	3	1	–	1	1	–	2	–	–	–
25	Brideville	–	2	–	–	–	–	–	2	–	–	–
26	St Francis	–	1	–	–	–	–	–	1	–	–	–
27	Jacobs	–	–	1	–	–	1	–	–	–	–	–

To the end of the 1991–92 season. The totals for Shelbourne and Bohemians include honours won in the All-Ireland League pre-1922.

different clubs called by 14 different names, in so far as it is possible to connect all the different teams.

With a good many professionals playing in England and Scotland, the Republic have always been 'on the verge' of becoming a good side. Their first match was in the 1924 Olympic Games in Paris and saw a 1–0 victory over Bulgaria. Holland, however, won the quarter-final tie, and although Ireland have entered the World Cup on every occasion since 1934, international fixtures were the exception rather than the rule until after the Second World War.

At times the results of these international matches were encouraging. West Germany for example were defeated twice in the late 1950s and early 1960s. West Ham and Manchester United's Noel Cantwell who played at this time emerged as perhaps the first major star from the Republic, but was followed soon by Johnny Giles, the linchpin of the very successful Leeds United side of the 1960s and early 1970s.

The depth of the squad was never quite there, however, to qualify for the final tournament of either the World Cup or European Championship. Despite the presence of Liam Brady and Frank Stapleton this trend continued right through to the late 1980s, when in a bold move the Football Association of Ireland appointed Jack Charlton as manager. Designing a set of tactics based very much on the more robust side of the English game, which all the players were used to, Charlton gave the team a belief in itself, and as a result – and with some good fortune – they qualified for the 1988 European Championship finals in West Germany.

Liam Brady was perhaps, with Giles, the best player to don the shirt of the Republic. In the twilight of his career he helped in achieving qualification for these finals, as he did for the World Cup in Italy two years later. It was ironic therefore that he played in neither of these tournaments, and the European stage which he had graced for many years at club level was denied his many talents at national level.

The Republic of Ireland have finally arrived on the European scene. Despite not qualifying for the 1992 European Championships, the interest in the sport looks set to remain. The next major task is to improve the quality of the club game. The best path would seem to lie in the unification of the game north and south of the border, though with political tensions often high this could be fraught with danger. Until the flow of players across the Irish Sea can be halted, however, at club level the future does not look very bright.

Population: 3 509 000
Area, sq km: 70 285
% in urban areas: 57.0%
Capital city: Dublin

The Football Association of Ireland
80 Merrion Square, South Dublin 2
Republic of Ireland
Tel: (010 353) 1 766864
Fax: (010 353) 1 610931
Telex: 91397 FAI EI
Cable: SOCCER DUBLIN
Languages for correspondence: English

Year of formation: 1921
Affiliation to FIFA: 1923
Affiliation to UEFA: 1954
Registered clubs: 2367
Registered players: 80 500
Professional players: 100
Registered coaches: 20
Registered referees: 895
National stadium: Dalymount Park 22 000
Other major stadia: Landsdowne Road (Irish Rugby Football Union) 49 000
National colours: Shirts: Green/Shorts: White/Socks: Green
Reserve colours: Shirts: White/Shorts: Green/Socks: White
Season: August–May

THE RECORD

WORLD CUP

1930 .... Did not enter
1934 .... QT 3rd/3 in group 11
1938 .... QT 2nd/2 in group 2
1950 .... QT 2nd/3 in group 5
1954 .... QT 2nd/3 in group 4
1958 .... QT 2nd/3 in group 1
1962 .... QT 3rd/3 in group 8
1966 .... QT 2nd/2 in group 9
1970 .... QT 4th/4 in group 2
1974 .... QT 2nd/3 in group 9
1978 .... QT 3rd/3 in group 5
1982 .... QT 3rd/5 in group 2
1986 .... QT 4th/5 in group 6
1990 .... QT 2nd/5 in group 6 – Final Tournament/Quarter-finalists

EUROPEAN CHAMPIONSHIP

1960 .... Preliminary round
1964 .... Quarter-finalists
1968 .... QT 4th/4 in group 1
1972 .... QT 4th/4 in group 6
1976 .... QT 2nd/4 in group 6
1980 .... QT 3rd/5 in group 1
1984 .... QT 3rd/5 in group 7
1988 .... QT 1st/5 in group 7 – Final Tournament/1st round
1992 .... QT 2nd/4 in group 7

OLYMPIC GAMES

1908–20 ..... Did not enter
1924 .... Quarter-finalists
1928 .... Did not enter
1936 .... Did not enter
1948 .... Preliminary round
1952 .... Did not enter
1956 .... Did not enter
1960 .... QT Failed to qualify
1964 .... Did not enter
1968 .... Did not enter
1972 .... QT Failed to qualify
1976 .... QT Failed to qualify
1980 .... QT Failed to qualify
1984 .... Did not enter
1988 .... QT Failed to qualify
1992 .... QT Failed to qualify

EUROPEAN CLUB COMPETITIONS

EUROPEAN CUP: 2nd round – Waterford 1971, Cork Celtic 1975, Bohemians 1979, Dundalk 1980

CUP WINNERS CUP: 2nd round – Shamrock Rovers 1963 1967 1979, Cork Hibernians 1973, Bohemians 1977, Waterford 1981, Dundalk 1982 UEFA Cup: 2nd round – Drumcondra 1963, Shelbourne 1965, Shamrock Rovers 1966 1983, Athlone Town 1976

CLUB DIRECTORY

DUBLIN (Population – 1 140 000)

Bohemians Football Club
Stadium: Dalymount Park 22 000
Founded: 1890
Colours: Red and black stripes/Black

Home Farm Football Club
Stadium: Tolka Park 15 000
Founded: 1928

Colours: Blue and white hoops/White
Previous name: Home Farm and Drumcondra merged in 1972 as Home Farm

St. James' Gate Football Club
Stadium: Iveagh Grounds
Founded: 1913
Colours: Black and white hoops/White

St. Patrick's Athletic Football Club
Stadium: Harold's Cross 13000
Founded: 1929
Colours: Red/White

Shamrock Rovers Football Club
Stadium: Royal Dublin Showgrounds 28000
Founded: 1899
Colours: Green and white hoops/White

Shelbourne Football Club
Stadium: Tolka Park 15000
Founded: 1895
Colours: Red/White
Previous name: Reds United 1934–36

University College Dublin Football Club
Stadium: Belfield 10000
Founded: 1895
Colours: Sky blue/White

CORK (Population – 173000)

Cork City Football Club
Stadium: Turner's Cross 20000
Founded: 1984
Colours: White/Green
There have been five other clubs from Cork all of which no longer exist.

1: Cork Athletic folded in 1957. They were previously known as Fordsons 1912–30, Cork FC 1930–38, Cork City 1938–40, Cork United 1940–48, Cork Athletic 1948–57
2: Cork Celtic folded in 1979. They were previously known as Evergreen United from 1935–59, Cork Celtic 1959–79
3: Cork United folded in 1982. They were previously known as Albert Rovers 1946–77, Cork Alberts 1977–79, Cork United 1979–82
4: Cork Bohemians 1920–34
5: Cork Hibernians folded in 1976. They were previously known as AOH. (Ancient Order of the Hibernians)

LIMERICK (Population – 76000)
Limerick City Football Club
Stadium: Rathbane 10000
Founded: 1983
Colours: Yellow with green sleeves/Green
Previous names: Limerick FC 1937–79, Limerick United 1979–83

GALWAY (Population – 47000)
Galway United Football Club
Stadium: Terryland Park 5000
Founded: 1976
Colours: Maroon/Maroon
Previous name: Galway Rovers 1976–81

WATERFORD (Population – 41000)
Waterford United Football Club
Stadium: Kilcohan Park 12000
Founded: 1921 Colours: Blue/Blue
Previous name: Waterford FC 1921–82

ATHLONE
Athlone Town Football Club
Stadium: St. Mels Park 15000
Founded: 1887
Colours: Blue/Black

BALLYBOFEY
Finn Harps Football Club
Stadium: Finn Park 10000
Founded: 1954
Colours: White/Blue

BRAY
Bray Wanderers Football Club
Stadium: Carlisle Grounds 10000
Founded: 1942
Colours: Green and white stripes/Green

DROGHEDA
Drogheda United Football Club
Stadium: United Park 10000
Founded: 1919
Colours: Claret with blue sleeves/Blue
Previous name: Drogheda FC 1919–75

DUNDALK
Dundalk Football Club
Stadium: Oriel Park 20000
Founded: 1919
Colours: White/Black

SLIGO
Sligo Rovers Football Club
Stadium: The Showgrounds 10000
Founded: 1908
Colours: Red and white stripes/Red

REPUBLIC OF IRELAND LEAGUE CHAMPIONSHIP

Year	Champions		Runners up		3rd	
1922	St James' Gate	23	Bohemians	21	Shelbourne	18
1923	Shamrock Rovers	39	Shelbourne	34	Bohemians	32
1924	Bohemians	32	Shelbourne	28	Jacobs	24
1925	Shamrock Rovers	31	Bohemians	28	Shelbourne	27
1926	Shelbourne	31	Shamrock Rovers	29	Fordsons	27
1927	Shamrock Rovers	32	Shelbourne	29	Bohemians	25
1928	Bohemians	31	Shelbourne	28	Shamrock Rovers	25
1929	Shelbourne	33	Bohemians	32	Shamrock Rovers	24
1930	Bohemians	30	Shelbourne	29	Shamrock Rovers	26
1931	Shelbourne	31	Dundalk	28	Bohemians	27
1932	Shamrock Rovers	32	Cork FC	29	Waterford	28
1933	Dundalk	29	Shamrock Rovers	24	Shelbourne	23
1934	Bohemians	27	Cork FC	26	Shamrock Rovers	22
1935	Dolphin	28	St James' Gate	27	Sligo Rovers	20
1936	Bohemians	36	Dolphin	33	Cork FC	31
1937	Sligo Rovers	34	Dundalk	24	Waterford	24
1938	Shamrock Rovers	32	Waterford	31	Dundalk	30
1939	Shamrock Rovers	36	Sligo Rovers	27	Dundalk	27
1940	St James' Gate	36	Shamrock Rovers	30	Sligo Rovers	28
1941	Cork United	30	Waterford	30	Bohemians	23
1942	Cork United	30	Shamrock Rovers	28	Shelbourne	21
1943	Cork United	27	Dundalk	26	Drumcondra	23
1944	Shelbourne	21	Limerick United	20	Shamrock Rovers	15
1945	Cork United	22	Limerick United	17	Shamrock Rovers	17
1946	Cork United	21	Drumcondra	19	Waterford	16

1947	Shelbourne 19	Drumcondra 18	Shamrock Rovers 17
1948	Drumcondra 18	Dundalk 17	Shelbourne 17
1949	Drumcondra 29	Shelbourne 23	Dundalk 23
1950	Cork Athletic 25	Drumcondra 24	Shelbourne 21
1951	Cork Athletic 26	Sligo Rovers 25	Drumcondra 23
1952	St Patrick's Athletic 34	Shelbourne 31	Shamrock Rovers 29
1953	Shelbourne 30	Drumcondra 29	Shamrock Rovers 27
1954	Shamrock Rovers 30	Evergreen United 28	Drumcondra 27
1955	St Patrick's Athletic 36	Waterford 33	Shamrock Rovers 28
1956	St Patrick's Athletic 34	Shamrock Rovers 31	Waterford 30
1957	Shamrock Rovers 36	Drumcondra 31	Sligo Rovers 29
1958	Drumcondra 33	Shamrock Rovers 31	Evergreen United 29
1959	Shamrock Rovers 34	Evergreen United 29	Waterford 29
1960	Limerick United 30	Cork Celtic 28	Shelbourne 28
1961	Drumcondra 33	St Patrick's Athletic 32	Waterford 29
1962	Shelbourne 35	Cork Celtic 35	Shamrock Rovers 31
1963	Dundalk 24	Waterford 23	Drumcondra 23
1964	Shamrock Rovers 35	Dundalk 30	Limerick United 30
1965	Drumcondra 32	Shamrock Rovers 31	Bohemians 27
1966	Waterford 36	Shamrock Rovers 34	Bohemians 27
1967	Dundalk 34	Bohemians 27	Sligo Rovers 27
1968	Waterford 34	Dundalk 30	Cork Celtic 30
1969	Waterford 36	Shamrock Rovers 33	Cork Hibernians 30
1970	Waterford 38	Shamrock Rovers 36	Cork Hibernians 35
1971	Cork Hibernians 35	Shamrock Rovers 35	Waterford 34
1972	Waterford 44	Cork Hibernians 40	Bohemians 37
1973	Waterford 42	Finn Harps 41	Bohemians 37
1974	Cork Celtic 42	Bohemians 38	Cork Hibernians 38
1975	Bohemians 42	Athlone Town 33	Finn Harps 30
1976	Dundalk 40	Finn Harps 36	Waterford 34
1977	Sligo Rovers 39	Bohemians 38	Drogheda United 35
1978	Bohemians 44	Finn Harps 42	Drogheda United 40
1979	Dundalk 45	Bohemians 43	Drogheda United 42
1980	Limerick United 47	Dundalk 46	Athlone Town 39
1981	Athlone Town 51	Dundalk 45	Limerick United 41
1982	Dundalk 80	Shamrock Rovers 76	Bohemians 72
1983	Athlone Town 65	Drogheda United 49	Dundalk 48
1984	Shamrock Rovers 42	Bohemians 36	Athlone Town 34
1985	Shamrock Rovers 49	Bohemians 43	Athlone Town 40
1986	Shamrock Rovers 33	Galway United 31	Dundalk 30
1987	Shamrock Rovers 39	Dundalk 30	Bohemians 29
1988	Dundalk 46	St Patrick's Athletic 45	Bohemians 45
1989	Derry City 53	Dundalk 51	Limerick City 45
1990	St Patrick's Athletic 52	Derry City 49	Dundalk 42
1991	Dundalk 52	Cork City 50	St Patrick's Athletic 44
1992	Shelbourne 49	Derry City 44	Cork City 43

REPUBLIC OF IRELAND CUP FINALS

Year	Winners	Score	Runners-up
1922	St James's Gate	1-1 1-0	Shamrock Rovers
1923	Alton United	1-0	Shelbourne
1924	Athlone Town	1-0	Fordsons
1925	Shamrock Rovers	2-1	Shelbourne
1926	Fordsons	3-2	Shamrock Rovers
1927	Drumcondra	1-1 1-0	Brideville
1928	Bohemians	2-1	Drumcondra
1929	Shamrock Rovers	0-0 3-0	Bohemians
1930	Shamrock Rovers	1-0	Brideville
1931	Shamrock Rovers	1-1 1-0	Dundalk
1932	Shamrock Rovers	1-0	Dolphin
1933	Shamrock Rovers	3-3 3-0	Dolphin
1934	Cork FC	2-1	St James's Gate
1935	Bohemians	4-3	Dundalk
1936	Shamrock Rovers	2-1	Cork FC
1937	Waterford	2-1	St James's Gate
1938	St James's Gate	2-1	Dundalk
1939	Shelbourne	1-1 1-0	Sligo Rovers
1940	Shamrock Rovers	3-0	Sligo Rovers
1941	Cork United	2-2 3-1	Waterford
1942	Dundalk	3-1	Cork United
1943	Drumcondra	2-1	Cork United
1944	Shamrock Rovers	3-2	Shelbourne
1945	Shamrock Rovers	1-0	Bohemians
1946	Drumcondra	2-1	Shamrock Rovers
1947	Cork United	2-2 2-0	Bohemians
1948	Shamrock Rovers	2-1	Drumcondra
1949	Dundalk	3-0	Shelbourne
1950	Transport	2-2 2-2 3-1	Cork Athletic
1951	Cork Athletic	1–1 1-0	Shelbourne
1952	Dundalk	1-1 3-0	Cork Athletic
1953	Cork Athletic	2-2 2-1	Evergreen United
1954	Drumcondra	1-0	St Patrick's Athletic
1955	Shamrock Rovers	1-0	Drumcondra
1956	Shamrock Rovers	3-2	Cork Athletic
1957	Drumcondra	2-0	Shamrock Rovers
1958	Dundalk	1-0	Shamrock Rovers

1959	St Patrick's Athletic	2-2 2-1	Waterford
1960	Shelbourne	2-0	Cork Hibernians
1961	St Patrick's Athletic	2-1	Drumcondra
1962	Shamrock Rovers	4-1	Shelbourne
1963	Shelbourne	2-0	Cork Hibernians
1964	Shamrock Rovers	1-1 2-1	Cork Celtic
1965	Shamrock Rovers	1-1 1-0	Limerick
1966	Shamrock Rovers	2-0	Limerick
1967	Shamrock Rovers	3-2	St Patrick's Athletic
1968	Shamrock Rovers	3-0	Waterford
1969	Shamrock Rovers	1-1 4-1	Cork Celtic
1970	Bohemians	0-0 0-0 2-1	Sligo Rovers
1971	Limerick	0-0 3-0	Drogheda United
1972	Cork Hibernians	3-0	Waterford
1973	Cork Hibernians	0-0 1-0	Shelbourne
1974	Finn Harps	3-1	St Patrick's
1975	Home Farm	1-0	Shelbourne
1976	Bohemians	1-0	Drogheda United
1977	Dundalk	2-0	Limerick
1978	Shamrock Rovers	1-0	Sligo Rovers
1979	Dundalk	2-0	Waterford
1980	Waterford	1-0	St Patrick's Athletic
1981	Dundalk	2-0	Sligo Rovers
1982	Limerick United	1-0	Bohemians
1983	Sligo Rovers	2-1	Bohemians
1984	University College	0–0 2-1	Shamrock Rovers
1985	Shamrock Rovers	1-0	Galway United
1986	Shamrock Rovers	2-0	Waterford
1987	Shamrock Rovers	3-0	Dundalk
1988	Dundalk	1-0	Derry City
1989	Derry City	0-0 1-0	Cork City
1990	Bray Wanderers	3-0	St Francis
1991	Galway United	1-0	Shamrock Rovers
1992	Bohemians	1–0	Cork City

INTERNATIONAL MATCHES PLAYED BY THE REPUBLIC OF IRELAND

Date	Opponents	Result		Venue	Compet	Scorers
28–05–1924	Bulgaria	W	1–0	Paris	OGr1	Duncan
2–06	Holland	L	1–2	Paris	OGqf	
3–06	Estonia	W	3–1	Paris	Fr	Duncan, Muldoon
16–06–1925	United States	W	3–1	Dublin	Fr	Brooks 3
21–03–1926	Italy	L	0–3	Turin	Fr	
12–02–1928	Belgium	W	4–2	Liege	Fr	White 2, Lacey, Sullivan
20–04–1929	Belgium	W	4–0	Dublin	Fr	Flood 3, Byrne
11–05–1930	Belgium	W	3–1	Brussels	Fr	Dunne 2, Flood
26–04–1931	Spain	D	1–1	Barcelona	Fr	Moore
13–12	Spain	L	0–5	Dublin	Fr	
8–05–1932	Holland	W	2–0	Amsterdam	Fr	O'Reilly, Moore
25–02–1934	Belgium	D	4–4	Dublin	WCq	Moore 4
8–04	Holland	L	2–5	Amsterdam	WCq	Moore, Squires
15–12	Hungary	L	2–4	Dublin	Fr	Donnelly, Bermingham
5–05–1935	Switzerland	L	0–1	Basle	Fr	
8–05	Germany	L	1–3	Dortmund	Fr	Dunne
8–12	Holland	L	3–5	Dublin	Fr	Ellis, Horlacher 2
17–03–1936	Switzerland	W	1–0	Dublin	Fr	Dunne
3–05	Hungary	D	3–3	Budapest	Fr	Dunne 2, Madden
9–05	Luxembourg	W	5–1	Luxembourg	Fr	Dunne 3, Donnelly, O'Reilly
17–10	Germany	W	5–2	Dublin	Fr	Davis 2, Donnelly 2, Geoghegan
6–12	Hungary	L	2–3	Dublin	Fr	Fallon, Davis
17–05–1937	Switzerland	W	1–0	Berne	Fr	Dunne
23–05	France	W	2–0	Paris	Fr	Jordan, Brown
10–10	Norway	L	2–3	Oslo	WCq	Geoghegan, Dunne
7–11	Norway	D	3–3	Dublin	WCq	Dunne, O'Flanagan, Duggan
18–05–1938	Czechoslovakia	D	2–2	Prague	Fr	Davis, Dunne
22–05	Poland	L	0–6	Warsaw	Fr	
18–09	Switzerland	W	4–0	Dublin	Fr	Bradshaw 2, Dunne, Donnelly
13–11	Poland	W	3–2	Dublin	Fr	Fallon, Carey, Dunne
19–03–1939	Hungary	D	2–2	Cork	Fr	Bradshaw, Carey
18–05	Hungary	D	2–2	Budapest	Fr	O'Flanagan 2
23–05	Germany	D	1–1	Bremen	Fr	Bradshaw
16–06–1946	Portugal	L	1–3	Lisbon	Fr	O'Reilly
23–06	Spain	W	1–0	Madrid	Fr	Sloan
30–09	England	L	0–1	Dublin	Fr	
2–03–1947	Spain	W	3–2	Dublin	Fr	Walshe 2, Coad
4–05	Portugal	L	0–2	Dublin	Fr	
23–05–1948	Portugal	L	0–2	Lisbon	Fr	
30–05	Spain	L	1–2	Barcelona	Fr	Walshe
5–12	Switzerland	L	0–1	Dublin	Fr	
24–04–1949	Belgium	L	0–2	Dublin	Fr	
22–05	Portugal	W	1–0	Dublin	Fr	Coad
2–06	Sweden	L	1–3	Stockholm	WCq	Walshe
12–06	Spain	L	1–4	Dublin	Fr	Martin
8–09	Finland	W	3–0	Dublin	WCq	Martin 2, Gavin

21–09	England	W	2–0	Liverpool	Fr	Martin, Farrell
9–10	Finland	D	1–1	Helsinki	WCq	Farrell
13–11	Sweden	L	1–3	Dublin	WCq	Martin
10–05–1950	Belgium	L	1–5	Brussels	Fr	Duffy
26–11	Norway	D	2–2	Dublin	Fr	Carey, Walshe
13–05–1951	Argentina	L	0–1	Dublin	Fr	
30–05	Norway	W	3–2	Oslo	Fr	Ringstead, Farrell, Coad
17–10	West Germany	W	3–2	Dublin	Fr	OG, Fitzsimons, Glynn
4–05–1952	West Germany	L	0–3	Cologne	Fr	
7–05	Austria	L	0–6	Vienna	Fr	
1–06	Spain	L	0–6	Madrid	Fr	
16–11	France	D	1–1	Dublin	Fr	Fallon
25–03–1953	Austria	W	4–0	Dublin	Fr	Ringstead 2, Eglinton, O'Farrell
4–10	France	L	3–5	Dublin	WCq	Ryan, Walsh, O'Farrell
28–10	Luxembourg	W	4–0	Dublin	WCq	Fitzsimons 2, Ryan, Eglinton
25–11	France	L	0–1	Paris	WCq	
7–03–1954	Luxembourg	W	1–0	Luxembourg	WCq	Cummins
8–11	Norway	W	2–1	Dublin	Fr	Martin, Ryan
1–05–1955	Holland	W	1–0	Dublin	Fr	Fitzgerald
25–05	Norway	W	3–1	Oslo	Fr	Cummins 2, Ringstead
28–05	West Germany	L	1–2	Hamburg	Fr	Fallon
19–09	Yugoslavia	L	1–4	Dublin	Fr	Fitzsimons
27–11	Spain	D	2–2	Dublin	Fr	Fitzsimons, Ringstead
10–05–1956	Holland	W	4–1	Rotterdam	Fr	Fitzsimons 2, Haverty, Ringstead
3–10	Denmark	W	2–1	Dublin	WCq	Curtis, Gavin
25–11	West Germany	W	3–0	Dublin	Fr	Cantwell, McCann, Haverty
8–05–1957	England	L	1–5	London	WCq	Curtis
19–05	England	D	1–1	Dublin	WCq	Ringstead
2–10	Denmark	W	2–0	Copenhagen	WCq	Fitzsimons, Cummins
11–05–1958	Poland	D	2–2	Chorzow	Fr	Curtis, Cummins
14–05	Austria	L	1–3	Vienna	Fr	Curtis
5–10	Poland	D	2–2	Dublin	Fr	Cantwell 2
5–04–1959	Czechoslovakia	W	2–0	Dublin	ECpr	Tuohy, Cantwell
10–05	Czechoslovakia	L	0–4	Bratislava	ECpr	
1–11	Sweden	W	3–2	Dublin	Fr	Giles, Curtis 2
30–03–1960	Chile	W	2–0	Dublin	Fr	Cantwell, Curtis
11–05	West Germany	W	1–0	Dusseldorf	Fr	Fagan
18–05	Sweden	L	1–4	Malmo	Fr	Fagan
28–09	Wales	L	2–3	Dublin	Fr	Fagan
6–11	Norway	W	3–1	Dublin	Fr	Fitzgerald 2, Fagan
3–05–1961	Scotland	L	1–4	Glasgow	WCq	Haverty
7–05	Scotland	L	0–3	Dublin	WCq	
8–10	Czechoslovakia	L	1–3	Dublin	WCq	Giles
29–10	Czechoslovakia	L	1–7	Prague	WCq	Fogarty
8–04–1962	Austria	L	2–3	Dublin	Fr	Cantwell, Tuohy
12–08	Iceland	W	4–2	Dublin	ECr1	Cantwell, Tuohy, Fogarty
2–09	Iceland	D	1–1	Reykjavik	ECr1	Tuohy
9–06–1963	Scotland	W	1–0	Dublin	Fr	Cantwell
25–09	Austria	D	0–0	Vienna	ECr2	
13–10	Austria	W	3–2	Dublin	ECr2	Cantwell 2, OG
11–03–1964	Spain	L	1–5	Seville	ECqf	McEvoy
8–04	Spain	L	0–2	Dublin	ECqf	
10–05	Poland	L	1–3	Krakow	Fr	Ambrose
13–05	Norway	W	4–1	Oslo	Fr	Hurley, McEvoy, Giles
24–05	England	L	1–3	Dublin	Fr	Strahan
25–10	Poland	W	3–2	Dublin	Fr	McEvoy 2, Mooney
24–03–1965	Belgium	L	0–2	Dublin	Fr	
5–05	Spain	W	1–0	Dublin	WCq	OG
27–10	Spain	L	1–4	Seville	WCq	McEvoy
10–11	Spain	L	0–1	Paris	WCq	
4–05–1966	West Germany	L	0–4	Dublin	Fr	
22–05	Austria	L	0–1	Vienna	Fr	
25–05	Belgium	W	3–2	Liege	Fr	Cantwell 2, Fullam
23–10	Spain	D	0–0	Dublin	ECq	
16–11	Turkey	W	2–1	Dublin	ECq	O'Neill, McEvoy
7–12	Spain	L	0–2	Valencia	ECq	
22–02–1967	Turkey	L	1–2	Ankara	ECq	Cantwell
21–05	Czechoslovakia	L	0–2	Dublin	ECq	
22–11	Czechoslovakia	W	2–1	Prague	ECq	Treacy, O'Connor

15-05-1968	Poland	D	2–2	Dublin	Fr	
30-10	Poland	L	0–1	Chorzow	Fr	
10-11	Austria	D	2–2	Dublin	Fr	Rogers, Hale
4-05-1969	Czechoslovakia	L	1–2	Dublin	WCq	Rogers
27-05	Denmark	L	0–2	Copenhagen	WCq	
8-06	Hungary	L	1–2	Dublin	WCq	Givens
21-09	Scotland	D	1–1	Dublin	Fr	Givens
7-10	Czechoslovakia	L	0–3	Prague	WCq	
15-10	Denmark	D	1–1	Dublin	WCq	Givens
5-11	Hungary	L	0–4	Budapest	WCq	
6-05-1970	Poland	L	1–2	Poznan	Fr	Givens
9-05	West Germany	L	1–2	Berlin	Fr	Mulligan
23-09	Poland	L	0–2	Dublin	Fr	
14-10	Sweden	D	1–1	Dublin	ECq	Carroll
28-10	Sweden	L	0–1	Stockholm	ECq	
8-12	Italy	L	0–3	Florence	ECq	
10-05-1971	Italy	L	1–2	Dublin	ECq	Conway
30-05	Austria	L	1–4	Dublin	ECq	Rogers
10-10	Austria	L	0–6	Linz	ECq	
11-06-1972	Iran	W	2–1	Recife	Clr1	Leech, Givens
18-06	Ecuador	W	3–2	Natal	Clr1	Rogers, Martin, O'Connor
21-06	Chile	L	1–2	Recife	Clr1	Rogers
25-06	Portugal	L	1–2	Recife	Clr1	Leech
18-10	Soviet Union	L	1–2	Dublin	WCq	Conroy
15-11	France	W	2–1	Dublin	WCq	Conroy, Treacy
13-05-1973	Soviet Union	L	0–1	Moscow	WCq	
16-05	Poland	L	0–2	Wroclaw	Fr	
19-05	France	D	1–1	Paris	WCq	Martin
6-06	Norway	D	1–1	Oslo	Fr	Dennehy
21-10	Poland	W	1–0	Dublin	Fr	Dennehy
5-05-1974	Brazil	L	1–2	Rio de Janerio	Fr	Mancini
8-05	Uruguay	L	0–2	Montevideo	Fr	
12-05	Chile	W	2–1	Santiago	Fr	Hand, Conway
30-10	Soviet Union	W	3–0	Dublin	ECq	Givens 3
20-11	Turkey	D	1–1	Izmir	ECq	Givens
10-05-1975	Switzerland	W	2–1	Dublin	ECq	Martin, Treacy
18-05	Soviet Union	L	1–2	Kiev	ECq	Hand
21-05	Switzerland	L	0–1	Berne	ECq	
29-10	Turkey	W	4–0	Dublin	ECq	Givens 4
24-03-1976	Norway	W	3–0	Dublin	Fr	Brady, Holmes, Walsh
26-05	Poland	W	2–0	Poznan	Fr	Givens 2
8-09	England	D	1–1	London	Fr	Daly
13-10	Turkey	D	3–3	Ankara	Fr	Stapleton, Daly, Waters
17-11	France	L	0–2	Paris	WCq	
9-02-1977	Spain	L	0–1	Dublin	Fr	
30-03	France	W	1–0	Dublin	WCq	Brady
24-04	Poland	D	0–0	Dublin	Fr	
1-06	Bulgaria	L	0–2	Sofia	WCq	
12-10	Bulgaria	D	0–0	Dublin	WCq	
5-04-1978	Turkey	W	4–2	Dublin	Fr	Giles, McGee, Treacy 2
12-04	Poland	L	0–3	Lodz	Fr	
21-05	Norway	D	0–0	Oslo	Fr	
24-05	Denmark	D	3–3	Copenhagen	ECq	Stapleton, Grealish, Daly
20-09	Nth. Ireland	D	0–0	Dublin	ECq	
25-10	England	D	1–1	Dublin	ECq	Daly
2-05-1979	Denmark	W	2–0	Dublin	ECq	Daly, Givens
19-05	Bulgaria	L	0–1	Sofia	ECq	
22-05	West Germany	L	1–3	Dublin	Fr	Ryan
29-05	Argentina	D	0–0	Dublin	Fr	
11-09	Wales	L	1–2	Swansea	Fr	OG
26-09	Czechoslovakia	L	1–4	Prague	Fr	McGee
17-10	Bulgaria	W	3–0	Dublin	ECq	Martin, Grealish, Stapleton

LEADING INTERNATIONAL APPEARANCES

1 Brady	72	3 O'Leary	68	5 Giles	60
2 Stapleton	70	4 Moran K	63		

LEADING INTERNATIONAL GOALSCORERS			
1 Stapleton	20	3 Dunne	14
2 Givens	19	Cantwell	14

29–10	United States	W	3–2	Dublin	Fr	Grealish, Givens, Anderson
21–11	Nth. Ireland	L	0–1	Belfast	ECq	
6–02–1980	England	L	0–2	London	ECq	
26–03	Cyprus	W	3–2	Nicosia	WCq	Lawrenson, McGee 2
30–04	Switzerland	W	2–0	Dublin	Fr	Givens, Daly
16–05	Argentina	L	0–1	Dublin	Fr	
10–09	Holland	W	2–1	Dublin	WCq	Daly, Lawrenson
15–10	Belgium	D	1–1	Dublin	WCq	Grealish
28–10	France	L	0–2	Paris	WCq	
19–11	Cyprus	W	6–0	Dublin	WCq	Daly 2, Grealish, Robinson, Stapleton, Hughton
24–02–1981	Wales	L	1–3	Dublin	Fr	Grealish
25–03	Belgium	L	0–1	Brussels	WCq	
29–04	Czechoslovakia	W	3–1	Dublin	Fr	Moran 2, Stapleton
24–05	Poland	L	0–3	Bydgoszcz	Fr	
9–09	Holland	D	2–2	Rotterdam	WCq	Robinson, Stapleton
14–10	France	W	3–2	Dublin	WCq	OG, Stapleton, Robinson
28–04–1982	Algeria	L	0–2	Algiers	Fr	
22–05	Chile	L	0–1	Santiago	Fr	
27–05	Brazil	L	0–7	Uberlandia	Fr	
30–05	Trinidad	L	1–2	Port of Spain	Fr	Brady
22–09	Holland	L	1–2	Rotterdam	ECq	Daly
13–10	Iceland	W	2–0	Dublin	ECq	Stapleton, Grealish
17–11	Spain	D	3–3	Dublin	ECq	Grimes, Stapleton 2
30–03–1983	Malta	W	1–0	Ta'Qali	ECq	Stapleton
27–04	Spain	L	0–2	Zaragoza	ECq	
21–09	Iceland	W	3–0	Reykjavik	ECq	Waddock, Robinson, Walsh
12–10	Holland	L	2–3	Dublin	ECq	Waddock, Brady
16–11	Malta	W	8–0	Dublin	ECq	Lawrenson 2, Brady 2, Stapleton, O'Callaghan, Sheedy, Daly
4–04–1984	Israel	L	0–3	Tel Aviv	Fr	
23–05	Poland	D	0–0	Dublin	Fr	
3–06	China	W	1–0	Sapporo	Fr	O'Keefe
8–08	Mexico	D	0–0	Dublin	Fr	
12–09	Soviet Union	W	1–0	Dublin	WCq	Walsh
17–10	Norway	L	0–1	Oslo	WCq	
14–11	Denmark	L	0–3	Copenhagen	WCq	
5–02–1985	Italy	L	1–2	Dublin	Fr	Waddock
27–02	Israel	D	0–0	Tel Aviv	Fr	
26–03	England	L	1–2	London	Fr	Brady
1–05	Norway	D	0–0	Dublin	WCq	
26–05	Spain	D	0–0	Cork	Fr	
2–06	Switzerland	W	3–0	Dublin	WCq	Stapleton, Grealish, Sheedy
11–09	Switzerland	D	0–0	Berne	WCq	
16–10	Soviet Union	L	0–2	Moscow	WCq	
13–11	Denmark	L	1–4	Dublin	WCq	Stapleton
26–03–1986	Wales	L	0–1	Dublin	Fr	
23–04	Uruguay	D	1–1	Dublin	Fr	Daly
27–04	Iraq	L	0–1	Baghdad	Fr	
25–05	Iceland	W	2–1	Reykjavik	Fr	Daly, McGrath
27–05	Czechoslovakia	W	1–0	Reykjavik	Fr	Stapleton
10–09	Belgium	D	2–2	Brussels	ECq	Stapleton, Brady
15–10	Scotland	D	0–0	Dublin	ECq	
12–11	Poland	L	0–1	Warsaw	Fr	
18–02–1987	Scotland	W	1–0	Glasgow	ECq	Lawrenson
1–04	Bulgaria	L	1–2	Sofia	ECq	Stapleton
29–04	Belgium	D	0–0	Dublin	ECq	
23–05	Brazil	W	1–0	Dublin	Fr	Brady
28–05	Luxembourg	W	2–0	Luxembourg	ECq	Galvin, Whelan
9–09	Luxembourg	W	2–1	Dublin	ECq	Stapleton, McGrath
14–10	Bulgaria	W	2–0	Dublin	ECq	McGrath, Moran
10–11	Israel	W	5–0	Dublin	Fr	Byrne, Kelly 3, Quinn

23-03-1988	Romania	W	2-0	Dublin	Fr	Moran, Kelly
27-04	Yugoslavia	W	2-0	Dublin	Fr	McCarthy, Moran
22-05	Poland	W	3-1	Dublin	Fr	Sheedy, Cascarino, Sheridan
1-06	Norway	D	0-0	Oslo	Fr	
12-06	England	W	1-0	Stuttgart	ECr1	Houghton
15-06	Soviet Union	D	1-1	Hanover	ECr1	Whelan
18-06	Holland	L	0-1	Gelsenkirchen	ECr1	
14-09	Nth. Ireland	D	0-0	Belfast	WCq	
19-10	Tunisia	W	4-0	Dublin	Fr	Cascarino 2, Aldridge, Sheedy
16-11	Spain	L	0-2	Seville	WCq	
7-02-1989	France	D	0-0	Dublin	Fr	
8-03	Hungary	D	0-0	Budapest	WCq	
26-04	Spain	W	1-0	Dublin	WCq	OG
28-05	Malta	W	2-0	Dublin	WCq	Houghton, Moran
4-06	Hungary	W	2-0	Dublin	WCq	McGrath, Cascarino
6-09	West Germany	D	1-1	Dublin	Fr	Stapleton
11-10	Nth. Ireland	W	3-0	Dublin	WCq	Whelan, Cascarino, Houghton
15-11	Malta	W	2-0	Ta'Qali	WCq	Aldridge 2
28-03-1990	Wales	W	1-0	Dublin	Fr	Slaven
25-04	Soviet Union	W	1-0	Dublin	Fr	Staunton
16-05	Finland	D	1-1	Dublin	Fr	Sheedy
27-05	Turkey	D	0-0	Izmir	Fr	
2-06	Malta	W	3-0	Ta'Qali	Fr	Quinn, Townsend, Stapleton
11-06	England	D	1-1	Cagliari	WCr1	Sheedy
17-06	Egypt	D	0-0	Palermo	WCr1	
21-06	Holland	D	1-1	Palermo	WCr1	Quinn
25-06	Romania	D	0-0 (5-4p)	Genoa	WCr2	
30-06	Italy	L	0-1	Rome	WCqf	
12-09	Morocco	W	1-0	Dublin	Fr	Kelly
17-10	Turkey	W	5-0	Dublin	ECq	Aldridge 3, O'Leary, Quinn
14-11	England	D	1-1	Dublin	ECq	Cascarino
6-02-1991	Wales	W	3-0	Wrexham	Fr	Quinn 2, Byrne
27-03	England	D	1-1	London	ECq	Quinn
1-05	Poland	D	0-0	Dublin	ECq	
22-05	Chile	D	1-1	Dublin	Fr	Kelly
1-06	United States	D	1-1	Boston	Fr	Cascarino
11-09	Hungary	W	2-1	Gyor	Fr	Kelly, Aldridge
16-10	Poland	D	3-3	Poznan	ECq	McGrath, Townsend, Cascarino
13-11	Turkey	W	3-1	Istanbul	ECq	Byrne 2, Cascarino
19-02-1992	Wales	L	0-1	Dublin	Fr	
25-03	Switzerland	W	2-1	Dublin	Fr	Coyne, Aldridge
29-04	USA	W	4-1	Dublin	Fr	Townsend, Irwin, Quinn, Cascarino
26-05	Albania	W	2-0	Dublin	WCq	Aldridge, McGrath
30-05	USA	L	1-3	Washington	Fr	McCarthy
4-06	Italy	L	0-2	Boston	Fr	
7-06	Portugal	W	2-0	Boston	Fr	Staunton, Coyne

ROMANIA

Romania took to football before most of her Balkan neighbours. The Federatia Romana de Fotbal was formed in 1908, a full 15 years before neighbours Bulgaria sought to do the same. The initial impulse to organise football came from the growing number of teams that were playing the game at that time, not only in Bucharest but in the rich oil fields of Ploiesti. Here a growing number of industries, such as textiles, had sprung up and many of them were run by English companies.

At first the indigenous population were hesitant about taking up the game, but in Prince Carol, the heir to the Romanian throne, they had a perfect role model, and it was at his instigation that the football federation was formed. In 1910, Prince Carol formed the larger Federation of Romanian Sports Societies, which the football body immediately joined. So keen was the Prince on sport, and football in particular, that he became the first General Secretary of the Federation.

A championship was started in 1910, and the first champions, Olimpia Bucharest, contained several Britons in their side, but the First World War nearly killed the game. As the popularity of the game declined, so did the popularity of Carol, who was by now King, and in 1925 he abdicated. The ethnically Hungarian Transylvania, in the north-west of the country, was left as the main area where football was still played. Timisoara in particular was a stronghold and remained so throughout the inter-war period.

In June 1922 a match was played against Yugoslavia in a game that represented Romania's first ever and Yugoslavia's first on home soil. The Yugoslavs provided regular opposition in the inter-war years, and in the 1930s the Balkan Cup gave a competitive edge to the games. Bulgaria and Greece also took part in these tournaments, and of the four nations, Romania was the most successful with three titles.

King Carol was back in business in 1930, and he insisted Romania take part in the first World Cup in Uruguay. He selected a squad of players and then persuaded their employers to allow them leave to travel to South America. As one of only four European teams to make the journey, they were given a splendid welcome by the hosts although the hospitality did not extend to the pitch. Having beaten Peru, Romania lost 4–0 to Uruguay in the crucial match of the group and so failed to qualify for the semi-finals.

Romania entered all of the first three World Cups, but luckily did not have to travel so far for the 1934 and 1938 tournaments because they did not reach the second round in either. The eventual finalists Czechoslovakia ended their hopes in 1934, but it was a much more unlikely source, Cuba, who knocked the Romanians out in 1938, even if they did need a replay. Two players stand out from this time, the captain Emeric Vogel and the prolific scorer Iuliu Bodola, who to this day remains the top scorer for the national side.

The communists took control of the government in 1944, and as was standard practice they reorganised the game from top to bottom. Of all the Eastern Bloc countries, however, Romania was the last to benefit from the new system. In fact, the extraordinary thing was that when its allies were at their strongest, Romania was at its weakest, and whilst football has fallen into disrepair in the late 1980s in Poland, Hungary, Bulgaria and Czechoslovakia, Romania has embarked on its most successful era ever.

Two clubs have dominated Romanian football in the post-war period, Dinamo Bucharest, the team of the despised Securitate police, and Steaua Bucharest, the team of the army. At no time was this dominance more marked than in the 1988 season, when out of 34 games, both won 30 and the only separating factor was that Steaua had beaten Dinamo at home and drawn away.

Steaua, known as CCA Bucharest in the 1950s, won their first championship in 1951, Dinamo in 1955. Since then, apart from the occasional success of provincial teams like Petrolul Ploiesti, UT Arad, Arges Pitesti and Universitatea Craiova, the championship has remained a stronghold for these Bucharest teams.

Until the 1980s Romanian football was generally unremarkable. A few good players such as Florea Dumitrache, who scored two goals in the 1970 World Cup Finals, did emerge but not in any great numbers. Qualification for the 1970 World Cup, their first post-war, was followed by their reaching the quarter-finals of the 1972 European Championships before losing to Hungary after a play-off, but the upswing in fortunes was only temporary. Despite the presence of Dudu Georgescu and Anghel Iordanescu, two of the great names in Romanian football, not until 1984 did the Romanians qualify for a major tournament again.

The early 1980s saw the government of Nicolae Ceausescu become even more murderous than before and the two implements of his power, the army and the police, both used their football clubs to enhance their reputations even further. If Steaua and Dinamo had been powerful before, they were now transformed into sides that were almost unbeatable. This helped the national side, and led by Ladislau Bölöni, Romania's most capped player, they pulled themselves out of the doldrums. Though the 1984 European Championship in France was not a success, it proved to be the launching pad for Romania's emergence as a first-class football nation.

The late 1980s were an extraordinary time for Steaua in particular. Not only did they remain unbeaten for three consecutive seasons but in 1986 they became the only

		All			League			Cup		Europe		
	Team	G	S	B	G	S	B	G	S	G	S	B
1	Steaua Bucuresti	33	17	7	14	9	6	18	7	1	1	1
2	Dinamo Bucuresti	22	26	6	15	16	4	7	10	–	–	2
3	Rapid Bucuresti	10	14	3	1	11	3	9	3	–	–	–
4	Universitatea Craiova	9	5	7	4	3	6	5	2	–	–	1
5	UT Arad	8	3	1	6	1	1	2	2	–	–	–
6	Venus Bucuresti	8	1	1	8	–	1	–	1	–	–	–
7	Ripensia Timisoara	6	4	2	4	2	2	2	2	–	–	–
8	Chinezul Timisoara	6	1	–	6	–	–	–	1	–	–	–
9	Petrolul Ploiesti	5	4	2	4	3	2	1	1	–	–	–
10	Polit Timisoara	2	4	5	–	–	5	2	4	–	–	–
11	FC Arges Pitesti	2	3	3	2	2	3	–	1	–	–	–
12	FC Bihor Oradea	2	3	1	1	2	1	1	1	–	–	–
13	CSM Resita	2	1	–	1	1	–	1	–	–	–	–
14	Colentina Bucuresti	2	–	–	2	–	–	–	–	–	–	–
	Olimpia Bucuresti	2	–	–	2	–	–	–	–	–	–	–
	Prahova Ploiesti	2	–	–	2	–	–	–	–	–	–	–
	Universitatea Cluj	1	4	1	–	1	1	1	3	–	–	–
18	Jiul Petroseni	1	3	1	–	2	1	1	1	–	–	–
	Progresul Bucuresti	1	1	2	–	–	2	1	1	–	–	–
20	Coltea Brasov	1	1	–	1	1	–	–	–	–	–	–
21	Chimea Vîlcea	1	–	–	–	–	–	1	–	–	–	–
	Ariesul Turda	1	–	–	–	–	–	1	–	–	–	–
	Romano–American Bucuresti	1	–	–	1	–	–	–	–	–	–	–
	Tirnu Severin	1	–	–	–	–	–	1	–	–	–	–
24	Sportul Studentesc	–	4	3	–	1	3	–	3	–	–	–
25	Victoria Cluj	–	3	–	–	3	–	–	–	–	–	–
26	CFR Timisoara	–	2	1	–	1	1	–	1	–	–	–
27	FC Maramures Baia Mare	–	2	–	–	–	–	–	2	–	–	–
28	AMEFA Arad	–	1	1	–	1	1	–	–	–	–	–
	Steagul Rosa Brasov	–	1	1	–	1	1	–	–	–	–	–
	ASA Tîrgu Mures	–	1	1	–	1	1	–	–	–	–	–
	15 teams with a record of	–	11	6	–	3	6	–	8	–	–	–

To the end of the 1991–92 season

team from behind the Iron Curtain to win Europe's top prize, the European Cup, beating Barcelona 2–0 on penalties in the final. Three years later they were back again, but were on the end of a sound thrashing by Milan.

Not only were Steaua rampant at this time, the national side enjoyed a renaissance which included qualification for the World Cup in 1990. Steaua players were well represented in the side as it was common practice for all the best players to be recruited into either the Dinamo or Steaua camps.

The best known Romanian player of the 1980s has been Gheorghe Hagi, but he has been well supported by players such as Silviu Lung in goal, Mircea Rednic, Micheal Klein, Dorin Mateut, Gheorghe Popescu, Rodion Camataru and Marius Lacatus, all of whom have been in demand in the West since the downfall of Ceausescu. Generally acknowledged to be one of the better sides in the World Cup in Italy, they were unlucky to lose on penalties in the second round to the Republic of Ireland.

The future is uncertain for Romanian football, especially at club level, but as Steaua and Dinamo Bucharest will no longer be on the receiving end of massive state support, the league could well become a far more open and therefore interesting affair.

Population: 23 265 000
Area, sq km: 237 500
% in urban areas: 51.3%
Capital city: Bucharest

Federatia Romana de Fotbal
Vasile Conta #16
Bucharest R-70130
Romania
Tel: (010 40) 0 107090
Fax: (010 40) 0 117075
Telex: 11180 SPORT R
Cable: SPORTROM BUCHARESTI – FOTBAL
Languages for correspondence: English & French

Year of formation: 1908
Affiliation to FIFA: 1930
Affiliation to UEFA: 1954
Registered clubs: 5453
Registered players: 187600
Registered coaches: 10346
Registered referees: 8212
National stadium: Stadionul 23 August, Bucharest, 65000
National colours: Shirts: Yellow/Shorts: Blue/Socks: Red
Reserve colours: Shirts: Blue/Shorts: Yellow/Socks: Red
Season: August–June with a mid season break in January and February

THE RECORD

WORLD CUP

1930 .... QT Automatic – Final Tournament/1st round
1934 .... QT 2nd/3 in group 10 – Final Tournament/1st round
1938 .... QT Walk-over – Final Tournament/1st round
1950 .... Did not enter
1954 .... QT 2nd/3 in group 8
1958 .... QT 2nd/3 in group 7
1962 .... Did not enter
1966 .... QT 3rd/4 in group 4
1970 .... QT 1st/4 in group 1 – Final Tournament/1st round
1974 .... QT 2nd/4 in group 4
1978 .... QT 2nd/3 in group 8
1982 .... QT 3rd/5 in group 4
1986 .... QT 3rd/5 in group 3
1990 .... QT 1st/4 in group 1 – Final Tournament/2nd round

EUROPEAN CHAMPIONSHIP

1960 .... Quarter-finalists
1964 .... 1st round
1968 .... QT 2nd/4 in group 6
1972 .... QT 1st/4 in group 1 – Final Tournament/Quarter-finalists
1976 .... QT 2nd/4 in group 4
1980 .... QT 3rd/4 in group 3
1984 .... QT 1st/5 in group 5 – Final Tournament/1st round
1988 .... QT 2nd/4 in group 1
1992 .... QT 3rd/5 in group 2

OLYMPIC GAMES

1908–20 ..... Did not enter
1924 .... 1st round
1928–48 ..... Did not enter
1952 .... Preliminary round
1956 .... Did not enter
1960 .... QT Failed to qualify
1964 .... Final Tournament/Quarter-finalists
1968 .... QT Failed to qualify
1972 .... QT Failed to qualify
1976 .... QT Failed to qualify
1980 .... QT Failed to qualify
1984 .... QT Failed to qualify
1988 .... QT Failed to qualify
1992 .... QT Failed to qualify

EUROPEAN CLUB COMPETITIONS

EUROPEAN CUP: Winners – Steaua Bucharest 1986
Finalists – Steaua Bucharest 1989

CUP WINNERS CUP: Semi-finalists – Dinamo Bucharest 1990

UEFA CUP: Semi-finalists – Universitatea Craiova 1983

MITROPA CUP: Quarter-finalists – Ripensia Timisoara 1938, Rapid Bucharest 1938

CLUB DIRECTORY

BUCHAREST (Population – 2250000)

Dinamo Bucuresti
Stadium: Dinamo 18000
Founded: 1948
Colours: Red/Red
Previous names: Merger of Unirea and Tricolor in 1926 to form Unirea Tricolor, who merged with Ciocanul in 1948 to form Dinamo

Rapid Bucuresti
Stadium: Giulesti 18000
Founded: 1923
Colours: White with a maroon band on chest/White
Previous names: Casa Ferovarilul Rapid 1923–36 1946–50, Rapid 1936–46, Locomotiva 1950–58

Sportul Studentesc Bucuresti
Stadium: Sportul Studentesc 15000
Founded: 1916
Colours: White/Black
Previous names: Universitar 1916–19, Sportul Studentesc 1919–44, Sparta 1944–48, Central Universitar 1948–54, Stiinta 1954–67, Politehnica 1967–69

Steaua Bucuresti
Stadium: Steaua 30000
Founded: 1947
Colours: Blue/Red
Previous names: Armata 1947–48, CSCA 1948–50, CCA 1950–62

Venus Bucuresti were formed in 1915 and folded in 1949

BRASOV (Population – 351000)
FC Brasov
Stadium: Municipal 30000
Founded: 1937
Colours: Yellow and black stripes/Yellow

CONSTANTA (Population – 327 000)
FC Farul Constanta
Stadium: 1 Mai 20 000
Founded: 1957
Colours: Blue and white stripes/White
Previous names: Locomotiva 1950–57, Farul 1957–72, FC Constanta 1972–90

TIMISOARA (Population – 325 000)
Poletehnica Timisoara
Stadium: 1 Mai 40 000
Founded: 1921
Colours: Violet and white stripes/White
Previous names: UCAS 1921–30, CSU 1930–50, Stiinta 1950–66

Clubs from Timisoara that are no longer in existance:
1: CAMT Timisoara 1913–48. Known as Chinezul 1913–29, RGMT 1929–33, Chinezul 1933–39, CAMT 1939–48
2: Ripensia 1928–48

IASI (Population – 313 000)
Politehnica Iasi
Stadium: 23 August
Founded: 1958
Colours: Blue/White
Previous names: CSMS Iasi 1958–67

CLUJ–NAPOCA (Population – 310 000)
Universitatea Cluj–Napoca
Stadium: Municipal 30 000
Founded: 1919
Colours: White/White
Previous names: CSR 1919–23, Universitatea 1923–48, CSU 1948–49, Stiinta 1949–66

Victoria Cluj 1920–47 were known as Romania Cluj from 1920–36

PLOIESTI (Population – 300 000)
Petrolul Ploiesti
Stadium: Petrolul 16 000
Founded: 1924
Colours: Yellow/Yellow
Previous names: Juventus Bucharest 1924–44, Distributia Bucharest 1944–48, Petrolul Bucharest 1948–49, Partizanul Bucharest 1949–50, Flacara Bucharest 1950–52, Flacara Ploiesti 1952–57, Energia Ploiesti 1957

Prahova Ploiesti
Stadium: Municipal
Founded: 1909
Colours: Red/White
Previous names: United Ploiesti 1909–14, Prahova 1914–47, Concordia 1947–50, Partizanul 1950–56, Metalul 1956–58

GALATI (Population – 295 000)
Otelul Galati
Stadium: Dunarea 20 000
Founded: 1964
Colours: Red and blue stripes/Red

CRAIOVA (Population – 281 000)
Electroputere Craivova
Stadium: Electroputere 15 000
Founded: 1946
Colours: Red/White

Universitatea Craiova
Stadium: Central 30 000
Founded: 1948
Colours: White with three blue stripes/white
Previous name: Stiinta 1950–66

BRAILA (Population – 235 000)
FCM Progresul Braila
Stadium: Municipal 8000
Founded: 1960
Colours: White/Blue

ORADEA (Population – 213 000)
FC Bihor Oradea
Stadium: Bihor 20 000
Founded: 1972
Colours: Blue and red stripes/Blue
Previous names: Nagyvarad 1911–20 1940–44, CAO 1920–40, Libertatea 1944–48, ICO 1948–51, Progresul 1951–57, CSO 1957–61, Crisana 1961–72

ARAD (Population – 187 000)
UT Arad
Stadium: UTA 17 000
Founded: 1943
Colours: Red/Red
Previous name: IT Arad 1943–50, Flamura Rosie 1950–58

BACAU (Population – 179 000)
FC Bacau
Stadium: 23 August 34 000
Founded: 1950
Colours: Red/White
Previous names: Dinamo Bacau 1950–70, SC Bacau 1970–90

SIBIU (Population – 177 000)
FC Inter Sibiu
Stadium: Municipal 14 000
Founded: 1982
Colours: Red and blue stripes/White

TIRGU MURES (Population – 158 000)
ASA Tîrgu Mures
Stadium: Municipal 12 000
Founded: 1962
Colours: Blue/Red

PITESTI (Population – 157 000)
FC Arges Pitesti
Stadium: 1 Mai 15 000
Founded: 1953
Colours: Violet/White
Previous name: Dinamo Pitesti 1953–67

BAIA MARE (Population – 139 000)
FC Maramures Baia Mare
Stadium: Baia Mare 13 000
Founded: 1962
Colours: Yellow/Blue
Previous names: Phoenix CSM 1938–40, Carpati 1940–56, Minerul 1956–62, FC Baia Mare 1962–85

RESITA (Population – 105 000)
CSM Resita
Stadium: Valea Domanului
Founded: 1922
Colours: Red/Black
Previous names: UDR 1922–45, Otelul 1945–48, Metalochimic 1948–50, Metalul 1950–58

RIMNICU VILCEA (Population – 96 000)
Chîmea Rimnicu Vîlcea
Stadium: 1 Mai 13 000
Founded: 1924
Colours: White/Blue
Previous names: Vilceana 1924–44, CSM 1944–55, Flamura Rosie 1955–57, Unirea 1957–58 1962–66, Saniterul 1958–59, Chîmea 1959–62, Oltul 1966–67

HUNEDOARA (Population – 88 000)
Corvinul Hunedoara
Stadium: Corvinul 15 000
Founded: 1921
Colours: Blue with white sleeves/Blue
Previous names: Corvinul 1921–46 1957–63, UF 1946–48, IMS 1948–52, Metalul 1952–57, 1964–70, Siderurgistul 1963–64

PETROSANI (Population – 74 000)
Jiul Petrosani
Stadium: Jiul 25 000
Founded: 1919
Colours: Black and white stripes/Black
Previous names: Minerilor 1919–24, UCAS 1924–30, Merger with CS Lupeni in 1930 to form Jiul 1930–50, Partizanul 1950, Flacara 1950–53, Minerul 1953–58

ROMANIAN LEAGUE CHAMPIONSHIP

Year	Champions
1910	Olimpia Bucuresti
1911	Olimpia Bucuresti
1912	United Ploiesti
1913	Colentina Bucuresti
1914	Colentina Bucuresti
1915	Romano–Americana
1916	Prahova Ploiesti
1917–19	–
1920	Venus Bucuresti
1921	Venus Bucuresti

Year	Champions		Runners–up
1922	Chinezul Timisoara	5–1	Victoria Cluj
1923	Chinezul Timisoara	3–0	Victoria Cluj
1924	Chinezul Timisoara	4–1	CAO Oradea
1925	Chinezul Timisoara	5–1	UCAS Petrosani
1926	Chinezul Timisoara	3–0	Juventus Bucuresti
1927	Chinezul Timisoara	2–2 4–3	Coltea Brasov

1928	Coltea Brasov	3–2	Jiul Lupeni
1929	Venus Bucuresti	3–2	Romania Cluj
1930	Juventus Bucuresti	3–0	Gloria CFR Arad
1931	UDR Resita	2–0	SG Sibiu
1932	Venus Bucuresti	3–0	UDR Resita
1933	Ripensia Timisoara	5–3 0–0	Universitatea Cluj
1934	Venus Bucuresti	3–2 5–3	Ripensia Timisoara

	Champions		Runners–up		3rd	
1935	Ripensia Timisoara	32	CAO Oradea	29	Venus Bucuresti	29
1936	Ripensia Timisoara	30	AMEFA Arad	28	Juventus Bucuresti	24
1937	Venus Bucuresti	32	Rapid Bucuresti	30	Ripensia Timisoara	27
1938	Ripensia Timisoara	2–0 2–0	Rapid Bucuresti			
1939	Venus Bucuresti	35	Ripensia Timisoara	26	AMEFA Arad	25
1940	Venus Bucuresti	31	Rapid Bucuresti	29	Sportul Studentesc	27
1941	Unirea Tricolor	38	Rapid Bucuresti	35	Ripensia Timisoara	32
1942–46	–					
1947	IT Arad	44	Carmen Bucuresti	33	CFR Timisoara	33
1948	IT Arad	50	CFR Timisoara	45	CFR Bucuresti	42
1949	ICO Oradea	37	CFR Bucuresti	32	Jiul Petrosani	30
1950	Flamura Rosie	28	Lokomotiva Buch.	28	Stiinta Timisoara	25
1951	CCA Bucuresti	32	Dinamo Bucuresti	32	Progresul Oradea	26
1952	CCA Bucuresti	36	Dinamo Bucuresti	34	Cimpulung Moldavia	25
1953	CCA Bucuresti	28	Dinamo Bucuresti	25	Flamura Rosie	24
1954	Flamura Rosie	35	CCA Bucuresti	34	Dinamo Bucuresti	33
1955	Dinamo Bucuresti	37	Flacara Ploiesti	34	Progresul Bucuresti	33
1956	CCA Bucuresti	33	Dinamo Bucuresti	29	Stiinta Timisoara	29
1957	–					
1958	Petrolul Ploiesti	27	CCA Bucuresti	27	Stiinta Timisoara	27
1959	Petrolul Ploiesti	31	Dinamo Bucuresti	30	CCA Bucuresti	29
1960	CCA Bucuresti	34	Steagul Rosu Brasov	27	Petrolul Ploiesti	24
1961	CCA Bucuresti	37	Dinamo Bucuresti	32	Rapid Bucuresti	30
1962	Dinamo Bucuresti	36	Petrolul Ploiesti	33	Progresul Bucuresti	31
1963	Dinamo Bucuresti	37	Steaua Bucuresti	34	Stiinta Timisoara	29
1964	Dinamo Bucuresti	40	Rapid Bucuresti	33	Steaua Bucuresti	31
1965	Dinamo Bucuresti	38	Rapid Bucuresti	37	Steaua Bucuresti	31
1966	Petrolul Ploiesti	38	Rapid Bucuresti	32	Dinamo Bucuresti	28
1967	Rapid Bucuresti	34	Dinamo Bucuresti	32	Universit. Craiova	30
1968	Steaua Bucuresti	35	FC Arges Pitesti	33	Dinamo Bucuresti	31
1969	UT Arad	38	Dinamo Bucuresti	35	Rapid Bucuresti	34
1970	UT Arad	39	Rapid Bucuresti	37	Steaua Bucuresti	34
1971	Dinamo Bucuresti	36	Rapid Bucuresti	35	Steaua Bucuresti	33
1972	FC Arges Pitesti	41	UT Arad	37	Universitatea Cluj	37
1973	Dinamo Bucuresti	39	Universit. Craiova	39	FC Arges Pitesti	35
1974	Universit. Craiova	45	Dinamo Bucuresti	44	Steagul Rosu Brasov	39
1975	Dinamo Bucuresti	43	ASA Tîrgu Mures	40	Universit. Craiova	39
1976	Steaua Bucuresti	51	Dinamo Bucuresti	44	ASA Tîrgu Mures	38
1977	Dinamo Bucuresti	49	Steaua Bucuresti	45	Universit. Craiova	41
1978	Steaua Bucuresti	41	FC Arges Pitesti	41	Politehnica Timis.	38
1979	FC Arges Pitesti	45	Dinamo Bucuresti	41	Steaua Bucuresti	40
1980	Universit. Craiova	44	Steaua Bucuresti	44	FC Arges Pitesti	39
1981	Universit. Craiova	46	Dinamo Bucuresti	43	FC Arges Pitesti	42
1982	Dinamo Bucuresti	47	Universit. Craiova	45	Corvinul Hunedoara	39
1983	Dinamo Bucuresti	49	Universit. Craiova	46	Sportul Studentesc	44
1984	Dinamo Bucuresti	49	Steaua Bucuresti	47	Universit. Craiova	43
1985	Steaua Bucuresti	54	Dinamo Bucuresti	52	Sportul Studentesc	48
1986	Steaua Bucuresti	57	Sportul Studentesc	48	Universit. Craiova	46
1987	Steaua Bucuresti	59	Dinamo Bucuresti	44	Victoria Bucuresti	38
1988	Steaua Bucuresti	64	Dinamo Bucuresti	63	Victoria Bucuresti	40
1989	Steaua Bucuresti	65	Dinamo Bucuresti	62	Victoria Bucuresti	45
1990	Dinamo Bucuresti	57	Steaua Bucuresti	56	Universit. Craiova	44
1991	Universit. Craiova	50	Steaua Bucuresti	50	Dinamo Bucuresti	43
1992	Dinamo Bucuresti	55	Steaua Bucuresti	48	Electroputere Craiova	39

ROMANIAN CUP FINALS

Year	Winners	Score	Runners–up
1934	Ripensia Timisoara	5–0	Universitatea Cluj
1935	CFR Bucuresti	6–5	Ripensia Timisoara
1936	Ripensia Timisoara	5–1	Unirea Tricolor
1937	Rapid Bucuresti	5–1	Ripensia Timisoara
1938	Rapid Bucuresti	3–2	CAMT Timisoara
1939	Rapid Bucuresti	2–0	Sportul Studentesc
1940	Rapid Bucuresti	2–1*	Venus Bucuresti

* After 2–2 4–4 and 2–2 draws

1941	Rapid Bucuresti	4–3	Unirea Tricolor
1942	Rapid Bucuresti	7–1	Universitatea Cluj
1943	Tirnu Severin	4–0	Sportul Studentesc
1944–47	–		
1948	IT Arad	3–2	CFR Timisoara
1949	CSCA Bucuresti	2–1	CSU Cluj
1950	CCA Bucuresti	3–1	Flamura Rosie
1951	CCA Bucuresti	3–1	Flacara Medias
1952	CCA Bucuresti	2–0	Flacara Ploiesti
1953	Flamura Rosie	1–0	CCA Bucuresti
1954	Metalul Resita	2–0	Dinamo Bucuresti
1955	CCA Bucuresti	6–3	Progresul Oradea
1956	Progresul Oradea	2–0	Metalul Turzii
1957	–		
1958	Stiinta Timisoara	1–0	Progresul Bucuresti
1959	Dinamo Bucuresti	4–0	Minerul Baia Mare
1960	Progresul Bucuresti	2–0	Dinamo Bucuresti
1961	Ariesul Turda	2–1	Rapid Bucuresti
1962	Steaua Bucuresti	5–1	Rapid Bucuresti
1963	Petrolul Ploiesti	6–1	Siderurgistul Galati
1964	Dinamo Bucuresti	5–3	Steaua Bucuresti
1965	Stiinta Cluj	2–1	Dinamo Pitesti
1966	Steaua Bucuresti	4–0	UT Arad
1967	Steaua Bucuresti	6–0	Foresta Falticeni
1968	Dinamo Bucuresti	3–1	Rapid Bucuresti
1969	Steaua Bucuresti	2–1	Dinamo Bucuresti
1970	Steaua Bucuresti	2–1	Dinamo Bucuresti
1971	Steaua Bucuresti	3–2	Dinamo Bucuresti
1972	Rapid Bucuresti	2–0	Jiul Petrosani
1973	Chimia Vîlcea	1–1 3–0	Constructorul Galatizi
1974	Jiul Petrosani	4–2	Polit. Timisoara
1975	Rapid Bucuresti	2–1	Universit. Craiova
1976	Steaua Bucuresti	1–0	CSU Galati
1977	Universit. Craiova	2–1	Steaua Bucuresti
1978	Universit. Craiova	3–1	Olimpia Satu Mare
1979	Steaua Bucuresti	3–0	Sportul Studentesc
1980	Polit. Timisoara	2–1	Steaua Bucuresti
1981	Universit. Craiova	6–0	Polit. Timisoara
1982	Dinamo Bucuresti	3–2	FC Baia Mare
1983	Universit. Craiova	2–1	Polit. Timisoara
1984	Dinamo Bucuresti	2–1	Steaua Bucuresti
1985	Steaua Bucuresti	2–1	Universit. Craiova
1986	Dinamo Bucuresti	1–0	Steaua Bucuresti
1987	Steaua Bucuresti	1–0	Dinamo Bucuresti
1988	Steaua Bucuresti	2–1	Dinamo Bucuresti
1989	Steaua Bucuresti	1–0	Dinamo Bucuresti
1990	Dinamo Bucuresti	6–4	Steaua Bucuresti
1991	Universit. Craiova	2–1	FC Bacau
1992	Steaua Bucuresti	1–1 (4–3p)	Polit. Timisoara

INTERNATIONAL MATCHES PLAYED BY ROMANIA

Date	Opponents	Result		Venue	Compet	Scorers
8-06-1922	Yugoslavia	W	2–1	Belgrade	Fr	Ronay, Guga
3-09	Poland	D	1–1	Czernowitz	Fr	Kozzovits
10-06-1923	Yugoslavia	L	1–2	Bucharest	Fr	Ronay
1-07	Czechoslovakia	L	0–6	Cluj	Fr	
2-09	Poland	D	1–1	Lwow	Fr	Guga
26-10	Turkey	D	2–2	Istanbul	Fr	Gansl 2
20-05-1924	Austria	L	1–4	Vienna	Fr	Ströck
27-05	Holland	L	0–6	Paris	OGr1	
31-05	Czechoslovakia	L	1–4	Prague	Fr	Semler
1-05-1925	Turkey	L	1–2	Bucharest	Fr	Brauchler
31-08	Bulgaria	W	4–2	Sofia	Fr	Wetzer 2, Semler 2
25-04-1926	Bulgaria	W	6–1	Bucharest	Fr	Guga, Gugelbauer 2, Csomag, Ströck, Auer I
7-05	Turkey	W	3–1	Istanbul	Fr	Semler 2, Matek
3-10	Yugoslavia	W	3–2	Zagreb	Fr	Semler, Kilianowici, Guga
10-05-1927	Yugoslavia	L	0–3	Bucharest	Fr	
19-06	Poland	D	3–3	Bucharest	Fr	Auer II 2, Tänzer
15-04-1928	Turkey	W	4–2	Arad	Fr	Wetzer, OG, Sepi, Csomag
6-05	Yugoslavia	L	1–3	Belgrade	Fr	Possak
21-04-1929	Bulgaria	W	3–0	Bucharest	Fr	Ciolac 3
10-05	Yugoslavia	L	2–3	Bucharest	Fr	Subasanu, Boross
15-09	Bulgaria	W	3–2	Sofia	Fr	Sepi, Kovacs N, Desu
6-10	Yugoslavia	W	2–1	Bucharest	BC	Sepi, Ciolac
4-05-1930	Yugoslavia	L	1–2	Belgrade	Fr	Desu
25-05	Greece	W	8–1	Bucharest	BC	Wetzer 5, Vogl, Raffinski, Dobay
14-07	Peru	W	3–1	Montevideo	WCr1	Desu, Stanciu, Kovacs N
20-07	Uruguay	L	0–4	Montevideo	WCr1	
12-10	Bulgaria	L	3–5	Sofia	BC	Wetzer 2, OG
10-05-1931	Bulgaria	W	5–2	Bucharest	BC	Sepi, Bodola 2, Stanciu 2
28-06	Yugoslavia	W	4–2	Zagreb	BC	Glanzman, Kovacs N, Bodola 2
23-08	Poland	W	3–2	Warsaw	Fr	Sepi 2, Kocsis
26-08	Lithuania	W	4–2	Kaunas	Fr	Bodola 3, Sepi
29-11	Greece	W	4–2	Athens	BC	Bodola 3, Sepi
12-06-1932	France	W	6–3	Bucharest	Fr	Bodola 2, Wetzer 2, Schwartz 2
26-06	Bulgaria	L	0–2	Belgrade	BC	
28-06	Greece	W	3–0	Belgrade	BC	Ciolac, Schwartz, Bodola
3-07	Yugoslavia	L	1–3	Belgrade	BC	Kovacs N
2-10	Poland	L	0–5	Bucharest	Fr	

4-06-1933	Bulgaria	W	7-0	Bucharest	BC	Vîlcov 2, Dobay 2, Ciolac 3
6-06	Greece	W	1-0	Bucharest	BC	Dobay
11-06	Yugoslavia	W	5-0	Bucharest	BC	Bindea, Ciolac, Bodola 2, Dobay
29-10	Switzerland	D	2-2	Berne	WCq	Sepi, Dobay
29-04-1934	Yugoslavia	W	2-1	Bucharest	WCq	Schwartz, Dobay
27-05	Czechoslovakia	L	1-2	Trieste	WCr1	Dobay
14-10	Poland	D	3-3	Lwow	Fr	Dobay 2, Ciolac
24-12	Greece	D	2-2	Athens	BC	Dobay, Ciolac
30-12	Bulgaria	W	3-2	Athens	BC	Bodola 2, Ciolac
1-01-1935	Yugoslavia	L	0-4	Athens	BC	
17-06	Yugoslavia	L	0-2	Sofia	BC	
19-06	Bulgaria	L	0-4	Sofia	BC	
24-06	Greece	D	2-2	Sofia	BC	Bodola, Gruim
25-08	Germany	L	2-4	Erfurt	Fr	Vîlcov 2
1-09	Sweden	L	1-7	Stockholm	Fr	Georgescu G
3-11	Poland	W	4-1	Bucharest	Fr	Schileru, Bindea 2, Sepi
10-05-1936	Yugoslavia	W	3-2	Bucharest	BC	Bodola 3
17-05	Greece	W	5-2	Bucharest	BC	Bodola 2, Schwartz 2, Dobay
24-05	Bulgaria	W	4-1	Bucharest	BC	Schwartz 2, Ciolac, Dobay
4-10	Hungary	L	1-2	Bucharest	Fr	Bindea
18-04-1937	Czechoslovakia	D	1-1	Bucharest	Fr	Bodola
10-06	Belgium	W	2-1	Bucharest	Fr	Baratky 2
27-06	Sweden	D	2-2	Bucharest	Fr	Baratky 2
4-07	Poland	W	4-2	Lodz	Fr	Dobay, Baratky 2, Bodola
9-07	Lithuania	W	2-0	Kaunas	Fr	Bogdan, Bodola
13-07	Latvia	D	0-0	Riga	Fr	
15-07	Estonia	L	1-2	Tallin	Fr	Bodola
6-09	Yugoslavia	L	1-2	Belgrade	Fr	Baratky
8-05-1938	Yugoslavia	L	0-1	Bucharest	Fr	
5-06	Cuba	D	3-3	Toulouse	WCr1	Bindea, Baratky, Dobay
9-06	Cuba	L	1-2	Toulouse	WCr1	Dobay
6-09	Yugoslavia	D	1-1	Belgrade	Fr	Bindea
25-09	Germany	L	1-4	Bucharest	Fr	Orza
4-12	Czechoslovakia	L	2-6	Prague	Fr	Baratky, Bodola
7-05-1939	Yugoslavia	W	1-0	Bucharest	Fr	Dobay
18-05	Latvia	W	4-0	Bucharest	Fr	Bodola 2, Dobay, OG
24-05	England	L	0-2	Bucharest	Fr	
11-06	Italy	L	0-1	Bucharest	Fr	
22-10	Hungary	D	1-1	Bucharest	Fr	Spielmann
31-03-1940	Yugoslavia	D	3-3	Bucharest	Fr	Bindea 2, Baratky
14-04	Italy	L	1-2	Rome	Fr	Baratky
19-05	Hungary	L	0-2	Budapest	Fr	
14-07	Germany	L	3-9	Frankfurt	Fr	Baratky 2, Ploesteanu
22-09	Yugoslavia	W	2-1	Belgrade	Fr	Popescu, Bogdan
1-06-1941	Germany	L	1-4	Bucharest	Fr	Niculescu
12-10	Slovakia	W	3-2	Bucharest	Fr	Humis, Bindea 2
16-08-1942	Germany	L	0-7	Bytom	Fr	
23-08	Slovakia	L	0-1	Bratislava	Fr	
11-10	Croatia	D	2-2	Bucharest	Fr	Florian, Bogdan
13-06-1943	Slovakia	D	2-2	Bucharest	Fr	Marian, Kovacs I
30-09-1945	Hungary	L	2-7	Budapest	Fr	Pecsovsky, Fabian
8-10-1946	Bulgaria	D	2-2	Tirana	BC	Reuter, Toth
11-10	Yugoslavia	W	2-1	Tirana	BC	Reuter, Fabian
13-10	Albania	L	0-1	Tirana	BC	
25-05-1947	Albania	W	4-0	Tirana	BCE	Farkas 3, Kovacs I
22-06	Yugoslavia	L	1-3	Bucharest	BCE	Farkas
6-07	Bulgaria	W	3-2	Sofia	BCE	Bacut, Pecsovsky
19-07	Poland	W	2-1	Warsaw	Fr	Spielmann 2
21-09	Czechoslovakia	L	2-6	Bucharest	Fr	Spielmann, Dumitrescu
12-10	Hungary	L	0-3	Bucharest	BCE	
26-10	Poland	D	0-0	Bucharest	Fr	
2-05-1948	Albania	L	0-1	Bucharest	BCE	
6-06	Hungary	L	0-9	Budapest	BCE	
20-06	Bulgaria	W	3-2	Bucharest	BCE	Farkas 2, Dumitrescu
4-07	Czechoslovakia	W	2-1	Bucharest	BCE	Iordache, Bartha
10-10	Poland	D	0-0	Chorzow	BCE	
24-10	Hungary	L	1-5	Bucharest	BCE	Pecsovsky
8-05-1949	Poland	W	2-1	Bucharest	Fr	Pecsovsky 2
22-05	Czechoslovakia	L	2-3	Prague	Fr	Vaczi, Lungu

LEADING INTERNATIONAL GOALSCORERS

1 Bodola 30	Balint 14	16 Dembrowski 9
2 Iordanescu 26	11 Baratky 13	Georgescu N 9
3 Bölöni 25	Ciolac 13	Lacatus 9
4 Camataru 22	Wetzer 13	Lucescu 9
5 Georgescu D 21	14 Constantin 12	22 Swartz 8
6 Dobai 20	Dumitru 12	Vaczi 8
7 Hagi 19	15 Bindea 11	Dridea 8
8 Dumitrache 15	Pecsovsky 11	Balaci 8
9 Sepi 14	17 Mateut 10	

23–10	Albania	D	1–1	Bucharest	Fr	Pecsovsky
29–11	Albania	W	4–1	Tirana	Fr	Lungu 2, Vaczi, Filote
14–05–1950	Poland	D	3–3	Wroclaw	Fr	Mircea, Vaczi, Bodo
21–05	Czechoslovakia	D	1–1	Bucharest	Fr	Bodo
8–10	Albania	W	6–0	Bucharest	Fr	Pecsovsky 2, Radulescu 2, Mercea, Suru
20–05–1951	Czechoslovakia	D	2–2	Prague	Fr	Vaczi 2
11–05–1952	Czechoslovakia	W	3–1	Bucharest	Fr	Paraschiva, Serfözö, Ozon
25–05	Poland	W	1–0	Bucharest	Fr	Paraschiva
15–07	Hungary	L	1–2	Turku	OGpr	Suru
26–10	East Germany	W	3–1	Bucharest	Fr	Vaczi 3
14–06–1953	Czechoslovakia	L	0–2	Prague	WCq	
28–06	Bulgaria	W	3–1	Bucharest	WCq	Pecsovsky 2, Ene
11–10	Bulgaria	W	2–1	Sofia	WCq	Serfözö, Calinoiu
25–10	Czechoslovakia	L	0–1	Bucharest	WCq	
8–05–1954	East Germany	W	1–0	Berlin	Fr	Ozon
19–09	Hungary	L	1–5	Budapest	Fr	Ozon
29–05–1955	Poland	D	2–2	Bucharest	Fr	Ozon, Georgescu N
12–06	Norway	W	1–0	Oslo	Fr	Ozon
15–06	Sweden	L	1–4	Gothenburg	Fr	Georgescu N
18–09	East Germany	L	2–3	Bucharest	Fr	Georgescu N
28–09	Belgium	W	1–0	Bucharest	Fr	Georgescu N
9–10	Bulgaria	D	1–1	Bucharest	Fr	Georgescu N
22–04–1956	Yugoslavia	W	1–0	Belgrade	Fr	Cacoveanu
17–06	Sweden	L	0–2	Bucharest	Fr	
26–06	Norway	W	2–0	Bucharest	Fr	Zaharia, David
10–09	Bulgaria	L	0–2	Sofia	Fr	
26–05–1957	Belgium	L	0–1	Brussels	Fr	
1–06	Soviet Union	D	1–1	Moscow	Fr	Ene
16–06	Greece	W	2–1	Athens	WCq	Ene, Ozon
29–09	Yugoslavia	D	1–1	Bucharest	WCq	Ene
3–11	Greece	W	3–0	Bucharest	WCq	Pecsovsky, Tataru I, Cacoveanu
17–11	Yugoslavia	L	0–2	Belgrade	WCq	
14–09–1958	East Germany	L	2–3	Leipzig	Fr	Constantin, Ene
26–10	Hungary	L	1–2	Bucharest	Fr	Dinulescu
2–11	Turkey	W	3–0	Bucharest	ECr1	Oaida, Constantin, OG
26–04–1959	Turkey	L	0–2	Istanbul	ECr1	
19–07	Soviet Union	L	0–2	Moscow	OGq	
2–08	Soviet Union	D	0–0	Bucharest	OGq	
30–08	Poland	W	3–2	Warsaw	Fr	Dridea 3
8–11	Bulgaria	W	1–0	Bucharest	OGq	Constantin
1–05–1960	Bulgaria	L	1–2	Sofia	OGq	Tataru I
22–05	Czechoslovakia	L	0–2	Bucharest	ECr1	
29–05	Czechoslovakia	L	0–3	Prague	ECr1	
14–05–1961	Turkey	W	1–0	Ankara	Fr	Dridea
8–10	Turkey	W	4–0	Bucharest	Fr	Seredai 2, Constantin 2
30–09–1962	Morocco	W	4–0	Bucharest	Fr	Voinea, Ozon, Seredai
14–10	East Germany	L	2–3	Dresden	Fr	Emil 2
1–11	Spain	L	0–6	Madrid	ECr1	
25–11	Spain	W	3–1	Bucharest	ECr1	Tataru I, Manolache, Constantin
23–12	Morocco	L	1–3	Casablanca	Fr	Constantin
12–05–1963	East Germany	W	3–2	Bucharest	Fr	Pavlovici, Haidu, Pîrcalab
2–06	Poland	D	1–1	Chorzow	Fr	Haidu
23–06	Denmark	W	3–2	Copenhagen	OGq	Constantin, Manolache 2
9–10	Turkey	D	0–0	Ankara	Fr	
27–10	Yugoslavia	W	2–1	Bucharest	Fr	Tircovnicu, Haidu

3–11	Denmark	L	2–3	Bucharest	OGq	Emil 2
28–11	Denmark	W	2–1	Turin	OGq	Creiniceanu, Sasu
3–05–1964	Bulgaria	W	2–1	Bucharest	OGq	Constantin 2
31–05	Bulgaria	W	1–0	Sofia	OGq	Kozska
17–06	Yugoslavia	W	2–1	Belgrade	Fr	Georgescu N, Ionescu I
11–10	Mexico	W	3–1	Omiya	OGr1	Creiniceanu, Pîrcalab, Ionescu I
13–10	East Germany	D	1–1	Omiya	OGr1	Pavlovici
15–10	Iran	W	1–0	Omiya	OGr1	Pavlovici
18–10	Hungary	L	0–2	Yokohama	OGqf	
2–05–1965	Turkey	W	3–0	Bucharest	WCq	Georgescu N, Mateianu, Creiniceanu
30–05	Czechoslovakia	W	1–0	Bucharest	WCq	Mateianu
13–06	Portugal	L	1–2	Lisbon	WCq	Avram
19–09	Czechoslovakia	L	1–3	Prague	WCq	Coe
23–10	Turkey	L	1–2	Ankara	WCq	Georgescu N
21–11	Portugal	W	2–0	Bucharest	WCq	Pîrcalab, Badea
1–06–1966	West Germany	L	0–1	Ludwigshafen	Fr	
19–06	Uruguay	W	1–0	Bucharest	Fr	Iancu
3–07	Portugal	L	0–1	Oporto	Fr	
21–09	East Germany	L	0–2	Gera	Fr	
2–11	Switzerland	W	4–2	Bucharest	ECq	Fratila 3, Dridea
17–11	Poland	W	4–3	Ploesti	Fr	OG, Gergely, Fratila, Coe
26–11	Italy	L	1–3	Naples	ECq	Dobrin
3–12	Cyprus	W	5–1	Nicosia	ECq	Dridea 2, Lucescu, Fratila 2
7–12	Israel	W	2–1	Tel Aviv	Fr	Badea, Pîrcalab
4–01–1967	Uruguay	D	1–1	Montevideo	Fr	OG
8–03	Greece	W	2–1	Athens	Fr	Ionescu I
22–03	France	W	2–1	Paris	Fr	Fratila, Dridea
23–04	Cyprus	W	7–0	Bucharest	ECq	Lucescu, Martinovici, Dumitriu 3, Ionescu I 2
24–05	Switzerland	L	1–7	Zurich	ECq	Dobrin
25–06	Italy	L	0–1	Bucharest	ECq	
29–10	Poland	D	0–0	Krakow	Fr	
18–11	East Germany	L	0–1	Berlin	OGq	
22–11	West Germany	W	1–0	Bucharest	Fr	Gergely
6–12	East Germany	L	0–1	Bucharest	OGq	
24–12	Zaire	D	1–1	Kinshasa	Fr	Sasu
1–05–1968	Austria	D	1–1	Linz	Fr	Kallo
5–06	Holland	D	0–0	Bucharest	Fr	
27–10	Portugal	L	0–3	Lisbon	WCq	
6–11	England	D	0–0	Bucharest	Fr	
23–11	Switzerland	W	2–0	Bucharest	WCq	Dumitrache, Domide
15–01–1969	England	D	1–1	London	Fr	Dumitrache
16–04	Greece	D	2–2	Athens	WCq	Dumitrache 2
14–05	Switzerland	W	1–0	Lausanne	WCq	OG
3–09	Yugoslavia	D	1–1	Belgrade	Fr	Dembrowski
12–10	Portugal	W	1–0	Bucharest	WCq	Dobrin
16–11	Greece	D	1–1	Bucharest	WCq	Dembrowski
9–02–1970	Peru	L	0–2	Lima	Fr	
8–04	West Germany	D	1–1	Stuttgart	Fr	Neagu
8–04	France	L	0–2	Reims	Fr	
6–05	Yugoslavia	D	0–0	Bucharest	Fr	
2–06	England	L	0–1	Guadalajara	WCr1	
6–06	Czechoslovakia	W	2–1	Guadalajara	WCr1	Neagu, Dumitrache
10–06	Brazil	L	2–3	Guadalajara	WCr1	Dumitrache, Dembrowski
11–10	Finland	W	3–0	Bucharest	ECq	Dumitrache, Nunweiller
11–11	Wales	D	0–0	Cardiff	ECq	
2–12	Holland	L	0–2	Amsterdam	Fr	
18–04–1971	Albania	W	2–1	Bucharest	OGq	Iordanescu, Salceanu

LEADING INTERNATIONAL APPEARANCES

1	Bölöni	108
2	Klein	90
3	Rednic	83
4	Lung	76
5	Dinu	75
	Camataru	75
7	Hagi	72
8	Lucescu	70
9	Balaci	69
10	Stefanescu	66
11	Iordanescu	64

21–04	Yugoslavia	W	1–0	Novi Sad	Fr	Dembrowski
16–05	Czechoslovakia	L	0–1	Bratislava	ECq	
26–05	Albania	W	2–1	Tirana	OGq	Tataru II 2
22–09	Finland	W	4–0	Helsinki	ECq	Iordanescu, Lupescu I, Dembrowski, Lucescu
10–10	Denmark	L	1–2	Copenhagen	OGq	Dembrowski
14–11	Czechoslovakia	W	2–1	Bucharest	ECq	Dembrowski, Dobrin
24–11	Wales	W	2–0	Bucharest	ECq	Lupescu I, Lucescu
31–01–1972	Morocco	W	4–2	Casablanca	Fr	Kun, Radu, Brosowski, Domide
8–04	France	W	2–0	Bucharest	Fr	Iordanescu, Dinu
23–04	Peru	D	2–2	Bucharest	Fr	Tataru II, Marcu
29–04	Hungary	D	1–1	Budapest	ECqf	Satmareanu
14–05	Hungary	D	2–2	Bucharest	ECqf	Dobrin, Neagu
17–05	Hungary	L	1–2	Belgrade	ECqf	Neagu
21–05	Denmark	L	2–3	Bucharest	OGq	Gyorfi, Dumitru
17–06	Italy	D	3–3	Bucharest	Fr	Dobrin, Hainal, OG
3–09	Austria	D	1–1	Craiova	Fr	Dembrowski
20–09	Finland	D	1–1	Helsinki	WCq	Nunweiller
29–10	Albania	W	2–0	Bucharest	WCq	Dobrin, Dembrowski
18–04–1973	Soviet Union	L	0–2	Kiev	Fr	
6–05	Albania	W	4–1	Tirana	WCq	Dumitru, Troi, Dumitrache, Taralunga
27–05	East Germany	W	1–0	Bucharest	WCq	Dumitrache
26–09	East Germany	L	0–2	Leipzig	WCq	
14–10	Finland	W	9–0	Bucharest	WCq	Marcu 2, Mircea 2, Dumitrache 2, Dumitru, Pantea, Georgescu D
23–03–1974	France	L	0–1	Paris	Fr	
17–04	Brazil	L	0–2	Sao Paulo	Fr	
22–04	Argentina	L	1–2	Buenos Aires	Fr	Kun
29–05	Greece	W	3–1	Bucharest	BC	Iordanescu 2, Lucescu
5–06	Holland	D	0–0	Rotterdam	Fr	
28–07	Japan	W	4–1	Constanza	Fr	Dumitrache 2, Dumitru, Hainal
25–09	Bulgaria	D	0–0	Sofia	Fr	
13–10	Denmark	D	0–0	Copenhagen	ECq	
4–12	Israel	W	1–0	Tel Aviv	Fr	Samas
19–03–1975	Turkey	D	1–1	Istanbul	Fr	Lucescu
31–03	Czechoslovakia	D	1–1	Prague	Fr	Kun
17–04	Spain	D	1–1	Madrid	ECq	Crisan
10–05	Denmark	W	6–1	Bucharest	ECq	Georgescu D 2, Crisan 2, Lucescu, Dinu
1–06	Scotland	D	1–1	Bucharest	ECq	Georgescu D
24–09	Greece	D	1–1	Salonika	BC	Dimitru
12–10	Turkey	D	2–2	Bucharest	Fr	Iordanescu, Dinu
16–11	Spain	D	2–2	Bucharest	ECq	Georgescu D, Iordanescu
29–11	Soviet Union	D	2–2	Bucharest	Fr	Troi, Hainal
17–12	Scotland	D	1–1	Glasgow	ECq	Crisan
12–05–1976	Bulgaria	L	0–1	Veliko Tarnovo	BC	
5–06	Italy	L	2–4	Milan	Fr	Lucescu, Georgescu D
2–07	Iran	D	2–2	Tehran	Fr	Bölöni, Sandu
22–09	Czechoslovakia	D	1–1	Bucharest	Fr	Georgescu D
6–10	Czechoslovakia	L	2–3	Prague	Fr	Balaci, Georgescu D
28–11	Bulgaria	W	3–2	Bucharest	BC	Troi 2, Multescu
23–03–1977	Turkey	W	4–0	Bucharest	BC	Georgescu D, Dumitru, Vigu, Iordanescu
16–04	Spain	W	1–0	Bucharest	WCq	OG
27–04	East Germany	D	1–1	Bucharest	Fr	Dumitru
8–05	Yugoslavia	W	2–0	Zagreb	WCq	Georgescu D, Iordanescu
5–08	Iran	D	0–0	Tehran	Fr	
21–09	Greece	W	6–1	Bucharest	Fr	Dumitru 3, Bölöni 2, Georgescu D
26–10	Spain	L	0–2	Madrid	WCq	
13–11	Yugoslavia	L	4–6	Bucharest	WCq	Vigu, Iordanescu, Bölöni, Georgescu D
22–03–1978	Turkey	D	1–1	Istanbul	BC	Georgescu D
5–04	Argentina	L	0–2	Buenos Aires	Fr	
3–05	Bulgaria	W	2–0	Bucharest	BC	Iordanescu, Balaci
14–05	Soviet Union	L	0–1	Bucharest	Fr	
31–05	Bulgaria	D	1–1	Sofia	BC	Iordanescu
11–10	Poland	W	1–0	Bucharest	Fr	Iordanescu
25–10	Yugoslavia	W	3–2	Bucharest	ECq	Sames 2, Iordanescu
15–11	Spain	L	0–1	Valencia	ECq	
13–12	Greece	L	1–2	Athens	Fr	Romila
19–12	Israel	D	1–1	Tel Aviv	Fr	Stan
21–03–1979	Greece	W	3–0	Bucharest	Fr	Dimitru, Balaci, Georgescu D

4–04	Spain	D	2–2	Craiova	ECq	Georgescu D 2
13–05	Cyprus	D	1–1	Limassol	ECq	Augustin
1–06	East Germany	L	0–1	Berlin	Fr	
29–08	Poland	L	0–3	Warsaw	Fr	
14–10	Soviet Union	L	1–3	Moscow	Fr	Nicolae
31–10	Yugoslavia	L	1–2	Kosovo	ECq	Raducanu
18–11	Cyprus	W	2–0	Bucharest	ECq	Raducanu, Multescu
16–02–1980	Italy	L	1–2	Naples	Fr	Bölöni
30–03	Yugoslavia	L	0–2	Belgrade	BC	
2–04	East Germany	D	2–2	Bucharest	Fr	Sandu, OG
16–05	Czechoslovakia	L	1–2	Brno	Fr	Ionescu
6–06	Belgium	L	1–2	Brussels	Fr	Camataru
27–08	Yugoslavia	W	4–1	Bucharest	BC	Iordanescu 3, Camataru
10–09	Bulgaria	W	2–1	Varna	Fr	Beldeanu, Iordanescu
24–09	Norway	D	1–1	Oslo	WCq	Iordanescu
15–10	England	W	2–1	Bucharest	WCq	Raducanu, Iordanescu
25–03–1981	Poland	W	2–0	Bucharest	Fr	Camataru, Iordanescu
8–04	Israel	L	1–2	Tel Aviv	Fr	Sandu
15–04	Denmark	L	1–2	Copenhagen	Fr	Camataru
29–04	England	D	0–0	London	WCq	
13–05	Hungary	L	0–1	Budapest	WCq	
3–06	Norway	W	1–0	Bucharest	WCq	Ticleanu
9–09	Bulgaria	L	1–2	Bucharest	Fr	Balaci
23–09	Hungary	D	0–0	Bucharest	WCq	
10–10	Switzerland	L	1–2	Bucharest	WCq	Balaci
11–11	Switzerland	D	0–0	Berne	WCq	
24–03–1982	Belgium	L	1–4	Brussels	Fr	Ticleanu
14–04	Bulgaria	W	2–1	Ruse	Fr	Camataru, Bölöni
1–05	Cyprus	W	3–1	Hunedoara	ECq	Vaetus, Camataru, Bölöni
12–05	Argentina	L	0–1	Rosario	Fr	
17–05	Peru	L	0–2	Lima	Fr	
19–05	Chile	W	3–2	Santiago	Fr	Klein 2, Augustin
14–07	Japan	W	4–0	Suceava	Fr	Klein, Turcu, Bölöni, Georgescu D
18–07	Japan	W	3–1	Bucharest	Fr	Georgescu D 2, Bölöni
1–09	Denmark	W	1–0	Bucharest	Fr	Balaci
8–09	Sweden	W	2–0	Bucharest	ECq	Andone, Klein
17–11	East Germany	L	1–4	Karl–Marx–Stadt	Fr	Bölöni
4–12	Italy	D	0–0	Florence	ECq	
29–01–1983	Turkey	D	1–1	Istanbul	Fr	Gabor
2–02	Greece	W	3–1	Larissa	Fr	Camataru 2, Bölöni
9–03	Turkey	W	3–1	Tirgu Mures	Fr	Balaci 2, Bölöni
30–03	Yugoslavia	L	0–2	Timisoara	Fr	
16–04	Italy	W	1–0	Bucharest	ECq	Bölöni
15–05	Czechoslovakia	L	0–1	Bucharest	ECq	
1–06	Yugoslavia	L	0–1	Sarajevo	Fr	
9–06	Sweden	W	1–0	Stockholm	ECq	Camataru
10–08	Norway	D	0–0	Oslo	Fr	
24–08	East Germany	W	1–0	Bucharest	Fr	Negrila
7–09	Poland	D	2–2	Krakow	Fr	Movila, Irimescu
12–10	Wales	L	0–5	Wrexham	Fr	
8–11	Israel	D	1–1	Tel Aviv	Fr	Coras
12–11	Cyprus	W	1–0	Limassol	ECq	Bölöni
30–11	Czechoslovakia	D	1–1	Bratislava	ECq	Geolgau
22–01–1984	Ecuador	W	3–1	Guayaquil	Fr	Bölöni, Iorgulescu, Camataru
7–02	Algeria	D	1–1	Algiers	Fr	OG
7–03	Greece	W	2–0	Craiova	Fr	Coras, Mateus
11–04	Israel	D	0–0	Oradea	Fr	
14–06	Spain	D	1–1	Saint Etienne	ECr1	Bölöni
17–06	West Germany	L	1–2	Lens	ECr1	Coras
20–06	Portugal	L	0–1	Nantes	ECr1	
29–07	China	W	4–2	Iasi	Fr	Rednic, Camataru, Orac, Balint
1–08	China	W	1–0	Buzau	Fr	Balint
29–08	East Germany	L	1–2	Dresden	Fr	Irimescu
12–09	Nth. Ireland	L	2–3	Belfast	WCq	Hagi, Geolgau
21–11	Israel	D	1–1	Tel Aviv	Fr	Lacatus
30–01–1985	Portugal	W	3–2	Lisbon	Fr	Lacatus 2, Hagi
27–03	Poland	D	0–0	Sibiu	Fr	
3–04	Turkey	W	3–0	Craiova	WCq	Camataru 2, Hagi
1–05	England	D	0–0	Bucharest	WCq	

6–06	Finland	D	1–1	Helsinki	WCq	Hagi
7–08	Soviet Union	L	0–2	Moscow	Fr	
28–08	Finland	W	2–0	Timisoara	WCq	Hagi, Mateut
11–09	England	D	1–1	London	WCq	Camataru
16–10	Nth. Ireland	L	0–1	Bucharest	WCq	
13–11	Turkey	W	3–1	Izmir	WCq	Iorgulescu, Coras, Iovan
28–02–1986	Egypt	D	2–2	Alexandria	Fr	Coras, Iorgulescu
2–03	Egypt	W	1–0	Alexandria	Fr	Gabor
14–03	Iraq	D	1–1	Baghdad	Fr	Augustin
17–03	Iraq	D	0–0	Baghdad	Fr	
26–03	Scotland	L	0–3	Glasgow	Fr	
23–04	Soviet Union	W	2–1	Timisoara	Fr	Hagi, Camataru
4–06	Norway	W	3–1	Bucharest	Fr	Piturca 2, Mateut
20–08	Norway	D	2–2	Oslo	Fr	Hagi, OG
10–09	Austria	W	4–0	Bucharest	ECq	Iovan 2, Lacatus, Hagi
8–10	Israel	W	4–2	Tel Aviv	Fr	Piturca 2, Bölöni, Camaratu
12–11	Spain	L	0–1	Seville	ECq	
4–03–1987	Turkey	W	3–1	Ankara	Fr	Belodedici, Bölöni, OG
11–03	Greece	D	1–1	Athens	Fr	Hagi
25–03	Albania	W	5–1	Bucharest	ECq	Piturca, Bölöni, Hagi, Belodedici, Bumbescu
8–04	Israel	W	3–2	Brasov	Fr	Cimpeanu, Belodedici, Kramer
29–04	Spain	W	3–1	Bucharest	ECq	Piturca, Mateut, Ungureanu
2–09	Poland	L	1–3	Bydgoszcz	Fr	Bölöni
7–10	Greece	D	2–2	Bucharest	Fr	Tîrlea, Bölöni
28–10	Albania	W	1–0	Vlore	ECq	Klein
18–11	Austria	D	0–0	Vienna	ECq	
3–02–1988	Israel	W	2–0	Haifa	Fr	Bölöni, Ciuca
6–02	Poland	D	2–2	Haifa	Fr	Coras, Sabau
23–03	Rep. Ireland	L	0–2	Dublin	Fr	
30–03	East Germany	D	3–3	Halle	Fr	Andone, Geolgau, Bölöni
1–06	Holland	L	0–2	Amsterdam	Fr	
20–09	Albania	W	3–0	Constanta	Fr	Belodedici, Hagi, Camataru
19–10	Bulgaria	W	3–1	Sofia	WCq	Mateut, Camataru 2
2–11	Greece	W	3–0	Bucharest	WCq	Mateut, Hagi, Sabau
23–11	Israel	W	3–0	Sibiu	Fr	Mateut 2, Camataru
29–03–1989	Italy	W	1–0	Sibiu	Fr	Sabau
12–04	Poland	L	1–2	Warsaw	Fr	Sabau
26–04	Greece	D	0–0	Athens	WCq	
10–05	Bulgaria	W	1–0	Bucharest	WCq	Popescu
31–08	Portugal	D	0–0	Setubal	Fr	
5–09	Czechoslovakia	L	0–2	Nitra	Fr	
11–10	Denmark	L	0–3	Copenhagen	WCq	
15–11	Denmark	W	3–1	Bucharest	WCq	Balint 2, Sabau
4–02–1990	Algeria	D	0–0	Algiers	Fr	
28–03	Egypt	W	3–1	Cairo	Fr	Timofte I 2, Balint
3–04	Switzerland	L	1–2	Lucerne	Fr	Hagi
25–04	Israel	W	4–1	Haifa	Fr	Hagi, Sabau, Balint, OG
21–05	Egypt	W	1–0	Bucharest	Fr	Camataru
26–05	Belgium	D	2–2	Brussels	Fr	Rednic, Lacatus
9–06	Soviet Union	W	2–0	Bari	WCr1	Lacatus 2
14–06	Cameroon	L	1–2	Bari	WCr1	Balint
18–06	Argentina	D	1–1	Naples	WCr1	Balint
25–06	Rep. Ireland	D	0–0 (4–5p)	Genoa	WCr2	
29–08	Soviet Union	W	2–1	Moscow	Fr	Lacatus, Lupescu
12–09	Scotland	L	1–2	Glasgow	ECq	Camaturu
26–09	Poland	W	2–1	Bucharest	Fr	Lazar, Rotariu
17–10	Bulgaria	L	0–3	Bucharest	ECq	
5–12	San Marino	W	6–0	Bucharest	ECq	Sabau, Mateut, Raducioiu, Lupescu, Badea, Petrescu
27–03–1991	San Marino	W	3–1	Serravalle	ECq	Hagi, Raducioiu, Timofte
3–04	Switzerland	D	0–0	Neuchatel	ECq	
17–04	Spain	W	2–0	Caceres	Fr	Timofte II, Balint
22–05	Norway	L	0–1	Oslo	Fr	
28–08	USA	L	0–2	Brasov	Fr	
16–10	Scotland	W	1–0	Bucharest	ECq	Hagi
13–11	Switzerland	W	1–0	Bucharest	ECq	Mateut
20–11	Bulgaria	D	1–1	Sofia	ECq	Popescu
25–12	Egypt	L	0–3	Cairo	Fr	

28–12	Egypt	D	1–1	Port Said	Fr	Munteanu
12–02–1992	Greece	L	0–1	Athens	Fr	
8–04	Latvia	W	2–0	Bucharest	Fr	Badea, Petrescu
6–05	Faeroe Islands	W	7–0	Bucharest	Fr	Balint 3, Hagi, Lacatus, Lupescu, Pana
20–05	Wales	W	5–1	Bucharest	WCq	Hagi 2, Lupescu 2, Balint

SAN MARINO

The official name of the country is the Most Serene Republic of San Marino, and it is located entirely within northern Italy, 50 miles east of Florence. With a population of just 22 000, it is also the smallest independent country in Europe, so it was to general surprise that San Marino entered the 1992 European Championship qualifiers. The experience was not a particularly happy one, but there were no rugby scores. Indeed, throughout the qualifiers their defending was tenacious and they even managed to score a goal.

A team called San Marino does play in the Italian league, although it has remained in the very lowest echelons. There is also a local league and cup competition, both of which have been running since 1986. Under the principle that allows every sovereign state the right to membership of FIFA, San Marino looks set to become a regular on the European football scene.

Population: 22 000
Area, sq km: 61
Capital city: San Marino

Federazione Sammarinese Giuoco Calcio
Via Ca dei Lunghi 18
Cailungo
47031 San Marino
Tel: (010 39) 549 902228
Fax: (010 39) 549 906226
Telex: 0505-284 COSMAR SO
Cable: FEDERCALCIO SAN MARINO
Languages for correspondence: French

Year of formation: 1931
Affiliation to FIFA: 1988
Affiliation to UEFA: 1988
Registered clubs: 17
Registered players: 1040
Registered referees: 26

National stadium: Seravalle 7000
National colours: Shirts: Sky Blue/Shorts: Sky Blue/Socks: Sky Blue
Season: Clubs take part in Italian league

THE RECORD

WORLD CUP

1930–90 ..... Did not enter

EUROPEAN CHAMPIONSHIP

1960–88 ..... Did not enter
1992 .... QT 5th/5 in group 2

OLYMPIC GAMES

1908–92 ..... Did not enter

EUROPEAN CLUB COMPETITIONS

Clubs from San Marino do not take part in the European club competitions

LEAGUE CHAMPIONS

1986 Faetano – 1987 Fiorita – 1988 Tre Fiori – 1989 Domagnano – 1990 Fiorita – 1991 Faetano – 1992 Domagnano

CUP WINNERS

1986 Fiorita – 1987 Libertas – 1988 Domagnano – 1989 Libertas – 1990 Domagnano – 1991 Libertas – 1992 Faetano

INTERNATIONAL MATCHES PLAYED BY SAN MARINO

Date	Opponents	Result		Venue	Compet
14–11–1990	Switzerland	L	0–4	Serravalle	ECq
5–12	Romania	L	0–6	Bucharest	ECq
27–03–1991	Romania *Scorer:* Pasolini	L	1–3	Serravalle	ECq
1–05	Scotland	L	0–2	Serravalle	ECq
22–05	Bulgaria	L	0–3	Serravalle	ECq
5–06	Switzerland	L	0–7	St Gallen	ECq
16–10	Bulgaria	L	0–4	Sofia	ECq
13–11	Scotland	L	0–4	Glasgow	ECq
19–02–1992	Italy	L	0–4	Cesena	Fr

SCOTLAND

Scotland may not have invented modern-day football, but the country was a huge contributing factor in the development, spread and rise in popularity of the game. More often than not it was Scottish immigrant workers who showed the locals how the game was played as it spread abroad, whilst in Britain, both Irish and English teams regularly featured large numbers of Scots in their teams before the turn of the century. England in particular has continued in this vein as Scottish players continue to go south to further their careers. From great early teams like Preston North End and Sunderland to modern-day Liverpool, Scots have made their mark not only as players but also as managers. Much of the current reputation of both Manchester United and Liverpool is due to two Scots, Matt Busby and Bill Shankly, and it is a tradition carried on by the likes of Dalglish and Souness at Liverpool, Ferguson at Manchester United and George Graham at Arsenal.

To look at Scottish football only in terms of its contribution in other countries, however, would be to miss out on a proud history within its own borders. Queen's Park Football Club, formed in 1867 by members of a Glasgow YMCA, was the first Scottish club to be formed. Named after the park in which the members used to play, Queen's Park were the standard bearers of football in Scotland before the turn of the century. Devoutly amateur, even to this day, their home, Hampden Park, remains the spiritual home of Scottish football.

A great many of the present-day clubs were formed in the 1870s and in 1873 it was felt necessary to form a Scottish Football Association to regulate the game north of the border. Although part of the United Kingdom, Scotland did not come under the control of the Football Association in London, and in respect of its contribution to the world game it has remained a separate entity to this date and still keeps its permanent seat on the world's rule-making body, the International Board.

Glasgow was chosen as the location for the association in preference to the capital Edinburgh, where the Scottish Rugby Union was founded in the same year. Over the years Glasgow has come to be regarded as the football capital of Scotland. Edinburgh on the other hand, with Murrayfield as the second 'National Stadium' and home to the Scottish rugby team, has never been regarded as a football city, despite the presence of Hibernian and Heart of Midlothian, the city's two football teams.

A year after its formation, the Scottish FA launched a cup competition based on the model south of the border in England. Naturally, Queen's Park were the first winners, and in the great amateur era before professionalism was adopted in 1893, they won the competition on ten occasions. Their victory in the 1893 tournament was a watershed in the development of the game. In the very year that professionalism was introduced, it was the last honour they won. Their opponents that day, Celtic, though defeated, had the last laugh. They represented the new face of Scottish football, and along with their fierce rivals Rangers soon started on a course of total domination of the domestic game.

This two-club domination has no comparison elsewhere in world football with the exception of the Montevideo giants, Peñarol and Nacional. The similarities with Uruguayan football do not end there either. Both countries have remarkably small populations in relation to their impact on the game. Though Scotland have never been crowned world champions like their South American counterparts, they were for 30 or so years the top national side in the world. Not until the turn of the century did England begin to match the Scots on the football pitch.

The England–Scotland rivalry on the international field dates back to 30 November 1872, when the first ever international match took place. England, represented by players from teams like the 1st Surrey Rifles, Oxford University, Wanderers and Sheffield Wednesday, faced a team of Scots who – surprise, surprise – all came from the Queen's Park club. The 0–0 scoreline seems somewhat surprising in that of the 22 players on the the pitch, 14 were forwards!

The England–Scotland game remained an annual encounter and apart from the war years, took place every year until 1990. Wales were added to the fixture list in 1876, and with the inclusion in 1884 of Ireland, the Home International Championship was launched. Although Scotland's total of 41 victories in this tournament is 13 less than England, it must be remembered that she has one-tenth of the population, and this figure ranks as a considerable achievement.

The matches against England provided the first tactical

		All			League			Cup		Europe			L Cup	
	Team	G	S	B	G	S	B	G	S	G	S	B	G	S
1	Rangers	85	46	18	42	23	16	25	15	1	2	2	17	6
2	Celtic	74	51	20	35	22	16	29	17	1	1	4	9	11
3	Aberdeen	17	22	7	4	11	6	7	6	1	–	1	4	5
4	Heart of Midlothian	13	19	11	4	13	11	5	5	–	–	–	4	1
5	Queen's Park	10	2	–	–	–	–	10	2	–	–	–	–	–
6	Hibernian	8	18	12	4	6	10	2	8	–	–	2	2	4
7	Dundee	5	9	3	1	4	1	1	3	–	–	2	3	2
8	Motherwell	4	9	5	1	4	5	2	4	–	–	–	1	1
9	East Fife	4	2	2	–	–	2	1	2	–	–	–	3	–
10	Kilmarnock	3	12	4	1	4	3	2	5	–	–	1	–	3
11	Dundee United	3	9	7	1	–	6	–	6	–	1	1	2	2
12	Third Lanark	3	5	2	1	–	2	2	4	–	–	–	–	1
13	Dumbarton	3	5	–	2	–	–	1	5	–	–	–	–	–
14	St Mirren	3	4	2	–	–	2	3	3	–	–	–	–	1
15	Vale of Levan	3	4	–	–	–	–	3	4	–	–	–	–	–
16	Clyde	3	3	3	–	–	3	3	3	–	–	–	–	–
17	Partick Thistle	2	4	3	–	–	3	1	1	–	–	–	1	3
18	Falkirk	2	3	1	–	2	1	2	–	–	–	–	–	1
19	Renton	2	3	–	–	–	–	2	3	–	–	–	–	–
20	Dunfermline Athletic	2	3	3	–	–	2	2	1	–	–	1	–	2
21	Airdrieonians	1	6	1	–	4	1	1	2	–	–	–	–	–
22	Morton	1	3	2	–	1	2	1	1	–	–	–	–	1
23	St Bernard's	1	–	1	–	–	1	1	–	–	–	–	–	–
24	Raith Rovers	–	2	1	–	–	1	–	1	–	–	–	–	1
25	St Johnstone	–	1	1	–	–	1	–	–	–	–	–	–	1
26	Hamilton Academicals	–	2	–	–	–	–	–	2	–	–	–	–	–
27	Albion Rovers	–	1	–	–	–	–	–	1	–	–	–	–	–
	Cambuslang	–	1	–	–	–	–	–	1	–	–	–	–	–
	Clydesdale	–	1	–	–	–	–	–	1	–	–	–	–	–
	Thornley Bank	–	1	–	–	–	–	–	1	–	–	–	–	–

Complete to the end of the 1991–92 season

breakthrough in the game, and it was a Scottish innovation. In the very early years, football consisted of a player receiving the ball and dribbling with it until he lost it or scored. In the 1870s, the Scottish national side introduced the concept of passing into the game, and the results in the international matches of this time show that they were the masters of this new style. The Scots were also at the forefront of the next great tactical leap in the 1880s, with the introduction of the 2–3–5 formation.

While the British Isles was the focus of world football Scotland played an important part in the development of the game, but by the end of the First World War they were becoming increasingly isolated. Scottish club sides had been amongst the first British sides to make tours abroad, especially to Scandinavia, but it was not until a tour in 1929 to Scandinavia and Germany that Scotland played an international match against anyone other than a British side.

It soon became apparent that valuable ground had been lost when in 1931, in the space of four days, they were beaten 5–0 by Austria and 3–0 by Italy. Three years previously a false light had been cast on the Scottish game when a team called the 'Wembley Wizards' had thrashed England 5–1 on their own territory. That Wembley team was a good one, but it highlighted a major problem that the Scots have had to deal with down the years: the loss of their best players to English clubs.

In that side were three of the greatest names of Scottish football: Hughie Gallacher, Alex James and Alec Jackson. Gallacher played for Newcastle, James for Preston and later notably for Arsenal, whilst Jackson plied his trade with Huddersfield. Between them they could only muster 45 caps. James in particular suffered through refusals to release him for internationals as well as an inbred reluctance of the Scottish FA to select 'Anglo-Scots'. His eight caps belie his reputation as one of the most influential figures in football at that time. The other of the giants of the Scottish game at the time, Alan 'the Wee Blue Devil' Morton, by contrast stayed in Scotland and won 31 caps.

Faced with an exodus on such a large scale, it is surprising that league football managed to survive in Scotland. That it did was largely the result of a continual flow of talented players and two clubs, Celtic and Rangers. In religion, Scotland is a divided country with very active Protestant and Catholic communities. Founded in 1888 to help finance soup kitchens for the poor of the city, Celtic is the standard bearer of the largely Irish-descended Catholic community, and the Irish tricolour is still flown at the ground today.

Rangers on the other hand have been fierce proponents of the Protestant community since they were founded in 1873. Only one recognised Catholic, Mo Johnston, has ever worn the blue of Rangers, and that took over a hundred years to happen. The rivalry is strong and its intensity is matched perhaps only elsewhere in the world by the Real Madrid–Barcelona encounters in Spain, and this has kept Scottish football on its feet, where in different circumstances it might have withered away.

Between them Rangers and Celtic have completely dominated the league and cup. Of 95 league competitions they have won 77, whilst they have faced each other in the Cup Final on 13 occasions. This hegemony has at various times been tested, most notably in recent years with the rise to prominence of Aberdeen and Dundee United and the continuing presence of Hearts and Hibs from Edinburgh, but it will never be broken as long as the set up in Scottish football remains as it is at present.

The post-war years were troubled ones for the international side. Despite qualifying for the 1950 World Cup, a tournament which up until that point they had refused to enter, in a fit of pique the Scots withdrew, feeling that as they had finished only second in their group a place was not merited. Such arrogance did not deter them from travelling to Switzerland four years later, as they again finished second behind England in the Home International tournament which was used as a qualifying group.

The Scots must have wished they had stayed away again after a 7–0 humiliation by Uruguay ensured an early exit from the tournament. Since then, the national side has been no more than a medium power in European football. Failure to qualify for the 1962, 1966 and 1970 World Cups has been followed by qualification for every tournament since, but once there they have never been able to progress beyond the first round. Qualification for the 1992 European Championship marked the first success in seven outings in that competition, but the best to be hoped for in the future is that Scotland will continue to make the final tournaments of either the World Cup or European Championship. To actually win either of them seems to be beyond their reach.

The same can be said of its club football. The late 1960s saw it at its strongest. In 1967, Celtic became the first British side to win the European Cup and were losing finalists three years later, whilst in 1972, Rangers won the Cup Winners Cup. In a country where all of the stars seemed to play abroad, Jimmy Johnstone, a crucial figure in the success at Celtic at the time, bucked the trend and stayed at home. The players of true international class who left, however, still outnumbered those who stayed and included such famous names as Denis Law at Manchester United, Ian St John and Kenny Dalglish at Liverpool, Billy Bremner at Leeds . . . the list goes on.

Scottish clubs inevitably suffered and although Aberdeen won the Cup Winners Cup in 1983 and Dundee United reached the final of the UEFA Cup in 1987, Scottish influence in European competitions has waned. In the late 1980s, Rangers, having set themselves up with one of the most modern stadiums in Europe, started to reverse the southward flow of players by not only buying English players, but also Dutch and Soviets in a bid to revitalise their European ambitions. In the long run the policy may work, but success has not been forthcoming as yet.

There is potential in Scottish football. An unusually high percentage of the population either follows or takes part in the game, and this is a key factor in helping to overcome the disadvantage of a relatively small population, but whether the lead given by Rangers in facing the future will bring any more success is open to debate.

Population: 5094000
Area, sq km: 78783
% in urban areas: 91.5%
Capital city: Edinburgh

The Scottish Football Association
6 Park Gardens
Glasgow, G3 7YF
Scotland
Tel: (010 44) 41 3326372
Fax: (010 44) 41 3327559
Telex: 778904 SFA G
Cable: EXECUTIVE GLASGOW
Languages for correspondence: English, French & German

Year of formation: 1873
Affiliation to FIFA: 1910–1920, 1924–1928, 1946
Affiliation to UEFA: 1954
Registered clubs: 6078
Registered players: 133400
Professional Players: 3200
Registered coaches: 260
Registered referees: 1783
National stadium: Hampden Park, Glasgow 74000
National colours: Shirts: Blue/Shorts: White/Socks: Red
Reserve colours: Shirts: White/Shorts: Blue/Socks: Red
Season: August–May

THE RECORD

WORLD CUP

1930–38 ..... Did not enter
1950 .... QT 2nd/4 in group 1
1954 .... QT 2nd/4 in group 3 – Final Tournament/1st round
1958 .... QT 1st/3 in group 9 – Final Tournament/1st round
1962 .... QT 2nd/3 in group 8
1966 .... QT 2nd/4 in group 8
1970 .... QT 2nd/4 in group 7
1974 .... QT 1st/3 in group 8 – Final Tournament/1st round
1978 .... QT 1st/3 in group 7 –Final Tournament/1st round
1982 .... QT 1st/5 in group 6 – Final Tourbament/1st round
1986 .... QT 2nd/4 in group 7 – Final Tournament/1st round
1990 .... QT 2nd/5 in group 5 – Final Tournament/1st round

EUROPEAN CHAMPIONSHIP

1960 .... Did not enter
1964 .... Did not enter
1968 .... QT 2nd/4 in group 8
1972 .... QT 3rd/4 in group 5
1976 .... QT 3rd/4 in group 4
1980 .... QT 4th/5 in group 2
1984 .... QT 4th/4 in group 1
1988 .... QT 4th/5 in group 7
1992 .... QT 1st/5 in group 2

EUROPEAN CLUB COMPETITIONS

EUROPEAN CUP: Winners – Glasgow Celtic 1967
Finalists – Glasgow Celtic 1970

CUP WINNERS CUP: Winners – Glasgow Rangers 1972, Aberdeen 1983
Finalists – Glasgow Rangers 1961, 1967

UEFA CUP: Finalists – Dundee United 1987

CLUB DIRECTORY

EDINBURGH (Population – 630000)

Heart of Midlothian Football Club
Stadium: Tynecastle Park 25000
Founded: 1874
Colours: Maroon/White

Hibernian Football Club
Stadium: Easter Road 22000
Founded: 1875
Colours: Green with white sleeves/White

GLASGOW (Population – 1800000)

The Celtic Football Club
Stadium: Celtic Park 53000
Founded: 1888
Colours: Green and white hoops/White

Clyde Football Club
Stadium: Firhill Park 20000
Founded: 1878
Colours: White/Black

Clydebank Football Club
Stadium: Kilbowie Park 9000
Founded: 1965
Colours: White with a red diagonal stripe/White

Hamilton Academical Football Club
Stadium: Douglas Park 14000
Founded: 1875
Colours: Red and white hoops/White

Motherwell Football Club
Stadium: Fir Park 18000
Founded: 1886
Colours: Yellow/Claret

Partick Thistle Football Club
Stadium: Firhill Park 20000
Founded: 1876
Colours: Yellow with red sleeves/Red

Queen's Park Football Club
Stadium: Hampden Park 74000
Founded: 1867
Colours: Black and white hoops/White

Rangers Football Club
Stadium: Ibrox 44000
Founded: 1873
Colours: Blue/White

St Mirren Football Club
Stadium: Love Street 21000
Founded: 1877
Colours: Black and white stripes/White

ABERDEEN (Population – 186000)

Aberdeen Football Club
Stadium: Pittodrie 21000
Founded: 1903
Colours: Red/Red

DUNDEE (Population – 172000)

Dundee Football Club
Stadium: Dens Park 22000
Founded: 1893
Colours: Blue/White

Dundee United Football Club
Stadium: Tannadice Park 22000
Founded: 1909
Colours: Tangerine/Black
Previous name: Dundee Hibernians 1909–23

FALKIRK (Population – 148000)

East Stirlingshire Football Club
Stadium: Firs Park 6000
Founded: 1881
Colours: White with black band on chest/Black

Falkirk Football Club
Stadium: Brockville Park 18000
Founded: 1876
Colours: Blue/White

KIRCALDY (Population – 148 000)
Raith Rovers Football Club
Stadium: Stark's Park 9000
Founded: 1883
Colours: Blue/White

DUNFERMLINE (Population – 125 000)
Dunfermline Athletic Football Club
Stadium: East End Park 19 000
Founded: 1885
Colours: Black and white stripes/Black

GREENOCK (Population – 101 000)
Greenock Morton Football Club
Stadium: Cappielow Park 16 000
Founded: 1874
Colours: Blue and white hoops

AYR (Population – 100 000)
Ayr United Football Club
Stadium: Sommerset Park 18 000
Founded: 1910
Colours: White with black band on chest/Black

KILMARNOCK (Population – 84 000)
Kilmarnock Football Club
Stadium: Rugby Park 17 000
Founded: 1869
Colours: Blue and white hoops/Blue

STIRLING (Population – 61 000)
Stirling Albion Football Club
Stadium: Annfield Park 4000
Founded: 1945
Colours: Red with white sleeves/White

COATBRIDGE (Population – 50 000)
Albion Rovers Football Club
Stadium: Clifton Hall 1000
Founded: 1882
Colours: Yellow/Red

PERTH (Population – 41 000)
St Johnstone Football Club
Stadium: McDiarmid Park 10 000
Founded: 1884 Colours: Blue/White

AIRDRIE
Airdrieonians Football Club
Stadium: Broomfield Park 11 000
Founded: 1878 Colours: White/White

DUMBARTON
Dumbarton Football Club
Stadium: Boghead Park 10 000
Founded: 1872
Colours: Gold with white band on chest/Black

METHIL FIFE
East Fife Football Club
Stadium: Bayview Park 14 000
Founded: 1903
Colours: Black and gold stripes/Black

SCOTTISH LEAGUE CHAMPIONSHIP

Year	Champions		Runners up		3rd	
1891	Dumbarton	29				
	Rangers	29			Celtic	21
1892	Dumbarton	37	Celtic	35	Heart of Midlothian	34
1893	Celtic	29	Rangers	28	St Mirren	20
1894	Celtic	29	Heart of Midlothian	26	St Bernard's	23
1895	Heart of Midlothian	31	Celtic	26	Rangers	22
1896	Celtic	30	Rangers	26	Hibernian	24
1897	Heart of Midlothian	28	Hibernian	26	Rangers	25
1898	Celtic	33	Rangers	29	Hibernian	22
1899	Rangers	36	Heart of Midlothian	26	Celtic	24
1900	Rangers	32	Celtic	25	Hibernian	24
1901	Rangers	35	Celtic	29	Hibernian	25
1902	Rangers	28	Celtic	26	Heart of Midlothian	22
1903	Hibernian	37	Dundee	31	Rangers	29
1904	Third Lanark	43	Heart of Midlothian	39	Celtic	38
1905	Celtic	41	Rangers	41	Third Lanark	35
1906	Celtic	49	Heart of Midlothian	43	Airdrieonians	38
1907	Celtic	55	Dundee	48	Rangers	45
1908	Celtic	55	Falkirk	51	Rangers	50
1909	Celtic	51	Dundee	50	Clyde	48
1910	Celtic	54	Falkirk	52	Rangers	46
1911	Rangers	52	Aberdeen	48	Falkirk	44
1912	Rangers	51	Celtic	45	Clyde	42
1913	Rangers	53	Celtic	49	Heart of Midlothian	41
1914	Celtic	65	Rangers	59	Heart of Midlothian	54
1915	Celtic	65	Heart of Midlothian	61	Rangers	50
1916	Celtic	67	Rangers	56	Morton	51
1917	Celtic	64	Morton	54	Rangers	53
1918	Rangers	56	Celtic	55	Kilmarnock	43
1919	Celtic	58	Rangers	57	Morton	47
1920	Rangers	71	Celtic	68	Motherwell	57
1921	Rangers	76	Celtic	66	Heart of Midlothian	50
1922	Celtic	67	Rangers	66	Raith Rovers	51
1923	Rangers	55	Airdrieonians	50	Celtic	46
1924	Rangers	59	Airdrieonians	50	Celtic	46
1925	Rangers	60	Airdrieonians	57	Hibernian	52
1926	Celtic	58	Airdrieonians	50	Heart of Midlothian	50
1927	Rangers	56	Motherwell	51	Celtic	49
1928	Rangers	60	Celtic	55	Motherwell	55
1929	Rangers	67	Celtic	51	Motherwell	50

1930	Rangers	60	Motherwell	55	Aberdeen	53
1931	Rangers	60	Celtic	58	Motherwell	56
1932	Motherwell	66	Rangers	61	Celtic	48
1933	Rangers	62	Motherwell	59	Heart of Midlothian	50
1934	Rangers	66	Motherwell	62	Celtic	47
1935	Rangers	55	Celtic	52	Heart of Midlothian	50
1936	Celtic	66	Rangers	61	Aberdeen	61
1937	Rangers	61	Aberdeen	54	Celtic	52
1938	Celtic	61	Heart of Midlothian	58	Rangers	49
1939	Rangers	59	Celtic	48	Aberdeen	46
1940–46	–					
1947	Rangers	46	Hibernian	44	Aberdeen	39
1948	Hibernian	48	Rangers	46	Partick Thistle	36
1949	Rangers	46	Dundee	45	Hibernian	39
1950	Rangers	50	Hibernian	49	Heart of Midlothian	43
1951	Hibernian	48	Rangers	38	Dundee	38
1952	Hibernian	45	Rangers	41	East Fife	37
1953	Rangers	43	Hibernian	43	East Fife	39
1954	Celtic	43	Heart of Midlothian	38	Partick Thistle	35
1955	Aberdeen	49	Celtic	46	Rangers	41
1956	Rangers	52	Aberdeen	46	Heart of Midlothian	45
1957	Rangers	55	Heart of Midlothian	53	Kilmarnock	42
1958	Heart of Midlothian	62	Rangers	49	Celtic	46
1959	Rangers	50	Heart of Midlothian	48	Motherwell	44
1960	Heart of Midlothian	54	Kilmarnock	50	Rangers	42
1961	Rangers	51	Kilmarnock	50	Third Lanark	42
1962	Dundee	54	Rangers	51	Celtic	46
1963	Rangers	57	Kilmarnock	48	Partick Thistle	46
1964	Rangers	55	Kilmarnock	49	Celtic	47
1965	Kilmarnock	50	Heart of Midlothian	50	Dunfermline	49
1966	Celtic	57	Rangers	55	Kilmarnock	45
1967	Celtic	58	Rangers	55	Clyde	46
1968	Celtic	63	Rangers	61	Hibernian	45
1969	Celtic	54	Rangers	49	Dunfermline	45
1970	Celtic	57	Rangers	45	Hibernian	44
1971	Celtic	56	Aberdeen	54	St Johnstone	44
1972	Celtic	60	Aberdeen	50	Rangers	44
1973	Celtic	57	Rangers	56	Hibernian	45
1974	Celtic	53	Hibernian	49	Rangers	48
1975	Rangers	56	Hibernian	49	Celtic	45
1976	Rangers	54	Celtic	48	Hibernian	43
1977	Celtic	55	Rangers	46	Aberdeen	43
1978	Rangers	55	Aberdeen	53	Dundee United	40
1979	Celtic	48	Rangers	45	Dundee United	44
1980	Aberdeen	48	Celtic	47	St Mirren	42
1981	Celtic	56	Aberdeen	49	Rangers	44
1982	Celtic	55	Aberdeen	53	Rangers	43
1983	Dundee United	56	Celtic	55	Aberdeen	55
1984	Aberdeen	57	Celtic	50	Dundee United	47
1985	Aberdeen	59	Celtic	52	Dundee United	47
1986	Celtic	50	Heart of Midlothian	50	Dundee United	47
1987	Rangers	69	Celtic	63	Dundee United	60
1988	Celtic	72	Heart of Midlothian	62	Rangers	60
1989	Rangers	56	Aberdeen	50	Celtic	46
1990	Rangers	51	Aberdeen	44	Heart of Midlothian	44
1991	Rangers	55	Aberdeen	53	Celtic	41
1992	Rangers	72	Heart of Midlothian	63	Celtic	62

SCOTTISH CUP FINALS

Year	Winners	Score	Runners-up
1874	Queen's Park	2–0	Clydesdale
1875	Queen's Park	3–0	Renton
1876	Queen's Park	1–1 2–0	Third Lanark
1877	Vale of Levan	0–0 1–1 3–2	Rangers
1878	Vale of Levan	1–0	Third Lanark
1879	Vale of Levan	1–1 W–O	Rangers
1880	Queen's Park	3–0	Thornley Bank
1881	Queen's Park	3–1	Dumbarton
1882	Queen's Park	2–2 4–1	Dumbarton
1883	Dumbarton	2–2 2–1	Vale of Levan
1884	Queen's Park	W–O	Vale of Levan
1885	Renton	0–0 3–1	Vale of Levan
1886	Queen's Park	3–1	Renton
1887	Hibernian	2–1	Dumbarton
1888	Renton	6–1	Cambuslang

1889	Third Lanark	2–1	Celtic
1890	Queen's Park	1–1 2–1	Vale of Levan
1891	Heart of Midlothian	1–0	Dumbarton
1892	Celtic	5–1	Queen's Park
1893	Queen's Park	2–1	Celtic
1894	Rangers	3–1	Celtic
1895	St Bernard's	2–1	Renton
1896	Heart of Midlothian	3–1	Hibernian
1897	Rangers	5–1	Dumbarton
1898	Rangers	2–0	Kilmarnock
1899	Celtic	2–0	Rangers
1900	Celtic	4–3	Queen's Park
1901	Heart of Midlothian	4–3	Celtic
1902	Hibernian	1–0	Celtic
1903	Rangers	1–1 0–0 2–0	Heart of Midlothian
1904	Celtic	3–2	Rangers
1905	Third Lanark	0–0 3–1	Rangers
1906	Heart of Midlothian	1–0	Third Lanark
1907	Celtic	3–0	Heart of Midlothian
1908	Celtic	5–1	St Mirren
1909	Cup withheld Celtic v Rangers 2–2 1–1		
1910	Dundee	2–2 0–0 2–1	Clyde
1911	Celtic	0–0 2–0	Hamilton Academicals
1912	Celtic	2–0	Clyde
1913	Falkirk	2–0	Raith Rovers
1914	Celtic	0–0 4–1	Hibernian
1915–19 –			
1920	Kilmarnock	3–2	Albion Rovers
1921	Partick Thistle	1–0	Rangers
1922	Morton	1–0	Rangers
1923	Celtic	1–0	Hibernian
1924	Airdrieonians	2–0	Hibernian
1925	Celtic	2–1	Dundee
1926	St Mirren	2–0	Celtic
1927	Celtic	3–1	East Fife
1928	Rangers	4–0	Celtic
1929	Kilmarnock	2–0	Rangers
1930	Rangers	0–0 2–1	Partick Thistle
1931	Celtic	2–2 4–2	Motherwell
1932	Rangers	1–1 3–0	Kilmarnock
1933	Celtic	1–0	Motherwell
1934	Rangers	5–0	St Mirren
1935	Rangers	2–1	Hamilton Academicals
1936	Rangers	1–0	Third Lanark
1937	Celtic	2–1	Aberdeen
1938	East Fife	1–1 4–2	Kilmarnock
1939	Clyde	4–0	Motherwell
1940–46 –			
1947	Aberdeen	2–1	Hibernian
1948	Rangers	1–1 1–0	Morton
1949	Rangers	4–1	Clyde
1950	Rangers	3–0	East Fife
1951	Celtic	1–0	Motherwell
1952	Motherwell	4–0	Dundee
1953	Rangers	1–1 1–0	Aberdeen
1954	Celtic	2–1	Aberdeen
1955	Clyde	1–1 1–0	Celtic
1956	Heart of Midlothian	3–1	Celtic
1957	Falkirk	1–1 2–1	Kilmarnock
1958	Clyde	1–0	Hibernian
1959	St Mirren	3–1	Aberdeen
1960	Rangers	2–0	Kilmarnock
1961	Dunfermline Ath	0–0 2–0	Celtic
1962	Rangers	2–0	St Mirren
1963	Rangers	1–1 3–0	Celtic
1964	Rangers	3–1	Dundee
1965	Celtic	3–2	Dunfermline Athletic
1966	Rangers	0–0 1–0	Celtic
1967	Celtic	2–0	Aberdeen
1968	Dunfermline Athletic	3–1	Heart of Midlothian
1969	Celtic	4–0	Rangers
1970	Aberdeen	3–1	Celtic
1971	Celtic	1–1 2–1	Rangers
1972	Celtic	6–1	Hibernian
1973	Rangers	3–2	Celtic
1974	Celtic	3–0	Dundee United
1975	Celtic	3–1	Airdrieonians
1976	Rangers	3–1	Heart of Midlothian
1977	Celtic	1–0	Rangers
1978	Rangers	2–1	Aberdeen
1979	Rangers	0–0 0–0 3–2	Hibernian
1980	Celtic	1–0	Rangers
1981	Rangers	0–0 4–1	Dundee United
1982	Aberdeen	4–1	Rangers
1983	Aberdeen	1–0	Rangers
1984	Aberdeen	2–1	Celtic
1985	Celtic	2–1	Dundee United
1986	Aberdeen	3–0	Heart of Midlothian
1987	St Mirren	1–0	Dundee United
1988	Celtic	2–1	Dundee United
1989	Celtic	1–0	Rangers
1990	Aberdeen	0–0 (9–8p)	Celtic
1991	Motherwell	4–3	Dundee United
1992	Rangers	2–1	Airdrieonians

SCOTTISH LEAGUE CUP FINALS

Year	Winners	Score	Runners–up
1947	Rangers	4–0	Aberdeen
1948	East Fife	0–0 4–1	Falkirk
1949	Rangers	2–0	Raith Rovers
1950	East Fife	3–0	Dunfermline Athletic
1951	Motherwell	3–0	Hibernian
1952	Dundee	3–2	Rangers
1953	Dundee	2–0	Kilmarnock
1954	East Fife	3–2	Partick Thistle
1955	Heart of Midlothian	4–2	Motherwell
1956	Aberdeen	2–1	St Mirren
1957	Celtic	0–0 3–0	Partick Thistle
1958	Celtic	7–1	Rangers
1959	Heart of Midlothian	5–1	Partick Thistle
1960	Heart of Midlothian	2–1	Third Lanark
1961	Rangers	2–0	Kilmarnock
1962	Rangers	1–1 3–1	Heart of Midlothian
1963	Heart of Midlothian	1–0	Kilmarnock
1964	Rangers	5–0	Morton
1965	Rangers	2–1	Celtic
1966	Celtic	2–1	Rangers
1967	Celtic	1–0	Rangers
1968	Celtic	5–3	Dundee
1969	Celtic	6–2	Hibernian
1970	Celtic	1–0	St Johnstone
1971	Rangers	1–0	Celtic
1972	Partick Thistle	4–1	Celtic
1973	Hibernian	2–1	Celtic
1974	Dundee	1–0	Celtic
1975	Celtic	6–3	Hibernian
1976	Rangers	1–0	Celtic
1977	Aberdeen	2–1	Celtic
1978	Rangers	2–1	Celtic
1979	Rangers	2–1	Aberdeen
1980	Dundee United	0–0 3–0	Aberdeen
1981	Dundee United	3–0	Dundee
1982	Rangers	2–1	Dundee United

1983	Celtic	2–1	Rangers
1984	Rangers	3–2	Celtic
1985	Rangers	1–0	Dundee United
1986	Aberdeen	3–0	Hibernian
1987	Rangers	2–1	Celtic
1988	Rangers	3–3 (5–3p)	Aberdeen
1989	Rangers	3–2	Aberdeen
1990	Aberdeen	2–1	Rangers
1991	Rangers	2–1	Celtic
1992	Hibernian	2–0	Dunfermline Athletic

INTERNATIONAL MATCHES PLAYED BY SCOTLAND

Date	Opponents	Result	Venue	Compet	Scorers
30–11–1872	England	D 0–0	Glasgow	Fr	
8–03–1873	England	L 2–4	London	Fr	Renny-Tailyour, Gibb
7–03–1874	England	W 2–1	Glasgow	Fr	McKinnon A, Anderson F
6–03–1875	England	D 2–2	London	Fr	McNeil, Andrews
4–03–1876	England	W 3–0	Glasgow	Fr	McKinnon W, McNeil, Highet
25–03	Wales	W 4–0	Glasgow	Fr	Ferguson, Lang, McKinnon W, McNeil
3–03–1877	England	W 3–1	London	Fr	Ferguson 2, Richmond
5–03	Wales	W 2–0	Wrexham	Fr	Campbell C, OG
2–03–1878	England	W 7–2	Glasgow	Fr	McDougall 3, McGregor, McNeil 2, McKinnon W
23–03	Wales	W 9–0	Glasgow	Fr	Campbell P, Weir J 2, Ferguson 3, Baird J, Watson, Anon
5–04–1879	England	L 4–5	London	Fr	McKinnon W 2, McDougall, Smith J (I)
7–04	Wales	W 3–0	Wrexham	Fr	Campbell P, Smith J (I) 2
13–03–1880	England	W 5–4	Glasgow	Fr	Ker 3, Baird J, Kay
27–03	Wales	W 5–1	Glasgow	Fr	Davidson D, Beveridge, Lindsay, McAdam, Campbell J (I)
12–03–1881	England	W 6–1	London	Fr	Smith J (I) 3, Ker 2, McGuire
14–03	Wales	W 5–1	Wrexham	Fr	Smith J (I) 2, Ker 2, Lindsay
11–03–1882	England	W 5–1	Glasgow	Fr	Harrower, Ker 2, Kay, McPherson R
25–03	Wales	W 5–0	Glasgow	Fr	Kay, Ker, Fraser 2, McAulay
10–03–1883	England	W 3–2	Sheffield	Fr	Smith J (I) 2, Fraser
12–03	Wales	W 3–0	Wrexham	Fr	Smith J (I), Fraser, Anderson W
26–01–1884	Ireland	W 5–0	Belfast	HC	Goudie, Harrower 2, Gossland 2
15–03	England	W 1–0	Glasgow	HC	Smith J (I)
29–03	Wales	W 4–1	Glasgow	HC	Kay 2, Lindsay, Shaw
14–03–1885	Ireland	W 8–2	Glasgow	HC	Higgins A (I) 4, Kelso, Barbour,\ McPherson J (I), Calderwood
21–03	England	D 1–1	London	HC	Lindsay
23–03	Wales	W 8–1	Wrexham	HC	Anderson W 3, Lindsay 2, Allan D 2, Calderwood
20–03–1886	Ireland	W 7–2	Belfast	HC	Heggie 5, Dunbar, Gourlay
27–03	England	D 1–1	Glasgow	HC	Somerville
10–04	Wales	W 4–1	Glasgow	HC	Harrower 2, Allan D 2
19–02–1887	Ireland	W 4–1	Glasgow	HC	Watt W, Jenkinson, Johnstone W, Lowe J (I)
19–03	England	W 3–2	Blackburn	HC	McCall, Allan J 2
21–03	Wales	W 2–0	Wrexham	HC	Robertson W, Marshall J
10–03–1888	Wales	W 5–1	Edinburgh	HC	Paul W 2, McPherson J (II) 2, Groves
17–03	England	L 0–5	Glasgow	HC	
24–03	Ireland	W 10–2	Belfast	HC	Dewar G, Dickson, Aitken, McCallum, Brackenridge, OG, Anon 4
9–03–1889	Ireland	W 7–0	Glasgow	HC	Watt F, McInnes 2, Black D, Groves 3
13–04	England	W 3–2	London	HC	McLaren J, Oswald, Munro N
15–04	Wales	D 0–0	Wrexham	HC	
22–03–1890	Wales	W 5–0	Glasgow	HC	Paul W 4, Wilson H
29–03	Ireland	W 4–1	Belfast	HC	Wylie, Rankin G 2, McPherson J (II)
5–04	England	D 1–1	Glasgow	HC	McPherson J (II)
21–03–1891	Wales	W 4–3	Wrexham	HC	Logan, Buchanan R, Boyd R 2
28–03	Ireland	W 2–1	Glasgow	HC	Waddell T, Lowe J (II)
6–04	England	L 1–2	Blackburn	HC	Watt F
19–03–1892	Ireland	W 3–2	Belfast	HC	Keillor, Lambie, Ellis
26–03	Wales	W 6–1	Edinburgh	HC	Thomson W, Hamilton J 2, McPherson J (II), Baird D 2
2–04	England	L 1–4	Glasgow	HC	Bell
18–03–1893	Wales	W 8–0	Wrexham	HC	Madden 4, Barker 3, Lambie
25–03	Ireland	W 6–1	Glasgow	HC	Sellar 2, Kelly, McMahon, Hamilton J, OG
1–04	England	L 2–5	London	HC	Sellar 2

24-03-1894	Wales	W	5-2	Kilmarnock	HC	Berry, Barker, Chambers, Alexander, Johnstone J (I)
31-03	Ireland	W	2-1	Belfast	HC	Taylor, OG
7-04	England	D	2-2	Glasgow	HC	Lambie, McMahon
23-03-1895	Wales	D	2-2	Wrexham	HC	Madden, Divers
30-03	Ireland	W	3-1	Glasgow	HC	Lambie, Walker J 2
6-04	England	L	0-3	Liverpool	HC	
21-03-1896	Wales	W	4-0	Dundee	HC	Neil 2, Keillor 2
28-03	Ireland	D	3-3	Belfast	HC	McColl 2, Drummond
4-04	England	W	2-1	Glasgow	HC	Lambie, Bell
20-03-1897	Wales	D	2-2	Wrexham	HC	Ritchie, OG
27-03	Ireland	W	5-1	Glasgow	HC	McPherson J (II) 2, Gibson N, McColl, King A
3-04	England	W	2-1	London	HC	Hyslop, Millar
19-03-1898	Wales	W	5-2	Motherwell	HC	Gillespie 3, McKie 2
26-03	Ireland	W	3-0	Belfast	HC	Robertson T, McColl, Stewart W
2-04	England	L	1-3	Glasgow	HC	Millar
18-03-1899	Wales	W	6-0	Wrexham	HC	Campbell J (II) 2, McColl 3, Marshall H
25-03	Ireland	W	9-1	Glasgow	HC	McColl 3, Hamilton R 2, Campbell J (II) 2, Bell, Christie
8-04	England	L	1-2	Birmingham	HC	Hamilton R
3-02-1900	Wales	W	5-2	Aberdeen	HC	Bell, Wilson D (I) 2, Hamilton R, Smith A
3-03	Ireland	W	3-0	Belfast	HC	Campbell J (III) 2, Smith A
7-04	England	W	4-1	Glasgow	HC	McColl 3, Bell
23-02-1901	Ireland	W	11-0	Glasgow	HC	Campbell J (III) 2, McMahon 4, Hamilton R 4, Russell
2-03	Wales	D	1-1	Wrexham	HC	Robertson J (I)
30-03	England	D	2-2	London	HC	Campbell J (III), Hamilton R
1-03-1902	Ireland	W	5-1	Belfast	HC	Hamilton R 3, Buick, Walker R
15-03	Wales	W	5-1	Greenock	HC	Smith A 3, Buick, Drummond
3-05	England	D	2-2	Birmingham	HC	Templeton, Orr R
9-03-1903	Wales	W	1-0	Cardiff	HC	Speedie
21-03	Ireland	L	0-2	Glasgow	HC	
4-04	England	W	2-1	Sheffield	HC	Speedie, Walker R
12-03-1904	Wales	D	1-1	Dundee	HC	Walker R
26-03	Ireland	D	1-1	Dublin	HC	Hamilton R
9-04	England	L	0-1	Glasgow	HC	
6-03-1905	Wales	L	1-3	Wrexham	HC	Robertson J (I)
18-03	Ireland	W	4-0	Glasgow	HC	Thomson C 2, Walker R, Quinn J
1-04	England	L	0-1	London	HC	
3-03-1906	Wales	L	0-2	Edinburgh	HC	
17-03	Ireland	W	1-0	Dublin	HC	Fitchie
7-04	England	W	2-1	Glasgow	HC	Howie J 2
4-03-1907	Wales	L	0-1	Wrexham	HC	
16-03	Ireland	W	3-0	Glasgow	HC	O'Rourke, Walker R, Thomson C
6-04	England	D	1-1	Newcastle	HC	OG
7-03-1908	Wales	W	2-1	Dundee	HC	Bennett, Lennie
14-03	Ireland	W	5-0	Dublin	HC	Quinn J 4, Galt
4-04	England	D	1-1	Glasgow	HC	Wilson A (I)
1-03-1909	Wales	L	2-3	Wrexham	HC	Walker R, Paul H
15-03	Ireland	W	5-0	Glasgow	HC	McMenemy 2, McFarlane, Thomson A, Paul H
3-04	England	L	0-2	London	HC	
5-03-1910	Wales	W	1-0	Kilmarnock	HC	Devine
19-03	Ireland	L	0-1	Belfast	HC	
2-04	England	W	2-0	Glasgow	HC	McMenemy, Quinn J
6-03-1911	Wales	D	2-2	Cardiff	HC	Hamilton R 2
18-03	Ireland	W	2-0	Glasgow	HC	Reid, McMenemy
1-04	England	D	1-1	Liverpool	HC	Higgins A (II)
2-03-1912	Wales	W	1-0	Edinburgh	HC	Quinn J
16-03	Ireland	W	4-1	Belfast	HC	Aitkenhead 2, Reid, Walker R
23-03	England	D	1-1	Glasgow	HC	Wilson A (I)
3-03-1913	Wales	D	0-0	Wrexham	HC	
15-03	Ireland	W	2-1	Dublin	HC	Reid, Bennett
5-04	England	L	0-1	London	HC	
28-02-1914	Wales	D	0-0	Glasgow	HC	
14-03	Ireland	D	1-1	Belfast	HC	Donnachie
4-04	England	W	3-1	Glasgow	HC	Thomson C, McMenemy, Reid
26-02-1920	Wales	D	1-1	Cardiff	HC	Cairns

13–03	Ireland	W	3–0	Glasgow	HC	Wilson A (II), Morton, Cunningham
10–04	England	L	4–5	Sheffield	HC	Miller T 2, Wilson A (II), Donaldson
12–02–1921	Wales	W	2–1	Aberdeeen	HC	Wilson A (II) 2
26–02	Ireland	W	2–0	Belfast	HC	Wilson A (II), Cassidy
9–04	England	W	3–0	Glasgow	HC	Wilson A (II), Morton, Cunningham
4–02–1922	Wales	L	1–2	Wrexham	HC	Archibald A
4–03	Ireland	W	2–1	Glasgow	HC	Wilson A (II) 2
8–04	England	W	1–0	Birmingham	HC	Wilson A (II)
3–03–1923	Ireland	W	1–0	Belfast	HC	Wilson A (II)
17–03	Wales	W	2–0	Glasgow	HC	Wilson A (II) 2
14–04	England	D	2–2	Glasgow	HC	Cunningham, Wilson A (II)
16–02–1924	Wales	L	0–2	Cardiff	HC	
1–03	Nth. Ireland	W	2–0	Glasgow	HC	Cunningham, Morris D
12–04	England	D	1–1	London	HC	OG
14–02–1925	Wales	W	3–1	Edinburgh	HC	Meiklejohn, Gallacher H 2
28–02	Nth. Ireland	W	3–0	Belfast	HC	Meiklejohn, Gallacher H, Dunn
4–04	England	W	2–0	Glasgow	HC	Gallacher H 2
31–10	Wales	W	3–0	Cardiff	HC	Duncan J, McLean A, Clunas
27–02–1926	Nth. Ireland	W	4–0	Glasgow	HC	Gallacher H 3, Cunningham
17–04	England	W	1–0	Manchester	HC	Jackson A
30–10	Wales	W	3–0	Glasgow	HC	Gallacher H, Jackson A 2
26–02–1927	Nth. Ireland	W	2–0	Belfast	HC	Morton 2
2–04	England	L	1–2	Glasgow	HC	Morton
29–10	Wales	D	2–2	Wrexham	HC	Gallacher H, Hutton
25–02–1928	Nth. Ireland	L	0–1	Glasgow	HC	
31–03	England	W	5–1	London	HC	Jackson A 3, James, Gibson J
27–10	Wales	W	4–2	Glasgow	HC	Gallacher H 3, Dunn
23–02–1929	Nth. Ireland	W	7–3	Belfast	HC	Gallacher H 4, Jackson A, James
13–04	England	W	1–0	Glasgow	HC	Cheyne
28–05	Norway	W	7–3	Oslo	Fr	Cheyne 3, Nisbet 2, Craig, Rankin
1–06	Germany	D	1–1	Berlin	Fr	Imrie
4–06	Holland	W	2–0	Amsterdam	Fr	Fleming J, Rankin R
26–10	Wales	W	4–2	Cardiff	HC	Gallacher H 2, James, Gibson J
22–02–1930	Nth. Ireland	W	3–1	Glasgow	HC	Gallacher H 2, Stevenson
5–04	England	L	2–5	London	HC	Fleming J 2
18–05	France	W	2–0	Paris	Fr	Gallacher H 2
25–10	Wales	D	1–1	Glasgow	HC	Battles
21–02–1931	Nth. Ireland	D	0–0	Belfast	HC	
28–03	England	W	2–0	Glasgow	HC	Stevenson, McGrory
16–05	Austria	L	0–5	Vienna	Fr	
20–05	Italy	L	0–3	Rome	Fr	
24–05	Switzerland	W	3–2	Geneva	Fr	Easson, Boyd W, Love
19–09	Nth. Ireland	W	3–1	Glasgow	HC	Stevenson, McGrory, McPhail R
31–10	Wales	W	3–2	Wrexham	HC	Stevenson, Thomson R, McGrory
9–04–1932	England	L	0–3	London	HC	
8–05	France	W	3–1	Paris	Fr	Dewar N 3
17–09	Nth. Ireland	W	4–0	Belfast	HC	McPhail R 2, King J, McGrory
26–10	Wales	L	2–5	Edinburgh	HC	Dewar N, Duncan D (I)
1–04–1933	England	W	2–1	Glasgow	HC	McGrory 2
16–09	Nth. Ireland	L	1–2	Glasgow	HC	McPhail R
4–10	Wales	L	2–3	Cardiff	HC	Duncan D (I), McFadyen
29–11	Austria	D	2–2	Glasgow	Fr	Meiklejohn, McFadyen
14–04–1934	England	L	0–3	London	HC	
20–10	Nth. Ireland	L	1–2	Belfast	HC	Gallacher P
21–11	Wales	W	3–2	Aberdeen	HC	Duncan D (I), Napier 2
6–04–1935	England	W	2–0	Glasgow	HC	Duncan D (I) 2
5–10	Wales	D	1–1	Cardiff	HC	Duncan D (I)
13–11	Nth. Ireland	W	2–1	Edinburgh	HC	Walker T, Duncan D (I)
4–04–1936	England	D	1–1	London	HC	Walker T
14–10	Germany	W	2–0	Glasgow	Fr	Delaney 2
31–10	Nth. Ireland	W	3–1	Belfast	HC	Napier, Munro A, McCulloch
2–12	Wales	L	1–2	Dundee	HC	Walker T
17–04–1937	England	W	3–1	Glasgow	HC	O'Donnell, McPhail R 2
9–05	Austria	D	1–1	Vienna	Fr	O'Donnell
22–05	Czechoslovakia	W	3–1	Prague	Fr	Simpson, McPhail R, Gillick
30–10	Wales	L	1–2	Cardiff	HC	Massie
10–11	Nth. Ireland	D	1–1	Aberdeen	HC	Smith J (II)
8–12	Czechoslovakia	W	5–0	Glasgow	Fr	McCulloch 2, Black A, Buchanan P, Kinnear
9–04–1938	England	W	1–0	London	HC	Walker T

21–05	Holland	W	3–1	Amsterdam	Fr	Black A, Murphy, Walker T
8–10	Nth. Ireland	W	2–0	Belfast	HC	Delaney, Walker T
9–11	Wales	W	3–2	Edinburgh	HC	Walker T 2, Gillick
7–12	Hungary	W	3–1	Glasgow	Fr	Black A, Walker T, Gillick
15–04–1939	England	L	1–2	Glasgow	HC	Dougall
23–01–1946	Belgium*	D	2–2	Glasgow	Fr	Delaney 2
15–05	Switzerland*	W	3–1	Glasgow	Fr	Liddell 2, Delaney
19–10	Wales	L	1–3	Wrexham	HC	Waddell W
27–11	Nth. Ireland	D	0–0	Glasgow	HC	
12–04–1947	England	D	1–1	London	HC	McLaren A
18–05	Belgium	L	1–2	Brussels	Fr	Steel
24–05	Luxembourg	W	6–0	Luxembourg	Fr	McLaren A 2, Steel 2, Flavell 2
4–10	Nth. Ireland	L	0–2	Belfast	HC	
12–11	Wales	L	1–2	Glasgow	HC	McLaren A
10–04–1948	England	L	0–2	Glasgow	HC	
28–04	Belgium	W	2–0	Glasgow	Fr	Combe, Duncan D (II)
17–05	Switzerland	L	1–2	Berne	Fr	Johnston L
23–05	France	L	0–3	Paris	Fr	
23–10	Wales	W	3–1	Cardiff	HC	Howie H, Waddell W 2
17–11	Nth. Ireland	W	3–2	Glasgow	HC	Houliston 2, Mason
9–04–1949	England	W	3–1	London	HC	Mason, Steel, Reilly
27–04	France	W	2–0	Glasgow	Fr	Steel 2
1–10	Nth. Ireland	W	8–2	Belfast	HC/WCq	Morris H 3, Waddell W 2, Steel, Reilly, Mason
9–11	Wales	W	2–0	Glasgow	HC/WCq	McPhail J, Linwood
15–04–1950	England	L	0–1	Glasgow	HC/WCq	
26–04	Switzerland	W	3–1	Glasgow	Fr	Bauld, Campbell R, Brown
21–05	Portugal	D	2–2	Lisbon	Fr	Brown, W Bauld
27–05	France	W	1–0	Paris	Fr	Brown
21–10	Wales	W	3–1	Cardiff	HC	Reilly 2, Liddell
1–11	Nth. Ireland	W	6–1	Glasgow	HC	McPhail J 2, Steel 4
13–12	Austria	L	0–1	Glasgow	Fr	
14–04–1951	England	W	3–2	London	HC	Johnstone R, Reilly, Liddell
12–05	Denmark	W	3–1	Glasgow	Fr	Steel, Reilly, Mitchell
16–05	France	W	1–0	Glasgow	Fr	Reilly
20–05	Belgium	W	5–0	Brussels	Fr	Hamilton G 3, Mason, Waddell W
27–05	Austria	L	0–4	Vienna	Fr	
6–10	Nth. Ireland	W	3–0	Belfast	HC	Johnstone R 2, Orr T
14–11	Wales	L	0–1	Glasgow	HC	
5–04–1952	England	L	1–2	Glasgow	HC	Reilly
30–04	USA	W	6–0	Glasgow	Fr	Reilly 3, McMillan 2, OG
25–05	Denmark	W	2–1	Copenhagen	Fr	Thornton, Reilly
30–05	Sweden	L	1–3	Stockholm	Fr	Liddell
18–10	Wales	W	2–1	Cardiff	HC	Brown, Liddell
5–11	Nth. Ireland	D	1–1	Glasgow	HC	Reilly
18–04–1953	England	D	2–2	London	HC	Reilly 2
6–05	Sweden	L	1–2	Glasgow	Fr	Johnstone R
3–10	Nth. Ireland	W	3–1	Belfast	HC/WCq	Fleming C 2, Henderson J
4–11	Wales	D	3–3	Glasgow	HC/WCq	Brown, Johnstone R, Reilly
3–04–1954	England	L	2–4	Glasgow	HC/WCq	Brown, OG
5–05	Norway	W	1–0	Glasgow	Fr	Hamilton G
19–05	Norway	D	1–1	Oslo	Fr	MacKenzie
25–05	Finland	W	2–1	Helsinki	Fr	Ormond, Johnstone R
16–06	Austria	L	0–1	Zurich	WCr1	
19–06	Uruguay	L	0–7	Basle	WCr1	
16–10	Wales	W	1–0	Cardiff	HC	Buckley
3–11	Nth. Ireland	D	2–2	Glasgow	HC	Davidson J, Johnstone R
8–12	Hungary	L	2–4	Glasgow	Fr	Ring, Johnstone R
2–04–1955	England	L	2–7	London	HC	Reilly, Docherty
4–05	Portugal	W	3–0	Glasgow	Fr	Reilly, Gemmell T (I), Liddell
15–05	Yugoslavia	D	2–2	Belgrade	Fr	Reilly, Smith G
19–05	Austria	W	4–1	Vienna	Fr	Robertson A, Smith G, Liddell, Reilly
29–05	Hungary	L	1–3	Budapest	Fr	Smith G
8–10	Nth. Ireland	L	1–2	Belfast	HC	Reilly
9–11	Wales	W	2–0	Glasgow	HC	Johnstone R
14–04–1956	England	D	1–1	Glasgow	HC	Leggat
2–05	Austria	D	1–1	Glasgow	Fr	Conn
20–10	Wales	D	2–2	Cardiff	HC	Fernie, Reilly
7–11	Nth. Ireland	W	1–0	Glasgow	HC	Scott

* Not full internationals

21–11	Yugoslavia	W	2–0	Glasgow	Fr	Mudie, Baird S
6–04–1957	England	L	1–2	London	HC	Ring
8–05	Spain	W	4–2	Glasgow	WCq	Mudie 3, Hewie
19–05	Switzerland	W	2–1	Basle	WCq	Mudie, Collins R
22–05	West Germany	W	3–1	Stuttgart	Fr	Collins R 2, Mudie
26–05	Spain	L	1–4	Madrid	WCq	Smith G
5–10	Nth. Ireland	D	1–1	Belfast	HC	Leggat
6–11	Switzerland	W	3–2	Glasgow	WCq	Robertson A, Mudie, Scott
13–11	Wales	D	1–1	Glasgow	HC	Collins R
19–04–1958	England	L	0–4	Glasgow	HC	
7–05	Hungary	D	1–1	Glasgow	Fr	Mudie
1–06	Poland	W	2–1	Warsaw	Fr	Collins R 2
8–06	Yugoslavia	D	1–1	Vasteraas	WCr1	Murray
11–06	Paraguay	L	2–3	Norrkoping	WCr1	Mudie, Collins R
15–06	France	L	1–2	Orebro	WCr1	Baird S
18–10	Wales	W	3–0	Cardiff	HC	Leggat, Law, Collins R
5–11	Nth. Ireland	D	2–2	Glasgow	HC	Herd, Collins R
11–04–1959	England	L	0–1	London	HC	
6–05	West Germany	W	3–2	Glasgow	Fr	White, Weir A, Leggat
27–05	Holland	W	2–1	Amsterdam	Fr	Collins R, Leggat
3–06	Portugal	L	0–1	Lisbon	Fr	
3–10	Nth. Ireland	W	4–0	Belfast	HC	Leggat, Hewie, White, Mulhall
14–11	Wales	D	1–1	Glasgow	HC	Leggat
9–04–1960	England	D	1–1	Glasgow	HC	Leggat
4–05	Poland	L	2–3	Glasgow	Fr	Law, St John
29–05	Austria	L	1–4	Vienna	Fr	Mackay D
5–06	Hungary	D	3–3	Budapest	Fr	Hunter, Herd, Young
8–06	Turkey	L	2–4	Ankara	Fr	Caldow, Young
22–10	Wales	L	0–2	Cardiff	HC	
9–11	Nth. Ireland	W	5–2	Glasgow	HC	Law, Caldow, Young, Brand 2
15–04–1961	England	L	3–9	London	HC	Mackay D, Wilson D (II), Quinn P
3–05	Rep. Ireland	W	4–1	Glasgow	WCq	Brand 2, Herd 2
7–05	Rep. Ireland	W	3–0	Dublin	WCq	Young 2, Brand
14–05	Czechoslovakia	L	0–4	Bratislava	WCq	
26–09	Czechoslovakia	W	3–2	Glasgow	WCq	St John, Law 2
7–10	Nth. Ireland	W	6–1	Belfast	HC	Wilson D (II), Scott 3, Brand 2
8–11	Wales	W	2–0	Glasgow	HC	St John 2
29–11	Czechoslovakia	L	2–4	Brussels	WCq	St John 2
14–04–1962	England	W	2–0	Glasgow	HC	Wilson D (II), Caldow
2–05	Uruguay	L	2–3	Glasgow	Fr	Baxter, Brand
20–10	Wales	W	3–2	Cardiff	HC	Caldow, Law, Henderson W
7–11	Nth. Ireland	W	5–1	Glasgow	HC	Law 4, Henderson W
6–04–1963	England	W	2–1	London	HC	Baxter 2
8–05	Austria	W	4–1	Glasgow	Fr	Wilson D (II) 2, Law 2,
	Abandoned after 79 mins					
4–06	Norway	L	3–4	Bergen	Fr	Law 3
9–06	Rep. Ireland	L	0–1	Dublin	Fr	
13–06	Spain	W	6–2	Madrid	Fr	St John, Wilson D (II), Law, Henderson W, Gibson D, McLintock
2–10	Nth. Ireland	L	1–2	Belfast	HC	St John
7–11	Norway	W	6–1	Glasgow	Fr	Law 4, Mackay D 2
20–11	Wales	W	2–1	Glasgow	HC	White, Law
11–04–1964	England	W	1–0	Glasgow	HC	Gilzean
12–05	West Germany	D	2–2	Hanover	Fr	Gilzean 2
3–10	Wales	L	2–3	Cardiff	HC	Chalmers, Gibson D
21–10	Finland	W	3–1	Glasgow	WCq	Law, Chalmers, Gibson D
25–11	Nth. Ireland	W	3–2	Glasgow	HC	Wilson D (II) 2, Gilzean
10–04–1965	England	D	2–2	London	HC	Law, St John
8–05	Spain	D	0–0	Glasgow	Fr	
23–05	Poland	D	1–1	Chorzow	WCq	Law
27–05	Finland	W	2–1	Helsinki	WCq	Wilson D (II), Greig
2–10	Nth. Ireland	L	2–3	Belfast	HC	Gilzean 2
13–10	Poland	L	1–2	Glasgow	WCq	McNeill
9–11	Italy	W	1–0	Glasgow	WCq	Greig
24–11	Wales	W	4–1	Glasgow	HC	Murdoch 2, Henderson W, Greig
7–12	Italy	L	0–3	Naples	WCq	
2–04–1966	England	L	3–4	Glasgow	HC	Law, Johnstone J (II) 2
11–05	Holland	L	0–3	Glasgow	Fr	
18–06	Portugal	L	0–1	Glasgow	Fr	

25–06	Brasil	D	1–1	Glasgow	Fr	Chalmers
22–10	Wales	D	1–1	Cardiff	HC/ECq	Law
16–11	Nth. Ireland	W	2–1	Glasgow	HC/ECq	Murdoch, Lennox
15–04–1967	England	W	3–2	London	HC/ECq	Law, Lennox, McCalliog
10–05	Soviet Union	L	0–2	Glasgow	Fr	
21–10	Nth. Ireland	L	0–1	Belfast	HC/ECq	
22–11	Wales	W	3–2	Glasgow	HC/ECq	Gilzean 2, McKinnon R
24–02–1968	England	D	1–1	Glasgow	HC/ECq	Hughes
30–05	Holland	D	0–0	Amsterdam	Fr	
16–10	Denmark	W	1–0	Copenhagen	Fr	Lennox
6–11	Austria	W	2–1	Glasgow	WCq	Law, Bremner
11–12	Cyprus	W	5–0	Nicosia	WCq	Gilzean 2, Stein 2, Murdoch
16–04–1969	West Germany	D	1–1	Glasgow	WCq	Murdoch
3–05	Wales	W	5–3	Wrexham	HC	McNeill, Stein, Gilzean, Bremner, McLean T
6–05	Nth. Ireland	D	1–1	Glasgow	HC	Stein
10–05	England	L	1–4	London	HC	Stein
17–05	Cyprus	W	8–0	Glasgow	WCq	Gray E, McNeill, Stein 4, Henderson W, Gemmell T (II)
21–09	Rep. Ireland	D	1–1	Dublin	Fr	Stein
22–10	West Germany	L	2–3	Hamburg	WCq	Johnstone J (II), Gilzean
5–11	Austria	L	0–2	Vienna	WCq	
18–04–1970	Nth. Ireland	W	1–0	Belfast	HC	O'Hare
22–04	Wales	D	0–0	Glasgow	HC	
25–04	England	D	0–0	Glasgow	HC	
11–11	Denmark	W	1–0	Glasgow	ECq	O'Hare
3–02–1971	Belgium	L	0–3	Liege	ECq	
21–04	Portugal	L	0–2	Lisbon	ECq	
15–05	Wales	D	0–0	Cardiff	HC	
18–05	Nth. Ireland	L	0–1	Glasgow	HC	
22–05	England	L	1–3	London	HC	Curran
9–06	Denmark	L	0–1	Copenhagen	ECq	
14–06	Soviet Union	L	0–1	Moscow	Fr	
13–10	Portugal	W	2–1	Glasgow	ECq	O'Hare, Gemmill
10–11	Belgium	W	1–0	Aberdeen	ECq	O'Hare
1–12	Holland	L	1–2	Amsterdam	Fr	Graham G
26–04–1972	Peru	W	2–0	Glasgow	Fr	O'Hare, Law
20–05	Nth. Ireland	W	2–0	Glasgow	HC	Law, Lorimer
24–05	Wales	W	1–0	Glasgow	HC	Lorimer
27–05	England	L	0–1	Glasgow	HC	
29–06	Yugoslavia	D	2–2	Belo Horizonte	Clr2	Macari 2
2–07	Czechoslovakia	D	0–0	Porto Alegre	Clr2	
5–07	Brazil	L	0–1	Rio de Janeiro	Clr2	
18–10	Denmark	W	4–1	Copenhagen	WCq	Macari, Bone, Harper, Morgan
15–11	Denmark	W	2–0	Glasgow	WCq	Dalglish, Lorimer
14–02–1973	England	L	0–5	Glasgow	Fr	
12–05	Wales	W	2–0	Wrexham	HC	Graham G 2
16–05	Nth. Ireland	L	1–2	Glasgow	HC	Dalglish
19–05	England	L	0–1	London	HC	
22–06	Switzerland	L	0–1	Berne	Fr	
30–06	Brazil	L	0–1	Glasgow	Fr	
26–09	Czechoslovakia	W	2–1	Glasgow	WCq	Holton, Jordan
17–10	Czechoslovakia	L	0–1	Bratislava	WCq	
14–11	West Germany	D	1–1	Glasgow	Fr	Holton
27–03–1974	West Germany	L	1–2	Frankfurt	Fr	Dalglish
11–05	Nth. Ireland	L	0–1	Glasgow	HC	
14–05	Wales	W	2–0	Glasgow	HC	Dalglish, Jardine
18–05	England	W	2–0	Glasgow	HC	Jordan, OG
1–06	Belgium	L	1–2	Bruges	Fr	Johnstone J (II)
6–06	Norway	W	2–1	Oslo	Fr	Jordan, Dalglish
14–06	Zaire	W	2–0	Dortmund	WCr1	Lorimer, Jordan
18–06	Brazil	D	0–0	Frankfurt	WCr1	
22–06	Yugoslavia	D	1–1	Frankfurt	WCr1	Jordan
30–10	East Germany	W	3–0	Glasgow	Fr	Hutchison, Burns, Dalglish
20–11	Spain	L	1–2	Glasgow	ECq	Bremner
5–02–1975	Spain	D	1–1	Valencia	ECq	Jordan
16–04	Sweden	D	1–1	Gothenburg	Fr	Macdougall
13–05	Portugal	W	1–0	Glasgow	Fr	OG
17–05	Wales	D	2–2	Cardiff	HC	Jackson C, Rioch

LEADING INTERNATIONAL GOALSCORERS					
1	Dalglish	30	7	McColl R	13
	Law	30		Wilson A	13
3	Gallacher H	23	9	Smith J	12
4	Reilly	22		Steel W	12
5	Hamilton R	14	11	Jordan	11
	Johnston M	14		McCoist	11

20–05	Nth. Ireland	W	3–0	Glasgow	HC	Macdougall, Dalglish, Parlane
24–05	England	L	1–5	London	HC	Rioch
1–06	Romania	D	1–1	Bucharest	ECq	McQueen
3–09	Denmark	W	1–0	Copenhagen	ECq	Harper
29–10	Denmark	W	3–1	Glasgow	ECq	Dalglish, Rioch, Macdougall
17–12	Romania	D	1–1	Glasgow	ECq	Rioch
7–04–1976	Switzerland	W	1–0	Glasgow	Fr	Pettigrew
6–05	Wales	W	3–1	Glasgow	HC	Pettigrew, Rioch, Gray E
8–05	Nth. Ireland	W	3–0	Glasgow	HC	Gemmill, Masson, Dalglish
15–05	England	W	2–1	Glasgow	HC	Masson, Dalglish
8–09	Finland	W	6–0	Glasgow	Fr	Rioch, Masson, Dalglish, Gray A 2, Gray E
13–10	Czechoslovakia	L	0–2	Prague	WCq	
17–11	Wales	W	1–0	Glasgow	WCq	OG
27–04–1977	Sweden	W	3–1	Glasgow	Fr	Hartford, Dalglish, Craig
28–05	Wales	D	0–0	Wrexham	HC	
1–06	Nth. Ireland	W	3–0	Glasgow	HC	Dalglish 2, McQueen
4–06	England	W	2–1	London	HC	McQueen, Dalglish
15–06	Chile	W	4–2	Santiago	Fr	Dalglish, Macari 2, Hartford
18–06	Argentina	D	1–1	Buenos Aires	Fr	Masson
23–06	Brazil	L	0–2	Rio de Janeiro	Fr	
7–09	East Germany	L	0–1	Berlin	Fr	
21–09	Czechoslovakia	W	3–1	Glasgow	WCq	Jordan, Hartford, Dalglish
12–10	Wales	W	2–0	Liverpool	WCq	Masson, Dalglish
22–02–1978	Bulgaria	W	2–1	Glasgow	Fr	Gemmill, Wallace
13–05	Nth. Ireland	D	1–1	Glasgow	HC	Johnstone D
17–05	Wales	D	1–1	Glasgow	HC	Johnstone D
20–05	England	L	0–1	Glasgow	HC	
3–06	Peru	L	1–3	Cordoba	WCr1	Jordan
7–06	Iran	D	1–1	Cordoba	WCr1	OG
11–06	Holland	W	3–2	Mendoza	WCr1	Dalglish, Gemmill 2
20–09	Austria	L	2–3	Vienna	ECq	McQueen, Gray A
25–10	Norway	W	3–2	Glasgow	ECq	Dalglish 2, Gemmill
29–11	Portugal	L	0–1	Lisbon	ECq	
19–05–1979	Wales	L	0–3	Cardiff	HC	
22–05	Nth. Ireland	W	1–0	Glasgow	HC	Graham A
26–05	England	L	1–3	London	HC	Wark
2–06	Argentina	L	1–3	Glasgow	Fr	Graham
7–06	Norway	W	4–0	Oslo	ECq	Jordan, Dalglish, Robertson J (II), McQueen
12–09	Peru	D	1–1	Glasgow	Fr	OG
17–10	Austria	D	1–1	Glasgow	ECq	Gemmill
21–11	Belgium	L	0–2	Brussels	ECq	
19–12	Belgium	L	1–3	Glasgow	ECq	Robertson J (II)
26–03–1980	Portugal	W	4–1	Glasgow	ECq	Dalglish, Gray A, Archibald S, Gemmill
16–05	Nth. Ireland	L	0–1	Belfast	HC	
21–05	Wales	W	1–0	Glasgow	HC	Miller W
24–05	England	L	0–2	Glasgow	HC	
28–05	Poland	L	0–1	Poznan	Fr	
31–05	Hungary	L	1–3	Budapest	Fr	Archibald S
10–09	Sweden	W	1–0	Stockholm	WCq	Strachan
15–10	Portugal	D	0–0	Glasgow	WCq	
25–02–1981	Israel	W	1–0	Tel Aviv	WCq	Dalglish
25–03	Nth. Ireland	D	1–1	Glasgow	WCq	Wark
28–04	Israel	W	3–1	Glasgow	WCq	Robertson J (II) 2, Provan
16–05	Wales	L	0–2	Swansea	HC	
19–05	Nth. Ireland	W	2–0	Glasgow	HC	Stewart R, Archibald S
23–05	England	W	1–0	London	HC	Robertson J (II) (p)
9–09	Sweden	W	2–0	Glasgow	WCq	Jordan, Robertson J (II)

14–10	Nth. Ireland	D	0–0	Belfast	WCq	
18–11	Portugal	L	1–2	Lisbon	WCq	Sturrock
24–02–1982	Spain	L	0–3	Valencia	Fr	
23–03	Holland	W	2–1	Glasgow	Fr	Gray F, Dalglish
28–04	Nth. Ireland	D	1–1	Belfast	HC	Wark
24–05	Wales	W	1–0	Glasgow	HC	Hartford
29–05	England	L	0–1	Glasgow	HC	
15–06	New Zealand	W	5–2	Malaga	WCr1	Dalglish, Wark 2, Robertson J (II), Archibald S
18–06	Brazil	L	1–4	Seville	WCr1	Narey
22–06	Soviet Union	D	2–2	Malaga	WCr1	Jordan, Souness
13–10	East Germany	W	2–0	Glasgow	ECq	Wark, Sturrock
17–11	Switzerland	L	0–2	Berne	ECq	
15–12	Belgium	L	2–3	Brussels	ECq	Dalglish 2
30–03–1983	Switzerland	D	2–2	Glasgow	ECq	Wark, Nicholas
24–05	Nth. Ireland	D	0–0	Glasgow	HC	
28–05	Wales	W	2–0	Cardiff	HC	Gray A, Brazil
1–06	England	L	0–2	London	HC	
12–06	Canada	W	2–0	Vancouver	Fr	Strachan, McGhee
16–06	Canada	W	3–0	Edmonton	Fr	Nicholas, Gough, Souness
20–06	Canada	W	2–0	Toronto	Fr	Gray A 2
21–09	Uruguay	W	2–0	Glasgow	Fr	Robertson J (II), Dodds
12–10	Belgium	D	1–1	Glasgow	ECq	Nicholas
16–11	East Germany	L	1–2	Halle	ECq	Bannon
13–12	Nth. Ireland	L	0–2	Belfast	HC	
28–02–1984	Wales	W	2–1	Glasgow	HC	Cooper, Johnston M
26–05	England	D	1–1	Glasgow	HC	McGhee
1–06	France	L	0–2	Marseille	Fr	
12–09	Yugoslavia	W	6–1	Glasgow	Fr	Souness, Dalglish, Sturrock, Johnston M, Cooper, Nicholas
17–10	Iceland	W	3–0	Glasgow	WCq	Nicholas, McStay 2
14–11	Spain	W	3–1	Glasgow	WCq	Dalglish, Johnston M 2
27–02–1985	Spain	L	0–1	Seville	WCq	
27–03	Wales	L	0–1	Glasgow	WCq	
25–05	England	W	1–0	Glasgow	Fr	Gough
28–05	Iceland	W	1–0	Reykjavik	WCq	Bett
10–09	Wales	D	1–1	Cardiff	WCq	Cooper
16–10	East Germany	D	0–0	Glasgow	Fr	
20–11	Australia	W	2–0	Glasgow	WCq	McAvennie, Cooper
4–12	Australia	D	0–0	Melbourne	WCq	
28–01–1986	Israel	W	1–0	Tel Aviv	Fr	McStay
26–03	Romania	W	3–0	Glasgow	Fr	Gough, Strachan, Aitken
23–04	England	L	1–2	London	Fr	Souness
29–04	Holland	D	0–0	Eindhoven	Fr	
4–06	Denmark	L	0–1	Nezahualcoyotl	WCr1	
8–06	West Germany	L	1–2	Queretaro	WCr1	Strachan
13–06	Uruguay	D	0–0	Nezahualcoyotl	WCr1	
10–09	Bulgaria	D	0–0	Glasgow	ECq	
15–10	Rep. Ireland	D	0–0	Dublin	ECq	
12–11	Luxembourg	W	3–0	Glasgow	ECq	Cooper 2, Johnston M
18–02–1987	Rep. Ireland	L	0–1	Glasgow	ECq	
1–04	Belgium	L	1–4	Brussels	ECq	McStay
23–05	England	D	0–0	Glasgow	Fr	
26–05	Brazil	L	0–2	Glasgow	Fr	
9–09	Hungary	W	2–0	Glasgow	Fr	McCoist 2
14–10	Belgium	W	2–0	Glasgow	ECq	McStay, McCoist
11–11	Bulgaria	W	1–0	Sofia	ECq	Mackay G

LEADING INTERNATIONAL APPEARANCES

1	Dalglish	102	9	Law	55		Strachan	50
2	McLeish A	76	10	Bremner	54	18	Evans R	48
3	Miller W	65		Souness	54	19	Greig	44
4	McGrain	62	12	Rough	53	20	Gemmill A	43
5	McStay P	60		Young G	53	21	McCoist	41
6	Gough	59	14	Jordan	52	22	Caldow	40
7	Leighton	58		Malpas	52			
8	Aitken R	57	16	Hartford	50			

2-12	Luxembourg	D	0-0	Esch	ECq	
17-02-1988	Saudi Arabia	D	2-2	Riyadh	Fr	Johnston M, Collins J
22-03	Malta	D	1-1	Ta'Qali	Fr	Sharp
27-04	Spain	D	0-0	Madrid	Fr	
17-05	Colombia	D	0-0	Glasgow	Fr	
21-05	England	L	0-1	London	Fr	
14-09	Norway	W	2-1	Oslo	WCq	McStay, Johnston M
19-10	Yugoslavia	D	1-1	Glasgow	WCq	Johnston M
22-12	Italy	L	0-2	Perugia	Fr	
8-02-1989	Cyprus	W	3-2	Limassol	WCq	Johnston M, Gough 2
8-03	France	W	2-0	Glasgow	WCq	Johnston M 2
26-04	Cyprus	W	2-1	Glasgow	WCq	Johnston M, McCoist
27-05	England	L	0-2	Glasgow	Fr	
30-05	Chile	W	2-0	Glasgow	Fr	McInally, Mcleod
6-09	Yugoslavia	L	1-3	Zagreb	WCq	Durie
11-10	France	L	0-3	Paris	WCq	
15-11	Norway	D	1-1	Glasgow	WCq	McCoist
28-03-1990	Argentina	W	1-0	Glasgow	Fr	McKimmie
25-04	East Germany	L	0-1	Glasgow	Fr	
16-05	Egypt	L	1-3	Aberdeen	Fr	McCoist
19-05	Poland	D	1-1	Glasgow	Fr	Johnston M
28-05	Malta	W	2-1	Ta'Qali	Fr	McInally 2
11-06	Costa Rica	L	0-1	Genoa	WCr1	
16-06	Sweden	W	2-1	Genoa	WCr1	McCall, Johnston M
20-06	Brazil	L	0-1	Turin	WCr1	
12-09	Romania	W	2-1	Glasgow	ECq	Robertson, McCoist
17-10	Switzerland	W	2-1	Glasgow	ECq	Robertson, McAllister
14-11	Bulgaria	D	1-1	Sofia	ECq	McCoist
6-02-1991	Soviet Union	L	0-1	Glasgow	Fr	
27-03	Bulgaria	D	1-1	Glasgow	ECq	Collins
1-05	San Marino	W	2-0	Serravalle	ECq	Strachan, Durie
11-09	Switzerland	D	2-2	Berne	ECq	Durie, McCoist
16-10	Romania	L	0-1	Bucharest	ECq	
13-11	San Marino	W	4-0	Glasgow	ECq	McStay, Gough, Durie, McCoist
19-02-1992	Nth. Ireland	W	1-0	Glasgow	Fr	McCoist
25-03	Finland	D	1-1	Glasgow	Fr	McStay
17-05	USA	W	1-0	Denver	Fr	Nevin
20-05	Canada	W	3-1	Toronto	Fr	McAllister, McCoist, Malpas
3-06	Norway	D	0-0	Oslo	Fr	
12-06	Holland	L	0-1	Gothenburg	ECr1	
15-06	Germany	L	0-2	Norrkoping	ECr1	
18-06	CIS	W	3-0	Norrkoping	ECr1	OG, McClair, McAllister

The former

SOVIET UNION

What the future holds for the former Soviet Union is not easy to predict. In September 1991 the three Baltic republics of Lithuania, Latvia and Estonia gained independence from the Union in time to enter the 1994 World Cup, but with the complete disintegration of the country not only Soviet football but world football faces an enormous shake up.

Instead of one country, there are now 15, all of whom would presumably like to join FIFA. The Baltic states, Georgia and the Ukraine had all taken steps to move away from the existing football structure before the political break-up, despite the efforts of the Football Federation to keep everyone together. As football is often considered a symbol of national self-expression, it was always doubtful how long the Soviet team could continue under the banner of the Commonwealth of Independent States.

The implications of this are enormous. With a membership of over 40 countries, UEFA will have to reconsider the structure of all their tournaments as will FIFA, although it would seem natural for some of the states like Kazakhstan to join the Asian Confederation rather than UEFA, given their geographic location.

Although vast tracts of the former Soviet Union lie in Asia, almost all of the football activity has been centred in the European area, and it was here that the game first took root. First played in the 1880s, football remained low key until over 70 years later, held back by political considerations, the vast size of the country and the harsh weather conditions throughout much of the year.

The first known side was formed by the English managers of the Morozov cotton mills in Orekhovo, Harry and Clement Charnock. Clad in the colours of Blackburn Rovers, the Charnocks' favoured team, Morozov were the leading light of football in the Moscow area, and when the whole of Soviet football was reorganised in 1923 they became Dynamo Moscow, the team of the Electrical Trades Union.

By the early years of the 20th century, leagues had sprung up in many of the major cities of the Russian Empire, most notably in St Petersburg which was then the capital. In 1897 the Amateur Sports Club of St Petersburg formed a football team which led to the creation of the league in that city. It was not until 1912 that the All Russian Football Union was created and a short–lived championship for representative sides introduced.

Though widely played, football was largely a pastime of the privileged classes, and as a result there was not much strength in depth nor an eagerness to develop the game. This was shown in the ill-fated trip to the Stockholm Olympics where in the consolation tournament, Germany scored 16 without any Russian reply.

Matters did not improve later in the same month when Hungary visited Moscow and scored 21 goals without reply over two games, but although four more games were played against Sweden and Norway, the First World War put an end to Russia's fledgling international career for the time being.

		All			League			Cup		Europe		
	Team	G	S	B	G	S	B	G	S	G	S	B
1	Dynamo Kiev	24	13	5	13	11	3	9	2	2	–	2
2	Spartak Moskva	22	17	10	12	12	9	10	5	–	–	1
3	Dynamo Moskva	17	17	7	11	11	5	6	5	–	1	2
4	CSKA Moskva	12	7	6	7	4	6	5	3	–	–	–
5	Torpedo Moskva	9	12	6	3	3	6	6	9	–	–	–
6	Dynamo Tbilisi	5	11	14	2	5	13	2	6	1	–	1
7	Shachter Donetsk	4	6	2	–	2	2	4	4	–	–	–
8	Ararat Yerevan	3	4	–	1	2	–	2	2	–	–	–
9	Dnepr Dnepropetrovsk	3	2	2	2	2	2	1	–	–	–	–
10	Zenit Leningrad	2	3	1	1	–	1	1	3	–	–	–
11	Lokomotiv Moskva	2	2	–	–	1	–	2	1	–	–	–
12	SKA Rostov-na-Donu	1	3	–	–	1	–	1	2	–	–	–
13	Zarja Lugansk	1	2	–	1	–	–	–	2	–	–	–
14	Dynamo Minsk	1	1	3	1	–	3	–	1	–	–	–
15	Metalist Kharkov	1	1	–	–	–	–	1	1	–	–	–
16	SKA Karpati Lvov	1	–	–	–	–	–	1	–	–	–	–
17	Kriliya Kuybyshev	–	2	–	–	–	–	–	2	–	–	–
18	Komanda Kalilin	–	1	–	–	–	–	–	1	–	–	–
	Pachtakor Tashkent	–	1	–	–	–	–	–	1	–	–	–
	ZT Orechevo Zujevo	–	–	–	–	–	1	–	–	–	–	–
21	Chernomorets Odessa	–	–	1	–	–	1	–	–	–	–	–
	Metallurg Moskva	–	–	1	–	–	1	–	–	–	–	–
	Neftchi Baku	–	–	1	–	–	1	–	–	–	–	–
	Zalgiris Vilnius	–	–	1	–	–	1	–	–	–	–	–

Complete to the end of the 1991 league season, the last in the history of the Soviet Union, and including the 1992 Cup competition played under the banner of the CIS.

After the revolution and ensuing civil war, the Committee of Physical Culture and Sport was formed and as the name suggests football was thoroughly organised along lines that were deemed suitable to the new political masters. Sports clubs were founded for the workers of various organisations and within them a whole host of sports were catered for. The idea was that sport would help in the cultural emancipation of the population, a fundamental tenet of communism.

In light of later events it seems strange that to start off with, the idea was not to build athletes capable of taking on the world. That came in the 1950s. In the meantime the Soviet Union became an international recluse. Football and other sports were used as a mechanism to build the character of individuals and train them in the benefits of working in a group, which was considered vital for the development of the country.

The main clubs in Moscow, which after the revolution had become the capital, were the Dynamo club, the Spartak club for the producers' cooperative (formed in 1922), the Torpedo club for workers in the automobile industry (1924), the Lokomotive club for the railway workers (1923) and the army club, known eventually as CSKA, formed in 1923. The same type of organisation was repeated over the whole country.

The development of these clubs was important, because although the idea of general sports clubs was not new, having long traditions in the German gymnastic clubs, the Soviet Union was the first country to actively promote them, and the system within which they functioned served as a role model for numerous countries around the world.

Competition did creep into this highly structured system in the 1930s and in 1936 a national football league was formed. Right from the start the clubs from Moscow dominated the competition, and it was not until Dynamo Kiev's win in 1961 that a club from outside the capital won the championship. Soviet sides did play in friendly matches whenever the occasion merited, but despite the increase in international competition in the rest of Europe, the Soviet Union remained aloof.

Quite how far they had developed became apparent when Dynamo Moscow toured Sweden and Great Britain in 1945 in a gesture of friendship and to celebrate the victory over Fascism. IFK Norrköping were beaten 5–0, the matches against Chelsea and Glasgow Rangers ended in draws, Cardiff City were beaten 10–1, whilst in the final match, Arsenal were beaten 4–3 on a foggy day at Highbury.

Dynamo were shown to be a methodical team and highly trained, if lacking in flair, and as the Soviet Union began to open up to the West, this type of approach was to become a familar sight. A team travelled to Finland for the 1952 Olympic Games, but after beating Bulgaria in the first round and drawing 5–5 with Yugoslavia in a remarkable game in Tampere, they lost the replay and disappeared from sight for a further two years.

Only in 1955 did the Soviet Federation start to organise a proper international fixture list. A tour was made of India and in August that year, in a historic match, West Germany, the world champions, travelled to Moscow and were beaten 3–2 in the Soviets' first meeting with a major Western power. The following year they won the gold medal in the Melbourne Olympic Games, but due to a very poor field, the title did not carry a great deal of weight.

Hopes were high for the 1958 World Cup, the first time they had entered the world's premier tournament. With a good if unspectacular side, they dumped England out of the competition before losing to the hosts Sweden in the quarter-finals. The most notable names in the side at the time were the captain Igor Netto, Valentin Ivanov, Nikita Simonyan and the brilliant Lev Yashin in goal.

This was the basis of the side that won the first European Championship two years later along with the talented Slava Metreveli and Viktor Ponedelnik. Having beaten Yugoslavia in the final of the 1956 Olympic Games, they consigned the poor Yugoslavs to yet another runners-up spot, this time by a score of 2–1 in Paris. This victory was to be the only major title ever won by the Soviet Union in its entire history.

With a remarkably stable side, which was perhaps to be expected from a country that took its sport so seriously, the Soviet Union did consistently well in the 1960s without ever shining, and it was this lack of extra sparkle that perhaps cost them the chance of more titles. They lost in the final of the 1964 European Championship to Spain, and again to West Germany in 1972, whilst reaching the semi-finals in between in 1968. Had the coin landed on the other side after the semi-final draw with Italy that year, they would have appeared in a remarkable four consecutive finals.

Finishing as quarter-finalists in the 1962 World Cup and semi-finalists in England four years later further reinforced the belief that the Soviets just did not have what it takes to win a tournament, and it should not be forgotten that none of the major powers took part in the first European Championship which they won.

At club level the 1960s saw the rise of teams from outside of Moscow, especially from the Ukraine which was establishing itself as a major football base. Leading the challenge were Dynamo Kiev and they have been the most successful side in the country since the mid-1960s. Also very successful have been the top side from Georgia, Dynamo Tbilisi, and they along with Kiev hold the honour of being the only Soviet sides to win a European club competition. Dynamo Moscow lost in the 1972 Cup Winners Cup final to Glasgow Rangers, but Kiev went one better in 1975 when they beat the Hungarians Ferencváros 3–0 in Basle.

Dynamo Tbilisi won the same tournament six years later before a poor crowd in Dusseldorf against Carl Zeiss Jena. Five years after that and once again in the Cup Winners Cup, Kiev won with an impressive 3–0 victory over Atlético Madrid in Lyon. The European Cup and UEFA Cup were different stories altogether and the record in both dismal. Three semi-final appearances in the European Cup is a record similar to a country like Switzerland, whilst in the UEFA Cup, the furthest a Soviet side has reached is the quarter-finals, and then only on three occasions.

Why they have performed so poorly, despite the capacity to generate huge crowds, is a mystery that can not be explained away with the same reasons as for the failure of the national side. Perhaps as clubs move towards a more professional set-up, fortunes might change, although the drift of players to the more settled states of Western Europe has already begun and is likely to continue to deplete teams of their star players.

The 1970s was a curious time for Soviet football, failing to qualify as they did for both the 1974 and 1978 World Cups. In 1974 they refused to play Chile in the Estadio Nacional in Santiago which had been used as a prison after the coup there in 1973, and were forced to withdraw, whilst in 1978 they finished second in their group behind Hungary.

In 1972 the first real star of Soviet football, Oleg Blokhin, made his debut for the national side, but despite missing out in 1974 and 1978, he was able to display his talents on the world stage in 1982 in Spain and again four years later in Mexico. Unless the Soviet team carries on under the banner of the Commonwealth of Independent States, he will remain as the most capped player in the history of the Soviet side as well as their top scorer. Voted European Footballer of the Year in 1975, along with Lev Yashin he is probably the finest footballer his country has ever produced.

In the 1988 European Championships, the Soviets once again reached the final and once again found themselves playing a minor role next to the real stars of the show. In 1964 it was the Spain of Suárez, Amancio and Zoco. In 1972 it was the Germans of Beckenbauer, Netzer and Müller, whilst in 1988 it was as sidekicks to Gullit, Van Basten and Rijkaard of Holland. Never again as the Soviet Union will they have the chance to prove that they can be the main event, but Russia or the Ukraine might cause a few surprises in the future. They will be two countries worth reckoning with.

Population: 282 279 000
Area, sq km: 22 228 200
% in urban areas: 65.7%
Capital city: Moscow

USSR Football Federation
Year of formation: 1912
Affiliation to FIFA: 1946
Affiliation to UEFA: 1954
Registered clubs: 50 198
Registered players: 4 800 300
National stadium: Centralny Stadion 100 000
National colours: Shirts: Red/Shorts: White/Socks: Red
Reserve colours: Shirts: White/Shorts: White/Socks: White
Season: April–October

THE RECORD

WORLD CUP

1930–54 ..... Did not enter
1958 .... QT 1st/3 in group 6 – Final Tournament/Quarter-finalists
1962 .... QT 1st/3 in group 5 – Final Tournament/Quarter-finalists
1966 .... QT 1st/4 in group 7 – Final Tournament/Semi-finalists/4th place
1970 .... QT 1st/3 in group 4 – Final Tournament/Quarter-finalists
1974 .... QT 1st/3 in group 9 (Withdrew)
1978 .... QT 2nd/3 in group 9
1982 .... QT 1st/5 in group 3 – Final Tournament/2nd round
1986 .... QT 2nd/5 in group 6 – Final Tournament/2nd round
1990 .... QT 1st/5 in group 3 – Final Tournament/1st round

EUROPEAN CHAMPIONSHIP

1960 .... Winners
1964 .... Finalists
1968 .... QT 1st/4 in group 3 – Final Tournament/Semi-finalists/4th place
1972 .... QT 1st/4 in group 4 – Final Tournament/Finalists
1976 .... QT 1st/4 in group 6 – Final Tournament/Quarter-finalists
1980 .... QT 4th/4 in group 6
1984 .... QT 2nd/4 in group 2
1988 .... QT 1st/5 in group 3 – Final Tournament/Finalists
1992 .... QT 1st/5 in group 3 – Final Tournament

OLYMPIC GAMES

1908–48 ..... Did not enter
1952 .... 1st round
1956 .... Winners
1960 .... QT Failed to qualify
1964 .... QT Failed to qualify
1968 .... QT Failed to qualify
1972 .... Final Tournament/2nd round/3rd place
1976 .... Final Tournament/Semi-finalists/3rd place
1980 .... Final Tournament/Semi-finalists/3rd place
1984 .... Final Tournament/withdrew
1988 .... Final Tournament/Winners
1992 .... QT Failed to qualify

EUROPEAN CLUB COMPETITIONS

EUROPEAN CUP: Semi-finalists – Dynamo Kiev 1977 1987, Spartak Moscow 1991

CUP WINNERS CUP: Winners – Dynamo Kiev 1975, 1986, Dynamo Tbilisi 1981
Finalists – Dynamo Moscow 1972

UEFA CUP: Quarter-finalists – Spartak Moscow 1984, Dynamo Minsk 1985, Torpedo Moscow 1991

CLUB DIRECTORY

RUSSIA
Population: 147 400 000
Area, sq km: 17 075 400
Capital city: Moscow

The Russian Football Federation
Luzhnetskaja Naberzhnaja #8
119871GSP–3 Moscow
Tel: (010 7) 095 2010834
Fax: (010 7) 095 2480814
Telex: 411287 PRIZ SU
Cable: None
Languages for correspondence: English

MOSCOW (Population – 13 100 000)

Centralnyi Sportivny Klub Armii (CSKA Moskva)
Stadium: Dynamo 51 000
Founded: 1923
Colours: Red and white hoops/Red
Previous names: Olls 1923, OPPV 1923–28, CDKA 1928–50, CDSA 1950–58, CSK–MO 1958–59

Dynamo Moskva
Stadium: Dynamo 51 000
Founded: 1923
Colours: White/Blue

Lokomotiv Moskva
Stadium: Lokomotiv 30 000
Founded: 1923
Colours: Red/White
Previous name: Kor 1923–36

Spartak Moskva
Stadium: Centralny Stadion 100 000
Founded: 1922
Colours: Red/Red
Previous name: Moskovski Klub Sporta 1922–35

Torpedo Moskva
Stadium: Torpedo 21 000
Founded: 1924
Colours: White/Black
Previous name: Proletarskkaja Kuznica 1924–36

ST PETERSBURG (Population – 5 825 000)
Zenit St Petersburg
Stadium: Kirova 75 000
Founded: 1931
Colours: Violet/White
Previous names: Stalin Leningrad 1931–40, Zent Leningrad 1940–91

NIZHNI NOVGOROD (Population – 2 025 000)
Volga Nizhni Novgorod
Stadium: Volga
Founded: 1963
Colours: White/White
Previous names: Merger in 1963 of Torpedo and Rakieta Sormovo, Volga Gorky 1963–91

YEKATERINBURG (Population – 1 620 000)
Uralmash Yekaterinburg
Stadium: Uralmash
Founded: 1950
Colours: Red/White
Previous names: ODO 1950–60, Uralmash Sverdlovsk 1960–91

SAMARA (Population – 1 505 000)
Kriliya Sovjetov Samara
Stadium: Metallurg
Founded: 1943
Colours: Blue/White
Previous name: Kriliya Sovjetov Kuybyshev 1943–91

VOLGOGRAD (Population – 1 360 000)
Rotor Volgograd
Stadium: Central 40 000
Founded: 1937
Colours: White/White
Previous names: Traktor Stalingrad 1933–48, Torpedo Stalingrad 1948–57, Stal Stalingrad 1957–61, Stal Volgograd 1961–71

ROSTOV-NA-DONU (Population – 1 165 000)
SKA Rostov-Na-Donu
Stadium: Central 35 000
Founded: 1938
Colours: Red/Green
Previous name: SKVO 1938–60

UKRAINE
Population: 51 707 000
Area, sq km: 60 378 200
Capital city: Kiev

KIEV (Population – 2 900 000)
Dynamo Kiev
Stadium: Central Republican 100 000
Founded: 1927
Colours: White/White

DONETSK (Population – 2 200 000)
Shachter Donetsk
Stadium: Lokomotiv 40 000
Founded: 1936
Colours: Orange and black stripes/Black
Previous names: Stachanovec Stalino 1935–47, Shachter Stalino 1947–61

KHARKOV (Population – 1 940 000)
Metalist Kharkov
Stadium: Metalist 37 000
Founded: 1944
Colours: White with blue shoulders and sleeves/Blue
Previous names: Lokomotiv 1944–56, Avangard 1956–66

DNEPROPETROVSK (Population – 1 600 000)
Dnepr Dnepropetrovsk
Stadium: Meteor 30 000
Founded: 1936
Colours: Red/Red

ODESSA (Population – 1 185 000)
Chernomorets Odessa
Stadium: Central 43 000
Founded: 1958
Colours: Blue/Blue

LVOV (Population – 790 000)
SKA Karpati Lvov
Stadium: Druzjba
Founded: 1963
Colours: Green/White

LUGANSK (Population – 497 000)
Zarja Lugansk
Stadium: Avangard
Founded: 1938
Colours: White/White
Previous name: Jerjinec 1938–64, Zarja Voroschilovgrad 1964–90

ARMENIA
Population: 3 288 000
Area, sq km: 29 800
Capital city: Yerevan

YEREVAN (Population – 1 315 000)
Ararat Yerevan
Stadium: Razdan 71 000
Founded: 1937
Colours: Red/Blue
Previous names: Dynamo 1937–54, Spartak 1954–62

AZERBAIJAN
Population: 7 038 000
Area, sq km: 86 600
Capital city: Baku

BAKU (Population – 2 020 000)
Neftchi Baku
Stadium: Republican 37 000
Founded: 1937
Colours: White/Maroon
Previous name: Neftjanik 1937–68

BELORUSSIA
Population: 10 200 000
Area, sq km: 207 600
Capital city: Minsk

MINSK (Population – 1 650 000)
Dynamo Minsk
Stadium: Dynamo 50 000
Founded: 1928
Colours: Violet with white sleeves/White
Previous names: Dynamo 1935–54, Spartak 1954–59, Belarus 1959–62

GEORGIA
Population: 5 443 000
Area, sq km: 69 700
Capital city: Tbilisi

TBILISI (Population – 1 460 000)
Iberya Tbilisi
Stadium: Dynamo 74 000
Founded: 1925
Colours: White/Blue
Previous name: Dynamo Tbilisi 1925–90

ESTONIA
Population: 1 571 000
Area, sq km: 45 100
Capital city: Tallinn

TALLINN (Population – 478 000)
Sport Tallinn
SKA Fosfarit Tallinn
FC Flora Tallinn

LATVIA
Population: 2 673 000
Area, sq km: 64 500
Capital city: Riga

RIGA (Population – 900 000)
Daugava Riga
LVFKI Riga
Torpedo Riga

DAUGAVPILS (Population – 128 000)
Stroitel Daugavpils

LIEPAJA (Population – 114 000)
Metalurg Liepaja

LITHUANIA
Population: 3 682 000
Area, sq km: 65 200
Capital city: Vilnius

VILNIUS (Population – 582 000)
Zalgiris Vilnius
Stadium: Zalgiris 15 000
Founded: 1947
Green and white stripes/White
Previous names: Dinamo 1947–48, Spartak 1948–62

Lietuvos Makabi Vilnius
Previous name: Neris Vilnius

Panerys Vilnius

KAUNAS (Population – 423 000)
Banga Kaunas
Vilija Kaunas
Vytis-Inkaras Kaunas

KLAIPEDA (Population 204 000)
Sirijus Klaipeda
Granitas Klaipeda

SIAULIAI (Population – 145 000)
Sakalas Siauliai
Tauras Siauliai

PANEVEZYS (Population – 126 000)
Ekrenas Panevezys

MOLDAVIA
Population: 4 338 000
Area, sq km: 33 700
Capital city: Kishinyov

KAZAKHSTAN
Population: 16 536 000
Area, sq km: 2 717 300
Capital city: Alma-Ata

ALMA-ATA (Population – 1 190 000)
Kairat Alma-Ata
Stadium: Kazakstan
Founded: 1954
Colours: Red/White

KIRGIZISTAN
Population: 4 290 000
Area, sq km: 198 500
Capital city: Pishpek

TADZHIKISTAN
Population: 5 109 000
Area, sq km: 143 100
Capital city: Dushanbe

TURKMENISTAN
Population: 3 534 000
Area, sq km: 488 100
Capital city: Ashkhabad

UZBEKISTAN
Population: 19 905 000
Area, sq km: 447 400
Capital city: Tashkent

TASHKENT (Population – 2 325 000)
Pachtakor Tashkent
Stadium: Pachtakor 60 000
Founded: 1956
Colours: Red/Black

SOVIET LEAGUE CHAMPIONSHIP

Year	Champions		Runners up		3rd	
1936	Dynamo Moskva	18	Dynamo Kiev	14	Spartak Moskva	13
1936	Spartak Moskva	17	Dynamo Moskva	16	Dynamo Tbilisi	16
1937	Dynamo Moskva	38	Spartak Moskva	37	Dynamo Kiev	36
1938	Spartak Moskva	39	CDKA Moskva	37	Metallurg Moskva	37
1939	Spartak Moskva	37	Dynamo Tbilisi	33	CDKA Moskva	32
1940	Dynamo Moskva	36	Dynamo Tbilisi	34	Spartak Moskva	31
1941–44 –						
1945	Dynamo Moskva	40	CDKA Moskva	39	Torpedo Moskva	27
1946	CDKA Moskva	37	Dynamo Moskva	33	Dynamo Tbilisi	33
1947	CDKA Moskva	40	Dynamo Moskva	40	Dynamo Tbilisi	33
1948	CDKA Moskva	41	Dynamo Moskva	40	Spartak Moskva	37
1949	Dynamo Moskva	57	CDKA Moskva	51	Spartak Moskva	49
1950	CDKA Moskva	53	Dynamo Moskva	50	Dynamo Tbilisi	47
1951	CDSA Moskva	43	Dynamo Tbilisi	36	Shachter Stalino	34
1952	Spartak Moskva	20	Dynamo Kiev	17	Dynamo Moskva	17
1953	Spartak Moskva	29	Dynamo Tbilisi	27	Torpedo Moskva	25
1954	Dynamo Moskva	35	Spartak Moskva	32	Spartak Minsk	31
1955	Dynamo Moskva	34	Spartak Moskva	33	CDSA Moskva	31
1956	Spartak Moskva	34	Dynamo Moskva	28	CDSA Moskva	25
1957	Dynamo Moskva	36	Torpedo Moskva	28	Spartak Moskva	28
1958	Spartak Moskva	32	Dynamo Moskva	31	CSK Moskva	27
1959	Dynamo Moskva	31	Lokomotiv Moskva	29	Dynamo Tbilisi	27
1960	Torpedo Moskva	14	Dynamo Kiev	11	Dynamo Moskva	11
1961	Dynamo Kiev	45	Torpedo Moskva	41	Spartak Moskva	40
1962	Spartak Moskva	32	Dynamo Moskva	29	Dynamo Tbilisi	28
1963	Dynamo Moskva	55	Spartak Moskva	52	Dynamo Minsk	48
1964	Dynamo Tbilisi	46	Torpedo Moskva	46	CSKA Moskva	43
1965	Torpedo Moskva	51	Dynamo Kiev	50	CSKA Moskva	38
1966	Dynamo Kiev	56	SKA Rostov–na–Donu	47	Neftchi Baku	45
1967	Dynamo Kiev	54	Dynamo Moskva	48	Dynamo Tbilisi	45
1968	Dynamo Kiev	57	Spartak Moskva	52	Torpedo Moskva	50
1969	Spartak Moskva	43	Dynamo Kiev	39	Dynamo Tbilisi	35
1970	CSKA Moskva	45	Dynamo Moskva	45	Spartak Moskva	38
1971	Dynamo Kiev	44	Ararat Yerevan	37	Dynamo Tbilisi	36
1972	Zarja Vorosch'grad	40	Dynamo Kiev	35	Dynamo Tbilisi	35
1973	Ararat Yerevan	39	Dynamo Kiev	36	Dynamo Moskva	33
1974	Dynamo Kiev	40	Spartak Moskva	39	Chernomorets Odessa	35
1975	Dynamo Kiev	43	Shachter Donetsk	38	Dynamo Moskva	38
1976	Dynamo Moskva	22	Ararat Yerevan	19	Dynamo Tbilisi	18
1976	Torpedo Moskva	20	Dynamo Kiev	18	Dynamo Tbilisi	17
1977	Dynamo Kiev	43	Dynamo Tbilisi	39	Torpedo Moskva	37
1978	Dynamo Tbilisi	42	Dynamo Kiev	38	Shachter Donetsk	37
1979	Spartak Moskva	50	Shachter Donetsk	48	Dynamo Kiev	47
1980	Dynamo Kiev	51	Spartak Moskva	45	Zenit Leningrad	42
1981	Dynamo Kiev	53	Spartak Moskva	46	Dynamo Tbilisi	42
1982	Dynamo Minsk	47	Dynamo Kiev	46	Spartak Moskva	41
1983	Dnepr Dnepropetrovsk	49	Spartak Moskva	45	Dynamo Minsk	43
1984	Zenit Leningrad	47	Spartak Moskva	45	Dnepr Dnepropetrovsk	42
1985	Dynamo Kiev	48	Spartak Moskva	46	Dnepr Dnepropetrovsk	42
1986	Dynamo Kiev	39	Dynamo Moskva	38	Spartak Moskva	37
1987	Spartak Moskva	42	Dnepr Dnepropetrovsk	39	Zalgiris Vilnius	36
1988	Dnepr Dnepropetrovsk	46	Dynamo Kiev	43	Torpedo Moskva	42
1989	Spartak Moskva	44	Dnepr Dnepropetrovsk	42	Dynamo Kiev	38
1990	Dynamo Kiev	34	CSKA Moskva	31	Dynamo Moskva	31
1991	CSKA Moskva	43	Spartak Moskva	41	Torpedo Moskva	36

SOVIET CUP FINALS

Year	Winners	Score	Runners–up
1936	Lokomotiv Moskva	2–0	Dynamo Tbilisi
1937	Dynamo Moskva	5–2	Dynamo Tbilisi
1938	Spartak Moskva	3–2	Elektrik Leningrad
1939	Spartak Moskva	3–1	Stalinets Leningrad
1940–43 –			
1944	Zenit Leningrad	2–1	CDKA Moskva
1945	CDKA Moskva	2–1	Dynamo Moskva
1946	Spartak Moskva	3–2	Dynamo Tbilisi
1947	Spartak Moskva	2–0	Torpedo Moskva
1948	CDKA Moskva	3–0	Spartak Moskva
1949	Torpedo Moskva	2–1	Dynamo Moskva
1950	Spartak Moskva	3–0	Dynamo Moskva

1951	CDSA Moskva	2–1	Komanda Kalinin
1952	Torpedo Moskva	1–0	Spartak Moskva
1953	Dynamo Moskva	1–0	Kriliya Kuybyshev
1954	Dynamo Kiev	2–1	Spartak Yerevan
1955	CDSA Moskva	2–1	Dynamo Moskva
1956	–		
1957	Lokomotiv Moskva	1–0	Spartak Moskva
1958	Spartak Moskva	1–0	Torpedo Moskva
1959	–		
1960	Torpedo Moskva	4–3	Dynamo Tbilisi
1961	Shachter Donetsk	3–1	Torpedo Moskva
1962	Shachter Donetsk	2–0	Znamia Truda O–Z
1963	Spartak Moskva	2–1	Shachter Donetsk
1964	Dynamo Kiev	1–0	Kriliya Kuybyshev
1965	Spartak Moskva	0–0 2–1	Dynamo Minsk
1966	Dynamo Kiev	2–0	Torpedo Moskva
1967	Dynamo Moskva	3–0	CSKA Moskva
1968	Torpedo Moskva	1–0	Pakhtakor Tashkent
1969	SKA Karpati Lvov	2–1	SKA Rostov-na-Donu
1970	Dynamo Moskva	2–1	Dynamo Tbilisi
1971	Spartak Moskva	2–1	SKA Rostov-na-Donu
1972	Torpedo Moskva	0–0 1–1 (4–1p)	Spartak Moskva
1973	Ararat Yerevan	2–1	Dynamo Kiev
1974	Dynamo Kiev	3–0	Zarja Voroshilovgrad
1975	Ararat Yerevan	2–1	Zarja Voroshilovgrad
1976	Dynamo Tbilisi	3–0	Ararat Yerevan
1977	Dynamo Moskva	1–0	Torpedo Moskva
1978	Dynamo Kiev	2–1	Shachter Donetsk
1979	Dynamo Tbilisi	0–0 (5–4p)	Dynamo Moskva
1980	Shachter Donetsk	2–1	Dynamo Tbilisi
1981	SKA Rostov-na-Donu	1–0	Spartak Moskva
1982	Dynamo Kiev	1–0	Torpedo Moskva
1983	Shachter Donetsk	1–0	Metalist Kharkov
1984	Dynamo Moskva	2–0	Zenit Leningrad
1985	Dynamo Kiev	2–1	Shachter Donetsk
1986	Torpedo Moskva	1–0	Shachter Donetsk
1987	Dynamo Kiev	3–3 (4–3p)	Dynamo Minsk
1988	Metalist Kharkov	2–0	Torpedo Moskva
1989	Dnepr Dnepropetrovsk	1–0	Torpedo Moskva
1990	Dynamo Kiev	6–1	Lokomotiv Moskva
1991	CSKA Moskva	3–2	Torpedo Moskva
1992	Spartak Moskva	2–0	CSKA Moskva

INTERNATIONAL MATCHES PLAYED BY THE SOVIET UNION

Date	Opponents	Result		Venue	Compet	Scorers
30–06–1912	Finland	L	1–2	Stockholm	OGqf	Batusov
1–07	Germany	L	0–16	Stockholm	OGct	
12–07	Hungary	L	0–9	Moscow	Fr	
14–07	Hungary	L	0–12	Moscow	Fr	
4–05–1913	Sweden	L	1–4	Moscow	Fr	
14–09	Norway	D	1–1	Moscow	Fr	
5–07–1914	Sweden	D	2–2	Stockholm	Fr	Zhitarev 2
12–07	Norway	D	1–1	Oslo	Fr	Krotov
16–11–1924	Turkey	W	3–0	Moscow	Fr	Butusov 2, Spakovski
15–05–1925	Turkey	W	2–1	Ankara	Fr	Selin, Butusov
15–07–1952	Bulgaria	W	2–1	Kotka	OGr1	Bobrov, Trofimov
20–07	Yugoslavia	D	5–5	Tampere	OGr2	Bobrov 3, Trofimov, Petrov
22–07	Yugoslavia	L	1–3	Tampere	OGr2	Bobrov
8–09–1954	Sweden	W	7–0	Moscow	Fr	Simonyan 2, Ilyin, OG, Gogoberidze, Salinikov 2
26–09	Hungary	D	1–1	Moscow	Fr	Salinikov
6–02–1955	India	W	4–0	Dehli	Fr	Kuznetsov U 3, Voinov
27–02	India	W	3–0	Bombay	Fr	Simonyan 2, Tatushin
2–03	India	W	3–0	Calcutta	Fr	Tatushin 2, Voinov
26–06	Sweden	W	6–0	Stockholm	Fr	Strelitsov 3, Tatushin, Salinikov, Ivanov V
21–08	West Germany	W	3–2	Moscow	Fr	Parshin, Maslenkin, Ilyin
16–09	India	W	11–1	Moscow	Fr	Shabrov 2, Strelitsov 3, Salinikov 3, Kuznetsov U 2, Netto
25–09	Hungary	D	1–1	Budapest	Fr	Kuznetsov U
23–10	France	D	2–2	Moscow	Fr	Strelitsov, Simonyan
23–05–1956	Denmark	W	5–1	Moscow	Fr	Ivanov V, Salinikov 2, Strelitsov, Ilyin
1–07	Denmark	W	5–2	Copenhagen	Fr	Ilyin 3, Isaev, Tatushin
11–07	Israel	W	5–0	Moscow	OGq	Tatushin, Ivanov V 2, Simonyan 2
31–07	Israel	W	2–1	Tel Aviv	OGq	Ilyin, Tatushin
15–09	West Germany	W	2–1	Hanover	Fr	Strelitsov, Ivanov V
23–09	Hungary	L	0–1	Moscow	Fr	
21–10	France	L	1–2	Paris	Fr	Isaev
29–11	Indonesia	D	0–0	Melbourne	OGqf	
1–12	Indonesia	W	4–0	Melbourne	OGqf	Salinikov 2, Ivanov V, Netto
5–12	Bulgaria	W	2–1	Melbourne	OGsf	Strelitsov, Tatushin
8–12	Yugoslavia	W	1–0	Melbourne	OGf	Ilyin
1–06–1957	Romania	D	1–1	Moscow	Fr	Strelitsov
23–06	Poland	W	3–0	Moscow	WCq	Tatushin, Simonyan, Ilyin
21–07	Bulgaria	W	4–0	Sofia	Fr	Strelitsov 2, Ilyin, Isaev
27–07	Finland	W	2–1	Moscow	WCq	Voinov, Netto
15–08	Finland	W	10–0	Helsinki	WCq	Netto, Simonyan 3, Isaev 2, Strelitsov 2, Ilyin 2

22–09	Hungary	W	2–1	Budapest	Fr	Tatushin, Strelitsov
20–10	Poland	L	1–2	Chorzow	WCq	Ivanov V
24–11	Poland	W	2–0	Leipzig	WCq	Strelitsov, Fedosov
18–05–1958	England	D	1–1	Moscow	Fr	Ivanov V
8–06	England	D	2–2	Gothenburg	WCr1	Simonyan, Ivanov A
11–06	Austria	W	2–0	Boras	WCr1	Ilyin, Ivanov V
15–06	Brazil	L	0–2	Gothenburg	WCr1	
17–06	England	W	1–0	Gothenburg	WCr1	Ilyin
19–06	Sweden	L	0–2	Stockholm	WCqf	
30–08	Czechoslovakia	W	2–1	Prague	Fr	Voroshilov, Voinov
28–09	Hungary	W	3–1	Moscow	ECr1	Ilyin, Metreveli, Ivanov V
22–10	England	L	0–5	London	Fr	
27–06–1959	Bulgaria	D	1–1	Moscow	OGq	Korolenkov
19–07	Romania	W	2–0	Moscow	OGq	Yurin, Metreveli
2–08	Romania	D	0–0	Bucharest	OGq	
6–09	Czechoslovakia	W	3–1	Moscow	Fr	Bubukin, Meshi, Ivanov V
13–09	Bulgaria	L	0–1	Sofia	OGq	
27–09	Hungary	W	1–0	Budapest	ECr1	Voinov
3–10	China	W	1–0	Peking	Fr	Ilyin
19–05–1960	Poland	W	7–1	Moscow	Fr	Ivanov 2, Bubukin, Ponedelnik 3, Metreveli
	Spain	W-O	*(Spain withdrew)*		ECqf	
6–07	Czechoslovakia	W	3–0	Marseille	ECsf	Ivanov V 2, Ponedelnik
10–07	Yugoslavia	W	2–1	Paris	ECf	Metreveli, Ponedelnik
17–08	East Germany	W	1–0	Leipzig	Fr	Ponedelnik
4–09	Austria	L	1–3	Vienna	Fr	Ponedelnik
21–05–1961	Poland	L	0–1	Warsaw	Fr	
18–06	Turkey	W	1–0	Moscow	WCq	Voronin
24–06	Argentina	D	0–0	Moscow	Fr	
1–07	Norway	W	5–2	Moscow	WCq	Metreveli, Ponedelnik, Bubukin 2, Meshi
23–08	Norway	W	3–0	Oslo	WCq	Ponedelnik, Meshi, Metreveli
10–09	Austria	L	0–1	Moscow	Fr	
12–11	Turkey	W	2–1	Istanbul	WCq	Gusarov, Mamikin
18–11	Argentina	W	2–1	Buenos Aires	Fr	Ponedelnik 2
22–11	Chile	W	1–0	Santiago	Fr	Mamikin
29–11	Uruguay	W	2–1	Montevideo	Fr	Gusarov, Ponedelnik
11–04–1962	Luxembourg	W	3–1	Luxembourg	Fr	Mamikin 2, Gusarov
18–04	Sweden	W	2–0	Stockholm	Fr	Ponedelnik, Mamikin
27–04	Uruguay	W	5–0	Moscow	Fr	Mamikin 3, Chislenko, Ivanov V
3–05	East Germany	W	2–1	Moscow	Fr	
31–05	Yugoslavia	W	2–0	Arica	WCr1	Ivanov V, Ponedelnik
3–06	Colombia	D	4–4	Arica	WCr1	Ivanov V 2, Chislenko, Ponedelnik
6–06	Uruguay	W	2–1	Arica	WCr1	Mamikin, Ivanov V
10–06	Chile	L	1–2	Arica	WCqf	Chislenko
22–05–1963	Sweden	L	0–1	Moscow	Fr	
22–09	Hungary	D	1–1	Moscow	Fr	Ivanov V
13–10	Italy	W	2–0	Moscow	ECr2	Ponedelnik, Chislenko
10–11	Italy	D	1–1	Rome	ECr2	Gusarov
1–12	Morocco	D	1–1	Casablanca	Fr	OG
13–05–1964	Sweden	D	1–1	Stockholm	ECqf	Ivanov V
20–05	Uruguay	W	1–0	Moscow	Fr	Mudrik
27–05	Sweden	W	3–1	Moscow	ECqf	Pondelnik 2, Voronin
17–06	Denmark	W	3–0	Barcelona	ECsf	Voronin, Pondelnik, Ivanov V
21–06	Spain	L	1–2	Madrid	ECf	Khusainov
11–10	Austria	L	0–1	Vienna	Fr	
4–11	Algeria	D	2–2	Algiers	Fr	Mateev, Khusainov
22–11	Yugoslavia	D	1–1	Belgrade	Fr	Serebrjanikov
29–11	Bulgaria	D	0–0	Sofia	Fr	
16–05–1965	Austria	D	0–0	Moscow	Fr	
23–05	Greece	W	3–1	Moscow	WCq	Kazakov, Ivanov V 2
30–05	Wales	W	2–1	Moscow	WCq	Ivanov V, OG
27–06	Denmark	W	6–0	Moscow	WCq	Khusainov, Metreveli, Voronin, Barkaj 2, Meshi
4–07	Brazil	L	0–3	Moscow	Fr	
4–09	Yugoslavia	D	0–0	Moscow	Fr	
3–10	Greece	W	4–1	Athens	WCq	Metreveli, Banishevski 3
17–10	Denmark	W	3–1	Copenhagen	WCq	Metreveli, Malofiev, Sabo
27–10	Wales	L	1–2	Cardiff	WCq	Banishevski
21–11	Brazil	D	2–2	Rio de Janeiro	Fr	Banishevski, Metreveli
1–12	Argentina	D	1–1	Buenos Aires	Fr	Banishevski

4–12	Uruguay	W	3–1	Montevideo	Fr	Khusainov, Banishevski, Osynin
23–02–1966	Chile	W	2–0	Santiago	Fr	Sabo 2
20–04	Switzerland	D	2–2	Basle	Fr	Chislenko, Ponedelnik
24–04	Austria	W	1–0	Vienna	Fr	Voronin
18–05	Czechoslovakia	W	2–1	Prague	Fr	Banishevski 2
22–05	Belgium	W	1–0	Brussels	Fr	Serebrjanikov
5–06	France	D	3–3	Moscow	Fr	Metreveli, Banishevski, Chislenko
12–07	North Korea	W	3–0	Middlesbrough	WCr1	Malofiev 2, Banishevski
16–07	Italy	W	1–0	Sunderland	WCr1	Chislenko
20–07	Chile	W	2–1	Sunderland	WCr1	Porkujan 2
23–07	Hungary	W	2–1	Sunderland	WCqf	Chislenko, Porkujan
25–07	West Germany	L	1–2	Liverpool	WCsf	Porkujan
28–07	Portugal	L	1–2	London	WC3p	Metreveli
18–09	Yugoslavia	W	2–1	Belgrade	Fr	Krasnitski, Mateev
16–10	Turkey	L	0–2	Moscow	Fr	
23–10	East Germany	D	2–2	Moscow	Fr	Strelitsov, Chislenko
1–11	Italy	L	0–1	Milan	Fr	
10–05–1967	Scotland	W	2–0	Glasgow	Fr	OG, Medvidi
28–05	Mexico	W	2–0	Leningrad	Fr	Chislenko, Byshovets
3–06	France	W	4–2	Paris	Fr	Chislenko 2, Byshovets, Strelitsov
11–06	Austria	W	4–3	Moscow	ECq	Malofiev, Byshovets, Chislenko, Strelitsov
16–07	Greece	W	4–0	Tbilisi	ECq	Banishevski 2, Sabo, Chislenko
20–07	Poland	W	1–0	Warsaw	OGq	Chislenko
4–08	Poland	W	2–1	Moscow	OGq	Chislenko, Banishevski
30–08	Finland	W	2–0	Moscow	ECq	Khurtzilava, Chislenko
6–09	Finland	W	5–2	Turku	ECq	Sabo 2, Maslov, Banishevski, Malofiev
1–10	Switzerland	D	2–2	Moscow	Fr	Khurtzilava, OG
8–10	Bulgaria	W	2–1	Sofia	Fr	Strelitsov, Banishevski
15–10	Austria	L	0–1	Vienna	ECq	
31–10	Greece	W	1–0	Athens	ECq	Malofiev
29–11	Holland	L	1–3	Rotterdam	Fr	Maslov
6–12	England	D	2–2	London	Fr	Chislenko 2
17–12	Chile	W	4–1	Santiago	Fr	OG, Strelitsov 3
3–03–1968	Mexico	D	0–0	Mexico City	Fr	
7–03	Mexico	D	1–1	Leon	Fr	Byshovets
10–03	Mexico	D	0–0	Mexico City	Fr	
24–04	Belgium	W	1–0	Moscow	Fr	Sabo
4–05	Hungary	L	0–2	Budapest	ECqf	
11–05	Hungary	W	3–0	Moscow	ECqf	OG, Khurtzilava, Byshovets
5–06	Italy	D	0–0	Naples	ECsf	*Italy won on toss of coin*
8–06	England	L	0–2	Rome	EC3p	
16–06	Austria	W	3–1	Leningrad	Fr	Vyun, Gershkovich, Asatiani
1–08	Sweden	D	2–2	Gothenburg	Fr	Gershkovich, Khurtzilava
20–02–1969	Colombia	W	3–1	Bogota	Fr	Gershkovich, Kmelnitski 2
25–07	East Germany	D	2–2	Leipzig	Fr	Puzach, Kmelnitski
6–08	Sweden	L	0–1	Moscow	Fr	
10–09	Nth. Ireland	D	0–0	Belfast	WCq	
24–09	Yugoslavia	W	3–1	Belgrade	Fr	Asatiani, Nodija, Byshovets
15–10	Turkey	W	3–0	Kiev	WCq	Muntjan 2, Nodija
22–10	Nth. Ireland	W	2–0	Moscow	WCq	Nodija, Byshovets
16–11	Turkey	W	3–1	Istanbul	WCq	Asianti 2, Kmelnitski
14–02–1970	Peru	D	0–0	Lima	Fr	
20–02	Peru	W	2–0	Lima	Fr	Byshovets 2
22–02	El Salvador	W	2–0	San Salvador	Fr	Puzach, Serebrjanikov
26–02	Mexico	D	0–0	Mexico City	Fr	
5–05	Bulgaria	D	3–3	Sofia	Fr	Evrushihin, Byshovets, Nodija
6–05	Bulgaria	D	0–0	Sofia	Fr	
31–05	Mexico	D	0–0	Mexico City	WCr1	
6–06	Belgium	W	4–1	Mexico City	WCr1	Byshovets 2, Asatiani, Kmelnitski
10–06	El Salvador	W	2–0	Mexico City	WCr1	Byshovets 2
14–06	Uruguay	L	0–1	Mexico City	WCqf	
28–10	Yugoslavia	W	4–0	Moscow	Fr	Shevchenko, Fedotov, Kolotov, Nodija
15–11	Cyprus	W	3–1	Nicosia	ECq	Kolotov, Evrushihin, Shevchenko
17–02–1971	Mexico	D	0–0	Guadalajara	Fr	
19–02	Mexico	D	0–0	Mexico City	Fr	
28–02	El Salvador	W	1–0	San Salvador	Fr	OG
28–04	Bulgaria	D	1–1	Sofia	Fr	Shevchenko
30–05	Spain	W	2–1	Moscow	ECq	Kolotov, Shevchenko
7–06	Cyprus	W	6–1	Moscow	ECq	Fedotov 2, Evrushihin 2, Kolotov,

						Banishevski
14–06	Scotland	W	1–0	Moscow	Fr	Evrushihin
18–09	India	W	5–0	Moscow	Fr	Kolotov 3, Kmelnitski 2
22–09	Nth. Ireland	W	1–0	Moscow	ECq	Muntjan
13–10	Nth. Ireland	D	1–1	Belfast	ECq	Byshovets
27–10	Spain	D	0–0	Seville	ECq	
29–03–1972	Bulgaria	D	1–1	Sofia	Fr	Kolotov
19–04	Peru	W	2–0	Kiev	Fr	Banishevski, Konkov
30–04	Yugoslavia	D	0–0	Belgrade	ECqf	
13–05	Yugoslavia	W	3–0	Moscow	ECqf	Kolotov, Banishevski, Kozinkevich
26–05	West Germany	L	1–4	Munich	Fr	Kolotov
7–06	Bulgaria	W	1–0	Moscow	Fr	Muntjan
14–06	Hungary	W	1–0	Brussels	ECsf	Konkov
18–06	West Germany	L	0–3	Brussels	ECf	
29–06	Uruguay	W	1–0	Sao Paulo	Clr2	Onishenko
2–07	Argentina	L	0–1	Belo Horizonte	Clr2	
6–07	Portugal	L	0–1	Belo Horizonte	Clr2	
16–07	Finland	D	1–1	Vaasa	Fr	Blokhin
6–08	Sweden	D	4–4	Stockholm	Fr	Yeliseev, Andreasjan, Semenov, Blokhin
28–08	Burma	W	1–0	Regensburg	OGr1	Kolotov
30–08	Sudan	W	2–1	Munich	OGr1	Evrushihin, Zanazanyan
1–09	Mexico*	W	4–1	Regensburg	OGr1	Blokhin 3, Semenov
3–09	Morocco	W	3–0	Munich	OGr2	Semenov, Kolotov, Yeliseev
5–09	Poland	L	1–2	Augsburg	OGr2	Blokhin
8–09	Denmark	W	4–0	Augsburg	OGr2	Kolotov, Semenov, Blokhin, Sabo
10–09	East Germany	D	2–2	Munich	OG3p	Blokhin, Khurtsilava
13–10	France	L	0–1	Paris	WCq	
18–10	Rep. Ireland	W	2–1	Dublin	WCq	Fedotov, Kolotov
28–03–1973	Bulgaria	L	0–1	Plovdiv	Fr	
18–04	Romania	W	2–0	Kiev	Fr	Onishenko, Muntjan
13–05	Rep. Ireland	W	1–0	Moscow	WCq	Onishenko
26–05	France	W	2–0	Moscow	WCq	Blokhin, Onishenko
10–06	England	L	1–2	Moscow	Fr	Muntjan
21–06	Brazil	L	0–1	Moscow	Fr	
5–08	Sweden	D	0–0	Moscow	Fr	
5–09	West Germany	L	0–1	Moscow	Fr	
26–09	Chile	D	0–0	Moscow	WCq	
17–10	East Germany	L	0–1	Leipzig	Fr	
21–11	Chile	L	0–2	Santiago	WCq	
	Soviet Union withdrew, Chile awarded game					
17–04–1974	Yugoslavia	W	1–0	Zenica	Fr	Kipiani
20–05	Czechoslovakia	L	0–1	Odessa	Fr	
30–10	Rep. Ireland	L	0–3	Dublin	ECq	
2–04–1975	Turkey	W	3–0	Kiev	ECq	Kolotov 2, Blokhin
18–05	Rep. Ireland	W	2–1	Kiev	ECq	Blokhin, Kolotov
8–06	Italy	W	1–0	Moscow	Fr	Konkov
12–10	Switzerland	W	1–0	Zurich	ECq	Muntjan
12–11	Switzerland	W	4–1	Kiev	ECq	Konkov, Onishenko 2, Veremejev
23–11	Turkey	L	0–1	Izmir	ECq	
29–11	Romania	D	2–2	Bucharest	Fr	Kolotov, Konkov
10–03–1976	Czechoslovakia	D	2–2	Kosice	Fr	Blokhin, Troshkin
20–03	Argentina	L	0–1	Kiev	Fr	
24–03	Bulgaria	W	3–0	Sofia	Fr	Onischenko, Minaev, Blokhin
24–04	Czechoslovakia	L	0–2	Bratislava	ECqf	
22–05	Czechoslovakia	D	2–2	Kiev	ECqf	Burjak, Blokhin
26–05	Hungary	D	1–1	Budapest	Fr	Nazarenko
23–06	Austria	W	2–1	Vienna	Fr	Minaev 2
19–07	Canada	W	2–1	Montreal	OGr1	Onishenko 2
23–07	North Korea	W	3–0	Ottawa	OGr1	Kolotov, Veremejev, Blokhin
25–07	Iran	W	2–1	Sherbrooke	OGqf	Minaev, Zvagintzev
27–07	East Germany	L	1–2	Montreal	OGsf	Kolotov
29–07	Brazil*	W	2–0	Montreal	OG3p	Onishenko, Nazarenko
28–11	Argentina	D	0–0	Buenos Aires	Fr	
1–12	Brazil	L	0–2	Rio de Janeiro	Fr	
10–12	Indonesia	D	0–0	Djakarta	Fr	
20–03–1977	Tunisia	W	3–0	Tunis	Fr	Maksimenkov, Lobchev, Onishenko
23–03	Yugoslavia	W	4–2	Belgrade	Fr	Blokhin 2, Kipiani, Burjak
24–04	Greece	W	2–0	Moscow	WCq	Konkov, Kipiani
30–04	Hungary	L	1–2	Budapest	WCq	Kipiani

10–05	Greece	L	0–1	Salonika	WCq	
18–05	Hungary	W	2–0	Tbilisi	WCq	Burjak, OG
28–07	East Germany	L	1–2	Leipzig	Fr	Bubnov
7–09	Poland	W	4–1	Volgograd	Fr	Burjak, Blokhin 2, Chesnokov
5–10	Holland	D	0–0	Rotterdam	Fr	
8–10	France	D	0–0	Paris	Fr	
26–02–1978	Morocco	W	3–2	Marrakech	Fr	Blokhin, Konkov, Chesnokov
8–03	West Germany	L	0–1	Frankfurt	Fr	
5–04	Finland	W	10–2	Erevan	Fr	Konkov, Kipiani, Chesnokov, Blokhin 3, Kolotov 2, Burjak, Petrakov
14–05	Romania	W	1–0	Bucharest	Fr	Blokhin
6–09	Iran	W	1–0	Tehran	Fr	Khidyatulin
20–09	Greece	W	2–0	Erevan	ECq	Chesnokov, Bessonov
5–10	Turkey	W	2–0	Ankara	Fr	Gutsaev, Blokhin
11–10	Hungary	L	0–2	Budapest	ECq	
19–11	Japan	W	4–1	Tokyo	Fr	Daraselia, Gazzaev 2, Gavrilov
23–11	Japan	W	4–1	Tokyo	Fr	Kipiani 2, Khidyatulin, Kostava
26–11	Japan	W	3–0	Osaka	Fr	Gazzaev, Gavrilov, Bessonov
28–03–1979	Bulgaria	W	3–1	Simferopol	Fr	Blokhin, Shengelia, Gavrilov
19–04	Sweden	W	2–0	Tbilisi	Fr	Shengelia, Khidyatulin
5–05	Czechoslovakia	W	3–0	Moscow	Fr	Koridze, Shengelia, Khidyatulin
19–05	Hungary	D	2–2	Tbilisi	ECq	Chesnokov, Shengelia
27–06	Denmark	W	2–1	Copenhagen	Fr	Daraselia, OG
4–07	Finland	D	1–1	Helsinki	ECq	Kapsalis
5–09	East Germany	W	1–0	Moscow	Fr	Gavrilov
12–09	Greece	L	0–1	Athens	ECq	
14–10	Romania	W	3–1	Moscow	Fr	Khidyatulin, Burjak, Yurchishin
31–10	Finland	D	2–2	Moscow	ECq	Andreev, Gavrilov
21–11	West Germany	L	1–3	Tbilisi	Fr	Makhovikov
26–03–1980	Bulgaria	W	3–1	Sofia	Fr	Cherenkov, Chelebadze 2
29–04	Sweden	W	5–1	Malmo	Fr	Andreev 2, Gavrilov, Chelebadze, Fedorenko
7–05	East Germany	D	2–2	Rostock	Fr	Gazzaev, Burkjak
23–05	France	W	1–0	Moscow	Fr	Cherenkov
15–06	Brazil	W	2–1	Rio de Janeiro	Fr	Cherenkov, Andreev
12–07	Denmark	W	2–0	Moscow	Fr	Cherenkov, Gassaev
20–07	Venezuela*	W	4–0	Moscow	OGr1	Andreev, Cherenkov, Gavrilov, Oganesian
22–07	Zambia*	W	3–1	Moscow	OGr1	Khidyatulin 2, Cherenkov
24–07	Cuba*	W	8–0	Moscow	OGr1	Andreev 3, Romantsev, Shavlo, Cherenkov, Gavrilov, Bessonov
27–07	Kuwait*	W	2–1	Moscow	OGqf	Cherenkov, Gavrilov
29–07	East Germany*	L	0–1	Moscow	OGsf	
1–08	Yugoslavia*	W	2–0	Moscow	OG3p	Oganesian, Andreev
27–08	Hungary	W	4–1	Budapest	Fr	Blokhin, Sulakvelidze, Burjak, Rodionov
3–09	Iceland	W	2–1	Reykjavik	WCq	Gavrilov, Andreev
15–10	Iceland	W	5–0	Moscow	WCq	Andreev 2, Oganesian 2, Bessanov
4–12	Argentina	D	1–1	Mar del Plata	Fr	Oganesian
30–05–1981	Wales	D	0–0	Wrexham	WCq	
23–09	Turkey	W	4–0	Moscow	WCq	Chivadze, Demyanenko, Blokhin, Shengelia
7–10	Turkey	W	3–0	Izmir	WCq	Shengelia, Blokhin 2
28–10	Czechoslovakia	W	2–0	Tbilisi	WCq	Shengelia 2
18–11	Wales	W	3–0	Tbilisi	WCq	Daraselia, Blokhin, Gavrilov
29–11	Czechoslovakia	D	1–1	Bratislava	WCq	Blokhin
10–03–1982	Greece	W	2–0	Athens	Fr	Cherenkov, Burjak
14–04	Argentina	D	1–1	Buenos Aires	Fr	Oganesian
5–05	East Germany	W	1–0	Moscow	Fr	Shengelia
3–06	Sweden	D	1–1	Stockholm	Fr	Blokhin
14–06	Brazil	L	1–2	Seville	WCr1	Bal
19–06	New Zealand	W	3–1	Malaga	WCr1	Gavrilov, Blokhin, Baltacha
22–06	Scotland	D	2–2	Malaga	WCr1	Chivadze, Shengelia
1–07	Belgium	W	1–0	Barcelona	WCr2	Oganesian
4–07	Poland	D	0–0	Barcelona	WCr2	
13–10	Finland	W	2–0	Moscow	ECq	Baltacha, Andreev
23–03–1983	France	D	1–1	Paris	Fr	Cherenkov
13–04	Switzerland	W	1–0	Lausanne	Fr	Blokhin
27–04	Portugal	W	5–0	Moscow	ECq	Cherenkov 2, Rodionov, Demyanenko, Larionov
17–05	Austria	D	2–2	Vienna	Fr	Rodionov, Blokhin
22–05	Poland	D	1–1	Chorzow	ECq	OG

* Not full internationals

1–06	Finland	W	1–0	Helsinki	ECq	Blokhin
26–07	East Germany	W	3–1	Leipzig	Fr	Blokhin, Oganesian, Yevtushenko
9–10	Poland	W	2–0	Moscow	ECq	Demyanenko, Blokhin
13–11	Portugal	L	0–1	Lisbon	ECq	
28–03–1984	West Germany	L	1–2	Hanover	Fr	Litovchenko
15–05	Finland	W	3–1	Kuovola	Fr	Rodionov, Chivadze, Protasov
2–06	England	W	2–0	London	Fr	Gotsmanov, Protasov
19–08	Mexico	W	3–0	Leningrad	Fr	Rodionov 2, Blokhin
12–09	Rep. Ireland	L	0–1	Dublin	WCq	
10–10	Norway	D	1–1	Oslo	WCq	Litovchenko
21–01–1985	China	W	3–2	Cochin	Fr	Stukasov, Litovchenko
25–01	Yugoslavia	L	1–2	Cochin	Fr	Larionov
28–01	Iran	W	2–0	Cochin	Fr	Sigmantovich, Protasov
2–02	Morocco	W	1–0	Cochin	Fr	Dmitriev
4–02	Yugoslavia	W	2–1	Cochin	Fr	Aleinikov, Kondratiev
27–03	Austria	W	2–0	Tbilisi	Fr	Demyanenko, Protasov
17–04	Switzerland	D	2–2	Berne	WCq	Gavrilov, Demyanenko
2–05	Switzerland	W	4–0	Moscow	WCq	Protasov 2, Kondratiev 2
5–06	Denmark	L	2–4	Copenhagen	WCq	Protasov, Gotsmanov
7–08	Romania	W	2–0	Moscow	Fr	Protasov, Cherenkov
28–08	West Germany	W	1–0	Moscow	Fr	Sigmantovic
25–09	Denmark	W	1–0	Moscow	WCq	Protasov
16–10	Rep. Ireland	W	2–0	Moscow	WCq	Cherenkov, Protasov
30–10	Norway	W	1–0	Moscow	WCq	Kondratiev
22–01–1986	Spain	L	0–2	Las Palmas	Fr	
19–02	Mexico	L	0–1	Mexico City	Fr	
26–03	England	L	0–1	Tbilisi	Fr	
23–04	Romania	L	1–2	Timisoara	Fr	Rodionov
7–05	Finland	D	0–0	Moscow	Fr	
2–06	Hungary	W	6–0	Irapuato	WCr1	Yakovenko, Aleinikov, Belanov, Yaremchuk, OG, Rodionov
5–06	France	D	1–1	Leon	WCr1	Rats
9–06	Canada	W	2–0	Irapuato	WCr1	Blokhin, Zavarov
15–06	Belgium	L	3–4	Leon	WCr2	Belanov 3
20–08	Sweden	D	0–0	Gothenburg	Fr	
24–09	Iceland	D	1–1	Reykjavik	ECq	Sulakvelidze
11–10	France	W	2–0	Paris	ECq	Belanov, Rats
29–10	Norway	W	4–0	Simferopol	ECq	Litovchenko, Belanov, Blokhin, Khidyatulin
18–02–1987	Wales	D	0–0	Swansea	Fr	
18–04	Sweden	L	1–3	Tbilisi	Fr	OG
29–04	East Germany	W	2–0	Kiev	ECq	Zavarov, Belanov
3–06	Norway	W	1–0	Oslo	ECq	Zavarov
29–08	Yugoslavia	W	1–0	Belgrade	Fr	Dobrovolski
9–09	France	D	1–1	Moscow	ECq	Mikhailichenko
23–09	Greece	W	3–0	Moscow	Fr	Dobrovolski, Protasov, Yaremchuk
10–10	East Germany	D	1–1	Berlin	ECq	Aleinikov
28–10	Iceland	W	2–0	Simferopol	ECq	Belanov, Protasov
20–02–1988	Italy	L	1–4	Bari	Fr	Litovchenko
23–03	Greece	W	4–0	Athens	Fr	Protasov 3, Litovchenko
31–03	Argentina	W	4–2	Berlin	Fr	Zavarov, Litovchenko, Protasov 2
2–04	Sweden	L	0–2	Berlin	Fr	
27–04	Czechoslovakia	D	1–1	Trnava	Fr	Protasov
1–06	Poland	W	2–1	Moscow	Fr	Litovchenko, Protasov
12–06	Holland	W	1–0	Cologne	ECr1	Rats
15–06	Rep. Ireland	D	1–1	Hanover	ECr1	Protasov
18–06	England	W	3–1	Frankfurt	ECr1	Aleinikov, Mikhailichenko, Pasulko
22–06	Italy	W	2–0	Stuttgart	ECsf	Litovschenko, Protasov
25–06	Holland	L	0–2	Munich	ECf	
17–08	Finland	D	0–0	Turku	Fr	
31–08	Iceland	D	1–1	Reykjavik	WCq	Litovschenko
21–09	West Germany	L	0–1	Dusseldorf	Fr	

LEADING INTERNATIONAL APPEARANCES

1	Blokhin	109	4	Bessonov	82
2	Dasayev	94	5	Demyanenko	80
3	Shesternev	89	6	Aleinikov	77

LEADING INTERNATIONAL GOALSCORERS					
1 Blokhin	39	3 Ivanov V	26	5 Kolotov	22
2 Protasov	29	4 Strelitsov	24	6 Ponedelnik	20

19–10	Austria	W	2–0	Kiev	WCq	Mikhailichenko, Zavarov
21–11	Syria	W	2–0	Damascus	Fr	Demyanenko, Gorlukovitch
23–11	Kuwait	W	1–0	Kuwait City	Fr	Mikhailichenko
27–11	Kuwait	W	2–0	Kuwait City	Fr	Protasov, Aleinikov
21–02–1989	Bulgaria	W	2–1	Sofia	Fr	Borodyuk, Rats
22–03	Holland	L	0–2	Eindhoven	Fr	
26–04	East Germany	W	3–0	Kiev	WCq	Dobrovolski, Litovchenko, Protasov
10–05	Turkey	W	1–0	Istanbul	WCq	Mikhailichenko
31–05	Iceland	D	1–1	Moscow	WCq	Dobrovolski
23–08	Poland	D	1–1	Lublin	Fr	Kiryakov
6–09	Austria	D	0–0	Vienna	WCq	
8–10	East Germany	L	1–2	Karl–Marx–Stadt	WCq	Litovchenko
15–11	Turkey	W	2–0	Simferopol	WCq	Protasov 2
22–02–1990	Costa Rica	W	2–1	Los Angeles	Fr	Litovchenko, Cherenkov
24–02	USA	W	3–1	Palo Alto	Fr	Bessonov, Cherenkov, Protasov
28–03	Holland	W	2–1	Kiev	Fr	Protasov, Lyuty
25–04	Rep. Ireland	L	0–1	Dublin	Fr	
16–05	Israel	L	2–3	Tel Aviv	Fr	Litovchenko, Mikhailichenko
9–06	Romania	L	0–2	Bari	WCr1	
13–06	Argentina	L	0–2	Naples	WCr1	
18–06	Cameroon	W	4–0	Bari	WCr1	Protasov, Zygmantovich, Zavarov, Dobrovolski
29–08	Romania	L	1–2	Moscow	Fr	Mikhailichenko
12–09	Norway	W	2–0	Moscow	ECq	Kanchelskis, Kuznetsov O
9–10	Israel	W	3–0	Moscow	Fr	Yuran 2, Litovchenko
3–11	Italy	D	0–0	Rome	ECq	
21–11	USA	D	0–0	Port of Spain	Fr	
24–11	Trinidad	W	2–0	Port of Spain	Fr	Shalimov, Tsveyba
30–11	Guatemala	W	3–0	Guatemala City	Fr	Mostovoy, Dobrovolski, Kolyvanov
6–02–1991	Scotland	W	1–0	Glasgow	Fr	Kuznetsov D
27–03	Germany	L	1–2	Frankfurt	Fr	Dobrovolski
17–04	Hungary	W	1–0	Budapest	ECq	Mikhailichenko
21–05	England	L	1–3	London	Fr	Tatarchuk
23–05	Argentina	D	1–1	Manchester	Fr	Kolyvanov
29–05	Cyprus	W	4–0	Moscow	ECq	Mostovoy, Mikhailichenko, Korneev, Aleinikov
13–06	Sweden	W	3–2	Gothenburg	Fr	Yuran, Kuznetsov D, Korneev
16–06	Italy	D	1–1	Stockholm	Fr	Korneev
28–08	Norway	W	1–0	Oslo	ECq	Mostovoy
25–09	Hungary	D	2–2	Moscow	ECq	Shalimov, Kanchelskis
12–10	Italy	D	0–0	Moscow	ECq	
13–11	Cyprus	W	3–0	Larnaca	ECq	Protasov, Yuran, Mikhailichenko

AS THE COMMONWEALTH OF INDEPENDENT STATES

25–01–1992	USA	W	1–0	Miami	Fr	Tsveyba
29–01	El Salvador	W	3–0	San Salvador	Fr	Chernishev 2, Khlestov
2–02	USA	L	1–2	Michigan	Fr	Sergeyev
12–02	Israel	W	2–1	Tel Aviv	Fr	Piatnitski, Kiriakov
19–02	Spain	D	1–1	Valencia	Fr	Kiriakov
8–03	Mexico	L	0–4	Mexico City	Fr	
11–03	Mexico	D	1–1	Tampico	Fr	Smirnov
29–04	England	D	2–2	Moscow	Fr	Chadadze, Kiriakov
3–06	Denmark	D	1–1	Copenhagen	Fr	Kolivanov
12–06	Germany	D	1–1	Norrkoping	ECr1	Dobrovolski
15–06	Holland	D	0–0	Gothenburg	ECr1	
18–06	Scotland	L	0–3	Norrkoping	ECr1	

SPAIN

Spain are one of the giants of football, though their fame largely rests on the laurels of a reputation built in the 1950s and 1960s as well as the continued excellence of the two major clubs, Real Madrid and Barcelona.

Football first made an appearance in Spain in the Basque region in the north of the country in the 1890s. British mining engineers were responsible according to some sources, British sailors according to others, but the game soon spread through the country, especially to the cities of Madrid, Barcelona and Valencia. The first club formed was the Athletic Club de Bilbao in 1898 and to this day they retain the English spelling in their name. Later in the same year Real Madrid were formed by students in the capital, though the club was not formalised until four years later and did not attain the Royal (Real) prefix until 1920 when it was granted by King Alfonso XIII.

By 1910 most of the major present-day clubs had been formed, spurred on by the presence of a cup competition that was introduced in 1902. Until the formation of a league in 1929, the Cup was the only national competition in the country and the winners were regarded as the champions of Spain. Unsurprisingly Athletic Bilbao featured strongly in the intial competitions. A combined Athletic Bilbao and Bilbao FC team called Vizcaya won the initial tournament, whilst Athletic won the next two and lost in the final of the following two.

The pattern for the future was beginning to emerge. First Real Madrid then Barcelona had dominant spells before the First World War, and neither have relinquished this pre-eminence since. Athletic Bilbao, Atlético Madrid, Valencia and to a lesser extent Sevilla have all challenged at one time or another, but the Real–Barcelona fixture remains the biggest of them all, compounded by the intense regional rivalry between Catalonia, in which Barcelona is located, and the capital city.

In 1913, nine years after Spain joined FIFA, the Real Federacion Española de Fútbol was formed, unifying all the regional organisations, but not until 1920 did it field a representative side. The programme of international matches remained light until well into the second half of the century even though the first signs were encouraging. Up until the outbreak of civil war in 1936, Spain's record was very good, and it included victories over some of Europe's stronger nations, most notably the 4–3 win in Madrid in 1929 over England. The Spaniards thus became the first nation outside of the British Isles to beat the English in a full international game. Star of that side was Ricardo Zamora, their goalkeeper, but Zamora could do nothing to help beat Spain's bogey team, Italy. In the 1924 and 1928 Olympics and in the 1934 World Cup, Spain's hopes were dashed every time by the Italians.

		All			League			Cup		Europe		
	Team	G	S	B	G	S	B	G	S	G	S	B
1	Real Madrid	49	35	14	25	13	6	16	17	8	5	8
2	Barcelona	41	31	14	12	18	10	22	8	7	5	4
3	Athletic Bilbao	31	18	10	8	6	10	23	11	–	1	–
4	Atlético Madrid	17	17	16	8	8	12	8	6	1	3	4
5	Valencia	12	14	5	4	5	5	5	8	3	1	–
6	Sevilla	4	6	2	1	4	2	3	2	–	–	–
7	Real Zaragoza	4	5	5	–	1	3	3	3	1	1	2
8	Real Sociedad	4	6	2	2	2	1	2	4	–	–	1
9	Real Union Irún	3	1	–	–	–	–	3	1	–	–	–
10	RCD Español	2	6	4	–	–	4	2	5	–	1	–
11	Real Betis Balompié	2	1	1	1	–	1	1	1	–	–	–
12	Arenas Guecho Bilbao	1	3	1	–	–	1	1	3	–	–	–
13	Vizcaya Bilbao	1	1	–	–	–	–	1	1	–	–	–
14	Racing Irún	1	–	–	–	–	–	1	–	–	–	–
15	Real Sporting Gijón	–	3	1	–	1	1	–	2	–	–	–
16	Las Palmas	–	2	1	–	1	1	–	1	–	–	–
17	Español Madrid	–	2	–	–	–	–	–	2	–	–	–
	Real Valladolid	–	2	–	–	–	–	–	2	–	–	–
19	Racing Santander	–	1	1	–	1	1	–	–	–	–	–
20	15 clubs with a record of	–	15	3	–	1	3	– 14	–	–		–

To the end of the 1991–92 season

The combination of the Civil War and then the Second World War effectively stopped international football for close to ten years, although club football carried on with an interruption only in the years when the fighting in the Civil War was at its worst. It was in the early years of the 1940s that the league competition grew in stature. Introduced in 1929 along with professionalism, it grew from 10 clubs in its first few years to 16 by 1951.

Political undertones helped reinforce the stature of the game. During the civil war, Catalonia, and Barcelona in particular, had been the main area of resistance to Franco's Fascist forces. Defeated, the Catalan people were banned from organising political meetings and the only place they could meet for such discussions was at football matches. The same was true for the Basques and other regions of Spain. The 1940s therefore were boom years for football.

The 1950s saw an even more rapid growth of the game as these rivalries intensified. Foreigners were brought in to help build winning teams, most notably Di Stéfano at Real and later the great Hungarian trio of Kubala, Kocsis and Czibor at Barcelona, and a trend was started that holds true to this day. Over the years many great players have been tempted into Spanish football by the wages and the level of competition on offer. Naturally there was concern about the effect on local players and after the initial influx a ban was imposed that lasted from 1963 to 1973, although many players in the league at this time were from South America and were considered, like Di Stéfano, as naturalised Spaniards.

Once the gates were opened again in 1973 the big names of world football reappeared in Spain, amongst them Cruyff and Neeskens at Barcelona, Breitner and Netzer at Real and Rep and Keita, the first winner of the African Footballer of the Year award, at Valencia. Only Athletic Bilbao and Real Sociedad, with their Basque-only rule, did not have any foreigners on their books. Since then players like Kempes, Maradona, Lineker, Schuster and Hugo Sanchez have all made their mark in the Spanish league.

After Real Madrid's European Cup exploits in the 1950s, the 1960s proved to be Spain's most successful era at both club and international level. Following on from their Fairs Cup victory in the initial tournament, Barcelona won the second edition in 1960 and triumphed again in 1966. In between these two victories it was twice won by Valencia and once by Real Zaragoza. Atlético Madrid won the 1962 Cup Winners Cup, whilst Real won the European Cup for the sixth time in 1966.

There then followed a strange slump in fortunes, both at club level and in the national side, in the 1970s. During the 1950s Spain had given little priority to the national side, a fact borne out by their elimination from both the 1954 and 1958 World Cups at the hands of Turkey and Scotland respectively in the qualifiers. Taken more seriously in the 1960s, the national side qualified for both Chile and England, and in between won the 1964 European Championship, beating the Soviet Union 2–1 in the final in Madrid. Central to that side were Luis Suárez, possibly the greatest Spanish footballer of all time and one of the very few Spaniards to have been signed by an Italian club, as well as Amancio, Zoco and Pereda.

Designed to improve the chances of the national side, the ban on foreigners seemed eventually to have the reverse effect. Failure to qualify for either the 1970 or 1974 World Cups was compounded by poor results at club level in the European competitions. Real's 1966 European Cup triumph was the last title won by a Spanish team until Barcelona won the Cup Winners Cup in 1979. The Spanish football association was persuaded to lift the ban in 1973 and although there was no tangible benefit at first, Spain has since clawed her way back up the international ladder.

Real Madrid, Barcelona and Valencia all had their share of success in the 1980s but most disappointing for the Spanish public was the dreadful failure in the World Cup of 1982, when as hosts they were amongst the favourites. Seldom has a host nation fared so badly as Spain did, and in five games they recorded only one victory.

Both Barcelona and Real Madrid remain at the forefront of European club football and will almost certainly continue to do so, but the national side is in danger of becoming an also-ran. So often a pioneer in the better aspects of football, Spain will have to come up with something to convince sceptics that she remains a world football power. Barcelona's victory in the 1992 European Cup, the first by a Spanish team for 26 years, provides some encouragement.

Population: 39 618 000
Area, sq km: 504 750
% in urban areas: 75.8%
Capital city: Madrid

Real Federación Española de Fútbol
Calle Alberto Bosch #13
Apartado Postal 347
E–28014 Madrid
Spain
Tel: (010 34) 1 4201362
Fax: (010 34) 1 4202094
Telex: 42420 RFEF E
Cable: FUTBOL MADRID
Languages for correspondence: Spanish, French & English

Year of formation: 1913
Affiliation to FIFA: 1904
Affiliation to UEFA: 1954
Registered clubs: 11 314
Registered players: 343 600
Professional players: 2300
Registered coaches: 4600
Registered referees: 8314
National Stadium: None
National colours: Shirts: Red/Shorts: Blue/Socks: Black
Reserve colours: Shirts: Blue/Shorts: Blue/Socks: Black
Season: September–June

THE RECORD

WORLD CUP

1930 .... Did not enter
1934 .... QT 1st/2 in group 6 – Final Tournament/Quarter-finalists
1938 .... Did not enter
1950 .... QT 1st/2 in group 6 – Final Tournament/2nd round/4th place
1954 .... QT 2nd/2 in group 6
1958 .... QT 2nd/3 in group 9
1962 .... QT 1st/5 in group 9 – Final Tournament/1st round
1966 .... QT 1st/2 in group 9 – Final Tournament/1st round
1970 .... QT 3rd/4 in group 6
1974 .... QT 2nd/3 in group 7
1978 .... QT 1st/3 in group 8 – Final Tournament/1st round
1982 .... QT Automatic – Final Tournament/2nd round
1986 .... QT 1st/4 in group 7 – Final Tournament/Quarter-finalists
1990 .... QT 1st/5 in group 6 – Final Tournament/2nd round

EUROPEAN CHAMPIONSHIP

1960 .... Quarter-finalists
1964 .... Winners
1968 .... QT 1st/4 in group 1 – Final Tournament/Quarter-finalists
1972 .... QT 2nd/4 in group 4
1976 .... QT 1st/4 in group 4 – Final Tournament/Quarter-finalists
1980 .... QT 1st/4 in group 3 – Final Tournament/1st round
1984 .... QT 1st/5 in group 7 – Final Tournament/Finalists
1988 .... QT 1st/4 in group 1 – Final Tournament/1st round
1992 .... QT 3rd/5 in group 1

OLYMPIC GAMES

1908 .... Did not enter
1912 .... Did not enter
1920 .... Quarter-finalists/3rd place
1924 .... Preliminary round
1928 .... Quarter-finalists
1936–60 ..... Did not enter
1964 .... QT Failed to qualify
1968 .... Final Tournament/Quarter-finalists
1972 .... QT Failed to qualify

1976 .... Final Tournament/1st round
1980 .... Final Tournament/1st round
1984 .... QT Failed to qualify
1988 .... QT Failed to qualify
1992 .... Final Tournament

EUROPEAN CLUB COMPETITIONS

EUROPEAN CUP: Winners – Real Madrid 1956 1957 1958 1959 1960 1966, Barcelona 1992
Finalists – Barcelona 1961 1986, Real Madrid 1962 1964 1981, Atlético Madrid 1974

CUP WINNERS CUP: Winners – Atlético Madrid 1962, Barcelona 1979 1982 1989, Valencia 1980
Finalists – Atlético Madrid 1963 1986, Barcelona 1969 1991, Real Madrid 1971 1983

UEFA CUP: Winners – Barcelona 1958 1960 1966, Valencia 1962 1963, Real Zaragoza 1964, Real Madrid 1985 1986
Finalists – Barcelona 1962, Valencia 1964, Real Zaragoza 1966, Athletic Bilbao 1977, Español 1988

CLUB DIRECTORY

MADRID (Population – 4 650 000)

Club Atlético de Madrid
Stadium: Vicente Calderón 70 000
Founded: 1903
Colours: Red and white stripes/Blue
Previous name: Atlético Aviación 1939–46
Reserve team: Atlético Madridleño Club de Fútbol (1963)

Real Madrid Club de Fútbol
Stadium: Santiago Bernabeu 90 000
Founded: 1902
Colours: White/White
Reserve team: Castilla Club de Fútbol (1942)

Asociación Deportiva Rayo Vallecano
Stadium: Nuevo Estadio de Vallecas 19 000
Founded: 1940
Colours: White with red sash/White

BARCELONA (Population – 4 040 000)

Fútbol Club Barcelona
Stadium: Camp Nou 115 000
Founded: 1899
Colours: Red and blue stripes/Blue
Reserve teams: Barcelona Atletic (1970) and Barcelona Amateur (1967)

Real Club Deportivo Español
Stadium: Sarriá 41 000 Founded: 1900
Colours: Blue and white stripes/Blue

Club Deportivo Europa
Stadium: Cerdena Founded: 1907
Colours: White with blue sleeves/Blue

Centre D'Esports Sabadell Fútbol Club
Stadium: Nova Creu Alta 20 000
Founded: 1903
Colours: Blue and white quarters/Blue

VALENCIA (Population – 1 270 000)

Levante Unión Deportiva
Stadium: Levante 29 000
Founded: 1909
Colours: Red and blue stripes/Blue

Valencia Club de Fútbol
Stadium: Luis Casanova 49 000
Founded: 1910
Colours: White/White

BILBAO (Population – 980 500)
Athletic Club de Bilbao
Stadium: San Mamés 46 000
Founded: 1898
Colours: Red and white stripes/Black
Reserve team: Bilbao Athletic Club (1918)

SEVILLE (Population – 945 000)

Real Betis Balompié
Stadium: Benito Villamarín 50 000
Founded: 1907
Colours: Green and white stripes/White
Reserve team: Betis Deportivo Balompié (1968)

Sevilla Fútbol Club
Stadium: Sánchez Pizjuán 70 000
Founded: 1905
Colours: White/White
Reserve team: Sevilla Atletico Club (1958)

ZARAGOZA (Population – 575 000)
Real Zaragoza Club Deportivo
Stadium: La Romareda 45 000
Founded: 1932
Colours: White/Blue
Reserve team: Club Deportivo Aragón (1966)

MALAGA (Population – 566 000)
Club Deportivo Málaga
Stadium: La Rosaleda 42 000
Founded: 1933
Colours: Sky blue and white stripes/Sky blue
Previous names: Merger in 1933 of Málaga and Malagueño

LAS PALMAS (Population – 358 000)
Unión Deportiva Las Palmas
Stadium: Insular 20 000
Founded: 1949
Colours: Yellow/Blue

VALLADOLID (Population – 329 000)
Real Valladolid Deportivo
Stadium: José Zorrilla 33 000
Founded: 1928
Colours: Violet and white stripes/White

MURCIA (Population – 305 000)
Real Murcia Club de Fútbol
Stadium: La Condomina 24 000
Founded: 1924
Colours: Red/White

CORDOBA (Population – 298 000)
Córdoba Club de Fútbol
Stadium: El Arcángel 18 000
Founded: 1951
Colours: Green and white stripes/White

PALMA (Population – 306 000)
Real Club Deportivo Mallorca
Stadium: Luis Sitjar 31 000
Founded: 1916
Colours: Red/Black

ALICANTE (Population – 258 000)
Hércules Club de Fútbol
Stadium: José Rico Pérez 40 000
Founded: 1922
Colours: Blue and white stripes/Black

VIGO (Population – 262 000)
Real Club Celta de Vigo
Stadium: Balaídos 33000
Founded: 1923
Colours: Sky blue/White

GRANADA (Population – 256 000)
Granada Club de Fútbol
Stadium: Los Cármenes 25 000
Founded: 1932
Colours: Red and white stripes/Blue

GIJON (Population – 255 000)
Real Sporting de Gijón
Stadium: El Molinón 45 000
Founded: 1905
Colours: Red and white stripes/Blue

LA CORUNA (Population – 242 000)
Real Club Deportivo de La Coruña
Stadium: Riazor 28 000
Founded: 1904
Colours: Blue and white stripes/Blue

CADIZ (population – 240 000)
Cádiz Club de Fútbol
Stadium: Ramón de Carranza 22 000
Founded: 1910
Colours: Yellow/Blue

SANTA CRUZ DE TENERIFE (Population – 211 000)
Club Deportivo Tenerife
Stadium: Heliodoro Rodríguez 20 000
Founded: 1922
Colours: White/Blue

SANTANDER (Population – 163 000)
Real Racing Club Santander
Stadium: El Sardinero 25 000
Founded: 1913
Colours: White/Black

OVIEDO (Population – 186 000)
Real Oviedo Club de Fútbol
Stadium: Carlos Tartiere 22 000
Founded: 1926
Colours: Blue/White
Reserve team: Real Oviedo Aficionados (1941)

PAMPLONA (Population – 178000)
Club Atlético Osasuna
Stadium: El Sadar 25000
Founded: 1920
Colours: Red/Blue
Reserve team: Osasuna Promesas (1962)

ELCHE (Population – 177000)
Elche Club de Fútbol
Stadium: Manuel Martínez Valero 38000
Founded: 1923
Colours: White with a green band on chest/White

SAN SEBASTIAN (Population – 176000)
Real Sociedad de Fútbol
Stadium: Atocha 27000
Founded: 1909
Colours: Blue and white stripes/White
Previous name: Ciclista de San Sebastián, Donostia 1931–40

LEON (Population – 159000)
Cultural y Deportiva Leonesa
Stadium: Antonio Amilibia 10000
Founded: 1928
Colours: White/White

BURGOS (Population – 158000)
Real Burgos Club de Fútbol
Stadium: El Plantío 20000
Founded: 1983
Colours: Red with a maroon stripe on left side/White
Previous name: Burgos Club de Fútbol 1922–83

SALAMANCA (Population – 155000)
Unión Deportiva Salamanca
Stadium: El Helmántico 25000
Founded: 1923
Colours: White/Black

ALMERIA (Population – 154000)
Club Polideportivo Almeirá
Stadium: Antonio Franco Navarro
Founded: 1982
Colours: Red and white stripes/Blue

HUELVA (Population – 135000)
Real Club Recreativo de Huelva
Stadium: Colombino 13000
Founded: 1880
Colours: Blue and white stripes/White

ALBACETE (Population – 125000)
Albacete Balompié
Stadium: Carlos Belmonte 14000
Founded: 1939
Colours: White/White

LOGRONO (Population – 116000)
Club Deportivo Logroñes
Stadium: Las Gaunas 16000
Founded: 1940
Colours: Red and white stripes/Black

LERIDA (Population – 108000)
Lleida Unió Esportiva
Stadium: Camp D'Esports 10000
Founded: 1939
Colours: Blue/White

TARRAGONA (Population – 107000)
Gimnasia de Tarragona
Stadium: Nou Estadi 15000
Founded: 1886
Colours: Red/White

JAEN (Population – 103000)
Real Jaén Club de Fútbol
Stadium: La Victoria 10000
Founded: 1922
Colours: White/White

ALCOY (Population – 66000)
Club Deportivo Alcoyano
Stadium: El Collao 7000
Founded: 1927
Colours: Blue and white stripes/Blue

IRUN (Population – 54000)
Real Union Irún
Stadium: Gal
Founded: 1915
Colours: White/Black

CASTELLON
Club Deportivo Castellón
Stadium: Castalia 14000
Founded: 1931
Colours: Black and white stripes/White

PONTEVEDRA
Pontevedra Club Fútbol
Stadium: Municipal Pasarón
Founded: 1941
Colours: Claret/Blue

SPANISH LEAGUE CHAMPIONSHIP

Year	Champions		Runners up		3rd	
1929	Barcelona	25	Real Madrid	23	Athletic Bilbao	20
1930	Athletic Bilbao	30	Barcelona	23	Arenas Guecho Bilbao	20
1931	Athletic Bilbao	22	Racing Santander	22	Real Sociedad	22
1932	Real Madrid	28	Athletic Bilbao	25	Barcelona	24
1933	Real Madrid	28	Athletic Bilbao	26	RCD Español	22
1934	Athletic Bilbao	24	Real Madrid	22	Racing Santander	19
1935	Real Betis	34	Real Madrid	33	Oviedo	26
1936	Athletic Bilbao	31	Real Madrid	29	Oviedo	28
1937–39 –						
1940	Atlético Aviación	29	Sevilla	28	Athletic Bilbao	26
1941	Atlético Aviación	33	Athletic Bilbao	31	Valencia	27
1942	Valencia	40	Real Madrid	33	Atlético Aviación	33
1943	Athletic Bilbao	36	Sevilla	33	Barcelona	32
1944	Valencia	40	Atlético Aviación	34	Sevilla	32
1945	Barcelona	39	Real Madrid	38	Atlético Aviación	31
1946	Sevilla	36	Barcelona	35	Athletic Bilbao	33
1947	Valencia	34	Athletic Bilbao	34	Atlético Madrid	32
1948	Barcelona	37	Valencia	34	Atlético Madrid	33
1949	Barcelona	37	Valencia	35	Real Madrid	34
1950	Atlético Madrid	33	La Coruña	32	Valencia	31
1951	Atlético Madrid	40	Sevilla	38	Valencia	37
1952	Barcelona	43	Athletic Bilbao	40	Real Madrid	38
1953	Barcelona	42	Valencia	40	Real Madrid	39
1954	Real Madrid	40	Barcelona	36	Valencia	34
1955	Real Madrid	46	Barcelona	41	Athletic Bilbao	39
1956	Athletic Bilbao	48	Barcelona	47	Real Madrid	38

1957	Real Madrid	44	Sevilla	39	Barcelona	39
1958	Real Madrid	45	Atlético Madrid	42	Barcelona	38
1959	Barcelona	51	Real Madrid	47	Athletic Bilbao	36
1960	Barcelona	46	Real Madrid	46	Athletic Bilbao	39
1961	Real Madrid	52	Atlético Madrid	40	Real Zaragoza	33
1962	Real Madrid	43	Barcelona	40	Atlético Madrid	36
1963	Real Madrid	49	Atlético Madrid	37	Oviedo	33
1964	Real Madrid	46	Barcelona	42	Real Betis	37
1965	Real Madrid	47	Atlético Madrid	43	Real Zaragoza	40
1966	Atlético Madrid	44	Real Madrid	43	Barcelona	38
1967	Real Madrid	47	Barcelona	42	RCD Español	37
1968	Real Madrid	42	Barcelona	39	Las Palmas	38
1969	Real Madrid	47	Las Palmas	38	Barcelona	36
1970	Atlético Madrid	42	Athletic Bilbao	41	Sevilla	35
1971	Valencia	43	Barcelona	43	Atlético Madrid	42
1972	Real Madrid	47	Valencia	45	Barcelona	43
1973	Atlético Madrid	48	Barcelona	46	RCD Español	45
1974	Barcelona	50	Atlético Madrid	42	Real Zaragoza	40
1975	Real Madrid	50	Real Zaragoza	38	Barcelona	37
1976	Real Madrid	48	Barcelona	43	Atlético Madrid	42
1977	Atlético Madrid	46	Barcelona	45	Athletic Bilbao	38
1978	Real Madrid	47	Barcelona	41	Athletic Bilbao	40
1979	Real Madrid	47	Sporting Gijón	43	Atlético Madrid	41
1980	Real Madrid	53	Real Sociedad	52	Sporting Gijón	39
1981	Real Sociedad	45	Real Madrid	45	Atlético Madrid	42
1982	Real Sociedad	47	Barcelona	45	Real Madrid	44
1983	Athletic Bilbao	50	Real Madrid	49	Atlético Madrid	46
1984	Athletic Bilbao	49	Real Madrid	49	Barcelona	48
1985	Barcelona	53	Atlético Madrid	43	Athletic Bilbao	41
1986	Real Madrid	56	Barcelona	45	Athletic Bilbao	43
1987	Real Madrid	66	Barcelona	63	RCD Español	51
1988	Real Madrid	62	Real Sociedad	51	Atlético Madrid	48
1989	Real Madrid	62	Barcelona	57	Valencia	49
1990	Real Madrid	62	Valencia	53	Barcelona	51
1991	Barcelona	57	Atlético Madrid	47	Real Madrid	46
1992	Barcelona	55	Real Madrid	54	Atlético Madrid	53

SPANISH CUP FINALS

Year	Winners	Score	Runners-up
1902	Vizcaya Bilbao	2–1	Barcelona
1903	Athletic Bilbao	3–2	Real Madrid
1904	Athletic Bilbao	W–O	
1905	Real Madrid	1–0	Athletic Bilbao
1906	Real Madrid	4–1	Athletic Bilbao
1907	Real Madrid	1–0	Vizcaya Bilbao
1908	Real Madrid	2–1	Vigo Sporting
1909	Ciclista San Sebast.	3–1	Español Madrid
1910	Athletic Bilbao	1–0	Basconia
1910	Barcelona	3–2	Español Madrid
1911	Athletic Bilbao	3–1	RCD Español
1912	Barcelona	2–0	Gimnástica Madrid
1913	Barcelona	2–2 0–0 2–1	Real Sociedad
1913	Racing Irún	2–2 1–0	Athletic Bilbao
1914	Athletic Bilbao	2–1	Espana Barcelona
1915	Athletic Bilbao	5–0	RCD Español
1916	Athletic Bilbao	4–0	Real Madrid
1917	Real Madrid	0–0 2–1	Arenas Guecho Bilbao
1918	Real Union Irún	2–0	Real Madrid
1919	Arenas Guecho Bilbao	5–2	Barcelona
1920	Barcelona	2–0	Athletic Bilbao
1921	Athletic Bilbao	4–1	Atlético Madrid
1922	Barcelona	5–1	Real Union Irún
1923	Athletic Bilbao	1–0	Europa Barcelona
1924	Real Union Irún	1–0	Real Madrid
1925	Barcelona	2–0	Arenas Guecho Bilbao
1926	Barcelona	3–2	Atlético Madrid
1927	Real Union Irún	1–0	Arenas Guecho Bilbao
1928	Barcelona	1–1 1–1 3–1	Real Sociedad
1929	RCD Español	2–1	Real Madrid
1930	Athletic Bilbao	3–2	Real Madrid
1931	Athletic Bilbao	3–1	Real Betis
1932	Athletic Bilbao	1–0	Barcelona
1933	Athletic Bilbao	2–1	Real Madrid
1934	Real Madrid	2–1	Valencia
1935	Sevilla	3–0	Sabadell
1936	Real Madrid	2–1	Barcelona
1937–38	–		
1939	Sevilla	6–2	Racing Ferrol
1940	RCD Español	3–2	Real Madrid
1941	Valencia	3–1	RCD Español
1942	Barcelona	4–3	Athletic Bilbao
1943	Athletic Bilbao	1–0	Real Madrid
1944	Athletic Bilbao	2–0	Valencia
1945	Athletic Bilbao	3–2	Valencia
1946	Real Madrid	3–1	Valencia
1947	Real Madrid	2–0	RCD Español
1948	Sevilla	4–1	Celta
1949	Valencia	1–0	Athletic Bilbao
1950	Athletic Bilbao	4–1	Valladolid
1951	Barcelona	3–0	Real Sociedad
1952	Barcelona	4–2	Valencia
1953	Barcelona	2–1	Athletic Bilbao
1954	Valencia	3–0	Barcelona
1955	Athletic Bilbao	1–0	Sevilla
1956	Athletic Bilbao	2–1	Atlético Madrid

1957	Barcelona	1–0	RCD Español
1958	Athletic Bilbao	2–0	Real Madrid
1959	Barcelona	4–1	Granada
1960	Atlético Madrid	3–1	Real Madrid
1961	Atlético Madrid	3–2	Real Madrid
1962	Real Madrid	2–1	Sevilla
1963	Barcelona	3–1	Real Zaragoza
1964	Real Zaragoza	2–1	Atlético Madrid
1965	Atlético Madrid	1–0	Real Zaragoza
1966	Real Zaragoza	2–0	Athletic Bilbao
1967	Valencia	2–1	Athletic Bilbao
1968	Barcelona	1–0	Real Madrid
1969	Athletic Bilbao	1–0	Elche
1970	Real Madrid	3–1	Valencia
1971	Barcelona	4–3	Valencia
1972	Atlético Madrid	2–1	Valencia
1973	Athletic Bilbao	2–0	Castellón
1974	Real Madrid	4–0	Barcelona
1975	Real Madrid	0–0 (4–3p)	Atlético Madrid
1976	Atlético Madrid	1–0	Real Zaragoza
1977	Real Betis	2–2 (11–9p)	Athletic Bilbao
1978	Barcelona	3–1	Las Palmas
1979	Valencia	2–0	Real Madrid
1980	Real Madrid	6–1	Castilla
1981	Barcelona	3–1	Sporting Gijón
1982	Real Madrid	2–1	Sporting Gijón
1983	Barcelona	2–1	Real Madrid
1984	Athletic Bilbao	1–0	Barcelona
1985	Atlético Madrid	2–1	Athletic Bilbao
1986	Real Zaragoza	1–0	Barcelona
1987	Real Sociedad	2–2 (4–3p)	Atlético Madrid
1988	Barcelona	1–0	Real Sociedad
1989	Real Madrid	1–0	Valladolid
1990	Barcelona	2–0	Real Madrid
1991	Atlético Madrid	1–0	Mallorca
1992	Atlético Madrid	2–0	Real Madrid

INTERNATIONAL MATCHES PLAYED BY SPAIN

Date	Opponents	Result		Venue	Compet	Scorers
28–08–1920	Denmark	W	1–0	Brussels	OGr1	Patricio
29–08	Belgium	L	1–3	Antwerp	OGqf	Arrate
1–09	Sweden	W	2–1	Antwerp	OGct	Belauste, Acedo
2–09	Italy	W	2–0	Antwerp	OGct	Sesúmaga 2
5–09	Holland	W	3–1	Antwerp	OG2p	Sesúmaga 2, Pichichi
9–10–1921	Belgium	W	2–0	Bilbao	Fr	Alcántara 2
18–12	Portugal	W	3–1	Madrid	Fr	Alcántara 2, Meana
30–04–1922	France	W	4–0	Bordeaux	Fr	Travieso 2, Alcántara 2
17–12	Portugal	W	2–1	Lisbon	Fr	Pieira, Monjardín
28–01–1923	France	W	3–0	San Sebastian	Fr	Monjardín 2, Zabala
4–02	Belgium	L	0–1	Antwerp	Fr	
16–12	Portugal	W	3–0	Seville	Fr	Zabala 3
9–03–1924	Italy	D	0–0	Milan	Fr	
25–05	Italy	L	0–1	Paris	OGr1	
21–12	Austria	W	2–1	Barcelona	Fr	Juantegui, Samieiter
15–05–1925	Portugal	W	2–0	Lisbon	Fr	Carmelo, Piera
1–06	Switzerland	W	3–0	Berne	Fr	Errazquin 3
14–06	Italy	W	1–0	Valencia	Fr	Errazquin
27–09	Austria	W	1–0	Vienna	Fr	Cubells
4–10	Hungary	W	1–0	Budapest	Fr	Carmelo
19–12–1926	Hungary	W	4–2	Vigo	Fr	Errazquin 2, Carmelo, Goiburu
17–04–1927	Switzerland	W	1–0	Santander	Fr	Oscar
22–05	France	W	4–1	Paris	Fr	Zaldúa 2, Yermo, Olaso
29–05	Italy	L	0–2	Bologna	Fr	
29–05	Portugal	W	2–0	Madrid	Fr	
8–01–1928	Portugal	D	2–2	Lisbon	Fr	Zaldúa, Goiburu
22–04	Italy	D	1–1	Gijon	Fr	Quesada
30–05	Mexico	W	7–1	Amsterdam	OGr1	Yermo 3, Regueiro 2, Marculeta, Mariscal
1–06	Italy	D	1–1	Amsterdam	OGqf	Zaldua
4–06	Italy	L	1–7	Amsterdam	OGqf	Yermo
17–03–1929	Portugal	W	5–0	Seville	Fr	Rubio 3, Padrón 2
14–04	France	W	8–1	Zaragoza	Fr	Rubio 4, Bienzobas 2, Goiburu 2
15–05	England	W	4–3	Madrid	Fr	Rubio 2, Lazcano, Goiburu
1–01–1930	Czechoslovakia	W	1–0	Barcelona	Fr	Sastre
14–06	Czechoslovakia	L	0–2	Prague	Fr	
22–06	Italy	W	3–2	Bologna	Fr	Luis Regueiro 2, Ventolra
30–11	Portugal	W	1–0	Oporto	Fr	Peña
19–04–1931	Italy	D	0–0	Bilbao	Fr	
26–04	Rep. Ireland	D	1–1	Barcelona	Fr	Arocha
9–12	England	L	1–7	London	Fr	Gorostiza
13–12	Rep. Ireland	W	5–0	Dublin	Fr	Luis Regueiro 2, Arocha, Samitier, Vantolrá
24–04–1932	Yugoslavia	W	2–1	Oviedo	Fr	Lángara, Luis Regueiro
2–04–1933	Portugal	W	3–0	Vigo	Fr	Elícegui 2, Larrinaga
23–04	France	L	0–1	Paris	Fr	
30–04	Yugoslavia	D	1–1	Belgrade	Fr	Goiburu

21–05	Bulgaria	W	13–0	Madrid	Fr	Chacho 6, Elícegui 3, Luis Regueiro 2, Bosch, OG
11–03–1934	Portugal	W	9–0	Madrid	WCq	Lángara 5, Luis Regueiro 2, Vantolrá, Chacho
18–03	Portugal	W	2–1	Lisbon	WCq	Lángara 2
27–05	Brazil	W	3–1	Genoa	WCr1	Lángara 2, Iraragorri
31–05	Italy	D	1–1	Florence	WCqf	Luis Regueiro
1–06	Italy	L	0–1	Florence	WCqf	
24–01–1935	France	W	2–0	Madrid	Fr	Luis Regueiro, Hilario
5–05	Portugal	D	3–3	Lisbon	Fr	Lángara 2, Gorostiza
12–05	Germany	W	2–1	Cologne	Fr	Lángara 2
19–01–1936	Austria	L	4–5	Madrid	Fr	Lángara 2, Luis Regueiro 2
23–02	Germany	L	1–2	Barcelona	Fr	Luis Regueiro
26–04	Czechoslovakia	L	0–1	Prague	Fr	
3–05	Switzerland	W	2–0	Berne	Fr	Lángara, Lecue
12–01–1941	Portugal	D	2–2	Lisbon	Fr	Campanal, Escolá
16–03	Portugal	W	5–1	Bilbao	Fr	Epi 2, Herrerita, Campanal, Campos
28–12	Switzerland	W	3–2	Valencia	Fr	Mundo 2, Campos
15–03–1942	France	W	4–0	Seville	Fr	Campos 2, Mundo, Epi
12–04	Germany	D	1–1	Berlin	Fr	Campos
19–04	Italy	L	0–4	Milan	Fr	
11–03–1945	Portugal	D	2–2	Lisbon	Fr	César, Epi
6–05	Portugal	W	4–2	La Coruna	Fr	Zarra 2, Herrerita, César
23–06–1946	Rep. Ireland	L	0–1	Madrid	Fr	
26–01–1947	Portugal	L	1–4	Lisbon	Fr	Iriondo
2–03	Rep. Ireland	L	2–3	Dublin	Fr	Zarra 2
21–03–1948	Portugal	W	2–0	Madrid	Fr	César, Gaínza
30–05	Rep. Ireland	W	2–1	Barcelona	Fr	Igoa 2
20–06	Switzerland	D	3–3	Zurich	Fr	Igoa 2, Pahíño
2–01–1949	Belgium	D	1–1	Barcelona	Fr	Silva
20–03	Portugal	D	1–1	Lisbon	Fr	Zarra
27–03	Italy	L	1–3	Madrid	Fr	Gaínza
12–06	Rep. Ireland	W	4–1	Dublin	Fr	Zarra 2, Basora, Igoa
19–06	France	W	5–1	Paris	Fr	Basora 3, Gaínza 2
2–04–1950	Portugal	W	5–1	Madrid	WCq	Zarra 2, Basora, Molowny, Panizo
9–04	Portugal	D	2–2	Lisbon	WCq	Zarra, Gaínza
25–06	USA	W	3–1	Curitiba	WCr1	Igoa, Basora, Zarra
29–06	Chile	W	2–0	Rio de Janeiro	WCr1	Basora, Zarra
2–07	England	W	1–0	Rio de Janeiro	WCr1	Zarra
9–07	Uruguay	D	2–2	Sao Paulo	WCr2	Basora 2
13–07	Brazil	L	1–6	Rio de Janeiro	WCr2	Igoa
16–07	Sweden	L	1–3	Sao Paulo	WCr2	Zarra
18–02–1951	Switzerland	W	6–3	Madrid	Fr	Zarra 4, Gaínza, César
10–06	Belgium	D	3–3	Brussels	Fr	Zarra 2, Gonzalvo (III)
17–06	Sweden	D	0–0	Stockholm	Fr	
1–06–1952	Rep. Ireland	W	6–0	Madrid	Fr	Basora 2, Coque, César, Panizo, Gaínza
8–06	Turkey	D	0–0	Istanbul	Fr	
7–12	Argentina	L	0–1	Madrid	Fr	
28–12	West Germany	D	2–2	Madrid	Fr	Gaínza, César
19–03–1953	Belgium	W	3–1	Barcelona	Fr	Marcet 2, Venancio
5–07	Argentina	L	0–1	Buenos Aires	Fr	
12–07	Chile	W	2–1	Santiago	Fr	Venancio, Kubala
8–11	Sweden	D	2–2	Bilbao	Fr	Venancio, Molowny
6–01–1954	Turkey	W	4–1	Madrid	WCq	Venancio, Gaínza, Miguel, Rafael Alsúa
14–03	Turkey	L	0–1	Istanbul	WCq	
17–03	Turkey	D	2–2	Rome	WCq	Arteche, Escudero
17–03–1955	France	L	1–2	Madrid	Fr	Gaínza
18–05	England	D	1–1	Madrid	Fr	Rial
19–06	Switzerland	W	3–0	Geneva	Fr	Collar, Arieta, Maguregui
27–11	Rep. Ireland	D	2–2	Dublin	Fr	Pahíño 2
30–11	England	L	1–4	London	Fr	Arieta
3–06–1956	Portugal	L	1–3	Lisbon	Fr	Peiró
30–01–1957	Holland	W	5–1	Madrid	Fr	Di Stéfano 3, Kubala, Garay
10–03	Switzerland	D	2–2	Madrid	WCq	Suárez, Miguel
31–03	Belgium	W	5–0	Brussels	Fr	Di Stéfano 2, Suárez, Mateos
8–05	Scotland	L	2–4	Glasgow	WCq	Kubala, Suárez
26–05	Scotland	W	4–1	Madrid	WCq	Basora 2, Mateos, Kubala
6–11	Turkey	W	3–0	Madrid	Fr	Kubala 3
24–11	Switzerland	W	4–1	Lausanne	WCq	Di Stéfano 2, Kubala 2

13-03-1958	France	D	2-2	Paris	Fr	Kubala, Suárez
19-03	West Germany	L	0-2	Frankfurt	Fr	
13-04	Portugal	W	1-0	Madrid	Fr	Di Stéfano
15-10	Nth. Ireland	W	6-2	Madrid	Fr	Tejada 4, Kubala, Suárez
28-02-1959	Italy	D	1-1	Rome	Fr	Di Stéfano
28-06	Poland	W	4-2	Chorzow	ECr1	Di Stéfano 2, Suárez 2
14-10	Poland	W	3-0	Madrid	ECr1	Di Stéfano, Gensana, Gento
22-11	Austria	W	6-3	Valencia	Fr	Di Stéfano 2, Suárez 2, Martínez, Mateos
17-12	France	L	3-4	Paris	Fr	Suárez, Martínez, Vergés
13-03-1960	Italy	W	3-1	Barcelona	Fr	Vergés, Di Stéfano, Martínez
15-05	England	W	3-0	Madrid	Fr	Martínez 2, Peiró
	Soviet Union	W-O		*Spain withdrew*	ECqf	
10-07	Peru	W	3-1	Lima	Fr	Suárez 2, Di Stéfano
14-07	Chile	W	4-0	Santiago	Fr	Di Stéfano 2, Martínez, Collar
17-07	Chile	W	4-1	Santiago	Fr	Di Stéfano 2, Pereda Peiró
24-07	Argentina	L	0-2	Buenos Aires	Fr	
26-10	England	L	2-4	London	Fr	Del Sol, Suárez
30-10	Austria	L	0-3	Vienna	Fr	
2-04-1961	France	W	2-0	Madrid	Fr	Gensana, Gento
19-04	Wales	W	2-1	Cardiff	WCq	Foncho, Di Stéfano
18-05	Wales	D	1-1	Madrid	WCq	Peiró
11-06	Argentina	W	2-0	Seville	Fr	Del Sol, Di Stéfano
12-11	Morocco	W	1-0	Casablanca	WCq	Del Sol
23-11	Morocco	W	3-2	Madrid	WCq	Marcelino, Di Stéfano, Collar
10-12	France	D	1-1	Paris	Fr	Félix Ruiz
31-05-1962	Czechoslovakia	L	0-1	Vina del Mar	WCr1	
3-06	Mexico	W	1-0	Vina del Mar	WCr1	Peiró
6-06	Brazil	L	1-2	Vina del Mar	WCr1	Adelardo
1-11	Romania	W	6-0	Madrid	ECr1	Guillot 3, Veloso, Collar, OG
25-11	Romania	L	1-3	Bucharest	ECr1	Veloso
2-12	Belgium	D	1-1	Brussels	Fr	Guillot
9-01-1963	France	D	0-0	Barcelona	Fr	
30-05	Nth. Ireland	D	1-1	Bilbao	ECr2	Amancio
13-06	Scotland	L	2-6	Madrid	Fr	Adelardo, Veloso
30-10	Nth. Ireland	W	1-0	Belfast	ECr2 Gento	
1-12	Belgium	L	1-2	Valencia	Fr	Zoco
11-03-1964	Rep. Ireland	W	5-1	Seville	ECqf	Amancio 2, Fusté, Marcelino 2
8-04	Rep. Ireland	W	2-0	Dublin	ECqf	Zaballa 2
17-06	Hungary	W	2-1	Madrid	ECsf	Pereda, Amancio
21-06	Soviet Union	W	2-1	Madrid	ECf	Pereda, Marcelino
15-11	Portugal	L	1-2	Oporto	Fr	Fusté
5-05-1965	Rep. Ireland	L	0-1	Dublin	WCq	
8-05	Scotland	D	0-0	Glasgow	Fr	
27-10	Rep. Ireland	W	4-1	Seville	WCq	Pereda 3, Lapetra
10-11	Rep. Ireland	W	1-0	Paris	WCq	Ufarte
8-12	England	L	0-2	Madrid	Fr	
23-06-1966	Uruguay	D	1-1	La Coruna	Fr	Gento
13-07	Argentina	L	1-2	Birmingham	WCr1	Pirri
15-07	Switzerland	W	2-1	Sheffield	WCr1	Sanchís, Amancio
20-07	West Germany	L	1-2	Birmingham	WCr1	Fusté
23-10	Rep. Ireland	D	0-0	Dublin	ECq	
7-12	Rep. Ireland	W	2-0	Valencia	ECq	José María, Pirri
1-02-1967	Turkey	D	0-0	Istanbul	ECq	
24-05	England	L	0-2	London	Fr	
31-05	Turkey	W	2-0	Bilbao	ECq	Grosso, Gento
1-10	Czechoslovakia	L	0-1	Prague	ECq	
22-10	Czechoslovakia	W	2-1	Madrid	ECq	Pirri, Garáte
28-02-1968	Sweden	W	3-1	Seville	Fr	Amancio 2, Rifé
3-04	England	L	0-1	London	ECqf	
2-05	Sweden	D	1-1	Malmo	Fr	Castellano
8-05	England	L	1-2	Madrid	ECqf	Amancio
17-10	France	W	3-1	Lyon	Fr	Pirri, Ufarte, Luis
27-10	Yugoslavia	D	0-0	Belgrade	WCq	
11-12	Belgium	D	1-1	Madrid	WCq	Gárate
23-02-1969	Belgium	L	1-2	Liege	WCq	Asensi
26-03	Switzerland	W	1-0	Valencia	Fr	Bustillo
23-04	Mexico	D	0-0	Seville	Fr	
30-04	Yugoslavia	W	2-1	Barcelona	WCq	Bustillo, Amancio
25-06	Finland	L	0-2	Helsinki	WCq	

15–10	Finland	W	6–0	La Concepcion	WCq	Gárate 2, Pirri, Velázquez, Amancio, Quino
11–02–1970	West Germany	W	2–0	Seville	Fr	Arieta 2
21–02	Italy	D	2–2	Madrid	Fr	Arieta 2
22–04	Switzerland	W	1–0	Lausanne	Fr	Rojo
28–10	Greece	W	2–1	Zaragoza	Fr	Luis, Quini
11–11	Nth. Ireland	W	3–0	Seville	ECq	Rexach, Pirri, Luis
20–02–1971	Italy	W	2–1	Cagliari	Fr	Pirri, Uriarte
17–03	France	D	2–2	Valencia	Fr	Pirri 2
9–05	Cyprus	W	2–0	Nicosia	ECq	Pirri, Violeta
30–05	Soviet Union	L	1–2	Moscow	ECq	Rexach
27–10	Soviet Union	D	0–0	Seville	ECq	
24–11	Cyprus	W	7–0	Granada	ECq	Pirri 2, Quini 2, Aguilar, Lora, Rojo
12–01–1972	Hungary	W	1–0	Madrid	Fr	Arieta
16–02	Nth. Ireland	D	1–1	Hull	ECq	Rojo
12–04	Greece	D	0–0	Salonica	Fr	
23–05	Uruguay	W	2–0	Madrid	Fr	Valdez, Gárate
11–10	Argentina	W	1–0	Madrid	Fr	Asensi
19–10	Yugoslavia	D	2–2	Las Palmas	WCq	Amancio, Asensi
17–01–1973	Greece	W	3–2	Athens	WCq	Valdez 2, Claramunt
21–02	Greece	W	3–1	Malaga	WCq	Claramunt, Sol, Roberto Martínez
2–05	Holland	L	2–3	Amsterdam	Fr	Valdez 2
17–10	Turkey	D	0–0	Istanbul	Fr	
21–10	Yugoslavia	D	0–0	Zagreb	WCq	
24–11	West Germany	L	1–2	Stuttgart	Fr	Claramunt
13–02–1974	Yugoslavia	L	0–1	Frankfurt	WCq	
23–02	West Germany	W	1–0	Barcelona	Fr	Asensi
25–09	Denmark	W	2–1	Copenhagen	ECq	Claramunt, Roberto Martínez
12–10	Argentina	D	1–1	Buenos Aires	Fr	Pirri
20–11	Scotland	W	2–1	Glasgow	ECq	Quini 2
5–02–1975	Scotland	D	1–1	Valencia	ECq	Megido
17–04	Romania	D	1–1	Madrid	ECq	Velázquez
12–10	Denmark	W	2–0	Barcelona	ECq	Pirri, Capón
16–11	Romania	D	2–2	Bucharest	ECq	Villar, Santillana
24–04–1976	West Germany	D	1–1	Madrid	ECqf	Santillana
22–05	West Germany	L	0–2	Munich	ECqf	
10–10	Yugoslavia	W	1–0	Seville	WCq	Pirri
9–02–1977	Rep. Ireland	W	1–0	Dublin	Fr	Satrústegui
27–03	Hungary	D	1–1	Alicante	Fr	Juanito
16–04	Romania	L	0–1	Bucharest	WCq	
21–09	Switzerland	W	2–1	Berne	Fr	Rubé Cano, López Ufarte
26–10	Romania	W	2–0	Madrid	WCq	Leal, Rubén Cano
30–11	Yugoslavia	W	1–0	Belgrade	WCq	Rubén Cano
25–01–1978	Italy	W	2–1	Madrid	Fr	Pirri, Dani
29–03	Norway	W	3–0	Gijon	Fr	Quini, Villar, Dani
26–04	Mexico	W	2–0	Granada	Fr	Quini, Dani
24–05	Uruguay	D	0–0	Montevideo	Fr	
3–06	Austria	L	1–2	Buenos Aires	WCr1	Dani
7–06	Brazil	D	0–0	Mar Del Plata	WCr1	
11–06	Sweden	W	1–0	Buenos Aires	WCr1	Asensi
4–10	Yugoslavia	W	2–1	Zagreb	ECq	Juanito, Santillana
8–11	France	L	0–1	Paris	Fr	
15–11	Romania	W	1–0	Valencia	ECq	Asensi
13–12	Cyprus	W	5–0	Salamanca	ECq	Santillana 2, Asensi, Rubén Cano, Del Bosque

LEADING INTERNATIONAL APPEARANCES

1	Camacho	81
2	Gordillo	75
3	Zubizarreta	69
4	Arconada	68
	Butragueño	68
6	Victor	60
7	Michel	63
	Santillana	56
9	Iribar	49
10	Sanchis (II)	48
11	Zamora R	46
12	Gento	43
13	Amancio	42
	Gallego R	42
15	Asensi	41
	Pirri	41
	Señor	41
18	Goioechea	39
19	Gallego F	36
	Maceda	36
21	Carasco	35
22	Quini	35
23	Ramallets	35
24	Alesanco	34
	Juanito	34
	Julio Alberto	34
27	Gainza	33
	Martin Vazquez	33

LEADING INTERNATIONAL GOALSCORERS

1	Butragueno	26	8	Santillana	15	15	Gaspar Rubio	9
2	Di Stefáno	23	9	Súarez	14		Manolo	9
3	Michel	21	10	Basora	13	16	Juanito	8
4	Zarra	20	11	Amancio	11		Julio Salinas	8
5	Lángara	17		Kubala	11		Quini	8
6	Luis Regueirdo	16	13	Dani	10		Satrústgui	8
	Pirri	16		Rincón	10			

21–12	Italy	L	0–1	Rome	Fr	
14–03–1979	Czechoslovakia	L	0–1	Bratislava	Fr	
4–04	Romania	D	2–2	Craiova	ECq	Dani 2
26–09	Portugal	D	1–1	Vigo	Fr	Dani
10–10	Yugoslavia	L	0–1	Valencia	ECq	
14–11	Denmark	L	1–3	Cadiz	Fr	Mesa
9–12	Cyprus	W	3–1	Limassol	ECq	Villar, Santillana, Saura
23–01–1980	Holland	W	1–0	Vigo	Fr	Dani
13–02	East Germany	L	0–1	Malaga	Fr	
26–03	England	L	0–2	Barcelona	Fr	
16–04	Czechoslovakia	D	2–2	Gijon	Fr	Migueli, Quini
21–05	Denmark	D	2–2	Copenhagen	Fr	Saura, Alexanco
12–06	Italy	D	0–0	Milan	ECr1	
15–06	Belgium	L	1–2	Milan	ECr1	Quini
18–06	England	L	1–2	Naples	ECr1	Dani
24–09	Hungary	D	2–2	Budapest	Fr	Juanito, Satrústegui
15–10	East Germany	D	0–0	Leipzig	Fr	
12–11	Poland	L	1–2	Barcelona	Fr	Dani
18–02–1981	France	W	1–0	Madrid	Fr	Juanito
25–03	England	W	2–1	London	Fr	Satrústegui, Zamora
15–04	Hungary	L	0–3	Valencia	Fr	
20–06	Portugal	L	0–2	Oporto	Fr	
24–06	Mexico	W	3–1	Mexico City	Fr	Juanito 2, Zamora
28–06	Venezuela	W	2–0	Caracus	Fr	Juanito, Satrústegui
2–07	Colombia	D	1–1	Bogota	Fr	Alexanco
5–07	Chile	D	1–1	Santiago	Fr	Satrústegui
8–07	Brazil	L	0–1	Bahia	Fr	
23–09	Austria	D	0–0	Vienna	Fr	
14–10	Luxembourg	W	3–0	Valencia	Fr	López Ufarte 2, Saura
18–11	Poland	W	3–2	Lodz	Fr	López Ufarte, Alexanco, Alonso
16–12	Belgium	W	2–0	Valencia	Fr	Satrústegui 2
24–02–1982	Scotland	W	3–0	Valencia	Fr	Víctor, Quini, Gallego
24–03	Wales	D	1–1	Valencia	Fr	Satrústegui
28–04	Switzerland	W	2–0	Valencia	Fr	Tendillo, Alexanco
16–06	Honduras	D	1–1	Valencia	WCr1	López Ufarte
20–06	Yugoslavia	W	2–1	Valencia	WCr1	Juanito, Saura
25–06	Nth. Ireland	L	0–1	Valencia	WCr1	
2–07	West Germany	L	1–2	Madrid	WCr2	Zamora
5–07	England	D	0–0	Madrid	WCr2	
27–10	Iceland	W	1–0	Malaga	ECq	Pedraza
17–11	Rep. Ireland	D	3–3	Dublin	ECq	Maceda, Víctor, OG
16–02–1983	Holland	W	1–0	Seville	ECq	Señor
27–04	Rep. Ireland	W	2–0	Zaragoza	ECq	Santillana, Rincón
15–05	Malta	W	3–2	Ta'Qali	ECq	Señor, Carrasco, Gordillo
29–05	Iceland	W	1–0	Reykjavik	ECq	Maceda
5–10	France	D	1–1	Paris	Fr	Señor
16–11	Holland	L	1–2	Rotterdam	ECq	Santillana
21–12	Malta	W	12–1	Sevilla	ECq	Santillana 4, Rincón 4, Maceda 2, Sarabia, Señor
18–01–1984	Hungary	L	0–1	Cadiz	Fr	
29–02	Luxembourg	W	1–0	Luxembourg	Fr	Maceda
2–04	Denmark	W	2–1	Valencia	Fr	Santillana, Señor
26–05	Switzerland	W	4–0	Geneva	Fr	Santillana 2, OG, Gallego
31–05	Hungary	D	1–1	Budapest	Fr	Rincón
7–06	Yugoslavia	L	0–1	La Linea	Fr	
14–06	Romania	D	1–1	Saint Etienne	ECr1	Carrasco
17–06	Portugal	D	1–1	Marseille	ECr1	Sousa
20–06	West Germany	W	1–0	Paris	ECr1	Maceda

24–06	Denmark	D	1–1	Lyon	ECsf	Maceda
27–06	France	L	0–2	Paris	ECf	
17–10	Wales	W	3–0	Seville	WCq	Rincón, Carrasco, Butragueño
14–11	Scotland	L	1–3	Glasgow	WCq	Goicoechea
23–01–1985	Finland	W	3–1	Alicante	Fr	Rincón, Butragueño 2
27–02	Scotland	W	1–0	Seville	WCq	Clos
27–03	Nth. Ireland	D	0–0	Palma	Fr	
30–04	Wales	L	0–3	Wrexham	WCq	
26–05	Rep. Ireland	D	0–0	Cork	Fr	
12–06	Iceland	W	2–1	Reykjavik	WCq	Sarabia, Marcos
25–09	Iceland	W	2–1	Seville	WCq	Rincón, Gordillo
20–11	Austria	D	0–0	Zaragoza	Fr	
18–12	Bulgaria	W	2–0	Valencia	Fr	Michel, Calderé
22–01–1986	Soviet Union	W	2–0	Las Palmas	Fr	Salinas, Eloy
19–02	Belgium	W	3–0	Elche	Fr	Butragueño, Salinas, Macedo
26–03	Poland	W	3–0	Cadiz	Fr	Butragueño, Calderé, Salinas
1–06	Brazil	L	0–1	Guadalajara	WCr1	
7–06	Nth. Ireland	W	2–0	Guadalajara	WCr1	Butragueño, Salinas
12–06	Algeria	W	3–0	Monterrey	WCr1	Calderé 2, Eloy
18–06	Denmark	W	5–1	Queretaro	WCr2	Butragueño 4, Goicoechea
22–06	Belgium	D	1–1	Puebla	WCqf	Señor
24–09	Greece	W	3–1	Gijon	Fr	Salinas, Víctor, Francisco
15–10	West Germany	D	2–2	Hanover	Fr	Butragueño, Goicoechea
12–11	Romania	W	1–0	Seville	ECq	Michel
3–12	Albania	W	2–1	Tirana	ECq	Arteche, Joaquín
21–01–1987	Holland	D	1–1	Barcelona	Fr	Calderé
18–02	England	L	2–4	Madrid	Fr	Butragueño, Ramón
1–04	Austria	W	3–2	Vienna	ECq	Eloy 2, Carrasco
29–04	Romania	L	1–3	Bucharest	ECq	Calderé
23–09	Luxembourg	W	2–0	Castellon	Fr	Carrasco, Butragueño
14–10	Austria	W	2–0	Seville	ECq	Michel, Sanchís
18–11	Albania	W	5–0	Seville	ECq	Baquero 3, Michel, Llorente
27–01–1988	East Germany	D	0–0	Valencia	Fr	
24–02	Czechoslovakia	L	1–2	Malaga	Fr	Salinas
23–03	France	L	1–2	Bordeaux	Fr	Calderé
27–04	Scotland	D	0–0	Madrid	Fr	
1–06	Sweden	L	1–3	Salamanca	Fr	Butragueño
5–06	Switzerland	D	1–1	Basle	Fr	Andrinúa
11–06	Denmark	W	3–2	Hannover	ECr1	Michel, Butragueño, Gordillo
14–06	Italy	L	0–1	Frankfurt	ECr1	
17–06	West Germany	L	0–2	Munich	ECr1	
14–09	Yugoslavia	L	1–2	Oviedo	Fr	Michel
12–10	Argentina	D	1–1	Seville	Fr	Butragueño
16–11	Rep. Ireland	W	2–0	Seville	WCq	Manolo, Butragueño
21–12	Nth. Ireland	W	4–0	Seville	WCq	OG, Butragueño, Michel, Roberto
22–01–1989	Malta	W	2–0	Ta'Qali	WCq	Michel, Beguiristain
8–02	Nth. Ireland	W	2–0	Belfast	WCq	Andrinúa, Manolo
23–03	Malta	W	4–0	Seville	WCq	Michel 2, Manolo
26–04	Rep. Ireland	L	0–1	Dublin	WCq	
20–09	Poland	W	1–0	La Coruna	Fr	Michel
11–10	Hungary	D	2–2	Budapest	WCq	Salinas, Michel
15–11	Hungary	W	4–0	Seville	WCq	Manolo, Butragueño, Juanito, Gomez
13–12	Switzerland	W	2–1	Tenerife	Fr	Michel, Minambres
21–02–1990	Czechoslovakia	W	1–0	Alicante	Fr	Manolo
28–03	Austria	L	2–3	Malaga	Fr	Manolo, Butragueño
26–05	Yugoslavia	W	1–0	Ljubljana	Fr	Butrageuño
13–06	Uruguay	D	0–0	Udine	WCr1	
17–06	South Korea	W	3–1	Udine	WCr1	Michel 3
21–06	Belgium	W	2–1	Verona	WCr1	Michel, Gorriz
26–06	Yugoslavia	L	1–2	Verona	WCr2	Salinas
12–09	Brazil	W	3–0	Gijon	Fr	Carlos, Fernando, Michel
10–10	Iceland	W	2–1	Seville	ECq	Butragueño, Carlos
14–11	Czechoslovakia	L	2–3	Prague	ECq	Roberto, Carlos
19–12	Albania	W	9–0	Seville	ECq	Amor, Carlos 2, Butragueño 4, Hierro, Baquero
16–01–1991	Portugal	D	1–1	Castellon	Fr	Moya
20–02	France	L	1–3	Paris	ECq	Baquero
27–03	Hungary	L	2–4	Santander	Fr	Manolo, Carlos
17–04	Romania	L	0–2	Caceres	Fr	

1-09	Uruguay	W	2-1	Oviedo	Fr	Martin Vazquez, Manolo
25-09	Iceland	L	0-2	Reykjavik	ECq	
12-10	France	L	1-2	Seville	ECq	Abelardo
13-11	Czechoslovakia	W	2-1	Seville	Ecq	Abelardo, Michel
15-01-1992	Portugal	D	0-0	Torres Novas	Fr	
19-02	CIS	D	1-1	Valencia	Fr	Hierro
11-03	USA	W	2-0	Valladolid	Fr	Beguiristain, Hierro
22-04	Albania	W	3-0	Seville	WCq	Michel 2, Hierro

SWEDEN

Though second best to Denmark in the early years of the century, by the 1920s Sweden had taken over the role of the leading Scandinavian football nation, a role that they have held onto despite the rebirth of the Danes in the 1980s. The edge that Sweden holds over Denmark is a stronger club scene that has seen IFK Göteborg crowned as UEFA Cup winners on two occasions, the only Scandinavian club to achieve such a feat.

Gothenburg was the early centre of Swedish football and it remains the city that is most passionate about the game; not surprisingly it is also the most successful. The oldest club in existence today, Örgryte IS were formed there in 1887, as was the game's first governing body, the Swedish Sports and Athletic Association in 1895. They organised a championship open only to Gothenburg clubs and in 1896 Örgryte became the first champions.

In 1900 the tournament was opened up to clubs from Stockholm, in 1902 an unofficial national body based in Stockholm was formed and in 1904, a few months after Sweden joined FIFA as one of the founding members, the current Swedish football association was formed. They took over the running of the championship which continued as a knock-out competition until 1925 when a national league was instituted. These early years of competition were dominated by clubs from Gothenburg and Stockholm, especially Örgryte, IFK, GAIS, AIK and Djurgårdens. Although IFK Eskilstuna became the first provincial club to win the championship in 1921, it was not until the 1930s and 40s that other provincial teams such Helsingborg IF, IFK Norrköping and Malmö FF made their presence felt.

Sweden's national side first took the field in July 1908 and recorded the most impressive international debut to date, beating Norway 11–3 in Gothenburg. Until 1920, however, results were mixed. A heavy defeat against the English amateurs at the 1908 Olympic Games was followed by another first round exit in the 1912 tournament. Despite hosting the games the Swedes lost 4–3 to Holland and it was left to Denmark to fly the flag for Scandinavia.

Once again, in the Antwerp games of 1920, the Dutch were responsible for Sweden's demise, this time in the quarter-finals. One thing the Swedes did not find difficult, however, was scoring goals. In the two games they played in the competition proper they scored 13! Seven were scored by Herbert Karlsson, who along with Karl Gustafsson was one of the early stars of the Swedish game.

Sweden has consistently produced good players, and few have been better than Sven Rydell, the Örgryte inside forward, whose 49 goals in 43 games between 1923 and 1932 remains a Swedish record. Along with players like Harry and Albin Dahl, Knut Kroon, Per Kaufeldt and Sigfrid Lindberg in goal, the Swedes built a strong reputation for themselves in the 1920s and early 1930s. In 1924 they laid the Dutch ghost to rest, beating them 3–1 to clinch a deserved bronze medal at the Paris Olympics, but it was not until the 1934 World Cup that another major competition was entered.

At this time the Scandinavian Championship was the major feature of the fixture list, though curiously the 1924–29 tournament was won by Denmark and the 1929–32 edition was won by Norway. Not until the third edition from 1933–36 did Sweden prove triumphant, when the national side was arguably inferior to the team of the 1920s and early 1930s. Sven Jonasson, Tore Keller and Eric Persson led the Swedes to fourth place in the 1938 World Cup, but this was achieved with a bye in the first round and a relatively easy quarter-final tie against Cuba.

The late 1940s saw Sweden at perhaps their best ever, boasting one of the most famous forward lines ever in football. Gunnar Gren, Gunnar Nordahl and Nils Liedholm formed the famous Gre-No-Li trio that was instrumental in winning the Swedes the gold medal at the 1948 Olympic Games in London. So impressed were the scouts of Milan that all three were signed up in 1949, and all three made a huge impact on the Italian game.

Suddenly Swedish players were fashionable and over the years the exodus to the major European leagues has continued unabated. Of the side that won the Olympic title with such style, only two remained in Sweden for the 1950 World Cup qualifiers, but with Karl Palmer and Nacka Skoglund drafted into the side, even without the exiles who were ineligible to play for their country due to the strict amateur rules of the Swedish association, they qualified and eventually finished third in the final tournament. On the way they defeated the defending champions

Italy 3–2 in Sao Paulo, which was good news for the players, eight of whom were signed up by Italian teams!

The supply of class players continued, among them Kurt Hamrin. He too made his name in Italy, and so it was with some relief that the football association overturned its rule forbidding the use of foreign-based players in time for the 1958 World Cup which Sweden had the honour of staging. A home side without all of these stars seemed unimaginable, and it seems unlikely that they would have reached the final as they did without them. Apart from Agne Simonsson and Gren, who had returned from Italy, the other forwards, Liedholm, Hamrin and Skogland, were all still based there.

		All			League			Cup		Europe		
	Team	G	S	B	G	S	B	G	S	G	S	B
1	Malmö FF	28	16	3	14	13	3	14	2	–	1	–
2	IFK Göteborg	19	8	12	13	7	11	4	1	2	–	1
3	IFK Norrköping	17	12	4	12	8	4	5	4	–	–	–
4	Örgryte IS Göteborg	14	5	4	14	5	4	–	–	–	–	–
5	AIK Stockholm	12	14	6	8	10	6	4	4	–	–	–
6	Djurgårdens IF Stockholm	9	13	7	8	10	7	1	3	–	–	–
7	GAIS Göteborg	7	5	3	6	4	3	1	1	–	–	–
8	Helsingborg IF	6	7	7	5	6	7	1	1	–	–	–
9	Östers IF Växjö	5	7	3	4	3	3	1	4	–	–	–
10	IF Elfsborg Borås	4	7	3	4	5	3	–	2	–	–	–
11	Åtvidabergs FF	4	5	–	2	2	–	2	3	–	–	–
12	Kalmar FF	2	1	1	–	–	1	2	1	–	–	–
13	Halmstad BK	2	1	–	2	1	–	–	–	–	–	–
14	IK Sleipner Norrköping	1	4	1	1	3	1	–	1	–	–	–
15	Landskrona BoIS	1	3	1	–	–	1	1	3	–	–	–
16	IFK Eskilstuna	1	1	–	1	1	–	–	–	–	–	–
	Råå IF Helsingborg	1	1	–	–	1	–	1	–	–	–	–
18	Brynäs IF Gävle	1	–	–	1	–	–	–	–	–	–	–
	Fassbergs IF	1	–	–	1	–	–	–	–	–	–	–
	Göteborg IF	1	–	–	1	–	–	–	–	–	–	–
21	Hammarby IF Stockholm	–	4	–	–	2	–	–	2	–	–	–
22	IFK Uppsala	–	3	–	–	3	–	–	–	–	–	–
23	Degerfors IF	–	2	2	–	2	2	–	–	–	–	–
24	Göteborg FF	–	2	–	–	2	–	–	–	–	–	–
	Örgryte II	–	2	–	–	2	–	–	–	–	–	–
26	Örebro SK	–	1	1	–	–	1	–	1	–	–	–
	Sandvikens IF	–	1	1	–	–	1	–	1	–	–	–
28	IK Brage Borlange	–	1	–	–	–	–	–	1	–	–	–
	Derby BK Linköping	–	1	–	–	1	–	–	–	–	–	–
	IV Göteborg	–	1	–	–	1	–	–	–	–	–	–
	Häcken BK Göteborg	–	1	–	–	–	–	–	1	–	–	–
	Jonköpings AIF	–	1	–	–	1	–	–	–	–	–	–
	Jonköping Södra	–	1	–	–	1	–	–	–	–	–	–
	BK Kenty Linköping	–	1	–	–	–	–	–	1	–	–	–
	IFK Malmö	–	1	–	–	1	–	–	–	–	–	–
	Sirius Uppsala	–	1	–	–	1	–	–	–	–	–	–
	IFK Stockholm	–	1	–	–	1	–	–	–	–	–	–

To the end of the 1991 season

A common factor running through the triumphant sides of 1948, 1950 and 1958 was George Raynor, their English manager, but there was nothing he could do in the final. Having surpassed themselves in beating the strong Soviets and West Germans in the quarter- and semi-finals, the Swedes found themselves facing Brazil and were simply no match for the talented South Americans, succumbing 5–2 despite taking a third-minute lead. The defeat still meant, however, that the Swedes remain as one of only ten countries to have appeared in a World Cup Final, an honour in itself.

Raynor remained as manager until Switzerland qualified for Chile at the Swedes' expense after a play-off between the two countries in Berlin, and the rest of the 1960s proved to be a big disappointment. Both the national and club sides did not find the new competitions that were springing up easy going.

The 1970s were far more successful with qualification for three World Cups. In 1974 a side including Ralf Edström and Ove Kindvall, both of whom were based in Holland, Ronnie Hellström in goal and Bjorn Nordqvist in defence, reached the second round of the World Cup in West Germany, but they were outclassed by the Germans and the Poles and finished third in the group. Though they qualified for Argentina in 1978 and Italy in 1990, the Swedes lack consistency. The 1992 European Championship finals saw them appear for the first time in seven attempts only because as hosts they were given a free passage.

One of the few pillars of stability was Nordqvist, who between 1963 and 1978 made a record 115 appearances for his country. In 1978 he overtook the world record held by Bobby Moore, a position he held until he in turn was overtaken by Pat Jennings, Peter Shilton and Heinz Hermann.

At club level, Malmö FF somewhat surprisingly reached the final of the 1979 European Cup but lost there to Nottingham Forest. Swedish clubs have never adopted full-time professionalism and virtually all the top names appear abroad, with Britain, Portugal, Holland, Belgium, Germany and Italy being the favoured destinations. IFK Göteborg did manage to go one better than Malmö by winning the UEFA Cup in 1982 and 1987 and lost to Barcelona in the semi-finals of the 1986 European Cup only after penalties, and all as a part-time side!

Sweden continues to produce quality players from fairly limited resources. The national side will always be there or thereabouts, but until full-time professionalism is introduced in the league, following the example of Denmark, clubs will not be able to hang on to the players they have nurtured, and it will be to the national team rather than club sides that the Swedish public will look for their thrills.

Population: 8 529 000
Area, sq km: 449 964
% in urban areas: 83.4%
Capital city: Stockholm

Svenska Fotbollfoerbundet
Box 1216
S–17123 Solna
Sweden
Tel: (010 46) 8 7350900
Fax: (010 46) 8 275147
Telex: 17711 FOTBOLL S
Cable: FOOTBALL S
Languages for correspondence: English, German & French

Year of formation: 1904
Affiliation to FIFA: 1904
Affiliation to UEFA: 1954
Registered clubs: 3430
Registered players: 188 100
Registered referees: 11 600
National stadium: Råsunda Stadion 41 000
National colours: Shirts: Yellow/Shorts: Blue/Socks: Yellow
Reserve colours: Shirts: Blue/Shorts: Blue/ Socks: Blue
Season: April–October

THE RECORD

WORLD CUP

1930 .... Did not enter
1934 .... QT 1st/3 in group 5 – Final Tournament/Quarter-finalists
1938 .... QT 2nd/4 in group 1 – Final Tournament/Semi-finalists/4th place
1950 .... QT 1st/3 in group 5 – Final Tournament/2nd round/3rd place
1954 .... QT 2nd/3 in group 2
1958 .... QT Automatic – Final Tournament/Finalists
1962 .... QT 2nd/3 in group 1
1966 .... QT 2nd/3 in group 2
1970 .... QT 1st/3 in group 5 – Final Tournament/1st round
1974 .... QT 1st/4 in group 1 – Final Tournament/2nd round
1978 .... QT 1st/3 in group 6 – Final Tournament/1st round
1982 .... QT 3rd/5 in group 6
1986 .... QT 3rd/5 in group 2
1990 .... QT 1st/4 in group 2 – Final Tournament/1st round

EUROPEAN CHAMPIONSHIP

1960 .... Did not enter
1964 .... Quarter-finalists
1968 .... QT 3rd/4 in group 2
1972 .... QT 3rd/4 in group 6
1976 .... QT 3rd/4 in group 3
1980 .... QT 3rd/4 in group 5
1984 .... QT 2nd/5 in group 5
1988 .... QT 2nd/5 in group 2
1992 .... QT Automatic – Final Tournament

OLYMPIC GAMES

1908 .... 1st round/4th place
1912 .... Preliminary round
1920 .... Quarter-finalists
1924 .... Semi-fianlists/3rd place
1928 .... Did not enter
1936 .... 1st round
1948 .... Winners
1952 .... Semi-finalists/3rd place
1956 .... Did not enter
1960 .... Did not enter
1964 .... QT Failed to qualify
1968–84 ..... Did not enter
1988 .... Final Tournament/Quarter-finalists
1992 .... Final Tournament

EUROPEAN CLUB COMPETITIONS

EUROPEAN CUP: Finalists – Malmö FF 1979

CUP WINNERS CUP: Quarter-finalists – Atvidabergs FF 1972, Malmö FF 1975 1987, IFK Göteborg 1980

UEFA CUP: Winners – IFK Göteborg 1982 1987

CLUB DIRECTORY

STOCKHOLM (Population – 1 449 000)

Allmänna Idrottsklubben (AIK Stockholm)
Stadium: Råsunda 27 000
Founded: 1891
Colours: Black/White

Djurgårdens Idrottsförening
Stadium: Stockholms Stadion 22 000
Founded: 1891
Colours: Light and dark blue stripes/Blue

Hammarby Idrottsförening
Stadium: Söderstadion 14 000
Founded: 1897
Colours: White/Green

GOTHENBURG (Population – 710 000)

Göteborgs Atlet & Idrottssälskap (GAIS Göteborg)
Stadium: Nya Ullevi 42 000
Founded: 1894
Colours: Green and black stripes/White

Häcken Bollklubben
Stadium: Rambergsvallen
Founded: 1940
Colours: Yellow/Black

Idrottsföreningen Kamraterna (IFK Göteborg)
Stadium: Nya Ullevi 42 000
Founded: 1904
Colours: Blue and white stripes/Blue

Örgryte Idrottssälskap
Stadium: Nya Ullevi 52 000
Founded: 1887
Colours: Red/Blue

MALMÖ (Population – 445 000)

Malmö Fotboll Förening
Stadium: Malmö 30 000
Founded: 1910
Colours: Sky blue/White

Idrottsföreningen Kamraterna (IFK Malmö)
Stadium: Malmö 30 000
Founded: 1899
Colours: Yellow/White

ÖREBRO (Population – 119 000)
Örebro Sportklubb
Stadium: Eyravallen 15 000
Founded: 1908
Colours: White/Black

NORRKÖPING (Population – 119 000)
Idrottsföreningen Kamraterna (IFK Nörrkoping)
Stadium: Idrottspark 23 000
Founded: 1897
Colours: White/Blue

HELSINGBORG (Population – 106 000)

Helsingborgs Idrottsförening
Stadium: Olympia
Founded: 1907
Colours: Red/Blue

Råå Idrottsförening
Stadium: Gamla Heden
Founded: 1921
Colours: Blue/White

BORÅS (Population – 100 000)
Idrottsförening Elfsborg
Stadium: Ryavallen 18 000
Founded: 1904
Colours: Yellow/Black

ESKILSTUNA (Population – 88 000)
Idrottsföreningen Kamraterna (IFK)
Stadium: Tunavallen
Founded: 1897
Colours: Blue/White

GÄVLE (Population – 87 000)
Brynäs Idrottsförening
Stadium: Geflering
Founded: 1912
Colours: Black/Black

HALMSTAD (Population – 77 000)
Halmstads Bollklubb
Stadium: Örjans Vall 20 000
Founded: 1914
Colours: Blue/White

VÄXJÖ (Population – 67 000)
Östers Idrottsförening
Stadium: Vårendsvallen 20 000
Founded: 1930
Colours: Red/Red

ÅTVIDABERG
Åtvidabergs Fotboll Förening
Stadium: Kopparvallen
Founded: 1907
Colours: Blue/White

BORLANGE
Idrottsklubben Brage
Stadium: Domnarvsvallen 12 000
Founded: 1925
Colours: Green/White

DEGERFORS
Degerfors Idrottsförening
Stadium: Storavalla
Founded: 1907
Colours: Red/White

KALMAR
Kalmar Fotboll Förening
Stadium: Fredriksskans 15 000
Founded: 1910
Colours: Red/Red

LANDSKRONA
Landskrona Boll & Idrottssälskap (BoIS)
Stadium: Idrottsparken
Founded: 1915
Colours: Black and white stripes/Black

SANDVIKEN
Sandvikens Idrottsförening
Stadium: Jernvallen 21 000
Founded: 1918
Colours: Red with white sleeves/White

SWEDISH LEAGUE CHAMPIONSHIP

Year	Champions		Runners up
1896	Örgryte IS	3–0	IV Göteborg
1897	Örgryte IS	1–0	Örgryte II
1898	Örgryte IS	3–0	AIK Stockholm
1899	Örgryte IS	4–0	Göteborg FF
1900	AIK Stockholm	1–0	Örgryte IS
1901	AIK Stockholm	W–O	Örgryte II
1902	Örgryte IS	9–0	Jonköpings AIF
1903	Göteborg IF	5–2	Göteborg FF
1904	Örgryte IS	2–1	Djurgårdens IF
1905	Örgryte IS	2–1	IFK Stockholm
1906	Örgryte IS	4–3	Djurgårdens IF
1907	Örgryte IS	4–1	IFK Uppsala
1908	IFK Göteborg	4–3	IFK Uppsala
1909	Örgryte IS	8–2	Djurgårdens IF
1910	IFK Göteborg	3–0	Djurgårdens IF
1911	AIK Stockholm	3–2	IFK Uppsala
1912	Djurgårdens IF	3–1	Örgryte IS
1913	Örgryte IS	3–2	Djurgårdens IF
1914	AIK Stockholm	7–2	Helsingborg IF
1915	Djurgårdens IF	4–1	Örgryte IS
1916	AIK Stockholm	3–1	Djurgårdens IF
1917	Djurgårdens IF	3–1	AIK Stockholm
1918	IFK Göteborg	5–0	Helsingborg IF
1919	GAIS Göteborg	4–1	Djurgårdens IF
1920	Djurgårdens IF	1–0	IK Sleipner
1921	IFK Eskilstuna	2–1	IK Sleipner
1922	GAIS Göteborg	3–1	Hammarby IF
1923	AIK Stockholm	5–1	IFK Eskilstuna
1924	Fassbergs IF	5–0	Sirius Uppsala
1925	Brynäs IF Gävle	4–2	Derby BK Linköping

	Champions		Runners–up		3rd	
1925	GAIS Göteborg	38	IFK Göteborg	36	Örgryte IS	35
1926	Örgryte IS	35	GAIS Göteborg	34	IFK Göteborg	33
1927	GAIS Göteborg	36	IFK Göteborg	33	Helsingborg IF	32
1928	Örgryte IS	33	Helsingborg IF	33	GAIS Göteborg	28
1929	Helsingborg IF	35	Örgryte IS	33	IFK Göteborg	32
1930	Helsingborg IF	31	IFK Göteborg	30	IK Sleipner	29
1931	GAIS Göteborg	36	AIK Stockholm	30	IFK Göteborg	30
1932	AIK Stockholm	33	Örgryte IS	31	GAIS Göteborg	30
1933	Helsingborg IF	35	GAIS Göteborg	34	IFK Göteborg	25
1934	Helsingborg IF	27	GAIS Göteborg	26	IFK Göteborg	25
1935	IFK Göteborg	33	AIK Stockholm	28	IF Elfsborg	28
1936	IF Elfsborg	34	AIK Stockholm	30	Sandvikens IF	27
1937	AIK Stockholm	36	IK Sleipner	27	Örgryte IS	25
1938	IK Sleipner	30	Helsingborg IF	26	Landskrona BoIS	26
1939	IF Elfsborg	34	AIK Stockholm	25	Malmö FF	25
1940	IF Elfsborg	32	IFK Göteborg	32	Helsingborg IF	27
1941	Helsingborg IF	31	Degerfors IF	29	AIK Stockholm	26
1942	IFK Göteborg	31	GAIS Göteborg	27	IFK Norrköping	26
1943	IFK Norrköping	31	IF Elfsborg	30	Helsingborg IF	30
1944	Malmö FF	37	IF Elfsborg	32	AIK Stockholm	32
1945	IFK Norrköping	37	IF Elfsborg	32	Malmö FF	28
1946	IFK Norrköping	35	Malmö FF	30	IFK Göteborg	30
1947	IFK Norrköping	36	AIK Stockholm	30	Malmö FF	28
1948	IFK Norrköping	33	Malmö FF	29	AIK Stockholm	27
1949	Malmö FF	29	Helsingborg IF	29	GAIS Göteborg	27
1950	Malmö FF	42	Jonköping Södra	27	Helsingborg IF	26
1951	Malmö FF	37	Råå IF Helsingborg	28	Degerfors IF	27
1952	IFK Norrköping	35	Malmö FF	32	Helsingborg IF	26
1953	Malmö FF	31	IFK Norrköping	27	Djurgårdens IF	26
1954	GAIS Göteborg	27	Helsingborg IF	26	Degerfors IF	25
1955	Djurgårdens IF	33	Halmstad BK	29	AIK Stockholm	28
1956	IFK Norrköping	35	Malmö FF	32	Djurgårdens IF	27
1957	IFK Norrköping	35	Malmö FF	28	Helsingborg IF	27
1958	IFK Göteborg	47	IFK Norrköping	47	Djurgårdens IF	42
1959	Djurgårdens IF	32	IFK Norrköping	31	IFK Göteborg	31
1960	IFK Norrköping	38	IFK Malmö	31	Örgryte IS	24

1961	IF Elfsborg 31	IFK Norrköping 26	IFK Göteborg 26
1962	IFK Norrköping 32	Djurgårdens IF 30	IFK Göteborg 24
1963	IFK Norrköping 31	Degerfors IF 29	AIK Stockholm 28
1964	Djurgårdens IF 31	Malmö FF 31	Örgryte IS 31
1965	Malmö FF 34	IF Elfsborg 32	AIK Stockholm 30
1966	Djurgårdens IF 33	IFK Norrköping 29	IF Elfsborg 29
1967	Malmö FF 33	Djurgårdens IF 28	Helsingborg IF 26
1968	Östers IF Växjö 27	Malmö FF 27	IFK Norrköping 27
1969	IFK Göteborg 31	Malmö FF 28	Djurgårdens IF 27
1970	Malmö FF 29	Åtvidabergs FF 28	Djurgårdens IF 24
1971	Malmö FF 30	Åtvidabergs FF 28	IFK Norrköping 26
1972	Åtvidabergs FF 33	AIK Stockholm 32	Östers IF Växjö 26
1973	Åtvidabergs FF 37	Östers IF Växjö 31	Djurgårdens IF 31
1974	Malmö FF 43	AIK Stockholm 34	Östers IF Växjö 33
1975	Malmö FF 42	Östers IF Växjö 37	Djurgårdens IF 34
1976	Halmstad BK 38	Malmö FF 35	Östers IF Växjö 42
1977	Malmö FF 38	IF Elfsborg 31	Kalmar FF 31
1978	Östers IF Växjö 38	Malmö FF 32	IFK Göteborg 31
1979	Halmstad BK 36	IFK Göteborg 35	IF Elfsborg 33
1980	Östers IF Växjö 37	Malmö FF 35	IFK Göteborg 34
1981	Östers IF Växjö 40	IFK Göteborg 36	IFK Norrköping 32

	Champions		Runners–up
1982	IFK Göteborg	1–2 3–1	Hammarby IF
1983	IFK Göteborg	1–1 3–0	Östers IF Växjö
1984	IFK Göteborg	5–1 2–0	IFK Norrköping
1985	Örgryte IS	4–2 2–3	IFK Göteborg
1986	Malmö FF	0–1 5–2	AIK Stockholm
1987	IFK Göteborg	1–0 1–2	Malmö FF
1988	Malmö FF	0–0 7–3	Djurgårdens IF
1989	IFK Norrköping	0–2 1–0 0–0 (4–3p)	Malmö FF
1990	IFK Göteborg	3–0 0–0	IFK Norrköping

1991	IFK Göteborg 36	IFK Norrköping 31	Örebro SK 28

SWEDISH CUP FINALS

Year	Winners	Score	Runners–up
1941	Helsingborg IF	3–1	IK Sleipner
1942	GAIS Göteborg	2–1	IF Elfsborg
1943	IFK Norrköping	0–0 5–2	AIK Stockholm
1944	Malmö FF	4–3	IFK Norrköping
1945	IFK Norrköping	4–1	Malmö FF
1946	Malmö FF	3–0	Åtvidabergs FF
1947	Malmö FF	3–2	AIK Stockholm
1948	Råå IF Helsingborg	6–0	BK Kenty Linköping
1949	AIK Stockholm	1–0	Landskrona BoIS
1950	AIK Stockholm	3–2	Helsingborg IF
1951	Malmö FF	2–1	Djurgårdens IF
1952	–		
1953	Malmö FF	3–2	IFK Norrköping
1954–66	–		
1967	Malmö FF	2–0	IFK Norrköping
1968	–		
1969	IFK Norrköping	1–0	AIK Stockholm
1970	Åtvidabergs FF	2–0	Sandvikens IF
1971	Åtvidabergs FF	3–2	Malmö FF
1972	Landskrona BoIS	0–0 3–2	IFK Norrköping
1973	Malmö FF	7–0	Åtvidabergs FF
1974	Malmö FF	2–0	Östers IF Växjö
1975	Malmö FF	1–0	Djurgårdens IF
1976	AIK Stockholm	1–1 3–0	Landskrona BoIS
1977	Östers IF Växjö	1–0	Hammarby IF
1978	Malmö FF	2–0	Kalmar FF
1979	IFK Göteborg	6–1	Åtvidabergs FF
1980	Malmö FF	3–3 4–3p	IK Brage
1981	Kalmar FF	4–0	IF Elfsborg
1982	IFK Göteborg	3–2	Östers IF Växjö
1983	IFK Göteborg	1–0	Hammarby IF
1984	Malmö FF	1–0	Landskrona BoIS
1985	AIK Stockholm	1–1 3–2p	Östers IF Växjö
1986	Malmö FF	2–1	IFK Göteborg
1987	Kalmar FF	2–0	GAIS Göteborg
1988	IFK Norrköping	3–1	Örebro SK
1989	Malmö FF	3–0	Djurgårdens IF
1990	Djurgårdens IF	2–0	Häcken BK Göteborg
1991	IFK Norrköping	4–1	Östers IF Växjö
1991	IFK Göteborg	3–2	AIK Stockholm

INTERNATIONAL MATCHES PLAYED BY SWEDEN

Date	Opponents	Result	Venue	Compet	Scorers
12–07–1908	Norway	W 11–3	Gothenburg	Fr	Gustafsson 2, Börjesson E 4, Bergström E 4, Lindman
8–09	England*	L 1–6	Gothenburg	Fr	Bergström E
20–10	England*	L 1–12	London	OGr1	Bergström G
23–10	Holland	L 0–2	London	OG3p	
25–10	Holland	L 3–5	The Hague	Fr	Gustafsson 2, Ohlson
26–10	Belgium	L 1–2	Brussels	Fr	Gustafsson
6–11–1909	England*	L 0–7	Hull	Fr	
11–09–1910	Norway	W 4–0	Oslo	Fr	Myhrberg 2, Gustafsson 2
18–06–1911	Germany	L 2–4	Stockholm	Fr	Gustafsson 2
17–09	Norway	W 4–1	Stockholm	Fr	Ekroth 2, Börjesson E, Dahlström
22–10	Finland	W 5–2	Helsinki	Fr	Eriksson, Persson K, Brolin 2, Andersson R

* Amateur side

29–10	Germany	W	3–1	Hamburg	Fr	Börjesson E 2, Olsson J
16–06–1912	Norway	W	2–1	Oslo	Fr	Ekroth 2
20–06	Hungary	D	2–2	Gothenburg	Fr	Bergström E, Swenson
27–06	Finland	W	7–1	Stockholm	Fr	Lorichs 3, Dahlström 2, Persson K 2
29–06	Holland	L	3–4	Stockholm	OGr1	Swenson 2, Börjesson E
1–07	Italy	L	0–1	Stockholm	OGct	
3–11	Norway	W	4–2	Gothenburg	Fr	Frykman, Swenson 2, Ekroth
4–05–1913	Tsarist Russia	W	4–1	Moscow	Fr	Howander 2, Gustafsson, Swenson
18–05	Hungary	L	0–2	Budapest	Fr	
25–05	Denmark	L	0–8	Copenhagen	Fr	
8–06	Norway	W	9–0	Stockholm	Fr	Swenson 2, Bergström R, Gustafsson 5, Ekroth
5–10	Denmark	L	0–10	Stockholm	Fr	
26–10	Norway	D	1–1	Oslo	Fr	Ohlsson C
24–05–1914	Finland	W	4–3	Stockholm	Fr	Bergström R, Swenson 2, Gunnarsson
10–06	England*	L	1–5	Stockholm	Fr	Börjesson E
21–06	Hungary	D	1–1	Stockholm	Fr	Börjesson E
28–06	Norway	W	1–0	Oslo	Fr	Hjelm
5–07	Tsarist Russia	D	2–2	Stockholm	Fr	Wicksell, Swenson
25–10	Norway	W	7–0	Stockholm	Fr	Ekroth 3, Söderberg 3, Johansson G
6–06–1915	Denmark	L	0–2	Copenhagen	Fr	
27–06	Norway	D	1–1	Oslo	Fr	Gunnarsson
24–10	Norway	W	5–2	Stockholm	Fr	Swenson 3, Gunnarsson 2
31–10	Denmark	L	0–2	Stockholm	Fr	
4–06–1916	Denmark	L	0–2	Copenhagen	Fr	
2–07	Norway	W	6–0	Stockholm	Fr	Karlstrand, Gustafsson 3, Wicksell, Swenson,
20–08	United States	L	2–3	Stockholm	Fr	Törnqvist 2
1–10	Norway	D	0–0	Oslo	Fr	
8–10	Denmark	W	4–0	Stockholm	Fr	Karlstrand, Gustafsson, Swenson, Bergström R
3–06–1917	Denmark	D	1–1	Copenhagen	Fr	Börjesson E
19–08	Norway	D	3–3	Halsingborg	Fr	Ström 2, Malm
16–09	Norway	W	2–0	Oslo	Fr	Ekroth, Gustafsson
14–10	Denmark	L	1–2	Stockholm	Fr	Gustafsson
26–05–1918	Norway	W	2–0	Stockholm	Fr	Gustafsson, Sterne
2–06	Denmark	L	0–3	Copenhagen	Fr	
15–09	Norway	L	1–2	Oslo	Fr	Börjesson E
20–10	Denmark	L	1–2	Gothenburg	Fr	Hjelm
29–05–1919	Finland	W	1–0	Stockholm	Fr	Svedberg
5–06	Denmark	L	0–3	Copenhagen	Fr	
9–06	Holland	L	1–3	Amsterdam	Fr	Karlsson H
29–06	Norway	L	3–4	Oslo	Fr	Karlsson H, OG, Bergström R
24–08	Holland	W	4–1	Stockholm	Fr	Karlsson H 3, Svedberg
14–09	Norway	L	1–5	Gothenburg	Fr	Svedberg
28–09	Finland	D	3–3	Helsinki	Fr	Kock 2, Arontzon
12–10	Denmark	W	3–0	Stockholm	Fr	Karlsson H 3
30–05–1920	Finland	W	4–0	Stockholm	Fr	Dahl A 2, Krantz 2
6–06	Switzerland	L	0–1	Stockholm	Fr	
27–06	Norway	W	3–0	Oslo	Fr	Karlsson H, Bergström R, Andersson S
28–08	Greece	W	9–0	Antwerp	OGr1	Olsson A 2, Karlsson H 5, Wicksell, Dahl A
29–08	Holland	L	4–5	Antwerp	OGqf	Karlsson H 2, Olsson A, Dahl A
1–09	Spain	L	1–2	Antwerp	OGct	Dahl A
19–09	Finland	L	0–1	Helsinki	Fr	
26–09	Norway	D	0–0	Stockholm	Fr	
10–10	Denmark	L	0–2	Stockholm	Fr	
25–03–1921	Austria	D	2–2	Vienna	Fr	Horndahl, Andersson E
29–05	Finland	L	0–3	Stockholm	Fr	
19–06	Norway	L	1–3	Oslo	Fr	Kock
22–07	Estonia	D	0–0	Tallin	Fr	
24–07	Austria	L	1–3	Stockholm	Fr	Dahl A
18–09	Norway	L	0–3	Stockholm	Fr	
9–10	Denmark	D	0–0	Stockholm	Fr	
6–11	Hungary	L	2–4	Budapest	Fr	Karlsson H 2
13–11	Czechoslovakia	D	2–2	Prague	Fr	Karlsson H, Edlund
28–05–1922	Poland	L	1–2	Stockholm	Fr	Svedberg
5–06	Finland	W	4–1	Helsinki	Fr	Edlund 2, Kaufeldt 2
9–07	Hungary	D	1–1	Stockholm	Fr	Börjesson E

13–08	Czechoslovakia	L	0–2	Stockholm	Fr	
23–08	Norway	D	0–0	Stockholm	Fr	
24–09	Norway	W	5–0	Oslo	Fr	Malm 2, Dahl A 3
1–10	Denmark	W	2–1	Copenhagen	Fr	Dahl H, Dahl A
21–05–1923	England	L	2–4	Stockholm	Fr	Dahl H 2
10–06	Austria	W	4–2	Gothenburg	Fr	Dahl H, Olsson G, Dahl A 2
20–06	Finland	W	5–4	Gavle	Fr	Rydell, Paulsson 3, Carlsson B
28–06	Germany	W	2–1	Stockholm	Fr	Dahl H, Dahl A
16–09	Norway	W	3–2	Oslo	Fr	Kaufeldy, Kock, Rydell
14–10	Denmark	L	1–3	Stockholm	Fr	Sundberg
28–10	Hungary	L	1–2	Budapest	Fr	Detter
1–11	Poland	D	2–2	Krakow	Fr	Dahl H, Helgesson
18–05–1924	Poland	W	5–1	Stockholm	Fr	Rydell 3, Olsson G, Svensson T
29–05	Belgium	W	8–1	Paris	OGr2	Kock 3, Rydell 3, Brommesson, Kaufeldt
1–06	Egypt	W	5–0	Paris	OGqf	Kaufeldt 2, Brommesson 2, Rydell
5–06	Switzerland	L	1–2	Paris	OGsf	Kock
8–06	Holland	D	1–1	Paris	OG3p	Kaufeldt
9–06	Holland	W	3–1	Paris	OG3p	Rydell 2, Lundquist
15–06	Denmark	W	3–2	Copenhagen	Fr	Kaufeldt, Rydell 2
29–06	Egypt	W	5–0	Stockholm	Fr	Keller, Rydell 4
25–07	Estonia	W	5–2	Stockholm	Fr	Haglund, Keller, Kaufeldt 2, Kock
28–07	Finland	W	7–5	Helsinki	Fr	Haglund 2, Kock 3, Karlsson B 2
31–08	Germany	W	4–1	Berlin	Fr	Wenzel, Malm, Rydberg, Carlsson B
21–09	Norway	W	6–1	Stockholm	Fr	Keller, Kaufeldt 2, Rydell 3
9–11	Austria	D	1–1	Vienna	Fr	Paulsson
16–11	Italy	D	2–2	Milan	Fr	Kaufeldt, Malm
9–06–1925	Finland	W	4–0	Gothenburg	Fr	Johansson F 4
14–06	Denmark	L	0–2	Stockholm	Fr	
21–06	Germany	W	1–0	Stockholm	Fr	Johansson F
5–07	Austria	L	2–4	Stockholm	Fr	Rydell, Keller
12–07	Hungary	W	6–2	Stockholm	Fr	Johansson F 3, Rydell 2, Kaufeldt
23–08	Norway	W	7–3	Oslo	Fr	Rydell 4, Kaufeldt 2, Haglund
1–11	Poland	W	6–2	Krakow	Fr	Dahl A 2, Johansson F 3, Rydberg
9–06–1926	Norway	W	3–2	Stockholm	Fr	Kaukeldt, Rydell 2
13–06	Czechoslovakia	D	2–2	Stockholm	Fr	Kaufeldt, Holmberg
20–06	Germany	D	3–3	Nuremberg	Fr	Hallbäck 2, Olsson G
3–07	Czechoslovakia	L	2–4	Prague	Fr	Johansson F, Holmberg
18–07	Italy	W	5–3	Stockholm	Fr	Rydberg, Holmberg, Kroon, Johansson F 2
20–07	Latvia	L	1–4	Riga	Fr	Hedström
23–07	Estonia	W	7–1	Tallin	Fr	Kling 3, Hedström 2, Lööf 2
26–07	Finland	W	3–2	Helsinki	Fr	Hedström 2, Sundberg
3–10	Denmark	L	0–2	Copenhagen	Fr	
3–10	Poland	W	3–1	Stockholm	Fr	Rydberg 2, Keller
7–11	Austria	L	1–3	Vienna	Fr	Rydberg
14–11	Hungary	L	1–3	Budapest	Fr	Svensson T
3–04–1927	Belgium	L	1–2	Brussels	Fr	Rydell
29–05	Latvia	W	12–0	Stockholm	Fr	Hallbäck 6, Rydell 3, Johansson T, Kaufeldt, Andersson K
12–06	Finland	W	6–2	Stockholm	Fr	Hallbäck 2, Kaufeldt, Johansson B 2, Dahl H
19–06	Denmark	D	0–0	Stockholm	Fr	
26–06	Norway	W	5–3	Oslo	Fr	Rydell 3, Olsson A 2
1–07	Estonia	W	3–1	Norrkoping	Fr	Keller 3
4–09	Belgium	W	7–0	Stockholm	Fr	Kroon 2, Kaufeldt 2, Brommesson, Persson J, Holmberg
6–11	Switzerland	D	2–2	Zurich	Fr	Rydell, Kroon
13–11	Holland	L	0–1	Amsterdam	Fr	
7–06–1928	Norway	W	6–1	Stockholm	Fr	Keller 2, Lundahl 2, Kroon 2
1–07	Poland	L	1–2	Katowice	Fr	Persson E
6–07	Latvia	W	4–0	Riga	Fr	Lööf 3, Pettersson
9–07	Estonia	W	1–0	Tallin	Fr	Pettersson
29–07	Austria	L	2–3	Stockholm	Fr	Lundahl 2
2–09	Finland	W	3–2	Helsinki	Fr	Andersson H 2, Bergström E
30–09	Germany	W	2–0	Stockholm	Fr	Lundahl, Olsson G
7–10	Denmark	L	1–3	Copenhagen	Fr	Rydell
9–06–1929	Holland	W	6–2	Stockholm	Fr	Dahl A, Rydell 3, OG, Nilsson J
14–06	Finland	W	3–1	Stockholm	Fr	Lundahl 2, Holmberg
16–06	Denmark	W	3–2	Gothenburg	Fr	Nilsson J, Kaufeldt, Kroon
23–06	Germany	L	0–3	Cologne	Fr	

7–07	Estonia	W	4–1	Landskrona	Fr	Lundahl 2, Kroon, Dahl H
28–07	Latvia	W	10–0	Malmo	Fr	Dahl A, Rydell, Kroon 2, Andersson R 3, Helgesson, Nilsson J
29–09	Norway	L	1–2	Oslo	Fr	Kroon
15–06–1930	Switzerland	W	1–0	Stockholm	Fr	Kroon
22–06	Denmark	L	1–6	Copenhagen	Fr	Nilsson J
6–07	Norway	W	6–3	Stockholm	Fr	Lundahl 3, Kroon 2, Dahl A
18–07	Estonia	W	5–1	Tallin	Fr	Sundberg 3, Thörn, Johansson K
22–07	Latvia	W	5–0	Riga	Fr	Nilsson A 2, Johansson K, Lööf, Dunker
28–09	Belgium	D	2–2	Liege	Fr	Dahl A 2
28–09	Finland	D	4–4	Helsinki	Fr	Karlsson B 3, Andersson A
28–09	Poland	L	0–3	Stockholm	Fr	
16–11	Austria	L	1–4	Vienna	Fr	Engdahl
17–06–1931	Germany	D	0–0	Stockholm	Fr	
28–06	Denmark	W	3–1	Stockholm	Fr	Gardtman, Rydell 2
3–07	Finland	W	8–2	Stockholm	Fr	Gardtman, Zetterberg 4, Hansson E 3
8–07	Estonia	W	3–1	Sandviken	Fr	Jacobsson R, Zetterberg 2
26–07	Latvia	W	6–0	Vasteras	Fr	Sundberg 3, Roos 2, Rydell
27–09	Norway	L	1–2	Oslo	Fr	Hansson E
8–11	Hungary	L	1–3	Budapest	Fr	Rydell
16–05–1932	Finland	W	7–1	Stockholm	Fr	Rydell 3, OG, Persson E, Nilsson J, Holmberg
10–06	Finland	W	3–1	Helsinki	Fr	Nilsson J, Holmberg, Gardtman
12–06	Belgium	W	3–1	Stockholm	Fr	Sundberg 2, Hansson E
19–06	Denmark	L	1–3	Copenhagen	Fr	Kroon
1–07	Norway	L	1–4	Gothenburg	Fr	Holmberg
10–07	Poland	L	0–2	Warsaw	Fr	
13–07	Latvia	D	0–0	Riga	Fr	
15–07	Estonia	W	3–1	Tallin	Fr	Johansson T 2, Dunker
17–07	Austria	L	3–4	Stockholm	Fr	Nilsson J (II) 2, Svensson G
25–09	Germany	L	3–4	Nuremberg	Fr	Lundahl, Kempe, Persson E
25–09	Lithuania	W	8–1	Stockholm	Fr	Gustavsson 2, Johansson H 2, Nilsson J (II) 4
6–11	Switzerland	L	1–2	Basle	Fr	Olsson G
11–06–1933	Estonia	W	6–2	Stockholm	WCq	Kroon, Bunke L, Ericsson 2, Bunke T, Andersson S
18–06	Denmark	L	2–3	Stockholm	Fr	Ericsson 2
29–06	Lithuania	W	2–0	Kaunas	WCq	Hansson K 2
2–07	Hungary	W	5–2	Stockholm	Fr	Persson E, Karlsson H, Bunke L 2, Nilsson J
4–07	Latvia	D	1–1	Riga	Fr	Hansson K
14–07	Finland	W	2–0	Stockholm	Fr	Kroon, Bunke L
24–09	Norway	W	1–0	Oslo	Fr	Dunker
23–05–1934	Poland	W	4–2	Stockholm	Fr	Jonasson S, Keller 3
27–05	Argentina	W	3–2	Bologna	WCr1	Jonasson S 2, Kroon
31–05	Germany	L	1–2	Milan	WCqf	Dunker
17–06	Denmark	W	5–3	Copenhagen	Fr	Ericsson 4, Persson E
1–07	Norway	D	3–3	Stockholm	Fr	Karlsson E, Andersson S, Ericsson
23–09	Finland	L	4–5	Helsinki	Fr	Persson E 3, Keller
23–09	Latvia	W	3–1	Stockholm	Fr	Andersson S, Carlsson R, Gustavsson
12–06–1935	Finland	D	2–2	Stockholm	Fr	Persson E, Nyberg
16–06	Denmark	W	3–1	Gothenburg	Fr	Grahn, Jonasson S, Hallman
30–06	Germany	W	3–1	Stockholm	Fr	Hallman 2, Jonasson S
5–07	Latvia	W	3–0	Riga	Fr	Carlsson R, Jonasson S, Samuelsson
9–07	Estonia	W	2–1	Tallin	Fr	Samuelsson 2
1–09	Romania	W	7–1	Stockholm	Fr	Bergsten, Keller, Nilsson A 3, Jonasson S, Persson E
22–09	Norway	W	2–0	Oslo	Fr	Nilsson A, Grahn
10–11	France	L	0–2	Paris	Fr	
17–11	Belgium	L	1–5	Brussels	Fr	Nilsson A
14–06–1936	Denmark	L	3–4	Copenhagen	Fr	OG Jonasson S, Josefsson
21–06	Switzerland	W	5–2	Stockholm	Fr	Hallman 2, Jonasson S 3
5–07	Norway	W	2–0	Gothenburg	Fr	Jonasson S 2
26–07	Norway	L	3–4	Stockholm	Fr	Persson E 2, Jonasson S
4–08	Japan	L	2–3	Berlin	OGr1	Persson E 2
27–09	Finland	W	2–1	Helsinki	Fr	Jonasson S, Ericsson
17–05–1937	England	L	0–4	Stockholm	Fr	
16–06	Finland	W	4–0	Stockholm	WCq	Bunke L 2, Persson E, Svanström
20–06	Estonia	W	7–2	Stockholm	WCq	Josefsson 2, Bunke L, Jonasson S,

						Wetterström 3
23–06	Poland	L	1–3	Warsaw	Fr	Wetterström
27–06	Romania	D	2–2	Bucharest	Fr	Jonasson S 2
19–09	Norway	L	2–3	Oslo	Fr	Bunke L, Johansson G
3–10	Denmark	L	1–2	Stockholm	Fr	Persson E
21–11	Germany	L	0–5	Hamburg	WCq	
10–06–1938	Latvia	D	3–3	Stockholm	Fr	Hansson K 2, Bergström G
12–06	Cuba	W	8–0	Antibes	WCqf	Wetterstrom 3, Andersson 3, Keller, Nyberg
15–06	Finland	W	2–0	Stockholm	Fr	Bergström G, Lagercrantz
16–06	Hungary	L	1–5	Paris	WCsf	Nyberg
19–06	Brazil	L	2–4	Bordeaux	WC3p	Jonasson S, Nyberg
21–06	Denmark	W	1–0	Copenhagen	Fr	Nyberg
4–07	Finland	W	4–2	Helsinki	Fr	Lagercrantz 2, Nyberg, Bergström G
7–08	Czechoslovakia	L	2–6	Stockholm	Fr	Nyberg, Bergström G
4–09	Norway	L	1–2	Oslo	Fr	Hansson K
2–10	Norway	L	2–3	Stockholm	Fr	Nyberg, Persson E
3–06–1939	Norway	W	3–2	Stockholm	Fr	Martinsson, Andersson A, Persson E
9–06	Finland	W	5–1	Stockholm	Fr	Andersson A, Persson E 3, Grahn
11–06	Lithuania	W	7–0	Karlstad	Fr	Larsson R, Hjelm 2, Nyström, Lundin, Karlsson W
14–06	Norway	L	0–1	Copenhagen	Fr	
17–09	Norway	W	3–2	Oslo	Fr	Nyström 2, Lennartsson
1–10	Denmark	W	4–1	Stockholm	Fr	Lennartsson, Johansson K, Nyström, Dahl G
29–08–1940	Finland	W	3–2	Helsinki	Fr	Johansson K 3
22–09	Finland	W	5–0	Stockholm	Fr	Persson E, Johansson K 3, Gren
6–10	Denmark	D	1–1	Stockholm	Fr	Emanuelsson
20–10	Denmark	D	3–3	Copenhagen	Fr	Jonasson S, Holmqvist E 2
14–09–1941	Denmark	D	2–2	Stockholm	Fr	Carlsson H, Jacobsson S
5–10	Germany	W	4–2	Stockholm	Fr	Carlsson H 3, Mårtensson
19–10	Denmark	L	1–2	Copenhagen	Fr	Holmqvist E
28–06–1942	Denmark	W	3–0	Copenhagen	Fr	OG, Nordahl, Carlsson H
20–09	Germany	W	3–2	Berlin	Fr	Nyberg, Carlsson H, Mårtensson
4–10	Denmark	W	2–1	Stockholm	Fr	Gren, Nordahl G
15–11	Switzerland	L	1–3	Zurich	Fr	Leander
14–06–1943	Switzerland	W	1–0	Stockholm	Fr	Sandberg
20–06	Denmark	L	2–3	Copenhagen	Fr	Gren, Nordahl G
12–09	Hungary	L	2–3	Stockholm	Fr	Nordahl G 2
3–10	Finland	D	1–1	Helsinki	Fr	Johansson K
7–11	Hungary	W	7–2	Budapest	Fr	Carlsson H, Nyberg 2, Nilsson S 2, Nordahl G 2
24–06–1945	Denmark	W	2–1	Stockholm	Fr	Nordahl G, Holmqvist
1–07	Denmark	W	4–3	Copenhagen	Fr	Åhlund 2, Nordahl G, Gren
26–08	Finland	W	7–2	Gothenburg	Fr	Nyberg 2, Gren 3, Carlsson H, Grahn
30–09	Denmark	W	4–1	Stockholm	Fr	Nordahl G, Carlsson H, OG, Nilsson S
30–09	Finland	W	6–1	Helsinki	Fr	Tapper 5, Holmqvist E
21–10	Norway	W	10–0	Stockholm	Fr	Persson V, Nordahl G 4, Carlsson H 2, Nyberg 2, Gren
25–11	Switzerland	L	0–3	Geneva	Fr	
24–06–1946	Denmark	L	1–3	Copenhagen	Fr	Gren
7–07	Switzerland	W	7–2	Stockholm	Fr	Gren 4, Nyström, Nordahl G, OG
15–09	Finland	W	7–0	Helsinki	Fr	Nilsson G 3, Jönsson E 2, Karlsson B, Rosén
15–09	Norway	W	3–0	Oslo	Fr	Nyberg, Gren, Karlsson E
6–10	Denmark	D	3–3	Gothenburg	Fr	Gren, Nordahl K, Nordahl G
15–06–1947	Denmark	W	4–1	Copenhagen	Fr	Nordahl G 2, Liedholm, Lindskog
26–06	Denmark	W	6–1	Stockholm	Fr	Leander 2, Andersson S, Nordahl G, Nyström, Mårtenson
28–06	Norway	W	5–1	Helsinki	Fr	Nordahl G 4, Persson S
24–08	Finland	W	7–0	Boras	Fr	Liedholm 2, Nordahl G 3, Gren, OG
14–09	Poland	W	5–4	Stockholm	Fr	Nordahl G 2, Nyström, Tapper, Liedholm
5–10	Norway	W	4–1	Stockholm	Fr	Liedholm, Nordahl G 2, Gren
19–11	England	L	2–4	London	Fr	Nordahl G Gren
9–06–1948	Holland	L	0–1	Amsterdam	Fr	
11–07	Austria	W	3–2	Stockholm	Fr	Liedholm, Gren 2
2–08	Austria	W	3–0	London	OGr1	Nordahl G 2, Rosén
5–08	Korea	W	12–0	London	OGqf	Liedholm 2, Nordahl G 4, Gren, Carlsson H 3, Rosén 2

10–08	Denmark	W	4–2	London	OGsf	Carlsson H 2, Rosén 2
13–08	Yugoslavia	W	3–1	London	OGf	Gren 2, Nordahl G
19–09	Norway	W	5–3	Oslo	Fr	Nordahl G 5
19–09	Finland	D	2–2	Helsinki	Fr	Tapper, Mårtensson
10–10	Denmark	W	1–0	Stockholm	Fr	Liedholm
14–11	Austria	L	1–2	Vienna	Fr	Gren
13–05–1949	England	W	3–1	Stockholm	Fr	Carlsson H, Jeppson, Johnsson E
2–06	Rep. Ireland	W	3–1	Stockholm	WCq	Andersson, Jeppson, Liedholm
19–06	Hungary	D	2–2	Stockholm	Fr	Jeppson, Gren
2–10	Finland	W	8–1	Malmo	Fr	Jönsson E 3, Rydell I 3, Palmér, Jakobsson
2–10	Norway	D	3–3	Stockholm	Fr	Lindskog, Jeppson, Simonsson C
23–10	Denmark	L	2–3	Copenhagen	Fr	Jeppson, Mellberg
13–11	Rep. Ireland	W	3–1	Dublin	WCq	Palmér 3
20–11	Hungary	L	0–5	Budapest	Fr	
8–06–1950	Holland	W	4–1	Stockholm	Fr	Jeppson 2, Palmér, Nilsson S
25–06	Italy	W	3–2	Sao Paulo	WCr1	Jeppson 2, Andersson S
29–06	Paraguay	D	2–2	Curitiba	WCr1	Sundkvist, Palmér
9–07	Brazil	L	1–7	Rio de Janeiro	WCr2	Andersson S
13–07	Uruguay	L	2–3	Sao Paulo	WCr2	Palmér, Sundkvist
16–07	Spain	W	3–1	Sao Paulo	WCr2	Sundkvist, Mellberg, Palmér
3–09	Yugoslavia	L	1–2	Stockholm	Fr	Lindskog
24–09	Finland	W	1–0	Helsinki	Fr	Rosén
24–09	Norway	W	3–1	Oslo	Fr	Jönsson E 2, Palmér
15–10	Denmark	W	4–0	Stockholm	Fr	Granqvist, Jönsson E, Bengtsson, OG
12–11	Switzerland	L	2–4	Geneva	Fr	Palmér, Leander
10–06–1951	Turkey	W	3–1	Stockholm	Fr	Sandin 2, Lundkvist
17–06	Spain	D	0–0	Stockholm	Fr	
29–06	Iceland	L	3–4	Reykjavik	Fr	Larsson P, Jönsson A
2–09	Yugoslavia	L	1–2	Belgrade	Fr	Rydell I
2–09	Finland	W	3–2	Stockholm	Fr	Lundkvist 2, Eriksson J
30–09	Norway	L	3–4	Gothenburg	Fr	Rydell I 2, Lindh
21–10	Denmark	L	1–3	Copenhagen	Fr	Jönsson E
11–11	Italy	D	1–1	Florence	Fr	Löfgren
14–11	Turkey	L	0–1	Istanbul	Fr	
26–03–1952	France	W	1–0	Paris	Fr	Westerberg
14–05	Holland	D	0–0	Amsterdam	Fr	
30–05	Scotland	W	3–1	Stockholm	Fr	Sandberg, Löfgren, Bengtsson
11–06	Denmark	W	2–0	Oslo	Fr	Löfgren, Brodd
13–06	Finland	L	1–3	Oslo	Fr	Lindh
22–06	Denmark	W	4–3	Stockholm	Fr	Bengtsson, Brodd, Sandberg, Sandell
21–07	Norway	W	4–1	Tammerfors	OGr1	Brodd 2, Rydell I, Bengtsson
	Austria*	W	3–1	Helsinki	OGqf	Sandberg, Brodd, Rydell
28–07	Hungary	L	0–6	Helsinki	OGsf	
	West Germany*	W	2–0	Helsinki	OG3p	Rydell I, Löfgren
21–09	Finland	W	8–1	Helsinki	Fr	Råberg 3, Persson H 3, Sandin, Sandberg
5–10	Norway	W	2–1	Oslo	Fr	Jakobsson K, Persson H
26–10	Italy	D	1–1	Stockholm	Fr	Persson H
6–05–1953	Scotland	W	2–1	Glasgow	Fr	Löfgren, Eriksson L
28–05	Belgium	L	2–3	Stockholm	WCq	Bengtsson, Selmosson
11–06	France	W	1–0	Stockholm	Fr	Sandell
21–06	Denmark	W	3–1	Copenhagen	Fr	Thillberg 2, Eriksson L
5–07	Hungary	L	2–4	Stockholm	Fr	Sandberg, Sandell
5–08	Finland	D	3–3	Helsinki	WCq	Sandell 2, Persson H
16–08	Finland	W	4–0	Stockholm	WCq	Sandberg, Sandell 2, Sandin
8–10	Belgium	L	0–2	Brussels	WCq	
18–10	Norway	D	0–0	Stockholm	Fr	
8–11	Spain	D	2–2	Bilbao	Fr	Eriksson J, Jacobsson F
15–11	Hungary	D	2–2	Budapest	Fr	Källgren, Hamrin
19–05–1954	Holland	W	6–1	Stockholm	Fr	Thillberg 2, Sandell 2, Svensson S 2
4–06	Finland	W	6–0	Gothenburg	Fr	Sandell, Svensson S 2, Liander, Hamrin, Jakobsson K
7–06	Norway	W	3–0	Stockholm	Fr	Svensson S, Jakobsson K, Sandell
15–08	Finland	W	10–1	Helsinki	Fr	Hamrin 3, Eklund 3, Thillberg 2, Eriksson J
24–08	Iceland	W	3–2	Kalmar	Fr	Eriksson J 2, Sandberg
8–09	Soviet Union	L	0–7	Moscow	Fr	
19–09	Norway	D	1–1	Oslo	Fr	Eriksson J
10–10	Denmark	W	5–2	Stockholm	Fr	Eriksson J, Sandell 3, OG
31–10	Austria	W	2–1	Stockholm	Fr	Sandell, Eriksson J
3–04–1955	France	L	0–2	Paris	Fr	

* Not full internationals

11-05	Hungary	L	3-7	Stockholm	Fr	Löfgren, Svensson S, Isgren
15-06	Romania	W	4-1	Gothenburg	Fr	Bengtsson, Hamrin 2, Svensson S
26-06	Soviet Union	L	0-6	Stockholm	Fr	
28-08	Finland	W	3-0	Halsingborg	Fr	Sandell 2, Lindskog
25-09	Norway	D	1-1	Stockholm	Fr	Nilsson B
16-10	Denmark	D	3-3	Copenhagen	Fr	Nilsson B, Sandell, Hamrin
13-11	Hungary	L	2-4	Budapest	Fr	Svensson S, Löfgren
20-11	Portugal	W	6-2	Lisbon	Fr	Hamrin, Nilsson B, Löfgren 2, Jonsson T, Sandell
16-05-1956	England	D	0-0	Stockholm	Fr	
10-06	Finland	W	3-1	Helsinki	Fr	Ekström, Löfgren, Sandell
17-06	Romania	W	2-0	Bucharest	Fr	Thillberg, Johansson A
30-06	West Germany	D	2-2	Stockholm	Fr	Sandberg, Bengtsson
16-09	Norway	L	1-3	Oslo	Fr	Sandberg
21-10	Denmark	D	1-1	Stockholm	Fr	Löfgren
5-05-1957	Austria	L	0-1	Vienna	Fr	
16-06	Hungary	D	0-0	Stockholm	Fr	
18-06	Norway	D	0-0	Turku	Fr	
19-06	Finland	W	5-1	Helsinki	Fr	Källgren 3, Sandberg, Löfgren
30-06	Denmark	W	2-1	Copenhagen	Fr	Källgren 2
22-09	Finland	W	5-1	Helsinki	Fr	OG 2, Källgren, Jonsson T, Gren
13-10	Norway	W	5-2	Stockholm	Fr	Simonsson A 2, Sandberg, Ekström, Gren
20-11	West Germany	L	0-1	Hamburg	Fr	
7-05-1958	Switzerland	W	3-2	Halsingborg	Fr	Löfgren, Simonsson A 2
8-06	Mexico	W	3-0	Stockholm	WCr1	Simonsson A 2, Liedholm
12-06	Hungary	W	2-1	Stockholm	WCr1	Hamrin 2
15-06	Wales	D	0-0	Stockholm	WCr1	
19-06	Soviet Union	W	2-0	Stockholm	WCqf	Hamrin, Simonsson A
24-06	West Germany	W	3-1	Gothenburg	WCsf	Skoglund, Gren, Hamrin
29-06	Brazil	L	2-5	Stockholm	WCf	Liedholm, Simonsson A
20-08	Finland	W	7-1	Helsinki	Fr	Jonsson T 3, Börjesson R 2, Källgren, Simonsson A
14-09	Norway	W	2-0	Oslo	Fr	Börjesson R, Simonsson A
26-10	Denmark	D	4-4	Stockholm	Fr	Berndtsson B, Börjesson R, Gren 2
21-05-1959	Portugal	W	2-0	Gothenburg	Fr	Simonsson A, Ohlsson O
21-06	Denmark	W	6-0	Copenhagen	Fr	Bild 2, Simonsson A, Berndtsson B 2, Backman
28-06	Hungary	L	2-3	Budapest	Fr	Jonsson T, Backman
2-08	Finland	W	3-1	Malmo	Fr	Bild, Börjesson R, Simonsson A
18-10	Norway	W	6-2	Gothenburg	Fr	Simonsson A 2, Berndtsson B, Börjesson R 2, Thillberg
28-10	England	W	3-2	London	Fr	Simonsson A 2, Salomonsson
1-11	Rep. Ireland	L	2-3	Dublin	Fr	Börjesson R, Berndtsson B
18-05-1960	Rep. Ireland	W	4-1	Malmo	Fr	OG 2, Simonsson A, Börjesson R
22-06	Finland	W	3-0	Helsinki	Fr	Börjesson R 2, Simonsson A
18-09	Norway	L	1-3	Oslo	Fr	Börjesson R
19-10	Belgium	W	2-0	Stockholm	WCq	Börjesson R, Brodd
23-10	Denmark	W	2-0	Gothenburg	Fr	Börjesson R, Bild
30-10	France	W	1-0	Stockholm	Fr	Jonsson T
26-03-1961	Czechoslovakia	L	1-2	Prague	Fr	Jonsson T
28-05	Switzerland	W	4-0	Stockholm	WCq	Jonsson T, Börjesson R 2, Simonsson A
18-06	Denmark	W	2-1	Copenhagen	Fr	Börjesson R 2
9-08	Finland	W	4-0	Norrkoping	Fr	Svahn 2, Bild, Backman
4-10	Belgium	W	2-0	Brussels	WCq	Brodd 2
22-10	Norway	W	2-0	Gothenburg	Fr	Råberg, Wendt
29-10	Switzerland	L	2-3	Berne	WCq	Simonsson A, Brodd
12-11	Switzerland	L	1-2	Berlin	WCq	Brodd
7-04-1962	Czechoslovakia	W	3-1	Gothenburg	Fr	Öberg 2, Bild
18-04	Soviet Union	L	0-2	Stockholm	Fr	
19-06	Finland	W	3-0	Helsinki	Fr	Grahn O, Brodd, Ohlsson O
21-06	Norway	W	2-0	Oslo	ECr1	Martinsson 2
16-09	Norway	L	1-2	Oslo	Fr	Skiöld
28-10	Denmark	W	4-2	Stockholm	Fr	Ohlsson O 2, Martinsson, Eriksson L
4-11	Norway	D	1-1	Malmo	ECr1	Eriksson L
13-11	Israel	W	4-0	Tel Aviv	Fr	Ohlsson O, Skiöld 3
16-11	Thailand	W	2-1	Bangkok	Fr	Ohlsson O, Nilsson B
5-05-1963	Hungary	W	2-1	Stockholm	Fr	Mild, Brodd
22-05	Soviet Union	W	1-0	Moscow	Fr	Martinsson
19-06	Yugoslavia	D	0-0	Belgrade	ECr2	

14–08	Norway	D	0–0	Gothenburg	Fr	
14–08	Finland	D	0–0	Stockholm	Fr	
18–09	Yugoslavia	W	3–2	Malmo	ECr2	Persson O 2, Bild
6–10	Denmark	D	2–2	Copenhagen	Fr	Bild, Öberg
3–11	West Germany	W	2–1	Stockholm	Fr	Simonsson A, Bild
29–04–1964	Holland	W	1–0	Rotterdam	Fr	Simonsson A
13–05	Soviet Union	D	1–1	Stockholm	ECqf	Hamrin
27–05	Soviet Union	L	1–3	Moscow	ECqf	Hamrin
28–06	Denmark	W	4–1	Malmo	Fr	Öberg, Bild, Martinsson, Magnusson R
2–08	Finland	L	0–1	Helsinki	Fr	
20–09	Norway	D	1–1	Oslo	Fr	Larsson B
7–10	Poland	D	3–3	Stockholm	Fr	Öberg, Magnusson R, Larsson B
4–11	West Germany	D	1–1	Berlin	WCq	Hamrin
5–05–1965	Cyprus	W	3–0	Norrkoping	WCq	Simonsson A 2, Jonsson T
16–05	England	L	1–2	Gothenburg	Fr	Eriksson L
16–06	Italy	D	2–2	Malmo	Fr	Larsson B, Persson O
20–06	Denmark	L	1–2	Copenhagen	Fr	Persson O
30–06	Brazil	L	1–2	Stockholm	Fr	Bild
22–08	Finland	D	2–2	Lulea	Fr	Bild, Simonsson A
26–09	West Germany	L	1–2	Stockholm	WCq	Jonsson T
31–10	Norway	D	0–0	Stockholm	Fr	
7–11	Cyprus	W	5–0	Famagusta	WCq	Granström 2, Kinvdall, Larsson B 2
27–04–1966	East Germany	L	1–4	Leipzig	Fr	Kindvall
18–05	Poland	D	1–1	Wroclaw	Fr	Larsson B
4–06	Finland	L	0–1	Helsinki	Fr	
27–06	Yugoslavia	D	1–1	Malmo	Fr	Nildén
30–06	Brazil	L	2–3	Gothenburg	Fr	Kindvall 2
18–09	Norway	W	4–2	Oslo	Fr	Karlsson J, Turesson 3
5–10	Austria	W	4–1	Stockholm	Fr	Lundblad, Kindvall, Turesson 2
6–11	Denmark	W	2–1	Stockholm	Fr	Simonsson A, Danielsson
13–11	Portugal	W	2–1	Lisbon	ECq	Danielsson 2
17–05–1967	East Germany	L	0–1	Halsingborg	Fr	
1–06	Portugal	D	1–1	Stockholm	ECq	Svensson I
11–06	Bulgaria	L	0–2	Stockholm	ECq	
25–06	Denmark	D	1–1	Copenhagen	Fr	Selander
10–08	Finland	W	2–0	Stockholm	Fr	Eriksson L, Danielsson
3–09	Norway	L	1–3	Oslo	ECq	Nordahl T
5–11	Norway	W	5–2	Stockholm	ECq	Turesson 2, Danielsson, Eriksson L 2
12–11	Bulgaria	L	0–3	Sofia	ECq	
19–02–1968	Israel	W	3–0	Tel Aviv	Fr	Ejderstedt 3
28–02	Spain	L	1–3	Seville	Fr	Ejderstedt
2–05	Spain	D	1–1	Malmo	Fr	Nordahl T
22–05	England	L	1–3	London	Fr	Andersson R
27–06	Denmark	W	2–1	Stockholm	Fr	Lindman, Nordahl T
1–08	Soviet Union	D	2–2	Gothenburg	Fr	Eriksson L, Grahn O
11–09	Finland	W	3–0	Helsinki	Fr	Eriksson L, Andersson R, Selander
15–09	Norway	D	1–1	Oslo	Fr	Eriksson L
9–10	Norway	W	5–0	Stockholm	WCq	Kindvall 3, Larsson B 2
19–02–1969	Israel	W	3–2	Tel Aviv	Fr	Ejderstedt, Selander, Andersson R
26–02	Yugoslavia	L	1–2	Split	Fr	Magnusson R
1–05	Mexico	W	1–0	Malmo	Fr	Kindvall
22–05	Finland	W	4–0	Vaxjo	Fr	Johansson H 2, Svensson T, OG
1–06	Norway	W	4–2	Gothenburg	Fr	Pålsson, Ejderstadt 2, Andersson R
19–06	Norway	W	5–2	Oslo	WCq	Persson O, Eriksson L, Kindvall, Grahn O, Grip
25–06	Denmark	W	1–0	Copenhagen	Fr	Eklund
6–08	Soviet Union	W	1–0	Moscow	Fr	Eklund
25–08	Israel	W	3–1	Stockholm	Fr	Danielsson 2, Eriksson L
24–09	Hungary	W	2–0	Stockholm	Fr	Nicklasson, Grahn O
15–10	France	W	2–0	Stockholm	WCq	Kindvall 2
1–11	France	L	0–3	Paris	WCq	
22–02–1970	Mexico	D	0–0	Mexico City	Fr	
1–03	Mexico	W	1–0	Puebla	Fr	Eriksson L
16–05	Hungary	W	2–1	Budapest	Fr	Persson O, Ejderstedt
3–06	Italy	L	0–1	Toluca	WCr1	
7–06	Israel	D	1–1	Toluca	WCr1	Turesson
10–06	Uruguay	W	1–0	Puebla	WCr1	Grahn O
25–06	Denmark	D	1–1	Gothenburg	Fr	Pålsson
26–08	Finland	W	2–1	Helsinki	Fr	Almqvist, Brzokoupil

13–09	Norway	W	4–2	Oslo	Fr	Danielsson, Brzokoupil, Svensson T
14–10	Rep. Ireland	D	1–1	Dublin	ECq	Brzokoupil
28–10	Rep. Ireland	W	1–0	Stockholm	ECq	Turesson
12–03–1971	Israel	L	1–2	Tel Aviv	Fr	Eklund
20–05	Finland	W	4–1	Boras	Fr	Larsson B, Svensson T, Persson O, Pålsson
26–05	Austria	W	1–0	Stockholm	ECq	Olsson J
9–06	Italy	D	0–0	Stockholm	ECq	
20–06	Denmark	W	3–1	Copenhagen	Fr	Grahn O 2, Eklund
27–06	West Germany	W	1–0	Gothenburg	Fr	Kindvall
8–08	Norway	W	3–0	Malmo	Fr	Sandberg, Pålsson, Larsson B
4–09	Austria	L	0–1	Vienna	ECq	
9–10	Italy	L	0–3	Milan	ECq	
26–04–1972	Switzerland	D	1–1	Geneva	Fr	Hult
14–05	Czechoslovakia	L	1–2	Gothenburg	Fr	Hult
25–05	Hungary	D	0–0	Stockholm	WCq	
10–06	Austria	L	0–2	Vienna	WCq	
29–06	Denmark	W	2–0	Malmo	Fr	Larsson B, Sandberg
6–08	Soviet Union	D	4–4	Stockholm	Fr	Edström 3, Pålsson
17–09	Norway	W	3–1	Oslo	Fr	Edström 2, Larsson B
15–10	Malta	W	7–0	Gothenburg	WCq	Edström 3, Larsson B 2, Sandberg, Szepanski
26–04–1973	Denmark	W	2–1	Copenhagen	Fr	Sandberg, Kindvall
23–05	Austria	W	3–2	Gothenburg	WCq	Sandberg 2, Grahn O
13–06	Hungary	D	3–3	Budapest	WCq	Kindvall, Sandberg, Edström
25–06	Brazil	W	1–0	Stockholm	Fr	Sandberg
8–07	Finland	D	1–1	Halmstad	Fr	Leback
11–07	Iceland	W	1–0	Uddevalla	Fr	Tapper
5–08	Soviet Union	D	0–0	Moscow	Fr	
29–08	Finland	W	2–1	Helsinki	Fr	Torstensson, Svensson H
29–09	Italy	L	0–2	Milan	Fr	
11–11	Malta	W	2–1	Gzira	WCq	Kindvall, Larsson B
27–11	Austria	W	2–1	Gelsenkirchen	WCq	Sandberg, Larsson B
1–05–1974	West Germany	L	0–2	Hamburg	Fr	
3–06	Denmark	W	2–0	Copenhagen	Fr	Sandberg, Torstensson
9–06	Switzerland	D	0–0	Malmo	Fr	
15–06	Bulgaria	D	0–0	Dusseldorf	WCr1	
19–06	Holland	D	0–0	Dortmund	WCr1	
23–06	Uruguay	W	3–0	Dusseldorf	WCr1	Edström 2, Sandberg
26–06	Poland	L	0–1	Stuttgart	WCr2	
30–06	West Germany	L	2–4	Dusseldorf	WCr2	Edström, Sandberg
3–07	Yugoslavia	W	2–1	Dusseldorf	WCr2	Edström, Torstensson
8–08	Norway	W	2–1	Gothenburg	Fr	Fredriksson, Tapper
4–09	Holland	L	1–5	Stockholm	Fr	Larsson B
13–10	Czechoslovakia	L	0–4	Bratislava	Fr	
30–10	Nth. Ireland	L	0–2	Stockholm	ECq	
16–04–1975	Scotland	D	1–1	Gothenburg	Fr	Sjöberg
19–05	Algeria	W	4–0	Halmstad	Fr	Edström, Sandberg, Grahn O, Sjöberg
4–06	Yugoslavia	L	1–2	Stockholm	ECq	Edström
30–06	Norway	W	3–1	Stockholm	ECq	Nordahl T 2, Grahn O
13–08	Norway	W	2–0	Oslo	ECq	Sandberg, Sjöberg
3–09	Nth. Ireland	W	2–1	Belfast	ECq	Sjöberg, Torstensson
25–09	Denmark	D	0–0	Malmo	Fr	
15–10	Yugoslavia	L	0–3	Zagreb	ECq	
28–02–1976	Tunisia	D	1–1	Tunis	Fr	Fredriksson

LEADING INTERNATIONAL APPEARANCES

1	Nordqvist	115
2	Bergmark	94
3	Ravelli	92
4	Hellström	77
5	Svensson K	73
6	Larsson B	70
7	Erlandsson	69
8	Hysen	68
9	Fredriksson	63

LEADING INTERNATIONAL GOALSCORERS

1	Rydell I	49
2	Nordahl G	43
3	Gren G	32
4	Simonsson A	27
5	Kaufeldt	23
6	Gustafsson	22
7	Dahl A	21
8	Sandell	20
	Persson E	20
	Johansson S	20

2–03	Algeria	W	2–0	Algiers	Fr	Fredriksson, Tapper
28–04	Austria	L	0–1	Vienna	Fr	
11–05	Denmark	L	1–2	Gothenburg	Fr	Sandberg
1–06	Finland	W	2–0	Helsinki	Fr	Torstensson, Linderoth
16–06	Norway	W	2–0	Stockholm	WCq	Andersson B, Sjöberg
11–08	Finland	W	6–0	Malmo	Fr	Sjöberg 2, Ljungberg, Werner, Nilsson T, Börjesson B
8–09	Hungary	D	1–1	Stockholm	Fr	Torstensson
22–09	Norway	L	2–3	Oslo	Fr	Torstensson, Sjöberg
9–10	Switzerland	W	2–1	Basle	WCq	Börjesson B, Sjöberg
27–04–1977	Scotland	L	1–3	Glasgow	Fr	Wendt
26–05	Norway	W	1–0	Gothenburg	Fr	Linderoth
8–06	Switzerland	W	2–1	Stockholm	WCq	Sjöberg, Börjesson B
15–06	Denmark	L	1–2	Copenhagen	Fr	Nordin
20–07	Iceland	W	1–0	Reykjavik	Fr	Johansson S
17–08	East Germany	L	0–1	Stockholm	Fr	
7–09	Norway	L	1–2	Oslo	WCq	Sjöberg
5–10	Denmark	W	1–0	Malmo	Fr	Larsson L
2–10	Hungary	L	0–3	Budapest	Fr	
12–11	Poland	L	1–2	Wroclaw	Fr	Åslund
4–04–1978	East Germany	W	1–0	Leipzig	Fr	Åslund
19–04	West Germany	W	3–1	Stockholm	Fr	OG, Larsson L 2
21–05	Czechoslovakia	D	0–0	Stockholm	Fr	
3–06	Brazil	D	1–1	Mar del Plata	WCr1	Sjöberg
7–06	Austria	L	0–1	Buenos Aires	WCr1	
11–06	Spain	L	0–1	Buenos Aires	WCr1	
28–06	Finland	W	2–1	Boras	Fr	Nilsson T, Andersson M
16–08	Denmark	L	1–2	Copenhagen	Fr	Berggren
1–09	France	D	2–2	Paris	ECq	Nordgren, Grönhagen
4–10	Czechoslovakia	L	1–3	Stockholm	ECq	Borg
19–04–1979	Soviet Union	L	0–2	Tbilisi	Fr	
9–05	Denmark	D	2–2	Copenhagen	Fr	Erlandsson, Ohlsson B
7–06	Luxembourg	W	3–0	Malmo	ECq	Grönhagen, Cervin, Borg
10–06	England	D	0–0	Stockholm	Fr	
28–06	Norway	W	2–0	Gothenburg	Fr	Borg, Nordin
15–08	Norway	L	0–2	Oslo	Fr	
5–09	France	L	1–3	Stockholm	ECq	Backe
26–09	Italy	L	0–1	Florence	Fr	
10–10	Czechoslovakia	L	1–4	Prague	ECq	Svensson J
23–10	Luxembourg	D	1–1	Esch	ECq	Grönhagen
14–11	Malaysia	W	3–1	Kuala Lumpur	Fr	Nilsson P, Grönhagen, Andersson M
17–11	Singapore	W	5–0	Singapore	Fr	Nilsson T 3, Svensson J 2
29–04–1980	Soviet Union	L	1–5	Malmo	Fr	Nordgren
7–05	Denmark	L	0–1	Gothenburg	Fr	
22–05	Finland	W	2–0	Helsinki	Fr	Nordgren, Sjöberg
18–06	Israel	D	1–1	Stockholm	WCq	Ramberg
17–07	Iceland	D	1–1	Halmstad	Fr	Backe
20–08	Hungary	L	0–2	Budapest	Fr	
10–09	Scotland	L	0–1	Stockholm	WCq	
24–09	Bulgaria	W	3–2	Burgas	Fr	Ramberg, Ohlsson B, Holmgren
15–10	Nth. Ireland	L	0–3	Belfast	WCq	
12–11	Israel	D	0–0	Tel Aviv	WCq	
28–02–1981	Norway	W	4–2	Lahti	Fr	Nilsson Tb, Rönnberg, Larsson L, Nilsson T
1–03	Finland	L	1–2	Lahti	Fr	Nilsson Tb
14–05	Denmark	L	1–2	Malmo	Fr	Börjesson B
3–06	Nth. Ireland	W	1–0	Stockholm	WCq	Borg
24–06	Portugal	W	3–0	Stockholm	WCq	Börjesson B, Hysén, Svensson J
29–07	Finland	W	1–0	Halmstad	Fr	Björklund
12–08	Bulgaria	W	1–0	Uddevalla	Fr	Sjöberg
9–09	Scotland	L	0–2	Glasgow	WCq	
23–09	Greece	L	1–2	Salonika	Fr	Larsson T
14–10	Portugal	W	2–1	Lisbon	WCq	Larsson T, Persson T
28–10	Saudi Arabia	W	2–1	Riyadh	Fr	Larsson T 2
20–02–1982	Finland	D	2–2	Lahti	Fr	Ahlström 2
21–02	Finland	L	1–2	Lahti	Fr	Dahlkvist
5–05	Denmark	D	1–1	Copenhagen	Fr	Larsson T
19–05	East Germany	D	2–2	Halmstad	Fr	Persson T, Larsson T
3–06	Soviet Union	D	1–1	Stockholm	Fr	Nilsson B

11–08	Norway	L	0–1	Oslo	Fr	
8–09	Romania	L	0–2	Bucharest	ECq	
6–10	Czechoslovakia	D	2–2	Bratislava	ECq	Jingblad, Eriksson U
13–11	Cyprus	W	1–0	Nicosia	ECq	Corneliusson
27–04–1983	Holland	W	3–0	Utrecht	Fr	Corneliusson 2, Prytz
15–05	Cyprus	W	5–0	Malmo	ECq	Prytz 2, Corneliusson, Hysén, Ravelli
29–05	Italy	W	2–0	Gothenburg	ECq	Sandberg, Strömberg
9–06	Romania	L	0–1	Stockholm	ECq	
22–06	Brazil	D	3–3	Gothenburg	Fr	Corneliusson 2, Hysén
17–08	Iceland	W	4–0	Reykjavik	Fr	Jingblad, Ramberg, Hysén, Fredriksson S
7–09	Finland	W	3–0	Helsinki	Fr	Eriksson U 2, Sunesson
21–09	Czechoslovakia	W	1–0	Stockholm	ECq	Corneliusson
15–10	Italy	W	3–0	Naples	ECq	Strömberg 2, Sunesson
16–11	Trinidad	W	5–0	Port of Spain	Fr	Dahlqvist, Jingblad 3, Sunesson
19–11	Barbados	W	4–0	Bridgetown	Fr	Dahlqvist, Jingblad 3
22–11	Mexico	L	0–2	Morelia	Fr	
2–05–1984	Switzerland	D	0–0	Berne	Fr	
23–05	Malta	W	4–0	Norrkoping	WCq	Sunesson 2, Corneliusson, Erlandsson
6–06	Denmark	L	0–1	Gothenburg	Fr	
22–08	Mexico	D	1–1	Malmo	Fr	Prytz
12–09	Portugal	L	0–1	Stockholm	WCq	
26–09	Italy	L	0–1	Milan	Fr	
17–10	West Germany	L	0–2	Cologne	WCq	
14–11	Portugal	W	3–1	Lisbon	WCq	Prytz 2, Nilsson Tb
1–05–1985	Israel	D	1–1	Tel Aviv	Fr	Prytz
22–05	Norway	W	1–0	Gothenburg	Fr	Prytz
5–06	Czechoslovakia	W	2–0	Stockholm	WCq	Prytz, Larsson L
21–08	Poland	W	1–0	Malmo	Fr	Ravelli
11–09	Denmark	W	3–0	Copenhagen	Fr	Prytz, Corneliusson, Magnusson M
25–09	West Germany	D	2–2	Stockholm	WCq	Corneliusson, Magnusson M
16–10	Czechoslovakia	L	1–2	Prague	WCq	Corneliusson
17–11	Malta	W	2–1	Ta'Qali	WCq	Prytz, Strömberg
1–05–1986	Greece	D	0–0	Malmo	Fr	
14–05	Austria	L	0–1	Salzburg	Fr	
6–08	Finland	W	3–1	Helsinki	Fr	Prytz 2, Ekström
20–08	Soviet Union	D	0–0	Gothenburg	Fr	
10–09	England	W	1–0	Stockholm	Fr	Ekström
24–09	Switzerland	W	2–0	Stockholm	ECq	Ekström 2
12–10	Portugal	D	1–1	Lisbon	ECq	Strömberg
16–11	Malta	W	5–0	Ta'Qali	ECq	Ekström 2, Magnusson M, Hysén, Fredriksson S
18–04–1987	Soviet Union	W	3–1	Tbilisi	Fr	Limpár, Magnusson M 2
24–05	Malta	W	1–0	Gothenburg	ECq	Ekström
3–06	Italy	W	1–0	Stockholm	ECq	Larsson P
17–06	Switzerland	D	1–1	Lausanne	ECq	Ekström
12–08	Norway	D	0–0	Oslo	Fr	
26–08	Denmark	W	1–0	Stockholm	Fr	Magnusson M
23–09	Portugal	L	0–1	Stockholm	ECq	
13–10	West Germany	D	1–1	Gelsenkirchen	Fr	Hysén
14–11	Italy	L	1–2	Naples	ECq	Larsson P
13–01–1988	East Germany	W	4–1	Las Palmas	Fr	Thern 2, Truedsson, Rehn
15–01	Finland	W	1–0	Las Palmas	Fr	Thern
31–03	West Germany	D	1–1 (4–2p)	Berlin	Fr	Truedsson
2–04	Soviet Union	W	2–0	Berlin	Fr	Eskilsson, Holmqvist H
27–04	Wales	W	4–1	Stockholm	Fr	Holmqvist H 2, Strömberg, Eskilsson
1–06	Spain	W	3–1	Salamanca	Fr	Nilsson J, Magnusson M, Hysén
31–07	Brazil	D	1–1	Stockholm	Fr	Hellstrom
31–08	Denmark	L	1–2	Stockholm	Fr	Pettersson
12–10	Portugal	D	0–0	Gothenburg	Fr	
19–10	England	D	0–0	London	WCq	
5–11	Albania	W	2–1	Tirana	WCq	Holmqvist, Ekstrom
26–04–1989	Wales	W	2–0	Wrexham	Fr	Schiller, OG
7–05	Poland	W	2–1	Stockholm	WCq	Ljung, Larsson N
31–05	Algeria	W	2–0	Orebro	Fr	Ingesson 2
14–06	Denmark	L	0–6	Copenhagen	Fr	
16–06	Brazil	W	2–1	Copenhagen	Fr	Ljung, Rehn
16–08	France	L	2–4	Malmo	Fr	Thern, Lindqvist
6–09	England	D	0–0	Stockholm	WCq	
8–10	Albania	W	3–1	Stockholm	WCq	Ingesson, Magnusson M, Engkvist
25–10	Poland	W	2–0	Chorzow	WCq	Larsson P, Ekström

14-02-1990	Arab Emirates	L	1-2	Dubai	Fr	Schwarz
17-02	Arab Emirates	W	2-0	Dubai	Fr	Rehn, Ingesson
21-02	Belgium	D	0-0	Brussels	Fr	
11-04	Algeria	D	1-1	Algiers	Fr	Schwarz
25-04	Wales	W	4-2	Stockholm	Fr	Brolin 2, Ingesson 2
27-05	Finland	W	6-0	Stockholm	Fr	Brolin 2, Magnusson M, Limpár, Larsson P, Thern
10-06	Brazil	L	1-2	Turin	WCr1	Brolin
16-06	Scotland	L	1-2	Genoa	WCr1	Strömberg
20-06	Costa Rica	L	1-2	Genoa	WCr1	Ekström
22-08	Norway	W	2-1	Stavanger	Fr	Engqvist, Fjellstrom
5-09	Denmark	L	0-1	Vasteras	Fr	
26-09	Bulgaria	W	2-0	Stockholm	Fr	Corneliusson, Andersson K
10-10	West Germany	L	1-3	Stockholm	Fr	Rehn
17-04-1991	Greece	D	2-2	Athens	Fr	Erlingburg, Mild
1-05	Austria	W	6-0	Stockholm	Fr	Andersson K 3, Rehn, Dahlin 2
5-06	Colombia	D	2-2	Stockholm	Fr	Brolin, Andersson K
13-06	Soviet Union	L	2-3	Gothenburg	Fr	Brolin 2
15-06	Denmark	W	4-0	Norrkoping	Fr	Dahlin 2, Andersson K, Brolin
8-08	Norway	W	2-1	Oslo	Fr	Nilsson R, Limpar
21-08	Poland	L	0-2	Gdynia	Fr	
4-09	Yugoslavia	W	4-3	Stockholm	Fr	Dahlin 2, Limpar, Thern
9-10	Switzerland	L	1-3	Lucerne	Fr	Eriksson
25-01-1992	Australia	D	0-0	Sydney	Fr	
29-01	Australia	L	0-1	Adelaide	Fr	
2-02	Australia	L	0-1	Melbourne	Fr	
22-04	Tunisia	W	1-0	Tunis	Fr	Andersson K
7-05	Poland	W	5-0	Stockholm	Fr	Andersson K, Ingesson, Dahlin, Pettersson
27-05	Hungary	W	2-1	Stockholm	Fr	Schwarz 2
10-06	France	D	1-1	Stockholm	ECr1	Eriksson J
14-06	Denmark	W	1-0	Stockholm	ECr1	Brolin
17-06	England	W	2-1	Stockholm	ECr1	Eriksson J, Brolin
21-06	Germany	L	2-3	Stockholm	ECsf	Brolin, Andersson K

SWITZERLAND

Switzerland are one of those countries who have not improved with age. Though never actually a force to be reckoned with, the Swiss were useful competitors in the first half of the century, but as a small and on the whole affluent society, they have not been able to keep pace with the larger and more successful European nations. The 1966 World Cup was the last occasion they qualified for a major tournament, and it may be many more years before they do so again.

The Swiss Football Association, formed in 1895, was one of the first on mainland Europe and over the years the Swiss have proved themselves adept in the organisational field. Noted for its neutrality and situated in central Europe, Switzerland, one of the founding members of FIFA, became one of the centres for world football when it was decided wisely to locate the FIFA organisation there and Zürich was chosen as the location. Fifty years later in 1954, the founders of UEFA decided that Switzerland should also be home to their body and so located themselves in Berne.

Football is recorded as having been played in Switzerland as early as 1869 by English students at La Châtelaine College in Geneva, and in 1879 St Gallen, the oldest surviving club, were formed. As the names of some of the clubs like Grasshoppers and Young Boys suggest, the British influence was strong.

Three years after the formation of the association a championship was instituted, and by this time the majority of the clubs still active today had been formed. The first competition was won by Grasshoppers after a play-off between the winners of the three regional leagues. This was the system used until the introduction of a single national league in 1934. Grasshoppers, Servette and Young Boys, representing Zürich, Geneva and Berne respectively were amongst the most successful teams in the early years and remain so. There is, however, a strong rivalry within the cities, and in recent years FC Zurich, FC Basel and regional clubs like Neuchâtel Xamax have all experienced periods of success at the expense of the established clubs.

In 1905 a national side was fielded for the first time with a match against France in Paris. Defeat that day was to become a familar experience, though notable victories were occasionally scored on home territory. Even the emergence of the amazing Abegglen footballing family could not alter the overall poor record of the national side. Max and André Abegglen were a feature of the side for nearly two decades and between them they scored over 60 goals for their country.

Although the overall results remained poor, Switzerland continually made her mark upon the major tournaments in the 1920s and 1930s. Max Abegglen inspired them to a silver medal in the 1924 Olympic Games in Paris, where they succumbed to the dazzling Uruguayans in the final. They also reached the quarter-finals of both the 1934 and

1938 World Cups. Their 4–2 victory over Germany in the first round in 1938, in which André, the younger Abegglen brother by seven years, scored twice, was particularly impressive.

The Swiss finished last in every Dr Gerö Cup that was played, in perhaps a truer indication of the level of the game, and were often on the end of some heavy defeats. Aside from the victory over Germany in the World Cup, their finest moment pre-war was the 3–2 victory over England a month before the German game.

Responsible for the national side at the time was one of the key figures in Swiss football history, Karl Rappan. The inventor of the 'Swiss Bolt' system, Rappan instigated a major tactical innovation which saw the initial use of a free man in defence, along the lines of a sweeper. Under him the Swiss experienced an immediate rise in their fortunes, and as their manager on and off until he retired in 1968, he was responsible for Switzerland's continued presence as a international force.

Helped by players like Hügi, Ballaman, Fatton and Bickel, Switzerland took part in four of the first five World Cups after the war. As hosts in 1954 they reached the quarter-finals before losing to Austria in one of the most bizarre games ever staged in the tournament. Three–nil up after 23 minutes, they eventually lost 7–5 with all of the goals being scored within the period of an hour.

The 1950, 1962 and 1966 tournaments all saw elimination in the first round, but not much more was expected of the team and in light of later achievements, reaching the final tournament was success in itself. Since 1966, the national side has not reached the finals of either the World Cup or European Championships. They have, however, always proved difficult opponents and in the 1992 European Championship came the closest yet to breaking the sequence, finishing a point behind Scotland after losing their final match against Romania in Bucharest.

		All			League			Cup		Europe		
	Team	G	S	B	G	S	B	G	S	G	S	B
1	Grasshopper-Club Zürich	39	24	11	22	16	10	17	8	–	–	1
2	Servette FC Genève	21	26	11	15	15	11	6	11	–	–	–
3	BSC Young Boys Bern	17	16	9	11	11	8	6	5	–	–	1
4	Lausanne-Sports	14	13	7	7	7	6	7	6	–	–	1
5	FC Zürich	14	9	8	9	8	6	5	1	–	–	2
6	FC Basel	13	9	3	8	3	3	5	6	–	–	–
7	FC La Chaux-de-Fonds	9	4	7	3	3	7	6	1	–	–	–
8	FC Sion	7	1	4	1	1	4	6	–	–	–	–
9	FC Lugano	5	7	8	3	3	8	2	4	–	–	–
10	Neuchâtel Xamax FC	3	6	6	3	2	6	–	4	–	–	–
11	FC Winterthur	3	4	1	3	2	1	–	2	–	–	–
12	FC Aarau	3	3	3	2	1	3	1	2	–	–	–
13	FC Luzern	3	1	1	1	1	1	2	–	–	–	–
14	FC St Gallen	2	2	2	1	–	2	1	2	–	–	–
15	FC Grenchen	1	7	1	–	4	1	1	3	–	–	–
16	Young Fellows Zürich	1	4	2	–	3	2	1	1	–	–	–
17	FC Bern	1	4	1	1	3	1	–	1	–	–	–
18	FC Biel	1	3	2	1	2	2	–	1	–	–	–
19	Urania Geneva Sport	1	2	1	–	1	1	1	1	–	–	–
20	AC Bellinzona	1	2	–	1	–	–	–	2	–	–	–
21	Etoile La Chaux-de-Fonds	1	1	–	1	1	–	–	–	–	–	–
22	Anglo–American FC Zürich	1	–	–	1	–	–	–	–	–	–	–
	SC Brühl St Gallen	1	–	–	1	–	–	–	–	–	–	–
24	Nordstern Basel	–	5	–	–	3	–	–	2	–	–	–
25	BSC Old Boys Basel	–	3	1	–	3	1	–	–	–	–	–
26	FC Chiasso	–	1	2	–	1	2	–	–	–	–	–
27	Chatelaine	–	1	–	–	1	–	–	–	–	–	–
	FC Fribourg	–	1	–	–	–	–	–	1	–	–	–
	FC Locarno	–	1	–	–	–	–	–	1	–	–	–
	FC Schaffhausen	–	1	–	–	–	–	–	1	–	–	–
	FC Thun	–	1	–	–	–	–	–	1	–	–	–
32	Blue Stars Zürich	–	–	1	–	–	1	–	–	–	–	–
	FC Etoile Carouge	–	–	1	–	–	1	–	–	–	–	–
	Villa Longchamp	–	–	1	–	–	1	–	–	–	–	–

To the end of the 1991–92 season

Swiss club football tends to have an even lower profile than the national side. For an important international match it is not unusual to see the Wankdorf stadium full to capacity, but the league does not have the glamour of those in neighbouring countries, though it does boast professionalism. The European club tournaments have not been particularly happy hunting grounds; FC Zürich have reached the semi-final of the European Cup twice, but on neither occasion were they serious contenders to win the tournament.

Population: 6 756 000
Area, sq km: 41 293
% in urban areas: 60.2%
Capital city: Berne

Schweizerischer Fussballverband
Laubeggstrasse #70
Postfach 24
CH-3000 Berne 32
Switzerland
Tel: (010 41) 31 435111

Fax: (010 41) 31 435081
Telex: 912910 SFV CH
Cable: SWISSFOOT BERNE
Languages for correspondence: German, French & English

Year of formation: 1895
Affiliation to FIFA: 1904
Affiliation to UEFA: 1954
Registered clubs: 1474
Registered players: 182 500

Professional Players: 150
Registered coaches: 7036
Registered referees: 4751

National stadium: Wankdorf, Berne 58 000
National colours: Shirts: Red/Shorts: White/Socks: Red
Reserve colours: Shirts: White/Shorts: White/Socks: Red
Season: August–June

THE RECORD

WORLD CUP

1930 .... Did not enter
1934 .... QT 1st/3 in group 10 – Final Tournament/Quarter-finalists
1938 .... QT 1st/2 in group 4 – Final Tournament/Quarter-finalists
1950 .... QT 1st/2 in group 4 – Final Tournament/1st round
1954 .... QT Automatic – Final Tournament/Quarter-finalists
1958 .... QT 3rd/3 in group 9
1962 .... QT 1st/3 in group 1 – Final Tournament/1st round
1966 .... QT 1st/4 in group 5 – Final Tournament/1st round
1970 .... QT 3rd/4 in group 1
1974 .... QT 3rd/4 in group 2
1978 .... QT 3rd/3 in group 6
1982 .... QT 4th/5 in group 4
1986 .... QT 3rd/5 in group 6
1990 .... QT 4th/5 in group 7

EUROPEAN CHAMPIONSHIP

1960 .... Did not enter
1964 .... 1st round
1968 .... QT 3rd/4 in group 6
1972 .... QT 2nd/4 in group 3
1976 .... QT 4th/4 in group 6
1980 .... QT 4th/5 in group 4
1984 .... QT 2nd/4 in group 1
1988 .... QT 4th/5 in group 2
1992 .... QT 2nd/5 in group 2

OLYMPIC GAMES

1908–20 ..... Did not enter
1924 .... Runners–up
1928 .... 1st round
1936–56 ..... Did not enter
1960 .... QT Failed to qualify
1964 .... QT Failed to qualify
1968 .... QT Failed to qualify
1972 .... QT Failed to qualify
1976–84 ..... Did not enter
1988 .... QT Failed to qualify
1992 .... QT Failed to qualify

DR GERÖ CUP

1929 .... 5th
1932 .... 5th
1935 .... 5th
1953 .... 5th
1960 .... 6th

EUROPEAN CLUB COMPETITIONS

EUROPEAN CUP: Semi-finalists – Young Boys Berne 1959, FC Zürich 1964 1977

CUP WINNERS CUP: Quarter-finalists – Lausanne-Sports 1965, Servette 1967 1979, FC Zürich 1974, FC Sion 1987, Young Boys Berne 1988, Grasshoppers 1990

UEFA CUP: Semi-finalists – Lausanne-Sports 1958, Grasshoppers 1978

MITROPA CUP: Quarter-finalists – Grasshoppers 1937

CLUB DIRECTORY

BERNE (Population – 298 000)
Berner Sportclub (BSC) Young Boys
Stadium: Wankdorf 58 000
Founded: 1898
Colours: Yellow/Black

ZÜRICH (Population – 860 000)

Grasshopper-Club Zürich
Stadium: Hardturm 32 000
Founded: 1886
Colours: Blue and white halves/White

Fussball-Club Zürich
Stadium: Letzigrund 27 000
Founded: 1896
Colours: White with blue upper half/White

BASLE (Population – 575 000)

Fussball-Club Basel
Stadium: St. Jakob 60 000
Founded: 1893
Colours: Blue and red halves/Blue

Basel Sportclub (BSC) Old Boys
Stadium: Schützenmatte 12 000
Founded: 1894
Colours: Yellow/Black

GENEVA (Population – 460 000)

Servette Football Club Genève
Stadium: Charmilles 30 000
Founded: 1890
Colours: Grenadine/Grenadine

Urania Genève Sport
Stadium: Frontenex 4000
Founded: 1896
Colours: Violet/White

LAUSANNE (Population – 259 000)
Lausanne-Sports
Stadium: Olympique 26 000
Founded: 1896
Colours: White with blue shoulders and sleeves/White
Previous name: Merger in 1920 of Montriond '96 and Hygrénique

LUCERNE (Population – 159 000)
Fussball-Club Luzern
Stadium: Allmend 24 000
Founded: 1901
Colours: White with blue shoulders and sleeves/White

ST GALLEN (Population – 125 000)
St Gallen Fussball-Club
Stadium: Espenmoos 13 000 Founded: 1879
Colours: Green and white stripes/Green

WINTERTHUR (Population – 107 000)
Fussball-Club Winterthur
Stadium: Schützenwiese 15 000
Founded: 1896 Colours: White/White

LUGANO (Population – 94 000)
Football-Club Lugano
Stadium: Comunale Cornaredo 26 000
Founded: 1908
Colours: Black with a broad white V on chest/White

BIEL (Population – 81 000)
Fussball-Club Biel
Stadium: Gorzellen Founded: 1896
Colours: Blue/Yellow

THUN (Population – 77 000)
Fussball-Club Thun
Stadium: Lachen Founded: 1898
Colours: Red/White

NEUCHATEL (Population – 65 000)
Neuchâtel Xamax Football Club
Stadium: Maladière 21 000
Founded: 1970
Colours: Red and black stripes/Black
Previous names: Merger in 1970 of Cantonal and FC Neuchâtel

AARAU (Population – 57 000)
Fussball-Club Aarau
Stadium: Brügglifeld 14 000 Founded: 1902
Colours: Black and white stripes/Black

SCHAFFHAUSEN (Population – 53 000)
Fussball-Club Schaffhausen
Stadium: Breite 7000 Founded: 1896
Colours: Yellow/Black

LOCARNO (Population – 42 000)
Football-Club Locarno
Stadium: Del Lido 11 000 Founded: 1906
Colours: White/Blue

LA CHAUX-DE-FONDS (Population 35 000)
Football-Club La Chaux-de-Fonds
Stadium: Charrière 14 000
Founded: 1894
Colours: Yellow/Blue

SION (Population – 23 000)
Football-Club Sion
Stadium: Tourbillon 13 000
Founded: 1909
Colours: White/White

BELLINZONA (Population 16 000)
Associazione Calcio Bellinzona
Stadium: Comunale 20 000
Founded: 1904
Colours: Red/Blue

WETTINGEN
Fussball-Club Wettingen
Stadium: Altenburg 9000
Founded: 1931
Colours: White/White

SWISS LEAGUE CHAMPIONSHIP

Year	Champions		Runners up		3rd	
REGIONAL LEAGUE PLAY-OFFS						
1898	Grasshopper-Club	4	Chatelaine	0	Villa Longchamp	0
1899	Anglo-American	7–0	Old Boys Basel			
1900	Grasshopper-Club	2–0	FC Bern			
1901	Grasshopper-Club	2–0	FC Bern			
1902	FC Zürich	4	BSC Young Boys	1	FC Bern	1
1903	BSC Young Boys	4	FC Zürich	0	FC Neuchâtel	0
1904	FC St Gallen	3	Old Boys Basel	1	Servette FC	1
1905	Grasshopper-Club	4	La Chaux-de-Fonds	1	BSC Young Boys	1
1906	FC Winterthur	4	Servette FC	2	BSC Young Boys	0
1907	Servette FC	4	Young Fellows Zürich	2	FC Basel	0
1908	FC Winterthur	4–1	BSC Young Boys			
1909	BSC Young Boys	1–0	FC Winterthur			
1910	BSC Young Boys	4	Servette FC	2	FC Aarau	0
1911	BSC Young Boys	4	FC Zürich	2	Servette FC	0
1912	FC Aarau	4	Et Chaux-de-Fonds	2	Servette FC	0
1913	Montriond Lausanne	4	Old Boys Basel	2	FC Aarau	0
1914	FC Aarau	3	BSC Young Boys	2	Cantonal Neuchâtel	1
1915	Brühl St Gallen	3–0	Servette FC			
1916	Cantonal Neuchâtel	4	FC Winterthur	1	Old Boys Basel	1
1917	FC Winterthur	4	La Chaux-de-Fonds	1	BSC Young Boys	1
1918	Servette FC	4	BSC Young Boys	2	FC St Gallen	0
1919	Et Chaux-de-Fonds	4	Servette FC	1	FC Winterthur	1
1920	BSC Young Boys	3	Servette FC	2	Grasshopper-Club	1
1921	Grasshopper-Club	4	BSC Young Boys	2	Servette FC	0
1922	Servette FC	4	FC Luzern	2	Blue Stars Zürich	0
1923	FC Bern	3	Young Fellows Zürich	2	Servette FC	1
1924	FC Zürich	4	Nordstern Basel	2	Servette FC	0
1925	Servette FC	3	FC Bern	2	Young Fellows Zürich	1
1926	Servette FC	3	Grasshopper-Club	3	BSC Young Boys	0
1927	Grasshopper-Club	4	Nordstern Basel	2	FC Biel	0
1928	Grasshopper-Club	4	Nordstern Basel	2	FC Etoile Carouge	0
1929	BSC Young Boys	3	Grasshopper-Club	2	Urania Genève	1
1930	Servette FC	8	Grasshopper-Club	5	FC Biel	5
1931	Grasshopper-Club	7	Urania Genève	6	La Chaux-de-Fonds	4
1932	Lausanne-Sports	4	FC Zürich	4	Grasshopper-Club	3
1933	Servette FC	5	Grasshopper-Club	5	BSC Young Boys	2
NATIONAL LEAGUE						
1934	Servette FC	49	Grasshopper-Club	46	FC Lugano	38
1935	Lausanne-Sports	41	Servette FC	40	FC Lugano	35
1936	Lausanne-Sports	41	Young Fellows Zürich	38	Grasshopper-Club	36
1937	Grasshopper-Club	36	BSC Young Boys	29	Young Fellows Zürich	28
1938	FC Lugano	30	Grasshopper-Club	29	BSC Young Boys	28
1939	Grasshopper-Club	31	FC Grenchen	27	FC Lugano	27
1940	Servette FC	41	FC Grenchen	28	Grasshopper-Club	26
1941	FC Lugano	37	BSC Young Boys	35	Servette FC	33
1942	Grasshopper-Club	36	FC Grenchen	36	Servette FC	35
1943	Grasshopper-Club	44	FC Lugano	35	Lausanne-Sports	34
1944	Lausanne-Sports	38	Servette FC	32	FC Lugano	30
1945	Grasshopper-Club	41	FC Lugano	34	BSC Young Boys	34
1946	Servette FC	36	FC Lugano	35	Lausanne-Sports	30
1947	FC Biel	36	Lausanne-Sports	35	FC Lugano	31
1948	AC Bellinzona	38	FC Biel	37	Lausanne-Sports	34
1949	FC Lugano	40	FC Basel	33	La Chaux-de-Fonds	29
1950	Servette FC	35	FC Basel	33	Lausanne-Sports	32
1951	Lausanne-Sports	34	FC Chiasso	31	La Chaux-de-Fonds	30
1952	Grasshopper-Club	38	FC Zürich	37	FC Chiasso	35
1953	FC Basel	42	BSC Young Boys	38	Grasshopper-Club	32
1954	La Chaux-de-Fonds	42	Grasshopper-Club	41	Lausanne-Sports	36
1955	La Chaux-de-Fonds	42	Lausanne-Sports	38	Grasshopper-Club	33
1956	Grasshopper-Club	42	La Chaux-de-Fonds	34	BSC Young Boys	32

1957	BSC Young Boys 45	Grasshopper-Club 41	La Chaux-de-Fonds 38
1958	BSC Young Boys 43	Grasshopper-Club 35	FC Chiasso 35
1959	BSC Young Boys 38	FC Grenchen 32	FC Zürich 30
1960	BSC Young Boys 42	FC Biel 36	La Chaux-de-Fonds 32
1961	Servette FC 46	BSC Young Boys 36	FC Zürich 35
1962	Servette FC 40	Lausanne-Sports 35	La Chaux-de-Fonds 34
1963	FC Zürich 44	Lausanne-Sports 40	La Chaux-de-Fonds 32
1964	La Chaux-de-Fonds 39	FC Zürich 38	FC Grenchen 38
1965	Lausanne-Sports 36	BSC Young Boys 32	Servette FC 31
1966	FC Zürich 42	Servette FC 35	Lausanne-Sports 32
1967	FC Basel 40	FC Zürich 39	FC Lugano 39
1968	FC Zürich 38	Grasshopper-Club 38	FC Lugano 38
1969	FC Basel 36	Lausanne-Sports 35	FC Zürich 30
1970	FC Basel 37	Lausanne-Sports 36	FC Zürich 34
1971	Grasshopper-Club 42	FC Basel 42	FC Lugano 31
1972	FC Basel 43	FC Zürich 39	Grasshopper-Club 38
1973	FC Basel 39	Grasshopper-Club 35	FC Sion 33
1974	FC Zürich 45	Grasshopper-Club 33	Servette FC 32
1975	FC Zürich 39	BSC Young Boys 33	Grasshopper-Club 33
1976	FC Zürich 44	Servette FC 39	FC Basel 34
1977	FC Basel 29	Servette FC 29	FC Zürich 27
1978	Grasshopper-Club 29	Servette FC 28	FC Basel 27
1979	Servette FC 35	FC Zürich 29	Grasshopper-Club 23
1980	FC Basel 33	Grasshopper-Club 31	Servette FC 31
1981	FC Zürich 40	Grasshopper-Club 34	Neuchâtel Xamax 34
1982	Grasshopper-Club 49	Servette FC 46	FC Zürich 46
1983	Grasshopper-Club 49	Servette FC 48	FC St Gallen 40
1984	Grasshopper-Club 44	Servette FC 44	FC Sion 43
1985	Servette FC 46	FC Aarau 42	Neuchâtel Xamax 39
1986	BSC Young Boys 44	Neuchâtel Xamax 42	FC Luzern 41
1987	Neuchâtel Xamax 48	Grasshopper-Club 43	FC Sion 42
1988	Neuchâtel Xamax 32	Servette FC 30	FC Aarau 30
1989	FC Luzern 33	Grasshopper-Club 30	FC Sion 29
1990	Grasshopper-Club 31	Lausanne-Sports 31	Neuchâtel Xamax 30
1991	Grasshopper-Club 33	FC Sion 29	Neuchâtel Xamax 29
1992	FC Sion 33	Neuchâtel Xamax 31	Grasshopper-Club 30

SWISS CUP FINALS

Year	Winners	Score	Runners-up
1926	Grasshopper-Club	2–1	FC Bern
1927	Grasshopper-Club	3–1	Young Fellows Zürich
1928	Servette FC	5–1	Grasshopper-Club
1929	Urania Genève	1–0	BSC Young Boys
1930	BSC Young Boys	1–0	FC Aarau
1931	FC Lugano	2–1	Grasshopper-Club
1932	Grasshopper-Club	5–1	Urania Genève
1933	FC Basel	4–3	Grasshopper-Club
1934	Grasshopper-Club	2–0	Servette FC
1935	Lausanne-Sports	10–0	Nordstern Basel
1936	Young Fellows Zürich	2–0	Servette FC
1937	Grasshopper-Club	10–0	Lausanne-Sports
1938	Grasshopper-Club	2–2 5–1	Servette FC
1939	Lausanne-Sport	2–0	Nordstern Basel
1940	Grasshopper-Club	3–0	FC Grenchen
1941	Grasshopper-Club	1–1 2–0	Servette FC
1942	Grasshopper-Club	0–0 2–1	FC Basel
1943	Grasshopper-Club	2–1	FC Lugano
1944	Lausanne-Sport	3–0	FC Basel
1945	BSC Young Boys	2–0	FC St Gallen
1946	Grasshopper-Club	3–0	Lausanne-Sports
1947	FC Basel	3–0	Lausanne-Sports
1948	La Chaux-de-Fonds	2–2 2–2 4–0	FC Grenchen
1949	Servette FC	3–0	Grasshopper-Club
1950	Lausanne-Sports	1–1 4–0	Cantonal Neuchâtel
1951	La Chaux-de-Fonds	3–2	FC Locarno
1952	Grasshopper-Club	2–0	FC Lugano
1953	BSC Young Boys	1–1 3–1	Grasshopper-Club
1954	La Chaux-de-Fonds	2–0	FC Fribourg
1955	La Chaux-de-Fonds	3–1	FC Thun
1956	Grasshopper-Club	1–0	BSC Young Boys
1957	La Chaux-de-Fonds	3–1	Lausanne-Sports
1958	BSC Young Boys	1–1 4–1	Grasshopper-Club
1959	FC Grenchen	1–0	Servette FC
1960	FC Lucern	1–0	FC Grenchen
1961	La Chaux-de-Fonds	1–0	FC Biel
1962	Lausanne-Sports	4–0	AC Bellinzona
1963	FC Basel	2–0	Grasshopper-Club
1964	Lausanne-Sports	2–0	La Chaux-de-Fonds
1965	FC Sion	2–1	Servette FC
1966	FC Zürich	2–0	Servette FC
1967	FC Basel	2–1*	Lausanne-Sports
1968	FC Lugano	2–1	FC Winterthur
1969	FC St Gallen	2–0	AC Bellinzona
1970	FC Zürich	4–1	FC Basel
1971	Servette FC	2–0	FC Lugano
1972	FC Zürich	1–0	FC Basel
1973	FC Zürich	2–0	FC Basel
1974	FC Sion	3–2	Neuchâtel Xamax
1975	FC Basel	2–1	FC Winterthur
1976	FC Zürich	1–0	Servette FC
1977	BSC Young Boys	1–0	FC St Gallen
1978	Servette FC	2–2 1–0	Grasshopper-Club
1979	Servette FC	1–1 3–2	BSC Young Boys
1980	FC Sion	2–1	BSC Young Boys
1981	Lausanne-Sports	4–3	FC Zürich
1982	FC Sion	1–0	FC Basel
1983	Grasshopper-Club	2–2 3–0	Servette FC

* FC Basel later awarded the game 3–0

1984	Servette FC	1–0	Lausanne-Sports	
1985	FC Aarau	1–0	Neuchâtel Xamax	
1986	FC Sion	3–1	Servette FC	
1987	BSC Young Boys	4–2	Servette FC	
1988	Grasshopper-Club	2–0	FC Schaffhausen	
1989	Grasshopper-Club	2–1	FC Aarau	
1990	Grasshopper-Club	2–1	Neuchâtel Xamax	
1991	FC Sion	3–2	BSC Young Boys	
1992	FC Luzern	3–1	FC Lugano	

INTERNATIONAL MATCHES PLAYED BY SWITZERLAND

Date	Opponents	Result		Venue	Compet	Scorers
12-02-1905	France	L	0–1	Paris	Fr	
8-03-1908	France	L	1–2	Geneva	Fr	Frenken
5-04	Germany	W	5–3	Basle	Fr	Pfeiffer 2, Kämpfer 2, Hug
4-04-1909	Germany	L	0–1	Karlsruhe	Fr	
20-05	England*	L	0–9	Basle	Fr	
3-04-1910	Germany	L	2–3	Basle	Fr	Müller, Renand
9-04	England*	L	1–6	London	Fr	Sydler H
8-01-1911	Hungary	W	2–0	Zurich	Fr	Wyss P, Collet
26-03	Germany	L	2–6	Stuttgart	Fr	Weiss, Collet
23-04	France	W	5–2	Geneva	Fr	Rubli 2, Wyss P 2, Sydler (III)
7-05	Italy	D	2–2	Milan	Fr	Hassler, Sydler (III)
21-05	Italy	W	3–0	Chaux de Fonds	Fr	Wyss P, Sydler H, Sydler (III)
25-05	England*	L	1–4	Berne	Fr	Wyss P
29-10	Hungary	L	0–9	Budapest	Fr	
18-02-1912	France	L	1–4	Paris	Fr	Wyss P
20-02	Belgium	L	2–9	Antwerp	Fr	Weiss, Wyss P
5-05	Germany	L	1–2	St Gallen	Fr	Weiss
9-03-1913	France	L	1–4	Geneva	Fr	Rubli
4-05	Belgium	L	1–2	Basle	Fr	Wydler
18-05	Germany	W	2–1	Freiburg	Fr	Märki, Collet
2-11	Belgium	L	0–2	Verviers	Fr	
8-03-1914	France	D	2–2	Paris	Fr	Schreyer, Albicker
5-04	Italy	D	1–1	Genoa	Fr	Wyss P
17-05	Italy	L	0–1	Berne	Fr	
31-01-1915	Italy	L	1–3	Turin	Fr	Wyss P
23-12-1917	Austria	L	0–1	Basle	Fr	
26-12	Austria	W	3–2	Zurich	Fr	Haas 2, Huber
9-05-1918	Austria	L	1–5	Vienna	Fr	Keller
12-05	Hungary	L	1–2	Budapest	Fr	Keller
29-02-1920	France	L	0–2	Geneva	Fr	
28-03	Italy	W	3–0	Berne	Fr	Merkt 2, Kramer
16-05	Holland	W	2–1	Basle	Fr	Friedrich, Merkt
6-06	Sweden	W	1–0	Stockholm	Fr	Martenet
27-06	Germany	W	4–1	Zurich	Fr	Meyer 2, Merkt, Afflerbach
6-03-1921	Italy	L	1–2	Milan	Fr	Fontana
28-03	Holland	L	0–2	Amsterdam	Fr	
1-05	Austria	D	2–2	St Gallen	Fr	Brand, Friedrich
6-11	Italy	D	1–1	Geneva	Fr	Pache
26-03-1922	Germany	D	2–2	Frankfurt	Fr	Sturzenegger, Merkt
11-06	Austria	L	1–7	Vienna	Fr	Leiber
15-06	Hungary	D	1–1	Budapest	Fr	Merkt
19-11	Holland	W	5–0	Berne	Fr	Abegglen M 3, Pache, Leiber
3-12	Italy	D	2–2	Bologna	Fr	Pache, Ramseyer
21-12	Austria	W	2–0	Geneva	Fr	Leiber, Pache
11-03-1923	Hungary	L	1–6	Lausanne	Fr	Abegglen M
22-04	France	D	2–2	Paris	Fr	Afflerbach 2
3-06	Germany	L	1–2	Basle	Fr	Pache
17-06	Denmark	L	2–3	Copenhagen	Fr	Pache, Abegglen M
21-06	Norway	D	2–2	Oslo	Fr	Afflerbach, Charpillod
25-11	Holland	L	1–4	Amsterdam	Fr	De Lavallaz
23-03-1924	France	W	3–0	Geneva	Fr	Krammer E, Pache, Dietrich
21-04	Denmark	W	2–0	Basle	Fr	Abegglen M, Dietrich
18-05	Hungary	W	4–2	Zurich	Fr	Abegglen M, Dietrich, Sturzenegger 2
25-05	Lithuania	W	9–0	Paris	OGpr	Sturzenegger 4, Abegglen M 3, Ramseyer, Dietrich
28-05	Czechoslovakia	D	1–1	Paris	OGr1	Dietrich
30-05	Czechoslovakia	W	1–0	Paris	OGr1	Pache
2-06	Italy	W	2–1	Paris	OGqf	Sturzenegger, Abegglen M
5-06	Sweden	W	2–1	Paris	OGsf	Abegglen M 2

9–06	Uruguay	L	0–3	Paris	OGf	
14–12	Germany	D	1–1	Stuttgart	Fr	Dietrich
22–03–1925	Austria	L	0–2	Vienna	Fr	
25–03	Hungary	L	0–5	Budapest	Fr	
19–04	Holland	W	4–1	Zurich	Fr	Hürzeler 2, Sturzenegger, Abegglen J
24–05	Belgium	D	0–0	Lausanne	Fr	
1–06	Spain	L	0–3	Berne	Fr	
25–10	Germany	L	0–4	Basle	Fr	
8–11	Austria	W	2–0	Berne	Fr	Abegglen M, Passello
28–03–1926	Holland	L	0–5	Amsterdam	Fr	
18–04	Italy	D	1–1	Zurich	Fr	Ehrenbolger
25–04	France	L	0–1	Paris	Fr	
9–05	Italy	L	2–3	Milan	Fr	Sturzenegger, Brand
10–10	Austria	L	1–7	Vienna	Fr	Poretti A
12–12	Germany	W	3–2	Munich	Fr	Brand, Weiler M, Fink
30–01–1927	Italy	L	1–5	Geneva	Fr	Weiler W
17–04	Spain	L	0–1	Santander	Fr	
29–05	Austria	L	1–4	Zurich	Fr	Jäggi W
6–11	Sweden	D	2–2	Zurich	Fr	Ramseyer, Abegglen M
1–01–1928	Italy	L	2–3	Genoa	DGC	Abegglen M 2
11–03	France	W	4–3	Lausanne	Fr	Jäggi W 3, Romberg
15–04	Germany	L	2–3	Berne	Fr	Jäggi W 2
6–05	Holland	W	2–1	Basle	Fr	Tschirren, Abegglen M
28–05	Germany	L	0–4	Amsterdam	OGr1	
14–10	Italy	L	2–3	Zurich	DGC	Abegglen M, Grimm
28–10	Austria	L	0–2	Vienna	DGC	
1–11	Hungary	L	1–3	Budapest	DGC	Weiler W
10–02–1929	Germany	L	1–7	Mannheim	Fr	Abegglen M
17–03	Holland	L	2–3	Amsterdam	Fr	Abegglen A, Grimm
14–04	Hungary	L	4–5	Berne	DGC	Abegglen A 2, Abegglen A, Weiler M
5–05	Czechoslovakia	L	1–4	Lausanne	DGC	Abegglen M
6–10	Czechoslovakia	L	0–5	Prague	DGC	
27–10	Austria	L	1–3	Berne	DGC	Passello
9–02–1930	Italy	L	2–4	Rome	Fr	Poretti A 2
23–03	France	D	3–3	Paris	Fr	Lehmann 2, Romberg
13–04	Hungary	D	2–2	Basle	Fr	Baumeister, Ramseyer
4–05	Germany	L	0–5	Zurich	Fr	
15–06	Sweden	L	0–1	Stockholm	Fr	
19–06	Norway	L	0–3	Oslo	Fr	
2–11	Holland	W	6–3	Zurich	Fr	Abegglen A 3, Jäggi W, Poretti A, Grassi
29–03–1931	Italy	D	1–1	Berne	DGC	Abegglen A
12–04	Hungary	L	2–6	Budapest	DGC	Abegglen A 2
24–05	Scotland	L	2–3	Geneva	Fr	Büche, Faugel
13–06	Czechoslovakia	L	3–7	Prague	DGC	Fasson, Büche, Springer
16–06	Austria	L	0–2	Vienna	Fr	
29–11	Austria	L	1–8	Basle	DGC	Abegglen A
6–12	Belgium	L	1–2	Brussels	Fr	Ehrismann
14–02–1932	Italy	L	0–3	Naples	DGC	
6–03	Germany	L	0–2	Leipzig	Fr	
20–03	France	D	3–3	Berne	Fr	Abegglen M, Abegglen A 2
17–04	Czechoslovakia	W	5–1	Zurich	DGC	Abegglen A 2, Abegglen M 2, Billeter
19–06	Hungary	W	3–1	Berne	DGC	Von Känel, Passello, Abegglen A
23–10	Austria	L	1–3	Vienna	DGC	Abegglen A
6–11	Sweden	W	2–1	Basle	Fr	Abegglen M 2
22–01–1933	Holland	W	2–0	Amsterdam	Fr	Jäggi W, Von Känel
12–03	Belgium	D	3–3	Zurich	Fr	Abegglen A 2, Abegglen M
2–04	Italy	L	0–3	Geneva	DGC	
7–05	Yugoslavia	W	4–1	Zurich	Fr	Abegglen M 2, Von Känel, Jaeck
20–05	England	L	0–4	Berne	Fr	
17–09	Hungary	L	0–3	Budapest	DGC	
24–09	Yugoslavia	D	2–2	Belgrade	WCq	Jäggi W, Frigerio
29–10	Romania	D	2–2	Berne	WCq	Hufschmid, Hochstrasser
19–11	Germany	L	0–2	Zurich	Fr	
3–12	Italy	L	2–5	Florence	DGC	Kielholz, Bossi
11–03–1934	France	W	1–0	Paris	Fr	Kielholz
25–03	Austria	L	2–3	Geneva	DGC	Bossi, Kielholz
27–05	Holland	W	3–2	Milan	WCr1	Kielholz 2, Abegglen A
31–05	Czechoslovakia	L	2–3	Turin	WCqf	Jäggi W, Kielholz
14–10	Czechoslovakia	D	2–2	Geneva	DGC	Kielholz 2

4–11	Holland	L	2–4	Berne	Fr	Spagnoli, Jäggi W
11–11	Austria	L	0–3	Vienna	DGC	
27–01–1935	Germany	L	0–4	Stuttgart	Fr	
17–03	Czechoslovakia	L	1–3	Prague	DGC	Bösch
14–04	Hungary	W	6–2	Zurich	DGC	Kielholz 3, Abegglen A 2, Jaeck
5–05	Rep. Ireland	W	1–0	Basle	Fr	Weiler W
30–05	Belgium	D	2–2	Brussels	Fr	Kielholz, OG
27–10	France	W	2–1	Geneva	Fr	Abegglen A, Jäggi W
3–11	Norway	W	2–0	Zurich	Fr	Stelzer, Jäggi W
10–11	Hungary	L	1–6	Budapest	Fr	Abegglen A
17–03–1936	Rep. Ireland	L	0–1	Dublin	Fr	
5–04	Italy	L	1–2	Zurich	Fr	Weiler W
3–05	Spain	L	0–2	Berne	Fr	
24–05	Belgium	D	1–1	Basle	Fr	Ciseri
18–06	Norway	W	2–1	Oslo	Fr	Abegglen M 2
21–06	Sweden	L	2–5	Stockholm	Fr	Aebi, Bickel
25–10	Italy	L	2–4	Milan	DGC	Bickel, Diebold
8–11	Austria	L	1–3	Zurich	DGC	OG
21–02–1937	Czechoslovakia	L	3–5	Prague	DGC	Bickel 2, Wagner
7–03	Holland	L	1–2	Amsterdam	Fr	Abegglen M
11–04	Hungary	L	1–5	Basle	DGC	Aeby G
18–04	Belgium	W	2–1	Brussels	Fr	Abegglen M, Bickel
2–05	Germany	L	0–1	Zurich	Fr	
17–05	Rep. Ireland	L	0–1	Berne	Fr	
19–09	Austria	L	3–4	Vienna	DGC	Walaschek, Aebi, Aeby G
10–10	France	L	1–2	Paris	Fr	Rupf
31–10	Italy	D	2–2	Geneva	DGC	Walaschek, Wagner
14–11	Hungary	L	0–2	Budapest	DGC	
6–02–1938	Germany	D	1–1	Cologne	Fr	Aeby G
13–03	Poland	D	3–3	Zurich	Fr	Amadò 2, Abegglen A
3–04	Czechoslovakia	W	4–0	Basle	DGC	Monnard, Grassi, Aeby G, Amadò
1–05	Portugal	W	2–1	Milan	WCq	Aeby G, Amadò
8–05	Belgium	L	0–3	Lausanne	Fr	
21–05	England	W	2–1	Zurich	Fr	Abey G, Abegglen A
4–06	Germany	D	1–1	Paris	WCr1	Abegglen A
9–06	Germany	W	4–2	Paris	WCr1	Abegglen A 2, Walaschek, Bickel
12–06	Hungary	L	0–2	Lille	WCqf	
18–09	Rep. Ireland	L	0–4	Dublin	Fr	
6–11	Portugal	W	1–0	Lausanne	Fr	Aebi P
20–11	Italy	L	0–2	Bologna	Fr	
12–02–1939	Portugal	W	4–2	Lisbon	Fr	Aeby G 2, Bickel, Sydler C
2–04	Hungary	W	3–1	Zurich	Fr	Aeby G, Aebi, Walaschek
7–05	Holland	W	2–1	Berne	Fr	Amadò 2
14–05	Belgium	W	2–1	Liege	Fr	Abegglen A, Amadò
4–06	Poland	D	1–1	Warsaw	Fr	Amadò
12–11	Italy	W	3–1	Zurich	Fr	Monnard, Aeby G
3–03–1940	Italy	D	1–1	Turin	Fr	Bickel
31–03	Hungary	L	0–3	Budapest	Fr	
9–03–1941	Germany	L	2–4	Stuttgart	Fr	Monnard, OG
20–04	Germany	W	2–1	Berne	Fr	Monnard, Amadò
16–11	Hungary	L	1–2	Zurich	Fr	Monnard
28–12	Spain	L	2–3	Valencia	Fr	Kappenburger, Aeby R
1–01–1942	Portugal	L	0–3	Lisbon	Fr	
1–02	Germany	W	2–1	Vienna	Fr	Kappenburger 2
8–03	France	W	2–0	Marseille	Fr	Amadò, Kappenburger
18–10	Germany	L	3–5	Berne	Fr	Bickel, Amadò, Kappenburger
1–11	Hungary	L	0–3	Budapest	Fr	
15–11	Sweden	W	3–1	Zurich	Fr	Friedländer, Amadò, Bickel
16–05–1943	Hungary	L	1–3	Geneva	Fr	Monnard
14–06	Sweden	L	0–1	Stockholm	Fr	
8–04–1945	France	W	1–0	Lausanne	Fr	Friedländer
21–05	Portugal	W	1–0	Basle	Fr	Friedländer
11–11	Italy	D	4–4	Zurich	Fr	Amadò 3, Aeby G
25–11	Sweden	W	3–0	Geneva	Fr	Amadò 2, Friedländer
11–05–1946	England*	L	1–4	London	Fr	Friedländer
25–05	Scotland*	L	1–3	Glasgow	Fr	Aeby G
7–07	Sweden	L	2–7	Stockholm	Fr	Lanz, Courtat
14–09	Czechoslovakia	L	2–3	Prague	Fr	Amadò 2
10–11	Austria	W	1–0	Berne	Fr	Pasteur

5-01-1947	Portugal	D	2-2	Lisbon	Fr	Fatton 2
27-04	Italy	L	2-5	Florence	Fr	Fatton, Bocquet
18-05	England	W	1-0	Zurich	Fr	Fatton
8-06	France	L	1-2	Lausanne	Fr	Fatton
21-09	Holland	L	2-6	Amsterdam	Fr	Maillard, Amadò
2-11	Belgium	W	4-0	Geneva	Fr	Tamini, Fatton, Lusenti, Maillard
18-04-1948	Austria	L	1-3	Vienna	Fr	Fatton
21-04	Hungary	L	4-7	Budapest	DGC	Lusenti, Amadò, Maillard, Tamini
17-05	Scotland	W	2-1	Berne	Fr	Maillard, Fatton
20-06	Spain	D	3-3	Zurich	Fr	OG, Friedländer, Antenen
10-10	Czechoslovakia	D	1-1	Basle	DGC	Friedländer
2-12	England	L	0-6	London	Fr	
5-12	Rep. Ireland	W	1-0	Dublin	Fr	Bickel
3-04-1949	Austria	L	1-2	Lausanne	DGC	Bickel
26-05	Wales	W	4-0	Berne	Fr	Fatton 2, Ballaman 2, Pasteur
4-06	France	L	2-4	Paris	Fr	Fatton 2
26-06	Luxembourg	W	5-2	Zurich	WCq	Fatton 2, Maillard, Ballaman, Antenen
18-09	Luxembourg	W	3-2	Luxembourg	WCq	Maillard, Oberer, Fatton
2-10	Belgium	L	0-3	Brussels	Fr	
19-03-1950	Austria	D	3-3	Vienna	DGC	Fatton, Tamini, Oberer
26-04	Scotland	L	1-3	Glasgow	Fr	Antenen
11-06	Yugoslavia	L	0-4	Berne	Fr	
25-06	Yugoslavia	L	0-3	Belo Horizonte	WCr1	
28-06	Brazil	D	2-2	Sao Paulo	WCr1	Fatton 2
2-07	Mexico	W	2-1	Porto Alegre	WCr1	Bader, Antenen
15-10	Holland	W	7-5	Basle	Fr	Fatton 3, Friedländer 2, Antenen 2
12-11	Sweden	W	4-2	Geneva	Fr	Fatton 2, Friedländer, Antenen
22-11	West Germany	L	0-1	Stuttgart	Fr	
18-02-1951	Spain	L	3-6	Madrid	Fr	Bickel 2, OG
15-04	West Germany	L	2-3	Zurich	Fr	Bocquet, Fatton
16-05	Wales	L	2-3	Wrexham	Fr	Ballaman, Antenen
24-06	Yugoslavia	L	3-7	Belgrade	Fr	Ballaman 2, Bickel
14-10	France	L	1-2	Geneva	Fr	Ballaman
25-11	Italy	D	1-1	Lugano	DGC	Riva
28-05-1952	England	L	0-3	Zurich	Fr	
1-06	Turkey	W	5-1	Ankara	Fr	Riva 2, Hügi J 2, Pasteur
22-06	Austria	D	1-1	Geneva	Fr	Riva
20-09	Hungary	L	2-4	Berne	DGC	Hügi J, Fatton
9-11	West Germany	L	1-5	Augsburg	Fr	Friedländer
28-12	Italy	L	0-2	Palermo	DGC	
22-03-1953	Holland	W	2-1	Amsterdam	Fr	Mauron, Hügi J
25-05	Turkey	L	1-2	Berne	Fr	Meier
27-06	Denmark	L	1-4	Basle	Fr	Hügi J
20-09	Czechoslovakia	L	0-5	Prague	DGC	
11-11	France	W	4-2	Paris	Fr	Antenen 3, Fatton
22-11	Belgium	D	2-2	Zurich	Fr	Fatton, Antenen
25-04-1954	West Germany	L	3-5	Basle	Fr	Fatton, Ballaman, Kernan
23-05	Uruguay	D	3-3	Lausanne	Fr	Casali, Ballaman, Antenen
30-05	Holland	W	3-1	Zurich	Fr	Vonlanthen 3
17-06	Italy	W	2-1	Lausanne	WCr1	Hügi J, Ballaman
20-06	England	L	0-2	Berne	WCr1	
23-06	Italy	W	4-1	Basle	WCr1	Hügi J 2, Ballaman, Fatton
26-06	Austria	L	5-7	Lausanne	WCqf	Hügi J 3, Ballaman 2
19-09	Denmark	D	1-1	Copenhagen	Fr	Antenen
10-10	Hungary	L	0-3	Budapest	Fr	

LEADING INTERNATIONAL APPEARANCES

1	Hermann H	117
2	Minelli	80
3	Geiger	74
4	Bickel	71
5	Abegglen M	68
	Wehrli	68
7	Egli	67
8	Botteron	65
9	Burgener	64
10	Kuhn	63
11	Ramseyer	59
12	Antenen	56
	Sutter B	56
14	Amadò	54
	Barberis	54
16	Fatton	53
17	Abegglen A	52
18	Ballaman	50
	Odermatt	50
20	Bocquet	48
21	Sulser	46
22	Eggimann	44
23	Schneiter	44
24	Künzli	42
	Luedi	42
	Meier	42
	Tacchella	42

1-05-1955	Austria	L	2-3	Berne	DGC	Hügi J, Vonlanthen
19-05	Holland	L	1-4	Rotterdam	Fr	Hügi J
19-06	Spain	L	0-3	Geneva	Fr	
26-06	Yugoslavia	D	0-0	Belgrade	DGC	
17-09	Hungary	L	4-5	Lausanne	DGC	Vonlanthen 2, Antenen 2
9-10	France	L	1-2	Basle	Fr	Mauron
11-03-1956	Belgium	W	3-1	Brussels	Fr	Pastega, Ballaman, Meier
11-04	Brazil	D	1-1	Zurich	Fr	OG
1-05	Saar	D	1-1	Saarbrucken	Fr	Riva
10-05	Czechoslovakia	L	1-6	Geneva	DGC	Ballaman
15-09	Holland	L	2-3	Lausanne	Fr	Antenen, Riva
11-11	Italy	D	1-1	Berne	DGC	Ballaman
21-11	West Germany	W	3-1	Frankfurt	Fr	Riva, Hügi J, Ballaman
10-03-1957	Spain	D	2-2	Madrid	WCq	Hügi J 2
14-04	Austria	L	0-4	Vienna	DGC	
19-05	Scotland	L	1-2	Basle	WCq	Vonlanthen
6-11	Scotland	L	2-3	Glasgow	WCq	Riva, Vonlanden
24-11	Spain	L	1-4	Lausanne	WCq	Ballaman
16-04-1958	France	D	0-0	Paris	Fr	
7-05	Sweden	L	2-3	Halsingborg	Fr	Allemann 2
26-05	Belgium	L	0-2	Zurich	Fr	
20-09	Czechoslovakia	L	1-2	Bratislava	DGC	Meier
2-11	Holland	L	0-2	Rotterdam	Fr	
26-04-1959	Yugoslavia	L	1-5	Basle	DGC	Rey
16-05	Portugal	W	4-3	Geneva	Fr	Burger 2, Hamel, Frey
4-10	West Germany	L	0-4	Berne	Fr	
25-10	Hungary	L	0-8	Budapest	DGC	
6-01-1960	Italy	L	0-3	Naples	DGC	
27-03	Belgium	L	1-3	Brussels	Fr	Allemann
6-04	Chile	W	4-2	Basle	Fr	OG, Hügi J, Allemann, Vonlanthen
18-05	Holland	W	3-1	Zurich	Fr	Allemann 2, Hügi J
12-10	France	W	6-2	Basle	Fr	Hügi J 5, Weber H
20-11	Belgium	W	4-2	Brussels	WCq	Antenen 3, Schneiter
20-05-1961	Belgium	W	2-1	Lausanne	WCq	Ballaman, OG
28-05	Sweden	L	0-4	Stockholm	WCq	
29-10	Sweden	W	3-2	Berne	WCq	Antenen, Wüthrich, Eschmann
12-11	Sweden	W	2-1	Berlin	WCq	Schneiter, Antenen
9-05-1962	England	L	1-3	London	Fr	Allemann
30-05	Chile	L	1-3	Santiago	WCr1	Wüthrich
3-06	West Germany	L	1-2	Santiago	WCr1	Schneiter
7-06	Italy	L	0-3	Santiago	WCr1	
11-11	Holland	L	1-3	Amsterdam	ECr1	Hertig
23-12	West Germany	L	1-5	Karlsruhe	Fr	Brodmann
13-01-1963	Morocco	L	0-1	Casablanca	Fr	
31-03	Holland	D	1-1	Berne	ECr1	Allemann
5-06	England	L	1-8	Basle	Fr	Bertschi
3-11	Norway	L	0-2	Zurich	Fr	
11-11	France	D	2-2	Paris	Fr	OG, Bosson
15-04-1964	Belgium	W	2-0	Geneva	Fr	Schindelholz, Bertschi
29-04	Portugal	L	2-3	Zurich	Fr	OG, Eschmann
10-05	Italy	L	1-3	Lausanne	Fr	Eschmann
1-07	Norway	L	2-3	Bergen	Fr	Grünig 2
4-10	Hungary	L	0-2	Berne	Fr	
14-10	Nth. Ireland	L	0-1	Belfast	WCq	
14-11	Nth. Ireland	W	2-1	Lausanne	WCq	Quentin, Kuhn
11-04-1965	Albania	W	2-0	Tirana	WCq	Quentin, Kuhn
2-05	Albania	W	1-0	Geneva	WCq	Kuhn
26-05	West Germany	L	0-1	Basle	Fr	
17-10	Holland	D	0-0	Amsterdam	WCq	
14-11	Holland	W	2-1	Berne	WCq	Allemann, Hosp
20-04-1966	Soviet Union	D	2-2	Basle	Fr	Hosp, Grobéty
5-06	Hungary	L	1-3	Budapest	Fr	Kuhn
19-06	Mexico	D	1-1	Lausanne	Fr	Odermatt
12-07	West Germany	L	0-5	Sheffield	WCr1	
15-07	Spain	L	1-2	Sheffield	WCr1	Quentin
19-07	Argentina	L	0-2	Sheffield	WCr1	
22-10	Belgium	L	0-1	Bruges	Fr	
2-11	Romania	L	2-4	Bucharest	ECq	Künzli, Odermatt
5-01-1967	Mexico	L	0-3	Mexico City	Fr	

3–05	Czechoslovakia	L	1–2	Basle	Fr	Odermatt
24–05	Romania	W	7–1	Zurich	ECq	Künzli 2, Blättler 2, Quentin, Odermatt, OG
1–10	Soviet Union	D	2–2	Moscow	Fr	Blättler, Perroud
8–11	Cyprus	W	5–0	Lugano	ECq	Blättler 2, Künzli, Dürr, Odermatt
18–11	Italy	D	2–2	Berne	ECq	Quentin, Künzli
23–12	Italy	L	0–4	Cagliari	ECq	
14–02–1968	Israel	L	1–2	Tel Aviv	Fr	Künzli, OG
17–02	Cyprus	L	1–2	Nicosia	ECq	OG
17–04	West Germany	D	0–0	Basle	Fr	
22–09	Austria	W	1–0	Berne	Fr	Quentin
12–10	Greece	W	1–0	Basle	WCq	Quentin
23–11	Romania	L	0–2	Bucharest	WCq	
26–03–1969	Spain	L	0–1	Valencia	Fr	
16–04	Portugal	W	2–0	Lisbon	WCq	Vuilleumier 2
14–05	Romania	L	0–1	Lausanne	WCq	
24–09	Turkey	L	0–3	Istanbul	Fr	
15–10	Greece	L	1–4	Salonika	WCq	Künzli
2–11	Portugal	D	1–1	Berne	WCq	Künzli
22–04–1970	Spain	L	0–1	Lausanne	Fr	
3–05	France	W	2–1	Basle	Fr	Blättler 2
17–10	Italy	D	1–1	Berne	Fr	Blättler
15–11	Hungary	L	0–1	Basle	Fr	
16–12	Greece	W	1–0	Athens	ECq	Müller K
20–12	Malta	W	2–1	Gzira	ECq	Quentin, Künzli
21–04–1971	Malta	W	5–0	Lucerne	ECq	Blättler, Künzli, Quentin, Citherlet, Müller K
5–05	Poland	L	2–4	Lausanne	Fr	Künzli, Kuhn
12–05	Greece	W	1–0	Berne	ECq	Odermatt
26–09	Turkey	W	4–0	Zurich	Fr	Boffi, Odermatt, Balmer, Blättler
13–10	England	L	2–3	Basle	ECq	Jeandupeux, Künzli
10–11	England	D	1–1	London	ECq	Odermatt
26–04–1972	Sweden	D	1–1	Geneva	Fr	Blättler
10–05	Poland	D	0–0	Poznan	Fr	
4–10	Denmark	D	1–1	Copenhagen	Fr	Balmer
21–10	Italy	D	0–0	Berne	WCq	
15–11	West Germany	L	1–5	Dusseldorf	Fr	Künzli
8–04–1973	Luxembourg	W	1–0	Luxembourg	WCq	Odermatt
9–05	Turkey	D	0–0	Basle	WCq	
22–06	Scotland	W	1–0	Berne	Fr	Mundschin
26–09	Luxembourg	W	1–0	Lucerne	WCq	Blättler
20–10	Italy	L	0–2	Rome	WCq	
18–11	Turkey	L	0–2	Izmir	WCq	
1–05–1974	Belgium	L	0–1	Geneva	Fr	
9–06	Sweden	D	0–0	Malmo	Fr	
4–09	West Germany	L	1–2	Basle	Fr	Müller K
9–10	Holland	L	0–1	Rotterdam	Fr	
13–11	Portugal	W	3–0	Berne	Fr	Jeandupeux, Pfister, Schild
1–12	Turkey	L	1–2	Izmir	ECq	Schild
4–12	Hungary	L	0–1	Szolnok	Fr	
30–04–1975	Turkey	D	1–1	Zurich	ECq	OG
10–05	Rep. Ireland	L	1–2	Dublin	ECq	Müller K
21–05	Rep. Ireland	W	1–0	Berne	ECq	Elsener
3–09	England	L	1–2	Basle	Fr	Müller K

LEADING INTERNATIONAL GOALSCORERS

1	Abegglen M	32
2	Abegglen A	30
3	Fatton	29
4	Hügi J	23
5	Antenen	22
6	Amadò	21
7	Ballaman	18
8	Künzli	15
	Bickel	15
10	Hermann H	14
	Türkyilmaz	14
12	Jäggi W	13
	Abey G	13
	Sulser	13
	Sutter B	12
16	Blättler	12
	Kielholz	12
18	Friedländer	11
19	Sturzenegger	10
	Odermatt	10
21	Allemann	9
	Quentin	9
	Wyss P	9
24	Pache	8
	Riva	8
	Vonlanthen	8
	Egli	8
28	Barberis	7
	Müller K	7
	Bregy	7

24-09	Czechoslovakia	D	1-1	Brno	Fr	Risi
12-10	Soviet Union	L	0-1	Zurich	ECq	
12-11	Soviet Union	L	1-4	Kiev	ECq	Risi
7-04-1976	Scotland	L	0-1	Glasgow	Fr	
30-04	Hungary	L	0-1	Lausanne	Fr	
11-05	Poland	W	2-1	Basle	Fr	Bizzini, Barberis
19-05	Finland	L	0-1	Kuopio	Fr	
17-08	Bulgaria	D	2-2	Lucerne	Fr	Müller K, Künzli
8-09	Norway	L	0-1	Oslo	WCq	
22-09	Austria	L	1-3	Linz	Fr	Trinchero
9-10	Sweden	L	1-2	Basle	WCq	Trinchero
30-03-1977	Portugal	L	0-1	Funchal	Fr	
23-04	France	L	0-4	Geneva	Fr	
24-05	Czechoslovakia	W	1-0	Basle	Fr	Müller K
8-06	Sweden	L	1-2	Stockholm	WCq	Risi
7-09	England	D	0-0	London	Fr	
21-09	Spain	L	1-2	Berne	Fr	Elsener
5-10	Finland	W	2-0	Zurich	Fr	Elsener, Küttel
30-10	Norway	W	1-0	Berne	WCq	Sulser
16-11	West Germany	L	1-4	Stuttgart	Fr	Meyer
8-03-1978	East Germany	L	1-3	Karl-Marx-Stadt	Fr	Sulser
4-04	Austria	L	0-1	Basle	Fr	
6-09	United States	W	2-0	Lucerne	Fr	Elsener, Schnyder
11-10	Holland	L	1-3	Berne	ECq	Tanner
15-11	Poland	L	0-2	Wroclaw	ECq	
28-03-1979	Holland	L	0-3	Eindhoven	ECq	
5-05	East Germany	L	0-2	St Gallen	ECq	
22-05	Iceland	W	2-0	Berne	ECq	Zappa, Hermann Hr
9-06	Iceland	W	2-1	Reykjavik	ECq	Hermann H, Ponte
12-09	Poland	L	0-2	Lausanne	ECq	
13-10	East Germany	L	2-5	Berlin	ECq	Barberis, Pfister
17-11	Italy	L	0-2	Udine	Fr	
26-03-1980	Czechoslovakia	W	2-0	Basle	Fr	Sulser, Barberis
1-04	Greece	W	2-0	Zurich	Fr	Schnyder 2
30-04	Rep. Ireland	L	0-2	Dublin	Fr	
27-08	Denmark	D	1-1	Lausanne	Fr	Pfister
10-09	West Germany	L	2-3	Basle	Fr	Pfister, Botteron
29-10	Norway	L	1-2	Berne	WCq	Barberis
19-11	England	L	1-2	London	WCq	Pfister
16-12	Argentina	L	0-5	Cordoba	Fr	
18-12	Uruguay	L	0-4	Montevideo	Fr	
21-12	Brazil	L	0-2	Cuiaba	Fr	
24-03-1981	Czechoslovakia	W	1-0	Bratislava	Fr	Botteron
28-04	Hungary	D	2-2	Lucerne	WCq	Sulser 2
30-05	England	W	2-1	Basle	WCq	Scheiwilder, Sulser
17-06	Norway	D	1-1	Oslo	WCq	Barberis
1-09	Holland	W	2-1	Zurich	Fr	Favre, Elia
10-10	Romania	W	2-1	Bucharest	WCq	Zappa, Lüthi
14-10	Hungary	L	0-3	Budapest	WCq	
11-11	Romania	D	0-0	Berne	WCq	
24-03-1982	Portugal	W	2-1	Lugano	Fr	Zappa, Egli
28-04	Spain	L	0-2	Valencia	Fr	
19-05	Brazil	D	1-1	Recife	Fr	Sulser
28-05	Italy	D	1-1	Geneva	Fr	Barberis
7-09	Bulgaria	W	3-2	St Gallen	Fr	Sulser, Elsener, OG
6-10	Belgium	L	0-3	Brussels	ECq	
27-10	Italy	W	1-0	Rome	Fr	Elsener
17-11	Scotland	W	2-0	Berne	ECq	Sulser, Egli
1-12	Greece	W	3-1	Athens	Fr	Sulser 2, Egli
7-03-1983	Bulgaria	D	1-1	Varna	Fr	Ponte
30-03	Scotland	D	2-2	Glasgow	ECq	Egli, Hermann H
13-04	Soviet Union	L	0-1	Lausanne	Fr	
14-05	East Germany	D	0-0	Berne	ECq	
17-06	Brazil	L	1-2	Basle	Fr	Koller
7-09	Czechoslovakia	D	0-0	Neuchatel	Fr	
12-10	East Germany	L	0-3	Berlin	ECq	
26-10	Yugoslavia	W	2-0	Basle	Fr	Sutter B, Brigger
9-11	Belgium	W	3-1	Berne	ECq	Schällibaum, Brigger, Geiger
30-11	Algeria	W	2-1	Algiers	Fr	Jaccard, Hermann H

2–12	Ivory Coast	L	0–1	Abidjan	Fr	
4–12	Zimbabwe	L	2–3	Harare	Fr	In-Albon, Lüdi
6–12	Kenya	D	0–0	Mombasa	Fr	
27–03–1984	Poland	D	1–1	Zurich	Fr	Hermann H
2–05	Sweden	D	0–0	Berne	Fr	
26–05	Spain	L	0–4	Geneva	Fr	
22–08	Hungary	L	0–3	Budapest	Fr	
1–09	Argentina	L	0–2	Berne	Fr	
12–09	Norway	W	1–0	Oslo	WCq	Egli
17–10	Denmark	W	1–0	Berne	WCq	Barberis
3–11	Italy	D	1–1	Lausanne	Fr	Bregy
1–02–1985	Colombia	D	2–2	Bogota	Fr	Hermann H, Schällibaum
5–02	Bulgaria	L	0–1	Queretaro	Fr	
6–02	Mexico	W	2–1	Queretaro	Fr	Geiger, Bregy
8–02	United States	D	1–1	Tampa	Fr	Hermann H
27–03	Czechoslovakia	W	2–0	Sion	Fr	Sulser 2
17–04	Soviet Union	D	2–2	Berne	WCq	Bregy, Egli
2–05	Soviet Union	L	0–4	Moscow	WCq	
2–06	Rep. Ireland	L	0–3	Dublin	WCq	
28–08	Turkey	D	0–0	St Gallen	Fr	
11–09	Rep. Ireland	D	0–0	Berne	WCq	
9–10	Denmark	D	0–0	Copenhagen	WCq	
13–11	Norway	D	1–1	Lucerne	WCq	Matthey
12–03–1986	Turkey	L	0–1	Adana	Fr	
9–04	West Germany	L	0–1	Basle	Fr	
6–05	Algeria	W	2–0	Geneva	Fr	Hermann H 2
19–08	France	W	2–0	Lausanne	Fr	Hermann H, Sutter B
27–08	Austria	D	1–1	Innsbruck	Fr	Bickel
24–09	Sweden	L	0–2	Stockholm	ECq	
29–10	Portugal	D	1–1	Berne	ECq	Bregy
15–11	Italy	L	2–3	Milan	ECq	Brigger, Webber
25–03–1987	Czechoslovakia	L	1–2	Bellinzona	Fr	Hermann H
15–04	Malta	W	4–1	Neuchatel	ECq	Egli, Bregy 3
19–05	Israel	W	1–0	Aarau	Fr	Bonvin
17–06	Sweden	D	1–1	Lausanne	ECq	Halter
18–08	Austria	D	2–2	St Gallen	Fr	Bonvin, Sutter B
17–10	Italy	D	0–0	Berne	ECq	
11–11	Portugal	D	0–0	Oporto	ECq	
15–11	Malta	D	1–1	Ta'Qali	ECq	Zwicker
16–12	Israel	W	2–0	Tel Aviv	Fr	Sutter B, Bonvin
2–02–1988	France	L	1–2	Toulouse	Fr	Sutter B
5–02	Austria	W	2–1	Monaco	Fr	Koller, Sutter B
27–04	West Germany	L	0–1	Kaiserslautern	Fr	
28–05	England	L	0–1	Lausanne	Fr	
5–06	Spain	D	1–1	Basle	Fr	Sutter B
24–08	Yugoslavia	L	0–2	Lucerne	Fr	
21–09	Luxembourg	W	4–1	Luxembourg	WCq	Sutter A, Türkyilmaz 2, Sutter B
19–10	Belgium	L	0–1	Brussels	WCq	
14–12	Egypt	W	3–1	Cairo	Fr	Zuffi 2, Hermann H
4–04–1989	Hungary	L	0–3	Budapest	Fr	
26–04	Portugal	L	1–3	Lisbon	WCq	Zuffi
7–06	Czechoslovakia	L	0–1	Berne	WCq	
21–06	Brazil	W	1–0	Basle	Fr	Türkyilmaz
20–09	Portugal	L	1–2	Neuchatel	WCq	Türkyilmaz
11–10	Belgium	D	2–2	Basle	WCq	Knup, Türkyilmaz
25–10	Czechoslovakia	L	0–3	Prague	WCq	
15–11	Luxembourg	W	2–1	St Gallen	WCq	Bonvin, Türkyilmaz
13–12	Spain	L	1–2	Tenerife	Fr	Knup
31–03–1990	Italy	L	0–1	Basle	Fr	
3–04	Romania	W	2–1	Lucerne	Fr	Hermann H, Chassot
8–05	Argentina	D	1–1	Berne	Fr	Türkyilmaz
2–06	United States	W	2–1	St Gallen	Fr	Schepull, Knup
21–08	Austria	W	3–1	Vienna	Fr	Türkyilmaz 2, Knup
12–09	Bulgaria	W	2–0	Geneva	ECq	Hottiger, Bickel
17–10	Scotland	L	1–2	Glasgow	ECq	Knup
14–11	San Marino	W	4–0	Serravalle	ECq	Sutter A, Chapuisat, Knup, Chassot
19–12	Germany	L	0–4	Stuttgart	Fr	
2–02–1991	United States	W	1–0	Miami	Fr	Knup
3–02	Colombia	W	3–2	Miami	Fr	Koller, Sutter B 2

12–03	Liechtenstein	W	6–0	Balzers	Fr	Hermann H, Knup 3, Türkyilmaz, Aeby
3–04	Romania	D	0–0	Neuchatel	ECq	
1–05	Bulgaria	W	3–2	Sofia	ECq	Knup 2, Türkyilmaz
5–06	San Marino	W	7–0	St Gallen	ECq	Knup 2, Hottiger, Sutter B, Hermann H, Ohrel, Türkyilmaz
21–08	Czechoslovakia	D	1–1	Prague	Fr	Türkyilmaz
11–09	Scotland	D	2–2	Berne	ECq	Chapuisat, Hermann H
9–10	Sweden	W	3–1	Lucerne	Fr	Chapuisat, Herr, Türkyilmaz
13–11	Romania	L	0–1	Bucharest	ECq	
29–01–1992	UAE	W	2–0	Dubai	Fr	Sutter B, Bonvin
25–03	Rep. Ireland	L	1–2	Dublin	Fr	OG
28–04	Bulgaria	L	0–2	Berne	Fr	
27–05	France	W	2–1	Lausanne	Fr	Bonvin

TURKEY

Turkey are Europe's major under-achievers. There is a football revolution just waiting to happen. The interest is there, and there is an enormous amount of talent to be unearthed. With a population of over 55 million Turkey should be at the forefront of the European game.

The vast majority of Turkey is in fact in Asia, but the fact that Istanbul, the major footballing city, is located partly in Europe has meant that the Turks have always looked to European countries for competition. Due to a poor record in the past, however, Turkey's task will not be easy as they are usually listed as a bottom seed and therefore drawn against the top sides in both the World Cup and European Championship. Qualification for either of these events will always be difficult until the duck is eventually broken.

		All			League			Cup		Europe		
	Team	G	S	B	G	S	B	G	S	G	S	B
1	Galatasaray Istanbul	17	9	13	8	7	12	9	2	–	–	1
2	Fenerbahçe Istanbul	16	14	4	12	11	4	4	3	–	–	–
3	Besiktas Istanbul	11	12	3	8	9	3	3	3	–	–	–
4	Trabzonspor	10	7	3	6	3	3	4	4	–	–	–
5	Altay Izmir	2	5	2	–	–	2	2	5	–	–	–
6	MKE Ankaragücü	2	3	–	–	–	–	2	3	–	–	–
7	Göztepe Izmir	2	1	2	–	–	1	2	1	–	–	1
8	Eskisehirspor	1	5	2	–	3	2	1	2	–	–	–
9	Bursaspor	1	3	–	–	–	–	1	3	–	–	–
10	Gençlerbirligi Ankara	1	–	1	–	–	1	1	–	–	–	–
11	Sakaryaspor Adapazari	1	–	–	–	–	–	1	–	–	–	–
12	Samsunspor	–	1	2	–	–	2	–	1	–	–	–
13	Boluspor	–	1	1	–	–	1	–	1	–	–	–
14	Adana Demirspor	–	1	–	–	–	–	–	1	–	–	–
	Adanaspor	–	1	–	–	1	–	–	–	–	–	–
	Mersin Idman Yurdu	–	1	–	–	–	–	–	1	–	–	–
17	Malatyaspor	–	–	1	–	–	1	–	–	–	–	–
	Zonguldakspor	–	–	1	–	–	1	–	–	–	–	–

To the end of the 1991–92 season. Does not include wins prior to the professional league formation in 1959

Football first came to Turkey along with the British and a game is recorded in 1895 between English and Greek residents in Izmir. At this time, however, the foundations of the Ottoman Empire were crumbling and in an attempt to reverse the decline, the authorities were quick to stamp out any movement they perceived as a threat and football was regarded as just that. In one bizarre incident, a group of players were arrested after soldiers discovered shirts which were described as uniforms, a ball which they assumed was a cannon ball and a set of the rules in English which they took to be subversive literature!

In 1905 eight boys of the Galatasaray High School formed a team and they along with Fenerbahçe, formed in 1907, and the oldest club of them all Besiktas, formed in 1903, remain the top clubs of today. Until 1908 and the Young Turk Revolution, all clubs in Turkey operated in near secrecy. Seen as less of a threat by the new regime, the game enjoyed a brief period of growth. A league of sorts had been started in 1905 in Istanbul, but the Balkan Wars, the First World War, Civil War and then war with Greece put paid to any real efforts to promote the game until a republic with the present boundaries was declared in 1923.

As some semblance of peace was restored to the country, the Turkish Football Federation was formed later that year. Proper regional championships were started the following year with a view to staging a tournament to find the national champions at the end of the season, but the latter was only ever a regular occurrence in the late 1930s and early 40s and the winners of the Istanbul league were regarded as the top club until the formation of the professional national league in 1959.

In 1923 the Turks took on Romania in Istanbul in their first international match, but it was not until the 1960s that any great prominence was given to the national side. One player perhaps more than any other was responsible for the increased awareness of the game: Lefter Kücükandonyadis, from the Greek quarter of Istanbul, was Turkey's first player of genuine international class, and from his first appearance in 1948 he helped change the fortunes of the game in his country.

Turkey had entered the 1924, 1928 and 1936 Olympic Games but were knocked out in the first round of each. During these years there had been a few wins against their Balkan neighbours, but the overall record was poor. It reached the stage that between 1932 and 1948 only three games were played. In 1948 fortunes changed as the Federation once more fielded a side. The quarter-finals of the 1948 Olympic Games in London were reached and the following year the Turks qualified for the World Cup finals in Brazil.

In the light of subsequent failures to qualify, their withdrawal before the tournament got underway, due to the high expenses anticipated and the time needed to make the trip to Brazil, seems ridiculous, but four years later they were present in Switzerland for the 1954 tournament.

The situation was helped by the introduction of professionalism in 1951, and in June of that year they pulled off the first of a remarkable series of victories for which they became famous down the years when they beat West Germany 2–1 in Berlin. Admittedly the German game had not fully recovered from the war, but in qualifying for the 1954 World Cup they defeated Spain in Istanbul and drew 2–2 with them in a play-off in Rome, where they won the ensuing lots.

They had beaten Switzerland in Berne in 1953 but on their return for the World Cup the following year, despite scoring seven against the South Koreans, they could not beat the Germans for a second time and bowed out of their sole World Cup Finals appearance after a play-off.

More good results were to follow, however. Portugal were beaten at home in 1955, whilst most impressive of all, and inspired by Lefter who scored two goals, the Turks ended Hungary's two-year unbeaten run with a 3–2 victory in Istanbul in 1956. Both Poland and Holland were defeated away from home before the end of the decade, and although not members of UEFA until 1962, Turkey were invited to take part in the initial European Championship and were unlucky to lose out to Romania in the first round on goal average.

Alongside Lefter in what still stand out as the best teams Turkey has fielded were players such as Metin Otkay and Burhan Sargin who between them scored 47 goals for the national side. Since the mid-1960s, however, instead of building on these foundations the national team has declined. Heavy defeats at home in recent years by both Hungary and England have not helped matters.

In the light of declining international fortunes, attention has focused on the very competitive national league. Although professionalism was legalised in 1951, it was not until eight years later that the regional leagues were replaced by a single national league. Galatasaray, Besiktas and Fenerbahçe have continued to be the leading clubs, but a unified structure has allowed provincial clubs as well as those from Izmir and Ankara to rise from obscurity. Trabzonspor, from the small town of Trabzon, have fared particularly well and along with the big three from Istanbul are part of an elite group which have managed to win the national league.

The 1960s saw the formation of many clubs in the smaller cities of Turkey, and as they gain more experience, they will undoubtedly challenge for honours as Trabzonspor have done. In the meantime, Turkey's main challenge for European club honours seems set to come from Istanbul. In 1989 Galatasaray reached the semi-finals of the European Cup, the best performance to date from a Turkish club. The question is how long will it be before one of them goes one further and reaches the final?

Population: 56 941 000
Area, sq km: 779 452
% in urban areas: 45.9%
Capital city: Ankara

Türkiye Futbol Federasyonu
Konur Sokak #10
Kizilay–Ankara
Turkey
Tel: (010 90) 4 1259182
Fax: (010 90) 41171090
Telex: 46308 BTFFTR
Cable: FUTBOLSPOR ANKARA
Languages for correspondence: English & French

Year of formation: 1923
Affiliation to FIFA: 1923
Affiliation to UEFA: 1962
Registered clubs: 3764
Registered players: 87 200
Professional players: 2000
Registered coaches: 5107
Registered referees: 4292
National stadium: Inönü Stadi, Ankara 30000
National colours: Shirts: White/Shorts: White/Socks: Red & White
Reserve colours: Shirts: Red/Shorts: White/ Socks: Red & White
Season: September–June

THE RECORD

WORLD CUP

1930–38 ..... Did not enter
1950 .... QT 1st/2 in group 2 – Withdrew
1954 .... QT 1st/2 in group 6 – Final Tournament/1st round
1958 .... Did not enter
1962 .... QT 2nd/3 in group 5
1966 .... QT 4th/4 in group 4
1970 .... QT 3rd/3 in group 4
1974 .... QT 2nd/4 in group 2
1978 .... QT 3rd/4 in group 3
1982 .... QT 5th/5 in group 3
1986 .... QT 5th/5 in group 3
1990 .... QT 3rd/5 in group 3

EUROPEAN CHAMPIONSHIP

1960 .... 1st round
1964 .... 1st round
1968 .... QT 3rd/4 in group 1
1972 .... QT 3rd/4 in group 8
1976 .... QT 3rd/4 in group 6
1980 .... QT 2nd/4 in group 7
1984 .... QT 4th/5 in group 6
1988 .... QT 4th/4 in group 4
1992 .... QT 4th/4 in group 7

OLYMPIC GAMES

1908–20 ..... Did not enter
1924 .... Preliminary round
1928 .... 1st round
1936 .... 1st round
1948 .... Quarter- finalists
1952 .... Quarter- finalists
1956 .... Did not enter
1960 .... 1st round
1964 .... QT Failed to qualify
1968 .... QT Failed to qualify
1972 .... QT Failed to qualify
1976 .... QT Failed to qualify
1980 .... QT Failed to qualify
1984 .... Did not enter
1988 .... QT Failed to qualify
1992 .... QT Failed to qualify

EUROPEAN CLUB COMPETITIONS

EUROPEAN CUP: Semi-finalists – Galatasaray 1989

CUP WINNERS CUP: Quarter-finalists – Fenerbahce 1964, Goztepe Izmir 1970, Bursaspor 1975

UEFA CUP: Semi-finalists – Goztepe Izmir 1969

CLUB DIRECTORY

ANKARA (Population – 2 400 000)

MKE Ankaragücü Kulübü
Stadium: 19 Mayis 24 000
Founded: 1910
Colours: Yellow/Blue

Genclerbirligi Spor Kulübü
Stadium: 19 Mayis 24 000
Founded: 1923
Colours: Red/Black

ISTANBUL (Population – 5 750 000)

Besiktas Jimnastik Kulübü
Stadium: Inönü 38 000
Founded: 1903
Colours: White/White

Fenerbahçe Spor Kulübü
Stadium: Fenerbahçe 32 000
Founded: 1907
Colours: Blue and yellow stripes/White

Galatasaray Spor Kulübü
Stadium: Ali Sami Yen 34 000
Founded: 1905
Colours: Red and yellow halves/Red

Sariyer Genclik Kulübü
Stadium: Yusuf Ziya Önis 8000
Founded: 1940
Colours: Blue/White

IZMIR (Population – 1 550 000)

Altay Spor Kulübü
Stadium: Alsancak 17 000
Founded: 1914
Colours: Black and white stripes/Black

Göztepe Spor Kulübü
Stadium: Alsancak 17 000
Founded: 1925
Colours: Yellow and black stripes/Black

Karsiyaka Spor Kulübü
Stadium: Alsancak 17000
Founded: 1912
Colours: Red/Green

ADANA (Population – 931 000)

Adana Demirspor Kulübü
Stadium: 5 Ocak 21 000
Founded: 1940
Colours: Blue/Blue

Adanaspor Kulübü
Stadium: 5 Ocak 21 000
Founded: 1954
Colours: Orange/White

BURSA (Population – 838 000)

Bursaspor Kulübü
Stadium: Atatürk 22 000
Founded: 1963
Colours: Green/White

GAZIANTEP (Population – 478 000)

Gaziantepspor Kulübü
Stadium: Kamil Ocak 20 000
Founded: 1965
Colours: Red and black stripes/White

KONYA (Population – 439 000)

Konyaspor Kulübü
Stadium: Atatürk 35 000
Founded: 1981
Colours: Green/Green

KAYSERI (Population – 373 000)

Kayserispor Kulübü
Stadium: Atatürk
Founded: 1966
Colours: Red and yellow stripes/White

ESKISEHIR (Population – 366 000)

Eskisehirspor Kulübü
Stadium: Atatürk 16 000
Founded: 1965
Colours: Red/Black

ICEL (Population – 314 000)

Mersin Idmanyurdu
Stadium: Tefvik Siri Gur
Founded: 1925
Colours: Red and blue stripes/White

DIYARBAKIR (Population – 305 000)

Diyarbakirspor Kulübü
Stadium: Atatürk
Founded: 1968
Colours: Red and green stripes/White

MALATYA (Population – 243 000)

Malatyaspor Kulübü
Stadium: Inönü 18000
Founded: 1966
Colours: Red/Red

SAMSUM (Population – 240 000)

Samsumspor Kulübü
Stadium: 19 Mayis 20 000
Founded: 1965
Colours: Red/Red

IZMIT (Population – 233 000)

Kocaelispor Kulübü
Stadium: Ismetpasa 20 000
Founded: 1966
Colours: Green and black stripes/Black

ZONGULDAK (Population – 210 000)

Zonguldakspor Kulübü
Stadium: Sehir 15 000
Founded: 1966
Colours: Red and blue stripes/Red

DENIZLI (Population – 169 000)

Denizlispor Kulübü
Stadium: Sehir 15000
Founded: 1966
Colours: Green and black stripes/Black

ADAPAZARI (Population – 152 000)

Sakaryaspor Kulübü
Stadium: Atatürk 15 000
Founded: 1965
Colours: White/White

TRABZON (Population – 142 000)

Tabzonspor Kulübü PK
Stadium: Avni Aker 27 000
Founded: 1967
Colours: Maroon and blue stripes/Blue

BOLU (Population – 50 000)

Boluspor Kulübü
Stadium: Sehir 12 000
Founded: 1965
Colours: Red and white hoops/White

REGIONAL LEAGUE PLAY-OFF WINNERS

1937 .... Fenerbahçe
1938 .... Günes
1939 .... Galatasaray
1940 .... Fenerbahçe
1941 .... Besiktas
1942 .... –
1943 .... Fenerbahçe
1944 .... Besiktas
1946 .... Fenerbahçe
1947 .... Besiktas
1948–49 .... –
1950 .... Fenerbahçe

ISTANBUL LEAGUE CHAMPIONSHIP

Year	Champions	Year	Champions	Year	Champions
1924	Besiktas	1936	Fenerbahçe	1948	Fenerbahçe
1925	Galatasaray	1937	Fenerbahçe	1949	Galatasaray
1926	Galatasaray	1938	Günes	1950	Besiktas
1927	Galatasaray	1939	Besiktas	1951	Besiktas
1928	–	1940	Besiktas	1952	Besiktas
1929	Galatasaray	1941	Besiktas	1953	Fenerbahçe
1930	Fenerbahçe	1942	Besiktas	1954	Besiktas
1931	Galatasaray	1943	Besiktas	1955	Galatasaray
1932	Istanbulspor	1944	Fenerbahçe	1956	Galatasaray
1933	Fenerbahçe	1945	Besiktas	1957	Galatasaray
1934	Besiktas	1946	Besiktas	1958	Galatasaray
1935	Fenerbahçe	1947	Fenerbahçe		

TURKISH CUP FINALS

Year	Winners	Score	Runners–up
1963	Galatasaray	2–1 2–1	Fenerbahçe
1964	Galatasaray	0–0*	Altay Izmir
1965	Galatasaray	0–0 1–0	Fenerbahçe
1966	Galatasaray	1–0	Besiktas
1967	Altay Izmir	2–2	Göztepe Izmir
1968	Fenerbahçe	2–0 0–1	Altay Izmir
1969	Göztepe Izmir	1–0 1–1	Galatasaray
1970	Göztepe Izmir	1–2 3–1	Eskisehirspor
1971	Eskisehirspor	0–1 2–0	Bursaspor
1972	MKE Ankaragücü	0–0 3–0	Altay Izmir
1973	Galatasaray	3–1 1–1	MKE Ankaragücü
1974	Fenerbahçe	0–1 3–0	Bursaspor
1975	Besiktas	0–1 2–0	Trabzonspor
1976	Galatasaray	0–1 1–0 (5–4p)	Trabzonspor
1977	Trabzonspor	1–0 0–0	Besiktas
1978	Trabzonspor	3–0 0–0	Adana Demirspor
1979	Fenerbahçe	1–2 2–0	Altay Izmir
1980	Altay Izmir	1–0 1–1	Galatasaray
1981	MKE Ankaragücü	2–1 0–0	Boluspor
1982	Galatasaray	3–0 1–2	MKE Ankaragücü
1983	Fenerbahçe	2–0 2–1	Mersin Idman Yurdu
1984	Trabzonspor	2–0	Besiktas
1985	Galatasaray	0–0 2–1	Trabzonspor
1986	Bursaspor	2–0	Altay Izmir
1987	Gençlerbirligi	5–0 1–2	Eskisehirspor
1988	Sakaryaspor	1–1 2–0	Samsunspor
1989	Besiktas	1–0 2–1	Fenerbahçe
1990	Besiktas	2–0	Trabzonspor
1991	Galatasaray	3–1	MKE Ankaragücü
1992	Trabzonspor	0–3 5–1	Bursaspor

* Galatasaray awarded the game

TURKISH NATIONAL LEAGUE

Year	Champions		Runners up		3rd	
1959	Fenerbahçe	*	Galatasaray			
1960	Besiktas	65	Fenerbahçe	60	Galatasaray	58
1961	Fenerbahçe	61	Galatasaray	60	Besiktas	55
1962	Galatasaray	57	Fenerbahçe	53	Besiktas	48
1963	Galatasaray	35	Besiktas	34	Fenerbahçe	28
1964	Fenerbahçe	53	Besiktas	52	Galatasaray	42
1965	Fenerbahçe	47	Besiktas	41	Galatasaray	39
1966	Besiktas	48	Galatasaray	42	Gençlerbirligi	38
1967	Besiktas	45	Fenerbahçe	43	Galatasaray	41
1968	Fenerbahçe	49	Besiktas	42	Galatasaray	36
1969	Galatasaray	46	Eskisehirspor	43	Besiktas	38
1970	Fenerbahçe	44	Eskisehirspor	37	Altay Izmir	36
1971	Galatasaray	42	Fenerbahçe	41	Göztepe Izmir	37
1972	Galatasaray	42	Eskisehirspor	39	Fenerbahçe	39
1973	Galatasaray	47	Fenerbahçe	42	Eskisehirspor	36
1974	Fenerbahçe	43	Besiktas	40	Boluspor	39
1975	Fenerbahçe	43	Galatasaray	38	Eskisehirspor	35
1976	Trabzonspor	43	Fenerbahçe	40	Galatasaray	37
1977	Trabzonspor	43	Fenerbahçe	39	Altay Izmir	35
1978	Fenerbahçe	42	Trabzonspor	41	Galatasaray	38
1979	Trabzonspor	42	Galatasaray	41	Fenerbahçe	38
1980	Trabzonspor	39	Fenerbahçe	35	Zonguldakspor	33
1981	Trabzonspor	39	Adanaspor	34	Galatasaray	34
1982	Besiktas	44	Trabzonspor	43	Fenerbahçe	41
1983	Fenerbahçe	49	Trabzonspor	47	Galatasaray	44
1984	Trabzonspor	50	Fenerbahçe	45	Galatasaray	44
1985	Fenerbahçe	50	Besiktas	50	Trabzonspor	42
1986	Besiktas	56	Galatasaray	56	Samsunspor	48
1987	Galatasaray	54	Besiktas	53	Samsunspor	49
1988	Galatasaray	90	Besiktas	78	Malatyaspor	62
1989	Fenerbahçe	90	Besiktas	80	Galatasaray	66
1990	Besiktas	75	Fenerbahçe	70	Trabzonspor	68
1991	Besiktas	69	Galatasaray	64	Trabzonspor	51
1992	Besiktas	76	Fenerbahçe	71	Galataaray	60

* Won play-off

INTERNATIONAL MATCHES PLAYED BY TURKEY

Date	Opponents	Result		Venue	Compet	Scorers
26-10-1923	Romania	D	2-2	Istanbul	Fr	Zeki Riza 2
25-05-1924	Czechoslovakia	L	2-5	Paris	OGr1	Bekir 2
17-06	Finland	W	4-2	Helsinki	Fr	Zeki Riza 4
19-06	Estonia	W	4-1	Tallin	Fr	Sabih, Bedri, Zeki Riza 2
22-06	Latvia	W	3-1	Riga	Fr	Zeki Riza 3
29-06	Poland	L	0-2	Lodz	Fr	
16-11	Soviet Union	L	0-3	Moscow	Fr	
10-04-1925	Bulgaria	W	2-1	Istanbul	Fr	Mehmet L, Sabih
1-05	Romania	W	2-1	Bucharest	Fr	Zeki Riza, Mehmet L
15-05	Soviet Union	L	1-2	Ankara	Fr	Sabih
2-10	Poland	L	1-2	Istanbul	Fr	Zeki Riza
7-05-1926	Romania	L	1-3	Istanbul	Fr	Muslih
2-10	Poland	L	1-6	Lwow	Fr	Alaaddin
17-07-1927	Bulgaria	D	3-3	Sofia	Fr	Latif 2, Kemal Faruki
14-10	Bulgaria	W	3-1	Istanbul	Fr	Zeki Riza 2, Nihat
8-04-1928	Yugoslavia	L	1-2	Zagreb	Fr	Latif
15-04	Romania	L	2-4	Arad	Fr	Kemal Faruki, Burham
28-05	Egypt	L	1-7	Amsterdam	OGr1	Bekir
27-09-1931	Bulgaria	L	1-5	Sofia	BC	Hakki
2-10	Yugoslavia	W	2-0	Sofia	BC	Rebii, Fikret B
5-11-1932	Bulgaria	L	2-3	Istanbul	Fr	Esref, Salahaddin
12-07-1936	Yugoslavia	D	3-3	Istanbul	Fr	Seref, Niyazi, Fikret B
3-08	Norway	L	0-4	Berlin	OGr1	
1-08-1937	Yugoslavia	L	1-3	Belgrade	Fr	Rasih
23-04-1948	Greece	W	3-1	Athens	Fr	Fikret K, Lefter, Sukru
30-05	Austria	L	0-1	Istanbul	Fr	
2-08	China	W	4-0	London	OGr1	Gunduz 2, Huseyin, Lefter
5-08	Yugoslavia	L	1-3	London	OGqf	Sukru
28-11	Greece	W	2-1	Istanbul	Fr	Reha 2
20-03-1949	Austria	L	0-1	Vienna	Fr	
13-05	Egypt	W	3-2	Athens	Fr	Bulent E, Sukru 2
15-05	Greece	W	2-1	Athens	Fr	Gunduz, Bulent E
20-11	Syria	W	7-0	Ankara	WCq	Fahreddin 3, Bulent U, Lefter, Erol, Gunduz
28-05-1950	Iran	W	6-1	Istanbul	Fr	Reha 3, Halit, Lefter 2
28-10	Israel	L	1-5	Tel Aviv	Fr	Reha
3-12	Israel	W	3-2	Istanbul	Fr	Halit, Isfendiyar, Lefter
10-06-1951	Sweden	L	1-3	Stockholm	Fr	Lefter
17-06	West Germany	W	2-1	Berlin	Fr	Recep, Muzaffer
14-11	Sweden	W	1-0	Istanbul	Fr	Muhtar
21-11	West Germany	L	0-2	Istanbul	Fr	
1-06-1952	Switzerland	L	1-5	Ankara	Fr	Garbis B
8-06	Spain	D	0-0	Istanbul	Fr	
25-05-1953	Switzerland	W	2-1	Berne	Fr	Garbis B 2
5-06	Yugoslavia	D	2-2	Istanbul	Fr	Burhan, Fikret K
6-01-1954	Spain	L	1-4	Madrid	WCq	Recep
14-03	Spain	W	1-0	Istanbul	WCq	Burhan
17-03	Spain	D	2-2	Rome	WCq	Burhan, Suat
17-06	West Germany	L	1-4	Berne	WCr1	Suat
20-06	South Korea	W	7-0	Geneva	WCr1	Suat 2, Lefter, Burhan 3, Erol
23-06	West Germany	L	2-7	Zurich	WCr1	Mustafa, Lefter
17-10	Yugoslavia	L	1-5	Sarajevo	Fr	Burhan
18-12-1955	Portugal	W	3-1	Istanbul	Fr	Lefter, Metin O, Nazmi
19-02-1956	Hungary	W	3-1	Istanbul	Fr	Lefter 2, Metin O
25-03	Portugal	L	1-3	Lisbon	Fr	Isfendiyar
1-05	Brazil	L	0-1	Istanbul	Fr	
16-11	Poland	D	1-1	Istanbul	Fr	Metin O
25-11	Czechoslovakia	D	1-1	Prague	Fr	Ergun
5-04-1957	Egypt	W	4-0	Cairo	Fr	Lefter 3, Hilmi
19-05	Poland	W	1-0	Warsaw	Fr	Ali B
6-11	Spain	L	0-3	Madrid	Fr	
8-12	Belgium	D	1-1	Ankara	Fr	Can
4-05-1958	Holland	W	2-1	Amsterdam	Fr	Metin O 2
26-10	Belgium	D	1-1	Brussels	Fr	Metin O
2-11	Romania	L	0-3	Bucharest	ECr1	

7–12	Bulgaria	D	0–0	Ankara	Fr	
18–12	Czechoslovakia	W	1–0	Istanbul	Fr	Seref
26–04–1959	Romania	W	2–0	Istanbul	ECr1	Lefter 2
10–05	Holland	D	0–0	Istanbul	Fr	
8–06–1960	Scotland	W	4–2	Ankara	Fr	Metin O, Lefter 2, Senol
27–11	Bulgaria	L	1–2	Sofia	Fr	Metin O
14–05–1961	Romania	L	0–1	Ankara	Fr	
1–06	Norway	W	1–0	Oslo	WCq	Metin O
18–06	Soviet Union	L	0–1	Moscow	WCq	
8–10	Romania	L	0–4	Bucharest	Fr	
18–10	South Korea	W	1–0	Ankara	Fr	Tarik
29–10	Norway	W	2–1	Istanbul	WCq	Aydin, Metin O
12–11	Soviet Union	L	1–2	Istanbul	WCq	Metin O
29–04–1962	Hungary	L	1–2	Budapest	Fr	Talat
16–05	Israel	W	1–0	Istanbul	Fr	Lefter
10–10	Ethiopia	W	3–0	Ankara	Fr	Metin O 3
25–11	Israel	W	2–0	Tel Aviv	Fr	Senol 2
2–12	Italy	L	0–6	Bologna	ECr1	
12–12	Denmark	D	1–1	Istanbul	Fr	Birol
16–12	Ethiopia	D	0–0	Addis Ababa	Fr	
27–03–1963	Italy	L	0–1	Istanbul	ECr1	
22–09	Poland	D	0–0	Poznan	Fr	
28–09	West Germany	L	0–3	Frankfurt	Fr	
9–10	Romania	D	0–0	Ankara	Fr	
27–09–1964	Poland	L	2–3	Istanbul	Fr	Aydin, Metin O
1–11	Tunisia	W	4–1	Ankara	Fr	Aydin, Metin O 2, Can
20–12	Bulgaria	D	0–0	Istanbul	Fr	
24–01–1965	Portugal	L	1–5	Lisbon	WCq	Fevzi
19–04	Portugal	L	0–1	Ankara	WCq	
2–05	Romania	L	0–3	Bucharest	WCq	
9–05	Bulgaria	L	1–4	Sofia	Fr	Metin
21–07	Pakistan	W	3–1	Tehran	Fr	Ogun 2, Gursel
25–07	Iran	D	0–0	Tehran	Fr	
9–10	Czechoslovakia	L	0–6	Istanbul	WCq	
23–10	Romania	W	2–1	Ankara	WCq	Fevzi, Nedim
21–11	Czechoslovakia	L	1–3	Brno	WCq	Ayhan
16–03–1966	Iran	D	0–0	Tehran	Fr	
30–05	Denmark	D	0–0	Copenhagen	Fr	
12–10	West Germany	L	0–2	Ankara	Fr	
16–10	Soviet Union	W	2–0	Moscow	Fr	Fevzi, Ayhan
16–11	Rep. Ireland	L	1–2	Dublin	ECq	Ogun
22–01–1967	Tunisia	D	0–0	Tunis	Fr	
1–02	Spain	D	0–0	Istanbul	ECq	
22–02	Rep. Ireland	W	2–1	Ankara	ECq	Ayhan, Ogun
31–05	Spain	L	0–2	Bilbao	ECq	
18–06	Czechoslovakia	L	0–3	Bratislava	ECq	
15–11	Czechoslovakia	D	0–0	Ankara	ECq	
26–11	Iran	W	1–0	Dacca	Fr	Nevzat
28–11	Pakistan	W	7–4	Dacca	Fr	Fevzi 2, Ergun 2, Ogun, Ayhan, Sanli
13–03–1968	Tunisia	D	0–0	Izmir	Fr	
24–04	Poland	L	0–8	Chorzow	Fr	
9–10	Bulgaria	L	0–2	Istanbul	Fr	
23–10	Nth. Ireland	L	1–4	Belfast	WCq	Ogun
11–12	Nth. Ireland	L	0–3	Istanbul	WCq	
17–01–1969	Saudi Arabia	W	2–1	Riyadh	Fr	Faruk, Mesut
30–04	Poland	L	1–3	Ankara	Fr	Ergun
14–09	Pakistan	W	4–2	Ankara	Fr	Fevzi, Can 2, Sanli
17–09	Iran	W	4–0	Ankara	Fr	Ender 2, Can, Metin
24–09	Switzerland	W	3–0	Istanbul	Fr	Metin, Nihat, Can
15–10	Soviet Union	L	0–3	Kiev	WCq	
16–11	Soviet Union	L	1–3	Istanbul	WCq	Ender
17–10–1970	West Germany	D	1–1	Cologne	ECq	Kamuran
13–12	Albania	W	2–1	Istanbul	ECq	Metin, Kemil
25–04–1971	West Germany	L	0–3	Istanbul	ECq	
22–09	Poland	L	1–5	Krakow	ECq	Nihat
26–09	Switzerland	L	0–4	Zurich	Fr	
14–11	Albania	L	0–3	Tirana	ECq	
5–12	Poland	W	1–0	Izmir	ECq	Cemil
4–10–1972	Algeria	L	0–1	Algiers	Fr	

22–10	Luxembourg	L	0–2	Esch	WCq	
10–12	Luxembourg	W	3–0	Istanbul	WCq	Osman 2, Koksal
13–01–1973	Italy	D	0–0	Naples	WCq	
14–02	Algeria	W	4–0	Izmir	Fr	Mehmet B, Cemil, Ziya, Osman
25–02	Italy	L	0–1	Istanbul	WCq	
18–04	Bulgaria	W	5–2	Izmir	BC	Mehmet B, Cemil 3, Metin
9–05	Switzerland	D	0–0	Basle	WCq	
17–10	Spain	D	0–0	Istanbul	Fr	
18–11	Switzerland	W	2–0	Izmir	WCq	Mehmet F, Metin
18–01–1974	Pakistan	D	2–2	Karachi	Fr	Melih 2
20–01	Iran	W	1–0	Karachi	Fr	Sinan
8–05	Bulgaria	L	1–5	Sofia	BC	Cemil
13–11	Austria	L	0–1	Istanbul	Fr	
20–11	Rep. Ireland	D	1–1	Izmir	ECq	OG
1–12	Switzerland	W	2–1	Izmir	ECq	Izmail, Mehmet B
19–03–1975	Romania	D	1–1	Istanbul	Fr	Cemil
2–04	Soviet Union	L	0–3	Kiev	ECq	
30–04	Switzerland	D	1–1	Zurich	ECq	Alpaslan
12–10	Romania	D	2–2	Bucharest	Fr	Cemil, Gokmen
29–10	Rep. Ireland	L	0–4	Dublin	ECq	
23–11	Soviet Union	W	1–0	Izmir	ECq	OG
20–12	West Germany	L	0–5	Istanbul	Fr	
8–02–1976	Iraq	D	0–0	Baghdad	Fr	
25–08	Finland	L	1–2	Helsinki	Fr	Resit
22–09	Bulgaria	D	2–2	Sofia	Fr	OG, Ali Kemal
13–10	Rep. Ireland	D	3–3	Ankara	Fr	Cemil 2, Isa
31–10	Malta	W	4–0	Istanbul	WCq	Mehmet K, Cemil 3
17–11	East Germany	D	1–1	Dresden	WCq	Cemil
16–02–1977	Bulgaria	W	2–0	Istanbul	BC	Ali Kemal, Cemil
23–03	Romania	L	0–4	Bucharest	BC	
6–04	Finland	L	1–2	Ankara	Fr	Mustafa B
17–04	Austria	L	0–1	Vienna	WCq	
7–09	Czechoslovakia	L	0–1	Bratislava	Fr	
21–09	Bulgaria	L	1–3	Sofia	BC	Sedat
30–10	Austria	L	0–1	Izmir	WCq	
16–11	East Germany	L	1–2	Izmir	WCq	Volkan
27–11	Malta	W	3–0	Gzira	WCq	Sedat 2, Cemil
22–03–1978	Romania	D	1–1	Istanbul	BC	Sedat
5–04	Rep. Ireland	L	2–4	Dublin	Fr	Cemil, Onder
23–09	Italy	L	0–1	Florence	Fr	
5–10	Soviet Union	L	0–2	Ankara	Fr	
29–11	Wales	L	0–1	Wrexham	ECq	
28–02–1979	Algeria	L	0–1	Bursa	Fr	
18–03	Malta	W	2–1	Izmir	ECq	Fatih, Sedat
1–04	West Germany	D	0–0	Izmir	ECq	
28–10	Malta	W	2–1	Gzira	ECq	Sedat, Mustafa B
21–11	Wales	W	1–0	Izmir	ECq	Onal
22–12	West Germany	L	0–2	Gelsenkirchen	ECq	
24–09–1980	Iceland	L	1–3	Izmir	WCq	Fatih
1–10	Libya	L	1–2	Izmir	Fr	Muharrem
3–10	Saudi Arabia	W	3–0	Izmir	Fr	Tuncay, OG, Ibrahim
5–10	Malaysia	W	3–0	Izmir	Fr	Metin B, Tuncay
15–10	Wales	L	0–4	Cardiff	WCq	
3–12	Czechoslovakia	L	0–2	Prague	WCq	
25–03–1981	Wales	L	0–1	Ankara	WCq	
15–04	Czechoslovakia	L	0–3	Istanbul	WCq	
9–09	Iceland	L	0–2	Reykjavik	WCq	
23–09	Soviet Union	L	0–4	Moscow	WCq	

LEADING INTERNATIONAL APPEARANCES

1	Fatih Terim	51	6	Metin Oktay	36
2	Turgay Seren	47	7	Turgay Semercioglu	35
3	Lefter Kucukandonyadis	46	8	Sedat Ozden	34
4	Cemil Turan	44	9	Ogün Altiparmak	32
5	Seref Has	39		Metin Tekin	32

LEADING INTERNATIONAL GOALSCORERS					
1	Lefter Kucukandonyadis	21		Sedat Ozden	7
2	Cemil Turan	19	8	Reha Eken	6
3	Metin Oktay	19		Ilyas Tufekci	6
4	Zeki Riza	15		Fevzi Zemzem	6
5	Tanju Colak	10		Can Bortu	6
6	Burhan Sargin	7		Ogün Altiparmak	6

7–10	Soviet Union	L	0–3	Izmir	WCq	
22–09–1982	Hungary	L	0–5	Gyor	Fr	
27–10	Albania	W	1–0	Izmir	ECq	Arif
17–11	Austria	L	0–4	Vienna	ECq	
29–01–1983	Romania	D	1–1	Istanbul	Fr	Selcuk
9–03	Romania	L	1–3	Tirgu Mures	Fr	Rasit
30–03	Nth. Ireland	L	1–2	Belfast	ECq	Hasan
23–04	West Germany	L	0–3	Izmir	ECq	
11–05	Albania	D	1–1	Tirana	ECq	Metin T
12–10	Nth. Ireland	W	1–0	Ankara	ECq	Selcuk
26–10	West Germany	L	1–5	Berlin	ECq	Hasan
16–11	Austria	W	3–1	Istanbul	ECq	Tufekci, Selcuk 2
20–01–1984	Egypt	L	0–1	Cairo	Fr	
22–01	Egypt	W	1–0	Port Said	Fr	Chinal
3–03	Italy	L	1–2	Istanbul	Fr	Tufekci
11–03	Luxembourg	W	3–1	Esch	Fr	Sedat, Tufekci 2
4–04	Hungary	L	0–6	Istanbul	Fr	
26–09	Poland	L	0–2	Slupsk	Fr	
16–10	Bulgaria	D	0–0	Istanbul	Fr	
31–10	Finland	L	1–2	Antalya	WCq	Tufekci
14–11	England	L	0–8	Istanbul	WCq	
22–12	Luxembourg	W	1–0	Istanbul	Fr	Ceyhun
28–03–1985	Albania	D	0–0	Tirana	Fr	
3–04	Romania	L	0–3	Craiova	WCq	
1–05	Nth. Ireland	L	0–2	Belfast	WCq	
28–08	Switzerland	D	0–0	St Gallen	Fr	
11–09	Nth. Ireland	D	0–0	Izmir	WCq	
25–09	Finland	L	0–1	Tampere	WCq	
6–10	England	L	0–5	London	WCq	
13–11	Romania	L	1–3	Izmir	WCq	Metin T
11–12	Poland	D	1–1	Adana	Fr	Tanju
12–03–1986	Switzerland	W	1–0	Adana	Fr	Yusef
29–10	Yugoslavia	L	0–4	Split	ECq	
12–11	Nth. Ireland	D	0–0	Izmir	ECq	
4–03–1987	Romania	L	1–3	Ankara	Fr	Tanju
25–03	East Germany	W	3–1	Istanbul	Fr	Keser, Kayhan, Tanju
29–04	England	D	0–0	Izmir	ECq	
14–10	England	L	0–8	London	ECq	
11–11	Nth. Ireland	L	0–1	Belfast	ECq	
16–12	Yugoslavia	L	2–3	Izmir	ECq	Yusef, Fejaz
16–03–1988	Hungary	L	0–1	Budapest	Fr	
21–09	Greece	W	3–1	Istanbul	Fr	Tanju, Ogriz, Ridvan
12–10	Iceland	D	1–1	Istanbul	WCq	Tanju
2–11	Austria	L	2–3	Vienna	WCq	Feyyaz, Tanju
30–11	East Germany	W	3–1	Istanbul	WCq	Tanju 2, Oguz
29–03–1989	Greece	W	1–0	Athens	Fr	Ridvan
12–04	East Germany	W	2–0	Magdeburg	WCq	Tanju, Ridvan
10–05	Soviet Union	L	0–1	Istanbul	WCq	
20–09	Iceland	L	1–2	Reykjavik	WCq	Feyyaz
25–10	Austria	W	3–0	Istanbul	WCq	Ridvan 2, Feyyaz
15–11	Soviet Union	L	0–2	Simferopol	WCq	
11–04–1990	Denmark	L	0–1	Copenhagen	Fr	
27–05	Rep. Ireland	D	0–0	Izmir	Fr	
5–09	Hungary	L	1–4	Budapest	Fr	Tanju
17–10	Rep. Ireland	L	0–5	Dublin	ECq	
14–11	Poland	L	0–1	Istanbul	ECq	
27–02–1991	Yugoslavia	D	1–1	Izmir	Fr	Ugur
27–03	Tunisia	D	0–0	Tunis	Fr	

17–04	Poland	L	0–3	Warsaw	ECq	
1–05	England	L	0–1	Izmir	ECq	
15–07	Faeroe Islands	D	1–1	Torshavn	Fr	Hami
17–07	Iceland	L	1–5	Reykjavik	Fr	Unal
21–08	Bulgaria	D	0–0	Stara Zagora	Fr	
4–09	USA	D	1–1	Istanbul	Fr	Erdal
16–10	England	L	0–1	London	ECq	
13–11	Rep. Ireland	L	1–3	Istanbul	ECq	Riza
12–02–1992	Finland	D	1–1	Adana	Fr	Orhan
25–03	Luxembourg	W	3–2	Luxembourg	Fr	Unal, Hami 2
8–04	Denmark	W	2–1	Ankara	Fr	Hami, Hakan
30–05	Germany	L	0–1	Gelsenkirchen	Fr	

WALES

Unlike England, Scotland and Northern Ireland, the other trio in the United Kingdom quartet, in Wales football is not the national sport. The national stadium is Cardiff Arms Park, the home of the Welsh Rugby Football Union, and until recent times at least, the oval ball has far outstripped the round one in popularity.

	Team	Cup G	Cup S
1	Wrexham	22	21
2	Cardiff City	21	8
3	Swansea City	10	8
4	Druids	8	5
5	Shrewsbury Town	6	3
6	Chirk	5	1
7	Chester City	3	10
8	Bangor City	3	6
9	Merthyr Tydfil	3	3
10	Oswestry	3	1
11	Wellington Town	3	–
12	Newtown	2	3
	Rhyl	2	3
14	Crewe Alexandra	2	–
15	Hereford United	1	3
16	Connah's Quay	1	2
	Newport County	1	2
18	Flint	1	1
	Lovell's Athletic	1	1
	Tranmere Rovers	1	1
21	Aberystwyth	1	–
	Barry Town	1	–
	Borough United	1	–
	Bristol City	1	–
	Ebbw Vale	1	–
	South Liverpool	1	–
27	Aberdare	–	3
	Pontypridd	–	3
29	Kidderminster Harriers	–	2
	Northwich Victoria	–	2
	Westminster Rovers	–	2
	Whitchurch	–	2
33	Aberaman	–	1
	Davenham	–	1
	Hednesford Town	–	1
	Llanelly	–	1
	Newtown White Stars	–	1
	Ruthin	–	1
	Stourbridge	–	1
	Ton Pentre	–	1

To the end of the 1991–92 season

Things may be changing, however. As the Welsh rugby side slips to levels unimaginable at the beginning of the 1980s, fans are turning in numbers to football, safe in the knowledge that it may be many years before the football team loses a match to Western Samoa, the fate suffered by the rugby side in the 1991 World Cup.

North Wales has always been more devoted to football than the South, and it was here that the first activity in Welsh football took place. A club called Druids, the first club in the country and based in Ruabon near Wrexham, were formed at some point before 1873, when the oldest club still in existence, Wrexham AFC, were formed. Three years later, also in the same city, the Football Association of Wales was instituted, three months after a match between a Scottish and Welsh team had taken place in Glasgow.

Wrexham was naturally the venue for the return game the following year, and although games against both Ireland and England followed it was not until 1894 that Wales played in the South, when they met Ireland in Swansea, and it was a further two years before Cardiff was considered.

The North's domination in these early years was complete. The Welsh Cup was introduced in 1878 and until 1912 it produced all of the winners. The major clubs of the time, Druids, Wrexham, Bangor City, Oswestry and Chirk all had to face up to the challenge that was rising in the South, however, especially from Cardiff City, Swansea Town as they were then known and Newport County. As the majority of the population lived in that part of the country, this was an inevitable trend.

The Cup has always been the premier event in Welsh football as there has never been a proper league in force. In the 1920s Wrexham, Cardiff, Swansea and Newport all joined the English league, and with the exception of Newport who folded in the 1980s, they remain there today. There is a Welsh league, but it does not even contain any of the semi-professional clubs that currently play in the minor English leagues like Merthyr Tydfil or Bangor City.

In a bid to exert itself as a fully independent football force, the Welsh Association has plans to create a fully-fledged league with all of the top clubs involved and the winners playing in the European Cup, but it is meeting with stiff resistance from the clubs who, on the whole, wish to stay in the English leagues. The winners of the Welsh Cup do have an entry into the Cup Winners Cup, although English teams from the borders which are allowed to take part are not allowed to enter if they win. It must be a Welsh team that enters.

It is perhaps fortunate that when Cardiff City won the FA Cup in 1927, there was not a Cup Winners Cup around to confuse Europe's administrators! Nor does it seem that this will be a problem in the future as all three remaining clubs in the English league have languished in the lower divisions for many years, with the exception of Swansea City who in the 1980s rose from the fourth division to the first in rapid succession under John Toshack, but when he departed they slid back from whence they came.

Despite a relatively low profile, Wales has produced some world class footballers. The first of these was Billy Meredith, a man who played for Wales when he was 46 in 1920, some 25 years after he made his debut, and this remains a world record to this day. Unfortunately for him, Wales' fixture list was composed entirely of Home International Championship games in these years. Not until the 1933 match with France in Paris did Wales play a foreign opponent. Had they done so when Meredith was playing he could have doubled his 48 caps, but this was still a remarkable figure for the time.

Success in these championships for both Meredith and Wales was not easy to come by, but they won their first title in 1907 and followed this up with victory in 1920, a fitting tribute to the retiring Meredith. The 1920 victory was the first of six during the 1920s and 30s, five of them outright. Although England won on seven occasions over the same period, only three of them were outright victories, a testament to the fact that the inter-war period was perhaps the most successful in the history of the game in Wales.

The national side left the borders of the British Isles for only the second time in 1939 for another match in Paris, but after the war a more concerted effort was made to take on opponents from abroad. After failing to qualify for the 1950 and 1954 World Cups, the qualifiers for which doubled up as matches in the Home International Championship, Wales somewhat fortuitously qualified for the tournament in Sweden in 1958 by beating Israel in a play-off. Czechoslovakia had come first in Wales' group, but when Israel were ordered to play-off for a place after all of their opponents had withdrawn, Wales were the lucky winners of the lottery.

Once in Sweden they progressed further than either Scotland or England, coming second in their group behind the hosts. In the quarter-finals the Welsh were rather unlucky to face Brazil. They gave the South Americans their hardest match in the competition, with Kelsey particularly brilliant in goal. The others stars of that that side were Ivor Allchurch, Trevor Ford and the great John Charles who found so much fame with Juventus in Italy.

Since 1958, however, Wales have struggled to keep pace with the best of Europe. After winning their qualifying group in the 1976 European Championships they fell at the quarter-final hurdle against Yugoslavia. Despite the presence of players such as John Toshack and most recently Ian Rush, Mark Hughes and Neville Southall in the team, further success has failed to materialise.

There is hope for the future, however. As Wales were being hounded out of the 1991 Rugby World Cup on their home territory, the Welsh Football Association was still basking in the glory of victories over Germany and Brazil in quick succession, and both on the sacred rugby turf at Cardiff Arms Park.

Population: 2857000
Area, sq km: 20768
% in urban areas: 91.5%
Capital city: Cardiff

The Football Association of Wales
Plymouth Chambers
3 Westgate Street
Cardiff CF1 1DD
Tel: (010 44) 222 372325
Fax: (010 44) 222 343961
Telex: 497 363 FAW G
Cable: WELSOCCER CARDIFF
Languages for correspondence: English
Year of formation: 1876
Affiliation to FIFA: 1910–1920, 1924–28, 1946
Affiliation to UEFA: 1954

Registered clubs: 1807
Registered players: 53 140
Professional players: 140
Registered referees: 901
National stadium: Cardiff Arms Park (Welsh Rugby Football Union) 58000
National colours: Shirts: Red/Shorts: Red/Socks: Red
Reserve colours: Shirts: Yellow/Shorts: Yellow/Socks: Yellow
Season: Welsh clubs play in the English league

THE RECORD

WORLD CUP

1930–38 ..... Did not enter
1950 .... QT 3rd/4 in group 1
1954 .... QT 4th/4 in group 3
1958 .... QT 2nd/3 in group 4 – Final Tournament/Quarter-finalists
1962 .... QT Rnd 1 in group 9
1966 .... QT 2nd/4 in group 7
1970 .... QT 3rd/3 in group 3
1974 .... QT 3rd/3 in group 5
1978 .... QT 3rd/3 in group 7
1982 .... QT 3rd/5 in group 3
1986 .... QT 3rd/4 in group 7
1990 .... QT 4th/4 in group 4

EUROPEAN CHAMPIONSHIP

1960 .... Did not enter
1964 .... 1st round

1968 .... QT 3rd/4 in group 8
1972 .... QT 3rd/4 in group 1
1976 .... QT 1st/4 in group 2 – Final Tournament/Quarter-finalists
1980 .... QT 3rd/4 in group 7
1984 .... QT 2nd/4 in group 4
1988 .... QT 3rd/4 in group 6
1992 .... QT 2nd/4 in group 5

EUROPEAN CLUB COMPETITIONS

EUROPEAN CUP: Ineligible to compete

CUP WINNERS CUP: Semi-finalists – Cardiff City 1968

UEFA CUP: Ineligible to compete

CLUB DIRECTORY

CARDIFF (Population – 625 000)
Cardiff City Football Club
Stadium: Ninian Park 42 000
Founded: 1899
Colours: Blue/White

SWANSEA (Population – 275 000)
Swansea City Football Club
Stadium: Vetch Field 26 000
Founded: 1900
Colours: White/White

WREXHAM (Population – 39 000)
Wrexham Association Football Club
Stadium: Racecourse Ground 28 000
Founded: 1873
Colours: Red/White

MERTHYR TYDFIL (Population – 38 000)
Merthyr Tydfil Football Club
Stadium: Penydarren Park 10 000
Founded: 1908
Colours: White/Black

BANGOR
Bangor City Football Club
Stadium: Farrar Road 10 000
Founded: 1876
Colours: Blue/Blue

WELSH CUP FINALS

Year	Winners	Score	Runners–up
1878	Wrexham	1–0	Druids
1879	Newtown	1–0	Wrexham
1880	Druids	2–1	Ruthin
1881	Druids	2–0	Newtown White Stars
1882	Druids	2–1	Northwich Victoria
1883	Wrexham	1–0	Druids
1884	Oswestry	3–2	Druids
1885	Druids	2–0	Oswestry
1886	Druids	5–2	Newtown
1887	Chirk	4–2	Davenham
1888	Chirk	5–0	Newtown
1889	Bangor City	2–1	Northwich Victoria
1890	Chirk	1–0	Wrexham
1891	Shrewsbury Town	5–2	Wrexham
1892	Chirk	2–1	Westminster Rovers
1893	Wrexham	2–1	Chirk
1894	Chirk	2–0	Westminster Rovers
1895	Newtown	3–2	Wrexham
1896	Bangor City	3–1	Wrexham
1897	Wrexham	2–0	Newtown
1898	Druids	1–1 2–1	Wrexham
1899	Druids	2–2 1–0	Wrexham
1900	Aberystwyth	3–0	Druids
1901	Oswestry	1–0	Druids
1902	Wellington	1–0	Wrexham
1903	Wrexham	8–0	Aberaman
1904	Druids	3–2	Aberdare
1905	Wrexham	3–0	Aberdare
1906	Wellington	3–2	Whitchurch
1907	Oswestry	2–0	Whitchurch
1908	Chester	3–1	Connah's Quay
1909	Wrexham	1–0	Chester
1910	Wrexham	2–1	Chester
1911	Wrexham	6–1	Connah's Quay
1912	Cardiff City	0–0 3–0	Pontypridd
1913	Swansea Town	0–0 1–0	Pontypridd
1914	Wrexham	0–0 3–0	Llanelly
1915	Wrexham	1–1 1–0	Swansea Town
1916–19 –			
1920	Cardiff City	2–1	Wrexham
1921	Wrexham	1–1 3–1	Pontypridd
1922	Cardiff City	2–0	Ton Pentre
1923	Cardiff City	3–2	Aberdare
1924	Wrexham	2–2 1–0	Merthyr Tydfil
1925	Wrexham	3–1	Flint
1926	Ebbw Vale	3–2	Swansea Town
1927	Cardiff City	2–0	Rhyl
1928	Cardiff City	2–0	Bangor City
1929	Connah's Quay	3–0	Cardiff City
1930	Cardiff City	0–0 4–2	Rhyl
1931	Wrexham	7–0	Shrewsbury Town
1932	Swansea Town	1–1 2–0	Wrexham
1933	Chester	2–0	Wrexham
1934	Bristol City	1–1 3–0	Tranmere Rovers
1935	Tranmere Rovers	1–0	Chester
1936	Crewe Alexandra	2–0	Chester
1937	Crewe Alexandra	1–1 3–1	Rhyl
1938	Shrewsbury Town	2–1	Swansea Town
1939	South Liverpool	2–1	Cardiff City
1940	Wellington Town	4–0	Swansea Town
1941–46 –			
1947	Chester	0–0 5–1	Merthyr Tydfil
1948	Lovell's Athletic	3–0	Shrewsbury Town
1949	Merthyr Tydfil	2–0	Swansea Town
1950	Swansea Town	4–1	Wrexham
1951	Merthyr Tydfil	1–1 3–2	Cardiff City
1952	Rhyl	4–3	Merthyr Tydfil
1953	Rhyl	2–1	Chester
1954	Flint	2–0	Chester
1955	Barry Town	1–1 4–3	Chester
1956	Cardiff City	3–2	Swansea Town
1957	Wrexham	2–1	Swansea Town
1958	Wrexham	1–1 2–0	Chester
1959	Cardiff City	2–0	Lovell's Athletic
1960	Wrexham	1–1 1–0	Cardiff City
1961	Swansea Town	3–1	Bangor City
1962	Bangor City	0–3 2–0 3–1	Wrexham
1963	Borough United	2–1 0–0	Newport County
1964	Cardiff City	0–2 3–1 2–0	Bangor City
1965	Cardiff City	5–1 0–1 3–0	Wrexham
1966	Swansea Town	3–0 0–1 2–1	Chester
1967	Cardiff City	2–2 2–1	Wrexham
1968	Cardiff City	2–0 4–1	Hereford United
1969	Cardiff City	3–1 2–0	Swansea Town
1970	Cardiff City	1–0 4–0	Chester
1971	Cardiff City	1–0 3–1	Wrexham
1972	Wrexham	2–1 1–1	Cardiff City
1973	Cardiff City	0–1 5–0	Bangor City
1974	Cardiff City	1–0 1–0	Stourbridge
1975	Wrexham	2–1 3–1	Cardiff City
1976	Cardiff City	3–3 3–2	Hereford United
1977	Shrewsbury Town	1–2 3–0	Cardiff City
1978	Wrexham	0–0 3–1	Bangor City
1979	Shrewsbury Town	1–1 1–0	Wrexham
1980	Newport County	2–1 3–0	Shrewsbury Town

1981	Swansea City	1–0 1–1	Hereford United
1982	Swansea City	0–0 2–1	Cardiff City
1983	Swansea City	2–0 2–1	Wrexham
1984	Shrewsbury Town	2–1 0–0	Wrexham
1985	Shrewsbury Town	3–1 2–0	Bangor City
1986	Wrexham	1–1 2–1	Kidderminster Harriers
1987	Merthyr Tydfil	2–2 1–0	Newport County
1988	Cardiff City	2–0	Wrexham
1989	Swansea City	5–0	Kidderminster Harriers
1990	Hereford United	2–1	Wrexham
1991	Swansea City	2–0	Wrexham
1992	Cardiff City	1–0	Hednesford Town

INTERNATIONAL MATCHES PLAYED BY WALES

Date	Opponents	Result		Venue	Compet	Scorers
25-03-1876	Scotland	L	0–4	Glasgow	Fr	
5-03-1877	Scotland	L	0–2	Wrexham	Fr	
23-03-1878	Scotland	L	0–9	Glasgow	Fr	
18-01-1879	England	L	1–2	London	Fr	Davies W (I)
7-04	Scotland	L	0–3	Wrexham	Fr	
15-03-1880	England	L	2–3	Wrexham	Fr	Roberts J (I), Roberts W (I)
27-03	Scotland	L	1–5	Glasgow	Fr	Roberts W (I)
26-02-1881	England	W	1–0	Blackburn	Fr	Vaughan
14-03	Scotland	L	1–5	Wrexham	Fr	Cross
25-02-1882	Ireland	W	7–1	Wrexham	Fr	Price J 4, Morgan, Owen W (I) 2
13-03	England	W	5–3	Wrexham	Fr	Owen W (I) 2, Morgan, Vaughan, OG
25-03	Scotland	L	0–5	Glasgow	Fr	
3-02-1883	England	L	0–5	London	Fr	
12-03	Scotland	L	0–3	Wrexham	Fr	
17-03	Ireland	D	1–1	Belfast	Fr	Roberts W (II)
9-02-1884	Ireland	W	6–0	Wrexham	HC	Owen W (I) 2, Shaw 2, Jones R, Eyton Jones
17-03	England	L	0–4	Wrexham	HC	
29-03	Scotland	L	1–4	Glasgow	HC	Roberts R
14-03-1885	England	D	1–1	Blackburn	HC	Wilding
23-03	Scotland	L	1–8	Wrexham	HC	Jones R
11-04	Ireland	W	8–2	Belfast	HC	Owen W (II), Burke, Sisson 3, Roach 2, Jones H
27-02-1886	Ireland	W	5–0	Wrexham	HC	Roberts W (III), Wilding, Hersee, Sisson, Bryan
29-03	England	L	1–3	Wrexham	HC	Lewis W (I)
10-04	Scotland	L	1–4	Glasgow	HC	OG
26-02-1887	England	L	0–4	London	HC	
12-03	Ireland	L	1–4	Belfast	HC	Sabine
21-03	Scotland	L	0–2	Wrexham	HC	
4-02-1888	England	L	1–5	Crewe	HC	Doughty J
3-03	Ireland	W	11–0	Wrexham	HC	Doughty J 4, Doughty R 2, Wilding 2, Howell 2, Pryce-Jones
10-03	Scotland	L	1–5	Edinburgh	HC	Doughty J
23-02-1889	England	L	1–4	Stoke	HC	Owen W (II)
15-04	Scotland	D	0–0	Wrexham	HC	
27-04	Ireland	W	3–1	Belfast	HC	Jarrett 3
8-02-1890	Ireland	W	5–2	Shrewsbury	HC	Lewis W 2 (I), Pryce-Jones 2, Owen W (II)
15-03	England	L	1–3	Wrexham	HC	Lewis W (I)
22-03	Scotland	D	0–0	Glasgow	HC	
7-02-1891	Ireland	L	2–7	Belfast	HC	Lewis W (I) 2
7-03	England	L	1–4	Sunderland	HC	Howell
21-03	Scotland	L	3–4	Wrexham	HC	Bowdler 2, Owen W (II)
27-02-1892	Ireland	D	1–1	Bangor	HC	Lewis B
5-03	England	L	0–2	Wrexham	HC	
26-03	Scotland	L	1–6	Edinburgh	HC	Lewis B
13-03-1893	England	L	0–6	Stoke	HC	
18-03	Scotland	L	0–8	Wrexham	HC	
5-04	Ireland	L	3–4	Belfast	HC	Owen G 2, OG
24-02-1894	Ireland	W	4–1	Swansea	HC	Lewis W (I) 2, James E 2
12-03	England	L	1–5	Wrexham	HC	Bowdler
24-03	Scotland	L	2–5	Kilmarnock	HC	Morris H 2
16-03-1895	Ireland	D	2–2	Belfast	HC	Trainer
18-03	England	D	1–1	London	HC	Lewis W (I)
23-03	Scotland	D	2–2	Wrexham	HC	Lewis W (I), Chapman
29-02-1896	Ireland	W	6–1	Wrexham	HC	Lewis W (I) 2, Meredith 2, Pugh, Morris A
16-03	England	L	1–9	Cardiff	HC	Chapman
21-03	Scotland	L	0–4	Dundee	HC	

6-03-1897	Ireland	L	3-4	Belfast	HC	Meredith 2, Jenkyns
20-03	Scotland	D	2-2	Wrexham	HC	Pugh, Morgan-Owen M
29-03	England	L	0-4	Sheffield	HC	
19-02-1898	Ireland	L	0-1	Llandudno	HC	
19-03	Scotland	L	2-5	Motherwell	HC	Thomas T, Morgan-Owen M
28-03	England	L	0-3	Wrexham	HC	
4-03-1899	Ireland	L	0-1	Belfast	HC	
18-03	Scotland	L	0-6	Wrexham	HC	
20-03	England	L	0-4	Bristol	HC	
3-02-1900	Scotland	L	2-5	Aberdeen	HC	Butler, Parry
24-02	Ireland	W	2-0	Llandudno	HC	Parry, Meredith
26-03	England	D	1-1	Cardiff	HC	Meredith
2-03-1901	Scotland	D	1-1	Wrexham	HC	Parry
18-03	England	L	0-6	Newcastle	HC	
23-03	Ireland	W	1-0	Belfast	HC	Jones J (I)
22-02-1902	Ireland	L	0-3	Cardiff	HC	
3-03	England	D	0-0	Wrexham	HC	
15-03	Scotland	L	1-5	Greenock	HC	Meredith
2-03-1903	England	L	1-2	Portsmouth	HC	Watkins
9-03	Scotland	L	0-1	Cardiff	HC	
28-03	Ireland	L	0-2	Belfast	HC	
29-02-1904	England	D	2-2	Wrexham	HC	Watkins, Davies L (I)
12-03	Scotland	D	1-1	Dundee	HC	Atherton
21-03	Ireland	L	0-1	Bangor	HC	
6-03-1905	Scotland	W	3-1	Wrexham	HC	Morris A, Meredith, Watkins
27-03	England	L	1-3	Liverpool	HC	Morris A
8-04	Ireland	D	2-2	Belfast	HC	Watkins, Atherton
3-03-1906	Scotland	W	2-0	Edinburgh	HC	Jones W, Jones J (II)
19-03	England	L	0-1	Cardiff	HC	
2-04	Ireland	D	4-4	Wrexham	HC	Green 3, Morgan-Owen H
23-02-1907	Ireland	W	3-2	Belfast	HC	Morris R, Meredith, Jones W
4-03	Scotland	W	1-0	Wrexham	HC	Morris A
18-03	England	D	1-1	London	HC	Jones W
7-03-1908	Scotland	L	1-2	Dundee	HC	Jones W
16-03	England	L	1-7	Wrexham	HC	Davies W (II)
11-04	Ireland	L	0-1	Aberdare	HC	
1-03-1909	Scotland	W	3-2	Wrexham	HC	Davies W (II) 2, Jones W
15-03	England	L	0-2	Nottingham	HC	
20-03	Ireland	W	3-2	Belfast	HC	Jones W, Wynn, Meredith
5-03-1910	Scotland	L	0-1	Kilmarnock	HC	
14-03	England	L	0-1	Cardiff	HC	
11-04	Ireland	W	4-1	Wrexham	HC	Evans R 2, Morris A 2
28-01-1911	Ireland	W	2-1	Belfast	HC	Davies W (II), Morris A
6-03	Scotland	D	2-2	Cardiff	HC	Morris A 2
13-03	England	L	0-3	London	HC	
2-03-1912	Scotland	L	0-1	Edinburgh	HC	
11-03	England	L	0-2	Wrexham	HC	
13-04	Ireland	L	2-3	Cardiff	HC	Davies W (II), Davies D
18-01-1913	Ireland	W	1-0	Belfast	HC	Roberts J (II)
3-03	Scotland	D	0-0	Wrexham	HC	
17-03	England	L	3-4	Bristol	HC	Davies W (III), Meredith, Peake
19-01-1914	Ireland	L	1-2	Wrexham	HC	Jones E
28-02	Scotland	D	0-0	Glasgow	HC	
16-03	England	L	0-2	Cardiff	HC	
14-02-1920	Ireland	D	2-2	Belfast	HC	Davies S 2
26-02	Scotland	D	1-1	Cardiff	HC	Evans J
15-03	England	W	2-1	London	HC	Davies S, Richards
12-02-1921	Scotland	L	1-2	Aberdeen	HC	Collier
14-03	England	D	0-0	Cardiff	HC	
9-04	Ireland	W	2-1	Swansea	HC	Hole, Davies S
4-02-1922	Scotland	W	2-1	Wrexham	HC	Davies S, Davies L (II)
13-03	England	L	0-1	Liverpool	HC	
1-04	Ireland	D	1-1	Belfast	HC	Davies L (II)
5-03-1923	England	D	2-2	Cardiff	HC	Keenor, Jones I
17-03	Scotland	L	0-2	Glasgow	HC	
14-04	Ireland	L	0-3	Wrexham	HC	
16-02-1924	Scotland	W	2-0	Cardiff	HC	Davies W (IV), Davies L (II)
3-03	England	W	2-1	Blackburn	HC	Davies W (IV), Vizard
15-03	Nth. Ireland	W	1-0	Belfast	HC	Russell

14-02-1925	Scotland	L	1-3	Edinburgh	HC	Williams W
28-02	England	L	1-2	Swansea	HC	OG
18-04	Nth. Ireland	D	0-0	Wrexham	HC	
31-10	Scotland	L	0-3	Cardiff	HC	
13-02-1926	Nth. Ireland	L	0-3	Belfast	HC	
1-03	England	W	3-1	London	HC	Fowler 2, Davies W (IV)
30-10	Scotland	L	0-3	Glasgow	HC	
12-02-1927	England	D	3-3	Wrexham	HC	Davies L (II) 2, Lewis W (II)
9-04	Nth. Ireland	D	2-2	Cardiff	HC	Williams R 2
29-10	Scotland	D	2-2	Wrexham	HC	Curtis E, OG
28-11	England	W	2-1	Burnley	HC	Lewis W (II), OG
4-02-1928	Nth. Ireland	W	2-1	Belfast	HC	Davies W (IV), Lewis W (II)
27-10	Scotland	L	2-4	Glasgow	HC	Davies W (IV) 2
17-11	England	L	2-3	Swansea	HC	Fowler, Keenor
2-02-1929	Nth. Ireland	D	2-2	Wrexham	HC	Mays, Warren
26-10	Scotland	L	2-4	Cardiff	HC	O'Callaghan, Davies L (II)
20-11	England	L	0-6	London	HC	
1-02-1930	Nth. Ireland	L	0-7	Belfast	HC	
25-10	Scotland	D	1-1	Glasgow	HC	Bamford
22-11	England	L	0-4	Wrexham	HC	
22-04-1931	Nth. Ireland	W	3-2	Wrexham	HC	Phillips C, Griffiths T, Warren
31-10	Scotland	L	2-3	Wrexham	HC	Curtis E 2
18-11	England	L	1-3	Liverpool	HC	Robbins
5-12	Nth. Ireland	L	0-4	Belfast	HC	
26-10-1932	Scotland	W	5-2	Edinburgh	HC	O'Callaghan 2, Griffiths T, Astley, OG
16-11	England	D	0-0	Wrexham	HC	
7-12	Nth. Ireland	W	4-1	Wrexham	HC	Astley 2, Robbins 2
25-05-1933	France	D	1-1	Paris	Fr	Griffiths T
4-10	Scotland	W	3-2	Cardiff	HC	Evans W, Robbins, Astley
4-11	Nth. Ireland	D	1-1	Belfast	HC	Glover
15-11	England	W	2-1	Newcastle	HC	Mills, Astley
29-09-1934	England	L	0-4	Cardiff	HC	
21-11	Scotland	L	2-3	Aberdeen	HC	Phillips C, Astley
27-03-1935	Nth. Ireland	W	3-1	Wrexham	HC	Jones C (I), Phillips C, Hopkins
5-10	Scotland	D	1-1	Cardiff	HC	Phillips C
5-02-1936	England	W	2-1	Wolverhampton	HC	Astley, Jones B (I)
11-03	Nth. Ireland	L	2-3	Belfast	HC	Astley, Phillips C
17-10	England	W	2-1	Cardiff	HC	Morris S, Glover
2-12	Scotland	W	2-1	Dundee	HC	Glover 2
17-03-1937	Nth. Ireland	W	4-1	Wrexham	HC	Glover 2, Jones B (I), Warren
30-10	Scotland	W	2-1	Cardiff	HC	Jones B (I), Morris S
17-11	England	L	1-2	Middlesbrough	HC	Perry
16-03-1938	Nth. Ireland	L	0-1	Belfast	HC	
22-10	England	W	4-2	Cardiff	HC	Astley 2, Hopkins, Jones B (I)
9-11	Scotland	L	2-3	Edinburgh	HC	Astley, Jones L
15-03-1939	Nth. Ireland	W	3-1	Wrexham	HC	Cumner, Glover, Boulter
20-05	France	L	1-2	Paris	Fr	Astley
19-10-1946	Scotland	W	3-1	Wrexham	HC	Jones B (I), Ford, OG
13-11	England	L	0-3	Manchester	HC	
16-04-1947	Nth. Ireland	L	1-2	Belfast	HC	Ford
18-10	England	L	0-3	Cardiff	HC	
12-11	Scotland	W	2-1	Glasgow	HC	Lowrie, Ford
10-03-1948	Nth. Ireland	W	2-0	Wrexham	HC	Lowrie, Edwards G
23-10	Scotland	L	1-3	Cardiff	HC	Jones B (I)
10-11	England	L	0-1	Birmingham	HC	
9-03-1949	Nth. Ireland	W	2-0	Belfast	HC	Edwards G, Ford
15-05	Portugal	L	2-3	Lisbon	Fr	Ford 2
22-05	Belgium	L	1-3	Liege	Fr	Ford
26-05	Switzerland	L	0-4	Berne	Fr	
15-10	England	L	1-4	Cardiff	HC/WCq	Griffiths M
9-11	Scotland	L	0-2	Glasgow	HC/WCq	
23-11	Belgium	W	5-1	Cardiff	Fr	Clarke, Paul, Ford 3
8-03-1950	Nth. Ireland	D	0-0	Wrexham	HC/WCq	
21-10	Scotland	L	1-3	Cardiff	HC	Powell A
15-11	England	L	2-4	Sunderland	HC	Ford 2
7-03-1951	Nth. Ireland	W	2-1	Belfast	HC	Clarke 2
12-05	Portugal	W	2-1	Cardiff	Fr	Griffiths M, Ford
16-05	Switzerland	W	3-2	Wrexham	Fr	Ford 2, Burgess
20-10	England	D	1-1	Cardiff	HC	Foulkes

14–11	Scotland	W	1–0	Glasgow	HC	Allchurch
19–03–1952	Nth. Ireland	W	3–0	Swansea	HC	Barnes, Allchurch, Clarke
18–10	Scotland	L	1–2	Cardiff	HC	Ford
12–11	England	L	2–5	London	HC	Ford 2
15–04–1953	Nth. Ireland	W	3–2	Belfast	HC	Charles J 2, Ford
14–05	France	L	1–6	Paris	Fr	Allchurch
21–05	Yugoslavia	L	2–5	Belgrade	Fr	Ford 2
10–10	England	L	1–4	Cardiff	HC/WCq	Allchurch
4–11	Scotland	D	3–3	Glasgow	HC/WCq	Charles J 2, Allchurch
31–03–1954	Nth. Ireland	L	1–2	Wrexham	HC/WCq	Charles J
9–05	Austria	L	0–2	Vienna	Fr	
22–09	Yugoslavia	L	1–3	Cardiff	Fr	Allchurch
16–10	Scotland	L	0–1	Cardiff	HC	
10–11	England	L	2–3	London	HC	Charles J 2
20–04–1955	Nth. Ireland	W	3–2	Belfast	HC	Charles J 3
22–10	England	W	2–1	Cardiff	HC	Tapscott, Jones C (II)
9–11	Scotland	L	0–2	Glasgow	HC	
23–11	Austria	L	1–2	Wrexham	Fr	Tapscott
11–04–1956	Nth. Ireland	D	1–1	Cardiff	HC	Clarke
20–10	Scotland	D	2–2	Cardiff	HC	Ford, Medwin
14–11	England	L	1–3	London	HC	Charles J
10–04–1957	Nth. Ireland	D	0–0	Belfast	HC	
1–05	Czechoslovakia	W	1–0	Cardiff	WCq	Vernon
19–05	East Germany	L	1–2	Leipzig	WCq	Charles M
26–05	Czechoslovakia	L	0–2	Prague	WCq	
25–09	East Germany	W	4–1	Cardiff	WCq	Palmer 3, Jones C (II)
19–10	England	L	0–4	Cardiff	HC	
13–11	Scotland	D	1–1	Glasgow	HC	Medwin
15–01–1958	Israel	W	2–0	Tel Aviv	WCq	Allchurch, Bowen
5–02	Israel	W	2–0	Cardiff	WCq	Allchurch, Jones C (II)
16–04	Nth. Ireland	D	1–1	Cardiff	HC	Hewitt
8–06	Hungary	D	1–1	Sandviken	WCr1	Charles J
11–06	Mexico	D	1–1	Stockholm	WCr1	Allchurch
15–06	Sweden	D	0–0	Stockholm	WCr1	
17–06	Hungary	W	2–1	Stockholm	WCr1	Allchurch, Medwin
19–06	Brazil	L	0–1	Gothenburg	WCqf	
18–10	Scotland	L	0–3	Cardiff	HC	
26–11	England	D	2–2	Birmingham	HC	Tapscott, Allchurch
22–04–1959	Nth. Ireland	L	1–4	Belfast	HC	Tapscott
17–10	England	D	1–1	Cardiff	HC	Moore
4–11	Scotland	D	1–1	Glasgow	HC	Charles J
6–04–1960	Nth. Ireland	W	3–2	Wrexham	HC	Medwin 2, Woosnam
28–09	Rep. Ireland	W	3–2	Dublin	Fr	Jones C (II) 2, Woosnam
22–10	Scotland	W	2–0	Cardiff	HC	Vernon, Jones C (II)
23–11	England	L	1–5	London	HC	Leek
12–04–1961	Nth. Ireland	W	5–1	Belfast	HC	Charles M, Jones C (II) 2, Allchurch, Leek
19–04	Spain	L	1–2	Cardiff	WCq	Woosnam
18–05	Spain	D	1–1	Madrid	WCq	Allchurch
28–05	Hungary	L	2–3	Budapest	Fr	Allchurch, Jones C (II)
14–10	England	D	1–1	Cardiff	HC	Williams G
8–11	Scotland	L	0–2	Glasgow	HC	
11–04–1962	Nth. Ireland	W	4–0	Cardiff	HC	Charles M 4
12–05	Brazil	L	1–3	Rio de Janeiro	Fr	Allchurch
16–05	Brazil	L	1–3	Sao Paulo	Fr	Leek
22–05	Mexico	L	1–2	Mexico City	Fr	Charles J
20–10	Scotland	L	2–3	Cardiff	HC	Allchurch, Charles J
7–11	Hungary	L	1–3	Budapest	ECr1	Medwin
21–11	England	L	0–4	London	HC	
20–03–1963	Hungary	D	1–1	Cardiff	ECr1	Jones C (II)
3–04	Nth. Ireland	W	4–1	Belfast	HC	Woosnam, Jones C (II) 3
12–10	England	L	0–4	Cardiff	HC	
20–11	Scotland	L	1–2	Glasgow	HC	Jones B (II)
15–04–1964	Nth. Ireland	L	2–3	Swansea	HC	Godfrey, Davies R (I)
3–10	Scotland	W	3–2	Cardiff	HC	Davies R (II), Leek 2
21–10	Denmark	L	0–1	Copenhagen	WCq	
18–11	England	L	1–2	London	HC	Jones C (II)
9–12	Greece	L	0–2	Athens	WCq	
17–03–1965	Greece	W	4–1	Cardiff	WCq	Allchurch 2, England, Vernon
31–03	Nth. Ireland	W	5–0	Belfast	HC	Vernon 2, Jones C (II), Williams G,

						Allchurch
1–05	Italy	L	1–4	Florence	Fr	Godfrey
30–05	Soviet Union	L	1–2	Moscow	WCq	Davies R (II)
2–10	England	D	0–0	Cardiff	HC	
27–10	Soviet Union	W	2–1	Cardiff	WCq	Vernon, Allchurch
24–11	Scotland	L	1–4	Glasgow	HC	Allchurch
1–12	Denmark	W	4–2	Wrexham	WCq	Vernon 2, Davies R (II), Rees
30–03–1966	Nth. Ireland	L	1–4	Cardiff	HC	Davies R (II)
14–05	Brazil	L	1–3	Rio de Janeiro	Fr	Davies R (I)
18–05	Brazil	L	0–1	Belo Horizonte	Fr	
22–05	Chile	L	0–2	Santiago	Fr	
22–10	Scotland	D	1–1	Cardiff	HC/ECq	Davies R (I)
16–11	England	L	1–5	London	HC/ECq	Davies R (II)
12–04–1967	Nth. Ireland	D	0–0	Belfast	HC/ECq	
21–10	England	L	0–3	Cardiff	HC/ECq	
22–11	Scotland	L	2–3	Glasgow	HC/ECq	Davies R (I), Durban
28–02–1968	Nth. Ireland	W	2–0	Wrexham	HC/ECq	Rees, Davies R (II)
8–05	West Germany	D	1–1	Cardiff	Fr	Davies R (II)
23–10	Italy	L	0–1	Cardiff	WCq	
26–03–1969	West Germany	D	1–1	Frankfurt	Fr	Jones B (II)
16–04	East Germany	L	1–2	Dresden	WCq	Toshack
3–05	Scotland	L	3–5	Wrexham	HC	Davies R (I) 2, Toshack
7–05	England	L	1–2	London	HC	Davies R (I)
10–05	Nth. Ireland	D	0–0	Belfast	HC	
22–10	East Germany	L	1–3	Cardiff	WCq	Powell D
4–11	Italy	L	1–4	Rome	WCq	England
18–04–1970	England	D	1–1	Cardiff	HC	Krzywicki
22–04	Scotland	D	0–0	Glasgow	HC	
25–04	Nth. Ireland	W	1–0	Swansea	HC	Rees
11–11	Romania	D	0–0	Cardiff	ECq	
21–04–1971	Czechoslovakia	L	1–3	Swansea	ECq	Davies R (I)
15–05	Scotland	D	0–0	Cardiff	HC	
19–05	England	D	0–0	London	HC	
22–05	Nth. Ireland	L	0–1	Belfast	HC	
26–05	Finland	W	1–0	Helsinki	ECq	Toshack
13–10	Finland	W	3–0	Swansea	ECq	Durban, Toshack, Reece
27–10	Czechoslovakia	L	0–1	Prague	ECq	
24–11	Romania	L	0–2	Bucharest	ECq	
20–05–1972	England	L	0–3	Cardiff	HC	
24–05	Scotland	L	0–1	Glasgow	HC	
27–05	Nth. Ireland	D	0–0	Wrexham	HC	
15–11	England	L	0–1	Cardiff	WCq	
24–01–1973	England	D	1–1	London	WCq	Toshack
28–03	Poland	W	2–0	Cardiff	WCq	James L, Hockey
12–05	Scotland	L	0–2	Wrexham	HC	
15–05	England	L	0–3	London	HC	
19–05	Nth. Ireland	L	0–1	Liverpool	HC	
26–09	Poland	L	0–3	Chorzow	WCq	
11–05–1974	England	L	0–2	Cardiff	HC	
14–05	Scotland	L	0–2	Glasgow	HC	
18–05	Nth. Ireland	W	1–0	Wrexham	HC	Smallman
4–09	Austria	L	1–2	Vienna	ECq	Griffiths A
30–10	Hungary	W	2–0	Cardiff	ECq	Griffiths A, Toshack
20–11	Luxembourg	W	5–0	Swansea	ECq	Toshack, England, Roberts P, Griffiths A, Yorath

LEADING INTERNATIONAL APPEARANCES

1	Nicolas	73		Ratcliffe	58	17	James R	47
2	Jones J	72	10	James L	54	18	England	44
	Allchurch	68	11	Rush	53	19	Williams S	43
4	Flynn	66	12	Davies D	52	20	Hughes	42
5	Southall	60	13	Mahoney	51	21	Kelsey	41
6	Jones C	59		Thomas M	51		Sherwwod	41
	Yorath	59	15	Thomas R	50	23	Rodrigues	40
8	Phillips	58	16	W Meredith	48		Toshack	40

16-04-1975	Hungary	W	2-1	Budapest	ECq	Toshack, Mahoney
1-05	Luxembourg	W	3-1	Luxembourg	ECq	Reece, James L 2
17-05	Scotland	D	2-2	Cardiff	HC	Toshack, Flynn
21-05	England	D	2-2	London	HC	Toshack, Griffiths A
23-05	Nth. Ireland	L	0-1	Belfast	HC	
19-11	Austria	W	1-0	Wrexham	ECq	Griffiths A
24-03-1976	England	L	1-2	Wrexham	Fr	Curtis A
24-04	Yugoslavia	L	0-2	Zagreb	ECqf	
6-05	Scotland	L	1-3	Glasgow	HC	Griffiths A
8-05	England	L	0-1	Cardiff	HC	
14-05	Nth. Ireland	W	1-0	Swansea	HC	James L
22-05	Yugoslavia	D	1-1	Cardiff	ECqf	Evans I
6-10	West Germany	L	0-2	Cardiff	Fr	
17-11	Scotland	L	0-1	Glasgow	WCq	
30-03-1977	Czechoslovakia	W	3-0	Wrexham	WCq	James L 2, Deacy
28-05	Scotland	D	0-0	Wrexham	HC	
31-05	England	W	1-0	London	HC	James L
3-06	Nth. Ireland	D	1-1	Belfast	HC	Deacy
6-09	Kuwait	D	0-0	Wrexham	Fr	
20-09	Kuwait	D	0-0	Kuwait City	Fr	
12-10	Scotland	L	0-2	Liverpool	WCq	
16-11	Czechoslovakia	L	0-1	Prague	WCq	
14-12	West Germany	D	1-1	Dortmund	Fr	Jones D
18-04-1978	Iran	W	1-0	Tehran	Fr	Dwyer
13-05	England	L	1-3	Cardiff	HC	Dwyer
17-05	Scotland	D	1-1	Glasgow	HC	OG
19-05	Nth. Ireland	W	1-0	Wrexham	HC	Deacy
25-10	Malta	W	7-0	Wrexham	ECq	Edwards R 4, O'Sullivan, Thomas M, Flynn
29-11	Turkey	W	1-0	Wrexham	ECq	Deacy
2-05-1979	West Germany	L	0-2	Wrexham	ECq	
19-05	Scotland	W	3-0	Cardiff	HC	Toshack 3
23-05	England	D	0-0	London	HC	
26-05	Nth. Ireland	D	1-1	Belfast	HC	James R
2-06	Malta	W	2-0	Gzira	ECq	Nicholas, Flynn
11-09	Rep. Ireland	W	2-1	Swansea	Fr	Walsh, Curtis A
17-10	West Germany	L	1-5	Cologne	ECq	Curtis A
21-11	Turkey	L	0-1	Izmir	ECq	
17-05-1980	England	W	4-1	Wrexham	HC	Thomas M, Walsh, James R, OG
21-05	Scotland	L	0-1	Glasgow	HC	
23-05	Nth. Ireland	L	0-1	Cardiff	HC	
2-06	Iceland	W	4-0	Reykjavik	WCq	Walsh 2, Giles, Flynn
15-10	Turkey	W	4-0	Cardiff	WCq	Flynn, James L 2, Walsh
19-11	Czechoslovakia	W	1-0	Cardiff	WCq	Giles
24-02-1981	Rep. Ireland	W	3-1	Dublin	Fr	Price P, Boyle, Yorath
25-03	Turkey	W	1-0	Ankara	WCq	Harris
16-05	Scotland	W	2-0	Swansea	HC	Walsh 2
20-05	England	D	0-0	London	HC	
30-05	Soviet Union	D	0-0	Wrexham	WCq	
9-09	Czechoslovakia	L	0-2	Prague	WCq	
14-10	Iceland	D	2-2	Swansea	WCq	James R, Curtis A
18-11	Soviet Union	L	0-3	Tbilisi	WCq	
24-03-1982	Spain	D	1-1	Valencia	Fr	James R
27-04	England	L	0-1	Cardiff	HC	
24-05	Scotland	L	0-1	Glasgow	HC	
27-05	Nth. Ireland	W	3-0	Wrexham	HC	Curtis A, Rush, Nicholas
2-06	France	W	1-0	Toulouse	Fr	Rush
22-09	Norway	W	1-0	Swansea	ECq	Rush
15-12	Yugoslavia	D	4-4	Titograd	ECq	Flynn, Rush, Jones J (III), James R
23-02-1983	England	L	1-2	London	HC	Rush
27-04	Bulgaria	W	1-0	Wrexham	ECq	Charles J (II)
28-05	Scotland	L	0-2	Cardiff	HC	
31-05	Nth. Ireland	W	1-0	Belfast	HC	Davies G
12-06	Brazil	D	1-1	Cardiff	Fr	Flynn
21-09	Norway	D	0-0	Oslo	ECq	
12-10	Romania	W	5-0	Wrexham	Fr	Rush 2, Thomas M, James R, Curtis A
16-11	Bulgaria	L	0-1	Sofia	ECq	
14-12	Yugoslavia	D	1-1	Cardiff	ECq	James R
28-02-1984	Scotland	L	1-2	Glasgow	HC	James R
2-05	England	W	1-0	Wrexham	HC	Hughes

LEADING INTERNATIONAL GOALSCORERS

1	Allchurch	23
	Ford	23
3	Rush	20
4	Jones C	16
5	Charles J	15
6	Toshack	12
	Astley	12
	Lewis W	12
9	Meredith	11
10	James L	10
	Saunders	10
12	Hughes	9
	Morris A	9
	Davies R	9
15	Vernon	8
16	Flynn	7
	Glover	7
	James R	7
	Walsh	7

22–05	Nth. Ireland	D	1–1	Swansea	HC	Hughes
6–06	Norway	L	0–1	Trondheim	Fr	
10–06	Israel	D	0–0	Tel Aviv	Fr	
12–09	Iceland	L	0–1	Reykjavik	WCq	
17–10	Spain	L	0–3	Seville	WCq	
14–11	Iceland	W	2–1	Cardiff	WCq	Thomas M, Hughes
26–02–1985	Norway	D	1–1	Wrexham	Fr	Rush
27–03	Scotland	W	1–0	Glasgow	WCq	Rush
30–04	Spain	W	3–0	Wrexham	WCq	Rush 2, Hughes
5–06	Norway	L	2–4	Bergen	Fr	Hughes, Lovell
10–09	Scotland	D	1–1	Cardiff	WCq	Hughes
16–10	Hungary	L	0–3	Cardiff	Fr	
25–02–1986	Saudi Arabia	W	2–1	Dhahran	Fr	Slatter, Davies G
26–03	Rep. Ireland	W	1–0	Dublin	Fr	Rush
21–04	Uruguay	D	0–0	Wrexham	Fr	
10–05	Canada	L	0–2	Toronto	Fr	
19–05	Canada	W	3–0	Vancouver	Fr	Saunders 2, Allen
10–09	Finland	D	1–1	Helsinki	ECq	Slatter
18–02–1987	Soviet Union	D	0–0	Swansea	Fr	
1–04	Finland	W	4–0	Wrexham	ECq	Rush, Hodges, Phillips D, Jones A
29–04	Czechoslovakia	D	1–1	Wrexham	ECq	Rush
9–09	Denmark	W	1–0	Cardiff	ECq	Hughes
14–10	Denmark	L	0–1	Copenhagen	ECq	
11–11	Czechoslovakia	L	0–2	Prague	ECq	
23–03–1988	Yugoslavia	L	1–2	Swansea	Fr	Saunders
27–04	Sweden	L	1–4	Stockholm	Fr	Hodges
1–06	Malta	W	3–2	Ta'Qali	Fr	Rush, Hughes, Horne
4–06	Italy	W	1–0	Brescia	Fr	Rush
14–09	Holland	L	0–1	Amsterdam	WCq	
19–10	Finland	D	2–2	Swansea	WCq	Saunders, OG
8–02–1989	Israel	D	3–3	Tel–Aviv	Fr	Allen, Horne, OG
26–04	Sweden	L	0–2	Wrexham	Fr	
31–05	West Germany	D	0–0	Cardiff	WCq	
6–09	Finland	L	0–1	Helsinki	WCq	
11–10	Holland	L	1–2	Wrexham	WCq	Bowen
15–11	West Germany	L	1–2	Cologne	WCq	Allen
28–03–1990	Rep. Ireland	L	0–1	Dublin	Fr	
25–04	Sweden	L	2–4	Stockholm	Fr	Saunders 2
19–05	Costa Rica	W	1–0	Cardiff	Fr	Saunders
11–09	Denmark	L	0–1	Copenhagen	Fr	
17–10	Belgium	W	3–1	Cardiff	ECq	Rush, Saunders, Hughes
14–11	Luxembourg	W	1–0	Luxembourg	ECq	Rush
6–02–1991	Rep. Ireland	L	0–3	Wrexham	Fr	
27–03	Belgium	D	1–1	Brussels	ECq	Saunders
1–05	Iceland	W	1–0	Cardiff	Fr	Bodin
29–05	Poland	D	0–0	Radom	Fr	
5–06	Germany	W	1–0	Cardiff	ECq	Rush
11–09	Brazil	W	1–0	Cardiff	Fr	Saunders
16–10	Germany	L	1–4	Nuremberg	ECq	Bodin
13–11	Luxembourg	W	1–0	Cardiff	ECq	Bodin
19–02–1992	Rep. Ireland	W	1–0	Dublin	Fr	Pembridge
29–04	Austria	D	1–1	Vienna	Fr	Coleman
20–05	Romania	L	1–5	Bucharest	WCq	Rush
30–05	Holland	L	0–4	Utrecht	Fr	
3–06	Argentina	L	0–1	Gifu	KC	
7–06	Japan	W	1–0	Matsuyama	KC	Bowen

The former
YUGOSLAVIA

The future of Yugoslavia is even more uncertain than that of the former Soviet Union in that whereas the Soviet Union fell apart through largely peaceful means, Yugoslavia is disintegrating violently as old nationalist tensions bubble to the surface. One of the first indications that this was going to happen came in the league games between Red Star Belgrade and Dinamo Zagreb in the years leading up to the civil war. These matches were constantly marred by fierce fighting between supporters of the Serbian Red Star and Croatian Dinamo.

Should the republics go their own way, it will mark the end of the road for a country loved the world over for its football. In the 1960s the phrase 'often the bridesmaid, but never the bride' summed up Yugoslavia's habit of finishing as runners-up rather than winners, but over the years they have dazzled the world with some beautiful football played by some of the world's most skilful players.

With the bitterness that exists between the warring factions at present, it is unlikely that they will have the chance to win that elusive championship. In future World Cups and European Championships we are likely to witness Serbia, Croatia and Bosnia taking the field, and hopefully they will not be drawn in the same group!

As in all of the Balkan nations, the development of the game was held up by the turbulent nature of the region at the beginning of the century. Yugoslavia did not exist as a state until after the First World War and it is to this pre-war situation that Yugoslavia seems to be returning as the patchwork of nationalities fight it out once again. Split, the Adriatic seaport in Croatia, saw the first club when Hajduk Split were formed in 1911, named after local fighters who had resisted the Ottoman Empire in the previous century.

It was eleven years before they could take part in a proper league. An association for the newly-formed state was founded in 1919 and a national league started four years later. The standard of the game was not particularly high and many of the clubs that took part in the new competition no longer exist.

In 1920 the Yugoslavs took on another newly-formed country, Czechoslovakia, in the Antwerp Olympic Games, but the difference in experience told as they lost 7–0. A 4–2 defeat at the hands of Egypt in the consolation tournament did little to raise spirits and it was not until the late 1920s that the team began to perform better. In the 1924 Olympic Games, Uruguay inflicted another 7–0 defeat on them, whilst in 1928 an inexperienced Portugal side made sure that it was three first round exits in a row in the the world's premier football tournament of the time.

The 1930 World Cup saw the first signs of development. As one of only four European countries to make the trip to Uruguay, Yugoslavia did commendably well to reach the semi-finals, but although the victory over Brazil looks good on paper, the Brazilians were not performing well at the time and were certainly not of the same calibre as the sides after the war. That Yugoslavia's success in Montevideo was a flash in the pan was proved by their failure to qualify for both the 1934 and 1938 tournaments, after defeats by Romania and Poland respectively.

In the early 1930s, the Balkan Cup provided much of the international interest and Yugoslavia's record was generally good, coming second in the first three editions and winning the fourth in 1934. It was not until after the Second World War that the Yugoslavs really began to make progress and move ahead of their Balkan neighbours. The war had once again caused a rift in the country as a German-backed government was installed in Croatia. A Croatian team was even able to travel widely during the war years and play international matches against Germany and her allies, but it did not last as communist guerillas under Tito eventually threw the Germans out.

		All			League			Cup		Europe		
	Team	G	S	B	G	S	B	G	S	G	S	B
1	Crvena Zvedza	31	17	11	18	8	7	12	8	1	1	4
2	Hajduk Split	18	15	12	9	10	10	9	5	–	–	2
3	Partizan Beograd	16	14	8	11	9	8	5	4	–	1	–
4	Dinamo Zagreb	13	21	7	4	12	6	8	8	1	1	1
5	OFK Beograd	9	6	5	5	6	4	4	–	–	–	1
6	Gradanski Zagreb	5	2	3	5	2	3	–	–	–	–	–
7	Velez Mostar	2	5	4	–	3	4	2	2	–	–	–
8	Vojvodina Novi Sad	2	4	1	2	3	1	–	1	–	–	–
9	FK Sarajevo	2	4	–	2	2	–	–	2	–	–	–
10	Yugoslavia Beograd	2	3	3	2	3	3	–	–	–	–	–
11	Concordia Zagreb	2	1	–	2	1	–	–	–	–	–	–
12	NK Rijeka	2	1	–	–	–	–	2	1	–	–	–
13	Zeljeznicar Sarajevo	1	2	3	1	1	2	–	1	–	–	1
14	Borac Banja Luka	1	1	–	–	–	–	1	1	–	–	–
15	HASK Zagreb	1	–	1	1	–	1	–	–	–	–	–
16	Vardar Skopje	1	–	–	–	–	–	1	–	–	–	–
17	Buducnost Titograd	–	2	–	–	–	–	–	2	–	–	–
	Nasa Krila Zemun	–	2	–	–	–	–	–	2	–	–	–
19	Radnicki Beograd	–	1	2	–	–	2	–	1	–	–	–
20	Slavia Sarajevo	–	1	1	–	1	1	–	–	–	–	–
	Sloboda Tuzla	–	1	1	–	–	1	–	1	–	–	–
22	FK Bor	–	1	–	–	–	–	–	1	–	–	–
	Olimpia Ljubljana	–	1	–	–	–	–	–	1	–	–	–
	SASK Sarajevo	–	1	–	–	1	–	–	–	–	–	–
	Spartak Subotica	–	1	–	–	–	–	–	1	–	–	–
	Trepca Mitrovica	–	1	–	–	–	–	–	1	–	–	–
	Varteks Varazdin	–	1	–	–	–	–	–	1	–	–	–
28	Radnicki Nis	–	–	3	–	–	2	–	–	–	–	1
29	Lokomotiva Zagreb	–	–	1	–	–	1	–	–	–	–	–
	Belgrade Select XI	–	–	1	–	–	–	–	–	–	–	1

To the end of the 1990–91 season

As a communist state Yugoslavia, reunited again, could have been expected to go the same way as all the other Eastern bloc countries, but like the policies of Tito, Yugoslav football followed a peculiarly independent line. In fact they could perhaps have done with some of the teamwork so renowned of the communist countries, for despite producing players with outstanding skill, the main criticism levelled was one of inconsistency, and it was this that led to so many runner-up positions.

After the war, club football was completely reorganised along the lines of that in the Soviet Union. In 1945 Gradanski Zagreb, the first ever champions, and their rivals HASK formed the basis of the Dinamo club that was to become a dominant power, whilst in Belgrade, BSK, champions on five occasions in the 1930s and along with Hajduk the oldest club in the country, were reorganised as OFK. A new army team called Partizan were formed in 1945 whilst perhaps the most famous team of them all, Crvena Zvezda or Red Star, were formed as the University club in the same year.

These five clubs have dominated the league, and the new cup competition introduced in 1947, ever since. The standard was quick to improve, though it was mainly for the achievements of the national side that the Yugoslavs became famous. As an 'amateur' country they entered the 1948 Olympic Games with their full international side, and by finishing as runners-up started a remarkable sequence.

In four consecutive Olympic tournaments, the Yugoslav team appeared in the final. Hungary beat them 2–0 in Helsinki in the 1952 final, the Soviet Union won 1–0 in 1956 in Melbourne before at last, in the 1960 Rome Olympics, the gold medal was won. Their opponents that day were poor Denmark, who in turn collected *their* third silver medal after having lost in the 1908 and 1912 finals.

That win was the only title at senior level to be won by the national side, but unfortunately it carries little weight due to the lack of any Western-based professionals in the tournament. Two months previously in a similarly depleted first European Championship, Yugoslavia attained her customary second place after losing 2–1 in the final to the Soviet Union in Paris, having beaten both Portugal and France along the way.

In the World Cup the habit was to reach the quarter-finals before bowing out to West Germany. This happened in both 1954 and 1958, but when they were paired with the Germans in the quarter-finals for the third successive tournament, in 1962 in Chile, it was third time lucky and they won 1–0. Czechoslovakia were generally considered the weaker of the two teams in the semi-finals, but once again a lack of consistency let Yugoslavia down as they lost 3–1 in Viña del Mar and had to settle for fourth place after losing the third place play-off to the hosts.

Many fine players represented Yugoslavia in these post-war years. Stejpan Bobek was instrumental in helping the team reach the first two Olympic finals, and the 38 goals he scored between 1946 and 1956 remains a record. Branco Zebec, a team-mate of Bobek for most of those years, was another great player and after he retired in 1961, his 65 caps remained a record for over 10 years until broken by Dragan Dzajic. The two most important goalscorers who took over the role vacated by Bobek were Milan Galic and Bora Kostic, the former falling just one short of his predecessor's goal tally.

Both were key elements in both the Olympic triumph of 1960 and the second place in the European Championship of that year. The outstanding player of the time though was Dragoslav Sekularac, and it was he who inspired his team to fourth place in the World Cup in Chile.

The mid-1960s were not a very happy time for the national side and they did not make the journey to England for the 1966 World Cup. Two years later, though, they defeated the world champions England in the semi-finals of the European Championship to reach yet another final. Surprise, surprise, it ended in defeat, though it took the hosts Italy two games seal the victory. The star of this side was Dzajic, the most capped Yugoslav of all time, but despite his presence in the side until the late 1970s Yugoslavia's form continued to baffle.

In 1970, for the second consecutive World Cup, the team failed to qualify. When they did in 1974, they were very disappointing despite reaching the second round and beating Zaire 9–0. The European Championships has always been a different story. They have never finished lower than second in their qualifying group and in 1976 had a glorious opportunity to win the tournament when it was staged in Yugoslavia. Home advantage could not be made to count and they lost to the powerful West Germany in the semi-final.

It is sad that just as the country was mounting a serious challenge for honours once again, it should start to fall apart to wreck these hopes. The 1991 win by Red Star in the European Cup, though not Yugoslavia's first in a European competition, was the first in the premier event. Despite a dreadful final, they had played some scintillating football to get that far and once again Yugoslav footballers have become the fashion.

For years they had been in high demand with clubs in the West, but the federation was always able to control the exodus, not allowing them to leave in most cases until they were past their prime. Now that has become impossible. Real Madrid signed Robert Prosinecki and many followed him abroad, often in the hope that they could actually start playing some football again, as the game ground to a halt in many regions of the country.

In 1992 the recognition of both Slovenia and Croatia as separate states saw the latter organising her first championship for nearly 50 years to celebrate independence. The withdrawal of the Croatian clubs effectively ended the Yugoslav championship in any recognisable form, and with the withdrawal of the Bosnian teams it became very much a Serbian affair.

The final ignominy for Yugoslav football came with the forced withdrawal of the national side from the 1992 European Championship finals. Most of the non-Serbian players had already withdrawn from the team, but it marked a sad end to a proud footballing history at a time when Yugoslav football was perhaps at its strongest.

Population: 23 861 000
Area, sq km: 255 804
% in urban areas: 46.5%
Capital city: Belgrade

Fudbalski Savez Jugoslavije
PO Box 263
Terazije #35
11000 Belgrade
Tel: (010 38) 11 333447
Fax: (010 38) 11 333433
Telex: 11666 FSJ YU
Cable: JUGOFUTBAL BELGRADE
Languages for correspondence: French, English, Spanish & German

Year of formation: 1919
Affiliation to FIFA: 1919
Affiliation to UEFA: 1954
Registered clubs: 6030
Registered players: 230 800
Professional players: 420
Registered coaches: 7479
Registered referees: 9570
National Stadium: No national stadium
National colours: Shirts: Blue/Shorts: White/Socks: Red
Reserve colours: Shirts: White/Shorts: White/Socks: White
Season: August–June

THE RECORD

WORLD CUP

1930 .... QT Automatic – Final Tournament/Semi-finalists
1934 .... QT 3rd/3 in group 10
1938 .... QT 2nd/2 in group 2
1950 .... QT 1st/3 in group 3 – Final Tournament/1st round
1954 .... QT 1st/3 in group 10– Final Tournament/Quarter-finalists
1958 .... QT 1st/3 in group 7 – Final Tournament/Quarter-finalists
1962 .... QT 1st/4 in group 10– Final Tournament/Semi-finalists/4th place
1966 .... QT 3rd/4 in group 3
1970 .... QT 2nd/4 in group 6
1974 .... QT 1st/3 in group 7 – Final Tournament/2nd round
1978 .... QT 3rd/3 in group 8
1982 .... QT 1st/5 in group 5 – Final Tournament/1st round
1986 .... QT 4th/5 in group 4
1990 .... QT 1st/5 in group 5 – Final Tournament/Quarter-finalists

EUROPEAN CHAMPIONSHIP

1960 .... Finalists
1964 .... 2nd round
1968 .... QT 1st/3 in group 4 – Final Tournament/Finalists
1972 .... QT 1st/4 in group 7 – Final Tournament/Quarter-finalists
1976 .... QT 1st/4 in group 3 – Final Tournament/Semi-finalists/4th place
1980 .... QT 2nd/4 in group 3
1984 .... QT 1st/4 in group 4 – Final Tournament/1st round
1988 .... QT 2nd/4 in group 4
1992 .... QT 1st/5 in group 4

OLYMPIC GAMES

1908 .... Did not enter
1912 .... Did not enter
1920 .... 1st round
1924 .... Preliminary round
1928 .... 1st round
1936 .... Did not enter
1948 .... Finalists
1952 .... Finalists
1956 .... Finalists
1960 .... Final Tournament/Winners
1964 .... Final Tournament/Quarter-finalists
1968 .... QT Did not qualify
1972 .... QT Did not qualify
1976 .... QT Did not qualify
1980 .... Final Tournament/Semi-finalists/4th place
1984 .... Final Tournament/Semi-finalists/3rd place
1988 .... Final Tournament/1st round
1992 .... QT Failed to qualify

DR GERÖ CUP

1929–53 ..... Did not enter
1960 .... 4th

EUROPEAN CLUB COMPETITIONS

EUROPEAN CUP: Winners – Crvena Zvezda 1991
Finalists – Partizan Beograd 1966

CUP WINNERS CUP: Semi-finalists – Dinamo Zagreb 1961, OFK Beograd 1963, Hajduk Split 1973, Crvena Zvezda 1975

UEFA CUP: Winners – Dinamo Zagreb 1967
Finalists – Dinamo Zagreb 1963, Crvena Zvezda 1979

MITROPA CUP: Semi-finalists – SK Beograd 1939

CLUB DIRECTORY

SERBIA
Population: 9 830 000
Area, sq km: 88 361
Capital city: Belgrade

BELGRADE (Population – 1 400 000)

OFK Beograd
Stadium: Omladinski 20 000
Founded: 1911
Colours: Blue and white stripes/Blue
Previous names: BSK 1911–40 & 1950–57, Metalac 1940–50

FK Crvena Zvezda (Red Star) Beograd
Stadium: Crvena Zvezda 97 000
Founded: 1945
Colours: Red and white stripes/Red

FK Partizan Beograd
Stadium: JNA 50 000
Founded: 1945
Colours: Black and white stripes/White

FK Rad Beograd
Stadium: Rad 13 000
Founded: 1958
Colours: Blue/White

NOVI SAD (Population – 266 000)
FK Vojvodina Novi Sad
Stadium: Gradski 22 000
Founded: 1914
Colours: Red and white halves/Red
Previous name: Sloga 1945–51

PRISTINA (Population – 244 000)
FK Pristina
Stadium: Gradski 30 000
Founded: 1922
Colours: Blue/White

NIS (Population – 240 000)
FK Radnicki Nis
Stadium: Cair 20 000
Founded: 1923
Colours: Blue with white sleeves/Blue

SUBOTICA (Population – 153 000)
Subotica is part of Vojvodina
FK Spartak Subotica
Stadium: Gradski 28 000
Founded: 1945
Colours: Blue/Blue

ZRENJANIN (Population – 140 000)
FK Proleter Zrenjanin
Stadium: Karadordevom 33 000
Founded: 1947
Colours: Red and white stripes/White

BOSNIA-HERCEGOVINA
Population: 4 479 000
Area, sq km: 51 129
Capital city: Sarajevo

SARAJEVO (Population – 479 000)
FK Sarajevo
Stadium: Kosevo 45 000
Founded: 1946
Colours: Claret/Claret

FK Zeljeznicar Sarajevo
Stadium: Grbavica 26 000
Founded: 1921
Colours: Sky Blue/Sky blue

BANJA LUKA (Population – 193 000)
FK Borac Banja Luka
Stadium: Gradski 18 000
Founded: 1926
Colours: Red/Blue

ZENICA (Population – 144 000)
FK Celik Zenica
Stadium: Bilino Polje 22 000
Founded: 1945
Colours: Red/Black

TUZLA (Population – 129 000)
FK Sloboda Tuzla
Stadium: Tusanj 11 000
Founded: 1919
Colours: Red and black stripes/Black

MOSTAR (Population – 110 000)
FK Velez Mostar
Stadium: Gradski 21 000
Founded: 1922
Colours: Red/Red

CROATIA
Population: 4 683 000
Area, sq km: 56 538
Capital city: Zagreb

ZAGREB (Population – 697 000)
HASK Gradanski Zagreb
Stadium: HASK Gradanski 55 000
Founded: 1945
Colours: Blue/Blue
Previous name: NK Dinamo Zagreb 1945–91

NK Zagreb
Stadium: Kranjcevicevoj
Founded: 1946
Colours: White/Blue
Previous name: Borac 1946–52

RIJEKA (Population – 199 000)
NK Rijeka
Stadium: Kantrida 20 000
Founded: 1946
Colours: White/White

SPLIT (Population – 191 000)
NK Hajduk Split
Stadium: Poljud 51 000
Founded: 1911
Colours: White/Blue

OSIJEK (Population – 162 000)
NK Osijek
Stadium: Gradski 35 000
Founded: 1945
Colours: Blue/Blue
Previous names: Merger in 1967 of Proleter and Slavija

MACEDONIA
Population: 2 111 000
Area, sq km: 25 713
Capital city: Skopje

SKOPJE (Population – 547 000)
FK Vardar Skoplje
Stadium: Gradski 28 000
Founded: 1947
Colours: Red/Black
Previous names: Gradjanski 1922–39, Pobeda 1939–47

MONTENEGRO
Population: 639 000
Area, sq km: 13 812
Capital city: Titograd

TITOGRAD (Population – 145 000)
FK Budocnost Titograd
Stadium: Pod Goricom 15 000
Founded: 1925
Colours: Blue/white

SLOVENIA
Population: 1 948 000
Area, sq km: 20 251
Capital city: Ljubljana

LJUBLJANA (Population – 316 000)
NK Olimpija Ljubljana
Stadium: Bezigrad 18 000
Founded: 1945
Colours: Green/Green
Previous names: Merger in 1962 of Enotnost and Odred

YUGOSLAV LEAGUE CHAMPIONSHIP

Year	Champions		Runners up		3rd	
1923	Gradanski Zagreb	1–1 4–2	SASK Sarajevo			
1924	Yugoslavia Beograd	2–1	Hajduk Split			
1925	Yugoslavia Beograd	3–2	Gradanski Beograd			
1926	Gradanski Zagreb	2–1	Yugoslavia Beograd			
1927	Hajduk Split	8	BSK Beograd	6	HASK Zagreb	5
1928	Gradanski Zagreb	9	Hajduk Split	6	BSK Beograd	6
1929	Hajduk Split	12	BSK Beograd	10	Yugoslavia Beograd	8
1930	Concordia Zagreb	15	Yugoslavia Beograd	13	Hajduk Split	13
1931	BSK Beograd	20	Concordia Zagreb	11	Gradanski Zagreb	10
1932	Concordia Zagreb	2–1 2–1	Hajduk Split			
1933	BSK Beograd	31	Hajduk Split	28	Yugoslavia Beograd	23
1934						–
1935	BSK Beograd	24	Yugoslavia Beograd	22	Gradanski Zagreb	22
1936	BSK Beograd	1–0 1–1	Slavia Sarajevo			
1937	Gradanski Zagreb	28	Hajduk Split	21	BSK Beograd	21
1938	HASK Zagreb	26	BSK Beograd	26	Gradanski Zagreb	25
1939	BSK Beograd	37	Gradanski Zagreb	32	Yugoslavia Beograd	28
1940	Gradanski Beograd	16	BSK Beograd	15	Slavia Sarajevo	14

1941–46	–					
1947	Partizan Beograd	47	Dinamo Zagreb	42	Crvena Zvezda	39
1948	Dinamo Zagreb	29	Hajduk Split	24	Partizan Beograd	24
1949	Partizan Beograd	29	Crvena Zvezda	26	Hajduk Split	25
1950	Hajduk Split	28	Crvena Zvezda	26	Partizan Beograd	26
1951	Crvena Zvezda	35	Dinamo Zagreb	35	Hajduk Split	32
1952	Hajduk Split	9	Crvena Zvezda	8	Lokomotiva Zagreb	4
1953	Crvena Zvezda	31	Hajduk Split	29	Partizan Beograd	25
1954	Dinamo Zagreb	42	Partizan Beograd	41	Crvena Zvezda	38
1955	Hajduk Split	38	BSK Beograd	36	Dinamo Zagreb	34
1956	Crvena Zvezda	40	Partizan Beograd	35	Radnicki Beograd	31
1957	Crvena Zvezda	39	Vojvodina Novi Sad	35	Hajduk Split	30
1958	Dinamo Zagreb	37	Partizan Beograd	33	Radnicki Beograd	28
1959	Crvena Zvezda	31	Partizan Beograd	31	Vojvodina Novi Sad	30
1960	Crvena Zvezda	33	Dinamo Zagreb	32	Partizan Beograd	27
1961	Partizan Beograd	32	Crvena Zvezda	31	Hajduk Split	30
1962	Partizan Beograd	31	Vojvodina Novi Sad	26	Dinamo Zagreb	25
1963	Partizan Beograd	40	Dinamo Zagreb	35	Zeljeznicar Sarajevo	29
1964	Crvena Zvezda	36	OFK Beograd	33	Dinamo Zagreb	33
1965	Partizan Beograd	43	FK Sarajevo	35	Crvena Zvezda	35
1966	Vojvodina Novi Sad	43	Dinamo Zagreb	35	Velez Mostar	35
1967	FK Sarajevo	42	Dinamo Zagreb	40	Partizan Beograd	38
1968	Crvena Zvezda	43	Partizan Beograd	38	Dinamo Zagreb	35
1969	Crvena Zvezda	48	Dinamo Zagreb	45	Partizan Beograd	40
1970	Crvena Zvezda	46	Partizan Beograd	44	Velez Mostar	43
1971	Hajduk Split	49	Zeljeznicar Sarajevo	45	Dinamo Zagreb	43
1972	Zeljeznicar Sarajevo	51	Crvena Zvezda	49	OFK Beograd	45
1973	Crvena Zvezda	52	Velez Mostar	46	OFK Beograd	45
1974	Hajduk Split	45	Velez Mostar	45	Crvena Zvezda	43
1975	Hajduk Split	48	Vojvodina Novi Sad	45	Crvena Zvezda	40
1976	Partizan Beograd	50	Hajduk Split	49	Dinamo Zagreb	44
1977	Crvena Zvezda	50	Dinamo Zagreb	41	Sloboda Tuzla	39
1978	Partizan Beograd	54	Crvena Zvezda	49	Hajduk Split	39
1979	Hajduk Split	50	Dinamo Zagreb	50	Crvena Zvezda	41
1980	Crvena Zvezda	48	FK Sarajevo	41	Radnicki Nis	39
1981	Crvena Zvezda	44	Hajduk Split	42	Radnicki Nis	41
1982	Dinamo Zagreb	49	Crvena Zvezda	44	Hajduk Split	44
1983	Partizan Beograd	45	Dinamo Zagreb	43	Hajduk Split	43
1984	Crvena Zvezda	44	Partizan Beograd	42	Zeljeznicar Sarajevo	42
1985	FK Sarajevo	48	Hajduk Split	44	Partizan Beograd	39
1986	Partizan Beograd	47	Crvena Zvezda	47	Velez Mostar	39
1987	Partizan Beograd	43	Velez Mostar	42	Crvena Zvezda	41
1988	Crvena Zvezda	45	Partizan Beograd	44	Velez Mostar	42
1989	Vojvodina Novi Sad	41	Crvena Zvezda	38	Hajduk Split	36
1990	Crvena Zvezda	51	Dinamo Zagreb	42	Hajduk Split	38
1991	Crvena Zvezda	54	Dinamo Zagreb	46	Partizan Beograd	41

YUGOSLAV CUP FINALS

Year	Winners	Score	Runners–up
1947	Partizan Beograd	2–0	Nasa Krila Zemun
1948	Crvena Zvezda	3–0	Partizan Beograd
1949	Crvena Zvezda	3–2	Nasa Krila Zemun
1950	Crvena Zvezda	3–0	Dinamo Zagreb
1951	Dinamo Zagreb	2–0 2–0	Vojvodina Novi Sad
1952	Partizan Beograd	6–0	Crvena Zvezda
1953	BSK Beograd	2–0	Hajduk Split
1954	Partizan Beograd	4–1	Crvena Zvezda
1955	BSK Beograd	2–0	Hajduk Split
1956	–		
1957	Partizan Beograd	5–3	Radnicki Belgrade
1958	Crvena Zvezda	4–0	Velez Mostar
1959	Crvena Zvezda	3–1	Partizan Belgrade
1960	Dinamo Zagreb	3–2	Partizan Beograd
1961	Vardar Skopje	2–1	Varteks Varazdin
1962	OFK Beograd	4–1	Spartak Subotica
1963	Dinamo Zagreb	4–1	Hajduk Split
1964	Crvena Zvezda	3–0	Dinamo Zagreb
1965	Dinamo Zagreb	2–1	Buducnost Titograd
1966	OFK Beograd	6–2	Dinamo Zagreb
1967	Hajduk Split	2–1	FK Sarajevo
1968	Crvena Zvezda	7–0	FK Bor
1969	Dinamo Zagreb	3–3 3–0	Hajduk Split
1970	Crvena Zvezda	2–2 1–0	Olimpia Ljubljana
1971	Crvena Zvezda	2–0 4–0	Sloboda Tuzla
1972	Hajduk Split	2–1	Dinamo Zagreb
1973	Dinamo Zagreb	2–1	Crvena Zvezda
1974	Hajduk Split	1–1 2–1	Crvena Zvezda
1975	Hajduk Split	1–0	Borac Banja Luka
1976	Hajduk Split	1–0	Dinamo Zagreb
1977	Hajduk Split	2–0	Buducnost Titograd
1978	NK Rijeka	1–0	Trepca Mitrovica
1979	NK Rijeka	0–0 2–1	Partizan Beograd
1980	Dinamo Zagreb	1–1 1–0	Crvena Zvezda
1981	Velez Mostar	3–2	Zeljeznicar Sarajevo
1982	Crvena Zvezda	2–2 4–2	Dinamo Zagreb
1983	Dinamo Zagreb	3–2	FK Sarajevo
1984	Hajduk Split	0–0 2–1	Crvena Zvezda
1985	Crvena Zvezda	1–1 2–1	Dinamo Zagreb

1986	Velez Mostar	3–1	Dinamo Zagreb
1987	Hajduk Split	1–1 (9–8p)	NK Rijeka
1988	Borac Banja Luka	1–0	Crvena Zvezda
1989	Partizan Beograd	6–1	Velez Mostar
1990	Crvena Zvezda	1–0	Hajduk Split
1991	Hajduk Split	1–0	Crvena Zvezda

INTERNATIONAL MATCHES PLAYED BY YUGOSLAVIA

Date	Opponents	Result		Venue	Compet	Scorers
28-08-1920	Czechoslovakia	L	0–7	Antwerp	OGr1	
2-09	Egypt	L	2–4	Antwerp	OGct	Dubravcic, Ruzic
28-10-1921	Czechoslovakia	L	1–6	Prague	Fr	Zinaja
8-06-1922	Romania	L	1–2	Belgrade	Fr	Sifer
28-06	Czechoslovakia	W	4–3	Zagreb	Fr	Saraz–Abraham 2, Zinaja 2
1-10	Poland	L	1–3	Zagreb	Fr	Vinek
3-06-1923	Poland	W	2–1	Krakow	Fr	Perska, Zinaja
10-06	Romania	W	2–1	Bucharest	Fr	Vinek 2
28-10	Czechoslovakia	D	4–4	Prague	Fr	Jovanovic 2, Petkovic, Babic
10-02-1924	Austria	L	1–4	Zagreb	Fr	Jovanovic
26-05	Uruguay	L	0–7	Paris	OGr1	
28-09	Czechoslovakia	L	0–2	Zagreb	Fr	
28-10-1925	Czechoslovakia	L	0–7	Prague	Fr	
4-11	Italy	L	1–2	Padua	Fr	Bencic
30-05-1926	Bulgaria	W	3–1	Zagreb	Fr	Cindric 3
13-06	France	L	1–4	Paris	Fr	Bonacic M
28-06	Czechoslovakia	L	2–6	Zagreb	Fr	Giler, Petkovic
3-10	Romania	L	2–3	Zagreb	Fr	Percl 2
10-04-1927	Hungary	L	0–3	Budapest	Fr	
10-05	Romania	W	3–0	Bucharest	Fr	Luburic, Bonacic A, Giler
15-05	Bulgaria	W	2–0	Sofia	Fr	Marjanovic 2
31-07	Czechoslovakia	D	1–1	Belgrade	Fr	Perska
28-10	Czechoslovakia	L	3–5	Prague	Fr	Bencic, Bonacic M, Jovanovic
25-03-1928	Hungary	L	1–2	Budapest	Fr	
8-04	Turkey	W	2–1	Zagreb	Fr	Babic, Giler
6-05	Romania	W	3–1	Belgrade	Fr	Sotirovic 2, Marjanovic
29-05	Portugal	L	1–2	Amsterdam	OGr1	Bonacic M
28-10	Czechoslovakia	L	1–7	Prague	Fr	Beleslin
10-05-1929	Romania	W	3–2	Bucharest	Fr	Pavelic, Hitrec, Lemesic
19-05	France	W	3–1	Paris	Fr	Hitrec, Marjanovic, Lajnert
28-06	Czechoslovakia	D	3–3	Zagreb	Fr	Marjanovic 2, Hitrec
6-10	Romania	L	1–2	Bucharest	BC	Marjanovic
28-10	Czechoslovakia	L	3–4	Prague	Fr	Hitrec 2, Lajnert
26-01-1930	Greece	L	1–2	Athens	BC	Vujadinovic
13-04	Bulgaria	W	6–1	Belgrade	Fr	Vujadinovic 2, Marjanovic 2, Tirnanic, Hrnjicek
4-05	Romania	W	2–1	Belgrade	Fr	Premeri, Bonacic A
15-06	Bulgaria	D	2–2	Sofia	Fr	Tirnanic, Najdanovic
14-07	Brazil	W	2–1	Montevideo	WCr1	Tirnanic, Bek
17-07	Bolivia	W	4–0	Montevideo	WCr1	Bek 2, Marjanovic, Vujadinovic
27-07	Uruguay	L	1–6	Montevideo	WCsf	Vujadinovic
3-08	Argentina	L	1–3	Buenos Aires	Fr	Marjanovic
10-08	Brazil	L	1–4	Rio de Janeiro	Fr	
16-11	Bulgaria	W	3–0	Sofia	BC	Lemesic, Marjanovic, Praunsberger
15-03-1931	Greece	W	4–1	Belgrade	BC	Tomasevic 3, Hitrec
19-04	Bulgaria	W	1–0	Belgrade	BC	Marjanovic
21-05	Hungary	W	3–2	Belgrade	Fr	Marjanovic, Hitrec, Lemesic
28-06	Romania	L	2–4	Zagreb	BC	Zecevic, Marjanovic
2-08	Czechoslovakia	W	2–1	Belgrade	Fr	Zivkovic, Marjanovic
2-10	Turkey	L	0–2	Sofia	Fr	
4-10	Bulgaria	L	2–3	Sofia	Fr	Tirnanic, Marjanovic
25-10	Poland	L	3–6	Poznan	Fr	Bek 2, Hitrec
24-04-1932	Spain	L	1–2	Oviedo	Fr	Vujadinovic
3-05	Portugal	L	2–3	Lisbon	Fr	Vujadinovic 2
29-05	Poland	L	0–3	Zagreb	Fr	
5-06	France	W	2–1	Belgrade	Fr	Glisovic 2
26-06	Greece	W	7–1	Belgrade	BC	Zivkovic 2, Zecevic 2, Tirnanic, Vujadinovic, Glisovic
30-06	Bulgaria	L	2–3	Belgrade	BC	Zivkovic 2
3-07	Romania	W	3–1	Belgrade	BC	Zecevic, Zivkovic, Vujadinovic

9–10	Czechoslovakia	L	1–2	Prague	Fr	Zivkovic
30–04–1933	Spain	D	1–1	Belgrade	Fr	Marjanovic
7–05	Switzerland	L	1–4	Zurich	Fr	Hitric
3–06	Greece	W	5–3	Bucharest	BC	Kodrnja 3, Zivkovic 2
7–06	Bulgaria	W	4–0	Bucharest	BC	Kokotovic 3, Zivkovic
11–06	Romania	L	0–5	Bucharest	BC	
6–08	Czechoslovakia	W	2–1	Zagreb	Fr	Kragic, Kodrnja
10–09	Poland	L	3–4	Warsaw	Fr	Vujadinovic 2, Tirnanic
24–09	Switzerland	D	2–2	Belgrade	WCq	Marjanovic, Kragic
18–03–1934	Bulgaria	W	2–1	Sofia	Fr	Marjanovic 2
1–04	Bulgaria	L	2–3	Belgrade	Fr	Kragic, Zivkovic
29–04	Romania	L	1–2	Bucharest	WCq	Kragic
3–06	Brazil	W	8–4	Belgrade	Fr	Marjanovic 3, Glisovic 2, Stevovic, Tirnanic, Petrak
26–08	Poland	W	4–1	Belgrade	Fr	Sekulic 3, Marjanovic
2–09	Czechoslovakia	L	1–3	Prague	Fr	Sekulic
16–12	France	L	2–3	Paris	Fr	Marjanovic, Vujadinovic
23–12	Greece	L	1–2	Athens	BC	Sekulic
25–12	Bulgaria	W	4–3	Athens	BC	Tirnanic 2, Sekulic, Tomasevic
1–01–1935	Romania	W	4–0	Athens	BC	Tomasevic 2, Tiranic, Marjanovic
17–06	Romania	W	2–0	Sofia	BC	Marjanovic, Sekulic
21–06	Greece	W	6–1	Sofia	BC	Zivkovic 2, Glisovic 2, Marjanovic, Vujadinovic
24–06	Bulgaria	D	3–3	Sofia	BC	Vujadinovic 2, Marjanovic
18–08	Poland	W	3–2	Katowice	Fr	Zivkovic 2, Sekulic
6–09	Czechoslovakia	D	0–0	Belgrade	Fr	
10–05–1936	Romania	L	2–3	Bucharest	Fr	Vujadinovic, Tomasevic
12–07	Turkey	D	3–3	Istanbul	Fr	Marjanovic, Tirnanic, Tomasevic
6–09	Poland	W	9–3	Belgrade	Fr	Marjanovic 4, Bozovic 2, Perlic 2, Tirnanic
13–12	France	L	0–1	Paris	Fr	
9–05–1937	Hungary	D	1–1	Budapest	Fr	Lesnik
6–06	Belgium	D	1–1	Belgrade	Fr	Lesnik
11–07	Bulgaria	L	0–4	Sofia	Fr	
1–08	Turkey	W	3–1	Belgrade	Fr	Plese, Bozovic, Lesnik
6–09	Romania	W	2–1	Belgrade	Fr	Vujadinovic, Lesnik
3–10	Czechoslovakia	L	4–5	Prague	Fr	Plese 2, Valjarevic, OG
10–10	Poland	L	0–4	Warsaw	WCq	
3–04–1938	Poland	W	1–0	Belgrade	WCq	Marjanovic
8–05	Romania	W	1–0	Bucharest	Fr	Matosic
22–05	Italy	L	0–4	Genoa	Fr	
29–05	Belgium	D	2–2	Brussels	Fr	Petrovic, Matosic
28–08	Czechoslovakia	L	1–3	Zagreb	Fr	Sipos
6–09	Romania	D	1–1	Belgrade	Fr	Petrovic
25–09	Poland	D	4–4	Warsaw	Fr	Velfl 2, Velker, Kokotovic
26–02–1939	Germany	L	2–3	Berlin	Fr	Petrovic, Klodt
7–05	Romania	L	0–1	Bucharest	Fr	
18–05	England	W	2–1	Belgrade	Fr	Glisovic, Perlic
4–06	Italy	L	1–2	Belgrade	Fr	Petrovic
15–10	Germany	L	1–5	Zagreb	Fr	Antolkovic
12–11	Hungary	L	0–2	Belgrade	Fr	
31–03–1940	Romania	D	3–3	Bucharest	Fr	Valjarevic 2, Bozovic
14–04	Germany	W	2–1	Vienna	Fr	Glisovic, Velfl
22–09	Romania	L	1–2	Belgrade	Fr	Petrovic
29–09	Hungary	D	0–0	Budapest	Fr	
3–11	Germany	W	2–0	Zagreb	Fr	Bozovic, Cimerancic
23–03–1941	Hungary	D	1–1	Belgrade	Fr	Valjarevik
9–05–1946	Czechoslovakia	W	2–0	Prague	Fr	Tomasevic, Mitic
29–09	Czechoslovakia	W	4–2	Belgrade	Fr	Matosic 2, Mitic, Bobek
7–10	Albania	W	3–2	Tirana	BC	Matosic, Bobek, Cajkovski
11–10	Romania	L	1–2	Tirana	BC	Simonovski
13–10	Bulgaria	W	2–1	Tirana	BC	Sandic 2
11–05–1947	Czechoslovakia	L	1–3	Prague	Fr	Bobek
22–06	Romania	W	3–1	Bucharest	BCE	Bobek 2, Jezerkic
29–06	Hungary	L	2–3	Belgrade	BCE	Cimermancic, Mihajlovic
14–09	Albania	W	4–2	Tirana	BCE	Bobek, Mitic, Krnic, Cimermancic
12–10	Bulgaria	W	2–1	Zagreb	BCE	Mihajlovic 2
19–10	Poland	W	7–1	Belgrade	Fr	Jezerkic 4, Bobek 2, Mitic
27–06–1948	Albania	D	0–0	Belgrade	BCE	

4–07	Bulgaria	W	3–1	Sofia	BCE	Velfl, Mitic, Cajkovski
31–07	Luxembourg	W	6–1	London	OGr1	Cajkovski 2, Stankovic, Mihajlovic, Mitic, Bobek
5–08	Turkey	W	3–1	London	OGqf	Cajkovski, Bobek, Velfl
11–08	Great Britain	W	3–1	London	OGsf	Mitic, Bobek, Velfl
13–08	Sweden	L	1–3	London	OGf	Bobek
25–08	Poland	W	1–0	Warsaw	BCE	Mitic
19–06–1949	Norway	W	3–1	Oslo	Fr	Mitic, Bobek, Cajkovski
21–08	Israel	W	6–0	Belgrade	WCq	Pajevic 3, Sencar, Cajkovski, Bobek
18–09	Israel	W	5–2	Tel Aviv	WCq	Valok 2, Bobek, Cajkovski, Cajkovski
9–10	France	D	1–1	Belgrade	WCq	Cajkovski
30–10	France	D	1–1	Paris	WCq	Bobek
13–11	Austria	L	2–5	Belgrade	Fr	Cajkovski, Bobek
11–12	France	W	3–2	Florence	WCq	Mihajlovic 2, Cajkovski
28–05–1950	Denmark	W	5–1	Belgrade	Fr	Mitic 3, Vukas, Hocevar
11–06	Switzerland	W	4–0	Berne	Fr	Cajkovski, Tomasevic, Bobek, Atanackovic
25–06	Switzerland	W	3–0	Belo Horizonte	WCr1	Mitic, Tomasevic, Ognjanov
29–06	Mexico	W	4–1	Porto Alegre	WCr1	Cajkovski 2, Bobek, Tomasevic
1–07	Brazil	L	0–2	Rio de Janeiro	WCr1	
3–09	Sweden	W	2–1	Stockholm	Fr	Valok, Herceg
7–09	Finland	L	2–3	Helsinki	Fr	Bobek, Vukas
10–09	Denmark	W	4–1	Copenhagen	Fr	Zivanovic, Bobek, Mitic, Herceg
8–10	Austria	L	2–7	Vienna	Fr	Mitic, Zivanovic
5–11	Norway	W	4–0	Belgrade	Fr	Ognjanov 2, Mitic, Rupnik
22–11	England	D	2–2	London	Fr	Zivanovic, OG
6–02–1951	France	L	1–2	Paris	Fr	Tomasevic
6–05	Italy	D	0–0	Milan	Fr	
24–06	Switzerland	W	7–3	Belgrade	Fr	Bobek 2, Mitic 2, Zebec 2, Rajkov
23–08	Norway	W	4–2	Oslo	Fr	Bobek 2, Vukas, Zebec
2–09	Sweden	W	2–1	Belgrade	Fr	Bobek, Ognjanov
25–06–1952	Norway	W	4–1	Zagreb	Fr	Vukas 2, Mitic, Zebec
15–07	India	W	10–1	Helsinki	OGr1	Zebec 4, Mitic 3, Vukas 2, Ognjanov
20–07	Soviet Union	D	5–5	Tampere	OGr2	Zebec 2, Ognjanov, Mitic, Bobek
22–07	Soviet Union	W	3–1	Tampere	OGr2	Mitic, Bobek, Cajkovski
25–07	Denmark	W	5–3	Helsinki	OGqf	Cajkovski, Bobek, Zebec, Ognjanovic, Vukas
29–07	West Germany*	W	3–1	Helsinki	OGsf	Mitic 2, Cajkovski
2–08	Hungary	L	0–2	Helsinki	OGf	
21–09	Austria	W	4–2	Belgrade	Fr	Bobek 3, Vukas
2–11	Egypt	W	5–0	Belgrade	Fr	Jocic 2, Rajkov, Cocic, Vukas
21–12	West Germany	L	2–3	Ludwigshafen	Fr	Cajkovski, Bobek
16–01–1953	Egypt	W	3–1	Cairo	Fr	Vukas 2, Mitic
9–05	Greece	W	1–0	Belgrade	WCq	Matosic
14–05	Belgium	W	3–1	Brussels	Fr	Vukas 2, Rajkov
21–05	Wales	W	5–2	Belgrade	Fr	Mitic 3, Vukas, Rajkov
5–06	Turkey	D	2–2	Istanbul	Fr	Rajkov, Mitic
18–10	France	W	3–1	Zagreb	Fr	Veselinovic, Rajkov, Dvornic
8–11	Israel	W	1–0	Skoplje	WCq	Milutinovic
21–03–1954	Israel	W	1–0	Tel Aviv	WCq	Zebec
28–03	Greece	W	1–0	Athens	WCq	Veselinovic
9–05	Belgium	L	0–2	Zagreb	Fr	
16–05	England	W	1–0	Belgrade	Fr	Mitic
16–06	France	W	1–0	Lausanne	WCr1	Milutinovic
19–06	Brazil	D	1–1	Lausanne	WCr1	Zebec
27–06	West Germany	L	0–2	Geneva	WCqf	
22–09	Wales	W	3–1	Cardiff	Fr	Veselinovic 3
26–09	Saar	W	5–1	Saarbrucken	Fr	Vukas 3, Bobek, Veselinovic
3–10	Austria	D	2–2	Vienna	Fr	Stankovic, Bobek
17–10	Turkey	W	5–1	Sarajevo	Fr	Bobek 3, Pasic, Markovic
15–05–1955	Scotland	D	2–2	Belgrade	Fr	Veselinovic, Vukas
29–05	Italy	W	4–0	Turin	DGC	Veselinovic, Zebec, Vukas, OG
26–06	Switzerland	D	0–0	Belgrade	DGC	
25–09	West Germany	W	3–1	Belgrade	Fr	Milutinovic, Rajkov, Veselinovic
19–10	Rep. Ireland	W	4–1	Dublin	Fr	Milutinovic 3, Veselinovic
30–10	Austria	L	1–2	Vienna	DGC	Milutinovic
11–11	France	D	1–1	Paris	Fr	Veselinovic
22–04–1956	Romania	L	0–1	Belgrade	Fr	
29–04	Hungary	D	2–2	Budapest	DGC	Vukas, Veselinovic
17–06	Austria	D	1–1	Zagreb	DGC	Rajkov

9–09	Indonesia	W	4–2	Belgrade	Fr	Milutinovic 3, Kostic
16–09	Hungary	L	1–3	Belgrade	DGC	Petakovic
30–09	Czechoslovakia	L	1–2	Belgrade	DGC	Stankovic
21–11	Scotland	L	0–2	Glasgow	Fr	
28–11	England	L	0–3	London	Fr	
28–11	USA	W	9–1	Melbourne	OGqf	Mujic 3, Veselinovic 3, Antic 2, Papec
4–12	India	W	4–1	Melbourne	OGsf	Papec 2, Veselinovic, OG
8–12	Soviet Union	L	0–1	Melbourne	OGf	
23–12	Indonesia	W	5–1	Djarkarta	Fr	Veselinovic 2, Liposinovic, Papec, Radovic
5–05–1957	Greece	D	0–0	Athens	WCq	
12–05	Italy	W	6–1	Zagreb	DGC	Milutinovic 2, Zebec, Liposinovic, Rajkov, Vukas
18–05	Czechoslovakia	L	0–1	Bratislava	DGC	
15–09	Austria	D	3–3	Belgrade	Fr	Rajkov, Milutinovic, OG
29–09	Romania	D	1–1	Bucharest	WCq	Mujic
10–11	Greece	W	4–1	Belgrade	WCq	Mujic 2, Petakovic, Krstic
17–11	Romania	W	2–0	Belgrade	WCq	Milutinovic 2
20–04–1958	Hungary	L	0–2	Budapest	Fr	
11–05	England	W	5–0	Belgrade	Fr	Petakovic 3, Milutinovic, Veselinovic
8–06	Scotland	D	1–1	Vasteras	WCr1	Petakovic
11–06	France	W	3–2	Vasteras	WCr1	Veselinovic 2, Petakovic
15–06	Paraguay	D	3–3	Eskilstuna	WCr1	Ognjanovic, Veselinovic, Rajkov
19–06	West Germany	L	0–1	Malmo	WCqf	
14–09	Austria	W	4–3	Vienna	Fr	Veselinovic 3, Mujic
5–10	Hungary	D	4–4	Zagreb	Fr	Zebec 2, Petakovic, Veselinovic
19–04–1959	Hungary	L	0–4	Budapest	Fr	
26–04	Switzerland	W	5–1	Basle	DGC	Sekularac 2, Veselinovic 2, Liposinovic
31–05	Bulgaria	W	2–0	Belgrade	ECr1	Galic, Tasic
11–10	Hungary	L	2–4	Belgrade	Fr	Mujic, Kostic
21–10	Israel	D	2–2	Tel Aviv	OGq	Kostic 2
25–10	Bulgaria	D	1–1	Sofia	ECr1	Mujic
15–11	Greece	W	4–0	Belgrade	OGq	Mujic 2, Mihajlovic, Kostic
20–12	West Germany	D	1–1	Hanover	Fr	Mujic
1–01–1960	Morocco	W	5–0	Casablanca	Fr	Kostic 2, Mihajlovic, Maravic, Ankovic
3–01	Tunisia	W	5–1	Tunis	Fr	Kostic, Knez, Maravic, Mihajlovic, Cebinac
8–01	Egypt	W	1–0	Cairo	Fr	Mihajlovic
10–04	Israel	L	1–2	Belgrade	OGq	Mujic
24–04	Greece	W	5–0	Athens	OGq	Kostic, Zanetic, Takac, Galic, Knez
8–05	Portugal	L	1–2	Lisbon	ECqf	Kostic
11–05	England	D	3–3	London	Fr	Galic 2, Kostic
22–05	Portugal	W	5–1	Belgrade	ECqf	Kostic 2, Sekularac, Cebinac, Galic
6–07	France	W	5–4	Paris	ECsf	Jerkovic 2, Galic, Zanetic, Knez
10–07	Soviet Union	L	1–2	Paris	ECf	Galic
6–08	Tunisia	W	7–0	Belgrade	Fr	Knez 3, Kostic 2, Galic, Maravic
26–08	Egypt	W	6–1	Pescara	OGr1	Kostic 4, Galic, Knez
29–08	Turkey*	W	4–0	Florence	OGr1	Kostic 2, Galic, Knez
1–09	Bulgaria	D	3–3	Rome	OGr1	Galic 3
5–09	Italy*	D	1–1	Naples	OGsf	Galic
10–09	Denmark	W	3–1	Rome	OGf	Galic, Matus, Kostic
9–10	Hungary	D	1–1	Budapest	Fr	Kostic
7–05–1961	Hungary	L	2–4	Belgrade	Fr	Kostic, Matus
4–06	Poland	W	2–1	Belgrade	WCq	Kaloperovic, Kostic
18–06	Morocco	W	3–2	Belgrade	Fr	Mujic 2, Matus
25–06	Poland	D	1–1	Chorzow	WCq	Galic
8–10	South Korea	W	5–1	Belgrade	WCq	Sekularac 2, Cebinac, Radakovic, Galic
19–11	Austria	W	2–1	Zagreb	Fr	Jerkovic 2
26–11	South Korea	W	3–1	Seoul	WCq	Galic 2, Jerkovic
29–11	Japan	W	1–0	Tokyo	Fr	Cebinac
2–12	Hong Kong	W	2–1	Hong Kong	Fr	Mujic, Bego
7–12	Indonesia	W	5–1	Djakarta	Fr	Radakovic, Galic, Sekularac, Mujic, Bego
14–12	Israel	W	2–0	Tel Aviv	Fr	Galic 2
16–05–1962	East Germany	W	3–1	Belgrade	Fr	Galic 2, Skoblar
31–05	Soviet Union	L	0–2	Arica	WCr1	
2–06	Uruguay	W	3–1	Arica	WCr1	Skoblar, Galic, Jerkovic
7–06	Colombia	W	5–0	Arica	WCr1	Galic 2, Jerkovic 2, Melic
10–06	West Germany	W	1–0	Santiago	WCqf	Radakovic
13–06	Czechoslovakia	L	1–3	Vina del Mar	WCsf	Jerkovic
16–06	Chile	L	0–1	Santiago	WC3p	
16–09	East Germany	D	2–2	Leipzig	Fr	Zambata, Jerkovic

19–09	Ethiopia	W	5–2	Belgrade	Fr	Matus 2, Zambata 2, Lukaric
30–09	West Germany	L	2–3	Zagreb	Fr	Galic 2
14–10	Hungary	W	1–0	Budapest	Fr	Galic
4–11	Belgium	W	3–2	Belgrade	ECr1	Skoblar 2, Vasovic
31–03–1963	Belgium	W	1–0	Brussels	ECr1	Galic
19–06	Sweden	D	0–0	Belgrade	ECr2	
18–09	Sweden	L	2–3	Malmo	ECr2	Galic, Zambata
6–10	Hungary	W	2–0	Belgrade	Fr	Skoblar, Samardzic
27–10	Romania	L	1–2	Bucharest	Fr	Smailovic
3–11	Czechoslovakia	W	2–0	Zagreb	Fr	Zambata, Skoblar
17–05–1964	Czechoslovakia	W	3–2	Prague	Fr	Skoblar, Samardzic, Zambata
17–06	Romania	L	1–2	Belgrade	Fr	Takac
20–09	Luxembourg	W	3–1	Belgrade	WCq	Kovacevic, Jerkovic, Galic
27–09	Austria	L	2–3	Vienna	Fr	Melic, Skoblar
13–10	Morocco	W	3–1	Tokyo	OGr1	Belin 2, Samardzic
15–10	Hungary*	L	5–6	Tokyo	OGr1	Belin 2, Osim 2, Zambata
18–10	East Germany*	L	0–1	Tokyo	OGqf	
20–10	Japan	W	6–1	Osaka	OG5p	Zambata 4, Osim 2
22–10	Romania	L	0–3	Osaka	OG5p	
25–10	Hungary	L	1–2	Budapest	Fr	Skoblar
28–10	Israel	L	0–2	Tel Aviv	Fr	
22–11	Soviet Union	D	1–1	Belgrade	Fr	Zambata
18–04–1965	France	W	1–0	Belgrade	WCq	Galic
9–05	England	D	1–1	Belgrade	Fr	Kovacevic
16–06	Norway	L	0–3	Oslo	WCq	
4–09	Soviet Union	D	0–0	Moscow	Fr	
19–09	Luxembourg	W	5–2	Luxembourg	WCq	Galic 2, Dzajic 2, Musovic
9–10	France	L	0–1	Paris	WCq	
7–11	Norway	D	1–1	Belgrade	WCq	Vasovic
4–05–1966	England	L	0–2	London	Fr	
8–05	Hungary	W	2–0	Zagreb	Fr	Gugleta, Skoblar
1–06	Bulgaria	L	0–2	Belgrade	Fr	
23–06	West Germany	L	0–2	Hanover	Fr	
27–06	Sweden	D	1–1	Malmo	Fr	Santrac
18–09	Soviet Union	L	1–2	Belgrade	Fr	Musovic
12–10	Israel	W	3–1	Tel Aviv	Fr	Bukal 2, Zambata
19–10	Czechoslovakia	W	1–0	Belgrade	Fr	Dzajic
6–11	Bulgaria	L	1–6	Sofia	Fr	Gugleta
23–04–1967	Hungary	L	0–1	Budapest	Fr	
3–05	West Germany	W	1–0	Belgrade	ECq	Skoblar
14–05	Albania	W	2–0	Tirana	ECq	Zambata 2?
7–10	West Germany	L	1–3	Hamburg	ECq	Zambata
1–11	Holland	W	2–1	Rotterdam	Fr	Belin, Osim
12–11	Albania	W	4–0	Belgrade	ECq	Osim 2, Lazarevic, Spreco
6–04–1968	France	D	1–1	Marseille	ECqf	Musemic
24–04	France	W	5–1	Belgrade	ECqf	Petkovic 2, Musemic 2, Dzajic
27–04	Czechoslovakia	L	0–3	Bratislava	Fr	
5–06	England	W	1–0	Florence	ECsf	Dzajic
8–06	Italy	D	1–1	Rome	ECf	Dzajic
10–06	Italy	L	0–2	Rome	ECf	
25–06	Brazil	L	0–2	Belgrade	Fr	

LEADING INTERNATIONAL GOALSCORERS

1	Bobek	38	14	Mujic	17
2	Galic	37		Zebec	17
3	Marjanovic	36		Pancev	17
4	Mitic	32	17	Milutinovic	16
5	Bajevic	29	18	Zivkovic A	15
6	Veselinovic	28	19	Cajkowski Ze	12
7	Kostic	26		Tirnanic	12
8	Vujovic Z	24	21	Jerkovic D	11
9	Dzajic	23		Rajkovic	11
10	Vukas	22		Skoblar	11
11	Susic	21	24	Bukal	10
	Zambata	21		Katalinski	10
13	Vujadinovic	18		Surjak	10

25–09	Finland	W	9–1	Belgrade	WCq	Zambata 3, Musemic 3, Dzajic 2, Osim
16–10	Belgium	L	0–3	Brussels	WCq	
27–10	Spain	D	0–0	Belgrade	WCq	
17–12	Brazil	D	3–3	Rio de Janeiro	Fr	Spasovski, Dzajic, Bukal
19–12	Brazil	L	2–3	Belo Horizonte	Fr	Musemic, Bjekovic
22–12	Argentina	D	1–1	Mar del Plata	Fr	Musemic
26–02–1969	Sweden	W	2–1	Split	Fr	Bjekovic, Musemic
30–04	Spain	L	1–2	Barcelona	WCq	Pavlovic
4–06	Finland	W	5–1	Helsinki	WCq	Bukal 2, Dzajic, Spreco, Piric
3–09	Romania	D	1–1	Belgrade	Fr	Mujkic
24–09	Soviet Union	L	1–3	Belgrade	Fr	Dzajic
19–10	Belgium	W	4–0	Skoplje	WCq	Spasovski 2, Belin, Dzajic
8–04–1970	Austria	D	1–1	Sarajevo	Fr	Bajevic
12–04	Hungary	D	2–2	Belgrade	Fr	Gracanin, OG
6–05	Romania	D	0–0	Bucharest	Fr	
13–05	West Germany	L	0–1	Hanover	Fr	
10–09	Austria	W	1–0	Graz	Fr	Bajevic
11–10	Holland	D	1–1	Rotterdam	ECq	Dzajic
14–10	Luxembourg	W	2–0	Luxembourg	ECq	Bukal 2
28–10	Soviet Union	L	0–4	Moscow	Fr	
18–11	West Germany	W	2–0	Zagreb	Fr	Bukal, Dzajic
4–04–1971	Holland	W	2–0	Split	ECq	Jerkovic, Dzajic
21–04	Romania	L	0–1	Novi Sad	Fr	
9–05	East Germany	W	2–1	Leipzig	ECq	Filipovic, Dzajic
18–07	Brazil	D	2–2	Rio de Janeiro	Fr	Dzajic, Jerkovic
1–09	Hungary	L	1–2	Budapest	Fr	Oblak
22–09	Mexico	W	4–0	Sarajevo	Fr	Bukal 2, Acimovic, Oblak
16–10	East Germany	D	0–0	Belgrade	ECq	
27–10	Luxembourg	D	0–0	Titograd	ECq	
30–04–1972	Soviet Union	D	0–0	Belgrade	ECqf	
13–05	Soviet Union	L	0–3	Moscow	ECqf	
14–06	Venezuela	W	10–0	Curitiba	Clr1	Bajevic 5, Popivoda, Dzajic, Acimovic, Stepanovic, Katalinski
18–06	Bolivia	D	1–1	Campo Grande	Clr1	Katalinski
22–06	Paraguay	W	2–1	Manaus	Clr1	Bajevic 2
25–06	Peru	W	2–1	Manaus	Clr1	Bajevic 2
29–06	Scotland	D	2–2	Belo Horizonte	Clr2	Bajevic, Jerkovic
2–07	Brazil	L	0–3	Sao Paulo	Clr2	
6–07	Czechoslovakia	W	2–1	Sao Paulo	Clr2	Bajevic, Dzajic
9–07	Argentina	W	4–2	Rio de Janeiro	Cl3p	Bajevic 2, Katalinski, Dzajic
20–09	Italy	L	1–3	Turin	Fr	Vukotic
11–10	England	D	1–1	London	Fr	Vladic
19–10	Spain	D	2–2	Las Palmas	WCq	Bajevic 2
19–11	Greece	W	1–0	Belgrade	WCq	Acimovic
4–02–1973	Tunisia	W	5–0	Tunis	Fr	Bajevic 2, Petkovic 2, Vladic
9–05	West Germany	W	1–0	Munich	Fr	Bajevic
13–05	Poland	D	2–2	Warsaw	Fr	Pavlovic, Bjekovic
26–09	Hungary	D	1–1	Belgrade	Fr	Bjekovic
21–10	Spain	D	0–0	Zagreb	WCq	
19–12	Greece	W	4–2	Athens	WCq	Karasi 2, Bajevic, Surjak
13–02–1974	Spain	W	1–0	Frankfurt	WCq	Katalinski
17–04	Soviet Union	L	0–1	Zenicar	Fr	
29–05	Hungary	L	0–3	Szekesfehervar	Fr	
5–06	England	D	2–2	Belgrade	Fr	Petkovic, Oblak
13–06	Brazil	D	0–0	Frankfurt	WCr1	
18–06	Zaire	W	9–0	Gelsenkirchen	WCr1	Bajevic 3, Dzajic, Surjak, Katalinski, Bogicevic, Oblak, Petkovic
22–06	Scotland	D	1–1	Frankfurt	WCr1	Karasi
26–06	West Germany	L	0–2	Dusseldorf	WCr2	
30–06	Poland	L	1–2	Frankfurt	WCr2	Karasi
3–07	Sweden	L	1–2	Dusseldorf	WCr2	Surjak
28–09	Italy	W	1–0	Zagreb	Fr	Surjak
30–10	Norway	W	3–1	Belgrade	ECq	Katalinski 2, Vukotic
16–03–1975	Nth. Ireland	L	0–1	Belfast	ECq	
31–05	Holland	W	3–0	Belgrade	Fr	Savic, Popivoda, Ivezic
4–06	Sweden	W	2–1	Stockholm	ECq	Katalinski, Ivezic
9–06	Norway	W	3–1	Oslo	ECq	Buljan, Bogicevic, Surjak
15–10	Sweden	W	3–0	Zagreb	ECq	Oblak, Vladic, Vabec
19–11	Nth. Ireland	W	1–0	Belgrade	ECq	Oblak

18–02–1976	Tunisia	L	1–2	Tunis	Fr	Surjak
24–02	Algeria	W	2–1	Algiers	Fr	Vukotic, Sljivo
17–04	Hungary	D	0–0	Banja Luka	Fr	
24–04	Wales	W	2–0	Zagreb	ECqf	Vukotic, Popivoda
22–05	Wales	D	1–1	Cardiff	ECqf	Katalinski
17–06	West Germany	L	2–4	Belgrade	ECsf	Popivoda, Dzajic
19–06	Holland	L	2–3	Zagreb	EC3p	Katalinski, Dzajic
25–09	Italy	L	0–3	Rome	Fr	
10–10	Spain	L	0–1	Seville	WCq	
30–01–1977	Colombia	W	1–0	Bogota	Fr	Bajevic
1–02	Mexico	L	1–5	Leon	Fr	Bajevic
8–02	Mexico	W	1–0	Monterrey	Fr	Bajevic
23–03	Soviet Union	L	2–4	Belgrade	Fr	Bajevic, Jerkovic
30–04	West Germany	L	1–2	Belgrade	Fr	Bajevic
8–05	Romania	L	0–2	Zagreb	WCq	
26–06	Brazil	D	0–0	Belo Horizonte	Fr	
3–07	Argentina	L	0–1	Buenos Aires	Fr	
5–10	Hungary	L	3–4	Budapest	Fr	Susic 2, Nikolic
13–11	Romania	W	6–4	Bucharest	WCq	Susic 3, Muzinic, Trifunovic, Filipovic
16–11	Greece	D	0–0	Salonika	BC	
30–11	Spain	L	0–1	Belgrade	WCq	
5–04–1978	Iran	D	0–0	Tehran	Fr	
18–05	Italy	D	0–0	Rome	Fr	
4–10	Spain	L	1–2	Zagreb	ECq	Halilhodzic
25–10	Romania	L	2–3	Bucharest	ECq	Petrovic, Desnica
15–11	Greece	W	4–1	Skoplje	BC	Halilhodzic 3, Savic
1–04–1979	Cyprus	W	3–0	Nicosia	ECq	Vujovic Z 2, Surjak
13–06	Italy	W	4–1	Zagreb	Fr	Susic 3, Zajec
16–09	Argentina	W	4–2	Belgrade	Fr	Susic 3, Sliskovic
10–10	Spain	W	1–0	Valencia	ECq	Surjak
31–10	Romania	W	2–1	Kosovo	ECq	Vujovic Z, Sliskovic
14–11	Cyprus	W	5–0	Novi Sad	ECq	Kranjcar 2, Vujovic Z, Petrovic, Savic
22–03–1980	Uruguay	W	2–1	Sarajevo	Fr	Klincarski, Vujovic Z
30–03	Romania	W	2–0	Belgrade	BC	Krsticevic, Susic
26–04	Poland	W	2–1	Borovo	Fr	Mirocevic 2
27–08	Romania	L	1–4	Bucharest	BC	Susic
10–09	Luxembourg	W	5–0	Luxembourg	WCq	Vujovic Z 2, Susic, Petrovic, Buljan
27–09	Denmark	W	2–1	Ljubjana	WCq	Vujovic Zo, Pantelic
15–11	Italy	L	0–2	Turin	WCq	
25–03–1981	Bulgaria	W	2–1	Subotica	Fr	Halilhodzic, Sliskovic
29–04	Greece	W	5–1	Split	WCq	Vujovic Z 2, Sljivo, Halilhodzic, Pantelic
9–09	Denmark	W	2–1	Copenhagen	WCq	Vujovic Z, Petrovic
17–10	Italy	D	1–1	Belgrade	WCq	Vujovic Z
21–11	Luxembourg	W	5–0	Novi Sad	WCq	Halilhodzic 2, Surjak, Pasic, Vujovic Z
29–11	Greece	W	2–1	Athens	WCq	Surjak, Jerkovic
17–06–1982	Nth. Ireland	D	0–0	Zaragoza	WCr1	
20–06	Spain	L	1–2	Valencia	WCr1	Gudelj
24–06	Honduras	W	1–0	Zaragoza	WCr1	Petrovic
13–10	Norway	L	1–3	Oslo	ECq	Savic
17–11	Bulgaria	W	1–0	Sofia	ECq	Stojkovic N,
15–12	Wales	D	4–4	Titograd	ECq	Cvetkovic, Zivkovic, Kranjcar, Jesic
30–03–1983	Romania	W	2–0	Timisoara	Fr	Dzeko, Trifunovic
23–04	France	L	0–4	Paris	Fr	
1–06	Romania	W	1–0	Sarajevo	Fr	OG
7–06	West Germany	L	2–4	Luxembourg	Fr	Jesic, Miljanovic
12–10	Norway	W	2–1	Belgrade	ECq	Vujovic Z, Susic
26–10	Switzerland	L	0–2	Basle	Fr	
12–11	France	D	0–0	Zagreb	Fr	
14–12	Wales	D	1–1	Cardiff	ECq	Bazdarevic
21–12	Bulgaria	W	3–2	Split	ECq	Susic 2, Radanovic
31–03–1984	Hungary	W	2–1	Subotica	Fr	Durovski, Radanovic
2–06	Portugal	W	3–2	Lisbon	Fr	Susic, Halilovic, Stojkovic D
7–06	Spain	W	1–0	La Linea	Fr	Susic
13–06	Belgium	L	0–2	Lens	ECr1	
16–06	Denmark	L	0–5	Lyon	ECr1	
19–06	France	L	2–3	St Etienne	ECr1	Sestic, Stojkovic D
12–09	Scotland	L	1–6	Glasgow	Fr	Vokri
29–09	Bulgaria	D	0–0	Belgrade	WCq	
20–10	East Germany	W	3–2	Leipzig	WCq	Bazdarevic, Vokri, Sestic

LEADING INTERNATIONAL APPEARANCES

1	Dzajic	85
2	Vujovic Z	70
3	Zebec	65
4	Bobek	63
5	Stankovic	61
6	Horvat	60
7	Vukas	59
	Mitic	59
	Beara	59
	Hadzibegic	59
11	Marjanovic	57
	Boskov	57
13	Acimovic	55
	Cajkovski Zl	55
	Jusufi	55
16	Surjak	54
	Bazdarevic	54
18	Arsenijevic	52
	Holcer	52
20	Crnkovic	51
	Galic	51

20-01-1985	Iran	W	3-1	Cochin	Fr	Baljic 2, Mlinaric
25-01	Soviet Union	W	2-1	Cochin	Fr	Hadzibegic, Vujovic Z
29-01	China	D	1-1	Cochin	Fr	Zivkovic
1-02	South Korea	W	3-1	Cochin	Fr	Vokri, Gudelj, Vujovic Zo
4-02	Soviet Union	L	1-2	Cochin	Fr	Hadzibegic
27-03	Luxembourg	W	1-0	Zenica	WCq	Gudelj
3-04	France	D	0-0	Sarajevo	WCq	
1-05	Luxembourg	W	1-0	Luxembourg	WCq	Vokri
1-06	Bulgaria	L	1-2	Sofia	WCq	Durovski
28-09	East Germany	L	1-2	Belgrade	WCq	Skoro
16-10	Austria	W	3-0	Linz	Fr	Vujovic Z 2, Mrkela
16-11	France	L	0-2	Paris	WCq	
30-04-1986	Brazil	L	2-4	Recife	Fr	Gracan, Jankovic
11-05	West Germany	D	1-1	Bochum	Fr	Skoro
19-05	Belgium	W	3-1	Brussels	Fr	Skoro, Gracan, Vujovic Z
29-10	Turkey	W	4-0	Split	ECq	Vujovic Z 3, Savicevic
12-11	England	L	0-2	London	ECq	
25-03-1987	Austria	W	4-0	Banja Luka	Fr	Pancev 2, Stojkovic D, Tuce
29-04	Nth. Ireland	W	2-1	Belfast	ECq	Stojkovic D, Vujovic Z
29-08	Soviet Union	L	0-1	Belgrade	Fr	
23-09	Italy	L	0-1	Pisa	Fr	
14-10	Nth. Ireland	W	3-0	Sarajevo	ECq	Vokri 2, Hadzibegic
11-11	England	L	1-4	Belgrade	ECq	Katanec
16-12	Turkey	W	3-2	Izmir	ECq	Radanovic, Katanec, Hadzibegic
23-03-1988	Wales	W	2-1	Swansea	Fr	Stojkovic D, Jakovljevic
31-03	Italy	D	1-1	Split	Fr	Jakovljevic
27-04	Rep. Ireland	L	0-2	Dublin	Fr	
4-06	West Germany	D	1-1	Bremen	Fr	Baljic
24-08	Switzerland	W	2-0	Lucerne	Fr	Mihajlovic, Djukic
14-09	Spain	W	2-1	Oviedo	Fr	Bazdarevic, Cvetkovic
19-10	Scotland	D	1-1	Glasgow	WCq	Katanec
19-11	France	W	3-2	Belgrade	WCq	Spasic, Susic, Stojkovic D
11-12	Cyprus	W	4-0	Belgrade	WCq	Savicevic 3, Hadzibegic
5-04-1989	Greece	W	4-1	Athens	Fr	Vujovic Z 2, Tuce, Jakovljevic
29-04	France	D	0-0	Paris	WCq	
27-05	Belgium	L	0-1	Brussels	Fr	
14-06	Norway	W	2-1	Oslo	WCq	Stojkovic D, Vujovic Z
23-08	Finland	D	2-2	Kuopio	Fr	Pancev, Savicevic
6-09	Scotland	W	3-1	Zagreb	WCq	Katanec, OG 2
20-09	Greece	W	3-0	Novi Sad	Fr	Brnovic, Prosinecki, Pancev
11-10	Norway	W	1-0	Sarajevo	WCq	Hadzibegic
28-10	Cyprus	W	2-1	Athens	WCq	Stanojkovic, Pancev
14-11	Brazil	D	0-0	Joao Pessoa	Fr	
13-12	England	L	1-2	London	Fr	Skoro
28-03-1990	Poland	D	0-0	Lodz	Fr	
26-05	Spain	L	0-1	Ljubljana	Fr	
3-06	Holland	L	0-2	Zagreb	Fr	
10-06	West Germany	L	1-4	Milan	WCr1	Jozic
14-06	Colombia	W	1-0	Bologna	WCr1	Jozic
19-06	UAE	W	4-1	Bologna	WCr1	Susic, Pancev 2, Prosinecki

26–06	Spain	W	2–1	Verona	WCr2	Stojkovic 2
30–06	Argentina	D	0–0 (2–3p)	Florence	WCqf	
12–09	Nth. Ireland	W	2–0	Belfast	ECq	Pancev, Prosinecki
31–10	Austria	W	4–1	Belgrade	ECq	Pancev 3, Katanec
14–11	Denmark	W	2–0	Copenhagen	ECq	Bazdarevic, Jarni
27–02–1991	Turkey	D	1–1	Izmir	Fr	Savicevic
27–03	Nth. Ireland	W	4–1	Belgrade	ECq	Binic, Pancev 3
1–05	Denmark	L	1–2	Belgrade	ECq	Pancev
16–05	Faeroe Islands	W	7–0	Belgrade	ECq	Najdoski, Prosinecki, Pancev 2, Vulic, Boban, Suker
4–09	Sweden	L	3–4	Stockholm	Fr	Savicevic 2, OG
16–10	Faeroe Islands	W	2–0	Landskrona	ECq	Jugovic, Savicevic
30–10	Brazil	L	1–3	Varginha	Fr	Lukic
13–11	Austria	W	2–0	Vienna	Fr	Lukic, Savicevic
25–03–1992	Holland	L	0–2	Amsterdam	Fr	

South America

Argentina v Uruguay, South American Championship 1989

WORLD SOCCER

SOUTH AMERICA

Known for many years in football parlance as the 'New World', South America is now very much part of the establishment of world football. CONMEBOL is the oldest continental confederation, having been in existence almost 40 years longer than UEFA, and through the organisation of the South American Championship it has played a crucial role in the development of the game on the continent.

Aside from the big three of Argentina, Brazil and Uruguay, until the last twenty years or so almost all of the competitive matches played by the other seven countries were in CONMEBOL-sponsored tournaments. At club level, CONMEBOL organises both the Copa Libertadores and the recently introduced Super Cup, a tournament reserved for the winners of the Copa Libertadores.

In 1992 a third tournament was introduced. The CONMEBOL Cup, like the UEFA Cup in Europe, is a 'best of the rest' competition. Countries are ranked according to their strength and size, and as a result Brazil has four places, Argentina three, Uruguay two and the seven other members one each.

Also at club level there is the Recopa, played between the winners of the Copa Libertadores and Super Cup. It has been held every year since 1988. In 1992 came the introduction of a further tournament, the Masters Cup. This is played between past winners of the Super Cup. Any excuse for a tournament! At national level, CONMEBOL's main responsibilities lie in organising the South American Championship, which she has done since 1916.

South America covers a very large area, of which Brazil and Argentina occupy a sizeable proportion. Due to trading and cultural links with the east coast of America and Europe, the countries on the Atlantic coastline have been more prosperous than their neighbours who border on the Pacific and this has helped make football in Brazil, Uruguay and Argentina more successful than in Chile, Peru, Paraguay, Bolivia or Ecuador.

In the other two members of CONMEBOL, Colombia and Venezuela, local factors have helped retard the growth of the game. In Venezuela, football is far less popular than a host of imported American sports, such as baseball, whilst Colombia are prone to flout the regulations of FIFA and have often found themselves ostracised from the world game; the presence of the drug cartels has not helped the situation there either. Though situated in South America, Guyana and Surinam are members of CONCACAF, whilst French Guiana are affiliated to the French Football Federation.

Eight World Cup victories are testament to the strength of the national sides of South America, but club football seems to be in a permanent state of crisis. The deteriorating economic state of the continent has meant a constant flow of players to Europe as clubs try to balance their books and players look for a secure living. Until clubs are in a position to keep their players and compete with the Europeans in the transfer market, the situation does not look like improving.

The basis is there, however. The biggest clubs can draw on large support, and the idea of a super league for the top 20 or so clubs is rapidly gaining momentum. Should that happen, who knows, we may yet witness a European moving to South America to play his football for a change.

SOUTH AMERICAN GOVERNING BODY

Confederación Sudamericana de Fútbol
Ed. Banco do Brasil - Piso 4
Nuestra Señora de la Asunción 540
Asunción
Paraguay
Tel: (010 595) 21 494628
Fax: (010 595) 21 492976
Telex: 328 PY CONMEBOL
Cable: CONMEBOL

Year of formation: 1916

Members: 10
Argentina – Bolivia – Brazil – Chile – Colombia – Ecuador – Paraguay – Peru – Uruguay – Venezuela

SOUTH AMERICAN FOOTBALLER OF THE YEAR

***From* El Mundo**

1971	Tostao	BRA
1972	Teofilo Cubillas	PER
1973	Pele	BRA
1974	Elias Figueroa	CHI
1975	Elias Figueroa	CHI
1976	Elias Figueroa	CHI
1977	Zico	BRA

1978	Mario Kempes	ARG
1979	Diego Maradona	ARG
1980	Diego Maradona	ARG
1981	Zico	BRA
1982	Zico	BRA
1983	Socrates	BRA
1984	Enzo Francescoli	URU
1985	Romero	PAR
1986	Alzamendi	URU
1987	Carlos Valderrama	COL
1988	Ruben Paz	URU
1989	Bebeto	BRA
1990	Diego Maradona	ARG
1991	Oscar Ruggeri	ARG

THE SOUTH AMERICAN CHAMPIONSHIP

The South American Championship is now the longest-running tournament in world football, and has been since the demise of the British Championship in 1984. Played by the national teams of the 10 members of CONMEBOL, the governing body for the continent, the Copa America, as it has been known since the 1975 edition, predates its European counterpart by nearly 50 years and has played a crucial part in facilitating the spread of football on the continent. Between 1916 and 1959 it was played on average once every two years but since then it has been the policy to hold it every four years. Since 1989, however, CONMEBOL have stated their intention to revert back to the biennial formula.

Given that South America is dominated by Argentina, Brazil and Uruguay, one would expect the honours to be evenly divided between the 'Big Three'. This has not, however, been the case. Since 1922, Brazil have won the tournament on only two occasions, in 1959 and 1989. As there have been 29 tournaments played in this time, it can be seen just how poor their record is. Instead, Argentina and Uruguay have dominated the competition, between them winning 27 of the 36 editions played.

The first South American Championship took place in 1910. Though not an official competition, taking place as it did six years before the founding of CONMEBOL, the newspapers of the time acclaimed it as such. With Montevideo just over the River Plate from Buenos Aires, matches between Argentina and Uruguay in the Lipton and Newton Cups had been a regular feature for nine years. As transport was rapidly improving, both countries looked further afield for opposition. The opening of the Transandine Railway between Argentina and Chile encouraged the Argentines to organise a tournament involving themselves, Uruguay, Brazil and Chile. Brazil withdrew, but at the end of May the tournament got underway with Uruguay defeating Chile, who had no experience of international football at all, by 3–0 on the grounds of the Gimnasia club at Palermo in Buenos Aires. Peñarol's Jose Piendibene, the star of Uruguayan football at that time, had the honour of scoring the first goal in the championship's history.

A week later Argentina defeated the Chileans with even more ease, setting up what over the years was to become the familar sight of Uruguay playing Argentina on the final day to decide the championship. Nearly 40000 spectators turned up to see the game, such was the interest, and the occasion showed that some things never change in football. Excited fans burnt down one of the stands at Gimnasia's ground and there were reports of shootings. The match was abandoned before it had even started, postponed until the following day and relocated to Racing Club's ground.

A much smaller crowd of 8000, strictly controlled by the police, saw Argentina crowned as the first unofficial champions of South America. Leading 2–0 at half-time, they completely dominated the game and won 4–1.

The second tournament is also listed as an unofficial event. Organised in 1916 to celebrate Argentina's centenary as an independent nation, it saw Uruguay gain revenge for the defeat of six years previously. In the entire history of the championships there have only ever been four proper final ties, in 1975, 1979, 1983 and 1987. All of the other tournaments have been played on a league basis, and 1916 again threw up an Argentina–Uruguay game in the last match of the tournament to decide the winners – it was a practice of the organisers to try to predict which game would be the decider and leave that fixture until last. This became more complicated as more countries entered the tournament, and over the years the 'deciding game' has often occurred early on in the tournament.

Uruguay were the early force in the tournament, winning six of the first 11 series, and they have carried on winning with surprising regularity ever since. Argentina really came into their own from the mid-1920s until the end of the 1950s, winning 11 of the 18 tournaments played. Brazil's record is lamentable. They have never won a championship outside their own country and have only won four overall.

There is a small element of truth in the suggestion that they do not take the tournament as seriously as other countries, in that they have only ever acted as hosts on four occasions compared to eight for Argentina, six for Uruguay, six for Chile and five for Peru. The lack of success, though, is probably a clear indication that before the 1950s, when the majority of these championships were played, the Brazilians were not as strong as either the Argentinians or Uruguayans, and it was their misfortune that when they were at their best – from the mid-1950s – there were not that many championships played.

The 1960s saw a decline in the championships as the Copa Libertadores began to become an ever more popular tournament, and this, combined with an increased desire of the Argentines, Uruguayans and Brazilians to play more lucrative friendlies in Europe, nearly killed off the tournament for good. Bolivia were chosen to host the 1963 tournament and they won it – a remarkable achievement, but although not weak, the Argentine and Brazilian sides were certainly not full-strength elevens.

An eight-year gap after the 1967 edition, the longest in its history, saw the series revamped in 1975 under a different format. Three qualifying groups were played, and for the first time the championship was not held in a single country as a home and away system was used to find the three qualifiers for the semi-finals, who were joined there by the previous winners. Peru and Paraguay seemed to adapt well to this new system, both winning the title for the second time in their histories in 1975 and 1979 respectively.

The 1975 edition was the first in which all 10 CONMEBOL members entered, a difficult number to work with – hence the bye to the semi-finals for the holders. In 1987 the same format was kept but the whole tournament held in a single country, Argentina. It was not a satisfactory arrangement and in 1989, two groups of five were used to qualify the top two in each group for a final round played on a league basis. The 1989 tournament provided Brazil with their first win in 40 years, whilst in 1991, Argentina won for the first time in 32 years.

THE SOUTH AMERICAN CHAMPIONSHIP

1910 Argentina	1925 Argentina	1945 Argentina	1959 Uruguay
1916 Uruguay	1926 Uruguay	1946 Argentina	1963 Bolivia
1917 Uruguay	1927 Argentina	1947 Argentina	1967 Uruguay
1919 Brazil	1929 Argentina	1949 Brazil	1975 Peru
1920 Uruguay	1935 Uruguay	1953 Paraguay	1979 Paraguay
1921 Argentina	1937 Argentina	1955 Argentina	1983 Uruguay
1922 Brazil	1939 Peru	1956 Uruguay	1987 Uruguay
1923 Uruguay	1941 Argentina	1957 Argentina	1989 Brazil
1924 Uruguay	1942 Uruguay	1959 Argentina	1991 Argentina

	Country	G	S	B
1	Argentina	14	10	4
2	Uruguay	13	6	6
3	Brazil	4	10	7
4	Paraguay	2	5	8
5	Peru	2	–	4
6	Bolivia	1	–	–
7	Chile	–	4	6
8	Colombia	–	1	1
		36	36	36

Correct to end of 1991 championship

FIRST EDITION

Buenos Aires, 29th May–12th June 1910

Not for the Copa America

Gimnasia Club, Buenos Aires, 29–05–1910, 5000
Uruguay 3 (Piendibene, Brachi, Buck)
Chile 0

Gimnasia Club, Buenos Aires, 5–06–1910
Argentina 5 (Brown E 2, Susan 2, Brown ER)
Chile 1 (Campbell)

Racing Club, Buenos Aires, 12–06–1910, 8000
Argentina 4 (Vialle, Hayes, Hutton, Susan)
Uruguay 1 (Piendibene)
Argentina – Wilson – Brown J, Brown G – Brown E, Ginocchio, Jacobs – Vialle, Hutton, Hayes, Susan, Gonzales
Uruguay – Saporiti – Bertone, Benincasa – Suazu, Apostegui, Pena – Brachi, Raymonda, Piendibene, Dacal, Buck

	Ar	Ur	Ch	Pl	W	D	L	F	A	Pts
ARGENTINA	–	4–1	5–1	2	2	0	0	9	2	4
URUGUAY	–	–	3–0	2	1	0	1	4	4	2
CHILE	–	–	–	2	0	0	2	1	8	0

Top scorer: Susan, Argentina 3

SECOND EDITION

Buenos Aires, 2nd–17th July 1916

Not for the Copa America

Gimnasia y Esgrima, Buenos Aires, 2–07–1916, 30 000
Uruguay 2 (Piendibene 2, Gradín 2)
Chile 0

Gimnasia y Esgrima, Buenos Aires, 6–07–1916, 15 000
Argentina 6 (Ohaco 2, Brown J 2, Marcovecchio 2)
Chile 1 (Báez)

Gimnasia y Esgrima, Buenos Aires, 8–07–1916, 15 000
Chile 1 (Salazar)
Brazil 1 (Demóstenes)

Gimnasia y Esgrima, Buenos Aires, 10–07–1916, 20 000
Argentina 1 (Laguna)
Brazil 1 (Aléncar)

Gimnasia y Esgrima, Buenos Aires, 12–07–1916, 20 000
Uruguay 2 (Gradín, Tognola)
Brazil 1 (Friedenreich)

Racing Club, Buenos Aires, 17–07–1916, 30 000. Referee: Fanta, Chile
Argentina 0
Uruguay 0
Argentina – Isola – Diaz, Reyes A – Martínez, Olazar, Badaracco – Heissinger, Ohaco, Hayes H, Reyes E, Perinetti
Uruguay – Saporiti – Benincasa, Foglino – Zibechi, Delgado, Varela – Somma, Tognola, Piendibene, Gradín, Mará

	Ur	Ar	Br	Ch	Pl	W	D	L	F	A	Pts
URUGUAY	–	0–0	2–1	4–0	3	2	1	0	6	1	5
ARGENTINA	–	–	1–1	6–1	3	1	2	0	7	2	4
BRAZIL	–	–	–	1–1	3	0	2	1	3	4	2
CHILE	–	–	–	–	3	0	1	2	2	11	1

Top scorer: Gradín, Uruguay 3

THIRD EDITION
Montevideo, 30th September–14th October 1917

Parque Central, Montevideo, 30–09–1917, 22000
Uruguay 4 (Romano 2, Scarone C 2)
Chile 0

Parque Central, Montevideo, 3–10–1917, 20000
Argentina 4 (Ohaco 2, Calomino, Blanco)
Brazil 2 (Neco, Lagreca)

Parque Central, Montevideo, 6–10–1917, 12000
Argentina 1 (OG)
Chile 0

Parque Central, Montevideo, 7–10–1917, 21000
Uruguay 4 (Romano 2, Scarone C, Scarone H)
Brazil 0

Parque Central, Montevideo, 12–10–1917, 10000
Brazil 5 (Haroldo 2, Amilcar, Caetano, Neco)
Chile 0

Parque Central, Montevideo, 14–10–1917, 40000. Referee: Livingstone, Chile
Uruguay 1 (Scarone H)
Argentina 0
Uruguay – Saporiti – Varela M, Foglino – Pacheco, Rodriguez G, Vanzzino – Pérez J, Scarone H, Romano, Scarone C, Somma
Argentina – Isola – Ferro, Reyes A – Mattozzi, Olazar, Martinez – Calomino, Ohaco, Martin, Hayes E, Perinetti

	Ur	Ar	Br	Ch	Pl	W	D	L	F	A	Pts
URUGUAY	–	1–0	4–0	4–0	3	3	0	0	9	0	6
ARGENTINA	–	–	4–2	1–0	3	2	0	1	5	3	4
BRAZIL	–	–	–	5–0	3	1	0	2	7	8	2
CHILE	–	–	–	–	3	0	0	3	0	10	0

Top scorer: Romano, Uruguay 4

FOURTH EDITION
Rio de Janeiro, 11th–29th May 1919

Alvaro Chaves, Rio de Janeiro, 11–05–1919, 25000
Brazil 6 (Friedenreich 3, Neco 2, Haroldo)
Chile 0

Alvaro Chaves, Rio de Janeiro, 13–05–1919, 25000
Uruguay 3 (Gradín, Scarone C, Scarone H)
Argentina 2 (Izaguirre, Calomino)

Alvaro Chaves, Rio de Janeiro, 17–05–1919, 7000
Uruguay 2 (Perez J, Scarone C)
Chile 0

Alvaro Chaves, Rio de Janeiro, 18–05–1919, 28000
Brazil 3 (Amilcar, Millon, Heitor Domingues)
Argentina 1 (Izaguirre)

Alvaro Chaves, Rio de Janeiro, 22–05–1919, 5000
Argentina 4 (Clarke 3, Izaguirre)
Chile 1 (France)

Alvaro Chaves, Rio de Janeiro, 26–05–1919, 25000
Uruguay 2 (Gradín, Scarone C)
Brazil 2 (Neco 2)

Play–off
Alvaro Chaves, Rio de Janeiro, 29–05–1919, 28000. Referee: Barbera, Argentina
Brazil 1 (Friedenreich)
Uruguay 0
Brazil – Marcos – Pindaro, Bianco – Sergio, Amilcar, Fortes – Millon, Neco, Friedenreich, Heitor Dominguez, Arnaldo
Uruguay – Saporiti – Varela M, Foglino – Naguil, Zibechi, Vanzzino – Pérez J, Scarone H, Romano, Gradin, Marín

	Br	Ur	Ar	Ch	Pl	W	D	L	F	A	Pts
BRAZIL	–	2–2	3–1	6–0	3	2	1	0	11	3	5
URUGUAY	–	–	3–2	2–0	3	2	1	0	7	4	5
ARGENTINA	–	–	–	4–1	3	1	0	2	7	7	2
CHILE	–	–	–	–	3	0	0	3	1	12	0

Top scorers: Neco, Brazil 4
Friedenreich, Brazil 4

FIFTH EDITION
Viña del Mar, 11th September–26th September 1920

Sporting Club, Viña del Mar, 11–09–1920, 15000
Brazil 1 (Alvariza)
Chile 0

Sporting Club, Viña del Mar, 12–09–1920, 20000. Referee: Fanta, Chile
Uruguay 1 (Piendibene)
Argentina 1 (Etcheverria)
Uruguay – Legnazzi – Urdinarán, Foglino – Ruotta, Zibechi, Ravera – Somma, Pérez J, Piendibene, Romano, Campolo
Argentina – Tesorieri – Cortella, Bearzotti – Frumento, Dellavalle, Uslenghi – Calomino, Libonatti, Badalini, Etcheverria, Miguel

Sporting Club, Viña del Mar, 17–09–1920, 16000
Argentina 1 (Dellavalle)
Chile 1 (Dominguez)

Sporting Club, Viña del Mar, 18–09–1920, 16000
Uruguay 6 (Romano 2, Pérez J 2, Urdinarán, Campolo)
Brazil 0

Sporting Club, Viña del Mar, 25–09–1920, 12000
Argentina 2 (Etchverria, Libonatti)
Brazil 0

Sporting Club, Viña del Mar, 26–09–1920, 16000
Uruguay 2 (Perez J, Romano)
Chile 1 (Bolados)

	Ur	Ar	Br	Ch	Pl	W	D	L	F	A	Pts
URUGUAY	–	1–1	6–0	2–1	3	2	1	0	9	2	5
ARGENTINA	–	–	2–0	1–1	3	1	2	0	4	2	4
BRAZIL	–	–	–	1–0	3	1	0	2	1	8	2
CHILE	–	–	–	–	3	0	1	2	2	4	1

Top scorers: Pérez J, Uruguay 4
Romano, Uruguay 4

SIXTH EDITION
Buenos Aires, 2nd–30th October 1921

Sportivo Barracas, Buenos Aires, 2–10–1921, 20000
Argentina 1 (Libonatti)
Brazil 0

Sportivo Barracas, Buenos Aires, 9–10–1921, 18000
Paraguay 2 (Rivas G, López E)
Uruguay 1 (Piendibene)

Sportivo Barracas, Buenos Aires, 12–10–1921, 25 000
Brazil 3 (Machado 2, Candiota)
Paraguay 0

Sportivo Barracas, Buenos Aires, 16–10–1921, 25 000
Argentina 3 (Libonatti, Etcheverria, Saruppo)
Paraguay 0

Sportivo Barracas, Buenos Aires, 23–10–1921, 18 000
Uruguay 2 (Romano 2)
Brazil 1 (Zezé I)

Sportivo Barracas, Buenos Aires, 30–10–1921, 30 000. Referee: Santos, Brazil
Argentina 1 (Libonatti)
Uruguay 0

Argentina – Tesorieri – Celli, Bearzotti – López A, Dellavalle, Solari – Calomino, Libonatti, Saruppo, Etcheverria, González V
Uruguay – Beloutas – Benincasa, Foglino – Molinari, Zibechi, Broncini – Somma, Romano, Pendibene, Casanello, Campolo

	Ar	Br	Ur	Pa	Pl	W	D	L	F	A	Pts
ARGENTINA	–	1–0	1–0	3–0	3	3	0	0	5	0	6
BRAZIL	–	–	1–2	3–0	3	1	0	2	4	3	2
URUGUAY	–	–	–	1–2	3	1	0	2	3	4	2
PARAGUAY	–	–	–	–	3	1	0	2	2	7	2

Top scorer: Libonatti, Argentina 3

SEVENTH EDITION

Rio de Janeiro, 17th September–22nd October 1922

Alvaro Chaves, Rio de Janeiro, 17–09–1922, 30 000
Brazil 1 (Tatú)
Chile 1 (Bravo)

Alvaro Chaves, Rio de Janeiro, 23–09–1922, 6000
Uruguay 2 (Heguy, Urdinarán)
Chile 0

Alvaro Chaves, Rio de Janeiro, 24–09–1922, 25 000
Brazil 1 (Amilcar)
Paraguay 1 (Rivas G)

Alvaro Chaves, Rio de Janeiro, 28–09–1922, 6000
Argentina 4 (Francia 2, Chiessa, Gaslini)
Chile 0

Alvaro Chaves, Rio de Janeiro, 1–10–1922, 30 000
Brazil 0
Uruguay 0

Alvaro Chaves, Rio de Janeiro, 5–10–1922, 1000
Paraguay 3 (Ramirez C, López E, Fretes)
Chile 0

Alvaro Chaves, Rio de Janeiro, 8–10–1922, 7000
Uruguay 1 (Buffoni)
Argentina 0

Alvaro Chaves, Rio de Janeiro, 12–10–1922, 3000
Paraguay 1 (Elizeche)
Uruguay 0

Alvaro Chaves, Rio de Janeiro, 15–10–1922, 25 000
Brazil 2 (Amilcar, Neco)
Argentina 0

Alvaro Chaves, Rio de Janeiro, 18–10–1922, 8000
Argentina 2 (Francia 2)
Paraguay 0

Play–off
Alvaro Chaves, Rio de Janeiro, 22–10–1922, 20 000. Referee: Guevara, Chile
Brazil 3 (Formiga 2, Neco)
Paraguay 1 (Rivas G)

Brazil – Kuntz – Palamone, Barto – Lais, Amilcar, Fortes – Formiga, Neco, Heitor Domingues, Tatú, Rodriguez
Paraguay – Denis – Mena, Porta – Miranda, Fleitas Solich, Benitez I – Capdevilla, Schaerer, Lopez I, Rivas G, Fretes

	Br	Pa	Ur	Ar	Ch	Pl	W	D	L	F	A	Pts
BRAZIL	–	1–1	0–0	2–0	1–1	4	1	3	0	4	2	5
PARAGUAY	–	–	1–0	0–2	3–0	4	2	1	1	5	3	5
URUGUAY	–	–	–	1–0	2–0	4	2	1	1	3	1	5
ARGENTINA	–	–	–	–	4–0	4	2	0	2	6	3	4
CHILE	–	–	–	–	–	4	0	1	3	1	10	1

Uruguay withdrew after the last match in protest over decisions in her match with Paraguay. This left a play-off between Brazil and Paraguay to decide the title

Top scorer: Francia, Argentina 4

EIGHTH EDITION

Montevideo, 29th October–2nd December 1923

Parque Central, Montevideo, 29–10–1923, 20 000
Argentina 4 (Aguirre 3, Seruppo)
Paraguay 3 (Rivas G, Zelada, Fretes)

Parque Central, Montevideo, 4–11–1923, 20 000
Uruguay 2 (Scarone H, Petrone)
Paraguay 0

Parque Central, Montevideo, 11–11–1923, 15 000
Paraguay 1 (López I)
Brazil 0

Parque Central, Montevideo, 18–11–1923, 15 000
Argentina 2 (Onzari, Saruppo)
Brazil 1 (Nilo)

Parque Central, Montevideo, 25–11–1923, 20 000
Uruguay 2 (Petrone, Cea)
Brazil 1 (Nilo)

Parque Central, Montevideo, 2–12–1923, 22 000. Referee: Campos, Brazil
Uruguay 2 (Petrone, Somma)
Argentina 0

Uruguay – Casella – Nasazzi, Uriarte – Andrade, Vidal, Ghierra – Pérez L, Petrone, Scarone H, Cea, Somma
Argentina – Tesorieri – Bidoglio, Iribarren – Médici, Vaccaro, Solari – Loizo, Miguel, Saruppo, Aguirre, Onzari

	Ur	Ar	Pa	Br	Pl	W	D	L	F	A	Pts
URUGUAY	–	2–0	2–0	2–1	3	3	0	0	6	1	6
ARGENTINA	–	–	4–3	2–1	3	2	0	1	6	6	4
PARAGUAY	–	–	–	1–0	3	1	0	2	4	6	2
BRAZIL	–	–	–	–	3	0	0	3	2	5	0

Top scorers: Aguirre, Argentina 3
Petrone, Uruguay 3

NINTH EDITION

Montevideo, 12th October–2nd November 1924

Parque Central, Montevideo. 12–10–1924, 8000
Paraguay 0
Argentina 0

Parque Central, Montevideo. 19–10–1924, 15 000
Uruguay 5 (Petrone 3, Zingone, Romano)
Chile 0

Parque Central, Montevideo. 25–10–1924, 4000
Argentina 2 (Loyarte, Sosa G)
Chile 0

Parque Central, Montevideo. 26–10–1924, 14 000
Uruguay 3 (Petrone, Romano, Cea)
Paraguay 1 (Sosa U)

Parque Central, Montevideo. 1–11–1924, 1000
Paraguay 3 (López I 2, Rivas G)
Chile 1 (Arellano)

Parque Central, Montevideo. 2–11–1924, 20 000. Referee: Fanta, Chile
Uruguay 0
Argentina 0

Uruguay – Mazzali – Nasazzi, Arispe – Alzugaray, Zibechi, Ghierra – Urdinarán, Barlocco, Petrone, Cea, Romano
Argentina – Tesorieri – Cochrane, Bearzotti – Médici, Bidoglio, Solari – Tarasconi, Loyarte, Sosa G, Seoane, Onzari

	Ur	Ar	Pa	Ch	Pl	W	D	L	F	A	Pts
URUGUAY	–	0–0	3–1	5–0	3	2	1	0	8	1	5
ARGENTINA	–	–	0–0	2–0	3	1	2	0	2	0	4
PARAGUAY	–	–	–	3–1	3	1	1	1	4	4	3
CHILE	–	–	–	–	3	0	0	3	1	10	0

Top scorer: Petrone, Uruguay 4

TENTH EDITION
Buenos Aires, 29th November–25th December 1925

Sportivo Barracas, Buenos Aires, 29–11–1925, 12 000
Argentina 2 (Seoane, Sánchez M)
Paraguay 0

La Bonbonera, Buenos Aires, 6–12–1925, 18 000
Brazil 5 (Lagarto 2, Friedenreich, Moderato, Nilo)
Paraguay 2 (Rivas G, Fretes)

Sportivo Barracas, Buenos Aires, 13–12–1925, 25 000
Argentina 4 (Seoane 3, Garasino)
Brazil 1 (Nilo)

La Bonbonera, Buenos Aires, 17–12–1925, 14 000
Brazil 3 (Lagarto 2, Nilo)
Paraguay 1 (Fretes)

Sportivo Barracas, Buenos Aires, 20–12–1925, 25 000
Argentina 3 (Tarasconi, Seoane, Irurierta)
Paraguay 1 (Fleitas Solich)

La Bonbonera, Buenos Aires, 25–12–1925, 18 000. Referee: Vallarino, Uruguay
Argentina 2 (Cerrutti, Seoane)
Brazil 2 (Friedenreich, Nilo)

Argentina – Tesorieri – Muttis, Bidoglio – Fortunato, Vaccaro, Médici – Tarascone, Cerrutti, Seoane, De Los Santos, Bianchi
Brazil – Tuffy – Penaforte, Helcio – Nascimeinto, Rueda, Pamplona – Filó, Lagarto, Friedenreich, Nilo, Moderato

	Ar	Br	Pa	Pl	W	D	L	F	A	Pts
ARGENTINA	–	4–1	2–0	4	3	1	0	11	4	7
BRAZIL	2–2	–	5–2	4	2	1	1	11	9	5
PARAGUAY	1–3	1–3	–	4	0	0	4	4	13	0

Top scorer: Seoane, Argentina 6

ELEVENTH EDITION
Santiago, 12th October–3rd November 1926

Sport de Nuñoa, Santiago, 12–10–1926, 12 000
Chile 7 (Arellano 3, Subiabre 2, Ramirez M, Moreno)
Bolivia 1 (Aguilar)

Sport de Nuñoa, Santiago, 16–10–1926, 8000
Argentina 5 (Cherro 2, Sosa G, Delgado, Miguel)
Bolivia 0

Sport de Nuñoa, Santiago, 17–10–1926, 13 000
Uruguay 3 (Borjas, Castro H, Scarone H)
Chile 1 (Subiabre)

Sport de Nuñoa, Santiago, 20–10–1926, 3000
Argentina 8 (Sosa G 4, Delgado 2, Cherro, Miguel)
Paraguay 0

Sport de Nuñoa, Santiago, 23–10–1926, 2000
Paraguay 6 (Ramirez J 3, Ramirez C 2, López I)
Bolivia 1 (Soto)

Sport de Nuñoa, Santiago, 24–10–1926, 15 000. Referee: Barba, Paraguay
Uruguay 2 (Castro H, Borjas)
Argentina 0

Uruguay – Batignani – Nasazzi, Recoba – Andrade, Fernández L, Vanzzino – Urdinarán, Scarone H, Borjas, Castro H, Saldombide
Argentina – Diaz – Bidoglio, Cochrane – Medici, Vaccaro, Monti – Tarasconi, Cherro, Sosa G, Miguel, Delgado

Sport de Nuñoa, Santiago, 24–10–1926, 8000
Uruguay 6 (Scarone H 5, Romano)
Bolivia 0

Sport de Nuñoa, Santiago, 31–10–1926, 8000
Chile 1 (Saavedra)
Argentina 1 (Tarasconi)

Sport de Nuñoa, Santiago, 1–11–1926, 12 000
Uruguay 6 (Castro H 4, Saldombide 2)
Paraguay 1 (Fretes)

Sport de Nuñoa, Santiago, 3–11–1926, 6000
Chile 5 (Subiabre 3, Arellano 2)
Paraguay 1 (Vargas)

	Ur	Ar	Ch	Pa	Bo	Pl	W	D	L	F	A	Pts
URUGUAY	–	2–0	3–1	6–1	6–0	4	4	0	0	17	2	8
Argentina	–	–	1–1	8–0	5–0	4	2	1	1	14	3	5
Chile	–	–	–	5–1	7–1	4	2	1	1	14	6	5
Paraguay	–	–	–	–	6–1	4	1	0	3	8	20	2
Bolivia	–	–	–	–	–	4	0	0	4	2	24	0

Top scorers: Scarone H, Uruguay 6
Castro H, Uruguay 6
Subiabre, Chile 6

TWELFTH EDITION
Lima, 30th October–27th November 1927

Estadio Nacional, Lima, 30–10–1927, 15 000
Argentina 7 (Carricaberry 2, Seoane 2, Luna 2, Recanattini)
Bolivia 1 (Algorta)

Estadio Nacional, Lima, 1–11–1927, 22 000
Uruguay 4 (Sacco, Castro H, OG)
Peru 0

Estadio Nacional, Lima, 6–11–1927, 6000
Uruguay 9 (Petrone 3, Figueroa 3, Arremón, Castro H, Scarone H)
Bolivia 0

Estadio Nacional, Lima, 13–11–1927, 15000
Peru 3 (Montellanos, Neyra, Sarmiento)
Bolivia 2 (Bustamante)

Estadio Nacional, Lima, 20–11–1927, 26000. Referee: Theurner, England
Argentina 3 (Recanattini, Luna, OG)
Uruguay 2 (Scarone H 2)
Argentina – Diaz – Recanattini, Bidoglio – Evaristo J, Zumelzú, Monti – Carricaberry, Maglio, Ferreira, Seoane, Luna
Uruguay – Capuccini – Canavessi, Tejera – Andrade, Fernández L, Vanzzino – Arremón, Scarone H, Petrone, Castro H, Figueroa

Estadio Nacional, Lima, 27–11–1927, 15000
Argentina 5 (Maglio 2, Ferreira, Orsi, Carricaberry)
Peru 1 (Villaneuva)

	Ar	Ur	Pe	Bo	Pl	W	D	L	F	A	Pts
ARGENTINA	–	3–2	5–1	7–1	3	3	0	0	15	4	6
URUGUAY	–	–	4–0	9–0	3	2	0	1	15	3	4
PERU	–	–	–	3–2	3	1	0	2	4	11	2
BOLIVIA	–	–	–	–	3	0	0	3	3	19	0

Top scorers: Carricaberry, Argentina 3
Luna, Argentina 3
Petrone, Uruguay 3
Figueroa, Uruguay 3
Scarone H, Uruguay 3

THIRTEENTH EDITION
Buenos Aires, 1st–17th November 1929

River Plate, Buenos Aires, 1–11–1929, 40000
Paraguay 3 (González A 2, Sosa L)
Uruguay 0

San Lorenzo, Buenos Aires, 3–11–1929, 20000
Argentina 3 (Zumelzú 2, Peucelle)
Peru 0

San Lorenzo, Buenos Aires, 10–11–1929, 20000. Referee: Bonelli, Peru
Argentina 4 (Ferreira 2, Evaristo, Cherro)
Paraguay 1 (Dominguez)
Argentina – Bossio – Tarrio, Paternóster – Evaristo J, Zumelzú, Chivirini – Peucelle, Rivarola, Ferreira, Cherro, Evaristo M
Paraguay – Brunetti – Olmedo, Flores – Viccini, Diaz, Etcheverry – Nessi, Dominguez, González A, Caceres, Sosa U

River Plate, Buenos Aires, 11–11–1929, 22000
Uruguay 4 (Fernández L 3, Andrade J)
Peru 1 (Bulnes)

Cordero, Buenos Aires, 16–11–1929, 8000
Paraguay 5 (González A 3, Nessi, Dominguez)
Peru 0

San Lorenzo, Buenos Aires, 17–11–1929, 60000
Argentina 2 (Ferreira, Evaristo M)
Uruguay 0

	Ar	Pa	Ur	Pe	Pl	W	D	L	F	A	Pts
ARGENTINA	–	4–1	2–0	3–0	3	3	0	0	9	1	6
PARAGUAY	–	–	3–0	5–0	3	2	0	1	9	4	4
URUGUAY	–	–	–	4–1	3	1	0	2	4	6	2
PERU	–	–	–	–	3	0	0	3	1	12	0

Top scorer: González, Paraguay 5

FOURTEENTH EDITION
Lima, 6th–27th January 1935

Not for the Copa America

Estadio Nacional, Lima, 6–01–1935, 25000
Argentina 4 (Lauri, Garcia D, Arrieta, Masantonio)
Chile 1 (Carmona)

Estadio Nacional, Lima, 13–01–1935, 28000
Uruguay 1 (Castro H)
Peru 0

Estadio Nacional, Lima, 18–01–1935, 13000
Uruguay 2 (Ciocca 2)
Chile 1 (Giúdici)

Estadio Nacional, Lima, 20–01–1935, 28000
Argentina 4 (Masantonio 3, Garcia D)
Peru 1 (Fernández T)

Estadio Nacional, Lima, 26–01–1935, 12000
Peru 1 (Montellanos)
Chile 0

Estadio Nacional, Lima, 27–01–1935, 25000. Referee: Reginatto, Chile
Uruguay 3 (Castro H, Taboada, Ciocca)
Argentina 0
Uruguay – Ballesteros – Nasazzi, Muñiz – Zunino (Denis), Fernandez L, Pérez M – Taboada, Ciocca, Castro H, Fernandez E, Castro B
Argentina – Bello (Gualco) – Wilson, Scarcella – De Jonge, Minella, Demare – Lauri, Sastre, Masantonio, Garcia D (Zito), Arrieta

	Ur	Ar	Pe	Ch	Pl	W	D	L	F	A	Pts
URUGUAY	–	3–0	1–0	2–1	3	3	0	0	6	1	6
ARGENTINA	–	–	4–1	4–1	3	2	0	1	8	5	4
PERU	–	–	–	1–0	3	1	0	2	2	5	2
CHILE	–	–	–	–	3	0	0	3	2	7	0

Top scorer: Masantonio, Argentina 4

FIFTEENTH EDITION
Buenos Aires, 27th December 1936–1st February 1937

San Lorenzo, Buenos Aires, 27–12–1936, 20000
Brazil 3 (Alfonsinho, Roberto, Niginho)
Peru 2 (Fernández T, Villaneuva)

San Lorenzo, Buenos Aires, 30–12–1936, 35000
Argentina 2 (Varallo 2)
Chile 1 (Toro)

San Lorenzo, Buenos Aires, 2–01–1937, 25000
Paraguay 4 (González A 2, Erico, Ortega A)
Uruguay 2 (Varela S 2)

La Bombonera, Buenos Aires, 3–01–1937, 20000
Brazil 6 (Luiz M Oliveira 2, Patesko 2, Carvalho Leite, Roberto)
Chile 4 (Toro 2, Avendaño, Riveros)

San Lorenzo, Buenos Aires, 6–01–1937, 20000
Uruguay 4 (Varela S 2, Piriz, Camaiti)
Peru 2 (Fernandez T, Magallanes)

La Bombonera, Buenos Aires, 9–01–1937, 25000
Argentina 6 (Zozaya 3, Scopelli 2, Garcia E)
Paraguay 1 (Gonzalez A)

San Lorenzo, Buenos Aires, 10–01–1937, 18 000
Chile 3 (Toro 2, Arancibia)
Uruguay 0

San Lorenzo, Buenos Aires, 13–01–1937, 20 000
Brazil 5 (Luiz M Oliveira 2, Patesko 2, Carvalho Leite)
Paraguay 0

San Lorenzo, Buenos Aires, 16–01–1937, 40 000
Argentina 1 (Zozaya)
Peru 0

San Lorenzo, Buenos Aires, 17–01–1937, 12 000
Paraguay 3 (Amarilla, Nuñez, Flor)
Chile 2 (Toro 2)

San Lorenzo, Buenos Aires, 19–01–1937, 35 000
Brazil 3 (Bahia, Niginho, Carvalho Leite)
Uruguay 2 (Villadoniga, Piriz)

San Lorenzo, Buenos Aires, 21–01–1937, 8000
Peru 2 (Alcade J 2)
Chile 2 (Torres, Carmona)

San Lorenzo, Buenos Aires, 23–01–1937, 70 000
Uruguay 3 (Villadóniga, Piriz, Varela S)
Argentina 2 (Varallo, Zozaya)

San Lorenzo, Buenos Aires, 24–01–1937, 8000
Peru 1 (Lavalle)
Paraguay 0

Monumental, Buenos Aires, 30–01–1937, 80 000
Argentina 1 (Garcia E)
Brazil 0

Play–off
San Lorenzo, Buenos Aires, 1–02–1937, 80 000. Referee: Macias, Argentina
Argentina 2 (De la Mata 2)
Brazil 0

Argentina – Bello – Tarrio, Fazio – Sastre, Lazzatti, Martinez – Guaita, Varallo (De La Mata), Zozaya (Ferreira), Cherro (Peucelle), Garcia E
Brazil – Jurandir – Carnera, Jaú – Britto, Brandao, Afonsinho – Roberto I (Carreiro), Luiz M Oliveira (Bahia), Cardeal (Carvalho Leite), Tim, Patesko

	Ar	Br	Ur	Pa	Ch	Pe	Pl	W	D	L	F	A	Pts
ARGENTINA	–	1–0	2–3	6–1	2–1	1–0	5	4	0	1	12	5	8
BRAZIL	–	–	3–2	5–0	6–4	3–2	5	4	0	1	17	9	8
URUGUAY	–	–	–	2–4	0–3	4–2	5	2	0	3	11	14	4
PARAGUAY	–	–	–	–	3–2	0–1	5	2	0	3	8	16	4
CHILE	–	–	–	–	–	2–2	5	1	1	3	12	13	3
PERU	–	–	–	–	–	–	5	1	1	3	7	10	3

Top scorer: Toro, Chile 7

SIXTEENTH EDITION
Lima, 15th January–12th February 1939

Estadio Nacional, Lima, 15–01–1939, 10 000
Paraguay 5 (Godoy 2, Barrios 2, Aquino)
Chile 1 (Sorrel)

Estadio Nacional, Lima, 15–01–1939, 10 000
Peru 5 (Fernández T 3, Alcalde J 2)
Ecuador 2 (Herrera, Suarez)

Estadio Nacional, Lima, 22–01–1939, 6000
Uruguay 6 (Varela S 3, Lago 2, Porta)
Ecuador 0

Estadio Nacional, Lima, 22–01–1939, 6000
Peru 3 (Fernández T 2, Alcalde J)
Chile 1 (Dominguez)

Estadio Nacional, Lima, 29–01–1939, 15 000
Uruguay 3 (Varela S, Camiati, Chirimini)
Chile 2 (Muñoz, Luco)

Estadio Nacional, Lima, 29–01–1939, 15 000
Peru 3 (Fernández T 2, Alcalde J)
Paraguay 0

Estadio Nacional, Lima, 5–02–1939, 10 000
Chile 4 (Avendaño 2, Toro, Sorrel
Ecudor 1 (Arenas)

Estadio Nacional, Lima, 5–02–1939, 10 000
Uruguay 3 (Lago, Varela S, Porta)
Paraguay 1 (Barrios)

Estadio Nacional, Lima, 12–02–1939, 15 000
Paraguay 3 (Mingo, Bareiro, Godoy)
Ecuador 1 (Herrera)

Estadio Nacional, Lima, 12–02–1939, 15 000. Referee: Vargas, Chile
Peru 2 (Alcalde J 7, Bielich 35)
Uruguay 1 (Porta 44)

Peru – Honores – Chapell, Fernandez A – Tovar, Pasache, Castillo – Alcade T, Fernandez T, Alcade J, Bielich (Ibanez) (Quispe), Paredes
Uruguay – Granero – Sanguinetti (Zaccour), Mascheroni – Zunino, Galvalisi, Viana – Porta, Ciocca (Camaiti), Lago, Varela S (Chirimini), Rodriguez

	Pe	Ur	Pa	Ch	Ec	Pl	W	D	L	F	A	Pts
PERU	–	2–1	3–0	3–1	5–2	4	4	0	0	13	4	8
URUGUAY	–	–	3–1	3–2	6–0	4	3	0	1	13	5	6
PARAGUAY	–	–	–	5–1	3–1	4	2	0	2	9	8	4
CHILE	–	–	–	–	4–1	4	1	0	3	8	12	2
ECUADOR	–	–	–	–	–	4	0	0	4	4	18	0

Top scorer: Fernández, Peru 7

SEVENTEENTH EDITION
Santiago, 2nd February–4th March 1941

Not for the Copa America

Estadio Nacional, Santiago, 2–02–1941, 40 000
Chile 5 (Sorrel 2, Toro, Contreras A, Pérez R)
Ecuador 0

Estadio Nacional, Santiago, 9–02–1941, 70 000
Uruguay 6 (Rivero 3, Porta, Gambetta, OG)
Ecuador 0

Estadio Nacional, Santiago, 9–02–1941, 70 000
Chile 1 (Pérez R)
Peru 0

Estadio Nacional, Santiago, 12–02–1941, 45 000
Argentina 2 (Moreno J 2)
Peru 1 (Socarraz)

Estadio Nacional, Santiago, 16–02–1941, 70 000
Argentina 6 (Marvezzi 5, Moreno J)
Ecuador 1 (Freire)

Estadio Nacional, Santiago, 16–02–1941, 70 000
Uruguay 2 (Cruche, Chirimini)
Chile 0

Estadio Nacional, Santiago, 23–02–1941, 48 000
Peru 4 (Fernández T 3, Vallejos)
Ecuador 0

Estadio Nacional, Santiago, 23–02–1941, 48 000. Referee: Vargas, Chile
Argentina 1 (Sastre 54)
Uruguay 0

Argentina – Estrada – Salomón (Coletta), Alberti – Sbarra, Minella (Videla), Colombo – Pedernera, Moreno J, Marvezzi, Sastre, Garcia E
Uruguay – Paz – Romero, Cadilla – Martinez, Varela O (González S), Gambetta – Medina (Chirimini), Porta, Rivero, Riephoff, Magliano

Estadio Nacional, Santiago, 26–02–1941, 20 000
Uruguay 2 (Riephoff, Varela O)
Peru 0

Estadio Nacional, Santiago, 4–03–1941, 70 000
Argentina 1 (Garcia E)
Chile 0

	Ar	Ur	Ch	Pe	Ec	Pl	W	D	L	F	A	Pts
ARGENTINA	–	1–0	1–0	2–1	6–1	4	4	0	0	10	2	8
URUGUAY	–	–	2–0	2–0	6–0	4	3	0	1	10	1	6
CHILE	–	–	–	1–0	5–0	4	2	0	2	6	3	4
PERU	–	–	–	–	4–0	4	1	0	3	5	5	2
ECUADOR	–	–	–	–	–	4	0	0	4	1	21	0

Top scorer: Marvezzi, Argentina 5

EIGHTEENTH EDITION
Montevideo, 10th January–7th February 1942

Estadio Centenario, Montevideo, 10–01–1942, 40 000
Uruguay 6 (Castro L 2, Varela O, Ciocca, Zapirain, Porta)
Chile 1 (Contreras)

Estadio Centenario, Montevideo, 11–01–1942, 20 000
Argentina 4 (Masantonio 2, Sandoval, Perucca)
Paraguay 3 (Aveiro 2, Sánchez V)

Estadio Centenario, Montevideo, 14–01–1942, 10 000
Brazil 6 (Pirilo 3, Patesko 2, Claudio C Pinto)
Chile 1 (Dominguez)

Estadio Centenario, Montevideo, 17–01–1942, 30 000
Argentina 2 (Garcia E, Masantonio)
Brazil 1 (Servílio I)

Estadio Centenario, Montevideo, 18–01–1942, 45 000
Uruguay 7 (Varela S 3, Porta 2, Zapirain, Gambetta)
Ecuador 0

Estadio Centenario, Montevideo, 18–01–1942, 45 000
Paraguay 1 (Barrios)
Peru 1 (Magallanes)

Estadio Centenario, Montevideo, 21–01–1942, 10 000
Brazil 2 (Amorim 2)
Peru 1 (Fernández L)

Estadio Centenario, Montevideo, 22–01–1942, 25 000
Paraguay 2 (Barrios, Franco)
Chile 0

Estadio Centenario, Montevideo, 22–01–1942, 25 000
Argentina 12 (Moreno J 5, Masantonio 4, Garcia E, Pedernera, Perucca)
Ecuador 0

Estadio Centenario, Montevideo, 24–01–1942, 55 000
Uruguay 1 (Varela S)
Brazil 0

Estadio Centenario, Montevideo, 25–01–1942, 12 000
Paraguay 3 (Franco, Mingo, Ibarrola)
Ecuador 1 (Herrera)

Estadio Centenario, Montevideo, 25–01–1942, 12 000
Argentina 3 (Moreno J 2, Heredia)
Peru 1 (Fernández T)

Estadio Centenario, Montevideo, 28–01–1942, 40 000
Peru 2 (Quiñones, Morales)
Ecuador 1 (Jiminez)

Estadio Centenario, Montevideo, 28–01–1942, 40 000
Uruguay 3 (Varela S, Porta, Ciocca)
Paraguay 1 (Barrios)

Estadio Centenario, Montevideo, 31–01–1942, 15 000
Argentina 0
Chile 0

Chile walked off the field after 43 minutes. Argentina were awarded the points.

Estadio Centenario, Montevideo, 31–01–1942, 40 000
Brazil 5 (Pirilo 3, Tim, Zizinho)
Ecuador 1 (Alvarez)

Estadio Centenario, Montevideo, 1–02–1942, 40 000
Uruguay 3 (Chirimini, Castro L, Porta)
Peru 0

Estadio Centenario, Montevideo, 5–02–1942, 15 000
Chile 2 (Dominguez, Armingol)
Ecuador 1 (Alcibar)

Estadio Centenario, Montevideo, 5–02–1942, 15 000
Brazil 1 (Zizinho)
Paraguay 1 (Franco)

Estadio Centenario, Montevideo, 7–02–1942, 70 000
Peru 0
Chile 0

Estadio Centenario, Montevideo, 7–02–1942, 70 000. Referee: Rojas, Paraguay
Uruguay 1 (Zapirain)
Argentina 0

Uruguay – Paz – Ramero, Muñiz – Rodriguez, Varela O, Gambetta – Castro, Varela S (Chirimini) (Faltando), Ciocca, Porta, Zapirain
Argentina – Gualco – Salomón, Valussi (Montañez) – Esperón, Perucca, Ramos – Heredia (Pedernera), Sandoval, Masantonio, Moreno, Garcia (Ferreyra)

	Ar	Br	Pa	Pe	Ch	Ec	Pl	W	D	L	F	A	Pts
URUGUAY	1–0	1–0	3–1	3–0	6–1	7–0	6	6	0	0	21	2	12
Argentina	–	2–1	4–3	3–1	0–0	12–0	6	5	0	1	21	6	10
Brazil	–	–	1–1	2–1	6–1	5–1	6	3	1	2	15	7	7
Paraguay	–	–	–	1–1	2–0	3–1	6	2	2	2	11	10	6
Peru	–	–	–	–	0–0	2–1	6	1	2	3	5	10	4
Chile	–	–	–	–	–	2–1	6	1	1	4	4	15	3
Ecuador	–	–	–	–	–	–	6	0	0	6	4	31	0

Top scorers: Moreno, Argentina 5
Masantonio, Argentina 5

NINETEENTH EDITION
Santiago, 14th January–28th February 1945

Not for the Copa America

Estadio Nacional, Santiago, 14–01–1945, 65 000
Chile 6 (Alcántara 2, Hormazábal, Vera, Clavero, Piñero)
Ecuador 3 (Raymondi 2, Mendoza)

Estadio Nacional, Santiago, 18–01–1945, 35 000
Argentina 4 (Pontoni, Martino, Loustau, De La Mata)
Bolivia 0

Estadio Nacional, Santiago, 21–01–1945, 60 000
Brazil 3 (Jorginho, Heleno de Freitas, Jaime)
Colombia 0

Estadio Nacional, Santiago, 24–01–1945, 70 000
Uruguay 5 (Garcia A 3, Porta, Varela O)
Ecuador 1 (Aguayo)

Estadio Nacional, Santiago, 24–01–1945, 70 000
Chile 5 (Clavero 2, Alcántara 2, Medina)
Bolivia 0

Estadio Nacional, Santiago, 28–01–1945, 28 000
Brazil 2 (Ademir de Menezes, Tesourinha)
Bolivia 0

Estadio Nacional, Santiago, 28–01–1945, 28 000
Uruguay 7 (Garcia A 2, Garcia J 2, Ortiz, Porta, Riephoff)
Colombia 0

Estadio Nacional, Santiago, 31–01–1945, 60 000
Argentina 4 (Pontoni, De La Mata, Martino, Pellegrina)
Ecuador 2 (Aguayo, Acevedo)

Estadio Nacional, Santiago, 31–01–1945, 60 000
Chile 2 (Medina, Piñero)
Colombia 0

Estadio Nacional, Santiago, 7–02–1945, 60 000
Argentina 9 (Pontoni 2, Méndez 2, Martino 2, Boyé 2, Ferraro 2, Loustau)
Colombia 1 (Mendoza)

Estadio Nacional, Santiago, 7–02–1945, 60 000
Brazil 3 (Heleno de Freitas 2, Rui)
Uruguay 0

Estadio Nacional, Santiago, 11–02–1945, 70 000
Bolivia 0
Ecuador 0

Estadio Nacional, Santiago, 11–02–1945, 70 000
Chile 1 (Medina)
Argentina 1 (Méndez)

Estadio Nacional, Santiago, 15–02–1945, 65 000
Uruguay 2 (Falero, Porta)
Bolivia 0

Estadio Nacional, Santiago, 15–02–1945, 65 000. Referee: Valentini, Uruguay
Argentina 3 (Méndez 3)
Brazil 1 (Ademir Menezes)
Argentina – Ricardo – Salomón, De Zorzi (Palma) – Sosa, Perucca, Colombo – Muñoz, Méndez (De la Mata), Pontoni, Martino (Farro), Loustau
Brazil – Oberdan – Domingos da Guia, Begliomini (Newton) – Biguá, Ruy, Jaime (Alfredo) – Tesourinha, Zizinho, Heleno de Freitas (Servilio), Jair R Pinto, Ademir Menezes

Estadio Nacional, Santiago, 18–02–1945, 65 000
Colombia 3 (Berdugo, Rubio, Gamez)
Ecuador 1 (Aguayo)

Estadio Nacional, Santiago, 18–02–1945, 65 000
Chile 1 (Medina)
Uruguay 0

Estadio Nacional, Santiago, 21–02–1945, 22 000
Bolivia 3 (Orozco, Romero, Fernández R)
Colombia 3 (Rubio, Berdugo, Gamez)

Estadio Nacional, Santiago, 21–02–1945, 22 000
Brazil 9 (Ademir Menezes 3, Heleno de Freitas 2, Jair R Pinto 2, Zizinho 2)
Ecuador 2 (Aguayo, Albornoz)

Estadio Nacional, Santiago, 25–02–1945, 45 000
Argentina 1 (Martino)
Uruguay 0

Estadio Nacional, Santiago, 28–02–1945, 80 000
Brazil 1 (Heleno de Freitas)
Chile 0

	Br	Ch	Ur	Co	Bo	Ec	Pl	W	D	L	F	A	Pts
ARGENTINA	3–1	1–1	1–0	9–1	4–0	4–2	6	5	1	0	22	5	11
BRAZIL	–	1–0	3–0	3–0	2–0	9–2	6	5	0	1	19	5	10
CHILE	–	–	1–0	2–0	5–0	6–3	6	4	1	1	15	5	9
URUGUAY	–	–	–	7–0	2–0	5–1	6	3	0	3	14	6	6
COLOMBIA	–	–	–	–	3–3	3–1	6	1	1	4	7	25	3
BOLIVIA	–	–	–	–	–	0–0	6	0	2	4	3	16	2
ECUADOR	–	–	–	–	–	–	6	0	1	5	9	27	1

Top scorers: Méndez, Argentina 6
De Freitas, Brazil 6

TWENTIETH EDITION
Buenos Aires, 12th January–10th February 1946

Not for the Copa America

Monumental, Buenos Aires, 12 01–1946, 70 000
Argentina 2 (De la Mata, Martino)
Paraguay 0

San Lorenzo, Buenos Aires, 16–01–1946, 70 000
Brazil 3 (Heleno de Freitas 2, Zizinho)
Bolivia 0

San Lorenzo, Buenos Aires, 16–01–1946, 70 000
Uruguay 1 (Medina)
Chile 0

San Lorenzo, Buenos Aires, 19–01–1946, 65 000
Chile 2 (Araya, Cremaschi)
Paraguay 1 (Rolón)

San Lorenzo, Buenos Aires, 19–01–1946, 65 000
Argentina 7 (Méndez 2, Labruna 2, Salvini 2, Loustau)
Bolivia 1 (Peredo)

San Lorenzo, Buenos Aires, 23–01–1946, 40 000
Brazil 4 (Jair R Pinto 2, Heleno de Freitas, Chico)
Uruguay 3 (Medina 2, Vázquez)

Monumental, Buenos Aires, 26–01–1946, 80 000
Paraguay 4 (Villalba 2, Genes, Benitez Cáceres)
Bolivia 2 (OG, Ortega)

Monumental, Buenos Aires, 26–01–1946, 80 000
Argentina 3 (Labruna 2, Pedernera)
Chile 1 (Alcantara)

Cordero, Buenos Aires, 29–01–1946, 30 000
Uruguay 5 (Medina 4, Garcia J)
Bolivia 0

Cordero, Buenos Aires, 29–01–1946, 30 000
Brazil 1 (Norival)
Paraguay 1 (Villalba)

San Lorenzo, Buenos Aires, 2–02–1946, 80 000
Argentina 3 (Pedernera, Labruna, Méndez)
Uruguay 1 (Riephoff)

San Lorenzo, Buenos Aires, 3–02–1946, 22 000
Brazil 5 (Zizinho 4, Chico)
Chile 1 (Salfate)

San Lorenzo, Buenos Aires, 8–02–1946, 18 000
Chile 4 (Araya 3, Cremaschi)
Bolivia 1 (OG)

San Lorenzo, Buenos Aires, 8–02–1946, 18 000
Paraguay 2 (Villalba, Rodriguez A)
Uruguay 1 (OG)

Monumental, Buenos Aires, 10–02–1946, 80 000. Referee: Valentini, Uruguay
Argentina 2 (Méndez 2)
Brazil 0
Argentina – Vacca – Salomón (Marante), Sobrero – Fonda, Strembell (Ongaro), Pescia – De la Mata, Méndez, Pedernera, Labruna, Loustau
Brazil – Luiz Borracha – Domingos da Guia, Norival – Zezé Procopio, Danilo Alvim, Jaime (Ruy) – Tesourinha (Eduardo Lima), Zizinho (Ademir Menezes), Heleno de Freitas, Jair R Pinto, Chico

	Ar	Br	Pa	Ur	Ch	Bo	Pl	W	D	L	F	A	Pts
ARGENTINA	–	2–0	2–0	3–1	3–1	7–1	5	5	0	0	17	3	10
BRAZIL	–	–	1–1	4–3	5–1	3–0	5	3	1	1	13	7	7
PARAGUAY	–	–	–	2–1	1–2	4–2	5	2	1	2	8	8	5
URUGUAY	–	–	–	–	1–0	5–0	5	2	0	3	11	9	4
CHILE	–	–	–	–	–	4–1	5	2	0	3	8	11	4
BOLIVIA	–	–	–	–	–	–	5	0	0	5	4	23	0

Top scorer: Medina, Uruguay 7

TWENTY-FIRST EDITION
Guayaquil, 30th November–30th December 1947

Capwell, Guayaquil, 30–11–1947, 30 000
Ecuador 2 (Jiménez J 2)
Bolivia 2 (Gutiérrez 2)

Capwell, Guayaquil, 2–12–1947, 20 000
Uruguay 2 (Falero, Britos)
Colombia 0

Capwell, Guayaquil, 2–12–1947, 20 000. Referee: Rivas, Chile
Argentina 6 (Pontoni 3, Moreno J, Loustau, Méndez)
Paraguay 0
Argentina – Cozzi – Marante (Colman), Sobrero – Yácono, Prucca, Pescia – Boyé, Méndez, Pontoni, Moreno, Loustau
Paraguay – Garcia S – Hugo, Caciano – Céspedes, Gavilán, Ocampos – Cantero, Fernández P, López Fretes (Rivas), Marin, Genés, Villalba

Capwell, Guayaquil, 4–12–1947, 30 000
Argentina 7 (Méndez 2, Boyé 2, Pontoni, Di Stéfano, Loustau)
Bolivia 0

Capwell, Guayaquil, 4–12–1947, 30 000
Ecuador 0
Colombia 0

Capwell, Guayaquil, 6–12–1947, 20 000
Peru 2 (Castillo, Mosquera)
Paraguay 2 (Villalba, Marin)

Capwell, Guayaquil, 6–12–1947, 20 000
Uruguay 6 (Sarro 2, Falero, Magliano, Gambetta, Puente)
Chile 0

Capwell, Guayaquil, 9–12–1947, 15 000
Chile 2 (Varela C, Busquets)
Peru 1 (López V)

Capwell, Guayaquil, 9–12–1947, 15 000
Uruguay 3 (Falero 2, Magliano)
Bolivia 0

Capwell, Guayaquil, 11–12–1947, 11 000
Chile 3 (López P 2, Peñaloza)
Ecuador 0

Capwell, Guayaquil, 11–12–1947, 11 000
Argentina 3 (Moreno J, Di Stéfano, Boyé)
Peru 2 (Gómez Sánchez, López.V)

Capwell, Guayaquil, 13–12–1947, 18 000
Colombia 0
Bolivia 0

Capwell, Guayaquil, 13–12–1947, 18 000
Paraguay 4 (Genés 2, Marin, Villalba)
Uruguay 2 (Magliano, Britos)

Capwell, Guayaquil, 16–12–1947, 30 000
Uruguay 6 (Falero 2, Sarro 2, Magliano, Puente)
Ecuador 1 (Garnica)

Capwell, Guayaquil, 16–12–1947, 30 000
Argentina 1 (Di Stéfano)
Chile 1 (Riera)

Capwell, Guayaquil, 18–12–1947, 12 000
Paraguay 3 (Marin, Avalos, Genés)
Bolivia 1 (Tapia)

Capwell, Guayaquil, 18–12–1947, 12 000
Argentina 6 (Di Stéfano 3, Fernandez M, Boyé, Loustau)
Colombia 0

Capwell, Guayaquil, 20–12–1947, 20 000
Ecuador 0
Peru 0

Capwell, Guayaquil, 20–12–1947, 20 000
Paraguay 2 (Villalba 2)
Colombia 0

Capwell, Guayaquil, 23–12–1947, 5000
Peru 5 (Mosquera 2, Valdivieso, López V, Guzmán)
Colombia 1 (Arango)

Capwell, Guayaquil, 23–12–1947, 5000
Paraguay 1 (Villalba)
Chile 0

Capwell, Guayaquil, 25–12–1947, 25 000
Argentina 2 (Moreno J, Méndez)
Ecuador 0

Capwell, Guayaquil, 26–12–1947, 6000
Uruguay 1 (Falero)
Peru 0

Capwell, Guayaquil, 27–12–1947, 5000
Peru 2 (Gómez Sánchez, Valdivieso)
Bolivia 0

Capwell, Guayaquil, 28–12–1947, 25 000
Argentina 3 (Méndez 2, Loustau)
Uruguay 1 (Britos)

Capwell, Guayaquil, 29–12–1947, 5000
Paraguay 4 (Marin 3, Genés)
Ecuador 0

Capwell, Guayaquil, 29–12–1947, 5000
Chile 4 (Sáenz, López P, Infante, Riera)
Colombia 1 (Rubio)

Capwell, Guayaquil, 31–12–1947, 5000
Chile 4 (OG, López P, Sáenz, Riera)
Bolivia 3 (Tapia 2, Orgaz)

	Pa	Ur	Ch	Pe	Ec	Bo	Co	Pl	W	D	L	F	A	Pts
ARGENTINA	6–0	3–1	1–1	3–2	2–0	7–0	6–0	7	6	1	0	28	4	13
PARAGUAY	–	4–2	1–0	2–2	4–0	3–1	2–0	7	5	1	1	16	11	11
URUGUAY	–	–	6–0	1–0	6–1	3–0	2–0	7	5	0	2	21	8	10
CHILE	–	–	–	2–1	3–0	4–3	4–1	7	4	1	2	14	13	9
PERU	–	–	–	–	0–0	2–0	5–1	7	2	2	3	12	9	6
ECUADOR	–	–	–	–	–	2–2	0–0	7	0	3	4	3	17	3
BOLIVIA	–	–	–	–	–	–	0–0	7	0	2	5	6	21	2
COLOMBIA	–	–	–	–	–	–	–	7	0	2	5	2	19	2

Top scorer: Falero, Uruguay 7

TWENTY-SECOND EDITION
Brazil, 3rd April–8th May 1949

Sao Januario, Rio de Janeiro, 3–04–1949, 70 000
Brazil 9 (Jair R Pinto 2, Simao 2, Tesourinha 2, Ademir Menezes, Otávio, Zizinho)
Ecuador 1 (Chuchuca)

Pacaembu, Sao Paulo, 6–04–1949, 60 000
Bolivia 3 (Mena, Algañaraz, Godoy B)
Chile 2 (Salamanca, López P)

Pacaembu, Sao Paulo, 6–04–1949, 60 000
Paraguay 3 (López Fretes 2, Benitez D)
Colombia 0

Sao Januario, Rio de Janeiro, 10–04–1949, 15 000
Peru 4 (Drago, Salinas, Pedraza 2)
Colombia 0

Sao Januario, Rio de Janeiro, 10–04–1949, 15 000
Paraguay 1 (Barrios R)
Ecuador 0

Pacaembu, Sao Paulo, 10–04–1949, 40 000
Brazil 10 (Nininho 3, Claudio C Pinho 2, Zizinho 2, Simao 2, Jair R Pinto)
Bolivia 1 (Ugarte)

Pacaembu, Sao Paulo, 13–04–1949, 35 000
Brazil 2 (Claudio C Pinho, Zizinho)
Chile 1 (López P)

Sao Januario, Rio de Janeiro, 13–04–1949, 30 000
Uruguay 3 (Castro R 2, Moreno)
Ecuador 2 (Arteaga, Vargas)

Sao Januario, Rio de Janeiro, 13–04–1949, 30 000
Paraguay 3 (Barrios R, Arce, López Fretes)
Peru 1 (Drago)

Pacaembu, Sao Paulo, 17–04–1949, 45 000
Brazil 5 (Ademir Menezes 2, Orlando, Tesourinha, Canhotinho)
Colombia 0

Sao Januario, Rio de Janeiro, 17–04–1949, 8000
Chile 1 (Rojas C)
Ecuador 0

Sao Januario, Rio de Janeiro, 17–04–1949, 8000
Bolivia 3 (Ugarte, Algañaraz, Gutierrez B)
Uruguay 2 (Moll, Suarez)

Sao Januario, Rio de Janeiro, 20–04–1949, 7000
Peru 4 (Drago 2, Gómez Sánchez, Castillo)
Ecuador 0

Sao Januario, Rio de Janeiro, 20–04–1949, 7000
Chile 1 (Cremaschi)
Colombia 1 (Pérez A)

Pacaembu, Sao Paulo, 20–04–1949, 20 000
Uruguay 2 (Garcia J 2)
Paraguay 1 (Vazquez)

Pacaembu, Sao Paulo, 24–04–1949, 14 000
Bolivia 2 (Algañaraz, Mena)
Ecuador 0

Pacaembu, Sao Paulo, 24–04–1949, 45 000
Colombia 2 (Gastelbondo, Pérez A)
Uruguay 2 (Martinez M, Ayala)

Sao Januario, Rio de Janeiro, 24–04–1949, 45 000
Brazil 7 (Jair R Pinto 2, Simao, OG, Augusto, Orlando, Ademir Menezes)
Peru 1 (Salinas)

Villa Belmiro, Santos, 27–04–1949, 12 000
Peru 3 (Salinas 2, Lavalle)
Bolivia 0

Pacaembu, Sao Paulo, 27–04–1949, 1000
Paraguay 4 (Arce 3, Benitez D)
Chile 2 (Cremaschi, Riera)

Sao Januario, Rio de Janeiro, 30–04–1949, 45 000
Paraguay 7 (Benitez D 4, Arce 2, Avalos)
Bolivia 0

Sao Januario, Rio de Janeiro, 30–04–1949, 45 000
Brazil 5 (Jair R Pinto 2, Danilo Alvim, Tesourinha, Zizinho)
Uruguay 1 (Castro R)

Pacaembu, Sao Paulo, 30–04–1949, 1000
Peru 3 (Castillo 2, Mosquera)
Chile 0

Sao Januario, Rio de Janeiro, 3–05–1949, 3000
Ecuador 3 (Cantos, Vargas, Maldonado)
Colombia 2 (Garcia R, Berdugo)

Caio Martins, Rio de Janeiro, 4–05–1949, 30 000
Peru 4 (Gómez Sánchez 2, Mosquera, Castillo)
Uruguay 3 (Moll, Castro R, Ayala)

Caio Martins, Rio de Janeiro, 6–05–1949, 12 000
Bolivia 4 (Godoy 3, Rojas N)
Colombia 0

America, Belo Horizonte, 8–05–1949, 5000
Chile 3 (Infante 2, Rojas C)
Uruguay 1 (Ayala)

Sao Januario, Rio de Janeiro, 8–05–1949, 50 000
Paraguay 2 (Avalos, Benitez D)
Brazil 1 (Tesourinha)

Play–off
Sao Januario, Rio de Janeiro, 11–05–1949, 55 000. Referee: Berrick, England
Brazil 7 (Ademir Menezes 3, Tesourinha 2, Jair R Pinto 2)
Paraguay 0

Brazil – Barbosa – Augusto, Mauro R Oliveira – Ely, Danilo Alvim, Noronha – Tesourinha, Zizinho, Ademir Menezes, Jair R Pinto, Simao
Paraguay – Garcia S – González, Céspedes – Gavilán, Nardelli, Cantero – Fernández (Barrios), López Fretes (Romero), Arce, Benitez D, Vázquez

	Pa	Pe	Bo	Ch	Ur	Ec	Co	Pl	W	D	L	F	A	Pts
BRAZIL	1–2	7–1	10–1	2–1	5–1	9–1	5–0	7	6	0	1	39	7	12
PARAGUAY	–	3–1	7–0	4–2	1–2	1–0	3–0	7	6	0	1	21	6	12
PERU	–	–	3–0	3–0	4–3	4–0	4–0	7	5	0	2	20	13	10
BOLIVIA	–	–	–	3–2	3–2	2–0	4–0	7	4	0	3	13	24	8
CHILE	–	–	–	–	3–1	1–0	1–1	7	2	1	4	10	14	5
URUGUAY	–	–	–	–	–	3–2	2–2	7	2	1	4	14	20	5
ECUADOR	–	–	–	–	–	–	3–2	7	1	0	6	6	22	2
COLOMBIA	–	–	–	–	–	–	–	7	0	2	5	5	22	2

Top scorer: Jair R Pinto, Brazil 9

TWENTY-THIRD EDITION
Lima, 22nd February–2nd April 1953

Estadio Nacional, Lima, 22–02–1953, 50 000
Bolivia 1 (OG)
Peru 0

Estadio Nacional, Lima, 25–02–1953, 45 000
Paraguay 3 (Fernández R 2, Berni)
Chile 0

Estadio Nacional, Lima, 25–02–1953, 45 000
Uruguay 2 (Puente, Romero C)
Bolivia 0

Estadio Nacional, Lima, 28–02–1953, 50 000
Peru 1 (Villamares)
Ecuador 0

Estadio Nacional, Lima, 1–03–1953, 45 000
Brazil 8 (Julinho 4, Pinga 2, Rodrigues 2)
Bolivia 1 (Ugarte)

Estadio Nacional, Lima, 1–03–1953, 45 000
Chile 3 (Molina 3)
Uruguay 2 (Morel, Balseiro)

Estadio Nacional, Lima, 4–03–1953, 45 000
Paraguay 0
Ecuador 0

Estadio Nacional, Lima, 4–03–1953, 45 000
Chile 0
Peru 0

Estadio Nacional, Lima, 8–03–1953, 45 000
Bolivia 1 (Alcón)
Ecuador 1 (Guzmán E)

Estadio Nacional, Lima, 8–03–1953, 45 000
Peru 2 (Gómez Sánchez, Terry)
Paraguay 2 (Fernández R, Berni)

Estadio Nacional, Lima, 12–03–1953, 35 000
Paraguay 2 (López A, Berni)
Uruguay 2 (Balseiro 2)

Estadio Nacional, Lima, 12–03–1953, 35 000
Brazil 2 (Ademir Menezes, Claudio C Pinho)
Ecuador 0

Estadio Nacional, Lima, 15–03–1953, 45 000
Brazil 1 (Ipojucan)
Uruguay 0

Estadio Nacional, Lima, 16–03–1953, 15 000
Paraguay 2 (Romero J, Berni)
Bolivia 1 (Ugarte)

Estadio Nacional, Lima, 19–03–1953, 55 000
Chile 3 (Molina 2, Diaz G)
Ecuador 0

Estadio Nacional, Lima, 19–03–1953, 55 000
Peru 1 (Navarrete)
Brazil 0

Estadio Nacional, Lima, 23–03–1953, 35 000
Brazil 3 (Baltazar, Julinho, Zizinho)
Chile 2 (Molina, Cremaschi)

Estadio Nacional, Lima, 23–03–1953, 35 000
Uruguay 6 (Méndez, Peláez, Morel, Romero C, Puente, Balseiro)
Ecuador 0

Estadio Nacional, Lima, 27–03–1953, 35 000
Paraguay 2 (López A, León)
Brazil 1 (Nilton Santos)

Estadio Nacional, Lima, 28–03–1953, 45 000
Chile 2 (Molina, Diaz.G)
Bolivia 2 (Alcón, Santos)

Estadio Nacional, Lima, 28–03–1953, 45 000
Uruguay 3 (Peláez 2, Romero C)
Peru 0

Play–off
Estadio Nacional, Lima, 1–04–1953, 35 000. Referee: Dean, England
Paraguay 3 (López A, Gavilán, Fernández R)
Brazil 2 (Baltazar 2)

Paraguay – Riquelme – Herrera, Olmedo, Gavilán, Leguizamón – Hermosilla, Berni – López A (Parodi), Fernández R, Romero (Lacasia), Gómez (González)
Brazil – Castilho – Djalma Santos, Haroldo II, Nilton Santos (Alfredo II) – Bauer, Brandaozinho, Didi – Julinho, Baltazar, Pinga (Ipojucan), Claudio C Pinho

	Br	Ur	Ch	Pe	Bo	Ec	Pl	W	D	L	F	A	Pts
PARAGUAY	2–1	2–2	3–0	2–2*	2–1	0–0	6	3	3	0	11	6	8
BRAZIL	–	1–0	3–2	0–1	8–1	2–0	6	4	0	2	15	6	8
URUGUAY	–	–	2–3	3–0	2–0	6–0	6	3	1	2	15	6	7
CHILE	–	–	–	0–0	2–2*	3–0	6	2	2	2	10	10	7
PERU	–	–	–	–	0–1	1–0	6	2	2	2	4	6	7
BOLIVIA	–	–	–	–	–	1–1	6	1	1	4	6	15	3
ECUADOR	–	–	–	–	–	–	6	0	2	4	1	13	2

* Chile awarded both points in 2–2 draw with Bolivia
* Peru awarded both points in 2–2 draw with Paraguay

Top scorer: Molina, Chile 7

TWENTY-FOURTH EDITION
Santiago, 27th February–30th March 1955

Estadio Nacional, Santiago, 27–02–1955, 40 000
Chile 7 (Hormazábal 3, Diaz G 2, Robledo J, Meléndez)
Ecuador 1 (Villacreces)

Estadio Nacional, Santiago, 2–03–1955, 35 000
Argentina 5 (Micheli 4, Borello)
Paraguay 3 (Rolón, Villalba), Parodi)

Estadio Nacional, Santiago, 6–03–1955, 50 000
Chile 5 (Robledo J 2, Hormazábal, Muñoz, Ramirez)
Peru 4 (Castillo, Barbadillo, Heredia, Gómez Sánchez)

Estadio Nacional, Santiago, 9–03–1955, 48 000
Uruguay 3 (Borges, Miguez, Abbadie)
Paraguay 1 (Rolón)

Estadio Nacional, Santiago, 9–03–1955, 48 000
Argentina 4 (Bonelli, Grillo, Micheli, Borello)
Ecuador 0

Estadio Nacional, Santiago, 13–03–1955, 50 000
Chile 2 (Muñoz, Hormazábal)
Uruguay 2 (Galván 2)

Estadio Nacional, Santiago, 13–03–1955, 50 000
Peru 4 (Gómez Sánchez 2, OG 2)
Ecuador 2 (Matute 2)

Estadio Nacional, Santiago, 16–03–1955, 35 000
Paraguay 2 (Rolón 2)
Ecuador 0

Estadio Nacional, Santiago, 16–03–1955, 35 000
Argentina 2 (Grillo, Cecconato)
Peru 2 (Gómez Sánchez 2)

Estadio Nacional, Santiago, 20–03–1955, 55 000
Chile 5 (Melendez 2, Muñoz 2, Hormazábal)
Paraguay 0

Estadio Nacional, Santiago, 23–03–1955, 25 000
Paraguay 1 (Rolón)
Peru 1 (Terry)

Estadio Nacional, Santiago, 23–03–1955, 25 000
Uruguay 5 (Abbadie 2, Galván, Miguez, Pérez)
Ecuador 1 (Matute)

Estadio Nacional, Santiago, 27–03–1955, 45 000
Argentina 6 (Labruna 3, Micheli 2, Borello)
Uruguay 1 (Miguez)

Estadio Nacional, Santiago, 30–03–1955, 65 000
Peru 2 (Castillo, Gómez Sánchez)
Uruguay 1 (Morel)

Estadio Nacional, Santiago, 30–03–1955, 65 000. Referee: Rodriguez, Uruguay
Argentina 1 (Micheli)
Chile 0

Argentina – Mussimessi – Dellacha, Balay, Vairo – Lombardo, Gutiérrez – Micheli (Vernazza), Cecconato, Borello, Labruna, Cucchiaroni
Chile – Escuti – Almeyda, Cortes, Carrasco – Alvarez, Robledo E – Hormazábal, Melendez (Espinoza), Robledo J, Muñoz (Diaz G), Ramirez

	Ar	Ch	Pe	Ur	Pa	Ec	Pl	W	D	L	F	A	Pts
ARGENTINA	–	1–0	2–2	6–1	5–3	4–0	5	4	1	0	18	6	9
CHILE	–	–	5–4	2–2	5–0	7–1	5	3	1	1	19	8	7
PERU	–	–	–	2–1	1–1	4–2	5	2	2	1	13	11	6
URUGUAY	–	–	–	–	3–1	5–1	5	2	1	2	12	12	5
PARAGUAY	–	–	–	–	–	2–0	5	1	1	3	7	14	3
ECUADOR	–	–	–	–	–	–	5	0	0	5	4	22	0

Top scorer: Micheli, Argentina 8

TWENTY-FIFTH EDITION
Montevideo, 24th January–15th February 1956

Estadio Centenario, Montevideo, 21–01–1956, 55 000
Uruguay 4 (Escalada 2, Miguez, Roque)
Paraguay 2 (Gómez A 2)

Estadio Centenario, Montevideo, 22–01–1956, 16 000
Argentina 2 (Sivori, Vairo)
Peru 1 (Drago)

Estadio Centenario, Montevideo, 24–01–1956, 18 000
Chile 4 (Hormazábal 2, Meléndez R, Sánchez L)
Brazil 1 (Maurinho)

Estadio Centenario, Montevideo, 28–01–1956, 70 000
Uruguay 2 (Escalada, Miguez O)
Peru 0

Estadio Centenario, Montevideo, 29–01–1956, 45 000
Brazil 0
Paraguay 0

Estadio Centenario, Montevideo, 29–01–1956, 45 000
Argentina 2 (Labruna 2)
Chile 0

Estadio Centenario, Montevideo, 1–02–1956, 20 000
Brazil 2 (Alvaro, Zezinho)
Peru 1 (Drago)

Estadio Centenario, Montevideo, 1–02–1956, 20 000
Argentina 1 (Cecconato)
Paraguay 0

Estadio Centenario, Montevideo, 5–02–1956, 25 000
Paraguay 1 (Rolón)
Peru 1 (Andrade)

Estadio Centenario, Montevideo, 5–02–1956, 25 000
Brazil 1 (Luizinho)
Argentina 0

Estadio Centenario, Montevideo, 6–02–1956, 30 000
Uruguay 2 (Miguez O, Borges)
Chile 1 (Ramirez J)

Estadio Centenario, Montevideo, 9–02–1956, 5000
Chile 4 (Hormazábal, Muñoz, Fernández J, Sánchez L)
Peru 3 (Castillo, Mosquera, Gómez Sánchez)

Estadio Centenario, Montevideo, 10–02–1956, 80 000
Uruguay 0
Brazil 0

Estadio Centenario, Montevideo, 12–02–1956, 4000
Chile 2 (Hormazábal, Ramirez J)
Paraguay 0

Estadio Centenario, Montevideo, 15–02–1956, 80 000. Referee: Nicola, Paraguay
Uruguay 1 (Ambrois)
Argentina 0
Uruguay – Maceiras – Martinez, Carranza, Brazionis – Rodriguez Andrade, Miramontes – Borges (Pirez), Ambrois, Miguez O, Escalada (Auscarriaga), Roque
Argentina – Mussimessi – Dellacha, Mouriño, Vairo – Lombardo, Gutiérrez – Pentrelli, Sivori, Grillo, Labruna, Zárate

	Ur	Ch	Ar	Br	Pa	Pe	Pl	W	D	L	F	A	Pts
URUGUAY	–	2–1	1–0	0–0	4–2	2–0	5	4	1	0	9	3	9
CHILE	–	–	0–2	4–1	2–0	4–3	5	3	0	2	11	8	6
ARGENTINA	–	–	–	0–1	1–0	2–1	5	3	0	2	5	3	6
BRAZIL	–	–	–	–	0–0	2–1	5	2	2	1	4	5	6
PARAGUAY	–	–	–	–	–	1–1	5	0	2	3	3	8	2
PERU	–	–	–	–	–	–	5	0	1	4	6	11	1

Top scorer: Hormazabal, Chile 4

TWENTY-SIXTH EDITION
Lima, 7th March–6th April 1957

Estadio Nacional, Lima, 7–03–1957, 50 000
Uruguay 5 (Ambrois 4, Sasia)
Ecuador 2 (Cantos, Larraz)

Estadio Nacional, Lima, 10–03–1957, 55 000
Peru 2 (Terry 2)
Ecuador 1 (Cantos)

Estadio Nacional, Lima, 13–03–1957, 42 000
Argentina 8 (Maschio 4, Angelillo 2, Cruz, Corbatta)
Colombia 2 (Gamboa, Valencia)

Estadio Nacional, Lima, 13–03–1957, 42 000
Brazil 4 (Didi 3, Pepe)
Chile 2 (Ramirez J, Fernández J)

Estadio Nacional, Lima, 16–03–1957, 60 000
Peru 1 (Mosquera)
Chile 0

Estadio Nacional, Lima, 17–03–1957, 50 000
Colombia 1 (Arango)
Uruguay 0

Estadio Nacional, Lima, 17–03–1957, 50 000
Argentina 3 (Angelillo 2, Sivori)
Ecuador 0

Estadio Nacional, Lima, 20–03–1957, 40 000
Argentina 4 (Maschio 2, Angelillo, Sanfilippo)
Uruguay 0

Estadio Nacional, Lima, 21–03–1957, 45 000
Brazil 7 (Evaristo 2, Joel 2, Indio, Pepe, Zizinho)
Ecuador 1 (Larraz)

Estadio Nacional, Lima, 21–03–1957, 45 000
Chile 3 (Verdejo 2, Espinoza S)
Colombia 2 (Arango, Carrillo)

Estadio Nacional, Lima, 23–03–1957, 55 000
Uruguay 5 (Ambrois 4, Carranza)
Peru 3 (Terry, Seminario, Mosquera)

Estadio Nacional, Lima, 24–03–1957, 45 000
Chile 2 (Ramirez J 2)
Ecuador 2 (Larraz, Cantos)

Estadio Nacional, Lima, 24–03–1957, 45 000
Brazil 9 (Evaristo 5, Didi 2, Zizinho, Pepe)
Colombia 0

Estadio Nacional, Lima, 27–03–1957, 55 000
Peru 4 (Rivera 2, Terry, Bassa)
Colombia 1 (Arango)

Estadio Nacional, Lima, 28–03–1957, 50 000
Argentina 6 (Angelillo 2, Maschio 2, Sivori, Corbatta)
Chile 2 (Fernández J 2)

Estadio Nacional, Lima, 28–03–1957, 50 000
Uruguay 3 (Campero 2, Ambrois)
Brazil 2 (Evaristo, Didi)

Estadio Nacional, Lima, 31–03–1957, 55 000
Brazil 1 (Didi)
Peru 0

Estadio Nacional, Lima, 1–04–1957, 40 000
Colombia 4 (Gamboa 2, Alvarez, Gutiérrez J)
Ecuador 1 (Larraz)

Estadio Nacional, Lima, 1–04–1957, 40 000
Uruguay 2 (Campero, Roque)
Chile 0

Estadio Nacional, Lima, 3–04–1957, 55 000. Referee: Turner, England
Argentina 3 (Angelillo, Maschio, Cruz)
Brazil 0
Argentina – Dóminguez – Dellacha, Vairo, Giménez – Rossi N, Schandlein – Corbatta, Maschio, Angelillo, Sivori, Cruz
Brazil – Gilmar (Castilho) – Djalma Santos, Edson, Olavo, Zózimo – Roberto Belangero, Didi – Joel, Evaristo (Indio), Zizinho (Dino Sani), Pepe

Estadio Nacional, Lima, 3–04–1957, 55 000
Peru 2 (Mosquera, Terry)
Argentina 1 (Sivori)

	Br	Ur	Pe	Co	Ch	Ec	Pl	W	D	L	F	A	Pts
ARGENTINA	3–0	4–0	1–2	8–2	6–2	3–0	6	5	0	1	25	6	10
BRAZIL	–	2–3	1–0	9–0	4–2	7–1	6	4	0	2	23	9	8
URUGUAY	–	–	5–3	0–1	2–0	5–2	6	4	0	2	15	12	8
PERU	–	–	–	4–1	1–0	2–1	6	4	0	2	12	9	8
COLOMBIA	–	–	–	–	2–3	4–1	6	2	0	4	10	25	4
CHILE	–	–	–	–	–	2–2	6	1	1	4	9	17	3
ECUADOR	–	–	–	–	–	–	6	0	1	5	7	23	1

Top scorers: Maschio, Argentina 9
Ambrosis, Uruguay 9

TWENTY-SEVENTH EDITION
Buenos Aires 7th March–4th April 1959

Monumental, Buenos Aires. 7–03–1959, 70 000
Argentina 6 (Manfredini 2, Pizzutti 2, Callá, Belén)
Chile 1 (Alvarez L)

Monumental, Buenos Aires. 8–03–1959, 35 000
Uruguay 7 (Borges, Sasia 2, Escalada, Guaglianone, Douksas, Pérez D)
Bolivia 0

Monumental, Buenos Aires. 10–03–1959, 45 000
Brazil 2 (Didi, Pelé)
Peru 2 (Seminario 2)

Monumental, Buenos Aires. 11–03–1959, 45 000
Paraguay 2 (Aveiro 2)
Chile 1 (Sánchez L)

Monumental, Buenos Aires. 11–03–1959, 45 000
Argentina 2 (Corbatta, Callá)
Bolivia 0

Monumental, Buenos Aires. 14–03–1959, 40 000
Peru 5 (Loayza 3, Joya, Gómez Sánchez)
Uruguay 3 (Demarco, Sasia, Douksas)

Monumental, Buenos Aires. 15–03–1959, 40 000
Paraguay 5 (Cayetano Ré 3, Sanabria I, Aveiro)
Bolivia 0

Monumental, Buenos Aires. 15–03–1959, 40 000
Brazil 3 (Pelé 2, Didi)
Chile 0

Monumental, Buenos Aires. 18–03–1959, 70 000
Uruguay 3 (Demarco, Douksas, Sasia)
Paraguay 1 (Aveiro)

Monumental, Buenos Aires. 18–03–1959, 70 000
Argentina 3 (Corbatta, Sosa R, OG)
Peru 1 (Loayza)

Monumental, Buenos Aires. 21–03–1959, 50 000
Brazil 4 (Paulo Valentim 2, Pelé, Didi)
Bolivia 2 (Garcia A, Alcón)

Monumental, Buenos Aires. 21–03–1959, 50 000
Chile 1 (Tobar)
Peru 1 (Loayza)

Monumental, Buenos Aires. 22–03–1959, 50 000
Argentina 3 (Corbatta, Sosa R, Cap)
Paraguay 1 (Sanabria C)

Monumental, Buenos Aires. 26–03–1959, 70 000
Chile 5 (Soto J 2, Soto M 2, Sánchez L)
Bolivia 1 (Alcócer 2)

Monumental, Buenos Aires. 26–03–1959, 70 000
Brazil 3 (Paulo Valentim 3)
Uruguay 1 (Escalada)

Monumental, Buenos Aires. 29–03–1959, 40 000
Peru 0
Bolivia 0

Monumental, Buenos Aires. 29–03–1959, 40 000
Brazil 4 (Pelé 3, Chinezinho)
Paraguay 1 (Parodi)

Monumental, Buenos Aires. 30–03–1959, 80 000
Argentina 4 (Belén 2, Sosa R 2)
Uruguay 1 (Demarco)

Monumental, Buenos Aires. 2–03–1959, 5000
Paraguay 2 (Aveiro 2)
Peru 1 (Gómez Sánchez)

Monumental, Buenos Aires. 2–03–1959, 5000
Chile 1 (Moreno)
Uruguay 0

Monumental, Buenos Aires. 4–04–1959, 100 000. Referee: Robles, Chile
Argentina 1 (Pizzuti)
Brazil 1 (Pele)
Argentina – Negri – Lombardo (Simeone), Griffa (Cardozo), Murúa – Mouriño, Cap – Nardiello, Pizzuti, Sosa, Calá (Rodriguez J), Belén
Brazil – Gilmar – Djalma Santos, Bellini, Orlando Pecanha, Coronel – Dino Sani, Didi – Garrincha, Paulo Valentim (Almir Albuquerque), Pelé, Chinezinho

	Br	Pa	Pe	Ch	Ur	Bo	Pl	W	D	L	F	A	Pts
ARGENTINA	1–1	3–1	3–1	6–1	4–1	2–0	6	5	1	0	19	5	11
BRAZIL	–	4–1	2–2	3–0	3–1	4–2	6	4	2	0	17	7	10
PARAGUAY	–	–	2–1	2–1	1–3	5–0	6	3	0	3	12	12	6
PERU	–	–	–	1–1	5–3	0–0	6	1	3	2	10	11	5
CHILE	–	–	–	–	1–0	5–2	6	2	1	3	9	14	5
URUGUAY	–	–	–	–	–	7–0	6	2	0	4	15	14	4
BOLIVIA	–	–	–	–	–	–	6	0	1	5	4	23	1

Top scorer: Pelé, Brazil 8

TWENTY-EIGHTH EDITION
Guayaquil, 5th–25th December 1959

Estadio Modelo, Guayaquil, 5–12–1959, 35 000
Brazil 3 (Paulo PE 2, Zé de Mello)
Paraguay 2 (Parodi, Benitez G)

Estadio Modelo, Guayaquil, 6–12–1959, 55 000
Uruguay 4 (Silveira, Escalada, Bergara, Pérez D)
Ecuador 0

Estadio Modelo, Guayaquil, 9–12–1959, 55 000
Argentina 4 (Sanfilippo 2, Sosa R, Pizzuti)
Paraguay 2 (Lezcano J, Cabral)

Estadio Modelo, Guayaquil, 12–12–1959, 55 000
Uruguay 3 (Escalada, Bergara, Sacia)
Brazil 0

Estadio Modelo, Guayaquil, 12–12–1959, 55 000
Ecuador 1 (Raffo)
Argentina 1 (Sosa R)

Estadio Modelo, Guayaquil, 16–12–1959, 50 000. Referee: Sobrinho, Brazil
Uruguay 5 (Silveira 2, Bergara, Sasia, Douksas)
Argentina 0
Uruguay – Sosa – Méndez, González, Troche – Mesias, Silveira – Pérez D, Bergara, Sasia, Douksas, Escalada
Argentina – Negri – Arredondo, Guidi, Grigoul – Murua, Bettinotti (Rattin) – Boggio, Pizzuti, Sosa (Ruiz), Sanfilippo (Rodriguez J), Belén

Estadio Modelo, Guayaquil, 19–12–1959, 55 000
Brazil 3 (Geraldo, Paulo PE, Zé de Mello)
Ecuador 1 (Raffo)

Estadio Modelo, Guayaquil, 22–12–1959, 45 000
Argentina 4 (Sanfilippo 3, Garcia O)
Brazil 1 (Geraldo)

Estadio Modelo, Guayaquil, 22–12–1959, 45 000
Uruguay 1 (Sasia)
Paraguay 1 (Parodi)

Estadio Modelo, Guayaquil, 25–12–1959, 50 000
Ecuador 3 (Spencer, Balseca, Cañarte)
Paraguay 1 (OG)

	Ur	Ar	Br	Ec	Pa	Pl	W	D	L	F	A	Pts
URUGUAY	–	5–0	3–0	4–0	1–1	4	3	1	0	13	1	7
ARGENTINA	–	–	4–1	1–1	4–2	4	2	1	1	9	9	5
BRAZIL	–	–	–	3–1	3–2	4	2	0	2	7	10	4
ECUADOR	–	–	–	–	3–1	4	1	0	3	5	9	2
PARAGUAY	–	–	–	–	–	4	0	1	3	6	11	1

Top scorer: Sanfilippo, Argentina 6

TWENTY-NINTH EDITION
Bolivia, 10th–31st March 1963

Hernán Siles, La Paz, 10–03–1963, 15 000
Bolivia 4 (Lopez R, Castillo, Camacho, Alcócer)
Ecuador 4 (Raymondi 2, Raffo, Bolaños)

Félix Capriles, Cochabamba, 10–03–1963, 18 000
Argentina 4 (Zárate 2, Rodriguez M, Fernández J)
Colombia 2 (Campillo, Aceros)

Félix Capriles, Cochabamba, 10–03–1963, 18 000
Brazil 1 (Flavio)
Peru 0

Félix Capriles, Cochabamba, 13–03–1963, 10 000
Peru 2 (Tenemás, Gallardo)
Argentina 1 (Zárate)

Hernán Siles, La Paz, 14–03–1963, 15 000
Paraguay 3 (Zarate E 2, Quiñones)
Ecuador 1 (Raffo)

Hernán Siles, La Paz, 14–03–1963, 15 000
Brazil 5 (Flavio 2, Marco Antônio, Oswaldo, Fernando)
Colombia 1 (Gamboa)

Félix Capriles, Cochabamba, 17–03–1963, 18 000
Bolivia 2 (Alcócer, Castillo)
Colombia 1 (Botero)

Hernán Siles, La Paz, 17–03–1963, 8000
Peru 2 (León, Mosquera)
Ecuador 1 (Raffo)

Hernán Siles, La Paz, 17–03–1963, 8000
Paraguay 2 (Navarte, Ayala)
Brazil 0

Félix Capriles, Cochabamba, 20–03–1963, 10 000
Paraguay 3 (Cabrera C 2, Valdez)
Colombia 2 (Campilo, Gamboa)

Félix Capriles, Cochabamba, 20–03–1963, 10 000
Argentina 4 (Savoy 2, Zárate, Rodriguez M)
Ecuador 2 (Pineda, Palacios)

Hernán Siles, La Paz, 21–03–1963, 20 000
Bolivia 3 (Camacho, Alcócer, Garcia A)
Peru 2 (Gallardo, León)

Hernán Siles, La Paz, 24–03–1963, 10 000
Peru 1 (Gallardo)
Colombia 1 (González F)

Hernán Siles, La Paz, 24–03–1963, 10 000
Argentina 3 (Rodriguez M, Savoy, Juárez)
Brazil 0

Félix Capriles, Cochabamba, 24–03–1963, 18 000
Bolivia 2 (Castillo, Garcia A)
Paraguay 0

Bolivia – López A – Ramirez M, Zabalaga, Cainzo – Camacho, Herbas – Garcia A, Aramayo (Blacutt), Alcócer, Ugarte (López R), Castillo
Paraguay – González V – Insfran A, Calonga (Cabrera), Bobadilla (Barbarolli) – Amarilla, Osorio – Martinez, Lezcano, Zárate (Valdéz), Insfrán E, Arambulo

Félix Capriles, Cochabamba, 27–03–1963, 20 000
Brazil 2 (Oswaldo 2)
Ecuador 2 (Gando, Raffo)

Félix Capriles, Cochabamba, 27–03–1963, 20 000
Paraguay 4 (Martinez D 2, Cabrera C, Zárate E)
Peru 1 (Gallardo)

Hernán Siles, La Paz, 28–03–1963, 20 000
Bolivia 3 (Castillo, Blacutt, Camacho)
Argentina 2 (Rodriguez M 2)

Hernán Siles, La Paz, 31–03–1963, 15 000
Ecuador 4 (Raffo 2, Raymondi, Bolaños)
Colombia 3 (Aceros, Bolero, González F)

Hernán Siles, La Paz, 31–03–1963, 15 000
Argentina 1 (Lallana)
Paraguay 1 (Cabrera C)

Félix Capriles, Cochabamba, 31–03–1963, 25 000
Bolivia 5 (Ugarte 2, Camacho, Garcia A, Alcócer)
Brazil 4 (Flavio 2, Almir, Marco Antônio)

	Bo	Pa	Ar	Br	Pe	Ec	Co	Pl	W	D	L	F	A	Pts
BOLIVIA	–	2–0	3–2	5–4	3–2	4–4	2–1	6	5	1	0	19	13	11
PARAGUAY	–	–	1–1	2–0	4–1	3–1	3–2	6	4	1	1	13	7	9
ARGENTINA	–	–	–	3–0	1–2	4–2	4–2	6	3	1	2	15	10	7
BRAZIL	–	–	–	–	1–0	2–2	5–1	6	2	1	3	12	13	5
PERU	–	–	–	–	–	2–1	1–1	6	2	1	3	8	11	5
ECUADOR	–	–	–	–	–	–	4–3	6	1	2	3	14	18	4
COLOMBIA	–	–	–	–	–	–	–	6	0	1	5	10	19	1

Top scorer: Raffo, Ecuador 6

THIRTIETH EDITION
Montevideo, 17th January–2nd February 1967

Estadio Centenario, Montevideo, 17–01–1967, 15 000
Uruguay 4 (Rocha, Castillo, OG, Oyarbide)
Bolivia 0

Estadio Centenario, Montevideo, 18–01–1967, 15 000
Chile 2 (Marcos 2)
Venezuela 0

Estadio Centenario, Montevideo, 18–01–1967, 15 000
Argentina 4 (Mas, Artime, Bernao, Albrecht)
Paraguay 1 (Mora)

Estadio Centenario, Montevideo, 21–01–1967, 9000
Uruguay 4 (Urruzmendi 2, Oyarbide, OG)
Venezuela 0

Estadio Centenario, Montevideo, 22–01–1967, 6000
Argentina 1 (Bernao)
Bolivia 0

Estadio Centenario, Montevideo, 22–01–1967, 6000
Chile 4 (Gallardo 3, Araya)
Paraguay 2 (Riveiro, Apocada)

Estadio Centenario, Montevideo, 25–01–1967, 5000
Paraguay 1 (Del Puerto)
Bolivia 0

Estadio Centenario, Montevideo, 25–01–1967, 5000
Argentina 5 (Artime 3, Carone, Marzolini)
Venezuela 1 (Santana)

Estadio Centenario, Montevideo, 26–01–1967, 30 000
Uruguay 2 (Rocha, Oyarbide)
Chile 2 (Gallardo, Marcos)

Estadio Centenario, Montevideo, 28–01–1967, 14 000
Venezuela 3 (Scovino, Santana, González P)
Bolivia 0

Estadio Centenario, Montevideo, 28–01–1967, 14 000
Argentina 2 (Sarnari, Artime)
Chile 0

Estadio Centenario, Montevideo, 29–01–1967, 17 000
Uruguay 2 (Pérez D, Urruzmendi)
Paraguay 0

Estadio Centenario, Montevideo, 1–02–1967, 1000
Bolivia 0
Chile 0

Estadio Centenario, Montevideo, 1–02–1967, 1000
Paraguay 5 (Rojas J 2, Garay, Mora 2)
Venezuela 3 (Mendoza, Santana, Scovino)

Estadio Centenario, Montevideo, 2–02–1967, 70 000. Referee: Gasc, Chile
Uruguay 1 (Rocha)
Argentina 0

Uruguay – Mazurkiewicz – Baeza, Paz J, Varela L – Cincunegui (Forlan), Mujica – Pérez D, Rocha, Oyarbide (Viera), Salvá (Techera), Urruzmendi
Argentina – Roma – Calics, Rattin, Marzolini – Acevedo, Albrecht – Bernao (Raffo), González A, Artime, Sarnari (Rojas A), Mas (Carone)

	Ur	Ar	Ch	Pa	Ve	Bo	Pl	W	D	L	F	A	Pts
URUGUAY	–	1–0	2–2	2–0	4–0	4–0	5	4	1	0	13	2	9
ARGENTINA	–	–	2–0	4–1	5–1	1–0	5	4	0	1	12	3	8
CHILE	–	–	–	4–2	2–0	0–0	5	2	2	1	8	6	6
PARAGUAY	–	–	–	–	5–3	1–0	5	2	0	3	9	13	4
VENEZUELA	–	–	–	–	–	3–0	5	1	0	4	7	16	2
BOLIVIA	–	–	–	–	–	–	5	0	1	4	0	9	1

Top scorer: Artime, Argentina 5

THIRTY-FIRST EDITION
July–October 1975

FIRST ROUND

Group 1

Olimpico, Caracas, 31–07–1975, 30 000
Venezuela 0
Brazil 4 (Palinha 2, Romeu, Danival)

Olimpico, Caracas, 3–08–1975, 30 000
Venezuela 1 (Iriarte)
Argentina 5 (Luque 3, Kempes, Ardiles)

Minerao, Belo Horizonte, 6–08–1975, 80 000
Brazil 2 (Nelinho 2)
Argentina 1 (Asad)

Rosario Central, Rosario, 10–08–1975, 50 000
Argentina 11 (Killer 3, Kempes 2, Zanabria 2, Gallego, Ardiles, Bóveda, Luque)
Venezuela 0

Minerao, Belo Horizonte, 13–08–1975, 32 000
Brazil 6 (Batata 2, Nelinho, Danival, Campos, Palinha)
Venezuela 0

Rosario Central, Rosario, 16–08–1975, 50 000
Argentina 0
Brazil 1 (Danival)

	Br	Ar	Ve	Pl	W	D	L	F	A	Pts
BRAZIL	–	2–1	6–0	4	4	0	0	13	1	8
ARGENTINA	0–1	–	11–0	4	2	0	2	17	4	4
VENEZUELA	0–4	1–5	–	4	0	0	4	1	26	0

Group 2

Estadio Nacional, Santiago, 17–07–1975, 50 000
Chile 1 (Crisosto)
Peru 1 (Rojas P)

Jesus Bermudez, Oruro, 20–07–1975, 18 000
Bolivia 2 (Mezza O 2)
Chile 1 (Gamboa)

Jesus Bermudez, Oruro, 27–07–1975, 18 000
Bolivia 0
Peru 1 (Ramirez O)

Estadio Nacional, Lima, 7–08–1975, 40 000
Peru 3 (Ramirez O, Cueto, Oblitas)
Bolivia 1 (Mezza O)

Estadio Nacional, Santiago, 13–08–1975, 15 000
Chile 4 (Araneda 2, Ahumada, Gamboa)
Bolivia 0

Villaneuva, Lima, 20–08–1975, 40 000
Peru 3 (Rojas P, Oblitas, Cubillas)
Chile 1 (Reinoso)

	Pe	Ch	Bo	Pl	W	D	L	F	A	Pts
PERU	–	3–1	3–1	4	3	1	0	8	3	7
CHILE	1–1	–	4–0	4	1	1	2	7	6	3
BOLIVIA	0–1	2–1	–	4	1	0	3	3	9	2

Group 3

El Campin, Bogota, 20–07–1975, 60 000
Colombia 1 (Diaz E)
Paraguay 0

Estadio Modelo, Guayaquil, 24–07–1975, 50 000
Ecuador 2 (Carrera, Lasso)
Paraguay 2 (Kiese H 2)

Atahualpa, Quito, 27–07–1975, 45 000
Ecuador 1 (Carrera)
Colombia 3 (Ortiz, Retat, Castro P)

Defensores del Chaco, Asuncion, 30–07–1975, 50 000
Paraguay 0
Colombia 1 (Diaz E)

Abandoned after 43 minutes

El Campin, Bogota, 7–08–1975, 50 000
Colombia 2 (Diaz E, Calero)
Ecuador 0

Defensores del Chaco, Asuncion, 10–08–1975
Paraguay 3 (Rolón 2, Baez)
Ecuador 1 (Castañeda)

	Co	Pa	Ec	Pl	W	D	L	F	A	Pts
COLOMBIA	–	1–0	2–0	4	4	0	0	7	1	8
PARAGUAY	0–1	–	3–1	4	1	1	2	5	5	3
ECUADOR	1–3	2–2	–	4	0	1	3	4	10	1

SEMI-FINALS

El Campin, Bogota, 21–09–1975, 55 000
Colombia 3 (Angulo, Ortiz, Diaz E)
Uruguay 0

Minerao, Belo Horizonte, 30–09–1975
Brazil 1 (Batata)
Peru 3 (Cubillas 2, Casaretto)

Estadio Centenario, Montevideo, 1–10–1975, 70 000
Uruguay 1 (Morena)
Colombia 0

Colombia qualified on goal difference

Villaneuva, Lima, 4–10–1975, 55 000
Peru 0
Brazil 2 (Ze Carlos, Campos)

Peru qualified on lots

FINAL

1st leg
El Campin, Bogota, 16–10–1975, 50 000
COLOMBIA 1 (Castro P)
PERU 0

Colombia – Zape – Segovia, Zárate (González), Escobar, Bolaños – Calero, Retat, Umaña – Rendón (Diaz E), Londero, Castro P
Peru – Sartor – Soria, Meléndez, Chumpitaz, Diaz T – Quesada, Ojeda, Rojas (Ruiz) – Barbadillo, Ramirez O (Casaretto), Oblitas

2nd leg
Estadio Nacional, Lima, 22–10–1975, 50 000
PERU 2 (Oblitas, Ramirez O)
COLOMBIA 0

Peru – Sartor – Soria, Meléndez, Chumpitaz, Diaz – Quesada, Ojeda, Rojas P – Barbadillo (Ruiz), Ramirez O, Oblitas
Colombia – Zape – Segovia, Zárate, Escobar, Bolaños – Calero, Retat, Umaña – Arboleda (Diaz), Londero, Castro P (Angulo)

Play-off
Olimpico, Caracus, 28–10–1975, 30 000. Referee: Barreto, Uruguay
PERU 1 (Sotil)
COLOMBIA 0

Peru – Sartor – Soria, Meléndez, Chumpitaz, Diaz – Cubillas, Ojeda, Quesada – Rojas P (Ramirez) Sotil, Oblitas
Colombia – Zape – Segovia, Zárate, Escobar, Bolaños – Ortiz, Calero, Umaña (Retat) – Arboleda, Diaz (Castro P), Campaz

Final positions:

1 Peru	2 Colombia	3 Brazil	4 Uruguay	5 Argentina
6 Chile	7 Paraguay	8 Bolivia	9 Ecuador	10 Venezuela

Top scorers: Diaz, Colombia 4
Luque, Argentina 4

THIRTY-SECOND EDITION
July–October 1979

FIRST ROUND

Group 1

Pueblo Neuvo, San Cristobal, 1–08–1979, 40 000
Venezuela 0
Colombia 0

Pueblo Nuevo, San Cristobal, 8–08–1979, 14 000
Venezuela 1 (Carbajal)
Chile 1 (Peredo)

El Campin, Bogota, 15–08–1979, 45 000
Colombia 1 (Diaz E)
Chile 0

El Campin, Bogota, 22–08–1979, 40 000
Colombia 4 (Iguarán, Valverde, Chaparro, Morón)
Venezuela 0

Estadio Nacional, Santiago, 29–08–1979, 70 000
Chile 7 (Peredo 2, Rivas 2, Veliz, Soto M, Yañez P)
Venezuela 0

Estadio Nacional, Santaigo, 5–09–1979, 85 000
Chile 2 (Caszely, Peredo)
Colombia 0

	Ch	Co	Ve	Pl	W	D	L	F	A	Pts
CHILE	–	2–0	7–0	4	2	1	1	10	2	5
COLOMBIA	1–0	–	4–0	4	2	1	1	5	2	5
VENEZUELA	1–1	0–0	–	4	0	2	2	1	12	2

Group 2

Hernán Siles, La Paz, 18–07–1979, 40 000
Bolivia 2 (Reynaldo 2)
Argentina 1 (López C)

Hernáan Siles, La Paz, 26–07–1979, 40 000
Bolivia 2 (Aragonés 2)
Brazil 1 (Roberto Dinamite)

Maracana, Rio de Janeiro, 2–08–1979, 130 000
Brazil 2 (Zico, Tita)
Argentina 1 (Coscia)

Jose Amalfitani, Buenos Aires, 8–08–1979, 30 000
Argentina 3 (Passarella, Gáspari, Maradona)
Bolivia 0

Morumbi, Sao Paulo, 16–08–1979, 50 000
Brazil 2 (Tita, Zico)
Bolivia 0

Monumental, Buenos Aires, 23–08–1979, 68 000
Argentina 2 (Passarella, Diaz R)
Brazil 2 (Sócrates 2)

	Br	Bo	Ar	Pl	W	D	L	F	A	Pts
BRAZIL	–	2–0	2–1	4	2	1	1	7	5	5
BOLIVIA	2–1	–	2–1	4	2	0	2	4	7	4
ARGENTINA	2–2	3–0	–	4	1	1	2	7	6	3

Group 3

Atahualpa, Quito, 29–08–1979, 45 000
Ecuador 1 (Torres Garcés)
Paraguay 2 (Talavera, Solalinde)

Atahualpa, Quito, 5–09–1979, 30 000
Ecuador 2 (Tenorio, Alarcón)
Uruguay 1 (Victorino)

Defensores del Chaco, Asuncion, 13–09–1979, 25 000
Paraguay 2 (Morel E, Osorio J)
Ecuador 0

Centenario, Montevideo, 16–09–1979, 25 000
Uruguay 2 (Bica, Victorino)
Ecuador 1 (Klinger)

Defensores del Chaco, Asuncion, 20–09–1979, 25 000
Paraguay 0
Uruguay 0

Centenario, Montevideo, 26–09–1979, 18 000
Uruguay 2 (Milar, Paz R)
Paraguay 2 (Morel E 2)

	Pa	Ur	Ec	Pl	W	D	L	F	A	Pts
Paraguay	–	0–0	2–0	4	2	2	0	6	3	6
Uruguay	2–2	–	2–1	4	1	2	1	5	5	4
Ecuador	1–2	2–1	–	4	1	0	3	4	7	2

SEMI-FINALS

Estadio Nacional, Lima, 17–10–1979, 50 000
Peru 1 (Mosquera)
Chile 2 (Caszely 2)

Estadio Nacional, Santiago, 24–10–1979, 75 000
Chile 0
Peru 0

Defensores del Chaco, Asuncion, 24–10–1979
Paraguay 2 (Morel E, Talavera)
Brazil 1 (Palinha)

Maracana, Rio de Janeiro, 31–10–1979, 80 000
Brazil 2 (Falcao, Sócrates)
Paraguay 2 (Morel M, Romero C)

FINAL

1st leg

Defensores del Chaco, Asuncion, 28–11–1979. Referee: Da Rosa, Uruguay
PARAGUAY 3 (Romero C 2, Morel M)
CHILE 0
Paraguay – Fernández R – Espinola, Sosa F, Paredes (Cibils), Torales – Torres (Florentin), Kiese C, Romero – Isasi, Morel M, Morel E
Chile – Osbén – Galindo, Quintano, Valenzuela, Escobar E – Rivas, Soto, Bonvallet (Estay) – Caszely, Fabbiani, Rojas M

2nd leg

Estadio Nacional, Santiago, 5–12–1979, 55 000. Referee: Barreto, Uruguay
CHILE 1 (Rivas)
PARAGUAY 0
Chile – Osbén – Galindo, Valenzuela, Figueroa, Escobar E – Rivas, Bonvallet, Rojas M (Neira) – Caszely, Fabbiani (Estay), Véliz
Paraguay – Fernández R – Solalinde, Sosa F, Paredes, Torales – Kiese (Florentin), Talavera, Romero C – Isasi, Morel M, Morel E

Play-off
Jose Amalfitani, Buenos Aires, 11–12–1979, 6000. Referee: Cesar Coelho, Brazil
PARAGUAY 0
CHILE 0
Paraguay – Fernández R – Espinola, Paredes, Sosa F, Torales – Florentin, Kiese, Romero C – Perez (Cibils), Morel M, Aquino (Torres)
Chile – Osbén – Galindo, Valenzuela, Figueroa, Escobar E – Rojas M, Dubó (Estay), Rivas – Caszely, Fabbiani (Yañez), Véliz
Paraguay won on goal difference

Final positions:
1 Paraguay 2 Chile 3 Brazil 4 Peru 5 Colombia
6 Uruguay 7 Bolivia 8 Argentina 9 Ecuador 10 Venezuela

Top scorers: Peredo, Chile 4
Morel, Paraguay 4

THIRTY-THIRD EDITION
August–November 1983

FIRST ROUND

Group 1

Atahualpa, Quito, 10–08–1983, 50 000
Ecuador 2 (Vázquez, Vega)
Argentina 2 (Burruchaga 2)

Atahualpa, Quito, 17–08–1983, 50 000
Ecuador 0
Brazil 1 (Roberto Dinamite)

Monumental, Buenos Aires, 24–08–1983, 56 000
Argentina 1 (Gareca)
Brazil 0

Serra Dourada, Gôiania, 1–09–1983, 35 000
Brazil 5 (Roberto Dinamite 2, Renato Gaucho, Éder, Tita)
Ecuador 0

Monumental, Buenos Aires, 7–09–1983, 20 000
Argentina 2 (Ramos, Burruchaga)
Ecuador 2 (Quiñones, Maldonado)

Maracana, Rio de Janeiro, 14–09–1983, 75 000
Brazil 0
Argentina 0

	Br	Ar	Ec	Pl	W	D	L	F	A	Pts
BRAZIL	–	0–0	5–0	4	2	1	1	6	1	5
ARGENTINA	1–0	–	2–2	4	1	3	0	5	4	5
ECUADOR	0–1	2–2	–	4	0	2	2	4	10	2

Group 2

Hernán Siles, La Paz, 14–08–1983, 40 000
Bolivia 0
Colombia 1 (Valderrama D)

Estadio Nacional, Lima, 17–08–1983, 30 000
Peru 1 (Navarro)
Colombia 0

Hernán Siles, La Paz, 21–08–1983, 45 000
Bolivia 1 (Romero E)
Peru 1 (Navarro)

El Campin, Bogota, 28–08–1983, 50 000
Colombia 2 (Prince, Fiorillo)
Peru 2 (Malásquez 2)

El Campin, Bogota, 31–08–1983, 45 000
Colombia 2 (Valderrama D, Molina)
Bolivia 2 (Melgar, Rojas S)

Estadio Nacional, Lima, 4–09–1983, 50 000
Peru 2 (Leguia, Caballero)
Bolivia 1 (Panaguía)

	Pe	Co	Bo	Pl	W	D	L	F	A	Pts
PERU	–	1–0	2–1	4	2	2	0	6	4	6
COLOMBIA	2–2	–	2–2	4	1	2	1	5	5	4
BOLIVIA	1–1	0–1	–	4	0	2	2	4	6	2

Group 3

Centenario, Montevideo, 1–09–1983, 30 000
Uruguay 2 (Acevedo, Moreno F)
Chile 1 (Orellana)

Centenario, Montevideo, 4–09–1983, 60 000
Uruguay 3 (Cabrera, Morena F, Luzardo)
Venezuela 0

Estadio Nacional, Santiago, 8–09–1983, 20 000
Chile 5 (Aravena 2, Arriza, Dubó, Letelier)
Venezuela 0

Estadio Nacional, Santiago, 11–09–1983, 55 000
Chile 2 (Dubó, Letelier)
Uruguay 0

Olimpico, Caracas, 18–09–1983, 3000
Venezuela 1 (Febles)
Uruguay 2 (Santelli, Aguilera)

Brigido Iriarte, Caracas, 21–09–1983, 3000
Venezuela 0
Chile 0

	Ur	Ch	Ve	Pl	W	D	L	F	A	Pts
URUGUAY	–	2–1	3–0	4	3	0	1	7	4	6
CHILE	2–0	–	5–0	4	2	1	1	8	2	5
VENEZUELA	1–2	0–0	–	4	0	1	3	1	10	1

SEMI-FINALS

Estadio Nacional, Lima, 13–10–1983, 28 000
Peru 0
Uruguay 1 (Aguilera)

Defensores del Chaco, Asuncion, 13–10–1983, 55 000
Paraguay 1 (Morel M)
Brazil 1 (Eder)

Centenario, Montevideo, 20–10–1983, 58 000
Uruguay 1 (Cabrera)
Peru 1 (Malásquez)

Parque de Sabia, Uberlandia, 20–10–1983, 75 000
Brazil 0
Paraguay 0

Brazil win on away goals

FINAL

1st leg
Centenario, Montevideo, 27–10–1983, 65 000. Referee: Ortiz, Paraguay
URUGUAY 2 (Francescoli 42, Diogo 80)
BRAZIL 0
Uruguay – Rodriguez R – Diogo, Gutiérrez, Acevedo, Agresta – González W, Barrios, Cabrera – Aguilera (Bossio), Francescoli, Acosta (Ramos)
Brazil – Leao – Leandro, Márcio, Mozer, Junior – Jorginho, China (Tita), Renato Frederico – Renato Gaúcho, Roberto Dinamite, Éder

2nd leg
Fonte Nova, Salvador, 4–11–1983, 95 000. Referee: Perez, Peru
BRAZIL 1 (Jorginho 23)
URUGUAY 1 (Aguilera 75)
Brazil – Leao – Paulo Roberto, Márcio, Mozer, Junior – Jorginho, China, Sócrates – Tita (Renato Gaúcho), Roberto Dinamite (Careca), Éder
Uruguay – Rodriguez R – Diogo, Gutiérrez, Acevedo, González W – Barrios, Agresta, Cabrera – Aguilera (Bossio), Francescoli, Acosta (Ramos)

Top scorers: Burruchaga, Argentina/Roberto Dinamite, Brazil/ Aguilera, Uruguay/Malasquez, Peru 3

Final positions:
1 Uruguay 2 Brazil 3 Paraguay 4 Peru 5 Chile
6 Argentina 7 Colombia 8 Bolivia 9 Ecuador 10 Venezuela

THIRTY-FOURTH EDITION
Argentina, 27th June–12th July 1987

FIRST ROUND

Group 1

Monumental, Buenos Aires, 27–06–1987, 40 000
Argentina 1 (Maradona)
Peru 1 (Reyna)

Monumental, Buenos Aires, 2–07–1987, 30 000
Argentina 3 (Canigga, Maradona 2)
Ecuador 0

Monumental, Buenos Aires, 4–07–1987, 10 000
Peru 1 (La Rosa)
Ecuador 1 (Cuvi)

	Ar	Pe	Ec	Pl	W	D	L	F	A	Pts
ARGENTINA	–	1–1	3–0	2	1	1	0	4	1	3
PERU	–	–	1–1	2	0	2	0	2	2	2
ECUADOR	–	–	–	2	0	1	1	1	4	1

Group 2

Estadio Cordoba, Cordoba, 28–06–1987, 8000
Brazil 5 (Edú Marangón, OG, Careca, Nelsinho, Romario)
Venezuela 0

Estadio Cordoba, Cordoba, 30–06–1987, 5000
Chile 3 (Letelier, Contreras, Salgado)
Venezuela 1 (Acosta)

Estadio Cordoba, Cordoba, 3–07–1989, 15 000

Chile	4	(Basay 2, Letelier 2)
Brazil	0	

	Ch	Br	Ve	Pl	W	D	L	F	A	Pts
Chile	–	4–0	3–1	2	2	0	0	7	1	4
Brazil	–	–	5–0	2	1	0	1	5	4	2
Venezuela	–	–	–	2	0	0	2	1	8	0

Group 3

Rosario Central, Rosario, 28–06–1987, 5000

Paraguay	0	
Bolivia	0	

Rosario Central, Rosario, 1–07–1987, 5000

Colombia	2	(Valderrama C, Iguarán)
Bolivia	0	

Rosario Central, Rosario, 5–07–1987, 10 000

Colombia	3	(Iguarán 3)
Paraguay	0	

	Co	Bo	Pa	Pl	W	D	L	F	A	Pts
COLOMBIA	–	2–0	3–0	2	2	0	0	5	0	4
BOLIVIA	–	–	0–0	2	0	1	1	0	2	1
PARAGUAY	–	–	–	2	0	1	1	0	3	1

SEMI-FINALS

Estadio Cordoba, Cordoba, 8–07–1987, 10 000

Chile	2	(Astengo, Vera)
Colombia	1	(Redin)

Monumental, Buenos Aires, 9–07–1987, 65 000

Uruguay 1 (Alzamendi)
Argentina 0

3RD PLACE

Monumental, Buenos Aires, 11–07–1987, 15 000

Colombia	2	(Gómez G, Galeano)
Argentina	1	(Canigga)

FINAL

Monumental, Buenos Aires, 12–07–1987, 35 000. Referee: Do Arppi, Brazil

URUGUAY	1	(Bengoechea 56)
CHILE	0	

Uruguay – Pereira – Dominguez, Gutiérrez, Trasante, Saldaña – Matosas, Perdomo, Bengoechea – Alzamendi (Peña), Francescoli, Sosa R

Chile – Rojas R – Reyes, Gomez E, Astengo, Hormazábal – Mardonez, Contreras, Puebla (Torro) (Rubio) – Letelier, Basay

Final Positions:
1 Uruguay 2 Chile 3 Colombia 4 Argentina 5 Brazil 6 Peru 7 Bolivia 8 Ecuador 9 Paraguay 10 Venezuela

Top scorer: Iguarán, Colombia 4

THIRTY-FIFTH EDITION

Brazil, 1st–16th July 1989

FIRST ROUND

Group 1

Fonte Nova, Salvador, 1–07–1989, 5000

Paraguay	5	(Cañete 2, Neffa, Mendoza, OG)
Peru	2	(Hirano, Reinoso)

Fonte Nova, Salvador, 1–07–1989, 18 000

Brazil	3	(Bebeto, Geovani, Baltazar)
Venezuela	1	(Maldonado)

Fonte Nova, Salvador, 3–07–1989, 4000

Colombia	4	(Higuita, Iguarán 2, De Avila)
Venezuela	2	(Maldonado 2)

Fonte Nova, Salvador, 3–07–1989, 8000

Brazil	0	
Peru	0	

Fonte Nova, Salvador, 5–07–1989, 1000

Peru	1	(Navarro)
Venezuela	1	(Maldonado)

Fonte Nova, Salvador, 5–07–1989, 1000

Paraguay	1	(Mendoza)
Colombia	0	

Fonte Nova, Salvador, 7–07–1989, 3000

Paraguay	3	(Neffa, Ferreira 2)
Venezuela	0	

Fonte Nova, Salvador, 7–07–1989, 9000

Brazil	0	
Colombia	0	

Arruda, Recife, 9–07–1989, 60 000

Colombia	1	(Iguarán)
Peru	1	(Hirano)

Arruda, Recife, 9–07–1989, 76 000

Brazil	2	(Bebeto 2)
Paraguay	0	

	Pa	Br	Co	Pe	Ve	Pl	W	D	L	F	A	Pts
PARAGUAY	–	0–2	1–0	5–2	3–0	4	3	0	1	9	4	6
BRAZIL	–	–	0–0	0–0	3–1	4	2	2	0	5	1	6
COLOMBIA	–	–	–	1–1	4–2	4	1	2	1	5	4	4
PERU	–	–	–	–	1–1	4	0	3	1	4	7	3
VENEZUELA	–	–	–	–	–	4	0	1	3	4	11	1

Group 2

Serra Dourada, Gôiania, 2–07–1989, 19 000

Ecuador	1	(Benitez)
Uruguay	0	

Serra Dourada, Gôiania, 2–07–1989, 40 000

Argentina	1	(Canigga)
Chile	0	

Serra Dourada, Gôiania, 4–07–1989, 8000

Uruguay	3	(Ostolaza 2, Sosa R)
Bolivia	0	

Serra Dourada, Gôiania, 4–07–1989, 12 000

Argentina	0	
Ecuador	0	

Serra Dourada, Gôiania, 6–07–1989, 3000

Ecuador	0	
Bolivia	0	

Serra Dourada, Gôiania, 6–07–1989, 3000

Uruguay	3	(Sosa R, Alzamendi, Francescoli)
Chile	0	

Serra Dourada, Gôiania, 8–07–1989, 3000

Chile	5	(Olmis, Ramirez J, Astengo, Pizarro, Reyes)
Bolivia	0	

Serra Dourada, Gôiania, 8–07–1989, 18 000
Argentina 1 (Canigga)
Uruguay 0

Serra Dourada, Gôiania, 10–07–1989, 2000
Chile 2 (Olmis, Letelier)
Ecuador 1 (Aviles)

Serra Dourada, Gôiania, 10–07–1989, 5000
Argentina 0
Bolivia 0

	Ar	Ur	Ch	Ec	Bo	Pl	W	D	L	F	A	Pts
ARGENTINA	–	1–0	1–0	0–0	0–0	4	2	2	0	2	0	6
URUGUAY	–	–	3–0	0–1	3–0	4	2	0	2	6	2	4
CHILE	–	–	–	2–1	5–0	4	2	0	2	7	5	4
ECUADOR	–	–	–	–	0–0	4	1	2	2	2	2	4
BOLIVIA	–	–	–	–	–	4	0	2	2	0	8	2

FINAL GROUP

Maracana, Rio de Janeiro, 12–07–1989, 60 000
Uruguay 3 (Francescoli, Alzamendi, Paz)
Paraguay 0

Maracana, Rio de Janeiro, 12–07–1989, 110 000
Brazil 2 (Bebeto, Romario)
Argentina 0

Maracana, Rio de Janeiro, 14–07–1989, 45 000
Uruguay 2 (Sosa R 2)
Argentina 0

Maracana, Rio de Janeiro, 14–07–1989, 64 000
Brazil 3 (Bebeto 2, Romario)
Paraguay 0

Maracana, Rio de Janeiro, 16–07–1989, 90 000
Argentina 0
Paraguay 0

Maracana, Rio de Janeiro. 16–07–1989, 170 000. Referee: Silva, Chile
Brazil 1 (Romario 49)
Uruguay 0

Brazil – Taffarel – Mazinho, Aldair, Mauro Galvao, Ricardo – Silas (Alemao), Dunga, Branco – Valdo (Josimar), Bebeto, Romario
Uruguay – Zeoli – Herrera, De León, Gutiérrez, Dominguez – Ostolaza (Correa), Perdomo, Francescoli – Paz R (Da Silva), Alzamendi, Sosa R

	Br	Ur	Ar	Pa	Pl	W	D	L	F	A	Pts
BRAZIL	–	1–0	2–0	3–0	3	3	0	0	6	0	6
URUGUAY	–	–	2–0	3–0	3	2	0	1	5	1	4
ARGENTINA	–	–	–	0–0	3	0	1	2	0	4	1
PARAGUAY	–	–	–	–	3	0	1	2	0	6	1

Top scorer: Bebeto, Brazil 6

Final Positions
1 Brazil 2 Uruguay 3 Argentina 4 Paraguay 5 Chile
6 Colombia 7 Ecuador 8 Peru 9 Bolivia 10 Venezuela

THIRTY-SIXTH EDITION
Chile, 6th–21st July 1991

FIRST ROUND

Group 1

Estadio Nacional, Santiago, 6–07–1991, 50 000
Chile 2 (Vilches, Zamorano)
Venezuela 0

Estadio Nacional, Santiago, 6–07–1991, 50 000
Paraguay 1 (Monzon)
Peru 0

Collado, Concepcion, 8–07–1991, 21 000
Chile 4 (Rubio, Contreras, Zamorano 2)
Peru 2 (Maestri, Del Solar)

Estadio Nacional, Santiago, 8–07–1991, 2000
Argentina 3 (Batistuta 2, Canigga)
Venezuela 0

Estadio Nacional, Santiago, 10–07–1991, 70 000
Paraguay 5 (Neffa, Guirland, Monzon 2, Sanabria)
Venezuela 0

Estadio Nacional, Santiago, 10–07–1991, 70 000
Argentina 1 (Batistuta)
Chile 0

Estadio Nacional, Santiago, 12–07–1991, 4000
Peru 5 (La Rosa 2, OG, Del Solar, Hirano)
Venezuela 1 (OG)

Collado, Concepcion, 12–07–1991, 4000
Argentina 4 (Batistuta, Simeone, Astrada, Caniggia)
Paraguay 1 (Cardozo)

Estadio Nacional, Santiago, 14–07–1991, 80 000
Argentina 3 (Latorre, Craviotto, Garcia)
Peru 2 (Yanez, Hirano)

Estadio Nacional, Santiago, 14–07–1991, 80 000
Chile 4 (Rubio, Zamorano, Estay, Vera)
Paraguay 0

	Ar	Ch	Pa	Pe	Ve	Pl	W	D	L	F	A	Pts
Argentina	–	1–0	4–1	3–2	3–0	4	4	0	0	11	3	8
Chile	–	–	4–0	4–2	2–0	4	3	0	1	10	3	6
Paraguay	–	–	–	1–0	5–0	4	2	0	2	7	8	4
Peru	–	–	–	–	5–1	4	1	0	3	9	9	2
Venezuela	–	–	–	–	–	4	0	0	4	1	15	0

Group 2

Playa Ancha, Valparaiso, 7–07–1991, 15 000
Colombia 1 (De Avila)
Ecuador 0

Playa Ancha, Valparaiso, 7–07–1991, 15 000
Bolivia 1 (Suarez J)
Uruguay 1 (Castro)

Sausalito, Viña del Mar, 9–07–1991, 17 000
Uruguay 1 (Mendez P)
Ecuador 1 (Aguinaga)

Sausalito, Viña del Mar, 9–07–1991, 17 000
Brazil 2 (Neto, Branco)
Bolivia 1 (Sanchez E)

Sausalito, Viña del Mar, 11–07–1991, 15 000
Colombia 0
Bolivia 0

Sausalito, Viña del Mar, 11–07–1991, 15 000
Brazil 1 (Joao Paulo)
Uruguay 1 (Mendez P)

Sausalito, Viña del Mar, 13–07–1991, 15 000
Ecuador 4 (Aguinaga, Aviles 2, Ramirez)
Bolivia 0

Sausalito, Viña del Mar, 13–07–1991, 15 000
Colombia 2 (De Avila, Iguarán)
Brazil 0

Sausalito, Viña del Mar, 15–07–1991, 30 000
Uruguay 1 (Mendez P)
Colombia 0

Sausalito, Viña del Mar, 15–07–1991, 30 000
Brazil 3 (Mazinho II, Santos, Henrique)
Ecuador 1 (Muñoz)

	Co	Br	Ur	Ec	Bo	Pl	W	D	L	F	A	Pts
Colombia	–	2–0	0–1	1–0	0–0	4	2	1	1	3	1	5
Brazil	–	–	1–1	3–1	2–1	4	2	1	1	6	5	5
Uruguay	–	–	–	1–1	1–1	4	1	3	0	4	3	5
Ecuador	–	–	–	–	4–0	4	1	1	2	6	5	3
Bolivia	–	–	–	–	–	4	0	2	2	2	7	2

FINAL ROUND

Estadio Nacional, Santiago, 17–07–1991, 50 000. Referee: Maciel, Paraguay
Argentina 3 (Franco 1 39, Batistuta 46)
Brazil 2 (Branco 4, Joao Paulo 52)
Argentina – Goycochea – Basualdo, Ruggeri, Vazquez, Enrique – Astrada, Simeone, Franco, Rodriguez L (Giunta) – Batistuta, Caniggia
Brazil – Taffarel – Mazinho I, Santos, Rocha, Branco – Henrique, Mauro Silva, Silvio Cesar (Renato), Neto – Marcio, Joao Paulo (Careca)

Estadio Nacional, Santiago, 17–07–1991, 50 000
Chile 1 (Zamorano)
Colombia 1 (Iguarán)

stadio Nacional, Santiago, 19–07–1991, 65 000
Chile 0
Argentina 0

Estadio Nacional, Santiago, 19–07–1991, 65 000
Brazil 2 (Renato, Branco)
Colombia 0

Estadio Nacional, Santiago, 21–07–1991, 50 000
Brazil 2 (Mazinho II, Henrique)
Chile 0

Estadio Nacional, Santiago, 21–07–1991, 50 000
Argentina 2 (Simeone, Batistuta)
Colombia 1 (De Avila)

	Ar	Br	Ch	Co	Pl	W	D	L	F	A	Pts
ARGENTINA	–	3–2	0–0	2–1	3	2	1	0	5	3	5
BRAZIL	–	–	2–0	2–0	3	2	0	1	6	3	4
CHILE	–	–	–	1–1	3	0	2	1	1	3	2
COLOMBIA	–	–	–	–	3	0	1	2	2	5	1

Top scorer: Batistuta, Argentina 6

Final positions
1 Argentina 2 Brazil 3 Chile 4 Colombia 5 Uruguay
6 Paraguay 7 Ecuador 8 Peru 9 Bolivia 10 Venezuela

SOUTH AMERICAN CLUB COMPETITIONS

The Copa Libertadores de América is the premier South American club event. Prior to its inception in 1960, there had been no continent-wide tournament organised by CONMEBOL. A still-born Campeonato Sudamericano de Campeones, organised by Colo Colo in Chile in 1948 and won by Vasco da Gama, attracted the champion teams from all but Colombia, Venezuela and Paraguay, but it was a financial disaster and was not organised the following year.

The success of the European Cup persuaded CONMEBOL to give the idea another try, and at a meeting in Brazil in 1958 the idea was approved in principle. That same year Henri Delaunay, the general secretary of UEFA, suggested to CONMEBOL an annual meeting between the winners of the European Cup and the winners of a South American tournament. The prospect of a World Club Championship was very appealing to the top clubs, and it was this more than anything else that got the idea off the ground.

The first series was organised in 1960, with seven of the continent's champions taking part. Missing were Ecuador, Peru and Venezuela. For the second tournament the following year all bar Venezuela entered, but despite a weak club scene, by 1964 they too found the lure of the competition too hard to resist and entered for the first time.

The Copa Libertadores has had a rich and varied history and has not been without its moments of high drama. It has always been dominated by clubs from around the River Plate, and as in the South American Championship, Brazil's record is lamentable. The first two tournaments were played on a knock-out basis with home and away legs in each tie, including the final. Although the format of the rounds prior to the final has since varied over the years, the final itself has always been played over two legs and is decided on a points basis, with goal difference only counting if the play-off has not produced a winner. Penalties have recently been introduced instead of the play-off.

The first two series were both won by Peñarol but did not set the continent on fire. In 1960 the Uruguayan champions beat Olimpia of Paraguay in the final, the decisive goal coming from Alberto Spencer, their Ecuadoran forward, who remains the top scorer in the Copa Libertadores with over 50 goals.

In 1961, Peñarol beat Palmeiras of Brazil and again Spencer scored the decisive goal. The following year they appeared in their third consecutive final, but this time faced Pelé and his Santos team. Santos gave the competition the boost it needed by winning in 1962 and 1963.

Their matches with Benfica and Milan in the World Club Championship also stirred up interest and in 1966 it was decided to increase the eligibility to include the champions and runners-up of each of the 10 nations. The knock-out system had been replaced in 1962 by three first round groups from which the top side qualified for the semi-finals where they were joined by the previous year's winners.

COPA LIBERTADORES MEDALS TABLE

	Team	Country	G	S	B
1	Independiente	ARG	7	–	5
2	Peñarol	URU	5	4	10
3	Nacional Montevideo	URU	3	3	6
4	Estudiantes La Plata	ARG	3	1	1
5	Olimpia	PAR	2	3	4
6	Boca Juniors	ARG	2	2	3
7	Santos FC	BRA	2	–	2
8	River Plate	ARG	1	2	6
9	Colo Colo	CHI	1	1	2
10	Cruzeiro	BRA	1	1	2
	Sao Paulo FC	BRA	1	1	1
	Gremio	BRA	1	1	–
13	Flamengo	BRA	1	–	2
	Atletico Nacional Medellin	COL	1	–	2
15	Racing Club Avellaneda	ARG	1	–	1
	Argentinos Juniors	ARG	1	–	1
17	America Calì	COL	–	3	4
18	Cobreloa	CHI	–	2	1
	Palmeiras	BRA	–	2	1
	Newell's Old Boys	ARG	–	2	–
21	Barcelona	ECU	–	1	5
22	Universitario	PER	–	1	3
23	Internacional P–A	BRA	–	1	2
	Deportivo Calì	COL	–	1	2
25	Union Española	CHI	–	1	1
26	Universidad Catolica	CHI	–	–	4
27	San Lorenzo de Almagro	ARG	–	–	3
	Millonarios	COL	–	–	3
29	Botafogo	BRA	–	–	2
	Alianza	PER	–	–	2
	Cerro Porteño	PAR	–	–	2
	LDU Quito	ECU	–	–	2
33	Atletico Mineiro	BRA	–	–	1
	Blooming	BOL	–	–	1
	Bolivar	BOL	–	–	1
	Danubio	URU	–	–	1
	Defensor Lima	PER	–	–	1
	Guarani Asuncion	PAR	–	–	1
	Guarani Campinas	BRA	–	–	1
	Huracan	ARG	–	–	1
	Jorge Wilsterman	BOL	–	–	1
	Libertad	PAR	–	–	1
	Nacional Quito	ECU	–	–	1
	O'Higgins	CHI	–	–	1
	Palestino	CHI	–	–	1
	Portuguesa	VEN	–	–	1
	Rosario Central	ARG	–	–	1
	Atlet. San Cristobal	VEN	–	–	1
	Independ. Santa Fé	COL	–	–	1
	Deportes Tolima	COL	–	–	1
	ULA Merida	VEN	–	–	1
	Universidad de Chile	CHI	–	–	1
	Velez Sarsfield	ARG	–	–	1

To the end of the 1992 Competition

The increase in numbers in 1966 meant a huge amount of games in the first round and so Brazil withdrew their clubs in protest until 1968 and again from 1969 to 1970. Only when the first round was reorganised into five groups of four clubs did they enter again. The dominant force after Santos relinquished their hold were the clubs from Argentina, most notably Independiente and Estudiantes.

Estudiantes, from the town of La Plata just south of Buenos Aires, became especially notorious for their rough tactics and gamesmanship. Winners for three successive years, based on one championship victory in 1967, their coach Osvaldo Zubeldia raised his team from an ordinary one to a winning combination by using tactics which found them no favour either among their South American or European opponents.

Defensively almost impenetrable, Estudiantes used to goad the opposition into being sent off by a whole host of dirty tricks, and it worked. Unfortunately for the Copa Libertadores, after the positive image put across by Santos, Estudiantes undid most of the good work, especially with their displays in the World Club Championship.

Though never as bad, Independiente did not do much to improve the image of the tournament with their four straight wins in the first half of the 1970s. Once again teamwork proved to be the key rather the outstanding brilliance of a few players. Independiente, not as successful as either River Plate or Boca Juniors at home, remain the most successful club in the history of the tournament with seven wins.

Boca Juniors eventually won in 1977 and again in 1978, but the second of those victories heralded a decline in Argentina's dominance. Between Boca's final defeat by Santos in 1963 and their final defeat against Olimpia in 1979, an Argentine club had appeared in all 17 finals winning 12 of them.

In 1979 Olimpia from Paraguay became the first club from one of the so-called smaller nations to win the title and they repeated their success in 1990. The tournament became more even in its distribution and the 1989, 1990 and 1991 finals were notable for the absence of teams from Argentina, Brazil and Uruguay, the longest period during which none of them has made a final appearance.

In 1988 the structure of the tournament was changed yet again. The formula of five first round groups of four was kept, but instead of only one club qualifying to make up two semi-final groups of 3 teams including the previous year's winner, as had been the practice since 1971, the top two now went forward. The semi-final group system was replaced by a knock-out competition from the second round. The following year, the quite ridiculous system of three teams from the first round groups qualifying was introduced to make the numbers up to a workable 16 teams for the second round. This means, however, that 60 games are played to eliminate just 5 teams!

The last few years have seen a proliferation of club tournaments in South America. In 1988 the South American Super Cup, or Trofeo Havelange as it is also known, was introduced for the first time. Played between former winners of the Copa Libertadores, the competition is

COPA LIBERTADORES BY COUNTRY

	Country	G	S	B	Finals	Semis
1	Argentina	15	7	23	22	45
2	Uruguay	8	7	17	15	32
3	Brazil	6	6	14	12	26
4	Paraguay	2	3	8	5	13
5	Colombia	1	4	13	5	18
6	Chile	1	4	11	5	16
7	Ecuador	–	1	8	1	9
8	Peru	–	1	6	1	7
9	Bolivia	–	–	3	–	3
	Venezuela	–	–	3	–	3

To the end of the 1992 Competition

gaining momentum. Dismissed to start with as just another excuse for a game, it has the advantage that only the continent's top sides are included. Though it falls short of the idea of a South American super league, the desperate financial position of many of the top sides may well see this competition take over as the number one tournament on the continent, and the possibilities are there that it will progress from a knock-out tournament to one based on a league format.

Though the top sides from Argentina and Uruguay are well represented in the Super Cup, Brazilian sides are not. Of the big Rio de Janeiro sides only Flamengo have won the Copa Libertadores. Apart from Sao Paulo FC and Santos, who play in the Sao Paulo league but are not from the city itself, the only other Brazilian clubs to have won the Copa Libertadores are Gremio from Porto Alegre and Cruzeiro from Belo Horizonte.

With the Super Cup has come the Recopa, a play-off between the winners of the Copa Libertadores and the Super Cup. There is every possibility that the Recopa will be expanded to include the winners of the CONMEBOL and Masters Cups introduced in 1992. The CONMEBOL Cup could prove to be the most interesting new development in South American club football since 1960. It is heavily weighted in favour of the 'Big Three', thus giving some of the larger clubs on the continent an outlet largely denied them at present. Brazilian clubs will especially welcome its arrival.

A major problem for the Copa Libertadores over the years has been the lack of the well-known South American stars who have moved to Europe. The tournament has undoubtedly lost some of the glamour of the early years when the likes of Pele were a regular feature. The irony of Argentinos Juniors' win in 1985 was that it was achieved with the money obtained from the sale of Maradona, who in all his time at the club never appeared in the competition with them.

Another feature has been the continued problems with violence on and off the field and the charges of bribery levelled at referees and officials. Despite these problems, however, it has survived as the premier tournament in South America and the future holds the possibility of clubs from outside the continent taking part. Mexico in particular would be well suited given their strong league set-up.

COPA LIBERTADORES

1960	Peñarol	1–0 1–1	Olimpia
1961	Peñarol	1–0 1–1	Palmeiras
1962	Santos	2–1 2–3 3–0	Peñarol
1963	Santos	3–2 2–1	Boca Juniors
1964	Independiente	0–0 1–0	Nacional Montevideo
1965	Independiente	1–0 1–3 4–1	Peñarol
1966	Peñarol	2–0 2–3 4–2	River Plate
1967	Racing Club	0–0 0–0 2–1	Nacional Montevideo
1968	Estudiantes LP	2–1 1–3 2–0	Palmeiras
1969	Estudiantes LP	1–0 2–0	Nacional Montevideo
1970	Estudiantes LP	1–0 0–0	Peñarol
1971	Nacional Montevideo	0–1 1–0 2–0	Estudiantes LP
1972	Independiente	0–0 2–1	Universitario
1973	Independiente	1–1 0–0 2–1	Colo Colo
1974	Independiente	1–2 2–0 1–0	Sao Paulo FC
1975	Independiente	0–1 3–1 2–0	Union Española
1976	Cruzeiro	4–1 1–2 3–2	River Plate
1977	Boca Juniors	1–0 0–1 0–0 (5–4p)	Cruzeiro
1978	Boca Juniors	0–0 4–0	Deportivo Cali
1979	Olimpia	2–0 0–0	Boca Juniors
1980	Nacional Montevideo	0–0 1–0	Internacional PA
1981	Flamengo	2–1 0–1 2–0	Cobreloa
1982	Peñarol	0–0 1–0	Cobreloa
1983	Gremio	1–1 2–1	Peñarol
1984	Independiente	1–0 0–0	Gremio
1985	Argentinos Juniors	1–0 0–1 1–1 (5–4p)	America Cali
1986	River Plate	2–1 1–0	America Cali
1987	Peñarol	0–2 2–1 1–0	America Cali
1988	Nacional Montevideo	0–1 3–0	Newell's Old Boys
1989	Nacional Medellin	0–2 2–0 (5–4p)	Olimpia
1990	Olimpia	2–0 1–1	Barcelona
1991	Colo Colo	0–0 3–0	Olimpia
1992	Sao Paulo FC	0–1 1–0 (3–2p)	Newell's Old Boys

SUPERCOPA

1988	Racing Club	2–1 1–1	Cruzeiro
1989	Boca Juniors	0–0 0–0 (5–3p)	Independiente
1990	Olimpia	3–0 3–3	Nacional Montevideo
1991	Cruzeiro	0–2 3–0	River Plate

RECOPA

1988	Nacional Montevideo	1–0 0–0	Racing Club
1989	Boca Juniors	1–0	Nacional Medellin
1990	Olimpia	*	
1991	Colo Colo	0–0 (5–4p)	Cruzeiro

* Olimpia won both the Copa Libertadores and Super Cup in 1990 and so were awarded the Recopa

1960

FIRST ROUND

Peñarol	7–1 1–1	Jorge Wilsterman
San Lorenzo	3–0 2–3	EC Bahia
Millonarios	1–0 6–0	Univ. de Chile
Olimpia	Bye	

SEMI-FINALS

Peñarol	0–0 1–1 2–1	San Lorenzo
Olimpia	5–1 0–0	Millonarios

FINAL

1st leg. Centenario, Montevideo, 12–06–1960. Referee: Robles, Chile

PENAROL 1 (Spencer)
OLIMPIA 0

Peñarol – Maidana – Martinez (Majewski), Pino – Salvador, Goncalvez, Aguerre – Cubilla, Linazza, Spencer, Crescio, Borges
Olimpia – Arias – Rojas S, Lezcano V – Rojas A, Lezcano C, Osorio – Rodriguez, Recalde, Roldan, Cabral, Melgarejo

2nd leg. Sajonia, Asuncion, 19–06–1960, 35 000. Referee: Praddaude, Argentina

OLIMPIA 1 (Recalde)
PENAROL 1 (Cubilla)

Olimpia – Arias – Arevalo, Peralta – Echague, Lezcano C, Rojas S – Rodriguez, Recalde, Roldan, Cabral, Malgarejo
Peñarol – Maidana – Martinez, Salvador – Pino, Goncalvez, Aguerre – Cubilla, Linazza, Spencer (Hoberg), Crescio, Borges

Top scorer: Spencer, Peñarol 7

1961

FIRST ROUND

Indep. Santa Fé	2–2 3–0	Barcelona

QUARTER-FINALS

Peñarol	5–0 0–2	Universitario
Olimpia	5–2 1–2	Colo Coll
Indep. Santa Fé	*1–0 2–3	Jorge Wilsterman
Palmeiras	2–0 1–0	Independiente

SEMI-FINALS

Peñarol	3–1 2–1	Olimpia
Palmeiras	4–1 2–2	Independiente Santa Fé

FINAL

1st leg. Centenario, Montevideo, 9–06–1961, 50 000. Referee: Praddaude, Argentina

PENAROL 1 (Spencer)
PALMEIRAS 0

Peñarol – Maidana – Martinez, Cano – Gonzalez, Matosas, Aguerre – Cubilla, Ledesma, Spencer, Sasia, Joya
Palmeiras – Waldir – Dernadziais, Djalma Santos – Waldemar, Geraldo, Zeuinha – Nilton Santos (Julinho), Humberto, Silva, Chinesinho, Romeiro

2nd leg. Pacaembú, Sao Paulo, 11–06–1961, 40 000. Referee: Praddaude, Argentina

PALMEIRAS 1 (Nardo)
PENAROL 1 (Sasia)

Palmeiras – Waldir – Djalma Santos, Waldemar – Geraldo, Zequinha, Aldemar – Julinho, Romeiro (Nardo), Silva, Chinesinho, Gildo
Peñarol – Maidana – Martinez, Cano – Gonzalez, Matosas, Aguerre – Cubilla, Ledesma, Sasia, Spencer, Joya

Top scorers: Sasia, Peñarol 3
Cubilla, Peñarol 3
Spencer, Peñarol 3

1962

FIRST ROUND

Group 1

	Sa	CP	Mu	Pl	W	D	L	F	A	Pts
Santos	–	9–1	4–3	4	3	1	0	20	6	7
Cerro Porteño	1–1	–	3–2	4	2	1	1	7	13	5
Deport. Municipal	1–6	1–2	–	4	0	0	4	7	15	0

Group 2

	Na	RC	SC	Pl	W	D	L	F	A	Pts
Nacional Mont'deo	–	3–2	2–1	4	3	1	0	8	5	7
Racing Club	2–2	–	2–1	4	1	1	2	7	8	3
Sporting Cristal	0–1	2–1	–	4	1	0	3	4	6	2

Group 3

	UC	Em	Mi	Pl	W	D	L	F	A	Pts
Univ. Catolica	–	3–0	4–1	4	2	1	1	10	9	5
Emelec	7–2	–	4–2	4	2	0	2	12	10	4
Millonarios	1–1	3–1	–	4	1	1	2	7	10	3

SEMI-FINALS

Santos	1–0 1–1	Universidad Catolica
Peñarol	3–1 1–2 1–1	Nacional Montevideo

FINAL

1st leg. Centenario, Montevideo, 28–07–1962, 50 000. Referee: Robles, Chile

PENAROL 1 (Spencer)
SANTOS 2 (Coutinho 2)

Peñarol – Maidana – Lezcano, Cano – Gonzalez, Matosas, Caetano – Carranza (Moacir), Rocha, Sasia, Spencer, Joya
Santos – Gilmar – Lima, Mauro – Dalmao, Zito, Calvet – Dorval, Mengalvio, Pagao, Coutinho, Pepe (Osvaldo)

2nd leg. Villa Belmiro, Santos, 2–08–1962, 30 000. Referee: Robles, Chile

SANTOS 2 (Dorval, Mengalvio)
PENAROL 3 (Spencer, Sasia 2)

Santos – Gilmar – Lima, Mauro – Dalmao, Zito, Calvet – Dorval, Mengalvio, Pagao, Coutinho, Pepe
Peñarol – Maidana – Lezcano, Cano – Gonzalez, Goncalvez, Caetano – Rocha, Matosas, Sasia, Spencer, Joya

Play–off. Monumental, Buenos Aires, 30–08–1962, 36 000. Referee: Horn, Holland

SANTOS 3 (Coutinho, Pelé 2)
PENAROL 0

Santos – Gilmar – Lima, Mauro – Dalmo, Zito, Calvet – Dorval, Mengalvio, Coutinho, Pelé, Pepe
Peñarol – Maidana – Lezcano, Cano – Gonzalez, Goncalvez, Caetano – Rocha, Matosas, Spencer, Sasia, Joya

Top scorers: Spencer, Peñarol 6
Coutinho, Santos 6

1963

FIRST ROUND

Group 1

	Bo	Al	Mi	Pl	W	D	L	F	A	Pts
Botafogo	–	2–1	*	4	4	0	0	5	1	8
Alianza	0–1	–	0–0	4	1	1	2	2	3	3
Millonarios	0–2	0–1	–	4	0	1	3	0	3	1

* Game awarded to Botafogo 2–0

Group 2

	Pe	Ev	Pl	W	D	L	F	A	Pts
Peñarol	–	9–1	2	2	0	0	14	1	4
Everest	0–5	–	2	0	0	2	1	14	0

Group 3

	BJ	Ol	UC	Pl	W	D	L	F	A	Pts
Boca Juniors	–	5–3	1–0	4	3	0	1	9	6	6
Olimpia	1–0	–	2–1	4	2	0	2	7	10	4
Univ. de Chile	2–3	4–1	–	4	1	0	3	7	7	2

SEMI-FINALS

Santos .... 1–1 4–0 .... Botafogo
Boca Juniors .... 2–1 1–0 .... Peñarol

FINAL

1st leg. Maracaná, Rio de Janeiro, 3–09–1963, 55 000. Referee: Bois, France

SANTOS 3 (Coutinho 2, Lima)
BOCA JUNIORS 2 (Sanfilippo 2)

Santos – Gilmar – Mauro, Geraldino – Dalmao, Zito, Calvet – Dorval, Lima, Coutinho, Pelé, Pepe
Boca Juniors – Errea – Magdalena, Marzolini (Orlando) – Simeone, Rattin, Silveyra – Grillo, Rojas, Menendez, Sanfilippo, Gonzalez

2nd leg. La Bombonera, Buenos Aires, 11–09–1963, 50 000. Referee: Bois, France

BOCA JUNIORS 1 (Sanfilippo)
SANTOS 2 (Coutinho, Pelé)

Boca Juniors – Errea – Magdalena, Orlando – Simeone, Rattin, Silveyra – Grillo, Rojas, Menendez, Sanfilippo, Gonzalez
Santos – Gilmar – Mauro, Geraldino – Dalmao, Zito, Calvet – Dorval, Lima, Coutinho, Pelé, Pepe

Top scorer: Sanfilippo, Boca Juniors 7

1964

PRELIMINARY ROUND

Deportivo Italia .... 0–0 2–1 .... EC Bahia

FIRST ROUND

Group 1

	Na	CP	Au	Pl	W	D	L	F	A	Pts
Nacional Mont'deo	–	2–0	2–0	4	3	1	0	9	2	7
Cerro Porteño	2–2	–	7–0	4	1	2	1	11	6	4
Aurora	0–3	2–2	–	4	0	1	3	2	14	1

Group 2

	In	Mi	Al	Pl	W	D	L	F	A	Pts
Independiente	–	5–1	4–0	4	3	1	0	11	3	7
Millonarios	*	–	3–2	4	2	0	2	6	8	4
Alianza	2–2	1–2	–	4	0	1	3	5	11	1

* Game awarded to Independiente

Group 3

	CC	Ba	DI	Pl	W	D	L	F	A	Pts
Colo Colo	–	3–2	4–0	4	3	0	1	9	7	6
Barcelona	4–0	–	1–0	4	2	0	2	7	6	4
Deportivo Italia	1–2	3–0	–	4	1	0	3	4	7	2

SEMI-FINALS

Independiente .... 3–2 2–1 ... Santos
Nacional Montevideo ..... 4–2 4–2 ... Colo Colo

FINAL

1st leg. Centenario, Montevideo, 6–08–1964

NACIONAL MONTEVIDEO 0
INDEPENDIENTE 0

Nacional – Sosa – Baeza, Alvarez Em – Ramos, Alvarez El, Méndez – Pérez, Douksas, Jaburu, Arias (Bergara), Urruzmendi
Independiente – Santoro – Zerrillo, Rolan – Ferreiro, Acevedo, Maldonado – Bernao, Mura, Suarez, Rodriguez, Savoy

2nd leg. Cordero, Avellaneda, 12–08–1964

INDEPENDIENTE 1 (Rodriguez)
NACIONAL MONTEVIDEO 0

Independiente – Santoro – Guzman, Rolan – Ferreiro, Acevedo, Maldonado – Bernao, Prospitti, Suarez, Rodriguez, Savoy
Nacional – Sosa – Baeza, Alvarez Em – Ramos, Alvarez El, Méndez – Oyarbide, Douksas, Jaburu, Pérez, Urruzmendi

Top scorers: Mora, Cerro Porteño 6
Rodriguez M, Independiente 6

1965

FIRST ROUND

Group 1

	BJ	TS	DQ	Pl	W	D	L	F	A	Pts
Boca Juniors	–	2–0	4–0	4	4	0	0	11	3	8
The Strongest	2–3	–	2–2	4	1	1	2	5	7	3
Deportivo Quito	1–2	0–1	–	4	0	1	2	3	9	1

Group 2

	Sa	UC	Un	Pl	W	D	L	F	A	Pts
Santos	–	1–0	2–1	4	4	0	0	10	3	8
Univ. de Chile	1–5	–	5–2	4	1	0	3	6	9	2
Universitario	1–2	1–0	–	4	1	0	3	5	9	2

Group 3

	Pe	Gu	Ga	Pl	W	D	L	F	A	Pts
Peñarol	–	2–0	2–0	4	3	1	0	5	2	7
Guarani Asuncion	2–1	–	2–0	4	3	0	1	6	4	6
Deportivo Galicia	0–0	1–2	–	4	0	1	3	1	6	1

SEMI-FINALS

Independiente .... 2–0 0–1 0–0 ..... Boca Juniors
Santos .... 5–4 2–3 1–2 ..... **Peñarol**

FINAL

1st leg. Cordero, Avellaneda, 9–04–1965

INDEPENDIENTE 1 (Bernao)
PENAROL 0

Independiente – Santoro – Navarro, Decaria – Ferreiro, Acevedo, Guzman – Bernao, Mura, Suarez (De la Mata), Avallay, Savoy
Peñarol – Mazurkiewicz – Pérez, Varela – Forlan, Goncalvez, Caetano – Ledesma, Rocha, Silva, Sasia, Joya

2nd leg. Centenario, Montevideo, 12–04–1965

PENAROL 3 (Goncalvez, Reznik, Rocha)
INDEPENDIENTE 1 (De la Mata)

Peñarol – Mazurkiewicz – Pérez, Varela – Forlan (Reznik), Goncalvez, Caetano – Ledesma, Rocha, Sasia, Silva, Joya
Independiente – Santoro – Navarro, Paflik – Ferreiro, Acevedo, Guzman – Bernao, Mura, Suarez, Avallay (De la Mata), Savoy

Play–off. Estadio Nacional, Santiago, 15–04–1965

INDEPENDIENTE 4 (Acevedo, Bernao, Avallay, Mura)
PENAROL 1 (Joya)

Independiente – Santoro – Navarro, Decaria – Ferreiro, Acevedo, Guzman – Bernao, Mura, De la Mata (Mori), Avallay, Savoy
Peñarol – Mazurkiewicz – Pérez, Varela – Forlan, Goncalvez, Caetano – Ledesma, Rocha, Reznik (Sasia), Silva, Joya

Top scorer: Pelé, Santos 7

1966

FIRST ROUND

Group 1

	RP	BJ	DI	Un	Al	La	Pl	W	D	L	F	A	Pts
River Plate	–	2–1	2–1	5–0	3–2	3–0	10	8	1	1	23	8	17
Boca Juniors	2–0	–	5–2	2–0	1–0	2–1	10	7	0	3	19	9	14
Deportivo Italia	0–3	1–2	–	2–2	3–1	1–1	10	4	2	4	15	18	10
Universitario	1–1	2–1	1–2	–	2–0	1–0	10	3	4	3	10	14	10
Alianza	0–2	1–0	1–2	1–1	–	3–0	10	2	1	7	10	16	5
Deportivo Lara	1–2	0–3	0–1	0–0	2–1	–	10	1	2	7	5	17	4

Group 2

	UC	Gu	Ol	UC	Pl	W	D	L	F	A	Pts
Univ. Catolica	–	2–0	4–0	2–2	6	2	3	1	9	4	7
Guarani Asuncion	2–1	–	2–0	1–1	6	2	2	2	8	9	6
Olimpia	0–0	3–3	–	2–0	6	2	2	2	7	10	6
Univ. de Chile	0–0	2–0	1–2	–	6	1	3	2	6	7	5

Play-off

Guarani .... 2–1 .... Olimpia

Group 3

	Pe	Na	Mu	JW	Em	NO	Pl	W	D	L	F	A	Pts
Peñarol	–	0–4	2–1	2–0	4–1	2–0	10	8	0	2	20	10	16
Nacional M.	0–3	–	4–1	3–0	2–0	3–1	10	7	1	2	22	10	15
Deport. Muni.	1–3	3–2	–	1–1	4–1	5–1	10	4	2	4	22	20	10
Jorge Wilster.	1–0	0–0	1–1	–	2–1	4–1	10	3	3	4	12	15	9
Emelec	1–2	0–1	2–1	3–1	–	2–1	10	4	0	6	16	18	8
Nueve de Oct.	1–2	2–3	3–4	3–2	0–5	–	10	1	0	9	13	32	2

SEMI-FINALS

Group 1

	RP	In	BJ	Gu	Pl	W	D	L	F	A	Pts
River Plate	–	4–2	2–2	3–1	6	3	2	1	13	8	8
Independiente	1–1	–	2–0	2–1	6	3	2	1	9	6	8
Boca Juniors	1–0	0–0	–	1–1	6	2	3	1	7	6	7
Guarani Asuncion	1–3	0–2	1–3	–	6	0	1	5	5	14	1

Play-off

River Plate .... 2–1 .... Independiente

Group 2

	Pe	UC	Na	Pl	W	D	L	F	A	Pts
Peñarol	–	2–0	3–0	4	3	0	1	6	1	6
Univ. Catolica	1–0	–	1–0	4	2	0	2	4	5	4
Nacional Montevideo	0–1	3–2	–	4	1	0	3	3	7	2

FINAL

1st leg. Centenario, Montevideo, 12–05–1966, 49 000. Referee: Goicoechea, Argentina

PENAROL 2 (Abbadie, Joya)

RIVER PLATE 0

Peñarol – Mazurkiewicz – Lezcano, Diaz – Forlan, Goncalves, Caetano – Abbadie, Rocha, Silva, Cortes, Joya

River Plate – Carrizo – Guzman, Vieytez – Sainz, Matosas, Bayo – Cubilla, Loayza (Onega E), Onega D, Sarnari, Solari

2nd leg. Monumental, Buenos Aires, 18–05–1966, 60 000. Referee: Codesal, Uruguay

RIVER PLATE 3 (Onega E, Onega D, Sarnari)

PENAROL 2 (Rocha, Spencer)

River Plate – Carrizo – Guzman, Vieytez – Sainz, Sarnari, Matosas – Cubilla, Solari, Onega D (Lallana), Onega E, Mas

Peñarol – Mazurkiewicz – Lezcano, Diaz – Forlan, Goncalvez, Caetano – Abbadie, Rocha, Spencer, Cortes, Joya

Play-off. Estadio Nacional, Santiago, 20–05–1966, 39 000. Referee: Vicuña, Chile

PENAROL 4 (Spencer 2, Rocha, Abbadie)

RIVER PLATE 2 (Onega D, Solari)

Peñarol – Mazurkiewicz – Lezcano, Diaz (Gonzalez) – Forlan, Goncalvez, Caetano – Abbadie, Cortes, Spencer, Rocha, Joya

River Plate – Carrizo – Grispo, Vieytez – Sainz (Solari), Matosas, Sarnari – Cubilla, Onega E, Lallana, Onega D, Mas

Top scorer: Onega D, River Plate 17

1967

FIRST ROUND

Group 1

	Cr	Un	SB	Ga	DI	Pl	W	D	L	F	A	Pts
Cruzeiro	–	4–1	3–1	3–1	3–0	8	7	1	0	22	6	15
Universitario	2–2	–	1–0	2–0	3–0	8	5	1	2	11	8	11
Sport Boys	1–2	0–1	–	2–0	5–2	8	2	1	5	10	11	5
Deportivo Galicia	0–1	2–0	2–1	–	0–0	8	2	1	5	5	10	5
Deportivo Italia	0–4	0–1	0–0	1–0	–	8	1	2	5	3	16	4

Group 2

	RC	RP	Me	Bo	SF	TO	Pl	W	D	L	F	A	Pts
Racing Club	–	2–0	5–2	6–0	4–1	6–0	10	8	1	1	29	7	17
River Plate	0–0	–	6–2	2–0	4–0	4–0	10	6	3	1	29	9	15
Independ. Medellín	0–2	0–1	–	2–2	4–0	3–0	10	4	1	5	17	19	9
Bolivar	0–2	3–3	0–2	–	2–2	1–0	10	2	4	4	12	22	8
Indep. Santa Fé	1–2	2–2	2–0	1–2	–	2–0	10	2	2	6	13	26	6
31 de Octubre	3–0	0–7	1–2	2–2	6–2	–	10	2	1	7	12	29	5

Group 3

	Na	CC	UC	Gu	Ba	Em	CP	Pl	W	D	L	F	A	Pts
Nacional Mont'deo	–	5–2	3–0	3–1	2–0	4–1	4–1	12	9	1	2	34	12	19
Colo Colo	3–2	–	4–2	1–0	3–2	3–2	5–1	12	7	1	4	30	28	15
Univ. Catolica	0–0	5–2	–	1–1	2–1	5–2	3–1	12	5	3	4	22	18	13
Guarani Asuncion	0–1	4–2	1–1	–	4–1	3–0	1–2	12	4	2	6	18	15	10
Barcelona	2–1	1–1	0–2	2–1	–	2–1	1–2	12	4	1	7	14	23	9
Emelec	0–3	4–3	2–1	0–2	3–0	–	2–1	12	4	1	7	18	28	9
Cerro Porteño	2–6	0–1	1–0	1–0	1–2	1–1	–	12	4	1	7	14	26	9

SEMI-FINALS

Group 1

	RC	Un	RP	CC	Pl	W	D	L	F	A	Pts
Racing Club	–	1–2	3–1	2–0	6	4	1	1	11	5	9
Universitario	1–2	–	2–2	3–0	6	4	1	1	10	5	9
River Plate	0–0	0–1	–	1–1	6	0	3	3	4	8	3
Colo Colo	1–3	0–1	1–0	–	6	1	1	4	3	10	3

Play–off:

Racing Club .... 2–1 .... Universitario

Group 2

	Na	Cr	Pe	Pl	W	D	L	F	A	Pts
Nacional Mon'deo	–	2–0	1–0	4	2	1	1	6	4	5
Cruzeiro	2–1	–	1–0	4	2	0	2	5	6	4
Peñarol	2–2	3–2	–	4	1	1	2	5	6	3

FINAL

1st leg. Mozart y Cuyo, Avellaneda, 15–08–1967, 54 000. Referee: Orozco, Peru

RACING CLUB 0

NACIONAL MONTEVIDEO 0

Racing – Cejas – Perfumo, Diaz – Martin, Mori, Basile – Martinoli, Rulli, Raffo, Rodriguez, Maschio

Nacional – Dominguez – Manicera, Alvarez Em – Ubinas, Montero Castillo, Mujica – Esparrago, Viera, Celio, Sosa, Urruzmendi

2nd leg. Centenario, Montevideo, 25–08–1967, 62 000. Referee: Orozco, Peru

NACIONAL MONTEVIDEO 0

RACING CLUB 0

Nacional – Dominguez – Manicera, Alvarez Em – Ubinas, Montero Castillo, Mujica – Esparrago, Viera, Celio, Sosa, Urruzmendi

Racing – Cejas – Perfumo, Diaz – Martin, Mori, Basile – Cardozo, Rulli, Cardenas, Raffo, Maschio

Play–off. Estadio Nacional, Santiago, 29–08–1967, 25 000. Referee: Orozco, Peru

RACING CLUB 2 (Cardozo, Raffo)

NACIONAL MONTEVIDEO 1 (Esparrago)

Racing – Cejas – Perfumo, Diaz – Martin, Mori, Basile – Cardozo (Parenti), Rulli, Cardenas, Raffo, Maschio

Nacional – Dominguez – Manicera, Alvarez Em – Ubinas, Montero Castillo, Mujica – Urruzmendi, Viera, Celio, Esparrago, Morales (Oyarbide)

Top scorer: Raffo, Racing Club 14

1968

FIRST ROUND

Group 1

	Es	In	DC	Mi	Pl	W	D	L	F	A	Pts
Estudiantes LP	–	2–0	3–0	0–0	6	5	1	0	12	3	11
Independiente	2–4	–	1–1	3–1	6	2	1	3	8	10	5
Deportivo Cali	1–2	1–0	–	1–0	6	2	1	3	6	10	5
Millonarios	0–1	1–2	4–2	–	6	1	1	4	6	9	3

Play–off for second place

Independiente .... 3–2 .... Deportivo Cali

Group 2

	Un	SC	JW	AR	Pl	W	D	L	F	A	Pts
Universitario	–	1–1	5–1	6–0	6	3	3	0	17	4	9
Sporting Cristal	2–2	–	2–0	1–1	6	3	3	0	11	5	9
Jorge Wilsterman	0–0	0–1	–	3–0	5	1	1	3	4	8	3
Always Ready	0–3	1–4	–	–	5	0	1	4	2	17	1

Group 3

	UC	Em	Na	UC	Pl	W	D	L	F	A	Pts
Univ. Catolica	–	1–1	2–0	2–1	6	4	1	1	11	7	9
Emelec	1–2	–	0–0	2–1	6	2	3	1	5	4	7
Nacional Quito	2–1	0–1	–	3–1	6	2	1	3	5	6	5
Univ. de Chile	2–3	0–0	1–0	–	6	1	1	4	6	10	3

Group 4

	Pe	Gu	Na	Li	Pl	W	D	L	F	A	Pts
Peñarol	–	2–0	1–0	4–0	6	3	2	1	8	2	8
Guarani Asuncion	1–1	–	2–1	1–1	6	2	3	1	8	7	7
Nacional Mont'deo	0–0	2–2	–	4–0	6	2	2	2	9	5	6
Libertad	1–0	0–2	0–2	–	6	1	1	4	2	13	3

Group 5

	Pa	PC	Ga	NR	Pl	W	D	L	F	A	Pts
Palmeiras	–	3–0	2–0	0–0	6	5	1	0	12	3	11
Portugues Caracus	1–2	–	1–0	1–1	6	2	1	3	5	11	5
Deportivo Galicia	1–2	2–0	–	2–1	6	2	0	4	5	7	4
Nautico Recife	1–3	3–2*	1–0	–	6	1	2	3	7	8	4

* Points awarded to Portugues. Nautico fielded ineligible players.

QUARTER-FINALS

Group 1

	Es	In	Un	Pl	W	D	L	F	A	Pts
Estudiantes LP	–	1–0	1–0	4	3	0	1	4	2	6
Independiente	1–2	–	3–0	4	2	0	2	7	3	4
Universitario	1–0	0–3	–	4	1	0	3	1	7	2

Group 2

	Pe	SC	Em	PC	Pl	W	D	L	F	A	Pts
Peñarol	–	1–1	2–0	4–0	6	4	2	0	11	1	11
Sporting Cristal	0–0	–	0–1	2–0	6	2	3	1	6	3	7
Emelec	0–1	0–2	–	2–0	6	1	1	4	3	7	4
Portugues Caracus	0–3	1–1	2–0	–	6	1	1	4	3	12	3

Group 3

	Pa	Gu	UC	Pl	W	D	L	F	A	Pts
Palmeiras	–	2–1	4–1	4	3	0	1	7	4	6
Guarani Asuncion	2–0	–	2–1	4	2	0	2	7	7	4
Univ. Catolica	0–1	4–2	–	4	1	0	3	6	9	2

SEMI-FINALS

Estudiantes LP .... 3–0 0–2 1–1 .... Racing Club

Palmeiras .... 1–0 2–1 .... Peñarol

FINAL

1st leg. Estadio La Plata, La Plata, 2–05–1968

ESTUDIANTES LP 2 (Veron, Flores)

PALMEIRAS 1 (Servilio)

Estudiantes – Poletti – Fucceneco, Spadaro – Madero, Malbernat, Pachamé – Bilardo, Flores, Ribaudo (Lavezzi), Conigliaro, Veron

Palmeiras – Waldir – Geraldo, Baldochi – Osmar, Gilberto, Ademir da Guia – Dudu, Singue, Tupazinho, Servilio, Rinaldo

2nd leg. Pacaembú, Sao Paulo, 7–05–1968

PALMEIRAS 3 (Tupazinho 2, Reinaldo)

ESTUDIANTES LP 1 (Veron)

Palmeiras – Waldir – Escalera, Baldochi – Osmar, Ferrari, Ademir da Guia – Dudu, Servilio (China), Tupazinho, Rinaldo, Singue

Estudiantes – Poletti – Spadaro, Madero – Fucceneco, Pachamé, Malbernat – Bilardo, Ribaudo, Flores (Togneri), Conigliaro, Veron

Play–off. Centenario, Montevideo, 16–05–1968

ESTUDIANTES LP 2 (Ribaudo, Veron)

PALMEIRAS 0

Estudiantes – Poletti – Aguirre Suarez, Madero – Malbernat, Pachamé, Medina – Bilardo, Flores, Ribaudo, Conigliaro, Veron

Palmeiras – Waldir – Escalera, Baldochi – Osmar, Ademir da Guia, Ferrari – Singue, Dudu, Tupazinho, Servilio (China), Rinaldo

Top scorer: Tupazinho, Palmeiras 11

1969

FIRST ROUND

Group 1

	DC	DI	UM	Ca	Pl	W	D	L	F	A	Pts
Deportivo Cali	–	3–0	3–1	2–0	6	3	2	1	12	6	8
Deportivo Italia	2–1	–	2–0	2–0	6	3	1	2	7	8	7
Union Magdalena	2–2	3–0	–	1–0	6	2	1	3	7	8	5
Canarias	1–1	1–1	1–0	–	6	1	2	3	3	7	4

Group 2

	Wa	SC	UC	JA	Pl	W	D	L	F	A	Pts
Wanderers	–	2–0	3–1	4–1	6	3	0	3	13	10	6
Sporting Cristal	2–1	–	2–0	2–2	6	2	2	2	11	11	6
Univ. Catolica	3–2	3–2	–	4–2	6	3	0	3	12	13	6
Juan Aurich	3–1	3–3	2–1	–	6	2	0	2	13	15	6

Group 2 play–off

	UC	Wa	SC	JA	Pl	W	D	L	F	A	Pts
Univ. Catolica	–	–	–	4–1	2	2	0	0	6	2	4
Wanderers	–	–	1–1	–	2	1	1	0	2	1	3
Sporting Cristal	1–2	–	–	–	2	0	1	1	2	3	1
Juan Aurich	–	0–1	–	–	2	0	0	2	1	5	0

Group 3

	CP	Ol	Bo	Li	Pl	W	D	L	F	A	Pts
Cerro Porteño	–	4–1	1–1	6–0	6	4	1	1	15	5	9
Olimpia	1–2	–	4–0	3–0	6	3	1	2	12	7	7
Bolivar	2–1	1–1	–	1–0	6	2	3	1	6	8	7
Litoral	0–1	0–2	1–1	–	6	0	1	5	1	14	1

Play-off

Olimpia .... 2–1 .... Bolivar

Group 4

	Pe	Na	DQ	Ba	Pl	W	D	L	F	A	Pts
Peñarol	–	1–1	5–2	5–2	6	3	3	0	16	8	9
Nacional Mont'deo	2–2	–	4–0	2–0	6	2	4	0	10	4	8
Deportivo Quito	1–1	0–0	–	1–0	6	1	3	2	4	10	5
Barcelona	0–2	1–1	0–0	–	6	0	2	4	3	11	2

QUARTER-FINALS

Group 1

	UC	CP	DI	Pl	W	D	L	F	A	Pts
Univ. Catolica	–	0–0	4–0	4	2	1	1	7	3	5
Cerro Porteño	0–1	–	1–0	4	1	2	1	1	1	4
Deportivo Italia	3–2	0–0	–	4	1	1	2	3	7	3

Group 2

	Na	DC	Wa	Pl	W	D	L	F	A	Pts
Nacional Mont'deo	–	2–0	2–0	4	3	1	0	10	2	7
Deportivo Cali	1–5	–	5–1	4	1	1	2	9	11	3
Wanderers	1–1	3–3	–	4	0	2	2	5	11	2

Group 3

	Pe	Ol	Pl	W	D	L	F	A	Pts
Peñarol	–	1–1	2	1	1	0	2	1	3
Olimpia	0–1	–	2	0	1	1	1	2	1

SEMI-FINALS

Estudiantes LP .... 3–1 3–1 .... Universidad Catolica
Nacional Montevideo ... 2–0 0–1 0–0 .... Peñarol

FINAL

1st leg. Centenario, Montevideo, 15–05–1969, 50 000. Referee: Massaro, Chile

NACIONAL MONTEVIDEO 0
ESTUDIANTES LP 1 (Flores 66)

Nacional – Manga – Ancheta, Alvarez Em – Ubinas, Montero Castillo, Mujija – Prieto, Maneiro (Esparrago), Cubilla, Celio, Morales (Taveira)
Estudiantes – Poletti – Togneri, Aguirre Suarez – Madero, Malbernat, Bilardo – Pachamé, Flores, Rudzki (Ribaudo), Conigliaro, Veron

2nd leg. Estadio La Plata, La Plata, 22–05–1969, 30 000. Referee: Delgado, Colombia

ESTUDIANTES LP 2 (Flores 31, Conigliaro 37)
NACIONAL MONTEVIDEO 0

Estudiantes – Poletti – Togneri, Aguirre Suarez – Madero, Malbernat, Bilardo – Pachamé, Flores, Rudzki, Conigliaro, Veron
Nacional – Manga – Ubinas, Ancheta – Alvarez Em, Mujica, Montero Castillo – Prieto, Esparrago, Cubilla, Garcia (Silveyra), Morales

Top scorers: Isella, Universidad Catolica 7
Ferrero, Wanderers Santiago 7
Iroldo, Deportivo Cali 7

1970

FIRST ROUND

Group 1

	BJ	RP	Bo	Un	Pl	W	D	L	F	A	Pts
Boca Juniors	–	2–1	2–0	4–0	6	5	1	0	14	4	11
River Plate	1–3	–	1–0	9–0	6	3	1	2	15	6	7
Bolivar	2–3	1–1	–	2–0	6	1	2	3	7	9	4
Universitario	0–0	0–2	2–2	–	6	0	2	4	2	19	2

Group 2

	Na	Pe	Va	Ga	Pl	W	D	L	F	A	Pts
Nacional Mont'.	–	1–1	1–0	2–0	6	4	2	0	13	3	10
Peñarol	0–0	–	11–2	4–1	6	3	3	0	17	4	9
Valencia	2–5	0–0	–	3–1	6	2	1	3	9	18	5
Deportivo Galicia	0–4	0–1	0–2	–	6	0	0	6	2	16	0

Group 3

	Un	LQ	DA	AQ	Pl	W	D	L	F	A	Pts
Universitario	–	2–0	2–1	3–0	6	4	1	1	11	4	9
LDU Quito	2–0	–	1–2	4–1	6	3	1	2	10	6	7
Defensor Arica	1–1	0–0	–	0–1	6	1	3	2	5	6	5
America Quito	0–3	1–3	1–1	–	6	1	1	4	4	14	3

Group 4

	GU	UC	Ol	DC	AC	Ra	Pl	W	D	L	F	A	Pts
Guarani Asuncion	–	1–0	1–0	1–1	4–1	2–0	10	5	5	0	12	4	15
Univ. de Chile	0–0	–	2–1	3–1	2–1	2–1	10	5	3	2	19	11	13
Olimpia	0–0	1–1	–	5–1	1–0	5–1	10	4	4	2	19	11	12
Deportivo Cali	0–0	2–0	0–1	–	4–2	3–2	10	5	2	3	18	16	12
America Cali	2–2	2–2	1–1	2–4	–	1–0	10	1	3	6	12	22	5
Rangers	0–1	1–7	4–4	0–2	2–0	–	10	1	1	8	11	27	3

QUARTER-FINALS

Group 1

	RP	BJ	Un	Pl	W	D	L	F	A	Pts
River Plate	–	1–1	5–3	4	3	1	0	9	5	7
Boca Juniors	0–1	–	1–0	4	2	1	1	5	3	5
Universitario	1–2	1–3	–	4	0	0	4	5	11	0

Group 2

	Pe	Gu	LQ	Pl	W	D	L	F	A	Pts
Peñarol	–	1–0	2–1	4	3	0	1	6	4	6
Guarani Asuncion	2–0	–	1–1	4	1	1	2	3	3	3
LDU Quito	1–3	1–0	–	4	1	1	2	4	6	3

Group 3

	UC	Na	Pl	W	D	L	F	A	Pts
Univ. de Chile	–	3–0	2	1	0	1	3	2	2
Nacional Montevideo	2–0	–	2	1	0	1	2	3	2

Play-off
Universidad de Chile .... 2–1 .... Nacional Montevideo

SEMI-FINALS

Estudiantes LP .... 3–1 1–0 .... River Plate
Peñarol .... 2–0 0–1 2–2 .... Universidad de Chile

FINAL

1st leg. Estadio La Plata, La Plata, 21–05–1970, 36 000. Referee: Robles, Chile

ESTUDIANTES LP 1 (Togneri 87)
PENAROL 0

Estudiantes – Errea – Pagnanini, Spadaro – Togneri, Pachamé, Solari – Bilardo, Echecopar, Conigliaro, Flores (Rudzki), Veron
Peñarol – Pintos – Soria (Gonzalez), Figueroa – Peralta, Martinez, Goncalvez – Viera, Lamas (Caceres), Acuna, Onega E, Lamberck

2nd leg. Centenario, Montevideo, 27–05–1970, 50 000. Referee: Larrosa, Paraguay

PENAROL 0
ESTUDIANTES LP 0

Peñarol – Pintos – Soria (Speranza), Figueroa – Peralta, Martinez, Viera – Goncalvez, Lamas, Onega E, Lamberck, Acuna
Estudiantes – Errea – Pagnanini, Spadaro – Togneri, Medina, Bilardo – Pachamé, Solari, Conigliaro (Aguilar), Echecopar (Rudzki), Veron

Top scorers: Mas, River Plate 9
Bertocchi, LDU Quito 9

1971

FIRST ROUND

Group 1

	Un	RC	BJ	SC	Pl	W	D	L	F	A	Pts
Universitario	–	3–2	0–0	0–0	6	3	3	0	8	4	9
Rosario Central	2–2	–	*	4–0	6	3	1	2	11	8	7
Boca Juniors	*	2–1	–	2–2	6	1	2	3	4	5	4
Sporting Cristal	0–3	1–2	2–0	–	6	1	2	3	5	11	4

* Boca Juniors withdrew. Their opponents were awarded the points

Group 2

	Na	Pe	CP	St	Pl	W	D	L	F	A	Pts
Nacional Mon'deo	–	2–1	3–0	5–0	6	5	1	0	14	2	11
Peñarol	0–2	–	1–0	9–0	6	3	1	2	14	6	7
Chaco Petrolero	0–1	1–1	–	3–1	6	1	1	4	5	9	3
The Strongest	1–1	1–2	2–1	–	6	1	1	4	5	21	3

Group 3

	Pa	Fl	DI	Ga	Pl	W	D	L	F	A	Pts
Palmeiras	–	3–1	1–0	3–0	6	5	0	1	13	5	10
Fluminense	2–0	–	6–0	3–1	6	4	0	2	16	6	8
Deportivo Italia	0–3	1–0	–	6–5	6	2	1	3	7	15	5
Deportivo Galicia	2–3	1–4	0–0	–	6	0	1	5	9	19	1

Group 4

	UE	CC	CP	Gu	Pl	W	D	L	F	A	Pts
Union Española	–	2–1	0–0	2–1	6	2	3	1	7	6	7
Colo Colo	1–1	–	1–0	3–2	6	2	2	2	6	7	6
Cerro Porteño	2–1	0–0	–	1–1	6	1	4	1	5	5	6
Guarani Asuncion	1–1	2–0	2–2	–	6	1	3	2	9	9	5

Group 5

	Ba	Em	DC	AJ	Pl	W	D	L	F	A	Pts
Barcelona	–	1–1	1–0	3–1	6	3	1	2	8	6	7
Emelec	1–0	–	3–1	1–1	6	2	3	1	6	4	7
Deportivo Cali	3–1	1–0	–	2–0	6	3	0	3	8	7	6
Atletico Junior	0–2	0–0	2–1	–	6	1	2	3	4	9	4

Play-off

Barcelona .... 3–0 .... Emelec

SEMI-FINALS

Group 1

	Na	Pa	Un	Pl	W	D	L	F	A	Pts
Nacional Mont'deo	–	3–1	3–0	4	3	1	0	9	1	7
Palmeiras	0–3	–	3–0	4	2	0	2	6	7	4
Universitario	0–0	1–2	–	4	0	1	3	1	8	1

Group 2

	Es	Ba	UE	Pl	W	D	L	F	A	Pts
Estudiantes LP	–	0–1	2–1	4	3	0	1	4	2	6
Barcelona	0–1	–	1–0	4	2	0	2	3	4	4
Union Española	0–1	3–1	–	4	1	0	3	4	5	2

FINAL

1st leg. Estadio La Plata, La Plata, 26–05–1971, 32 000

ESTUDIANTES LP 1 (Romeo)
NACIONAL MONTEVIDEO 0

Estudiantes – Leone – Aguirre Suarez, Togneri – Malbernat, Pachamé, Medina – Romeo, Echecopar, Rudzki (Bedogni), Verde, Veron

Nacional – Manga – Blanco, Ancheta – Masnik, Mujica, Montero Castillo – Esparrago (Mameli), Maneiro, Prieto (Bareno), Artime, Morales

2nd leg. Centenario, Montevideo, 2–06–1971, 62 000

NACIONAL MONTEVIDEO 1 (Masnik 17)
ESTUDIANTES LP 0

Nacional – Manga – Ubinas, Anchetta – Masnik, Blanco, Montero Castillo – Esparrago, Maneiro, Cubilla (Prieto), Artime, Morales

Estudiantes – Leone – Malbernat, Aguirre Suarez – Togneri, Medina, Pachamé – Echecopar, Romeo, Verde, Rudzki (Bedogni), Veron

Play-off. Estadio Nacional, Lima, 9–06–1971, 42 000

NACIONAL MONTEVIDEO 2 (Esparrago 22, Artime 65)
ESTUDIANTES LP 0

Nacional – Manga – Ubinas, Anchetta – Masnik, Blanco, Montero Castillo – Esparrago, Maneiro (Mujica), Cubilla, Artime, Morales (Mameli)

Estudiantes – Pezzano – Malbernat, Aguirre Suarez – Togneri, Medina, Pachamé – Romeo, Echecopar, Rudzki, Verde, Veron (Bedogni)

Top scorers: Artime, Nacional Montevideo 10
Castronovo, Peñarol 10

1972

FIRST ROUND

Group 1

	In	RC	SF	NM	Pl	W	D	L	F	A	Pts
Independiente	–	2–0	4–2	2–0	6	4	2	0	13	5	10
Rosario Central	2–2	–	2–0	1–0	6	3	2	1	8	4	8
Indep. Santa Fé	0–2	0–0	–	1–1	6	1	2	3	4	9	4
Nacional Medellín	1–1	0–3	0–1	–	6	0	2	4	2	9	2

Group 2

	Ba	AQ	OP	Pe	Pl	W	D	L	F	A	Pts
Barcelona	–	3–1	1–1	3–0	6	3	3	0	9	3	9
America Quito	0–0	–	3–0	1–0	6	3	1	2	9	8	7
Oriente Petrolero	0–0	4–2	–	5–0	6	2	2	2	10	7	6
Chaco Petrolero	1–2	1–2	1–0	–	6	1	0	5	2	12	2

Group 3

	SP	Ol	CP	AM	Pl	W	D	L	F	A	Pts
Sao Paulo FC	–	3–1	4–0	0–0	6	3	2	1	12	6	8
Olimpia	0–1	–	1–1	2–2*	6	1	3	2	7	8	6
Cerro Porteño	3–2	1–3	–	1–0	6	2	2	2	7	11	6
Atletico Mineiro	2–2	0–0	1–1	–	6	0	5	1	5	6	4

* Olimpia awarded the points

Group 4

	Un	UC	Al	US	Pl	W	D	L	F	A	Pts
Universitario	–	2–1	2–1	3–1	6	3	2	1	9	6	8
Univ. de Chile	1–0	–	2–3	2–1	6	3	0	3	12	12	6
Alianza	2–2	3–4	–	1–0	6	2	2	2	10	10	6
Union San Felipe	0–0	3–2	0–0	–	6	1	2	3	5	8	4

Group 5

	Pe	DI	Va	Pl	W	D	L	F	A	Pts
Peñarol	–	1–0	2–1	4	4	0	0	12	3	8
Deportivo Italia	1–5	–	2–0	4	1	1	2	4	7	3
Valencia	1–4	1–1	–	4	1	0	3	3	9	1

SEMI-FINALS

Group 1

	Un	Na	Pe	Pl	W	D	L	F	A	Pts
Universitario	–	3–0	2–3	4	1	2	1	9	7	4
Nacional Montevideo	3–3	–	1–1	4	1	2	1	7	7	4
Peñarol	1–1	0–3	–	4	1	2	1	5	7	4

Group 2

	In	SP	Ba	Pl	W	D	L	F	A	Pts
Independiente	–	2–0	1–0	4	2	1	1	4	2	5
Sao Paulo FC	1–0	–	1–1	4	1	2	1	2	3	4
Barcelona	1–1	0–0	–	4	0	3	1	2	3	3

FINAL

1st leg. Estadio Nacional, Lima, 17–05–72, 45 000

UNIVERSITARIO 0
INDEPENDIENTE 0

Universitario – Ballesteros – Soria, Cuellar – Chumpitaz, Luna, Techera – Carbonell, Castaneda, Ramirez, Rojas, Bailette

Independiente – Santoro – Comisso, Sa – Garisto, Pavoni, Pastoriza – Raymundo, Semenewicz, Balbuena, Mircoli, Saggioratto

2nd leg. Cordero, Avellaneda, 24–05–72, 65 000

INDEPENDIENTE 2 (Maglioni 2)
UNIVERSITARIO 1 (Rojas)

Independiente – Santoro – Comisso, Sa – Garisto, Pavoni, Pastoriza – Raymundo, Semenewicz, Balbuena, Maglioni, Saggioratto

Universitario – Ballesteros – Soria, Cuellar – Chumpitaz, Luna, Techera (Alva) – Cruzado, Castaneda, Munante, Rojas, Ramirez

Top scorer: Toninho, Sao Paulo FC 7

1973

FIRST ROUND

Group 1

	SL	JW	RP	OP	Pl	W	D	L	F	A	Pts
San Lorenzo	–	3–0	1–0	2–0	6	5	0	1	15	1	10
Jorge Wilsterman	1–0	–	1–0	1–0	6	3	1	2	6	8	7
River Plate	0–4	2–2	–	7–1	6	2	1	3	12	10	5
Oriente Petrolero	0–4	3–1	1–3	–	6	1	0	5	5	19	2

Group 2

	Bo	Pa	Na	Pe	Pl	W	D	L	F	A	Pts
Botafogo	–	2–0	3–2	4–1	6	4	1	1	15	9	9
Palmeiras	3–2	–	1–1	2–0	6	4	1	1	10	6	9
Nacional Mont'deo	1–2	1–2	–	2–0	6	1	2	3	8	9	4
Peñarol	2–2	0–2	1–1	–	6	0	2	4	4	13	2

Play-off

Botafogo .... 2–1 .... Palmeiras

Group 3

	CC	Em	NQ	UE	Pl	W	D	L	F	A	Pts
Colo Colo	–	5–1	5–1	5–0	6	3	2	1	16	4	8
Emelec	1–0	–	2–0	1–0	6	3	1	2	6	7	7

					Pl	W	D	L	F	A	Pts
Nacional Quito	1–1	1–0	–	1–0	6	2	1	3	5	10	5
Union Española	0–0	1–1	2–1	–	6	1	2	3	3	9	4

Group 4

	Mi	DC	Pl	W	D	L	F	A	Pts
Millonarios	–	6–2	2	1	1	0	6	2	3
Deportivo Cali	0–0	–	2	0	1	1	2	6	1

The Venezuelan entrants withdrew

Group 5

	CP	Ol	SC	Un	Pl	W	D	L	F	A	Pts
Cerro Porteño	–	4–2	5–0	1–0	6	4	1	1	14	5	9
Olimpia	2–1	–	1–0	1–0	6	3	0	3	7	8	6
Sporting Cristal	1–1	1–0	–	1–0	6	2	2	2	5	9	6
Universitario	0–2	2–1	2–2	–	6	1	1	4	4	8	3

SEMI-FINALS

Group 1

	In	SL	Mi	Pl	W	D	L	F	A	Pts
Independiente	–	1–0	2–0	4	2	1	1	5	3	5
San Lorenzo	2–2	–	2–0	4	1	2	1	4	3	4
Millonarios	1–0	0–0	–	4	1	1	2	1	4	3

Group 2

	CC	CP	Bo	Pl	W	D	L	F	A	Pts
Colo Colo	–	4–0	3–3	4	2	1	0	10	9	5
Cerro Porteño	5–1	–	3–2	4	2	0	2	8	9	4
Botafogo	1–2	2–0	–	4	1	1	2	8	8	3

FINAL

1st leg. Cordero, Avellaneda, 22–05–1973, 65 000. Referee: Lorenzo, Uruguay

INDEPENDIENTE 1 (Mendoza 75)
COLO COLO 1 (OG 71)

Independiente – Santoro – Comisso, Sa – Lopez, Pavoni, Semenewicz – Raymundo, Martinez, Balbuena (Bertoni), Giachello (Maglioni), Mendoza

Colo Colo – Neff – Galindo, Herrera – Gonzales, Silva, Paez – Valdés, Osorio (Caszely), Messen, Ahumada, Véliz

2nd leg. Estadio Nacional, Santiago, 29–05–1973, 77 000. Referee: Arpi Filho, Brazil

COLO COLO 0
INDEPENDIENTE 0

Colo Colo – Neff – Galindo, Herrera – Gonzales, Silva, Paez – Valdés, Osorio, Caszely, Messen, Véliz

Independiente – Santoro – Comisso, Sa – Lopez, Pavoni, Semenewicz – Raymundo, Martinez, Balbuena (Bertoni), Giachello (Maglioni), Mendoza

Play–off. Centenario, Montevideo, 6–06–1973, 45 000. Referee: Romei, Paraguay

INDEPENDIENTE 2 (Mendoza 25, Giachello 107)
COLO COLO 1 (Caszely 39)

Independiente – Santoro – Comisso, Sa – Lopez, Pavoni, Semenewicz – Raymundo, Galvan, Bertoni, Maglioni (Bochini), Mendoza (Giachello)

Colo Colo – Neff – Galindo, Herrera – Gonzales, Silva (Castaneda), Valdés – Paez, Messen, Caszely, Ahumada, Véliz (Lara)

Top scorer: Caszely, Colo Colo 9

1974

FIRST ROUND

Group 1

	Hu	RC	UE	CC	Pl	W	D	L	F	A	Pts
Huracan	–	1–0	3–1	2–1	6	5	0	1	13	4	10
Rosario Central	1–0	–	4–0	2–0	6	5	0	1	11	2	10
Union Española	1–5	0–1	–	2–1	6	2	0	4	6	14	4
Colo Colo	0–2	1–3	0–2	–	6	0	0	6	3	13	0

Play-off
Huracan .... 4–0 .... Rosario Central

Group 2

	SP	Pa	JW	Mu	Pl	W	D	L	F	A	Pts
Sao Paulo FC	–	2–0	5–0	1–1	6	4	2	0	14	5	10
Palmeiras	1–2	–	2–0	3–0	6	3	0	3	7	5	6
Jorge Wilsterman	0–1	1–0	–	1–0	5	2	0	3	2	8	4
Deport. Municipal	3–3	0–1	–	–	5	0	2	3	4	9	2

Group 3

	Mi	NM	Po	Va	Pl	W	D	L	F	A	Pts
Millonarios	–	3–0	2–1	2–1	6	4	1	1	10	6	9
Nacional Medellín	1–2	–	3–0	2–1	6	3	1	2	8	7	7
Portuguesa	2–0	0–0	–	0–0	6	2	2	2	4	5	6
Valencia	1–1	1–2	0–1	–	6	0	2	4	4	8	2

Group 4

	DL	NQ	UC	SC	Pl	W	D	L	F	A	Pts
Defensor Lima	–	2–1	1–0	2–0	6	4	1	1	7	2	9
Nacional Quito	0–0	–	2–0	3–0	6	3	2	1	9	3	8
Univ. Catolica	1–0	0–0	–	0–0	6	1	2	3	2	5	4
Sporting Cristal	0–2	1–3	2–1	–	6	1	1	4	3	11	3

Group 5

	Pe	CP	Ol	Na	Pl	W	D	L	F	A	Pts
Peñarol	–	1–0	0–0	1–0	6	3	2	1	5	3	8
Cerro Porteño	1–1	–	1–0	2–1	6	2	3	1	7	6	7
Olimpia	0–2	1–1	–	2–0	6	1	3	2	4	5	5
Nacional Mont'deo	2–0	2–2	1–1	–	6	1	2	3	6	8	4

SEMI-FINALS

Group 1

	In	Pe	Hu	Pl	W	D	L	F	A	Pts
Independiente	–	3–2	3–0	4	2	2	0	8	4	6
Peñarol	1–1	–	1–1	4	1	2	1	7	5	4
Huracan	1–1	0–3	–	4	0	2	2	2	8	2

Group 2

	SP	Mi	DL	Pl	W	D	L	F	A	Pts
Sao Paulo FC	–	4–0	4–0	4	3	1	0	9	0	7
Millonarios	0–0	–	1–0	4	2	1	1	5	5	5
Defensor Lima	0–1	1–4	–	4	0	0	4	1	10	0

FINAL

1st Leg. Morumbí, Sao Paulo, 12–10–1974, 51 000. Referee: Perex, Peru

SAO PAULO FC 2 (Rocha 48, Mirandinha 50)
INDEPENDIENTE 1 (Saggioratto 28)

Sao Paulo – Valdir Peres – Nelson, Paranhos – Arlindo, Gilberto, Ademir da Guia – Zé Carlos (Mauro), Rocha, Terto, Mirandinha, Piau

Independiente – Gay – Comisso, Sa – Lopez, Pavoni, Galvan – Raymundo, Saggioratto, Balbuena, Bochini, Bertoni

2nd leg. Cordero, Avellaneda , 16–10–1974, 48 000. Referee: Barreto, Uruguay

INDEPENDIENTE 2 (Bochini 34, Balbuena 48)
SAO PAULO FC 0

Independiente – Gay – Comisso, Sa – Lopez, Pavoni, Galvan – Raymundo, Saggioratto, Balbuena, Bochini, Bertoni (Semenewicz)

Sao Paulo – Valdir Peres – Nelson, Paranhos – Arlindo, Gilberto, Chicao – Zé Carlos, Rocha (Mauro), Terto, Mirandinha, Piau

Play–off. Estadio Nacional, Santiago, 19–10–1974, 27 000. Orozco, Peru

INDEPENDIENTE 1 (Pavoni 37)
SAO PAULO FC 0

Independiente – Gay – Comisso, Sa – Lopez, Pavoni, Galvan – Raymundo, Semenewicz, Balbuena (Carrica), Bochini, Bertoni (Giribert)

Sao Paulo – Valdir Peres – Forlan, Paranhos – Arlindo, Gilberto (Nelson), Chicao – Zé Carlos (Silva), Rocha, Mauro, Mirandinha, Piau

Top scorers: Terti, Sao Paulo FC 7
Rocha, Sao Paulo FC 7

1975

FIRST ROUND

Group 1

	RC	Ne	Ol	CP	Pl	W	D	L	F	A	Pts
Rosario Central	–	1–1	1–1	2–1	6	2	4	0	8	5	8
Newell's Old Boys	1–1	–	3–2	1–0	6	3	2	1	9	8	8
Olimpia	0–0	2–0	–	2–1	6	2	3	1	7	5	7
Cerro Porteño	1–3	2–3	0–0	–	6	0	1	5	5	11	1

Play-off

Rosario Central .... 1–0 ...... Newell's Old Boys

Group 2

	UE	Hu	St	JW	Pl	W	D	L	F	A	Pts
Union Española	–	7–2	4–0	4–1	6	3	3	0	17	5	9
Huachipato	0–0	–	4–2	4–0	6	2	2	2	10	10	6
The Strongest	1–1	1–0	–	3–1	6	2	2	2	8	11	6
Jorge Wilsterman	1–1	0–0	1–1	–	6	0	3	3	4	13	3

Group 3

	Cr	DC	NM	VG	Pl	W	D	L	F	A	Pts
Cruzeiro	–	2–1	2–3	3–2	6	3	1	2	10	9	7
Deportivo Cali	1–0	–	0–0	2–1	6	2	2	2	5	5	6
Nacional Medellín	1–2	2–1	–	1–1	6	2	2	2	7	8	6
Vasco da Gama	1–1	0–0	2–0	–	6	1	3	2	7	7	5

Group 4

	LQ	Po	Ga	NQ	Pl	W	D	L	F	A	Pts
LDU Quito	–	1–1	4–2	3–1	6	3	3	0	11	6	9
Portuguesa	1–1	–	1–1	1–0	6	1	4	1	5	8	6
Deportivo Galicia	0–1	0–0	–	4–0	6	1	3	2	7	6	5
Nacional Quito	1–1	5–1	0–0	–	6	1	2	3	7	10	4

Group 5

	Un	Pe	Wa	UH	Pl	W	D	L	F	A	Pts
Universitario	–	3–2	3–1	1–1	6	4	2	0	12	6	10
Peñarol	0–1	–	1–0	5–2	6	4	0	2	13	7	8
Wanderers	0–2	1–2	–	4–0	6	1	1	4	8	10	3
Union Huaral	2–2	0–3	2–2	–	6	0	3	3	7	17	3

SEMI-FINALS

Group 1

	In	RC	Cr	Pl	W	D	L	F	A	Pts
Independiente	–	2–0	3–0	4	2	0	2	5	4	4
Rosario Central	2–0	–	3–1	4	2	0	2	5	5	4
Cruzeiro	2–0	2–0	–	4	2	0	2	5	6	4

Group 2

	UE	Un	LQ	Pl	W	D	L	F	A	Pts
Union Española	–	2–1	2–0	4	2	1	1	7	6	5
Universitario	1–1	–	2–1	4	1	2	1	4	4	4
LDU Quito	4–2	0–0	–	4	1	1	2	5	6	3

FINAL

1st leg. Estadio Nacional, Santiago, 18–06–1975, 43 000. Referee: Bazan, Uruguay

UNION ESPANOLA 1 (Ahumada 87)
INDEPENDIENTE 0

Union Española – Vallejos – Machuca, Soto – Arias, Palacios, Las Heras – Hinostroza, Trujillo, Spedaletti, Ahumada, Hoffman (Miranda)
Independiente – Pérez – Comisso, Sa – Semenewicz, Pavoni, Galvan – Bochini, Rojas, Balbuena, Ruiz Moreno, Bertoni (Giribert)

2nd leg. Cordero, Avellaneda , 25–06–1975, 52 000. Referee, Barreto, Uruguay

INDEPENDIENTE 3 (Rojas 1, Pavoni 58, Bertoni 83)
UNION ESPANOLA 1 (Las Heras)

Independiente – Pérez – Comisso, Sa – Semenewicz, Pavoni, Galvan – Bochini, Balbuena, Ruiz Moreno, Rojas, Bertoni
Union Española – Vallejos – Machuca, Berly – Soto, Arias, Palacios – Las Heras (Maldonado), Hinostroza, Spedaletti, Ahumada, Veliz (Trujillo)

Play–off. Defensores del Chaco, Asuncion, 29–06–1975, 45 000. Referee: Perez, Peru

INDEPENDIENTE 2 (Ruiz Moreno 29, Bertoni 65)
UNION ESPANOLA 0

Independiente – Pérez – Comisso, Sa – Lopez, Pavoni, Semenewicz – Galvan, Bochini, Balbuena, Ruiz Moreno, Bertoni (Saggioratto)
Union Española – Vallejos – Machuca, Maldonado – Gaete, Arias, Palacios – Hinostroza (Las Heras), Veliz, Spedaletti, Trujillo, Ahumada

Top scorers: Morena F, Peñarol 8
Ramirez C, Universitario 8

1976

FIRST ROUND

Group 1

	RP	Es	Po	DG	Pl	W	D	L	F	A	Pts
River Plate	–	1–0	2–1	4–1	6	5	0	1	10	3	10
Estudiantes LP	1–0	–	3–0	4–0	6	4	1	1	11	3	9
Portuguesa	0–2	2–2	–	3–1	6	2	1	3	8	11	5
Deportivo Galicia	0–1	0–1	1–2	–	6	0	0	6	3	15	0

Group 2

	LQ	DC	Bo	Gu	Pl	W	D	L	F	A	Pts
LDU Quito	–	1–1	2–1	4–0	6	3	2	1	10	5	8
Deportivo Cuenca	0–0	–	3–1	1–0	6	3	2	1	9	6	8
Bolivar	3–2	4–2	–	7–1	6	3	0	3	16	11	6
Guabirà	0–1	0–2	1–0	–	6	1	0	5	2	15	2

Play-off

LDU Quito .... 2–1 ...... Deportivo Cuenca

Group 3

	Cr	IP	Ol	SL	Pl	W	D	L	F	A	Pts
Cruzeiro	–	5–4	4–1	4–1	6	5	1	0	20	9	11
Internacional PA	0–2	–	1–0	3–0	6	3	1	2	10	8	7
Olimpia	2–2	1–1	–	2–3	6	1	2	3	7	11	4
Sportivo Luqueño	1–3	0–1	0–1	–	6	1	0	5	5	14	2

Group 4

	Al	Mi	AU	SF	Pl	W	D	L	F	A	Pts
Alianza	–	2–1	0–0	3–0	6	3	2	1	8	4	8
Millonarios	1–0	–	4–0	0–1	6	2	2	2	8	5	6
Alfonso Ugarte	0–0	1–1	–	2–1	6	1	4	1	5	8	6
Indep. Santa Fé	2–3	1–1	2–2	–	6	1	2	3	7	11	4

Group 5

	Pe	UE	Pa	Na	Pl	W	D	L	F	A	Pts
Peñarol	–	2–0	2–1	1–1	6	3	2	1	7	4	8
Union Española	0–0	–	1–0	2–0	6	3	2	1	5	3	8
Palestino	1–0	0–1	–	2–1	6	2	1	3	5	6	5
Nacional Mont'deo	1–2	1–1	1–1	–	6	0	3	3	5	9	3

SEMI-FINALS

Group 1

	Cr	LQ	Al	Pl	W	D	L	F	A	Pts
Cruzeiro	–	4–1	7–1	4	4	0	0	18	3	8
LDU Quito	1–3	–	2–1	4	1	0	3	4	10	2
Alianza	0–4	2–0	–	4	1	0	3	4	13	2

Group 2

	RP	In	Pe	Pl	W	D	L	F	A	Pts
River Plate	–	0–0	3–0	4	2	1	1	4	1	5
Independiente	0–1	–	1–0	4	2	1	1	2	1	5
Peñarol	1–0	0–1	–	4	1	0	3	1	5	2

Play-off

River Plate .... 1–0 ...... Independiente

FINAL

1st leg. Mineirao, Belo Horizonte, 21–07–76, 58 000. Referee: Llobregat, Venezuela

CRUZEIRO 4 (Nelinho, Palinha 2, Waldo)
RIVER PLATE 1 (Mas)
Cruzeiro – Raul – Nelinho, Morais – Menezes, Vanderlay, Wilson Piazza (Waldo) – Zé Carlos, Eduardo (Ronaldo), Palinha, Jairzinho, Joazinho
River Plate – Fillol (Landaburu) – Comelles, Perfumo – Lonardi, Lopez H, Merlo – Lopez J, Gonzalez, Sabella, Luque, Mas

2nd leg. Monumental, Buenos Aires, 28–07–76, 45 000. Referee: Bazan, Uruguay
RIVER PLATE 2 (Lopez J, Gonzalez)
CRUZEIRO 1 (Palinha)
River Plate – Landaburu – Comelles, Perfumo – Pasarella, Lopez H (Artico), Lopez J – Merlo, Alonso, Gonzalez, Luque, Mas (Sabella)
Cruzeiro – Raul – Nelinho, Morais – Menezes, Vanderlay, Zé Carlos – Wilson Piazza, Jairzinho, Eduardo (Ronaldo), Palinha, Joazinho

Play–off. Estadio Nacional, Santiago, 30–07–76, 35 000. Referee: Martinez, Chile
CRUZEIRO 3 (Nelinho, Ronaldo, Joazinho)
RIVER PLATE 2 (Mas, Urquiza)
Cruzeiro – Raul – Nelinho, Morais – Menezes, Vanderlay, Eduardo – Wilson Piazza (Osiris), Zé Carlos, Ronaldo, Palinha, Joazinho
River Plate – Landaburu – Comelles, Lonardi – Artico, Urquiza, Sabella – Merlo, Alonso, Gonzalez, Luque, Mas (Crespo)

Top scorer: Jairzinho, Cruzeiro 14

1977

FIRST ROUND

Group 1

	BJ	RP	De	Pe	Pl	W	D	L	F	A	Pts
Boca Juniors	–	1–0	2–0	1–0	6	4	2	0	5	0	10
River Plate	0–0	–	1–1	2–1	6	1	4	1	5	5	6
Defensor	0–0	0–0	–	2–4	6	1	3	2	5	7	5
Peñarol	0–1	2–2	0–2	–	6	1	1	4	7	10	3

Group 2

	DC	Bo	OP	NM	Pl	W	D	L	F	A	Pts
Deportivo Cali	–	3–0	3–0	3–1	6	4	0	2	12	5	8
Bolivar	3–0	–	1–0	3–0	6	3	1	2	7	4	7
Oriente Petrolero	1–0	0–0	–	4–0	6	2	1	3	6	7	5
Nacional Medellín	0–3	1–0	3–1	–	6	2	0	4	5	14	4

Group 3

	IP	NQ	Co	DC	Pl	W	D	L	F	A	Pts
Internacional PA	–	2–0	1–0	3–1	6	4	1	1	9	4	9
Nacional Quito	2–0	–	2–1	0–0	6	3	1	2	6	6	7
Corinthians	1–1	3–0	–	4–0	6	2	1	3	10	6	5
Deportivo Cuenca	0–2	0–2	2–1	–	6	1	1	4	3	12	3

Group 4

	Li	UC	Ev	Ol	Pl	W	D	L	F	A	Pts
Libertad	–	3–0	2–1	2–2	6	3	2	1	10	5	8
Univ. de Chile	1–0	–	1–0	1–0	6	3	0	3	3	6	6
Everton	1–3	2–0	–	1–0	6	2	1	3	7	8	5
Olimpia	0–0	1–0	2–2	–	6	1	3	2	5	6	5

Group 5

	Po	UH	EM	SB	Pl	W	D	L	F	A	Pts
Portuguesa	–	2–0	3–0	0–0	6	4	2	0	10	2	10
Union Huaral	1–1	–	2–1	1–0	6	2	2	2	4	5	6
Estudiantes Merida	0–2	1–0	–	1–0	6	3	0	3	6	8	6
Sport Boys	1–2	0–0	1–3	–	6	0	2	4	2	7	2

SEMI-FINALS

Group 1

	BJ	DC	Li	Pl	W	D	L	F	A	Pts
Boca Juniors	–	1–1	1–0	4	2	2	0	4	2	6
Deportivo Cali	1–1	–	0–0	4	0	3	1	3	4	3
Libertad	0–1	2–1	–	4	1	1	2	2	3	3

Group 2

	Cr	IP	Po	Pl	W	D	L	F	A	Pts
Cruzeiro	–	0–0	2–1	4	3	1	0	7	1	7
Internacional PA	0–1	–	2–1	4	1	1	2	2	5	3
Portuguesa	0–4	3–0	–	4	1	0	3	5	8	2

FINAL

1st leg. La Bonbonera, Buenos Aires, 6–09–77, 50 000. Referee: Cerullo, Uruguay
BOCA JUNIORS 1 (Veglio 3)
CRUZEIRO 0
Boca Juniors – Gatti – Pernia, Sa (Tesare) – Mouzo, Tarantini, Veglio – Suné, Zanabria, Mastrangelo, Pavon (Bernabitti), Felman
Cruzeiro – Raul – Nelinho, Morais – Menezes, Vanderlay, Zé Carlos – Eduardo, Eli Carlos, Méndez, Neca, Jaozinho

2nd leg. Mineirao, Belo Horizonte, 11–09–77, 55 000. Referee: Orozco, Peru
CRUZEIRO 1 (Nelinho 76)
BOCA JUNIORS 0
Cruzeiro – Raul – Nelinho, Morais – Menezes, Vanderlay, Zé Carlos – Eduardo, Eli Carlos (Livio), Méndez, Neca, Jaozinho
Boca Juniors – Gatti – Pernia, Tesare – Mouzo, Tarantini, Ribolzi – Suné, Veglio (Pavon), Zanabria, Mastrangelo, Felman (Ortiz)

Play-off. Centenario, Montevideo, 14–09–77, 45 000. Referee: Llobregat, Venezuela
BOCA JUNIORS 0
CRUZEIRO 0
Boca Juniors won 5–4 on penalties
Boca Juniors – Gatti – Pernia, Tesare – Mouzo, Tarantini, Benitez (Ribolzi) (Pavon) – Suné, Zanabria, Mastrangelo, Veglio, Felman
Cruzeiro – Raul – Nelinho (Mariano), Morais – Menzezs, Vanderlay, Eduardo – Eli Carlos (Livio), Zé Carlos, Méndez, Neca, Jaozinho

Top scorers: Scotta, Deportivo Cali 5
Silva, Portuguesa Acarigua 5

1978

FIRST ROUND

Group 1

	RP	In	LQ	NQ	Pl	W	D	L	F	A	Pts
River Plate	–	0–0	4–0	2–0	6	2	4	0	7	1	8
Independiente	0–0	–	2–0	2–0	6	3	2	1	6	2	8
LDU Quito	0–0	1–0	–	3–2	6	2	1	3	4	10	5
Nacional Quito	1–1	1–2	2–0	–	6	1	1	4	6	10	3

Play-off
River Plate .... 4–1 .... Independiente

Group 2

	Al	SC	St	OP	Pl	W	D	L	F	A	Pts
Alianza	–	4–1	2–0	5–1	6	5	1	0	19	5	11
Sporting Cristal	2–2	–	3–0	1–0	6	3	1	2	9	9	7
The Strongest	1–2	3–1	–	2–0	6	2	0	4	6	12	4
Oriente Petrolero	0–4	0–1	4–0	–	6	1	0	5	5	13	2

Group 3

	AM	UE	SP	Pa	Pl	W	D	L	F	A	Pts
Atletico Mineiro	–	5–1	2–1	2–0	6	4	2	0	16	8	10
Union Española	1–1	–	1–1	0–0	6	1	4	1	7	10	6
Sao Paulo FC	1–1	1–1	–	1–2	6	1	3	2	6	7	5
Palestino	4–5	2–3	0–1	–	6	1	1	4	8	12	3

Group 4

	DC	Pe	AJ	Da	Pl	W	D	L	F	A	Pts
Deportivo Cali	–	1–0	0–0	2–0	6	3	2	1	5	3	8
Peñarol	0–2	–	1–0	4–2	6	3	0	3	7	7	6
Atletico Junior	0–0	1–0	–	0–0	6	1	4	1	1	1	6
Danubio	3–0	1–2	0–0	–	6	1	2	3	6	8	4

Group 5

	CP	Po	EM	Li	Pl	W	D	L	F	A	Pts
Cerro Porteño	–	1–0	3–2	1–0	6	3	3	0	7	4	9
Portuguesa	1–1	–	1–2	2–1	6	2	2	2	5	5	6
Estudiantes Merida	1–1	0–0	–	1–1	6	1	3	2	7	8	5
Libertad	0–0	0–1	2–1	–	6	1	2	3	4	6	4

SEMI-FINALS

Group 1

	BJ	RP	AM	Pl	W	D	L	F	A	Pts
Boca Juniors	–	0–0	3–1	4	3	1	0	7	2	7
River Plate	0–2	–	1–0	4	1	1	2	1	3	3
Atletico Mineiro	1–2	1–0	–	4	1	0	3	3	6	2

Group 2

	DC	CP	Al	Pl	W	D	L	F	A	Pts
Deportivo Cali	–	1–1	3–2	4	3	1	0	12	4	7
Cerro Porteño	0–4	–	3–1	4	1	1	2	4	9	3
Alianza	1–4	3–0	–	4	1	0	3	7	10	2

FINAL

1st leg. Pascual Guerrero, Cali, 23–11–78. Referee: Ortiz, Paraguay

DEPORTIVO CALI 0
BOCA JUNIORS 0

Deportivo Cali – Zape – Ospina, Caicedo, Escobar, Castro (Correa) – Otero (Jaramillo), Landucci, Valverde – Torres, Scotta, Benitez

Boca Juniors – Rodriguez – Pernia, Sa, Mouzo, Bordon – Benitez, Suné, Zanabria – Mastrangelo, Salinas, Perotti

2nd leg. La Bombonera, Buenos Aires, 28–11–78. Referee: Nuñez, Peru

BOCA JUNIORS 4 (Perotti 15 85, Mastrangelo 60, Salinas 71)
DEPORTIVO CALI 0

Boca Juniors – Gatti – Pernia, Sa, Mouzo, Bordon – Benitez (Veglio), Suné, Zanabria – Mastrangelo, Salinas, Perotti

Deportivo Cali – Zape – Ospina (Castro), Caicedo, Escobar, Correa – Otero (Umana), Landucci, Valverde – Torres, Scotta, Benitez

Top scorers: Larrosa, Alianza 8
Scotta, Deportivo Cali 8

1979

FIRST ROUND

Group 1

	In	DC	Mi	Qu	Pl	W	D	L	F	A	Pts
Independiente	–	1–0	4–1	2–0	6	4	1	1	12	6	9
Deportivo Cali	1–0	–	2–0	3–2	6	3	1	2	8	7	7
Millonarios	3–3	1–1	–	1–0	6	2	2	2	8	11	6
Quilmes	1–2	3–1	1–2	–	6	1	0	5	7	11	2

Group 2

	Ol	Bo	SA	JW	Pl	W	D	L	F	A	Pts
Olimpia	–	3–0	1–0	4–2	6	5	0	1	12	4	10
Bolivar	2–1	–	4–1	4–0	6	4	1	1	18	7	9
Sol de America	0–1	2–2	–	2–1	6	2	1	3	8	11	5
Jorge Wilsterman	0–2	0–6	2–3	–	6	0	0	6	5	21	0

Group 3

	Gu	Un	Pa	Al	Pl	W	D	L	F	A	Pts
Guarani Campinas	–	6–1	1–0	2–1	6	5	0	1	16	6	10
Universitario	3–0	–	2–5	1–0	6	4	0	2	15	15	8
Palmeiras	1–4	1–2	–	4–0	6	3	0	3	15	11	6
Alianza	0–3	3–6	2–4	–	6	0	0	6	6	20	0

Group 4

	Pa	OH	Po	Ga	Pl	W	D	L	F	A	Pts
Palestino	–	1–0	6–0	5–0	6	4	2	0	16	2	10
O'Higgins	1–1	–	1–1	6–0	6	2	3	1	10	4	7
Portuguesa	0–2	1–1	–	1–1	6	0	4	2	4	12	4
Deportivo Galicia	1–1	0–1	1–1	–	6	0	3	3	3	15	3

Group 5

	Pe	Na	NQ	TU	Pl	W	D	L	F	A	Pts
Peñarol	–	1–1	2–1	4–0	6	4	2	0	10	2	10
Nacional Mont'deo	0–0	–	3–0	2–0	6	2	3	1	7	3	7
Nacional Quito	0–2	1–0	–	2–1	6	2	1	3	6	10	5
Tecnico Universit.	0–1	1–1	2–2	–	6	0	2	4	4	12	2

SEMI-FINALS

Group 1

	Ol	Gu	Pa	Pl	W	D	L	F	A	Pts
Olimpia	–	2–1	3–0	4	3	1	0	8	2	7
Guarani Campinas	1–1	–	2–2	4	0	3	1	4	5	3
Palestino	0–2	0–0	–	4	0	2	2	2	7	2

Group 2

	BJ	In	Pe	Pl	W	D	L	F	A	Pts
Boca Juniors	–	2–0	1–0	4	2	1	1	3	1	5
Independiente	1–0	–	1–0	4	2	1	1	2	2	5
Peñarol	0–0	0–0	–	4	0	2	2	0	2	2

Play-off
Boca Juniors .... 1–0 .... Independiente

FINAL

1st leg. Defensores del Chaco, Asuncion, 22–07–1979, 45 000. Referee: Castro, Chile

OLIMPIA 2 (Aquino 3, Piazza)
BOCA JUNIORS 0

Olimpia – Almeida – Solalinde, Paredes, Giménez, Piazza – Torres, Kiese, Talavera – Isasi, Villalba, Aquino

Boca Juniors – Gatti – Pernia, Capurro, Sa, Bordon – Benitez (Palacios), Suné, Salinas – Mastrangelo, Salguero, Rocha

2nd leg. La Bombonera, Buenos Aires, 27–07–1979, 50 000. Referee: Gardelino, Uruguay

BOCA JUNIORS 0
OLIMPIA 0

Boca Juniors – Gatti – Pernia, Sa, Capurro, Bordon – Benitez, Suné, Zanabria (Salguero) – Mastrangelo, Salinas, Rocha (Palacios)

Olimpia – Almeida – Solalinde, Paredes, Giménez, Piazza – Torres (Guasch), Kiese, Talavera – Isasi, Villalba, Aquino (Delgado)

Top scorer: Talavera, Olimpia 9

1980

FIRST ROUND

Group 1

	VS	RP	SC	AC	Pl	W	D	L	F	A	Pts
Velez Sarsfield	–	0–0	2–0	5–2	6	4	2	0	10	2	10
River Plate	0–0	–	3–2	3–0	6	4	2	0	10	3	10
Sporting Cristal	0–1	1–2	–	0–0	6	1	1	4	5	8	3
Atletico Chalaco	0–2	0–2	0–2	–	6	0	1	5	2	14	1

Play-off
Velez Sarsfield .... 1–1 .... River Plate

Velez Sarsfield qualify on goal difference

Group 2

	Na	St	De	OP	Pl	W	D	L	F	A	Pts
Nacional Mon'deo	–	2–0	1–0	5–0	6	5	0	1	14	4	10
The Strongest	3–0	–	2–0	3–2	6	3	1	2	9	6	7
Defensor	0–3	1–1	–	1–1	6	1	2	3	3	8	4
Oriente Petrolero	1–3	1–0	0–1	–	6	1	1	4	5	13	3

Group 3

	IP	VG	Ga	Ta	Pl	W	D	L	F	A	Pts
Internacional PA	–	2–1	2–0	4–0	6	4	1	1	10	3	9
Vasco da Gama	0–0	–	4–0	1–0	6	3	2	1	7	2	8
Deportivo Galicia	2–1	0–0	–	1–0	6	3	1	2	4	7	7
Deportivo Tachira	0–1	0–1	0–1	–	6	0	0	6	0	9	0

Group 4

	AC	UC	SF	Em	Pl	W	D	L	F	A	Pts
America Cali	–	1–0	1–0	4–1	6	4	1	1	11	7	9
Univ. Catolica	4–2	–	1–0	5–0	6	3	0	3	10	5	6
Indep. Santa Fé	1–1	1–0	–	1–2	6	2	1	3	5	5	5
Emelec	1–2	1–0	0–2	–	6	2	0	4	5	14	4

Group 5

	OH	CP	CC	SA	Pl	W	D	L	F	A	Pts
O'Higgins	–	0–0	1–3	2–0	6	2	2	2	8	6	6
Cerro Porteño	1–0	–	5–3	0–0	6	2	2	2	8	7	6
Colo Colo	1–1	2–1	–	1–1	6	2	2	2	11	11	6
Sol de America	1–4	2–1	2–1	–	6	2	2	2	6	9	6

SEMI-FINALS

Group 1

	Na	Ol	OH	Pl	W	D	L	F	A	Pts
Nacional Mon'deo	–	1–1	2–0	4	3	1	0	5	1	7
Olimpia	0–1	–	2–0	4	2	1	1	4	2	5
O'Higgins	0–1	0–1	–	4	0	0	4	0	6	0

Group 2

	IP	AC	VS	Pl	W	D	L	F	A	Pts
Internacional PA	–	0–0	3–1	4	2	2	0	4	1	6
America Cali	0–0	–	0–0	4	0	4	0	0	0	4
Velez Sarsfield	0–1	0–0	–	4	0	2	2	1	4	2

FINAL

1st leg. Beira–Rio, Porto Alegre, 30–07–80, 80 000. Referee: Romero, Argentina

INTERNACIONAL PORTO ALEGRE 0
NACIONAL MONTEVIDEO 0

Internacional – Gasperim – Toninho, Mauro Pastor, Mauro Galvao, Andrés – Tonho, Falcao, Batista, Jair – Chico Espina (Aldison), Mario Sergio

Nacional – Rodriguez – Moreira, De Leon, Blanco, Gonzalez – Luzardo, Esparrago, De la Pena – Bica, Victorino, Pérez

2nd leg. Centenario, Montevideo, 6–08–80, 75 000. Referee: Perez, Peru

NACIONAL MONTEVIDEO 1 (Victorino 35)
INTERNACIONAL PORTO ALEGRE 0

Nacional – Rodriguez – Moreira, Blanco, De Leon, Gonzalez – Esparrago, De la Pena, Luzardo – Bica, Victorino, Morales

Internacional – Gasperim – Tonho, Mauro Pastor, Mauro Galvao, Mineiro – Jair (Bereta), Batista, Falcao, Chico Espina – Aldison, Mario Sergio

Top scorer: Victorino, Nacional Montevideo 6

1981

FIRST ROUND

Group 1

	DC	RP	RC	AJ	Pl	W	D	L	F	A	Pts
Deportivo Cali	–	2–1	1–0	4–1	6	4	0	2	10	6	8
River Plate	1–2	–	3–2	3–0	6	3	1	2	9	6	7
Rosario Central	2–1	0–1	–	5–0	6	3	0	3	11	7	6
Atletico Junior	1–0	0–0	1–2	–	6	1	1	4	3	14	5

Group 2

	Co	SC	UC	AT	Pl	W	D	L	F	A	Pts
Cobreloa	–	6–1	1–0	6–1	6	3	3	0	14	3	9
Sporting Cristal	0–0	–	3–2	2–1	6	3	2	1	9	10	8
Univ. de Chile	0–0	1–1	–	3–0	6	2	2	2	8	6	6
Atletico Torino	1–1	0–2	1–2	–	6	0	1	5	4	16	1

Group 3

	Fl	AM	CP	Ol	Pl	W	D	L	F	A	Pts
Flamengo	–	2–2	5–2	1–1	6	2	4	0	14	9	8
Atletico Mineiro	2–2	–	1–0	1–0	6	2	4	0	8	6	8
Cerro Porteño	2–4	2–2	–	0–0	6	1	2	3	9	12	4
Olimpia	0–0	0–0	0–3	–	6	0	4	2	1	5	4

Play-off
Flamengo .... 0–0 * ..... Atletico Mineiro

* Abandoned after 35 mins. Game awarded to Flamengo

Group 4

	JW	St	Ba	TU	Pl	W	D	L	F	A	Pts
Jorge Wilsterman	–	3–2	1–0	3–1	6	4	0	2	9	9	8
The Strongest	2–0	–	1–0	4–2	6	4	0	2	13	9	8
Barcelona	3–0	2–1	–	2–1	6	3	0	3	8	8	6
Tecnico Universit.	1–2	2–3	4–1	–	6	1	0	5	11	15	2

Play-off
Jorge Wilsterman .... 4–1 ... The Strongest

Group 5

	Pe	BV	EM	Po	Pl	W	D	L	F	A	Pts
Peñarol	–	3–1	4–2	3–0	6	5	1	0	13	3	11
Bella Vista	0–0	–	3–1	4–0	6	4	1	1	16	5	9
Estudiantes Merida	0–2	1–4	–	1–1	6	0	2	4	5	14	2
Portuguesa	0–1	0–4	0–0	–	6	0	2	4	1	13	2

SEMI-FINALS

Group 1

	Co	Na	Pe	Pl	W	D	L	F	A	Pts
Cobreloa	–	2–2	4–2	4	3	1	0	9	5	7
Nacional Montevideo	1–2	–	1–1	4	0	3	1	5	6	3
Peñarol	0–1	1–1	–	4	0	2	2	4	7	2

Group 2

	Fl	DC	JW	Pl	W	D	L	F	A	Pts
Flamengo	–	3–0	4–1	4	4	0	0	10	2	8
Deportivo Cali	0–1	–	1–0	4	1	1	2	2	5	3
Jorge Wilsterman	1–2	1–1	–	4	0	1	3	3	8	1

FINAL

1st leg. Maracaná, Rio de Janeiro, 13–11–1981, 114 000. Referee: Esposito, Argentina

FLAMENGO 2 (Zico 12 30)
COBRELOA 1 (Merello 65)

Flamengo – Raul – Leandro, Figueiredo, Mozer, Junior – Andrade, Adilio, Zico – Lico (Varoninho), Nunes, Tita

Cobreloa – Wirth – Tabilo, Rojas, Soto, Escobar – Alarcón, Jiménez, Merello – Muñoz (Gómez), Siviero, Puebla

2nd leg. Estadio Nacional, Santiago, 20–11–1981, 61 000. Referee: Barreto, Urug

COBRELOA 1 (Merello 79)
FLAMENGO 0

Cobreloa – Wirth – Tabilo, Jiménez, Soto, Escobar – Merello, Alarcón, Gómez R – Puebla, Siviero, Olivera

Flamengo – Raul – Leandro, Figueiredo, Mozer, Junior – Adilio, Andrade, Zico – Lico, Nunes, Tita

Play–off. Centenario, Montevideo, 23–11–1981 35 000. Referee: Cerullo, Uruguay

FLAMENGO 2 (Zico 18 79)
COBRELOA 0

Flamengo – Raul – Leandro, Marinho, Mozer, Junior – Andrade, Adilio, Zico – Tita, Nunes (Anselmo), Lico

Cobreloa – Wirth – Tabilo, Páez (Munoz), Soto, Escobar – Merello, Jiménez, Alarcón – Puebla, Siviero, Olivera

Top scorer: Zico, Flamengo 12

1982

FIRST ROUND

Group 1

	RP	St	BJ	JW	Pl	W	D	L	F	A	Pts
River Plate	–	4–1	1–0	3–0	6	4	1	1	9	2	11
The Strongest	1–0*	–	1–0	1–1	6	3	1	2	6	7	5

					Pl	W	D	L	F	A	Pts
Boca Juniors	0–0	1–0	–	2–2	6	1	2	3	3	5	4
Jorge Wilsterman	0–1	1–2	1–0	–	6	1	2	3	5	9	4

* Points awarded to River Plate

Group 2

	Pe	SP	Gr	De	Pl	W	D	L	F	A	Pts
Peñarol	–	1–0	1–0	0–0	6	4	1	1	7	3	9
Sao Paulo FC	0–1	–	2–2	2–1	6	2	2	2	7	6	6
Gremio	3–1	0–0	–	–	5	1	3	1	5	4	5
Defensor	0–3	1–3	0–0	–	5	0	2	3	2	8	2

Group 3

	To	NM	EM	Ta	Pl	W	D	L	F	A	Pts
Deportes Tolima	–	0–0	1–0	2–2	6	3	3	0	9	3	9
Nacional Medellín	0–3	–	2–0	1–0	6	3	2	1	6	4	8
Estudiantes Merida	1–1	1–3	–	1–0	6	1	2	3	3	7	4
Deportivo Tachira	0–2	0–0	0–0	–	6	0	3	3	2	6	3

Group 4

	Co	CC	LQ	Ba	Pl	W	D	L	F	A	Pts
Cobreloa	–	2–0	3–1	3–0	6	3	3	0	9	2	9
Colo Colo	0–0	–	1–0	2–0	6	3	2	1	8	5	8
LDU Quito	0–0	2–2	–	4–2	6	1	2	3	8	12	4
Barcelona	1–1	1–3	4–1	–	6	1	1	4	8	14	3

Group 5

	Ol	Me	SA	DM	Pl	W	D	L	F	A	Pts
Olimpia	–	4–0	1–1	1–0	6	4	2	0	12	3	10
Mariano Melgar	0–3	–	3–2	2–1	6	4	0	2	9	10	8
Sol de America	1–1	0–2	–	2–1	6	2	2	2	9	8	6
Deport. Municipal	1–2	0–2	0–3	–	6	0	0	6	3	12	0

SEMI-FINALS

Group 1

	Pe	Fl	RP	Pl	W	D	L	F	A	Pts
Peñarol	–	1–0	2–1	4	4	0	0	8	3	8
Flamengo	0–1	–	4–2	4	2	0	2	7	4	4
River Plate	2–4	0–3	–	4	0	0	4	5	13	0

Group 2

	Co	Ol	To	Pl	W	D	L	F	A	Pts
Cobreloa	–	1–0	3–0	4	2	1	1	5	2	5
Olimpia	1–1	–	2–0	4	1	2	1	4	3	4
Deportes Tolima	1–0	1–1	–	4	1	1	2	2	6	3

FINAL

1st leg. Centenario, Montevideo, 26–11–82, 70 000

PENAROL 0
COBRELOA 0

Peñarol – Fernández – Diogo, Olivera, Gutiérrez, Morales – Saralegui, Bossio, Jair – Walkir Silva (Rodriguez), Morena, Ramos

Cobreloa – Wirth – Tabilo, Gómez E, Soto, Escobar – Alarcón, Merello (Puebla), Gómez R – Siviero, Letelier, Olivera (Rubio)

2nd leg. Estadio Nacional, Santiago, 30–11–82, 70 000

COBRELOA 0
PENAROL 1 (Morena 89)

Cobreloa – Wirth – Tabilo (Martinez), Soto, Gómez E, Escobar – Alarcón, Merello, Gómez R – Rubio, Siviero, Olivera (Letelier)

Peñarol – Fernández – Diogo, Gutiérrez, Olivera, Morales – Bossio, Saralegui, Jair – Vargas, Morena, Ramos (Rodriguez)

Top scorers: Morena F, Peñarol 6
Vargas, Peñarol 6

1983

FIRST ROUND

Group 1

	Es	Co	CC	FO	Pl	W	D	L	F	A	Pts
Estudiantes LP	–	2–0	4–1	0–0	6	3	1	2	8	6	7
Cobreloa	3–0	–	2–0	2–1	6	3	0	3	8	6	6
Colo Colo	1–0	2–1	–	1–0	6	3	0	3	5	8	6
Ferrocarril Oeste	1–2	1–0	1–0	–	6	2	1	3	4	5	5

Group 2

	Gr	Fl	Bo	Bl	Pl	W	D	L	F	A	Pts
Gremio	–	1–1	3–1	2–0	6	5	1	0	13	4	11
Flamengo	1–3	–	5–2	7–1	6	2	2	2	15	10	6
Bolivar	1–2	3–1	–	6–0	6	2	0	4	13	14	4
Blooming	0–2	0–0	3–0	–	6	1	1	4	4	17	3

Group 3

	AC	To	Un	Al	Pl	W	D	L	F	A	Pts
America Cali	–	1–1	2–0	2–0	6	4	2	0	10	3	10
Deportes Tolima	0–2	–	1–1	0–0	6	1	4	1	5	6	6
Universitario	1–1	2–2	–	0–0	6	0	4	2	5	8	4
Alianza	1–2	0–1	2–1	–	6	1	2	3	3	6	4

Group 4

	SC	NQ	Ba	Ta	Pl	W	D	L	F	A	Pts
At. San Cristobal	–	1–0	2–0	2–0	6	3	2	1	8	4	8
Nacional Quito	1–0	–	3–1	3–0	6	3	1	2	7	4	7
Barcelona	3–3	2–0	–	–	5	1	2	2	7	9	4
Deportivo Tachira	0–0	0–0	1–1	–	5	0	3	2	1	6	3

Group 5

	Na	Wa	NA	Ol	Pl	W	D	L	F	A	Pts
Nacional Mon'deo	–	1–1	4–2	3–0	6	4	1	1	12	4	9
Wanderers	1–0	–	3–1	0–0	6	3	3	0	9	5	9
Nacional Asuncion	0–3	1–1	–	2–1	6	1	2	3	6	12	4
Olimpia	0–1	2–3	0–0	–	6	0	2	4	3	9	2

Play-off
Nacional Montevideo .... 2–0 .... Wanderers

SEMI-FINALS

Group 1

	Pe	Na	SC	Pl	W	D	L	F	A	Pts
Peñarol	–	2–0	1–0	4	3	1	0	5	1	7
Nacional Montevideo	1–2	–	5–1	4	2	0	2	8	6	4
Atletico San Cristobal	0–0	1–2	–	4	0	1	3	2	8	1

Group 2

	Gr	Es	AC	Pl	W	D	L	F	A	Pts
Gremio	–	2–1	2–1	4	2	1	1	7	6	5
Estudiantes LP	3–3	–	2–0	4	1	2	1	6	5	4
America Cali	1–0	0–0	–	4	1	1	2	2	4	3

FINAL

1st leg. Centenario, Montevideo, 22–07–83, 65 000. Referee: Nitti, Argentina

PENAROL 1 (Morena 35)
GREMIO 1 (Tita 12)

Peñarol – Fernández – Montelongo, Olivera, Gutiérrez, Diogo – Salazar, Bossio, Saralegui – Walkir Silva (Villareal), Morena, Ramos

Gremio – Mazaropi – Paulo Roberto, Baidek, De León, Casemiro – China, Osvaldo, Tita – Renato, Caio (César), Tarciso

2nd leg. Olimpico, Porto Alegre, 28–07–83, 75 000. Referee: Perez, Peru

GREMIO 2 (Caio 9, Cesar 87)
PENAROL 1 (Morena 70)

Gremio – Mazaropi – Paulo Roberto, Baidek, De León, Casemiro – Osvaldo, China, Tita – Renato, Caio (César), Tarciso

Peñarol – Fernández – Montelongo, Olivera, Gutiérrez, Diogo – Saralegui, Bossio, Salazar – Walkir Silva (Peirano), Morena, Ramos

Top scorers: Luzardo, Nacional Montevideo 8
Cabbera, Nacional Montevideo 8

1984

FIRST ROUND

Group 1

	In	Ol	SL	Es	Pl	W	D	L	F	A	Pts
Independiente	–	3–2	2–0	4–1	6	4	1	1	11	5	9
Olimpia	1–0	–	0–0	2–1	6	4	1	1	8	5	9

					Pl	W	D	L	F	A	Pts
Sportivo Luqueño	0–1	1–2	–	0–0	6	0	3	3	2	6	3
Estudiantes LP	1–1	0–1	1–1	–	6	0	3	3	4	9	3

Group 2

	UC	Bl	Bo	OH	Pl	W	D	L	F	A	Pts
Univ. Catolica	–	0–0	3–1	2–0	6	4	1	1	11	5	9
Blooming	1–2	–	2–1	3–0	6	3	2	1	10	6	8
Bolivar	3–2	0–0	–	5–1	6	2	2	2	10	8	6
O'Higgins	0–2	3–4	0–0	–	6	0	1	5	4	16	1

Group 3

	Fl	AC	AJ	Sa	Pl	W	D	L	F	A	Pts
Flamengo	–	4–2	3–1	4–1	6	5	1	0	19	6	11
America Cali	1–1	–	2–0	1–0	6	3	1	2	8	9	7
Atletico Junior	1–2	4–1	–	0–3	6	2	0	4	9	12	4
Santos	0–5	0–1	1–3	–	6	1	0	5	5	14	2

Group 4

	Na	NQ	Da	NO	Pl	W	D	L	F	A	Pts
Nacional Mon'deo	–	1–1	1–0	6–0	6	4	1	1	13	5	9
Nacional Quito	3–1	–	3–0	3–1	6	3	2	1	12	6	8
Danubio	0–1	1–0	–	5–1	6	2	1	3	8	8	5
Nueve de Octubre	1–3	2–2	2–2	–	6	0	2	4	7	21	2

Group 5

	UM	SC	Po	Me	Pl	W	D	L	F	A	Pts
ULA Merida	–	0–1	2–0	1–0	6	4	0	2	6	4	8
Sporting Cristal	2–0	–	2–1	3–2	6	4	0	2	8	6	8
Portuguesa	1–2	1–0	–	4–0	6	3	0	3	9	7	6
Mariano Melgar	0–1	2–0	1–2	–	6	1	0	5	5	11	2

Play-off
ULA Merida .... 2–1 .... Sporting Cristal

SEMI-FINALS

Group 1

	In	Na	UC	Pl	W	D	L	F	A	Pts
Independiente	–	1–0	2–1	4	2	2	0	4	2	6
Nacional Montevideo	1–1	–	2–0	3	1	1	1	3	2	3
Universidad Catolica	0–0	–	–	3	0	1	2	1	4	1

Group 2

	Gr	Fl	UM	Pl	W	D	L	F	A	Pts
Gremio	–	5–1	6–1	4	3	0	1	14	5	6
Flamengo	3–1	–	2–1	4	3	0	1	9	7	6
ULA Merida	0–2	0–3	–	4	0	0	4	2	13	0

Play-off
Gremio .... 0–0 .... Flamengo

Gremio qualify due to a better goal difference

FINAL
1st leg. Olimpico, Porto Alegre, 24–07–84, 55 000
GREMIO 0
INDEPENDIENTE 1 (Burruchaga 24)

Gremio – Joao Marcos – Casemiro, Baidek, De León, Paulo César – China, Luis Carlos, Osvaldo – Renato, Guilherme (Gilson), Tarciso

Independiente – Goyén – Clausen, Villaverde, Trossero, Enrique – Giusti, Marangoni, Bochini, Burruchaga – Bufarini, Barberón (Reinoso)

2nd leg. Cordero, Avellaneda, 27–07–84, 75 000
INDEPENDIENTE 0
GREMIO 0

Independiente – Goyén – Clausen, Villaverde, Trossero, Enrique – Giusti, Marangoni, Bochini (Zimmermann) – Bufarini, Burruchaga, Barberón

Gremio – Joao Marcos – Casemiro, Baidek, De León, Paulo César – China, Luis Carlos, Osvaldo – Renato, Guilherme, Tarciso

Top scorer: Tita, Flamengo 8

1985

FIRST ROUND

Group 1

	AJ	FO	Fl	VG	Pl	W	D	L	F	A	Pts
Argentinos Jun.	–	0–1	1–0	2–2	6	4	1	1	9	5	9
Ferrocarril Oeste	1–3	–	1–0	2–0	6	4	1	1	7	3	9
Fluminense	0–1	0–0	–	0–0	6	0	3	3	3	6	3
Vasco da Gama	1–2	0–2	3–3	–	6	0	3	3	6	11	3

Play-off
Argentinos Juniors .... 3–1 .... Ferrocarril Oeste

Group 2

	Bl	OP	Ta	DI	Pl	W	D	L	F	A	Pts
Blooming	–	1–1	6–3	8–0	6	5	1	0	20	4	11
Oriente Petrolero	0–1	–	3–2	3–1	6	3	2	1	11	6	8
Deportivo Tachira	0–1	1–1	–	0–0	6	1	2	3	9	12	4
Deportivo Italia	0–3	0–3	1–3	–	6	0	1	5	2	20	1

Group 3

	Pe	CC	Ma	BV	Pl	W	D	L	F	A	Pts
Peñarol	–	3–1	1–0	1–0	6	5	1	0	10	3	11
Colo Colo	1–2	–	2–0	2–0	6	3	0	3	10	8	6
Magallanes	1–1	1–3	–	2–1	6	2	1	3	5	8	5
Bella Vista	0–2	2–1	0–1	–	6	1	0	5	3	9	2

Group 4

	AC	CP	Mi	Gu	Pl	W	D	L	F	A	Pts
America Cali	–	2–0	0–0	2–1	6	2	4	0	5	2	8
Cerro Porteño	0–0	–	0–0	3–1	6	2	3	1	5	3	7
Millonarios	0–0	0–2	–	5–1	6	1	3	2	5	5	5
Guarani Asuncion	1–1	0–0	2–0	–	6	1	2	3	6	11	4

Group 5

	NQ	NO	Un	SB	Pl	W	D	L	F	A	Pts
Nacional Quito	–	3–1	4–1	2–0	5	5	0	0	12	3	10
Nueve de Octubre	0–1	–	1–0	4–0	4	2	0	2	6	4	4
Universitario	–	–	–	4–0	4	2	0	2	7	5	4
Sport Boys	1–2	–	0–2	–	5	0	0	5	1	14	0

SEMI-FINALS

Group 1

	AJ	In	Bl	Pl	W	D	L	F	A	Pts
Argentinos Juniors	–	2–2	1–0	4	2	2	0	6	4	6
Independiente	1–2	–	2–0	4	1	2	1	6	5	4
Blooming	1–1	1–1	–	4	0	2	2	2	5	2

Group 2

	AC	NQ	Pe	Pl	W	D	L	F	A	Pts
America Cali	–	5–0	4–0	4	2	1	1	10	3	5
Nacional Quito	2–0	–	2–0	4	2	0	2	4	7	4
Peñarol	1–1	2–0	–	4	1	1	2	3	7	3

FINAL
1st leg. Monumental, Buenos Aires, 17–10–85, 50 000. Referee: Escobar, Paraguay
ARGENTINOS JUNIORS 1 (Comisso 40)
AMERICA CALI 0

Argentinos – Vidallé – Villalba, Pavoni, Olguin, Domenech – Comisso, Batista, Corsi, Castro – Borghi, Ereros (Pellegrini)

America – Falcioni – Porras (Chaparro), Soto, Viafara, Valencia – Gonzáles Aquino, Cabañas, Penagos (Escobar) – De Avila, Ortiz, Gareca

2nd leg. Pascual Guerrero, Cali, 22–10–85, 50 000. Referee: Felix, Brazil
AMERICA CALI 1 (Ortiz 3)
ARGENTINOS JUNIORS 0

America – Falcioni – Valencia, Soto, Viafara, Chaparro – Sarmiento, Gonzáles Aquino, Cabanas – Ortiz (De Avila), Gareca, Bataglia (Herrera)

Argentinos – Vidallé – Villalba, Pavoni, Olguin, Domenech – Videla, Batista, Comisso – Castro (Lopez J) – Borghi, Ereros (Valdez)

Play–off. Defensores del Chaco, Asuncion, 24–10–85, 35 000. Referee: Silva, Chile

ARGENTINOS JUNIORS	1	(Comisso 37)
AMERICA	1	(Gareca 42)

Argentinos Juniors won 5–4 on penalties

Argentinos – Vidallé – Villalba (Mayor), Pellegrini (Lemme), Pavoni, Domenech – Olguin, Batista, Corsi, Comisso – Borghi, Videla
America – Falcioni – Valencia, Soto, Viafara, Chaparro – Sarmiento, Gonzáles Aquino, Cabañas – Ortiz (De Avila), Gareca, Bataglia (Herrera)

1986

FIRST ROUND

Group 1

	RP	Wa	BJ	Pe	Pl	W	D	L	F	A	Pts
River Plate	–	4–2	1–0	3–1	6	5	1	0	13	4	11
Wanderers	0–2	–	2–0	1–0	6	3	0	3	10	10	6
Boca Juniors	1–1	3–2	–	1–1	6	2	2	2	7	8	6
Peñarol	0–2	1–3	1–2	–	6	0	1	5	4	12	1

Group 2

	AC	DC	Co	UC	Pl	W	D	L	F	A	Pts
America Cali	–	0–0	0–0	2–1	6	3	3	0	8	4	9
Deportivo Cali	0–1	–	1–1	3–1	6	2	3	1	8	5	7
Cobresal	2–2	1–1	–	1–1	6	1	5	0	6	5	7
Univ. Catolica	1–3	1–3	0–1	–	6	0	1	5	5	13	1

Group 3

	Bo	JW	Un	UC	Pl	W	D	L	F	A	Pts
Bolivar	–	2–0	4–0	2–1	6	4	1	1	12	7	9
Jorge Wilsterman	1–2	–	4–0	2–0	6	3	0	3	11	8	6
Universitario	3–0	1–2	–	2–0	6	3	0	3	9	11	6
Univ. Cajamarca	2–2	3–2	1–3	–	6	1	1	4	7	13	3

Group 4

	Ba	DQ	Co	Ba	Pl	W	D	L	F	A	Pts
Barcelona	–	3–3	1–1	1–0	6	2	4	0	7	5	8
Deportivo Quito	0–0	–	2–1	3–1	6	2	3	1	12	11	7
Coritiba	0–0	3–1	–	–	5	1	3	1	6	5	5
Bangu	1–2	3–3	1–1	–	5	0	2	3	6	10	2

Group 5

	Ol	NA	Pl	W	D	L	F	A	Pts
Olimpia	–	3–1	2	2	0	0	5	2	4
Nacional Asuncion	1–2	–	2	0	0	2	2	5	0

The Venezuelan entrants withdrew

SEMI-FINALS

Group 1

	RP	AJ	Ba	Pl	W	D	L	F	A	Pts
River Plate	–	0–2	4–1	4	2	1	1	7	3	5
Argentinos Juniors	0–0	–	1–0	4	2	1	1	3	1	5
Barcelona	0–3	1–0	–	4	1	0	3	2	8	2

Play-off
River Plate .... 0–0 .... Argentinos Juniors
River Plate win due to a better goal difference

Group 2

	AC	Ol	Bo	Pl	W	D	L	F	A	Pts
America Cali	–	1–0	2–1	4	2	1	1	4	4	5
Olimpia	1–1	–	3–1	4	1	2	1	5	4	4
Bolivar	2–0	1–1	–	4	1	1	2	5	6	3

FINAL

1st leg. Pascual Guerrero, Cali, 22–10–1986, 55 000. Referee: Cardellino, Urug

AMERICA CALI	1	(Cabanas 47)
RIVER PLATE	2	(Funes 22, Alonso 25)

America – Falcioni – Valencia, Espinoza, Esterilla, Porras – Gonzáles Aquino, Ischia (De Avila), Cabañas – Ortiz (Escobar), Gareca, Bataglia
River Plate – Pumpido – Gordillo, Gutiérrez, Ruggeri, Montenegro – Enrique, Gallego, Alonso (Sperandio) – Alfaro (Troglio), Alzamendi, Funes

2nd leg. Monumental, Buenos Aires, 29–10–1986, 85 000. Referee: Wright, Brazil

RIVER PLATE	1	(Funes 70)
AMERICA CALI	0	

River Plate – Pumpido – Gordillo, Gutiérrez, Ruggeri, Montenegro – Enrique, Gallego, Alonso – Alfaro (Gomez), Alzamendi (Sperandio), Funes
America – Falcioni – Valencia (De Avila), Espinoza, Luna, Porras – Gonzáles Aquino (Escobar), Ischia, Cabañas – Ortiz, Gareca, Bataglia

1987

FIRST ROUND

Group 1

	In	RC	Ta	EM	Pl	W	D	L	F	A	Pts
Independiente	–	3–1	5–0	2–0	6	4	1	1	13	4	9
Rosario Central	0–0	–	3–2	5–2	6	3	2	1	12	7	8
Deportivo Tachira	3–2	0–0	–	3–2	6	3	1	2	11	12	7
Estudiantes Merida	0–1	0–3	0–3	–	6	0	0	6	4	17	0

Group 2

	AC	DC	St	OP	Pl	W	D	L	F	A	Pts
America Cali	–	1–0	6–0	3–1	6	3	2	1	13	5	8
Deportivo Cali	2–1	–	4–0	5–1	6	4	0	2	13	5	8
The Strongest	1–1	2–1	–	3–2	6	2	1	3	7	16	5
Oriente Petrolero	1–1	0–1	2–1	–	6	1	1	4	7	14	3

Play-off
America Cali .... 0–0 (4–2p) .... Deportivo Cali

Group 3

	Co	CC	Gu	SP	Pl	W	D	L	F	A	Pts
Cobreloa	–	1–0	3–1	3–1	6	3	2	1	8	4	8
Colo Colo	0–0	–	2–0	2–2	6	2	3	1	6	4	7
Guarani Campinas	0–0	0–0	–	3–1	6	1	3	2	6	8	5
Sao Paulo FC	2–1	1–2	2–2	–	6	1	2	3	9	13	4

Group 4

	Ba	Ol	NQ	SA	Pl	W	D	L	F	A	Pts
Barcelona	–	3–2	2–1	1–0	6	4	0	2	8	7	8
Olimpia	1–0	–	2–0	2–1	6	3	1	2	9	10	7
Nacional Quito	2–0	4–0	–	4–1	6	3	0	3	12	7	6
Sol de America	1–2	2–2	2–1	–	6	1	1	4	7	12	3

Group 5

	Pe	Pr	Al	SA	Pl	W	D	L	F	A	Pts
Peñarol	–	3–2	2–0	2–0	6	4	2	0	10	4	10
Progreso	1–1	–	0–0	3–0	6	1	3	2	7	7	5
Alianza	0–1	0–0	–	0–0	6	1	3	2	2	4	5
Colégio San Augst.	1–1	3–1	1–2	–	6	1	2	3	5	9	4

SEMI-FINALS

Group 1

	Pe	RP	In	Pl	W	D	L	F	A	Pts
Peñarol	–	0–0	3–0	4	2	1	1	7	3	5
River Plate	1–0	–	0–0	4	1	2	1	2	2	4
Independiente	2–4	2–1	–	4	1	1	2	4	8	3

Group 2

	AC	Co	Ba	Pl	W	D	L	F	A	Pts
America Cali	–	1–1	4–0	4	2	2	0	9	3	6
Cobreloa	2–2	–	3–0	4	2	2	0	8	3	6
Barcelona	0–2	0–2	–	4	0	0	4	0	11	0

FINAL

1st leg. Pascual Guerrero, Cali, 21–10–87, 45 000. Referee: Writh, Brazil

AMERICA CALI	2	(Bataglia, Cabañas)
PENAROL	0	

America – Falcioni – Valencia, Espinosa, Aponte, Porras – Luna, Santin, Herrera (Escobar) – Cabañas, Gareca (Maturana), Bataglia
Peñarol – Preyra – Herrera, Trasante, Rotti, Dominguez – Perdomo, Matosas (Da Silva), Viera, Vidal (Villar) – Aguirre, Cabrera

2nd leg. Centenario, Montevideo, 28–10–87, 70 000. Referee: Calabria, Argentina
PENAROL 2 (Aguirre 58, Villar 86)
AMERICA CALI 1 (Cabañas 19)
Peñarol – Preyra – Rotti (Goncalvez), Trasante, Herrera, Perdomo – Dominguez, Vidal, Da Silva – Aguirre, Viera, Cabrera (Villar)
America – Falcioni – Aponte, Espinosa, Valencia, Luna – Porras, Bataglia, Santin – Gareca, Cabañas, Ortiz (Herrera)

Play-off. Estadio Nacional, Santiago, 31–10–87, 30 000. Referee: Silva, Chile
PENAROL 1 (Aguirre 119)
AMERICA CALI 0
Peñarol – Pereyra – Rotti, Trasante, Herrera, Dominguez – Da Silva, Perdomo (Goncalves), Viera, Vidal (Villar) – Aguirre, Cabrera
America – Falcioni – Valencia, Espinoza, Aponte, Ampudia – Luna, Santin, Cabañas – Ortiz, Gareca (Esterilla), Bataglia

1988

COPA LIBERTADORES

FIRST ROUND

Group 1

	UC	CC	Ma	Ta	Pl	W	D	L	F	A	Pts
Univ. Catolica	–	1–0	2–1	3–1	6	4	2	0	9	4	10
Colo Colo	2–2	–	1–0	2–0	6	4	1	1	7	3	9
Maritimo	0–0	0–1	–	1–1	6	0	3	3	2	5	3
Deportivo Tachira	0–1	0–1	0–0	–	6	0	2	4	2	8	2

Group 2

	Ne	SL	Ba	Fi	Pl	W	D	L	F	A	Pts
Newell's Old Boys	–	0–0	3–0	1–0	6	2	4	0	5	1	8
San Lorenzo	0–0	–	2–1	2–0	6	3	2	1	6	4	8
Barcelona	0–0	2–0	–	4–2	6	3	1	2	9	8	7
Filanbanco	1–1	1–2	1–2	–	6	0	1	5	5	12	1

Play-off to determine second round placement
Newell's Old Boys .... 1–0 .... San Lorenzo

Group 3

	AC	Na	Mi	Wa	Pl	W	D	L	F	A	Pts
America Cali	–	0–0	2–1	1–0	6	4	1	1	8	6	9
Nacional Mon'deo	2–0	–	4–1	1–0	6	3	2	1	8	7	8
Millonarios	2–3	6–1	–	3–0	6	2	0	4	14	12	4
Wanderers	1–2	0–0	2–1	–	6	1	1	4	3	8	3

Group 4

	OP	Bo	CP	Ol	Pl	W	D	L	F	A	Pts
Oriente Petrolero	–	2–1	2–2	1–0	6	3	1	2	8	8	7
Bolivar	3–1	–	2–0	2–0	6	3	0	3	12	10	6
Cerro Porteño	1–0	3–2	–	0–0	6	2	2	2	6	7	6
Olimpia	1–2	4–2	1–0	–	6	2	1	3	6	7	5

Group 5

	Gu	Un	SR	Al	Pl	W	D	L	F	A	Pts
Guarani Campinas	–	1–1	4–1	1–0	6	3	2	1	9	5	8
Universitario	1–1	–	1–0	2–0	6	2	4	0	5	2	8
Sport Recife	0–1	0–0	–	5–0	6	2	1	3	7	6	5
Alianza	2–1	0–0	0–1	–	6	1	1	4	2	10	3

SECOND ROUND

Universidad Catolica .... 1–1 0–0 .... **Nacional Montevideo**
America Cali .... 1–0 2–2 .... Universitario
Oriente Petrolero .... 2–1 0–0 .... Colo Colo
San Lorenzo .... 1–1 1–0 .... Guarani Campinas
Bolivar .... 1–0 0–1 (2–3p) .... **Newell's Old Boys**
Peñarol .... Bye

QUARTER-FINALS

Newell's Old Boys .... 1–1 1–2 .... **Nacional Montevideo**
San Lorenzo .... 1–0 0–0 .... Peñarol
America Cali .... 2–0 1–1 .... America Cali

SEMI-FINALS

Nacional Montevideo ..... 1–0 1–1 .... America Cali
Newell's Old Boys .... 1–0 2–1 .... San Lorenzo

FINAL

1st leg. Cordoviola, Rosario, 19–10–88, 45 000. Referee: Silva, Chile
NEWELL'S OLD BOYS 1 (Gabrich 60)
NACIONAL MONTEVIDEO 0
Newell's – Scoponi – Llop, Theiler, Pautasso, Sensini – Martino (Fullana), Franco, Alfaro, Rossi – Batistuta, Almiron (Gabrich)
Nacional – Seré – Pintos Saldanha, Revelez, De León, Soca – Lemos, Ostolaza, Cardaccio, Castro – Vargas (Carreño), De Lima

2nd leg. Centenario, Montevideo, 26–10–88, 75 000. Referee: Coelho, Brazil
NACIONAL MONTEVIDEO 3 (Vargas 10, Ostolaza 30, De Leon 81)
NEWELL'S OLD BOYS 0
Nacional – Seré – Pintos Saldanha, Revelez, De León, Soca – Lemos, Ostolaza, Cardaccio, Castro (Moran) – Vargas (Carreño), De Lima
Newell's – Scoponi – Llop (Ramos), Theiler, Pautasso, Sensini – Martino, Alfaro (Almiron), Franco, Rossi – Batistuta, Gabrich

SUPERCOPA

FIRST ROUND

Racing Club .... 2–0 0–0 .. Santos
Boca Juniors .... 1–0 0–2 .. **Gremio**
Olimpia .... 2–0 0–4 .. **River Plate**
Nacional Mon'deo .... Bye
Estudiantes LP .... 1–0 0–3 .. **Flamengo**
Peñarol .... 1–0 0–2 .. **Argentinos Juniors**
Independiente .... 1–2 0–1 .. **Cruzeiro**

QUARTER-FINALS

Racing Club .... Bye
Gremio .... 1–0 1–3 ... **River Plate**
Nacional Montevideo ..... 3–0 2–0 ... Flamengo
Cruzeiro .... 1–0 1–0 ... Argentinos Juniors

SEMI-FINALS

Racing Club .... 2–1 1–1 ... River Plate
Nacional Montevideo .... 3–2 0–1 ... **Cruzeiro**

FINAL

1st leg. Mozart y Cuyo, Buenos Aires, 13–06–1988, 50 000
RACING CLUB 2 (Fernandez 44, Colombatti 89)
CRUZEIRO 1 (Robson 36)
Racing – Fillol – Vázquez, Fabbri, Acuña (Perez), Costas – Ludueña, Olarán, Fernandez – Colombatti, Paz, Catálan (Bello)
Cruzeiro – Wellington – Ronaldo, Heraldo, Heriberto, Gilmar – Ademir, Vladimir, Anderson (Denilson) – Eder, Careca II, Robson

2nd leg. Mineirao, Belo Horizonte, 18–06–1988
CRUZEIRO 1 (Robson 82)
RACING CLUB 1 (Catalan 44)
Cruzeiro – Wellington – Balu, Heraldo, Gilmar, Ademir – Eder, Vladimir, Anderson – Heriberto (Ramondal), Robson, Careca
Racing – Fillol – Vázquez, Fabbri, Acuña, Costas – Ludueña, Olarán, Fernandez – Colombatti, Paz (Perez), Catálan (Bello)

RECOPA

1st leg, Centenario, Montevideo, 31–01–1989
Nacional Montevideo 1 (Fonseca)
Racing Club 0

2nd leg, Mozart y Cuyo, Buenos Aires, 6–02–1989
Racing Club 0
Nacional Montevideo 0

1989

COPA LIBERTADORES

FIRST ROUND

Group 1

	Co	SA	Ol	CC	Pl	W	D	L	F	A	Pts
Cobreloa	–	1–0	2–0	2–0	6	3	2	1	7	4	8
Sol de America	0–0	–	5–4	1–0	6	2	2	2	7	8	6
Olimpia	2–0	0–0	–	2–0	6	2	1	3	8	9	5
Colo Colo	2–2	3–1	2–0	–	6	2	1	3	7	8	5

Group 2

	Ba	Ta	IP	Ma	Pl	W	D	L	F	A	Pts
EC Bahia	–	4–1	1–0	3–2	6	4	2	0	11	5	10
Deportivo Tachira	1–1	–	1–0	2–0	6	3	1	2	7	8	7
Internacional PA	1–2	3–1	–	3–0	6	2	1	3	8	6	5
Maritimo	0–0	0–1	1–1	–	6	0	2	4	3	10	2

Group 3

	Mi	NM	DQ	Em	Pl	W	D	L	F	A	Pts
Millonarios	–	1–1	3–1	4–1	6	4	2	0	12	3	10
Nacional Medellín	0–2	–	2–1	3–1	6	2	3	1	8	7	7
Deportivo Quito	0–0	1–1	–	1–0	6	1	2	3	4	7	4
Emelec	0–2	1–1	1–0	–	6	1	1	4	4	11	3

Group 4

	BJ	RC	Un	SC	Pl	W	D	L	F	A	Pts
Boca Juniors	–	3–2	2–0	4–3	6	3	1	2	9	7	7
Racing Club	0–0	–	2–0	2–0	6	3	1	2	9	6	7
Universitario	1–0	2–1	–	4–0	6	3	0	3	7	6	6
Sporting Cristal	1–0	1–2	1–0	–	6	2	0	4	6	12	4

Play–off for second round placement
Boca Juniors .... 3–1 .... Racing Club

Group 5

	Pe	Da	Bo	St	Pl	W	D	L	F	A	Pts
Peñarol	–	2–0	5–0	1–1	6	3	1	2	11	9	7
Danubio	4–1	–	1–0	1–0	6	3	0	3	7	7	6
Bolivar	3–0	3–1	–	0–0	6	2	2	2	6	7	6
The Strongest	1–2	1–0	0–0	–	6	1	3	2	3	4	5

SECOND ROUND

At. Nacional Medellín .... 2–0 1–2 ... Racing Club
Bolivar .... 1–0 2–3 (3–4p) **Millonarios**
Deportivo Quito .... 0–0 0–1 ... **Cobreloa**
Nacional Montevideo .... 1–3 0–0 ... **Danubio**
Internacional PA .... 6–2 2–1 ... Peñarol
Universitario .... 1–1 1–2 ... **EC Bahia**
Sol de America .... 3–0 0–3 (3–2p) Deportivo Tachira
Olimpia .... 2–0 3–5 (7–6p) Boca Juniors

QUARTER-FINALS

At. Nacional Medellín .... 1–0 1–1 ... Millonarios
Cobreloa .... 0–2 1–2 ... **Danubio**
Internacional PA .... 1–0 0–0 ... EC Bahia
Olimpia .... 2–0 4–4 ... Sol de America

SEMI-FINALS

Danubio .... 0–0 0–6 ... **At. Nacional Medellín**
Olimpia .... 0–1 3–2 (5–3p) Internacional Porto Alegre

FINAL

1st leg. Defensores del Chaco, Asuncion, 24–05–89, 50 000. Referee: Wright, Braz

OLIMPIA 2 (Bobadilla 36, Sanabria 60)
AT. NACIONAL MEDELLIN 0

Olimpia – Almeida – Miño, Benitez, Chamas, Krausemann – Sanabria (Balbuena), Guasch, Neffa, Bobadilla – Amarilla, Mendoza (Gonzalez)
Nacional – Higuita – Gómez, Perea, Escobar, Villa (Carmona) – Pérez, Alvárez, Fajardo, Garcia – Arango (Arboleda), Usurriaga

2nd leg. El Campin, Bogotá, 31–05–89, 50 000. Referee: Loustau, Argentina

AT. NACIONAL MEDELLIN 2 (OG 46, Usurriaga 64)
OLIMPIA 0

Nacional won 5–4 on penalties

Nacional – Higuita – Carmona, Perea, Escobar, Gómez – Alvárez, Garcia, Fajardo (Arboleda) – Arango (Pérez), Usurriaga, Trellez
Olimpia – Almeida – Miño, Benitez, Chamas, Krausemann – Sanabria, Guasch, Bobadilla (Balbuena), Neffa – Amarilla, Mendoza
Top scorer: Amarilla, Olimpia 11

SUPERCOPA

FIRST ROUND

Boca Juniors .... Bye
Racing Club .... Bye
Estudiantes LP .... 3–0 0–2 .... Peñarol
River Plate .... 2–1 1–2 (1–4p) . **Gremio**
Flamengo .... 0–1 1–2 .... **Argentinos Juniors**
Olimpia .... 2–0 0–3 .... **Cruzeiro**
Nacional Mont'deo .... 2–1 0–2 .... **Nacional Medellín**
Santos .... 1–2 0–2 .... **Independiente**

QUARTER-FINALS

Boca Juniors .... 0–0 2–1 .... Racing Club
Gremio .... 0–1 3–0 .... Estudiantes LP
Cruzeiro .... 1–1 0–2 .... **Argentinos Juniors**
At. Nacional Medellín .... 2–2 0–2 .... **Independiente**

SEMI-FINALS

Gremio .... 0–0 0–2 .... **Boca Juniors**
Argentinos Juniors .... 0–1 1–2 .... **Independiente**

FINAL

1st leg. La Bombonera, Buenos Aires, 23–11–1989, 23 000

BOCA JUNIORS 0
INDEPENDIENTE 0

Boca Juniors – Navarro – Montoya, Simon, Cuciuffo, Stafuza – Giunta, Marchesini, Latorre – Marangoni, Graciani, Perazzo (Berti)
Independiente – Pereira – Morales, Delgado (Lozano), Bianco, Monzon – Ludueña, Altamirano, Moreno – Giusti, Insua, Reggiardo (Ubaldi)

2nd leg. Cordero, Buenos Aires, 29–11–1989, 60000

INDEPENDIENTE 0
BOCA JUNIORS 0

Independiente – Pereira – Morales, Delgado, Bianco, Monzon – Ludueña, Altamirano, Moreno (Artime) – Giusti, Insua, Reggiardo (Bochini)
Boca Juniors – Navarro – Montoya, Simon, Cuciuffo, Stafuza – Giunta, Marchesini, Perazzo (Berti) – Marangoni, Latorre, Graciani

Boca Juniors won 5–3 on penalties

RECOPA

Orange Bowl, Miami, 17–03–1990, 9000

Boca Juniors 1 (Latorre)
At. Nacional Medellin 0

1990

COPA LIBERTADORES

FIRST ROUND

Group 1

	Em	St	Ba	OP	Pl	W	D	L	F	A	Pts
Emelec	–	1–0	3–1	2–2	6	2	2	2	9	8	6
The Strongest	4–3	–	2–1	2–0	6	3	0	3	8	7	6
Barcelona	0–0	1–0	–	2–1	6	2	2	2	6	7	6
Oriente Petrolero	1–0	1–0	1–1	–	6	2	2	2	6	7	6

Play-off
Barcelona .... 3–1 2–3 ... Oriente Petrolero

Group 2

	In	RP	Pl	W	D	L	F	A	Pts
Independiente	–	1–0	2	1	1	0	1	0	3
River Plate	0–0	–	2	0	1	1	0	1	1

The Colombian representatives withdrew

Group 3

	CC	UC	UH	SC	Pl	W	D	L	F	A	Pts
Colo Colo	–	0–0	3–1	2–0	6	3	2	1	9	5	8
Univ. Catolica	2–1	–	2–2	2–0	6	2	3	1	6	4	7
Union Huaral	1–1	1–0	–	0–3	6	1	3	2	5	9	5
Sporting Cristal	1–2	0–0	0–0	–	6	1	2	3	4	6	4

Group 4

	Pr	De	Pe	MG	Pl	W	D	L	F	A	Pts
Progreso	–	1–1	2–0	1–1	6	2	3	1	7	4	7
Defensor	0–0	–	1–0	3–1	6	2	3	1	5	3	7
Pepeganga	1–0	1–0	–	2–1	6	3	0	3	4	5	6
Mineros Guyana	1–3	0–0	1–0	–	6	1	2	3	5	9	4

Play-off to determine second round placement
Progreso .... 4–0 .... Defensor

Group 5

	Ol	CP	VG	Gr	Pl	W	D	L	F	A	Pts
Olimpia	–	2–1	2–1	1–0	6	3	1	2	9	8	7
Cerro Porteño	3–2	–	1–1	3–1	6	2	2	2	8	8	6
Vasco da Gama	1–0	2–0	–	0–0	6	2	2	2	5	5	6
Gremio	2–2	0–0	2–0	–	6	1	3	2	5	6	5

SECOND ROUND

Olimpia .... Bye
Universidad Catolica ..... 3–1 1–1 .... The Strongest
Vasco da Gama .... 0–0 3–3 (5–4p) .. Colo Colo
Cerro Porteño .... 0–0 0–1 .... **At. Nacional Medellín**
Defensor .... 1–2 1–2 .... **River Plate**
Pepeganga .... 0–6 0–3 .... **Independiente**
Union Huaral .... 1–0 0–2 .... **Emelec**
Barcelona .... 2–0 2–2 .... Progreso

QUARTER-FINALS

Olimpia .... 2–0 4–4 .... Universidad Catolica
Vasco da Gama .... 0–0 0–1 .... **At. Nacional Medellín**
River Plate .... 2–0 1–1 .... Independiente
Emelec .... 0–0 0–1 .... **Barcelona**

SEMI-FINALS

At. Nacional Medellín .... 1–2 3–2 (1–2p) .. **Olimpia**
River Plate .... 1–0 0–1 (3–4p) .. **Barcelona**

FINAL

1st leg. Defensores del Chaco, Asuncion, 3–10–90, 35 000. Referee: Cardellino, Uruguay
OLIMPIA 2 (Amarilla 47, Samaniego 65)
BARCELONA 0

Olimpia – Almeida – Ramirez J, Fernandez, Ramirez M, Suarez – Guasch, Balbuena (Cubilla), Monzon, Gonzalez – Samaniego, Amarilla
Barcelona – Morales – Izquierdo, Martinez, Nacias, Bravo F – Saralegui, Munoz (Maldonado), Proano (Bravo D), Trobbiani – Jimenez, Acosta

2nd leg. Modelo, Guayaquil, 10–10–90, 55 000. Referee: Montalban, Peru
BARCELONA 1 (Trobbiani 61)
OLIMPIA 1 (Amarilla 80)

Barcelona – Morales – Izquierdo, Bravo.F, Macias, Guzman (Proano) – Saralegui, Bravo D, Trobbiani, Munoz – Uquillas, Acosta
Olimpia – Almeida – Ramirez J, Ramirez M, Suarez, Fernandez (Gonzalez) – Guasch, Balbuena, Jara, Monzon – Amarilla (Sanabria), Samaniego

Top scorer: Samaniego, Olimpia 7

SUPERCOPA

FIRST ROUND

River Plate .... 3–0 0–3 (3–4p) .... **Olimpia**
Cruzeiro .... 1–0 0–1 (2–4p) .... **Racing Club**
Boca Juniors .... Bye
Peñarol .... 0–0 2–2 (4–2p) .... Santos
Gremio .... 1–0 0–2 .... **Estudiantes LP**
Argentinos Jun. .... 3–1 1–3 (4–3p) .... Flamengo
Independiente .... 1–1 1–2 .... **Nacional Montevideo**

QUARTER-FINALS

Olimpia .... 1–1 3–0 .... Racing Club
Peñarol .... 0–1 2–0 .... Boca Juniors
Estudiantes LP .... Bye
Argentinos Juniors .... 2–1 1–3 .... **Nacional Montevideo**

SEMI-FINALS

Peñarol .... 2–1 0–6 .... **Olimpia**
Estudiantes LP .... 0–0 0–0 (3–5p) .... **Nacional Montevideo**

FINAL

1st leg. Montevideo, 5–01–1991, 45 000. Referee: Wright, Brazil
NACIONAL MONTEVIDEO 0
OLIMPIA 3 (Gonzalez 55, Amarilla 81, Samaniego 87)

Nacional – Sere – Gomez T, Gomez M, Revelez, Soca – Moran, Cardaccio, Lemos – Valdez D, Cabrera (Baez), Vargas (Ramos)
Olimpia – Almeida – Caceres, Ramirez, Fernandez, Suarez – Balbuena, Guasch, Monzon – Gonzalez, Amarilla, Samaniego

2nd leg. Asuncion, 11–01–1991, 40 000. Referee: Loustau, Argentina
OLIMPIA 3 (Samaniego 27, Amarilla 50, Monzon 69)
NACIONAL MONTEVIDEO 3 (Cardaccio 5, Moran 31, Wilson Nunez 34)

Olimpia – Almeida – Caceres, Ramirez, Fernandez, Suarez – Balbuena, Guasch, Monzon – Gonzalez (Villalba), Amarilla, Samaniego
Nacional – Sere – Maristal, Sarabia, Revelez, Mozo – Pena, Cardaccio, Moran – Miranda (Cabrera), Wilson Nunez, Garcia (Ramos)

RECOPA

Olimpia were declared automatic winners after winning both the Libertadores and Super Cups

1991

COPA LIBERTADORES

FIRST ROUND

Group 1

	Bo	BJ	OP	RP	Pl	W	D	L	F	A	Pts
Bolivar	–	2–0	2–0	4–1	6	3	1	2	9	5	7
Boca Juniors	0–0	–	0–0	4–3	6	2	2	2	6	6	6
Oriente Petro.	2–1	1–0	–	1–1	6	2	3	1	5	7	6
River Plate	2–0	0–2	3–1	–	6	2	1	3	10	12	5

Group 2

	CC	LQ	DC	Ba	Pl	W	D	L	F	A	Pts
Colo Colo	–	3–0	2–0	3–1	6	3	3	0	10	3	9
LDU Quito	0–0	–	4–0	0–0	6	2	2	2	5	6	6
Deport. Concep.	0–0	3–0	–	1–0	6	2	2	2	6	8	6
Barcelona	2–2	0–1	2–2	–	6	0	3	3	5	9	3

Group 3

	Fl	Co	Na	BV	Pl	W	D	L	F	A	Pts
Flamengo	–	2–0	4–0	1–1	6	3	3	0	11	4	9
Corinthians	1–1	–	0–0	4–1	6	1	4	1	7	6	6
Nacional Mon'deo	0–1	1–1	–	3–0	6	2	2	2	7	6	6
Bella Vista	2–2	1–1	0–3	–	6	0	3	3	5	14	3

Group 4

	CP	AC	Un	SB	Pl	W	D	L	F	A	Pts
Cerro Porteño	–	1–1	0–0	3–0	6	2	4	0	9	4	8
Atlet. Colegiales	1–1	–	2–0	4–1	6	2	4	0	10	5	8
Universitario	1–1	0–0	–	1–3	6	1	3	2	4	6	5
Sport Boys	1–3	2–2	0–2	–	6	1	1	4	7	15	3

Play-off to determine second round placement
Cerro Porteño .... 1–0 .... Atletico Colegiales

Group 5

	AC	NM	Ta	Ma	Pl	W	D	L	F	A	Pts
America Cali	–	1–0	3–2	2–0	6	5	1	0	10	3	11
Nacional Med'lín	0–2	–	0–0	2–2	6	2	2	2	7	7	6
Deport. Tachira	1–1	1–2	–	2–1	6	1	3	2	6	7	5
Maritimo	0–1	1–3	0–0	–	6	0	2	4	4	10	2

SECOND ROUND

Universitario .... 0–0 1–2 ... **Colo Colo**
Nacional Montevideo ..... 4–1 1–1 ... Bolivar
Deportivo Tachira .... 2–3 0–5 ... **Flamengo**
Boca Juniors .... 3–1 1–1 ... Corinthians
LDU Quito .... 2–2 0–2 ... **At. Nacional Medellin**
Deportivo Concepcion .... 0–3 3–3 ... **America Cali**
Oriente Petrolero .... 1–1 0–2 ... **Cerro Porteño**
Atletico Colegiales .... 1–1 1–3 ... **Olimpia**

QUARTER-FINALS

Colo Colo .... 4–0 0–2 ... Nacional Montevideo
Flamengo .... 2–1 0–3 ... **Boca Juniors**
America Cali .... 0–0 0–2 ... **At. Nacional Medellin**
Cerro Porteño .... 1–0 0–3 ... **Olimpia**

SEMI-FINALS

Boca Juniors .... 1–0 1–3 ... **Colo Colo**
At. Nacional Medellin .... 0–0 0–1 ... **Olimpia**

FINAL

1st leg. Defensores del Chaco, Asuncion, 29–05–1991, 48 000. Referee: Filippi, Uruguay

OLIMPIA 0
COLO COLO 0

Olimpia – Battaglia – Caceres, Fernandez, Castro, Suarez – Balbuena, Guasch, Monzon, Guirland (Cubilla) – Samaniego, Gonzalez (Villalba)
Colo Colo – Moron – Garrido, Margas, Ramirez, Vilchez – Mendoza, Espinoza, Pizarro, Peralta – Barticciotto, Martinez

2nd leg. Estadio Nacional, Santiago, 5–06–1991, 64 000. Referee: Wright, Brazil

COLO COLO 3 (Perez 13 18, Herrera 85)
OLIMPIA 0

Colo Colo – Moron – Garrido, Ramirez, Margas, Vilchez – Peralta, Espinoza, Pizarro, Mendoza (Herrera) – Perez, Barticciotto
Olimpia – Battaglia – Ramirez, Castro, Fernandez, Suarez – Jara (Guirland), Balbuena (Cubilla), Guasch, Monzon – Torres, Gonzalez

Top scorer: Gaucho, Flamengo 8

SUPERCOPA

FIRST ROUND

Cruzeiro .... 0–0 0–0 (5–4p) ... Colo Colo
Boca Juniors .... 1–1 0–2 .... **Nacional Montevideo**
Argentinos Juniors .... 1–2 0–0 .... **Santos**
Peñarol .... 3–2 0–0 .... Racing Club
Flamengo .... 1–1 2–0 .... Estudiantes LP
River Plate .... 2–2 1–1 (5–4p) ... Gremio

QUARTER-FINALS

Cruzeiro .... 4–0 0–3 .... Nacional Montevideo
Independiente .... 1–1 0–2 .... **Olimpia**
Peñarol .... 3–2 0–0 .... Santos
River Plate .... 1–0 1–2 (4–3p) ... Flamengo

SEMI-FINALS

Cruzeiro .... 1–1 0–0 (5–3p) ... Olimpia
River Plate .... 2–0 3–1 .... Peñarol

FINAL

1st leg. Monumental, Buenos Aires, 13–11–1991, 60 000. Referee: Orellana Ecuador

RIVER PLATE 2 (Rivarola 30, Higuain 90)
CRUZEIRO 0

River Plate – Comizzo – Gordillo, Higuain, Rivarola, Enrique – Diaz H, Astrada (Zapata), Borrelli, Medina Bello – Diaz R, Silvani
Cruzeiro – Paulo Cesar – Zelao, Vanderci, Adilson, Donato – Andrade, Ademir, Boiadeiro, Luis Fernando – Tilico (Paulinho), Charles (Macale)

2nd leg. Mineirao, Belo Horizonte, 20–11–1991, 80 000. Referee: Silva, Chile

CRUZEIRO 3 (Ademir 34, Tilico 52, Marquinhos 76)
RIVER PLATE 0

Cruzeiro – Paulo Cesar – Donato, Paulao, Adilson, Celio Gaucho – Ademir, Boiadeiro, Luis Fernando (Macale), Tilico – Charles, Marquinhos
River Plate – Comizzo – Gordillo, Higuain, Rivarola, Enrique – Diaz H (Berti), Astrada, Borrelli, Zapata (Toresani) – Medina Bello, Diaz R

RECOPA

Kobe, Japan, 19–04–1992

Colo Colo 0
Cruzeiro 0

Colo Colo won 5–4 on penalties

1992

COPA LIBERTADORES

FIRST ROUND

Group 1

	NO	UC	SL	CC	Co	Pl	W	D	L	F	A	Pts
Newell's Old Boys	–	0–0	0–6	3–1	3–0	8	4	3	1	11	10	11
Univ. Catolica	1–1	–	4–0	0–0	5–1	8	2	5	1	15	8	9
San Lorenzo	0–1	2–2	–	1–0	3–0	8	4	1	3	13	8	9
Colo Colo	1–1	1–1	1–0	–	1–0	8	2	4	2	6	7	8
Coquimbo	1–2	3–2	0–1	1–1	–	8	1	1	6	6	18	3

Group 2

	Cr	SP	Bo	SJ	Pl	W	D	L	F	A	Pts
Criciuma	–	3–0	2–1	5–0	6	4	1	1	13	7	9
Sao Paulo FC	4–0	–	2–0	1–1	6	3	2	1	11	5	8
Bolivar	1–1	1–1	–	2–1	6	2	2	2	9	9	6
San Jose	1–2	0–3	2–4	–	6	0	1	5	5	17	1

Group 3

	Ba	Va	Ma	UM	Pl	W	D	L	F	A	Pts
Barcelona	–	0–0	3–1	5–1	6	4	2	0	11	3	10
Valdez	0–1	–	2–1	1–1	6	2	2	2	5	4	6
Maritimo	1–1	1–0	–	1–2	6	1	2	3	5	8	4
ULA Merida	0–1	0–2	0–0	–	6	1	2	3	4	10	4

Group 4

	NM	AC	SC	SB	Pl	W	D	L	F	A	Pts
Nacional Medellin	–	3–0	1–0	2–2	6	4	1	1	15	4	9
America Cali	2–0	–	1–0	2–0	6	4	0	2	8	7	8
Sporting Cristal	0–3	3–1	–	2–0	6	2	1	3	6	7	5
Sport Boys	0–6	1–2	1–1	–	6	0	2	4	4	15	2

Group 5

	CP	Na	De	SA	Pl	W	D	L	F	A	Pts
Cerro Porteño	–	1–1	1–1	2–0	6	3	3	0	9	4	9
Nacional Mont'deo	0–0	–	1–0	2–2	6	2	3	1	9	7	6
Defensor	2–3	3–2	–	1–2	6	1	2	3	7	9	5
Sol de America	0–2	1–3	0–0	–	6	1	2	3	5	10	4

SECOND ROUND

Defensor .... 1–1 0–1 .... **Newell's Old Boys**
Sporting Cristal .... 1–2 2–3 .... **Criciuma**
Colo–Colo .... 1–0 0–2 .... **Barcelona**
Maritimo .... 0–0 0–3 .... **At. Nacional**
Bolivar .... 2–0 0–3 .... **Cerro Porteño**
Universidad Catolica .... 0–0 0–1 .... **America Cali**
Nacional Montevideo .... 0–2 0–2 .... **Sao Paulo FC**
San Lorenzo .... 2–0 0–2 (6–5p) ... Valdez

QUARTER-FINALS

Sao Paulo FC .... 1–0 1–1 .... Criciuma
Barcelona .... 1–1 1–1 (4–3p) ... Cerro Porteño
Newell's Old Boys .... 4–0 1–1 .... San Lorenzo
At. Nacional Medellin .... 0–1 2–4 .... **America Cali**

SEMI-FINALS

Sao Paulo FC .... 3–0 0–2 .... Barcelona
Newell's Old Boys .. 1–1 1–1 (11–10p) . America Cali

FINAL

1st leg. Cordoviola, Rosario, 10–06–1992, 45 000. Referee: Silva, Chile
NEWELL'S OLD BOYS 1 (Berizzo 38)
SAO PAULO FC 0

Newell's - Scoponi - Raggio, Gamboa, Pochettino, Saldanha - Berti, Berizzo, Martino (Garfagnoli) - Zamora, Lunari, Mendoza (Domizzi)
Sao Paulo - Zetti - Cafu, Antonio Carlos, Ronaldo, Ivan - Adilson, Pintado, Rai - Muller, Palinha (Macedo), Elivelton

2nd leg. Morumbi, Sao Paulo, 17–06–1992, 105 000. Referee: Cadena, Colombia
SAO PAULO FC 1 (Rai 65)
NEWELL'S OLD BOYS 0

Sao Paulo won 3–2 on penalties

Sao Paulo - Zetti - Cafu, Antonio Carlos, Ronaldo, Ivan - Adilson, Pintado, Rai - Palinha, Muller (Macedo), Elivelton
Newell's - Scoponi - Saldana, Gamboa, Pochettino, Berizzo - Llop, Berti, Martino (Domizzi), Lunari - Zamora, Mendoza

THE SOUTH AMERICAN YOUTH CUP

Since the introduction of the World Youth Cup in 1977, the South American Youth Cup has been used as a qualifying group for the world event. The first edition, however, was played for as early as 1954.

Year	Winners
1954	Uruguay
1958	Uruguay
1964	Uruguay
1967	Argentina
1971	Paraguay
1974	Brazil
1975	Uruguay
1977	Uruguay
1979	Uruguay
1981	Uruguay
1983	Brazil
1985	Brazil
1987	Colombia
1988	Brazil
1991	Brazil

THE PANAMERICAN CHAMPIONSHIPS

The Confederación Panamericana de Football was formed in 1946 in Barranquilla, Colombia in an attempt to unite all of the countries of the Americas. The motivation was more from the states of Central and North America in a bid to be associated with the more famous countries in South America. The body did not serve a particularly useful function aside from organising three championships before disappearing from sight in the 1960s. The three tournaments do, however, represent the only continent-wide competition for the Americas, given that the football tournament of the Pan-American Games is only open to amateurs, in a continent where professionalism is widespread.

1st Panamerican Championship
Santiago, 16th March–20th April 1952

	Br	Ch	Ur	Pe	Me	Pa	Pl	W	D	L	F	A	Pts
BRAZIL	–	3–0	4–2	0–0	2–0	5–0	5	4	1	0	14	2	9
CHILE	–	–	2–0	3–2	4–0	6–1	5	4	0	1	15	6	8
URUGUAY	–	–	–	5–2	3–1	6–1	5	3	0	2	16	10	6
PERU	–	–	–	–	3–0	7–1	5	2	1	2	14	9	5
MEXICO	–	–	–	–	–	4–2	5	1	0	4	5	14	2
PANAMA	–	–	–	–	–	–	5	0	0	5	5	28	0

2nd Panamerican Championship
Mexico City, 26th February–18th March 1956

	Br	Ar	CR	Pe	Me	Ch	Pl	W	D	L	F	A	Pts
BRAZIL	–	2–2	7–1	1–0	2–1	2–1	5	4	1	0	14	5	9
ARGENTINA	–	–	4–3	0–0	0–0	3–0	5	2	3	0	9	5	7
COSTA RICA	–	–	–	4–2	1–1	2–1	5	2	1	2	11	15	5
PERU	–	–	–	–	2–0	2–2	5	1	2	2	6	7	4
MEXICO	–	–	–	–	–	2–1	5	1	2	2	4	6	4
CHILE	–	–	–	–	–	–	5	0	1	4	5	11	1

3rd Panamerican Championship
San Jose, 7th–20th March 1960

	Ar	Br	Me	CR	Pl	W	D	L	F	A	Pts
ARGENTINA	–	2–1	3–2	2–0	6	4	1	1	9	4	9
BRAZIL	1–0	–	2–1	4–0	6	3	1	2	10	8	7
MEXICO	0–2	2–2	–	3–0	6	1	2	3	9	10	4
COSTA RICA	0–0	3–0	1–1	–	6	1	2	3	4	10	4

THE PANAMERICAN GAMES

Open to all the countries of North, South and Central America, these Games include a football tournament which is for amateurs only. Despite their sending only amateur selections, countries from South America have still dominated the competition.

Year .... Winners
1937 .... Argentina
1951 .... Argentina
1955 .... Argentina
1959 .... Argentina
1963 .... Brazil
1967 .... Mexico
1971 .... Argentina
1975 .... Mexico
1979 .... Brazil
1983 .... Uruguay
1987 .... Brazil
1991 .... United States

THE ATLANTIC CUP

The Atlantic Cup is an occasional series played between those countries which border onto the Atlantic Ocean. Of all the minor tournaments played in South America, this was the most important of the lot because it was the only one that involved all three of Brazil, Argentina and Uruguay. Though not strictly an Atlantic nation, Paraguay were invited to take part in the second and third editions due to their proximity to the other three nations.

1st Atlantic Cup
24th June–8th July 1956

	Br	Ar	Ur	Pl	W	D	L	F	A	Pts
BRAZIL	–	0–0	2–0	2	1	1	0	2	0	3
ARGENTINA	–	–	2–1	2	1	1	0	2	1	3
URUGUAY	–	–	–	2	0	0	2	1	4	0

2nd Atlantic Cup
3rd–17th August 1960

	Br	Ar	Ur	Pa	Pl	W	D	L	F	A	Pts
BRAZIL	–	5–1	0–1	2–1	3	2	0	1	7	3	4
ARGENTINA	–	–	4–0	1–0	3	2	0	1	6	5	4
URUGUAY	–	–	–	2–1	3	2	0	1	3	5	4
PARAGUAY	–	–	–	–	3	0	0	3	2	5	0

3rd Atlantic Cup
25th February–9th June 1976

	Br	Ar	Pa	Ur	Pl	W	D	L	F	A	Pts
BRAZIL	–	2–0	3–1	2–1	6	5	1	0	12	5	11
ARGENTINA	1–2	–	2–2	4–1	6	3	1	2	13	9	7
PARAGUAY	1–1	2–3	–	1–0	6	1	3	2	9	11	5
URUGUAY	1–2	0–3	2–2	–	6	0	1	5	5	14	1

THE LIPTON AND NEWTON CUPS

Donated by the English tea baron Sir Thomas Lipton, the Lipton Cup was the first regular tournament outside the British Isles and was contested between the national sides of Argentina and Uruguay. From 1905 until 1927 it was held on a regular basis, but since 1937 it has been played for only eight times, as the fixture lists of both countries grew.

The Newton Cup named after Richard Newton, a famous English settler in the mid-1800s, was introduced a year after the Lipton Cup. It too was played for by the national sides of Argentina and Uruguay, and like the Lipton Cup was a regular event until the late 1920s and has been played on only eight occasions since 1937.

LIPTON CUP

1905 .... Shared
1906 .... Argentina
1907 .... Argentina
1908 .... Shared
1909 .... Argentina
1910 .... Uruguay
1911 .... Uruguay
1912 .... Uruguay
1913 .... Argentina
1915 .... Argentina
1916 .... Argentina
1917 .... Argentina
1918 .... Shared
1919 .... Uruguay
1922 .... Uruguay
1923 .... Shared
1927 .... Uruguay
1928 .... Shared
1929 .... Shared
1937 .... Argentina
1942 .... Shared
1945 .... Shared
1957 .... Shared
1962 .... Argentina
1968 .... Uruguay
1971 .... Shared
1973 .... Shared

NEWTON CUP

1906 .... Argentina
1907 .... Argentina
1908 .... Argentina
1909 .... Shared
1911 .... Argentina
1912 .... Shared
1913 .... Uruguay
1915 .... Uruguay
1916 .... Argentina
1917 .... Uruguay
1918 .... Argentina
1919 .... Uruguay
1920 .... Uruguay
1922 .... Shared
1924 .... Uruguay
1924 .... Argentina
1927 .... Argentina
1928 .... Argentina
1929 .... Uruguay
1930 .... Shared
1937 .... Argentina
1942 .... Argentina
1945 .... Argentina
1957 .... Shared
1968 .... Argentina
1971 .... Argentina
1973 .... Shared
1975 .... Argentina

At the beginning of the century, Argentina and Uruguay played each other several times a year. Alongside the Lipton and Newton Cups, representative league sides regularly played for two trophies presented by the Argentine and Uruguayan Education Ministries.

Four other trophies have featured in the fixture list. In 1912 Argentina won the Montevideo Cup and in 1913 they also won the Saenz Piena Cup. In the 1930s and 1940s the Hector Gomez and Juan Mignaburu Cups were competed for.

MINISTRY OF EDUCATION, ARGENTINA

1908 .... Uruguay
1909 .... Argentina
1910 .... Uruguay
1911 .... Argentina
1912 .... Uruguay
1913 .... Argentina
1914 .... Argentina
1916 .... Argentina
1918 .... Argentina
1919 .... Argentina
1920 .... Argentina
1923 .... Shared

MINISTRY OF EDUCATION, URUGUAY

1911 .... Uruguay
1912 .... Uruguay
1913 .... Uruguay
1914 .... Uruguay
1915 .... Argentina
1916 .... Argentina
1918 .... Uruguay
1919 .... Uruguay
1920 .... Uruguay
1922 .... Uruguay
1923 .... Argentina

HECTOR GOMEZ CUP

1935 .... Shared
1936 .... Uruguay
1938 .... Argentina
1940 .... Uruguay
1943 .... Argentina

JUAN MIGNABURU CUP

1935 .... Argentina
1936 .... Argentina
1938 .... Argentina
1940 .... Argentina
1943 .... Shared

THE ROCA CUP

Introduced in 1914, the Roca Cup is played for between the national sides of Brazil and Argentina. The last occasion on which it was played for was 1971. It is named after the Argentine General, Julio Roca.

THE ROCA CUP WINNERS

1914 .... Brazil
1922 .... Brazil
1923 .... Argentina
1939 .... Argentina
1940 .... Argentina
1945 .... Brazil
1957 .... Brazil
1960 .... Brazil
1963 .... Brazil
1971 .... Shared

THE RIO BRANCA CUP

The Rio Branco Cup is played for between the national sides of Uruguay and Brazil. The first of the eight editions was in 1931, the last in 1967. It is named after the main border town between the two countries.

1931 .... Brazil
1932 .... Brazil
1940 .... Uruguay
1946 .... Uruguay
1947 .... Brazil
1948 .... Uruguay
1950 .... Brazil
1967 .... Shared

OTHER SOUTH AMERICAN TOURNAMENTS

Of all the other irregular tournaments between South American countries the most notable involve Chile and Paraguay. Chile have played in the Carlos Dittborn Cup against Argentina, the Bernardo O'Higgins Cup against Brazil and the Juan Pinto Durán Cup against Uruguay.

Paraguay have also played in the Rosa Chevallier Boutell Cup against Argentina, the Oswaldo Cruz Cup against Brazil and the Artigas Cup against Uruguay. Others include the Pacific Cup between Chile and Peru and the Roque Gomez Pena Cup between Peru and Argentina. The least known perhaps is the Paz del Chaco Cup between Bolivia and Paraguay played to celebrate the resolution of a border dispute between the two countries.

ARGENTINA

Nobody apart from the British have been playing the game longer, and only a few have ever played it better, than the Argentines. A championship was played in 1891, a full five years before Sweden and Belgium, the first to do so on mainland Europe, whilst their record of two World Cup victories is bettered only by Brazil, Germany and Italy.

Had the Italians not continually swiped their best players to play not only for their clubs but also for the national side until the rules were changed to forbid this, this figure would almost certainly be higher. Not until 1958 was a serious bid made to take part in the World Cup after their initial entry in 1930, and that collapsed around them as one of the best sides they had managed to put together was broken up by the unscrupulous Italian agents.

Argentina has produced more players of natural talent than any other country, with the possible exception of Brazil, as well as two of the greatest players ever in Alfredo di Stefano and Diego Maradona. Both symbolise the excitement and the trauma Argentine football followers have had to endure. Di Stefano left during the players' strike of 1948, never returned and ended up playing for Spain, whilst Maradona left but returned a broken man. On their day they were supreme footballers. Di Stefano guided Real Madrid to countless honours in the 1950s whilst Maradona not only guided Argentina to a World Cup victory in 1986, but single-handedly transformed Napoli into one of the strongest teams in Europe.

The tragedy for Argentina is that these two were not the only ones to leave and as a result the league, which by all rights should be amongst the very best, often resembles the leftovers that the European clubs have rejected. Unfortunately, persistent economic pressures help reinforce this trend as players seek the security of a regular wage packet in a currency that is not worthless by the end of the month. It is an unequal struggle and one that does not look like getting any more even in the near future.

Football was brought to Argentina by the British, with whom the Argentines had very close links, and in May 1865 a team called Buenos Aires Football Club was founded. For many years the game was played exclusively by British residents in the capital, but by the end of the century it had begun to spread and was taken up by the locals. In 1887 Quilmes FC was formed by British railway workers, and they along with Gimansia y Esgrima, formed five months previously in La Plata 30 miles to the south of Buenos Aires, remain the two oldest clubs in the country. Not until after the turn of the century, however, did Gimnasia form a football section, a policy that had led disgruntled members to form Estudiantes de La Plata in 1905.

Many of the names of the clubs reflect the British involvement in the game. In 1889 Rosario Central were formed, not 'Centro Rosario' as the indigenous language would have had it, whilst their great rivals from the same city are called Newell's Old Boys; 1901 saw the formation of River Plate, 1903 Racing Club, 1905 Boca Juniors and Independiente and 1908 Huracan, and all had their origins in one or other of the migrant communities for which Argentina was famous.

Boca Juniors, though founded by an Irishman, had their roots in the Italian community, whilst Racing were named after the Paris-based club of the same name and wore the same light blue colours. River Plate were formed by Englishmen and of this 'big five' only Independiente were formed by Argentines, all of whom worked for a store called City of London. The store already had a team but the Argentines wanted to play for a separate team, hence the name.

In 1891 Alexander Hutton, the director of the English High School, formed the Argentine Association Football League, and two years later this league was reformed as the Argentine Football Association. The winners of the first league in 1891, St Andrews, have since faded into the mists of time, as have Lomas Athletic and Alumni, the major powers until after the turn of the century. Alumni, made up of old boys from the English High School, were instrumental in the popularising of the game, but by the time of Racing's first championship in 1913, only a few British players remained, and most teams were comprised of Argentinians.

The Argentine championship was not a truly national competition. Only clubs from Buenos Aires, La Plata, Rosario and Santa Fe were ever invited to take part. The rest of the country had to make do with their own leagues, the first of which, the Liga Santiaguena de Futbol, was formed in 1906. Buenos Aires is, however, a large city, made up of 22 municipalities within which there are 50 *barrios*, or neighbourhoods. The identification of teams with either a municipality or *barrio* has ensured the survival of so many clubs in such a concentrated area, and the development of fierce rivalry between teams.

Not only was there a vibrant domestic scene in Argentine football, but along with Uruguay, Argentina were at the forefront of the international game in South America. In 1901 a representative side took on a side from Uruguay and a long rivalry was started that has seen more games than any other 'derby' encounter throughout the world. The match on May 16 was the first international played anywhere outside Great Britain. In 1905 these games were given a competitive edge when a cup was donated by Sir Thomas Lipton, the English tea baron. In these early years of international competition, the two countries played together as often as four times a year.

In 1910, Argentina organised a tournament between herself, Uruguay and Chile, and although not strictly a South American Championship it was regarded as such at the time. Not until six years later, in celebration of her centenary, did the first recognised championship take place, and there started another rivalry with the Uruguayans to add to that of the Lipton and Newton Cups. Brazil very rarely threatened the Argentine–Uruguay hegemony, except when the tournament was played on their territory.

The game remained an amateur sport until the adoption of professionalism in 1931, but the years leading up to this event were often fraught with trouble as various different governing bodies were set up at the merest hint of an argument. In this pre-professional era, the most successful clubs were Racing Club and Huracan, the former a bastion of the amateur ideals.

Neither adapted well to the new situation after 1931, and this was a factor that helped forge the success of both River Plate and Boca Juniors, the two most famous Argentine clubs. After 1931 the new professional league was the lifeblood of Argentine football until the 1960s when the Copa Libertadores caught the imagination. During this period the programme of the international side was very light, especially during the 1930s and 1950s when hardly any matches were played at all, further increasing the importance of the league.

The Boca Juniors side of the first half of the 1930s and the River Plate side of the 1940s are considered to be amongst the greatest teams that have ever played in Argentina. Boca's side contained players such as Juan Evaristo, Cherro, Francisco Varallo, and the Brazilian Domingos da Guia, but perhaps the River Plate side was even better.

At one time or another during the 1940s famous players like Bernabe Ferreyra, Carlos Peucelle, Angel Labruna, Jose Moreno and Adolfo Pedernera made the club the most famous on the South American continent. The forward line containing Muñoz, Moreno, Pedernera and Loustau was referred to as *la máquina* – the machine – whilst the forward line of the 1947 championship winning side consisting of Reyes, Moreno, Di Stéfano, Labruna and Loustau was regarded as one of the best ever.

Up until the late 1950s Argentina remained an isolationist within the world game. Uruguay, Brazil and Paraguay were their only regular opponents outside of the South American Championship which, along with Uruguay, they dominated from the start. Had they entered more than just the 1928 Olympic Games and the 1930 World Cup, Argentina might well have been world champions many years before they finally were in 1978.

The national side's first excursion to Europe came in the 1928 Amsterdam Olympic Games. Domingo Tarasconi

		Total			League	Nat champ	Copa Lib		
		G	S	B	G	G	G	S	B
1	River Plate	23	2	6	19	3	1	2	6
2	Boca Juniors	23	2	3	18	3	2	2	3
3	Independiente	21	–	5	11	3	7	–	5
4	Racing Club Avellaneda	16	–	1	15	–	1	–	1
5	San Lorenzo de Almagro	10	–	3	8	2	–	–	3
6	Alumni	9	–	–	9	–	–	–	–
7	Estudiantes La Plata	7	1	1	3	1	3	1	1
8	Lomas Athletic	7	–	–	7	–	–	–	–
9	Hurucan	5	–	1	5	–	–	–	1
10	Rosario Central	4	–	1	1	3	–	–	1
11	Estudiantil Porteño	4	–	–	4	–	–	–	–
12	Newell's Old Boys	3	1	–	3	–	–	1	–
13	Argentinos Juniors	3	–	1	1	1	1	–	1
14	Belgrano Athletic	3	–	–	3	–	–	–	–
15	Quilmes	2	–	–	2	–	–	–	–
	Ferrocarril Oeste	2	–	–	–	2	–	–	–
17	Velez Sarsfield	1	–	1	–	1	–	–	1
18	Gimnasia y Esgrima LP	1	–	–	1	–	–	–	–
	Chacarita Juniors	1	–	–	1	–	–	–	–
	English High School	1	–	–	1	–	–	–	–
	Sportivo Dock Sud	1	–	–	1	–	–	–	–
	Sportivo Barracas	1	–	–	1	–	–	–	–
	St Andrew's	1	–	–	1	–	–	–	–

To end of 1990–91 season

was in tremendous form and scored an amazing 12 goals in three games leading up to the final. It was Argentina's misfortune to meet Uruguay there, two sides who knew each other inside out. Tarasconi could not reproduce his form in the final and the Argentines lost after a replay. Two years later, Uruguay completed a double over them by winning the first World Cup final. This time Stabile was scoring the goals for Argentina, but despite taking a 2–1 half-time lead in Montevideo they succumbed to three second-half goals and went home runners-up yet again.

A team did travel to the 1934 World Cup in Italy, but for fear of losing more players like Monti and Orsi to the Italian game, a third-rate side was sent that did not survive the first round. Not until the late 1950s did the national side resurface with any great enthusiasm.

The 1957 South American Championship saw the birth of a very good side containing another of Argentina's famous forward lines. Corbatta, Maschio, Angelillo, Sivori and Cruz caused a sensation in Lima, so much so that as soon as the tournament finished, Bologna signed Maschio, Juventus signed Sivori and Internazionale signed Angelillo. All three never played for Argentina again, appearing instead briefly for Italy.

With a severely depleted side, the Argentines made the journey to Sweden for the 1958 World Cup and were promptly eliminated in the first round. Argentine football has now come to terms with the constant flow of players moving abroad and has used the extra experience gained by these players to its advantage. The rule introduced by FIFA forbidding the practice of playing for more than one country was crucial in this respect.

Argentina is lucky, though, in that there seems to be a huge reservoir of very talented players in the country, and often the national side has not needed to rely on the foreign-based players. This was especially true in 1978 when at last Argentina won the World Cup. Of the winning side, only Mario Kempes played his football abroad.

Argentina was awarded the tournament after many failed attempts, but the deteriorating political situation nearly saw its relocation to the Low Countries. Although sympathy often lies with Holland for losing two consecutive finals, Argentina were worthy winners, and it was just reward for all the fine footballers that they had produced in the past who had never had the opportunity to shine on the world stage.

Since 1978, along with West Germany, Argentina have been the most potent force in international football. They have appeared in three of the last four World Cup Finals, and in 1986 won the title for the second time. Central to the side was Diego Maradona, who along with Di Stéfano, Pele and Cruyff ranks among the very best footballers the world has ever produced.

The side that won in Mexico contained some excellent players like Burruchaga, Valdano, Ruggeri and Pumpido, but Maradona was the undoubted star and it was to him that they looked for inspiration in their time of need. His second goal against England in the quarter-finals is one of the best witnessed in any final tournamament, though his first, the notorious 'hand of God', will be remembered for different reasons. With him Argentina appeared unstoppable, and although West Germany caused them a few heart-stopping moments towards the end of the final, it was no surprise that they finally won.

Four years later saw a repeat of the 1986 final when the Germans again faced Maradona and his Argentine side in the final, though this time they beat them in what is generally regarded as the worst final in the history of the tournament. Despite their reaching the final, Italy was not a particularly happy experience for Argentina. Their tactics were roundly criticised and they used penalty-kicks to excellent effect to reach a final that their form did not merit. They were up against the odds, however. Pumpido was carried off in the second game of the tournament with a broken leg, whilst Maradona was at half-speed due to injury.

Club football has remained remarkably buoyant despite the exodus of players. This has been helped by the Copa

Libertadores in which Argentine clubs have a record second to none. Although they were slow to take to the competition, between 1964 and 1978 only three clubs from elsewhere could prise the trophy from Argentine hands. Two clubs have been especially pre-eminent, and surprisingly they were not Boca and River Plate but Independiente and Estudiantes de La Plata, neither of whom were particularly strong in the league at the time of their successes.

Estudiantes were responsible for showing the world the dark side of Argentine football epitomised by their poor sportsmanship in the 1966 World Cup. It got to the stage where police were starting to arrest players after the match for poor behaviour during it, and this happened after the World Club Championship between Estudiantes and Milan in 1969 when three players from Estudiantes were imprisoned.

Independiente won the title four times in a row in the 1970s with a side including Ricardo Bochini, Daniel Bertoni and Ruben Galvan, the latter two playing a crucial part in Argentina's 1978 World Cup victory, and they remain the top club in the history of the competition with their record seven wins.

There was a major reorganisation of the league in 1967. Up until then the championship, though including all the major clubs, was not open to every team. It was renamed the Metropolitan League and a national championship was started to run alongside which was open to all of the clubs around the country.

Since the beginning of the 1970s the stranglehold of the big Buenos Aires clubs has gradually been broken down as the two Rosario clubs and some of the less well-known Buenos Aires clubs have begun to make their presence felt. Further reorganisation in 1985 saw, for the first time, a single national first division, as the national championship in its previous form was scrapped. There now exists a second division beneath which there are 32 regional leagues and three further leagues for clubs from Buenos Aires.

Argentina is here to stay as a world power. The league is the strongest in South America and the national side can draw on a large pool of talented players. With a largely home-based side they won the 1991 South American Championship, but some things never change in football: half of that side is now playing in Europe.

Population: 31963000
Area, sq km: 2780092
% in urban areas: 85%
Capital city: Buenos Aires

Asociación del Fútbol Argentino
Viamonte #1366–76
1053 Buenos Aires
Argentina
Tel: (010 54) 1 404276
Fax: (010 54) 1 9533469
Telex: 22710 AFA AR
Cable: FUTBOL BUENOS AIRES
Languages for correspondence: Spanish, English & French

Year of formation: 1893
Affiliation to FIFA: 1912
Affiliation to CONMEBOL: 1916
Registered clubs: 3035
Registered players: 386200
Professional players: 3320
Registered coaches: 5125
Registered referees: 360
National stadium: Antonio Liberti 'Monumental' de Nunez 76000
National colours: Shirts: Light Blue and White Stripes/Shorts: Black/Socks: White
Reserve colours: Shirts: Blue/Shorts: Black/ Socks: White
Season: August–June

THE RECORD

WORLD CUP

1930 .... QT Automatic – Final Tournament/Runners-up
1934 .... QT W–O in group 3 – Final Tournament/1st round
1938–54 ..... Did not enter
1958 .... QT 1st/3 in group 2 – Final Tournament/1st round
1962 .... QT 1st/2 in group 1 – Final Tournament/1st round
1966 .... QT 1st/3 in group 3 – Final Tournament/Quarter-finalists
1970 .... QT 3rd/3 in group 1
1974 .... QT 1st/3 in group 2 – Final Tournament/2nd round
1978 .... QT Automatic – Final Tournament/Winners
1982 .... QT Automatic – Final Tournament/2nd round
1986 .... QT 1st/4 in group 1 – Final Tournament/Winners
1990 .... QT Automatic – Final Tournament/Finalists

SOUTH AMERICAN CHAMPIONSHIP

1910 .... 1st/3 – Winners
1916 .... 2nd/4
1917 .... 2nd/4
1919 .... 3rd/4
1920 .... 2nd/4
1921 .... 1st/4 – Winners
1922 .... 4th/5
1923 .... 2nd/4
1924 .... 2nd/4
1925 .... 1st/3 – Winners
1926 .... 2nd/5
1927 .... 1st/4 – Winners
1929 .... 1st/4 – Winners
1935 .... 2nd/4
1937 .... 1st/6 – Winners
1939 .... –
1941 .... 1st/5 – Winners
1942 .... 2nd/7
1945 .... 1st/7 – Winners
1946 .... 1st/6 – Winners
1947 .... 1st/8 – Winners
1949 .... –
1953 .... –
1955 .... 1st/6 – Winners
1956 .... 3rd/6
1957 .... 1st/7 – Winners
1959 .... 1st/7 – Winners
1959 .... 2nd/5
1963 .... 3rd/7
1967 .... 2nd/6
1975 .... 5th/10/1st round
1979 .... 8th/10/1st round
1983 .... 6th/10/1st round
1987 .... 4th/10/Semi-finalists
1989 .... 3rd/10/2nd round
1991 .... 1st/10 – Winners

OLYMPIC GAMES

1908–24 ..... Did not enter
1928 .... Runners-up
1936–56 ..... Did not enter
1960 .... Final Tournament/1st round
1964 .... Final Tournament/1st round
1968 .... Did not enter
1972 .... QT Failed to qualify
1976 .... QT Failed to qualify
1980 .... Qualified but withdrew
1984 .... Did not enter
1988 .... Final Tournament/Quarter-finalists
1992 .... QT Failed to qualify

COPA LIBERTADORES

Winners – Independiente 1964, 1965, 1972, 1973, 1974, 1975, 1984. Racing Club 1967. Estudiantes LP 1968, 1969, 1970. Boca Juniors 1977, 1978. Argentinos Juniors 1985. River Plate 1986
Finalists – Boca Juniors 1963, 1979. River Plate 1966, 1976. Estudiantes LP 1971. Newell's Old Boys 1988, 1992

SUPERCOPA: Winners – Racing Club 1988. Boca Juniors 1989
Finalists – River Plate 1991

CLUB DIRECTORY

BUENOS AIRES (Population – 10750000)

Club Almirante Brown
Stadium: San Petesburgo 17000
Founded: 1922
Colours: Yellow with black sleeves/Black

Asociacion Atletica Argentinos Juniors
Stadium: Martin de Gainza 24000
Founded: 1904
Colours: Red/Red

Club Deportivo Armenio
Stadium: Vicente Lopez 15000
Founded: 1962
Colours: Green/Black

Club Atletico Atlanta
Stadium Humboldt 35000
Founded: 1904
Colours: Blue and yellow stripes/Sky blue

Club Atletico Banfield
Stadium Pena y Arenales 18000
Founded: 1896
Colours: Green and white stripes/green

Club Atletico Boca Juniors
Stadium La Bombonera 58000
Founded: 1905
Colours: Blue with Yellow Band on chest/Blue

Club Atletico Chacarita Juniors
Stadium San Lartin 25000
Founded: 1906
Colours: Red, black and white thin stripes/Black

Club Deportivo Espanol
Stadium Espana 18000
Founded: 1956
Colours: Red/Blue

Club Estudiantes La Plata
Stadium Estadio La Plata 26000
Founded: 1905
Colours: Red and white stripes/Black

Club Ferrocarril Oeste
Stadium Martin de Gainza 24000
Founded: 1904
Colours: Green/White

Gimnasia y Esgrima La Plata
Stadium Del Bosque 25000
Founded: 1887
Colours: White with blue hoop on chest/Blue

Club Atletico Huracan
Stadium Estadio Tomas Aldolfo Duco 48000
Founded: 1908
Colours: White/Blue

Club Atletico Independiente
Stadium Cordero 68000
Founded: 1905
Colours: Red/Blue

Club Deportivo Italiano
Stadium Humbolt 35000
Founded: 1957
Colours: Blue/Blue

Club Atletico Lanus
Stadium General Arias 15000
Founded: 1916
Colours: Maroon/Maroon

Club Atletico Platense
Stadium Vicente Lopez 15000
Founded: 1905
Colours: Maroon/Maroon

Quilmes Atletico Club
Stadium Sarmiento 20000
Founded: 1887
Colours: White/Blue

Racing Club
Stadium Mozart y Cuyo 70000
Founded: 1903
Colours: Sky blue and white stripes/Black

Club Atletico River Plate
Stadium Antonio Liberti 'Monumental' de Nunez 76000
Founded: 1901
Colours: White with red sash/Black

Club Atletico San Lorenzo de Almagro
Stadium Estadio Tomas Aldolfo Duco 48000
Founded: 1908
Colours: Red and blue stripes/Blue

Club Atletico Temperley
Stadium Temperley 15000
Founded: 1912
Colours: Sky blue/Sky blue

Club Atletico Tigre
Stadium Victoria 25000
Founded: 1902
Colours: Red/Blue

Club Atletico Velez Sarsfield
Stadium José Amalfitani 49000
Founded: 1910
Colours: White with a blue V/Blue

CORDOBA (Population – 1070000)

Club Atletico Belgrano
Stadium Belgrano 20000
Founded: 1925
Colours: Sky Blue/Black

Instituto Atletico Central
Stadium Instituto 21000
Founded: 1918
Colours: Red and white stripes/Black

Club Atletico Racing
Stadium Barrio Italia 20000
Founded: 1924
Colours: Sky blue and white stripes/Black

Club Atletico Talleres
Stadium Chateau Carreras 46000
Founded: 1913
Colours: Blue and white stripes/Blue

ROSARIO (Population – 1045000)

Club Atletico Newell's Old Boys
Stadium Parque Independencia 31000
Founded: 1903
Colours: Red and black halves/Black

Club Atletico Rosario Central
Stadium Cordoviola 41000
Founded: 1889
Colours: Blue and yellow stripes/Blue

MENDOZA (Population – 650000)
Deportivo Maipu
Stadium Estadio Mendoza 50000
Colours: Red with white sash/Black

SAN MIGUEL DE TUCUMAN (Population – 525000)

Atletico Tucumán
Stadium La Ciudadela 20000
Founded: 1902
Colours: Sky blue and white stripes/Blue

San Martin Tucumán
Stadium La Ciudadela 20000
Founded: 1909
Colours: Red and white stripes/White

SANTA FE (Population – 292000)

Club Atletico Colon Santa Fe
Stadium Centenario de los Elefantes 35000
Founded: 1905
Colours: Red and black halves/white

Club Atletico Union Santa Fe
Stadium Lopez y Planes 22000
Founded: 1907
Colours: Red and white stripes/Black

ARGENTINIAN LEAGUE CHAMPIONSHIP

Year .... Champions

1891 .... St Andrew's
1892 .... Lomas Athletic
1893 .... Lomas Athletic
1894 .... Lomas Athletic
1895 .... Lomas Athletic
1896 .... Lomas Athletic
1897 .... Lomas Athletic
1898 .... Lomas Athletic
1899 .... Belgrano Athletic
1900 .... English High School
1901 .... Alumni

1902 .... Alumni
1903 .... Alumni
1904 .... Belgrano Athletic
1905 .... Alumni
1906 .... Alumni
1907 .... Alumni
1908 .... Belgrano
1909 .... Alumni
1910 .... Alumni
1911 .... Alumni
1912 .... Quilmes
1913 .... Racing Club
1914 .... Racing Club
1915 .... Racing Club
1916 .... Racing Club
1917 .... Racing Club
1918 .... Racing Club
1919 .... Boca Juniors
1920 .... Boca Juniors
1921 .... Huracan
1922 .... Huracan
1923 .... Boca Juniors
1924 .... Boca Juniors
1925 .... Huracan
1926 .... Boca Juniors
1927 .... San Lorenzo
1928 .... Huracan
1929 .... Gimnasia y Esgrima
1930 .... Boca Juniors

PROFESSIONAL LEAGUE

1931 .... Boca Juniors
1932 .... River Plate
1933 .... San Lorenzo
1934 .... Boca Juniors
1935 .... Boca Juniors
1936 .... River Plate
1937 .... River Plate
1938 .... Independiente
1939 .... Independiente
1940 .... Boca Juniors
1941 .... River Plate
1942 .... River Plate
1943 .... Boca Juniors
1944 .... Boca Juniors
1945 .... River Plate
1946 .... San Lorenzo
1947 .... River Plate
1948 .... Independiente
1949 .... Racing Club
1950 .... Racing Club
1951 .... Racing Club
1952 .... River Plate
1953 .... River Plate
1954 .... Boca Juniors
1955 .... River Plate
1956 .... River Plate
1957 .... River Plate
1958 .... Racing Club
1959 .... San Lorenzo
1960 .... Independiente
1961 .... Racing Club
1962 .... Boca Juniors
1963 .... Independiente
1964 .... Boca Juniors
1965 .... Boca Juniors
1966 .... Racing Club

METROPOLITAN CHAMPIONSHIP

1967 .... Estudiantes LP
1968 .... San Lorenzo
1969 .... Chacarita Juniors
1970 .... Independiente
1971 .... Independiente
1972 .... San Lorenzo
1973 .... Huracan
1974 .... Newell's Old Boys
1975 .... River Plate
1976 .... Boca Juniors
1977 .... River Plate
1978 .... Quilmes
1979 .... River Plate
1980 .... River Plate
1981 .... Boca Juniors
1982 .... Estudiantes LP
1983 .... Independiente
1984 .... Argentinos Juniors

NATIONAL LEAGUE CHAMPIONSHIP

1986 .... River Plate
1987 .... Rosario Central
1988 .... Newell's Old Boys
1989 .... Independiente
1990 .... River Plate
1991 .... Newell's Old Boys

NATIONAL CHAMPIONSHIP

1967 .... Independiente
1968 .... Velez Sarsfield
1969 .... Boca Juniors
1970 .... Boca Juniors
1971 .... Rosario Central
1972 .... San Lorenzo
1973 .... Rosario Central
1974 .... San Lorenzo
1975 .... River Plate
1976 .... Boca Juniors
1977 .... Independiente
1978 .... Independiente
1979 .... River Plate
1980 .... Rosario Central
1981 .... River Plate
1982 .... Ferrocarril Oeste
1983 .... Estudiantes LP
1984 .... Ferrocarril Oeste
1985 .... Argentinos Juniors

PRE LIBERTADORES LIGUILLA

1986 .... Boca Juniors
1987 .... Independiente
1988 .... Racing Club
1989 .... River Plate
1990 .... Boca Juniors
1991 .... San Lorenzo

RIVAL LEAGUES

FEDERACION ARGENTINA DE FOOTBALL

1912 .... Estudiantil Porteño
1913 Estudiantes LP
1914 .... Estudiantil Porteño

ASOCIACIÓN AMATEURS

1919 .... Racing Club
1920 .... River Plate
1921 .... Racing Club
1922 .... Independiente
1923 .... San Lorenzo
1924 .... San Lorenzo
1925 .... Racing Club
1926 .... Independiente

ASOCIACIÓN AMATEUR ARGENTINA

1931 .... Estudiantil Porteño
1932 .... Sportivo Barracas
1933 .... Sportivo Dock Sud
1934 .... Estudiantil Porteño

PROVINCIAL LEAGUES OF ARGENTINA

MESOPOTAMIA – The North-East

Liga Paranaense de Futbol (1942–86)
Province – Entre Rios. Main city – Paraná 161 000

Patronato	15
Atletico Paraná	13
Belgrano	6
Ministerio	5
Penarol	2
Sportivo Urquiza	1

Liga Posadena (1934–86)
Province – Misiones. Main city – Posadas 143 000

Guarani Antonio Franco	26
Bartolome Mitre	11
Union	6
Atletico Posasdes	5
America For Ever	1
JG Brown	1

THE CHACO – North

Liga Chaquena de Futbol (1925–86)
Province – Chaco. Main city – Resistencia 220 000

Chaco For Ever	23
Sarmiento	23
Don Oriene	5
Regional	4
Independiente Tirol	3
Central Norte	1
Fontana	1
Velez Sarsfield	1

Liga Santiaguena de Futbol (1906–86)
Province – Santiago del Estero. Main city – Santiago del Estero 200 000

Union Santiago	22
Central Cordoba	20
Estudiantes	10
Mitre	8
Sarmiento	7
Central Argentino	5
Comercio Unidos	3
Atletico	2
Agua y Energia	1
La Banda	1
Guemes	1

THE NORTH–WEST

Liga Jujena de Futbol (1975–86)

Province – Jujuy. Main city – San Salvador 124 000

Gimnasia y Esgrima	6
Altos Hornos Zapla	5
Juventud Celulosa	1

Liga Saltena de Futbol (1921–86)

Province – Salta. Main city – Salta 260 000

Central Norte	27
Juventud Antoniana	16
Gimnasia y Tiro	14
Telecomunicaciones	4
Sportivo Commercio	1
Argentinos del Norte	1

Liga Tucamana de Futbol (1919–86)

Province – Tucuman. Main city – San Miguel de Tucuman 525 000

Atletico Tucuman	26
San Martin	25
Central Cordoba	4
Central Norte	4
All Boys	4
San Pablo	3
Sportivo Guzman	2

THE PAMPAS – Central

Liga Pampeana de Futbol (1926–86)

Province – La Pampa. Main cities – Santa Rosa and General Pico

Spotivo Independiente	11
Cultural Argentino	8
Ferrocarril Oeste	8
Alvear FC	7
Costa Brava	7
Racing Club	7
Ferrocarril Oeste Alvear	5
Pico FC	4
Miguel Cane	1
Sportivo Realico	1
Estudiantes	1

Asociacion Cordobesa de Futbol (1913–85)

Province – Córdoba. Main city – Córdoba 1 070 000

Atletico Belgrano	26
Talleres Córdoba	25
Instituto Córdoba	7
Sportivo Belgrano	3
Central Córdoba	2
General Paz Juniors	2
Union San Vicente	2
Universitario	1

Liga del Sur (1908–86)

Province – Buenos Aires. Main city – Bahia Blanca

Olimpo	24
Puerto Commercial	16
Pacifico	10
Rosario PB	7
Liniers	5
Bella Vista	3
Porteno	2
Villa Mitre	2
Huracan	2
Ferrocarril Sud	1
Sansinena	1
Libertad	1

Liga Deportiva Confluencia de Rio Negro (1975–86)

Province – Buenos Aires. Main city – Cipoletti

Atletico Cipolletti	7
Deportivo Roca	4
Atletico Regina	1

Liga Deportiva del Oeste (1917–86)

Province – Buenos Aires. Main city – Junin

Sarmiento	18
Jorge Newbery	14
Mariano Moreno	13
Rivadavia Junin	6
River Plate	4
El Linqueno	3
Buenos Aires al Pacifico	3
Rivadavia de Lincoln	2
Ambos Mundos	2
Junin	1
Villa Belgrano	1

Liga Marplatense de Futbol (1909–86)

Province – Buenos Aires. Main city – Mar del Plata

Quilmes	12
Kimberley	11
San Lorenzo	11
Atletico Mar del Plata	9
Nacional	7
Circulo Deportivo	4
Independiente	4
General Mitre	3
Aldosivi	3
River Plate	3
Penarol	2

7 clubs with one victory

Liga Necochea de Futbol (1930–86)

Province – Buenos Aires. Main city – Necochea

Rivadavia	21
Independiente	9
Estancion Quequen	8
Huracan	7
Defensores	3
Jorge Newbery	2
Villa del Parque	2
Ameghino	2
Palermo	1
Barracas	1
Ministerio	1

Liga de Futbol de Olavarria (1926–86)

Province – Buenos Aires. Main city – Olavarria

Estudiantes	18
Racing	12
San Martin	12
Loma Negra	8
Ferrocarril Sud	6
Sierra Chica	2
El Fortin	1

Liga Tandilense de Futbol (1919–86)

Province – Buenos Aires. Main city – Tandil

Ramon Santamarina	27
Ferrocarril Sud	15
Excursionistas	5
Newbery	4
Independiente	4
Racing	3
Loma Negra	2

7 teams with one victory

THE PAMPEAN SIERRAS AND CUJO – West

Liga Mendocina de Futbol (1922–86)

Province – Mendoza. Main city – Mendoza 650 000

Independiente Rivadavia	21
Gimnasia y Esgrima	17
Godoy Cruz	6
Atletico San Martin	5
Andes Talleres	4
Nacional	4
Deportivo Maipu	3
Atletico Argentino	2
Palmira	1
Boca Juniors	1
Huracan Las Heras	1

Liga Riojana de Futbol (1919–86)

Province – La Rioja. Main city – La Rioja 67 000

Atletico Riojjana	10
Americo Tesorieri	10
Rioja Juniors	10
Independiente	6
Sportivo Firpo	5
Andino	5
Union	5
Sportivo San Vincente	4
Tiro Federal	3
Atletico San Isidro	2
Estudiantes	2
San Lorenzo de Vargas	2
Defensor	1
Almirante Brown	1
Penarol	1
Sportivo San Francisco	1

Liga Sanjuanina de Futbol (1922–86)

Province – San Juan. Main city – San Juan 300 000

San Martin	24
Atletico de la Juventud	17
Sportivo Desamporados	8
Atletico Graffigna	4
Los Andes	4
Penarol	3
Independiente	1

PATAGONIA – South

Liga Rionegrina de Futbol (1985)

Province – Rio Negro. Main city – Viedma

In 1986 the first truly national league was set up and so all the provincial leagues lost their status as the premier league in their region. All the leagues have remained but are now in effect a regionalised sixth division beneath five national divisions.

INTERNATIONAL MATCHES PLAYED BY ARGENTINA

Date	Opponents	Result	Venue	Compet	Scorers
16–05–1901	Uruguay	W 3–2	Montevideo	Fr	
20–07–1902	Uruguay	W 6–0	Montevideo	Fr	Dickinson, Brown G, Moore, Sardeson, Buchanan, Duggan
13–09–1903	Uruguay	L 2–3	Buenos Aires	Fr	Brown G 2
15–08–1905	Uruguay	D 0–0	Buenos Aires	LC	
9–07–1906	South Africa	L 0–1	Buenos Aires	Fr	
15–08	Uruguay	W 2–0	Montevideo	LC	Brown A, Gonzalez T
21–10	Uruguay	W 2–1	Buenos Aires	NC	Watson-Hutton, Brown E
15–08–1907	Uruguay	W 2–1	Buenos Aires	LC	Brown E, Jacobs
6–10	Uruguay	W 2–1	Montevideo	NC	Malbran 2
15–08–1908	Uruguay	D 2–2	Montevideo	LC	Brown EA, Susan
13–09	Uruguay	W 2–1	Buenos Aires	NC	Brown E, Watson-Hutton
4–10	Uruguay	L 0–1	Buenos Aires	MEA	
15–08–1909	Uruguay	W 2–1	Buenos Aires	LC	Watson-Hutton, Brown E
19–09	Uruguay	D 2–2	Montevideo	NC	Viale, OG
10–10	Uruguay	W 3–1	Buenos Aires	MEA	Fernandez E, Brown G, Brown A
27–05–1910	Chile	W 3–1	Buenos Aires	Fr	Viale, Susan, Hayes H
5–06	Chile	W 5–1	Buenos Aires	SC	Brown E 2, Susan 2, Brown EA
12–06	Uruguay	W 4–1	Buenos Aires	SC	Viale, Hayes H, Watson-Hutton, Susan
15–08	Uruguay	L 1–3	Montevideo	LC	
11–09	Chile	W 3–0	Viña del Mar	Fr	
13–11	Uruguay	D 1–1	Buenos Aires	MEA	Gonzalez T
27–11	Uruguay	L 2–6	Buenos Aires	MEA	Gonzalez M, Viale
30–04–1911	Uruguay*	W 2–1	Montevideo	Fr	
15–08	Uruguay	L 0–2	Buenos Aires	LC	
17–09	Uruguay	W 3–2	Montevideo	NC	Brown A, Brown E
8–10	Uruguay	D 1–1	Montevideo	MEU	
22–10	Uruguay	W 2–0	Buenos Aires	MEA	
29–10	Uruguay	L 0–3	Montevideo	MEU	
25–02–1912	Uruguay*	W 2–0	Buenos Aires	Fr	
15–08	Uruguay	L 0–2	Montevideo	LC	
25–08	Uruguay	L 0–3	Montevideo	MEU	
22–09	Uruguay	L 0–1	Buenos Aires	MEA	
6–10	Uruguay	D 3–3	Buenos Aires	NC	
1–12	Uruguay	W 3–1	Montevideo	MC	
27–04–1913	Uruguay*	D 0–0	Buenos Aires	Fr	
15–06	Uruguay	D 1–1	Buenos Aires	SPC	Gonzalez M
9–07	Uruguay	W 2–1	Buenos Aires	SPC	
13–07	Uruguay*	L 4–5	Montevideo	Fr	
15–08	Uruguay	W 4–0	Buenos Aires	LC	
31–08	Uruguay	W 2–0	Buenos Aires	MEA	
21–09	Chile	W 2–0	Viña del Mar	Fr	
28–09	Uruguay*	W 4–0	Buenos Aires	Fr	
5–10	Uruguay	L 0–1	Montevideo	MEU	
26–10	Uruguay	L 0–1	Montevideo	NC	
30–08–1914	Uruguay	L 2–3	Montevideo	MEU	
13–09	Uruguay	W 2–1	Buenos Aires	MEA	Gallardo, Lozcano
20–09	Brazil	W 3–0	Buenos Aires	Fr	Izaguirre 2, Molfino
27–09	Brazil	L 0–1	Buenos Aires	RC	
18–07–1915	Uruguay	W 3–2	Montevideo	MEU	Marcovecchio 2, Hayes E
15–08	Uruguay	W 2–1	Buenos Aires	LC	
12–09	Uruguay	L 0–2	Montevideo	NC	
6–07–1916	Chile	W 6–1	Buenos Aires	SC	Ohaco 2, Brown J 2, Marcovecchio 2
10–07	Brazil	D 1–1	Buenos Aires	SC	Laguna
12–07	Chile	W 1–0	Buenos Aires	Fr	Marcovecchio
17–07	Uruguay	D 0–0	Buenos Aires	SC	
15–08	Uruguay	W 2–1	Montevideo	LC	Hayes E, Laiolo
15–08	Uruguay	W 3–1	Buenos Aires	NC	Ohaco 2, Hiller
1–10	Uruguay	W 1–0	Montevideo	MEU	Badalini
1–10	Uruguay	W 7–2	Buenos Aires	MEA	
29–10	Uruguay	L 1–3	Montevideo	Fr	
18–07–1917	Uruguay	W 2–0	Montevideo	MEU	Marcovecchio, Vivaldi
15–08	Uruguay	W 1–0	Buenos Aires	LC	Calomino
2–09	Uruguay	L 0–1	Montevideo	NC	
3–10	Brazil	W 4–2	Montevideo	SC	Calomino, Ohaco 2, Blanco

6-10	Chile	W	1-0	Montevideo	SC	OG
14-10	Uruguay	L	0-1	Montevideo	SC	
22-10	Chile	D	1-1	Buenos Aires	Fr	Matozzi
18-07-1918	Uruguay	D	1-1	Montevideo	MEU	Laiolo
28-07	Uruguay	L	1-3	Montevideo	MEU	Laiolo
15-08	Uruguay	D	0-0	Buenos Aires	MEA	
25-08	Uruguay	W	2-1	Buenos Aires	MEA	
20-09	Uruguay	D	1-1	Montevideo	LC	
29-09	Uruguay	W	2-0	Buenos Aires	NC	
11-05-1919	Paraguay	W	5-1	Asuncion	Fr	Laguna 2, OG 2, Ochandio
13-05	Uruguay	L	2-3	Rio de Janeiro	SC	Izaguirre, Calomino
18-05	Paraguay	W	2-0	Asuncion	Fr	
18-05	Brazil	L	1-3	Rio de Janeiro	SC	Izaguirre
21-05	Paraguay	W	2-1	Asuncion	Fr	
22-05	Chile	W	4-1	Rio de Janeiro	SC	Clarke 3, Izaguirre
24-05	Paraguay	W	2-1	Asuncion	Fr	
1-06	Brazil	D	3-3	Rio de Janeiro	Fr	
18-07	Uruguay	L	1-4	Montevideo	MEU	
24-08	Uruguay	L	1-2	Montevideo	NC	
7-09	Uruguay	L	1-2	Buenos Aires	LC	
19-10	Uruguay	W	6-1	Buenos Aires	MEA	
7-12	Uruguay	L	2-4	Montevideo	Fr	
18-07-1920	Uruguay	L	0-2	Montevideo	MEU	
25-07	Uruguay	L	1-3	Buenos Aires	NC	
8-08	Uruguay	W	1-0	Buenos Aires	MEA	
12-09	Uruguay	D	1-1	Viña del Mar	SC	Etcheverria
17-09	Chile	D	1-1	Viña del Mar	SC	Dellavella
25-09	Brazil	W	2-0	Viña del Mar	SC	Etcheverria, Libonatti
12-10	Brazil	W	3-1	Buenos Aires	Fr	
7-04-1921	Paraguay*	L	1-3	Asuncion	Fr	
14-04	Paraguay*	D	2-2	Asuncion	Fr	
25-09	Chile	W	4-1	Viña del Mar	Fr	
2-10	Chile	D	1-1	Santiago	Fr	
2-10	Brazil	W	1-0	Buenos Aires	SC	Libonatti
16-10	Paraguay	W	3-0	Buenos Aires	SC	Libonatti, Saruppo, Etcheverria
30-10	Uruguay	W	1-0	Buenos Aires	SC	Libonatti
22-01-1922	Uruguay*	L	1-3	Buenos Aires	Fr	
22-07	Uruguay	D	2-2	Montevideo	Fr	
27-08	Uruguay*	D	3-3	Buenos Aires	Fr	
28-09	Chile	W	4-0	Rio de Janeiro	SC	Francia 2, Chiessa, Gaslini
8-10	Uruguay	L	0-1	Rio de Janeiro	SC	
15-10	Brazil	L	0-2	Rio de Janeiro	SC	
18-10	Paraguay	W	2-0	Rio de Janeiro	SC	Francia 2
22-10	Brazil	L	1-2	Sao Paulo	RC	Chiessa
22-10	Uruguay*	W	3-2	Buenos Aires	Fr	
22-10	Chile	W	1-0	Buenos Aires	Fr	
11-11	Uruguay*	W	4-0	La Plata	Fr	
12-11	Uruguay	L	0-1	Montevideo	LC	
10-12	Uruguay	L	0-1	Montevideo	MEU	
17-12	Uruguay	D	2-2	Buenos Aires	NC	
20-05-1923	Paraguay	L	0-2	Buenos Aires	RCB	
25-05	Paraguay	W	1-0	Buenos Aires	RCB	Izaguirre
25-05	Uruguay*	L	0-2	Montevideo	Fr	
24-06	Uruguay	D	0-0	Buenos Aires	LC	
15-07	Uruguay	D	2-2	Buenos Aires	MEA	
22-07	Uruguay	D	2-2	Montevideo	MEU	
25-08	Uruguay*	D	1-1	Montevideo	Fr	
30-09	Uruguay	W	2-0	Montevideo	MEU	
29-10	Paraguay	W	4-3	Montevideo	SC	Saruppo, Aguirre 3
18-11	Brazil	W	2-1	Montevideo	SC	Onzari, Saruppo
2-12	Uruguay	L	0-2	Montevideo	SC	
2-12	Brazil	L	0-2	Buenos Aires	RC	
3-12	Chile	W	6-0	Buenos Aires	Fr	
8-12	Uruguay	L	2-3	Buenos Aires	Fr	
9-12	Brazil	W	2-0	Buenos Aires	RC	
15-05-1924	Paraguay	W	3-1	Asuncion	RCB	Onzari, Tarasconi, Seoane
18-05	Paraguay	L	1-2	Asuncion	RCB	Tarasconi
25-05	Uruguay	W	4-0	Buenos Aires	NC	
25-05	Uruguay	L	0-2	Montevideo	LC	

10–08	Uruguay	D	0–0	Buenos Aires	Fr	
31–08	Uruguay	W	3–2	Montevideo	MEU	
21–09	Uruguay	D	1–1	Montevideo	Fr	
2–10	Uruguay	W	2–1	Buenos Aires	Fr	
12–10	Paraguay	D	0–0	Montevideo	SC	
25–10	Chile	W	2–0	Montevideo	SC	Loyarte, Sosa
2–11	Uruguay	D	0–0	Montevideo	SC	
16–11	Uruguay	L	0–1	Montevideo	Fr	
5–01–1925	Uruguay	W	1–0	Buenos Aires	Fr	
9–07	Paraguay	D	1–1	Buenos Aires	RCB	Evaristo J
12–07	Paraguay	D	1–1	Buenos Aires	RCB	Gaslini
29–11	Paraguay	W	2–0	Buenos Aires	SC	Seoane, Sanchez
13–12	Brazil	W	4–1	Buenos Aires	SC	Seoane 3, Garasino
20–12	Paraguay	W	3–1	Buenos Aires	SC	Tarasconi, Seoane, Irurieta
25–12	Brazil	D	2–2	Buenos Aires	SC	Cerroti, Seoane
29–05–1926	Paraguay	W	2–1	Asuncion	RCB	Cherro, Stanaro
3–06	Paraguay	W	2–1	Asuncion	RCB	Cesarini, Villagra
16–10	Bolivia	W	5–0	Santiago	SC	Cherro 2, Sosa, Delgado, Miguel
20–10	Paraguay	W	8–0	Santiago	SC	Sosa 4, Delgado 2, Cherro, Miguel
24–10	Uruguay	L	0–2	Santiago	SC	
31–10	Chile	D	1–1	Santiago	SC	Tarasconi
14–07–1927	Uruguay	W	1–0	Montevideo	NC	Carricaberry
30–08	Uruguay	L	0–1	Buenos Aires	LC	
30–10	Bolivia	W	7–1	Lima	SC	Luna 2, Carricaberry 2, Recanattini, Seoane 2
20–11	Uruguay	W	3–2	Lima	SC	Recanattini, Luna
27–11	Peru	W	5–1	Lima	SC	Ferreira, Maglio 2, Orsi, Carricaberry
1–04–1928	Portugal	D	0–0	Lisbon	Fr	
29–05	United States	W	11–2	Amsterdam	OGr1	Tarasconi 4, Cherro 3, Orsi 2, Ferreira, Findlay
2–06	Belgium	W	6–3	Amsterdam	OGqf	Tarasconi 4, Cherro, Orsi
6–06	Egypt	W	6–0	Amsterdam	OGsf	Tarasconi 4, Ferreira, Cherro
10–06	Uruguay	D	1–1	Amsterdam	OGf	Ferreira
13–06	Uruguay	L	1–2	Amsterdam	OGf	Monti
30–08	Uruguay	W	1–0	Buenos Aires	NC	Seoane
21–09	Uruguay	D	2–2	Montevideo	LC	Maglio, Alonso
16–06–1929	Uruguay	W	2–0	Buenos Aires	Fr	
16–06	Uruguay	D	1–1	Montevideo	Fr	
20–09	Uruguay	L	1–2	Montevideo	NC	Maglio
28–09	Uruguay	D	0–0	Buenos Aires	LC	
3–11	Peru	W	3–0	Buenos Aires	SC	Zumelzu 2, Peucelle
10–11	Paraguay	W	4–1	Buenos Aires	SC	Ferreira 2, Evaristo M, Cherro
17–11	Uruguay	W	2–0	Buenos Aires	SC	Ferreira, Evaristo
25–05–1930	Uruguay	D	1–1	Buenos Aires	NC	Varallo
15–07	France	W	1–0	Montevideo	WCr1	Monti
19–07	Mexico	W	6–3	Montevideo	WCr1	Stabile 3, Varallo 2, Zumelzu
22–07	Chile	W	3–1	Montevideo	WCr1	Stabile 2, Evaristo M
26–07	United States	W	6–1	Montevideo	WCsf	Monti, Scopelli, Stabile 2, Peucelle 2
30–07	Uruguay	L	2–4	Montevideo	WCf	Peucelle, Stabile
3–08	Yugoslavia	W	3–1	Buenos Aires	Fr	Sponda 2, Trulillo
19–04–1931	Paraguay	W	1–0	Asuncion	Fr	
25–04	Paraguay	D	1–1	Asuncion	Fr	
4–07	Paraguay	D	1–1	Buenos Aires	RCB	Monti
9–07	Paraguay	W	3–1	Buenos Aires	RCB	Castro 2, Spadaro
15–05–1932	Uruguay	W	2–0	Buenos Aires	Fr	
18–05	Uruguay	L	0–1	Montevideo	Fr	
21–01–1933	Uruguay	L	1–2	Montevideo	Fr	
5–02	Uruguay	W	4–1	Buenos Aires	Fr	
14–12	Uruguay	W	1–0	Montevideo	Fr	
27–05–1934	Sweden	L	2–3	Bologna	WCr1	Belis, Galateo
18–07	Uruguay	D	2–2	Montevideo	Fr	
15–08	Uruguay	W	1–0	Buenos Aires	Fr	
6–01–1935	Chile	W	4–1	Lima	SC	Lauri, Garcia D, Arrieta, Masantonio
20–01	Peru	W	4–1	Lima	SC	Masantonio 3, Garcia D
20–01	Uruguay*	D	2–2	Buenos Aires	Fr	
27–01	Uruguay	L	0–3	Lima	SC	
18–07	Uruguay	D	1–1	Montevideo	HGC	Peucelle
15–08	Uruguay	W	3–0	Buenos Aires	JMC	Zozaya 2, Garcia D
9–08–1936	Uruguay	W	1–0	Buenos Aires	JMC	Zozaya

20–09	Uruguay	L	1–2	Montevideo	HGC	Garcia D
30–12	Chile	W	2–1	Buenos Aires	SC	Varallo F 2
9–01–1937	Paraguay	W	6–1	Buenos Aires	SC	Zozaya 3, Scopelli 2, Garcia E
16–01	Peru	W	1–0	Buenos Aires	SC	Zozaya
23–01	Uruguay	L	2–3	Buenos Aires	SC	Varallo F, Zozaya
30–01	Brazil	W	1–0	Buenos Aires	SC	Garcia E
1–02	Brazil	W	2–0	Buenos Aires	SC	De La Matta 2
10–10	Uruguay	W	3–0	Montevideo	NC	Marvezzi, Fidel, Moreno
11–11	Uruguay	W	5–1	Buenos Aires	LC	Masantonio 3, Fidel, Garcia E
18–06–1938	Uruguay	W	1–0	Buenos Aires	JMC	Moreno
12–10	Uruguay	W	3–2	Montevideo	HGC	Garcia E, Cosso, Cavadini
15–01–1939	Brazil	W	5–1	Rio de Janeiro	RC	Masantonio 2, Moreno 2, Garcia E
22–01	Brazil	L	2–3	Rio de Janeiro	RC	Rodolfi, Garcia E
14–08	Paraguay	W	1–0	Asuncion	RCB	Fabrini
16–08	Paraguay	D	2–2	Asuncion	RCB	Sarlanga, Arrieta
18–02–1940	Brazil	D	2–2	Sao Paulo	RC	Cassán, Baldonedo
18–02	Paraguay	W	3–1	Buenos Aires	RCB	Ballesteros, Pedernera, Leguizamón
25–02	Paraguay	W	4–0	Buenos Aires	RCB	Laferrara 2, Masantonio 2
25–02	Brazil	W	3–0	Sao Paulo	RC	Baldonedo, Fidel, Sastre
2–03	Chile*	W	4–1	Buenos Aires	Fr	Laferrara 3, Maril
5–03	Brazil	W	6–1	Buenos Aires	RC	Peucelle 3, Masantonio 2, Baldonedo
9–03	Chile*	W	3–2	Buenos Aires	Fr	Arrieta 3
10–03	Brazil	L	2–3	Buenos Aires	RC	Baldonedo 2
17–03	Brazil	W	5–1	Buenos Aires	RC	Baldonedo 2, Masantonio, Peucelle, Cassán
18–07	Uruguay	L	0–3	Montevideo	HGC	
15–08	Uruguay	W	5–0	Buenos Aires	JMC	Sarlanga, Esperón, Moreno, Marvezzi 2
5–01–1941	Chile*	W	2–1	Santiago	Fr	Sastre, Arregui
9–01	Chile*	W	5–2	Santiago	Fr	Sastre 2, Arrieta 2, Arregui
19–01	Peru	D	1–1	Lima	RGP	Moreno
26–01	Peru	D	1–1	Lima	RGP	Belén
29–01	Peru	W	3–0	Lima	RGP	Moreno, Sastre, Marvezzi
12–02	Peru	W	2–1	Santiago	SC	Moreno 2
16–02	Ecuador	W	6–1	Santiago	SC	Marvezzi 5, Moreno
23–02	Uruguay	W	1–0	Santiago	SC	Sastre
4–03	Chile	W	1–0	Santiago	SC	Garcia E
11–01–1942	Paraguay	W	4–3	Montevideo	SC	Masantonio 2, Sandoval, Perucca
17–01	Brazil	W	2–1	Montevideo	SC	Garcia E, Masantonio
22–01	Ecuador	W	12–0	Montevideo	SC	Moreno 5, Masantonio 4, Garcia E, Pedernera, Perucca
25–01	Peru	W	3–1	Montevideo	SC	Moreno 2, Heredia
31–01	Chile	D	0–0	Montevideo	SC	*Abandoned 43 mins*
7–02	Uruguay	L	0–1	Montevideo	SC	
25–05	Uruguay	W	4–1	Buenos Aires	NC	Alberti, Pontoni, Martino
25–08	Uruguay	D	1–1	Montevideo	LC	Muñoz
6–01–1943	Uruguay*	W	1–0	Buenos Aires	Fr	
9–01	Uruguay*	L	2–6	Montevideo	Fr	
28–03	Uruguay	D	3–3	Buenos Aires	JMC	Pontoni 2, Martino
4–04	Uruguay	W	1–0	Montevideo	HGC	Canteli
10–07	Paraguay	W	5–2	Asuncion	RCB	Sarlanga 2, Pellegrina, Martino, De La Mata
11–07	Paraguay	L	1–2	Asuncion	RCB	Sarlanga
5–01–1944	Uruguay*	W	3–1	Montevideo	Fr	
8–01	Uruguay*	D	3–3	Buenos Aires	Fr	
29–01	Uruguay*	L	1–2	Montevideo	Fr	
29–01	Uruguay*	W	6–2	Buenos Aires	Fr	
6–01–1945	Paraguay	W	5–2	Buenos Aires	RCB	Muñoz, Pontoni 2, Loustau, Martino
9–01	Paraguay	W	5–3	Buenos Aires	RCB	Pontoni 4, Martino
18–01	Bolivia	W	4–0	Santiago	SC	Pontoni, Martino, Loustau, De La Mata
31–01	Ecuador	W	4–2	Santiago	SC	Pontoni, De La Mata, Martino, Pellegrina
7–02	Colombia	W	9–1	Santiago	SC	Pontoni 2, Mendez N 2, Martino 2, Boyé 2, Ferraro 2, Loustau
11–02	Chile	D	1–1	Santiago	SC	Mendez N
15–02	Brazil	W	3–1	Santiago	SC	Mendez N 3
25–02	Uruguay	W	1–0	Santiago	SC	Martino
7–07	Paraguay	L	1–5	Asuncion	RCB	Pontoni
9–07	Paraguay	W	3–1	Asuncion	RCB	Martino 2, Sued
18–07	Uruguay	D	2–2	Montevideo	LC	Martino, OG
15–08	Uruguay	W	6–2	Buenos Aires	NC	Loustau, Ferraro, Mendez N, Martino 2, Pedernera
16–12	Brazil	W	4–3	Sao Paulo	RC	Pedernera, Boyé, Sued, Labruna

20–12	Brazil	L	2–6	Rio de Janeiro	RC	Pedernera, Martino
23–12	Brazil	L	1–3	Rio de Janeiro	RC	Martino
29–12	Uruguay*	D	1–1	Montevideo	Fr	
12–01–1946	Paraguay	W	2–0	Buenos Aires	SC	De La Mata, Martino
19–01	Bolivia	W	7–1	Buenos Aires	SC	Mendez N 2, Labruna 2, Salvini 2, Loustau
26–01	Chile	W	3–1	Buenos Aires	SC	Labruna 2, Pedernera
2–02	Uruguay	W	3–1	Buenos Aires	SC	Pedernera, Labruna, Mendez N
10–02	Brazil	W	2–0	Buenos Aires	SC	Mendez N 2
2–03–1947	Uruguay*	W	2–1	Buenos Aires	Fr	
9–03	Uruguay*	D	4–4	Montevideo	Fr	
2–12	Paraguay	W	6–0	Guayaquil	SC	Pontoni 3, Moreno, Loustau, Mendez N
4–12	Bolivia	W	7–0	Guayaquil	SC	Mendez N 2, Boyé 2, Pontoni, Di Stéfano, Loustau
11–12	Peru	W	3–2	Guayaquil	SC	Moreno, Di Stéfano, Boyé
16–12	Chile	D	1–1	Guayaquil	SC	Di Stéfano
18–12	Colombia	W	6–0	Guayaquil	SC	Di Stéfano 3, Fernandez M, Boyé, Loustau
25–12	Ecuador	W	2–0	Guayaquil	SC	Moreno, Mendez N
28–12	Uruguay	W	3–1	Guayaquil	SC	Mendez N 2, Loustau
18–05–1948	Uruguay*	W	1–0	Montevideo	Fr	
25–05	Uruguay*	L	0–2	Buenos Aires	Fr	
25–03–1950	Paraguay	D	2–2	Buenos Aires	RCB	Bravo, Vernazza
29–03	Paraguay	W	4–0	Buenos Aires	RCB	Labruna 2, Uñate 2
9–05–1951	England	L	1–2	London	Fr	Boyé
13–05	Rep. Ireland	W	1–0	Dublin	Fr	Labruna
7–12–1952	Spain	W	1–0	Madrid	Fr	Infante
14–12	Portugal	W	3–1	Lisbon	Fr	Loustau, Labruna
14–05–1953	England*	W	3–1	Buenos Aires	Fr	
17–05	England	D	0–0	Buenos Aires	Fr	*Abandoned after 23 mins*
5–07	Spain	W	1–0	Buenos Aires	Fr	Grillo
28–11–1954	Portugal	W	3–1	Lisbon	Fr	Micheli, Grillo, Cruz
5–12	Italy	L	0–2	Rome	Fr	
2–03–1955	Paraguay	W	5–3	Santiago	SC	Micheli 4, Borello
9–03	Ecuador	W	4–0	Santiago	SC	Bonelli, Grillo, Micheli, Borelo
16–03	Peru	D	2–2	Santiago	SC	Grillo, Cecconato
27–03	Uruguay	W	6–1	Santiago	SC	Labruna 3, Micheli 2, Borello
30–03	Chile	W	1–0	Santiago	SC	Micheli
22–01–1956	Peru	W	2–1	Montevideo	SC	Sivori, Vairo
29–01	Chile	W	2–0	Montevideo	SC	Labruna 2
1–02	Paraguay	W	1–0	Montevideo	SC	Cecconato
5–02	Brazil	L	0–1	Montevideo	SC	
15–02	Uruguay	L	0–1	Montevideo	SC	
28–02	Peru	D	0–0	Mexico City	PAC	
6–03	Costa Rica	W	4–3	Mexico City	PAC	Sivori 3, Maschio
11–03	Chile	W	3–0	Mexico City	PAC	Maschio 2, Sivori
13–03	Mexico	D	0–0	Mexico City	PAC	
18–03	Brazil	D	2–2	Mexico City	PAC	Yudica, Sivori
24–06	Italy	W	1–0	Buenos Aires	Fr	Conde
1–07	Uruguay	W	2–1	Montevideo	CA	Grillo 2
8–07	Brazil	D	0–0	Buenos Aires	CA	
15–08	Paraguay	W	1–0	Asuncion	RCB	Cross
19–08	Czechoslovakia	W	1–0	Buenos Aires	Fr	Angelillo
10–10	Uruguay	W	2–1	Paysandu	Fr	Garabal 2
14–11	Uruguay	D	2–2	Buenos Aires	Fr	Corbatta, Angelillo
13–03–1957	Colombia	W	8–2	Lima	SC	Maschio 4, Angelillo 2, Cruz O, Corbatta
17–03	Ecuador	W	3–0	Lima	SC	Angelillo 2, Sivori
20–03	Uruguay	W	4–0	Lima	SC	Maschio 2, Angelillo, Sanfilippo
28–03	Chile	W	6–2	Lima	SC	Angelillo 2, Maschio 2, Sivori, Corbatta
3–04	Brazil	W	3–0	Lima	SC	Angelillo, Maschio, Cruz O
6–04	Peru	L	1–2	Lima	SC	Sivori
9–04	Peru	W	4–1	Lima	Fr	Angelillo, Juarez, Sanfilippo, Brookes
23–05	Uruguay	D	0–0	Montevideo	NC	
5–06	Uruguay	D	1–1	Buenos Aires	LC	
7–07	Brazil	W	2–1	Rio de Janeiro	RC	Labruna, Juarez
10–07	Brazil	L	0–2	Sao Paulo	RC	
6–10	Bolivia	L	0–2	La Paz	WCq	
13–10	Chile	W	2–0	Santiago	WCq	Conde, Menendez
20–10	Chile	W	4–0	Buenos Aires	WCq	Corbatta, Prado, Menendez, Zarate
27–10	Bolivia	W	4–0	Buenos Aires	WCq	Corbatta 2, Prado, Menendez
6–04–1958	Uruguay	L	0–1	Montevideo	Fr	

20–04	Paraguay	L	0–1	Asuncion	Fr	
26–04	Paraguay	W	2–0	Buenos Aires	Fr	
30–04	Uruguay	W	2–0	Buenos Aires	Fr	
8–06	West Germany	L	1–3	Malmo	WCr1	Corbatta
11–06	Nth. Ireland	W	3–1	Halmstad	WCr1	Corbatta, Menendez, Avio
15–06	Czechoslovakia	L	1–6	Halsingborg	WCr1	Corbatta
7–03–1959	Chile	W	6–1	Buenos Aires	SC	Manfredini 2, Pizzutti 2, Calla, Belen
11–03	Bolivia	W	2–0	Buenos Aires	SC	Corbatta, Calla
18–03	Peru	W	3–1	Buenos Aires	SC	Corbatta, Sosa R, OG
22–03	Paraguay	W	3–1	Buenos Aires	SC	Corbatta, Sosa R, Cap
30–03	Uruguay	W	4–1	Buenos Aires	SC	Belen 2, Sosa R 2
4–04	Brazil	D	1–1	Buenos Aires	SC	Pizzutti
18–11	Chile	L	2–4	Santiago	Fr	Ruiz, Sanfilippo
9–12	Paraguay	W	4–2	Guayaquil	SC	Sanfilippo 2, Sosa R, Pizzutti
12–12	Ecuador	D	1–1	Guayaquil	SC	Sosa R
16–12	Uruguay	L	0–5	Guayaquil	SC	
22–12	Brazil	W	4–1	Guayaquil	SC	Sanfilippo 3, Garcia O
8–03–1960	Costa Rica	D	0–0	San Jose	PAC	
10–03	Mexico	W	3–2	San Jose	PAC	Belén 2, Nardiello
13–03	Brazil	W	2–1	San Jose	PAC	Belén, Nardiello
15–03	Costa Rica	W	2–0	San Jose	PAC	Onega, D'Ascenso
17–03	Mexico	W	2–0	San Jose	PAC	Jimenez, Nardiello
20–03	Brazil	L	0–1	San Jose	PAC	
26–05	Brazil	W	4–2	Buenos Aires	RC	Nardiello 2, D'Ascenso, Belén
29–05	Brazil	L	1–4	Buenos Aires	RC	Sosa
9–07	Paraguay	W	1–0	Buenos Aires	CA	Sosa
12–07	Brazil	L	1–5	Rio de Janeiro	CA	Sosa
24–07	Spain	W	2–0	Buenos Aires	Fr	Sanfilippo 2
17–08	Uruguay	W	4–0	Buenos Aires	CA	Sanfilippo 3, Jimenez
4–12	Ecuador	W	6–3	Guayaquil	WCq	Corbatta 2, Pando, Sosa, Belén, Ramaciotti, Pando
17–12	Ecuador	W	5–0	Buenos Aires	WCq	OG, Sanfilippo, Corbatta, Sosa, Pando
17–05–1961	Paraguay	D	0–0	Asuncion	Fr	
4–06	Portugal	W	2–0	Lisbon	Fr	Pando, Sanfilippo
11–06	Spain	L	0–2	Seville	Fr	
15–06	Italy	L	1–4	Florence	Fr	Sacchi
19–06	Czechoslovakia	D	3–3	Brno	Fr	Sanfilippo 2, Artime
24–06	Soviet Union	D	0–0	Moscow	Fr	
12–10	Paraguay	W	5–1	Buenos Aires	Fr	Corbatta 2, Artime, Pagani, Sanfilippo
18–11	Soviet Union	L	1–2	Buenos Aires	Fr	Belén
13–03–1962	Uruguay	D	1–1	Montevideo	Fr	Sosa
28–03	Mexico	W	1–0	Buenos Aires	Fr	OG
30–05	Bulgaria	W	1–0	Rancagua	WCr1	Facundo
2–06	England	L	1–3	Rancagua	WCr1	Sanfilippo
6–06	Hungary	D	0–0	Rancagua	WCr1	
15–08	Uruguay	W	3–1	Buenos Aires	LC	Pagani, Willington, Gonzalez A
7–11	Chile	D	1–1	Santiago	CDC	Artime
21–11	Chile	W	1–0	Buenos Aires	CDC	Artime
10–03–1963	Colombia	W	4–2	Cochabamba	SC	Zarate 2, Rodriguez M, Fernandez J
13–03	Peru	L	1–2	Cochabamba	SC	Zarate
20–03	Ecuador	W	4–2	Cochabamba	SC	Savoy 2, Zarate, Rodriguez M
24–03	Brazil	W	3–0	La Paz	SC	Rodriguez M, Savoy, Juarez
28–03	Bolivia	L	2–3	La Paz	SC	Rodriguez M 2
31–03	Paraguay	D	1–1	La Paz	SC	Lallana
13–04	Brazil	W	3–2	Sao Paulo	RC	Lallana 2, Juarez
16–04	Brazil	L	2–5	Rio de Janeiro	RC	Fernandez
15–10	Paraguay	W	4–0	Asuncion	RCB	Artime 2, Savoy, Onega
29–10	Paraguay	L	2–3	Buenos Aires	RCB	Menotti, Artime
31–05–1964	Portugal	W	2–0	Rio de Janeiro	CN	Rojas A, Rendo
3–06	Brazil	W	3–0	Sao Paulo	CN	Onega, Telch 2
6–06	England	W	1–0	Rio de Janeiro	CN	Rojas A
24–09	Chile	W	5–0	Buenos Aires	CDC	Artime 2, Onega, Rendo, Bielli
14–10	Chile	D	1–1	Santiago	CDC	Rattin
25–11	Paraguay	L	0–3	Asuncion	RCB	
8–12	Paraguay	W	8–1	Buenos Aires	RCB	Artime 4, Onega 2, Prospitti 2
3–06–1965	France	D	0–0	Paris	Fr	
9–06	Brazil	D	0–0	Rio de Janeiro	Fr	
14–07	Chile	W	1–0	Buenos Aires	CDC	Rojas A
21–07	Chile	D	1–1	Santiago	CDC	Mas

1-08	Paraguay	W	3-0	Buenos Aires	WCq	OG, Onega, Artime
8-08	Paraguay	D	0-0	Asuncion	WCq	
17-08	Bolivia	W	4-1	Buenos Aires	WCq	Bernao 2, Onega 2
29-08	Bolivia	W	2-1	La Paz	WCq	Artime 2
1-12	Soviet Union	D	1-1	Buenos Aires	Fr	Onega
11-06-1966	Poland	D	1-1	Buenos Aires	Fr	Mas
17-06	Denmark*	W	2-0	Copenhagen	Fr	
22-06	Italy	L	0-3	Turin	Fr	
13-07	Spain	W	2-1	Birmingham	WCr1	Artime 2
16-07	West Germany	D	0-0	Birmingham	WCr1	
19-07	Switzerland	W	2-0	Sheffield	WCr1	Artime, Onega
23-07	England	L	0-1	London	WCqf	
18-01-1967	Paraguay	W	4-1	Montevideo	SC	Mas, Artime, Bernao, Albrecht
22-01	Bolivia	W	1-0	Montevideo	SC	Bernao
25-01	Venezuela	W	5-1	Montevideo	SC	Artime 3, Carone, Marzolini
28-01	Chile	W	2-0	Montevideo	SC	Sarnari, Artime
2-02	Uruguay	L	0-1	Montevideo	SC	
15-08	Chile	L	0-1	Santiago	Fr	
22-08	Mexico	L	1-2	Mexico City	Fr	Gennoni
13-10	Paraguay	D	1-1	Asuncion	Fr	Pardo
8-11	Chile	L	1-3	Santiago	Fr	Carone
15-05-1968	Paraguay	L	0-2	Asuncion	Fr	
5-06	Uruguay	W	2-0	Buenos Aires	NC	Avallay, Fischer
20-06	Uruguay	L	1-2	Montevideo	LC	Fischer
7-08	Brazil	L	1-4	Rio de Janeiro	Fr	Basile
11-08	Brazil	L	2-3	Belo Horizonte	Fr	
18-08	Colombia	W	1-0	Cali	Fr	Savoy
29-08	Peru	D	2-2	Lima	Fr	Yazalde, Savoy
1-09	Peru	D	1-1	Lima	Fr	Veglio
27-11	Chile	W	4-0	Rosario	CDC	Veglio, Fischer 2, Minnitti
4-12	Chile	L	1-2	Santiago	CDC	Rendo
22-12	Yugoslavia	D	1-1	Mar del Plata	Fr	Olmedo
19-03-1969	Paraguay	D	1-1	Rosario	Fr	Cocco
9-04	Paraguay	D	0-0	Asuncion	Fr	
28-05	Chile	D	1-1	Santiago	Fr	OG
11-06	Chile	W	2-1	La Plata	Fr	Fischer, Brindisi
27-07	Bolivia	L	1-3	La Paz	WCq	Tarabini
3-08	Peru	L	0-1	Lima	WCq	
24-08	Bolivia	W	1-0	Buenos Aires	WCq	Albrecht
31-08	Peru	D	2-2	Buenos Aires	WCq	Albrecht, Rendo
4-03-1970	Brazil	W	2-0	Porto Alegre	Fr	Mas, Conigliaro
8-03	Brazil	L	1-2	Rio de Janeiro	Fr	Brindisi
8-04	Uruguay	W	2-1	Buenos Aires	Fr	Conigliaro, Mas
15-04	Uruguay	L	1-2	Montevideo	Fr	Giribet
22-10	Paraguay	D	1-1	Asuncion	Fr	Brindisi
8-01-1971	France	L	3-4	Buenos Aires	Fr	Brindisi, Nicolau, Madurga
13-01	France	W	2-0	Mar del Plata	Fr	Laraignee, Madurga
4-07	Paraguay	D	1-1	Asuncion	RCB	Marcos
9-07	Paraguay	W	1-0	Rosario	RCB	Laraignee
14-07	Uruguay	W	1-0	Buenos Aires	NC	Madurga
18-07	Uruguay	D	1-1	Montevideo	LC	
21-07	Chile	D	2-2	Santiago	CDC	Bianchi 2
28-07	Brazil	D	1-1	Buenos Aires	RC	Madurga
31-07	Brazil	D	2-2	Buenos Aires	RC	Fischer 2
4-08	Chile	W	1-0	Buenos Aires	CDC	Fischer
25-05-1972	Paraguay	D	0-0	Salta	Fr	
31-05	Chile	W	4-3	Santiago	CDC	Mas 2, Raimondo, Mastrangelo
22-06	Colombia	W	4-1	Salvador	Clr1	Bianchi 3, Bargas
25-06	France	D	0-0	Salvador	Clr1	
29-06	Portugal	L	1-3	Rio de Janeiro	Clr2	
2-07	Soviet Union	W	1-0	Belo Horizonte	Clr2	Pastoriza
6-07	Uruguay	W	1-0	Porto Alegre	Clr2	
9-07	Yugoslavia	L	2-4	Rio de Janeiro	Cl3p	Brindisi 2
25-09	Chile	W	2-0	Buenos Aires	CDC	Brindisi, Ayala
11-10	Spain	L	0-1	Madrid	Fr	
25-10	Peru	W	2-0	Lima	RCC	Ayala 2
6-02-1973	Mexico	L	0-2	Mexico City	Fr	
14-02	West Germany	W	3-2	Munich	Fr	Ghiso, Alonso, Brindisi
20-02	Israel	D	1-1	Tel Aviv	Fr	Heredia

17–05	Uruguay	D	1–1	Buenos Aires	LC	Brindisi
23–05	Uruguay	D	1–1	Montevideo	NC	Babington
13–07	Chile	W	5–4	Buenos Aires	CDC	Guerini, Ayala 2, Brindisi 2
18–07	Chile	L	1–3	Santiago	CDC	Brindisi
27–07	Peru	W	3–1	Buenos Aires	RCC	Guerini 2, Brindisi
9–09	Bolivia	W	4–0	Buenos Aires	WCq	Brindisi 2, Ayala 2
16–09	Paraguay	D	1–1	Asuncion	WCq	Ayala
23–09	Bolivia	W	1–0	La Paz	WCq	Fornari
7–10	Paraguay	W	3–1	Buenos Aires	WCq	Ayala 2, Guerini
22–04–1974	Romania	W	2–1	Buenos Aires	Fr	Houseman, Kempes
18–05	France	W	1–0	Paris	Fr	Kempes
22–05	England	D	2–2	London	Fr	Kempes 2
26–05	Holland	L	1–4	Amsterdam	Fr	Wolf
15–06	Poland	L	2–3	Stuttgart	WCr1	Heredia, Babington
19–06	Italy	D	1–1	Stuttgart	WCr1	Houseman
23–06	Haiti	W	4–1	Munich	WCr1	Yazalde 2, Houseman, Ayala
26–06	Holland	L	0–4	Gelsenkirchen	WCr2	
30–06	Brazil	L	1–2	Hanover	WCr2	Brindisi
3–07	East Germany	D	1–1	Gelsenkirchen	WCr2	Houseman
12–10	Spain	D	1–1	Buenos Aires	Fr	Rogel
6–11	Chile	W	2–0	Santiago	CDC	Lopez, Ferrero
20–11	Chile	D	1–1	Buenos Aires	CDC	Galletti
27–06–1975	Bolivia*	W	2–1	Cochabamba	Fr	
18–07	Uruguay	W	3–2	Montevideo	NC	Alonso, Valdano 2
3–08	Venezuela	W	5–1	Caracus	SCr1	Luque 3, Kempes, Ardiles
6–08	Brazil	L	1–2	Belo Horizonte	SCr1	Asad
10–08	Venezuela	W	11–0	Rosario	SCr1	Killer 3, Kempes 2, Gallego, Ardiles, Zanabria 2, Boveda, Luque
16–08	Brazil	L	0–1	Rosario	SCr1	
21–08	United States	W	6–0	Mexico City	Fr	Ardiles 2, Cardemas, Coscia 2, Valencia
24–08	Costa Rica	W	2–0	Mexico City	Fr	
31–08	Mexico	D	1–1	Mexico City	Fr	Coscia
25–02–1976	Paraguay	W	3–2	Asuncion	CA	Scotta 3
27–02	Brazil	L	1–2	Buenos Aires	CA	Kempes
20–03	Soviet Union	W	1–0	Kiev	Fr	Kempes
24–03	Poland	W	2–1	Chorzow	Fr	Scotta, Houseman
27–03	Hungary	L	0–2	Budapest	Fr	
8–04	Uruguay	W	4–1	Buenos Aires	CA	Kempes 2, Luque, Scotta
28–04	Paraguay	D	2–2	Buenos Aires	CA	Kempes 2
19–05	Brazil	L	0–2	Rio de Janeiro	CA	
9–06	Uruguay	W	3–0	Montevideo	CA	Luque, Kempes, Houseman
13–10	Chile	W	2–0	Buenos Aires	CDC	Ardiles, Bertoni
28–10	Peru	W	3–1	Lima	RCC	Houseman 2, Passarella
10–11	Peru	W	1–0	Buenos Aires	RCC	Passarella
28–11	Soviet Union	D	0–0	Buenos Aires	Fr	
27–02–1977	Hungary	W	5–1	Buenos Aires	Fr	Bertoni 3, Luque 2
22–03	Iran	D	1–1	Madrid	Fr	Bertoni
29–05	Poland	W	3–1	Buenos Aires	Fr	Bertoni 2, Luque
5–06	West Germany	L	1–3	Buenos Aires	Fr	Passarella
12–06	England	D	1–1	Buenos Aires	Fr	Bertoni
18–06	Scotland	D	1–1	Buenos Aires	Fr	Passarella
26–06	France	D	0–0	Buenos Aires	Fr	
3–07	Yugoslavia	W	1–0	Buenos Aires	Fr	Passarella
12–07	East Germany	W	2–0	Buenos Aires	Fr	Houseman, Carrascosa
24–08	Paraguay	W	2–1	Buenos Aires	Fr	Luque 2
31–08	Paraguay	L	0–2	Asuncion	Fr	
4–03–1978	Uruguay	D	0–0	Mar del Plata	Fr	
19–03	Peru	W	2–1	Buenos Aires	RCC	Houseman, Pagnanini

LEADING INTERNATIONAL GOALSCORERS

1	Maradona	29
2	Artime	24
	Passarella	24
4	Luque	22
5	Moreno J	20
	Kempes	20
	Masantonio	20

LEADING INTERNATIONAL APPEARANCES

1	Maradona	82
2	Gallego	71
3	Passarella	69
4	Ruggeri	68
5	Tarantini	60
6	Olguin	58
7	Fillol	56

23-03	Peru	W	3-1	Lima	RCC	Luque, Passarella, Houseman
29-03	Bulgaria	W	3-1	Buenos Aires	Fr	Gallego, Ortiz, Ardiles
5-04	Romania	W	2-0	Buenos Aires	Fr	Passarella 2
19-04	Rep. Ireland*	W	3-1	Buenos Aires	Fr	Luque, Ortiz, Villa
25-04	Uruguay	L	0-2	Montevideo	Fr	
3-05	Uruguay	W	3-0	Buenos Aires	Fr	Luque, Ardiles, Alonso
2-06	Hungary	W	2-1	Buenos Aires	WCr1	Luque, Bertoni
6-06	France	W	2-1	Buenos Aires	WCr1	Passarella, Luque
10-06	Italy	L	0-1	Buenos Aires	WCr1	
14-06	Poland	W	2-0	Rosario	WCr2	Kempes 2
18-06	Brazil	D	0-0	Rosario	WCr2	
21-06	Peru	W	6-0	Rosario	WCr2	Kempes 2, Luque 2, Tarantini, Houseman
25-06	Holland	W	3-1	Buenos Aires	WCf	Kempes 2, Bertoni
25-04-1979	Bulgaria	W	2-1	Buenos Aires	Fr	Houseman, Passarella
22-05	Holland	D	0-0	Berne	Fr	
26-05	Italy	D	2-2	Rome	Fr	Valencia, Passarella
29-05	Rep. Ireland*	D	0-0	Dublin	Fr	
2-06	Scotland	W	3-1	Glasgow	Fr	Luque 2, Maradona
18-07	Bolivia	L	1-2	La Paz	SCr1	Lopez C
2-08	Brazil	L	1-2	Rio de Janeiro	SCr1	Coscia
8-08	Bolivia	W	3-0	Buenos Aires	SCr1	Passarella, Gaspari, Maradona
23-08	Brazil	D	2-2	Buenos Aires	SCr1	Passarella, Diaz R
12-09	West Germany	L	1-2	Berlin	Fr	Castro
16-09	Yugoslavia	L	2-4	Belgrade	Fr	Passarella, Diaz R
13-05-1980	England	L	1-3	London	Fr	Passarella
16-05	Rep. Ireland	W	1-0	Dublin	Fr	Valencia
21-05	Austria	W	5-1	Vienna	Fr	Maradona 3, Santamaria, Luque
18-09	Chile	D	2-2	Mendoza	Fr	Valencia, Diaz R
9-10	Bulgaria	W	2-0	Buenos Aires	Fr	Maradona, Diaz R
12-10	Poland	W	2-1	Buenos Aires	Fr	Passarella, Maradona
15-10	Czechoslovakia	W	1-0	Buenos Aires	Fr	Diaz R
4-12	Soviet Union	D	1-1	Mar del Plata	Fr	Maradona
16-12	Switzerland	W	5-0	Cordoba	Fr	Diaz R, Luque, Valencia, Maradona, Passarella
1-01-1981	West Germany	W	2-1	Montevideo	ML	OG, Diaz R
4-01	Brazil	D	1-1	Montevideo	ML	Maradona
28-10	Poland	L	1-2	Buenos Aires	Fr	Passarella
11-11	Czechoslovakia	D	1-1	Buenos Aires	Fr	Gallego
9-03-1982	Czechoslovakia	D	0-0	Mar del Plata	Fr	
24-03	West Germany	D	1-1	Buenos Aires	Fr	Calderon
14-04	Soviet Union	D	1-1	Buenos Aires	Fr	Diaz R
5-05	Bulgaria	W	2-1	Buenos Aires	Fr	Diaz R, Passarella
12-05	Romania	W	1-0	Rosario	Fr	Diaz R
13-06	Belgium	L	0-1	Barcelona	WCr1	
18-06	Hungary	W	4-1	Alicante	WCr1	Maradona 2, Bertoni, Ardiles
23-06	El Salvador	W	2-0	Alicante	WCr1	Passarella, Bertoni
29-06	Italy	L	1-2	Barcelona	WCr2	Passarella
2-07	Brazil	L	1-3	Barcelona	WCr2	Diaz R
12-05-1983	Chile	D	2-2	Santiago	Fr	Alonso, Gareca
23-06	Chile	W	1-0	Buenos Aires	Fr	Morete
14-07	Paraguay	L	0-1	Asuncion	Fr	
21-07	Paraguay	D	0-0	Buenos Aires	Fr	
10-08	Ecuador	D	2-2	Quito	SCr1	Burruchaga 2
24-08	Brazil	W	1-0	Buenos Aires	SCr1	Gareca
7-09	Ecuador	D	2-2	Buenos Aires	SCr1	Ramos, Burruchaga
14-09	Brazil	D	0-0	Rio de Janeiro	SCr1	
14-01-1984	India	W	1-0	Calcutta	Fr	Gareca
17-01	Poland	D	1-1	Calcutta	Fr	Ponce
20-01	China	L	0-1	Calcutta	Fr	
17-06	Brazil	D	0-0	Sao Paulo	Fr	
18-07	Uruguay	L	0-1	Montevideo	Fr	
2-08	Uruguay	D	0-0	Buenos Aires	Fr	
24-08	Colombia	L	0-1	Bogota	Fr	
1-09	Switzerland	W	2-0	Berne	Fr	Ponce, Dertycia
5-09	Belgium	W	2-0	Brussels	Fr	Trobbiani, Ruggeri
12-09	West Germany	W	3-1	Dusseldorf	Fr	Garre, Ponce, Burruchaga
18-09	Mexico	D	1-1	Monterrey	Fr	Burruchaga
25-10	Mexico	D	1-1	Buenos Aires	Fr	Gareca
28-04-1985	Paraguay	L	0-1	Asuncion	Fr	

5–05	Brazil	L	1–2	Salvador	Fr	Burruchaga
9–05	Paraguay	D	1–1	Buenos Aires	Fr	Maradona
15–05	Chile	W	2–0	Buenos Aires	Fr	Maradona, Burruchaga
26–05	Venezuela	W	3–2	San Cristobal	WCq	Maradona 2, Passarella
2–06	Colombia	W	3–1	Bogota	WCq	Pasculli 2, Burruchaga
9–06	Venezuela	W	3–0	Buenos Aires	WCq	Russo, Clausen, Maradona
16–06	Colombia	W	1–0	Buenos Aires	WCq	Valdano
23–06	Peru	L	0–1	Lima	WCq	
30–06	Peru	D	2–2	Buenos Aires	WCq	Pasculli, Gareca
14–11	Mexico	D	1–1	Los Angeles	Fr	Maradona
17–11	Mexico	D	1–1	Puebla	Fr	Ruggeri
26–03–1986	France	L	0–2	Paris	Fr	
30–04	Norway	L	0–1	Oslo	Fr	
4–05	Israel	W	7–2	Tel Aviv	Fr	Almiron 3, Maradona 2, Borghi, Tapia
2–06	South Korea	W	3–1	Irappuato	WCr1	Valdano 2, Ruggeri
5–06	Italy	D	1–1	Puebla	WCr1	Maradona
10–06	Bulgaria	W	2–0	Mexico City	WCr1	Valdano, Burruchaga
16–06	Uruguay	W	1–0	Puebla	WCr2	Pasculli
22–06	England	W	2–1	Mexico City	WCqf	Maradona 2
25–06	Belgium	W	2–0	Mexico City	WCsf	Maradona 2
29–06	West Germany	W	3–2	Mexico City	WCf	Brown, Valdano, Burruchaga
10–06–1987	Italy	L	1–3	Zurich	Fr	Maradona
20–06	Paraguay	L	0–1	Buenos Aires	Fr	
27–06	Peru	D	1–1	Buenos Aires	SCr1	Maradona
2–07	Ecuador	W	3–0	Buenos Aires	SCr1	Maradona 2, Caniggia
9–07	Uruguay	L	0–1	Buenos Aires	SCsf	
11–07	Colombia	L	1–2	Buenos Aires	SC3p	Caniggia
16–12	West Germany	W	1–0	Buenos Aires	Fr	Burruchaga
31–03–1988	Soviet Union	L	2–4	Berlin	Fr	Troglio, Maradona
2–04	West Germany	L	0–1	Berlin	Fr	
6–07	Saudi Arabia	D	2–2	Adelaide	Fr	Diaz R 2
10–07	Brazil	D	0–0	Melbourne	Fr	
14–07	Australia	L	1–4	Sydney	Fr	Ruggeri
16–07	Saudi Arabia	W	2–0	Canbera	Fr	Simeone, Dertifcia
12–10	Spain	D	1–1	Seville	Fr	Caniggia
9–03–1989	Colombia	L	0–1	Barranquilla	Fr	
13–04	Ecuador	D	2–2	Guayaquil	Fr	Moreno 2
20–04	Chile	D	1–1	Santiago	Fr	Airez
2–07	Chile	W	1–0	Goiania	SCr1	Caniggia
4–07	Ecuador	D	0–0	Goiania	SCr1	
8–07	Uruguay	W	1–0	Goiania	SCr1	Caniggia
10–07	Bolivia	D	0–0	Goiania	SCr1	
12–07	Brazil	L	0–2	Rio de Janeiro	SCr2	
14–07	Uruguay	L	0–2	Rio de Janeiro	SCr2	
16–07	Paraguay	D	0–0	Rio de Janeiro	SCr2	
21–12	Italy	D	0–0	Cagliari	Fr	
14–01–1990	Guatemala*	D	0–0	Guatemala	Fr	
17–01	Mexico	L	0–2	Los Angeles	Fr	
28–03	Scotland	L	0–1	Glasgow	Fr	
3–05	Austria	D	1–1	Vienna	Fr	Burruchaga
8–05	Switzerland	D	1–1	Berne	Fr	Balbo
22–05	Israel	W	2–1	Tel Aviv	Fr	Maradona, Caniggia
8–06	Cameroon	L	0–1	Milan	WCr1	
13–06	Soviet Union	W	2–0	Naples	WCr1	Troglio, Burruchaga
18–06	Romania	D	1–1	Naples	WCr1	Monzon
24–06	Brazil	W	1–0	Turin	WCr2	Caniggia
30–06	Yugoslavia	D	0–0 (3–2p)	Florence	WCqf	
3–07	Italy	D	1–1 (4–3p)	Naples	WCsf	Caniggia
8–07	West Germany	L	0–1	Rome	WCf	
19–02–1991	Hungary	W	2–0	Rosario	Fr	Franco, Mohamed
13–03	Mexico	D	0–0	Buenos Aires	Fr	
27–03	Brazil	D	3–3	Buenos Aires	Fr	Ferreyra, Franco, Bisconti
19–05	USA	W	1–0	Palo Alto	Fr	Franco
23–05	Soviet Union	D	1–1	Manchester	Fr	Ruggeri
25–05	England	D	2–2	London	Fr	Garcia, Franco
27–06	Brazil	D	1–1	Curitiba	Fr	Caniggia
8–07	Venezuela	W	3–0	Santiago	SCr1	Batistuta 2, Caniggia
10–07	Chile	W	1–0	Santiago	SCr1	Batistuta
12–07	Paraguay	W	4–1	Concepcion	SCr1	Batistuta, Simeone, Astrada, Caniggia
14–07	Peru	W	3–2	Santiago	SCr1	Latorre, Craviotto, Garcia
17–07	Brazil	W	3–2	Santiago	SCr2	Franco 2, Batistuta
19–07	Chile	D	0–0	Santiago	SCr2	
21–07	Colombia	W	2–1	Santiago	SCr2	Simeone, Batistuta

* Matches of disputed official status

BOLIVIA

Bolivia are on the lowest rung of the South American ladder, but have the pleasure knowing that they have at least taken part in two World Cup final tournaments and in 1963 were crowned South American champions, a feat that not even Chile can boast of.

A Chilean, Leoncio Zuaznabar, founded the first club in Bolivia, Oruro Royal Club in 1896, but the game spread slowly throughout the rest of the country. The major cities are mostly located in the mountains of the Andes so perhaps the slow growth is not surprising. The Federación Boliviana de Fútbol was formed in Cochabamba in 1925 and the following year it launched a national championship for representative sides, but the real power lay high up in the mountains in the capital La Paz.

In 1908 The Strongest were formed, and they remain the oldest senior club. Six years later the La Paz league was founded and it came to be regarded as the national league. Until clubs from outside La Paz were invited to take part in the league in the early 1950s, it was dominated by The Strongest and Bolivar. Since that time, however, clubs from Cochabamba and Santa Cruz have begun to make their mark, especially Jorge Wilsterman and Oriente Petrolero.

A major reorganisation took place in 1977 with the formation of a truly national league for the first time to replace the Campeonato Professional de Fútbol, as the La Paz league had become known. The standard has remained fairly low overall as the record in the Copa Libertadores shows: three semi-final appearances is equal to that of Venezuela, and together they stand at the bottom of overall standings in the competition.

The national side made its debut in the 1926 South American Championships but it was not an auspicious introduction to international football. Two goals were scored and 24 conceded in the four matches played. The experience the following year was not much dissimilar, and the 19 goals against in three matches effectively put an end to their participation until 1945.

The lure of the 1930 World Cup in Uruguay was too hard to resist and surprisingly the games against Brazil and Yugoslavia were not the heavy defeats many expected them to be. Bolivia lost 4–0 on both occasions, results that were better than all bar one of their scores in the previous South American Championship excursions.

Entry into the Bolivarian Games in 1938, in which they finished an encouraging second to Peru, was followed by four successive appearances in the South American Championships in the 1940s. As expected the results were not good to start with but in the 1949 tournamment in Brazil, the Bolivians finished an astonishing fourth out of the eight entries. Victories over Chile, Uruguay, Ecuador and Colombia gave Bolivia real hope for the World Cup the following year in the same country.

		Total			League	Copa Lib		
		G	S	B	G	G	S	B
1	The Strongest	21	–	–	21	–	–	–
2	Bolivar	15	–	1	15	–	–	1
3	Jorge Wilsterman	8	–	1	8	–	–	1
4	Litoral	4	–	–	4	–	–	–
5	Deportivo Municipal	3	–	–	3	–	–	–
	Oriente Petrolero	3	–	–	3	–	–	–
	Universitario	3	–	–	3	–	–	–
8	Always Ready	2	–	–	2	–	–	–
	Chaco Petrolero	2	–	–	2	–	–	–
10	Blooming	1	–	1	1	–	–	1
11	Ayacucho	1	–	–	1	–	–	–
	Colegio Militar	1	–	–	1	–	–	–
	Deportivo Militar	1	–	–	1	–	–	–
	Ferroviario	1	–	–	1	–	–	–
	Guabira	1	–	–	1	–	–	–
	Nimbles Sport	1	–	–	1	–	–	–
	Nimbles Rail	1	–	–	1	–	–	–
	San Jose Oruro	1	–	–	1	–	–	–

To the end of the 1991 season

Any thoughts of a repeat victory over Uruguay, their only first round opponents, were quickly dashed with an 8–0 thrashing. Undeterred, Bolivia entered the 1953 South American Championships in Lima and spoilt the party by beating the hosts in the opening game, but it was downhill from then on and they finished next from bottom. Since then the national side has regularly taken part in the tournaments open to them.

The World Cup, in particular, has always been a favoured hunting ground, and although 1950 was their last finals appearance, Bolivia's overall record is good because of one overwhelming advantage, the altitude of La Paz. Situated at over 12 000 feet above sea level, La Paz is the highest capital city in the world.

The advantage to the Bolivian players who are used to the thin air is enormous, and they have used this to great effect in the World Cup. Argentina and Chile were beaten in 1957 and since then, had it not been for a poor away record, the world would have seen a lot more of the Bolivians than they have done.

The 1963 South American Championship held in La Paz and Cochabamba was another case in point, as Bolivia won their only title to date. Although not as high as La Paz, at 8000 feet altitude is still a significant factor in Cochabamba. Víctor Ugarte, captain of the side and the most famous Bolivian footballer of all time, utilised this as he lead his team on an extraordinary run of results culminating in a 5–4 win over the Brazilians in Cochabamba.

Whenever a tournament involves the Bolivians playing at home, they are always in with a shout. They finished above Argentina in the 1970 World Cup qualifiers, won their group in 1978, finishing above Uruguay, only to lose to Hungary in a play-off, and in 1979 beat both Brazil and Argentina at home in the South American Championship only to lose to both of them away and finish a point behind Brazil at the end.

It is noticeable that their performances in this tournament improved when it was held on a home and away basis from 1975 until 1983 and have slumped again since it reverted back to single country location. If Bolivia are to win another tournament it is essential they persuade CONMEBOL that La Paz is just the place to spend two weeks in the summer!

Population: 7 322 000
Area, sq km: 1 098 581
% in urban areas: 50%
Capital city: La Paz

Federación Boliviana de Fútbol
Avda. 16 de Julio #782
Casilla Postal 484
Cochabamba
Bolivia
Tel: (010 591) 42 45064
Fax: (010 591) 42 47951
Telex: 6239 FEDBOL
Cable: FEDFUTBOL COCHABAMBA
Languages for correspondence: Spanish

Year of formation: 1925
Affiliation to FIFA: 1926
Affiliation to CONMEBOL: 1926
Registered clubs: 305
Registered players: 15 200
Professional players: 300
Registered referees: 322
National stadium: Estadio Nacional Olimpico 55000
National colours: Shirts: Green Shorts: White Socks: Green
Reserve colours: Shirts: White Shorts: White Socks: Green
Season: May–December (1st stage May–Sep, 2nd Sep–Dec)

THE RECORD

WORLD CUP

1930 .... QT Automatic – Final Tournament/1st round
1934 .... Did not enter
1938 .... Did not enter
1950 .... QT W-O in group 7 – Final Tournament/1st round
1954 .... Did not enter
1958 .... QT 2nd/3 in group 2
1962 .... QT 2nd/2 in group 2
1966 .... QT 3rd/3 in group 3
1970 .... QT 2nd/3 in group 1
1974 .... QT 3rd/3 in group 2
1978 .... QT 1st/3 in group 2
1982 .... QT 2nd/3 in group 1
1986 .... QT 3rd/3 in group 3
1990 .... QT 2nd/3 in group 1

SOUTH AMERICAN CHAMPIONSHIP

1910–25 ..... –
1926 .... 5th/5
1927 .... 4th/4
1929–42 ..... –
1945 .... 6th/7
1946 .... 6th/6
1947 .... 7th/8
1949 .... 4th/8
1953 .... 6th/7
1955–57 ..... –
1959 .... 7th/7
1959 .... –
1963 .... 1st/7 – Winners
1967 .... 6th/6
1975 .... 8th/10/1st round
1979 .... 7th/10/1st round
1983 .... 8th/10/1st round
1987 .... 7th/10/1st round
1989 .... 9th/10/1st round
1991 .... 9th/10/1st round

OLYMPIC GAMES

1908–68 ..... Did not enter
1972 .... QT Failed to qualify
1976 .... Did not enter
1980 .... QT Failed to qualify
1984 .... Did not enter
1988 .... QT Failed to qualify
1992 .... QT Failed to qualify

COPA LIBERTADORES

Semi-finalists – Jorge Wilsterman 1981, Blooming 1985, Bolivar 1986

CLUB DIRECTORY

LA PAZ (Population – 992 000)

Bolivar Independiente Unificada
Stadium: Estadio Nacional Olimpico 55 000
Founded: 1925
Colours: Sky blue/Sky blue

Chaco Petrolero
Stadium: Estadio Nacional Olimpico 55 000
Founded: 1944
Colours: White and green stripes

Deportivo Municipal
Stadium: Luis Lastra 10 000
Founded: 1944
Colours: Maroon/White

The Strongest
Stadium: Rafael Mendoza Castellon 40 000
Founded: 1908
Colours: Yellow and black stripes

Club Always Ready
Stadium: Achumani 40 000
Colours: White with red sash/White

Club Litoral
Stadium: Achumani 40000
Colours: White/White

SANTA CRUZ DE LA SIERRA (Population – 441 000)

Club Blooming
Stadium: Ramon Tauhichi Aguilera 40 000
Founded: 1946
Colours: Sky blue/White

Guabira
Stadium: Ramon Tauhichi Aguilera 40 000
Founded: 1962 Colours: Red/Blue

Oriente Petrolero
Stadium: Ramon Tauhichi Aguilera 40 000
Founded: 1955
Colours: Green/White

COCHABAMBA (Population – 317 000)

Club Aurora
Stadium: Felix Capriles 35 000
Founded: 1935
Colours: Sky blue/White

Club Jorge Wilsterman
Stadium: Felix Capriles 35 000
Founded: 1949
Colours: Red/Blue

Petrolero
Stadium: Felix Capriles 35 000
Founded: 1950
Colours: Red and white stripes/Black

ORURO (Population – 187 000)
San Jose
Stadium: Jesus Bermudez 40 000
Colours: White with a sky blue V on the front/Sky blue

BOLIVIAN LEAGUE CHAMPIONS

1914	The Strongest	1955	San Jose Oruro
1915	Colegio Militar	1956	Bolivar
1916	The Strongest	1957	Always Ready
1917	The Strongest	1958	Jorge Wilsterman
1918–19	–	1959	Jorge Wilsterman
1920	The Strongest	1960	Deportivo Municipal
1921–22	–	1961	Deportivo Municipal
1923	Universitario	1962	Chaco Petrolero
1924	The Strongest	1963	The Strongest
1925	–	1964	The Strongest
1926	Universitario	1965	Deportivo Municipal
1927	Nimbles Sport	1966	Jorge Wilsterman
1928	Deportivo Militar	1967	Jorge Wilsterman
1929	The Strongest	1968	Bolivar
1930	The Strongest	1969	Universitario
1931	Nimbles Rail	1970	Chaco Petrolero
1932	The Strongest	1971	Oriente Petrolero
1933–34	–	1972	Jorge Wilsterman
1935	The Strongest	1973	Jorge Wilsterman
1936	Ayacucho	1974	The Strongest
1937	The Strongest	1975	Guabira
1938	The Strongest	1976	Bolivar
1939	Bolivar	1977	The Strongest
1940	Bolivar	1978	Bolivar
1941	Bolivar	1979	Oriente Petrolero
1942	Bolivar	1980	Jorge Wilsterman
1943	The Strongest	1981	Jorge Wilsterman
1944	Ferroviario	1982	Bolivar
1945	The Strongest	1983	Bolivar
1946	–	1984	Blooming
1947	Litoral	1985	Bolivar
1948	Litoral	1986	The Strongest
1949	Litoral	1987	Bolivar
1950	Bolivar	1988	The Strongest
1951	Always Ready	1989	The Strongest
1952	The Strongest	1990	Oriente Petrolero
1953	Bolivar	1991	Bolivar
1954	Litoral		

INTERNATIONAL MATCHES PLAYED BY BOLIVIA

Date	Opponents	Result		Venue	Compet
12-10-1926	Chile	L	1–7	Santiago	SC
16–10	Argentina	L	0–5	Santiago	SC
23–10	Paraguay	L	1–6	Santiago	SC
28–10	Uruguay	L	0–6	Santiago	SC
30-10-1927	Argentina	L	1–7	Lima	SC
6–11	Uruguay	L	0–9	Lima	SC
13–11	Peru	L	2–3	Lima	SC
17-07-1930	Yugoslavia	L	0–4	Montevideo	WCr1
22–07	Brazil	L	0–4	Montevideo	WCr1
8-08-1938	Ecuador	D	1–1	Bogota	BG
11–08	Venezuela	W	3–1	Bogota	BG
14–08	Peru	L	0–3	Bogota	BG
16–08	Colombia	W	2–1	Bogota	BG
22–08	Ecuador	W	2–1	Bogota	BG
18-01-1945	Argentina	L	0–4	Santiago	SC
24–01	Chile	L	0–5	Santiago	SC
28–01	Brazil	L	0–2	Santiago	SC
11–02	Ecuador	D	0–0	Santiago	SC
15–02	Uruguay	L	0–2	Santiago	SC
21–02	Colombia	D	3–3	Santiago	SC
16-01-1946	Brazil	L	0–3	Buenos Aires	SC
19–01	Argentina	L	1–7	Buenos Aires	SC
26–01	Paraguay	L	2–4	Buenos Aires	SC
29–01	Uruguay	L	0–5	Buenos Aires	SC
8–02	Chile	L	1–4	Buenos Aires	SC
30-11-1947	Ecuador	D	2–2	Guayaquil	SC
4–12	Argentina	L	0–7	Guayaquil	SC
9–12	Uruguay	L	0–3	Guayaquil	SC
13–12	Colombia	D	0–0	Guayaquil	SC
18–12	Paraguay	L	1–3	Guayaquil	SC
27–12	Peru	L	0–2	Guayaquil	SC
31–12	Chile	L	3–4	Guayaquil	SC
5-01-1948	Venezuela	D	2–2	Lima	BG
6-04-1949	Chile	W	3–2	Sao Paulo	SC
10–04	Brazil	L	1–10	Sao Paulo	SC
17–04	Uruguay	W	3–2	Rio de Janeiro	SC
24–04	Ecuador	W	2–0	Sao Paulo	SC
27–04	Peru	L	0–3	Santos	SC
30–04	Paraguay	L	0–7	Rio de Janeiro	SC
6–05	Colombia	W	4–0	Rio de Janeiro	SC
26-02-1950	Chile	W	2–0	La Paz	WCq
12–03	Chile	L	0–5	Santiago	WCq
2–07	Uruguay	L	0–8	Belo Horizonte	WCr1
22-02-1953	Peru	W	1–0	Lima	SC
25–02	Uruguay	L	0–2	Lima	SC
1–03	Brazil	L	1–8	Lima	SC
8–03	Ecuador	D	1–1	Lima	SC
16–03	Paraguay	L	1–2	Lima	SC
28–03	Chile	D	2–2	Lima	SC
6-06-1957	Paraguay	L	2–5	Asuncion	PDC
13–06	Paraguay	W	1–0	Asuncion	PDC
18–08	Paraguay	D	3–3	La Paz	PDC
21–08	Paraguay	W	2–1	La Paz	PDC
22–09	Chile	L	1–2	Santiago	WCq
29–09	Chile	W	3–0	La Paz	WCq
6–10	Argentina	W	2–0	La Paz	WCq
27–10	Argentina	L	0–4	Buenos Aires	WCq
8-03-1959	Uruguay	L	0–7	Buenos Aires	SC
11–03	Argentina	L	0–2	Buenos Aires	SC
15–03	Paraguay	L	0–5	Buenos Aires	SC
21–03	Brazil	L	2–4	Buenos Aires	SC
26–03	Chile	L	2–5	Buenos Aires	SC
29–03	Peru	D	0–0	Buenos Aires	SC
15-07-1961	Uruguay	D	1–1	La Paz	WCq
30–07	Uruguay	L	1–2	Montevideo	WCq
10-08-1962	Paraguay	W	3–1	Cochabamba	PDC
12–08	Paraguay	W	3–2	La Paz	PDC
17-02-1963	Paraguay	L	0–3	Asuncion	PDC
19–02	Paraguay	L	1–5	Asuncion	PDC
10–03	Ecuador	D	4–4	La Paz	SC
17–03	Colombia	W	2–1	Cochabamba	SC
21–03	Peru	W	3–2	La Paz	SC
24–03	Paraguay	W	2–0	Cochabamba	SC
28–03	Argentina	W	3–2	La Paz	SC
31–03	Brazil	W	5–4	Cochabamba	SC
25-07-1965	Paraguay	L	0–2	Asuncion	WCq
17–08	Argentina	L	1–4	Buenos Aires	WCq
22–08	Paraguay	W	2–1	La Paz	WCq
29–08	Argentina	L	1–2	La Paz	WCq
17-01-1967	Uruguay	L	0–4	Montevideo	SC
22–01	Argentina	L	0–1	Montevideo	SC
25–01	Paraguay	L	0–1	Montevideo	SC
28–01	Venezuela	L	0–3	Montevideo	SC
1–02	Chile	D	0–0	Montevideo	SC
27-07-1969	Argentina	W	3–1	La Paz	WCq
10–08	Peru	W	2–1	La Paz	WCq
17–08	Peru	L	0–3	Lima	WCq
24–08	Argentina	L	0–1	Buenos Aires	WCq
15-08-1971	Chile*	L	3–4	La Paz	Fr

11-06-1972	Peru	L	0–3	Curitiba	Clr1
18-06	Yugoslavia	D	1–1	Campo Grande	Clr1
21-06	Venezuela	D	2–2	Manaus	Clr1
25-06	Paraguay	L	1–6	Manaus	Clr1
24-03-1973	Peru	L	0–2	Lima	Fr
31-03	Paraguay	D	1–1	La Paz	Fr
29-04	Ecuador	D	3–3	La Paz	Fr
6-05	Ecuador	D	0–0	Quito	Fr
27-05	Brazil	L	0–5	Rio de Janeiro	Fr
15-07	Peru	W	2–0	La Paz	Fr
24-07	Chile	L	0–3	Santiago	Fr
2-09	Paraguay	L	1–2	La Paz	WCq
9-09	Argentina	L	0–4	Buenos Aires	WCq
23-09	Argentina	L	0–1	La Paz	WCq
30-09	Paraguay	L	0–4	Asuncion	WCq
27-06-1975	Argentina*	L	1–2	Cochabamba	Fr
7-07	Paraguay	L	1–2	Cochabamba	Fr
9-07	Ecuador	W	1–0	Cochabamba	Fr
20-07	Chile	W	2–1	La Paz	SCr1
27-07	Peru	L	0–1	Oruro	SCr1
7-08	Peru	L	1–3	Lima	SCr1
13-08	Chile	L	0–4	Santiago	SCr1
6-02-1977	Paraguay	L	0–1	La Paz	PDC
9-02	Paraguay	D	2–2	La Paz	PDC
27-02	Uruguay	W	1–0	La Paz	WCq
6-03	Venezuela	W	3–1	Caracas	WCq
13-03	Venezuela	W	2–0	La Paz	WCq
27-03	Uruguay	D	2–2	Montevideo	WCq
12-06	Poland	L	1–2	La Paz	Fr
14-07	Brazil	L	0–8	Cali	WCq
17-07	Peru	L	0–5	Cali	WCq
29-10	Hungary	L	0–6	Budapest	WCq
30-11	Hungary	L	2–3	La Paz	WCq
10-07-1979	Paraguay	W	3–1	La Paz	PDC
12-07	Paraguay	D	1–1	Cochabamba	Fr
18-07	Argentina	W	2–1	La Paz	SCr1
26-07	Brazil	W	2–1	La Paz	SCr1
1-08	Paraguay	L	0–2	Asuncion	PDC
8-08	Argentina	L	0–3	Buenos Aires	SCr1
16-08	Brazil	L	0–2	Sao Paulo	SCr1
2-07-1980	Poland	L	0–1	Santa Cruz	Fr
26-08	Paraguay	D	1–1	La Paz	PDC
28-08	Paraguay	L	1–3	Santa Cruz	Fr
18-09	Paraguay	L	1–2	Asuncion	PDC
9-11	Uruguay	L	1–3	Cochabamba	Fr
30-11	Finland	W	3–0	La Paz	Fr
4-12	Finland	D	2–2	Santa Cruz	Fr
11-12	Uruguay	L	0–5	Montevideo	Fr
25-01-1981	Czechoslovakia	W	2–1	La Paz	Fr
29-01	Czechoslovakia	L	2–5	Santa Cruz	Fr
1-02	Bulgaria	L	1–3	La Paz	Fr
15-02	Venezuela	W	3–0	La Paz	WCq
22-02	Brazil	L	1–2	La Paz	WCq
15-03	Venezuela	L	0–1	Caracas	WCq
22-03	Brazil	L	1–3	Rio de Janeiro	WCq
19-07-1983	Chile	L	1–2	La Paz	Fr
3-08	Paraguay	W	2–1	La Paz	Fr
5-08	Paraguay	L	1–3	Santa Cruz	Fr
14-08	Colombia	L	0–1	La Paz	SCr1
21-08	Peru	D	1–1	La Paz	SCr1
24-08	Chile	L	2–4	Arica	Fr
31-08	Colombia	D	2–2	Bogota	SCr1
4-09	Peru	L	1–2	Lima	SCr1
3-02-1985	East Germany	W	2–1	La Paz	Fr
6-02	Uruguay	L	0–1	Cochabamba	Fr
17-02	Peru	L	0–3	Lima	Fr
21-02	Ecuador	L	0–3	Quito	Fr
24-02	Venezuela	L	0–5	Caracas	Fr
21-04	Venezuela	W	4–0	Santa Cruz	Fr
1-05	Peru	D	0–0	Santa Cruz	Fr
26-05	Paraguay	D	1–1	Santa Cruz	WCq
2-06	Brazil	L	0–2	Santa Cruz	WCq
9-06	Paraguay	L	0–3	Asuncion	WCq
30-06	Brazil	D	1–1	Sao Paulo	WCq
14-06-1987	Paraguay	L	0–2	Santa Cruz	Fr
23-06	Uruguay	L	1–2	Montevideo	Fr
28-06	Paraguay	D	0–0	Rosario	SCr1
1-07	Colombia	L	0–2	Rosario	SCr1
25-05-1989	Paraguay	W	3–2	Cochabamba	Fr
1-06	Paraguay	L	0–2	Asuncion	Fr
8-06	Uruguay	D	0–0	Santa Cruz	Fr
14-06	Uruguay	L	0–1	Montevideo	Fr
22-06	Chile	L	0–1	La Paz	Fr
27-06	Chile	L	1–2	Santiago	Fr
4-07	Uruguay	L	0–3	Goiania	SCr1
6-07	Ecuador	D	0–0	Goiania	SCr1
8-07	Chile	L	0–5	Goiania	SCr1
10-07	Argentina	D	0–0	Goiania	SCr1
20-08	Peru	W	2–1	La Paz	WCq
3-09	Uruguay	W	2–1	La Paz	WCq
10-09	Peru	W	2–1	Lima	WCq
17-09	Uruguay	L	0–2	Montevideo	WCq
14-06-1991	Paraguay	L	0–1	Santa Cruz	PDC
16-06	Paraguay	D	0–0	Asuncion	PDC
7-07	Uruguay	D	1–1	Valparaiso	SCr1
9-07	Brazil	L	1–2	Vina del Mar	SCr1
11-07	Colombia	D	0–0	Vina del Mar	SCr1
13-07	Ecuador	L	0–4	Vina del Mar	SCr1

* Matches of disputed official status

BRAZIL

Though no longer the 'golden boys' of world football, Brazil will always retain a special place in the hearts of football lovers around the world. In the 1950s and 1960s, Brazilian football was blessed with so many players of outstanding talent that in six World Cups they reached the final on four occasions and won three of them. For a country of an estimated 150 million inhabitants, perhaps this should not be surprising, but size of population is never a guarantee of success in football.

Brazil were so popular and successful because they combined supreme footballing skills with a carefree arrogance that left their opponents in awe of them, especially when those opponents came from outside of South America. To Europeans, players such as Pele and Garrincha attained an almost mystical quality because they never plied their trade in Europe as so many Argentines and Uruguayans did. Instead the only glimpses they caught of these players were at World Cups or when the Brazilian national team or teams like Santos came to Europe on tours.

Away from Europe, and beyond the gaze of those who admired them so much, the story of Brazilian football is a different matter altogether. Success has been limited for both the national side in the South American Championships and the club sides in the Copa Libertadores, so much so that the River Plate estuary, encompassing both Buenos Aires and Montevideo, is seen as the real home of football on the continent.

The structure of Brazilian football is certainly the reason why it has suffered in comparison to Uruguay and Argentina. The huge size of the country – it is the fifth biggest in the world and takes up more than half of the South American continent – has meant that only in recent years has there been any semblance of a national competition for club sides.

Politically the country is divided into 27 states, many of which are larger in size and have bigger populations than an average size European country. Each state therefore has its own governing body for football and organises its own state league. The idea of a national league was just not feasible. Such a system, however, has left a legacy of chaos and infighting between the different organisations as they all vie for a say in how the game should be run.

Football is said to have been introduced into Brazil by Charles Miller, a worker with the Sao Paulo Railway Company at the end of the 19th century. As is the case with other South American countries, British residents in Brazil had formed sports clubs in which they spent much of their spare time playing cricket. Miller succeeded in persuading the Sao Paulo Athletic Club to start a football section, and soon other clubs followed suit.

Sao Paulo and Rio de Janeiro were the first cities to start playing football on a large scale and in 1901, the Campeonato Paulista de Futebol was founded in Sao Paulo, based on a strong British contingent. The first tournament was completed in 1902 and won by Charles Miller's Sao Paulo Athletic Club. Miller himself finished top scorer with 10 goals.

It was not long before Rio got in on the act and formed the Liga Metropolitana de Football do Rio de Janeiro in 1905. Again the British presence was strong. Fluminense, another club founded by an Englishman, Oscar Cox, won the first tournament. Very quickly Brazilians of European descent other than the British took up the game. By 1914 all of the major clubs had been formed in Rio and Sao Paulo, and all in one way or another had links to one of the white European communities.

Vasco da Gama were a Portuguese-based sailing club formed in 1898. Corinthians, though they were named after the famous English amateur side who made a tour of the country in 1910, were founded by five Brazilians of Portuguese descent. The Italians were not left out. Palestra Italia, later to become SE Palmeiras, was formed by Italian workers in the aftermath of an exhibition match played by Pro Vercelli and Torino in 1914, whilst Germania, as the name suggests, were the team of the German community.

Football also spread to other cities, most notably Belo Horizonte, Porto Alegre, Bahia, Recife, Curitiba and Fortaleza and by 1920 there were 15 state leagues in operation. Although under the jurisdiction of the Federacao Brasileira de Sports – later to become the Confederacao Brasileira de Desportes (CBD) – these leagues were run by state governing bodies who over the years built up a strong power base, which eventually led to much controversy in the 1970s as they began to flex their muscles.

Until the 1970s, however, the leagues in Rio de Janeiro and Sao Paulo were the most important competitions in the country. Although Rio select teams played Sao Paulo state selections every year in the Taca Correio de Manha from 1913 to 1923, and from 1923 to 1963 in the Campeonato Brasileiro de Selecoes, in which other state selections could enter, there was no national championship for clubs until 1950. Even then the Rio–Sao Paulo Championship, as the tournament was called, was not open to teams outside of the big two. Given that the Campeonato Selecoes was won by either Rio or Sao Paulo every year bar 1934 when Bahia were the winners, this is perhaps not surprising.

Both the Rio and Sao Paulo leagues remained amateur and largely closed to the coloured population until the 1920s when a series of events changed the face of Brazilian football. Vasco da Gama emerged from the shadows of the more famous Rio clubs in 1923 when, playing a team containing coloured players, they ran away with the Rio title. Other clubs, realising the benefits of this untapped source of footballers, soon followed suit with the result that in terms of football at least, Brazil became the first racially integrated country.

Administrative struggles also marked the early years of football in Rio but more especially in Sao Paulo where it was not uncommon to have two different leagues in operation. Professionalism was the cause that in the end united football in each of the cities, despite initially causing further splits. By the early 1940s, Brazil had emerged as a strong, racially integrated, professional footballing nation capable of taking on the strongest of opponents. As the results of the national team show, before this time this had not been the case.

Brazil was rather slow in taking up international football. The difficulties in selecting a team from all of the different leagues were compounded by the huge distances involved in travelling to games. Therefore it was not until 1913 that any Brazilian representative side left the country to play a game.

Surprisingly Brazil's first registered representative match was played by a Bahia selection against a North American selection in August 1903 in Salvador. In 1906 a Sao Paulo selection lost heavily to the touring South African side, and in 1908 a touring Argentine combination played three matches against a Sao Paulo selection and one each against a Rio, Santos and a combined Brazilian selection. An Argentine combination toured again in 1912 whilst a

		All			Nat champ		Cup		State champ	Libertad cup		
		G	S	B	G	S	G	S	G	G	S	B
	Federaçao Carioca de Futebol. Rio de Janeiro.											
1	Fluminense FC	31	1	–	4	1	–	–	27	–	–	–
2	Flamengo	29	2	2	6	1	1	1	21	1	–	2
3	Vasco da Gama	20	8	–	4	7	–	1	16	–	–	–
4	Botafogo	19	5	2	3	4	1	1	15	–	–	2
5	America FC	7	–	–	–	–	–	–	7	–	–	–
6	Bangu	2	1	–	–	1	–	–	2	–	–	–
7	Paissandu	1	–	–	–	–	–	–	1	–	–	–
	Sao Cristovao	1	–	–	–	–	–	–	1	–	–	–
	Federaçao Paulista de Futebol. Sao Paulo.											
1	Santos FC	27	3	2	5	1	5	2	15	2	–	2
2	SE Palmeiras	26	7	1	6	5	2	–	18	–	2	1
3	SC Corinthians	25	3	–	5	3	–	–	20	–	–	–
4	Sao Paulo FC	19	7	1	3	6	–	–	16	–	1	1
5	Paulistano	11	–	–	–	–	–	–	11	–	–	–
6	Portuguesa	5	1	–	2	1	–	–	3	–	–	–
7	Sao Paulo Atletic	4	–	–	–	–	–	–	4	–	–	–
8	AA das Palmeiras	3	–	–	–	–	–	–	3	–	–	–
	Internacional Limeira	3	–	–	–	–	–	–	3	–	–	–
10	Americano	2	–	–	–	–	–	–	2	–	–	–
	Germania	2	–	–	–	–	–	–	2	–	–	–
	Sao Bento	2	–	–	–	–	–	–	2	–	–	–
13	Bragantino	1	1	–	–	1	–	–	1	–	–	–
	Guarani Campinas	1	1	1	1	1	–	–	–	–	–	1
	Federaçao Mineira de Futebol. Minas Gerais.											
1	Atletico Mineiro	35	2	1	1	2	–	–	34	–	–	1
2	EC Cruzeiro	26	4	2	–	3	1	–	24	1	1	2
3	America FC	13	–	–	–	–	–	–	13	–	–	–
4	Vila Nova AC	5	–	–	–	–	–	–	5	–	–	–
5	Siderurgica	2	–	–	–	–	–	–	2	–	–	–
	Federaçao Gaucha de Futebol. Rio Grande do Sul.											
1	SC Internacional	33	3	2	3	3	–	–	30	–	1	2
2	Gremio	31	3	–	1	1	1	1	28	1	1	–
3	Guarani de Bage	2	–	–	–	–	–	–	2	–	–	–
	Rio Grande	2	–	–	–	–	–	–	2	–	–	–
5	Americano	1	–	–	–	–	–	–	1	–	–	–
	Brasil	1	–	–	–	–	–	–	1	–	–	–
	Cruzeiro	1	–	–	–	–	–	–	1	–	–	–
	Farroupilha	1	–	–	–	–	–	–	1	–	–	–
	Gremio Bage	1	–	–	–	–	–	–	1	–	–	–
	Gremio Santanense	1	–	–	–	–	–	–	1	–	–	–
	Pelotas	1	–	–	–	–	–	–	1	–	–	–
	Sao Paulo	1	–	–	–	–	–	–	1	–	–	–

To the end of the 1992 national championships and the 1991 state leagues

Portuguese combination made the trip across the Atlantic in 1913.

With the formation of the Federacao Brasileira de Sports, a truly national team was picked for the first time on 21 July 1914 for a match against Exeter City, but the first full international was not played until two months later with a friendly match against Argentina in Buenos Aires, followed a week later by the first edition of the Roca Cup, an irregular competition played between the two countries.

Brazil entered a team for the first South American Championship in 1916, but as in future editions, it did not prove to be a happy hunting ground. Over the next forty years the majority of the games played were in this competition and out of over twenty tournaments played, only three were won and in each case on Brazilian soil.

Despite the relative lack of success in the early years, Brazil produced many fine players, the most famous of whom were Artur Friedenreich, Leonidas da Silva, Domingos da Guia, Romeu, Tim and Fausto. Players like Leonidas would have won more caps for their country but for the chaos on the home front and disputes with neighbouring countries restricting the number of games played during the whole of the 1930s to just 22. Friedenreich, however, still found plenty of opportunities to score goals in domestic competitions and the 1329 goals he scored between 1909 and 1934 is a world record that will surely never be equalled.

Brazil entered the first World Cup in Montevideo, and in a result symptomatic of their fortunes at the time were knocked out by Yugoslavia in the first round. Since then the winning of the World Cup has become an obsession for everybody involved in Brazilian football. They have entered and qualified for every tournament held, the only country to do so. The 1934 tournament was no less disastrous than the first, losing to Spain in the first round.

In 1938 Brazil showed their true potential for the first time, reaching the semi-finals, but overconfidence, not for the last time, lost them the semi-final against Italy. Inexplicably, Leonidas was rested for what the selectors assumed would be the final, but instead turned out to be the third place play-off!

The golden age of Brazilian football came between 1950 and 1970 and it is for this period that the Brazilians are best remembered. In 1949, in preparation for the 1950 World Cup which they had been given the responsibility of hosting, Brazil staged the South American Championship and won it despite being taken to a play-off by Paraguay. No less than 46 goals were scored in just 8 games as Ademir and Jair Pinto, to name just two, ran riot in their opponents' penalty area.

This form was repeated the following year in the World Cup, and perhaps there have never been more clear-cut favourites than Brazil that year. Twenty-one goals en route to the final game had many Brazilians celebrating before the game against Uruguay had begun. Brazil needed just a draw from the game to top the second round group and win the World Cup. When Friaca scored early in the second half they looked to be there, but in one of the greatest upsets in the history of the tournament, Uruguay scored twice to snatch the title from the hosts.

Perhaps the result should not be considered that surprising. Consistently the masters of Brazil in the South American Championship, Uruguay knew the Brazilian style inside out and exploited that knowledge, even though they could not match them for skill or flair.

By 1954 the basis of a much more stable side was growing. In defence both Nilton and Djalma Santos were proving very effective whilst the midfield was being run effectively by Didi, but once again the World Cup was to prove elusive. In the famous quarter-final with Hungary, Brazil lost to the best team in the tournament, but not before violence flared on and off the field in a game that has become known as the 'Battle of Berne'.

Four years later the inevitable happened when Brazil finally won the tournament they had set their hearts on. The forward line of Garrincha, Vavá, Pelé and Zagalo was the clinching factor. Pelé was especially vital. His presence at only 17 caused a huge stir and he became an instant hero and a household name around the world after his performance against Sweden in the final. Most would class Pelé as the greatest footballer ever, above even Maradona, Di Stéfano or Cruyff, and for over a decade he came to epitomise Brazilian football.

He appeared for Brazil in the 1958, 1962, 1966 and 1970 World Cup finals, though injury meant he did not appear in the final itself against Czechoslovakia in 1962. Instead it was Garrincha who was the driving force in a team that was almost identical to that of 1958.

The 1966 side that lost its crown in England was in a transitional stage and again Pelé did not have a happy time as he was continually fouled. He even threatened to give up football in the face of such treatment. Gone from the side were Didi, Nilton Santos, Vavá, Zito, Zózimo and Zagalo, whilst in had come Tostao, Gérson and Jairzinho. Portugal and Hungary qualified from the group and Brazil went home after the first round for only the third time in their history.

The 1970 side that won the World Cup in Mexico has been described as the best football team ever to take the field in a World Cup. At the back, Carlos Alberto marshalled a defence that liked to attack and so consequently relied on scoring more goals than they let in, but the mix worked. In attack, Pelé was back to his most masterful self and he, Jairzinho, Rivelino and Tostao were a potent force to match that of the 1958 forward line.

No-one except England came close to matching the Brazilians in Mexico and their performance in the final against Italy was one of the best displays the World Cup has ever seen. A good Italian side were simply not in the same class, especially in the second half when the Brazilians seemed to toy with them as a cat would with a mouse. Their fourth goal, scored by the captain Carlos Alberto, typified the versatility of their game. The move involved nine passes both long and short, a mazy dribble and a lightning finish that had the Italian defence looking on in admiration.

Since 1970 the national side has never reached the same heights and has had to live in the shadow of the performances of the 1950–70 era. Only once, in 1982, did they come close, when the likes of Sócrates, Falcao, Junior and Zico played a brand of football reminiscent of 1970. Instead, the side has tended to ape the rigid tactical approach of the Europeans and this has not stood them in good stead. This was especially true in the 1990 World Cup, and in a dreadful game against Argentina, the team lost in the second round to howls of derision back in Brazil.

The club scene in Brazil has also suffered since 1970. The big clubs from Rio and Sao Paulo had introduced an annual tournament in 1950 between the best teams from the two cities, the winners of which were regarded as national champions. Pressure from the other state leagues to be involved led to the Roberto Gomez Pedrosa tournament in 1967. Minas Gerais, Rio Grande do Sul and Parana were involved for the first time that year whilst the following year Bahia and Pernambuco were invited to send sides.

The ball had started to roll and soon all the states in the country were anxious to take part, and as the Confederacao Brasileira de Futebol is in effect controlled by the various state governing bodies, they started a national championship in 1971. Throughout the 1970s the number of participants rose as even the smallest states demanded to take part, and by 1979 the national league consisted of 94 teams.

It has been the practice for the Brazilian season to be divided in half. The national championship now occupies the first half of the year, and the state leagues the second half. Football is thus played all year round with hardly a break. Increasingly the big clubs from Rio and Sao Paulo have become unhappy with the status quo, not just because of the number of games they play but also the long distances they have to travel to play the small teams in the national league.

Threats of breakaways and the like have never materialised and club football continues on in its confused way. The mechanisms used for deciding the champions in either the national or the state leagues vary from year to year and have often been decided on after the tournament has started. Roughly speaking, it involves various stages leading up to a final tournament played on a knock-out basis, resulting in a grand final.

Amid so much confusion it is perhaps not surprising that the Copa Libertadores has not been a favoured hunting ground for Brazilian clubs. The first difficulty in the 1960s was who should qualify, so a Brazilian Cup was introduced to find an entrant. From 1971 the national champions and runners-up qualified but in 1989 the Cup was re-introduced to qualify one team to join the national champions.

Only two teams from either Rio or Sao Paulo have ever won the Copa Libertadores and only five Brazilian teams have won it at all. Pelé's Santos won it twice in the early 1960s, but since then only Flamengo, Sao Paulo FC, Gremio from Porto Alegre and Cruzeiro from Belo Horizonte have won it.

This is all the more extraordinary considering the fact that until the 1980s, unlike the rest of South America, Brazilians did not tend to move abroad to play their football. Pelé, Tostao, Rivelino, Didi, Garrincha and Zico, for example, played almost all of their football at home. Didi spent one unsuccessful season at Real Madrid, whilst Zico returned home from Italy after two.

There is no doubt that Brazilian football is in need of an urgent overhaul and this must start at club level. If they do have anything to learn from Europe it is the benefit of a stable club structure. The case for abandoning the state leagues and implementing a streamlined national league is strong. The game in Brazil needs a focus and at present does not have one. Until it does and the clubs can woo back supporters that have almost disappeared except for the very big games, football in Brazil will continue to decline.

With a never-ending stream of talented players and the basic club structure already there, it is not an impossible task; but until someone takes the bull by the horns, do not expect to see Brazil win the World Cup again in a hurry.

Population: 150 368 000
Area, sq km: 8 511 965
% in urban areas: 75%
Capital city: Brasília

Confederacao Brasileira de Futebol
Rua da Alfandega #70
PO Box 1078
20.070 Rio de Janeiro
Tel: (010 55) 21 2215937
Fax: (010 55) 21 252 9294
Telex: 2121509 CBDS BR
Cable: DESPORTOS RIO DE JANEIRO
Languages for correspondence: Spanish & English

Year of formation: 1914
Affiliation to FIFA: 1923
Affiliation to CONMEBOL: 1916
Registered clubs: 12 987
Registered players: 551 300
Professional players: 13 000
Registered coaches: 4324
Registered referees: 4950
National stadium: Maracaná, Rio de Janeiro 200 000
National colours: Shirts: Yellow/Shorts: Green/Socks: White
Reserve colours: Shirts: Blue/Shorts: White/Socks: White
Season: National Championship January–June, State leagues August–December

THE RECORD

WORLD CUP

1930 .... QT Automatic – Final Tournament/1st round
1934 .... QT W-O in group 2 – Final Tournament/1st round
1938 .... QT W-O in group 9 – Final Tournament/Semi-finalists/3rd place
1950 .... QT Automatic – Final Tournamrnt/Runners–up
1954 .... QT 1st/3 in group 12 – Final Tournament/Quarter-finalists
1958 .... QT 1st/2 in group 1 – Final Tournament/Winners
1962 .... QT Automatic – Final Tournament/Winners
1966 .... QT Automatic – Final Tournament/1st round
1970 .... QT 1st/4 in group 2 – Final Tournament/Winners
1974 .... QT Automatic – Final Tournament/2nd round/4th place
1978 .... QT 1st/3 in group 1 – Final Tournament/2nd round/3rd place
1982 .... QT 1st/3 in group 1 – Final Tournament/2nd round
1986 .... QT 1st/3 in group 3 – Final Tournament/Quarter-finalists
1990 .... QT 1st/3 in group 3 – Final Tournament/2nd round

SOUTH AMERICAN CHAMPIONSHIP

1910 .... –
1916 .... 3rd/4
1917 .... 3rd/4
1919 .... 1st/4 – Winners
1920 .... 3rd/4
1921 .... 2nd/4
1922 .... 1st/5 – Winners
1923 .... 4th/4
1924 .... –
1925 .... 2nd/3
1926–35 ..... –
1937 .... 2nd/6
1939 .... –
1941 .... –
1942 .... 3rd/7
1945 .... 2nd/7
1946 .... 2nd/6
1947 .... –
1949 .... 1st/8 – Winners
1953 .... 2nd/7
1955 .... –
1956 .... 4th/6
1957 .... 2nd/7
1959 .... 2nd/7
1959 .... 3rd/5
1963 .... 4th/7
1967 .... –
1975 .... 3rd/10 – Semi-finalists
1979 .... 3rd/10 – Semi-finalists
1983 .... 2nd/10 – Finalists
1987 .... 5th/10 – 1st round
1989 .... 1st/10 – Winners
1991 .... 2nd/10 – 2nd round

OLYMPIC GAMES

1908–48 ..... Did not enter
1952 .... Quarter-finalists
1956 .... Did not enter
1960 .... Final Tournament/1st round
1964 .... Final Tournament/1st round
1968 .... Final Tournament/1st round

1972	Final Tournament/1st round	
1976	Final Tournament/Semi-finalists/4th place	
1980	QT Failed to qualify	
1984	Final Tournament/Finalists	
1988	Final Tournament/ Finalists	
1992	QT Failed to qualify	

COPA LIBERTADORES

Winners – Santos 1962, 1963, Cruzeiro 1976, Flamengo 1981, Gremio 1983, Sao Paulo FC 1992

Finalists – Palmeiras 1961 1968, Sao Paulo FC 1974, Cruzeiro 1977, Internacional 1980, Gremio 1984

SUPER CUP: Winners – Cruzeiro 1991
Finalists – Cruzeiro 1988

RIO-SAO PAULO TOURNAMENT

Year	Winners	Runners-up
1950	Corinthians	Vasco da Gama
1951	Palmeiras	Corinthians
1952	Portuguesa	Vasco da Gama
1953	Corinthians	Vasco da Gama
1954	Corinthians	Fluminense
1955	Portuguesa	Palmeiras
1956	-	
1957	Fluminense	Vasco da Gama
1958	Vasco da Gama	Flamengo
1959	Santos	Vasco da Gama
1960	Fluminense	Botafogo
1961	Flamengo	Botafogo
1962	Botafogo	Palmeiras
1963	Santos	Corinthians
1964	Santos/Botafogo	
1965	Palmeiras	Portuguesa/Sao Paulo FC
1966	Corinthians/Santos/ Vasco da Gama/Botafogo	

NATIONAL CHAMPIONSHIP

1971	Atletico Mineiro	Sao Paulo FC
1972	Palmeiras	Botafogo
1973	Palmeiras	Sao Paulo FC
1974	Vasco Da Gama	Cruzeiro
1975	Internacional PA	Cruzeiro
1976	Internacional PA	Corinthians
1977	Sao Paulo FC	Atletico Mineiro
1978	Guarani	Palmeiras
1979	Internacional PA	Vasco da Gama
1980	Flamengo	Atletico Mineiro
1981	Gremio	Sao Paulo FC
1982	Flamengo	Gremio
1983	Flamengo	Santos
1984	Fluminense	Vasco da Gama
1985	Coritiba FC	Bangu
1986	Sao Paulo FC	Guarani
1987	Flamengo	Internacional PA
1988	EC Bahia	Internacional PA
1989	Vasco da Gama	Sao Paulo FC
1990	Corinthians	Sao Paulo FC
1991	Sao Paulo FC	Bragantino
1992	Flamengo	Botafogo

ROBERTO GOMEZ PEDROZA TOURNAMENT

1967	Palmeiras	Internacional PA
1968	Santos	Palmeiras
1969	Palmeiras	Cruzeiro
1970	Fluminense	Palmeiras

BRAZILIAN CUP

1959	EC Bahia	Santos
1960	Palmeiras	Fortaleza
1961	Santos	EC Bahia
1962	Santos	Botafogo
1963	Santos	EC Bahia
1964	Santos	Flamengo
1965	Santos	Vasco da Gama
1966	Cruzeiro	Santos
1967	Palmeiras	Nautico
1968	Botafogo	Fortaleza
1969-88	–	
1989	Gremio	Sport Recife
1990	Flamengo	AC Goiâs FC
1991	Criciuma	Gremio

SAO PAULO
State capital - Sao Paulo
State populataion - 33 069 000
State area - 248 256 sq km

Governing body - Federaçao Paulista de Futebol
Number of professional teams: 128

SAO PAULO (Population 15 175 000)

Sao Paulo Futebol Clube
Stadium: Morumbi 150000
Founded: 1930
Colours: White with a red and black hoop/White

Sport Club Corinthians Paulista
Stadium: Parque Sao Jorge 30000
Founded: 1910
Colours: White/Black

Sociedade Esportiva Palmeiras
Stadium: Parque Antartica 35000
Founded: 1914
Colours: Green/White
Previous Name: Palestra Italia 1914-42

Portuguesa de Deportes
Stadium: Osvaldo Teixeira Duarte (Canindé) 22 000
Founded: 1920
Colours: Red with green sleeves/White

CAMPINAS (Population - 1 125 000)

Guarani Futebol Clube
Stadium: Brinco de Ouro de Princesa 35 000
Founded: 1911
Colours: Green/White

AA Ponte Preta
Stadium: Moises Lucaelli 30 000
Founded: 1900
Colours: White with a black sash/Black

SANTOS (Population - 1 065 000)
Santos Futebol Clube
Stadium: Vila Belmiro 20 000
Founded: 1912
Colours: White/White

LIMEIRA (Population - 186 000)
AA Internacional Limeira
Stadium: Major José Levi Sobrinho 15 000
Founded: 1913
Colours: Black and white stripes/Black

BRAGANCA PAULISTA (Population – 105 000)
CA Bragantino
Founded: 1928
Colours: White/Black

STATE CHAMPIONS

1902 Sao Paulo Atletic
1903 Sao Paulo Atletic
1904 Sao Paulo Atletic
1905 Paulistano
1906 Germania
1907 Internacional Limeira
1908 Paulistano
1909 AA das Palmeiras
1910 AA das Palmeiras
1911 Sao Paulo Atletic
1912 Americano
1913 Americano
Rival League: Paulistano
1914 Corinthians
Sao Bento
1915 Germania
AA das Palmeiras
1916 Corinthians
Paulistano
1917 Paulistano
1918 Paulistano
1919 Paulistano
1920 Palestra Italia
1921 Paulistano
1922 Corinthians
1923 Corinthians
1924 Corinthians
1925 Sao Bento
1926 Palestra Italia
Paulistano
1927 Palestra Italia
Paulistano
1928 Corinthians
Internacional Limeira
1929 Corinthians
Paulistano
1930 Corinthians
1931 Sao Paulo FC
1932 Palestra Italia
1933 Palestra Italia
1934 Palestra Italia
1935 Santos
Portuguesa
1936 Palestra Italia
Portuguesa
1937 Corinthians
1938 Corinthians
1939 Corinthians
1940 Palestra Italia
1941 Corinthians
1942 Palmeiras
1943 Sao Paulo FC
1944 Palmeiras
1945 Sao Paulo FC
1946 Sao Paulo FC
1947 Palmeiras
1948 Sao Paulo FC
1949 Sao Paulo FC
1950 Palmeiras
1951 Corinthians
1952 Corinthians
1953 Sao Paulo FC
1954 Corinthians
1955 Santos
1956 Santos
1957 Sao Paulo FC
1958 Santos
1959 Palmeiras
1960 Santos
1961 Santos
1962 Santos
1963 Palmeiras
1964 Santos
1965 Santos
1966 Palmeiras
1967 Santos
1968 Santos
1969 Santos
1970 Sao Paulo FC
1971 Sao Paulo FC
1972 Palmeiras
1973 Santos/Portuguesa
1974 Palmeiras
1975 Sao Paulo FC
1976 Palmeiras
1977 Corinthians
1978 Santos
1979 Corinthians
1980 Sao Paulo FC
1981 Sao Paulo FC
1982 Corinthians
1983 Corinthians
1984 Santos
1985 Sao Paulo FC
1986 Internacional Limeira
1987 Sao Paulo FC
1988 Corinthians
1989 Sao Paulo FC
1990 Bragantino
1991 Sao Paulo FC

RIO DE JANEIRO
State capital - Rio de Janeiro
State population - 14 133 000
State size - 43653 sq km

Governing body - Federaçao Carioca de Futebol
Number of professional teams: 18

RIO DE JANEIRO - Population 10 150 000

Club de Regatas Flamengo
Stadium: Estádio da Gavea 20 000 or Maracaná
Founded: 1895. Football team in 1911
Colours: Red and black hoops/White

Fluminense Football Club
Stadium: Laranjeiras 10000, or Maracaná
Founded: 1902
Colours: Thin maroon, green and white stripes/White

Vasco da Gama Clube de Regatas
Stadium: Sao Januario 40000 or Maracaná
Founded: 1898
Colours: White/White

Botafogo de Futebol e Regatas
Stadium: Caio Martins 20000 or Maracaná
Founded: 1904
Colours: Black and white stripes/Black

Atletico Club Bangu
Stadium: Moca Bonita 15000 or Maracaná
Founded: 1904
Colours: Red and white stripes/White

America Futebol Clube
Stadium: Caio Martins 20000 or Maracana
Founded: 1905
Colours: Red/White

STATE CHAMPIONS

1906 Fluminense
1907 Fluminense/Botafogo
1908 Fluminense
1909 Fluminense
1910 Botafogo
1911 Fluminense
1912 Paissandu
1913 America FC
1914 Flamengo
1915 Flamengo
1916 America FC
1917 Fluminense
1918 Fluminense
1919 Fluminense
1920 Flamengo
1921 Flamengo
1922 America FC
1923 Vasco da Gama
1924 Vasco da Gama
Rival League: Fluminense
1925 Flamengo
1926 Sao Cristovao
1927 Flamengo
1928 America FC
1929 Vasco da Gama
1930 Botafogo
1931 America FC
1932 Botafogo
1933 Bangu
Botafogo
1934 Vasco da Gama
Botafogo
1935 America FC
Botafogo
1936 Fluminense
1937 Fluminense
1938 Fluminense
1939 Flamengo
1940 Fluminense
1941 Fluminense
1942 Flamengo
1943 Flamengo
1944 Flamengo
1945 Vasco da Gama
1946 Fluminense
1947 Vasco da Gama
1948 Botafogo
1949 Vasco da Gama
1950 Vasco da Gama
1951 Fluminense
1952 Vasco da Gama
1953 Flamengo
1954 Flamengo
1955 Flamengo
1956 Vasco da Gama
1957 Botafogo
1958 Vasco da Gama
1959 Fluminense
1960 America FC
1961 Botafogo
1962 Botafogo
1963 Flamengo
1964 Fluminense
1965 Flamengo
1966 Bangu

1967	Botafogo
1968	Botafogo
1969	Fluminense
1970	Vasco da Gama
1971	Fluminense
1972	Flamengo
1973	Fluminense
1974	Flamengo
1975	Fluminense
1976	Fluminense
1977	Vasco da Gama
1978	Flamengo
1979	Flamengo
1980	Fluminense
1981	Flamengo
1982	Vasco da Gama
1983	Fluminense
1984	Fluminense
1985	Fluminense
1986	Flamengo
1987	Vasco da Gama
1988	Vasco da Gama
1989	Botafogo
1990	Botafogo
1991	Flamengo

MINAS GERAIS

State capital – Belo Horizonte
State population – 15831000
State area – 586624 sq km

Governing body – Federaçao Mineira de Futebol
Number of professional teams – 22

BELO HORIZONTE (Population – 2950000)

Clube Atletico Mineiro
Stadium: Magalhaes Pinto–Mineirao 110000
Founded: 1908
Colours: Black and white stripes/Black

Esporte Clube Cruzeiro
Stadium: Magalhaes Pinto–Mineirao 110000
Founded: 1902
Colours: Blue/White
Previous names: Società Sportiva Palestra Italia 1902–42

STATE CHAMPIONS

1916	America FC
1917	America FC
1918	America FC
1919	America FC
1920	America FC
1921	America FC
1922	America FC
1923	America FC
1924	America FC
1925	America FC
1926	Atletico Mineiro
1927	Atletico Mineiro
1928	Palestra Italia
1929	Palestra Italia
1930	Palestra Italia
1931	Atletico Mineiro
1932	Atletico Mineiro/Vila Nova AC
1933	Vila Nova AC
1934	Vila Nova AC
1935	Vila Nova AC
1936	Atletico Mineiro
1937	Siderurgica
1938	Atletico Mineiro
1939	Atletico Mineiro
1940	Cruzeiro
1941	Atletico Mineiro
1942	Atletico Mineiro
1943	Cruzeiro
1944	Cruzeiro
1945	Cruzeiro
1946	Atletico Mineiro
1947	Atletico Mineiro
1948	America FC
1949	Atletico Mineiro
1950	Atletico Mineiro
1951	Vila Nova AC
1952	Atletico Mineiro
1953	Atletico Mineiro
1954	Atletico Mineiro
1955	Atletico Mineiro
1956	Atletico Mineiro/ Cruzeiro
1957	America FC
1958	Atletico Mineiro
1959	Cruzeiro
1960	Cruzeiro
1961	Cruzeiro
1962	Atletico Mineiro
1963	Atletico Mineiro
1964	Siderurgica
1965	Cruzeiro
1966	Cruzeiro
1967	Cruzeiro
1968	Cruzeiro
1969	Cruzeiro
1970	Atletico Mineiro
1971	America FC
1972	Cruzeiro
1973	Cruzeiro
1974	Cruzeiro
1975	Cruzeiro
1976	Atletico Mineiro
1977	Cruzeiro
1978	Atletico Mineiro
1979	Atletico Mineiro
1980	Atletico Mineiro
1981	Atletico Mineiro
1982	Atletico Mineiro
1983	Atletico Mineiro
1984	Cruzeiro
1985	Atletico Mineiro
1986	Atletico Mineiro
1987	Cruzeiro
1988	Atletico Mineiro
1989	Atletico Mineiro
1990	Cruzeiro
1991	Atletico Mineiro

RIO GRANDE DO SUL

State capital – Pôrto Alegre
State populataion – 9163000
State area – 280674 sq km

Governing body – Federaçao Gaucha de Futebol
Number of professional teams: 40

PORTO ALEGRE (Population – 2600000)

Gremio Foot–Ball Porto–Alegrense
Stadium: Olimpico 100000
Founded: 1903
Colours: Thin black, blue and white stripes/Black

Sport Club Internacional Porto Alegre
Stadium: Beira–Rio 100000
Founded: 1909
Colours: Red/Red

STATE CHAMPIONS

1919	Brasil
1920	Guarani
1921	Gremio
1922	Gremio
1923–24	–
1925	Gremio Bage
1926	Gremio
1927	Internacional
1928	Americano
1929	Cruzeiro
1930	Pelotas
1931	Gremio
1932	Gremio
1933	Sao Paulo
1934	Internacional
1935	Farroupilha
1936	Rio Grande
1937	Gremio Santanense
1938	Guarani
1939	Rio Grande
1940	Internacional
1941	Internacional
1942	Internacional
1943	Internacional
1944	Internacional
1945	Internacional
1946	Gremio
1947	Internacional
1948	Internacional
1949	Gremio
1950	Internacional
1951	Internacional
1952	Internacional
1953	Internacional
1954	Renner
1955	Internacional
1956	Gremio
1957	Gremio
1958	Gremio
1959	Gremio
1960	Gremio
1961	Internacional
1962	Gremio
1963	Gremio
1964	Gremio
1965	Gremio
1966	Gremio
1967	Gremio
1968	Gremio
1969	Internacional
1970	Internacional
1971	Internacional
1972	Internacional
1973	Internacional
1974	Internacional
1975	Internacional
1976	Internacional

1977	Gremio
1978	Internacional
1979	Gremio
1980	Gremio
1981	Internacional
1982	Internacional
1983	Internacional
1984	Internacional
1985	Gremio
1986	Gremio
1987	Gremio
1988	Gremio
1989	Gremio
1990	Gremio
1991	Internacional

ACRE

State capital – Rio Branco 145 000
State populataion – 417 000
State area – 153 698 sq km

STATE CHAMPIONS

1989	Juventos
1990	Juventos
1991	Atletico Acreano

ALGOAS

State capital – Maceió 482 000
State populataion – 2 420 000
State area – 29 107 sq km

Governing body – Federaçao Alagoana de Desportos
Number of professional teams – 8
Major clubs – Maceió – CSA, CRB

STATE CHAMPIONS

1927	CRB
1928	CSA
1929	CSA
1930	CRB
1931–32	–
1933	CSA
1934	–
1935	CSA
1936	CSA
1937	CRB
1938	CRB
1939	CRB
1940	CRB
1941	CSA
1942	CSA
1943	–
1944	CSA
1945	Santa Cruz
1946	Barroso
1947	Alexandria
1948	Santa Cruz
1949	CSA
1950	CRB
1951	CRB
1952	CSA
1953	Ferroviario AC
1954	Ferroviario AC
1955	CSA
1956	CSA
1957	CSA
1958	CSA
1959	EC Capelense
1960	CSA
1961	CSA
1962	EC Capelense
1963	CSA
1964	CRB
1965	CSA
1966	CSA
1967	CSA
1968	CSA
1969	CRB
1970	CRB
1971	CSA
1972	CRB
1973	CRB
1974	CSA
1975	CSA
1976	CRB
1977	CRB
1978	CSA
1979	CRB
1980	CSA
1981	CSA
1982	CSA
1983	CRB
1984	CSA
1985	CSA
1986	CRB
1987	CRB
1988	CSA
1989	EC Capelense
1990	CSA
1991	CSA

1	CS Algoana (CSA)	33
2	CR Brasil (CRB)	19
3	EC Capelense	3
4	Ferroviario AC	2
	Santa Cruz	2
6	Alexandria	1
	Barroso	1

AMAZONIA

State capital – Manaus 809 000
State populataion – 2 001 000
State area – 1 567 954 sq km

Governing body – Federaçao Amazonense de Futebol
Number of professional teams – 9
Major Clubs – Manaus – Nacional, Rio Negro, Fast Club

STATE CHAMPIONS

1914	Manaus Atletic
1915	Manaus Atletic
1916	Nacional
1917	Nacional
1918	Nacional
1919	Nacional
1920	Nacional
1921	Rio Negro
1922	Nacional
1923	Nacional
1924–26	–
1927	Rio Negro
1928	Cruzeiro do Sul
1929	Manaus Sporting
1930	Cruzeiro do Sul
1931	Rio Negro
1932	Rio Negro
1933	Nacional
1934	Portuguesa
1935	Portuguesa
1936	Nacional
1937	Nacional
1938	Rio Negro
1939	Nacional
1940	Rio Negro
1941	Nacional
1942	Nacional
1943	Rio Negro
1944	Olimpico
1945	Nacional
1946	Nacional
1947	Olimpico
1948	Fast
1949	Fast
1950	Nacional
1951	America
1952	America
1953	America
1954	Fast
1955	Fast
1956	Auto Esporte
1957	Nacional
1958	Santos
1959	Auto Esporte
1960	Fast
1961	Sao Raimundo
1962	Rio Negro
1963	Nacional
1964	Nacional
1965	Rio Negro
1966	Olimpico
1967	Olimpico
1968	Nacional
1969	Nacional
1970	Fast
1971	Fast
1972	Nacional
1973	Rodoviaria
1974	Nacional
1975	Rio Negro
1976	Nacional
1977	Nacional
1978	Nacional
1979	Nacional
1980	Nacional
1981	Nacional
1982	Rio Negro
1983	Nacional
1984	Nacional
1985	Nacional
1986	Nacional
1987	Rio Negro
1988	Rio Negro
1989	Rio Negro
1990	Rio Negro
1991	Nacional

1	Nacional FC	34
2	Rio Negro	15
3	Fast Club	7
4	Olimpico	4
5	America	3
6	Auto Esporte	2

	Cruzeiro do Sul	2
	Portuguesa	2
	Manaus Atletic	2
10	Manaus Sporting	1
	Rodoviaria	1
	Santos	1
	Sao Raimundo	1

BAHIA

State capital – Salvador
State populataion – 11 738 000
State area – 566 979 sq km

Governing body – Federaçao Bahiana de Futebol
Number of professional teams – 18

SALVADOR (Population – 2 050 000)

Esporte Clube Bahia
Stadium: Fonte Nova 80 000
Founded: 1931
Colours: White/Blue

Esporte Clube Vitoria
Stadium: Fonte Nova 80 000
Founded: 1899
Colours: Red and black hoops/White

STATE CHAMPIONS

1905	Internacional
1906	Sao Salvador
1907	Sao Salvador
1908	Vitoria
1909	Vitoria
1910	Santos Dumont
1911	SC Bahia
1912	Atletico
1913	Fluminense
1914	Internacional
1915	Fluminense
1916	Republica
1917	Ypiranga
1918	Ypiranga
1919	Botafogo
1920	Ypiranga
1921	Ypiranga
1922	Botafogo
1923	Botafogo
1924	AA de Bahia
1925	Ypiranga
1926	Botafogo
1927	Baiano de Tenis
1928	Ypiranga
1929	Ypiranga
1930	Botafogo
1931	EC Bahia
1932	Ypiranga
1933	EC Bahia
1934	EC Bahia
1935	Botafogo
1936	EC Bahia
1937	Galicia
1938	Botafogo/EC Bahia
1939	Ypiranga
1940	EC Bahia
1941	Galicia
1942	Galicia
1943	Galicia
1944	EC Bahia
1945	EC Bahia
1946	Guarani
1947	EC Bahia
1948	EC Bahia
1949	EC Bahia
1950	EC Bahia
1951	Ypiranga
1952	EC Bahia
1953	Vitoria
1954	EC Bahia
1955	Vitoria
1956	EC Bahia
1957	Vitoria
1958	EC Bahia
1959	EC Bahia
1960	EC Bahia
1961	EC Bahia
1962	EC Bahia
1963	Fluminense
1964	Vitoria
1965	Vitoria
1966	Leonico
1967	EC Bahia
1968	Galicia
1969	Fluminense
1970	EC Bahia
1971	EC Bahia
1972	Vitoria
1973	EC Bahia
1974	EC Bahia
1975	EC Bahia
1976	EC Bahia
1977	EC Bahia
1978	EC Bahia
1979	EC Bahia
1980	Vitoria
1981	EC Bahia
1982	EC Bahia
1983	EC Bahia
1984	EC Bahia
1985	Vitoria
1986	EC Bahia
1987	EC Bahia
1988	EC Bahia
1989	Vitoria
1990	Vitoria
1991	EC Bahia

1	EC Bahia	38
	+ 1 National Championship	
	+ 1 Brazil Cup	
	+ 2 Brazil Cup runners–up	
2	Vitoria	12
3	Ypiranga	10
4	Botafogo SC	7
5	Galicia	5
6	Fluminense	4
7	Internacional	2
	Sao Salvador	2
9	AA de Bahia	1
	Atletico	1
	Baiano de Tenis	1
	Guarani	1
	Leonico	1
	Republica	1
	Santos Dumont	1
	SC Bahia	1

CEARA

State capital – Fortaleza 1 825 000
State populataion – 6 471 000
State area – 145694 sq km

Governing body – Federaçao Cearense de Futebol
Number of professional teams – 10
Major clubs – Fortaleza – Ceara SC, Fortaleza FC, Ferroviaro

STATE CHAMPIONS

1920	Fortaleza FC
1921	Fortaleza FC
1922	Ceara SC
1923	Fortaleza FC
1924	Fortaleza FC
1925	Ceara SC
1926	Fortaleza FC
1927	Fortaleza FC
1928	Fortaleza FC
1929	Maguari
1930	Orion
1931	Ceara SC
1932	Ceara SC
1933	Fortaleza FC
1934	Fortaleza FC
1935	America
1936	Maguari
1937	Fortaleza FC
1938	Fortaleza FC
1939	Ceara SC
1940	Tramways
1941	Ceara SC
1942	Ceara SC
1943	Maguari
1944	Maguari
1945	Ferroviario AC
1946	Fortaleza FC
1947	Fortaleza FC
1948	Ceara SC
1949	Fortaleza FC
1950	Ferroviario AC
1951	Ceara SC
1952	Ferroviario AC
1953	Fortaleza FC
1954	Fortaleza FC
1955	Calouros do Ar
1956	Gentilandia
1957	Ceara SC
1958	Ceara SC
1959	Fortaleza FC
1960	Fortaleza FC
1961	Ceara SC
1962	Ceara SC
1963	Ceara SC
1964	Fortaleza FC
1965	Fortaleza FC
1966	America
1967	Fortaleza FC
1968	Ferroviario AC
1969	Fortaleza FC
1970	Ferroviario AC
1971	Ceara SC
1972	Ceara SC
1973	Fortaleza FC
1974	Fortaleza FC
1975	Ceara SC

1976 Ceara SC
1977 Ceara SC
1978 Ceara SC
1979 Ferroviario AC
1980 Ceara SC
1981 Ceara SC
1982 Fortaleza FC
1983 Fortaleza FC
1984 Ceara SC
1985 Fortaleza FC
1986 Ceara SC
1987 Fortaleza FC
1988 Ferroviario AC
1989 Ceara SC
1990 Ceara SC
1991 Fortaleza FC

1 Fortaleza FC 29
+2 Brazil Cup runners–up
2 Ceara SC 26
3 Ferroviario AC 7
4 Maguari 4
5 America 2
6 Colouros do Ar 1
Gentilandia 1
Orion 1
Tramways 1

DISTRITO FEDERAL

State capital – Brasilia 1 567 000
State populataion – 1 567 000
State area – 5794 sq km

Governing body – Federaçao Desportiva de Brasilia
Number of professional teams – 9

STATE CHAMPIONS

1973 CEUB
1974 Pioneira
1975 –
1976 Brasilia EC
1977 Brasilia EC
1978 Brasilia EC
1979 Gama
1980 Brasilia EC
1981 Taguatinga
1982 Brasilia EC
1983 Brasilia EC
1984 Brasilia EC
1985 Sobradinho
1986 Sobradinho
1987 Brasilia EC
1988 Tiradentes
1989 Taguatinga
1990 Taguatinga
1991 Taguatinga

1 Brasilia EC 8
2 Taguatinga 4
3 Sobradinho 2
4 CEUB 1
Gama 1
Pioneira 1
Tiradentes 1

ESPIRITO SANTO

State capital – Vitória 735 000
State populataion – 2 523 000
State area – 45733 sq km

Governing body – Federaçao Desportiva Espiritosantense
Number of professional teams – 16
Major Clubs – Vitória – Rio Branco AC, Desportiva Ferroviaria

STATE CHAMPIONS

1940 Americano
1941 Rio Branco AC
1942 Rio Branco AC
1943 Vitoria
1944 Caxias
1945 Rio Branco AC
1946 Rio Branco AC
1947 Rio Branco AC
1948 Vale de Rio Doce
1949 Rio Branco AC
1950 Vitoria
1951 Rio Branco AC
1952 Vitoria
1953 Santo Antonio
1954 Santo Antonio
1955 Santo Antonio
1956 Vitoria
1957 Rio Branco AC
1958 Rio Branco AC
1959 Rio Branco AC
1960 Santo Antonio
1961 Santo Antonio
1962 Santo Antonio
1963 Rio Branco AC
1964 Desportiva Ferroviaria
1965 Desportiva Ferroviaria
1966 Rio Branco AC
1967 Desportiva Ferroviaria
1968 Rio Branco AC
1969 Rio Branco AC
1970 Rio Branco AC
1971 –
1972 Desportiva Ferroviaria
1973 Rio Branco AC
1974 Desportiva Ferroviaria
1975 Rio Branco AC
1976 Vitoria
1977 Desportiva Ferroviaria
1978 Rio Branco AC
1979 Desportiva Ferroviaria
1980 Desportiva Ferroviaria
1981 Desportiva Ferroviaria
1982 Rio Branco AC
1983 Rio Branco AC
1984 Desportiva Ferroviaria
1985 Rio Branco AC
1986 Desportiva Ferroviaria
1987 Guarapari
1988 Ibiracu
1989 Desportiva Ferroviaria
1990 Colatina
1991 Muniz Freire

1 Rio Branco AC 21
2 Desportivo Ferroviaria 12
3 Santo Antonio 6
4 Vitoria 5
5 Americano 1
Caxias 1
Colatina 1
Guarapari 1
Ibiracu 1
Muniz Freire 1
Vale do Rio Doce 1

GOIAS

State capital – Goiânia 990 000
State populataion – 3 983 000
State area – 340 166 sq km

Governing body – Federaçao Goiana de Desportos
Number of professional teams – 18
Major clubs – Goiânia – Atletico Goiâniense, Goiânia, Goiâs AC, Villa Nova FC

STATE CHAMPIONS

1944 Atletico Goiâniense
1945 Goiânia
1946 Goiânia
1947 Atletico Goiâniense
1948 Goiânia
1949 Atletico Goiâniense
1950 Goiânia
1951 Goiânia
1952 Goiânia
1953 Goiânia
1954 Goiânia
1955 Atletico Goiâniense
1956 Goiânia
1957 Atletico Goiâniense
1958 Goiânia
1959 Goiânia
1960 Goiânia
1961 Vila Nova FC
1962 Vila Nova FC
1963 Vila Nova FC
1964 Atletico Goiâniense
1965 Anapolis
1966 Goiâs AC
1967 CRAC
1968 Goiânia
1969 Vila Nova FC
1970 Atletico Goiâniense
1971 Goiâs AC
1972 Goiâs AC
1973 Vila Nova FC
1974 Goiânia
1975 Goiâs AC
1976 Goiâs AC
1977 Vila Nova FC
1978 Vila Nova FC
1979 Vila Nova FC
1980 Vila Nova FC
1981 Goiâs AC
1982 Vila Nova FC
1983 Goiâs AC
1984 Vila Nova FC
1985 Atletico Goiâniense
1986 Goiâs AC
1987 Goiâs AC
1988 Atletico Goiâniense
1989 Goiâs AC
1990 Goiâs AC
1991 Goiâs AC

1 Goiania 14
2 Goias AC12 +1 Brazil Cup runners–up

3	Vila Nova FC	11
4	Atletico Goianiense	9
5	Anapolis	1
	CRAC	1

MARANHAO

State capital – Sao Luis 600 000
State populataion – 5 181 000
State area – 329 556 sq km

Governing body – Federaçao Maranhaense de Desportos
Number of professional teams – 10
Major clubs – Sao Luis – Moto Clube, Sampaio Correa FC, Maranhao FC

STATE CHAMPIONS

1918	Fenix
1919	Luso
1920	Luso
1921	FAC
1922	Fenix
1923	FAC
1924	Luso
1925	Luso
1926	Luso
1927	Luso
1928	Vasco
1929	–
1930	Sampaio Correa
1931	Sirio
1932	Tupa
1933	Sampaio Correa
1934	Sampaio Correa
1935	Tupa
1936	–
1937	Maranhao AC
1938	Tupa
1939	Maranhao AC
1940	Sampaio Correa
1941	Maranhao AC
1942	Sampaio Correa
1943	Maranhao AC
1944	Moto
1945	Moto
1946	Moto
1947	Moto
1948	Moto
1949	Moto
1950	Moto
1951	Maranhao AC
1952	Vitoria do Mar
1953	Sampaio Correa
1954	Sampaio Correa
1955	Moto
1956	Sampaio Correa
1957	Ferroviario
1958	Ferroviario
1959	Moto
1960	Moto
1961	Sampaio Correa
1962	Sampaio Correa
1963	Maranhao AC
1964	Sampaio Correa
1965	Sampaio Correa
1966	Moto
1967	Moto
1968	Moto
1969	Maranhao AC
1970	Maranhao AC
1971	Ferroviario
1972	Sampaio Correa
1973	Ferroviario
1974	Moto
1975	Sampaio Correa
1976	Sampaio Correa
1977	Moto
1978	Sampaio Correa
1979	Maranhao AC
1980	Sampaio Correa
1981	Moto
1982	Moto
1983	Moto
1984	Sampaio Correa
1985	Sampaio Correa
1986	Sampaio Correa
1987	Sampaio Correa
1988	Sampaio Correa
1989	Moto
1990	Moto
1991	Sampaio Correa

1	Sampiao Correa	23
2	Moto	20
3	Maranhao AC	9
4	Luso	6
5	Ferroviario	4
6	Tupa	3
7	FAC	2
	Fenix	2
9	Sirio	1
	Vasco	1
	Vitoria do Mar	1

MATO GROSSO

State capital – Cuiabá 279 000
State populataion – 1 727 000
State area – 901 421 sq km

Governing body – Federaçao Matogrossense de Desportes
Number of professional teams – 10
Major clubs – Cuiabá – Mixto EC, Vareza Grande – CE Operario

STATE CHAMPIONS

1974	Operario FC
1975	Comercial EC
1976	Operario FC
1977	Operario FC
1978	Operario FC
1979	Mixto
1980	Mixto
1981	Mixto
1982	Mixto
1983	CE Operario
1984	Mixto
1985	CE Operario
1986	CE Operario
1987	CE Operario
1988	Mixto
1989	Mixto
1990	Mixto
1991	Dom Bosco

1	Mixto	8
2	CE Operario	4

In 1979 the Federaçao Matogrossense do Sul was formed. Both Operario EC and Comercial EC joined this new body

MATO GROSSO DO SUL

State capital – Campo Grande 384 000
State populataion – 1 797 000
State area – 357 472 sq km

Governing body – Federaçao Matogrossense do Sul de Desportes
Number of professional teams – 8
Major clubs – Campo Grande – Operario FC, Comercial EC

STATE CHAMPIONS

1979	Operario FC
1980	Operario FC
1981	Operario FC
1982	Comercial EC
1983	Operario FC
1984	Corumbaense
1985	Comercial EC
1986	Operario FC
1987	Comercial EC
1988	Operario FC
1989	Operario FC
1990	Ubiratan
1991	Operario FC

1	Operario FC	12
2	Comercial EC	4
3	Corumbaense	1
	Ubiraton	1

PARA

State capital – Belém 1 200 000
State populataion – 5 001 000
State area – 1 246 833 sq km

Governing body – Federaçao Paraense de Futebol
Number of professional teams – 7
Major clubs – Belém – Paysandu, Club do Remo, Tuna Luso Brasileira

STATE CHAMPIONS

1913	Remo
1914	Remo
1915	Remo
1916	Remo
1917	Remo
1918	Remo
1919	Remo
1920	Paysandu
1921	Paysandu
1922	Paysandu
1923	Paysandu
1924	Remo
1925	Remo
1926	Remo
1927	Paysandu
1928	Paysandu
1929	Paysandu
1930	Remo
1931	Paysandu
1932	Remo

1933	Remo
1934	Paysandu
1935	–
1936	Remo
1937	Tuna Luso
1938	Tuna Luso
1939	Tuna Luso
1940	Remo
1941	Tuna Luso
1942	Paysandu
1943	Paysandu
1944	Paysandu
1945	Paysandu
1946	–
1947	Paysandu
1948	Tuna Luso
1949	Remo
1950	Remo
1951	Tuna Luso
1952	Remo
1953	Remo
1954	Remo
1955	Tuna Luso
1956	Paysandu
1957	Paysandu
1958	Tuna Luso
1959	Paysandu
1960	Remo
1961	Paysandu
1962	Paysandu
1963	Paysandu
1964	Remo
1965	Paysandu
1966	Paysandu
1967	Paysandu
1968	Remo
1969	Paysandu
1970	Tuna Luso
1971	Remo
1972	Paysandu
1973	Remo
1974	Remo
1975	Remo
1976	Paysandu
1977	Remo
1978	Remo
1979	Remo
1980	Paysandu
1981	Paysandu
1982	Paysandu
1983	Tuna Luso
1984	Paysandu
1985	Paysandu
1986	Remo
1987	Paysandu
1988	–
1989	–
1990	Remo
1991	Remo

1	Remo	33
2	Paysandu	32
3	Tuna Luso	10

PARAIBA

State capital – Joao Pessoa 550000
State populataion – 3247000
State area – 53958 sq km

Governing body – Federaçao Paraibana de Futebol
Number of professional teams – 9
Major clubs – Joao Pessoa – Botafogo, Campina Grande – Campinense Clube, Treze FC

STATE CHAMPIONS

1917	Colegio Pio
1918	Cabo Branco
1919	Palmeiras
1920	Cabo Branco
1921	Palmeiras
1922	Pytaguares
1923	America
1924	Cabo Branco
1925	America
1926	Cabo Branco
1927	Cabo Branco
1928	Palmeiras
1929	Cabo Branco
1930	–
1931	Cabo Branco
1932	Cabo Branco
1933	Palmeiras
1934	Cabo Branco
1935	Palmeiras
1936	Botafogo
1937	Botafogo
1938	Botafogo
1939	Auto Esporte
1940	Treze
1941	Treze
1942	Astrea
1943	Astrea
1944	Botafogo
1945	Botafogo
1946	Filipeia
1947	Botafogo
1948	Botafogo
1949	Botafogo
1950	Treze
1951	–
1952	Red Cross
1953	Botafogo
1954	Botafogo
1955	Botafogo
1956	Auto Esporte
1957	Botafogo
1958	Auto Esporte
1959	Estrela do Mar
1960	Campinense
1961	Campinense
1962	Campinense
1963	Campinense
1964	Campinense
1965	Campinense
1966	Treze
1967	Campinense
1968	Botafogo
1969	Botafogo
1970	Botafogo
1971	Campinense
1972	Campinense
1973	Campinense
1974	Campinense
1975	Botafogo/Treze
1976	Botafogo
1977	Botafogo
1978	Botafogo
1979	Botafogo
1980	Campinense
1981	Treze
1982	Treze
1983	Treze
1984	Botafogo
1985	No title awarded
1986	Botafogo
1987	Auto Esporte
1988	Botafogo
1989	Treze
1990	Auto Esporte
1991	Campinense

1	Botafogo Joao Pessoa	23
2	Campinense	13
3	Cabo Branco	9
	Treze	9
5	Auto Esporte	5
	Palmeiras	5
7	America	2
	Astrea	2
9	Colegio Pio	1
	Estrela	1
	Filipeia	1
	Red Cross	1
	Pytaguares	1

PARANA

State capital – Curitiba
State populataion – 9137000
State area – 199324 sq km

Governing body – Federaçao Paranaense de Futebol
Number of professional teams – 30

CURITIBA (Population – 1700000)

Coritiba Football Club
Stadium: Antonio do Pereira 80000 and Pinherao 130000
Founded: 1909
Colours: White with two green hoops/Black

Clube Atletico Paranaense
Stadium: Antonio do Pereira 80000 and Pinherao 130000
Founded: 1924
Colours: Red and black hoops/White

STATE CHAMPIONS

1915	Internacional
1916	Coritiba FC
1917	America
1918	Britania
1919	Britania
1920	Britania
1921	Britania
1922	Britania
1923	Britania
1924	Palestra Italia
1925	Atletico Paranaense
1926	Palestra Italia
1927	Coritiba FC
1928	Britania

1929 Atletico Paranaense
1930 Atletico Paranaense
1931 Coritiba FC
1932 Palestra Italia
1933 Coritiba FC
1934 Atletico Paranaense
1935 Coritiba FC
1936 Atletico Paranaense
1937 Ferroviario
1938 Ferroviario
1939 Coritiba FC
1940 Atletico Paranaense
1941 Coritiba FC
1942 Coritiba FC
1943 Atletico Paranaense
1944 Ferroviario
1945 Atletico Paranaense
1946 Coritiba FC
1947 Coritiba FC
1948 Ferroviario
1949 Atletico Paranaense
1950 Ferroviario
1951 Coritiba FC
1952 Coritiba FC
1953 Ferroviario
1954 Coritiba FC
1955 Monte Alegre
1956 Coritiba FC
1957 Coritiba FC
1958 Atletico Paranaense
1959 Coritiba FC
1960 Coritiba FC
1961 Comercial
1962 Londrina
1963 Maringa
1964 Maringa
1965 Ferroviario
1966 Ferroviario
1967 Agua Verde
1968 Coritiba FC
1969 Coritiba FC
1970 Atletico Paranaense
1971 Coritiba FC
1972 Coritiba FC
1973 Coritiba FC
1974 Coritiba FC
1975 Coritiba FC
1976 Coritiba FC
1977 Maringa
1978 Coritiba FC
1979 Coritiba FC
1980 Cascavel
1981 Londrina
1982 Atletico Paranaense
1983 Atletico Paranaense
1984 Pinheiros
1985 Atletico Paranaense
1986 Coritiba FC
1987 Pinheiros
1988 Atletico Paranaense
1989 Coritiba FC
1990 Atletico Paranaense
1991 Atletico Paranaense

1 Coritiba FC 29
+1 National Championship
2 Atletico Paranaense 17
3 Ferroviario 8
4 Britania 7
5 Maringa 3
Palestra Italia 3
6 Londrina 2
Pinheiros 2
8 Agua Verde 1
America 1
Cascavel 1
Comercial 1
Internacional 1
Monte Alegre 1

PERNAMBUCO

State capital – Recife
State populataion – 7 360 000
State area – 101 023 sq km

Governing body – Federaçao Pernambucana de Futebol
Number of professional teams – 10

RECIFE (Population – 2 625 000)

Sport Club Recife
Stadium: Ilha do Retiro 50 000
Founded: 1905
Colours: Red and black hoops/Black

Santa Cruz Futebol Clube
Stadium: José do Rego Maciel – Arudao 150 000
Founded: 1914
Colours: White with a black, white and red band on chest/black

Nautico Clube Capibaribe
Stadium: Estadio dos Aflitos
Founded:
Colours: Red and white stripes/White

STATE CHAMPIONS

1915 Flamengo
1916 Sport Recife
1917 Sport Recife
1918 America CF
1919 America CF
1920 Sport Recife
1921 America CF
1922 America CF
1923 Sport Recife
1924 Sport Recife
1925 Sport Recife
1926 Torre
1927 America CF
1928 Sport Recife
1929 Torre
1930 Torre
1931 Santa Cruz
1932 Santa Cruz
1933 Santa Cruz
1934 Nautico
1935 Santa Cruz
1936 Tramways
1937 Tramways
1938 Sport Recife
1939 Nautico
1940 Santa Cruz
1941 Sport Recife
1942 Sport Recife
1943 Sport Recife
1944 America CF
1945 Nautico
1946 Santa Cruz
1947 Santa Cruz
1948 Sport Recife
1949 Sport Recife
1950 Nautico
1951 Nautico
1952 Nautico
1953 Sport Recife
1954 Nautico
1955 Sport Recife
1956 Sport Recife
1957 Santa Cruz
1958 Sport Recife
1959 Santa Cruz
1960 Nautico
1961 Sport Recife
1962 Sport Recife
1963 Nautico
1964 Nautico
1965 Nautico
1966 Nautico
1967 Nautico
1968 Nautico
1969 Santa Cruz
1970 Santa Cruz
1971 Santa Cruz
1972 Santa Cruz
1973 Santa Cruz
1974 Nautico
1975 Sport Recife
1976 Santa Cruz
1977 Sport Recife
1978 Santa Cruz
1979 Santa Cruz
1980 Sport Recife
1981 Sport Recife
1982 Sport Recife
1983 Santa Cruz
1984 Nautico
1985 Nautico
1986 Santa Cruz
1987 Santa Cruz
1988 Sport Recife
1989 Nautico
1990 Santa Cruz
1991 Sport Recife

1 Sport Recife 26
+1 Brazil Cup runners–up
2 Santa Cruz 21
3 Nautico 18
+1 Brazil Cup runners–up
4 FC America 6
5 Torre 3
6 Tramways 2
7 Flamengo 1

PIAUI

State capital – Teresina 525 000
State populataion – 2 666 000
State area – 251 273 sq km

Governing body – Federaçao Piauiense de Desportos
Number of professional teams – 8
Major clubs – Teresina – Flamengo, River AC, Piaui EC, AE Tiradentes

STATE CHAMPIONS

1918 Palmeiras
1919 Teresinense
1920 Artistico
1921 Militar
1922 Teresinense
1923 Artistico
1924 AE Tiradentes
1925 AE Tiradentes
1926 AE Tiradentes
1927 AE Tiradentes
1928 AE Tiradentes
1929 Artistico
1930 Artistico
1931 Militar
1932 Militar
1933 Artistico
1934 AE Tiradentes
1935 Militar
1936 Militar
1937 Militar
1938 Botafogo
1939 Flamengo
1940 Botafogo
1941 Botafogo
1942 Flamengo
1943 Botafogo
1944 Flamengo
1945 Flamengo
1946 Flamengo
1947 Botafogo
1948 River AC
1949 Botafogo
1950 River AC
1951 River AC
1952 River AC
1953 River AC
1954 River AC
1955 River AC
1956 River AC
1957 Botafogo
1958 River AC
1959 River AC
1960 River AC
1961 River AC
1962 River AC
1963 River AC
1964 Flamengo
1965 Flamengo
1966 Piaui EC
1967 Piaui EC
1968 Piaui EC
1969 Piaui EC
1970 Flamengo
1971 Flamengo
1972 AE Tiradentes
1973 River AC
1974 AE Tiradentes
1975 River AC/AE Tiradentes
1976 Flamengo
1977 River AC
1978 River AC
1979 Flamengo
1980 River AC
1981 River AC
1982 AE Tiradentes
1983 Auto Esporte
1984 Flamengo
1985 Piaui EC
1986 Flamengo
1987 Flamengo
1988 Flamengo
1989 River AC
1990 AE Tiradentes
1991 SE Picos

1 River AC 21
2 Flamengo 15
3 AE Tiradentes 11
4 Botafogo 7
5 Militar 6
6 Artistico 5
Piaui EC 5
8 Teresinense 2
9 Auto Esporte 1
Palmeiras 1
SE Picos 1

RIO GRANDE DO NORTE

State capital – Natal 510000
State populataion – 2318000
State area – 53 167 sq km

Governing body – Federaçao Norte Riograndense de Desportos
Number of professional teams – 10
Major clubs – Natal – ABC, Alecrim, America

STATE CHAMPIONS

1920 ABC
1921 ABC
1922 America
1923 ABC
1924 America
1925 ABC
1926 ABC
1927 America
1928 ABC
1929 ABC
1930 America
1931 America
1932 ABC
1933 ABC
1934 ABC
1935 ABC
1936 ABC
1937 ABC
1938 ABC
1939 ABC
1940 ABC
1941 ABC
1942 –
1943 America
1944 ABC
1945 ABC
1946 Santa Cruz
1947 ABC
1948 America
1949 America
1950 ABC
1951 –
1952 America
1953 ABC
1954 ABC
1955 ABC
1956 America
1957 America
1958 ABC
1959 ABC
1960 ABC
1961 ABC
1962 ABC
1963 America
1964 Alecrim
1965 ABC
1966 ABC
1967 Alecrim
1968 Alecrim
1969 America
1970 ABC
1971 ABC
1972 ABC
1973 ABC
1974 America
1975 America
1976 ABC
1977 America
1978 ABC
1979 America
1980 America
1981 America
1982 America
1983 ABC
1984 ABC
1985 Alecrim
1986 Alecrim
1987 America
1988 America
1989 America
1990 ABC
1991 America

1 ABC 40
2 America 24
3 Alecrim 5
4 Santa Cruz 1

SANTA CATARINA

State capital – Florianópolis 365000
State populataion – 4461000
State area – 95318 sq km

Governing body – Federaçao Catarinense de Futebol
Number of professional teams – 15
Major clubs – Florianópolis – Avai FC, Joinville – Joinville

STATE CHAMPIONS

1927 Avai
1928 Avai
1929 Caxias
1930 Avai
1931 Lauro Muller
1932 Figueirense
1933 –
1934 Atletico Florianopolis
1935 Figueirense
1936 Figueirense
1937 Figueirense
1938 CIP
1939 Figueirense
1940 Ipiranga
1941 Figueirense

1942	Avai
1943	Avai
1944	Avai
1945	Avai
1946	–
1947	America
1948	America
1949	Olimpico
1950	Carlos Renaux
1951	America
1952	America
1953	Carlos Renaux
1954	Caxias
1955	Caxias
1956	Operario
1957	Hercilio Luz
1958	Hercilio Luz
1959	Paulo Ramos
1960	Metropol
1961	Metropol
1962	Metropol
1963	Marcilio Diaz
1964	Olimpico
1965	Internacional
1966	Perdigao
1967	Metropol
1968	Comerciario
1969	Metropol
1970	Ferroviario
1971	America
1972	Figueirense
1973	Avai
1974	Figueirense
1975	Avai
1976	Joinville
1977	Chapecoense
1978	Joinville
1979	Joinville
1980	Joinville
1981	Joinville
1982	Joinville
1983	Joinville
1984	Joinville
1985	Joinville
1986	Criciuma
1987	Joinville
1988	Avai
1989	Criciuma
1990	Criciuma
1991	Criciuma

1	Avai	10
	Joinville	10
3	Figueirense	8
4	Criciuma	5
	+1 Brazil Cup	
5	America	5
	Metropol	5
7	Caxias	3
8	Carlos Renaux	2
	Hercilio Luz	2
	Olimpico	2
11	Atletico Florianopolis	1
	Chapcoense	1
	CIP	1
	Ferroviario	1
	Internacional	1
	Ipiranga	1
	Lauro Muller	1
	Marcilio Dias	1
	Operario Joinville	1
	Paula Ramos	1
	Perdigao	1

SERGIPE

State capital – Aracaju 360 000
State populataion – 1 416 000
State area – 21 863 sq km

Governing body – Federaçao Sergipana de Desportos
Number of professional teams – 12
Major clubs – Aracaju – CS Sergipe, Confianca

STATE CHAMPIONS

1918	Cotinguiba
1919	–
1920	Cotinguiba
1921	Industrial
1922	CS Sergipe
1923	Cotinguiba
1924	CS Sergipe
1925–26	–
1927	CS Sergipe
1928	CS Sergipe
1929	CS Sergipe
1930–31	–
1932	CS Sergipe
1933	CS Sergipe
1934	Palestra
1935	Palestra
1936	Cotinguiba
1937	CS Sergipe
1938	–
1939	Ipiranga
1940	CS Sergipe
1941	Riachuelo
1942	Cotinguiba
1943	CS Sergipe
1944	Vasco
1945	Ipiranga
1946	Olimpico
1947	Olimpico
1948	Vasco
1949	Palestra
1950	Passagem
1951	Confianca
1952	Cotinguiba
1953	Vasco
1954	Confianca
1955	CS Sergipe
1956	Santa Cruz
1957	Santa Cruz
1958	Santa Cruz
1959	Santa Cruz
1960	Santa Cruz
1961	CS Sergipe
1962	Confianca
1963	Confianca
1964	CS Sergipe
1965	Confianca
1966	America
1967	CS Sergipe
1968	Confianca
1969	Itabaiana
1970	CS Sergipe
1971	CS Sergipe
1972	CS Sergipe
1973	Itabaiana
1974	CS Sergipe
1975	CS Sergipe
1976	Confianca
1977	Confianca
1978	Itabaiana
1979	Itabaiana
1980	Itabaiana
1981	Itabaiana
1982	CS Sergipe/Itabaiana
1983	Confianca
1984	CS Sergipe
1985	CS Sergipe
1986	Confianca
1987	Vasco
1988	Confianca
1989	CS Sergipe
1990	Confianca
1991	CS Sergipe

1	CS Sergipe	24
2	Confianca	12
3	Itabaiana	7
4	Cotinguiba	6
5	Santa Cruz	5
6	Vasco	4
7	Palestra	3
8	Ipiranga	2
	Olimpico	2
10	America	1
	Industrial	1
	Riachuelo	1
	Passagem	1

INTERNATIONAL MATCHES PLAYED BY BRAZIL

Date	Opponents	Result		Venue	Compet	Scorers
20-09-1914	Argentina	L	0–3	Buenos Aires	Fr	
27–09	Argentina	W	1–0	Buenos Aires	RC	Rubens Salles
8–07–1916	Chile	D	1–1	Buenos Aires	SC	Demóstenes
10–07	Argentina	D	1–1	Buenos Aires	SC	Alencar
12–07	Uruguay	L	1–2	Buenos Aires	SC	Friedenreich
18–07	Uruguay	W	1–0	Montevideo	Fr	Mimi

3-10-1917	Argentina	L	2-4	Montevideo	SC	Lagreca, Neco
7-10	Uruguay	L	0-4	Montevideo	SC	
12-10	Chile	W	5-0	Montevideo	SC	Haroldo 2, Amilcar, Caetano, Neco
16-10	Uruguay	L	1-3	Montevideo	Fr	Neco
11-05-1919	Chile	W	6-0	Rio de Janeiro	SC	Neco 2, Friedenreich 3, Haroldo
18-05	Argentina	W	3-1	Rio de Janeiro	SC	Amilcar, Millon, Heitor Dominguez
25-05	Uruguay	D	2-2	Rio de Janeiro	SC	Neco 2
29-05	Uruguay	W	1-0	Rio de Janeiro	SCpo	Friedenreich
1-06	Argentina	D	3-3	Rio de Janeiro	Fr	Arlindo I, Haroldo
11-09-1920	Chile	W	1-0	Viña del Mar	SC	Alvariza
18-09	Uruguay	L	0-6	Viña del Mar	SC	
25-09	Argentina	L	0-2	Viña del Mar	SC	
12-10	Argentina	L	1-3	Buenos Aires	Fr	Osvaldo
2-10-1921	Argentina	L	0-1	Buenos Aires	SC	
12-10	Paraguay	W	3-0	Buenos Aires	SC	Machado 2, Candiotta
23-10	Uruguay	L	1-2	Buenos Aires	SC	Zezé I
17-09-1922	Chile	D	1-1	Rio de Janeiro	SC	Tatú
24-09	Paraguay	D	1-1	Rio de Janeiro	SC	Amilcar
1-10	Uruguay	D	0-0	Rio de Janeiro	SC	
15-10	Argentina	W	2-0	Rio de Janeiro	SC	Amilcar, Neco
22-10	Paraguay	W	3-1	Rio de Janeiro	SCpo	Formiga 2, Neco
22-10	Argentina	W	2-1	Sao Paulo	RC	Gamba 2
29-10	Paraguay	W	3-1	Sao Paulo	Fr	Imparatinho 2, Gamba
11-11-1923	Paraguay	L	0-1	Montevideo	SC	
18-11	Argentina	L	1-2	Montevideo	SC	Nilo
22-11	Paraguay	W	2-0	Montevideo	Fr	Zezé I, Nilo
25-11	Uruguay	L	1-2	Montevideo	SC	Nilo
2-12	Argentina	W	2-0	Buenos Aires	RC	Zezé I, Nilo
9-12	Argentina	L	0-2	Buenos Aires	RC	
6-12-1925	Paraguay	W	5-2	Buenos Aires	SC	Lagarto 2, Friedenreich, Filó, Nilo
13-12	Argentina	L	1-4	Buenos Aires	SC	Nilo
17-12	Paraguay	W	3-1	Buenos Aires	SC	Lagarto 2, Nilo
25-12	Argentina	D	2-2	Buenos Aires	SC	Nilo, Friedenreich
14-07-1930	Yugoslavia	L	1-2	Montevideo	WCr1	Preguinho
22-07	Bolivia	W	4-0	Montevideo	WCr1	Carvalho Leite, Preguinho 3
1-08	France	W	3-2	Rio de Janeiro	Fr	Heitor Dominguez 2, Friedenreich
10-08	Yugoslavia	W	4-1	Rio de Janeiro	Fr	Carvalho Leite 2, Benedicto II, Russinho
17-08	USA	W	4-3	Rio de Janeiro	Fr	Doca, Carvalho Leite, Preguinho, Teóphilo
6-09-1931	Uruguay	W	2-0	Rio de Janeiro	RBC	Nilo 2
4-12-1932	Uruguay	W	2-1	Montevideo	RBC	Leônidas da Silva 2
27-05-1934	Spain	L	1-3	Genoa	WCr1	Leônidas da Silva
3-06	Yugoslavia	L	4-8	Belgrade	Fr	Leônidas da Silva 2, Armandinho, Valdemar de Brito
27-12-1936	Peru	W	3-2	Buenos Aires	SC	Alfonsinho, Roberto I, Niginho
3-01-1937	Chile	W	6-4	Buenos Aires	SC	Patesko 2, Carvalho Leite, Luiz M Oliveira 2, Roberto I
13-01	Paraguay	W	5-0	Buenos Aires	SC	Patesko 2, Luiz M Oliveira 2, Carvalho Leite
19-01	Uruguay	W	3-2	Buenos Aires	SC	Bahia, Carvalho Leite, Niginho
30-01	Argentina	L	0-1	Buenos Aires	SC	
1-02	Argentina	L	0-2	Buenos Aires	SCpo	
5-06-1938	Poland	W	6-5	Strasbourg	WCr1	Leônidas da Silva 4, Perácio, Romeu Pelliciari
12-06	Czechoslovakia	D	1-1	Bordeaux	WCqf	Leônidas da Silva
14-06	Czechoslovakia	W	2-1	Bordeaux	WCqf	Leônidas da Silva, Roberto I
16-06	Italy	L	1-2	Marseille	WCsf	Romeu Pelliciari
19-06	Sweden	W	4-2	Bordeaux	WC3p	Leônidas da Silva 2, Romeu Pelliciari, Perácio
15-01-1939	Argentina	L	1-5	Rio de Janeiro	RC	Leônidas da Silva
22-01	Argentina	W	3-2	Rio de Janeiro	RC	Adilson, Leônidas da Silva, Perácio
18-02-1940	Argentina	D	2-2	Sao Paulo	RC	Leônidas da Silva 2
25-02	Argentina	L	0-3	Sao Paulo	RC	
5-03	Argentina	L	1-6	Buenos Aires	RC	Jair R Pinto
10-03	Argentina	W	3-2	Buenos Aires	RC	Hércules 2, Leônidas da Silva
17-03	Argentina	L	1-5	Buenos Aires	RC	Leônidas da Silva
24-03	Uruguay	L	3-4	Rio de Janeiro	RBC	Pedro Amorim, Leônidas da Silva, Hércules
31-03	Uruguay	D	1-1	Rio de Janeiro	RBC	Leônidas da Silva
14-01-1942	Chile	W	6-1	Montevideo	SC	Pirilo 3, Patesko 2, Cláudio C Pinho

17–01	Argentina	L	1–2	Montevideo	SC	Servílio I
21–01	Peru	W	2–1	Montevideo	SC	Pedro Amorim
24–01	Uruguay	L	0–1	Montevideo	SC	
1–02	Ecuador	W	5–1	Montevideo	SC	Pirilo 3, Tim, Zizinho
5–02	Paraguay	D	1–1	Montevideo	SC	Zizinho
14–05–1944	Uruguay	W	6–1	Rio de Janeiro	Fr	Eduardo Lima 2, Tesourinha, Isaías, Lelé, Rui
17–05	Uruguay	W	4–0	Sao Paulo	Fr	Jair R Pinto 3, Heleno de Freitas
21–01–1945	Colombia	W	3–0	Santiago	SC	Heleno de Freitas, Jaime, Jorginho
28–01	Bolivia	W	2–0	Santiago	SC	Ademir Menezes, Tesourinha
7–02	Uruguay	W	3–0	Santiago	SC	Heleno de Freitas 2, Rui
15–02	Argentina	L	1–3	Santiago	SC	Ademir Menezes
21–02	Ecuador	W	9–2	Santiago	SC	Ademir Menezes 3, Jair R Pinto 2, Heleno de Freitas 2, Zizinho 2
28–02	Chile	W	1–0	Santiago	SC	Heleno de Freitas
16–12	Argentina	L	3–4	Sao Paulo	RC	Zizinho, OG, Ademir Menezes
20–12	Argentina	W	6–2	Rio de Janeiro	RC	Ademir Menezes 2, Heleno de Freitas, Chico, Leônidas da Silva, Zizinho
23–12	Argentina	W	3–1	Rio de Janeiro	RC	OG, Heleno de Freitas, Eduardo Lima
5–01–1946	Uruguay	L	3–4	Montevideo	RBC	Jair R Pinto 2, Zizinho
9–01	Uruguay	D	1–1	Montevideo	RBC	Heleno de Freitas
16–01	Bolivia	W	3–0	Buenos Aires	SC	Heleno de Freitas 2, Zizinho
23–01	Uruguay	W	4–3	Buenos Aires	SC	Jair R Pinto, Heleno de Freitas, Chico
29–01	Paraguay	D	1–1	Buenos Aires	SC	Norival
3–02	Chile	W	5–1	Buenos Aires	SC	Zizinho 4, Chico
10–02	Argentina	L	0–2	Buenos Aires	SC	
29–03–1947	Uruguay	D	0–0	Sao Paulo	RBC	
1–04	Uruguay	W	3–2	Rio de Janeiro	RBC	Heleno de Freitas 2, Tesourinha
4–04	Uruguay	D	1–1	Rio de Janeiro	Fr	
4–04–1948	Uruguay	D	1–1	Montevideo	RBC	Danilo Alvim
11–04	Uruguay	L	2–4	Montevideo	RBC	Canhotinho, Carlyle
3–04–1949	Ecuador	W	9–1	Rio de Janeiro	SC	Jair R Pinto 2, Simao 2, Tesourinha 2, Ademir Menezes, Otávio, Zizinho
10–04	Bolivia	W	10–1	Sao Paulo	SC	Nininho 3, Cláudio C Pinho 2, Zizinho 2, Simao 2, Jair R Pinto
13–04	Chile	W	2–1	Sao Paulo	SC	Cláudio C Pinto, Zizinho
17–04	Colombia	W	5–0	Sao Paulo	SC	Ademir Menezes 2, Orlando de Ouro, Tesourinha, Canhotinho
24–04	Peru	W	7–1	Rio de Janeiro	SC	Jair R Pinto 2, OG, Augusto, Orlando de Ouro, Ademir Menezes
30–04	Uruguay	W	5–1	Rio de Janeiro	SC	Jair R Pinto 2, Danilo Alvim, Tesourinha, Zizinho
8–05	Paraguay	L	1–2	Rio de Janeiro	SC	Tesourinha
11–05	Paraguay	W	7–0	Rio de Janeiro	SC	Ademir Menezes 3, Jair R Pinto, Tesourinha 2
6–05–1950	Uruguay	L	3–4	Sao Paulo	RBC	Ademir Menezes 2, Zizinho
7–05	Paraguay	W	2–0	Rio de Janeiro	OCC	Pinga I 2
13–05	Paraguay	D	3–3	Sao Paulo	OCC	Maneca, Baltazar I, Pinga I
14–05	Uruguay	W	3–2	Rio de Janeiro	RBC	Ademir Menezes 2, Chico
18–05	Uruguay	W	1–0	Rio de Janeiro	RBC	Ademir Menezes
24–06	Mexico	W	4–0	Rio de Janeiro	WCr1	Ademir Menezes 2, Jair R Pinto, Baltazar I
28–06	Switzerland	D	2–2	Sao Paulo	WCr1	Alfredo II, Baltazar I
1–07	Yugoslavia	W	2–0	Rio de Janeiro	WCr1	Ademir Menezes, Zizinho
9–07	Sweden	W	7–1	Rio de Janeiro	WCr2	Ademir Menezes 4, Chico 2, Maneca
13–07	Spain	W	6–1	Rio de Janeiro	WCr2	Ademir Menezes 2, Chico 2, Zizinho, Jair R Pinto
16–07	Uruguay	L	1–2	Rio de Janeiro	WCf	Friaca
6–04–1952	Mexico	W	2–0	Santiago	PAC	Baltazar I 2
10–04	Peru	D	0–0	Santiago	PAC	
13–04	Panama	W	5–0	Santiago	PAC	Rodrigues II 2, Pinga I, Baltazar I, Julinho I
16–04	Uruguay	W	4–2	Santiago	PAC	Baltazar I, Rodrigues II, Didi, Pinga I
20–04	Chile	W	3–0	Santiago	PAC	Ademir Menezes 2, Pinga I
17–07	Holland	W	5–1	Turku	OGr1	Larry 2, Humberto, Jansen, Vavá
21–07	Luxembourg	W	2–1	Kotka	OGr2	Larry, Humberto
1–03–1953	Bolivia	W	8–1	Lima	SC	Julinho I 4, Pinga I 2, Rodrigues II 2
12–03	Ecuador	W	2–0	Lima	SC	Ademir Menezes, Cláudio C Pinho
15–03	Uruguay	W	1–0	Lima	SC	Ipojucan
19–03	Peru	L	0–1	Lima	SC	
23–03	Chile	W	3–2	Lima	SC	Baltazar I, Julinho I, Zizinho

27–03	Paraguay	L	1–2	Lima	SC	Nilton Santos
1–04	Paraguay	L	2–3	Lima	SCpo	Baltazar I 2
28–02–1954	Chile	W	2–0	Santiago	WCq	Baltazar I 2
7–03	Paraguay	W	1–0	Asuncion	WCq	Baltazar I
14–03	Chile	W	1–0	Rio de Janeiro	WCq	Baltazar I
21–03	Paraguay	W	4–1	Rio de Janeiro	WCq	Julinho I 2, Baltazar I, Maurinho
16–06	Mexico	W	5–0	Geneva	WCr1	Pinga I 2, Baltazar I, Didi, Julinho I
19–06	Yugoslavia	D	1–1	Lausanne	WCr1	Didi
27–06	Hungary	L	2–4	Berne	WCqf	Djalma Santos, Julinho I
18–09–1955	Chile	D	1–1	Rio de Janeiro	OHC	Pinheiro
20–09	Chile	W	2–1	Sao Paulo	OHC	Maurinho, Alvaro
13–11	Paraguay	W	3–0	Rio de Janeiro	OCC	Zizinho 2, Sabará
17–11	Paraguay	D	3–3	Sao Paulo	OCC	Maurinho, Canhoteiro, Humberto
24–01–1956	Chile	L	1–4	Montevideo	SC	Maurinho
29–01	Paraguay	D	0–0	Montevideo	SC	
1–02	Peru	W	2–1	Montevideo	SC	Alvaro, Zezinho
5–02	Argentina	W	1–0	Montevideo	SC	Luiz Trujilo
10–02	Uruguay	D	0–0	Montevideo	SC	
1–03	Chile	W	2–1	Mexico City	PAC	Luizinho RS, Raul
6–03	Peru	W	1–0	Mexico City	PAC	Larry
8–03	Mexico	W	2–1	Mexico City	PAC	Bodinho 2
13–03	Costa Rica	W	7–1	Mexico City	PAC	Chinezinho 3, Larry 3, Bodinho
18–03	Argentina	D	2–2	Mexico City	PAC	Enio Andrade, Chinezinho
8–04	Portugal	W	1–0	Lisbon	Fr	Gino
11–04	Switzerland	D	1–1	Zurich	Fr	Gino
15–04	Austria	W	3–2	Vienna	Fr	Didi, Gino, Zózimo
21–04	Czechoslovakia	D	0–0	Prague	Fr	
25–04	Italy	L	0–3	Milan	Fr	
1–05	Turkey	W	1–0	Istanbul	Fr	Djalma Santos
9–05	England	L	2–4	London	Fr	Paulinho V
12–06	Paraguay	W	2–0	Asuncion	OCC	Ferreira 2
17–06	Paraguay	W	5–2	Asuncion	OCC	Zizinho 2, Ferreira, Leônidas II, Ilton
24–06	Uruguay	W	2–0	Rio de Janeiro	CA	Canário, Zizinho
1–07	Italy	W	2–0	Rio de Janeiro	Fr	Ferreira, Canário
8–07	Argentina	D	0–0	Buenos Aires	CA	
5–08	Czechoslovakia	L	0–1	Rio de Janeiro	Fr	
8–08	Czechoslovakia	W	4–1	Sao Paulo	Fr	Pepe 2, Zizinho 2
13–03–1957	Chile	W	4–2	Lima	SC	Didi 3, Pepe
21–03	Ecuador	W	7–1	Lima	SC	Evaristo 2, Joel 2, Indio, Pepe, Zizinho
24–03	Colombia	W	9–0	Lima	SC	Evaristo 5, Didi 2, Zizinho, Pepe
28–03	Uruguay	L	2–3	Lima	SC	Evaristo, Didi
31–03	Peru	W	1–0	Lima	SC	Didi
3–04	Argentina	L	0–3	Lima	SC	
13–04	Peru	D	1–1	Lima	WCq	Indio
21–04	Peru	W	1–0	Rio de Janeiro	WCq	Didi
11–06	Portugal	W	2–1	Rio de Janeiro	Fr	Didi, Tite
16–06	Portugal	W	3–0	Sao Paulo	Fr	Zito, Altafini, Del Vecchio
7–07	Argentina	L	1–2	Rio de Janeiro	RC	Pelé
10–07	Argentina	W	2–0	Sao Paulo	RC	Pelé, Altafini
15–09	Chile	L	0–1	Santiago	OHC	
18–09	Chile	D	1–1	Santiago	OHC	Matos
4–05–1958	Paraguay	W	5–1	Rio de Janeiro	OCC	Zagalo 2, Dida, Vavá, Pelé
7–05	Paraguay	D	0–0	Sao Paulo	OCC	
14–05	Bulgaria	W	4–0	Rio de Janeiro	Fr	Moacir 2, Dida, Joel
18–05	Bulgaria	W	3–1	Sao Paulo	Fr	Pelé 2, Pepe
8–06	Austria	W	3–0	Uddevalla	WCr1	Altafini 2, Nilton Santos
11–06	England	D	0–0	Gothenberg	WCr1	
15–06	Soviet Union	W	2–0	Gothenberg	WCr1	Vavá 2
19–06	Wales	W	1–0	Gothenberg	WCqf	Pelé
24–06	France	W	5–2	Stockholm	WCsf	Pelé 3, Vavá, Didi
29–06	Sweden	W	5–2	Stockholm	WCf	Vavá 2, Pelé 2, Zagalo
10–03–1959	Peru	D	2–2	Buenos Aires	SC	Didi, Pelé
15–03	Chile	W	3–0	Buenos Aires	SC	Pelé 2, Didi
21–03	Bolivia	W	4–2	Buenos Aires	SC	Paulo Valentim 2, Pelé, Didi
26–03	Uruguay	W	3–1	Buenos Aires	SC	Paulo Valentim 3
29–03	Paraguay	W	4–1	Buenos Aires	SC	Pelé 3, Chinezinho
4–04	Argentina	D	1–1	Buenos Aires	SC	Pelé
13–05	England	W	2–0	Rio de Janeiro	Fr	Julinho I, Henrique
17–09	Chile	W	7–0	Rio de Janeiro	OHC	Pelé 3, Quarentinha 2, Dino Sani, Dorval

20-09	Chile	W	1-0	Sao Paulo	OHC	Quarentinha
5-12	Paraguay	W	3-2	Guayaquil	SC	Paulo PE 2, Zé de Mello
12-12	Uruguay	L	0-3	Guayaquil	SC	
19-12	Ecuador	W	3-1	Guayaquil	SC	Geraldo II, Paulo PE, Zé de Mello
22-12	Argentina	L	1-4	Guayaquil	SC	Geraldo II
27-12	Ecuador	W	2-1	Guayaquil	Fr	Traçaia, Zé de Mello
6-03-1960	Mexico	D	2-2	San Jose	PAC	Élton, Gilberto
10-03	Costa Rica	L	0-3	San Jose	PAC	
13-03	Argentina	L	1-2	San Jose	PAC	Juarez
15-03	Mexico	W	2-1	San Jose	PAC	Mengálvio, Alfeu
17-03	Costa Rica	W	4-0	San Jose	PAC	Juarez 2, Élton 2
20-03	Argentina	W	1-0	San Jose	PAC	Mílton I
29-04	Egypt	W	5-0	Cairo	Fr	Pepe 2, Quarentinha 2, Garrincha
1-05	Egypt	W	3-1	Alexandria	Fr	Pelé 3
6-05	Egypt	W	3-0	Cairo	Fr	Quarentinha 2, Garrincha
10-05	Denmark*	W	4-3	Copenhagen	Fr	Quarentinha 2, Chinezinho, Pepe
25-05	Argentina	L	2-4	Buenos Aires	RC	Djalma Santos, Delem
26-05	Argentina	W	4-1	Buenos Aires	RC	Delem 2, Servílio II, Julinho I
29-06	Chile	W	4-0	Rio de Janeiro	Fr	Valdo I 2, Dida, Vavá
3-07	Paraguay	W	2-1	Asuncion	CA	Delem, Almir Albuquerque
9-07	Uruguay	L	0-1	Montevideo	CA	
12-07	Argentina	W	5-1	Rio de Janeiro	CA	Pepe 2, Pelé, Delem, Chinezinho
30-04-1961	Paraguay	W	2-0	Asuncion	OCC	Coutinho, Pepe
3-05	Paraguay	W	3-2	Asuncion	OCC	Coutinho 2, Quarentinha
7-05	Chile	W	2-1	Santiago	OHC	Garrincha, Didi
11-05	Chile	W	1-0	Santiago	OHC	Gérson
29-06	Paraguay	W	3-2	Rio de Janeiro	Fr	Joel, Dida, Henrique
21-04-1962	Paraguay	W	6-0	Rio de Janeiro	OCC	Didi, Pelé, Coutinho, Vavá, Garrincha, Nilton Santos
24-04	Paraguay	W	4-0	Sao Paulo	OCC	Pelé 2, Pepe, Vavá
6-05	Portugal	W	2-1	Sao Paulo	Fr	Zagalo, Zequinha
9-05	Portugal	W	1-0	Rio de Janeiro	Fr	Pelé
12-05	Wales	W	3-1	Rio de Janeiro	Fr	Garrincha, Coutinho, Pelé
16-05	Wales	W	3-1	Sao Paulo	Fr	Pelé 2, Vavá
30-05	Mexico	W	2-0	Vina del Mar	WCr1	Zagalo, Pelé
2-06	Czechoslovakia	D	0-0	Vina del Mar	WCr1	
6-06	Spain	W	2-1	Vina del Mar	WCr1	Amarildo 2
10-06	England	W	3-1	Vina del Mar	WCqf	Garrincha 2, Vavá
13-06	Chile	W	4-2	Santiago	WCsf	Garrincha 2, Vavá 2
17-06	Czechoslovakia	W	3-1	Santiago	WCf	Amarildo, Zito, Vavá
3-03-1963	Paraguay	D	2-2	Asuncion	Fr	Flávio, Hilton Chaves
10-03	Peru	W	1-0	Cochabamba	SC	Flávio
14-03	Colombia	W	5-1	La Paz	SC	Flávio 2, Marco Antônio, Oswaldo, Fernando
17-03	Paraguay	L	0-2	La Paz	SC	
24-03	Argentina	L	0-3	La Paz	SC	
27-03	Ecuador	D	2-2	Cochabamba	SC	Oswaldo 2
31-03	Bolivia	L	4-5	Cochabamba	SC	Flávio, Almir, Marco Antônio
13-04	Argentina	L	2-3	Sao Paulo	RC	Pepe 2
16-04	Argentina	W	5-2	Rio de Janeiro	RC	Pelé 3, Amarildo 2
21-04	Portugal	L	0-1	Lisbon	Fr	
24-04	Belgium	L	1-5	Brussels	Fr	Quarentinha
28-04	France	W	3-2	Paris	Fr	Pelé 3
2-05	Holland	L	0-1	Amsterdam	Fr	
5-05	West Germany	W	2-1	Hamburg	Fr	Coutinho, Pelé
8-05	England	D	1-1	London	Fr	Pepe
12-05	Italy	L	0-3	Milan	Fr	
17-05	Egypt	W	1-0	Cairo	Fr	Quarentinha
19-05	Israel	W	5-0	Tel Aviv	Fr	Quarentinha 2, Amarildo 2, Zequinha
30-05-1964	England	W	5-1	Rio de Janeiro	CN	Rinaldo 2, Pelé, Julinho I, Roberto Dias
3-06	Argentina	L	0-3	Sao Paulo	CN	
7-06	Portugal	W	4-1	Rio de Janeiro	CN	Pelé, Jairzinho, Gérson 2
2-06-1965	Belgium	W	5-0	Rio de Janeiro	Fr	Pelé 3, Flávio, Rinaldo
6-06	West Germany	W	2-0	Rio de Janeiro	Fr	Flávio, Pelé
9-06	Argentina	D	0-0	Rio de Janeiro	Fr	
17-06	Algeria	W	3-0	Oran	Fr	Pelé, Dudu I, Gérson
24-06	Portugal	D	0-0	Oporto	Fr	
30-06	Sweden	W	2-1	Stockholm	Fr	Pelé, Gérson
4-07	Soviet Union	W	3-0	Moscow	Fr	Pelé 2, Flávio

7–09	Uruguay	W	3–0	Belo Horizonte	Fr	Rinaldo, Tupazinho, Germano
21–11	Soviet Union	D	2–2	Rio de Janeiro	Fr	Gérson, Pelé
17–04–1966	Chile	W	1–0	Santiago	OHC	Joao Carlos
20–04	Chile	L	1–2	Vina del Mar	OHC	Joao Carlos
14–05	Wales	W	3–1	Rio de Janeiro	Fr	Silva I, Servílio II, Garrincha
15–05	Chile	D	1–1	Sao Paulo	Fr	Rinaldo
18–05	Wales	W	1–0	Belo Horizonte	Fr	Lima
19–05	Chile	W	1–0	Rio de Janeiro	Fr	Gérson
4–06	Peru	W	4–0	Sao Paulo	Fr	Lima 2, Pelé, Paraná
5–06	Poland	W	4–1	Belo Horizonte	Fr	Tostao, Alcindo, Denilson
8–06	Poland	W	2–1	Rio de Janeiro	Fr	Silva I, Garrincha
8–06	Peru	W	3–1	Belo Horizonte	Fr	Fidélis, Tostao, Edu
12–06	Czechoslovakia	W	2–1	Rio de Janeiro	Fr	Pelé 2
15–06	Czechoslovakia	D	2–2	Rio de Janeiro	Fr	Pelé, Zito
25–06	Scotland	D	1–1	Glasgow	Fr	Servílio II
30–06	Sweden	W	3–2	Gothenberg	Fr	Tostao 2, Gérson
12–07	Bulgaria	W	2–0	Liverpool	WCr1	Pelé, Garrincha
15–07	Hungary	L	1–3	Liverpool	WCr1	Tostao
19–07	Portugal	L	1–3	Liverpool	WCr1	Rildo
25–06–1967	Uruguay	D	0–0	Montevideo	RBC	
28–06	Uruguay	D	2–2	Montevideo	RBC	Paulo Borges 2
1–07	Uruguay	D	1–1	Montevideo	RBC	Dirceu Lopes
19–09	Chile	W	1–0	Santiago	Fr	Roberto Miranda
9–06–1968	Uruguay	W	2–0	Sao Paulo	Fr	Tostao, Sadí
12–06	Uruguay	W	4–0	Rio de Janeiro	Fr	Paulo Borges, Tostao, Gérson, Jairzinho
16–06	West Germany	L	1–2	Stuttgart	Fr	Tostao
20–06	Poland	W	6–3	Warsaw	Fr	Natal, Rivelino 2, Jairzinho 2, Tostao
23–06	Czechoslovakia	L	2–3	Bratislava	Fr	Natal, Carlos Alberto Torres
25–06	Yugoslavia	W	2–0	Belgrade	Fr	Carlos Alberto Torres, Tostao
30–06	Portugal	W	2–0	Lourenco Marquez	Fr	Rivelino, Tostao
7–07	Mexico	W	2–0	Mexico City	Fr	Jairzinho 2
10–07	Mexico	L	1–2	Mexico City	Fr	Rivelino
14–07	Peru	W	4–3	Lima	Fr	Natal, Roberto Miranda, Jairzinho, Carlos Alberto Torres
17–07	Peru	W	4–0	Lima	Fr	Rivelino, Gérson, Tostao, Jairzinho
25–07	Paraguay	W	4–0	Asuncion	OCC	Pelé 2, Toninho Guerreiro, Eduardo I
28–07	Paraguay	L	0–1	Asuncion	OCC	
7–08	Argentina	W	4–1	Rio de Janeiro	Fr	Valtencir, Roberto Miranda, Paulo César Lima, Jairzinho
11–08	Argentina	W	3–2	Belo Horizonte	Fr	Evaldo, Rodrigues III, Dirceu Lopes
31–10	Mexico	L	1–2	Rio de Janeiro	Fr	Carlos Alberto Torres
3–11	Mexico	W	2–1	Belo Horizonte	Fr	Pelé, Jairzinho
14–12	West Germany	D	2–2	Rio de Janeiro	Fr	Edu 2
17–12	Yugoslavia	D	3–3	Rio de Janeiro	Fr	Carlos Alberto Torres, Pelé, Babá II
19–12	Yugoslavia	W	3–2	Belo Horizonte	Fr	Vaguinho, Amauri, Ronaldo
7–04–1969	Peru	W	2–1	Porto Alegre	Fr	Jairzinho, Gérson
9–04	Peru	W	3–2	Rio de Janeiro	Fr	Pelé, Tostao, Edu
12–06	England	W	2–1	Rio de Janeiro	Fr	Tostao, Jairzinho
6–08	Colombia	W	2–0	Bogota	WCq	Tostao 2
10–08	Venezuela	W	5–0	Caracas	WCq	Tostao 3, Pelé 2
17–08	Paraguay	W	3–0	Asuncion	WCq	OG, Edu, Jairzinho
21–08	Colombia	W	6–2	Rio de Janeiro	WCq	Pelé, Tostao 2, Jairzinho, Edu, Rivelino
24–08	Venezuela	W	6–0	Rio de Janeiro	WCq	Tostao 3, Pelé 2, Jairzinho
31–08	Paraguay	W	1–0	Rio de Janeiro	WCq	Pelé
4–03–1970	Argentina	L	0–2	Porto Alegre	Fr	
8–03	Argentina	W	2–1	Rio de Janeiro	Fr	Jairzinho, Pelé
22–03	Chile	W	5–0	Sao Paulo	Fr	Gérson, Roberto Miranda 2, Pelé 2

LEADING INTERNATIONAL GOALSCORERS

1	Pelé	77
2	Zico	54
3	Jairzinho	38
4	Rivelino	26
5	Tostao	32
6	Ademir Menezes	31
7	Zizinho	30
8	Careca I	27
9	Gérson	23
10	Leônidas da Silva	22
	Socrates	22
13	Jair R Pinto	21
14	Romário	20
	Roberto Dinamite	20
	Didi	20
16	Pepe	16
	Baltazar I	16
18	Quarentinha	15
	Heleno de Freitas	15
	Vavá	15

26–03	Chile	W	2–1	Rio de Janeiro	Fr	Carlos Alberto Torres, Rivelino
12–04	Paraguay	D	0–0	Rio de Janeiro	Fr	
26–04	Bulgaria	D	0–0	Sao Paulo	Fr	
29–04	Austria	W	1–0	Rio de Janeiro	Fr	Rivelino
3–06	Czechoslovakia	W	4–1	Guadalajara	WCr1	Rivelino, Pelé, Jairzinho 2
7–06	England	W	1–0	Guadalajara	WCr1	Jairzinho
10–06	Romania	W	3–2	Guadalajara	WCr1	Jairzinho, Pelé 2
14–06	Peru	W	4–2	Guadalajara	WCqf	Rivelino, Tostao 2, Jairzinho
17–06	Uruguay	W	3–1	Guadalajara	WCsf	Clodoaldo, Jairzinho, Rivelino
21–06	Italy	W	4–1	Mexico City	WCf	Pelé, Gérson, Jairzinho, Carlos Alberto Torres
30–09	Mexico	W	2–1	Rio de Janeiro	Fr	Tostao, Jairzinho
4–10	Chile	W	5–1	Santiago	Fr	Roberto Miranda, Pelé, Jairzinho 2, Paulo César Lima
11–07–1971	Austria	D	1–1	Sao Paulo	Fr	Pelé
14–07	Czechoslovakia	W	1–0	Rio de Janeiro	Fr	Tostao
18–07	Yugoslavia	D	2–2	Rio de Janeiro	Fr	Rivelino, Gérson
21–07	Hungary	D	0–0	Rio de Janeiro	Fr	
24–07	Paraguay	W	1–0	Rio de Janeiro	Fr	Claudiomiro
28–07	Argentina	D	1–1	Buenos Aires	RC	Paulo César Lima
31–07	Argentina	D	2–2	Buenos Aires	RC	Tostao, Paulo César Lima
26–04–1972	Paraguay	W	3–2	Porto Alegre	Fr	Carlos Alberto Torres, Tostao, Dirceu Lopes
28–06	Czechoslovakia	D	0–0	Rio de Janeiro	Clr2	
2–07	Yugoslavia	W	3–0	Sao Paulo	Clr2	Leivinha 2, Jairzinho
5–07	Scotland	W	1–0	Rio de Janeiro	Clr2	Jairzinho
9–07	Portugal	W	1–0	Rio de Janeiro	Clf	Jairzinho
27–05–1973	Bolivia	W	5–0	Rio de Janeiro	Fr	Rivelino 2, Valdomiro, Leivinha 2
3–06	Algeria	W	2–0	Algiers	Fr	Rivelino, Paulo César Lima
6–06	Tunisia	W	4–1	Tunis	Fr	Paulo César Lima 2, Valdomiro, Leivinha
9–06	Italy	L	0–2	Rome	Fr	
13–06	Austria	D	1–1	Vienna	Fr	Jairzinho
16–06	West Germany	W	1–0	Berlin	Fr	Dirceu II
21–06	Soviet Union	W	1–0	Moscow	Fr	Jairzinho
25–06	Sweden	L	0–1	Stockholm	Fr	
30–06	Scotland	W	1–0	Glasgow	Fr	OG
31–03–1974	Mexico	D	1–1	Rio de Janeiro	Fr	Jairzinho
7–04	Czechoslovakia	W	1–0	Rio de Janeiro	Fr	Marinho Chagas
14–04	Bulgaria	W	1–0	Rio de Janeiro	Fr	Jairzinho
17–04	Romania	W	2–0	Sao Paulo	Fr	Leivinha, Edu
21–04	Haiti	W	4–0	Brasilia	Fr	Paulo César Lima, Rivelino, Marinho Chagas, Edu
28–04	Greece	D	0–0	Rio de Janeiro	Fr	
1–05	Austria	D	0–0	Sao Paulo	Fr	
5–05	Rep. Ireland	W	2–1	Rio de Janeiro	Fr	Leivinha, Rivelino
12–05	Paraguay	W	2–0	Rio de Janeiro	Fr	Marinho Perez, Rivelino
13–06	Yugoslavia	D	0–0	Frankfurt	WCr1	
18–06	Scotland	D	0–0	Frankfurt	WCr1	
22–06	Zaire	W	3–0	Gelsenkirchen	WCr1	Jairzinho, Rivelino, Valdomiro
26–06	East Germany	W	1–0	Hanover	WCr2	Rivelino
30–06	Argentina	W	2–1	Hanover	WCr2	Rivelino, Jairzinho
3–07	Holland	L	0–2	Dortmund	WCr2	
6–07	Poland	L	0–1	Munich	WC3p	
30–07–1975	Venezuela	W	4–0	Caracas	SCr1	Romeu, Danival, Palhinha 2
6–08	Argentina	W	2–1	Belo Horizonte	SCr1	Nelhino 2
13–08	Venezuela	W	6–0	Belo Horizonte	SCr1	Roberto Batata 2, Nelhino, Danival, Campos, Palhinha
16–08	Argentina	W	1–0	Rosario	SCr1	Danival
30–09	Peru	L	1–3	Belo Horizonte	SCsf	Roberto Batata
4–10	Peru	W	2–0	Lima	SCsf	Zé Carlos, Campos
25–02–1976	Uruguay	W	2–1	Montevideo	CA	Nelinho, Rivelino
27–02	Argentina	W	2–1	Buenos Aires	CA	Lula, Zico
7–04	Paraguay	D	1–1	Asuncion	CA	Eneas
28–04	Uruguay	W	2–1	Rio de Janeiro	CA	Rivelino, Zico
19–05	Argentina	W	2–0	Rio de Janeiro	CA	Lula, Neca
23–05	England	W	1–0	Los Angeles	Fr	Roberto Dinamite
31–05	Italy	W	4–1	New Haven	Fr	Gil 2, Zico, Roberto Dinamite
4–06	Mexico	W	3–0	Guadalajara	Fr	Roberto Dinamite 2, Gil
9–06	Paraguay	W	3–1	Rio de Janeiro	CA	Roberto Dinamite 2, Zico

1–12	Soviet Union	W	2–0	Rio de Janeiro	Fr	Falcao, Zico
23–01–1977	Bulgaria	W	1–0	Sao Paulo	Fr	Roberto Dinamite
20–02	Colombia	D	0–0	Bogota	WCq	
9–03	Colombia	W	6–0	Rio de Janeiro	WCq	Roberto Dinamite 2, Zico, Marinho Chagas 2, Rivelino
13–03	Paraguay	W	1–0	Asuncion	WCq	OG
20–03	Paraguay	D	1–1	Rio de Janeiro	WCq	Roberto Dinamite
8–06	England	D	0–0	Rio de Janeiro	Fr	
12–06	West Germany	D	1–1	Rio de Janeiro	Fr	Rivelino
19–06	Poland	W	3–1	Sao Paulo	Fr	Paulo Isidoro, Reinaldo, Rivelino
23–06	Scotland	W	2–0	Rio de Janeiro	Fr	Zico, Toninho Cerezo
26–06	Yugoslavia	D	0–0	Belo Horizonte	Fr	
30–06	France	D	2–2	Rio de Janeiro	Fr	Edinho, Roberto Dinamite
10–07	Peru	W	1–0	Cali	WCq	Gil
14–07	Bolivia	W	8–0	Cali	WCq	Zico 4, Roberto Dinamite, Gil, Toninho Cerezo, Marcelo
1–04–1978	France	L	0–1	Paris	Fr	
5–04	West Germany	W	1–0	Hamburg	Fr	Nunes
19–04	England	D	1–1	London	Fr	Gil
1–05	Peru	W	3–0	Rio de Janeiro	Fr	Zico, Reinaldo 2
17–05	Czechoslovakia	W	2–0	Rio de Janeiro	Fr	Reinaldo, Zico
3–06	Sweden	D	1–1	Mar del Plata	WCr1	Reinaldo
7–06	Spain	D	0–0	Mar del Plata	WCr1	
11–06	Austria	W	1–0	Mar del Plata	WCr1	Roberto Dinamite
14–06	Peru	W	3–0	Mendoza	WCr2	Dirceu II 2, Zico
18–06	Argentina	D	0–0	Rosario	WCr2	
21–06	Poland	W	3–1	Mendoza	WCr2	Nelinho, Roberto Dinamite 2
24–06	Italy	W	2–1	Buenos Aires	WC3p	Nelinho, Dirceu II
17–05–1979	Paraguay	W	6–0	Rio de Janeiro	Fr	Éder, Zico 3, Nílton Batata
31–05	Uruguay	W	5–1	Rio de Janeiro	Fr	Edinho, Sócrates 2, Nílton Batata, Éder
26–07	Bolivia	L	1–2	La Paz	SCr1	Roberto Dinamite
2–08	Argentina	W	2–1	Rio de Janeiro	SCr1	Zico, Tita
16–08	Bolivia	W	2–0	Sao Paulo	SCr1	Tita, Zico
23–08	Argentina	D	2–2	Buenos Aires	SCr1	Sócrates 2
24–10	Paraguay	L	1–2	Asuncion	SCsf	Palhinha
31–10	Paraguay	D	2–2	Rio de Janeiro	SCsf	Falcao, Sócrates
8–06–1980	Mexico	W	2–0	Rio de Janeiro	Fr	Zé Sérgio, Serginho
15–06	Soviet Union	L	1–2	Rio de Janeiro	Fr	Nunes
24–06	Chile	W	2–1	Belo Horizonte	Fr	Zico, Toninho Cerezo
29–06	Poland	D	1–1	Sao Paulo	Fr	Zico
27–08	Uruguay	W	1–0	Fortaleza	Fr	Getúlio
25–09	Paraguay	W	2–1	Asuncion	Fr	Zé Sérgio, Reinaldo
30–10	Paraguay	W	6–0	Goiania	Fr	Zé Sérgio, Tita, Zico 2, Sócrates, Luizinho
21–12	Switzerland	W	2–0	Cuiaba	Fr	Sócrates, Zé Sérgio
4–01–1981	Argentina	D	1–1	Montevideo	ML	Edvaldo
7–01	West Germany	W	4–1	Montevideo	ML	Júnior, Toninho Cerezo, Serginho, Zé Sérgio
10–01	Uruguay	L	1–2	Montevideo	ML	Sócrates
1–02	Colombia	D	1–1	Bogota	Fr	Serginho
8–02	Venezuela	W	1–0	Caracas	WCq	Zico
14–02	Ecuador	W	6–0	Quito	Fr	Reinaldo 2, Sócrates 2, OG, Zico
22–02	Bolivia	W	2–1	La Paz	WCq	Sócrates, Reinaldo
14–03	Chile	W	2–1	Ribeirao Preto	Fr	Zico, Reinaldo
22–03	Bolivia	W	3–1	Rio de Janeiro	WCq	Zico 3
29–03	Venezuela	W	5–0	Goiania	WCq	Tita 2, Sócrates, Zico, Júnior
12–05	England	W	1–0	London	Fr	Zico
15–05	France	W	3–1	Paris	Fr	Zico, Reinaldo, Sócrates
19–05	West Germany	W	2–1	Stuttgart	Fr	Toninho Cerezo, Júnior
8–07	Spain	W	1–0	Salvador	Fr	Baltazar II
26–08	Chile	D	0–0	Santiago	Fr	
23–09	Rep. Ireland	W	6–0	Maceio	Fr	Eder, Roberto PE, Zico 4
28–10	Bulgaria	W	3–0	Porto Alegre	Fr	Roberto Dinamite, Zico, Leandro
26–01–1982	East Germany	W	3–1	Natal	Fr	Paulo Isidoro, Renato, Serginho
3–03	Czechoslovakia	D	1–1	Sao Paulo	Fr	Zico
21–03	West Germany	W	1–0	Rio de Janeiro	Fr	Júnior
5–05	Portugal	W	3–1	Sao Luiz	Fr	Júnior, Éder, Zico
19–05	Switzerland	D	1–1	Recife	Fr	Zico
27–05	Rep. Ireland	W	7–0	Uberlandia	Fr	Falcao, Sócrates 2, Serginho 2, Luizinho, Zico

LEADING INTERNATIONAL APPEARANCES

1	Djalma Santos	100		Júnior	74	19	Batista	54
2	Gilmar I	95	11	Edinho	68	20	Éder	53
3	Rivelino	94		Didi	68		Zizinho	53
4	Pelé	92	13	Oscar	60	22	Piazza	52
5	Jairzinho	87		Sócrates	60	23	Carlos	51
6	Gérson	83	15	Paulo César Lima	59		Bellini	51
7	Leao	82	16	Carlos Alberto	58	25	Garrincha	50
8	Zico	78		Toninho Cerezo	58			
9	Nilton Santos	74	18	Tostao	55			

14–06	Soviet Union	W	2–1	Seville	WCr1	Sócrates, Éder
18–06	Scotland	W	4–1	Seville	WCr1	Zico, Oscar, Éder, Falcao
23–06	New Zealand	W	4–0	Seville	WCr1	Zico 2, Falcao, Serginho
2–07	Argentina	W	3–1	Barcelona	WCr2	Zico, Serginho, Júnior
5–07	Italy	L	2–3	Barcelona	WCr2	Sócrates, Falcao
28–04–1983	Chile	W	3–2	Rio de Janeiro	Fr	Careca I, Éder, Renato
8–06	Portugal	W	4–0	Coimbra	Fr	Careca I 2, Sócrates, Pedrinho
12–06	Wales	D	1–1	Cardiff	Fr	Paulo Isidoro
17–06	Switzerland	W	2–1	Basle	Fr	Sócrates, Careca I
22–06	Sweden	D	3–3	Gothenburg	Fr	Marcio, Careca I, Jorginho II
28–07	Chile	D	0–0	Santiago	Fr	
17–08	Ecuador	W	1–0	Quito	SCr1	Roberto Dinamite
24–08	Argentina	L	0–1	Buenos Aires	SCr1	
1–09	Ecuador	W	5–0	Goiania	SCr1	Renato Gaúcho, Roberto Dinamite 2, Éder, Tita
14–09	Argentina	D	0–0	Rio de Janeiro	SCr1	
13–10	Paraguay	D	1–1	Asuncion	SCsf	Éder
20–10	Paraguay	D	0–0	Uberlandia	SCsf	
27–10	Uruguay	L	0–2	Montevideo	SCf	
4–11	Uruguay	D	1–1	Salvador	SCf	Jorginho II
10–06–1984	England	L	0–2	Rio de Janeiro	Fr	
17–06	Argentina	D	0–0	Sao Paulo	Fr	
21–06	Uruguay	W	1–0	Curitiba	Fr	Arturzinho
25–04–1985	Colombia	W	2–1	Belo Horizonte	Fr	Alemao, Casagrande
28–04	Peru	L	0–1	Brasilia	Fr	
2–05	Uruguay	W	2–0	Recife	Fr	Alemao, Careca I
5–05	Argentina	W	2–1	Salvador	Fr	Careca I, Alemao
15–05	Colombia	L	0–1	Bogota	Fr	
21–05	Chile	L	1–2	Santiago	Fr	Casagrande
2–06	Bolivia	W	2–0	Santa Cruz	WCq	Casagrande, OG
8–06	Chile	W	3–1	Porto Alegre	Fr	Zico 2, Leandro
16–06	Paraguay	W	2–0	Asuncion	WCq	Casagrande, Zico
23–06	Paraguay	D	1–1	Rio de Janeiro	WCq	Sócrates
30–06	Bolivia	D	1–1	Sao Paulo	WCq	Careca I
12–03–1986	West Germany	L	0–2	Frankfurt	Fr	
16–03	Hungary	L	0–3	Budapest	Fr	
1–04	Peru	W	4–0	Sao Luis	Fr	Casagrande 2, Alemao, Careca I
8–04	East Germany	W	3–0	Goiania	Fr	Müller, Alemao, Careca I
17–04	Finland	W	3–0	Brasilia	Fr	Marinho I, Oscar, Casagrande
30–04	Yugoslavia	W	4–2	Recife	Fr	Zico 3, Careca I
7–05	Chile	D	1–1	Curitiba	Fr	Casagrande
1–06	Spain	W	1–0	Guadalajara	WCr1	Sócrates
6–06	Algeria	W	1–0	Guadalajara	WCr1	Careca I
12–06	Nth. Ireland	W	3–0	Guadalajara	WCr1	Careca I 2, Josimar
16–06	Poland	W	4–0	Guadalajara	WCr2	Sócrates, Josimar, Edinho, Careca I
21–06	France	D	1–1 (3–4p)	Guadalajara	WCqf	Careca I
19–05–1987	England	D	1–1	London	Fr	Mirandinha II
23–05	Rep. Ireland	L	0–1	Dublin	Fr	
26–05	Scotland	W	2–0	Glasgow	Fr	Raí, Valdo II
28–05	Finland	W	3–2	Helsinki	Fr	Romário, Valdo II, Müller
1–06	Israel	W	4–0	Tel Aviv	Fr	Romário 2, Dunga, Joao Paulo II
21–06	Ecuador	W	4–1	Florianopolis	Fr	Raí, Careca I, Müller, Jorginho
24–06	Paraguay	W	1–0	Porto Alegre	Fr	Valdo II
28–06	Venezuela	W	5–0	Cordoba	SCr1	Edu, OG, Careca I, Nelsinho, Romário
3–07	Chile	L	0–4	Cordoba	SCr1	
9–12	Chile	W	2–1	Uberlandia	Fr	Valdo II, Renato

12–12	West Germany	D	1–1	Brasilia	Fr	Batista
7–07–1988	Australia	W	1–0	Melbourne	Fr	Romário
10–07	Argentina	D	0–0	Melbourne	Fr	
13–07	Saudi Arabia	W	4–1	Melbourne	Fr	Geovani 2, Jorginho, Edmar
17–07	Australia	W	2–0	Sydney	Fr	Romário, Müller
28–07	Norway	D	1–1	Oslo	Fr	Edmar
31–07	Sweden	D	1–1	Stockholm	Fr	Jorginho
3–08	Austria	W	2–0	Vienna	Fr	Edmar, Andrade
12–10	Belgium	W	2–1	Antwerp	Fr	Geovani 2
15–03–1989	Ecuador	W	1–0	Cuiaba	Fr	Washington II
12–04	Paraguay	W	2–0	Teresina	Fr	Cristovao, Vivinho
10–05	Peru	W	4–1	Fortaleza	Fr	Zé do Carmo, Bebeto, Charles 2
24–05	Peru	D	1–1	Lima	Fr	Cristovao
8–06	Portugal	W	4–0	Rio de Janeiro	Fr	Bebeto, OG, Ricardo II, Charles
16–06	Sweden	L	1–2	Copenhagen	Fr	Cristovao
18–06	Denmark	L	0–4	Copenhagen	Fr	
21–06	Switzerland	L	0–1	Basle	Fr	
1–07	Venezuela	W	3–1	Salvador	SCr1	Bebeto, Geovani, Baltazar II
3–07	Peru	D	0–0	Salvador	SCr1	
7–07	Colombia	D	0–0	Salvador	SCr1	
9–07	Paraguay	W	2–0	Recife	SCr1	Bebeto 2
12–07	Argentina	W	2–0	Rio de Janeiro	SCr2	Bebeto, Romário
14–07	Paraguay	W	3–0	Rio de Janeiro	SCr2	Bebeto 2, Romário
16–07	Uruguay	W	1–0	Rio de Janeiro	SCf	Romário
23–07	Japan	W	1–0	Rio de Janeiro	Fr	Bismark
30–07	Venezuela	W	4–0	Caracas	WCq	Branco, Romário, Bebeto 2
13–08	Chile	D	1–1	Santiago	WCq	OG
20–08	Venezuela	W	6–0	Sao Paulo	WCq	Careca I 4, Silas, OG
3–09	Chile	W	2–0	Rio de Janeiro	WCq	Careca I *Abandoned after 65 mins*
Game awarded to Brazil by 2–0						
14–10	Italy	W	1–0	Bologna	Fr	André Cruz
14–11	Yugoslavia	D	0–0	Joao Pessao	Fr	
20–12	Holland	W	1–0	Rotterdam	Fr	Careca I
28–03–1990	England	L	0–1	London	Fr	
5–05	Bulgaria	W	2–1	Campinas	Fr	Müller, Aldair
13–05	East Germany	D	3–3	Rio de Janeiro	Fr	Alemao, Careca I, Dunga
10–06	Sweden	W	2–1	Turin	WCr1	Careca I 2
16–06	Costa Rica	W	1–0	Turin	WCr1	Müller
20–06	Scotland	W	1–0	Turin	WCr1	Müller
24–06	Argentina	L	0–1	Turin	WCr2	
12–09	Spain	L	0–3	Gijon	Fr	
17–10	Chile	D	0–0	Santiago	Fr	
8–11	Chile	D	0–0	Belem	Fr	
13–12	Mexico	D	0–0	Los Angeles	Fr	
27–02–1991	Paraguay	D	1–1	Campo Grande	Fr	Neto
27–03	Argentina	D	3–3	Buenos Aires	Fr	Renato Gaúcho, Luis Henrique, Careca II
28–05	Bulgaria	W	3–0	Uberlandia	Fr	Neto 2, Joao Paulo II
27–06	Argentina	D	1–1	Curitiba	Fr	Neto
9–07	Bolivia	W	2–1	Viña del Mar	SCr1	Neto, Branco
11–07	Uruguay	D	1–1	Viña del Mar	SCr1	Joao Paulo II
13–07	Colombia	L	0–2	Viña del Mar	SCr1	
15–07	Ecuador	W	3–1	Viña del Mar	SCr1	Mazinho II, Santos, Luis Henrique
17–07	Argentina	L	2–3	Santiago	SCr2	Branco, Joao Paulo II
19–07	Colombia	W	2–0	Santiago	SCr2	Renato, Branco
21–07	Chile	W	2–0	Santiago	SCr2	Mazinho II, Luis Henrique
11–09	Wales	L	0–1	Cardiff	Fr	
30–10	Yugoslavia	W	3–1	Varginha	Fr	Luis Henrique, Rai, Müller
18–12	Czechoslovakia	W	2–1	Goiaia	Fr	Elivelton, Rai
26–02–1992	USA	W	3–0	Fortaleza	Fr	Antonio Carlos, Rai 2
15–04	Finland	W	3–1	Cuiaba	Fr	Bebeto 2, Paulo Sergio
30–04	Uruguay	L	0–1	Montevideo	Fr	
17–05	England	D	1–1	London	Fr	Bebeto

CHILE

After the 'big three', Chile is often regarded as the fourth strongest nation on the South American continent. It is somewhat surprising, therefore, that its first ever honour came in 1991 when Colo Colo won the Copa Libertadores. Until then Chile's history had been a tale of nearly but not quite.

The British in the port of Valparaiso and the neighbouring resort of Viña del Mar first introduced football to Chile, and the first club, Valparaiso FC, were formed in 1889. In 1895 nine clubs of mainly British origin formed the Football Association of Chile, after Argentina the second oldest on the continent.

Chile is a thin, elongated country and although roughly in the centre, the capital Santiago is a good distance from many of the major towns in the rest of Chile, so as football spread around the country regional associations were set up to administer the game. From 1910 until 1933 the Copa Arturo Allesandri was the main competition in the country. Played for by representative sides of the regional associations, all of which ran their own league, it was supplanted by the new professional national league in 1933.

Prime motivators for the new league were Colo Colo, formed in 1925 by dissident members of Magallanes. The Liga Metropolitana in Santiago formed the basis of the new national league, and from the start Colo Colo have been the dominant force. The area around Santiago has always been the most powerful, and until Huachipato from Talcahuano in the Concepcion area won the title in 1974, the Santiago–Valparaiso axis remained unbroken.

Along with Colo Colo the most prominent sides have been the two university clubs, Universidad de Chile and Universidad Catolica, as well as Union Española. Recently, however, provincial clubs have begun to challenge the supremacy of Santiago, none more so than Cobreloa from the small mining town of Calama in the north. Four times winners of the championship, they twice reached the final of the Copa Libertadores in the early 1980s.

The national side first took the field when they travelled to Buenos Aires for the unofficial South American Championship in 1910, although their first game was a friendly match against Argentina two days before the tournament got under way. Not until 1926, however, 23 matches later, did Chile win a game, despite the 1922 tournament being held in Valparaiso.

In 1926 Santiago staged the competition and spurred on by David Arellano who had founded Colo Colo the previous year, Chile beat both Bolivia and Paraguay to finish third out of the five entrants, the first occasion on which they had not finished bottom. Also in good form was Guillermo Subiabre who finished the tournament as top scorer.

Chile made the trip to the Amsterdam Olympics in 1928 and luckily for them a consolation tournament for the first round losers had been arranged, so after losing to Portugal they did not have to go home after just one match. They fared much better in this tournament, beating Mexico and then drawing 2–2 with the hosts Holland.

		Total			League	Copa Lib		
		G	S	B	G	G	S	B
1	Colo Colo	19	1	2	18	1	1	2
2	Universidad de Chile	7	–	1	7	–	–	1
3	Universidad Catolica	6	–	4	6	–	–	4
4	Union Española	5	1	1	5	–	1	1
5	Cobreloa	4	2	1	4	–	2	1
6	Audax Italiano	4	–	–	4	–	–	–
	Magallanes	4	–	–	4	–	–	–
8	Everton	3	–	–	3	–	–	–
9	Palestino	2	–	1	2	–	–	1
10	Wanderers Valparaiso	2	–	–	2	–	–	–
11	Green Cross	1	–	–	1	–	–	–
	Huachipato	1	–	–	1	–	–	–
	Santiago Morning	1	–	–	1	–	–	–
	Union San Felipe	1	–	–	1	–	–	–
15	O'Higgins	–	–	1	–	–	–	1

Correct to the end of the 1991 season

Entry into the 1930 World Cup nearly proved fruitful, but a 3–1 loss to Argentina in the final first round group match meant they were eliminated despite having beaten both France and Mexico. Once again their top player was Subiabre, but unfortunately for him there was a five-year gap before the next match.

The 1937 South American Championship in Buenos Aires produced another Chilean hero in Raul Toro, and he finished as the top scorer with 7 goals in 4 games. It did not do his side much good, however, as their poor showings in the tournament continued. They were generally weak in the tournaments played away from Chile but played well when they hosted the series, such as in 1945 and 1955.

Regular though not particularly successful competitors in the World Cup from 1950 onwards, Chile have taken part in five final tournaments out of the 11 held since that date. Only once have they progressed beyond the first round, and that was as hosts in 1962.

Based in Santiago in the first round, Chile beat both Switzerland and Italy in their first two matches, though the latter has become known as the 'Battle of Santiago' as tempers flared between the two sides. Relations between Italy and the hosts were not good. A series of articles written by Italian journalists criticising Chile had not gone down well in Santiago and the hostility spilled over onto the pitch. Italy's Argentinian, Maschio, had his nose broken, two Italians were sent off and all hell broke loose in a match that was nearly abandoned.

The victory over Italy qualified Chile for a quarter-final tie against the Soviet Union in far away Arica. Leonel Sanchez, the top Chilean footballer of the time, gave his side the lead after 11 minutes, and a minute after Chislenko equalised Eladio Rojas scored the winner in what was without question the best result in the history of the country.

The hosts were no match for the Brazilians in the semi-finals and bowed out of the tournament, although they had some consolation in winning the third place play-off against Yugoslavia. The 1962 World Cup was Chile's finest hour. Home advantage had played a large part in their third place and it is unlikely that the national side will ever reach the same heights again.

Further controversy erupted in the 1974 World Cup qualifying tournament. By beating Peru, Chile qualified to play the Soviet Union in a play-off for a place in West Germany. After drawing 0–0 in Moscow, the Soviet Union refused to play in the Estadio Nacional in Santiago. In 1973, Chile's left-wing government of President Allende had been overthrown by General Pinochet and the army, and when they rounded up all the left-wing and communist activists they were kept in the stadium. Few of them ever left. The Soviet Union did not feel able to play under such conditions, and after failing to turn up on the day were disqualified.

Since then Chile have continued on their unremarkable way. In 1979 they reached the final of the South American Championships, but the route was not exactly perilous. Colombia and Venezuela were overcome in the first round and Peru in the semi-finals before they lost to Paraguay over three games in the final. They reached the final again in 1987, losing this time to Uruguay, and despite hosting the tournament could do no better than finish third in 1991.

Chileans were all in good heart for the 1991 tournament, coming as it did on the heels of Colo Colo's win in the Copa Libertadores. Chile has suffered, like most countries in South America, the sight of her best players leaving to play in Europe and the top South American leagues, and this has had an effect on performances in the Copa. Colo Colo's appearance in the 1991 final was their second and Chile's fifth in all, which puts them in the same bracket as Paraguay and Colombia.

It was heartening for the supporters to see the most popular club in the country start to sign players like Yañez, back from his club in Spain, and this policy paid off with the triumph. Whether they can repeat this performance and translate success to the national team is another question. Certainly few other Chilean clubs can afford to do the same.

Population: 13 173 000
Area, sq km: 756 626
% in urban areas: 80%
Capital city: Santiago

Federación de Fútbol de Chile
Calle Erasmo Escala #1872
Casilla 3733, Santiago de Chile
Tel: (010 56) 2 6965381
Fax: (010 56) 2 6987082
Telex: 440474 FEBOL CZ
Cable: FEDFUTBOL SANTIAGO DE CHILE
Languages for correspondence: Spanish & English

Year of formation: 1895
Affiliation to FIFA: 1912
Affiliation to CONMEBOL: 1916
Registered clubs: 8071
Registered players: 635 800
Professional players: 770
Registered coaches: 990
Registered referees: 6435
National stadium: Estadio Nacional, Santiago 74 000
National colours: Shirts: Red/Shorts: Blue/Socks: White
Reserve colours: Shirts: White/Shorts: White/Socks: White
Season: May–December

THE RECORD

WORLD CUP

1930 .... QT Automatic – Final Tournament/1st round
1934 .... Did not enter
1938 .... Did not enter
1950 .... QT W-O in group 7– Final Tournament/1st round
1954 .... Did not enter
1958 .... QT 3rd/3 in group 2
1962 .... QT Automatic – Final Tournament/Semi-finalists/3rd place
1966 .... QT 1st/3 in group 2 – Final Tournament/1st round
1970 .... QT 2nd/3 in group 3
1974 .... QT 1st/2 in group 3 – Final Tournament/1st round
1978 .... QT 2nd/3 in group 3
1982 .... QT 1st/3 in group 3 – Final Tournament/1st round
1986 .... QT 2nd/3 in group 2
1990 .... QT 2nd/3 in group 3

SOUTH AMERICAN CHAMPIONSHIP

1910 .... 3rd/3
1916 .... 4th/4
1917 .... 4th/4
1919 .... 4th/4
1920 .... 4th/4
1921 .... –
1922 .... 5th/5
1923 .... –
1924 .... 4th/4
1925 .... –
1926 .... 3rd/5
1927 .... –
1929 .... –
1935 .... 4th/4
1937 .... 5th/6
1939 .... 4th/5
1941 .... 3rd/5
1942 .... 6th/7
1945 .... 3rd/7
1946 .... 5th/6
1947 .... 4th/8
1949 .... 5th/8
1953 .... 4th/7
1955 .... 2nd/6
1956 .... 2nd/6
1957 .... 6th/6
1959 .... 4th/7
1959 .... –
1963 .... –
1967 .... 3rd/6
1975 .... 6th/10/1st round
1979 .... 2nd/10/Finalists
1983 .... 5th/10/1st round
1987 .... 2nd/10/Finalists
1989 .... 5th/10/1st round
1991 .... 3rd/10/2nd round

OLYMPIC GAMES

1908–48 ..... Did not enter
1952 .... Preliminary round
1956 .... Did not enter
1960 .... QT Failed to qualify
1964 .... QT Failed to qualify
1968 .... QT Failed to qualify
1972 .... QT Failed to qualify
1976 .... QT Failed to qualify
1980 .... QT Failed to qualify
1984 .... Final Tournament/Quarter-finalists
1988 .... QT Failed to qualify
1992 .... QT Failed to qualify

COPA LIBERTADORES

Winners – Colo Colo 1991
Finalists – Colo Colo 1973, Union Espanola 1975, Cobreloa 1981, 1982

CLUB DIRECTORY

SANTIAGO (Population – 4 100 000)

Audax Italiano
Stadium: Estadio Municipal de la Florida 20 000
Founded: 1910
Colours: Green/White

Colo Colo
Stadium: Estadio Monumental David Arellano 62 000
Founded: 1925
Colours: White/Black

Magallanes San Bernardo
Stadium: Vulco 15 000
Founded: 1897
Colours: Sky blue and white stripes/Black

Club Palestino
Stadium: La Cisterna 20 000
Founded: 1920
Colours: Red, Green and white stripes/Black

Union Espanola
Stadium: San Carlos 12 000
Founded: 1909
Colours: Red/Blue

Universidad Catolica
Stadium: Santa Laura 35 000
Founded: 1937
Colours: White with a blue U on the front/Blue

Universidad de Chile
Stadium: Santa Laura 35 000
Founded: 1911
Colours: Blue with a white U on the front/Blue

CONCEPCION (Population – 675 000)

Deportes Concepción
Stadium: Estadio Regional de Concepción 36 000
Colours: Violet/White

Club Deportivo Fernandezez Vial
Stadium: Estadio Regional de Concepción 36 000
Founded:
Colours: Yellow and Black stripes/Black

Deportes Huachipato Talcahuano
Stadium: Estadio Las Higueras 12 000
Founded: 1947
Colours: Black and blue stripes/Blue

Deportivo Naval Talcahuano
Stadium: El Morro de Talcahuano 15 000
Founded: 1932
Colours: White/White

VALPARAISO (Population – 675 000)

Everton Viña del Mar
Stadium: Sausalito 25 000
Founded: 1909
Colours: Blue and yellow stripes/Blue

Santiago Wanderers Valparaíso
Stadium: Playa Ancha 16 000
Founded: 1892
Colours: Green/White

ANTOFAGASTA (Population – 185 000)
Deportes Antofagasta
Stadium: Estadio regional de Antofagasta 26 000
Founded: 1966
Colours: Sky blue and white halves/Sky blue

TEMUCO (Population – 157 000)
Deportes Temuco
Stadium: Estadio Municipal 10 000
Founded: 1916
Colours: White/White
Previous names: Green Cross

RANCAGUA (Population – 139 000)
O'Higgins
Stadium: El Teniente 20 000
Founded: 1955
Colours: Sky blue/Sky blue

TALCA (Population – 128 000)
Rangers Talca
Stadium: Estadio Fiscal 10 000
Founded: 1955
Colours: Red and black hoops

IQUIQUE (Population – 110 000)
Deportivo Iquique
Stadium: Municipal de Iquique
Founded: 1979
Colours: Blue/White

VALDIVIA (Population – 100 000)
Club Deportes Valdívia
Stadium: Parque Municipal 15 000
Colours: Red and white stripes/Red

LA SERENA (Population – 83 000)
Deportes La Serena
Stadium: La Portada 20 000
Founded: 1955
Colours: Red and White/Red

CALAMA (Population – 81 000)
Club de Deportes Cobreloa
Stadium: Municipal de Calama 20 000
Founded: 1977
Colours: Orange/Orange

COQUIMBO (Population – 62 000)
Coquimbo Unido
Stadium: Francisco Sanchez 15 000
Founded: 1897
Colours: Yellow/Black

SAN FELIPE (Population – 31 000)
Union San Felipe
Stadium: Estadio Municipal 12 000
Founded: 1956
Colours: White/White

EL SALVADOR
Cobresal
Stadium: El Cobre 10 000
Founded: 1979
Colours: White and orange stripes/Orange

CHILEAN LEAGUE CHAMPIONS

1933	Magallanes
1934	Magallanes
1935	Magallanes
1936	Audax Italiano
1937	Colo Colo
1938	Magallanes
1939	Colo Colo
1940	Universidad de Chile
1941	Colo Colo
1942	Santiago Morning
1943	Union Española
1944	Colo Colo
1945	Green Cross
1946	Audax Italiano
1947	Colo Colo
1948	Audax Italiano
1949	Universidad Catolica
1950	Everton
1951	Union Española
1952	Everton
1953	Colo Colo
1954	Universidad Catolica
1955	Palestino
1956	Colo Colo
1957	Audax Italiano
1958	Wanderers
1959	Universidad de Chile
1960	Colo Colo
1961	Universidad Catolica
1962	Universidad de Chile
1963	Colo Colo
1964	Universidad de Chile
1965	Universidad de Chile
1966	Universidad Catolica
1967	Universidad de Chile
1968	Wanderers
1969	Universidad de Chile
1970	Colo Colo
1971	Union San Felipe
1972	Colo Colo
1973	Union Española
1974	Huachipato
1975	Union Española
1976	Everton
1977	Union Española
1978	Palestino
1979	Colo Colo
1980	Cobreloa
1981	Colo Colo
1982	Cobreloa
1983	Colo Colo
1984	Universidad Catolica
1985	Cobreloa
1986	Colo Colo
1987	Universidad Catolica
1988	Cobreloa
1989	Colo Colo
1990	Colo Colo
1991	Colo Colo

INTERNATIONAL MATCHES PLAYED BY CHILE

Date	Opponents	Result		Venue	Compet	Scorers
27-05-1910	Argentina	L	1-3	Buenos Aires	Fr	Acuna
29-05	Uruguay	L	0-3	Buenos Aires	SC	
5-06	Argentina	L	1-5	Buenos Aires	SC	Sturgess
11-09	Argentina	L	0-3	Viña del Mar	Fr	
21-09-1913	Argentina	L	0-2	Viña del Mar	Fr	
2-07-1916	Uruguay	L	0-4	Buenos Aires	SC	
6-07	Argentina	L	1-6	Buenos Aires	SC	Báez
8-07	Brazil	D	1-1	Buenos Aires	SC	Salazar
12-07	Argentina	L	0-1	Buenos Aires	Fr	
14-07	Uruguay	L	1-4	Montevideo	Fr	
30-09-1917	Uruguay	L	0-4	Montevideo	SC	
6-10	Argentina	L	0-1	Montevideo	SC	
12-10	Brazil	L	0-5	Montevideo	SC	
22-10	Argentina	D	1-1	Buenos Aires	Fr	Muñoz
11-05-1919	Brazil	L	0-6	Rio de Janeiro	SC	
17-05	Uruguay	L	0-2	Rio de Janeiro	SC	
22-05	Argentina	L	1-4	Rio de Janeiro	SC	France
11-09-1920	Brazil	L	0-1	Viña del Mar	SC	
17-09	Argentina	D	1-1	Viña del Mar	SC	Dominguez A
3-10	Uruguay	L	1-2	Viña del Mar	SC	Bolados
25-09-1921	Argentina	L	1-4	Viña del Mar	Fr	
2-10	Argentina	D	1-1	Santiago	Fr	
17-09-1922	Brazil	D	1-1	Rio de Janeiro	SC	Bravo
23-09	Uruguay	L	0-2	Rio de Janeiro	SC	
28-09	Argentina	L	0-4	Rio de Janeiro	SC	
5-10	Paraguay	L	0-3	Rio de Janeiro	SC	
22-10	Argentina	L	0-1	Buenos Aires	Fr	
25-11-1923	Uruguay	L	1-2	Montevideo	Fr	
3-12	Argentina	L	0-6	Buenos Aires	Fr	
12-10-1924	Uruguay	L	0-1	Santiago	Fr	
19-10	Uruguay	L	0-5	Montevideo	SC	
25-10	Argentina	L	0-2	Montevideo	SC	
1-11	Paraguay	L	1-3	Montevideo	SC	Arellano
12-10-1926	Bolivia	W	7-1	Santiago	SC	Arellano 3, Subiabre 2, Ramirez M, Moreno
17-10	Uruguay	L	1-3	Santiago	SC	Subiabre
31-10	Argentina	D	1-1	Santiago	SC	Saavedra
3-11	Paraguay	W	5-1	Santiago	SC	Subiabre 3, Arellano 2
10-12-1927	Uruguay	L	2-3	Viña del Mar	Fr	
27-05-1928	Portugal	L	2-4	Amsterdam	OGr1	
5-06	Mexico	W	3-1	Arnhem	OGct	
8-06	Holland	D	2-2	Rotterdam	OGct	Lost on lots
16-07-1930	Mexico	W	3-0	Montevideo	WCr1	Vidal, Subiabre 2
19-07	France	W	1-0	Montevideo	WCr1	Subiabre
22-07	Argentina	L	1-3	Montevideo	WCr1	Subiabre
6-01-1935	Argentina	L	1-4	Lima	SC	Carmona
18-01	Uruguay	L	1-2	Lima	SC	Giudici
26-01	Peru	L	0-1	Lima	SC	
30-12-1936	Argentina	L	1-2	Buenos Aires	SC	Toro
3-01-1937	Brazil	L	4-6	Buenos Aires	SC	Toro 2, Avendaño, Riveros
10-01	Uruguay	W	3-0	Buenos Aires	SC	Toro 2, Arancibia
17-01	Paraguay	L	2-3	Buenos Aires	SC	Toro 2
21-01	Peru	D	2-2	Buenos Aires	SC	Torres, Carmona
15-01-1939	Paraguay	L	1-5	Lima	SC	Sorrel
22-01	Peru	L	1-3	Lima	SC	Dominguez Al
29-01	Uruguay	L	2-3	Lima	SC	Muñoz, Luco
5-02	Ecuador	W	4-1	Lima	SC	Aveñdano 2, Toro, Sorrel
26-02	Paraguay	W	4-2	Santiago	Fr	
2-03-1940	Argentina*	L	1-4	Buenos Aires	Fr	Sorrel
9-03	Argentina*	L	2-3	Buenos Aires	Fr	Pizzaro, Muñoz
12-03	Uruguay	L	2-3	Montevideo	Fr	
5-01-1941	Argentina*	L	1-2	Santiago	Fr	Alonso
9-01	Argentina*	L	2-5	Santiago	Fr	Sorrel, Balbuena
2-02	Ecuador	W	5-0	Santiago	SC	Sorrel 2, Toro, Contreras, Pérez R
9-02	Peru	W	1-0	Santiago	SC	Pérez R

16-02	Uruguay	L	0-2	Santiago	SC	
4-03	Argentina	L	0-1	Santiago	SC	
10-01-1942	Uruguay	L	1-6	Montevideo	SC	Contreras
14-01	Brazil	L	1-6	Montevideo	SC	Dominguez Al
22-01	Paraguay	L	0-2	Montevideo	SC	
31-01	Argentina	D	0-0	Montevideo	SC	*Abandoned 43 mins*
5-02	Ecuador	W	2-1	Montevideo	SC	Dominguez Al, Armingol
7-02	Peru	D	0-0	Montevideo	SC	
14-01-1945	Ecuador	W	6-3	Santiago	SC	Alcantara 2, Hormazábal F, Vera, Clavero, Piñero
24-01	Bolivia	W	5-0	Santiago	SC	Clavero 2, Alcantára 2, Medina
31-01	Colombia	W	2-0	Santiago	SC	Medina, Piñero
11-02	Argentina	D	1-1	Santiago	SC	Medina
18-02	Uruguay	W	1-0	Santiago	SC	Medina
28-02	Brazil	L	0-1	Santiago	SC	
16-01-1946	Uruguay	L	0-1	Buenos Aires	SC	
19-01	Paraguay	W	2-1	Buenos Aires	SC	Araya, Cremaschi
26-01	Argentina	L	1-3	Buenos Aires	SC	Alcantara
3-02	Brazil	L	1-5	Buenos Aires	SC	Salfate
8-02	Bolivia	W	4-1	Buenos Aires	SC	Araya 3, Cremaschi
6-12-1947	Uruguay	L	0-6	Guayaquil	SC	
9-12	Peru	W	2-1	Guayaquil	SC	Varela C, Busquets
11-12	Ecuador	W	3-0	Guayaquil	SC	López PH 2, Peñaloza
16-12	Argentina	D	1-1	Guayaquil	SC	Riera
23-12	Paraguay	L	0-1	Guayaquil	SC	
29-12	Colombia	W	4-1	Guayaquil	SC	Sáenz, López PH, Infante, Riera
31-12	Bolivia	W	4-3	Guayaquil	SC	OG, López PH, Sáenz, Riera
6-04-1949	Bolivia	L	2-3	Sao Paulo	SC	Salamanca, López PH
13-04	Brazil	L	1-2	Sao Paulo	SC	López PH
17-04	Ecuador	W	1-0	Rio de Janeiro	SC	Rojas C
20-04	Colombia	D	1-1	Rio de Janeiro	SC	Cremaschi
27-04	Paraguay	L	2-4	Sao Paulo	SC	Cremaschi, Riera
30-04	Peru	L	0-3	Sao Paulo	SC	
8-05	Uruguay	W	3-1	Belo Horizonte	SC	Infante 2, Rojas C
26-02-1950	Bolivia	L	0-2	La Paz	WCq	
12-03	Bolivia	W	5-0	Santiago	WCq	
7-04	Uruguay	L	1-5	Santiago	Fr	
9-04	Uruguay	W	2-1	Santiago	Fr	
25-06	England	L	0-2	Rio de Janeiro	WCr1	
29-06	Spain	L	0-2	Rio de Janeiro	WCr1	
2-07	United States	W	5-2	Recife	WCr1	Cremaschi 3, Robledo G, Prieto
16-03-1952	Panama	W	6-1	Santiago	PAC	
26-03	Mexico	W	4-0	Santiago	PAC	
2-04	Peru	W	3-2	Santiago	PAC	
13-04	Uruguay	W	2-0	Santiago	PAC	
20-04	Brazil	L	0-3	Santiago	PAC	
25-02-1953	Paraguay	L	0-3	Lima	SC	
1-03	Uruguay	W	3-2	Lima	SC	Molina 3
4-03	Peru	D	0-0	Lima	SC	
19-03	Ecuador	W	3-0	Lima	SC	Molina 2, Diaz G
23-03	Brazil	L	2-3	Lima	SC	Molina, Cremaschi
28-03	Bolivia	D	2-2	Lima	SC	Molina, Diaz G
24-05	England	L	1-2	Santiago	Fr	
12-07	Spain	L	1-2	Santiago	Fr	Muñoz
26-07	Peru	W	2-1	Lima	PC	Hormazábal, Robledo G
28-07	Peru	L	0-5	Lima	PC	
14-02-1954	Paraguay	L	0-4	Asuncion	WCq	
21-02	Paraguay	L	1-3	Santiago	WCq	
28-02	Brazil	L	0-2	Santiago	WCq	
14-03	Brazil	L	0-1	Rio de Janeiro	WCq	
17-09	Peru	W	2-1	Santiago	PC	Meléndez, Musso
19-09	Peru	L	2-4	Santiago	PC	Meléndez 2
27-02-1955	Ecuador	W	7-1	Santiago	SC	Hormazábal 3, Diaz G 2, Robledo J, Meléndez
6-03	Peru	W	5-4	Santiago	SC	Robledo J 2, Hormazábal, Muñoz, Ramirez J
13-03	Uruguay	D	2-2	Santiago	SC	Muñoz, Hormazábal
20-03	Paraguay	W	5-0	Santiago	SC	Meléndez 2, Muñoz 2, Hormazábal
30-03	Argentina	L	0-1	Santiago	SC	

18–09	Brazil	D	1–1	Rio de Janeiro	OHC	
20–09	Brazil	L	1–2	Sao Paulo	OHC	
24–01–1956	Brazil	W	4–1	Montevideo	SC	Hormazábal 2, Meléndez, Sanchez L
29–01	Argentina	L	0–2	Montevideo	SC	
6–02	Uruguay	L	1–2	Montevideo	SC	Ramirez J
9–02	Peru	W	4–3	Montevideo	SC	Hormazábal, Muñoz, Fernandez J, Sanchez L
12–02	Paraguay	W	2–0	Montevideo	SC	Hormazábal, Ramirez J
1–03	Brazil	L	1–2	Mexico City	PAC	
8–03	Costa Rica	L	1–2	Mexico City	PAC	
11–03	Argentina	L	0–3	Mexico City	PAC	
15–03	Peru	D	2–2	Mexico City	PAC	
18–03	Mexico	L	1–2	Mexico City	PAC	
26–08	Czechoslovakia	W	3–0	Santiago	Fr	
13–03–1957	Brazil	L	2–4	Lima	SC	Ramirez J, Fernandez J
16–03	Peru	L	0–1	Lima	SC	
21–03	Colombia	W	3–2	Lima	SC	Verdejo 2, Espinoza
24–03	Ecuador	D	2–2	Lima	SC	Ramirez J 2
28–03	Argentina	L	2–6	Lima	SC	Fernandez J 2
1–04	Uruguay	L	0–2	Lima	SC	
15–09	Brazil	W	1–0	Santiago	OHC	
18–09	Brazil	D	1–1	Santiago	OHC	
22–09	Bolivia	W	2–1	Santiago	WCq	Ramirez, Hormazábal
29–09	Bolivia	L	0–3	La Paz	WCq	
13–10	Argentina	L	0–2	Santiago	WCq	
20–10	Argentina	L	0–4	Buenos Aires	WCq	
7–03–1959	Argentina	L	1–6	Buenos Aires	SC	Alvarez
11–03	Paraguay	L	1–2	Buenos Aires	SC	Sanchez L
15–03	Brazil	L	0–3	Buenos Aires	SC	
21–03	Peru	D	1–1	Buenos Aires	SC	Tobar
26–03	Bolivia	W	5–2	Buenos Aires	SC	Soto J 2, Soto M 2, Sanchez L
2–04	Uruguay	W	1–0	Buenos Aires	SC	Moreno
17–09	Brazil	L	0–7	Rio de Janeiro	OHC	
20–09	Brazil	L	0–1	Sao Paulo	OHC	
18–11	Argentina	W	4–2	Santiago	Fr	Bello 2, Sanchez L, Rios
16–03–1960	France	L	0–6	Paris	Fr	
23–03	West Germany	L	1–2	Stuttgart	Fr	
30–03	Rep. Ireland	L	0–2	Dublin	Fr	
6–04	Switzerland	L	2–4	Basle	Fr	
13–04	Belgium	D	1–1	Brussels	Fr	
1–06	Uruguay	L	2–3	Santiago	Fr	
5–06	Uruguay	D	2–2	Montevideo	Fr	
29–06	Brazil	L	0–4	Rio de Janeiro	Fr	
14–07	Spain	L	0–4	Santiago	Fr	
17–07	Spain	L	1–4	Santiago	Fr	Musso
18–12	Paraguay	W	4–1	Santiago	Fr	
21–12	Paraguay	W	3–1	Valparaiso	Fr	
19–03–1961	Peru	W	5–2	Santiago	Fr	Toro, Betta, Soto 2, Sanchez L
26–03	West Germany	W	3–1	Santiago	Fr	Sanchez L, Rojas E
7–05	Brazil	L	1–2	Santiago	OHC	Soto
11–05	Brazil	L	0–1	Santiago	OHC	
12–10	Uruguay	L	2–3	Santiago	Fr	Fouilloux, Moreno
22–11	Soviet Union	L	0–1	Santiago	Fr	
9–12	Hungary	W	5–1	Santiago	Fr	Landa, Fouilloux, Sanchez L 2, Sepulveda
13–12	Hungary	D	0–0	Santiago	Fr	
30–05–1962	Switzerland	W	3–1	Santiago	WCr1	Sanchez L 2, Ramirez
2–06	Italy	W	2–0	Santiago	WCr1	Ramirez, Toro
6–06	West Germany	L	0–2	Santiago	WCr1	
10–06	Soviet Union	W	2–1	Arica	WCqf	Sanchez L, Rojas E
13–06	Brazil	L	2–4	Santiago	WCsf	Toro, Sanchez L
16–06	Yugoslavia	W	1–0	Santiago	WC3p	Rojas E
7–11	Argentina	D	1–1	Santiago	CDC	Landa
21–11	Argentina	L	0–1	Buenos Aires	CDC	
23–03–1963	Uruguay	L	2–3	Montevideo	PDC	
24–07	Uruguay	D	0–0	Santiago	PDC	
24–09–1964	Argentina	L	0–5	Buenos Aires	CDC	
14–10	Argentina	D	1–1	Santiago	CDC	Verdejo
15–04–1965	Peru	W	4–1	Santiago	PC	Lando 2, Araya 2
28–04	Peru	W	1–0	Lima	PC	Araya

9–05	Uruguay	D	0–0	Santiago	PDC	
16–05	Uruguay	D	1–1	Montevideo	PDC	Sanchez L
14–07	Argentina	L	0–1	Buenos Aires	CDC	
21–07	Argentina	D	1–1	Santiago	CDC	Sanchez L
1–08	Colombia	W	7–2	Santiago	WCq	Fouilloux 2, Mendez 2, Sanchez L, Campos, Prieto
7–08	Colombia	L	0–2	Barranquilla	WCq	
15–08	Ecuador	D	2–2	Guayaquil	WCq	Sanchez L, Prieto
22–08	Ecuador	W	3–1	Santiago	WCq	
12–10	Ecuador	W	2–1	Lima	WCq	Sanchez L, Marcos
23–02–1966	Soviet Union	L	0–2	Santiago	Fr	
17–04	Brazil	L	0–1	Santiago	OHC	
20–04	Brazil	W	2–1	Viña del Mar	OHC	
11–05	Mexico	L	0–1	Mexico City	Fr	
15–05	Brazil	D	1–1	Sao Paulo	Fr	
19–05	Brazil	L	0–1	Rio de Janeiro	Fr	
22–05	Wales	W	2–0	Santiago	Fr	Marcos, Tobar
29–05	Mexico	L	0–1	Santiago	Fr	
2–07	East Germany	L	2–5	Leipzig	Fr	Tobar, Marcos
13–07	Italy	L	0–2	Sunderland	WCr1	
15–07	North Korea	D	1–1	Middlesbrough	WCr1	Marcos
20–07	Soviet Union	L	1–2	Sunderland	WCr1	Marcos
30–11	Colombia	W	5–2	Santiago	SCq	Castro 2, Araya, Prieto, Saavedra
11–12	Colombia	D	0–0	Bogota	SCq	
18–01–1967	Venezuela	W	2–0	Montevideo	SC	Marcos 2
22–01	Paraguay	W	4–2	Montevideo	SC	Gallardo 3, Araya
26–01	Uruguay	D	2–2	Montevideo	SC	Gallardo, Marcos
28–01	Argentina	L	0–2	Montevideo	SC	
1–02	Bolivia	D	0–0	Montevideo	SC	
15–08	Argentina	W	1–0	Santiago	Fr	Araya
19–09	Brazil	L	0–1	Santiago	Fr	
8–11	Argentina	W	3–1	Santiago	Fr	Fouilloux 2, Reynoso
17–12	Soviet Union	L	1–4	Santiago	Fr	Reynoso
18–08–1968	Peru	W	2–1	Lima	PC	Valdez 2
21–08	Peru	D	0–0	Lima	PC	
28–08	Mexico	L	1–3	Mexico City	Fr	
23–10	Mexico	W	3–1	Santiago	Fr	Araya, Olivares 2
27–11	Argentina	L	0–4	Rosario	CDC	
4–12	Argentina	W	2–1	Santiago	CDC	Fouilloux, Olivares
18–12	West Germany	W	2–1	Santiago	Fr	Araya, Fouilloux
28–05–1969	Argentina	D	1–1	Santiago	Fr	Velez
8–06	Paraguay	W	1–0	Asuncion	Fr	Araya
11–06	Argentina	L	1–2	La Plata	Fr	Olivares
15–06	Colombia	D	3–3	Bogota	Fr	Fouilloux, Reynoso, Laube
22–06	East Germany	W	1–0	Magdeburg	Fr	Javar
6–07	Paraguay	D	0–0	Santiago	Fr	
13–07	Uruguay	D	0–0	Santiago	WCq	
15–07	Colombia	D	3–3	Bogota	Fr	Alube, Fouilloux, Reynoso
27–07	Ecuador	W	4–1	Santiago	WCq	Olivares 2, Valdes 2
3–08	Ecuador	D	1–1	Guayaquil	WCq	Olivares
10–08	Uruguay	L	0–2	Montevideo	WCq	
22–03–1970	Brazil	L	0–5	Sao Paulo	Fr	
26–03	Brazil	L	1–2	Rio de Janeiro	Fr	OG
4–10	Brazil	L	1–5	Santiago	Fr	Messen
2–02–1971	East Germany	L	0–1	Santiago	Fr	
14–07	Paraguay	W	3–2	Santiago	Fr	Osorio, Castro 2
21–07	Argentina	D	2–2	Santiago	CDC	Viveros, Castro
4–08	Argentina	L	0–1	Buenos Aires	CDC	
8–08	Paraguay	L	0–2	Asuncion	Fr	
11–08	Peru	L	0–1	Lima	PC	
15–08	Bolivia*	W	4–3	La Paz	Fr	
18–08	Peru	W	1–0	Santiago	PC	Vivero
27–10	Uruguay	L	0–3	Montevideo	PDC	
3–11	Uruguay	W	5–0	Santiago	PDC	
27–01–1972	Mexico	L	0–2	Mexico City	Fr	
9–02	Haiti	L	0–1	Port au Prince	Fr	
31–05	Argentina	L	3–4	Santiago	CDC	Caszely, Valdez 2
14–06	Ecuador	W	2–1	Natal	ClrI	
18–06	Portugal	L	1–4	Recife	ClrI	

21–06	Rep. Ireland	W	2–1	Recife	Clr1	
25–06	Iran	W	2–1	Recife	Clr1	
16–08	Mexico	L	0–2	Santiago	Fr	
25–09	Argentina	L	0–2	Buenos Aires	CDC	
14–04–1973	Haiti	D	1–1	Port-au-Prince	Fr	
21–04	Mexico	D	1–1	Mexico City	Fr	
24–04	Ecuador	D	1–1	Guayaquil	Fr	
29–04	Peru	L	0–2	Lima	WCq	
13–05	Peru	W	2–0	Santiago	WCq	Crisosto, Ahumada
13–07	Argentina	L	4–5	Buenos Aires	CDC	Ahumada 2, Crisosto, Caszely
18–07	Argentina	W	3–1	Santiago	CDC	Caszely 2, Crisosto
24–07	Bolivia	W	3–0	Santiago	Fr	
5–08	Peru	W	2–1	Montevideo	WCq	Valdez, Reinoso
20–09	Mexico	W	2–1	Mexico City	Fr	
26–09	Soviet Union	D	0–0	Moscow	WCq	
21–11	Soviet Union		W–O	Santiago	WCq	*Soviet Union refused to play*
24–04–1974	Haiti	W	1–0	Port au Prince	Fr	
26–04	Haiti	D	0–0	Port au Prince	Fr	
12–05	Rep. Ireland	L	1–2	Santiago	Fr	Valdez
14–06	West Germany	L	0–1	Berlin	WCr1	
18–06	East Germany	D	1–1	Berlin	WCr1	Ahumada
22–06	Australia	D	0–0	Berlin	WCr1	
6–11	Argentina	L	0–2	Santiago	CDC	
20–11	Argentina	D	1–1	Buenos Aires	CDC	Mendez
22–12	Paraguay	W	1–0	Santiago	Fr	
4–06–1975	Uruguay	L	0–1	Montevideo	PDC	
25–06	Uruguay	L	1–3	Santiago	PDC	Pinto
16–07	Peru	D	1–1	Santiago	SCr1	Crisosto
20–07	Bolivia	L	1–2	La Paz	SCr1	Gamboa
13–08	Bolivia	W	4–0	Santiago	SCr1	
20–08	Peru	L	1–3	Lima	SCr1	Reinoso
6–10–1976	Uruguay	D	0–0	Santiago	PDC	
13–10	Argentina	L	0–2	Buenos Aires	CDC	
26–01–1977	Paraguay	W	4–0	Santiago	Fr	Crisosto 3, Rojas
30–01	Uruguay	L	0–3	Montevideo	PDC	
2–02	Paraguay	L	0–2	Asuncion	Fr	
27–02	Ecuador	W	1–0	Guayaquil	WCq	Gamboa
6–03	Peru	D	1–1	Santiago	WCq	Ahumada
20–03	Ecuador	W	3–0	Santiago	WCq	Figueroa 2, Castro
26–03	Peru	L	0–2	Lima	WCq	
15–06	Scotland	L	2–4	Santiago	Fr	Crisosto 2
13–06–1979	Ecuador	D	0–0	Santiago	Fr	
21–06	Ecuador	L	1–2	Guayaquil	Fr	
11–07	Uruguay	W	1–0	Santiago	PDC	Figueroa
18–07	Uruguay	L	1–2	Montevideo	PDC	
8–08	Venezuela	D	1–1	San Cristobal	SCr1	Peredo
15–08	Colombia	L	0–1	Bogota	SCr1	
29–08	Venezuela	W	7–0	Santiago	SCr1	Peredo 2, Rivas 2, Veliz, Soto M, Yañez
5–09	Colombia	W	2–0	Santiago	SCr1	Caszely, Peredo
17–10	Peru	W	2–1	Lima	SCsf	Caszely 2
24–10	Peru	D	0–0	Santiago	SCsf	
28–11	Paraguay	L	0–3	Asuncion	SCf	
5–12	Paraguay	W	1–0	Santiago	SCf	Rivas
11–12	Paraguay	D	0–0	Buenos Aires	SCf	
24–06–1980	Brazil	L	1–2	Belo Horizonte	Fr	
21–08	Uruguay	D	0–0	Montevideo	PDC	
18–09	Argentina	D	2–2	Mendoza	Fr	Vargas, Castec
10–03–1981	Colombia	W	1–0	Santiago	Fr	Herrera
14–03	Brazil	L	1–2	Ribeirao Preto	Fr	Caszely
19–03	Colombia	W	2–1	Bogota	Fr	Caszely 2
19–04	Peru	W	3–0	Santiago	Fr	Moscoso 2, Caszely
29–04	Uruguay	L	1–2	Santiago	PDC	Rojas
24–05	Ecuador	D	0–0	Guayaquil	WCq	
7–06	Paraguay	W	1–0	Asuncion	WCq	Yañez
14–06	Ecuador	W	2–0	Santiago	WCq	Rivas, Caszely
21–06	Paraguay	W	3–0	Santiago	WCq	Caszely, Yañez, Neyra
5–07	Spain	D	1–1	Santiago	Fr	Caszely
15–07	Uruguay	D	0–0	Montevideo	PDC	
5–08	Peru	W	2–1	Lima	Fr	Caszely 2

26–08	Brazil	D	0–0	Santiago	Fr	
23–03–1982	Peru	W	2–1	Santiago	Fr	Letelier, Neyra
30–03	Peru	L	0–1	Lima	Fr	
19–05	Romania	L	2–3	Santiago	Fr	Bigorra, Caszely
22–05	Rep. Ireland	W	1–0	Santiago	Fr	Gamboa
17–06	Austria	L	0–1	Oviedo	WCr1	
20–06	West Germany	L	1–4	Gijon	WCr1	Moscoso
24–06	Algeria	L	2–3	Oviedo	WCr1	Neyra, Letelier
28–04–1983	Brazil	L	2–3	Rio de Janeiro	Fr	Orellana 2
12–05	Argentina	D	2–2	Santiago	Fr	Orellana, Dubo
23–06	Argentina	L	0–1	Buenos Aires	Fr	
14–07	Colombia	D	2–2	Bogota	Fr	Aravena, Hurtado
19–07	Bolivia	W	2–1	La Paz	Fr	
21–07	Peru	W	1–0	Lima	Fr	Soto M
24–07	Paraguay	L	0–1	Asuncion	Fr	
28–07	Brazil	D	0–0	Santiago	Fr	
3–08	Peru	W	2–0	Arica	Fr	Letelier 2
17–08	Paraguay	W	3–2	Santiago	Fr	Aravena, Letelier, Hurtado
24–08	Bolivia	W	4–2	Arica	Fr	
1–09	Uruguay	L	1–2	Montevideo	SCr1	Orellana
8–09	Venezuela	W	5–0	Santiago	SCr1	Aravena 2, Arriza, Dubo, Espinoza
11–09	Uruguay	W	2–0	Santiago	SCr1	Dubo, Letelier
21–09	Venezuela	D	0–0	Caracas	SCr1	
17–06–1984	England	D	0–0	Santiago	Fr	
25–07	Canada	D	0–0	Edmonton	Fr	
28–10	Mexico	W	1–0	Santiago	Fr	Aravena
6–02–1985	Paraguay	W	1–0	Viña del Mar	Fr	Aravena
8–02	Finland	W	2–0	Viña del Mar	Fr	Letelier, Aravena
21–02	Colombia	D	1–1	Santiago	Fr	Letelier
24–02	Peru	L	1–2	Santiago	Fr	Rubio
3–03	Ecuador	D	1–1	Quito	WCq	Letelier
9–03	Peru	D	1–1	Lima	Fr	Aravena
17–03	Ecuador	W	6–2	Santiago	WCq	Puebla, Cazsely 2, Hisis, Aravena 2
24–03	Uruguay	W	2–0	Santiago	WCq	Rubio, Aravena
7–04	Uruguay	L	1–2	Montevideo	WCq	Aravena
15–05	Argentina	L	0–2	Buenos Aires	Fr	
21–05	Brazil	W	2–1	Santiago	Fr	Rubio, Caszely
8–06	Brazil	L	1–3	Porto Alegre	Fr	
9–10	Paraguay	D	0–0	Asuncion	Fr	
17–10	Uruguay	W	1–0	Santiago	Fr	Neyra
27–10	Peru	W	4–2	Santiago	WCq	Aravena 2, Rubio, Hisis
29–10	Paraguay	D	0–0	Santiago	Fr	
3–11	Peru	W	1–0	Lima	WCq	Aravena
10–11	Paraguay	L	0–3	Asuncion	WCq	
17–11	Paraguay	D	2–2	Santiago	WCq	Rubio, Nunoz
7–05–1986	Brazil	D	1–1	Curitiba	Fr	Puyal
19–06–1987	Peru	W	3–1	Lima	Fr	Rodriguez, Basay, Zamorano
21–06	Peru	L	0–2	Lima	Fr	
24–06	Peru	W	1–0	Santiago	Fr	Hurtado
30–06	Venezuela	W	3–1	Cordoba	SCr1	Letelier, Contreras, Salgado
3–07	Brazil	W	4–0	Cordoba	SCr1	Basay 2, Letelier 2
8–07	Colombia	W	2–1	Cordoba	SCsf	Astengo, Vera
12–07	Uruguay	L	0–1	Buenos Aires	SCf	
9–12	Brazil	L	1–2	Uberlandia	Fr	Martinez
23–05–1988	Greece	L	0–1	Toronto	Fr	
25–05	Canada	L	0–1	Toronto	Fr	
1–06	United States	D	1–1	Stockton	Fr	
3–06	United States	W	3–1	San Diego	Fr	Hurtado, Salgado, Rojas O
5–06	United States	W	3–0	Fresno	Fr	
13–09	Ecuador	W	3–1	La Serena	Fr	Salgado, Alvarez, Rodriguez
27–09	Paraguay	L	0–2	Asuncion	Fr	
29–09	Ecuador	D	0–0	Asuncion	Fr	
25–10	Peru	W	2–0	Arica	Fr	Espinoza, Gonzalez
1–11	Uruguay	D	1–1	Santiago	PDC	Espinoza
9–11	Uruguay	L	1–3	Montevideo	PDC	Espinoza
23–11	Peru	D	1–1	Lima	Fr	Mardones
29–01–1989	Ecuador	L	0–1	Guayaquil	Fr	
1–02	Peru	D	0–0	Armenia	Fr	
5–02	Colombia	L	0–1	Armenia	Fr	

20–04	Argentina	D	1–1	Santiago	Fr	Espinoza
5–05	Guatemala	W	1–0	Los Angeles	Fr	Martinez
7–05	El Salvador	W	1–0	Los Angeles	Fr	Cormeno
23–05	England	D	0–0	London	Fr	
26–05	Nth. Ireland	W	1–0	Belfast	Fr	Astengo
30–05	Scotland	L	0–2	Glasgow	Fr	
3–06	Egypt	L	0–2	Cairo	Fr	
19–06	Uruguay	D	2–2	Montevideo	Fr	Gonzalez, Pizarro
22–06	Bolivia	W	1–0	La Paz	Fr	Covarrubias
27–06	Bolivia	W	2–1	Santiago	Fr	Covarrubias, Pizarro
2–07	Argentina	L	0–1	Goiania	SCr1	
6–07	Uruguay	L	0–3	Goiania	SCr1	
8–07	Bolivia	W	5–0	Goiania	SCr1	Olmis, Ramirez, Astengo, Pizarro, Reyes
10–07	Ecuador	W	2–1	Goiania	SCr1	Olmis, Letelier
25–07	Peru	W	2–1	Arica	Fr	Tudor, Aravena
6–08	Venezuela	W	3–1	Caracas	WCq	Aravena 2, Zamorano
13–08	Brazil	D	1–1	Santiago	WCq	Basay
27–08	Venezuela	W	5–0	Mendoza	WCq	Letelier 3, Yañez, Vera
3–09	Brazil	L	0–2	Rio de Janeiro	WCq	*Abandoned after 65 mins*
17–10–1990	Brazil	D	0–0	Santiago	Fr	
8–11	Brazil	D	0–0	Belem	Fr	
9–04–1991	Mexico	L	0–1	Veracruz	Fr	
22–05	Rep. Ireland	D	1–1	Dublin	Fr	Estay
30–05	Uruguay	W	2–1	Santiago	Fr	Vega, Gonzalez
19–06	Ecuador	L	1–2	Quito	Fr	Vera
26–06	Uruguay	L	1–2	Montevideo	Fr	Rubio
30–06	Ecuador	W	3–1	Santiago	Fr	Rubio 2, Zamorano
6–07	Venezuela	W	2–0	Santiago	SCr1	Vilches, Zamorano
8–07	Peru	W	4–2	Concepcion	SCr1	Rubio, Contreras, Zamorano 2
10–07	Argentina	L	0–1	Santiago	SCr1	
14–07	Paraguay	W	4–0	Santiago	SCr1	Rubio, Zamorano, Estay, Vera
17–07	Colombia	D	1–1	Santiago	SCr2	Zamorano
19–07	Argentina	D	0–0	Santiago	SCr2	
21–07	Brazil	L	0–2	Santiago	SCr2	

COLOMBIA

To find a country with a more turbulent football history than Colombia would be a difficult task. From shooting referees to paying players with money laundered from the drugs business, Colombia has it all. They have enraged other nations by their flagrant disregard of the rules set down by FIFA, but despite all of this, after years of achieving little, Colombia is emerging as the biggest threat to the established powers of Argentina, Brazil and Uruguay.

As was common in South America, a port, Barranquilla, was the first place football really took a hold. Until the introduction of professionalism in 1948, Barranquilla was the centre of football in the country. The first ruling body of any kind in the country, the Liga de Football del Atlantico was founded there in 1924. Affiliation to FIFA occurred seven years later, but the fact that both these events happened some forty years after the first recorded game was played gives an indication as to how disjointed progress was.

Colombia is a very large country. Roughly half of the total area comprises the northern boundary of the Amazon basin, whilst much of the rest of the country is taken up by the northern reaches of the Andes. A majority of the cities are located in these mountains, so it is not surprising that communications were not good.

The first game adhering to the proper rules is said to have taken place in Bogota, the capital, in 1887, but for many years football was played on an ad hoc basis with no proper organisation. A national body was finally formed in 1938 and known as the Asociacion Colombiana de Futbol, but clubs in all the different provinces were under the control of various regional associations not the ACF.

An annual tournament for representative teams from the various regional leagues was introduced, but the main role of the ACF was to put together a national side and in 1938, Colombia joined the Confederacion Centro-americano y del Caribe de Futbol and later that year made their international debut in the Central American and Caribbean Games. Bogota then hosted the Bolivar games at the end of the year, but neither tournament proved successful for the Colombians and it was five years before they played another game.

In 1940 the ACF decided to join the South American confederation in apparent contradiction to its membership of the CCCF, but from that time Colombia has stuck with South America and eventually gave up membership of the Central American body.

The early 1940s saw major developments at club level and they were ultimately to lead to notoriety for Colombia at the end of the decade. Professionalism was becoming a major issue and in 1939 the club that was to represent the new era in Colombian football was founded by two wealthy businessmen in Bogota. Known initially as Deportivo Municipal, in 1947 they officially adopted their nickname, 'Los Millonarios', a reference to the size of their bank balance.

Wealthy patrons became involved with other clubs also. The amateur era passed into history with the creation of a new professional league in 1948, but instead of making this a platform from which to build, Colombia hit the self-destruct button. Players were imported from all over South America and the league was an instant hit. In 1950 the DiMayor, as the league was known, broke away form the ACF, and there followed four years of turmoil that put Colombia on the world football map.

Known as the 'El Dorado' period, it saw Colombia assemble some of the world's best talent, much to the dismay of the rest of the world. After the breakaway, Colombia had been suspended from FIFA which meant that transfer fees did not have to be paid. At the same time a players' strike in both Argentina and Uruguay meant many of the continent's best players were available for transfer. Signing-on fees and wages higher than anywhere else meant that soon there were up to 70 Argentinians, 15 Uruguayans and six Britons, among others, playing in the DiMayor.

Among those tempted to Colombia were Alfredo Di Stefano, Nestor Rossi and Adolfo Pedernera, all major stars with River Plate before they came to Colombia. Even England was raided and Neil Franklin, the England centre-half at the time, was signed up by Millonarios' major cross-town rivals, Santa Fe.

El Dorado was not to last long, however. In 1954 FIFA accepted Colombia back into the fold, whilst most of the major stars had by then departed, in many cases to Europe. The bubble had well and truly burst, leaving many clubs in severe financial trouble. There had been 18 clubs in the DiMayor at its peak; by 1955 the number had shrunk to just 10. The reliance on foreign players, and the high standard they set, had left a dearth of home-grown talent. Spectator interest waned and Colombia slipped firmly into the international football backwaters from which it had briefly risen.

The national team proved a fairer indication of the standard of Colombian footballers. They had entered three editions of the South American Championship in the 1940s, and out of 20 games played only won one. Many of the defeats were substantial, and from 1949 until 1957 no further international matches were played. There was a brief flurry of international activity in 1957 which included a victory over Uruguay in the South American Championships, as well as a first attempt to qualify for the World Cup, but with a group containing Uruguay and Paraguay, Colombia placed comfortably last behind the other vastly more experienced sides.

It was a great surprise, therefore, when the Colombians did qualify for the 1962 finals, but with both Chile and Brazil qualifying automatically, all that involved was two games with Peru. A 1–0 win in Bogota was sufficient to see them through. Very much the unknown quantity, their 2–1 and 5–0 defeats by Uruguay and Yugoslavia respectively were redeemed by a superb display against the Soviet Union in their finest performance to that date. Losing 4–1 at one point, they fought back to draw 4–4. The experience was not built upon and the team faded back into obscurity until the mid-1970s.

At home, the DiMayor had struggled on after El Dorado. Millonarios briefly rose again in the late 1950s and early 1960s but the team did not have the same aura about it as before. In 1965, the self-destruct button was pushed once again with the creation of the Federacion del Futbol Colombiana as a direct challenge to the authority of the ACF. FIFA was called in to mediate in the dispute and ended up directly running the game until 1971 when a wholly new Federacion Colombiana de Futbol was formed. Meanwhile, 1968 saw a complete reorganisation of the league competition in response to the post El Dorado depression that had enveloped the game. A simple, European-style league was replaced by what can seem an unbelievably complicated structure.

Three phases were introduced, the Apertura, the Finalizacion and finally the Serie Definitiva. The precise system has varied from year to year since, but broadly speaking the first two phases are used to select a final group of clubs to play in the last stage, in which they start from scratch. There is no promotion or relegation, as the current 16 clubs are the only professional sides in the

		Total			League	Copa Lib		
		G	S	B	G	G	S	B
1	Millonarios Bogotá	13	–	3	13	–	–	3
2	America Cali	7	3	3	7	–	3	3
3	At. Nacional Medellín	6	–	2	5	1	–	2
4	Independiente Santa Fé	6	–	1	6	–	–	1
5	Deportivo Cali	5	1	2	5	–	1	2
6	Independiente Medellín	2	–	–	2	–	–	–
	Atletico Junior	2	–	–	2	–	–	–
8	Atletico Quindio	1	–	–	1	–	–	–
	Deportes Caldas	1	–	–	1	–	–	–
	Union Magdalena	1	–	–	1	–	–	–
11	Deportes Tolima	–	–	1	–	–	–	1

Correct to the end of the 1991 season

country. Since 1968 the league has been relatively stable and has improved in standard.

Much of this has been due to the progress made by the city of Cali. From 1968 until 1990 the city won the title on 12 occasions either through Deportivo Cali or America Cali. Both were also the first Colombian clubs to make inroads in the Copa Libertadores. Deportivo were losing finalists in 1978, whilst America were losing finalists three years running in the mid-1980s. How much of this progress has been due to the Cali drug cartel helping to fund the game has never been proved, but more than one judge has been assassinated trying to find out!

Careful control on the number of foreigners in the league meant that in the 1970s local talent began to develop. Atletico Nacional of Medellin, another city with a large drugs cartel, even have a policy of only playing Colombian players, and this paid off in May 1989 when the event all Colombians had been waiting for occurred. Nacional won the Copa Libertadores, the first international trophy in the history of the country, amid scenes of unprecedented celebrations.

The fortunes of the national team have also risen in the corresponding period. In the 1975 South American Championship, Paraguay, Ecuador and Uruguay were beaten on the way to the final where the Colombians met Peru. Peru eventually won after a play-off in Caracas, but the signs were there that matters were improving. Players of the class of Willington Ortiz were starting to emerge, and by the 1980s the basis of a good national side was there. Under the leadership of Francisco Maturano, who also led Nacional to their Copa Libertadores success, Colombia finished third in the 1987 South American Championships in Argentina.

In 1990, with players like Carlos Valderrama, Alberto Iguaran, Bernardo Redin and the eccentric Rene Higuita in goal, Colombia qualified for the World Cup finals and when pressed, showed they were capable of living with the best. They certainly made their mark on the tournament, especially Higuita who showed goalkeepers how to win over the crowds, if not managers, with his interpretation of a goalkeeping sweeper.

Naturally the 1970s and 1980s have not been without their problems. Originally the 1986 World Cup was to be held in Colombia as recognition of the progress that was being made, but to the disappointment of all Colombians they had to pull out as the facilities and communications were not considered sufficient for a 24-team event.

The drugs problem has been a consistent source of worry, however, not just because of the money aspect. In November 1989, Daniel Ortega made a terrible mistake: he refereed a game honestly, and was assassinated outside the ground for his trouble, as one of the drug gangs had made a large bet on the game and had lost their money. This it seemed was just the tip of the iceberg. Many strange refereeing decisions have been put down to bribery. Faced with the sort of threat they are under, perhaps it is not surprising.

The league was immediately suspended and a clear-up ordered, but it is difficult to do little more than scratch at the surface. Other South American teams are refusing to travel to Colombia for fear of their safety, but it would be a shame if when at last it seems Colombia can live with the best on the continent, progress should be ruined by forces outside of the grasp of football. The time is long overdue for international recognition on the playing field rather than off it.

Population: 32 978 000
Area, sq km: 1 141 748
% in urban areas: 67%
Capital city: Bogotá

Federación Colombiana de Fútbol
Avenida 32, #16-22
Apartado Aéreo 17.602
Bogotá
Colombia
Tel: (010 57) 1 2455370
Fax: (010 57) 1 2854340
Telex: 45598 COLFU CO
Cable: COLFUTBOL BOGOTA
Languages for correspondence: Spanish, English & French

Year of formation: 1924
Affiliation to FIFA: 1936
Affiliation to CONMEBOL: 1940
Registered clubs: 3805
Registered players: 209 500
Professional players: 460
Registered coaches: 80
Registered referees: 3098

National stadium: El Campin, Bogota 52 000
National colours: Shirts: Red/Shorts: Blue/Socks: Yellow
Reserve colours: Shirts: Blue/Shorts: White/Socks: Blue
Season: March–December (1st stage Mar–May, 2nd May–Jun, 3rd Jun–Oct, 4th Oct–Dec)

THE RECORD

WORLD CUP

1930–54 ..... Did not enter
1958 .... QT 3rd/3 in group 3
1962 .... QT 1st/2 in group 3 – Final Tournament/1st round
1966 .... QT 3rd/3 in group 2
1970 .... QT 3rd/4 in group 2
1974 .... QT 2nd/3 in group 1
1978 .... QT 3rd/3 in group 1
1982 .... QT 3rd/3 in group 2
1986 .... QT 3rd/4 in group 1
1990 .... QT 1st/3 in group 2 – Final Tournament/2nd round

SOUTH AMERICAN CHAMPIONSHIP

1910–42 ..... –
1945 .... 5th/7
1946 .... –
1947 .... 8th/8
1949 .... 8th/8
1953–56 ..... –
1957 .... 5th/7
1959 .... –
1959 .... –
1963 .... 7th/7
1967 .... –
1975 .... 2nd/10/Finalists
1979 .... 5th/10/1st round
1983 .... 7th/10/1st round
1987 .... 3rd/10/Semi-finals
1989 .... 6th/10/1st round
1991 .... 4th/10/2nd round

OLYMPIC GAMES

1908–56 ..... Did not enter
1960 .... QT Failed to qualify
1964 .... QT Failed to qualify
1968 .... Final Tournament/1st round
1972 .... Final Tournament/1st round
1976 .... QT Failed to qualify
1980 .... Final Tournament/1st round
1984 .... QT Failed to qualify
1988 .... QT Failed to qualify
1992 .... Final Tournament

COPA LIBERTADORES

Winners – At. Nacional Medellin 1989
Finalists – Deportivo Cali 1978. America de Cali 1985, 1986, 1987

CLUB DIRECTORY

BOGOTA (Population – 4260000)

Deportivo Club Los Millonarios
Stadium: El Campin 52000
Founded: 1938
Colours: Blue/White
Previous name: Deportivo Municipal 1938–46

Club Independiente Santa Fé
Stadium: El Campin 52000
Founded: 1941
Colours: Red with white sleeves/White

MEDELLIN (Population – 2095000)

Club Deportivo Independiente Medellín
Stadium: Antanasio Girardot 36000
Founded: 1914
Colours: Red/Blue

Club Atletico Nacional Medellín
Stadium: Antanasio Girardot 36000
Founded: 1936
Colours: Green and white stripes/White

CALI (Population – 1400000)

Club Deportivo América Cali
Stadium: Pascual Guerrero 61000
Founded: 1924
Colours: Red/Red

Asociacion Deportivo Cali
Stadium: Pascual Guerrero 61000
Founded: 1918
Colours: Green/White
Previous name: Cali Futebol Club 1908–47

BARRANQUILLA (Population – 1140000)
Club Atletico Junior
Stadium: Romelito Martinez 20000 or Metropolitano 60000
Founded: 1948
Colours: Red and white stripes/Blue

BUCARAMANGA (Population – 550000)
Deportiva Atletico Bucaramanga
Stadium: Alfonso Lopez 20000
Founded: 1949
Colours: Yellow/Green

CARTAGENA (Population – 531000)
Real Cartagena
Stadium: Cartagena 8000
Founded: 1949
Colours: Black and yellow stripes/Black
Previous name: Club Deportivo Sporting Barranquilla 1949–91

CUCUTA (Population – 445000)
Corporacion Nuevo Cúcuta Deportivo
Stadium: General Santander 10000
Founded: 1949
Colours: Black and red halves/White

PEREIRA (Population – 390000)
Corporacion Social y Cultural de Pereira
Stadium: Hernan Ramirez Villegas 42000
Founded: 1944
Colours: Yellow/Red

MANIZALES (Population – 330000)
Club Once Philips
Stadium: Fernando Londono y Londono 17000
Founded: 1947
Colours: White/White
Previous names: Deportes Caldas, Once Caldas, Crystal Caldas

IBAGUE (Population – 292000)
Club Deportes Tolima
Stadium: Manuel Murillo Toro 20000
Founded: 1954
Colours: Yellow with white sleeves/Red

ARMENIA (Population – 187000)
Corporacion Centenario Deportes Quindio
Stadium: Centenario 35000
Founded: 1951
Colours: Green with a yellow V on the front/White

SANTA MARTA (Population – 177000)
Asociacion Deportiva Union Magdalena
Stadium: Eduardo Santos 18000
Founded: 1950
Colours: Blue and red stripes/Blue

COLOMBIAN LEAGUE CHAMPIONSHIP

1948	Independiente Santa Fé
1949	Millonarios
1950	Deportes Caldas
1951	Millonarios
1952	Millonarios
1953	Millonarios
1954	At. Nacional Medellín
1955	Independiente Medellín
1956	Atletico Quindio
1957	Independiente Medellín
1958	Independiente Santa Fé
1959	Millionarios
1960	Independiente Santa Fé
1961	Millonarios
1962	Millonarios
1963	Millonarios
1964	Millonarios
1965	Deportivo Cali
1966	Independiente Santa Fé
1967	Deportivo Cali
1968	Union Magdalena
1969	Deportivo Cali
1970	Deportivo Cali
1971	Independiente Santa Fé
1972	Millonarios
1973	At. Nacional Medellín
1974	Deportivo Cali
1975	Independiente Santa Fé
1976	At. Nacional Medellín
1977	Atletico Junior
1978	Millonarios
1979	America Cali
1980	Atletico Junior
1981	At. Nacional Medellín
1982	America Cali
1983	America Cali
1984	America Cali
1985	America Cali
1986	America Cali
1987	Millonarios
1988	Millonarios
1989	–
1990	America Cali
1991	At. Nacional Medellín

INTERNATIONAL MATCHES PLAYED BY COLOMBIA

Date	Opponents	Result		Venue	Compet	Scorers
10–02–1938	Mexico	L	1–3	Panama City	CG	
12–02	Panama	W	4–0	Panama City	CG	
14–02	Costa Rica	L	1–3	Panama City	CG	
18–02	El Salvador	W	3–2	Panama City	CG	
22–02	Venezuela	L	1–2	Panama City	CG	
8–08	Peru	L	2–4	Bogota	BG	Botto 2
10–08	Ecuador	L	1–2	Bogota	BG	
13–08	Venezuela	W	2–0	Bogota	BG	Umana, Torres
16–08	Bolivia	L	1–2	Bogota	BG	Mejia
21–01–1945	Brazil	L	0–3	Santiago	SC	
28–01	Uruguay	L	0–7	Santiago	SC	
31–01	Chile	L	0–2	Santiago	SC	
7–02	Argentina	L	1–9	Santiago	SC	Mendoza
18–02	Ecuador	W	3–1	Santiago	SC	Mendoza, Berdugo, Granados
21–02	Bolivia	D	3–3	Santiago	SC	Berdugo, Granados, Gamez
9–12–1946	Curacao	W	4–2	Barranquilla	CG	Rubio, Granados 2, Berdugo
12–12	Venezuela	W	3–1	Barranquilla	CG	
14–12	Guatemala	W	4–2	Barranquilla	CG	
16–12	Puerto Rico	W	4–1	Barranquilla	CG	
18–12	Costa Rica	W	4–1	Barranquilla	CG	Rubio 2, Garcia, Granados
20–12	Panama	W	2–1	Barranquilla	CG	Rubio, Arango
2–12–1947	Uruguay	L	0–2	Guayaquil	SC	
4–12	Ecuador	D	0–0	Guayaquil	SC	
13–12	Bolivia	D	0–0	Guayaquil	SC	
18–12	Argentina	L	0–6	Guayaquil	SC	
20–12	Paraguay	L	0–2	Guayaquil	SC	
23–12	Peru	L	1–5	Guayaquil	SC	Arango
29–12	Chile	L	1–4	Guayaquil	SC	Granados
6–04–1949	Paraguay	L	0–3	Sao Paulo	SC	
10–04	Peru	L	0–4	Rio de Janeiro	SC	
17–04	Brazil	L	0–5	Sao Paulo	SC	
20–04	Chile	D	1–1	Rio de Janeiro	SC	Berdugo
24–04	Uruguay	D	2–2	Sao Paulo	SC	Castelbondo, Perez
3–05	Ecuador	L	1–4	Rio de Janeiro	SC	Rubio
6–05	Bolivia	L	0–4	Rio de Janeiro	SC	
13–03–1957	Argentina	L	2–8	Lima	SC	Gamboa, Valencia
17–03	Uruguay	W	1–0	Lima	SC	Arango
21–03	Chile	L	2–3	Lima	SC	Arango, Carrillo
24–03	Brazil	L	0–9	Lima	SC	
27–03	Peru	L	1–4	Lima	SC	Arango
1–04	Ecuador	W	4–1	Lima	SC	Alvarez, Gutierrez, Gamboa 2
16–06	Uruguay	D	1–1	Bogota	WCq	Arango
20–06	Paraguay	L	2–3	Bogota	WCq	Gutierrez, Diaz R
23–06	Paraguay	L	1–2	Medellin	Fr	Panesso
30–06	Uruguay	L	0–1	Montevideo	WCq	
7–07	Paraguay	L	0–3	Asuncion	WCq	
30–04–1961	Peru	W	1–0	Bogota	WCq	Escobar
7–05	Peru	D	1–1	Lima	WCq	Gonzalez H
1–04–1962	Mexico	L	0–1	Bogota	Fr	
4–04	Mexico	D	2–2	Cali	Fr	Klinger, Gamboa
25–04	Mexico	L	0–1	Mexico City	Fr	
30–05	Uruguay	L	1–2	Arica	WCr1	Zuluaga
3–06	Soviet Union	D	4–4	Arica	WCr1	Aceros, Coll, Rada, Klinger
7–06	Yugoslavia	L	0–5	Arica	WCr1	
10–03–1963	Argentina	L	2–4	Cochabamba	SC	Campillo, Aceros
14–03	Brazil	L	1–5	La Paz	SC	Gamboa
17–03	Bolivia	L	1–2	Cochabamba	SC	Botero
20–03	Paraguay	L	2–3	Cochabamba	SC	OG, Campillo
24–03	Peru	D	1–1	La Paz	SC	Salla
31–03	Ecuador	L	3–4	La Paz	SC	Salla 2, Gamboa
1–09	Costa Rica	L	4–5	Bogota	Fr	
4–09	Costa Rica	W	1–0	Cali	Fr	
20–07–1965	Ecuador	L	0–1	Barranquilla	WCq	
25–07	Ecuador	L	0–2	Guayaquil	WCq	
1–08	Chile	L	2–7	Santiago	WCq	Segrera 2

7–08	Chile	W	2–0	Barranquilla	WCq	Rada 2
30–11–1966	Chile	L	2–5	Santiago	SCq	Gamboa, Canon
11–12	Chile	D	0–0	Bogota	SCq	
18–08–1968	Argentina	L	0–1	Cali	Fr	
16–10	Mexico	L	0–1	Bogota	Fr	
4–02–1969	Mexico	L	0–1	Leon	Fr	
20–02	Soviet Union	L	1–3	Bogota	Fr	Santa
8–05	Peru	L	1–3	Bogota	Fr	Gonzalez J
15–06	Chile	D	3–3	Bogota	Fr	Gonzalez J 2, Gallego
18–06	Peru	D	1–1	Lima	Fr	Gallego
22–06	Ecuador	L	1–4	Guayaquil	Fr	Gonzalez J
2–07	Uruguay	L	0–1	Cali	Fr	
15–07	Chile	D	3–3	Bogota	Fr	Gonzalez J 2, Gallego
27–07	Venezuela	W	3–0	Bogota	WCq	Gonzalez J 2, Segrera
2–08	Venezuela	D	1–1	Caracas	WCq	Tamayo
6–08	Brazil	L	0–2	Bogota	WCq	
10–08	Paraguay	L	0–1	Bogota	WCq	
21–08	Brazil	L	2–6	Rio de Janeiro	WCq	Mesa, Gallego
24–08	Paraguay	L	1–2	Asuncion	WCq	Segrera
20–05–1970	England	L	0–4	Bogota	Fr	
29–03–1972	Peru	D	1–1	Bogota	Fr	Moron
3–06	Venezuela	L	1–2	Caracas	Fr	Brand
6–06	Peru	D	0–0	Lima	Fr	
18–06	France	L	2–3	Salvador	Clr1	Pineros, Mesa
22–06	Argentina	L	1–4	Salvador	Clr1	Moron
15–02–1973	East Germany	L	0–2	Bogota	Fr	
27–05	Haiti	W	2–1	Port-au-Prince	Fr	Moron, Diaz E
29–05	Haiti	L	1–2	Port-au-Prince	Fr	Moron
21–06	Ecuador	D	1–1	Bogota	WCq	Ortiz
24–06	Uruguay	D	0–0	Bogota	WCq	
28–06	Ecuador	D	1–1	Guayaquil	WCq	Ortiz
1–07	Peru	L	1–3	Lima	Fr	Moron
5–07	Uruguay	W	1–0	Montevideo	WCq	Ortiz
20–07–1975	Paraguay	W	1–0	Bogota	SCr1	Diaz E
27–07	Ecuador	W	3–1	Quito	SCr1	Ortiz, Retat, Castro
30–07	Paraguay	W	1–0	Asuncion	SCr1	Diaz E
7–08	Ecuador	W	2–0	Bogota	SCr1	Diaz E, Calero
21–09	Uruguay	W	3–0	Bogota	SCsf	Angulo, Ortiz, Diaz E
1–10	Uruguay	L	0–1	Montevideo	SCsf	
16–10	Peru	W	1–0	Bogota	SCf	Castro
22–10	Peru	L	0–2	Lima	SCf	
28–10	Peru	L	0–1	Caracas	SCf	
15–10–1976	Uruguay	L	1–2	Bogota	Fr	Rios
16–01–1977	Ecuador	L	0–1	Cali	Fr	
26–01	Ecuador	L	1–4	Quito	Fr	Retat
30–01	Yugoslavia	L	0–1	Bogota	Fr	
20–02	Brazil	D	0–0	Bogota	WCq	
24–02	Paraguay	L	0–1	Bogota	WCq	
6–03	Paraguay	D	1–1	Asuncion	WCq	Vilarete E
9–03	Brazil	L	0–6	Rio de Janeiro	WCq	
18–07–1979	Peru	W	1–0	Lima	Fr	Ortiz
25–07	Peru	L	1–2	Bogota	Fr	Ortiz
1–08	Venezuela	D	0–0	San Cristobal	SCr1	
15–08	Chile	W	1–0	Bogota	SCr1	Diaz E
22–08	Venezuela	W	4–0	Bogota	SCr1	Iguaran, Valverde, Chaparro, Moron
5–09	Chile	L	0–2	Santiago	SCr1	
5–01–1980	Venezuela	D	0–0	Caracas	Fr	
9–07	Poland	L	1–4	Bogota	Fr	Herrera
1–02–1981	Brazil	D	1–1	Bogota	Fr	Vilarete E
10–03	Chile	L	0–1	Santiago	Fr	
15–03	Paraguay	W	2–0	Asuncion	Fr	Vilarete E 2
19–03	Chile	L	1–2	Bogota	Fr	Ortiz
2–07	Spain	D	1–1	Bogota	Fr	Herrera
26–07	Peru	D	1–1	Bogota	WCq	Herrera
9–08	Uruguay	L	2–3	Montevideo	WCq	Sarmiento, Herrera
16–08	Peru	L	0–2	Lima	WCq	
13–09	Uruguay	D	1–1	Bogota	WCq	Herrera
14–07–1983	Chile	D	2–2	Bogota	Fr	Valderrama D 2
26–07	Ecuador	D	0–0	Quito	Fr	

29–07	Ecuador	D	0–0	Bogota	Fr	
14–08	Bolivia	W	1–0	La Paz	SCr1	Valderrama D
17–08	Peru	L	0–1	Lima	SCr1	
28–08	Peru	D	2–2	Bogota	SCr1	Prince, Fiorillo
31–08	Bolivia	D	2–2	Bogota	SCr1	Valderrama D, Molina
23–01–1984	El Salvador	W	1–0	San Salvador	Fr	
26–07	Peru	D	1–1	Medellin	Fr	Prince
9–08	Peru	D	0–0	Lima	Fr	
24–08	Argentina	W	1–0	Bogota	Fr	Prince
9–10	Mexico	L	0–1	Los Angeles	Fr	
11–10	United States	L	0–1	Los Angeles	Fr	
1–02–1985	Switzerland	D	2–2	Bogota	Fr	Valderrama, Sarmiento
10–02	Poland	L	1–2	Bogota	Fr	Cordoba
14–02	Poland	W	1–0	Cali	Fr	Sarmiento
21–02	Chile	D	1–1	Santiago	Fr	Vilarete E
24–02	Uruguay	L	0–3	Montevideo	Fr	
28–02	Paraguay	W	3–0	Asuncion	Fr	Cordoba, Iguaran, Vilarete E
17–04	Paraguay	W	1–0	Pereira	Fr	Herrera
19–04	Paraguay	D	2–2	Bogota	Fr	Iguaran, Ortiz
25–04	Brazil	L	1–2	Belo Horizonte	Fr	Prince
28–04	Uruguay	W	2–1	Bogota	Fr	Ortiz, Iguaran
15–05	Brazil	W	1–0	Bogota	Fr	Lugo
26–05	Peru	W	1–0	Bogota	WCq	Prince
2–06	Argentina	L	1–3	Bogota	WCq	Prince
9–06	Peru	D	0–0	Lima	WCq	
16–06	Argentina	L	0–1	Buenos Aries	WCq	
23–06	Venezuela	D	2–2	San Cristobal	WCq	Ortiz, Herrera
30–06	Venezuela	W	2–0	Bogota	WCq	Cordoba, Herrera
27–10	Paraguay	L	0–3	Asuncion	WCq	
3–11	Paraguay	W	2–1	Cali	WCq	Angulo, Ortiz
11–06–1987	Ecuador	W	1–0	Medellin	Fr	Alvarez
14–06	Ecuador	L	0–3	Guayaquil	Fr	
1–07	Bolivia	W	2–0	Rosario	SCr1	Valderrama C, Iguaran
5–07	Paraguay	W	3–0	Rosario	SCr1	Iguaran 3
8–07	Chile	L	1–2	Cordoba	SCsf	Redin
11–07	Argentina	W	2–1	Buenos Aries	SC3p	Gomez, Galleano
30–03–1988	Canada	W	3–0	Armenia	Fr	Perea, Valderrama C, Trellez
14–05	United States	W	2–0	Miami	Fr	Iguaran 2
17–05	Scotland	D	0–0	Glasgow	Fr	
19–05	Finland	W	3–1	Helsinki	Fr	Arango, Higuita, Iguaran
24–05	England	D	1–1	London	Fr	Escobar
7–08	Uruguay	W	2–1	Bogota	Fr	Iguaran, Redin
3–02–1989	Peru	W	1–0	Pereira	Fr	Higuita
5–02	Chile	W	1–0	Armenia	Fr	Redin
9–03	Argentina	W	1–0	Barranquilla	Fr	Iguaran
24–06	United States	W	1–0	Miami	Fr	Valderrama C
27–06	Haiti	W	4–0	Miami	Fr	Trellez, Iguaran, Valderrama C, De Avila
3–07	Venezuela	W	4–2	Salvador	SCr1	Higuita, Iguaran 2, De Avila
5–07	Paraguay	L	0–1	Salvador	SCr1	
7–07	Brazil	D	0–0	Salvador	SCr1	
9–07	Peru	D	1–1	Recife	SCr1	Iguaran
6–08	Uruguay	D	0–0	Montevideo	Fr	
20–08	Ecuador	W	2–0	Barranquilla	WCq	Iguaran 2
27–08	Paraguay	L	1–2	Asuncion	WCq	Iguaran
3–09	Ecuador	D	0–0	Guayaquil	WCq	
17–09	Paraguay	W	2–1	Barranquilla	WCq	Iguaran, Hernandez
15–10	Israel	W	1–0	Barranquila	WCq	Usuriaga
30–10	Israel	D	0–0	Tel Aviv	WCq	
2–02–1990	Uruguay	L	0–2	Miami	Fr	
4–02	United States	D	1–1	Miami	Fr	Fajardo
20–02	Soviet Union	D	0–0	Los Angeles	Fr	
17–04	Mexico	L	0–2	Los Angeles	Fr	
22–04	United States	W	1–0	Miami	Fr	Guerrero
4–05	Poland	W	2–1	Chicago	Fr	Estrada, Iguaran
26–05	Egypt	D	1–1	Cairo	Fr	Rincon
2–06	Hungary	L	1–3	Budapest	Fr	Rincon
9–06	UAE	W	2–0	Bologna	WCr1	Redin, Valderrama
14–06	Yugoslavia	L	0–1	Bologna	WCr1	
19–06	West Germany	D	1–1	Milan	WCr1	Rincon

23–06	Cameroon	L	1–2	Naples	WCr2	Redin
29–01–1991	Mexico	D	0–0	Leon	Fr	
3–02	Switzerland	L	2–3	Miami	Fr	De Avila, Rincon
5–06	Sweden	D	2–2	Stockholm	Fr	Rincon, Iguaran
25–06	Costa Rica	W	1–0	San Jose	Fr	De Avila
7–07	Ecuador	W	1–0	Valparaiso	SCr1	De Avila
11–07	Bolivia	D	0–0	Vina del Mar	SCr1	
13–07	Brazil	W	2–0	Vina del Mar	SCr1	De Avila, Iguaran
15–07	Uruguay	L	0–1	Vina del Mar	SCr1	
17–07	Chile	D	1–1	Santiago	SCr2	Iguaran
19–07	Brazil	L	0–2	Santiago	SCr2	
21–07	Argentina	L	1–2	Santiago	SCr2	De Avila

ECUADOR

'Thank goodness for Colombia' would be a good motto for Ecuadorian football, for if it had not been for victories over their South American neighbours in the Bolivaran Games of 1938 and South American Championships of 1949, Ecuador would have been left without a win in their first twenty years of international football.

Guayaquil, the economic capital and chief port of Ecuador, unsurprisingly saw the first football, and in 1925 the Federación Deportiva Guayaquil was formed, a name later changed to the Federación Deportiva Nacional del Ecuador. This body controlled football as well as other sports, and it was not until 1957, with the creation of the Asociación Ecuatoriana de Fútbol, that football was governed by a separate body. Up until this time there was not much need for one. Regional associations oversaw competitions in all of the major cities, and outings for the international side were restricted to the South American Championships after their debut in the 1938 Bolivaran Games.

The formation of the national championship in 1957 was an effort to bring the clubs of Guayaquil and Quito, the capital, into regular competition with each other. There is a fierce rivalry between the two cities, not just in sport, and between them they have won just about every championship played, with the exception of 1961 and 1962 when Everest won the title twice.

The major clubs from Guayaquil are Barcelona and Emelec, whilst in Quito, high up in the Andes, Deportivo Quito and Nacional Quito are joined by the last of the big five, Liga Deportivo Universitaria. They may dominate Ecuadorian football but their impact on South American football on the whole has been limited. Though semi-finalists in the Copa Libertadores on eight occasions, this has more to do with being grouped in the first round with clubs from either Venezuela or Bolivia than football prowess, with one notable exception.

In 1990, Barcelona made it right the way to the final after beating Progreso from Uruguay, Emelec and most impressively River Plate from Argentina on the way. The semi-final win over River Plate is perhaps the best performance to date by a team from Ecuador even if it did need penalties to separate the teams after the two legs had ended in 1–0 victories for the home sides.

In the final against Olimpia from Paraguay, Barcelona lost the tie in the second half of the first match in Asuncion. There was no way back from a two-goal deficit despite a capacity crowd in the home leg in Guayaquil and they went down 3–1 on aggregate.

Their final appearance does show that football in Ecuador is not stagnating and is showing signs of progress. From being the whipping boys at the South American Championships, though they are not seriously challenging for honours, they are no longer automatic walkovers and in 1989 and 1991 finished above Peru, Bolivia and Venezuela in the final championship rankings. They have come a long way since winning just eight games between 1938 and 1975.

Ecuador's first entry into the World Cup was not at all successful as they lost heavily to Argentina in the two games played in 1962, but the attempt to qualify for England in 1966 proved to be the closest they have ever

		Total			League	Copa Lib		
		G	S	B	G	G	S	B
1	Barcelona SC	10	1	4	10	–	1	4
2	CD Nacional	9	–	1	9	–	–	1
3	CS Emelec	6	–	–	6	–	–	–
4	LD Universitaria	4	–	2	4	–	–	2
5	Deportivo Quito	2	–	–	2	–	–	–
	Everest	2	–	–	2	–	–	–

Correct to the end of the 1991 season

come to qualifying. Two of the eight aforementioned wins came against Colombia within the space of five days, and a 2–2 draw with Chile at home meant a draw in Santiago would have seen them through. The 3–1 defeat still meant, however, that they would have to play off. Hopes were high for victory in neutral Lima, but it was not to be as they went down 2–1. Since then they have never seriously threatened to qualify, finishing last in their group on all but one occasion.

Playing that day for Ecuador was their most famous player of all time, Alberto Spencer. He, like most Ecuadorians of repute, ended up playing his football abroad. He made a great reputation for himself throughout South America and Europe with Peñarol, a team he helped to many honours. He also holds the distinctive record of being the record goalscorer in the Copa Libertadores with over 50 goals, a record, like Di Stéfano's in European competitions, that is unlikely to be beaten.

Uruguay may have complained in the past of Italians poaching their players and then playing them in the national side, but they were quite capable of doing the same. Spencer ended up not only playing his club football in Uruguay, but he also appeared in the Uruguay national team.

Population: 10 782 000
Area, sq km: 269 178
% in urban areas: 54%
Capital city: Quito

Asociación Ecuatoriana de Fútbol
Calle Jose Mascote #1.103
Castilla 7447
Guayaquil
Ecuador
Tel: (010 593) 4 371674
Fax: (010 593) 4 373320
Telex: 42970 FEECFU ED
Cable: ECUAFUTBOL GUAYAQUIL
Languages for correspondence: Spanish

Year of formation: 1925
Affiliation to FIFA: 1926
Affiliation to CONMEBOL: 1930
Registered clubs: 170
Registered players: 31 000
Professional players: 470
Registered coaches: 87
Registered referees: 170
National stadium: Modelo, Guayaquil 48000
National colours: Shirts: Yellow/Shorts: Blue/Socks: Red
Reserve colours: Shirts: White/Shorts: White/Socks: White
Season: March–December

THE RECORD

WORLD CUP

1930–58 ..... Did not enter
1962 .... QT 2nd/2 in group 1
1966 .... QT 2nd/3 in group 2
1970 .... QT 3rd/3 in group 3
1974 .... QT 3rd/3 in group 1
1978 .... QT 3rd/3 in group 3
1982 .... QT 2nd/3 in group 3
1986 .... QT 3rd/3 in group 2
1990 .... QT 3rd/3 in group 2

SOUTH AMERICAN CHAMPIONSHIP

1910–37 ..... –
1939 .... 5th/5
1941 .... 5th/5
1942 .... 7th/7
1945 .... 7th/7
1946 .... –
1947 .... 6th/8
1949 .... 7th/8
1953 .... 7th/7
1955 .... 6th/6
1956 .... –
1957 .... 7th/7
1959 .... –
1959 .... 4th/7
1963 .... 6th/7
1967 .... –
1975 .... 9th/10/1st round
1979 .... 9th/10/1st round
1983 .... 9th/10/1st round
1987 .... 8th/10/1st round
1989 .... 7th/10/1st round
1991 .... 7th/10/1st round

OLYMPIC GAMES

1908–60 ..... Did not enter
1964 .... QT Failed to qualify
1968 .... Did not enter
1972 .... QT Failed to qualify
1976 .... Did not enter
1980 .... Did not enter
1984 .... QT Failed to qualify
1988 .... QT Failed to qualify
1992 .... QT Failed to qualify

COPA LIBERTADORES

Finalists – Barcelona 1990

CLUB DIRECTORY

QUITO (Population – 1 050 000)

Club Deportivo America
Stadium: Olimpico de Batan 25 000
Founded: 1939
Colours: Green/White

Sociedad Deportivo Aucas
Stadium: Chillogallo 20 000
Founded: 1945
Colours: Yellow/Yellow

Sociedad Deportivo Quito
Stadium: Atahualpa 40 000
Founded: 1955
Colours: Blue and red stripes/White

Liga Deportivo Universitaria (LDU)
Stadium: Atahualpa 40 000
Founded: 1930
Colours: White with a red U on the front/White

Club Deportivo Nacional
Stadium: Atahualpa 40 000
Founded: 1963
Colours: Grey with a red, blue and sky blue sash/Red

Universidad Catolica Club Deportivo
Stadium: Atahualpa 40 000
Founded: 1965
Colours: Sky blue with a white U on the front/Blue

GUAYAQUIL (Population – 1 255 000)

Barcelona Sporting Club
Stadium: Monumental 55 000
Founded: 1925
Colours: Yellow/Black

Club Sport Emelec
Stadium: Capwell 25 000
Founded: 1929
Colours: Blue with grey sash/Blue

Deportivo Filabanco
Stadium: Modelo 48 000
Founded: 1979
Colours: Orange/Orange

Asociacion Deportivo Nueve De Octubre
Stadium: Los Chirijos 10 000
Founded: 1926
Colours: Red/White

CUENCA (Population – 157 000)
Club Deportivo Cuenca
Stadium: Serrano Aguilar 15 000
Founded: 1971
Colours: Red/Black

MACHALA (Population – 108 000)
Club Deportivo Audax Octubrino
Stadium: Estadio 9 de Mayo 25 000

Founded: 1948
Colours: White/White

PORTOVIEJO (Population – 102 000)
Liga Deportivo Universitaria Portoviejo
Stadium: Reales Tamarindos 25 000
Founded: 1969
Colours: White with a green U on the front/White

AMBATO (Population – 100 000)
Macara Ambato
Stadium: Bellavista 20 000
Founded: 1939
Colours: Sky Blue/Blue

Club Tecnico Universitario
Stadium: Bellavista 20 000
Founded: 1971
Colours: Red with white sleeves/Red

ESMERALDAS (Population – 91 000)
Juventus
Stadium: Teodoro Folke Anderson 25 000
Founded: 1979
Colours: Red and white stripes/Red

Club Deportivo Esmeraldas Petrolero
Stadium: Teodoro Folke Anderson 25 000
Founded: 1977
Colours: White/Blue

RIOBAMBA (Population – 75 000)
River Plate
Stadium: Olimpico 25 000
Founded: 1950
Colours: White with red sash/Black

QUEVEDO (Population – 67 000)
Deportivo Quevedo
Stadium: 7 de Octubre 20 000
Founded: 1950
Colours: Red with a blue band on chest/Blue

ECUADORIAN LEAGUE CHAMPIONS

1957	Emelec
1958–59	–
1960	Emelec
1961	Everest
1962	Everest
1963	Barcelona
1964	Deportivo Quito
1965	Emelec
1966	Barcelona
1967	Nacional Quito
1968	Deportivo Quito
1969	Liga Deportiva Universitaria
1970	Barcelona
1971	Barcelona
1972	Emelec
1973	Liga Deportivo Universitaria
1974	Nacional Quito
1975	Liga Deportivo Universitaria
1976	Nacional Quito
1977	Nacional Quito
1978	Nacional Quito
1979	Emelec
1980	Barcelona
1981	Barcelona
1982	Nacional Quito
1983	Nacional Quito
1984	Nacional Quito
1985	Barcelona
1986	Nacional Quito
1987	Barcelona
1988	Emelec
1989	Barcelona
1990	Liga Deportivo Universitaria
1991	Barcelona

INTERNATIONAL MATCHES PLAYED BY ECUADOR

Date	Opponents		Result	Venue	
8-08-1938	Bolivia	D	1–1	Bogota	BG
10–08	Colombia	W	2–1	Bogota	BG
11–08	Peru	L	1–9	Bogota	BG
19–08	Venezuela	L	2–5	Bogota	BG
22–08	Bolivia	L	1–2	Bogota	BG
15–01–1939	Peru	L	2–5	Lima	SC
22–01	Uruguay	L	0–6	Lima	SC
5–02	Chile	L	1–4	Lima	SC
12–02	Paraguay	L	1–3	Lima	SC
2–02–1941	Chile	L	0–5	Santiago	SC
9–02	Uruguay	L	0–6	Santiago	SC
16–02	Argentina	L	1–6	Santiago	SC
23–02	Peru	L	0–4	Santiago	SC
18–01–1942	Uruguay	L	0–7	Montevideo	SC
22–01	Argentina	L	0–12	Montevideo	SC
25–01	Paraguay	L	1–3	Montevideo	SC
28–01	Peru	L	1–2	Montevideo	SC
1–02	Brazil	L	1–5	Montevideo	SC
5–02	Chile	L	1–2	Montevideo	SC
14–01–1945	Chile	L	3–6	Santiago	SC
24–01	Uruguay	L	1–5	Santiago	SC
31–01	Argentina	L	2–4	Santiago	SC
11–02	Bolivia	D	0–0	Santiago	SC
18–02	Colombia	L	1–3	Santiago	SC
21–02	Brazil	L	2–9	Santiago	SC
30–11–1947	Bolivia	D	2–2	Guayaquil	SC
4–12	Colombia	D	0–0	Guayaquil	SC
11–12	Chile	L	0–3	Guayaquil	SC
16–12	Uruguay	L	1–6	Guayaquil	SC
20–12	Peru	D	0–0	Guayaquil	SC
25–12	Argentina	L	0–2	Guayaquil	SC
29–12	Paraguay	L	0–4	Guayaquil	SC
3–04–1949	Brazil	L	1–9	Rio de Janeiro	SC
10–04	Paraguay	L	0–1	Rio de Janeiro	SC
13–04	Uruguay	L	2–3	Rio de Janeiro	SC
17–04	Chile	L	0–1	Rio de Janeiro	SC
20–04	Peru	L	0–4	Rio de Janeiro	SC
24–04	Bolivia	L	0–2	Sao Paulo	SC
3–05	Colombia	W	4–1	Rio de Janeiro	SC
28–02–1953	Peru	L	0–1	Lima	SC
4–03	Paraguay	D	0–0	Lima	SC
8–03	Bolivia	D	1–1	Lima	SC
12–03	Brazil	L	0–2	Lima	SC
19–03	Chile	L	0–3	Lima	SC
23–03	Uruguay	L	0–6	Lima	SC
27–02–1955	Chile	L	1–7	Santiago	SC
9–03	Argentina	L	0–4	Santiago	SC
13–03	Peru	L	2–4	Santiago	SC
16–03	Paraguay	L	0–2	Santiago	SC
23–03	Uruguay	L	1–5	Santiago	SC
7–03–1957	Uruguay	L	2–5	Lima	SC
10–03	Peru	L	1–2	Lima	SC
17–03	Argentina	L	0–3	Lima	SC
21–03	Brazil	L	1–7	Lima	SC
24–03	Chile	D	2–2	Lima	SC
1–04	Colombia	L	1–4	Lima	SC
6–12–1959	Uruguay	L	0–4	Guayaquil	SC
12–12	Argentina	D	1–1	Guayaquil	SC
19–12	Brazil	L	1–3	Guayaquil	SC
25–12	Paraguay	W	3–1	Guayaquil	SC
27–12	Brazil	L	1–2	Guayaquil	Fr
4–12–1960	Argentina	L	3–6	Guayaquil	WCq
17–12	Argentina	L	0–5	Buenos Aires	WCq
10–03–1963	Bolivia	D	4–4	La Paz	SC
14–03	Paraguay	L	1–3	La Paz	SC
17–03	Peru	L	1–2	La Paz	SC
20–03	Argentina	L	2–4	Cochabamba	SC
27–03	Brazil	D	2–2	Cochabamba	SC
31–03	Colombia	W	4–3	La Paz	SC
20–07–1965	Colombia	W	1–0	Barranquilla	WCq
25–07	Colombia	W	2–0	Guayaquil	WCq
15–08	Chile	D	2–2	Guayaquil	WCq
22–08	Chile	L	1–3	Santiago	WCq
12–10	Chile	L	1–2	Lima	WCq
21–12–1966	Paraguay	D	2–2	Guayaquil	SCq

28–12	Paraguay	L	1–3	Asuncion	SCq
22–06–1969	Colombia	W	4–1	Guayaquil	Fr
6–07	Uruguay	L	0–2	Guayaquil	WCq
20–07	Uruguay	L	0–1	Montevideo	WCq
27–07	Chile	L	1–4	Santiago	WCq
3–08	Chile	D	1–1	Guayaquil	WCq
29–04–1970	Mexico	L	2–4	Leon	Fr
3–05	Mexico	L	2–3	Mexico City	Fr
24–05	England	L	0–2	Quito	Fr
11–06–1972	Portugal	L	0–3	Natal	Clr1
14–06	Chile	L	1–2	Natal	Clr1
18–06	Rep. Ireland	L	2–3	Natal	Clr1
21–06	Iran	D	1–1	Recife	Clr1
18–02–1973	East Germany	D	1–1	Quito	Fr
24–04	Chile	D	1–1	Guayaquil	Fr
29–04	Bolivia	D	3–3	La Paz	Fr
6–05	Bolivia	D	0–0	Quito	Fr
12–05	Haiti	W	2–1	Port au Prince	Fr
15–05	Haiti	L	0–1	Port au Prince	Fr
21–06	Colombia	D	1–1	Bogota	WCq
28–06	Colombia	D	1–1	Guayaquil	WCq
1–07	Uruguay	L	1–2	Quito	WCq
8–07	Uruguay	L	0–4	Montevideo	WCq
22–06–1975	Peru	W	6–0	Quito	Fr
25–06	Peru	W	1–0	Guayaquil	Fr
1–07	Peru	L	0–2	Lima	Fr
9–07	Bolivia	L	0–1	Cochabamba	Fr
24–07	Paraguay	D	2–2	Guayaquil	SCr1
27–07	Colombia	L	1–3	Quito	SCr1
7–08	Colombia	L	0–2	Bogota	SCr1
10–08	Paraguay	L	1–3	Asuncion	SCr1
20–10–1976	Uruguay	D	2–2	Quito	Fr
4–01–1977	Uruguay	D	1–1	Montevideo	Fr
9–01	Paraguay	L	0–2	Asuncion	Fr
16–01	Colombia	W	1–0	Cali	Fr
20–01	Venezuela	L	0–1	Caracas	Fr
26–01	Colombia	W	4–1	Quito	Fr
13–02	Paraguay	W	2–1	Quito	Fr
20–02	Peru	D	1–1	Quito	WCq
27–02	Chile	L	0–1	Guayaquil	WCq
12–03	Peru	L	0–4	Lima	WCq
20–03	Chile	L	0–3	Santiago	WCq
13–06–1979	Chile	D	0–0	Santiago	Fr
21–06	Chile	W	2–1	Guayaquil	Fr
11–07	Peru	L	1–2	Lima	Fr
8–08	Peru	W	2–1	Quito	Fr
29–08	Paraguay	L	1–2	Quito	SCr1
5–09	Uruguay	W	2–1	Guayaquil	SCr1
13–09	Paraguay	L	0–2	Asuncion	SCr1
16–09	Uruguay	L	1–2	Montevideo	SCr1
27–01–1981	Bulgaria	L	1–3	Quito	Fr
14–02	Brazil	L	0–6	Quito	Fr
17–05	Paraguay	W	1–0	Guayaquil	WCq
24–05	Chile	D	0–0	Guayaquil	WCq
31–05	Paraguay	L	1–3	Asuncion	WCq
14–06	Chile	L	0–2	Santiago	WCq
26–07–1983	Colombia	D	0–0	Quito	Fr
29–07	Colombia	D	0–0	Bogota	Fr
10–08	Argentina	D	2–2	Quito	SCr1
17–08	Brazil	L	0–1	Quito	SCr1
1–09	Brazil	L	0–5	Goiania	SCr1
7–09	Argentina	D	2–2	Buenos Aires	SCr1
22–01–1984	Romania	L	1–3	Guayaquil	Fr
30–11	United States	D	0–0	New York	Fr
2–12	United States	D	2–2	Miami	Fr
4–12	Mexico	L	2–3	Los Angeles	Fr
7–12	Honduras	D	0–0	Tegucigalpa	Fr
9–12	Guatemala	L	0–1	Guatemala City	Fr
12–12	El Salvador	D	0–0	San Salvador	Fr
6–02–1985	East Germany	L	2–3	Guayaquil	Fr
17–02	Finland	W	3–1	Ambato	Fr
21–02	Bolivia	W	3–0	Quito	Fr
3–03	Chile	D	1–1	Quito	WCq
10–03	Uruguay	L	1–2	Montevideo	WCq
17–03	Chile	L	2–6	Santiago	WCq
21–03	Peru	L	0–1	Lima	Fr
31–03	Uruguay	L	0–2	Quito	WCq
27–02–1987	Cuba	L	1–2	Havana	Fr
2–03	Cuba	D	0–0	Havana	Fr
11–06	Colombia	L	0–1	Medellin	Fr
14–06	Colombia	W	3–0	Guayaquil	Fr
19–06	Uruguay	L	1–2	Montevideo	Fr
21–06	Brazil	L	1–4	Florianopolis	Fr
2–07	Argentina	L	0–3	Buenos Aires	SCr1
4–07	Peru	D	1–1	Buenos Aires	SCr1
2–06–1988	Canada	W	2–1	Guayaquil	Fr
7–06	United States	W	1–0	Albuquerque	Fr
10–06	United States	W	2–0	Houston	Fr
12–06	United States	D	0–0	Fort Worth	Fr
15–06	Honduras	D	1–1	Tegucigalpa	Fr
17–06	Honduras	W	1–0	Tegucigalpa	Fr
19–06	Costa Rica	L	0–1	San Jose	Fr
7–09	Paraguay	L	1–5	Guayaquil	Fr
13–09	Chile	L	1–3	La Serena	Fr
27–09	Uruguay	L	1–2	Asuncion	Fr
29–09	Chile	D	0–0	Asuncion	Fr
29–01–1989	Chile	W	1–0	Guayaquil	Fr
15–03	Brazil	L	0–1	Cuiaba	Fr
13–04	Argentina	D	2–2	Guayaquil	Fr
3–05	Uruguay	L	1–3	Montevideo	Fr
23–05	Uruguay	D	1–1	Quito	Fr
18–06	Nth. Ireland	D	1–1	Port of Spain	Fr
20–06	Peru	L	1–2	Port of Spain	Fr
2–07	Uruguay	W	1–0	Goiania	SCr1
4–07	Argentina	D	0–0	Goiania	SCr1
6–07	Bolivia	D	0–0	Goiania	SCr1
10–07	Chile	L	1–2	Goiania	SCr1
20–08	Colombia	L	0–2	Barranquilla	WCq
3–09	Colombia	D	0–0	Guayaquil	WCq
10–09	Paraguay	L	1–2	Asuncion	WCq
24–09	Paraguay	W	3–1	Guayaquil	WCq
6–06–1991	Peru	W	1–0	Lima	Fr
19–06	Chile	W	2–1	Quito	Fr
25–06	Peru	D	2–2	Quito	Fr
30–06	Chile	L	1–3	Santiago	Fr
7–07	Colombia	L	0–1	Valparaiso	SCr1
9–07	Uruguay	D	1–1	Viña del Mar	SCr1
13–07	Bolivia	W	4–0	Viña del Mar	SCr1
15–07	Brazil	L	1–3	Viña del Mar	SCr1
24–05–1992	Guatemala	D	1–1	Guatemala City	Fr
27–05	Costa Rica	L	1–2	San Jose	Fr

PARAGUAY

Traditional links with Argentina, Uruguay and Brazil meant that football developed relatively early in Paraguay despite its poverty and isolation, though strangely enough for South America, it is a Dutchman who is credited with first bringing the game to the country.

The Liga Paraguaya de Fútbol, the game's governing body, was formed in 1906 and as the name suggests it was

		Total G	Total S	Total B	League G	Copa Lib G	Copa Lib S	Copa Lib B
1	Olimpia	35	3	4	33	2	3	4
2	Cerro Porteño	21	–	2	21	–	–	2
3	Guarani	8	–	1	8	–	–	1
	Libertad	8	–	1	8	–	–	1
5	Nacional	6	–	–	6	–	–	–
6	Sol de America	2	–	–	2	–	–	–
	Sportivo Luqueño	2	–	–	2	–	–	–
8	Presidente Hayes	1	–	–	1	–	–	–

To the end of the 1991 season

founded to run the league from which it takes its name. Based in Asuncion, the league has been completely dominated by clubs from the capital. Foremost is Olimpia, formed in 1902, the oldest club in the country and by far the most successful. In them Paraguay can boast the fifth most successful club in the Copa Libertadores.

Cerro Porteño, Guarani, Libertad and Nacional are the only other clubs that have done well in a league that has seen a remarkably small shift in power over the years. Only Nacional and Libertad have fallen away, the former winning their last title in 1946. Like the leagues of other small South American countries, Paraguay has been susceptible to the advances of clubs from Brazil, Uruguay and Argentina as they seek to replace players lost to Europe.

Professionalism was introduced in 1935 but has not been a barrier to the flow of players abroad. Asuncion is simply not big enough to support a prosperous club structure. An indication of the uphill struggle clubs in Paraguay face is the fact that with grounds boasting a total capacity of nearly 300 000 within the city, almost half of the present-day population can be accommodated within them at any one time.

The Liga Paraguaya de Fútbol is also responsible for running the national team, though as it took 13 years for a Paraguayan side to take to the field, to begin with its priorities obviously lay with the league. In 1921 Paraguay was the fifth nation to take part in the South American Championships, but despite this long record of participation, along with Colombia and Venezuela they have never hosted the event. Their record in the tournament, though never outstanding, has been consistently good. Their initial match in the 1921 tournament saw a victory over Uruguay, whilst the following year they took Brazil to a play-off before finishing the tournament in second place. History repeated itself in 1949 when Paraguay again forced a play-off against Brazil by beating them on the last day of the tournament. Once again, however, the Brazilians were too strong for the normally resilient Paraguayans and they won 7–0 in convincing fashion.

Aside from the period when they were at war with Bolivia from 1932 until 1935, the national side regularly undertook international games outside the South American Championships. Their debut was made with four friendly games against Argentina in 1919 and that rivalry has continued down the years in the Rosa Chevalier Boutell Cup. Links with Brazil have been maintained through the Oswaldo Cruz Cup and with Uruguay in the Artigas Cup. Matches like these have helped keep the standard of the game up despite the relatively small population.

Paraguay finally made their mark in the 1953 South American Championships, winning it for the first time, and were responsible for a tactical innovation that was to change world football. For the 1953 tournament the Paraguayan coach, Fleitas Solich, implemented a 4–2–4 system and they used it to good effect, winning the series after yet another play-off against the Brazilians. So impressed was Feola, the Brazilian coach, that he copied and perfected the system which eventually won the Brazilians the 1958 World Cup.

The irony of the situation was that Paraguay qualified for the tournament in Sweden as well but were knocked out in the first round despite beating Scotland and drawing with Yugoslavia. The late 1940s and 1950s were undoubtedly Paraguay's most successful era at international level and it was not until 1979 that the national side again caught the imagination.

That year turned out to be a memorable one for the country. As well as beating Chile to win the South American Championship for the second time, Olimpia won the Copa Libertadores, the first club from outside of the continent's big three to achieve such a feat. Boca Juniors, the reigning champions, were beaten 2–0 over two legs and to complete an amazing quadruple, Olimpia won the ensuing Inter-American club championship by beating Deportivo FAS of El Salvador as well as the World Club Championship against Malmö of Sweden, deputising for Nottingham Forest. Paraguay was therefore in possession of every continental trophy available.

Olimpia have continued to do well in the Copa Libertadores. Having been finalists in the first competition in 1960, they appeared in their third final in 1989, this time losing to Nacional Medellin of Colombia. They were back again in 1990 and won for the second time by beating Barcelona 3–1 on aggregate. That year also saw Olimpia win the South American Super Cup and as a result they were awarded the Recopa, a trophy for the winners of the annual game between the Copa Libertadores and Super Cup winners. There was a third consecutive final appearance in 1991 but once again it was to prove a disappointing experience as Colo Colo became the first Chilean club to win the tournament.

Should a South American Super League ever become a reality, Olimpia would undoubtedly be involved. Despite the national side's qualification for the 1986 World Cup in Mexico, their first appearance since 1958, it is Olimpia that all Paraguayans look to in the search for honours.

Population: 4 279 000
Area, sq km: 406 752
% in urban areas: 43%
Capital city: Asunción

Liga Paraguaya de Fútbol
Estadio de Sajonia
Calles Mayor Martínez y Alejo García
Asunción
Paraguay
Tel: (010 595) 21 81743
Fax: (010 595) 21 81743
Telex: 38009 PY FUTBOL
Cable: None
Languages for correspondence: Spanish

Year of formation: 1906
Affiliation to FIFA: 1921
Affiliation to CONMEBOL: 1921
Registered clubs: 1500
Registered players: 257 300
Registered coaches: 150
Registered referees: 302
National stadium: Defensores del Chaco, Asuncion 60 000
National colours: Shirts: Red and white stripes/Shorts: Blue/Socks: Blue
Reserve colours: Shirts: White/Shorts: White/Socks: White
Season: May–December

THE RECORD

WORLD CUP

1930 .... QT Automatic – Final Tournament/1st round
1934 .... Did not enter
1938 .... Did not enter
1950 .... QT W-O in group 8 – Final Tournament/1st round
1954 .... Did not enter
1958 .... QT 1st/3 in group 3 – Final Tournament/1st round
1962 .... QT 2nd in CONCACAF
1966 .... QT 2nd/3 in group 3
1970 .... QT 2nd/4 in group 2
1974 .... QT 2nd/3 in group 2
1978 .... QT 2nd/3 in group 1
1982 .... QT 3rd/3 in group 3
1986 .... QT 2nd/3 in group 3 – Final Tournament/2nd round
1990 .... QT 2nd/3 in group 2

SOUTH AMERICAN CHAMPIONSHIP

1910–20 ..... –
1921 .... 4th/4
1922 .... 2nd/5
1923 .... 3rd/4
1924 .... 3rd/4
1925 .... 3rd/3
1926 .... 4th/5
1927 .... –
1929 .... 2nd/4
1935 .... –
1937 .... 3rd/6
1939 .... 3rd/5
1941 .... –
1942 .... 4th/7
1945 .... –
1946 .... 3rd/6
1947 .... 2nd/8
1949 .... 2nd/8
1953 .... 1st/7 – Winners
1955 .... 5th/6
1956 .... 5th/6
1957 .... –
1958 .... 3rd/7
1959 .... 5th/5
1963 .... 2nd/7
1967 .... 4th/6
1975 .... 7th/10/1st round
1979 .... 1st/10 – Winners
1983 .... 3rd/10/Semi-finalists
1987 .... 9th/10/1st round
1989 .... 4th/10/2nd round
1991 .... 6th/10/1st round

OLYMPIC GAMES

1908–64 ..... Did not enter
1968 .... QT Failed to qualify
1972 .... QT Failed to qualify
1976 .... Did not enter
1980 .... Did not enter
1984 .... QT Failed to qualify
1988 .... QT Failed to qualify
1992 .... Final Tournament

COPA LIBERTADORES

Winners – Olimpia 1979, 1990
Finalists – Olimpia 1960, 1989, 1991

SUPER CUP: Winners – Olimpia 1990

CLUB DIRECTORY

ASUNCION (Population – 700 000)

Club Cerro Porteño
Stadium: Adriano Irala 30 000
Founded: 1912
Colours: Blue and red stripes/White

Atletico Colegiales
Stadium: Luciano Zacarias 20 000
Colours: Red/Blue

Club Guarani
Stadium: Lorenzo Livieres 20 000
Founded: 1903
Colours: Black and yellow stripes/Black

Club Libertad
Stadium: Alfredo Stroessner 45 000
Founded: 1905
Colours: Black and white stripes

Sportivo Luqueño
Stadium: Feliciano Caceres 38 000
Founded: 1921
Colours: Blue and yellow stripes/Blue

Club Nacional
Stadium: Arsenio Erico 10 000
Founded: 1904
Colours: White/Blue

Club Olimpia
Stadium: Manuel Ferreira 40 000
Founded: 1902
Colours: White with a single black hoop/White

Club Presidente Hayes
Stadium: Villa Hayes 20 000
Colours: Red and white stripes/Blue

Club Sol de America
Stadium: Estadio Sol 8000
Founded: 1909 Colours: Blue/Blue

PARAGUYUAN LEAGUE CHAMPIONS

1906	Guarani
1907	Guarani
1908	–
1909	Nacional Asuncion
1910	–
1911	Nacional Asuncion
1912	Olimpia
1913	Cerro Porteño
1914	Olimpia
1915	Cerro Porteño
1916	Olimpia
1917	Libertad
1918	Cerro Porteño
1919	Cerro Porteño
1920	Libertad
1921	Guarani
1922	–
1923	Guarani
1924	Nacional Asuncion
1925	Olimpia
1926	Nacional Asuncion
1927	Olimpia
1928	Olimpia
1929	Olimpia
1930	Libertad
1931	Olimpia
1932–34	–
1935	Cerro Porteño
1936	Olimpia
1937	Olimpia
1938	Olimpia
1939	Cerro Porteño
1940	Cerro Porteño
1941	Cerro Porteño
1942	Nacional Asuncion
1943	Libertad
1944	Cerro Porteño
1945	Libertad
1946	Nacional Asuncion
1947	Olimpia
1948	Olimpia
1949	Guarani
1950	Cerro Porteño
1951	Sportivo Luqueño
1952	Presidente Hayes
1953	Sportivo Luqueño
1954	Cerro Porteño
1955	Libertad
1956	Olimpia
1957	Olimpia
1958	Olimpia
1959	Olimpia
1960	Olimpia
1961	Cerro Porteño
1962	Olimpia
1963	Cerro Porteño
1964	Guarani
1965	Olimpia

1966	Cerro Porteño	1979	Olimpia
1967	Guarani	1980	Olimpia
1968	Olimpia	1981	Olimpia
1969	Olimpia	1982	Olimpia
1970	Cerro Porteño	1983	Olimpia
1971	Olimpia	1984	Guarani
1972	Cerro Porteño	1985	Olimpia
1973	Cerro Porteño	1986	Sol de America
1974	Cerro Porteño	1987	Cerro Porteño
1975	Olimpia	1988	Olimpia
1976	Libertad	1989	Olimpia
1977	Cerro Porteño	1990	Cerro Porteño
1978	Olimpia	1991	Sol de America

LEADING INTERNATIONAL GOALSCORERS

1	Arrua	13
	Romero	13
3	Rivas G	12

LEADING INTERNATIONAL APPEARANCES

1	Fernandez R	78
2	Torales	77
3	Delgado R	61

INTERNATIONAL MATCHES PLAYED BY PARAGUAY

Date	Opponents	Result		Venue	Compet	Scorers
11-05-1919	Argentina	L	1-5	Asuncion	Fr	
18-05	Argentina	L	0-2	Asuncion	Fr	
21-05	Argentina	L	1-2	Asuncion	Fr	
24-05	Argentina	L	1-2	Asuncion	Fr	
7-04-1921	Argentina*	W	3-1	Asuncion	Fr	
14-04	Argentina*	D	2-2	Asuncion	Fr	
9-10	Uruguay	W	2-1	Buenos Aires	SC	Rivas G, López E
12-10	Brazil	L	0-3	Buenos Aires	SC	
16-10	Argentina	L	0-3	Buenos Aires	SC	
2-11	Uruguay	L	2-4	Montevideo	Fr	
24-09-1922	Brazil	D	1-1	Rio de Janeiro	SC	Rivas G
5-10	Chile	W	3-0	Rio de Janeiro	SC	Ramirez C, López E, Fretes A
12-10	Uruguay	W	1-0	Rio de Janeiro	SC	Elizeche
18-10	Argentina	L	0-2	Rio de Janeiro	SC	
22-10	Brazil	L	1-3	Rio de Janeiro	SC	Rivas G
29-10	Brazil	L	1-3	Sao Paulo	Fr	
20-05-1923	Argentina	W	2-0	Buenos Aires	RCB	Centurion, Lima
25-05	Argentina	L	0-1	Buenos Aires	RCB	
29-10	Argentina	L	3-4	Montevideo	SC	Rivas G, Zelada, Fretes A
4-11	Uruguay	L	0-2	Montevideo	SC	
11-11	Brazil	W	1-0	Montevideo	SC	López I
22-11	Brazil	L	0-2	Montevideo	Fr	
15-05-1924	Argentina	L	1-3	Asuncion	RCB	Solich
18-05	Argentina	W	2-1	Asuncion	RCB	Solich, Rivas G
12-10	Argentina	D	0-0	Montevideo	SC	
26-10	Uruguay	L	1-3	Montevideo	SC	Sosa U
1-11	Chile	W	3-1	Montevideo	SC	López I 2, Rivas G
9-07-1925	Argentina	D	1-1	Buenos Aires	RCB	Fretes A
12-07	Argentina	D	1-1	Buenos Aires	RCB	Fretes A
14-07	Uruguay	W	1-0	Montevideo	Fr	
18-07	Uruguay	W	1-0	Montevideo	Fr	
15-08	Uruguay	W	1-0	Asuncion	Fr	
19-08	Uruguay	L	0-1	Asuncion	Fr	
23-08	Uruguay	D	0-0	Asuncion	Fr	
29-11	Argentina	L	0-2	Buenos Aires	SC	
6-12	Brazil	L	2-5	Buenos Aires	SC	Rivas, Fretes A
17-12	Brazil	L	1-3	Buenos Aires	SC	Fretes A
20-12	Argentina	L	1-3	Buenos Aires	SC	Solich
29-05-1926	Argentina	L	1-2	Asuncion	RCB	López I
3-06	Argentina	L	1-2	Asuncion	RCB	Fretes A
20-10	Argentina	L	0-8	Santiago	SC	
23-10	Bolivia	W	6-1	Santiago	SC	Ramirez J 3, Ramirez C 2, López I
1-11	Uruguay	L	1-6	Santiago	SC	Fretes L
3-11	Chile	L	1-5	Santiago	SC	Vargas
15-08-1928	Uruguay	W	3-1	Asuncion	Fr	
19-08	Uruguay	D	1-1	Asuncion	Fr	
1-11-1929	Uruguay	W	3-0	Buenos Aires	SC	Gonzalez A 2, Lagos
10-11	Argentina	L	1-4	Buenos Aires	SC	Dominguez
16-11	Peru	W	5-0	Buenos Aires	SC	Gonzalez A 3, Lino Nessi, Dominguez
17-07-1930	United States	L	0-3	Montevideo	WCr1	

20–07	Belgium	W	1–0	Montevideo	WCr1	Pena
19–04–1931	Argentina	L	0–1	Asuncion	Fr	
25–04	Argentina	D	1–1	Asuncion	Fr	
4–07	Argentina	D	1–1	Buenos Aires	RCB	Gonzalez A
9–07	Argentina	L	1–3	Buenos Aires	RCB	Laterza
2–01–1937	Uruguay	W	4–2	Buenos Aires	SC	Gonzalez A 2, Erico, Ortega
9–01	Argentina	L	1–6	Buenos Aires	SC	Gonzalez A
13–01	Brazil	L	0–5	Buenos Aires	SC	
17–01	Chile	W	3–2	Buenos Aires	SC	Amarillo, Nuñez, Flor
24–01	Peru	L	0–1	Buenos Aires	SC	
15–01–1939	Chile	W	5–1	Lima	SC	Godoy 2, Barrios 2, Aquino
29–01	Peru	L	0–3	Lima	SC	
5–02	Uruguay	L	1–3	Lima	SC	Barrios
12–02	Ecuador	W	3–1	Lima	SC	Mingo, Bareiro, Godoy
26–02	Chile	L	2–4	Santiago	Fr	
14–08	Argentina	L	0–1	Asuncion	RCB	
16–08	Argentina	D	2–2	Asuncion	RCB	Espindola, Diaz
18–02–1940	Argentina	L	1–3	Buenos Aires	RCB	Mingo
25–02	Argentina	L	0–4	Buenos Aires	RCB	
11–01–1942	Argentina	L	3–4	Montevideo	SC	Aveiro 2, Sanchez V
18–01	Peru	D	1–1	Montevideo	SC	Barrios
22–01	Chile	W	2–0	Montevideo	SC	Barrios, Franco
25–01	Ecuador	W	3–1	Montevideo	SC	Franco, Mingo, Ibarrola
28–01	Uruguay	L	1–3	Montevideo	SC	Barrios
5–02	Brazil	D	1–1	Montevideo	SC	Franco
10–07–1943	Argentina	L	2–5	Asuncion	RCB	Benega, Mellone
11–07	Argentina	W	2–1	Asuncion	RCB	Marin, Alvarez
6–01–1945	Argentina	L	2–5	Buenos Aires	RCB	Fernandez, Benitez Cáceres
9–01	Argentina	L	3–5	Buenos Aires	RCB	Benitez Cáceres 2, Esquiel
7–07	Argentina	W	5–1	Asuncion	RCB	Sanchez V, OG, Benitez Cáceres, Villalba, Sosa
9–07	Argentina	L	1–3	Asuncion	RCB	Fernandez
12–01–1946	Argentina	L	0–2	Buenos Aires	SC	
19–01	Chile	L	1–2	Buenos Aires	SC	Rolón
26–01	Bolivia	W	4–2	Buenos Aires	SC	Villalba 2, Genes, Benitez Cáceres
29–01	Brazil	D	1–1	Buenos Aires	SC	Villalba
8–02	Uruguay	W	2–1	Buenos Aires	SC	Villalba, Rodriguez A
2–12–1947	Argentina	L	0–6	Guayaquil	SC	
6–12	Peru	D	2–2	Guayaquil	SC	Villalba, Márin
13–12	Uruguay	W	4–2	Guayaquil	SC	Genes 2, Márin, Villalba
18–12	Bolivia	W	3–1	Guayaquil	SC	Márin, Avalos, Genes
20–12	Colombia	W	2–0	Guayaquil	SC	Villalba 2
23–12	Chile	W	1–0	Guayaquil	SC	Villalba
29–12	Ecuador	W	4–0	Guayaquil	SC	Márin 3, Genes
6–04–1949	Colombia	W	3–0	Sao Paulo	SC	López Fretes 2, Benitez D
10–04	Ecuador	W	1–0	Rio de Janeiro	SC	Barrios R
13–04	Peru	W	3–1	Rio de Janeiro	SC	Barrios R, Arce, López Fretes
20–04	Uruguay	L	1–2	Sao Paulo	SC	Vazquez
27–04	Chile	W	4–2	Sao Paulo	SC	Arce 3, Benitez D
30–04	Bolivia	W	7–0	Rio de Janeiro	SC	Benitez D 4, Arce 2, Avalos
8–05	Brazil	W	2–1	Rio de Janeiro	SC	Avalos, Benitez D
11–05	Brazil	L	0–7	Rio de Janeiro	SCpo	
25–03–1950	Argentina	D	2–2	Buenos Aires	RCB	OG, Sosa
29–03	Argentina	L	0–4	Buenos Aires	RCB	
30–04	Uruguay	W	3–2	Rio de Janeiro	Fr	
7–05	Brazil	L	0–2	Rio de Janeiro	OCC	
13–05	Brazil	D	3–3	Sao Paulo	OCC	
29–06	Sweden	D	2–2	Curitiba	WCr1	López A, López Fretes
2–07	Italy	L	0–2	Sao Paulo	WCr1	
25–02–1953	Chile	W	3–0	Lima	SC	Fernandez R 2, Berni
4–03	Ecuador	D	0–0	Lima	SC	
8–03	Peru	D	2–2	Lima	SC	Fernandez R, Berni
12–03	Uruguay	D	2–2	Lima	SC	López A
16–03	Bolivia	W	2–1	Lima	SC	Romero J, Berni
27–03	Brazil	W	2–1	Lima	SC	López A, León
1–04	Brazil	W	3–2	Lima	SCpo	López A, Gavilán, Fernandez R
14–02–1954	Chile	W	4–0	Asuncion	WCq	
21–02	Chile	W	3–1	Santiago	WCq	
7–03	Brazil	L	0–1	Asuncion	WCq	
21–03	Brazil	L	1–4	Rio de Janeiro	WCq	

10–04	Uruguay	W	4–1	Montevideo	Fr	
18–04	Uruguay	D	1–1	Asuncion	Fr	
2–03–1955	Argentina	L	3–5	Santiago	SC	Rólon, Villalba, Parodi
9–03	Uruguay	L	1–3	Santiago	SC	Rólon
16–03	Ecuador	W	2–0	Santiago	SC	Rólon 2
20–03	Chile	L	0–5	Santiago	SC	
23–03	Peru	D	1–1	Santiago	SC	Rólon
13–11	Brazil	L	0–3	Rio de Janeiro	OCC	
17–11	Brazil	D	3–3	Sao Paulo	OCC	
21–01–1956	Uruguay	L	2–4	Montevideo	SC	Gómez A 2
29–01	Brazil	D	0–0	Montevideo	SC	
1–02	Argentina	L	0–1	Montevideo	SC	
5–02	Peru	D	1–1	Montevideo	SC	Rólon
12–02	Chile	L	0–2	Montevideo	SC	
12–06	Brazil	L	0–2	Asuncion	OCC	
17–06	Brazil	L	2–5	Asuncion	OCC	
15–07	Uruguay	D	2–2	Asuncion	Fr	
15–08	Argentina	L	0–1	Asuncion	RCB	
6–06–1957	Bolivia	W	5–2	Asuncion	PDC	
13–06	Bolivia	L	0–1	Asuncion	PDC	
20–06	Colombia	W	3–2	Bogota	WCq	Jara A 2, OG
23–06	Colombia	W	2–1	Medellin	Fr	Amarilla, Aguero
7–07	Colombia	W	3–0	Asuncion	WCq	Jara E 2, Aguero
14–07	Uruguay	W	5–0	Asuncion	WCq	Amarilla 3, Aguero, Jara A
28–07	Uruguay	L	0–2	Montevideo	WCq	
18–08	Bolivia	D	3–3	La Paz	PDC	
21–08	Bolivia	L	1–2	La Paz	PDC	
20–04–1958	Argentina	W	1–0	Asuncion	Fr	
26–04	Argentina	L	0–2	Buenos Aires	Fr	
4–05	Brazil	L	1–5	Rio de Janeiro	OCC	
7–05	Brazil	D	0–0	Sao Paulo	OCC	
8–06	France	L	3–7	Norrkoping	WCr1	Amarilla 2, Romero
11–06	Scotland	W	3–2	Norrkoping	WCr1	Aguero, Re, Parodi
15–06	Yugoslavia	D	3–3	Eskilstuna	WCr1	Parodi, Aguero, Romero
11–03–1959	Chile	W	2–1	Buenos Aires	SC	Aveiro 2
15–03	Bolivia	W	5–0	Buenos Aires	SC	Ré 3, Sanabria I, Aveiro
18–03	Uruguay	L	1–3	Buenos Aires	SC	Aveiro
22–03	Argentina	L	1–3	Buenos Aires	SC	Sanabria C
29–03	Brazil	L	1–4	Buenos Aires	SC	Parodi
2–04	Peru	W	2–1	Buenos Aires	SC	Aveiro 2
1–05	Uruguay	W	3–1	Montevideo	Fr	
5–12	Brazil	L	2–3	Guayaquil	SC	Parodi, Benitez G
9–12	Argentina	L	2–4	Guayaquil	SC	Lezcano, Cabral
22–12	Uruguay	D	1–1	Guayaquil	SC	Parodi
25–12	Ecuador	L	1–3	Guayaquil	SC	OG
3–07–1960	Brazil	L	1–2	Asuncion	CA	
9–07	Argentina	L	0–1	Buenos Aires	CA	
13–07	Uruguay	L	1–2	Montevideo	CA	Cabral
18–12	Chile	L	1–4	Santiago	Fr	
21–12	Chile	L	1–3	Valparaiso	Fr	
30–04–1961	Brazil	L	0–2	Asuncion	OCC	
3–05	Brazil	L	2–3	Asuncion	OCC	
17–05	Argentina	D	0–0	Asuncion	Fr	
29–06	Brazil	L	2–3	Rio de Janeiro	Fr	
12–10	Argentina	L	1–5	Buenos Aires	Fr	
29–10	Mexico	L	0–1	Mexico City	WCq	
5–11	Mexico	D	0–0	Asuncion	WCq	
21–04–1962	Brazil	L	0–6	Rio de Janeiro	OCC	
24–04	Brazil	L	0–4	Sao Paulo	OCC	
10–08	Bolivia	L	1–3	Cochabamba	PDC	
12–08	Bolivia	L	2–3	La Paz	PDC	
17–02–1963	Bolivia	W	3–0	Asuncion	PDC	
19–02	Bolivia	W	5–1	Asuncion	PDC	
3–03	Brazil	D	2–2	Asuncion	Fr	
14–03	Ecuador	W	3–1	La Paz	SC	Zárate 2, Quiñones
17–03	Brazil	W	2–0	La Paz	SC	Navarate, Ayala
20–03	Colombia	W	3–2	Cochabamba	SC	Cabrera 2, Valdez
24–03	Bolivia	L	0–2	Cochabamba	SC	
27–03	Peru	W	4–1	Cochabamba	SC	Martinez D 2, Cabrera, Zárate
31–03	Argentina	D	1–1	La Paz	SC	Cabrera
15–10	Argentina	L	0–4	Asuncion	RCB	

29–10	Argentina	W	3–2	Buenos Aires	RCB	Pavon, Ayala, Rojas B
25–11–1964	Argentina	W	3–0	Asuncion	RCB	Candia, Ivaldi, Garcia
8–12	Argentina	L	1–8	Buenos Aires	RCB	Pavon
10–03–1965	Guatemala	W	4–1	Guatemala City	Fr	
14–03	Guatemala	W	3–0	Guatemala City	Fr	
17–03	Costa Rica	L	0–1	San Jose	Fr	
19–03	Costa Rica	D	0–0	San Jose	Fr	
3–04	Peru	W	1–0	Lima	Fr	Riquelme
25–04	Uruguay	W	2–1	Asuncion	AC	Riquelme, Caceres
1–05	Uruguay	L	0–4	Montevideo	AC	
25–07	Bolivia	W	2–0	Asuncion	WCq	Rodriguez, Rojas J
1–08	Argentina	L	0–3	Buenos Aires	WCq	
8–08	Argentina	D	0–0	Asuncion	WCq	
22–08	Bolivia	L	1–2	La Paz	WCq	Mora C
24–04–1966	Mexico	L	0–4	Mexico City	Fr	
15–05	Uruguay	D	2–2	Asuncion	AC	
18–05	Uruguay	L	1–3	Montevideo	AC	
21–12	Ecuador	D	2–2	Guayaquil	SCq	
28–12	Ecuador	W	3–1	Asuncion	SCq	
18–01–1967	Argentina	L	1–4	Montevideo	SC	Mora C
22–01	Chile	L	2–4	Montevideo	SC	Rivero, Apocada
25–01	Bolivia	W	1–0	Montevideo	SC	Del Puerto
29–01	Uruguay	L	0–2	Montevideo	SC	
1–02	Venezuela	W	5–3	Montevideo	SC	Rojas J 2, Garay, Mora C 2
13–10	Argentina	D	1–1	Asuncion	Fr	
15–05–1968	Argentina	W	2–0	Asuncion	Fr	
2–06	Uruguay	D	0–0	Asuncion	AC	*Abandoned after 70 mins*
25–07	Brazil	L	0–4	Asuncion	OCC	
28–07	Brazil	W	1–0	Asuncion	OCC	
19–03–1969	Argentina	D	1–1	Rosario	Fr	Valdez
9–04	Argentina	D	0–0	Asuncion	Fr	
8–06	Chile	L	0–1	Asuncion	Fr	
6–07	Chile	D	0–0	Santiago	Fr	
9–07	Peru	L	1–2	Lima	Fr	Mora C
18–07	Peru	L	1–2	Lima	Fr	Sosa
7–08	Venezuela	W	2–0	Caracas	WCq	Rojas 2
10–08	Colombia	W	1–0	Bogota	WCq	Martinez
17–08	Brazil	L	0–3	Asuncion	WCq	
21–08	Venezuela	W	1–0	Asuncion	WCq	Gimenez
24–08	Colombia	W	2–1	Asuncion	WCq	Arrua 2
31–08	Brazil	L	0–1	Rio de Janeiro	WCq	
12–04–1970	Brazil	D	0–0	Rio de Janeiro	Fr	
22–10	Argentina	D	1–1	Asuncion	Fr	Irala
4–07–1971	Argentina	D	1–1	Asuncion	RCB	Arrua
9–07	Argentina	L	0–1	Rosario	RCB	
14–07	Chile	L	2–3	Santiago	Fr	
24–07	Brazil	L	0–1	Rio de Janeiro	Fr	
27–07	Peru	D	0–0	Lima	Fr	
8–08	Chile	W	2–0	Asuncion	Fr	
15–08	Peru	W	2–0	Asuncion	Fr	
26–04–1972	Brazil	L	2–3	Porto Alegre	Fr	Escobar, Diarte
25–05	Argentina	D	0–0	Salta	Fr	
11–06	Venezuela	W	4–1	Campo Grande	Clr1	
14–06	Peru	W	1–0	Campo Grande	Clr1	
21–06	Yugoslavia	L	1–2	Manaus	Clr1	
25–06	Bolivia	W	6–1	Manaus	Clr1	
28–03–1973	Peru	L	0–1	Lima	Fr	
31–03	Bolivia	D	1–1	La Paz	Fr	Giminez
8–04	Peru	D	1–1	Asuncion	Fr	Maldonado
2–09	Bolivia	W	2–1	La Paz	WCq	Escobar, Insfran
16–09	Argentina	D	1–1	Asuncion	WCq	Arrua
30–09	Bolivia	W	4–0	Asuncion	WCq	Insfran, Bareiro, Osorio, Arrua
7–10	Argentina	L	1–3	Buenos Aires	WCq	Escobar
12–05–1974	Brazil	L	0–2	Rio de Janeiro	Fr	
22–12	Chile	L	0–1	Santiago	Fr	
12–06–1975	Uruguay	L	0–1	Asuncion	AC	
19–06	Uruguay	W	1–0	Montevideo	AC	Rolón
7–07	Bolivia	W	2–1	Cochabamba	Fr	
10–07	Peru	L	0–2	Lima	Fr	
20–07	Colombia	L	0–1	Bogota	SCr1	

24-07	Ecuador	D	2-2	Guayaquil	SCr1	Kiese H 2
30-07	Colombia	L	0-1	Asuncion	SCr1	*Abandoned at half-time*
10-08	Ecuador	W	3-1	Asuncion	SCr1	Rolón 2, Baez
25-02-1976	Argentina	L	2-3	Asuncion	CA	Aquino, Diaz
10-03	Uruguay	D	2-2	Montevideo	CA	Pesoa, Paniagua
7-04	Brazil	D	1-1	Asuncion	CA	Aquino
28-04	Argentina	D	2-2	Buenos Aires	CA	Rivera, Aquino
19-05	Uruguay	W	1-0	Asuncion	CA	Solalinde
9-06	Brazil	L	1-3	Rio de Janeiro	CA	Diaz
9-01-1977	Ecuador	W	2-0	Asuncion	Fr	Calman, Aquino
12-01	Uruguay	D	1-1	Asuncion	AC	
23-01	Uruguay	L	1-2	Montevideo	AC	Villalba
26-01	Chile	L	0-4	Santiago	Fr	
2-02	Chile	W	2-0	Asuncion	Fr	Baez, Aifuche
6-02	Bolivia	W	1-0	La Paz	PDC	Bareiro
9-02	Bolivia	D	2-2	La Paz	PDC	
13-02	Ecuador	L	1-2	Quito	Fr	Spinola
24-02	Colombia	W	1-0	Bogota	WCq	Jara-Saguier
6-03	Colombia	D	1-1	Asuncion	WCq	Jara-Saguier
13-03	Brazil	L	0-1	Asuncion	WCq	
20-03	Brazil	D	1-1	Rio de Janeiro	WCq	Baez
24-08	Argentina	L	1-2	Buenos Aires	Fr	Escobar
31-08	Argentina	W	2-0	Asuncion	Fr	OG, Espinola
17-05-1979	Brazil	L	0-6	Rio de Janeiro	Fr	
10-07	Bolivia	L	1-3	La Paz	PDC	Overal
12-07	Bolivia	D	1-1	Cochabamba	Fr	
1-08	Bolivia	W	2-0	Asuncion	PDC	
29-08	Ecuador	W	2-1	Quito	SCr1	Talavera, Solalinde
13-09	Ecuador	W	2-0	Asuncion	SCr1	Morel E, Osorio
20-09	Uruguay	D	0-0	Asuncion	SCr1	
26-09	Uruguay	D	2-2	Montevideo	SCr1	Morel E 2
10-10	Peru	W	3-2	Lima	Fr	Espinola, Morel E, Lobaton
24-10	Brazil	W	2-1	Asuncion	SCsf	Morel E, Talavera
31-10	Brazil	D	2-2	Rio de Janeiro	SCsf	Morel M, Romero
28-11	Chile	W	3-0	Asuncion	SCf	Romero 2, Morel M
5-12	Chile	L	0-1	Santiago	SCf	
11-12	Chile	D	0-0	Buenos Aires	SCf	
26-08-1980	Bolivia	D	1-1	La Paz	PDC	
28-08	Bolivia	W	3-1	Santa Cruz	Fr	Florentin, Issasi, Michelagnoli
18-09	Bolivia	W	2-1	Asuncion	PDC	Mino, Lopez
25-09	Brazil	L	1-2	Asuncion	Fr	Benitez
30-10	Brazil	L	0-6	Goiania	Fr	
15-03-1981	Colombia	L	0-2	Asuncion	Fr	
17-05	Ecuador	L	0-1	Guayaquil	WCq	
31-05	Ecuador	W	3-1	Asuncion	WCq	Michelagnoli, Morel, Romero
7-06	Chile	L	0-1	Asuncion	WCq	
21-06	Chile	L	0-3	Santiago	WCq	
2-06-1983	Uruguay	D	0-0	Asuncion	AC	
9-06	Uruguay	L	0-3	Montevideo	AC	
14-07	Argentina	W	1-0	Asuncion	Fr	Delgado
21-07	Argentina	D	0-0	Buenos Aires	Fr	
24-07	Chile	W	1-0	Asuncion	Fr	Hicks
3-08	Bolivia	L	1-2	La Paz	Fr	Florentin
5-08	Bolivia	W	3-1	Santa Cruz	Fr	Florentin 2, Delgado
17-08	Chile	L	2-3	Santiago	Fr	Olmedo, Delgado
25-08	Uruguay	D	0-0	Montevideo	Fr	
5-10	Peru	W	2-0	Lima	Fr	Romero, Torrales
7-10	Peru	W	4-1	Asuncion	Fr	Cabanas 2, Romero 2
13-10	Brazil	D	1-1	Asuncion	SCsf	Morel M
20-10	Brazil	D	0-0	Uberlandia	SCsf	
3-02-1985	Uruguay	L	0-1	Montevideo	AC	
6-02	Chile	L	0-1	Viña del Mar	Fr	
10-02	Uruguay	L	1-3	Asuncion	AC	Benitez
28-02	Colombia	L	0-3	Asuncion	Fr	
17-04	Colombia	L	0-1	Pereira	Fr	
19-04	Colombia	D	2-2	Bogota	Fr	Bobadilla, Ferreira
28-04	Argentina	W	1-0	Asuncion	Fr	
9-05	Argentina	D	1-1	Buenos Aires	Fr	Zabala
26-05	Bolivia	D	1-1	Santa Cruz	WCq	Nunez

9–06	Bolivia	W	3–0	Asuncion	WCq	Mendoza, Jacquet, Romero
16–06	Brazil	L	0–2	Asuncion	WCq	
23–06	Brazil	D	1–1	Rio de Janeiro	WCq	Romero
9–10	Chile	D	0–0	Asuncion	Fr	
16–10	Peru	W	1–0	Lima	Fr	Ferreira
27–10	Colombia	W	3–0	Asuncion	WCq	Hicks, Romero, Cabanas
29–10	Chile	D	0–0	Santiago	Fr	
3–11	Colombia	L	1–2	Cali	WCq	Ferreira
10–11	Chile	W	3–0	Asuncion	WCq	Cabanas 2, Delgado
17–11	Chile	D	2–2	Santiago	WCq	Schettina, Romero
29–01–1986	Canada	D	0–0	Vancouver	Fr	
5–02	Jamaica	W	4–1	Miami	Fr	
11–02	Hong Kong	D	1–1	Hong Kong	Fr	Delgado
14–02	South Korea	W	3–1	Hong Kong	Fr	OG, Sandoval, Schetlina
16–02	Indonesia	W	3–2	Djakarta	Fr	Ramon, Zabala, Canete
26–02	Qatar	D	1–1	Doha	Fr	Delgado
1–03	Qatar	W	3–0	Doha	Fr	
8–03	Bahrain	W	2–1	Manama	Fr	Roman, Ordinario
12–03	Saudi Arabia	D	0–0	Dhahran	Fr	
20–05	Denmark	W	2–1	Bogota	Fr	Cabanas 2
4–06	Iraq	W	1–0	Toluca	WCr1	Romero
7–06	Mexico	D	1–1	Mexico City	WCr1	Romero
11–06	Belgium	D	2–2	Toluca	WCr1	Cabanas 2
18–06	England	L	0–3	Mexico City	WCr2	
14–06–1987	Bolivia	W	2–0	Santa Cruz	Fr	Palacios, Jacqet
20–06	Argentina	W	1–0	Buenos Aires	Fr	OG
24–06	Brazil	L	0–1	Porto Alegre	Fr	
28–06	Bolivia	D	0–0	Rosario	SCr1	
5–07	Colombia	L	0–3	Rosario	SCr1	
7–09–1988	Ecuador	W	5–1	Guayaquil	Fr	Roman B, Almirom, Rivarola, Roman A, Ferreira
12–09	Honduras	D	0–0	San Pedro Sula	Fr	
15–09	Honduras	W	2–0	Tegucigalpa	Fr	
17–09	El Salvador	W	1–0	San Salvador	Fr	
21–09	Peru	W	1–0	Lima	Fr	Roman
27–09	Chile	W	2–0	Asuncion	Fr	Roman, OG
29–09	Uruguay	W	3–1	Asuncion	Fr	Palacios, Franco, Jacqet
12–10	Uruguay	L	0–2	Montevideo	Fr	
12–03–1989	Jamaica	W	3–0	Kingston	Fr	Jacqet, Palacios, Roman G
15–03	Martinique*	W	2–0	Fort de France	Fr	
17–03	Guadeloupe*	W	2–0	Basse Terre	Fr	
19–03	Trinidad	D	2–2	Port of Spain	Fr	Caceres, Palacios
22–03	Trinidad	D	1–1	Arima	Fr	Franco
26–03	Venezuela	W	2–1	Caracas	Fr	Ferreira, Franco
30–03	Venezuela	D	0–0	Maturin	Fr	
12–04	Brazil	L	0–2	Teresina	Fr	
5–05	El Salvador	W	2–1	Los Angeles	Fr	
7–05	Guatemala	W	2–1	Los Angeles	Fr	Roman B, Ferreyra
15–05	Peru	D	1–1	Asuncion	Fr	Roman B
25–05	Bolivia	L	2–3	Cochabamba	Fr	Rojas, Franco
1–06	Bolivia	W	2–0	Asuncion	Fr	Ferreira 2
1–07	Peru	W	5–2	Salvador	SCr1	Canete 2, Neffa, Mendoza, OG
5–07	Colombia	W	1–0	Salvador	SCr1	Mendoza
7–07	Venezuela	W	3–0	Salvador	SCr1	Neffa, Ferreira 2
9–07	Brazil	L	0–2	Recife	SCr1	
12–07	Uruguay	L	0–3	Rio de Janeiro	SCr2	
14–07	Brazil	L	0–3	Rio de Janeiro	SCr2	
16–07	Argentina	D	0–0	Rio de Janeiro	SCr2	
27–08	Colombia	W	2–1	Asuncion	WCq	Ferreira, Chilavert
10–09	Ecuador	W	2–1	Asuncion	WCq	Cabanas, Ferreira
17–09	Colombia	L	1–2	Barranquilla	WCq	Mendoza
24–09	Ecuador	L	1–3	Guayaquil	WCq	Neffa
27–02–1991	Brazil	D	1–1	Campo Grande	Fr	Samaniego
14–06	Bolivia	W	1–0	Santa Cruz	PDC	Gonzalez
16–06	Bolivia	D	0–0	Asuncion	PDC	
6–07	Peru	W	1–0	Santiago	SCr1	Monzon
10–07	Venezuela	W	5–0	Santiago	SCr1	Neffa, Guirland, Monzon 2, Sanabria
12–07	Argentina	L	1–4	Santiago	SCr1	Cardozo
14–07	Chile	L	0–4	Santiago	SCr1	

PERU

Peru are a middle-ranking South American power noted most for the fine teams they fielded during the 1970s. The rest of their footballing history has been largely undistinguished, and as one of the poorest nations on the continent with bad political problems, the future does not look very rosy for the Peruvians.

Though football was played at the turn of the century by British residents and a league of sorts formed in Lima in 1912, it was not until 1922 that the Federación Peruana de Fútbol was founded in the same city. Four years later the Liga Nacional de Football was introduced, though it was not strictly a national league as only clubs from the Lima area were invited to take part.

Until the introduction of a proper national league in 1966, the league in Lima was the strongest and its winners were regarded as national champions. In 1972, further changes were introduced. A metropolitan league for the area around Lima was instituted and a complex network of regional leagues set up to qualify teams for a final decentralised tournament to find the national champions.

The strongest teams have traditionally been from Lima and include Alianza, Universitario, Sporting Cristal and from nearby Callao, Sport Boys, though since the league has opened up, teams from the regions have begun to make their presence felt more and more, even if as yet they do not constitute a great threat to the capital.

The national side made its debut in the 1927 South American Championships which the Peruvian federation had been given the privilege of organising. Home advantage counted for little although Bolivia, who had made their debut in the previous year's tournament, were beaten. Lima was often used as a venue for the tournament and in 1939 Peru made home advantage count.

Spurred on by their greatest player of these early years, Teodoro 'Lolo' Fernández, the Peruvians beat all four of their opponents to win the tournament, although of the big three only Uruguay were present. Entry into the initial World Cup did not result in any progress, but three years before their South American Championship success, and again with Fernandez at the helm, Peru had made an impact, though not of the right kind, at the 1936 Olympic Games in Berlin.

Professionalism had been introduced in 1931, but the Peru team that made the journey to Berlin was the strongest at their disposal. They comprehensively beat Finland in the first round but were then involved in an extraordinary game against Austria. With Peru winning 4–2 near the end of extra-time, the game was abandoned after a melee stemming from a misunderstanding over an Austrian substitution. The game was ordered to be replayed but the Peru team were told not to turn up to the game by their embassy who considered the decision unjust, and they returned home.

There was little progress made in the game and even the emergence of a number of great players in the late 1950s including Gomez Sanchez, Mosquera, Loyaza, Seminario and Joya did little to help the cause. A famous victory over England in 1959 only helped speed up the flow of players to Europe and other South American countries where the conditions for players were much better. Seminario and Mosquera made names for themselves in Spain and Portugal, whilst Joya, Gomez Sanchez and Loyaza were very successful in Argentina.

Peru will primarily be remembered for the great sides of the 1970s. Guided by the greatest Peruvian footballer of all time, Teofilo Cubillas, Peru were in great form in the 1970 World Cup, and if they had not met Brazil in the quarter-finals they might have progressed further. Surprisingly eliminated in the 1974 qualifiers after a play-off with Chile, they made up for that defeat by winning the 1975 South American Championships, beating Brazil in the semi-finals and Colombia in the final.

Qualification for the 1978 and 1982 World Cup finals did not see the team perform as well as they had done in the first half of the 1970s, especially in Spain in 1982. Cubillas was still in the team but it was his swansong in the international game. The 1978 tournament will be remembered for the Peru–Argentina game in the second round. The Peruvians had played some excellent football in the first round, but collapsed in the second, especially against Argentina against whom they lost 6–0. The result was greeted with cries of 'cheat' from Brazil who were eliminated as a result, though it seems unlikely that Peru actually threw the game. The result had more to do with inept organisation which saw Brazil's game with Poland and the Peru–Argentina game scheduled for different times, thereby allowing the Argentines the advantage of knowing exactly how many goals they needed to score to proceed to the final.

		Total			League	Copa Lib		
		G	S	B	G	G	S	B
1	Universitario	18	1	3	18	–	1	3
2	Alianza	16	–	2	16	–	–	2
3	Sporting Cristal	10	–	–	10	–	–	–
4	Sport Boys	6	–	–	6	–	–	–
5	Deportivo Municipal	4	–	–	4	–	–	–
6	Atletico Chalaco	2	–	–	2	–	–	–
	Mariscal Sucre	2	–	–	2	–	–	–
	Union Huaral	2	–	–	2	–	–	–
9	Defensor Lima	1	–	1	1	–	–	1
10	Centro Iqueno	1	–	–	1	–	–	–
	Colegio San Agustin	1	–	–	1	–	–	–
	CS Progreso	1	–	–	1	–	–	–
	Mariano Melgar	1	–	–	1	–	–	–

The 1980s have on the whole been a very poor time for the country as political violence has gone hand in hand with economic stagnation. Peru are in danger of losing their traditional standing in South America and joining the likes of Venezuela as also-rans. The 1990 World Cup qualifiers saw them finish bottom of their group, whilst in the Copa Libertadores, never a happy hunting ground for Peruvian clubs, since 1984 the Peruvian entrants have occupied the bottom two places of their first round group on every occasion bar one.

Population: 22 332 000
Area, sq km: 1 285 216
% in urban areas: 69%
Capital city: Lima

Federación Peruana de Fútbol
Estadio Nacional, Puerta #4
Calle José Díaz
Lima
Perú
Tel: (010 51) 14 337070
Fax: (010 51) 14 320646
Telex: 20066 FEPEFUT PE
Cable: FEPEFUTBOL LIMA
Languages for correspondence: Spanish, French & English

Year of formation: 1922
Affiliation to FIFA: 1924
Affiliation to CONMEBOL: 1926
Registered clubs: 10 000
Registered players: 510 600
Professional players: 650
Registered coaches: 110
Registered referees: 156
National stadium: Estadio Nacional, Lima 45 000
National colours: Shirts: White with red sash/Shorts: White/Socks: White
Reserve colours: Shirts: Red/Shorts: White/Socks: White
Season: Regional championships March–November, National Championship November–January

THE RECORD

WORLD CUP

1930 .... QT Automatic – Final Tournament/1st round
1934–54 ..... Did not enter
1958 .... QT 2nd/2 in group 1
1962 .... QT 2nd/2 in group 3
1966 .... QT 2nd/3 in group 1
1970 .... QT 1st/3 in group 1 – Final Tournament/Quarter-finalists
1974 .... QT 2nd/2 in group 3
1978 .... QT 1st/3 in group 3 – Final Tournament/2nd round
1982 .... QT 1st/3 in group 2 – Final Tournament/1st round
1986 .... QT 2nd/4 in group 1
1990 .... QT 3rd/3 in group 1

SOUTH AMERICAN CHAMPIONSHIP

1910–26 ..... –
1927 .... 3rd/4
1929 .... 4th/4
1935 .... 3rd/4
1937 .... 6th/6
1939 .... 1st/5 – Winners
1941 .... 4th/5
1942 .... 5th/7
1945 .... –
1946 .... –
1947 .... 5th/8
1949 .... 3rd/8
1953 .... 5th/7
1955 .... 3rd/6
1956 .... 6th/6
1957 .... 4th/7
1959 .... 5th/7
1959 .... –
1963 .... 5th/7
1967 .... –
1975 .... 1st/10 – Winners
1979 .... 4th/10/Semi-finalists
1983 .... 4th/10/Semi-finalists
1987 .... 6th/10/1st round
1989 .... 8th/10/1st round
1991 .... 8th/10/1st round

OLYMPIC GAMES

1908–28 ..... Did not enter
1936 .... Quarter-finalists
1948–56 ..... Did not enter
1960 .... Final Tournament/1st round
1964 .... QT Failed to qualify
1968 .... QT Failed to qualify
1972 .... QT Failed to qualify
1976 .... QT Failed to qualify
1980 .... QT Failed to qualify
1984 .... Did not enter
1988 .... QT Failed to qualify
1992 .... QT Failed to qualify

COPA LIBERTADORES

Finalists – Universitario 1972

CLUB DIRECTORY

LIMA (Population – 4 608 000)

Club Alianza
Stadium: Alejandro Villanueva 34 000
Founded: 1901
Colours: Blue and white stripes/Blue

Atletico Chalaco Callao
Stadium: Telmo Carbajo
Founded: 1902
Colours: Red and white stripes/White

Deportivo Colegio San Agustin
Stadium: Estadio Matute 8000
Founded: 1982
Colours: Yellow/Red
Previous names: Club Huracan San Isidro 1982–86

Club Atletico Defensor
Stadium: San Martin de Porres
Colours: Maroon/White

Club Centro Deportivo Municipal
Stadium: Estadio Nacional 45 000
Founded: 1935
Colours: White with a red sash/Blue

Circolo Sportivo Internazionale
Stadium: Municipal 10 000
Founded: 1986
Colours: Blue/White
Previous name: Deportivo Cantolao until 1986

Sport Boys Callao
Stadium: Telmo Carbajo 15 000
Founded: 1927
Colours: Pink/Black

Club Sporting Cristal-Backus
Stadium: Alejandro Villanueva 34 000
Founded: 1922
Colours: Sky blue/White
Previous name: Sporting Tabacco 1922–55

Club Universitario de Deportes
Stadium: Teodoro 'Lolo' Fernandez 15 000
Founded: 1924
Colours: Cream/Cream

AREQUIPA (Population – 446 000)
Mariano Melgar FC
Stadium: IV Centenario 25 000
Founded: 1915
Colours: Red and black halves/Black

TRUJILLO (Population – 354 000)

Club Carlos Mannucci
Stadium: Mansische 20 000
Colours: Blue/Blue

Club Sport Libertad
Stadium: Mansische 20 000
Founded: 1887
Colours: Blue/Blue

PIURA (Population – 207 000)

Club Atletico Grau
Stadium: Miguel Grau 25 000
Founded: 1919
Colours: White/Black

Club Alianza Atletico
Stadium: Estadio Municipal 6000
Founded: 1920
Colours: White with a black sash/White

CUZCO (Population – 184 000)
Atletico Cienciano
Stadium: Estadio Inca Carcilasco de la Vega (12 000)

Founded: 1894
Colours: Red/White

IQUITOS (Population – 178000)

Colegio Nacional de Iquitos (CNI)
Stadium: Max Agustin 20000
Colours: White/White

Hungaritos Augustinos
Stadium: Max Agustin 20000
Colours: Green/Green

HUANCAYO (Population – 164000)
Club Deportivo Junin
Stadium: IV Centenario 15000
Founded: 1962
Colours: Green and white stripes/White

ICA (Population – 114000)
Octavio Espinoza Ica
Stadium: Picasso Peralta 6000
Founded: 1923
Colours: Red/White

TACNA (Population – 97000)
Club Deportivo Coronel Bolognesi
Stadium: Guillermo Briceno 25000
Founded: 1929
Colours: Red/Red

PUNO (Population – 67000)
Club Alfonso Ugarte
Stadium: Enrique Torres 25000
Founded: 1929
Colours: White with a red sash/Red

TALARA (Population – 57000)
Atletico Torino
Stadium: Campeonisimo 10000
Founded: 1952
Colours: Maroon with two white stripes/Maroon

CAJAMARCA (Population – 62000)
Universidad Tecnica de Cajamarca (UTC)
Stadium: Estadio Municipal 'Heroes de San Ramon' 30000
Founded: 1964
Colours: Cream/Black

HUANACO (Population – 61000)
Leon de Huánaco
Stadium: Baraclito Tapia
Founded: 1949
Colours: White/White

HUACHO (Population – 43000)
Juventud La Palma
Stadium: Segundo Torres Aranado 15000
Colours: Sky blue/Black

MOQUEGUA (Population – 31000)

Club Los Angeles
Stadium: 25 de Noviembre 15000
Colours: Red/Red

Atletico Hurucan
Stadium: 25 de Noviembre 15000
Colours: White/Blue

CHANCAY
La Joya-Iqueno
Stadium: Victor Raul Haya 15000
Founded: 1987
Colours: White with a black sash/Black
Previous names: Formed when Centro Iqueno and Juventus La Joya merged

CHICLANA
Club Juan Aurich
Stadium: Elias Aguirre 20000
Founded: 1922 Colours: Red/White

HUARAL
Sport Union Huaral
Stadium: Julio Lores Colan 10000
Founded: 1947
Colours: Red and white stripes/Black

TARMA
Asociacion Deportiva Tarma
Stadium: Estadio Union 15000
Founded: 1929 Colours: Sky blue/White

PERUVIAN LEAGUE CHAMPIONS

1926	CS Progreso
1927	Alianza
1928	Alianza
1929	Universitario
1930	Atletico Chalaco
1931	Alianza
1932	Alianza
1933	Alianza
1934	Alianza
1935	Sport Boys
1936	–
1937	Sport Boys
1938	Deportivo Municipal
1939	Universitario
1940	Deportivo Municipal
1941	Universitario
1942	Sport Boys
1943	Deportivo Municipal
1944	Sucre
1945	Universitario
1946	Universitario
1947	Atletico Chalaco
1948	Alianza
1949	Universitario
1950	Deportivo Municipal
1951	Sport Boys
1952	Alianza
1953	Mariscal Sucre
1954	Alianza
1955	Alianza
1956	Sporting Cristal
1957	Centro Iqueno
1958	Sport Boys
1959	Universitario
1960	Universitario
1961	Sporting Cristal
1962	Alianza
1963	Alianza
1964	Universitario
1965	Alianza
1966	Universitario
1967	Universitario
1968	Sporting Cristal
1969	Universitario
1970	Sporting Cristal
1971	Universitario
1972	Sporting Cristal
1973	Defensor Lima
1974	Universitario
1975	Alianza
1976	Union Huaral
1977	Alianza
1978	Alianza
1979	Sporting Cristal
1980	Sporting Cristal
1981	Mariano Melgar
1982	Universitario
1983	Sporting Cristal
1984	Sport Boys
1985	–
1986	Universitario
1987	Colegio San Augustin
1988	Universitario
1989	Sporting Cristal
1990	Union Huaral
1991	Universitario
1992	Sporting Cristal

INTERNATIONAL MATCHES PLAYED BY PERU

Date	Opponents	Result		Venue	Compet	Scorers
1-11-1927	Uruguay	L	0-4	Lima	SC	
13-11	Bolivia	W	3-2	Lima	SC	Neira, Sarmiento, Montellanos
27-11	Argentina	L	1-5	Lima	SC	Villanueva
3-11-1929	Argentina	L	0-3	Buenos Aires	SC	
11-11	Uruguay	L	1-4	Buenos Aires	SC	Lizarbe
16-11	Paraguay	L	0-5	Buenos Aires	SC	
14-07-1930	Romania	L	1-3	Montevideo	WCr1	Ferreira
18-07	Uruguay	L	0-1	Montevideo	WCr1	
13-01-1935	Uruguay	L	0-1	Lima	SC	
20-01	Argentina	L	1-4	Lima	SC	Fernandez T
26-01	Chile	W	1-0	Lima	SC	Montellanos

6-08-1936	Finland	W	7-3	Berlin	OGr1	Fernandez T 5, Villanueva 2
9-08	Austria	W	4-2	Berlin	OGqf	Alcalde, Villanueva 2, Fernandez T
27-12	Brazil	L	2-3	Buenos Aires	SC	Fernandez T, Villanueva
6-01-1937	Uruguay	L	2-4	Buenos Aires	SC	Fernandez T, Magallanes
16-01	Argentina	L	0-1	Buenos Aires	SC	
21-01	Chile	D	2-2	Buenos Aires	SC	Alcalde 2
24-01	Paraguay	W	1-0	Buenos Aires	SC	Magallanes
8-08-1938	Colombia	W	4-2	Bogota	BG	Ibanez 2, Fernandez T, Alcalde
11-08	Ecuador	W	9-1	Bogota	BG	Espinar 3, Alcalde 4, Bielich 2
14-08	Bolivia	W	3-0	Bogota	BG	Fernandez T 2, Alcalde
17-08	Venezuela	W	2-1	Bogota	BG	Bielich, Parades
15-01-1939	Ecuador	W	5-2	Lima	SC	Fernandez T 2, Alcalde 2, Ibanez
22-01	Chile	W	3-1	Lima	SC	Fernandez T 3
29-01	Paraguay	W	3-0	Lima	SC	Fernandez T 2, Alcalde
12-02	Uruguay	W	2-1	Lima	SC	Alcalde, Bielich
19-01-1941	Argentina	D	1-1	Lima	RGP	Hurtado
26-01	Argentina	D	1-1	Lima	RGP	Magallanes
29-01	Argentina	L	0-3	Lima	RGP	
9-02	Chile	L	0-1	Santiago	SC	
12-02	Argentina	L	1-2	Santiago	SC	Socarraz
23-02	Ecuador	W	4-0	Santiago	SC	Fernandez T 3, Vallejas
26-02	Uruguay	L	0-2	Santiago	SC	
18-01-1942	Paraguay	D	1-1	Montevideo	SC	Magallanes
21-01	Brazil	L	1-2	Montevideo	SC	Fernandez T
25-01	Argentina	L	1-3	Montevideo	SC	Fernandez T
28-01	Ecuador	W	2-1	Montevideo	SC	Quinonez, Guzman
1-02	Uruguay	L	0-3	Montevideo	SC	
7-02	Chile	D	0-0	Montevideo	SC	
6-12-1947	Paraguay	D	2-2	Guayaquil	SC	Castillo, Mosquera M
9-12	Chile	L	1-2	Guayaquil	SC	Lopez V
11-12	Argentina	L	2-3	Guayaquil	SC	Gomez C, Lopez V
20-12	Ecuador	D	0-0	Guayaquil	SC	
23-12	Colombia	W	5-1	Guayaquil	SC	Gomez C 2, Mosquera M, Guzman 2
25-12	Uruguay	L	0-1	Guayaquil	SC	
27-12	Bolivia	W	2-0	Guayaquil	SC	Guzman, Castillo
10-04-1949	Colombia	W	4-0	Rio de Janeiro	SC	Pedraza 2, Drago, Castillo
13-04	Paraguay	L	1-3	Rio de Janeiro	SC	Colunga
20-04	Ecuador	W	4-0	Rio de Janeiro	SC	Salinas, OG, Castillo, Pedraza
24-04	Brazil	L	1-7	Rio de Janeiro	SC	Salinas
27-04	Bolivia	W	3-0	Santos	SC	Drago 2, Heredia
30-04	Chile	W	3-0	Sao Paulo	SC	Mosquera A 2, Castillo
4-05	Uruguay	W	4-3	Rio de Janeiro	SC	Mosquera A, Castillo, Gomez C 2
23-03-1952	Panama	W	7-1	Santiago	PAC	Lopez V 5, Drago, Morales
30-03	Uruguay	L	2-5	Santiago	PAC	Barbadillo, Lopez V
2-04	Chile	L	2-3	Santiago	PAC	Barbadillo, Lopez V
10-04	Brazil	D	0-0	Santiago	PAC	
20-04	Mexico	W	3-0	Santiago	PAC	Rivera, Drago, Torres
22-02-1953	Bolivia	L	0-1	Lima	SC	
28-02	Ecuador	W	1-0	Lima	SC	Gomez C
4-03	Chile	D	0-0	Lima	SC	
8-03	Paraguay	D	2-2	Lima	SC	Terry, Villamares
19-03	Brazil	W	1-0	Lima	SC	Navarrete
28-03	Uruguay	L	0-3	Lima	SC	
26-07	Chile	L	1-2	Lima	PC	Navarrete
28-07	Chile	W	5-0	Lima	PC	Terry 2, Heredia 2, Drago
17-09-1954	Chile	L	1-2	Santiago	PC	Gomez Sanchez
19-09	Chile	W	4-2	Santiago	PC	Terry, OG, Gomez Sanchez 2
6-03-1955	Chile	L	4-5	Santiago	SC	Castillo, Barbadillo, Heredia, Gomez Sanchez
13-03	Ecuador	W	4-2	Santiago	SC	Gomez Sanchez 2, OG, Mosquera M
16-03	Argentina	D	2-2	Santiago	SC	Gomez Sanchez 2
23-03	Paraguay	D	1-1	Santiago	SC	Terry
30-03	Uruguay	W	2-1	Santiago	SC	Castillo, Gomez Sanchez
22-01-1956	Argentina	L	1-2	Montevideo	SC	Drago
28-01	Uruguay	L	0-2	Montevideo	SC	
1-02	Brazil	L	1-2	Montevideo	SC	Drago
5-02	Paraguay	D	1-1	Montevideo	SC	Lazon
9-02	Chile	L	3-4	Montevideo	SC	Castillo, Mosquera M, Gomez Sanchez
28-02	Argentina	D	0-0	Mexico City	PAC	

4–03	Mexico	W	2–0	Mexico City	PAC	Drago, Gomez Sanchez
6–03	Brazil	L	0–1	Mexico City	PAC	
15–03	Chile	D	2–2	Mexico City	PAC	Lamas, Mosquera M
17–03	Costa Rica	L	2–4	Mexico City	PAC	Salinas 2
10–03–1957	Ecuador	W	2–1	Lima	SC	Terry 2
16–03	Chile	W	1–0	Lima	SC	Mosquera M
23–03	Uruguay	L	3–5	Lima	SC	Terry, Seminario, Mosquera M
27–03	Colombia	W	4–1	Lima	SC	Terry, Rivera 2, Bassa
31–03	Brazil	L	0–1	Lima	SC	
6–04	Argentina	W	2–1	Lima	SC	Mosquera M, Terry
9–04	Argentina	L	1–4	Lima	Fr	Minaya
13–04	Brazil	D	1–1	Lima	WCq	Terry
21–04	Brazil	L	0–1	Rio de Janeiro	WCq	
10–03–1959	Brazil	D	2–2	Buenos Aires	SC	Seminario 2
14–03	Uruguay	W	5–3	Buenos Aires	SC	Loayza 3, Gomez Sanchez, Joya
18–03	Argentina	L	1–3	Buenos Aires	SC	Terry
21–03	Chile	D	1–1	Buenos Aires	SC	Loayza
29–03	Bolivia	D	0–0	Buenos Aires	SC	
2–04	Paraguay	L	1–2	Buenos Aires	SC	Gomez Sanchez
17–05	England	W	4–1	Lima	Fr	Seminario 3, Joya
10–07–1960	Spain	L	1–3	Lima	Fr	Carrasco
19–03–1961	Chile	L	2–5	Santiago	Fr	Flores, Carrasco
30–04	Colombia	L	0–1	Bogota	WCq	
7–05	Colombia	D	1–1	Lima	WCq	Delgado
20–05–1962	England	L	0–4	Lima	Fr	
10–03–1963	Brazil	L	0–1	Cochabamba	SC	
13–03	Argentina	W	2–1	Cochabamba	SC	Tenemas, Zegarra
17–03	Ecuador	W	2–1	La Paz	SC	Leon, Mosquera N
21–03	Bolivia	L	2–3	La Paz	SC	Gallardo, Leon
24–03	Colombia	D	1–1	La Paz	SC	Gallardo
27–03	Paraguay	L	1–4	Cochabamba	SC	Gallardo
3–04–1965	Paraguay	L	0–1	Lima	Fr	
15–04	Chile	L	1–4	Santiago	PC	Zegarra
28–04	Chile	L	0–1	Lima	PC	
16–05	Venezuela	W	1–0	Lima	WCq	Zegarra
2–06	Venezuela	W	6–3	Caracas	WCq	Mosquera N, Zavalla 2, Leon 3
6–06	Uruguay	L	0–1	Lima	WCq	
13–06	Uruguay	L	1–2	Montevideo	WCq	Uribe A
4–06–1966	Brazil	L	0–4	Sao Paulo	Fr	
8–06	Brazil	L	1–3	Belo Horizonte	Fr	Herera
28–07–1967	Uruguay	L	0–1	Lima	Fr	
30–07	Uruguay	L	1–2	Lima	Fr	Uribe A
14–07–1968	Brazil	L	3–4	Lima	Fr	Leon 2, Zegarra
17–07	Brazil	L	0–4	Lima	Fr	
18–08	Chile	L	1–2	Lima	PC	Bailleti
21–08	Chile	D	0–0	Lima	PC	
29–08	Argentina	D	2–2	Lima	Fr	Casaretto 2
1–09	Argentina	D	1–1	Lima	Fr	Casaretto
20–10	Mexico	D	3–3	Lima	Fr	Casaretto 3
7–04–1969	Brazil	L	1–2	Porto Alegre	Fr	Gallardo
9–04	Brazil	L	2–3	Rio de Janeiro	Fr	Gallardo, Baylon
8–05	Colombia	W	3–1	Bogota	Fr	Ramirez O, Cubillas, Leon
14–05	El Salvador	W	4–1	San Salvador	Fr	OG, Ramirez O 2, Castaneda
20–05	Mexico	W	1–0	Mexico City	Fr	Leon
22–05	Mexico	L	0–3	Leon	Fr	
18–06	Colombia	D	1–1	Lima	Fr	Chumpitaz
27–06	Uruguay	W	1–0	Lima	Fr	Leon
9–07	Paraguay	W	2–1	Lima	Fr	Cubillas 2
18–07	Paraguay	W	2–1	Lima	Fr	OG, Leon
3–08	Argentina	W	1–0	Lima	WCq	Leon
10–08	Bolivia	L	1–2	La Paz	WCq	Challe
17–08	Bolivia	W	3–0	Lima	WCq	Cubillas, Cruzado, Gallardo
31–08	Argentina	D	2–2	Buenos Aires	WCq	Ramirez O 2
9–02–1970	Romania	D	1–1	Lima	Fr	Cubillas
14–02	Soviet Union	D	0–0	Lima	Fr	
20–02	Soviet Union	L	0–2	Lima	Fr	
21–02	Bulgaria	L	1–3	Lima	Fr	Sotil
24–02	Bulgaria	W	5–3	Lima	Fr	Sotil 3, Challe, Cubillas
5–03	Mexico	L	0–1	Lima	Fr	

8-03	Mexico	W	1-0	Lima	Fr	Gallardo
15-03	Mexico	L	1-3	Mexico City	Fr	Challe
18-03	Mexico	D	3-3	Leon	Fr	Leon 2, Baylon
31-03	Uruguay	L	0-2	Montevideo	Fr	
18-04	Uruguay	W	4-2	Lima	Fr	Reyes 2, Leon, Gallardo
21-04	El Salvador	W	3-0	Lima	Fr	Gallardo, Sotil, Del Castillo
2-06	Bulgaria	W	3-2	Leon	WCr1	Gallardo, Chumpitaz, Cubillas
6-06	Morocco	W	3-0	Leon	WCr1	Cubillas 2, Challe
10-06	West Germany	L	1-3	Leon	WCr1	Cubillas
14-06	Brazil	L	2-4	Guadalajara	WCqf	Gallardo, Cubillas
27-07-1971	Paraguay	D	0-0	Lima	Fr	
11-08	Chile	W	1-0	Lima	PC	Sotil
15-08	Paraguay	L	0-2	Asuncion	Fr	
18-08	Chile	L	0-1	Santiago	PC	
29-03-1972	Colombia	D	1-1	Bogota	Fr	Munante
5-04	Mexico	L	1-2	Mexico City	Fr	Cubillas
19-04	Soviet Union	L	0-2	Kiev	Fr	
23-04	Romania	D	2-2	Bucharest	Fr	Rojas P, Cubillas
26-04	Scotland	L	0-2	Glasgow	Fr	
3-05	Holland	L	0-3	Rotterdam	Fr	
6-06	Colombia	D	0-0	Lima	Fr	
11-06	Bolivia	W	3-0	Curitiba	Clr1	Gallardo, Castenada, Sotil
14-06	Paraguay	L	0-1	Campo Grande	Clr1	
18-06	Venezuela	W	1-0	Manaus	Clr1	Ramirez O
25-06	Yugoslavia	L	1-2	Manaus	Clr1	Ramirez O
9-08	Mexico	W	3-2	Lima	Fr	Munante, Fernandez J 2
25-10	Argentina	L	0-2	Lima	RCC	
4-03-1973	Guatemala	W	5-1	Lima	Fr	Cubillas 2, Munante 2, Sotil
24-03	Bolivia	W	2-0	Lima	Fr	OG, Sotil
28-03	Paraguay	W	1-0	Lima	Fr	Sotil
8-04	Paraguay	D	1-1	Asuncion	Fr	Sotil
23-04	Panama	W	4-0	Lima	Fr	Cubillas, Munante, Ramirez O, Mayorga
29-04	Chile	W	2-0	Lima	WCq	Sotil 2
13-05	Chile	L	0-2	Santiago	WCq	
1-07	Colombia	W	3-1	Lima	Fr	Bailetti 2, Ramirez O
15-07	Bolivia	L	0-2	La Paz	Fr	
27-07	Argentina	L	1-3	Buenos Aires	RCC	Bailetti
5-08	Chile	L	1-2	Montevideo	WCq	Bailetti
22-06-1975	Ecuador	L	0-6	Quito	Fr	
25-06	Ecuador	L	0-1	Guayaquil	Fr	
1-07	Ecuador	W	2-0	Lima	Fr	Oblitas, Diaz R
10-07	Paraguay	W	2-0	Lima	Fr	Ramirez O 2
16-07	Chile	D	1-1	Santiago	SCr1	Rojas P
27-07	Bolivia	W	1-0	Oruro	SCr1	Ramirez O
7-08	Bolivia	W	3-1	Lima	SCr1	Ramirez O, Cueto, Oblitas
20-08	Chile	W	3-1	Lima	SCr1	Rojas P, Oblitas, Cubillas
30-09	Brazil	W	3-1	Belo Horizonte	SCsf	Casaretto 2, Cubillas
4-10	Brazil	L	0-2	Lima	SCsf	
16-10	Colombia	L	0-1	Bogota	SCf	
22-10	Colombia	W	2-0	Lima	SCf	Oblitas, Ramirez O
28-10	Colombia	W	1-0	Caracas	SCf	Sotil
12-10-1976	Uruguay	D	0-0	Lima	Fr	
28-10	Argentina	L	1-3	Lima	RCC	Quesada
10-11	Argentina	L	0-1	Buenos Aires	RCC	
24-11	Uruguay	D	0-0	Montevideo	Fr	
9-02-1977	Hungary	W	3-2	Lima	Fr	Velasquez 2, Sotil
20-02	Ecuador	D	1-1	Quito	WCq	Oblitas
6-03	Chile	D	1-1	Santiago	WCq	Munante
12-03	Ecuador	W	4-0	Lima	WCq	Velasquez, Oblitas 2, Luces
26-03	Chile	W	2-0	Lima	WCq	Sotil, Oblitas
17-05	Mexico	D	1-1	Mexico City	Fr	Ramirez O
24-05	Mexico	L	1-2	Monterrey	Fr	OG
26-05	Haiti	W	2-1	Port-au-Prince	Fr	Sotil, Luces
29-05	Haiti	D	2-2	Port-au-Prince	Fr	Velasquez, Ramirez O
10-06	Poland	L	1-3	Lima	Fr	Luces
10-07	Brazil	L	0-1	Cali	WCq	
17-07	Bolivia	W	5-0	Cali	WCq	Cubillas 2, Velasquez 2, Rojas P
19-03-1978	Argentina	L	1-2	Buenos Aires	RCC	Rojas P
23-03	Argentina	L	1-3	Lima	RCC	Oblitas

1–04	Bulgaria	D	1–1	Lima	Fr	Ramirez O
11–04	Mexico	W	1–0	Los Angeles	Fr	Goritti
22–04	China	W	2–1	Lima	Fr	Mosquera R, Rojas P
1–05	Brazil	L	0–3	Rio de Janeiro	Fr	
3–06	Scotland	W	3–1	Mendoza	WCr1	Cueto, Cubillas 2
7–06	Holland	D	0–0	Mendoza	WCr1	
11–06	Iran	W	4–1	Cordoba	WCr1	Velasquez, Cubillas 3
14–06	Brazil	L	0–3	Mendoza	WCr2	
18–06	Poland	L	0–1	Mendoza	WCr2	
21–06	Argentina	L	0–6	Rosario	WCr2	
11–07–1979	Ecuador	W	2–1	Lima	Fr	Ore, Mosquera R
18–07	Colombia	L	0–1	Lima	Fr	
25–07	Colombia	W	2–1	Bogota	Fr	Duarte, Cueto
8–08	Ecuador	L	1–2	Quito	Fr	Ravello
30–08	Uruguay	W	2–0	Lima	Fr	Mosquera R, Leguia
12–09	Scotland	D	1–1	Glasgow	Fr	Leguia
10–10	Paraguay	L	2–3	Lima	Fr	Chumpitaz, Lobaton
17–10	Chile	L	1–2	Lima	SCsf	Mosquera R
24–10	Chile	D	0–0	Santiago	SCsf	
1–11	Mexico	L	0–1	Monterrey	Fr	
18–07–1980	Uruguay	D	0–0	Montevideo	Fr	
12–11	Uruguay	D	1–1	Lima	Fr	Uribe J
4–02–1981	Czechoslovakia	L	1–3	Lima	Fr	Uribe J
11–02	Bulgaria	L	1–2	Lima	Fr	Correa
19–04	Chile	L	0–3	Santiago	Fr	
26–07	Colombia	D	1–1	Bogota	WCq	La Rosa
5–08	Chile	L	1–2	Lima	Fr	Olaechea
16–08	Colombia	W	2–0	Lima	WCq	Barbadillo, Uribe J
23–08	Uruguay	W	2–1	Montevideo	WCq	La Rosa, Uribe J
6–09	Uruguay	D	0–0	Lima	WCq	
23–03–1982	Chile	L	1–2	Santiago	Fr	OG
30–03	Chile	W	1–0	Lima	Fr	Navarro
18–04	Hungary	W	2–1	Budapest	Fr	Uribe J 2
25–04	Algeria	D	1–1	Algiers	Fr	Cueto
28–04	France	W	1–0	Paris	Fr	Oblitas
17–05	Romania	W	2–0	Lima	Fr	Uribe J, Velasquez
15–06	Cameroon	D	0–0	La Coruna	WCr1	
18–06	Italy	D	1–1	Vigo	WCr1	OG
22–06	Poland	L	1–5	La Coruna	WCr1	La Rosa
18–07–1983	Uruguay	D	1–1	Montevideo	Fr	Caballero
21–07	Chile	L	0–1	Lima	Fr	
3–08	Chile	L	0–2	Arica	Fr	
11–08	Uruguay	D	1–1	Lima	Fr	Navarro
17–08	Colombia	W	1–0	Lima	SCr1	Navarro
21–08	Bolivia	D	1–1	La Paz	SCr1	Navarro
28–08	Colombia	D	2–2	Bogota	SCr1	Malasquez 2
4–09	Bolivia	W	2–1	Lima	SCr1	Leguia, Caballero
5–10	Paraguay	L	0–2	Lima	Fr	
7–10	Paraguay	L	1–4	Asuncion	Fr	Caballero
13–10	Uruguay	L	0–1	Lima	SCsf	
20–10	Uruguay	D	1–1	Montevideo	SCsf	Malasquez
26–02–1984	Honduras	L	1–3	Lima	Fr	Hirano
2–08	Colombia	D	1–1	Medellin	Fr	Lobaton
9–08	Colombia	D	0–0	Lima	Fr	
19–09	Uruguay	L	0–2	Montevideo	Fr	
3–10	Uruguay	L	1–3	Lima	Fr	Lobaton
17–02–1985	Bolivia	W	3–0	Lima	Fr	Navarro 3
24–02	Chile	W	2–1	Santiago	Fr	Velasquez, Navarro
27–02	Uruguay	D	2–2	Montevideo	Fr	Navarro, Velasquez
9–03	Chile	D	1–1	Lima	Fr	Hirano
21–03	Ecuador	W	1–0	Lima	Fr	Hirano
23–04	Uruguay	W	2–1	Lima	Fr	Velasquez, Cueto
28–04	Brazil	W	1–0	Brasilia	Fr	Uribe J
1–05	Bolivia	D	0–0	Santa Cruz	Fr	
26–05	Colombia	L	0–1	Bogota	WCq	
2–06	Venezuela	W	1–0	San Cristobal	WCq	Uribe J
9–06	Colombia	D	0–0	Lima	WCq	
16–06	Venezuela	W	4–1	Lima	WCq	Navarro, Barbadillo, Hirano, Cueto
23–06	Argentina	W	1–0	Lima	WCq	Oblitas

30–06	Argentina	D	2–2	Buenos Ares	WCq	Velasquez, Barbadillo
20–09	Mexico	D	0–0	Los Angeles	Fr	
22–09	Mexico	L	0–1	San Jose	Fr	
16–10	Paraguay	L	0–1	Lima	Fr	
27–10	Chile	L	2–4	Santiago	WCq	Navarro 2
3–11	Chile	L	0–1	Lima	WCq	
23–01–1986	South Korea*	W	2–1	Trivandrum	JNC	
28–01	China*	L	1–3	Trivandrum	JNC	
30–01	India*	W	1–0	Trivandrum	JNC	
1–04	Brazil	L	0–4	Sao Luis	Fr	
19–06–1987	Chile	L	1–3	Lima	Fr	Navarro
21–06	Chile	W	2–0	Lima	Fr	Soto, Hirano
24–06	Chile	L	0–1	Santiago	Fr	
27–06	Argentina	D	1–1	Buenos Aires	SCr1	Reyna
4–07	Ecuador	D	1–1	Buenos Aires	SCr1	La Rosa
21–09–1988	Paraguay	L	0–1	Lima	Fr	
25–10	Chile	L	0–2	Arica	Fr	
23–11	Chile	D	1–1	Lima	Fr	Farfan
14–12	Uruguay	L	0–3	Montevideo	Fr	
1–02–1989	Chile	D	0–0	Armenia	Fr	
3–02	Colombia	L	0–1	Pereira	Fr	
10–05	Brazil	L	1–4	Fortaleza	Fr	Torres
15–05	Paraguay	D	1–1	Asuncion	Fr	Requena
18–05	Venezuela	W	2–1	Lima	Fr	Zegarra, Rey
24–05	Brazil	D	1–1	Lima	Fr	Dall'Orso
4–06	United States	L	0–3	New York	Fr	
16–06	Trinidad	L	1–2	Port of Spain	Fr	Manassero
20–06	Ecuador	W	2–1	Port of Spain	Fr	Olaechea, Navarro
25–06	Venezuela	L	1–3	San Cristobal	Fr	Rodriguez C
1–07	Paraguay	L	2–5	Salvador	SCr1	Hirano, Manassero
3–07	Brazil	D	0–0	Salvador	SCr1	
5–07	Venezuela	D	1–1	Salvador	SCr1	Navarro
9–07	Colombia	D	1–1	Recife	SCr1	Hirano
25–07	Chile	L	1–2	Arica	Fr	Reynoso
20–08	Bolivia	L	1–2	La Paz	WCq	Del Solar
27–08	Uruguay	L	0–2	Lima	WCq	
10–09	Bolivia	L	1–2	Lima	WCq	Gonzalez
24–09	Uruguay	L	0–2	Montevideo	WCq	
6–06–1991	Ecuador	L	0–1	Lima	Fr	
12–06	Uruguay	W	1–0	Lima	Fr	Hirano
20–06	Uruguay	D	0–0	Montevideo	Fr	
25–06	Ecuador	D	2–2	Quito	Fr	Hirano, Rodriguez
6–07	Paraguay	L	0–1	Santiago	SCr1	
8–07	Chile	L	2–4	Concepcion	SCr1	Maestri, Del Solar
12–07	Venezuela	W	5–1	Santiago	SCr1	La Rosa 2, OG, Del Solar, Hirano
14–07	Argentina	L	2–3	Santiago	SCr1	Yanez, Hirano

URUGUAY

Uruguay would seem to be in the dying throes of its status as a world power. Colombia looks set to replace it as one of the big three on the continent, and with a population that is ten times as large, perhaps this should not be too surprising. It would be wrong to write the Uruguayans off, however. Two World Cup titles, two Olympic titles at a time that they were in effect the world championships, and continuing success in the South American Championships is not a record to be trifled with.

Football in Uruguay is really football in Montevideo, as all the major clubs are located within the city. Montevideo is just across the River Plate estuary from Buenos Aires, and these two cities formed the heartland of South American football at the beginning of the century. Like in Argentina, the English introduced the game to Uruguay. William Poole, an English professor at Montevideo University, formed Albion Football Club in 1886, whilst English workers on the Central Uruguayan Railway formed in 1891 a club that became known by the name of the district within which it was located, Peñarol. Then 1899 saw the merger of two clubs, Montevideo FC and Defensa, under the name of Nacional, and they along with Peñarol have dominated the game in a manner matched perhaps only by Rangers and Celtic in Scotland. Out of 88 league championships they have won all bar 15 and finished in second spot in all bar 17, a remarkable achievement. In the period from 1915 to 1977, only Rampla Juniors in 1927 and Wanderers in 1931 managed to wrest the title from them.

Given the predictability of much of the domestic fare, international football has always been of prime importance to the Uruguayans. The formation of a football association in 1900, at the behest of Peñarol and Nacional, saw not only the start of a league championship but also the formation of a national selection. On 16 May 1901 a representative side met an Argentine combination in Montevideo for the first ever international match played outside the British Isles.

Uruguay and Argentina have met more times than any other international pairing over the years due to their proximity and relative isolation. The Lipton and Newton Cups were an almost annual event and two trophies donated by each country's Ministry of Education were another source for friendly games. The most notable rivalry, however, has been in the South American Championships.

Though not an official championship, the tournament in 1910 set the standard for future events as both Argentina and Uruguay easily saw off the challenge of Chile to set up a deciding last game. The rivalry even then was huge and the original game had to be postponed until the following day as excited fans burnt down one of the grandstands!

		Total			League			Copa Lib		
		G	S	B	G	S	B	G	S	B
1	Peñarol	43	40	15	38	36	5	5	4	10
2	Nacional	38	37	18	35	34	12	3	3	6
3	River Plate Buenos Aires	4	1	1	4	1	1	–	–	–
4	Wanderers	3	4	14	3	4	14	–	–	–
5	Defensor	3	1	8	3	1	8	–	–	–
6	Rampla Juniors	1	5	13	1	5	13	–	–	–
7	Danubio	1	2	3	1	2	2	–	–	1
8	Bella Vista	1	1	2	1	1	2	–	–	–
9	Central Espanol	1	–	4	1	–	4	–	–	–
10	Progreso	1	–	–	1	–	–	–	–	–
11	Cerro	–	1	6	–	1	6	–	–	–
12	Universal	–	1	4	–	1	4	–	–	–
13	Albion	–	1	1	–	1	1	–	–	–
14	Fénix	–	–	3	–	–	3	–	–	–
	Liverpool	–	–	3	–	–	3	–	–	–
16	Deutscher	–	–	2	–	–	2	–	–	–
	River Plate Montevideo	–	–	2	–	–	2	–	–	–
18	Dublin	–	–	1	–	–	1	–	–	–
	Huracan	–	–	1	–	–	1	–	–	–
	Miramar	–	–	1	–	–	1	–	–	–
	Racing	–	–	1	–	–	1	–	–	–
	Uruguay	–	–	1	–	–	1	–	–	–

Correct to the end of the 1991 season

Uruguay lost the match 4–1 to an in-form Argentine side, their goal scored by their most famous player in these early years, José Piendibene, the Peñarol centre-forward who played for the club from 1908 to 1930 and for the national side until 1921. Indeed he was the motivating force behind Uruguay's win in the next South American Championship, held in Buenos Aires again in 1916.

The golden age of Uruguayan football came just after Piendibene's retirement from international football when for over a decade Uruguay reigned supreme in the world. The 'Celeste', as they were known on account of their sky blue shirts, won the equivalent of three world championships with their victories in the 1924 and 1928 Olympic Games and their triumph in the first World Cup in 1930. The side that achieved these incredible feats was in essence the same throughout the whole period.

Captain and mentor was José Nasazzi and he was joined in defence by Pedro Arispe. In front of them they could rely on a midfield known as 'la costilla metalica', the iron curtain, consisting of José Andrade, Lorenzo Fernandez and Alvaro Gestido, whilst their attack was the most potent in the world with four of the most outstanding goalscorers of the time, Hector Castro, Pedro Petrone, Pedro Cea and most importantly Hector Scarone.

The Uruguayans took Europe by storm in 1924, delighting the Parisian crowds with their skill. They never looked in danger, beating Yugoslavia, America, France, Holland and then Switzerland in the final, scoring 20 goals in the process and conceding only two. In 1928 Europe knew what to expect but still could not cope, and just to emphasise the superiority of the River Plate Uruguay met their rivals Argentina in the final. Taken to a replay, the Celeste made no mistake in the second game and were crowned as Olympic Champions for the second time.

The 1930 World Cup triumph was the crowning glory of the side as they won the first edition on their own soil. Despite a poor European turn-out, it is generally agreed that Uruguay would have won whoever had made the trip. In the magnificent new Centenario stadium, built for the World Cup and to celebrate 100 years of independence, neither Peru or Romania were a match for the hosts in the first round. Neither were Yugoslavia in the semi-finals and they were brushed aside 6–1, setting the stage for a repeat of the 1928 Olympic final.

Once again the Uruguayans were triumphant, winning 4–2 after having been 2–1 down at half-time, and José Nasazzi became the first recipient of the Jules Rimet Cup. The victory signalled an extraordinary hiatus in the fixtures of the national side. Uruguay refused to make the journey to Italy to defend their title four years later and also declined to take part in 1938. There was not much action in the South American Championships either during the 1930s, and it was not until the early 1940s that the national side began playing regularly again.

This may have been due in part to the chaos at club level in the early 1930s caused by professionalism. As an issue, professionalism had been simmering since 1922 when Peñarol caused a split in the Association over payments to their players, and the situation was not resolved until 1932 when professionalism was legalised.

Professionalism has been a bitter-sweet pill for Uruguayan football. Without it they would have fallen behind their rivals, but it caused many disputes. All the clubs except Peñarol and Nacional could not afford it, and even the big two were hard pushed to pay the high wages expected by the players. A strike in 1949 lead to a large exodus, primarily to Colombia, whilst in the same year Peñarol would not release their players for the South American Championship, and the national team consequently finished a miserable sixth out of the eight teams taking part.

All was forgiven the following year as the national side, back at full strength, won the World Cup in neighbouring Brazil against all the odds. Bolivia were dispatched in the first round but in the final pool Uruguay were not expected to match the form of the Brazilians, who were scoring freely. The omens were not good after a draw with Spain in the first game, and despite a close win over Sweden, the Uruguayans had to beat Brazil in the Maracana to top the table and win the title.

When they fell behind to a Friaca goal early in the second half all looked lost, but in one of the most spirited comebacks of all time, first Schiaffino and then Ghiggia turned the Brazilians' world upside down to secure the victory. Uruguay were World Cup winners for a second time and had yet to lose a match in the tournament.

Four years later they travelled to Europe for the first time in the World Cup, and along with Hungary were regarded as the best team in the tournament. Indeed their semi-final defeat at the hands of the Magyars is often regarded as one of the best games of football ever played and would have made a perfect final. The stars of the early 1950s and the second great team that Uruguay had built were Juan Schiaffino, probably the most famous Uruguayan player ever, Victor Andrade, nephew of the great José Andrade of the 1930 team, Roque Maspoli in goal, Obdulio Varela, at centre half the linchpin of the side and Omar Miguez, the team's main goalscorer.

The sides of the 1920s and early 1950s have proved a heavy burden since as successive Uruguayan sides have failed to live up to this pedigree. The 1970 World Cup side containing Luis Cubilla, Ladislao Mazurkiewicz, Juan Mujica, Roberto Matosas and Pedro Rocha came close, but the reputation of that team lay more in the roots of club football than in the national side.

The year 1960 was a crucial one in Uruguayan football, for the new Copa Libertadores gave a new lease of life to both Peñarol and Nacional. All of a sudden they found themselves in the international spotlight. Peñarol have qualified for all but six of the editions played, whilst Nacional have missed out on only 12, and between them they have appeared in 15 finals, winning eight of them. Peñarol were the inaugural winners and after Independiente are the second most successful club in the history of the tournament. Nacional, winners for the first time in 1971, rank third on the list.

Though often a shop window for the agents of the big European clubs, the Copa Libertadores has added spice to a somewhat predictable Uruguayan championship. All of the major clubs are located within Montevideo and until the 1970s clubs from outside did not take part in the the league. Since the reorganisation of the league the power of both Nacional and Peñarol has been slowly curtailed. Winners every season between 1932 and 1975, their stranglehold was first broken in 1976 by Defensor, but the decline has been most notable in the second half of the 1980s. Peñarol last won the championship in 1985 and Nacional the year after.

With many of the best players moving abroad due to the perilous financial state of most Uruguayan clubs, the national team has struggled to retain its position at the top of the football hierarchy. Despite winning the 1983 and 1987 South Amercan Championships thanks to players of the calibre of Enzo Francescoli and Carlos Aguilera, the famous Celeste will have their work cut out not to be remembered only as the country that won a few world championships in the distant past.

Population: 3 033 000
Area, sq km: 176 215
% in urban areas: 86%
Capital city: Montevideo

Asociación Uruguaya de Fútbol
Guayabo 1531
Montevideo
Tel: (010 598) 2 407101
Fax: (010 598) 2 407873
Telex: AUF UY 22607
Cable: FOOTBALL MONTEVIDEO

Languages for correspondence: Spanish, English & French
Year of formation: 1900
Affiliation to FIFA: 1923
Affiliation to CONMEBOL: 1916
Registered clubs: 1102
Registered players: 163 600
Professional players: 740
Registered coaches: 378
Registered referees: 132
National stadium: Estadio Centenario, Montevideo 75 000

National colours: Shirts: Sky Blue/Shorts: Black/Socks: Black
Reserve colours: Shirts: White/Shorts: White/Socks: White
Season: April–December

THE RECORD

WORLD CUP

1930 .... QT Automatic – Final Tournament/Winners

1934 .... Did not enter
1938 .... Did not enter
1950 .... QT W-O in group 8 – Final Tournament/Winners
1954 .... QT Automatic – Final Tournament/Semi-finalists/4th place
1958 .... QT 2nd/3 in group 3
1962 .... QT 1st/2 in group 2 – Final Tournament/1st round
1966 .... QT 1st/3 in group 1 – Final Tournament/Quarter-finalists
1970 .... QT 1st/3 in group 3 – Final Tournament/Semi-finalists/4th place
1974 .... QT 1st/3 in group 1 – Final Tournament/1st round
1978 .... QT 2nd/3 in group 2
1982 .... QT 2nd/3 in group 2
1986 .... QT 1st/3 in group 2 – Final Tournament/2nd round
1990 .... QT 1st/3 in group 1 – Final Tournament/2nd round

SOUTH AMERICAN CHAMPIONSHIP

1910 .... 2nd/3
1916 .... 1st/4 – Winners
1917 .... 1st/4 – Winners
1919 .... 2nd/4
1920 .... 1st/4 – Winners
1921 .... 3rd/4
1922 .... 3rd/5
1923 .... 1st/4 – Winners
1924 .... 1st/4 – Winners
1925 .... –
1926 .... 1st/5 – Winners
1927 .... 2nd/4
1929 .... 3rd/4
1935 .... 1st/4 – Winners
1937 .... 4th/6
1939 .... 2nd/5
1941 .... 2nd/5
1942 .... 1st/7 – Winners
1945 .... 4th/7
1946 .... 4th/6
1947 .... 3rd/8
1949 .... 6th/8
1953 .... 3rd/7
1955 .... 4th/6
1956 .... 1st/6 – Winners
1957 .... 3rd/7
1959 .... 6th/7
1959 .... 1st/5 – Winners
1963 .... –
1967 .... 1st/6 – Winners
1975 .... 4th/10 / Semi-finalists
1979 .... 6th/10 / 1st round
1983 .... 1st/10 – Winners
1987 .... 1st/10 – Winners
1989 .... 2nd/10 – Second round
1991 .... 5th/10 – 1st round

OLYMPIC GAMES

1908–20 ..... Did not enter
1924 .... Winners
1928 .... Winners
1936–56 ..... Did not enter
1960 .... QT Failed to qualify
1964 .... QT Failed to qualify
1968 .... QT Failed to qualify
1972 .... QT Failed to qualify
1976 .... QT Failed to qualify
1980 .... Did not enter
1984 .... Did not enter
1988 .... QT Failed to qualify
1992 .... QT Failed to qualify

COPA LIBERTADORES

Winners – Peñarol 1960, 1961, 1966, 1982, 1987. Nacional 1971, 1980, 1988
Finalists – Peñarol 1962, 1965, 1970, 1983. Nacional 1964, 1967, 1969

SUPER CUP: Finalists – Nacional 1990

CLUB DIRECTORY

MONTEVIDEO (1 550 000)

Club Atletico Bella Vista
Stadium: Parque José Nasazzi 20 000
Founded: 1920
Colours: Gold and white halves/Blue

Central Espanol
Stadium: Palermo 10 000
Founded: 1905
Colours: Red and white stripes/Blue
Previous name: Central FC 1905–71

Club Atletico Cerro
Stadium: Luis Troccoli 30 000
Founded: 1922
Colours: Sky Blue and white stripes/Blue

Danubio Futbol Club
Stadium: Jardins del Hipodromo 18 000
Founded: 1932
Colours: White with black sash/White

Club Atletico Defensor
Stadium: Luis Frazzini 15 000
Founded: 1913
Colours: Violet/White

Liverpool Futbol Club
Stadium: Belvedere 10 000
Founded: 1915
Colours: Black and blue stripes/White

Club Nacional de Football
Stadium: Parque Central 20 000
Founded: 1899
Colours: White/Blue

Club Atletico Peñarol
Stadium: Las Acacias, 'Pocitos' 15 000
Founded: 1891
Colours: Black and yellow stripes/Black
Previous names: Central Uruguayan Railways Cricket Club 1891–1913

Club Atletico Progreso
Stadium: Parque Abraham Paladino 10 000
Founded: 1917
Colours: Yellow and red stripes/Red

Club Atletico River Plate
Stadium: Parque Federico Saroldi 10 000
Founded: 1932
Colours: Red and white stripes/Blue

Rampla Juniors Futbol Club
Stadium: Olimpico 10 000
Founded: 1914
Colours: Green and red stripes/Black

Montevideo Wanderers Futbol Club
Stadium: Parque Alfredo Viera 12 000
Founded: 1902
Colours: Black and white stripes/Black

URUGUAYAN LEAGUE CHAMPIONSHIP

Year	Champions					
1900	Peñarol	12	Albion	8	Uruguay	2
1901	Peñarol	15	Nacional	12	Albion	8
1902	Nacional	20	Peñarol	16	Deutscher	9
1903	Nacional	24	Peñarol	22	Deutscher	10
1904	–					
1905	Peñarol	16	Nacional	12	Wanderers	10
1906	Wanderers	18	Peñarol	14	Nacional	10
1907	Peñarol	17	Wanderers	13	Nacional	12
1908	River Plate B-A	31	Nacional	26	Dublin	24
1909	Wanderers	35	Peñarol	34	River Plate B-A	32
1910	River Plate B-A	26	Peñarol	24	Nacional	22

1911	Peñarol 25	River Plate B-A 17	Wanderers 17
1912	Nacional 25	Peñarol 19	Wanderers 18
1913	River Plate B-A 22	Nacional 19	Central 14
1914	River Plate B-A 26	Peñarol 24	Nacional 21
1915	Nacional 29	Peñarol 27	Universal 23
1916	Nacional 30	Peñarol 18	Wanderers 17
1917	Nacional 34	Peñarol 32	Universal 21
1918	Peñarol 32	Nacional 31	Universal 22
1919	Nacional 31	Universal 27	Peñarol 26
1920	Nacional 40	Peñarol 36	Central 25
1921	Peñarol 39	Nacional 37	Universal 31
1922	Nacional 36	Wanderers 35	Peñarol 28
1923	Nacional 37	Rampla Juniors 33	Bella Vista 30
1924	Nacional 39	Bella Vista 33	Rampla Juniors 29
1925	–		
1926	Peñarol		
1927	Rampla Juniors 57	Peñarol 54	Wanderers 50
1928	Peñarol 45	Rampla Juniors 37	Nacional 35
1929	Peñarol 47	Nacional 36	Rampla Juniors 29
1930	–		
1931	Wanderers 39	Nacional 37	Rampla Juniors 31

PROFESSIONAL LEAGUE

1932	Peñarol 40	Rampla Juniors 35	Nacional 32
1933	Nacional 46	Peñarol 46	Rampla Juniors 32
1934	Nacional 41	Peñarol 38	Wanderers 35
1935	Peñarol 31	Nacional 29	Wanderers 25
1936	Peñarol 30	Nacional 27	Rampla Juniors 24
1937	Peñarol 29	Nacional 28	Wanderers 21
1938	Peñarol 34	Nacional 31	Central 25
1939	Nacional 28	Peñarol 28	Wanderers 22
1940	Nacional 35	Rampla Juniors 25	Wanderers 24
1941	Nacional 40	Peñarol 31	Rampla Juniors 22
1942	Nacional 28	Peñarol 25	Wanderers 24
1943	Nacional 32	Peñarol 27	Miramar 17
1944	Peñarol 27	Nacional 27	Defensor 25
1945	Peñarol 31	Nacional 25	Defensor 22
1946	Nacional 32	Peñarol 28	River Plate 21
1947	Nacional 27	Peñarol 21	Rampla Juniors 21
1948	–		
1949	Peñarol 34	Nacional 28	Rampla Juniors 23
1950	Nacional 30	Peñarol 28	Rampla Juniors 22
1951	Peñarol 29	Nacional 27	Rampla Juniors 22
1952	Nacional 31	Peñarol 31	Rampla Juniors 19
1953	Peñarol 32	Nacional 25	Rampla Juniors 22
1954	Peñarol 32	Danubio 24	Nacional 22
1955	Nacional 31	Peñarol 27	Danubio 18
1956	Nacional 32	Peñarol 29	Cerro 24
1957	Nacional 24	Peñarol 21	Defensor 20
1958	Peñarol 24	Nacional 23	Rampla Juniors 23
1959	Peñarol 26	Nacional 26	Racing 22
1960	Peñarol 28	Cerro 28	Nacional 24
1961	Peñarol 30	Nacional 27	Defensor 23
1962	Peñarol 33	Nacional 27	Fénix 18
1963	Nacional 31	Peñarol 30	Wanderers 21
1964	Peñarol 34	Rampla Juniors 22	Nacional 21
1965	Peñarol 32	Nacional 27	Cerro 25
1966	Nacional 28	Peñarol 26	Cerro 23
1967	Peñarol 33	Nacional 27	Cerro 21
1968	Peñarol 33	Nacional 27	Cerro 21
1969	Nacional 43	Peñarol 39	River Plate 28
1970	Nacional 45	Peñarol 38	Huracan 30
1971	Nacional 40	Peñarol 39	Liverpool 34
1972	Nacional 36	Peñarol 28	Defensor 26
1973	Peñarol 35	Nacional 29	Danubio 28
1974	Peñarol 36	Nacional 31	Liverpool 31
1975	Peñarol 38	Nacional 29	Liverpool 28
1976	Defensor 32	Peñarol 31	Nacional 28

1977	Nacional	36	Peñarol	35	Defensor	30
1978	Peñarol	39	Nacional	36	Fénix	24
1979	Peñarol	41	Nacional	38	Fénix	27
1980	Nacional	41	Wanderers	35	Peñarol	32
1981	Peñarol	44	Nacional	41	Wanderers	35
1982	Peñarol	39	Defensor	36	Nacional	32
1983	Nacional	38	Danubio	29	Defensor	29
1984	Central Espanol	35	Peñarol	34	Nacional	32
1985	Peñarol	32	Wanderers	28	Cerro	27
1986	Nacional	35	Peñarol	34	Central Espanol	28
1987	Defensor	33	Nacional	30	Bella Vista	28
1988	Danubio	40	Peñarol	31	Defensor	31
1989	Progreso	20	Nacional	15	Peñarol	15
1990	Bella Vista	39	Nacional	32	Peñarol	31
1991	Defensor	34	Nacional	33	Wanderers	31

Championship play-offs

1933	Nacional	0–0 0–0 3–2	Peñarol
1939	Nacional	3–2	Peñarol
1944	Peñarol	0–0 3–2	Nacional
1952	Nacional	4–2	Peñarol
1959	Peñarol	2–0	Nacional
1960	Peñarol	3–1	Cerro

INTERNATIONAL MATCHES PLAYED BY URUGUAY

Date	Opponents	Result		Venue	Compet	Scorers
16-05-1901	Argentina	L	2–3	Montevideo	Fr	Cespedes B, Poole
20-07-1902	Argentina	L	0–6	Montevideo	Fr	
13-09-1903	Argentina	W	3–2	Buenos Aires	Fr	Cespedes B 2, Cespedes C
15-08-1905	Argentina	D	0–0	Buenos Aires	LC	
15-08-1906	Argentina	L	0–2	Montevideo	LC	
21-10	Argentina	L	1–2	Buenos Aires	NC	OG
15-08-1907	Argentina	L	1–2	Buenos Aires	LC	Zibecchi
6-10	Argentina	L	1–2	Montevideo	NC	Zumarin
15-08-1908	Argentina	D	2–2	Montevideo	LC	Bertone J, Zumaran
13-09	Argentina	L	1–2	Buenos Aires	NC	Brachi
4-10	Argentina	W	1–0	Buenos Aires	MEA	Brachi
15-08-1909	Argentina	L	1–2	Buenos Aires	LC	Zumaran
19-09	Argentina	D	2–2	Montevideo	NC	Raymonda, Buck
10-10	Argentina	L	1–3	Buenos Aires	MEA	Raymonda
29-05-1910	Chile	W	3–0	Buenos Aires	SC	Piendibene, Brachi, Buck
12-06	Argentina	L	1–4	Buenos Aires	SC	Piendibene
15-08	Argentina	W	3–1	Montevideo	LC	Dacal, Scarone C, Zibecchi
13-11	Argentina	D	1–1	Buenos Aires	MEA	Piendibene
27-11	Argentina	W	6–2	Buenos Aires	MEA	Seoanne 2, Scarone C 2, Piendibene, Quaglia
30-04-1911	Argentina*	L	1–2	Montevideo	Fr	Canavessi
15-08	Argentina	W	2–0	Buenos Aires	LC	Piendibene, Dacal
17-09	Argentina	L	2–3	Montevideo	NC	Romano, Canavessi
8-10	Argentina	D	1–1	Montevideo	MEU	Piendibene
22-10	Argentina	L	0–2	Buenos Aires	MEA	
29-10	Argentina	W	3–0	Montevideo	MEU	Piendibene 2, Canavessi
25-02-1912	Argentina*	L	0–2	Buenos Aires	Fr	
15-08	Argentina	W	2–0	Montevideo	LC	Scarone C, Dacal
25-08	Argentina	W	3–0	Montevideo	MEU	Scarone C, Romano, Dacal
22-09	Argentina	W	1–0	Buenos Aires	MEA	Piendibene
6-10	Argentina	D	3–3	Buenos Aires	NC	Scarone C, Romano, Dacal
1-12	Argentina	L	1–3	Montevideo	MC	Scarone C
27-04-1913	Argentina*	D	0–0	Buenos Aires	Fr	
15-06	Argentina	D	1–1	Buenos Aires	SPC	Dacal
9-07	Argentina	L	1–2	Buenos Aires	SPC	Piendibene
13-07	Argentina*	W	5–4	Montevideo	Fr	
15-08	Argentina	L	0–4	Buenos Aires	LC	
31-08	Argentina	L	0–2	Buenos Aires	MEA	
28-09	Argentina*	L	0–4	Buenos Aires	Fr	
5-10	Argentina	W	1–0	Montevideo	MEU	Vallarino
26-10	Argentina	W	1–0	Montevideo	NC	Gorla
30-08-1914	Argentina	W	3–2	Montevideo	MEU	Vallarino, Dacal, OG
13-09	Argentina	L	1–2	Buenos Aires	MEA	Vallarino
18-07-1915	Argentina	L	2–3	Montevideo	MEU	Dacal, Lazaro

15–08	Argentina	L	1–2	Buenos Aires	LC	Piendibene
12–09	Argentina	W	2–0	Montevideo	NC	Piendibene 2
2–07–1916	Chile	W	4–0	Buenos Aires	SC	Piendibene 2, Gradin 2
12–07	Brazil	W	2–1	Buenos Aires	SC	Gradin, Tognola
14–07	Chile	W	4–1	Montevideo	Fr	
17–07	Argentina	D	0–0	Buenos Aires	SC	
18–07	Brazil	L	0–1	Montevideo	Fr	
15–08	Argentina	L	1–3	Buenos Aires	NC	Farinasso
15–08	Argentina	L	1–2	Montevideo	LC	Gradin
1–10	Argentina	L	0–1	Montevideo	MEU	
1–10	Argentina	L	2–7	Buenos Aires	MEA	Mongelar, Harley
29–10	Argentina	W	3–1	Montevideo	Fr	
18–07–1917	Argentina	L	0–2	Montevideo	MEU	
15–08	Argentina	L	0–1	Buenos Aires	LC	
2–09	Argentina	W	1–0	Montevideo	NC	Scarone C
30–09	Chile	W	4–0	Montevideo	SC	Romano 2, Scarone C 2
7–10	Brazil	W	4–0	Montevideo	SC	Romano 2, Scaorne H, Scarone C
14–10	Argentina	W	1–0	Montevideo	SC	Scarone H
16–10	Brazil	W	3–1	Montevideo	Fr	
18–07–1918	Argentina	D	1–1	Montevideo	MEU	Gradin
28–07	Argentina	W	3–1	Montevideo	MEU	Romano 2, Gradin
15–08	Argentina	D	0–0	Buenos Aires	MEA	
25–08	Argentina	L	1–2	Buenos Aires	MEA	Somma
20–09	Argentina	D	1–1	Montevideo	LC	Perez J
29–09	Argentina	L	0–2	Buenos Aires	NC	
13–05–1919	Argentina	W	3–2	Rio de Janeiro	SC	Scarone C, Scarone H, Gradin
17–05	Chile	W	2–0	Rio de Janeiro	SC	Scarone C, Perez J
25–05	Brazil	D	2–2	Rio de Janeiro	SC	Gradin, Scarone C
29–05	Brazil	L	0–1	Rio de Janeiro	SCpo	
18–07	Argentina	W	4–1	Montevideo	MEU	Scarone H 2, Perez O, Romano
24–08	Argentina	W	2–1	Montevideo	NC	Romano, Villar
7–09	Argentina	W	2–1	Buenos Aires	LC	Scarone H 2
19–10	Argentina	L	1–6	Buenos Aires	MEA	Fraga
7–12	Argentina	W	4–2	Montevideo	Fr	
18–07–1920	Argentina	W	2–0	Montevideo	MEU	Scarone H, Romano
25–07	Argentina	W	3–1	Buenos Aires	NC	Piendibene, Romano, Somma
8–08	Argentina	L	0–1	Buenos Aires	MEA	
12–09	Argentina	D	1–1	Viña del Mar	SC	Piendebene
18–09	Brazil	W	6–0	Viña del Mar	SC	Romano, Somma, Perez J, Campolo, Urdinarian
26–09	Chile	W	2–1	Viña del Mar	SC	Romano, Perez J
9–10–1921	Paraguay	L	1–2	Buenos Aires	SC	Piendibene
23–10	Brazil	W	2–1	Buenos Aires	SC	Romano 2
30–10	Argentina	L	0–1	Buenos Aires	SC	
2–11	Paraguay	W	4–2	Montevideo	Fr	Buffoni 2, Campolo, Foglino
22–01–1922	Argentina*	W	3–1	Buenos Aires	Fr	
22–07	Argentina	D	2–2	Montevideo	Fr	
27–08	Argentina*	D	3–3	Buenos Aires	Fr	
23–09	Chile	W	2–0	Rio de Janeiro	SC	Urdinaran, Heguy
1–10	Brazil	D	0–0	Rio de Janeiro	SC	
8–10	Argentina	W	1–0	Rio de Janeiro	SC	Buffoni
12–10	Paraguay	L	0–1	Rio de Janeiro	SC	
22–10	Argentina*	L	2–3	Buenos Aires	Fr	
11–11	Argentina*	L	0–4	La Plata	Fr	
12–11	Argentina	W	1–0	Montevideo	LC	Romano
10–12	Argentina	W	1–0	Montevideo	MEU	Scarone C
17–12	Argentina	D	2–2	Buenos Aires	NC	Scarone C, Saldombide
25–05–1923	Argentina*	W	2–0	Montevideo	Fr	
24–06	Argentina	D	0–0	Buenos Aires	LC	
15–07	Argentina	D	2–2	Buenos Aires	MEA	Romano, Oliveiri
22–07	Argentina	D	2–2	Montevideo	MEU	Romano, Saldombide
25–08	Argentina*	D	1–1	Montevideo	Fr	
30–09	Argentina	L	0–2	Montevideo	MEU	
4–11	Paraguay	W	2–0	Montevideo	SC	Scarone H, Petrone
25–11	Brazil	W	2–1	Montevideo	SC	Petrone, Cea
25–11	Chile	W	2–1	Montevideo	Fr	
2–12	Argentina	W	2–0	Montevideo	SC	Petrone, Somma
8–12	Argentina	W	3–2	Buenos Aires	Fr	
25–05–1924	Argentina	L	0–4	Buenos Aires	NC	

25–05	Argentina	W	2–0	Montevideo	LC	
26–05	Yugoslavia	W	7–0	Paris	OGr1	Petrone 2, Cea 2, Scarone H, Vidal
29–05	United States	W	3–0	Paris	OGr2	Petrone 3
1–06	France	W	5–1	Paris	OGqf	Petrone 2, Scarone H 2, Romano
6–06	Holland	W	2–1	Paris	OGsf	Cea, Scarone H
9–06	Switzerland	W	3–0	Paris	OGf	Petrone, Cea, Romano
10–08	Argentina	D	0–0	Buenos Aires	Fr	
31–08	Argentina	L	2–3	Montevideo	MEU	
21–09	Argentina	D	1–1	Montevideo	Fr	Petrone
2–10	Argentina	L	1–2	Buenos Aires	Fr	Cea
12–10	Chile	W	1–0	Santiago	Fr	
19–10	Chile	W	5–0	Montevideo	SC	Petrone 3, Romano, Zingone
26–10	Paraguay	W	3–1	Montevideo	SC	Petrone, Romano, Cea
2–11	Argentina	D	0–0	Montevideo	SC	
16–11	Argentina	W	1–0	Montevideo	Fr	
5–01–1925	Argentina	L	0–1	Buenos Aires	Fr	
14–07	Paraguay	L	0–1	Montevideo	Fr	
18–07	Paraguay	L	0–1	Montevideo	Fr	
15–08	Paraguay	L	0–1	Asuncion	Fr	
19–08	Paraguay	W	1–0	Asuncion	Fr	Fernandez L
23–08	Paraguay	D	0–0	Asuncion	Fr	
17–10–1926	Chile	W	3–1	Santiago	SC	Borjas, Castro H, Scarone H
24–10	Argentina	W	2–0	Santiago	SC	Borjas, Scarone H
28–10	Bolivia	W	6–0	Santiago	SC	Scarone H 5, Romano
1–11	Paraguay	W	6–1	Santiago	SC	Castro H 4, Saldombide 2
14–07–1927	Argentina	L	0–1	Montevideo	NC	
30–08	Argentina	W	1–0	Buenos Aires	LC	Scarone H
1–11	Peru	W	4–0	Lima	SC	Sacco 2, Castro H, OG
6–11	Bolivia	W	9–0	Lima	SC	Petrone 3, Figueroa 3, Arremon, Castro H, Scarone H
20–11	Argentina	L	2–3	Lima	SC	Scarone H 2
10–12	Chile	W	3–2	Viña del Mar	Fr	Scarone H, Castro H, Petrone
30–05–1928	Holland	W	2–0	Amsterdam	OGr1	Scarone H, Urdinaran
3–06	Germany	W	4–1	Amsterdam	OGqf	Petrone 3, Castro H
7–06	Italy	W	3–2	Amsterdam	OGsf	Cea, Scarone H, Campolo
10–06	Argentina	D	1–1	Amsterdam	OGf	Petrone
13–06	Argentina	W	2–1	Amsterdam	OGf	Figueroa, Scarone H
15–08	Paraguay	L	1–3	Asuncion	Fr	
19–08	Paraguay	D	1–1	Asuncion	Fr	
30–08	Argentina	L	0–1	Buenos Aires	NC	
21–09	Argentina	D	2–2	Montevideo	LC	Petrone, Piriz
16–06–1929	Argentina	L	0–2	Buenos Aires	Fr	
16–06	Argentina	D	1–1	Montevideo	Fr	Carbone
20–09	Argentina	W	2–1	Montevideo	NC	Castro H, Fernandez L
28–09	Argentina	D	0–0	Buenos Aires	LC	
1–11	Paraguay	L	0–3	Buenos Aires	SC	
11–11	Peru	W	4–1	Buenos Aires	SC	Fernandez E 3, Andrade J
17–11	Argentina	L	0–2	Buenos Aires	SC	
25–05–1930	Argentina	D	1–1	Buenos Aires	NC	Petrone
18–07	Peru	W	1–0	Montevideo	WCr1	Castro H
22–07	Rumania	W	4–0	Montevideo	WCr1	Dorado, Scarone H, Anselmo, Cea
27–07	Yugoslavia	W	6–1	Montevideo	WCsf	Cea 3, Anselmo 2, Iriarte
30–07	Argentina	W	4–2	Montevideo	WCf	Dorado, Cea, Iriarte, Castro
6–09–1931	Brazil	L	0–2	Rio de Janeiro	RBC	
15–05–1932	Argentina	L	0–2	Buenos Aires	Fr	
18–05	Argentina	W	1–0	Montevideo	Fr	Dorado
4–12	Brazil	L	1–2	Montevideo	RBC	Castro H
21–01–1933	Argentina	W	2–1	Montevideo	Fr	Fernandez E, Haebrili
5–02	Argentina	L	1–4	Buenos Aires	Fr	Matta
14–12	Argentina	L	0–1	Montevideo	Fr	
18–07–1934	Argentina	D	2–2	Montevideo	Fr	Garcia J, Ciocca
15–08	Argentina	L	0–1	Buenos Aires	Fr	
13–01–1935	Peru	W	1–0	Lima	SC	Castro H
18–01	Chile	W	2–1	Lima	SC	Ciocca 2
20–01	Argentina*	D	2–2	Buenos Aires	Fr	Amarillo, Castaldo
27–01	Argentina	W	3–0	Lima	SC	Castro H, Taboada, Ciocca
18–07	Argentina	D	1–1	Montevideo	HGC	Piriz
15–08	Argentina	L	0–3	Buenos Aires	JMC	
9–08–1936	Argentina	L	0–1	Buenos Aires	JMC	

20–09	Argentina	W	2–1	Montevideo	HGC	Lago, Villdonica
2–01–1937	Paraguay	L	2–4	Buenos Aires	SC	Varela S 2
6–01	Peru	W	4–2	Buenos Aires	SC	Varela S 2, Camaiti 2
10–01	Chile	L	0–3	Buenos Aires	SC	
19–01	Brazil	L	2–3	Buenos Aires	SC	Piriz, Villadonica
23–01	Argentina	W	3–2	Buenos Aires	SC	Piriz, Varela S, Ithurbide
10–10	Argentina	L	0–3	Montevideo	NC	
11–11	Argentina	L	1–5	Buenos Aires	LC	Muniz
18–06–1938	Argentina	L	0–1	Buenos Aires	JMC	
12–10	Argentina	L	2–3	Montevideo	HGC	Varela S, Ciocca
22–01–1939	Ecuador	W	6–0	Lima	SC	Varela S 3, Lago 2, Porta
29–01	Chile	W	3–2	Lima	SC	Lago, Chirmini, Camaiti
5–02	Paraguay	W	3–1	Lima	SC	Porta, Lago, Varela S
12–02	Peru	L	1–2	Lima	SC	Porta
12–03–1940	Chile	W	3–2	Montevideo	Fr	Lago 2, Varela S
24–03	Brazil	W	4–3	Rio de Janeiro	RBC	Varela S 2, Perez R, Rodriguez R
31–03	Brazil	D	1–1	Rio de Janeiro	RBC	Varela S
18–07	Argentina	W	3–0	Montevideo	HGC	Rivero 2, Porta
15–08	Argentina	L	0–5	Buenos Aires	JMC	
9–02–1941	Ecuador	W	6–0	Santiago	SC	Rivero 3, Gambetta, Porta, OG
16–02	Chile	W	2–0	Santiago	SC	Rivero, Magliano
23–02	Argentina	L	0–1	Santiago	SC	
26–02	Peru	W	2–0	Santiago	SC	Riephoff, Varela O
10–01–1942	Chile	W	6–1	Montevideo	SC	Castro L 2, Varela O, Ciocca, Zapirain, Porta
18–01	Ecuador	W	7–0	Montevideo	SC	Varela S 3, Porta 2, Zapirain, Gambetta
24–01	Brazil	W	1–0	Montevideo	SC	Varela S
28–01	Paraguay	W	3–1	Montevideo	SC	Varela S, Ciocca, Porta
1–02	Peru	W	3–0	Montevideo	SC	Castro L, Chirmini, Porta
7–02	Argentina	W	1–0	Montevideo	SC	Zapirain
25–05	Argentina	L	1–4	Buenos Aires	NC	Zapirain
25–08	Argentina	D	1–1	Montevideo	LC	Alvarez
6–01–1943	Argentina*	L	0–1	Buenos Aires	Fr	
9–01	Argentina*	W	6–2	Montevideo	Fr	
28–03	Argentina	D	3–3	Buenos Aires	JMC	Medina 2, Castro L
4–04	Argentina	L	0–1	Montevideo	HGC	
5–01–1944	Argentina*	L	1–3	Montevideo	Fr	
8–01	Argentina*	D	3–3	Buenos Aires	Fr	
29–01	Argentina*	W	2–1	Montevideo	Fr	Zapirain, Medina
29–01	Argentina*	L	2–6	Buenos Aires	Fr	Porta, Chirmini
14–05	Brazil	L	1–6	Rio de Janeiro	Fr	Tejera
17–05	Brazil	L	0–4	Sao Paulo	Fr	
24–01–1945	Ecuador	W	5–1	Santiago	SC	Garcia A 3, Varela O, Porta
28–01	Colombia	W	7–0	Santiago	SC	Garcia A 2, Garcia J 2, Ortiz, Porta, Riephoff
7–02	Brazil	L	0–3	Santiago	SC	
15–02	Bolivia	W	2–0	Santiago	SC	Porta, Falero
18–02	Chile	L	0–1	Santiago	SC	
25–02	Argentina	L	0–1	Santiago	SC	
18–07	Argentina	D	2–2	Montevideo	LC	Varela O 2
15–08	Argentina	L	2–6	Buenos Aires	NC	Ortiz, Falero
29–12	Argentina*	D	1–1	Montevideo	Fr	
5–01–1946	Brazil	W	4–3	Montevideo	RBC	Riephoff 2, Medina, Volpi
9–01	Brazil	D	1–1	Montevideo	RBC	Medina
16–01	Chile	W	1–0	Buenos Aires	SC	Medina
23–01	Brazil	L	3–4	Buenos Aires	SC	Medina, Volpi, Vasquez
29–01	Bolivia	W	5–0	Buenos Aires	SC	Medina 4, Garcia J
2–02	Argentina	L	1–3	Buenos Aires	SC	Riephoff
8–02	Paraguay	L	1–2	Buenos Aires	SC	OG
2–03–1947	Argentina*	L	1–2	Buenos Aires	Fr	
9–03	Argentina*	D	4–4	Montevideo	Fr	
29–03	Brazil	D	0–0	Sao Paulo	RBC	
1–04	Brazil	L	2–3	Rio de Janeiro	RBC	Medina, Pini
4–04	Brazil	D	1–1	Rio de Janeiro	Fr	Castro L
2–12	Colombia	W	2–0	Guayaquil	SC	Falero, Britos
6–12	Chile	W	6–0	Guayaquil	SC	Garcia J 2, Magliano 2, Britos, Sarro
9–12	Bolivia	W	3–0	Guayaquil	SC	Sarro, Falero, Riephoff
13–12	Paraguay	L	2–4	Guayaquil	SC	Magliano, Britos
16–12	Ecuador	W	6–1	Guayaquil	SC	Falero 2, Magliano, Puente, Sarro, Garcia J

25–12	Peru	W	1–0	Guayaquil	SC	Falero
28–12	Argentina	L	1–3	Guayaquil	SC	Britos
4–04–1948	Brazil	D	1–1	Montevideo	RBC	Falero
11–04	Brazil	W	4–2	Montevideo	RBC	Magliano, Falero, Britos
18–05	Argentina*	L	0–1	Montevideo	Fr	
25–05	Argentina•	W	2–0	Buenos Aires	Fr	
13–04–1949	Ecuador	W	3–2	Rio de Janeiro	SC	Castro R 2, Moreno N
17–04	Bolivia	L	2–3	Rio de Janeiro	SC	Moll, Suarez E
20–04	Paraguay	W	2–1	Sao Paulo	SC	Garcia JM 2
24–04	Colombia	D	2–2	Sao Paulo	SC	Martinez M, Ayala
30–04	Brazil	L	1–5	Rio de Janeiro	SC	Castro R
4–05	Peru	L	3–4	Rio de Janeiro	SC	Castro R, Ayala, Moll
8–05	Chile	L	1–3	Belo Horizonte	SC	Ayala
7–04–1950	Chile	W	5–1	Santiago	Fr	Carambula 2, Romero C, Perez J, OG
9–04	Chile	L	1–2	Santiago	Fr	Romero C
30–04	Paraguay	L	2–3	Rio de Janeiro	Fr	Schiaffino, Miguez
6–05	Brazil	W	4–3	Sao Paulo	RBC	Schiaffino 2, Miguez 2
14–05	Brazil	L	2–3	Rio de Janeiro	RBC	Vilamide
18–05	Brazil	L	0–1	Rio de Janeiro	RBC	
2–07	Bolivia	W	8–0	Belo Horizonte	WCr1	Schiaffino 4, Miguez 2, Vidal, Ghiggia
9–07	Spain	D	2–2	Sao Paulo	WCr2	Ghiggia, Varela O
13–07	Sweden	W	3–2	Sao Paulo	WCr2	Miguez 2, Ghiggia
16–07	Brazil	W	2–1	Rio de Janeiro	WCf	Schiaffino, Ghiggia
23–03–1952	Mexico	W	3–1	Santiago	PAC	Miguez, Perez J
30–03	Peru	W	5–2	Santiago	PAC	Miguez 3, Perez J, Vidal
6–04	Panama	W	6–1	Santiago	PAC	Abbadie 3, Santamaria, Miguez, Britos
13–04	Chile	L	0–2	Santiago	PAC	
16–04	Brazil	L	2–4	Santiago	PAC	Ghigggia, Loureiro
25–02–1953	Bolivia	W	2–0	Lima	SC	Romero C, Puente
1–03	Chile	L	2–3	Lima	SC	Morel, Balseiro
12–03	Paraguay	D	2–2	Lima	SC	Romero C, Pelaez
15–03	Brazil	L	0–1	Lima	SC	
23–03	Ecuador	W	6–0	Lima	SC	Mendez, Pelaez, Morel, Romero, Puente, Balseiro
28–03	Peru	W	3–0	Lima	SC	Pelaez 2, Romero C
31–05	England	W	2–1	Montevideo	Fr	Miguez, Abaddie
10–04–1954	Paraguay	L	1–4	Montevideo	Fr	Miguez
18–04	Paraguay	D	1–1	Asuncion	Fr	Abbadie
23–05	Switzerland	D	3–3	Lausanne	Fr	Borges, Ambrois, Martinez W
5–06	Saar	W	7–1	Saarbrucken	Fr	Ambrois 3, Schiaffino, Varela O, OG 2
16–06	Czechoslovakia	W	2–0	Berne	WCr1	Miguez, Schiaffino
19–06	Scotland	W	7–0	Basle	WCr1	Borges 3, Miguez 2, Abbadie 2
26–06	England	W	4–2	Basle	WCqf	Borges, Varela O, Schiaffino, Ambrois
30–06	Hungary	L	2–4	Lausanne	WCsf	Hohberg 2
3–07	Austria	L	1–3	Zurich	WC3p	Hohberg
9–03–1955	Paraguay	W	3–1	Santiago	SC	Borges, Miguez, Abbadie
13–03	Chile	D	2–2	Santiago	SC	Galvan 2
23–03	Ecuador	W	5–1	Santiago	SC	Abbadie 2, Perez J, Galvan, Miguez
27–03	Argentina	L	1–6	Santiago	SC	Miguez
30–03	Peru	L	1–2	Santiago	SC	Morel
21–01–1956	Paraguay	W	4–2	Montevideo	SC	Escalada 2, Galvan, Roque
28–01	Peru	W	2–0	Montevideo	SC	Escalada, Miguez
6–02	Chile	W	2–1	Montevideo	SC	Borges, Miguez
10–02	Brazil	D	0–0	Montevideo	SC	
15–02	Argentina	W	1–0	Montevideo	SC	Ambrois
24–06	Brazil	L	0–2	Rio de Janeiro	CA	
1–07	Argentina	L	1–2	Montevideo	CA	Abbadie
15–07	Paraguay	D	2–2	Asuncion	Fr	Auscarriaga, OG
12–08	Czechoslovakia	W	2–1	Montevideo	Fr	Borges, Mendez
10–10	Argentina	L	1–2	Paysandu	Fr	Ambrois
14–11	Argentina	D	2–2	Buenos Aires	Fr	Ambrois, Miguez
7–03–1957	Ecuador	W	5–2	Lima	SC	Ambrois 4, Sasia J
17–03	Colombia	L	0–1	Lima	SC	
20–03	Argentina	L	0–4	Lima	SC	
23–03	Peru	W	5–3	Lima	SC	Ambrois 4, Carranza
28–03	Brazil	W	3–2	Lima	SC	Campero 2, Ambrois
1–04	Chile	W	2–0	Lima	SC	Roque
23–05	Argentina	D	0–0	Montevideo	NC	
5–06	Argentina	D	1–1	Buenos Aires	LC	Correa

16–06	Colombia	D	1–1	Bogota	WCq	Ambrois
30–06	Colombia	W	1–0	Montevideo	WCq	Miguez
14–07	Paraguay	L	0–5	Asuncion	WCq	
28–07	Paraguay	W	2–0	Montevideo	WCq	Martinez W, Benitez
6–04–1958	Argentina	W	1–0	Montevideo	Fr	Miguez
30–04	Argentina	L	0–2	Buenos Aires	Fr	
8–03–1959	Bolivia	W	7–0	Buenos Aires	SC	Sasia J 2, Borges, Escalada, Guaglianone, Douksas, Perez D
14–03	Peru	L	3–5	Buenos Aires	SC	De Marco, Sasia J, Douksas
18–03	Paraguay	W	3–1	Buenos Aires	SC	De Marco, Sasia J, Douksas
26–03	Brazil	L	1–3	Buenos Aires	SC	Escalada
30–03	Argentina	L	1–4	Buenos Aires	SC	De Marco
2–04	Chile	L	0–1	Buenos Aires	SC	
1–05	Paraguay	L	1–3	Montevideo	Fr	Escalada
6–12	Ecuador	W	4–0	Guayaquil	SC	Escalada, Perez D, Silveira, Bergara
12–12	Brazil	W	3–0	Guayaquil	SC	Sasia J 2, Escalada
16–12	Argentina	W	5–0	Guayaquil	SC	Bergara 2, Silveira 2, Sasia J
22–12	Paraguay	D	1–1	Guayaquil	SC	Sasia J
1–06–1960	Chile	W	3–2	Santiago	Fr	Bergara 2, Guaglianone
5–06	Chile	D	2–2	Montevideo	Fr	Guaglianone 2
9–07	Brazil	W	1–0	Montevideo	CA	Perez D
13–07	Paraguay	W	2–1	Montevideo	CA	Rodriguez H, Escalada
17–08	Argentina	L	0–4	Buenos Aires	CA	
15–07–1961	Bolivia	D	1–1	La Paz	WCq	Cubila L
30–07	Bolivia	W	2–1	Montevideo	WCq	Cabrera, Escalada
12–10	Chile	W	3–2	Santiago	Fr	Pintos 2, Cubila
29–11	Soviet Union	L	1–2	Montevideo	Fr	Cubila
23–12	Hungary	D	1–1	Montevideo	Fr	Escalada
13–03–1962	Argentina	D	1–1	Montevideo	Fr	Alvarez
11–04	West Germany	L	0–3	Hamburg	Fr	
18–04	Hungary	D	1–1	Budapest	Fr	Silva
22–04	Czechoslovakia	L	1–3	Prague	Fr	Sasia J
27–04	Soviet Union	L	0–5	Moscow	Fr	
2–05	Scotland	W	3–2	Glasgow	Fr	Sasia J, Cubila 2
30–05	Colombia	W	2–1	Arica	WCr1	Cubila, Sacia J
2–06	Yugoslavia	L	1–3	Arica	WCr1	Cabrera
6–06	Soviet Union	L	1–2	Arica	WCr1	Sacia J
15–08	Argentina	L	1–3	Buenos Aires	LC	Mattera
23–03–1963	Chile	W	3–2	Montevideo	PDC	Pintos 2, Sasia J
24–07	Chile	D	0–0	Santiago	PDC	
25–04–1964	Morocco	W	1–0	Casablanca	Fr	Castro M
29–04	Nth. Ireland	L	0–3	Belfast	Fr	
6–05	England	L	1–2	London	Fr	Spencer
14–05	Austria	W	2–0	Vienna	Fr	Castro M 2
20–05	Soviet Union	L	0–1	Moscow	Fr	
3–01–1965	East Germany	L	0–2	Montevideo	Fr	
25–04	Paraguay	L	1–2	Asuncion	AC	Toja
1–05	Paraguay	W	4–0	Montevideo	AC	Urrusmendi 2, Silva 2
9–05	Chile	D	0–0	Santiago	PDC	
16–05	Chile	D	1–1	Montevideo	PDC	Toja
23–05	Venezuela	W	5–0	Montevideo	WCq	Alvarez 3, Rocha, Meneses
30–05	Venezuela	W	3–1	Caracas	WCq	Rocha 2, Silva
6–06	Peru	W	1–0	Lima	WCq	Urruzmendi
13–06	Peru	W	2–1	Montevideo	WCq	Silva, Rocha
7–09	Brazil	L	0–3	Belo Horizonte	Fr	
4–12	Soviet Union	L	1–3	Montevideo	Fr	Rocha
15–05–1966	Paraguay	D	2–2	Asuncion	AC	Salva 2
18–05	Paraguay	W	3–1	Montevideo	AC	Morales, Perez D
15–06	Israel	W	2–1	Tel Aviv	Fr	Abbadie 2
19–06	Romania	L	0–1	Bucharest	Fr	
23–06	Spain	D	1–1	La Coruna	Fr	Perez D
26–06	Portugal	L	0–3	Lisbon	Fr	
11–07	England	D	0–0	London	WCr1	
15–07	France	W	2–1	London	WCr1	Rocha, Cortes
19–07	Mexico	D	0–0	London	WCr1	
23–07	West Germany	L	0–4	Sheffield	WCqf	
4–01–1967	Rumania	D	1–1	Montevideo	Fr	Urrusmendi
17–01	Bolivia	W	4–0	Montevideo	SC	Rocha, Castillo, OG, Oyarbide
21–01	Venezuela	W	4–0	Montevideo	SC	Urrusmendi 2, Oyarbide, OG

26–01	Chile	D	2–2	Montevideo	SC	Oyarbide, Rocha
29–01	Paraguay	W	2–0	Montevideo	SC	Perez D, Urrusmendi
2–02	Argentina	W	1–0	Montevideo	SC	Rocha
25–06	Brazil	D	0–0	Montevideo	RBC	
28–06	Brazil	D	2–2	Montevideo	RBC	Rocha 2
1–07	Brazil	D	1–1	Montevideo	RBC	Urrusmendi
28–07	Peru	W	1–0	Lima	Fr	Rocha
30–07	Peru	W	2–1	Lima	Fr	Rocha, Bareno
21–05–1968	Mexico	D	3–3	Mexico City	Fr	Morales, Rocha, Mujica
28–05	Mexico	D	2–2	Mexico City	Fr	Mujica, Morales
2–06	Paraguay	D	0–0	Asuncion	AC	Abandoned after 70 mins
5–06	Argentina	L	0–2	Buenos Aires	NC	
9–06	Brazil	L	0–2	Sao Paulo	RBC	
12–06	Brazil	L	0–4	Rio de Janeiro	RBC	
20–06	Argentina	W	2–1	Montevideo	LC	Zubia, Morales
26–10	Mexico	L	0–2	Montevideo	Fr	
8–06–1969	England	L	1–2	Montevideo	Fr	Cubila L
27–06	Peru	L	0–1	Lima	Fr	
2–07	Colombia	W	1–0	Cali	Fr	Bareno
6–07	Ecuador	W	2–0	Guayaquil	WCq	Bareno, Ancheta
13–07	Chile	D	0–0	Santiago	WCq	
20–07	Ecuador	W	1–0	Montevideo	WCq	Ancheta
10–08	Chile	W	2–0	Montevideo	WCq	Cortes, Rocha
31–03–1970	Peru	W	2–0	Montevideo	Fr	Maneiro, Cubila
8–04	Argentina	L	1–2	Buenos Aires	Fr	Zubia
15–04	Argentina	W	2–1	Montevideo	Fr	Rocha, Ubina
18–04	Peru	L	2–4	Lima	Fr	Barreno, Ancheta
2–06	Israel	W	2–0	Puebla	WCr1	Maneiro, Mujica
6–06	Italy	D	0–0	Puebla	WCr1	
10–06	Sweden	L	0–1	Puebla	WCr1	
14–06	Soviet Union	W	1–0	Mexico City	WCqf	Esparrago
17–06	Brazil	L	1–3	Guadalajara	WCsf	Cubila
20–06	West Germany	L	0–1	Mexico City	WC3p	
8–02–1971	East Germany	L	0–3	Montevideo	Fr	
10–02	East Germany	D	1–1	Montevideo	Fr	Zubia
14–07	Argentina	L	0–1	Buenos Aires	NC	
18–07	Argentina	D	1–1	Montevideo	LC	Bertocchi
27–10	Chile	W	3–0	Montevideo	PDC	Repetto, OG 2
3–11	Chile	L	0–5	Santiago	PDC	
23–05–1972	Spain	L	0–2	Madrid	Fr	
27–05	East Germany	L	0–1	Leipzig	Fr	
31–05	East Germany	D	0–0	Rostock	Fr	
14–06	Norway	W	1–0	Oslo	Fr	Lattuada
29–06	Soviet Union	L	0–1	Sao Paulo	Clr2	
2–07	Portugal	D	1–1	Sao Paulo	Clr2	Pavoni
6–07	Argentina	L	0–1	Porto Alegre	Clr2	
17–05–1973	Argentina	D	1–1	Buenos Aires	LC	Morena F
23–05	Argentina	D	1–1	Montevideo	NC	Rey
6–06	Haiti	D	0–0	Port au Prince	Fr	
24–06	Colombia	D	0–0	Bogota	WCq	
1–07	Ecuador	W	2–1	Quito	WCq	Cubila, Morena F
5–07	Colombia	L	0–1	Montevideo	WCq	
8–07	Ecuador	W	4–0	Montevideo	WCq	Morena F 2, Cubila, Milar
19–07	Israel	W	2–1	Tel Aviv	Fr	Morena F, Milar
23–03–1974	Haiti	W	1–0	Port au Prince	Fr	Morena F
25–03	Haiti	D	0–0	Port au Prince	Fr	
28–03	Jamaica	W	3–0	Kingston	Fr	Morena F 2, Mantegazza
21–04	Indonesia	W	3–2	Djarkarta	Fr	Morena F 2, Milar
26–04	Australia	D	0–0	Sydney	Fr	
28–04	Australia	L	0–2	Melbourne	Fr	
8–05	Rep. Ireland	W	2–0	Montevideo	Fr	Morena F 2
15–06	Holland	L	0–2	Hanover	WCr1	
19–06	Bulgaria	D	1–1	Hanover	WCr1	Pavoni
23–06	Sweden	L	0–3	Dusseldorf	WCr1	
4–06–1975	Chile	W	1–0	Montevideo	PDC	Unanue
12–06	Paraguay	W	1–0	Asuncion	AC	Jimenez
19–06	Paraguay	L	0–1	Montevideo	AC	
25–06	Chile	W	3–1	Santiago	PDC	Revetria, Peruena, OG
18–07	Argentina	L	2–3	Montevideo	NC	Morena F 2

21–09	Colombia	L	0–3	Bogota	SCsf	
1–10	Colombia	W	1–0	Montevideo	SCsf	Morena F
25–02–1976	Brazil	L	1–2	Montevideo	CA	Ocampo
10–03	Paraguay	D	2–2	Montevideo	CA	Ocampo, Pereyra
8–04	Argentina	L	1–4	Buenos Aires	CA	Pereyra
28–04	Brazil	L	1–2	Rio de Janeiro	CA	Torres
19–05	Paraguay	L	0–1	Asuncion	CA	
9–06	Argentina	L	0–3	Montevideo	CA	
6–10	Chile	D	0–0	Santiago	PDC	
12–10	Peru	D	0–0	Lima	Fr	
15–10	Colombia	W	2–1	Bogota	Fr	
20–10	Ecuador	D	2–2	Quito	Fr	Victoriano 2
24–11	Peru	D	0–0	Montevideo	Fr	
4–01–1977	Ecuador	D	1–1	Montevideo	Fr	Rodriguez R
12–01	Paraguay	D	1–1	Asuncion	AC	
23–01	Paraguay	W	2–1	Montevideo	AC	
30–01	Chile	W	3–0	Montevideo	PDC	
9–02	Venezuela	D	1–1	Caracas	WCq	Carrasco
27–02	Bolivia	L	0–1	La Paz	WCq	
17–03	Venezuela	W	2–0	Montevideo	WCq	Morena F, Pereyra
27–03	Bolivia	D	2–2	Montevideo	WCq	Pereyra 2
8–06	West Germany	L	0–2	Montevideo	Fr	
15–06	England	D	0–0	Montevideo	Fr	
4–03–1978	Argentina	D	0–0	Mar del Plata	Fr	
25–04	Argentina	W	2–0	Montevideo	Fr	Maneiro, Morena F
3–05	Argentina	L	0–3	Buenos Aires	Fr	
24–05	Spain	D	0–0	Montevideo	Fr	
31–05–1979	Brazil	L	1–5	Rio de Janeiro	Fr	Victorino
11–07	Chile	L	0–1	Santiago	PDC	
18–07	Chile	W	2–1	Montevideo	PDC	Victorino, Unanue
30–08	Peru	L	0–2	Lima	Fr	
5–09	Ecuador	L	1–2	Guayaquil	SCr1	Victorino
16–09	Ecuador	W	2–1	Montevideo	SCr1	Bica, Victorino
20–09	Paraguay	D	0–0	Asuncion	SCr1	
26–09	Paraguay	D	2–2	Montevideo	SCr1	Milar, Paz
15–03–1980	Italy	L	0–1	Milan	Fr	
18–03	Belgium	L	0–2	Brussels	Fr	
22–03	Yugoslavia	L	1–2	Sarajevo	Fr	OG
26–03	Luxembourg	W	1–0	Esch	Fr	Victorino
18–07	Peru	D	0–0	Montevideo	Fr	
21–08	Chile	D	0–0	Montevideo	PDC	
27–08	Brazil	L	0–1	Fortaleza	Fr	
9–11	Bolivia	W	3–1	Cochabamba	Fr	Victorino, Morales J, De La Pena
12–11	Peru	D	1–1	Lima	Fr	Krasouski
8–12	Finland	W	6–0	Montevideo	Fr	Krasouski, Morales 2, Vargas, Siviero, Falero M
11–12	Bolivia	W	5–0	Montevideo	Fr	Morales J 2, Paz, Ramos, Victorino
18–12	Switzerland	W	4–0	Montevideo	Fr	Oliviera, Paz 3
30–12	Holland	W	2–0	Montevideo	ML	Ramos, Victorino
3–01–1981	Italy	W	2–0	Montevideo	ML	Morales,J, Victorino
10–01	Brazil	W	2–1	Montevideo	ML	Barrios, Victorino
29–04	Chile	W	2–1	Santiago	PDC	Nunez, Agresta
15–07	Chile	D	0–0	Montevideo	PDC	
9–08	Colombia	W	3–2	Montevideo	WCq	Paz, Morales J 2
23–08	Peru	L	1–2	Montevideo	WCq	Victorino
6–09	Peru	D	0–0	Lima	WCq	
13–09	Colombia	D	1–1	Bogota	WCq	Victorino
20–02–1982	South Korea*	D	2–2	Calcutta	JNC	
22–02	China*	D	0–0	Calcutta	JNC	
25–02	India*	W	3–1	Calcutta	JNC	
28–02	China*	W	2–0	Calcutta	JNC	
2–06–1983	Paraguay	D	0–0	Asuncion	AC	
9–06	Paraguay	W	3–0	Montevideo	AC	Cabrera 2, Morena F
18–07	Peru	D	1–1	Montevideo	Fr	Luzardo
11–08	Peru	D	1–1	Lima	Fr	Muhletaler
25–08	Paraguay	D	0–0	Montevideo	Fr	
1–09	Chile	W	2–1	Montevideo	SCr1	Acevedo, Morena F
4–09	Venezuela	W	3–0	Montevideo	SCr1	Cabrera, Morena F, Luzardo
11–09	Chile	L	0–2	Santiago	SCr1	

18–09	Venezuela	W 2–1	Caracas	SCr1	Santelli, Aguilera
21–09	Scotland	L 0–2	Glasgow	Fr	
26–09	Israel	D 2–2	Tel Aviv	Fr	Aguilera 2
13–10	Peru	W 1–0	Lima	SCsf	Aguilera
20–10	Peru	D 1–1	Montevideo	SCsf	Cabrera
27–10	Brazil	W 2–0	Montevideo	SCf	Francescoli, Diogo
4–11	Brazil	D 1–1	Salvador	SCf	Aguilera
13–06–1984	England	W 2–0	Montevideo	Fr	Acosta, Cabrera
21–06	Brazil	L 0–1	Curitiba	Fr	
18–07	Argentina	W 1–0	Montevideo	Fr	Barrios
2–08	Argentina	D 0–0	Buenos Aires	Fr	
19–09	Peru	W 2–0	Montevideo	Fr	Aguilera, Salazar
3–10	Peru	W 3–1	Lima	Fr	Barrios, Santin, Nadal
31–10	Mexico	D 1–1	Montevideo	Fr	Nadal
29–01–1985	East Germany	W 3–0	Montevideo	Fr	Aguilera, Da Silva, Francescoli
3–02	Paraguay	W 1–0	Montevideo	AC	Francescoli
6–02	Bolivia	W 1–0	Cochabamba	Fr	Pereyra
10–02	Paraguay	W 3–1	Asuncion	AC	Nadal 3
14–02	Finland	W 2–1	Montevideo	Fr	Aguilera, Nadal
24–02	Colombia	W 3–0	Montevideo	Fr	Aguilera, Francescoli, Nadal
27–02	Peru	D 2–2	Montevideo	Fr	Nadal, Cabrera
10–03	Ecuador	W 2–1	Montevideo	WCq	Aguilera, Ramos
24–03	Chile	L 0–2	Santiago	WCq	
31–03	Ecuador	W 2–0	Quito	WCq	Saralegui, Francescoli
7–04	Chile	W 2–1	Montevideo	WCq	Batista, Ramos
23–04	Peru	L 1–2	Lima	Fr	Carrasco
28–04	Colombia	L 1–2	Bogota	Fr	Aguilera
2–05	Brazil	L 0–2	Recife	Fr	
25–05	Japan	W 4–1	Tokyo	Fr	Aguilera 2, Da Silva 2
1–06	Malaysia	W 6–0	Kuala Lumpur	Fr	Carrasco, Alzugaray, Aguilera, Barrios,
					Pereyra, Cabrera
21–08	France	L 0–2	Paris	AFT	
17–10	Chile	L 0–1	Santiago	Fr	
2–02–1986	Canada	W 3–1	Miami	Fr	Aguilera, Ostolaza, Salazar
7–02	United States	D 1–1	Miami	Fr	Aguilera
16–02	Poland	D 2–2	Montevideo	Fr	Bossio, Salazar
13–04	Mexico	L 0–1	Los Angeles	Fr	
21–04	Wales	D 0–0	Wrexham	Fr	
23–04	Rep. Ireland	D 1–1	Dublin	Fr	OG
4–06	West Germany	D 1–1	Queretaro	WCr1	Alzamendi
8–06	Denmark	L 1–6	Nezahualcoyotl	WCr1	Francescoli
13–06	Scotland	D 0–0	Nezahualcoyotl	WCr1	
16–06	Argentina	L 0–1	Puebla	WCr2	
19–06–1987	Ecuador	W 2–1	Montevideo	Fr	Perdomo 2
23–06	Bolivia	W 2–1	Montevideo	Fr	Matosas, Alzamendi
9–07	Argentina	W 1–0	Buenos Aires	SCsf	Alzamendi
12–07	Chile	W 1–0	Buenos Aires	SCf	Bengoechea
7–08–1988	Colombia	L 1–2	Bogota	Fr	Herrera
27–09	Ecuador	W 2–1	Asuncion	Fr	Dalto, Herrera
29–09	Paraguay	L 1–3	Asuncion	Fr	Da Silva
12–10	Paraguay	W 2–0	Montevideo	Fr	Da Silva, Pereyra
1–11	Chile	D 1–1	Santiago	PDC	Vidal
9–11	Chile	W 3–1	Montevideo	PDC	Da Silva, Baez, Martinez S
14–12	Peru	W 3–0	Montevideo	Fr	Francescoli 2, Sosa
22–04–1989	Italy	D 1–1	Verona	Fr	Aguilera
3–05	Ecuador	W 3–1	Montevideo	Fr	Martinez S, Aguilera 2
23–05	Ecuador	D 1–1	Quito	Fr	Herrera
8–06	Bolivia	D 0–0	Santa Cruz	Fr	
14–06	Bolivia	W 1–0	Montevideo	Fr	Aguilera
19–06	Chile	D 2–2	Montevideo	Fr	Correa 2
2–07	Ecuador	L 0–1	Goiânia	SCr1	
4–07	Bolivia	W 3–0	Goiânia	SCr1	Ostolaza 2, Sosa
6–07	Chile	W 3–0	Goiânia	SCr1	Sosa, Alzamendi, Francescoli
8–07	Argentina	L 0–1	Goiânia	SCr1	
12–07	Paraguay	W 3–0	Rio de Janeiro	SCr2	Francescoli, Alzamendi, Paz
14–07	Argentina	W 2–0	Rio de Janeiro	SCr2	Sosa 2
16–07	Brazil	L 0–1	Rio de Janeiro	SCf	
6–08	Colombia	D 0–0	Montevideo	Fr	
27–08	Peru	W 2–0	Lima	WCq	Sosa, Alzamendi

3–09	Bolivia	L	1–2	La Paz	WCq	Sosa
17–09	Bolivia	W	2–0	Montevideo	WCq	Sosa, Francescoli
24–09	Peru	W	2–0	Montevideo	WCq	Sosa 2
2–02–1990	Colombia	W	2–0	Miami	Fr	Pedrucci, Castro
4–02	Costa Rica	W	2–0	Miami	Fr	Castro, Martinez S
20–03	Mexico	L	1–2	Los Angeles	Fr	Suarez
25–04	West Germany	D	3–3	Stuttgart	Fr	Aguilera, Ostolaza, Revelez
18–05	Nth. Ireland	L	0–1	Belfast	Fr	
22–05	England	W	2–1	London	Fr	Ostolaza, Perdomo
13–06	Spain	D	0–0	Udine	WCr1	
17–06	Belgium	L	1–3	Verona	WCr1	Bengoechea
21–06	South Korea	W	1–0	Udine	WCr1	Fonseca
25–06	Italy	L	0–2	Rome	WCr2	
5–05–1991	United States	L	0–1	Denver	Fr	
7–05	Mexico	W	2–0	Los Angeles	Fr	Lopez V, Ferreira
13–05	Costa Rica	W	1–0	San Jose	Fr	Cedres
30–05	Chile	L	1–2	Santiago	Fr	OG
12–06	Peru	L	0–1	Lima	Fr	
20–06	Peru	D	0–0	Montevideo	Fr	
26–06	Chile	W	2–1	Montevideo	Fr	Baez, Mendez
7–07	Bolivia	D	1–1	Valparaiso	SCr1	Castro
9–07	Ecuador	D	1–1	Viña del Mar	SCr1	Mendez
11–07	Brazil	D	1–1	Viña del Mar	SCr1	Mendez
15–07	Colombia	W	1–0	Viña del Mar	Scr1	Mendez
4–09	Spain	L	1–2	Oviedo	Fr	Gutierrez
20–11	Mexico	D	1–1	Veracruz	Fr	Cedres
30–04–1992	Brazil	W	1–0	Montevideo	Fr	Paz
21–06	Australia	W	2–0	Montevideo	Fr	Martinez, Larrea

VENEZUELA

Venezuela is the weakest of all the ten South American countries and the only one in which football is not the national sport, that accolade falling to baseball. Oil resources mean that Venezuela is a relatively prosperous country, but although there is now a professional league, progress has been slow and the standard does not look like matching that of either Ecuador or Bolivia in the near future.

Historically Venezuela has more in common with football in Central America than in South America and it was to the Confederacion Centroamericano y del Caribe de Futbol that she affiliated in 1938. The Federación Venezolana de Fútbol had been founded 12 years previously in Caracas, although the first organised competition stretches back five years prior to that.

In 1921 a group of Caracas-based clubs set up their own league which was taken over by the new federation in 1926, and despite a break-away in 1929 when two leagues were in operation, the national amateur league continued to operate until the major reorganisation of 1956, the date when professionalism was legalised.

The national side made its debut in the 1938 Central American and Caribbean Games and later in the same year took part in the Bolivaran Games in Barranquilla but did not play regularly until the mid-1960s, reflecting the low priority attached to the game by the population as a whole.

The professional league gave rise to a whole new breed of clubs, which as their names suggest – Portugues, Deportivo Italia – are run loosely along ethnic lines, a factor that further alienates the sport from the general public. There are a surprising number of foreign players in the league, but attendances remain low. Success in the Copa Libertadores has been restricted to three semi-final appearances between 1977 and 1984, but on each occasion the Venezuelan team has finished bottom of their semi-final group.

Honours have been spread evenly among the clubs and, surprisingly, among the cities in Venezuela. Caracas has found its dominant position challenged in particular by San Cristobal and Mérida, especially since the beginning of the 1980s as teams like Deportivo Tachira and

		Total			League	Copa Lib		
		G	S	B	G	G	S	B
1	Portuguesa	5	–	1	5	–	–	1
2	Deportivo Galicia	4	–	–	4	–	–	–
	Deportivo Italia	4	–	–	4	–	–	–
	Deportivo Portugues	4	–	–	4	–	–	–
5	Deportivo Tachira	3	–	–	3	–	–	–
	Sport Maritimo	3	–	–	3	–	–	–
7	Estudiantes Merida	2	–	–	2	–	–	–
	ULA Merida	2	–	1	2	–	–	1
9	Atletico San Cristobal	1	–	1	1	–	–	1
10	Banco Obrero	1	–	–	1	–	–	–
	Deportivo Espanol	1	–	–	1	–	–	–
	Deportivo Lara	1	–	–	1	–	–	–
	Mineros de Guyana	1	–	–	1	–	–	–
	Union Deportiva Canarias	1	–	–	1	–	–	–
	Universidad Central	1	–	–	1	–	–	–
	Valencia	1	–	–	1	–	–	–

Estudiantes Mérida have forced the Caracas teams like Deportivo Italia, Galicia and Portugues into the background.

Entry into the 1966 World Cup was the country's first real taste of international competition, and was followed the year after by their first appearance in the South American Championships. They surprisingly finished above Bolivia in that tournament but have been last in every tournament since. Fixtures are almost exclusively in both of these competitions, for which Venezuela are now regular entrants.

If Venezuela are to make any strides in world football they will have to improve on a record that shows just one win in the South American Championships, against Bolivia in 1967, and one win in the World Cup qualifiers, also against Bolivia, this time in 1981.

Population: 19735000
Area, sq km: 912000
% in urban areas: 84%
Capital city: Caracas

Federación Venezolana de Fútbol
Ave. Este Estadio Nacional
Quinta Claret #28
El Paraíso, Apartado Postal 14160
Candelaria, Caracus
Venezuela
Tel: (010 58) 2 4618010
Fax: (010 58) 2 4618010
Telex: 26 140 FVFCS VC
Cable: FEVEFUTBOL CARACUS
Languages for correspondence: Spanish, French & English

Year of formation: 1926
Affiliation to FIFA: 1952
Affiliation to CONMEBOL: 1952
Registered clubs: 1483
Registered players: 80300
Professional players: 570
Registered coaches: 475
Registered referees: 391
National stadium: Estadio Olimpico, Caracas 25000
National colours: Shirts: Dark red/Shorts: White/Socks: White
Reserve colours: Shirts: White/Shorts: White/Socks: White
Season: September–June

THE RECORD

WORLD CUP

1930–62 ..... Did not enter
1966 .... QT 3rd/3 in group 1
1970 .... QT 4th/4 in group 2
1974 .... Did not enter
1978 .... QT 3rd/3 in group 2
1982 .... QT 3rd/3 in group 1
1986 .... QT 4th/4 in group 1
1990 .... QT 3rd/3 in group 3

SOUTH AMERICAN CHAMPIONSHIP

1910–63 ..... Did not enter
1967 .... 5th/6
1975 .... 10th/10/1st round
1979 .... 10th/10/1st round
1983 .... 10th/10/1st round
1987 .... 10th/10/1st round
1989 .... 10th/10/1st round
1991 .... 10th/10/1st round

OLYMPIC GAMES

1908–64 ..... Did not enter
1968 .... QT Failed to qualify
1972 .... QT Failed to qualify
1976 .... Did not enter
1980 .... Final Tournament/1st round
1984 .... QT Failed to qualify
1988 .... QT Failed to qualify
1992 .... QT Failed to qualify

COPA LIBERTADORES

Semi-finalists – Portuguesa Acarigua 1977. Deportivo San Cristobal 1983, ULA Merida 1984

CLUB DIRECTORY

CARACAS (Population – 3600000)

Deportivo Italia
Stadium: Estadio Olimpico 25000
Founded: 1952 Colours: Blue/White

Deportivo Galicia
Stadium: Estadio Olimpico 25000
Founded: 1926 Colours: White/White

Club Maritimo
Stadium: Estadio Olimpico 25000
Colours: Blue/Blue

Club Deportivo Portugues
Stadium: Estadio Olimpico
Founded: 1950
Colours: Red and green stripes/White

Universidad Central Venezoelana
Stadium: Estadio Olimpico 25000
Colours: Green and white stripes/White

Caracas Futbol Club
Stadium: Estadio Olimpico
Colours: White/White

BARQUISIMENTO (Population – 497000)
Deportivo Lara
Stadium: Estadio Faris Richa 10000
Founded: 1951 Colours: Red/Red

CIUDAD GUAYANA (Population – 314000)
Minerven Puerto Ordaz
Stadium: Polideportivo Venalum 15000
Colours: Black and white stripes/White

SAN CRISTOBAL (Population – 198000)

Deportivo Tachira
Stadium: Tachira 12000
Founded: 1978
Colours: Red/White

Atletico San Cristobal
Stadium: Estadio San Cristobal 20000
Founded: 1981
Colours: Green and white stripes/White
Previous names: Deportivo San Cristobal

CIUDAD BOLIVAR (Population – 182000)
Mineros de Guyana
Stadium: Estadio Olimpico 10000
Founded: 1981
Colours: Sky blue and white stripes/Black

MERIDA (Population – 143000)

Estudiantes Mérida
Stadium: Guillermo Rosa Soto 10000
Founded: 1952
Colours: Red and white stripes/Red

Universidad de Los Andes (ULA) Mérida
Stadium: Guillermo Rosa Soto 10000
Founded: 1977 Colours: White/White

BARINAS (Population – 110000)
Atletico Zamora
Stadium: Estadio Barinas 15000
Founded: 1976
Colours: Black and white stripes/White

CORO (Population – 96000)
Atletico Universitario Falco
Stadium: Universitario 10000
Founded: 1977 Colours: Violet/White

ACARIGUA (Population – 91000)

FC Portuguesa
Stadium: José Antonio Paez 10000
Founded: 1926
Colours: White with red sleeves with a green and red band on chest/White

Valencia FC
Stadium: José Antonio Paez 10000
Founded: 1960 Colours: Green/White

PUERTO LA CRUZ (Population – 53000)
Atletico Anzoategui
Stadium: Luis Ramos 15000
Colours: Red/Red

PORLAMAR (Isl de Margarita) (Population – 51000)
Atletico Pepeganda
Stadium: Guatemare 15000
Founded: 1987
Colours: White/White

VENEZUELAN LEAGUE CHAMPIONS

1921	America
1922	Centro Atlético
1923	America
1924	Centro Atlético
1925	Loyola SC
1926	Centro Atlético
1927	Venzoleo FC
1928	Deportivo Venezuela
1929	Deportivo Venezuela & Centro Atlético
1930	Centro Atlético
1931	Deportivo Venezuela
1932	Union SC
1933	Deportivo Venezuela
1934	Union SC
1935	Union SC
1936	Dos Caminos SC
1937	Dos Caminos SC
1938	Dos Caminos SC
1939	Union SC
1940	Union SC
1941	Litoral FC
1942	Dos Caminos SC
1943	Loyola SC
1944	Loyola SC
1945	Dos Caminos SC
1946	Deportivo Espanol
1947	Union SC
1948	Loyola SC
1949	Dos Caminos SC
1950	Union SC
1951	Universidad Central
1952	Le Salle
1953	Universidad Central
1954	Deportivo Vasco
1955	Le Salle

PROFESSIONAL LEAGUE

1956	Banco Obrero
1957	Universidad Central
1958	Deportivo Portugues
1959	Deportivo Espanol
1960	Deportivo Portugues
1961	Deportivo Italia
1962	Deportivo Portugues
1963	Deportivo Italia
1964	Deportivo Galicia
1965	Deportivo Lara
1966	Deportivo Italia
1967	Deportivo Portugues
1968	Union Dep. Canarias
1969	Deportivo Galicia
1970	Deportivo Galicia
1971	Valencia
1972	Deportivo Italia
1973	Portuguesa
1974	Deportivo Galicia
1975	Portuguesa
1976	Portuguesa
1977	Portuguesa
1978	Portuguesa
1979	Deportivo Tachira
1980	Estudiantes Merida
1981	Deportivo Tachira
1982	Atletico San Cristobal
1983	ULA Merida
1984	Tachira
1985	Estudiantes Merida
1986	–
1987	Maritimo
1988	Maritimo
1989	Mineros de Guyana
1990	Maritimo
1991	ULA Merida

INTERNATIONAL MATCHES PLAYED BY VENEZUELA

Date	Opponents	Result		Venue	Compet
10–02–1938	Panama	L	1–2	Panama City	CG
14–02	Mexico	L	0–1	Panama City	CG
17–02	Costa Rica	L	0–5	Panama City	CG
20–02	El Salvador	L	2–3	Panama City	CG
22–02	Colombia	W	2–1	Panama City	CG
11–08	Bolivia	L	1–3	Bogota	BG
13–08	Colombia	L	0–2	Bogota	BG
17–08	Peru	L	1–2	Bogota	BG
19–08	Ecuador	W	5–2	Bogota	BG
12–12–1946	Colombia	L	1–3	Barranquilla	CG
14–12	Curacao	L	0–1	Barranquilla	CG
17–12	Panama	L	1–2	Barranquilla	CG
20–12	Costa Rica	L	2–4	Barranquilla	CG
23–12	Guatemala	W	3–2	Barranquilla	CG
26–12	Puerto Rico	W	6–0	Barranquilla	CG
5–01–1948	Bolivia	D	2–2	Lima	BG
8–03–1956	Panama	W	1–0	Port-au-Prince	Fr
10–03	Haiti	D	1–1	Port-au-Prince	Fr
14–03	Panama	W	4–2	Port-au-Prince	Fr
16–03	Haiti	L	0–3	Port-au-Prince	Fr
16–05–1965	Peru	L	0–1	Lima	WCq
23–05	Uruguay	L	0–5	Montevideo	WCq
30–05	Uruguay	L	1–3	Caracas	WCq
2–06	Peru	L	3–6	Caracas	WCq
18–01–1967	Chile	L	0–2	Montevideo	SC
21–01	Uruguay	L	0–4	Montevideo	SC
25–01	Argentina	L	1–5	Montevideo	SC
28–01	Bolivia	W	3–0	Montevideo	SC
1–02	Paraguay	L	3–5	Montevideo	SC
27–07–1969	Colombia	L	0–3	Bogota	WCq
2–08	Colombia	D	1–1	Caracas	WCq
7–08	Paraguay	L	0–2	Caracas	WCq
10–08	Brazil	L	0–5	Caracas	WCq
21–08	Paraguay	L	0–1	Asuncion	WCq
24–08	Brazil	L	0–6	Rio de Janeiro	WCq
13–11–1971	Trinidad	W	1–0	Caracas	Fr
3–06–1972	Colombia	W	2–1	Caracas	Fr
11–06	Paraguay	L	1–4	Campo Grande	Clr1
14–06	Yugoslavia	L	0–10	Curitiba	Clr1
18–06	Peru	L	0–1	Manaus	Clr1
21–06	Bolivia	D	2–2	Manaus	Clr1
16–12–1973	Dominican Rep.	W	1–0	Caracas	Fr
30–07–1975	Brazil	L	0–4	Caracas	SCr1
3–08	Argentina	L	1–5	Caracas	SCr1
10–08	Argentina	L	0–11	Rosario	SCr1
13–08	Brazil	L	0–6	Belo Horizonte	SCr1
20–01–1977	Ecuador	W	1–0	Caracas	Fr
9–02	Uruguay	D	1–1	Caracas	WCq
6–03	Bolivia	L	1–3	Caracas	WCq
13–03	Bolivia	L	0–2	La Paz	WCq
17–03	Uruguay	L	0–2	Montevideo	WCq
31–03–1978	China	L	0–1	Caracas	Fr
1–08–1979	Colombia	D	0–0	San Cristobal	SCr1
8–08	Chile	D	1–1	San Cristobal	SCr1
22–08	Colombia	L	0–4	Bogota	SCr1
29–08	Chile	L	0–7	Santiago	SCr1
5–01–1980	Colombia	D	0–0	Caracas	Fr
5–07	Costa Rica	D	1–1	Valera	Fr
11–01–1981	Neth. Antilles	L	1–2	Curacao	Fr
18–01	Neth. Antilles	W	1–0	Caracas	Fr
8–02	Brazil	L	0–1	Caracas	WCq
15–02	Bolivia	L	0–3	La Paz	WCq
15–03	Bolivia	W	1–0	Caracas	WCq
29–03	Brazil	L	0–5	Goiania	WCq
28–06	Spain	L	0–2	Caracas	Fr
4–09–1983	Uruguay	L	0–3	Montevideo	SCr1
8–09	Chile	L	0–5	Santiago	SCr1
18–09	Uruguay	L	1–2	Caracas	SCr1
21–09	Chile	D	0–0	Caracas	SCr1
24–01–1984	Mexico	L	0–3	Iraputo	Fr
24–02–1985	Bolivia	W	5–0	Caracas	Fr
21–04	Bolivia	L	0–4	Santa Cruz	Fr
26–05	Argentina	L	2–3	San Cristobal	WCq
2–06	Peru	L	0–1	San Cristobal	WCq
9–06	Argentina	L	0–3	Buenos Aires	WCq
16–06	Peru	L	1–4	Lima	WCq
23–06	Colombia	D	2–2	San Cristobal	WCq
30–06	Colombia	L	0–2	Bogota	WCq
28–06–1987	Brazil	L	0–5	Cordoba	SCr1
30–06	Chile	L	1–3	Cordoba	SCr1
26–03–1989	Paraguay	L	1–2	Caracas	Fr
30–03	Paraguay	D	0–0	Maturin	Fr
18–05	Peru	L	1–2	Lima	Fr
25–06	Peru	W	3–1	San Cristobal	Fr
1–07	Brazil	L	1–3	Salvador	SCr1
3–07	Colombia	L	2–4	Salvador	SCr1
5–07	Peru	D	1–1	Salvador	SCr1
7–07	Paraguay	L	0–3	Salvador	SCr1
30–07	Brazil	L	0–4	Caracas	WCq
6–08	Chile	L	1–3	Caracas	WCq
20–08	Brazil	L	0–6	Sao Paulo	WCq
27–08	Chile	L	0–5	Mendoza	WCq
6–07–1991	Chile	L	0–2	Santiago	SCr1
8–07	Argentina	L	0–3	Santiago	SCr1
10–07	Paraguay	L	0–5	Santiago	SCr1
12–07	Peru	L	1–5	Santiago	SCr1

AFRICA

Cameroon v Nigeria, African Cup of Nations 1988

AFRICA

Africa can safely be regarded as the 'New Continent' of world football. If the 20th century was a tale of Europe and South America, the 21st could well see Africa rise to the top of the pile. In the early 1960s it was predicted that an African country would win the World Cup by the end of the century. One still might, but the likelihood would have been greatly increased had a fairer number of places been allotted to the continent in the finals. The allocation has increased from one to two in 1982 and three for the 1994 competition, but with over 40 countries taking an active interest in the game, this falls way short of a fair system.

Football in Africa is really a tale of the second half of the century, for not until the shackles of colonialism had been thrown off in the 1960s was there any serious movement to organise the game. Until that point, football in sub-Saharan Africa especially was organised from the Football Association in London or the French Federation in Paris, England and France being the two major colonial powers on the continent.

Football in Africa has traditionally been strongest north of the Sahara desert. Egypt, for instance, has had a football association since 1921 and qualified for the World Cup finals as long ago as 1934. Six years previously they even reached the semi-finals of the football tournament at the Olympic Games. Egypt, Morocco, Algeria and Tunisia all have leagues dating from the 1920s. Only Ghana, Nigeria and Zaire, formerly the Belgian Congo, can claim the same for 'Black Africa'.

The year 1957 was a key one for African football. Not only was the Confédération Africaine de Football formed, but Ghana under Kwame Nkrumah lit the torch of African awareness when the country gained independence from Britain. As nation after nation broke away from their European rulers, a football revolution was triggered, the ramifications of which are just beginning to be felt.

The highlight to date must be the achievement of Cameroon in the 1990 World Cup in Italy when they reached the quarter-finals, although their performance was not the first outstanding one by an African country in a World Cup. Algeria were good enough to beat the eventual finalists, West Germany, in 1982 in Spain, whilst Morocco four years later won their first round group ahead of England, Portugal and Poland, before going out to a last-minute goal against the West Germans in the second round.

The population in Africa is growing fast. Nigeria, for example, currently has a population of just under 120 million, but by the year 2010 it will have grown to an estimated 220 million. The population of the continent as a whole is expected to rise from the present 600 million to over 1600 million by the year 2025. This, coupled with the fact that football is unrivalled in the affections of the majority of Africans, makes for an exciting scenario.

Perhaps more than any other regional body, the African Football Confederation has been crucial to the development of football in the countries under its wing. The concept of forming the CAF was first realised at the 1954 World Cup and it came to fruition in 1957 at the Grand Hotel in Khartoum. The Charter members were the four African countries who by that stage had independent football associations: Egypt, Ethiopia, South Africa and Sudan.

At the same time as this meeting, the first African Cup of Nations was held in the new stadium in Khartoum and one of the three pillars of CAF policy was established. The African Cup of Champion Clubs followed seven years later, and the African Cup Winners Cup 11 years after that. These three competitions have been vital in helping the spread of football in Africa, and in overcoming the barriers that both poverty and the great distances involved in travelling to matches present. A fourth competition, the CAF Cup, was introduced in 1992, for those not in the Champions or Cup Winners Cup.

Poverty is an ever-increasing factor in African life. Famine has swept through areas of the north-east as well as other parts of the continent. Added to this is the fact that, as the initial enthusiasm after independence has worn away, bloody civil wars have erupted. This makes for an often harsh environment for football to operate in.

Club football is crucial to the development of the game. Already there is a comprehensive club structure in most countries that can accommodate the large number of excellent players that are being produced. The next challenge is to keep these players from being tempted abroad in vast numbers by creating the wealth in the game to reward them. Far too many go to France and Belgium and end up playing for second-rate clubs just to earn a living. For every Pelé playing for Marseille there are scores of other Africans wasting away in the mediocrity of the French second division.

There is a case that the exodus does have positive effects. First, it brings more tactical awareness to the national sides when the exiles return for competitions like the Cup of Nations, and second, it also provides the basis of a future generation of African coaches. Of the 12 teams taking part in the 1992 Cup of Nations, half were coached by foreigners. If a proportion of the 250 Africans currently employed by European clubs can return at some stage and help develop the game in their homeland, perhaps it will all have been worthwile.

No one is expecting every African country to produce teams capable winning the World Cup, but in Algeria, Cameroon, Egypt, Ghana, Ivory Coast, Kenya, Morocco, Nigeria, Senegal, Zaire, Zambia, Zimbabwe and now South Africa, Africa already has a very strong frontline of states ready to challenge for honours worldwide.

AFRICAN GOVERNING BODY

CONFÉDÉRATION AFRICAINE DE FOOTBALL
5 Shareh Gabalaya
Guezira, Cairo
Egypt
Tel: (010 20) 2 3412497
Fax: (010 20) 2 3420114
Telex: 93162 CAF UN
Cable: AFROBAL CAIRO

Year of formation: 1957

Members: 50
Algeria – Angola – Benin – Botswana – Burkina Faso – Burundi – Cameroon – Cape Verde Islands – Central African Republic – Chad – Congo – Côte d'Ivoire – Egypt – Equatorial Guinea – Ethiopia – Gabon – Gambia – Ghana – Guinea – Guinea-Bissau – Kenya – Lesotho – Liberia – Libya – Madagascar – Malawi – Mali – Mauritania – Mauritius – Morocco – Mozambique – Namibia – Niger – Nigeria – Rwanda – Sao Tomé e Principe – Senegal – Seychelles – Sierra Leone – Somalia – South Africa – Sudan – Swaziland – Tanzania – Togo – Tunisia – Uganda – Zaire – Zambia – Zimbabwe

Non Members: 4
Comros – Djibouti – Mayotte – Réunion

AFRICAN FOOTBALLER OF THE YEAR

From 'France Football'

1970

1	Salif Keita	Saint-Étienne	MLI	54
2	Laurent Pokou	ASEC Abidjan	CIV	28
	Ubugreisha	Al Ismaili	EGY	28
4	Kalala	TP Englebert	ZAI	19
5	Lalmas	CR Belcourt	ALG	15
6	Petit Sory	Hafia FC Conakry	GUI	9
7	Allal	FAR Rabat	MAR	5
	Robert Mensah	Asante Kotoko	GHA	5
	Ossey Coffie	Asante Kotoko	GHA	5
10	4 players on 4 points			

1971

1	Ibrahim Sunday	Asante Kotoko	GHA	29
2	Robert Mensah	Asante Kotoko	GHA	15
3	Lea	Canon Yaoundé	CMR	13
4	Laurent Pokou	ASEC Abidjan	CIV	8
	Attouga	Club Africain	TUN	8
6	Kibonge	Victoria Club	ZAI	6
	François M'Pele	AC Ajaccio	CGO	6
	Koum	AS Monaco	CMR	6
	Lalmas	CR Belcourt	ALG	6
	Kallet	Africa Sports	CIV	6

1972

1	Cherif Souleymane	Hafia FC Conakry	GUI	21
2	Tshimen Bwanga	TP Mazembe	ZAI	16
3	Petit Sory	Hafia FC Conakry	GUI	14
4	Hanni	Al Ahly	EGY	12
5	Ahmed Faras	Mohammedia	MAR	11
	Hadfi		ALG	11
7	Malik		GHA	10
8	Abougreisha		EGY	8
	Minga		CGO	8
	N'Tumba		ZAI	8

1973

1	Tshimen Bwanga	TP Mazembe	ZAI	49
2	Mwamba Kazadi	TP Mazembe	ZAI	44
3	Laurent Pokou	ASEC Abidjan	CIV	41
4	Kakoko		ZAI	29
5	Ahmed Faras		MAR	18
6	Yaw Sam		GHA	16
7	Kembo		ZAI	15
8	Cherif Souleymane		GUI	9
9	Moheddine		TUN	8
	Kibonge		ZAI	8
	Attouga		TUN	8

1974

1	Paul Moukila	CARA Brazzaville	CGO	57
2	Lobilo	AS Vita Kinshasa	ZAI	32
3	Chehata		EGY	28
4	Chama		ZAM	16
5	Ahmed Faras		MAR	14
6	N'Daye		ZAI	10
7	Kakoko		ZAI	8
8	Yanghat		CGO	6
	Mwamba Kazadi		ZAI	6
	Mana		ZAI	6
	Amasha		EGY	6
	Mambo Sasa		TAN	6

1975

1	Ahmed Faras	Chabab Mohammedia	MAR	28
2	N'Jolea	Hafia FC Conakry	GUI	24
	Roger Milla	Canon Yaoundé	CMR	24
4	Tarak Dhiab		TUN	16
5	Sagna		SEN	15
6	Petit Sory		GUI	10
7	Larbi		MAR	9
8	Gaafar		EGY	7
	Attouga		TUN	7
10	3 players on 5 points			

1976

1	Roger Milla	Canon Yaoundé	CMR	33
2	Papa Camara	Hafia FC Conakry	GUI	32
3	Ali Bencheikh	MC Algiers	ALG	27
4	Bengally Sylla	Hafia FC Conakry	GUI	26
5	Ahmed Faras	Chabab Mohammedia	MAR	12
	Betroumi		ALG	12
7	Lalbi		MAR	11
	Attouga		TUN	11
9	Tarak Dhiab		TUN	10
	Petit Sory		GUI	10

1977

1	Tarak Dhiab	ES Tunis	TUN	45
2	Papa Camara	Hafia FC Conakry	GUI	33
3	Odegbami	IICC Shooting Stars	NGR	29
4	Mohamed Polo		GHA	15
5	Bwalya		ZAM	6

6	Ali Bencheikh		ALG	5
7	Attouga		TUN	4
8	Gaafar		EGY	3
	Bahamboula		CGO	3
	Cherif Souleymane		GUI	3

1978

1	Karim Abdoul Razak	Asante Kotoko	GHA	58
2	Ali Bencheikh	MP Algiers	ALG	33
3	Thomas N'Kono	Canon Yaoundé	CMR	29
4	Christian Chukwu	Enugu Rangers	NGR	25
5	Bengally Sylla	Hafia FC Conakry	GUI	20
6	Tarak Dhiab	Al Ahly Jeddah	TUN	18
7	Temime Lahzani		TUN	12
8	Manga Onguene	Canon Yaoundé	CMR	10
9	Philip Omondi		UGA	9
10	4 players on 4 points			

1979

1	Thomas N'Kono	Canon Yaoundé	CMR	55
2	Adolf Armah	Hearts of Oak	GHA	23
3	Kerfalla Bangoura	Horoya AC Conakry	GUI	15
4	Abdoulaye Campaore	Bobo Dioulasso	BFA	13
5	Nahashion Oluoch	Gor Mahia	KEN	9
6	Kiyika		ZAI	8
7	Felix Agbonifo		NGR	7
8	Pascal Miezan	ASEC Abidjan	CIV	6
9	Muda Lawal	IICC Shooting Stars	NGR	5
10	4 players on 4 points			

1980

1	Manga Onguene	Canon Yaoundé	CMR	64
2	Segun Odegbami	IICC Shooting Stars	NGR	41
3	Théophile Abega	Canon Yaoundé	CMR	18
4	Lakhdar Belloumi	GCR Mascara	ALG	13
5	Ayel Mayele	AS Bilima	ZAI	12
	Thomas N'Kono	Canon Yaoundé	CMR	12
7	Mustapha Kouici	CR Belcourt	MAR	11
8	Elunga Massengo	TP Mazembe	ZAI	7
9	Tadj Bensaoula	Mouloudia Oran	ALG	6
	Mwamba Kazadi	TP Mazembe	ZAI	6

1981

1	Lakhdar Belloumi	GCR Mascara	ALG	78
2	Thomas N'Kono	Canon Yaoundé	CMR	54
3	Ali Fergani	JE Tizi-Ouzou	ALG	26
4	Eugène Ekoule	Union Douala	CMR	18
5	Théophile Abega	Canon Yaoundé	CMR	16
	Aziz Bouderbala	WAC Casablanca	MAR	16
7	Segun Odegbami	IICC Shooting Stars	NGR	8
8	Cheik Keita	AS Kaloum Stars	GUI	6
9	Koffi Kouadio	ASEC Abidjan	CIV	4
10	Badou Zaki	WAC Casablanca	MAR	4

1982

1	Thomas N'Kono	Español	CMR	83
2	Salah Assad	FC Mulhouse	ALG	54
3	Lakhdar Belloumi	GCR Mascara	ALG	36
4	Mahmoud Al Khatib	Al Ahly Cairo	EGY	28
5	Théophile Abega	Canon Yaoundé	CMR	23
	Peter Kaumba	Power Dynamos	ZAM	23
7	Albert Asase	Asante Kotoko	GHA	22
8	Opoku Afriyie	Asante Kotoko	GHA	13
9	Rabah Madjer	MA Hussein Dey	ALG	9
10	Chaabane Merzekane	MA Hussein Dey	ALG	8

1983

1	Mahmoud Al Khatib	Al Ahly Cairo	EGY	98
2	Opoku N'Ti	Asante Kotoko	GHA	89
3	Rafiou Moutairou	Agaza Lomé	TOG	19
4	Théophile Abega	Canon Yaoundé	CMR	18
	Antoine Bell	Al Makaouloum	CMR	18
	Karim Abdul Razak	Al Makaouloum	GHA	18
7	Cheikh Seck	ASC Diaraf Dakar	SEN	11
8	Mohamed Ali Nasser	Al Ahly Cairo	EGY	7
	Mustapha Haddaoui	Raja Casablanca	MAR	7
	Rabah Madjer	Racing Club Paris	ALG	7

1984

1	Théophile Abega	FC Toulouse	CMR	124
2	Ibrahim Youssef	Zamalek	EGY	65
	Antoine Bell	Al Makaouloum	CMR	61
4	Henry Nwosu	New Nigerian Bank	NGR	47
5	Taher Abou Zeid	Al Ahly Cairo	EGY	28
	Youssouf Fofana	AS Cannes	CIV	28
	Mahmoud Al Khatib	Al Ahly Cairo	EGY	28
8	Stephen Keshi	New Nigerian Bank	NGR	16
9	Lakhdar Belloumi	GCR Mascara	ALG	12
10	Clifton Msiya	Berrick Power	MAW	12

1985

1	Mohamed Timoumi	FAR Rabat	MAR	113
2	Rabah Madjer	FC Porto	ALG	45
3	Djamel Menad	JE Tizi-Ouzou	ALG	39
	Ibrahim Youssef	Zamalek	EGY	39
5	Badou Zaki	WAC Casablanca	MAR	33
6	Youssouf Fofana	AS Monaco	CIV	31
7	Lakhdar Belloumi	GCR Mascara	ALG	20
8	Abedi Pelé	Dragons de l'Ouème	GHA	19
9	Francois Bocande	FC Metz	SEN	17
10	Roger Milla	Saint-Étienne	CMR	16
	Wa Mbati Mobati	AS Bilima	ZAI	16

1986

1	Badou Zaki	Real Mallorca	MAR	125
2	Aziz Bouderbala	FC Sion	MAR	88
3	Roger Milla	Montpellier	CMR	80
4	Taher Abou Zeid	Al Ahly	EGY	47
5	Mohamed Timoumi	Real Murcia	MAR	35
6	Francois Bocande	Paris Saint Germain	SEN	13
	Abdelmajid Dolmy	Raja Casablanca	MAR	13
	Abedi Pelé	Chamois Niortais	GHA	13
9	Efford Chabala	Nkana Red Devils	ZAM	11
	Nacer Drid	MP Oran	ALG	11

1987

1	Rabah Madjer	FC Porto	ALG	130
2	Youssouf Fofana	AS Monaco	CIV	63
3	Francois Oman-Biyik	Stade Lavallois	CMR	52
4	Magdi Abdelghani	Al Ahly Cairo	EGY	37
5	Taher Abou Zeid	Al Ahly Cairo	EGY	25
6	Kennedy Malunga	Club Brugge	MAW	24
7	Peter Dawo	Gor Mahia	KEN	21
8	Abedi Pelé	Olympique Mareseille	GHA	17
9	Ambrose Ayoyi	AFC Leopards	KEN	15
10	Roger Milla	Montpellier	CMR	14

1988

1	Kalusha Bwalya	Cercle Brugge	ZAM	111
2	Roger Milla	Montpellier	CMR	68
3	Youssouf Fofana	AS Monaco	CIV	40
4	George Weah	AS Monaco	LBR	32
5	Aziz Bouderbala	Matra Racing Paris	MAR	27
	Peter Rufai	SC Lokeren	NGR	27
7	Stephen Keshi	RSC Anderlecht	NGR	14
	Emmanuel Kunde	Stade de Reims	CMR	14
9	Jacques Kingambo	St. Truidense	ZAI	13
10	Antoine Bell	SC Toulon	CMR	12

1989

1	George Weah	AS Monaco	LBR	133
2	Antoine Bell	Girondins Bordeaux	CMR	105
3	Kalusha Bwalya	PSV Eindhoven	ZAM	49
4	Abedi Pelé	Lille OSC	GHA	40
5	Francois Oman-Biyik	Stade Lavallois	CMR	31
6	Magdi Abdelghani	Beira Mar	EGY	30
7	Ahmed Shoubeir	Al Ahly Cairo	EGY	28
8	Stephen Tataw	Tonnerre Yaoundé	CMR	19
9	Stephen Keshi	RSC Anderlecht	NGR	18
10	Hossam Hassan	Al Ahly Cairo	EGY	17

1990

1	Roger Milla		CMR	209
2	Cherif El Ouazani	Aydinspor	ALG	64
3	Rabah Madjer	FC Porto	ALG	60
	Francois Oman-Biyik	Stade Rennais	CMR	60
5	Ahmed Shoubeir	Al Ahly Cairo	EGY	49
6	Hany Ramzy	Neuchâtel Xamax	EGY	41
7	Cyrille Makanaky	Málaga	CMR	34
8	George Weah	AS Monaco	LBR	26
9	Abedi Pelé	Olympique Marseille	GHA	23
10	Hossam Hassn	PAOK Salonika	EGY	22

1991

1	Abedi Pelé	Olympique Marseile	GHA	159
2	George Weah	AS Monaco	LBR	106
3	Francois Oman-Biyik	AS Cannes	CMR	52
4	Kalusha Bwalya	PSV Eindhoven	ZAM	30
5	Nii Lampety	RSC Anderlecht	GHA	29
6	Antony Yeboah	Eintracht Frankfurt	GHA	20
7	Roger Mendy	AS Monaco	SEN	18
8	Abdoulaye Traoré	ASEC Abidjan	CIV	16
9	Youssouf Fofana	AS Monaco	CIV	14
10	Aziz Bouderbala	Olympique Lyonnais	EGY	13

THE AFRICAN CUP OF NATIONS

The African Cup of Nations is the showpiece of African football and is held every two years in a designated country. For many years a simple knock-out qualifying tournament was used to reduce the number of entrants to just eight finalists, but for the 1992 tournament in Senegal it was decided to increase the number of finalists to 12. The hosts and previous winners have on each occasion received a bye into the final tournament.

The first finals took place in Khartoum at the same time as the formation of the Confédération Africaine de Football. South Africa were initially involved and were drawn against Ethiopia in the semi-finals, but only agreed to send either an all-black or all-white team. CAF insisted on a multi-racial one and so the South Africans withdrew and until they were readmitted to the confederation in 1992 they played no part in African football.

The first five editions were confined to only ten different entrants and did not involve any qualifying rounds. Egypt won the first two tournaments and reached the final of the third having played only six matches, so small was the number of entries at the time.

AFRICAN CUP OF NATIONS MEDALS TABLE

	Country	G	S	B	Finals	Semis
1	Ghana	4	3	–	7	5
2	Egypt	3	1	3	3	7
3	Cameroon	2	1	1	3	4
4	Zaire	2	–	–	2	3
5	Nigeria	1	3	2	4	5
6	Sudan	1	3	–	3	2
7	Algeria	1	1	2	2	5
8	Côte d'Ivoire	1	–	3	1	4
9	Ethiopia	1	–	2	1	3
10	Morocco	1	–	1	–	3
11	Congo	1	–	–	1	2
12	Zambia	–	1	2	1	3
13	Tunisia	–	1	1	1	2
14	Uganda	–	1	–	1	2
15	Guinea	–	1	–	–	–
	Libya	–	1	–	1	1
	Mali	–	1	–	1	1
18	Senegal	–	–	–	–	1

Ghana won the fourth tournament in 1963, and for the rest of the decade they were the dominant power, winning again in 1965 and reaching the final in 1968 and 1970. In 1965 a regulation was passed allowing each nation to play only two overseas-based players. This rule remained in force until 1982 when, due to the increasing numbers of players earning their living abroad, it was felt that the value of the tournament was being undermined.

In 1968 the formula for the tournament was changed to cope with the increasing number of countries wishing to take part. A qualifying round was introduced and the number of finalists increased to eight. The countries surrounding the river Congo were the first to make their mark in the new-style tournament. Congo Kinshasa, as Zaire was previously known, won in 1968; their smaller neighbours, the Congo, were victorious in 1972, and in 1974 not only did Zaire qualify for the World Cup but they went to West Germany as African champions after winning their second title a few months before.

The biggest surprise of the 1970s was the failure of Guinea to add an international honour to the many club honours won. They came close in 1976 finishing second behind Morocco, who themselves have never really shone despite qualifying for the World Cup on two occasions. Their 1976 win is their only triumph, and is in line with a poor showing by the North African countries, the real powers in club football. Egypt in 1986 and Algeria in 1990 both won on home ground, but neither they nor Morocco or Tunisia seem to travel well.

Since the late 1970s, West Africa has been the dominant force. Ghana regained some of their previous form by winning two further titles, which leaves them, with four titles, as clear overall leaders, whilst Cameroon and Nigeria have been especially powerful in the 1980s. The Nigerians have won once and lost in the final three times, twice against Cameroon who, had they not lost to Egypt on penalties in 1986, would have been the first team to win on three consecutive occasions.

Release of players from European clubs has often been a problem, but by moving the tournament to January, when much of Europe is in a mid-season break, the problem has been alleviated. Television companies around the world are now beginning to take the Cup of Nations seriously. The presence of famous names in European football has undoubtedly been the spur and the future of the competition looks brighter than ever.

1957	Egypt	4–0	Ethiopia
1959	Egypt	2–1	Sudan
1962	Ethiopia	4–2	Egypt
1963	Ghana	3–0	Sudan
1965	Ghana	3–2	Tunisia
1968	Congo Kinshasa	1–0	Ghana
1970	Sudan	1–0	Ghana
1972	Congo	3–2	Mali
1974	Zaire	2–2 2–0	Zambia
1976	Morocco	1–1	Guinea
1978	Ghana	2–0	Uganda
1980	Nigeria	3–0	Algeria
1982	Ghana	1–1 (7–6p)	Libya
1984	Cameroon	3–1	Nigeria
1986	Egypt	0–0 (5–4p)	Cameroon
1988	Cameroon	1–0	Nigeria
1990	Algeria	1–0	Nigeria
1992	Côte d'Ivoire	0–0 (11–10p)	Ghana

FIRST EDITION
Sudan, 10th–16th February 1957

SEMI-FINALS

Ethiopia received a walk over after South Africa were forced to withdraw

Khartoum Stadium, Khartoum, 10–02–1957
Egypt 2 (Raafat 21, El Diba 72)
Sudan 1 (Manzul 58)

FINAL

Khartoum Stadium, Khartoum, 16–02–1957. Referee: Youssef, Sudan
EGYPT 4 (El Diba 4)
ETHIOPIA 0

Egypt – Brascos – Mossaad, Dali – Fanaguili, Hanafi, Kotb – Tewfik, El Diba, Attia, Alaa, Hamdi

Ethiopia – Gila – Ayele, Adale – Adamu, Asefaw, Berthe – Kebede, Zewode, Abreha, Netsere, Berhane

Top Scorer: El Diba, Egypt 5

SECOND EDITION
Egypt, 22nd–29th May 1959

Al Ahli Stadium, Cairo, 22–05–1959
Egypt 4 (Gohri 29 42 73, Cherbini 64)
Ethiopia 0

Al Ahli Stadium, Cairo, 25–05–1959
Sudan 1 (Drissa 40)
Ethiopia 0

Al Ahli Stadium, Cairo, 29–05–1959. Referee: Guisebatic, Yugoslavia
EGYPT 2 (Issam 12 89)
SUDAN 1 (Manzul 65)

Egypt – Heykal – Yakin, Tarek Selim – Fanaguili, Al-Hamouli, Ismail – Bahig, Cherif El-Far, Salah Selim, Gohri, Cherbini

Sudan – Samir – Mutawakil, Bashir – Syam, Hassan Abd, Mahina – Kabir, Zoubeir, Drissa, Seddik Manzul, Wahaga

	Eg	Su	Et	Pl	W	D	L	F	A	Pts
EGYPT	–	2–1	4–0	2	2	0	0	6	1	4
SUDAN	–	–	1–0	2	1	0	1	2	2	2
ETHIOPIA	–	–	–	2	0	0	2	0	5	0

Top Scorer: Gohri, Egypt 3

THIRD EDITION
Ethiopia, 14th–21st January 1962

1ST ROUND/SEMI-FINALS

Haile Selassie Stadium, Addis Ababa, 14–01–1962
Ethiopia 4 (Luciano 2, Girma, Menguistou)
Tunisia 2 (Marrichko, Moncef Cherif)

Haile Selassie Stadium, Addis Ababa, 18–01–1962
Egypt 2 (Abdelfattah Badawi 50, Salah Selim)
Uganda 1 (Jonathan 16)

3RD PLACE

Haile Selassie Stadium, Addis Ababa, 20–01–1962
Tunisia 3 (Djedidi, Moncef Cherif, Meddeb)
Uganda 0

FINAL

Haile Selassie Stadium, Addis Ababa, 21–01–1962. Referee: Brooks, Uganda
ETHIOPIA 4 (Girma 74, Menguistou 84 117, Italo 101)
EGYPT 2 (Abdelfattah Badawi 35 75)

Ethiopia – Gila – Kiflom, Asmelash, Berhe, Awade – Tesfaye, Luciano – Girma, Menguistou, Italo, Guetacheou

Egypt – Heykal – Ahmed Mostafa, Raafat, Tarak – Fanaguili, Badawi.M – Salah Selim, Taha, Cherbini, Chehta, Abdelfattah Badawi

Top scorers: Badawi, Egypt 3
Menguistou, Ethiopia 3

FOURTH EDITION
Ghana, 24th November–1st December 1963

FIRST ROUND

Group 1

Accra Stadium, Accra, 24–11–1963
Ghana 1 (Mfum 9)
Tunisia 1 (Djedidi 36)

Accra Stadium, Accra, 26–11–1963
Ghana 2 (Acquah 2)
Ethiopia 0

Accra Stadium, Accra, 28–11–1963
Ethiopia 4
Tunisia 2

	Gh	Et	Tu	Pl	W	D	L	F	A	Pts
GHANA	–	2–0	1–1	2	1	1	0	3	1	3
ETHIOPIA	–	–	4–2	2	1	0	1	4	4	2
TUNISIA	–	–	–	2	0	1	1	3	5	1

Group 2

Kumasi Stadium, Kumasi, 24–11–1963
Egypt 6 (Chazli 42 44 81 87, Riza 30 32)
Nigeria 3 (Okepe 78, Bassey 82, Onya 89)

Kumasi Stadium, Kumasi, 26–11–1963
Sudan 2 (Djaksa 60 75)
Egypt 2 (Chazli 5, Riza 7)

Kumasi Stadium, Kumasi, 28–11–1963
Sudan 4
Nigeria 0

	Su	Eg	Ni	Pl	W	D	L	F	A	Pts
SUDAN	–	2–2	4–0	2	1	1	0	6	2	3
EGYPT	–	–	6–3	2	1	1	0	8	5	3
NIGERIA	–	–	–	2	0	0	2	3	10	0

3RD PLACE

Accra Stadium, Accra, 30–01–1963
Egypt 3 (Riadh, Taha, Chazli)
Ethiopia 0

FINAL

Accra Stadium, Accra, 1–12–1963. Referee: Abdelkader, Tunisia
GHANA 3 (Aggrey–Fynn 62, Mfum 72 82)
SUDAN 0

Ghana – Ankrah – Crentsil, Aggrey-Fynn, Odametey, Simmons – Obiley, Adarkwa – Ofei Dodo, Mfum, Acquah, Salisu
Sudan – Sabbit – Samir, Kabir, Amin, Omar – Zarzour, Magid – Ibrahima, Djaksa, Nagy, Jagdoul

Top scorer: Chazli, Egypt 6

FIFTH EDITION
Tunisia, 12th–21st November 1965

FIRST ROUND

Group 1

Zouiten, Tunis, 12–11–1965
Tunisia 4 (Chaibi 32, Djedidi 62, Delhoum 80, Lahmar 84)
Ethiopia 0

Zouiten, Tunis, 14–11–1965
Senegal 0
Tunisia 0

Zouiten, Tunis, 19–11–1965
Senegal 5 (Louis Camara 3 52, Gueye 37, Matar Niang 48 53)
Ethiopia 1 (Luciano 12)

	Tu	Se	Et	Pl	W	D	L	F	A	Pts
TUNISIA	–	0–0	4–0	2	1	1	0	4	0	3
SENEGAL	–	–	5–1	2	1	1	0	5	1	3
ETHIOPIA	–	–	–	2	0	0	2	1	9	0

Group 2

Maarouf, Sousse, 12–11–1965
Ghana 5 (Osei Kofi 13, Ben Acheampong 18 59, Jones 84 89)
Congo Kinshasa 2 (Kalala 43 45)

Maarouf, Sousse, 14–11–1965
Côte d'Ivoire 3 (Mangle 14 59 80)
Congo Kinshasa 0

Maarouf, Sousse, 19–11–1965
Ghana 4 (Ben Acheampong 20, Kwamenti 43, Lutdrot 52, Osei Kofi 70)
Côte d'Ivoire 1 (Bleziri 66)

	Gh	IC	CK	Pl	W	D	L	F	A	Pts
GHANA	–	4–1	5–2	2	2	0	0	9	3	4
CÔTE D'IVOIRE	–	–	3–0	2	1	0	1	4	4	2
CONGO KINSHASA	–	–	–	2	0	0	2	2	8	0

3RD PLACE

Zouiten, Tunis, 21–11–1965
Côte d'Ivoire 1 (Yoboue 35)
Senegal 0

FINAL

Zouiten, Tunis, 21–11–1965. Referee: Chekaimi, Algeria
GHANA 3 (Odoi 37 96, Kofi 79)
TUNISIA 2 (Chetali 47, Chaibi 67)

Ghana – Naawu – Ben Kusi, Acquah, Odametey, Evans – Kwamenti, Mensah – Osei Kofi, Jones, Kofi Pare, Odoi
Tunisia – Attouga – Benzerti, Douiri, Habacha, Lamine – Chetali, Chaibi – Sassi, Gribaa, Delhoum, Djedidi

Top scorers: Kofi, Ghana 3
Ben Acheampong, Ghana 3
Mangle, Côte d'Ivoire 3

SIXTH EDITION
1967–1968

QUALIFYING TOURNAMENT

Group 1

	Se	Gu	Lb	Pl	W	D	L	F	A	Pts
SENEGAL	–	4–1	4–1	4	2	1	1	9	6	5
GUINEA	3–0	–	3–0	4	2	1	1	9	6	5
LIBERIA	1–1	2–2	–	4	0	2	2	4	10	2

Play–off
Senegal .... 2–1 .... Guinea

Group 2

	Al	Ml	BF	Pl	W	D	L	F	A	Pts
ALGERIA	–	1–0	3–1	4	4	0	0	9	2	8
MALI	0–3	–	4–0	4	2	0	2	5	4	4
UPPER VOLTA	1–2	0–1	–	4	0	0	4	2	10	0

Group 3

	IC	Ng	To	Pl	W	D	L	F	A	Pts
COTE D'IVOIRE	–	2–0	3–0	4	3	1	0	7	0	7
NIGERIA	0–0	–	4–2	4	1	1	2	4	5	3
TOGO	0–2	1–0	–	4	1	0	3	3	9	2

Group 4
Egypt .... 3–2 2–2 .... Libya
Uganda .... 2–1 3–3 .... Kenya
Uganda .... 0–1 .... Egypt

UGANDA qualified after Egypt withdrew

Group 5

	CB	Tu	Ca	Pl	W	D	L	F	A	Pts
CONGO BRAZZAVILLE	–	W-O	2–1	3	2	1	0	3	2	5

TUNISIA	1–1	–	4–0	4	1	1	2	5	3	3
CAMEROON	–	2–0	–	3	1	0	2	3	6	2

Group 6

Congo Kinsh. .... 3–2 0–1 2–1 ... Sudan
Tanzania .... 1–0 1–1 .... Mauritius
CONGO KINSHASA ... W-O .... Tanzania

FINAL TOURNAMENT

Ethiopia, 12th–21st January 1968

FIRST ROUND

Group 1

Haile Selassie Stadium, Addis Ababa, 12–01–1968
Ethiopia 2 (Girma, Luciano)
Uganda 1 (Ouma)

Haile Selassie Stadium, Addis Ababa, 12–01–1968
Côte d'ivoire 3 (Pokou 25 65, Bozon 15)
Algeria 0

Haile Selassie Stadium, Addis Ababa, 14–01–1968
Ethiopia 1 (Bekouresion 86)
Côte d'Ivoire 0

Haile Selassie Stadium, Addis Ababa, 14–01–1968
Algeria 4 (Lalmas 15 25 70, Khalem 60)
Uganda 0

Haile Selassie Stadium, Addis Ababa, 16–01–1968
Côte d'Ivoire 2 (Pokou, Mangle)
Uganda 1 (Obua)

Haile Selassie Stadium, Addis Ababa, 16–01–1968
Ethiopia 3 (Menguistou 16, Shewangezaw 19, Luciano 27)
Algeria 1 (Amirouche 68)

	Et	IC	Al	Ug	Pl	W	D	L	F	A	Pts
ETHIOPIA	–	1–0	3–1	2–1	3	3	0	0	6	2	6
CÔTE D'IVOIRE	–	–	3–0	2–1	3	2	0	1	5	2	4
ALGERIA	–	–	–	4–0	3	1	0	2	5	6	2
UGANDA	–	–	–	–	3	0	0	3	2	8	0

Group 2

Saba, Asmara, 12–01–1968
Ghana 2 (Osei Kofi 63, Mfum 87)
Senegal 2 (Diongue 10, Diop 65)

Saba, Asmara, 12–01–1968
Congo Kinshasa 3 (Muwawia 19, Kabamba 27)
Congo Brazzaville 0

Saba, Asmara, 14–01–1968
Senegal 2 (Diop 27, Diock 86)
Congo Brazzaville 1 (Foutika 31)

Saba, Asmara, 14–01–1968
Ghana 2 (Osei Kofi 17, Mfum 84)
Congo Kinshasa 1 (Mokili 42)

Saba, Asmara, 16–01–1968
Congo Kinshasa 2 (Kidumu, Tshimanga)
Senegal 1 (Diouck)

Saba, Asmara, 16–01–1968
Ghana 3
Congo Brazzaville 1

	Gh	CK	Se	CB	Pl	W	D	L	F	A	Pts
GHANA	–	2–1	2–2	3–1	3	2	1	0	7	4	5
ZAIRE	–	–	2–1	3–0	3	2	0	1	6	3	4
SENEGAL	–	–	–	2–1	3	1	1	1	5	5	3
CONGO BRAZZAVILLE	–	–	–	–	3	0	0	3	2	8	0

SEMI-FINALS

Haile Selassie Stadium, Addis Ababa, 19–01–1968
Congo Kinshasa 3 (Kidumu 3, Mungamuni 16 100)
Ethiopia 2 (Luciano 25, Menguistou 65)

Saba, Asmara, 19–01–1968
Ghana 4 (Mfum 2, Sunday, Odoi)
Côte d'Ivoire 3 (Pokou 2, Konan Henri)

3RD PLACE

Haile Selassie Stadium, Addis Ababa, 21–01–1968
Côte d'Ivoire 1 (Pokou 28)
Ethiopia 0

FINAL

Haile Selassie Stadium, Addis Ababa, 21–01–1968. Referee: El Diba, Egypt
CONGO KINSHASA 1 (Kalala 66)
GHANA 0

Congo Kinshasa – Kazadi – Mange, Katumba, Tshimanga, Mukombo – Kibonge, Kassongo – Kalala, Kidumu, Kembo, Mungamuni
Ghana – Naawu – Crentsil, Eshun, Odametey, Kusi – Sunday, Odoi – Kofi, Attuquayefio, Mfum, Malik

Top scorer: Pokou, Côte d'Ivoire 6

SEVENTH EDITION

1969–1970

QUALIFYING TOURNAMENT

FIRST ROUND

Algeria .... 2–0 0–1 .... Morocco
Egypt .... W-O .... Somalia
Guinea .... 4–0 1–1 .... Togo
Kenya .... 0–1 1–1 .... **Tanzania**
Mali .... W-O .... Upper Volta
Mauritius .... 2–3 2–2 .... **Zambia**
Niger .... W-O .... Nigeria
Senegal .... W-O .... Sierra Leone
Uganda .... 1–1 0–2 .... **Cameroon**

SECOND ROUND

EGYPT .... 1–0 1–1 .... Algeria
ETHIOPIA .... 7–0 2–1 .... Tanzania
GHANA .... 6–0 9–1 .... Niger
Mali .... 0–0 0–4 .... COTE D'IVOIRE
Senegal .... 1–1 3–4 .... GUINEA
Zambia .... 2–2 1–2 .... CAMEROON

FINAL TOURNAMENT

Sudan, 6th–16th February 1970

FIRST ROUND

Group 1

Municipal Stadium, Khartoum, 6–02–1970, 14 000
Cameroon 3 (Koum 57 66, Ndoga 60)
Côte d'Ivoire 2 (Pokou 25 45)

Municipal Stadium, Khartoum, 6–02–1970, 14 000
Sudan 3 (Gagarine 43, Hasabu 47, Djaksa 85)
Ethiopia 0

Municipal Stadium, Khartoum, 8–02–1970, 9000
Cameroon 3 (Tsebo 21, Manga 43, Ndoga 70)
Ethiopia 2 (Menguistou 12 75)

Municipal Stadium, Khartoum, 8–02–1970, 9000
Côte d'Ivoire 1 (Tahi 89)
Sudan 0

Municipal Stadium, Khartoum, 10–02–1970, 9000
Côte d'Ivoire 6 (Losseni 16, Pokou 21 60 71 80 87)
Ethiopia 1 (Menguistou 33)

Municipal Stadium, Khartoum, 10–02–1970, 9000
Sudan 2 (Djaksa 20, Hasabu 60)
Cameroon 1 (Tsebo 34)

	IC	Su	Ca	Et	Pl	W	D	L	F	A	Pts
CÔTE D'IVOIRE	–	1–0	2–3	6–1	3	2	0	1	9	4	4
SUDAN	–	–	2–1	3–0	3	2	0	1	5	2	4
CAMEROON	–	–	–	3–2	3	2	0	1	7	6	4
ETHIOPIA	–	–	–	–	3	0	0	3	3	12	0

Group 2
Municipal Stadium, Wad Madani, 7–02–1970, 7000
Ghana 2 (Owusu 29 32)
Congo Kinshasa 0

Municipal Stadium, Wad Madani, 7–02–1970, 7000
Egypt 4 (Abugreisha 5 10, Chazli 73, Taha Bisri 65)
Guinea 1 (Edente 25)

Municipal Stadium, Wad Madani, 9–02–1970, 3000
Congo Kinshasa 2 (Kalonzo 70, Mungamuni 72)
Guinea 2 (Petit Sory 5, Edente 55)

Municipal Stadium, Wad Madani, 9–02–1970, 3000
Egypt 1 (Abdelrazak 70)
Ghana 1 (Sunday 60)

Municipal Stadium, Wad Madani, 11–02–1970, 3000
Ghana 1 (Owusu 50)
Guinea 1 (Tolo 10)

Municipal Stadium, Wad Madani, 11–02–1970, 3000
Egypt 1 (Abugreisha 71)
Congo Kinshasa 0

	Eg	Gh	Gu	CK	Pl	W	D	L	F	A	Pts
EGYPT	–	1–1	4–2	1–0	3	2	1	0	6	3	5
GHANA	–	–	1–1	2–0	3	1	2	0	4	2	4
GUINEA	–	–	–	2–2	3	0	2	1	5	7	2
CONGO KINSHASA	–	–	–	–	3	0	1	2	2	5	1

SEMI-FINALS

Municipal Stadium, Khartoum, 14–02–1970, 12 000
Sudan 2 (El Issed 83 102)
Egypt 1 (Chazli 84)

Municipal Stadium, Khartoum, 14–02–1970, 12 000
Ghana 2 (Sunday 21, Malik 100)
Côte d'Ivoire 1 (Losseni 78)

3RD PLACE

Municipal Stadium, Khartoum, 16–02–1970, 12 000
Egypt 3 (Chazli 3 14 50)
Côte d'Ivoire 1 (Pokou 72)

FINAL

Municipal Stadium, Khartoum, 16–02–1970, 12 000. Referee: Tesfaye, Ethiopia
SUDAN 1 (El Issed 12)
GHANA 0

Sudan – Aziz – Kaunda, Suliman, Amin, Samir – Bushara, Bushra – El Issed, Djaksa, Dahish, Hasabu
Ghana – Mensah – Boye, Mingle, Eshun, Acquah – Ghartey, Attuquayafio, Sunday – Folley, Owusu, Malik

Top scorer: Pokou, Côte d'Ivoire 8

EIGHTH EDITION
1971–1972

QUALIFYING TOURNAMENT

FIRST ROUND

Algeria	3–1 0–3	**Morocco**
Gabon	1–2 0–1	**Côte d'Ivoire**
Ghana	W–O	Upper Volta
Guinea	1–0 0–0	Senegal
Libya	0–1 1–2	**Egypt**
Kenya	2–0 1–0	Ethiopia
Madagascar	2–1 1–4	**Mauritius**
Niger	0–1 1–3	**Mali**
Nigeria	0–0 1–2	**Congo**
Tanzania	1–1 1–5	**Zambia**
Togo	2–1 0–0	Dahomey
Uganda	1–4 0–1	**Zaire**

SECOND ROUND

Guinea	0–0 1–3	MALI
Côte d'Ivoire	3–2 0–2	CONGO
KENYA	2–1 0–0	Mauritius
MOROCCO	3–0 2–3	Egypt
TOGO	0–0 1–0	Ghana
Zambia	2–1 0–3	ZAIRE

FINAL TOURNAMENT
Cameroon, 23rd February–5th March 1972

FIRST ROUND

Group 1

Omnisports, Yaounde, 23–02–1972
Cameroon 2 (Ndoga 7, Ndongo 20)
Kenya 1 (Niva 44)

Omnisports, Yaounde, 24–02–1972
Mali 3 (Bakary Traoré 10, Keita.F 46, Bako Traoré 49)
Togo 3 (Kaolo 45 60 81)

Omnisports, Yaounde, 26–02–1972, 45 000
Mali 1 (Touré)
Kenya 1 (Ouma 60)

Omnisports, Yaounde, 26–02–1972, 45 000
Cameroon 2 (Joseph 64, Mve 79)
Togo 0

Omnisports, Yaounde, 28–02–1972, 45 000
Togo 1 (Kaolo 60)
Kenya 1 (Makunda 30)

Omnisports, Yaounde, 28–02–1972, 45 000
Cameroon 1 (Lea 67)
Mali 1 (Keita F 43)

	Ca	Ml	Ke	To	Pl	W	D	L	F	A	Pts
CAMEROON	–	1–1	2–1	2–0	3	2	1	0	5	2	5
MALI	–	–	1–1	3–3	3	0	3	0	5	5	3
KENYA	–	–	–	1–1	3	0	2	1	3	4	2
TOGO	–	–	–	–	3	0	2	1	4	6	2

Group 2

Omnisports, Douala, 25–02–1972, 40 000
Congo 1 (Moukila 45)
Morocco 1 (Maaroufi 34)

Omnisports, Douala, 25–02–1972, 40 000
Zaire 1 (Mayanga 53)
Sudan 1 (Hasabu 55)

Omnisports, Douala, 27–02–1972
Morocco 1 (Faras 32)
Sudan 1 (Bushara 49)

Omnisports, Douala, 27–02–1972
Zaire 2 (Ntumba 15 61)
Congo 0

Omnisports, Douala, 29–02–1972, 20 000
Zaire 1 (Mayanga 36)
Morocco 1 (Faras)

Omnisports, Douala, 29–02–1972, 20 000
Congo 4 (Mbono 8 55, M'Pele 32, Banamboula 46)
Sudan 2 (Kamal 37 44)

	Zr	Co	Mr	Su	Pl	W	D	L	F	A	Pts
ZAIRE	–	2–0	1–1	1–1	3	1	2	0	4	2	4
CONGO	–	–	1–1	4–2	3	1	1	1	5	5	3
MOROCCO	–	–	–	1–1	3	0	3	0	3	3	3
SUDAN	–	–	–	–	3	0	2	1	4	6	2

SEMI-FINALS

Omnisports, Douala, 2–03–1972
Congo 1 (Minga 31)
Cameroon 0

Omnisports, Douala, 2–03–1972
Mali 4 (Traoré A 17, Touré 68, Keita F 48 92)
Zaire 3 (Ntumba 6, Kakoko 61, Ngassebe 78)

3RD PLACE

Omnisports, Yaounde, 4–03–1972
Cameroon 5 (Akono 4, Ndongo 31, Owona 32, Mouthe 34, Ndoga 42)
Zaire 2 (Kakoko 13, Mayanga 17)

FINAL

Omnisports, Yaounde, 5–03–1972. Referee: Aouissi, Algeria
CONGO 3 (M'Bono 57 59, M'Pele 63)
MALI 2 (Diakhite 42, Traoré M 75)

Congo – Matsima – Dengaky, Ngassaki, Ndolou, Niangou – Minga, Balekita, M'Pele – Bahamboula, Matongo (Ongania), M'Bono (Moukila).
Mali – Keita M – Moctar, Sangare, Kidian, Cheikna – Bakary Traoré, Traoré O – Touré (Traoré M), Keita S (Traoré A), Keita F, Diakhité.

Top scorer: Keita F, Mali 5

NINTH EDITION
1973–1974

QUALIFYING TOURNAMENT

PRELIMINARY ROUND

Cent. Af. Rep. .... W–O .... Gabon
Sierra Leone .... W–O .... Benin
Somalia .... 2–0 0–5 .... **Uganda**

FIRST ROUND

Algeria .... W–O .... Libya
Cameroon .... W–O .... Niger
Cent. Af. Rep. .... 4–2 1–2* .... **Côte d'Ivoire**
Ethiopia .... 2–1 0–3 .... **Tanzania**
Ghana .... 3–2 0–1 (5–3p) .... Senegal
Guinea .... W–O .... Togo
Lesotho .... 0–0 1–5 .... **Mauritius**
Sierra Leone .... 1–1 2–4 .... **Mali**
Sudan .... 1–1 1–2 .... **Nigeria**
Uganda .... 1–0 2–1 .... Kenya
Upper Volta .... 0–5 1–4 .... **Zaire**
Zambia .... 3–1 1–2 .... Madagascar

* Central African Republic disqualified

SECOND ROUND

Cameroon .... 2–1 0–2 .... ZAIRE
Ghana .... 0–3 0–1 .... COTE D'IVOIRE
Mali .... 2–2 1–1* .... GUINEA
Tanzania .... 1–1 0–0* .... MAURITIUS
UGANDA .... 2–1 1–1 .... Algeria
ZAMBIA .... 5–1 2–3 .... Nigeria

* Won on penalties

FINAL TOURNAMENT

Egypt, 1st–14th March 1974

FIRST ROUND

Group 1

International Stadium, Cairo, 1–03–1974
Egypt 2 (Abugreisha 6, Khalil 52)
Uganda 1 (Mubiru 28)

Mehalla Stadium, Mehalla, 2–03–1974, 4000
Zambia 1 (Kaushi 2)
Côte d'Ivoire 0

International Stadium, Cairo, 4–03–1974, 40000
Egypt 3 (Abdel Azim 4, Taha Basri 18, Abugreisha 53)
Zambia 1 (Chitalu 10)

Mehalla Stadium, Mehalla, 3,000, 4–03–1974, 3000
Côte d'Ivoire 2 (Kobinan 2)
Uganda 2 (Mubiru 2)

International Stadium, Cairo, 6–03–1974, 10 000
Egypt 2 (Chazli 1, Khalil 44)
Côte d'Ivoire 0

Mehalla Stadium, Mehalla, 6–03–1974, 2000
Zambia 1 (Kapita)
Uganda 0

	Eg	Zm	Ug	IC	Pl	W	D	L	F	A	Pts
EGYPT	–	3–1	2–1	2–0	3	3	0	0	7	2	6
ZAMBIA	–	–	1–0	1–0	3	2	0	1	3	3	4

					Pl	W	D	L	F	A	Pts
UGANDA	–	–	–	2–2	3	0	1	2	3	5	1
CÔTE D'IVOIRE	–	–	–	–	3	0	1	2	2	5	1

Group 2

Damanhour Stadium, Damanhour, 3–03–1974

Zaire 2 (Ndaye 18 65)
Guinea 1 (Sylla B 25)

Municipal Stadium, Alexandria, 3–03–1974, 5000

Congo 2 (Moukila, Lakou)
Mauritius 0

Municipal Stadium, Alexandria, 5–03–1974, 8000

Congo 2 (M'Bono 70, Minga 81)
Zaire 1 (Mayanga 25)

Damanhour Stadium, Damanhour, 5–03–1974, 1000

Guinea 2 (Morcire 2)
Mauritius 1 (Imbert)

Municipal Stadium, Alexandria, 7–03–1974, 7000

Guinea 1 (Edente 60)
Congo 1 (Ndomba 65)

Damanhour Stadium, Damanhour, 7–03–1974

Zaire 4 (Mayanga 2, Ndaye, Kakoko)
Mauritius 1 (Imbert)

	Co	Zr	Gu	Mr	Pl	W	D	L	F	A	Pts
CONGO	–	2–1	1–1	2–0	3	2	1	0	5	2	5
ZAIRE	–	–	2–1	4–1	3	2	0	1	7	4	4
GUINEA	–	–	–	2–1	3	1	1	1	4	4	3
MAURITIUS	–	–	–	–	3	0	0	3	2	8	0

SEMI-FINALS

International Stadium, Cairo, 9–03–1974, 50 000

Zaire 3 (Ndaye 55 72, Kidumu 61)
Egypt 2 (OG 41, Abugreisha 54)

Municipal Stadium, Alexandria, 9–03–1974, 2000

Zambia 4 (Chanda 3, Mapulanga)
Congo 2 (Ndomba, M'Pele)

3RD PLACE

International Stadium, Cairo, 11–03–1974, 5000

Egypt 4 (Mostafa Abdou 5, Chehata 18 80, Abugreisha 62)
Congo 0

FINAL

International Stadium, Cairo, 12–03–1974. Referee: Gamar, Libya

ZAIRE 2 (Ndaye 65 117)
ZAMBIA 2 (Kaushi 40, Sinyangwe 120)

Zaire – Kazadi – Mwepu, Bwanga, Lobilo, Ngoie – Mavuba, Mana – Mayanga, Ndaye, Kidumu, Kakoko

Zambia – Mwape – Musenge, Chama, Makwaza, Mbaso – Simutowe, Simulambo – Mapulanga, Chanda, Kaushi, Sinyangwe

Replay. International Stadium, Cairo, 14–03–1974, 1000. Referee: Gamar, Libya

ZAIRE 2 (Ndaye 30 76)
ZAMBIA 0

Zaire – Kazadi – Mwepu, Mukombo, Bwanga, Lobilo – Mavuba, Mana, Mayanga – Ndaye, Kidumu, Kakoko

Zambia – Mwape – Musenge, Chama, Makwaza, Mbaso – Simutowe, Simulambo, Mapulanga – Chanda, Kaushi, Sinyangwe

Top scorer: Ndaye, Zaire 9

TENTH EDITION
1975–1976

QUALIFYING TOURNAMENT

PRELIMINARY ROUND

Mali .... W-O .... Lesotho
Morocco .... 3–0 3–0 .... Gambia
Niger .... W–O .... Benin
Somali .... 0–2 1–0 .... **Burundi**
Togo .... 1–0 2–0 .... Liberia
Tunisia .... *1–0 0–1 .... Libya
* Won on penalties

FIRST ROUND

Burundi .... 0–3 0–2 .... **Egypt**
Cameroon .... 3–0 0–4 .... **Togo**
Congo .... 1–0 1–2 .... Côte d'Ivoire
Mali .... 3–1 0–4 .... **Ghana**
Morocco .... 4–0 1–2 .... Senegal
Niger .... 2–4 0–3 .... **Guinea**
Nigeria .... W–O .... Cent. Af. Rep.
Sudan .... 1–0 2–0 .... Kenya
Tanzania .... W–O .... Madagascar
Tunisia .... 1–1 2–1 .... Algeria
Uganda .... 4–0 1–1 .... Mauritius
Zambia .... 3–3 6–1 .... Malawi

SECOND ROUND

Congo .... 0–1 1–2 .... NIGERIA
Ghana .... 2–0 0–2* .... MOROCCO
Tanzania .... 1–1 2–5 .... EGYPT
Togo .... 2–2 0–2 .... GUINEA
Tunisia .... 3–2 1–2 .... SUDAN
Zambia .... 2–1 0–3 .... UGANDA
* Won on penalties

FINAL TOURNAMENT

Ethiopia, 29th February–14th March 1976

FIRST ROUND

Group 1

Addis Ababa Stadium, Addis Ababa, 29–02–1976

Ethiopia 2 (Sheferaw 2, Tesfaye 83)
Uganda 0

Addis Ababa Stadium, Addis Ababa, 29–02–1976

Egypt 1 (Taha Basri 43)
Guinea 1 (Sylla B 44)

Addis Ababa Stadium, Addis Ababa, 3–03–1976

Egypt 2 (Abdou 26, Taha Basri 32)
Uguanda 1 (Obua 21)

Addis Ababa Stadium, Addis Ababa, 3–03–1976

Guinea 2 (N'Jo Léa 15, Petit Sory 85)
Ethiopia 1 (Sheferaw 40)

Addis Ababa Stadium, Addis Ababa, 5–03–1976

Guinea 2 (N'Jo Léa 2, Sylla.B 20)
Uganda 1 (Muguwa 85)

Addis Ababa Stadium, Addis Ababa, 5–03–1976

Egypt 1 (Chehata 28)
Ethiopia 1 (Mohamed Ali 46)

	Gu	Eg	Et	Ug	Pl	W	D	L	F	A	Pts
GUINEA	–	1–1	2–1	2–1	3	2	1	0	5	3	5
EGYPT	–	–	1–1	2–1	3	1	2	0	4	3	4

Ethiopia	–	–	–	2–0	3	1	1	1	4	3	3
Uganda	–	–	–	–	3	0	0	3	2	6	0

Group 2

Dire Dawa Stadium, Dire Dawa, 1–03–1976
Nigeria 4 (Baba Otu 28 44, Ojebode 37, Usiyan 90)
Zaire 2 (Kabasu 2)

Dire Dawa Stadium, Dire Dawa, 1–03–1976
Morocco 2 (Cherif 1, Abouali 58)
Sudan 2 (Gagrine 9 79)

Dire Dawa Stadium, Dire Dawa, 4–03–1976
Nigeria 1 (Usiyan 8)
Sudan 0

Dire Dawa Stadium, Dire Dawa, 4–03–1976
Morocco 1 (Zahraoui 80)
Zaire 0

Dire Dawa Stadium, Dire Dawa, 6–03–1976
Morocco 3 (Faras 8, Tazi 19, Larbi 81)
Nigeria 1 (Ojebode 5)

Dire Dawa Stadium, Dire Dawa, 6–03–1976
Zaire 1 (Ndaye 41)
Sudan 1 (Gagarine 14)

	Mr	Ng	Su	Zr	Pl	W	D	L	F	A	Pts
Morocco	–	3–1	2–2	1–0	3	2	1	0	6	3	5
Nigeria	–	–	1–0	4–2	3	2	0	1	6	5	4
Sudan	–	–	–	1–1	3	0	2	1	3	4	2
Zaire	–	–	–	–	3	0	1	2	3	6	1

FINAL ROUND

Addis Ababa Stadium, Addis Ababa, 9–03–1976
Guinea 1 (Papa Camara 88)
Nigeria 1 (Lawal 52)

Addis Ababa Stadium, Addis Ababa, 9–03–1976
Morocco 2 (Faras 23, Zahraoui 88)
Egypt 1 (Abu Rehab 34)

Addis Ababa Stadium, Addis Ababa, 11–03–1976
Morocco 2 (Faras 82, Guezzar 87)
Nigeria 1 (Baba Otu 50)

Addis Ababa Stadium, Addis Ababa, 11–03–1976
Guinea 4 (N'Jo Léa 24 65, OG 53, Morcire 62)
Egypt 2 (Abdou 33, Siaguy 86)

Addis Ababa Stadium, Addis Ababa, 14–03–1976
Nigeria 3 (Llerika 35, 62, Lawal 82)
Egypt 2 (Khatib 7, Ussama 41)

Addis Ababa Stadium, Addis Ababa, 14–03–1976. Referee: Chayu, Zambia
MOROCCO 1 (Baba 86)
GUINEA 1 (Cherif 33)

Morocco – Hazzaz – Cherif, Baba, Claoua, Mehdi (Guezzar), Larbi – Semmat, Zahraoui – Tazi, Faras, Abouali (Dolmy)

Guinea – Sylla – Bangoura, Morcire, Cherif, Diarra – Sylla I, Papa Camara – Jansky, Petit Sory, N'Jo Léa, Sylla B (Mory Kone)

	Mr	Gu	Ng	Eg	Pl	W	D	L	F	A	Pts
Morocco	–	1–1	2–1	2–1	3	2	1	0	5	3	5
Guinea	–	–	1–1	4–2	3	1	2	0	6	4	4
Nigeria	–	–	–	3–2	3	1	1	1	5	5	3
Egypt	–	–	–	–	3	0	0	3	5	9	0

Top scorer: N'Jo Léa, Guinea 4

ELEVENTH EDITION
1977–1978

QUALIFYING TOURNAMENT

PRELIMINARY ROUND

Malawi	1–1 2–3	**Mauritius**

FIRST ROUND

Algeria	4–1 1–2	Kenya
Upper Volta	0–1 1–4	**Côte d'Ivoire**
Cameroon	2–0 0–4	**Congo**
Egypt	2–2 2–3	**Tunisia**
Gabon	Bye	
Guinea	3–0 2–0	Libya
Mali	W–O	Niger
Mauritius	2–3 0–1	**Ethiopia**
Senegal	2–1 1–0	Togo
Sierra Leone	1–1 0–2	**Nigeria**
Uganda	W–O	Tanzania
Zambia	W–O	Sudan

SECOND ROUND

Algeria	2–0 0–2**	ZAMBIA
CONGO	3–2 3–3	Gabon
Ethiopia	0–0 1–2	UGANDA
Senegal	3–1 0–3	NIGERIA
TUNISIA	3–0 2–3	Guinea
Côte d'Ivoire	*	Mali

* Both teams were disqualified. Upper Volta were given a place in the finals, having been beaten by Côte d'Ivoire in the second round.
** Won on penalties

FINAL TOURNAMENT

Ghana, 5th–18th March 1978

FIRST ROUND

Group 1

Accra Stadium, Accra, 5–03–1978, 50 000
Ghana 2 (Afriye 21, Abdul Razak 55)
Zambia 1 (Kapita 8)

Accra Stadium, Accra, 5–03–1978, 50 000
Nigeria 4 (Chukwu 17, Adekiye 31, Odegbami 44 82)
Upper Volta 2 (Hien 50, Koita 52)

Accra Stadium, Accra, 8–03–1978, 60 000
Zambia 2 (Phiri P 20, Phiri B)
Upper Volta 0

Accra Stadium, Accra, 8–03–1978, 60 000
Ghana 1 (Kluste 76)
Nigeria 1 (Odegbami 33)

Accra Stadium, Accra, 10–03–1978, 25 000
Zambia 0
Nigeria 0

Accra Stadium, Accra, 10–03–1978, 25 000
Ghana 3 (Alhassan 3 59, Mohamed)
Upper Volta 0

	Gh	Ng	Zm	BF	Pl	W	D	L	F	A	Pts
Ghana	–	1–1	2–1	3–0	3	2	1	0	6	2	5
Nigeria	–	–	0–0	4–2	3	1	2	0	5	3	4
Zambia	–	–	–	2–0	3	1	1	1	3	2	3
Upper Volta	–	–	–	–	3	0	0	3	2	9	0

Group 2

Kumasi Stadium, Kumasi, 6–03–1978
Morocco 1 (Amcharrat 29)
Tunisia 1 (Kaabi 63)

Kumasi Stadium, Kumasi, 6–03–1978
Uganda 3 (Omondi 1, Semwanga 31, Kisitu 81)
Congo 1 (Mamounoubala 80)

Kumasi Stadium, Kumasi, 9–03–1978, 50 000
Tunisia 3 (Kamates 36, Ben Aziza 38 83)
Uganda 1 (Musenze 71)

Kumasi Stadium, Kumasi, 9–03–1978, 50 000
Morocco 1 (Amcharrat 28)
Congo 0

Kumasi Stadium, Kumasi, 11–03–1978, 20 000
Congo 0
Tunisia 0

Kumasi Stadium, Kumasi, 11–03–1978, 20 000
Uganda 3 (Kisitu 13, Msereko 32, Omondi 36)
Morocco 0

	Ug	Tu	Mr	Co	Pl	W	D	L	F	A	Pts
UGANDA	–	1–3	3–0	3–1	3	2	0	1	7	4	4
TUNISIA	–	–	1–1	0–0	3	1	2	0	4	2	4
MOROCCO	–	–	–	1–0	3	1	1	1	2	4	3
CONGO	–	–	–	–	3	0	1	2	1	4	1

SEMI-FINALS

Accra Stadium, Accra, 14–03–1978, 10 000
Ghana 1 (Razak 57)
Tunisia 0

Kumasi Stadium, Kumasi, 14–03–1978
Uganda 2 (Nasur 11, Omondi 58)
Nigeria 1 (Eyo 54)

3RD PLACE

Match abandoned after 30 minutes with the score at 1–1. Nigeria were awarded the match 2–0 over Tunisia

FINAL

Accra Stadium, Accra, 18–03–1978, 40 000. Referee: El Ghoul, Egypt
GHANA 2 (Afriye 38 64)
UGANDA 0

Ghana – Carr – Paha, Quaye, Acquaye, Dadzie – Kyenkyehen, Yawson, Seidi – Afriye, Razak, Ahmed
Uganda – Ssali – Semwanga, Musenze, Lwanga, Kirundu – Kiganda, Nasur, Nsereko – Omondi, Kisitu, Isabirye (Lubega)

Top scorer: Omondi, Uganda 4

TWELFTH EDITION
1979–1980

QUALIFYING TOURNAMENT

PRELIMINARY ROUND

Madagascar 2–1 1–5 **Malawi**
Mauritius 0–1 2–1 Lesotho
Benin W-O Niger

FIRST ROUND

Benin 1–0 1–4 **Côte d'Ivoire**
Congo 4–2 1–4 **Zaire**
Guinea 3–0 0–3* Cameroon
Libya 2–1 1–1 Ethiopia
Malawi 0–2 0–2 **Zambia**
Mauritania 2–2 1–4 **Morocco**
Mauritius 3–2 0–4 **Tanzania**
Togo 2–0 0–1 Gambia
Algeria W-O Burundi
Egypt W-O Somalia
Kenya W-O Tunisia
Sudan W-O Uganda
* Guinea won on penalties

SECOND ROUND

ALGERIA 3–1 0–1 Libya
Kenya 3–1 0–3 EGYPT
MOROCCO 7–0 1–2 Togo
Sudan 2–0 0–4 COTE D'IVOIRE
TANZANIA 1–0 1–1 Zambia
Zaire 3–2 1–3 GUINEA

FINAL TOURNAMENT
Nigeria, 8th–22nd March 1980

FIRST ROUND

Group 1

Surulere, Lagos, 8–03–1980, 80 000
Nigeria 3 (Lawal 11, Onyedika 35, Odegbami 85)
Tanzania 1 (Mkambi 54)

Surulere, Lagos, 8–03–1980, 80 000
Egypt 2 (Hammam 8, Mokhtar 20)
Côte d'Ivoire 1 (Ani Gome 7)

Surulere, Lagos, 12–03–1980, 55 000
Egypt 2 (Chehata 32, Nour 38)
Tanzania 1 (Wazir 86)

Surulere, Lagos, 12–03–1980, 55 000
Nigeria 0
Côte d'Ivoire 0

Surulere, Lagos, 15–03–1980, 70 000
Tanzania 1 (Wazir 59)
Côte d'Ivoire 1 (Kobenan 7)

Surulere, Lagos, 15–03–1980, 70 000
Nigeria 1 (Isima 15)
Egypt 0

	Ng	Eg	IC	Ta	Pl	W	D	L	F	A	Pts
NIGERIA	–	1–0	0–0	3–1	3	2	1	0	4	1	5
EGYPT	–	–	2–1	2–1	3	2	0	1	4	3	4
CÔTE D'IVOIRE	–	–	–	1–1	3	0	2	1	2	3	2
TANZANIA	–	–	–	–	3	0	1	2	3	6	1

Group 2

Liberty Stadium, Ibadan, 9–03–1980, 40 000
Ghana 0
Algeria 0

Liberty Stadium, Ibadan, 9–03–1980, 40 000
Guinea 1 (Moussa Camara 8)
Morocco 1 (Tahir Mustapha 7)

Liberty Stadium, Ibadan, 13–03–1980, 20 000
Algeria 1 (Belloumi 90)
Morocco 0

Liberty Stadium, Ibadan, 13–03–1980, 20000
Ghana 1 (Klutse 69)
Guinea 0

Liberty Stadium, Ibadan, 16–03–1980, 20000
Algeria 3 (Bensaoula 12 49, Benmiloudi 37)
Guinea 2 (Diawara 82, Bangoura 90)

Liberty Stadium, Ibadan, 16–03–1980, 20000
Morocco 1 (Labied 44)
Ghana 0

	Al	Mr	Gh	Gu	Pl	W	D	L	F	A	Pts
ALGERIA	–	1–0	0–0	3–2	3	2	1	0	4	2	5
MOROCCO	–	–	1–0	1–1	3	1	1	1	2	2	3
GHANA	–	–	–	1–0	3	1	1	1	1	1	3
GUINEA	–	–	–	–	3	0	1	2	3	5	1

SEMI-FINALS

Surulere, Lagos, 19–03–1980, 70000
Nigeria 1 (Owolabi 9)
Morocco 0

Liberty Stadium, Ibadan, 19–03–1980, 5000
Algeria 2 (Assad 55, Benmiloudi 62)
Egypt 2 (Khatib 32, Sayed 47)

Algeria won 4–2 on penalties

3RD PLACE

Surulere, Lagos, 21–03–1980, 5000
Morocco 2 (Labied 9 78)
Egypt 0

FINAL

Surulere, Lagos, 22–03–1980, 80000. Referee: Tesfaye, Ethiopia
NIGERIA 3 (Odegbami 2 42, Lawal 50)
ALGERIA 0

Nigeria – Best – Adiele, Chukwu, Tunde, Isima – Atuegbu, Odiye, Owolabi – Odegbami, Lawal, Amiesemaka

Algeria – Cerbah – Merzekane, Horr, Khedis, Kouici – Mahyouz, Fergani, Belloumi – Bensaoula (Madjer), Benmiloudi (Guemri), Assad

Top scorer: Odegbami, Nigeria 3
Labied, Morocco 3

THIRTEENTH EDITION
1981–1982

QUALIFYING TOURNAMENT

PRELIMINARY ROUND

Angola .... 1–1 0–0 .... **Congo**
Liberia .... 0–0 1–1 .... Gambia
Madagascar .... 0–0 1–1 .... Mauritius
Malawi .... 0–1 1–1 .... **Zimbabwe**
Mali .... 2–0 1–2 .... Mauritania
Mozambique .... 6–1 1–2 .... Lesotho
Senegal .... 2–0 2–1 .... Sierra Leone
Upper Volta .... W-O .... Gabon
Guinea Equat. .... W-O .... Benin
Rwanda .... W-O .... Uganda

FIRST ROUND

Algeria .... 5–1 0–3 .... Mali
Cameroon .... 4–0 2–2 .... Togo
Ethiopia .... 1–0 0–1 (4–3p) .... Rwanda
Ghana .... 1–1 1–0 .... Congo
Morocco .... 3–1 5–0 .... Liberia
Tunisia .... 1–0 0–0 .... Senegal
Zaire .... 2–1 3–3 .... Mozambique
Zimbabwe .... 0–1 0–2 .... **Zambia**
Kenya .... 3–5 0–2 .... **Egypt**
Guinea .... W-O .... Guinea Equat.
Madagascar .... W-O .... Tanzania

SECOND ROUND

ALGERIA .... 7–0 1–1 .... Upper Volta
CAMEROON .... 5–1 1–2 .... Madagascar
GHANA .... 2–2 2–1 .... Zaire
Guinea .... 2–2 1–1 .... ETHIOPIA
Morocco .... 2–1 0–2 .... ZAMBIA
TUNISIA .... W-O .... Egypt

FINAL TOURNAMENT
Libya, 5th–19th March 1982

FIRST ROUND

Group 1

11th June Stadium, Tripoli, 5–03–1982, 40000
Libya 2 (Garana 58, Issawi 76)
Ghana 0 (Al Hassan 28, Opoku Nti 89)

11th June Stadium, Tripoli, 5–03–1982, 40000
Cameroon 1 (Mbida 50)
Tunisia 1 (Gabsi 49)

11th June Stadium, Tripoli, 9–03–1982, 40000
Cameroon 0
Ghana 0

11th June Stadium, Tripoli, 9–03–1982, 40000
Libya 2 (OG 42, El Borosi 83)
Tunisia 0

11th June Stadium, Tripoli, 12–03–1982, 40000
Ghana 1 (Essien 28)
Tunisia 0

11th June Stadium, Tripoli, 12–03–1982, 40000
Libya 0
Cameroon 0

	Ly	Gh	Ca	Tu	Pl	W	D	L	F	A	Pts
LIBYA	–	2–2	0–0	2–0	3	1	2	0	4	2	4
GHANA	–	–	0–0	1–0	3	1	2	0	3	2	4
CAMEROON	–	–	–	1–1	3	0	3	0	1	1	3
TUNISIA	–	–	–	–	3	0	1	2	1	4	1

Group 2

28th March Stadium, Benghazi, 7–03–1982, 5000
Nigeria 3 (Keshi 27 84, Ademola 40)
Ethiopia 0

28th March Stadium, Benghazi, 7–03–1982, 5000
Algeria 1 (Merzekane 85)
Zambia 0

28th March Stadium, Benghazi, 10–03–1982, 5000
Zambia 1 (Munshya 68)
Ethiopia 0

28th March Stadium, Benghazi, 10–03–1982, 5000
Algeria 2 (OG 44, Assad 65)
Nigeria 1 (Osigwe 40)

28th March Stadium, Benghazi, 13–03–1982, 5000
Algeria 0
Ethiopia 0

28th March Stadium, Benghazi, 13–03–1982, 5000
Zambia 3 (Kaumba 25, Njovu 80, OG 81)
Nigeria 0

	Al	Zm	Ng	Et	Pl	W	D	L	F	A	Pts
ALGERIA	–	1–0	2–1	0–0	3	2	1	0	3	1	5
ZAMBIA	–	–	3–0	1–0	3	2	0	1	4	1	4
NIGERIA	–	–	–	3–0	3	1	0	2	4	5	2
ETHIOPIA	–	–	–	–	3	0	1	2	0	4	1

SEMI-FINALS

28th March Stadium, Benghazi, 16–03–1982, 5000
Ghana 3 (Al Hassan 4 103, Opoku Nti 90)
Algeria 2 (Zidane 29, Assad 62)

11th June Stadium, Tripoli, 16–03–1982, 50 000
Libya 2 (Beshari 38 84)
Zambia 1 (Kaumba 29)

3RD PLACE

11th June Stadium, Tripoli, 18–03–1982, 2000
Zambia 2 (Kaumba 2, Munshya 25)
Algeria 0

FINAL

11th June Stadium, Tripoli, 19–03–1982, 50 000. Referee: Ramlochun, Mauritius
GHANA 1 (Al Hassan 35)
LIBYA 1 (Beshari 70)

Ghana won 7–6 on penalties

Ghana – Owusu – Haruna Yusif, Sampson L, Paha, Sampson K – Asase, Quarshie, Kofi Badu (Abedi Pele) – Essein (Opoku Nti), Al Hassan, Abbrey Kofi

Libya – Kouafi – El Ageli, Zeiw, Sola, Beshari – Majdoub (El Borosi), Garana, El Fergami (Abubaker), Ferjani – Issawi, Gonaim

Top scorer: Al Hassan, Ghana 4

FOURTEENTH EDITION
1983–1984

QUALIFYING TOURNAMENT

PRELIMINARY ROUND

Gabon 2–2 0–4 **Angola**
Malawi 2–0 2–0 Zimbabwe
Mali 3–1 0–1 Gambia
Niger 0–0 0–1 **Senegal**
Somalia 0–1 **Rwanda**
Tanzania 1–1 2–3 **Uganda**
Togo 3–0 1–0 Sierra Leone
Benin W-O Liberia
Mauritius W-O Lesotho
Mozambique W-O Swaziland

FIRST ROUND

Algeria 6–2 1–1 Benin
Congo 2–0 0–2* **Egypt**
Ethiopia 1–0 0–1* Mauritius
Guinea 0–1 0–2 **Togo**
Libya 2–1 0–1 **Senegal**
Madagascar 1–0 1–2 Uganda
Morocco 4–0 0–2 Mali
Mozambique 3–0 0–4 **Cameroon**
Nigeria 2–0 0–1 Angola
Sudan 2–1 0–0 Zambia
Tunisia 5–0 1–0 Rwanda
Malawi W-O Zaire

* Egypt and Ethiopia won on penalties

SECOND ROUND

CAMEROON 5–0 0–2 Sudan
EGYPT 1–0 0–0 Tunisia
Ethiopia 2–1 0–3 TOGO
Madagascar 0–1 1–1 MALAWI
NIGERIA 0–0 0–0 4–3p Morocco
Senegal 1–1 0–2 ALGERIA

FINAL TOURNAMENT

Côte d'Ivoire, 4th–18th March 1984

FIRST ROUND

Group 1

Houphouet Boigny, Abidjan, 4–03–1984, 50 000
Côte d'Ivoire 3 (Koffi T 27, Fofana 62, Goba 75)
Togo 0

Houphouet Boigny, Abidjan, 4–03–1984, 50 000
Egypt 1 (Abou Zeid 75)
Cameroon 0

Houphouet Boigny, Abidjan, 7–03–1984, 40 000
Cameroon 4 (Djonkep 6, Abega 21 60, Aoudou 45)
Togo 1 (Moutairou 54)

Houphouet Boigny, Abidjan, 7–03–1984, 40 000
Egypt 2 (Abou Zeid 66 72)
Côte d'Ivoire 1 (Miezan 53)

Houphouet Boigny, Abidjan, 10–03–1984, 40 000
Egypt 0
Togo 0

Houphouet Boigny, Abidjan, 10–03–1984, 40 000
Cameroon 2 (Milla 42, Djonkep 61)
Côte d'Ivoire 0

	Eg	Ca	IC	To	Pl	W	D	L	F	A	Pts
EGYPT	–	1–0	2–1	0–0	3	2	1	0	3	1	5
CAMEROON	–	–	2–0	4–1	3	2	0	1	6	2	4
CÔTE D'IVOIRE	–	–	–	3–0	3	1	0	2	4	4	2
TOGO	–	–	–	–	3	0	1	2	1	7	1

Group 2

Municipal Stadium, Bouaké, 5–03–1984, 10 000
Nigeria 2 (Nwosu 13, Ehilegbu 31)
Ghana 1 (Opoku Nti 19)

Municipal Stadium, Bouaké, 5–03–1984, 10 000
Algeria 3 (Bouiche 29, Belloumi 36, Fergani 38)
Malawi 0

Municipal Stadium, Bouaké, 8–03–1984, 15 000
Malawi 2 (Waya 7, Msiya 35)
Nigeria 2 (Temile 39 41)

Municipal Stadium, Bouaké, 8–03–1984, 15 000
Algeria 2 Menad 75, Bensaoula 85)
Ghana 0

Municipal Stadium, Bouaké, 11–03–1984, 3000
Algeria 0
Nigeria 0

Municipal Stadium, Bouaké, 11–03–1984, 3000
Ghana 1 (Ampadu 32)
Malawi 0

	Al	Ng	Gh	Mw	Pl	W	D	L	F	A	Pts
ALGERIA	–	0–0	2–0	3–0	3	2	1	0	5	0	5
NIGERIA	–	–	2–1	2–2	3	1	2	0	4	3	4
GHANA	–	–	–	1–0	3	1	0	2	2	4	2
MALAWI	–	–	–	–	3	0	1	2	2	6	1

SEMI-FINALS

Houphouet Boigny, Abidjan, 14–03–1984, 15000
Nigeria 2 (Keshi 43, Ali Bala 75)
Egypt 2 (Soliman 25, Abou Zeid 38)

Nigeria won 8–7 on penaties

Municipal Stadium, Bouaké, 14–03–1984, 15000
Cameroon 0
Algeria 0

Cameroon won 5–4 on penalties

3RD PLACE

Houphouet Boigny, Abidjan, 17–03–1984, 1000
Algeria 3 (Madjer 67, Belloumi 70, Yahi 88)
Egypt 1 (Abdelghani 74)

FINAL

Houphouet Boigny, Abidjan, 18–03–1984, 50000. Referee: Bennaceur, Tunisia
CAMEROON 3 (Ndjeya 32, Abega 79, Ebongué 84)
NIGERIA 1 (Lawal 10)
Cameroon – Bell – Toubé, Ndjeya, Doumbé Léa, Sinkot – Abega, Mbida, Aoudou – Ebongué, Milla, Djonkep (Kundé)
Nigeria – Okala – Kingsley, Keshi, Eboigbe, Shofoluwe – Lawal, Adesina (Okoku), Edobor – Ali Bala (Temile), Nwosu, Etokebe

Top scorer: Abou Zeid, Egypt 4

FIFTEENTH EDITION
1985–1986

QUALIFYING TOURNAMENT

PRELIMINARY ROUND

Gambia	3–2 0–2	**Sierra Leone**
Liberia	3–1 0–3	**Mauritania**
Mali	1–0 2–2	Benin
Mauritius	0–0 0–3	**Mozambique**
Somalia	1–0 0–1 (3–4p)	**Kenya**
Tanzania	0–1 3–1	Uganda
Zaire	2–0 1–1	Gabon
Zimbabwe	3–0 5–1	Swaziland

FIRST ROUND

Algeria	4–0 1–1	Mauritania
Congo	2–5 0–0	**Zaire**
Ghana	1–1 4–1	Guinea
Côte d'Ivoire	6–0 1–1	Mali
Libya	2–0 0–1	Tunisia
Madagascar	0–1 2–5	**Zimbabwe**
Malawi	1–1 1–1 (5–6p)	**Mozambique**
Togo	0–1 1–1	**Senegal**
Kenya	W-O	Sudan
Morocco	W-O	Sierra Leone
Nigeria	W-O	Tanzania
Zambia	W-O	Ethiopia

SECOND ROUND

COTE D'IVOIRE	2–0 0–0	Ghana
Kenya	0–0 0–3	ALGERIA
Libya	2–1 1–2 (3–4p)	MOZAMBIQUE
MOROCCO	1–0 0–0	Zaire
Nigeria	0–0 0–1	ZAMBIA
Zimbabwe	1–0 0–3	SENEGAL

FINAL TOURNAMENT
Egypt, 7th–21st March 1986

FIRST ROUND

Group 1

International Stadium, Cairo, 7–03–1986, 45000
Senegal 1 (Youm 66)
Egypt 0

International Stadium, Cairo, 7–03–1986, 45000
Côte d'Ivoire 3 (Traoré A 24 52, Pascal 85)
Mozambique 0

International Stadium, Cairo, 10–03–1986, 50000
Senegal 2 (Pape Fall 27, Bocande 83)
Mozambique 0

International Stadium, Cairo, 10–03–1986, 50000
Egypt 2 (Shawky 72, Abdel Hamid 83)
Côte d'Ivoire 0

International Stadium, Cairo, 13–03–1986, 55000
Côte d'Ivoire 1 (Traoré A 71)
Senegal 0

International Stadium, Cairo, 13–03–1986, 55000
Egypt 2 (Abou Zeid 13 15)
Mozambique 0

	Eg	IC	Se	Mz	Pl	W	D	L	F	A	Pts
EGYPT	–	2–0	0–1	2–0	3	2	0	1	4	1	4
CÔTE D'IVOIRE	–	–	1–0	3–0	3	2	0	1	4	2	4
SENEGAL	–	–	–	2–0	3	2	0	1	3	1	4
MOZAMBIQUE	–	–	–	–	3	0	0	3	0	7	0

Group 2

Alexandria Stadium, Alexandria, 8–03–1986, 20000
Cameroon 3 (Milla 48, Mfede 81 88)
Zambia 2 (Chabala 68, Kalusha 85)

Alexandria Stadium, Alexandria, 8–03–1986, 20 000
Algeria 0
Morocco 0

Alexandria Stadium, Alexandria, 11–03–1986, 10 000
Zambia 0
Algeria 0

Alexandria Stadium, Alexandria, 11–03–1986, 10000
Cameroon 1 (Milla 89)
Morocco 1 (Karim 72)

Alexandria Stadium, Alexandria, 14–03–1986, 15 000
Morocco 1 (Karim 20)
Zambia 0

Alexandria Stadium, Alexandria, 14–03–1986, 15 000
Cameroon 3 (Kana 65 70, Milla 72)
Algeria 2 (Madjer 61, Maroc 74)

	Ca	Mr	Al	Zm	Pl	W	D	L	F	A	Pts
CAMEROON	–	1–1	3–2	3–2	3	2	1	0	7	5	5
MOROCCO	–	–	0–0	1–0	3	1	2	0	2	1	4
ALGERIA	–	–	–	0–0	3	0	2	1	2	3	2
ZAMBIA	–	–	–	–	3	0	1	2	2	4	1

SEMI-FINALS

International Stadium, Cairo, 17–03–1986, 90 000
Egypt 1 (Abou Zeid 80)
Morocco 0

Alexandria Stadium, Alexandria, 17–03–1986, 10 000
Cameroon 1 (Milla 46)
Côte d'Ivoire 0

3RD PLACE

International Stadium, Cairo, 20–03–1986, 1000
Côte d'Ivoire 3 (Ben Salah 8, Kouadiou 38 66)
Morocco 2 (Rhiati 44, Sahil 85)

FINAL

International Stadium, Cairo, 21–03–1986, 100 000. Referee: Bennaceur, Tunisia
EGYPT 0
CAMEROON 0

Egypt won 5–4 on penalties
Egypt – Batal – Yassine, Chehata, Omar (Mayhoub), Sedki – Kassem, Abdelghani, Abou Zeid (Yehia), Abdelhamid – Abdou, Khatib
Cameroon – N'Kono – N'Dip, Aoudou, Kundé, Sinkot – Mbouh, Kana, Mbida – Ebongue (Oumarou), Milla, Mfédé
Top scorers: Milla, Cameroon, ... 4
Traoré A, Côte d'Ivoire 4

SIXTEENTH EDITION
1987–1988

QUALIFYING TOURNAMENT

PRELIMINARY ROUND

Angola	1–0 0–1 (5–3p)	Gabon
Cent. Af. Rep.	1–2 1–5	**Congo**
Ethiopia	4–2*	**Tanzania**
Guinea	2–1 1–0	Gambia
Sierra Leone	2–1 1–1	Liberia
Uganda	5–0 0–0	Somalia
Madagascar	W-O	Mauritius
Rwanda	W-O	Lesotho
Togo	W-O	Guinea Equat.
Tunisia	W-O	Mali

* Ethiopia withdrew

FIRST ROUND

Algeria	1–0 1–1	Tunisia
Cameroon	5–1 1–3	Uganda
Ghana	1–2 0–0	**Sierra Leone**
Côte d'Ivoire	2–0 2–1	Congo
Kenya	2–0 1–2	Madagascar
Mozambique	1–1 2–3	**Zimbabwe**
Nigeria	2–0 1–1	Togo
Senegal	4–0 0–0	Guinea
Sudan	1–0 1–1	Tanzania
Zaire	3–0 0–1	Angola
Libya	W-O	Zambia
Malawi	W-O	Rwanda

SECOND ROUND

ALGERIA	W-O	Libya
CAMEROON	2–0 0–1	Sudan
Malawi	1–2 0–2	COTE D'IVOIRE
NIGERIA	3–0 0–2	Sierra Leone
Senegal	0–0 0–0 (2–4p)	ZAIRE
Zimbabwe	1–1 0–0	KENYA

FINAL TOURNAMENT

Morocco, 13th–27th March 1988

FIRST ROUND

Group 1

Mohammed V, Casablanca, 13–03–1988, 70 000
Morocco 1 (Krimau 43)
Zaire 1 (Lutonadio 88)

Mohammed V, Casablanca, 13–03–1988, 70 000
Algeria 1 (Belloumi 16)
Côte d'Ivoire 1 (Traoré A 48)

Mohammed V, Casablanca, 16–03–1988, 10 000
Côte d'Ivoire 1 (Traoré A 74)
Zaire 1 (Kabongo 37)

Mohammed V, Casablanca, 16–03–1988, 40 000
Morocco 1 (Haddaoui 52)
Algeria 0

Mohammed V, Casablanca, 19–03–1988, 80 000
Algeria 1 (Ferhaoui 36)
Zaire 0

Mohammed V, Casablanca, 19–03–1988, 90 000
Morocco 0
Côte d'Ivoire 0

	Mr	Al	IC	Zr	Pl	W	D	L	F	A	Pts
MOROCCO	–	1–0	0–0	1–1	3	1	2	0	2	1	4
ALGERIA	–	–	1–1	1–0	3	1	1	1	2	2	3
CÔTE D'IVOIRE	–	–	–	1–1	3	0	3	0	2	2	3
ZAIRE	–	–	–	–	3	0	2	1	2	3	2

Algeria qualified on drawing of lots.

Group 2

Moulay Abdullah, Rabat, 14–03–1988, 7000
Cameroon 1 (Milla 5)
Egypt 0

Moulay Abdullah, Rabat, 14–03–1988, 7000
Nigeria 3 (Yekini 6, Edobor 13, Okosieme 33)
Kenya 0

Moulay Abdullah, Rabat, 17–03–1988, 15 000
Cameroon 1 (Milla 21)
Nigeria 1 (Okwaraji 2)

Moulay Abdullah, Rabat, 17–03–1988, 15 000
Egypt 3 (Abdelhamid 2 65, Younis 58)
Kenya 0

Moulay Abdullah, Rabat, 20–03–1988, 25 000
Cameroon 0
Kenya 0

Moulay Abdullah, Rabat, 20–03–1988, 25 000
Egypt 0
Nigeria 0

	Ng	Ca	Eg	Ke	Pl	W	D	L	F	A	Pts
NIGERIA	–	1–1	0–0	3–0	3	1	2	0	4	1	4
CAMEROON	–	–	1–0	0–0	3	1	2	0	2	1	4
EGYPT	–	–	–	3–0	3	1	1	1	3	1	3
KENYA	–	–	–	–	3	0	1	2	0	6	1

SEMI-FINALS

Mohammed V, Casablanca, 23–03–1988, 45 000
Cameroon 1 (Makanaky 78)
Morocco 0

Moulay Abdullah, Rabat, 23–03–1988, 35 000
Nigeria 1 (OG 39)
Algeria 1 (Maatar 86)

Nigeria won 9–8 on penalties

3RD PLACE

Mohammed V, Casablanca, 26–03–1988, 40 000
Morocco 1 (Nader 67)
Algeria 1 (Belloumi 87)

Morocco won 4–3 on penalties

FINAL

Mohammed V, Casablanca, 27–03–1988, 50 000. Referee: Idrissa, Senegal
CAMEROON 1 (Kundé 55)
NIGERIA 0

Cameroon – Bell – Massing, Kundé, Ntamark – Tataw, Mbouh, M'Fede, Biyik K – Makanaky, Milla, Olleolle (Abena)

Nigeria – Rufai – Sofoluwe, Keshi, Eboigbe, Omokaro – Nwosu, Okosieme, Eguavon – Folorunso (Edobor), Okwaraji, Yekini

Top scorers: Abdelhamid, Egypt 2
Belloumi, Algeria 2
Milla, Cameroon 2
Traoré A, Côte d'Ivoire 2

SEVENTEENTH EDITION
1989–1990

QUALIFYING TOURNAMENT

PRELIMINARY ROUND

Angola .... 4–1 0–0 .... Guinea Equat.
Gabon .... 3–0 0–1 .... Burkina Faso
Liberia .... 0–1 0–3 .... **Mali**
Mauritius .... 3–0 0–1 .... Seychelles
Tanzania .... 1–1 1–1 (1–3p) .... **Swaziland**
Ethiopia .... W-O .... Uganda
Guinea .... W-O .... Gambia
Libya .... W-O .... Mauritania
Mozambique .... W-O .... Madagascar

FIRST ROUND

Angola .... 0–2 1–4 .... **Côte d'Ivoire**
Ethiopia .... 1–0 1–6 .... **Egypt**
Gabon .... 1–0 0–1 (5–3p) .... Ghana
Guinea .... 1–1 0–3 .... **Nigeria**
Mali .... 0–0 1–1 .... Morocco
Mauritius .... 1–4 0–1 .... **Zimbabwe**
Mozambique .... 0–1 0–3 .... **Zambia**
Sudan .... 1–0 0–1 (5–6p) .... **Kenya**
Swaziland .... 0–2 1–1 .... **Malawi**
Senegal .... W-O .... Togo
Tunisia .... W-O .... Libya
Zaire .... W-O .... Sierra Leone

SECOND ROUND

EGYPT .... 2–0 0–0 .... Zaire
NIGERIA .... 3–0 1–1 .... Zimbabwe
Malawi .... 2–3 0–0 .... KENYA
Mali .... 2–2 1–3 .... COTE D'IVOIRE
SENEGAL .... 3–0 1–0 .... Tunisia
ZAMBIA .... 3–0 1–2 .... Gabon

FINAL TOURNAMENT

Algeria, 2nd–16th March 1990

FIRST ROUND

Group 1

Stade Olympique, Algiers, 2–03–1990, 65 000
Algeria 5 (Madjer 36 58, Menad 69 72, Amani 88)
Nigeria 1 (Okocha 82)

Stade Olympique, Algiers, 3–03–1990
Côte d'Ivoire 3 (Traoré A 53 60, Kagui 73)
Egypt 1 (Abdel 75)

Stade Olympique, Algiers, 5–03–1990, 45 000
Nigeria 1 (Yekini 8)
Egypt 0

Stade Olympique, Algiers, 5–03–1990, 45 000
Algeria 3 (Menad 23, El Ouazani 81, Oudjani 82)
Côte d'Ivoire 0

Stade Olympique, Algiers, 8–03–1990, 80 000
Nigeria 1 (Yekini 3)
Côte d'Ivoire 0

Stade Olympique, Algiers, 8–03–1990, 80 000
Algeria 2 (Amani 39, Saib 43)
Egypt 0

	Al	Ng	IC	Eg	Pl	W	D	L	F	A	Pts
ALGERIA	–	5–1	3–0	2–0	3	3	0	0	10	1	6
NIGERIA	–	–	1–0	1–0	3	2	0	1	3	5	4
CÔTE D'IVOIRE	–	–	–	3–1	3	1	0	2	3	5	2
EGYPT	–	–	–	–	3	0	0	3	1	6	0

Group 2

Annaba, 3–03–1990
Zambia 1 (Chikabala 58)
Cameroon 0

Annaba, 3–03–1990
Senegal 0
Kenya 0

Annaba, 6–03–1990
Zambia 1 (Makwaza 40)
Kenya 0

Annaba, 6–03–1990
Senegal 2 (Diallo 45, Ndao 56)
Cameroon 0

Annaba, 9–03–1990
Zambia 0
Senegal 0

Annaba, 9–03–1990

Cameroon 2 (Maboang 28 69)
Kenya 0

	Zm	Se	Ca	Ke	Pl	W	D	L	F	A	Pts
ZAMBIA	–	0–0	1–0	1–0	3	2	1	0	2	0	5
SENEGAL	–	–	2–0	0–0	3	1	2	0	2	0	4
CAMEROON	–	–	–	2–0	3	1	0	2	2	3	2
KENYA	–	–	–	–	3	0	1	2	0	3	1

SEMI-FINALS

Stade Olympique, Algiers, 12–03–1990, 80 000

Algeria 2 (Menad 4, Amani 62)
Senegal 1 (OG 20)

Annaba, 12–03–1990, 35 000

Nigeria 2 (Okechukwu 18, Yekini 77)
Zambia 0

3RD PLACE

Stade Olympique, Algiers, 15–03–1990, 8000

Zambia 1 (Chikabala 73)
Senegal 0

FINAL

Stade Olympique, Algiers, 16–03–1990, 80 000

ALGERIA 1 (Oudjani 38)
NIGERIA 0

Algeria – Demani – Benhalima, Kegharia, Serrar, Ait-Abderrahmane – El Ouazani (Neftah), Amani, Saib – Madjer, Oudjani (Rahim), Menad
Nigeria – Agui – Okechukwu, Anijekwu, Semitoje – Uwe (Aminu), Adesina, Kpakor, Oliha, Ogunlana (Omokachi) – Yekini, Elahor

Top scorer: Menad, Algeria 4

EIGHTEENTH EDITION
1991–1992

QUALIFYING TOURNAMENT

Group 1

	Cm	SL	Gu	Ma	Pl	W	D	L	F	A	Pts
CAMEROON	–	1–0	1–0	0–0	6	3	3	0	5	1	9
SIERRA LEONE	1–1	–	0–1	2–0	6	2	2	2	5	4	6
GUINEA	0–0	1–2	–	2–1	6	2	2	2	5	5	6
MALI	0–2	0–0	1–1	–	6	0	3	3	2	7	3

Group 2

	Eg	Tu	Ch	Et	Pl	W	D	L	F	A	Pts
EGYPT	–	2–2	5–1	2–0	4	3	3	0	13	5	9
TUNISIA	2–2	–	2–1	2–0*	4	3	3	0	10	5	9
CHAD	0–0	0–0	–	2–0*	4	2	2	2	6	7	6
ETHIOPIA	0–2*	0–2	0–2*	–	4	0	0	6	0	12	0

* Ethiopia withdrew after 2 games. The unplayed games were all awarded to their opponents 2–0

Group 3

	CI	Ma	Ni	Ma	Pl	W	D	L	F	A	Pts
COTE D'IVOIRE	–	2–0	1–0	2–0	6	5	0	1	9	3	10
MOROCCO	3–1	–	2–0	4–0	6	4	0	2	11	4	8
NIGER	0–1	1–0	–	7–1	5	2	0	3	8	5	4
MAURITANIA	0–2*	0–2	–	–	6	0	0	5	1	17	0

Liberia withdrew
* Côte d'Ivoire awarded the match 2–0

Group 4

	Gh	Ng	BF	To	Be	Pl	W	D	L	F	A	Pts
GHANA	–	1–0	2–0	2–0	4–0	8	5	2	1	11	2	12
NIGERIA	0–0	–	7–1	3–0	3–0	8	4	3	1	15	3	11
BURKINA FASO	2–1	1–1	–	2–0	2–0	8	4	1	3	10	13	9
TOGO	0–1	0–0	1–0	–	2–0	8	2	2	4	4	9	6
BENIN	0–0	0–1	1–2	1–1	–	8	0	2	6	2	15	2

Group 5

	Zm	Md	Sw	An	Pl	W	D	L	F	A	Pts
ZAMBIA	–	2–1	5–0	1–0	6	4	1	1	11	4	9
MADAGASCAR	0–0	–	–	0–0	5	2	2	1	3	2	6
SWAZILAND	2–1	0–1	–	1–1	5	1	2	2	4	9	4
ANGOLA	1–2	0–1	1–1	–	6	0	3	3	3	6	3

Group 6

	Ke	Mz	Su	Pl	W	D	L	F	A	Pts
KENYA	–	1–0	2–1	4	2	0	2	4	4	4
MOZAMBIQUE	2–1	–	1–0	4	2	0	2	3	3	4
SUDAN	1–0	1–0	–	4	2	0	2	3	3	4

Mauritius withdrew

Group 7

	Co	Zi	Ml	Pl	W	D	L	F	A	Pts
CONGO	–	2–0	2–1	4	3	1	0	7	3	7
Zimbabwe	2–2	–	4–0	4	1	2	1	8	6	4
Malawi	0–1	2–2	–	4	0	1	3	3	9	1

Seychelles withdrew

Group 8

	Zr	Ga	Ug	Ta	Pl	W	D	L	F	A	Pts
ZAIRE	–	2–1	1–0	2–0	6	3	1	2	6	4	7
Gabon	0–0	–	1–0	1–0	6	2	3	1	3	2	7
Uganda	2–1	0–0	–	3–2	6	2	2	2	6	6	6
Tanzania	1–0	0–0	1–1	–	6	1	2	3	4	7	4

FINAL TOURNAMENT

Senegal, 12th–26th January 1992

FIRST ROUND

Group 1

Stade de l'Amitie, Dakar, 12–01–1992, 75000

Nigeria 2 (Siasia 13, Keshi 88)
Senegal 1 (Bocande 38)

Stade de l'Amitie, Dakar, 14–01–1992, 8000

Nigeria 2 (Yekini 7 15)
Kenya 1 (Weche 89)

Stade de l'Amitie, Dakar, 16–01–1992, 45000

Senegal 3 (Sane 46, Bocande 68, Diagre 89)
Kenya 0

	Ng	Se	Ke	Pl	W	D	L	F	A	Pts
NIGERIA	–	2–1	2–1	2	2	0	0	4	2	4
SENEGAL	–	–	3–0	2	1	0	1	4	2	2
KENYA	–	–	–	2	0	0	2	1	5	0

Group 2

Stade de l'Amitie, Dakar, 12–01–1992, 70000

Cameroon 1 (Kana Biyik 22)
Morocco 0

Stade de l'Amitie, Dakar, 14–01–1992, 11000

Zaire 1 (Kana 90)
Morocco 1 (Rokbi 89)

Stade de l'Amitie, Dakar, 16–01–1992, 18000
Cameroon 1 (Oman Biyik 16)
Zaire 1 (Tueba 2)

	Cm	Za	Ma	Pl	W	D	L	F	A	Pts
CAMEROON	–	1–1	1–0	2	1	1	0	2	1	3
ZAIRE	–	–	1–1	2	0	2	0	2	2	2
MOROCCO	–	–	–	2	0	1	2	1	2	1

Group 3

Stade Aline Sitoe Diatta, Ziguinchor, 13–01–1992, 7000
Côte d'Ivoire 3 (Traoré A 14, Fofana 37, Tiehi 90)
Algeria 0

Stade Aline Sitoe Diatta, Ziguinchor, 15–01–1992, 6000
Côte d'Ivoire 0
Congo 0

Stade Aline Sitoe Diatta, Ziguinchor, 17–01–1992, 7000
Congo 1 (Tchibota 7)
Algeria 1 (Bouiche 44)

	CI	Co	Al	Pl	W	D	L	F	A	Pts
CÔTE D'IVOIRE	–	0–0	3–0	2	1	1	0	3	0	3
CONGO	–	–	1–1	2	0	2	0	1	1	2
ALGERIA	–	–	–	2	0	1	1	1	4	1

Group 4

Stade Aline Sitoe Diatta, Ziguinchor, 13–01–1992, 7000
Zambia 1 (Bwalya 60)
Egypt 0

Stade Aline Sitoe Diatta, Ziguinchor, 15–01–1992, 6000
Ghana 1 (Pelé 64)
Zambia 0

Stade Aline Sitoe Diatta, Ziguinchor, 17–01–1992, 7000
Ghana 1 (Yeboah 90)
Egypt 0

	Gh	Zm	Eg	Pl	W	D	L	F	A	Pts
GHANA	–	1–0	1–0	2	2	0	0	2	0	4
ZAMBIA	–	–	1–0	2	1	0	1	1	1	2
EGYPT	–	–	–	2	0	0	2	0	2	0

QUARTER-FINALS

Stade de l'Amitie, Dakar, 20–01–1992, 6000
Côte d'Ivoire 1 (OG 90)
Zambia 0

Stade de l'Amitie, Dakar, 19–01–1992, 45 000
Cameroon 1 (Ebongue 86)
Senegal 0

Stade de l'Amitie, Dakar, 19–01–1992, 30 000
Nigeria 1 (Yekini 22)
Zaire 0

Stade de l'Amitie, Dakar, 20–01–1992, 7000
Ghana 2 (Yeboah 26, Pelé 51)
Congo 1 (Tchibota 55)

SEMI-FINALS

Stade de l'Amitie, Dakar, 23–01–1992, 25 000
Côte d'Ivoire 0
Cameroon 0

Côte d'Ivoire won 3–1 on penalties

Stade de l'Amitie, Dakar, 23–01–1992, 30 000
Ghana 2 (Pelé 44 Opoku 53)
Nigeria 1 (Adepoju 11)

3RD PLACE

Stade de l'Amitie, Dakar, 25–01–1992, 2000
Nigeria 2 (Ekpo 76, Yekini 89)
Cameroon 1 (Maboang 81)

FINAL

Stade de l'Amitie, Dakar, 26–01–1992, 60 000. Referee: Séné, Senegal
COTE D'IVOIRE 0
GHANA 0
Côte d'Ivoire – Gouaméné – Aka, Sam, Sekana, Hobou – Gadji–Celi, Magui, Otokoré (Traoré M), Sié – Traoré A (Kassy–Kouadio), Tiéni
Ghana – Ansah – Armah, Ampeah, Baffoe, Asare – Abroah, Gyamfi (Naawu), Lampety, Mensah – Opoku, Yeboah

Côte d'Ivoire won 11–10 on penalties

Top Scorer – Yekini, Nigeria 4

ALL AFRICAN GAMES

The football tournament of the All Africa Games is a four yearly affair in theory, but never in practice. Originally only open to amateurs, this never mattered in the early years but the 1991 tournament in Cairo was turned into an age-restricted tournament in the wake of a similar decision for the football tournament of the Olympic Games.

1965	Congo	0–0 (10–1c)	Ethiopia
1973	Nigeria	2–0	Guinea
1978	Algeria	1–0	Nigeria
1987	Egypt	1–0	Kenya
1991	Cameroon	1–0	Tunisia

FIRST FOOTBALL TOURNAMENT

Brazzaville, 18th–25th July 1965

FIRST ROUND

Group 1

	IC	Al	Md	Za	Pl	W	D	L	F	A	Pts
IVORY COAST	–	1–0	5–0	1–1	3	2	1	0	7	1	5
ALGERIA	–	–	0–0	4–1	3	1	1	1	4	2	3
MADAGASCAR	–	–	–	1–0	3	1	1	1	1	5	3
ZAIRE	–	–	–	–	3	0	1	2	2	6	1

Group 2

	Ml	Co	To	Ug	Pl	W	D	L	F	A	Pts
MALI	–	1–1	3–1	5–1	3	2	1	0	9	3	5
CONGO	–	–	1–1	2–1	3	1	2	0	4	3	4
TOGO	–	–	–	1–1	3	0	2	1	3	5	2
UGANDA	–	–	–	–	3	0	1	2	3	8	1

SEMI-FINALS

Congo	1–0	Ivory Coast
Mali	2–1	Algeria

3RD PLACE

Ivory Coast .... 1–0 .... Algeria

FINAL

Brazzaville, 25–07–1965

CONGO 0
MALI 0

Congo won 10–1 on corner kicks

SECOND FOOTBALL TOURNAMENT

Lagos, 8th–17th January 1973

FIRST ROUND

Group 1

	Ng	Gh	Al	Ta	Pl	W	D	L	F	A	Pts
Nigeria	–	4–2	2–2	2–1	3	2	1	0	8	5	5
Ghana	–	–	2–0	1–0	3	2	0	1	5	4	4
Algeria	–	–	–	4–2	3	1	1	1	6	6	3
Tanzania	–	–	–	–	3	0	0	3	3	7	0

Group 2

	Gu	Eg	Co	BF	Pl	W	D	L	F	A	Pts
Guinea	–	4–1	5–1	3–2	3	3	0	0	12	4	6
Egypt	–	–	3–1	4–2	3	2	0	1	8	7	4
Congo	–	–	–	3–0	3	1	0	2	5	8	2
Upper Volta	–	–	–	–	3	0	0	3	4	10	0

SEMI-FINALS

Nigeria .... 4–2 .... Egypt
Guinea .... 2–1 .... Ghana

3RD PLACE

Egypt .... 2–1 .... Ghana

FINAL

Surulere, Lagos, 17–01–1973

NIGERIA 2
GUINEA 0

THIRD FOOTBALL TOURNAMENT

Algiers, 13th–28th July 1978

FIRST ROUND

Group 1

	Eg	Al	Lb	Mw	Pl	W	D	L	F	A	Pts
Egypt	–	1–1	1–0	4–1	3	2	1	0	6	2	5
Algeria	–	–	2–1	3–0	3	2	1	0	6	2	5
Libya	–	–	–	2–1	3	1	0	2	3	4	2
Malawi	–	–	–	–	3	0	0	3	2	9	0

Egypt placed above Algeria on the drawing of lots, but then withdrew. As Libya had been disqualified Malawi qualified for the semi-finals

Group 2

	Ng	Gh	Cm	Ml	Pl	W	D	L	F	A	Pts
Nigeria	–	0–0	0–0	3–1	3	1	2	0	3	1	4
Ghana	–	–	2–1	1–1	3	1	2	0	3	2	4
Cameroon	–	–	–	1–1	3	0	2	1	2	3	2
Mali	–	–	–	–	3	0	2	1	3	5	2

SEMI-FINALS

Algeria .... 2–0 .... Ghana
Nigeria .... 3–2 .... Malawi

3RD PLACE

Ghana .... 1–0 .... Malawi

FINAL

5th July Stadium, Algiers, 28–07–1978

ALGERIA 1
NIGERIA 0

FOURTH FOOTBALL TOURNAMENT

Nairobi, 1st–12th August 1987

FIRST ROUND

Group 1

	Cm	Ke	Md	Tu	Pl	W	D	L	F	A	Pts
Cameroon	–	3–3	3–0	3–1	3	2	1	0	9	4	5
Kenya	–	–	2–1	1–0	3	2	1	0	6	4	5
Madagascar	–	–	–	3–0	3	1	0	2	4	5	2
Tunisia	–	–	–	–	3	0	0	3	1	7	0

Group 2

	Mw	Eg	IC	Se	Pl	W	D	L	F	A	Pts
Malawi	–	2–1	0–1	2–0	3	2	0	1	4	2	4
Egypt	–	–	2–1	1–0	3	2	0	1	4	3	4
Ivory Coast	–	–	–	1–0	3	2	0	1	3	2	4
Senegal	–	–	–	–	3	0	0	3	0	4	0

7TH/8TH PLACE

Senegal .... 1–0 .... Tunisia

5TH/6TH PLACE

Ivory Coast .... 1–1 (3–2p) .... Madagascar

SEMI-FINALS

Egypt .... 1–1 (4–3p) .... Cameroon
Kenya .... 1–1 (4–3p) .... Malawi

3RD PLACE

Malawi .... 3–1 .... Cameroon

FINAL

Nyayo National Stadium, Nairobi, 12–08–1987

EGYPT 1
KENYA 0

FIFTH FOOTBALL TOURNAMENT

Cairo, 16th–30th September 1991

FIRST ROUND

Group 1

	Ng	Zi	Eg	Ug	Pl	W	D	L	F	A	Pts
Nigeria	–	1–0	2–1	8–1	3	3	0	0	11	2	6
Zimbabwe	–	–	3–2	2–1	3	2	0	1	5	4	4
Egypt	–	–	–	1–0	3	1	0	2	4	5	2
Uganda	–	–	–	–	3	0	0	3	2	11	0

Group 2

	Tu	Cm	Ml	Mt	Pl	W	D	L	F	A	Pts
TUNISIA	–	1–0	0–0	3–0	3	2	1	0	4	0	5
CAMEROON	–	–	1–0	1–0	3	2	0	1	2	1	4
MALI	–	–	–	5–0	3	1	1	1	5	1	3
MAURITIUS	–	–	–	–	3	0	0	3	0	9	0

SEMI-FINALS

Cameroon .... 1–0 .... Nigeria
Tunisia .... 3–1 .... Zimbabwe

FINAL

Cairo, 30–09–1991, 5000
CAMEROON 1
TUNISIA 0

AFRICAN CLUB COMPETITIONS

African club competitions centre around two CAF-organised tournaments, the African Cup of Champion Clubs and the African Cup Winners Cup. They are open to the league champions and the winners of the main knock-out competition in each country as is the case in Europe, and are held every year. In each case the previous year's winners are entitled to defend their title.

COMBINED CLUB HONOURS BY COUNTRY

	Country	G	S	B	Finals	Semis
1	Egypt	10	2	9	12	21
2	Cameroon	8	3	7	11	18
3	Zaire	4	5	5	9	14
4	Guinea	4	2	5	6	11
5	Algeria	4	2	3	6	9
6	Nigeria	3	8	9	11	20
7	Ghana	2	6	8	8	16
8	Tunisia	2	2	1	4	5
9	Morocco	2	–	2	2	4
10	Côte d'Ivoire	1	3	3	4	7
11	Zambia	1	2	7	3	10
12	Kenya	1	1	4	2	6
13	Sudan	1	1	2	2	4
14	Congo	1	–	1	1	2
15	Mali	–	2	3	2	5
	Togo	–	2	3	2	5
17	Uganda	–	2	–	2	2
18	Gabon	–	1	–	1	1
19	Senegal	–	–	5	–	5
20	Burkina Faso	–	–	2	–	2
	Ethiopia	–	–	2	–	2
	Libya	–	–	2	–	2
23	Benin	–	–	1	–	1
	Burundi	–	–	1	–	1
	Madagascar	–	–	1	–	1
	Mozambique	–	–	1	–	1
	Tanzania	–	–	1	–	1

To the end of the 1991 tournaments

The African Cup of Champion Clubs is now a major feature on the calendar of world football. It had always been the intention of the African Football Confederation to promote club football, but in 1957 not many clubs were in a position to play teams from other cities, let alone other countries.

Not until 1964 did a Champions' cup seem remotely feasible. Leagues were springing up in every country following independence, and representatives of 14 of them played off for the right to be represented in the first tournament, to be staged in Ghana. In that historic three-day tournament in Accra, Oryx Douala from Cameroon beat not only the hosts Real Republicans, who were in effect the Ghana national side, but also Stade Malien to win the first title.

Very much influenced by the organisation of the European Cup, the format was changed for the second edition two years later. Each tie was to be contested on a home and away basis with the highest aggregate scorers qualifying for the next round. In the event of these being tied, the number of away goals would be the deciding factor, and in the final resort, penalties. Unlike the European Cup, however, the final was to be staged over two legs as a neutral venue was thought unlikely to pull in a big enough crowd.

The early years of the competition were dominated by the clubs of West and Central Africa. TP Englebert, later renamed TP Mazembe, appeared in four of the first six finals and another club from Zaire, Vita Kinshasa, won the tournament in 1973. Ghana was also well represented, particularly by the great Asante Kotoko who, like TP Englebert, also appeared in four finals although they only emerged victorious once.

The competition really came to life in the early 1970s, and so encouraged were CAF that they introduced a second tournament, for the winners of what in most cases were fledgling cup competitions. Cameroon and Guinea were the major forces of the time. Canon Yaoundé, Union Douala and Tonnerre Yaoundé from Cameroon, and Hafia and Horoya Conakry from Guinea, all made their names at this time.

Hafia Conakry were especially dominant, appearing in five finals between 1972 and 1978 with a team that was feared throughout the continent. The attacking line-up of Petit Sory, Papa Camara, Bangaly Sylla, Cherif Soulayeman, N'Jolea, Tollo and Jansky has perhaps yet to be equalled in African club football.

Until the 1980s, clubs from North Africa had shown little interest in the two competitions. Al Ismaili had won the Champions' cup in 1969 but they were not regarded as the best Egyptian team, whilst Mouloudia Algiers won the cup for Algeria in 1976. In the 1980s, however, they began to realise what they were missing out on, and fairly soon made their mark. Asante Kotoko's win in the 1983 Champions' cup marks the last occasion on which the cup was held by a sub-Saharan nation.

The Cup Winners Cup, too, has been the domain of the North Africans since the early 1980s. Al Ahly from Cairo have emerged as one of the finest clubs Africa has produced. They won the competition three years on the trot, the only club to have achieved such a feat, and on the third occasion gave up their place in the Champions' cup to take part. They returned to the Champions' cup the following year and promptly won that as well. This was all on top of a victory and a final appearance in the Champions' cup in 1981 and 1982. Six years, six final appearances and five victories!

They were not the only North Africans to enjoy success. Zamalek, their great Cairo rivals, won the Champions' cup twice, whilst their compatriots Al Makaouloum won the Cup Winners Cup twice. Tunisia, Algeria and Morocco have also contributed to this phenomenal success.

In a bid to increase the number of clubs taking part in continental tournaments, the CAF Cup was introduced in 1992, along the same lines as the UEFA Cup in Europe and CONMEBOL Cup in South America. There is only one representative for each country but a weighted entry for countries such as Nigeria and Egypt may be introduced in the future.

The hope is that the African champions will soon be asked to take part in the World Club Championship with the winners of the European Cup and Copa Libertadores. There is little reason for their continued exclusion.

COMBINED CLUB MEDALS TABLE

	Team	Country	G	S	B
1	Al Ahly Cairo	EGY	5	1	2
2	Canon Yaoundé	CMR	4	2	2
3	TP Mazembe	ZAI	3	2	1
4	Hafia FC Conakry	GUI	3	2	–
5	Asante Kotoko	GHA	2	4	3
6	Zamalek	EGY	2	–	2
7	Al Mokaoulum	EGY	2	–	1
	JS Kabylie	ALG	2	–	1
	Union Douala	CMR	2	–	1
10	Enugu Rangers	NGR	1	1	3
11	AS Vita Club Kinshasa	ZAI	1	1	2
12	IICC Shooting Stars	NGR	1	1	1
	Gor Mahia	KEN	1	1	1
	Tonnerre Yaoundé	CMR	1	1	1
	BCC Lions	NGR	1	1	–
	Club Africain	TUN	1	1	–
	Power Dynamos	ZAM	1	1	–
18	FAR Rabat	MAR	1	–	2
	Horoya AC Conakry	GUI	1	–	2
	Al Ismaili	EGY	1	–	2
21	Al Merreikh	SUD	1	–	1
	Oryx Douala	CMR	1	–	1
	ES Setif	ALG	1	–	1
24	CA Bizerte	TUN	1	–	–
	CARA Brazzaville	CGO	1	–	–
	MC Algiers	ALG	1	–	–
	Raja Casablanca	MAR	1	–	–
	Stade Abidjan	CIV	1	–	–
29	Hearts of Oak	GHA	–	2	2
30	Africa Sports	CIV	–	2	–
	AS Bilima	ZAI	–	2	–
32	Nkana Red Devils	ZAM	–	1	4
	Iwuanyanwu Owerri	NGR	–	1	2
34	Al Hilal	SUD	–	1	1
	NA Hussein–Dey	ALG	–	1	1
	Mehalla Al Kubra	EGY	–	1	1
37	Agaza Lomé	TOG	–	1	–
	Bendel United	NGR	–	1	–
	Etoile Filante	TOG	–	1	–
	ES Tunis	TUN	–	1	–
	Leventis United	NGR	–	1	–
	MC Oran	ALG	–	1	–
	Nakivubo Villa	UGA	–	1	–
	Ranchers Bees	NGR	–	1	–
	AS Real Bamako	MLI	–	1	–
	Simba FC	UGA	–	1	–
	AS Sogara	GAB	–	1	–
	Stade Malien	MLI	–	1	–
	Stationary Stores	NGR	–	1	–
	Stella Abidjan	CIV	–	1	–
51	ASEC Abidjan	CIV	–	–	3
	Djoliba AC	MLI	–	–	3
	Mufulira Wanderers	ZAM	–	–	3
54	Bendel Insurance	NGR	–	–	2
	US Goree	SEN	–	–	2
	ASC Jeanne d'Arc	SEN	–	–	2
	Kadiogo	BFA	–	–	2
	AS Kalum Star	GUI	–	–	2
	AFC Leopards	KEN	–	–	2
	Lomé I	TOG	–	–	2

To the end of 1991 tournaments

THE AFRICAN CUP OF CHAMPION CLUBS

1964	Oryx Douala	CMR	2–1	Stade Malien	MLI
1965	–				
1966	Stade Abidjan	CIV	1–3 4–1	AS Real Bamako	MLI
1967	TP Englebert	ZAI	1–1 2–2	Asante Kotoko	GHA
1968	TP Englebert	ZAI	5–0 1–4	Etoile Filante	TOG
1969	Al Ismaili	EGY	2–2 3–1	TP Englebert	ZAI
1970	Asante Kotoko	GHA	1–1 2–1	TP Englebert	ZAI
1971	Canon Yaoundé	CMR	0–3 2–0 1–0	Asante Kotoko	GHA
1972	Hafia FC Conakry	GUI	4–2 3–2	Simba FC	UGA
1973	AS Vita Kinshasa	ZAI	2–4 3–0	Asante Kotoko	GHA
1974	CARA Brazzaville	CGO	4–2 2–1	Mehalla Al Kubra	EGY
1975	Hafia FC Conakry	GUI	1–0 2–1	Enugu Rangers	NGR
1976	MC Algiers	ALG	3–0 0–3 (4–1p)	Hafia FC Conakry	GUI
1977	Hafia FC Conakry	GUI	1–0 3–2	Hearts of Oak	GHA
1978	Canon Yaoundé	CMR	0–0 2–0	Hafia FC Conakry	GUI
1979	Union Douala	CMR	0–1 1–0 (5–3p)	Hearts of Oak	GHA
1980	Canon Yaoundé	CMR	2–2 3–0	AS Bilima	ZAI
1981	JE Tizi–Ouzou	ALG	4–0 1–0	AS Vita Kinshasa	ZAI

CUP OF CHAMPION CLUBS BY COUNTRY

	Country	G	S	B	Finals	Semis
1	Egypt	5	2	5	7	12
2	Cameroon	5	–	6	5	11
3	Algeria	4	1	1	5	6
4	Zaire	3	5	4	8	12
5	Guinea	3	2	3	5	8
6	Ghana	2	6	6	8	14
7	Morocco	2	–	2	2	4
8	Côte d'Ivoire	1	1	2	2	4
9	Congo	1	–	–	1	1
	Tunisia	1	–	–	1	1
11	Nigeria	–	3	6	3	9
12	Mali	–	2	1	2	3
13	Uganda	–	2	–	2	2
14	Zambia	–	1	5	1	6
15	Togo	–	1	3	1	4
16	Sudan	–	1	1	1	2
17	Senegal	–	–	4	–	4
18	Ethiopia	–	–	2	–	2
	Kenya	–	–	2	–	2
20	Tanzania	–	–	1	–	1

To the end of the 1991 tournament

1982	Al Ahly Cairo	EGY	3–0 1–1		Asante Kotoko	GHA
1983	Asante Kotoko	GHA	0–0 1–0		Al Ahly Cairo	EGY
1984	Zamalek	EGY	2–0 0–0		Shooting Stars	NGR
1985	FAR Rabat	MAR	5–2 1–1		AS Bilima	ZAI
1986	Zamalek	EGY	2–0 0–2	(4–2p)	Africa Sports	CIV
1987	Al Ahly Cairo	EGY	0–0 2–0		Al Hilal	SUD
1988	EP Setif	ALG	0–1 4–0		Iwuanyanwu Owerri	NGR
1989	Raja Casablanca	MAR	1–0 0–1	(4–2p)	MP Oran	ALG
1990	JS Kabylie	ALG	1–0 0–1	(5–3p)	Nkana Red Devils	ZAM
1991	Club Africain	TUN	5–1 1–1		Nakivubo Villa	UGA

CHAMPIONS CUP MEDALS TABLE

	Team	Country	G	S	B
1	Hafia FC Conakry	GUI	3	2	–
2	Canon Yaoundé	CMR	3	–	2
3	Asante Kotoko	GHA	2	4	3
4	TP Mazembe	ZAI	2	2	1
5	Al Ahly Cairo	EGY	2	1	2
6	JS Kabylie	ALG	2	–	1
	Zamalek	EGY	2	–	1
8	AS Vita Club Kinshasa	ZAI	1	1	1
9	FAR Rabat	MAR	1	–	2
10	Al Ismaili	EGY	1	–	1
	Oryx Douala	CMR	1	–	1
	Union Douala	CMR	1	–	1
13	CARA Brazzaville	CGO	1	–	–
	MC Algiers	ALG	1	–	–
	Raja Casablanca	MAR	1	–	–
	Club Africain	TUN	1	–	–
	ES Setif	ALG	1	–	–
	Stade Abidjan	CIV	1	–	–
19	Hearts of Oak	GHA	–	2	1
20	AS Bilima	ZAI	–	2	–
21	Nkana Red Devils	ZAM	–	1	4
22	Enugu Rangers	NGR	–	1	3
23	Al Hilal	SUD	–	1	1
	Iwuanyanwu Owerri	NGR	–	1	1
	Mehalla Al Kubra	EGY	–	1	1
26	Africa Sports	CIV	–	1	–
	Etoile Filante	TOG	–	1	–
	Nakivubo Villa	UGA	–	1	–
	MC Oran	ALG	–	1	–
	AS Real Bamako	MLI	–	1	–
	IICC Shooting Stars	NGR	–	1	–
	Simba FC	UGA	–	1	–
	Stade Malien	MLI	–	1	–
34	ASEC Abidjan	CIV	–	–	2
	US Goree	SEN	–	–	2
	AS Kalum Star	GUI	–	–	2
	Lomé I	TOG	–	–	2
38	Bendel Insurance	NGR	–	–	1
	Kenya Breweries	KEN	–	–	1
	Cotton Club	ETH	–	–	1
	ASC Diaraf	SEN	–	–	1
	Djoliba AC	MLI	–	–	1
	Great Olympics	GHA	–	–	1
	CS Imana	ZAI	–	–	1
	ASC Jeanne d'Arc	SEN	–	–	1
	Kakimbo FC	GUI	–	–	1
	Leopard Douala	CMR	–	–	1
	AFC Leopards	KEN	–	–	1
	FC Lupopo	ZAI	–	–	1
	Mufulira Wanderers	ZAM	–	–	1
	Real Republicans	GHA	–	–	1
	St Georges	ETH	–	–	1
	Semassi Sokode	TOG	–	–	1
	SC Simba	TAN	–	–	1
	Tonnerre Yaoundé	CMR	–	–	1

To the end of the 1991 tournament

THE AFRICAN CUP WINNERS CUP

1975	Tonnerre Yaoundé	CMR	1–0 4–1		Stella Abidjan	CIV
1976	Shooting Stars	NGR	4–1 0–1		Tonn. Yaoundé	CMR
1977	Enugu Rangers	NGR	4–1 1–1		Canon Yaoundé	CMR
1978	Horoya AC Con'ry	GUI	3–1 2–1		MA Hussein-Dey	ALG
1979	Canon Yaoundé	CMR	2–0 6–0		Gor Mahia	KEN
1980	TP Mazembe	ZAI	3–1 1–0		Africa Sports	CIV
1981	Union Douala	CMR	2–1 0–0		Stationary Stores	NGR
1982	Al Mokaoulum	EGY	2–0 2–0		Power Dynamos	ZAM
1983	Al Mokaoulum	EGY	1–0 0–0		Agaza Lomé	TOG
1984	Al Ahly Cairo	EGY	1–0 0–1	(4–2p)	Canon Yaoundé	CMR
1985	Al Ahly Cairo	EGY	2–0 0–1		Leventis United	NGR
1986	Al Ahly Cairo	EGY	3–0 0–2		AS Sogara	GAB
1987	Gor Mahia	KEN	2–2 1–1		ES Tunis	TUN
1988	CA Bizerte	TUN	0–0 1–0		Ranchers Bees	NGR
1989	Al Merreikh	SUD	1–0 0–0		Bendel United	NGR
1990	BCC Lions	NGR	3–0 1–1		Club Africain	TUN
1991	Power Dynamos	ZAM	2–3 3–1		BCC Lions	NGR

CUP WINNERS CUP MEDALS TABLE

	Team	Country	G	S	B
1	Al Ahly Cairo	EGY	3	–	–
2	Al Mokaoulum	EGY	2	–	1
3	Canon Yaoundé	CMR	1	2	–
4	Gor Mahia	KEN	1	1	1

CUP WINNERS CUP BY COUNTRY

	Country	G	S	B	Finals	Semis
1	Egypt	5	–	4	5	9
2	Nigeria	3	5	3	8	11
3	Cameroon	3	3	1	6	7
4	Tunisia	1	2	1	3	4
5	Kenya	1	1	2	2	4
	Zambia	1	1	2	2	4
7	Guinea	1	–	2	1	3
8	Sudan	1	–	1	1	2
	Zaire	1	–	1	1	2
10	Côte d'Ivoire	–	2	1	2	3
11	Algeria	–	1	2	1	3
12	Gabon	–	1	–	1	1
	Togo	–	1	–	1	1
14	Burkina Faso	–	–	2	–	2
	Ghana	–	–	2	–	2
	Libya	–	–	2	–	2
	Mali	–	–	2	–	2
18	Benin	–	–	1	–	1
	Burundi	–	–	1	–	1
	Congo	–	–	1	–	1
	Madagascar	–	–	1	–	1
	Mozambique	–	–	1	–	1
	Senegal	–	–	1	–	1

To the end of the 1991 tournament

5	BCC Lions	NGR	1	1	–
	Power Dynamos	ZAM	1	1	–
7	Tonnerre Yaoundé	CMR	1	1	–
8	Horoya AC Conakry	GUI	1	–	2
9	Al Merreikh	SUD	1	–	1
	IICC Shooting Stars	NGR	1	–	1
11	CA Bizerte	TUN	1	–	–
	Enugu Rangers	NGR	1	–	–
	TP Mazembe	ZAI	1	–	–
	Union Douala	CMR	1	–	–
15	ES Tunis	TUN	–	1	1
	NA Hussein-Dey	ALG	–	1	1
17	Africa Sports	CIV	–	1	–
	Agaza Lomé	TOG	–	1	–
	Bendel United	NGR	–	1	–
	Club Africain	TUN	–	1	–
	Leventis United	NGR	–	1	–
	Ranchers Bees	NGR	–	1	–
	AS Sogara	GAB	–	1	–
	Stationary Stores	NGR	–	1	–
	Stella Abidjan	CIV	–	1	–
26	Djoliba AC	MLI	–	–	2
	Kadiogo	BFA	–	–	2
	Mufulira Wanderers	ZAM	–	–	2
29	Abiola Babes	NGR	–	–	1
	ASEC Abidjan	CIV	–	–	1
	Bendel Insurance	NGR	–	–	1
	BFV FC	MAD	–	–	1
	Diamant Yaoundé	CMR	–	–	1
	Dragons de l'Ouème	BEN	–	–	1
	Al Ahly Tripoli	LBA	–	–	1
	Al Ittihad	EGY	–	–	1
	Al Nasr	LBA	–	–	1
	CS Hammam-Lif	TUN	–	–	1
	Hearts of Oak	GHA	–	–	1
	Inter Club	CGO	–	–	1
	International FC	BUR	–	–	1
	Al Ismaili	EGY	–	–	1
	ASC Jeanne d'Arc	SEN	–	–	1
	AFC Leopards	KEN	–	–	1
	Desportivo Maputo	MOZ	–	–	1
	Sekondi Hasaacas	GHA	–	–	1
	AS Vita Club Kinshasa	ZAI	–	–	1
	Zamalek	EGY	–	–	1

To the end of the 1991 tournament

AFRICAN CLUB CUPS

1964

CHAMPIONS CUP

SEMI-FINALS

Oryx Douala	CMR	2–1	Real Republicans	GHA
Stade Malien	MLI	3–1	Cotton Club	ETH

FINAL

Accra Stadium, Accra, 7–02–1964

ORYX DOUALA 2
STADE MALIEN 1

1966

CHAMPIONS CUP

FIRST ROUND

Etoile Filante	VOL	2–0 1–4	**Stade Abidjan**	CIV
Etoile Filante	TOG	0–3 0–3	**Asante Kotoko**	GHA
Diables Noirs	CGO	1–2 2–0	Dragons	ZAI
Ethio-Cement	ETH	1–4 0–6	**Al Hilal**	SUD
Oryx Douala	CMR	Bye		
Conakry I	GUI	W-O	US Goree	SEN
Invincible Eleven	LBR	2–3 0–6	**AS Real Bamako**	MLI

QUARTER-FINALS

Asante Kotoko	0–1 2–2	**Stade Abidjan**
Al Hilal	6–1 4–1	Diables Noirs
Oryx Douala	Bye	
AS Real Bamako	2–1 3–2	Conakry I

SEMI-FINALS

Al Hilal	1–0 2–4	**Stade Abidjan**
Oryx Douala	2–4 2–3	**AS Real Bamako**

FINAL

1st leg

Omnisport, Bamako, 11–12–1966

AS REAL BAMAKO 3
STADE ABIDJAN 1

2nd leg

Houphouet Boigny, Abidjan, 25–12–1966

STADE ABIDJAN 4
AS REAL BAMAKO 1

1967

CHAMPIONS CUP

PRELIMINARY ROUND

Secteur 6	NIG	3–2 1–3	**Al Ittihad**	LBA
AS Fonctionnaires	VOL	W-O	Augustinians	GAM

FIRST ROUND

TP Englebert	ZAI	2–0 1–3	Abeilles FC	CGO
Al Ittihad	LBA	W-O	Diamant Yaoundé	CMR

Al Hilal	SUD	0–1 1–3	**Olympic Alexandria**	EGY
St Georges	ETH	W-O	Bitumastic	UGA
Djoliba AC	MLI	W-O	Invincible Eleven	LBR
AS Fonctionnaires	VOL	0–2 1–1	**Conakry II**	GUI
Stade Abidjan	CIV	2–1 0–0	Modela Lomé	TOG
AS St Louisienne	SEN	2–3 0–3	**Asante Kotoko**	GHA

QUARTER-FINALS

TP Englebert	W-O	Al Ittihad
St Georges	3–2	Olympic Alexandria
Djoliba AC	2–1 0–0	Conakry II
Stade Abidjan	1–3 2–5	**Asante Kotoko**

SEMI-FINALS

TP Englebert	3–1 1–2	St Georges
Asante Kotoko	1–1 2–1	Djoliba AC

FINAL

1st leg

Kumasi Stadium, Kumasi, 19–11–1967

ASANTE KOTOKO 1
TOUT PUISSANT ENGLEBERT 1

2nd leg

20th May stadium, Kinshasa, 26–11–1967

TP ENGLEBERT 2
ASANTE KOTOKO 2

TP Englebert were awarded the cup after Asante Kotoko refused to take part in a play off

1968

CHAMPIONS CUP

PRELIMINARY ROUND

Secteur 6	NIG	1–1 1–3	**US Ouagadougou**	VOL
Police Mogadishu	SOM	W-O	Cosmopolitans	TAN
FAR Rabat	MAR	W-O	Augustinians	GAM
Etoile du Congo	CGO	W-O	Mighty Blackpool	SLE

FIRST ROUND

Africa Sports	CIV	2–0 4–4**	**TP Englebert**	ZAI
Etoile du Congo	CGO	1–2 3–4	**Oryx Douala**	CMR
Stationary Stores	NGR	3–2 1–2*	Cape Coast Dwarfs	GHA
FAR Rabat	MAR	2–0 1–0	Foyer France	SEN
Police Mogadishu	SOM	1–1 1–3	**Al Mourada**	SUD
Abaluhya FC	KEN	1–1 3–1	St Georges	ETH
Mighty Barolle	LBR	1–2	**Conakry II**	GUI
US Ouagadougou	VOL	1–4 0–2	**Etoile Filante**	TOG

** Africa Sports disqualified * Stores won on lots

QUARTER-FINALS

TP Englebert	3–0 2–0	Oryx Douala
FAR Rabat	1–0 1–2 2–2*	Stationary Stores
Abaluhya FC	3–0 1–3	Al Mourada
Etoile Filante	3–0	Conakry II

* FAR Rabat won on penalties

SEMI-FINALS

TP Englebert	1–1 3–1	FAR Rabat
Abaluhya FC	2–0 0–4	**Etoile Filante**

FINAL

1st leg

20th May Stadium, Kinshasa, 16–03–1969

TOUT PUISSANT ENGLEBERT 5
ETOILE FILANTE 0

2nd leg

Eyadema Stadium, Lome, 30–03–1969

ETOILE FILANTE 4
TOUT PUISSANT ENGLEBERT 1

1969

CHAMPIONS CUP

PRELIMINARY ROUND

Africa Sports	CIV	5–1 2–0	Olympique Sportif	GAB
Hoga Mogadishu	SOM	2–0 1–4	**Burri**	SUD
Young Africans	TAN	4–1 0–2	Fitarikandro	MAD
St Eloi	ZAI	W-O	US Cattin	CAR

FIRST ROUND

TP Englebert	ZAI	2–1 2–2	Africa Sports	CIV
Secteur 6	NIG	1–5 0–3	**Etoile Filante**	TOG
Caiman Douala	CMR	0–0 1–3	**St Eloi**	ZAI
USFRAN	VOL	2–7	**Conakry II**	GUI
St Georges	ETH	0–0 0–5	**Young Africans**	TAN
Asante Kotoko	GHA	5–1 1–1	Patronage St Anne	CGO
Burri	SUD	2–4 1–0	**Gor Mahia**	KEN
Al Tahadi	LBA	0–5 0–3	**Al Ismaili**	EGY

QUARTER-FINALS

TP Englebert	4–1 0–1	Etoile Filante
Conakry II	7–2 3–1	St Eloi
Asante Kotoko	1–1 1–1*	Young Africans
Al Ismaili	3–1 1–1	Gor Mahia

* Asante won on lots

SEMI-FINALS

TP Englebert	4–0 3–5	Conakry II
Asante Kotoko	2–2 2–3	**Al Ismaili**

FINAL

1st leg

20th May Stadium, Kinshasa, 22–12–1969

TOUT PUISSANT ENGLEBERT 2
AL ISMAILI 2

2nd leg

International Stadium, Cairo, 9–01–1970

AL ISMAILI 3
TOUT PUISSANT ENGLEBERT 1

1970

CHAMPIONS CUP

FIRST ROUND

Asante Kotoko	GHA	Bye		
Stationary Stores	NGR	3–1 3–2	Forces Armees	DAH
Nakuru All Stars	KEN	Bye		
Young Africans	TAN	4–0 2–4	US Fonctionnaires	MAD
Lavori Publici	SOM	2–1 2–4	**Prisons FC**	UGA
Tele SC Asmara	ETH	Bye		
Al Hilal	SUD	Bye		
Al Ismaili	EGY	Bye		
AS Kaloum Star	GUI	Bye		
CR Belcourt	ALG	5–3**	**ASC Jeanne d'Arc**	SEN
AS Real Bamako	MLI	3–0 2–2	AS Fonctionnaires	VOL
Stade Abidjan	CIV	Bye		
Modele Lomé	TOG	Bye		
Secteur 6	NIG	0–2 2–1	**Union Douala**	CMR
Aigle Royal	GAB	0–3 5–2	**CARA Brazzaville**	CGO
TP Englebert	ZAI	Bye		

** CR Belcourt withdrew, Jeanne d'Arc qualified

SECOND ROUND

Stationary Stores	3–2 0–1**	**Asante Kotoko**
Nakuru All Stars	1–0 1–3	**Young Africans**
Prisons FC	3–2 1–2*	Tele SC Asmara
Al Ismaili	1–0 0–0	Al Hilal
AS Kaloum Star	3–1 1–2	ASC Jeanne d'Arc
AS Real Bamako	2–3 2–6	**Stade Abidjan**
Union Douala	0–0 1–1*	**Modele Lomé**
TP Englebert	3–0 2–2	CARA Brazzaville

** 2nd match abandoned. Stationary Stores disqualified
* Prisons and Modele won on lots

QUARTER-FINALS

Young Africans	1–1 0–2	**Asante Kotoko**
Al Ismaili	4–1 2–1	Prisons FC
Stade Abidjan	1–1 3–4	**AS Kaloum Star**
Modele Lomé	0–0 1–3	**TP Englebert**

SEMI-FINALS

Al Ismaili	0–0 0–2	**Asante Kotoko**
AS Kaloum Star	1–2 1–3	**TP Englebert**

FINAL

1st leg

Kumasi Stadium, Kumasi, 10–01–1971

ASANTE KOTOKO 1
TOUT PUISSANT ENGLEBERT 1

2nd leg

20th May Stadium, Kinshasa, 24–01–1971

TOUT PUISSANT ENGLEBERT 1
ASANTE KOTOKO 2

1971

CHAMPIONS CUP

FIRST ROUND

Canon Yaoundé	CMR	7–3 2–1	AS Solidarite	GAB
AS Vita Club	ZAI	Bye		
AS Porto Novo	DAH	0–1 0–2	**Victoria Mokanda**	CGO
Dynamic Togolais	TOG	Bye		
Secteur 6	NIG	1–1 0–1	**Enugu Rangers**	NGR
AS Kaloum Star	GUI	Bye		
ASC Diaraf	SEN	3–0 0–4	**Stade Malien**	MLI
ASEC Abidjan	CIV	Bye		
Abaluhya FC	KEN	0–0 1–3	**Great Olympics**	GHA
Maseru United	LES	1–2 2–3	**MMM Tamatave**	MAD
Young Africans	TAN	2–0 0–0	Lavori Publici	SOM
Coffee FC	UGA	Bye		
Al Ismaili	EGY	Bye		
ES Tunis	TUN	0–0 1–0	Al Ahly Benghazi	LBA
Al Merreikh	SUD	2–1 0–1 (5–4p)	Tele SC Asmara	ETH
Asante Kotoko	GHA	Bye		

SECOND ROUND

AS Vita Club	2–0 1–3 (3–4p)	**Canon Yaoundé**
Victoria Mokanda	1–2 0–2	**Dynamic Togolaise**
AS Kaloum Star	3–3 1–2	**Enugu Rangers**
Stade Malien	2–2 1–2	**ASEC Abidjan**
MMM Tamatave	2–1 0–4	**Great Olympics**
Coffee FC	W-O	Young Africans
Al Ismaili	W-O	ES Tunis
Al Merreikh	2–1 0–1 (4–5p)	**Asante Kotoko**

QUARTER-FINALS

Dynamic Togolaise	1–2 3–4	**Canon Yaoundé**
Enugu Rangers	0–1 0–2	**ASEC Abidjan**
Coffee FC	0–0 0–2	**Great Olympics**
Al Ismaili	0–0 0–3	**Asante Kotoko**

SEMI-FINALS

ASEC Abidjan	2–1 1–4	**Canon Yaoundé**
Great Olympics	1–1 0–1	**Asante Kotoko**

FINAL

1st leg

Kumasi Stadium, Kumasi, 5–12–1971

ASANTE KOTOKO 3
CANON YAOUNDE 0

2nd leg

Militaire Garoua, Yaoundé, 19–12–1971

CANON YAOUNDE 2
ASANTE KOTOKO 0

Play-off. Militaire Garoua, Yaoundé, 21–12–1971

CANON YAOUNDE 1
ASANTE KOTOKO 0
Match abandoned but the result stood

1972

CHAMPIONS CUP

FIRST ROUND

Hafia FC	GUI	4–1 1–1	ASFAN Niamey	NIG
Canon Yaoundé	CMR	Bye		
ASFA Dakar	SEN	3–0 3–2	AS Cotonou	DAH
ASFA Ouagadougou	VOL	1–3 0–1	**Djoliba AC**	MLI
Aigle Nkongsamba	CMR	3–1 0–1	Olympique Real	CAR
Dynamic Togolaise	TOG	Bye		
Africa Sports	CIV	Bye		
TP Mazembe	ZAI	2–0 1–1	AS Police	GAB
Hearts of Oak	GHA	W-O	Abaluhya FC	KEN
WNDC Ibadan	NGR	Bye		
AS St Michael	MAD	2–0 0–1	Young Africans	TAN
Majantja Maseru	LES	2–2 0–9	**Kabwe Warriors**	ZAM
Al Ahly Tripoli	LBA	W-O	Al Merreikh	SUD
Al Ismaili	EGY	Bye		
St Georges	ETH	3–1 1–1	Lavori Publici	SOM
Simba FC	UGA	Bye		

SECOND ROUND

Canon Yaoundé	3–2 1–4	**Hafia FC**
ASFA Dakar	2–0 0–2*	**Djoliba AC**
Dynamic Togolaise	1–1 3–4	**Aigle Nkongsamba**
Africa Sports	1–2 2–5	**TP Mazembe**
WNDC Ibadan	1–0 0–3	**Hearts of Oak**
Kabwe Warriors	2–1 3–0	AS St Michael
Al Ismaili	0–1 2–1 (3–4p)	**Al Ahly Tripoli**
Simba FC	4–0 1–1	St Georges

* Forces Armees withdrew

QUARTER-FINAL

Hafia FC	3–0 1–2	Djoliba AC
TP Mazembe	4–1 2–1	Aigle Nkongsamba
Hearts of Oak	7–2 1–2	Kabwe Warriors
Al Ahly Tripoli	1–1 0–3	**Simba FC**

SEMI-FINALS

TP Mazembe	3–2*	**Hafia FC**
Hearts of Oak	1–1 0–1	**Simba FC**

* TP Mazembe withdrew

FINAL

1st leg

28th September Stadium, Conakry, 10–12–1972

HAFIA CONAKRY 4
SIMBA FOOTBALL CLUB 2

2nd leg

Nakivubo, Kampala, 22–12–1972

SIMBA FOOTBALL CLUB 2
HAFIA CONAKRY 3

1973

CHAMPIONS CUP

FIRST ROUND

AS Vita Club	ZAI	Bye		
Mighty Jets	NGR	2–1 0–1*	Jeanne d'Arc	VOL
ASFA Dakar	SEN	2–2 2–4	**Modele Lomé**	TOG
Stade Malien	MLI	Bye		
Hafia FC	GUI	Bye		
ASEC Abidjan	CIV	2–1 3–1	Mighty Barolle	LBR

CARA Brazzaville CGO 1–0 2–2 Sports Dynamic BUR
Leopards Douala CMR Bye
FC Horsed SOM 3–1 0–5 **Al Ismaili** EGY
Al Ahly Benghazi LBA Bye
Simba FC UGA Bye
Kenya Breweries KEN 1–1 1–1 (5–4p) Tele SC Asmara ETH
Kabwe Warriors ZAM Bye
Fortior Mahajanga MAD 5–1 1–2 Maseru Police LES
Young Africans TAN 1–2 1–1 **Al Merreikh** SUD
Asante Kotoko GHA Bye
* Jeanne d'Arc withdrew, Mighty Jets qualified

SECOND ROUND

AS Vita Club W-O Mighty Jets
Stade Malien 2–1 0–0 Modele Lomé
Hafia FC 2–1 3–4 (3–2p) ASEC Abidjan
Leopards Douala 2–0 0–1 CARA Brazzaville
Al Ismaili 4–1 1–0 Al Ahly Benghazi
Kenya Breweries 3–1 1–2 Simba FC
Kabwe Warriors 4–0 3–0 Fortior Mahajanga
Al Merreikh 1–1 0–3 **Asante Kotoko**

QUARTER-FINALS

Stade Malien 0–3 1–4 **AS Vita Club**
Hafia FC 2–4 3–2 Leopards Douala
Kenya Breweries 0–0 1–2* Al Ismaili
Kabwe Warriors 2–1 0–2 **Asante Kotoko**
* Ismaili withdrew, Breweries qualified

SEMI-FINALS

AS Vita Club 3–0 1–3 Leopards Douala
Kenya Breweries 0–2 1–2 **Asante Kotoko**

FINAL

1st leg
Kumasi Stadium, Kumasi, 25–11–1973
ASANTE KOTOKO 4
AS VITA CLUB 2

2nd leg
20th May Stadium, Kinshasa, 16–12–1973
AS VITA CLUB 3
ASANTE KOTOKO 0

1974

CHAMPIONS CUP

FIRST ROUND

CARA Brazzaville CGO 3–1 4–0 Zalang GAB
AS Vita Club ZAI Bye
Bendel Insurance NGR 7–0 0–1 Secteur 7 NIG
Djoliba AC MLI Bye
Mighty Barolle LBR 0–0 0–2 **ASEC Abidjan** CIV
Modele Lomé TOG 3–0 0–1 AS Porto Novo DAH
Hafia FC GUI Bye
Ports Authority SLE 3–2 1–3 **ASC Jeanne d'Arc** SEN
Linare FC LES 1–3 1–2 **SC Simba** TAN
Green Buffaloes ZAM 4–1 2–1 JS Antalaha MAD
Olympique Real CAR 4–0 0–1 Simba FC UGA
Hearts of Oak GHA Bye
Abaluhya FC KEN Bye
Tele SC Asmara ETH W-O FC Horsed SOM
Al Ahly Tripoli LBA 2–2 0–3 **Al Hilal** SUD
Mehalla Al Kubra EGY Bye

SECOND ROUND

CARA Brazzaville 4–0 0–3 AS Vita Club
Djoliba AC 2–0 0–1 Bendel Insurance
ASEC Abidjan 3–0 Modele Lomé
ASC Jeanne d'Arc W-O Hafia FC
Green Buffaloes 1–2 0–1 **SC Simba**
Hearts of Oak 6–1 3–3 Olympique Real
Abaluhya FC 2–0 0–1 Tele SC Asmara
Mehalla Al Kubra 4–1 1–4 (4–2p) Al Hilal

QUARTER-FINALS

Djoliba AC 0–0 0–3 **CARA Brazzaville**
ASEC Abidjan 2–1 0–1 **ASC Jeanne d'Arc**
Hearts of Oak 1–2 0–0 **SC Simba**
Mehalla Al Kubra 3–0 1–1 Abaluhya FC

SEMI-FINALS

CARA Brazzaville 2–0 4–1 ASC Jeanne d'Arc
SC Simba 1–0 0–1 (0–3p) **Mehalla Al Kubra**

FINAL

1st leg
Revolution Stadium, Brazzaville, 29–11–1974
CARA BRAZZAVILLE 4
MEHALLA AL KUBRA 2

2nd leg
Mehalla Stadium, Mehalla, 13–12–1974
MEHALLA AL KUBRA 1
CARA BRAZZAVILLE 2

1975

CHAMPIONS CUP

FIRST ROUND

Hafia FC GUI W-O Real Banjul GAM
AS Vita Club ZAI 4–0 1–1 Petrosport FC GAB
Silures VOL 3–2 2–0 Etoile Porto Novo DAH
CARA Brazzaville CGO Bye
Olympic Niamey NIG 0–2 1–4 **ASEC Abidjan** CIV
ASFA Dakar SEN Bye
Djoliba AC MLI 2–0 1–0 Mighty Blackpool SLE
Bame Monrovia LBR 0–1 1–3 **Lome I** TOG
Mehalla Al Kubra EGY Bye
Uganda Exp. FC UGA 1–0 0–0 FC Horsed SOM
Embassoria ETH 1–1 0–2 **International FC** BUR
ASDR Fatima CAR 3–0 0–2* **Al Merreikh** SUD
Green Buffaloes ZAM W-O Corps Enseignant MAD
Bata Bullets MAW W-O Matlama FC LES
Young Africans TAN Bye
Great Olympics GHA 0–2 1–2 **Enugu Rangers** NGR
* Fatima withdrew during the second match

SECOND ROUND

AS Vita Club 2–0 0–3 **Hafia FC**
CARA Brazzaville 4–0 5–4 Silures
ASEC Abidjan 1–1 1–1 (6–5p) ASFA Dakar
Djoliba AC 1–1 2–3 **Lome I**
Uganda Express FC 1–1 0–1 **Mehalla Al Kubra**
International FC 0–0 2–4 **Al Merreikh**
Bata Bullets 0–2 2–3 **Green Buffaloes**
Enugu Rangers 0–0 1–1 Young Africans

QUARTER-FINALS

CARA Brazzaville 2–0 0–2 (3–4p) **Hafia FC**
ASEC Abidjan 1–0 1–3 **Lome I**
Mehalla Al Kubra 2–1 0–0 Al Merreikh
Green Buffaloes 2–2 1–2 **Enugu Rangers**

SEMI-FINALS

Hafia FC 1–0 1–1 Lome I
Mehalla Al Kubra 3–1 0–3 **Enugu Rangers**

FINAL

1st leg
28th September Stadium, Conakry, 7–12–1975
HAFIA CONAKRY 1
ENUGU RANGERS 0

2nd leg
Surulere, Lagos, 20–12–1975

ENUGU RANGERS	1
HAFIA CONAKRY	2

CUP WINNERS CUP

FIRST ROUND

Mighty Jets	NGR	2–2 0–0	**Tonnerre Yaoundé**	CMR
Al Ittihad	EGY	2–0 0–0	St Georges	ETH
Fortior Mahajanga	MAD	Bye		
Mufulira Wanderers	ZAM	3–0 3–1	Jeshi Zanzibar	TAN
Wallidan	GAM	0–0 0–2	**ASC Jeanne d'Arc**	SEN
Postel Sport	DAH	1–0 0–3	**AS Tempete Mocaf**	CAR
Ifodje Atakpame	TOG	1–0 2–2	Sahel SC	NIG
Stella Abidjan	CIV	1–0 1–0	Mighty Barolle	LBR

QUARTER-FINALS

Al Ittihad	4–0 0–3*	**Tonnerre Yaoundé**
Mufulira Wanderers	W-O	Fortior Mahajanga
ASC Jeanne d'Arc	1–1 3–1	AS Tempete Mocaf
Ifodje Atakpame	0–1 0–4	**Stella Abidjan**

* Al Ittihad withdrew during the second match

SEMI-FINALS

Tonnerre Yaoundé	1–0 2–2	Mufulira Wanderers
ASC Jeanne d'Arc	2–2 1–2	**Stella Abidjan**

FINAL

1st leg
Houphouet Boigny, Abidjan, 30–11–1975

STELLA ABIDJAN	0
TONNERRE YAOUNDE	1

2nd leg
Omnisport, Yaoundé, 14–12–1975

TONNERRE YAOUNDE	4
STELLA ABIDJAN	1

1976

CHAMPIONS CUP

FIRST ROUND

Al Ahly Benghazi	LBA	3–2 1–3	**MC Algiers**	ALG
Al Ahly Cairo	EGY	Bye		
Al Merreikh	SUD	Bye		
Luo Union	KEN	3–1 2–0	St Georges	ETH
Green Buffaloes	ZAM	Bye		
Corps Enseignant	MAD	4–2 1–4	**SC Simba**	TAN
Uganda Ex. FC	UGA	1–0 0–1 (4–3p)	Caiman Douala	CMR
Enugu Rangers	NGR	Bye		
ASEC Abidjan	CIV	Bye		
Silures	VOL	W-O	ASFAN Niamey	NIG
CARA Brazzaville	CGO	4–0 0–2	CS Imana	ZAI
Asante Kotoko	GHA	W-O	Okoume	GAB
ASC Diaraf	SEN	6–1 4–1	Balantas Mansoa	BIS
Lome I	TOG	Bye		
Real Banjul	GAM	0–2 0–2	**Djoliba AC**	MLI
Hafia FC	GUI	Bye		

SECOND ROUND

MC Algiers	3–0 0–1	Al Ahly Cairo
Luo Union	W-O	Al Merreikh
Green Buffaloes	3–2 1–0	SC Simba
Enugu Rangers	0–0 2–2	Uganda Express FC
ASEC Abidjan	2–0 2–0	Silures
Asante Kotoko	1–0 1–2	CARA Brazzaville
Lome I	1–1 0–1	**ASC Diaraf**
Djoliba AC	2–1 0–2	**Hafia FC**

QUARTER-FINALS

MC Algiers	6–3 1–0	Luo Union
Green Buffaloes	3–1 0–3	**Enugu Rangers**
Asante Kotoko	2–1 0–1	**ASEC Abidjan**
ASC Diaraf	2–2 0–4	**Hafia FC**

SEMI-FINALS

Enugu Rangers	2–0 0–3	**MC Algiers**
ASEC Abidjan	3–0 0–5	**Hafia FC**

FINAL

1st leg
28th September Stadium, Conakry, 5–12–1976

HAFIA CONAKRY	3
MOULOUDIA CHALLIA ALGIERS	0

2nd leg
5th July Stadium, Algiers, 18–12–1976

MOULOUDIA CHALLIA ALGIERS	3
HAFIA CONAKRY	0

MC Algiers won 4–1 on penalties

CUP WINNERS CUP

PRELIMINARY ROUND

Bata Bullets	MAW	2–4 4–0	Fortior Mahajanga	MAD
Liberté FC	NIG	0–5 1–4	**Al Ahly Tripoli**	LBA
Canon Yaoundé	CMR	3–0 3–1	Petrosport FC	GAB
Ports Authority	GAM	1–4 1–2	**Kadiogo**	VOL

FIRST ROUND

Shooting Stars	NGR	3–0 2–0	Kenya Breweries	KEN
Bata Bullets	MAW	1–0 0–4	**Rokana United**	ZAM
Mechal Army	ETH	5–2 1–2	Youth League	TAN
Zamalek	EGY	3–0 1–2	Al Ahly Tripoli	LBA
Canon Yaoundé	CMR	2–1 0–1	**AS Vita Club**	ZAI
US Goree	SEN	1–0 2–6	**Stella Abidjan**	CIV
Kadiogo	VOL	1–0 0–7	**AS Kaloum Star**	GUI
CS Lama Kara	TOG	1–2 0–3	**Tonnerre Yaoundé**	CMR

QUARTER-FINALS

Shooting Stars	3–2 1–1	Rokana Utd
Mechal Army	2–0 0–6	**Zamalek**
AS Vita Club	2–0 3–3	US Goree
Tonnerre Yaoundé	0–0 2–1	AS Kaloum Star

SEMI-FINALS

Zamalek	2–0 0–2 (3–5p)	**Shooting Stars**
AS Vita Club	1–1 1–3	**Tonnerre Yaoundé**

FINAL

1st leg
Surulere, Lagos, 27–11–1976

SHOOTING STARS	4
TONNERRE YAOUNDE	1

2nd leg
Omnisport, Yaoundé, 12–12–1976

TONNERRE YAOUNDE	1
SHOOTING STARS	0

1977

CHAMPIONS CUP

FIRST ROUND

Hafia FC	GUI	Bye		
Vautour Club M'gou	GAB	2–4 2–4	**Diables Noirs**	CGO
SC Simba	TAN	W-O	Highlanders	SWZ
Water Corp.	NGR	Bye		
UDIB Bissau	BIS	0–1 0–5	**Djoliba AC**	MLI
SC Gagnoa	CIV	W-O	AS Tempete Mocaf	CAR
Union Douala	CMR	2–0 1–0	Silures	VOL
TP Mazembe	ZAI	1–1 0–3	**Lome I**	TOG

Mufulira Wand.	ZAM	1–1 2–2	Maseru United	LES
Gor Mahia	KEN	1–2 2–1 (5–3p)	Yamaha Wanderers	MAW
Kampala CC	UGA	1–0 3–0	Mechal Army	ETH
MC Algiers	ALG	Bye		
FC Horsed	SOM	1–1 0–3	**Al Ahly Cairo**	EGY
Olympic Niamey	NIG	2–4 2–2	**Al Medina**	LBA
ASC Diaraf	SEN	3–0 2–0	ASC Garde National	MRT
St Joseph	LBR	1–3 1–2	**Hearts of Oak**	GHA

SECOND ROUND

Diables Noirs	0–1 1–1	**Hafia FC**
Water Corporation	0–0 1–0	SC Simba
SC Gagnoa	1–3 1–1	**Djoliba AC**
Union Douala	1–1 1–1 (3–4p)	**Lome I**
Gor Mahia	2–1 2–4	**Mufulira Wanderers**
Kampala CC	1–1 2–3	**MC Algiers**
Al Ahly Cairo	7–2 0–1	Al Medina
ASC Diaraf	1–1 1–2	**Hearts of Oak**

QUARTER-FINALS

Water Corporation	4–2 0–3	**Hafia FC**
Djoliba AC	2–0 0–1*	**Lome I**
MC Algiers	2–1 0–2	**Mufulira Wanderers**
Al Ahly Cairo	1–0 0–3	**Hearts of Oak**

* Djoliba suspended, Lome I qualified

SEMI-FINALS

Lome I	2–1 0–2	**Hafia FC**
Mufulira Wanderers	5–2 0–3	**Hearts of Oak**

FINAL

1st leg

Accra Stadium, Accra, 4–12–1977

HEARTS OF OAK 0
HAFIA CONAKRY 1

2nd leg

28th September Stadium, Conakry, 18–12–1977

HAFIA CONAKRY 3
HEARTS OF OAK 2

CUP WINNERS CUP

FIRST ROUND

Enugu Rangers	NGR	0–0 1–1	Al Ahly Tripoli	LBA
Electric Sports	ETH	Bye		
CS Lama Kara	TOG	1–0 1–3	**Anges ABC**	GAB
ASF Police	SEN	Bye		
Stade Abidjan	CIV	Bye		
Wallidan	GAM	1–1 0–0	**Espoirs Nouakchott**	MRT
Bata Bullets	MAW	4–1 1–2	Gangama United	UGA
Shooting Stars	NGR	Bye		
Al Ittihad	EGY	Bye		
Luo Union	KEN	1–0*	**MP Constantine**	ALG
Ndola United	ZAM	Bye		
Matlama FC	LES	2–5 2–6	**Rangers Intern'al**	TAN
Liberté FC	NIG	1–1 1–6	**Kadiogo**	VOL
AS Kaloum Star	GUI	Bye		
Cedar United	LBR	1–1 0–1	**Sporting Clube**	BIS
Canon Yaoundé	CMR	W-O	Red Star Bangui	CAR

* Luo Union withdrew before the second game. MP Constantine qualified

SECOND ROUND

Enugu Rangers	4–0 2–0	Electric Sports
ASF Police	8–1 0–0	Anges ABC
Stade Abidjan	3–0 1–3	Espoirs Nouakchott
Shooting Stars	4–1 0–1	Bata Bullets
MP Constantine	1–0 1–3	**Al Ittihad**
Ndola United	1–2 1–1	**Rangers International**
Kadiogo	2–1 1–1	AS Kaloum Star
Sporting Clube Bissau	0–4 1–7	**Canon Yaoundé**

QUARTER-FINALS

Enugu Rangers	0–0 2–1	ASF Police
Stade Abidjan	2–0 0–3	**Shooting Stars**
Al Ittihad	2–0 0–0	Rangers International
Kadiogo	2–1 1–4	**Canon Yaoundé**

SEMI-FINALS

Shooting Stars	0–0 0–0 (2–4p)	**Enugu Rangers**
Al Ittihad	1–0 0–2	**Canon Yaoundé**

FINAL

1st leg

Surulere, Lagos, 26–11–1977

ENUGU RANGERS 4
CANON YAOUNDE 1

2nd leg

Omnisports, Yaoundé, 14–12–1977

CANON YAOUNDE 1
ENUGU RANGERS 1

1978

CHAMPIONS CUP

FIRST ROUND

Canon Yaoundé	CMR	Bye		
Hardware Stars	MAW	1–1 0–4	**Al Merreikh**	SUD
Corps Enseignant	MAD	1–2	**Matlama FC**	LES
Green Buffaloes	ZAM	Bye		
Kampala CC	UGA	1–1 2–0	FC Horsed	SOM
Al Ahly Cairo	EGY	Bye		
SCAF Tocages	CAR	1–3 1–1	**Olympic Niamey**	NIG
Enugu Rangers	NGR	Bye		
AS Vita Club	ZAI	Bye		
SC Simba	TAN	2–0 0–1	Vautour Club M'gou	GAB
Al Tahadi	LBA	3–1 2–3	Medr Babur	ETH
JE Tizi-Ouzou	ALG	Bye		
Silures	VOL	7–0 3–2	Benfica	BIS
Africa Sports	CIV	Bye		
ASC Garde Nat.	MRT	3–1 2–2	Wallidan	GAM
Hafia FC	GUI	Bye		

SECOND ROUND

Canon Yaoundé	2–0 1–2	Al Merreikh
Green Buffaloes	1–0 0–0	Matlama FC
Kampala CC	W-O	Al Ahly Cairo
Enugu Rangers	W-O	Olympic Niamey
AS Vita Club	1–0 1–0	SC Simba
JE Tizi-Ouzou	1–0 2–0	Al Tahadi
Africa Sports	2–1 1–3	**Silures**
Hafia FC	5–0 1–0	ASC Garde National

QUARTER-FINALS

Canon Yaoundé	2–0 1–1	Green Buffaloes
Enugu Rangers	3–1 1–0	Kampala CC
JE Tizi-Ouzou	3–2 0–1	**AS Vita Club**
Silures	0–4 1–4	**Hafia FC**

SEMI-FINALS

Canon Yaoundé	0–0 0–0 (6–5p)	Enugu Rangers
Hafia FC	2–0 1–3	AS Vita Club

FINAL

1st leg

28th September Stadium, Conakry, 3–12–1978, 35 000

HAFIA CONAKRY 0
CANON YAOUNDE 0

2nd leg

Omnisport, Yaoundé, 17–12–1978, 80 000

CANON YAOUNDE 2
HAFIA CONAKRY 0

CUP WINNERS CUP

PRELIMINARY ROUND

Zumunta AC	NIG	0–3 0–5	**Horoya AC**	GUI
Lavori Publici	SOM	0–1 0–1	**Al Hilal**	SUD
UDIB Bissau	BIS	3–1 0–2	**Espoirs Nouakchott**	MRT
Sucoma Chikwawa	MAW	1–1 0–1	**Fortior Mahajanga**	MAD
Simba FC	UGA	1–1 1–1 (5–4p)	St Georges	ETH
Al Medina	LBA	W-O	Sodiam Bangui	CAR

FIRST ROUND

Shooting Stars	NGR	3–1 0–3	**Horoya AC**	GUI
Caiman Douala	CMR	2–0 1–3	FC 105 Libreville	GAB
Zamalek	EGY	1–1 2–1	Al Hilal	SUD
Kadiogo	VOL	2–0 0–0	Espoirs Nouakchott	MRT
Mufulira Wand.	ZAM	3–1 1–1	Fortior Mahajanga	MAD
KMKM Zanzibar	TAN	2–0 1–1	Simba FC	UGA
Inter Club	CGO	0–0 4–1	SC Alliance	CIV
MA Hussein-Dey	ALG	2–1 1–1	Al Medina	LBA

QUARTER-FINALS

Horoya AC	4–1 3–3	Caiman Douala
Zamalek	2–1 0–1	**Kadiogo**
Mufulira Wanderers	W-O	KMKM Zanzibar
MA Hussein-Dey	3–0 2–1	Inter Club

SEMI-FINALS

Kadiogo	3–2 0–1	**Horoya AC**
Mufulira Wanderers	2–1 0–1	**MA Hussein-Dey**

FINAL

1st leg

5th July Stadium, Algiers, 24–11–1978

MILAHA ATHLETIC HUSSEIN-DEY 1
HOROYA ATHLETIC CLUB CONAKRY 3

2nd leg

28th September Stadium, Conakry, 10–12–1978

HOROYA ATHLETIC CLUB CONAKRY 2
MILAHA ATHLETIC HUSSEIN–DEY 1

1979

CHAMPIONS CUP

FIRST ROUND

Union Douala	CMR	Bye		
Al Ahly Tripoli	LBA	1–2 0–2	**MP Algiers**	ALG
Kenya Breweries	KEN	*	Al Merreikh	SUD
Desportivo Maputo	MOZ	3–2 0–1	**Matlama FC**	LES
Zamalek	EGY	2–1	Simba FC	UGA
Ogaden Anbassa	ETH	W-O	Bata Bullets	MAW
Dragons de l'Ouème	BEN	0–2 1–3	**Africa Sports**	CIV
CS Imana	ZAI	Bye		
US Goree	SEN	2–0 1–1	ASC Garde National	MRT
Etoile du Congo	CGO	2–0 1–1	FC 105 Libreville	GAB
SC Simba	TAN	0–4 5–0	Mufulira Wanderers	ZAM
Raccah Rovers	NGR	Bye		
Hafia FC	GUI	Bye		
ASDR Fatima	CAR	1–1 1–1 (4–5p)	**Silures**	VOL
St Joseph	LBR	0–0 0–1	**Real Banjul**	GAM
Mighty Blackpool	SLE	2–0 0–2 (2–4p)	**Hearts of Oak**	GHA

* Both clubs withdrew

SECOND ROUND

MP Algiers	2–0 0–2 (1–2p)	**Union Douala**
Matlama FC	Bye	
Zamalek	W-O	Ogaden Anbassa
Africa Sports	1–0 0–2	**CS Imana**
Etoile du Congo	2–3 0–1	**US Goree**
SC Simba	0–0 0–2	**Raccah Rovers**
Hafia FC	1–0 0–1 (1–0p)	Silures
Hearts of Oak	2–0 1–1	Real Banjul

QUARTER-FINALS

Matlama FC	1–3 0–2	**Union Douala**
Zamalek	3–1 0–1*	**CS Imana**
US Goree	2–0 0–1	Raccah Rovers
Hafia FC	2–0 0–3	**Hearts of Oak**

* 2nd match abandoned. CS Imana qualified

SEMI-FINALS

CS Imana	1–2 0–1	**Union Douala**
US Goree	1–2 1–4	**Hearts of Oak**

FINAL

1st leg

Accra Stadium, Accra, 2–12–1979

HEARTS OF OAK 1
UNION DOUALA 0

2nd leg

Omnisports, Yaoundé, 16–12–1979

UNION DOUALA 1
HEARTS OF OAK 0

Union Douala won 5–3 on penalties

CUP WINNERS CUP

FIRST ROUND

Sportive Mongomo	EQG	1–3 1–5	**Canon Yaoundé**	CMR
Espoirs Nouakchott	MRT	1–0 0–1 (4–5p)	**Wallidan**	GAM
Pan African	TAN	0–1 1–0 (5–4p)	Omedla	ETH
AS Vita Club	ZAI	Bye		
Maxaquene Maputo	MOZ	0–3 0–1	**AC Sotema**	MAD
Maseru United	LES	2–1 4–5	FC Notwane	BOT
SC Gagnoa	CIV	3–1 1–0	Cedar United	LBR
Bendel Insurance	NGR	1–0 5–1	Petrosport FC	GAB
Horoya AC	GUI	Bye		
UDIB Bissau	BIS	1–1 1–2	**Bai-Bureh Warriors**	SLE
Al Nasr	LBA	W-O	USCA Bangui	CAR
CM Belcourt	ALG	Bye		
Kadiogo	VOL	0–1 1–0 (4–2p)	Asante Kotoko	GHA
Requins de l'At'q	BEN	Bye		
Nsambya FC	UGA	W-O	Al Nil Khartum	SUD
Gor Mahia	KEN	W-O	Al Ittihad	EGY

SECOND ROUND

Wallidan	1–2 0–1	**Canon Yaoundé**
Pan African	2–1 0–1	**AS Vita Club**
Maseru United	0–1 1–4	**AC Sotema**
Bendel Insurance	1–0 1–0	SC Gagnoa
Bai-Bureh Warriors	0–1 0–3	**Horoya AC**
CM Belcourt	4–2 1–0	Al Nasr
Kadiogo	3–1 1–1	Requins de l'Atlantique
Gor Mahia	0–0 1–1	Nsambya FC

QUARTER-FINALS

AS Vita Club	3–1 1–6	**Canon Yaoundé**
AC Sotema	0–2 2–0 (3–5p)	**Bendel Insurance**
CM Belcourt	0–3 1–3	**Horoya AC**
Kadiogo	1–2 1–2	**Gor Mahia**

SEMI-FINALS

Canon Yaoundé	1–0 0–0	Bendel Insurance
Gor Mahia	1–0 2–0	Horoya AC

FINAL

1st leg

Kasarani Stadium, Nairobi, 25–11–1979

GOR MAHIA 0
CANON YAOUNDE 2

2nd leg

Omnisport, Yaoundé, 9–12–1979

CANON YAOUNDE 6
GOR MAHIA 0

1980

CHAMPIONS CUP

FIRST ROUND

Canon Yaoundé	CMR	3–0 4–3	Primeiro de Agosto	ANG
Wallidan	GAM	1–1 0–1	**Silures**	VOL
Benfica	BIS	0–4 2–3	**Stella Abidjan**	CIV
Dragons de l'Ouème	BEN	0–0 0–3	**MP Algiers**	ALG
Olympique Real	CAR	0–1 1–3	**Etoile du Congo**	CGO
ASC Garde National	MRT	1–1 0–2	**Hafia FC**	GUI
FC Horsed	SOM	0–0 0–2	**Gor Mahia**	KEN
Bendel Insurance	NGR	W–O	Commercial Bank	UGA
Union Douala	CMR	Bye		
Linare FC	LES	2–1 0–3	**SC Simba**	TAN
Ela Nguema	EQG	1–0 0–4	**Semassi Sokodé**	TOG
Mighty Blackpool	SLE	1–2 0–2	**ASF Police**	SEN
AS Niamey	NIG	0–1 0–2	**Djoliba AC**	MLI
Anges ABC	GAB	2–3 2–2	**Hearts of Oak**	GHA
Fortior Mahajanga	MAD	W–O	**Limbe Leaf Wand.**	MAW
Costa do Sol	MOZ	0–0 1–3	**AS Bilima**	ZAI

SECOND ROUND

Silures	0–1 0–3	**Canon Yaoundé**
Stella Abidjan	4–2 1–3	**MP Algiers**
Etoile du Congo	0–1 1–0 (3–1p)	Hafia FC
Bendel Insurance	1–2 3–2	Gor Mahia
SC Simba	2–4 0–1	**Union Douala**
Semassi Sokodé	1–1 0–1	**ASF Police**
Djoliba AC	1–1 0–1	**Hearts of Oak**
AS Bilima	3–0 1–1	Fortior Mahajanga

QUARTER-FINALS

Canon Yaoundé	2–0 1–3	MP Algiers
Etoile du Congo	3–2 0–1	**Bendel Insurance**
ASF Police	0–3 3–2	**Union Douala**
Hearts of Oak	1–3 0–1	**AS Bilima**

SEMI-FINALS

Canon Yaoundé	0–0 4–2	Bendel Insurance
Union Douala	1–0 1–5	**AS Bilima**

FINAL

1st leg

Militare Garoua, Yaoundé, 30–11–1980

CANON YAOUNDE 2
AS BILIMA 2

2nd leg

20th May Stadium, Kinshasa, 14–12–1980

AS BILIMA 0
CANON YAOUNDE 3

CUP WINNERS CUP

FIRST ROUND

Township Rollers	BOT	2–2 1–4	**TP Mazembe**	ZAI
Kampala CC	UGA	3–1 2–1	Marine Club	SOM
Pan African	TAN	4–3 1–1	AC Sotema	MAD
Shooting Stars	NGR	Bye		
Ramogi Momb'a	KEN	Bye		
Matlama FC	LES	2–0 3–2	Palmeiras Beira	MOZ
ES Tunis	TUN	W–O	Ader Club	NIG
Kadiogo	VOL	4–1 1–4 (4–2p)	Wulum Stars	SLE
MA Hussein-Dey	ALG	7–0 0–1	ASC Ksar	MRT
Casa Sports	SEN	5–1 1–0	Bula FC	BIS
Dynamo Douala	CMR	Bye		
Eleven Wise FC	GHA	3–0 1–0	Sodiam Bangui	CAR
Buffles de Borgou	BEN	1–2 3–5	**Agaza Lomé**	TOG
Horoya AC	GUI	Bye		
Atletico Malabo	EQG	2–2 1–3	**US Mbila-Nzambi**	GAB
Africa Sports	CIV	W–O	Dingareh	GAM

SECOND ROUND

TP Mazembe	1–0 2–2	Kampala CC
Pan African	0–1 1–1	**Shooting Stars**
Matlama FC	1–1 0–0	**Ramogi Mombassa**
Kadiogo	W-O	ES Tunis
Casa Sports	1–1 0–2	**MA Hussein-Dey**
Eleven Wise FC	2–1 1–1	Dynamo Douala
Agaza Lomé	0–0 0–0 (2–1p)	Horoya AC
Africa Sports	3–2 1–1*	US Mbila-Nzambi

* 2nd match abandoned. Africa Sports qualified

QUARTER-FINALS

TP Mazembe	2–1 1–2 (3–0p)	Shooting Stars
Ramogi Mombassa	0–3 0–1	**Kadiogo**
Eleven Wise FC	1–1 1–4	**MA Hussein-Day**
Agaza Lomé	1–1 0–1	**Africa Sports**

SEMI-FINALS

TP Mazembe	2–0 1–1	Kadiogo
Africa Sports	1–0 2–2	MA Hussein-Dey

FINAL

1st leg

Houphouet Boigny, Abidjan, 25–11–1980

AFRICA SPORTS 1
TOUT PUISSANT MAZEMBE 3

2nd leg

20th May Stadium, Kinshasa, 7–12–1980

TOUT PUISSANT MAZEMBE 1
AFRICA SPORTS 0

1981

CHAMPIONS CUP

FIRST ROUND

Al Ahly Tripoli	LBA	0–0 1–2	**JE Tizi-Ouzou**	ALG
FC Horsed	SOM	W–O	SC Simba	TAN
Shooting Stars	NGR	7–1 0–2	Township Rollers	BOT
Dynamos Harare	ZIM	5–0 1–1	Linare FC	LES
Agaza Lomé	TOG	W–O	Benfica	BIS
US Mbila-Nzambi	GAB	1–0 0–1 (4–2p)	AS Real Bamako	MLI
Nile Breweries FC	UGA	2–1	USCA Bangui	CAR
Al Ahly Cairo	EGY	3–1 1–1	Abaluhya FC	KEN
AS Kaloum Star	GUI	2–1 1–0	Starlight	GAM
Asante Kotoko	GHA	3–0 1–1	Invincible Eleven	LBR
Canon Yaoundé	CMR	Bye		
SEIB Diourbel	SEN	2–1 1–2 (3–4p)	**ASEC Abidjan**	CIV
Nchanga Rangers	ZAM	1–0 4–0	Highlanders	SWZ
MMM Tamatave	MAD	2–4 0–2	**Costa do Sol**	MOZ
East End Lions	SLE	1–1 0–1	**Silures**	VOL
Primeiro de Agosto	ANG	1–1 1–2	**AS Vita Club**	ZAI

SECOND ROUND

FC Horsed	1–2	**JE Tizi-Ouzou**
Shooting Stars	1–2 0–3	**Dynamos Harare**
US Mbila-Nzambi	2–0 0–1	Agaza Lomé
Nile Breweries FC	2–0 0–5	**Al Ahly Cairo**
Asante Kotoko	1–0 1–3	**AS Kaloum Star**
Canon Yaoundé	0–0 1–3	**ASEC Abidjan**
Costa do Sol	1–3 1–3	**Nchanga Rangers**
Silures	0–1 3–3	**AS Vita Club**

QUARTER-FINALS

JE Tizi-Ouzou	3–0 2–2	Dynamos Harare
US Mbila-Nzambi	1–1 0–3	**Al Ahly Cairo**
AS Kaloum Star	2–1 2–1	ASEC Abidjan
AS Vita Club	4–1 0–2	**Nchanga Rangers**

SEMI-FINALS

JE Tizi-Ouzou	W-O	Al Ahly Cairo
AS Vita Club	1-0 0-0	AS Kaloum Star

FINAL

1st leg

Omnisport, Tizi-Ouzou, 27-11-1981

JEUNESSE ELECTRONIQUE TIZI-OUZOU	4
AS VITA CLUB	0

2nd leg

20th May Stadium, Kinshasa, 13-12-1981

AS VITA CLUB	0
JEUNESSE ELECTRONIQUE TIZI-OUZOU	1

CUP WINNERS CUP

FIRST ROUND

Nacional Benguela	ANG	1-7 0-6	**Union Douala**	CMR
Lubumbashi Sport	ZAI	4-3 0-1	**FC 105 Libreville**	GAB
Zindourma	NIG	*	ES Tunis	TUN
Kampala CC	UGA	1-0 0-2	**EP Setif**	ALG
Palmeiras Beira	MOZ	W-O	Highlanders	SWZ
Matlama FC	LES	1-1 0-2	**Power Dynamos**	ZAM
TP Mazembe	ZAI	5-0 2-0	ASDR Fatima	CAR
Sekondi Hasaacas	GHA	W-O	CS Nere	EQG
Reveil Daloa	CIV	2-1 0-1	**Djoliba AC**	MLI
Kadiogo	VOL	3-2 1-2	**Semassi Sokodé**	TOG
Gor Mahia	KEN	W-O	Coastal Union	TAN
Lavori Publici	SOM	W-O	Zamalek	EGY
Real Republicans	SLE	2-0 1-2	ASC Jeanne d'Arc	SEN
Gbessia AC	GUI	W-O	Estrela Negra	BIS
CAPS United	ZIM	8-1	AS St Michael	MAD
Stationary Stores	NGR	1-0 0-1 (5-4p)	Al Ahly Benghazi	LBA

* Both clubs withdrew

SECOND ROUND

FC 105 Libreville	1-3 0-1	**Union Douala**
EP Setif	Bye	
Palmeiras Beira	1-1 0-5	**Power Dynamos**
Sekondi Hasaacas	2-1 1-0	TP Mazembe
Djoliba AC	3-0 1-0	Semassi Sokodé
Gor Mahia	3-0 0-1	Lavori Publici
Real Republicans	1-2 0-2	**Gbessia AC**
CAPS United	1-0 0-1 (1-3p)	**Stationary Stores**

QUARTER-FINALS

Union Douala	5-0 1-1	EP Setif
Power Dynamos	1-0 1-3	**Sekondi Hasaacas**
Djoliba AC	2-0 0-1	Gor Mahia
Gbessia AC	0-1 1-3	**Stationary Stores**

SEMI-FINALS

Union Douala	2-1 2-3	Sekondi Hasaacas
Stationary Stores	0-0 1-0	Djoliba AC

FINAL

1st leg

Omnisport Yaoundé, 22-11-1981

UNION DOUALA	0
STATIONARY STORES	0

2nd leg

Surulere, Lagos, 5-12-1981

STATIONARY STORES	1
UNION DOUALA	2

1982

CHAMPIONS CUP

PRELIMINARY ROUND

AS Police	MRT	0-2 1-1	**Adjidjas FAP**	BEN
Atletico Malabo	EQG	0-1 1-3	**Sporting Moura**	CAR
Mhlume Peacemakers	SWZ	1-0 2-2	Maseru Brothers	LES
Vital'O	BUR	3-1 0-1	Rayon Sports	RWA

FIRST ROUND

Lavori Publici	SOM	0-0 0-1	**Al Ahly Cairo**	EGY
Textile Pungue	MOZ	1-2 0-2	**Young Africans**	TAN
Green Buffaloes	ZAM	0-0 2-0	Vital'O	BUR
AS Somasud	MAD	4-0 0-2	Mhlume Peacemakers	SWZ
Adjidjas FAP	BEN	1-3 1-3	**Stella Abidjan**	CIV
RS Kouba	ALG	1-1 3-1	KAC Kenitra	MAR
AS Kaloum Star	GUI	3-0 0-1	Real Republicans	SLE
Primeiro de Agosto	ANG	1-1 0-3	**Enugu Rangers**	NGR
FC Lupopo	ZAI	4-2 3-0	Sporting Moura	CAR
Dynamos Harare	ZIM	2-2 2-1	Defence Force	BOT
US Mbila-Nzambi	GAB	W-O	US Goree	SEN
Etoile du Congo	CGO	1-1 0-1	**AS Real Bamako**	MLI
Al Hilal	SUD	1-0 0-1 (4-1p)	JE Tizi-Ouzou	ALG
Kampala CC	UGA	3-0 1-4	AFC Leopards	KEN
Invincible Eleven	LBR	1-0 1-1	Tonnerre Yaoundé	CMR
Semassi Sokodé	TOG	3-2 0-2	**Asante Kotoko**	GHA

SECOND ROUND

Al Ahly Cairo	5-0 1-1	Young Africans
Green Buffaloes	3-0 3-1	AS Somasud
Stella Abidjan	1-0 0-1 (3-4p)	**RS Kouba**
Enugu Rangers	0-0 1-0	AS Kaloum Star
FC Lupopo	0-0 1-1	Dynamos Harare
US Mbila-Nzambi	1-0 0-2	**AS Real Bamako**
Al Hilal	0-2 1-3	**Kampala CC**
Invincible Eleven	0-0 0-3	**Asante Kotoko**

QUARTER-FINALS

Al Ahly Cairo	3-1 0-1	Green Buffaloes
Enugu Rangers	5-0 2-1	RS Kouba
FC Lupopo	2-0 2-3	AS Real Bamako
Asante Kotoko	6-0 1-1	Kampala CC

SEMI-FINALS

Enugu Rangers	1-0 0-4	**Al Ahly Cairo**
FC Lupopo	1-2 0-2	**Asante Kotoko**

FINAL

1st leg

International Stadium, Cairo, 28-11-1982

AL AHLY CAIRO	3
ASANTE KOTOKO	0

2nd leg

Kumasi Stadium, Kumasi, 12-12-1982

ASANTE KOTOKO	1
AL AHLY CAIRO	1

CUP WINNERS CUP

PRELIMINARY ROUND

Zindourma	NIG	3-0 0-4	**ASC Garde National**	MRT

FIRST ROUND

Hay el Arab	SUD	1-1 1-3	**Al Mokaoulum**	EGY
Desport. Maputo	MOZ	W-O	Printing Agency	SOM
ASC Garde National	MRT	0-1 0-2	**Dynamo Douala**	CMR
Kamboi Eagles	SLE	0-4 0-6	**Africa Sports**	CIV
CARA Brazzaville	CGO	1-0 0-2	**USK Algiers**	ALG
Bendel Insurance	NGR	2-0 1-0	Agaza Lomé	TOG
Mighty Barolle	LBR	0-0 0-1	**ASF Police**	SEN
Wallidan	GAM	1-0 1-4	**Hearts of Oak**	GHA
Requins de l'Atl'q	BEN	0-1 0-0	**Djoliba AC**	MLI
Ela Nguema	EQG	0-2 1-6	**Union Douala**	CMR
FC 105 Libreville	GAB	1-1 2-2	Gbessia AC	GUI
TAAG Luanda	ANG	0-0 0-0 (4-5p)	**AS Vita Club**	ZAI
Maseru Rovers	LES	0-1 0-1	**CAPS United**	ZIM
Gor Mahia	KEN	2-3	**Dynamo Fima**	MAD
Mukura VS	RWA	0-4 0-4	**Pan African**	TAN
Coffee FC	UGA	0-0 0-2	**Power Dynamos**	ZAM

SECOND ROUND

Al Mokaoulum .... 3–2 2–0 .... Desportivo Maputo
Dynamo Douala .... 1–2 0–1 .... **Africa Sports**
Bendel Insurance.................... 3–1 0–2 .... **USK Algiers**
ASF Police .... 1–0 0–1 (3–4p) .. **Hearts of Oak**
Union Douala .... 0–1 0–3 .... **Djoliba AC**
AS Vita Club .... 4–0 0–0 .... FC 105 Libreville
CAPS United .... 1–1 3–2 .... Dynamo Fima
Pan African .... 1–0 0–1 (3–5p) .. **Power Dynamos**

QUARTER-FINALS

Africa Sports .... 2–0 0–3 .... **Al Mokaoulum**
USK Algiers .... 2–1 0–2 .... **Hearts of Oak**
AS Vita Club .... 0–0 0–1 .... **Djoliba AC**
CAPS United .... 1–2 0–3 .... **Power Dynamos**

SEMI-FINALS

Al Mokaoulum .... 1–1 2–1 .... Hearts of Oak
Power Dynamos .... 2–1 0–0 .... Djoliba AC

FINAL

1st leg

Independence Stadium, Lusaka, 21–11–1982

POWER DYNAMOS 0
AL MOKAOULUM 2

2nd leg

International Stadium, Cairo, 3–12–1982

AL MOKAOULUM 2
POWER DYNAMOS 0

1983

CHAMPIONS CUP

PRELIMINARY ROUND

AS Police .... MRT .. 1–3 0–1 ... **Sierra Fisheries** .... SLE
ASC Diaraf .... SEN ... 4–0 2–0 ... Ports Authority .... GAM
Fantastique .... BUR .. 2–1 0–1 ... **Olympique Real** .... CAR
Highlanders .... SWZ . 2–1 1–0 ... Township Rollers .... BOT

FIRST ROUND

FC 105 Libreville .... GAB .. 1–2 0–2 ... **Asante Kotoko** .... GHA
CARA Brazzaville CGO . 6–1 2–0 ... Dragons FC .... EQG
AS Bilima .... ZAI .... 5–1 3–4 ... Semassi Sokodé .... TOG
Enugu Rangers .... NGR . 0–1 0–1 ... **Sierra Fisheries** .... SLE
KAC Kenitra .... MAR .... W–O ..... Benfica .... BIS
Djoliba AC .... MLI ... 0–0 0–1 ... **Hafia FC** .... GUI
Al Ahly Tripoli .... LBA ... 0–1 0–2 ... **JE Tizi-Ouzou** .... ALG
Africa Sports .... CIV0–0 0–0 (0–3p)**ASC Diaraf** .... SEN
Nkana Red Devils ZAM . 2–2 1–0 ... Highlanders .... SWZ
Wagad Mogadishu .... SOM .. 1–2 0–0 . **Pan African** .... TAN
Matlama FC .... LES ..... 1–2 1–3 . **Ferrovario Maputo** . MOZ
Nakivubu Villa ...... UGA .. 4–2 1–1 . Dynamo Fima .... MAD
Petro Atletico ...... ANG .. 3–1 3–2 . Olympique Real .... CAR
Canon Yaoundé ... CMR .. 2–0 0–1 . Dragons de l'Ouème ...... BEN
Dynamos Harare ZIM ..... 5–1 0–3 . AFC Leopards .... KEN
Al Ahly Cairo .... EGY ... 1–0 0–0 ... Al Merreikh .... SUD

SECOND ROUND

CARA Brazzaville .... 3–2 0–2 .... **Asante Kotoko**
AS Bilima .... 1–0 1–1 .... Sierra Fisheries
KAC Kenitra .... 4–0 0–0 .... Hafia FC
JE Tizi-Ouzou .... 0–1 0–0 .... **ASC Diaraf**
Nkana Red Devils ...... 0–0 0–0 (4–2p) .. Pan African
Ferrovario Maputo .... 1–2 0–3 .... **Nakivubu Villa**
Petro Atletico .... 0–0 3–4 .... **Canon Yaoundé**
Al Ahly Cairo .... 4–1 2–1 .... Dynamos Harare

QUARTER-FINALS

Asante Kotoko .... 3–0 0–2 .... AS Bilima
KAC Kenitra .... 1–1 1–2 .... **ASC Diaraf**
Nkana Red Devils .... 4–0 1–2 .... Nakivubu Villa
Al Ahly Cairo .... 5–0 0–1 .... Canon Yaoundé

SEMI-FINALS

ASC Diaraf .... 2–1 0–2 .... **Asante Kotoko**
Nkana Red Devils .... 0–0 0–2 .... **Al Ahly Cairo**

FINAL

1st leg

International Stadium, Cairo, 27–11–1983

AL AHLY CAIRO 0
ASANTE KOTOKO 0

2nd leg

Kumasi Stadium, Kumasi, 11–12–1983

ASANTE KOTOKO 1
AL AHLY CAIRO 0

CUP WINNERS CUP

PRELIMINARY ROUND

Maseru Rovers ..... LES .... 2–1 1–1 ... Young Aces .... SWZ
Vital'O .... BUR .. 1–2 3–0 ... Gor Mahia .... KEN

FIRST ROUND

Vital'O .... BUR .. 0–0 1–6 ... **Al Mokaoulum** .... EGY
Kampala CC .... UGA . 2–0 0–1 ... FC Horsed .... SOM
UBAC Bangui .... CAR .. 0–0 0–2 ... **Al Ahly Wad Medani** SUD
KMKM Zanzibar .... TAN .. 2–3 0–4 ... **CAPS United** .... ZIM
Green Buffaloes ... ZAM . 5–1 1–1 ... Maxaquene Maputo ..... MOZ
Maseru Rovers .... LES .... 3–2 0–2 ... **AC Sotema** .... MAD
ASF Police .... SEN ... 1–0 0–0 ... Raja Casablanca .... MAR
Bai-Bureh Warriors . SLE .... 0–1 2–3 ... **Horoya AC** .... GUI
ASEC Abidjan .... CIV .... 4–1 1–2 ... Buffles du Borgou .... BEN
CAP Owendo .... GAB .. 0–1 0–0 ... **Stationary Stores** .... NGR
Trarza Rosso .... MRT .. 0–0 1–8 ... **DNC Algiers** .... ALG
Stade Malien .... MLI ...... W–O ..... Ajuda Sports .... BIS
Ela Nguema .... EQG .. 0–1 0–4 ... **AS Vita Club** .... ZAI
Primeiro de Maio ...... ANG . 3–2 0–2 ... **AS Cheminots** .... CGO
Al Nasr .... LBA ... 1–1 0–4 ... **Sekondi Hasaacas** ... GHA
Dragons Yaoundé ..... CMR . 0–3 1–4 ... **Agaza Lomé** .... TOG

SECOND ROUND

Al Mokaoulum .... 2–2 2–2 (3–1p) . Kampala CC
Al Ahly Wad Medani .... 0–2 0–5 .... **CAPS United**
Green Buffaloes .... 2–0 0–0 .... AC Sotema
Horoya AC .... 2–1 1–0 .... ASF Police
ASEC Abidjan .... W–O .... Stationary Stores
DNC Algiers .... 2–0 1–2 .... Stade Malien
AS Cheminots .... 1–2 0–2 .... **AS Vita Club**
Sekondi Hasaacas .... 0–0 1–4 .... **Agaza Lomé**

QUARTER-FINALS

CAPS United .... 2–1 0–2 .... **Al Mokaoulum**
Green Buffaloes .... 1–0 0–2 .... **Horoya AC**
DNC Algiers .... 1–2 0–1 .... **ASEC Abidjan**
Agaza Lomé .... 2–0 0–2 (4–2p) . AS Vita Club

SEMI-FINALS

Horoya AC .... 0–1 0–3 .... **Al Mokaoulum**
ASEC Abidjan .... 2–2 0–0 .... **Agaza Lomé**

FINAL

1st leg

Eyadema, Lome, 20–11–1983

AGAZA LOME 0
AL MOKAOULUM 1

2nd leg

International Stadium, Cairo, 2–12–1983

AL MOKAOULUM 0
AGAZA LOME 0

1984

CHAMPIONS CUP

PRELIMINARY ROUND

Township Rollers	BOT	0–2 1–1	**LPF Maseru**	LES
Desport. Maputo	MOZ	1–1 1–0	Manzini Wanderers	SWZ
Real Banjul	GAM	0–0 0–2	**Sporting Clube**	BIS
Real Republicans	SLE	1–0 0–0	Invincible Eleven	LBR
Atletico Malabo	EQG	2–0 1–6	**Primeiro de Maio**	ANG
Kiyovu Sports	RWA	W–O	ADMARC Tigers	MAW
US Ouagadougou	VOL	0–2 1–3	**Dragons de l'Ouème**	BEN

FIRST ROUND

Zamalek	EGY	3–0 1–1	CS Sfax	TUN
Young Africans	TAN	1–1 0–1	**Gor Mahia**	KEN
Al Hilal	SUD	1–1 0–1	**Printing Agency**	SOM
Nkana Red Devils	ZAM	5–0 1–0	LPF Maseru	LES
Kampala CC	UGA	6–1 3–2	Desportivo Maputo	MOZ
HTMF Mahajanga	MAD	0–3	**Dynamos Harare**	ZIM
Sporting Clube	BIS	W–O	Hafia FC	GUI
JE Tizi-Ouzou	ALG	1–0 2–1	Real Republicans	SLE
Africa Sports	CIV	2–1 2–4	**Semassi Sokodé**	TOG
Asante Kotoko	GHA	1–1 1–2	**Primeiro de Maio**	ANG
Sanga Balende	ZAI	2–1 4–1	Kiyovu Sports	RWA
FC 105 Libreville	GAB	3–1 5–1	ASDR Fatima	CAR
Al Medina	LBA	0–0 1–2	**MAS Fès**	MAR
AS Real Bamako	MLI	2–2 0–2	**Dragons de l'Ouème**	BEN
Vital'O	BUR	1–0 0–3	**Tonnerre Yaoundé**	CMR
Shooting Stars	NGR	2–0 0–1	SEIB Diourbel	SEN

SECOND ROUND

Zamalek	1–0*	Gor Mahia
Printing Agency	2–1 0–3	**Nkana Red Devils**
Kampala CC	0–0 1–2	**Dynamos Harare**
JE Tizi-Ouzou	W–O	Sporting Clube Bissau
Primeiro de Maio	2–0 0–2 (3–4p)	**Semassi Sokodé**
Sanga Balende	2–0 0–2**	**FC 105 Libreville**
MAS Fès	3–0 0–1	Dragons de l'Ouème
Shooting Stars	4–0 0–4 (5–4p)	Tonnerre Yaoundé

* Match abandoned. Tie awarded to Zamalek

** 2nd match abandoned. FC 105 qualify

QUARTER-FINALS

Nkana Red Devils	1–1 1–5	**Zamalek**
Dynamos Harare	2–0 0–2 (2–3p)	**JE Tizi-Ouzou**
Semassi Sokodé	W–O	FC 105 Libreville
MAS Fès	1–1 1–4	**Shooting Stars**

SEMI-FINALS

JE Tizi-Ouzou	3–1 0–3	**Zamalek**
Shooting Stars	5–1 1–2	Semassi Sokodé

FINAL

1st leg

International Stadium, Cairo, 23–11–1984

ZAMALEK 2
SHOOTING STARS 0

2nd leg

Surulere, Lagos, 8–12–1984

SHOOTING STARS 0
ZAMALEK 0

CUP WINNERS CUP

PRELIMINARY ROUND

Avia Sports	CAR	0–0 0–1*	GD Lage	EQG
Mighty Barolle	LBR	3–0 0–0	Hawks	GAM
Pantheres Noires	RWA	0–0 1–1	International FC	BUR

* 2nd match abandoned after 80 minutes. Tie awarded to Avia

FIRST ROUND

Al Ahly Cairo	EGY	3–1 2–0	CLAS Casablanca	MAR
MP Algiers	ALG	4–0 0–2	Racing Club	VOL
Pantheres Noires	RWA	0–3 1–3	**Scarlets Nakuru**	KEN
Costa do Sol	MOZ	0–2 1–0	**Nakivubu Villa**	UGA
Requins de l'Atl'q	BEN	2–1 0–3	**ASEC Abidjan**	CIV
Great Olympics	GHA	0–0 4–0	Djoliba AC	MLI
Al Merreikh	SUD	1–0 1–0	KMKM Zanzibar	TAN
Al Mokaoulum	EGY	7–0 0–2	FC Horsed	SOM
ES du Sahel	TUN	1–1 0–1	**Al Ahly Tripoli**	LBA
ASC Diaraf	SEN	2–0 1–2	Mighty Blackpool	SLE
Red Arrows	ZAM	9–1 3–1	Linare FC	LES
Mighty Barolle	LBR	2–1 1–3	**AS Vita Club**	ZAI
Agaza Lomé	TOG	W–O	CAP Owendo	GAB
Enugu Rangers	NGR	W–O	Horoya AC	GUI
Dynamo Fima	MAD	6–1 0–1	Highlanders	SWZ
Canon Yaoundé	CMR	3–0 1–1	Avia Sports	CAR

SECOND ROUND

MP Algiers	1–0 1–3	**Al Ahly Cairo**
Scarlets Nakuru	0–3 1–2	**Nakivubu Villa**
Great Olympics	2–1 0–2	**ASEC Abidjan**
Al Merreikh	0–0 0–2	**Al Mokaoulum**
ASC Diaraf	2–1 0–3	**Al Ahly Tripoli**
AS Vita Club	2–1 0–1	**Red Arrows**
Enugu Rangers	1–0 1–0	Agaza Lomé
Dynamo Fima	0–1 0–1	**Canon Yaoundé**

QUARTER-FINALS

Al Ahly Cairo	1–0 1–2	Nakivubu Villa
ASEC Abidjan	2–1 1–3	**Al Mokaoulum**
Red Arrows	2–0 0–3	**Al Ahly Tripoli**
Canon Yaoundé	5–0 0–3	Enugu Rangers

SEMI-FINALS

Al Ahly Cairo	0–0 1–1	Al Mokaoulum
Canon Yaoundé	1–0 0–1 (4–5p)	*Al Ahly Tripoli

* Al Ahly Tripoli withdrew before the final and were replaced by Canon

FINAL

1st leg

International Stadium, Cairo, 30–11–1984

AL AHLY CAIRO 1
CANON YAOUNDE 0

2nd leg

Omnisport, Yaoundé, 30–12–1984

CANON YAOUNDE 1
AL AHLY CAIRO 0

Al Ahly Cairo won 4–2 on penalties

1985

CHAMPIONS CUP

PRELIMINARY ROUND

ASC Garde Nat'l	MRT	1–0 2–1	Sporting Clube	BIS
Ground Force	ETH	1–2 0–2	**Vital'O**	BUR
Highlanders	SWZ	4–1 0–2	LFP Maseru	LES
Petro Atletico	ANG	4–1 1–1	AS Tempete Mocaf	CAR
Ports Authority	GAM	W–O	ASFA Ouagadougou	BFA

FIRST ROUND

FAR Rabat	MAR	8–0	Ports Authority	GAM
CA Bizerte	TUN	1–0 1–1	ASC Garde National	MRT
Enugu Rangers	NGR	2–0 2–1	Petro Atletico	ANG
AS Kaloum Star	GUI	1–0 2–2	Real Republicans	SLE
Scarlets Nakuru	KEN	2–1 0–1	**Vital'O**	BUR
Tonnerre Yaoundé	CMR	2–1 0–1	**AS Sogara**	GAB
Nakivubu Villa	UGA	4–2 0–2	**Al Hilal**	SUD
Zamalek	EGY	W–O	Marine Club	SOM
Stella Abidjan	CIV	1–1 0–3	**US Goree**	SEN

Lions de l'Atakory	BEN	0–1 0–3	**Hearts of Oak**	GHA
Power Dynamos	ZAM	4–0 2–1	KMKM Zanzibar	TAN
Black Rhinos	ZIM	1–0 3–1	Highlanders	SWZ
GCR Mascara	ALG	4–0 0–3	Al Ittihad	LBA
Invincible Eleven	LBR	3–0 1–1*	**Stade Malien**	MLI
Agaza Lomé	TOG	0–1 1–2	**CARA Brazzaville**	CGO
AS Bilima	ZAI	3–0 1–0	Township Rollers	BOT

* Invincible Eleven disqualified. Tie awarded to Stade Malien

SECOND ROUND

CA Bizerte	1–4 1–0	**FAR Rabat**
AS Kaloum Star	2–0 1–3	Enugu Rangers
Vital'O	3–1 1–1	AS Sogara
Zamalek	4–0 1–1	Al Hilal
US Goree	3–0 0–1	Hearts of Oak
Power Dynamos	0–2 1–1	**Black Rhinos**
Stade Malien	2–0 0–3	**GCR Mascara**
AS Bilima	1–1 1–0	CARA Brazzaville

QUARTER-FINALS

FAR Rabat	3–0 0–3 (3–1p)	AS Kaloum Star
Vital'O	1–0 2–5	**Zamalek**
Black Rhinos	2–0 0–3	**US Goree**
GCR Mascara	0–0 0–3	**AS Bilima**

SEMI-FINALS

Zamalek	1–0 0–1 (3–4p)	**FAR Rabat**
AS Bilima	2–0 0–1	US Goree

FINAL

1st leg

Moulay Abdallah Stadium, Rabat, 30–11–1985

FORCES ARMEES ROYAL RABAT 5
AS BILIMA 2

2nd leg

Mobuto Stadium, Lubumbashi, 22–12–1985

AS BILIMA 1
FORCES ARMEES ROYAL RABAT 1

CUP WINNERS CUP

PRELIMINARY ROUND

Drag. de l'Ouème	BEN	8–0 2–1	Atletico Malabo	EQG
International FC	BUR	3–1 0–2*	**Waxool**	SOM
Trarza Rosso	MRT	W-O	Racing Club	BFA

* Waxool disqualified. Tie awarded to International FC

FIRST ROUND

AS Marsa	TUN	0–0 0–4	**Al Ahly Cairo**	EGY
SC Simba	TAN	5–0 0–1	Shoe Factory	ETH
Primeiro de Agosto	ANG	1–0 0–3	**Dihep di Nkam**	CMR
Drag. de l'Ouème	BEN	3–1 0–1	CS Imana	ZAI
International FC	BUR	1–2 0–3	**Kampala CC**	UGA
Lioli FC	LES	1–1 1–2	**Gweru United**	ZIM
Stade Abidjan	CIV	3–1 1–5	**FC 105 Libreville**	GAB
Trarza Rosso	MRT	1–1 0–2	**Al Nasr**	LBA
AFC Leopards	KEN	2–0 1–2	Al Merreikh	SUD
Manzini Wanderers	SWZ	0–0 0–2	**Mufulira Wanderers**	ZAM
Mighty Barolle	LBR	1–0 0–3	**Asante Kotoko**	GHA
SCAF Tocages	CAR	3–2 0–2	**ASFOSA Lomé**	TOG
ASC Jeanne d'Arc	SEN	1–0 1–0	RS Kenitra	MAR
Djoliba AC	MLI	0–0 0–2	**MP Oran**	ALG
Horoya AC	GUI	2–0 0–1	Wallidan	GAM
Old Edwardians	SLE	0–0 1–4	**Leventis United**	NGR

SECOND ROUND

SC Simba	2–1 0–2	**Al Ahly Cairo**
Dragons de l'Ouème	1–0 1–2	Dihep di Nkam
Kampala CC	3–1 1–1	Gweru United
FC 105 Libreville	2–1 1–3	**Al Nasr**
Mufulira Wanderers	1–1 1–1 (3–5p)	**AFC Leopards**
ASFOSA Lomé	1–1 0–0	**Asante Kotoko**
ASC Jeanne d'Arc	0–0 1–1	MP Oran
Leventis United	0–0 1–1	Horoya AC

QUARTER-FINALS

Dragons de l'Ouème	1–1 0–4	**Al Ahly Cairo**
Kampala CC	1–0 0–1 (2–4p)	**Al Nasr**
Asante Kotoko	2–0 0–2 (4–5p)	**AFC Leopards**
ASC Jeanne d'Arc	0–1 0–1	**Leventis United**

SEMI-FINALS

Al Ahly Cairo	W-O	Al Nasr
Leventis United	2–0 0–1	AFC Leopards

FINAL

1st leg

International Stadium, Cairo, 22–11–1985

AL AHLY CAIRO 2
LEVENTIS UNITED 0

2nd leg

Surulere, Lagos, 7–12–1985

LEVENTIS UNITED 1
AL AHLY CAIRO 0

1986

CHAMPIONS CUP

PRELIMINARY ROUND

UDIB Bissau	BIS	W-O	East End Lions	SLE
Etoile Filante	BFA	W-O	ASC Ksar	MRT
Lioli FC	LES	2–3 0–4	**Maji Maji**	TAN
Manzini Wanderers	SWZ	1–3 2–3	**AC Sotema**	MAD
Pantheres Noires	RWA	3–0 2–1	Wagad Mogadishu	SOM
SCAF Tocages	CAR	4–1 2–1	Juvenil Reyes	EQG

FIRST ROUND

Zamalek	EGY	5–1 1–1	Pantheres Noires	RWA
Dynamos Harare	ZIM	5–1	Maji Maji	TAN
FC Darnah	LBA	2–1 0–2	**Kampala CC**	UGA
International FC	BUR	2–1 1–1	US Tshinkunku	ZAI
FAR Rabat	MAR	W-O	UDIB Bissau	BIS
FC 105 Libreville	GAB	1–0 0–2	**SCAF Tocages**	CAR
ASC Jeanne d'Arc	SEN	0–0 0–2	**MAS Fès**	MAR
Canon Yaoundé	CMR	3–0 0–2	Primeiro de Maio	ANG
Nkana Red Devils	ZAM	4–1 1–2	AC Sotema	MAD
Kenya Breweries	KEN	0–0 1–2	**Brewery Jimma**	ETH
Horoya AC	GUI	4–0 1–3	Invincible Eleven	LBR
Hearts of Oak	GHA	2–0 0–1	Wallidan	GAM
Al Merreikh	SUD	2–1 0–1	**ES Tunis**	TUN
JE Tizi-Ouzou	ALG	5–0 1–1	Etoile Filante	BFA
ASFOSA Lomé	TOG	0–2 0–2	**New Nigeria Bank**	NGR
Africa Sports	CIV	1–0 0–1 (4–3p)	Requins de l'Atl'q	BEN

SECOND ROUND

Zamalek	2–1 2–0	Dynamos Harare
Kampala CC	1–1 1–2	**International FC**
SCAF Tocages	0–1 1–6	**FAR Rabat**
MAS Fès	1–0 0–3	**Canon Yaoundé**
Brewery Jimma	0–0 0–0 (3–4p)	**Nkana Red Devils**
Horoya AC	1–2 0–2	**Hearts of Oak**
JE Tizi–Ouzou	2–1 0–1	**ES Tunis**
Africa Sports	5–0 0–2	New Nigeria Bank

QUARTER-FINALS

International FC	1–0 0–3	**Zamalek**
Canon Yaoundé	2–0 0–1	FAR Rabat
Nkana Red Devils	2–0 1–1	Hearts of Oak
Africa Sports	1–0 1–2	ES Tunis

SEMI-FINALS

Canon Yaoundé	2–1 0–2	**Zamalek**
Nkana Red Devils	1–1 0–0	**Africa Sports**

FINAL

1st leg

International Stadium, Cairo, 28–11–1986

ZAMALEK 2
AFRICA SPORTS 0

2nd leg

Houphouet Boigny, Abidjan, 21–12–1986

AFRICA SPORTS 2
ZAMALEK 0

Zamalek won 4–2 on penalties

CUP WINNERS CUP

PRELIMINARY ROUND

Kamboi Eagles	SLE	W–O		AS Police	MRT
Ela Nguemb	EQG	0–0	1–3	**AS Fonct. Bobo-D**	BFA
Al Merreikh	SUD	1–1	0–1	**AS Tempete Mocaf**	CAR
LPF Maseru	LES	0–0	2–3	**Fortior Mahajanga**	MAD
Highlanders	SWZ	4–2	1–2	Kiyovu Sports	RWA
Starlight	GAM	3–1	1–1	Benfica	BIS
Vital'O	BUR	1–0	1–2	Petrolium	SOM

FIRST ROUND

Al Ahly Cairo	EGY	2–0	0–1	Uganda Express FC	UGA
Highlanders	SWZ	1–1	2–2	Shoe Factory	ETH
Fortior Mahajanga	MAD	2–2	0–1	**Miembeni**	TAN
Highlanders	ZIM	1–3	0–2	**Power Dynamos**	ZAM
Ferroviaro Huila	ANG	1–3	0–0	**FC Kalamu**	ZAI
Vital'O	BUR	1–1	0–1	**AFC Leopards**	KEN
MP Oran	ALG	W–O		Kamboi Eagles	SLE
AS Tempete Mocaf	CAR	2–0	0–3	**Al Ismaili**	EGY
CS Hammam-Lif	TUN	Bye			
Starlight	GAM	1–1	1–1 (3–4p)	**ASC Diaraf**	SEN
AS Kaloum Star	GUI	1–0	0–2	**DHJ Jadida**	MAR
AS Fonct. Bobo–D	BFA	1–0	1–5	**Al Ahly Tripoli**	LBA
Foadan Dapaong	TOG	3–0	1–2	SC Gagnoa	CIV
Mighty Barolle	LBR	2–1	0–0	Union Douala	CMR
Dragons de l'Ouème	BEN	2–0 *		Abiola Babes	NGR
AS Sogara	GAB	3–0	0–1	Sekondi Hasaacas	GHA

* Match abandoned. Both teams disqualified

SECOND ROUND

Highlanders	0–5	0–3	**Al Ahly Cairo**
Miembeni	1–1	0–5	**Power Dynamos**
AFC Leopards	1–1	1–3	**FC Kalamu**
Al Ismaili	1–0	0–0	MP Oran
ASC Diaraf	2–1	0–1	**CS Hammam-Lif**
DHJ Jadida	W-O		Al Ahly
Mighty Barolle	3–2	0–2	**Foadan Dapaong**
AS Sogara	Bye		

QUARTER-FINALS

Al Ahly Cairo	2–0	0–1	Power Dynamos
FC Kalamu	2–0	0–3	**Al Ismaili**
DHJ Jadida	0–0	0–0 (3–4p)	**CS Hammam-Lif**
AS Sogara	3–1	2–1	Foadan Dapaong

SEMI-FINALS

Al Ahly Cairo	0–0	1–1	Al Ismaili
CS Hammam-Lif	0–0	0–3	**AS Sogara**

FINAL

1st leg

International Stadium, Cairo, 21–11–1986

AL AHLY CAIRO 3
AS SOGARA 0

2nd leg

Omar Bongo, Libreville, 7–12–86

AS SOGARA 2
AL AHLY CAIRO 0

1987

CHAMPIONS CUP

PRELIMINARY ROUND

BTM Antananarivo	MAD	1–1	1–2	**Maji Maji**	TAN
Juvenil Reyes	EQG	W-O		Sporting Moura	CAR
Matlama FC	LES	1–0	2–0	Gaborone United	BOT
Municipality	SOM	1–0	0–2	**Pantheres Noires**	RWA
Sporting Clube	BIS	W–O		Old Edwardians	SLE
Petro Atletico	ANG	3–1	1–0	Maxaquene Maputo	MOZ
Tamil Cadets SC	MRI	3–2	1–2	**Highlanders**	SWZ

FIRST ROUND

Al Ahly Cairo	EGY	4–0	1–1	Pantheres Noires	RWA
AFC Leopards	KEN	1–0	1–0	Maji Maji	TAN
Mighty Barolle	LBR	2–1	0–0	Horoya AC	GUI
Africa Sports	CIV	2–1	1–0	ASFOSA Lome	TOG
Nkana Red Devils	ZAM	1–1	1–0	Petro Atletico	ANG
Zamalek	EGY	W-O		Juvenil Reyes	EQG
WAC Casablanca	MAR	3–1*		AS Police	MRT
Asante Kotoko	GHA	W-O		Sporting Clube	BIS
Requins de l'Atl'q	BEN	0–0	0–7	**Canon Yaoundé**	CMR
ASC Jeanne d'Arc	SEN	2–1	0–2	**EP Setif**	ALG
Dynamos Harare	ZIM	6–1	2–1	Highlanders	SWZ
FC Lupopo	ZAI	1–0	0–0	FC 105 Libreville	GAB
ES Ham.-Sousse	TUN	W–O		Al Ittihad	LBA
AS Real Bamako	MLI	0–0	0–4	**Leventis United**	NGR
Nakivubu Villa	UGA	4–0	1–0	Matlama FC	LES
Al Hilal	SUD	2–0	1–0	International FC	BUR

* AS Police disqualified. Tie awrded to WAC

SECOND ROUND

Al Ahly Cairo	6–0	1–2	AFC Leopards
Africa Sports	2–1	1–1	Mighty Barolle
Nkana Red Devils	1–0	0–2	**Zamalek**
WAC Casablanca	1–1	0–2	**Asante Kotoko**
EP Setif	0–0	1–2	**Canon Yaoundé**
Dynamos Harare	3–1	1–1	FC Lupopo
ES Hammam-Sousse	2–1	0–1	**Leventis United**
Nakivubu Villa	2–1	0–1	**Al Hilal**

QUARTER-FINALS

Africa Sports	2–0	0–2 (2–4p)	**Al Ahly Cairo**
Zamalek	2–0	1–5	**Asante Kotoko**
Canon Yaoundé	2–1	1–1	Dynamos Harare
Al Hilal	2–1	0–0	Leventis United

SEMI-FINALS

Al Ahly Cairo	2–0	0–1	Asante Kotoko
Al Hilal	1–0	0–1 (4–1p)	Canon Yaoundé

FINAL

1st leg

The Stadium, Khartum, 29–11–1987

AL HILAL 0
AL AHLY CAIRO 0

2nd leg

International Stadium, Cairo, 18–12–1987

AL AHLY CAIRO 2
AL HILAL 0

CUP WINNERS CUP

PRELIMINARY ROUND

Stade Malien	MLI	W–O		Real Republicans	SLE
RLDF Maseru	LES	1–1	1–1 (5–3p)	Swallows FC	SWZ

FIRST ROUND

Marine Club	SOM	0–2	0–3	**Gor Mahia**	KEN
Al Merreikh	SUD	2–0	1–0	Blue Bats	UGA
Okwahu United	GHA	2–0	1–1	FC Kalamu	ZAI

LPRC Oilers	LBR	1–1 0–0	**Entente II Lomé**	TOG
Inter Club Luanda	ANG	1–1 0–2	**Vital'O**	BUR
Highlanders	ZIM	1–0 0–1 (2–5p)	**Miembeni**	TAN
Rail Douala	CMR	1–0 0–2	**US Mbila-Nzambi**	GAB
CO Kakande Boke	GUI	0–3 1–4	**Dragons de l'Ouème**	BEN
Abiola Babes	NGR	W–O	Ela Nguema	EQG
ASF Douanes	SEN	2–0 1–4	**ASEC Abidjan**	CIV
RLDF Maseru	LES	3–2 0–2	**HTMF Mahajanga**	MAD
Estrela Vemelha	MOZ	0–1 0–3	**Nchanga Rangers**	ZAM
WKF Collo	ALG	W–O	FC Batafa	BIS
Stade Malien	MLI	0–1 0–4	**FAR Rabat**	MAR
Mukura VS	RWA	1–1 0–5	**Al Tersana**	EGY
ASC Garde National	MRT	1–3 0–4	**ES Tunis**	TUN

SECOND ROUND

Al Merreikh	1–1 0–0	**Gor Mahia**
Entente II Lomé	2–0 0–0	Okwahu United
Miembeni	0–1 1–3	**Vital'O**
Dragons de l'Ouème	1–0 0–1 (4–2p)	US Mbila-Nzambi
Abiola Babes	2–0 0–2 (4–2p)	ASEC Abidjan
HTMF Mahajanga	2–2 1–2	**Nchanga Rangers**
WKF Collo	3–2 1–5	**FAR Rabat**
Al Tersana	0–0 0–2	**ES Tunis**

QUARTER-FINALS

Gor Mahia	4–1 0–0	Entente II Lomé
Dragons de l'Ouème	2–0 0–1	Vital'O
Nchanga Rangers	1–1 1–2	**Abiola Babes**
FAR Rabat	1–0 1–3	**ES Tunis**

SEMI-FINALS

Dragons de l'Ouème	0–0 2–3	**Gor Mahia**
Abiola Babes	1–0 0–2	**ES Tunis**

FINAL

1st leg

El Mensah, Tunis, 21–11–1987

ESPERANCE SPORTIVE TUNIS 2
GOR MAHIA 2

2nd leg

Kasarani, Nairobi, 5–12–1987

GOR MAHIA 1
ESPERANCE SPORTIVE TUNIS 1

Gor Mahia won on away goals

1988

CHAMPIONS CUP

PRELIMINARY ROUND

Ela Nguema	EQG	0–1 0–4	**Etoile du Congo**	CGO
Manzini Wand.	SWZ	2–0 4–1	Township Rollers	BOT
Pantheres Noires	RWA	2–2 0–1	**Wagad Mogadishu**	SOM
RLDF Maseru	LES	2–0 0–3	**Sunrise FC**	MRI
Sierra Fisheries	SLE	0–1 0–0	**AS Police**	MRT

FIRST ROUND

Stade Malien	MLI	1–1 0–4	**EP Setif**	ALG
ES Ham.-Sousse	TUN	W–O	Al Nasr	LBA
Etoile de Congo	CGO	0–0 0–2	**International FC**	BUR
Asante Kotoko	GHA	2–0 0–2 (2–4p)	**FC 105 Libreville**	GAB
Sunrise FC	MRI	2–1 2–2	Black Rhinos	ZIM
Matchedje Maputo	MOZ	3–1 1–2	Jos Nosy Be	MAD
Manzini Wanderers	SWZ	1–4 1–1	**Nakivubu Villa**	UGA
Young Africans	TAN	0–0 0–4	**Al Ahly Cairo**	EGY
Invincible Eleven	LBR	0–1 0–0	**FAR Rabat**	MAR
AS Police	MRT	2–0 0–2 (9–10p)	**SEIB Diourbel**	SEN
Shabana Kisii	KEN	1–0 1–4	**Kabwe Warriors**	ZAM
Wagad Mogadishu	SOM	1–1 0–6	**Al Hilal**	SUD
AS Kaloum Star	GUI	0–2 1–3	**Africa Sports**	CIV
Petro Atletico	ANG	2–1 1–0	TP Mazembe	ZAI
Doumbe Sans' Mango	TOG	0–1 0–1	**Tonnerre Yaoundé**	CMR
Iwuan'nwu Owerri	NGR	2–0 1–0	Requins de l'Atl'q	BEN

SECOND ROUND

ES Hammam-Sousse	2–1 0–2	**EP Setif**
FC 105 Libreville	2–1 1–1	International FC
Sunrise FC	2–0 1–5	**Matchedje Maputo**
Nakivubu Villa	2–3 1–3	**Al Ahly Cairo**
FAR Rabat	5–0 1–2	AS Police Dakar
Kabwe Warriors	0–0 1–3	**Al Hilal**
Africa Sports	3–0 1–2	Petro Atletico
Iwuanyanwu Owerri	2–0 2–3	Tonnerre Yaoundé

QUARTER-FINALS

FC 105 Libreville	3–1 0–3	**EP Setif**
Al Ahly Cairo	2–0 0–1	Matchedje Maputo
Al Hilal	1–0 0–3	**FAR Rabat**
Iwuanyanwu Owerri	2–0 1–2	Africa Sports

SEMI-FINALS

EP Setif	2–0 0–2 (4–2p)	Al Ahly Cairo
Iwuanyanwu Owerri	4–1 1–4 (5–3p)	FAR Rabat

FINAL

1st leg

Liberty Stadium, Ibadan, 26–11–1988, 25 000

IWUANYANWU OWERRI 1
ENTENTE PLASTICIENS SETIF 0

2nd leg

Constantine, 9–12–1988, 40 000

ENTENTE PLASTICIENS SETIF 4
IWUANYANWU OWERRI 0

CUP WINNERS CUP

PRELIMINARY ROUND

Matlama FC	LES	2–1 0–4	**Maxaquene Maputo**	MOZ
Mukura VS	RWA	5–1 0–3	Highlanders	SWZ
AS Sigui Kayes	MLI	0–0 0–0 (3–4)	**Real Republicans**	SLE
Wallidan	GAM	3–0 *	AS Douanes	MRT

* Match abandoned after 64 minutes. Tie awarded to Wallidan

FIRST ROUND

CA Bizerte	TUN	0–1 1–0 (6–5p)	USM El Harrach	ALG
FC Horsed	SOM	0–0 1–1	Al Mourada	SUD
Real Republicans	SLE	W–O	Al Medina	LBA
Wallidan	GAM	W–O	KAC Marrakech	MAR
AFC Leopards	KEN	1–1 4–0	CAPS United	ZIM
Kampala CC	UGA	0–1 0–1	**FC Kalamu**	ZAI
ASC Jeanne d'Arc	SEN	3–0 2–1	ASKO Kara	TOG
Atletico Malabo	EQG	3–1 0–5	**Diamant Yaoundé**	CMR
US Mbila-Nzambi	GAB	1–1 0–0*	**Inter Club**	CGO
ASC Bouaké	CIV	W–O	Dragons de l'Ouéme	BEN
Mukura VS	RWA	0–1 0–1	**Gor Mahia**	KEN
BTM Antana'rivo	MAD	3–1 0–0	Miembeni	TAN
Muzinga	BUR	0–1 1–1	**Ferroviaro Lubango**	ANG
Maxaquene Maputo	MOZ	1–3 0–1	**Power Dynamos**	ZAM
ASFAG Conakry	GUI	W–O	Hearts of Oak	GHA
Ranchers Bees	NGR	4–1 1–1	Mighty Barolle	LBR

* 2nd match abandoned. Tie awarded to Inter Club

SECOND ROUND

FC Horsed	0–2 0–7	**CA Bizerte**
Real Republicans	0–0 0–1	**Wallidan**
AFC Leopards	4–1 0–2	FC Kalamu
ASC Jeanne d'Arc	1–2 1–2	**Diamant Yaoundé**
Inter Club	1–0 1–1	ASC Bouaké
Gor Mahia	2–1 1–0	BTM Antananarivo
Power Dynamos	1–0 2–5	**Ferroviaro Lubango**
Ranchers Bees	1–0 1–1	ASFAG Conakry

QUARTER-FINALS

CA Bizerte	W-O	Wallidan
AFC Leopards	1–0 0–1 (4–5p)	**Diamant Yaoundé**
Gor Mahia	2–1 1–4	**Inter Club**
Ferroviaro Lubango	1–1 2–4	**Ranchers Bees**

SEMI-FINALS

Diamant Yaoundé	1–0 0–3	**CA Bizerte**
Inter Club	1–0 0–2	**Ranchers Bees**

FINAL

1st leg

Liberty Stadium, Ibadan, 19–11–1988, 20 000

RANCHERS BEES 0
CLUB ATHLETIQUE BIZERTE 0

2nd leg

El Menzah, Tunis, 3–12–1988, 40 000

CLUB ATHLETIQUE BIZERTE 1
RANCHERS BEES 0

1989

CHAMPIONS CUP

PRELIMINARY ROUND

Ela Nguema	EQG	1–0 0–4	**ASDR Fatima**	CAR
Highlanders	SWZ	2–0	Pan African	TAN
Matlama FC	LES	0–1 1–4	**Defence Force**	BOT
Mighty Blackpool	SLE	W-O	Benfica	BIS
St Louis	SEY	0–0 1–0	COSFAP Ant'arivo	MAD
Zumunta AC	NIG	0–2 1–1	**Etoile Filante**	BFA

FIRST ROUND

Raja Casablanca	MAR	2–0 0–1	ASC Jeanne d'Arc	SEN
JAC Port-Gentil	GAB	1–0 0–1 (5–3p)	Africa Sports	CIV
Iwuan'wu Owerri	NGR	4–1 0–0	Mighty Barolle	LBR
Inter Club	CGO	2–1 2–2	Petro Atletico	ANG
EP Setif	ALG	1–0 0–1 (3–5p)	**Mighty Blackpool**	SLE
Djoliba AC	MLI	1–0 0–0	Horoya AC	GUI
AS Vita Club	ZAI	4–0 2–1	Mukungwa	RWA
Tonnerre Yaoundé	CMR	2–0 3–0	ASDR Fatima	CAR
Nkana Red Devils	ZAM	4–1 1–1	Defence Force	BOT
Fire Brigade SC	MRI	1–0 1–0	St Louis	SEY
Uganda Ex. FC	UGA	4–0 1–2	Highlanders	SWZ
Desportivo Maputo	MOZ	2–2 1–1	**Zimbabwe Saints**	ZIM
Zamalek	EGY	2–1 0–1	**Al Mourada**	SUD
AFC Leopards	KEN	0–0 1–1	International FC	BUR
ES Tunis	TUN	2–1 0–0	Etoile Filante	BFA
MP Oran	ALG	W-O	Al Ittihad	LBA

SECOND ROUND

Raja Casablanca	0–0 1–1	JAC Port-Gentil
Iwuanyanwu Owerri	2–1 1–2 (4–5p)	**Inter Club**
Mighty Blackpool	2–1 0–0	Djoliba AC
AS Vita Club	1–1 1–3	**Tonnerre Yaoundé**
Nkana Red Devils	5–1 3–2	Fire Brigade SC
Zimbabwe Saints	0–1 1–0 (4–3p)	Uganda Express FC
AFC Leopards	1–0 0–3	**Al Mourada**
MP Oran	2–3 3–1	ES Tunis

QUARTER-FINALS

Raja Casablanca	2–0 0–1	Inter Club
Mighty Blackpool	0–1 1–3	**Tonnerre Yaoundé**
Zimbabwe Saints	0–0 1–2	**Nkana Red Devils**
Al Mourada	1–0 0–4	**MP Oran**

SEMI-FINALS

Raja Casablanca	2–0 2–2	Tonnerre Yaoundé
Nkana Red Devils	1–0 2–5	**MP Oran**

FINAL

1st leg

Mohammed V, Casablanca, 3–12–1989, 40000

RAJA CLUB ATHLETIQUE CASABLANCA 1
MOULOUDIA PETROLIERS ORAN 0

2nd leg

Oran, 15–12–1989, 25000

MOULOUDIA PETROLIERS ORAN 1
RAJA CLUB ATHLETIQUE CASABLANCA 0

Raja won 4–2 on penalties

CUP WINNERS CUP

PRELIMINARY ROUND

Moneni Pirates	SWZ	2–0 0–1	RLDF Maseru	LES

FIRST ROUND

Al Merreikh	SUD	W-O	Al Ahly Tripoli	LBA
CO Kakande Boke	GUI	0–0 0–1	**CA Bizerte**	TUN
Vautour Club M'gou	GAB	1–0 1–3	**Sagrada Esperanca**	ANG
Union Vesper	EQG	0–1 0–2	**Patronage St Anne**	CGO
Panthère Bangangte	CMR	0–0 1–2	**LPRC Oilers**	LBR
ASI Abengourou	CIV	W-O	UDIB Bissau	BIS
Coastal Union	TAN	2–3 0–2	**Costa do Sol**	MOZ
Gor Mahia	KEN	W-O	Nakivubu Villa	UGA
Dynamos Harare	ZIM	0–1 1–1	**BFV FC**	MAD
Moneni Pirates	SWZ	1–1 0–5	**Power Dynamos**	ZAM
Stade Malien	MLI	3–0 0–0	COT Tunis	TUN
Liberté FC	NIG	1–0 0–4	**USK Algiers**	ALG
USCA Bangui	CAR	3–3 0–2	**FC Kalamu**	ZAI
Etincelles	RWA	1–0 1–1	Vital'O	BUR
AS Fonction.	BFA	1–0 1–2	ASC Linguère	SEN
Diamond Stars		0–0 0–2	**Bendel United**	NGR

SECOND ROUND

CA Bizerte	1–0 0–2	**Al Merreikh**
Patronage Saint Anne	2–1 0–0	Sagrada Esperanca
ASI Abengourou	3–2 0–2	**LPRC Oilers**
Costa do Sol	1–2 0–0	**Gor Mahia**
BFV FC	1–2 3–1	Power Dynamos
Stade Malien	1–0 0–1 (3–4p)	**USK Algiers**
Etincelles	0–0 0–1	**FC Kalamu**
AS Fonctionnaires	1–3 0–2	**Bendel United**

QUARTER-FINALS

Al Merreikh	2–0 1–1	Patronage Saint Anne
Gor Mahia	0–0 3–1	LPRC Oilers
USK Algiers	1–3	**BFV FC**
Bendel United	2–0 1–0	FC Kalamu

SEMI-FINALS

Gor Mahia	1–0 0–2	**Al Merreikh**
Bendel United	4–1 0–0	BFV FC

FINAL

1st leg

Khartoum, 25–11–1989, 40 000

AL MERREIKH 1
BENDEL UNITED 0

2nd leg

Benin, 9–12–1989, 30 000

BENDEL UNITED 0
AL MERREIKH 0

1990

CHAMPIONS CUP

PRELIMINARY ROUND

ASKO Kara	TOG	1–0 2–0	ASFA Yennega	BFA
AC Sotema	MAD	1–0 1–2	Defence Force	BOT
MBC	SOM	1–0 2–4	**St Louis**	SEY
Malindi	TAN	0–0 1–2	**Mukungwa**	RWA
International FC	BUR	2–0 0–3	**Petro Atletico**	ANG
AS Kaloum Star	GUI	2–0 1–0	Benfica	BIS

Al Ittihad	LBA	6–1 0–2	Olympic Niamey	NIG
Renaissance	CHD	2–2 0–1	**SCAF Tocages**	CAR
Dragons de l'Ouème	BEN	0–0 0–3	**Mighty Barolle**	LBR
Arsenals	LES	1–0 3–0	Denver Sundowns	SWA

FIRST ROUND

JS Kabylie	ALG	6–0 4–0	ASKO Kara	TOG
AS Sogara	GAB	0–2 0–1	**Etoile du Congo**	CGO
Sunrise FC	MRI	4–1 0–2	AC Sotema	MAD
AFC Leopards	KEN	4–2 3–3	St Louis	SEY
Al Hilal	SUD	4–0 2–0	Mukungwa	RWA
Dynamos Harare	ZIM	1–1 1–1 (5–4p)	Petro Atletico	ANG
FAR Rabat	MAR	4–0 1–1	AS Kaloum Star	GUI
Asante Kotoko	GHA	4–0 1–1	Freetown United	SLE
ASC Diaraf	SEN	1–0 0–3	**Iwuanyanwu Owerri**	NGR
CS Imana	ZAI	1–0 0–3	**Africa Sports**	CIV
Al Ahly Cairo	EGY	5–0 3–0	Al Ittihad	LBA
ES Tunis	TUN	2–0 1–0	Stade Malien	MLI
Racing Bafoussam	CMR	2–1 0–0	SCAF Tocages	CAR
Raja Casablanca	MAR	2–0 1–2	Mighty Barolle	LBR
Ferroviario Maputo	MOZ	1–0 0–2	**Arsenals**	LES
Nkana Red Devils	ZAM	3–1 1–0	Uganda Express FC	UGA

SECOND ROUND

Etoile du Congo	2–2 0–2	**JS Kabylie**
Sunrise FC	1–1 0–3	**AFC Leopards**
Dynamos Harare	2–1 0–1	**Al Hilal**
FAR Rabat	3–3 0–1	**Asante Kotoko**
Africa Sports	1–1 2–3	**Iwuanyanwu Owerri**
Al Ahly Cairo	0–0 0–0 (2–4p)	**ES Tunis**
Racing Bafoussam	W-O	Raja Casablanca
Arsenals	0–3 1–5	**Nkana Red Devils**

QUARTER-FINALS

AFC Leopards	2–1 0–3	**JS Kabylie**
Al Hilal	2–1 1–2	**Asante Kotoko**
Iwuanyanwu Owerri	2–1 1–1	ES Tunis
Racing Bafoussam	0–1 1–2	**Nkana Red Devils**

SEMI-FINALS

Asante Kotoko	1–0 0–2	**JS Kabylie**
Nkana Red Devils	1–0 1–0	Iwuanyanwu Owerri

FINAL

1st leg

Stade Olympique, Algiers, 30–11–1990

JEUNESSE SPORTIVE KABYLIE 1
NKANA RED DEVILS 0

2nd leg

Independence Stadium, Lusaka, 22–12–1990

NKANA RED DEVILS 1
JEUNESSE SPORTIVE KABYLIE 0

JS Kabylie won 5–3 on penalties

CUP WINNERS CUP

PRELIMINARY ROUND

Anse Boileau	SEY	0–5 1–12	**Pamba SC**	TAN
Desportivo Maputo	MOZ	2–0 2–0	RLDF Maseru	LES
Liberté FC	NIG	0–0 1–2	**FC Tourbillon**	CHA
Moneni Pirates	SWZ	0–0 1–6	**Vital'O**	BUR

FIRST ROUND

BCC Lions	NGR	1–0 1–1	Entente II Lome	TOG
Rayon Sports	RWA	1–0 0–3	**Diables Noirs**	CGO
Olympique Real	CAR	1–0 0–1 (3–4p)	**Requins de l'Atl'q**	BEN
US Ouakam	SEN	2–0 1–0	Tonnerre Yaoundé	CMR
Vital'O	BUR	1–1 1–1 (5–3p)	FC Kalamu	ZAI
LPRC Oilers	LBR	0–0 0–1	**East End Lions**	SLE
Darryn Textiles	ZIM	1–4 0–1	**Red Arrows**	ZAM
Des. Maputo	MOZ	0–1 1–0 (5–3p)	Ferroviaro Lubango	ANG
Al Merreikh	SUD	3–0	Al Suguar	LBA
FC Tourbillon	CHA	0–0 0–2	**Petrosport FC**	GAB
Kenya Breweries	KEN	0–0 2–1	Nakivubu Villa	UGA
Pamba SC	TAN	0–0 1–2	**BTM Antananarivo**	MAD
AS Real Bamako	MLI	1–2 0–2	**Hearts of Oak**	GHA
Mankona Guedeckou	GUI	0–2 0–2	**AS Sotra**	CIV
AS Fonctionnaires	BFA	0–1 0–2	**MAS Fès**	MAR
Relizane	ALG	1–4 0–2	**Club Africain**	TUN

SECOND ROUND

Diables Noirs	2–0 0–3	**BCC Lions**
Requins de l'Atlantique	0–0 0–1	**US Ouakam**
East End Lions	0–0 0–2	**Vital'O**
Desportivo Maputo	3–2 0–0	Red Arrows
Petrosport FC	2–0 0–2 (3–4p)	**Al Merreikh**
Kenya Breweries	1–1 0–0	**BTM Antananarivo**
AS Sotra	1–1 1–2	**Hearts of Oak**
MAS Fès	1–0 0–4	**Club Africain**

QUARTER-FINALS

US Ouakam	0–1 1–3	**BCC Lions**
Desportivo Maputo	1–0 1–2	Vital'O
BTM Antananarivo	0–0 0–1	**Al Merreikh**
Hearts of Oak	2–0 0–2 (5–6p)	**Club Africain**

SEMI-FINALS

Desportivo Maputo	2–1 1–6	**BCC Lions**
Al Merreikh	1–0 0–1 (3–4p)	**Club Africain**

FINAL

1st leg

Surulere, Lagos, 24–11–1990

BCC LIONS 3
CLUB AFRICAIN 0

2nd leg

El Menzah, Tunis, 8–12–1990

CLUB AFRICAIN 1
BCC LIONS 1

1991

CHAMPIONS CUP

PRELIMINARY ROUND

ASF Fianarantsoa	MAD	4–1 0–0	St Louis	SEY
Brewery Addis	ETH	W–0	Jadidka	SOM
RLDF Maseru	LES	0–3 0–0	**Pamba SC**	TAN
Denver Sundowns	SWZ	0–1 1–0 (4–2p)	Gaborone United	BOT
Ifodje Atakpeme	TOG	0–0 1–3	**FC Sahel Niamey**	NIG
AS Tempete Mocafe	CAR	2–4 0–4	**Petro Atletico**	ANG

FIRST ROUND

Club Africain	TUN	5–1 2–1	Requins de l'Atl'q	BEN
Port Autonome	SEN	0–0 0–1	**Djoliba AC**	MLI
JS Kabylie	ALG	6–0 0–1	TPES	CHD
FC Sahel Niamey	NIG	0–0 1–3	**WAC Casablanca**	MAR
Union Douala	CMR	3–0 2–1	Etoile Filante	BFA
Inter Club	CGO	2–1 0–1	**Vital'O**	BUR
Sunrise FC	MRI	6–0 1–2	Denver Sundowns	SWZ
Nkana Red Devils	ZAM	6–0	ASF Fianarantsoa	MAD
Iwuan'wu Owerri	NGR	3–0 0–2	Old Edwardians	SLE
FC Lupopo	ZAI	1–1 0–0	**JAC Port-Gentil**	GAB
Hearts of Oak	GHA	4–2 1–3	**Petro Atletico**	ANG
Al Ittihad	LBA	0–2 0–0	**ASEC Abidjan**	CIV
Al Ahly Cairo	EGY	W–O	Brewery Addis	ETH
Gor Mahia	KEN	1–0 0–4	**Highlanders**	ZIM
Matchedje Maputo	MOZ	1–1 0–1	**Pamba SC**	TAN
Al Merreikh	SUD	1–0 0–1 (7–8p)	**Nakivubo Villa**	UGA

SECOND ROUND

Club Africain	2–0 0–0	Djoliba AC
JS Kabylie	1–0 0–3	**WAC Casablanca**
Union Douala	2–0 0–0	Vital'O
Nkana Red Devils	4–1 0–2	Sunrise FC
Iwuanyanwu Owerri	5–0 2–1	JAC Port-Gentil

Petro Atletico	1–0 0–1 (1–3p)	**ASEC Abidjan**
Al Ahly Cairo	3–1 1–0	Highlanders
Nakivubo Villa	4–1 1–2	Pamba SC

QUARTER-FINALS

Club Africain	2–0 0–1	WAC Casablanca
Union Douala	2–1 0–1	**Nkana Red Devils**
Iwuanyanwu Owerri	3–0 0–3 (6–5p)	AESC Abidjan
Al Ahly Cairo	2–0 0–2 (2–4p)	**Nakivubo Villa**

SEMI-FINALS

Club Africain	3–0 1–4	Nkana Red Devils
Nakivubo Villa	3–2 1–1	Iwuanyanwu Owerri

FINAL

1st leg

El Menzah, Tunis, 23–11–1991, 40000

CLUB AFRICAIN 5
NAKIVUBO VILLA 1

2nd leg

Nakivubo Stadium, Kampala, 14–12–1991, 25000

NAKIVUBO VILLA 1
CLUB AFRICAIN 1

CUP WINNERS CUP

PRELIMINARY ROUND

Prim. de Agosto	ANG	7–0 2–1	Nashua Black Af'ns	NAM
Small Simba	TAN	1–0 1–3	**Highlanders**	SWZ
Olympic Niamey	NIG	5–1 3–1	Faca FC	CAR
Plaisance	SEY	1–3 0–3	**Rivatex**	KEN

FIRST ROUND

Rivatex	KEN	1–0 2–4	**Power Dynamos**	ZAM
Highlanders	SWZ	1–1 0–0	**Al Ittihad**	SUD
AS Marsa	TUN	5–0	Ports Authority	SLE
ASFA Yennega	BFA	1–0 0–1 (3–2p)	Asante Kotoko	GHA
Renaissance	CHD	0–1 0–3	**Al Mokaoulum**	EGY
BFV FC	MAD	1–0 1–3	**Kampala CC**	UGA
Shell FC	GAB	2–0 1–1	Stationary Stores	NGR
Arsenals	LES	2–0	**International FC**	BUR
ASC Linguère	SEN	1–0 1–7	**EP Setif**	ALG
SC Gagnoa	CIV	2–0 0–2 (5–4p)	Stade Malien	MLI
Olympic Niamey	NIG	2–0 1–3	Prevoyance FC	CMR
Semassi Sokodé	TOG	0–0 1–2	**CS Daring**	ZAI
Dynamos Harare	ZIM	5–1 2–0	Maxaquene Maputo	MOZ
Primeiro de Agosto	ANG	0–0 1–2	**Diables Noirs**	CGO
Al Medina	LBA	W–O	Ground Force	ETH
Dragons de l'Ouème	BEN	2–0 0–3	**BCC Lions**	NGR

SECOND ROUND

Power Dynamos	2–1 2–0	Al Ittihad
ASFA Yennega	3–1 0–2	AS Marsa
Al Mokaoulum	2–0 0–1	Kampala CC
Shell FC	1–0 1–3	**International FC**
EP Setif	4–0 1–2	SC Gagnoa
CS Daring	2–1 1–2 (4–3p)	Olympic Niamey
Diables Noirs	0–2 1–1	**Dynamos Harare**
BCC Lions	2–0 0–0	Al Medina

QUARTER-FINALS

ASFA Yennega	1–1 0–0	**Power Dynamos**
International FC	0–0 0–0 (5–4p)	Al Mokaoulum
CS Daring	2–1 0–2	**EP Setif**
Dynamos Harare	1–1 0–3	**BCC Lions**

SEMI-FINALS

Power Dynamos	2–1 2–2	International FC
BCC Lions	1–0 1–1	EP Setif

FINAL

1st leg

Surelere, Lagos, 17–12–1991, 40000

BCC LIONS 3
POWER DYNAMOS 2

2nd leg

Independence Stadium, Lusaka, 1–12–1991, 20000

POWER DYNAMOS 3
BCC LIONS 1

NORTH AFRICA

North Africa has for many years been the closest link the rest of the world has had with African football. Their leagues are amongst the oldest on the continent, their national teams have been playing longer, and in players like Larbi Ben Barek, Just Fontaine and Rachid Mekhloufi, North Africa provided Europe with some fine players before the floodgates opened in the 1970s.

Proximity to Europe has also been a telling factor in the organisation of football in Egypt, Libya, Algeria, Morocco and Tunisia, the countries which make up the region. Egypt entered the 1920 Olympic Games and featured regularly in competitions before the Second World War, whilst French North Africa, though excluded from international competition, had a lively domestic scene.

Egypt was the first African country to join FIFA, two years after the founding of its Football Association in 1921, and as the only independent nation on the continent apart from the remote Liberia, it continued to be the only African representative until Sudan joined in 1948.

Few would doubt that club football in Egypt is the strongest in Africa. A year after the Egyptian Football Association was formed, the Farouk Cup was introduced and until the arrival of the national league in 1949 this was the main competition. After 1949 it simply became known as Cup of Egypt and has been dominated, as has the league, by the clubs from Cairo and in particular Al Ahly and Zamalek.

Zamalek and Al Ahly regularly attract crowds of 100 000 to the International Stadium for matches against each other, and it is because of support like this that they have been able to prosper. In its entire history the Egyptian league has been won by another team on only six occasions. To emphasise their superiority, between them they have won seven African club titles. Only Arab Contractors have risen to challenge this hegemony, and they too have won an African club title.

Algeria has a good league set-up though the composition of clubs differs greatly from when the league started, unlike in Egypt. Algeria was the largest state in French North Africa and had three leagues operational in its territory, based in Algiers, Oran and Constantine. Along with the leagues in Morocco and Tunisia, the other two states under French rule, the winners of the five league and five cup competitions used to take part in the North African Club Championship and the North African Cup respectively.

Since independence there has only been one league in Algeria and it has produced the top team in Africa on four occasions. JS Kabylie (twice), ES Setif and Mouloudia Challia from Algiers have all won the African Cup of Champion Clubs.

Club names are prone to change in Algeria depending on the political mood. JS Kabylie, for instance, were known as JE Tizi-Ouzou for many years in an attempt to curb regional sentiments. Kabylie is the area of the Berbers in Algeria, and they were using the club to vent their feelings. Politics in Algerian football is not new. At the time of the struggle for independence many of the great Algerian footballers of the time joined up with the FLN team which acted as a focus for anti-French feeling by touring Africa and playing matches.

In 1977 a massive reorganisation was undertaken whereby all clubs were attached to a major industrial concern. Mouloudia Challia thereby became known as Mouloudia Petrioliers as they were attached to the national oil company, though all the clubs have recently reverted to their pre-1977 names.

Nowhere in Africa can match the political interference that has taken place in Libyan football as two examples serve to show. In the 1984 Cup Winners Cup, Al Ahly of Tripoli, against the odds, reached the final where they were due to meet their namesakes from Cairo. At the time though, Egypt and Libya were not on good terms and so the Libyans refused to turn up in Cairo, forfeiting their place to Canon Yaounde. On the other hand, in a case perhaps unique in football, Libya withdrew from a qualifying tie in the 1988 Cup of Nations against Algeria as a token of gratitude for Algerian support after the bombing of Tripoli by the United States. Quite what the public in Libya thought about such a magnanimous gesture is open to question.

Both Morocco and Tunisia, the remaining North African countries, can lay claim to excellent club sides. Tunisia, despite its small size, won the Champions' cup with Club Africain in 1991, the Cup Winners Cup in 1988 with CA Bizerte, though neither is as popular or successful at home as ES Tunis.

In Morocco the network of clubs is extremely well balanced around the country. Unlike most of Africa where all of the big clubs tended to be located in the capital and perhaps the second largest city, there are major clubs in all of the big cities. Marrakech, Rabat, Casablanca, Kenitra, Oujda, Fes and Mohammedia can all boast championship winning sides. Only two of these, though, have ever gone on to win the African Cup of Champion Clubs, FAR Rabat in 1985 and Raja Casablanca in 1989.

It was not only with club sides that North Africa won renown. Morocco in 1970 and 1986, Tunisia in 1978, Algeria in 1982 and 1986 and Egypt in 1990 have all qualified for the World Cup finals. Only Cameroon and Zaire have managed to do the same in the whole of the rest of Africa. Once there, the North Africans have generally made their mark on the tournament.

In 1970 Morocco gave the West Germans a shock in the first round before losing 2–1 and also managed to hold Bulgaria to a draw. Sixteen years later in Mexico they qualified for the second round, winning their group ahead of England, Poland and Portugal before West Germany once again beat them. Again the Germans did not find it easy, relying on a goal from a free-kick right at the death to sneak a victory.

Tunisia kept up the good work in 1978, finishing above Mexico in their group after convincingly beating the Central Americans and holding West Germany to a draw. Only an unlucky 1–0 defeat at the hands of Poland denied them a second round place.

Algeria gave perhaps the best performance of the lot with their display in 1982, and again the West Germans were involved. In a thrilling match in Gijón, inspired by Lakdar Belloumi and Rabah Madjer, two of the finest African footballers of all time, the Algerians beat West Germany 2–1. A further victory over Chile almost assured them of a second round place, which they were denied by a wicked piece of gamesmanship by the Austrians and Germans who contrived to see all three teams finish on four points. Algeria, with the worst goal difference, lost out and went home justifiably crying foul.

With this success in the World Cup, it is very surprising that the North Africans have not done better in the Cup of Nations. Egypt have won on three occasions but two of these were in the first two tournaments when there were only three participants. Since then they have won only once, on home soil in 1986. Algeria did likewise in 1990, their only win to date, whilst Morocco's sole triumph came in Ethiopia in 1976.

For so long the major force in African football, there can be no doubt that the region is beginning to lose its grip on the reigns of power. West Africa and South Africa seem set to challenge the position of the North, and nowhere was this more evident than at the 1992 Cup of Nations. All three North African representatives finished bottom of their first round groups and were eliminated, leaving all eight quarter-finalists hailing from south of the Sahara.

ARAB FOOTBALL UNION
PO Box 5844, Riyadh,
Saudi Arabia

Year of formation: 1974

THE NORTH AFRICAN CLUB CHAMPIONSHIP

1919	Racing Club Tunis	TUN
1920	AS Maritime Oran	ALG
1921	SC Bel Abbes Oran	ALG
1922	FC Blideen Alger	ALG
1923	SC Bel Abbes Oran	ALG
1924	SC Bel Abbes Oran	ALG
1925	SC Bel Abbes Oran	ALG
1926	SC Bel Abbes Oran	ALG
1927	Gallia Sports Alger	ALG
1928	FC Blideen Alger	ALG
1929	AS Saint Eugene Alger	ALG
1930	Club des Joyeusetes Oran	ALG
1931	US Marocaine	MAR
1932	US Marocaine	MAR
1933	US Marocaine	MAR
1934	Racing Universitaire Alger	ALG
1935	Gallia Club Oran	ALG
1936	Gallia Sports Alger	ALG
1937	Jeun. Bone AC Constantine	ALG
1938	Racing Univ. Constantine	ALG
1939–40 –		
1941	US Marocaine	MAR
1942–45 –		
1946	Gallia Sports Alger	ALG
1947	WAC Casablanca	MAR
1948	WAC Casablanca	MAR
1949	WAC Casablanca	MAR

THE NORTH AFRICAN CUP

1930	Club des Joyeusetes Oran	ALG
1931	Racing Universitaire Alger	ALG
1932	Club des Joyeusetes Oran	ALG
1933	Club des Joyeusetes Oran	ALG
1934	Club des Joyeusetes Oran	ALG
1935	Italia de Tunis	TUN
1936	Racing Universitaire Alger	ALG
1937	Olympique Marocaine	MAR
1938	Stade AM Casablanca	MAR
1939–45 –		
1946	US Marocaine	MAR
1947	US Athletique Casablanca	MAR
1948	WAC Casablanca	MAR
1949	AS Saint Eugene Alger	ALG

MAGHREB CHAMPIONS CUP

1970	CR Belcourt	ALG
1971	CR Belcourt	ALG
1972	CR Belcourt	ALG
1973	ES Sahel	TUN
1974	Club Africain	TUN
1975	Club Africain	TUN

ALGERIA

Population: 25 337 000
Area, sq km: 2 381 741
% in urban areas: 49%
Capital city: Algiers

Fédération Algérienne de Football
Route Ahmed Ouaked
BP 39
Algiers–Dely–Ibrahim
Algeria
Tel: (010 213) 2 799443
Fax: None
Telex: 61378
Cable: FAFOOT ALGER
Languages for correspondence: French

Year of formation: 1962
Affiliation to FIFA: 1963
Affiliation to CAF: 1964
Registered clubs: 1066
Registered players: 91 000
Registered coaches: 2800
Registered referees: 2100
National stadium: Stade Olympique, Algiers 80000
National colours: Shirts: Green/Shorts: Green/Socks: Red
Reserve colours: Shirts: White/Shorts: White/Socks: White
Season: September–June

THE RECORD

WORLD CUP

1930–66 ..... Did not enter
1970 .... QT 1st round
1974 .... QT 1st round
1978 .... QT 2nd round
1982 .... QT Qualified – Final tournament/1st round
1986 .... QT Qualified – Final tournament/1st round
1990 .... QT 3rd round

OLYMPIC GAMES

1908–64 ..... Did not enter
1968 .... QT 2nd round
1972 .... QT 1st round
1976 .... QT 1st round
1980 .... QT Qualified – Final Tournament/Quarter-finalists
1984 .... QT 3rd round
1988 .... QT 3rd round
1992 .... QT 1st round

AFRICAN CUP OF NATIONS

1957–65 ..... Did not enter
1968 .... QT Qualified – Final tournament/1st round
1970 .... QT 2nd round
1972 .... QT 1st round
1974 .... QT 2nd round
1976 .... QT 1st round
1978 .... QT 2nd round
1980 .... QT Qualified – Final tournament/Finalists
1982 .... QT Qualified – Final tournament/Semi-finalists/4th place
1984 .... QT Qualified – Final tournament/Semi-finalists/3rd place
1986 .... QT Qualified – Final tournament/1st round
1988 .... QT Qualified – Final tournament/Semi-finalists/4th place
1990 .... QT Automatic – Final tournament/Winners
1992 .... QT Automatic – Final tournament/1st round

AFRICAN GAMES

Winners 1978

AFRICAN CLUB COMPETITIONS

AFRICAN CUP: Winners – MC Algiers 1976, JS Kabylie 1981 1990, ES Setif 1988
Finalists – MC Oran 1989
CUP WINNERS CUP: Finalists – NA Hussein–Dey 1978

ALGIERS LEAGUE CHAMPIONS

1920	FC Blideen
1921	FC Blideen
1922	FC Blideen
1923	FC Blidden
1924	AS Boufarik
1925	US Blideenne
1926	GS d'Orleansville
1927	Gallia Sports
1928	FC Blideen
1929	AS Saint Eugene
1930	AS Boufarik
1931	Gallia Sports
1932	AS Boufarik
1933	Racing Universitaire
1934	Racing Universitaire
1935	AS Saint Eugene
1936	Gallia Sports
1937	AS Boufarik
1938	AS Boufarik
1939–40 –	
1941	AS Boufarik
1942	AS Saint Eugene
1943	AS Saint Eugene
1944	AS Saint Eugene & Mouloudia Algiers
1945	Racing Universitaire
1946	Galiia Sports
1947	Olympique Hussein-Dey
1948	Olympique Hussein-Dey
1949	Olympique Hussein-Dey

ALGERIAN NATIONAL LEAGUE CHAMPIONS

1963	USM Algiers
1964	USM Annaba
1965	CR Belcourt
1966	CR Belcourt
1967	NA Hussein–Dey
1968	ES Setif
1969	CR Belcourt
1970	CR Belcourt
1971	MC Oran
1972	MC Algiers
1973	JS Kabylie
1974	JS Kabylie
1975	MC Algiers
1976	MC Algiers
1977	JS Kabylie
1978	MP Algiers
1979	MP Algiers
1980	JE Tizi-Ouzou
1981	RS Kouba
1982	JE Tizi-Ouzou
1983	JE Tizi-Ouzou
1984	GCR Mascara
1985	JE Tizi-Ouzou
1986	JE Tizi-Ouzou
1987	EP Setif
1988	MP Oran
1989	JS Kabylie
1990	JS Kabylie
1991	MC Algiers

ALGERIAN CUP WINNERS

1963	ES Setif
1964	ES Setif
1965	MC Saida
1966	CR Belcourt
1967	ES Setif
1968	ES Setif
1969	CR Belcourt
1970	CR Belcourt
1971	MC Algiers
1972	HAMR-Annaba
1973	MC Algiers
1974	USM El-Harrach
1975	MC Oran
1976	MC Algiers
1977	JS Kabylie
1978	CM Belcourt
1979	MA Hussein-Dey
1980	EP Setif
1981	USK Algiers
1982	DNC Algiers
1983	MP Algiers
1984	MP Oran
1985	MP Oran
1986	JE Tizi-Ouzou
1987	USM El-Harrach
1988	USK Algiers
1989	ES Setif
1990	Sidi Bel Abbes
1991	MC Algiers
1992	JS Kabylie

CONSTANTINE LEAGUE CHAMPIONS

1922	AS Bonoise
1923	US Constantine
1924	US Constantine
1925	US Constantine
1926	JS Philippeville
1927	Racing Philippeville
1928	Stade Olympique Setif
1929	AS Bonoise
1930	Stade Olympique Setif
1931	Racing Philippeville
1932	JS Guelmoise
1933	JS Guelmoise
1934	JS Guelmoise
1935	Jeunesse Bone AC
1936	–
1937	Jeunesse Bone AC
1938	Jeunesse Bone AC
1939	MO Constantine
1940–44	–
1945	USFMS
1946	USMB
1947	JSD
1948	MO Constantine
1949	ASB
1950	USFMS

ORAN LEAGUE CHAMPIONS

1920	AS Maritime
1921	SC Bel Abbes
1922	SC Bel Abbes
1923	SC Bel Abbes
1924	SC Bel Abbes
1925	SC Bel Abbes
1926	SC Bel Abbes
1927	SC Bel Abbes
1928	AS Maritime
1929	Club Joyeusetes
1930	Gallia Club Oran
1931	Club Joyeusetes
1932	USM Oran
1933	Club Joyeusetes
1934	–
1935	Gallia Club Oran
1936	Club Joyeusetes
1937	Club Joyeusetes
1938	Club Joyeusetes
1939	–
1940	AS Maritime
1941	Club Joyeusetes
1942	USM Oran
1943	USM Oran
1944	USM Oran
1945	USM Oran
1946	SC Bel Abbes
1947	FC Oran
1948	USM Oran
1949	USM Oran
1950	GC Mascara

CLUB DIRECTORY

ALGIERS (Population – 1 507 000)

MC Algiers (Mouloudia Challia) – Formerly MP Algiers

CR Belcourt – Formerly CM Belcourt

NA Hussein-Dey – Formerly MAHD

USK Algiers

JHD Algiers – Formerly DNC Algiers

USM El Harrach

ORAN (Population – 628 000)

MC Oran – Formerly MP Oran

ASM Oran – Formerly ASCO

CONSTANTINE (Population – 440 000)
MO Constantine – Formerly MP Constantine

ANNABA – (Population – 305 000)
USM Annaba – Formerly HAMR Annaba

SETIF (Population – 117 000)
ES Setif (Entente Setif) – Formerly EP Setif

MASCARA (Population – 64 000)
GC Mascara – Formerly GCR Mascara

TIZI-OUZOU – (Population 61 000)
JS Kabylie – Formerly JE Tizi-Ouzou

EGYPT

Population: 53 170 000
Area, sq km: 997 739
% in urban areas: 43%
Capital city: Cairo

All Ettihad el Masri li Korat el Kadam
Egyptian Football Association
5 Shareh Gabalaya, Guezira
Al Borg Post Office
Cairo
Egypt
Tel: (010 20) 2 3401793
Fax: (010 20) 2 3417817
Telex: 23504 KORA
Cable: KORA CAIRO
Languages for correspondence: English

Year of formation: 1921
Affiliation to FIFA: 1923
Affiliation to CAF: 1957
Registered clubs: 247
Registered players: 19 700
Registered Coaches: 841
Registered referees: 843
National stadium: International Stadium, Cairo 100 000

National colours: Shirts: Red/Shorts: White/Socks: Black
Reserve colours: Shirts: Green/Shorts: Green/Socks: Green
Season: September–June

THE RECORD

WORLD CUP

1930 .... Did not enter
1934 .... QT 1st/4 in group 4 – Final tournament/1st round
1938 .... Did not enter
1950 .... Did not enter
1954 .... QT 2nd/2 in group 9
1958–70 ..... Did not enter
1974 .... QT 1st round
1978 .... QT 4th round
1982 .... QT 3rd round
1986 .... QT 3rd round
1990 .... QT Qualified – Final tournament/1st round

OLYMPIC GAMES

1908 .... Did not enter
1912 .... Did not enter
1920 .... 1st round
1924 .... Quarter-finalists
1928 .... Semi-finalists/4th place
1936 .... 1st round
1948 .... 1st round
1952 .... 1st round
1956 .... QT Qualified/withdrew
1960 .... QT Qualified – Final tournament/1st round
1964 .... QT Qualified – Final tournament/Semi-finalists/4th place
1968 .... Did not enter
1972 .... QT 1st round
1976 .... QT 1st round
1980 .... QT Qualified/withdrew
1984 .... QT Qualified – Final tournament/Quarter-finalists
1988 .... QT 2nd round
1992 .... QT Qualified

AFRICAN CUP OF NATIONS

1957 .... Winners
1959 .... Winners
1962 .... Finalists
1963 .... 3rd place
1965 .... Did not enter
1968 .... QT 1st/4 in group 4 – withdrew
1970 .... QT Qualified – Final tournament/Semi-finalists/3rd place
1972 .... QT 2nd round
1974 .... QT Automatic – Final tournament/Semi-finalists/3rd place
1976 .... QT Qualified – Final tournament/2nd round/4th place
1978 .... QT 1st round
1980 .... QT Qualified – Final tournament/Semi-finalists/4th place
1982 .... QT 2nd round
1984 .... QT Qualified – Final tournament/Semi-finalists/4th place
1986 .... QT Automatic – Final tournament/Winners
1988 .... QT Automatic – Final tournament/1st round
1990 .... QT Qualified – Final tournament/1st round
1992 .... QT 1st/4 in group 2 – Final tournament/1st round

AFRICAN GAMES

Winners 1987

AFRICAN CLUB COMPETITIONS

AFRICAN CUP: Winners – Ismaili 1969, Al Ahly 1982 1987, Zamalek 1984 1986
Finalists – Mehalla 1974, Al Ahly 1983
CUP WINNERS CUP: Winners – Arab Contractors 1982 1983, Al Ahly 1984 1985 1986

EGYPTIAN LEAGUE CHAMPIONS

1949	Al Ahly
1950	Al Ahly
1951	Al Ahly
1952	–
1953	Al Ahly
1954	Al Ahly
1955	–
1956	Al Ahly
1957	Al Ahly
1958	Al Ahly
1959	Al Ahly
1960	Zamalek
1961	Al Ahly
1962	Al Ahly
1963	Al Tersana
1964	Zamalek
1965	Zamalek
1966	Olympia
1967	Ismaili
1968–72	–
1973	Mehalla Al Kubra
1974	–
1975	Al Ahly
1976	Al Ahly
1977	Al Ahly
1978	Zamalek
1979	Al Ahly
1980	Al Ahly
1981	Al Ahly
1982	Al Ahly
1983	Al Mokaoulum
1984	Zamalek
1985	Al Ahly
1986	Al Ahly
1987	Al Ahly
1988	Zamalek
1989	Al Ahly
1990	Al Ahly
1991	Ismaili

FAROUK CUP

1922	Cairo International SC
1923	Cairo International SC
1924	Al Ahly
1925	Al Ahly
1926	Al Ittihad
1927	Al Ahly
1928	Al Ahly
1929	Al Tersana
1930	Al Ahly
1931	Al Ahly
1932	Zamalek
1933	Olympia
1934	Olympia
1935	Zamalek
1936	Al Ittihad
1937	Al Ahly
1938	Zamalek
1939	Al Teram SC
1940	Al Ahly
1941	Zamalek
1942	Al Ahly
1943	Al Ahly & Zamalek
1944	Zamalek
1945	Al Ahly
1946	Al Ahly
1947	Al Ahly
1948	Al Ittihad

CUP OF EGYPT

1949	Al Ahly
1950	Al Ahly
1951	Al Ahly
1952	Zamalek
1953	Al Ahly
1954	Al Tersana
1955	Zamalek
1956	Al Ahly
1957	Zamalek
1958	Zamalek & Al Ahly
1959	Zamalek
1960	Zamalek
1961	Al Ahly
1962	Zamalek
1963	Al Ittihad
1964	Suez Canal
1965	Al Tersana
1966	Al Ahly
1967	Al Tersana
1968–72	–
1973	Al Ittihad
1974	–
1975	Zamalek
1976	Al Ittihad
1977	Zamalek
1978	Al Ahly
1979	Zamalek
1980	–
1981	Al Ahly
1982	–
1983	Al Ahly
1984	Al Ahly
1985	Al Ahly
1986	Al Tersana
1987	Zamalek

1988 Zamalek
1989 Zamalek
1990 Al Mokaoulum
1991 Al Ahly

CLUB DIRECTORY

CAIRO (Population – 6052000)
Al Ahly Sporting Club (National)

Zamalek Sporting Club

Al Mokaouloum (Arab Contractors)

Al Tersana (Arsenal)

ALEXANDRIA (Population – 2917000)
Olympic Sporting Club

Al Ittihad (Union Recreation)

PORT SAID (Population – 399000)
Al Mesri Sporting Club

MAHALLAH AL KUBRA (Population – 385000)
Mehalla Sporting Club

MANSURAH (Population – 375000)
Al Mansurah Sporting Club

TANTA (Population – 334000)
Tanta Sporting Club

ISMAILI (Population – 235000)
Al Ismaili Sporting Club

LIBYA

Population: 4 206 000
Area, sq km: 1 757 000
% in urban areas: 75%
Capital city: Tripoli

Libyan Arab Jamahiriya Football Federation
PO Box 5137
Tripoli
Libya
Tel: (010 218) 21 46610
Fax: (010 218) 21 46610
Telex: 20896 KURATP LY
Cable: ALKURA TRIPOLI
Languages for correspondence: English

Year of formation: 1962
Affiliation to FIFA: 1963
Affiliation to CAF: 1965
Registered clubs: 1578
Registered players: 39 400
Registered coaches: 1578
Registered referees: 721
National stadium: 11 June Stadium, Tripoli 70 000
National colours: Shirts: Green/Shorts: White/Socks: Green
Reserve colours: Shirts: White/Shorts: Green/Socks: White
Season: September–April

THE RECORD

WORLD CUP

1930–66 ..... Did not enter
1970 .... QT 1st round
1974 .... Did not enter
1978 .... QT 1st round
1982 .... QT 2nd round
1986 .... QT 4th round
1990 .... QT 2nd round

OLYMPIC GAMES

1908–64 ..... Did not enter
1968 .... QT 1st round
1972 .... Did not enter
1976 .... QT 1st round
1980 .... QT 3rd round
1984 .... QT 2nd round
1988 .... QT 2nd round
1992 .... Did not enter

AFRICAN CUP OF NATIONS

1957–65 ..... Did not enter
1968 .... QT 1st round
1970 .... Did not enter
1972 .... QT 1st round
1974 .... Did not enter
1976 .... QT pr round
1978 .... QT 1st round
1980 .... QT 2nd round
1982 .... QT Automatic – Final tournament/Finalists
1984 .... QT 1st round
1986 .... QT 2nd round
1988 .... QT 2nd round
1990 .... QT 1st round
1992 .... Did not enter

AFRICAN CLUB COMPETITIONS

AFRICAN CUP: Quarter-finalists – Al Ittihad 1967, Al Ahly Tripoli 1972
CUP WINNERS CUP: Semi-finalists – Al Ahly Tripoli 1984, Al Nasr 1985

LIBYAN LEAGUE CHAMPIONS

1964 Al Ahly Tripoli
1965 Al Ittihad
1966 –
1967 Al Tahaddy
1968 –
1969 Al Ittihad
1970 Al Ahly Benghazi
1971 Al Ahly Tripoli
1972 Al Ahly Benghazi
1973 Al Ahly Tripoli
1974 Al Ahly Tripoli
1975 Al Ahly Benghazi
1976 Al Medina
1977 Al Tahaddy
1978 Al Ahly Tripoli
1979 –
1980 Al Ahly Tripoli
1981 –
1982 Al Ahly Tripoli
1983 Al Medina
1984 Al Ahly Tripoli
1985 Al Adhara
1986 Al Ahly Tripoli
1987 Al Nasr
1988 Al Ittihad
1989 Al Ittihad
1990 Al Ittihad
1991 Al Ittihad

CLUB DIRECTORY

TRIPOLI (Population – 990000)
Al Ahly (National)

Al Ittihad – Al Medina – Municipal

BENGHAZI (Population – 435000)
Al Ahly (National)

Al Tahaddy – Al Nasr – Municipal

MOROCCO

Population: 25 113 000
Area, sq km: 458 730
% in urban areas: 45%
Capital city: Rabat

Fédération Royale Marocaine de Football
Av Ibn Sina, CNS Bellevue
BP 51
Rabat
Morocco
Tel: (010 212) 7 672706
Fax: (010 212) 7 671070
Telex: 32940 FERMFOOT M
Cable: FERMAFOOT RABAT
Languages for correspondence: French

Year of formation: 1955
Affiliation to FIFA: 1956
Affiliation to CAF: 1966
Registered clubs: 394
Registered players: 20 700
Registered coaches: 272
Registered referees: 897
National stadium: Mohamed V, Casablanca 80 000
National colours: Shirts: Red/Shorts: Red/Socks: Red
Reserve colours: Shirts: Green/Shorts: Green/Socks: Green
Season: September–June

THE RECORD

WORLD CUP

1930–58 ..... Did not enter
1962 .... QT 3rd round
1966 .... Did not enter
1970 .... QT Qualified – Final tournament/1st round

1974 .... QT 4th round
1978 .... QT 1st round
1982 .... QT 4th round
1986 .... QT Qualified – Final tournament/2nd round
1990 .... QT 2nd round

OLYMPIC GAMES

1908–56 ..... Did not enter
1960 .... QT 1st round
1964 .... QT Qualified – Final tournament/1st round
1968 .... QT Qualified/withdrew
1972 .... QT Qualified – Final tournament/2nd round
1976 .... QT 3rd round
1980 .... QT 2nd round
1984 .... QT Qualified – Final tournament/1st round
1988 .... QT 3rd round
1992 .... QT 3rd round

AFRICAN CUP OF NATIONS

1957–68 ..... Did not enter
1970 .... QT 1st round
1972 .... QT qualified – Final tournament/1st round
1974 .... Did not enter
1976 .... QT Qualified – Final tournament/Winners
1978 .... QT Automatic – Final tournament/1st round
1980 .... QT Qualified – Final tournament/Semi-finalists/3rd place
1982 .... QT 2nd round
1984 .... QT 2nd round
1986 .... QT Qualified – Final tournament/Semi-finalists/4th place
1988 .... QT Automatic – Final tournament/Semi-finalists/3rd place
1990 .... QT 1st round
1992 .... QT 2nd/4 in group 3 – Final tournament/1st round

AFRICAN CLUB COMPETIONS

AFRICAN CUP: Winners – FAR Rabat 1985, Raja Casablanca 1989
CUP WINNERS CUP: Quarter–finalists – DHJ Jadida 1986, FAR Rabat 1987

MOROCCAN LEAGUE CHAMPIONS

1916	CA Casablanca
1917	US Marocaine
1918	US Marocaine
1919	US Marocaine
1920	Olympique Marocaine
1921	Olympique Marocaine
1922	Olympique Marocaine
1923	US Fes
1924	Olympique Marocaine
1925	US Fes
1926	US Athletique
1927	Stade Marocaine
1928	–
1929	US Athletique
1930	Olympique Marocaine
1931	Stade Marocaine
1932	US Marocaine
1933	US Marocaine
1934	US Marocaine
1935	US Marocaine
1936	Olympique Marocaine
1937	Olympique Marocaine
1938	US Marocaine
1939	US Marocaine
1940	US Marocaine
1941	US Marocaine
1942	US Marocaine
1943	US Marocaine
1944	Stade Marocaine
1945	Racing Avant-Garde
1946	US Marocaine
1947	US Athletique
1948	WAC Casablanca
1949	WAC Casablanca
1950	WAC Casablanca
1951–56	–
1957	WAC Casablanca
1958	KAC Marrakech
1959	EJS Casablanca
1960	KAC Kenitra
1961	FAR Rabat
1962	FAR Rabat
1963	FAR Rabat
1964	FAR Rabat
1965	MAS Fès
1966	WAC Casablanca
1967	FAR Rabat
1968	FAR Rabat
1969	WAC Casablanca
1970	FAR Rabat
1971	RS Settat
1972	ADM Casablanca
1973	KAC Kenitra
1974	RBM Beni Mellal
1975	MC Oujda
1976	WAC Casablanca
1977	WAC Casablanca
1978	WAC Casablanca
1979	MAS Fès
1980	Chabab Mohammedia
1981	KAC Kenitra
1982	KAC Kenitra
1983	MAS Fès
1984	FAR Rabat
1985	MAS Fès
1986	WAC Casablanca
1987	FAR Rabat
1988	Raja Casablanca
1989	FAR Rabat
1990	WAC Casablanca
1991	WAC Casablanca

MOROCCAN CUP WINNERS

1957	MC Oujda
1958	MC Oujda
1959	FAR Rabat
1960	MC Oujda
1961	KAC Kenitra
1962	MC Oujda
1963	KAC Marrakech
1964	KAC Marrakech
1965	KAC Marrakech
1966	COD Meknes
1967	FUS Rabat
1968	Raja Casablanca
1969	RS Settat
1970	WAC Casablanca
1971	FAR Rabat
1972	Chabab Mohammedia
1973	FUS Rabat
1974	Raja Casablanca
1975	Chabab Mohammedia
1976	FUS Rabat
1977	Raja Casablanca
1978	WAC Casablanca
1979	WAC Casablanca
1980	MAS Fès
1981	WAC Casablanca
1982	Raja Casablanca
1983	CLAS Casablanca
1984	FAR Rabat
1985	FAR Rabat
1986	FAR Rabat
1987	KAC Marrakech

CLUB DIRECTORY

RABAT (Population – 980 000)
Forces Armees Royales (FAR Rabat)

Fatah Union Sportive (FUS Rabat)

Stade Marocaine

CASABLANCA (Population – 2 475 000)
Wydad Athletic Club (WAC Casablanca)

Raja Club Athletique

Centrale Laitiere Association Sportive (CLAS Casablanca)

Olympique Casablanca

FES (Population 535 000)
Maghreb Athletique Sport (MAS Fès)

MARRAKECH (Population – 535 000)
Kawkab Athletique Club (KAC Marrakech)

TANGIERS (Population – 370 000)
Ittihad Tanger

OUJDA (Population – 260 000)
Molodiat Club Oujda (MC Oujda)

KENITRA (Population – 188 000)
Kenitra Athletique Club

MOHAMMEDIA (Population – 105 000)
Chabab Mohammedia

TUNISIA

Population: 8 182 000
Area, sq km: 154 530

% in urban areas: 53%
Capital city: Tunis

Fédération Tunisienne de Football
2 Rue Hamza Abdelmottaleb
El Menzah VI
Tunis
Tunisia
Tel: (010 216) 1 233303
Fax: (010 216) 1 767929
Telex: 14783 FTFOOT TN
Cable: FOOTBALL TUNIS
Languages for correspondence: French

Year of formation: 1956
Affiliation to FIFA: 1960
Affiliation to CAF: 1960
Registered clubs: 215
Registered players: 18300
Registered referees: 590
National stadium: El Menzah, Tunis 50000
National colours: Shirts: Red/Shorts: White/Socks: Red
Reserve colours: Shirts: White/Shorts: White/Socks: White
Season: September–June

THE RECORD

WORLD CUP

1930–58 ..... Did not enter
1962 .... QT 1st round
1966 .... Did not enter
1970 .... QT 2nd round
1974 .... QT 2nd round
1978 .... QT Qualified – Final tournament/1st round
1982 .... QT 1st round
1986 .... QT 4th round
1990 .... QT 3rd round

OLYMPIC GAMES

1908–56 ..... Did not enter
1960 .... QT Qualified – Final tournament/1st round
1964 .... QT 2nd round
1968 .... QT 1st round
1972 .... QT 2nd round
1976 .... QT 2nd round
1980 .... QT 1st round
1984 .... QT 2nd round
1988 .... QT Qualified – Final tournament/1st round
1992 .... QT 2nd round

AFRICAN CUP OF NATIONS

1957 .... Did not enter
1959 .... Did not enter
1962 .... 3rd place
1963 .... 1st round
1965 .... Finalists
1968 .... QT 2nd/3 in group 5
1970–74 ..... Did not enter
1976 .... QT 2nd round
1978 .... QT Qualified – Final tournament/Semi-finalists/4th place
1980 .... Did not enter
1982 .... QT Qualified – Final tournament/1st round
1984 .... QT 2nd round
1986 .... QT 1st round
1988 .... QT 1st round
1990 .... QT 2nd round
1992 .... QT 2nd/4 in group 2

AFRICAN CLUB COMPETITIONS

AFRICAN CUP: Winners – Club Africain 1991
CUP WINNERS CUP: Winners – CA Bizerte 1988
Finalists – ES Tunis 1987, Club Africain 1990

TUNISIAN LEAGUE CHAMPIONS

1921 Racing Club
1922 Stade Gaulois
1923 Stade Gauloise
1924 Racing Club
1925 Sporting Club
1926 Stade Gauloise
1927 Sporting Club
1928 Avant Garde
1929 US Tunisienne
1930 US Tunisienne
1931 Italia de Tunis
1932 US Tunisienne
1933 Sfax Railway
1934 Italia de Tunis
1935 Italia de Tunis
1936 Italia de Tunis
1937 Savoia de la Goulette
1938 CS Gabesien
1939–40 –
1941 ES Tunis
1942–43 –
1944 CA Bizerte
1945 CA Bizerte
1946 Club Africain
1947 Club Africain
1948 CA Bizerte
1949 ES Sahel
1950 CS Hammam-Lif
1951–55 –
1956 CS Hammam-Lif
1957 Stade Tunisiene
1958 ES Sahel
1959 ES Tunis
1960 ES Tunis
1961 Stade Tunisiene
1962 Stade Tunisiene
1963 ES Sahel
1964 Club Africain
1965 Stade Tunisienne
1966 ES Sahel
1967 Club Africain
1968 Sfax Railway
1969 CS Sfax
1970 ES Tunis
1971 CS Sfax
1972 ES Sahel
1973 Club Africain
1974 Club Africain
1975 ES Tunis
1976 ES Tunis
1977 JS Kairouan
1978 CS Sfax
1979 Club Africain
1980 Club Africain
1981 CS Sfax
1982 ES Tunis
1983 CS Sfax
1984 CA Bizerte
1985 ES Tunis
1986 ES Sahel
1987 ES Sahel
1988 ES Tunis
1989 ES Tunis
1990 Club Africain
1991 ES Tunis
1992 Club Africain

CUP OF TUNIS

1922 Avant Garde
1923 Racing Club
1924 Stade Gauloise
1925 Sporting Club
1926 Stade Gauloise
1927–28 –
1929 US Tunisiene
1930 US Tunisiene
1931 Racing Club
1932 US Tunisiene
1933 US Tunisiene
1934 US Tunisiene
1935 Italia de Tunis
1936 Stade Gauloise
1937 Sporting Club
1938 ES Tunis
1939–40 –
1941 US Ferryville
1942–43 –
1944 Olympique Tunis
1945 Patrie FC Bizerte
1946 CS Hammam-Lif
1947 CS Hammam-Lif
1948 CS Hammam-Lif
1949 CS Hammam-Lif
1950 CS Hammam-Lif
1951–55 –
1956 Stade Tunisien
1957 ES Tunis
1958 Stade Tunisien
1959 ES Sahel
1960 Stade Tunisien
1961 AS Marsa
1962 Stade Tunisien
1963 ES Sahel
1964 ES Tunis
1965 Club Africain
1966 Stade Tunisien
1967 Club Africain
1968 Club Africain
1969 Club Africain
1970 Club Africain
1971 CS Sfax
1972 Club Africain
1973 Club Africain
1974 ES Sahel
1975 ES Sahel
1976 Club Africain
1977 AS Marsa
1978 –
1979 ES Tunis

1980	ES Tunis
1981	ES Sahel
1982	CA Bizerte
1983	ES Sahel
1984	AS La Marsa
1985	CS Hammam-Lif
1986	ES Tunis
1987	CA Bizerte
1988	COT Tunis
1989	Club Africain
1990	AS Marsa
1991	ES Sahel

CLUB DIRECTORY

TUNIS (Population – 1 225 000)
Club Africain

Esperance Sportive (ES Tunis)

Stade Tunisien

Club Sportif Cheminots

Club Olympique des Transports
(COT Tunis)

Club Sportif Hammam-Lif

SFAX (Population – 310 000)
Club Sportif (CS Sfax)

Sfax Railway Sports

SOUSSE (Population – 160 000)
Etoile Sportive du Sahel (ES Sahel)

BIZERTE (Population – 94 000)
Club Athletique (CA Bizerte)

WEST AFRICA

West Africa is a patchwork of large and small nations consisting of 16 countries, although CAF sub-divides the area in two with a West Africa zone A and zone B. There are five powerful football states among these nations: the Ivory Coast, Guinea, Ghana, Nigeria and Senegal. The rest are by no means football outcasts, but as yet have not proved themselves either in the club tournaments or in the Cup of Nations.

Ghana and Nigeria are the most celebrated of all the nations in the region and remain the only African countries who have won world titles at any level. Nigeria were world under-17 champions in 1985, whilst Ghana won the same title six years later. Football came with British rule and was quick to spread through both countries – by the 1920s it was popular enough amongst the locals for leagues to be formed in many of the towns, helped along by British organisation.

In Ghana, the most famous of the teams formed around this time were Hearts of Oak (1911) in Accra, Asante Kotoko (1926) based in Kumasi and Eleven Wise (1919) based in Sekondi. Due to the poor communications, competitions did not take on a nationwide character until the late 1950s when a national league and cup competition were introduced for the first time. Instead, tournaments were played for teams in a town or region. Asante Kotoko for instance made their name in the Asanthene Cup where they had a great rivalry with Cornerstones of Kumasi. In Accra, the City Championship Cup was the domain of both Hearts of Oak and Steadfast.

Independence saw the creation of the Ghana Football Association, which took over from the Gold Coast Football Association formed in 1922. It was responsible for the implementation of the new league and cup and for fielding a national side. Because of the head start Ghana had had, they were the most successful nation in Africa in the 1960s.

In an age of footballing innocence, Ghanaian footballers such as Baba Yara, Ibrahim Sunday, Robert Mensah and Wilberforce Mfum were the toast of African football, but it is a legacy that has been hard to live up to. The 'Black Stars', as the national side is known, have managed to do reasonably well and despite some lapses – and the surprising failure to qualify for a World Cup – have remained at the forefront of the game. Cup of Nations wins in 1978 and 1982 are testament to this.

Nigeria on the other hand have not found the task so easy. With their vast population and huge oil resources, the Nigerians were expected to be leading the pack by a long way. Unlike Ghana, however, Nigeria did not have a well-founded club structure from the beginning and clubs are still prone to fade away from the limelight. There have been no Asante Kotokos to blaze a trail for the rest to follow behind.

Another factor was the late formation of the Nigeria Football Association which in 1945 came 23 years after its counterpart in Ghana. The Challenge Cup was introduced in the same year and until the national league was formed some thirty years later it remained the only nationwide competition, and is still regarded by some as the premier competition in the country. This may perhaps help explain the success of Nigerian teams in the Cup Winners Cup compared to the Champions Cup.

Only since the 1970s has Nigerian football begun to develop rapidly. Outside of Lagos, representative teams had always entered the Challenge Cup but in 1970, due to the huge increase in the number of clubs being formed throughout the country, it became a clubs-only competition. In 1972 the next important step was taken when the national league was formed and it has always been well represented by clubs from most of the major towns. Both the national side and the club sides have profited from this new-found stability, especially in the 1980s.

After not qualifying for the final tournament of the Cup of Nations until 1976, Nigeria have since reached the final itself on four occasions, although they have lost three of them. Their only triumph came in 1980 on home territory. The most famous of Nigeria's footballers in the 1950s was Tesilimi Balogun who did much to spread the gospel of the game, but it has not been until the recent upsurge that other Nigerians such as Stephen Keshi, Rashidi Yekini and Muda Lawal have made their mark on

African football. It will not be long before Nigeria translate their superiority in Africa to the world stage, and few would argue that it is Nigeria who will most likely be the first African team to lift the World Cup.

The other successful West African nations were all French colonies and they include Guinea, the Ivory Coast, or Côte d'Ivoire as they prefer to be called, and Senegal. Guinea, though very strong in the 1970s at both club and national level, have faded alarmingly from the scene. At the height of their power they possessed the best team Africa had seen. Petit Sory, Papa Camara, Bangaly Sylla, Cherif Soulayeman, N'Jolea, Tollo and Jansky will not be forgotten in a hurry, but unfortunately for Guinea they have not been replaced by players of equal quality.

The Ivory Coast have inherited their mantle as the top Francophile nation in the region. Also blessed with oil and a sound club structure based around the Abidjan quartet of ASEC, Africa Sports, Stella and Stade Abidjan, they have a healthy if unremarkable record. Until their victory in the 1992 Cup of Nations, they were often likened to Yugoslavia; always there displaying great skill, but never quite consistent enough to actually win titles.

The league in the Ivory Coast is one of the most stable on the continent, though the French league is too much of a temptation for many of their top footballers, the most famous of which, Youssouf Fofana and Abdoulaye Traoré in recent years and Laurent Pokou in the past, have all played there. Although the league has been dominated by Abidjan clubs, teams like SC Ganoa, Reveil Doloa and ASC Bouaké are starting to make more of an impact, though it could be some time before they break the dominance of Abidjan.

Senegal are the last of the West African powers, though they have never been as strong as the other four, not having won a title at club or national level. They do produce good footballers such as Francoise Bocande and Souleyman Sane, the majority of whom end up in France, and it is from this base that the national team is built. The 1992 Cup of Nations was a good pointer as to how far they have still to go to catch up. On home territory they could do no more than reach the quarter-finals.

Of the rest of the region, one or two of the nations have occasionally made their presence felt. Mali reached the final of the All-Africa Games in 1965, a year after Stade Malien had reached the final of the initial African Cup of Champion Clubs, whilst two years later Real Bamoko lost to Stade Abidjan in the second Champions Cup. Since 1972 when the national side were runners-up to Congo in the Cup of Nations, the only time they have managed to qualify for the finals, Mali has almost disappeared off the the map.

The only other performances of note have come from Togo. In 1968 Etoile Filante lost in the final of the Champions Cup to TP Englebert and in 1983 Agaza Lomé reached the final of the Cup Winners Cup before losing to the Arab Contractors.

There are four regional tournaments in West Africa. At club level the West African Club Championship is disputed between the runners-up of the national leagues of the region, not the champions. For the national teams the CEDEAO tournament, named after the economic trade grouping in West Africa, was supposed to be a regional championship but there has never been much enthusiasm for it.

Neither has there been much enthusiasm for the Zone 3 tournament for which Ghana, Nigeria, Benin, Burkina Faso (formerly Upper Volta), Ivory Coast, Liberia, Niger and Togo qualify. Only the Zone 2 tournament has proved popular, and mostly because of the intense rivalry between Senegal and Guinea. Other nations entitled to take part are Cape Verde, Gambia, Guinea-Bissau, Mali, Mauritania and Sierra Leone.

THE WEST AFRICAN CLUB CHAMPIONSHIP

1977	Stade Abidjan	CIV			
1978	AS Forces Armees	SEN			
1979	ASF Police	SEN			
1980	ASF Police	SEN			
1981	Stella Abidjan	CIV	1–3 4–0	ASF Police	SEN
1982	Sekondi Hassacas	GHA	1–0 0–0	Spartans Owerri	NGR
1983	New Nigeria Bank	NGR	2–0 0–0	Sekondi Hassacas	GHA
1984	New Nigeria Bank	NGR	3–2 1–0	Stade Malien	MLI
1985	Africa Sports	CIV	3–0 2–0	New Nigeria Bank	NGR
1986	Africa Sports	CIV	2–0 0–2 (6–5p)	Asante Kotoko	GHA
1987	Cornerstone	GHA	1–1 1–1 (4–2p)	Stella Abidjan	CIV
1988	ASFAG Conakry	GUI	1–2 1–0	New Nigeria Bank	NGR
1989	Ranchers Bees	NGR	3–1 1–2	ASEC Abidjan	CIV
1990	ASEC Abidjan	CIV	1–0 1–1	Djoliba AC	MLI
1991	Africa Sports	CIV	1–1 2–1	Lobi Bank	NGR

WEST AFRICAN FOOTBALL UNION
BP V 307
Abidjan
Côte d'Ivoire

Founded: 1975

ZONE 2 THE AMILCAR CABRAL CUP

1979	Senegal	1–0	Mali
1980	Senegal	1–0	Gambia
1981	Guinea	0–0 (6–5p)	Mali
1982	Guinea	3–0	Senegal
1983	Senegal	3–0	Guinea–Bissau
1984	Senegal	0–0 (5–4p)	Sierra Leone
1985	Senegal	1–0	Gambia
1986	Senegal	3–1	Sierra Leone
1987	Guinea	1–0	Mali
1988	Guinea	0–0 (4–2p)	Mali
1989	Mali	3–0	Guinea
1990	–		
1991	Senegal	1–0	Cape Verde

ZONE 3

1982	Ghana	2–1	Togo
1983	Ghana	3–1	Togo
1984	Ghana	1–1*	Togo
1986	Ghana	1–0	Togo
1987	Ghana	2–1	Liberia
1988–92	–		

* Ghana won on penalties

CEDEAO TOURNAMENT

1983	Côte d'Ivoire	1–0	Togo
1985	Senegal	2–0	Côte d'Ivoire
1987	Côte d'ivoire	2–1	Liberia
1989	Nigeria	0–0*	Senegal
1991	Côte d'Ivoire	1–0	Senegal

* Nigeria won on penalties

BENIN

Population: 4 741 000
Area, sq km: 112 600
% in urban areas: 19%
Capital city: Luanda

Fédération Béninoise de Football
BP 965
Cotonou
Benin
Tel: (010 229) 330537
Fax: (010 229) 312485
Telex: 5245 SONACOP COTONOU
Cable: FEBEFOOT COTONOU
Languages for correspondence: French & English

Year of formation: 1968
Affiliation to FIFA: 1969
Affiliation to CAF: 1969
Registered clubs: 117
Registered players: 6700
Registered referees: 61
National stadium: Cotonou II 7000
National colours: Shirts: Green/Shorts: Green/Socks: Green
Reserve colours: Shirts: Red/Shorts: Green/Socks: Green
Season: November–June

THE RECORD

WORLD CUP

1930–70	Did not enter
1974	QT 1st round
1978	Did not enter
1982	Did not enter
1986	QT 1st round
1990	Did not enter

OLYMPIC GAMES

1908–60	Did not enter
1964	QT 1st round
1968–80	Did not enter
1984	QT 1st round
1988	Did not enter
1992	Did not enter

AFRICAN CUP OF NATIONS

1957–70	Did not enter
1972	QT 1st round
1974–78	Did not enter
1980	QT 1st round
1982	Did not enter
1984	QT 1st round
1986	QT 1st round
1988	Did not enter
1990	Did not enter
1992	QT 5th/5 in group 4

AFRICAN CLUB COMPETITIONS

AFRICAN CUP: 2nd round – Dragons de l'Ouème 1984
CUP WINNERS CUP: Semi-finalists – Dragons de l'Ouème 1987

BENIN LEAGUE CHAMPIONS

1969	FAD
1970	AS Porto Novo
1971	AS Cotonou
1972	AS Porto Novo
1973	AS Porto Novo
1974	Etoile Sportive Porto Novo
1975–77	–
1978	Dragons de l'Ouème
1979	Dragons de l'Ouème
1980	Buffles de Borgou
1981	Adjidjas FAP
1982	Dragons de l'Ouème
1983	Dragons de l'Ouème
1984	Lions de l'Atakory
1985	Requins de l'Atlantique
1986	Dragons de l'Ouème
1987	Requins de l'Atlantique
1988	–
1989	Dragons de l'Ouème
1990	Requins de l'Atlantique
1991	Postel Sport

CLUB DIRECTORY

COTONOU (Population – 478 000)
Requins de l'Atlantique

Association Sportive Cotonou

Adjidjas FAP

PORT NOVO (Population – 164 000)
Dragons de l'Ouème

Postel Sport

Etoile Sportive

AS Porto Novo

PARAKOU (Population – 92 000)
Buffles de Borgou

BURKINA FASO

(Formerly Upper Volta)

Population: 9 012 000
Area, sq km: 274 200
% in urban areas: 8%
Capital city: Ouagadougou

Fédération Burkinabe de Football
BP 57
Ouagadougou
Burkina Faso
Tel: (010 226) 302850
Fax: None
Telex: None
Cable: FEDEFOOT OUAGADOUGOU
Languages for correspondence: French

Year of formation: 1960
Affiliation to FIFA: 1964
Affiliation to CAF: 1964
Registered clubs: 42
Registered players: 4000

Registered referees: 71
National stadium: Municipal, Ouagadougou 4000
National colours: Shirts: Red/Shorts: Green/Socks: Red
Reserve colours: Shirts: White/Shorts: White/Socks: White
Season: October–July

THE RECORD

WORLD CUP

1930–74 ..... Did not enter
1978 .... QT 1st round
1982 .... Did not enter
1986 .... Did not enter
1990 .... QT 1st round

OLYMPIC GAMES

1908–72 ..... Did not enter
1976 .... QT 1st round
1980–92 ..... Did not enter

AFRICAN CUP OF NATIONS

1957–65 ..... Did not enter
1968 .... QT 3rd in group
1970 .... Did not enter
1972 .... Did not enter
1974 .... QT 1st round
1976 .... QT 1st round
1978 .... QT Qualified – Final tournament/1st round
1980 .... Did not enter
1982 .... QT 2nd round
1984–88 ..... Did not enter
1990 .... QT pr round
1992 .... QT 3rd/5 in group 4

AFRICAN CLUB COMPETITIONS

AFRICAN CUP: Quarter-finalists – Silures 1978
CUP WINNERS CUP: Semi-finalists – Kadiogo 1978 1980

BURKINA FASO LEAGUE CHAMPIONS

1965	Etoile Filante
1966	AS Fonctionnaires Ouagadougou
1967	US Ouagadougou
1968	USFERAN
1969	AS Fonctionnaires Ouagadougou
1970	ASFA Ouagadougou
1971	ASFA Ouagadougou
1972	Jeanne d'Arc
1973	Jeanne d'Arc
1974	Silures
1975	Silures
1976	Silures
1977	Silures
1978	Silures
1979	Silures
1980	Silures
1981	Silures
1982	–
1983	US Ouagadougou
1984	ASFA Ouagadougou
1985	Etoile Filante
1986	–
1987	–
1988	Etoile Filante
1989	ASFA Yennega
1990	Etoile Filante
1991	Etoile Filante

CLUB DIRECTORY

OUAGADOUGOU (Population – 441 000)
ASFA Ouagadougou

Etoile Filante

Jeanne d'Arc

Union Sportive Ouagadougou

Association Sportive Fonctionnaires

ASFA Yennega

Silures – Folded 1982

BOBO DIOULASSO (Population – 228 000)
Union Sportive Foyer Rails National (USFRAN)

Racing Club

Association Sportive Bobo–Dioulasso

Kadiogo – Folded 1982

CAPE VERDE

Population: 339 000 Area, sq km: 4033
% in urban areas: 33% Capital city: Praia

Federacao Cabo-Verdiana de Futebol
CP 234 Praia
Cape Verde Islands
Tel: (010 238) 611362
Fax: None
Telex: 6030 MICD – CV
Cable: FCF – CV
Languages for correspondence: French & Spanish

Year of formation: 1982
Affiliation to FIFA: 1986
Affiliation to CAF: 1986
Registered clubs: 60
Registered players: 2000
Registered Coaches: 10
Registered referees: 66
National stadium: Estadio da Varzea, Praia 8000
National colours: Shirts: Green/Shorts: Green/Socks: Green
Reserve colours: Shirts: White/Shorts: White/Socks: White
Season: October–July

THE RECORD

WORLD CUP

1930–90 ..... Did not enter

OLYMPIC GAMES

1908–92 ..... Did not enter

AFRICAN CUP OF NATIONS

1957–92 ..... Did not enter

AFRICAN CLUB COMPETITIONS

AFRICAN CUP: First round – Sporting Praia 1992
CUP WINNERS CUP: Have never entered

CLUB DIRECTORY

PRAIA (Population – 37 000)
Sporting Praia

Desportivo Praia

Boavista Praia

Santacruz Praia

Vitoria Praia

MINDELO (Population – 36 000)
Academica Mindelo

Derby Mindelo

CÔTE D'IVOIRE

Population: 12 657 000
Area, sq km: 320 763
% in urban areas: 43%
Capital city: Abidjan and Yamoussoukro

Fédération Ivoirienne de Football
Av 1 Treichville
BP 1202 Abidjan 01
Côte d'Ivoire
Tel: (010 225) 240027
Fax: None
Telex: 22722 FIF CI
Cable: FIF ABIDJAN
Languages for correspondence: French

Year of formation: 1960
Affiliation to FIFA: 1960
Affiliation to CAF: 1960
Registered clubs: 110
Registered players: 3500
Registered coaches: 16
Registered referees: 250
National stadium: Felix Houphouet–Boigny, Abidjan 36 000
National colours: Shirts: White/Shorts: Orange/Socks: Green

Reserve colours: Shirts: Orange/Shorts: White/Socks: Orange
Season: December–August

THE RECORD

WORLD CUP

1930–70 ..... Did not enter
1974 .... QT 3rd round
1978 .... QT 3rd round
1982 .... Did not enter
1986 .... QT 2nd round
1990 .... QT 2nd round

OLYMPIC GAMES

1908–84 ..... Did not enter
1988 .... QT 2nd round
1992 .... Did not enter

AFRICAN CUP OF NATIONS

1957–63 ..... Did not enter
1965 .... 3rd place
1968 .... QT 1st/3 in group 3 – Final tournament/Semi-finalists/3rd place
1970 .... QT Qualified – Final tournament/Semi-finalists/4th place
1972 .... QT 2nd round
1974 .... QT Qualified – Final tournament/1st round
1976 .... QT 1st round
1978 .... QT 2nd round
1980 .... QT Qualified – Final tournament/1st round
1982 .... Did not enter
1984 .... QT Automatic – Final tournament/1st round
1986 .... QT Qualified – Final tournament/Semi-finalists/3rd place
1988 .... QT Qualified – Final tournament/1st round
1990 .... QT Qualified – Final tournament/1st round
1992 .... QT 1st/4 in group 3 – Final tournament/Winners

AFRICAN CLUB COMPETITIONS

AFRICAN CUP: Winners – Stade Abidjan 1966
Finalists – Africa Sports 1986
CUP WINNERS CUP: Finalists – Stella Abidjan 1975, Africa Sports 1980

CÔTE D'IVOIRE LEAGUE CHAMPIONS

1960 Onze Freres
1961 –
1962 Stade Abidjan
1963 Stade Abidjan
1964 ASEC Abidjan
1965 Stade Abidjan
1966 Stade Abidjan
1967 Africa Sports
1968 Africa Sports
1969 Stade Abidjan
1970 ASEC Abidjan
1971 Africa Sports
1972 ASEC Abidjan
1973 ASEC Abidjan
1974 ASEC Abidjan
1975 ASEC Abidjan
1976 SC Gagnoa
1977 Africa Sports
1978 Africa Sports
1979 Stella Club
1980 ASEC Abidjan
1981 Stella Club
1982 Africa Sports
1983 Africa Sports
1984 Stella Club
1985 Africa Sports
1986 Africa Sports
1987 Africa Sports
1988 Africa Sports
1989 Africa Sports
1990 ASEC Abidjan
1991 ASEC Abidjan

CÔTE D'IVOIRE CUP WINNERS

1960 Espoir de Man
1961 Africa Sports
1962 ASEC Abidjan
1963 Jeunesse
1964 Africa Sports
1965 –
1966 –
1967 ASEC Abidjan
1968 ASEC Abidjan
1969 ASEC Abidjan
1970 ASEC Abidjan
1971 Stade Abidjan
1972 ASEC Abidjan
1973 ASEC Abidjan
1974 Stella Club
1975 Stella Club
1976 Stade Abidjan
1977 Africa Sports
1978 Africa Sports
1979 Africa Sports
1980 Reveil Daloa
1981 Africa Sports
1982 Africa Sports
1983 ASEC Abidjan
1984 Stade Abidjan
1985 Africa Sports
1986 Africa Sports
1987 ASC Bouake
1988 ASI Abengouron
1989 Africa Sports
1990 SC Gagnoa
1991 Africa Sports

CLUB DIRECTORY

ABIDJAN (Population – 1 950 000)
Association Sportive Employeés Commercial (ASEC Abidjan)

Stade Abidjan

Africa Sports

Association Sportive Sotra

Stella Club

BOUAKE (Population – 275 000)
Association Sportive Culturelle (ASC Bouaké)

Sporting Club Alliance

DALOA (Population – 85 000)
Reveil Club

GAGNOA (Population – 42 000)
Sporting Club Gagnoa

Onze Freres

THE GAMBIA

Population: 860 000
Area, sq km: 10 689
% in urban areas: 20%
Capital city: Banjul

Gambia Football Association
PO Box 523
Banjul
The Gambia
Tel: (010 220) 95834
Fax: (010 220) 29837
Telex: 2262 FISCO GV
Cable: SPORTS GAMBIA BANJUL
Languages for correspondence: English

Year of formation: 1952
Affiliation to FIFA: 1966
Affiliation to CAF: 1962
Registered clubs: 24
Registered players: 860
Registered referees: 27
National stadium: Box Bar Stadium, Banjul 10 000
National colours: Shirts: White/Shorts: White/Socks: White
Reserve colours: Shirts: Blue/Shorts: Blue/ Socks: White
Season: November–July

THE RECORD

WORLD CUP

1930–78 ..... Did not enter
1982 .... QT 1st round
1986 .... QT 1st round
1990 .... Did not enter

OLYMPIC GAMES

1908–72 ..... Did not enter
1976 .... QT pr round
1980 .... Did not enter
1984 .... QT 1st round
1988–92 ..... Did not enter

AFRICAN CUP OF NATIONS

1957–74 ..... Did not enter
1976 .... QT pr round
1978 .... Did not enter
1980 .... QT 1st round
1982 .... QT pr round
1984 .... QT pr round
1986 .... QT pr round
1988 .... QT pr round
1990 .... Did not enter
1992 .... Did not enter

AFRICAN CLUB COMPETITIONS

AFRICAN CUP: 2nd round – Real Banjul 1979
CUP WINNERS CUP: 2nd round – Wallidan 1979

GAMBIAN LEAGUE CHAMPIONS

1973 Ports Authority
1974 Wallidan
1975 Real Banjul
1976 –
1977 Wallidan
1978 Real Banjul
1979 Wallidan
1980 Starlight
1981 Starlight
1982 Ports Authority
1983 Real Banjul
1984 Ports Authority
1985 Wallidan
1986 Ports Authority
1987–91 –

CLUB DIRECTORY

BANJUL (Population – 95 000)
Real Banjul

Wallidan

Ports Authority

Starlight

Augustinians

Hawks

GHANA

Population: 15 020 000
Area, sq km: 238 533
% in urban areas: 31%
Capital city: Accra

Ghana Football Association
PO Box 1272
Accra
Ghana
Tel: (010 233) 21 663924
Fax: (010 233) 21 662019
Telex: 2519 SPORTS GH
Cable: GFA ACCRA
Languages for correspondence: English

Year of formation: 1957
Affiliation to FIFA: 1958
Affiliation to CAF: 1958
Registered clubs: 185
Registered players: 11 200
Registered referees: 376
National stadium: Accra Sports Stadium 34 000
National colours: Shirts: White/Shorts: White/Socks: White
Reserve colours: Shirts: Yellow/Shorts: Yellow/Socks: Yellow
Season: January–November

THE RECORD

WORLD CUP

1930–58 ..... Did not enter
1962 .... QT 2nd round
1966 .... Did not enter
1970 .... QT 2nd round
1974 .... QT 3rd round
1978 .... QT 1st round
1982 .... Did not enter
1986 .... QT 3rd round
1990 .... QT 1st round

OLYMPIC GAMES

1908–56 ..... Did not enter
1960 .... QT 1st round
1964 .... QT Qualified – Final tournament/Quarter-finalists
1968 .... QT Qualified – Final tournament/1st round
1972 .... QT Qualified – Final tournament/1st round
1976 .... QT Qualified/withdrew
1980 .... QT Qualified/withdrew
1984 .... QT 2nd round
1988 .... QT 3rd round
1992 .... QT Qualified

AFRICAN CUP OF NATIONS

1957–62 ..... Did not enter
1963 .... Winners
1965 .... Winners
1968 .... QT Automatic – Final tournament/Finalists
1970 .... QT Qualified – Final tournament/Finalists
1972 .... QT 2nd round
1974 .... QT 2nd round
1976 .... QT 2nd round
1978 .... QT Automatic – Final tournament/Winners
1980 .... QT Automatic – Final tournament/1st round
1982 .... QT Qualified – Final tournament/Winners
1984 .... QT Automatic – Final tournament/1st round
1986 .... QT 2nd round
1988 .... QT 1st round
1990 .... QT 1st round
1992 .... QT 1st/5 in group 4 – Final tournament/Finalists

AFRICAN CLUB COMPETITIONS

AFRICAN CUP: Winners – Asante Kotoko 1970 1983
Finalists – Asante Kotoko 1967 1971 1973 1982, Hearts of Oak 1977 1979
CUP WINNERS CUP: Semi-finalists – Sekondi Hasaacas 1981, Hearts of Oak 1982

GHANAIAN LEAGUE CHAMPIONS

1957 Hearts of Oak
1958 Hearts of Oak
1959 Asante Kotoko
1960 Eleven Wise FC
1961 –
1962 Hearts of Oak
1963 Asante Kotoko
1964 Asante Kotoko
1965 Asante Kotoko
1966 Real Republicans
1967 Asante Kotoko
1968 Cape Coast Dwarfs
1969 Asante Kotoko
1970 Asante Kotoko
1970 Great Olympics
1971 Hearts of Oak
1972 Asante Kotoko
1973 Hearts of Oak
1974 Great Olympics
1975 Asante Kotoko
1976 Hearts of Oak
1977 Hearts of Oak
1978 Hearts of Oak
1979 Hearts of Oak
1980 Asante Kotoko
1981 Asante Kotoko
1982 Asante Kotoko
1983 Asante Kotoko
1984 Hearts of Oak
1985 Hearts of Oak
1986 Asante Kotoko
1987 Asante Kotoko
1988 –
1989 Asante Kotoko
1990 Hearts of Oak
1991 Asante Kotoko

GHANAIAN CUP WINNERS

1958 Asante Kotoko
1959 Cornerstones
1960 Asante Kotoko
1961 –
1962 Real Republicans
1963 Real Republicans
1964 Real Republicans
1965 Real Republicans
1966–68 –
1969 Cape Coast Dwarfs
1970–72 –

1973	Hearts of Oak
1974	Hearts of Oak
1975	Great Olympics
1976	Asante Kotoko
1977	–
1978	Asante Kotoko
1979	Hearts of Oak
1980	–
1981	Hearts of Oak
1982	Eleven Wise FC
1983	Great Olympics
1984	Asante Kotoko
1985	Sekondi Hasaacas
1986	Okwahu United
1987	Hearts of Oak
1988	–
1989	Hearts of Oak
1990	Hearts of Oak
1991	–

CLUB DIRECTORY

ACCRA (Population – 1 250 000)
Hearts of Oak

Great Olympics

Real Republicans (Folded 1966)

KUMASI (Population – 600 000)
Asante Kotoko

Cornerstones

SEKONDI (Population – 175 000)
Sekondi Hasaacas

Eleven Wise FC

TAMALE (Population – 168 000)
Real Tamale United

OBUASI (Population – 60 000)
Obuasi Goldfields

NKAWKAW
Okwahu United

GUINEA-BISSAU

Population: 973 000
Area, sq km: 36 125
% in urban areas: 28%
Capital city: Bissau

Federacao de Football da Guinea-Bissau
Apartado 75
1035 Bissau – Codex
Guinea–Bissau
Tel: (010 245) 212545
Fax: None
Telex: PAIGC 230 BI
Cable: FUTEBOL BISSAU
Languages for correspondence: Spanish & French

Year of formation: 1974
Affiliation to FIFA: 1986
Affiliation to CAF: 1986
Registered clubs: 16
Registered players: 900
Registered coaches: 29
Registered referees: 31
National stadium: Lino Correia 12 000
National colours: Shirts: Green/Shorts: Green/Socks: Green
Reserve colours: Shirts: Yellow/Shorts: Yellow/Socks: Yellow
Season: October–July

THE RECORD

WORLD CUP

1930–90 ..... Did not enter

OLYMPIC GAMES

1908–92 ..... Did not enter

AFRICAN CUP OF NATIONS

1957–92 ..... Did not enter

AFRICAN CLUB COMPETITIONS

AFRICAN CUP: 2nd round – Sporting Clube Bissau 1984
CUP WINNERS CUP: 2nd round – Sporting Club Bissau 1977

GUINEA BISSAU LEAGUE CHAMPIONS

1975	Balantes
1976	UDIB Bissau
1977	Benfica
1978	–
1979	Benfica
1980	Benfica
1981	–
1982	Benfica
1983	Sporting Clube Bissau
1984	Sporting Clube Bissau
1985	UDIB Bissau
1986	Sporting Clube Bissau
1987	Sporting Clube Batafa
1988	Benfica
1989	Benfica
1990	Sporting Clube Bissau

CLUB DIRECTORY

BISSAU (Population – 109 000)
Benfica

Uniao Deportiva Internacional Bissau (UDIB)

Sporting Clube

Ajuda Sport

BATAFA
Sporting Clube

MANSOA
Balantas

GUINEA

Population: 6 876 000
Area, sq km: 245 857
% in urban areas: 23%
Capital city: Conakry

Fédération Guinéenne de Football
PO Box 262
Conakry
Guinea
Tel: (010 224) 445041
Fax: None
Telex: 22302 MJ GE
Cable: GUINEFOOT CONAKRY
Languages for correspondence: French

Year of formation: 1959
Affiliation to FIFA: 1961
Affiliation to CAF: 1962
Registered clubs: 46
Registered players: 8500
Registered coaches: 48
Registered referees: 136
National stadium: Stade du 28 septembre, Conakry 40 000
National colours: Shirts: Red/Shorts: Yellow/Socks: Green
Reserve colours: Shirts: White/Shorts: White/Socks: White
Season: November–July

THE RECORD

WORLD CUP

1930–70 ..... Did not enter
1974 .... QT 2nd round
1978 .... QT 3rd round
1982 .... QT 3rd round
1986 .... QT 2nd round
1990 .... QT 1st round

OLYMPIC GAMES

1908–64 ..... Did not enter
1968 .... QT Qualified – Final tournament/1st round
1972 .... QT 1st round
1976 .... QT 2nd round
1980 .... Did not enter
1984 .... QT 1st round
1988–92 ..... Did not enter

AFRICAN CUP OF NATIONS

1957–65 ..... Did not enter
1968 .... QT 2nd in group
1970 .... QT Qualified – Final tournament/1st round
1972 .... QT 2nd round
1974 .... QT Qualified – Final tournament/1st round
1976 .... QT Qualified – Final tournament/2nd round/2nd place
1978 .... QT 2nd round

1980 .... QT Qualified – Final tournament/1st round
1982 .... QT 2nd round
1984 .... QT 1st round
1986 .... QT 1st round
1988 .... QT 1st round
1990 .... QT 1st round
1992 .... QT 3rd/4 in group 1

AFRICAN CLUB COMPETITIONS

AFRICAN CUP: Winners – Hafia FC Conakry 1972 1975 1977
Finalists – Hafia FC Conakry 1976 1978
CUP WINNERS CUP: Winners – Horoya AC Conakry 1978

GUINEA LEAGUE CHAMPIONS

1965	Conakry I
1966	Conakry II
1967	Conakry II
1968	Conakry II
1969	Conakry I
1970	Conakry I
1971	Hafia FC
1972	Hafia FC
1973	Hafia FC
1974	Hafia FC
1975	Hafia FC
1976	Hafia FC
1977	Hafia FC
1978	Hafia FC
1979	Hafia FC
1980	Kalum Star
1981	Kalum Star
1982	Hafia FC
1983	Hafia FC
1984	Kalum Star
1985	Hafia FC
1986	Horoya AC
1987	Kalum Star
1988	Horoya AC
1989	Horoya AC
1990	Horoya AC
1991	Horoya AC

CLUB DIRECTORY

CONAKRY (Population – 800 000)
Hafia FC (Formerly Conakry II)

Horoya AC

Kalum Star (Formerly Conakry I)

Gbessia AC

Kakimbo FC

ASFAG Conakry

LIBERIA

Population: 2 595 000
Area, sq km: 99 067
% in urban areas: 39%
Capital city: Monrovia

The Liberia Football Association
PO Box 1066
Monrovia 1000
Liberia
Tel: (010 231) 222177
Fax: None
Telex: 44508 IFALI
Cable: LIBFOTASS MONROVIA
Languages for correspondence: English

Year of formation: 1936
Affiliation to FIFA: 1962
Affiliation to CAF: 1962
Registered clubs: 60
Registered players: 2100
Registered coaches: 48
Registered referees: 50
National stadium: National Sports Complex, Monrovia 35 000
National colours: Shirts: Red/Shorts: White/Socks: Blue
Reserve colours: Shirts: Blue/Shorts: White/Socks: Red
Season: January–October

THE RECORD

WORLD CUP

1930–78 ..... Did not enter
1982 .... QT 2nd round
1986 .... QT 1st round
1990 .... QT 2nd round

OLYMPIC GAMES

1908–60 ..... Did not enter
1964 .... QT 1st round
1968 .... Did not enter
1972 .... QT 1st round
1976 .... QT 1st round
1980 .... QT 3rd round
1984 .... Did not enter
1988 .... QT 1st round
1992 .... Did not enter

AFRICAN CUP OF NATIONS

1957–65 ..... Did not enter
1968 .... QT 3rd in group
1970–74 ..... Did not enter
1976 .... QT pr round
1978 .... Did not enter
1980 .... Did not enter
1982 .... QT 1st round
1984 .... Did not enter
1986 .... QT pr round
1988 .... QT pr round
1990 .... QT pr round
1992 .... Did not enter

AFRICAN CLUB COMPETITIONS

AFRICAN CUP: 2nd round – Invincible Eleven 1982. Mighty Barolle 1987
CUP WINNERS CUP: Quarter-finalists – LPRC Oilers 1989

LIBERIAN LEAGUE CHAMPIONS

1965	Invincible Eleven
1966	Invincible Eleven
1967	Mighty Barolle
1968–71	–
1972	Mighty Barolle
1973	Mighty Barolle
1974	Mighty Barolle
1975	–
1976	St Joseph
1977	–
1978	St Joseph
1979	St Joseph
1980	Invincible Eleven
1981	Invincible Eleven
1982	–
1983	Invincible Eleven
1984	Invincible Eleven
1985	Invincible Eleven
1986	Mighty Barolle
1987	Invincible Eleven
1988	Mighty Barolle
1989	Mighty Barolle
1990	–
1991	LPRC Oilers

CLUB DIRECTORY

MONROVIA (Population – 465 000)
Mighty Barolle

St Joseph Warriors

Invincible Eleven

Cedar United

LPRC Oilers

Bame Monrovia

MALI

Population: 8 151 000
Area, sq km: 1 240 192
% in urban areas: 22%
Capital city: Bamako

Fédération Malienne de Football
Stade Mamadou Konate
BP 1020
Bamako
Mali
Tel: (010 223) 224152
Fax: None
Telex: 09851200
Cable: MALIFOOT BAMAKO
Languages for correspondence: French
Year of formation: 1960
Affiliation to FIFA: 1962
Affiliation to CAF: 1963
Registered clubs: 205
Registered players: 12 000
Registered coaches: 65
Registered referees: 145

National stadium: Omnisports, Bamako 25 000
National colours: Shirts: Green/Shorts: Yellow/Socks: Red
Reserve colours: Shirts: White/Shorts: Red/Socks: White
Season: October–June

THE RECORD

WORLD CUP

1930–90 ..... Did not enter

OLYMPIC GAMES

1908–68 ..... Did not enter
1972 .... QT 2nd round
1976 .... QT 2nd round
1980 .... QT 1st round
1984–92 ..... Did not enter

AFRICAN CUP OF NATIONS

1957–65 ..... Did not enter
1968 .... QT 2nd in group
1970 .... QT 2nd round
1972 .... QT Qualified – Final tournament/Finalists
1974 .... QT 2nd round
1976 .... QT 1st round
1978 .... QT 2nd round
1980 .... Did not enter
1982 .... QT 1st round
1984 .... QT 1st round
1986 .... QT 1st round
1988 .... Did not enter
1990 .... QT 2nd round
1992 .... QT 4th/4 in group 1

AFRICAN CLUB COMPETITIONS

AFRICAN CUP: Finalists – Stade Malien 1964, AS Real Bamako 1966
CUP WINNERS CUP: Semi-finalists – Djoliba AC 1981 1982

MALI LEAGUE CHAMPIONS

1966	Djoliba AC
1967	Djoliba AC
1968	Djoliba AC
1969	AS Real Bamako
1970	Stade Malien
1971	Djoliba AC
1972	Stade Malien
1973	Djoliba AC
1974	Djoliba AC
1975	Djoliba AC
1976	Djoliba AC
1977	–
1978	–
1979	Djoliba AC
1980	AS Real Bamako
1981	AS Real Bamako
1982	Djoliba AC
1983	AS Real Bamako
1984	Stade Malien
1985	Djoliba AC
1986	AS Real Bamako
1987	Stade Malien
1988	Djoliba AC
1989	Stade Malien
1990	Djoliba AC
1991	AS Real Bamako
1992	Sahel SC

CLUB DIRECTORY

BAMAKO (Population – 646 000)
Djoliba Athletic Club

Association Sportive Real Bamako

Stade Malien

MAURITANIA

Population: 1 999 000
Area, sq km: 1 030 700
% in urban areas: 34%
Capital city: Nouakchott

Fédération de Football de la République de Mauritanie
BP 566
Nouakchott
Mauritania
Tel: (010 222) 2 51860
Fax: None
Telex: 577 MTN NKTT RIM
Cable: FOOTRIM NOUAKCHOTT
Languages for correspondence: French

Year of formation: 1961
Affiliation to FIFA: 1964
Affiliation to CAF: 1968
Registered clubs: 29
Registered players: 1500
Registered coaches: 44
Registered referees: 97
National stadium: Stade National, Nouakchott 6000
National colours: Shirts: Yellow/Shorts: Blue/Socks: Green
Reserve colours: Shirts: Green/Shorts: Yellow/Socks: Yellow
Season: November–July

THE RECORD

WORLD CUP

1930–74 ..... Did not enter
1978 .... QT pr round
1982–90 ..... Did not enter

OLYMPIC GAMES

1908–72 ..... Did not enter
1976 .... QT 1st round
1980 .... Did not enter
1984 .... QT pr round
1988 .... Did not enter
1992 .... QT 1st round

AFRICAN CUP OF NATIONS

1957–78 ..... Did not enter
1980 .... QT 1st round
1982 .... QT pr round
1984 .... Did not enter
1986 .... QT 1st round
1988 .... Did not enter
1990 .... Did not enter
1992 .... QT 4th/4 in group 3

AFRICAN CLUB COMPETITIONS

AFRICAN CUP: 2nd round – Espoirs Nouakchott 1977
CUP WINNERS CUP: 2nd round – ASC Garde Nationale 1978

MAURITANIAN LEAGUE CHAMPIONS

1976	ASC Garde Nationale
1977	ASC Garde Nationale
1978	ASC Garde Nationale
1979	ASC Garde Nationale
1980	–
1981	AS Police
1982	AS Police
1983	AS Ksar
1984	ASC Garde Nationale
1985	AS Ksar
1986	AS Police
1987	AS Police
1988	AS Police
1989	–
1990	AS Police
1991	AS Police

CLUB DIRECTORY

NOUAKCHOTT (Population – 285 000)
Association Sportive Culturelle Garde Nationale

Association Sportive Police

Association Sportive Culturelle Ksar

Association Sportive Forces Armees

Espoirs Nouakchott

NIGER

Population: 7 779 000
Area, sq km: 1 186 408
% in urban areas: 21%
Capital city: Niamey

Fédération Nigerienne de Football
Stade National Niamey
BP 10299 Niamey
Niger
Tel: (010 227) 734705
Fax: (010 227) 735512
Telex: 975 5527
Cable: FEDERFOOT NIGER NIAMEY
Languages for correspondence: French

Year of formation: 1967
Affiliation to FIFA: 1967
Affiliation to CAF: 1967
Registered clubs: 64
Registered players: 1500
Registered referees: 74
National stadium: Stade National 7000
National colours: Shirts: Orange/Shorts: White/Socks: Green
Reserve colours: Shirts: Green/Shorts: White/Socks: Orange
Season: October–July

THE RECORD

WORLD CUP

1930–74 ..... Did not enter
1978 .... QT pr round
1982 .... QT 3rd round
1986 .... Did not enter
1990 .... Did not enter

OLYMPIC GAMES

1908–64 ..... Did not enter
1968 .... QT pr round
1972 .... QT 1st round
1976–92 ..... Did not enter

AFRICAN CUP OF NATIONS

1957–68 ..... Did not enter
1970 .... QT 2nd round
1972 .... QT 1st round
1974 .... Did not enter
1976 .... QT 1st round
1978–82 ..... Did not enter
1984 .... QT pr round
1986–90 ..... Did not enter
1992 .... QT 3rd/4 in group 3

AFRICAN CLUB COMPETITIONS

AFRICAN CUP: 2nd round – Olympic Niamey 1978
CUP WINNERS CUP: 2nd round – Olympic Niamey 1991

NIGER LEAGUE CHAMPIONS

1966	Secteur 6
1967	Secteur 6
1968	Secteur 6
1969	Secteur 6
1970	Secteur 6
1971	ASFAN Niamey
1972	–
1973	Secteur 7
1974	Olympic FC
1975	ASFAN Niamey
1976	Olympic FC
1977	Olympic FC
1978	Olympic FC
1979	–
1980	AS Niamey
1981	AS Niamey
1982	AS Niamey
1983	Djan-Gorzo Maradi
1984	Espoir FC Zinder
1985	Zumunta AC
1986	–
1987	Sahel SC
1988	Zumunta AC
1989	Olympic FC
1990	Olympic FC
1991	Sahel SC

CLUB DIRECTORY

NIAMEY (Population – 398 000)
Liberté FC

Secteur 6

Association Sportive Niamey

Association Sportive Forces Armees (ASFAN Niamey)

Sahel Sporting Club

Olympic Niamey FC

Zumunta Athletic Club

ZINDER (Population – 120 000)
Espoir FC Zinder
Zindourma

MARADI (Population – 112 000)
Djan-Gorzo FC

NIGERIA

Population: 119 812 000
Area, sq km: 923 768
% in urban areas: 31%
Capital city: Lagos

Nigeria Football Association
National Stadium
PO Box 466
Lagos
Nigeria
Tel: (010 234) 1 835265
Fax: (010 234) 1 824912
Telex: 26570 NFA NG
Cable: FOOTBALL LAGOS
Languages for correspondence: English

Year of formation: 1945
Affiliation to FIFA: 1959
Affiliation to CAF: 1959
Registered clubs: 521
Registered players: 21 100
Registered referees: 1384
National stadium: National Stadium, Lagos 50 000
National colours: Shirts: Green/Shorts: Green/Socks: Green
Reserve colours: Shirts: White/Shorts: White/Socks: White
Season: February–November

THE RECORD

WORLD CUP

1930–58 ..... Did not enter
1962 .... QT 1st round
1966 .... Did not enter
1970 .... QT 3rd round
1974 .... QT 2nd round
1978 .... QT 4th round
1982 .... QT 4th round
1986 .... QT 3rd round
1990 .... QT 2nd round

OLYMPIC GAMES

1908–56 ..... Did not enter
1960 .... QT 1st round
1964 .... QT 1st round
1968 .... Qualified – Final tournament/1st round
1972 .... QT 1st round
1976 .... QT Qualified/withdrew
1980 .... QT Qualified – Final tournament/1st round
1984 .... QT 3rd round
1988 .... QT 1st round
1992 .... Did not enter

AFRICAN CUP OF NATIONS

1957–62 ..... Did not enter
1963 .... 1st round
1965 .... Did not enter
1968 .... QT 2nd/3 in group 3
1970 .... Did not enter
1972 .... QT 1st round
1974 .... QT 2nd round
1976 .... QT Qualified – Final tournament/2nd round/3rd place
1978 .... QT Qualified – Final tournament/Semi-finalists/3rd place
1980 .... QT Automatic – Final tournament/Winners
1982 .... QT Automatic – Final tournament/1st round
1984 .... QT Qualified – Final tournament/Finalists
1986 .... QT 2nd round
1988 .... QT Qualified – Final tournament/Finalists
1990 .... QT Qualified – Final tournament/Finalists
1992 .... QT 2nd/5 in group 4 – Final tournament/3rd place

AFRICAN GAMES

Winners 1973

AFRICAN CLUB COMPETITIONS

AFRICAN CUP: Finalists – Enugu Rangers 1975, IICC Shooting Stars 1984, Iwuanyanwu Owerri 1988
CUP WINNERS CUP: Winners – IICC Shooting Stars 1976, Enugu Rangers 1977, BCC Lions 1990

Finalists – Stationary Stores 1981, Leventis United 1985, Ranchers Bees 1988, Bendel United 1989, BCC Lions 1991

NIGERIAN LEAGUE CHAMPIONS

1972	Mighty Jets
1973	Bendel Insurance
1974	Enugu Rangers
1975	Enugu Rangers
1976	IICC Shooting Stars
1977	Stationary Stores
1978	Racca Rovers
1979	Bendel Insurance
1980	IICC Shooting Stars
1981	Enugu Rangers
1982	Enugu Rangers
1983	IICC Shooting Stars
1984	Enugu Rangers
1985	New Nigeria Bank
1986	Leventis United
1987	Iwuanyanwu Owerri
1988	Iwuanyanwu Owerri
1989	Iwuanyanwu Owerri
1990	Iwuanyanwu Owerri
1991	Julius Berger

NIGERIAN FA CHALLENGE CUP WINNERS

1945	Marine
1946	Lagos Railways
1947	Marine
1948	Lagos Railways
1949	Lagos Railways
1950	GO Urion
1951	Lagos Railways
1952	Lagos Pan Bank
1953	Kano
1954	Calabar
1955	Port Harcourt
1956	Lagos Railways
1957	Lagos Railways
1958	Port Harcourt
1959	Ibadan Lions
1960	Lagos EDN
1961	Ibadan Lions
1962	Police
1963	Port Harcourt
1964	Lagos Railways
1965	Lagos EDN
1966	Ibadan Lions
1967	Stationary Stores
1968	Stationary Stores
1969	Ibadan Lions
1970	Lagos EDN
1971	IICC Shooting Stars
1972	Bendel Insurance
1973	–
1974	Enugu Rangers
1975	Enugu Rangers
1976	Enugu Rangers
1977	IICC Shooting Stars
1978	Bendel Insurance
1979	IICC Shooting Stars
1980	Bendel Insurance
1981	Enugu Rangers
1982	Stationary Stores
1983	Enugu Rangers
1984	Leventis United
1985	Abiola Babes
1986	Leventis United
1987	Abiola Babes
1988	Iwuanyanwu Owerri
1989	BCC Lions
1990	Stationary Stores
1991	El Kanemi Warriors

CLUB DIRECTORY

LAGOS (Population – 1213000)
Stationary Stores FC

Water Corporation FC

Julius Berger

IBADAN (Population – 1144000)
Leventis United

IICC Shooting Stars

KANO (Population – 538000)
Raccah Rovers

PORT HARCOURT (Population 327000)
Nigerian Ports Authority

KADUNA (Population – 273000)
Ranchers Bees

ENUGU (Population – 252000)
Enugu Rangers International

BENIN CITY (Population – 183000)
Bendel Insurance FC

New Nigerian Bank FC

JOS (Population – 164000)
Mighty Jets

GBOKO (Population – 49000)
BCC Lions

OWERRI (Population – 32000)
Iwuanyanwu National

SENEGAL

Population: 7277000
Area, sq km: 196722
% in urban areas: 38%
Capital city: Dakar

Fédération Sénégalaise de Football
Stade de l'Amite
Route de l'Aeroport de Yoff
BP 13021
Dakar
Senegal
Tel: (010 221) 243524
Fax: (010 221) 220241
Telex: 21741
Cable: SENEFOOT DAKAR

Languages for correspondence: French & English

Year of formation: 1960
Affiliation to FIFA: 1962
Affiliation to CAF: 1963
Registered clubs: 75
Registered players: 7000
Registered referees: 179
National stadium: Stade de l'Amitè, Dakar 60000
National colours: Shirts: Green/Shorts: Yellow/Socks: Red
Reserve colours: Shirts: Red/Shorts: Yellow/Socks: Green
Season: October–July

THE RECORD

WORLD CUP

1930–66 ..... Did not enter
1970 .... QT 1st round
1974 .... QT 1st round
1978 .... QT 1st round
1982 .... QT 1st round
1986 .... QT 1st round
1990 .... Did not enter

OLYMPIC GAMES

1908–68 ..... Did not enter
1972 .... QT 2nd round
1976 .... QT 3rd round
1980 .... QT 1st round
1984 .... QT 2nd round
1988 .... QT 1st round
1992 .... QT 1st round

AFRICAN CUP OF NATIONS

1957–62 ..... Did not enter
1965 .... 4th place
1968 .... QT 1st/3 in group 1 – Final tournament/1st round
1970 .... QT 2nd round
1972 .... QT 1st round
1974 .... QT 1st round
1976 .... QT 1st round
1978 .... QT 2nd round
1980 .... Did not enter
1982 .... QT 1st round
1984 .... QT 2nd round
1986 .... QT Qualified – Final tournament/1st round
1988 .... QT 2nd round
1990 .... QT Qualified – Final tournament/Semi-finalists/4th place
1992 .... QT Automatic – Final tournament/Quarter-finalists

AFRICAN CLUB COMPETITIONS

AFRICAN CUP: Semi-finalists – ASC Jeanne d'Arc 1974, US Goree 1979 1985, ASC Diaraf 1983
CUP WINNERS CUP: Semi-finalists – ASC Jeanne d'Arc 1975

SENEGAL LEAGUE CHAMPIONS

1966	Olympique Thies
1967	Espoir St Louis
1968	Foyer France
1969	Jeanne d'Arc
1970	ASC Diaraf
1971	ASFA Dakar
1972	ASFA Dakar
1973	ASC Jeanne d'Arc
1974	ASFA Dakar
1975	ASC Diaraf
1976	ASC Diaraf
1977	ASC Diaraf
1978	US Goree
1979	AS Police
1980	SEIB Diourbel
1981	US Goree
1982	ASC Diaraf
1983	SEIB Diourbel
1984	US Goree
1985	ASC Jeanne d'Arc
1986	ASC Jeanne d'Arc
1987	SEIB Diourbel
1988	ASC Jeanne d'Arc
1989	ASC Diaraf
1990	Port Autonome
1991	Port Autonome

SENEGAL CUP WINNERS

1961	Espoir St Louis
1962	ASC Jeanne d'Arc
1963	US Rail
1964	US Ouakam
1965	US Goree
1966	AS St Louisienne
1967	Foyer France
1968	Foyer France
1969	ASC Jeanne d'Arc
1970	ASC Diaraf
1971	ASC Linguère
1972	US Goree
1973	ASC Diaraf
1974	ASC Jeanne d'Arc
1975	ASC Diaraf
1976	AS Police
1977	Saltigues
1978	AS Police
1979	Casa Sport
1980	ASC Jeanne d'Arc
1981	AS Police
1982	ASC Diaraf
1983	ASC Diaraf
1984	ASC Jeanne d'Arc
1985	ASC Diaraf
1986	AS Douanes
1987	ASC Jeanne d'Arc
1988	ASC Linguère
1989	US Ouakam
1990	ASC Linguère
1991	ASC Diaraf

CLUB DIRECTORY

DAKAR (Population – 1 248 000)
Association Sportive Culturelle Jeanne d'Arc (ASC Jeanne d'Arc Dakar)

Association Sportive Culturelle Diaraf (ASC Diaraf Dakar)

Association Sportive Police Dakar (AS Police Dakar)

Association Sportive Douanes Dakar (AS Douanes Dakar)

Union Sportive Goree (US Goree Dakar)

Association Sportive Forces Armees (ASFA Dakar)

Union Sportive Ouakam (US Ouakam)

Port Autonome

THIES (Population – 156 000)
Union Sportive Rail (US Rail)

SAINT LOUIS (Population – 91 000)
Association Sportive Saint Louisienne (AS St Louisienne)

Association Sportive Culturelle Linguère (ASC Linguère)

ZINGUINCHOR (Population – 106 000)
Casa Sports

DIOURBEL (Population – 76 000)
Societe Electrique Industrial de Baol (SEIB Diourbel)

SIERRA LEONE

Population: 4 151 000
Area, sq km: 71 740
% in urban areas: 28%
Capital city: Freetown

Sierra Leone Amateur Football Association
Siaka Stevens Stadium
Brookfields
PO Box 672
Freetown
Sierra Leone
Tel: (010 232) 22 41872 Fax: None
Telex: 3210 BOOTH SL
Cable: SLFA FREETOWN
Languages for correspondence: English

Year of formation: 1923
Affiliation to FIFA: 1967
Affiliation to CAF: 1967
Registered clubs: 40
Registered players: 2000
Registered coaches: 51
Registered referees: 109
National stadium: Siaka Stevens, Freetown 30 000
National colours: Shirts: Green/Shorts: White/Socks: Blue
Reserve colours: Shirts: Blue/Shorts: White/Socks: Blue
Season: February–December

THE RECORD

WORLD CUP

1930–70 ..... Did not enter
1974 .... QT 1st round
1978 .... QT 1st round
1982 .... QT 1st round
1986 .... QT 1st round
1990 .... Did not enter

OLYMPIC GAMES

1908–76 ..... Did not enter
1980 .... QT 2nd round
1984 .... Did not enter
1988 .... QT 1st round
1992 .... QT 2nd round

AFRICAN CUP OF NATIONS

1957–72 ..... Did not enter
1974 .... QT 1st round
1976 .... Did not enter
1978 .... QT 1st round
1980 .... Did not enter
1982 .... QT pr round
1984 .... QT pr round
1986 .... QT 1st round
1988 .... QT 2nd round
1990 .... Did not enter
1992 .... QT 2nd/4 in group 1

AFRICAN CLUB COMPETITIONS

AFRICAN CUP: Quarter-finalists – Mighty Blackpool 1989
CUP WINNERS CUP: 2nd round – Bai-Bureh Warriors 1979. Real Republicans 1981 1988. East End Lions 1990

SIERRA LEONE LEAGUE CHAMPIONS

1978	Mighty Blackpool
1979	Mighty Blackpool
1980	East End Lions
1981	Real Republicans
1982	Sierra Fisheries
1983	Real Republicans
1984	Real Republicans
1985	East End Lions
1986	Sierra Fisheries
1987	Sierra Fisheries
1988	Mighty Blackpool
1989	Freetown United
1990	Old Edwardians
1991	Mighty Blackpool

CLUB DIRECTORY

FREETOWN (Population – 525 000)
Real Republicans

Mighty Blackpool Sports Club

Sierra Fisheries

Ports Authority

Freetown United

Old Edwardians St Edwards

East End Lions

KENEMA (Population – 52 000)
Kamboi Eagles

BONBALI
Walum Stars

PORT LOKO
Bai-Bureh Warriors

TOGO

Population: 3764000
Area, sq km: 56785
% in urban areas: 23%
Capital city: Lomé

Fédération Togolaise de Football
CP 5
Lomé
Togo
Tel: (010 228) 212698
Fax: None
Telex: 5015 CNOT TG
Cable: TOGOFOOT LOME
Languages for correspondence: French

Year of formation: 1960
Affiliation to FIFA: 1962
Affiliation to CAF: 1963
Registered clubs: 24
Registered players: 7000
Registered referees: 147
National stadium: Stade Général Eyadema, Lomé 20000
National colours: Shirts: Red/Shorts: White/Socks: Red
Reserve colours: Shirts: White/Shorts: White/Socks: White
Season: October–July

THE RECORD

WORLD CUP

1930–70 ..... Did not enter
1974 .... QT 1st round
1978 .... QT 2nd round
1982 .... QT 2nd round
1986 .... Did not enter
1990 .... Did not enter

OLYMPIC GAMES

1908–68 ..... Did not enter
1972 .... QT 2nd round
1976 .... QT 1st round
1980 .... Did not enter
1984 .... QT 1st round
1988–92 ..... Did not enter

AFRICAN CUP OF NATIONS

1957–65 ..... Did not enter
1968 .... QT 3rd/3 in group 3
1970 .... QT 1st round
1972 .... QT Qualified – Final tournament/1st round
1974 .... Did not enter
1976 .... QT 2nd round
1978 .... QT 1st round
1980 .... QT 2nd round
1982 .... QT 1st round
1984 .... QT Qualified – Final tournament/1st round
1986 .... QT 1st round
1988 .... QT 1st round
1990 .... Did not enter
1992 .... QT 4th/5 in group 4

AFRICAN CLUB COMPETITIONS

AFRICAN CUP: Finalists – Etoile Filante 1968
CUP WINNERS CUP: Finalists – Agaza Lomé 1983

TOGOLESE LEAGUE CHAMPIONS

1965	Etoile Filante
1966	Modele Lomé
1967	Etoile Filante
1968	Etoile Filante
1969	Modele Lomé
1970	Dynamic Lomé
1971	Dynamic Lomé
1972	Modele Lomé
1973	Modele Lomé
1974	Lomé I
1975	Lomé I
1976	Lomé I
1977	–
1978	–
1979	Semassi Sokodé
1980	Agaza Lomé
1981	Semassi Sokodé
1982	Semassi Sokodé
1983	Semassi Sokodé
1984	Agaza Lomé
1985	ASFOSA
1986	ASFOSA
1987	Doumbe Sausanné-Mango
1988	ASKO Kara
1989	ASKO Kara
1990	Ifodje Atakpame

CLUB DIRECTORY

LOME (Population – 400 000)
Agaza Omnisports Club

Aiglons de Lomé

Association Sportive de la Foret Sacree (ASFOSA Lomé)

Entente II

AC Modele (Folded 1974)

Etoile Filante (Folded 1974)

Dynamic Togolais (Folded 1974)

SOKODE (Population – 48 000)
Semassi de Sokode

LAMA KARA
Association Sportive de Kozah (ASKO Kara)
Club Sportive Lama Kara

SANSANNE MANGO
Doumbe

ATAKPAME
Ifodje

CENTRAL AFRICA

Central Africa is made up of eight countries, although in the Central African Games, Angola, Burundi and Rwanda are invited to take part despite not being classified in the region by the CAF. The big three are Cameroon, Congo and Zaire, though the latter two have seen their influence decline in recent years. In Cameroon, the region has the most celebrated of all Africa's teams.

In the 1990 World Cup, Cameroon were ten minutes away from reaching the semi-finals, but two penalties carelessly given away let England off the hook in what was undoubtedly the best match of the tournament. That performance earned Africa a third slot in future finals. Eight years previously, again with Roger Milla as their star player, Cameroon had impressed in the World Cup in Spain. Italy, the eventual winners, only qualified for the second round at Cameroon's expense by virtue of having scored more goals.

Cameroon was a relative late developer in football. It was the only country under French rule which was not affiliated to the French Football Federation and the situation was made even more complicated by the division of the country into a British and French Protectorate. This was only finally solved in 1961 when the northern part of the British-controlled territory voted to join Nigeria, and the south Cameroon.

Oryx Douala, one of the famous pre-independence clubs, were quick to take up the challenge of the new African Cup of Champion Clubs, and they hold a special place in African football as the first winners. Since then, however, other clubs from Yaounde and Douala have emerged, most notably Canon and Tonnerre from the former and Union from the latter. These three clubs have dominated both the league and cup since the 1970s.

In African club competitions in the 1970s, Canon, Tonnerre and Union were unstoppable, winning eight titles and appearing in a further three finals. Since Union's win in the 1981 Cup Winners Cup, however, the titles have dried up and the focus has switched to the national side. The North Africans may have dimmed the challenge of clubs from the Cameroon, but the 'Indomitable Lions', as the national side are known, have swept all before them. On three consecutive occasions from 1984 to 1988 they appeared in the final of the Cup of Nations and were only denied a hat-trick of titles when Egypt won the 1986 competition on penalties.

Although Roger Milla has stolen much of the limelight with his displays for the side, especially in the 1990 World Cup, Cameroon has been represented by many fine players in the 1980s. Thomas N'Kono and Antoine Bell are two of the best goalkeepers not only in Africa but also in European club football, the destination of most of the top Cameroon players. Players like Emmanuel Kunde, Paul M'Fede, Cyril Makanaky and Emile M'Bouh have all helped put Cameroon on the map. Such is their reputation now that despite a relatively small population, it will take some knocking to get them off the perch on which they currently stand.

Zaire is the biggest country of the region both in terms of population and size, and so it was no surprise when they became the first sub-Saharan African country to reach the World Cup finals in 1974. Humiliated 9–0 against Yugoslavia in the final tournament, they have suffered deeply since that outing and have only recently emerged from among the shadows again.

Football has a long history in Zaire. They were the only colony that Belgium ever aspired to and the influence of that country is strong. Under Belgian guidance, the Association Royale Sportive Congolaise was founded in Leopoldville (later Kinshasa) in 1919, making it after South Africa the second oldest association on the continent. There was a thriving league, started three years earlier and confined at first to Leopoldville.

A league was started also in Elizabethville (later Lubumbashi), but for many years the main focus was the Pool Championship. Stanley Pool, the lake which separated the Belgian Congo from the French Congo and its capital Brazzaville, gave its name to a championship played between sides from the two countries which lasted from 1923 until independence.

From the late 1960s until 1974, Zaire was the most powerful country in Africa. Twice winners of the Cup of Nations, her main clubs, AS Vita from Kinshasa and TP Englebert from Lubumbashi, collected three continental club honours between them. Although TP Mazembe, as Englebert are now known, won the Cup Winners Cup in 1980, teams from Zaire have not been as prominent as they were before. The contrast is far more marked for the national side. Since winning the Cup of Nations in 1974 they have only managed to qualify for the final tournament on three occasions.

The French Congo, known for a while as Congo Brazzaville but now simply as Congo, have suffered much the same fate. Winners of the 1972 Cup of Nations, thanks in no small measure to Francois M'Pele, Congo's most famous player, and of the Champions Cup in 1974 with CARA Brazzaville, the country's most famous club, the future looked rosy. Since then, however, very little of substance has been achieved.

With a population of only two million it is perhaps unsurprising that this should be the case. One would expect a country like Gabon, with a similar population but vast oil resources, to be in a much better position to succeed, and in the UDEAC tournament this has indeed been the case. Of the rest of the countries, the Central African Republic has been too racked with poverty to pay much attention to football, whilst the football authorities in Chad do not take too kindly to paying their dues to FIFA or CAF and have spent many years in the wilderness.

UNION OF FOOTBALL ASSOCIATIONS OF CENTRAL AFRICA
BP 1363
Yaoundé
Cameroon

Founded: 1979

UDEAC TOURNAMENT

1984	Cameroon	2–2 (5–4p)	Congo
1985	Gabon	3–0	Congo
1986	Cameroon	4–1	Chad
1987	Cameroon	1–0	Chad
1988	Gabon	1–0	Cameroon
1989	Cameroon	2–1	Cent. Af. Rep.
1990	Congo	2–1	Cameroon

CENTRAL AFRICAN GAMES FOOTBALL TOURNAMENT

1976	Cameroon	3–2	Congo
1981	Zaire		
1987	Cameroon	2–0	Angola

CAMEROON

Population: 11 900 000
Area, sq km: 465 458
% in urban areas: 42%
Capital city: Yaoundé

Fédération Camérounaise de Football
BP 1116
Yaoundé
Cameroon
Tel: (010 237) 202538
Fax: None
Telex: 8568 JEUNESPO KN
Cable: FECAFOOT YAOUNDE
Languages for correspondence: French

Year of formation: 1960
Affiliation to FIFA: 1962
Affiliation to CAF: 1963
Registered clubs: 200
Registered players: 9300
Registered Coaches: 15
Registered referees: 381
National stadium: Omnisport, Yaoundé 70 000
National colours: Shirts: Green/Shorts: Red/Socks: Yellow
Reserve colours: Shirts: Yellow/Shorts: Green/Socks: Red
Season: November–July

THE RECORD

WORLD CUP

1930–66 ..... Did not enter
1970 .... QT 1st round
1974 .... QT 2nd round
1978 .... QT 1st round
1982 .... QT Qualified – Final tournament/1st round
1986 .... QT 2nd round
1990 .... QT Qualified – Final tournament/Quarter-finalists

OLYMPIC GAMES

1908–64 ..... Did not enter
1968 .... QT 1st round
1972 .... QT 2nd round
1976 .... Did not enter
1980 .... Did not enter
1984 .... QT Qualified – Final tournament/1st round
1988 .... QT 2nd round
1992 .... QT Qualified

AFRICAN CUP OF NATIONS

1957–65 ..... Did not enter
1968 .... QT 3rd/3 in group 5
1970 .... QT Qualified – Final tournament/1st round
1972 .... QT Automatic – Final tournament/Semi-finalists/3rd place
1974 .... QT 2nd round
1976 .... QT 1st round
1978 .... QT 1st round
1980 .... QT 1st round
1982 .... QT Qualified – Final tournament/1st round
1984 .... QT Qualified – Final tournament/Winners
1986 .... QT Automatic – Final tournament/Finalists
1988 .... QT Qualified – Final tournament/Winners
1990 .... QT Automatic – Final tournament/1st round
1992 .... QT 1st/4 in group 1 – Final tournament/4th place

AFRICAN CLUB COMPETITIONS

AFRICAN CUP: Winners – Oryx Douala 1964, Canon Yaoundé 1971 1978 1980 Union Douala 1979
CUP WINNERS CUP: Winners – Tonnerre Yaoundé 1975, Canon Yaoundé 1979, Union Douala 1981
Finalists – Tonnerre Yaoundé 1976, Canon Yaoundé 1977 1984

CAMEROON LEAGUE CHAMPIONS

1961	Oryx Douala
1962	Caiman Douala
1963	Oryx Douala
1964	Oryx Douala
1965	Oryx Douala
1966	Diamant Yaoundé
1967	Oryx Douala
1968	Caiman Douala
1969	Union Douala
1970	Canon Yaoundé
1971	Aigle Nkongsamba
1972	Leopards Douala
1973	Leopards Douala
1974	Canon Yaoundé
1975	Caiman Douala
1976	Union Douala
1977	Canon Yaoundé
1978	Union Douala
1979	Canon Yaoundé
1980	Canon Yaoundé
1981	Tonnerre Yaoundé
1982	Canon Yaoundé
1983	Tonnerre Yoaunde
1984	Tonnerre Yaoundé
1985	Canon Yaoundé
1986	Canon Yaoundé
1987	Tonnerre Yaoundé
1988	Tonnerre Yaoundé
1989	Racing Bafoussam
1990	Union Douala
1991	Canon Yaoundé

CAMEROON CUP WINNERS

1960	Lions Yaoundé
1961	Union Douala
1962	Lions Yaoundé
1963	Oryx Douala
1964	Diamant Yaoundé
1965	Lions Yaoundé
1966	Lions Yaoundé
1967	Canon Yaoundé
1968	Oryx Yaoundé
1969	Union Douala
1970	–
1971	Diamant Yaoundé
1972	Diamant Yaoundé
1973	Canon Yaoundé
1974	Tonnerre Yaoundé
1975	Canon Yaoundé
1976	Canon Yaoundé
1977	Canon Yaoundé
1978	Canon Yaoundé
1979	Dynamo Douala
1980	Union Douala
1981	Dynamo Douala
1982	Dragons Yaoundé
1983	Canon Yaoundé
1984	Dihep de Nkam
1985	Union Douala
1986	Canon Yaoundé
1987	Tonnerre Yaoundé
1988	Panthère Bangangte
1989	Tonnerre Yaoundé
1990	Prevoyance FC Yaoundé
1991	Tonnerre Yaoundé

CLUB DIRECTORY

DOUALA (Population – 1 029 000)
Caiman – Oryx – Leopard – Union – Rail – Dynamo

YAOUNDE (Population – 653 000)
Tonnerre – Dragons – Lions – Canon – Diamant – Prevoyance FC

BAFOUSSAM (Population – 89 000)
Racing Club

YABASSI
Dihep di Nkam

NKONGSAMBA
Aigle

BANGANGTE
Panthère

CENTRAL AFRICAN REPUBLIC

Population: 2 875 000
Area, sq km: 622 436
% in urban areas: 33%
Capital city: Bangui

Fédération Centrafricaine de Football
BP 334
Bangui
Central African Republic

Tel: (010 236) 61 2141
Fax: None Telex: None
Cable: FOOTBANGUI BANGUI
Languages for correspondence: French

Year of formation: 1937
Affiliation to FIFA: 1963
Affiliation to CAF: 1965
Registered clubs: 256
Registered players: 7200
Registered Coaches: 12
Registered referees: 92
National stadium: Barthèlemy Boganda, Bangui 35 000
National colours: Shirts: Sky blue/Shorts: White/Socks: Red
Reserve colours: Shirts: Red/Shorts: Red/Socks: Red
Season: October–July

THE RECORD

WORLD CUP

1930–90 ..... Did not enter

OLYMPIC GAMES

1908–92 ..... Did not enter

AFRICAN CUP OF NATIONS

1957–72 ..... Did not enter
1974 .... QT 1st round
1976–86 ..... Did not enter
1988 .... QT pr round
1990 .... Did not enter
1992 .... Did not enter

AFRICAN CLUB COMPETITIONS

AFRICAN CUP: 2nd round – Olympique Real 1974, SCAF Tocages 1985
CUP WINNERS CUP: Quarter-finalists – AS Tempete Mocaf 1975

CENTRAL AFRICAN REPUBLIC LEAGUE CHAMPIONS

1973	Olympique Real
1974	ASDR Fatima
1975	Olympique Real
1976	AS Tempete Mocaf
1977	SCAF Tocages
1978	ASDR Fatima
1979	Olympique Real
1980	USCA Bangui
1981	Sporting Moura
1982	Olympique Real
1983	ASDR Fatima
1984	AS Tempete Mocaf
1985	SCAF Tocages
1986	Sporting Moura
1987	–
1988	ASDR Fatima
1989	SCAF Tocages
1990	AS Tempete Mocaf
1991	FACA FC

CLUB DIRECTORY

BANGUI (Population – 473 000)
Stade Central Africaine Tocages (SCAF Tocages)

Union Sportive Central Africaine (USCA Bangui)

Association Sportive Tempete Mocaf

Sporting Moura

Sodiam

Association Sportive Diables Rouges Fatima

Olympique Real

Avia Sports

FACA FC

THE CONGO

Population: 2 326 000
Area, sq km: 342 000
% in urban areas: 51%
Capital city: Brazzaville

Fédération Congolaise de Football
BP 4041
Brazzaville
Congo
Tel: (010 242) 82 815101
Fax: None
Telex: 5210 KG
Cable: FECOFOOT BRAZZAVILLE
Languages for correspondence: French

Year of formation: 1962
Affiliation to FIFA: 1962
Affiliation to CAF: 1966
Registered clubs: 132
Registered players: 3900
Registered Coaches: 43
Registered referees: 136
National stadium: Stade de la Révolution, Brazzaville 50 000
National colours: Shirts: Red/Shorts: Red/Socks: Red
Reserve colours: Shirts: White/Shorts: Red/Socks: White
Season: November–August

THE RECORD

WORLD CUP

1930–70 ..... Did not enter
1974 .... QT 1st round
1978 .... QT 2nd round
1982–90 ..... Did not enter

OLYMPIC GAMES

1908–92 ..... Did not enter

AFRICAN CUP OF NATIONS

1957–65 ..... Did not enter
1968 .... QT 1st/4 in group 6 – Final tournament/1st round
1970 .... Did not enter
1972 .... QT Qualified – Final tournament/Winners
1974 .... QT Automatic – Final tournament/Semi-finalists/4th place
1976 .... QT 2nd round
1978 .... QT Qualified – Final tournament/1st round
1980 .... QT 1st round
1982 .... QT 1st round
1984 .... QT 1st round
1986 .... QT 1st round
1988 .... QT 1st round
1990 .... Did not enter
1992 .... QT 1st/3 in group 7 – Final tournament/Quarter-finalists

AFRICAN GAMES

Winners 1965

AFRICAN CLUB COMPETITIONS

AFRICAN CUP: Winners – CARA Brazzaville 1974
CUP WINNERS CUP: Semi-finalists – Inter Club 1988

CONGO LEAGUE CHAMPIONS

1965	Diables Noirs
1966	Abeilles FC
1967	Etoile du Congo
1968	Patronage
1969	CARA Brazzaville
1970	Victoria Club Mokanda
1971	CARA Brazzaville
1972	CARA Brazzaville
1973	CARA Brazzaville
1974	CARA Brazzaville
1975	CARA Brazzaville
1976	Diables Noirs
1977	Inter Club
1978	Etoile du Congo
1979	Etoile du Congo
1980	CARA Brazzaville
1981	Etoile du Congo
1982	CARA Brazzaville
1983	Kotoko Mfoa
1984	CARA Brazzaville
1985	Etoile du Congo
1986	Patronage
1987	Etoile du Congo
1988	Inter Club
1989	Etoile du Congo
1990	Inter Club
1991	Diables Noirs

CLUB DIRECTORY

BRAZZAVILLE (Population – 585 000)
Club Athletique Renaissance Aiglons (CARA)

Etoile du Congo

Diables Noirs

Inter Club

POINTE-NOIR (Population – 294 000)
Abeilles FC

Patronage Sainte Anne

LUBOMO
AS Cheminots

KOUILOU
Victoria Club Mokanda

GABON

Population: 1 171 000
Area, sq km: 267 667
% in urban areas: 40%
Capital city: Libreville

Fédération Gabonaise de Football
BP 181
Libreville
Gabon
Tel: (010 241) 744747
Fax: None
Telex: 5526 GO
Cable: FEGAFOOT LIBREVILLE
Languages for correspondence: French

Year of formation: 1962
Affiliation to FIFA: 1963
Affiliation to CAF: 1967
Registered clubs: 300
Registered players: 10 000
Registered referees: 90
National stadium: Omnisport, Libreville 50 000
National colours: Shirts: White/Shorts: White/Socks: White
Reserve colours: Shirts: Blue/Shorts: Yellow/Socks: Green
Season: October–July

THE RECORD

WORLD CUP

1930–86 ..... Did not enter
1990 .... QT 2nd round

OLYMPIC GAMES

1908–64 ..... Did not enter
1968 .... QT pr round
1972 .... QT 1st round
1976 .... Did not enter
1980 .... Did not enter
1984 .... QT 1st round
1988 .... Did not enter
1992 .... QT 1st round

AFRICAN CUP OF NATIONS

1957–70 ..... Did not enter
1972 .... QT 1st round
1974 .... Did not enter
1976 .... Did not enter
1978 .... QT 2nd round
1980 .... Did not enter
1982 .... Did not enter
1984 .... QT pr round
1986 .... QT pr round
1988 .... QT pr round
1990 .... QT 2nd round
1992 .... QT 2nd/4 in group 8

AFRICAN CLUB COMPETITIONS

AFRICAN CUP: Quarter-finalists – US Mbila Nzambi 1981. FC 105 1984 1988
CUP WINNERS CUP: Finalists – AS Sogara 1986

GABON LEAGUE CHAMPIONS

1968	Olympique Sportif
1969	Aigle Royal
1970	Aigle Royal
1971	AS Solidarite
1972	Olympique Sportif
1973	AS Police
1974	Zalang COC
1975	Petrosports FC
1976	Vautour Club Mangoungou
1977	Vautour Club Mangoungou
1978	FC 105
1979	Anges ABC
1980	US Mbila Nzambi
1981	US Mbila Nzambi
1982	FC 105
1983	FC 105
1984	AS Sogara
1985	FC 105
1986	FC 105
1987	FC 105
1988	JAC Port Gentil
1989	AS Sogara
1990	JAC Port Gentil
1991	AS Sogara

CLUB DIRECTORY

LIBREVILLE (Population – 235 000)
Football Canon 105 (FC 105 Libreville)

Union Sportive Mbila Nzambi

Olympique Sportif

Aigle Royal

Vautour Club Mangounou

Association Sportive Solidarite

Anges ABC

Zalang

Cercle Athletique Professionel Owendo (CAPO)

Okoume

PORT GENTIL (Population – 124 000)
Association Sportive Sogara

Petrosport FC

Shell FC

JAC Port Gentil

EQUATORIAL GUINEA

Population: 350 000
Area, sq km: 28 051
% in urban areas: 60%
Capital city: Malabo

Federacion Equatoguineana de Futbol
BP 471
Malabo
Equatorial Guinea
Tel: (010 240) 2653
Fax: None
Telex: 999 1111 EG
Cable: FEGUIFUT/MALABO
Languages for correspondence: Spanish

Year of formation: 1976
Affiliation to FIFA: 1986
Affiliation to CAF: 1986
Registered clubs: 42
Registered players: 2400
Registered coaches: 27
Registered referees: 67
National stadium: Estadio La Paz, Malabo 15 000
National colours: Shirts: Red/Shorts: Red/Socks: Red
Reserve colours: Shirts: Green/Shorts: Green/Socks: Green

THE RECORD

WORLD CUP

1930–90 ..... Did not enter

OLYMPIC GAMES

1908–92 ..... Did not enter

AFRICAN CUP OF NATIONS

1957–80 ..... Did not enter
1982 .... QT 1st round
1984–88 ..... Did not enter
1990 .... QT pr round
1992 .... Did not enter

EQUATORIAL GUINEA LEAGUE CHAMPIONS

1979 Real Rebola
1980 FC Mongomo
1981 Atletico Malabo
1982 Atletico Malabo
1983 FC Dragons
1984 CD Ela Nguema
1985 CD Ela Nguema
1986 CD Ela Nguema
1987 CD Ela Nguema
1988 CD Ela Nguema
1989 CD Ela Nguema
1990 CD Ela Nguema
1991 CD Ela Nguema

CLUB DIRECTORY

MALABO (Population – 30 000)
Atletico Malabo

GD Lage

ELA NGUEMA
Clube Deportivo Ela Nguema

Atletico Ela Nguema

BATA
Dragons FC

Union Vesper

SAO TOMÉ AND PRINCIPE

Population: 121 000
Area, sq km: 1001
% in urban areas: 39%
Capital city: Sao Tomé

Federacion Santomense de Futebol
PO Box 42 Sao Tomé
Sao Tomé and Príncipe
Tel: (010 23 912) 22311
Telex: 213 PUBLICO STP
Cable: None
Languages for correspondence: French

Year of formation: 1975
Affiliation to FIFA: 1986
Affiliation to CAF: 1986
Registered clubs: 40
Registered players: 880
Registered coaches: 15
Registered referees: 30
National stadium: Estadio 12 de Julho, Sao Tomé 5000
National colours: Shirts: Green/Shorts: Green/Socks: Green
Reserve colours: Shirts: Yellow/Shorts: Yellow/Socks: Yellow
Season: April–March

THE RECORD

WORLD CUP

1930–90 ..... Did not enter

OLYMPIC GAMES

1908–92 ..... Did not enter

AFRICAN CUP OF NATIONS

1957–92 ..... Did not enter

AFRICAN GAMES

Never qualified for the final tournament

AFRICAN CLUB COMPETITIONS

AFRICAN CUP: Have never entered
CUP WINNERS CUP: Have never entered

SAO TOME LEAGUE CHAMPIONS

1977 Vitoria Riboque
1978 Vitoria Riboque
1979 Vitoria Riboque
1980 Desportivo Guadelupe
1981 Desportivo Guadelupe
1982 Praia Cruz
1983 –
1984 Andorinhas
1985 Praia Cruz
1986 Vitoria Riboque
1987 –
1988 6 de Setembro
1989 Vitoria Riboque
1990 OS Operacios

CLUB DIRECTORY

SAO TOME (Population – 17 000)
Vitoria Riboque

Praia Cruz

6 de Setembro

Desportivo Guadelupe

ZAIRE

Population: 34 138 000
Area, sq km: 2 345 095
% in urban areas: 44%
Capital city: Kinshasa

Fédération Zaireoise de Football-Association
BP 1284
Rue Dima #10
Kinshasa 1
Zaire
Tel: None Fax: None
Telex: 098 221 605
Cable: FEZAFA KINSHASA
Languages for correspondence: French

Year of formation: 1919
Affiliation to FIFA: 1964
Affiliation to CAF: 1963
Registered clubs: 297
Registered players: 7500
Registered coaches: 600
Registered referees: 2850
National stadium: Stade 20 Mai, Kinshasa 60 000
National colours: Shirts: Green/Shorts: Yellow/Socks: Yellow
Reserve colours: Shirts: Yellow/Shorts: Green/Socks: Green
Season: August–May

THE RECORD

WORLD CUP

1930–70 ..... Did not enter
1974 .... QT Qualified – Final tournament/1st round
1978 .... QT 2nd round
1982 .... QT 3rd round
1986 .... Did not enter
1990 .... QT 2nd round

OLYMPIC GAMES

1908–72 ..... Did not enter
1976 .... QT 2nd round
1980–92 ..... Did not enter

AFRICAN CUP OF NATIONS

1957–63 ..... Did not enter
1965 .... 1st round
1968 .... QT 1st/4 in group 6 – Final tournament/Winners
1970 .... QT Qualified – Final tournament/1st round
1972 .... QT Qualified – Final tournament/Semi-finalists/4th place
1974 .... QT Qualified – Final tournament/Winners
1976 .... QT Automatic – Final tournament/1st round
1978 .... Did not enter
1980 .... QT 2nd round
1982 .... QT 2nd round
1984 .... Did not enter
1986 .... QT 2nd round
1988 .... QT Qualified – Final tournament/1st round
1990 .... QT 2nd round
1992 .... QT 1st/4 in group 8 – Final tournament/Quarter-finalists

AFRICAN CLUB COMPETITIONS

AFRICAN CUP: Winners – TP Mazembe 1967 1968, Vita Club Kinshasa 1973

Finalists – TP Mazembe 1969 1970, AS Bilima 1980 1985, Vita Club Kinshasa 1981
CUP WINNERS CUP: Winners – TP Mazembe 1980

THE POOL CHAMPIONSHIP

1923	CO Kinshasa
1924	CO Kinshasa
1925	CO Kinshasa
1926	CO Kinshasa
1927	AS Kinshasa
1928	AS Kinshasa
1929	ES Congolaise
1930	CO les Nomades Kinshasa
1931	CA Brazzavillois
1932	AS Kinshasa
1933	AS Portuguesa
1934	AS Portuguesa
1935	AS Portuguesa
1936	CS Belge Leopoldville
1937	CA Brazzavillois
1938	CS Belge Leopoldville
1939	AS Portuguesa
1940	AS Portuguesa
1941	CA Brazzavillois
1942	Nomades FC
1943	Nomades FC
1944	AS Portuguesa
1945	CA Brazzavillois
1946	Nomades FC
1947	CS Belge Leopoldville
1948	CS Belge Leopoldville
1949	CA Brazzavillois
1950	CS Belge Leopoldville

CUP DE LEOPOLDVILLE

1928	ES Congolaise
1929	CO les Nomades Kinshasa
1930	ES Congolaise
1931	AS Kinshasa
1932	Diables Rouge
1933	–
1934	AS Portuguesa
1935	AS Portuguesa
1936	CS Belge Leopoldville
1937	CA Brazzavillois
1938	CS Belge Leopoldville

CHAMPIONS OF ZAIRE

1958	FC Lupopo
1959–62	–
1963	CS Imana
1964	CS Imana
1965	AS Bilima
1966	TP Mazembe
1967	TP Mazembe
1968	FC Lupopo
1969–70	–
1971	AS Vita Club
1972	AS Vita Club
1973	AS Vita Club
1974	CS Imana
1975	AS Vita Club
1976	TP Mazembe
1977	AS Vita Club
1978	CS Imana
1979	AS Bilima
1980	AS Vita Club
1981	FC Lupopo
1982	AS Bilima
1983	Sanga Balende
1984	AS Bilima
1985	US Tshinkunku Kalamu
1986	FC Lupopo
1987	TP Mazembe
1988	AS Vita Club
1989	CS Imana
1990	FC Lupopo
1991	Mikishi

CLUB DIRECTORY

KINSHASA (Population – 3 000 000)
Club Omnisport Daring Motema Pemba

Amicale Sportive Bilima

Association Sportive Vita Club

Club Sportive Imana

FC Kalamu

LUBUMBASHI (Population – 543 000)
Toute Puissant Mazembe (TP Mazembe) – Formerly TP Englebert

FC Lubumbashi Sport

MBUJI–MAYI (Population – 423 000)
Sanga Balende

KANANGA (Population – 290 000)
FC Lupopo
Union Sportive Tshinkunku

MBANDAKA (Population – 125 000)
Club Sportif Mokanda

EAST AFRICA

East Africa was the main area of British control during the first half of the century, and so it is surprising to learn that it is the weakest of all the regions in Africa at football. The area does, after all, produce some of the finest athletes in the world.

One reason put forward for the lack of success has been the importance of the regional tournaments, which are often more keenly contested than the continental cups. Another factor is the lack of experience of football outside of the region. Very few players from Burundi, Ethiopia, Kenya, Rwanda, Somalia, the Sudan, Tanzania or Uganda, the nations which make up East Africa, ever ply their trade elsewhere. Though this benefits the local leagues in that there is no player drain, it does mean that new ideas and tactics are not easy to come by.

Ethiopia and Sudan were among the early shakers and movers in African football, but have seen their role steadily diminish over the years, due in no small part to the disastrous effects of famine and civil war that have plagued both countries. Both have won the Cup of Nations, Ethiopia in 1962 when it was held in Addis Ababa and Sudan in 1970 when Khartoum hosted the event for the second time.

Along with Egypt and South Africa, Ethiopia and Sudan were founder members of the CAF. Sudan had had a football association since 1936, Ethiopia since 1943. It was perhaps a good job for the survival of football in Ethiopia that Italian rule was brief. In the period of occupation from 1936–41, the Italians ran a 'Sports Office for the Indigenous' which strictly forbade any inter-racial matches and designated certain sports fields as out of bounds for the locals. This was hardly a generous attitude for the world champions of the time to take, when they were in an excellent position to help the spread of the game.

Club football has never been strong in Ethiopia, but in Sudan two clubs, Al Hilal and Al Merreikh, stand head and shoulders above the rest and both have known success in the African club competitions. Against all the odds, Sudanese football found its feet again in the late 1980s. Merreikh won the Cup Winners Cup in 1989, following on from Hilal's Champions cup final appearance of two years previously.

Kenya, Uganda and Tanzania have a long football rivalry, dating back to the 1930s in the form of the Gossage Cup, a tournament named after a Governor of the time and played by representative sides of each country. In the 1970s it took on a new form as the East and Central African Challenge Cup, and the entrants have over the years expanded to include Malawi, Zambia, Zimbabwe, Sudan, Ethiopia and Somalia. Uganda's football association dates back to 1924, Kenya's to 1932 and Tanzania's to 1930, although in the latter case Zanzibar, which remained an independent nation from Tanzania until 1964, still fields a side in the East and Central African Challenge Cup.

Neither the national nor club sides from these three nations have been very successful. There is an intense rivalry in Kenya between Gor Mahia and AFC Leopards (formerly Abaluhya), and the former remain Kenya's only major title winners after winning the Cup Winners Cup in 1987. Simba FC from Uganda managed to reach the Champions cup final in 1972 as did their compatriots Nakivubo Villa in 1991, but these achievements are few and far between.

In the Cup of Nations, the story is no different. Uganda's appearance in the 1978 final which they lost to Ghana in Accra marks the only significant impact the three countries have made on the tournament. Tanzania are the weakest of the trio, having made the final tournament on only one occasion.

The remaining two nations, Burundi and Rwanda, are keen competitors but little more. Both are among the most remote countries in the world, and this will always hold them back. Both International FC and Vital'O from Burundi, however, have gained from the experience of continental competition and in 1991 the former managed to reach the semi-finals of the Cup Winners Cup.

In the region as a whole there is tremendous potential for football. It is a popular sport, and there are many fine athletes about. Perhaps for once a strong case could be made for encouraging players to play in Europe. The experience could be the impetus the area needs to start challenging the rest of Africa for honours.

THE EAST AND CENTRAL AFRICAN CLUB CHAMPIONSHIP

1974	SC Simba	TAN			
1975	Young Africans	TAN	2–0	SC Simba	TAN
1976	Luo Union	KEN	2–1	Young Africans	TAN
1977	Luo Union	KEN	1–0	FC Horsed	SUD
1978	Kampala CC	UGA	0–0*	SC Simba	TAN
1979	Abaluhya FC	KEN	1–0	Kampala CC	UGA
1980	Gor Mahia	KEN	3–2	Abaluhya FC	KEN
1981	Gor Mahia	KEN	1–0	SC Simba	TAN
1982	AFC Leopards	KEN	1–0	Rio Tinto	ZIM
1983	AFC Leopards	KEN	2–1	ADMARC Tigers	MAW
1984	AFC Leopards	KEN	2–1	Gor Mahia	KEN
1985	Gor Mahia	KEN	2–0	AFC Leopards	KEN
1986	El Merreikh	SUD	2–2 (4–2p)	Young Africans	TAN
1987	Nakivubu Villa	UGA	1–0	El Merreikh	SUD
1988	Kenya Breweries	KEN	2–0	El Merreikh	SUD
1989	Kenya Breweries	KEN	3–0	Coastal Union	TAN
1990	SC Simba	TAN	3–0	Nakivubo Villa	UGA

* Kampala won on penalties

CONFEDERATION OF EAST AND CENTRAL AFRICAN FOOTBALL ASSOCIATIONS
PO Box 49295, Nairobi, Kenya
Founded: 1970

GOSSAGE CUP

Winners 1927–72: Uganda 26, Kenya 12, Tanzania 4, Zanaibar 1

THE FRIENDSHIP CUP OF THE EAST AFRICAN ZONE

1966	Ethiopia			
1967	Sudan	1–1 5–3	Ethiopia	
1969	Sudan	1–0	Ethiopia	

THE EAST AFRICAN CHALLENGE CUP

1965	Tanzania
1966	Tanzania
1967	Kenya
1968	Uganda
1969	Uganda
1970	Uganda
1971	Kenya

EAST AND CENTRAL AFRICAN CHALLENGE CUP

1973	Uganda	2–1	Tanzania
1974	Tanzania	1–1 (5–3p)	Uganda
1975	Kenya	0–0 (4–3p)	Malawi
1976	Uganda	2–0	Zambia
1977	Uganda	0–0 (5–3p)	Zambia
1978	Malawi	3–2	Zambia
1979	Malawi	3–2	Kenya
1980	Sudan	1–0	Tanzania
1981	Kenya	1–0	Tanzania
1982	Kenya	1–1 (5–3p)	Uganda
1983	Kenya	1–0	Zimbabwe
1984	Zambia	0–0 3–0	Malawi
1985	Zimbabwe	2–0	Kenya
1986	–		
1987	Ethiopia	1–1 (5–4p)	Zimbabwe
1988	Malawi	3–1	Zambia
1989	Uganda	3–3 (2–1p)	Malawi
1990	Uganda	2–0	Sudan
1991	Zambia	2–0	Kenya

BURUNDI

Population: 5 451 000
Area, sq km: 27 834
% in urban areas: 7%
Capital city: Bujumbura

Fédération de Football du Burundi
BP 3426
Bujumbura
Burundi
Tel: (010 257) 225160
Fax: (010 257) 228283
Telex: None
Cable: FFB BUJA
Languages for correspondence: French

Year of formation: 1948
Affiliation to FIFA: 1972
Affiliation to CAF: 1972
Registered clubs: 25
Registered players: 3900
Registered referees: 125
National stadium: FFB, Bujumbura 6000
National colours: Shirts: Red/Shorts: White/Socks: Green
Season: October–July

THE RECORD

WORLD CUP

1930–90 ..... Did not enter

OLYMPIC GAMES

1908–92 ..... Did not enter

AFRICAN CUP OF NATIONS

1957–74 ..... Did not enter
1976 .... QT 1st round
1978–92 ..... Did not enter

AFRICAN CLUB COMPETITIONS

AFRICAN CUP: Quarter-finalists – Vital'O 1985, International FC 1986
CUP WINNERS CUP: Semi-finalists – International FC 1991

BURUNDI LEAGUE CHAMPIONS

1972	Sports Dynamic
1973	Sports Dynamic
1974	International FC
1975–80	–
1981	Prince Louis
1982	Fantastique
1983	Vital'O
1984	Vital'O
1985	International FC
1986	International FC
1987	International FC
1988	International FC
1989	International FC
1990	Vital'O
1991	International FC

CLUB DIRECTORY

BUJUMBURA (Population – 273 000)
International FC – Vital'O – Burundi – Sports Dynamic – Fantastique – Prince Louis FC – Muzinga

ETHIOPIA

Population: 50 341 000
Area, sq km: 1 223 500
% in urban areas: 10%
Capital city: Addis Ababa

Yeitiopia Football Federechin
Addis Ababa Stadium
PO Box 1080 Addis Ababa
Ethiopia
Tel: (010 251) 1 514453
Fax: (010 251) 1 513345
Telex: 21377 NESCO ET
Cable: FOOTBALL ADDIS ABABA
Languages for correspondence: English

Year of formation: 1943
Affiliation to FIFA: 1953
Affiliation to CAF: 1957
Registered clubs: 169
Registered players: 53 700
Registered coaches: 1016
Registered referees: 5484
National stadium: Addis Ababa Stadium 30 000
National colours: Shirts: Green/Shorts: Yellow/Socks: Red
Reserve colours: Shirts: Red/Shorts: Green/ Socks: Yellow
Season: September–June

THE RECORD

WORLD CUP

1930–58 ..... Did not enter
1962 .... QT 2nd round
1966 .... Did not enter
1970 .... QT 2nd round
1974 .... QT 2nd round
1978 .... QT 1st round
1982 .... QT 1st round
1986 .... QT 1st round
1990 .... Did not enter

OLYMPIC GAMES

1908–52 ..... Did not enter
1956 .... QT Failed to qualify
1960 .... QT 1st round
1964 .... QT 2nd round
1968 .... QT 2nd round
1972 .... QT 2nd round
1976 .... QT 1st round
1980 .... QT 1st round
1984 .... QT 3rd round
1988–92 ..... Did not enter

AFRICAN CUP OF NATIONS

1957 .... Finalists
1959 .... 3rd place
1962 .... Winners
1963 .... 4th place
1965 .... 1st round
1968 .... QT Automatic – Final tournament/Semi-finalists/4th place
1970 .... QT Qualified – Final tournament/1st round
1972 .... QT 1st round
1974 .... QT 1st round
1976 .... QT Automatic – Final tournament/1st round
1978 .... QT 2nd round
1980 .... QT 1st round
1982 .... QT Qualified – Final tournament/1st round
1984 .... QT 2nd round
1986 .... Did not enter
1988 .... QT 1st round
1990 .... QT 1st round
1992 .... QT 4th/4 in group 2

AFRICAN CLUB COMPETITIONS

AFRICAN CUP: Semi-finalists – Cotton Club 1964, St Georges 1967
CUP WINNERS CUP: Quarter-finalists – Mechal Army 1976

ETHIOPIAN LEAGUE CHAMPIONS

1943–64	–
1965	Ethio-cement
1966	St Georges
1967	St Georges
1968	St Georges
1969	Tele Asmara
1970	Tele Asmara
1971	St Georges
1972	Tele Asmara
1973	Tele Asmara
1974	Embassoria
1975	St Georges
1976	Mechal Army
1977	Medr Babur
1978	Ogaden Anbassa
1979–83	–
1984	Ground Force
1985	Brewery Jimma
1986	Brewery Jimma
1987–89	–
1990	Brewery Addis
1991	St Georges

CLUB DIRECTORY

ADDIS ABABA (Population – 1 500 000)
Saint Georges Sports Association

Cotton Club

Mechal Army

Ground Force

Electric Sports

ASMARA (Population – 275 000)
Eritrea Shoe Factory

Tele Sporting Club

DIRE DAWA (Population – 98 000)
Ogaden Anbassa

Ethio-Cement

KENYA

Population: 24 872 000
Area, sq km: 582 646
% in urban areas: 19%
Capital city: Nairobi

Kenya Football Federation
Nyayo National Stadium
PO Box 40234
Nairobi
Kenya

Tel: (010 254) 2 501853
Fax: (010 254) 2 501120
Telex: 25784 KFF
Cable: KEFF NAIROBI
Languages for correspondence: English

Year of formation: 1932
Affiliation to FIFA: 1960
Affiliation to CAF: 1968
Registered clubs: 500
Registered players: 18000
Registered referees: 1300
National stadium: Nyayo, Nairobi 35000
National colours: Shirts: Red/Shorts: Red/Socks: Red
Reserve colours: Shirts: Green/Shorts: Green/Socks: Green
Season: February–November

THE RECORD

WORLD CUP

1930–70 ..... Did not enter
1974 .... QT 3rd round
1978 .... QT 2nd round
1982 .... QT 1st round
1986 .... QT 2nd round
1990 .... QT 2nd round

OLYMPIC GAMES

1908–60 ..... Did not enter
1964 .... QT 1st round
1968–76 ..... Did not enter
1980 .... QT 2nd round
1984 .... QT 1st round
1988 .... QT 1st round
1992 .... Did not enter

AFRICAN CUP OF NATIONS

1957–65 ..... Did not enter
1968 .... QT 1st round
1970 .... QT 1st round
1972 .... QT Qualified – Final tournament/1st round
1974 .... QT 1st round
1976 .... QT 1st round
1978 .... QT 1st round
1980 .... QT 2nd round
1982 .... QT 1st round
1984 .... Did not enter
1986 .... QT 2nd round
1988 .... QT Qualified – Final tournament/1st round
1990 .... QT Qualified – Final tournament/1st round
1992 .... QT 1st/3 in group 6 – Final tournament/First round

AFRICAN CLUB COMPETITIONS

AFRICAN CUP: Semi-finalists – AFC Leopards 1968, Kenya Breweries 1973
CUP WINNERS CUP: Winners – Gor Mahia 1987
Finalists – Gor Mahia 1979

KENYAN LEAGUE CHAMPIONS

1963 .... Nakuru All Stars
1964 .... Luo Union
1965 .... Liverpool
1966 .... Abaluhya United
1967 .... Abaluhya United
1968 .... –
1969 .... Gor Mahia
1970 .... Abaluhya United
1971 .... –
1972 .... Kenya Breweries
1973 .... Abaluhya
1974 .... Gor Mahia
1975 .... Luo Union
1976 .... Gor Mahia
1977 .... Kenya Breweries
1978 .... Kenya Breweries
1979 .... Gor Mahia
1980 .... Abaluhya
1981 .... AFC Leopards
1982 .... AFC Leopards
1983 .... Gor Mahia
1984 .... Gor Mahia
1985 .... Gor Mahia
1986 .... AFC Leopards
1987 .... Shabana Kissi
1988 .... AFC Leopards
1989 .... AFC Leopards
1990 .... Gor Mahia
1991 .... Gor Mahia

CLUB DIRECTORY

NAIROBI (Population – 1286000)
Gor Mahia

AFC Leopards – Formerly Abaluhya United and Abaluhya

Kenya Breweries Nairobi

MOMBASSA (Population – 442000)
Luo Union

Ramogi

NAKURU (Population – 101000)
Nakuru All Stars

Scarlets

KISII
Shabana Kisii

RWANDA

Population: 7232000 Area, sq km: 26338
% in urban areas: 6% Capital city: Kigali

Fédération Rwandaise de Football Amateur
BP 2000, Kigali, Rwanda
Tel: (010 250) 82605 Fax: (010 250) 76574
Telex: 22504 PUBLIC RW
Cable: FERWAFA KIGALI
Languages for correspondence: French

Year of formation: 1972
Affiliation to FIFA: 1976
Affiliation to CAF: 1976
Registered clubs: 47
Registered players: 4500
Registered coaches: 191
Registered referees: 321
National stadium: Stade Amahoro, Kigali 25000
National colours: Shirts: Red/Shorts: Green/Socks: Yellow
Reserve colours: Shirts: Green/Shorts: Red/Socks: Yellow
Season: August–March

THE RECORD

WORLD CUP

1930–90 ..... Did not enter

OLYMPIC GAMES

1908–84 ..... Did not enter
1988 .... QT Prelim round
1992 .... Did not enter

AFRICAN CUP OF NATIONS

1957–80 ..... Did not enter
1982 .... QT 1st round
1984 .... QT 1st round
1986 .... Did not enter
1988 .... QT 1st round
1990 .... Did not enter
1992 .... Did not enter

AFRICAN CLUB COMPETITIONS

AFRICAN CUP: Never past the first round
CUP WINNERS CUP: 2nd round – Etincelles 1989

RWANDA LEAGUE CHAMPIONS

1981 Rayon Sports
1982 –
1983 Kiyovou Sports
1984 Pantheres Noires
1985 Pantheres Noires
1986 Pantheres Noires
1987 Pantheres Noires
1988 Mukungwa Ruhengeri
1989 Mukungwa Ruhengeri

CLUB DIRECTORY

KIGALI (Population – 181000)
Pantheres Noires – Kiyovou Sports

BUTARE
Rayon Sports – Mukura Victory Sports

RUHENGERI
Mukungwa

GISENYI
Etincelles

SOMALIA

Population: 7 555 000 Area, sq km: 637 000
% in urban areas: 35% Capital city: Mogadishu

Somali Football Federation
Ministry of Sports, CP 247, Mogadishu, Somalia
Tel: (010 252) 20501
Telex: 3061 SONOC SM
Cable: SOMALIA FOOTBALL MOGADISHU
Languages for correspondence: English

Year of formation: 1951
Affiliation to FIFA: 1961
Affiliation to CAF: 1968
Registered clubs: 10
Registered players: 2200
Registered coaches: 122
Registered referees: 251
National stadium: Mogadishu Stadium, Mogadishu 40 000
National colours: Shirts: Sky blue/Shorts: White/Socks: White
Reserve colours: Shirts: White/Shorts: White/Socks: White
Season: November–July

THE RECORD

WORLD CUP

1930–78 ..... Did not enter
1982 .... QT 1st round
1986 .... Did not enter
1990 .... Did not enter

OLYMPIC GAMES

1908–88 ..... Did not enter
1992 .... Prelim round

AFRICAN CUP OF NATIONS

1957–72 ..... Did not enter
1974 .... QT pr round
1976 .... QT pr round
1978–82 ..... Did not enter
1984 .... QT pr round
1986 .... QT pr round
1988 .... QT pr round
1990 .... Did not enter
1992 .... Did not enter

AFRICAN CLUB COMPETITIONS

AFRICAN CUP: 2nd round – FC Horsed 1981. Printing Agency 1984
CUP WINNERS CUP: 2nd round – Lavori Publici 1981. FC Horsed 1988

SOMALIAN LEAGUE CHAMPIONS

1967	Somali Police
1968	Hoga Mogadishu
1969	Lavori Publici
1970	Lavori Publici
1971	Lavori Publici
1972	Horsed
1973	Horsed
1974	Horsed
1975	Mogadishu Municipality
1976	Horsed
1977	Horsed
1978	Horsed
1979	Horsed
1980	Horsed
1981	Lavori Publici
1982	Wagad
1983	Printing Agency
1984	Marine Club
1985	Wagad
1986	Mogadishu Municipality
1987	Wagad

CLUB DIRECTORY

MOGADISHU (Population – 600 000)
Horsed – Printing Agency – Marine Club – Somali Police – Wagad

SUDAN

Population: 28 311 000
Area, sq km: 2 503 890
% in urban areas: 29%
Capital city: Khartoum

Sudan Football Association
PO Box 437
Khartoum
Sudan
Tel: (010 249) 11 76633
Fax: None
Telex: 23007 KORA SD
Cable: ALKOURA KHARTOUM
Languages for correspondence: English

Year of formation: 1936
Affiliation to FIFA: 1948
Affiliation to CAF: 1956
Registered clubs: 750
Registered players: 42 200
Registered coaches: 85
Registered referees: 1412
National stadium: Merreikh, Khartoum 45 000
National colours: Shirts: White/Shorts: White/Socks: White
Reserve colours: Shirts: Green/Shorts: White/Socks: White
Season: July–June

THE RECORD

WORLD CUP

1930–54 ..... Did not enter
1958 .... QT 3rd round
1962 .... Did not enter
1966 .... Did not enter
1970 .... QT 3rd round
1974 .... QT 1st round
1978 .... Did not enter
1982 .... QT 2nd round
1986 .... QT 2nd round
1990 .... QT 1st round

OLYMPIC GAMES

1908–56 ..... Did not enter
1960 .... QT 2nd round
1964 .... QT 2nd round
1968 .... QT 1st round
1972 .... QT Qualified – Final tournament/1st round
1976 .... QT 3rd round
1980 .... Did not enter
1984 .... QT 1st round
1988 .... QT 1st round
1992 .... QT 1st round

AFRICAN CUP OF NATIONS

1957 .... 3rd place
1959 .... 2nd place
1962 .... Did not enter
1963 .... Finalists
1965 .... Did not enter
1968 .... QT 1st round
1970 .... QT Qualified – Final tournament/Winners
1972 .... QT Automatic – Final tournament/1st round
1974 .... QT 1st round
1976 .... QT Qualified – Final tournament/1st round
1978 .... Did not enter
1980 .... QT 2nd round
1982 .... Did not enter
1984 .... QT 2nd round
1986 .... Did not enter
1988 .... QT 2nd round
1990 .... QT 1st round
1992 .... QT 3rd in group

AFRICAN CLUB COMPETITIONS

AFRICAN CUP: Finalists – Al Hilal 1987
CUP WINNERS CUP: Winners – Al Merreikh 1989

SUDANESE LEAGUE CHAMPIONS

1964	Al Hilal
1965	Al Hilal
1966	Al Hilal
1967	Al Hilal
1968	Al Mourada
1969	Burri
1970	Al Merreikh
1971	Al Merreikh
1972	Al Merreikh
1973	Al Merreikh
1974	Al Hilal
1974	Al Merreikh
1975	Al Merreikh

1976	–
1977	Al Merreikh
1978	Al Merreikh
1979	–
1980	–
1981	Al Hilal
1982	Al Merreikh
1983	Al Hilal
1984	Al Hilal
1985	Al Merreikh
1986	Al Hilal
1987	Al Hilal
1988	Al Hilal
1989	Al Hilal
1990	Al Merreikh
1991	Al Hilal

CLUB DIRECTORY

KHARTOUM (Population – 924 000)
Al Hilal – Al Nil – Al Mourada – Burri

UMM DURMAN (Population – 526 000)
Al Merreikh

PORT SUDAN (Population – 206 000)
Hay el Arab

WAD MADANI (Population – 141 000)
Al Ahly Wad Madani

TANZANIA

Population: 24 403 000
Area, sq km: 942 799
% in urban areas: 17%
Capital city: Dodoma

Football Association of Tanzania
PO Box 1574
Dar es Salaam
Tanzania
Tel: (010 255) 51 32334
Fax: None
Telex: 41873 TZ
Cable: FAT DAR ES SALAAM
Languages for correspondence: English

Year of formation: 1930
Affiliation to FIFA: 1964
Affiliation to CAF: 1960
Registered clubs: 420
Registered players: 9400
Registered coaches: 50
Registered referees: 320
National stadium: National Stadium, Dar es Salaam 25 000
National colours: Shirts: Yellow/Shorts: Yellow/Socks: Yellow
Reserve colours: Shirts: Green/Shorts: Black/Socks: Green
Season: September–August

THE RECORD

WORLD CUP

1930–70 ..... Did not enter
1974 .... QT 1st round
1978 .... Did not enter
1982 .... QT 2nd round
1986 .... QT 1st round
1990 .... Did not enter

OLYMPIC GAMES

1908–64 ..... Did not enter
1968 .... QT pr round
1972 .... Did not enter
1976 .... QT 2nd round
1980–92 ..... Did not enter

AFRICAN CUP OF NATIONS

1957–65 ..... Did not enter
1968 .... QT 2nd/4 in group 6
1970 .... QT 2nd round
1972 .... QT 1st round
1974 .... QT 2nd round
1976 .... QT 2nd round
1978 .... Did not enter
1980 .... QT Qualified – Final tournament/1st round
1982 .... Did not enter
1984 .... QT pr round
1986 .... QT 1st round
1988 .... QT 1st round
1990 .... QT pr round
1992 .... QT 4th/4 in group 8

AFRICAN CLUB COMPETITIONS

AFRICAN CUP: Semi-finalists – SC Simba 1974
CUP WINNERS CUP: Quarter-finalists – Rangers International 1977. KMKM Zanzibar 1977

TANZANIAN LEAGUE CHAMPIONS

1965	Dar Sunderland
1966	Dar Sunderland
1967	Cosmopolitans
1968	Young Africans
1969	Young Africans
1970	Young Africans
1971	Young Africans
1972	SC Simba
1973	SC Simba
1974	Young Africans
1975	Mseto
1976	SC Simba
1977	SC Simba
1978	SC Simba
1979	SC Simba
1980	SC Simba
1981	Young Africans
1982	Pan African
1983	Young Africans
1984	KMKM Zanzibar
1985	Maji Maji
1986	Maji Maji
1987	Young Africans
1988	Pan African
1989	Malindi
1990	Pamba SC
1991	Young Africans

CLUB DIRECTORY

DAR ES SALAAM (Population – 1 300 000)
Young Africans (Yanga)

Pan African Sports Club

Sports Club Simba – Previously Dar Sunderland

Rangers International

Youth League

ZANZIBAR (Population – 119 000)
Small Simba

KMKM Zanzibar (Zanzibar Navy)

Miembeni

TANGA (Population – 121 000)
Coastal Union

SONGEA
Maji Maji

SHINYANGA
Pamba Sports Club

UGANDA

Population: 16 928 000
Area, sq km: 241 040
% in urban areas: 9%
Capital city: Kampala

Federation of Uganda Football Associations
PO Box 20077
Kampala
Uganda
Tel: (010 256) 41254478
Fax: (010 256) 41255288
Cable: FUFA KAMPALA
Languages for correspondence: English

Year of formation: 1924
Affiliation to FIFA: 1959
Affiliation to CAF: 1959
Registered clubs: 400
Registered players: 18 500
Registered referees: 910
National stadium: Nakivubo, Kampala 35 000
National colours: Shirts: Yellow and black stripes/Shorts: Black/Socks: Yellow
Reserve colours: Shirts: Red/Shorts: Red/Socks: Black
Season: January–November

THE RECORD

WORLD CUP

1930–74 ..... Did not enter
1978 .... QT 2nd round
1982 .... Did not enter
1986 .... QT 1st round
1990 .... QT 1st round

OLYMPIC GAMES

1908–60 ..... Did not enter
1964 .... QT 1st round
1968 .... Did not enter
1972 .... QT 1st round
1976 .... Did not enter
1980 .... Did not enter
1984 .... QT 1st round
1988 .... QT 2nd round
1992 .... QT 2nd round

AFRICAN CUP OF NATIONS

1957 .... Did not enter
1959 .... Did not enter
1962 .... 4th place
1963 .... Did not enter
1965 .... Did not enter
1968 .... QT 2nd/4 in group 4 – Final tournament/1st round
1970 .... QT 1st round
1972 .... QT 1st round
1974 .... QT Qualified – Final tournament/1st round
1976 .... QT Qualified – Final tournament/1st round
1978 .... QT Qualified – Final tournament/Finalists
1980 .... Did not enter
1982 .... Did not enter
1984 .... QT 1st round
1986 .... QT pr round
1988 .... QT 1st round
1990 .... Did not enter
1992 .... QT 3rd/4 in group 8

AFRICAN CLUB COMPETITIONS

AFRICAN CUP: Finalists – Simba FC 1972. Nakivubu Villa 1991
CUP WINNERS CUP: Quarter-finalists – Nakivubo Villa 1984. Kampala CC 1985

UGANDAN LEAGUE CHAMPIONS

1966	Express FC
1967	Bitumastic
1968	–
1969	Prisons FC
1970	Coffee FC
1971	Simba FC
1972	Simba FC
1973	Simba FC
1974	Express FC
1975	Express FC
1976	Kampala CC
1977	Kampala CC
1978	Kampala CC
1979	Commercial Bank
1980	Nile FC
1981	Kampala CC
1982	Nakivubo Villa
1983	Kampala CC
1984	Nakivubo Villa
1985	Kampala CC
1986	Kampala CC
1987	Nakivubo Villa
1988	Express FC
1989	Express FC
1990	Nakivubo Villa
1991	Kampala CC

CLUB DIRECTORY

KAMPALA (Population – 460 000)
Kampala City Council Sports Club

Uganda Express FC

Nakivubo Villa Sports Club

Prisons Football Club

Coffee Football Club

Gangama United

Nsambya Football Club

JINJA (Population – 55 000)
Nile Breweries Football Club

SOUTHERN AFRICA

Few doubt that Southern Africa could well become one of the growth regions of world football. Now that apartheid has all but crumbled away in South Africa, more and more attention will be focused on the region, which has for many years been a backwater of the game. South Africa may have been a founder member of CAF but it has never played a part in African football. Only recently has its northern neighbour, Zimbabwe, been able to join in, whilst both Angola and Mozambique have been fighting fierce civil wars. Namibia was also an international outcast, as a puppet state of the South Africans, until its independence in 1990.

The rump of active football nations left consisted of Zambia, Malawi, Botswana, Lesotho, Swaziland, Madagascar, the Seychelles, the Comoros Islands and Mauritius, hardly a task force to take on the world. In the new order that is likely to emerge, South Africa, Zimbabwe, Zambia, Angola and Mozambique look set to be the strongest.

Most attention will unavoidably fall on South Africa in the future. As a nation they have a sporting history to match even the strongest nations in the world. Before their international exile because of apartheid, both their rugby union and cricket teams were world beaters. The Springboks, as the rugby side is called, were especially feared, but like everything in South Africa rugby was run along racial lines and has remained a sport that is largely a preserve of the white minority population.

The exciting aspect about the future of South African football is that for the first time the black majority will be able to make their mark on international sport, for it is football, not rugby or cricket, that is their passion, a factor commonly ignored by supporters of the other sports.

Football did not escape the horrors of apartheid and its roots are deeply entrenched in the country's colonial past. In 1882 the British province of Natal founded an association for the game, three years after South Africa's first club, Pietermaritzburg County, was formed. Along with the association in New South Wales in Australia, this body was the first of its kind outside Britain. Cape Province, the other British territory, soon followed suit and in 1892 the two were the prime movers behind the new South African Football Association, the oldest national body in Africa.

The Dutch areas of Transvaal and Orange Free State quickly took to the game too. In 1892 the Currie Cup was introduced for representative teams of the four provinces and it has been dominated by both Transvaal and Natal. In 1959 professionalism was introduced and the National

Professional Football League (NPFL) started. Until this point there had been a variety of local leagues and tournaments, but the NPFL, later known simply as the NFL, was the first to be open to the whole country, although only clubs from Johannesburg and Pretoria were at first represented.

An all-white league from the start, the NFL suffered greatly when in 1972 the non-white National Professional Soccer League was founded. It was an instant hit among the black population. Faced with this stiff competition, the NFL agreed to merge with the NPSL in 1978 and the new body became known as the National Soccer League. Since that time, on the playing field at least, football has been one of the few racially integrated activities in the country.

There have been problems regarding who actually controls the game, but in January 1992 the CAF were sufficiently confident that a single governing body was in place that they welcomed South Africa back into the fold.

For many years Zimbabwe was in a similar position to that of South Africa. As Rhodesia and before that as Southern Rhodesia, they had become outcasts as a result of the racial policies of the government. Rhodesia became an independent country after the declaration of UDI in 1965 and immediately joined FIFA, but the CAF would have nothing to do with them until the advent of black majority rule in 1980.

After a brief flirtation with the World Cup in 1970, Rhodesia were suspended from FIFA and did not take part again until 1982, but their form since becoming Zimbabwe has not been particularly impressive either at international or club level. They have yet to qualify for the Cup of Nations whilst the club sides have found it impossible to progress beyond the quarter-finals of the African club championships.

Zimbabwe's neighbours Zambia, known before independence as Northern Rhodesia, have fared slightly better and in 1991 won their first continental honour when Power Dynamos won the Cup Winners Cup. A Northern Rhodesia Football Association had been formed in 1929 and was affiliated to the Nyasaland Football Association in present-day Malawi. After independence in 1964, the Zambians had no neighbours to the south to play with and so concentrated their efforts on the tournaments played by the East and Central African Confederation.

Zambia have always threatened to do well and in 1974 lost to Zaire in the final of the Cup of Nations. Since then they have qualified for an average of one out of every two tournaments and reached the semi-finals twice. In 1988 at the Seoul Olympics they caused a sensation by defeating a fully-fledged professional Italian side 4–0 to reach the quarter-finals before losing to West Germany.

Zambia and later Zimbabwe's lack of nearby quality opposition was not helped by the unstable situations in three neighbouring countries. Mozambique may have produced two of the greatest footballers ever in Eusebio and Mario Coluña, but since the Portuguese upped and left both it and Angola in 1975, both countries have produced nothing but bloody conflicts, while Namibia has been involved in yet another civil war, although with independence in 1990 Namibians can look forward to taking part in African football for the first time.

None of the other nations of the region have contributed much to the game. The vast, under-populated Botswana, the tiny kingdoms of Lesotho and Swaziland, Mauritius and Madagascar are all keen competitors but have achieved little of note. Only Malawi, in the East and Central African competitions, have made their presence felt occasionally.

The region may not have had much of a history but changes are under way and only Mozambique still remains at war. It is possible that a regional championship of sorts could emerge to help get all of the countries on their feet, but in the future Southern Africans will have their eyes very much on the African and world titles at stake, and along with Nigeria, South Africa can be regarded as co-favourites to be the first African country to win the World Cup.

SOUTHERN AFRICAN FOOTBALL CONFEDERATION
PO Box 22121
Kitwe
Zambia

Founded: 1982

ANGOLA

Population: 10 002 000 Area, sq km: 1 246 000
% in urban areas: 26% Capital city: Luanda

Federacao Angolana de Futebol
BP 3449 Luanda
Angola
Tel: (010 244) 2 338635 Fax: None
Telex: 4072 CIAM AN
Cable: FUTANGOLA
Languages for correspondence: French & English

Year of formation: 1977
Affiliation to FIFA: 1980
Affiliation to CAF: 1980
Registered clubs: 177
Registered players: 8800
Registered coaches: 15
Registered referees: 297
National stadium: Cidadela, Luanda 35 000
National colours: Shirts: Red/Shorts: Black/Socks: Red
Reserve colours: Shirts: White/Shorts: White/Socks: White
Season: April–January

THE RECORD

WORLD CUP

1930–82 ..... Did not enter
1986 .... QT 2nd round
1990 .... QT 2nd round

OLYMPIC GAMES

1908–80 ..... Did not enter
1984 .... QT 1st round
1988–92 ..... Did not enter

AFRICAN CUP OF NATIONS

1957–80 ..... Did not enter
1982 .... QT pr round
1984 .... QT 1st round
1986 .... Did not enter
1988 .... QT 1st round
1990 .... QT 1st round
1992 .... QT 4th/4 in group 5

AFRICAN CLUB COMPETITIONS

AFRICAN CUP: 2nd round – Petro Atletico 1983 1988 1991. Primeiro de Maio 1984
CUP WINNERS CUP: Quarter-finals – Ferroviario Lubango 1988

ANGOLAN LEAGUE CHAMPIONS

1979	Primeiro de Agosto
1980	Primeiro de Agosto
1981	Primeiro de Agosto
1982	Petro Atletico
1983	Primeiro de Maio
1984	Petro Atletico
1985	Primeiro de Maio
1986	Petro Atletico
1987	Petro Atletico
1988	Petro Atletico
1989	Petro Atletico
1990	Petro Atletico
1991	Primeiro de Agosto

CLUB DIRECTORY

LUANDA (Population – 1 458 000)
Petro Atletico

Primeiro de Agosto

Desportivo TAAG

Inter Club

Sagrada Esperanca

BENGUELA (Population – 155 000)
FC Nacional

Primeiro de Maio

LUBANGO (Population – 95 000)
Ferroviario Lubango

BOTSWANA

Population: 1 295 000
Area, sq km: 581 730
% in urban areas: 21%
Capital city: Gaborone

Botswana Football Association
PO Box 1396, Gaborone, Botswana
Tel: (010 267) 300279
Fax: (010 267) 300280
Telex: 2977 BD
Cable: BOTSBALL GABORONE
Languages for correspondence: English

Year of formation: 1970
Affiliation to FIFA: 1976
Affiliation to CAF: 1976
Registered clubs: 168
Registered players: 4500
Registered Coaches: 8
Registered referees: 23
National stadium: National Stadium, Gaborone 20 000
National colours: Shirts: Sky blue/Shorts: White/Socks: Sky blue
Reserve colours: Shirts: White/Shorts: White/Socks: White
Season: February–October

THE RECORD

WORLD CUP

1930–90 ..... Did not enter

OLYMPIC GAMES

1908–84 ..... Did not enter
1988 .... QT 1st round
1992 .... Prelim round

AFRICAN CUP OF NATIONS

1957–92 ..... Did not enter

AFRICAN CLUB COMPETITIONS

AFRICAN CUP: Never past the 1st round

BOTSWANAN LEAGUE CHAMPIONS

1978	FC Notwane
1979	Township Rollers
1980	Township Rollers
1981	Defence Force
1982	Township Rollers
1983	Township Rollers
1984	Township Rollers
1985	Township Rollers
1986	Gaborone United
1987	Township Rollers
1988	Defence Force
1989	Defence Force
1990	Gaborone United
1991	Defence Force

CLUB DIRECTORY

GABORONE (Population – 95 000)
Botswana Defence Force

Gaborone United

FC Notwane

Township Rollers

LESOTHO

Population: 1 760 000
Area, sq km: 30 355
% in urban areas: 16%
Capital city: Maseru

Lesotho Sports Council
PO Box 138, Maseru 100, Lesotho
Tel: (010 266) 311291
Fax: (010 266) 310194
Telex: 4493 SPORTS LO
Cable: LIPAPALI MASERU
Languages for correspondence: English

Year of formation: 1932
Affiliation to FIFA: 1964
Affiliation to CAF: 1964
Registered clubs: 172
Registered players: 5000
Registered referees: 21
National stadium: National Stadium, Maseru 20 000
National colours: Shirts: Blue/Shorts: White/Socks: Blue
Reserve colours: Shirts: White/Shorts: Blue/Socks: Blue
Season: January–October

THE RECORD

WORLD CUP

1930–70 ..... Did not enter
1974 .... QT 1st round
1978 .... Did not enter
1982 .... QT 1st round
1986 .... Did not enter
1990 .... Did not enter

OLYMPIC GAMES

1908–76 ..... Did not enter
1980 .... QT 2nd round
1984 .... QT pr round
1988–92 ..... Did not enter

AFRICAN CUP OF NATIONS

1957–72 ..... Did not enter
1974 .... QT 1st round
1976 .... Did not enter
1978 .... Did not enter
1980 .... QT pr round
1982 .... QT pr round
1984–92 ..... Did not enter

AFRICAN CLUB COMPETITIONS

AFRICAN CUP: Quarter-finalists – Matlama FC 1979
CUP WINNERS CUP: 2nd round – Maseru United 1979. Matlama FC 1980

LESOTHO LEAGUE CHAMPIONS

1970	Maseru United
1971	Majantja
1972	Police
1973	Linare
1974	Matlama
1975	FC Maseru
1976	Maseru United
1977	Matlama
1978	Matlama
1979	Linare
1980	Linare
1981	Maseru Brothers
1982	Matlama
1983	LPF Maseru
1984	LPF Maseru
1985	Lioli Teyateyaneng
1986	Matlama
1987	RLDF Maseru
1988	Matlama
1989	Arsenal
1990	RLDF Maseru
1991	Arsenal

CLUB DIRECTORY

MASERU (Population – 109 000)
Matlama FC

Linare FC

Maseru Brothers

Maseru United

Maseru Rovers
Royal Lesotho Defence Force (RLDF Maseru)

Lesotho Paramilitary Force (LPF Maseru)

Arsenal

MADAGASCAR

Population: 11 980 000
Area, sq km: 587 041
% in urban areas: 21%
Capital city: Antananarivo

Fédération Malagasy de Football
BP 4409
Antananarivo 101
Madagascar
Tel: (010 261) 2 28051
Telex: 22393 MOTEL MG
Languages for correspondence: French

Year of formation: 1961
Affiliation to FIFA: 1962
Affiliation to CAF: 1963
Registered clubs: 445
Registered players: 9200
Registered coaches: 15
Registered referees: 477
National stadium: Municipal de Mahamasina, Antananarivo 15 000
National colours: Shirts: Red/Shorts: White/Socks: Green
Reserve colours: Shirts: White/Shorts: Red/ Socks: Green
Season: February–November

THE RECORD

WORLD CUP

1930–78 ..... Did not enter
1982 .... QT 2nd round
1986 .... QT 2nd round
1990 .... Did not enter

OLYMPIC GAMES

1908–64 ..... Did not enter
1968 .... QT 1st round
1972 .... QT 2nd round
1976 .... Did not enter
1980 .... QT 2nd round
1984–92 ..... Did not enter

AFRICAN CUP OF NATIONS

1957–70 ..... Did not enter
1972 .... QT 1st round
1974 .... QT 1st round
1976 .... Did not enter
1978 .... Did not enter
1980 .... QT pr round
1982 .... QT 2nd round
1984 .... QT 2nd round
1986 .... QT 1st round
1988 .... QT 1st round
1990 .... Did not enter
1992 .... QT 2nd/4 in group 5

AFRICAN CLUB COMPETITIONS

AFRICAN CUP: 2nd round – MMM Tamatave 1971. Fortior 1973. AS Somasud 1982
CUP WINNERS CUP: Semi-finalists – BFV FC 1989

MADAGASCAR LEAGUE CHAMPIONS

1968	Fitarikandro
1969	US Fonctionnaries
1970	MMM Tamatave
1971	AS St Michael
1972	Fortior Mahajanga
1973	Antalaha
1974	Corps Enseignant
1975	Corps Enseignant
1976	–
1977	Corps Enseignant
1978	AS St Michael
1979	Fortior Mahajunga
1980	MMM Tamatave
1981	AS Somasud
1982	Dinamo Fima
1983	Dinamo Fima
1984	–
1985	AC Sotema
1986	BTM Antananarivo
1987	Jos Nosy Be
1988	COSFAP Antananarivo
1989	AC Sotema
1990	ASF Fianarantsoa
1991	AC Sotema

CLUB DIRECTORY

ANTANANARIVO (Population – 663 000)
COSFAP Antananarivo

Dinamo Fima

BTM Antananarivo

Union Sportive Fonctionnaires

BFV FC

FIANARANTSOA (Population – 130 000)
ASF Fianarantsoa

TOAMASINA (Population – 100 000)
MMM Tamatave

MAHAJUNGA (Population – 85 000)
Athletic Club Sotema

Fortior Cote Ouest

HTMF Mahajunga

TOLARIA (Population – 55 000)
Association Sportive Somasud

Association Sportive Corps Enseignant

HELL-VILLE
Jos Nosy Be

MALAWI

Population: 8 831 000
Area, sq km: 118z484
% in urban areas: 11%
Capital city: Lilongwe

Football Association of Malawi
PO Box 865
Blantyre
Malawi
Tel: (010 265) 636686
Fax: None
Telex: 4526 SPORTS MI
Cable: FOOTBALL BLANTYRE
Languages for correspondence: English

Year of formation: 1966
Affiliation to FIFA: 1967
Affiliation to CAF: 1968

Registered clubs: 29
Registered players: 6200
Registered coaches: 150
Registered referees: 290
National stadium: Kamjizu, Blantyre 50 000
National colours: Shirts: Red/Shorts: Red/Socks: Red
Reserve colours: Shirts: White/Shorts: White/Socks: White
Season: March–December

THE RECORD

WORLD CUP

1930–74 ..... Did not enter
1978 .... QT 1st round
1982 .... QT 1st round
1986 .... QT 2nd round
1990 .... QT 2nd round

OLYMPIC GAMES

1908–68 ..... Did not enter
1972 .... QT 1st round
1976 .... QT 2nd round
1980 .... Did not enter
1984 .... Did not enter
1988 .... QT 1st round
1992 .... QT 2nd round

AFRICAN CUP OF NATIONS

1957–74 ..... Did not enter
1976 .... QT 1st round
1978 .... QT Pr round
1980 .... QT 1st round
1982 .... QT pr round
1984 .... QT Qualified – Final tournament/1st round
1986 .... QT 1st round
1988 .... QT 2nd round
1990 .... QT 2nd round
1992 .... QT 3rd/3 in group 7

AFRICAN CLUB COMPETITIONS

AFRICAN CUP: 2nd round – Bata Bullets 1975
CUP WINNERS CUP: 2nd round – Bata Bullets 1977

CLUB DIRECTORY

BLANTYRE (Population – 331 000)
Bata Bullets

ADMARC Tigers

Hardware Stars

LILONGWE (Population – 233 000)
Silver Strikers

LIMBE
Limbe Leaf Wanderers – Formerly Yamaha Wanderers

MAURITIUS

Population: 1 080 000
Area, sq km: 2040
% in urban areas: 40%
Capital city: Port Louis

Mauritius Football Association
2nd Floor #303–305, Chancery House
14 Lislet Geoffroy Street
Port Louis
Mauritius
Tel: (010 230) 2121418
Fax: (010 230) 2084100
Telex: 4427 MSA IW
Cable: MFA PORT LOUIS
Languages for correspondence: English & French

Year of formation: 1952
Affiliation to FIFA: 1962
Affiliation to CAF: 1963
Registered clubs: 600
Registered players: 30 100
Registered coaches: 130
Registered referees: 57
National stadium: King George V Stadium, Curepipe 19 000
National colours: Shirts: Red/Shorts: White/Socks: Red
Reserve colours: Shirts: White/Shorts: White/Socks: Red
Season: September–June

THE RECORD

WORLD CUP

1930–70 ..... Did not enter
1974 .... QT 2nd round
1978 .... Did not enter
1982 .... Did not enter
1986 .... QT 1st round
1990 .... Did not enter

OLYMPIC GAMES

1908–72 ..... Did not enter
1976 .... QT 1st round
1980 .... QT 1st round
1984 .... QT 1st round
1988 .... Did not enter
1992 .... QT 3rd round

AFRICAN CUP OF NATIONS

1957–65 ..... Did not enter
1968 .... QT 4th/4 in group 6
1970 .... QT 1st round
1972 .... QT 2nd round
1974 .... QT Qualified – Final tournament/1st round
1976 .... QT 1st round
1978 .... QT 1st round
1980 .... QT 1st round
1982 .... QT pr round
1984 .... QT 1st round
1986 .... QT pr round
1988 .... Did not enter
1990 .... QT 1st round
1992 .... Did not enter

AFRICAN CLUB COMPETITIONS

AFRICAN CUP: 2nd round – Sunrise FC 1988 1990 1991. Fire Brigade 1989
CUP WINNERS CUP: Have never entered

MAURITIUS LEAGUE CHAMPIONS

1970	FC Dodo
1971	Police Club
1972	Police Club
1973	Fire Brigade
1974	Fire Brigade
1975	Hindu Cadets
1976	Muslim Scouts
1977	Hindu Cadets
1978	Racing Club
1979	Hindu Cadets
1980	Fire Brigade
1981	Police Club
1982	Police Club
1983	Fire Brigade
1984	Fire Brigade
1985	Fire Brigade
1986	Tamil Cadets
1987	Sunrise FC
1988	Fire Brigade
1989	Sunrise FC
1990	Sunrise FC
1991	Sunrise FC

CLUB DIRECTORY

PORT LOUIS (Population – 139 000)
Fire Brigade Sports Club

Police Club

Tamil Cadets Sports Club

Muslim Scouts Sports Club

Hindu Cadets United

Racing Club de Maurice

CUREPIPE (Population – 64 000)
Sunrise FC

FC Dodo

MOZAMBIQUE

Population: 15 696 000
Area, sq km: 812 379
% in urban areas: 13%
Capital city: Maputo

Federacao Mocambicana de Futebol
Avenue Samora Machel 11–2
Caixa Postal 1467
Maputo
Mozambique
Tel: (010 258) 1 26475 Fax: None

Telex: 6–575 PERCO MO
Cable: MOCAMBOLA MAPUTO
Languages for correspondence: English & French

Year of formation: 1975
Affiliation to FIFA: 1978
Affiliation to CAF: 1978
Registered clubs: 128
Registered players: 2800
Registered coaches: 264
Registered referees: 73
National stadium: Estadio de Machava, Maputo 35 000
National colours: Shirts: Red/Shorts: Red/Socks: Black
Reserve colours: Shirts: Yellow/Shorts: Black/Socks: Yellow
Season: February–November

THE RECORD

WORLD CUP

1930–78 ..... Did not enter
1982 .... QT 1st round
1986 .... Did not enter
1990 .... Did not enter

OLYMPIC GAMES

1908–80 ..... Did not enter
1984 .... QT 1st round
1988 .... QT 1st round
1992 .... QT 1st round

AFRICAN CUP OF NATIONS

1957–80 ..... Did not enter
1982 .... QT 1st round
1984 .... QT 1st round
1986 .... QT Qualified – Final tournament/1st round
1988 .... QT 1st round
1990 .... QT 1st round
1992 .... QT 2nd/3 in group 6

AFRICAN CLUB COMPETITIONS

AFRICAN CUP: Quarter-finalists – Matchadje 1988
CUP WINNERS CUP: Semi-finalists – Desportivo Maputo 1990

MOZAMBIQUE LEAGUE CHAMPIONS

1976	Textafrica
1977	Desportivo Maputo
1978	Desportivo Maputo
1979	Costa do Sol
1980	Costa do Sol
1981	Textil Pungue Beira
1982	Ferroviario Maputo
1983	Desportivo Maputo
1984	Maxaquene
1985	Maxaquene
1986	Maxaquene
1987	Matchedje
1988	Desportivo Maputo
1989	Ferroviario Maputo
1990	Matchadje
1991	Costa do Sol

CLUB DIRECTORY

MAPUTO (1 069 000)
Matchedje

Desportos da Costa do Sol

Club Desportos Maxaquene

Clube Ferroviario

Estrela Vermehla

BEIRA (Population – 291 000)
Textil Pungue

Club Palmeiras

SEYCHELLES

Population: 68 000 Area, sq km: 453
% in urban areas: 47% Capital city: Victoria

Seychelles Football Federation
PO Box 580, Mont Fleuri, Victoria, Seychelles
Tel: (010 248) 24126
Fax: (010 248) 23518
Telex: 2240 CULSPT SZ
Languages for correspondence: English

Year of formation: 1976
Affiliation to FIFA: 1986
Affiliation to CAF: 1986
Registered clubs: 28
Registered players: 1300
Registered referees: 44
National stadium: People's Stadium, Victoria 7000
National colours: Shirts: Red/Shorts: White/Socks: Red
Reserve colours: Shirts: White/Shorts: Red/Socks: White
Season: July–May

THE RECORD

WORLD CUP

1930–90 ..... Did not enter

OLYMPIC GAMES

1908–92 ..... Did not enter

AFRICAN CUP OF NATIONS

1957–88 ..... Did not enter
1990 .... QT pr round
1992 .... Did not enter

AFRICAN CLUB COMPETITIONS

AFRICAN CUP: Never past the first round
CUP WINNERS CUP: Never past the first round

SEYCHELLES LEAGUE CHAMPIONS

1986	St Louis
1987	St Louis
1988	St Louis
1989	St Louis
1990	St Louis
1991	St Louis

CLUB DIRECTORY

VICTORIA (Population – 23 000)
St Louis

ANSE BOILEAU
Anse Boileau FC

PLAISANCE
Plaisance FC

SOUTH AFRICA

Population: 30 797 000
Area, sq km: 1 123 226
% in urban areas: 56%
Capital city: Pretoria

South African Football Association
PO Box 910
Johannesburg 2000
South Africa
Fax: (010 027) 11 4943447
Languages for correspondence: English

Year of formation: 1892
Affiliation to FIFA: 1952–1976 (Suspended 1964–76) 1992
Affiliation to CAF: 1957 and 1992
National stadium: Soccer City, Soweto 80 000
National colours: Shirts: Gold/Shorts: Black/Socks: White
Season: January–November

THE RECORD

WORLD CUP

1930–90 ..... Did not enter

OLYMPIC GAMES

1908–92 ..... Did not enter

AFRICAN CUP OF NATIONS

1957–92 ..... Did not enter

SOUTH AFRICAN LEAGUE CHAMPIONS

1971 Orlando Pirates
1972 AmaZulu
1973 Orlando Pirates
1974 Kaizer Chiefs
1975 Orlando Pirates
1976 Orlando Pirates
1977 Kaizer Chiefs
1978 Lusitano
1979 Kaizer Chiefs
1980 Dion Highlands
1981 Kaizer Chiefs
1982 Durban City
1983 Durban City
1984 Kaizer Chiefs
1985 Bush Bucks
1986 Rangers
1987 Jomo Cosmos
1988 Mamelodi Sundowns
1989 Kaizer Chiefs
1990 Mamelodi Sundowns
1991 Kaizer Chiefs

SOUTH AFRICAN CUP WINNERS

1970 Kaizer Chiefs
1972 Orlando Pirates
1973 Kaizer Chiefs
1974 Orlando Pirates
1975 Orlando Pirates
1976 Kaizer Chiefs
1977 Orlando Pirates
1978 Moroka Swallows
1979 Kaizer Chiefs
1980 Orlando Pirates
1981 Kaizer Chiefs
1982 Kaizer Chiefs
1983 –
1984 Kaizer Chiefs
1985 Bloemfontein Celtic
1986 Mamelodi Sundowns
1987 Kaizer Chiefs
1988 Orlando Pirates
1989 Moroka Swallows
1990 Jomo Cosmos
1991 Moroka Swallows

JPS CUP

1984 Kaizer Chiefs
1985 Wits University
1986 Kaizer Chiefs
1987 Bush Bucks
1988 Kaizer Chiefs
1989 Kaizer Chiefs
1990 Mamelodi Sundowns
1991 Dynamos

BP TOP EIGHT

1972 Orlando Pirates
1973 Kaizer Chiefs
1974 Kaizer Chiefs
1975 Moroka Swallows
1976 Kaizer Chiefs
1977 Kaizer Chiefs
1978 Orlando Pirates
1979 Moroka Swallows
1980 Witbank Black Aces
1981 Kaizer Chiefs
1982 Kaizer Chiefs
1983 Orlando Pirates
1984 Wits University
1985 Kaizer Chiefs
1986 Arcadia
1987 Kaizer Chiefs
1988 Mamelodi Sundowns
1989 Kaizer Chiefs
1990 Mamelodi Sundowns
1991 Kaizer Chiefs

CASTLE CHAMPION OF CHAMPIONS CHALLENGE

1980 Kaizer Chiefs
1981 Kaizer Chiefs
1982 Arcadia
1983 Kaizer Chiefs
1984 Orlando Pirates
1985 Arcadia
1986 Kaizer Chiefs
1987 Kaizer Chiefs
1988 Mamelodi Sundowns
1989 Kaizer Chiefs
1990 Kaizer Chiefs
1991 Kaizer Chiefs

NATIONAL FOOTBALL LEAGUE

1959 Durban City
1960 Highlands Park
1961 Durban City
1962 Highlands Park
1963 Addington
1964 Highlands Park
1965 Highlands Park
1966 Highlands Park
1967 Port Elizabeth City
1968 Highlands Park
1969 Durban Spurs
1970 Durban City
1971 Hellenic
1972 Durban City
1973 Cape Town City
1974 Arcadia Shepherds
1975 Highlands Park
1976 Cape Town City
1977 Highlands Park

NATIONAL FOOTBALL LEAGUE CUP

1959 Rangers
1960 Durban City
1961 Highlands Park
1962 Durban City
1963 Addington
1964 Durban City
1965 Highlands Park
1966 Highlands Park
1967 Highlands Park
1968 Durban City
1969 Maritzburg
1970 Cape Town City
1971 Cape Town City
1972 Durban United
1973 Highlands Park
1974 Arcadia Shepherds
1975 Highlands Park
1976 Cape Town City
1977 Highlands Park

CLUB DIRECTORY

JOHANNESBURG (Population – 3650000)

Jomo Cosmos
Stadium: Vosloorus
Founded: 1983
Colours: White/Orange
Previous names: Merger in 1983 of Germiston Callies and Highlands Park. Highlands Park were a result of the merger of Highlands Park, Balfour Park and Powerlines

Kaizer Chiefs
Stadium: Ellis Park
Founded: 1970
Colours: Gold/Black
Previous names: Kaizer XI

Moroka Swallows
Stadium: Ellis Park
Founded: 1947
Colours: Maroon/White
Previous names: Corrugated FC, Moroka Swallows, Big XV and Real Moroha

Orlando Pirates
Stadium: Orlando
Founded: 1937
Colours: Black/White
Previous names: Orlando Boys Club

Grinaker PUBS
Founded: 1900
Previous names: Imperial Military Railways, Rangers

Wits University
Stadium: Milpark
Founded: 1922
Colours: Blue/White

CAPE TOWN (Population – 1 790 000)

Cape Town Spurs
Stadium: Hartleyvale
Colours: Red/White
Previous names: Merged with Cape Town City

Hellenic
Stadium: Hartleyvale
Founded: 1958
Colours: Blue/White

Santos
Stadium: Athlone
Colours: White/White

DURBAN (Population – 1 550 000)

AmaZulu
Stadium: Glebelands
Founded: 1939
Colours: Green/White
Previous names: Zulu Royals and Amandhla AmaZulu

Bush Bucks
Stadium: Glebelands
Colours: Black/Gold

Manning Rangers
Stadium: Chatsworth
Founded: 1928

PRETORIA (Population – 960 000)

Dynamos
Stadium: Lenasia
Founded: 1902
Colours: Red/White
Previous names: Arcadia Shepherds, Arcadia and Arcadia United

Mamelodi Sundowns
Stadium: Pitje
Founded: 1970
Colours: Green/Yellow
Previous names: Mamelodi United

Pretoria City
Stadium: Koedoes Park
Colours: Red/White

PORT ELIZABETH (Population – 690 000)

Blackpool
Stadium: Boet Erasmus

BLOEMFONTEIN (Population – 235 000)

Bloemfontein Celtic
Stadium: Seisa Ramabodu
Colours: Green/White
Previous names: Bloemfontein City, Frasers Celtic, Magic Curl Celtic, Phunya sele-Sele

PIETERMARITZBURG (Population – 230 000)

Real Taj
Stadium: Northdale

SWAZILAND

Population: 770 000
Area, sq km: 17 364
% in urban areas: 22%
Capital city: Mbabane

National Football Association of Swaziland
PO Box 641
Mbabane
Swaziland
Tel: (010 268) 46852
Fax: None
Telex: 2245 EXP WD
Cable: None
Languages for correspondence: English

Year of formation: 1964
Affiliation to FIFA: 1976
Affiliation to CAF: 1976
Registered clubs: 16
Registered players: 880
Registered coaches: 6
Registered referees: 41
National stadium: Somholo, Mbabane 20 000
National colours: Shirts: Blue/Shorts: White/Socks: Blue
Reserve colours: Shirts: White/Shorts: White/Socks: White

THE RECORD

WORLD CUP

1930–90 ..... Did not enter

OLYMPIC GAMES

1908–84 ..... Did not enter
1988 .... QT 1st round
1992 .... Prelim round

AFRICAN CUP OF NATIONS

1957–84 ..... Did not enter
1986 .... QT pr round
1988 .... Did not enter
1990 .... QT 1st round
1992 .... QT 3rd/4 in group 5

AFRICAN CLUB COMPETITIONS

AFRICAN CUP: Never past the first round
CUP WINNERS CUP: 2nd round – Highlanders 1986

SWAZILAND LEAGUE CHAMPIONS

1980	Highlanders
1981	Peacemakers
1982	Highlanders
1983	Manzini Wanderers
1984	Highlanders
1985	Manzini Wanderers
1986	Highlanders
1987	Manzini Wanderers
1988	Highlanders
1989	Denver Sundowns
1990	Denver Sundowns
1991	Highlanders

CLUB DIRECTORY

MBABANE (Population – 38 000)
Mbabane Highlanders

Swallows FC

MANZINI (Population – 30 000)
Manzini Wanderers

MHLUME
Peacemakers

ZAMBIA

Population: 8 456 000
Area, sq km: 752 614
% in urban areas: 44%
Capital city: Lusaka

Football Association of Zambia
PO Box 34751
Lusaka
Zambia
Tel: (010 260) 1 221145
Fax: None
Telex: 40204 FAZ ZA
Cable: FOOTBALL LUSAKA
Languages for correspondence: English

Year of formation: 1929
Affiliation to FIFA: 1964
Affiliation to CAF: 1964
Registered clubs: 194
Registered players: 4900
Professional players: 350
Registered referees: 290
National stadium: Independence Stadium, Lusaka 30 000
National colours: Shirts: Green/Shorts: Copper/Socks: Copper
Reserve colours: Shirts: Copper/Shorts: Copper/Socks: Green
Season: March–November

THE RECORD

WORLD CUP

1930–66 ..... Did not enter
1970 .... QT 1st round
1974 .... QT 4th round
1978 .... QT 3rd round
1982 .... QT 2nd round
1986 .... QT 3rd round
1990 .... QT 2nd round

OLYMPIC GAMES

1908–68 ..... Did not enter
1972 .... QT 1st round
1976 .... QT Qualified/withdrew
1980 .... QT Qualified – Final tournament/1st round
1984 .... QT 2nd round
1988 .... QT Qualified – Final tournament/Quarter-finalists
1992 .... Did not enter

AFRICAN CUP OF NATIONS

1957–68 ..... Did not enter
1970 .... QT 2nd round
1972 .... QT 2nd round
1974 .... QT Qualified – Final tournament/Finalists
1976 .... QT 2nd round
1978 .... QT Qualified – Final tournament/1st round
1980 .... QT 2nd round
1982 .... QT Qualified – Final tournament/Semi-finalists/3rd place
1984 .... QT 1st round
1986 .... QT Qualified – Final tournament/1st round
1988 .... Did not enter
1990 .... QT Qualified – Final tournament/Semi-finalists/3rd place
1992 .... QT 1st/4 in group 5 – Final tournament/Quarter-finalists

AFRICAN CLUB COMPETITIONS

AFRICAN CUP: Finalists – Nkana Red Devils 1990
CUP WINNERS CUP: Winners – Power Dynamos 1991
Finalists – Power Dynamos 1982

ZAMBIAN LEAGUE CHAMPIONS

1962 City of Lusaka
1963 Mufulira Wanderers
1964 Roan United
1965 Mufulira Wanderers
1966 Mufulira Wanderers
1967 Mufulira Wanderers
1968 Kabwe Warriors
1969 Mufulira Wanderers
1970 Kabwe Warriors
1971 Kabwe Warriors
1972 Kabwe Warriors
1973 Zambia Army
1974 Zambia Army
1975 Green Buffaloes
1976 Mufulira Wanderers
1977 Green Buffaloes
1978 Mufulira Wanderers
1979 Green Buffaloes
1980 Nchanga Rangers
1981 Green Buffaloes
1982 Nkana Red Devils
1983 Nkana Red Devils
1984 Power Dynamos
1985 Mufulira Wanderers
1986 Nkana Red Devils
1987 Kabwe Warriors
1988 Nkana Red Devils
1989 Nkana Red Devils
1990 Nkana Red Devils
1991 Nkana Red Devils

CLUB DIRECTORY

LUSAKA (Population – 535 000)
City of Lusaka

Red Arrows

Green Buffaloes

KITWE (Population – 283 000)
Rokana United

Power Dynamos

Nkana Red Devils

NDOLA (Population – 250 000)
Ndola United

MUFULIRA (Population 138 000)
Mufulira Wanderers

KABWE (Population – 127 000)
Kabwe Warriors

ZIMBABWE

Population: 9 369 000
Area, sq km: 390 759
% in urban areas: 25%
Capital city: Harare

Zimbabwe Football Association
PO Box 8343
Causeway
Harare
Zimbabwe
Tel: (010 263) 4 791275
Fax: (010 263) 4 793320
Telex: 22299 SOCCER ZW
Cable: SOCCER HARARE
Languages for correspondence: English

Year of formation: 1950
Affiliation to FIFA: 1965
Affiliation to CAF: 1980
Registered clubs: 610
Registered players: 12 000
National stadium: Rufaro Stadium, Harare 32 000
National colours: Shirts: White/Shorts: Black/Socks: Black
Reserve colours: Shirts: Green/Shorts: Green/Socks: Green
Season: January–November

THE RECORD

WORLD CUP

1930–66 ..... Did not enter
1970 .... QT 2nd round (As Rhodesia)
1974 .... Did not enter
1978 .... Did not enter
1982 .... QT 2nd round
1986 .... QT 1st round
1990 .... QT 2nd round

OLYMPIC GAMES

1908–80 ..... Did not enter
1984 .... QT 2nd round
1988 .... QT 2nd round
1992 .... QT 3rd round

AFRICAN CUP OF NATIONS

1957–80 ..... Did not enter
1982 .... QT 1st round
1984 .... QT pr round
1986 .... QT 2nd round
1988 .... QT 2nd round
1990 .... QT 2nd round
1992 .... QT 2nd/4 in group 7

AFRICAN CLUB COMPETITIONS

AFRICAN CUP: Quarter-finalists – Dynamos 1981 1984 1987. Black Rhinos 1985. Zimbabwe Saints 1989
CUP WINNERS CUP: Quarter-finalists – CAPS United 1982 1983. Dynamos 1991

ZIMBABWE LEAGUE CHAMPIONS

1963 Dynamos
1964 Bulawayo Rovers
1965 Dynamos
1966 St. Pauls
1967 Tornados
1968 Bulawayo Sables
1969 Bulawayo Sables
1970 Dynamos
1971 Arcadia United
1972 Salisbury Sables
1973 Metal Box
1974 Highlanders
1975 Chibuku
1976 Dynamos
1977 Zimbabwe Saints
1978 Dynamos

1979	CAPS United
1980	Dynamos
1981	Dynamos
1982	Dynamos
1983	Dynamos
1984	Black Rhinos
1985	Dynamos
1986	Dynamos
1987	Zimbabwe Saints
1988	Dynamos
1989	Dynamos
1990	Bulawayo Highlanders
1991	Dynamos

CASTLE CUP WINNERS

1962	Bulawayo Rovers
1963	Salisbury Callies
1964	–
1965	Salisbury City
1966	Mangula
1967	Salisbury Callies
1968	Arcadia United
1969	Arcadia United
1970	Wankie
1971	Chibuku
1972	Mangula
1973	Wankie
1974	Chibuku
1975	Salisbury Callies
1976	Dynamos
1977	Zimbabwe Saints
1978	Zisco
1979	Zimbabwe Saints
1980	CAPS United
1981	CAPS United
1982	CAPS United
1983	CAPS United
1984	Black Rhinos
1985	Dynamos
1986	Highlanders
1987	Zimbabwe Saints
1988	Dynamos
1989	Dynamos
1990	Bulawayo Highlanders
1991	Dynamos

CLUB DIRECTORY

HARARE (Population – 890 000)

CAPS United

Dynamos

Arcadia United

State House Tornados

BULAWAYO (Population – 413 000)

Zimbabwe Saints

Bulawayo Highlanders

Bulawayo Wanderers

GWERU (Population – 78 000)

Gweru United

MUTARE (Population – 69 000)
Black Rhinos

CONCACAF

Costa Rica v Brazil, World Cup 1990

CONCACAF

The Confederación Norte-Centroamericana y del Caribe de Fútbol, or CONCACAF for short, is with the exception of Oceania the weakest of the continental confederations, and for many years seemed only to exist in order that Mexico could be given a World Cup berth.

The present body dates only from 1961 but before then there had been a confusion of bodies claiming responsibility over the game in the region or various parts of it. Part of the problem is that CONCACAF is not a recognisable geographical entity. By right there should be a confederation for all the countries of the Americas as existed in the 1950s, but this body never had any jurisdictional power and the South American confederation was unwilling to see its control weakened.

In 1924 the Congreso Deportivo Centroamericano was founded and this became the Organización Deportiva Centroamericana y del Caribe and its primary function was to organise the Central American and Caribbean Games which started in 1930, and in which there was a football tournament.

Before the 1938 edition of those games it was decided to found a football-only governing body and so the Confederación Centroamericana y del Caribe de Fútbol, or the CCCF, came into being. Its charter members included Colombia, Venezuela, most of the Central American nations as well as Haiti, Puerto Rico and Jamaica from the Caribbean. It was to organise the football tournament of the Central American and Caribbean Games and a new tournament, the Championship of the CCCF, which was open to amateurs and professionals.

In 1939 a short-lived North American Football Confederation containing the United States, Cuba and Mexico was founded and two championships played, but by 1961, Mexico in particular were keen to revitalise the international game in the region, which the CCCF had never really got to grips with, and they were one of the founding members of CONCACAF along with Cuba, Guatemala, Honduras and the Netherlands Antilles.

Other members soon followed and by 1970 there were 14 in all. Since then the number has risen to 29 as the tiny islands of the Caribbean have made the effort to join. CONCACAF's major role has been to organise a championship for both clubs and national sides, but two factors have always dominated the confederation's activities.

Firstly Mexico is by far and away the strongest of all the nations affiliated. When their clubs take the tournament seriously, clubs from other nations in the club championship do not really stand a chance. Even worse for CONCACAF has been Mexico's total indifference to the championship for international sides, so much so that it was abandoned as a separate event in the 1970s and the winners of the World Cup qualifying competition were regarded as champions.

The other problem has been the attitude of the United States, whose national and club sides have shunned both competitions. The New York Cosmos and the like had more important matters on their mind than playing in some backwater tournament, or so it seemed.

Matters have changed since the 1994 World Cup was awarded to the United States, and for the first time since the formation of the first governing body in 1924, a true representative continental championship was held in 1991 under the banner of the CONCACAF Gold Cup. American support was crucial in getting the tournament off the ground, and the region can now look forward to more prosperous times with their backing, especially as CONCACAF's offices have moved to America.

Regional Governing Body

CONFEDERACIÓN NORTE-CENTROAMERICANA Y DEL CARIBE DE FÚTBOL
717 Fifth Avenue, 13th Floor
New York
NY 10022
USA
Tel: (0101) 212 3080044
Fax: (0101) 212 3081851
Telex: 49605089 CONCACAF
Cable: CONCACAF NYC

Year of formation: 1961

Members: 27
Antigua and Barbuda – Aruba – Bahamas – Barbados – Belize – Bermuda – Canada – Cayman Islands – Costa Rica – Cuba – Dominican Republic – El Salvador – Grenada – Guatemala – Guyana – Haiti – Honduras – Jamaica – Mexico – Netherlands Antilles – Nicaragua – Panama – Puerto Rico – Saint Lucia – Saint Kitts and Nevis – Saint Vincent and the Grenadines – Suriname – Trinidad and Tobago – United States of America

Associate Members: 2
Dominica – Virgin Islands of the US

Non Members: 8
Anguilla – British Virgin Islands – French Guiana – Guadeloupe – Martinique – Montserrat – St Pierre and Miquelon – Turks and Caicos Islands

THE CENTRAL AMERICAN CHAMPIONSHIPS

Year	Winners	Year	Winners
1941	Costa Rica	1965	Mexico
1943	El Salvador	1967	Guatemala
1946	Costa Rica	1969	Costa Rica
1948	Costa Rica	1971	Mexico
1951	Panama	1973	Haiti
1953	Costa Rica	1977	Mexico
1955	Costa Rica	1981	Honduras
1957	Haiti	1985	Canada
1960	Costa Rica	1989	Costa Rica
1961	Costa Rica	1991	United States
1963	Costa Rica		

CCCF FIRST CHAMPIONSHIP
San Jose, Costa Rica, 8th–18th May 1941

	CR	ES	Cu	Pa	Ni	Pl	W	D	L	F	A	Pts
COSTA RICA	–	3–1	6–2	7–0	7–2	4	4	0	0	23	5	8
EL SALVADOR	–	–	2–2	4–3	8–0	4	2	1	1	15	8	5
CURACAO	–	–	–	3–3	9–1	4	1	2	1	16	12	4
PANAMA	–	–	–	–	5–2	4	1	1	2	11	16	3
NICARAGUA	–	–	–	–	–	4	0	0	4	5	29	0

CCCF SECOND CHAMPIONSHIP
San Salvador, 5th–19th December 1943

	ES	CR	Gu	Ni	Pl	W	D	L	F	A	Pts
EL SALVADOR	–	4–3	2–2	10–1	6	4	1	1	28	12	9
COSTA RICA	4–2	–	2–3	7–0	6	3	0	3	21	15	6
GUATEMALA	1–2	4–2	–	–	4	2	1	1	10	8	5
NICARAGUA	1–8	2–3	–	–	4	0	0	4	4	28	0

CCCF THIRD CHAMPIONSHIP
San Jose, Costa Rica , 23rd Feb–13th March 1946

	CR	Gu	ES	Ho	Pa	Ni	Pl	W	D	L	F	A	Pts
COSTA RICA	–	1–4	4–0	5–0	7–0	7–1	5	4	0	1	24	5	8
GUATEMALA	–	–	W	L	D	W	5	3	1	1			7
EL SALVADOR	–	–	–	3–1	W	W	5	3	0	2			6
HONDURAS	–	–	–	–	L	W	5	2	0	3			4
PANAMA	–	–	–	–	–	L	5	1	1	3			3
NICARAGUA	–	–	–	–	–	–	5	1	0	4			2

CCCF FOURTH CHAMPIONSHIP
Guatemala City 1948

Winners – Costa Rica

CCCF FIFTH CHAMPIONSHIP 1951

Winners – PANAMA

CCCF SIXTH CHAMPIONSHIP 1953

Winners – COSTA RICA

CCCF SEVENTH CHAMPIONSHIP 1955

Winners – COSTA RICA

CCCF EIGHTH CHAMPIONSHIP
Curacao, 11th–25th Aug 1957

	Ha	Cu	Ho	Pa	Cu	Pl	W	D	L	F	A	Pts
HAITI	–	3–1	2–1	3–1	6–1	4	4	0	0	14	4	8
CURACAO	–	–	1–1	3–0	2–0	4	2	1	1	7	4	5
HONDURAS	–	–	–	2–1	2–0	4	2	1	1	6	4	5
PANAMA	–	–	–	–	1–0	4	1	0	3	3	8	2
CUBA	–	–	–	–	–	4	0	0	4	1	11	0

CCCF NINTH CHAMPIONSHIP
Havana, Cuba, 14th–28th Feb 1960

	CR	NA	Ho	Su	Cu	Pl	W	D	L	F	A	Pts
COSTA RICA	–	1–1	1–1	3–1	5–0	4	2	2	0	10	3	6
NETH. ANTILES	–	–	3–3	1–0	4–3	4	2	2	0	9	7	6
HONDURAS	–	–	–	1–1	1–2	4	0	3	1	6	7	3
SURINAME	–	–	–	–	2–0	4	1	1	2	4	5	3
CUBA	–	–	–	–	–	4	0	0	4	5	12	0

CCCF TENTH CHAMPIONSHIP
San Jose, Costa Rica, March 1961

FIRST ROUND

Group 1

	CR	Ha	Gu	Pa	Cu	Pl	W	D	L	F	A	Pts
Costa Rica	–	3–0	4–2	6–1	–	4	4	0	0	17	4	8
Haiti	–	–	–	3–1	2–1	4	3	0	1	8	6	6
Guatemala	–	1–3	–	–	2–0	4	2	0	2	7	7	4
Panama	–	–	0–2	–	1–0	4	1	0	3	3	11	2
Cuba	1–4	–	–	–	–	4	0	0	4	2	9	0

Group 2

	ES	Ho	NA	Ni	Pl	W	D	L	F	A	Pts
El Salvador	–	1–0	–	10–2	3	2	1	0	11	2	5
Honduras	–	–	4–2	–	3	2	0	1	10	3	4
Neth. Antilles	0–0	–	–	2–1	3	1	1	1	4	5	3
Nicaragua	–	0–6	–	–	3	0	0	3	3	18	0

FINAL ROUND

	CR	ES	Ho	Ha	Pl	W	D	L	F	A	Pts
COSTA RICA	–	4–0	3–0	8–0	3	3	0	0	15	0	6
EL SALVADOR	–	–	5–1	2–0	3	2	0	1	7	5	4
HONDURAS	–	–	–	2–0	3	1	0	2	3	8	2
HAITI	–	–	–	–	3	0	0	3	0	12	0

CONCACAF FIRST CHAMPIONSHIP
San Salvador , 23rd–7th April 1963

FIRST ROUND

Group 1

	Ho	ES	Pa	Gu	Ni	Pl	W	D	L	F	A	Pts
Honduras	–	2–2	1–0	2–1	1–0	4	3	1	0	6	3	7
El Salvador	–	–	1–1	1–1	6–1	4	1	3	0	10	5	5
Panama	–	–	–	2–2	5–0	4	1	2	1	8	4	4
Guatemala	–	–	–	–	3–1	4	1	2	1	7	6	4
Nicaragua	–	–	–	–	–	4	0	0	4	2	15	0

Group 2

	CR	NA	Me	Ja	Pl	W	D	L	F	A	Pts
Costa Rica	–	1–0	0–0	6–0	3	2	1	0	7	0	5
Neth. Antilles	–	–	2–1	2–1	3	2	0	1	4	3	4

					Pl	W	D	L	F	A	Pts
Mexico	–	–	–	8–0	3	1	1	1	9	2	3
Jamaica	–	–	–	–	3	0	0	3	1	16	0

FINAL ROUND

	CR	ES	NA	Ho	Pl	W	D	L	F	A	Pts
COSTA RICA	–	4–1	1–0	2–1	3	3	0	0	7	2	6
El Salvador	–	–	3–2	3–0	3	2	0	1	7	6	4
Neth. Antilles	–	–	–	4–1	3	1	0	2	6	5	2
Honduras	–	–	–	–	3	0	0	3	2	9	0

CONCACAF SECOND CHAMPIONSHIP

Guatemala City, 28th March–11th April 1965

	Me	Gu	CR	ES	NA	Ha	Pl	W	D	L	F	A	Pts
MEXICO	–	2–1	1–1	2–0	5–0	3–0	5	4	1	0	13	2	9
Guatemala	–	–	0–0	4–1	3–2	3–0	5	3	1	1	11	5	7
Costa Rica	–	–	–	1–2	6–0	3–1	5	2	2	1	11	4	6
El Salvador	–	–	–	–	1–1	3–1	5	2	1	2	7	9	5
Neth. Antilles	–	–	–	–	–	1–1	5	0	2	3	4	16	2
Haiti	–	–	–	–	–	–	5	0	1	4	3	13	1

CONCACAF THIRD CHAMPIONSHIP

Tegucigalpa, Honduras, 5th–9th March 1967

	Gu	Me	Ho	Tr	Ha	Ni	Pl	W	D	L	F	A	Pts
GUATEMALA	–	1–0	0–0	2–0	2–1	2–0	5	4	1	0	7	1	9
Mexico	–	–	1–0	4–0	1–0	4–0	5	4	0	1	10	1	8
Honduras	–	–	–	1–0	2–0	1–1	5	2	2	1	4	2	6
Trinidad	–	–	–	–	3–2	3–1	5	2	0	3	6	10	4
Haiti	–	–	–	–	–	2–1	5	1	0	4	5	9	2
Nicaragua	–	–	–	–	–	–	5	0	1	4	3	12	1

CONCACAF FOURTH CHAMPIONSHIP

San Jose, Costa Rica, 23rd Nov–8th Dec 1969

	CR	Gu	NA	Me	Tr	Ja	Pl	W	D	L	F	A	Pts
COSTA RICA	–	1–1	2–1	2–0	5–0	3–0	5	4	1	0	13	2	9
Guatemala	–	–	6–1	1–0	2–0	0–0	5	3	2	0	10	2	8
Neth. Antilles	–	–	–	2–2	3–1	2–1	5	2	1	2	9	12	5
Mexico	–	–	–	–	0–0	2–0	5	1	2	2	4	5	4
Trinidad	–	–	–	–	–	3–2	5	1	1	3	4	12	3
Jamaica	–	–	–	–	–	–	5	0	1	4	3	10	1

CONCACAF FIFTH CHAMPIONSHIP

Port of Spain, Trinidad, 20th Nov–5th Dec 1971

	Me	Ha	CR	Cu	Tr	Ho	PL	W	D	L	F	A	Pts
MEXICO	–	0–0	1–0	1–0	2–0	2–1	5	4	1	0	6	1	9
Haiti	–	–	0–0	0–0	6–0	3–1	5	2	3	0	9	1	7
Costa Rica	–	–	–	3–0	1–3	2–1	5	2	1	2	6	5	5
Cuba	–	–	–	–	2–2	3–1	5	1	2	2	5	7	4
Trinidad	–	–	–	–	–	1–1	5	1	2	2	6	12	4
Honduras	–	–	–	–	–	–	5	0	1	4	5	11	1

CONCACAF SIXTH CHAMPIONSHIP 1973

Winners – HAITI

CONCACAF SEVENTH CHAMPIONSHIP 1977

Winners – MEXICO

CONCACAF EIGHTH CHAMPIONSHIP 1981

Winners – HONDURAS

CONCACAF NINTH CHAMPIONSHIP 1985

Winners – CANADA

CONCACAF TENTH CHAMPIONSHIP 1989

Winners – COSTA RICA

FIRST CONCACAF GOLD CUP 1991

QUALIFYING ROUNDS

CARIBBEAN

For the Shell Caribbean Cup

Qualifying round

Group 1

	SL	Mo	An	Pl	W	D	L	F	A	Pts
St Lucia	–	3–0	6–0	2	2	0	0	9	0	4
Montserrat	–	–	1–1	2	0	1	1	1	4	1
Anguilla	–	–	–	2	0	1	1	1	7	1

Group 2

	DR	Ha	PR	Pl	W	D	L	F	A	Pts
Dominican Rep	–	1–1	3–1	2	1	1	0	4	2	3
Haiti	–	–	3–2	2	1	1	0	4	3	3
Puerto Rico	–	–	–	2	0	0	2	3	6	0

Group 3

	CI	SK	VI	Pl	W	D	L	F	A	Pts
Cayman Islands	–	1–1	2–1	2	1	1	0	3	2	3
St Kitts	–	–	0–0	2	0	2	0	1	1	2
Br. Virgin Is	–	–	–	2	0	1	1	1	2	1

Group 4

	Gu	Su	NA	Pl	W	D	L	F	A	Pts
Guyana	–	1–1	4–0	2	1	1	0	5	1	3
Suriname	–	–	1–0	2	1	1	0	2	1	3
Neth. Antilles	–	–	–	2	0	0	2	0	5	0

Group 5

1 Martinique
2 French Guyana

FINAL TOURNAMENT

Held in Jamaica, 23rd May–2nd June 1991

Group 1

	Tr	SL	Ma	DR	Pl	W	D	L	F	A	Pts
Trinidad	–	1–2	1–0	7–0	3	2	0	1	9	2	4
St Lucia	–	–	0–0	0–0	3	1	2	0	2	1	4
Martinique	–	–	–	4–1	3	1	1	1	4	2	3
Dominican Rep	–	–	–	–	3	0	1	2	1	11	1

Group 2

	Ja	Gu	CI	Pl	W	D	L	F	A	Pts
Jamaica	–	6–0	3–2	2	2	0	0	9	2	4
Guyana	–	–	2–1	2	1	0	1	2	7	2
Cayman Islands	–	–	–	2	0	0	2	3	5	0

Semi-finals
Jamaica .... 2–0 .... St Lucia
Trinidad .... 3–1 .... Guyana

3rd Place
St Lucia .... 4–1 .... Guayana

Final
Jamaica .... 2–0 .... Trinidad
Jamaica and Trinidad qualify for the CONCACAF Gold Cup

CENTRAL AMERICA
For the Central American Championship

Qualifying round
Panama .... 2–0 0–3 .... Honduras
Nicaragua .... 2–3 0–2 .... El Salvador

FINAL TOURNAMENT
Held in San Jose, Costa Rica from 26th May–29th 1991

	CR	Ho	Gu	ES	Pl	W	D	L	F	A	Pts
Costa Rica	–	2–0	1–0	7–1	3	3	0	0	10	1	6
Honduras	–	–	0–0	2–1	3	1	1	1	2	3	3
Guatemala	–	–	–	0–0	3	0	2	1	0	1	2
El Salvador	–	–	–	–	3	0	1	2	2	9	1

Costa Rica, Honduras and Guatemala qualify for the CONCACAF Gold Cup

NORTH AMERICA
For the North American Championship

	Me	US	Ca	Pl	W	D	L	F	A	Pts
Mexico	–	2–2	3–0	2	1	1	0	5	2	3
United States	–	–	2–0	2	1	1	0	4	2	3
Canada	–	–	–	2	0	0	2	0	5	0

All three take part in the CONCACAF Gold Cup Finals

FINAL TOURNAMENT
held in Los Angeles, 28th June–7th July 1991

FIRST ROUND

Group 1

	Ho	Me	Ca	Ja	Pl	W	D	L	F	A	Pts
Honduras	–	1–1	4–2	5–0	3	2	1	0	10	3	5
Mexico	–	–	3–1	4–1	3	2	1	0	8	3	5
Canada	–	–	–	3–2	3	1	0	2	6	9	2
Jamaica	–	–	–	–	3	0	0	3	3	12	0

Group 2

	US	CR	Tr	Gu	Pl	W	D	L	F	A	Pts
United States	–	3–2	2–1	3–0	3	3	0	0	8	3	6
Costa Rica	–	–	1–2	2–0	3	1	0	2	5	5	2
Trinidad	–	–	–	0–1	3	1	0	2	3	4	2
Guatemala	–	–	–	–	3	1	0	2	1	5	2

SEMI-FINALS

United States .... 2–0 .... Mexico
Honduras .... 2–0 .... Costa Rica

3RD PLACE

Mexico .... 2–0 .... Costa Rica

FINAL

Coliseum, Los Angeles, 7–07–1991, 39 000
UNITED STATES 0
HONDURAS 0

USA won 4–3 on penalties

USA – Meola – Caligiuri, Balboa, Doyle, Clavijo – Quinn, Henderson, Murray (Kinnear), Perez – Vermes, Wynalda (Eck)
Honduras – Rivera (Cruz) – Castro, Martinez, Flores, Zapata – Anariba, Yearwood, Funez, Espinoza – Calix, Bennett (Vallejo)

CONCACAF CHAMPIONS CUP

1962 Guadalajara CD .... MEX ... 1–0 5–0 ... Comunicaciones .. GUA
1963 Racing Club .... HAI . Walk-over
1964 Not completed
1965 Not completed
1966 –
1967 Alianza .... ELS 1–2 3–0 5–3 Jong Colombia ..... AHO
1968 Toluca .... MEX . Walk-over
1969 Cruz Azul .... MEX ... 0–0 1–0 ... Comunicaciones .. GUA
1970 Cruz Azul .... MEX North winners
Deportivo SaprissaCRC Central winners
Transvaal .... SUR Caribbean winners
1971 Cruz Azul .... MEX .... 5–1 .... LD Alajuelense ..... CRC
1972 Olimpia .... HON ... 0–0 2–0 ... Robin Hood .... SUR
1973 Transvaal .... SUR . Walk-over
1974 Municipal .... GUA ... 2–1 2–1 ... Transvaal .... SUR
1975 Atletico Español ... MEX ... 3–0 2–1 ... Transvaal .... SUR
1976 Aguila .... MEX . Walk-over . Robin Hood .... SUR
1977 América .... MEX ... 1–0 0–0 ... Robin Hood .... SUR
1978 Univ. Guadalajara . MEX North winners
Comunicaciones .. GUA Central winners
Defence Force .... TRI Caribbean winners
1979 Deportivo FAS .... ELS ... 1–0 8–0 ... Young Colombia . AHO
1980 UNAM .... MEX .... 2–0 .... Univ. Honduras ... HON
1981 Transvaal .... SUR ... 1–0 1–1 ... Atletico Marte .... ELS
1982 UNAM .... MEX ... 2–2 3–0 ... Robin Hood .... SUR
1983 Atlante .... MEX ... 1–1 5–0 ... Robin Hood .... SUR
1984 Violette .... HAI Walk-over
1985 Defence Force .... TRI ... 2–0 0–1 ... Olimpia .... HON
1986 LD Alajuelense ..... CRC ... 4–1 1–1 ... Transvaal .... SUR
1987 América .... MEX ... 2–0 1–1 ... Defence Force .... TRI
1988 Olimpia .... HON ... 2–0 2–0 ... Defence Force .... TRI
1989 UNAM .... MEX ... 1–1 3–1 ... Piñar del Rio .... CUB
1990 América .... MEX ... 2–2 6–0 ... Piñar del Rio .... CUB
1991 Puebla .... MEX ... 3–1 1–1 ... Police Force .... TRI

CONCACAF CHAMPIONS CUP MEDALS TABLE

	Team	Country	G	S
1	Transvaal	SUR	3	3
2	América	MEX	3	–
	Cruz Azul	MEX	3	–
	UNAM	MEX	3	–
5	Defence Force	TRI	2	2
6	Olimpia	HON	2	2
7	Comunicaciones	GUA	1	2
8	Guadalajara CD	MEX	1	1
	LD Alajuelense	CRC	1	1
10	Eleven teams		1	–

CONCACAF YOUTH CHAMPIONSHIP

1962	Mexico	1980	Mexico
1964	El Salvador	1983	United States
1970	Mexico	1984	Mexico
1973	Mexico	1986	Canada
1974	Mexico	1988	Costa Rica
1976	Mexico	1990	Mexico
1978	Mexico	1992	Mexico

CONCACAF UNDER-17 CHAMPIONSHIP

1983	United States	1988	Chile
1985	Mexico	1990	Mexico
1987	Mexico		

FOOTBALL TOURNAMENTS OF THE CENTRAL AMERICAN AND CARIBBEAN GAMES

1926	Mexico	1962	Neth. Antilles
1930	Cuba	1966	Mexico
1935	Mexico	1970	Cuba
1938	Mexico	1974	Cuba
1946	Colombia	1978	Cuba
1950	Neth. Antilles	1982	Venezuela
1954	El Salvador	1986	Cuba
1959	Mexico	1990	Mexico

COPA INTER AMERICA

1968 *1st leg. Mexico City, 13–02–1969*
Toluca 1 (Linares)
Estudiantes LP 2 (Conigliaro, Bilardo)
2nd leg. La Plata, 19–02–1969
Estudiantes LP 1 (Veron)
Toluca 2 (Linares, Albino)
Play-off. Montevideo, 21–02–1969
Estudiantes LP 3 (Conigliaro 2, Flores E)
Toluca 0

1971 *1st leg. Mexico City, 15–07–1972*
Cruz Azul 1 (Pulido)
Nacional Montevideo 1 (Mamelli)
2nd leg. Montevideo, 7–11–1972
Nacional Montevideo 2 (Mamelli, Castro B)
Cruz Azul 1 (Bustos)

1972 *1st leg. San Pedro Sula, 17–06–1973*
Olimpia 1 (Brand)
Independiente 2 (Semenewicz, Maglioni)
2nd leg. Tegucigalpa, 20–06–1972
Olimpia 0
Independiente 2 (Maglioni, Balbuena)

1974 *1st leg. Guatemala City, 24–11–1974*
Municipal 0
Independiente 1 (Bochini)
2nd leg. Guatemala City, 26–11–1974
Municipal 1 (Mitrovich)
Independiente 0
Independiente won 4–2 on penalties

1976 *1st leg. Caracus, 26–08–1976*
Independiente 2 (Bochini, Villaverde)
Atletico Español 2 (Ramirez, Borbolla)
2nd leg. Caracus, 29–08–1976
Independiente 0
Atletico Español 0
Independiente won 4–2 on penalties

1977 *1st leg. Buenos Aires, 28–03–1978*
Boca Juniors 3 (Salinas 2, Mastrangelo)
América 0
2nd leg. Mexico City, 17–04–1978
América 1 (Kiese)
Boca Juniors 0
Play-off. Mexico City, 19–04–1978
América 2 (Acevedo, Reynoso)
Boca Juniors 1 (Pavon)

1979 *1st leg. San Salvador, 18–02–1980*
Deportivo FAS 3 (Casadei 2, Abraham)
Olimpia 3 (Solalinde, Yaluk, Isasi)
2nd leg. Asuncion, 17–03–1980
Olimpia 5 (Aquino, Michelagnoli 2, Ortiz 2)
Deportivo FAS 0

1980 *1st leg. Mexico City, 25–03–1981*
UNAM 3 (Sanchez 2, Ferreti)
Nacional Montevideo 1 (Esparrago)
2nd leg. Montevideo, 8–04–1981
Nacional Montevideo 3 (Cabrera J 2, Cabrera W)
UNAM 1 (Vargas)
Play-off. Los Angeles, 15–05–1981
UNAM 2 (Ferretti, Vargas)
Nacional Montevideo 1 (Cabrera J)

1985 *Port of Spain, 11–12–1986, 30 000*
Argentinos Juniors 1 (Valdez)
Defence Force 0

1986 *1st leg. San Jose, 21–07–1987, 16 000*
LD Alajuelense 0
River Plate 0
2nd leg. Buenos Aries, 16–08–1987, 20 000
River Plate 3 (Villazan, Funes, Enrique)
LD Alajeulense 0

1988 *1st leg. Tegucigalpa, 5–03–1989, 30 000*
Olimpia 1 (Rivera)
Nacional Montevideo 1 (Fonseca)
2nd leg. Montevideo, 30–03–1989, 30 000
Nacional Montevideo 4 (Fonseca, Ostolaza, Noe 2)
Olimpia 0

1989 *1st leg. Medellin, 25–07–1990, 26 000*
At. Nacional Medellin 2 (Fajardo, Galeano)
UNAM 0
2nd leg. Mexico City, 1–08–1990, 15 000
UNAM 1 (Negrete)
At. Nacional Medellin 4 (OG, Restrepo, Galeano, Arango)

1990 *1st leg. Asuncion, 1–10–1991, 40 000*
Olimpia 1 (Gonzalez)
América 1 (Edu)
2nd leg. Mexico City, 12–10–1991, 60 000
América 2 (Toninho 2)
Olimpia 1 (Gonzalez)

CANADA

Canada curiously have their football headquarters in James Naismith Drive, a street named after the Canadian inventor of basketball, a fact which neatly symbolises the way the indigenous North American sports have overshadowed football. Only once have Canada made a mark and that was in the 1986 World Cup for which they managed to qualify.

Football is not high on their list of priorities. Ice hockey is the national pastime, in which they have few equals. A distinctive brand of American football called, would you believe it, Canadian football is also played and Canadian teams also take part in North America's Major League for baseball.

Following the pattern of both baseball and ice hockey in which the United States and Canada take part in the same league, Canadian soccer teams took part in the great NASL experiment of the 1970s through the Vancouver Whitecaps, the Edmonton Drillers and Toronto Blizzard. Toronto appeared in three Soccer Bowl finals, the first in 1976 as Toronto Metros, which they won, and in 1983 and 1984 as Toronto Blizzard, both of which they lost.

A club called Montreal Football Club was founded in 1868 and in these early years the Association code was played in a number of universities in the country. McGill University in Montreal, however, were ultimately to determine the destiny of the game and unfortunately for football they favoured rugby. In a famous match with Harvard University in 1874, McGill won over their American counterparts to the oval ball code and the North American continent has not looked back since. The game eventually developed into the present-day American and Canadian gridiron football, and soccer as it is known there has not stood a chance.

The Association code did not die altogether and in 1886 a team representing Canada travelled to Newark to play the United States in a challenge match, a journey they repeated the following year. Though some have doubted the validity of the matches as full internationals, they do represent a landmark in world football history. If treated as full internationals they are the first such games to be played anywhere outside the British Isles.

In 1888 a Canadian team travelled to Scotland and three years later another made the same journey and played games against representative sides from England, Scotland and Wales, in what marked the first visit to Britain by a foreign team. In 1904 Galt Football Club, from Ontario, a major centre of football at the time, played the United States in the St Louis Olympic Games. Although football was only an exhibition sport, the Canadian side beat two representative sides from America to win the title and this remains the country's only honour to date.

In 1912 the Dominion of Canada Football Association was formed, the predecessor of the current Canadian Soccer Association. They introduced a cup competition for the champion team of each province and a trophy was donated by the Duke of Connaught. Until the late 1980s this remained the only national tournament for clubs in the country.

Football, though it had made encouraging progress, continued to fall behind the indigenous sports in popularity. A tour was made to Australia in 1924 and a second to New Zealand three years later but this was the only international activity until 1957 apart from three games against the United States in between the two tours.

Various provinces attempted to introduce professionalism at one time or another during this period, aided by the European immigrant communities that were swelling the population of Canada, but none were lastingly successful. Due to the enormous size of the country there was no cohesive structure to the game, and it was only played with any great enthusiasm in British Colombia, Ontario and Quebec.

A national eleven was put together to enter the 1958 World Cup and in June 1957 Canada eventually played their first game on home soil with a 5-1 victory over the United States. Though the Americans were beaten in both qualifying matches, Mexico won twice in Mexico City to end Canada's first venture into the World Cup.

The 1960s saw a reappraisal of the game in Canada. In 1961 the Eastern Canada Professional Soccer League was formed and this lasted until 1966. The following year Canadian clubs joined the fledgling North American Soccer League, and until 1984 when the NASL collapsed, football in Canada was represented by teams from Montreal, Toronto, Edmonton and Vancouver at various times, the highlight of which was Vancouver's victory in the Soccer Bowl in 1979 when the NASL was at its peak.

The demise of the NASL was a serious blow to football in the country, but the World Cup qualification in 1986 may well be seen as a knock-on effect from the 18 years of professional football, as the majority of the team had played for NASL clubs. The Canadian Soccer Associa-

CANADIAN SOCCER LEAGUE

1987	Calgary Kickers	2–1	Hamilton Steelers
1988	Vancouver 86ers	4–1	Hamilton Steelers
1989	Vancouver 86ers	3–2	Hamilton Steelers
1990	Vancouver 86ers	6–1	Hamilton Steelers
1991	Vancouver 86ers	5–3	Toronto Blizzard

tion also deserves credit for implementing a plan for the national side in the early 1970s which saw for the first time in the history of the country a regular fixture list.

Apart from the World Cup qualification, success has not been easy to come by. Even when the Olympic Games were held in Montreal in 1976 the national side could not get past the North Koreans in the first round and since 1986, despite the introduction of the Canadian Soccer League in 1987, the national side has not shown much form. In the 1991 North American Championship Canada placed a poor third behind Mexico and the United States, and could not get past the first round of the CONCACAF Gold Cup in Los Angeles later on in the year.

Population: 26 620 000
Area, sq km: 9 970 610
% in urban areas: 75%
Capital city: Ottawa 819 000

The Canadian Soccer Association
1600 James Naismith Drive
Gloucester, Ontario, ONT. K1B 5N4
Tel: (010 1) 613 7485667
Fax: (010 1) 613 7451938
Telex: 053-3350
Cable: SOCCANADA OTTAWA
Languages for correspondence: English, French

Year of formation: 1912
Affiliation to FIFA: 1912
Affiliation to CONCACAF: 1978
Registered clubs: 1600
Registered players: 285 200
Professional players: 200
Registered Coaches: 25 300
Registered Referees: 3057
National stadium: Olympic Stadium, Montreal 64 000
National colours: Shirts: Red/Shorts: Red/Socks: Red
Reserve colours: Shirts: White/Shorts: White/Socks: White
Season: May–November

THE RECORD

WORLD CUP

1930-54 ...... Did not enter
1958 .... QT 1st round
1962 .... Did not enter
1966 .... Did not enter
1970 .... QT 1st round
1974 .... QT 1st round
1978 .... QT 2nd round
1982 .... QT 2nd round
1986 .... QT Qualified – Final tournament/1st round
1990 .... QT 2nd round

OLYMPIC GAMES

1904 .... Winners (Galt FC Ontario)
1908-64 ...... Did not enter
1968 .... QT 1st round
1972 .... QT 1st round
1976 .... QT Automatic – Final tournament/1st round
1980 .... QT 1st round
1984 .... QT Qualified – Final tournament/Quarter-finalists
1988 .... QT 1st round
1992 .... QT 3rd round

CANADIAN CUP

1913	Norwood Wanderers
1914	Norwood Wanderers
1915	Winnipeg Scots
1916–18	–
1919	Grand Trunk Quebec
1920	Westinghouse Ontario
1921	Toronto Scots
1922	Hillhurst Calgary
1923	Nanaimo
1924	Weston University
1925	Toronto Ulsters
1926	Weston University
1927	Nanaimo
1928	New Westminster Royals
1929	CNR Montreal
1930	New Westminster Royals
1931	New Westminster Royals
1932	Toronto Scots
1933	Toronto Scots
1934	Verduns Montreal
1935	Aldreds Montreal
1936	New Westminster Royals
1937	Johnston Nationals
1938	North Shore Vancouver
1939	Radials Vancouver
1940–45	–
1946	Toronto Ulsters
1947	St Andrews Vancouver
1948	Carsteel Montreal
1949	North Shore Vancouver
1950	Vancouver City
1951	Ulster United Toronto
1952	Steelco Montreal
1953	New Westminster Royals
1954	Scottish Winnipeg
1955	New Westminster Royals
1956	Halecos Vancouver
1957	Ukrainia SC Montreal
1958	New Westminster Royals
1959	Alouetts Montreal
1960	New Westminster Royals
1961	Concordia Montreal
1962	Scottish Winnipeg
1963	–
1964	Columbus Vancouver
1965	Firefighters Vancouver
1966	Firefighters Vancouver
1967	Toronto
1968	Toronto Royals
1969	Columbus Vancouver
1970	Manitoba Selects
1971	Eintracht Vancouver
1972	New Westminster Blues
1973	Firefighters Vancouver
1974	Calgary Springer Kickers
1975	London Boxing Club Victoria
1976	Victoria West SC
1977	Columbus Vancouver
1978	Columbus Vancouver
1979	Victoria West SC
1980	St John Drydock
1981	Toronto Ciociario
1982	Victoria West SC
1983	Vancouver Firefighters
1984	Victoria West SC
1985	Vancouver Croatia
1986	Hamilton Steelers
1987	Lucania SC
1988	Holy Cross
1989	Scarborough Azzurri
1990	Vancouver Firefighters
1991	Norvan SC

INTERNATIONAL MATCHES PLAYED BY CANADA

Date	Opponents	Result		Venue	Compet	Scorers
28-11-1885	United States	W	1–0	Newark	Fr	Gibson
25-11-1886	United States	L	2–3	Newark	Fr	Doll 2
16-11-1904	United States	W	7–0	St Louis	OGf	Hall 3, Steep, McDonald 2, Taylor
17-11	United States	W	4–0	St Louis	OGf	Taylor 2, OG
7-06-1924	Australia	L	2–3	Brisbane	Fr	Linning, Forrest
14-06	Australia	W	1–0	Sydney	Fr	Stobbart
23-06	Australia	L	1–4	Sydney	Fr	Forrest

28–06	Australia	D	0–0	Newcastle	Fr	
12–07	Australia	W	4–1	Adelaide	Fr	Wilson 2, Linning, Stobbart
26–07	Australia	L	0–1	Sydney	Fr	
5–08	New Zealand	D	1–1	Auckland	Fr	
27–06–1925	United States	W	1–0	Montreal	Fr	McLaine
8–11	United States	L	1–6	Brooklyn	Fr	Burness
6–11–1926	United States	L	2–6	Brooklyn	Fr	Faulkner, Graham
25–06–1927	New Zealand	D	2–2	Dunedin	Fr	OG, Williams
2–07	New Zealand	W	2–1	Christchurch	Fr	Archibald, Turner
9–07	New Zealand	L	0–1	Wellington	Fr	
23–07	New Zealand	W	4–1	Auckland	Fr	Davidson, Archibald 2, Gibson
22–06–1957	United States	W	5–1	Toronto	WCq	PhilleyB, Hughes 2, Stewart, McLeodN
30–06	Mexico	L	0–3	Mexico City	WCq	
4–07	Mexico	L	0–2	Mexico City	WCq	
6–07	United States	W	3–2	St Louis	WCq	
21–06–1967	Cuba	D	1–1	Edmonton	OGq	Hansen
24–06	Cuba	L	1–2	Edmonton	OGq	Hansen
6–10–1968	Bermuda	W	4–0	Toronto	WCq	Vigh, Zanatta, Papadakis 2
17–10	United States	W	4–2	Toronto	WCq	McPate 2, Patterson, Vigh
20–10	Bermuda	D	0–0	Hamilton	WCq	
26–10	United States	L	0–1	Atlanta	WCq	
30–05–1971	Bermuda	W	3–0	Hamilton	OGq	Zanatta, Parsons, Schepers
13–06	Bermuda	D	1–1	Toronto	OGq	Schepers
20–08–1972	United States	W	3–2	St John's	WCq	Parsons, Twamley, Johnson
24–08	Mexico	L	0–1	Toronto	WCq	
29–08	United States	D	2–2	Baltimore	WCq	MacKay, Douglas
2–09	Guatemala	D	2–2	Guatemala City	Fr	Young, Schiraldi
5–09	Mexico	L	1–2	Mexico City	WCq	Robinson
1–08–1973	Poland	L	1–3	Toronto	Fr	Aubert
5–08	United States	L	0–2	Windsor	Fr	
28–09	Malta	L	0–2	Gzira	Fr	
7–10	Luxembourg	W	2–0	Luxembourg	Fr	Parsons, Schiraldi
10–11	Haiti	L	1–5	Port au Prince	Fr	Parsons
12–11	Haiti	W	1–0	Port au Prince	Fr	Bennett
12–04–1974	Bermuda	D	0–0	Hamilton	Fr	
9–10	East Germany	L	0–2	Frankfurt	Fr	
31–10	Poland	L	0–2	Warsaw	Fr	
5–01–1975	Cuba	L	0–4	Havana	Fr	
6–07	Poland	L	1–8	Montreal	Fr	Douglas
9–07	Poland	L	1–4	Toronto	Fr	Bennett
29–07	East Germany	L	0–3	Toronto	Fr	
31–07	East Germany	L	1–7	Ottawa	Fr	Rose
19–07–1976	Soviet Union	L	1–2	Montreal	OGr1	Douglas
21–07	North Korea	L	1–3	Toronto	OGr1	Douglas
24–09	United States	D	1–1	Vancouver	WCq	Bolitho
10–10	Mexico	W	1–0	Vancouver	WCq	Parsons
20–10	United States	L	0–2	Seattle	WCq	
27–10	Mexico	D	0–0	Toluca	WCq	
22–12	United States	W	3–0	Port au Prince	WCq	
11–09–1977	Trinidad	D	1–1	Port of Spain	Fr	
8–10	El Salvador	L	1–2	Monterrey	WCq	Roe
12–10	Surinam	W	2–1	Mexico City	WCq	Parsons, Bakic
16–10	Guatemala	W	2–1	Mexico City	WCq	Parsons, Lenarduzzi
20–10	Haiti	D	1–1	Monterrey	WCq	Bakic
22–10	Mexico	L	1–3	Monterrey	WCq	Parsons
1–04–1979	Bermuda	L	0–3	Hamilton	OGq	
27–05	Bermuda	L	2–5	Ottawa	OGq	Burke, Sweeney
15–09–1980	New Zealand	W	4–0	Vancouver	Fr	Mitchell 2, Stojanovic, Lenarduzzi
17–09	New Zealand	W	3–0	Edmonton	Fr	Miller 2, Lenarduzzi
18–10	Mexico	D	1–1	Toronto	WCq	Stojanovic
25–10	United States	D	0–0	Fort Lauderdale	WCq	
1–11	United States	W	2–1	Vancouver	WCq	Iarusci, Segota
9–11	Honduras	L	0–2	Tegucigalpa	Fr	
11–11	Guatemala	W	1–0	Guatemala City	Fr	Mitchell
16–11	Mexico	D	1–1	Mexico City	WCq	Gray
12–10–1981	Trinidad	W	4–2	Port of Spain	Fr	Mitchell 2, Stojanovic, Segota
2–11	El Salvador	W	1–0	Tegucigalpa	WCq	Stojanovic
6–11	Haiti	D	1–1	Tegucigalpa	WCq	Stojanovic
12–11	Honduras	L	1–2	Tegucigalpa	WCq	Bridge

15–11	Mexico	D	1–1	Tegucigalpa	WCq	Bridge
21–11	Cuba	D	2–2	Tegucigalpa	WCq	McLeod, Iarusci
8–05–1983	Bermuda	W	6–0	Burnaby	OGq	Felix 2, Sudeyko, Pakos, Connor, McNally
15–05	Bermuda	D	1–1	Hamilton	OGq	Pakos
12–06	Scotland	L	0–2	Vancouver	Fr	
16–06	Scotland	L	0–3	Edmonton	Fr	
20–06	Scotland	L	0–2	Toronto	Fr	
6–12	Mexico	L	0–5	Iraputo	Fr	
11–12	Honduras	L	1–3	San Pedro Sula	Fr	Pakos
14–12	Honduras	L	0–1	Tegucigalpa	Fr	
28–03–1984	Haiti	W	1–0	Port au Prince	Fr	Bridge
26–05	Italy	L	0–2	Toronto	Fr	
25–07	Chile	D	0–0	Edmonton	Fr	
30–07	Iraq	D	1–1	Cambridge	OGr1	Gray
1–08	Yugoslavia*	L	0–1	Annapolis	OGr1	
3–08	Cameroon	W	3–1	Cambridge	OGr1	Mitchell 2, Vrablic
6–08	Brazil*	D	1–1	Palo Alto	OGqf	Mitchel *Lost on pens*
16–10	Algeria	L	0–1	Algiers	Fr	
21–10	Tunisia	L	0–2	Tunis	Fr	
24–10	Morocco	L	2–3	Rabat	Fr	James, Miller
30–10	Cyprus	D	0–0	Nicosia	Fr	
2–11	Egypt	L	0–1	Cairo	Fr	
10–03–1985	Trinidad	W	2–1	Port of Spain	Fr	Vrablic, DeLuca
13–03	Jamaica	D	1–1	Montego Bay	Fr	Vrablic
17–03	Jamaica	D	0–0	Kingston	Fr	
21–03	Costa Rica	L	0–1	San Jose	Fr	
24–03	Costa Rica	D	0–0	San Jose	Fr	
2–04	United States	W	2–0	Vancouver	Fr	Vrablic 2
4–04	United States	D	1–1	Portland	Fr	Pakos
13–04	Haiti	W	2–0	Victoria	WCq	Vrablic, Sweeney
20–04	Guatemala	W	2–1	Victoria	WCq	Mitchell 2
5–05	Guatemala	D	1–1	Guatemala City	WCq	Mitchell
8–05	Haiti	W	2–0	Port au Prince	WCq	Mitchell, Vrablic
2–06	Ghana	W	2–1	Seoul	PC	Mitchell, Norman
9–06	Iraq	L	1–6	Kwangju	PC	Catliff
17–08	Costa Rica	D	1–1	Toronto	WCq	James
25–08	Honduras	W	1–0	Tegucigalpa	WCq	Pakos
1–09	Costa Rica	D	0–0	San Jose	WCq	
14–09	Honduras	W	2–1	St John's	WCq	Pakos, Vrablic
29–01–1986	Paraguay	D	0–0	Vancouver	Fr	
2–02	Uruguay	L	1–3	Miami	Fr	Pakos
5–02	United States	D	0–0	Miami	Fr	
27–04	Mexico	L	0–3	Mexico City	Fr	
10–05	Wales	W	2–0	Toronto	Fr	Vrablic, Gray
19–05	Wales	L	0–3	Vancouver	Fr	
24–05	England	L	0–1	Burnaby	Fr	
1–06	France	L	0–1	Leon	WCr1	
6–06	Hungary	L	0–2	Iraputo	WCr1	
9–06	Soviet Union	L	0–2	Iraputo	WCr1	
24–08	Singapore	W	1–0	Singapore	MLC	Vrablic
25–08	Malaysia	W	5–0	Singapore	MLC	Hooper, Vrablic 2, Ianiero, Cubellis
27–08	North Korea	D	0–0	Singapore	MLC	
30–08	Indonesia	W	4–0	Singapore	MLC	Vrablic, Chueden, Bunbury, Ianiero
31–08	China	L	0–1	Singapore	MLC	
4–09	North Korea	L	0–2	Singapore	MLC	
6–09	Singapore	W	1–0	Singapore	MLC	Bunbury
30–09–1987	El Salvador	L	1–2	San Salvador	Fr	Bunbury
2–10	Honduras	D	1–1	Tegucigalpa	Fr	Catliff
6–10	Mexico	L	0–4	Toluca	Fr	
18–02–1988	Bermuda	D	0–0	Hamilton	Fr	
26–03	Peru	W	3–1	Lima	Fr	Hooper, DeSantis, Catliff
30–03	Colombia	L	0–3	Armenia	Fr	
5–04	Jamaica	W	4–0	Kingston	Fr	Catliff 3
7–04	Jamaica	D	0–0	Montego Bay	Fr	
12–04	Mexico	W	1–0	Victoria	Fr	
14–04	Mexico	D	1–1	Vancouver	Fr	
19–05	Greece	L	0–1	Montreal	Fr	
21–05	Greece	L	0–3	Toronto	Fr	
25–05	Chile	W	1–0	Toronto	Fr	Bridge

28-05	Greece	D	0-0	Toronto	Fr	
2-06	Ecuador	L	1-2	Guayaquil	Fr	
17-06	Costa Rica	L	0-1	Montreal	Fr	
15-07	Poland	L	1-2	Toronto	Fr	Sweeney
1-10	Trinidad	W	2-1	Port of Spain	Fr	Catliff, Mitchell
9-10	Guatemala	L	0-1	Guatemala City	WCq	
15-10	Guatemala	W	3-2	Burnaby	WCq	Bridge, Mitchell
12-04-1989	Denmark	L	0-2	Aalborg	Fr	
8-06	Belgium	L	0-2	Ottawa	Fr	
13-05-1990	Mexico	W	2-1	Burnaby	Fr	Catliff 2
14-03-1991	Mexico	L	0-3	Los Angeles	NAC	
16-03	United States	L	0-2	Torrance	NAC	
28-06	Honduras	L	2-4	Los Angeles	CCr1	Mitchell 2
30-06	Mexico	L	1-3	Los Angeles	CCr1	Lowery
3-07	Jamaica	W	3-2	Los Angeles	CCr1	
19-05-1992	Scotland	L	1-3	Toronto	Fr	Catliff

MEXICO

Unfortunately for Mexican football, the country is situated in a footballing no man's land. To the north is the uninterested United States, to the south the small states of Central America and to the east the islands of the Caribbean. With a strong tradition in football that has seen it stage two World Cups, Mexico appears out on a limb, never maximising the potential that undoubtedly exists there.

Football came to Mexico at the end of the 19th century and in particular to Mexico City, already at that time one of the world's largest cities. Now, with its population conservatively estimated at 14 million, it *is* the largest. It was not long before a league was founded and in 1903 Mexico saw its first championship played. Based as it was in the capital it remained the domain of clubs from Mexico City until the 1940s.

The most famous of these clubs were España, Reforma and América. España were the most successful and they remain the leading championship winners with 14 titles despite the fact that none of them have come after 1945. They and Reforma flourished in an age of amateurism but like South America, Mexico was not exempt from the rise of professionalism and the organisational squabbles that went with it.

In 1927, some 24 years after the league had started, and primarily to organise a national team and gain recognition from FIFA, the Federación Mexicana de Fútbol Asociación was formed. It immediately ran into trouble over professionalism and in 1931 was replaced by another governing body which was prepared to sanction payment.

The composition of the league has changed greatly since its introduction as clubs from the other large cities have entered the fray, most notably from Guadalajara, but also from Monterrey, Puebla, Leon and the small city of Toluca. Mexico has over one million registered players, one of the largest figures in the world, so its club base is very strong. Clubs like Leon and Deportivo Guadalajara tapped into these resources and built teams capable of taking on those from the capital.

Leon's triumph in 1948 marked a watershed in Mexican club football and was followed by the complete domination of the late 1950s and 1960s by Deportivo Guadalajara. Although América remain a powerful force in the capital, Cruz Azul and UNAM, formed after the introduction of professionalism, have joined them as the major focus of attention.

In one concession to their northern neighbours, the Mexican league, after being run on a straight league basis for many years, has adopted the system so favoured of the major American sports. Four divisions of five teams, the members of which play all the teams from the other leagues, qualify two teams each for the end of season play-offs ending with a grand final. It is a system that seems to work and is popular with the fans, and compared to some of the complicated systems used in the South American countries, it has a lot to recommend it.

The formation of the federation in 1927 saw the national side take the field for the first time in the 1928 Olympic Games. Mexico's Olympic adventure lasted just one game as Spain, their first opponents, defeated them heavily. So as not to return home after just one game, the side entered the consolation tournament, but here too they were handed a first round defeat, this time at the hands of Chile.

Two years later Mexico entered the first World Cup in Montevideo. Over the years the tournament has provided Mexico with the only focus of their fixture list, given the lack of competitive games in any other competition. Their nine finals appearances equal those of England, France, Hungary and Uruguay. Taking part in all but four of them was Antonio Carbajal, one of Mexico's most celebrated players. The famous goalkeeper played in every

World Cup from 1950 to 1966, five tournaments in all, a feat never yet equalled.

Nine qualifications shows the true strength of Mexico vis-a-vis their Central American neighbours, but their performances once there show their lack of competitive edge. Not until a 3–1 victory over Czechoslovakia in 1962 did Mexico win a game. Had it not been for the advantage of being hosts in 1970 and 1986, when five games were won, the Czechoslovakia win would probably have remained their sole victory.

It is easy to decry Mexico's record in the World Cup finals, but in friendly matches against European and South American touring sides, or whilst on tour themselves, victories have been scored against all of the top nations. Prior to the late 1960s, apart from the World Cup, international games were organised on a very haphazard basis. The Mexicans threw a lot of support behind the Panamerican Confederation in the 1950s as it sought to end its isolation, but the organisation faded away in the early 1960s and Mexico has had to be content with being a part of CONCACAF.

Many believe Mexico's future lies with the South Americans in CONMEBOL and in the past there have been attempts to join, but they have always been blocked on geographical grounds. Mexican clubs would especially benefit from taking part in the Copa Libertadores, as at present they take part in the wholly unsatisfactory CONCACAF Club Championship. Club football is not strong in CONCACAF and the Mexican league sticks out like a sore thumb in the region.

The league even tempts foreigners into its ranks, most notably from Argentina and Brazil, but it is still prone to lose its best players, the best example being Hugo Sanchez, the star of the Real Madrid side in the 1980s. Its relative isolation does keep the flow at a minimum, however.

Mexico has twice been at the centre of world football by staging the World Cup in 1970 and 1986, both of which proved to be excellent tournaments. Indeed, the 1970 edition is often regarded as the finest ever staged. The country as a result has some of the finest stadiums in the world, none more so than the magnificent Azteca in Mexico City. With its 110 000 capacity fitted tightly around the pitch as opposed to the more usual elongated stadia such as the Olympiastadion in Munich or Wembley, the scenes of the 1966 and 1974 World Cup Finals, for spectators at least there is probably no better place to watch football.

The quarter-final placings in 1970 and 1986 represent Mexico's best achievements in international football to date. The 1986 side was especially good. Led by Sanchez, they almost reached the semi-finals but lost out to the uninspiring West Germans on penalties after extra-time. Unfortunately for Mexico they were not allowed to enter for the 1990 tournament, as they were suspended by FIFA for fielding an over-age player in a youth tournament.

Population: 81 883 000
Area, sq km: 1 958 201
% in urban areas: 72%
Capital city: Mexico City

Federación Mexicana de Fútbol Asociación A.C.
Abraham Gonzalez #74
CP 06600, Col. Juarez
Mexico 6 D.F
Mexico
Tel: (010 52) 5 5662155
Fax: (010 52) 5 5667580
Telex: 1771678 MSUTME
Cable: MEXFUTBOL MEXICO
Languages for correspondence: Spanish, English & French

Year of formation: 1927
Affiliation to FIFA: 1929
Affiliation to CONCACAF: 1961
Registered clubs: 117
Registered players: 1 402 000
Professional Players: 2800
Registered referees: 25 170
National stadium: Azteca, Mexico City 110 000
National colours: Shirts: Green/Shorts: White/Socks: Red
Reserve colours: Shirts: Red/Shorts: Blue/Socks: Blue
Season: September–June

THE RECORD

WORLD CUP

1930 .... QT Automatic – Final tournament/1st round
1934 .... QT 3rd round
1938 .... Did not enter
1950 .... QT 1st/3 in group 9 – Final tournament/1st round
1954 .... QT 1st/3 in group 11 – Final tournament/1st round
1958 .... QT Qualified – Final tournament/1st round
1962 .... QT Qualified – Final tournament/1st round
1966 .... QT Qualified – Final tournament/1st round
1970 .... QT Automatic – Final tournament/Quarter-finalists
1974 .... QT 2nd round
1978 .... QT Qualified – Final tournament/1st round
1982 .... QT 2nd round
1986 .... QT Automatic – Final tournament/Quarter-finalists
1990 .... Did not enter

OLYMPIC GAMES

1908–24 ..... Did not enter
1928 .... 1st round
1936 .... Did not enter
1948 .... 1st round
1952 .... Did not enter
1956 .... Did not enter
1960 .... QT 2nd round
1964 .... QT Qualified – Final tournament/1st round
1968 .... QT Automatic – Final tournament/Semi-finalists/4th place
1972 .... QT Qualified – Final tournament/2nd round
1976 .... QT Qualified – Final tournament/1st round
1980 .... QT 1st round
1984 .... QT 2nd round
1988 .... QT Qualified – withdrew
1992 .... QT Qualified

CENTRAL AMERICA COMPETITIONS

CONCACAF Championship: Winners – 1965, 1971, 1977
CONCACAF Club Championship: Winners – Guadalajara CD 1962, Toluca 1968, Cruz Azul 1969 1970 1971, Atlético Español 1975, América 1977 1987 1990, Universidad Guadalajara 1978, UNAM 1980 1982 1989, Atlante 1983, Puebla 1991
Runners-up – Guadalajara CD 1963

Mexican League Champions

1903	Orizaba
1904	Mexico Country Club
1905	Pachuca
1906	Reforma
1907	Reforma
1908	British Club
1909	Reforma
1910	Reforma
1911	Reforma
1912	Reforma
1913	Mexico Country Club
1914	España
1915	España
1916	España
1917	España
1918	Pachuca
1919	España
1920	España
1921	España
1922	España
1923	Asturias
1924	América
1925	América
1926	América
1927	América
1928	América
1929	Marte
1930	–
1931	España
1932	Atlante
1933	Necaxa
1934	España
1935	Necaxa
1936	España
1937	Necaxa
1938	Necaxa
1939	Asturias
1940	España
1941	Atlante
1942	España
1943	Marte
1944	Asturias
1945	España
1946	Veracruz
1947	Atlante
1948	León
1949	León
1950	Veracruz
1951	Atlas & Guadalajara CD
1952	León
1953	Tampico
1954	Marte
1955	Zacatepec
1956	León
1957	Guadalajara CD
1958	Zacatepec
1959	Guadalajara CD
1960	Guadalajara CD
1961	Guadalajara CD
1962	Guadalajara CD
1963	Oro Jalisco
1964	Guadalajara CD
1965	Guadalajara CD
1966	América
1967	Toluca
1968	Toluca
1969	Guadalajara CD
1970	Cruz Azul
1971	América
1972	Cruz Azul
1973	Cruz Azul
1974	Cruz Azul
1975	Toluca
1976	América
1977	UNAM
1978	Universidad Nuevo Leon
1979	Cruz Azul
1980	Cruz Azul
1981	UNAM
1982	Universidad Neuvo Leon
1983	Puebla
1984	América
1985	América
1986	Monterrey
1987	Guadalajara CD
1988	América
1989	América
1990	Puebla
1991	UNAM
1992	León

CHAMPIONSHIP WINS

España	14
América	12
Guadalajara CD	10
Cruz Azul	6
Reforma	6
León	5
Necaxa	4
Asturias	3
Atlante	3
Marte	3
Toluca	3
UNAM	3
Mexico Country Club	2
Puebla	2
Pachuca	2
Univ. Nuevo León	2
Veracruz	2
Zacatepec	2
Atlas Guadalajara	1
British Club	1
Monterrey	1
Orizaba	1
Oro Jalisco	1
Tampico	1

Club Directory

MEXICO CITY (Population – 14 100 000)
Club de Fútbol de América
Stadium: Azteca 110 000
Founded: 1906
Colours: Yellow/Blue

Club de Fútbol Atlante
Stadium: Azulgrana 52 000
Founded: 1916
Colours: Red and blue stripes/Blue

Club Deportivo Social y Cultural Cruz Azul
Stadium: Azteca 110 000
Founded: 1932
Colours: White/White

Necaxa
Stadium: Azteca 110 000
Founded: 1925
Colours: Red and white stripes/White

Universidad Nacional Autónoma de Mexico (UNAM)
Stadium: Olimpico 65 000
Founded: 1940
Colours: Blue/Blue

GUADALAJARA (Population – 2 325 000)
Club Deportivo Guadalajara
Stadium: Jalisco 70 000
Founded: 1908
Colours: Red and white stripes/Blue

Universidad Autonoma Guadalajara (UAG)
Stadium: 3 de Marzo 30 000

Atlas Guadalajara
Stadium: Jalisco 70 000

Universidad de Guadalajara
Stadium: Jalisco 70 000

MONTERREY (Population – 2 015 000)
Monterrey
Stadium: Estadio Tecnologico 33 000

Universidad Nuevo León
Stadium: Universitario 43 000

PUEBLA (Population – 1 055 000)
Puebla Unido
Stadium: Cuauhtemoc 40 000
Founded: 1944
Colours: White with a sky blue sash/White

LEON (Population – 593 000)
Club Social y Deportivo León
Stadium: Nou Camp 39 000
Founded: 1944
Colours: Green/White

TOLUCA (Population – 199000)
Club Deportivo Toluca
Stadium: Luis Dosal 30000
Founded: 1925
Colours: Red and white stripes/White

INTERNATIONAL MATCHES PLAYED BY MEXICO

Date	Opponents	Result	Venue	Compet
30–05–1928	Spain	L 1–7	Amsterdam	OGr1
5–06	Chile	L 1–3	Arnhem	OGct
13–07–1930	France	L 1–4	Montevideo	WCr1
16–07	Chile	L 0–3	Montevideo	WCr1
19–07	Argentina	L 3–6	Montevideo	WCr1
4–03–1934	Cuba	W 3–2	Mexico City	WCq
11–03	Cuba	W 5–0	Mexico City	WCq
18–03	Cuba	W 4–1	Mexico City	WCq
24–05	United States	L 2–4	Rome	WCq
27–03–1935	El Salvador	W 8–2	San Salvador	CG
28–03	Guatemala	W 5–1	San Salvador	CG
30–03	Cuba	W 6–1	San Salvador	CG
1–04	Honduras	W 8–2	San Salvador	CG
2–04	Costa Rica	W 2–0	San Salvador	CG
10–02–1938	Colombia	W 3–1	Panama City	CG
14–02	Venezuela	W 1–0	Panama	CG
18–02	El Salvador	W 6–0	Panama	CG
20–02	Panama	D 2–2	Panama	CG
22–02	Costa Rica	W 2–1	Panama	CG
13–07–1947	United States	W 5–0	Havana	NAC
17–07	Cuba	W 3–1	Havana	NAC
2–08–1948	Korea	L 3–5	London	OGr1
4–09–1949	United States	W 6–0	Mexico City	NAC/WCq
11–09	Cuba	W 2–0	Mexico City	NAC/WCq
18–09	United States	W 6–2	Mexico City	NAC/WCq
25–09	Cuba	W 3–0	Mexico City	NAC/WCq
27–02–1950	Honduras	W 2–1	Guatemala City	Fr
4–03	Guatemala	D 0–0	Guatemala City	Fr
7–03	Guatemala	D 3–3	Guatemala City	Fr
8–03	Guatemala	D 0–0	Guatemala City	Fr
10–03	Guatemala	L 1–2	Guatemala City	Fr
24–06	Brazil	L 0–4	Rio de Janeiro	WCr1
29–06	Yugoslavia	L 1–4	Porto Alegre	WCr1
2–07	Switzerland	L 1–2	Porto Alegre	WCr1
23–03–1952	Uruguay	L 1–3	Santiago	PAC
26–03	Chile	L 0–4	Santiago	PAC
6–04	Brazil	L 0–2	Santiago	PAC
10–04	Panama	W 4–2	Santiago	PAC
20–04	Peru	L 0–3	Santiago	PAC
19–07–1953	Haiti	W 8–0	Mexico City	WCq
27–12	Haiti	W 4–0	Port au Prince	WCq
10–01–1954	United States	W 4–0	Mexico City	WCq
14–01	United States	W 3–1	Mexico City	WCq
9–03	Cuba	W 4–0	Mexico City	Fr
11–03	Panama	W 4–0	Mexico City	Fr
12–03	El Salvador	L 2–3	Mexico City	Fr
16–06	Brazil	L 0–5	Geneva	WCr1
19–06	France	L 2–3	Geneva	WCr1
26–02–1956	Costa Rica	D 1–1	Mexico City	PAC
4–03	Peru	L 0–2	Mexico City	PAC
8–03	Brazil	L 1–2	Mexico City	PAC
13–03	Argentina	D 0–0	Mexico City	PAC
18–03	Chile	W 2–1	Mexico City	PAC
7–04–1957	United States	W 6–0	Mexico City	WCq
28–04	United States	W 7–2	Long Beach	WCq
30–06	Canada	W 3–0	Mexico City	WCq
4–07	Canada	W 2–0	Mexico City	WCq
20–10	Costa Rica	W 2–0	Mexico City	WCq
27–10	Costa Rica	D 1–1	San Jose	WCq
8–06–1958	Sweden	L 0–3	Stockholm	WCr1
11–06	Wales	D 1–1	Stockholm	WCr1
15–06	Hungary	L 0–4	Sandviken	WCr1
1–03–1959	Costa Rica	W 3–1	Mexico City	Fr
8–03	Costa Rica *Abandoned*	W 2–1	San Jose	Fr
24–05	England	W 2–1	Mexico City	Fr
6–03–1960	Brazil	D 2–2	San Jose	PAC
10–03	Argentina	L 2–3	San Jose	PAC
12–03	Costa Rica	D 1–1	San Jose	PAC
15–03	Brazil	L 1–2	San Jose	PAC
17–03	Argentina	L 0–2	San Jose	PAC
20–03	Costa Rica	W 3–0	San Jose	PAC
26–06	Holland	W 3–1	Mexico City	Fr
6–11	United States	D 3–3	Los Angeles	WCq
13–11	United States	W 3–0	Mexico City	WCq
22–03–1961	Costa Rica	L 0–1	San Jose	WCq
5–04	Neth Antilles	W 7–0	Mexico City	WCq
12–04	Costa Rica	W 4–1	Mexico City	WCq
19–04	Holland	W 2–1	Amsterdam	Fr
29–04	Czechoslovakia	L 1–2	Ostrava	Fr
10–05	England	L 0–8	London	Fr
16–05	Norway	D 1–1	Bergen	Fr
21–05	Neth Antilles	D 0–0	Willemstad	WCq
29–10	Paraguay	W 1–0	Mexico City	WCq
5–11	Paraguay	D 0–0	Asuncion	WCq
–03–1962	Haiti	D 1–1	Port au Prince	Fr
28–03	Argentina	L 0–1	Buenos Aires	Fr
1–04	Colombia	W 1–0	Bogota	Fr
4–04	Colombia	D 2–2	Cali	Fr
25–04	Colombia	W 1–0	Mexico City	Fr
22–05	Wales	W 2–1	Mexico City	Fr
30–05	Brazil	L 0–2	Vina del Mar	WCr1
3–06	Spain	L 0–1	Vina del Mar	WCr1
7–06	Czechoslovakia	W 3–1	Vina del Mar	WCr1
24–03–1963	Neth Antilles	L 1–2	San Salvador	CCr1
28–03	Jamaica	W 8–0	San Salvador	CCr1
30–03	Costa Rica	D 0–0	San Salvador	CCr1
28–02–1965	Honduras	W 1–0	San Pedro	WCq
4–03	Honduras	W 3–0	Mexico City	WCq
7–03	United States	D 2–2	Los Angeles	WCq
12–03	United States	W 2–0	Mexico City	WCq
28–03	El Salvador	W 2–0	Guatemala City	CC
1–04	Neth Antilles	W 5–0	Guatemala City	CC
4–04	Haiti	W 3–0	Guatemala City	CC
7–04	Costa Rica	D 1–1	Guatemala City	CC
11–04	Guatemala	W 2–1	Guatemala City	CC
25–04	Costa Rica	D 0–0	San Jose	WCq
3–05	Jamaica	W 3–2	Kingston	WCq
7–05	Jamaica	W 8–0	Mexico City	WCq
16–05	Costa Rica	W 1–0	Mexico City	WCq
24–04–1966	Paraguay	W 4–0	Mexico City	Fr
11–05	Chile	W 1–0	Mexico City	Fr
29–05	Chile	W 1–0	Santiago	Fr
19–06	Switzerland	D 1–1	Lausanne	Fr
22–06	Nth. Ireland	L 1–4	Belfast	Fr
29–06	Italy	L 0–5	Florence	Fr
13–07	France	D 1–1	London	WCr1
16–07	England	L 0–2	London	WCr1
19–07	Uruguay	D 0–0	London	WCr1
5–01–1967	Switzerland	W 3–0	Mexico City	Fr
6–03	Nicaragua	W 4–0	Tegucigalpa	CC
10–03	Guatemala	L 0–1	Tegucigalpa	CC
12–03	Trinidad	W 4–0	Tegucigalpa	CC
14–03	Haiti	W 1–0	Tegucigalpa	CC
19–03	Honduras	W 1–0	Tegucigalpa	CC
28–05	Soviet Union	L 0–2	Leningrad	Fr
22–08	Argentina	W 2–1	Mexico City	Fr
3–03–1968	Soviet Union	D 0–0	Mexico City	Fr
7–03	Soviet Union	D 1–1	Leon	Fr
10–03	Soviet Union	D 0–0	Mexico City	Fr
21–05	Uruguay	D 3–3	Mexico City	Fr
28–05	Uruguay	D 2–2	Mexico City	Fr

7–07	Brazil	L	0–2	Mexico City	Fr
10–07	Brazil	W	2–1	Mexico City	Fr
28–08	Chile	W	3–1	Mexico City	Fr
16–10	Colombia	W	1–0	Bogota	Fr
20–10	Peru	D	3–3	Lima	Fr
23–10	Chile	L	1–3	Santiago	Fr
26–10	Uruguay	W	2–0	Montevideo	Fr
31–10	Brazil	W	2–1	Rio de Janeiro	Fr
3–11	Brazil	L	1–2	Belo Horizonte	Fr
22–12	West Germany	D	0–0	Mexico City	Fr
1–01–1969	Italy	L	2–3	Mexico City	Fr
5–01	Italy	D	1–1	Mexico City	Fr
22–01	Denmark	W	3–0	Mexico City	Fr
4–02	Colombia	W	1–0	Leon	Fr
6–04	Portugal	D	0–0	Lisbon	Fr
10–04	Luxembourg	L	1–2	Luxembourg	Fr
16–04	Belgium	L	0–2	Brussels	Fr
23–04	Spain	D	0–0	Seville	Fr
1–05	Sweden	L	0–1	Malmo	Fr
6–05	Denmark	L	1–3	Copenhagen	Fr
8–05	Norway	W	2–0	Oslo	Fr
20–05	Peru	L	0–1	Mexico City	Fr
22–05	Peru	W	3–0	Leon	Fr
1–06	England	D	0–0	Mexico City	Fr
2–11	Bermuda	L	1–2	Hamilton	Fr
5–11	Belgium	W	1–0	Mexico City	Fr
11–11	Norway	W	4–0	Mexico City	Fr
28–11	Jamaica	W	3–0	San Jose	CC
2–12	Costa Rica	L	0–2	San Jose	CC
4–12	Guatemala	L	0–1	San Jose	CC
6–12	Neth Antilles	D	2–2	San Jose	CC
8–12	Trinidad	D	0–0	San Jose	CC
15–02–1970	Bulgaria	D	1–1	Mexico City	Fr
18–02	Bulgaria	W	2–0	Leon	Fr
22–02	Sweden	D	0–0	Mexico City	Fr
26–02	Soviet Union	D	0–0	Mexico City	Fr
1–03	Sweden	L	0–1	Puebla	Fr
5–03	Peru	W	1–0	Lima	Fr
8–03	Peru	L	0–1	Lima	Fr
15–03	Peru	W	3–1	Mexico City	Fr
18–03	Peru	D	3–3	Leon	Fr
29–04	Ecuador	W	4–2	Leon	Fr
3–05	Ecuador	W	3–2	Mexico City	Fr
31–05	Soviet Union	D	0–0	Mexico City	WCr1
7–06	El Salvador	W	4–0	Mexico City	WCr1
11–06	Belgium	W	1–0	Mexico City	WCr1
14–06	Italy	L	1–4	Toluca	WCqf
30–09	Brazil	L	1–2	Rio de Janeiro	Fr
2–12	Australia	W	3–0	Mexico City	Fr
17–02–1971	Soviet Union	D	0–0	Guadalajara	Fr
19–02	Soviet Union	D	0–0	Mexico City	Fr
21–04	Haiti	L	1–3	Port au Prince	Fr
7–07	Greece	D	1–1	Mexico City	Fr
16–08	East Germany	L	0–1	Guadalajara	Fr
8–09	West Germany	L	0–5	Hannover	Fr
12–09	Morocco	L	1–2	Casablanca	Fr
18–09	East Germany	D	1–1	Leipzig	Fr
22–09	Yugoslavia	L	0–4	Sarajevo	Fr
25–09	Italy	L	0–2	Genoa	Fr
3–10	Greece	L	0–1	Salonica	Fr
16–10	Bermuda	W	4–0	Mexico City	Fr
21–11	Haiti	D	0–0	Port of Spain	CC
26–11	Trinidad	W	2–0	Port of Spain	CC
28–11	Cuba	W	1–0	Port of Spain	CC
2–12	Costa Rica	W	1–0	Port of Spain	CC
4–12	Honduras	W	2–1	Port of Spain	CC
27–01–1972	Chile	W	2–0	Mexico City	Fr
5–04	Peru	W	2–1	Mexico City	Fr
6–08	Costa Rica	L	0–1	San Jose	Fr
9–08	Peru	L	2–3	Lima	Fr
16–08	Chile	W	2–0	Santiago	Fr
24–08	Canada	W	1–0	Toronto	WCq
3–09	United States	W	3–1	Mexico City	WCq
5–09	Canada	W	2–1	Mexico City	WCq
10–09	United States	W	2–1	Los Angeles	WCq
12–10	Costa Rica	W	3–0	Mexico City	Fr
6–02–1973	Argentina	W	2–0	Mexico City	Fr
21–04	Chile	D	1–1	Mexico City	Fr
5–08	Poland	L	0–1	Los Angeles	Fr
8–08	Poland	L	1–2	Monterrey	Fr
20–09	Chile	L	1–2	Mexico City	Fr
16–10	United States	W	2–0	Puebla	Fr
30–11	Guatemala	D	0–0	Port au Prince	WCq
3–12	Honduras	D	1–1	Port au Prince	WCq
8–12	Neth Antilles	W	8–0	Port au Prince	WCq
14–12	Trinidad	L	0–4	Port au Prince	WCq
18–12	Haiti	W	1–0	Port au Prince	WCq
12–03–1974	Bermuda	L	0–3	Mexico City	Fr
31–03	Brazil	D	1–1	Rio de Janeiro	Fr
5–09	United States	W	3–1	Monterrey	Fr
8–09	United States	W	1–0	Dallas	Fr
9–04–1975	Jamaica	L	1–3	Kingston	Fr
17–08	Costa Rica	W	7–0	Mexico City	Fr
24–08	United States	W	2–0	Mexico City	Fr
31–08	Argentina	D	1–1	Mexico City	Fr
20–10	Israel	L	0–1	Tel Aviv	Fr
11–02–1976	El Salvador	D	0–0	San Salvador	Fr
4–06	Brazil	L	0–3	Guadalajara	Fr
3–10	United States	D	0–0	Los Angeles	WCq
10–10	Canada	L	0–1	Vancouver	WCq
15–10	United States	W	3–0	Puebla	WCq
27–10	Canada	D	0–0	Toluca	WCq
1–02–1977	Yugoslavia	W	5–1	Leon	Fr
8–02	Yugoslavia	L	0–1	Monterrey	Fr
22–02	Hungary	D	1–1	Mexico City	Fr
17–05	Peru	D	1–1	Mexico City	Fr
24–05	Peru	W	2–1	Monterrey	Fr
14–06	West Germany	D	2–2	Mexico City	Fr
27–09	United States	W	3–0	Monterrey	Fr
9–10	Haiti	W	4–1	Mexico City	WCq
12–10	El Salvador	W	3–1	Mexico City	WCq
15–10	Surinam	W	8–1	Monterrey	WCq
19–10	Guatemala	W	2–1	Mexico City	WCq
22–10	Canada	W	3–1	Monterrey	WCq
15–02–1978	El Salvador	W	5–1	San Salvador	Fr
5–04	Bulgaria	W	3–0	Mexico City	Fr
11–04	Peru	L	0–1	Los Angeles	Fr
26–04	Spain	L	0–2	Granada	Fr
3–05	Finland	W	1–0	Helsinki	Fr
2–06	Tunisia	L	1–3	Rosario	WCr1
6–06	West Germany	L	0–6	Cordoba	WCr1
10–06	Poland	L	1–3	Rosario	WCr1
17–10	Honduras	L	1–4	Guadalajara	Fr
28–10	Costa Rica	L	1–3	San Jose	Fr
1–04–1979	Guatemala	D	0–0	Guatemala City	Fr
1–05	El Salvador	W	1–0	San Salvador	Fr
31–05	Costa Rica	D	0–0	San Jose	Fr
1–11	Peru	W	1–0	Monterrey	Fr
21–11	Finland	D	1–1	Mexico City	Fr
4–12	El Salvador	W	2–0	San Salvador	Fr
23–01–1980	Czechoslovakia	W	1–0	Leon	Fr
8–06	Brazil	L	0–2	Rio de Janeiro	Fr
20–08	New Zealand	L	0–4	Auckland	Fr
24–08	Australia	D	2–2	Sydney	Fr
26–08	Australia	D	1–1	Melbourne	Fr
30–08	Fiji	W	2–0	Suva	Fr
18–10	Canada	D	1–1	Toronto	WCq
9–11	United States	W	5–1	Mexico City	WCq

6–11	Canada	D	1–1	Mexico City	WCq
23–11	United States	L	1–2	Lauderdale	WCq
20–01–1981	Bulgaria	D	1–1	Mexico City	Fr
10–02	South Korea	W	4–0	Mexico City	Fr
24–06	Spain	L	1–3	Mexico City	Fr
1–11	Cuba	W	4–0	Tegucigalpa	WCq
6–11	El Salvador	L	0–1	Tegucigalpa	WCq
11–11	Haiti	D	1–1	Tegucigalpa	WCq
15–11	Canada	D	1–1	Tegucigalpa	WCq
22–11	Honduras	D	0–0	Tegucigalpa	WCq
22–11–1983	Sweden	W	2–0	Morelia	Fr
6–12	Canada	W	5–0	Iraputo	Fr
4–02–1984	Italy	L	0–5	Rome	Fr
22–07	Guatemala	W	3–1	Guatemala City	Fr
8–08	Rep. Ireland	D	0–0	Dublin	Fr
11–08	East Germany	D	1–1	Berlin	Fr
16–08	Finland	W	3–0	Helsinki	Fr
19–08	Soviet Union	L	0–3	Leningrad	Fr
22–08	Sweden	D	1–1	Malmo	Fr
25–08	Hungary	W	2–0	Budapest	Fr
18–09	Argentina	D	1–1	Monterrey	Fr
9–10	Colombia	W	1–0	Los Angeles	Fr
11–10	El Salvador	W	1–0	Los Angeles	Fr
17–10	United States	W	2–1	Mexico City	Fr
25–10	Argentina	D	1–1	Buenos Aires	Fr
28–10	Chile	L	0–1	Santiago	Fr
31–10	Uruguay	D	1–1	Montevideo	Fr
11–11	Trinidad	W	2–0	Port of Spain	Fr
4–12	Ecuador	W	3–2	Los Angeles	Fr
5–02–1985	Poland	W	5–0	Queretaro	Fr
6–02	Switzerland	L	1–2	Queretaro	Fr
26–02	Finland	W	2–1	Acapulco	Fr
2–06	Italy	D	1–1	Mexico City	Fr
9–06	England	W	1–0	Mexico City	Fr
15–06	West Germany	W	2–0	Mexico City	Fr
27–08	Bulgaria	D	1–1	Los Angeles	Fr
20–09	Peru	D	0–0	Los Angeles	Fr
22–09	Peru	W	1–0	San Jose	Fr
14–11	Argentina	D	1–1	Los Angeles	Fr
17–11	Argentina	D	1–1	Puebla	Fr
3–12	South Korea	W	2–1	Los Angeles	Fr
7–12	Algeria	W	2–0	Mexico City	Fr
10–12	South Korea	W	2–1	Guadalajara	Fr
14–12	Hungary	W	2–0	Mexico City	Fr
15–02–1986	East Germany	L	1–2	San Jose	Fr
19–02	Soviet Union	W	1–0	Mexico City	Fr
13–04	Uruguay	W	1–0	Los Angeles	Fr
27–04	Canada	W	3–0	Mexico City	Fr
17–05	England	L	0–3	Los Angeles	Fr
3–06	Belgium	W	2–1	Mexico City	WCr1
7–06	Paraguay	D	1–1	Mexico City	WCr1
11–06	Iraq	W	1–0	Mexico City	WCr1
15–06	Bulgaria	W	2–0	Mexico City	WCr2
21–06	West Germany	D	0–0 (1–4p)	Monterrey	WCqf
13–01–1987	El Salvador	W	3–1	Los Angeles	Fr
6–10	Canada	W	4–0	Toluca	Fr
12–04–1988	Canada	L	0–1	Victoria	Fr
14–04	Canada	D	1–1	Vancouver	Fr
14–02–1989	Poland	W	3–1	Puebla	Fr
21–02	Guatemala	W	2–1	Los Angeles	Fr
23–02	El Salvador	W	2–0	Los Angeles	Fr
8–08	South Korea	W	4–2	Los Angeles	Fr
17–01–1990	Argentina	W	2–0	Los Angeles	Fr
20–03	Uruguay	W	2–1	Los Angeles	Fr
17–04	Colombia	W	2–0	Los Angeles	Fr
13–05	Canada	L	1–2	Burnaby	Fr
2–06	Belgium	L	0–3	Brussels	Fr
13–12	Brazil	D	0–0	Los Angeles	Fr
29–01–1991	Colombia	D	0–0	Leon	Fr
12–03	United States	D	2–2	Los Angeles	NAC
13–03	Argentina	D	0–0	Buenos Aires	Fr
14–03	Canada	W	3–0	Los Angeles	NAC
9–04	Chile	W	1–0	Veracruz	Fr
17–04	Costa Rica	D	0–0	San Jose	Fr
7–05	Uruguay	L	0–2	Los Angeles	Fr
28–06	Jamaica	W	4–1	Los Angeles	CCr1
30–06	Canada	W	3–1	Los Angeles	CCr1
3–07	Honduras	D	1–1	Los Angeles	CCr1
5–07	United States	L	0–2	Los Angeles	CCsf
7–07	Costa Rica	W	2–0	Los Angeles	CC3p
20–11	Uruguay	D	1–1	Veracruz	Fr
27–11	Costa Rica	D	1–1		Fr
4–12	Hungary	W	3–0	Leon	Fr
8–03–1992	CIS	D	4–0	Mexico City	Fr
11–03	CIS	D	1–1	Tampico	Fr

UNITED STATES OF AMERICA

If it had not been for two games played in 1874 between Harvard University and McGill University of Montreal, football today might be the national sport in the United States. In the second of these two games, Harvard were persuaded to use an oval ball instead of the usual round ball, and immediately took to it. From that they developed the handling code, and what Harvard do, others usually follow.

Had the United States stuck with the Association rules, who knows, they might well have become the strongest football nation in the world. With all of the resources that are presently channelled into baseball and American football, it would have been surprising if they had not. Instead they have the barest rump of the game, very popular at school level we are always reminded, but with no infrastructure for developing the talent once it has left school.

The first club in America was Oneida Football Club which was formed in 1862 in Boston by Gerritt Smith Miller, and it is interesting to note that its foundation predates any club outside of England. No club in Scotland had even been formed by that time. All of its members came from the substantial English community located in Boston, but unfortunately the club no longer exists.

Prior to the Harvard–McGill games, the round ball had found favour with most of the major universities on the East coast of the country. The Princeton rules, based on the 1863 Football Association rules, were drawn up in 1873 by Yale, Colombia, Rutgers and Princeton Universities, but they were superseded in 1876 when Harvard, Yale and Colombia met to form the Intercollegiate Football Association and the rugby code was adopted as the basis for the rules of the game.

Once no longer played in the universities, football became the pastime of the numerous ethnic communities and often was centred around the factories which sponsored the teams and provided the grounds on which they played. Despite the formation in 1884 of the American Football Association by a group of Britons, the organisation of the game on a country-wide basis was haphazard. Numerous regional associations appeared in what is a vast country, some adhering to amateurism, others allowing semi-professionalism.

Particular hotspots of the game at this time included St Louis, New York, Philadelphia, New Jersey and Fall River. Four international games were organised in these early years, two matches against Canada in Newark in 1885 and 1886 and the two exhibition matches at the St Louis Olympic Games in 1904, also against Canada.

The validity of these matches as full internationals is open to some debate, but they do represent the first games played outside the British Isles which could be considered as such. The 1904 sides were actually two separate teams from St Louis called the St Rose Kickers and the Christian Brothers College, but who went under the banner of the United States.

The American Football Association, which had affiliated to the association in London, was eventually superseded in 1913 by the rival American Amateur Football Association under the banner of the United States Football Association, later known as the United States Soccer Federation, and it was admitted to FIFA the same year. Its first task involved the organising of the first nationwide competition for all of the clubs that were now under its control.

The National Open Challenge Cup introduced the following year is the yardstick by which football in America can be measured until the formation of the North American Soccer League in the late 1960s. It was joined in 1924 by the National Amateur Cup and both these competitions still run today. Part of football's problem in America is its association with ethnic communities as a look at the winners of both competitions show.

From the New York Greek Americans to the Philadelphia Ukrainians, and the Los Angeles Armenians to the German–Hungarian Soccer Club from Brooklyn, one is left in little doubt as to the composition of the teams. This has tended to alienate Americans even further from what they already consider a foreign sport.

Efforts were made in the 1920s to enter the national team in international competitions. Teams took part in the 1924 and 1928 Olympic Games, and in the first World Cup in 1930 the United States beat both Belgium and Paraguay in the first round in Montevideo to qualify for the semi-finals. Once there they faced Argentina, who had bundled them out of the Olympics two years previously with an 11–2 thrashing. It was not so bad this time but they still lost 6–1.

Five of the team were former Scottish professionals so perhaps reaching the semi-final should not be seen as too surprising. Back in the United States the achievements of the team were barely even noted as the baseball season was in full swing.

Four years later the team was represented again in the final tournament, but had the misfortune to meet the hosts Italy in the first round and lost 1–0. There then followed a 13-year hiatus. As members of the North American Confederation, two series with Mexico and Cuba were played in the late 1940s for the North American Championship, neither of which proved successful. They did however prepare the American side for one of the biggest upsets the world has ever seen in the 1950 World Cup.

Unlike the 1930 side, the team representing the United States in Brazil was made up almost entirely of American born and bred players. In the first match, despite leading 1–0 with only 10 minutes remaining, the team contrived to lose 3–1 against Spain, but their second match against England in Belo Horizonte is indelibly etched into history. One of their few 'foreigners', Larry Gaetjens from Haiti, scored a goal that saw the mighty English humbled. So surprising was the result to those back in England that one newspaper thought there had been a mistake in the telegram and printed the result as 10–1!

Defeat against Chile in the final match meant that the team returned home after the first round, but unfortunately there were no crowds to welcome them back. Once again the World Cup had passed the country by. Not until the late 1960s did the population of America stand up and take note of what was by then far and away the most popular sport in the world.

Talk of football in the United States and the two things that first come to mind are the 1950 defeat of England and the North American Soccer League, or NASL for short. For nearly 20 years, the United States conducted an experiment in winning over the American public to football, and the only conclusion that could be reached at the end was that Americans simply did not like the game and probably never would.

Aside from the two national cup competitions, there were numerous local leagues spread around the country, one even calling itself the American Soccer League, or ASL for short, which had full-time professionalism. In 1960 the International Soccer League was set up consisting of 11 foreign teams and the New York Americans and was won in the first year by Bangu from Brazil in the final against Kilmarnock from Scotland.

Unfortunately not many teams took it seriously and in 1965 the league folded. Two years later, however, business began looking into the possibility of the growth of football. If successful in winning over Americans they stood to make a lot of money. The United States Soccer Federation, realising the growing interest, sanctioned the United Soccer Association as the controlling body of this new national league and in 1967 it got off the ground.

Ten franchises were sold and teams imported wholesale to represent these cities. The first winners were the Los Angeles Wolves with a team composed entirely of players from Wolverhampton Wanderers in England. A rival league was also set up at the same time but in 1968 the two leagues were persuaded to merge, and at last the United States had a truly national league which included Canada as well.

The NASL, as it was known from 1968, was modelled on those that existed in American football and baseball, from the system of franchising down to the cheerleaders. New clubs were created in an attempt to get away from the ethnic image of the game and to spread it around the country to cities like Miami, Atlanta and Kansas to whom it was new.

Although the number of Americans taking part in the league grew over the years it was always dominated by foreigners even if they were relatively well known. The best known of these were Pelé and Franz Beckenbauer, both of whom played for the best known and most popular of the clubs created, the New York Cosmos, backed by Warner Communications. For a while it seemed as if the experiment was working. The money was there, gates were high, especially in New York, and the level of play was to a good standard. It was not to last, however.

One by one clubs folded as the owners, disappointed by profit levels, pulled the plug on their teams, and in 1984 the NASL itself folded. The major problem was that the game was built up on an artificial basis. Clubs will only survive and even thrive if they have a history that players, supporters and owners can identify with. None of the NASL clubs had that, and so from the very start the idea was doomed to failure. Football was simply not allowed to grow naturally, and no matter how much money was thrown at it, the conditions were not right.

All the ethnic leagues still survive in the United States and as these represent the only areas where there is any tradition in the American game, perhaps the NASL should have paid more attention to them as should administrators in the future.

FIFA, despite the failure of the NASL, has long regarded the United States as unconquered virgin territory full of dollars that could make their way into its coffers, and so in a decision roundly condemned at the time, they awarded the 1994 World Cup to America, in an attempt to give the game another boost.

Whether this tactic will work or not is open to question. Certainly the United States Soccer Federation has adopted the right approach of letting the game grow naturally at grass roots. The American Soccer League and the Western Soccer League, both founded in 1985 after the demise of the NASL, are on a much smaller scale than their predecessor and represent hope for the future, but the suspicion is that once the World Cup is over, Americans will carry on watching and playing baseball, American football, basketball and ice hockey, leaving football once again in the shadows.

Population: 251 394 000
Area, sq km: 9 529 063
% in urban areas: 76%
Capital city: Washington D.C.

United States Soccer Federation
US Soccer House
1801–1811 S. Prairie Ave.
Chicago Il 60616
Tel: (010 1) 312 808 1300
Fax: (010 1) 312 808 9566
Telex: 450024 US SOCCER FED
Languages for correspondence: English, Spanish & German
Year of formation: 1913
Affiliation to FIFA: 1913
Affiliation to CONCACAF: 1961
Registered clubs: 5375
Registered players: 3 189 100
Professional players: 700
Registered coaches: 12 000
Registered referees: 30 449
National stadium: Rose Bowl, Los Angeles 104 000
National colours: Shirts: White/Shorts: Blue/Socks: White
Reserve colours: Shirts: Red/Shorts: White/Socks: Blue
Season: April–September

THE RECORD

WORLD CUP

1930 .... QT Automatic – Final tournament/Semi-finalists
1934 .... QT 1st/4 in group 1 – Final tournament/1st round
1938 .... Did not enter
1950 .... QT 2nd/3 in group 9 – Final tournament/1st round
1954 .... QT 2nd/3 in group 11
1958 .... QT 1st round
1962 .... QT 1st round
1966 .... QT 1st round
1970 .... QT 2nd round
1974 .... QT 1st round
1978 .... QT 1st round
1982 .... QT 2nd round
1986 .... QT 2nd round
1990 .... QT Qualified – Final tournament/1st round

OLYMPIC GAMES

1908–20 ..... Did not enter
1924 .... 1st round
1928 .... 1st round
1936 .... 1st round
1948 .... 1st round
1952 .... 1st round
1956 .... 1st round
1960 .... QT 1st round
1964 .... QT 2nd round
1968 .... QT 1st round
1972 .... QT Qualified – Final tournament/1st round
1976 .... QT 2nd round
1980 .... QT Qualified – withdrew
1984 .... QT Automatic – Final tournament/1st round
1988 .... QT Qualified – Final tournament/1st round
1992 .... QT Qualified

CONCACAF Championship: Winners – 1991

NASL Soccer Bowl Finals

1967	Los Angeles Wolves	6–5	Washington Whips
1967	Oakland Clippers	0–1 4–1	Baltimore Bays
1968	Atlanta Chiefs	0–0 3–0	San Diego Toros
1969	Kansas City Spurs	*	Atlanta Chiefs
1970	Rochester Lancers	3–0 1–3	Washington Darts
1971	Dallas Tornado	1–2 4–1 2–0	Atlanta Chiefs
1972	New York Cosmos	2–1	St Louis Stars
1973	Philadelphia Atoms	2–0	Dallas Tornado
1974	Los Angeles Aztecs	4–3	Miami Toros
1975	Tampa Bay Rowdies	2–0	Portland Timbers
1976	Toronto Metros	3–0	Minnesota Kicks
1977	New York Cosmos	2–1	Seattle Sounders
1978	New York Cosmos	3–1	Tampa Bay Rowdies
1979	Vancouver Whitecaps	2–1	Tampa Bay Rowdies
1980	New York Cosmos	3–0	Fort Lauderdale Strikers
1981	Chicago Sting	1–0	New York Cosmos
1982	New York Cosmos	1–0	Seattle Sounders
1983	Tulsa Roughnecks	2–0	Toronto Blizzard
1984	Chicago Sting	2–1 3–2	Toronto Blizzard

* Run Solely on a league basis

American Professional Soccer League

1989	Fort Laud. Strikers	3–2	San Diego Nomads
1990	Maryland Bays	1–1 (4–3p)	San Fran. Blackhawks
1991	San Fran. Blackhawks	1–3 2–0 (4–2p)	Albany Capitals

United States National Open Challenge Cup

1914	Brooklyn Field Club	2–1	Brooklyn Celtic
1915	Bethlehem Steel Co.	3–1	Brooklyn Celtic
1916	Bethlehem Steel Co.	1–0	Fall River Rovers
1917	Fall River Rovers	1–0	Bethlehem Steel Co.
1918	Bethlehem Steel Co.	2–2 3–0	Fall River Rovers
1919	Bethlehem Steel Co.	2–0	Paterson New Jersey
1920	Benn Miller FC St Louis	2–1	Fore River
1921	Robins Dry Dock Br'lyn	4–2	Scullin Steel St Louis
1922	Scullin Steel St Louis	3–2	Todd Shipyard
1923	Paterson N.J.	2–2 W-O	Scullin Steel St Louis
1924	Fall River FC	4–2	Vesper Buick
1925	Shawsheen SC	3–0	Canadian Club
1926	Bethlehem Steel Co.	7–2	Benn Miller St Louis
1927	Fall River FC	7–0	Holley Carburetor
1928	New York Nationals	2–2 3–0	Bricklayers
1929	Hakoah All Stars NY	2–0 3–0	Madison Kennels
1930	Fall River FC	7–2 2–7	Bruell Insurance
1931	Fall River FC	6–2 1–1	Bricklayers
1932	New Bedford St Louis	3–3 5–2	Stix, Baer & Fuller SL
1933	Stix, Baer & Fuller SL	1–0 2–1	New York Americans
1934	Stix, Baer & Fuller SL	4–2 2–3 5–0	Pawtucket Rangers
1935	Central Breweries	5–0 1–1 1–3	Pawtucket Rangers
1936	1st Ger.-Amer. Phil.	2–2 3–1	St Louis Shamrocks
1937	N.Y. Americans	0–2 4–2	St Louis Shamrocks
1938	Sparta ABA Chicago	4–0 4–2	St Mary's Celtic Brooklyn
1939	St Mary's Celtic Br'lyn	1–0 4–1	Manhatten Beer
1940	Sparta ABA Chicago	0–0 2–2	Baltimore DC
1941	Pawtucket FC	4–2 4–3	Chrysler
1942	Gallatin Pittsburgh	2–1 4–2	Pawtucket FC
1943	Brooklyn Hispano	2–2 4–2	Morgan-Strasser Pitts.
1944	Brooklyn Hispano	4–0	Morgan-Strasser Pitts.
1945	Brookhattan N.Y.	4–1 2–1	Cleveland Americans
1946	Vikings Chicago	1–1 2–1	Ponta Delgada Fall River
1947	Ponta Delgada Fall Riv.	6–2 3–2	Sparta ABA Chicago
1948	Joe Simpkins St Louis	3–1	Brookhattan N.Y.
1949	Morgan-Strasser Pitts.	2–0 4–0	Philadelphia Nats
1950	Joe Simpkins St Louis	2–1 1–4	Ponta Delgada Fall River
1951	Ger.-Hung. Brooklyn	2–2 6–2	Heidelberg
1952	Harmarville Pennsyl.	3–1 4–1	Philadelphia Nats
1953	Chicago Falcons	2–0 1–1	Harmarville Pennsylvania
1954	New York Americans	1–0 2–0	Kutis St Louis
1955	Eintracht Astoria	2–1	Americans
1956	Harmarville Pennsyl.	0–1 3–1	Chicago Schwaben
1957	Kutis St Louis	3–0 3–1	Hakoah New York
1958	Los Angeles Kickers	2–1	Pompei Baltimore
1959	San Pedro Canvasbacks	4–3	Fall River FC
1960	Ukranian Nationals Phil.	5–3	Los Angeles Kickers
1961	Ukranian Nationals Phil.	2–2 5–2	Los Angeles Scots
1962	New York Hungarians	3–2	San Francisco Scots
1963	Philadelphia Ukrainians	1–0	Los Angeles Americans
1964	Los Angeles Kickers	2–2 2–0	Philadelphia Ukranians
1965	New York Ukranians	1–1 3–0	Hansa Chicago
1966	Philadelphia Ukrainians	1–0 3–0	Orange County
1967	Greek-Americans N.Y.	4–2	Orange County
1968	Greek-Americans N.Y.	1–1 1–0	Chicago Olympic
1969	Greek-Americans N.Y.	1–0	Montebello Armenians
1970	Elizabeth SC	2–1	Los Angeles Croatia
1971	New York Hota	6–4	San Pedro Yugoslavs
1972	Elizabeth SC	1–0	San Pedro Yugoslavs
1973	Maccabee Los Ang.	5–3	Cleveland Inter
1974	Greek-Americans N.Y.	2–0	Chicago Croatians
1975	Maccabee Los Ang.	1–0	Inter-Giuliana
1976	San Francisco AC	1–0	Inter-Giuliana
1977	Maccabee Los Ang.	5–0	United German-Hung.
1978	Maccabee Los Ang.	2–0	V. da Gama Bridgeport
1979	Brooklyn Dodgers	2–1	Chicago Croatians
1980	New York Freedoms	3–2	Maccabee Los Ang.
1981	Maccabee Los Ang.	5–1	Brooklyn Dodgers
1982	New York Freedoms	4–3	Maccabee Los Ang.
1983	New York Freedoms	4–3	Kutis St Louis

1984	AO Krete NY	1988	Busch St Louis
1985	Greek-Ams SF	1989	Kickers St Peters.
1986	Kutis St Louis	1990	Chicago Eagles
1987	Espana Wash.	1991	Brooklyn Italians

United States National Amateur Challenge Cup

1924	Fleisher Yarn Phil.	3–0	Swedeish-Americans
1925	Toledo FC	3–1	McLeod Council
1926	Defenders New Bed.	1–0	Heidelberg Pittsburgh
1927	Heidelburg Pittsburgh		
1928	–		
1929	Heidelburg Pittsburgh	9–0	1st German Phil.
1930	Raffies Fall River	3–3 W-O	Gallatin Pittsburgh
1931	Goodyear Akron	1–1 2–0	Black Cats
1932	Shamrock Cleveland	2–1	Santo Christo
1933	German-Amer. Phil.	5–1	McKnight Beverage
1934	German-Amer. Phil.	1–1	Heidelburg Pittsburgh
1935	WW Riehl C'le Shan.	3–0	All American Cafe
1936	1st German Brooklyn	2–1	Castle Shannon
1937	Highlander Trenton	1–0	Castle Shannon
1938	Ponta Delgada Fall River	2–0	Heidelburg Pittsburgh
1939	St Michael's Fall River	3–1	Gallatin Pittsburgh
1940	Morgan-Strasser Pitts.	1–0	Firestone
1941	Fall River FC	2–1	Chrysler

1942	Fall River FC	4–3	Morgan USCO
1943	Morgan–Strasser Pitts.	4–1	Santa Maria
1944	Eintracht Astoria	5–2	Morgan Strasser Pitts.
1945	Eintracht Astoria	1–0	Raffertys
1946	Ponta Delgada Fall R.	5–0	Castle Shannon
1947	Ponta Delgada Fall R	4–1	Curry Vets
1948	Ponta Delgada Fall R.	4–1	Curry Vets
1949	Elizabeth SC	6–1	Zenthoefer
1950	Ponta Delgada Fall R.	0–1 4–1	Harmarville Pennsylvania
1951	German-Hung. Brooklyn	4–3	Harmarville Pennsylvania
1952	St Louis Raiders	3–1	Lusitano
1953	Ponta Delgada Fall River	2–0	Chicago Slovaks
1954	Beadling Pittsburgh	2–5 5–1	Joe Simpkins St Louis
1955	Heidelburg Torn. Pitt.	2–2 5–0	Chicago Eagles
1956	Kutis St Louis	1–0	Philadelphia Ukrainians
1957	Kutis St Louis	1–1	Rochester Ukrainians
1958	Kutis St Louis	2–1	Beadling SC Pittsburgh
1959	Kutis St Louis	5–0 2–2	St Andrew Scots
1960	Kutis St Louis	4–0	Patchogue New York
1961	Kutis St Louis	1–0 3–3	Ital.-Amer. Stars Hartford
1962	Carpathia Kickers De'oit	4–0	American-Hungarian
1963	Ital.–Americans Rochester	1–0	St Ambrose
1964	Schwaben Chicago	4–0	German-Hungarians Phil.
1965	German-Hungarians Phil.	6–0	St Ambrose
1966	Chicago Kickers	5–2	Ital.-Americans Hartford
1967	Ital.-Americans Hartford	2–0	Kutis St Louis
1968	Chicago Kickers	2–1	Carpathia Kickers Detroit
1969	British Lions Washington	4–1	Kutis St Louis
1970	Chicago Kickers	6–5	German-Hungarians Phil.
1971	Kutis St Louis	4–1	Cleveland Inter-Italian
1972	Busch St Louis	1–0	New Bedford Portuguese
1973	Inter Philadelphia	3–2	San Jose Grenadiers
1974	Inter Philadelphia	4–3	Big 4 Chevrolet
1975	Chicago Kickers	1–0	Scotland SC
1976	Bavarian BR Milwaukee	3–2	Trenton Extension
1977	Denver Kickers SC	3–1	United German-Hung. SC
1978	Denver Kickers	8–3	Cleveland Inter
1979	Atlanta Datagraphic	1–0	San Francisco Glens
1980	Busch Bavarians	3–2	Atlanta Datagraphic
1981	Busch St Louis	3–2	Philadelphia Bayern
1982	Seattle Croatia	1–0	Virginia Kickers
1983	Denver Kickers	5–0	Detroit Ukrainian
1984	Mean Green Richardson		
1985	Espana Wash.		
1986	Fairfax Spartans		
1987	Polish-Am Eagles NY		
1988	Mean Green Dallas		
1989	Chcago Eagles		
1990	Kickers St Peters.		
1991	Scott Gallagher Mo.		

INTERNATIONAL MATCHES PLAYED BY THE UNITED STATES OF AMERICA

Date	Opponents	Result		Venue	Compet	Scorers
28–11–1885	Canada	L	0–1	Newark	Fr	
25–11–1886	Canada	W	3–2	Newark	Fr	Swarbuck, Gray, McGurck
16–11–1904	Canada	L	0–7	St Louis	OGf	
17–11	Canada	L	0–4	St Louis	OGf	
20–08–1916	Sweden	W	3–2	Stockholm	Fr	
3–09	Norway	D	1–1	Oslo	Fr	
26–05–1924	Estonia	W	1–0	Paris	OGr1	
29–05	Uruguay	L	0–3	Paris	OGqf	
10–06	Poland	W	3–2	Warsaw	Fr	
16–06	Rep. Ireland	L	1–3	Dublin	Fr	
27–06–1925	Canada	L	0–1	Montreal	Fr	
8–11	Canada	W	6–1	Brooklyn	Fr	Brown 3, Stark 3
6–11–1926	Canada	W	6–2	Brooklyn	Fr	Brown 2, Auld 2, Marshall, Florrie
29–05–1928	Argentina	L	2–11	Amsterdam	OGr1	Findley 2
10–06	Poland	D	3–3	Warsaw	Fr	
13–07–1930	Belgium	W	3–0	Montevideo	WCr1	McGhee 2, Patenaude
17–07	Paraguay	W	3–0	Montevideo	WCr1	Patenaude 2, Florie
26–07	Argentina	L	1–6	Montevideo	WCsf	Brown
17–08	Brazil	L	3–4	Rio de Janeiro	Fr	Patenaude 2
24–05–1934	Mexico	W	4–2	Rome	WCq	
27–05	Italy	L	1–7	Rome	WCr1	Donelli
13–07–1947	Mexico	L	0–5	Havana	NAC	
20–07	Cuba	L	2–5	Havana	NAC	
6–08–1948	Norway	L	0–11	Oslo	Fr	
11–08	NIreland	L	0–5	Belfast	Fr	
4–09–1949	Mexico	L	0–6	Mexico City	NAC/WCq	
14–09	Cuba	D	1–1	Mexico City	NAC/WCq	
18–09	Mexico	L	2–6	Mexico City	NAC/WCq	
21–09	Cuba	W	5–2	Mexico City	NAC/WCq	Matevich 2, Souza, Wallace, Bahr
25–06–1950	Spain	L	1–3	Curtiba	WCr1	Souza
29–06	England	W	1–0	Belo Horizonte	WCr1	Gaetjens
2–07	Chile	L	2–5	Recife	WCr1	Pariani, Souza
30–04–1952	Scotland	L	0–6	Glasgow	Fr	
8–06–1953	England	L	3–6	New York	Fr	Decker 2, Atheneos
10–01–1954	Mexico	L	0–4	Mexico City	WCq	
14–01	Mexico	L	1–3	Mexico City	WCq	Looby
3–04	Haiti	W	3–2	Port au Prince	WCq	Looby, Casey, Chachurian
4–04	Haiti	W	3–0	Port au Prince	WCq	Looby, Mendoza
25–08–1955	Iceland	L	2–3	Reykjavik	Fr	Looby
7–04–1957	Mexico	L	0–6	Mexico City	WCq	
28–04	Mexico	L	2–7	Long Beach	WCq	MurphyE

22–06	Canada	L	1–5	Toronto	WCq	Keough
6–07	Canada	L	2–3	St Louis	WCq	MurphyJ, Mendoza
28–05–1959	England	L	1–8	Los Angeles	Fr	MurphyE
6–11–1960	Mexico	D	3–3	Los Angeles	WCq	Bicek, Zerhusen, Fister
13–11	Mexico	L	0–3	Mexico City	WCq	
27–05–1964	England	L	0–10	New York	Fr	
7–03–1965	Mexico	D	2–2	Los Angeles	WCq	Bicek, Shmotoolocha
12–03	Mexico	L	0–2	Mexico City	WCq	
17–03	Honduras	W	1–0	San Pedro	WCq	MurphyE
21–03	Honduras	D	1–1	Tegucigalpa	WCq	MurphyE
15–09–1968	Israel	D	3–3	New York	Fr	Millar, Roy
25–09	Israel	L	0–4	Philadelphia	Fr	
17–10	Canada	L	2–4	Toronto	WCq	Roy, Stritzl
20–10	Haiti	W	6–3	Port au Prince	Fr	
21–10	Haiti	L	2–5	Port au Prince	Fr	
23–10	Haiti	W	1–0	Port au Prince	Fr	
26–10	Canada	W	1–0	Atlanta	WCq	Albrecht
2–11	Bermuda	W	6–2	Kansas City	WCq	Millar 3, Baker 2, Roy
10–11	Bermuda	W	2–0	Hamilton	WCq	Roy, OG
20–04–1969	Haiti	L	0–2	Port au Prince	WCq	
11–05	Haiti	L	0–1	San Diego	WCq	
20–08–1972	Canada	L	2–3	St John's	WCq	Roy, Getzinger
29–08	Canada	D	2–2	Baltimore	WCq	Roy, Geimer
3–09	Mexico	L	1–3	Mexico City	WCq	Roy
10–09	Mexico	L	1–2	Los Angeles	WCq	Geimer
17–03–1973	Bermuda	L	0–4	Hamilton	Fr	
20–03	Poland	L	0–4	Lodz	Fr	
3–08	Poland	L	0–1	Chicago	Fr	
5–08	Canada	W	2–0	Windsor	Fr	Grgurev, Liveric
10–08	Poland	L	0–4	San Francisco	Fr	
12–08	Poland	W	1–0	New Britain	Fr	Trost
9–09	Bermuda	W	1–0	Hartford	Fr	Brewster
16–10	Mexico	L	0–2	Puebla	Fr	
3–11	Haiti	L	0–1	Port au Prince	Fr	
5–11	Haiti	L	0–1	Port au Prince	Fr	
13–11	Israel	L	1–3	Tel Aviv	Fr	Roy
15–11	Israel	L	0–2	Beersheba	Fr	
5–09–1974	Mexico	L	1–3	Monterrey	Fr	Vaninger
8–09	Mexico	L	0–1	Dallas	Fr	
26–03–1975	Poland	L	0–7	Poznan	Fr	
24–06	Poland	L	0–4	Seattle	Fr	
19–08	Costa Rica	L	1–3	Mexico City	Fr	McCully
21–08	Argentina	L	0–6	Mexico City	Fr	
24–08	Mexico	L	0–2	Mexico City	Fr	
24–09–1976	Canada	D	1–1	Vancouver	WCq	Bandov
3–10	Mexico	D	0–0	Los Angeles	WCq	
15–10	Mexico	L	0–3	Puebla	WCq	
20–10	Canada	W	2–0	Seattle	WCq	Rys, Veee
10–11	Haiti	D	0–0	Port au Prince	Fr	
12–11	Haiti	D	0–0	Port au Prince	Fr	
14–11	Haiti	D	0–0	Port au Prince	Fr	
22–12	Canada	L	0–3	Port au Prince	WCq	
15–09–1977	El Salvador	W	2–1	San Salvador	Fr	Davis, Villa
18–09	Guatemala	L	1–3	Guatemala City	Fr	Bellinger
22–09	El Salvador	W	1–0	San Salvador	Fr	Davis
25–09	Guatemala	L	0–2	Guatemala City	Fr	
27–09	Mexico	L	0–3	Monterrey	Fr	
30–09	El Salvador	D	0–0	Los Angeles	Fr	
6–10	China	D	1–1	Washington	Fr	Villa
10–10	China	W	1–0	Atlanta	Fr	
16–10	China	W	2–1	San Francisco	Fr	Villa, Nanchoff G
3–09–1978	Iceland	D	0–0	Reykjavik	Fr	
6–09	Switzerland	L	0–2	Lucerne	Fr	
20–09	Portugal	L	0–1	Setubal	Fr	
2–05–1979	France	L	0–6	New York	Fr	
7–10	Bermuda	W	3–1	Hamilton	Fr	Liveric, Bandov, Makowski
10–10	France	L	0–3	Paris	Fr	
26–10	Hungary	W	2–0	Budapest	Fr	Nanchoff L, Di Bernardo
29–10	Rep. Ireland	L	2–3	Dublin	Fr	Villa, Di Bernardo

4–10–1980	Luxembourg	W	2–0	Dudelange	Fr	Davis, Hulcer
7–10	Portugal	D	1–1	Lisbon	Fr	Davis
25–10	Canada	D	0–0	Fort Lauderdale	WCq	
1–11	Canada	L	1–2	Vancouver	WCq	Villa
9–11	Mexico	L	1–5	Mexico City	WCq	Davis
23–11	Mexico	W	2–1	Lauderdale	WCq	Moyers 2
21–03–1982	Trinidad	W	2–1	Port of Spain	Fr	Davis, Veee
8–04–1983	Haiti	W	2–0	Port au Prince	Fr	Borja, Durgan
30–05–1984	Italy	D	0–0	New York	Fr	
29–09	Neth Antilles	D	0–0	Curacao	WCq	
6–10	Neth Antilles	W	4–0	St Louis	WCq	Coker 2, Di Bernardo, Kapp
9–10	El Salvador	W	3–1	Los Angeles	Fr	Davis, Ladouceur, Hooker
11–10	Colombia	W	1–0	Los Angeles	Fr	Coker
14–10	Guatemala	L	0–4	Guatemala City	Fr	
17–10	Mexico	L	1–2	Mexico City	Fr	Van der Beck
30–11	Ecuador	D	0–0	New York	Fr	
2–12	Ecuador	D	2–2	Miami	Fr	Ladouceur, Sharp
8–02–1985	Switzerland	D	1–1	Tampa	Fr	Van der Beck
2–04	Canada	L	0–2	Vancouver	Fr	
4–04	Canada	D	1–1	Portland	Fr	Perez
15–05	Trinidad	W	2–1	St Louis	WCq	Borja, Peterson
19–05	Trinidad	W	1–0	Torrance	WCq	Caligiuri
26–05	Costa Rica	D	1–1	San Jose	WCq	Kerr
31–05	Costa Rica	L	0–1	Torrance	WCq	
16–06	England	L	0–5	Los Angeles	Fr	
5–02–1986	Canada	D	0–0	Miami	Fr	
7–02	Uruguay	D	1–1	Miami	Fr	Murray
8–06–1987	Egypt	L	1–3	Seoul	Fr	Hantak
12–06	South Korea	L	0–1	Pusan	Fr	
16–06	Thailand	W	1–0	Chongju	Fr	Hantak
10–08	Trinidad	W	3–1	Indianapolis	Fr	Hantak 2, Klopas
12–08	El Salvador	D	0–0	Indianapolis	Fr	
5–09	Trinidad	W	4–1	St Louis	Fr	Goulet 3, Stollmeyer
20–09	Trinidad	W	1–0	Port of Spain	Fr	Perez
18–10	El Salvador	W	4–2	San Salvador	Fr	Perez 2, Goulet, Klopas
10–01–1988	Guatemala	L	0–1	Guatemala City	Fr	
13–01	Guatemala	W	1–0	Guatemala City	Fr	Agoos
14–05	Colombia	L	0–2	Miami	Fr	
25–05	El Salvador	W	4–1	Indianapolis	Fr	Goulet 2, Davis, OG
1–06	Chile	D	1–1	Stockton	Fr	Eichmann
3–06	Chile	L	1–3	San Diego	Fr	Borja
5–06	Chile	L	0–3	Fresno	Fr	
7–06	Ecuador	L	0–1	Alburquerque	Fr	
10–06	Ecuador	L	0–2	Houston	Fr	
12–06	Ecuador	D	0–0	Fort Worth	Fr	
14–06	Costa Rica	W	1–0	San Antonio	Fr	Ryerson
13–07	Poland	L	0–2	New Britan	Fr	
24–07	Jamaica	D	0–0	Kingston	WCq	
13–08	Jamaica	W	5–1	St Louis	WCq	Klopas 2, Bliss, Krumpe, Perez
16–04–1989	Costa Rica	L	0–1	San Jose	WCq	
30–04	Costa Rica	W	1–0	St Louis	WCq	Ramos
13–05	Trinidad	D	1–1	Torrance	WCq	Trittschuh
4–06	Peru	W	3–0	New York	Fr	Murray, Ramos, Bliss
17–06	Guatemala	W	2–1	Connecticut	WCq	Murray, Eichmann
24–06	Colombia	L	0–1	Miami	Fr	
13–08	South Korea	L	1–2	Los Angeles	Fr	Harkes
17–09	El Salvador	W	1–0	Tegucigalpa	WCq	Perez
8–10	Guatemala	D	0–0	Guatemala City	WCq	
5–11	El Salvador	D	0–0	St Louis	WCq	
14–11	Bermuda	W	2–1	Cocoa Beach	Fr	Eichmann, Doyle
19–11	Trinidad	W	1–0	Port of Spain	WCq	Caligiuri
2–02–1990	Costa Rica	L	0–2	Miami	Fr	
4–02	Colombia	D	1–1	Miami	Fr	Wynalda
13–02	Bermuda	W	1–0	Hamilton	Fr	Sullivan
24–02	Soviet Union	L	1–3	Palo Alto	Fr	Harkes
10–03	Finland	W	2–1	Tampa	Fr	Murray, Caligiuri
20–03	Hungary	L	0–2	Budapest	Fr	
28–03	East Germany	L	2–3	Berlin	Fr	Murray, Vermes
8–04	Iceland	W	4–1	St Louis	Fr	Wynalda, Murray, Trittschuh

22–04	Colombia	L	0–1	Miami	Fr	
5–05	Malta	W	1–0	Piscataway	Fr	Wynalda
10–05	Poland	W	3–1	Hershey	Fr	Murray, Vermes, Sullivan
30–05	Liechtenstein	W	4–1	Eschen	Fr	Vermes, Balboa, Wynalda, Henderson
2–06	Switzerland	L	1–2	St Gallen	Fr	Murray
10–06	Czechoslovakia	L	1–5	Florence	WCr1	Caligiuri
14–06	Italy	L	0–1	Rome	WCr1	
19–06	Austria	L	1–2	Florence	WCr1	Murray
28–07	East Germany	L	1–2	Milwaukee	Fr	Eck
15–09	Trinidad	W	3–0	Charlotte	Fr	Vermes, Murray, Eichmann
10–10	Poland	W	3–2	Warsaw	Fr	Murray, Vermes 2
18–11	Trinidad	D	0–0	Port of Spain	Fr	
21–11	Soviet Union	D	0–0	Port of Spain	Fr	
19–12	Portugal	L	0–1	Oporto	Fr	
2–02–1991	Switzerland	L	0–1	Miami	Fr	
21–02	Bermuda	L	0–1	Hamilton	Fr	
12–03	Mexico	D	2–2	Los Angeles	NAC	Washington, Murray
16–03	Canada	W	2–0	Torrance	NAC	Washington, Murray
5–05	Uruguay	W	1–0	Denver	Fr	Vermes
19–05	Argentina	L	0–1	Palo Alto	Fr	
1–06	Rep. Ireland	D	1–1	Foxboro	Fr	Wynalda
29–06	Trinidad	W	2–1	Los Angeles	CCr1	Murray, Balboa
1–07	Guatemala	W	3–0	Los Angeles	CCr1	Murray, Quinn, Wynalda
3–07	Costa Rica	W	3–2	Los Angeles	CCr1	Vermes, Perez, OG
5–07	Mexico	W	2–0	Los Angeles	CCsf	Doyle, Vermes
7–07	Honduras	D	0–0 (4–3p)	Los Angeles	CCf	
28–08	Romania	W	2–0	Brasov	Fr	Balboa, Murray
4–09	Turkey	D	1–1	Istanbul	Fr	Klopas
14–09	Jamaica	W	1–0	High Point	Fr	Gjonbalaj
19–10	North Korea	L	1–2	Washington	Fr	Murray
24–11	Costa Rica	D	1–1	Dallas	Fr	Kinnear
25–01–1992	CIS	K	0–1	Miami	Fr	
2–02	CIS	W	2–1	Detroit	Fr	Wynalda, Balboa
12–02	Costa Rica	D	0–0	San Jose	Fr	
19–02	El Salvador	L	0–2	San Salvador	Fr	
26–02	Brazil	L	0–3	Fortaleza	Fr	
11–03	Spain	L	0–2	Valladolid	Fr	
18–03	Morocco	L	1–3	Casablanca	Fr	Perez
29–04	Rep. Ireland	L	1–4	Dublin	Fr	Wynalda
17–05	Scotland	L	0–1	Denver	Fr	
31–05	Rep. Ireland	W	3–1	Washington	Fr	Balboa, Ramos, Harkes
3–06	Portugal	W	1–0	Chicago	Fr	Wegerle
6–06	Italy	D	1–1	Chicago	Fr	Harkes

CENTRAL AMERICA

Central America has traditionally been the stronghold of CONCACAF. Costa Rica, Guatemala, Honduras and El Salvador are the strongest of the seven nations although all operate under the shadow of Mexico. The political turmoil that has characterised the area has not helped either. Civil war has been waged in El Salvador for many years as it has in Nicaragua. The most famous incident relating to football remains the Fútbol War between El Salvador and Honduras in 1969.

The countries faced each other in the semi-finals of the CONCACAF World Cup qualifying group in June 1969 and rioting followed each of the games, particularly after the second game which El Salvador won to force a play-off. Salvadorean migrant workers were at the centre of the dispute and after their national side defeated the Hondurans in the play-off tension reached boiling point and the El Salvador army invaded Honduras to protect their nationals from persecution.

Costa Rica are perhaps the best of the Central American nations so it was surprising that the 1990 World Cup was the first time they had made it to the final tournament. During the 1940s, 50s and 60s, they won nine continental titles to El Salvador's one, Guatemala's one, Panama's one and Honduras' none, but never seemed to make it to the World Cup. Instead both Honduras and El Salvador qualified before they did, though none met with the eventual success of the Costa Ricans.

In Italy they defeated both Scotland and Sweden to qualify for the second round before going down to Czechoslovakia. El Salvador on the other hand lost all three of their games in the 1970 tournament and again in 1982, including a 10–1 thrashing at the hands of Hungary, whilst Honduras' only final appearance in 1982 resulted in two draws with Spain and Northern Ireland and a loss to Yugoslavia.

Costa Rica also has a good club structure. A championship was started in 1921, before any of her rivals, in which the top clubs have been Herediano, Liga Deportivo Alajuelense and since the war Deportivo Saprissa. The other major clubs in the region are Alianza, Deportivo FAS, Luis Angel Firpo and Atletico Marte from El Salvador, Comunicaciones in Guatemala and Olimpia in Honduras.

Until the CONCACAF Club Championship can develop into an internationally recognised tournament in place of the rather shabby event at present, progress is likely to be limited in all of these countries. Political stability would also be a useful asset, but in an area where football has caused one war already, don't count on it.

BELIZE

Population: 189 000
Area, sq km: 22 965
% in urban areas: 51%
Capital city: Belmopan 3000
Major Cities: Belize City 49 000, Orange Walk 10 000

Belize National Football Association
PO Box 1742
Belize City
Belize
Tel: (010 501) 2 082609
Fax: (010 501) 2 77416
Telex: 102 FOREIGN BZ
Cable: None
Languages for correspondence: English

Year of formation: 1980
Affiliation to FIFA: 1986
Affiliation to CONCACAF: 1986
Registered Clubs: 45
Registered players: 4400
Registered Coaches: 20
Registered Referees: 55
National Stadium: People's Stadium, Orange Walk 10 000
National colours: Shirts: Blue/Shorts: White/Socks: Blue

THE RECORD

WORLD CUP

1930–90 ..... Did not enter

OLYMPIC GAMES

1908–88 ..... Did not enter
1992 .... QT 1st round

COSTA RICA

Population: 3 015 000
Area, sq km: 51 100
% in urban areas: 51%
Capital city: San José 1 040 000

Federacion Costarricense de Futbol
Apartado 670–1000
Calle 40–Ave.Ctl 1
San José
Costa Rica
Tel: (010 506) 221544
Fax: (010 506) 552674
Telex: 3394 DIDER CR
Cable: FEDEFUTBOL SAN JOSE
Languages for correspondence: Spanish

Year of formation: 1921
Affiliation to FIFA: 1921
Affiliation to CONCACAF: 1962
Registered clubs: 28
Registered players: 6900
Professional players: 500
Registered coaches: 28
Registered referees: 85
National stadium: Estadio Nacional, San José 30 000
National colours: Shirts: Red/Shorts: Blue/Socks: White
Reserve colours: Shirts: White/Shorts: White/Socks: White
Season: October–July

THE RECORD

WORLD CUP

1930–54 ..... Did not enter
1958 .... QT 2nd round
1962 .... QT 2nd round
1966 .... QT 2nd round
1970 .... QT 1st round
1974 .... QT 1st round
1978 .... QT 1st round
1982 .... QT 1st round
1986 .... QT 3rd round
1990 .... QT Qualified – Final tournament/2nd round

OLYMPIC GAMES

1908–64 ..... Did not enter
1968 .... QT 3rd round
1972 .... Did not enter
1976 .... QT 2nd round
1980 .... QT Qualified – Final tournament/1st round
1984 .... QT Qualified – Final tournament/1st round
1988–92 ..... Did not enter

CCCF and CONCACAF Championship:
Winners – 1941, 1946, 1948, 1953, 1955, 1960, 1961, 1963, 1969, 1989
CONCACAF Club Championship:
Winners – Deportivo Saprissa 1970. LD Alajeulense 1986
Finalists – Deportivo Saprissa 1978

COSTA RICAN LEAGUE CHAMPIONS

1921	CS Herediano
1922	CS Herediano
1923	CS Cartagines
1924	CS Herediano
1925	CS La Libertad
1926	CS La Libertad
1927	CS Herediano
1928	LD Alajuelense
1929	CS LA Libertad
1930	CS Herediano
1931	CS Herediano
1932	CS Herediano
1933	CS Herediano
1934	CS La Libertad
1935	CS Herediano
1936	CS Cartagines
1937	CS Herediano
1938	Orion FC
1939	LD Alajeulense
1940	CS Cartagines
1941	LD Alajeulense
1942	CS La Libertad
1943	Universidad Nacional
1944	Orion FC
1945	LD Alajeulense
1946	CS La Libertad
1947	CS Herediano
1948	CS Herediano
1949	LD Alajeulense
1950	LD Alajeulense
1951	CS Herediano
1952	Deportivo Saprissa
1953	Deportivo Saprissa
1954	–
1955	CS Herediano

1956	–
1957	CS Herediano
1958	LD Alajeulense
1959	LD Alajeulense
1960	LD Alajeulense
1961	CS Herediano
1962	Deportivo Saprissa
1963	CS Uruguay
1964	Deportivo Saprissa
1965	Deportivo Saprissa
1966	LD Alajeulense
1967	Deportivo Saprissa
1968	Deportivo Saprissa
1969	Deportivo Saprissa
1970	LD Alajeulense
1971	LD Alajeulense
1972	Deportivo Saprissa
1973	Deportivo Saprissa
1974	Deportivo Saprissa
1975	Deportivo Saprissa
1976	Deportivo Saprissa
1977	Deportivo Saprissa
1978	CS Herediano
1979	CS Herediano
1980	LD Alajeulense
1981	CS Herediano
1982	Deportivo Saprissa
1983	LD Alajeulense
1984	LD Alajeulense
1985	CS Herediano
1986	ML Puntarenas
1987	CS Herediano
1988	Deportivo Saprissa
1989	Deportivo Saprissa
1990	–
1991	LD Alajeulense
1992	LD Alajeulense

EL SALVADOR

Population: 5 221 000
Area, sq km: 21 041
% in urban areas: 48%
Capital city: San Salvador 459 000

Federacion Salvadorena de Futbol
Av J.M. Delgado, Col. Escalon
Centro Espanol, Apartado 1029
San Salvador
El Salvador
Tel: (010 503) 237362
Fax: (010 503) 235893
Telex: 20484 FESFUT SAL
Cable: FESFUT SAN SALVADOR
Languages for correspondence: Spanish

Year of formation: 1935
Affiliation to FIFA: 1938
Affiliation to CONCACAF: 1962
Registered clubs: 885
Registered players: 22 200
Professional players: 3000
Registered coaches: 14
Registered referees: 60
National stadium: Estadio Nacional de Flor Blanca, San Salvador 60000 National colours: Shirts: Blue Shorts: White Socks: Blue
Reserve colours: Shirts: White Shorts: White Socks: White
Season: September–June

THE RECORD

WORLD CUP

1930–66 ..... Did not enter
1970 .... QT Qualified – Final tournament/1st round
1974 .... QT 1st round
1978 .... QT 2nd round
1982 .... QT Qualified – Final tournament/1st round
1986 .... QT 2nd round
1990 .... QT 3rd round

OLYMPIC GAMES

1908–64 ..... Did not enter
1968 .... QT Qualified – Final tournament/1st round
1972 .... QT 1st round
1976 .... QT 1st round
1980 .... QT 1st round
1984 .... QT 1st round
1988 .... QT 2nd round
1992 .... QT 2nd round

CCCF Championship: Winners – 1943
CONCACAF Cub Championship:
Winners – Alianza 1967. Aguila 1976.
Deportivo FAS 1979
Finalists – Atletico Marte 1981

EL SALVADOR LEAGUE CHAMPIONS

1972	Aguila
1973	Juventud
1974	Platense
1975	Aguila
1976	Aguila
1977	Deportivo FAS
1978	Deportivo FAS
1979	Deportivo FAS
1980	Santiagueño
1981	Atletico Marte
1982	Deportivo FAS
1983	Atletico Marte
1984	Aguila
1985	Deportivo FAS
1986	Atletico Marte
1987	Alianza
1988	Cojutepeque
1989	LA Firpo
1990	LA Firpo
1991	LA Firpo

GUATEMALA

Population: 9 197 000
Area, sq km: 108 889
% in urban areas: 38%
Capital city: Guatemala City 1 057 000

Federacion Nacional de Futbol de Guatemala
Palacio de los Deportes
Segundo Nivel, Zona 4
Guatemala Ciudad
Guatemala
Tel: (010 502) 2 362211
Fax: (010 502) 367268
Telex: None
Cable: FEDFUTBOL GUATEMALA
Languages for correspondence: Spanish

Year of formation: 1926
Affiliation to FIFA: 1933
Affiliation to CONCACAF: 1961
Registered clubs: 2710
Registered players: 59 300
Professional players: 220
Registered coaches: 77
Registered referees: 250
National stadium: Mateo Flores, Guatemala City 50000
National colours: Shirts: White with blue diagonal stripe/Shorts: Blue/Socks: White
Reserve colours: Shirts: White/Shorts: Blue/Socks: White
Season: January–December

THE RECORD

WORLD CUP

1930–54 ..... Did not enter
1958 .... QT 1st round
1962 .... QT 1st round
1966 .... Did not enter
1970 .... QT 1st round
1974 .... QT 2nd round
1978 .... QT 2nd round
1982 .... QT 1st round
1986 .... QT 2nd round
1990 .... QT 3rd round

OLYMPIC GAMES

1908–64 ..... Did not enter
1968 .... QT Qualified – Final tournament/Quarter-finalists
1972 .... QT 2nd round
1976 .... QT Qualified – Final tournament/1st round
1980 .... QT 2nd round
1984 .... QT 2nd round
1988 .... QT Qualified – Final tournament/1st round
1992 .... QT 1st round

CONCACAF Championship: Winners – 1967
CONCACAF Club Championship:
Winners – Municipal 1974.
Comunicaciones 1978
Finalists – Comunicaciones 1962, 1969

HONDURAS

Population: 4674000
Area, sq km: 112088
% in urban areas: 40%
Capital city: Tegucigalpa 551000

Federacion Nacional Autonoma de Futbol de Honduras
Apartado Postal 827
Costa Oeste del Estadio Nacional
Tegucigalpa D.C.
Honduras
Tel: (010 504) 321897
Fax: (010 504) 311428
Telex: None
Cable: FENAFUTH TEGUCIGALPA
Languages for correspondence: Spanish & English

Year of formation: 1935
Affiliation to FIFA: 1946
Affiliation to CONCACAF: 1961
Registered clubs: 125
Registered players: 23100
Professional players: 900
National stadium: Norte e Sur, Tegucigalpa 50000
National colours: Shirts: Blue/Shorts: Blue/ Socks: Blue
Reserve colours: Shirts: White/Shorts: White/Socks: White
Season: September–June

THE RECORD

WORLD CUP

1930–58 ..... Did not enter
1962 .... QT 1st round
1966 .... QT 1st round
1970 .... QT 2nd round
1974 .... QT 2nd round
1978 .... Did not enter
1982 .... QT Qualified – Final tournament/1st round
1986 .... QT 3rd round
1990 .... QT 1st round

OLYMPIC GAMES

1908–72 ..... Did not enter
1976 .... QT 1st round
1980 .... Did not enter
1984 .... QT 1st round
1988 .... QT 1st round
1992 .... QT 3rd round

CONCACAF Championship: Winners 1981

CONCACAF Club championship:
Winners – Olimpia 1972, 1988
Finalists – Universidad de Honduras 1980, Olimpia 1985

NICARAGUA

Population: 3871000
Area, sq km: 130700
% in urban areas: 60%
Capital city: Managua 682000

Federacion Nicaraguense de Futbol
Instituto Nicaraguense de Desportes
Apartado Postal 976 0 383
Managua
Nicaragua
Tel: (010 505) 2 52271
Fax: None
Telex: 2156 IND NK
Cable: FEDEFOOT MANAGUA
Languages for correspondence: Spanish & English

Year of formation: 1931
Affiliation to FIFA: 1950
Affiliation to CONCACAF: 1968
Registered clubs: 16
Registered players: 2000
Registered referees: 14
National stadium: Estadio Nacional, Managua 30000
National colours: Shirts: Blue/Shorts: Blue/ Socks: Blue
Reserve colours: Shirts: White/Shorts: White/Socks: White
Season: September–June

THE RECORD

WORLD CUP

1930–90 ..... Did not enter

OLYMPIC GAMES

1908–72 ..... Did not enter
1976 .... QT pr round
1980–92 ..... Did not enter

PANAMA

Population: 2418000
Area, sq km: 75517
% in urban areas: 52%
Capital city: Panama City 411000

Federacion Nacional de Futbol de Panama
Estadio Revolucion
Apartado Postal 1523
Panama 1
Tel: (010 507) 335726
Fax: (010 507) 620289
Telex: 2534 INDE PG
Cable: PANAOLIMPIC PANAMA
Languages for correspondence: Spanish

Year of formation: 1937
Affiliation to FIFA: 1938
Affiliation to CONCACAF: 1960
Registered clubs: 219
Registered players: 18300
Registered coaches: 36
Registered referees: 73
National stadium: Estadio Revolución, Panama City 22000
National colours: Shirts: Red and white Stripes/Shorts: Blue/Socks: Red
Reserve colours: Shirts: Blue and white Stripes/Shorts: White/Socks: White
Season: September–June

THE RECORD

WORLD CUP

1930–90 ..... Did not enter

OLYMPIC GAMES

1908–60 ..... Did not enter
1964 .... QT 2nd round
1968–88 ..... Did not enter
1992 .... QT 2nd round

CCCF Championship: Winners – 1951

THE CARIBBEAN

The Caribbean is the birthplace of some of the best sportsmen in the world and has a rich tradition in sporting circles. The reason? Cricket. The West Indies cricket team has for decades been the best in the world and even an island as small as Antigua has produced the finest cricketer of recent years in Viv Richards, whilst Barbados, only marginally bigger, has produced the greatest cricketer of all time in Sir Garfield Sobers.

The result is that football is almost non-existent as an organised sport, especially in the islands that were former British colonies. Jamaica, Barbados, Antigua, Guyana and Trinidad are all major Test cricket locations and so the base is just not there to support anything like a proper football structure capable of making any kind of impact.

Cricket is not the only distraction. American influence in the area is obviously marked and so it is not surprising to learn that sports such as baseball are popular in Cuba and

Puerto Rico whilst other sports such as American football are also popular with television viewers in the region as a whole.

Haiti remain the only Caribbean side to have qualified for the final tournament of the World Cup since the war, although Trinidad have come close on two occasions. In 1974 a dubious refereeing decision cost them the game against Haiti and in 1990 a surprise defeat by the United States in the final game at home saw them miss out on the trip to Italy.

Cuba qualified in 1938 but did not have to play any games to get there, although they did beat Romania once in France. At national level the only other achievement of note was Haiti's victory in the 1957 championship of the CCCF, but this was in a dreadfully weak field in a tournament held in Curacao.

At club level, Transvaal from Curacao, Defence Force from Trinidad and Violette and Racing Club from Haiti have all won the CONCACAF Club Championship – indeed Transvaal are the most successful side in the history of the competition – but this is not symptomatic of any great strength in the respective leagues, more a reflection on the weakness of the tournament as a whole.

The 1991 Shell Caribbean Cup may well mark a new era in football in the Caribbean. For the first time a sizeable proportion of the countries in the region got together in a tournament, and by beating Trinidad in the final, Jamaica became the first champions of the Caribbean. Both finalists then qualified for the CONCACAF Gold Cup in Los Angeles, but did not proceed beyond the first round. If the islands of the Caribbean can be persuaded to carry on participating in future editions the effect on football can only be beneficial.

Antigua and Barbuda

Population: 80 600
Area, sq km: 441
% in urban areas: 32%
Capital city: Saint John's 36 000

The Antigua Football Association
PO Box 773
St. John's
Antigua
Tel: (010 1 809) 4623945
Fax: (010 1 809) 4622649
Telex: 2177 SIDAN AK
Cable: AFA ANTIGUA
Languages for correspondence: English

Year of formation: 1928
Affiliation to FIFA: 1970
Affiliation to CONCACAF: 1980
Registered clubs: 28
Registered players: 1000
Registered Referees: 61
National stadium: Recreation Ground 25 000
National colours: Shirts: Gold/Shorts: Black/Socks: Black
Reserve colours: Shirts: White/Shorts: Gold/Socks: Red
Season: August–December

The Record

World Cup

1930–70 ..... Did not enter
1974 .... QT 1st round
1978 .... Did not enter
1982 .... Did not enter
1986 .... QT 1st round
1990 .... QT 1st round

Olympic Games

1908–80 ..... Did not enter
1984 .... QT pr round
1988 .... QT pr round
1992 .... QT pr round

Aruba

Population: 62 000
Area, sq km: 193
Capital city: Oranjestad 19 000

Arubaanse Voetbal Bond
Schoenerstraat 2
PO Box 376
Oranjestad
Aruba
Tel: (010 2 978) 28016
Fax: (010 2 978) 38438
Telex: None
Cable: AVB ARUBA
Languages for correspondence: English and Spanish

Year of formation: 1932
Affiliation to FIFA: 1988
Affiliation to CONCACAF: 1988
Registered clubs: 50
Registered players: 1000
National colours: Shirts: Yellow/Shorts: Blue/Socks: Yellow

The Record

World Cup

1930–90 ..... Did not enter

Olympic Games

1908–88 ..... Did not enter
1992 .... QT pr round

The Bahamas

Population: 253000 Area, sq km: 13939
% in urban areas: 59%
Capital city: Nassau 168000

The Bahamas Football Association
PO Box N 8434
Nassau NP, The Bahamas
Tel: (010 1 809) 3266895
Fax: (010 1 809) 3226017
Telex: None
Cable: BAHSOCA NASSAU
Languages for correspondence: English

Tear of formation: 1967
Affiliation to FIFA: 1968
Affiliation to CONCACAF: 1981
Registered clubs: 13
Registered players: 300
Registered Coaches: 6
Registered Referees: 8
National stadium: Thomas Robinson, Nassau 15000
National colours: Shirts: Yellow/Shorts: Black/Socks: Yellow
Reserve colours: Shirts: Red/Shorts: White/Socks: Red
Season: October–May

The Record

World Cup

1930–90 ..... Did not enter

Olympic Games

1908–80 ..... Did not enter
1984 .... QT 1st round
1988 .... QT pr round
1992 .... Did not enter

BARBADOS

Population: 257 000
Area, sq km: 430
% in urban areas: 44%
Capital city: Bridgetown 102 000

Barbados Football Association
PO Box 1362
Bridgetown
Barbados
Tel: (010 1 809) 4244413
Fax: (010 1 809) 4360130
Telex: None
Cable: FOOTBALL BRIDGETOWN
Languages for correspondence: English

Year of formation: 1910
Affiliation to FIFA: 1968
Affiliation to CONCACAF: 1968
Registered clubs: 92
Registered players: 1100
Registered Referees: 63
National stadium: National Stadium, Bridgetown 12 000
National colours: Shirts: Blue/Shorts: Gold/ Socks: Blue
Reserve colours: Shirts: Gold/Shorts: Blue/ Socks: Gold
Season: January–May

THE RECORD

WORLD CUP

1930–74 ..... Did not enter
1978 .... QT 1st round
1982–90 ..... Did not enter

OLYMPIC GAMES

1908–68 ..... Did not enter
1972 .... QT 1st round
1976 .... QT pr round
1980 .... QT 2nd round
1984 .... QT pr round
1988 .... QT 1st round
1992 .... QT 1st round

BERMUDA

Population: 59 000
Area, sq km: 54
% in urban areas: 100%
Capital city: Hamilton 1000

The Bermuda Football Association
PO Box HM 745
Hamilton 5 HM CX
Bermuda
Tel: (010 1 809) 2952199
Fax: (010 1 809) 2950773
Telex: 3441 BFA BA
Cable: FOOTBALL BERMUDA
Languages for correspondence: English

Year of formation: 1928
Affiliation to FIFA: 1962
Affiliation to CONCACAF: 1966
Registered clubs: 23
Registered players: 1600
Registered Coaches: 9
Registered Referees: 39
National stadium: National Stadium, Hamilton 10 000
National colours: Shirts: Blue/Shorts: White/Socks: White
Reserve colours: Shirts: Red/Shorts: White/ Socks: White
Season: September–April

THE RECORD

WORLD CUP

1930–66 ..... Did not enter
1970 .... QT 1st round
1974–90 ..... Did not enter

OLYMPIC GAMES

1908–64 ..... Did not enter
1968 .... QT 2nd round
1972 .... QT 1st round
1976 .... QT 1st round
1980 .... QT 2nd round
1984 .... QT 1st round
1988 .... QT 1st round
1992 .... Did not enter

CUBA

Population: 10 603 000
Area, sq km: 110861
% in urban areas: 72%
Capital city: Havana 2 077 938

Asociacion de Futbol de Cuba
C/O Comite Olimpico Cubano
Calle 13 #601 Esq C. Vedado
La Habana ZP 4
Cuba
Tel: (010 53) 7403581
Fax: None
Telex: 511332 INDER CU
Cable: FOOTBALL HABANA
Languages for correspondence: Spanish

Year of formation: 1924
Affiliation to FIFA: 1932
Affiliation to CONCACAF: 1961
Registered clubs: 164
Registered players: 12 900
Registered referees: 160
National stadium: Juan Abrantes, Havana 18 000
National colours: Shirts: White/Shorts: Blue/Socks: White
Reserve colours: Shirts: Red/Shorts: White/ Socks: White
Season: July–November

THE RECORD

WORLD CUP

1930 .... Did not enter
1934 .... QT 2nd round
1938 .... QT W-O in group 9 – Final tournament/Quarter-finalists
1950 .... QT 3rd/3 in group 9
1954–62 ..... Did not enter
1966 .... QT 1st round
1970 .... Did not enter
1974 .... Did not enter
1978 .... QT 1st round
1982 .... QT 1st round
1986 .... Did not enter
1990 .... QT 1st round

OLYMPIC GAMES

1908–64 ..... Did not enter
1968 .... QT 2nd round
1972 .... Did not enter
1976 .... QT Qualified – Final tournament/1st round
1980 .... QT Qualified – Final tournament/Quarter-finalists
1984 .... QT 3rd round
1988 .... Did not enter
1992 .... QT pr round

CONCACAF Club Championship: Finalists – Piñar del Rio 1989, 1990

DOMINICAN REPUBLIC

Population: 7 170 000
Area, sq km: 48 443
% in urban areas: 60%
Capital city: Santo Domingo 1 600 000

Federacion Dominicana de Futbol
Apartado de Correos #1953
Santo Domingo
Dominican Republic
Tel: (010 1 809) 5426923
Fax: (010 1 809) 5359451
Telex: 817240
Cable: FEDOFUTBOL SANTO DOMINGO
Languages for correspondence: Spanish

Year of formation: 1953
Affiliation to FIFA: 1958
Affiliation to CONCACAF: 1964
Registered clubs: 200
Registered players: 2500
Registered referees: 64
National stadium: Olimpico Juan Pablo Duarte, Santo Domingo 30 000
National colours: Shirts: Blue/Shorts: White/Socks: Red
Reserve colours: Shirts: White/Shorts: White/Socks: Red
Season: March–December

The Record

WORLD CUP

1930–74 ..... Did not enter
1978 .... QT 1st round
1982–90 ..... Did not enter

OLYMPIC GAMES

1908–64 ..... Did not enter
1968 .... QT 1st round
1972 .... Did not enter
1976 .... QT pr round
1980 .... QT 1st round
1984 .... Did not enter
1988 .... QT 1st round
1992 .... Did not enter

GRENADA

Population: 101 000
Area, sq km: 345
Capital city: St George's 7000

Grenada Football Association
2 Hillsborough Street
PO Box 326
St George's
Grenada
Tel: (010 1 809) 4401986
Fax: (010 1 809) 4402123
Telex: 3431 CW BUR
Cable: GRENBALL GRENADA
Languages for correspondence: English

Year of formation: 1924
Affiliation to FIFA: 1976
Affiliation to CONCACAF: 1976
Registered clubs: 26
Registered players: 1000
Registered coaches: 9
Registered referees: 16
National stadium: Queen's Park, St George's 8000
National colours: Shirts: Green and Yellow Stripes/Shorts: Red/Socks: Green
Reserve colours: Shirts: Green/Shorts: Yellow/Socks: Red
Season: July–December

The Record

WORLD CUP

1930–78 ..... Did not enter
1982 .... QT 1st round
1986 .... Did not enter
1990 .... Did not enter

OLYMPIC GAMES

1908–92 ..... Did not enter

GUYANA

Population: 756 000
Area, sq km: 215 083
% in urban areas: 28%
Capital city: Georgetown 150 000

Guyana Football Association
PO Box 10727
Georgetown
Guyana
Tel: (010 592) 2 59454
Fax: (010 592) 2 52169
Telex: 2266 RICEBRD GY
Cable: FOOTBALL GUYANA
Languages for correspondence: English

Year of formation: 1904
Affiliation to FIFA: 1968
Affiliation to CONCACAF: 1969
Registered clubs: 34
Registered players: 1600
Registered coaches: 6
Registered referees: 40
National stadium: Cricket Club, Georgetown 15 000
National colours: Shirts: Green/Shorts: Green/Socks: Yellow
Reserve colours: Shirts: Yellow/Shorts: Green/Socks: Yellow
Season: March–December

The Record

WORLD CUP

1930–74 ..... Did not enter
1978 .... QT 1st round
1982 .... QT 1st round
1986 .... QT 1st round
1990 .... QT 1st round

OLYMPIC GAMES

1908–84 ..... Did not enter
1988 .... QT 2nd round
1992 .... Did not enter

HAITI

Population: 5 862 000
Area, sq km: 27 400
% in urban areas: 27%
Capital city: Port-au-Prince 514 000

Fédération Haitienne de Football
BP 2258
Stade Sylvio Cator
Port–au–Prince
Haiti
Tel: (010 509) 1 223237
Fax: None
Telex: None
Cable: FEDHAFOOB PORT-AU-PRINCE
Languages for correspondence: French

Year of formation: 1904
Affiliation to FIFA: 1933
Affiliation to CONCACAF: 1957
Registered clubs: 40
Registered players: 4000
Registered referees: 41
National stadium: Sylvio Cator 25 000
National colours: Shirts: Red/Shorts: Black/Socks: Red
Reserve colours: Shirts: White/Shorts: Black/Socks: Red
Season: November–May

The Record

WORLD CUP

1930 .... Did not enter
1934 .... QT 1st round
1938 .... Did not enter
1950 .... Did not enter
1954 .... QT 3rd/3 in group 11
1958–66 ..... Did not enter
1970 .... QT 3rd round
1974 .... QT Qualified – Final tournament/1st round
1978 .... QT 2nd round
1982 .... QT 2nd round
1986 .... QT 2nd round
1990 .... Did not enter

OLYMPIC GAMES

1908–64 ..... Did not enter
1968 .... QT 2nd round
1972 .... Did not enter
1976 .... Did not enter
1980 .... QT 3rd round
1984 .... Did not enter
1988 .... Did not enter
1992 .... QT 2nd round

CCCF Championship: Winners – 1957, 1973
CONCACAF Club Championship: Winners – Racing Club 1963. Violette 1984

JAMAICA

Population: 2 391 000
Area, sq km: 10 991
% in urban areas: 51%
Capital city: Kingston 524 000

Jamaica Football Federation
Room 8, INSPORTS
Independence Park
Kingston 6, Jamaica
Tel: (010 1 809) 9290483
Fax: (010 1 809) 9622858
Telex: 2224 FEDLASCO JA
Cable: FOOTBALL JAMAICA KINGSTON
Languages for correspondence: English
Year of formation: 1910
Affiliation to FIFA: 1962
Affiliation to CONCACAF: 1963
Registered clubs: 16

Registered players: 45 200
Registered referees: 122
National stadium: National Stadium, Kingston 40 000
National colours: Shirts: Green/Shorts: Black/Socks: Green
Reserve colours: Shirts: Gold/Shorts: Black/ Socks: Gold
Season: August–April

THE RECORD

WORLD CUP

1930–62 ..... Did not enter
1966 .... QT 2nd round
1970 .... QT 1st round
1974 .... Did not enter
1978 .... QT 1st round
1982 .... Did not enter
1986 .... Did not enter
1990 .... QT 2nd round

OLYMPIC GAMES

1908–68 ..... Did not enter
1972 .... Did not enter
1976 .... QT 2nd round
1980 .... QT 1st round
1984 .... QT pr round
1988 .... QT pr round
1992 .... QT 1st round

NETHERLANDS ANTILLES

Population: 196 000
Area, sq km: 800
% in urban areas: 92%
Capital city: Willemstad 125 000

Nederlands Antiliaanse Voetbal Unie
PO Box 341
Curacao
Netherlands Antilles
Tel: (010 599) 9 617960
Fax: (010 599) 9 617488
Telex: 1046 ENNIA NA
Cable: NAVU CURACAO
Languages for correspondence: English & Spanish

Year of formation: 1921
Affiliation to FIFA: 1932
Affiliation to CONCACAF: 1961
Registered clubs: 42
Registered players: 2800
Professional players: 300
Registered Coaches: 17
Registered Referees: 35
National stadium: Korsou, Curacao 12 000
National colours: Shirts: White with red and blue stripes/Shorts: White/Socks: Red
Reserve colours: Shirts: Blue/Shorts: Blue/ Socks: Red
Season: August–February

THE RECORD

WORLD CUP

1930–54 ..... Did not enter
1958 .... QT 1st round
1962 .... QT 2nd round
1966 .... QT 1st round
1970 .... QT 1st round
1974 .... QT 2nd round
1978 .... QT 1st round
1982 .... QT 1st round
1986 .... QT 1st round
1990 .... QT 2nd round

OLYMPIC GAMES

1908–48 ..... Did not enter
1952 .... 1st round
1956 .... Did not enter
1960 .... QT 1st round
1964 .... QT 1st round
1968 .... QT 2nd round
1972 .... QT 1st round
1976 .... Did not enter
1980 .... QT 1st round
1984 .... Did not enter
1988 .... Did not enter
1992 .... QT pr round

CONCACAF Club Championship: Finalists – Jong Colombia 1967, 1979

PUERTO RICO

Population: 3 336 000
Area, sq km: 9104
% in urban areas: 70%
Capital city: San Juan 431 000

Federacion Puertorriquena de Futbol
Coliseo Roberto Clemente
PO Box 4355
Hato Rey, 00919–4355
Puerto Rica
Tel: (010 1 809) 7642025
Fax: (010 1 809) 7642025
Telex: 0206 3450296
Cable: BORIKENFPF
Languages for correspondence: Spanish & English

Year of formation: 1940
Affiliation to FIFA: 1960
Affiliation to CONCACAF: 1962
Registered clubs: 175
Registered players: 4200
Registered referees: 135
National stadium: Sixto Escobar, San Juan 12 000
National colours: Shirts: Red and White stripes/Shorts: Blue/Socks: Blue
Reserve colours: Shirts: White/Shorts: Blue/Socks: Red
Season: March–June

THE RECORD

WORLD CUP

1930–70 ..... Did not enter
1974 .... QT 1st round
1978 .... Did not enter
1982 .... Did not enter
1986 .... QT 1st round
1990 .... QT 1st round

OLYMPIC GAMES

1908–88 ..... Did not enter
1992 .... QT pr round

SAINT LUCIA

Population: 151 000
Area, sq km: 617
% in urban areas: 46%
Capital city: Castries 55 000

St. Lucia National Football Union
PO Box 255
Castries
St. Lucia
Tel: (010 1 809) 31519
Fax: (010 1 809) 31614
Telex: 6394 FOR AFF LC
Cable: NFU ST LUCIA
Languages for correspondence: English

Year of formation: Unknown
Affiliation to FIFA: 1988
Affiliation to CONCACAF: 1988
Registered clubs: 100
Registered players: 4000
National colours: Shirts: Blue and white stripes/Shorts: Black/ Socks: Blue

THE RECORD

WORLD CUP

1930–90 ..... Did not enter

OLYMPIC GAMES

1908–88 ..... Did not enter
1992 .... QT 1st round

SAINT VINCENT AND THE GRENADINES

Population: 115 000
Area, sq km: 389
% in urban areas: 25%
Capital city: Kingstown 19 000

St Vincent and the Grenadines Football Federation
PO Box 1278
Kingstown
St Vincent
Languages for correspondence: English

Affiliation to FIFA: 1988
Affiliation to CONCACAF: 1988
Registered clubs: 500
Registered players: 5000

THE RECORD

WORLD CUP

1930–90 ..... Did not enter

OLYMPIC GAMES

1908–92 ..... Did not enter

SURINAM

Population: 411 000
Area, sq km: 163 820
% in urban areas: 65%
Capital city: Paramaribo 67 000

Surinaamse Voetbal Bond
Cultuuruinlaan 7
PO Box 1223
Paramaribo
Suriname
Tel: (010 597) 73112
Fax: None
Telex: None
Cable: SVB PARAMARIBO
Languages for correspondence: English & French

Year of formation: 1920
Affiliation to FIFA: 1929
Affiliation to CONCACAF: 1961
Registered clubs: 42
Registered players: 16 300
Registered coaches: 56
Registered referees: 218
National stadium: Surinam Stadion, Paramaribo 21 000
National colours: Shirts: Red/Shorts: White/Socks: White
Reserve colours: Shirts: Green/Shorts: Green/Socks: Green
Season: March–December

THE RECORD

WORLD CUP

1930–58 ..... Did not enter
1962 .... QT 1st round
1966 .... QT 1st round
1970 .... QT 1st round
1974 .... QT 1st round
1978 .... QT 2nd round
1982 .... QT 1st round
1986 .... QT 2nd round
1990 .... Did not enter

OLYMPIC GAMES

1908–56 ..... Did not enter
1960 .... QT 2nd round
1964 .... QT 2nd round
1968 .... QT 1st round
1972 .... QT 1st round
1976 .... QT 2nd round
1980 .... QT 4th round
1984 .... QT 1st round
1988 .... Did not enter
1992 .... QT 2nd round

CONCACAF Club Championship:
Winners – Transvaal 1970, 1973, 1981
Finalists – Transvaal 1974, 1975, 1986. Robin Hood 1972, 1976, 1977, 1982, 1983

TRINIDAD AND TOBAGO

Population: 1 233 000
Area, sq km: 5128
% in urban areas: 51%
Capital city: Port of Spain 58 000

Trinidad and Tobago Football Association
Cor. Duke & Scott, Bushe Street
PO Box 400
Port of Spain
Trinidad
Tel: (010 1 809) 6245183
Fax: (010 1 809) 6277661
Telex: 22652 TRAFA
Cable: TRAFA PORT OF SPAIN
Languages for correspondence: English

Year of formation: 1906
Affiliation to FIFA: 1963
Affiliation to CONCACAF: 1964
Registered clubs: 114
Registered players: 4900
Registered coaches: 114
Registered referees: 296
National stadium: Queen's Park Oval, Port of Spain 25 000
National colours: Shirts: Red/Shorts: Black/Socks: Red
Reserve colours: Shirts: Black/Shorts: Red/Socks: Black
Season: January–December

THE RECORD

WORLD CUP

1930–62 ..... Did not enter
1966 .... QT 1st round
1970 .... QT 1st round
1974 .... QT 2nd round
1978 .... QT 1st round
1982 .... QT 1st round
1986 .... QT 2nd round
1990 .... QT 3rd round

OLYMPIC GAMES

1908–64 ..... Did not enter
1968 .... QT 3rd round
1972 .... Did not enter
1976 .... QT 1st round
1980 .... QT 2nd round
1984 .... QT 2nd round
1988 .... QT 2nd round
1992 .... QT 2nd round

CONCACAF Club Championship:
Winners – Defence Force 1978, 1985
Finalists – Defence Force 1987, 1988, Police Force 1991

ASIA

South Korea v Bulgaria, World Cup 1986

ASIA

Considering that Asia contains over half of the world's population, it has made a surprisingly feeble impact on football at world level. Within Asia itself, however, the game thrives with a multitude of tournaments and events. Some countries, however, are more keen than others. The two biggest, China and India, who between them account for 2 billion of the 5 billion people on this earth, have shown little interest, whilst the Middle East, backed up by large oil revenues, has taken to the game in a big way.

Football is largely a post-war phenomenon, and has had to fight off competition from other sports. Cricket and hockey remain the main passions for the people of the Indian sub-continent, whilst American influence in the Far East has meant the widespread popularity of baseball most notably in Japan, Korea, Taiwan and the Philippines.

Due to the weakness of club football in all bar a few countries, the national sides are often the focus of the game, and there are plenty of tournaments to occupy their time. The two main ones are the Asian Cup, started in 1956, and the football tournament of the Asian Games, first played in 1951. There is also a vast array of non-AFC sponsored events, the most notable of which are the Merdeka Cup organised by the FA of Malaysia since 1957 and the President's Cup held in South Korea since 1971.

The first international match on Asian soil dates back to February 1913 in Manila. As part of the Far Eastern Games, the Philippines challenged China to a match which they won 2–1. Two years later in Shanghai a second game was played which China this time won. Japan then joined in for the third Games in Tokyo but were beaten so heavily by both China and the Philippines that they did not enter the fourth tournament. From the 1921 Games in Shanghai, all three countries entered until the final edition in 1934, but on only one occasion, in 1930 when Japan shared the title with the Chinese, did the latter not emerge as outright winners.

Football was played elsewhere in Asia at this time as both English and French colonists introduced the game. India, for example, has a national football federation dating from 1937 and a league in Calcutta dating from 1898, before even most Europeans had organised one. Other countries too had some semblance of organised football and by 1940, seventeen had a national football association. The game remained marginalised and small scale throughout the continent, however, and was mainly played by the numerous foreigners resident.

In 1951 the first progress was made when India organised the first Asian Games. Eleven nations gathered in the newly constructed New Dehli National Stadium on 4 March 1951. Six of these countries had brought teams for the football tournament, but it was no surprise that the standard of the football played was not of the highest quality.

With home advantage India were obvious favourites as of all the nations taking part they had the most organised football set-up. They dispatched Indonesia in the opening round with some ease and Afghanistan in the semi-final. In the final the Indians met Iran and were extremely lucky to win, relying on a fine defensive display and an opportunist goal by Mewalal four minutes into the second half. It is interesting to note that in these early years of Asian football, most games were played over 80 and not 90 minutes.

The second Asian Games in Manila built upon the success of the first and the football tournament doubled in size. The tournament opened in spectacular style in the newly built Rizal Memorial stadium with a 3–3 draw between South Korea and Hong Kong, two of the strongest sides who had unfortunately been drawn together in the same group. South Korea won the group and reached the final at their first attempt. In later years they would be a familar sight fighting it out in a final and losing, as they did on this occasion.

Taiwan won the tournament but this did not reflect the standard of the football in that country. The side consisted exclusively of players from Hong Kong who chose to represent a team that was simply labelled 'China'. At that time the Football Association in Taipei claimed responsibility for football on mainland China and this theoretically included Hong Kong.

The Taiwan issue was to be a major focus of attention in Asia over the years, but in Manila they were worthy winners. The Games also saw the birth of the Asian Football Confederation. Delegates travelling with Afghanistan, Burma, Hong Kong, India, Indonesia, Japan, the Republic of Korea, Malaysia, Pakistan, the Philippines, Singapore, Taiwan and the Republic of Vietnam put in place an organisation that was to play a key role in the development of the game on the continent.

The first task the AFC undertook was to organise a championship of their own. Unlike the football tournament of the Asian Games, the Asian Cup as it was called was open to both amateurs and professionals, though in reality this has never been an issue given the tiny number of professional Asian footballers. Also unlike the Asian Games, qualifying groups were organised on a geographical basis to produce four finalists.

Hong Kong was awarded the staging of the first tournament in 1956 given its pioneering role in founding the Asian Confederation. Along with Israel they did not have to play any games to qualify. The hosts were given a bye, but in Israel's case both Pakistan and Afghanistan refused to play them, setting the tone for what what was to be, along with Taiwan, the AFC's second pressing problem.

The finals were very well attended by an enthusiastic Hong Kong public who gathered in the Government Stadium for the six matches which were played totally on a league basis. Hong Kong opened the tournament with a game against Israel which they were unlucky to lose, but Israel were generally disappointing, and much more was expected of them. In the crucial game with South Korea they were 2–0 down before they started to test the Koreans but by then it was too late.

The pattern was set for future years. With both the Asian Cup and the football tournament of the Asian Games occurring every four years, Asia in effect had a continental championship every two years.

In Tokyo in 1958 the Asian Games began to lose their innocence. In all of the sports there were acrimonious accusations of biased refereeing as well as sheer incompetence on the part of the officials. Football did not escape, but despite the referees, the standard of the play continued to improve. For the second Games on the trot it was the Taiwanese and the Koreans who contested the final, and again it was won by Taiwan, who as in 1954 were represented by footballers based in Hong Kong.

The fourth Games in Djakarta, Indonesia in 1962 were again the scene of bitter confrontations, not on the pitch but among the administrators. Indonesia's decision to rescind the invitations to Taiwan and Israel had the Indian delegation up in arms; they even tried to have the name changed from the Asian Games, arguing that they were nothing of the sort. Taiwan's absence meant that the football tournament was without the reigning champions, but still South Korea could not take advantage and win the tournament for the first time. After again playing the best football in the tournament, they lost their third final in a row, this time to the champions of the first tournament, India.

Taiwan and Israel continued to pose the authorities problems until they were both expelled from the AFC in 1975. Nowhere was this more evident than at the 1974 Asian Games in Tehran. Israel reached the final thanks to both North Korea and Kuwait's refusal to play them in the semi-final group. As the Arab nations joined the AFC, sheer force of numbers weighed against Israel, who have since wandered the world in search of a footballing home. Taiwan on the other hand have recently been accepted back into the fold.

The South Koreans have always been the strongest nation in Asia along with Iran, and these two countries dominated the Asian Cup until the 1980 edition. The Koreans won the first two editions, the second of which was at home in 1960. The number of entrants increased from 7 to 11, but the formula for the final tournament remained the same as in the first edition. It was not until 1972 that it was changed. As the number of entrants continued to grow, the league system was replaced with a combination of league and knock-out, and it now consists of eight teams divided into two groups of four, from which four teams qualify for the semi-finals.

Played in Seoul's Hyochang Park Stadium, the crucial game of the 1960 tournament was again the South Korea–Israel encounter. In an example of how popular the game was becoming, the match witnessed chaotic scenes. The ground was overlooked by a hill which in effect doubled the capacity to 40 000, and still boisterous fans broke down gates and overran the police to gain access to the stadium. The Korean Prime Minister, attending the game as guest of honour, was even forced to leave during the first half because he could not see! Israel, who were still regarded as the strongest side in Asia, could not resist the Koreans who ran out 3–0 winners.

The third Asian Cup was the poorest tournament of the first three. Though played to big crowds in Haifa, Jerusalem, Jaffa and Ramat Gan, the standard of football was certainly not as high as it had been in Seoul four years previously. Sir Stanley Rous, attending the tournament on FIFA's behalf, also commented on the relatively poor levels of sportsmanship shown by the teams. Israel in purely practical terms was not a wise choice of venue, coming hard on the heels of the furore at the Asian Games in Djakarta.

That they won was partly due to the fact that the holders South Korea did not send their strongest team. That was kept at home for the Olympic qualifying game against

ASIAN CUP HONOURS

	Country	G	S	B	Finals	Semis
1	Iran	3	–	2	2	5
2	South Korea	2	3	1	3	3
3	Saudi Arabia	2	–	–	2	2
4	Israel	1	2	1	–	–
5	Kuwait	1	1	1	2	3
6	China	–	1	1	1	3
7	Myanmar	–	1	–	–	–
	India	–	1	–	–	–
9	Hong Kong	–	–	1	–	–
	Taiwan	–	–	1	–	–
	Thailand	–	–	1	–	1
12	North Korea	–	–	–	–	1
	Iraq	–	–	–	–	1
	Cambodia	–	–	–	–	1

South Vietnam which was being played at the same time in Seoul. The decisive game of the tournament was played between India and Israel early on, but if the Koreans had beaten Israel by three clear goals in the final match before 40 000 spectators in Ramat Gan, they would have won the title for the third time in succession. Instead Israel won 2–1 to take the title and the Koreans had to settle for third place.

The 1960s saw the rise of Iran as the major power. They succeeded in achieving what the South Koreans failed to do, winning three Asian Cups in a row, in 1968, 1972 and 1976. In addition to this they appeared in the final of the 1966 Asian Games and won the gold medal in 1974. To cap over a decade of success they made the journey to Argentina for the 1978 World Cup, before the fall of the Shah the following year brought a temporary end to their period of dominance. Their Asian Cup success was remarkable in that they won every single match they played in the competition from 1968 to 1976. Even since then their record has been good and in the three tournaments played they have reached the semi-finals on each occasion.

In the late 1960s Burma (now Myanmar) was on the verge of challenging the supremacy of Iran and Korea, winning the Asian Games twice and finishing runners-up to Iran in the 1968 Asian Cup, but the military regime then clamped down on contacts with the outside world and the country has been in isolation since.

The 1970s saw a major shift in the balance of power in Asia. Petrodollars encouraged the emergence of the Arab nations of the Middle East. The Gulf states were soon spending massive amounts of money on facilities and coaches, and by the end of the decade the results were beginning to show. Kuwait reached the 1976 Asian Cup final and in 1980 they won the title. Two years later in the Asian Games they reached their third final before losing to neighbours Iraq.

Saudi Arabia were also becoming a force and in 1984 and 1988 they confirmed their supremacy by winning the Asian Cup. Oil revenues were the telling factor. Of the four Asian countries who have qualified for the World Cup since 1982, three have been oil-rich Gulf States: Kuwait, Iraq and the United Arab Emirates. Only South Korea, who have continued to be strong throughout the years, have managed to break the monopoly.

In the future China will undoubtedly emerge as the strongest force on the continent if not the world. Sheer force of numbers indicates that this is likely to be the case. After years of isolation due to the presence of Taiwan in the AFC, China joined that body in 1974 and then FIFA in 1979.

Those who expected China to make an immediate impact were disappointed. In three attempts they have failed to qualify for the World Cup, and although they have reached three semi-finals in the Asian Cup, the title still eludes them. As coaching methods become more widespread and more experience is gained, they should still pose a threat for the future.

The overall level of the game in Asia continues to lag behind the rest of the world, a fact recognised by FIFA when it awarded an extra place to Africa for the 1994 World Cup but not to Asia. With so many tournaments played, this is something of a mystery. According to one commentator the problems can be attributed to 'finance, diet, religious customs, political infighting, corruption and administrative imcompetence', but many of these problems exist elsewhere in the world.

Asia perhaps faces the hardest job of any continent in establishing itself as a force to be reckoned with, and at the present time it is not succeeding very well. There is a strong case for dividing Asia up into Middle East, Central Asia and Far East given the huge distances involved in travelling to games, an idea that will be reinforced as the Central Asian states of the former Soviet Union swell the numbers of the AFC even further. From Seoul to Riyadh and Alma Ata to Hong Kong: it does not make much sense to have everything under one regional confederation.

ASIAN GOVERNING BODY

ASIAN FOOTBALL CONFEDERATION
Wisma Olympic Council of Malaysia
1st Jalan Hang Jebat
50150 Kuala Lumpur
Malaysia
Tel: (010 60) 3 2384860
Fax: (010 60) 3 2384861
Telex: MA 30837 AFC
Cable: AFC KUALA LUMPUR

Year of formation: 1954

Members: 33
Afghanistan – Bahrain – Bangladesh – Brunei – China – Chinese Taipei – Hong Kong – India – Indonesia – Iran – Iraq – Japan – Jordan – North Korea – South Korea – Kuwait – Lebanon – Macao – Malaysia – Maldives – Myanmar – Nepal – Oman – Pakistan – Philippines – Qatar – Saudi Arabia – Singapore – Sri Lanka – Syria – Thailand – United Arab Emirates – Yemen

Members of FIFA but not of the AFC: 3
Kampuchea – Laos – Vietnam

Provisional Members: 1
Guam

Non Members: 2
Bhutan – Mongolia

THE ASIAN CUP

1956	South Korea	2–1*	Isreal
1960	South Korea	3–0*	Isreal
1964	Isreal	2–0*	India
1968	Iran	3–1*	Burma
1972	Iran	2–1	South Korea
1976	Iran	1–0	Kuwait
1980	Kuwait	3–0	South Korea
1984	Saudi Arabia	2–0	China
1988	Saudi Arabia	0–0 (4–3p)	South Korea

* As the tournament was decided on a league basis, technically there was no final tie. The matches listed are those between the first and second placed teams.

FIRST EDITION
1956

QUALIFYING COMPETITION

Group 1

ISRAEL qualified after Afghanistan and Pakistan withdrew

Group 2

1 SOUTH KOREA
2 TAIWAN
3 PHILIPPINES

Group 3

1 SOUTH VIETNAM
2 MALAYSIA
3 CAMBODIA

HONG KONG qualify as hosts

FINAL TOURNAMENT
Hong Kong, 1st–15th September

	SK	Is	HK	SV	Pl	W	D	L	F	A	Pts
South Korea	–	2–1	2–2	5–3	3	2	1	0	9	6	5
Israel	–	–	3–2	2–1	3	2	0	1	6	5	4
Hong Kong	–	–	–	2–2	3	0	2	1	6	7	2
South Vietnam	–	–	–	–	3	0	1	2	6	9	1

Government Stadium, Hong Kong, 8–09–1956, 25 000
SOUTH KOREA 2 (Woo Sang-Koon 53, Soung Rak-woon 65)
ISRAEL 1 (Stelmach 71)

SECOND EDITION
1960

QUALIFYING COMPETITION

Group 1
Tournament in Calcutta and Cochin

1 ISRAEL
2 IRAN
3 PAKISTAN
4 INDIA

Group 2
Tournament in Singapore

	SV	Ma	Si	Pl	W	D	L	F	A	Pts
SOUTH VIETNAM	–	1–0	4–1	2	2	0	0	5	1	4
MALAYSIA	–	–	5–2	2	1	0	1	5	3	2
SINGAPORE	–	–	–	2	0	0	2	3	9	0

Group 3
Tournament in Manilla

Winners – TAIWAN

SOUTH KOREA qualified as hosts

FINAL TOURNAMENT
South Korea, 14th–23rd October 1960

	SK	Is	Ta	SV	Pl	W	D	L	F	A	Pts
South Korea	–	3–0	1–0	5–1	3	3	0	0	9	1	6
Israel	–	–	1–0	5–1	3	2	0	1	6	4	4
Taiwan	–	–	–	3–1	3	1	0	2	3	3	2
South Vietnam	–	–	–	–	3	0	0	3	3	13	0

Deciding game. Hyochang Park, Seoul, 17–10–1960, 20 000
SOUTH KOREA 3
ISRAEL 0

THIRD EDITION
1964

QUALIFYING COMPETITION

Group 1	*Group 2*	*Group 3*
INDIA	HONG KONG	SOUTH KOREA

ISRAEL qualify as hosts

FINAL TOURNAMENT
Israel, 26th May–3rd June 1964

	Is	In	SK	HK	Pl	W	D	L	F	A	Pts
Israel	–	2–0	2–1	1–0	3	3	0	0	5	1	6
India	–	–	2–0	3–1	3	2	0	1	5	3	4
South Korea	–	–	–	1–0	3	1	0	2	2	4	2
Hong Kong	–	–	–	–	3	0	0	3	1	5	0

Deciding game. Bloomfield, Tel-Aviv, 29–05–64, 20 000
ISRAEL 2 (Spiegler 27, Aharoni 77)
INDIA 0

FOURTH EDITION
1968

QUALIFYING COMPETITION

Group 1
Tournament in Burma

	Bu	Ca	Pa	In	Pl	W	D	L	F	A	Pts
BURMA	–	1–0	2–0	2–0	3	3	0	0	5	0	6
CAMBODIA	–	–	1–0	3–1	3	2	0	1	4	2	4
PAKISTAN	–	–	–	1–1	3	0	1	2	1	4	1
INDIA	–	–	–	–	3	0	1	2	2	6	1

Group 2
Tournament in Hong Kong

	HK	Th	SV	Ma	Si	Pl	W	D	L	F	A	Pts
HONG KONG	–	2–0	2–0	3–1	2–0	4	4	0	0	9	1	8
THAILAND	–	–	0–1	1–0	4–1	4	2	0	2	5	4	4
SOUTH VIETNAM	–	–	–	0–2	3–0	4	2	0	2	4	4	4
MALAYSIA	–	–	–	–	1–1	4	1	1	2	4	5	3
SINGAPORE	–	–	–	–	–	4	0	1	3	2	10	1

Group 3

Tournament in Taipei

	Ta	Ja	SK	In	Ph	Pl	W	D	L	F	A	Pts
TAIWAN	–	2–2	1–0	3–2	9–0	4	3	1	0	15	4	7
JAPAN	–	–	2–1	2–1	2–0	4	3	1	0	8	4	7
SOUTH KOREA	–	–	–	1–1	7–0	4	1	1	2	9	4	3
INDONESIA	–	–	–	–	6–0	4	1	1	2	10	6	3
PHILIPPINES	–	–	–	–	–	4	0	0	4	0	24	0

IRAN qualified as hosts

ISRAEL qualified as holders

FINAL TOURNAMENT

Iran, 10th–19th May 1968

	Ir	Bu	Is	Ta	HK	Pl	W	D	L	F	A	Pts
Iran	–	3–1	2–1	4–0	2–0	4	4	0	0	11	2	8
Burma	–	–	1–0	1–1	2–0	4	2	1	1	5	4	5
Israel	–	–	–	4–1	6–1	4	2	0	2	11	5	4
Taiwan	–	–	–	–	1–1	4	0	2	2	3	10	2
Hong Kong	–	–	–	–	–	4	0	1	3	2	11	1

Deciding game. Amjadieh, Tehran, 16–05–1968, 30000

IRAN 3 (I Kalani 2, Bahzadi)

BURMA 1 (Aung Khin 49)

FIFTH EDITION
1972

QUALIFYING COMPETITION

Group 1

Winners – IRAQ

Group 2

Winners – KUWAIT

Group 3

Winners – CAMBODIA

Group 4

Winners – SOUTH KOREA

THAILAND qualified as hosts

IRAN qualified as holders

FINAL TOURNAMENT

Thailand, 7th–19th May 1972

PRELIMINARY GAMES

South Korea .... 0–0 .... Iraq

Iran .... 2–0 .... Cambodia

Kuwait .... 2–0 .... Thailand

FIRST ROUND

Group 1

	Ir	Th	Iq	Pl	W	D	L	F	A	Pts
Iran	–	3–2	3–0	2	2	0	0	6	2	4
Thailand	–	–	1–1	2	0	1	1	3	4	1
Iraq	–	–	–	2	0	1	1	1	4	1

Group 2

	SK	Ca	Ku	Pl	W	D	L	F	A	Pts
South Korea	–	4–1	1–2	2	1	0	1	5	3	2
Cambodia	–	–	4–0	2	1	0	1	5	4	2
Kuwait	–	–	–	2	1	0	1	2	5	2

SEMI-FINALS

Iran .... 2–1 .... Cambodia

South Korea .... 1–1 (2–1p) ..... Thailand

3RD PLACE

Thailand .... 2–2 (5–3p) ..... Cambodia

FINAL

Suphachalasai, Bangkok, 19–05–1972, 8000

IRAN 2 (Jabary 48, Khalany 107)

SOUTH KOREA 1 (Lee Whae–taek 65)

SIXTH EDITION
1976

QUALIFYING COMPETITION

Group 1

KUWAIT and SOUTH YEMEN qualified. Bahrain, Lebanon, Pakistan and Syria withdrew

Group 2

Tournament in Baghdad

	Iq	SA	Qa	Af	Pl	W	D	L	F	A	Pts
IRAQ	–	1–1	1–0	3–1	6	5	1	0	14	3	11
SAUDI ARABIA	1–2	–	2–1	2–0	6	3	1	2	12	5	7
QATAR	0–3	1–0	–	2–1	6	2	1	3	5	8	5
AFGHANISTAN	0–4	0–6	1–1	–	6	0	1	5	3	18	1

Group 3

Tournament in Bangkok

	Ma	Th	SK	In	SV	Pl	W	D	L	F	A	Pts
MALAYSIA	–	1–0	2–1	0–0	3–0	4	3	1	0	6	1	7
THAILAND	–	–	1–0	3–1	4–0	4	3	0	1	8	2	6
SOUTH KOREA	–	–	–	1–0	1–0	4	2	0	2	3	3	4
INDONESIA	–	–	–	–	2–1	4	1	1	2	3	5	3
SOUTH VIETNAM	–	–	–	–	–	4	0	0	4	1	10	0

Group 4

Tournament in Hong Kong

FIRST ROUND

	Ch	HK	NK	Ja	Si	Br	Pl	W	D	L	F	A	Pts
China	–	1–0	1–0	–	–	10–1	3	3	0	0	12	1	6
Hong Kong	–	–	–	0–0*	–	3–0	3	2	0	1	3	1	4
North Korea	–	–	–	1–0	1–0	–	3	2	0	1	2	1	4
Japan	–	–	–	–	2–1	–	3	1	0	2	2	2	2
Singapore	–	–	–	–	–	6–0	3	1	0	2	7	3	2
Brunei	–	–	–	–	–	–	3	0	0	3	1	19	0

* Hong Kong won 4–3 on penalties

SEMI-FINALS

China .... 2–1 .... Japan

North Korea .... 3–3 (11–10p) ... Hong Kong

FINAL
NORTH KOREA .... 2–0 .... CHINA

IRAN qualified as hosts and holders

FINAL TOURNAMENT
Iran, 3rd–13th June 1976

North Korea, Saudi Arabia and Thailand withdrew

FIRST ROUND

Group 1

	Ku	Ch	Ma	Pl	W	D	L	F	A	Pts
Kuwait	–	1–0	2–0	2	2	0	0	3	0	4
China	–	–	1–1	2	0	1	1	1	2	1
Malaysia	–	–	–	2	0	1	1	1	3	1

Group 2

	Ir	Iq	SY	Pl	W	D	L	F	A	Pts
Iran	–	2–0	8–0	2	2	0	0	10	0	4
Iraq	–	–	1–0	2	1	0	1	1	2	2
South Yemen	–	–	–	2	0	0	2	0	9	0

SEMI-FINAL
Iran .... 2–0 .... China
Kuwait .... 3–2 .... Iraq

3RD PLACE
China .... 1–0 .... Iraq

FINAL
Azadi, Tehran, 13–06–1976
IRAN 1
KUWAIT 0

SEVENTH EDITION
1980

QUALIFYING COMPETITION

Group 1
Tournament in Abu Dhabi

1 ARAB EMIRATES
2 SYRIA
3 BAHRAIN
4 LEBANON

Group 2
Tournament in Dacca
1 QATAR
2 BANGLADESH
3 AFGHANISTAN

Group 3
Tournament in Bangkok

PRELIMINARY GAMES
Thailand .... 3–1 .... Indonesia
Malaysia .... 3–1 .... Sri Lanka
North Korea .... 3–0 .... Hong Kong

Group 1

	Ma	NK	In	Pl	W	D	L	F	A	Pts
Malaysia	–	1–1	4–1	2	1	1	0	5	2	3
North Korea	–	–	3–1	2	1	1	0	4	2	3
Indonesia	–	–	–	2	0	0	2	2	7	0

Group 2

	Th	HK	SL	Si	Pl	W	D	L	F	A	Pts
Thailand	–	1–0	4–0	4–0	3	3	0	0	9	0	6
Hong Kong	–	–	5–0	3–1	3	2	0	1	8	2	4
Sri Lanka	–	–	–	4–0	3	1	0	2	4	9	2
Singapore	–	–	–	–	3	0	0	3	1	11	0

SEMI-FINALS
Malaysia .... 0–0 (5–4p) ..... Hong Kong
North Korea .... 1–0 .... Thailand

3RD PLACE
Hong Kong .... 2–1 .... Thailand

FINAL
NORTH KOREA .... 1–0 .... MALAYSIA

Group 4
Tournament in Manila

	SK	Ch	Ma	Ph	Pl	W	D	L	F	A	Pts
SOUTH KOREA	–	1–0	4–1	5–0	3	3	0	0	10	1	6
CHINA	–	–	2–1	5–0	3	2	0	1	7	2	4
MACAO	–	–	–	2–1	3	1	0	2	4	7	2
PHILIPPINES	–	–	–	–	3	0	0	3	1	12	0

KUWAIT qualified as hosts

IRAN qualified as holders

FINAL TOURNAMENT
Kuwait, 15th–30th September 1980

FIRST ROUND

Group 1

	Ir	NK	Sy	Ch	Ba	Pl	W	D	L	F	A	Pts
Iran	–	3–2	0–0	2–2	7–0	4	2	2	0	12	4	6
North Korea	–	–	2–1	2–1	3–2	4	3	0	1	9	7	6
Syria	–	–	–	1–0	1–0	4	2	1	0	3	2	5
China	–	–	–	–	6–0	4	1	1	2	9	5	3
Bangladesh	–	–	–	–	–	4	0	0	4	2	17	0

Group 2

	SK	Ku	Ma	Qa	Em	Pl	W	D	L	F	A	Pts
South Korea	–	3–0	1–1	2–0	4–1	4	3	1	0	10	2	7
Kuwait	–	–	3–1	4–0	1–1	4	2	1	1	8	5	5
Malaysia	–	–	–	1–1	2–0	4	1	2	1	5	5	4
Qatar	–	–	–	–	2–1	4	1	1	2	3	8	3
Arab Emirates	–	–	–	–	–	4	0	1	3	3	9	1

SEMI-FINALS
Kuwait .... 2–1 .... Iran
South Korea .... 2–1 .... North Korea

3RD PLACE
Iran .... 3–0 .... North Korea

FINAL
Kuwait City, 28–09–1980
KUWAIT 3
SOUTH KOREA 0

EIGHTH EDITION
1984

QUALIFYING COMPETITION

Group 1
Tournament in Jakarta
1 IRAN
2 SYRIA
3 INDONESIA
4 THAILAND
5 BANGLADESH
6 PHILIPPINES

Group 2
Tournament in Jeddah
1 SAUDI ARABIA
2 ARAB EMIRATES
3 OMAN
4 SRI LANKA
5 NEPAL

Group 3
Tournament in Calcutta

	SK	In	Ma	Pa	NY	Pl	W	D	L	F	A	Pts
SOUTH KOREA	–	1–0	0–0	6–0	6–0	4	3	1	0	13	0	7
INDIA	–	–	2–1	2–0	4–0	4	3	0	1	8	2	6
Malaysia	–	–	–	5–0	4–1	4	2	1	1	10	3	5
Pakistan	–	–	–	–	4–1	4	1	0	3	4	14	2
North Yemen	–	–	–	–	–	4	0	0	4	2	18	0

Group 4
Tournament in Guangzhou

	Ch	Qa	Jo	HK	Af	Pl	W	D	L	F	A	Pts
CHINA	–	1–0	6–0	2–0	6–0	4	4	0	0	15	0	8
QATAR	–	–	2–0	1–0	8–0	4	3	0	1	11	1	6
Jordan	–	–	–	1–1	6–1	4	1	1	2	7	10	3
Hong Kong	–	–	–	–	0–0	4	0	2	2	1	4	2
Afghanistan	–	–	–	–	–	4	0	1	3	1	20	1

SINGAPORE qualified as hosts

KUWAIT qualified as holders

FINAL TOURNAMENT
Singapore, 1st–1th December 1984

FIRST ROUND

Group 1

	SA	Ku	Qa	Sy	SK	Pl	W	D	L	F	A	Pts
Saudi Arabia	–	1–0	1–1	1–0	1–1	4	2	2	0	4	2	6
Kuwait	–	–	1–0	3–1	0–0	4	2	1	1	4	2	5
Qatar	–	–	–	1–1	1–0	4	1	2	1	3	3	4
Syria	–	–	–	–	1–0	4	1	1	2	3	5	3
South Korea	–	–	–	–	–	4	0	2	2	1	3	2

Group 2

	Ch	Ir	Em	Si	In	Pl	W	D	L	F	A	Pts
China	–	0–2	5–0	2–0	3–0	4	3	0	1	10	2	6
Iran	–	–	3–0	1–1	0–0	4	2	2	0	6	1	6
UAE	–	–	–	1–0	2–0	4	2	0	2	3	8	4
Singapore	–	–	–	–	2–0	4	1	1	2	3	4	3
India	–	–	–	–	–	4	0	1	3	0	7	1

SEMI-FINALS

Saudi Arabia .... 1–1 (5–4p) ..... Iran
China .... 1–0 .... Kuwait

3RD PLACE

Kuwait .... 1–1 (5–3p) ..... Iran

FINAL

National Stadium, Singapore, 16–12–1984, 40000
SAUDI ARABIA 2 (Shaye Nafisah 10, Majed Abdullah 47)
CHINA 0

NINTH EDITION
1988

QUALIFYING COMPETITION

Group 1
Tournament in Abu Dhabi

	Ch	NY	Th	Ba	In	Pl	W	D	L	F	A	Pts
ARAB EMIRATES	0–0	2–1	3–0	4–0	3–0	5	4	1	0	12	1	9
CHINA	–	0–0	5–0	4–0	1–1	5	2	3	0	10	1	7
North Yemen	–	–	3–3	0–0	1–0	5	1	3	1	5	5	5
Thailand	–	–	–	1–1	1–0	5	1	2	2	5	12	4
Bangladesh	–	–	–	–	0–0	5	0	3	2	1	9	3
India	–	–	–	–	–	5	0	2	3	1	6	2

Group 2
Tournament in Kuala Lumpur

	Ku	Ja	Jo	Ma	Pa	Pl	W	D	L	F	A	Pts
KUWAIT	–	1–0	0–0	5–0	3–0	4	3	1	0	9	0	7
JAPAN	–	–	1–1	1–0	4–1	4	2	1	1	6	3	5
Jordan	–	–	–	0–0	1–0	4	1	3	0	2	1	5
Malaysia	–	–	–	–	4–0	4	1	1	2	4	6	3
Pakistan	–	–	–	–	–	4	0	0	4	1	12	0

Group 3
Tournament in Katmandu

	Sy	Ir	NK	HK	Ne	Pl	W	D	L	F	A	Pts
SYRIA	–	1–1	2–1	2–0	3–0	4	3	1	0	8	2	7
IRAN	–	–	0–0	2–0	3–0	4	2	2	0	6	1	6
North Korea	–	–	–	1–0	1–0	4	2	1	1	3	2	5
Hong Kong	–	–	–	–	0–0	4	0	1	3	0	5	1
Nepal	–	–	–	–	–	4	0	1	3	0	7	1

Group 4
Tournament in Jakarta

	Ba	SK	In	SY	Pl	W	D	L	F	A	Pts
BAHRAIN	–	2–0	0–0	2–0	3	2	1	0	4	0	5
SOUTH KOREA	–	–	4–0	1–1	3	1	1	1	5	3	3
Indonesia	–	–	–	1–0	3	1	1	1	1	4	3
South Yemen	–	–	–	–	3	0	1	2	1	4	1

QATAR qualified as hosts

SAUDI ARABIA qualified as holders

FINAL TOURNAMENT
Qatar, 2nd–18th December 1988

FIRST ROUND

Group 1

	SK	Ir	Qa	Em	Ja	Pl	W	D	L	F	A	Pts
South Korea	–	3–0	3–2	1–0	2–0	4	4	0	0	9	2	8
Iran	–	–	2–0	1–0	0–0	4	2	1	1	3	3	5

							Pl	W	D	L	F	A	Pts
Qatar	–	–	–	2–1	3–0		4	2	0	2	7	6	4
UAE	–	–	–	–	1–0		4	1	0	3	2	4	2
Japan	–	–	–	–	–		4	0	1	3	0	6	1

Group 2

	SA	Ch	Sy	Ku	Ba	Pl	W	D	L	F	A	Pts
Saudi Arabia	–	1–0	2–0	0–0	1–1	4	2	2	0	4	1	6
China	–	–	3–0	2–2	1–0	4	2	1	1	6	3	5
Syria	–	–	–	1–0	1–0	4	2	0	2	2	5	4
Kuwait	–	–	–	–	0–0	4	0	3	1	2	3	3
Bahrain	–	–	–	–	–	4	0	2	2	1	3	2

SEMI-FINALS

Saudi Arabia .... 1–0 .... Iran
South Korea .... 2–1 .... China

3RD PLACE

Iran .... 0–0 (3–0p) ..... China

FINAL

Khalifa, Doha, 18–12–1988
SAUDI ARABIA 0
SOUTH KOREA 0

Saudi Arabia won 4–3 on penalties

THE ASIAN GAMES

1951	India	1–0	Iran
1954	Taiwan	5–2	South Korea
1958	Taiwan	3–2	South Korea
1962	India	2–1	South Korea
1966	Burma	1–0	Iran
1970	Burma	0–0*	South Korea
1974	Iran	1–0	Israel
1978	North Korea	0–0*	South Korea
1982	Iraq	1–0	Kuwait
1986	South Korea	2–0	Saudi Arabia
1990	Iran	0–0 (4–1p)	North Korea

* In 1970 and 1978 the gold medal was shared between the two finalists

ASIAN GAMES MEDALS TABLE

	Country	G	S	B	Finals	Semis
1	South Korea	3	3	1	6	7
2	Iran	2	2	–	4	4
3	India	2	–	1	2	4
4	Myanmar	2	–	1	2	3
5	Taiwan	2	–	–	2	2
6	North Korea	1	1	–	2	4
7	Iraq	1	–	–	1	2
8	Kuwait	–	1	1	1	2
	Saudi Arabia	–	1	1	1	2
10	Israel	–	1	–	1	1
11	Japan	–	–	2	–	3
12	Malaysia	–	–	2	–	2
13	Indonesia	–	–	1	–	3
14	Afghanistan	–	–	1	–	1
	China	–	–	1	–	1
16	Singapore	–	–	–	–	1
	Thailand	–	–	–	–	1
	South Vietnam	–	–	–	–	1

FIRST ASIAN GAMES
New Delhi, 4th–11th March 1951

FIRST ROUND

India .... 3–0 .... Indonesia
Afghanistan .... Bye
Japan .... Bye
Iran .... 2–0 .... Burma

SEMI-FINALS

India .... 3–0 .... Afghanistan
Iran .... 3–2 .... Japan

FINAL

National Stadium, New Delhi, 11–05–1951
INDIA 1 (Mewalal 44)
IRAN 0

SECOND ASIAN GAMES
Manila, 1st–8th May 1954

FIRST ROUND

Group 1

	Ta	Vi	Ph	Pl	W	D	L	F	A	Pts
Taiwan	–	3–2	4–0	2	2	0	0	7	2	4
Vietnam	–	–	3–2	2	1	0	1	5	5	2
Philippines	–	–	–	2	0	0	2	2	7	0

Group 2

	Bu	Pa	Si	Pl	W	D	L	F	A	Pts
Burma	–	2–1	1–1	2	1	1	0	3	2	3
Pakistan	–	–	6–2	2	1	0	1	7	4	2
Singapore	–	–	–	2	0	1	1	3	7	1

Group 3

	In	In	Ja	Pl	W	D	L	F	A	Pts
Indonesia	–	4–0	5–3	2	2	0	0	9	3	4
India	–	–	3–2	2	1	0	1	3	6	2
Japan	–	–	–	2	0	0	2	5	8	0

Group 4

	SK	HK	Af	Pl	W	D	L	F	A	Pts
South Korea	–	3–3	8–2	2	1	1	0	11	5	3
Hong Kong	–	–	4–2	2	1	1	0	7	5	3
Afghanistan	–	–	–	2	0	0	2	4	12	0

SEMI-FINALS

Taiwan .... 4–2 .... Indonesia
South Korea .... *2–2 .... Burma

* South Korea won on lots

3RD PLACE

Burma .... 5–4 .... Indonesia

FINAL

Rizal Memorial Stadium, Manila, 8–05–1954
TAIWAN 5 (Yiu Cheuk-yin 8, Chu Wing-keung 20 62, Szeto Man 43, Ho Ying–fun 77)
SOUTH KOREA 2 (Choi Tur–min 33, Pakil Kap 66)

THIRD ASIAN GAMES
Tokyo, 25th May–1st June 1958

FIRST ROUND

Group 1

	Ta	SV	Pa	Ma	Pl	W	D	L	F	A	Pts
Taiwan	–	–	3–1	2–1	2	2	0	0	5	2	4
South Vietnam	–	–	1–1	6–1	2	1	1	0	7	2	3
Pakistan	–	–	–	–	2	0	1	1	2	4	1
Malaysia	–	–	–	–	2	0	0	2	2	8	0

Group 2

	In	In	Bu	Pl	W	D	L	F	A	Pts
Indonesia	–	2–1	4–2	2	2	0	0	6	3	4
India	–	–	3–2	2	1	0	1	4	4	2
Burma	–	–	–	2	0	0	2	4	7	0

Group 3

	HK	Ph	Ja	Pl	W	D	L	F	A	Pts
Hong Kong	–	4–1	2–0	2	2	0	0	6	1	4
Philippines	–	–	1–0	2	1	0	1	2	4	2
Japan	–	–	–	2	0	0	2	0	3	0

Group 4

	SK	Is	Si	Ir	Pl	W	D	L	F	A	Pts
South Korea	–	–	2–1	5–0	2	2	0	0	7	1	4
Israel	–	–	2–1	4–0	2	2	0	0	6	1	4
Singapore	–	–	–	–	2	0	0	2	2	4	0
Iran	–	–	–	–	2	0	0	2	0	9	0

QUARTER-FINALS

Taiwan .... 2–0 .... Israel
Indonesia .... 5–2 .... Philippines
India .... 5–2 .... Hong Kong
South Korea .... 3–1 .... South Vietnam

SEMI-FINALS

Taiwan .... 1–0 .... Indonesia
South Korea .... 3–1 .... India

3RD PLACE

Indonesia .... 4–1 .... India

FINAL

National Stadium, Tokyo, 1–06–1958
TAIWAN 3 (Mok Chun-wah 55, Lau Yee 75, Chan Fai-hung 98)
SOUTH KOREA 2 (Lee 16, Choi 76)

FOURTH ASIAN GAMES
Djakarta, 25th August–4th September 1962

FIRST ROUND

Group 1

	SK	In	Ja	Th	Pl	W	D	L	F	A	Pts
South Korea	–	2–0	1–0	3–2	3	3	0	0	6	2	6
India	–	–	2–0	4–1	3	2	0	1	6	3	4
Japan	–	–	–	3–1	3	1	0	2	3	4	2
Thailand	–	–	–	–	3	0	0	3	4	10	0

Group 2

	Ma	SV	In	Ph	Pl	W	D	L	F	A	Pts
Malaysia	–	0–3	3–2	15–1	3	2	0	1	18	6	4
South Vietnam	–	–	0–1	6–0	3	2	0	1	9	1	4
Indonesia	–	–	–	6–0	3	2	0	1	9	3	4
Philippines	–	–	–	–	3	0	0	3	1	27	0

SEMI-FINALS

India .... 3–2 .... South Vietnam
South Korea .... 2–1 .... Malaysia

3RD PLACE

Malaysia .... 4–1 .... South Vietnam

FINAL

Djakarta, 4–09–1962
INDIA 2
SOUTH KOREA 1

FIFTH ASIAN GAMES
Bangkok, 10th–20th December 1966

FIRST ROUND

Group 1

	Th	Bu	SK	Pl	W	D	L	F	A	Pts
Thailand	–	1–1	3–0	2	1	1	0	4	1	3
Burma	–	–	1–0	2	1	1	0	2	1	3
South Korea	–	–	–	2	0	0	2	0	4	0

Group 2

	Ja	Ir	In	Ma	Pl	W	D	L	F	A	Pts
Japan	–	3–1	2–1	1–0	3	3	0	0	6	2	6
Iran	–	–	4–1	2–0	3	2	0	1	7	4	4
India	–	–	–	2–1	3	1	0	2	4	7	2
Malaysia	–	–	–	–	3	0	0	3	1	5	0

Group 3

	In	Si	SV	Ta	Pl	W	D	L	F	A	Pts
Indonesia	–	3–0	0–0	3–1	3	2	1	0	6	1	5
Singapore	–	–	5–0	3–3	3	1	1	1	8	6	3
South Vietnam	–	–	–	2–1	3	1	1	1	2	6	3
Taiwan	–	–	–	–	3	0	1	2	5	8	1

QUARTER-FINALS

Group A

	Ja	Si	Th	Pl	W	D	L	F	A	Pts
Japan	–	5–1	5–1	2	2	0	0	10	2	4
Singapore	–	–	2–0	2	1	0	1	3	5	2
Thailand	–	–	–	2	0	0	2	1	7	0

Group B

	Bu	Ir	In	Pl	W	D	L	F	A	Pts
Burma	–	1–0	2–2	2	1	1	0	3	2	3
Iran	–	–	1–0	2	1	0	1	1	1	2
Indonesia	–	–	–	2	0	1	1	2	3	1

SEMI-FINALS

Iran .... 1–0 .... Japan
Burma .... 2–0 .... Singapore

3RD PLACE

Japan .... 2–0 .... Singapore

FINAL

Suphachalasai, Bangkok, 20–12–1966
BURMA 1 (Aung Khin 66)
IRAN 0

SIXTH ASIAN GAMES
Bangkok, 10th–20th December 1970

FIRST ROUND

Group 1

	SK	In	Ir	Pl	W	D	L	F	A	Pts
South Korea	–	0–0	1–0	2	1	1	0	1	0	3
Indonesia	–	–	2–2	2	0	2	0	2	2	2
Iran	–	–	–	2	0	1	1	2	3	1

Group 2

	Ja	Bu	Ca	Ma	Pl	W	D	L	F	A	Pts
Japan	–	2–1	1–0	1–0	3	3	0	0	4	1	6
Burma	–	–	2–1	1–0	3	2	0	1	4	3	4
Cambodia	–	–	–	2–0	3	1	0	2	3	3	2
Malaysia	–	–	–	–	3	0	0	3	0	4	0

Group 3

	In	Th	SV	Pl	W	D	L	F	A	Pts
India	–	2–2	2–0	2	1	1	0	4	2	3
Thailand	–	–	1–0	2	1	1	0	3	2	3
South Vietnam	–	–	–	2	0	0	2	0	3	0

QUARTER-FINALS

Group A

	Ja	In	In	Pl	W	D	L	F	A	Pts
Japan	–	1–0	2–1	2	2	0	0	3	1	4
India	–	–	3–0	2	1	0	1	3	1	2
Indonesia	–	–	–	2	0	0	2	1	5	0

Group B

	Bu	SK	TH	Pl	W	D	L	F	A	Pts
Burma	–	1–0	2–2	2	1	1	0	3	2	3
South Korea	–	–	2–1	2	1	0	1	2	2	2
Thailand	–	–	–	2	0	1	1	3	4	1

SEMI-FINALS

Burma .... 2–0 .... India
South Korea .... 2–1 .... Japan

3RD PLACE

India .... 1–0 .... Japan

FINAL

Suphachalasai, Bangkok, 20–12–1970, 35 000
BURMA 0
SOUTH KOREA 0

Gold medal shared

SEVENTH ASIAN GAMES
Tehran, 2nd–15th September 1974

FIRST ROUND

Group 1

	Ku	SK	Th	Pl	W	D	L	F	A	Pts
Kuwait	–	4–0	3–2	2	2	0	0	7	2	4
South Korea	–	–	1–0	2	1	0	1	1	4	2
Thailand	–	–	–	2	0	0	2	2	4	0

Group 2

	Ir	NK	Ch	In	Pl	W	D	L	F	A	Pts
Iraq	–	1–0	1–0	3–0	3	3	0	0	5	0	6
North Korea	–	–	2–0	4–1	3	2	0	1	6	2	4
Taiwan	–	–	–	7–1	3	1	0	2	7	4	2
India	–	–	–	–	3	0	0	3	2	14	0

Group 3

	Is	Ma	Ja	Ph	Pl	W	D	L	F	A	Pts
Israel	–	8–3	3–0	6–0	3	3	0	0	17	3	6
Malaysia	–	–	1–1	11–0	3	1	1	1	15	9	3
Japan	–	–	–	4–0	3	1	1	1	5	4	3
Philippines	–	–	–	–	3	0	0	3	0	21	0

Group 4

	Ir	Bu	Pa	Ba	Pl	W	D	L	F	A	Pts
Iran	–	2–1	7–0	6–0	3	3	0	0	15	1	6
Burma	–	–	5–1	4–0	3	2	0	1	10	3	4
Pakistan	–	–	–	5–1	3	1	0	2	6	13	2
Bahrain	–	–	–	–	3	0	0	3	1	15	0

SEMI-FINALS

Group A

	Ir	Ma	Iq	SK	Pl	W	D	L	F	A	Pts
Iran	–	1–0	1–0	2–0	3	3	0	0	4	0	6
Malaysia	–	–	0–0	3–2	3	1	1	1	3	3	3
Iraq	–	–	–	1–1	3	0	2	1	1	2	2
South Korea	–	–	–	–	3	0	1	2	3	6	1

Group B

	Is	NK	Ku	Bu	Pl	W	D	L	F	A	Pts
Israel	–	2–0*	2–0*	3–0	3	3	0	0	7	0	6
North Korea	–	–	2–0	2–2	3	1	1	1	4	4	3
Kuwait	–	–	–	5–2	3	1	0	2	5	6	2
Burma	–	–	–	–	3	0	1	2	4	10	1

* Games awarded to Israel after opponents refused to play

3RD PLACE

Malaysia .... 2–1 .... North Korea

FINAL

Aryamehr Stadium, Tehran, 15–09–1974, 100 000
IRAN 1 (OG 23)
ISRAEL 0

EIGHTH ASIAN GAMES
Bangkok, 9th–20th December 1978

FIRST ROUND

Group 1

	Ir	Ch	SA	Qa	Pl	W	D	L	F	A	Pts
Iraq	–	2–0	1–1	2–1	3	2	1	0	5	2	5
China	–	–	1–0	3–0	3	2	0	1	4	2	4
Saudi Arabia	–	–	–	2–2	3	0	2	1	3	4	2
Qatar	–	–	–	–	3	0	1	2	3	7	1

Group 2

	Ma	In	Ba	Pl	W	D	L	F	A	Pts
Malaysia	–	1–0	1–0	2	2	0	0	2	0	4
India	–	–	3–0	2	1	0	1	3	1	2
Bangladesh	–	–	–	2	0	0	2	0	4	0

Group 3

	SK	Ku	Ja	Ba	Pl	W	D	L	F	A	Pts
South Korea	–	2–0	3–1	5–1	3	3	0	0	10	2	6
Kuwait	–	–	2–0	3–0	3	2	0	1	5	2	4
Japan	–	–	–	4–0	3	1	0	2	5	5	2
Bahrain	–	–	–	–	3	0	0	3	1	12	0

Group 4

	NK	Th	Bu	Pl	W	D	L	F	A	Pts
North Korea	–	3–0	3–0	2	2	0	0	6	0	4
Thailand	–	–	2–1	2	1	0	1	2	4	2
Burma	–	–	–	2	0	0	2	1	5	0

SEMI-FINALS

Group A

	SK	Ch	Th	Ma	Pl	W	D	L	F	A	Pts
South Korea	–	1–0	3–1	1–0	3	3	0	0	5	1	6
China	–	–	4–1	7–1	3	2	0	1	11	3	4
Thailand	–	–	–	2–1	3	1	0	2	4	8	2
Malaysia	–	–	–	–	3	0	0	3	2	10	0

Group B

	NK	Ir	Ku	In	Pl	W	D	L	F	A	Pts
North Korea	–	1–0	2–2	3–1	3	2	1	0	6	3	5
Iraq	–	–	3–0	3–0	3	2	0	1	6	1	4
Kuwait	–	–	–	6–1	3	1	1	1	8	6	3
India	–	–	–	–	3	0	0	3	2	12	0

3RD PLACE

China .... 1–0 .... Iraq

FINAL

Suphachalasai, Bangkok, 20–12–1978

SOUTH KOREA 0
NORTH KOREA 0

Gold medal shared

NINTH ASIAN GAMES
New Delhi, 19th November–4th December 1982

FIRST ROUND

Group 1

	In	Ch	Ba	Ma	Pl	W	D	L	F	A	Pts
India	–	2–2	2–0	1–0	3	2	1	0	5	2	5
China	–	–	1–0	1–0	3	2	0	1	4	2	4
Bangladesh	–	–	–	2–1	3	1	0	2	2	4	2
Malaysia	–	–	–	–	3	0	0	3	1	4	0

Group 2

	NK	SA	Th	Sy	Pl	W	D	L	F	A	Pts
North Korea	–	2–2	3–0	1–1	3	1	2	0	6	3	4
Saudi Arabia	–	–	1–0	1–1	3	1	2	0	4	3	4
Thailand	–	–	–	3–1	3	1	0	2	3	5	2
Syria	–	–	–	–	3	0	2	1	3	5	2

Group 3

	Ja	Ir	SK	SY	Pl	W	D	L	F	A	Pts
Japan	–	1–0	2–1	3–1	3	3	0	0	6	2	6
Iran	–	–	1–0	2–0	3	2	0	1	3	1	4
South Korea	–	–	–	3–0	3	1	0	2	4	3	2
South Yemen	–	–	–	–	3	0	0	3	1	8	0

Group 4

	Ku	Ir	Bu	Ne	Pl	W	D	L	F	A	Pts
Kuwait	–	2–1	4–0	3–0	3	3	0	0	9	1	6
Iraq	–	–	4–0	3–0	3	2	0	1	8	2	4
Burma	–	–	–	3–0	3	1	0	2	3	8	2
Nepal	–	–	–	–	3	0	0	3	0	9	0

QUARTER-FINALS

Iraq .... 1–0 .... Japan
Saudi Arabia .... 1–0 .... India
North Korea .... 1–0 .... China
Kuwait .... 1–0 .... Iran

SEMI-FINALS

Iraq .... 1–0 .... Saudi Arabia
Kuwait .... 3–2 .... North Korea

FINAL

National Stadium, New Delhi, 4–12–1982

IRAQ 1
KUWAIT 0

TENTH ASIAN GAMES
Seoul, 20th September–5th October 1986

FIRST ROUND

Group 1

	Em	Ir	Om	Th	Pa	Pl	W	D	L	F	A	Pts
UAE	–	2–1	0–0	2–1	1–0	4	3	1	0	5	2	7
Iraq	–	–	4–0	2–1	5–1	4	3	0	1	12	4	6
Oman	–	–	–	0–0	3–1	4	1	2	1	3	5	4
Thailand	–	–	–	–	6–0	4	1	1	2	8	4	3
Pakistan	–	–	–	–	–	4	0	0	4	2	15	0

Group 2

	SK	Ch	Ba	In	Pl	W	D	L	F	A	Pts
South Korea	–	4–2	0–0	3–0	3	2	1	0	7	2	5
China	–	–	5–1	2–1	3	2	0	1	9	6	4
Bahrain	–	–	–	3–0	3	1	1	1	4	5	3
India	–	–	–	–	3	0	0	3	1	8	0

Group 3

	SA	In	Qa	Ma	Pl	W	D	L	F	A	Pts
Saudi Arabia	–	2–0	1–0	3–1	3	3	0	0	6	1	6
Indonesia	–	–	1–1	1–0	3	1	1	1	2	3	3
Qatar	–	–	–	1–1	3	0	2	1	2	3	2
Malaysia	–	–	–	–	3	0	1	2	2	5	1

Group 4

	Ku	Ir	Ja	Ba	Ne	Pl	W	D	L	F	A	Pts
Kuwait	–	1–0	2–0	4–0	5–0	4	4	0	0	12	0	8
Iran	–	–	2–0	4–0	6–0	4	3	0	1	12	1	6
Japan	–	–	–	4–0	5–0	4	2	0	2	9	4	4
Bangladesh	–	–	–	–	1–0	4	1	0	3	1	12	2
Nepal	–	–	–	–	–	4	0	0	4	0	17	0

QUARTER-FINALS

South Korea .... 1–1 (5–4p) ..... Iran
Indonesia .... 2–2 (4–3p) ..... UAE
Kuwait .... 1–1 (5–4p) ..... China
Saudi Arabia .... 1–1 (9–8p) ..... Iraq

SEMI-FINALS

South Korea .... 4–0 .... Indonesia
Saudi Arabia .... 2–2 (5–4p) ..... Kuwait

3RD PLACE

Kuwait .... 5–0 .... Indonesia

FINAL

Olympic Stadium, Seoul, 5–10–1986, 75 000

SOUTH KOREA 2 (Cho Kwang-rae 8, Byun Byung-joo 85)
SAUDI ARABIA 0

ELEVENTH ASIAN GAMES
Beijing, 22nd September–6th October 1990

FIRST ROUND

Group 1

	SK	Ch	Si	Pa	Pl	W	D	L	F	A	Pts
South Korea	–	2–0	7–0	7–0	3	3	0	0	16	0	6
China	–	–	5–1	3–0	3	2	0	1	8	3	4
Singapore	–	–	–	6–1	3	1	0	2	7	13	2
Pakistan	–	–	–	–	3	0	0	3	1	16	0

Group 2

	Ir	NK	Ma	Pl	W	D	L	F	A	Pts
Iran	–	2–1	3–0	2	2	0	0	5	1	4
North Korea	–	–	0–0	2	0	1	1	1	2	1
Malaysia	–	–	–	2	0	1	1	0	3	1

Group 3

	Th	Ku	HK	Ye	Pl	W	D	L	F	A	Pts
Thailand	–	2–1	2–0	0–0	3	2	1	0	4	1	5
Kuwait	–	–	2–1	0–0	3	1	1	1	3	3	3
Hong Kong	–	–	–	2–0	3	1	0	2	3	4	2
Yemen	–	–	–	–	3	0	2	1	0	2	2

Group 4

	SA	Ja	Ba	Pl	W	D	L	F	A	Pts
Saudi Arabia	–	2–0	4–0	2	2	0	0	6	0	4
Japan	–	–	3–0	2	1	0	1	3	2	2
Bangladesh	–	–	–	2	0	0	2	0	7	0

QUARTER-FINALS

Iran .... 1–0 .... Japan
South Korea .... 1–0 .... Kuwait
Thailand .... 1–0 .... China
North Korea .... 0–0 (4–3p) ..... Saudi Arabia

SEMI-FINALS

Iran .... 1–0 .... South Korea
North Korea .... 1–0 .... Thailand

3RD PLACE

South Korea .... 1–0 .... Thailand

FINAL

Workers Stadium, Beijing, 6–10–1990, 70 000
IRAN 0
NORTH KOREA 0

Iran won 4–1 on penalties

THE FAR EASTERN GAMES

1st Football Tournament. Manila. February 1913
Philippines .... 2–1 .... China

2nd Football Tournament. Shanghai. May 1915
China .... 1–0 .... Philippines

3rd Football Tournament. Tokyo. 9th–10th May 1917

	Ch	Ph	Ja	Pl	W	D	L	F	A	Pts
China	–	3–0	8–0	2	2	0	0	11	0	4
Philippines	–	–	15–2	2	1	0	1	15	5	2
Japan	–	–	–	2	0	0	2	2	23	0

4th Football Tournament. Manila. 12th–15th May 1919
China .... 2–1 1–2 3–2 ... Philippines

5th Football Tournament. Shanghai. 1st–2nd June 1921

	Ch	Ph	Ja	Pl	W	D	L	F	A	Pts
China	–	1–0	4–1	2	2	0	0	5	1	4
Philippines	–	–	3–0	2	1	0	1	3	1	2
Japan	–	–	–	2	0	0	2	1	7	0

6th Football Tournament. Osaka. 22nd–23rd May 1923

	Ch	Ph	Ja	Pl	W	D	L	F	A	Pts
China	–	3–0	5–1	2	2	0	0	8	1	4
Philippines	–	–	2–1	2	1	0	1	2	4	2
Japan	–	–	–	2	0	0	2	2	7	0

7th Football Tournament. Manila. 16th–23rd May 1925

	Ch	Ph	Ja	Pl	W	D	L	F	A	Pts
China	–	5–1	2–0	2	2	0	0	7	1	4
Philippines	–	–	4–0	2	1	0	1	5	5	2
Japan	–	–	–	2	0	0	2	0	6	0

8th Football Tournament. Shanghai. 27th August–3rd September 1927

	Ch	Ja	Ph	Pl	W	D	L	F	A	Pts
China	–	5–1	3–1	2	2	0	0	8	2	4
Japan	–	–	2–1	2	1	0	1	3	6	2
Philippines	–	–	–	2	0	0	2	2	5	0

9th Football Tournament. Tokyo. 25th–29th May 1930

	Ch	Ja	Ph	Pl	W	D	L	F	A	Pts
China	–	3–3	5–0	2	1	1	0	8	3	3
Japan	–	–	7–2	2	1	1	0	10	5	3
Philippines	–	–	–	2	0	0	2	2	12	0

China and Japan shared the title

10th Football Tournament. Manila. 5th–20th May 1934

	Ch	DI	Ph	Ja	Pl	W	D	L	F	A	Pts
China	–	2–0	2–0	4–3	3	3	0	0	8	3	6
Dutch E Indies	–	–	2–3	7–1	3	1	0	2	9	6	2
Philippines	–	–	–	3–4	3	1	0	2	6	8	2
Japan	–	–	–	–	3	1	0	2	8	14	2

ASIAN CLUB FOOTBALL

Club football is not strong in Asia, though efforts are being made to rectify this situation through the reintroduction of the Asian Champion Teams' Cup and more recently the Asian Cup Winners Cup. It is hoped that these tournaments will be an incentive for an increased awareness of club football. Many put the lack of progress of the continent down to the lack of a well-founded club structure in the majority of countries.

First played for at the end of the 1960s for four editions, the Champions Cup was resumed in 1985, has been held each year since and looks set to stay. It does, however, face enormous logistical problems, the most basic being the enormous size of Asia. After all, Riyadh and Seoul are as far apart as Madrid and Rio de Janeiro. A second problem the tournament faces is just who qualifies to take part, as some countries cannot admit to having a national league, and in some which do, representative rather than club sides take part.

This is not to decry Asian club football totally. South Korea, Japan, Bangladesh, India, Hong Kong and the majority of the Gulf states do have well-established leagues that, given the right circumstances, do capture the attention of the public, but it is a hard battle as a look at the television screens of the continent will tell you. Wherever you look there is Italian, English, German and Spanish football, but little of the local variety.

In the early editions of the tournament, an Israeli club appeared in all of the four finals and were three times victorious. Their monopoly was broken once by the Taj club from Iran. As Israel does not take part anymore and none of the Iranian clubs of the time exist any longer, the links between the old tournament and the new are patchy. The victorious team in the 1991 edition, Esteghlal, are the team of the Iranian army, as were Taj, but there the similarity ends.

Japan and Saudi Arabia have been the dominant countries since the competition's reintroduction with three final appearances each, and these two leagues are arguably amongst the strongest in Asia as both can afford the facilities and the coaches. Others included would be South Korea who in 1983 introduced a professional superleague of teams attached to some of the countries biggest industrial concerns. It has proved to be successful enough for Japan to follow suit in 1992, although most of the franchises taken up in Japan's case are by clubs that already exist.

Above all the others, however, stands Hong Kong, whose league for many years was the only professional one in Asia. It not only attracted most of the best Asian players but also a good number of Europeans and South Americans who were seeking to make some money at the end of their careers. Given that it still is a colony of Great Britain, the link with players from the English and Scottish leagues has been strong.

There is a long way to go before Asian club football catches up with even that in Africa. The ultimate aim would be for the Asian champions to take part in a four-way club championship of the world with the European champions, Copa Libertadores winners and African champions; but don't hold your breath.

THE ASIAN CHAMPION TEAMS' CUP

Year	Winners		Score	Runners–up	
1967	Hapoel Tel Aviv	ISR	2–1	FA Selangor	MAL
1968	Maccabi Tel Aviv	ISR	1–0	Yangzee	KOR
1969	–				
1970	Taj Club	IRN	2–1	Hapoel Tel Aviv	ISR
1971	Maccabi Tel Aviv	ISR	W-O	Police Club	IRQ
1972–84	–				
1985	Daewoo Royals	KOR	3–1	Al Ahli	ARS
1986	Furukawa	JAP	4–3	Al Hilal	ARS
1987	Yomiuri	JAP	W-O	Al Hilal	ARS
1988	Al Saad	QAT	2–3 1–0	Al Rasheed	IRQ
1989	Liaoning	PRC	2–1 1–1	Nissan	JAP
1990	Esteghlal SC	IRN	2–1	Liaoning	PRC

1967
Tournament in Bangkok

FIRST ROUND

Hapoel Tel–Aviv	ISR	Bye		
Tungsten Mining	KOR	Bye		
South China	HKG	1–0 0–2	Bangkok Bank	THA
FA Selangor	MAL	0–0 2–1	Vietnam Customs	SVM

SECOND ROUND

Hapoel Tel-Aviv	Bye	
Tungsten Mining	Bye	
FA Selangor	1–0 0–0	Bangkok Bank

SEMI-FINALS

Hapoel Tel-Aviv	Bye	
Tungsten Mining	0–0 0–1	FA Selangor

FINAL

HAPOEL TEL-AVIV	2
FA SELANGOR	1

1968
Tournament in Bangkok

FIRST ROUND

Group A

		My	BB	VP	ML	W	D	L	F	A	Pts
Yangzee	KOR	5–0	1–0	4–1	7–0	4	0	0	17	1	8
Mysore State	IND	–	1–1	2–1	2–1	2	1	1	5	8	5
Bangkok Bank	THA	–	–	1–1	4–0	1	2	1	6	3	4
Vietnam Police	SVT	–	–	–	7–0	1	1	2	10	7	3
Manila Lions	PHI	–	–	–	–	0	0	4	1	20	0

Group B

		TK	TC	Pe	Ko	W	D	L	F	A	Pts
Maccabi Tel-Aviv	ISR	3–2	0–0	1–1	5–0	2	2	0	9	3	6
Toyo Kogyo	JAP	–	1–0	2–0	1–0	3	0	1	6	3	6
Tehran Club	IRN	–	–	4–2	4–0	2	1	1	8	3	5
Perak AFA	MAL	–	–	–	6–2	1	1	2	9	9	3
K'loon Motor Bus	HKG	–	–	–	–	0	0	4	2	16	0

SEMI-FINALS

Maccabi Tel-Aviv .... 6–1 .... Mysore State
Yangzee .... 2–0 .... Toyo Kogyo

3RD PLACE

Toyo Kogyo .... 2–0 .... Mysore State

FINAL

Bangkok

MACCABI TEL-AVIV	1
YANGZEE	0

1970

Tournament in Tehran, 1st – 10th April 1970

FIRST ROUND

Group A

	TC	CH	FA	W	D	L	F	A	Pts
Taj Club .... IRN	–	3–0	3–0	2	0	0	6	0	4
Club Homenetmen ... LIB	–	–	4–2	1	0	1	4	5	2
FA Selangor .... MAL	–	–	–	0	0	2	2	7	0

Group B

	Ha	PS	WB	Po	W	D	L	F	A	Pts
Hapoel Tel-Aviv .... ISR	–	3–1	3–1	5–0	3	0	0	11	2	6
PSMS .... INA	–	–	1–0	4–0	2	0	1	6	3	4
West Bengal .... IND	–	–	–	2–1	1	0	2	3	5	2
Police .... THA	–	–	–	–	0	0	3	1	11	0

SEMI-FINALS

Hapoel Tel-Aviv .... W-O ..... Club Homenetmen
Taj Club .... 2–0 .... PSMS

3RD PLACE

Club Homenetmen .... 1–0 .... PSMS

FINAL

Tehran

TAJ CLUB	2
HAPOEL TEL-AVIV	1

1971

Tournament in Bangkok, 21st March – 2nd April 1971

FIRST ROUND

Inter group games

ROK Army .... 2–1 .... Bangkok Bank
Al Schurta .... 3–2 .... Taj Club
Al Arabi .... 8–1 .... Punjab FA
Maccabi Tel–Aviv .... 1–0 .... Perak AFA
Al Arabi .... 3–0 .... Perak AFA
Taj Club .... 2–1 .... ROK Army
Bangkok Bank .... 2–0 .... Punjab FA
Maccabi Tel–Aviv .... W-O .... Al Schurta
ROK Army .... 3–0 .... Perak AFA
Taj Club .... 0–0 .... Al Arabi
Maccabi Tel–Aviv .... 4–1 .... Punjab FA
Al Schurta .... 2–0 .... Bangkok Bank
Taj Club .... 3–0 .... Perak AFA
ROK Army .... 1–0 .... Al Arabi
Al Schurta .... 6–1 .... Punjab FA
Maccabi Tel-Aviv .... 4–1 .... Bangkok Bank

Group A

	W	D	L	F	A	Pts
ROK Army .... KOR	3	0	1	7	3	6
Taj Club .... IRN	2	1	1	7	4	5
Al Arabi .... KUW	2	1	1	11	2	5
Perak AFA .... MAL	0	0	4	0	10	0

Group B

	W	D	L	F	A	Pts
Maccabi Tel-Aviv .... ISR	4	0	0	9	2	8
Al Schurta .... IRQ	3	0	1	11	3	6
Bangkok Bank .... THA	1	0	3	4	8	2
Punjab FA .... IND	0	0	4	3	20	0

SEMI-FINALS

Maccabi Tel–Aviv .... 2–0 .... ROK Army
Al Schurta .... 2–0 .... Taj Club

THIRD PLACE

Taj Club .... 3–2 .... ROK Army

FINAL

Maccabi Tel-Aviv were declared the winners after Al Schurta from Iraq refused to play Maccabi

1972 to 1984

No competition

1985

QUALIFYING COMPETITION

Group 1

First round

Al Ittihad .... SYR ...... W-O
Al Rasheed .... IRQ .... 4–0 .... Amman Club .... JOR

Second round

Ittihad Club beat Al Rasheed to qualify

Group 2

Tournament in Dubai with Al Ahli ARS, Al Arabi KUW, Al Fanja OMN, Muharraq BAH, Al Rayyan QAT and Al Ain UAE

Final

Al Ahli .... 2–1 .... Al Arabi
Both clubs qualified, but Al Arabi withdrew from the final tournament

Group 3

Tournament in Colombo

	AK	Sa	Pl	NR	Va	W	D	L	F	A	Pts
East Bengal .... IND	1–0	1–0	2–0	7–0	9–0	5	0	0	20	0	10
Abah. Krira Ch. ...... BAN	–	4–1	3–0	2–1	8–1	4	0	1	17	4	8
Saunders SC .... SRI	–	–	2–2	2–1	7–0	2	1	2	12	8	5
Pakistan Int. Air. ...... PAK	–	–	–	0–0	6–1	1	2	2	8	8	4
New Road Team ..... NEP	–	–	–	–	6–0	1	1	3	8	11	3
Valencia .... MLD	–	–	–	–	–	0	0	5	2	36	0

East Bengal qualified

Group 4

Tournament in Jakarta

	BB	TB	MA	AP	Pl	W	D	L	F	A	Pts
Tiga Berlian .... INA	1–1	5–0	2–0	7–0	4	3	1	0	15	1	7
Bangkok Bank .... THA	–	2–0	5–1	1–0	4	3	1	0	9	2	7
Tiong Bahru .... SIN	–	–	0–0	2–0	4	1	1	2	2	7	3
Malacca AFA .... MAL	–	–	–	1–0	4	1	1	2	2	7	3
Angkata Persenjata . BRU	–	–	–	–	4	0	0	4	0	11	0

Play–off

Bankok Bank .... 1–0 .... Tiga Berlian
Both clubs qualified

Group 5

	Se	Ap	Li	Pl	W	D	L	F	A	Pts
Seiko .... HKG	–	2–1	2–1	4	3	0	1	6	6	6
April 25 .... PRK	4–1	–	3–1	4	2	1	1	8	4	5
Liaoning .... PRC	0–1	0–0	–	4	0	1	3	2	6	1

Seiko qualified, but withdrew from the final tournament

Group 6

Daewoo Royals .... KOR . 9–0 5–1* .. Wa Seng .... MAC
* Both games in Seoul

FINAL TOURNAMENT

Jeddah, 19th–29th October 1985

FIRST ROUND

Group A

		AA	TB	EB	W	D	L	F	A	Pts
Al Ahli	ARS	–	1–0	2–1	2	0	0	3	1	4
Tiga Berlian	INA	–	–	2–0	1	0	1	2	1	2
East Bengal	IND	–	–	–	0	0	2	1	4	0

Group B

		DR	IC	BB	W	D	L	F	A	Pts
Daewoo Royals	KOR	–	1–0	3–1	2	0	0	4	1	4
Ittihad Club	SYR	–	–	3–0	1	0	1	3	1	2
Bangkok Bank	THA	–	–	–	0	0	2	1	6	0

SEMI-FINALS

Daewoo Royals .... 3–0 .... Tiga Berlian
Al Ahli .... 1–0 .... Ittihad Club

3RD PLACE

Tiga Berlian .... 1–0 .... Ittihad Club

FINAL

Al Ahli stadium, Jeddah, 24–01–1986

DAEWOO ROYALS 3 (Byung-joo, Yang-ha, Sin-woo)
AL AHLI 1 (Dabu)

1986

QUALIFYING TOURNAMENT

FIRST ROUND

Group 1

Police FC .... SYM ..... W-O

Group 2

Al Talabah .... IRQ ...... 2–1* ...... Al Wahda .... NYM
* Played in Saan'a

Group 3

Tournament in Bahrain

Al Hilal, ARS and Al Arabi, QAT, qualified at the expense of teams from the United Arab Emirates, Oman and Kuwait

Group 4

Tournament in Colombo

Malavan SC, IRN and Saunders, SRL, qualified at the expense of Habib Bank, PAK and Victory SC, MDV

Group 5

Selangor FA .... MAL . 1–0 1–0* .. Port Authority .... THA
* Both Games in Kuala Lumpur

Group 6

Tournament in Brunei

Tiga Berlian, INA qualified for the second round at the expense of Air Force, PHI and Daerah Brunei, BRU

Group 7

April 25 .... PRK ... 0–0 0–1 ... Liaoning .... PRC
Furukawa .... JAP .... Bye

Group 8

Tournament in Hong Kong

South China .... HKG ..... 1–0 .... Hap Kuan .... MAC
Hap Kuan .... MAC .... W-O ..... Lucky Goldstar .... KOR

SECOND ROUND

Group A

Tournament in Baghdad

		AT	AA	Sa	Pl	W	D	L	F	A	Pts
Al Talabah	IRQ	–	2–0	4–0	2	2	0	0	6	0	4
Al Arabi	QAT	–	–	9–0	2	1	0	1	9	2	2
Saunders	SRL	–	–	–	2	0	0	2	0	13	0

Al Talabah qualified

Group B

Tournament in Saudi Arabia

		AH	Po	Pl	W	D	L	F	A	Pts
Al Hilal	ARS	–	5–0	2	2	0	0	7	0	4
Police FC	SYM	0–2	–	2	0	0	2	0	7	0

Malavan withdrew, Al Hilal qualified

Group C

Tournament in Hong Kong

		Li	TB	SC	Pl	W	D	L	F	A	Pts
Liaoning	PRC	–	0–0	1–0	2	1	1	0	1	0	3
Tiga Berlian	INA	–	–	1–1	2	0	2	0	1	1	2
South China	HKG	–	–	–	2	0	1	1	1	2	1

Liaoning qualified

Group D

Tournament in Kuala Lumpur

		Fu	Se	HK	Pl	W	D	L	F	A	Pts
Furukawa	JAP	–	2–1	3–1	2	2	0	0	5	2	4
Selangor FA	MAL	–	–	5–0	2	1	0	1	6	2	2
Hap Kuan	MAC	–	–	–	2	0	0	2	1	8	0

Furukawa qualified

FINAL TOURNAMENT

Riyadh, 26th–30th December 1986

		Fu	AH	Li	AT	W	D	L	F	A	Pts
Furukawa	JAP	–	4–3	1–0	2–0	3	0	0	7	3	6
Al Hilal	ARS	–	–	2–1	2–1	2	0	1	7	6	4
Liaoning	PRC	–	–	–	2–2	0	1	2	3	5	1
Al Talaba	IRQ	–	–	–	–	0	1	2	3	6	1

Decisive game. Riyadh, 26–12–1986

FURUKAWA 4
AL HILAL 3

1987

FIRST ROUND

Group 1

Tournament in Kuwait

		AH	AM	AN	AF	Pl	W	D	L	F	A	Pts
Al Kazma	KUW	0–1	3–0	1–0	2–0	4	3	0	0	6	1	6
Al Hilal	ARS	–	2–3	0–0	3–0	4	2	1	1	6	3	5
Al Muharraq	BAH	–	–	0–1	2–1	4	2	0	2	5	7	4
Al Nasr	UAE	–	–	–	2–3	4	1	1	2	3	4	3
Al Fanja	OMN	–	–	–	–	4	1	0	3	4	9	2

Kazma and Hilal qualified for the semi–finals

Group 2

Tournament in Bangladesh

		MB	Mo	MM	AF	Pl	W	D	L	F	A	Pts
Al Rasheed	IRQ	2–0	5–1	6–1	10–0	4	4	0	0	23	2	8
Mohun Bagan	IND	–	2–2	6–1	4–1	4	2	1	1	12	6	5
Mohammedan	BAN	–	–	6–2	3–1	4	2	1	1	12	10	5
Manang Marsy'di	NEP	–	–	–	4–1	4	1	0	3	8	19	2
Air Force	PAK	–	–	–	–	4	0	0	4	3	21	0

Al Rasheed qualified for the semi-finals

Group 3

Tournament in Male, Maldives

		BB	AF	Vi	Pl	W	D	L	F	A	Pts
Bangkok Bank	THA	–	0–0	7–0	2	1	1	0	7	0	3
Air Force	SRL	–	–	1–1	2	0	2	0	1	1	2
Victory SC	MDV	–	–	–	2	0	1	1	1	8	1

Bangkok Bank qualified for the semi-finals

Group 4
Tournament in Bandung, Indonesia

	FT	TB	TB	KR	Pl	W	D	L	F	A	Pts
Federal Territory ... MAL	–	2–0	0–0	8–1	3	2	1	0	10	1	5
Tiga Berlian .... INA	–	–	3–0	5–1	3	2	0	1	8	3	4
Tiong Baru .... SIN	–	–	–	3–2	3	1	1	1	3	5	3
Kota Rangers .... BRU	–	–	–	–	3	0	0	3	4	16	0

Federal Territory qualified for the semi-finals

Group 5
Tournament in Dalian, China

	Au	Ap	HK	Pl	W	D	L	F	A	Pts
August 1st .... PRC	–	2–0	3–0	2	2	0	0	5	0	4
April 25th .... PRK	–	–	2–1	2	1	0	1	2	3	2
Hap Kuan .... MAC	–	–	–	2	0	0	2	1	5	0

August 1st qualified for the semi-finals

Group 6

South China .... HKG . 1–0 0–2 ... Yomiuri .... JAP

Yomiuri qualified for the semi-finals

SEMI-FINALS

Group A
Tournament in Riyadh

	AH	AR	BB	Pl	W	D	L	F	A	Pts
Al Hilal	–	2–1	4–0	2	2	0	0	6	1	4
Al Rasheed	–	–	6–1	2	1	0	1	7	3	2
Bangkok Bank	–	–	–	2	0	0	2	1	10	0

Hilal qualified for the final

Group B
Tournament in Kuala Lumpur

	Yo	FT	AK	Au	Pl	W	D	L	F	A	Pts
Yomiuri	–	0–1	2–1	2–0	3	2	0	1	4	2	4
Federal Territory	–	–	1–1	1–1	3	1	2	0	3	2	4
Al Kazma	–	–	–	1–0	3	1	1	1	3	3	3
August 1st	–	–	–	–	3	0	1	2	1	4	1

Yomiuri qualified for the final

FINAL

Yomiuri declared champions after Al Hilal withdrew

1988

FIRST ROUND

Group 1
Tournament in Doha

	AR	AS	AF	AA	Pl	W	D	L	F	A	Pts
Al Rasheed .... IRQ	–	0–0	3–0	6–0	3	2	1	0	9	0	5
Al Saad .... QAT	–	–	4–1	1–0	3	2	1	0	5	1	5
Al Futuwa .... SYR	–	–	–	1–0	3	1	0	2	2	7	2
Al Ansar .... LIB	–	–	–	–	3	0	0	3	0	8	0

Al Rasheed and Al Saad qualified for the semi-finals

Group 2
Tournament in Sharjah, United Arab Emirates

	AI	AK	AS	AF	AR	Pl	W	D	L	F	A	Pts
Al Ittifaq .... ARS	–	1–1	1–0	1–0	3–1	4	3	1	0	6	2	7
Al Kazma .... KUW	–	–	3–0	3–1	2–0	4	3	1	0	9	2	7
Al Sharjah .... UAE	–	–	–	4–1	2–0	4	2	0	2	6	5	4
Al Fanja .... OMN	–	–	–	–	1–0	4	1	0	3	3	8	2
Al Rifaa .... BAH	–	–	–	–	–	4	0	0	4	1	8	0

Al Itifaq and Al Kazma qualified for the semi–finals

Group 3
Tournament in Calcutta

	MB	AF	CT	Ka	Pl	W	D	L	F	A	Pts
Mohun Bagan .... IND	–	1–0	8–0	4–2	3	3	0	0	13	2	6
Al Fanja .... OMN	–	–	8–1	5–1	3	2	0	1	13	3	4
Cresent Textile .... PAK	–	–	–	2–1	3	1	0	2	3	17	2
Kathmandu SC .... NEP	–	–	–	–	3	0	0	2	4	11	0

Mohun Bagan qualified for the semi–finals

Group 4
Tournament in Dacca, Bangladesh

	Mo	Pi	Sa	Pl	W	D	L	F	A	Pts
Mohammedan .... BAN	–	2–1	0–0	2	1	1	0	2	1	3
Piroozi .... IRN	–	–	5–0	2	1	0	1	6	2	2
Saunders SC .... SRL	–	–	–	2	0	1	1	0	5	1

Mohammedan qualified for the semi-finals

Group 5
Tournament in Bangkok

	AF	Pa	NM	Ge	Be	Pl	W	D	L	F	A	Pts
Air Force .... THA	–	2–1	2–1	9–0	9–0	4	4	0	0	22	2	8
Pahang FA .... MAL	–	–	0–0	2–1	5–1	4	2	1	1	8	4	5
Niac Mitra .... INA	–	–	–	1–1	3–1	4	1	2	1	5	4	4
Geylang Inter. ... SIN	–	–	–	–	3–1	4	1	1	2	5	13	3
Belait .... BRU	–	–	–	–	–	4	0	0	4	3	20	0

Air Force and Pahang FA qualified for the semi-finals but Air Force later withdrew

Group 6
Tournament in Guangzhou

	Ap	WB	Ya	SC	WS	Pl	W	D	L	F	A	Pts
April 25th .... PRK	–	1–0	3–1	3–0	4–0	4	4	0	0	11	1	8
Wan Bao .... PRC	–	–	3–1	1–0	7–1	4	3	0	1	11	3	6
Yamaha .... JAP	–	–	–	1–1	9–2	4	1	1	2	12	9	3
South China .... HKG	–	–	–	–	3–0	4	1	1	2	4	5	3
Wa Seng .... MAC	–	–	–	–	–	4	0	0	4	3	23	0

April 25th and Wan Bao qualified for the semi-finals

SEMI-FINALS

Group A
Tournament in Guangzhou

	AR	WB	AK	MB	Pl	W	D	L	F	A	Pts
Al Rasheed	–	1–1	2–0	4–0	3	2	1	0	7	1	5
Wan Bao	–	–	1–1	6–0	3	1	2	0	8	2	4
Al Kazma	–	–	–	1–0	3	1	1	1	2	3	3
Mohun Bagan	–	–	–	–	3	0	0	3	0	11	0

Al Rasheed qualified for the final

Group B
Tournament in Kuantan, Malaysia

	AS	AI	Ap	Mo	Pa	Pl	W	D	L	F	A	Pts
Al Saad	–	2–1	2–1	2–2	2–0	4	3	1	0	8	4	7
Al Itifaq	–	–	1–1	3–1	4–1	4	2	1	1	9	5	5
April 25th	–	–	–	0–1	2–0	4	1	1	2	4	4	3
Mohammedan	–	–	–	–	1–2	4	1	1	2	5	7	3
Pahang FA	–	–	–	–	–	4	1	0	3	3	9	2

Al Saad qualified for the final

FINAL

1st Leg

Baghdad, 31–03–1989, 10000

AL RASHEED 3 (Radhi, Kadhum 2)
AL SAAD 2 (Salman K, Ghanim)

2nd Leg

Doha, 6–04–1989, 5000

AL SAAD 1 (Salman K)
AL RASHEED 0

Al Saad won on away goals

1989

FIRST ROUND

Group 1
Tournament in Amman, Jordan

	AD	AR	AA	AS	AA	Pl	W	D	L	F	A	Pts
Al Deffatain ...... JOR	–	2–1	0–0	3–0	2–0	4	3	1	0	7	1	7
Al Rasheed .... IRQ	–	–	0–0	3–0	1–0	4	2	1	1	5	2	5
Al Ansar .... LIB	–	–	–	0–2	2–1	4	1	2	1	2	3	4
Al Saad .... QAT	–	–	–	–	0–0	4	1	1	2	2	6	3
Al Ahli .... NYM	–	–	–	–	–	4	0	1	3	1	5	1

Al Deffatain and Al Rasheed qualified for the semi-finals but Al Deffatain later withdrew

Group 2
Tournament in Bahrain

		AA	AM	AF	AW	AH	Pl	W	D	L	F	A	Pts
Al Arabi	KUW	–	1–2	1–1	2–1	4–2	4	2	1	1	8	6	5
Al Muharraq	BAH	–	–	2–0	1–2	1–1	4	2	1	1	6	4	5
Al Fanja	OMN	–	–	–	3–0	2–1	4	2	1	1	6	4	5
Al Wasl	UAE	–	–	–	–	1–0	4	2	0	2	4	6	4
Al Hilal	ARS	–	–	–	–	–	4	0	1	3	4	8	1

Al Muharraq and Al Arabi qualified for the semi-finals but both later withdrew

Group 3
Tournament in Muscat, Oman

		AF	Sa	Pu	Ka	Pl	W	D	L	F	A	Pts
Al Fanja	OMN	–	3–1	2–0	5–0	3	3	0	0	10	1	6
Salgaocar SC	IND	–	–	0–0	3–0	3	1	1	1	4	3	3
Punjab FC	PAK	–	–	–	1–1	3	0	2	1	1	3	2
Kathmandu SC	NEP	–	–	–	–	3	0	1	2	1	9	1

Al Fanja qualified for the semi–finals

Group 4
Tournament in Ahwaz, Iran

		Sh	Mo	OB	Vi	Pl	W	D	L	F	A	Pts
Shahin FC	IRN	–	1–0	5–0	5–0	3	3	0	0	11	0	6
Mohammedan	BAN	–	–	3–1	7–2	3	2	0	1	10	4	4
Old Bens SC	SRL	–	–	–	3–1	3	1	0	2	4	9	2
Victory SC	MDV	–	–	–	–	3	0	0	3	3	15	0

Shahin qualified for the semi-finals

Group 5
Tournament in Kuala Lumpur, Malaysia

		KL	PJ	Ge	AF	Mu	Pl	W	D	L	F	A	Pts
Kuala Lum. FA	MAL	–	2–1	4–2	6–0	7–1	4	4	0	0	19	4	8
Pelita Jaya FC	INA	–	–	4–1	3–0	2–1	4	3	0	1	10	4	6
Geylang Inter.	SIN	–	–	–	3–0	5–1	4	2	0	2	11	9	4
Air Force	PHI	–	–	–	–	1–0	4	1	0	3	1	12	2
Muara FC	BRU	–	–	–	–	–	4	0	0	4	3	15	0

Kuala Lumpur and Pelita Jaya qualified for the semi-finals

Group 6
Tournament in Shenyang, China

		Li	Ni	Ch	HK	Pl	W	D	L	F	A	Pts
Liaoning	PRC	–	1–0	1–1	5–1	3	2	1	0	7	2	5
Nissan	JAP	–	–	2–0	9–0	3	2	0	1	11	1	4
Chadongcha FC	PRK	–	–	–	2–0	3	1	1	1	3	3	3
Hap Kuan	MAC	–	–	–	–	3	0	0	3	1	16	0

Liaoning and Nissan qualify for the semi-finals

SEMI-FINALS

Group A
Tournament in Kuala Lumpur

		Ni	KL	AF	Pl	W	D	L	F	A	Pts
Nissan	JAP	–	2–1	1–0	2	2	0	0	3	1	4
Kuala Lumpur FA	MAL	–	–	2–0	2	1	0	1	3	2	2
Al Fanja	OMN	–	–	–	2	0	0	2	0	3	0

Nissan qualified for the final

Group B
Tournament in Jakarta, Indonesia

		Li	AR	Sh	PJ	Pl	W	D	L	F	A	Pts
Liaoning	PRC	–	0–0	2–0	1–0	3	2	1	0	3	0	5
Al Rasheed	IRQ	–	–	5–0	1–1	3	1	2	0	6	1	4
Shahin FC	IRN	–	–	–	2–0	3	1	0	2	2	7	2
Pelita Jaya FC	INA	–	–	–	–	3	0	1	2	1	4	1

Liaoning qualified for the final

FINAL

1st leg
Yokohama, 22–04–1990
NISSAN 1 (Sandoro)
LIAONING 2 (Fu Bo, Sandoro)

2nd leg
Shenyang, 29–04–1990
LIAONING 1 (Xu Hui)
NISSAN 1 (Kazushi Kimura)

1990

QUALIFYING TOURNAMENT

Group 1
Tournament in Baghdad

		AR	AR	AY	Pl	W	D	L	F	A	Pts
Al Rasheed	IRQ	–	2–1	1–0	2	2	0	0	3	1	4
Al Ramtha	JOR	–	–	3–1	2	1	0	1	4	3	2
Al Yarmouk	YEM	–	–	–	2	0	0	2	1	4	0

Al Rasheed qualified for the final tournament but withdrew

Group 2
Al Saad .... QAT . 1–1 0–1 ... Esteghlal SC IRN
Esteghlal qualified for the final tournament

Group 3
The Gulf Cooperation Council Club Tournament was cancelled due to the political crisis in the region

Group 4
Tournament in Quetta, Pakistan

		AN	PA	Ra	Pl	W	D	L	F	A	Pts
Al Nasr	OMN	–	0–0	2–0	2	1	1	0	2	0	3
Pakistan Airlines	PAK	–	–	1–0	2	1	1	0	1	0	3
Ranipokhari	NEP	–	–	–	2	0	0	2	0	3	0

Al Nasr qualified for the final tournament

Group 5
Tournament in Dhaka, Bangladesh

		Mo	Sa	CL	Pl	W	D	L	F	A	Pts
Mohammedan	BAN	–	2–1	5–0	2	2	0	0	7	1	4
Salgaocar SC	IND	–	–	3–1	2	1	0	1	4	3	2
Club Lagoons	MDV	–	–	–	2	0	0	2	1	8	0

Mohammedan qualified for the final tournament

Group 6
Tournament in Singapore

		PJ	BB	Ge	Pl	W	D	L	F	A	Pts
Pelita Jaya FC	INA	–	2–1	0–0	2	1	1	0	2	1	3
Bangkok Bank	THA	–	–	2–1	2	1	0	1	3	3	2
Geylang Internat.	SIN	–	–	–	2	0	1	1	1	2	1

Pelita Jaya and Bangkok Bank qualified for the final tournament

Group 7
Tournament in Pyongyang, North Korea

		Ap	Li	Ni	Pl	W	D	L	F	A	Pts
April 25th	PRK	–	1–0	1–0	2	2	0	0	2	0	4
Liaoning	PRC	–	–	3–2	2	1	0	1	3	3	2
Nissan	JAP	–	–	–	2	0	0	2	2	4	0

April 25th and Liaoning qualified for the final tournament

FINAL TOURNAMENT

Dhaka, Bangladesh, 19th–29th July 1991

FIRST ROUND

Group 1

		Li	PJ	AN	Pl	W	D	L	F	A	Pts
Liaoning	PRC	–	1–0	1–1	2	1	1	0	2	1	3
Pelita Jaya	INA	–	–	3–0	2	1	0	1	3	1	2
Al Nasr	OMN	–	–	–	2	0	1	1	1	4	1

Group 2

		Es	Ap	Mo	BB	Pl	W	D	L	F	A	Pts
Esteghlal	IRN	–	2–1	1–1	2–0	3	2	1	0	5	2	5
April 25th	PRK	–	–	0–0	4–3	3	1	1	1	5	5	3

Mohammedan	BAN	–	–	–	1–1	3	0	3	0	2	2	3
Bangkok Bank	THA	–	–	–	–	3	0	1	2	4	7	1

SEMI-FINALS

Esteghlal .... 2–0 .... Pelita Jaya
Liaoning .... 3–0 .... April 25th

3RD PLACE

April 25th .... 2–2 (7–6p) Pelita Jaya

FINAL

Dhaka Stadium, Dhaka, 29–07–1991
ESTEGHLAL SPORTS CLUB 2 (Barvagh, Marfavy)
LIAONING 1 (Xu-hui)

ASIAN CUP WINNERS CUP

1990

SEMI-FINALS

Muharraq .... BAH .... 1–0 2–2 ... Al Shabab .... UAE
Al Hilal .... ARS .... 0–0 0–1 ... Pirouzi .... IRN

FINAL

Pirouzi .... 0–0 1–0 ... Muharraq

1991

SEMI-FINALS

Nissan .... JPN .... 2–0 0–0 ... Pupuk Kaltim ... INA
Al Ramtha .... JOR .... 0–1 1–2 ... Al Nasser .... ARS

FINAL

Nissan .... 1–1 5–0 ... Al Nasser

OTHER ASIAN TOURNAMENTS

Apart from the Asian Cup and the football tournament of the Asian Games, there are many tournaments catering for the national sides of the region. Almost every country hosts an event of some sort, and so worried was the AFC at the proliferation that they recently insisted that instead of being held annually, such tournaments could only take place once every two years.

The dubious status of some of these minor tournaments as 'A' grade internationals has led to much debate as to the true number of international matches played by Asian countries and especially the number of caps won by some of the leading players. It is common practice to play an Olympic team or an under-21 team without making it clear and added to this is the fact that many of the European sides who take part are listed as representing their country when in fact they are club sides on tour.

The most famous of these tournaments are the Merdeka Cup and the President's Cup. First played in 1957, the Merdeka is the longest running of all, and for many years was an annual event in the fixture lists of countries from South East Asia. Held in the Malaysian capital of Kuala Lumpur and occasionally in Ipoh as part of that country's independence celebrations, it was instrumental in the development of football in Asia as it provided an ideal annual opportunity for courses on coaching, refereeing and so on.

Its importance has been diminished in the 1980s due to the proliferation of other tournaments and this can be seen from the contestants, many of whom are no more than average European club sides. Taking over in the prestige stakes has been the President's Cup held in South Korea. As the major football and economic power in the region, Korea has been able to maintain a high standard of entrant in the cup, unlike the Merdeka.

The late 1960s and early 1970s saw the initial burst of new tournaments following in the footsteps of the Merdeka. In 1968 the King's Cup, held annually in Thailand, was introduced and was followed in 1970 by the Jakarta Anniversary Tournament. South Vietnam also held an annual competition, but the real growth has occurred in the 1980s. The Jawaharal Nehru Gold Cup made its first appearance in 1982, fielding in the first few years the best sides any Asian tournament has managed to assemble to date. China, Pakistan, Bangladesh, Singapore and even Brunei and Nepal have all got in on the act.

On top of all these tournaments are three regional tournaments of some import: the football tournaments of both the South Asian Federation Games and the South East Asian Games as well as the Arabian Gulf Tournament. The first involves Bangladesh, Bhutan, India, Maldives, Nepal, Pakistan and Sri Lanka, and is held every second year as part of a bigger tournament. The same is also true for the South East Asian Games whose participants include Brunei, Indonesia, Malaysia, Myanmar, Philippines, Singapore and Thailand. The Arabian Gulf Tournament has gained a reputation as the focus for the emerging Arab nations and its entrants include Bahrain, Iraq, Kuwait, Oman, Qatar, Saudi Arabia and the United Arab Emirates.

ASIAN YOUTH CUP

1959 .... South Korea
1960 .... South Korea
1961 .... Indonesia & Burma
1962 .... Thailand
1963 .... South Korea & Burma
1964 .... Burma & Israel
1965 .... Israel
1966 .... Israel & Thailand
1967 .... Israel
1968 .... Burma
1969 .... Burma & Thailand
1970 .... Burma
1971 .... Israel
1972 .... Israel
1973 .... Iran
1974 .... Iran & India
1975 .... Iran & Iraq
1976 .... Iran & North Korea
1977 .... Iraq
1978 .... Iraq & South Korea
1980 .... South Korea
1982 .... South Korea
1984 .... China
1986 .... Saudi Arabia
1988 .... Iraq
1990 .... South Korea

AFRO-ASIAN CUP OF NATIONS

1985 Cameroon .... 4–1 1–2 .... Saudi Arabia
1987 South Korea .... 1–1 (4–3p) .... Egypt

ARAB NATIONS CUP

1963 ...... Tunisia
1964 ...... Iraq
1986 ...... Iraq
1985 ...... Iraq
1988 ...... Iraq

ASIAN UNDER-16 CUP

1984 ...... Saudi Arabia
1986 ...... South Korea
1988 ...... Saudi Arabia

THE MERDEKA FOOTBALL TOURNAMENT

FIRST EDITION
1st August–7th September 1957

FIRST ROUND

Hong Kong .... 6–2 .... Cambodia
Indonesia .... 4–0 .... Thailand
South Vietnam .... 5–5 2–1 .... Singapore
Malaysia .... 5–2 .... Burma

SECOND ROUND

Winners Group

	HK	Id	SV	Ma	Pl	W	D	L	F	A	Pts
Hong Kong	–	2–1	3–1	3–3	3	2	1	0	8	5	5
Indonesia	–	–	3–1	4–2	3	2	0	1	8	5	4
South Vietnam	–	–	–	4–1	3	1	0	2	6	7	2
Malaysia	–	–	–	–	3	0	1	2	6	11	1

Losers Group

	Si	Bu	Th	Ca	Pl	W	D	L	F	A	Pts
Singapore	–	3–2	6–0	1–1	3	2	1	0	10	3	5
Burma	–	–	5–2	2–0	3	2	0	1	9	5	4
Thailand	–	–	–	3–0	3	1	0	2	5	11	2
Cambodia	–	–	–	–	3	0	1	2	1	6	1

SECOND EDITION
30th August–4th September 1958

	Ma	HK	Id	Si	SV	Pl	W	D	L	F	A	Pts
Malaysia	–	3–0	3–2	0–0	2–0	4	3	1	0	8	2	7
Hong Kong	–	–	2–1	2–0	5–3	4	3	0	1	9	7	6
Indonesia	–	–	–	2–0	4–1	4	2	0	2	9	6	4
Singapore	–	–	–	–	4–4	4	0	2	2	4	8	2
South Vietnam	–	–	–	–	–	4	0	1	3	8	15	1

THIRD EDITION
30th August–7th September 1959

FIRST ROUND

Malaysia .... 4–1 .... South Korea
India .... 2–0 .... Singapore
South Vietnam .... 3–2 .... South Korea
Hong Kong .... 1–1 4–2 .... Japan

SECOND ROUND

Winners Group

	Ma	In	SV	HK	Pl	W	D	L	F	A	Pts
Malaysia	–	1–1	4–3	2–1	3	2	1	0	7	5	5
India	–	–	2–2	2–0	3	1	2	0	5	3	4
South Vietnam	–	–	–	4–1	3	1	1	1	9	7	3
Hong Kong	–	–	–	–	3	0	0	3	2	8	0

Losers Group

	SK	Ja	Si	Pl	W	D	L	F	A	Pts
South Korea	–	0–0	4–1	2	1	1	0	4	1	3
Japan	–	–	4–1	2	1	1	0	4	1	3
Singapore	–	–	–	2	0	0	2	2	8	0

South Korea won a third place play-off 3–1 against Japan

FOURTH EDITION
5th–14th August 1960

FIRST ROUND

Group 1

	Ma	Pa	Ja	Th	Pl	W	D	L	F	A	Pts
Malaysia	–	1–0	3–0	8–2	3	3	0	0	12	2	6
Pakistan	–	–	3–1	7–0	3	2	0	1	10	2	4
Japan	–	–	–	3–1	3	1	0	2	4	7	2
Thailand	–	–	–	–	3	0	0	3	3	18	0

Group 2

	SK	Id	HK	SV	Si	Pl	W	D	L	F	A	Pts
South Korea	–	2–0	3–1	0–0	3–3	4	2	2	0	8	4	6
Indonesia	–	–	3–1	5–3	8–3	4	3	0	1	16	9	6
Hong Kong	–	–	–	3–1	3–2	4	2	0	2	8	9	4
South Vietnam	–	–	–	–	2–1	4	1	1	2	6	9	3
Singapore	–	–	–	–	–	4	0	1	3	9	16	1

3RD PLACE

Indonesia .... 4–0 .... Pakistan

FINAL

Malaysia .... 0–0 .... South Korea

Title shared

FIFTH EDITION
2nd–13th August 1961

FIRST ROUND

Group 1

	Ma	SV	Ja	In	Pl	W	D	L	F	A	Pts
Malaysia	–	3–1	3–2	1–2	3	2	0	1	7	5	4
South Vietnam	–	–	3–2	2–1	3	2	0	1	6	6	4
Japan	–	–	–	3–1	3	1	0	2	7	7	2
India	–	–	–	–	3	1	0	2	4	6	2

Group 2

	Id	Si	SK	HK	Th	Pl	W	D	L	F	A	Pts
Indonesia	–	1–0	1–1	2–2	2–1	4	2	2	0	6	4	6
Singapore	–	–	1–0	4–3	5–3	4	3	0	1	10	7	6
South Korea	–	–	–	1–1	3–1	4	1	2	1	5	4	4
Hong Kong	–	–	–	–	2–1	4	1	2	1	8	8	4
Thailand	–	–	–	–	–	4	0	0	4	6	12	0

3RD PLACE

Vietnam .... 2–1 .... Singapore

FINAL

Indonesia .... 2–1 .... Malaysia

SIXTH EDITION
8th–19th September 1962

FIRST ROUND

Group 1

	Id	SK	SV	Si	Ph	Pl	W	D	L	F	A	Pts
Indonesia	–	3–0	2–1	2–0	9–0	4	4	0	0	16	1	8
South Korea	–	–	3–0	2–0	3–2	4	3	0	1	8	5	6
South Vietnam	–	–	–	2–2	6–0	4	1	1	2	9	7	3
Singapore	–	–	–	–	5–0	4	1	1	2	7	6	3
Philippines	–	–	–	–	–	4	0	0	4	2	23	0

Group 2

	Pa	Ma	Bu	Ja	Pl	W	D	L	F	A	Pts
Pakistan	–	0–0	1–0	1–1	3	1	2	0	2	1	4
Malaysia	–	–	3–2	2–2	3	1	2	0	5	4	4
Burma	–	–	–	3–1	3	1	0	2	5	5	2
Japan	–	–	–	–	3	0	2	1	4	6	2

3RD PLACE

Malaysia .... 3–1 .... South Korea

FINAL

Indonesia .... 2–1 .... Pakistan

SEVENTH EDITION
8th–18th August 1963

	Ja	SK	SV	Ma	Fo	Th	Pl	W	D	L	F	A	Pts
Taiwan	2–0	1–0	1–1	3–2	2–0	2–2	6	4	2	0	11	5	10
Japan	–	1–1	5–1	4–3	6–1	4–1	6	4	1	1	20	9	9
South Korea	–	–	3–1	2–3	1–0	5–1	6	3	1	2	12	7	7
South Vietnam	–	–	–	5–0	3–1	3–2	6	3	1	2	14	12	7
Malaysia	–	–	–	–	3–1	2–2	6	2	1	3	13	17	5
Forces XI	–	–	–	–	–	4–0	6	1	0	5	7	15	2
Thailand	–	–	–	–	–	–	6	0	2	4	8	20	2

EIGHTH EDITION
22nd August–5th Sept 1964

PRELIMINARY GAMES

South Korea .... 1–0 .... Burma
Malaysia .... 3–0 .... Thailand
Vietnam .... 2–0 .... Japan
Taiwan .... 4–0 .... Cambodia
Malaysia .... 1–1 .... India
India .... 0–0 .... South Korea

FIRST ROUND

Group 1

	In	SK	Ja	Th	Ca	Pl	W	D	L	F	A	Pts
India	–	2–1	3–2	2–1	4–0	4	4	0	0	11	4	8
South Korea	–	–	3–0	2–0	2–2	4	2	1	1	8	4	5
Japan	–	–	–	2–2	4–0	4	1	1	2	8	8	3
Thailand	–	–	–	–	1–0	4	1	1	2	4	6	3
Cambodia	–	–	–	–	–	4	0	1	3	2	11	1

Group 2

	Bu	SV	Ta	Ma	Pl	W	D	L	F	A	Pts
Burma	–	1–0	2–4	3–0	3	2	0	1	6	4	4
South Vietnam	–	–	0–0	2–1	3	1	1	1	2	2	3
Taiwan	–	–	–	2–5	3	1	1	1	6	7	3
Malaysia	–	–	–	–	3	1	0	2	6	7	2

MINOR PLACINGS

Malaysia .... 1–0 .... Thailand
Taiwan .... 2–2 .... Japan

3RD PLACE

South Korea .... 2–1 .... South Vietnam

FINAL

Burma .... 1–0 .... India

NINTH EDITION
14th–28th August 1965

PRELIMINARY GAMES

Thailand .... 3–2 .... South Korea
Malaysia .... 2–2 .... Japan
South Vietnam .... 5–2 .... Taiwan
Burma .... 4–2 .... Hong Kong
India .... 1–1 .... Japan

FIRST ROUND

Group 1

	SK	In	SV	HK	Ma	Pl	W	D	L	F	A	Pts
South Korea	–	1–0	0–0	1–0	2–0	4	3	1	0	4	0	7
India	–	–	2–0	2–2	2–0	4	2	1	1	6	3	5
South Vietnam	–	–	–	2–1	3–3	4	1	2	1	5	6	4
Hong Kong	–	–	–	–	3–1	4	1	1	2	6	6	3
Malaysia	–	–	–	–	–	4	0	1	3	4	10	1

Group 2

	Ta	Bu	Ja	Th	Pl	W	D	L	F	A	Pts
Taiwan	–	1–3	4–0	3–2	3	2	0	1	8	5	4
Burma	–	–	1–3	1–1	3	1	1	1	5	5	3
Japan	–	–	–	0–0	3	1	1	1	3	5	3
Thailand	–	–	–	–	3	0	2	1	3	4	2

MINOR PLACINGS

Thailand .... 1–1 .... Hong Kong
Japan .... 2–1 .... South Vietnam

3RD PLACE

Burma .... 1–1 .... India

FINAL

South Korea .... 1–1 .... Taiwan

Title shared

TENTH EDITION
13th–18th August 1966

PRELIMINARY GAMES

Malaysia .... 5–2 .... South Vietnam
Burma .... 2–2 .... Singapore

India .... 2–0 .... Hong Kong
South Korea .... 2–0 .... Japan
Taiwan .... 2–1 .... Thailand

FIRST ROUND

Group 1

	SV	In	Si	Ja	Ta	Pl	W	D	L	F	A	Pts
South Vietnam	–	0–1	2–1	2–0	3–0	4	3	0	1	7	2	6
India	–	–	0–1	3–0	1–0	4	3	0	1	5	1	6
Singapore	–	–	–	0–1	4–1	4	2	0	2	6	4	4
Japan	–	–	–	–	5–2	4	2	0	2	6	7	4
Taiwan	–	–	–	–	–	4	0	0	4	3	13	0

Group 2

	Bu	SK	Ma	Th	HK	Pl	W	D	L	F	A	Pts
Burma	–	2–0	0–0	3–0	2–0	4	3	1	0	7	0	7
South Korea	–	–	2–1	2–1	1–0	4	3	0	1	5	4	6
Malaysia	–	–	–	0–0	1–0	4	1	2	1	2	2	4
Thailand	–	–	–	–	2–2	4	0	2	2	3	7	2
Hong Kong	–	–	–	–	–	4	0	1	3	2	6	1

3RD PLACE

South Korea .... 1–0 .... India

FINAL

South Vietnam .... 1–0 .... Burma

ELEVENTH EDITION
10th–26th August 1967

FIRST ROUND

Group 1

	SV	Ma	In	HK	Au	Th	Pl	W	D	L	F	A	Pts
South Vietnam	–	1–1	1–0	5–0	3–0	5–2	5	4	1	0	15	3	9
Malaysia	–	–	0–0	3–0	3–2	1–0	5	3	2	0	8	3	8
India	–	–	–	4–0	3–1	1–1	5	2	2	1	8	3	6
Hong Kong	–	–	–	–	3–2	1–0	5	2	0	3	4	14	4
Australian XI	–	–	–	–	–	3–1	5	1	0	4	8	13	2
Thailand	–	–	–	–	–	–	5	0	1	4	4	11	1

Group 2

	SK	Bu	Id	Ta	Si	Pl	W	D	L	F	A	Pts
South Korea	–	1–0	3–1	2–1	3–0	4	4	0	0	9	2	8
Burma	–	–	5–0	1–2	3–0	4	2	0	2	9	3	4
Indonesia	–	–	–	2–1	4–1	4	2	0	2	7	10	4
Taiwan	–	–	–	–	3–3	4	1	1	2	7	8	3
Singapore	–	–	–	–	–	4	0	1	3	4	13	1

MINOR PLACINGS

Australian XI .... 5–3 .... Singapore
India .... 1–1 .... Taiwan
Hong Kong .... 2–1 .... Indonesia
Taiwan .... 4–2 .... Hong Kong
Indonesia .... 3–0 .... India

SEMI-FINALS

South Korea .... 3–1 .... Malaysia
Burma .... 3–0 .... South Vietnam

3RD PLACE

South Vietman .... 2–1 .... Malaysia

FINAL

South Korea .... 0–0 .... Burma

TWELFTH EDITION
9th–25th August 1968

FIRST ROUND

Group 1

	Au	SK	Ja	Ta	Si	Pl	W	D	L	F	A	Pts
Indonesia	4–5	4–2	7–0	10–1	4–0	5	4	0	1	29	8	8
Australian XI	–	3–0	0–1	3–2	4–4	5	3	1	1	15	11	7
South Korea	–	–	2–0	2–1	3–2	5	3	0	2	9	10	6
Japan	–	–	–	1–0	2–1	5	3	0	2	4	10	6
Taiwan	–	–	–	–	2–0	5	1	0	4	6	16	2
Singapore	–	–	–	–	–	5	0	1	4	7	15	1

Group 2

	Bu	In	Th	SV	HK	Pl	W	D	L	F	A	Pts
Malaysia	1–1	2–1	4–1	4–0	1–1	5	3	2	0	12	4	8
Burma	–	1–3	0–0	3–0	3–0	5	2	2	1	8	4	6
India	–	–	0–1	3–2	1–1	5	2	1	2	8	7	5
Thailand	–	–	–	2–3	0–0	5	1	2	2	4	7	4
South Vietnam	–	–	–	–	3–1	5	2	0	3	8	13	4
Hong Kong	–	–	–	–	–	5	0	3	2	3	8	3

MINOR PLACINGS

South Korea .... 2–1 .... Thailand
India .... 1–0 .... Japan
South Korea .... 1–0 .... India
Japan .... 2–1 .... Thailand

SEMI-FINALS

Malaysia .... 4–3 .... Australian XI
Burma .... 2–1 .... Indonesia

3RD PLACE

Australian XI .... 3–1 .... Indonesia

FINAL

Malaysia .... 3–0 .... Burma

THIRTEENTH EDITION
30th October–9th November 1969

FIRST ROUND

Group 1

	Id	Ma	SK	Th	Pl	W	D	L	F	A	Pts
Indonesia	–	3–1	3–0	4–0	3	3	0	0	10	1	6
Malaysia	–	–	4–1	1–0	3	2	0	1	6	4	4
South Korea	–	–	–	3–0	3	1	0	2	4	7	2
Thailand	–	–	–	–	3	0	0	3	0	8	0

Group 2

	Bu	Si	In	Au	Pl	W	D	L	F	A	Pts
Burma	–	3–1	6–0	5–2	3	3	0	0	14	3	6
Singapore	–	–	0–3	4–2	3	1	0	2	5	8	2
India	–	–	–	0–1	3	1	0	2	3	7	2
Australian XI	–	–	–	–	3	1	0	2	5	9	2

MINOR PLACINGS

South Korea .... 3–2 .... Australian XI
Thailand .... 1–0 .... India

SEMI-FINALS

Indonesia .... 9–2 .... Singapore
Malaysia .... 3–1 .... Burma

3RD PLACE

Burma .... 9–0 .... Singapore

FINAL

Indonesia .... 3–2 .... Malaysia

FOURTEENTH EDITION
30th July–16th August 1970

FIRST ROUND

Group 1

	In	Ma	Ta	Au	SV	Pl	W	D	L	F	A	Pts
Burma	2–0	2–1	1–1	1–0	4–2	5	4	1	0	10	4	9
India	–	3–1	0–1	2–0	2–1	5	3	0	2	7	5	6
Malaysia	–	–	3–1	4–1	0–0	5	2	1	2	9	7	5
Taiwan	–	–	–	1–3	2–1	5	2	1	2	6	8	5
Australian XI	–	–	–	–	3–1	5	2	0	3	7	9	4
South Vietnam	–	–	–	–	–	5	0	1	4	5	11	1

Group 2

	HK	Id	Ja	Th	Si	Pl	W	D	L	F	A	Pts
South Korea	0–0	2–1	1–1	0–0	4–0	5	2	3	0	7	2	7
Hong Kong	–	1–3	2–1	2–0	3–2	5	3	1	1	8	6	7
Indonesia	–	–	3–4	6–3	3–1	5	3	0	2	16	11	6
Japan	–	–	–	0–0	4–0	5	2	2	1	10	6	6
Thailand	–	–	–	–	5–4	5	1	2	2	8	12	4
Singapore	–	–	–	–	–	5	0	0	5	7	19	0

MINOR PLACINGS

South Vietnam .... 4–0 .... Singapore
Thailand .... 2–0 .... Australian XI
Japan .... 3–2 .... Thailand
Malaysia .... 4–0 .... Indonesia

SEMI-FINALS

South Korea .... 3–2 .... India
Burma .... 5–0 .... Hong Kong

3RD PLACE

India .... 3–2 .... Hong Kong

FINAL

South Korea .... 1–0 .... Burma

FIFTEENTH EDITION
August 1971

FIRST ROUND

Group 1

	SK	Ta	Ma	SV	Ja	Th	Pl	W	D	L	F	A	Pts
South Korea	–	0–1	1–0	1–0	3–0	4–0	5	4	0	1	9	1	8
Taiwan	–	–	0–0	3–2	0–2	4–0	5	3	1	1	8	4	7
Malaysia	–	–	–	2–0	4–1	0–2	5	2	1	2	6	4	5
South Vietnam	–	–	–	–	2–0	4–2	5	2	0	3	8	8	4
Japan	–	–	–	–	–	3–2	5	2	0	3	6	11	4
Thailand	–	–	–	–	–	–	5	1	0	4	6	15	2

Group 2

	Id	Bu	Si	HK	In	Ph	Pl	W	D	L	F	A	Pts
Indonesia	–	2–2	4–0	3–0	3–1	3–1	5	4	1	0	15	4	9
Burma	–	–	0–1	4–0	9–1	2–0	5	3	1	1	17	4	7
Singapore	–	–	–	2–1	2–2	4–4	5	2	2	1	9	11	6
Hong Kong	–	–	–	–	2–1	2–1	5	2	0	3	5	11	4
India	–	–	–	–	–	5–1	5	1	1	3	10	17	3
Philippines	–	–	–	–	–	–	5	0	1	4	7	16	1

MINOR PLACINGS

Philippines .... 3–1 .... Thailand
Japan .... 1–0 .... India
South Vietnam .... 3–1 .... Hong Kong
Malaysia .... 4–2 .... Singapore

SEMI-FINALS

Burma .... 1–0 .... South Korea
Indonesia .... 1–0 .... Taiwan

3RD PLACE

South Korea .... 2–0 .... Taiwan

FINAL

Burma .... 1–0 .... Indonesia

SIXTEENTH EDITION
July 1972

FIRST ROUND

Group 1

	Ma	Ja	Ca	Ph	Bu	SL	Pl	W	D	L	F	A	Pts
Malaysia	–	3–1	6–1	1–0	4–0	4–1	5	5	0	0	18	3	10
Japan	–	–	4–1	5–1	6–1	5–0	5	4	0	1	21	6	8
Cambodia	–	–	–	2–2	2–1	6–1	5	2	1	2	12	14	5
Philippines	–	–	–	–	1–1	4–1	5	1	2	3	8	10	4
Burma	–	–	–	–	–	5–2	5	1	1	3	8	15	3
Sri Lanka	–	–	–	–	–	–	5	0	0	5	5	24	0

Group 2

	SK	Ma	HK	Th	Id	Si	Pl	W	D	L	F	A	Pts
South Korea	–	3–1	0–0	2–0	2–0	4–1	5	4	1	0	11	2	9
Malaysia B	–	–	4–1	2–0	2–1	2–0	5	4	0	1	11	5	8
Hong Kong	–	–	–	2–2	1–0	4–1	5	2	2	1	8	7	6
Thailand	–	–	–	–	2–3	2–0	5	1	1	3	6	9	3
Indonesia	–	–	–	–	–	0–0	5	1	1	3	4	7	3
Singapore	–	–	–	–	–	–	5	0	1	4	2	12	1

MINOR PLACINGS

Singapore .... 6–1 .... Sri Lanka
Indonesia .... 3–2 .... Burma
Thailand .... 4–0 .... Philippines
Cambodia .... 1–0 .... Hong Kong

SEMI-FINALS

South Korea .... 3–0 .... Japan
Malaysia .... 4–0 .... Malaysia B

3RD PLACE

Japan .... 1–0 .... Malaysia B

FINAL

South Korea .... 2–1 .... Malaysia

SEVENTEENTH EDITION
26th July–12th August 1973

PRELIMINARY ROUND

Malaysia .... 0–0 (3–2p) ..... Kuwait
Singapore .... 1–1 (1–0p) ..... Cambodia
Thailand .... 2–2 (1–0p) ..... Bangladesh
Burma .... 0–0 (5–4p) ..... South Korea
India .... 2–1 .... South Vietnam

FIRST ROUND

Group 1

	SK	Ma	In	Th	Ca	Pl	W	D	L	F	A	Pts
South Korea	–	2–1	0–0	0–0	1–0	4	2	2	0	3	1	6
Malaysia	–	–	4–0	2–2	1–0	4	2	1	1	8	4	5
India	–	–	–	2–0	3–0	4	2	1	1	5	4	5
Thailand	–	–	–	–	4–1	4	1	2	1	6	5	4
Cambodia	–	–	–	–	–	4	0	0	4	1	9	0

Group 2

	Bu	Ku	SV	Ba	Si	Pl	W	D	L	F	A	Pts
Burma	–	2–0	2–1	6–0	1–0	4	4	0	0	11	1	8
Kuwait	–	–	2–1	2–1	2–0	4	3	0	1	6	4	6
South Vietnam	–	–	–	1–1	1–0	4	1	1	2	4	5	3
Bangladesh	–	–	–	–	1–1	4	0	2	2	3	10	2
Singapore	–	–	–	–	–	4	0	1	3	1	5	1

MINOR PLACINGS

Singapore .... 3–0 .... Cambodia
Thailand .... 2–0 .... Bangladesh
South Vietnam .... 1–1 (5–4p) ..... India

SEMI-FINALS

Malaysia .... 2–1 .... Burma
Kuwait .... 1–0 .... South Korea

3RD PLACE

Burma .... 2–1 .... South Korea

FINAL

Malaysia .... 3–1 .... Kuwait

EIGHTEENTH EDITION
23rd July–4th August 1974

PRELIMINARY ROUND

Malaysia .... 1–0 .... South Korea
India .... 4–2 .... Thailand
Indonesia .... 5–2 .... Hong Kong

FIRST ROUND

Group 1

	Ma	HK	In	Pl	W	D	L	F	A	Pts
Malaysia	–	1–0	4–1	2	2	0	0	5	1	4
Hong Kong	–	–	2–2	2	0	1	1	2	3	1
India	–	–	–	2	0	1	1	3	6	1

Group 2

	SK	Th	Id	Si	Pl	W	D	L	F	A	Pts
South Korea	–	1–1	0–0	1–0	3	1	2	0	2	1	4
Thailand	–	–	2–1	1–1	3	1	2	0	4	3	4
Indonesia	–	–	–	5–0	3	1	1	1	6	2	3
Singapore	–	–	–	–	3	0	1	2	1	7	1

MINOR PLACINGS

Indonesia .... 4–2 .... India

SEMI-FINALS

Malaysia .... 3–2 .... Thailand
South Korea .... 3–3 (5–4p) ..... Hong Kong

3RD PLACE

Hong Kong .... 1–0 .... Thailand

FINAL

Malaysia .... 1–0 .... South Korea

NINETEENTH EDITION
29th July–17th August 1975

	Ma	Bu	Ja	HK	Id	Th	Ba	Pl	W	D	L	F	A	Pts
S. Korea	3–1	3–2	3–1	1–0	5–1	6–0	4–0	7	7	0	0	25	5	14
Malaysia	–	2–1	2–0	3–1	2–1	1–0	3–0	7	6	0	1	14	6	12
Burma	–	–	0–2	5–0	2–0	1–0	7–1	7	4	0	3	18	8	8
Japan	–	–	–	0–2	4–1	4–0	3–0	7	4	0	3	14	8	8
H. Kong	–	–	–	–	2–3	3–0	9–1	7	3	0	4	17	13	6
Indonesia	–	–	–	–	–	2–1	4–0	7	3	0	4	12	16	6
Thailand	–	–	–	–	–	–	1–1	7	0	1	6	2	18	1
Bangladesh	–	–	–	–	–	–	–	7	0	1	6	3	31	1

FINAL

South Korea .... 1–0 .... Malaysia

TWENTIETH EDITION
7th–20th August 1976

	Ja	SK	Bu	Th	In	Id	Pl	W	D	L	F	A	Pts
Malaysia	2–2	2–1	3–1	0–0	5–1	7–1	6	4	2	0	19	6	10
Japan	–	0–0	2–2	2–2	5–1	6–0	6	2	4	0	17	7	8
South Korea	–	–	2–2	2–1	8–0	2–0	6	3	2	1	15	5	8
Burma	–	–	–	1–0	2–2	5–1	6	2	3	1	13	10	7
Thailand	–	–	–	–	6–2	1–0	6	2	2	2	10	7	6
India	–	–	–	–	–	3–1	6	1	1	4	9	27	3
Indonesia	–	–	–	–	–	–	6	0	0	6	3	24	0

FINAL

Malaysia .... 2–0 .... Japan

TWENTY-FIRST EDITION
16th–31st July 1977

	Iq	Ma	Lb	Bu	Th	Id	Pl	W	D	L	F	A	Pts
South Korea	1–1	1–1	4–0	4–0	4–1	5–1	6	4	2	0	19	4	10
Iraq	–	0–0	0–0	3–0	5–0	2–0	6	3	3	0	11	1	9
Malaysia	–	–	1–1	1–0	3–0	5–1	6	3	3	0	11	3	9
Libya	–	–	–	1–3	2–2	4–0	6	1	3	2	8	10	5
Burma	–	–	–	–	1–1	1–1	6	1	2	3	5	11	4
Thailand	–	–	–	–	–	1–0	6	1	2	3	5	15	4
Indonesia	–	–	–	–	–	–	6	0	1	5	3	18	1

FINAL

South Korea .... 1–0 .... Iraq

TWENTY-SECOND EDITION
12th–29th July 1978

	Iq	Ma	Th	Ja	Si	Id	Sy	Pl	W	D	L	F	A	Pts
S. Korea	2–0	3–1	3–0	4–0	2–0	2–0	2–0	7	7	0	0	18	1	14
Iraq	–	2–1	1–0	0–0	3–0	4–0	2–1	7	5	1	1	12	4	11
Malaysia	–	–	2–0	4–1	6–0	1–0	5–2	7	5	0	2	20	8	10
Thailand	–	–	–	0–4	2–1	3–0	3–1	7	3	0	4	8	12	6
Japan	–	–	–	–	1–2	1–2	3–2	7	2	1	4	10	14	5
Singapore	–	–	–	–	–	0–0	4–1	7	2	1	4	7	15	5
Indonesia	–	–	–	–	–	–	1–0	7	2	1	4	3	11	5
Syria	–	–	–	–	–	–	–	7	0	0	7	7	20	0

FINAL

South Korea .... 2–0 .... Iraq

TWENTY-THIRD EDITION
27th June–15th July 1979

	Ma	Ja	Bu	Id	Si	Ma	Th	Pl	W	D	L	F	A	Pts
S. Korea	4–1	1–0	3–2	6–0	1–1	3–1	2–1	7	6	1	0	20	6	13
Malaysia	–	1–1	4–1	1–1	3–0	3–1	4–2	7	4	2	1	17	10	10
Japan	–	–	1–0	0–0	3–1	0–0	2–0	7	3	3	1	7	3	9
Burma	–	–	–	4–0	4–1	3–1	2–0	7	4	0	3	16	10	8
Indonesia	–	–	–	–	0–0	1–1	2–1	7	1	4	2	4	13	6
Singapore	–	–	–	–	–	2–1	1–1	7	1	3	3	6	13	5
Malaysia B	–	–	–	–	–	–	2–2	7	0	3	4	7	14	3
Thailand	–	–	–	–	–	–	–	7	0	2	5	7	15	2

FINAL

South Korea .... 0–0 .... Malaysia

TWENTY-FOURTH EDITION
15th October–2nd November 1980

	Mo	SK	Th	NZ	Bu	Id	Ku	Pl	W	D	L	F	A	Pts
Malaysia	2–0	1–1	2–2	2–0	3–2	1–1	2–1	7	4	3	0	13	7	11
Morocco	–	1–1	2–1	3–0	2–2	2–0	3–0	7	4	2	1	13	6	10
S. Korea	–	–	0–0	1–2	1–1	1–0	3–0	7	2	4	1	8	5	8
Thailand	–	–	–	1–1	2–1	1–1	1–0	7	2	4	1	8	7	8
New Zeal.	–	–	–	–	1–1	0–0	5–1	7	2	3	2	9	9	7
Burma	–	–	–	–	–	1–0	1–3	7	1	3	3	9	12	5
Indonesia	–	–	–	–	–	–	2–1	7	1	3	3	4	7	5
Kuwait	–	–	–	–	–	–	–	7	1	0	6	6	17	2

FINAL

Morocco .... 2–1 .... Malaysia

TWENTY-FIFTH EDITION
30th August–20th September 1981

FIRST ROUND

Group 1

	Ja	In	NZ	Em	Id	Ma	Pl	W	D	L	F	A	Pts
Japan	–	3–2	0–1	3–2	2–0	2–0	5	4	0	1	10	5	8
India	–	–	0–0	2–0	1–0	2–2	5	2	2	1	7	5	6
New Zealand	–	–	–	0–1	0–0	1–0	5	2	2	1	2	1	6
Arab Emirates	–	–	–	–	2–5	1–0	5	2	0	3	6	10	4
Indonesia	–	–	–	–	–	0–2	5	1	1	3	5	7	3
Malaysia	–	–	–	–	–	–	5	1	1	3	4	6	3

Group 2

	Br	Iq	SK	Th	Si	Pl	W	D	L	F	A	Pts
Brazilian XI	–	2–1	2–0	5–1	3–0	4	4	0	0	12	2	8
Iraq	–	–	1–1	7–1	4–0	4	2	1	1	13	4	5
South Korea	–	–	–	1–1	2–0	4	1	2	1	4	4	4
Thailand	–	–	–	–	3–1	4	1	1	2	6	14	3
Singapore	–	–	–	–	–	4	0	0	4	1	12	0

SEMI-FINALS

Iraq .... 2–0 .... Japan
Brazilian XI .... 2–0 .... India

FINAL

Iraq .... 1–0 .... Brazilian XI

TWENTY-SIXTH EDITION
5th–22nd August 1982

FIRST ROUND

Group 1

	SK	Se	Ma	Id	Em	Pl	W	D	L	F	A	Pts
South Korea	–	0–2	2–1	4–0	3–2	4	3	0	1	9	5	6
Senegal	–	–	0–1	2–2	3–1	4	2	1	1	7	4	5
Malaysia	–	–	–	0–2	1–0	4	2	0	2	3	4	4
Indonesia	–	–	–	–	1–2	4	1	1	2	5	8	3
Arab Emirates	–	–	–	–	–	4	1	0	3	5	8	2

Group 2

	Br	Gh	Si	In	Th	Pl	W	D	L	F	A	Pts
Brazilian XI	–	1–1	4–1	1–0	4–0	4	3	1	0	10	2	7
Ghana	–	–	3–0	1–0	4–1	4	3	1	0	9	2	7
Singapore	–	–	–	3–0	2–0	4	2	0	2	6	7	4
India	–	–	–	–	0–0	4	0	1	3	0	5	1
Thailand	–	–	–	–	–	4	0	1	3	1	10	1

SECOND ROUND

	Br	Gh	Se	SK	Pl	W	D	L	F	A	Pts
Brazilian XI	–	2–0	2–0	2–0	3	3	0	0	6	0	6
Ghana	–	–	2–2	1–0	3	1	1	1	3	4	3
Senegal	–	–	–	1–1	3	0	2	1	3	5	2
South Korea	–	–	–	–	3	0	1	2	1	4	1

FINAL

Brazilian XI .... 3–0 .... Ghana

TWENTY-SEVENTH EDITION
14th September–2nd October 1983

FIRST ROUND

Group 1

	Ar	Al	SK	Ma	Ba	Ne	Pl	W	D	L	F	A	Pts
Argentine XI	–	1–0	1–3	2–1	5–2	1–0	5	4	0	1	10	6	8
Algeria	–	–	3–1	0–0	1–0	2–0	5	3	1	1	6	2	7
South Korea	–	–	–	1–1	3–1	1–0	5	3	1	1	9	6	7
Malaysia	–	–	–	–	1–0	7–0	5	2	2	1	10	3	6
Bangladesh	–	–	–	–	–	1–0	5	1	0	4	4	10	2
Nepal	–	–	–	–	–	–	5	0	0	5	0	12	0

Group 2

	Gh	Br	SK	Th	Ma	US	Pl	W	D	L	F	A	Pts
Ghana	–	1–0	1–1	2–1	1–1	1–0	5	3	2	0	6	3	8
Brazilian XI	–	–	1–1	2–0	5–1	4–0	5	3	1	1	12	3	7
South Korea XI	–	–	–	2–3	3–1	2–0	5	2	2	1	9	6	6

Thailand	–	–	–	–	–	1–2	2–1	5	2	0	3	7	9	4
Malaysian XI	–	–	–	–	–	–	0–2	5	1	1	3	5	12	3
USA XI	–	–	–	–	–	–	–	5	1	0	4	3	9	2

SEMI-FINALS

Argentine XI .... 3–1 .... Brazilian XI
Algeria .... 1–0 .... Ghana

FINAL

Argentine XI .... 2–1 .... Algeria

TWENTY-EIGHTH EDITION
21st August–9th September 1984

FIRST ROUND

Group 1

	Br	Ma	Pa	Li	Id	Th	Pl	W	D	L	F	A	Pts
Brazilian XI	–	4–0	7–0	3–2	2–0	9–2	5	5	0	0	25	4	10
Malaysia	–	–	5–1	3–1	2–2	1–0	5	3	1	1	11	8	7
P. New Guinea	–	–	–	2–1	1–0	4–1	5	3	0	2	8	14	6
Liberia	–	–	–	–	2–1	2–1	5	2	0	3	8	10	4
Indonesia	–	–	–	–	–	5–1	5	1	1	3	8	8	3
Thailand	–	–	–	–	–	–	5	0	0	5	5	21	0

Group 2

	SK	Ch	Ma	Ar	Al	Pa	Pl	W	D	L	F	A	Pts
South Korea	–	0–1	3–0	4–0	4–1	6–1	5	4	0	1	17	3	8
China	–	–	1–1	2–0	1–1	6–1	5	3	2	0	11	3	8
Malaysian XI	–	–	–	1–1	2–0	2–0	5	2	2	1	6	5	6
Argentine XI	–	–	–	–	0–0	2–1	5	1	2	2	3	8	4
Algeria XI	–	–	–	–	–	0–2	5	0	2	3	2	9	2
Pakistan	–	–	–	–	–	–	5	1	0	4	5	16	2

SEMI-FINALS

South Korea .... 3–1 .... Malaysia
Brazilian XI .... 2–0 .... China

FINAL

South Korea .... 2–0 .... Brazilian XI

TWENTY-NINTH EDITION
24th July–3rd August 1985

FIRST ROUND

Group 1

	Ma	Gh	Id	Wa	Pl	W	D	L	F	A	Pts
Malaysia	–	1–0	1–1	3–1	3	2	1	0	5	2	5
Ghana	–	–	4–0	3–1	3	2	0	1	7	2	4
Indonesia	–	–	–	2–2	3	0	2	1	3	7	2
Welsh XI	–	–	–	–	3	0	1	2	4	8	1

Group 2

	Br	SK	Th	Ma	Pl	W	D	L	F	A	Pts
Brazilian XI	–	0–2	5–0	4–0	3	2	0	1	9	2	4
South Korea	–	–	2–3	4–0	3	2	0	1	8	3	4
Thailand	–	–	–	2–4	3	1	0	2	5	11	2
Malaysian XI	–	–	–	–	3	1	0	2	4	10	2

SEMI-FINALS

South Korea .... 3–0 .... Malaysia
Brazilian XI .... 2–1 .... Ghana

FINAL

South Korea .... 7–4 .... Brazilian XI

THIRTIETH EDITION
22nd July–3rd August 1986

FIRST ROUND

Group 1

	Ma	In	Th	SK	Id	Pl	W	D	L	F	A	Pts
Malaysia	–	3–0	2–0	1–0	3–0	4	4	0	0	9	0	8
India	–	–	3–1	4–3	1–1	4	2	1	1	8	8	5
Thailand	–	–	–	1–0	1–0	4	2	0	2	3	5	4
South Korea	–	–	–	–	4–0	4	1	0	3	7	6	2
Indonesia	–	–	–	–	–	4	0	1	3	1	9	1

Group 2

	Cz	Ja	Sy	Ch	Pl	W	D	L	F	A	Pts
Czechoslovak XI	–	2–1	2–0	3–2	3	3	0	0	7	3	6
Japan	–	–	2–1	4–2	3	2	0	1	7	5	4
Syria	–	–	–	3–0	3	1	0	2	4	4	2
China	–	–	–	–	3	0	0	3	4	10	0

SEMI FINALS

Malaysia .... 2–1 .... Japan
Czechoslovak XI .... 1–0 .... India

FINAL

Malaysia .... 3–0 .... Czechoslovak XI

THIRTY-FIRST EDITION
8th–19th December 1987

FIRST ROUND

Group 1

	Cz	Ma	De	Sd	Pl	W	D	L	F	A	Pts
Czechoslovak XI	–	2–0	2–0	3–0	3	3	0	0	7	0	6
Malaysia	–	–	3–1	0–1	3	1	0	2	3	4	2
Danish XI	–	–	–	3–1	3	1	0	2	4	6	2
Swedish XI	–	–	–	–	3	1	0	2	2	6	2

Group 2

	SK	Yu	SU	Hu	Pl	W	D	L	F	A	Pts
South Korea	–	2–1	2–1	2–0	3	3	0	0	6	2	6
Yugoslav XI	–	–	3–1	4–0	3	2	0	1	8	3	4
Soviet XI	–	–	–	2–0	3	1	0	2	4	5	2
Hungarian XI	–	–	–	–	3	0	0	3	0	8	0

SEMI-FINALS

Czechoslovak XI .... 3–0 .... Yugoslav XI
South Korea .... 1–0 .... Malaysia

FINAL

Czechoslovak XI .... 3–2 .... South Korea

THIRTY-SECOND EDITION
8th–17th December 1988

FIRST ROUND

Group 1

	SU	Id	Ma	Th	Pl	W	D	L	F	A	Pts
Soviet XI	–	1–1	3–1	4–1	3	2	1	0	8	3	5
Indonesia	–	–	0–0	0–0	3	0	3	0	1	1	3
Malaysia	–	–	–	0–0	3	0	2	1	1	3	2
Thailand	–	–	–	–	3	0	2	1	1	4	2

Group 2

	WG	Au	Si	Om	Pl	W	D	L	F	A	Pts
West German XI	–	2–1	2–1	4–0	3	3	0	0	8	2	6
Austrian XI	–	–	2–0	4–0	3	2	0	1	7	2	4
Singapore	–	–	–	3–1	3	1	0	2	4	5	2
Oman	–	–	–	–	3	0	0	3	1	11	0

SEMI-FINALS

West German XI .... 6–0 .... Indonesia
Austrian XI .... 2–1 .... Soviet XI

FINAL

West German XI .... 1–0 .... Austrian XI

THIRTY-THIRD EDITION
4th–13th February 1991

FIRST ROUND

Group 1

	Au	Ch	Ma	Id	Pl	W	D	L	F	A	Pts
Austrian XI	–	2–1	2–3	2–0	3	2	0	1	6	4	4
China	–	–	2–2	3–1	3	1	1	1	6	5	3
Malaysia	–	–	–	1–2	3	1	1	1	6	6	3
Indonesia	–	–	–	–	3	1	0	2	3	6	2

Group 2

	De	Cz	Ma	Th	Pl	W	D	L	F	A	Pts
Danish XI	–	3–1	1–1	2–0	3	2	1	0	6	2	5
Czeckoslovak XI	–	–	2–0	2–0	3	2	0	1	5	3	4
Malaysian XI	–	–	–	2–1	3	1	1	1	3	4	3
Thailand	–	–	–	–	3	0	0	3	1	6	0

SEMI-FINALS

Austrian XI .... 3–1 .... Czechoslovak XI
China .... 1–0 .... Danish XI

FINAL

Austrian XI .... 3–0 .... China

PRESIDENT'S CUP

1971	South Korea & Burma
1972	Burma
1973	Burma & Cambodia
1974	South Korea
1975	South Korea
1976	South Korea & Brazilian XI (Sao Paulo U-21 Selection)
1977	Brazilian XI (Sao Paulo U-21 Selection)
1978	South Korea
1979	Brazilian XI (Sao Paulo U-21 Selection)
1980	South Korea
1981	South Korea & Argentine XI (Racing Cordoba)
1982	South Korea & Brazilian XI (Atletico Mineiro)
1983	Dutch XI (PSV Eindhoven)
1984	Brazilian XI (Bangu)
1985	South Korea
1986	–
1987	South Korea
1988	Czechoslovak XI
1989	Czechoslovak XI
1990	–
1991	South Korea

FIRST EDITION
2nd–15th May 1971

FIRST ROUND

Group 1

	SK	Ma	Th	Ca	Pl	W	D	L	F	A	Pts
South Korea	–	5–1	1–0	2–0	3	3	0	0	8	1	6
Malaysia	–	–	4–1	3–1	3	2	0	1	8	7	4
Thailand	–	–	–	4–3	3	1	0	2	5	8	2
Cambodia	–	–	–	–	3	0	0	3	4	9	0

Group 2

	Bu	In	HK	SV	Pl	W	D	L	F	A	Pts
Burma	–	3–1	2–0	2–0	3	3	0	0	7	1	6
Indonesia	–	–	2–1	9–1	3	2	0	1	12	5	4
Hong Kong	–	–	–	2–0	3	1	0	2	3	4	2
South Vietnam	–	–	–	–	3	0	0	3	1	13	0

SEMI-FINALS

South Korea .... 3–0 .... Indonesia
Burma .... 6–1 .... Malaysia

3RD PLACE

Indonesia .... 4–2 .... Malaysia

FINAL

South Korea .... 0–0 0–0 .... Burma

SECOND EDITION
20th–30th September 1972

FIRST ROUND

Group 1

	SK	Ma	Th	Ca	Pl	W	D	L	F	A	Pts
South Korea	–	2–0	3–0	3–1	3	3	0	0	8	1	6
Malaysia	–	–	1–1	1–0	3	1	1	1	2	3	3
Thailand	–	–	–	0–0	3	0	2	1	1	4	2
Cambodia	–	–	–	–	3	0	1	2	1	4	1

Group 2

	In	Bu	Si	Ph	Pl	W	D	L	F	A	Pts
Indonesia	–	1–1	2–1	12–0	3	2	1	0	15	2	5
Burma	–	–	1–0	4–0	3	2	1	0	6	1	5
Singapore	–	–	–	5–0	3	1	0	2	6	3	2
Philippines	–	–	–	–	3	0	0	3	0	21	0

MINOR PLACINGS

Thailand .... 4–1 .... Singapore
Cambodia .... 1–0 .... Philippines

SEMI-FINALS

Burma .... 1–0 .... South Korea
Indonesia .... 3–1 .... Malaysia

3RD PLACE

South Korea .... 1–0 .... Malaysia

FINAL

Burma .... 3–1 .... Indonesia

THIRD EDITION
22nd–30th September 1973

FIRST ROUND

Group 1

	SK	Ca	In	Pl	W	D	L	F	A	Pts
South Korea	–	6–0	3–1	2	2	0	0	9	1	4
Cambodia	–	–	3–2	2	1	1	0	3	8	2
Indonesia	–	–	–	2	0	0	2	3	6	0

Group 2

	Ma	Bu	Th	Pl	W	D	L	F	A	Pts
Malaysia	–	3–1	5–1	2	2	0	0	8	2	4
Burma	–	–	2–2	2	0	1	1	3	5	1
Thailand	–	–	–	2	0	1	1	3	7	1

SEMI-FINALS

Burma .... 1–0 .... South Korea
Cambodia .... 2–0 .... Malaysia

3RD PLACE

South Korea .... 2–0 .... Malaysia

FINAL

Burma .... 0–0 .... Cambodia

FOURTH EDITION
11th–20th May 1974

FIRST ROUND

Group 1

	SK	Ca	Ja	Ma	Pl	W	D	L	F	A	Pts
South Korea	–	0–1	3–0	4–0	3	2	0	1	7	1	4
Cambodia	–	–	1–1	1–1	3	1	2	0	3	2	4
Japan	–	–	–	2–2	3	0	2	1	3	6	2
Malaysia	–	–	–	–	3	0	2	1	3	7	2

Group 2

	Bu	In	Th	Pl	W	D	L	F	A	Pts
Indonesia	–	2–1	0–0	2	1	1	0	2	1	3
Burma	–	–	2–1	2	1	0	1	3	3	2
Thailand	–	–	–	2	0	1	1	1	2	1

SEMI-FINALS

South Korea .... 3–0 .... Burma
Indonesia .... 1–1 (3–2p) ..... Cambodia

3RD PLACE

Burma .... 6–0 .... Cambodia

FINAL

South Korea .... 7–1 .... Indonesia

FIFTH EDITION
10th–22nd May 1975

FIRST ROUND

Group 1

	SK	Ja	Le	In	Pl	W	D	L	F	A	Pts
South Korea	–	1–0	1–0	3–0	3	3	0	0	5	0	6
Japan	–	–	1–0	1–1	3	1	1	1	2	2	3
Lebanon	–	–	–	4–0	3	1	0	2	4	2	2
Indonesia	–	–	–	–	3	0	1	2	1	8	1

Group 2

	Bu	Ir	Th	Ma	Pl	W	D	L	F	A	Pts
Burma	–	1–1	4–1	2–0	3	2	1	0	7	2	5
Iran	–	–	1–1	3–0	3	1	2	0	5	2	4
Thailand	–	–	–	3–3	3	0	2	1	5	8	2
Malaysia	–	–	–	–	3	0	1	2	3	8	1

SEMI-FINALS

South Korea .... 1–0 .... Iran
Burma .... 1–0 .... Japan

3RD PLACE

Iran .... 3–0 .... Japan

FINAL

South Korea .... 1–0 .... Burma

SIXTH EDITION
11th–25th September 1976

FIRST ROUND

Group 1

	Br	SK	Ma	Si	In	Pl	W	D	L	F	A	Pts
Brazilian XI	–	1–1	2–0	4–0	2–0	4	3	1	0	9	1	7
South Korea	–	–	4–4	7–0	4–0	4	2	2	0	16	5	6
Malaysia	–	–	–	4–1	4–0	4	2	1	1	12	7	5
Singapore	–	–	–	–	2–1	4	1	0	3	3	16	2
India	–	–	–	–	–	4	0	0	4	1	12	0

Group 2

	NZ	SK	Bu	Th	In	Pl	W	D	L	F	A	Pts
New Zealand	–	1–0	2–0	3–1	0–0	4	3	1	0	6	1	7
South Korea B	–	–	1–0	1–1	2–0	4	2	1	1	4	2	5
Burma	–	–	–	2–0	2–0	4	2	0	2	4	3	4
Thailand	–	–	–	–	1–1	4	0	2	2	3	7	2
Indonesia	–	–	–	–	–	4	0	2	2	1	5	2

SEMI-FINALS

South Korea .... 2–0 .... New Zealand
Brazilian XI .... 3–0 .... South Korea B

3RD PLACE

South Korea B .... 1–0 .... New Zealand

FINAL

South Korea .... 0–0 .... Brazilian XI

SEVENTH EDITION
3rd–15th September 1977

FIRST ROUND

Group 1

	SK	Th	Le	En	In	Pl	W	D	L	F	A	Pts
South Korea	–	3–1	4–1	6–1	3–0	4	4	0	0	16	3	8
Thailand	–	–	5–3	2–1	4–0	4	3	0	1	12	7	6
Lebanon	–	–	–	2–1	2–4	4	1	0	3	8	14	2
English XI	–	–	–	–	1–0	4	1	0	3	4	10	2
India	–	–	–	–	–	4	1	0	3	4	10	2

Group 2

	Br	Ma	Sk	Ba	Pl	W	D	L	F	A	Pts
Brazilian XI	–	3–1	1–1	4–0	3	2	1	0	8	2	5
Malaysia	–	–	1–1	3–1	3	1	1	1	5	5	3
South Korea B	–	–	–	1–1	3	0	3	0	3	3	3
Bahrain	–	–	–	–	3	0	1	2	2	8	1

SEMI-FINALS

Brazilian XI .... 4–0 .... Thailand
South Korea .... 3–0 .... Malaysia

3RD PLACE

Malaysia .... 1–1 .... Thailand

FINAL

Brazilian XI .... 1–0 .... South Korea

Eighth Edition
9th–21st September 1978

FIRST ROUND

Group 1

	SK	US	Ma	Ba	Pl	W	D	L	F	A	Pts
South Korea	–	3–2	2–2	3–1	3	2	1	0	8	5	5
USA Pro XI	–	–	2–0	3–2	3	2	0	1	7	5	4
Malaysia	–	–	–	2–1	3	1	1	1	4	5	3
Bahrain	–	–	–	–	3	0	0	3	4	8	0

Group 2

	Ir	Mo	NZ	WG	Pl	W	D	L	F	A	Pts
Iran	–	2–0	2–1	3–1	3	3	0	0	7	2	6
Morocco	–	–	3–0	1–1	3	1	1	1	4	3	3
New Zealand	–	–	–	3–0	3	1	0	2	4	5	2
West German XI	–	–	–	–	3	0	1	2	2	7	1

Group 3

	Me	US	Le	Pl	W	D	L	F	A	Pts
Mexico XI	–	2–0	7–1	2	2	0	0	9	1	4
USA Oly XI	–	–	6–1	2	1	0	1	6	3	2
Lebanon	–	–	–	2	0	0	2	2	13	0

Group 4

	Br	SK	Th	In	Pl	W	D	L	F	A	Pts
Brazilian XI	–	4–0	2–0	3–0	3	3	0	0	9	0	6
South Korea B	–	–	4–2	1–1	3	1	1	1	5	7	3
Thailand	–	–	–	2–0	3	1	0	2	4	6	2
Indonesia	–	–	–	–	3	0	1	2	1	6	1

QUARTER-FINALS

South Korea .... 4–1 .... USA Olympic XI
South Korea B .... 2–1 .... Iran
Morocco .... 1–0 .... Brazilian XI
USA Pro XI .... 3–0 .... Mexico XI

SEMI–FINALS

South Korea .... 1–0 .... South Korea B
USA Pro XI .... 3–1 .... Morocco

3RD PLACE

South Korea B .... 2–1 .... Morocco

FINAL

South Korea .... 6–2 .... USA Pro XI

Ninth Edition
8th–21st September 1979

FIRST ROUND

Group 1

	SK	Ba	Su	Ba	SL	Pl	W	D	L	F	A	Pts
South Korea	–	5–1	8–0	9–0	6–0	4	4	0	0	28	1	8
Bahrain	–	–	1–0	2–0	1–0	4	3	0	1	5	5	6
Sudan	–	–	–	4–1	1–0	4	2	0	2	5	10	4
Bangladesh	–	–	–	–	3–1	4	1	0	3	4	16	2
Sri Lanka	–	–	–	–	–	4	0	0	4	1	11	0

Group 2

	Br	SK	Th	Ma	In	Pl	W	D	L	F	A	Pts
Brazilian XI	–	2–1	6–0	5–0	3–1	4	4	0	0	16	2	8
South Korea B	–	–	1–0	4–0	2–0	4	3	0	1	8	2	6
Thailand	–	–	–	1–1	2–1	4	1	1	2	3	9	3
Malaysia	–	–	–	–	3–2	4	1	1	2	4	12	3
Indonesia	–	–	–	–	–	4	0	0	4	4	10	0

SEMI-FINALS

Brazilian XI .... 2–2 .... Bahrain
South Korea .... 4–1 .... South Korea B

3RD PLACE

Bahrain .... 1–0 .... South Korea B

FINAL

Brazilian XI .... 2–1 .... South Korea

Tenth Edition
23rd August–2nd September 1980

FIRST ROUND

	SK	In	SK	Th	Ma	Ba	Pl	W	D	L	F	A	Pts
South Korea	–	3–0	3–0	4–0	2–0	5–0	5	5	0	0	17	0	10
Indonesia	–	–	1–1	2–1	1–1	3–2	5	2	2	1	7	8	6
South Korea B	–	–	–	1–1	1–0	1–0	5	2	2	1	4	5	6
Thailand	–	–	–	–	4–1	1–0	5	2	1	2	7	8	5
Malaysia	–	–	–	–	–	1–1	5	0	2	3	3	9	2
Bahrain	–	–	–	–	–	–	5	0	1	4	3	11	1

FINAL

South Korea .... 2–0 .... Indonesia

Eleventh Edition
13th–26th June 1981

FIRST ROUND

Group 1

	SK	WG	Ja	Ma	Fr	Pl	W	D	L	F	A	Pts
Argentine XI	1–1	3–0	1–0	6–0	4–3	5	4	1	0	15	4	9
South Korea	–	4–1	2–0	2–0	1–1	5	3	2	0	10	3	8
W. German XI	–	–	1–0	2–1	3–1	5	3	0	2	7	9	6
Japan	–	–	–	2–0	2–0	5	2	0	3	4	4	4
Malaysia	–	–	–	–	2–0	5	1	0	4	3	12	2
French XI	–	–	–	–	–	5	0	1	4	5	12	1

Group 2

	Br	Ma	Th	Li	In	Pl	W	D	L	F	A	Pts
Uruguayan XI	1–1	1–0	3–2	1–0	3–1	5	4	1	0	9	4	9
Brazilian XI	–	0–0	1–0	2–0	4–0	5	3	2	0	8	1	8

Malta	–	–	2–0	1–1	1–0	5	2	2	1	4	2	6
Thailand	–	–	–	2–0	3–1	5	2	0	3	7	7	4
Liechtenstein	–	–	–	–	3–2	5	1	1	3	4	8	3
Indonesia	–	–	–	–	–	5	0	0	5	4	14	0

SEMI-FINALS

South Korea .... 2–0 .... Uruguayan XI
Argentine XI .... 2–0 .... Brazilian XI

3RD PLACE

Brazilian XI .... 1–0 .... Uruguayan XI

FINAL

South Korea .... 2–2 .... Argentine XI

TWELFTH EDITION
5th–18th June 1982

FIRST ROUND

Group 1

	SK	In	In	Ba	Pl	W	D	L	F	A	Pts
Dutch XI	2–0	4–0	1–1	8–1	4	3	1	0	15	2	7
South Korea	–	3–0	1–0	3–0	4	3	0	1	7	2	6
Indonesia	–	–	1–0	1–1	4	1	1	2	2	8	3
India	–	–	–	0–0	4	0	2	2	1	3	2
Bahrain	–	–	–	–	4	0	2	2	2	12	2

Group 2

	SK	Th	Ma	WG	Pl	W	D	L	F	A	Pts
Brazilian XI	3–0	1–0	3–1	2–0	4	4	0	0	9	1	8
South Korea XI	–	2–1	1–0	4–0	4	3	0	1	7	4	6
Thailand	–	–	1–1	10–0	4	1	1	2	12	4	3
Malaysia	–	–	–	2–1	4	1	1	2	4	6	3
West German XI	–	–	–	–	4	0	0	4	1	18	0

SEMI–FINALS

South Korea .... 2–1 .... South Korea XI
Brazilian XI .... 4–3 .... Dutch XI

3RD PLACE

Dutch XI .... 5–0 .... South Korea XI

FINAL

South Korea .... 0–0 .... Brazilian XI

THIRTEENTH EDITION
4th–17th June 1983

FIRST ROUND

Group 1

1 South Korea
2 USA XI
3 Italian XI
4 Nigeria
5 Thailand

Group 2

	Du	Gh	SK	NZ	Su	Pl	W	D	L	F	A	Pts
Dutch XI	–	1–0	3–1	3–0	4–0	4	4	0	0	11	1	8
Ghana	–	–	3–1	0–2	3–1	4	2	0	2	6	5	4
South Korea XI	–	–	–	2–0	0–0	4	1	1	2	4	6	3
New Zealand	–	–	–	–	1–1	4	1	1	2	3	6	3
Sudan	–	–	–	–	–	4	0	2	2	2	8	2

SEMI-FINALS

South Korea .... 5–0 .... Ghana
Dutch XI .... 2–1 .... USA XI

3RD PLACE

Ghana .... 5–0 .... USA XI

FINAL

Dutch XI .... 3–2 .... South Korea

FOURTEENTH EDITION
30th May–8th June 1984

FIRST ROUND

Group 1

	SK	WG	Pe	Gu	Pl	W	D	L	F	A	Pts
South Korea	–	3–2	2–2	0–0	3	1	2	0	5	4	4
West German XI	–	–	1–1	2–0	3	1	1	1	5	4	3
Peru XI	–	–	–	0–0	3	0	3	0	3	3	3
Guatemala	–	–	–	–	3	0	2	1	0	2	2

Group 2

	Br	SK	Be	Th	Pl	W	D	L	F	A	Pts
Brazilian XI	–	0–0	4–0	4–0	3	2	1	0	8	0	5
South Korea XI	–	–	1–1	2–0	3	1	2	0	3	1	4
Belgian XI	–	–	–	1–1	3	0	2	1	2	6	2
Thailand	–	–	–	–	3	0	1	2	1	7	1

SEMI–FINALS

Brazilian XI .... 1–1 (4–2p) ..... West German XI
South Korea XI .... 2–1 .... South Korea

3RD PLACE

South Korea .... 2–1 .... West German XI

FINAL

Brazilian XI .... 2–1 .... South Korean XI

FIFTEENTH EDITION
1st–17th June 1985

FIRST ROUND

Group 1

	SK	Ba	Ma	Pl	W	D	L	F	A	Pts
South Korea XI	–	4–2	6–0	2	2	0	0	10	2	4
Bahrain	–	–	3–1	2	1	0	1	5	5	2
Malaysia	–	–	–	2	0	0	2	1	9	0

Group 2

	Ir	Br	Be	Pl	W	D	L	F	A	Pts
Iraq	–	2–2	5–3	2	1	1	0	7	5	3
Brazilian XI	–	–	3–2	2	1	1	0	5	4	3
Belgian XI	–	–	–	2	0	0	2	5	8	0

Group 3

	SK	Ar	Th	Pl	W	D	L	F	A	Pts
South Korea	–	1–1	3–2	2	1	1	0	4	3	3
Argentine XI	–	–	1–0	2	1	1	0	2	1	3
Thailand	–	–	–	2	0	0	2	2	4	0

Group 4

	Ur	Ca	Gh	Pl	W	D	L	F	A	Pts
Uruguayan XI	–	0–0	3–1	2	1	1	0	3	1	3
Canada	–	–	2–1	2	1	1	0	2	1	3
Ghana	–	–	–	2	0	0	2	2	5	0

SECOND ROUND

Group 1

	SK	Br	Ur	Ba	Pl	W	D	L	F	A	Pts
South Korea	–	1–1	2–1	3–0	3	2	1	0	6	2	5
Brazilian XI	–	–	0–0	3–0	3	1	2	0	4	1	4
Uruguayan XI	–	–	–	1–1	3	0	2	1	2	3	2
Bahrain	–	–	–	–	3	0	1	2	1	7	1

Group 2

	SK	Ir	Ca	Ar	Pl	W	D	L	F	A	Pts
South Korea XI	–	1–0	1–0	4–1	3	3	0	0	6	1	6
Iraq	–	–	6–1	6–1	3	2	0	1	12	3	4
Canada	–	–	–	2–1	3	1	0	2	3	8	2
Argentine XI	–	–	–	–	3	0	0	3	3	12	0

SEMI-FINALS

South Korea .... 2–0 .... Iraq
South Korea XI .... 1–1 (4–2p) ..... Brazilian XI

3RD PLACE

Iraq .... 1–1 (5–2p) ..... Brazilian XI

FINAL

South Korea .... 1–0 .... South Korea XI

SIXTEENTH EDITION
8th–21st June 1987

FIRST ROUND

Group 1

	Eg	Hu	Ar	US	Th	Pl	W	D	L	F	A	Pts
South Korea	0–0	1–0	3–0	1–0	4–2	5	4	1	0	9	2	9
Egypt	–	2–1	3–2	3–1	1–1	5	3	2	0	9	5	8
Hungarian XI	–	–	1–1	3–2	0–0	5	1	2	2	5	6	4
Argentine XI	–	–	–	2–2	1–0	5	1	2	2	6	9	4
USA	–	–	–	–	1–0	5	1	1	3	6	9	3
Thailand	–	–	–	–	–	5	0	2	3	3	7	2

Group 2

	SK	Du	Mo	Ch	Ir	Pl	W	D	L	F	A	Pts
Australia	5–0	1–1	1–0	2–0	1–0	5	4	1	0	10	1	9
South Korea B	–	4–0	1–0	0–0	1–0	5	3	1	1	6	5	7
Dutch XI	–	–	3–2	1–1	0–0	5	1	3	1	5	8	5
Morocco	–	–	–	3–1	1–0	5	2	0	3	6	6	4
Chilean XI	–	–	–	–	1–0	5	1	2	2	3	6	4
Irish XI	–	–	–	–	–	5	0	1	4	0	4	1

SEMI-FINALS

South Korea .... 3–1 .... South Korea B
Australia .... 0–0 (4–3p) ..... Egypt

FINAL

South Korea .... 0–0 (5–4p) ..... Australia

SEVENTEENTH EDITION
16th–28th June 1988

FIRST ROUND

Group 1

	Me	SK	Za	It	Pl	W	D	L	F	A	Pts
Mexico	–	2–1	2–0	1–1	3	2	1	0	5	2	5
South Korea XI	–	–	4–0	5–1	3	2	0	1	10	3	4
Zambia	–	–	–	2–1	3	1	0	2	2	7	2
Italian XI	–	–	–	–	3	0	1	2	3	8	1

Group 2

	Yu	Cz	Tu	Pe	Pl	W	D	L	F	A	Pts
Yugoslav XI	–	3–2	1–1	4–2	3	2	1	0	8	5	5
Czechoslovak XI	–	–	2–0	1–1	3	1	1	1	5	4	3
Turkish XI	–	–	–	2–1	3	1	1	1	3	4	3
Peruvian XI	–	–	–	–	3	0	1	2	4	7	1

Group 3

	SU	Ng	En	US	Pl	W	D	L	F	A	Pts
Soviet XI	–	1–0	3–0	1–0	3	3	0	0	5	0	6
Nigeria	–	–	1–1	3–2	3	1	1	1	4	4	3
English XI	–	–	–	1–1	3	0	2	1	2	5	2
USA XI	–	–	–	–	3	0	1	2	3	5	1

Group 4

	Ir	Hu	SK	Ar	Pl	W	D	L	F	A	Pts
Iraq	–	2–1	2–0	3–1	3	3	0	0	7	2	6
Hungarian XI	–	–	1–0	0–0	3	1	1	1	2	2	3
South Korea	–	–	–	2–1	3	1	0	2	2	4	2
Argentine XI	–	–	–	–	3	0	1	2	2	5	1

QUARTER-FINALS

Czechoslovak XI .... 3–2 .... Mexico
South Korea XI .... 1–0 .... Yugoslav XI
Nigeria .... 2–1 .... Iraq
Soviet XI .... 2–0 .... Hungarian XI

SEMI-FINALS

Czechoslovak XI .... 4–3 .... South Korea XI
Soviet XI .... 1–0 .... Nigeria

3RD PLACE

South Korea XI .... 3–2 .... Nigeria

FINAL

Czechoslovak XI .... 2–1 .... Soviet XI

EIGHTEENTH EDITION
17th–26th June 1989

	Pl	W	D	L	F	A	Pts
Czechoslovak XI	5	4	1	0	12	4	9
Danish XI	5	3	0	2	8	4	6
South Korea	5	2	2	1	6	3	6
Portugal XI	5	2	0	3	6	11	4
Uruguay XI	3	1	0	2	2	3	2
South Korea B	3	1	0	2	4	7	2
Hungarian XI	3	1	0	2	1	5	2
USA XI	3	0	1	2	2	4	1

NINETEENTH EDITION
7th–16th June 1991

FIRST ROUND

Group 1

	Eg	SK	Ma	In	Pl	W	D	L	F	A	Pts
Egypt	–	0–0	5–2	6–0	3	2	1	0	11	2	5
South Korea	–	–	1–1	3–0	3	1	2	0	4	1	4
Malta	–	–	–	3–0	3	1	1	1	6	6	3
Indonesia	–	–	–	–	3	0	0	3	0	12	0

Group 2

	Au	SU	SK	US	Pl	W	D	L	F	A	Pts
Australia	–	2–1	2–0	4–2	3	3	0	0	8	3	6
Soviet XI	–	–	1–0	1–1	3	1	1	1	3	3	3
South Korea B	–	–	–	2–1	3	1	0	2	2	4	2
USA XI	–	–	–	–	3	0	1	2	4	7	1

SEMI-FINALS

South Korea .... 4–3 .... Australia
Egypt .... 2–1 .... Soviet XI

FINAL

South Korea .... 2–0 .... Egypt

THE SOUTH ASIAN FEDERATION GAMES

1984 Nepal
1985 India
1987 Pakistan
1989 Pakista
1991 Pakistan

THE SOUTH EAST ASIAN GAMES

1959 South Vietnam
1961 Malaysia
1965 Burma & Thailand
1967 Burma
1969 Burma
1971 Burma
1973 Burma
1975 Thailand
1977 Malaysia
1979 Malaysia
1981 Thailand
1983 Thailand
1985 Thailand
1987 Indonesia
1989 Malaysia
1991 Indonesia

THE ARABIAN GULF TOURNAMENT

1970 Kuwait
1972 Kuwait
1974 Kuwait
1976 Kuwait
1979 Iraq
1982 Kuwait
1984 Iraq
1986 Kuwait
1988 Iraq
1990 Kuwait

KING'S CUP
Bangkok, Thailand

1968 Indonesia
1969 South Korea
1970 South Korea
1971 South Korea
1972 Malaysia
1973 South Korea
1974 South Korea
1975 South Korea
1976 Thailand & Malaysia
1977 Malaysia & South Korea
1978 Malaysia
1979 Thailand
1980 Thailand & South Korea
1981 Thailand & South Korea
1982 Thailand
1983 Thailand
1984–85 –
1986 North Korea
1987 –
1988 Danish XI
1989 Thailand
1990 Thailand
1991 China

JAKARTA ANNIVERSARY TOURNAMENT
Indonesia

1970 Malaysia
1971 Burma
1972 Indonesia
1973 Burma
1974 Burma
1975 Burma
1976 South Korea
1977 –
1978 South Korea

PIALA KEMERDEKAAN INDEPENDENCE CUP
Jakarta, Indonesia

1985 Chilean XI
1986 Algerian XI
1987 Indonesia
1988 China
1989 –
1990 Australia

KIRIN CUP
Tokyo, Japan

1978 B. Mönchengladbach & Palmeiras
1979 Tottenham Hotspur
1980 Middlesbrough
1981 Club Brugge
1982 Werder Bremen
1983 Newcastle United
1984 Internacional PA
1985 Santos
1986 Werder Bremen
1987 Fluminense
1988 Flamengo
1991 Japan
1992 Argentina

JAWAHARLAL NEHRU GOLD CUP
India

1982 Uruguay
1983 Hungarian XI
1984 Poland
1985 Soviet Union
1986 Soviet Union XI
1987 Soviet Union XI
1988 Soviet Union XI
1989 Hungarian XI
1990 Paraguayan XI *
1991 Romanian XI

* Jawaharlal Nehru Centenary Gold Cup

PRESIDENT'S GOLD CUP
Dhaka, Bangladesh

1981 South Korea
1982 China
1983 Malaysian XI
1984–85 –
1986 Swiss XI
1987 Syria
1988 –
1989 Bangladesh

MERLION CUP
Singapore

1982 Australia
1983 Australia
1984 Iraq
1985 Yugoslav XI
1986 China

MARAH HALIM CUP
Medan, Indonesia

1972	Medan XI
1973	Medan XI
1974	Japan
1975	Australian XI
1976	Australian XI
1977	Indonesian XI
1978	Burma
1979	Burma
1980	Dutch XI
1981	South Korea
1982	West German XI
1983	South Korea
1984	Iraqi XI
1985	South Korea
1986	South Korea
1987	–
1988	Japan
1989	Dutch XI
1990	–
1991	China

AFGHANISTAN

Population: 15 592 000
Area, sq km: 652 225
% in urban areas: 18%
Capital city: Kabul 1 424 000

The Football Federation of the National Olympic Committee
PO Box 756
Kabul
Afghanistan
Tel: Kabul 20579
Fax: None
Telex: None
Cable: OLYMPIC KABUL
Languages for correspondence: English & French

Year of formation: 1922
Affiliation to FIFA: 1948
Affiliation to AFC: 1954
Registered clubs: 30
Registered players: 4800
Registered Coaches: 20
Registered referees: 18
National stadium: National Stadium, Kabul 25 000
National colours: Shirts: White/Shorts: White/Socks: White
Reserve colours: Shirts: Green/Shorts: White/Socks: Green
Season: September–January

THE RECORD

WORLD CUP

1930–90 ..... Did not enter

OLYMPIC GAMES

1908–36 ..... Did not enter
1948 .... Preliminary round
1952 .... Did not enter
1956 .... Did not enter
1960 .... QT 1st round
1964–92 ..... Did not enter

ASIAN CHAMPIONSHIP

1956–68 ..... Did not enter
1972
1976 .... QT 4th/4 in group 2
1980 .... QT 3rd/3 in group 2
1984 .... QT 5th/5 in group 4
1988 .... Did not enter

ASIAN GAMES

1951 .... Semi-finalists
1954 .... 1st round
1958–90 ..... Did not enter

BAHRAIN

Population: 503 000
Area, sq km: 692
% in urban areas: 82%
Capital city: Manama 151 000

Bahrain Football Association
PO Box 5464
Bahrain
Tel: (010 973) 728218
Fax: (010 973) 729361
Telex: 9040 FAB BN
Cable: BAHKORA BAHRAIN
Languages for correspondence: English
Year of formation: 1951
Affiliation to FIFA: 1966
Affiliation to AFC: 1970
Registered clubs: 25
Registered players: 2000
Registered Coaches: 180
Registered referees: 55
National stadium: Isa Town Stadium, Manama 16 000
National colours: Shirts: White/Shorts: Red/Socks: Red
Reserve colours: Shirts: Blue/Shorts: Blue/Socks: Blue
Season: October–June

THE RECORD

WORLD CUP

1930–74 ..... Did not enter
1978 .... QT R1 2nd/3 in group 4
1982 .... QT R1 4th/5 in group 2
1986 .... QT R1 1st/2 in group 4, R2 2nd/2
1990 .... Did not enter

OLYMPIC GAMES

1908–72 ..... Did not enter
1976 .... QT R1 5th/5 in group 1
1980 .... Did not enter
1984 .... QT R1 2nd/3 in group 2, R2 4th/5 in group 2
1988 .... QT R1 2nd/3 in group 1
1992 .... QT R1 1st/4 in group 3, R2 6th/6

ASIAN CHAMPIONSHIP

1956–68 ..... Did not enter
1972
1976 .... Did not enter
1980 .... QT 3rd/4 in group 1
1984 .... Did not enter
1988 .... QT 1st/4 in group 4 – Final tournament/1st round

ASIAN GAMES

1951–70 ..... Did not enter
1974 .... 1st round
1978 .... 1st round
1982 .... Did not enter
1986 .... 1st round
1990 .... Did not enter

LEAGUE CHAMPIONS OF BAHRAIN

1957	Muharraq
1958	Muharraq
1959	Al Nasr
1960	Muharraq
1961	Muharraq
1962	Muharraq
1963	Muharraq
1964	Muharraq
1965	Muharraq
1966	Muharraq
1967	Muharraq
1968	Bahrain Club
1969	Al Ahli
1970	Muharraq
1971	Muharraq
1972	Al Ahli
1973	Muharraq
1974	Muharraq
1975	Al Arabi
1976	Muharraq
1977	Al Ahli
1978	Bahrain Club
1979	Al Hala
1980	Muharraq
1981	Bahrain Club
1982	West Riffa
1983	Muharraq
1984	Muharraq
1985	Bahrain Club
1986	Muharraq
1987	West Riffa
1988	Muharraq

BANGLADESH

Population: 113 005 000
Area, sq km: 143 998
% in urban areas: 24%
Capital city: Dhaka 5 300 000

Bangladesh Football Federation
Stadium, Dhaka–1000
Bangladesh
Tel: (010 880) 2 252034
Fax: (010 880) 2 863191
Telex: 642460 BHL BJ
Cable: FOOTBALFED DHAKA
Languages for correspondence: English

Year of formation: 1972
Affiliation to FIFA: 1974
Affiliation to AFC: 1974
Registered clubs: 1265
Registered players: 30 300
Registered Coaches: 20
Registered referees: 996
National stadium: Dhaka Stadium 55 000
National colours: Shirts: Orange/Shorts: White/Socks: Green
Reserve colours: Shirts: White/Shorts: White/Socks: Green
Season: March–November

THE RECORD

WORLD CUP

1930–82 ..... Did not enter
1986 .... QT R1 4th/4 in group 6
1990 .... QT R1 3rd/4 in group 5

OLYMPIC GAMES

1908–88 ..... Did not enter
1992 .... QT R1 4th/5 in group 4

ASIAN CHAMPIONSHIP

1956–76 ..... Did not enter
1980 .... QT 2nd/3 in group 2 – Final tournament/1st round
1984 .... QT th/6 in group 1
1988 .... QT 5th/6 in group 1

ASIAN GAMES

1951–74 ..... Did not enter
1978 .... 1st round
1982 .... 1st round
1986 .... 1st round
1990 .... 1st round

DHAKA LEAGUE CHAMPIONSHIP

1948	Victoria Sporting
1949	East Pakistan Gymkhana
1950	Dhaka Wanderers
1951	Dhaka Wanderers
1952	Bengal Government Press
1953	Dhaka Wanderers
1954	Dhaka Wanderers
1955	Dhaka Wanderers
1956	Dhaka Wanderers
1957	Mohammedan Sporting
1958	Azad Sporting
1959	Mohammedan Sporting
1960	Dhaka Wanderers
1961	Mohammedan Sporting
1962	Victoria Sporting
1963	Mohammedan Sporting
1964	Victoria Sporting
1965	Mohammedan Sporting
1966	Mohammedan Sporting
1967	East Pakistan IDC
1968	East Pakistan IDC
1969	Mohammedan Sporting
1970	East Pakistan IDC
1971–72	–
1973	Bangladesh IDC
1974	Abahani Krira Chakra
1975	Mohammedan Sporting
1976	Mohammedan Sporting
1977	Abahani Krira Chakra
1978	Mohammedan Sporting
1979	Bangladesh Jute Mill Corp.
1980	Mohammedan Sporting
1981	Abahani Krira Chakra
1982	Mohammedan Sporting
1983	Abahani Krira Chakra
1984	Abahani Krira Chakra
1985	Abahani Krira Chakra
1986	Mohammedan Sporting
1987	Mohammedan Sporting
1988	Mohammedan Sporting
1989	Mohammedan Sporting
1990	Abahani Krira Chakra

CLUB DIRECTORY

DHAKA (Population – 3 430 000)
Abahani Krira Chakra – Arambagh – Azad Sporting – BPWD – Brothers Union – BRTC – Dhaka Wanderers – Dhanmondi Club – East End Club – Farashganj Sporting – Mohammedan Sporting – Muktijadha Sangshad – Rahmatganj MFS – Sadharan Bima – Victoria Sporting – Wari Club

BRUNEI

Population: 259 000 Area, sq km: 5765
% in urban areas: 63%
Capital city: Bandar Seri Begawan 52 000

Brunei Amateur Football Association
PO Box 2010
1920 Bandar Seri Begawan, Brunei
Tel: (010 673) 242283
Fax: (010 673) 242300
Telex: BU 2575
Cable: BAFA BRUNEI
Languages for correspondence: English

Year of formation: 1959
Affiliation to FIFA: 1969
Affiliation to AFC: 1970
Registered clubs: 22
Registered players: 2500
Registered Coaches: 21
Registered referees: 50
National stadium: Hassanal Bolkiah, Bandar Seri Begawan 40 000
National colours: Shirts: Gold/Shorts: Black/Socks: Gold
Reserve colours: Shirts: Red/Shorts: White/Socks: Red
Season: September–March

THE RECORD

WORLD CUP

1930–82 ..... Did not enter
1986 .... QT R1 4th/4 in group 7
1990 .... Did not enter

OLYMPIC GAMES

1908–76 ..... Did not enter
1980 .... QT 4th/6 in group 2
1984–92 ..... Did not enter

ASIAN CHAMPIONSHIP

1956–72 ..... Did not enter
1976 .... QT 6th/6 in group 4
1980–88 ..... Did not enter

ASIAN GAMES

1951–90 ..... Did not enter

PEOPLE'S REPUBLIC OF CHINA

Population: 1 133 683 000
Area, sq km: 9 572 900
% in urban areas: 51%
Capital city: Beijing 6 800 000

Football Association of the People's Republic of China
9 Tiyuguan Road, Beijing, China
Tel: (010 86) 1 7017018
Fax: (010 86) 1 5112533
Telex: 22034 ACSF CN
Cable: SPORTSCHINE BEIJING
Languages for correspondence: English & French

Year of formation: 1924
Affiliation to FIFA: 1931–58 & 1979

Affiliation to AFC: 1974
Registered clubs: 1045
Registered players: 2250000
Registered Coaches: 950
Registered referees: 2584
National stadium: Workers Stadium, Beijing 63000
National colours: Shirts: Red/Shorts: White/Socks: Red
Reserve colours: Shirts: White/Shorts: White/Socks: White
Season: February–September

THE RECORD

WORLD CUP

1930–78 ..... Did not enter
1982 .... QT R1 1st/6 in group 4, R2 3rd/4
1986 .... QT R1 2nd/4 in group 7
1990 .... QT R1 1st/4 in group 5, R2 4th/6

OLYMPIC GAMES

1908–28 ..... Did not enter
1936 .... 1st round
1948 .... 1st round
1952 .... Did not enter
1956 .... Qualified but withdrew
1960–76 ..... Did not enter
1980 .... QT 3rd/6 in group 3
1984 .... QT R1 3rd/4 in group 4
1988 .... QT R1 1st/3 in group 4, R2 1st/4 – Final tournament/1st round
1992 .... QT R1 1st/5 in group 5, R2 4th/6

ASIAN CHAMPIONSHIP

1956–72 ..... Did not enter
1976 .... QT 2nd/6 in group 4 – Final tournament/Semi-finalists/3rd place
1980 .... QT 2nd/4 in group 4 – Final tournament/1st round
1984 .... QT 1st/5 in group 4 – Final tournament/Finalists
1988 .... QT 2nd/6 in group 1 – Final tournament/Semi-finalists/4th place

ASIAN GAMES

1951–74 ..... Did not enter
1978 .... Semi-finalists/3rd place
1982 .... Quarter-finalists
1986 .... Quarter-finalists
1990 .... Quarter-finalists

ASIAN CHAMPION TEAMS' CUP

Winners – Liaoning 1989
Finalists – Liaoning 1990

NATIONAL CHAMPIONSHIP

1953 August 1st
1954 North East China
1955 Central Institute of Physical Culture
1956 –
1957 Tianjin
1958 Beijing
1959 August 1st
1960 Tianjin
1961 Shanghai
1962 Shanghai
1963 Beijing Youth
1964 Beijing Physical Culture Institute
1965 Jilin
1966–72 –
1973 Beijing
1974 August 1st
1975 Guangxi
1976 Beijing
1977 August 1st
1978 Liaoning
1979 Guangtung
1980 Tianjin
1981 August 1st
1982 Beijing
1983 Shanghai
1984 Beijing
1985 Liaoning
1986 August 1st
1987 Guandong
1988 Liaoning
1989 Liaoning
1990 Liaoning
1991 Liaoning

CLUB DIRECTORY

SHANGHAI (Population – 9300000)
Shanghai Football Club

BEIJING (Population – 6450000)
Beijing Football Club – Beijing Army Unit – August 1st Football Club

TIANJIN (Population – 5460000)
Tianjin Football Club

SHENYANG (Population – 4290000)
Liaoning Football Club – Shenyang Army Unit

WUHAN (Population – 3490000)
Hebei Football Club

GUANGZHOU (Population – 3050000)
Guangzhou Football Club

NANJING (Population – 2290000)
Nanjing Army Unit

DALIAN (Population – 1680000)
Dalian Football Club

KUNMING (Population – 1520000)
Kunming Army Unit

JILIN (Population – 1170000)
Jilin Football Club

HONG KONG

Population: 5841000
Area, sq km: 1074
% in urban areas: 100%
Capital city: Victoria

The Hong Kong Football Association Ltd
55 Fat Kwong Street, Homantin
Kowloon
Hong Kong
Tel: (010 852) 7129122
Fax: (010 852) 7604303
Telex: 405 18 FAHKG HX
Cable: FOOTBALL HONG HONG
Languages for correspondence: English

Year of formation: 1914
Affiliation to FIFA: 1954
Affiliation to AFC: 1954
Registered clubs: 85
Registered players: 3700
Professional players: 300
Registered Coaches: 142
Registered referees: 161
National stadium: Government Stadium 28000
National colours: Shirts: Red/Shorts: White/Socks: Red
Reserve colours: Shirts: White/Shorts: White/Socks: White
Season: September–May

THE RECORD

WORLD CUP

1930–70 ..... Did not enter
1974 .... QT R1 4th/7 in group A
1978 .... QT R1 1st/5 in group 1, R2 5th/5
1982 .... QT R1 3rd/6 in group 4
1986 .... QT R1 1st/4 in group 7, R2 2nd/2
1990 .... QT R1 4th/4 in group 6

OLYMPIC GAMES

1908–80 ..... Did not enter
1984 .... QT R1 4th/4 in group 4
1988 .... QT R1 2nd/3 in group 4
1992 .... QT R1 2nd/4 in group 6

ASIAN CHAMPIONSHIP

1956 .... QT Automatic – Final tournament/3rd place
1960 .... –
1964 .... QT 1st/in group 2 – Final tournament/4th place
1968 .... QT 1st/5 in group 2 – Final tournament/5th place
1972 .... –
1976 .... QT 3rd/6 in group 4
1980 .... QT 3rd/7 in group 3
1984 .... QT 4th/5 in group 4
1988 .... QT 4th/5 in group 3

ASIAN GAMES

1951 .... Did not enter
1954 .... 1st round
1958 .... Quarter-finalists
1962–86 ..... Did not enter
1990 .... 1st round

HONG KONG LEAGUE CHAMPIONS

1946	Royal Air Force
1947	Sing Tao
1948	Kitchee
1949	South China
1950	Kitchee
1951	South China
1952	South China
1953	South China
1954	Kowloon Motor Bus Co.
1955	South China
1956	Eastern
1957	South China
1958	South China
1959	South China
1960	South China
1961	South China
1962	South China
1963	Yuen Long
1964	Kitchee
1965	Happy Valley
1966	South China
1967	Kowloon Motor Bus Co.
1968	South China
1969	South China
1970	Jardines
1971	Rangers
1972	South China
1973	Seiko
1974	South China
1975	Seiko
1976	South China
1977	South China
1978	South China
1979	Seiko
1980	Seiko
1981	Seiko
1982	Seiko
1983	Seiko
1984	Seiko
1985	Seiko
1986	South China
1987	South China
1988	South China
1989	Happy Valley
1990	South China
1991	South China

INDIA

Population: 853 373 000
Area, sq km: 3 166 414
% in urban areas: 27%
Capital city: New Dehli 8 156 000

All India Football Federation
Green Lawns
Talap, PO Box 429
Cannanore 670 002
Kerala
India
Tel: (010 91) 3497 67799
Fax: (010 91) 3497 67724
Telex: 805 286
Cable: SOCCER
Languages for correspondence: English

Year of formation: 1937
Affiliation to FIFA: 1948
Affiliation to AFC: 1954
Registered clubs: 2000
Registered players: 56 000
Registered referees: 4300
National stadium: Jawaharlal Nehru Stadium, New Dehli 75 000
National colours: Shirts: Sky blue Shorts: White Socks: Blue
Reserve colours: Shirts: White Shorts: Blue Socks: White

THE RECORD

WORLD CUP

1930–82 ..... Did not enter
1986 .... QT R1 2nd/4 in group 6
1990 .... Did not enter

OLYMPIC GAMES

1908–36 ..... Did not enter
1948 .... 1st round
1952 .... Preliminary round
1956 .... Semi-finalists/3rd place
1960 .... QT Qualified – Final tournament/1st round
1964 .... QT 2nd round
1968 .... Did not enter
1972 .... QT 5th/6 in group 2
1976 .... Did not enter
1980 .... QT 5th/6 in group 3
1984 .... QT R1 3rd/5 in group 3
1988 .... Did not enter
1992 .... QT 5th/5 in group 2

ASIAN CHAMPIONSHIP

1956 .... Did not enter
1960 .... QT 4th/4 in group 1
1964 .... QT 1st/in group 1 – Final tournament/2nd place
1968 .... QT 4th/4 in group 1
1972–80 ..... Did not enter
1984 .... QT 2nd/5 in group 3 – Final tournament/1st round
1988 .... QT 6th/6 in group 1

ASIAN GAMES

1951 .... Winners
1954 .... 1st round
1958 .... Semi-finalists/4th place
1962 .... Winners
1966 .... 1st round
1970 .... Semi-finalists/3rd place
1974 .... 1st round
1978 .... Semi-finalists/4th in group
1982 .... Quarter-finalists
1986 .... 1st round
1990 .... Did not enter

CALCUTTA LEAGUE CHAMPIONS

1898	Gloucestershire Regiment
1899	Calcutta Football Club
1900	Royal Irish Rifles
1901	Royal Irish Rifles
1902	King's Own Scottish Borderers
1903	93rd Highlanders
1904	King's Own Regiment
1905	King's Own Regiment
1906	Highland Light Infantry
1907	Calcutta Football Club
1908	Gordon Light Infantry
1909	Gordon Light Infantry
1910	Dalhousi
1911	70th Company RGA
1912	Black Watch
1913	Black Watch
1914	91st Highlanders
1915	10th Middlesex Regiment
1916	Calcutta Football Club
1917	Lincolnshire Regiment
1918	Calcutta Football Club
1919	12th Special Service Battalion
1920	Calcutta Football Club
1921	Dalhousi
1922	Calcutta Football Club
1923	Calcutta Football Club
1924	Cameron Highlanders
1925	Calcutta Football Club
1926	North Staffordshire Regiment
1927	North Staffordshire Regiment
1928	Dalhousi
1929	Dalhousi
1930	–
1931	Durham Light Infantry
1932	Durham Light Infantry
1933	Durham Light Infantry
1934	Mohammedan Sporting
1935	Mohammedan Sporting
1936	Mohammedan Sporting
1937	Mohammedan Sporting
1938	Mohammedan Sporting
1939	Mohon Bagan
1940	Mohammedan Sporting
1941	Mohammedan Sporting
1942	East Bengal
1943	Mohon Bagan
1944	Mohon Bagan
1945	East Bengal
1946	East Bengal
1947	–
1948	Mohammedan Sporting
1949	East Bengal
1950	East Bengal
1951	Mohon Bagan
1952	East Bengal
1953	–
1954	Mohon Bagan

1955	Mohon Bagan
1956	Mohon Bagan
1957	Mohammedan Sporting
1958	Eastern Railway
1959	Mohon Bagan
1960	Mohon Bagan
1961	East Bengal
1962	Mohon Bagan
1963	Mohon Bagan
1964	Mohon Bagan
1965	Mohon Bagan
1966	East Bengal
1967	Mohammedan Sporting
1968	–
1969	Mohon Bagan
1970	East Bengal
1971	East Bengal
1972	East Bengal
1973	East Bengal
1974	East Bengal
1975	East Bengal
1976	Mohon Bagan
1977	East Bengal
1978	Mohon Bagan
1979	Mohon Bagan
1980	–
1981	Mohammedan Sporting
1982	East Bengal
1983	Mohon Bagan
1984	Mohon Bagan
1985	East Bengal
1986	Mohon Bagan
1987	East Bengal
1988	East Bengal
1989	East Bengal
1990	Mohon Bagan
1991	East Bengal

SANTOSH TROPHY WINNERS

1941	Bengal	1966	Railways
1942	–	1967	Mysore
1943	–	1968	Mysore
1944	Dehli	1969	Bengal
1945	Bengal	1970	Punjab
1946	Mysore	1971	Bengal
1947	Bengal	1972	Bengal
1948	–	1973	Kerala
1949	Bengal	1974	Punjab
1950	Bengal	1975	Bengal
1951	Bengal	1976	Bengal
1952	Mysore	1977	Bengal
1953	Bengal	1978	Bengal
1954	Bombay (Maharashtra)	1979	Bengal
1955	Bengal	1980	Punjab
1956	Hyderabad (Andrha Pradesh)	1981	Bengal
		1982	–
		1983	Bengal & Goa
1957	Hyderabad (Andrha Pradesh)	1984	Goa
		1985	Punjab
1958	Bengal	1986	Punjab
1959	Bengal	1987	Bengal
1960	Services	1988	Punjab
1961	Railways	1989	Bengal
1962	Bengal	1990	Bengal
1963	Maharashtra	1991	Maharashtra
1964	Railways	1992	Kerala
1965	Andrha Pradesh		

FEDERATION CUP

1977	ITI Bangalore
1978	East Bengal/Mohon Bagan
1979	BSF Jullundur
1980	Mohon Bagan/East Bengal
1981	Mohon Bagan
1982	Mohon Bagan
1983	Mohammedan Sporting
1984	Mohammedan Sporting
1985	East Bengal
1986	Mohon Bagan
1987	Mohon Bagan
1988	Salgacor
1989	Salgacor
1990	Kerala Police
1991	Kerala Police
1992	Mohon Bagan

INDONESIA

Population: 180 763 000
Area, sq km: 1 948 732
% in urban areas: 26%
Capital city: Jakarta 7 829 000

All Indonesia Football Federation
Main Stadium Senayan, Gate VII
PO Box 2305
Jakarta 10001
Indonesia
Tel: (010 62) 21 581541
Fax: (010 62) 21 584386
Telex: 44439 PSSI IA
Cable: PSSI JAKARTA
Languages for correspondence: English

Year of formation: 1930
Affiliation to FIFA: 1952
Affiliation to AFC: 1954
Registered clubs: 334
Registered players: 307 000
Registered coaches: 1019
Registered referees: 337
National stadium: Senayan, Jakarta 110 000
National colours: Shirts: Red/Shorts: White/Socks: Red
Reserve colours: Shirts: White/Shorts: White/Socks: Red
Season: June–June

THE RECORD

WORLD CUP

1930	Did not enter
1934	Did not enter
1938	QT W–O in group 10 – Final tournament/1st round
1950	Did not enter
1954	Did not enter
1958	QT R1 1st/2 in group 1, R2 withdrew
1962–70	Did not enter
1974	QT R1 6th/8 in group B
1978	QT R1 4th/5 in group 1
1982	QT R1 3rd/5 in group 1
1986	QT R1 1st/4 in group 6, R2 2nd/2
1990	QT R1 3rd/4 in group 6

OLYMPIC GAMES

1908–52	Did not enter
1956	1st round
1960	QT 2nd round
1964	Did not enter
1968	QT 3rd/3 in group 2
1972	QT 4th/6 in group 2
1976	QT 2nd/5 in group 2
1980	QT 5th/6 in group 2
1984	QT R1 5th/5 in group 3
1988	QT R1 3rd/3 in group 3
1992	QT R1 3rd/4 in group 6

ASIAN CHAMPIONSHIP

1956	Did not enter
1960	
1964	
1968	QT 4th/5 in group 3
1972	
1976	QT 4th/5 in group 3
1980	QT 6th/7 in group 3
1984	QT /6 in group 1
1988	QT 3rd/4 in group 4

ASIAN GAMES

1951	1st round
1954	Semi-finalists/4th place
1958	Semi-finalists/3rd place
1962	1st round
1966	Quarter-finalists
1970	Quarter-finalists
1974–82	Did not enter
1986	Semi-finalists/4th place
1990	Did not enter

INDONESIAN NATIONAL CHAMPIONS

1981	Warna Agung
1982	NIAC Mitra
1983	NIAC Mitra
1984	Yanita Utama Bogor
1984	Yanita Utama Bogor
1985	Tiga Berlian
1986	Tiga Berlian
1987	–
1988	NIAC Mitra

IRAN

Population: 56 293 000
Area, sq km: 1 948 732
% in urban areas: 26%
Capital city: Tehran 6 042 000

Football Federation of the Islamic Republic of Iran
Ave Varzandeh #10

PO Box 11/1642, Tehran, Iran
Tel: (010 98) 21 825534
Fax: (01098) 21833272
Telex: 212691 VARZ IR
Cable: FOOTBALL IRAN – TEHRAN
Languages for correspondence: English

Year of formation: 1920
Affiliation to FIFA: 1948
Affiliation to AFC: 1958
Registered clubs: 6326
Registered players: 306000
Registered Coaches: 1200
Registered referees: 2000
National stadium: Azadi, Tehran 100000
National colours: Shirts: Green/Shorts: White/Socks: Red
Reserve colours: Shirts: White/Shorts: White/Socks: White
Season: March–January

THE RECORD

WORLD CUP

1930–70 ..... Did not enter
1974 .... QT R1 2nd/8 in group B
1978 .... QT R1 1st/3 in group 3, R2 1st/5 – Final tournament/1st round
1982 .... Did not enter
1986 .... Did not enter
1990 .... QT R1 2nd/4 in group 5

OLYMPIC GAMES

1908–60 ..... Did not enter
1964 .... QT Qualified – Final tournament/1st round
1968 .... Did not enter
1972 .... QT 1st/6 in group 3 – Final tournament/1st round
1976 .... QT 1st/5 in group 1 – Final tournament/Quarter–finalists
1980 .... QT 1st/6 in group 3 – Withdrew
1984 .... Did not enter
1988 .... QT R1 2nd/2 in group 4
1992 .... QT R1 2nd/5 in group 1

ASIAN CHAMPIONSHIP

1956 .... Did not enter
1960 .... QT 2nd/4 in group 1
1964 .... –
1968 .... QT Automatic – Final tournament/Winners
1972 .... QT Automatic – Final tournament/Winners
1976 .... QT Automatic – Final tournament/Winners
1980 .... QT Automatic – Final tournament/Semi-finalists/3rd place
1984 .... QT 1st/6 in group 1 – Final tournament/Semi-finalists/3rd place
1988 .... QT 2nd/5 in group 3 – Final tournament/3rd place

ASIAN GAMES

1951 .... Finalists
1954 .... Did not enter
1958 .... 1st round
1962 .... Did not enter
1966 .... Finalists
1970 .... 1st round
1974 .... Winners
1978 .... Did not enter
1982 .... Quarter-finalists
1986 .... Quarter-finalists
1990 .... Winners

ASIAN CHAMPION TEAMS' CUP

Winners – Taj Club 1970. Esteghlal SC 1990

IRANIAN LEAGUE CHAMPIONS

1974 Persepolis
1975 Taj
1976 Persepolis
1977 Persepolis
1978 Pas
1979 Shahbaz
1980 Persepolis
1981–85 –
1986 Malavan SC
1987 –
1988 Peroozi
1989 Shanin FC
1990 Esteghlal SC

IRAQ

Population: 17754000
Area, sq km: 435052
% in urban areas: 70%
Capital city: Baghdad 5348000

Iraqi Football Association
Olympic Committee Building
Palestine Street, Baghdad, Iraq
Tel: (010 964) 1 7748261
Fax: (010 964) 1 7728424
Telex: 214074 IRFA IK
Cable: BALL BAGHDAD
Languages for correspondence: English

Year of formation: 1948
Affiliation to FIFA: 1951
Affiliation to AFC: 1971
Registered clubs: 40
Registered players: 1900
Registered Coaches: 120
Registered referees: 190
National stadium: Sha'ab 50000
National colours: Shirts: White/Shorts: Green/Socks: White
Reserve colours: Shirts: Green/Shorts: White/Socks: White
Season: October–May

THE RECORD

WORLD CUP

1930–70 ..... Did not enter
1974 .... QT R1 3rd/8 in group B
1978 .... Did not enter
1982 .... QT R1 2nd/5 in group 2
1986 .... QT R1 1st/3 in group 6, R2 1st/2, R3 1st/2 – Final tournament/1st round
1990 .... QT R1 2nd/4 in group 1

OLYMPIC GAMES

1908–56 ..... Did not enter
1960 .... QT Failed to qualify
1964 .... QT 1st round
1968 .... QT 2nd/3 in group 2
1972 .... QT 3rd/6 in group 3
1976 .... QT 3rd/5 in group 1
1980 .... QT 1st/5 in group 1 – Final tournament/Quarter–finalists
1984 .... QT R1 1st/3 in group 2, R2 1st/5 in group 2 – Final tournament/1st round
1988 .... QT R1 1st/3 in group 2, R2 1st/4 – Final tournament/1st round
1992 .... Did not enter

ASIAN CHAMPIONSHIP

1956–68 ..... Did not enter
1972 .... QT 1st/in group 1 – Final tournament/1st round
1976 .... QT 1st/4 in group 2 – Final tournament/Semi-finalists/4th place
1980–88 ..... Did not enter

ASIAN GAMES

1951–70 ..... Did not enter
1974 .... Semi-finalists/3rd in group
1978 .... Semi-finalists/4th place
1982 .... Winners
1986 .... Quarter-finalists
1990 .... Did not enter

ASIAN CHAMPION TEAMS' CUP

Finalists – Police Club 1971. Al Rasheed 1988

IRAQI LEAGUE CHAMPIONS

1974 Al Tayeran
1975 Al Tayeran
1976 Al Zewra
1977 Al Zewra
1978 Al Mena
1979 Al Zewra
1980 Al Schurta
1981 Al Talaba
1982 Al Talaba
1983 Sal-el-Deen
1984 Al Jaische

1985 Al Rasheed
1986 Al Talaba
1987 Al Rasheed
1988 Al Rasheed
1989 Al Rasheed
1990 Al Rasheed
1991 Al Zewra

JAPAN

Population: 123 692 000
Area, sq km: 377 835
% in urban areas: 76%
Capital city: Tokyo 8 278 000

The Football Association of Japan
Kishi Memorial Hall
1-1-1 Jinnan, Shibuya-Ku
Tokyo
Japan
Tel: (010 81) 3 3481 2311
Fax: (010 81) 3 3481 0976
Telex: 2422975 FOTJPN J
Cable: SOCCERJAPAN TOKYO
Languages for correspondence: English

Year of formation: 1921
Affiliation to FIFA: 1929–45 & 1950
Affiliation to AFC: 1954
Registered clubs: 4523
Registered players: 641 900
Registered Coaches: 394
Registered referees: 6100
National stadium: National Stadium, Tokyo 62 000
National colours: Shirts: Blue/Shorts: White/Socks: Blue
Reserve colours: Shirts: White/Shorts: Blue/Socks: White
Season: October–May

THE RECORD

WORLD CUP

1930–50 ..... Did not enter
1954 .... QT 2nd/2 in group 13
1958 .... Did not enter
1962 .... QT 3rd/4 in group 10
1966 .... Did not enter
1970 .... QT R1 3rd/3 in group 1
1974 .... QT R1 4th/4 in group A
1978 .... QT R1 3rd/3 in group 2
1982 .... QT R1 4th/7 in group 4
1986 .... QT R1 1st/3 in group 8, R2 1st/2, R3 2nd/2
1990 .... QT R1 2nd/4 in group 6

OLYMPIC GAMES

1908–28 ..... Did not enter
1936 .... Quarter-finalists
1948 .... Did not enter
1952 .... Did not enter
1956 .... Preliminary round
1960 .... QT 1st round
1964 .... QT Automatic – Final tournament/Quarter-finalists
1968 .... QT 1st/6 in group 1 – Final tournament/Semi-finalists/3rd place
1972 .... QT 3rd/5 in group 1
1976 .... QT 3rd/3 in group 3
1980 .... QT 3rd/6 in group 2
1984 .... QT R1 2nd/4 in group 5, R2 5th/5 in group 2
1988 .... QT R1 1st/3 in group 3, R2 2nd/4
1992 .... QT R1 1st/4 in group 6, R2 5th/6

ASIAN CHAMPIONSHIP

1956 .... Did not enter
1960 .... –
1964 .... –
1968 .... QT 2nd/5 in group 3
1972 .... –
1976 .... QT 4th/6 in group 4
1980 .... QT Did not enter
1984 .... QT Did not enter
1988 .... QT 2nd/5 in group 2 – Final tournament/1st round

ASIAN GAMES

1951 .... Semi-finalists
1954 .... 1st round
1958 .... 1st round
1962 .... 1st round
1966 .... Semi-finalists/3rd place
1970 .... Semi-finalists/4th place
1974 .... 1st round
1978 .... 1st round
1982 .... Quarter-finalists
1986 .... 1st round
1990 .... Quarter-finalists

ASIAN CHAMPION TEAMS' CUP

Winners – Furukawa 1986. Yomuri 1987
Finalists – Nissan 1989

JAPANESE NATIONAL CHAMPIONS

1965 Toyo Kogyo
1966 Toyo Kogyo
1967 Toyo Kogyo
1968 Toyo Kogyo
1969 Mitsubishi
1970 Toyo Kogyo
1971 Yanmar Diesel
1972 Hitachi
1973 Mitsubishi
1974 Yanmar Diesel
1975 Yanmar Diesel
1976 Furukawa
1977 Fujita
1978 Mitsubishi
1979 Fujita
1980 Yanmar Diesel
1981 Fujita
1982 Mitsubishi
1983 Yomiuri
1984 Yomiuri
1985 Furukawa
1986 Furukawa
1987 Yomiuri
1988 Yamaha
1989 Nissan
1990 Nissan
1991 Yomiuri

JAPAN SOCCER LEAGUE CUP

1976 Hitachi
1977 Furukawa
1978 Mitsubishi
1979 Yomiuri
1980 Nippon Kohan
1981 Mitsubishi/Toshiba
1982 Furukawa
1983 Yanmar Diesel
1984 Yanmar Diesel
1985 Yomiuri
1986 Furukawa
1987 Nippon Kohan
1988 Nissan
1989 Nissan
1990 Nissan
1991 Yomiuri

ENGLISH F.A. CUP

1921 Tokyo FC
1922 Nagoya FC
1923 Astra
1924 Rijyo Club
1925 Rijyo Club
1926 –
1927 Kobe High School
1928 Waseda University
1929 Kansei Gakuin University
1930 Kansei Gakuin University
1931 Tokyo Imperial University
1932 Keio Club
1933 Tokyo OB
1934 –
1935 All Keijyo FC
1936 Keio BRB
1937 Keio University
1938 Waseda University
1939 Keio BRB
1940 Keio BRB

EMPEROR'S CUP

1946 Tokyo University
1947–48 –
1949 Tokyo University
1950 All Kansei Gakuin
1951 Keio BRB
1952 All Keio
1953 All Kansei Gakuin
1954 Keio BRB
1955 All Kansei Gakuin

1956	Keio BRB
1957	Chuo University
1958	Kansei Gakuin Club
1959	Kansei Gakuin Club
1960	Furukawa Electric
1961	Furukawa Electric
1962	Chuo University
1963	–
1964	Waseda University
1965	Yawata Steel
1966	Toyo Kogyo
1967	Waseda University
1968	Toyo Kogyo
1969	Yanmar Diesel
1970	Toyo Kogyo
1971	Yanmar Diesel
1972	Mitsubishi
1973	Hitachi
1974	Mitsubishi
1975	Yanmar Diesel
1976	Hitachi
1977	Furukawa
1978	Fujita
1979	Mitsubishi
1980	Fujita
1981	Mitsubishi
1982	Nippon Kokan
1983	Yamaha
1984	Nissan
1985	Yomiuri
1986	Nissan
1987	Yomiuri
1988	Yomiuri
1989	Nissan
1990	Nissan
1991	Matsushita
1992	Nissan

CLUB DIRECTORY

TOKYO (Population – 27700000)
Fujita Football Club
Stadium: Komazawa 20000
Founded: 1968
Colours: Yellow/Green

JR East Furukawa Football Club
Stadium: Ichihara 15000
Colours: Yellow/Green

Mitsubishi Motors Football Club
Stadium: Komaba 15000
Colours: Red/White

Nissan Football Club Yokohama Marinos
Stadium: Mitsuzawa 15000
Colours: Blue/White

Yomiuri Nippon Soccer Club
Stadium: Todoroki 15000
Colours: Green/White

OSAKA (Population – 16450000)
Yanmar Diesel Football Club
Stadium: Kobe 20000
Colours: Red/Red

Panasonic Gamba Osaka
Stadium: World Expo Memorial 23000
Colours: Blue/Black

NAGOYA (population – 1575000)
Nagoya Grampus Eight
Stadium: Mizuho 30000
Colours: Red/Red

HIROSHIMA (Population – 1575000)
Mazda Football Club
Stadium: Municipal 20000
Colours: White/White
Previous name: Toyo Kogyo 1938–81

Sanfrecce Hiroshoma Football Club
Stadium: Hiroshoma 15000
Colours: Purple/White

JORDAN

Population: 3169000
Area, sq km: 88946
% in urban areas: 69%
Capital city: Amman 936000

Jordan Football Association
PO Box 1054, Amman, Jordan
Tel: (010 962) 6 624481
Fax: (010 962) 6 624454
Telex: 22415 FOBALL JO
Cable: JORDAN FOOTBALL ASSOCIATION AMMAN
Languages for correspondence: English

Year of formation: 1949
Affiliation to FIFA: 1958
Affiliation to AFC: 1970
Registered clubs: 140
Registered players: 8900
Registered Coaches: 133
Registered referees: 114
National stadium: International Stadium, Amman 30000
National colours: Shirts: White/Shorts: White/Socks: White
Reserve colours: Shirts: Sky blue/Shorts: Sky blue/Socks: Sky blue
Season: June–December

THE RECORD

WORLD CUP

1930–82 ..... Did not enter
1986 .... QT R1 3rd/3 in group 2
1990 .... QT R1 3rd/4 in group 1

OLYMPIC GAMES

1908–76 ..... Did not enter
1980 .... QT 5th/5 in group 1
1984 .... QT R1 4th/4 in group 1
1988 .... QT R1 3rd/3 in group 2
1992 .... QT R1 3rd/4 in group 3

ASIAN CHAMPIONSHIP

1956–80 ..... Did not enter
1984 .... QT 3rd/5 in group 4
1988 .... QT 3rd/5 in group 2

ASIAN GAMES

1951–90 ..... Did not enter

JORDANIAN LEAGUE CHAMPIONS

1959	Al Faisaly
1960	Al Faisaly
1961	Al Faisaly
1962	Al Faisaly
1963	Al Faisaly
1964	Al Faisaly
1965	Al Faisaly
1966	Al Faisaly
1967	–
1968	Al Faisaly
1969	Al Faisaly
1970	Al Faisaly
1971	Al Faisaly
1972	Al Faisaly
1973	Al Faisaly
1974	Al Faisaly
1975	Al Ahli
1976	Al Faisaly
1977	Al Faisaly
1978	Al Ahli
1979	Al Ahli
1980	Al Wehdat
1981	Al Ramta
1982	Al Ramta
1983	Al Faisaly
1984	Amman Club
1985	–
1986	–
1987	Al Deffatain
1988	–
1989	Al Ramta

KAMPUCHEA

Population: 8592000
Area, sq km: 181916
% in urban areas: 12%
Capital city: Phnom Penh 564000

Fédération Khmère de Football Association
CP 101
Complex Sportif National
Phnom Penh
Kampuchea
Tel: (010 855) 23 22469 Fax: None
Telex: None
Cable: FKFA PHNOMPENH
Languages for correspondence: French & English

Year of formation: 1933
Affiliation to FIFA: 1953
Affiliation to AFC: 1957
Registered clubs: 30
Registered players: 2400
Registered Coaches: 50
Registered referees: 93
National stadium: CSN (Complex Sportif National), Phnom Penh 170000
National colours: Shirts: Red/Shorts: White/Socks: Red

Reserve colours: Shirts: Blue/Shorts: White/Socks: Blue
Season: November–October

THE RECORD

WORLD CUP

1930–90 ..... Did not enter

OLYMPIC GAMES

1908–52 ..... Did not enter
1956 .... QT Failed to qualify
1960–92 ..... Did not enter

ASIAN CHAMPIONSHIP

1956 .... QT 3rd/3 in group 3
1960
1964
1968 .... QT 2nd/4 in group 1
1972 .... QT 1st/in group 3 – Final tournament/Semi-finalists/4th place
1976–88 ..... Did not enter

ASIAN GAMES

1951–66 ..... Did not enter
1970 .... 1st round
1974–90 ..... Did not enter

KUWAIT

Population: 2 143 000
Area, sq km: 17 818
% in urban areas: 95%
Capital city: Kuwait City

Kuwait Football Association
Udailiyya, Bl 4
Al-Ittihad Street
PO Box 2029
13021 Safat
Kuwait
Tel: (010 965) 2555851
Fax: (010 965) 2563737
Telex: 22600 KT
Cable: FOOTKUWAIT
Languages for correspondence: English

Year of formation: 1952
Affiliation to FIFA: 1962
Affiliation to AFC: 1964
Registered clubs: 14
Registered players: 1200
Registered Coaches: 42
Registered referees: 49
National stadium: Al Qadesseyah 25 000
National colours: Shirts: Blue/Shorts: Blue/Socks: Blue
Reserve colours: Shirts: Red/Shorts: White/Socks: Red
Season: October–May

THE RECORD

WORLD CUP

1930–70 ..... Did not enter
1974 .... QT R1 7th/8 in group B
1978 .... QT R1 1st/3 in group 4, R2 3rd/5
1982 .... QT R1 1st/4 in group 3, R2 1st/4 – Final tournament/1st round
1986 .... QT R1 2nd/3 in group 3
1990 .... QT R1 2nd/3 in group 3

OLYMPIC GAMES

1908–68 ..... Did not enter
1972 .... QT 4th/6 in group 3
1976 .... QT 2nd/5 in group 1
1980 .... QT 1st/5 in group 1 – Final tournament/Quarter-finalists
1984 .... QT R1 1st/4 in group 1, R2 3rd/5 in group 1
1988 .... QT R1 1st/2 in group 4, R2 2nd/4
1992 .... QT R1 1st/5 in group 2, R2 3rd/6

ASIAN CHAMPIONSHIP

1956–68 ..... Did not enter
1972 .... QT 1st/in group 2 – Final tournament/1st round
1976 .... QT W-O in group 1 – Final tournament/Finalists
1980 .... QT Automatic – Final tournament/Winners
1984 .... QT Automatic – Final tournament/Semi-finalists/3rd place
1988 .... QT 1st/5 in group 2 – Final tournament/1st round

ASIAN GAMES

1951–70 ..... Did not enter
1974 .... Semi-finalists/3rd in group
1978 .... Semi-finalists/3rd in group
1982 .... Finalists
1986 .... Semi-finalists/3rd place
1990 .... Quarter-finalists

KUWAITI LEAGUE CHAMPIONS

1962 Al Arabi
1963 Al Arabi
1964 Al Arabi
1965 Al Kuwait
1966 Al Arabi
1967 Al Arabi
1968 Al Kuwait
1969 Al Qadesseyah
1970 Al Arabi
1971 Al Qadesseyah
1972 Al Kuwait
1973 Al Qadesseyah
1974 Al Kuwait
1975 Al Qadesseyah
1976 Al Qadesseyah
1977 Al Kuwait
1978 Al Qadesseyah
1979 Al Kuwait
1980 Al Arabi
1981 Al Salmiyah
1982 Al Arabi
1983 Al Arabi
1984 Al Arabi
1985 Al Arabi
1986 Al Kazmah
1987 Al Kazmah
1988 Al Arabi
1989 Al Arabi
1990 Al Jabaa

LAOS

Population: 4 024 000
Area, sq km: 236 800
% in urban areas: 16%
Capital city: Vientiane 377 000

Fédération de Foot-Ball Lao
C/O Direction des Sports-Education Physique et artistique
BP 268, Vientiane, Laos
Tel: (010 856) 2741
Fax: None Telex: None
Cable: FOOTBALL VIENTAINE
Languages for correspondence: French

Year of formation: 1951
Affiliation to FIFA: 1952
Affiliation to AFC: 1968
Registered clubs: 20
Registered players: 2000
Registered referees: 64
National stadium: Stade National, Vientaine 11000
National colours: Shirts: Red/Shorts: White/Socks: Blue
Reserve colours: Shirts: Blue/Shorts: White/Socks: Red
Season: October–May

THE RECORD

WORLD CUP

1930–90 ..... Did not enter

OLYMPIC GAMES

1908–92 ..... Did not enter

ASIAN CHAMPIONSHIP

1956–88 ..... Did not enter

ASIAN GAMES

1951–90 ..... Did not enter

LEBANON

Population: 2 965 000
Area, sq km: 10 230
% in urban areas: 80%
Capital city: Beirut 200 000

Fédération Libanaise de Football Association
PO Box 4732
Verdun Street Bristol
Radwan Center Bldg
Beirut, Lebanon
Tel: (010 961) 1868099
Fax: (010 961) 1 868099
Telex: 23001 ALABAL
Cable: FOOTBALL BEIRUT
Languages for correspondence: French & English

Year of formation: 1933
Affiliation to FIFA: 1935
Affiliation to AFC: 1964
Registered clubs: 105
Registered players: 8100
Registered referees: 87
National stadium: Camille Champum, Beirut 60 000
National colours: Shirts: Red/Shorts: White/Socks: Red
Reserve colours: Shirts: White/Shorts: White/Socks: Red
Season: October–June

THE RECORD

WORLD CUP

1930–90 ..... Did not enter

OLYMPIC GAMES

1908–64 ..... Did not enter
1968 .... QT 3rd/6 in group 1
1972 .... QT 5th/6 in group 3
1976–88 ..... Did not enter
1992 .... QT R1 4th/5 in group 2

ASIAN CHAMPIONSHIP

1956–76 ..... Did not enter
1980 .... QT 4th/4 in group 1
1984–88 ..... Did not enter

ASIAN GAMES

1951–90 ..... Did not enter

LEBANESE LEAGUE CHAMPIONS

1934	DPHB
1935	Al Nahda
1936	American University
1937	Sika
1938	American University
1939	American University
1940	Sika
1941	–
1942	Sika
1943	Al Nahda
1944	Homentmen
1945	Homentmen
1946	Homentmen
1947	Homentmen
1948	Al Nahda
1949	Homentmen
1950	Al Nahda
1951	–
1952	Homentmen
1953	–
1954	–
1955	Homentmen
1956	Homentmen
1957	Racing
1958	Homentmen
1959–61	–
1962	Homentmen
1963	–
1964	Homentmen
1965	–
1966	Racing
1967	–
1968	Chabiba Mazraa
1969	–
1970	Homentmen
1971	Racing
1972	–
1973	–
1974	Al Nejmeh
1975	–
1976	Al Nejmeh
1977–87	–
1988	Al Ansar
1989	Al Ansar

MACAU

Population: 461 000
Area, sq km: 17
Capital city: Macau 416 000

Associacao de Futebol de Macau
PO Box 920
Macau
Tel: (010 853) 71996
Fax: (010 853) 260148
Telex: None
Cable: FOOTBALL MACAU
Languages for correspondence: English & French

Year of formation: 1939
Affiliation to FIFA: 1976
Affiliation to AFC: 1976
Registered clubs: 23
Registered players: 450
Registered Coaches: 6
Registered referees: 27
National stadium: Campo Desportivo, Macau 12 000
National colours: Shirts: Green/Shorts: White/Socks: Green
Reserve colours: Shirts: White/Shorts: White/Socks: Red
Season: September–June

THE RECORD

WORLD CUP

1930–78 ..... Did not enter
1982 .... QT R1 6th/6 in group 4
1986 .... QT R1 3rd/4 in group 7
1990 .... Did not enter

OLYMPIC GAMES

1908–92 ..... Did not enter

ASIAN CHAMPIONSHIP

1956–76 ..... Did not enter
1980 .... QT 3rd/4 in group 4
1984–88 ..... Did not enter

ASIAN GAMES

1951–90 ..... Did not enter

MALAYSIA

Population: 17 886 000
Area, sq km: 330 442
% in urban areas: 38%
Capital city: Kuala Lumpur 1 103 000

Persatuan Bolasepak Malaysia
Wisma Fam, Tingkat 3
Jalan SS5A/9, Kelana Jaya
47301 Petaling Jaya, Selangor, Malaysia
Tel: (010 60) 3 7763766
Fax: (010 60) 3 7757984
Telex: FAM PJ MA 35701
Cable: FOOTBALL PETALING JAYA SELANGO
Languages for correspondence: English

Year of formation: 1933
Affiliation to FIFA: 1956
Affiliation to AFC: 1954
Registered clubs: 450
Registered players: 11 200
Registered Coaches: 480
Registered referees: 1223
National stadium: Merdeka, Kuala Lumpur 37 000
National colours: Shirts: Yellow/Shorts: Black/Socks: Yellow
Reserve colours: Shirts: White/Shorts: White/Socks: White
Season: February–September

THE RECORD

WORLD CUP

1930–70 ..... Did not enter
1974 .... QT R1 5th/7 in group A

1978 .... QT R1 3rd/5 in group 1
1982 .... QT R1 3rd/4 in group 3
1986 .... QT R1 2nd/3 in group 5
1990 .... QT R1 2nd/4 in group 4

OLYMPIC GAMES

1908–60 ..... Did not enter
1964 .... QT pr round
1968 .... Did not enter
1972 .... QT 1st/5 in group 1 – Final tournament/1st round
1976 .... QT 3rd/5 in group 2
1980 .... QT 1st/6 in group 2 – withdrew
1984 .... QT R1 2nd/5 in group 3, R2 4th/5 in group 2
1988 .... QT R1 2nd/2 in group 2
1992 .... QT R1 3rd/5 in group 4

ASIAN CHAMPIONSHIP

1956 .... QT 2nd/3 in group 3
1960 .... QT 2nd/3 in group 2
1964
1968 .... QT 4th/5 in group 2
1972
1976 .... QT 1st/5 in group 3 – Final tournament/1st round
1980 .... QT 2nd/7 in group 3 – Final tournament/1st round
1984 .... QT 3rd/5 in group 3
1988 .... QT 4th/5 in group 2

ASIAN GAMES

1951 .... Did not enter
1954 .... Did not enter
1958 .... 1st round
1962 .... Semi-finalists/3rd place
1966 .... 1st round
1970 .... 1st round
1974 .... Semi-finalists/3rd place
1978 .... Semi-finalists/4th in group
1982 .... 1st round
1986 .... 1st round
1990 .... 1st round

ASIAN CHAMPION TEAMS' CUP

Finalists – Selangor 1967

MALAYSIA CUP WINNERS

1921 Singapore
1922 Selangor
1923 Singapore
1924 Singapore
1925 Singapore
1926 Perak
1927 Selangor
1928 Singapore & Selangor
1929 Singapore & Selangor
1930 Singapore
1931 Perak
1932 Singapore
1933 Singapore
1934 Singapore
1935 Selangor
1936 Selangor
1937 Singapore
1938 Selangor
1939 Singapore
1940 Singapore
1941–47 –
1948 Negri Sembilan
1949 Selangor
1950 Singapore
1951 Singapore
1952 Singapore
1953 Penang
1954 Penang
1955 Singapore
1956 Selangor
1957 Perak
1958 Penang
1959 Selangor
1960 Singapore
1961 Selangor
1962 Selangor
1963 Selangor
1964 Singapore
1965 Singapore
1966 Selangor
1967 Perak
1968 Selangor
1969 Selangor
1970 Perak
1971 Selangor
1972 Selangor
1973 Selangor
1974 Penang
1975 Selangor
1976 Selangor
1977 Singapore
1978 Selangor
1979 Selangor
1980 Singapore
1981 Selangor
1982 Selangor
1983 Pahang
1984 Selangor
1985 Johore
1986 Selangor
1987 Kuala Lumpur
1988 Kuala Lumpur
1989 Kuala Lumpur

MALDIVES

Population: 214 000
Area, sq km: 298
% in urban areas: 25%
Capital city: Male 46 000

Football Association of Maldives
Sports Division
Male 20–04
Maldives
Tel: (010 960) 325758
Fax: (010 960) 324739
Telex: 77039 MINHOM MF
Cable: None
Languages for correspondence: English

Year of formation: 1983
Affiliation to FIFA: 1986
Affiliation to AFC: 1983
Registered clubs: 32
Registered players: 2000
Registered Coaches: 2
Registered referees: 30
National stadium: National Stadium, Male
National colours: Shirts: Green/Shorts: Red/Socks: White
Season: November–February

THE RECORD

WORLD CUP

1930–90 ..... Did not enter

OLYMPIC GAMES

1908–88 ..... Did not enter
1992 .... QT R1 4th/5 in group 5

ASIAN CHAMPIONSHIP

1956–88 ..... Did not enter

ASIAN GAMES

1951–90 ..... Did not enter

MALDIVES LEAGUE CHAMPIONS

1983 Valencia
1984 Valencia
1985 Valencia
1986 Victory SC
1987 Victory SC
1988 Victory SC
1989 Club Lagoons

MYANMAR

Population: 41 675 000
Area, sq km: 676 577
% in urban areas: 23%
Capital city: Rangoon 2 513 000

Myanmar Football Federation
Aung San Memorial Stadium
Kandawgalay Post Office
Rangoon
Tel: (010 95) 1 75249
Fax: None
Telex: 21218 BRCROS BM
Cable: BFF RANGOON
Languages for correspondence: English

Year of formation: 1947
Affiliation to FIFA: 1947
Affiliation to AFC: 1958
Registered clubs: 600
Registered players: 21 000
Registered Coaches: 60

Registered referees: 1840
National stadium: Aung San Memorial Stadium, Rangoon 45 000
National colours: Shirts: Red/Shorts: White/Socks: Red
Reserve colours: Shirts: White/Shorts: White/Socks: White
Season: May–February

THE RECORD

WORLD CUP

1930–90 ..... Did not enter

OLYMPIC GAMES

1908–60 ..... Did not enter
1964 .... QT 1st round
1968 .... Did not enter
1972 .... QT 1st/6 in group 2 – Final tournament/1st round
1976–92 ..... Did not enter

ASIAN CHAMPIONSHIP

1956 .... Did not enter
1960 .... –
1964 .... –
1968 .... QT 1st/4 in group 1 – Final tournament/2nd place
1972 .... –
1976–88 ..... Did not enter

ASIAN GAMES

1951 .... 1st round
1954 .... Semi-finalists/3rd place
1958 .... 1st round
1962 .... Did not enter
1966 .... Winners
1970 .... Winners
1974 .... Semi-finalists/4th in group
1978 .... 1st round
1982 .... 1st round
1986 .... Did not enter
1990 .... Did not enter

NEPAL

Population: 18 910 000
Area, sq km: 147 181
% in urban areas: 8%
Capital city: Kathmandu 235 000

All Nepal Football Association
Desareth Rangashala
Tripureshwor
Kathmandu
Nepal
Tel: (010 977) 1 15703
Fax: None
Telex: 2390 NSC NP
Cable: ANFA KATHMANDU
Languages for correspondence: English

Year of formation: 1951
Affiliation to FIFA: 1970
Affiliation to AFC: 1971
Registered clubs: 90
Registered players: 6900
Registered Coaches: 43
Registered referees: 77
National stadium: Dasarath Rangashala, Kathmandu 35 000
National colours: Shirts: Red/Shorts: Blue/Socks: White
Season: April–November

THE RECORD

WORLD CUP

1930–92 ..... Did not enter
1986 .... QT R1 3rd/3 in group 5
1990 .... QT R1 4th/4 in group 4

OLYMPIC GAMES

1908–84 ..... Did not enter
1988 .... QT R1 1st/2 in group 1, R2 4th/4
1992 .... QT R1 5th/5 in group 5

ASIAN CHAMPIONSHIP

1956–80 ..... Did not enter
1984 .... QT 5th/5 in group 2
1988 .... QT 5th/5 in group 3

ASIAN GAMES

1951–78 ..... Did not enter
1982 .... 1st round
1986 .... 1st round
1990 .... Did not enter

NEPALESE LEAGUE CHAMPIONS

1985 New Road Team
1986 Menang Marsyangdi
1987 Kathmandu SC
1988 Kathmandu SC
1989 Ranipokhari

NORTH KOREA

Population: 22 937 000
Area, sq km: 122 400
% in urban areas: 64%
Capital city: Pyongyang 2 000 000

Football Association of the Democratic People's Republic of Korea
Munsin-Dong 2
Dongdaewon District
Pyongyang, North Korea
Tel: (010 850) 2 3998
Fax: (010 850) 2 814403
Telex: 5472 KP
Cable: DPR KOREA FOOTBALL PYONGYANG
Languages for correspondence: English, French, German and Spanish

Year of formation: 1945
Affiliation to FIFA: 1958
Affiliation to AFC: 1974
Registered clubs: 50
Registered players: 3400
Registered referees: 720
National stadium: Moranbong, Pyongyang 90 000
National colours: Shirts: Red/Shorts: White/Socks: Red
Reserve colours: Shirts: White/Shorts: Green/Socks: White
Season: March–November

THE RECORD

WORLD CUP

1930–62 ..... Did not enter
1966 .... QT 1st/2 – Final tournament/Quarter-finalists
1970 .... Did not enter
1974 .... QT R1 5th/8 in group B
1978 .... Did not enter
1982 .... QT R1 2nd/6 in group 4
1986 .... QT R1 2nd/3 in group 8
1990 .... QT R1 1st/4 in group 6, R2 6th/6

OLYMPIC GAMES

1908–60 ..... Did not enter
1964 .... QT Qualified – withdrew
1968 .... Did not enter
1972 .... QT 2nd/6 in group 3
1976 .... QT 1st/5 in group 2 – Final tournament/Quarter-finalists
1980 .... QT 4th/6 in group 3
1984 .... Did not enter
1988 .... Did not enter
1992 .... QT R1 2nd/5 in group 5

ASIAN CHAMPIONSHIP

1956–68 ..... Did not enter
1972 .... –
1976 .... QT 1st/6 in group 2 – Withdrew
1980 .... QT 1st/7 in group 3 – Final tournament/Semi-finalists/4th place
1984 .... Did not enter
1988 .... QT 3rd/5 in group 3

ASIAN GAMES

1951–70 ..... Did not enter
1974 .... Semi-finalists/4th place
1978 .... Winners
1982 .... Semi-finalists/4th place
1986 .... Did not enter
1990 .... Finalists

OMAN

Population: 1 468 000
Area, sq km: 300 000
% in urban areas: 9%
Capital city: Muscat 85 000

Oman Football Association
PO Box 6462
Ruwi, Muscat, Oman
Tel: (010 968) 707885
Fax: (010 968) 707829
Telex: 3760 FOOTBALL ON
Cable: FOOTBALL MUSCAT
Languages for correspondence: English

Year of formation: 1978
Affiliation to FIFA: 1980
Affiliation to AFC: 1979
Registered clubs: 47
Registered players: 2300
Registered referees: 95
National stadium: El Shorta, Muscat 45 000
National colours: Shirts: White/Shorts: Red/Socks: White
Reserve colours: Shirts: Red/Shorts: White/Socks: Red
Season: October–May

THE RECORD

WORLD CUP

1930–86 ..... Did not enter
1990 .... QT R1 4th/4 in group 1

OLYMPIC GAMES

1908–84 ..... Did not enter
1988 .... QT R1 3rd/3 in group 1
1992 .... QT R1 3rd/5 in group 2

ASIAN CHAMPIONSHIP

1956–80 ..... Did not enter
1984 .... QT 3rd/5 in group 2
1988 .... Did not enter

ASIAN GAMES

1951–82 ..... Did not enter
1986 .... 1st round
1990 .... Did not enter

PAKISTAN

Population: 122 666 000
Area, sq km: 796 095
% in urban areas: 32%
Capital city: Islamabad 204 000
Major city: Karachi 5208000

Pakistan Football Federation
43 Rettigon Road
Lahore–54000, Pakistan
Tel: (010 92) 42 233348
Fax: (010 92) 42 237927
Telex: 52369 PCOPE PK
Cable: FOOTBALL PESHAWAR
Languages for correspondence: English

Year of formation: 1948
Affiliation to FIFA: 1948
Affiliation to AFC: 1960
Registered clubs: 2730
Registered players: 5000
Registered Coaches: 23
Registered referees: 1109
National stadium: Karachi Stadium 86 000
National colours: Shirts: Green/Shorts: Green/Socks: Green
Reserve colours: Shirts: White/Shorts: White/Socks: White
Season: October–April

THE RECORD

WORLD CUP

1930–86 ..... Did not enter
1990 .... QT R1 3rd/3 in group 3

OLYMPIC GAMES

1908–60 ..... Did not enter
1964 .... QT pr round
1968–84 ..... Did not enter
1988 .... QT R1 2nd/2 in group 1
1992 .... QT R1 5th/5 in group 1

ASIAN CHAMPIONSHIP

1956 .... Did not enter
1960 .... QT 3rd/4 in group 1
1964 .... QT 3rd in group 1
1968 .... QT 3rd/4 in group 1
1972 .... Did not enter
1976 .... Did not enter
1980 .... Did not enter
1984 .... QT 4th/5 in group 3
1988 .... QT 5th/5 in group 2

ASIAN GAMES

1951 .... Did not enter
1954 .... 1st round
1958 .... 1st round
1962–70 ..... Did not enter
1974 .... 1st round
1978 .... Did not enter
1982 .... Did not enter
1986 .... 1st round
1990 .... 1st round

PAKISTAN NATIONAL CHAMPIONS

1948	Karachi Red
1949	–
1950	Baluchistan
1951	–
1952	Punjab
1953	Punjab
1954	Punjab
1955	Punjab
1956	Baluchistan
1957	Punjab
1958	Punjab Blue
1959	Baluchistan
1960	Dacca
1961	Dacca
1962	Dacca
1963	Karachi
1964	Karachi
1965	–
1966	Karachi
1967	–
1968	Peshawar
1969	Pakistan Railways
1970	Chittagong
1971	Pakistan International Airlines
1972	Pakistan International Airlines
1973	Karachi Yellow
1974	Pakistan International Airlines
1975	Sind Red
1976	Pakistan International Airlines
1977	–
1978	Pakistan International Airlines
1979	Karachi Red
1980	Karachi Red
1981	Pakistan International Airlines
1982	Habib Bank
1983	WAPDA
1984	Pakistan Railways
1985	Quetta
1986	Pakistan Air Force
1987	–
1988	–
1989	Punjab Red
1990	Punjab Red
1991	WAPDA

PAKISTAN INTER-PROVINCIAL CHAMPIONSHIP

1984	Pakistan International Airlines
1985	Habib Bank
1986	–
1987	Crescent Textiles

PHILIPPINES

Population: 64 480 000
Area, sq km: 300 000
% in urban areas: 42%
Capital city: Manila 1 876 000

Philippine Football Federation
Room 207, Administration Building
Rizal Memorial Sports Complex
Vito Cruz
Metro Manilla
Philippines
Tel: (010 63) 2 594655
Fax: (010 63) 2 588317

Telex: 65014 POCPACA PN
Cable: FOOTBALL MANILLA
Languages for correspondence: English & Spanish

Year of formation: 1907
Affiliation to FIFA: 1928
Affiliation to AFC: 1954
Registered clubs: 410
Registered players: 29 700
Registered Coaches: 600
Registered referees: 1230
National stadium: Jose Rizal Memorial, Manila 30 000
National colours: Shirts: Blue/Shorts: White/Socks: Blue
Reserve colours: Shirts: White/Shorts: Blue/Socks: Red
Season: July–April

THE RECORD

WORLD CUP

1930–90 ..... Did not enter

OLYMPIC GAMES

1908–64 ..... Did not enter
1968 .... QT 6th/6 in group 1
1972 .... QT 4th/5 in group 1
1976 .... QT 5th/5 in group 3
1980 .... QT 6th/6 in group 2
1984 .... QT R1 4th/4 in group 5
1988 .... QT R1 3rd/3 in group 4
1992 .... QT R1 5th/5 in group 4

ASIAN CHAMPIONSHIP

1956 .... QT 3rd/3 in group 2
1960
1964
1968 .... QT 5th/5 in group 3
1972
1976 .... Did not enter
1980 .... QT 4th/4 in group 4
1984 .... QT 6th/6 in group 1
1988 .... Did not enter

ASIAN GAMES

1951 .... Did not enter
1954 .... 1st round
1958 .... Quarter-finalists
1962 .... 1st round
1966 .... Did not enter
1970 .... Did not enter
1974 .... 1st round
1978–90 ..... Did not enter

QATAR

Population: 444 000
Area, sq km: 11 427
% in urban areas: 88%
Capital city: Doha 217 000

Qatar Football Association
PO Box 5333
Doha
Qatar
Tel: (010 974) 351641
Fax: (010 974) 411660
Telex: 4749 QATFOT DH
Cable: FOOTQATAR DOHA
Languages for correspondence: English

Year of formation: 1960
Affiliation to FIFA: 1970
Affiliation to AFC: 1972
Registered clubs: 12
Registered players: 830
Registered Coaches: 54
Registered referees: 40
National stadium: Khalifa, Doha 40 000
National colours: Shirts: White/Shorts: Maroon/Socks: White
Reserve colours: Shirts: Maroon/Shorts: White/Socks: Maroon
Season: October–May

THE RECORD

WORLD CUP

1930–74 ..... Did not enter
1978 .... QT R1 3rd/3 in group 4
1982 .... QT R1 3rd/5 in group 2
1986 .... QT R1 2nd/3 in group 2
1990 .... QT R1 1st/4 in group 1, R2 3rd/6

OLYMPIC GAMES

1908–80 ..... Did not enter
1984 .... QT R1 2nd/4 in group 1, R2 1st/5 in group 2 – Final tournament/1st round
1988 .... QT R1 1st/2 in group 3, R2 3rd/4
1992 .... QT R1 1st/5 in group 1, R2 1st/6

ASIAN CHAMPIONSHIP

1956–72 ..... Did not enter
1976 .... QT 3rd/4 in group 2
1980 .... QT 1st/3 in group 2 – Final tournament/1st round
1984 .... QT 2nd/5 in group 4 – Final tournament/1st round
1988 .... QT Automatic – Final tournament/1st round

ASIAN GAMES

1951–74 ..... Did not enter
1978 .... 1st round
1982 .... Did not enter
1986 .... 1st round
1990 .... Did not enter

ASIAN CHAMPION TEAMS' CUP

Winners – Al Saad 1988

QATARI LEAGUE CHAMPIONS

1973 Al Esteklal
1974 Al Saad
1975 –
1976 Al Rayyan
1977 Al Esteklal
1978 Al Rayyan
1979 Al Saad
1980 Al Saad
1981 Al Saad
1982 Al Rayyan
1983 Al Arabi
1984 Al Rayyan
1985 Al Arabi
1986 Al Rayyan
1987 Al Saad
1988 Al Saad
1989 Al Saad
1990 Al Rayyan
1991 Al Arabi

SAUDI ARABIA

Population: 14 131 000
Area, sq km: 2 240 000
% in urban areas: 73%
Capital city: Riyadh 1 308 000

Saudi Arabian Football Federation
North Al-Morabbaa Quarter
PO Box 5844
Riyadh 11432
Saudi Arabia
Tel: (010 966) 1 4022699
Fax: (010 966) 1 4021276
Telex: 404300 SAFOTB SJ
Cable: KORA RIYADH
Languages for correspondence: English

Year of formation: 1959
Affiliation to FIFA: 1959
Affiliation to AFC: 1972
Registered clubs: 154
Registered players: 9600
Registered Coaches: 309
Registered referees: 504
National stadium: Malaz, Riyadh 30 000
National colours: Shirts: Green/Shorts: White/Socks: Green
Reserve colours: Shirts: White/Shorts: WhiteSocks: White
Season: September–March

THE RECORD

WORLD CUP

1930–74 ..... Did not enter
1978 .... QT R1 2nd/3 in group 3
1982 .... QT R1 1st/5 in group 2, R2 4th/4
1986 .... QT R1 2nd/2 in group 1
1990 .... QT R1 1st/3 in group 2, R2 5th/6

OLYMPIC GAMES

1908–72 ..... Did not enter
1976 .... QT 4th/5 in group 1
1980 .... Did not enter
1984 .... QT R1 1st/5 in group 3, R2 1st/5 in group 1 – Final tournament/1st round
1988 .... QT R1 1st/3 in group 1, R2 4th/4
1992 .... QT R1 2nd/4 in group 3

ASIAN CHAMPIONSHIP

1956–72 ..... Did not enter
1976 .... QT 2nd/4 in group 1 – Withdrew
1980 .... Did not enter
1984 .... QT 1st/5 in group 2 – Final tournament/Winners
1988 .... QT Automatic – Final tournament/Winners

ASIAN GAMES

1951–74 ..... Did not enter
1978 .... 1st round
1982 .... Semi-finalists/3rd place
1986 .... Finalists
1990 .... Quarter-finalists

ASIAN CHAMPION TEAMS' CUP

Finalists – Al Ahli 1985. Al Hilal 1986, 1987

SAUDI ARABIAN LEAGUE CHAMPIONS

1979	Al Hilal
1980	Al Nasr
1981	Al Nasr
1982	Al Ittihad
1983	Al Ittifaq
1984	Al Ahli
1985	Al Hilal
1986	Al Hilal
1987	Al Ittifaq
1988	Al Hilal
1989	Al Nasr
1990	Al Hilal

KING'S CUP WINNERS

1957	Al Wehda
1958	Al Ittihad
1959	Al Ittihad
1960	Al Ittihad
1961	Al Hilal
1962	Al Ahli
1963	Al Ittihad
1964	Al Hilal
1965	Al Ahli
1966	Al Wehda
1967	Al Ittihad
1968	Al Ittifaq
1969	Al Ahli
1970	Al Ahli
1971	Al Ahli
1972	Al Ahli
1973	Al Ahli
1974	Al Nasr
1975	–
1976	Al Nasr
1977	Al Ahli
1978	Al Ahli
1979	Al Ahli
1980	Al Hilal
1981	Al Nasr
1982	Al Ittihad
1983	Al Ittifaq
1984	Al Ahli
1985	Al Hilal
1986	Al Nasr
1987	
1988	
1989	Al Hilal
1990	Al Nasr

SINGAPORE

Population: 2 718 000
Area, sq km: 622
% in urban areas: 100%
Capital city: Singapore City State 2 718 000

Football Association of Singapore
Jalan Besar Stadium, Tyrwhitt Road
Singapore 0820
Tel: (010 65) 2931477
Fax: (010 65) 2933728
Telex: SINFA RS 37683
Cable: SOCCER SINGAPORE
Languages for correspondence: English

Year of formation: 1892
Affiliation to FIFA: 1952
Affiliation to AFC: 1954
Registered clubs: 120
Registered players: 8800
Registered Coaches: 359
Registered referees: 125
National stadium: National Stadium 65 000
National colours: Shirts: Sky blue/Shorts: Sky blue/Socks: Sky blue
Reserve colours: Shirts: White/Shorts: White/Socks: White
Season: March–December

THE RECORD

WORLD CUP

1930–74 ..... Did not enter
1978 .... QT R1 2nd/5 in group 1
1982 .... QT R1 5th/6 in group 4
1986 .... QT R1 3rd/3 in group 8
1990 .... QT R1 3rd/4 in group 4

OLYMPIC GAMES

1908–72 ..... Did not enter
1976 .... QT 4th/5 in group 2
1980 .... QT 2nd/6 in group 3
1984 .... QT R1 4th/5 in group 3
1988 .... QT R1 2nd/3 in group 3
1992 .... QT R1 3rd/5 in group 5

ASIAN CHAMPIONSHIP

1956 .... Did not enter
1960 .... QT 3rd/3 in group 2
1964
1968 .... QT 5th/5 in group 2
1972
1976 .... QT 5th/6 in group 4
1980 .... QT 7th/7 in group 7
1984 .... QT Automatic – Final tournament/1st round
1988 .... Did not enter

ASIAN GAMES

1951 .... Did not enter
1954 .... 1st round
1958 .... 1st round
1962 .... Did not enter
1966 .... Semi-finalists/4th place
1970–86 ..... Did not enter
1990 .... 1st round

SINGAPORE LEAGUE CHAMPIONS

1975	Geylang International
1976	Geylang International
1977	Geylang International
1978	SAFSA
1979	Tampines Rovers
1980	Tampines Rovers
1981	SAFSA
1982	Farrer Park United
1983	Tiong Bahru
1984	Tampines Rovers
1985	Police SA
1986	Tiong Bahru
1987	Geylang International
1988	Geylang International
1989	Geylang International
1990	Geylang International

SOUTH KOREA

Population: 42 793 000
Area, sq km: 99 237
% in urban areas: 69%
Capital city: Seoul 10 726 000

Korea Football Association
110–39 Kyeonji-Dong
Chongro-Ku, Seoul, South Korea
Tel: (010 82) 2 7336764
Fax: (010 82) 2 7352755
Telex: KFASEL K25373
Cable: FOOTBALL KOREA SEOUL
Languages for correspondence: English

Year of formation: 1928
Affiliation to FIFA: 1948
Affiliation to AFC: 1954
Registered clubs: 78
Registered players: 11 400
Registered Coaches: 526
Registered referees: 485
National stadium: Olympic Stadium, Seoul 100 000
National colours: Shirts: Red/Shorts: Red/ Socks: Red
Reserve colours: Shirts: Blue/Shorts: Blue/ Socks: Blue
Season: March–November

THE RECORD

WORLD CUP

1930–50 ..... Did not enter
1954 .... QT 1st/2 in group 13 – Final tournament/1st round
1958 .... Did not enter
1962 .... QT 2nd/4 in group 10
1966 .... Did not enter
1970 .... QT 2nd/3 in group 1
1974 .... QT R1 1st/7 in group 1, R2 2nd/2
1978 .... QT R1 1st/3 in group 2, R2 2nd/5
1982 .... QT R1 2nd/4 in group 3
1986 .... QT R1 1st/3 in group 5, R2 1st/2, R3 1st/2 – Final tournament/1st round
1990 .... QT R1 1st/4 in group 4, R2 1st/6 – Final tournament/1st round

OLYMPIC GAMES

1908–36 ..... Did not enter
1948 .... Quarter-finalists
1952 .... Did not enter
1956 .... QT Failed to qualify
1960 .... QT 2nd round
1964 .... QT Qualified – Final tournament/1st round
1968 .... QT 2nd/6 in group 1
1972 .... QT 2nd/5 in group 1
1976 .... QT 2nd/3 in group 3
1980 .... QT 2nd/6 in group 2
1984 .... QT R1 2nd/4 in group 4, R2 2nd/5 in group 1
1988 .... QT Automatic – Final tournament/1st round
1992 .... QT R1 1st/5 in group 4, R2 2nd/6

ASIAN CHAMPIONSHIP

1956 .... QT 1st/3 in group 2 – Final tournament/Winners
1960 .... QT Automatic – Final tournament/Winners
1964 .... QT Automatic – Final tournament/3rd place
1968 .... QT 3rd/5 in group 3
1972 .... QT 1st in group 4 – Final tournament/Finalists
1976 .... QT 3rd/5 in group 3
1980 .... QT 1st/4 in group 4 – Final tournament/Finalists
1984 .... QT 1st/5 in group 3 – Final tournament/1st round
1988 .... QT 2nd/4 in group 4 – Final tournament/Finalists

ASIAN GAMES

1951 .... Did not enter
1954 .... Finalists
1958 .... Finalists
1962 .... Finalists
1966 .... 1st round
1970 .... Winners
1974 .... Semi-finalists/4th in group
1978 .... Winners
1982 .... 1st round
1986 .... Winners
1990 .... Semi-finalists/3rd place

ASIAN CHAMPION TEAMS' CUP

Winners – Daewoo Royals 1985
Finalists – Yangzee 1968

SOUTH KOREAN PRO-FOOTBALL LEAGUE

Year	Champions		Runners up		3rd	
1983	Halleluyah Eagles	20	Daewoo Royals	19	Yukong Elephants	17
1984	Daewoo Royals	*	Yukong Elephants			
1985	Lucky Goldstar	27	POSCO Atoms	25	Daewoo Royals	25
1986	Hyundai Tigers	23	Daewoo Royals	16	Yukong Elephants	15
1987	Daewoo Royals	46	POSCO Atoms	40	Yukong Elephants	27
1988	POSCO Atoms	27	Hyundai Tigers	25	Yukong Elephants	24
1989	Yukong Elephants	49	Lucky Goldstar	47	Daewoo Royals	42
1990	Lucky Goldstar	39	Daewoo Royals	35	Posco Atoms	28
1991	Daewoo Royals		Hyundai Tigers		Po-hang Dolphins	

* Play-off
Daewoo Royals .... 1–0 1–1 Yukong Elephants

INTERNATIONAL MATCHES PLAYED BY SOUTH KOREA

Date	Opponents	Result		Venue	Compet
2-08-1948	Mexico	W	5–3	London	OGr1
5-08	Sweden	L	0–12	London	OGqf
1-01-1949	Hong Kong	W	5–2	Hong Kong	Fr
2-01	China	L	2–3	Hong Kong	Fr
9-01	Hong Kong	W	4–2	Hong Kong	Fr
16-01	Vietnam	D	3–3	Saigon	Fr
15-04-1950	Hong Kong	W	6–3	Hong Kong	Fr
16-04	Hong Kong	W	3–1	Hong Kong	Fr
5-04-1953	Singapore	W	3–2	Hong Kong	Fr
-04	Hong Kong	L	0–3	Hong Kong	Fr
-04	Malaysia	W	3–2	Hong Kong	Fr
-04	Singapore	L	1–3	Hong Kong	Fr
-04	Singapore	W	3–1	Hong Kong	Fr
-04	Singapore	D	0–0	Hong Kong	Fr
-04	Hong Kong	L	3–5	Singapore	Fr
-04	Indonesia	W	3–1	Singapore	Fr
7-03-1954	Japan	W	5–1	Tokyo	WCq
14-03	Japan	D	2–2	Tokyo	WCq
1-05	Hong Kong	D	3–3	Manila	AGr1
-05	Afghanistan	W	8–2	Manila	AGr1
-05	Burma	D	2–2	Manila	AGsf
	Won on lots				
8-05	Taiwan	L	2–5	Manila	AGf
17-06	Hungary	L	0–9	Zurich	WCr1

20–06	Turkey	L	0–7	Geneva	WCr1
25–02–1956	Philippines	W	2–0	Manila	ACq
21–04	Philippines	W	3–0	Seoul	ACq
3–06	Japan	L	0–2	Tokyo	OGq
10–06	Japan	W	2–0	Tokyo	OGq
	Lost on lots				
26–08	Taiwan	W	2–0	Seoul	ACq
2–09	Taiwan	W	2–1	Taipei	ACq
6–09	Hong Kong	D	2–2	Hong Kong	AC
8–09	Israel	W	2–1	Hong Kong	AC
15–09	Vietnam	W	5–3	Hong Kong	AC
18–02–1958	Hong Kong	L	2–3	Hong Kong	Fr
26–05	Singapore	W	2–1	Tokyo	AGr1
28–05	Iran	W	5–0	Tokyo	AGr1
30–05	Vietnam	W	3–1	Tokyo	AGqf
31–05	India	W	3–1	Tokyo	AGsf
1–06	Taiwan	L	2–3	Tokyo	AGf
08–1959	3rd Merdeka Cup				
13–09	Singapore	W	4–0	Singapore	Fr
13–12	Japan	W	2–0	Tokyo	OGq
20–12	Japan	L	0–1	Tokyo	OGq
25–04–1960	Taiwan	W	2–1	Taipei	OGq
1–05	Taiwan	L	0–1	Taipei	OGq
Match awarded to Taiwan					
08	4th Merdeka Cup				
14–10	South Vietnam	W	5–1	Seoul	AC
17–10	Israel	W	3–0	Seoul	AC
21–10	Taiwan	W	1–0	Seoul	AC
6–11	Japan	W	2–1	Seoul	WCq
11–06–1961	Japan	W	2–0	Tokyo	WCq
08	5th Merdeka Cup				
8–10	Yugoslavia	L	1–5	Belgrade	WCq
18–10	Turkey	L	0–1	Ankara	Fr
22–10	Israel	D	1–1	Tel Aviv	Fr
–10	Burma	W	3–0	Rangoon	Fr
4–11	Thailand	W	4–1	Bangkok	Fr
26–11	Yugoslavia	L	1–3	Seoul	WCq
24–08–1962	India	W	2–0	Djakarta	AGr1
27–08	Thailand	W	3–2	Djakarta	AGr1
30–08	Japan	W	1–0	Djakarta	AGr1
1–09	Malaysia	W	2–1	Djakarta	AGsf
4–09	India	L	1–2	Djakarta	AGf
09	6th Merdeka Cup				
08–1963	7th Merdeka Cup				
27–11	Taiwan	W	2–1	Seoul	OGq
7–12	Taiwan	L	0–1	Taipei	OGq
–05–1964	India	W	2–0	Haifa	AC
–05	Hong Kong	W	1–0	Jerusalem	AC
3–06	Israel	L	1–2	Tel Aviv	AC
31–05	South Vietnam	W	3–0	Seoul	OGq
28–06	South Vietnam	D	2–2	Saigon	OGq
08	8th Merdeka Cup				
12–10	Czechoslovakia	L	1–6	Tokyo	OGr1
14–10	Brazil*	L	0–4	Tokyo	OGr1
16–10	Egypt	L	0–10	Tokyo	OGr1
08–1965	9th Merdeka Cup				
08–1966	10th Merdeka Cup				
9–12	Thailand	L	0–3	Bangkok	AGr1
11–12	Burma	L	0–1	Bangkok	AGr1
29–07–1967	Indonesia	D	1–1	Taipei	ACq
1–08	Japan	L	1–2	Taipei	ACq
5–08	Philippines	W	7–0	Taipei	ACq
7–08	Taiwan	L	0–1	Taipei	ACq
08	11th Merdeka Cup				
28–09	Taiwan	W	4–2	Tokyo	OGq
1–10	Lebanon	W	2–0	Tokyo	OGq
4–10	South Vietnam	W	3–0	Tokyo	OGq
7–10	Japan	D	3–3	Tokyo	OGq
9–10	Philippines	W	5–0	Tokyo	OGq

5–11	Hong Kong	W	1–0	Saigon	Fr
7–11	Thailand	W	3–1	Saigon	Fr
11–11	Malaysia	W	2–1	Saigon	Fr
12–11	South Vietnam	W	3–0	Saigon	Fr
14–11	Australia	L	2–3	Saigon	Fr
08–1968	12th Merdeka Cup				
27–08	Singapore	L	3–4	Singapore	Fr
–	Indonesia	D	1–1	Jakarta	ACq
–	Japan	L	1–2	Tokyo	ACq
–	Philippines	W	7–0	Seoul	ACq
–	Taiwan	L	0–1	Taipei	ACq
12–10–1969	Japan	D	2–2	Seoul	WCq
14–10	Australia	L	1–2	Seoul	WCq
18–10	Japan	W	2–0	Seoul	WCq
20–10	Australia	D	1–1	Seoul	WCq
10	13th Merdeka Cup				
11	1st King's Cup				
07–1970	14th Merdeka Cup				
11	2nd King's Cup				
11–12	Iran	W	1–0	Bangkok	AGr1
13–12	Indonesia	D	0–0	Bangkok	AGr1
15–12	Thailand	W	2–1	Bangkok	AGr2
17–12	Burma	L	0–1	Bangkok	AGr2
18–12	Japan	W	2–1	Bangkok	AGsf
20–12	Burma	D	0–0	Bangkok	AGf
05–1971	1st President's Cup				
08	15th Merdeka Cup				
27–08	Philippines	W	2–1		Fr
28–08	Singapore	W	4–1		Fr
10–09	Iran	W	2–0	Seoul	Fr
12–09	Iran	L	0–2	Seoul	Fr
25–09	Malaysia	L	0–1	Seoul	OGq
30–09	Philippines	W	6–0	Seoul	OGq
2–10	Japan	W	2–1	Seoul	OGq
4–10	Taiwan	W	8–0	Seoul	OGq
11	3rd King's Cup				
7–05–1972	Iraq	D	0–0	Bangkok	ACr1
10–05	Cambodia	W	4–1	Bangkok	ACr1
12–05	Kuwait	L	1–2	Bangkok	ACr1
17–05	Thailand	D	1–1	Bangkok	ACsf
	Won on pens				
19–05	Iran	L	1–2	Bangkok	ACf
06	3rd Jakarta Tournament				
07	16th Merdeka Cup				
14–09	Japan	D	2–2	Tokyo	Fr
09	2nd President's Cup				
22–10	Australia	D	1–1	Seoul	Fr
24–10	Australia	L	0–2	Seoul	Fr
11	4th King's Cup				
19–05–1973	Thailand	W	4–0	Seoul	WCq
21–05	Malaysia	D	0–0	Seoul	WCq
23–05	Israel	D	0–0	Seoul	WCq
26–05	Hong Kong	W	3–1	Seoul	WCq
28–05	Israel	W	1–0	Seoul	WCq
23–06	Japan	W	2–0	Seoul	Fr
07	17th Merdeka Cup				
09	3rd President's Cup				
28–10	Australia	D	0–0	Sydney	WCq
10–11	Australia	D	2–2	Seoul	WCq
13–11	Australia	L	0–1	Hong Kong	WCq
11	5th King's Cup				
05–1974	4th President's Cup				
07	18th Merdeka Cup				
4–09	Thailand	W	1–0	Tehran	AGr1
6–09	Kuwait	L	0–4	Tehran	AGr1
10–09	Iraq	D	1–1	Tehran	AGr2
12–09	Iran	L	0–2	Tehran	AGr2
14–09	Malaysia	L	2–3	Tehran	AGr2
28–09	Japan	L	1–4	Tokyo	Fr

12	6th King's Cup				
25–12	Indonesia	W	3–1	Hong Kong	Fr
16–03–1975	Malaysia	L	1–2	Bangkok	ACq
19–03	South Vietnam	W	1–0	Bangkok	ACq
22–03	Indonesia	W	1–0	Bangkok	ACq
24–03	Thailand	L	0–1	Bangkok	ACq
05	5th President's Cup				
06	6th Jakarta Tournament				
08	19th Merdeka Cup				
14–12	Taiwan	W	2–0	Taipei	OGq
12	7th King's Cup				
6–03–1976	Taiwan	W	3–0	Seoul	OGq
21–03	Japan	W	2–0	Tokyo	OGq
27–03	Japan	W	2–0	Seoul	OGq
4–04	Israel	L	1–3	Seoul	OGq
28–04	Israel	D	0–0	Tel Aviv	OGq
06	7th Jakarta Tournament				
08	20th Merdeka Cup				
09	6th President's Cup				
4–11	Japan	W	2–1	Tokyo	Fr
12	8th King's Cup				
14–02–1977	Singapore	W	4–0	Singapore	Fr
18–02	Bahrein	W	4–1	Manama	Fr
20–02	Bahrein	D	1–1	Manama	Fr
27–02	Israel	D	0–0	Tel Aviv	WCq
20–03	Israel	W	3–1	Seoul	WCq
26–03	Japan	D	0–0	Tokyo	WCq
3–04	Japan	W	1–0	Seoul	WCq
15–06	Japan	W	2–1	Seoul	Fr
26–06	Hong Kong	W	1–0	Hong Kong	WCq
3–07	Iran	D	0–0	Pusan	WCq
07	21st Merdeka Cup				
27–08	Australia	L	1–2	Sydney	WCq
09	7th President's Cup				
9–10	Kuwait	W	1–0	Seoul	WCq
23–10	Australia	D	0–0	Seoul	WCq
11	9th King's Cup				
5–11	Kuwait	D	2–2	Kuwait	WCq
11–11	Iran	D	2–2	Tehran	WCq
4–12	Hong Kong	W	5–2	Pusan	WCq
4–05–1978	Kenya	D	2–2	Riyadh	Fr
7–05	Pakistan	W	5–0	Riyadh	Fr
10–05	Saudi Arabia	W	2–0	Riyadh	Fr
25–05	Japan	W	3–0	Tokyo	Fr
06	9th Jakarta Tournament				
07	22nd Merdeka Cup				
09	8th President's Cup				
10–12	Bahrain	W	5–1	Bangkok	AGr1
12–12	Kuwait	W	2–0	Bangkok	AGr1
14–12	Japan	W	3–1	Bangkok	AGr1
16–12	China	W	1–0	Bangkok	AGr2
18–12	Malaysia	W	1–0	Bangkok	AGr2
20–12	Thailand	W	3–1	Bangkok	AGr2
22–12	North Korea	D	0–0	Bangkok	AGf
25–12	Macao	W	4–1	Manila	ACq
27–12	Philippines	W	5–0	Manila	ACq
29–12	China	W	1–0	Manila	ACq
4–03–1979	Japan	L	1–2	Tokyo	Fr
27–04	Burma	L	0–1	Medan	MHC
05	11th King's Cup				
16–06	Japan	W	4–1	Seoul	Fr
07	23rd Merdeka				
09	9th President's Cup				
28–01–1980	Saudi Arabia	W	3–1	Jeddah	Fr
30–01	Saudi Arabia	L	0–1	Riyadh	Fr
22–03	Japan	W	1–0	Kuala Lumpur	OGq
25–03	Malaysia	L	0–3	Kuala Lumpur	OGq
27–03	Philippines	W	8–0	Kuala Lumpur	OGq
31–03	Brunei	W	3–0	Kuala Lumpur	OGq
3–04	Indonesia	W	1–0	Kuala Lumpur	OGq
6–04	Malaysia	L	1–2	Kuala Lumpur	OGq
07	24th Merdeka Cup				
08	10th President's Cup				
9–09	Singapore	W	2–0	Singapore	Fr
16–09	Malaysia	D	1–1	Kuwait	ACr1
19–09	Qatar	W	2–0	Kuwait	ACr1
21–09	Kuwait	W	3–0	Kuwait	ACr1
24–09	Arab Emirates	W	4–1	Kuwait	ACr1
28–09	North Korea	W	2–1	Kuwait	ACsf
30–09	Kuwait	L	0–3	Kuwait	ACf
11–02–1981	Mexico	L	0–4	Mexico City	Fr
8–03	Japan	W	1–0	Tokyo	Fr
21–04	Malaysia	W	2–1	Kuwait	WCq
24–04	Thailand	W	5–1	Kuwait	WCq
29–04	Kuwait	L	0–2	Kuwait	WCq
06	11th President's Cup				
09	25th Merdeka Cup				
18–02–1982	India	D	2–2	Calcutta	Fr
1–03	China	D	1–1	Calcutta	Fr
7–03	Iraq	L	0–3	Baghdad	Fr
10–03	Iraq	D	1–1	Baghdad	Fr
21–03	Japan	W	3–0	Seoul	Fr
06	12th President's Cup				
08	26th Merdeka Cup				
19–11	South Yemen	W	3–0	New Dehli	AGr1
23–11	Japan	L	1–2	New Dehli	AGr1
25–11	Iran	L	0–1	New Dehli	AGr1
6–03–1983	Japan	D	1–1	Tokyo	Fr
06	13th President's Cup				
29–07	Guatemala	D	1–1	Guatemala	Fr
3–08	Guatemala	L	1–2	Guatemala	Fr
9–08	Costa Rica	D	1–1	San Jose	Fr
09	27th Merdeka Cup				
1–11	Thailand	L	1–2	Bangkok	OGq
3–11	China	D	3–3	Bangkok	OGq
5–11	Hong Kong	W	4–0	Bangkok	OGq
8–11	China	D	0–0	Bangkok	OGq
10–11	Hong Kong	W	2–0	Bangkok	OGq
12–11	Thailand	W	2–0	Bangkok	OGq
17–04–1984	Kuwait	D	0–0	Singapore	OGq
19–04	Bahrain	W	1–0	Singapore	OGq
22–04	New Zealand	W	2–0	Singapore	OGq
24–04	Saudi Arabia	L	4–5	Singapore	OGq
29–04	Iraq	L	0–1	Singapore	OGq
06	14th President's Cup				
08	28th Merdeka Cup				
30–09	Japan	L	1–2	Seoul	Fr
4–10	Cameroon	W	5–0	Seoul	Fr
10–10	Yeman AR	W	6–0	Calcutta	ACq
13–10	Pakistan	W	6–0	Calcutta	ACq
16–10	Malaysia	D	0–0	Calcutta	ACq
19–10	India	W	1–0	Calcutta	ACq
2–12	Saudi Arabia	D	1–1	Singapore	ACr1
5–12	Kuwait	D	0–0	Singapore	ACr1
7–12	Syria	L	0–1	Singapore	ACr1
10–12	Qatar	L	0–1	Singapore	ACr1
2–03–1985	Nepal	W	2–0	Katmandu	WCq
7–03	Bahrain	W	5–1	Manama	Fr
10–03	Malaysia	L	0–1	Kuala Lumpur	WCq
6–04	Nepal	W	4–0	Seoul	WCq
19–05	Malaysia	W	2–0	Seoul	WCq
06	15th President's Cup				
07	29th Merdeka Cup				
21–07	Indonesia	W	2–0	Seoul	WCq
30–07	Indonesia	W	4–1	Jakarta	WCq
26–11	Japan	W	2–1	Tokyo	WCq
3–11	Japan	W	1–0	Seoul	WCq
3–12	Mexico	L	1–2	Los Angeles	Fr

8–12	Hungary	L	0–1	Iraputo	Fr
10–12	Mexico	L	1–2	Guadalajara	Fr
14–12	Algeria	W	2–0	Mexico City	Fr
9–02–1986	Hong Kong	W	2–0	Hong Kong	Fr
16–02	Paraguay	L	1–3	Hong Kong	Fr
2–06	Argentina	L	1–3	Mexico City	WCr1
5–06	Bulgaria	D	1–1	Mexico City	WCr1
10–06	Italy	L	2–3	Puebla	WCr1
07	30th Merdeka Cup				
20–09	India	W	3–0	Seoul	AGr1
24–09	Bahrain	D	0–0	Seoul	AGr1
28–09	China	W	4–2	Seoul	AGr1
1–10	Iran	D	1–1(5–4p)	Seoul	AGqf
3–10	Indonesia	W	4–0	Seoul	AGsf
5–10	Saudi Arabia	W	2–0	Seoul	AGf
06	16th President's Cup				
12	31st Merdeka Cup				
1–06–1988	Egypt	D	1–1(4–3p)	Doha	Fr
06	17th President's Cup				
17–06	Bahrain	L	0–2	Jakarta	ACq
19–06	Yemen PDR	D	1–1	Jakarta	ACq
22–06	Indonesia	W	4–0	Jakarta	ACq
19–09	Soviet Union*	D	0–0	Pusan	OGr1
20–09	United States	D	0–0	Pusan	OGr1
22–09	Argentina*	L	1–2	Pusan	OGr1
26–10	Japan	W	1–0	Tokyo	Fr
3–12	Arab Emirates	W	1–0	Doha	ACr1
6–12	Japan	W	2–0	Doha	ACr1
9–12	Qatar	W	3–2	Doha	ACr1
11–12	Iran	W	3–0	Doha	ACr1
14–12	China	W	2–1	Doha	ACsf
18–12	Saudi Arabia	D	0–0(3–4p)	Doha	ACf
5–05–1989	Japan	W	1–0	Seoul	Fr
23–05	Singapore	W	3–0	Seoul	WCq
25–05	Nepal	W	9–0	Seoul	WCq
27–05	Malaysia	W	3–0	Seoul	WCq
3–06	Nepal	W	4–0	Singapore	WCq
5–06	Malaysia	W	3–0	Singapore	WCq
7–06	Singapore	W	3–0	Singapore	WCq
06	18th President's Cup				
10–08	Mexico	L	2–4	Los Angeles	Fr
13–08	USA	W	2–1	Los Angeles	Fr
16–09	Egypt	W	1–0	Seoul	Fr
13–10	Qatar	D	0–0	Singapore	WCq
16–10	North Korea	W	1–0	Singapore	WCq
20–10	China	W	1–0	Singapore	WCq
25–10	Saudi Arabia	W	2–0	Singapore	WCq
28–10	Arab Emirates	D	1–1	Singapore	WCq
4–02–1990	Norway	L	2–3	Ta'Qali	Fr
10–02	Malta	W	2–1	Ta'Qali	Fr
15–02	Iraq	D	0–0	Baghdad	Fr
18–02	Egypt	D	0–0	Cairo	Fr
12–06	Belgium	L	0–2	Verona	WCr1
17–06	Spain	L	1–3	Udine	WCr1
21–06	Uruguay	L	0–1	Udine	WCr1
6–09	Australia	W	1–0	Seoul	Fr
9–09	Australia	W	1–0	Pusan	Fr
23–09	Singapore	W	7–0	Beijing	AGr1
25–09	Pakistan	W	7–0	Beijing	AGr1
27–09	China	W	2–0	Beijing	AGr1
1–10	Kuwait	W	1–0	Beijing	AGqf
3–10	Iran	L	0–1	Beijing	AGsf
5–10	Thailand	W	1–0	Beijing	AG3p
11–10	North Korea	L	1–2	Pyongyang	Fr
23–10	North Korea	W	1–0	Seoul	Fr

* Not Full Internationals

SRI LANKA

Population: 17 103 000 Area, sq km: 65 610
% in urban areas: 21%
Capital city: Colombo 609 000

Football Federation of Sri Lanka
2 Old Grandstand, Race Course,
Reid Avenue, Colombo 7
Tel: (010 94) 1 696179
Fax: (010 94) 1 580721
Telex: 21537 METALIX CE
Cable: SOCCER COLOMBO
Languages for correspondence: English
Year of formation: 1939
Affiliation to FIFA: 1950
Affiliation to AFC: 1958
Registered clubs: 600
Registered players: 18 800
Registered referees: 347
National stadium: Sugathadasa, Colombo 25 000
National colours: Shirts: Maroon/Shorts: White/Socks: White
Reserve colours: Shirts: White/Shorts: White/Socks: Maroon
Season: September–March

THE RECORD

WORLD CUP

1930–90 ..... Did not enter

OLYMPIC GAMES

1908–60 ..... Did not enter
1964 .... QT pr round
1968 .... QT 2nd/2 in group 3
1972 .... QT 6th/6 in group 2
1976 .... Did not enter
1980 .... QT 6th/6 in group 3
1984 .... Did not enter
1988 .... Did not enter
1992 .... QT 4th/4 in group 3

ASIAN CHAMPIONSHIP

1956–76 ..... Did not enter
1980 .... QT 5th/7 in group 3
1984 .... QT 4th/5 in group 2
1988 .... QT Did not enter

ASIAN GAMES

1951–90 ..... Did not enter

SYRIA

Population: 12 116 000
Area, sq km: 185 180
% in urban areas: 50%
Capital city: Damascus 1 361 000

Association Arabe Syrienne de Football
General Sport Federation Building
October Stadium
Baremke, Damascus
Syria
Tel: (010 963) 11 335866
Fax: None
Telex: HOTECH 411935
Cable: FOOTBALL DAMASCUS
Languages for correspondence: English & French

Year of formation: 1936
Affiliation to FIFA: 1937
Affiliation to AFC: 1970
Registered clubs: 102
Registered players: 30 600
Registered Coaches: 532
Registered referees: 490
National stadium: Al Abbassiyne, Damascus 45 000
National colours: Shirts: White/Shorts: White/Socks: White
Reserve colours: Shirts: Red/Shorts: Red/Socks: Red
Season: September–June

THE RECORD

WORLD CUP

1930–38 ..... Did not enter
1950 .... QT 2nd/2 in group 2

1954 .... Did not enter
1958 .... QT R1 2nd/2 in group 4
1962–70 ..... Did not enter
1974 .... QT R1 4th/8 in group B
1978 .... QT R1 3rd/3 in group 3
1982 .... QT R1 5th/5 in group 2
1986 .... QT R1 1st/3 in group 3, R2 1st/2, R3 2nd/2
1990 .... QT R1 2nd/3 in group 2

OLYMPIC GAMES

1908–68 ..... Did not enter
1972 .... QT 6th/6 in group 3
1976 .... Did not enter
1980 .... QT 3rd/5 in group 1 – Final tournament/1st round
1984 .... QT R1 3rd/4 in group 1
1988 .... QT R1 2nd/2 in group 3
1992 .... QT R1 2nd/5 in group 2

ASIAN CHAMPIONSHIP

1956–76 ..... Did not enter
1980 .... QT 2nd/4 in group 1 – Final tournament/1st round
1984 .... QT 2nd/6 in group 1 – Final tournament/1st round
1988 .... QT 1st/5 in group 3 – Final tournament/1st round

ASIAN GAMES

1951–78 ..... Did not enter
1982 .... 1st round
1986 .... Did not enter
1990 .... Did not enter

TAIWAN

Population: 20221000
Area, sq km: 36000
% in urban areas: 73%
Capital city: Taipei 2702000

Chinese Taipei Football Association
100 Kuang–Fu South Road
Taipei
Taiwan
Tel: (010 886) 27117710
Fax: (010 886) 27117713
Telex: 24195 EDUCA TAIPEI
Cable: CTFA TAIPEI
Languages for correspondence: English

Year of formation: 1936
Affiliation to FIFA: 1954
Affiliation to AFC: 1955–76 & 1990
Registered clubs: 55
Registered players: 18300
Registered Coaches: 423
Registered referees: 447
National stadium: Taipei Municipal 30000
National colours: Shirts: Blue/Shorts: White/Socks: Red
Reserve colours: Shirts: White/Shorts: White/Socks: White
Season: January–December

THE RECORD

WORLD CUP

1930–54 ..... Did not enter
1958 .... QT R1 2nd/2 in group
1962–74 ..... Did not enter
1978 .... QT R1 3rd/3 in Oceania group
1982 .... QT R1 4th/5 in group 1
1986 .... QT R1 4th/4 in Oceania group
1990 .... QT R1 2nd/2 in Oceania group

OLYMPIC GAMES

1908–56 ..... Did not enter
1960 .... QT Qualified – Final tournament/1st round
1964 .... QT pr round
1968 .... QT 5th/6 in group 1
1972 .... QT 5th/5 in group 1
1976 .... QT 4th/5 in group 3
1980 .... Did not enter
1984 .... QT R1 3rd/4 in group 5
1988 .... QT R1 3rd/4 in Oceania group, R2 4th/4
1992 .... QT R1 4th/4 in group 6

ASIAN CHAMPIONSHIP

1956 .... QT 2nd/3 in group 2
1960 .... QT 1st/in group 3 – Final tournament/3rd place
1964
1968 .... QT 1st/5 in group 3 – Final tournament/4th place
1972
1976–88 ..... Did not enter

ASIAN GAMES

1951 .... Did not enter
1954 .... Winners
1958 .... Winners
1962 .... Did not enter
1966 .... 1st round
1970 .... Did not enter
1974 .... 1st round
1978–90 ..... Did not enter

THAILAND

Population: 56217000
Area, sq km: 513115
% in urban areas: 19%
Capital city: Bangkok 5716000

The Football Association of Thailand
C/O National Stadium
Rama 1 Road
Bangkok
Thailand
Tel: (010 66) 2 2141058
Fax: (010 66) 2 2154494
Telex: 20211 FAT TH
Cable: FOOTBALL BANGKOK
Languages for correspondence: English

Year of formation: 1916
Affiliation to FIFA: 1925
Affiliation to AFC: 1957
Registered clubs: 168
Registered players: 15000
Registered referees: 150
National stadium: Suphachalasai, Bangkok 45000
National colours: Shirts: Crimson/Shorts: White/Socks: Crimson
Reserve colours: Shirts: White/Shorts: White/Socks: White
Season: November–April

THE RECORD

WORLD CUP

1930–70 ..... Did not enter
1974 .... QT R1 7th/7 in group A
1978 .... QT R1 5th/5 in group 1
1982 .... QT R1 4th/5 in group 1
1986 .... QT R1 3rd/4 in group 6
1990 .... QT R1 4th/4 in group 5

OLYMPIC GAMES

1908–52 ..... Did not enter
1956 .... QT Qualified – Final tournament/Preliminary round
1960 .... QT 1st round
1964 .... QT 2nd round
1968 .... QT 1st/3 in group 2 – Final tournament/1st round
1972 .... QT 4th/6 in group 2
1976 .... Did not enter
1980 .... Did not enter
1984 .... QT R1 1st/4 in group 4, R2 3rd/5 in group 2
1988 .... QT R1 1st/2 in group 2, R2 3rd/4
1992 .... QT R1 2nd/5 in group 4

ASIAN CHAMPIONSHIP

1956 .... Did not enter
1960
1964
1968 .... QT 2nd/5 in group 2
1972 .... QT Automatic – Final tournament/Semi-finalists/3rd place
1976 .... QT 2nd/5 in group 3 – Withdrew
1980 .... QT 4th/7 in group 3
1984 .... QT 4th/6 in group 1
1988 .... QT 4th/6 in group 1

ASIAN GAMES

1951–58 ..... Did not enter
1962 .... 1st round

1966 .... Quarter-finalists
1970 .... Quarter-finalists
1974 .... 1st round
1978 .... Semi-finalists/3rd in group
1982 .... 1st round
1986 .... 1st round
1990 .... Semi-finalists/3rd place

UNITED ARAB EMIRATES

Population: 1 903 000
Area, sq km: 77 700
% in urban areas: 86%
Capital city: Abu Dhabi 243 000

United Arab Emirates Football Association
PO Box 5458
Dubai
United Arab Emirates
Tel: (010 971) 4 245636
Fax: (010 971) 4 245559
Telex: 47623 UAEFA EM
Cable: FOOTBALL EMIRATES DUBAI
Languages for correspondence: English

Year of formation: 1971
Affiliation to FIFA: 1972
Affiliation to AFC: 1974
Registered clubs: 25
Registered players: 3400
Registered Coaches: 57
Registered referees: 109
National stadium: Zayed Sports City, Dubai 60 000
National colours: Shirts: White/Shorts: White/Socks: White
Reserve colours: Shirts: Red/Shorts: Red/Socks: Red
Season: December–May

THE RECORD

WORLD CUP

1930–82 ..... Did not enter
1986 .... QT R1 1st/2 in group 1, R2 2nd/2
1990 .... QT R1 1st/3 in group 3, R2 2nd/6 – Final tournament/1st round

OLYMPIC GAMES

1908–80 ..... Did not enter
1984 .... QT R1 3rd/3 in group 2
1988 .... QT R1 2nd/3 in group 2
1992 .... QT R1 3rd/5 in group 1

ASIAN CHAMPIONSHIP

1956–76 ..... Did not enter
1980 .... QT 1st/4 in group 1 – Final tournament/1st round
1984 .... QT 2nd/5 in group 2 – Final tournament/1st round
1988 .... QT 1st/6 in group 1 – Final tournament/1st round

ASIAN GAMES

1951–82 ..... Did not enter
1986 .... Quarter-finalists
1990 .... Did not enter

UNITED ARAB EMIRATES LEAGUE CHAMPIONS

1975	Al Ahli
1976	Al Ahli
1977	Al Ain
1978	Al Nasr
1979	Al Nasr
1980	Al Ahli
1981	Al Ain
1982	Al Wasl
1983	Al Wasl
1984	Al Ain
1985	Al Wasl
1986	Al Nasr
1987	Al Sharjah
1988	Al Wasl
1989	Al Sharjah
1990	Al Shabab

VIETNAM

Population: 66 128 000
Area, sq km: 329 566
% in urban areas: 20%
Capital city: Hanoi 1 088 000
Major city: Ho Chi Minh City (Prev. Saigon) 3169000

Association de Football de la Republique du Vietnam
36 Boulevard Tran-phu
Hanoi
Vietnam
Tel: (010 84) 44867
Fax: None
Telex: None
Cable: AFBVN, 36, TRAN-PHU HANOI
Languages for correspondence: French

Year of formation: 1962
Affiliation to FIFA: 1964
Affiliation to AFC: 1954
Registered clubs: 20
Registered players: 16 000
Registered referees: 181
National stadium: Stade Hang Day, Hanoi 40 000
National colours: Shirts: Red/Shorts: White/Socks: Red
Reserve colours: Shirts: White/Shorts: White/Socks: Red
Season: November–May

THE RECORD

WORLD CUP

1930–70 ..... Did not enter
1974 .... QT R1 6th/7 in group A
1978–90 ..... Did not enter

OLYMPIC GAMES

1908–52 ..... Did not enter
1956 .... QT Qualified – withdrew
1960 .... Did not enter
1964 .... QT 2nd round
1968 .... QT 4th/6 in group 1
1972–92 ..... Did not enter

ASIAN CHAMPIONSHIP

1956 .... QT 1st/3 in group 3 – Final tournament/4th place
1960 .... QT 1st/3 in group 2 – Final tournament/4th place
1964
1968 .... QT 3rd/5 in group 2
1972
1976 .... QT 5th/5 in group 3
1980–88 ..... Did not enter

ASIAN GAMES

1951 .... Did not enter
1954 .... 1st round
1958 .... Quarter-finalists
1962 .... Semi-finalists/4th place
1966 .... 1st round
1970 .... 1st round
1974–90 ..... Did not enter

VIETNAMESE NATIONAL CHAMPIONS

1981	Tong Cuc Duong Sat
1982	Cau Lac Bo Quan Doi
1983	Cau Lac Bo Quan Doi
1984	Cong An Hanoi
1985	Cong Nghiep Ham Nam Ninh
1986	Cang Siagon
1987	Cau Lac Bo Quan Doi
1988	Cong An Hanoi
1989	Dong Thap

YEMEN

Population: 11 546 000
Area, sq km: 472 099
% in urban areas: 24%
Capital city: Sana'a and Aden

Republic of Yemen Football Association
PO Box 908
Sana'a
Yemen

Tel: (010 967) 2 215720
Fax: None
Telex: 2710 YOUTH YE
Cable: SANA'A FOOTBALL
Languages for correspondence: English

Year of formation: 1940 (South) 1976 (North)
Affiliation to FIFA: 1967 (South) 1980 (North)
Affiliation to AFC: 1967 (South) 1980 North)
Registered clubs: 83
Registered players: 4600
Registered Coaches: 27
Registered referees: 120
National stadium: National Stadium, Sana'a 50 000
National colours: Shirts: Green/Shorts: Green/Socks: Green
Season: October–April

THE RECORD

WORLD CUP

1930–82 ..... Did not enter
1986 .... QT R1 3rd/3 in group 3 (North) & 2nd/2 in group 4 (South)
1990 .... QT R1 3rd/3 in group 2 (North)

OLYMPIC GAMES

1908–76 ..... Did not enter
1980 .... QT 4th/5 in group 1 (South)
1984 .... Did not enter
1988 .... Did not enter
1992 .... QT 4th/5 in group 1

ASIAN CHAMPIONSHIP

1956–72 ..... Did not enter
1976 .... QT W-O in group 1 – Final tournament/1st round (South)
1980 .... Did not enter
1984 .... QT 5th/5 in group 3 (North)
1988 .... QT 3rd/6 in group 1 (North) & 4th/4 in group 4 (South)

ASIAN GAMES

1951–78 ..... Did not enter
1982 .... 1st round (South)
1986 .... Did not enter
1990 .... 1st round

OCEANIA

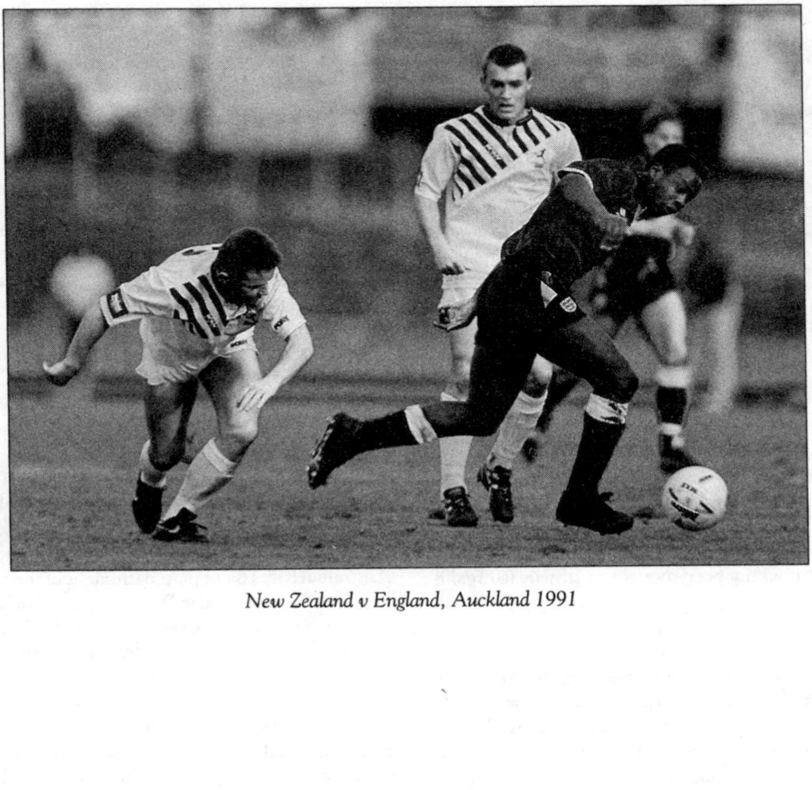

New Zealand v England, Auckland 1991

OCEANIA

Although the Oceania Football Confederation governs football in more than one sixth of the area of the world, it is not considered important enough by FIFA to grant it a permanent place on its executive committee. The two major countries in the Oceania confederation are Australia and New Zealand, and they are joined by six of the larger nations among the many Pacific islands. The problem is that few of them can claim football to be the major sport in their respective countries.

New Zealand won the first rugby World Cup in 1987, and Australia followed them as winners four years later, but rugby is even more deeply engrained in the culture of the region. Both Fiji and Western Samoa have reached the quarter-finals of that event, the former in 1987 and the latter in 1991, whilst both Papua New Guinea, the Solomon Islands and Tonga are regarded as strong opponents on their day.

Only in the former French territories of Tahiti, New Caledonia and Vanuatu is football the main pastime and their small populations severely limit their prospects. Not to be underestimated either is the American influence in the region which has ensured the spread of baseball and American football especially in Guam and American Samoa.

Due to the enormous distances involved, international activity is extremely restricted, even for New Zealand and Australia. An Oceania tournament has been played on two occasions, but neither was a conspicuous success and since 1980 it has not been thought worthwile to organise a third. A similar tournament for clubs is simply out of the question.

Oceania's future was put in jeopardy in the early 1970s when Australia sought affiliation with the Asian Football Confederation in an attempt to increase the level of competition, but their approaches were rejected. Instead both they and New Zealand have had to be content with entries into both the World Cup and Olympic Games as well as friendly matches against touring European sides.

Only Australia, Fiji and New Zealand have entered the World Cup in the past, although Tahiti, the Solomon Islands, Vanuatu and Western Samoa are making their first appearance in the 1994 tournament. Australia and New Zealand have qualified for the final tournament once each but on both occasions they have done so through the Asian qualifying tournament.

Neither team was particularly remarkable and they relied on their larger physique to overcome their opponents as well as their greater experience. In 1974 Australia beat both Iran and South Korea in crucial matches, whilst in 1982 New Zealand beat the Chinese in a play-off in Singapore. Since then a separate qualifying group has been set aside for Oceania, although the winners are not guaranteed a place in the finals.

In 1986 the winners were forced to play-off against a European side, in 1990 against a South American opponent, whilst in 1994 they will have to first win their group matches, then play-off against the other Oceania group winner for the right to play the runner-up in CONCACAF and, if successful in that match, a final game against the runners-up of group B in South America. If there is an Oceania entrant present at the 1994 finals, it will be a remarkable achievement.

Australia has the best football set-up in the region due mainly to the large number of ethnic communities present in the country. Team names like St George Budapest, Sydney Croatia and Brunswick Juventus leave no doubt as to their origin, but this has hampered the growth of the game amongst native Australians who see it largely as an alien sport. So worried were the authorities and the clubs that briefly in the early 1980s teams dropped their ethnic tags, but this proved unpopular and they were restored.

Football faces stiff competition from a host of sports in Australia. The national game is Australian Rules, a hybrid of rugby, football and Gaelic football played on a pitch that often doubles up as a cricket field, hence its enormous size. In typical Australian fashion, however, Australian Rules is not played throughout the country but largely in the south and in Western Australia, but particularly in Victoria. In Queensland rugby league is the number one code, whilst rugby union remains popular mainly in New South Wales.

Also competing for the attention of the public there is cricket as well as individual sports like athletics and swimming. Football has therefore taken a back seat, and until the 1960s, played very little part in the national life of the country at all.

Between 1946 and 1960, 1.6 million immigrants made their way to Australia, mainly from Europe, and this was the initial boost the game needed. An association had been in existence since 1882 but it was replaced in 1961 by the current federation in order to run the game in a more organised fashion, as well as to revive the national side which had lain dormant for many years.

From the late 1950s until 1976 each state ran its own league, the best being in New South Wales, Victoria and

South Australia. In 1977 Australia finally got a national league beneath which the state leagues continue to operate. The national league has never had an easy path. Gates are invariably low except for the play-offs at the end of the season and travel expenses are high, given the vast size of the country. Though it is called the national league, no teams from either Tasmania or Western Australia are included. In the latter's case travel expenses would be prohibitive.

In recent years the league has seen the rise of a number of Australian players who continue their careers in Europe, the most famous being Craig Johnston who won many honours with Liverpool. Others include Frank Farina who has done exceptionally well in Belgium and Italy. Other players like Tony Dorigo of Leeds United have been persuaded to play for other countries due to their parentage. Though born and bred in Australia, Dorigo is now a regular in the England squad.

In New Zealand, which can safely be regarded as the second power in the region, football faces much more clear-cut opposition to football than in Australia. Rugby union dominates the national sporting life to the almost complete exclusion of everything else. Only amongst the British community is football played with any great vigour.

Formed in 1891, the New Zealand Football Association supervised a competition called the Brown Shield, but the most important development came in 1923 when a cup presented by the English Navy ship HMS Chatham was introduced as an annual knockout competition for club sides. This still remains as a major feature on the fixture list and it was joined in 1970 by a national championship.

Despite very poor attendances, the national league has given a boost to the clubs in New Zealand who up until that point had played in poorly organised local leagues. It undoubtedly also helped the 'All Whites', as the national side is known in order to distinguish it from rugby's 'All Blacks', to qualify for the 1982 World Cup where they helped make their group one of the most entertaining of the tournament.

The future does not look very bright though, for either New Zealand or the rest of the Oceania members. Unless Oceania is given a regular berth in an expanded World Cup, the Pacific island states in particular will continue to flounder. The incentive is simply not there. Support for football in the region can be strong, as both Australia in 1974 and New Zealand in 1982 showed, but for this there has to be a real chance of qualification for the final tournament. Until that happens, as Western Samoa showed in the 1991 rugby World Cup, the oval ball will increase in popularity at the expense of the round one.

THE PACIFIC BASIN

Oceania Football Confederation
Mount Smart Stadium, PO Box 35-210, Brown's Bay, Auckland 10, New Zealand
Tel: (010 64) 9 590705 Fax: (010 64) 9 4138074
Telex: 63007 NZFAOFC Cable: None

Year of formation: 1966

Members: 8
Australia – Fiji – French Polynesia "Tahiti" – New Zealand – Papua New Guinea – Solomon Islands – Vanuatu – Western Samoa

Associate Members: 6
American Samoa – Cook Islands – New Caledonia – Niue Island – Northern Marianas – Tonga

Non Members: 12
Christmas Island – Cocos Islands – Kiribati – Marshall Islands – Micronesia – Nauru – Norfolk Island – Palau – Pitcairn Island – Tokelau – Tuvalu – Wallis and Fotuna

FIRST OCEANIA CUP
New Zealand, 17th –24th Feb 1973

	NZ	Ta	NC	NH	Fi	Pl	W	D	L	F	A	Pts
New Zealand	–	1–1	2–1	3–1	5–1	4	3	1	0	11	4	7
Tahiti	–	–	2–1	0–0	4–0	4	2	2	0	7	2	6
New Caledonia	–	–	–	4–1	2–0	4	2	0	2	8	5	4
New Hebrides	–	–	–	–	2–1	4	1	1	0	4	8	3
Fiji	–	–	–	–	–	4	0	0	4	2	13	0

3RD PLACE

New Caledonia .... 2–1 .... New Hebrides

FINAL

New Zealand .... 2–0 .... Tahiti

SECOND OCEANIA CUP
Numea, New Caledonia, 22nd Feb–3rd March 1980

Group 1

	Ta	Fi	NZ	SI	Pl	W	D	L	F	A	Pts
Tahiti	–	6–3	3–1	12–1	3	3	0	0	21	5	6
Fiji	–	–	4–0	3–1	3	2	0	1	10	7	4
New Zealand	–	–	–	6–1	3	1	0	2	7	8	2
Solomon Islands	–	–	–	–	3	0	0	3	3	21	0

Group 2

	Au	NC	PN	NH	Pl	W	D	L	F	A	Pts
Australia	–	8–0	11–2	1–0	3	3	0	0	20	2	6
New Caledonia	–	–	8–0	4–3	3	2	0	1	12	11	4
Papua N. Guinea	–	–	–	4–3	3	1	0	2	6	22	2
New Hebrides	–	–	–	–	3	0	0	3	6	9	0

3RD PLACE

New Caledonia .... 2–1 .... Fiji

FINAL

Australia .... 4–2 .... Tahiti

AUSTRALIA

Population: 17 073 000
Area, sq km: 7 682 300
% in urban areas: 85%
Capital city: Canberra

Australia Soccer Federation
1st Floor, 23–25 Frederick Street
Rockdale, NSW 2216, Australia
Tel: (010 61) 2 5976611
Fax: (010 61) 2 5993593
Telex: AA 170512
Cable: FOOTBALL SYDNEY
Languages for correspondence: English, German & Spanish

Year of formation: 1961
Affiliation to FIFA: 1963
Affiliation to OFC: 1966
Registered clubs: 1860
Registered players: 459 400
Registered referees: 3020
National stadium: National Stadium, Canberra 30 000
National colours: Shirts: Gold/Shorts: Green/Socks: White
Reserve colours: Shirts: Green/Shorts: White/Socks: Green
Season: March–October

THE RECORD

WORLD CUP

1930–62 ..... Did not enter
1966 .... QT 2nd/2
1970 .... QT R1 1st/3 in group 1, R2 2nd/2
1974 .... QT R1 1st/8 in group B, R2 1st/2 – Final tournament/1st round
1978 .... QT R1 1st/3 in Oceania group, R2 4th/5
1982 .... QT R1 2nd/5 in group 1
1986 .... QT 1st/4 in Oceania group. Lost European – Oceania play-off
1990 .... QT 2nd/5 in Oceania group

OLYMPIC GAMES

1908–52 ..... Did not enter
1956 .... QT Automatic – Final tournament/1st round
1960–84 ..... Did not enter
1988 .... QT 1st/5 in Oceania group – Final tournament/Quarter-finalists
1992 .... QT 1st/4 in Oceania group – Won play-off with Europe

AUSTRALIAN NATIONAL CHAMPIONS

1977 Sydney City Hakoah
1978 West Adelaide Hellas
1979 Marconi
1980 Sydney City Hakoah
1981 Sydney City Hakoah
1982 Sydney City Hakoah
1983 St George Budapest
1984 South Melbourne Hellas
1985 Brunswick Juventus
1986 Adelaide City Juventus
1987 APIA-Leichhardt
1988 Marconi
1989 Marconi
1990 Sydney Olympic
1991 South Melbourne Hellas
1992 Adelaide City Juventus

AUSTRALIAN CUP WINNERS

1977 Brisbane City
1978 Brisbane City
1979 Adelaide City Juventus
1980 Marconi
1981 Brisbane Lions
1982 APIA Leichhardt
1983 Sydney Olympic
1984 Newcastle Rosebud
1985 Sydney Olympic
1986 Sydney City Hakoah
1987 Sydney Olympic
1988 APIA Leichhardt
1989 Adelaide City Juventus
1990 South Melbourne Hellas
1991 Melita Eagles
1992 Adelaide City Juventus

CLUB DIRECTORY

SYDNEY (Population – 3 364 000)
Sydney City Hakoah
Sydney Olympic
Sydney Croatia
APIA Leichhardt
St George Budapest
Marconi

MELBOURNE (Population – 2 832 000)
South Melbourne Hellas
Melbourne Croatia
Heidelberg Alexander
Footscray JUST
Brunswick Juventus

BRISBANE (Population – 1 149 000)
Brisbane City
Brisbane Lions

ADELAIDE (Population – 977 000)
Adelaide City Juventus
West Adelaide Hellas

NEWCASTLE (Population – 405 000)
Newcastle KB United
Newcastle Rosebud United

NEW SOUTH WALES STATE CHAMPIONS

1957 Canterbury Marrickville
1958 Corrimal
1959 Prague
1960 Prague
1961 Prague
1962 St George Budapest
1963 Prague
1964 APIA Leichhardt
1965 South Coast
1966 APIA Leichhardt
1967 APIA Leichhardt
1968 Sydney City Hakoah
1969 South Coast
1970 Sydney City Hakoah
1971 Sydney City Hakoah
1972 St George Budapest
1973 Sydney City Hakoah
1974 Sydney City Hakoah
1975 APIA Leichhardt
1976 St George Budapest

VICTORIA STATE CHAMPIONS

1958 Brunswick Juventus
1959 Wilhelmina
1960 Polonia
1961 Polonia
1962 South Melbourne Hellas
1963 Footscray JUST
1964 South Melbourne Hellas
1965 South Melbourne Hellas
1966 South Melbourne Hellas
1967 Melbourne
1968 Melbourne Croatia
1969 Footscray JUST
1970 Brunswick Juventus
1971 Footscray JUST
1972 South Melbourne Hellas
1973 Footscray JUST
1974 South Melbourne Hellas
1975 Heidelberg Alexander
1976 South Melbourne Hellas

SOUTH AUSTRALIA STATE CHAMPIONS

1953 Adelaide City Juventus
1954 Adelaide City Juventus
1955 Polonia
1956 Adelaide City Juventus
1957 Adelaide City Juventus
1958 Adelaide City Juventus
1959 Adelaide City Juventus
1960 Budapest
1961 Budapest
1962 Budapest
1963 Adelaide City Juventus
1964 Adelaide City Juventus
1965 West Adelaide Hellas

1966 West Adelaide Hellas
1967 Adelaide City Juventus
1968 West Adelaide Hellas
1969 West Adelaide Hellas
1970 Adelaide City Juventus
1971 West Adelaide Hellas
1972 Adelaide City Juventus
1973 West Adelaide Hellas
1974 Adelaide City Juventus
1975 Polonia

FIJI

Population: 740 000
Area, sq km: 18 274
% in urban areas: 38%
Capital city: Suva 69 000

Fiji Football Association
Government Buildings
PO Box 2514, Suva, Fiji
Tel: (010 679) 300453
Fax: (010 679) 304642
Telex: 2366 FJ
Cable: FOOTSOCCER SUVA
Languages for correspondence: English

Year of formation: 1938
Affiliation to FIFA: 1963
Affiliation to OFC: 1963
Registered clubs: 22
Registered players: 10 200
National stadium: National Sports Stadium, Suva 25 000
National colours: Shirts: White/Shorts: Black/Socks: Black
Reserve colours: Shirts: Black and white hoops/Shorts: Black/Socks: Black
Season: February–October

THE RECORD

WORLD CUP

1930–78 ..... Did not enter
1982 .... QT R1 5th/5 in Asia group 1
1986 .... Did not enter
1990 .... QT R1 4th/5 in Oceania group

OLYMPIC GAMES

1908–88 ..... Did not enter
1992 .... QT 3rd/4 in Oceania group

NEW ZEALAND

Population: 3 389 000
Area, sq km: 270 534
% in urban areas: 83%
Capital city: Wellington

New Zealand Football Association
PO Box 62–532
Central Park
Auckland 6
New Zealand
Tel: (010 64) 9 5256120
Fax: (010 64) 9 5256123
Telex: NZ 63007 NZFAOFC
Cable: None
Languages for correspondence: English

Year of formation: 1891
Affiliation to FIFA: 1948
Affiliation to OFC: 1966
Registered clubs: 343
Registered players: 81 100
Registered coaches: 91
Registered referees: 872
National stadium: Mt. Smart, Auckland 45 000
National colours: Shirts: White/Shorts: White/Socks: White
Reserve colours: Shirts: Black/Shorts: White/Socks: White
Season: March–October

THE RECORD

WORLD CUP

1930–66 ..... Did not enter
1970 .... QT R1 2nd/2 in group 2
1974 .... QT R1 8th/8 in group B
1978 .... QT R1 2nd/3 in Oceania group
1982 .... QT R1 1st/5 in group 1, R2 2nd/4 – Final tournament/1st round
1986 .... QT R1 3rd/4 in Oceania group
1990 .... QT R1 3rd/5 in Oceania group

OLYMPIC GAMES

1908–80 ..... Did not enter
1984 .... QT R1 1st/4 in Asia group 5
1988 .... QT 3rd/5 in Oceania group
1922 .... QT 2nd/4 in Oceania group

NEW ZEALAND NATIONAL CHAMPIONS

1970 Blockhouse Bay
1971 Eastern Suburbs
1972 Mount Wellington
1973 Christchurch United
1974 Mount Wellington
1975 Christchurch United
1976 Wellington Diamond United
1977 North Shore United
1978 Christchurch United
1979 Mount Wellington
1980 Mount Wellington
1981 Wellington Diamond United
1982 Mount Wellington
1983 Manurewa
1984 Gisbourne City
1985 Wellington Diamond United
1986 Mount Wellington
1987 Christchurch United
1988 Christchurch United
1989 Napier City Rovers
1990 Waitakere City
1991 Christchurch United

CHATHAM CUP WINNERS

1923 Seacliff
1924 Auckland Harbour Board
1925 Wellington YMCA
1926 Sunnyside
1927 Ponsonby
1928 Petone
1929 Tramways
1930 Petone
1931 Tramurewa
1932 Wellington Marist
1933 Ponsonby
1934 Auckland Thistle
1935 Wellington Hospital
1936 Western
1937 –
1938 Waterside
1939 Waterside
1940 Waterside
1941–44 –
1945 Western
1946 Wellington Marist
1947 Waterside
1948 Christchurch Technical
1949 Petone
1950 Eden
1951 Eastern Suburbs
1952 North Shore United/Western
1953 Eastern Suburbs
1954 Onehunga
1955 Western
1956 Stop Out
1957 Seatoun
1958 Seatoun
1959 Northern
1960 North Shore United
1961 Northern
1962 Hamilton Technical
1963 North Shore United
1964 Mount Roskill
1965 Eastern Suburbs
1966 Miramar Rangers
1967 North Shore United
1968 Eastern Suburbs
1969 Eastern Suburbs
1970 Blockhouse Bay
1971 Western Suburbs
1972 Christchurch United
1973 Mount Wellington
1974 Christchurch United
1975 Christchurch United
1976 Christchurch United
1977 Nelson United
1978 Manurewa
1979 North Shore United
1980 Mount Wellington
1981 Dunedin City
1982 Mount Wellington

1983 Mount Wellington
1984 Manurewa
1985 Napier City Rovers
1986 North Shore United
1987 Gisbourne City
1988 Waikato United
1989 Christchurch United
1990 Mount Wellington
1991 Christchurch United

PAPUA NEW GUINEA

Population: 3 671 000
Area, sq km: 462 840
% in urban areas: 14%
Capital city: Port Moresby 152 000

Papua New Guinea Football Association
PO Box 337
Goroka
Papua New Guinea
Tel: (010 675) 722391
Fax: (010 675) 721941
Telex: TOTOTRA NE 23436
Cable: None
Languages for correspondence: English

Year of formation: 1962
Affiliation to FIFA: 1963
Affiliation to OFC: 1963
Registered clubs: 250
Registered players: 8200
Registered referees: 20
National stadium: Sir Hubert Murray stadium, Port Moresby 20 000
National colours: Shirts: Red/Shorts:/Black Socks:/Red
Reserve colours: Shirts: White/Shorts: White/Socks: White
Season: February–November

THE RECORD

WORLD CUP

1930–90 ..... Did not enter

OLYMPIC GAMES

1908–72 ..... Did not enter
1976 .... QT 5th/5 in Asia group 2
1980–88 ..... Did not enter
1992 .... QT 4th/4 in Oceania group

SOLOMON ISLANDS

Population: 319 000
Area, sq km: 28 370
% in urban areas: 15%
Capital city: Honiara 30 000

Solomon Islands Football Federation
PO Box 532, Honiara, Solomon Islands
Tel: (010 677) 23553
Fax: (010 677) 20391
Telex: HQ 66349
Languages for correspondence: English
Affiliation to FIFA: 1988
Affiliation to OFC: 1988
National stadium: Lawson Tawa, Honiara 3000
National colours: Shirts: Blue/Shorts: White/Socks: White
Season: May–December

THE RECORD

WORLD CUP

1930–90 ..... Did not enter

OLYMPIC GAMES

1908–92 ..... Did not enter

FRENCH POLYNESIA

Population: 197 000 Area, sq km: 4000
% in urban areas: 55%
Capital city: Papeete 103 000

Fédération Tahitienne de Football
BP 650, Papeete, Tahiti, French Polynesia
Tel: (010 689) 420410
Fax: (010 689) 421679
Telex: 454 FP
Cable: FOOTBALL TAHITI
Languages for correspondence: French
Year of formation: 1938
Affiliation to FIFA: 1990
Affiliation to OFC:
National stadium: Stade Olympique, Papeete
National colours: Shirts: Red/Shorts: White/Socks: White
Season: February–October

THE RECORD

WORLD CUP

1930–90 ..... Did not enter

OLYMPIC GAMES

1908–92 ..... Did not enter

VANUATU

Population: 147 000 Area, sq km: 12 190
% in urban areas: 18%
Capital city: Port Vila 19 000

Vanuatu Football Federation
PO Box 226, Port Vila, Vanuatu
Tel: (010 678) 22009
Fax: (010 678) 23579
Cable: FUTBOL BLONG VANUATU
Languages for correspondence: English
Year of formation: 1934
Affiliation to FIFA: 1988
Affiliation to OFC: 1988
National colours: Shirts: Gold/Shorts: Black/Socks: Gold
Season: March–September

THE RECORD

WORLD CUP

1930–90 ..... Did not enter

OLYMPIC GAMES

1908–92 ..... Did not enter

WESTERN SAMOA

Population: 165 000
Area, sq km: 2831
% in urban areas: 21%
Capital city: Apia 33 000

Western Samoa Football Association
Ministry of Youth, Sports and Culture
Private bag, Apia, Western Samoa
Tel: (010 685) 21420
Fax: (010 685) 24166
Telex: 230 SAMGAMES SX Cable: None
Languages for correspondence: English

Year of formation: 1968
Affiliation to FIFA: 1986
Affiliation to OFC: 1986
Registered clubs: 33
Registered players: 1750
Registered coaches: 2
Registered referres: 28
National stadium: Apia Park 12 000
National colours: Shirts: Blue/Shorts: White/Socks: Blue
Season: June–September

THE RECORD

WORLD CUP

1930–90 ..... Did not enter

OLYMPIC GAMES

1908–84 ..... Did not enter
1988 .... QT 5th/5 in Oceania group
1992 .... Did not enter

BIBLIOGRAPHY

Alaway RB (1948), *Football: All round the world* (Newservice Ltd).

Arlott J (1977), *The Oxford Companion to Sports and Games* (Paladin).

Asian Football Confederation (1984), *AFC 1954–1984*.

Asian Football Confederation (1989), *Achievements 1979–1989*.

Baker B (1992), *South African Soccer*.

Barrett N (1973), *World Soccer from A to Z.* (Rainbird).

Barrett N (1980), *Purnell's New Encyclopedia of Association Football* (Purnell).

Batty E (1980), *Soccer Coaching: The European Way* (Souvenir).

Beccantini R (1990), *Dizionario del Calcio* (BUR)

Beltrami A (1988), *Almanacco Illustrato del Calcio* (Panini).

Bestard M (1991), *Football in South America* (BPPC Wheatons).

Bulgarian FA (1982), *10 year review* (BFA).

Bulgarian FA (1988), *Yearbook* (BFA).

Burgisser N (1990), *Handbuch der National-Liga* (Swiss National League).

Butler B (1987), *The Football League 1888–1988* (Queen Anne Press).

Camkin J (1958), *World Cup 1958* (Rupert Hart-Davis).

Cazal J & Oreggia M (1989), *Israel 1948–1989* (AFSF).

Clayton D & Buitenga J (1991), *Football in Europe* (Soccer Book Publishing).

Clayton D & Buitenga J (1990), *The International Matches of Greece*.

Confédération Africaine de Football (1987), *1957–1987*.

Dougan D & Murphy P (1984), *Matches of the Day 1958–83* (JM Dent & Sons Ltd).

Ebneter H (1989), *Jahresberichte Rapports Annuels* (Schweizerischer Fussballverband).

Edelston M & Delaney T (1960), *Masters of Soccer* (The Naldrett Press).

Ellis AE (1954), *Refereeing round the World* (Hutchinson).

Fabian AH & Green G (eds) (1961), *Association Football* (Four volumes) (Caxton).

Faeroe FA (1991), *Handbook*.

FIFA (1950), *Handbook*.

FIFA (1953 onwards), *FIFA News*.

Freddi C (1991), *England Football Fact Book* (Guinness).

Gibson A & Pickford W (1906), *Association Football and the Men who Made it* (Four volumes) (Caxton. Reprint 1988).

Glanville B (1969), *Soccer: A Panorama* (Eyre & Spottiswoode).

Glanville B (1984), *The Puffin Book of the World Cup* (Puffin).

Glanville B (1970), *The Puffin Book of Football* (Puffin).

Glanville B (1978), *The Puffin Book of Footballers* (Puffin).

Glanville B (1967), *People in Sport* (Secker & Warburg).

Glanville B (1980), *The History of the World Cup* (Faber & Faber).

Glanville B (1963 onwards), *World Football Handbook* (Hodder/Mayflower).

Golesworthy M (1957), *The Encyclopaedia of Association Football* (Robert Hale).

Golesworthy M (1964), *Soccer Who's Who* (Robert Hale).

Green G (1954), *Soccer: The World Game. A popular History*.

Green G (1972), *Great Moments in Sport: Soccer* (Pelham)

Green G (1974), *Soccer in the 1950s* (Ian Allan)

Hammond M (1988), *The European Football Yearbook* (Facer).

Hammond M (1991), *The European Football Handbook* (Sports Projects Ltd).

Hammond M (1991), *Eurosoccer Statistics* (Sports Projects Ltd).

Harvey C (1960), *Sport International* (Sampson Low).

Harvey C (1966), *Encyclopedia of Sport and Sportsmen* (Sampson Low).

Heimann K & Jens K (1991), *Kicker Almanach* (Copress).

Henshaw R (1979), *The Encyclopedia of World Soccer* (New Republic Books).

Hereng J (1990), *Annuaire Footbal 1989–1990* (Vumpress).

Hill J, *Great Soccer Stars* (Hamlyn).

Hockings R (1988), *European Cups* (Kenneth Mason).

Hockings R (1991), *South American Cups* (Articulate).

Hopcraft A (1968), *The Football Man* (Collins).

Iceland Football Association (1990), *Handbok og Motaskra 1990*.

Inarsa T (1989), *Anuario de Futbol 1989–1990* (Todosport).

Inglis S (1985), *The Football Grounds of England and Wales* (Willow Books).

Inglis S (1987), *The Football Grounds of Great Britain* (Willow Books).

Inglis S (1988), *League Football and the Men who Made it* (Willow Books).

Inglis S (1990), *The Football Grounds of Europe* (Willow Books).

Jeffrey G (1963), *European International Football* (Nicholas Kaye).

Joy B (1963), *Soccer tactics: A New Appraisal* (Phoenix).

Kelly S (1988), *Back Page Football* (Macdonald Queen Anne).

Korea Football Association (1991), *The 19th President's Cup*.

Korea Football Association (1990), *Handbook*.

Kukulski J (1986), *Swiatowa Pilka Nozna 1977–1983* (Wydawnictwo).

KNVB (1973), *Voetbalhandboek 1968–1973*.

Laszlo M (1987), *Futball–adattar II* (Sportpropaganda).

Ledbrooke A & Turner E (1950), *Soccer from the Press Box* (Nicholas Kaye).

Libotte A (1985), *Almanacco Calcistico Svizzero*.

Lo Presti S (1991), *Annuario del Calcio Mondiale* (ERG).

Lowndes W (1952), *The Story of Football* (Thorsons).

Marples M (1954), *A History of Football* (Secker & Warburg).

Mason T (1981), *Association Football and English Society 1863–1915* (Harvester Press).

Macdonald R & Batty E (1971), *Scientific Soccer in the 1970s* (Pelham).

McIlvanney H (1966), *World Cup 1966* (Eyre and Spottiswoode).

McIlvanney H & Hopcraft A. (1970), *World Cup 1970* (Eyre & Spottiswoode).

Meisl W (1956), *Soccer Revolution* (Phoenix).

Meyer S (1986), *Europa: 1889–1986*.

Midwinter E (1986), *Fair Game: Myth and Reality in Sport* (Allen & Unwin).

Moon P & Burns P (1985), *The Asia–Oceania Soccer Handbook*.

Moon P & Burns P (1986), *The Asia–Oceania Soccer Yearbook*.

Moore B & Tyler M (1980), *The Big Matches* (Queen Anne Press).

Morris D (1981), *The Soccer Tribe* (Jonathan Cape).

Morrison I (1990), *The World Cup* (Breedon).

Motson J (1972), *Second to None* (Pelham).

Moynihan J (1987), *The Soccer Syndrome* (Simon & Schuster).

Mraz I et al (1980), *Svet Devadesati minut*, 2 vols. (Olimpia).

Parkinson M & Hall W (1974), *Football Classified* (William Luscombe).

Parkinson M & Hall W (1975), *Football Final* (Pelham).

Pele & Fish R (1977), *My Life and the Beautiful Game* (New English Library).

Portelli L (1990), *The Football Year Book. Malta 1990–91* (Progress Press).

Radnedge K (1984), *World Club Football Directory 1984–85* (Queen Anne Press).

Radnedge K (1985), *World Club Football Directory 1985–86* (Queen Anne Press).

Radnedge K *World Soccer* (monthly magazine, Oct 1960 onwards).

Ramirez G (1991), *Football in Ecuador* (Soccer Book Publishing).

Rethacker J (1989), *Football 1989* (L'Equipe).

Riordan J (1981), *Sport Under Communism* (Hurst).

Rippon A (1980), *European Cup. 1955–1980* (Mirror).

Robinson J (1988), *The European Championship. 1958–1988.* (Marksman).

Rohr B & Simon G (1988), *Lexikon Fussball* (VEB).

Rollin J (1981), *Guinness Book of Soccer Facts and Feats* (Guinness).

Rostkowski D (1988), *Short History of Polish Football*.

Rothmans (1970–92), *Football Yearbook* (Queen Anne Press).

Rous S (1978), *Football Worlds* (Faber & Faber).

Saunders D (1963), *World Cup 1962* (Heinemann).

Schwab L (1985), *National Soccer Annual* (Newspress).

Sharpe I (1952), *40 Years in Football* (Hutchinson).

Signy D (1970), *A Pictorial History of Soccer* (Hamlyn).

Soar P & Tyler M (1979), *Encyclopedia of British Football* (Cavendish).

Soar P (ed) (1984), *The Hamlyn World Encyclopedia of Football* (Hamlyn).

Stramare R (1989), *Sud America I*.

Taylor J & Jones D (1976), *World Soccer Referee* (Pelham).

Ticher M then Lyons A *When Saturday Comes* (monthly magazine).

Thomas M (1988), *African Football Handbook*.

Tomlinson A & Whannel G (1986), *Off the Ball* (Pluto).

United States Soccer Federation (1990), *United States Soccer*.

Wolstenholme K (1958), *Sports Special* (Stanley Paul).

Van Dijk F (1988), *100 Years of League Football in Europe*.

Van Hoof S & Guerra T (1989), *Encyclopedia of Peruvian Football*.

Van Hoof S & Villareal J (1991), *Colombia. 1938–1991*.

Van Hoof S & Sandoval J (1991), *La Celeste Uruguay 1901–91*.

Versi A (1986), *Football in Africa* (Collins).

Yasin I (1984), *Futbol Almanak '84*.

Young P (1953), *The Appreciation of Football* (Dennis Dobson).

COUNTRIES OF TEAMS LISTED IN EUROPEAN CLUB COMPETITIONS

Clubs A–Z	Country
AAB Aalborg	DEN
FC Aarau	SUI
AGF Aarhus	DEN
Aberdeen	SCO
Abo IFK	FIN
Academica Coimbra	POR
Adanaspor	TUR
Admira Wacker	AUT
Admira Wien	AUT
Ajax Amsterdam	HOL
Akademic Sofia	BUL
Akademisk Kobenhavn	DEN
IA Akranes	ISL
IBA Akureyri	ISL
KA Akureyri	ISL
AZ 67 Alkmaar	HOL
Alliance Dudelange	LUX
Altay Izmir	TUR
DWS Amsterdam	HOL
FC Amsterdam	HOL
RSC Anderlecht	BEL
SC Angers	FRA
AS Angouleme	FRA
MKE Ankaragucu	TUR
Anorthosis Famagusta	CYP
Royal Antwerp FC	BEL
Apoel Nicosia	CYP
Apollon Limassol	CYP
Apolonia Fier	ALB
UT Arad	ROM
Ararat Yerevan	URS
Ards	NIR
FC Arges Pitesti	ROM
Aries Bonnevoie	LUX
Aris Salonica	GRE
Arka Gdynia	POL
Arsenal	ENG
Aston Villa	ENG
Atalanta	ITA
AEK Athens	GRE
Athletic Bilbao	ESP
Athlone Town	IRE
Atletico Madrid	ESP
Atvidabergs FF	SWE
Austria Salzburg	AUT
FK Austria	AUT
AJ Auxerre	FRA
Avenir Beggen	LUX
FC Bacau	ROM
FC Baia Mare	ROM
Chemnitzer FC	GDR
Chernomorets Burgas	BUL
Chernomorets Odessa	URS
Chimea Vilcea	ROM
Cliftonville	NIR
Club Brugge	BEL
Coleraine	NIR
Cork Celtic	IRE
Cork City	IRE
Cork Hibernians	IRE
Corvinul Hunedoara	ROM
Coventry City	ENG
OFI Crete	GRE
Crvena Zvezda Beograd	YUG
Csepel SC	HUN
Crusaders	NIR
GD CUF Barreiro	POR
Daring CB	BEL
ADO Den Haag	HOL
FC Den Haag	HOL
Derby County	ENG
Derry City	NIR
Digenis Morphou	CYP
Diosgyori VTK	HUN
Distillery	NIR
Djurgardens IF	SWE
Dnepr Dnepropetrovsk	URS
Drogheda United	IRE
Drumcondra	IRE
Stade Dudelange	LUX
Dinamo Bacau	ROM
Dinamo Berlin	GDR
Dinamo Bucuresti	ROM
Dinamo Dresden	GDR
Dinamo Kiev	URS
Dinamo Minsk	URS
Dinamo Moskva	URS
Dinamo Pitesti	ROM
Dinamo Tbilisi	URS
Dinamo Tirane	ALB
Dinamo Zagreb	YUG
Dinamo Zilina	TCH
MSV Duisburg	FRG
Dukla Banska Bystrica	TCH
Dukla Praha	TCH
Dunajska Streda	TCH
Dunav Ruse	BUL
Dundalk	IRE
Dundee United	SCO
Dunfermline Athletic	SCO
Eintracht Braunschweig	FRG
Eintracht Frankfurt	FRG
IF Elfsborg Boras	SWE
Esbjerg FB	DEN
Eskisehirspor	TUR
RCD Espanol	ESP
Estrella da Amadora	POR
Etar Veliko Tirnova	BUL
Everton	ENG
Fenerbahce	TUR
Ferencvaros	HUN
Feyenoord	HOL
Finn Harps	IRE
Fiorentina	ITA
First Vienna	AUT
Flacara Moreni	ROM
Flamurtari Vlore	ALB
Floriana	MLT
Fola Esch	LUX
Fortuna Dusseldorf	FRG
Fortuna Geleen	HOL
Fortuna Sittard	HOL
Fram Reykjavik	ISL
Fredrikstad	NOR
Frem Kobenhavn	DEN
Fremad Amager	DEN
Frigg SK Oslo	NOR
Fyllingen IL	NOR
Galatasaray	TUR
CSU Galati	ROM
Galway United	IRE
Genclerbirligi	TUR
AA Gent	BEL
Genoa 1893	ITA
Germin Ekeren	BEL
Girondins Bordeaux	FRA
Gjovik Lyn	NOR
Glasgow Celtic	SCO
Glasgow Rangers	SCO
Glenavon	NIR
Glentoran	NIR
Go Ahead Deventer	HOL
Gornik Zabrze	POL
GAIS Goteborg	SWE
IFK Goteborg	SWE
TJ Gottwaldov	TCH
Goztepe Izmir	TUR
HASK Gradanski	YUG
Grasshopper-Club	SUI
Grazer AK	AUT
FC Groningen	HOL
Gwardia Warszawa	POL
Gyor Vasas ETO	HUN
Gzira United	MLT
Haarlem	HOL
FH Hafnarfjordur	ISL
Halmstad BK	SWE
Hamburger SV	FRG
Hajduk Split	YUG
Haka Valkeakoski	FIN
Haladas VSE	HUN
Hallescher FC	GER
Hammarby IF	SWE
Hamrun Spartans	MLT
Hannover 96	FRG
Hansa Rostock	GDR
SK Hauger	NOR
Heart of Midlothian	SCO
Hellas-Verona	ITA
HPS Helsinki	FIN
Hertha BSC Berlin	FRG
Hibernian	SCO
Hibernians Paola	MLT
HIFK Helsinki	FIN
HJK Helsinki	FIN
Holbaek BK	DEN
Honved	HUN
Hvidrove BK	DEN
Ikast BK	DEN
Ilves Tampere	FIN
TJ Internacional	TCH
Internazionale	ITA
Ipswich Town	ENG
Iraklis Salonica	GRE
Jeunesse Esch	LUX
Jeunesse Hautcharage	LUX
Jiul Petrosani	ROM
Juventus	ITA
I.FC Kaiserslautern	FRG
Kalmar FF	SWE
Karl-Marx-Stadt	GDR
SKA Karpati Lvov	URS
Kastoria	GRE
GKS Katowice	POL
IBK Keflavik	ISL
Kickers Offenbach	FRG
Kilmarnock	SCO
Kispest-Honved	HUN
B 1903 Kobenhavn	DEN

KB Kobenhavn	DEN
Koge BK	DEN
KPV Kokkola	FIN
Kolmo Banyasz	HUN
I.FC Koln	FRG
Koparit Kuopio	FIN
VSS Kosice	TCH
KTP Kotka	FIN
Kremser SC	AUT
KuPS Kuopio	FIN
Kuusysi Lahti	FIN
Labinoti Elbasan	ALB
Lanerossi-Vicenza	ITA
Landskrona BoIS	SWE
Larissa	GRE
EPA Larnaka	CYP
Las Palmas	ESP
Lausanne-Sports	SUI
Stade Lavallois	FRA
Lazio	ITA
Lech Poznan	POL
Leeds United	ENG
Lechia Gdansk	POL
Legia Warszawa	POL
Leicester City	ENG
Leixoes SC	POR
RC Lens	FRA
Bayer Leverkusen	FRG
Levski Sofia	BUL
Levski Spartak	BUL
RFC Liege	BEL
Lierse SK	BEL
Lillestrom SK	NOR
AEL Limassol	CYP
Limerick	IRE
Limerick City	IRE
Linfield	NIR
Linzer ASK	AUT
Liverpool	ENG
KSC Lokeren	BEL
Lokomotiv Kosice	TCH
Lokomotiv Leipzig	GDR
Lokomotiv Plovdiv	BUL
Lokomotiv Sofia	BUL
FC Lugano	SUI
FC Luzern	SUI
SOFK Lyn Oslo	NOR
Lyngby BK	DEN
Olympique Lyon	FRA
I.FC Magdeburg	GDR
KV Mechelen	BEL
Malmo FF	SWE
Manchester City	ENG
Manchester United	ENG
Marek St Dimitrov	BUL
Marsa	MLT
Mersin Idman Yurdu	TUR
Merthyr Tydfil	WAL
Metalist Kharkov	URS
FC Metz	FRA
MP Mikkeli	FIN
Milan	ITA
Mjondalen IF	NOR
Molde FK	NOR
RWD Molenbeek	BEL
AS Monaco	FRA
SCP Montpellier	FRA
Morton	SCO
CSKA Moskva	URS
Moss FK	NOR
Motherwell	SCO
Motor Jena	GDR
Motor Zwickau	GDR
TSV 1860 Munchen	FRG
NAC Breda	HOL
Naestved IF	DEN
AS Nancy-Lorraine	FRA
FC Nantes	FRA
Napoli	ITA
Napredak Krusevac	YUG
17 Nentori Tirane	ALB
Neuchatel Xamax	SUI
Newcastle United	ENG
Newport County	WAL
OCG Nice	FRA
NEC Nijmegen	HOL
Nîmes Olympique	FRA
IFK Norrkoping	SWE
Nottingham Forest	ENG
I.FC Nurnberg	FRG
B 1901 Nykobing	DEN
B 1909 Odense	DEN
B 1913 Odense	DEN
OB Odense	DEN
Odra Opole	POL
Orgryte IS Goteborg	SWE
Osters IF Vaxjo	SWE
Olimpia Ljubljana	YUG
Olympiakos	GRE
Olympiakos Nicosia	CYP
Olympique Marseille	FRA
Omonia Nicosia	CYP
Orduspor	TUR
Orebro SK	SWE
Osasuna	ESP
Otelul Galati	ROM
OPS Oulu	FIN
Panahaiki Patras	GRE
Panathinaikos	GRE
Panionios	GRE
Union Paralimni	CYP
Paris Saint-Germain	FRA
Parma	ITA
Partick Thistle	SCO
Partizan Beograd	YUG
Partizani Tirane	ALB
Pecsi Dozsa	HUN
Pecsi MSC	HUN
Perugia	ITA
Petrolul Ploiesti	ROM
Pezoporikos Larnaka	CYP
Pirin Blagoevgrad	BUL
Plastica Nitra	TCH
Politehnica Timisoara	ROM
Pogon Szczecin	POL
Polonia Bytom	POL
Portadown	NIR
Portimonense SC	POR
FC Porto	POR
Progres Niedercorn	LUX
Progresul Oradea	ROM
Queen's Park Rangers	ENG
Raba Gyor ETO	HUN
Rabat Ajax	MLT
Racing White	BEL
Rad Beograd	YUG
Radnicki Nis	YUG
Randers Freja	DEN
Rapid Bucuresti	ROM
Rapid Heerlen	HOL
SK Rapid Wien	AUT
Real Betis	ESP
Real Madrid	ESP
Real Oviedo	ESP
Real Sociedad	ESP
Real Valladolid	ESP
Red Boys Differdange	LUX
Red Star Brno	TCH
Reipas Lahti	FIN
KR Reykjavik	ISL
NK Rijeka	YUG
Roda JC Kerkrade	HOL
Roma	ITA
Rosenborg BK Trondheim	NOR
SKA Rostovna Donu	URS
Rot-Weiss Erfurt	GDR
FC Rouen	FRA
RoPS Rovaniemi	FIN
Ruch Chorzow	POL
US Rumelange	LUX
I.FC Saarbrucken	FRG
Sabadell	ESP
Sachsenring Zwickau	GDR
AS Saint-Etienne	FRA
FC St Gallen	SUI
St Johnstone	SCO
St Mirren	SCO
St Patrick's Athletic	IRE
Sakaryaspor	TUR
SC Salgueiros	POR
PAOK Salonica	GRE
Sampdoria	ITA
NEA Salamis	CYP
Salgotarjan BTC	HUN
FK Sarajevo	YUG
FK Sarpsborg	NOR
Shachter Donetsk	URS
FC Schalke 04	FRG
PSV Schwerin	GDR
FC Sedan	FRA
Servette FC	SUI
Sevilla	ESP
Shamrock Rovers	IRE
Sheffield Wednesday	ENG
Shelbourne	IRE
Sigma Olomouc	TCH
Siofoki Banyasz	HUN
FC Sion	SUI
SK Skeid Oslo	NOR
Skoda Plzen	TCH
Slask Wroclaw	POL
Slavia Praha	TCH
Slavia Sofia	BUL
Sliema Wanderers	MLT
Sligo Rovers	IRE
Sliven	BUL
Sloboda Tuzla	YUG
Slovan Bratislava	TCH
FC Sochaux	FRA
CFKA Sofia	BUL
CSKA Sofia	BUL
Southampton	ENG
Sparta Praha	TCH
Sparta Rotterdam	HOL
Spartak Hradec Kralove	TCH
Spartak Moskva	URS
Spartak Plovdiv	BUL

Spartak Trnava	TCH
Spartak Varna	BUL
AC Spora	LUX
Sporting Clube Braga	POR
Sporting Gijon	ESP
Sporting CP	POR
Sportul Studentesc	ROM
Sredets Sofia	BUL
Stade Français	FRA
Stade de Reims	FRA
Stade de Rennes	FRA
Staevnet	DEN
Stahl Brandenburg	GDR
Stahl Eisenhuttenstadt	GER
Stal Mielec	POL
Stal Rzeszow	POL
Standard CL	BEL
IK Start Kristiansand	NOR
Steagul Rosu Brasov	ROM
Steaua Bucuresti	ROM
Stijnta Cluj	ROM
SV Stockerau	AUT
AIK Stockholm	SWE
Stoke City	ENG
RC Strasbourg	FRA
IF Stromgodset	NOR
Sturm Graz	AUT
VfB Stuttgart	FRG
Sunderland	ENG
Swansea City	WAL
Swift Hesperange	LUX
Szombierki Bytom	POL
Tasmania Berlin	FRG
Tatabanya Banyasz	HUN
Tatran Presov	TCH
SK Tirane	ALB
ASA Tirgu Mures	ROM
FC Tirol	AUT
Torino	ITA
Torpedo Moskva	URS
FC Toulouse	FRA
TPS Turku	FIN
Trakia Plovdiv	BUL
Tromso IL	NOR
Trabzonspor	TUR
Tresnjevka Zagreb	YUG
FC Twente Enschede	HOL
GKS Tychy	POL
Udinese	ITA
Bayer Uerdingen	FRG
Ujpesti Dozsa	HUN
Union Luxembourg	LUX
Union Teplice	TCH
University College	IRE
Universitatea Craiova	ROM
Universitatea Cluj	ROM
DOS Utrecht	HOL
FC Utrecht	HOL
Vaci Izzo MTE	HUN
Valencia	ESP
Valerengens IF Oslo	NOR
Valletta	MLT
Valur Reykjavik	ISL
Vanlose BK	DEN
Vardar Skopje	YUG
Vasas Budapest	HUN
Vejle BK	DEN
Velez Mostar	YUG
IBV Vestmarnaeyjar	ISL
Victoria Bucuresti	ROM
Videoton SC	HUN
Viking FK Stavanger	NOR
Vikingur Reykjavik	ISL
Viktoria Koln	FRG
TJ Vitkovice	TCH
Vitesse Arnhem	HOL
Vitoria SC Guimaraes	POR
Vitoria FC Setubal	POR
Vitosha Sofia	BUL
Vllaznia Shkoder	ALB
VOEST Linz	AUT
Vojvodina Novi Sad	YUG
Voros Lobogo	HUN
Vorwarts Berlin	GDR
Vorwarts Frankfurt Oder	GDR
Wacker Innsbruck	AUT
KSV Waregem	BEL
Waterford	IRE
Waterschei THOR	BEL
Watford	ENG
Werder Bremen	FRG
West Bromwich Albion	ENG
West Ham United	ENG
FC Wettingen	SUI
Widzew Lodz	POL
Wiener Neustadt	AUT
Wiener Sportklub	AUT
Willem II Tilburg	HOL
Winterslag	BEL
Wisla Krakow	POL
Wismut Aue	GDR
Wolverhampton Wanderers	ENG
Wrexham	WAL
Wuppertaler SV	FRG
BSC Young Boys	SUI
Zaglebie Lublin	POL
Zaglebie Sosnowiec	POL
Zaglebie Walbrzych	POL
Zalgiris Vilnius	URS
NK Zagreb	YUG
Zarja Voroschilovgrad	URS
Zbrojovka Brno	TCH
Zeljeznicar Sarajevo	YUG
Zenit Leningrad	URS
FC Zurich	SUI
Zurrieq	MLT

Countries Of Teams Listed In South American Club Competitions

Clubs A–Z	Country
Alfonso Ugarte	PER
Alianza	PER
Always Ready	BOL
America Cali	COL
America Quito	ECU
Argentinos Juniors	ARG
Atletico Chalaco	PER
Atletico Colegiales	PAR
Atletico Junior	COL
Atletico Mineiro	BRA
Atletico Nacional Medellin	COL
Atletico San Cristobal	VEN
Atletico Torino	PER
Aurora	BOL
EC Bahia	BRA
Bangu	BRA
Barcelona	ECU
Bella Vista	URU
Blooming	BOL
Boca Juniors	ARG
Bolivar	BOL
Botafogo	BRA
Canarias	VEN
Cerro Porteño	PAR
Chaco Petrolero	BOL
Cobreloa	CHI
Cobresal	CHI
Colo Colo	CHI
Corinthians	BRA
Coritiba FC	BRA
Cruzeiro	BRA
Defensor	URU
Danubio	URU
Defensor Arica	PER
Defensor Lima	PER
Deportivo Cali	COL
Deportivo Concepcion	CHI
Deportivo Galica	VEN
Deportivo Italia	VEN
Deportivo Lara	VEN
Deportivo Municipal	BOL
Deportivo Municipal Lima	PER
Deportivo Quito	ECU
Deportivo Tachira	VEN
Emelec	ECU
Estudiantes LP	ARG
Estudiantes Merida	VEN
Everest	ECU
Everton	CHI
Ferrocarril Oeste	ARG
Filanbanco	ECU
Flamengo	BRA
Fluminense	BRA
Gremio	BRA
Guarani Campinas	BRA
Guarani Asuncion	PAR
Huracan	ARG
Independiente	ARG
Independiente Medellin	COL
Independiente Sante Fe	COL
Internacional PA	BRA
Jorge Wilsterman	BOL
Juan Aurich	PER
LDU Quito	ECU
Libertad	PAR
Litoral	BOL
Magallanes	CHI
Mariano Melgar	PER
Maritimo	VEN
Millonarios	COL
Mineros Guyana	VEN
Nacional Asuncion	PAR
Nacional Montevideo	URU
Nacional Quito	ECU
Nautico Recife	BRA
Nueve de Octubre	ECU
Newell's Old Boys	ARG
O'Higgins	CHI
Olimpia	PAR
Oriente Petrolero	BOL
Palestino	CHI
Palmeiras	BRA
Peñarol	URU
Pepeganda	VEN
Petrolero	BOL
Portugues Caracas	VEN
Progreso	URU
Quilmes	ARG
Racing Club	ARG
Rangers Tolca	CHI
River Plate	ARG
Rosario Central	ARG
San Augustin	PER
San Lorenzo	ARG
Santos	BRA
Sao Paulo FC	BRA
Sol de America	PAR
Sport Boys	PER
Sporting Cristal	PER
Sportivo Luqueño	PAR
Sport Recife	BRA
Tecnico Universitario	ECU
The Strongest	BOL
31 de Octubre	BOL
Tolima	COL
ULA Merida	VEN
Union Española	CHI
Union Huaral	PER
Union Magdalena	COL
Union San Felipe	CHI
Universidad Cajamarca	PER
Universidad Catolica	CHI
Universidad Catolica Quito	ECU
Universidad de Chile	CHI
Universitario	PER
Universitario La Paz	BOL
Valencia	VEN
Velez Sarsfield	ARG
Wanderers Valparaiso	CHI
Wanderers Montevideo	URU